Freshwater Fishes of Virginia

Support for the publication of this book
was provided by

VIRGINIA DEPARTMENT OF GAME AND INLAND FISHERIES

THE GREENSTONE FOUNDATION

Freshwater Fishes of Virginia

Robert E. Jenkins and Noel M. Burkhead

Roanoke College
Salem, Virginia

With special thanks to William H. Haxo

American Fisheries Society
Bethesda, Maryland

Suggested Citation Format

Jenkins, R. E., and N. M. Burkhead. 1993. Freshwater fishes of
Virginia. American Fisheries Society, Bethesda, Maryland.

©Copyright 1994 by the American Fisheries Society

All rights reserved

99 98 97 96 95 94 93   5 4 3 2 1

Library of Congress Catalog Card Number 93-073704

ISBN 0-913235-87-3

Printed in the United States of America
This book is printed on acid-free paper

Address orders to

American Fisheries Society
5410 Grosvenor Lane, Suite 110
Bethesda, Maryland 20814-2199, USA
Telephone (301) 897-8616

Dedication

To the people of Virginia, many of whom made this treatise possible, and who
   are the protectors of our rich natural heritage.
To Jack M. Hoffman in gratitude for his support during preparation of this book.
To our families and friends for their interest and patience, as we performed the
   pleasurable study of Virginia fishes.
And lastly, to those who can hear the song of a stream, who still get excited at
   the sight of clear water, and who want their grandchildren to know the same
   experience.

TABLE OF CONTENTS

COLOR PLATES

TABLES

ACKNOWLEDGMENTS

Without the generous aid and encouragement readily given to us by many ichthyologists, fishery scientists, administrators, students, and other interested persons, the level of this study would have been impossible to attain. That aid extended to virtually every facet of preparing this book, and we are extremely grateful for all of the help.

COAUTHORS

Eight sections or groups of accounts benefitted markedly by coauthorship with Joseph C. Desfosse, Virginia Institute of Marine Science (VIMS); Richard A. Dietz; William H. Haxo; Amy R. McCune, Cornell University; Stephen P. McIninch, University of Maryland; Thomas A. Munroe, VIMS; and John A. Musick, VIMS.

REVIEWERS

Much of the manuscript was technically reviewed by colleagues; they are listed in the topical sequence of the text. Absence of a parenthetical qualifier denotes that the entirety of a topical section or the accounts of all included taxa were reviewed. The affiliation of a reviewer is noted only at the first listing of the reviewer; an acronym is given (in parentheses) only when the agency or institution is repeated.

History of Virginia Freshwater Ichthyology—Joseph C. Mitchell, William S. Woolcott, University of Richmond (UR). *Estuarine Fishes*—Joseph C. Desfosse, VIMS. *Biogeography* (New and Tennessee drainages)—Richard J. Neves, Cooperative Fish and Wildlife Research Unit, Virginia Polytechnic Institute and State University (VPISU). *Endangered Fishes*—J. C. Mitchell; R. J. Neves; Karen A. Terwilliger, Virginia Department of Game and Inland Fisheries (VDGIF). *Introduced Fishes*—Paul H. Bugas, Larry O. Mohn, VDGIF. *Hybridization*—Karen P. Adkisson, Roanoke College (RC); Ernest A. Lachner, U.S. National Museum of Natural History (USNM). *Photography of Fishes*—Elizabeth Koesters Heil, RC. *Introduction to Accounts*—Herbert T. Boschung, University of Alabama (UA).

Petromyzontidae—Fred C. Rohde, North Carolina Division of Marine Fisheries. Petromyzontidae (family account)—F. W. H. Beamish, University of Guelph. Acipenseridae, Polyodontidae, and Amiidae—Amy R. McCune, Cornell University. Polyodontidae—Lance Grande, Field Museum of Natural History. Anguillidae—Gene S. Helfman, University of Georgia; Charles A. Wenner, South Carolina Marine Resources Institute. Esocidae—Edward J. Crossman, Royal Ontario Museum. *Esox masquinongy*—Daniel L. Brewer, Lewis E. Kornman, Kentucky Department of Fish and Wildlife Resources; David K. Whitehurst, VDGIF.

Margariscus, Semotilus—Eugene G. Maurakis, UR; Michael R. Ross, University of Massachusetts. *Campostoma anomalum*—Robert C. Cashner, University of New Orleans. *Exoglossum, Nocomis*—E. A. Lachner. *Erimystax dissimilis, E. insignis*—J. L. Harris, Arkansas Highway Department. *Phenacobius*—David A. Etnier, University of Tennessee (UT). *Hybopsis amblops, H. hypsinotus*—Miles M. Coburn, John Carroll University; E. G. Maurakis. *Cyprinella* (generic account)—Reeve M. Bailey, University of Michigan, Museum of Zoology (UMMZ); Donald G. Cloutman, Duke Power Company; Richard L. Mayden, UA. *Cyprinella labrosa, C. monacha*—D. G. Cloutman, M. M. Coburn, R. L. Mayden. *Luxilus*—E. A. Lachner. *Lythrurus*—Franklin F. Snelson, University of Central Florida. *Notropis* (*Hydrophlox*)—E. A. Lachner. *Notropis scabriceps*—Charles H. Hocutt, University of Maryland. *Hybognathus, Pimephales*—Lawrence M. Page, Illinois Natural History Survey.

Catostomidae—Lee A. Fuiman, University of Michigan. *Thoburnia rhothoeca*—C. H. Hocutt. *Moxostoma lacerum*—Arthur E. Bogan, Academy of Natural Sciences, Philadelphia. Ictaluridae—Brooks M. Burr, Southern Illinois University at Carbondale. *Ameiurus* (generic account)—John G. Lundberg, Duke University; Robert R. Miller, UMMZ. *Ictalurus furcatus, I. punctatus, Ameiurus catus, Pylodictis olivaris*—Edward L. Steinkoenig, VDGIF. *Noturus flavipinnis*—Peggy W. Shute, Tennessee Valley Authority.

Salmonidae—Robert A. Bachman, Maryland Department of Natural Resources; P. H. Bugas, L. O. Mohn. Salmonidae (family account, *Oncorhynchus mykiss*)—Robert J. Behnke, Colorado State University. *Oncorhynchus* (generic account)—R. R. Miller. Percopsidae, Aphredoderidae—Jay R. Stauffer, Pennsylvania State University. Aphredoderidae—John S. Brill, Livingston, New Jersey; Edward O. Murdy, USNM; Thomas L. Poulson, University of Illinois, Chicago Circle; F. C. Rohde. Amblyopsidae—T. L. Poulson, F. C. Rohde. Fundulidae—R. R. Miller. Poeciliidae—F. F. Snelson. Cottidae—Robert A. Daniels, New York State Museum; James D. Williams, U.S. Fish and Wildlife Service (USFWS). *Cottus* species (bluestone sculpin)—Henry W. Robison, Southern Arkansas University; J. R. Stauffer.

Moronidae—George C. Grant, VIMS. Moronidae (family account)—G. David Johnson, USNM; D. K. Whitehurst. Moronidae (key)—Dan A. Cincotta, West Virginia Department of Natural Resources. *Morone saxatilis*—William N. Cochran, *Roanoke Times and World-News*; Charles C. Coutant, Oak Ridge National Laboratory; John A. Musick, VIMS; William E. Neal, VDGIF; Robert E. Stevens, USFWS; D. K. Whitehurst. *Morone chrysops*—W. N. Cochran; D. K. Whitehurst.

Centrarchidae—R. C. Cashner. *Ambloplites cavifrons*—Gregory C. Garman, Virginia Commonwealth University. *Ambloplites cavifrons, Acantharchus pomotis, Centrarchus macropterus, Enneacanthus*—Mitchell D. Norman, VDGIF. *Pomoxis*—Arthur L. LaRoche, VDGIF. *Micropterus*—R. J. Neves. *Micropterus punctulatus, M. salmoides*—A. L. LaRoche. *Micropterus dolomieu, Lepomis auritus, L. microlophus*—John W. Kauffman, VDGIF. *Lepomis macrochirus*—A. L. LaRoche. *Lepomis megalotis*—Robert E. Wollitz, VDGIF.

Percidae (family account)—L. M. Page. *Stizostedion, Perca flavescens*—John J. Ney, VPISU. *Stizostedion vitreum*—D. K. Whitehurst. *Percina* (*Alvordius*)—W. S. Woolcott. *Percina* (all except six *Alvordius*)—Bruce A. Thompson, Louisiana State University. *Percina evides*—Robert F. Denoncourt, York College of Pennsylvania. *Etheostoma* (*Boleosoma*)—J. Randy Shute, UT. *Etheostoma* (*Catonotus*)—Steven R. Layman, UA. *Etheostoma* (*Hololepis*)—Bruce B. Collette, National Marine Fisheries Service.

ICHTHYOLOGICAL AID

A myriad of small and large tasks lies behind any major study; continually we had to rely on help from colleagues and others to accomplish these. The aid included access to specimens and records of collections, sharing anatomical data, sleuthing locality data, locating obscure literature, copying and allowing citation of unpublished manuscripts, and many other courtesies. A testimony to the support we have had is the following list of persons who helped in these endeavors. The institutions, agencies, and firms of many of these persons are listed in *Appendix 2*.

Tom M. Abbott, William Adams, W. Bruce Aitkenhead, Paul L. Angermeier, Vernon C. Applegate, Michael P. Armstrong, Joseph R. Bailey, Reeve M. Bailey, W. Donald Baker, K. E. Balliet, Roger W. Barbour, Daniel G. Bardarik, Bruce A. Bauer, Robert T. Bay, Eugene C. Beckham, Hal A. Beecher, Robert J. Behnke, Ray S. Birdsong, R. David Bishop, Charles R. Blem, Lawrence S. Blumer, Arthur E. Bogan, Eugenia B. Böhlke, James E. Böhlke, John W. Bolin, George W. Bond, Richard I. Bonn, Herbert T. Boschung, Branley A. Branson, Alvin L. Braswell, John S. Brill, Timothy D. Brush, Paul H. Bugas, George H. Burgess, Jimmy Burkholder, Robert G. Burnley, Brooks M. Burr.

Paul Calhoun, Robert C. Cashner, Ted M. Cavender, William Y. B. Chang, Labbish N. Chao, Donald S. Cherry, Mark E. Chittenden, Dan A. Cincotta, Jeffrey M. Clayton, Glenn H. Clemmer, Donald G. Cloutman, Brian W. Coad, Miles M. Coburn, Al Cockrell, Brian Cohen, Peter S. Coleman, Bruce B. Collette, A. Carter Cooke, Edwin L. Cooper, John E. Cooper, James Cox, Robert A. Cromer, Steven Q. Croy, Michael D. Dahlberg, Robert F. Denoncourt, Joseph C. Desfosse, R. Thomas Dews, William C. Dickinson, Allan J. Dietemann, Neil H. Douglas, Jerry F. Downhower, Michael C. Duvall.

Bruce W. Easley, Gwen A. Edwards, Edward C. Enamait, William N. Eschmeyer, R. Donald Estes, William S. Estes, David A. Etnier, Joseph C. Feeman, Norma Feinberg, T. M. Felvey, Carl J. Ferraris, William J. Fisk, Richard B. Fitz, John M. Fitzsimmons, E. David Frankensteen, Jean M. Fulton, William F. Gale, James N. Galloway, Gregory C. Garman, Bruce Gebhardt, Diane J. Giessler, Carter R. Gilbert, Ronnie J. Gilbert, John Gillenwater, Curt A. Gleason, Janet R. Gomon, John T. Goodin, John Gourley, John H. Graham, Larry A. Greenberg, David A. Griffin, Mart R. Gross, C. Richard Guier, Alice Guilday, Thomas P. Gunter.

Courteney T. Hackney, Timothy N. Hall, Patrick S. Hambrick, John L. Harris, Larry G. Hart, Karsten E. Hartel, Robert W. Hastings, William H. Haxo, Louis A. Helfrich, Charles H. Hocutt, John Homa, E. Terry Houston, W. Michael Howell, Melvin T. Huish, Michael Humphreys, Julian M. Humphries, Bruce E. Ingram, Daniel L. James, Susan L. Jewett, James E. Johnson, Jhil Kar, C. Lynn Keiser, Donald P. Kelso, George E. Krantz, Robert A. Kuehne, Ernest A. Lachner, Arthur L. LaRoche, Steven R. Layman, David S. Lee, Richard S. Lee, David Lindquist, Richard Lindsay, M. Delbert Lobb, Jules J. Loos, John G. Lundberg.

D. E. Marchette, Douglas F. Markle, Gary F. Martel, William H. Martin, Michael T. Masnik, Frank Massie, Richard E. Matheson, William J. Matthews, O. Eugene Maughan, Mitchell D. Maulfair, Morris Mauney, Eugene G. Maurakis, Richard L. Mayden, David A. Mayhew, Don E. McAllister, Amy R. McCune, John D. McEachran, J. J. McHugh, Stephen P. McIninch, Carole C. McIvor, D. Michael McLeod, Edward F. Menhinick, Linda P. Mercer, Robert R. Miller, Joseph C. Mitchell, Larry O. Mohn, G. Andrew Moser, Gregory H. Moser, S. Mudre, Patrick J. Mulholland, Thomas A. Munroe, John A. Musick.

Richard J. Neves, John J. Ney, Max A. Nickerson, David L. Nieland,

Arnold W. Norden, Mitchell D. Norman, W. Hank Norton, Michael Novachek, John K. Novak, Michael C. Odom, James Oland, J. R. Orgain, Donald J. Orth, Lawrence M. Page, Christopher A. Pague, William M. Palmer, Garland B. Pardue, C. W. Paulk, Elgin Perry, Harold J. Petrimoulx, Gerald B. Pottern, David Propst, Robert F. Raleigh, John S. Ramsey, Edward C. Raney, James R. Reed, Luis A. Revelle, C. Richard Robins, Jeffrey Robinson, Larry H. Robinson, Donn E. Rosen, Robert D. Ross, Thomas C. Ryan.

William G. Saul, Charles F. Saylor, Robert Schoknecht, Frank J. Schwartz, Monte E. Seehorn, Diane M. Shamel, Darrell Shanks, Robert J. Sheehan, Michael H. Shelor, Jack R. Sheridan, Daniel J. Shuber, J. Randy Shute, Peggy W. Shute, Andrew M. Simons, Timothy D. Simonson, Robert C. Simpson, Timothy J. Sinnott, Charles A. Sledd, C. Lavett Smith, DeWitt Smith, Gerald R. Smith, Philip W. Smith, William F. Smith-Vaniz, Leonard A. Smock, Roy A. Smoger, Franklin F. Snelson, Blaine D. Snyder, Pearl Sonoda, Debra S. Sorensen, Ronald Southwick, Harley J. Spear, Victor G. Springer, Paul E. Stacey, Richard W. Standage, Wayne C. Starnes, Jay R. Stauffer, Edward L. Steinkoenig, Robert A. Stiles, Joseph N. Stoeckel, Richard E. Strauss, John M. Stubbs, Royal D. Suttkus, Camm C. Swift.

William H. Tanger, Stephen H. Taub, W. Ralph Taylor, Allan J. Temple, Terry Teppen, Bruce A. Thompson, Robert L. Vadas, Henry van der Schalie, Donald L. Van Hoose, William D. Voiers, J. Bruce Wallace, Melvin L. Warren, Ronald E. Watson, Stanley H. Weitzman, Stanford R. Wells, Charles A. Wenner, Jerry L. West, Christopher P. White, Gregory White, John C. White, David K. Whitehurst, Shirley K. Whitt, Walter R. Whitworth, James C. Widlak, Jeffrey T. Williams, Robert E. Wollitz, Kenneth V. Wood, William S. Woolcott, and Timothy Zorach.

For many years we have been fortunate to be apprised of the distribution and status of gamefishes and their habitats in Virginia through conversation with and writings of William N. Cochran, outdoor writer of the *Roanoke Times and World-News*. Bill gave much-valued encouragement to the book project.

ROANOKE COLLEGE

Our home institution made a strong community effort in seeing this work to press by providing work space, facilities, personnel, reduction in teaching time, and sustained encouragement. Our administrators Gary A. Clarke, Jan Douglas, Norman D. Fintel, Gerald W. Gibson, Margaret S. Hudson, C. Freeman Sleeper, Jesse C. Thompson, Jack M. Turner, and William R. Walton smoothed the way for our work. Gary A. Clarke and Gene Grubitz relinquished laboratory space as our operation expanded. James R. Dalton and Terri M. Austin expedited our use of personal computers and the Academic Computer Center.

In the library, George E. Craddock, Elinor W. Coleman, W. Thomas Davidson, Kimberly D. Hickson, Patricia W. Scott, Andrea Svetson, and Stanley F. Umberger were frequently helpful. Elizabeth Koesters Heil advised on artwork; Peter Bogan aided in initial efforts at black-and-white photography. Joe E. Williamson and James W. Henderson reduced drawings. Zebulon V. Hooker, English Department, facilitated use of early American literature.

Our esteemed field and laboratory personnel William H. Haxo, Elizabeth H. Knicely, Stephen P. McIninch, and Bonnie J. Woffenden eagerly tackled and competently handled any task presented.

Drawings were executed by Sheila E. Herzog, Elizabeth H. Knicely, and especially Fred M. Odum and Sandra Jordan. We are particularly pleased to have had Sandy aboard, for she is a descendent of the great ichthyologist David Starr Jordan. The jacket watercolor was painted by Lora L. Giessler. Many of the maps were inked by Diane J. Giessler, Katherine S. Jenkins, Stacey A. Quigg, Francis T. Smigelsky, and Warren M. Thompson. Our typists were James P. Akowski, Jennifer L. Barger, Peggy A. Frank, Diane J. Giessler, Leslie A. Goodwin, Glenn R. Jenkins, Katherine S. Jenkins, Elizabeth H. Knicely, Karen L. Millan, Elizabeth J. Tucker, Bonnie J. Woffenden, and Linette D. Wray. We thank Christine B. Cable and her staff of the Word Processing Center for initial typing of the keys and tables.

Students of the Roanoke College aquatic biology course performed food-habits studies; written reports by the following are cited in species accounts: R. Carl Bumgarner, Andrew H. Campbell, A. Ross Clarke, Kimberly A. Cronin, Leslie A. Goodwin, Scott W. Hipple, Thomas E. Inman, Elizabeth H. Knicely, Rhonda K. Law, Melissa G. Pflegar, Hank J. Rolfs, Rosemary L. Steele, Craig M. Stephens, Kathryn M. Sullivan, Karen A. Tyler, and V. Lynn Webb. Also cited are senior student research reports by Samuel R. Crockett (Clinch sculpin); Elizabeth C. Diggs, Philip H. Lahrmann, and Nancy A. Mudrick (bigeye jump-rock); Mark A. Hartman and (Hollins College) Gail D. Maxey (glassy darter), and Stephen B. Harvey (mountain redbelly dace). Thanks go also to the many students who helped with the tedious task of testing the keys.

VIRGINIA AGENCIES

The Virginia Department of Game and Inland Fisheries gave the book enthusiastic support beginning with early study stages in 1973; it added comprehensive financial and logistical aid from 1983 to 1989. Thus we thank Frances Anderson, Raymond V. Corning, Richard H. Cross, Harry L. Gillam, Jack M. Hoffman, William E. Neal, John P. Randolph, Charles A. Sledd, Melvin M. White, and David K. Whitehurst, all of the Richmond office. Help was also given by regional biologists of the VDGIF (cited above).

When he was with the Virginia State Water Control Board, David S. Bailey made resources available to us. James Coles of the Virginia Highway Department helped us locate sites of old collections whose locality descriptors involved road number changes.

BOVA

The BOVA (Biota of Virginia) system, a computerized information bank, organized our distributional data into summaries of records by species and drainages; it also computer-plotted maps from which we adapted most of our maps. The data processing occurred mostly in the Department of Fisheries and Wildlife Sciences of VPISU with support by the VDGIF. For that effort we sincerely thank Robert H. Giles, who organized and early directed BOVA; Mark A. Howard, for programming and many other operations; David Barnes, Brenda Eves, Susan C. Hamilton, A. Blair Jones, Andrea Odom, and Cathie Vouchilas. Virgil E. Kopf, BOVA Coordinator in the Richmond office of the VDGIF, filled subsequent needs for data summary. An interim computer summary of distributional data was made for us at Berry Dail and Co., Salem, courtesy of Jack Randall; the service was rendered by Diane J. Giessler and Boyd Hale.

NOMENCLATURAL ADVICE

Timely apprisals and discussions on proposed changes of fish names were given by Reeve M. Bailey, Ernest A. Lachner, and C. Richard Robins of the American Fisheries Society's and the American Society of Ichthyologists and Herpetologists' joint Committee on Names of Fishes. Several other workers already cited gave us information from their studies that would result in no-menclatural changes. To help with accommodating in our key several generic changes, we thank David A. Etnier for allowing us to use the minnow key for his book on the fishes of Tennessee, which he coauthored with Wayne C. Starnes.

ILLUSTRATION CREDITS

For photographs of ichthyologists and permission to publish these, we acknowledge Sylva S. Baker, Academy of Natural Sciences, Philadelphia (E. D. Cope); Stanford University (D. S. Jordan); John Homa, Ichthyological Associates, Inc. (E. C. Raney); Mary H. Ross (R. D. Ross); Ernest A. Lachner; and William S. Woolcott. Don E. McAllister, National Museum of Canada, allowed use of a print of the shortnose sturgeon. We are pleased that William N. Roston let us include his underwater photographs of a paddlefish, brook silversides, and white bass. The photograph of James River in the Fall Zone (Plate 3) is by Dwight Dyke of Blackhawk Productions. The base map of rivers of North America (Map 6) was made available by the University of Michigan, Museum of Zoology. William Tanger, Image Advertising and Friends of the Roanoke River, gave advice on black-and-white printing.

LANDOWNERS AND FIELD HANDS

Many landowners graciously gave us and our entourages access to collecting, photographing, and camping sites. Many students, colleagues, and friends pulled an end of the seine. They are remembered for these essential contributions.

FUNDING

Generous financial support made this treatise possible, for which we are indebted to John A. Mulheren (Roanoke College alumnus), Roanoke College, the U.S. Fish and Wildlife Service, the Virginia Department of Game and Inland Fisheries, the Virginia Environmental Endowment, the Virginia Power Company, and the Virginia Water Control Board.

GALLEY PROOFING

The last onerous task of proofing galleys was made easier with the generous assistance of William Smith-Vaniz, Stephen J. Walsh, and James D. Williams (National Biological Survey, Gainesville).

AMERICAN FISHERIES SOCIETY

We and the readers of this book are immensely fortunate to have had the meticulous and extensive services of the contract editors and staff of the American Fisheries Society. In Oak Ridge, Tennessee, Clyde W. Voigtlander edited two drafts of the manuscript, and Bonnie M. Voigtlander performed most of the final wordprocessing. In the Bethesda office, the text was further honed, the pages were designed, and production was handled by Robert L. Kendall, Sally M. Kendall, Elizabeth A. Mitchell, Elizabeth D. Staehle, and Amy E. M. Wassmann.

PREFACE

This book is intended for students, teachers, fishery scientists, ichthyologists, consulting biologists, naturalists, planners, anglers, aquarists, and any other persons curious about the freshwater fish fauna of Virginia. The book has much wider use; many of Virginia's fish species occur more widely in North America. It contains more detail than needed by some, not enough for others, but plenty that is useful for many. We trust that continued emphasis on conservation and preservation of aquatic organisms and habitats is a clear message of this treatise.

A major purpose of this volume is to provide a reliable means to accurately identify species all of the freshwater fishes of Virginia. To this end we include keys, illustrations, descriptions, and—for species that look much alike and often are collected together—comparisons. The keys have been tested by many students. Under *Identifying Fishes* we describe the procedures of keying and alternative methods of identifying fishes. We would like to believe that now there is no excuse for misidentifying an inland Virginia fish. We recognize that as students we were sometimes confused by the many similar species, but we learned that mistakes were avoidable by using caution and patience.

Other primary objectives are to acquaint the reader with the ways of life and habitats of Virginia species and to provide a detailed picture of their historical and current distributions. At the end of each species account is a *Remarks* section containing comments on conservation status, anecdotes, or impressions we brought back from visits to streams.

This book has its roots in an unpublished annotated list of the freshwater fishes of Virginia compiled by Robert E. Jenkins in 1967 at Cornell University. The authors arrived at Roanoke College the year after, R.E.J. on the faculty, Noel M. Burkhead as a student. In early 1973 the Virginia Department of Game and Inland Fisheries provided this book's first direct financial support, allowing drafting of the stream base map and a strong start in the acquisition and synthesis of distributional data. Data gathering and synthesis continued intermittently during 1974–1979.

Our first major funding was granted in fall 1979 through the Virginia Water Control board. During 1968–1982 much of our research was on other projects, but generally it was undertaken because it would make valuable contributions to the book. In 1983–1990 our preparation of the manuscript and illustrations, and the assistance by our associates Bill Haxo and Steve McIninch and many students, was financially supported chiefly by Roanoke College and the Virginia Department of Game and Inland Fisheries. The editing by the American Fisheries Society and the printing were generously supported by the Virginia Department of Game and Inland Fisheries.

Our fieldwork in Virginia, R.E.J. starting in 1961, N.M.B. in 1968, comprises 1,160 collections or detailed observations; the majority occurred in the western half of the state but significant forays were made into the southeastern and other parts. Fieldwork was also conducted in northern North Carolina, eastern Tennessee, and southern Kentucky. We extensively canvassed fish collections in museums and other institutions for data on fishes of Virginia and those of adjacent areas. In all, distributional data from slightly over 10,000 collections from Virginia were used.

The original writing of the manuscript occurred from early 1983 to early 1987; revisions and updates were made during 1988–1991. The original writing was interspersed with field trips aimed to survey critical areas, to collect poorly known species, and to photograph these and nearly all others shown herein. The fieldwork afforded a fresh view of almost all species and many habitats in the state. Our methods of gathering, treating, and reporting data are described in *History of Virginia Freshwater Ichthyology, Anatomy and Color of Fishes,* and *Introduction to Accounts.*

Before starting to write, we naively believed that the manuscript would amount to about 500 typed pages; the typescript is more than quadruple that. We wanted each species account to be as complete as possible within the scope of the book. To this end, we incorporated extensive unpublished data from our studies and those of colleagues; the latter are cited as *in press, in litt.,* or *personal communication* (defined in the *Glossary*). We regret that we were unable to include all papers in the benchmark volume edited by R. L. Mayden (1992) and the final manuscript by E. F. Menhinick now published as *The Freshwater Fishes of North Carolina* (1991, North Carolina Wildlife Resources Commission). Many technical reviewers helped to hone the manuscript during 1984–1987, as did Clyde Voigtlander, our Technical Editor in 1988–1991.

Although we tended to work relatively little in the laboratory with game fishes, we are avid freshwater anglers and understand problems of fishery management; accounts of game fishes tend to be the longest. Some of the lengthy accounts of nongame fishes concern species that we have studied in considerable depth. The life history of some nongame species is so poorly known that little can be written.

To help the reader find facts in the species accounts, the sequence of topics and subtopics in each section is standardized, as indicated in *Introduction to Accounts.* That section also treats some principles of systematics and life history study.

Four sets of illustrations—maps, figures, fish, and plates—are intermixed in this book; numbering within each set begins with 1. Some aspects of map symbols and legends are explained in the *Introduction to Accounts.* Figures are line drawings; nearly all are located in the section *Anatomy and Color* and in the keys. The word Fish followed by a number refers to black-and-white photographs of specimens plus the drawings of a shortnose sturgeon, pike, and muskellunge. Plates contain color photographs of fishes or habitats; documentary data are in *Appendix 1.*

This book is relatively heavy on systematics when compared with most books on the fishes of a state. We treat interrelations of taxa to further the understanding of why species appear and act similarly or differently; this is the realm of comparative biology (Funk and Brooks 1990). The descriptions depart from the state-book norm by reference to materials (specimens and literature) used for descriptions.

The accounts of sculpins, family Cottidae, are particularly detailed. *Cottus* species have been among the poorest known and most difficult to identify of Virginia fishes. Among the eight species are three undescribed species and (counting the form of *C. cognatus*) two undescribed subspecies; they are separated here for the first time. We introduce standardized terminology for many taxonomic characters of sculpins.

Many scientific and a few common names that we use for family, genus, or species taxa may be unfamiliar (Table 1). They depart from the analogous names formerly or currently adopted by the joint Committee on Names of Fishes of the American Fisheries Society and the American Society of Ichthyologists and Herpetologists (Robins et al. 1980, 1991). Although name changes often are unpopular, they generally reflect improved perception of the interrelations or status of the organisms involved. Most of the changes resulted from phylogenetic (cladistic) analyses, as opposed to purely evolutionary or phenetic studies; these types of studies are compared in *Introduction to Accounts*.

Phylogenetic inquiry on fishes is a dynamic field and much remains to be learned. In truth, a new era of studying interrelations of fishes has just been entered, hence the names of many taxa are uncertain. We strove to follow or anticipate nomenclature that appeared to have the best chances of becoming stable; we initiated some of the name changes. Specific reasons for making or deferring name changes are given or cited in the accounts.

Some of the distribution sections are very detailed. Extensive historical and other esoteric or intricate data were used to determine the original status (either native or introduced) of species in drainages, and to verify or reject critical locality records.

This volume is a time capsule of the Virginia ichthyofauna in the late 20th century. We hope it promotes understanding and respect for our wonderful aquatic heritage, and that it fosters a desire to learn more about it. We hope that in the not too distant future, another treatise will document the recovery and health everywhere of our fishes.

Robert E. Jenkins
Roanoke College
Salem, Virginia 24153

Noel M. Burkhead
National Biological Survey
7920 N.W. 71st Street
Gainesville, Florida 32606

Table 1 Differences in scientific and common names herein (in sequence of accounts) from those in the 1980 or 1991 or both names lists of the American Fisheries Society (Robins et al. 1980, 1991); most differences are from the 1980 list. Differences from the 1991 list include: retention of *Hybopsis* as a genus, substitution of the common names turquoise shiner and thicklip shiner, elevation of *Thoburnia* and *Scartomyzon* to genus, placement of *Lagochila* in *Moxostoma*, and recognition of Fundulidae and Moronidae as families. Reasons for differences from the AFS lists are given in text.

Scientific name herein	Formerly	Common name herein	Formerly
Margariscus margarita	*Semotilus margarita*	pearl dace	same
Erimystax cahni	*Hybopsis cahni*	slender chub	same
Erimystax dissimilis	*Hybopsis dissimilis*	streamline chub	same
Erimystax insignis	*Hybopsis insignis*	blotched chub	same
Cyprinella labrosa	*Hybopsis labrosa*	thicklip shiner	thicklip chub
Cyprinella monacha	*Hybopsis monacha*	spotfin shiner	turquoise chub
Cyprinella galactura	*Notropis galacturus*	whitetail shiner	same
Cyprinella whipplei	*Notropis whipplei*	steelcolor shiner	same
Cyprinella analostana	*Notropis analostanus*	satinfin shiner	same
Cyprinella spiloptera	*Notropis spilopterus*	spotfin shiner	same
Luxilus coccogenis	*Notropis coccogenis*	warpaint shiner	same
Luxilus cerasinus	*Notropis cerasinus*	crescent shiner	same
Luxilus albeolus	*Notropis albeolus*	white shiner	same
Luxilus cornutus	*Notropis cornutus*	common shiner	same
Luxilus chrysocephalus	*Notropis chrysocephalus*	striped shiner	same
Lythrurus lirus	*Notropis lirus*	mountain shiner	same
Lythrurus ardens	*Notropis ardens*	rosefin shiner	same
Notropis buccatus	*Ericymba buccata*	silverjaw minnow	same
Thoburnia rhothoeca	*Moxostoma rhothoecum*	torrent sucker	same
Thoburnia hamiltoni	*Moxostoma hamiltoni*	rustyside sucker	same
Scartomyzon robustus	*Moxostoma robustum*	smallfin redhorse	same
Scartomyzon cervinus	*Moxostoma cervinum*	black jumprock	same
Scartomyzon ariommus	*Moxostoma ariommum*	bigeye jumprock	same
Moxostoma pappillosum	same	V-lip redhorse	suckermouth redhorse
Moxostoma lacerum	*Lagochila lacera*	harelip sucker	same
Ameiurus catus	*Ictalurus catus*	white catfish	same
Ameiurus platycephalus	*Ictalurus platycephalus*	flat bullhead	same
Ameiurus brunneus	*Ictalurus brunneus*	snail bullhead	same
Ameiurus natalis	*Ictalurus natalis*	yellow bullhead	same
Ameiurus nebulosus	*Ictalurus nebulosus*	brown bullhead	same
Ameiurus melas	*Ictalurus melas*	black bullhead	same
Oncorhynchus mykiss	*Salmo gairdneri*	rainbow trout	same
Fundulidae	Cyprinodontidae (part)	killifishes	same
Gambusia holbrooki	*Gambusia affinis*	eastern mosquitofish	mosquitofish
Moronidae	Percichthyidae (part)	striped basses	temperate basses
Micropterus dolomieu	*Micropterus dolomieui*	smallmouth bass	same
Percina oxyrhynchus	*Percina oxyrhyncha*	sharpnose darter	same
Etheostoma osburni	same	candy darter	finescale saddled darter
Etheostoma simoterum	same	snubnose darter	Tennessee snubnose darter
Etheostoma stigmaeum	*Etheostoma jessiae*	speckled darter	same
Etheostoma serrifer	*Etheostoma serriferum*	sawcheek darter	same

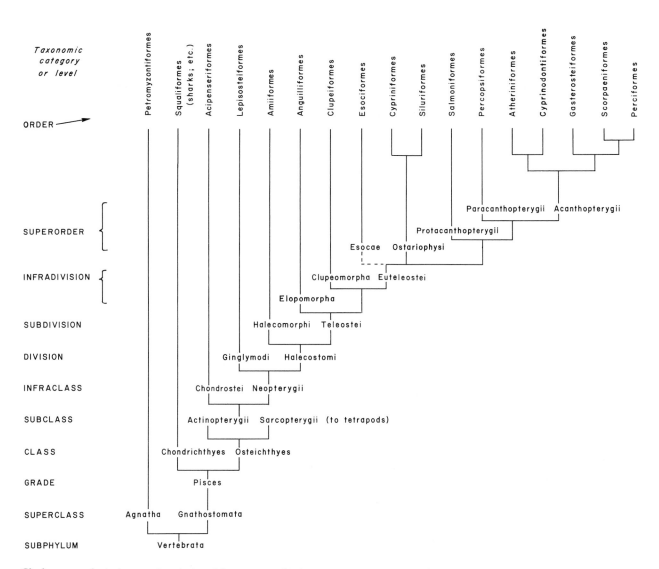

Cladogram of phylogenetic relationships among higher taxonomic groups of freshwater fishes treated in this book. Chondrichthyes and Squaliformes are added to show the evolutionary position of the major groups that include sharks and their allies. Sarcopterygii indicates the linkage of tetrapods (amphibians and higher vertebrates) to fishes. Dashed line indicates much uncertainty of placement of pikes and mudminnows (Esocae). Based chiefly on Patterson (1981), Lauder and Liem (1983), Nelson (1984), and Rosen (1985).

Histories and
Faunal Settings

INTRODUCTION

The Old Dominion is blessed with a diverse and rich aquatic heritage. Tumbling clear Blue Ridge brooks, the broad ancient New River, fertile streams of the Great Valley, the darkened Dismal Swamp, and the bountiful estuarine Chesapeake Bay and its riverine tributaries are a few of Virginia's features that collectively house a host of fishes. This treatise is the first synthetic and analytic catalogue of that fascinating piscine assemblage. We hope it fosters awareness, appreciation, and respect for our aquatic resources.

Presently 210 species of freshwater fishes are known to occur or have formerly resided within and along the boundaries of Virginia; adding subspecies, 230 taxa are tallied. Eleven of the species typically extend through estuaries, some of these into the Atlantic Ocean; all except the American eel spawn in fresh water. Six fishes are endemic to (i.e., known only from) Virginia—the roughhead shiner, rustyside sucker, Clinch sculpin, Roanoke logperch, and one subspecies each of the margined madtom and tessellated darter.

Eighteen of the 210 species are either clearly or possibly introduced, most of them to provide game or food. At least 10 more species were stocked but did not become established and thus are not included in the total. The absence of a formal description and hence lack of a scientific name for four species (a shiner and three sculpins) and four subspecies (a madtom, two sculpins, and a darter) indicates the imperfection of our knowledge of the fauna.

The 210 species are divided among 24 families; 78% of all species are minnows (67 species), suckers (18), catfishes (15), sunfishes (19), and perches (45, all but three of which are darters). The fauna includes primitive and advanced forms. Archaic fishes such as the lampreys, the paddlefish, and the longnose gar, whose near ancestors shared the planet with dinosaurs, live in some of the same streams with darters—small, evolutionarily advanced fishes fascinating in habit and splendid in color.

Most Virginia freshwater fishes are small and adapted to warm clear streams. Yet the fauna exhibits broad ranges of morphology, color, and life styles. The smallest species is the captivating orange, red, and blue Tippecanoe darter, an advanced fish whose adults are 25–35 mm (1.0–1.4 inches) in length and weigh less than one gram. The darter is a speck next to Virginia's largest fish, the primitive Atlantic sturgeon, whose adults typically attain 880–2,000 mm (2.9–6.6 feet) in length and 20–130 kg (40–290 pounds) in weight. The sight-feeding darter lives for only about one year in brawling current of clear upland rivers. The sturgeon is known to attain 60 years of age; it uses taste-bud-laden barbels to find food on murky estuary and ocean floors.

The diversity of the Virginia freshwater ichthyofauna reflects the wide variety of habitats, the geographic location of the state, and the partitioning of the fauna among 10 major separate drainages. Faunas of northern Atlantic drainages mix, particularly in the James and Roanoke drainages, with the more speciose southern assemblages. Many of the still greater variety of species in the Mississippi basin occupy the New and Tennessee drainages of western Virginia. Prehistoric modifications of the drainages have been an impetus to speciation; five drainages have fishes that occur nowhere else in the world.

The 210 Virginia species constitute one of the richest state faunas in North America. Of adjacent states, Maryland has 107 species (Lee et al. 1981; plus one sculpin), West Virginia 164 (Cincotta et al. 1986a), North Carolina 199 (E. F. Menhinick, in litt.; our adjustment), and Kentucky 242 (Burr and Warren 1986). The richest North American freshwater fish fauna is that of Tennessee, about 307 species including those introduced (D. A. Etnier, personal communication). In all, some 950 freshwater fishes occupy North America, south to southern Mexico (Gilbert 1976); this total includes many species which occur in estuarine habitats of Virginia but which are neither included in the 210 species nor treated herein.

The abodes and ecological roles of Virginia fishes are diverse. Fishes populate cold tumbling mountain streams, tepid dark-stained coastal swamps, and any healthy aquatic habitat in between. Some can tolerate quite inhospitable conditions whereas others are dependent on pristine environments. Few aquatic animal and plant species go uneaten by fishes.

Most Virginia fishes are of value to humans or to other species. About 25 species are important as game or food; accordingly, along with nonindigenous species, many native species have had their ranges greatly augmented by stocking. Although this book does not tell how to hook them, it reveals their habits and habitat preferences and may lend understanding to angling ventures. Nongame fishes serve as links in food webs; many of them are gaining favor as aquarium fishes. Undoubtedly some species have beneficial uses that await discovery.

Conservation is a theme of this book. Early literature, canvases of museums for fish records, and re-
cent surveys jointly reveal that, owing to the degradation of Virginia waterways, many fishes have been critically afflicted or endangered. Within the state, 45 species or subspecies—21% of the 217 native taxa—are precariously localized, very rare, extirpated (six taxa), or extinct (one). The Virginia populations of several other species are at lesser but still substantial risk. Twenty-one of the extant taxa are federally designated with or worthy of protective status over their full ranges. There is an urgent need for increased protection of biotas and their habitats.

This volume may seem to pose a final chapter to natural history study of inland Virginia fishes, but this is very far from true. We hope it stimulates and guides the further research needed. Careful observations by nature enthusiasts can contribute new knowledge of the fishes.

Virginia is indeed fortunate to have had its waters sampled by many prominent ichthyologists. Two of the greatest natural historians, Edward Drinker Cope and David Starr Jordan, seined here in the late 1800s. We have spent weeks studying Cope's and Jordan's words and specimens. In tracing their paths, maybe we have stood in the same place as they, eagerly searching a stream. We hope we have passed on what they so richly gave us, a spirit of inquiry.

HISTORY OF VIRGINIA
FRESHWATER ICHTHYOLOGY

The Old Dominion is rich in history, for its roots are deep in colonial time, beginning in 1607. The written record of its foodfishes begins with the writings of the early settlers. This literature and archeological studies (Rostlund 1952) indicate that fishes were important sustenance also for Native Americans in Virginia. Virginia's fishes have yielded to the nets of many of the greatest North American ichthyologists.

The formal study of Virginia fishes spans a relatively brief period, 125 years, compared with the 385-year nonnative peopling of the state (as of 1991). The biologist Andrews (1971) and zooarcheologist McDonald (1986) considered that Virginia, although having an early wealth of leaders and education, long remained impoverished in knowledge of the fauna and flora. However, the situation in Virginia's early times was little different from that prevalent in other areas; settlement and survival were utmost concerns. Over much of the world there also has been a major lag between early exploration or development of written communication on one hand and accurate recording of biotas on the other.

COLONIAL SETTLEMENT AND EXPANSION PERIOD, THROUGH 1866

Recorded knowledge of Virginia fishes probably stems from the first attempts by the English to settle North America—the "Lost Colony" on Roanoke Island behind North Carolina's Outer Banks. Promoted by Sir Walter Raleigh, five expeditions reached the island during 1584–1590 (Lefler and Newsome 1954; Quinn 1977). The last two attempts to maintain a colony ended with the mysterious disappearance of

all the settlers. Those of the first colony, 1585–1586, had all returned to England.

Included in the first group of returnees was the scientist Thomas Harriot (1560–1621). In reconnoitering the Outer Banks region, one of his journeys extended up the Chowan River into Virginia, thence to the Elizabeth River, a southern tributary of Chesapeake Bay. Harriot's report, *A Briefe and True Report of the New Found Land of Virginia*, was published in 1588 (Quinn 1977). Along with then-familiar types of fishes, mostly marine, he mentioned a true gar, obviously the longnose gar *Lepisosteus osseus* (Goode 1884–1886). Although Harriot may not have seen that fish in Virginia, that species is the first freshwater fish described from the state (in 1758).

The first Virginia colony was founded at Jamestown on the James River estuary in 1607. Its early leader, Captain John Smith (1580–1631), was a good observer and reporter. His map and description of Virginia were printed in 1612, his *General History* in 1624. An abundance of fishes was frequently noted during exploration from the James to the head of Chesapeake Bay (Arber and Bradley 1910). Among the fishes Smith mentioned were lamprey, sturgeon, eel, herring, shad, catfish, striped bass, and perches.

Late in the 17th century, John Banister (1650–1692) ventured through southeastern Virginia, studying primarily plants, mollusks, and insects. Goode (1884–1886) considered him to be one of the earliest and greatest representatives of the new school of naturalists in North America. One of Banister's botanic papers is the first systematic treatise of natural history to emanate from America. However, much of his work was appropriated and published piecemeal by others. His publications and manuscripts were brought to light and analyzed by Ewan and Ewan

(1970). Banister considered the fisheries of the lower James to be bounteous and briefly commented on habits, habitats, migrations, and harvesting of several species, these identified by folk names. Among these, E. C. Raney (*in* Ewan and Ewan 1970) recognized some 13 freshwater genera or species.

An improved list of fishes in middle eastern United States was authored by the explorer and naturalist John Lawson (?–1711) in 1709. The fishes were encountered on his sojourns within and his "long trail" through the Coastal Plain and Piedmont of North and South Carolina. He mentioned some mountain fishes, presumably on the word of other persons. He traveled as far north as the Tar River, the first major drainage south of the Roanoke (Lefler 1967). We recognize Lawson's contribution for the clues furnished to determining the native distribution of some species (e.g., largemouth bass and yellow perch). Some 23 freshwater genera or species are decipherable with varying degrees of certainty; Fowler (1945) made a separate analysis. Our study of the fishes section in John Brickell's *Natural History of North Carolina*, first published in 1737 (Parramore 1968), leaves no doubt that the writing was taken without credit from Lawson's treatise.

Mark Catesby (1683–1749), considered the most outstanding figure in American herpetology during the pre-Linnaean era (Martof et al. 1980), drew a longnose gar in Virginia sometime in the period 1712–1719 (Goode 1884–1886). Although he reached the foot of the Blue Ridge via the James River in 1714 (Frick and Stearns 1961), Catesby probably saw the gar in southeastern Virginia, where he resided. Peter Artedi, a Swede, based his description of a gar in 1738 on Catesby's rendition (Jordan and Evermann 1896). Finally, in the official start of binomial zoological nomenclature—10th edition of the *Systema naturae* (1758) by the Swedish naturalist Caroli Linnaeus (1707–1778)—Artedi's description was adopted and *Lepisosteus osseus* became the first freshwater fish named from Virginia.

In passing from the colonial and settlement periods, we note the great hiatus in time, some 150 years, from Catesby's gar to the beginning of solid contributions to knowledge of inland Virginia fishes by Edward Drinker Cope in 1867. Catesby's large folio, appearing in the period 1731–1743, remained the great work on natural history of North America for about 80 years (Myers 1964), but it chiefly concerned faunas south of Virginia. Through 1866, 123 of the 210 Virginia freshwater fishes had been described, but only the gar had been described as new from Virginia.

It is perhaps fortunate that the limited survey in the Ohio River basin by the naturalist Constantine Samuel Rafinesque did not extend into Virginia. Many of his sketchy descriptions in the 1820 *Ichthyologia Ohiensis* were long in nomenclatural litigation or are unidentifiable to species. However, the stories told by his biographers—earlier Jordan (1882) and others, recently Pearson and Krumholz (1984)—provide a glimpse of the conduct of science in what was then the frontier of Kentucky and environs.

FISHERIES AND OTHER AGENCIES

Since the 1870s, federal and Virginia state agencies have had major roles in the culture, dissemination, and management of game and foodfishes, but only in recent decades have they strongly influenced the development of knowledge of the Virginia ichthyofauna as a whole. The most notable early exception is the report of David Starr Jordan's survey in 1888.

The United States Fish Commission (USFC) had its beginning in 1870 under Spencer Fullerton Baird (1823–1887), its first Commissioner. The agency was the forerunner of the U.S. Bureau of Fisheries, now the U.S. Fish and Wildlife Service and the separate National Marine Fisheries Service. George Brown Goode (1851–1896), colleague of Baird and Assistant Secretary of the Smithsonian Institution in charge of the natural history museum, wrote extensively on systematics and economics of marine fishes. In 1876 the U.S. National Museum (USNM) was constituted within the Smithsonian with full federal financial support. It is now known as the National Museum of Natural History (Goode 1901a, 1901b).

In its early years the USFC sent out expeditions to all parts of the country and seas to accurately determine the nature and constituents of faunas. Many journeys were led or aided by ichthyologists from academic institutions. Collections forming the base of information for large areas literally flowed into the USNM. Many collections, notably those from Virginia by Jordan, were divided between the USNM and a few universities. However, USNM ichthyologists did not begin surveying Virginia beyond the national capitol region until the 1930s.

The federal Tennessee Valley Authority (TVA) was created in 1933 to control and develop water resources of that region (Anonymous 1964). Alvin R. Cahn directed its initial biological surveys (Cahn 1938a, 1938b), which reached into southwestern Virginia in 1937–1938. The great significance of the surveys in the 1930s and 1940s and the deposition of the resulting fish collections at the University of Michigan Museum of Zoology are noted in the account of *Erimystax cahni*. A small fraction of the specimens was passed by C. L. Hubbs of Michigan to the USNM. In 1968–1988 a wealth of information on Virginia fishes was obtained from intensive TVA surveys, many under the direction of Richard B. Fitz.

Since the 1970s the data base for this book has been augmented by fieldwork conducted by biologists of three other federal agencies—the Army Corps of Engineers, the Forest Service, and the Soil Conservation Service. Most of these efforts have occurred in areas of proposed or realized water-resource projects.

The variously titled Virginia Fish Commission (VFC) was inaugurated in 1875. Its early annual reports (VFC 1876–1882) mainly concern the status of foodfish resources and efforts to enhance these resources by culturing and stocking fish, building fishways, and enacting legislation. Considerable effort was expended by the VFC, in some cases jointly with the USFC, in introducing or transplanting exotic species, western salmonids, black basses, and others. Emphasis of the VFC was on foodfishes but angling for some species was occasionally noted in reports.

Early in its tenure the Virginia Fish Commission published little on details of foodfish and gamefish distribution; practically nothing was known of nongame species. Many comments in VFC reports are from correspondents or hearsay; there is no mention of Cope's benchmark survey in 1867. The two faunal reports, each a few lines long, are on fishes in the Blackwater and Nottoway rivers and those in the vicinity of Norfolk (VFC 1877a, 1877b). The VFC reports published after 1882 contain little of interest to freshwater ichthyology. Marine finfish and shellfish progressively dominated the work of the Commission, judging by reports through 1918 (fiscal year 1916–1917), the last of which we are aware.

In 1916 the Virginia Department of Game and Inland Fisheries was created as an adjunct of the VFC. In 1926 it was separated from the VFC and retitled the Commission of Game and Inland Fisheries (Stras 1949), and in 1987 again named the Virginia Department of Game and Inland Fisheries (VDGIF). The early reorganizations stemmed partly from public demand for augmented management of game animals and freshwater sport fishes, and from needs of other wildlife, hunters, and anglers.

The Fish Division of the VDGIF embarked to improve fisheries, acquire fishing waters, and to conduct river-pollution studies. It was chiefed by Gay W. Buller from 1930 to 1960, by Robert G. Martin during 1960–1967, by Jack M. Hoffman in 1967–1990, and is now headed by David K. Whitehurst. To our knowledge, its first distributed reports containing significant fish-distribution data are those authored by Martin (1953, 1954, 1955). The VDGIF financially supports

some research programs of the federal Cooperative Fish and Wildlife Research Unit (Fishery Unit) at Virginia Polytechnic Institute and State University (VPISU or Virginia Tech).

Much of the information on fish-community composition in this book was derived from surveys by the VDGIF and the Fishery Unit. Particularly valuable data sets were generated from western Virginia by Robert E. Wollitz (1965–1975b) and Robert F. Raleigh et al. (1978); from the upper James drainage in 1972–1973 (R. F. Raleigh, in litt.) and from the state trout survey during 1975–1978 by Larry O. Mohn, Paul H. Bugas, David A. Griffin, and others (Mohn and Bugas 1980); and from the Chowan drainage survey in 1982–1986 by Mitchell D. Norman and Ronald Southwick (1985, and later unpublished data). The statewide warmwater stream survey, directed by Paul L. Angermeier originally through the Fishery Unit, had its first fieldwork season in 1987; we include certain range extensions from the survey. The VDGIF financially supported some of the 1950s surveys by R. D. Ross.

Two salmonid hatcheries ("hatching houses") began operation in the first year of the VFC, 1875. Both were associated with schools at which the theory and practice of fish culture were taught. The Blacksburg Hatchery at VPISU was managed by Professor M. G. Ellzey and Fred Mather; apparently it operated briefly because we found no mention of it after 1877. Mather went on to achieve fame by rearing brown trout eggs in New York during 1883. The Lexington Hatchery at Virginia Military Institute was tended by Professor and Colonel Marshall McDonald. It produced fish at least into January 1880 (VFC 1882). In late 1877 or early 1878, McDonald became the only Commissioner of the VFC (three had shared the title since its inception), and soon his interest turned to the Wytheville hatchery.

The Wytheville hatchery began by rearing rainbow trout during the winter of 1881–1882. Ponds for raising warmwater fishes were added in 1884 or 1885 (VFC 1885). Under cooperative operation by the VFC and USFC, the hatchery quickly grew to be one of the best equipped of its time in America (VFC 1888; McDonald 1889). McDonald planned and guided the Wytheville facility while employed by the VFC and, by 1885, as a member (and soon Commissioner) of the USFC. In that year he also made an important series of fish collections in central and western Virginia.

Early reports of the VFC (1876–1882) list fish stockings made by both the VFC and USFC; scattered earlier stockings were noted by Milner (1874). From the 1880s into the early 1900s, warmwater and coldwater fishes were being distributed from the Central

Station Hatchery and the Fish Ponds (sometimes termed Carp Ponds), both operated by the USFC in Washington, D.C. (USFC 1876–1936).

FAUNAL INVENTORY AND STUDY

In 1876 Virginia was in an enviable position for the advancement of knowledge about its fishes. The just-founded U.S. National Museum was on its border, post-Civil War reconstruction was well underway, and Cope's entry to the field in 1867 had revealed a wealth of beautiful fishes. However, the USNM and USFC had a whole country and adjacent seas to explore, and the VFC soon turned its attention largely to marine resources.

Also in 1876 a one-column commentary entitled *The Freshwater Fish of Virginia* appeared in *Forest and Stream* (which became the venerable *Field and Stream* magazine), authored by Richard Whig. Fishes of mountains, estuaries, and intervening areas are mentioned by common name only; some 28 genera or species are decipherable. The list essentially is no improvement over Lawson's 1709 list.

It remained until 1960 for a nearly complete list (for the time) of the fishes of Virginia to be compiled by Hester C. Harrison and Robert G. Martin of the VDGIF. The list has 142 of the 210 species now known; a few others are erroneously reported.

The inventory of Virginia freshwater fishes is divisible into five periods (Maps 1–5). The earliest ichthyologists generally made the fewest collections, but we cannot overemphasize the importance of their archival material to the determination of native ranges and changes in distribution of species. Unfortunately many early (and recent) collections have sketchy, questionable, or apparently erroneous locality data.

1867–1899, Discovery Phase   Map 1

Few of the 123 Virginia freshwater fishes described through 1866 actually were known then from the state. The Discovery Phase incorporated the first plans for the collection and scientific study of inland Virginia fishes. As in many later surveys, the collections were examined elsewhere, there being no resident ichthyologist until 1951.

Edward Drinker Cope's (1840–1897) multipurpose sojourn, primarily zoological and geological, in Virginia during July–October 1867 marks the real start of scientific survey, description, and analysis of our fishes. Cope was associated with the Academy of Natural Sciences of Philadelphia and the University of Pennsylvania. For his many penetrating contributions to knowledge of fossil and living vertebrates,

Edward Drinker Cope

from fishes to mammals, he earned the title of "Master Naturalist." The journal *Copeia* of the American Society of Ichthyologists and Herpetologists is named for him. Some of Cope's fame derives from an often bitter rivalry with O. C. Marsh of Yale University, most notably involving the study of dinosaurs. Cope's life and writings are chronicled by Gill (1897), Frazer (1900), Osborn (1931), Case (1940), Myers (1940), Hubbs (1964a), and Romer (1964).

Cope's papers—*On the Distribution of Fresh-Water Fishes in the Allegheny Region of South-Western Virginia* (Cope 1868b), his other papers that consider Virginia fishes (Cope 1867, 1868a, 1869), and a treatise on the North Carolina ichthyofauna (1870)—have long been scrutinized by ichthyologists, principally for taxonomic and nomenclatural purposes. The proper dates of publication of these works were determined by Gilbert (1971). However, many of Cope's distributional records remained for us to verify, clarify, or reject, an opportunity afforded by Cope's maintenance of much of his fish collections, at times under difficult conditions (Böhlke 1984). Unfortunately a small amount of the locality data, some of it not in Cope's writing, is faulty, thus enforcing our cautious attitude to all of the data.

Cope took residence at apparently five places in Virginia, at least three of them being resorts associated with major springs. These spas were vacation and social centers of the time; some served later as lodging to McDonald and Jordan. We determined Cope's path from his 1868b report, letters to members of his family that were printed by Osborn (1931), and photocopies of original copies of the letters.

Cope collected almost entirely in montane streams: one or two each in the lower James, upper James, and upper Roanoke drainages; at least five in the New drainage; three in the Middle Fork Holston system; and two in the North Fork Holston system. His seining efforts at some sites were intensive: " . . . many times . . ." and " . . . for some miles at a time," (1868b). He learned of large-sized species by interviewing fishers. Cope reported 72 species or subspecies, the latter he termed varieties; at least 79 taxa (77 species, 2 with 2 subspecies each) occur in his preserved collections. Thirty-one taxa were described as new, of which only 13 still stand as species and 2 others may be valid subspecies. The other 16 taxa had previously been described from beyond Virginia, but this was not recognized by Cope.

Cope's enthusiasm for the uniqueness and beauty of the piscine riches of Virginia effuses from his letters and publications; his color illustrations are further testimony (Cope 1868b). He was particularly struck by the strange suckermouth minnows of western Virginia and mailed a description to the Philadelphia Academy; it was published separately as the inauguration of the genus *Phenacobius*.

It is a reflection of Cope's analytic and synthetic mind that, based on one foray in Virginia plus his keen awareness of fish distribution rudimentarily known in other regions, he (1868b) hypothesized ecological, geographical, and geological foundations for distribution patterns. He suggested that stream captures opened temporary aquatic routes of dispersal between headwaters of opposed drainages. Contrary to the statement by Jenkins et al. (1972), Cope did grasp the zoogeographical significance of capture, even though he lacked specific geological evidence in Virginia (see *Biogeography*). Cope was far ahead of his time.

Leaving Cope, we note that the 1876 report of the Maryland Commissioners of Fisheries contains a list and descriptions of the fishes of that state, authored by P. R. Uhler and Otto Lugger. Some 51 freshwater species are recognizable, the majority shared with Virginia. Some statements on the occurrence of species aid in determining the native fish fauna of Virginia; others cloud the issue because some of Uhler and Lugger's fishes came from fish markets, their actual origin unknown.

Among the early USNM collections are records from at least 15 Virginia or Washington, D.C., sites

David Starr Jordan

("others" on Map 1). Some of them were reported by Hugh M. Smith of the USFC and Tarleton H. Bean of the USNM (Smith and Bean 1899).

The second fish-collecting journey into Virginia was made in the summer of 1885 by Marshall McDonald, who had recently left the employ of Virginia to join the U.S. Fish Commission. Following the custom of federal workers at the time, McDonald placed his collections in the USNM. A letter from him dated 24 November 1885, now in the USNM accession files, affirms his interest in the distribution of species according to drainage and water temperature. At least 15 streams in four drainages were sampled, some of the sites more than once. Most sites were in small streams, which typically have fewer species than do large ones. We determined 42 species among the collections.

McDonald's collections represent important ichthyological pioneering, but in attempting to use the data it sometimes has been difficult to judge their validity. Apparently the collections were received by the USNM in four shipments; some were identified and cataloged in 1888, some not until 1945 (Miller 1946; our study). Locality data often are hazy; some data obviously are faulty, possibly caused by misinterpretation of labels at the USNM.

David Starr Jordan (1851–1931), first President of Stanford University, was one of the greatest American

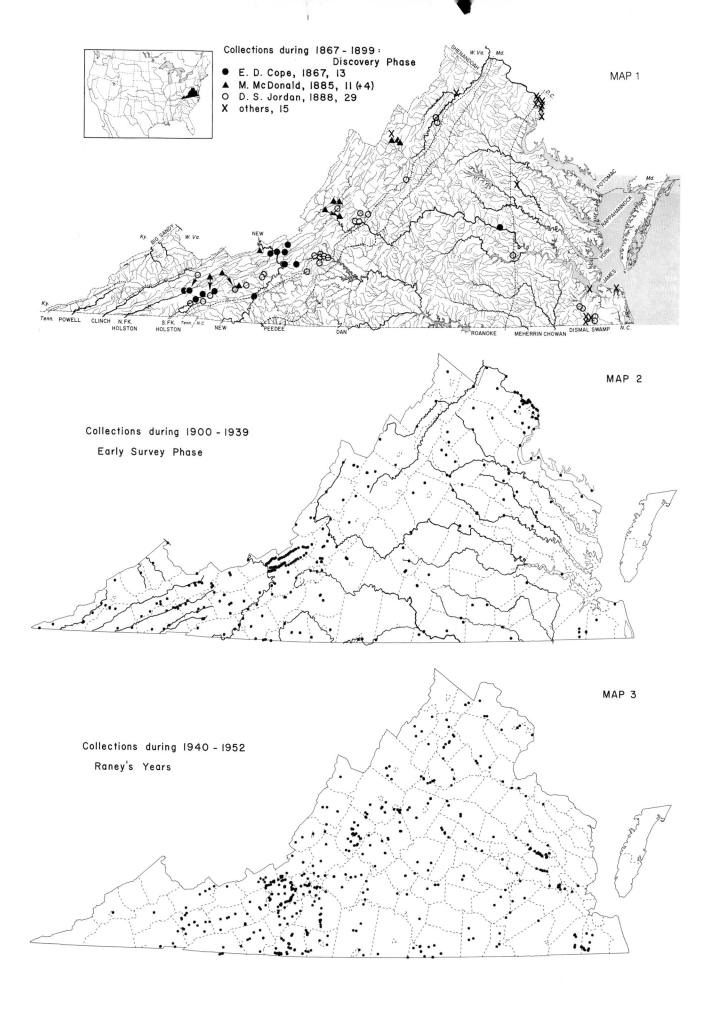

Collections during 1867 - 1899:
Discovery Phase

● E. D. Cope, 1867, 13
▲ M. McDonald, 1885, 11 (+4)
○ D. S. Jordan, 1888, 29
X others, 15

MAP 1

Collections during 1900 - 1939
Early Survey Phase

MAP 2

Collections during 1940 - 1952
Raney's Years

MAP 3

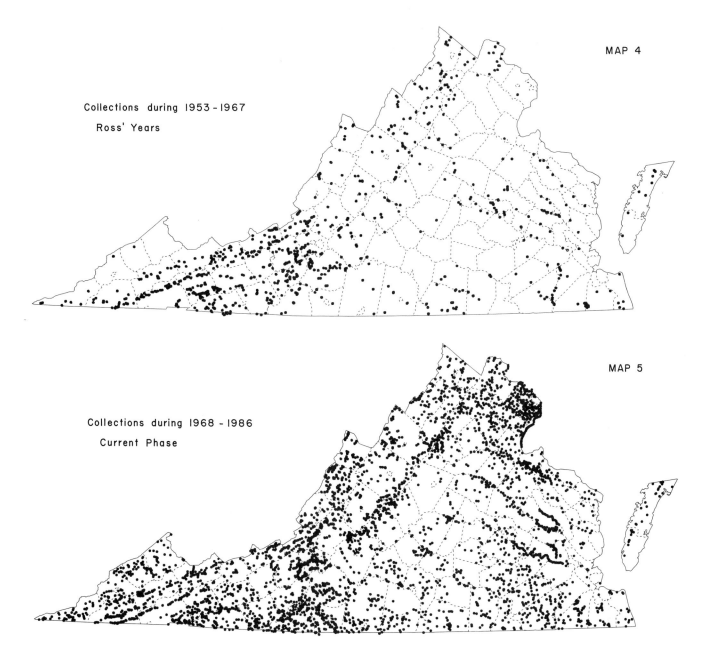

MAP 4

Collections during 1953–1967

Ross' Years

MAP 5

Collections during 1968 – 1986

Current Phase

Maps 1–5 Freshwater and estuarine sites represented by 9,821 fish collections from Virginia and a few immediately adjacent areas. Collections are divided among five periods of ichthyological survey (the full ranges of Raney's and Ross' years of collecting actually overlap, and Ross' also overlap with the current phase). Burton and Odum's (1945) collections (strings of dots on 1900–1939 map) were made in 1938–1941 but the exact year of most cannot be determined. On Map 1, the year of collecting and the number of collections follow the collector's name. Four of McDonald's 15 sites could not be located; several of his and a few other sites on Map 1 are located only approximately. Three twice-sampled sites in the western third of Map 1 are indicated by two symbols connected by an arrow point. In the upper James drainage, the arrow points to the fourth stream sampled by McDonald. Maps 2–5 were computer-printed by the BOVA (Biota of Virginia) system of the VDGIF, based on our data computerized through 1984. Map 5 includes several hand-plotted sites sampled in 1985–1987.

ichthyologists (Myers 1951; Hubbs 1964a, 1964b). Much of his life is expressed in the autobiography *The Days of a Man* (Jordan 1922). Jordan early plunged into the study of fishes and, unlike Cope, stayed almost entirely with it as his primary research. He was a

great teacher and attracted many bright students to ichthyology; he published with many of them. His *Manual of the Vertebrates*, aimed at students and the interested public, was first published in 1876 and went through 13 editions.

During the three summers of 1876–1878, Jordan and students set out from Butler University, Indiana, to explore the ichthyologically neglected streams of the southeastern United States. They traveled mostly by wagon and foot, crossing the western point of Virginia via Cumberland Gap, but likely did not collect in the state there. On the third trip while traversing Dismal Swamp on a small steamer, the party found the peculiar swampfish *Chologaster cornuta*, a tiny dark-water dweller whose closest relatives include the white eyeless cavefishes of the Mississippi basin.

During his tenure at Indiana University, Jordan was charged by G. B. Goode of the U.S. Fish Commission to begin a series of explorations of riverine fish faunas. Jordan carried this out with colleagues during the summers of 1884–1889, and (Jordan 1922) "By 1890 I had personally visited every considerable river basin in the United States."

Jordan's primary contribution to Virginia ichthyology stems from the journey made in 1888 for the USFC, then directed by M. McDonald. Jordan's party worked in the Potomac, James, Chowan, Dismal Swamp, Roanoke, and New drainages, and in the three branches of the Holston system. The 29 collecting sites shown in Map 1 allow that at least 3 were worked on the Roanoke River within current Roanoke or Salem city limits.

Jordan typically seined hard (Hubbs 1964b). The results compare well (in relatively unchanged streams) with the best of recent time. Thus his collections are exceptionally valuable in considering faunal changes during the past century. Jordan found numerous rare fishes and he and two colleagues were the only scientists to see the extinct harelip sucker *Moxostoma lacerum* in Virginia.

Jordan's venture yielded 111 species in Virginia, as determined by our analysis of his report and museum specimens. With colleagues or under sole authorship, he (1888, 1889a, 1889b) described 11 of these fishes as new, of which 2 were already named and 2 were hybrids. Jordan's species count is higher than Cope's 77 because he worked more than twice as many sites, sampled seven drainages compared with Cope's four, and his party was the first to sample the blackwaters of extreme southeastern Virginia.

In 1896–1900 the monumental four-volume work by Jordan and Barton W. Evermann entitled *The Fishes of North and Middle America* was published. This brought the North American fish fauna into a reasonable degree of order and completeness (Hubbs 1964a). Thus ended the "Golden Era" (1841–1892) of North American freshwater ichthyology, as revealed by the taxonomic history of the speciose darters and

shiners (Collette 1967; Gilbert 1978b). Jordan and colleagues then turned their primary attention away from North American fishes (Hubbs 1964a), ushering in a period of inactivity that lasted some 25 years.

During the Discovery Phase of Virginia ichthyology, 122 species had been captured by Cope, McDonald, or Jordan, although some were not recognized as species by them. Another 10 species were taken by other collectors. At least 72 collections had been made. Twenty-two valid species had been described as new from the state. Of the 210 (including 4 undescribed) freshwater species presently known from Virginia, 180 were described by 1899.

1900–1939, Early Survey Phase   Map 2

The term "Doldrums" applies to the largest part of this period, for of the 315 collections made in Virginia during 1900–1939, only 29 were in the first 28 years.

The early efforts include two collections from just within Virginia by William P. Hay, who during 1899–1900 directed a survey of West Virginia streams for the U.S. Bureau of Fisheries (Goldsborough and Clark 1908). Other early faunal reports, chiefly on lower Potomac drainage fishes by Bureau of Fisheries and USNM personnel, are by Evermann and Hildebrand (1910), Bean and Weed (1911), McAtee and Weed (1915), Truitt et al. (1929), and Radcliffe (1932). Hildebrand and Schroeder's (1928) benchmark *Fishes of Chesapeake Bay* includes many Virginia freshwater records. One of the most prolific ichthyologists ever, Henry Weed Fowler (1878–1965) of the Academy of Natural Sciences of Philadelphia, published (1918, 1922, 1923, 1945) species lists from Virginia collections made during 1915–1941, as well as a reanalysis of Cope's and others' materials. Some of the collecting into 1927 constituted detailed local canvases, but broad inland explorations had not been attempted since Jordan.

Carl Leavitt Hubbs (1894–1979), a student of Charles H. Gilbert and Jordan at Stanford, headed the "Reawakening" period of North American freshwater systematic ichthyology. While at the University of Michigan, with his many students and his wife Laura, he untangled many long-buried taxonomic problems, recognized and solved many new ones, and pioneered studies in geographic variation and hybridization. He had an incredibly keen taxonomic eye and was a great thinker and synthesizer (Norris 1974). His *Fishes of the Great Lakes Region* with Karl F. Lagler is a standard for that area.

As a small but significant part of his far-reaching expeditions, Hubbs made 31 collections from seven drainages in Virginia during 1928–1936. Apparently he also instructed Harold R. Becker to collect at Cope's and Jordan's North Fork Holston River site in 1928, so that fresh specimens could be compared with original descriptions of the species. Hubbs probably imbued the spirit of survey in D. Ameel and E. C. Sensening, who in 1931 and 1936 respectively each made eight collections and brought the samples to Michigan. Hubbs described three minnows and two darters and renamed another darter from materials obtained partly in Virginia.

The 1930s also saw a surge of interest in Virginia by Smithsonian ichthyologists. George Sprague Myers (1905–1985) left Stanford University in 1933 after close association with Jordan and colleagues and worked at the USNM before returning to Stanford in 1936. Myers was to gain fame especially from the study of South American freshwater fishes, from higher classification of fishes, and from worldwide zoogeographic studies (Cox 1988).

In 1933 and 1935 Myers made 22 collections from 10 Virginia drainages, missing only the Clinch–Powell system of the Tennessee drainage and the Big Sandy drainage. Apparently it was then generally recognized that wide-spaced efforts would more likely reveal the nature of a regional fauna than would concentrated sampling. Collaborating with Myers were Stuart Abraham and Earl D. Reid, who each made 11 separate collections during 1933–1935.

Leonard P. Schultz followed Myers at the National Museum and into Virginia. In 1937–1938 with Reid, he took 51 samples, skipping the Potomac drainage but collecting in the Powell and Big Sandy. Schultz (1939) wrote a short paper on highlights of the trips. Around this time he was obtaining records of Virginia fishes from Hubbs and summarizing National Museum holdings and literature in preparation for a treatise on the freshwater and marine fishes of Virginia. Eventually Schultz turned over his data to E. C. Raney, who passed them to us in 1976.

Closing the first 40 years of the present century, one of the initial attempts to determine distributional patterns of fishes within individual streams was conducted in the James and New drainages by George W. Burton, a Danville, Virginia, high school principal. He studied under Eugene P. Odum at the Mountain Lake Biological Station, and they published jointly (Burton and Odum 1945). The fieldwork, at 64 sites in 5 streams, took place during 1938–1941. Most collections are not specifically dated; all are plotted, resembling lines of dots, on Map 2. Hubbs studied some of the fishes; Burton and Odum identified the rest, using as comparative material specimens determined by Hubbs. Burton and Odum's paper has been widely cited as an early model analysis of local fish

Edward Cowden Raney

distribution, but their collecting techniques did not result in a strong data base (Lachner and Jenkins 1971a; Matthews 1986a; *Scartomyzon cervinus* account).

The Early Survey Phase is the period of the most even-spread collecting in Virginia. All major drainages were sampled and all physiographic provinces were represented. Still, and as would follow, most of the effort was expended in the mountains and in the Washington, D.C., area. The overall effort since collecting began in 1867 remained quite light—about 387 collections.

1940–1952, Raney's Years   Map 3

Edward Cowden Raney (1909–1984) is synonymous with the renowned ichthyology program which he built at Cornell University after taking graduate degrees there (Anonymous 1984). He is part of the Jordan lineage through collaboration with Hubbs at the University of Michigan. Raney attracted many students; 56 took advanced degrees under him, many of whom made their own ichthyological mark. As a tribute to Raney, and in allusion to the prominence both of the man in his field and of a large Virginia minnow over its nest, Lachner and Jenkins (1971a) named that fish the bull chub *Nocomis raneyi*.

Raney began his higher academic program with the investigation of the fishes of the upper Ohio basin and soon recognized that unsettled systematic problems and fertile fields of discovery lay south. From 1940 to 1956, interrupted only by the war years, he journeyed south with students in spring or summer to collect and observe fishes. In the early years considerable emphasis was on Virginia, in some of the mid-years emphasis was farther south. During 1953–1956 his efforts in the state were largely devoted to estuarine striped bass.

Raney made 216 of the 408 collections taken in Virginia during 1940–1952 and made 51 more in the state through 1956. Mostly with coauthors, he described three suckers from the upper Roanoke drainage, a minnow, and a darter as new species; to clarify the nomenclature of the stripeback darter, he renamed it. His 1950 treatise on the freshwater fishes of the James drainage is the first comprehensive drainage-wide treatment for Virginia. As was Hubbs, Raney was widely known as an expert identifier of fishes, and many scientists sent him fishes for that service.

Ernest Albert Lachner (1915–) collaborated on Raney's first three Virginia trips and, chiefly to collect *Nocomis* chubs, made other forays through Virginia. Lachner made 100 collections during 1940–1952, 3 more into 1958, and in 1964 he began intensive observations of the nest-building *Nocomis*. Since 1947 he has advised many ichthyologists who visited his office in the USNM.

Organized in 1944, the Virginia Fisheries Laboratory (Newcombe 1946), now the Virginia Institute of Marine Science (VIMS), had begun by 1949 to explore the upper ends of estuaries. Through 1952, Jay D. Andrews and William H. Massmann made at least 19 and 37 collections applicable to our study, many of them from Dismal Swamp in which they had special interest (Andrews 1971). Data from Andrews' preimpoundment survey of Kerr Reservoir tributaries are particularly valuable. Much of the estuarine data we used are from a few recent years of the VIMS Trawl Survey.

Several other persons made collections during 1940–1952 and usually deposited them at Cornell or Michigan. The list of these persons and those in later periods has grown too long to cite all but the main contributors. By the mid-1950s the estuarine and Piedmont faunas had become much better known, but the freshwater Virginia portion of the Delmarva Peninsula had not been sampled and the rich fauna of the Clinch–Powell system remained largely untouched. The Clinch–Powell was being missed partly because Highway Route 11 shunted collectors from the Holston system into the faunally rich streams of Tennessee. The Big Sandy drainage was being dev-

Ernest Albert Lachner

astated by coal mining; several species probably were becoming extirpated without trace.

1953–1967, Ross' Years   Map 4

Robert Donald Ross (1910–1983) studied under E. C. Raney at Cornell University, arrived at the Department of Biology of VPISU in 1951, and quickly began amassing the first major in-state collection of freshwater fishes—the VPI collection, as separate from the VPIFU (Fishery Unit) collection. In 1952 he joined Raney and his class in forays radiating from the Mountain Lake Biological Station. Of Virginia collections, we have records of 810 made by Ross with Raney in 1946 and 1952 and with other colleagues and students during 1951–1973. Some 364 more collections were taken separately by his students, thus totaling 1,174 samples from the state.

Ross was an energetic collector into the early 1970s; his general strategy was to "find most fishes that are here" and to gather specimens for taxonomic analysis. His fieldwork was concentrated in the mountainous areas of Virginia and the upper Piedmont, but he made a substantial number of collections in the lower Piedmont and Coastal Plain in the southern one-third of the state. Although he disfavored working in mucky Coastal Plain conditions, Dismal Swamp

Robert Donald Ross

William Starnold Woolcott

fishes were an allure. In the late 1960s his program became partly geared to others at VPISU, such as pollution and preimpoundment studies.

Ross was generous with his fish collection; he donated to or exchanged much material with other institutions, chiefly Cornell and the USNM. After he retired from VPISU, the bulk of the collection was transferred to the American Museum of Natural History (AMNH). Records of the earlier transfers often were not kept, and one must hunt beyond the AMNH for some material.

Ross was in particular a historical zoogeographer. His inspiring seminars often concerned stream capture and speciation of fishes, of which abundant evidence exists in the region (Map 12). Ross' geological leaning led him to recognize or interpret much of the physiographic evidence of captures (e.g., Ross 1969, 1972a; Ross and Carico 1963). Many of his students were drawn to zoogeography (e.g., Jenkins et al. 1972; Hocutt 1979a, 1979b; Hocutt et al. 1978, 1986). The monumental synthesis *The Zoogeography of North American Freshwater Fishes* edited by C. H. Hocutt and E. O. Wiley (1986) was dedicated to Ross.

William Starnold Woolcott (1922–) gained a solid introduction to Virginia fishes during 1952–1955 while making 93 collections in the state with Raney. Since 1956 Woolcott has directed a program in life history and systematics of fishes at the University of Richmond. From there he made 191 collections and his students made 88 others that we have used. For the first time in a major field program, collections were concentrated in the mid-latitudes of Virginia's Piedmont. Also, during the early 1970s Woolcott directed a study for the Virginia Institute of Scientific Research on the middle James River in the vicinity of the Bremo Power Station. Some 285 transect samples were made at nine sites, revealing for the first time the true composition of a Piedmont reach of Virginia's longest river (Woolcott et al. 1974; White et al. 1977; Maurakis and Woolcott 1984).

1968–1990, Current Phase   Map 5

Some 2,100 collections had been made in Virginia during the 101-year period ending in 1967. Over the next 23 years somewhat over 7,900 more were made. The increase in effort was precipitated partly by the sharp increase in environmental awareness. As a result, pre- and post-construction surveys (e.g., in relation to impoundment and channelization projects) and pollution monitoring have been undertaken more frequently. Public demand for enhanced recreational fisheries has led to greater emphasis on general stream and lake sampling in order to comprehend entire fish communities of which gamefishes are only part. Concern for endangered species prompted surveying by several governmental agencies; funding of endangered species projects extended to the academic sector (Burkhead and Jenkins 1991). A clear need remained to collect and observe fishes in systematic studies. These activities yielded distributional data on entire ichthyofaunas of particular bodies of water.

Robert Ellis Jenkins (1940–) studied under R. D. Ross at VPISU during 1961–1963, worked with E. A. Lachner on *Nocomis* at the USNM for one year, and then was a student under E. C. Raney at Cornell. In 1968 he returned to his undergraduate school, Roanoke College. He and his former wife Diane, who aided early stages of this book, first settled along Back Creek at Poages Mill, where Jordan had collected 81 years before. They made a collection as soon as the seine was uncovered in the moving van. While at Cornell, R. Jenkins projected, if properly located and feasible, to undertake a major treatise on the freshwater fishes of Virginia. He was fortunate to land at Roanoke College, for it is nearly centrally located in the state, within a 2-hour drive of six major drainages.

Noel Martin Burkhead (1950–) entered Roanoke College as a freshman in 1968, expressed interest in biological fieldwork of most any kind, and immediately teamed with Jenkins. Subtracting Burkhead's years at the University of Tennessee for a Master's degree, and working for Ichthyological Associates, Inc. (headed by Raney), he was at Roanoke for 13 years.

In 1968, undescribed forms were known in Virginia, large gaps in distributional information existed, and some species seemed to be declining. The tasks were set at Roanoke College for a program in systematics, zoogeography, and life history of fishes with emphasis on scarce species. Thus (beginning modestly in 1961) Jenkins made 897 collections or observations in Virginia. The observations comprise careful identification (from above or under water) of fishes; most of them include recording of habitat associations, feeding behavior, or reproductive activity. Burkhead shared on 382 of these occasions, and at 263 other times he separately made collections or observations. Our former students and later collaborators at Roanoke, William H. Haxo and Stephen P.

McIninch, took 86 more collections. These efforts amount to 1,246 collections through 1990.

Through 1982 many of the efforts from Roanoke College were centered on a few streams or areas, or on one or a few species. However, in nearly all of these cases we attempted to obtain a complete or nearly complete species inventory at the sites. This strategy left many data gaps for several parts of the state, to which we had been pointing other workers since 1970 (and studying their collections). During 1983–1986 we filled in some of the few remaining gaps.

During the two academic years 1977–1979, Jenkins was at Virginia Commonwealth University, and with students D. L. James and H. P. Petrimoulx surveyed southeastern and south-central Virginia streams. In that period, William J. Matthews and students at Roanoke College conducted detailed ecological studies of upper Roanoke drainage fishes, thus providing much of the basis for understanding the biology of that fauna.

The more intensive sampling from 1968 onward added relatively few species to the Virginia list, now standing at 210. Harrison and Martins' (1960) compilation included 142 of the species, and by the end of 1967, 41 more had been added. Thus 27 species were discovered or otherwise recognized in the state during the 23 years through 1990.

Many of the recent collections are from intensive surveys of particular streams and reservoirs, but much of the sampling has remained exploratory. Overall, our knowledge greatly deepened. Now, instead of simply knowing that a species occupies a drainage, generally we are able to recognize its pattern of distribution and abundance; often we can relate these to historical and current factors. The progression in regional distributional knowledge is documented by Jenkins et al. (1972), Stauffer et al. (1982), Hocutt et al. (1986), Table 2, and *Appendix 2.*

Forty-one valid species were described as new from Virginia, 22 of them prior to 1900. Three of these were announced during 1930–1939, seven in 1940–1959, four during 1960–1969, three in 1970–1980, and two after the first complete draft for this book was finished, in early 1987. Four species remain undescribed. Of the 210 species recorded from the state, 1 is extinct and 5 (and 1 subspecies) are extirpated. We hope that Virginia loses no more and that no undesirable nonnative fishes are gained.

Harrells Mill Pond, Blackwater River system, Chowan River drainage, Sussex County. An impoundment of Coppahaunk Swamp, on the Coastal Plain; lined by bald cypress and populated by swampfish, lined topminnow, bluespotted sunfish, and blackbanded sunfish.

PLATE 1

Unnamed tributary of Nottoway Swamp, Chowan River drainage, Southampton County. A dense black-gum swamp on the Coastal Plain; home to the pirate perch, swampfish, mud sunfish, and swamp darter.

Appomattox River, James River drainage, Amelia County. A sluggish medium-sized Piedmont river; occupied by swallowtail shiner, black crappie, redbreast sunfish, and an expanding population of the introduced spotted bass.

PLATE 2

Namozine Creek, Appomattox River system, James River drainage, Amelia County. A small, muck- and sand-bottomed, Piedmont creek; inhabited by chain pickerel, mosquitofish, flier, and pumpkinseed.

James River in the Fall Zone, Richmond. An ecological "island" of upland habitat and home of trophy smallmouth bass.

PLATE 3

Upper James River, Botetourt County. The magnificent James in the Valley and Ridge Province; resided by bull chub, channel catfish, white catfish, flathead catfish, rock bass, redbreast sunfish, and smallmouth bass.

Lower Craig Creek, James River drainage, Craig County. A nearly pristine stream in the Valley and Ridge Province; inhabited by chain pickerel, bull chub, roughhead shiner, creek chubsucker, black jumprock, orangefin madtom, and smallmouth bass.

PLATE 4

Upper Roanoke River, Roanoke County, in the Valley and Ridge Province. Supports the crescent and white shiners, bigeye jumprock, orangefin madtom, and Roanoke logperch.

Roaring Run, Smith River system, Roanoke drainage, Franklin County. A "dace-sized" stream in the Blue Ridge housing native brook trout and a naturalized population each of brown and rainbow trout.

PLATE 5

Lower Wolf Creek, New River drainage, Giles County, in the Valley and Ridge Province. Home to the tonguetied minnow, bigmouth chub, northern hogsucker, mottled and banded sculpins, and smallmouth bass.

PLATE 6

Big Stony Creek, New River drainage, Giles County, at the fringe of the Valley and Ridge and the Appalachian Plateau provinces. Prime residence of the brilliantly colored candy darter; also fine habitat for the longnose dace, rosyside dace, mottled sculpin, and stocked trouts.

Clinch River, Tennessee River drainage, Scott County, at Speers Ferry in the Valley and Ridge Province. Supports the most species-rich fauna in Virginia—more than 50 fish species, some jeopardized, live here.

PLATE 7

Mossy Creek, Shenandoah River system, Potomac drainage, Augusta County. A heavily vegetated, long, high-volume spring run, harboring an abundance of pearl dace, brown trout, and slimy sculpin.

Tributary of Pound River, Big Sandy River drainage, Wise County. A highly modified stream in the coal-mining area of the Appalachian Plateau; banks exposed and covered with strip-mine spoilage; the bottom severely silted; populated by stoneroller, creek chub, and blacknose dace.

PLATE 8

DRAINAGES, PHYSIOGRAPHY, AND FISH HABITATS OF VIRGINIA

Virginia's waters are carried by 10 major drainages and, in the eastern part of the state, many minor drainages. Five physiographic provinces are drained, which as a whole have diverse topography, lithology, geochemistry, hydrology, and climate. Bodies of water range from cold, cascading, mountain brooks to warm, wide, and deep estuaries; the majority are warm, moderate-gradient streams. The state has only two natural lakes, but thousands of farm ponds and mill ponds, many medium-sized impoundments, and 13 large reservoirs have been created. There are a few special habitats, such as Dismal Swamp and large springs. The habitats available to Virginia fishes comprise about as many different kinds as are found in any other area of similar size in North America.

Descriptions of drainages, physiographic provinces, and aquatic habitats are given below. The drainages, provinces, some large streams and rivers, the natural lakes and larger impoundments, and principal political units are identified in Maps 6–11. Characteristic habitats of the physiographic provinces are shown in Plates 1–8. The *Biogeography* section couples further descriptions of drainages with interpretive analyses of fish distribution. Under *References* at the end of *Biogeography* are citations of ichthyofaunal papers that include descriptions of drainages and streams. Characteristics and water-resource history of the drainages of Virginia are treated in detail in two series of water-supply bulletins (VDCED 1966–1972; VSWCB 1988a), which are summarized by Sevebeck et al. (1986) and the VSWCB (1988b).

Three terms are hierarchically used for hydrographic entities (Jenkins et al. 1972):

Basin—A major group of interconnected drainages; for example, the Mississippi basin. The Ohio River with its tributary drainages, one of the largest divisions of the Mississippi basin, is also considered a basin.

Drainage—A group of interconnected streams whose main channel enters an ocean, an estuary, or the main stem of a basin; for example, the New River drainage (of the Ohio River basin). Small drainages such as those entirely on the outer Coastal Plain are classed as minor drainages.

System—A division of a drainage; for example, the Reed Creek system (of the New River drainage). A subsystem is a division of a system; for example, the South Fork Reed Creek subsystem. Where clarity is not compromised, subsystems are called systems. The modifier "proper" often is applied to a division of a drainage that includes the main stem of the drainage; for example, the Roanoke system proper, which excludes the Dan River system of the Roanoke drainage.

The term watershed refers to the land and waters, both surface and underground, of a hydrographic unit. Thus a watershed is all water-collecting and water-distributing parts of a basin, drainage, or system, within the horizontal and vertical limits of its divides.

SETTING AND CLIMATE

A central Atlantic coastal state, Virginia lies between 36° and 40° north latitude and 75° and 84° west longitude. Its maximum east–west length is 684 km (425 miles); maximum north–south length is 322 km (200 miles). The total area of 105,716 km^2 (40,817

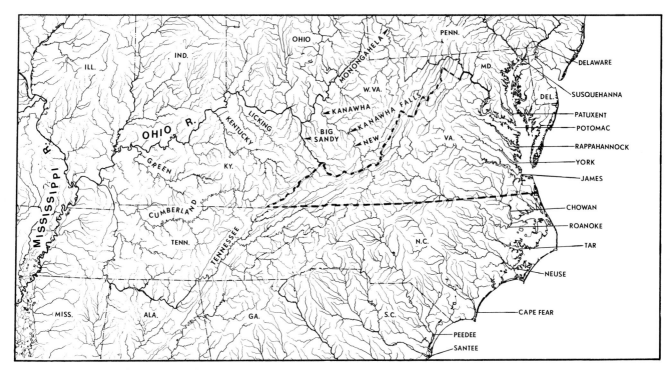

Map 6   Drainages of Virginia and adjacent regions.

miles²) includes 2,686 km² (2.5%) of inland waters. Elevation peaks at 1,746 m (5,729 feet); mean elevation is 290 m (950 feet).

The climate is moderate temperate; winters generally are mild, summers are humid and warm to hot. Mean seasonal temperatures are 3°C (37°F) in winter and 23°C (74°F) in summer. Mean annual precipitation is 1,090 mm (43 inches); the state is well watered by surface channels. The growing season ranges from 240 days in southeastern Virginia to 150 days in the mountains.

The dominant forest types are the southeastern pine in the southeastern part of the state, pine and deciduous hardwood over much of the Piedmont, and deciduous hardwood on the upper Piedmont and westward. Some higher mountains have stands of spruce, some with fir.

The 1982 estimate of 5,500,000 human inhabitants in Virginia averages to 52 persons/km² (135/mile²) (Colliers Encyclopedia 1984; Tiner 1987; Encyclopedia Americana 1986).

The following descriptions refer only to the Virginia portion of drainages and physiographic provinces, unless stated otherwise. Extralimital parts of the drainages are shown in Map 6.

DRAINAGES OF VIRGINIA   Maps 6 and 7

The Atlantic–Gulf divide in Virginia separates major drainages that flow generally eastward to the At-

lantic Ocean from those that flow northward or westward to the Ohio River. Of the 10 major drainages in the state, 7 are on the Atlantic slope; from north to south, they are the Potomac, Rappahannock, York, James, Chowan, Roanoke, and Pee Dee. The first four are part of the Chesapeake Bay basin. The three drainages of the Ohio River basin are the New, Tennessee, and Big Sandy.

Potomac Drainage

The portion of the Potomac watershed in Virginia is 14,778 km² in surface area, 39% of the whole Potomac watershed; the remainder is in Pennsylvania, Maryland, and West Virginia. The Coastal Plain section is quite narrow in Virginia, distinctly larger in Maryland. The tidal lower Potomac River is 230 rkm in length; the middle section is 88 rkm, through the Piedmont to the Shenandoah River mouth just above the Blue Ridge. Several middle Potomac tributaries in the Piedmont arise on the east front of the Blue Ridge.

The Shenandoah system is the largest division of the Potomac in Virginia. Almost entirely in the Valley and Ridge Province, it has a series of small tributaries tumbling off the west side of the Blue Ridge. The Shenandoah system is partitioned into the large North Fork and South Fork subsystems and the smaller lower Shenandoah subsystem. The system meanders through the Valley and Ridge for 330 rkm, from the headwaters of the North River of the South Fork through the lower segment of the Shenandoah River in West Virginia.

Two Valley and Ridge portions of the upper Potomac system proper (above the Shenandoah mouth) drain Virginia and cross into West Virginia. The portion in the small northern area just west of the lower Shenandoah River flows directly to the Potomac River. The few short, cool or cold streams heading in Highland County go to the South Branch Potomac River.

Rappahannock and York Drainages

Of all the major Virginia drainages, only the Rappahannock (7,032 km^2) and York (6,892 km^2) occur entirely within the state. Both drain the Coastal Plain and Piedmont; only the Rappahannock heads in the Blue Ridge and has true montane habitat. The tidewater portion of the Rappahannock River extends 172 rkm; another 23 rkm of the river is in the Fall Zone or Piedmont. The head of the Rapidan River, the large southerly tributary, is 129 rkm above its mouth. The York River is formed by union of the Mattaponi and Pamunkey rivers, and the Pamunkey River by juncture of the North Anna and South Anna rivers. From the source of the South Anna, the drainage flows 351 rkm.

James Drainage

This drainage is nearly wholly within Virginia; only a short segment of each of two streams originates in West Virginia. The watershed encompasses 26,164 km^2, just over 25% of the total area of Virginia. The main channel of 696 rkm is the longest in the state. The James River takes its name at the confluence of the Cowpasture and Jackson rivers near Clifton Forge; 151 rkm of the Jackson are included in the total length. Major portions of the drainage are in the Coastal Plain (including 171 rkm of the James River), Piedmont, and Valley and Ridge; many tributaries drop from the Blue Ridge.

The lower James has two large tributaries. The 132-rkm Chickahominy River is almost entirely on the Coastal Plain. The 258-rkm Appomattox River, the largest southern tributary, arises in hills of the upper Piedmont, flows almost entirely through that province, and has a short section on the Coastal Plain.

Chowan Drainage

This watershed has three major systems jointly covering 10,518 km^2 of southeastern Virginia. The Blackwater River system lies entirely on the Coastal Plain; the Nottoway and Meherrin river systems arise in the central Piedmont. The Blackwater (143 rkm) and Nottoway (249 rkm) rivers join at the North Carolina line to form the Chowan River. After traversing 201 rkm of Virginia and 61 rkm of North Carolina, the Meherrin meets the Chowan River at Rkm 66 of the Chowan. The mouth of the Chowan in Albemarle Sound is near that of the Roanoke River; zoogeographically the Chowan sometimes has been considered part of the Roanoke drainage.

Roanoke Drainage

The 16,276 km^2 of the Roanoke watershed in south-central Virginia represent about 16% of the area of the state and 64% of the total watershed area shared with North Carolina. The Roanoke River flows from the head of its South Fork for 449 rkm in Virginia, then 262 rkm in North Carolina to Albemarle Sound. The Coastal Plain reach of the Roanoke is entirely in North Carolina; in Virginia the drainage occupies a wide portion of the Piedmont, much more than in North Carolina. The Blue Ridge and Valley and Ridge divisions of the upper Roanoke are entirely in Virginia. The name Staunton River has been long applied to the reach of the Roanoke River between the Dan River mouth and the Blue Ridge (Ginther 1968); however, we refer to all of the river from the upper forks at Lafayette, Montgomery County, Virginia, to the mouth as the Roanoke River.

The large southern division of the Roanoke drainage, the approximately 193-rkm Dan River system, has four major tributary systems that we often refer to separately. From east to west they are the Banister River, Smith River, Mayo River, and upper Dan River systems. The Smith, Mayo, and Dan head on the Blue Ridge; the Hyco River is the largest tributary entering the lower Dan River from the south; it is mostly in North Carolina.

Pee Dee Drainage

This drainage is almost entirely in North and South Carolina, having only 303 km^2 in the Blue Ridge and extreme upper Piedmont of south-central Virginia. The Virginia tributaries are part of the Ararat River system, which is the eastern end of an arc of streams that arises on the Blue Ridge Escarpment and feeds the Yadkin River. Owing to its small area in Virginia, this part of the Pee Dee does not qualify as a major drainage in the state; it is given that status because of the overall large size of the drainage and because five or more taxa occupy Virginia only in the Pee Dee.

Minor Atlantic Drainages

Delmarva Peninsula and the "necks" of the western Chesapeake basin have separate minor drainages, the longest being the 99-rkm Piankatank River drainage between the Rappahannock and York. Dismal Swamp, in the southeastern corner of the state, is a distinctive entity but is not considered a separate drainage; its waters presently flow north, east, and south into other drainages or basins.

New Drainage

The New River arises in North Carolina, cuts overall north across Virginia, and flows northwestward through southern West Virginia. Its continuation in West Virginia from the mouth of the Gauley River to the confluence with the Ohio River is named the Kanawha River. However, in ichthyological literature Kanawha Falls just below the Gauley River mouth marks the downstream end of the New River and its distinctive fish fauna. The New drains 7,951 km² of Virginia, a much lesser area of North Carolina, and a major portion of West Virginia; the total area is 18,085 km². Lengths include 121 rkm for the South Fork and 6 rkm for the uppermost New River in North Carolina, 245 rkm for the New River in Virginia (including the short loop back into North Carolina), and 127 rkm for the New in West Virginia.

In Virginia much of the upper (southern) half of the watershed is on the New River Plateau. Smaller sections of that half drain other, higher-relief divisions of the Blue Ridge (see *Blue Ridge*, below) (Map 7). The rest of the drainage in Virginia courses the Valley and Ridge, except for two tributary systems. Laurel Fork, a Bluestone River tributary west of the New River, heads on the Appalachian Plateau escarpment; feeders of Big Stony Creek, an eastern tributary, also drain that escarpment.

Tennessee Drainage

Flowing from southwestern Virginia are the upper portions of the Holston River and Clinch River systems, the uppermost of several large tributaries of the 1,050-rkm Tennessee River. The Tennessee watershed has 8,109 km² of its area in Virginia. The Holston has three primary branches, the South, Middle, and North forks; their lengths in Virginia are 84, 92, and 217 rkm.

The Middle Fork joins the South Fork at about the upper end of South Holston Reservoir. The South Fork continues into Tennessee and receives the Watauga River system of North Carolina and Tennessee,

then turns north to merge with the North Fork a few rkm below the Virginia line, thereby forming the Holston River. The forks lie in the Valley and Ridge except for southern tributaries of the South Fork which arise in the highest portion of the Blue Ridge in the state and in a north-fringing, high-relief area.

In the Virginia portion of the Clinch system, the Clinch River is 251 rkm long and the Powell River is 182 rkm. The Powell loses its name to the Clinch River at their juncture in Tennessee, where they are impounded as Norris Reservoir. The system courses largely through the Valley and Ridge; many northern feeders arise on the escarpment of the Appalachian Plateau.

Big Sandy Drainage

Flowing northwestward to the Ohio River, this watershed in the Appalachian Plateau comprises 2,613 km² of Virginia. The four main trunks in the state or along the West Virginia line are, west to east, the Russell Fork, Levisa Fork, Knox Creek, and Tug Fork. The Russell Fork system is the longest in the state; its 126-rkm length includes the Pound River.

PHYSIOGRAPHIC PROVINCES AND HABITATS   Map 7

From east to west, the five physiographic (or geomorphic) provinces of inland Virginia are the Coastal Plain, Piedmont, Blue Ridge, Valley and Ridge, and Appalachian Plateau. The Fall Zone also is recognized as a distinct topographic unit. Geologically, all of these provinces except the Coastal Plain are part of the Appalachian Mountains. Whether of high or low relief, the Appalachians are that belt in eastern North America where Precambrian and Paleozoic rocks were deformed in Paleozoic time. They lie between the flat-bedded Paleozoic rocks of the interior, and the Coastal Plain where undeformed Cretaceous and younger sediments bury the older rocks.

The descriptions of provinces and habitats are from our field experience, map study, and the following mostly comprehensive papers: Broad references—Fenneman 1938; Thornbury 1965; Hoffman 1969; Dietrich 1970a; Rodgers 1970; Hunt 1974; Simmons and Heath 1979; Woodward and Hoffman 1991. Coastal Plain—Clark and Miller 1912; Wentworth 1930; Richards and Judson 1965; Richards 1967, 1974, 1975; Brown et al. 1972; Oaks and Coch 1973; Onuschak 1973; Teifke 1973; Newell 1985. Fall Zone—Hack 1982. Piedmont and Blue Ridge—Dietrich 1959; Hack 1969, 1980, 1982; Judson 1975; King 1975; Rankin 1975; Conley 1978; Pavich 1985. Valley and

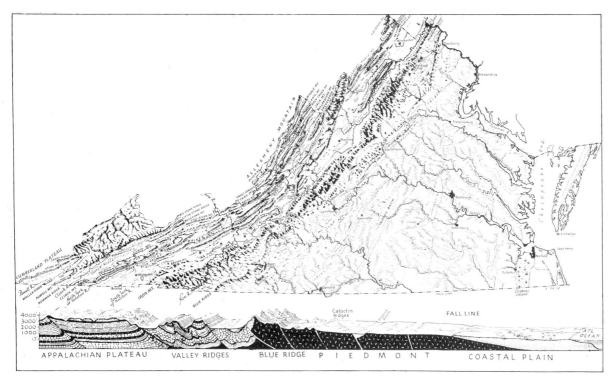

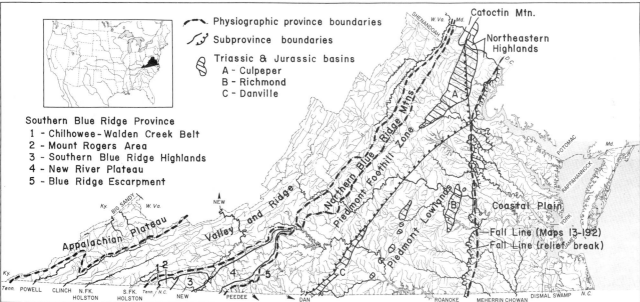

Map 7   Physiographic provinces, subprovinces, and other major geologic or topographic features of Virginia. Upper map: The physiography of Virginia by Erwin Raisz (Copyright permission: Physiographic map of Virginia, Hammond Incorporated, Maplewood, New Jersey). Lower map: Differences between two Fall Lines noted in text. Dismal Swamp outlined by dotted line. Northeastern Highlands and Triassic and Jurassic basins are parts of Piedmont. Catoctin Mountain is a spur of the Blue Ridge. Adapted mainly from VDMR (1963), USGS (1965, 1970), Oaks and Whitehead (1979), and Hack (1982).

Ridge—Butts 1940; Hack 1965, 1969. Habitats in one or two provinces—Garman and Nielsen 1992; Mulholland and Lenat 1992; Smock and Gilinsky 1992; Wallace et al. 1992.

Topography of the physiographic provinces, par-

ticularly the contrasts between the provinces, is well shown on the shaded relief map of Virginia (USGS 1965); surficial rock formations are depicted by the geologic map of Virginia (VDMR 1963). Province boundaries are shown on Map 7 and, by the heaviest dashed lines, on all but one of the species distribution maps (Maps 13–188, 190–192). Subprovinces are delineated only on Map 7.

Boundaries of some provinces on the distribution maps are emended on Map 7, which shows the Fall Line as on the distribution maps, and also has a Fall Line redrawn based upon topography instead of geology. The redrawn Fall Line generally conforms to the foot of the most downstream relief break in large rivers and major tributaries, as determined from the USGS (1965) map and several USGS 7.5-minute series topographic quadrangles. Thus the redrawn Fall Line indicates some stream incisions and other natural irregularities. On Map 7, the northern edge of the Southern Blue Ridge Province is moved in two places to accord with the geologic map of Virginia (VDMR 1963).

To have adjusted the 179 distribution maps would have been prohibitive and, at the level of habitat ranking of species we use, biologically insignificant. Reexamination of fish distributions relative to adjustments on Map 7 did not change our opinion of any distribution pattern or habitat classification of any species.

Coastal Plain

This outer province extends from New England south, along the Gulf of Mexico, and up the lower Mississippi Valley. It is moderately wide in Virginia and is much wider farther south. In Virginia it generally grades from virtually flat in tidewater areas to slightly rolling inland. Relief features include low scarps and rises of fluvial or marine littoral origin, and divides. Elevation and topographic diversity in Virginia are greatest in the northern portion, where some divides are about 100 m above mean sea level. Average elevation of the province in the state is approximately 30 m.

The Coastal Plain is veneered with unconsolidated or semiconsolidated gravel, sand, clay, and marl. These and underlying sedimentary formations bury the basement rocks shallowly in the innermost portion of the province and to more than 1,000 m at the Virginia coast. The sediments were eroded and transported from the Appalachians and continue out onto the Continental Shelf.

The Coastal Plain surrounds the great open estuary, Chesapeake Bay; its width from the bay west to the Fall Line is crossed by four riverine estuaries—the Potomac, Rappahannock, York, and James rivers—which are tidal up to the Fall Line. These estuaries and other waterways including small bays have been embayed or drowned by a postglacial rise in sea level, effecting a fringe of peninsulas (necks) along the western side of Chesapeake Bay. South of the James the Coastal Plain is coursed by the Chowan drainage and, in North Carolina, by the Roanoke drainage; Dismal Swamp lies east of the Chowan and is nontidal.

Freshwater streams on the Coastal Plain generally are sluggish; many are bordered by pondlike backwaters, marshes, and swamps. Locally near the Fall Line some streams have riffles and runs with bottoms of gravel and, rarely, rubble. Reaches of some larger Coastal Plain streams have moderate to strong currents but lack white water.

Streams and ponds entirely in the Coastal Plain range from clear (whether stained or not) to turbid. Alluvial streams draining onto the Coastal Plain from the Piedmont and those adjacent to cleared land are the most frequently and heavily turbid. Substrates in calm waters usually are mud, clay, silt, finely divided detritus, sticks, and logs. In well-flowing reaches the bottom is chiefly shifting sand and, often, logs. Debris dams and snags are prominent features of many channels; owing to the general absence of stable inorganic substrates such as rocks, these structures assume ecologic importance (Smock et al. 1989). Unshaded shallow bodies of water, even darkly stained ones, on the Coastal Plain often are well vegetated by aquatic macrophytes; well-shaded waters generally have few higher plants.

Most Coastal Plain waters are slightly to markedly dark-stained ("blackwater"), caused chiefly by organic acids (predominantly humic and fulvic) released in plant decomposition and leached from swamp soils. The pH generally is 6.0–6.9 but occasionally is as low as 5.5. Some waters, notably those draining areas of carbonate bedrock, are alkaline (pH 7.1–8.0). Lake Drummond and some of its feeders in the peat-based Dismal Swamp are of pH 4.0–5.0, to which few fishes are adapted. Desiccating cutoff pools in the swamp may have pH as low as 3.5 (Matta 1973), which would not be expected to support fish life.

Fall Zone

Although the Fall Zone (sometimes called Fall Belt, Fall Line) is not a physiographic province, it is a geologic zone that has major effects on fish distribution. It distinctly divides the Coastal Plain and Piedmont. Here, the resistant metamorphic rocks underlying the outer Piedmont increase in slope and often are exposed along streams, standing in contrast to softer Coastal Plain sedimentary formations beneath which they extend.

Topographically, the Fall Zone varies considerably in width and slope. Owing to its 7–18-km width in Virginia drainages, we refer to it as a zone and restrict the term Fall Line to its eastern edge. Elevations of the upstream limits of the Fall Zone, where crossed by major rivers in Virginia, vary from 20 to 45 m above mean sea level.

The steepest main-river crossings of the Fall Zone in Virginia are the Potomac (16.2 rkm length, 2.8 m/rkm average drop), Rappahannock (7.5 rkm, 2.6 m/rkm), and James (12.0 rkm, 2.1 m/rkm). Here the Fall Line marks the natural upstream limit of passage by sizeable boats, thus the adjoining areas became centers of human settlement (in the above rivers, respectively, Washington, D.C., Fredericksburg, and Richmond; also, Petersburg on the Appomattox River, and Emporia on the Meherrin River).

The Fall Zone is relatively gentle in the York and Chowan drainages. In the Chowan it drops 1.0 m/rkm in 17.5 rkm of the Nottoway River, and 0.9 m/rkm through 12.9 rkm of the Meherrin River (Jenkins et al. 1975). The 50-rkm long Fall Zone of the Roanoke River is in North Carolina and is a high-gradient area famous as spawning grounds of striped bass.

Aquatic habitats vary greatly within the Fall Zone. Pools are common, but rapids typically are more frequent, longer, and faster than in adjacent portions of the Piedmont and Coastal Plain. In most main Virginia rivers the Fall Zone includes islands, cascades, and, most notably in the Potomac, Rappahannock, and the Little River of the York drainage, one or a few falls. Thus the Fall Zone has pockets of habitat suited to many rheophilic upper Piedmont and montane fishes. These conditions are ecologic barriers to lowland, calm-water species. Chemical composition of Fall Zone streams essentially is that of the outermost Piedmont portion of the same streams.

In some places the Fall Zone deters or, during low water, fully blocks upstream movement of fishes. Of natural obstructions in Virginia, likely only Great Falls, near the head of the Potomac River Fall Zone, has nearly continuously barred fishes from ascending onto the Piedmont. Great Falls is a series of major free falls and cascades comprising a total drop of 23 m through 1.2 rkm. However, it is fully covered during large floods. Great Falls is pictured with normal flow by Anonymous (1973); Garrett and Garrett (1987) show it at normal flow and during its submergence in the 100-year flood of 1987.

Piedmont

The Piedmont (or Piedmont Plateau, Piedmont Upland) is an erosionally much-reduced subdivision or belt of the Appalachian Mountains group. It reaches from southern New York to central Alabama and generally extends from the Fall Zone to the Blue Ridge. The inner boundary is approximately where metamorphic Piedmont rocks end against upthrust Precambrian Blue Ridge formations. The width of the province in southern Virginia is three to four times that in northern Virginia. The elevation of the Piedmont in Virginia generally is 50–100 m above sea level near the Fall Zone and 200–400 m in inner areas; the southern portion tends to be the highest, with some summits being 450–600 m in elevation. Geographic divisions of the Piedmont often used in describing fish distribution are the outer (lower), middle (central), and inner (upper).

The Piedmont is underlain largely by resistant metamorphic and igneous (crystalline) rocks. Its mantle of saprolite and covering soil (chiefly clay and silt) is produced by weathering of parent rock and importation of sediments. Only a moderate to thin cover of modern soil is maintained in the Piedmont because of erosion. The Piedmont is the largest area of North America that drains to the Atlantic and is undergoing denudation (Pavich 1985).

Physiographically, the Piedmont of Virginia is divisible into three subprovinces: Piedmont Lowlands, Northeastern Highlands, and Foothill Zone (Hack 1982; Map 7). The Piedmont Lowlands is dominated by a monotonous topography of low rounded ridges and shallow ravines; ranges of low hills are scattered across the region. Its relief increases westward; the demarcation from adjacent regions on the west is vague in central Virginia. The outer edge of this subprovince may have marked the eastern edge of the North American continent in early Paleozoic time, and at later times was a coastal shore.

The Northeastern Highlands and the Foothill Zone, outlying the Blue Ridge, typically have substantially higher relief than the Piedmont Lowlands. Terrain varies from mountains and ranges of hills to extensive rolling lowlands. The Foothill Zone encloses the southern end of the Culpeper Triassic and Jurassic Basin, a region of typically lower relief than the Foothill Zone and Northeastern Highlands proper. The eastern front of the highlands is well cut by the Potomac River and dissected by a band of Potomac tributaries that descend to the Coastal Plain. Evidence exists that the highlands were uplifted or tilted at least twice, followed each time by rejuvenated erosion. The highlands probably represent part

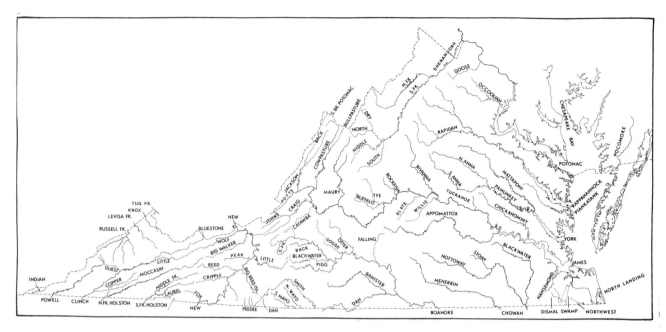

Map 8 Major streams of Virginia.

of the eastern margin of the Appalachian Mountain chain (Hack 1980, 1982). Catoctin Mountain is a spur of the Blue Ridge that is separated from the Blue Ridge by the northernmost sector of the Foothill Zone.

The Triassic and Jurassic basins (or Triassic basins) of the Virginia Piedmont comprise a series of filled fault troughs whose sediments were converted to rock, predominantly sandstone and shale (see *Fossil Fishes*). Igneous rocks commonly are associated with these basins. Relief of the basins generally is lower than that of surrounding crystalline rock areas (Roberts 1928; Hack 1982). The partly metamorphosed Danville Triassic Basin has higher average relief than the adjacent terrain; the Roanoke River drops steeply just below its crossing of the basin (Meyertons 1963; Hack 1982).

Piedmont habitats vary considerably in relation to gradient. Outer Piedmont streams tend to be moderately slow; runs and riffles are infrequent and short, and substrates are chiefly sand, silt, clay, and detritus. Some streams near the Fall Zone have many traits of typical Coastal Plain streams, including the presence of swampy margins and stained water. Upper Piedmont streams have somewhat low to moderate gradient; silt, sand (including shifting beds), gravel, and rubble are common, boulder less so; bedrock occasionally is exposed. Gravel and rubble usually is interbedded by sand. Moderate-gradient Piedmont streams resemble larger streams in the Valley and Ridge Province, but generally are more silty and sandy.

Piedmont streams may have been the most silted in Virginia over geologic time, but likely they did not have nearly the major extent of siltation prevalent today. The heavy siltation of many Piedmont streams is related to modest land relief, tilling for more than two centuries, and soil erosion into streams. In sluggish Piedmont streams, silt removal is a slow process and turbidity has long duration; the problem is compounded by unabated influx of silt. The majority of Piedmont streams we frequently cross are clear about one-third to one-half of the days in a year, but the mobile silt remains. In some ways, many Piedmont streams resemble the fluctuating harsh streams of today's Plains (Matthews 1988).

Blue Ridge

This montane–upland province extends northeast–southwest from southern Pennsylvania to northern Georgia. It has acquired several meanings, ranging from being restricted to the striking eastern frontal escarpment, to including many mountains in the upper Piedmont and all peaks and ridges in the chain east of the Valley and Ridge. We apply it in the sense of physiographers to include all contiguous high mountains underlain by crystalline rocks from south-central Pennsylvania to northeastern Georgia; the Great Smoky Mountains are included (Hack 1982). The Blue Ridge has two primary divisions—the Northern Blue Ridge Mountains extending south to the Roanoke River, and the Southern Blue Ridge Province beginning at the Roanoke (Map 7).

The narrow Northern Blue Ridge is an irregular chain of mountains one to a few peaks wide, about 3–20 km wide overall; its maximum elevation of 1,245 m occurs in Virginia. It is effectively the frontal mountain range of the adjacent Valley and Ridge Province. Together they apparently represent an erosional system that had been uplifted (Hack 1982).

The Southern Blue Ridge Province broadens markedly toward the south, to nearly 100 km wide by the Virginia line, and generally also increases in height southward. It is divisible topographically into five areas in Virginia: Blue Ridge Escarpment, New River Plateau, Chilhowee–Walden Creek Belt, Southern Blue Ridge Highlands, and Mount Rogers Area.

The Blue Ridge Escarpment is narrow, steep, and drains east. Hypotheses on the origin and history of the escarpment (Dietrich 1959; Hack 1982) involve faulting, uplift, erosion, and stream capture; the last two processes caused westward retreat of the divide.

The New River Plateau, or Blue Ridge Upland (Dietrich 1959), comprises about half the area of the Southern Blue Ridge Province in Virginia and includes a long reach of the New River. Compared with other divisions of the Blue Ridge, the plateau has relatively low relief and an overall appearance of late maturity; it is slightly to moderately dissected, the landscape typically rolling and agricultural, and mostly less than 900 m altitude. Monadnocks and ridges are scattered; where they are absent the relief is higher than that of the Piedmont but less than that in other parts of the province. Maintenance of the plainlike terrain is related to the extensive outcrops of resistant rocks in the Appalachian Plateau of West Virginia, where the gradient of the lower New River steepens in the New River Gorge. These strata cause a high base level for the extensive drainage upstream (Hack 1969, 1980, 1982).

The Chilhowee–Walden Creek Belt, on the northern margin of the province, is an elongate zone of mountain ridges and valleys. In Virginia it drains to the South Fork Holston River, crosses the New drainage, and just extends into the upper Roanoke.

The Southern Blue Ridge Highlands is the largest division of its province; only a small section lies in Virginia. It consists of ranges of high mountains including the loftiest peak in eastern United States, Mount Mitchell, North Carolina (2,040 m). In Virginia it lacks wide intermontane valleys and is drained by the South Fork Holston and the New.

The Mount Rogers Area, its south edge at common corners of North Carolina, Tennessee, and Virginia, embodies the two highest mountains in Virginia, Mount Rogers (1,746 m) and Whitetop Mountain (1,630 m). The area owes its distinctiveness to volcanic rock types (particularly rhyolite) that are more resistant than those nearby (Hack 1982). Both mountains are drained by the South Fork Holston and the New.

Use of the term Blue Ridge elsewhere in this book refers to both the Northern Blue Ridge Mountains and all divisions of the Southern Blue Ridge Province, unless a division is specified or clearly implicit. The term "Highlands" refers to the Mount Rogers Area and the Southern Blue Ridge Highlands including its portion southwest of Virginia.

The rocks of the Blue Ridge are largely resistant types; carbonate strata typical of the Valley and Ridge partly floor some valleys of the Chilhowee–Walden Creek Belt. Thus Blue Ridge streams tend to be the softwater type. A chief feature of small Blue Ridge streams is high gradient, reflected by a high frequency of rapids, by cascades and falls in many headwaters, and by bottoms chiefly of large gravel, rubble, boulder, and bedrock. Small streams are cool or cold during summer; rain-caused turbidity clears quickly. These traits are least developed, and in some areas absent, in the New River Plateau. Many streams in the Plateau are considerably sandy and silted, some being "Piedmont" in character (Ross and Perkins 1959). Most of the large streams of the New drainage in the Blue Ridge have moderate gradient; except for often sandy substrate, they physically resemble large Valley and Ridge streams. Gradients of the Potomac, James, and Roanoke rivers steepen where the Blue Ridge is breached.

Valley and Ridge

This province, termed the Ridge and Valley by ichthyologists and, often formerly, by geologists, adjoins the northwest border of the Blue Ridge. It extends northeast–southwest from eastern New York through Virginia to central Alabama. This province is marked by long narrow parallel ridges oriented with the long axis of the province. Consequently its streams form a rectilinear trellis drainage pattern of parallel-flowing streams in the valleys that are connected by right-angle valleys through the ridges.

The intermontane valleys tend to be widest in the belt that adjoins the Blue Ridge. Much of the Shenandoah system and the New and Tennessee drainages have coalesced broad valleys; here the name "Great Valley" is merited. The largest of the relatively low-relief divisions in the Virginia Valley and Ridge is the Shenandoah Valley proper; its most prominent break in topography, Massanutten Mountain, separates the forks of the Shenandoah River.

The province is underlain by a diversified sequence

of Paleozoic sedimentary rocks that have been strongly folded and faulted; with little exception the rocks are not metamorphosed. Mountain ridges of the province are capped by protruding edges of resistant sandstone and quartzite formations; the tops of many are 1,000–1,250 m in elevation. Intermontane valleys are floored by easily erodible carbonate (limestone and dolomite) and shale rocks; in transecting the province, carbonate valleys often alternate with shale valleys. Many of the limestone valleys are fertile farming areas; some have a karst landscape of knoblike hills with many sinks and caves. Shale valleys are less productive. Elevations of the main valley plains are about 150–250 m in northern Virginia, rise to 730–800 m in the area of the New–Holston divide, and descend to 530–675 m near the Tennessee line.

Small montane streams of the Valley and Ridge closely resemble the tumbling streams at similar elevations in the Blue Ridge. Streams in the valleys are of moderate gradient; shoals, runs, and riffles usually compose one-third to one-sixth or less of the length. In valley streams, gravel, rubble, and boulder bottoms are characteristic of both pools and riffles; bedrock is a common substrate. Substrates in calm pools of most valley streams often are quite silted; notable patches of sand are rare throughout the province. Montane streams of the province tend to carry soft water, whereas valley streams typically are the hardwater type. Almost all streams generally are clear but become heavily turbid from moderate or heavy rain. The Valley and Ridge is noted for watered caves and high-volume spring streams (see below).

Appalachian Plateau

This province extends through most of eastern United States between the Valley and Ridge and, on the west, the Interior Plateaus and Interior Plains. Its several divisions sometimes are collectively termed the Appalachian Plateaus; the part in Virginia, lying in the northern sector of the southwestern portion of the state, is the Cumberland Plateau. Portions of its south front in Virginia form an escarpment rising to 600–1,000 m altitude—the Allegheny Front; the plateau declines in altitude toward the northwest. In and near Virginia the province is a rugged mountainous region whose predominant sandstones and shales have been deeply dissected by dendritic streams.

In Virginia the plateau is drained mostly north via the Big Sandy drainage and, to very small extent, the New. All northern tributaries of the Powell River and most of those of the Clinch River flow south from the province. Standing east of the New River along the West Virginia line is the south edge of the unglaciated Allegheny Plateau section of the Appalachian Plateaus, cresting at 1,235 m. It is drained to a very limited extent in Virginia by the New and James drainages. Within West Virginia just west of James headwaters flows the Greenbrier system of the New, which has Valley and Ridge characteristics (Dietrich 1970b).

Appalachian Plateau streams in Virginia are of moderate or high gradient. Before exploitation of the abundant coal beds in the province, the stream substrates of gravel, rubble, and boulder probably were generally clean, a far cry from the deplorable siltation that exists today as a result of extensive underground and surface mining. The lack of carbonate rocks allows acid wastes from mines to go largely unbuffered.

NATURAL LAKES   Map 9

The two natural lakes of Virginia—Lake Drummond and Mountain Lake—both of uncertain origin, are opposites in many ways. Lake Drummond is an acidic (pH 4.2–4.8), brownwater lake lying near sea level in the heart of Dismal Swamp in extreme southeastern Virginia. Rimmed by bald cypress and gum trees, it is almost circular, 4.3 km wide, and 1.8–2.1 m deep. The bottom was clean sand before ditching of the surrounding swamp (Jordan 1889b); now it is mostly laden with detritus, silt, and mud. Lake waters remain turbid owing to substrate disturbance by wind (Marshall and Robinson 1979).

Mountain Lake nestles in deciduous forest near the top of Salt Pond Mountain, Giles County; its 1,180 m surface elevation is more than 600 m above that of the New River, only 10 km away. It is the only natural lake in the extensive nonglaciated portion of the Appalachians and one of the highest east of the Rockies. The lake is small (0.9 km length), deep (average 9.8 m, maximum 31.5 m), and rocky, and has clear, very soft water (Roth and Neff 1964; Simmons and Neff 1973; Parker et al. 1975; Sevebeck et al. 1986).

IMPOUNDMENTS   Map 9

Mill dams were built in Virginia as early as 1646, but large dams were first constructed much later (Mussey 1948). Since 1939, 13 major impoundments created in Virginia have increased electrical power generation, flood control, and water-based recreation. They and other reservoirs are home to transplanted high-profile gamefishes such as muskellunge, striped bass, black basses, and walleye. However, impoundments have also changed riverine environments to lacustrine ones, substantially re-

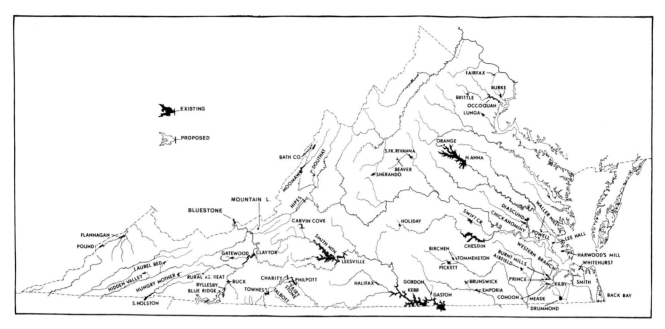

Map 9 Natural lakes (Lake Drummond and Mountain Lake) and larger impoundments (greater than 202 hectares or 500 acres of surface area) of Virginia.

duced living space for many stream fishes, and have blocked spawning migrations. A list and history of some of Virginia's older major and minor reservoirs is by Mussey (1948). The location and fishing opportunities of many Virginia impoundments are described by Anonymous (1990).

The major impoundments (in downstream-to-upstream order, main river first) and the years in which the dams were closed or the lakes were filled are as follows: Potomac—Occoquan Reservoir 1957; York—Lake Anna 1972; James—Lake Moomaw (Gathright Dam) 1981, Lake Chesdin ca. 1970; Roanoke—Gaston Reservoir 1964, Kerr Reservoir (often called Buggs Island Lake) 1952, Leesville Reservoir 1963, Smith Mountain Lake 1963, Philpott Reservoir 1951; New—Bluestone Reservoir (in West Virginia, ponding up to the Virginia line) 1949, Claytor Lake 1939; Tennessee—South Holston Reservoir 1951; Big Sandy—Flannagan Reservoir 1964.

DISMAL SWAMP   Maps 6–8

This large, outer Coastal Plain tract of forested wetland is also known as the Great Dismal Swamp; part of it is now a national wildlife refuge. It is centered on the Virginia–North Carolina state line. A volume recently was published on its scientific study (Kirk 1979), and a natural history of the swamp was authored by Meanley (1973); both references omit fishes. Owing to ditching, the present 850 km² of true swamp represent much less than the original (Lichtler and Walker 1979).

In Virginia the swamp is 16–18 km wide (east to west) and about 24 km long. Lying at elevations of 1.5–8 m above sea level, it has very slight relief (Oaks and Whitehead 1979). The only significant open body of water in the swamp is Lake Drummond (see above). The fauna and developmental history of the swamp are treated in *Biogeography*.

BIG SPRINGS

In the limestone belts of the Valley and Ridge Province in Virginia, there are many medium and large cold springs which are special habitats for fishes (Matthews et al. 1985). The largest springs emerge from aquifers (sometimes caves) as sizeable creeks or streams, as wide as 10 m. In Virginia outside of the Valley and Ridge, there are fewer medium-sized spring runs, and we are unaware of large ones.

Constant flow, temperature, and chemical content are dominant characteristics of many of Virginia's larger springs whose watersheds have been little modified. The usual temperature of groundwater in the state ranges from approximately 17°C in the southeastern corner to 11°C in the mountains (Vannote and Sweeney 1980), hence the springs that lack geothermal heating are about 10–19°C and their variation through time is about 1°C. Other characteristics

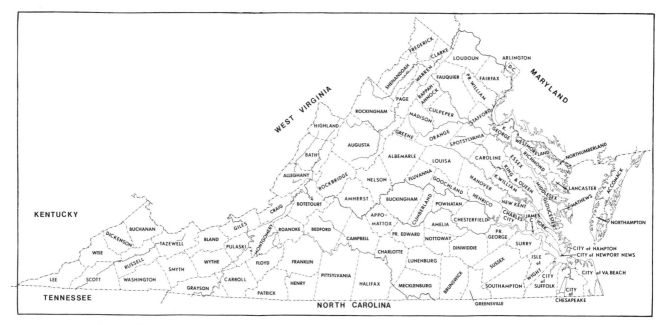

Map 10   Counties of Virginia.

of Virginia springs are reported by Collins et al. (1930) and Helfrich et al. (1990).

Mossy Creek, which flows through largely unshaded Shenandoah Valley meadows, is one of the largest spring-run streams in the state (Plate 8). Its fine trout water issues from a voluminous head spring at Mount Solon and is fed along approximately 10 rkm by numerous seepages and springs. This stream probably derives headflow via a subterranean connection with the nearby North River. During an extraordinary flood in 1949, the North River spilled over its divide into Mossy Creek, flooding Mount Solon (Hack 1965).

Some of the larger cold springs, and particularly the warm (16–40°C) mineral springs (Reeves 1932), were social and health centers for vacationers in the 1800s and early 1900s (Reniers 1941; Cohen 1981; Sevebeck et al. 1986). Some remain so.

Many of Virginia's springs have been adversely modified by humans and livestock (Helfrich et al. 1990); they merit protection for the continuance of their multiple use and that of receiving waterways.

CAVES

Virginia's limestone belts of the Valley and Ridge Province are riddled with subterranean passageways, some spacious; several caves (caverns) are major tourist attractions. Many of the caves contain standing or flowing water; considerable volumes occur in some (Douglas 1964; Holsinger 1975; Holsinger and Culver 1988). Although fishes often abound in alkaline waters just outside caves, the underground channels of Virginia rarely yield fishes.

The only fishes that may regularly occur underground in Virginia probably are trogloxenes—species that often are found in caves but which do not complete the life cycle there (Holsinger 1964; Holsinger and Culver 1988). The surface-dwelling fish perhaps most commonly encountered in caves, near the entrances, is the banded sculpin *Cottus carolinae*. It was once found to spawn in a Kentucky cave just inside the entrance (Craddock 1965). We suspect that its close relative the Potomac sculpin *C. girardi* inhabits caves. Holsinger (1964, in litt.) noted that mottled sculpins *C. bairdi* have been collected in caves of the Tennessee drainage in southwestern Virginia, but these probably were *C. carolinae*. An undescribed species most closely related to *C. carolinae* is known by one specimen from a West Virginia cave; it is colorless and appears to be a troglobite—an obligatory cave species (see *C. carolinae* account).

Other fishes seen in Virginia caves are suckers, catfish, and trout (Holsinger 1964). We heard a report of a "blind white catfish" in a cave in the Cowpasture River valley. J. E. Cooper (in litt.) also heard such rumors, but when investigated, the fish always proved to be sculpins. The apparent absence in Virginia of true cave-dwelling members of the cavefish family Amblyopsidae is discussed near the end of *Biogeography*.

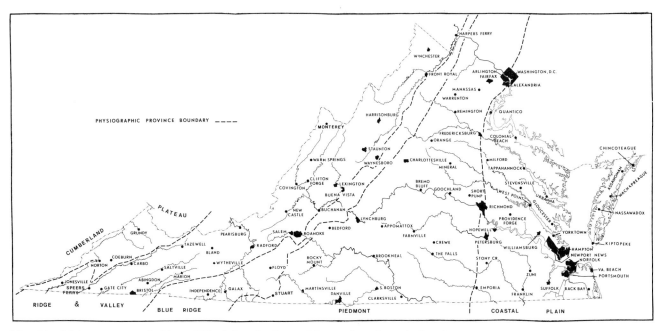

Map 11   Major towns and cities of Virginia; physiographic province boundaries shown.

ESTUARIES
BY ROBERT E. JENKINS AND THOMAS A. MUNROE

Estuaries are semi-enclosed bodies of water that are coastal or reach inland, that have a free connection to an open sea, and within which seawater is measurably diluted by freshwater runoff derived from land drainage (Pritchard 1967). Virginia has extensive estuarine systems, comprising areas behind the barrier islands along the Atlantic Coast of Delmarva, the many major riverine and multitudinous minor tributaries of Chesapeake Bay, and the bay itself. Most of these are heavily used for recreational and commercial fishing, as well as shipping; they provide sport and food for near and distant areas. Parts of some Virginia estuaries are remote and little visited. As a whole the estuaries support many fish species. Some estuarine fishes extend—as did others before damming—into Virginia via the Chowan and Roanoke rivers, whose waters enter Albemarle Sound, North Carolina.

A primary factor influencing the distributional patterns of animals and plants in estuaries is salinity. Salinity is expressed as the number of parts of salt per 1,000 (‰) parts of water. Estuaries are divisible into four salinity zones: tidal fresh water, 0.0–0.5‰; oligohaline, 0.5–5‰; mesohaline, 5–18‰; and polyhaline, 18–30‰. The zonal boundaries generally fluctuate depending on the amount of river inflow, tides, and weather factors. The distribution of mobile fishes also tends to be dynamic in response to changes in salinity.

Estuaries support a highly diverse assemblage of fishes and other aquatic organisms. Species differ markedly in their use of estuaries. Some that are considered freshwater species occur sporadically as waifs in brackish water, whereas many others typically extend well out into estuaries. Species that are adapted to a wide range of salinity are termed euryhaline. Diadromous species, those which migrate between fresh and salt water to spawn, traverse estuaries. Many marine fishes make other directed movements or wander into low salinity and, some, into fresh water. Estuaries serve as nurseries for young stages of numerous marine species. There are relatively few truly, exclusively estuarine fishes.

Estuaries present a gray zone to the student of typical freshwater fishes; we have taken a conservative approach and excluded several species from treatment in this book. Estuarine records are plotted where appropriate for the species given full treatment. Publications cited provide an introduction to the literature on regional estuaries; their bibliographies provide further leads.

We treat 11 species (4 of the herring family Clupeidae) which typically occupy estuaries at some life stage. Some of them enter the oceanic realm but all spawn in fresh water, except the eel, which breeds in the Sargasso Sea near Bermuda. The 11 are the sea lamprey, shortnose sturgeon, Atlantic sturgeon, American eel, blueback herring, alewife, hickory shad, American shad, banded killifish, white perch, and striped bass.

Chesapeake Bay is the largest estuary in the United States and one of the most useful in the world (Lippson 1973). The total number of fish species, 286, recorded in the Chesapeake system (Musick 1972; amended below) is substantially higher than that of inland Virginia fresh waters, but the number is misleading. Among the total are some 174 marine species, 93 of which occur rarely or sporadically in the bay during summer, and 16 of which are rare or occasional winter visitors. Only 27 of the 286 are ranked as estuarine and 11 as diadromous (including 3 also listed as estuarine). Musick (1972) also included 78 freshwater species as members of the Chesapeake fauna based on occurrence in the Coastal Plain. (One of these, *Erimyzon sucetta*, should be dropped from the Chesapeake list based on reidentifications.)

Although the bay is rich, we would be remiss to overlook that it has critical ecological problems, caused by a multitude of land-use and water-use practices (Bird 1985). Some headway is being made in correcting these but much remains to be done.

Introductions to the life and conditions in Chesapeake Bay have been written by Lippson (1973), Lippson and Lippson (1984), and White (1989). An excellent ecological treatment of tidal freshwater marshes is that of Odum et al. (1984). Use by fishes of a tidal Virginia marsh was analyzed by Rozas and Odum (1987a). The chemistry of Virginia's major estuaries was studied by Brehmer (1972). The time-honored *Fishes of the Chesapeake Bay* by Hildebrand and Schroeder (1928) has been reprinted. The field guide to Atlantic Coast fishes by Robins et al. (1986) is an invaluable aid to identification of fishes. For identification and references to the biology of many estuarine species of Virginia, Smith's (1985) book on New York fishes is useful. Several major works on larval fishes include life history information on the juvenile and adult stages of estuarine species; see, for example, Mansueti and Hardy (1967), Lippson and Moran (1974), Fritzche (1978), Johnson (1978), Jones et al. (1978), Hardy (1978a, 1978b), and Wang and Kernehan (1979). The salinity distribution of fishes in regional estuaries was studied by Keup and Bayless (1964), Schwartz (1964, 1981b), and Musick (1972). A broad and detailed treatise on estuaries was edited by Lauff (1967).

Table 2 Distribution by drainage and habitat of the 210 freshwater fish species in Virginia, in sequence of species accounts (phylogenetic). There are 230 taxa (species, subspecies, undescribed forms); the number of Virginia taxa in the 16 species with more than one taxon is indicated in parentheses after the name. The number of Virginia species in each family is given in brackets after the family name. **Habitat Abbreviations** (sequence of column head): **Lac**—lacustrine; **Low**—lowland; **Upl**—upland; **Mtn**—montane; **Riv**—river; **Str**—stream; **Crk**—creek. Habitats refer to those typically or frequently occupied in Virginia (denoted by **X**); they are characterized in *Biogeography* and *Drainages*. **Hydrographic Abbreviations** (sequence of column head): **Del**—Delmarva; **Pot**—Potomac; **Rap**—Rappahannock; **Yrk**—York; **Jam**—James; **Cho**—Chowan; **Roa**—Roanoke; **PD**—Pee Dee; **New** drainage; **Hol**—Holston; **C–P**—Clinch-Powell; **BS**—Big Sandy. **Status Abbreviations**: E—endemic; i.e., a single drainage is the total native range; taxa indicated to be endemic to the Holston and/or Clinch-Powell systems are endemic to the Tennessee drainage. **Ep**—population native but extirpated from Virginia (or entire drainage). **Ex**—extinct species. **I**—introduced. **IP**—regarded as introduced, but possibly native. **Ma**—marine or estuarine species with native and/or introduced freshwater occurrence or population. **N**—native. **NI**—regarded as native, but possibly introduced. *—occurs or formerly occurred in extralimital portion of the drainage, but there is no Virginia record of native occurrence in the drainage (entirely extralimital status is indicated only for the Potomac, Chowan, Roanoke, and New drainages). [1]—native to Virginia portion, but now occurs only extralimitally in, or is extirpated throughout the drainage. [i]—introduced to Virginia portion, native extralimitally in the drainage. A taxon may have more than one status in a drainage, sometimes indicated by two symbols; e.g., **EEp** means endemic, extirpated. In other cases of double (or triple) symbols for a drainage, different subspecific taxa are indicated. See *Appendix 2* for further documentation.

Family [number of species] and species (number of subspecies)	Habitat							Atlantic slope								Ohio River basin			
	Lac	Low	Upl	Mtn	Riv	Str	Crk	Del	Pot	Rap	Yrk	Jam	Cho	Roa	PD	New	Hol	C-P	BS
Petromyzontidae [5]																			
Ichthyomyzon bdellium	-	-	X	-	X	X	-	-	-	-	-	-	-	-	-	-	N	N	-
I. greeleyi	-	-	X	-	-	X	X	-	-	-	-	-	-	-	-	-	N	N	-
Petromyzon marinus	-	X	X	-	X	X	-	Ma	Ma	Ma	Ma	Ma	Ma	Ma¹	-	-	-	-	-
Lampetra appendix	-	X	X	-	-	X	X	-	N*	N	N	N	N	-	-	-	N	-	-
L. aepyptera	-	X	X	-	-	X	X	N	N	N	N	N	-	-	-	NI*	-	-	-
Acipenseridae [2]																			
Acipenser brevirostrum	-	X	-	-	X	-	-	-	Ma¹	-	-	-	Ma*	-	-	-	-	-	-
A. oxyrhynchus	-	X	-	-	X	-	-	-	Ma	Ma	Ma	Ma	Ma*	Ma*	-	-	-	-	-
Polyodontidae [1]																			
Polyodon spathula	-	-	X	-	X	-	-	-	-	-	-	-	-	-	-	-	-	N	-
Lepisosteidae [1]																			
Lepisosteus osseus	X	X	X	-	X	X	-	-	N	N	N	N	N	N	-	-	Ep	N	-
Amiidae [1]																			
Amia calva	X	X	X	-	X	X	-	-	N	N	N	N	N	N	-	I	-	-	-
Anguillidae [1]																			
Anguilla rostrata	-	X	X	-	X	X	X	Ma	Ma	Ma	Ma	Ma	Ma	Ma	-	Ma	-	-	-
Clupeidae [6]																			
Dorosoma cepedianum	X	X	X	-	X	X	-	-	N	N	N	N	N	N	-	-	N	N	N
D. petenense	X	X	X	-	X	X	-	-	I	I	I	I	I*	I	-	I	I	I	-
Alosa aestivalis	X	X	-	-	X	X	-	Ma	Ma	Ma	Ma	Ma	Ma	Ma^i	-	-	-	-	-
A. pseudoharengus	X	X	-	-	X	-	-	Ma	Ma	Ma	Ma	Ma	Ma	Ma^i	-	I	-	-	I
A. mediocris	-	X	-	-	X	-	-	Ma	Ma	Ma	Ma	Ma	Ma*	Ma*	-	-	-	-	-
A. sapidissima	-	X	X	-	X	X	-	Ma	Ma	Ma	Ma	Ma	Ma	Ma¹	-	-	-	-	-
Esocidae [4]																			
Esox lucius	X	(X)	-	-	-	-	-	-	I	I	I	I	-	I	-	-	I	-	-
E. masquinongy	X	-	X	-	X	-	-	-	I	I	-	I	-	I	-	I	I	I	-
E. niger	X	X	X	-	X	X	X	N	N	N	N	N	N	N	-	-	-	-	-
E. americanus	X	X	X	-	X	X	X	N	N	N	N	N	N	N	-	-	-	-	-
Umbridae [1]																			
Umbra pygmaea	X	X	-	-	-	X	X	N	N	N	N	N	N	N	-	-	-	-	-
Cyprinidae [67]																			
Cyprinus carpio	X	X	X	-	X	X	-	-	I	I	I	I	I	I	-	I	I	I	I
Carassius auratus	X	X	X	-	X	-	-	-	I	-	I	I	I	-	-	-	I	I	I
Ctenopharyngodon idella	X	X	X	-	X	-	-	-	I	-	I	I	-	-	-	-	-	I	-
Notemigonus crysoleucas	X	X	X	-	X	X	X	N	N	N	N	N	N	N	-	I	I	-	-
Phoxinus tennesseensis	-	-	X	-	-	-	X	-	-	-	-	-	-	-	-	-	E	-	-
P. oreas	-	-	X	X	-	X	X	-	IP	IP	NI	N	N	N	IP	N	IP	-	-
Clinostomus funduloides	-	-	X	X	-	-	X	-	N	N	N	N	N	N	N	N	N	N	N
Rhinichthys cataractae	-	-	X	X	X	X	X	-	N	N	-	N	-	IP	-	N	N	-	-
R. atratulus (2)	-	-	X	X	-	X	X	-	N	N	N	NN	N	NN	N	N	N	N	N

Table 2 Continued

Family [number of species] and species (number of subspecies)	Habitat							Atlantic slope								Ohio River basin			
	Lac	Low	Upl	Mtn	Riv	Str	Crk	Del	Pot	Rap	Yrk	Jam	Cho	Roa	PD	New	Hol	C-P	BS
Campostoma anomalum (2)	-	-	X	X	X	X	X	-	N	-	-	N	N	N	IP	-	N	N	N
Margariscus margarita	-	-	X	-	-	X	X	-	N	-	-	-	-	-	-	-	-	-	-
Semotilus corporalis	-	-	X	-	X	X	-	-	N	N	N	N	-	IP	-	-	-	-	-
S. atromaculatus	-	-	X	X	-	X	X	-	N	N	N	N	N	N	N	N	N	N	N
Exoglossum laurae	-	-	X	-	-	X	X	-	-	-	-	-	-	-	-	N	-	-	-
E. maxillingua	-	-	X	-	X	X	X	-	N	N	N	N	N	N	-	IP	-	-	-
Nocomis platyrhynchus	-	-	X	-	X	X	-	-	-	-	-	-	-	-	-	E	-	-	-
N. micropogon	-	-	X	-	X	X	-	-	N	N	N	-	-	-	-	-	N	N	N
N. raneyi	-	X	X	-	X	X	-	-	-	-	-	NI	N	N	-	-	-	-	-
N. leptocephalus	-	-	X	X	X	X	X	-	NI	IP	NI	N	N	N	N	N	-	-	-
Erimystax cahni	-	-	X	-	X	-	-	-	-	-	-	-	-	-	-	-	-	E	-
E. dissimilis	-	-	X	-	X	X	-	-	-	-	-	-	-	-	-	Ep*	N	N	-
E. insignis (2)	-	-	X	-	X	X	X	-	-	-	-	-	-	-	-	-	EN	EN	-
Phenacobius mirabilis	-	-	X	-	X	X	-	-	-	-	-	-	-	-	-	-	-	-	N
P. teretulus	-	-	X	-	X	X	X	-	-	-	-	-	-	-	-	E	-	-	-
P. crassilabrum	-	-	X	-	-	X	-	-	-	-	-	-	-	-	-	-	E	-	-
P. uranops	-	-	X	-	-	X	-	-	-	-	-	-	-	-	-	-	N	N	-
Hybopsis amblops	-	-	X	-	X	X	X	-	-	-	-	-	-	-	-	-	N	N	Ep
H. hypsinotus	-	-	X	-	-	X	X	-	-	-	-	-	-	-	N	-	-	-	-
Cyprinella labrosa	-	-	X	-	-	X	-	-	-	-	-	-	-	-	Ep	-	-	-	-
C. monacha	-	-	X	-	X	X	-	-	-	-	-	-	-	-	-	-	E	-	-
C. galactura	-	-	X	-	X	X	X	-	-	-	-	-	-	-	-	IP	N	N	IP
C. whipplei	-	-	X	-	X	-	-	-	-	-	-	-	-	-	-	-	-	N	-
C. analostana	-	X	X	-	X	X	-	-	N	N	N	N	N	N	-	-	-	-	-
C. spiloptera	X	-	X	-	X	X	-	-	N	-	-	-	-	IP	-	N	N	N	N
Luxilus coccogenis	-	-	X	X	X	X	X	-	-	-	-	-	-	-	-	IP*	N	N	-
L. cerasinus	-	-	X	X	-	X	X	-	-	IP	N	N	-	-	-	IP	-	-	-
L. albeolus	-	-	X	-	X	X	X	-	-	-	-	-	N	N	-	NI	-	-	-
L. cornutus	-	-	X	X	-	X	X	-	N	N	N	N	-	-	-	NI	N	N	N
L. chrysocephalus	-	-	X	-	X	X	X	-	-	-	-	-	-	-	-	NI	N	N	N
Lythrurus lirus	-	-	X	-	-	X	X	-	-	-	-	-	-	-	-	-	-	N	-
L. ardens (2)	-	-	X	-	X	X	X	-	-	IP	N	N	N	-	-	NI	N	N	-
Notropis rubellus (2)	-	-	X	-	X	X	-	-	N	N	N	N	-	-	-	N	N	N	N
N. leuciodus	-	-	X	-	X	X	X	-	-	-	-	-	-	-	-	IP*	N	N	-
N. rubricroceus	-	-	X	X	-	X	X	-	-	-	-	-	-	-	-	IP	N	N	-
N. chiliticus	-	-	X	X	-	X	X	-	-	-	-	-	-	NI	N	IP	-	-	-
N. atherinoides	-	-	X	-	X	-	-	-	-	-	-	-	-	-	-	-	-	-	N
N. amoenus	-	X	X	-	X	X	-	-	N	N	N	N	N	N	-	-	-	-	-
N. photogenis	-	-	X	-	X	X	-	-	-	-	-	-	-	-	-	N	N	N	N
N. semperasper	-	-	X	-	X	X	-	-	-	-	-	-	-	E	-	-	-	-	-
N. ariommus	-	-	X	-	X	X	-	-	-	-	-	-	-	-	-	-	N	N	-
N. telescopus	-	-	X	-	X	X	X	-	-	-	-	-	-	IP	-	IP	N	N	-
N. hudsonius	X	X	X	-	X	X	X	-	N	N	N	N	N	N	N	IP	-	-	-
N. scabriceps	-	-	X	-	X	X	X	-	-	-	-	-	-	-	-	E	-	-	-
N. volucellus	-	-	X	-	X	X	-	-	-	-	-	NI	N	N	-	N	N	N	N
N. sp., sawfin shiner	-	-	X	-	X	X	-	-	-	-	-	-	-	-	-	-	N	N	-
N. spectrunculus	-	-	X	X	-	X	X	-	-	-	-	-	-	-	-	-	N	N	-
N. stramineus	-	-	X	-	X	X	-	-	-	-	-	-	-	-	-	N	-	-	N
N. procne (2)	-	X	X	-	X	X	X	-	N	N	N	N	N	N	-	IP	-	-	-
N. alborus	-	-	X	-	-	X	X	-	-	-	-	-	Ep?	N	-	-	-	-	-
N. bifrenatus	-	X	X	-	-	X	X	-	N	Ep?	N	N	-	-	-	-	-	-	-
N. chalybaeus	-	X	-	-	-	X	X	-	N*	-	-	N	N	N*	-	-	-	-	-
N. altipinnis	-	X	X	-	-	X	X	-	-	-	-	-	N	N	-	-	-	-	-
N. buccatus	-	-	X	-	X	X	X	-	NI	NI	-	-	-	-	-	N	-	IP	N
Hybognathus regius	-	X	X	-	X	X	X	-	N	N	N	N	N	N	-	-	-	-	-
Pimephales promelas	X	-	X	-	X	X	X	-	I	-	I	-	-	I	-	I	IP	IP	IP
P. vigilax	-	-	X	-	X	-	-	-	-	-	-	-	-	-	-	-	NI	NI	-
P. notatus	X	-	X	-	X	X	X	-	IP	IP	I	IP	-	IP	-	NI	NI	NI	NI
Catostomidae [18]																			
Carpiodes cyprinus	X	X	X	-	X	X	-	-	N	-	-	N	N	N	-	-	N	N	-
Erimyzon sucetta	X	X	-	-	-	X	X	-	-	-	-	-	-	N	N*	-	-	-	-
E. oblongus	X	X	X	-	X	X	X	N	N	N	N	N	N	N	-	-	-	-	-
Hypentelium nigricans	-	-	X	X	X	X	X	-	N	N	N	N	N	N	-	N	N	N	N
H. roanokense	-	-	X	X	-	X	X	-	-	-	-	-	-	E	-	-	-	-	-
Thoburnia rhothoeca	-	-	X	X	-	X	X	-	NI	IP	-	N	NI	NI	-	Ep	-	-	-
T. hamiltoni	-	-	X	X	-	X	X	-	-	-	-	-	-	E	-	-	-	-	-
Scartomyzon robustus	-	-	X	-	-	X	X	-	-	-	-	-	-	-	N	-	-	-	-
S. cervinus	-	-	X	-	X	X	X	-	-	-	-	IP	N	N	-	IP	-	-	-
S. ariommus	-	-	X	-	-	X	X	-	-	-	-	-	-	E	-	-	-	-	-

Table 2 Continued

Family [number of species] and species (number of subspecies)	Habitat							Atlantic slope								Ohio River basin			
	Lac	Low	Upl	Mtn	Riv	Str	Crk	Del	Pot	Rap	Yrk	Jam	Cho	Roa	PD	New	Hol	C-P	BS
Moxostoma duquesnei	-	-	X	X	X	X	X	-	-	-	-	-	-	-	-	-	N	N	-
M. macrolepidotum (2)	X	X	X	-	X	X	-	-	N	N	N	N	N	N	-	-	N	N	-
M. erythrurum	X	-	X	-	X	X	X	-	IP	-	-	N	N	N	-	IP*	N	N	N
M. carinatum	-	-	X	-	X	X	-	-	-	-	-	-	-	-	-	-	N	N	-
M. anisurum	X	-	X	-	X	X	-	-	-	-	-	-	N	N	N	-	-	N	-
M. pappillosum	X	-	X	-	X	X	-	-	-	-	-	-	N	N	-	-	-	-	-
M. lacerum	-	-	X	-	-	X	-	-	-	-	-	-	-	-	-	-	Ex	-	-
Catostomus commersoni	X	-	X	X	X	X	X	-	N	N	N	N	N	N	N	N	N	N	N
Ictaluridae [15]																			
Ictalurus furcatus	-	X	-	-	X	-	-	-	I	I	-	I	-	-	-	-	-	-	-
I. punctatus	X	X	X	-	X	X	-	-	I	I	I	I	I	I	-	N	N	N	N
Ameiurus catus	X	X	X	-	X	X	-	N	N	N	N	N	N	N	-	-	-	-	-
A. platycephalus	X	-	X	-	X	X	X	-	-	-	-	NI	N	N	N	-	-	-	-
A. brunneus	-	-	X	-	X	X	-	-	-	-	-	-	-	IP	-	-	-	-	-
A. natalis	X	X	X	-	X	X	X	-	N	N	N	N	N	N	-	IP*	N	N	NI
A. nebulosus	X	X	X	-	X	X	X	N	N	N	N	N	N	N	-	IP	IP	IP	-
A. melas	X	-	X	-	X	X	-	-	-	-	-	-	-	I	-	IP	-	NI	-
Noturus flavus	-	-	X	-	X	X	-	-	-	-	-	-	-	-	-	NI*	N	N	-
N. gilberti	-	-	X	-	-	X	-	-	-	-	-	IP	-	E	-	-	-	-	-
N. insignis (2)	-	X	X	-	X	X	X	-	N	N	N	N	N	NE	N	N	IP	-	-
N. gyrinus	X	X	-	-	X	X	X	-	N	N	N	N	N	N*	-	-	-	-	-
N. flavipinnis	-	-	X	-	-	X	-	-	-	-	-	-	-	-	-	-	EEp	E	-
N. eleutherus	-	-	X	-	X	X	-	-	-	-	-	-	-	-	-	-	N	N	-
Pylodictis olivaris	X	-	X	-	X	X	-	-	I	-	-	I	-	I	-	N	N	N	N
Salmonidae [3]																			
Salvelinus fontinalis	X	-	X	X	-	X	X	-	N	N	-	N	-	NI	IP	N	N	IP	Ep
Salmo trutta	X	-	X	X	-	X	X	-	I	I	-	I	-	I	I	I	I	I	I
Oncorhynchus mykiss	X	-	X	X	-	X	X	-	I	I	-	I	-	I	I	I	I	I	I
Percopsidae [1]																			
Percopsis omiscomaycus	-	-	X	-	X	-	-	-	Ep										
Aphredoderidae [1]																			
Aphredoderus sayanus	X	X	X	-	X	X	X	N	N	N	N	N	N	N	-	-	-	-	-
Amblyopsidae [1]																			
Chologaster cornuta	X	X	-	-	-	X	X	-	-	-	-	N	N	N*	-	-	-	-	-
Atherinidae [1]																			
Labidesthes sicculus	-	-	X	-	X	-	-	-	I*	-	-	-	-	-	-	I*	-	N	-
Fundulidae [4]																			
Fundulus diaphanus	X	X	X	-	X	X	X	Ma	Ma	Ma	Ma	Ma	Ma*	Ma*	-	-	-	-	-
F. rathbuni	-	-	X	-	-	X	X	-	-	-	-	-	-	N	-	-	-	-	-
F. catenatus	-	-	X	-	X	X	-	-	-	-	-	-	-	-	-	-	N	N	-
F. lineolatus	-	X	-	-	-	X	X	-	-	-	-	N	N	N*	-	-	-	-	-
Poeciliidae [1]																			
Gambusia holbrooki	X	X	X	-	X	X	X	N	N	N	N	N	N	N	-	-	-	-	-
Cottidae [8]																			
Cottus bairdi	-	-	X	X	-	X	X	-	N	N	-	N	-	N	-	N	-	-	N
C. baileyi	-	-	X	X	-	X	X	-	-	-	-	-	-	-	-	-	E	E	-
C. cognatus	-	-	X	-	-	X	X	-	E	-	-	-	-	-	-	-	-	-	-
C. sp., Holston sculpin	-	-	X	X	X	X	X	-	-	-	-	-	-	-	-	-	E	-	-
C. sp., Clinch sculpin	-	-	X	X	-	X	X	-	-	-	-	-	-	-	-	-	-	E	-
C. sp., Bluestone sculpin	-	-	X	-	-	-	X	-	-	-	-	-	-	-	-	E	-	-	-
C. carolinae (2)	-	-	X	X	X	X	X	-	-	-	-	-	-	-	-	N	N	N	-
C. girardi	-	-	X	X	X	X	X	-	N	-	-	NI	-	-	-	-	-	-	-
Moronidae [3]																			
Morone americana	X	X	-	-	X	X	-	Ma	Ma	Ma	Ma	Ma	Ma	Ma[i]	-	-	-	-	-
M. saxatilis	X	X	X	-	X	-	-	Ma	Ma	Ma	Ma	Ma	Ma	Ma	-	I	-	-	-
M. chrysops	X	-	X	-	X	X	-	-	I	-	I	-	-	I	-	I	NI	NI	I
Centrarchidae [19]																			
Ambloplites rupestris	X	-	X	X	X	X	X	-	I	I	-	I	-	I	-	I	N	N	N
A. cavifrons	-	X	X	-	X	X	-	-	-	-	-	-	N	N	-	-	-	-	-

Table 2 Continued

Family [number of species] and species (number of subspecies)	Habitat							Atlantic slope								Ohio River basin			
	Lac	Low	Upl	Mtn	Riv	Str	Crk	Del	Pot	Rap	Yrk	Jam	Cho	Roa	PD	New	Hol	C-P	BS
Acantharchus pomotis	X	X	-	-	-	X	X	-	-	N	N	N	N	N*	-	-	-	-	-
Centrarchus macropterus	X	X	-	-	X	X	X	-	I*	N	N	N	N	N	-	-	-	-	-
Pomoxis nigromaculatus	X	X	X	-	X	X	X	IP	IP	IP	IP	N	N	N	-	I	IP	IP	IP
P. annularis	X	-	X	-	X	X	-	-	I	I	I	I	I	I	-	I	IP	IP	IP
Enneacanthus obesus	X	X	-	-	-	X	X	-	-	-	NI	N	N	N*	-	-	-	-	-
E. gloriosus	X	X	-	-	-	X	X	N	N	N	N	N	N	N	-	-	-	-	-
E. chaetodon	X	X	-	-	-	X	X	-	-	-	-	-	N	N*	-	-	-	-	-
Micropterus dolomieu	X	-	X	X	X	X	X	-	I	I	I	I	I	I	-	I	N	N	N
M. punctulatus	X	-	X	-	X	X	-	-	-	-	I	I	-	I	-	I	N	N	N
M. salmoides	X	X	X	-	X	X	X	I	I	I	I	IP	IP	IP	-	I	NI	NI	NI
Lepomis gulosus	X	X	X	-	X	X	X	-	IP	IP	IP	NI	N	N	-	I	I	-	-
L. cyanellus	X	-	X	-	X	X	X	-	I	I	-	I	I	I	I	N	NI	NI	NI
L. auritus	X	X	X	-	X	X	X	-	N	N	N	N	N	N	N	I	I	I	I
L. megalotis	X	-	X	-	X	X	-	-	I	-	-	-	-	-	-	I	N	N	N
L. macrochirus	X	X	X	-	X	X	X	I	I	I	I	I	I	I	NI	I	N	N	N
L. gibbosus	X	X	X	-	X	X	X	NI	N	N	N	N	N	N	-	I	I	I	-
L. microlophus	X	X	X	-	X	X	X	-	I	I	I	I	I	I	-	-	-	-	I
Percidae [45]																			
Stizostedion vitreum	X	X	X	-	X	X	-	-	I	-	I	I	IP	IP	-	I	N	N	N
S. canadense	X	-	X	-	X	-	-	-	-	-	-	-	-	-	-	-	N	N	-
Perca flavescens	X	X	X	-	X	X	X	-	N	N	N	N	N	N	-	I	-	-	-
Percina sciera	-	-	X	-	X	X	-	-	-	-	-	-	-	-	-	-	-	N	-
P. oxyrhynchus	-	-	X	-	X	X	-	-	-	-	-	-	-	-	-	N	-	-	N
P. burtoni	-	-	X	-	X	X	-	-	-	-	-	-	-	-	-	-	N	N	-
P. rex	-	-	X	-	X	X	-	-	-	-	-	-	N	N	-	-	-	-	-
P. caprodes (2)	X	-	X	-	X	X	-	-	Ep	-	-	-	-	-	-	N	N	N	N
P. macrocephala	-	-	X	-	-	X	-	-	-	-	-	-	-	-	-	-	N	N	-
P. maculata	-	-	X	-	-	X	-	-	-	-	-	-	-	-	-	-	-	-	Ep
P. notogramma (2)	-	-	X	-	X	X	X	-	N	N	N	NE	-	-	-	-	-	-	-
P. gymnocephala	-	-	X	-	X	X	-	-	-	-	-	-	-	-	-	E	-	-	-
P. peltata (2)	-	X	X	-	X	X	X	-	N	N	N	N	N	N	-	-	-	-	-
P. crassa	-	-	X	-	X	X	-	-	-	-	-	-	-	-	N	-	-	-	-
P. roanoka	-	-	X	-	X	X	X	-	-	-	-	IP	N	N	-	IP	-	-	-
P. evides	-	-	X	-	X	X	-	-	-	-	-	-	-	-	-	-	N	N	-
P. aurantiaca	-	-	X	-	X	X	-	-	-	-	-	-	-	-	-	-	E	E	-
P. copelandi	-	-	X	-	X	-	-	-	-	-	-	-	-	-	-	-?	-	N	-
Ammocrypta clara	-	-	X	-	X	-	-	-	-	-	-	-	-	-	-	-	-	N	-
Etheostoma cinereum	-	-	X	-	X	-	-	-	-	-	-	-	-	-	-	-	-	Ep	-
E. swannanoa	-	-	X	X	X	X	X	-	-	-	-	-	-	-	-	-	E	E	-
E. variatum	-	-	X	-	-	X	X	-	-	-	-	-	-	-	-	-	-	-	N
E. kanawhae	-	-	X	X	X	X	X	-	-	-	-	-	-	-	-	E	-	-	-
E. osburni	-	-	X	X	X	X	X	-	-	-	-	-	-	-	-	E	-	-	-
E. blennioides (2)	-	-	X	-	X	X	-	-	IP	-	-	-	-	-	-	N	N	N	N
E. zonale	-	-	X	-	X	X	-	-	-	-	-	-	-	-	-	-	N	N	N
E. simoterum	-	-	X	-	X	X	X	-	-	-	-	-	-	-	-	NI	N	N	NI
E. stigmaeum (2)	-	-	X	-	X	X	-	-	-	-	-	-	-	-	-	-	EEp	NE	-
E. longimanum	-	-	X	X	-	X	X	-	-	-	-	E	-	-	-	-	-	-	-
E. podostemone	-	-	X	X	X	X	X	-	-	-	-	-	-	E	-	-	-	-	-
E. nigrum	-	-	X	-	X	X	X	-	-	-	-	N	N	N	-	N	-	-	N
E. olmstedi (4)	-	X	X	-	X	X	X	N	NN	NN	NNN	NN	NN	NN*	N	I*	-	-	-
E. vitreum	-	X	X	-	X	X	X	-	N*	N	N	N	N	N	-	-	-	-	-
E. camurum	-	-	X	-	X	X	-	-	-	-	-	-	-	-	-	-	N	N	-
E. chlorobranchium	-	-	-	X	-	X	-	-	-	-	-	-	-	-	-	-	E	-	-
E. rufilineatum	-	-	X	-	X	X	X	-	-	-	-	-	-	-	-	-	N	N	-
E. tippecanoe	-	-	X	-	X	-	-	-	-	-	-	-	-	-	-	-	-	N	-
E. acuticeps	-	-	X	-	X	-	-	-	-	-	-	-	-	-	-	-	E	-	-
E. vulneratum	-	-	X	-	X	X	-	-	-	-	-	-	-	-	-	-	E	E	-
E. caeruleum	-	-	X	-	X	X	X	-	NI*	-	-	-	-	-	-	NI	-	N	N
E. flabellare (4)	-	-	X	X	X	X	X	-	N	-	-	N	N	N	N	N	N	N	N
E. percnurum	-	-	X	-	-	X	-	-	-	-	-	-	-	-	-	-	-	N	-
E. serrifer	-	X	-	-	-	X	X	-	-	-	-	N	N	N*	-	-	-	-	-
E. fusiforme	X	X	X	-	-	X	X	-	N	-	-	N	N	N*	-	-	-	-	-
E. collis	-	-	X	-	-	-	X	-	-	-	-	-	-	N	-	-	-	-	-
Sciaenidae [1]																			
Aplodinotus grunniens	-	-	X	-	X	-	-	-	-	-	-	-	-	-	-	-	-	N	-

BIOGEOGRAPHY

BY ROBERT E. JENKINS

How many fish species inhabit the Roanoke River drainage? Why do six kinds of fishes occur only in the Roanoke; conversely, why are many Roanoke species widespread in the eastern United States? How did fishes cross montane drainage divides to reach the Roanoke? Why are some Roanoke species more closely related to fishes living west of the Atlantic slope–Ohio basin divide than to any of those occupying Atlantic drainages adjacent to the Roanoke? Why are some species found mainly in mountain streams, and others restricted to lowland swampy habitat?

These are some of the kinds of questions addressed by biogeographers. Answers often constitute hypotheses, qualified conclusions, and predictions, some highly speculative. They stem partly from present ecologic conditions of a region and from physiology, habitat requirements, functional anatomy, and other traits of species. Phylogenetic relationships often must also be known in order to understand distribution patterns. Phylogeny and geology are the essence of historical biogeography, which attempts to explain distribution based on past, often ancient events. The full biogeographic story may unfold only from reconstructing the past; biohistory is tied to geohistory (Rosen 1985b).

Other common aims of biogeography are to compare species richness and quantitatively assess faunal relationships among different land and water areas. Developing the requisite data base may demand categorizing all pertinent taxa as native or introduced, an effort often confounded by undocumented introductions. Our conclusions on original distributional status represent a best estimate (Tables 2, 3; *Appendix 2*).

SOME APPROACHES TO BIOGEOGRAPHY
Stream Capture and Speciation

Zoogeographic interpretation of Virginia's inland fishes began with Cope's quest during 1867 (*History*). In an embryonic time of evolutionary thinking, he (1868b) indicated that after formation of the Appalachians and their principal drainages, fishes had opportunity for "descent with modification" in separate drainages. He explained trans-divide distributions of headwater species with rudiments of the stream capture theory of fish dispersal.

Jordan (1877b) noted that headwater faunas of adjacent montane drainages have species in common which are absent in low elevations. Based partly on his collecting through Virginia in 1888, he (1905, 1908) penned a "law of geminate species"—a species is not likely found in the same drainage as its phylogenetically closest relative, but in a neighboring one. Jordan (1902, 1928) also pioneered the thinking of drainages as "islands"—areas where species are isolated and may differentiate and adapt to local conditions. As a mode by which fishes may become isolated, he (1928) mentioned the mechanism of stream capture, but like Cope, he did not use the term and instead emphasized floods and marshes as routes for crossing divides.

Often called stream piracy, capture is a natural process by which a stream (the captor) eroded headward into a divide, contacted an adjacent stream or aquifer (the captive), and diverted it into the captor. The captor had an erosional advantage by having a steeper gradient or by flowing on softer rocks than the captive. Thus an aquatic biota could be transferred directly from the captive stream to the captor; two-way exchanges probably occurred less often. Autopiracy is the capture of a stream by another of the

43

same drainage. Such intradrainage piracies probably occurred more frequently than the interdrainage captures, which are believed to have been more significant to fish dispersal and speciation.

In alluding to stream capture, Cope and Jordan addressed elements of the allopatric speciation model: upon subdivision of a population, one or more descendent populations diverged genetically in isolation and became separate taxa. Stream capture and speciation are prehistorical events; today we can see only the evidence of their occurrence.

Geologists were writing on stream capture in the late 1800s (Ross 1972a). By 1900, students of mollusks and crustaceans were considering species distributions relative to drainage modifications, including capture (Adams 1901; Johnson 1905; Ortmann 1908, 1913). Bailey (1938a, 1945, 1948) and Myers (1938) briefly mentioned capture relative to fish distribution. Ross broadly applied stream capture theory to fish zoogeography, particularly in Virginia (Ross 1952, 1962, 1969, 1972a; Ross and Carico 1963). In a classic paper, Kuehne and Bailey (1961) analyzed stream piracy and fish speciation in a Kentucky area.

Until recently, most inquiries of historical biogeography had been approached with an essentially dispersalistic outlook, dispersal being an active or passive movement of individuals or populations into areas formerly uninhabited by that species (Wiley 1981). Thus much of the interpretive effort on eastern North American montane and upland fishes rested on stream capture theory; extended rivers and glacial outlets were more important in lowland or northerly areas.

Vicariance Biogeography

The recently developed vicariance approach emphasizes the recognition of congruent biogeographic tracks; a track is a line that defines the geographic range of a species or a higher monophyletic taxon (Wiley 1981). By using analytical techniques to determine the correspondence of tracks with cladograms (phylogenetic trees), general factors that affected the coevolution and distribution of a biota can be seen; then aspects of the geologic history of the region involved may be indicated (Nelson 1978; Nelson and Platnick 1981; Wiley 1981, 1988; Humphries and Parenti 1986; Funk and Brooks 1990).

A tenet of vicariance is that differentiation of organisms is related to the formation of a barrier that subdivided the range of the ancestral taxon. Depending on the taxa, barriers can include heavily turbid and silted rivers, harsh climates, glacial ice sheets, low drainage divides formed by upwarping, and newly upthrusted mountain ranges. Thus, in vicariance a *barrier was imposed* within the range of a taxon (the formation of the barrier being a vicariant event), whereas in dispersal, a *barrier was crossed* and one taxon (or more) founded a new population.

Vicariant patterns are recognized among the freshwater ichthyofaunas of eastern United States (e.g., Mayden 1985a, 1987a, 1987b, 1988a; Wiley and Mayden 1985) and elsewhere in North America (e.g., Hocutt and Wiley 1986). Numerous tracks involve species of Virginia fishes; most of those identified lie fully west of the Atlantic slope. The formation of most of the montane–upland, trans-Atlantic divide tracks in Virginia (and south) undoubtedly involved stock dispersal via stream capture. The origin of the Appalachian divide barrier has no relevance to the genesis of the modern fish fauna because it greatly antedates that fauna. Subsequent uplift of the Appalachians may be viewed as a vicariant event—it was an impetus to the occurrence of captures. Barriers related to glacial climate and sea level changes after (and perhaps during) the Miocene probably were factors in the evolution of modern Atlantic slope fishes from ancestors previously on the slope. Vicariance analysis of Atlantic slope fishes will lag until the phylogenetic linkages among many more of its species and to those westward are elucidated.

Most vicariance biogeographers acknowledge dispersal to be important in speciation, but explanations using dispersal should be a conclusion, not a first-order assumption (Wiley 1981, 1988; Mayden 1987b). A partial fusion of vicariance and dispersalistic approaches is indicated also by allowing that post-vicariant "secondary" dispersal has led to speciation, and by categorizing stream capture as a vicariant event.

Ecological Biogeography

Ecogeography concerns the distribution of organisms, often on the local population level, and the mechanisms which affect this distribution (Wiley 1981). Although molded by genetic and geographic prehistory, the essence of species distributions is recent ecological conditions. Often varying by life stage, most fish species prefer or closely associate with certain habitats; for example, streams of a certain range in size, substrate, and water chemistry (Matthews and Heins 1987). Ecological distribution may be analyzed at many levels; for example, by resource partitioning at particular sites (Ross 1986), variations through watersheds and ecoregions (Lyons 1989; Frissell et al. 1986), and the dynamics in entire streams—the river continuum concept (Vannote et al. 1980; Minshall et al. 1983).

DATA SET

In the following treatments the sequence of serially listed taxa is that of the species accounts, hence that of the distribution maps and Table 2.

Coverage

The history of fish inventory in Virginia is described under *History*; collection sites are depicted by year groups in Maps 1–5. Most of the state has been moderately to intensively sampled, especially during 1968–1987. The few collections made during 1867–1899 sketch the fauna in the late 1800s and thus are critical for recognizing faunal changes. The composition of the fish community in streams where few or no collections have been made generally can be estimated from data on adjacent parts of the same drainage.

The most intensively sampled areas or streams of Virginia (Map 5) include: Fairfax County, adjacent to Washington, D.C. (Kelso and Bright 1976; later by R. E. Watson, in litt.); large riverine estuaries from the Potomac to the James (annual trawl surveys by the Virginia Institute of Marine Science); the Blue Ridge Province, particularly by the Virginia Trout Survey (Mohn and Bugas 1980); the extreme upper Roanoke drainage (Jenkins 1979a; Burkhead 1983); the North Fork Holston River (Ross and Carico 1963; Jenkins and Burkhead 1984; Feeman 1986); and Copper Creek, a tributary of the Clinch River near the Tennessee line (Jenkins and Burkhead 1973).

We have scant data on the fishes of all nontidal sections of the James River, except for one short segment and one site. Our understanding of the middle James River fauna is derived principally from concentrated sampling in the Bremo Bluff area on the middle Piedmont. Another well-sampled site is the upper James River just above Craig Creek (Leonard et al. 1986). An extensive fish survey of the James River above the Fall Line was begun in 1987 by G. C. Garman, but few data were available when this section was written.

Drainage Occurrence Status

The status of taxa in the principal Virginia drainages, including extralimital portions of some, is listed in Table 2 and summarized in Table 3. These tables and *Appendix 2* revise the faunal lists by Jenkins et al. (1972), Stauffer et al. (1982), Hocutt et al. (1986), and Starnes and Etnier (1986). Many of the new or revised listings in those references were not documented in print; those applicable to the present work are docu-

mented in distribution sections of our species accounts. For many species the original distribution status in one or more drainages remains uncertain; some cases are noted below, where status changes could alter zoogeographic perspective.

Problematic Records

Many species lists that we obtained had problematic data (e.g., suspect or clearly faulty locality descriptors and species identifications). We attempted to decipher the problems because of the possible worth of the data; for example, as indicators of relict populations, of fading species, or simply because the data were usable if clarified. We often encountered conflicting evidence from specimen labels, field notes, and maps, and many dead ends. In the end a problem was either rectified or the information was rejected. Rejected ("problematic," "questionable," or "unverified") records that are critical are shown on distribution maps by special symbols. Many of the vexatious records are important; often these are old and unique, and some may be validated in the future. A few of the more pervasive cases are noted here.

Some records in Cope's (1868b) species accounts do not align with those in his distribution table, notably for *Exoglossum maxillingua, Ambloplites cavifrons, Micropterus dolomieu*, and *Etheostoma longimanum*. Some of the problems are exacerbated by Fowler's (1907, 1910, 1923, 1924) treatments of Cope's specimens. Some of McDonald's collections made in 1885, on the first foray after Cope's, are plagued by missing or tangled data (e.g., some of his collections of *Hybognathus regius* and *Thoburnia rhothoeca*).

We do not accept the one record each of seven species listed by Jordan (1889b) from Shingle Creek at the mouth of Jericho Ditch, on the north edge of Dismal Swamp. Habitat at the Shingle Creek site grades sharply from freshwater swamp to brackish tidal (Jordan 1889b; M. D. Norman, in litt.). Both biotopes are distinctly inappropriate for some species reported by Jordan or reidentified from his collection: *Notropis amoenus, N. procne, Moxostoma anisurum, Noturus insignis, Percina peltata*, and *Etheostoma vitreum*; his record of *Notropis chalybaeus* is questioned. Jordon's site was sampled in 1984, and yielded none of the above species and few others (M. D. Norman, in litt.).

Many problems have existed with locality data for collections made before 1968 and stored at VPISU. (These collections, subsequent holdings, and associated data were transferred to the AMNH in 1983.) Many problems were resolved; many records were rejected; for example, *Campostoma anomalum, Luxilus cerasinus*, *Pimephales notatus*, *Scartomyzon ariommus*, and *Moxostoma erythrurum* in the Chowan drainage.

Seeking support for peculiar records is often rewarding. For example, we doubted that Jordan had taken in the Blackwater River at Zuni—in the middle Coastal Plain—the many Piedmont or farther inland-dwelling species he reported there. Nearly a century later at or near Zuni, M. D. Norman (in litt.) found all the species reported by Jordan, plus an isolated population of *Notropis altipinnis*.

Future Collecting

Field-workers with a bent for exploration should survey the following waters that are among the least sampled in the state: most Coastal Plain tributaries of the four major drainages of the Chesapeake basin, particularly the southern tributaries of the James River estuary; warm streams of the upper North Fork Shenandoah system; Piedmont sections of James River tributaries; the Banister River system, a tributary of the lower Dan River in the Roanoke drainage Piedmont; and southern tributaries of the middle and lower Piedmont reach of the Roanoke River (from the head of Kerr Reservoir up to Leesville Dam).

Other areas where survey results would be of particular interest include many tributaries of the Shenandoah system and the New and Big Sandy drainages. Several species have a peculiar distribution there, perhaps owing to their waning or recent introduction. An objective of such surveys should be to discern changes in species ranges.

ECOLOGICAL DISTRIBUTION PATTERNS

Fish distribution is governed by obvious and subtle biological, chemical, and physical conditions. Some of these are considered below in reference to the inland Virginia ichthyofauna; many related terms are defined in *Introduction to Accounts* and the *Glossary*.

Lotic and Lentic Habitats

Running water, whether rapidly or barely flowing, defines the lotic environment—streams in general. Lentic (or lacustrine) environments such as ponds, lakes, and still swamps have standing water. Virginia's freshwater fish fauna is primarily lotic, for this environment forms most of the habitat long available. Of the 210 species in the state, 68 (32%) frequently or typically occupy lentic habitats (Table 2), many of them only in recently created impoundments. The most notable lentic-adapted families are the pikes (Esocidae, all four species) and sunfishes (Cen-

trarchidae, 18 of 19 species). All 68 lentic fish species have been found in at least one Virginia stream.

Pool, Run, and Riffle Habitats

Pools and slow areas along margins of faster current probably comprise more surface area than do riffles in Virginia streams; thus it is not surprising that most stream species are found most frequently in pools, backwaters, and slow runs. Based on habitat associations of large juveniles and adults of the 210 species during spring, summer, and fall, 91 (43%) chiefly inhabit pools; 47 (22%) typically occupy both pools and runs; and 29 (14%) are found nearly equally in pools, runs, and riffles. Only 41 species (20%) are characterized as run–riffle fishes; none is an obligate riffle dweller. Two species—*Erimystax cahni* and *Ammocrypta clara*—were recorded only in runs; although they are quite rare in the state, runs are their typical habitat elsewhere. Percentages of fishes living in swift water increase westward from the typically sluggish waters of the Coastal Plain into the high-gradient montane streams.

The disproportionate partitioning of stream habitats by fishes is not surprising. Although riffles tend to be most productive of benthic invertebrate fish foods, rapid turbulent current is a rigorous environment. Swift-water species—chiefly certain chubs, small suckers, sculpins, and many darters—are largely benthic. They tend to be small, have a reduced or vestigial gas bladder, and live under or in the lee of stones; thus they can avoid the displacing and energy-sapping effects of swift current. Pool and slow-run species include many minnows, larger suckers, larger catfishes, and sunfishes. They feed on aquatic organisms that drift from riffles, those produced in pools, terrestrial forms, or detritus. Some pool inhabitants, notably most suckers, spawn in runs and riffles where substrates are swept relatively free of egg-smothering silt; these were not counted as typical occupants of runs and riffles unless they often feed there as well.

Gradient and Physiography

The degree of slope (gradient) of streams determines the amounts of slow and swift habitats, substrate types, and many related factors. The physiography of an area is a primary determinant of gradient, thus the distribution of most Virginia fishes reflects to some extent the locations of the physiographic provinces (e.g., Jenkins and Burkhead 1975a).

The distribution of species by general gradients and terrains is indicated in Table 2. "Lowland" refers to the typical, moderately to very sluggish conditions on the Coastal Plain and certain parts of the lower Piedmont. "Upland," the category with the largest extent in Virginia, indicates streams of moderate gradient; runs and riffles form 10–50% of the length. Upland streams characterize the middle and upper Piedmont and the larger streams in the Blue Ridge and west. "Montane" connotes rapid and tumbling streams, 50% or more of which is riffles; these streams are on higher, steeper slopes of the Valley and Ridge and the Blue Ridge provinces.

Of the 210 species, 20 are characteristic of lowland habitats; 49 typically occupy both lowlands and uplands; 104 are restricted to uplands; and 36 are upland–montane forms. Only *Etheostoma chlorobranchium*, known in Virginia only from one stream, seems confined to montane conditions in the state.

Lowland fishes that are virtually restricted to the Coastal Plain include *Notropis chalybaeus*, *Erimyzon sucetta*, *Chologaster cornuta*, *Fundulus lineolatus*, *Enneacanthus obesus*, and *E. chaetodon* (Maps 80, 88, 122, 127, 143, 145). Most other lowland species occur predominantly or widely on the Coastal Plain but in one or more drainages also inhabit the Piedmont, most of them only the lower section; for example, *Esox americanus*, *Aphredoderus sayanus*, *Acantharchus pomotis*, *Centrarchus macropterus*, *Enneacanthus gloriosus*, *Etheostoma serrifer*, and *E. fusiforme* (Maps 33, 121, 139, 140, 144, 190, 191).

Chiefly or strictly Piedmont species include *Notropis alborus*, *N. altipinnis*, *Fundulus rathbuni*, *Etheostoma vitreum*, and *E. collis* (Maps 78, 81, 126, 181, 191). Most of the Atlantic slope species categorized as strictly upland inhabitants or which have upland affinity extend from mountainous provinces to well into the Piedmont or lower. A few species exhibit marked fidelity to only one of the three mountainous physiographic provinces; for example, *Notropis semperasper* and the *Cottus carolinae* group in the Valley and Ridge Province (Maps 70, 133). Some species found largely in mountainous areas have a disjunct population in and near the Fall Zone, indicating the localized, relatively high-gradient nature of the zone; these include *Exoglossum maxillingua* and *Percina rex* (Maps 47, 161). Other montane and upland fishes may have denser populations in the Fall Zone than in the lower Piedmont and upper Coastal Plain, but quantitative data are unavailable.

Several species occur largely, or clearly are most successful in the Blue Ridge Province; some of these extend south to Georgia in this mountain chain. Blue Ridge species include *Phenacobius teretulus*, *P. crassilabrum*, *Notropis scabriceps*, *N. spectrunculus*, *Etheostoma kanawhae*, and *E. chlorobranchium* (Maps 53, 74, 76, 174, 182). The influence of gradient on these patterns is discussed by Gilbert (1980); in some cases temperature, alkalinity, stream size, and competition from close relatives may also be involved. An example of a distribution-modifying effect of temperature concerns *Etheostoma swannanoa*, a coolwater fish that occurs largely in moderate to high-gradient Blue Ridge streams; it has recently been found in Valley and Ridge streams that are markedly influenced by large cold springs (Map 173).

No species is confined to the Fall Zone or its vicinity; this area is narrow and has a mixture of habitat types characteristic of more inland provinces and, to a lesser extent, the Coastal Plain.

Substrate, Siltation, and Turbidity

Many species prefer bottoms of clean loose gravel, rubble, or boulder, which are assumed to have been the dominant substrate types (along with bedrock in many streams) from the Fall Line west before deforestation. Loose coarse substrate has abundant spaces between and under stones to support the invertebrate foods of many fishes and to serve as egg deposition sites and cover from predators. Small species generally avoid open flat bedrock, where shelter essentially is nonexistent; irregular bedrock outcroppings often serve as foraging and hiding places.

Siltation and turbidity probably are the most pervasive deleterious factors to the Virginia ichthyofauna, much as they have been shown to be elsewhere (Berkman and Rabeni 1987). Siltation occurs when suspended solids, which cause turbidity, settle from the water column. The fine sediment tends to smother gravel and rubble and to fill interstices around boulders, and thus reduces benthic biota and buries breeding sites. Turbidity reduces the food-finding ability of sight-feeding fishes, of which there are many in Virginia. Many pool and backwater-inhabiting species commonly occur over silt bottom, but the food of many of these is drift from harder substrate or the terrestrial realm, and most or all of the species spawn on harder substrate or attach eggs above the bottom.

A few species have specific substrate requirements; when the substrate is a firm or hard type, such fishes tend to be the rarest or most localized of all. For example, *Erimystax cahni* and *Etheostoma tippecanoe* occur mainly on major beds of pea-sized gravel in runs of large streams and rivers (Maps 50, 184). The burrowing *Etheostoma vitreum* may be an obligate sand dweller. Some fishes that live in swift montane streams may spawn in sandy patches scattered among rubble and boulder substrates. Sizeable areas of sand are rare in rapids of montane streams in Virginia. Sandy patches in calm portions of streams above the Fall Line generally are overlain with silt.

Temperature

Water temperatures are related to latitude, altitude, season, weather, shade, and proximity to springs. Thermal requirements of some species vary by life stage; different life processes may be tuned to different temperature regimes. Difficulties of categorizing fish species by temperature relations are noted under *Introduction to Accounts*. Based mainly on temperature at capture during warmer parts of the year, 124 (59%) of the 210 Virginia fishes are found exclusively in warmwater types of habitat; 54 (26%) in warm and cool situations; 1 seemingly strictly in cool water (*Etheostoma swannanoa*); 11 in cool to cold situations; 1 almost entirely in cold water (*Cottus cognatus*); and 19 in all three types. Many temperature associations may be related to other factors that tend to coincide with a certain range of temperature.

Stream Size and Longitudinal Zonation

It has been repeatedly demonstrated that most fish species occupy streams or stream reaches of particular size ranges, thus their distributions are longitudinally zoned. Longitudinal zonation is documented in Virginia by Burton and Odum (1945), Flemer and Woolcott (1966), Jenkins and Freeman (1972), Hambrick (1973), Jenkins and Burkhead (1973), Masnik (1974), Stauffer et al. (1975), Garman et al. (1982), Feeman (1986), Matthews (1986a), and Maurakis et al. (1987). An analysis of studies on longitudinal zonation relative to stream order is by Matthews (1986a). The stream order system in our region classifies stream segments according to tributary union pattern, hence by size.

Zonation is related to many factors; for example, water temperature, permanency of flow, depth, cover, and substrate, all of which usually vary with distance from headwaters. Fishes are roughly classifiable longitudinally by the range of size (width) of streams typically inhabited. In our three-category system (Table 2), a "creek" is 10 m (33 feet) or less in width; a "river" is generally broader than 50 m (165 feet); a "stream" is intermediate.

In Virginia, 22 species are characteristic of rivers only; 61 are river and stream fish; 9 are confined to streams; 44 occupy streams and creeks; 4 typically or exclusively inhabit only creeks (*Phoxinus tennesseensis*, *Clinostomus funduloides*, *Etheostoma collis*, and Bluestone sculpin); and about 69 species are frequently encountered in all three types.

Species richness (number of species) in stream reaches is related to longitudinal zonation (Hynes 1970). Headwaters nearly universally have fewer species than do medium and large streams in the same system; progressing downstream, headwater species disappear and more-speciose assemblages take their place. Species richness in lakes also tends to increase directly with the size of the lake (Barbour and Brown 1974). However, faunal enrichment of large bodies of water often may be limited by factors other than size; for example, large but heavily turbid and silted North American rivers generally have fewer species than somewhat smaller, clear rivers.

There are many more creeks than rivers in eastern North America, but the summed lengths, areas, or volumes of each waterway type tend to be similar. Thus small- and medium-sized river-dwelling species may have about the same amount of available habitat as do those of creeks. By their size, rivers naturally tend to be the most stable; they ameliorate effects of catastrophic conditions (e.g., floods) in creeks. This inequality is nullified, however, by the prevalent siting on rivers of large population centers, major industries, and big dams. Thus species confined to rivers tend to be the most frequently endangered by adverse changes.

pH

The acid–base balance of water affects the geographic range of many species. Some species seem to be prohibited from very low-pH (highly acidic) water, as indicated by their avoidance of certain sections of the Coastal Plain, notably the interior Dismal Swamp. Very low pH, below about 5.0, has been regarded as a natural pollutant.

Species that appear tolerant of moderate to rather high acidity (pH of 4.5–6.0), include *Lepisosteus osseus*, *Amia calva*, *Esox niger*, *E. americanus*, *Umbra pygmaea*, *Notemigonus crysoleucas*, *Notropis chalybaeus*, *Erimyzon sucetta*, *Ameiurus natalis*, *A. nebulosus*, *Salvelinus fontinalis*, *Aphredoderus sayanus*, *Chologaster cornuta*, *Fundulus lineolatus*, *Gambusia holbrooki*, *Acantharchus pomotis*, *Centrarchus macropterus*, all three *Enneacanthus*, *Lepomis gulosus*, *L. macrochirus*, *L. gibbosus*, *Perca flavescens*, *Etheostoma serrifer*, and *E. fusiforme*. All of these except *S. fontinalis* are lowland dwellers in Virginia; many are identified as acid tolerant in the New Jersey Pine Barrens, Okefenokee Swamp, and elsewhere (Smith 1953; Collette 1962; Hastings 1979, 1984). The brook trout is adapted to moderately low pH but, with its associated biota, may be declining in some Virginia streams owing to acid precipitation shocks.

The concentration of populations of some other species in limestone-based streams of the Valley and Ridge Province may be related in part to the generally high pH and considerable hardness of those waters. The *Cottus carolinae* group (Map 133) affords perhaps the best examples.

Salinity

Several species generally regarded as strictly freshwater inhabitants, or which belong to so-classified families, extend downstream in estuaries into varying degrees of brackish water. Eleven species that typically occupy or migrate in medium or high salinities are denoted by "Ma" (marine) in Table 2; some of them usually do not inhabit the ocean.

Strictly freshwater species have been widely termed "primary division" freshwater fishes; "secondary division" species are considered relatively salt tolerant, at least for short periods (Myers 1938, 1949). Rosen (1974) advocated rejection of this system and reapplication of the terms "continental" and "oceanic" to the salinity distribution of fishes.

Vegetation and Other Cover

Cover is a chief commodity to most fishes. It serves as a substrate for food organisms, and it is important to many small species and juveniles of large species for predator avoidance. Adults of large species may be imprinted on cover, and cover is important to many ambushing predators. Cover may be used year-long or as breeding sites. Various types of natural cover are used, including plants, logs, rocks, and the banks. The increase of sunken trash such as cans, crockery, and boards has favored some species, notably certain madtoms, sculpins, and darters. The areas most often barren of fishes tend to be open and floored largely by sand, silt, or bedrock.

GEOGRAPHIC DISTRIBUTION PATTERNS: SINGLE SPECIES

Although labeled single-species patterns, it is unlikely that any distribution or habitat-use pattern is not shaped to some extent by the presence or absence of other species.

Widespread; Generally Distributed

Widespread species are those that occur within a large area of Virginia. They may also have a general distribution; that is, they may be regularly found in suitable habitat that is widely available. Examples are

Semotilus atromaculatus (in creeks only), *Nocomis leptocephalus*, *Catostomus commersoni*, *Noturus insignis*, and *Etheostoma flabellare* (Maps 46, 49, 102, 112, 188). Some other species are confined to one or few drainages but are generally distributed there; for example, *Notropis leuciodus*, *N. telescopus*, *Hypentelium roanokense*, and *Etheostoma rufilineatum* (Maps 66, 72, 91, 183).

Localized and Relict Species

A localized species may have a small or wide dispersion. The entire species is localized when the range is particularly small. For localized species with a wide range, some or all populations are disjunct and small. Localized fishes include *Ichthyomyzon greeleyi* (localized over its entire wide range); *Exoglossum maxillingua* (localized in several parts of its wide range); *Cottus baileyi* (localized over its entire small range, to cool and cold streams); *Ambloplites cavifrons* (localized in much of its moderate-sized range); and *Percina macrocephala* (localized in its entire wide range) (Maps 14, 47, 130, 138, 163).

Localized populations and species often are termed distributional relicts, but the term relict more correctly means reduction of range to a small fraction of its former size. The concept of distributional relicts differs from that of phylogenetic relicts; both may apply to the same species. Examples include the dwindled range of some of the many species adversely affected by recent habitat alteration: *Cyprinella monacha*, *Noturus gilberti*, and *Percina rex* (Maps 56, 111, 161). Relict distribution of the cool- and coldwater inhabitants *Margariscus margarita* and *Cottus cognatus* apparently has a natural cause—postglacial warming of streams—but has been furthered by deforestation (Maps 44, 131).

Endemism

Endemic taxa are taxa that live in only one drainage. The meaning of the term can be broadened (e.g., endemic to a larger hydrographic entity or to a political unit) or narrowed (found only in one system within a drainage). Endemic taxa are often thought to have originated in the drainage of their present occurrence; however, some may have arisen elsewhere but were extirpated there.

Of Virginia's 230 species and subspecies, 33 are endemic (Tables 2, 3). The most endemic taxa (16) are in the Tennessee drainage; numbers sharply decline eastward and northward—the New has 7, Roanoke 6, James 3, Potomac 1, and the other drainages none. Of the endemic taxa, four are known only from the Virginia portion of their drainage: *Notropis semperasper*,

Thoburnia hamiltoni, spotted madtom, and Clinch sculpin (*T. hamiltoni* and perhaps an intergrade of the madtom may just extend into North Carolina). Endemic taxa that barely range beyond the state are *Cottus baileyi*, into Tennessee; and Bluestone sculpin *Etheostoma longimanum* and *Percina notogramma montuosa*, into West Virginia.

Considering the full extent of drainages, the New drainage has the second highest percentage of endemic taxa (17.4%) among eastern and central North American drainages—8 of its 46 native nondiadromous fishes. The Tennessee drainage has 14.4% endemism (32 of 222 taxa). The large southerly Mobile drainage (or basin), flowing to the Gulf of Mexico, leads in relative endemism east of the Rockies (and leads the whole continent in numbers of endemic taxa), with 25.4% (43 of 169 taxa), as compiled chiefly from Swift et al. (1986), Boschung (1989), Mettee et al. (1989), and Pierson et al. (1989). On the Atlantic slope, peak endemism occurs in the Albemarle basin, comprising the Roanoke, Chowan, and minor drainages—8.2% (7 of 85 taxa).

Two entirely Virginia taxa often considered endemic to one drainage are here regarded as exclusively shared taxa: *Percina rex* occupies two drainages and *Etheostoma olmstedi vexillare* is genetically represented in two; their distributional status is explained below and in *Appendix 2*.

Unusual Patterns

Some species skip one or more drainages; that is, they apparently are absent from one or two drainages having seemingly favorable habitat but occur in surrounding drainages. Most notable are *Campostoma anomalum, Carpiodes cyprinus,* and *Etheostoma flabellare* (absent in Rappahannock and York; Maps 43, 87, 188); *Lampetra aepyptera* (Chowan and Roanoke; Map 17); *Notropis bifrenatus* (Roanoke and south; Map 79). Some lowland species have a large range hiatus comprising much or all of the western Chesapeake basin: *Notropis chalybaeus, Acantharchus pomotis, Enneacanthus obesus, E. chaetodon,* and *Etheostoma fusiforme* (Maps 80, 139, 143, 145, 191). Most of the range gaps result from the lack of ingress routes to the drainages or from extirpation. Other cases of absentee or missing species are discussed under drainage faunas.

Several instances exist of putative native populations which occur distinctly out of their normal range, or where the absence of a species from a major part of a drainage is peculiar; for example, *Esox niger* in the upper James and Roanoke, *E. americanus* in the Potomac and James, *Notropis volucellus* in the James and Roanoke, *Pimephales notatus* in the Tennessee, *Ameiurus platycephalus* in the James, *A. natalis* in the middle Roanoke, and *Aphredoderus sayanus* in the Potomac (Maps 32, 33, 75, 81, 86, 106, 108, 121). Some of these cases may have stemmed from introduction.

Contracting Ranges and Extirpations

Many fish species recently have suffered partial range loss in, or have been extirpated from Virginia by human-caused modifications of aquatic and riparian systems. Some long-term natural causes of range constriction include postglacial warming of waters and drowning of lowland waterways; reduction of water temperature during glacial times probably was also a factor.

Of particular interest are natural extinctions that create gaps in the phylogenetic record. Such extinctions are indicated by the distribution of, for example, *Notropis semperasper, N. scabriceps,* the genus *Thoburnia, Scartomyzon ariommus, Noturus gilberti, Ambloplites cavifrons* (possibly), and the subgenus *Percina*. The Maryland endemic species *Etheostoma sellare* belongs in this group, to which Mayden (1987b) adds *Luxilus cerasinus*. The New drainage is involved in most of these cases, usually as the gap.

Expanding Ranges

Many species are expanding their range in Virginia, mostly owing to recent introduction (*Introduced Species;* species accounts) and to habitat changes. Concerning habitat changes, *Phenacobius mirabilis, Notropis stramineus,* and *N. buccatus* apparently recently entered the Virginia portion of the Big Sandy drainage (Maps 53, 77, 82), probably in response to an increase in sandy substrate and attrition of competitors. *Notropis telescopus* appears poised to explosively spread in the upper James drainage (Map 72); it probably was introduced recently. Many species that were reduced or eliminated from the North Fork Holston and Clinch rivers by pollution are returning.

GEOGRAPHIC DISTRIBUTION PATTERNS: SHARED

Patterns that are shared, in the sense of being produced by a pair or small group of closely related taxa, are among the most interesting distribution patterns. Often they help to identify the point in the speciation process reached by the taxa.

Allopatry

Allopatric taxa occupy distinctly separate ranges. For those living in the same drainage, the gap between them may mean either that the intervening habitat is unsuitable or that insufficient time has elapsed for colonization of the gap. An example of allopatry within a single drainage that involves intimately related taxa may not exist in Virginia, although some of the first eight species pairs listed under *Parapatry* may qualify.

Allopatric freshwater fish taxa more typically are separated by a physical barrier, usually a drainage divide. Often the resultant geminate distribution pattern indicates the barrier that caused isolation and allowed evolutionary divergence of the taxa. Some examples of allopatry are (map numbers in parentheses): *Nocomis platyrhynchus* allopatric to *N. micropogon* and *N. raneyi* (48); *Luxilus albeolus* and *L. cornutus* (62); *Thoburnia rhothoeca* and *T. hamiltoni* (92); *Cottus bairdi* group (130); perhaps the Bluestone sculpin and *C. carolinae* (132, 133); *C. carolinae* group (133); and *Etheostoma longimanum* and *E. podostemone* (179).

Parapatry

Parapatric fishes occupy the same drainage but essentially live separately; their ranges abut or overlap very slightly. The taxa typically are intimately related species (e.g., those in the same subgenus or species group); many qualify as sibling, sister, or cognate species. Often they have not distinctly diverged ecologically, thus they may be unable to inhabit the same area without one displacing the other. Alternatively, the species may be ecologically segregated; often this is indicated by the coinciding of a range boundary with a break in habitat. Major ecologic breaks include the Fall Zone and the boundary between the Blue Ridge and the Valley and Ridge provinces (Jenkins et al. 1972; Gilbert 1980; Starnes and Etnier 1986).

Parapatric taxa in Virginia, some with interdigitating ranges, are *Nocomis micropogon* and *N. raneyi* (48); *Phenacobius crassilabrum* and *P. uranops* (53, Tennessee also); sawfin shiner and *Notropis spectrunculus* (76); *Etheostoma kanawhae* and *E. osburni* (174); *E. camurum* and *E. chlorobranchium* (182; perhaps before impoundment; now parapatric in Tennessee); *E. flabellare* and *E. percnurum* (188, 189); and *E. collis* and *E. fusiforme* (191; possibly in the Roanoke drainage and the Carolinas). Another case involves species apparently introduced to the New drainage, *Notropis rubricroceus* and *N. chiliticus* (67). The basis for range separation is not certain in any of these cases. The pattern of the *Nocomis* and the first and third pairs of *Etheostoma* may stem from competition; within the pairs, both species have very similar habits and habitat preferences. Some cases may be due to recent habitat modification.

Sympatry and Zones of Secondary Contact

After spatial separation and evolutionary divergence of populations, one or both forms may expand their ranges such that they become sympatric; that is, they substantially overlap geographically. Often the zone of sympatry, or secondary contact, becomes a zone of hybridization (infrequent interbreeding between species) or intergradation (massive interbreeding between subspecies and less-distinctive forms). Examples (some related to recent introduction) involve *Rhinichthys atratulus* subspecies (42); *Exoglossum laurae* and *E. maxillingua* (47); *Ambloplites rupestris* and *A. cavifrons* (137, 138); possibly *Percina notogramma* subspecies (164); *Etheostoma stigmaeum* subspecies (178); and *Etheostoma nigrum* and *E. olmstedi* (180).

Virginia has many examples of fairly closely related species that have developed differences (or encountered such abundant resources) as to enable wide sympatry: *Ichthyomyzon bdellium* and *I. greeleyi* (13, 14); *Nocomis leptocephalus* with the other three *Nocomis* (48, 49); *Luxilus coccogenis* and *L. chrysocephalus* (60, 62); *Notropis ariommus* and *N. telescopus* (71, 72); *N. procne* and *N. alborus* (77, 78); *Hypentelium nigricans* and *H. roanokense* (90, 91); *Percina burtoni* and *P. caprodes* (161, 162); *P. notogramma* and *P. peltata* (164, 166); *Etheostoma longimanum* and *E. podostemone* with *E. nigrum* (179, 180); *Etheostoma* (*Nothonotus*) (182–186); and *E. serrifer* and *E. fusiforme* (190, 191). In some of these cases the species occupy even the same habitat within the sympatric zone; that is, they are syntopic.

SPECIES RICHNESS

Species richness (or taxa richness) is the number of taxa occurring in a habitat, drainage, or some other hydrographic, geographic, or political unit. It tends to increase with increasing size of drainages and lakes, and with the number of physiographic provinces drained. Each Virginia drainage is a separate fluvifaunal unit with a distinctive ichthyofauna. The faunas show varied relationships according to ecologic conditions, geographic proximity, and long-past drainage interconnections.

An overview of species richness is given here; detailed broader analyses for Virginia are by Jenkins et al. (1972) and Hocutt et al. (1986). Discussions are based on the 230 freshwater fish taxa in Virginia plus all extralimital ("non-Va.") taxa of Virginia drainages (Tables 2, 3; *Appendix 2*; Map 6). Data for some systems or drainages are combined under either Delmarva Peninsula, Chesapeake basin, Albemarle Sound,

Table 3 Summary of drainage occurrence status of species, subspecies, and undescribed forms of Virginia drainages, including extralimital (non-Va.) portions, based on Table 2, *Appendix 2*, and text. Hydrographic abbreviations are given in Table 2; also: **Del**—Delmarva Peninsula; **Chp**—Chesapeake basin; **Alb**—Albemarle basin; **Ten**—Tennessee drainage. Status abbreviations are explained in Table 2. Numbers in non-Va. rows are entirely of taxa not in the Virginia portion of the drainage. "All" refers to total taxa in all portions (Va. and non-Va.) of a drainage. Hyphen (-) means not applicable, as the Rappahannock and York drainages are entirely in Virginia; a very small part of the James drainage is extralimital and has no additional species.

Status	Place	Atlantic slope										Ohio River basin				
		Del	Pot	Rap	Yrk	Jam	Chp	Cho	Roa	Alb	PD	New	Hol	C–P	Ten	BS
1. N	Va.	12	51	47	46	65	67	68	59	72	16	28	60	71	74	34
	Non-Va.	27	3	-	-	-	1	1	12	2	59	0	14	21	105	42
2. NI	Va.	1	3	1	3	5	6	1	5	3	1	6	5	6	6	5
	Non-Va.	0	1	-	-	-	0	0	0	1	0	2	0	1	0	0
3. E	Va.	0	1	0	0	3	5	0	6	7	0	7	13	10	16	0
	Non-Va.	0	0	-	-	-	1	0	0	0	1	1	1	4	16	0
4. Ep	Va.	0	2	1	0	0	2	1	0	0	1	1	1	1	1	3
	Non-Va.	1	0	-	-	-	0	0	0	0	0	1	1	3	3	0
5. Ex	Va.	0	0	0	0	0	0	0	0	0	0	0	1	0	1	0
	Non-Va.	0	0	-	-	-	0	0	0	0	0	0	0	0	0	0
6. I	Va.	2	22	15	15	19	22	8	18	18	3	24	11	9	12	8
	Non-Va.	4	2	-	-	-	0	1	1	1	15	2	1	2	5	4
7. Ip	Va.	1	6	6	3	7	8	2	8	8	3	12	6	6	7	4
	Non-Va.	1	0	-	-	-	0	0	0	0	3	4	0	0	1	1
8. Ma	Va.	9	11	10	10	10	12	7	7	7	0	1	0	0	0	0
	Non-Va.	0	0	-	-	-	0	4	3	4	8	0	0	0	1	1
Totals																
9. N (1–5)	Va.	13	57	49	49	73	80	70	70	82	18	42	80	88	98	42
10. N	All	41	61	49	49	73	82	71	82	85	78	46	96	118	222	86
11. I (6+7)	Va.	3	28	21	18	26	30	10	26	26	6	36	17	15	19	12
12. I	All	8	30	21	18	26	30	11	27	26	24	42	18	16	25	15
13. Freshwater (10+12)	All	49	91	70	67	99	112	82	109	112	102	88	114	134	247	101
14. Marine (8)	Va.	9	11	10	10	10	12	7	7	7	0	1	0	0	0	0
15. Marine	All	9	11	10	10	10	12	11	10	11	8	1	0	0	1	1
Grand totals																
16. (9+11+14)	Va.	25	96	80	77	109	122	87	103	115	24	79	97	103	117	54
17. (13+15)	All	58	102	80	77	109	124	93	119	123	110	89	114	134	248	102
% Introduced freshwater I (12)/N+I (13)	All	16.3	33.0	30.0	26.9	26.3	26.8	13.4	24.8	23.2	23.5	47.7	15.8	11.9	10.1	14.8

or Tennessee drainage. Unless specified otherwise, reference is only to species considered native (Table 2: N, NI, E, Ep, Ex) and freshwater (i.e., not Ma).

Interslope and Interdrainage Comparisons

The drainages of Virginia are divisible into those on the Atlantic slope and those tributary to the Ohio River of the Mississippi basin. Species richness in the seven separate Atlantic drainages ranges from 49 to 82 species (mean, 66; range in Virginia only, 49–70); in the three drainages of the Ohio basin the range is 46–222 species (mean, 118; Virginia range, 42–98). The much higher mean for the Ohio is biased by the Tennessee drainage, by far the largest drainage considered (and having over 90% of its area beyond Virginia). The Mississippi basin, of which the Ohio is a subbasin, is considered by many to be the greatest center of fish speciation in North America.

The greater richness of the Ohioan fauna is exemplified by the three drainages of the Ohio basin in Virginia which collectively drain only 17.7% of the state's area. Considering the in-state distribution of Virginia taxa relative to the Atlantic–Ohio divide, 82 species or subspecies occur only on the east side, and 95 only on the west; only 29 taxa are common to both.

On the Atlantic slope the most speciose fauna among Virginia drainages is in the Roanoke drainage—82 taxa (70 in the Virginia portion) including 6 endemic taxa. The total is exceeded elsewhere on the slope, south of the St. Lawrence drainage, only by the Santee and Savannah faunas of the Carolinas and Georgia, with 92 and 88 taxa including 4 and 2 endemic species (Hocutt et al. 1986; Swift et al. 1986; R.E.J.'s adjustments). These faunas contribute strongly to the southward trend of increasing species richness. The Roanoke fauna is enriched by narrowly distributed fishes whose direct ancestors came from the Ohio basin. To lesser extents, the faunas of other major central and south Atlantic slope drainages also exhibit trans-divide patterns.

The smallest Virginia Atlantic slope faunas are in the relatively small Rappahannock and York drainages (49 taxa each), Dismal Swamp (29), other minor Atlantic drainages (total 33, maximally 21 in a drainage), the piece of the Pee Dee in the state (18), and the southern end of the Delmarva Peninsula (13).

Extremes of species richness in the entire Ohio basin are marked by the faunas of the New and Tennessee drainages. The New has only 46 apparently native fishes (42 in Virginia), the Tennessee 222 (98). Adding introduced and euryhaline forms, the Tennessee with 248 taxa is the richest North American fish fauna. The New lacks lowland habitat and is isolated by Kanawha Falls in West Virginia. The Tennessee drains a large extent of diverse terrain, from the highest Appalachians to Mississippi Valley lowlands. The Big Sandy fauna of 86 fishes (42 in Virginia) probably is underestimated. Overall the Tennessee has 32 endemic taxa, the New 8, and the Big Sandy 0.

How Many Fish Species Occupy A Stream Site?

Only a relatively few fish species in a drainage occupy a given stream site or reach. Based on our efforts to capture most species present at most sites that were sampled, small creeks typically have 2–10 species, medium-sized streams 15–30, and rivers 20–40.

Occasionally we attempted to fully inventory the species present at sites with varied habitat by sampling intensively for about 300–600 m, under good conditions (normal or low water level), and with a variety of methods. The following efforts yielded the largest numbers of species of any of our collections from the drainages; likely not all rare and deep-pool fishes were taken. The sequence is north to south, then west.

In middle Craig Creek (James drainage, Valley and Ridge Province, Craig County, 17 May 1984)—32 species.

In the lower Falling River (Roanoke drainage, middle Piedmont, Campbell County, below the lowermost dam when suckers were immigrating, 29 April 1983)—38 species, perhaps the highest number for an Atlantic slope collection (cf. Hocutt et al. 1973).

In middle Big Reed Island Creek (New drainage, Blue Ridge Province, Carroll County, 3 June 1984)—23 species.

In lowermost Copper Creek (Tennessee drainage, Valley and Ridge, Scott County, 20–21 May 1971)—44 species.

In the Clinch River (Tennessee drainage, Valley and Ridge, Tennessee, Hancock County, Frost Ford–Brooks Island area, 25–26 September 1971)—55 species. This site is in extreme eastern Tennessee; its fauna is nearly the same as that of the lower section of the Clinch River in Virginia before the 1967 fish kill.

Intensive efforts in the lower (Valley and Ridge Province) and upper (Blue Ridge) sections of the New River in Virginia, which has a depauperate native fauna, yielded 23–30 and 18–25 species (Hocutt et al. 1973; Benfield and Cairns 1974; M. T. Masnik, in litt.).

The collections from Virginia with the largest numbers of species are from the Clinch River in the Valley and Ridge Province of Scott County, the first county above Tennessee. Masnik (1974, in litt.) took 47 species at the Virginia–Tennessee line in 1972, by applying rotenone upstream of a block net stretched across the river. The middle Scott County reach of the Clinch River (Craft Mill, Pendleton Island, and Fort Blackmore) yielded 51, 46, and 52 species; the sampling was done by Tennessee Valley Authority biologists, sometimes with other agencies, for 2–3 days at each site during 1980–1984 (C. F. Saylor, in litt.).

Most of these numbers are quite high for North American fresh waters, but are distinctly below that from a Duck River site (lower Tennessee drainage in western Tennessee) where several collections yielded a total of more than 90 species (Etnier and Jenkins 1980). A Tombigbee River, Mississippi, station sampled over 1963–1980 yielded 92 species (Boschung 1989).

The ranges of percentages of species by family in our five collections listed above are: minnows 32–44% (mostly shiners); percids 16–29 (mostly darters); sunfishes 9–21; suckers 7–16; and catfishes 2–9. Overall these families contributed 86–97% of the species.

The truly estuarine and marine fish fauna of Chesapeake Bay is about as equally diverse as is Virginia's inland fauna (*Estuaries* under *Drainages*). However, many bay species occur only rarely or sporadically during summer.

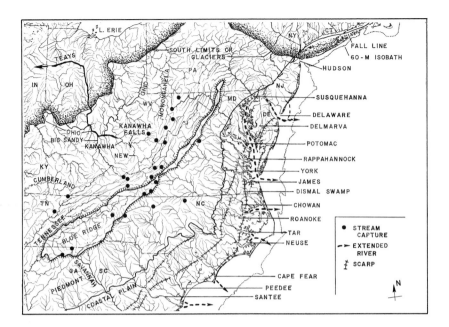

Map 12 Some means of dispersal and (or) isolation of freshwater fishes. All events and drainage patterns shown were not synchronous. The preglacial Teays River was the master stream of the huge Teays basin, now represented largely by the Mississippi basin; from central Illinois the Teays flowed to the Gulf of Mexico through the present Mississippi Valley. Some theaters of stream capture had more than one capture; others are quite tenuously recognized. Southern glacial limits are combined for the last two Pleistocene glaciations (Illinoan and Wisconsinan). Coastal rivers extended seaward as sea level dropped during glaciations; some now separate drainages became connected. Extended drainages include the Greater Susquehanna (through present Chesapeake Bay), Greater Roanoke (or Ancestral Albemarle; Chowan and Roanoke rivers; through Albemarle Sound), Greater Pamlico (Tar and Neuse rivers; through Pamlico Sound; not supported geologically), and Greater Santee (Pee Dee and Santee rivers). Also during glaciations, lowland freshwater and estuarine refugia developed off the present coast, some at least as far out as the present 60-m isobath. Scarps are relict shorelines of ocean high stands during interglacial times of the Pleistocene and earlier. See *Biogeography* for details and literature references.

MEANS OF FISH DISPERSAL   Map 12

An understanding of fish distribution often involves identification of the avenues or agents by which these organisms crossed or bypassed drainage divides. In Virginia and environs these are largely prehistorical events of stream capture, river extension, local inland flooding, estuarine flooding, and human actions (e.g., introductions and canals).

Drainage modifications accompanying glaciation and deglaciation had profound effects on fish distribution in the Great Lakes and their formerly connected drainages north of Virginia (e.g., Bailey and Smith 1981). In Virginia, which was not glaciated, the effects of glaciation relevant to ichthyogeography are water temperature depression, river extension, and development of coastal refugia.

Stream Capture

The process of capture and its implications to fish dispersal are outlined in the introduction to this sec-

tion and are discussed by Jenkins et al. (1972) and Burr and Warren (1986). Capture, recognized as the principal means by which montane–upland fishes traversed drainage divides (Gilbert 1980; Burr and Warren 1986), is considered from the geological standpoint by Hack (1969, 1982) and others, and more broadly by Lauder (1968).

Theaters of capture are shown in Map 12. Clear evidence for other possible captures in the region has been obliterated by subsequent erosion. Virtually all recognized surface-stream captures are undated; presumably, most occurred more than 10,000 years ago. Some subterranean stream connections, particularly those in areas of carbonate strata such as limestone, likely are quite recent and have been used by fishes in Virginia (*James Drainage Fauna*; possibly *Cottus baileyi*) and elsewhere (e.g., Nelson and Paetz 1974).

Extended Rivers

At various times lowland rivers extended beyond their present mouths. Some of the rivers joined, allowing freshwater fishes to disperse between drainages that presently are separated by estuarine or oceanic conditions. Many of the river extensions served biota as refugia from cold climate and glaciers.

The river extensions developed during cold times of the Pleistocene epoch, when much more of Earth's water than now was locked in extensive northern continental glaciers and smaller montane glaciers. The larger ice sheets averaged 2 km (1.2 miles) in thickness; maximally they were about 3.5 km high (Bowen 1978; Porter 1983). Sea levels were lowered in reciprocal proportion to the volume of water added to the ice sheets (Bloom 1983b). Alternating periods of waxing and waning of ice effected a series of eustatic fluctuations in sea level whose stages are termed, respectively, regression (emergence of land) and transgression (submergence).

River extension and inundation accompanied each regression–transgression cycle. From 17 to as many as 30 cycles occurred globally during the 1.6-million-year-long Pleistocene, a frequency much higher than that suggested by the classical recognition of four major glacial–interglacial episodes in the epoch (Emiliani and Shackleton 1974; Shackleton and Opdyke 1976; Bowen 1978; Barry 1983). The complex of eustatic fluctuations is partly indicated by relief features and sediment plains of marine origin on the Coastal Plain (e.g., Colquhoun and Johnson 1968; Oaks and DuBar 1974).

Although the Pleistocene often is termed the "glacial epoch," the Earth's climatic regime actually has been in a cool or glacial mode since the Middle Miocene (Kennett 1982). Glacio-eustatic fluctuations also occurred during parts of the Pliocene and in Late Miocene; the respective entire durations of these epochs were about 1.6–5 million years ago and 5–24 million years ago. Glacio-eustatic sea level oscillations may also have occurred late in the Oligocene epoch, about 24–36 million years ago. Hence it is appropriate to refer to the "late-Cenozoic ice ages," for glaciation occurred in much of the Late Cenozoic era (Bowen 1978). Sea level changes during some of the cycles were minor; the largest oscillations apparently occurred in the Late Pleistocene (Shackleton and Opdyke 1977).

In attempting to link present aspects of fish distribution with regression or transgression, those of the last and most researched of the Pleistocene glaciations—the Wisconsinan—would be the primary focus. However, the extent of sea level reduction during even the Late Wisconsinan low stand is uncertain. A maximum drop of about 120 m (394 feet) below current mean sea level often has been cited (e.g., Curray 1965; Emiliani and Shackleton 1974),

which may have an error range of ±60 m (Bloom 1983a); a fall of some 145 m has also been given (e.g., Mercer 1968). The consensus appears to be at least −85 m (McIntyre et al. 1976a, 1976b).

Somewhat after the peak of the Late Wisconsinan glaciation, relative sea levels of the Virginia coast were estimated as −61 m at 16,000 years B.P. (before present) and −75 m at 11,000 years B.P. (Clark 1981). Map 12 conservatively shows the mouths of maximally extended rivers off Virginia to have been at the present 60-m isobath (depth below mean sea level)—the lower extreme of the 50% error range associated with estimates of −120 m (Bloom 1983a). On Virginia's present 90–110-km wide Continental Shelf (Uchupi 1968; USGS 1970), the 60-m isobath is close to the shelf break at 100 m depth. Whatever the actual depths of sea level lowering were, authorities agree that most of the central western North Atlantic shelf was exposed during Late Wisconsinan time.

During major regressions, Coastal Plain estuaries and much of the Continental Shelf progressively became land. Rivers extended through emerged parts of these provinces; with their feeders, spacious marsh and stream systems were formed. Some valleys cut by these rivers align with the head of submarine canyons on the Continental Slope (Pratt 1967; Swift et al. 1972; Kennett 1982; McGregor 1984). Upper sections of small valleys, such as those off Delmarva Peninsula, apparently were formed by erosion during the Pleistocene; their streams constituted separate drainages (McGregor 1979). Now, after transgression, these shortened streams remain separate, and many formerly joined large rivers north and south independently enter a sound, a bay, or the ocean.

As a general model of drainage regression, when sea level began dropping, gradient first increased and excavation of soft sediments began at the high-stand mouths of streams. With the continued fall of base level, formerly separate tributaries intermittently joined the seaward-lengthening reach of the master stream. Above high-stand mouths, gradient would have steepened progressively upstream; the erosion-resistant Fall Line may have been the upper limit of renewed downcutting. Moderate and, perhaps, swift current occurred in rejuvenated reaches, exposing gravel. The distance between the rejuvenated zone in each tributary and the mouth of the master stream would have increased with time. Lowermost reaches, particularly in the high-gradient area near the shelf break (if exposed), had the briefest duration for colonization by freshwater biota. Synchronously, regressed areas probably had a mosaic of marshes and sluggish streams and some had higher-gradient reaches.

Chesapeake Bay and environs are an example. Gradient profiles of apparently Wisconsinan paleochannels of major tributaries steepened through reaches of 15 to 80 rkm that descended to the Late Wisconsinan Susquehanna River paleochannel. The rivers uncovered gravel and, very locally, larger substrate (Hack 1957). With increased gradient and straightening, the Rappahannock River and its tributaries rapidly entrenched in their present estuary (Newell 1985). Later (about 8,000 years B.P.), well after the onset of the last deglaciation, the present area of the bay's mouth was a floodplain, brackish-water environment (Harrison et al. 1965).

In the Delaware River extension (one of the best traced extended valleys between Cape Cod and Cape Hatteras), on the middle Continental Shelf the valley was broad and flat-bottomed; on the outer shelf it was V-shaped, narrower and deeper, and had a steeper gradient (Twichell et al. 1977).

Drainage extensions are named for their estuary or master river and are prefixed by the term "Ancestral" or "Greater." Excepting references to certain literature, a Greater *river* applies to an extended river, (e.g., the Greater Susquehanna River). A Greater *drainage* denotes the composite of the extended section of a river, its section above the extension, and all tributaries of both sections; for example, the Greater Susquehanna drainage includes the presently separate drainages from the Susquehanna to the James.

Present Chesapeake Bay—a classic example of a drowned river basin—and a broad, now offcoast area were traversed by interconnected drainages whose master stream was the Greater Susquehanna River (Map 12). The encompassed waterways of the present bay and seaward area served as the Chesapeake refugium for freshwater fishes during colder times of the Pleistocene. Fishes could have dispersed between the unglaciated lower section of the Susquehanna drainage in Pennsylvania and the James drainage. The lower Greater Susquehanna drainage is best known from the last glaciation (Hack 1957), but many uncertainties exist. Older paleochannels are poorly known. Lower portions of the Susquehanna, Potomac, York, James, and other Chesapeake basin rivers may have had a different course before the last glaciation than during it (Schlee 1957; Harrison et al. 1965; White 1966; Schubel and Zambawa 1973; Hunt 1974; Oaks et al. 1974). The extended James River was depicted (Swift 1975, 1976b) as separate from the Greater Susquehanna at some stage.

The combined Chowan and Roanoke rivers had a long freshwater extension beyond their present mouths at the head of Albemarle Sound. The extension has been variously termed the Greater Roanoke River (Lachner and Jenkins 1971a; Jenkins et al. 1972; Hocutt et al. 1986), the Ancestral Albemarle River (Swift et al. 1972), and the Albemarle River (McGregor 1979).

The Tar River and Neuse River drainages in North Carolina, having headwaters just south of the lower Roanoke drainage, were assumed to have been united; the common waterway was named the Greater Pamlico River (Jenkins et al. 1972; Hocutt et al. 1986). The assumption was based on present proximity of their mouths in Pamlico Sound and on the close similarity of their faunas. However, the Ancestral Pamlico River, an extension of the Tar River, may not have been connected to the Ancestral Neuse River during the Late Pleistocene (Swift et al. 1972; Swift 1976a, 1976b).

The Pee Dee River, some of whose Ararat River headwaters arise in Virginia, apparently was joined with the Santee River off South Carolina (Swift et al. 1972; Swift 1976a, 1976b). The combined channel was called the Greater Santee River by Hocutt et al. (1986). Today the mouths of the Pee Dee and Santee are less than 10 km apart, but any former trough on the Continental Shelf has been obscured by erosion (Hack 1982).

A grand union of extended rivers comprising the drainages from the Susquehanna to the Neuse was postulated by White (1966). The discharge of this basin was suggested to have cut the Hatteras Canyon, one of the largest submarine canyons on the Continental Slope south of the Hudson Canyon. White did not state how such a drainage would have aligned in place and time with the northeastward-flowing, primarily Piedmont drainage that he (1953) thought joined parts of the drainages from the Santee to the Rappahannock or Potomac, or farther north. Ichthyofaunal support for the latter drainage—"White's River" (Yerger and Relyea 1968)—and for a "Hatteras River" is too weak to consider them to have been contemporaneous with most elements of the present fauna (Jenkins et al. 1972; Hocutt et al. 1986). A Hatteras River is not supported geologically (Pratt 1967; McGregor 1979).

Local Inland Flooding

Also termed cross-grading, this is the overtopping of interstream divides by flood water. Small streams of the same drainage typically are involved and the process may lead to micropiracy, a consequence of breaking down the divide (Leopold et al. 1964). Its significance to fish dispersal in Virginia is unknown, but it may have been important in the south-central United States (Conner and Suttkus 1986).

Estuarine Flooding

Movements of freshwater fishes through areas whose salinities have been temporarily and substantially reduced by extended periods of rain were discussed by Conner and Suttkus (1986). Such low-salinity "bridges" undoubtedly occurred commonly; large-river lowland fishes probably have been thus interchanged between the Chowan and Roanoke drainages during the last 200 years. It is uncertain that the much wider gaps between the major drainages of the Chesapeake basin have been so traversed. Williams (1985) gave a scenario for freshwater faunal exchange in coastal drainages north and south of Chesapeake Bay, through plumes of outflow from the Greater Susquehanna River during deglaciation.

Natural Accidents

Phenomena such as tornado-induced "rains of fishes" (Dees 1961) and transfer of fish eggs by birds probably are of little or no significance in freshwater fish dispersal (Myers 1938; Ramsey 1965).

Introduction

Intentional and accidental releases of nonnative fishes have been frequent (*Introduced Fishes*). Introduced species comprise an array of game, food, bait, and forage fishes. In 11 drainages of Virginia, 8–42 taxa (mean, 22.4) are considered to be introduced (Table 3); these comprise 10.1–47.7% (mean, 24.3) of the fish taxa in the drainages.

The lowest percentage of nonindigenous fishes is from the drainage with the richest native fauna, the Tennessee. The highest percentage is from the New drainage, which has the smallest native fauna among drainages with a large area in Virginia. The number of transplanted and exotic fishes established in a drainage is related to the original number of species present. Factors promoting introduction include presence of large impoundments (fishing opportunities), proximity to cities (anglers), and the number of adjacent drainages (sources of baitfish transplants) (Maps 6, 9, 11). Thus the large number (42) of introduced species in the New is related to its two large impoundments in or fringing Virginia, its location near the populous upper Roanoke Valley, and by being bordered by nine other drainages.

Records of stocking activities often are buried in old literature; about as commonly, stockings are scantily documented or not at all. The natural range limits of several gamefishes are uncertain (e.g., *Micropterus dolomieu*, *M. salmoides*, and *Stizostedion vitreum*). Particularly troublesome to biogeographic analysis are suspected (cryptic) interdrainage transplants of small nongame species (Jenkins 1987).

First records of a species in a drainage can be interpreted either as resulting from release of a nonnative species or the discovery of a localized native population; rarely are we certain which. Most cases concern fishes likely used for bait and released in a different drainage at the end of the fishing trip; see, for example, accounts of *Noturus gilberti* and *N. insignis*. Sometimes forage fishes are purposefully or inadvertently transported with gamefishes; they may also escape from holding ponds. Further, some persons transfer fishes to streams simply because they want them there. Cryptic introductions probably occur more frequently in Virginia than is obvious; our direct evidence for them is largely from a few chance encounters with anglers and landowners who have transported and released fishes.

The uncertainty attending decisions on drainage occurrence status (native or introduced) is evident in Tables 2 and 3; the symbols NI (native but possibly introduced) and IP (the converse) are frequently used. The case of each pertinent species is discussed in the species accounts; see, for example, *Amia calva*, *Luxilus albeolus*, *Notropis rubricroceus*, *N. chiliticus*, *N. hudsonius*, *N. procne*, and *Noturus insignis*. Major problematic situations are treated under the *James Drainage* and *New Drainage* faunas.

Canals

Canals have been an important agent of fish passage through divides in many regions. Inland lock-and-dam canal systems were constructed early in Virginia to transport people and freight around main-river barriers such as rapids and falls, from overland routes on the Atlantic slope–Ohio basin divide, or through low drainage divides. Due partly to the railroad boom, use and maintenance of most canals became uneconomical during post–Civil War reconstruction. Most canals fell to ruins, although portions remain in recreational use.

The Patowmack Canal (or Great Falls Canal), a series of five locks bypassing Great Falls of the Potomac River, was opened in 1802. Side routes around lesser barriers had been in use by boat traffic long before. The Chesapeake and Ohio Canal succeeded the Patowmack Canal in 1830; along the north bank of the Potomac River and the North Branch Potomac River, it reached 314 rkm from Washington, D.C., to Cumberland, Maryland (VDCED 1968; Garrett and Garrett 1987).

The Rappahannock Navigation Canal, completed

in 1840, ran 83 rkm and had 47 locks from the Fall Line at Fredericksburg to Waterloo near the base of the Blue Ridge (VDCED 1970).

The James and Kanawha Canal project was remarkable. Along the James River from Bosher Dam (completed in 1795 at the Fall Line in Richmond), the canal reached Lynchburg on the upper Piedmont in 1840 and Buchanan in the eastern Valley and Ridge Province in 1851. The goal to reach the foot of the James–New drainage divide was not met, but the system extended along some major James tributaries, including the Appomattox River. The system's 738-rkm length included 235 locks, 79 dams, 20 aqueducts, and 2 tunnels. Many dams were destroyed in 1887; some others were converted to power production (Mussey 1948; VDCED 1969).

The Roanoke Navigation Company used a canal to transport freight around a fall of the Dan River during 1816–1862 (Beck 1971).

The Dismal Swamp Canal, just east of Lake Drummond, went into operation in 1822 to connect Chesapeake Bay with Albemarle Sound in North Carolina (Mussey 1948). Now it is well traveled by recreational craft. The Albemarle and Chesapeake Canal is the more easterly alternate route of the Intracoastal Waterway system.

Canals apparently have not affected fish distribution in Virginia to the extent that they have in the Great Lakes region (Hubbs and Lagler 1958; Bailey and Smith 1981; C. Smith 1985). Canals may be primary routes for upstream passage around the higher falls in eastern Virginia by the catadromous *Anguilla rostrata*; this tolerant eel lives in locks. More likely, the dominant overall effect of Virginia's canal systems has been detrimental. Dams associated with locks have long blocked anadromous fishes from ascending the Fall Line in the Rappahannock and James (Atran et al. 1983; see *Alosa sapidissima, Morone saxatilis*).

EVENTS AND SETTINGS OF VIRGINIA

The geological history of Virginia has shaped the evolution and distribution of its modern ichthyofauna. Former climates have strongly influenced this fauna as well.

Ancient to Pliocene

During 800–600 million years ago, in the Late Precambrian era, before fishes had originated, the coast of ancestral eastern North America was bathed by the Proto-Atlantic Ocean. Near shore were a microcontinent and an island arc, both sites of volcanic orogenies. In the period 400–350 million years ago (Devo-

nian period of the Middle Paleozoic era), by which time archaic fishes were present, the Proto-Atlantic was closed by migration and collision of the continental plates, forming the supercontinent Pangaea. The microcontinent, island arc, and part of the Proto-Atlantic floor were united with the North American plate and connected to Eurasia and Africa. The microcontinent and arc became the present area of the eastern Appalachians, which included the present Piedmont. Compression related to plate movement faulted and folded the Blue Ridge orogen and, to a lesser extent, the ancestral Valley and Ridge Province and Appalachian Plateaus to the west.

During 210–140 million years ago (Jurassic period of the Mesozoic era), the North Atlantic Ocean formed as the continents separated and moved from the present Mid-Atlantic Ridge. By about 20 million years ago (Early Miocene epoch of the Cenozoic era), the ocean basins had essentially attained their modern shapes. Highlands had been eroded to largely subdued surfaces, the deeper sediments converted to rock, and Virginia and eastern North America in general approached their present configurations (Rankin 1975; Hatcher 1972, 1978; Cook et al. 1979; Oliver 1980; Dott and Batten 1981; Ollier 1981; Kennett 1982).

Major features of ancient drainage development in eastern North America were determined by these tectonic events (Judson 1975). During the Late Precambrian era and Early Paleozoic era, low-gradient rivers flowed southeast from the Canadian Shield to the Proto-Atlantic Ocean. Following the collision of continental plates and with mountain building centered in or east of the present Appalachian highlands, most streamflow was reversed toward the west and northwest. Thus the ancient northwesterly course of the New River originated. As the continents later moved apart, the eastern margin of North America subsided, the major flowage began reversing again eastward, and ancestral Atlantic drainages lengthened headward. This scenario may not be confirmable (Dietrich 1959) and is ". . . best left alone by zoögeographers" of the modern ichthyofauna (Ross 1969).

The subsequent sculpting of Virginia's landscape was dominated by erosional adjustment of streams to uplifting and changes in base (sea) level (Ollier 1981). Accompanying the wearing down of the Appalachians, the Atlantic slope–Mississippi basin divide migrated west with the capture of west-flowing streams by Atlantic streams (Thompson 1939; Dietrich 1959, 1970b; Hack 1969; Ross 1969). Marked asymmetry of the divide favored the shorter, higher-gradient Atlantic slope drainages as captors; water of those arising on the divide in Virginia maximally flows only 15–20% of the distance that New River water takes to the Gulf of Mexico (Thompson 1939). The New-to-Gulf distance was much greater when the former Teays River continuation of the New River was a conduit.

"The stream contest" (Davis 1903) among opposed drainages along the Blue Ridge may not have involved capture as frequently nor divide migration as far in late geologic time as thought by some. In stating that, Hack (1982) and Ollier (1985) may have referred only to the Southern Blue Ridge (Map 7). Nonetheless, the Northern Blue Ridge was breached by the Susquehanna, Potomac, James, and Roanoke rivers; headwaters of the first three arise far west in the Valley and Ridge Province. The inception of the lower courses of drainages in the southeastern United States probably occurred during early post-Miocene time, when an arid episode ended and the sea retreated from the Coastal Plain (Alt 1974).

Many largely marine lineages of fishes, including some teleosts, were present in the Mesozoic era, but most are extinct; contemporaneous freshwater faunas were relatively archaic and impoverished (Patterson 1975, 1981; Cavender 1986). Because the fossil record is incomplete, the determination of the geographic history of ancient freshwater groups can be approached only on a continental or broad regional level. Exceptional is the detail afforded in eastern North America by the semionotid fishes of Triassic and Jurassic basins, whose formation was related to rupturing of Pangaea (*Fossil Fishes*). Today these sedimentary rock basins uniquely affect the ranges of some fishes in Virginia.

Five archaic (pre-teleost) families (10 species) persist in Virginia—the lamprey, sturgeon, paddlefish, gar, and bowfin families. The earliest known lampreys are from the Late Paleozoic of North America (Janvier and Lund 1983), where the family probably originated (Cavender 1986). In the Early Mesozoic, some of the other four families may have originated on Pangaea when it was intact or partly subdivided, as indicated by occurrence of fossils on two or more continental plates (Wiley 1976; Patterson and Longbottom 1989; Grande and Bemis 1991). However, the sturgeon family and perhaps others may have attained Holarctic ranges partly via the sea.

Most of the freshwater teleost families of Virginia also are very old, some dating to the Late Mesozoic. The phylogeny of many of these indicate trans-Atlantic or trans-Pacific dispersals. For example, ancestral darters probably reached North America from Europe via a pre-Eocene North Atlantic land bridge; minnows probably arrived relatively late, in or a little before the Oligocene by a connection with Asia. The suckers diversified in North America, leaving a primitive relict in China. Five endemic North American families likely originated there: bullhead catfishes, trout-perches, pirate perches, cavefishes, and sunfishes (Patterson 1981; Cavender 1986; Grande 1989).

The modern Virginia ichthyofauna is diverse, but owing to the paucity of unearthed fossils of its members in eastern North America, at best we have only cloudy ideas of the length of residency of most members (Smith 1981; Cavender 1986). The origin of many living genera and subgroups of eastern North American fishes probably dates no earlier than the Miocene (Miller 1965; Gilbert 1976). Cavender (1986) stated that by the Late Miocene, many extant genera are recognizable in the fossil record. However, it is unknown that extant species are as old as the Miocene or Pliocene; today's species are recognized chiefly by nonfossilized characters.

Much of the fish diversity now in eastern and central United States probably existed in the Pliocene (Mayden 1985a, 1987b; Wiley and Mayden 1985; Burr and Page 1986; Burr and Warren 1986; Cross et al. 1986; Swift et al. 1986). In the Mississippi basin during the Late Cenozoic, some lineages show species changes (pseudoextinction) but little true extinction has been demonstrated (Miller 1965; Smith 1981). Hence it appears that extant Virginia species can be considered in context of the Late Pleistocene, if not individually then as ecogeographic assemblages.

Pleistocene

The Pleistocene and Holocene (Recent) epochs (collectively the current Quaternary period) presented manifold conditions which caused adaptation, dispersal, extirpation, or extinction of species. Lacking an adequate fossil record, the clues to the composition and range shifts of the freshwater ichthyofauna of Virginia during the Pleistocene come largely from climate, drainage modifications, and present distribution patterns.

Virginia was not reached by the northerly Pleistocene glaciers but associated climatic changes were strongly felt. These glaciations were more extreme and their effects on Earth more severe than those of the Pliocene and Miocene (Wright and Porter 1983). Within the 1.6-million-year Pleistocene (Berggren and Van Couvering 1974, 1978; Haq et al. 1977), glacial periods occurred much longer than did interglacial periods; the last two continental glaciations were the most extensive. The Pleistocene ended only 10,000 years ago, hence many Virginia fishes may be more cool-adapted than is evident.

As classically but misleadingly construed, the Pleistocene had four major glacial episodes, each separated by a warmer interglacial interval. These intervals and their stages are named for places of characteristic deposits. Quite likely we are now in an interglacial period. Interglacial climate as warm as the present occurred infrequently; each such period lasted only some 10,000 years, about 10% of each glacial–interglacial cycle. Some rapid cooling events spanned only a few hundred years (Shackleton and Opdyke 1977; Bowen 1978; Barry 1983). Climatic events within cycles were complex; in the last major glacial episode the climate varied geographically at similar latitude and altitude, and several advances and retreats of ice sheets occurred (Andrews 1979; John 1979; Mickelson et al. 1983).

The Wisconsinan—the last major glacial interval—began 118,000–115,000 years B.P., following the Sangamonian interglacial of 125,000–118,000 years B.P.; its last major temperature decrement (the Late Wisconsinan minimum) occurred between 23,000 and 18,000 years B.P. (Emiliani and Shackleton 1974; Bowen 1978; Barry 1983). At full extent in the East (18,000 years B.P.), the Wisconsinan (Laurentide) ice sheet extended southward to Long Island, northern New Jersey, well into Pennsylvania, and through most of Ohio and Indiana (Flint 1957; Mickelson et al. 1983; Map 12). Climatic temperature reduction south of the ice sheet had a steep latitudinal gradient (Schumm 1965).

Virginia, lying well south of the Laurentide ice sheet, does not appear to have had permafrost during this time (Péwé 1983). The mean annual position of the Polar Frontal Zone apparently crossed the United States somewhat south of Virginia (Delcourt and Delcourt 1984). Virginia's inland full-glacial Late Wisconsinan air temperatures may have been 7°C (Barry 1983) or 10–15°C (Conners 1986) colder than today. Very cold winters accounted for most of the difference; the air probably was drier than today. As now, the Labrador Current bathed the Virginia coast and the Gulf Stream veered northeastward from Cape Hatteras. Virginia's nearshore sea surface temperatures, along a regressed Coastal Plain, were some 3–4°C colder than now during August, but only about 1–2°C colder in February (CLIMAP 1976; McIntyre et al. 1976b; Imbrie et al. 1983).

Stream temperatures during glacial times may be estimated on the basis that in the United States, groundwater is generally within 1°C of mean annual air temperature of a region, varies little seasonally, and has a well-defined latitudinal gradient (Vannote and Sweeney 1980). Thus as ground temperatures were lowered by long-standing cold climate, so too would those of aquifers and springs. Surface stream temperatures below headwaters vary more than in springs; in cold climates they likely exhibited similar diel and seasonal patterns as today, but were colder. Judging from present day groundwater isotherms (Vannote and Sweeney 1980), full-glacial stream temperatures in Virginia probably were similar to those which now occur in the middle Great Lakes–middle New England zone.

The piscine record for the Pleistocene of Virginia is meager; acceptable identifications usually are generic at best (*Fossil Fishes*). However, the summary at the end of the previous section, and many speciation and present distribution patterns of Virginia fishes, suggest that the Late Pleistocene Virginia ichthyofauna was essentially that of today.

Could many Virginia fishes have withstood Pleistocene temperature depression at moderate or low elevations in the state? They do so now during winter freezes. Were glacial temperature regimes in some Virginia areas sufficiently warm for maturation of gametes? Indirect evidence indicates this to be so; the northerly east–west zone that includes the northeastern United States contains many coolwater and warmwater fish species which also occupy Virginia. Based on the long duration of the Pleistocene and on the relative brevity of warm periods, fishes already in or then entering Virginia likely adapted to temperatures colder than currently prevalent. Eurythermality also would have been genetically selected; temperature change was a norm in the Pleistocene.

An intrinsic ability to disperse is well developed in most freshwater fish species, but the extrinsic constraints on doing so may render them as *in situ* indicators of individual Late Pleistocene drainage faunas. During that time most Virginia species probably were confined to drainages by falls, divides, salinity, and other factors. Interdrainage dispersal depended on connections that were rare (stream capture) or often hostile (extended rivers). Benign climate or local adaptation to climatic change is assumed to have been in effect for most species.

The present coldwater members of the Virginia fauna could have persisted during full-glacial climate in the drainages in which they presently occur. Brook trout, white sucker, sculpins, and other cool to cold-loving species probably thrived; the lowered temperature would have allowed them to range considerably below springs.

Warmwater species probably were displaced farther downstream than the coldwater assemblage; those that lived in mountains likely departed them (Cope 1868b). Those in east- and north-trending drainages may have been trapped, unable to emigrate south to a milder climate. Southerly Virginia drainages—the Chowan, Roanoke, and Pee Dee, which flow southeast, and the Tennessee drainage, which courses southwest (Map 6)—would have offered the warmest refugia.

Extinction relating to climatic rigor most probably occurred in the north-flowing montane New drainage, which arises in the North Carolina Highlands. Several lines of evidence for cold-induced extinctions (and adaptation) exist (*New Drainage Fauna*). However, even in the New, most warmwater fishes probably found refuge at moderate elevations, judging from present distributions and sparse (for the region) fossil evidence.

The Fall Zone likely was an oasis for cold-displaced upland fishes. It is situated between and has higher gradient than the Coastal Plain and lower Piedmont. Its streams probably were less silted than today, suiting lithophilic species. Lowland fishes undoubtedly extended into Coastal Plain and Continental Shelf areas that now are drowned by estuarine or oceanic conditions (Jenkins and Zorach 1970; Jenkins et al. 1972; Hocutt et al. 1986). Upland rheophilic fishes also may have occurred in some lowland refugia (*Extended Rivers*). The use of downslope refugia (Fall Zone and lower) by upland Virginia fishes is plausible owing to present drainage occurrences. Further, stream capture is not known to have occurred late enough, that is, in post-Wisconsinan time, for species to have then entered a drainage.

Full-glacial climate that was overly severe to fishes in all Atlantic drainages of Virginia would indicate subsequent recruitment to those drainages by large-scale dispersal from southerly refugia, involving several divide crossings along the way. Interconnections caused by stream capture and divide flooding probably occurred more frequently in lowlands than in uplands. Moreover, coastal divides could have been bypassed via low-salinity bridges. Such routes may have been heavily used by lowland fishes. Northward recruitment of upland fishes via these routes and extended rivers likely occurred to a much lesser extent.

A wave of postglacial reoccupation of northerly fresh waters (Delaware drainage and north), starting from Coastal Plain–Continental Shelf refugia in Virginia or North Carolina latitudes, was supported by Schmidt (1986). He considered that numerous lowland fishes took coastal routes, and that few upland species took inland paths northward from Virginia.

Retardation of both local adaptation and speciation may have been a dominant process in Virginia during glacial times. Extended rivers and other lowland interconnections would have allowed dispersal and genetic melding of formerly isolated, differentiating populations that had not become reproductively isolated. Expatriation of warmwater fishes and range expansion of coolwater forms from headlands would have had a similar effect. On the other hand, forced parapatry or sympatry could have resulted in refinement of earlier developed, intrinsic species-isolating mechanisms.

Warm climates during Pleistocene interglacial periods and warming trends within glacial episodes had effects on fishes opposite some of those of full-glacial times. Cold-adapted species contracted in range; some segregated into subpopulations within a drainage. Increased temperature allowed warmwater fishes to expand ranges. Lowland fishes were extirpated from outer refugia by rising sea level. With the severance of lowland river interconnections, species were divided into separate drainage populations, allowing evolutionary divergence in isolation. Sea levels as high to higher than today may have occurred 12 times during the Pleistocene (van Donk 1976). A stand of +6 m is a commonly accepted estimate for Sangamonian time, the last interglacial period; the alleged Middle Wisconsinan high transgression is invalid (Bloom 1983a). The Sangamonian and post-Wisconsinan transgressions may have been the highest during the Quaternary (Kennett 1982).

Transgression periods, with compression of the ranges of lowland species toward the Fall Zone, may have been primary times of adaptation by some species to higher-gradient areas on the outer Piedmont. Piedmont populations of more-typically Coastal Plain species seem to be more common in Virginia (and north), particularly in the considerably drowned Chesapeake basin, than farther south (judged by shared species). South of Virginia, wider Coastal Plain areas remained during transgressions; their inner, Fall Zone altitudes are higher than those to the north, and scarps of marine origin stand well east of the Fall Zone (Colquhoun and Johnson 1968; Oaks and DuBar 1974; Hack 1982). The greater extent of waterways remaining east of the Fall Zone in southern drainages during the Pleistocene may have precluded Piedmont adaptation.

Upland adaptation may also date back to the high transgression in the Miocene and the somewhat lower one in the Pliocene, when sea level was much higher than during the Pleistocene high stands. During the Middle Miocene, the oceans had more water partly because the northern continents were not glaciated (Mercer 1968; Bowen 1978; Kennett 1982). During the Miocene high stand much of the southeastern Virginia Coastal Plain was transgressed. The Orangeburg (Citronelle) Scarp (former shoreline), juxtaposed about the Fall Line in much of North Carolina and well east of it in South Carolina and south, passes inland from the Fall Line in Virginia (Alt 1974; Oaks and DuBar 1974). Estuarine conditions existed in lagoons behind scarps (some of which formed barrier islands) and extended farther inland along main rivers nearly or fully to the Fall Line (Oaks and Coch 1973; Oaks et al. 1974) (Map 12).

Surely the alternations of extended and transgressed drainages created the potential for species multiplication, but biotic evidence for this is ambiguous. For example, divergence within *Nocomis*, *Luxilus*, and *Percina* (*Alvordius*) seems better correlated to upland stream capture. Differentiation within *Etheostoma olmstedi* may be tied to eustasy or the result of parallel evolution. Some vicariant patterns and endemism on the eastern Gulf slope may be related to eustatic drainage modifications (Swift et al. 1986; Gilbert 1987).

Holocene

The Holocene (or Recent) epoch "officially" began 10,000 years B.P., a time between the coldest part of the last glaciation and the postglacial thermal optimum. The Wisconsinan ice sheets fluctuated through 18,000–6,000 years B.P.; 10,000 years B.P. is a good compromise for the onset of the Holocene in the region that includes Virginia (Bowen 1978). The trend of rising temperature that initiated deglaciation accelerated through much of the Holocene (Schumm 1965; Emiliani and Shackleton 1974). The postglacial Hypsithermal interval within 9,000–2,000 years B.P. in Europe and parts of North America was warmer and drier than today (Deevey and Flint 1957), but paleobotanical evidence of a Hypsithermal interval was not found in a Shenandoah Valley study (Craig 1970).

Relative sea level rose as deglaciation began, approximately 18,000 years B.P.; it may have oscillated. On the central north Atlantic coast the rise slowed pronouncedly during 7,000–4,000 years B.P., with sea level about 20 to 10 m below present level; then it was quite slow to the present (Curray 1965; Emery and Garrison 1967; Clark and Lingle 1979; Bloom 1983b). It is generally believed that today's sea level is at its highest Holocene stand (Kennett 1982).

Freshwater fish populations in the Pleistocene refuges that now constitute the Continental Shelf and Chesapeake Bay system were displaced or extirpated by increasing salinity. The early rate of sea level rise was quite rapid in a geological sense—about 1 cm per year (Bloom 1983b), but the landward advance of salinity certainly was slow enough to allow fishes to avoid it. Climatic amelioration allowed upland spe-

cies to reinvade higher-elevation areas before the salt front reached them, but it may have been difficult for some species to find congenial habitat. As indicated by presently localized lowland distributions, many species probably were not generally distributed within individual refugia. Some populations sequestered in minor outer drainages may have been trapped and extirpated by salinity, a process intensified by postglacial seaward tilting and sinking of the coast. Higher-elevation, minor-drainage populations were spared inundation, but may have suffered chance extirpation or shifts in range due to other habitat alterations; reestablishment via recruitment was prevented by salinity.

Modern humans originated in the Pleistocene. North America was peopled by Paleolithic pioneers from Asia who crossed the Beringian land bridge to Alaska no later than 15,000–14,000 years ago, a time of sea level regression. Paleo-Indians spread across the continent, occupying Virginia as early as 13,000–11,000 years B.P. (Williams and Stoltman 1965; Martin 1973; West 1983; McCary 1986).

Environmental effects by Indians in Virginia likely paralleled those reconstructed by Chapman et al. (1989) from a Cherokee village area in eastern Tennessee, where some land practices caused substantial soil erosion. Extensive tracts in the Rappahannock and Shenandoah valleys were transformed by burning into grasslands to allow cultivation and attract game animals (Braun 1950; Dabney 1971; Carrier 1975; Williams 1989). Zooarcheological studies of Indian settlements indicate an abundance of fishes in the Late Holocene of Virginia (e.g., Whyte 1989). Overall, the impacts of early Americans on aquatic habitats were slight compared with those of the past four centuries.

European colonists arrived in southeastern Virginia in the early 1600s; they brought the axe. Valleys of main rivers and larger tributaries were the focus of pioneering; extensive deforestation began. By 1800, settlement had pushed through the west end of the state; many valleys and gentle slopes were cleared by 1850 (Summers 1903; Gowing 1974; Rouse 1975; Johnson 1983).

As Virginia's population expanded to 6.2 million by 1990, many streams were warmed by loss of shade and made turbid and heavily silted from soil erosion. Clearing of the forest may have been the greatest single activity in the evolution of the rural landscape of the United States (Williams 1989). Streams were polluted particularly as an industrial base was added to the economy; small and large dams were erected. Some fishes were overexploited, others introduced. Many of the adverse changes have been long-standing, notably within and below major population centers (Map 11). Other changes have been brief, but catastrophic (e.g., the Clinch River fish kill of 1967).

The ichthyological literature contains few specific records of early conditions of inland streams. Cope's (1868b) account does not describe the quality of the few waters sampled and Jordan (1889b) noted only widely varying conditions of water clarity, turbidity, and siltation. Both found a few species in places where they no longer occur. One of the most detailed early accounts concerns the lower Roanoke and Dan rivers in south-central Virginia (VFC 1877a). The habitat degradations and fish depredations must have been typical of many areas: "No dams that would stop fish . . . [now there are six]. A few shad run now to Clarksville and above. . . . The catch as compared to twenty years ago and to sixty, comparatively trifling. . . . Rock fish [striped bass] abundant to Clarksville ninety years ago, not fifty . . . [downstream netting was reducing anadromous fish populations]. Thirty, forty, and fifty years ago, river clear all the time; now muddy six or eight months in the year." Today the middle and lower Dan River is so turbid during much of the year that it appears plowable. In 1882 the VFC noted that Southside and Piedmont streams were muddy and that edible native species had been exterminated; the proposed remedy was to stock common carp.

Perhaps turbidity and siltation are generally reduced in some areas now as compared with 50–150 years ago, owing to soil conservation practices, return of farmland to forest, and erosion-reduction measures taken during construction. However, old sources of siltation remain and new ones are continually opened.

DISTRIBUTION AND DISPERSAL: COMMENTARY

Many Virginia species probably originated on the central Atlantic slope; the ancestral stocks of most of them apparently reached the Atlantic slope from the faunally richer Mississippi–Ohio basin. Other species dispersed east to the Atlantic slope in their present form; still others probably reached Virginia from northerly or southerly areas of the Atlantic slope. Most Virginia fishes likely survived the Pleistocene glacial climate in Virginia; modest or minor distributional shifts probably were a norm for those times.

Distributions are linked to past and present ecologic and geologic events and factors. The uncertainty of correctly associating species distributions with these events and factors tends to increase with the age of the events. It is difficult to experimentally

confront and confirm even presently perceived distributional relationships; rarely are we afforded rigorous tests of hypotheses of prehistorical distributions. Alternative interpretations generally exist for the origin of a given distribution pattern (e.g., by stream capture versus extended rivers).

The occurrence of a fish species in montane or upland sections of opposed drainages often has been interpreted as evidence of dispersal via stream capture. This is readily acceptable for most trans-Atlantic-divide patterns of montane and upland species in the central and southern Appalachians. Capture may have been less important to the formation of upland distributions of species that are shared by drainages connected in lowlands by the Ohio River, or which are shared by formerly extended drainages. Dispersal through extended rivers and other lowland connections seems the best explanation of many lower Piedmont and Coastal Plain distributions.

Specific capture routes have been postulated for the ingress of "marker" species; that is, those confined to a small area near a divide or whose range appears to have expanded from a hub adjoining a divide (e.g., Schwartz 1965b; Lachner and Jenkins 1971a; Cincotta et al. 1986b). This can be perilous; distributions have shifted and localizations have developed in adjustment to changing conditions over geological time (Jenkins et al. 1972; Burr and Warren 1986). It is of little relevance that only one capture may be documented on a divide; geological evidence of other piracies may have been erased by erosion.

Some species that are widely distributed on the Atlantic slope may have reached the slope via multiple captures across the Atlantic–Ohio divide (e.g., *Hypentelium nigricans*). This scenario, however, does not accord with the present distribution of several other widespread taxa; for example, *Notropis hudsonius*, *Hybognathus regius*, and *Moxostoma m. macrolepidotum*, which are either absent from the Ohio basin or their ranges and habitat preferences preclude their occurrence in the Ohio near capture theaters on the Atlantic divide. Instead, their wide Atlantic slope ranges indicate relatively long-term residence there, in order to have accessed combinations of north-to-south (intraslope) large-stream captures and extended rivers. Clearly it would have taken much more time to achieve an extensive range on the Atlantic slope compared with that in the Mississippi basin, where many drainage interconnections have been long-standing.

Remaining unclear is which kind of intra-Atlantic-slope route has most facilitated the development of wide ranges there. Indicating dispersal via extended rivers, Jenkins et al. (1972) believed that in the central eastern United States, lowland fishes tend to have wider ranges than montane and upland fishes. The range size difference may be less tenable for the southeastern ichthyofauna, which has a greater number of lowland species of limited range on the widened Piedmont and Coastal Plain.

In the following sections the numbers of taxa refer to native freshwater species and subspecies of entire drainages or basins, unless specified otherwise (Tables 2, 3; *Appendix 2*). Map 6 shows the extralimital extent of Virginia drainages. Most statements of faunal relationships are based on similarity coefficients of Hocutt et al. (1986). The coefficients change somewhat with our revisions of distribution status, but the relationships remain essentially the same.

DELMARVA PENINSULA FAUNA

The large low-lying Delmarva Peninsula (the name is a compound of Delaware, Maryland, and Virginia) is bounded on the east by Delaware Bay and the Atlantic Ocean and on the west by Chesapeake Bay. Nearly entirely in the Coastal Plain, the peninsula is crossed by the Fall Line at about 15 km north of the Chesapeake and Delaware Canal; maximum elevation southward is less than 40 m. Major Delmarva streams are generally sluggish and marshy or swampy through their lower or full course; they are tidal for an average of about 48 rkm from Chesapeake Bay (Jordan 1974).

Fauna

The Delmarva fish fauna (north as far as the Chesapeake and Delaware Canal) comprises 41 native freshwater species: 8 introduced and 9 migratory or estuarine (Lee et al. 1975, 1980, 1981; Lee 1976; Wang and Kernehan 1979; Hocutt et al. 1986; our data). The poverty of the native freshwater fauna is indicative of meager variety and size of present habitats. The lack of an endemic species is related to the general youth of the present freshwater biotopes.

Extirpation and Repatriation

Cyclicly the Delmarva freshwater fauna was reduced by compression, and perhaps emigration and extirpation during high marine transgressions—the present case—and renewed during regressions. Compared with major mainland drainages that have higher elevations, proportionately much larger extents of freshwater habitat were affected.

During the transgressive Sangamonian interglacial interval, much of the southern portion of Delmarva was inundated and its valleys were filled with sediment (Jordan 1974; Rice et al. 1976; Shideler et al. 1984). Major reaches of streams in the northern sector were salty (Richards and Judson 1965; Sirkin 1977). Perhaps only a few fish species persisted in the nontransgressed small headland streams. The present transgression is about 6 m less than the Sangamonian high stand; its effects are much less pervasive to the inland biota.

Many insular biotas are depauperate as a consequence of isolation. Owing to the narrowness of its connection with the mainland, Delmarva presently is insular for freshwater fishes. However, it was not secluded during sea level regressions; it was the backbone between the Chesapeake and Delaware refugia, which were fresh water but now are mostly estuarine. These two refugia had their land areas contiguous with the now-submerged Atlantic refugium off the southeast edge of the Peninsula, although the major drainages apparently were not connected (Hack 1957; Twichell et al. 1977; Kraft and Belknap 1986) (Map 12).

Repatriation occurred progressively as the sea regressed during glacial advances. Delmarva tributaries were incised (Jordan 1974); the localized gradient increments favored support of a fauna more diverse than at present. The increase in species richness probably was modest. The Greater Susquehanna and Greater Delaware rivers intermittently carried great volumes of glacial meltwater and probably were generally turbid, limiting access to Delmarva tributaries. Cool to cold conditions (Sirkin et al. 1977; Lee 1987) also may have suppressed the fauna. Perhaps the pool of potential repatriates that occurred in much of the adjoining lowland refugia had only a few more species than the present Delmarva fauna.

Species Richness: East–West

In accordance with the distinctly asymmetric drainage of the peninsula, faunal differences exist between the east and west sides of the main Delmarva divide. The northern two-thirds of the divide is situated well east of the midline of the peninsula; all east-flowing (Delaware and direct Atlantic) drainages are quite small and many are mostly estuarine. The west (Chesapeake) slope includes far larger, southwesterly trending drainages, the four longest being the Chester, Choptank, Nanticoke, and Pocomoke (Map 6). Judged largely from maps in Lee et al. (1980), 12 native freshwater species are known only from the west slope; only *Lampetra appendix* is restricted to the east slope and 28 occur on both slopes.

The larger west-slope fauna reflects the availability

through the Holocene of large streams. Interslope faunal differences stem mainly from localizations in the largest west-flowing drainages, where based on drainage size alone, the chances of species survival would be higher. It is unlikely that the interslope difference resulted from distinctly different rates of climatically induced extirpation. Although the Chesapeake refugium was more southerly centered than the Delaware refugium, most Delmarva fishes presently occur also in northerly areas of the Delaware drainage, and many extend much farther north (Schmidt 1986).

Upland-predilected species account for most of the interslope difference. The concept of "Piedmont upland" and "non-Coastal Plain" fishes on Delmarva merits emendation. Seven of the 10 species so identified (e.g., Franz and Lee 1976; Lee and Norden 1976) are instead classifiable (Table 2) as upland–lowland types, based on their occurrence also in the Coastal Plain of the Virginia mainland: *Lampetra aepyptera*, *Cyprinella analostana*, *Notropis amoenus*, *N. hudsonius*, *N. procne*, *Noturus insignis*, and *Percina peltata*. The other three species essentially are upland or montane–upland types—*Rhinichthys atratulus*, *Semotilus corporalis*, and *Cottus bairdi*—but even the first two of these occur in a few streams on the outer Coastal Plain of Virginia. With the broader habitat classifications, perhaps only the *Cottus* would not be expected to inhabit Delmarva. Still, the populations are relict or otherwise notable, as are those of certain other Delmarva species (e.g., *Clinostomus funduloides*).

Modest topographic relief has been considered a factor favoring persistence of some fishes on the west slope of Delmarva. However, the short east-slope drainages arise on the same divide and thus have higher average gradients. Regardless, none of the above 11 species are strictly riffle dwellers or seem dependent at some stage on more than moderate current, except perhaps the *Cottus*.

Species Richness: North–South

No latitudinal trend in species richness occurs on much of Delmarva. The localized species tend to concentrate in tributaries near the mouths of the Delaware and Susquehanna rivers and in the larger drainages on the middle third of the peninsula. Through the Virginia one-third the fauna diminishes southward. Only 13 native freshwater fishes are recorded in the Virginia portion; all of them occupy its northern half and only 7 are known in the southern half. The Virginia portion is quite narrow and has little surface-flowing fresh water; it would not have offered appreciable habitat for many regional freshwater fishes to have used to escape rising sea level.

CHESAPEAKE BASIN FAUNA

The freshwater fish fauna of the Chesapeake basin, including the full extent of its component drainages except for the Susquehanna drainage above Conowingo Dam (near the mouth), comprises 124 taxa: 82 native, 30 alien, and 12 diadromous or estuarine.

Most species of the Chesapeake fauna are widespread in eastern North America, notably in the Susquehanna drainage and north; some Chesapeake lowland and upland areas have several southern faunal elements. Most of the limitedly distributed, central Appalachian taxa that extend into or occur strictly in the basin inhabit only the upper James. Five of the six endemic taxa of the basin as a whole live in Virginia. The other endemic taxon, the endangered Maryland darter *Etheostoma sellare*, is confined to a lower Susquehanna tributary and a minor system feeding the head of the Chesapeake Bay in Maryland. This enigmatic fish is a relict of Ohio basin stock (Knapp 1976; Wiley and Mayden 1985; Mayden 1987b). *Cottus girardi* almost qualifies as endemic to the basin as defined here; in addition to the James and Potomac drainages, it inhabits a Susquehanna tributary above Conowingo Dam.

The native nonmigratory gamefish portion of the Chesapeake fauna is not notable for diversity or size of the species. Most species are panfishes; the largest is the moderate-sized white catfish.

POTOMAC DRAINAGE FAUNA

The Potomac drainage, the most northern in Virginia and lying also in Maryland, Pennsylvania, and West Virginia, has a central position in the Chesapeake basin. After the Susquehanna River, the Potomac River is the longest of U.S. Atlantic slope rivers south of the St. Lawrence River. Most major Potomac tributaries including the Shenandoah system arise in the Valley and Ridge Province; many small streams drop from the Blue Ridge and the front of the Allegheny Plateau. A modest portion of the drainage is in the Piedmont; after descending Great Falls and lesser structures, the drainage is quite narrow through the Coastal Plain.

Fauna

The Potomac drainage has 61 native, 30 introduced, and 11 diadromous or estuarine taxa—102 in all. Its endemic taxon is an undescribed sculpin, either a subspecies of *Cottus cognatus* or a closely related species. The fauna is intimately related to that of the Rappahannock, very similar to the Susquehanna and James faunas, and distantly related to those of the Monongahela and New drainage faunas of the Ohio basin.

Lowland Fishes

The Potomac has a dearth of Coastal Plain species. Absence of some lowland species reflects northern range terminations south of the Potomac: *Centrarchus macropterus* and *Pomoxis nigromaculatus*. Other Coastal Plain species are missing from the Potomac (and one or more adjacent drainages) but occur to the north and south: *Acantharchus pomotis*, *Enneacanthus obesus*, and *E. chaetodon*. Several species that normally inhabit Coastal Plain tributaries have restricted distributions in the Potomac: *Notropis bifrenatus*, *Noturus gyrinus*, and *Aphredoderus sayanus* in Virginia and at least the first two species in Maryland; *Lampetra appendix*, *Notropis chalybaeus*, and *Etheostoma vitreum* live only in the Maryland section; *Etheostoma fusiforme* has been recorded in the Maryland Coastal Plain but only in the Piedmont of Virginia; and *Esox americanus* is scarce on the Coastal Plain but thriving on the Piedmont in the Occoquan system in Virginia.

The paucity and erratic distributions of Coastal Plain species in the Potomac is a result of limited suitable habitat—a reflection of the narrowness of the province in Virginia and its only slightly greater width in Maryland. Large streams are absent, other than the estuarine part of the Potomac River and its drowned tributaries. Some outer coastal populations may have been extirpated by the Holocene transgression that formed Chesapeake Bay.

Unusual Coastal Plain patterns among species that avoid large rivers may be relatively common in the Chesapeake basin; the lowlands are proportionately more inundated than are many of those farther south. Several of the unusual patterns involve centrarchids, fishes generally perceived as adaptable and wide ranging. A few such centrarchid distributions also occur farther south (Rohde et al. 1979; Gilbert 1987). Pollution in the lower Potomac seems to have severely affected *Notropis bifrenatus* and may have caused the disappearance of *Percopsis omiscomaycus* and *Percina caprodes semifasciata* from the drainage.

Great Falls

This prominent falls at the head of the Fall Zone just above Washington, D.C., is the largest physical main-river barrier of natural origin in Virginia. It de-

scends 11–12 m at the main rock mass and has a total fall of 24–27 m in 2.4 rkm (Stevenson 1899). It is insurmountable to fishes at low and normal river levels. However, judging from a photograph (Garrett and Garrett 1987) made during a major flood when the falls was fully submerged, fishes can bypass it by swimming "through the trees." The falls has long barred access of anadromous fishes to potential spawning grounds and it may have curtailed the distribution of Coastal Plain species that typically also populate the Piedmont (e.g., some of the above-named species localized in the Coastal Plain; *James Drainage Fauna*). Lesser falls and rapids below Great Falls may synergistically impede upstream movement, as evidenced in other rivers (McPhail and Lindsey 1970; Tweddle et al. 1979; Burr and Warren 1986).

Piedmont Cottus

A unique Piedmont distribution is that of *Cottus girardi*, which characteristically occurs in Valley and Ridge streams that drain carbonate strata. An exceptional population occupies the Goose Creek system in the Foothill Zone and the Culpeper Triassic and Jurassic basin (Maps 7, 133). Most streams in and around the Culpeper basin have low flow; some streams in the area drain predominantly carbonate rocks, but most or all of those containing *C. girardi* have low alkalinity and acidic to circumneutral pH (Cady 1938; Toewe 1966; Parker 1968; Lynch et al. 1987). *Cottus girardi* is apparently absent from the adjacent Catoctin Creek system, whose basement is poorly water-bearing granite and greenstone.

Shenandoah System

The Shenandoah River system has a montane and upland fauna that basically is typical of other western Chesapeake basin faunas; however, several species unexpectedly are localized or missing. This large southern tributary of the Potomac lies nearly entirely in the Valley and Ridge of Virginia. The fauna of the small lower portion in West Virginia is known only from one main stem collection (Cincotta et al. 1986a).

The 58 Shenandoah taxa comprise the catadromous *Anguilla*, the euryhaline *Fundulus diaphanus*, 38 native freshwater species and subspecies, and 18 introduced species. Of those native, 24 are generally distributed; the small range of some of these is related to a preference for large streams. Thus 14 putatively native fishes, plus the *Fundulus*, have a peculiar distribution, a high percentage (37%) for a native fish fauna in the East. Some of these 15 oddly distributed fishes may be introduced: *Notemigonus crysoleucas*, *Nocomis leptocephalus, Thoburnia rhothoeca,* and *Ameiurus nebulosus.*

Of the 15 species, some are highly localized on a system-wide basis, but are moderately or widely dispersed in certain other uplands of the Chesapeake basin: *N. crysoleucas, Erimyzon oblongus, T. rhothoeca, Percina peltata,* and *Etheostoma olmstedi* (two intergraded taxa). Other species are absent from or highly localized in one or two of the three main divisions of the system (North Fork, South Fork, the lower system): *Clinostomus funduloides, Campostoma anomalum, N. leptocephalus, Hybognathus regius, A. nebulosus,* and *Fundulus diaphanus.* Some species occur in all three divisions but are sporadic or localized in at least one: *Semotilus corporalis* (in upper South Fork), *Notropis procne,* and *Noturus insignis.* Additional large-stream collecting may change the picture for only some of these species and may add others to the list of oddities (e.g., *Cyprinella spiloptera*).

The Shenandoah is further notable for the absence of species that occur widely in either or both the Potomac system proper and the Valley and Ridge of the adjacent upper James: *Notropis buccatus, Moxostoma erythrurum, Percina notogramma,* and *Etheostoma blennioides,* the last of which we regard as probably introduced. In this, we differ from Schwartz (1965b) and subsequent workers who postulated a stream capture entry of *E. blennioides* to the Potomac. Colonization of the Shenandoah, or failure to do so, by this darter will be interesting. *Percina notogramma,* clearly native to the Potomac, does not fare well anywhere in the Potomac drainage. No darter is obviously successful in the Shenandoah except for the ubiquitous *Etheostoma flabellare.*

No consistent basis was discerned for any of the odd Shenandoah patterns except for that of *Etheostoma olmstedi,* which is attributable to the influx of a lowland-adapted genome (species account). Long-term chemical contamination of the South Fork Shenandoah River and its tributary the South River (Carter 1977; Kauffman 1980) does not affect most of the patterns, which are observed largely in tributaries. Long-standing deforestation of the broad divisions of the fertile valley may be involved. The system may have suffered higher silt levels earlier than most others in Virginia. Indians had kept the valley burned; settlers found it to be a huge, partly cultivated prairie (Dabney 1971; Williams 1989). The siltation associated with extensive tilling during Caucasian settlement certainly worsened stream conditions.

Margariscus margarita and the endemic form of *Cottus cognatus* have localized patterns in the Shenandoah (and elsewhere in the Potomac) that are equatable with natural conditions; both have their southern range limit in the Shenandoah. These Pleistocene relicts occur in isolated cool or cold limestone-based streams; most of these streams drain open valleys. The brook trout now has taken refuge in the higher mountains; the Piedmont population is questionably native.

Introduced Fishes

Introduced, established fishes make up 33% of the Potomac freshwater taxa, the highest such percentage among major central Atlantic slope faunas and second only to the New drainage fauna among those of Virginia. The composition of the original fauna is uncertain; several of our decisions rest on interpretations of an early report on Maryland fishes (Uhler and Lugger 1876). Introductions stemmed particularly from federal fish-rearing activities that centered in Washington, D.C., just after Uhler and Lugger's study (*History*).

A burgeoning human population and the scarcity of sizeable species provided a strong impetus for stocking; an experimental attitude toward faunal manipulation seems also to have prevailed. Apparently the only native, upland, or montane freshwater fishes present and valued as game or food were chain pickerel, white catfish, yellow and brown bullheads, brook trout, pumpkinseed, redbreast sunfish, and yellow perch. Some of these originally may have occurred only below Great Falls, which blocked anadromous species. Other larger predators above Great Falls are the fallfish and the catadromous American eel.

Stocking of larger fishes may have begun with the famous introduction of smallmouth bass in 1854; perhaps largemouth bass were added earlier. Recently the flathead catfish was established in a lower Potomac reservoir and the blue catfish was noted in the Potomac River. The drainage may have only a few cryptically introduced species, mainly bait fishes.

RAPPAHANNOCK AND YORK DRAINAGE FAUNAS

The Rappahannock and York are the only major drainages lying entirely within Virginia. Only the Rappahannock heads on the Blue Ridge; both transect a moderately wide Piedmont area and have a long course through the Coastal Plain.

Faunas

Both drainages have 49 native freshwater fish taxa and a typical Chesapeake complement (10) of estuarine and diadromous forms. There are 21 introduced species in the Rappahannock and 18 in the York; most are game or foodfishes. Drainage totals are 80 and 77 taxa, respectively. No endemic taxon inhabits either. The only exclusively shared taxon, *Etheostoma olmstedi vexillare*, apparently evolved in Rappahannock uplands and is shared owing to the occurrence of intergrades in the York.

The relatively small number of native species is related to the surrounding of the two drainages on three sides by the Potomac or James, thus being disjunct from Ohio (Teays) basin faunas. (The Teays is considered under *New Drainage Fauna*.) The Rappahannock and York gained fishes from the Potomac and James via stream capture, and likely by ingress from the Greater Susquehanna River or general Chesapeake refugium. Not all Potomac and James species reached or survived in the Rappahannock and York, which have 12 fewer taxa than the Potomac and 24 fewer than the James.

Range Terminations

Other than the exclusively shared darter, only three species have full-range terminations (discounting range gaps; see below) in the two-drainage area: *Notropis buccatus* ending south and *Centrarchus macropterus* stopping north in the Rappahannock, and *Phoxinus oreas* ending north in the York (likely native there, probably introduced in the Rappahannock). Two upland species that have a termination in this area have a limited or moderate central Atlantic slope range; their historical zoogeographic significance is nullified by their current introduced status. These species are *Lythrurus ardens*, presumably transplanted to the York, and *Thoburnia rhothoeca*, most likely introduced in the Rappahannock.

Interdrainage Comparison

The relationship between the native Rappahannock and York faunas is the most intimate among pairs of Virginia drainages, reflecting similarities in prehistorical drainage development and prevailing ecological conditions (Hocutt et al. 1986; Maurakis et al. 1987). The differences are related to disparate habitats and adjacency to the Potomac or James. *Salvelinus fontinalis*, *Rhinichthys cataractae*, and *Cottus bairdi*—montane fishes confined to or prospering in cool to cold water—are present in the Rappahannock but not the York. The Rappahannock gained *Notropis buccatus* from the Potomac; this species is absent from the York, whose headwaters are separated from the Potomac by the Rappahannock and James.

Two of the three species considered native to the York but not the Rappahannock—*Phoxinus oreas* and *Nocomis leptocephalus*—probably were gained from the James. The third York species *Enneacanthus obesus* is considered below. The widespread *Etheostoma o. olmstedi*, present in the York, is replaced in the Rappahannock by *E. o. vexillare*.

Differing from the York, the Rappahannock River above the Fall Line has lacked anadromous fishes, due to Embrey Dam built at Falmouth Falls, Fredericksburg in 1860 (McDonald 1884b; Stevenson 1899).

Absentees

Several species are conspicuously absent from both the Rappahannock and York. Of these, *Campostoma anomalum* and *Etheostoma flabellare* are extensively distributed in mountains and uplands of Virginia and elsewhere. Stream capture corridors to the Rappahannock and York may have postdated the entry of these two fishes to the Potomac and James (Hocutt et al. 1986). However, if these species were present in the Potomac or James at the time of such captures, they probably had not spread to the capture theater. The avoidance today by *Campostoma* of Blue Ridge streams in the Shenandoah system indicates that stream capture chronology in that area may be irrelevant.

The absence of the riverine silt-tolerant *Carpiodes cyprinus* from the Rappahannock and York, and its presence in the Susquehanna, Potomac, James, and Roanoke is anomalous. Hocutt et al. (1986) considered that in addition to reaching the Atlantic slope by stream capture, *C. cyprinus* may have used only part of the Greater Susquehanna River extension. Cincotta et al. (1986b) added that *Carpiodes* may have been introduced to the Atlantic slope; I doubt that this would apply to all four drainages.

Although the Rappahannock and York have ample area on the Coastal Plain, their lowland faunas are fairly small; both lack three widespread inhabitants of that province elsewhere: *Notropis chalybaeus*, *Enneacanthus chaetodon*, and *Etheostoma fusiforme*. The absence of *E. chaetodon* from the Potomac and the hiatus in the range of all three species farther north on the western side of Chesapeake Bay has been noted above. Thus it is surprising that *N. chalybaeus* and *E. fusiforme* are present in the relatively small Piankatank drainage on the Coastal Plain between the Rappahannock and York. Among other lowland fishes, *Acantharchus pomotis* recommences its range in the Rappahannock from a large northwestern Chesapeake basin hiatus and *Enneacanthus obesus* reappears as extremely localized in the York.

Range terminations, unexpected absences, and localizations of lowland species could have resulted from differential use of the Greater Susquehanna, localization within the Chesapeake and Continental Shelf refugia, or varying survival of briny transgression. It is likely that the Late Pleistocene to Middle Holocene fauna of this region was not homogeneously distributed.

Intradrainage Patterns

Distribution patterns in the main branches of the Rappahannock and York show similar trends according to habitat changes that extend from headwaters into estuaries. In the York, more species are known from the large Piedmont branches—the North and South Anna rivers—of the Pamunkey system than from the Mattaponi system. This reflects the availability of suitable habitat—the Mattaponi drains little of the Piedmont—and limited sampling of the Mattaponi.

Among fairly widespread species, the most obvious nonuniform pattern is that of *Cottus bairdi* in the Rappahannock, where this species extends the farthest east among the *Cottus* of Virginia. This sculpin is widespread in the Blue Ridge and has a few outlying populations on the upper Piedmont; then there is a substantial range hiatus, below which populations are clustered on the lower Piedmont in a corner of the Foothill Zone (Maps 7, 130). Much of the hiatus lies in the Culpeper Triassic and Jurassic basin—an area of lower relief, relatively few springs, and low flow (Roberts 1928; Furcron 1939; Hack 1982; Lynch et al. 1987). Four other species have somewhat fewer populations in and near the Culpeper basin than upstream and downstream: *Clinostomus funduloides*, *Rhinichthys cataractae*, *R. atratulus*, and *Semotilus atromaculatus*; most of them are typical of cool small streams.

JAMES DRAINAGE FAUNA

The James River is the longest river in Virginia and, except for headwaters of two tributaries, the drainage courses entirely in the state. It is the southernmost major Chesapeake tributary. The James drainage is narrow but lengthy in the Coastal Plain and has a much larger portion in the Piedmont. Like the Potomac but differing from the Rappahannock and York, the James breaches the Blue Ridge and drains a major part of the Valley and Ridge Province. The large southern tributary on the Piedmont is the Appomattox River system.

Fauna

The James ichthyofauna is fairly speciose for an Atlantic slope drainage, with 109 total taxa: 73 indigenous (3 endemic), 26 introduced, and 10 estuarine or diadromous taxa. Its high number of natives accrues mainly from southern Coastal Plain elements, from upland and montane species of direct affinity with species in the Roanoke drainage or Ohio (Teays) basin, and from the three endemic taxa. The James fauna is more similar to those of the York, Rappahannock, and Potomac than to the Chowan and Roanoke faunas on the south (*Chowan Drainage Fauna*). Many range terminations fall in and adjacent to the James, as identified just below and under *Albemarle Basin Fauna*.

The native game and foodfish fauna of the James above the Fall Zone was impoverished as were those farther north in Virginia; most species present are listed under *Potomac Drainage Fauna*. Unlike in the Potomac, which has a formidable natural Fall Zone barrier (Great Falls), striped bass ascended the James River well into the Piedmont and the American shad migrated far into the Valley and Ridge. Dams in the Fall Zone and at many points upstream have more recently blocked these migrants.

Lowland Fishes

The fauna of the Coastal Plain section of the James is augmented by five species having the north end of their native Atlantic slope range there: *Chologaster cornuta*, *Fundulus lineolatus*, *Pomoxis nigromaculatus*, *Lepomis gulosus*, and *Etheostoma serrifer*. *Fundulus lineolatus* and *E. serrifer* are regarded as native to the James owing to their occurrence in the Nansemond system of the lower James estuary, but the two site records of each are at the Dismal Swamp periphery and may reflect recent northward dispersal via a ditch. *Chologaster cornuta* was long known as far north as the Nansemond; recently it was found in the Chickahominy system, the large northern Coastal Plain tributary of the James. *Pomoxis nigromaculatus* and *L. gulosus* may be introduced to the James. Four species are known from the James by only one Coastal Plain record: *Lampetra appendix*, *Esox americanus*, *Notropis chalybaeus*, and *Enneacanthus obesus*; localization of the *Esox* is particularly puzzling. The James is part of the western Chesapeake hiatus in the range of *Enneacanthus chaetodon*. Some fishes typically restricted to the Coastal Plain (on a full-range basis) have invaded the lower Piedmont in the James: *Acantharchus pomotis*, *Centrarchus macropterus*, *Enneacanthus gloriosus*, and *Etheostoma fusiforme*. Similar tendencies for these species occur in some other Virginia drainages.

Extended-River Dispersal

The James may be the drainage least enriched by species that used the Greater Susquehanna River to disperse south within the Chesapeake basin. With varying sea levels, it would have been the last drainage to connect with the Susquehanna and the first to be severed. However, if species had reached the junction of the extended James and Susquehanna from upstream in the James or southerly lowland refugia, dispersal up the Greater Susquehanna would have been possible, even when sea level was rising.

Ichthyofaunal support for this two-way dispersal model is weak, corroborating other indications that the main paleochannels generally had hostile habitat for and were little used by upland and many lowland fishes. Several fishes (listed below) have their southern Atlantic slope terminus in the James, indicating possible use of the Greater Susquehanna to reach the James. However, nearly all are upland or montane species—those least likely to have used the Greater Susquehanna. Further, seven upland fishes (listed below) whose northern boundary is in the James apparently did not use the Greater Susquehanna. At least two of the five lowland species noted above whose northern limit is the James apparently used small-stream routes or swamps to reach the James recently. The many differences between the Chesapeake and Albemarle faunas (below) suggest the absence of a lowland sweepstakes route between these basins.

Instead of extended rivers, the moderate or wide ranges of many lowland fishes in the Chesapeake basin may be related chiefly to using smaller interdrainage connections in inner Coastal Plain areas during the Pleistocene. A direct freshwater connection between the James and the Susquehanna may not have existed during some sea level regressions (*Extended Rivers*).

Upland, Ohioan, and Endemic Fishes

Most of the distinctiveness of the James fauna owes to upland and montane fishes, including the three taxa endemic to the drainage: *Notropis semperasper*, *Percina notogramma montuosa*, and *Etheostoma longimanum*. Eight upland taxa have their southern range terminus (on the central Atlantic slope) in the James: *Rhinichthys cataractae*, *Semotilus corporalis*, *Nocomis micropogon*, *Luxilus cornutus*, *Notropis rubellus*, *N. p. procne*, *Percina n. notogramma*, and *P. p. peltata*. Northern limits occur in the James for eight upland dwellers: *Rhinichthys atratulus obtusus*, *Campostoma anomalum michauxi*, *Nocomis raneyi*, *Lythrurus ardens*,

Notropis volucellus, *Moxostoma erythrurum*, *Ameiurus platycephalus*, and *Etheostoma nigrum*; of these eight taxa, all except *Ameiurus* are closely related to Ohioan taxa or live in the Ohio basin, and they occupy only three to five central Atlantic slope drainages. *Notropis semperasper*, *Cottus girardi*, and *Percina notogramma* also may have their sister taxa in the Ohio basin.

The uncertainty of the original distribution status of several upper James taxa exemplifies problems in recognizing shared patterns that are relevant to historical biogeography. *Nocomis raneyi*, *N. volucellus*, and *A. platycephalus* are only tentatively regarded as native to the James. Considered introduced, *Luxilus cerasinus*, *Pimephales notatus*, *Scartomyzon cervinus*, *Noturus gilberti*, and *Percina roanoka* may be native.

Stream Capture

Major enrichment of the upper James fauna is related to headland stream captures. Stream capture and speciation scenarios involving "Fincastle River" and "Old Gauley River"—precursors of parts of the James, Roanoke, or New (Teays) drainages—have been debated without consensus (Ross 1969; Jenkins et al. 1972; Hocutt 1979a, 1979b; Hocutt et al. 1986).

Part of the debate concerns the extent and chronologic sequence of captures. If the principal dispersal event to this part of the central Atlantic slope was New-to-Roanoke, a subsequent Roanoke-to-James avenue would seem to have involved smaller streams or otherwise was less used by fishes. If instead the James first robbed a large portion of the New, then the transferred New fauna likely was underdeveloped or localized compared with that later gained from the New by the Roanoke. In either case, the James fauna may have suffered more extinctions than did the southerly Roanoke, particularly during the Pleistocene. The startling discovery of evidence that the James River was draining areas west of the present Blue Ridge by the Late Miocene (Weems 1990)—much earlier than previously known—has uncertain bearing on the problem.

Subterranean Dispersal

Three upper James taxa have especially small ranges so situated as to suggest that the drainage was colonized recently via subterranean routes. *Rhinichthys atratulus obtusus* is confined to Meadow Creek. *Fundulus diaphanus* is known only from Big Spring and Lick Run, far disjunct from estuarine populations. *Cottus girardi* occurs only in the Bullpasture and Cowpasture rivers. The Meadow Creek population of *R. a. obtusus* was derived from that in Sinking Creek of the New drainage; the aquifer system of the opposed headwaters of these creeks is dissolving the terrain—both streams are "sinking creeks" (Matthews et al. 1982; Conners 1986; Holsinger and Culver 1988). The James populations of *F. diaphanus* and *C. girardi* adjoin those in the upper Shenandoah system; they occur near limestone sink- and cave-riddled divides, and some of the subterranean passages are aquifers.

Downslope Extension

The common extension of Valley and Ridge and Blue Ridge species into the Piedmont is typified in the James. Piedmont populations of such species tend to concentrate in mountains and high hills outlying the Blue Ridge, becoming sporadic or waning eastward in areas of lesser relief and heavier siltation. As an index of downslope extension, most native montane and montane–upland James fishes have been found, some only sparingly, in the intensively surveyed Bremo Bluff reach of the James River, in the middle Piedmont (Woolcott et al. 1974; White et al. 1977; Maurakis and Woolcott 1984; Map 11). Unknown here are fishes whose ranges end much upstream: *Notropis semperasper*, *N. volucellus*, *Cottus bairdi*, and *C. girardi*; or which are confined to colder water: *Salvelinus fontinalis*. Also not found in the middle James River reach are *Nocomis micropogon*, which is replaced by *N. raneyi*, and *Etheostoma longimanum* of headwater tributaries in the area.

Appomattox System

Parallel downslope extension occurs in the Appomattox system. The headwaters arise from the front of the Piedmont Foothill Zone (Map 7) and are well inclined; they accommodate an isolated concentration of upland fishes (e.g., *Rhinichthys cataractae*, *Campostoma anomalum*, *Exoglossum maxillingua*, and *Etheostoma longimanum*). However, three species of the upper James system proper apparently are truant from the Appomattox above the Lake Chesdin impoundment on the lower Piedmont: *Moxostoma erythrurum*, *Ameiurus catus*, and *Cottus bairdi*. These are considered to be clearly native to the drainage; they live near the Appomattox. Also unknown in the Appomattox are seven of the eight upland species noted above whose native drainage occurrence status is questioned. One of the suspectedly introduced populations of *Luxilus cerasinus* also occupies the upper Appomattox.

Many lowland fishes extend above the Fall Zone in the Appomattox, some about as far as they do in the James proper. Others go farthest up in the Appomattox: *Notropis bifrenatus*, *Acantharchus pomotis*, *Centrarchus macropterus*, *Enneacanthus gloriosus*, *Etheostoma fusiforme*, and *E. olmstedi* (or intergrade). In the James proper, lowland fishes are most concentrated in Tuckahoe Creek, just above the Fall Zone. This small, partly swampy system is bedded largely in a relatively low-lying portion of the Richmond Triassic basin (Map 7). Cope's (1868b) sample from Tuckahoe Creek provides important evidence of the native status of some centrarchids in the James drainage. Above Tuckahoe Creek, we sampled little of the lower Piedmont of the James proper; I am unable to discern a basis for differential upslope colonization of the James and Appomattox systems.

MINOR WESTERN CHESAPEAKE BASIN FAUNAS

Grouped here are the small drainages found in approximately the outer half of the peninsulas (necks) that separate the major western Chesapeake subestuaries of Virginia. In composite, the number of native freshwater species known (33) is 80% of that on the whole of Delmarva. The number is much greater than that in the Virginia portion of Delmarva, owing to the presence of a lengthy stream (the Piankatank River–Dragon Swamp) on one neck; connection of some minor drainages to large oligohaline rivers of major drainages; and on the bayward end of the necks, interjacency to major drainages. Most freshwater members of the minor-drainage faunas are characteristic of the Coastal Plain; no endemic taxon is present. Euryhaline species constitute a chief share of each fauna.

Species occurrences on the necks are related to survival in higher reaches of the drainages during marine transgressions or to reestablishment of populations by ingress from refugia during sea level regressions. Interdrainage exchange also may have occurred via headwater capture and by straying or directed dispersal through low-salinity bridges.

Piankatank Drainage

The richest fauna occupies the Piankatank, the largest of the minor drainages situated between the Rappahannock and York. The main-stem freshwater section of the Piankatank, most of it a sluggish blackwater flowage (Dragon Swamp), arises at elevation 47 m; with its long estuary the drainage stretches 99 rkm. The Piankatank is the longest of the minor drainages of Virginia, but is somewhat smaller than the larger of the Delmarva drainages. The Piankatank fauna (21 native freshwater species) is known from Merriner et al. (1976) and nine samples (some of one species) from above their sites.

Piankatank natives unknown from any other peninsula-end tributary between the James and Potomac rivers are *Lepisosteus osseus, Rhinichthys atratulus, Semotilus atromaculatus, Notropis amoenus, N. hudsonius, N. chalybaeus, Ameiurus catus, Noturus gyrinus,* and *Etheostoma fusiforme; N. chalybaeus* and *E. fusiforme* apparently are absent also from the surrounding Rappahannock and York. Piankatank fishes of wider but still limited outer distribution are *Lampetra aepyptera, Esox niger, Umbra pygmaea, Notemigonus crysoleucas, Cyprinella analostana, Aphredoderus sayanus, Enneacanthus gloriosus, Lepomis auritus, L. gibbosus,* and *Perca flavescens.* Somewhat more widely distributed are *Erimyzon oblongus* and *Etheostoma olmstedi.*

Lepomis gulosus is present and may be native in the Piankatank, but it is considered probably introduced based on that status just north and south. Notable absence of records, some likely artifactual, for the Piankatank concern *Amia calva, Dorosoma cepedianum, Esox americanus, Hybognathus regius, Ameiurus natalis, A. nebulosus, Gambusia holbrooki, Acantharchus pomotis, Centrarchus macropterus,* and *Enneacanthus obesus. Hybognathus regius,* of wide Coastal Plain occurrence in major drainages, may not have found the Piankatank to be of sufficient size.

Other Drainages

In other minor drainages, the extreme eastern site of the upland-dwelling *Semotilus corporalis* is in the Ingram Bay drainage, just south of the Potomac mouth. Similarly, *Clinostomus funduloides* was disjunctively recorded in a tributary of the lower Potomac estuary, along with *Rhinichthys atratulus, S. corporalis,* and *Ameiurus nebulosus.* Surprisingly, *A. nebulosus* was found in only one direct minor western Chesapeake tributary.

DISMAL SWAMP FAUNA

Dismal Swamp, a large wet wilderness in southeastern Virginia and northeastern North Carolina, is a geologically and biotically diverse area (Kirk 1979). Except for Lake Drummond in its midst, the swamp was solid forest when first viewed by settlers. It is a northern outpost for bald cypress, Tupelo gum, and Spanish moss (Meanley 1973). The fish fauna is impressive primarily for its persistence in conditions adverse to most fishes.

Fauna

The Dismal Swamp ichthyofauna comprises only 28 native freshwater species, none endemic. Five of these occur strictly on the periphery: *Noturus gyrinus, Fundulus lineolatus, Lepomis auritus, Etheostoma olmstedi,* and *E. serrifer.* The diadromous American eel is present; channel catfish, largemouth bass, and bluegill have been introduced, but only the bass and bluegill remain. The swamp population of *Ameiurus catus* may have been stocked or might have entered via a ditch or Dismal Swamp Canal. Common in Lake Drummond, this catfish is known elsewhere in the swamp by one specimen from a ditch near the lake and one from the North Carolina section of the canal.

The species composition is known primarily from Smith and Baker (1965: 4A1, 4B2, 4B4), records summarized by Jenkins et al. (1975), and records from VPISU including some by Brady (1969). The fauna of the North Carolina portion is poorly known but likely duplicates that of Virginia. The six North Carolina species lists add only *Noturus gyrinus* to the fauna (from one site). The Dismal Swamp list of Jenkins et al. (1975) is updated in *Appendix 2.* Seven species reported only by Jordan (1889b) are excluded (*Data Set*).

Distribution patterns within the swamp are not clearly determined; homogeneity probably was typical before the swamp was extensively modified. Most of the collections were made in Lake Drummond and a few ditch sites; a few samples are from Dismal Swamp Canal and one is from the Pasquotank River. Fishes are concentrated inshore in Lake Drummond (Brady 1969). Shallow woodland pools of the interior may have few species, some perhaps only the pioneering mosquitofish.

Swamp Development and Faunal Depauperacy

This entirely freshwater swamp is youthful. Succeeding a late-glacial climate and flora, extensive marshes progressively formed along low-gradient dendritic stream systems that were being ponded by a rising water table. Forest eventually dominated. Accumulation of the Dismal Swamp Peat began about 8,900 years ago. By 3,500 years B.P., the peat mantled all originally contiguous parts of Dismal Swamp. Lake Drummond originated no earlier than 4,000 years B.P., probably from a depression formed by a peat burn.

The primary original direction of flow was southeasterly from the Suffolk Scarp–Sand Ridge, marking the western divide of the swamp, to the Little and Pasquotank rivers of the Albemarle Sound basin and to the Northwest River of the Currituck Sound basin (Maps 6, 7, 12). Minor drainage of the north edge of the swamp may have occurred north to the Nansemond River system and, more likely, northeast to the Elizabeth River system; both are tributaries of the lower James River estuary. Natural drainage became poorer with maturation of the swamp (Whitehead 1972; Oaks and Coch 1973; Oaks et al. 1974; Oaks and Whitehead 1979; Whitehead and Oaks 1979).

The swamp was extensively ditched starting in the 1760s, chiefly to drain it for farming and logging. Dismal Swamp Canal was dug east of Lake Drummond during the early 1800s. The swamp became well connected to the James drainage via Jericho Ditch to Shingle Creek of the Nansemond system and by Portsmouth Ditch to Deep Creek of the Elizabeth system. Dismal Swamp Canal conducts the principal surface water outflow of the swamp to the Elizabeth and Pasquotank rivers. Its main water source is the Feeder Ditch from Lake Drummond, which in turn taps much of the swamp (Lichtler and Walker 1979).

The Dismal Swamp ichthyofauna is about that expected for a somewhat isolated, lowland area having rather homogeneous, essentially lentic habitats. Most swamp species also occur to the immediate north, east, and south of the swamp; 90% or more of this fauna probably was shared with the late-glacial Albemarle and lower Chesapeake refugia.

Centrarchids dominate the Dismal Swamp fauna in number of species (eight). The two suckers are members of the low-gradient genus *Erimyzon*. Two darters, *Etheostoma serrifer* and *E. fusiforme*, are members of the "swamp darter" subgenus *Hololepis*; a third, *Etheostoma olmstedi*, lives on the swamp fringe. Three species have their northern range limits immediately north in the Nansemond (*Fundulus lineolatus* and *E. serrifer*) or somewhat farther in the Chickahominy system of the James (*Chologaster cornuta*). The range of *Erimyzon sucetta* terminates north on the Atlantic slope in the swamp and Chowan.

Absentees

The Dismal Swamp fauna is notable for what is missing (Jenkins et al. 1975). It bears comparison in this respect to the native freshwater fauna of the Blackwater River system, which flows entirely in the Coastal Plain on the west of the Dismal Swamp system. The Blackwater fauna is the most speciose of those adjacent to Dismal Swamp, but it is the least so in the Chowan drainage, of which it is part. The swampy Blackwater system is much larger than Dismal Swamp and its main channel has reaches of moderate current. It has 12 species that are absent from

Dismal Swamp, several of which (chiefly minnows and darters) are rheophils at least when spawning. The Dismal Swamp ditches with artificially hastened flow may suit a few of the missing species, but access to them from outside the swamp is difficult or lacking. Another Dismal Swamp truant is *Enneacanthus chaetodon*, a Blackwater fish that is extremely rare in Virginia.

Limiting Factors

Impoverishment of the Dismal Swamp fauna is a result of poor natural flow, the cloaking forests, and the light-quenching "black" (but clear) water of the swamp. Lake Drummond is open, shallow, and turbid ("brown"); it yields acceptable catches of some gamefishes (Rosebery and Bowers 1952; Brady 1969), but is not noted for angling. Stocked channel catfish, largemouth bass, and bluegill have had moderate to no success (Andrews 1971); *Ameiurus* catfishes and yellow perch are dwarfed there.

Low pH, owing to leaching of organic acids from peat deposits and to other decomposition products, also depresses biotic diversity. Ditches with primary drainage from outside the swamp are the least acidic, pH 6.0–7.0 in some areas; these values probably are not limiting to most species of the area. Ditches draining large portions of the swamp are quite acidic, 4.0–5.0. Lake Drummond typically measures 4.2–4.8 and declines to 3.5 (Smith and Baker 1965; Lichtler and Walker 1979; Marshall 1979; Gregory-Phillips and Marshall 1990). The more acidic waters generally support scant rooted vegetation (Matta 1979), a cover type important to many Coastal Plain fishes.

The list of species tolerant of low acidity in Virginia, although based largely on distribution patterns in (and beyond) the state and generally not on physiological study, is a near match of the Dismal Swamp fauna. Two Dismal Swamp species not on the list, *Lepomis auritus* and *Etheostoma olmstedi*, are peripheral in the swamp. The single record of *Noturus gyrinus*, from the Pasquotank River at the edge of the swamp, is from water of pH 5.6. Moderate acid tolerance may not allow certain species to live in the swamp interior; three other species on the list occur only on the edge of the swamp. Okefenokee Swamp in Georgia parallels Dismal Swamp ecologically; at an average pH of 3.7, it is devoid of minnows and depauperate of fishes in general (Laerm and Freeman 1986).

Cypress Swamp

This flowage probably was a primary contributor of fishes to Dismal Swamp. It drains part of the Isle of

Wight Plain in Virginia, then passes through the low Suffolk Scarp, thereby entering the west edge of Dismal Swamp; above the scarp it encompasses more than 61% of the higher area that drains into Dismal Swamp (Lichtler and Walker 1979). Formerly the system extended east across the swamp to the Northwest River; Washington Ditch presently conveys Cypress Swamp water from the scarp to Lake Drummond.

The present Cypress Swamp fauna is an indicator of the Dismal Swamp fauna before the latter was stocked. Based on 12 collections from the scarp and upstream, Cypress Swamp is occupied by 22 species, all of which are regarded as native in Dismal Swamp except for *Lepomis macrochirus*. Not recorded in Cypress Swamp are the interior Dismal Swamp natives *Lepisosteus osseus* and *Erimyzon oblongus*; all five peripheral Dismal Swamp species (see above); the possibly nonnative *Ameiurus catus*; and the probably or clearly introduced largemouth bass and bluegill. The apparent absence of the largemouth bass in Cypress Swamp lends credence to its introduced status throughout southeastern Virginia. None of the seven species accredited to Jordan's problematic collection in 1888 from the periphery of Dismal Swamp were found in Cypress Swamp.

FAUNAS NORTH AND EAST OF DISMAL SWAMP

Arcing from just northwest to east of Dismal Swamp in extreme southeastern Virginia is a series of minor drainages—Nansemond River to Northwest River—that are tributary to either the lower James River estuary, the mouth area of Chesapeake Bay, the Atlantic Ocean, or the northern arm of Currituck Sound. The depauperacy of the composite native freshwater ichthyofauna—about 29 species—reflects availability of only low-gradient and often quite acidic habitats. The species are largely those of Dismal Swamp.

Most species are sparsely distributed in the area; *Esox niger*, *E. americanus*, *Umbra pygmaea*, *Aphredoderus sayanus*, and *Chologaster cornuta* seem notably localized, the latter in a cypress swamp in Seashore State Park near Virginia Beach. That swamp may be a remnant of a small eastward-flowing drainage network that has been nearly obliterated by headland retreat of the coast (Andrews 1971; Oaks and Coch 1973). Some localized patterns may be artifacts of insufficient collecting, but extensive degradation of habitat has been caused by human population sprawl, industrialization, and naval military development.

Back Bay, a large backbarrier lagoon narrowly con-

tiguous with Currituck Sound at the North Carolina border, has had salinity fluctuations caused by tides, storm washovers from the Atlantic Ocean, and in-pumping of sea water (Oaks and Coch 1973). It has a low-diversity freshwater fauna typical of the area; the best sport fishing occurs where the environment is freshwater. Several game and forage species have been introduced to the many small or medium-sized impoundments north of Dismal Swamp (e.g., Norman 1985).

ALBEMARLE BASIN FAUNA

Albemarle Sound, North Carolina, is fed at its head by the broad sluggish Chowan River and the relatively narrow, fluvial Roanoke River, and along its north and south shores by several minor drainages (Map 12). Its fauna of 123 taxa comprises 85 native freshwater, 26 introduced, and 11 diadromous or estuarine taxa (Smith 1893; Lee et al. 1980; E. F. Menhinick, in litt.). Included are seven endemic taxa, all of which inhabit the Roanoke drainage (including *Percina rex*, which is exclusively shared by the Chowan and Roanoke). The Chowan and Roanoke drainages have much larger faunas than do the minor drainages, owing to their much greater habitat heterogeneity.

The one species that inhabits only a minor drainage of the basin is the Waccamaw killifish *Fundulus waccamensis*. The records are from Lake Phelps of the Scuppernong drainage, on the south side of Albemarle Sound; the Scuppernong erringly was considered part of the Roanoke drainage by Hocutt et al. (1986). The Lake Phelps population may be introduced. This species is known elsewhere only from the Lake Waccamaw area in southeastern North Carolina (Shute et al. 1981).

Southern Faunal Beginnings

The freshwater fish fauna of the Albemarle basin manifests a major commencement of the highly speciose southeastern United States ichthyofaunas (Miller 1959: Figure 1). The Albemarle fauna is most closely related to those just south in the Tar and Neuse drainages of the Pamlico Sound basin of North Carolina. These Piedmont–Coastal Plain drainages lack many upland and montane species of the Albemarle basin; fewer differences exist among the lowland faunas of the Albemarle and Pamlico basins (Jenkins et al. 1972; Rohde et al. 1979; Hocutt et al. 1986). The Albemarle fauna is slightly richer than that of the Chesapeake basin—85 versus 82 indigenous freshwater taxa.

Range Terminations

Its seven endemic taxa and range boundaries of many other taxa render the Albemarle fauna highly distinctive. The boundaries are set by the divide on the north between the Roanoke–Chowan and James drainages, by the south divide shared with the Tar, Neuse, Cape Fear, and Pee Dee drainages, and the western divide with the New drainage (Ohio basin).

Northern range terminations in the Roanoke–Chowan involve 17 taxa (other than endemic taxa): *Luxilus albeolus, L. cerasinus, Notropis chiliticus, N. procne longiceps, N. alborus, N. altipinnis, Erimyzon sucetta, Scartomyzon cervinus, Moxostoma anisurum, M. pappillosum, Fundulus rathbuni, Ambloplites cavifrons, Elassoma zonatum, Percina rex, P. peltata nevisense, P. roanoka,* and *Etheostoma collis.*

Southern range terminations in the Roanoke–Chowan are made by five forms (plus endemic taxa): *Lampetra appendix, Rhinichthys a. atratulus, Exoglossum maxillingua, Thoburnia rhothoeca,* and *Cottus b. bairdi.* Accentuating the uniqueness of the Albemarle fauna are the 11 taxa including 3 endemic taxa with southern range terminations in the James (listed under that fauna). Also, *Rhinichthys atratulus obtusus, Campostoma anomalum michauxi, Carpiodes cyprinus,* and *Enneacanthus chaetodon* have a major range hiatus beginning just north or south of the Albemarle basin.

Some of the full-range breaks may have been caused by latitudinally related climatic effects, notably for lowland species with large southerly ranges—*Erimyzon sucetta* and *Elassoma zonatum.* These two species may have been extirpated from Atlantic drainages north of the Albemarle by glacial climate; their occurrence in the central Mississippi basin north of Virginia latitudes would have stemmed from postglacial dispersal. Most range breaks around the Albemarle basin concern upland forms and probably involve stock dispersal via stream capture, particularly from the Ohio basin. Curiously, *Lampetra aepyptera* occurs just north and south but is unknown from the Albemarle basin.

Sport Fishes

There are slightly more native freshwater gamefish species in the Albemarle fauna than in the Chesapeake basin. A notable addition is the Roanoke bass *Ambloplites cavifrons.* Several redhorse suckers, often used as food, supplement the Albemarle fauna. Several gamefishes including three species of black basses were introduced to the Albemarle.

CHOWAN DRAINAGE FAUNA

The Chowan and Roanoke drainages of Virginia and North Carolina often have been combined in ichthyology papers as the Roanoke or Roanoke–Chowan drainage. Their mouths at the head of Albemarle Sound are only about 10 km apart; Schwartz (1981b) considered virtually all of the sound to typically have freshwater habitats during most of the year. We consider the Chowan, an entirely Piedmont and Coastal Plain drainage, to be a separate drainage partly to contrast its fauna with the faunas of other drainages.

Fauna

After most of the Chowan fauna was identified (Jenkins et al. 1975), extensive data for the Virginia portion were provided by Norman and Southwick (1985, in litt.) and others. The Chowan contains 93 fish taxa—71 native, 11 introduced, and 11 estuarine or diadromous; none are endemic. Comparing shared native freshwater taxa, the Chowan fauna is more closely related to that of the Roanoke than to that of the James, whose greater affinities are with the other faunas in the Virginia portion of the Chesapeake basin. Pairwise comparisons of the data (Table 2; *Appendix 2*) yielded the following coefficients of faunal similarity: Chowan–Roanoke 0.821; Chowan–James 0.655; James–Roanoke 0.598.

Occupying the Coastal Plain and the Lowlands division of the Piedmont, the Chowan fauna is dominated by species characteristic of one or both of these provinces, particularly of those parts south of the Albemarle basin. The other major faunal component comprises fishes more common to uplands, most of which apparently were derived from the Roanoke drainage.

Interdrainage Comparison

Only two freshwater species occupy the Chowan and not the Roanoke—*Lampetra appendix* and *Notropis bifrenatus.* The Chowan appears to be a natural southern range limit of the lamprey. The shiner likely was extirpated from the Roanoke before it was recorded; it occurs south of the Roanoke. The estuarine *Acipenser brevirostrum,* recorded in the lower Chowan River in 1881, probably ascended the Roanoke before its extirpation from the Albemarle basin.

Ten of the 13 native Roanoke taxa not shared with the Chowan are upland or montane–upland types: the 6 endemic taxa of the Roanoke and *Rhinichthys atratulus obtusus, Notropis chiliticus, Salvelinus fontina-*

lis, and *Cottus b. bairdi*. Most of the 10 would have found adequate (moderate) gradient and gravel–rubble substrate in the upper Chowan had they had access to the drainage. However, judging from present ranges, 9 of the 10 (*Hypentelium roanokense* excepted) may have lacked proximity to Roanoke–Chowan stream capture theaters when they were open. Had the brook trout colonized the Chowan during glacial climate, it would have perished with postglacial warming.

Of the other three Roanoke species absent from the Chowan, *Elassoma zonatum* has its northern limit on the Atlantic slope in lowermost Roanoke tributaries, where it is localized. *Fundulus rathbuni* and *Etheostoma collis* form a unique middle and lower Piedmont biogeographic track that has its northern end in the Albemarle basin. (*Notropis alborus*, known only from one Chowan site, has the same track; *N. altipinnis*, widespread in the Chowan, has a very similar track.)

Interdrainage Dispersal

Dispersal between the Roanoke and Chowan was afforded by the Greater Roanoke River interconnection during sea level regressions. Some lowland freshwater species probably interchange between the two drainages today. Because ecological conditions in the lower Roanoke and Chowan main stems have long been unsuited to upland species, stream capture likely transferred most upland species to the Chowan. Many Chowan upland species are shared with the James as well as the Roanoke, but no clear evidence exists as to whether these species reached the Chowan from only the James, only the Roanoke, or from both. The restriction of *Thoburnia rhothoeca* in the Chowan to a few Nottoway River headwaters adjacent to the James supports a James-to-Chowan path, but the population is either naturally relict or introduced and its source not directly traceable.

Fall Zone

The Chowan Fall Zone is fairly gentle; typically, long pools are interspersed with short riffles and, rarely, low cascades. Its ecological boundaries are indistinct; in some streams, habitats typical of the upper Coastal Plain occur distinctly above the Fall Zone and the converse ensues below the zone. Hence, the range of many species in the Chowan extends appreciably beyond provinces typically occupied. Anadromous fishes can easily traverse the Chowan Fall Zone, except for the dam on the Meherrin Fall Line at Emporia.

Intradrainage Patterns

The varied distribution patterns in the Chowan reflect differing relationships to the Fall Zone and attest to the habitat differences among the three main branches of the Chowan River—east to west, the Blackwater, Nottoway, and Meherrin systems. All of the Blackwater and much of the Nottoway and Meherrin drain the Coastal Plain; the Piedmont sections of the Nottoway and Meherrin include upland habitat.

Sixteen Chowan species appear to be typical Piedmont–upper Coastal Plain inhabitants: *Cyprinella analostana*, *Hybognathus regius*, *Erimyzon oblongus*, *Moxostoma macrolepidotum*, *M. anisurum*, *M. pappillosum*, *Ameiurus natalis*, *A. nebulosus*, *Noturus insignis*, *Aphredoderus sayanus*, *Pomoxis nigromaculatus*, *Enneacanthus gloriosus*, *Lepomis gulosus*, *L. auritus*, *L. gibbosus*, and *Etheostoma olmstedi*.

Six species are widespread only in, and are generally restricted to, the Coastal Plain: *Amia calva*, *Notropis chalybaeus*, *Erimyzon sucetta*, *Chologaster cornuta*, *Fundulus lineolatus*, and *Enneacanthus obesus*. Ten others are widespread on the Coastal Plain but extend somewhat farther into the Piedmont: *Lepisosteus osseus*, *Esox americanus*, *Ameiurus catus*, *Noturus gyrinus*, *Gambusia holbrooki*, *Acantharchus pomotis*, *Centrarchus macropterus*, *Perca flavescens*, *Etheostoma serrifer*, and *E. fusiforme*. A few of these species (Table 2) are known from the Meherrin Coastal Plain only in North Carolina; only a small part of the Meherrin Coastal Plain is in Virginia. Reaching farther into the Piedmont are *Esox niger*, *Umbra pygmaea*, and *Notemigonus crysoleucas*; these three are more abundant in the lower Piedmont and Coastal Plain than above.

Nine upland taxa are generally distributed in the Piedmont (and Fall Zone for some), but are absent or virtually so from the Coastal Plain: *Clinostomus funduloides*, *Semotilus atromaculatus*, *Nocomis leptocephalus*, *Lythrurus ardens*, *Notropis volucellus*, *N. altipinnis*, *Catostomus commersoni*, *Ameiurus platycephalus*, and *Etheostoma flabellare*.

Twelve Piedmont fishes extend well into the Coastal Plain of either or both the Nottoway or Meherrin, but only in the main stem: *Nocomis raneyi*, *Luxilus albeolus*, *Notropis amoenus*, *N. procne*, *Hypentelium nigricans*, *Scartomyzon cervinus*, *Ambloplites cavifrons*, *Percina rex*, *P. peltata nevisense*, *P. roanoka*, *Etheostoma vitreum*, and the introduced smallmouth bass. For 7 of the 12 species, the continuations below the Fall Zone occur only in the Nottoway River; the Fall Zone impoundment on the Meherrin River may limit downstream extension. The upper portions of the Coastal Plain sections of these rivers are essentially Piedmontane chemically; their physical habitats are similar to those of the lower Piedmont. The Coastal Plain extension of *Nocomis raneyi* contrasts with the distinct halt made at the Fall Line by its congener *N. leptocephalus*, perhaps due to the preference by *N. leptocephalus* for smaller streams than those occupied by *N. raneyi*. Over their full ranges, the other 11 species exhibit the same stream-size preferences as does *N. raneyi*.

Seven Piedmont species have disjunct populations in the middle Blackwater River: *Notropis amoenus, N. hudsonius, N. procne, N. altipinnis, Percina peltata, P. roanoka,* and *Etheostoma vitreum*. In the Blackwater, most of these are known only, and have long persisted, at or near Zuni, a reach having a few fast runs. This reach is blackwater and mostly sluggish, swampy, and sandy, a habitat combination perhaps characteristic only of *N. altipinnis*. A few other species are restricted in the Blackwater system to the main stem, but occur more widely on the Coastal Plain than do the above seven.

Seven fishes occur principally in upstream sections of the Piedmont: *Phoxinus oreas, Rhinichthys a. atratulus, Campostoma anomalum, Luxilus cerasinus, Thoburnia rhothoeca, Moxostoma erythrurum,* and (in the upper Meherrin) an *Etheostoma nigrum*-like population of the taxonomically problematic johnny darter group.

Among other localizations, *Exoglossum maxillingua* is confined to the Fall Zone and somewhat above in the Nottoway system and *Percina rex* occurs only in that area and slightly below. *Carpiodes cyprinus* is known from only one Chowan site in the Meherrin Piedmont. Its apparent rarity is surprising because this deepwater riverine species is tolerant of turbidity. Oddly too, *Notropis hudsonius* seems to be localized; in other drainages it generally is widespread in rivers (and often caught in shallows). Two shiners each known from one Nottoway system locality may be extirpated—*Notropis alborus* from the Piedmont and *N. bifrenatus* from the Fall Zone. The lentic *Enneacanthus chaetodon* is extremely localized in the Coastal Plain.

The availability of habitat accounts for the strong faunal similarity and greater species richness of the Nottoway and Meherrin, which drain both the Coastal Plain and Piedmont, when compared with the entirely Coastal Plain Blackwater. Particularly notable is the absence from the Blackwater of gravel-nest-building minnows and their breeding associates, and the redd-spawning *Moxostoma* species, *Hypentelium nigricans,* and *Catostomus commersoni*. The general lack of exposed gravel militates against establishment of these species in the Blackwater. The pH of the Blackwater River—typically 6.5–7.1—is not particularly low. The usual pH of Blackwater tributaries is 6.0–6.6, Nottoway Coastal Plain tributaries are 5.8–6.5, and Nottoway Piedmont tributaries (including some Coastal Plain-like swamps) are 5.7–7.0 (Corning and Prosser 1969; M. D. Norman, in litt.).

Distributional anomalies of five upland species may be due to their entry of the Chowan via headwater capture at only one place, or more than once into a single system. Recorded from only one of two systems are *Campostoma anomalum, Luxilus cerasinus,* and *Moxostoma erythrurum* in the Meherrin and *Thoburnia rhothoeca* and *Percina rex* in the Nottoway. Their restriction to (and localization within) one system may be related to lack of suitable habitat below the species ranges, such that the vacant system could not be reached by filtering through the Coastal Plain.

ROANOKE DRAINAGE FAUNA

With source streams descending a modest-sized segment of the Blue Ridge, a small but species-rich section in the Valley and Ridge Province, and major extents in the Piedmont and Coastal Plain, the Roanoke drainage has offered a wide variety of habitats for the development of a large fauna. The drainage has a large southern tributary, the Dan River.

Fauna

The Roanoke contains 119 piscine taxa—82 native, 27 introduced, and 10 estuarine or diadromous; its six endemic taxa are *Hypentelium roanokense, Thoburnia hamiltoni, Scartomyzon ariommus, Noturus gilberti,* the undescribed spotted madtom (tentatively a subspecies of *N. insignis*), and *Etheostoma podostemone*.

The native Roanoke fauna has been considered the most speciose and distinctive on the Atlantic slope of the United States south of the St. Lawrence drainage (Jenkins et al. 1972). With adjustment of species lists (*Appendix 2*), the Roanoke fauna has fewer native freshwater taxa than do the southerly Santee (92) and Savannah faunas (88), but remains the most distinctive based on its higher numbers of endemic taxa and range terminations in and adjacent to the drainage. With a larger number of introduced species (25% of freshwater forms) and estuarine or diadromous types, the Roanoke has a higher total of taxa than do the Santee (114) and Savannah (99).

The Roanoke fauna is particularly enriched by suckers—10 species of *Moxostoma* and allies, 14 in all. As many as 11 sucker species have been seen at one Roanoke site. Three of the species endemic to the Roanoke are catostomids, the largest complement of endemic suckers among drainages east of the Rocky Mountains.

Intradrainage Patterns

Most members of the Roanoke fauna are identified and their distributional patterns and range terminations discussed under the Albemarle or Chowan faunas. As exemplified in the Chowan, many characteristic Coastal Plain forms inhabit the extreme lower Piedmont of the Roanoke and nearly all upland species in the Roanoke extend well into the Piedmont. Most upland species become progressively less common and their populations tend to become increasingly sporadic downslope through the Piedmont.

Downslope Extension

Contrasting with the many upland Chowan species that extend down into the Fall Zone or upper Coastal Plain, most upland fishes in the Roanoke have the lower end of their ranges in the middle Piedmont. Reasons for the paucity of upland fishes in the lower Piedmont, Fall Zone, and upper Coastal Plain include: (1) the much larger size of the Roanoke River in the lower Piedmont and below, compared with the Nottoway and Meherrin rivers, diminishes use of the Roanoke River as a thoroughfare by species preferring small and medium streams; (2) high turbidity and siltation in the Roanoke and Dan rivers and their lower Piedmont tributaries are hostile conditions for sight-feeders or lithophilic spawners; (3) five mainstem reservoirs, created within the period 1952–1964, have obliterated more than half of the Piedmont–Fall Zone reach of the Roanoke River and the lowermost Dan River (Map 9; one reservoir entirely in North Carolina), and they also impeded movement of stream fishes among tributaries; (4) water releases from the two upper Piedmont, Roanoke River impoundments—an electric power generating complex—produce fluctuating conditions down to the lower series of reservoirs, including high and heavily turbid water during the spawning season of many species; and (5) four small dams on the Dan River in Danville block upstream fish movements.

Headland Isolates

In further contrast to the Chowan, the Roanoke drainage arises partly in the Blue Ridge and the Valley and Ridge provinces. Here occur high-gradient and cold water; the so-localized taxa which are absent from the Chowan are *Salvelinus fontinalis*, *Rhinichthys*

atratulus obtusus, *Thoburnia hamiltoni*, the spotted madtom, and *Cottus bairdi*.

Roanoke–Dan Comparison

Few distributional differences exist between the Virginia portion of the Roanoke system proper (above the Dan River mouth) and the Dan system; the habitats of the two are similar. The four species having a lower-to-middle Piedmont track (*Chowan Drainage Fauna*) reach upstream limits in the lower portions of one or both of these systems. *Notropis altipinnis* barely extends into the Dan and is absent in the Roanoke (assuming the upper Piedmont population to be introduced). *Fundulus rathbuni* has a similar range in the area; there are more Dan records in Virginia than for *N. altipinnis*, but the records are tightly clustered. *Notropis alborus* and *Etheostoma collis* limitedly inhabit both the Roanoke proper and Dan.

Other differences between the Roanoke and Dan concern species that are inclined to live in mountains or are wider ranging. *Notropis volucellus*, unknown from the Dan, has a broad gap in its Roanoke range, being noted only in the Valley and Ridge and from one record far downstream in North Carolina. Restriction of *Notropis chiliticus* to the Dan may have resulted from insufficient time for it to move to the Roanoke after having reached the Dan via capture of the Pee Dee drainage, or from introduction. *Thoburnia hamiltoni* and the spotted madtom, both endemic, are known only from extreme upper, montane portions of the Dan. The former is replaced in the upper Roanoke proper by *T. rhothoeca*. The range of *Noturus insignis* encloses the minuscule confines of the spotted madtom within the Dan. The locally distributed brook trout is assumed to be native to both systems.

Intra-Roanoke Comparison

Notable distributional differences within the Roanoke system proper include presence or absence in the five uppermost subsystems of certain endemic and other localized species. These subsystems are the only ones in the upper Roanoke proper that drain the Blue Ridge: the Roanoke River above its gap in the Blue Ridge; the Blackwater and Pigg rivers, which head on the Blue Ridge south of the Roanoke gap; and Goose and Otter creeks, which arise on the Blue Ridge north of the gap. The relevant species predominate in the medium or large channels with moderately frequent riffles, typically clear water, and little-silted substrate. The uppermost Roanoke River and its forks course the Valley and Ridge Province, have the greatest extent of such conditions, and harbor the most speciose fauna, including *Exoglossum maxillingua*, *Notropis volucellus*, *Scartomyzon ariommus*, *Noturus gilberti*, *Ambloplites cavifrons* (extirpated), and the endangered *Percina rex*.

The other four subsystems essentially are Piedmontane. Of the above six species, only *S. ariommus* has been recorded in the two most silted and chronically turbid of the subsystems—Goose and Otter creeks, at only one site in each. *Ambloplites cavifrons*, the only other of the six found in either the Goose or Otter, is found at one place in the Otter. Of the six species, *S. ariommus* and *A. cavifrons* are known from the Blackwater; they are modestly distributed there. It is discordant that the Pigg, being lower on the Piedmont than the Blackwater, has four of the six species and the Blackwater only two.

Intra-Dan Comparison

Distributional differences within the upper Dan system chiefly concern presence or absence of species in one or two of the three main upper branches—the Dan River proper, Mayo River, and Smith River subsystems. Some differences may be related to the cooler water of the reach of the upper Dan River below two dams. It is surprising that *Notropis hudsonius* and *Cottus bairdi* have not been seen in the Mayo. *Percina rex* is present in the Smith but absent from the Dan and Mayo; this species has waned widely, much as has *N. gilberti*, which occurs in all three branches of the Dan.

Upland, Ohioan, and Endemic Fishes

Upland taxa of Ohio (Teays) basin affinity on the central Atlantic slope have been mentioned previously, particularly under the James and Chowan drainage faunas. The Roanoke drainage has been implied to be the point of entry of many stocks to the Atlantic slope; some of them (notably the Roanoke endemic taxa) may have gone no further. With the New drainage lying on the west of Roanoke headwaters, many of the taxa or their ancestors are believed to have entered the Atlantic slope from the New. Some lineages, absent today from the New, are considered to have gone extinct there.

Which taxa exemplify these trans-Atlantic–Ohio divide patterns? Many have been discussed (e.g., Ross 1969; Jenkins et al. 1972; Hocutt 1979b; Hocutt et al. 1986), but rigorous phylogenetic study remains to be done. The fishes in the following categories 1–4 appear to have direct Ohioan ancestry; most of them have a limited range on the central Atlantic slope, such that they are zoogeographic markers. Species in categories 5 and 6 may have close Ohioan affinity, but the relationships are uncertain.

(1) Nine Roanoke taxa occur in the New (or their sister lineages still live or occurred historically, natively in the New): *Phoxinus oreas*, *Campostoma anomalum michauxi*, *Nocomis raneyi* (sister of *N. micropogon* plus *N. platyrhynchus*), *Luxilus albeolus*, *Lythrurus a. ardens*, *Hypentelium roanokense* (derived from *H. nigricans*-like stock), *Thoburnia rhothoeca* (extirpated from the New), *T. hamiltoni* (derivative of *T. rhothoeca*), and spotted madtom (*Noturus insignis* lineage).

(2) Seven Roanoke taxa are conspecific with or most closely related to Ohio basin occupants; they are considered nonnative (historically) to the New and may indicate extirpations there: *Luxilus cerasinus* (its ancestor an early *cornutus*-group stock), *Notropis procne* (see 4), *Scartomyzon ariommus* (affinity perhaps with *Thoburnia atripinnis* of the Green drainage of Kentucky and Tennessee), *Moxostoma erythrurum* (considered introduced to the New), *Noturus gilberti* (relationship uncertain), *Ambloplites cavifrons* (*A. rupestris* stock), and *Percina rex* (lineage with *P. burtoni*).

(3) Two Roanoke taxa may have reached the Atlantic slope from the New via both the James and Roanoke, based on indigenous status in each: *Notropis volucellus* and *Etheostoma nigrum*. A New-to-Roanoke ingress only is more probable because they occur no farther north than the James and inhabit the southerly Tar and Neuse. *Rhinichthys a. obtusus* is so sharply restricted to headlands in the Roanoke and James that certainly it used both routes.

(4) Two endemic taxa of Atlantic slope uplands exhibit a subspecific break between the Roanoke–Chowan and James: *Notropis procne* and *Percina peltata*. *Notropis procne* is linked to the Ohio basin through its undescribed sister taxon in the Tennessee and Cumberland drainages. *Percina peltata* is a member of the subgenus *Alvordius*, which has two species in the New. However, because *Alvordius* has radiated on the central Atlantic slope, *P. peltata* may best be placed in the next group.

(5) Some Roanoke species that do not appear directly linked to Ohioan species may have originated from ancestors long on the central Atlantic slope: *Scartomyzon cervinus*, *Percina roanoka*, *Etheostoma podostemone*, and *E. vitreum*.

(6) Other taxa have the north end of their ranges in the Roanoke–Chowan, but because they occur southward to at least the Santee drainage, their place of origin or entry to the Atlantic slope is unrecognized: *Moxostoma anisurum* and *M. pappillosum*, for example.

Stream Capture

Both the Roanoke system proper (North Fork, South Fork, and possible Blackwater River theaters) and the Dan system (Dan River theater) captured the New (e.g., Wright 1934; Thompson 1939; Ross 1969; Masnik 1971; Hocutt 1979b). Capture of the New by the Dan contributes to the uncertainties about the sequence of captures involving the Roanoke, James, and New (Hocutt et al. 1986; *James Drainage Fauna*). The Dan may have been as much or more a center of differentiation as the Roanoke proper. All seven endemic taxa of the Albemarle basin occupy the Dan system; two of them (discussed above) are confined to the Dan.

Geologic evidence of multiple capture in the New–South Fork Roanoke theater is impressive (e.g., Dietrich 1954, 1959). Most major South Fork tributaries are "barbed"—the westward direction of flow of their upper courses toward the New is of ancient duration, but their middle or lower courses now bend sharply (at "elbows of capture") to flow east. The reversals occurred with headward erosion and piracy by the new master stream (South Fork) and its tributary trunks. The diverted streams attacked resistant rock formations, dissecting the area into maximum relief exceeded in few other parts of Virginia. Gorges and V-shaped valleys, bare-rock walls, high waterfalls, and hanging tributaries accent the youth of the landscape; lower Bottom Creek and Lick Fork of the South Fork system are particularly good examples. The Blue Ridge section of the Blackwater River may have been involved in piracy with either or both the South Fork and New.

The Roanoke robbed its North Fork watershed from the New. The barbed North Fork valley is relatively broad and gentle-sloped to the head of its divide; its floor of relatively soft strata could have been beveled comparatively quickly. Some small western North Fork tributaries may have had recent contact with the New.

The New–Dan theater of capture is youthful. Arising in the Meadows of Dan—an upland surface formerly drained by the New—the Dan River then plunges past the Pinnacles of Dan and through the Dan River Gorge onto the Piedmont. Two small Smith River tributaries also tapped the New in this theater, but the interconnections may not have included surface flow (Hack 1982).

Physiographic evidence, fish distributions of varied extent, and intraspecific-variation patterns ranging from minor to strong differentiation indicate that captures spanned geologically recent to fairly old times. Multiple invasion of the central Atlantic slope from the New raises the possibility of asynchronous periods of differentiation on the slope, particularly in the Roanoke.

Faunal Age

The most recent entrants to the Roanoke drainage probably were montane small-stream dwellers; some probably invaded the drainage more than once. The Roanoke system and Dan system populations of *Rhinichthys a. obtusus* clearly entered separately from the New. The few populations are strongly localized to certain headwaters above the gorges of the South Fork (Lick Fork) and Dan systems, and to upper Smith River tributaries. They are replaced by *R. a. atratulus* elsewhere in the drainage (Matthews et al. 1982; Map 42).

Variation of *Clinostomus funduloides* and *Cottus bairdi* in the Roanoke indicates that some headwater populations entered the Roanoke from the New after the first establishment of the species in the Roanoke (Robins 1954; Masnik 1971). *Etheostoma flabellare* has a similar pattern of variation, *contra* McGeehan (1985). The spotted madtom, with its tiny range in the Dan River Gorge area and typical *Noturus insignis* living in the system, may be another example.

Fishes widespread on the Atlantic slope may have had a longer history in the Roanoke than some of the above taxa. Based on a range hiatus in the Roanoke–Chowan and the habitat differences between its upstream and downstream populations, *Notropis volucellus* may have twice entered the Roanoke from the New. The genus *Hypentelium* probably twice entered the Roanoke; the endemic *H. roanokense* may be younger than *H. nigricans*.

The question of age of the endemic taxa need not focus only on the Roanoke drainage; they could have originated in the New, been transferred to the Roanoke, and then been extirpated in the New. Their present restriction in range may be evidence either of compression of former ranges or of rather recent origin with insufficient time to spread further.

Danville Triassic Basin

An isolated ancient group of rock formations—the Danville Triassic Basin (Hack 1982; Map 7)—promotes faunal diversity in the middle Roanoke River today. The relatively erosion-resistant rocks of the Danville Basin "hold up" the Roanoke River and produce a steep gradient for several kilometers below. This reach, from Long Island to near Brookneal, is an outpost for several swift-water fishes that are characteristic of the Valley and Ridge and the Blue

Ridge provinces. Its fish diversity probably is suppressed by fluctuating flow from Leesville Dam and by turbidity and siltation. The Dan River also crosses the Danville basin, a few kilometers above Danville. The diversity of its fauna there and below is much reduced because of extensive turbidity and siltation.

PEE DEE DRAINAGE FAUNA

In the small sector of the Yadkin system in Virginia, tributaries descend sharply from the Blue Ridge Escarpment; their gradients are much lower on the Piedmont, and they depart the state as six main trunks. This portion of the Pee Dee comprises less than 1% of Virginia's area and less than 1% of the entire drainage, the remainder being in North and South Carolina.

Fauna

The 18 fish species native to the Virginia section of the Pee Dee constitute 23% of the 78 indigenous freshwater Pee Dee taxa. The Pee Dee fauna is most similar to those surrounding most of the drainage—the Cape Fear and Santee faunas. The one species endemic to the Pee Dee, a Coastal Plain darter *Etheostoma mariae*, lives distant from Virginia.

Six taxa populate Virginia only in the Pee Dee: *Hybopsis hypsinotus*, *Cyprinella labrosa* (extirpated), *Scartomyzon robustus*, *Percina crassa*, *Etheostoma olmstedi maculaticeps*, and *E. flabellare brevispina*. The blue-bodied nuptial male form of *Nocomis leptocephalus* also inhabits Virginia only in the Pee Dee. Three species of shiners widespread in the Pee Dee may barely extend into Virginia (*Fishes of Possible Occurrence*).

Limiting Factors

Environmental factors limiting species richness in the Pee Dee of Virginia include the small size of the watershed, high gradient and low fertility of headwaters, and siltation. Although many species have long lived in and adapted to sandy and somewhat silty conditions on the Piedmont, some appear intolerant of the intensified siltation that has developed over the past 250 years. Small stream size is another confining factor; the largest stream (Ararat River) typically is only about 10 m wide at the state line.

Stream Capture

Most Virginia headwaters of the Pee Dee oppose New drainage tributaries. Hack (1982) stated that the Ararat River captured a tiny parcel of terrain formerly drained by the New, but that no geologic evidence exists of recent piracy of surface waters. However, the former occurrence of a surface water, New-to-Pee Dee transit route is indicated by the presence of the Ohioan form *Rhinichthys atratulus obtusus* in the Pee Dee of Virginia. Because this fish inhabits streamlets, extremely heavy rainfall may enable it to swim across narrow, normally dry divides. A similar claim may be made for the brook trout, perhaps misclassified here as probably introduced in the Pee Dee. *Notropis chiliticus* may have entered the Dan system via an Ararat–Dan theater of capture in the Blue Ridge.

NEW DRAINAGE FAUNA

The name New River dates from early colonial time when the New River territory was designated New Brittaine or New Virginia (Givens 1983), but the river should be called Old River, for it is one of the oldest major streams of eastern United States. The river has retained a course through periods of slow uplift of the Appalachian surface that its drainage had planed. Although enduring maybe 300 million years from Late Paleozoic time (Branson 1912; Shuler 1945; Dietrich 1959), claims of the New being one of the oldest channels, or *the* oldest in North America, and one of the oldest on Earth do not seem solidly supported. Still, the New is the only river that heads in the Blue Ridge Province and arcs northwesterly, completely across the long axis of the Valley and Ridge Province and far into the Appalachian Plateau Province (Fridley 1950; Thornbury 1965).

Arising in the Blue Ridge Highlands of northwestern North Carolina, the New winds generally northward in Virginia across the New River Plateau and the Valley and Ridge, cutting narrow gaps through major mountain ridges (Maps 6, 7). With about doubled gradient it flows through the 106-km-long New River Gorge in the Appalachian Plateau of south-central West Virginia (Hack 1969; Givens 1983). The gorge (average depth about 300 m) is one of the deepest in eastern North America (Neves 1983). Just above its head or within the gorge, the New River receives the largest systems of the drainage—the Bluestone, Greenbrier, and Gauley. Descending Kanawha Falls at 3 rkm below the Gauley mouth and thereafter named the Kanawha River, the now low-gradient channel courses a well-developed floodplain and subdued topography while flowing northwesterly to the middle Ohio River. Varying nomenclature of the New River in the area of Kanawha Falls is noted under *Drainages*.

Despite its insularity owing to Kanawha Falls (Sheldon 1988), the New drainage and its fauna have many relationships to those surrounding. The drainage is bounded by nine others, the highest number for a Virginia drainage (the Roanoke and Tennessee each are adjoined by seven). The New drains against headwaters of four southwest- to northwest-flowing drainages of the Ohio basin—the Tennessee, Big Sandy, Guyandotte, and Kanawha. On its north fringe are another section of the Kanawha and the northbound Monongahela of the Ohio. Four northeasterly to southeasterly Atlantic slope drainages lie to the east—the Potomac, James, Roanoke, and Pee Dee.

Teays River

New River waters formerly took a much longer route from somewhat below Kanawha Falls to the Gulf of Mexico (Janssen 1953; Rhodehamel and Carlston 1963; Burr and Page 1986; Hocutt et al. 1986; Map 12). Before its obstruction by northern glaciers, the continuation of the New–Kanawha channel coursed west, then northwest through Ohio, arced south through northern Indiana and central Illinois, and emptied into the Gulf of Mexico. This great precursor of the Mississippi River is named the Teays River (pronounced Tayz). The ancestral Ohio River headed within the arc and was much shorter than today. Some aspects of the middle Teays basin are unclear, and at times the pattern may have differed drastically from this outline. Nonetheless, the Teays basin of many subdivisions was a primary center of origin and dispersal of aquatic biota.

Fauna

The New (upper Teays) fauna of 89 fish taxa comprises 46 native freshwater species or subspecies including 8 endemic species, plus the catadromous American eel and 42 introduced species. The extant fauna is composed essentially of modern genera and is not notably old; no clearly archaic species is historically native.

The number of aquatic zoogeographic problems concerning the New is high relative to the low richness of the fauna. The ichthyofauna was discussed in a series of papers by Ross and Perkins (1959), Jenkins et al. (1972), Hocutt et al. (1978, 1979, 1986), Hocutt (1979b), and Neves (1983). What follows is a fresh perspective afforded by recent survey and compilation of detailed species-distribution maps for the whole drainage (e.g., Lee et al. 1980).

Depauperacy

Having only 46 native freshwater fish species, the New fauna contrasts markedly in species richness with nearly all adjacent faunas, notably the James with 73 taxa, the Roanoke with 82, the Kanawha with 90 (Ross 1959c; VPISU 1985b; Hocutt et al. 1986), and the Virginia portion of the Tennessee with 98. The New fauna is 25% smaller than the Potomac fauna (61 taxa), but it has three more native stenohaline fishes than do the Rappahannock and York drainages and has more than any Pacific basin of western North America. Comparing numbers of taxa relative to drainage area for 26 drainages of eastern United States, the New fauna ranks the lowest (Sheldon 1988).

Only two suckers are clearly native to the New, *Hypentelium nigricans* and *Catostomus commersoni*; another, *Thoburnia rhothoeca*, may have been native but is extirpated. Surprisingly, only one centrarchid, *Lepomis cyanellus*, appears to be indigenous. The New has a relative wealth of sculpins—four taxa of the genus *Cottus*.

Depauperacy of the New fauna has been variously accredited to impoundment, natural water chemistry, montane character of the drainage, falls and cataracts, and Pleistocene temperature depression. Ross and Perkins (1959) considered that these factors, as well as loss of surface water to subterranean flow and by stream capture, and nonnatural perturbations, may have interacted to reduce the fauna.

Water loss probably has not been a significant factor in the development and retention of the fauna. Coal mine pollution (chiefly in the Appalachian Plateau), timbering, unnaturally high levels of siltation, and other disturbances probably before the 1900s depleted some populations (e.g., Goldsborough and Clark 1908). Adverse impacts continue to be documented (England and Cumming 1972; Cincotta 1978; Leonard and Orth 1983; Orth and Helfrich 1983), but none of these factors are known to have extirpated any species from the New. Five of the factors listed above merit further consideration:

Impoundment.—Four major impoundments exist in the drainage, three of which occur on the New River. Claytor Lake, a hydropower reservoir completed in 1939, is in the midportion of the Virginia section. Bluestone Dam, a flood-control dam in West Virginia between the mouths of the Bluestone and Greenbrier rivers, was closed in 1947; at times Bluestone Reservoir backs the New River just into Virginia (Lady 1983; Larkin and Nagy 1983). Hawks Nest Dam in the lower New River Gorge went into continuous operation in 1937. It diverts water for hydroelectric power generation from the 6.9-rkm Hawks Nest Lake through a 6.5-km tunnel and returns it to the river 8.1 rkm downstream from the dam (EMC 1984; Lobb 1986). Summersville Lake on the Gauley River began filling in 1965 (D. A. Cincotta, personal communication); it provides water for hydroelectric generation (and tailwater whitewater recreation). Four smaller dams span the New River in Virginia above Claytor Lake (Givens 1983).

Reservoirs segregated some fish populations, but it is unlikely that any impoundment directly extirpated a species from the drainage. Only *Erimystax dissimilis* may have been extirpated indirectly by impoundment. It was recorded only in 1935 from the lower New River Gorge, where its occurrence would be unexpected (Hocutt et al. 1986). If native, it had survived widespread "navigational improvements" (Lady 1983) made during 1877–1883. The other species regarded as extirpated in the 1900s, *Thoburnia rhothoeca*, is a tributary fish and probably was not affected by impoundments.

Bluestone Reservoir, a fjord-like, run-of-river lake with an epilimnetic release (VPISU 1985a; Lobb 1986), apparently allowed passage of *Notropis telescopus*, *N. hudsonius*, and *Percina roanoka*, all of which are believed to have been introduced upstream. Hawks Nest Lake was traversed by *N. telescopus*.

Water Chemistry.—Natural water chemistry may not have adversely affected species richness. Chemical characteristics naturally vary within and among the three physiographic provinces of the drainage (Ross and Perkins 1959; Jenkins et al. 1972). More than half of the drainage, in the Blue Ridge and Appalachian Plateau, typically has low-to-moderate inherent productivity, which perhaps curtailed population sizes and speciation. The remainder of the drainage, in the intervening, relatively fertile Valley and Ridge Province, has high chemical diversity, which enhances the fishes' opportunity to partition the drainage according to their differing chemical preferences.

Montane Aspect.—Characterization of the whole New drainage as montane (Ross and Perkins 1959) may give a misleading impression of fairly uniform, rigorous habitats. Addair (1944) described the Appalachian Plateau portion as prevalently narrow floodplains, steep gradient, scoured hard bottom, and few or no higher aquatic plants. Such conditions characterize many Appalachian Plateau streams and most Blue Ridge Highlands and smaller Valley and Ridge waters.

In contrast, many other streams in the Appalachian Plateau have moderate gradient or are nearly base-leveled; some are in karst-like areas (Hocutt et al. 1978, 1979). Many reaches of medium to large streams in the Blue Ridge Plateau and the Valley and Ridge Province resemble those of adjacent drainages; their ample pools with hard and soft bottoms are suited to support moderately diverse sucker and sunfish faunas. Several introduced sunfishes inhabit the drainage. Still, the New lacks habitats like those in much of the lower Piedmont and Coastal Plain and this explains some of the differences in species richness observed between the New and Atlantic slope drainages.

Structural Barriers.—Hindrants to colonization of, or dispersal through, the New River Gorge are imposed by Kanawha Falls and, in the gorge, tumultuous rapids, cascades, and lesser main-channel falls (e.g., Hocutt 1979b; Hocutt et al. 1986). Analogous conditions have been effective barriers elsewhere (*Potomac Drainage Fauna*). However, for any species living above Kanawha Falls, it is uncertain that over time the gorge would have fully barred them from swimming its length in either direction. Pools alternate with rough reaches; the falls essentially are cascades. Major rapids in the Breaks of Sandy did not prevent small minnow species, two of them gentle-flow inhabitants, from spreading into the upper Big Sandy drainage of Virginia.

Glacial Cooling.—Low temperature during glaciations probably was a chief natural depressant of piscine faunal richness in the somewhat high-altitude New drainage. Ross and Perkins' (1959) presumption that glacial regimes were severe in the New is well corroborated. New River headwaters arise at elevations of 1,300 m in North Carolina and 1,500 m in Virginia; the North and South forks join in North Carolina at near 760 m. The lower end of the drainage, Kanawha Falls at 200 m, was near the front of some ice sheets.

Recurrent cold climate probably extirpated species and prevented others from approaching (the rarely open) capture routes of entry to the drainage. Successful range shifts to lower, sufficiently warm elevations likely were impossible for some warmwater species. Downslope retreat would have been northward into colder latitudes and could have led to exiting the drainage over Kanawha Falls.

Ichthyofaunal indicators of Pleistocene climatic severity in the New include presence of a relatively high number of heterogeneous, coolwater and coldwater taxa, and absence or localization of many warmwater species that are widespread in adjacent drainages.

(1) The four taxa of *Cottus* in the New constitute the most diverse sculpin fauna (relative to the totals of native species in the drainages) of any drainage east of the Rocky Mountains (Jenkins et al. 1972). Of all groups in the New (discounting brook trout), the cold- to cool-adapted sculpins likely would have best withstood reduced temperatures. The two (or three) endemic *Cottus* almost certainly survived the Late Pleistocene there.

(2) Five of the other six endemic species of the New (excluding sculpins) are cold-tolerant. Coupled with endemism, this suggests evolutionary adaptation in a formerly periglacial climate. Moreover, the five endemic species apparently are eurythermal, expectable if trapped in a drainage with cyclic frigid to mild conditions. The avoidance of cool streams by the endemic *Nocomis platyrhynchus* is perhaps related only to the preference of this species for larger waters.

(3) Many regional warmwater catostomids are absent from the New, notably most of those that occur in the Kanawha or upper Roanoke drainages; some are included in paragraph 4. The two suckers widespread in the New, particularly the white sucker, are cold-tolerant.

(4) Several authors considered that the absence from the New of certain lineages having a trans-Atlantic–Ohio track is best explained by extirpation in the New. Exemplary, partly "ghost" lineages include coolwater–warmwater or exclusively warmwater inhabitants that are listed in numbered paragraph (2) under *Roanoke Drainage Fauna*. *Notropis semperasper* (endemic to the James) and *Percina notogramma* (of the James and limitedly northward) may also be eastern warmwater constituents of Atlantic–lower Ohio tracks which lack a taxon in the New.

(5) Localizations in the New to relatively low-elevation portions of the Gauley system may be evidence of extirpation from the drainage during glaciation and reentry in Holocene time. The species involved seem to prefer warm water: *Lampetra aepyptera*, *Moxostoma erythrurum*, *Ameiurus natalis*, *A. nebulosus*, and *Noturus flavus* (Hocutt 1979b; Hocutt et al. 1979). However, because of suspected introductions and range extensions, Hocutt et al. (1986) disqualified some of the localizations (and other species) as supporting similar scenarios concerning Kanawha Falls and the New River Gorge.

In summarizing faunal depauperacy in the New (including bivalve mollusks), Neves (1983) concluded that environmental changes caused by glaciation and the inception of Kanawha Falls had the greatest effects. The New lost several lineages that it earlier donated to the Atlantic slope (Hocutt 1979b), but no longer are the losses perplexing. In some ways both the river and the remaining fauna are relics.

Recruitment

Accrual of the New's presently limited faunal diversity was accredited by Neves (1983), after Wallace (1973a) and Hocutt (1979b), to upstream passage of species around or over Kanawha Falls during inundation by periglacial Teays Lake (Lake Tight) and extreme floods. Teays Lake developed from blockage by an ice sheet of the main channel below Kanawha Falls during the Late Pleistocene; it may have existed during other Pleistocene glaciations (Hocutt 1979b; Hocutt et al. 1986). However, even with the lake present during Late Wisconsinan time, climatic severity may have prohibited its use by most fishes. Rheophilic recruits would have dispersed in it slowly at best. Thus river-margin navigation during Holocene floods may best explain most postglacial returns of fish taxa to the New.

Endemism

The New fauna is a distinctive subunit of the Ohioan fauna; 8 of 46 taxa are endemic. Although high rates of endemism are typical of many western drainages, the 17.4% rate in the New is exceeded only in the Mobile drainage (25.4%) among eastern and central North America drainages. The absolute number of endemic taxa also is high in the New, more than in any Atlantic slope drainage; the Kanawha drainage lacks an endemic taxon.

Species endemic to the New are *Nocomis platyrhynchus*, *Phenacobius teretulus*, *Notropis scabriceps*, Bluestone sculpin, cave sculpin (pigmentless form, first recognized here as a species; see *Cottus carolinae*), *Percina gymnocephala*, *Etheostoma kanawhae*, and *E. osburni*. When better known taxonomically, the Kanawha sculpin may be regarded as endemic (see *C. carolinae*).

Evolutionary development of a major endemic complement indicates strong isolation of the New. Kanawha Falls generally has been thought to have played a main role or the crucial isolating role in fish evolution in the New. Kanawha Falls normally varies from 23 to 25 feet (7.0–7.6 m) in natural height; the uneven crest varies 646–648 feet (196.9–197.5 m) in elevation (E. J. Boyle, in litt.). The Glen Ferris power-production development modifies the falls somewhat. The first low dam, built during 1898–1901 fully across the top of the falls, raised and evened the crest of the falls to elevation 198.4 m. It was replaced in

1920 by a dam varying 0.9–3.7 m above the river bed; the 869-m-wide spillway also crests at elevation 198.4 m (EMC 1984). Normal river-surface level at the foot of the falls is 189.9 m. (ACE 1943; EMC 1984; E. J. Boyle, in litt.). Photographs of the falls (Givens 1983; Hocutt et al. 1986) reveal that the shelving sandstone forms not a single free fall, but a series of 2–4 main steps.

The time of inception of Kanawha Falls is unknown; the late Pliocene or early Pleistocene have been suggested by ichthyologists (R. V. Miller 1968; Neves 1983; Hocutt et al. 1986). Over time the height and position of the falls probably varied; perhaps a true falls did not always exist. In any event, floods may have allowed fishes to swim up over the falls (Gilbert 1980).

Teays Lake and the New River Gorge may also have isolated stocks (Hocutt 1979b). Sandstone Falls in the gorge may be as formidable an obstacle as Kanawha Falls (cover photo, Neves 1983; Hocutt et al. 1986). The American eel apparently rarely negotiates Kanawha Falls and the gorge.

Presumably some barrier in the main channel barred invasion of ancestral gene pools via the Kanawha River. The present ranges of three members of the *Etheostoma variatum* group yield the best (perhaps only) clue that Kanawha Falls (or its antecedent) was a decisive isolating agent. The falls separates the *E. kanawhae–E. osburni* species pair (which is widespread in the New, including the Gauley system), from *E. variatum* of the upper Kanawha drainage and elsewhere in the Ohio basin; *E. variatum* represents the basal stock of the species pair (McKeown et al. 1984; Wiley and Mayden 1985; Hocutt et al. 1986).

The birthplace systems of four of the other six endemic species—*Nocomis platyrhynchus, Phenacobius teretulus, Notropis scabriceps,* and *Percina gymnocephala*—are in no way indicated; these species range from the Gauley system to North Carolina tributaries. *Notropis scabriceps* surely is a relict in the New; its nearest relative occurs in the Ozarks. The remaining two endemic species, the Bluestone and cave sculpins, are distant from the falls and highly localized. The origin of these and the Kanawha sculpin apparently had no relation to the falls; these taxa sharply avoid the Appalachian Plateau except for calcareous fringes.

Speciation by fracture of populations within the New may have occurred. The rigor of the New River Gorge may have been sufficiently intense to cause isolation between the Gauley and above-gorge tributary systems. The gorge, perhaps in concert with Teays Lake, may have been a primary factor in divi-

sion of the stock that diverged into the intimately related endemic *Etheostoma kanawhae* and *E. osburni.* Autopiracy of the Gauley by the Greenbrier system would have allowed *E. osburni* to later skirt the gorge and move farther up the drainage (McKeown et al. 1984; Wiley and Mayden 1985; Hocutt et al. 1986). Under this hypothesis and with records clarified here (Map 174), the adjoining edges of the complementary ranges of these two darters—each occupies approximately a different half of the drainage—have adjusted considerably since *E. osburni* reached the New River from the Greenbrier.

Inbound Dispersal

Ascent and bypass of Kanawa Falls and the New River have been considered as primary modes of ingress to the New. However, several biogeographic tracks indicate that the southwestern divide of the New, that is, its breachment by stream captures (e.g., Ross and Carico 1963; Ross 1972a; Map 12), may have had greater influence on the development of the New fauna. Several southwest-extending tracks are shared by the New with Appalachian sections of either or both the Tennessee and Cumberland drainages of the lower Ohio basin. Many of the tracks are not shared with any of the four drainages of the middle or upper Ohio that are adjacent to the New, a pattern indicated quantitatively by Mayden (1988a) and Sheldon (1988).

Lower Ohio–New tracks include *Phoxinus, Phenacobius,* and *Percina (Swaina)* (e.g., Wiley and Mayden 1985; Mayden 1989). The *Cottus carolinae* group forms a similar track, with *C. c. carolinae* in the Tennessee and Cumberland and three allopatric taxa in the New (tentatively including the Bluestone sculpin). Adding *C. girardi* to the sculpin track extends it into the Potomac drainage. Other tracks, some with taxa extant in the New and others with missing ("ghost") members there, reach from the lower Ohio onto the central Atlantic slope. However, the sharp faunal differences between upland faunas of the lower Ohio and New, if not related chiefly to differential extirpation in the New, indicate that interchanges among these Ohio drainages generally were infrequent.

Relative isolation of the New from the drainages fringing its lower section is signified by 12, mostly upland, taxa that occur in one or more places above the Big Sandy drainage and that occur little or not at all outside the Ohio basin. These fishes, whose histories (but not necessarily origins) likely are tied to the middle or upper Ohio basin but not the New, are *Erimystax x-punctatus trautmani, Lythrurus ardens fasciolaris, Notropis ariommus, N. wickliffi* (may occur widely outside the Ohio basin), *Moxostoma macrolepi-*

dotum breviceps, Noturus stigmosus, N. trautmani, Percina macrocephala, Etheostoma variatum, and three members of the subgenus *Nothonotus*—*Etheostoma tippecanoe, E. camurum,* and *E. maculatum.* The near absence of endemic taxa in the middle and upper Ohio, except for the New (Burr and Page 1986; Hocutt et al. 1986), is evidence of the harshness of glaciations in the region; it may also indicate that the New gained a substantial share of its fauna from southwesterly areas.

Relatively high frequencies of ingress to the New are suspected for widespread montane and upland creek fishes such as *Rhinichthys* species, *Semotilus atromaculatus, Cottus bairdi,* and *Etheostoma flabellare.* The mode of entry to the New of another headwater fish, the much-localized *Etheostoma simoterum,* is questionable owing to its uncertain original distributional status.

The fishes most likely to have entered the New from the central Atlantic slope are those which in the Ohio basin are nearly or fully restricted to the New; for example, *Phoxinus oreas, Nocomis leptocephalus, Luxilus albeolus,* and *Noturus insignis* (Lachner and Jenkins 1971a). *Phoxinus oreas* may instead have had its origin and a long tenure in the New, based on endemism in the Tennessee drainage of its closest kin and its tolerance of coldness. Other taxa that may have taken a capture route from the Atlantic slope to the New were more likely introduced to the New: *Exoglossum maxillingua, Luxilus cerasinus, Notropis chiliticus, N. hudsonius, N. procne, Scartomyzon cervinus, Percina roanoka,* and *Etheostoma olmstedi.*

Outbound Dispersal

A case for general isolation of the New has been built, but with encompassment by nine drainages, surely it has donated fauna to other drainages. The narrowness of the New in North Carolina and Virginia indicates that it has been shorn of tributaries. Captures of the New served as direct or indirect corridors to the central Atlantic slope; dispersal was dominantly egress from the higher-elevation New.

No endemic species of the New have been found in the Kanawha drainage. Had they passed Kanawha Falls, low-gradient habitat of the upper Kanawha River would have thwarted them from reaching favorable conditions in the Elk system of the Kanawha; so too would the long-term stream degradation about and below Charleston, West Virginia, at the mouth of the Elk. Notably, the invasive pool-dwelling *Notropis telescopus* recently became established in the Kanawha River and tributaries after dispersing from the Virginia portion of the New.

A Greenbrier–Monongahela capture apparently injected New drainage species into the Monongahela, even though the Greenbrier was the pirate (Denoncourt et al. 1977a; Hocutt et al. 1978; Hocutt 1979b). The ability to recognize transfer in the opposite direction may be reduced by the lack of obvious marker taxa (Hocutt et al. 1986).

Introduced Fishes

Nearly half—42 of 88—of the freshwater taxa of the New apparently have been introduced, the largest number and proportion of all major eastern and central North American drainages (Jenkins 1987). Several nonindigenous game or foodfishes flourish in the New. Many forage and bait species became established via intentional or accidental releases; some of them have spread explosively (e.g., *Notropis rubricroceus, N. telescopus,* and *Percina roanoka*).

Low species richness has been regarded a major factor allowing the establishment and spread of introduced fishes. The native New fauna has been labeled "unsaturated," in the sense that "many ecological niches remain unfilled" (Gilbert 1980). However, the concept of "vacant niche" and the existence in natural systems of such niches were assailed by Herbold and Moyle (1986). "Opportunistic"—the taking advantage of unused resources—was applied to invasion of the New by *Percina roanoka* (Hocutt and Hambrick 1973), but proliferation of this darter and other introduced species may be partly at the expense of indigenous fishes. Herbold and Moyle (1986) concluded that the most successful fish introductions are made into highly disturbed habitats, and that introductions made into undisturbed habitats usually result in replacement of native species, often through competition. Characteristics of aquatic ecosystems that are susceptible to invasion by nonnative fishes were listed by Laurenson and Hocutt (1986); most of them typify the New drainage.

Many introductions were made because the New originally had few medium or large predatory fishes. Based on his collecting and the word of anglers, Cope (1868b) noted a paucity of gamefishes; the Virginia Fish Commission (VFC 1877a) stated that the New "has in its mainstream little else [of gamefish] than the cat fish." We regard as native only the American eel, channel catfish, flathead catfish, and green sunfish; 23 food or gamefishes are introduced: bowfin, common carp, muskellunge, 3 bullhead catfishes, 2 trouts, 2 moronid basses, 11 centrarchid basses or sunfishes, walleye, and yellow perch. Forage fishes were added to the drainage to serve the burgeoning gamefish population. Introduced species that have fared the least in the New, outside of impoundments, generally are low-gradient dwellers.

Uncertainties of original distributional status have plagued the study of historical zoogeography of the New fauna (Ross and Carico 1963; Ross 1969; Jenkins and Hambrick 1972; Jenkins et al. 1972). Documentation of stocking exists for only about half of the species regarded as introduced. Of the 42 taxa listed as introduced, 16 are ranked as probably introduced (IP; as opposed to clearly introduced, I); of the 47 regarded as native, 8 are possibly introduced (NI) (Tables 2, 3; *Appendix 2*). A slim line separates ranking some species as native and others as introduced; for example, *Luxilus albeolus* and *Lythrurus ardens* versus *Luxilus cerasinus*. The strengths of cases form a continuum from clearly native to certainly introduced. I considered (*in* Hocutt et al. 1986) that errors may have been made in status assignments, but that percentages of taxa judged native and those as introduced likely are close to correct. The latter statement may be closer to accurate with the switching here, from Hocutt et al. (1986), of six taxa from native (N or NI) to introduced (IP), and only two from IP to NI (*Appendix 2*).

With one to possibly four members introduced, the genus *Exoglossum* (1 nonnative), the genus *Luxilus* (4), and the subgenus *Hydrophlox* of *Notropis* (3) create interesting systematic problems. The New should serve as a large laboratory for studying varied interactions of introduced fishes.

Intradrainage Patterns

Most distributional patterns of native fishes in the New are categorized on the basis of a combination of physiographic provinces occupied, water chemistry (i.e., soft versus hard water according mainly to province) (Ross and Perkins 1959), stream-size preference, or water temperature. The patterns of distribution and abundance of several putative natives are in discord with these factors; the number of putative anomalous patterns in the New is relatively high for Virginia drainages. A numbered catalog of distribution patterns follows.

Widespread, mostly nonanomalous patterns exist for 24 species; deviations are given in parentheses. (1) Widespread, typically in small to large streams and the New River, are *Rhinichthys cataractae* (rare in Walker, Wolf, and Bluestone systems), *Campostoma anomalum*, *Luxilus albeolus* (rare in Reed Creek system and a few other major tributaries), *Catostomus commersoni*, and *Hypentelium nigricans*. (2) Widespread, typically in small to medium streams, are *Salvelinus fontinalis* (restricted to cold water), *Clinostomus fundu-*

loides, *Rhinichthys atratulus*, *Semotilus atromaculatus*, *Cottus bairdi*, and *Etheostoma flabellare*. (3) Widespread, typically in medium and large streams and the New River or chiefly the river, are *Exoglossum laurae*, *Nocomis platyrhynchus*, *Cyprinella spiloptera*, *Notropis photogenis*, *N. rubellus*, *N. volucellus*, *Pimephales notatus*, *Ictalurus punctatus*, *Pylodictis olivaris*, *Percina oxyrhynchus*, *P. caprodes*, *P. gymnocephala*, and *Etheostoma blennioides* (oddly, there is no record of latter species from some streams).

Somewhat restricted, mostly nonanomalous patterns involve seven taxa. (4) Restricted or almost so to the Blue Ridge province is *Etheostoma kanawhae* (complementary to *E. osburni*). (5) Restricted or nearly so to the Blue Ridge and Appalachian Plateau are *Phenacobius teretulus* (Valley and Ridge population extirpated; fares poorly in Appalachian Plateau) and *Notropis scabriceps* (also in the Reed Creek system of Valley and Ridge). (6) Restricted to the Valley and Ridge and Appalachian Plateau is *Etheostoma osburni* (complementary to *E. kanawhae*). (7) Restricted or virtually so to either or both the Valley and Ridge and the calcareous district of the Appalachian Plateau near the Virginia–West Virginia line are *Lythrurus a. ardens* (also in the Reed Island Creek system of Blue Ridge), *Noturus insignis* (also in the Reed Island Creek system), and *Cottus carolinae* subspecies.

Anomalous patterns concern 14 species. (8) West Virginia occupants only, or almost so, are *Lampetra aepyptera* (lower Gauley system only), *Erimystax dissimilis* (New River gorge only; extirpated), *Luxilus chrysocephalus* (sporadic; complementary to other *Luxilus*?), *Notropis stramineus* (sporadic), *N. buccatus* (sporadic), *Noturus flavus* (Gauley system only), and *Etheostoma nigrum* (sporadic; Virginia Blue Ridge population probably introduced). High gradient in much of West Virginia may account for sporadic occurrence there, but the reason these species extended barely or not at all into Virginia is not clear.

(9) Nearly restricted to Virginia, but widespread in the Valley and Ridge and Blue Ridge are *Phoxinus oreas* (also sharply localized in some Virginia systems), and *Nocomis leptocephalus*. Entry of these to the New via stream capture in Virginia should have occurred sufficiently long ago for dispersal far into West Virginia.

(10) Sharply localized are *Thoburnia rhothoeca* (Wolf and Greenbrier systems; extirpated?), Bluestone sculpin (calcareous upper Bluestone system; complementary to *Cottus carolinae* subspecies), *Cottus* species (one West Virginia cave), *Etheostoma simoterum* (upper Bluestone and Wolf systems), and *E. caeruleum* (East River, lower Gauley system, and, rarely, interjacent New River). (11) *Lepomis cyanellus*, the one cen-

trarchid regarded as native, extends through the Valley and Ridge into the upper Greenbrier system; possibly the Gauley population is introduced.

Epilogue

Ongoing survey of the New drainage continues to yield surprises. Late in our fieldwork for this book, we took *Etheostoma nigrum* in Big Reed Island Creek, far from its nearest population. Later, the Virginia Warmwater Survey under the direction of P. L. Angermeier found a peculiarly isolated population of *Etheostoma simoterum* and caught *Scartomyzon cervinus* in the drainage for the first time. In North Carolina, *Etheostoma olmstedi* was first recorded in the drainage by D. A. Etnier. Too late for inclusion elsewhere in this book is the discovery by Jenkins' ichthyology class of the apparently extirpated *Thoburnia rhothoeca* in the Little River of Virginia in 1991; the precursors of this strong population may have been transported there in a bait bucket.

TENNESSEE DRAINAGE FAUNA

Flowing southwest through eastern Tennessee, the Tennessee River acquires major tributary systems that arise in southwestern Virginia, western North Carolina, eastern Tennessee, and northern Georgia. The river bends through northern Alabama, edges Mississippi, and flows north to join the lower Ohio River at the Kentucky–Illinois line (Map 12). With a 1,050-rkm-long main stem and a basin in parts of seven states, the Tennessee drainage is the largest tributary of the Ohio River basin.

The Tennessee drainage houses the most diverse ichthyofauna in North America. It is home particularly to a great variety of minnows and darters, many of dazzling colors. The faunal diversity reflects widely varied habitats—high Appalachians to Ohio Valley lowlands. Many species are found in few of the major systems of the drainage, and some are restricted to one or two streams.

The Virginia portion of the Tennessee is the uppermost; it comprises the upper Holston River and Clinch River systems. The Holston system includes the South, Middle, and North forks of Holston River; its other major tributary, the Watauga River, arises in North Carolina and joins the South Fork in Tennessee. The Clinch River system contains that river and the Powell River.

The fish fauna of the Tennessee drainage was described by Jenkins et al. (1972) and Starnes and Etnier (1986). Major ichthyofaunal studies of individual tributary systems in the upper drainage include Ross and Carico (1963), Masnik (1974), Feeman (1986), and Saylor et al. (1988). Many important new records of fishes were announced by Feeman (1987); the history of sampling in parts of the upper drainage was documented by Jenkins and Burkhead (1984). The prehistorical development of the drainage was discussed by many (e.g., Ross 1972a; Masnik 1974; Braasch and Mayden 1985; Fitzpatrick 1986; Starnes and Etnier 1986). Information on principal streams, environs, and biota of the Holston and Clinch systems is presented by Helfrich et al. (1986).

Fauna

Of the 248 fish taxa known from the Tennessee, 223 are native including 32 that are endemic plus the catadromous American eel, and 25 that are introduced (Table 3). The ensuing analysis is largely restricted to the Virginia fraction, composed of 117 taxa of which 98 are native, 16 endemic, and 19 introduced. Thus 44% of the total native fauna and 50% of the endemic taxa populate the 7.5% (VDCED 1972 [231]) of the Tennessee River watershed in Virginia. This is the most diverse freshwater ichthyofauna of Virginia; the next largest is that of the James drainage, with 73 native taxa in the state. Comparing the small, ecologically similar streams of the Clinch and the adjacent Big Sandy drainage, the Clinch has the richer fauna (Masnik and Knollenberg 1972).

Species richness in the Tennessee drainage of Virginia reflects the large pool of species in the upper half of the drainage. Habitat diversity in the Virginia portion is modest compared with that encompassed by the whole drainage. In Virginia, the drainage is almost entirely in the Valley and Ridge Province; some streams arise in the fringing Blue Ridge or Appalachian Plateau provinces. Tumbling cold and cool tributaries flow in all of these provinces. The five largest rivers are in the Valley and Ridge and are of the upland type, having frequent runs and riffles. Four of the five are mostly or entirely warmwater rivers; only the South Fork Holston River remains somewhat cool (to its impoundment straddling the state line). Uniquely among Virginia rivers, the North Fork Holston, Clinch, and Powell rivers have large shoals composed mainly of loose, small to medium gravel, to which *Erimystax cahni*, *Notropis ariommus*, *Ammocrypta clara*, and *Etheostoma tippecanoe* are essentially restricted.

Several big-river species typical of downstream main channels of the drainage are rare or absent in Virginia; the three largest streams freely flowing from the state are not notably large. The North Fork Holston and Clinch rivers are 40–60 m wide near the state line; the lower Powell River and the lower free-flowing reaches of the South Fork and Middle Fork are 25–40 m.

The lack of a major impoundment in the Virginia portion of these rivers has spared the fauna. The only sizeable impoundment extending into the state, South Holston Reservoir, was filled in 1951; it inundates approximately the lower 17 rkm of the South Fork Holston River in Virginia and barely floods into the Middle Fork. In contrast, the Tennessee River is a chain of impoundments, and long reaches of most major tributaries are inundated. Most of the dams were built by the Tennessee Valley Authority, whose program began in the 1930s. Extensive extirpation of native aquatic biota has resulted from impoundment (Etnier et al. 1979; Jenkins and Burkhead 1984).

The upper impoundments on the Holston, South Fork Holston, and Clinch rivers (Cherokee, South Holston, and Norris reservoirs) in Tennessee may have facilitated the population expansion and extension of some species into Virginia; for example, paddlefish and several gamefishes such as largemouth bass, bluegill (both tentatively ranked as native in Virginia), white bass, walleye, and sauger. Habitat alteration and its effects on the upper Tennessee fish fauna are reviewed by Neves and Angermeier (1990).

Endemism

Stream captures and the intradrainage isolation of stocks by unfavorable habitat and perhaps distance have promoted the origin of endemic taxa. The 16 endemic taxa of the drainage that occupy Virginia are *Phoxinus tennesseensis*, *Erimystax cahni*, *E. insignis eristigma*, *Phenacobius crassilabrum*, *Cyprinella monacha*, *Noturus flavipinnis*, *Cottus baileyi*, two undescribed *Cottus* (the Holston and Clinch sculpins), *Percina aurantiaca*, *Etheostoma swannanoa*, *E. stigmaeum jessiae*, *E. s. meadiae*, *E. chlorobranchium*, *E. acuticeps*, and *E. vulneratum*. The Clinch sculpin is restricted to Virginia and the Holston sculpin and *C. baileyi* are nearly so.

Intradrainage Patterns

The relatively modest habitat heterogeneity of the Virginia portion of the Tennessee drainage precludes the major extent of geographic succession of species assemblages that occurs in large central Atlantic slope drainages. Most individual species patterns are restricted to or well represented in main stems (including headwaters). The patterns in tributaries often are irregular; as a result of dissolution in the limestone basement of many valleys, the surface network of tributaries in the drainage is among the least developed in Virginia.

Patterns of faunal replacement relative to stream size (or stream order) in the upper Tennessee drainage were indicated by Masnik (1974), Garman et al. (1982), and Feeman (1986). For example, small-stream forms such as blacknose dace and creek chub "drop out" in lower headwaters; restricted to large streams are the large paddlefish and the tiny Tippecanoe darter. Some species typically transcend nearly all stream sizes available in the Virginia portion of the drainage; for example, the telescope shiner, black redhorse, and snubnose darter.

It is often difficult to separate the effects of gradient and temperature on distribution of aquatic organisms. The taxa with a distinct affinity for cool or cold water, judging by confinement largely or entirely to high-volume spring streams or high-elevation headwaters, are *Salvelinus fontinalis*, *Phoxinus tennesseensis*, *Phenacobius crassilabrum*, *Notropis rubricroceus*, *N. spectrunculus*, *Cottus baileyi*, Clinch sculpin, Holston sculpin (borderline case), *Etheostoma swannanoa*, and *E. chlorobranchium*. Most of these species are endemic to the Tennessee.

Among this cool-adapted group, only *Notropis rubricroceus* and *N. spectrunculus* are native to all five systems of the drainage in Virginia. Most are more widely distributed in the South Fork Holston system than elsewhere in the state; *Phenacobius crassilabrum* and *Etheostoma chlorobranchium* (also *E. acuticeps*) occur in Virginia only in this system. The South Fork Holston system is the only Virginia portion of the drainage that heads on the Blue Ridge (Map 7); the populations occur within or just outside the fringe of the province. The suggested ecological restraint on some of these taxa may be competition with close relatives (see *Parapatry*).

Intersystem Comparison: Holston and Clinch

Paralleling each other in a trellis drainage pattern and seemingly physically and geochemically similar, the Holston and Clinch (or Clinch–Powell) systems have distinctly different faunas. In Virginia, 80 native fishes have been recorded from the Holston and 88 from the Clinch, but the differences actually concern 28 taxa. Reducing the disparity, 14 of the 28 taxa (5 in the Holston, 9 in the Clinch) occur only in the extralimital sections of the systems. Of the other 14 taxa, 5 inhabit only the Holston: *Rhinichthys cataractae*, *Phenacobius crassilabrum*, Holston sculpin, *Etheostoma chlorobranchium*, and *E. acuticeps*. The nine found only in the Clinch are *Cyprinella whipplei*, *Lythrurus lirus*, *Labidesthes sicculus*, Clinch sculpin, *Ammocrypta clara*,

Percina copelandi, Etheostoma cinereum, E. stigmaeum meadiae, and *E. tippecanoe.*

The intersystem faunal differences are related to the cooler, moderately high-gradient water of the upper South Fork system, the larger size of the Clinch River (in Virginia), the backing of South Holston Reservoir into Virginia, and perhaps a greater extirpation rate in the Holston system owing to chronic pollution. For the sculpins and *Etheostoma stigmaeum,* differentiation of an ancestral stock on either or both sides of the Holston–Clinch divide may have occurred. Why *Lythrurus lirus* is not shared between systems is enigmatic; its mesohabitat in the Clinch is also widely available in the Holston.

Intrasystem Comparison: Holston Branches

Ecologic and faunistic differences exist among the three branches. Water-quality problems compromise comparison of the faunas. The North Fork Holston River has been the most degraded; the Middle Fork and the South Fork Holston rivers also have been affected (Wollitz 1972; Jenkins and Burkhead 1975b; Saylor et al. 1988).

The South Fork Holston River in Virginia is decidedly montane in character; it has moderately high gradient and cool water, and most of the watershed is forested. Its southern tributaries arise in the Mount Rogers Area, a geologically distinct division of the Blue Ridge Province encompassing the two highest peaks in Virginia (Map 7). The lower South Fork Holston River is chilled by the influx of Laurel (Whitetop Laurel) Creek, which arises in the Mount Rogers Area and is one of the finest larger wild-trout streams in the state.

The South Fork system has a distinctive fauna; several members restricted in Virginia to this system are clustered in the lower main stem and Laurel Creek. Two coolwater species (*Phenacobius crassilabrum* and *Etheostoma chlorobranchium*) were noted to occur only there in Virginia; *E. acuticeps* has a very similar range in Virginia but occupies warm water beyond Virginia. Also found only in the South Fork system (within the Virginia portion) is *Rhinichthys cataractae.* Although ranging widely in warm water in other drainages, this torrent-adapted fish is largely confined in the Tennessee to the Blue Ridge. *Erimystax insignis* inhabits large warm streams in the Clinch system, but it is confined in the Holston of Virginia to the lower South Fork Holston River. This population has been regarded as an intergrade, as in the Clinch, but its habitat use resembles that of typical *E. insignis eristigma,* which populates Blue Ridge streams south of Virginia. It is odd that *Phoxinus tennesseensis* has not been collected in the South Fork system of Virginia. This dace occupies a small cool tributary in each of the Middle and North forks and lives just within Tennessee in a South Fork tributary that flows into Virginia (Map 39).

The warmwater fauna of the upper Tennessee is underrepresented in the South Fork system of Virginia. Some warmwater species seem restricted and rare or uncommon in the lower unimpounded reach of the main river; they mix with several coolwater fishes. Examples are *Cyprinella spiloptera, Phenacobius uranops, Notropis volucellus, Noturus flavus* (extirpated?), *Percina evides, P. aurantiaca, Etheostoma zonale,* and *E. vulneratum.* Also having restricted ranges and perhaps belonging to the warmwater category are, as noted above, *Rhinichthys cataractae, Erimystax insignis eristigma,* and *Etheostoma acuticeps.*

Several other warmwater species were recorded about 40 years ago in the South Fork Holston River in Tennessee; they may have populated Virginia but died out when South Holston Reservoir was filled (Jenkins and Burkhead 1984). These are *Erimystax dissimilis, Cyprinella monacha, Notropis rubellus,* sawfin shiner, *Noturus eleutherus, Percina burtoni, P. macrocephala, Etheostoma camurum,* and *E. percnurum.*

The Middle Fork Holston River has a moderate gradient throughout and is largely pastoral. The upper portion receives cold, high-elevation tributaries and many limestone springs, whereas the lower main stem lacks notable tributaries. The Middle Fork system is faunistically transitional among the three branches. Warmwater main-stem constituents of the fauna that are unknown in the unimpounded Virginia reach of the South Fork are *Erimystax dissimilis, Cyprinella monacha* (recently discovered), *Notropis rubellus* (extirpated?), sawfin shiner (extirpated?), *Ictalurus punctatus* (rare; Saylor et al. 1988), *Ameiurus natalis, Pylodictis olivaris, Lepomis megalotis,* and *Percina macrocephala* (extirpated?). Rare in the system are some of the warmwater species listed as rare or uncommon in the South Fork of Virginia.

The coolwater fauna of the Middle Fork system extends diminishingly downstream through almost half the main stem, judging from the "marker" ranges of *Notropis rubricroceus,* Holston sculpin, and *Etheostoma swannanoa.* Notable absentees from the system are the warmwater species *Ichthyomyzon bdellium, Noturus flavus, N. eleutherus, Fundulus catenatus, Percina burtoni, P. aurantiaca,* and *Etheostoma camurum* (all except *N. flavus* are also absent from the South Fork system of Virginia), and the species having a range termination in the South Fork.

The North Fork Holston River is entirely of moderate gradient and is warm (often very) in nearly all of its extensively cleared valley. The few substantial tributaries that drop from ridges negligibly affect the temperature of the main channel; the large lower tributary, Big Moccasin Creek, also is warm.

Having the largest main stem of the three Holston branches, the North Fork system supports the most species. It has (or had) the six named Middle Fork system absentees (five of them also missing in the South Fork system) and 10 more that are known only from the North Fork within the Holston of Virginia: *Lepisosteus osseus* (extirpated), *Lythrurus ardens*, *Notropis ariommus*, *Pimephales vigilax*, *Carpiodes cyprinus*, *Moxostoma lacerum* (extinct), *Noturus flavipinnis* (extirpated), *Fundulus catenatus*, *Micropterus punctulatus*, and *Etheostoma stigmaeum jessiae* (extirpated?). All 16 are warmwater fishes and all but two of those extant are essentially confined to the main stem. *Cyprinella spiloptera*, *Lythrurus ardens*, and *Notropis volucellus*, generally common in many areas, are rare in the North Fork system. The curious broad hiatus in the range of *Pimephales notatus* suggests that this fish, often ubiquitous elsewhere, is introduced.

Apparently lacking from the North Fork system are three coolwater species: *Notropis spectrunculus* (extirpated, if the one record is valid), Holston sculpin, and *Etheostoma swannanoa* (one unverified record). For the darter, cooler streams of the system may be too small and the main channel too warm.

Intrasystem Comparison: Clinch and Powell

The bounteous fish fauna of the upper Tennessee is best represented in Virginia in the Clinch–Powell system. The two divisions generally are similar ecologically; however, the Clinch system is larger, has two large tributaries (Little River, Big Cedar Creek) that are fed by big springs, and has the richest fauna. The Clinch system also includes the speciose fauna of Copper Creek, a major tributary at 15.3 rkm above the state line. The Clinch system yielded the single collections with the largest number of fish species taken in Virginia—44 in Copper Creek and as many as 52 in the Clinch River (*Species Richness*).

Only one species, the riverine *Erimystax cahni*, is known in Virginia from the Powell system and not the Clinch system proper. It barely extends into the state in the Powell River and probably was extirpated from the lower reach of the Clinch River in Virginia. By contrast, 12 species are known from the Clinch system in Virginia but not the Powell: *Clinostomus funduloides*, *Cyprinella whipplei*, *Lythrurus ardens*, *Ameiurus melas*, *Noturus flavus*, *N. flavipinnis* (lives in the Powell near Virginia), *Cottus baileyi*, Clinch

sculpin, *Percina burtoni*, *P. macrocephala*, *Etheostoma tippecanoe*, and *E. percnurum*. About equal numbers of the 12 species are categorized as typical inhabitants of creeks, streams, or rivers.

Riverine fishes generally extend farther into Virginia in the Clinch River than in the Powell River. The Clinch system harbors more relict populations of species that favor low temperatures. The cool-adapted species known in the Clinch but not the Powell are *Clinostomus funduloides*, *Cottus baileyi*, and the Clinch sculpin. Also affiliated with cool water, *Notropis rubricroceus* and *N. spectrunculus* are known from both systems. The Powell population of each is known from one site in the coal-industry district; apparently they are extirpated. The brook trout has been stocked in Clinch and Powell tributaries; it may not be native historically to either system.

A comparison of the ichthyofaunas of the Little River and Copper Creek (Map 8) illustrates differences in distributional patterns in the upper Tennessee drainage. Both tributary systems are of moderate gradient and course limestone valleys of similar lengths (the long headstream, Maiden Spring Creek, is included for the Little River). Their agricultural valleys lack major industry. The streams are well apart, the Little River being the uppermost large tributary of the Clinch and Copper Creek the lowest in Virginia. The full 98-rkm length of Copper Creek is warm, whereas only the lower 25 rkm of the Little River heats sufficiently to host a warmwater fauna. Voluminous springs, some issuing from caves, depress the temperature of the mid-reach of the Little River (see Clinch sculpin).

The Little River has at least 42 indigenous species; 63 natives are recorded from Copper Creek, by far the most known for any Virginia tributary of the Clinch–Powell (Jenkins and Burkhead 1973). Of the five species found in the Little River and not Copper Creek, four are coolwater isolates in the Clinch system. It is uncertain whether the warmwater fauna of the lower Little River is temperature-depressed. Of the 26 species recorded solely in Copper Creek (among the two streams), several are visitors from the Clinch River; others occupy the creek only in its lower section, to which they may be recruited from the Clinch River. Hence species richness in Copper Creek is differentially augmented by proximity to a Clinch River reach that has more species than the Clinch at the mouth of the Little River.

Copper Creek is well noted for having species that are localized, relict, or threatened. Best demonstrating this are *Ichthyomyzon bdellium*, *I. greeleyi*, *Notropis ariommus*, *Noturus flavus* (Tennessee drainage form), *N. flavipinnis*, *N. eleutherus*, *Percina burtoni*, *P. macro-*

cephala, Etheostoma tippecanoe, and *E. percnurum* (see *Endangered Fishes*). *Notropis ariommus* and *E. tippecanoe* may have been only visitors of the creek. Of the 10 species, only *N. flavus, P. burtoni,* and *P. macrocephala* also inhabit the Little River. Surprisingly, *Fundulus catenatus,* a moderately widespread and often common species outside of Virginia, is nearly confined in the Clinch system proper to Copper Creek and is extremely localized in the upper Powell.

Starkly contrasting with the Copper Creek and Little River faunas is the impoverished one of the Guest River system, also a major Clinch tributary. Unlike the former two tributaries, the Guest system is in a coal-mined area of the Appalachian Plateau and includes centers of human population (Map 8). The fauna has been sparingly sampled, partly because it has seemed relatively uninteresting, as attested by the eight collections (one in 1947, seven in 1972–1978). Thirteen native species and the introduced rainbow trout were recorded; *Percina aurantiaca* was the only species found that has a limited total range. The lowermost sampling site, 2 rkm below Coeburn, was heavily polluted by sewage in 1972; the entire system is afflicted with sediment and perhaps acid mine drainage.

Pollution in the North Fork Holston River

This river was ranked in the early 1970s as one of the most polluted in the United States. In 1970 a ban was imposed on taking fish from the North Fork for eating. The chief culprits were wastes issuing from outfalls and settling lagoons of a large Olin Mathieson Corporation chemical plant located at Saltville (Map 11). Lying just above the Smyth–Washington county line, the plant is 126 rkm above the Virginia–Tennessee state line and 134 rkm above the North Fork–South Fork junction. River contamination stemmed from heavy releases of dissolved solids and "prodigious" amounts of mercury (Bailey 1974; Toole and Ruane 1976; Carter 1977; Milligan and Ruane 1978; Neves and Angermeier 1990; T. M. Felvey, Virginia Water Control Board, in litt.).

Commercial production of salt had commenced in the area by the 1760s (McDonald 1984). Harmful effects were noted on aquatic biota at Saltville in the early 1900s (Adams 1915). Degradation became chronic and extensive, and at times was catastrophic (e.g., the large chemical-sludge pond spill in 1924). Fish kills were extending through the lower, Scott County reach in Virginia and into Tennessee by the 1940s (Jenkins and Burkhead 1984). An early 1950s study found the North Fork to be severely altered near Saltville, and a normal well-balanced biota was absent down to the state line (Anonymous 1955).

Following abatement of toxic releases in the late 1960s and closing of the plant in 1972, the fauna has recovered steadily, despite erosion and seepage of orphaned (but covered) chemical deposits into the river (Hill et al. 1975; Feeman 1986). Riverine species exhibiting substantial recovery below Saltville include *Cyprinella monacha* (federally listed as threatened), *Notropis ariommus,* sawfin shiner, *Percina aurantiaca, P. burtoni, P. evides, Etheostoma zonale,* and *E. camurum.* The evidence for earlier depletion of some of these species is unclear. Although no tributary record exists for some of them in the North Fork system, they may have survived the chemically severe periods by taking refuge in the lowermost section of feeders. Notably absent below Saltville is the parasitic *Ichthyomyzon bdellium*; it currently lives above Saltville. *Cyprinella monacha* has not been found above Saltville during the past 35 years; that population may have been marginal or sustained by recruitment from below Saltville.

Four strictly riverine species, *Moxostoma carinatum, Stizostedion vitreum, S. canadense,* and *Aplodinotus grunniens,* may have been extirpated from the entire Virginia reach before they could be recorded. *Stizostedion* species were depleted essentially by changed hydrologic regimes owing to hydroelectric operations and a detention dam at the head of Cherokee Reservoir in Tennessee (C. W. Voigtlander, in litt.). The occurrence of these species in the upper Holston River would be limited also by pollution from Kingsport, at the junction of the North and South forks. *Carpiodes cyprinus* and *Moxostoma macrolepidotum* apparently make incursions into Virginia from that area. Some of these species are migratory; their movements would be blocked by a mill dam in middle Scott County. Notably, in 1943 a mass migration of common carp, thousands at a time, moved some 50 rkm from Cherokee Reservoir into the lower North Fork (Shields 1944).

Long gone from the North Fork are *Lepisosteus osseus, Moxostoma lacerum* (the extinct harelip sucker), and *Noturus flavipinnis* (federally listed as threatened). They were recorded but once, in 1867 or 1888, and only in the Saltville vicinity (Cope 1868b; Jordan 1889b).

In passing from the Holston, I note that naturally saline water entered the North Fork at Saltville. The water created a barrier sufficient to separate some of the upper river's fauna from that below (Cooper 1966 *in* McDonald 1984).

Fish Kills in the Clinch River

In 1967 the Clinch River was ravaged by an immense chemical spill whose effects still pervade considerations of the fauna. The spill was caused by rupture of the dike of a waste-settling pond at the Appalachian Power Company plant at Carbo, in Russell County, Virginia (Map 11). The pond contained a highly alkaline slurry of fly ash, a residue of coal burned at the plant. Large quantities of fly ash produced daily were removed from the plant's furnace hoppers by pumping in river water, then pumping the mixture to settling ponds. The supernatant water of the ponds was recycled to remove more fly ash from the furnaces. In the ponds the free lime (CaO) of the fly ash reacted with water to form calcium hydroxide (CaOH$_2$) and the alkalinity of the pond water became highly elevated, to pH 12.0–12.7; the pH of the Clinch River normally was 7.8–8.5.

When the dike broke, almost 500 million liters of the slurry went into Dumps Creek in less than an hour, flowed 0.8 rkm, and entered the Clinch River as a "slug." The river was low; the caustic intrusion equalled 40% of the river's daily flow and raised the river level at Carbo a meter or so; some of the waste was forced about 0.8 rkm upriver.

The spill happened on 10 June 1967 at 1000 hours; the waste mass flowed at an average rate of 1.5 rkm/hour through Russell and Scott counties. It reached the Tennessee line, 106 rkm below Dumps Creek, on 13 June at approximately 0930 hours; the waste plume had lengthened to some 13 rkm and pH was elevated maximally to about 11.0. The severe kill continued to near Kyles Ford, 20 rkm below the state line; mortalities were slight near Sneedville, another 20 rkm downstream. When the contaminant reached Norris Reservoir, about 41 rkm below Sneedville, on 15 June at 2330 hours, it had been buffered and diluted to pH 8.9 (Jaco 1967; Tackett 1967; Crossman et al. 1973).

State agencies estimated the numbers of sport and "rough" fish killed as 162,000 in Virginia and 54,600 in Tennessee. Surely this represents only the tip of the iceberg, as larger moribund fish are disproportionately more noticed and counted; small fishes (and redhorse suckers) had numerically dominated the fauna.

The acute alkaline "shock" caused a virtually complete kill of fishes in the Virginia reach. At 8 rkm above the state line at midday, 13 June, the clear low water and little-sedimented bottom afforded notice of carcasses ranging from lampreys to darters and mudpuppies; most were redhorses. Twenty-five fish species were found, less than half the natural fauna; few small fishes were evident. Only two fish were sighted alive at the site, a nearly expired gar (others were dead) and a centrarchid (health unknown). The only other animals that seemed alive were mussels that had "clammed" shut.

In 1970 the faunal recovery in the 20-rkm reach below Carbo was retarded by a spill of sulphuric acid from the APCO plant (Soukup 1970). The effect of an oil spill in 1973 on a few rkm of the upper Clinch River was minimal (Masnik et al. 1976); the spill occurred in Plum Creek, whose mouth is 124 rkm above Carbo.

Stockings of four native gamefishes and the non-native muskellunge and redbreast sunfish were made in Virginia after the first kill, mainly in 1967–1969; muskellunge stocking continued afterward. Local residents evidently also stocked fish in 1967 (Wollitz 1972).

The 1967 kill evoked a spate of study on recovery of the river (Wollitz 1968b, 1970, 1972; Cairns et al. 1971; Crossman et al. 1973; Raleigh et al. 1978) and a survey of the Clinch–Powell system ichthyofauna (Masnik 1974). Documentation of continued recovery has stemmed chiefly from collections through 1984 by TVA biologists (Feeman 1987; C. F. Saylor, in litt.).

Geochronographic analysis of the fauna for this book indicates substantial to full recovery for most members of the main-stem ichthyofauna. Although the prekill distribution and abundance of many species, particularly small ones, is virtually unknown, in most cases the lack or occurrence of recovery can be inferred from current distributional patterns in the Clinch, Powell, and similar rivers of Virginia and Tennessee. Rates of movement and colonization by small fishes in large streams are largely unknown. One tends to think that their rates would be slow, but the converse is also tenable judging by the rapidity of spread of introduced fishes in the New drainage and of *Etheostoma zonale* in the Susquehanna River. Recovery is discussed in the most detail in accounts of certain species that are nearly or fully restricted in Virginia to the Clinch River: *Polyodon spathula, Notropis ariommus, Moxostoma carinatum, Noturus eleutherus, Ammocrypta clara, Etheostoma camurum,* and *E. tippecanoe.*

Fish foods and many fish returned locally to the Clinch River in less than a month after the 1967 kill. A fully productive food base for fishes was widely reestablished by the summer of 1969, although recovery was incomplete immediately downstream from Carbo (Crossman et al. 1973). Most species probably moved in first from above Carbo and from the many small Virginia tributaries; recruitment must have occurred also by upstream expansion of the fauna from Tennessee. In 1970, T. Zorach and I took 30 species by small seine at the site near Tennessee where I witnessed the kill. In 1972 with an intensive collecting effort, Masnik (1974; see *Species Richness*) tallied 47 species at the state line.

Recovery of the Clinch River in the vicinity of St. Paul, 17–25 rkm below Carbo was studied during 1972–1974 by Raleigh et al. (1978). Their chief conclusions were that general recovery was rapid; the number of species had become similar to that before the kill (46 taken postkill including 2–3 nonnatives introduced then); relative abundance differed significantly between the periods; 30 species could have reinvaded from tributaries of the reach; and natural restocking from the nearest tributary often occurred to a minor extent.

The data sets of Raleigh et al. (1978) are vital to understanding the Clinch River recovery. The prekill data are from Wollitz (1965, 1967a, 1967b); I examined his relatively few preserved collections. In these collections, riffle fishes and small-sized occupants of pools were underrepresented; Wollitz's study had focused on gamefishes. The postkill samples were examined by Masnik (1974) and some by me; the original report was transmitted to me (R. F. Raleigh, in litt.). The postkill river-sampling techniques may have been inadequate to inventory small fishes, particularly in pools. Several collections had few specimens, reflecting locally unsuitable habitat or adverse collecting conditions.

The seven tributaries sampled by Raleigh et al. (1978) were small (the largest averaged 4 m wide) and most were polluted from domestic, coal mining, or other industrial sources. The larger species lists from them (range, 4–20 species) were from at or near the mouths. In assessing tributary contributions to the river, Raleigh et al. (1978) separately compared the species found in each tributary with only those found at the nearest river site. However, the apparent difference in completeness of the data set from the river compared with those from tributaries renders the interpretations of relative recruitment suspect; because of the mobility of many riverine species, the seven tributaries should be regarded as a single recruitment pool for the 8-km river reach.

Most species now in the Clinch River probably reached it from combinations of sources. Species typical of medium-sized tributaries had many points of reentry to the river; seemingly they recovered the most rapidly. It appears that into the mid-1980s, recovery of these and more typically riverine species had proceeded well in the 41-rkm section from the state line upstream to the head of the Pendleton Island–Fort Blackmore area in middle Scott County. The latter area yielded 56 species within 1981–1985 (*Species Richness*; my data). However, I know of no collections made after 1974 in the 65-rkm reach from Fort Blackmore upstream to Carbo.

Large tributaries would be important recruitment sources for most Clinch system species and particularly crucial for fishes generally confined to lower reaches of large streams and the Clinch River. Copper Creek is the only tributary of the Virginia reach of the Clinch River directly effected in 1967 that would seem to have had major emigration of riverine species. The other sizeable tributary to that reach, the Guest River, would have dispensed few species to the river because of its depauperate fauna. Surely Copper Creek well served a reach of the river initially (*Moxostoma carinatum* and *Etheostoma tippecanoe* accounts).

Copper Creek above its mouth likely was not the source of several Clinch River recruits—the species unknown from the intensively sampled lower creek. Two examples are instructively disparate. The mobile paddlefish restocked itself almost certainly from Tennessee. The western sand darter *Ammocrypta clara* has been known in the Clinch River only since 1980, and only from three sites in Virginia and Tennessee. It, too, probably swam in from Tennessee, but back in geologic time. Its refuge from the toxic spill could have been any tributary mouth, regardless of tributary size, close to main-stem sites that it inhabited before the 1967 spill. The 1969 record of the riverine *Cyprinella whipplei* in Stock Creek (near Copper Creek) immediately above its mouth probably exemplifies sporadic occurrences pivotal to recovery of populations from crises in main rivers.

Apparently extirpated from the Clinch River in Virginia, and thus from the entire system in the state, are *Moxostoma anisurum* and *Etheostoma cinereum*. They were known at only one or two sites; the records shortly predated the 1967 spill. *Moxostoma anisurum* is expected to reinvade Virginia from the small population in Tennessee above Norris Reservoir. *Etheostoma cinereum*, however, was not found above the reservoir except for the Virginia record (Shepard and Burr 1984). *Moxostoma lacerum* probably extended into Virginia via the Clinch as it considerably did in the North Fork Holston, but probably was ousted long before 1967.

Other species that probably occupied the Clinch River of Virginia include *Cyprinella monacha*, *Erimystax cahni*, and *Noturus stanauli*. They could have been victims of the kill in Virginia; *E. cahni* and *N. stanauli* persist in the Tennessee reach. *Erimystax cahni* likely would be the first to reenter Virginia; it (presumably) recently did so in the Powell River. The closest Tennessee record site in the Clinch is 20 rkm below Virginia. The recently described, waning *N. stanauli* is known in the upper Tennessee from only two Clinch

River shoals within 30–34 rkm below Virginia (Etnier and Jenkins 1980; Feeman 1987; *Fishes of Possible Occurrence*). This pygmy madtom probably disperses slowly and may never reach Virginia. Owing to impoundment, the Clinch population of *C. monacha* may have gone the way of the harelip sucker (Jenkins and Burkhead 1984).

Sedimentation in the Clinch and Powell Systems

Sedimentation of streambeds does not produce the dramatic effects of a big fish kill, but it has long-term effects. Siltation of streams is often viewed in this book as a chief factor limiting aquatic life in Virginia. The Clinch and Powell watersheds have the normal sources of erosion of inorganic silt into its waterways. These systems locally have also accumulated extraordinary amounts of silt as a result of stripmining for coal in the northerly fringing Appalachian Plateau. The whole series of northern tributaries of the Powell and nearly all of those of the Clinch arise in the coal-bearing plateau.

Adding to sediment loads are "coal fines"—dust and somewhat larger particles of coal that enter streams (along with other sediments) from coal-washing operations (Helfrich et al. 1986; Biggins 1989). The potential for coal-fine sedimentation is attested by the mining of 56% of Virginia's coal from the counties drained by the Clinch and Powell rivers (Tackett 1963). In the early 1960s the Clinchfield Coal Company operated the world's largest coal preparation plant on Dumps Creek. The combined sediment load of coal and typical forms of silt is heaviest in Powell River headwaters (Dennis 1981).

Unlike many coal-mined areas, the Clinch and Powell rivers did not have a serious problem with acid mine wastes during Tackett's (1963) study. The water is well buffered by dissolution of the limestone bed of surface streams and underground aquifers. However, many tributaries of these rivers have been degraded by mine wastes.

The amounts of sedimentation now in the lower reaches of the Clinch and Powell rivers in Virginia and into Tennessee are similar to those in montane regions of most other Virginia drainages. I have not seen "blackwater," caused by suspended coal dust, in these Clinch and Powell reaches during any fieldwork, which started there essentially in 1970. Indications are that entry of coal into streams has been curtailed from levels noted by Tackett (1963) and Wollitz (1967b, 1968b). However, small pieces of coal often are found mixed with inorganic silt and detritus in backwaters (Wolcott 1990); these beds are quite mobile during high water.

The Powell River seems to be in a state of recovery concerning fishes, which may be at an advanced stage in the lower (western Lee County) reach of Virginia and in Tennessee above Norris Reservoir. Encouragingly, paddlefish, *Erimystax cahni*, *Pimephales vigilax*, *Noturus eleutherus*, and *Ammocrypta clara* now extend (barely) into Virginia; *Noturus flavipinnis* lives not far below (Feeman 1987; our data). Several other riverine species extend much farther upstream, some into Wise County. However, other species known from the Clinch River in either or both Virginia and Tennessee probably were extirpated from the Powell in Virginia: *Cyprinella monacha*, *C. whipplei*, *Moxostoma lacerum*, *Percina burtoni*, *P. macrocephala*, *Etheostoma tippecanoe*, and *E. percnurum* (Jenkins and Burkhead 1984). *Notropis atherinoides* and *Moxostoma anisurum*, both known from one Powell River, Virginia site in 1968, also seem to be missing.

Epilogue

It was partly mussels that drew me to the Clinch River. In 1967 while I was studying fishes at the Ohio State University Museum of Zoology, the malacologist D. H. Stansbery gave me a glimpse of the startling diversity of unionid mussels in the Clinch and Powell rivers (Dennis 1985; Starnes and Bogan 1988). Rich mollusk and fish faunas often co-occur in prime habitat; the relationship includes the requirement of unionid larvae for living in gill or skin tissue of fishes (Neves et al. 1985; Neves and Widlak 1988). Dr. Stansbery apprised me of good sampling sites above Norris Reservoir.

With a growing interest in Virginia fishes and aware that the big-water ichthyofauna of the Clinch River was poorly known, my interest in collecting there was honed. On the first opportunity, F. F. Snelson and I entered the river at a splendid island site, set to make a "killing"; we were a day late for live fishes. Initially we were unaware that a river kill was in progress, the peak just passed. It was mystifying to not capture a minnow in several seine hauls, and then astounding to have specimens that constituted first state records drift into hand. However, a glance at a backwater revealed a flotilla of bloated bodies, the wake of massive mortality that was duplicated up and down the river.

A rare opportunity to inventory the fauna was presented. Unfortunately, after two weeks of fieldwork as far west as Oklahoma, we had little time, and our car already was overloaded with specimens. We inventoried carcasses at the site, preserved some of them in formalin, queried game wardens and residents, checked a huge paddlefish upriver (which appeared on the CBS national news with Walter Cronkite), and returned to Cornell University, the car reeking with fishes to be skeletonized.

WHY DON'T CAVEFISHES OCCUPY WESTERN VIRGINIA?

The absence of the cavefish family Amblyopsidae in the limestone district of the Valley and Ridge Province of western Virginia and eastern Tennessee, in the upper Tennessee drainage, is puzzling. Amblyopsids have been carefully sought but not detected in that area and eastward by the expert cave biologists J. E. Cooper (in litt.) and J. R. Holsinger (in litt.; Holsinger and Culver 1988), and by many others looking for such species. In contrast, three amblyopsids inhabit the lower Tennessee drainage; altogether, five species occupy the central Mississippi basin, particularly the Interior Low Plateaus east of the Mississippi River.

The absence of cavefishes in western Virginia is made more enigmatic by the presence of the swampfish *Chologaster cornuta* in southeastern Virginia and south to central Georgia on the outer Atlantic slope. This small secretive, surface-water-inhabiting amblyopsid is the sister species of the spring-and-cave dweller *Chologaster agassizi* of the lower Tennessee and slightly northwest. The combined distributions of the cave species and the wide range hiatus separating them from the swampfish are shown in Map 122.

The basis for the range hiatus has been variously hypothesized; each scenario involves major extirpation. In reviewing the biogeography of cave animals, Poulson and White (1969) suggested that chances of extinction have been higher in Valley and Ridge cave systems than in the generally larger, more contiguous systems of the Interior Low Plateaus.

One scheme is that a swampfish-like stock dispersed eastward from the interior by skirting the southern end of the Appalachians and then died out in southern lowlands owing either to habitat desiccation (Woods and Inger 1957) or inundation by rising sea level (Gilbert 1987). However, amblyopsids may have spread in the opposite direction, an eastern stock having given rise to lineages of the interior. A difficulty of a southern-track dispersal or vicariance hypothesis is the absence of amblyopsids in Florida. Florida has abundant habitat that seemingly is suited for the swampfish. It could also support cave dwellers; portions of Florida are riddled with underground aquifers, and some are at higher elevation than Pliocene–Pleistocene sea inundation levels (Gilbert 1987).

Alternatively, Willis and Brown (1985) proposed that a swampfish-like ancestor of the Mississippi basin amblyopsids occupied swampy areas near or north of southern glacial limits during wet times of the Pleistocene. It and its derivatives became cave-adapted during drier periods; with further drying, the east–west range gap was produced by extirpations.

As another hypothesis, I offer that amblyopsids may have ranged directly east–west from the central Mississippi basin to the central Atlantic slope in the Valley and Ridge limestone belt. Supporting an early trans-Appalachian track are the interconnections, by stream captures or subterranean interflueves, of pairs of drainages comprising the upper Tennessee, New, Roanoke, James, and Potomac. Some captures almost certainly involved underground flow (e.g., Matthews et al. 1982). The *Cottus carolinae* group spans four of these drainages; one of its taxa is a troglobite and others may be trogloxenes.

Regardless of whether amblyopsids extended directly east–west, why don't they today occupy major springs and subterranean fluvial systems in the Valley and Ridge karst of the upper Tennessee drainage above Waldens Ridge? They seem to stop in northwestern Georgia, just short of that area, at approximately a finger of the southern portion of the Appalachian Plateau (Map 122). I suggest that because most drainage of the plateau is toward the west, the plateau probably causes a gradient or divide barrier to cavefishes. Also, the plateau is composed primarily of sandstone and shale, and hence lacks subterranean aquatic systems comparable in extent and productivity to those of limestone belts east and west.

The narrow gap through Waldens Ridge that is breached by the Tennessee River west of Chattanooga, Tennessee, may be a major breakpoint between faunal segments of the Tennessee drainage (Jenkins et al. 1972; Mayden 1988a). The ridge forms a surface bottleneck, probably interrupts underground aquifers, and thus may have prevented amblyopsids from moving into the upper Tennessee.

BIG SANDY DRAINAGE FAUNA

The Big Sandy drainage is a major southern tributary of the middle Ohio River. Gathering headwaters in the Appalachian Plateau of Kentucky, Virginia, and West Virginia, the Big Sandy River and its Tug Fork form the Kentucky–West Virginia line (Map 12). The Virginia portion is in the northern spur of the southwestern part of the state; its three major systems comprising four main trunks are, from west to east and in decreasing size: Russell Fork, Levisa Fork,

Knox Creek, and Tug Fork. Knox Creek joins Tug Fork, the stream along the northeasternmost edge of the drainage (and state line) in Virginia. The Tug Fork system in Virginia also includes a few small streams—Dry Fork and tributaries—that join Tug Fork in West Virginia; Dry Fork is indicated on pertinent distribution maps by an arrow pointing toward Tug Fork (e.g., Map 48).

In Virginia the dendritic drainage has an upland to montane topography that is typical of the highly stream-dissected southern portion of the Appalachian Plateau. The main stems and larger tributaries characteristically have moderate gradient. An exceptional feature is the Breaks of Sandy cut by Russell Fork as it crosses into Kentucky; this gorge is nearly 8 rkm long and in places almost 300 m deep (Dietrich 1970a). Most of the drainage in Virginia is rural and wooded; there are no major cities. The two sizeable impoundments, Flannagan and North Fork Pound reservoirs, are on the Pound River branch of Russell Fork.

The name Big Sandy is appropriate, but the drainage might just as well be called the Big Silty; few sizeable streams lack an overload of this sediment. Gravel, rubble, boulder, and bedrock substrates are typical in Virginia, but the first two commonly are interbedded or fully overlain with fine sediment. The bottom of many Big Sandy streams is Piedmontane. Contributing to the silt load are tillage of the well-sloped land and, particularly, the pervasive strip mining for coal. These and other conditions are reviewed by Evenhuis (1973), Howell (1981), Hess et al. (1985), and Burr and Warren (1986).

Fauna

The number of species composing the Big Sandy fauna is typical for the size and location of the drainage; 87 native (none endemic) and 15 introduced species have been recorded (Burr and Warren 1986; Hocutt et al. 1986). Nearly all the species are widespread in eastern central United States. Known from the Virginia portion of the drainage are 42 (48%) of the native species and 12 of those introduced, which may seem normal for an upper watershed that constitutes only about 16% (Burr and Warren 1986) of the total area of the drainage's watershed. However, because of environmental degradation, the Virginia contingent apparently has been substantially reduced in number of species; many populations of those present are depleted.

The present fauna is described from 105 stream collections made during 1972–1989 (by system—Russell Fork, 58; Levisa Fork, 33; Tug Fork, 14); from 14 reservoir samples taken in 1966–1973 (Wollitz 1972, 1973, 1975a, 1975b); and from 3 strip-mine ponds inventoried in 1976 (Peltz and Maughan 1979). Only five collections were made before 1972: one in a small stream in 1900, and one each from four different streams during 1937; each of the three systems is represented.

Faunal Decline

In reporting the 1900 collection, among many from throughout West Virginia, Goldsborough and Clark (1908) emphasized that the fauna was being decimated by abuses of land and water. Some of the species found in 1937 have since disappeared from the Virginia section; others are reduced.

Among the 42 native species in the drainage in Virginia, the number of those that are generally distributed is small for a drainage section having relatively high habitat homogeneity. The 14 generally distributed species are *Rhinichthys atratulus*, *Campostoma anomalum*, *Semotilus atromaculatus*, *Luxilus chrysocephalus*, *Notropis rubellus*, *N. stramineus*, *N. buccatus*, *Pimephales notatus*, *Hypentelium nigricans*, *Ictalurus punctatus*, *Ambloplites rupestris*, *Micropterus dolomieu*, *M. punctulatus*, and *Stizostedion vitreum*.

Recognition of some of the 14 as generally distributed takes into account stream-size zonation; for example, *I. punctatus* is a big-water fish and is expected to be confined to lower main stems (and stocked reservoirs). However, the general distribution status of some of these species is further qualified. For example, *L. chrysocephalus* and *H. nigricans* seemingly are rare in Levisa and Tug forks, respectively. Also, the state-line records of *S. vitreum* in Russell and Levisa forks may have stemmed from introductions in Virginia and Kentucky reservoirs.

All of the other 28 putative natives deviate conspicuously from having a general distribution in Virginia; habitat degradation appears to be the principal cause. Three of the 28 species are believed to be extirpated from the entire Virginia section: *Hybopsis amblops*, *Percina maculata*, and *Salvelinus fontinalis*. The first two were present during 1937 in Tug Fork and the darter also in Levisa Fork. We have no record of stream-bred brook trout for the Big Sandy; its hypothesized extirpation rests on native status accredited (arbitrarily) more than 100 years ago.

For the remaining 25 of the 42 native species, there are 75 possible "system occurrences" in Virginia (3 systems for each species, independent of the actual number of records of a species for a system). Of the 75 during 1972–1989, there are 28 "system nonoccurrences" among 21 species, indicating extensive extirpation (or for *Phenacobius mirabilis*, perhaps failure to colonize one system). The nonoccurrences are about equally divided among the systems: 11 in Russell Fork, 9 in Levisa Fork, and 8 in Tug Fork. A few of these nonoccurrences may be artifacts of unevenly dispersed stockings of gamefishes; a few occurrences may represent cryptic introductions of small species regarded as native. Early records of "dropouts" are few; only in 1937 were *Nocomis micropogon* and *Moxostoma erythrurum* recorded in Levisa Fork.

Localization and rarity is typical within systems. Subtracting the 28 nonoccurrences from the 75 possible occurrences gives 47 system occurrences that were detected during 1972–1989. Of the 47, 28 are based on only three or fewer records from a system. Among the 17 so-recorded species, 4 inhabit the Russell Fork, 11 the Levisa Fork, and 13 the Tug Fork systems.

In summary, of the 42 putative native species, 3 are fully extirpated. Recently, among 25 of the 42 species, the rate of extirpation from systems is 37% (28 of 75 possible nonoccurrences); among system residents the rate of localization or rarity is 60% (28 of 47 system occurrences). Only 14 species (33%) have an essentially general distribution. Extirpations are subequally divided among the systems; recognition of the smallest system as having the most localizations or rarities may reflect only the size of the system in Virginia. Extirpation, localization, and rarity befall creek dwellers about as often as river inhabitants.

Absentees

The Big Sandy fauna of Virginia is notable for absentees—unrecorded species that probably existed there before the onset of settlement and mining; surveying for native fishes essentially began in 1972. The number of absentees is at least 24, as judged by their habitat use and proximity in the extralimital portion of the drainage (e.g., Lee et al. 1980; Burr and Warren 1986) Seven species are considered under *Fishes of Possible Occurrence*. Although the Breaks of Sandy reach of Russell Fork is high gradient and mostly hard-bottomed, it appears insufficiently rigorous to prevent upstream invasion of even slow-water species. Virginia would have been easily accessible via the other systems. However, some of the species are faring little if any better in Kentucky and West Virginia than in Virginia.

Faunal Recovery?

The extent of depletion of the upper Big Sandy fauna is startling because most of the so-affected species are widespread and often common elsewhere in the Ohio basin. The species have successfully competed in the evolutionary arena, but siltation appears to have been an insurmountable adversary. Many species still present in Virginia seem to be barely persisting in marginal conditions, or they occupy isolated pockets of suitable habitat.

Reduction of silt would facilitate recovery of the Virginia fauna. However, because of the long time needed for natural means of silt removal to be effective, and from continued input of silt, it seems more likely that biotically destructive levels of sedimentation will outlast many species populations in the upper Big Sandy. Coal mining is one of the chief contributors of siltation. Although the coal industry is critical to the economy of the region that includes the Big Sandy, the cost in degradation of aquatic resources has been great.

Recent Entrants?

Three small minnows that typically occupy sand and small gravel substrate appear to have been spreading in the Big Sandy of Virginia: *Phenacobius mirabilis*, *Notropis stramineus*, and *N. buccatus*. The latter two are generally distributed in the Big Sandy. All three may have entered the Virginia section of the drainage recently. *Notropis buccatus* was first seen in the Virginia section in 1972 and it is the most widespread; the other two were found initially in 1982. *Phenacobius mirabilis* may have the smallest distribution, owing to a greater proclivity for larger streams. The three species may have responded positively to sedimentation resembling that in parts of the Great Plains.

REFERENCES

Gathered here are references primarily to publications on geographic and ecologic distribution of assemblages of Virginia fishes, ranging from those of one stream to the whole ichthyofauna. Included are gray literature (e.g., Dingell–Johnson reports of the VDGIF) on game and forage fish surveys that have locality data sufficient to allow accurate plotting of records. Many other unpublished reports used in this study for distributional data are not included below; the species lists in these reports are included (often with modifications) with the rest of the lists that we contributed (through late 1984) to the computerized BOVA data bank of the VDGIF. Under each drainage the references are listed alphabetically by author, to facilitate title searching in the main *References* section.

General.—Listed are zoogeographic treatises, comprehensive species lists for the Virginia region or broader, or lists for three or more Virginia drainages. Bowman et al. (1959); Cope (1868b); Fowler (1918, 1922, 1923, 1945); Gilbert (1976, 1980); Harrison and Martin (1960); Hildebrand and Schroeder (1928); Hocutt (1979b); Hocutt et al. (1986); Hoener (1969); Jenkins and Musick (1979); Jenkins et al. (1972); Jordan (1889b); Lee et al. (1980); Massmann (1957); McHugh and Steinkoenig (1980); Miller (1959); Mohn and Bugas (1980); Musick (1972); Ross (1969); Stauffer et al. (1982).

Potomac Drainage.—Bean and Weed (1911); Davis and Enamait (1982); Evermann and Hildebrand (1910); Hoffman (1960); Kauffman (1975); Kelso and Bright (1976); Lee et al. (1981); Manville (1968); Martin et al. (1963); Matheson (1979); McAtee and Weed (1915); Potter et al. (1981); Prosser (1972a, 1972b, 1973); Radcliffe and Welsh (1916); Ross (1959a, 1959b, 1972b); Seagle and Hendricks (1979); Smith and Bean (1899); Stauffer et al. (1978a, 1978b); Steinkoenig (1975); Surber (1970, 1972); Truitt et al. (1929); Uhler and Lugger (1876); Vadas (1990).

Rappahannock Drainage.—Massmann et al. (1952); Maurakis et al. (1987); Sheridan (1962).

York Drainage.—Corning (1967b); Patrick (1961); Prosser (1972a, 1972b); Raney and Massmann (1953); Reed (1980); Reed and Simmons (1976); Sledd and Shuber (1981); Steinkoenig (1975); VEPCO (1982).

James Drainage.—Flemer and Woolcott (1966); Leonard et al. (1986); Martin (1953, 1954); Martin et al. (1963); Neves and Pardue (1983); Norman (1972, 1973, 1974); Norman and LaRoche (1975); Raney (1950); Rozas and Odum (1987a, 1987c); Schontz (1962); Sheridan (1962, 1963); Shuber and Sledd (1981); VIMS (1977); White (1976); White et al. (1977); Woolcott et al. (1974).

Minor Chesapeake and Atlantic Drainages.—Merriner et al. (1976); Norman (1972, 1973, 1974, 1981); Norman and LaRoche (1975); Wollitz (1963).

Dismal Swamp.—Andrews (1971); Brady (1969); Jenkins et al. (1975); Rosebery and Bowers (1952); Russell (1976).

Chowan Drainage.—Corning (1967a); Jenkins et al. (1975); Norman and Southwick (1985); Sheridan (1963).

Roanoke Drainage.—Cairns et al. (1971); Domrose (1963); Garman and Nielsen (1982); Hambrick (1973); Hart (1978); Jackson and Henderson (1942); James (1979); Jenkins (1979a, 1979b, 1981); Jenkins and Freeman (1972); LaRoche (1985); Martin (1953, 1954); Matthews (1986a, 1990); Mauney and Maughan (1986); Neal (1967, 1968, 1973); Ney and Mauney (1981); Prince and Brouha (1975).

New Drainage.—References to the extralimital portions are included. Addair (1944); Benfield and Cairns (1974); Boaze and Lackey (1974); Brandt and Schreck (1975); Breder and Breder (1923); Burton and Odum (1945); England and Cumming (1972); Goldsborough and Clark (1908); Hambrick (1973); Hart (1981); Hess (1983); Hocutt et al. (1973, 1978, 1979); Leonard and Orth (1983); Lobb (1986); Lobb and Orth (1988); Neves (1983); Raney (1941); Richardson and Carnes (1964); Rosebery (1950a, 1950b); Ross (1959c, 1973); Ross and Perkins (1959); Stauffer et al. (1975, 1976); Whitehurst (1985); Wollitz (1968a).

Tennessee Drainage.—Denoncourt (1969a); Feeman (1980, 1986, 1987); Garman et al. (1982); Hill et al. (1975); Masnik (1974); Masnik and Knollenberg (1972); Masnik et al. (1976); Neves and Widlak (1988); Novak (1968); Patrick (1961); Peltz and Maughan (1979); Raleigh et al. (1978); Ross and Carico (1963); Saylor et al. (1988); TVA (1970); Wollitz (1965, 1967a, 1967b, 1968b, 1970, 1972, 1973).

Big Sandy Drainage.—Howell (1981); Masnik and Knollenberg (1972); Peltz and Maughan (1979); Wollitz (1972, 1973).

ENDANGERED FISHES

Starting with the environmental movement in the early 1970s, the protection of endangered biota has received much increased attention. Endangered species issues often are sociopolitically controversial. Proponents of healthy biotas and natural environments tend to be conservationists and preservationists. Their aims frequently clash with those of developers and industries whose activities may seriously affect or eliminate species and habitats. Environmentalists often have lost legal–environmental battles, and the decline of our living resource heritage is real. Virginia has a major share of sensitive and waning animals and plants that warrant protection, as determined in the 1978 and 1989 symposia on the state's endangered species (Linzey 1979; Terwilliger 1991).

The need for protection of species has been long present, but general awareness of that need is relatively recent. Field efforts during the first century of ichthyological study in Virginia (1867–1967) generally were too sparse to detect the decline of many species. However, in the last 20 years, surveys often were specifically designed to determine the status of sensitive and rare fishes. The now extensive data base indicates that the abundance and distribution of many fish species have been sharply curtailed in historical time.

Burkhead and Jenkins (1991) consider that 45 species or subspecies of Virginia fishes—21% of the 217 native taxa treated herein—are in varied degrees of jeopardy at the state level, on a national (total-range) basis, or have already vanished (Table 4). Some anadromous species not recommended for protective status are much depleted. The alarmingly high rate of biotic attrition accents the need to couple this knowledge with enforcement of the recently established endangered species laws.

Jenkins and Musick (1979) and Burkhead and Jenkins (1991) removed several fishes from the Virginia list of species recommended for protection in Virginia, but in most cases this stemmed from better knowledge of populations, not from improved biotic status. For true upgrading of status to become prevalent, the emphasis on endangered biota must shift to rigorous defense of habitat quality.

The many recommendations for protection of Virginia fishes and streams (Burkhead and Jenkins 1991) have begun to be addressed by the Virginia Department of Game and Inland Fisheries (VDGIF), the Virginia Division of Natural Heritage, The Nature Conservancy, and other agencies. The downward trend of some species has been stemmed. The road to partial or full recovery for many species will be long, difficult, and costly.

LEGISLATION AND DEFINITIONS

The Endangered Species Act of 1973, as amended in 1978 and 1979, provides for the protection and enhancement of endangered species (J. Williams 1976, 1981). Such species are prohibited from being taken without a permit issued by the U.S. Fish and Wildlife Service (USFWS). The act mandates reviews of federal programs and projects that may affect endangered and threatened species. It also allows federal funding of species and habitat enhancement programs, including those of states such as the Nongame and Endangered Species Program of the VDGIF. Endangered species legislation of Virginia has the proviso to protect species not federally listed (Code of Virginia §29.1-521 to -570 [1993]; VDGIF 1987; Terwilliger 1991).

The term endangered species is frequently used as a catchall for organisms that need help to survive. Thus in a general sense, the term endangered can refer to species warranting or legally assigned that status, to species having threatened status, and sometimes to those having a lesser classification,

Table 4 Fishes warranting protection in Virginia (as recommended by Burkhead and Jenkins 1991 or having legally designated status) or which no longer occur in the state. Status categories (defined in text): **E**—endangered; **Exp**—extirpated; **Ext**—extinct; **SC**—special concern; **T**—threatened; **U**—undetermined. *—legal Virginia or legal federal status. Legal Virginia status takes precedence for Virginia when it indicates greater level of jeopardy than federal status. In cases of two status categories for Virginia, the first is that recommended by Burkhead and Jenkins (1991). Nonlegal national status (Federal column, not asterisked) is that recommended herein or by Williams et al. (1989) or Burkhead and Jenkins (1991). c—Clinch River species known also from Copper Creek.

Family, species, and common name	Status Virginia	Status Federal	Drainage, system, or stream (possibly occurs in) [formerly in]
Acipenseridae			
Acipenser brevirostrum shortnose sturgeon	Exp/E*	E*	[Chesapeake estuaries]
Acipenser oxyrhynchus Atlantic sturgeon	SC	SC	Chesapeake estuaries
Polyodontidae			
Polyodon spathula paddlefish	T	SC	Clinch, Powell
Cyprinidae			
Cyprinella labrosa thicklip shiner	Exp	-	[Peedee]
Cyprinella monacha turquoise shiner	E/T*	T*	Middle Fork and North Fork Holston
Cyprinella whipplei steelcolor shiner	T	-	Clinch
Erimystax cahni slender chub	E/T*	T*	Powell (Clinch)
Notropis alborus whitemouth shiner	T	-	Lower Roanoke (Chowan)
Notropis ariommus popeye shiner	SC	-	North Fork Holston, Clinch^c, Powell
Notropis atherinoides emerald shiner	T	-	Clinch, Powell
Notropis bifrenatus bridle shiner	SC	SC	York, James [Potomac, Rappahannock, Chowan]
Notropis semperasper roughhead shiner	SC	SC	Upper James
Notropis spectrunculus mirror shiner	SC	-	Tennessee
Phenacobius crassilabrum fatlips minnow	SC	-	South Fork Holston
Phoxinus tennesseensis Tennessee dace	E	SC?	Middle Fork and North Fork Holston
Catostomidae			
Moxostoma carinatum river redhorse	SC	-	Tennessee^c [? North Fork Holston]
Moxostoma lacerum harelip sucker	Ext	Ext	[Tennessee]
Thoburnia hamiltoni rustyside sucker	SC	SC	Upper Dan
Ictaluridae			
Noturus flavipinnis yellowfin madtom	E/T*	T*	Copper [North Fork Holston]
Noturus flavus undescribed form of stonecat	SC	-	South Fork and North Fork Holston, Clinch^c
Noturus gilberti orangefin madtom	T	T	Craig, upper Roanoke, upper Dan
Noturus insignis spotted form of margined madtom	U	U	Upper Dan
Percopsidae			
Percopsis omiscomaycus trout-perch	Exp	-	[Potomac]
Fundulidae			
Fundulus rathbuni speckled killifish	SC	-	Lower Dan
Atherinidae			
Labidesthes sicculus brook silverside	SC	-	Clinch, Powell [? Holston]
Centrarchidae			
Ambloplites cavifrons Roanoke bass	SC	SC	Chowan, middle and upper Roanoke
Enneacanthus chaetodon blackbanded sunfish	T/E*	-	Chowan
Percidae			
Ammocrypta clara western sand darter	T	-	Clinch, Powell
Etheostoma acuticeps sharphead darter	E*	SC	South Fork Holston
Etheostoma camurum bluebreast darter	SC	-	North Fork Holston, Clinch^c, Powell
Etheostoma chlorobranchium greenfin darter	T	-	Whitetop Laurel
Etheostoma cinereum ashy darter	Exp	SC	[Clinch]
Etheostoma collis Carolina darter	SC/E*	-	Lower Roanoke
Etheostoma osburni candy darter	SC	SC	Lower New
Etheostoma stigmaeum jessiae blueside speckled darter	U/E*	-	North Fork Holston
Etheostoma tippecanoe Tippecanoe darter	T/E*	SC	Clinch [Copper]
Etheostoma variatum variegate darter	E	-	Big Sandy
Etheostoma percnurum duskytail darter	E	T	Clinch, Copper
Percina burtoni blotchside logperch	SC	SC	North Fork Holston, Clinch, Copper
Percina caprodes semifasciata northern logperch	Exp	-	[Potomac]
Percina copelandi channel darter	SC	-	Clinch, Powell [? New]
Percina macrocephala longhead darter	T	T	Middle Fork and North Fork Holston, Clinch^c
Percina maculata blackside darter	Exp	-	[Big Sandy]
Percina rex Roanoke logperch	E*	E*	Nottoway, upper Roanoke, upper Dan
Stizostedion canadense sauger	SC	-	South Fork Holston, Clinch, Powell

(e.g., special concern or rare). In a strict sense these protective or conservation categories are mutually exclusive. They have been rigidly defined in many quarters for the last 20 years, and have been so employed by us during that period and throughout this volume.

Endangered—Any species, subspecies, or race that is in danger of extinction throughout all or a significant portion of its range is termed endangered.

Threatened—Any species, subspecies, or race that is likely to become an endangered species within the foreseeable future throughout all or a significant portion of its range is termed threatened.

Special Concern—The special concern category is often applied (consistently so herein) to taxa that approach but do not clearly merit threatened status, or which have recently declined sharply in a major part of their range. It was applied by the Endangered Species Committee of the American Fisheries Society (Deacon et al. 1979; Williams et al. 1989) to species that could become threatened or endangered as a result of relatively minor disturbances of their habitats.

Undetermined—The special concern category sometimes is extended to include species that require additional information to determine their status; alternatively, such species may be placed in the undetermined category. Our knowledge of Virginia fishes has improved in the last 10 years such that all five species considered to have undetermined status by Jenkins and Musick (1979) are now allocated to other categories; we add two other species to the category.

Other Categories—Two more categories are needed to round out the list of primary terms we employ. *Extirpated* refers to species that no longer occupy a river drainage, major ecosystem, or political unit (e.g., Virginia) but which survive elsewhere. *Extinct* species no longer live anywhere.

Much controversy has developed on the merit of formally recognizing and protecting "peripheral" populations; that is, those that occur at the edge of the geographical range of a species or which inhabit a very small part of a state (Burkhead and Jenkins 1991). The term peripheral often has been appended to the special concern status of a species in a state. However, as a qualifier it may erroneously convey that some populations in critical need of protection are relatively unimportant to the overall survival of the species. Geographically peripheral populations

may be among the strongest of a wide-ranging but localized or depleted species (e.g., popeye shiner and bluebreast darter in Virginia). Peripheral populations may occupy a substantial portion of the total range (e.g., fatlips minnow and blotchside logperch). They may be slightly divergent or taxonomically distinct (e.g., stonecat and Tippecanoe darter).

The "rare" category sometimes is employed to connote localization or endangerment of species. However, we use it only in the sense of species or populations which exist at very low densities, whether relating or not to endangerment.

Critical Habitat—At the time an endangered and threatened species is listed by the USFWS, critical habitat may also be defined on the basis that such habitat is essential to the conservation of the species and thus may require special management or protection. Critical habitat designations extend protection to entire ecosystems; those in Virginia protect its most diverse ichthyofaunas.

In southwestern Virginia, critical habitat has been legally designated in the Tennessee drainage for the slender chub, turquoise shiner (formerly spotfin chub), and yellowfin madtom. The designated streams, varying by species, are the North Fork Holston River in Scott and Washington counties; the Clinch River and Copper Creek in Scott and Russell counties; and the Powell River in Lee County. Unfortunately, critical habitat was not designated for the Roanoke logperch.

APPLICATIONS TO VIRGINIA FISHES

Since the early 1970s a variable number of Virginia fishes have appeared on lists of waning species. National lists include Miller (1972), Anonymous (1977, 1989a, 1989b), Deacon et al. (1979), Williams (1981), Ono et al. (1983), Dodd et al. (1985), and Williams et al. (1989). Regional lists were prepared by Parker and Dixon (1980) and White (1982). Virginia lists are those of Anonymous (1974), Jenkins and Musick (1979), Goodin (1985), VDGIF (1987), VNHP (1989), and Burkhead and Jenkins (1991).

The state of Virginia (VDGIF 1987) conferred the protective status of endangered or threatened to species according to their legal federal status; five fishes are affected including the Roanoke logperch, which was federally listed in 1989. In the same regulation, the state designated five more fish species as endangered in Virginia. For most of these species the legal status differs from the status that we recommend for Virginia (Burkhead and Jenkins 1991; Table 4). The differences are being resolved by the VDGIF. Although the official Virginia designations have legal precedence over our recommendations, the following discussion reflects our recommendations.

In the Federal column of Table 4, the overall (total range) status of taxa is indicated in either one of two ways: on an unofficial basis (connoted below and in species accounts by "national"), or by the legal ("federal") status. We use the term national status when there is no corresponding federal listing.

Our list of species that are afflicted in Virginia is founded on current data and perspectives from the state and all adjacent ones (Bailey 1977; Starnes and Etnier 1980; Lee et al. 1984; Warren et al. 1986b; Braswell 1991; D. A. Cincotta, personal communication). The basis for status recommendations or designations is stated under *Remarks* in species accounts and, for some species, in greater detail by Burkhead and Jenkins (1991). We have attempted to consistently apply the same criteria to each species.

Some species seem to fall between two categories; even with much data at hand, it is often difficult to decide their status. Status decisions involve knowledge of the biology of species, their preferred and marginal habitats, recent distributional history, abundance trends, vulnerability to habitat changes, and present and projected human-induced perturbations. Predicting reactions of species to changes often can be done with confidence, but at other times this is an uncertain endeavor.

Some species which have been assigned status may appear to the reader to be unworthy of protective status owing to a goodly number of records along one or a few main rivers (e.g., river redhorse, Roanoke logperch). The larger rivers of Virginia tend to support the greatest diversity of fishes, a general trend in North America (Sheldon 1988). Species that are confined to main rivers may be eliminated by a single major accident such as spillage of a toxic substance. Hence we regard main rivers in Virginia to be critical threads of life; this weighs heavily when considering protection of particular riverine species.

Species that lack status but which nearly merit special concern in Virginia are so indicated by Jenkins and Musick (1979), Burkhead and Jenkins (1991), or in species accounts here (e.g., *Scartomyzon ariommus*, native brook trout, the undescribed Clinch and Bluestone sculpins, *Percina aurantiaca*, and species confined in Virginia to the Pee Dee drainage).

SPECIES STATUS AND CHARACTERISTICS

There are 45 freshwater fish species or subspecies with recommended or designated status in Virginia

(Table 4): endangered 8; threatened 10; special concern 18; undetermined 2; extirpated 6; and extinct 1.

The number of species listed per family is roughly proportional to the diversity of the family in the state; Percidae (darters) are represented by 18 taxa, Cyprinidae (minnows) by 12. Two of the taxa are undescribed. Thirty-eight of the fishes are small species. Only two, both of special concern, are gamefishes—Roanoke bass and sauger; the two sturgeons are foodfishes, although the shortnose sturgeon is prohibited from being taken.

Most of the 45 taxa occupy upland and montane areas; they prefer medium or large streams and rivers that typically are clear and little silted. In such rivers, the slender chub and Tippecanoe darter are further confined to areas of small gravel in swift current; the popeye shiner has similar but less rigid habitat affinities. Contrastingly, the blackbanded sunfish is restricted to calm, heavily vegetated, darkly stained, acidic waters in a very small segment of the Coastal Plain.

The numbers of recommended or designated species by drainage are: Potomac 5; Rappahannock 2; York 1; James 4; Chowan 5; Roanoke 8; Pee Dee 1; New 1; Tennessee 26; and Big Sandy 2. The numbers tend to parallel the southward and westward trend of increasing species richness and degrees of endemism or localization. Endemic and localized species are relatively more prone to endangerment. The low numbers in the Pee Dee and New drainages reflect small drainage size or original faunal depauperacy.

Eastern Virginia has many more people and major industries, hence potentially greater adverse impact on aquatic systems, than in the central and western portions. However, a few central or western towns or industries have had devastative long-term or long-distance effects on riverine faunas. Examples are the chemical degradation of the North Fork Holston River and the 1967 fish kill in the Clinch River (*Biogeography*). The low number of species listed for the Big Sandy drainage does not seem to fit the geographic trend. However, because the Big Sandy has been so modified by coal mining and other factors, and only recently has been well surveyed, many species probably were extirpated without record.

The Tennessee drainage has the most diverse ichthyofauna in North America; concordantly, numbers of species that we list for Virginia peak here—26 of the 45. These are distributed among the five systems as follows: South Fork Holston 7; Middle Fork Holston 5; North Fork Holston 10; Clinch 19; and Powell 11. Singling out the most critical tributary among these systems, Copper Creek supports resident populations of six species with protective status and has been visited or spawned in by at least three others that live in the Clinch River.

THREATS TO FISHES

There are many threats to fishes; problems facing individual species are treated in species accounts.

Habitat Alteration

Habitat change is the most frequent threat; it includes siltation, turbidity, pollution, channelization, impoundment (inundation of flowing water and thermal modification of tailwaters), water diversions, and flow reduction. All of these factors except possibly water diversion have negatively affected some Virginia fishes.

Siltation probably is the most widespread and insidious depressant of many species. The virgin Virginia forests served as a cushion and sponge for rainfall in the watersheds they covered; streams certainly were much less sedimented and more clear than today. Silt fills in and covers shelter and foraging spaces between and under stones that otherwise are used by small benthic and other fishes and by invertebrates that are important food sources. Siltation also reduces the quality of, or fully buries spawning sites. Siltation problems are serious in most of Virginia, and are acute in the Piedmont, the Big Sandy drainage, and many local areas. Turbidity—the clouding of water by suspended silt and other particles—places the many sight-feeding fishes at a disadvantage.

Chemical pollution problems emanate from the release of organic and inorganic wastes in and near waterways. It occurs widely in Virginia, typically in areas of high human population density (Map 11), but also in many agricultural and isolated industrial areas. Acidification of natural waters and entire watersheds only recently has been recognized as a major threat. Major declines in aquatic biota associated with reductions in pH from near neutral (7.0) to 5.1 have been detected in Virginia (P. E. Bugas, Jr., J. Kauffman, L. O. Mohn, and J. R. Webb, in litt.). Relatively unbuffered streams in the Blue Ridge are particularly sensitive to acidification.

We are unaware if channelization and existing impoundments have by themselves placed a species in jeopardy in Virginia, but the building of dams has contributed to downward trends of species and would have much more impact if existing project proposals are realized. Reduction of streamflow, resulting in increase of water temperature, has affected coolwater and coldwater fishes such as brook trout and some of the sculpins.

Restricted Natural Range

The smaller the range—on the basis of the number of streams or stream length occupied—the more vulnerable a species is to extirpation and extinction. We list several species which inhabit only three to five streams in the state, some only one. For species of such small range, all populations need protective consideration.

Overutilization

Many native brook trout populations were greatly diminished prior to legal protection, and sturgeons may have been overharvested in estuaries. A primary concern today is the collecting of localized species for fishing bait (e.g., the orangefin madtom in the upper Roanoke Valley) and overzealous taking of fishes for home aquaria.

Introduction

Introduction of exotic or other nonnative fishes can adversely affect native species by increased predation, competition for food and space, or loss of genetic purity or extirpation by hybridization. An apparent example of competition and hybridization concerns the demise of the Roanoke bass from the extreme upper Roanoke drainage owing to the introduction of the locally less-valued rock bass.

WHY PROTECT SPECIES?

There are many practical and philosophical reasons for protecting all kinds of organisms; see, for example, the excellent discussion by Ono et al. (1983). Some species are of direct benefit to us for recreation and food. All species are links in food webs, many of which include highly valued species. Many of our minnows, sunfishes, darters, and others are beautiful animals; others not adorned with brilliant colors are still attractive or have interesting habits. People visit museums and zoos because they provide pleasure and education. By the same token, we should protect species in their natural habitats, only partly because that is their source. Formerly unknown uses and products of organisms are continually being recognized to serve humankind; loss of a species may be more than just that.

Perhaps the most compelling reason for preserving

living species is to demonstrate the importance of restraint. We have a moral obligation to refrain from imperiling species even though they may lack apparent value or may interfere with a presumed quality of life. The significance of any species is much too complex to be measured only by its use to humans, especially in current economic terms. Ono et al. (1983) remarked that "Surely we are intelligent enough to solve our pressing space and resource requirements without large-scale habitat destruction. . . ." Habitat destruction is the greatest threat to our biota.

It is sometimes true that protection of species can cost money, especially when projects must be designed or altered to accommodate rare organisms. We simply believe that it is better to protect something rare than to destroy it.

SPECIAL CASES

In any study of the fishes of a state or other geographic area, certain special cases or categories of fishes are recognized. This section comprises our thoughts and findings on the fossil record, fishes that may occur in Virginia (and those that don't, but have been reported to), fishes that have been introduced, and hybrids.

FOSSIL FISHES

BY AMY REID MCCUNE AND ROBERT E. JENKINS

Fossils are continually being formed through geological processes of deposition, burial, and transformation of sediments into rock. Fish bones lying on a beach today or covered in silt or gravel in the bed of a lake or stream may eventually become fossilized, but in the end these fossils will represent only a tiny fragment of the fish fauna now living. This also has been true in the past; the fossil record of fishes provides only an inkling of the fishes that have lived during Earth's long history.

The fossils we do find give us a unique view of past organisms, revealing structure and function (sometimes bizarre) and clues about the ecology of these organisms. Fossils, especially relatively recent ones or even subfossil bones, can indicate prehistoric shifts in the distributions of living species and provide leads to the probable causes of these shifts.

Virginia has a wealth of "living fossil" species of freshwater fishes—five lampreys, two sturgeons, and one species each of paddlefish, gar, and bowfin; most of these groups are reviewed in Eldredge and Stanley (1984). However, the fossil record of fishes for the last 65 million years (the Cenozoic era) in Virginia is confined to the Late Pleistocene of 10,000–20,000 years ago. No earlier Cenozoic records are reported for Virginia in reviews of Cenozoic fishes (Uyeno and Miller 1963; Miller 1965; Smith 1981). Pleistocene fos-

sil fishes have been found in the Cowpasture River and North Fork Holston River valleys (Guilday et al. 1977; McDonald and Bartlett 1983). They are associated with far northern animals and plants that occupied Virginia just before the close of the last glacial period. Unfortunately, among the fish remains only the American eel seems clearly identified to species (e.g., see *Nocomis raneyi* account).

The paucity of fossil freshwater Cenozoic records in Virginia is related to the scarcity of exposed Cenozoic freshwater sediments. Such fossils are scarce because they have been modified by geological forces or buried deeply beneath more recent sediments. Moreover, most of the state has been an erosional rather than a depositional area. In much of its past, Virginia has been mountainous, a condition under which dead fish tend to be washed away and decay rather than be buried and preserved.

In contrast to the Cenozoic record of freshwater fishes in Virginia, the Mesozoic (66–245 million years ago) record is quite spectacular. Beginning some 210 million years ago, just before the African and North American continental plates began to move apart and form the Atlantic Ocean, great cracks developed in the Earth's crust along what is now the east coast of North America. These rift valleys—the Triassic and Jurassic basins (Map 7)—filled with fresh water and became large deep lakes, which endured intermittently for about 45 million years. The climate was tropical or subtropical. From the sediments that were deposited in these lakes, a number of very primitive ray-finned fishes and lobe-finned fishes have been recovered, along with tracks left by dinosaurs.

Lobe-finned (or fleshy-finned) fishes are kin to the fishes that gave rise to terrestrial vertebrates (Cladogram). The species found in the Mesozoic of Virginia (Culpeper and Richmond basins) is called *Diplurus longicaudatus* (Figure 1); although it lived in

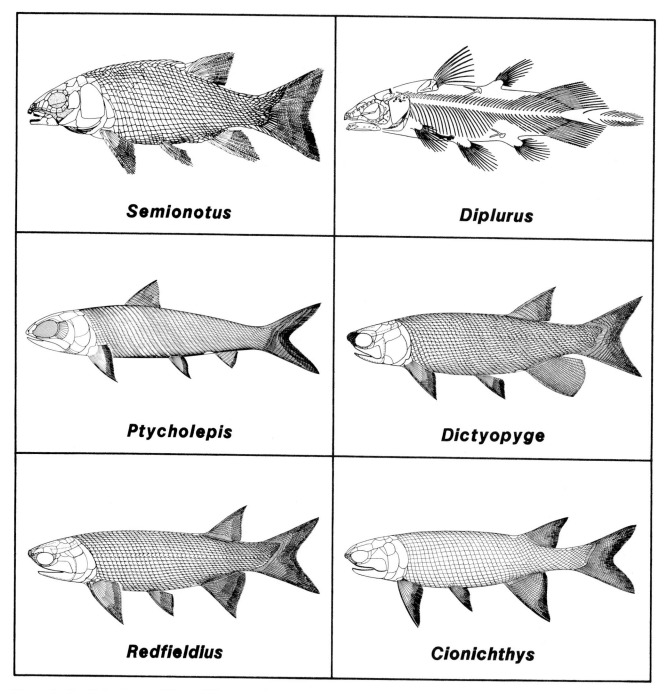

Semionotus

Diplurus

Ptycholepis

Dictyopyge

Redfieldius

Cionichthys

Figure 1 Fossil freshwater fishes of Virginia: *Semionotus*, a "holostean" fish related to freshwater gars (modified from McCune et al. 1984). *Diplurus*, a lobe-finned fish of the coelacanth group (drawing courtesy Department of Library Services, American Museum of Natural History). *Ptycholepis, Dictyopyge, Redfieldius,* and *Cionichthys*, "chondrostean" fishes related to sturgeons (*Ptycholepis* from Fieldiana: Geology, Volume 33, Number 12, Field Museum of Natural History; other three courtesy AMNH).

freshwater lakes, it is very similar to the famous coelacanth found in deep water off the coast of Madagascar. Four genera of chondrostean-like fishes—*Dictyopyge, Cionichthys, Ptycholepis,* and *Redfieldius*—found in these lacustrine deposits (Olsen et al. 1982)

are among the most primitive of the ray-finned fishes and are related to the sturgeon and paddlefish that now inhabit Virginia fresh waters.

Perhaps the most interesting fossil fishes in Virginia are the semionotids, allied to the gars and bowfin among living species. These fishes appear to have been quite diverse (Olsen et al. 1982; McCune et al. 1984), but most of the species have not yet been described. We do know that there are representatives of at least three species complexes, the *Semionotus elegans* group, the *S. micropterus* group, and the *S. tenuiceps* group. Assemblages of semionotid fishes are known also from related lake sediments in North Carolina, New Jersey, Connecticut, Massachusetts, and Nova Scotia (e.g., McCune 1987), but the Virginia fauna appears to be among the richest in species.

The Mesozoic fishes from Virginia usually are preserved as complete, articulated specimens (bones and scales still interconnected). The fossil scales of semionotids and the other fossil ray-finned fishes are shiny and black and have a structure very similar to human teeth—layers of bone and dentine covered with an enamel-like substance. The fine structure of these scales is so well preserved that it has been possible to determine the age of individual fishes by counting growth rings in their scales (Thomson and McCune 1984), just as ichthyologists age living fishes or botanists age trees.

Much remains to be done in the study of fossil fishes from Virginia. Many species on museum shelves remain undescribed, and surely there are undiscovered beds of fossils which could yield new and important information.

FISHES OF POSSIBLE OCCURRENCE IN VIRGINIA

We have identified 18 species that may now occur in Virginia or may appear in the future. The likely drainages where most of these fishes would occur are the Pee Dee, Tennessee, or Big Sandy. The probability of occurrence of some of the species is low. Most of them are included in their family key; otherwise, diagnostic characters or literary references for identification are given below. We also record three tropical "aquarium" species, including a piranha, that recently turned up in the wild in Virginia.

Unanticipated species may also surprise us. Species not treated below could be introduced to Virginia, have a relict population here, or extend well inland via an estuary. Seven taxa treated in species accounts as possibly or clearly extirpated from Virginia may be found again: shortnose sturgeon, thicklip shiner, trout-perch, blackside darter, ashy darter, a subspecies of the speckled darter, and the northern subspecies of the logperch.

Records of several species seemingly mapped (e.g., Lee et al. 1980) in Virginia near the Kentucky border

actually are in the upper Cumberland drainage, none of which courses Virginia. These records and, similarly, several for the Kentucky portion of the Big Sandy drainage are clearly plotted by Burr and Warren (1986).

Ichthyomyzon fossor (Reighard and Cummins), northern brook lamprey.—A few localized populations of this nonparasitic lamprey inhabit the Big Sandy drainage in Kentucky; the upper record is about 25 rkm below the Virginia line (Burr 1980; Rohde and Lanteigne-Courchene *in* Lee et al. 1980). Possibly extirpated in Virginia, this species may occur in some relatively unmodified streams. It is included in the key to lampreys.

Cyprinella lutrensis (Baird and Girard), red shiner.— Use of *Cyprinella* instead of *Notropis* as the genus for this minnow is discussed in the generic account. The red shiner often is called "redhorse minnow" or "rainbow dace" in aquarium literature and pet stores. This species ranges widely from the north-central United States into Mexico (Matthews *in* Lee et al. 1980).

Cyprinella lutrensis is a small but aggressive rapid colonizer adapted to harsh plains and some other biotopes (Matthews and Hill 1977; Farringer et al. 1979; Matthews 1986b). It has been expanding its range in Illinois, partly by mass hybridization and competitive displacement of *C. spiloptera* (Page and R. Smith 1970). It apparently was introduced in Alabama and hybridizes there with *C. callitaenia* (Wallace and Ramsey 1982). It is a major competitor of the endangered woundfin shiner *Plagopterus argentissimus* in whose southwestern range it was introduced (Anonymous 1989c). The red shiner is a potentially dangerous alien to some native Virginia fishes and to the many endemic species of *Cyprinella* farther south.

If not already in Virginia, the red shiner is expected to show up and gain a foothold, particularly in Piedmont waters. In Davidson County, North Carolina, it was found in High Rock Lake and Abbotts Creek of the Yadkin system, upper Pee Dee drainage during 1974 and 1975 (Moore et al. 1976; E. F. Menhinick, personal communication). In 1980 R. H. Moore (in litt.) informed us that *C. lutrensis* was under propagation as a bait fish in a quarry pond farther up the Yadkin. This may be the Windmill Fish Hatchery, Kernersville, Forsyth County, North Carolina, where the red shiner is raised as an aquarium fish, chiefly for export to Denmark (C. W. Paulk, in litt.). Kernersville is on the divide between the Yadkin system and Belews Creek of the Dan system, Roanoke drainage.

In 1976 an adult *C. lutrensis* (DPC 30407-04) was

taken in Belews Creek above Belews Lake in the Dan system, Roanoke drainage, North Carolina. Belews Creek is a tributary of the long upper loop that the Dan River makes into North Carolina from Virginia (Map 6). Three other apparently introduced fishes, the common bait minnow *Pimephales promelas* and the bullheads *Ameiurus brunneus* and *A. melas*, were also found in Belews Creek or Belews Lake, Rockingham and Stokes counties (Burkhead et al. 1980). In 1986 *C. lutrensis* was found in Rattlesnake Creek, Caswell County, North Carolina (D. A. Etnier, in litt.), a stream that enters the Dan in the lower loop. These records indicate either separate introductions or that the fish has spread from one point of introduction through the Virginia portion of the Dan between the two loops.

Cyprinella lutrensis could also become a bait bucket escapee within Virginia. It may also be introduced most anywhere as an unwanted aquarium pet; it is widely sold as a "tropical" fish in Virginia. It is included in the key to cyprinids.

Cyprinella nivea (Cope), whitefin shiner; *Cyprinella pyrrhomelas* (Cope), fieryblack shiner; and *Notropis scepticus* (Jordan and Gilbert), sandbar shiner.—These three native southeastern Atlantic-slope minnows populate Piedmont and Blue Ridge foothill tributaries of the Yadkin River, Pee Dee drainage, North Carolina (Harrell and Cloutman 1978; Lee et al. 1980) (Map 6). They are good candidates, *C. pyrrhomelas* the best, for residence or movement into the Virginia portion of one or more Ararat River tributaries on the extreme upper Piedmont. The Ararat system of the upper Yadkin is the only Virginia tributary of the Pee Dee.

The Ararat River (8–12 m wide at the state line) seems inhabitable by these species but its tributaries in Virginia may be too small. During 1972–1984 we made seven collections in Virginia from the Ararat River and its three largest tributaries, at sites within 3 rkm of the state line. R. E. Watson similarly sought these species in 1983 and 1985. Although the Ararat River is moderately silted, and *Cyprinella labrosa* appears to be extirpated from its Virginia portion, these three shiners seem to tolerate at least slight siltation. The three species are included in the key to cyprinids.

Macrhybopsis aestivalis (Girard), speckled chub.— This minnow recently was transferred from the genus *Hybopsis* to *Macrhybopsis* (Robins et al. 1991; Coburn and Cavender 1992). Mayden (1989) instead recognized the genus *Extrarius* for it. Native to the Mississippi basin and Gulf slope, *M. aestivalis* comprises a number of forms (Wallace *in* Lee at al. 1980), some of which are to be elevated as separate species (C. R.

Gilbert, in litt.). In much of its range it is restricted to large streams and big rivers; it occupies gravel shoals with substantial current. It may extend into Virginia in the Clinch and Powell rivers of the Tennessee drainage and in the Big Sandy drainage.

In the Tennessee drainage, *M. aestivalis* occurs in the lower Tennessee River and the lower main channel of several of the largest tributaries including the Holston and Clinch rivers. None of the Holston records are near Virginia; however, one specimen was taken in 1973 from the Clinch River at Frost Ford, Hancock County, 33.6 rkm below Virginia. In the Powell River, the largest Clinch tributary, *M. aestivalis* was taken at Rkm 105.1 during 1939–1973 and at Rkm 107.8 in 1975; the latter is 78.4 rkm below Virginia. The speckled chub is extremely rare in the Clinch–Powell system.

In the Big Sandy drainage, the speckled chub was found about 25 rkm below Virginia in Levisa Fork, Pike County, Kentucky, apparently during the late 1950s (Kirkwood 1957; Turner 1961; Burr and Warren 1986). It may no longer occupy the upper drainage because of habitat degradation.

Macrhybopsis aestivalis is included in the key to cyprinids. This small shinerlike fish is immediately recognizable by scattered bold round spots on the body and a barbel at the corners of the mouth.

Scardinius erythrophthalmus (Linnaeus), rudd.—This Eurasian minnow has become established in Indiana, New York, and Maine; is cultured as a bait fish in Arkansas; and is being disseminated further (Williams and Jennings 1988). It has the biotic potential to become established in much of the country including Virginia. Some states recently adopted regulations prohibiting its importation.

In 1989 N. M. Burkhead, who is studying the rudd for the U.S. Fish and Wildlife Service, was sent specimens that were found during 1988 by R. Southwick, VDGIF, in a bait bucket at Lake Meade, southeastern Virginia. The rudd were obtained nearby from a minnow farm in Windsor, where this species has been raised for the last 15 years. Many bait dealers in southeastern Virginia sell *S. erythrophthalmus*, often as "redfins" (R. Southwick, personal communication). This species may merit full membership in the Virginia ichthyofauna; it has reproduced, wintered, and summered at the minnow farm. However, currently it is unknown whether escapees have established a population; likely many are in stress when released.

The rudd is slab-sided, deep-bodied, and mostly silvery. Sometimes it reaches 400 mm TL but usually is much smaller. The rudd is quite similar to the golden shiner *Notemigonus crysoleucas*, with which it can hybridize (Burkhead and Williams 1991). The rudd can be recognized by tooth counts 3,5–5,3 vs. 0,5–5,0 in the golden shiner.

Carpiodes velifer (Rafinesque), highfin carpsucker.— This species has distant chances of reaching Virginia via the Clinch River. It was taken in the Clinch River impoundment Norris Reservoir during 1958–1959 and later (Carroll et al. 1963; R. D. Bishop, personal communication). However, it has not been recorded recently from Norris by TVA biologists (J. C. Feeman, personal communication), indicating its rarity or misidentifications as the quillback *Carpiodes cyprinus*.

The highfin carpsucker is distinguishable from the quillback by having a rounded, often nipplelike protuberance on the median of the lower lip.

Cycleptus elongatus (Lesueur), blue sucker.—This large divergent sucker is listed here on the very slight chance that it reaches Virginia and because of the interest that would attend its discovery. The basis for mention is an apparently small population in Norris Reservoir and the lower section of its two large tributaries, the Clinch and Powell rivers, Tennessee. Three blue suckers were among the 7,425 fishes commercially harvested from the reservoir during 1958–1959 (Carroll et al. 1963). The population, trapped by impoundment in 1936, is extant; a few *Cycleptus* have been taken in recent years in Norris and in the Clinch and Powell just above the reservoir (R. D. Bishop and J. C. Feeman, personal communications). The species would have to migrate 81 rkm from Norris to reach Virginia via the Clinch, and 102 rkm via the Powell. The Powell in Virginia is somewhat smaller than streams normally occupied by *Cycleptus*.

The blue sucker has a long-based dorsal fin (28–33 rays), similar among suckers only to that of buffalofishes (*Ictiobus*) and carpsuckers (*Carpiodes*). Contrasting with these genera, *Cycleptus* is elongate and low-backed.

Ictiobus bubalus (Rafinesque), smallmouth buffalo.—This large sucker is known in the Clinch system as far upstream as Norris Reservoir, where one was caught in 1958–1959 (Carroll et al. 1963). A few have been seen from Norris in recent years by biologists of the Tennessee Wildlife Resources Agency (R. D. Bishop, personal communication) but not by TVA biologists (J. C. Feeman, personal communication). We regard statements made by anglers and residents that "buffalo" occur in the Clinch River, Virginia, to be based on carpsuckers. The smallmouth buffalo could turn up in the Big Sandy of Virginia; of three records for the drainage in Kentucky, none recent, one is about 15 rkm below Virginia (Burr and Warren 1986).

Buffalofishes can be discerned from carpsuckers by their leaden shade (carpsuckers are silvery) and nearly semicircular subopercle (somewhat triangular in carpsuckers).

Noturus miurus Jordan, brindled madtom; *Noturus nocturnus* Jordan and Gilbert, freckled madtom; and *Noturus stigmosus* Taylor, northern madtom.—These three madtoms are known from Pike County, Kentucky, in the upper Big Sandy drainage (Turner 1961; Clay 1975; Burr and Warren 1986). Although Pike County is adjacent to Virginia, the chances of the madtoms occupying Virginia are low because they tend to avoid gradients and habitat degradation typical of the Virginia section. It is likely that two other madtoms, *N. eleutherus* and *N. flavus*, have been extirpated from the Virginia portion of the Big Sandy. Any madtom caught in the Big Sandy of Virginia would be a unique record; see Taylor (1969) and Page and Burr (1991) for species identification.

Noturus stanauli Etnier and Jenkins, pygmy madtom.—This is the most diminutive ictalurid catfish and one of the smallest North American freshwater fishes; the largest specimen known is 36 mm SL. It was discovered in 1971 and described from two gravel shoals of moderate and swift current in two tributaries of the Tennessee River in Tennessee (Etnier and Jenkins 1980). One site is in the Duck River, the other being 1,056 rkm upstream, in the Clinch River at Frost Ford, Rkm 291.6. In 1979, TVA biologists found two pygmy madtoms in the Clinch just above Brooks Island, 4.0 rkm above Frost Ford (Feeman 1987). *Noturus stanauli* usually is not taken at any of the three sites; when seen at Frost Ford, generally it is rare, much less numerous than *N. eleutherus*.

The gap between the Clinch and Duck sites is one of the widest known for an eastern North American freshwater fish. Because the Brooks Island site is 29.6 rkm below the Virginia line, collectors should be alert for *N. stanauli* in the Clinch River of Scott County. It probably occurred there but was extirpated in the 1967 fish kill. Recruitment from the unaffected downstream section probably would be slow. This species could also show up in the Powell River, Lee County, Virginia, which is physically, chemically, and biotically similar to the Clinch. *Noturus stanauli* was considered to be threatened in Tennessee (Starnes and Etnier 1980, as *Noturus* sp.); its candidacy for federal listing is under review.

The pygmy madtom can be recognized by its color pattern: upper two-thirds of head and body very dark, contrasting sharply with immaculate lower parts; a pale area on nape, at base of dorsal fin posteriorly, and at the base of adipose fin anteriorly and posteriorly; caudal peduncle with dark, somewhat wedge-shaped pattern laterally; pectoral and dorsal spines dusky or dark basally, remainder of these and other fins except caudal immaculate; caudal fin with basal, medial, and submarginal dark markings. Photographs of *N. stanauli* are in Etnier and Jenkins (1980) and Starnes and Etnier (1980).

Salmo letnica (Karaman), Ohrid trout.—This lake-spawning trout has been introduced to the United States from the Balkans. Some initial success occurred in Watauga Reservoir, on a branch of the South Fork Holston River in eastern Tennessee (Pistono 1975). Ohrid trout were liberated in the Tennessee portion of South Holston Reservoir in 1979, but we are unaware of any catches in the Virginia portion. Robins et al. (1980) reported that no reproductive success had been noted. Behnke (1962) commented on this species in its native land.

Ohrid trout are very similar to brown trout, differing by having asymmetrical red spots on the body (spots round in brown trout; Lawrence 1976) and averaging more gill rakers (19–25 *vs.* 17–22 in brown trout) and pyloric caeca (45–85 *vs.* 25–60) (Behnke 1968).

Elassoma zonatum Jordan, banded pygmy sunfish.—This bantam centrarchid-like fish, maximally 45 mm SL (Böhlke and Rohde *in* Lee et al. 1980), may be sequestered in heavily vegetated, calm darkwaters of the Chowan and Dismal Swamp drainages. It is widespread in the Coastal Plain of central and eastern United States. Its northern range limit on the Atlantic slope is the extreme lower Roanoke drainage of northeastern North Carolina: two sites in Martin County sampled in 1924 (Fowler 1945, as *E. evergladei*); rare in Hoggard Mill Creek, Bertie County during 1972–1975 (Pardue and Huish 1981). We do not believe that this species extends into Virginia via the Roanoke drainage as the gradient seems too high. We are skeptical of its occurrence in the lower Chowan and Dismal Swamp, because despite vigilance, it has not been collected during recent surveys.

The biology of *E. zonatum* is described by Walsh and Burr (1984). This species is distinguished from Virginia centrarchids by: lateral line absent on the body in *Elassoma vs.* lateral line present (incomplete in some adults of *Enneacanthus* and small young of other centrarchid genera); branchiostegal membranes broadly united *vs.* membranes separate. Many other differences exist. Although *Elassoma* often has been

considered a centrarchid, apparently it constitutes a separate family (Branson and Moore 1962; Moore 1968; Johnson 1984).

Ammocrypta pellucida (Putnam), eastern sand darter.—This darter occupies sandy raceways of streams and rivers of the Ohio and Great Lakes–St. Lawrence basins. It was collected within about 10 rkm below the Virginia line in the Levisa (1937) and Russell (1960) forks of the Big Sandy drainage, Kentucky (Clay 1975).

The eastern sand darter is similar to *A. clara* (see account). *Ammocrypta clara* has a well-developed opercular spine, and is less scaled, usually having three or fewer scale rows below the lateral line, as counted toward the anal fin origin (*vs.* usually four–seven scale rows) (Williams 1975).

Percina squamata (Gilbert and Swain), olive darter.—This species inhabits certain tributaries of the middle Cumberland and upper Tennessee river drainages. The population in the Watauga River of Tennessee indicates that the olive darter may have occupied the South Fork Holston River in Tennessee prior to impoundment, and that possibly it resides in the lower nonimpounded section of the South Fork in Virginia.

The olive darter closely resembles the sharpnose darter *P. oxyrhynchus* and is included in the key to percids. Other slight differences between these species are described by Thompson (1977).

Other Species

Some exotic aquarium fishes tend to outgrow their homes, and for this and other reasons they often are released into natural bodies of water. Occasionally (but actually relatively frequently, assuming a small number of releases) these fish survive and are captured. The following cases recently came to our attention.

In early fall 1987, two large (1.1, 1.4 kg) pacus (family Characidae, subfamily Serrasalminae) were landed in the Roanoke River, Roanoke; one of them was examined by Jenkins (Cochran 1987). Pacus are South American fishes closely related to and much resembling piranhas, but they are vegetarians; the Roanoke specimens were hooked on doughballs. A pacu was also caught in the Virginia Beach area, southeastern Virginia, during spring 1987, in fresh water of about 16°C (R. Southwick, personal communication).

A true piranha *Pygocentrus* sp. and an oscar *Astronotus ocellatus* were taken in a Virginia Beach area pond during 1987 (R. Southwick, personal communication). The oscar is somewhat similar to certain centrarchid basses but is a member of the family Cichlidae, several species of which have been introduced from the tropics into the United States (Courtenay and Stauffer 1984). Most or all of these species are not expected to survive cold winters in Virginia.

FISHES ERRONEOUSLY REPORTED IN VIRGINIA

Eleven species have been incorrectly reported or indicated by museum specimens to inhabit Virginia. Other synonymized or taxonomically reinterpreted forms that are no longer recognized, or that probably never lived in Virginia, are treated in pertinent species accounts.

Ichthyomyzon castaneus Girard, chestnut lamprey.— The report from the Clinch River (Wollitz 1965) is considered to be based on Ohio lamprey *I. bdellium* (see species account).

Clinostomus elongatus (Kirtland), redside dace.— The listing of this northerly species by Harrison and Martin (1960) clearly represents a lapse from intent to record the rosyside dace *C. funduloides*, which is widespread in Virginia but not listed by those authors.

Opsopoeodus emiliae Hay, pugnose shiner.—This species, until recently called *Notropis emiliae*, occurs west and south of, but not near Virginia. Harrison and Martin (1960) compiled it for Virginia from Ross (1959c), who only expected it to inhabit the New–Kanawha drainage (where it remains unknown [Gilbert and Bailey 1972]), and from reports to the VDGIF from two collectors whose materials we examined and found to lack *O. emiliae*.

Lythrurus umbratilus (Girard), redfin shiner.—The inclusion in the Virginia fauna of this Mississippi basin species, as *Notropis umbratilus*, by Harrison and Martin (1960) is credited to Ross (1959c), but Ross reported it from only the Kanawha drainage, West Virginia.

Phoxinus erythrogaster (Rafinesque), southern redbelly dace.—A series of this widespread cyprinid is labeled Indian Creek at Walnut Hill, Lee County, Virginia; it was taken in 1953 by F. G. Thompson (ANSP 83178). Indian Creek is a tributary of the Powell River. Evidence that the collection is not from the Virginia or Tennessee portions of the Powell system accrues from the would-be uniqueness of the record of the dace, and also the record each of *Pimephales promelas* and *Etheostoma kennicotti*, which are cataloged from the same collection (see *E. kennicotti*, below). These three species are not documented to occur anywhere in the Powell; Masnik (1974) and we unsuccessfully searched Indian Creek for them.

The only species of *Phoxinus* known in the Clinch–Powell system above the Emory River, Tennessee, is *P. tennesseensis*; it and *P. erythrogaster* appear to replace each other (Starnes and Jenkins 1988). We suspect that the *P. erythrogaster* specimens were taken elsewhere in one of the several collections (ANSP) by Thompson during the 1950s, and that the specimens or locality data were transposed.

Osmerus mordax (Mitchill), rainbow smelt.—This anadromous–freshwater species formerly extended south on the Atlantic slope in limited degree from a northeastern center of abundance to the lower Delaware River (Bigelow and Schroeder 1964). These authors and Kendall (1927), McAllister (1963), and Musick (1972) found no evidence for repeated early statements that smelt range south to Virginia. Bigelow and Schroeder (1964) considered those statements as "Based seemingly on Jordan and Gilbert . . . [1883]." Virginia was included in the range even in one of Jordan's earliest works (1876).

Jordan's initial record may derive from Captain John Smith of the Jamestown Colony (on the James River), who noted in 1622 that "of Smelts there is such abundance" (Kendall 1927). However, by that year Smith also had explored coastal New England, where he saw smelt (Arber and Bradley 1910). Jordan's (1876) record may stem instead from a prepublication copy of Uhler and Lugger (1876), who in one passage seemingly were believed by Goode (1884) to have referred to the minnow *Hybognathus regius* as a smelt. Further, silversides (Atherinidae) were called sand smelts in part of Jordan's and Goode's time.

Separate from the above considerations, the rainbow smelt was introduced but did not become established in Virginia fresh waters.

Lepomis humilis (Girard), orangespotted sunfish.— The report (Sledd and Shuber 1981) from the York drainage of this small central United States sunfish is almost certainly based on the pumpkinseed *Lepomis gibbosus*, which also has yellow to orange markings on the body. There is no voucher specimen.

Etheostoma kennicotti (Putnam), stripetail darter.—A series (ANSP 83177) of this lower Ohio basin species, indicated to be from Indian Creek, a Powell River tributary, is refuted as a valid Virginia record for most of the reasons applied above to *Phoxinus erythrogaster*. The collector sampled near documented populations of *E. kennicotti* in the Cumberland drainage and may have secured the species there instead.

If valid, the uppermost record of *E. kennicotti* in the Tennessee drainage, from Panther Creek, Tennessee (Page and Smith 1976; Page and Schemske 1978), would indicate that this species may reach Virginia. However, the record is based on unretained specimens (D. A. Etnier, in litt.). We found only the very similar fantail darter *E. flabellare* in Panther Creek; these species apparently do not occur together in the upper Tennessee drainage, where *E. flabellare* is widespread.

Three records of *E. kennicotti* plotted by Lee et al. (1980) seem to be located in the upper Powell of Virginia, but they are from the upper Cumberland drainage, Kentucky. Collection FMNH 6843, supposedly from Cumberland Cap, Kentucky, in the Powell very near Virginia, includes *E. kennicotti* and two forms of *E. flabellare*, rendering the collection an apparent collage from at least two sites, none of which may be in the Powell. The listing of *E. kennicotti* at five Powell River sites in Tennessee and Virginia (TVA 1970) probably is based entirely on *E. flabellare*. The only extant specimens are from one of the Virginia sites; they are *E. flabellare*, which occurs widely in the Powell.

Etheostoma maculatum Kirtland, spotted darter.—The report from the New River drainage (Ross and Perkins 1959: VPI 449, 536) apparently represents a slip from an intent to list *Percina maculata*. At that time *P. maculata* was considered to occupy the New drainage, but the population has since been described as *P. gymnocephala*. Collection VPI 499 includes *P. gymnocephala* but not *E. maculatum*. Specimens of neither species were located for VPI 536; the original list has only *P. maculata*. Ross (1959c) excluded *E. maculatum* from the New drainage fauna. *Etheostoma maculatum* may have occupied the Big Sandy drainage, but if so, it has been extirpated. Reports of this species from the Tennessee drainage are probably the wounded darter *E. vulneratum*.

Etheostoma spectabile (Agassiz), orangethroat darter.—This central United States species was reported (Distler 1968) from a collection made in the North Fork Holston River by H. R. Becker in 1928, but the locality data are obviously in error. This is supported by correspondence (UMMZ accession file) from C. L. Hubbs to Becker indicating that there may have been a mix-up in locality labels for Becker's collections.

This, and the confinement of *E. spectabile* in the Tennessee drainage to the lower section, refute its occurrence in Virginia.

Percina squamata (Gilbert and Swain), olive darter.—This species of the Tennessee and Cumberland drainages was reported as common in the Clinch River by Wollitz (1965), who indicated that identifications of some species were tentative. No Virginia specimen is extant. The olive darter is essentially a Blue Ridge and Appalachian Plateau species, and likely would not have been common in the upper Clinch system if present there. It may reside in the South Fork Holston River of Virginia.

INTRODUCED FISHES

Virginia's inland waters have received more than 28 fish species that are unknown to have originally occurred here. Some of the species have been long gone from the state; others are irrevocably established. Introduced species are categorized as either exotic or transplanted. Exotics emanate from a foreign land. Transplanted species are those moved within their source country or continent to places where they are nonnative, such as a different region, state, drainage, or ecosystem (Lachner et al. 1970; Courtenay and Stauffer 1984). Another system of terminology for invasive species is given by Laurenson and Hocutt (1986).

Modes of introduction and the composition of nonindigenous faunas in Virginia are discussed in *Biogeography*. Native and introduced ranges of exotic and transplanted fishes in North America are mapped in Lee et al. (1980). Characteristics and impacts of introduced species are reviewed by Courtenay and Taylor (1984), Courtenay et al. (1984), Laurenson and Hocutt (1986), and Moyle (1986). An analysis of exotic fishes on a worldwide basis was edited by Courtenay and Stauffer (1984).

Introductions are made intentionally or accidentally but the results may be the same—beneficial, adverse, or mixed; introductions tend to be controversial. Purposes and unanticipated direct or indirect benefits of introductions include enhancement of foodfisheries, sporting opportunities, bait supply, gamefish forage, and biological control; they extend to aesthetic or ornamental reasons. Adverse effects include habitat modification, displacement of native and valuable introduced species, and genetic alteration of native species by hybridization.

Documented introductions to Virginia began in the early 1800s; most first-time stockings of game or foodfishes fell in two periods. Those of 1875–1890 were made chiefly by the U.S. Fish Commission (USFC). Many of these were made with little knowledge of the ecology of introduced fishes or regard for native species, and often were unsuccessful.

Introductions of gamefishes during 1953–1972, including second attempts to establish some species, were made mainly by the Virginia Department of Game and Inland Fisheries. These recent liberations generally were planned to support specific management objectives. Notable success often resulted when the species found a "vacant niche" (e.g., the large predatory muskellunge and striped bass).

Some species such as certain trouts, sunfishes, and basses have a long history of release by federal and state agencies and the private sector. Unrecorded ("cryptic") releases, particularly by anglers, of game, bait, and forage fishes have greatly confounded biogeographic analyses.

Thirteen species currently living in the wild in Virginia are either clearly or probably introduced to the state (symbols I and IP, respectively, in Table 2). Of the 13, 9 are established; that is, they have at least one wild, self-sustaining population: threadfin shad, common carp, goldfish, fathead minnow, snail bullhead, brown trout, rainbow trout, white crappie, and redear sunfish. Three species are maintained essentially or entirely by repeated stocking: northern pike, muskellunge, and grass carp. The reproductive status of the other—blue catfish—is uncertain.

Five other species are considered to be questionably native to Virginia (NI in Table 2); all are established: bullhead minnow, bluntnose minnow, black bullhead, white bass, and largemouth bass. These and the 13 above species are treated by full species accounts in this book.

Introductions of 10 other species (reviewed below) to Virginia were unsuccessful. Another species treated, silver carp, is slated for introduction. Six of the 11 belong to the trout family Salmonidae; three are minnows; a sucker and a smelt round out the list. These stockings comprise transplantation of seven native North American fishes, introduction of three Eurasian species, and the release of the Atlantic salmon, which is indigenous to both continents. Recent translocations of other exotic species are noted in *Fishes of Possible Occurrence*.

Hypophthalmichthys molitrix (Valenciennes), silver carp.—As of early 1986, by permission of the VDGIF, the Craig County–New Castle Public Service Authority intended to soon use this large Asian minnow to consume algae in a wastewater treatment pond. The effluent is to be released into Craig Creek of the upper James drainage. Retention of the fish in the pond is to

be attempted (Anonymous 1986). The bighead carp *Hypophthalmichthys nobilis* (Richardson) may also become introduced in Virginia.

Leuciscus idus (Linnaeus), ide.—This medium-sized, sometimes gold-colored Eurasian minnow was imported in 1877 by the USFC. It is popular with European anglers and used as bait in Tennessee (Courtenay et al. 1984). Almost all ide held in the Washington, D.C., Fish Ponds in 1889 escaped during a flood, and the species was present in the Potomac River for some time after. Ide were consigned to applicants in Virginia during 1892–1894 (USFC 1894, 1896a), the last we know of their presence in Virginia. Courtenay et al. (1984) were unaware of an established population in the United States, but noted that the species was still being distributed.

Tinca tinca (Linnaeus), tench.—This large Eurasian minnow used for food and sport was first imported to North America in 1877 from Germany by the USFC. Local populations are established in some areas, mostly in the western United States (Courtenay et al. 1984). In 1877, 450 tench were shipped from the USFC Fish Ponds, Washington, D.C., to the Wytheville hatchery; some of these were liberated in nearby South Fork Reed Creek (USFC 1889). Tates Run near Wytheville received tench in 1895. The lower Appomattox River was stocked in 1892 and unspecified applicants were given *Tinca* during 1894–1895 (USFC 1894, 1896a, 1896b). Almost all tench escaped the Fish Ponds in 1889 owing to flooding by the Potomac River (USFC 1893). Apparently the species has had no notable success in Virginia. Most introductions to Maryland were unsuccessful, although it may occur in isolated Piedmont areas (Lee et al. 1984).

Ictiobus cyprinellus (Valenciennes), bigmouth buffalo.—This large sucker of the Mississippi basin, a commercial foodfish in some regions, was listed as a possible escapee from the VDGIF hatchery at Stevensville in the York drainage (Corning 1967b). The bigmouth buffalo is not known to have been held there in recent years.

Osmerus mordax (Mitchill), rainbow smelt.—The small tasty, troutlike rainbow smelt is abundant in the Great Lakes region and eastward through the Maritime Provinces of Canada. In 1891, 400,000 smelt were stocked in the Potomac River at Washington, D.C. (USFC 1893). Also, a cryptic note was found in the VPI catalog indicating that 150 adults were placed in Occoquan Reservoir of the lower Potomac drainage during 1957, presumably by the VDGIF. The only other mention of smelt in Virginia possibly traces to the misinterpretation of a statement by Capt. John Smith (see *Fishes Erroneously Reported*).

Oncorhynchus clarki (Richardson), cutthroat trout.— Use of the generic name *Oncorhynchus* for this western trout is explained under that genus in the Salmonidae section. During 1890–1894, eggs and adults of cutthroat trout were shipped from Leadville, Colorado, to the Wytheville hatchery (USFC 1893–1896a). Limited propagation was achieved and some 2,000 fry escaped the hatchery, but cutthroat trout are unknown to have become established in a Virginia stream.

Oncorhynchus kisutch (Walbaum), coho salmon.— This Pacific salmon was a late entrant to Virginia. Eggs acquired from Oregon by the VDGIF in late 1968 were hatched at the Marion hatchery. In November 1969 the fish were 200–260 mm in length and were liberated in the lower portion of one tributary each of Philpott Reservoir (2,400 fish) and Smith Mountain Lake (5,000). The intent to create a put-and-take fishery had modest success; the coho salmon fed largely on shad. The first angling return was a 432-mm fish in July 1970. Several other catches were announced in newspapers, most of them in 1970–1971 from the more salmonid-suited Philpott Reservoir. The largest recorded was a 4-kg (8-pound, 12-ounce) fish taken in December 1971. The last of which we have a record, 3.1 kg, was landed in late 1972 or January 1973; it may have been a chinook salmon.

Oncorhynchus tshawytscha (Walbaum), chinook salmon.—As an apparently collaborative venture of the USFC and the former Virginia Fish Commission (VFC), this largest of the Pacific salmons was stocked, sometimes in large numbers, during 1875–1880 under the names California salmon and Quinnat salmon. It was liberated in several tributaries and main rivers from the forks of the Holston in the mountains to the middle Piedmont of the Potomac drainage, and in high-elevation Mountain Lake and a reservoir near the Fall Line in Richmond (VFC 1877a–1882; USFC 1878, 1884a).

A 2-kg chinook salmon, thought to have been stocked at Lynchburg two years earlier, was caught in the James River at Richmond during 1877. Several of about 250 mm length were taken at about the same time in the lower James estuary. Lacking authenticated return of an adult, the VFC (1882) regarded the program a failure. The USFC (1900) made two stockings in 1899.

In spring 1972 approximately 9,000 Washington State chinook salmon 55–80 mm in length were stocked in four tributaries of Philpott Reservoir. No recaptures are known, although some of the last "coho" salmon caught in Philpott may have been chinook salmon.

Salmo salar Linnaeus, Atlantic salmon.—Anadromous and landlocked varieties of this noble game and foodfish have a brief but geographically extensive stocking history in Virginia that is essentially the same as for chinook salmon (VFC 1877a–1882; USFC 1879, 1884a–1893, 1900). No Atlantic salmon seem to have been recaptured.

Salvelinus namaycush (Walbaum), lake trout.—This large salmonid, a true char, is restricted to clear, deep, cold, rocky lakes as in the Great Lakes and Finger Lakes regions, the southern portion of its range. During 1885–1889, eggs from Michigan were reared at the Wytheville hatchery; the fish were stocked in nearby Reed Creek and five unspecified bodies of water (USFC 1885, 1889). In 1889, 575 lake trout were placed in "Salt Ponds, Giles County" (USFC 1892); we believe Salt Ponds to be Mountain Lake on Salt Pond Mountain. This small, natural, high-elevation (1,180 m) lake has rocky shores and well-oxygenated cold water in its clear depths during summer (Roth and Neff 1964), but despite the apparently favorable habitat, the trout vanished.

Lake trout had a brief stay in the two-story fishery of Philpott Reservoir. In December 1963, 10,000 fish of about 100 mm in length were stocked by the VDGIF. We saw a photograph of two angler-caught lake trout—0.9 kg and 2.4 kg (5 pounds, 6 ounces)— landed in mid-1966.

Thymallus arcticus (Pallas), Arctic grayling.—Twelve adults of this salmonid were shipped out of state from the Wytheville hatchery in 1889 (USFC 1892). Forty specimens were received in excellent condition at Wytheville in 1894 (USFC 1896a). The next entry of grayling to Virginia of which we are aware occurred in 1972, when 10,000 fertilized eggs were flown from Alaska to Utah, then to the VDGIF hatchery at Marion. The eggs were obtained in a trade with Utah for Virginia-produced striped bass. The hatched grayling were stocked in the upper 4.5 rkm of the Smith River below Philpott Dam. The upper reach of this tailwater is thermally and in other ways suited for grayling; it rarely exceeds 15°C. The grayling were not seen thereafter; some probably served as forage for the strong population of brown trout.

HYBRIDIZATION

In a general sense, the term hybridization means crossbreeding. When applied to intermating of individuals of the same species, it is labeled intraspecific hybridization. More frequently in ichthyology, the substantial interbreeding between subspecies or races of the same species is classed as intergradation. We restrict our discussion of hybridization to the interbreeding between different species—interspecific hybridization. If the species are in the same genus, we have intrageneric hybridization; if they are in different genera, then it is termed intergeneric.

Hybrids differ from their parents in biochemical makeup and usually appearance. The differences allow recognition of hybrids that were produced in nature and identification of their parentage. Interspecific crossings may result in gamete wastage because the zygotes often die before hatching or birth, and surviving hybrids often are less fit than are the parental species. However, by backcrossing, hybrids may transmit new alleles to the gene pool of the parental species.

In a review of hybridization in fishes, Hubbs (1955) noted that many early workers believed that species almost never crossbred. Hence early in ichthyological history, but rarely today, hybrids have been recognized as undescribed species. Two hybrids described as species from Virginia (*in* Jordan 1889a), but not now recognized as species, are *Notropis kanawha* (a cross between *Notropis rubellus* and *N. volucellus*) and *N. macdonaldi* (*Luxilus cornutus* × *N. rubellus*). The large number of hybrids now known and the extensive literature on hybridization are testimony to the lability and sometimes proclivity of many species to interbreed in nature.

Characteristics of Hybrids

Hybrids may exhibit a wide range of forms depending on the type of cross. First filial generation (F_1) hybrids are progeny of the two parental species; F_2 hybrids result from interbreeding of F_1 individuals. Backcrosses stem from mating of hybrids with parental stock. Each crossing may result in increased variability due to the production of new genetic combinations, particularly in backcrosses where parents other than those that produced the F_1 are involved.

All F_1 hybrids were long thought to be intermediate or nearly so in characteristics between the parents, a concept stemming much from extensive research by Carl L. Hubbs and colleagues (Hubbs 1955). Recent studies, however, have frequently found that hybrids closely resemble one parent or are extreme in some character expressions (e.g., Hubbs 1956; Ross and Cavender 1981; Leary et al. 1985).

Hybrids often exhibit other differences from parental stocks. They may have an unbalanced sex ratio and one or both sexes may exhibit low fertility or sterility. They may be selected against in other ways too, by being less adapted to the habitat favored by the parents. However, some hybrids are noted for superior vigor (heterosis), as shown by their adaptability to a wider range of habitats, or in higher activity and growth rates, than the parents. Such vitality may serve as a basis for programs of artificial hybridization of game and foodfishes. Hatchery culture of the tiger muskellunge *Esox lucius* × *E. masquinongy* is an example.

Identification of Hybrids

Most hybrids are first recognized by differences in morphology and color from known species. The parental species are identified at least tentatively by expressions in the suspected hybrid of intermediacy or by a mixture of parental traits. The choices of potential parental species can be narrowed by knowing which species inhabit the area of the hybrid collection, and coupled with knowledge of breeding habits, by determining which are likely to have interbred. Unfortunately, information gaps and circularity of reasoning impose limits on these intuitive methods. The methods are discussed, along with mathematical approaches to hybrid identification, by Smith (1973) and Neff and Smith (1979). Biochemical and phylogenetic analyses are now making headway in hybridization problems, particularly with cryptic species (e.g., Buth 1984; Funk and Brooks 1990). Experimental crossing as a tool in identifying hybrids is treated by Ross and Cavender (1981).

Any literature survey of hybrids should employ the worldwide compilations by Schwartz (1972, 1981a), but with caution and reference to original literature; certain crosses are erroneously included. In the original papers, some crosses are explicitly identified as only hypothetical; their original presentation in hybrid format (species × species) is the apparent basis for their inclusion by Schwartz. For example, compare Schwartz (1981a) with Ross and Cavender (1977 [*Notropis cornutus* × *Rhinichthys atratulus*]) and with McAllister and Coad (1978 [a multitude of unknown crosses]).

The Process of Hybridization

The occurrence and frequency of hybridization is related to environmental settings and reproductive

Table 5 Natural hybrids whose two parental species occur in Virginia. Families are listed in phylogenetic sequence; genera and species are alphabetic. + = known; - = not known; * = first reported herein.

Family, hybrid	Known from:	
	Virginia	Elsewhere
Clupeidae		
Dorosoma cepedianum × *Dorosoma petenense*	-	+
Esocidae		
Esox americanus × *Esox lucius*	-	+
Esox americanus × *Esox niger*	+	+
Esox lucius × *Esox masquinongy*	-	+
Esox lucius × *Esox niger*	-	+
Cyprinidae		
Campostoma anomalum × *Luxilus cornutus*	-	+
Campostoma anomalum × *Nocomis leptocephalus*	+	-
Campostoma anomalum × *Nocomis micropogon*	-	+
Campostoma anomalum × *Nocomis platyrhynchus*	-	+
Campostoma anomalum × *Rhinichthys cataractae*	-	+
Campostoma anomalum × *Semotilus atromaculatus*	-	+
Carassius auratus × *Cyprinus carpio*	-	+
Clinostomus funduloides × *Luxilus cornutus*	+	-
Clinostomus funduloides × *Nocomis leptocephalus*	+	+
Clinostomus funduloides × *Nocomis micropogon*	+	-
Clinostomus funduloides × *Notropis rubellus*	-	+
Clinostomus funduloides × *Phoxinus oreas*	+	-
Clinostomus funduloides × *Semotilus atromaculatus*	+*	-
Clinostomus funduloides × *Semotilus corporalis*	+*	-
Cyprinella analostana × *Cyprinella spiloptera*	-	+
Cyprinella galactura × *Cyprinella monacha*	-	+
Cyprinella galactura × *Cyprinella spiloptera*	+	+
Exoglossum laurae × *Exoglossum maxillingua*	+	
Luxilus albeolus × *Lythrurus ardens*	-	+
Luxilus albeolus × *Nocomis leptocephalus*	+	-
Luxilus albeolus × *Nocomis platyrhynchus*	-	+*
Luxilus albeolus × *Notropis rubellus*	+	-
Luxilus albeolus × *Notropis rubricroceus*	+*	-
Luxilus cerasinus × *Luxilus cornutus*	+	
Luxilus cerasinus × *Lythrurus ardens*	+*	+
Luxilus cerasinus × *Nocomis leptocephalus*	+*	+
Luxilus cerasinus × *Phoxinus oreas*	+	-
Luxilus chrysocephalus × *Luxilus coccogenis*	+*	-
Luxilus chrysocephalus × *Luxilus cornutus*	-	+
Luxilus chrysocephalus × *Nocomis micropogon*	-	+
Luxilus chrysocephalus × *Nocomis platyrhynchus*	-	+
Luxilus chrysocephalus × *Notropis leuciodus*	+	-
Luxilus chrysocephalus × *Notropis photogenis*	-	+
Luxilus chrysocephalus × *Notropis rubellus*	-	+
Luxilus coccogenis × *Nocomis leptocephalus*	-	+
Luxilus cornutus × *Lythrurus ardens*	+*	-
Luxilus cornutus × *Nocomis leptocephalus*	+	-
Luxilus cornutus × *Nocomis micropogon*	-	+
Luxilus cornutus × *Notropis rubellus*	+	+
Luxilus cornutus × *Phoxinus oreas*	+	-
Luxilus cornutus × *Rhinichthys cataractae*	-	+
Luxilus cornutus × *Semotilus atromaculatus*	-	+
Luxilus cornutus × *Semotilus corporalis*	-	+
Nocomis leptocephalus × *Nocomis micropogon*	+	+
Nocomis leptocephalus × *Nocomis platyrhynchus*	+	-
Nocomis leptocephalus × *Nocomis raneyi*	+	-
Nocomis leptocephalus × *Phoxinus oreas*	+*	-
Nocomis micropogon × *Nocomis raneyi*	+	-
Nocomis micropogon × *Rhinichthys cataractae*	-	+
Nocomis platyrhynchus × *Rhinichthys cataractae*	-	+
Notropis atherinoides × *Notropis volucellus*	-	+
Notropis leuciodus × *Notropis rubricroceus*	+*	-
Notropis rubellus × *Notropis rubricroceus*	+*	-
Notropis rubellus × *Notropis volucellus*	+	+
Pimephales notatus × *Pimephales promelas*	-	+
Pimephales notatus × *Pimephales vigilax*	-	+
Rhinichthys cataractae × *Semotilus atromaculatus*	-	+

Table 5   Continued

Family, hybrid	Known from:	
	Virginia	Elsewhere
Catostomidae		
Erimyzon oblongus × Erimyzon sucetta	-	+
Hypentelium nigricans × Hypentelium roanokense	+*	-
Moxostoma erythrurum × Moxostoma macrolepidotum	+*	-
Ictaluridae		
Ameiurus melas × Ameiurus nebulosus	-	+
Salmonidae		
Salmo trutta × Salvelinus fontinalis	+	+
Cyprinodontidae		
Fundulus diaphanus × Fundulus heteroclitus	-	+
Cottidae		
Cottus baileyi × Cottus carolinae	+*	-
Cottus bairdi × Cottus cognatus	-	+
Moronidae		
Morone americana × Morone chrysops	-	+
Morone chrysops × Morone saxatilis	+	+
Centrarchidae		
Ambloplites cavifrons × Ambloplites rupestris	+	-
Centrarchus macropterus × Pomoxis annularis	-	+
Enneacanthus gloriosus × Enneacanthus obesus	?	+
Lepomis auritus × Lepomis cyanellus	-	+
Lepomis auritus × Lepomis gibbosus	+	+
Lepomis auritus × Lepomis macrochirus	+	+
Lepomis auritus × Lepomis microlophus	-	+
Lepomis cyanellus × Lepomis gibbosus	-	+
Lepomis cyanellus × Lepomis gulosus	-	+
Lepomis cyanellus × Lepomis macrochirus	+	+
Lepomis cyanellus × Lepomis megalotis	-	+
Lepomis cyanellus × Lepomis microlophus	-	+
Lepomis gibbosus × Lepomis gulosus	-	+
Lepomis gibbosus × Lepomis macrochirus	+	+
Lepomis gibbosus × Lepomis megalotis	-	+
Lepomis gulosus × Lepomis macrochirus	-	+
Lepomis gulosus × Lepomis microlophus	-	+
Lepomis macrochirus × Lepomis megalotis	-	+
Lepomis macrochirus × Lepomis microlophus	-	+
Micropterus dolomieu × Micropterus punctulatus	-	+
Micropterus dolomieu × Micropterus salmoides	-	+
Pomoxis annularis × Pomoxis nigromaculatus	-	+
Percidae		
Etheostoma caeruleum × Etheostoma zonale	-	+
Etheostoma camurum × Etheostoma tippecanoe	-	+
Etheostoma chlorobranchium × Etheostoma rufilineatum	-	+
Etheostoma nigrum × Etheostoma olmstedi	+	+
Percina caprodes × Percina maculata	-	+
Percina caprodes × Percina sciera	-	+
Percina notogramma × Percina peltata	+	-
Percina oxyrhynchus × Percina roanoka	+	-
Stizostedion canadense × Stizostedion vitreum	-	+

ways of the parental species (Hubbs 1955). Hybridization often is associated with habitat disturbances such as ditching, channelization, and impoundment, whereby two or more species may be forced into atypically close proximity during breeding, thus increasing the chances of mismating. Turbidity may reduce the ability of a fish to visually discriminate other species from conspecific mates. Hybridization tends to occur also when one species is relatively rare; a proper mate may be difficult to locate. Introduced species often hybridize with native fishes, not infrequently to the detriment of the native population.

Cross-fertilization may occur in two ways. (1) In mismating, a female may choose a male of the wrong species, with or without being courted. Males may err too, by courting the wrong female. Flurries of spawning activity likely blur species differences (e.g., nuptial color and behavior) that otherwise serve for species recognition. Mistakes of identity may occur relatively commonly between species of quite similar color and profile (e.g., the two *Exoglossum* species). (2) Accidental fertilization can occur when two species, particularly those aggregated on a nest, spawn in the same current path, the eggs of one being carried a short distance downstream and fertilized by sperm of the other, and vice versa.

Frequencies of hybridization vary greatly. Most hybrids are extremely rare, or they rarely live long enough to reach sufficient size for capture and identification by the average collector. Perhaps the most common hybrid in Virginia is *Nocomis leptocephalus* × *N. micropogon*, whose parents (and possible backcrosses) mismate extensively in zones of range overlap (Lachner and Jenkins 1971a). The two species are assigned to different species groups, but their hybridization indicates a close affinity, and to the uninitiated that perhaps they are conspecific. However, they maintain separate gene pools (species identities)—*N. leptocephalus* in upstream sections and *N. micropogon* well below—and are regarded as biological species.

Virginia Hybrids

A long list of naturally produced hybrids has been developed for Virginia; 13 of them and 1 from West Virginia are first reported here (Table 5). The parental species of each cross are listed alphabetically. In other studies, when the sexes of the parents are known, the male parental species generally is given first. The basis for the identifications is not provided in this book other than by citing literature or deposition of specimens; these are noted in species accounts. One exception, made to exemplify some of the thinking involved in identifying hybrids, concerns a rare sculpin hybrid (see *Cottus carolinae*). A sunfish hybrid is also depicted (Plate 30). Table 5 excludes apparent hybrids when at least one of the parents could not be identified; certain cases are noted in species accounts.

Forty-four (perhaps 45) hybrid crosses are identified from Virginia, involving 47 (or 49) parental species distributed among 8 families. Twenty (45%) of the 44 are intergeneric hybrids. Of the other 17 families covered here, 12 have only 1 species in Virginia. In 2 of the 17 families (lampreys and sturgeons) no hybrids between the Virginia species are known any-

where. The remaining three families (clupeids, catfishes, and killifishes) are represented by hybrids produced elsewhere by pairs of species which occur in Virginia. The potential for hybridization in the state is much greater; 58 more crosses between Virginia species have been identified elsewhere. As expected, the 30 minnow combinations among 23 species much dominate the Virginia list; sunfishes are second with 5 (or 6) hybrids from 6 (or 8) species.

Hybridization at Nests

The large majority of natural hybrids produced in Virginia and environs involve species with specialized breeding habits, such as nest building, and other species associated with the nests. The 57 minnow hybrids known from Virginia and extralimital populations of Virginia species have been produced by 33 species. Nine of them are chubs and allies that build gravel-pit or gravel-mound nests: one *Campostoma*, two *Exoglossum*, four *Nocomis*, and two *Semotilus*. Twelve are reproductive associates of one or more of the gravel-nest builders: shiners—all five Virginia members of the genus *Luxilus*, three of the four in the subgenus *Hydrophlox*, and *Lythrurus ardens*; and daces—*Clinostomus funduloides*, *Phoxinus oreas*, and *Rhinichthys cataractae*. Seven others are crevice spawners or egg attachers: four satinfin shiners (*Cyprinella*) and three bluntnose minnows (*Pimephales*). Thus only 5 of the 33 hybridizing minnow species are unknown to spawn at gravel nests or other specific sites. All of the centrarchids, a commonly hybridizing group, are pit nesters.

Nest-associated species usually are common and are strongly attracted to breed at nests, hence the nests often are tightly crowded with spawning minnows. Suitable spawning habitat and, likely, social facilitation are cues for grouping at nests; the typical localization of nesting habitat further induces aggregation. We have seen *Nocomis leptocephalus* nests with a flock of up to six other minnow species over them concurrently.

There is little wonder that most of the natural hybridization recorded here involves nesters and aggregating associates. Likely much of the interfertilization is accidental. The benefits of nest building and nest association probably outweigh the cost of gamete wastage on hybrids, and limits to hybridization at nests may be set only by genetic incompatibility. The ecological significance of nesting and nest association is discussed in the introduction to the Cyprinidae and in the account of *Nocomis leptocephalus*.

Systematics and Hybrids

The study of hybridization can aid in assessing evolutionary interrelationships. An evolutionary tree may be constructed on the premise that the greater the degree of interfertility of species and viability of their hybrid, the closer the kinship (e.g., Hubbs 1967). However, such interpretations often are confounded by a relatively high proportion of intergeneric hybrids.

No member of three assemblages or genera of minnows with specialized spawning habits—*Nocomis*, other gravel-nest builders, and associates; *Cyprinella*; and *Pimephales*—is clearly known to interbreed between these groups or with other groups. However, a phylogenetic tree of these (and related) taxa would be poorly founded on hybridization. Reproductive compatibility is a primitive trait, nullifying its use in phylogenetic analysis; diverging lineages tend to lose the ability to interbreed, and the loss may occur at different rates (Rosen 1979).

Some species are thought to be of hybrid origin. They may have arisen by genetic modification (introgression) of a population through interbreeding with a different species, or by fusion of two populations. They persist by reproducing with their own kind. An example in Virginia is *Luxilus albeolus*, apparently a product of hybridization between the *L. cerasinus* and *L. cornutus* lineages. A currently debated possible hybrid species, the Cheat minnow *"Rhinichthys bowersi,"* is a product of hybridization between *Nocomis micropogon* and *R. cataractae*.

THE STUDY OF FISHES

The following sections tell how to collect, observe, and photograph fishes, and explain the methods of describing and identifying fishes that we used in the development of this book.

COLLECTING AND OBSERVING FISHES

The study of Virginia's freshwater fishes can be interesting, enjoyable, and informative. Certainly, much remains to be learned. Careful collection and observation, using one or more of the methods we discuss, can be important contributions to Virginia ichthyology.

Collecting with Nets

The straight or "common sense" seine is the time-honored implement for freshwater fish collecting. It consists of a rectangular net (usually nylon) strung between two poles (brails). Floats are arranged along the top of the seine and lead weights on the bottom. The seine length and depth selected usually depend on the size of the stream to be sampled. Small seines are always used for small streams and in swift portions of large ones. Large seines are more effective in slow open sections of large streams.

The selection of mesh size is based on the size of the smallest fishes sought. A one-eighth-inch mesh is suitable for very small specimens, whereas three-sixteenth- or one-fourth-inch mesh is preferred for general collecting. (English units are given because most manufacturers do not use the metric system.) The smaller mesh sizes are not useful for general collecting because their increased surface area creates more drag. We prefer a 10- or 12-foot-long × 6-foot-deep seine of three-sixteenth- or one-fourth-inch mesh for most of our collecting. A small seine can be operated by one person, but a 10-foot or larger seine and a field crew of two, preferably at least three people, is more efficient. In a three-person crew there are two seiners and a "kicker" or "wing."

Two basic seining techniques, with several variations, are employed: the "set-and-kick" and the "haul." For both, seining is done in the downstream direction; it is considerably easier and usually more fruitful.

The set-and-kick is used primarily in riffles and swift runs, particularly for catching darters and sculpins. The seiners hold the seine perpendicular to the current, the brails about three-fourths of the seine length apart in order to form a bag in the seine. They place the brail ends on the substrate and ensure that the lead line is not elevated above the bottom. As soon as the seine is down, the kicker, starting 1–2 m upstream from the seine, moves towards the seine, kicking and dislodging rocks. A kicker should move in a zig-zag or lateral fashion to cover much of the immediate area in front of the net. Two or more kickers may work side-by-side towards the net. As soon as the kicker reaches the net, it is lifted. With a two-person crew, the seiners also do the kicking.

The haul is used in slow or standing water, often for midwater fishes (e.g., many shiner species). A third person may help in ways depending on the particular type of haul. A bag is first formed in the seine by grabbing the float line, lifting the middle portion of the net from the water, and tossing the slack net upstream. The seiners then proceed downstream, keeping the lead line on or just above the substrate. Too quick a pace may cause the lead line to travel well above the bottom; too slow can cause loss of the bag. For a midstream lift of the seine, a third person usually acts as a wing, flanking one of the brails to herd fishes toward the seine. Just prior to lifting the net, the wing charges the net with considerable commotion, scaring fishes into it. Immediately before lifting the net, the seiners thrust the bottom brail ends forward, causing the lead line to extend under fishes in front of the net. The length of the haul and whether it is done parallel or obliquely to the current depends on the particular situation. Short hauls of 4–6 m generally are most efficient.

Common haul variations are the "shore haul" or "bank trap," effective for some catfishes and sunfishes. Here the seiners terminate the haul on a sloping shore or against a cut bank. For a haul to the left bank (left and right are determined facing downstream), the seiner on the right moves slightly faster; the other seiner acts as a pivot. A specific spot usually is selected for landing; when it is almost reached, the outside seiner has swung the net around so that it parallels the shore. A third person can act as an outside wing, preventing retreat of fishes. In cases of vegetated or undercut banks, the third may wait at the landing point and, as the net approaches, kick vegetation, tree roots, etc., to chase fishes toward it. If agile, the third person may wing and kick on the same haul.

Other nets commonly used are bag seines and gill nets. Bag seines have a deep pouch of netting in the center. When hauled the bag balloons open, creating a fish trap. Bag seines rarely are used in swift water. Gill nets generally have mesh sizes much larger than seines, allowing a fish to pass its head but not its body through the mesh. Upon attempting to retreat, the fish frequently ensnares its gill cover or fins. Mesh size usually is determined by the species or fish size sought. General survey collecting may require the use of several mesh sizes in the same net (an experimental gill net). Deployment of gill nets in streams usually is perpendicular or oblique to the current, often stretched fully across a stream. Nets should be inspected every three or four hours as fishes left in the net for longer periods usually die, yielding poor specimens.

Collecting with Electroshockers

The use of electroshockers, which stun and immobilize fish for capture, has developed over recent decades. It is the standard collecting method used in many studies and in much of ours. An electrofishing unit basically consists of an electrical current generator connected to electrodes. The electrodes are probed into fish habitats, creating an electrical field. Suitable generators are battery-powered or gasoline motor-driven. Depending on generator size and habitat, generators are placed on the bank, in a boat, or mounted on a backpack frame. For small to medium-sized streams we prefer the mobility of a gas-driven

backpack unit, and now use a generator that produces 110–115 volts and 2.3 amps of alternating current, but that is also capable of producing direct current. We do not alter the current from our generator because most Virginia streams have sufficient conductivity. Some shockers have controls that increase voltage, regulate frequency, and vary the electrical field in other ways.

Shockers are particularly effective in riffles, by shocking downstream to a set seine or blocknet, and in working around seine-obstructive fish shelter such as undercut banks, logs, and boulders. Shocking in slow currents and standing waters usually demands recovery by dip nets that are rapidly and accurately wielded, particularly for fishes exposed to only the periphery of the electrical field, which they quickly exit.

Seining and shocking often are selective for particular species. Frequently we use both methods at a site. We further enhance the success of qualitative inventory by selecting sites that include a variety of habitats, and by avoidance of high water conditions. It is easy to collect a sample of common species in a small stream, but a hard 1- or 2-hour coordinated team effort usually is required to collect 80–90% of the species present in a medium or large stream. Examples of collecting techniques and equipment, evaluations of these, or bibliographies are by Paloumpis (1958), Ming (1964), McAllister (1965), Calhoun (1966), Ricker (1971), Hocutt et al. (1973), Schwartz and Howland (1978), Corcoran (1979), Heidinger et al. (1983), and Wiley and Tsai (1983).

Collecting with Ichthyocides

The use of ichthyocides (fish poisons) is strictly regulated in Virginia. These chemicals are relatively unselective of species and are of great potential danger to the fish fauna beyond the targeted sample site. The use of sodium cyanide (NaCN) is illegal in the state, and rotenone may be applied only in the presence of a state fisheries biologist.

Collecting by Angling

This method enabled our capture of many valuable specimens, particularly the larger, wary, nongamefishes such as the bull chub and fallfish.

Collecting Permits

All fish collecting for scientific purposes in Virginia (and all other states) must be done under a permit. The permit is free of charge in Virginia. An application for a permit may be obtained from the Virginia Department of Game and Inland Fisheries (address below). The collection of state and federally endangered or threatened species is prohibited except under very specific permits—see *Endangered Fishes*.

Preserving Fishes

Ichthyologists have a much easier task in preserving specimens than do students of the other vertebrate groups. Herpetologists, ornithologists, and mammalogists must spend hours injecting or stuffing relatively few specimens; ichthyologists can quickly preserve large samples of specimens as soon as they are collected.

Initial field preservation consists of placing the fish in a jar containing a 10% solution of 37% aqueous (full strength, saturated) formaldehyde, a fixative of tissue. A solution of formaldehyde is called formalin (a 100% formalin solution is 37% formaldehyde). The volume of formalin should be enough to cover all specimens. We generally use 2- or 4-liter (0.05 or 1 gallon) glass jars in the field for most collecting. To allow thorough fixation of all specimens, they should not be tightly packed in jars.

Some workers advocate the use of opaque plastic jars in the field. However, we have broken only three glass jars in the field during the past 20 years, and prefer to see in the field, often studying "through the jar" what we have caught. Swiss army medic packs, available in most military surplus stores, make excellent jar carrying bags.

Specimens larger than 200 mm in length should be slit on the lower right side to allow formalin to enter the abdominal cavity. A slit 2–3 cm long will suffice; care should be taken not to penetrate viscera. To avoid cutting valuable specimens, formalin may be injected with a syringe. Preservation of fishes by "pinning" is described under *Photography*.

Specimens should be kept in formalin for 5–7 days. Then the formalin is discarded and the collection is soaked in tap water which is changed once or twice daily until the odor of formalin is barely perceptible (usually 4–5 days). After the rinse phase, the specimens are covered with either 45–50% isopropyl alcohol or 70% ethyl alcohol. Concentrations weaker or stronger than these will lead, respectively, to soft or hard and shrunken specimens. Specimens kept in airtight jars (such as "canning jars") with the prescribed concentration of alcohol may be kept indefinitely.

WARNING: Specimens can be studied while they are in formalin, but lengthy exposure to this chemical should be avoided. Formaldehyde is a carcinogen and an extreme skin irritant. Rubber gloves should be worn when handling specimens; repeated skin contact can produce an allergic reaction. If formalin is splashed in the face, one should immediately and copiously flush the face with water. Untreated eye contact with formalin can result in blindness.

Observing Fishes

Lately, following the development of equipment and techniques for working underwater in marine environments, qualitative and quantitative pioneer studies have been made in fresh water with snorkel and scuba (e.g., Moyle 1973; Emery 1973; Goldstein 1978; Whitworth and Schmidt 1980; Griffith 1983). A snorkel is a J-shaped tube that allows breathing while the face is under water. "Scuba" stands for self-contained underwater breathing apparatus. We have employed both to much advantage and delight in Virginia waters. The adults of nearly all species, and juveniles of many, in a stream are distinguishable underwater with prior experience. Underwater observations reveal species and habitat associations and feeding and breeding habitats often otherwise unnoticed. Important observations may also be made from banks, particularly with polarizing sunglasses and binoculars.

Locality Data, Labels, and Field Notes

A collection that lacks precise locality data is almost worthless. This can mean that all time and money spent on the collection were wasted, and unfortunately the waste often does not end with the collecting effort. While compiling data for this volume, we spent many weeks attempting to locate or verify collection sites described by sketchy or apparently erroneous locality data. For example, the only Virginia record of the ashy darter *Etheostoma cinereum* bears the data "Clinch River, Scott or Russell County, 1970 or 1971." After considerable efforts, we still were unable to determine the actual site of capture.

To record useful locality data, one needs maps of sufficient detail to accurately portray stream courses, to provide names of most tributaries, and to show secondary road crossings and the location of small towns. We rely heavily on Virginia county route maps and U.S. Geological Survey 7.5-minute topographic quadrangles; state highway maps usually do not provide sufficient detail. Except for local forays, we endeavor to take the necessary maps on field trips; they are almost as important as the seines.

Good locality data must contain the following minimum information: state and county (or other appropriate political boundaries) of collection site; specific name of body of water (if unnamed, state the stream or lake into which it empties); exact descriptor(s) of locality; date; and collectors. Precise locality descriptors generally are easy to take. Traceable descriptors include: the route number of a bridge crossing; distance from the junction of two routes, center of a town, or a county line; air-line bearings and distances from a stable reference point; elevation. A road may cross a stream several times, thus it is advisable to supplement the bridge route number with a distance bearing from another reference point. Short distances are preferred. Some biologists argue that latitude and longitude coordinates should always be given.

The following is an example of good locality data:

CHOWAN (Meherrin) drainage, VA, Greensville Co.
Fontaine Cr. at Co. Rt. 629 bridge, 5.5 air km SSW Emporia.
5 July 1983.
N. M. Burkhead (801), W. H. Haxo (139),
R. E. Jenkins (1014), S. P. McIninch (100)

The example provides the drainage (and system within the drainage), state, county, stream name, two site descriptors (one a bearing), a concise date (month spelled), collectors, and (parenthetically) their field numbers.

A jar label written on notebook paper with nonpermanent ink will usually become illegible or disintegrate by the time the collection is washed. Standard practice is to use 100% cotton rag paper and black permanent ink; a label written with a soft (2H) pencil will temporarily suffice. The label should be kept in the jar, not taped to the lid or outside; lids and jars can be mixed when washing and sorting collections. Locality data should be associated with *specimens*, not jars.

We strongly advocate developing the habit of recording field notes. We have found our notes to be invaluable to us and colleagues. In addition to locality data, notes include descriptions of habitats and impressions of the quality of the collection site. We use a standard field form which has space for a species list and, for each species, observations on specific habitat, relative abundance, size, life stages, color, and behavior. A different field number is assigned to each collection and is recorded on the field note sheet, jar labels, photographs, and any data taken from specimens. Our field numbers are consecutive through years; some collectors use a year–number system, for example, JAM 78-40 (J. A. Musick, 40th collection in 1978).

When pushed for time during fieldwork, we sometimes do not compose a species list, but concise locality data in field notes and specimen jars are mandatory. Unique observations are always recorded. Many seemingly insignificant bits of information generally are added; often they are important in later analyses. We do not list species not positively identified in the field, except by genus; such specimens are critically examined later.

Permits and Supplies

The following are addresses of state agencies and sources of field gear; this is not an endorsement for supplies, but simply the sources we have used.

Scientific Collector Permit
   Virginia Department of Game and Inland Fisheries
   P.O. Box 11104
   Richmond, VA 23230-1104

Maps
   County Route Maps:
   Virginia Department of Highways and Transportation
   1221 E. Broad St.
   Richmond, VA 23219

   Topographic Recreational Maps:
   Virginia Atlas & Gazetteer
   DeLorme Mapping Co.
   P.O. Box 298
   Freeport, ME 04032

   USGS Topographic Maps:
   Virginia Division of Mineral Resources
   P.O. Box 3667
   Charlottesville, VA 22903

Nets
   Mid-Lakes Manufacturing Co.
   3300 Rifle Range Rd.
   Knoxville, TN 37918

   Sterling Net and Twine Co.
   18 Label St.
   Montclair, NJ 07042

Shocker Engine-Generator
   Tanaka Kogyo (USA) Ltd.
   7509 S. 228th St.
   Kent, WA 98032

PHOTOGRAPHY OF FISHES

Until the last three decades most of the published high-quality color photographs of fishes were of exotic species and were taken by aquarists; photography was a small part of scientific ichthyological endeavor. Recently a relatively greater number of ichthyologists have become photographers, particularly of coral reef fishes. Nongame North American freshwater fishes, most notably the brilliantly colored darters and sunfishes, have increasingly become camera subjects. For example, the *Fishes of Missouri* (Pflieger 1975) and *The Audubon Society Field Guide to North American Fishes, Whales and Dolphins* (Boschung et al. 1983) portray many native freshwater fishes in color. Aquarium journals and natural history magazines publish articles on nongame North American species which include photographs and discussion of habits, habitats, and distribution. Fine examples are treatments of madtom catfishes (Mayden 1983) and the fish faunas of the Appomattox River and of New York (Taylor 1982, 1983; Smith 1983).

Prior to our work many Virginia freshwater fishes had never been photographed in color. We provide the first published color photos of some 30 species, but several others remain undepicted in color, and color variation, behavior, and habitat associations of these and many more species are yet to be captured on film. Thus photographic efforts by aquarists, divers (who greatly outnumber ichthyologists), and others can substantially contribute to the body of scientific knowledge.

Specimen Preparation

The first step toward obtaining a high-quality photograph is to capture and properly preserve a high-quality specimen—one with fins spread and untorn, all scales intact, body straight, and mouth not markedly gaped. A photograph of a specimen that is bent, partly descaled, or with torn or depressed fins will appear as such. For example, note the black-and-white photo of the extinct harelip sucker *Moxostoma lacerum* from the best specimen known (Fish 144).

To maintain high-quality specimens while collecting, we keep fishes alive and uncrowded in a bucket; water is changed frequently. While setting up the photo system or when transporting fishes to the laboratory, the water is aerated by a baitfish aerator.

We strove to photograph undamaged specimens in peak nuptial color, by seeking fishes that were spawning or in some other phase of reproductive behavior, and by selecting the most colorful, typically the larger specimens. Of course, many of our photos are of nonbreeding specimens. Some spawning minnows (particularly mountain redbelly dace) were rushed from stream to phototank because certain colors (notably reds and blacks) quickly become subdued when those fishes are removed from the spawning site. Some sculpins were maintained in aquaria and allowed to spawn, and thus develop nuptial color (darkening) before they were photographed. Some other sculpins were kept in aquaria with black gravel; sometimes this stimulated onset or intensification of nuptial color. Other sculpins were kept over variegated gravel to influence the assumption or stronger development of mottled and blotched patterns. Many sculpins and most other fishes were photographed at streamside. None of our transparencies are of unnatural colors or patterns, although orange and red often are not as bright in photos as in living specimens (perhaps due to photographing through thick plate-glass aquaria).

Intensity of color and lack of damage of specimens are checked by placing one or a few fishes at a time in a glass viewing jar filled with water. Usually we work on two specimens at a time, one being killed and prepared for the phototank, the other being positioned in the tank and photographed.

Several options are available for sacrificing and preparing specimens for photographing. "Pinning" refers to the practice of holding fins spread with pins ("minuten" and larger insect pins) after the specimen is killed and while it is hardening in formalin. Generally we do not use pins; pinholes can show in a photo. We kill specimens quickly in a jar of strong (30–50%) formalin. Immediately upon death the specimen is placed in a flat pan containing just enough formalin to cover about two-thirds of the body width. Because the left side is customarily photographed (unless damaged), it is placed down. This allows the left side of the body to remain straight while hardening, thus allowing more of the fish to be in sharp focus. All adjustments to the head and body, if necessary, are done quickly by hand: the body is straightened, flared gill covers are compressed, and a wide gape to the mouth is reduced or closed. Then while holding the specimen with one hand, small forceps are used to grasp the leading (anterior) spines or rays and spread the fins. Caution should be taken not to tear delicate membranes. By alternating between fins, holding each spread for about 10–30 seconds at a time (2–4 times for each fin), the fins usually will fix erect in 2–10 minutes. We scrupulously use clean formalin and rinse specimens to avoid introducing unwanted matter to the phototank.

With this technique a specimen may be photographed within 3–15 minutes of death, soon enough to capture most ephemeral structural colors on film. Unlike pigmentary colors (e.g., most reds and yellows), which absorb all wave lengths but those of the pigment, the structural hues (e.g., blue, green, and gold sheens or iridescences) are caused by refracted light. The iridescences are the most rapidly lost—within 10–15 minutes of cellular death, often much sooner. Because loss of sheen occurs throughout the preparation process, we work as quickly as possible. Our best coordinated effort culminated in photographing a splendid tangerine darter *Percina aurantiaca* (Plate 33) just 65 seconds after it was removed from the live bucket.

Alternative methods are used to prepare some specimens. To further reduce loss of iridescence, specimens are killed with an overdose of an anesthetic instead of formalin. To compensate for relaxed fins, we lay the specimen photo-side up in a pan of formalin whose level covers only the opposite side, and then briefly spread fins in formalin. Or, we place the drug-stilled specimen in a wax-bottom pan, hold fins erect by insect pins, and with an eyedropper place 100% formalin only on the fins. Still, some intensity or occasionally entire colors are lost, notably the blues. We rarely use an anesthetic because it often causes excessive darkening in fishes. Some fishes, particularly minnows, die in photographic posture, but we often spread their fins farther.

To prevent erection of pectoral fin spines of catfishes, the fins are hand-held against the body when the fish is dying in formalin. (See the warning regarding protection from formalin, page 125.)

Photographic System

Our system consists of an aquarium, background, camera and lens, electronic flashes, and supporting equipment such as a collapsible table, tripod, and flash stands (Figure 2). We use Kodachrome 64 for color slides and Kodak Plus-X for black-and-white work. With minor modifications, we use the same system in the field and laboratory. Our system is similar to that of Emery and Winterbottom (1980). The salient feature of our system is that the specimen is photographed underwater in a customized aquarium.

Some authors (Flescher 1983; Kuehne and Barbour 1983; Page 1983; Page and Cummings 1984) have photographed specimens out of water in specially designed boxes. The results of out-of-water photography generally can be good, whether or not a photobox is used; for example, see the photos and description of techniques by Wydoski and Whitney (1979). However, flashes reflected from the skin sometimes

Figure 2 Our photographic system.

obscure aspects of color patterns, and overall color saturation generally is inferior to shots of submerged specimens. Fishes appear more lifelike when submerged.

Dimensions (cm) of our phototank are 77 length × 38 height × 12.5 width. The tank is made of 5.5 mm thick pieces of plate glass bonded together with silicone adhesive. The inside of the bottom and side-pieces are painted flat black to reduce interior tank reflections. The fish is held against the frontpiece by a glass plate behind the fish, a method pioneered by G. Timmerman in the 1950s (Axelrod 1970). The glass plate (73 × 44 cm, 5.5 mm thick) is held in place by attaching alligator clips to the upper edge of the sides of the tank; the plate rests back against the clips. Depending on size and form of the fish, the plate is held at various distances and angles from the frontpiece by changing the position of the clips.

Backgrounds for fishes smaller than 200 mm in length are spray-painted plexiglass plates. Flat gray automobile primer paints are used; the two shades correspond approximately to numbers 5 and 8 on the Kodak Gray Scale. Gray backgrounds do not obscure dark pigmentation of fin membranes, a fault of black backgrounds, and pale fins tend to be better distinguished with gray than with white or clear backgrounds. We mount this background 14 cm behind the phototank, between small L-brackets screwed to a wood base that underlies the tank. The background for larger fishes is a pale blue fitted bedsheet held smooth by a collapsible frame and positioned 3 m behind the tank.

We use a Nikon FM2 body and a 105 mm f4 Micro Nikkor AI lens for all aquarium photography. A Nikon PN-11 ring is used for macrophotography (1:1).

A Nikon DG-2 2× eyepiece magnifier and a B (matte) focusing screen aid in critical focusing. Other high-quality single-lens reflex cameras can be just as effective. We recommend the use of a fixed focal length macro lens rather than a zoom lens with a macro setting; the macro lens provides better resolution and contrast. Long focal lengths provide more working space between the camera and the phototank, useful when making final adjustments of the position of the fish.

Reflection from the tank and tripod is eliminated by a 30 × 40-cm piece of dark gray posterboard placed over the front of the camera. The posterboard has a center hole to accommodate the lens; it is held to the camera body by long rubber bands taped at their ends to the back of the board. The lens has a built-in hood to eliminate other light flare.

We use electronic flashes because lighting is always available and controlled; smaller aperture openings, which provide greater depth of field, may be used; and flashes are easily portable. We use two Vivitar 3700 flashes with a guide number of 120 at ASA 100. The diffusers supplied with the flashes soften the hot spot. We bracket from f8 to f16, and sometimes a half-stop on each side and half-stops between these apertures. The depth of field at these f-stops is very small and is approximately one-third in front of and two-thirds behind the focal point.

The flash-to-subject distance is determined with the aid of a Vivitar flash meter calibrated at the desired f-stop range. Actual bracketing depends on the reflectivity of the subject; for example, silvery minnows require a smaller aperture range than dark non-shiny fishes. The angle of each flash to the subject is 45°. The flashes are aimed at the end of the fish furthest from the flash. The resultant crossing light paths reduce both harsh highlighting of the head and shadow behind the pectoral fin. The flashes are synchronized with equal-length PC cords. When shooting in the field, it is best to avoid bright overhead sunlight as the specimen may exhibit undesirable contrast, even when flashes are used.

The phototank is centered on a black-painted wood base to which the plexiglass background is secured as described above. The base permits moving the full tank without stressing its joints. In the field the base is centered on a small four-legged (collapsible) table. The front of the tank has center reference marks at the top and bottom edges. The marks aid in centering the fish in the tank horizontally; when the specimen is positioned, it is at equal angles and equidistant from the flashes. Tools for positioning specimens are long forceps and, particularly for small fishes, a fine stiff wire with a hooked end.

To avoid troublesome gas bubbles forming on the tank glass and on specimens, we use the hottest tap water available after it has cooled to ambient temperature in tightly sealed containers. For field photography, we carry four 20-liter jerry cans of water, enough for two photo sessions per day, one tank filling for each session. Normally with travel, collecting, and specimen preparation, two sessions are the most accomplished in a day. We never use stream or lake water; rarely does it approach the clarity of tap water.

Most of our color photography was done in the field, occasionally under inhospitable conditions. Differences (or advantages) of photographing in the laboratory are: the tank is placed on a solid bench; reference points for flash stand legs are marked on the floor to ensure consistency of angles and distances; flashes are operated, with a power converter, from the electrical supply of the building; lighting and weather are controlled; and disconcerting noxious insects are absent. However, some of our most pleasurable and exciting photo sessions were held at streamside.

Underwater Photography

Certainly the most interesting photographs of fishes are those taken underwater, because these portray behavior and habitat associations. Persons interested in this topic should consult some of the many books available on the subject. (For a book list, write Helix, 325 W. Huron St., Chicago IL 60610; inquire at a dive shop about an underwater photography course; browse diving magazines for underwater photo tips.) A good working knowledge of the photographic principles necessary to consistently produce high-quality pictures should be obtained before taking a camera underwater. The following suggestions are intended to aid the equipped and knowledgeable underwater photographer in photographing fishes underwater, particularly in streams.

Water clarity is one of the most critical factors; the clarity of Virginia and many other inland waters rarely approaches that of the clearer tropical oceans and springs. About the best horizontal clarity for Virginia waters (i.e., where fine details still can be seen) is 3–4 m. Thus working distances often are restricted to close-up and macrophotography. Entering a stream with mask and snorkel allows the determination of clarity. Clarity can also be assessed from the bank; sufficient clarity probably is present when details of the bottom can be clearly seen in a pool of 1.5–2 m depth. If the exposure guide for strobes was calibrated in a swimming pool or other clear water, then photography in water of about 2-m clarity requires the aperture be opened 1.5 to 2 f-stops or the strobes be moved closer to the subject. Pictures taken in poor clarity will have poor resolution; ASA 64 will look like ASA 1600.

When working in a stream, photographers should try to position themselves to a side of or downstream from the subject. These positions will prevent silt raised by the photographer from sweeping down over the subject. Because of the potential for raising silt (and to avoid disturbing fishes), photographers should move slowly and deliberately.

Runoff from rain is the most common cause of cloudy water in typically clear streams. A heavy rain may render photographic conditions unsuitable for a week. Clarity in a stream can differ between sections at the same time. A section with unvegetated banks may be quite turbid but upstream conditions may be ideal. Most streams in rural areas are crossed by fords; work above the fords because crossing vehicles can quickly ruin suitable conditions. Geographic location and time of year affect the clarity of streams. Mountain streams generally are clearer than those of the Piedmont or Coastal Plain; streams draining forested areas usually are clearer than those in farmlands. Streams usually are clearest from late October to late May. In warmer months clarity often is reduced by plankton blooms.

Specific goals should be set for each photographic foray. They may center on one species or several of a certain size range. Underwater photography requires concentration. The strain of flitting back and forth between potential subjects, or wondering whether to change lenses or adjust strobes, can lead to loss of attention and photographs of reduced quality.

The species accounts in this book may be used to learn the size range of the subject, the area where it is most likely found, and its particular habitat. When diving, pay special attention to behavior; you may detect something that will allow a closer approach to a certain fish. Some species can be enticed within range by feeding. In general, small fishes will ignore a motionless photographer. William R. Roston, an excellent underwater photographer of North American fishes, is an avid proponent of photographing at night.

The most spectacular time to photograph underwater in Virginia generally is from early May through mid-June, when many species sport wonderful nuptial colors. These fishes provide dramatic subjects, and with persistence (or luck) one might be able to record the spawning act.

For serious underwater photographers, we recommend that a photographic logbook be kept. At mini-

mum, the date and location where photographs were taken should be recorded. Narratives of habitat conditions, species associations, and behavior will be useful when photographs are displayed, and perhaps for other purposes. Some slides taken by nonscientists prove to be of immense value to ichthyology.

ANATOMY AND COLOR OF FISHES, AND METHODS OF STUDY

This section explains many of the characters that we use to describe fishes; their application in identifying fishes is treated in the next section. Some basic aspects of fish anatomy are shown in Figures 3–6. Specialized characters are described in introductions to the appropriate keys. Formats used for expressing meristic (counts) and morphometric (measurements) data, and the meaning of subjective qualifiers are explained in *Introduction to Accounts*. The *Glossary* defines many characters not treated below. More comprehensive descriptions of piscine characters are given by Hubbs and Lagler (1958), Trautman (1981), and Cailliet et al. (1986). Examples of anatomical compendia on single species are by Grizzle and Rogers (1976) and Fremling (1978).

Counts and measurements of fishes are standardly made on the left side of specimens unless the left side has been damaged; a few exceptions are indicated below or in figures. For small fishes, counts and dissections are made under a dissecting microscope. Any part that is dissected from a specimen should be placed in a labeled vial and the vial put in the specimen jar. Or, removed parts may be returned to their natural cavities.

Scales   Figure 7

For small thin-scaled species, partial drying by blotting or with a fine air stream may be needed to render the scales sufficiently evident. If scales are lost, the scale pockets (one per scale) may be counted. If scale pockets are uncountable but the adjacent scales are uniform in size, the size of the descaled area gives a clue to the number of missing scales.

Lateral Line Scales   Figures 7A and B, 8, 62.—A horizontal count is made of body scales that overlay the lateral line sensory canal. The scales to be counted extend from the shoulder (pectoral) girdle to the structural base of the caudal fin (the posterior end of the hypural plate, composed of hypural bones [Figure 5]). In some fishes the lateral line extends onto the caudal fin, but that portion is excluded in our counts.

PLANES and ORIENTATIONS

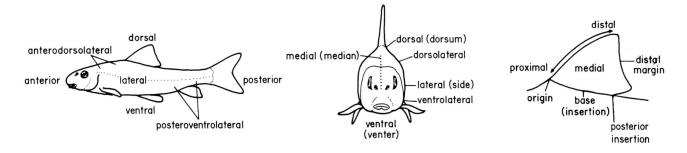

BODY FORMS

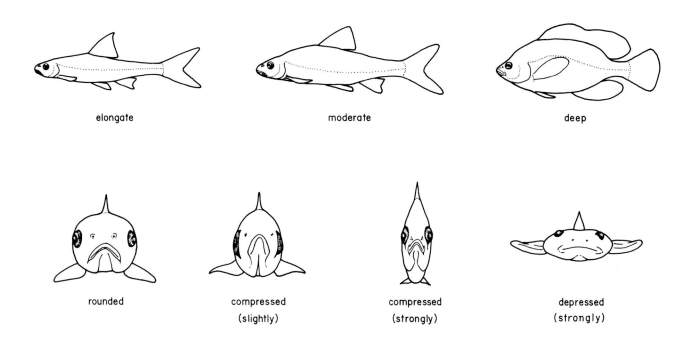

elongate

moderate

deep

rounded

compressed (slightly)

compressed (strongly)

depressed (strongly)

MOUTH POSITIONS and ORIENTATIONS

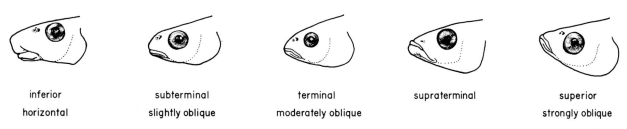

inferior
horizontal

subterminal
slightly oblique

terminal
moderately oblique

supraterminal

superior
strongly oblique

Figure 3 (Top) Anatomical planes, orientations, points, and areas commonly used in descriptions. (Row 2) Body forms in lateral profile. (Row 3) Body forms in anterior profile. (Bottom) Mouth positions and orientations with mouth closed, left to right: sucker, *Nocomis* chub, common shiner, killifish, golden shiner. The inferior mouth is markedly so; the subterminal mouth shown here can be also be construed as slightly inferior; the mouth labeled supraterminal may be considered slightly superior.

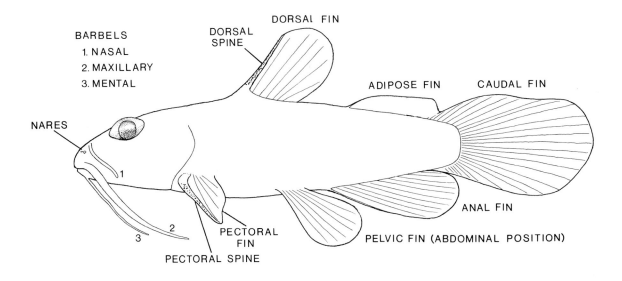

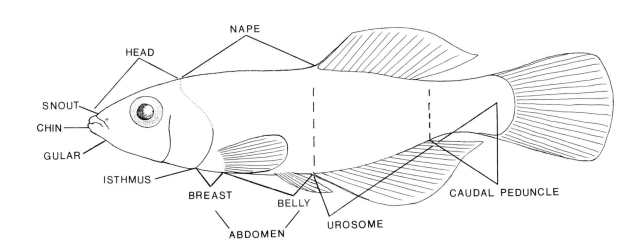

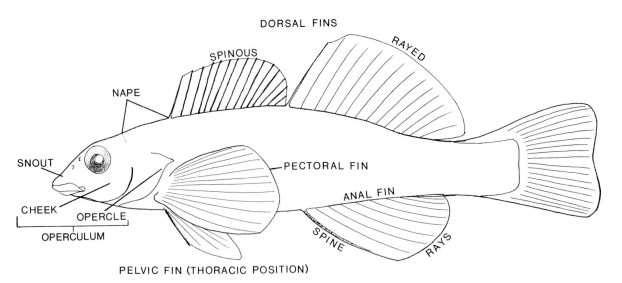

Figure 4 Areas and appendages. In lower panel: spinous dorsal fin = first dorsal fin; rayed (soft) dorsal fin = second dorsal fin; these fins may be broadly joined.

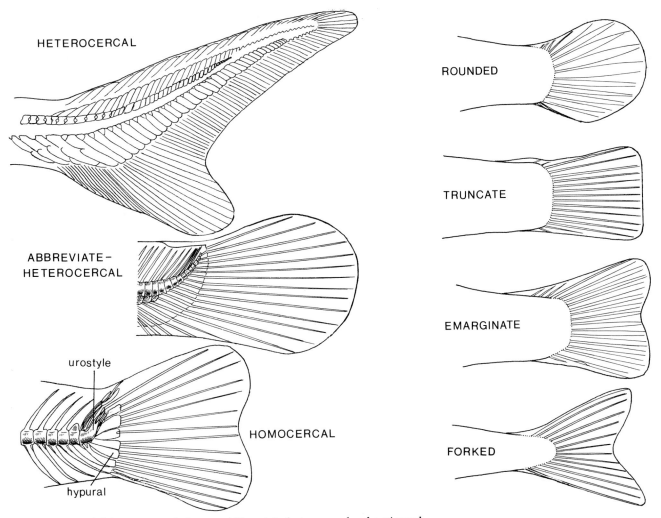

HETEROCERCAL

ABBREVIATE-
HETEROCERCAL

urostyle

HOMOCERCAL

hypural

ROUNDED

TRUNCATE

EMARGINATE

FORKED

Figure 5 Caudal fin types and shapes. Abbreviate-heterocercal = hemicercal.

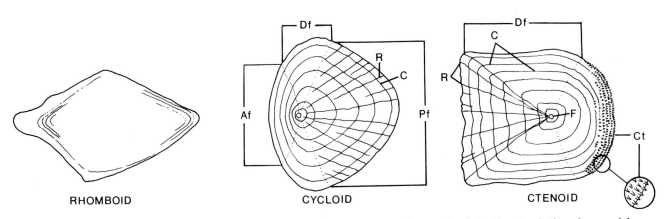

RHOMBOID

CYCLOID

CTENOID

Figure 6 Basic types of scales. Right margin is posterior margin of scales. Af—anterior field; C—circuli (few shown of those present); Ct—ctenii; Df—dorsal field (one of the two "lateral" fields in scale terminology, the ventral field is the other "lateral" field); F—focus; Pf—posterior field; R—radii.

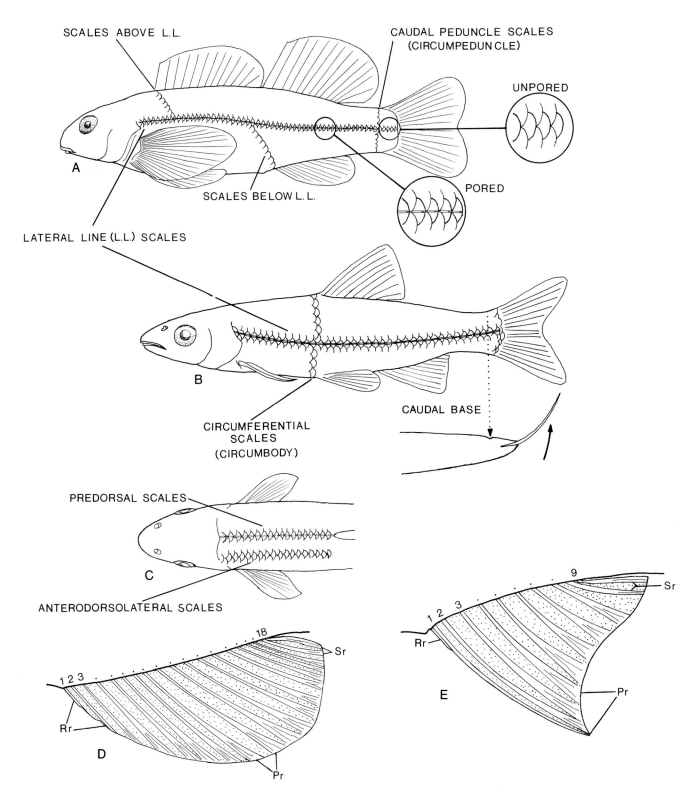

Figure 7 Counts of scales and median fin rays: (A) Pored and unpored lateral line scales shown. Scales above and below lateral line follow natural oblique rows. Caudal peduncle scales (circumpeduncle scales in text) are counted at the least depth of the caudal peduncle. (B) Delineation of caudal base for lateral line scale count is shown by caudal flexure. Circumferential scales (circumbody scales in text) may not be in the same vertical plane if the dorsal fin origin is not directly above the pelvic fin origin. (C) Anterodorsolateral scales counted in *Luxilus* shiners. (D) Anal fin with all rays counted, as in catfishes; last 2 ray elements [Sr] counted as 1 ray. Types of rays: Rr—rudimentary; Pr—principal; Sr—split ray. (E) Anal fin with only principal rays counted; Sr counted as 1 ray. See *Anatomy and Color* and Table 6 for criteria for counting or excluding rudimentary rays.

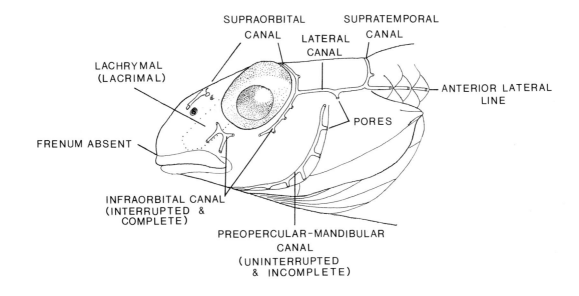

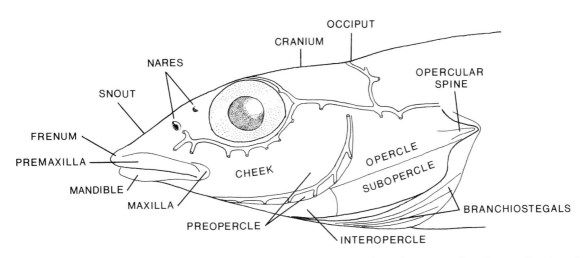

Figure 8 Areas and parts of the head, including the canals of the cephalic lateralis system. See Figures 60, 61, and 82 for other views of parts of the cephalic lateralis system.

The count generally is made of the scales that have a pored opening of the lateral line. In most fishes the lateral line is complete—all scales in the scale row overlying the lateral line are pored. Many fishes have an incomplete lateral line—one or more posterior scales are unpored (Figure 76). In this case the lateral line count is continued posteriad from the last pored scale (i.e., to the caudal base as usual).

For species with an incomplete lateral line, often the number of pored or unpored midlateral scales is used to identify them; the particular count is specified. The sum of pored and unpored scales is still termed the lateral line count, or often the midlateral scale row (or series) count. Some fishes (e.g., chub-

suckers and killifishes) lack pored body scales; the scales in the row along midheight of the body are counted (i.e., the midlateral row). Sculpins are scaleless but the lateral line pores are countable (Figure 62).

It is important to properly locate the anterior and posterior end-points for the lateral line count. The count usually is best begun by determining the most posterior scale or pore to be counted and then count forward.

To determine the posterior end-point, gently flex the caudal fin toward you to produce a vertical crease along the posterior end of the hypural plate (Figures 5, 7B). Flexing the fin excessively may cause an unwanted crease to develop in the musculature anterior to the posterior end of the hypural plate. Sometimes one or two scales over the posterior end of the hypural plate buckle upward when flexing the tail; by pushing these down, the proper crease may be produced. As an alternative, the posterior end of the hypural plate may be determined by probing through caudal base musculature; see *Key to Suckers*.

The most posterior scale to be counted must then be determined relative to the crease. If the crease forms at the posterior margin of a scale, that scale is the last one included. If the crease forms under a scale, the scale is included only if the crease lies at or posterior to midlength of the exposed portion of the scale.

The most anterior scale enumerated is the one that, in counting forward, is the first to touch the shoulder girdle (Hubbs and Lagler 1958). This scale is followed posteriorly by the first scale that is clearly separated, in exterior view, from the girdle by a scale in the row just below.

Circumbody Scales (Circumferential Scales) Figure 7B.—A count is made around the body of the horizontal scale rows in the vertical plane just anterior to the dorsal and pelvic fins. The count typically is made only on fishes with pelvic fins in the abdominal (posterior) position (e.g., minnows and suckers). Natural scale rows are counted; relatively small, irregularly shaped scales at the fin origins are excluded.

The count generally is made by counting the scale rows around the back (all rows above the lateral line), rows around the belly (those below the lateral line), summing these, and adding two for the lateral line scales (one scale on each side). If the dorsal and pelvic fin origins are not vertically aligned, the count is made along separate vertical planes, still passing just anterior to each fin origin.

Scales Above Lateral Line Figure 7A.—A count is made of scales on one side of the body above the lateral line. The count begins with the scale at the side of the dorsal fin origin, and scales are counted downward and backward along the natural oblique row, ending with the scale just above the lateral line scale row.

Scales Below Lateral Line Figure 7A.—A count is made of scales on one side of the body below the lateral line. The count begins at the side of the origin of a ventral fin. In relatively primitive fishes (e.g., shads and pikes), with posteriorly inserted pelvic fins (abdominal position), the count begins by the pelvic fin origin. In advanced fishes (e.g., sunfishes and

darters), with an anteriorly placed pelvic fin (thoracic position), it begins by the anal fin origin. Scales are counted upward and forward along the natural oblique row, to the scale just below the lateral line scale row.

Scales Around (Across) Back.—A count is made of horizontal scale rows from the first row above the lateral line on one side to that on the opposite side. The count is made by the same method as the upper body count for circumbody scales.

Scales Around (Across) Belly.—A count is made of horizontal scale rows from the first row below the lateral line on one side to that on the opposite side. The count is made by the same method as the lower body count for circumbody scales.

Circumpeduncle Scales (Caudal Peduncle Scales) Figure 7A.—A count is made of scales around the caudal peduncle at its least depth, hence nearly or actually the least count. We counted all natural horizontal scale rows except in the moxostomatin suckers and *Enneacanthus* sunfishes, in which the least count was always made (see *Key to Suckers*).

Predorsal Scales and Predorsal Scale Rows Figure 7C.—Counts of middorsal scales anterior to the dorsal fin are made. The predorsal scale count includes each scale, however small its portion, that contacts or crosses the middorsal line. In many fishes the predorsal scale *row* count is slightly lower than the predorsal scale count, because it enumerates only natural scale rows that extend onto the middorsum from the upper side, and excludes individual scales that may lie middorsally between two rows.

Fin Rays and Spines Figures 7D, E

Two basic types of fin-support elements occur in fishes: rays (soft rays) and spines (hard or spinous rays). Rays are bilateral (two closely bound units), flexible, and segmented; they are branched or unbranched. Principal rays are those whose tips reach the distal fin margin; in many fishes the first principal ray is unbranched. The small unbranched rays in the anterior portion (leading edge) of median fins whose tips do not reach the distal fin margin are termed rudimentary or procurrent rays.

Spines are unsegmented, unbranched, usually pointed at the tip, horny or bony in composition, and usually stiff. Highly flexible spines are termed soft spines (e.g., all fin spines in sculpins). Care must be exercised in distinguishing flexible anal spines from

Table 6 Methods of counting fin rays.

Fins	Rays counted
Pectoral, pelvic	All rays, both branched and unbranched, are counted.
Dorsal, anal	In Esocidae, Umbridae, Ictaluridae, and Salmonidae, count all anterior rudimentary and principal rays. In other families, count only principal rays. The last two rays generally are counted as one; often these can be seen, without dissection, to arise from the same point on the body. See Figure 7D, E. See text for variant methods of recognizing the last dorsal and anal fin rays.
Caudal	All principal rays are counted unless "branched rays" are specified. The principal ray count is the number of branched rays + 2.

anal rays, particularly in small darters (Figure 81). Spines may support an entire fin or occur only in the anterior portion of a fin.

Methods of counting fin rays are indicated partly in Table 6 and Figure 7D, E. Generally it is necessary to spread a fin to expose all supporting elements, but the interconnecting membranes should not be torn. Background or substage lighting often aids counting. The one or two tiny rays in the posterior portion of the pectoral fin must be sought carefully. The rudimentary rays in the median fins of most families are not counted (Table 6); in the exceptional families they are counted because they are numerous and grade in size with no clear distinction between them and the principal rays. The dorsal and anal fins in catfishes have basal fatty deposits; slitting along the fin base and peeling away the skin will expose the rays.

In the anal fin and dorsal fin (second dorsal when there are two), almost invariably we count the last two ray elements as one ray (split ray—Figure 7E). Some workers have counted both elements in the killifishes (Brown 1958; Thomerson 1969; Williams and Etnier 1982). For the subgenus *Boleosoma* of *Etheostoma*—the johnny darter group—we counted the last two elements as one, as did Cole (1967, 1972), but question that this method portrays the actual number of rays. For the logperches, subgenus *Percina*, the last two rays were counted as two when they appeared to have separate bases, which usually was the case; thus we agree in method with Thompson (1985). Complete separation of the last two ray elements may be more common in darters than generally believed (Thompson 1977). Methods of recognizing the last ray are further considered under *Systematics and Identification of Sculpins, Cottus*.

Branchiostegal Rays   Figure 8

A count is made of the splintlike bones in the branchiostegal membrane on the ventral surface of the head, beneath the operculum (gill cover). To flare the branchiostegals, flex the operculum dorsad. Be sure to count the branchiostegal closely adjoining the ventral margin of the operculum.

Cephalic Lateralis System   Figures 8, 60, 81, 83

This, the lateral line network on the head, comprises bilaterally paired, narrow canals containing sensory structures; the canals open to the exterior via pores. An incomplete canal is not connected to the lateral canal. An interrupted canal lacks a segment at a point other than at the junction with the lateral canal.

Counts of pores include those on the main canal or at the end of short branches (canaliculi) of the canal. A fine stream of compressed air (see *Identifying Fishes*) aids in observing the canals and pores; a partly dried canal often appears paler than adjacent areas of the skin, and pores can be detected as fluids exit them. It sometimes is necessary to alternately moisten and dry an area. Pore counts from only two of the cephalic lateralis canals are used in our keys.

Infraorbital (IO) Canal.—Pore counts of this canal are used for species identification in the darter genus *Etheostoma*. The anterior pore of the IO canal is situated anterior to the eye (orbit). The canal follows the ventral orbital rim, then rises along the posterior orbital rim. The IO canal unites with the supraorbital canal (canal above the eye) and lateral canal (a postorbital canal). Infraorbital pores are counted beginning with the anterior pore; a pore at the canal junction is excluded. Where the IO canal is interrupted, the count of the anterior segment is given first and separated from that of the posterior segment by a plus sign (e.g., 4+3; Figure 81A).

Preopercular-mandibular (POM) Canal.—This canal follows the posterior margin of the preopercle ventrally onto the underside of the mandible (lower jaw), terminating on the chin. All pores of the canal are counted. Mandibular pores of the POM occur entirely on the mandible. Right and left mandibular canals usually are not united on the chin except in some sculpins (Figure 61).

Gill Rakers   Figure 9

Gill rakers are customarily counted on the first gill (branchial) arch of one side (usually the right to avoid

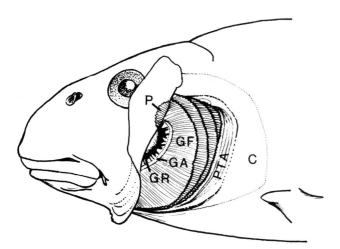

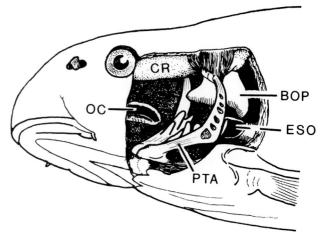

Figure 9 Head of *Nocomis leptocephalus* with operculum abducted forward; C—cleithrum bone of pectoral (shoulder) girdle; GA—gill arch; GF—gill filaments; GR—gill rakers; P—pseudobranchium; PTA—position of pharyngeal (tooth) arch, under tissue.

Figure 10 Relationships in *Nocomis leptocephalus* of the two pharyngeal tooth arches (PTA) to the masticatory (chewing) pad on the basioccipital process (BOP) of the cranium (CR). Removed are the operculum, gills, pharyngeal (branchial) cavity wall (ends of oral cavity [OC] and esophagus [ESO] are cut), thick epithelium over and some muscles inserted on the pharyngeal arch, and lateral part of the pectoral girdle.

damaging the left). In some species, particularly those with numerous crowded rakers, it may be necessary to remove the arch. All rakers including distinctly formed rudiments are counted. The count may be subdivided into rakers on the lower and upper limbs. Rakers on the lower limb are those below the angle of the gill arch; rakers on the upper limb are those dorsal to the angle. A raker at the angle of the limbs is included in the lower limb count.

Pharyngeal Teeth   Figures 9–11

Counts or shapes of pharyngeal teeth are particularly important in the identification of many minnows and one sucker. The first step is to locate and carefully remove the pharyngeal arches, which bear the teeth.

Pharyngeal arches are modified fifth (most posterior) gill arches. To locate them, the operculum is turned outward (Figure 9). This is assisted by cutting opercular muscles, but with experience, cutting is not necessary. Then a fine-point forceps (tips held together) or a narrow-blade scalpel is inserted into the pharyngeal cavity and held against the anterior edge of the cleithrum—the large, lateral, somewhat sickle-shaped bone of the shoulder girdle, which normally is overlapped by the posterior margin of the operculum. Next, the tool is moved slightly anteriad, away from the cleithrum. The hard structure offering resistance is the pharyngeal arch. One may have to probe somewhat deeper than the anterior surface of the cleithrum to feel the arch.

To remove an arch, the tip of the tool is moved

dorsad and ventrad along the arch, tearing or cutting the tissues that bind the arch. After the posterior margin of the arch is freed, the dorsal, ventral, and anterior points of attachment are located, and the arch is further freed by tearing or cutting. The arch is grasped alternately by its dorsal and ventral limbs and worked back and forth until it comes out; additional cutting may be needed. Teeth may be broken if the middle of the arch is grabbed. Arches of small minnows are frail, but firm pressure is needed to remove them. Arches of large minnows and suckers are robust and can withstand more force, but teeth can easily be lost. Finally, remaining tissue is carefully removed from the arch and teeth.

All teeth are counted in minnows (Figure 11A, B). Some may be broken off in dissection or may have been undergoing natural replacement. Tooth loss can be detected by a stub, socket, or distinctly rough spot on the arch. Well-cleaned arches, magnification, and strong light are needed to detect missing teeth on small arches.

In minnows, a pharyngeal arch bears one, two, or three rows of teeth (Figure 11A, B). In a dentition formula the number of teeth on the left arch is listed first, then a hyphen, then the teeth on the right arch; for example, for five teeth on the left arch and four on the right, the formula is five–four. When minor (outer) row teeth occur, they are separated from major (inner) row teeth on the same arch by a comma. The formula for one minor row tooth and four major row

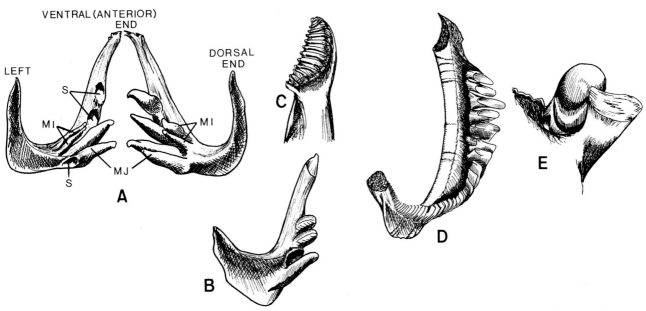

Figure 11 Pharyngeal arches and teeth: (A) *Semotilus corporalis*, dental formula 2,5–4,2 (three teeth missing on left major row, these represented by S—sockets); MI—minor row tooth; MJ—major row tooth. (B) Left arch of *Nocomis raneyi*, four teeth, one of which is missing. (C) Tooth cusp of *Ctenopharyngodon idella*. (D) Left arch of a typical redhorse sucker, *Moxostoma*. (E) Lower two teeth of *Moxostoma carinatum*, the rounded one in process of ankylosis (attachment to arch), the flat-crowned one showing wear.

teeth on both arches is 1,4–4,1. Minor row teeth are smaller and fewer than major row teeth. If one arch of a specimen has more teeth or tooth rows, it usually is the left. Often we remove only the left arch from a specimen.

The tooth formulae employed in the keys are modal counts; like other characters, they may vary. It is desirable to examine two or three specimens to ascertain the modal count.

In some minnows the shape, not the formula, of the teeth is diagnostic (Figure 11A–C). In a redhorse sucker the stoutness of the teeth and arch are discriminatory (Figure 11D–E). A method of discerning without dissection the thickness of the pharyngeal arch in suckers is described in the *Key to Suckers*.

Measurements

Dimensions of parts often are expressed as proportions of the standard length (SL) of the fish (e.g., head length 25% SL). We cite proportional data sparingly; see *Identifying Fishes*. Morphometric characters used in the keys are defined here or are illustrated in keys.

Dial calipers that are used for measuring should be in good working order. The needle points should just touch when the instrument is zeroed. Some dial calipers accurately measure to 0.1 mm, but they are

fairly expensive. Dividers and a rule (1-mm or smaller units) may be used instead.

All measurements are made along a straight line, point to point. It is preferable to measure specimens that are preserved with the body straight. Those that are curved should be forced straight when measuring.

Standard Length (SL).—Standard length is the distance from the anteriormost point on the head (usually front of upper lip or snout tip) to the caudal fin base. See the description of the lateral line scale count for the method of determining the caudal base. Standard length is the most common body–length measurement in ichthyology.

Total Length (TL).—Total length is the distance from the anteriormost point on the head to the posterior end of the longest caudal fin lobe. Typically the caudal lobes are folded together and aligned with the midhorizontal body axis. Total length is commonly used by fishery scientists, especially in the field.

Fork Length (FL).—Fork length is the distance from the anteriormost point on the head to the anteriormost point on the posterior margin of the caudal fin (usually the deepest point of the caudal fin notch).

Fork length is the least used body–length measurement.

Head Length.—Head length is the distance from the anteriormost point of the head (excluding lips for suckers) to either the posteriormost bony or fleshy (membranous) margin of the operculum. Authors often fail to state which posterior point is used; we used the bony margin.

Eye (Orbit) Diameter.—The diameter of the eye is measured from either the fleshy or bony orbital rim. Horizontal fleshy diameter was measured in *Cottus*.

Postorbital Length.—The distance from the posteriormost point on the orbital rim to either the posteriormost bony or fleshy margin of the operculum is measured. The bony rim to tip of the opercular spine was measured in *Cottus*.

Gape Width.—The distance across the mouth is measured between the jaw or lip angles. Lip angles were used for *Nocomis*.

Caudal Peduncle Length.—The distance from the posterior end of the anal fin base to midheight of the bony caudal fin base is measured.

Caudal Peduncle Depth.—The least depth of the caudal peduncle is measured.

Other Commonly Used Anatomical Characters

Several other anatomical features are commonly used to characterize fish species. These are defined below or cross-referenced to definitions or figures elsewhere.

Body Form   Figure 3.

Snout Form   Figure 74.

Frenum   Figures 8, 27, 73.—The frenum is a narrow or wide area of skin that bridges the snout tip to the upper lip; it impedes protrusion of the upper jaw when the mouth is opened. If a groove separates the snout tip and upper lip, a frenum is absent.

Mouth Position   Figure 3.—The position of the anterior end of the mouth is determined with the mouth closed. Terms are inferior (distinctly on ventral aspect of head), subterminal, terminal, supraterminal, and superior; see also *Glossary*.

Lips   Figures 25, 38, 42.—Lips are elaborated or specialized in size, shape, and surface texture in many fishes, particularly bottom feeders. For terminology, see *Key to Suckers* and Figure 42.

Barbels   Figures 4, 25, 27.—The number, point of origin, and size of sensory barbels are diagnostic in minnows. A terminal barbel originates at the posterior end of the lips. A preterminal barbel arises just anterior to the posterior end of the upper lip; often it is largely or entirely hidden in the groove along (just above) the upper lip; it sometimes is called a subterminal barbel. Some minnows have a small flaplike structure positioned similar to a preterminal barbel; we term it a supralabial flap (Figure 38D). In catfishes, a maxillary barbel is attached to the upper lip (applicable also to some minnows); a mental barbel arises on the chin; a nasal barbel originates on the snout near a nare (nostril).

Tubercles and Contact Organs   Figure 33.—These are conic or spinelike structures that occur in certain families and often are restricted to breeding males. They may develop on the head, body, or fins. See discussions under the introductions to the minnow and killifish families, and the key to *Nocomis*. Terms denoting tuberculate areas of the head are shown in Figure 32. Tuberculation generally varies with fish size and sex; tubercles are more numerous and widespread in larger males.

Fin Types and Shapes   Figures 5, 48, 57.—Descriptors of fin margins include convex (rounded outward), straight, concave (rounded inward), and falcate (deeply concave, Figure 29).

Dorsal Fin Position.—The position of the dorsal fin origin relative to the pelvic fin origin (Figure 24C) is often employed in the identification of minnows and is used in some other families.

Scale Types and Parts   Figures 6, 28, 43, 72.—The rhomboid scale is characteristic of gars. Cycloid scales are variously shaped, but not rhomboid, and lack ctenii (tiny spinelike projections); they occur mainly in lower fishes. Ctenoid scales also are variously shaped, but have ctenii on the posterior surface; they occur mostly in higher fishes. Sculpins lack true scales but some have prickles on the head and body (Figure 58).

Genital Papilla   Figures 15, 63, 70, 77.—The papilla is a protuberance through which gametes pass to the exterior; it develops in the male, female, or both sexes depending on the species.

Color Characters

Coloration is important in many aspects of the life of fishes (e.g., as camouflage), for species and sex recognition, and for reproductive signaling. Virtually all Virginia fish species are distinguishable by hues and patterns, sometimes only subtly. We emphasize color by detailed descriptions, extensive use in keys, and through photographs and drawings.

Although color patterns are species-specific, they vary ontogenetically, changing through the larval stage and often in the young and juvenile stages. Many species are sexually dichromatic—adult males differ from adult females. Color may also vary intraspecifically with habitat. Fish living in turbid water or over a pale sandy bottom typically are pallid, whereas those in clear water over a dark bottom or in dark-stained Coastal Plain water are darker.

Living fishes present a greater variety of hues than do preserved fishes because after several days in preservative, usually only the black-gray-pale components of patterns remain. These patterns are caused by the presence and concentration of melanin-bearing cells (melanophores or melanocytes).

We have adopted the following terminology of color patterns. A *stripe* is a long horizontal mark. *Body bars* are long vertical or oblique marks. *Ocular (orbital) bars* radiate from the orbit. *Blotches* are medium or large marks. *Saddles* are medium or large marks on the dorsum; they may connect with lateral bars or blotches. *Band* usually is applied to a mark or zone that crosses a fin parallel to the distal margin; it may also apply to a bar that encircles the upper, lower, or both portions of the body. *Fin streaks* occur on membranes and are parallel to spines and rays. *Fin tessellations* are short, alternating dark and pale marks on spines and rays. *Mottling* refers to a scrawl-like or reticulate pattern composed of many small intermixed dark and pale areas in which many dark marks are interconnected. *Spotted, dotted, flecked,* and *speckled* patterns have small dark marks which are largely or entirely separate. Spots and dots are round or oval, flecks linear, and speckles irregular. *Peppered* or *stippled* describe an area in which melanophores are separate or nearly so. *Stitched* refers to the effect of a pair of dark punctations or short dashes at each lateral line scale pore (e.g., Fish 109). The shade or intensity of a mark, pattern, or area is described as *colorless, immaculate,* or *pale* (very few or no melanophores), *dusky* (moderately concentrated melanophores), *dark* (heavily concentrated), and *black*.

The following figures depict general or specialized color characters: many marks, Figure 12; fin patterns, Figures 34, 40, 44, 49, 51, 55, 56, 67, 69; scale patterns, Figure 45; snout, lip, and chin pigmentation, Figures 36, 37, 53; opercular flaps, Figure 68; saddle-bars in sculpins, Figures 54, 62; peritoneum, Figures 26, 41.

IDENTIFYING FISHES

Accurate identification of species is a prerequisite to accumulating biological knowledge of species. The keys, comparison sections, and illustrations provided herein allow the accurate identification of all adults and most juveniles of the freshwater fishes of Virginia.

Tools of Identification

A few basic implements are needed to identify fishes: a dissecting (binocular or stereo) microscope with 10× to 30× magnification; fine-point forceps; fine-point scissors; scalpel; and dividers and a metric rule or dial calipers.

Some fishes require detailed inspection of the lateral line pored canal system. This is best accomplished with the application of a fine stream of compressed air, which renders the pores and canals more visible. The air source can be a central laboratory supply or an aquarium pump. A hose is connected to the air supply; an eye dropper (bulb removed) fitted to the other end narrows the air stream. Compressed air also aids in partially drying body scales (sometimes helpful when counting scales on small fishes) and for examining small nuptial tubercles. Blotting specimens with a smooth towel serves to make scales more obvious. Toweling, however, may cause loss of tubercles.

Sorting

Sorting involves arranging specimens into groups of similar-appearing specimens. The easiest steps should be done first. For example, soft-rayed fishes can be segregated from spiny-rayed ones, and highly distinctive species can be sorted. Preference is given to larger specimens; then juveniles are aligned with the larger specimens already sorted. Changes in shape and color pattern through a size series are noted. The residue of specimens bears closer scrutiny for differences in position and shape of fins, scale size, mouth orientation, and details of pigmentation. The beginning student is usually able to sort specimens into groups of one family each and these into

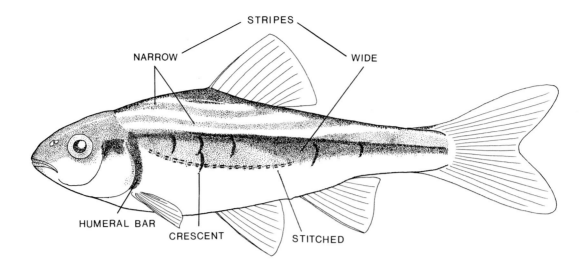

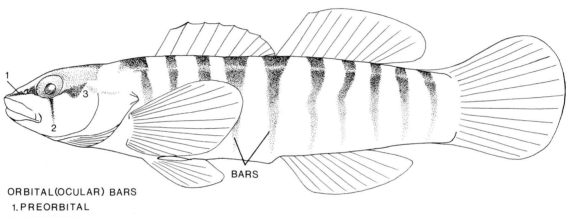

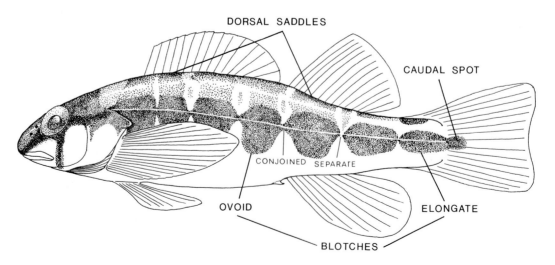

Figure 12 Types of melanistic pigmentary color patterns and markings. See also Figures 55, 56, and 69. ''Orbital'' usually is termed ocular in text.

genera; sometimes even many species may be segregated.

It should not come as a surprise that the sexes of a sexually dimorphic or dichromatic species have not been grouped together. Basic form and color pattern generally are quite similar or alike in the sexes of such species, but males tend to be darker and often have larger fins. Sorting fishes is a skill that improves with experience as one gains an eye for characters and differences. Sorting helps one discern variations in diagnostic characters, whose recognition is crucial in identifying species.

Using the Keys

It has been stated that "keys are made by biologists who don't need them for those who can't use them" (Edmunds et al. 1976). This derives partly from the difficulty that specialist biologists sometimes have in translating their skill in identifying organisms into a written and generally easy-to-use key. Specialists often use esoteric methods and subtle characters. Difficulties of keying are also related to the close similarity between species of many groups, and to the variation in characters that occurs within species.

Keys often appear formidible because of the many technical terms. We hope that we have softened such impressions by the many illustrations. Each step (couplet) of the key involves a decision at its end; the success of the keys hinges on the care and patience exercised in making those decisions.

Organization.—The keys are divided into a key to the families (which follows *Introduction to Accounts*) and keys to genera and species (found after the introductory account of most families). Families and genera that are monotypic in Virginia (represented by only one species) are indicated by inclusion of the species names in the family or generic keys. No key is given for sculpins (Cottidae), as explained in *Systematics and Identification of Cottus*. A few species of minnows and darters appear more than once in a key because of their variability.

The keys are in the form of dichotomous (two-branched) couplets. Each couplet has two parts (e.g., 1a and 1b); each part of a couplet contains one or more statements that are opposed to those in the corresponding part of that couplet. The statements give diagnostic (distinguishing) characteristics (e.g., anatomy, color). All statements in only one part of a couplet should fit the fish at hand.

Many couplets have an unpaired statement which follows the paired statement and is in parentheses. These supplementary statements apply to all taxa to which that part of the couplet applies, and usually apply to some but never all taxa to which the opposing part of the couplet applies.

Keying.—Keying involves sequential comparison of a specimen with a series of paired opposing statements (the parts of the couplets). The process continues, following the applicable statements (those that characterize the fish), until one ends at an identification. One begins at the first couplet, and determines which of its two parts fits the specimen. At the end of each part of a couplet is found either a number or a name. If the part that applies to the specimen ends in a number, then go to the couplet so numbered. If the part that applies to the specimen ends in a name, then the fish has been identified to the taxonomic level (family, genus, or species) in that key. If the fish is identified to family, then go to the key to genera for that family, and likewise from genus to species.

If one reaches a dead end in the key—the specimen fits neither part of a couplet, or it does not closely resemble the species determined (judging by illustrations)—then one should back-track through the couplets to where an error likely was made. During keying, it is useful to record character states determined for the fish at hand, partly to render back-tracking easier.

One should not finesse (bypass by guessing) any couplet. All characters given and the figures cited in the couplet should be considered. Our decisions to include illustrations were based on the aid they would give to users of the keys.

Key Characters.—Diagnostic characters are selected for discriminatory power and relative ease of observation. Generally the more useful characters are listed first within each couplet. Major emphasis is given to qualitative characters (e.g., a body part present or absent), the more readily examined meristic characters such as fin ray number, and specific aspects of color patterns.

The keys are based on the most frequently observed and other typical states (traits, values, expressions) of characters. "Usually" refers to the state found in about 80% or more of the specimens studied. (This percentage differs from that connoted in the species accounts, where the "usually" occurring state or range of states may occur in as few as 50% of the fish; see *Introduction to Accounts*.) Many expressions of meristic data in the keys indicate both the typical and extreme values; for example, "lateral line scales (40)42–45(47)" means that at least 80% of the specimens have 42 to 45 scales and that the known extremes are 40 and 47. Individual values or ranges of values lacking a qualifier indicate all known values for the populations treated. Because of variability within species, we recommend that, if possible, 3–5 specimens be considered to determine typical character states.

Key characters apply primarily to larger juveniles and adults. Exceptions are in the keys to the lampreys (larvae are included) and black basses (a separate key to the young is given). Larger young and small juveniles of many species are keyable by the same characters as adults, but often they are best identified by matching them with identified adults.

Color patterns or marks produced by melanophores are widely used in the keys because they are retainable in preservative. Patterns may vary in intensity and size; for example, marks often are bolder and more widespread in breeding males. However, the center of development of marks rarely varies.

Well-preserved specimens should be selected for identification. Those that were preserved well after death often are unnaturally pallid and their diagnostic marks may be modified or lacking. Few nonmelanistic color characters are used in our keys because they are ephemeral in preservative. Those included are important; specimens should be observed in life or very shortly after.

Black-spot parasites, which may occur in the skin of the head, body, or fins, should not be confused with normal color. The embedded parasites cause fishes to form distinct small black spots; some specimens may be heavily spotted.

Geographic distribution—presence or absence of a species in a drainage—is included in some couplets to supplement anatomical and color characters; it is used exclusively when diagnostic characters are too subtle or problematic. This particularly occurs for speciose genera and very similar species; only the Virginia portion of the species' range is given. The large distributional data base for this book clearly establishes details of distributional patterns; we are confident of their use as cues for identification. It has been our experience that in cases of putative range extensions, the species usually were misidentified. However, range extensions will occur, for which the identifier should be alert.

Perusal Method

Perusal means to go through, to inspect in detail; in this case, illustrations are examined and specimens of unknown identity are matched with them. Some students and professional biologists often do only that to identify organisms. This method is founded partly in the exquisite field guides available for many groups of animals and plants. Perusal of illustrations can be a quick and accurate method of identifying specimens; it circumvents much of the often lengthy and tedious process of keying. Hence we recommend the field guide by Page and Burr (1991).

The specimens in our black-and-white photographs were selected for typical proportions and melanophore color patterns. However, for some species it is nearly impossible to find a photographable specimen combining the typical states of all characters.

Verification

Identifications can be verified by comparing specimens with those in an institutional collection that has been curated by a competent ichthyologist; or by requesting the direct assistance of an ichthyologist. Most ichthyologists are interested in helping others identify fishes. We suggest this as a last step for certain identification, particularly for species to be published on. A regional ichthyologist listed under Acknowledgements may be consulted; a sizeable job may warrant a fee. Voucher specimens should be preserved, particularly for unique or otherwise important records. They should be accompanied by full and accurate locality data, and they should be deposited in a museum or other stable fish collection (Crossman 1980; *Collecting and Observing Fishes*).

Species New to Virginia?

In the event of a possible first record of a species from Virginia, see the section titled *Fishes of Possible Occurrence in Virginia*. Some species are diagnosed there; others are included in keys.

Learning the Species

The process of learning to identify the members of a regional ichthyofauna tends to occur in steps, generally by common species first, then newly encountered ones. Nearly all Virginia species are instantly recognizable by external features; upon learning them, they rarely would need to be keyed. Learn species by *looking* at them. Gestalt criteria for identifying fishes are engendered in the "art of seeing well" (Douglas et al. 1989). Many very similar fishes can be distinguished by the "expressions on their faces" (P. W. Smith *in* Burr and Page 1987).

INTRODUCTION TO FAMILY, GENUS, AND SPECIES ACCOUNTS

The following identifies the topics addressed and their sequence in accounts of families, genera, and species, and states our criteria for selecting, methods of summarizing, and formats of presenting data. Some often used terms are explained below, others are defined in the *Glossary*. For broader treatment and additional details on biology of fishes, we recommend M. Brown (1957), Herald (1961), Ommanney (1964), Marshall (1965), Grosvenor (1965), Norman and Greenwood (1975), Lagler et al. (1977), Bond (1979), Moyle and Cech (1982), Wootton (1990), and the continuing series of *Fish Physiology* edited by W. S. Hoar and D. J. Randall. The book by Cailliet et al. (1986) is a solid response to the long need for a broad ichthyology manual that includes modern laboratory and field methods.

Many species have a tangled taxonomic and nomenclatural history. To facilitate the correct use of the literature and to provide a partial background of practices in the field of systematic biology, some principles of systematics are discussed. Comprehensive introductions to the methods of taxonomy and nomenclature, which are included in the wider field of systematics, are by Mayr (1969), H. Ross (1974), and Wiley (1981). Our nomenclatural deliberations follow the rules of the International Code of Zoological Nomenclature (ICZN 1985).

The sequence of accounts of orders, families, genera, and species is phylogenetic, as well as knowledge permits. The most primitive (lower) fishes are treated first, then those of intermediate and advanced (higher) status (*Cladogram*; Table 2).

PHYLOGENETIC SYSTEMATICS

With the advent in the last two decades of phylogenetic (cladistic) methodology, formerly proposed evolutionary relationships often have been doubted or revised. The word clade means a branch. A primary objective of the cladistic school is to construct hierarchically arranged diagrams (cladograms or phylogenetic trees), whose branches represent natural groups or lineages of organisms or taxa. A taxon is a formal or informal grouping of organisms into a species or higher unit.

The branching points in cladograms ideally are only bifurcated (two-forked). Each lineage immediately beyond a branching point is regarded as the sister group of the other; that is, the two lineages are more closely related to each other genealogically than to any other lineage. Two sister groups (and each sister group by itself) form a monophyletic group—a group composed only of the organisms which share a unique common history. For example (*Cladogram*), the orders Cypriniformes (minnows, suckers, and allies) and Siluriformes (catfishes and allies) each constitute a monophyletic group. They are sister groups within the also monophyletic superorder Ostariophysi; they are more closely related to each other than to non-ostariophysan fishes.

When more than two lineages are drawn as stemming from one branching point, generally their exact interrelations are unresolved. For example, a trifurcation may indicate that the three advanced lineages are equally related to each other and to the ancestral stock; such an occurrence is unlikely.

The delineation of a monophyletic group is founded on the sharing by its members of one or more evolutionarily advanced (derived or apomorphic) character states (traits) that are unique to the group. Character states are polarized (i.e., postulated as either primitive or advanced) by the following criteria: (1) their distribution in outgroups (closely related taxa); the advanced states are those absent in outgroups; (2) their position in a transformation series (a character with at least three states each in a different species, indicating successional change); the advanced state tends to be the most specialized one; (3) their geological sequence; the advanced state tends to occur in the youngest fossils; (4) their ontogenetic sequence; the state that develops last embryonically or postembryonically tends to be the advanced one.

Primitive (ancestral or plesiomorphic) states are rejected for defining monophyletic groups. Their origin preceded that of the group; by themselves they do not indicate the advancement of lineages and they often have been lost evolutionarily by some members of a lineage. (That loss is an advanced state.)

Shared advanced character states (synapomorphies) are used to discern the sequence of branching of lineages; the sequence is presumed to be correlated to evolutionary time. Generally the less-shared states occur in the most recently evolved lineages. The states unique to a species (autapomorphies) can not be used for sequencing; they are assumed to have originated in that species and to have not been passed on. A cladogram fitting the character-state sequencing then can be drawn and translated into a classification of the group.

Principles of phylogenetic systematics are discussed by Mayr (1981) and Cohen (1984), in detail by Wiley (1981), and with broad application to North American freshwater fishes, in the volume edited by Mayden (1992). Papers that demonstrate phylogenetic methods for the general student of fisheries are by Smith (1988) and Smith and Stearley (1989). Examples of the acceptance of phylogenetic approaches are the adoption of cladistic classifications in the 1989 edition of *Vertebrate Life* (Pough et al. 1989), the recent acceptance by the American Fisheries Society of several name changes, and Table 1.

Our comments on the status and interrelations of taxa are phylogenetically based, at least in spirit. Some are handicapped by uncertainty of the polarity of character states. Many groups of freshwater fishes have not been phylogenetically analyzed; our statements on their interrelations are from classifications in the literature whose viewpoint is primarily phenetic or evolutionary.

Differing from phylogenetic systematics are the phenetic and evolutionary taxonomic approaches. Phenetic (or numerical) classifications are based on overall similarity among taxa as determined usually by large numbers of relatively unselected characters. Here, phylogenetic relationships may be obscured by evolutionary convergence of taxa; thus, superficially similar but distantly related taxa may be taxonomically clustered. An extreme example would be classi-

fying together the lampreys and true eels based on body form. Some pheneticists do not ascribe phylogenetic significance to their groupings.

Evolutionary taxonomy has a long history; generally it is a more subjective approach than phenetic taxonomy. Its many tenets for hypothesizing evolutionary history and constructing classifications include the weighing of both the assumed importance of characters and the degrees of difference among taxa, and using primitive character states.

FAMILY ACCOUNTS

The family is a category or level of higher classification that unites monophyletically related subfamilies and subordinate taxa. Some families are monogeneric (have only one genus) or monotypic (one species). We introduce families generally with a statement of the number of species; a brief anatomical description; phylogenetic relationships; an estimate of the geological age of the family; a synopsis of biology, habitat, and distribution; mention often of prominent genera, subgenera, and species groups; an overview of current taxonomic problems; and a consideration of economic and other importance of the group.

Name.—In zoology all formal family names are plural and end in -idae; the adjectival -id is also used. The stem of the scientific name is formed from the name of the type genus of the family. For example, the type genus of the minnow family is *Cyprinus* (for the common carp), hence the family name Cyprinidae or cyprinid fishes. The meaning of the scientific family name is also indicated in this section. Sometimes we state the basis of the accepted common name of the family, that in the heading; additional common names are given when in wide use.

KEY TO SPECIES

The introduction to each family is followed by a key to the Virginia genera and species, unless the family is monogeneric or monotypic. Introductions to characters used in the keys and to the process of identification are contained in *Anatomy and Color*, *Identifying Fishes*, and the *Glossary*. Specialized aspects of anatomy and methods of keying that pertain to particular families are explained in the introduction to the key for those families.

GENERIC ACCOUNTS

Genera are introduced by a common name, an indication of diversity (number of total and Virginia species), a brief statement of some major characteristics, and sometimes a consideration of their closest relatives and taxonomic problems. Genera have authorship; the format *Boleosoma* DeKay signifies that this taxon was validly described first by DeKay.

Many large genera are partitioned into subgenera. Genera and subgenera constitute the genus-group level. Subgenera are enclosed by parentheses when written after genera; for example, the name *Etheostoma* (*Boleosoma*) *longimanum* indicates that the species *longimanum* is in the subgenus *Boleosoma* of the genus *Etheostoma*.

Genera and subgenera can change in status (level of recognition); they may be lumped or split. Lumping means that two or more genus groups have been combined (synonymized) to one. When a genus group is split, one or more of its members take separate status. In either case, the selection of the name for a newly constituted genus group is governed by rules of priority in the ICZN (1985); the oldest valid genus-group name that has been applied to a member is used. For example, in the elevation of the satinfin shiner group from a subgenus of *Notropis* to a genus, *Cyprinella* (whose type species is a satinfin shiner) has priority over generic names later described for any satinfin shiner.

When two or more names that are the oldest for a genus group were proposed on the same date (usually in the same publication), then the valid name is chosen by the first reviser. For example, both *Cyprinella* and *Moniana* were based on satinfin shiners and were described in the same paper; *Cyprinella* was selected.

When a genus group is to be split from another but has not had a genus-group name described for any member, or if a generically or subgenerically distinct species is discovered, then a new genus group is named. Another kind of change concerns the shifting of species between genus groups without altering the level of either group. In most cases, shifts in status and composition of genus groups (and other taxa) are based on new information or on new interpretations of formerly available data that bear on the distinctiveness or relationships of taxa.

Name.—The meaning of the scientific name, and sometimes the origin of the common name, are stated. Common names of genera often are not standardized; we propose several.

SPECIES ACCOUNTS

Scientific Name

The heading of the species accounts includes the scientific name of the species and the last name of its describer(s) (author). The author is placed in parentheses when the species is currently assigned to a genus other than that in which it was first described. The scientific name is a latinized binomen (two names) with the generic name given first. If the species name (epithet) is an adjective, it must agree in gender with the generic name. The official starting point for scientific names of animals is the 10th edition of the *Systema Naturae*, published in 1758 by the Swedish naturalist Carl von Linné (now known by his latinized name Linnaeus). The names we use are largely those accepted by the joint Committee on Names of Fishes of the American Fisheries Society and the American Society of Ichthyologists and Herpetologists (Robins et al. 1980, 1991). Exceptions are listed in Table 1 (*Preface*).

Scientific names occasionally are changed. No two species (or subspecies) in the same genus can have the same specific (or subspecific) epithet. Name duplication (homonymy) may result when species are shifted between genera or when genera are lumped. Homonymy is rectified by applying the next oldest valid name to the later described species, or if another name does not exist, by giving that species a new name. If an earlier valid name is discovered to apply to a species, the rules of priority of the International Code dictate (with exceptions) that the earliest name is to be used. When two species-group names for the same taxon have the same date of publication, the rule of first reviser again applies.

Among other kinds of name changes, a form or population recognized as a species may later be considered insufficiently distinct from another species. In such cases the later described form is synonymized with (takes the species name of) the earlier known one. However, the synonymized form may still be recognized as a subspecies, in which case it retains its original authorship and is written as a trinomen. For example, the tessellated darter *Etheostoma olmstedi* was described from Connecticut in 1842 by Storer. A Virginia population was described as a species *Boleosoma vexillare* by Jordan in 1880. The Virginia population is now considered to be only subspecifically distinct from the tessellated darter. Thus the names are written and authored (and abbreviated) as follows: *Etheostoma olmstedi* Storer (or *E. olmstedi*) refers to the entire species; *E. olmstedi olmstedi* Storer (or *E. o. olmstedi*) applies only to the populations of the nominate subspecies (that bearing the species name); *E. olmstedi vexillare* (Jordan) (or *E. o. vexillare*) refers only to the population identified as *vexillare*.

Sometimes a group of populations regarded as a single species is later found to include more than one distinct form. These may be recognized as separate subspecies or species. The original subspecies or species epithets remain with the populations to which they were first applied. Such is the case with the Roanoke darter *Percina roanoka*, first described as a species. In a subsequent period it was considered a subspecies *P. crassa roanoka* of the Piedmont darter *Percina crassa*; later *P. roanoka* was reelevated to species status.

Considerable time often intervenes between discovery and formal (published) description of organisms. The lag frequently is related to the length of time needed to complete comprehensive, comparative, and revisionary studies of groups to which newly recognized organisms belong. It is briefly woeful but scientifically advancing that new species often reveal taxonomic problems of their relatives which formerly were believed to be clearly understood.

Undescribed taxa are treated in this volume. In addition to a common name, most undescribed taxa have had a manuscript (unpublished) scientific name proposed as the specific or subspecific epithet. However, manuscript scientific names should not appear in print before the description is published. Publication of a name lacking proper description makes the name a *nomen nudum*. We include undescribed forms (by common name) to allow their separation from similar, formally named species or subspecies, and to provide comprehensive coverage of the Virginia ichthyofauna.

Major criteria for determining whether two forms should be recognized at the species or infraspecific (below species) level include their degree of similarity in anatomy and coloration, and their reproductive interaction. When two distinct forms with overlapping geographic ranges interbreed freely in the zone of overlap, they are said to intergrade. Characteristics of intergrade populations usually are quite variable. The presence of intergrades indicates that the forms are not reproductively isolated, hence not "biological species," and are best regarded as subspecies or as a lower category (race or deme). Conversely, infrequent hybridization or a complete lack of interbreeding would indicate that one or more barriers to intermating exist, and that the forms are species. Potential barriers or isolation mechanisms are many, among them different reproductive timing, spawning site selection, courtship behavior, and gamete sterility and other cytological imbalances. When two closely related forms do not occur in sufficient geographic proximity to allow interbreeding, decisions on their status are more restrictedly made on the basis of, for example, appearance, cytology, or biochemistry.

Reproductive criteria often present problems, as when the frequency of interbreeding lies between common and rare. Thus systematists often must make a rather subjective decision on whether intergradation or hybridization has occurred; that is, on whether the forms are subspecies or species. Partly to circumvent such deliberations, the evolutionary species concept is being increasingly adopted—two taxa or lineages may be considered species despite potential or actual interbreeding if they maintain separate identities and evolutionary tendencies.

Common Name

Often called vernacular names, these are chosen on the basis of appropriateness (e.g., a reference to a physical feature or geographic range), uniqueness (no two species should have the same name), and long-term use (to stabilize nomenclature). Patronymic common names (named for a person) are not recognized by Robins et al. (1991). Some species are referred to by anglers, commercial fishers, and others by more than one common (or folk or local) name, often confusingly so. The many origins of names are discussed by Cohen (1969) and Robins et al. (1991); Cloutman and Olmsted (1983) list alternate common names of southeastern U.S. fishes.

Photographs

At least one black-and-white photograph, generally of an adult, is given for each species (except that a sturgeon and two pikes are shown by drawings). These illustrations are captioned "Fish" and numbered. A male and female are shown for many species that have obvious sexual dimorphism (usually differences in lengths of fins) and dichromatism (different color patterns or intensities). In many sexually dichromatic species the color differences are size-related, being most notable in adults when small females are compared to large males; we show the extreme sexual differences for many species.

Larger young or small juveniles are shown with adults for many common species in which these stages differ markedly. For some species, such as the spottail shiner *Notropis hudsonius*, we show more than one adult color morph, whose differences are independent of sex. When possible we selected well-preserved typical adults whose basic color pattern was not masked by excessive dark or silver pigment. Other variations are shown in the color plates.

Systematics

Many of the working principles and procedures of systematic biology that apply in this section have been introduced above. In this section we give the body of water, general location, and the year in which the species was originally described; if from Virginia, a citation of the original description is included. Subspecies and races are noted mainly for Virginia populations. In addition to being of academic interest, infraspecific differentiation (development of differences within a species) has a biological basis and can have relevance to management. Phylogenetic relationships and, when recognized, the subgenus and species group to which the species belong are considered. We also discuss some aspects of taxonomic history and current systematic problems. The history often is a key for the allocation of literature to species whose names have varied. The consideration of taxonomic problems helps to identify worthy study subjects and possible future name changes.

Description

A basic description of the species is given; for many species it contains original data. This section also serves as a checklist of character states (characteristics) of species to aid in their identification.

Character states often are described with modifiers that indicate their frequency of presence or absence. In species accounts we consistently use the following as defined: rarely—the character state occurs in 1–5% of the specimens; occasionally—6–20%; often—21–50%; usually—51–95% (see also *Identifying Fishes*); almost always—96–99%.

Materials.—The terms series and lot, as used in species accounts, refer to a sample of one or more specimens of a species collected at one place and time. For poorly known species virtually all significant literature sources were used. For well-known, widespread, or rather variable species, the choice of data often was narrowed to those bearing on Virginia and nearby populations.

Anatomy.—The description focuses on external characters. The first sentence gives one or a few diagnostic characteristics and the typical size range of adults. The amount of subsequent information varies by species; for some it is little more than a diagnosis. Detailed descriptions are given for some poorly known species which we have studied in some depth. Proportional measurements generally are included only where they are critical for species identification; their format is described in *Anatomy and Color*.

Meristics.—The general format for reporting meristic data—for example, "lateral line scales (35)37–

40(42)"—indicates that 80–90% of the specimens have 37 to 40 scales, and that the full known range is 35 to 42 scales. Ranges of values without parenthetical values or qualifiers indicate the full ranges. In lamprey accounts, meristic data are given in the *Anatomy* and *Dentition* sections.

Color in Preservative.—Descriptions refer to shades and patterns produced by melanophores. In describing fins, we apply the term pale to the absence of distinctive markings or notable shading, although vague pigmentation may occur in the fin or along its base. Absence of pigmentation from the venter often is not mentioned, nor are browns and yellows when they are caused by discoloration by fats.

The series of terms used for increasing intensity of pigmentation (concentration of melanophores) is: colorless (immaculate or pale), dusky, dark, and black; most of these terms are subject to the same qualifiers noted above. Specific descriptors of patterns are treated under *Anatomy and Color*, in the *Glossary*, and under the family Cottidae. An analysis of color patterns in fishes is by Breder (1972).

Color in Life.—Descriptions are largely of colors that are lost in preservative.

Larvae.—Identification of fish larvae is a specialized field. We provide references only to keys and descriptions of larvae; these are lacking for many Virginia species. Descriptions of larvae often have been compiled in series of publications; for many species we cite only the later papers.

Comparison

Emphasis is placed on comparing species that are very similar and which often live near each other or together. The comparison generally is found in the account of the species treated first in the sequence of accounts; the account of the other species refers to the location of a comparison. Sometimes this section lists, without a comparative statement, characteristics not included in the key but which promote quick recognition of a species.

The general format is the statement of a character and then in brackets, the character state of each species. The first listed character state always pertains to the species in whose account the comparison appears; next is the abbreviation *vs.* (*versus*); last is the character state of the second species. When the term "usually" applies to the character state of both species, it precedes the bracketed statements. An example is "Lateral line scales usually [40–45 *vs.* 34–39]."

Here the character is the lateral line scale count; the usual states (typical counts) are given for each species; 40–45 scales pertains to the species in whose account the comparison occurs.

Biology

This section treats life history (natural history) aspects including food habits, age or size at attainment of sexual maturity, longevity, age and growth, maximum size, and reproductive aspects such as spawning migration, season, temperature, habitat, nest-building and spawning behavior, parental care, and fecundity. Curious habits and interspecific hybridization are noted for some species. In general, we omit life history variations from the adult norm. In cases of abundant literature on a species, we emphasize that from Virginia and nearby. Life history aspects are unknown or poorly known for many Virginia fishes, particularly the smaller species.

Food Habits.—Generally only major food items are listed. Some detail is given to food habits, as well as other life history aspects, based on original data from our studies and those by students under our direction. We use the term larva for the nymphal (immature) stages of lower insect orders.

Maturity, Longevity, Growth, and Life Stages.—Mature refers to adult fish, those capable of reproducing. We recognized maturity by one or more of the following criteria: large fish size, large gonads, the presence of breeding tubercles and nuptial color, and behavior. Longevity is the length of the life span.

Most fishes have an indeterminate growth pattern; that is, growth continues throughout life. Relatively rapid growth is typical of young and juveniles; in some species it may be sustained during much of adulthood in environments with abundant food and other favorable conditions. Information on growth is variously presented depending often on the amount, manner of presentation, and geographic origin of published data. Usually only lengths that pertain to a single age-group, generally an adult age commonly reached, are reported. For example, length at age 2 is often cited for species whose maximum longevity is 4 years. Lengths may refer either to those calculated for the time of annulus formation (see below), or to any portion of the year of the age-group.

In our reporting of age and growth, many original references were used, as well as the detailed compilations by Carlander (1969, 1977) which have a wide geographic data base. Smith and Kauffman (1982) compiled age and growth of gamefishes in Virginia

from unpublished Dingell–Johnson reports; generally we cite only the most recent and inclusive versions of the original reports available to us. The volume edited by Hall (1987) is a synthesis of the current revolution in techniques of determining age and growth of fishes. It indicates that much published data, particularly concerning older specimens, are suspect.

Maximum size in the state that is given for most nongame species generally is based on specimens in the Roanoke College collection; we did not canvas museums for larger specimens. For game species, two kinds of size records are recognized by the VDGIF—the historical record and the state record; the distinction began with fish caught in July 1985. We cite only the larger record, or only the state record if informed by a VDGIF biologist that a larger historical record is questionable. For most species, the largest known individual from beyond Virginia is noted if larger than the Virginia record.

Metric units of measurement are used throughout; English units are secondarily given (usually in parentheses) for some species, mostly for maximum size of gamefishes. Metric data are presented first, regardless of which are the original. Conversion factors are listed at the back of the book. Fish length may be expressed as standard length (SL), fork length (FL), or total length (TL); we use the one that is conventional for the species. In some cases authors provided equations for converting between two of these length categories; we often used them to render data comparable with the majority of studies.

Life stages were defined by Lagler (1956). *Larva* refers to developmental stages after hatching and preceding the young stage. The change from the larva to the young stage is termed transformation or metamorphosis. *Young* refers to members of age-group 0, beginning just after transformation and extending through December 31 of the year of hatching; this stage also is termed young-of-the-year. *Juvenile* refers to fish between young and adult stages. Among the many systems of terminology for larval and postlarval stages of fishes (Kendall et al. 1984), the trend is to not recognize the young stage, but to include it in the juvenile stage. Juveniles often are characterized as having the appearance of small adults. However, because age-0 individuals of many Virginia species differ distinctly from older juveniles, we retain the use of the young stage. *Adult* refers to mature fish, able to spawn, spawning, spent (just spawned), or living to spawn again. Often it is difficult to distinguish small adults from large juveniles when small adults lack obvious development of reproductive characteristics (gonadal and external nuptial features). Lamprey stages have a partly different life-stage terminology; this is explained in the introduction to that family.

Age-group 0—As defined above for young; also often termed age-class 0 or age 0. *Age-group 1*—Fish in the first calendar year after that of hatching. Fish of older ages are reported similarly. A growing number of investigators report ages according to months or 12-month intervals beginning with hatching (as we do for some species), as opposed to the above system in which age changes on January 1. *Year-class*—all individuals of a population of a species hatched in a single calendar year, defined by that year (e.g., the 1986 year-class). *Annulus*—year mark on scales or other hard parts, formed each year usually upon resumption of rapid growth in spring or summer; termed annulus 1 for the first-year mark, etc.

Reproduction.—When easily summarized by family or genus, the descriptions of certain reproductive aspects (e.g., nest building), often are restricted to those sections. Broad summaries and analyses of reproduction of fishes are by Breder and Rosen (1966), Loiselle and Barlow (1978), and Blumer (1982).

The timing of spawning generally varies geographically within a species, occurring earlier and often for a longer period in the southerly latitudes and lower elevations (Hubbs 1985). Many Virginia species have not been observed spawning or performing other reproductive behaviors; we estimated the probable breeding period based on data from other regions or on some of the following criteria.

Reproductive periods were estimated from dates of capture of males having well-developed nuptial color and tubercles, and by the gonadal condition of preserved females. A sure sign of close imminence of spawning is the "running ripe" condition of females—extrusion of mature eggs without application of pressure to the abdomen or with slight pressure. In many species the release of milt by males may occur long before or after the spawning period, hence often it is only a general index of spawning time.

Fecundity (the number of mature eggs or ripe ova produced by a female in one year) is expressed as a numerical range. Fecundity is directly related to size of females and size of mature ova. Published fecundity estimates from fractionally or intermittently spawning species almost always have been lower than realized fecundity (Gale and Deutsch 1985; Heins and Rabito 1986).

Hybridization.—The summary of natural hybrids of Virginia fishes in an earlier section is based on crosses listed in species accounts. Many natural hybrid combinations and a few successful artificial crosses are reported. Generally the hybrids listed are those for which both parental species occur in Virginia, whether the hybrid is known from the state or not.

Habitat

This section describes the types, widths, depths, and gradients of bodies of water that are occupied. It includes associations with substrates, vegetation, and other cover; temperature, acidity, and salinity preferences or tolerances are noted. The information applies to juveniles and adults during warmer months (i.e., April through October) unless specified otherwise. The term "preferred" habitat is used in a loose sense to indicate habitats typically occupied, based on our observations and collections. Habitat summaries are found in *Drainages, Biogeography*, and Table 2. The proceedings of a symposium on habitat and other ecologic aspects of North American stream fishes was edited by Matthews and Heins (1987).

A riffle is characterized by a notable drop in elevation, hence the current is rapid; riffles are relatively shallow and the surface has white water. However, pockets of reduced current caused by rough substrate usually occur in riffles. We use the term run for sections of moderate or swift current, usually of greater depth than riffles, and with little or no white water; runs are often called raceways or glides by others (Winn 1958b). Runs are distinguished by Hatch (1986) as being deeper and slower than raceways. Pools are slower and generally deeper than runs. Pool-like calm backwaters may occur at edges of runs and riffles.

Definitions of stream-size categories are given in *Biogeography*.

Substrate (bottom material) categories include silt, sand, gravel, rubble, boulder, and bedrock; their definitions essentially follow Lagler (1956). The Wentworth system of substrate classification has gained prominence (Cummins and Lauff 1969; Hynes 1970); some of its categories are compared under the former categories in the *Glossary*. We use the term hard bottom for largely unsilted substrates of gravel or larger materials. Soft bottoms are chiefly composed of silt or sand.

Concerning temperature relations, fishes often are loosely categorized as coldwater, coolwater, and warmwater species, but limits of categories rarely are stated. Temperature relations of organisms are complex, often varying by life stage, function, and season (Hokanson 1977; see *Biology* in the account of the brook trout). According to the summary by Casselman (1978), coldwater fishes, when juveniles and adults, have physiological optima of about 12–17°C.

Very generally, coolwater fishes may be defined as those with optima of 18–25°C as subadults and adults. Hokanson (1977) defined temperature classes of temperate-climate fishes in greater detail, applying the terms stenotherm, mesotherm, and eurytherm. These terms translate respectively to narrow, moderate, and wide concerning the breadth of temperature adaptation. Most of our thermal categorizations of species are based on summer temperatures of waters yielding numerous records; several are from Coutant (1977). Characteristics of coldwater and warmwater streams are contrasted by Winger (1981); the temperature separating these is between 20 and 24°C. Most streams vary longitudinally in temperature (e.g., Moyle and Li 1979).

Salinity and pH relations often are founded on chemical values associated with species records and distribution patterns. The pH is an important ecologic factor, particularly on the Coastal Plain. Now, with acid precipitation, it may become a critical factor in many other areas. Much of our pH data for eastern Virginia is from Corning (1967a, 1967b), Corning and Prosser (1969), and Norman and Southwick (1985). Frequently consulted sources for other central eastern areas are Smith (1953), Collette (1962), and Hastings (1979, 1984). Primary references for maximum salinity records in Virginia and vicinity are Hildebrand and Schroeder (1928), Keup and Bayless (1964), Schwartz (1964, 1981b), and Musick (1972). Problems of defining natural salinity relations are addressed by Schwartz (1981b). Adults of many freshwater species are found in salinities higher than would be tolerable for reproduction and by early life stages; many extreme records probably are of waifs.

Distribution

Maps and the text document the overall distribution pattern, specific aspects of the pattern, and important individual records. An analysis of distribution patterns of the Virginia fish fauna is presented in *Biogeography*.

Text.—The total and Virginia ranges are stated. Virginia ranges are given by drainage, often by major subdivisions of drainages, and usually by physiographic provinces; for some species, physiographic distribution is considered only under *Habitat*. Ranges in extralimital portions of Virginia drainages are noted when they contribute substantially to our understanding of distribution patterns in Virginia. Numbers and years of records are given when ranges have expanded or contracted, or when the species is rare or extirpated (for some species these data are given under *Abundance*).

Questions of native or introduced status of populations of many species—their original drainage occurrence status—are examined chronologically from stocking records, population establishment, or first records for the drainage. Records of years of stocking cited from governmental publications often are fiscal years. A summary of the drainage occurrence status of Virginia species is given in Tables 2 and 3 and *Appendix 2*.

We discuss important records that are unverified, problematic, dubious, or that initially were misidentified, in order to clarify them. When involving more than one species, the discussion generally appears only in the account of one of them. Acronyms (abbreviations) of institutions, agencies, and collectors used when referring to particular collections are defined in *Appendix 2*.

Map of Virginia Range.—A spot-type map portrays the distribution of each species; the native and introduced portions are identified only in the text. Documented angling records were added to maps of gamefishes generally only when few or no other records were available for an area. Records are lacking for many small streams and artificial ponds.

Base Map and Symbols.—The base map was drafted from the U.S. Geological Survey Base Map of Virginia, scale 1:500,000, 1957 edition. Symbols on maps represent the capture of at least one specimen at the site indicated. Some individual symbols represent sites sampled 10–50 times and yielding thousands of specimens of a species. The center of a symbol (projected center for crescentic symbols) indicates the collection site. Many records were omitted because of immediate proximity to other records. Unless otherwise defined in a map or legend, circles signify records from running and saline waters; on lakes they refer to preimpoundment collections. Triangles depict records from ponds and lakes.

Distributional Relationships.—Twenty-six maps show the range of a pair or small group of closely related species; each species is indicated by a different symbol. Generally a solid circle is used for the most widespread species in the state, an open circle for the next so. The sequence of listing species names and symbols on maps generally is that in which the accounts of the species are presented.

For these 26 maps the distributional relationships generally can be categorized as allopatric (the range of each species is separated by a large or small gap), or parapatric (range borders are in contact but with very narrow or no overlap). A few slightly sympatric species (ranges distinctly overlapping) also are shown on the same map, but broadly sympatric species are on separate maps. These patterns are further defined and exemplified in *Biogeography*.

To discriminate between different types of range overlap, syntopic species are so called because they occur at some of the same general sites (e.g., a short reach of stream), or even in the same habitat (e.g., rubble bottom in swift riffles). Allotopic species largely segregate into separate areas or distinctly different habitats within an overlap zone.

Data Base.—The large majority of the data base for fish distribution in Virginia is from our collecting and museum searches, collections from other surveys brought to us for identification, information from colleagues, and the primary scientific literature. We also used "gray" literature, for example unpublished theses and sparingly distributed reports of institutions, agencies, and consultants. The localities for species lists from some 9,821 fish collections from Virginia are shown on Maps 1–5; overall, slightly more than 10,000 species lists were treated through 1990. In determining geographic and ecologic ranges of species, we agree that ". . . an obsession with spots [locality plots] should be matched with an obsession for their absence" (F. W. Schueler *in* Coad 1987).

We did not attempt to verify (by specimen examination) many of the plotted records; these records were used only when we were confident of correct identifications. Questionable records are plotted only if they are particularly important, for example, if they are unique or nearly so for a drainage or physiographic province, or they otherwise extend a range. Such records are identified in maps and legends as questionable, problematic, dubious, or unverified, and should not be accepted unless substantiated; most of them are noted in appropriate accounts or in *Biogeography*.

Data Synthesis.—Locality data, species lists, and documentation were filed by collector; that is, a person, institution, or agency. A unique acronym was available or assigned to each collector, and a collection number (generally the original field or station number) was given to each collection. All collection numbers were unique when coupled with their collector acronym. Separately for each collector, exact collection sites were marked on one or more fixed-scale copies of our base map; the collection number was written by each site on these collector maps.

In 1976 the data from approximately 5,100 collec-tions then available were punched onto computer cards. The data input, mostly encoded, for each collection was: acronym, collection number, species taken, drainage subdivision, name of body of water, whether the body is a stream or lake, county, and year of collection. The data were computer-sorted and printed by species and, under each species, by drainage subdivisions. A distribution map for each species was hand-plotted during 1976–1980 according to the numbered sites on the collector maps whose numbers were computer-listed for the species.

Acquisition of data from approximately 4,600 additional collections continued into late 1984. The data were treated much as before except for the methods of inputting site data and plotting the species maps. We had gained the service of the BOVA (Biota of Virginia) system at Virginia Tech and the Richmond office of the VDGIF. The data already on computer cards were transferred to computer tape. The more recently acquired species lists and associated information were input directly onto computer tape. All sites on the collector maps were digitized by compass coordinates to which collection numbers were associated. A single collection-site map for each collector was computer-printed and cross-checked for accuracy against the original collector maps.

In November 1984 the species distribution maps were computer-printed. We constructed inked maps by tracing symbols from the computer-printed maps onto blank maps. Comparing the new maps with those hand-plotted earlier provided a partial cross-check. Important records from collections made from late 1984 to mid-1990 were added to maps.

Use of the BOVA distributional data set is made available to qualified persons by the VDGIF. An expanded version of the data set, with ecologic data, will be deposited with the Virginia Division of Natural Heritage (Department of Conservation and Recreation, Richmond) and in Archives of the Roanoke College Library. Other examples of computer storage and retrieval systems designed to handle distributional data on aquatic organisms are described by McAllister (1978) and McDowall and Richardson (1983).

Total Range Maps.—Total North American ranges are shown on inset maps, except for portions of ranges that extend beyond the limits of the map and where adequate data are lacking for northern Mexico. The maps generally do not depict far-offshore distribution in the Great Lakes and marine realm. The ranges are based largely on Lee et al. (1980), but other information was used for nearly all species. The full range of certain widely introduced species (e.g., some centrarchids and larger catfishes) is not shown because of the unavailability of accurate range descriptions.

The overall intent was to be conservative; that is, to not fill in between putative gaps within ranges. This results in the portrayal of specific distribution patterns, for example, those of species that are widespread but locally concentrated, or that are restricted to large rivers.

Abundance.—We use the general descriptors rare, uncommon, common, and abundant. Abundance statements are based on numbers of individuals captured by normal efforts, taking into consideration the relative ease of capturing particular species. The statements also are based on a sliding scale according to adult body size, recognizing that relatively large species usually occur in lower population density than small ones. Thus, abundance statements loosely reflect local population densities. A very localized species may be rare on a statewide basis (considering uninhabited areas), but if it generally is common where found it is considered common. Patterns of abundance that vary by drainage, physiographic province, or other divisions of the state are noted. Numbers of collections or specimens often are cited for those species which are rare or whose conservation status is discussed in *Remarks*.

Remarks

The topics treated here vary widely with the species. They may include the value of the fish as sport and food; its role in the aquatic ecosystem; beauty, oddities, anecdotes, and trivia of the species; special phylogenetic significance; service as a biological indicator; and its conservation or protective status at the state or federal level.

Name.—The basis or meaning of specific and subspecific epithets is given. Sometimes common names are explained and alternate ones are noted.

Key to Families of Freshwater Fishes of Virginia

An outline drawing of one or two typical members of each family is shown in Figure 13. See Figures 3–11 for body areas and parts. Keys to genera and species are found after the introduction to each family (except for monotypic families).

1a Paired fins absent; jaws absent, mouth on an oral disk (the disk mostly represented by a fleshy hood in larvae); 7 external gill openings present in row behind eye .... LAMPREYS—Petromyzontidae p. 161
1b Paired fins present (at least 1 set); jaws present; 1 external gill opening per side 2

2a Caudal fin heterocercal or abbreviate heterocercal (Figure 5) 3
2b Caudal fin protocercal-like (Figure 13, Part 1, upper) or homocercal (Figure 5) 6

3a Snout having a long paddlelike structure; opercular flap long, flexible, and pointed posteriorly .... PADDLEFISHES—Polyodontidae p. 191
3b Snout lacking a long paddlelike structure; opercular flap short 4

4a Body having rows of large bony plates; barbels present on underside of snout; mouth ventral .... STURGEONS—Acipenseridae p. 183
4b Body lacking rows of large bony plates; barbels absent; mouth terminal 5

5a Jaws very long, beaklike; dorsal fin located far posteriorly on body and having a short base, the base much less than half the body length; scales rhomboid (Figure 6) .... GARS—Lepisosteidae p. 195
5b Jaws normal length, not beaklike; dorsal fin having a long base, more than half the body length; scales cycloid .... BOWFINS—Amiidae p. 199

6a   Pelvic fins absent 7
6b   Pelvic fins present (may appear reduced to a spine) 8

7a   Body extremely elongate, eel-like; dorsal, caudal, and anal fins
      continuous .... FRESHWATER EELS—Anguillidae   p. 203
7b   Body not eel-like; dorsal, caudal, and anal fins separate ..... CAVEFISHES—Amblyopsidae   p. 597

8a   Adipose fin present 9
8b   Adipose fin absent 11

9a   Body not scaled; barbels present above and below mouth ... BULLHEAD CATFISHES—Ictaluridae   p. 527
9b   Body scaled; barbels absent 10

10a   Dorsal fin with 2 weak spines; pelvic and anal fins with 1 weak
      spine; scales ctenoid (Figure 6) .... TROUT-PERCHES—Percopsidae   p. 589
10b   Fins lacking spines; scales cycloid .... TROUTS—Salmonidae   p. 571

11a   Belly very compressed or keel-like in cross section, its margin
      serrate or having sharp-ridged imbricated scutes .... HERRINGS—Clupeidae   p. 209
11b   Belly flat or round, or if compressed, not keel-like, nor having
      serrate margin, nor having sharp imbricated scutes 12

12a   Snout duckbill shaped .... PIKES—Esocidae   p. 229
12b   Snout not duckbill shaped 13

13a   Anus located just behind head, anterior to pelvic fin base (except in
      young) .... PIRATE PERCHES—Aphredoderidae   p. 593
13b   Anus located just in front of anal fin, posterior to pelvic fin base 14

14a   One dorsal fin present; dorsal fin spines, if present, always less
      than 4 15
14b   Two dorsal fins present (first dorsal may be composed of well-
      separated spines and discontinuous membranes), or apparently 1
      dorsal fin present which is composed anteriorly of spines (4 or
      more) and posteriorly of rays 19

15a   Caudal fin rounded 16
15b   Caudal fin forked or emarginate 18

16a   Upper jaw broadly bound to snout by wide bridge of tissue
      (frenum), mouth not protractile .... MUDMINNOWS—Umbridae   p. 247
16b   Upper jaw not bound to snout (frenum absent), mouth protractile 17

17a   Third anal ray branched; anal fin of same form in both sexes .... KILLIFISHES—Fundulidae   p. 605
17b   Third anal ray not branched; anal fin of mature male modified into
      a long intromittent organ (gonopodium) .... LIVEBEARERS—Poeciliidae   p. 617

18a   Dorsal fin with 9 or less rays (except for goldfish and carp, which
      also have an anterior spinelike serrate ray); branched caudal rays
      17; pharyngeal arch with 6 or less teeth in major row .... MINNOWS—Cyprinidae   p. 251
18b   Dorsal fin with 10 or more rays (none spinelike nor serrate);
      branched caudal rays 16; pharyngeal arch with 10 or more teeth
      (teeth in 1 row only) .... SUCKERS—Catostomidae   p. 459

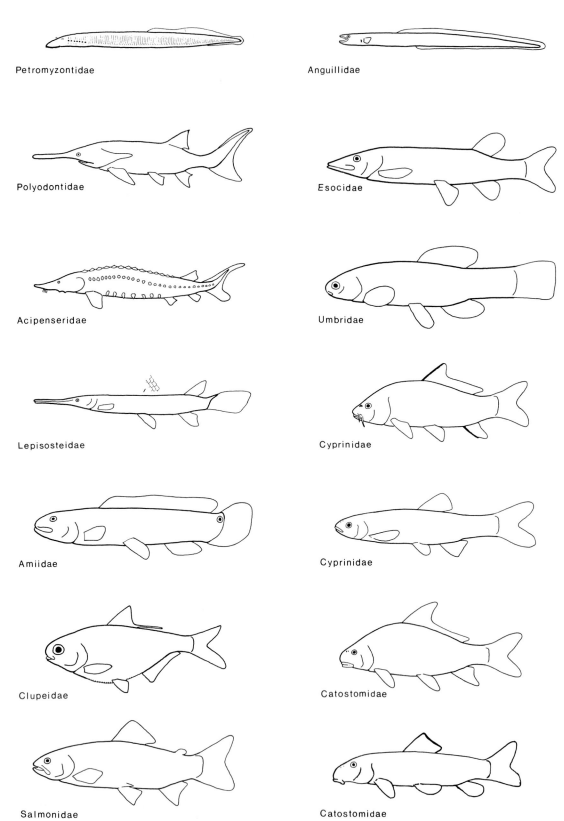

Figure 13 (Part 1)   Outlines of representatives of families; fin spines shown, fin rays omitted. Sequence (top to bottom, left column first) is approximately phylogenetic; notable exceptions are Anguillidae (eel shown next to lamprey) and Salmonidae (trout shown nearly in classical position). Some drawings adapted from Smith (1979). Opposite: **Figure 13 (Part 2)** Outlines of representatives of families; fin spines shown except for some soft spines in Cottidae; fin rays omitted.

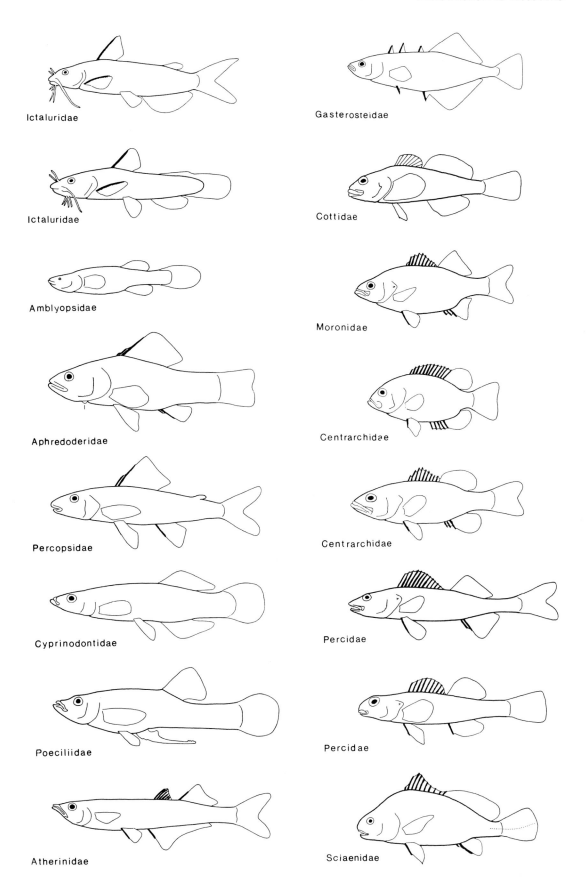

Ictaluridae

Ictaluridae

Amblyopsidae

Aphredoderidae

Percopsidae

Cyprinodontidae

Poeciliidae

Atherinidae

Gasterosteidae

Cottidae

Moronidae

Centrarchidae

Centrarchidae

Percidae

Percidae

Sciaenidae

19a   Pelvic fin basically a single prominent spine, and having 1–2
        rudimentary rays; first dorsal fin with widely separated spines,
        each with a separate membrane .... STICKLEBACKS—Gasterosteidae   p. 623
19b   Pelvic fin lacking a spine, or with 1 spine and 3 or more well-
        developed rays; first dorsal fin membranes continuous through fin 20

20a   Pelvic fin in abdominal position; first and second dorsal fins well
        separated .... SILVERSIDES—Atherinidae   p. 601
20b   Pelvic fin in thoracic position; first and second dorsal fins conjoined
        or narrowly separated 21

21a   Body not scaled; pelvic fin with 3–4 rays .... SCULPINS—Cottidae   p. 625
21b   Body scaled; pelvic fin with 5 or more rays 22

22a   Anal fin with 1–2 spines 23
22b   Anal fin with 3 or more spines 24

23a   Second anal spine broad and long, much more so than first spine;
        lateral line extends onto caudal fin .... DRUMS—Sciaenidae   p. 891
23b   Second anal spine, if present, about as thin and long as first spine;
        lateral line does not extend onto caudal fin .... PERCHES—Percidae   p. 755

24a   First and second dorsal fins narrowly separated or very slightly
        conjoined; pseudobranchae present (Figure 9) .... STRIPED BASSES—Moronidae   p. 675
24b   First and second dorsal fins moderately or broadly conjoined;
        pseudobranchae absent .... SUNFISHES—Centrarchidae   p. 691

Family, Genus, and Species Accounts

LAMPREYS
Family Petromyzontidae

The casual observer is generally unaware that parasitic lampreys spend most of their lives as larvae burrowed in sediments, feeding on small algae, and that there are many nonparasitic species which appear as adults only briefly to spawn and die. Lampreys are fascinating because of the great antiquity of their lineage and their survival in highly specialized form and function (e.g., Janvier 1981; Halstead 1982).

Lampreys are freshwater and marine fishes (or fishlike vertebrates) with an eel-like body, externally obvious body-muscle segmentation (myomeres), a cartilaginous skeleton, a notochord persistent through life, seven pairs of external gill openings, and a single median nostril. Adults have an oval or circular oral disk with horny, keratinoid teeth. Lampreys lack jaws, paired fins, scales, bone, and a complete vertebral column. Adults range in size from the diminutive least brook lamprey *Lampetra aepyptera*, recorded as small as 52 mm TL, to the sea lamprey *Petromyzon marinus* which sometimes reaches 1 m or more.

Lampreys, together with marine hagfishes and several long-extinct groups, form the most primitive superclass or branch of vertebrates, the Agnatha (meaning "without jaws"). Lampreys and hagfishes are often called cyclostomes in reference to their somewhat rounded mouths. All other living vertebrate subgroups, including true fishes, are placed in the more advanced Gnathostomata ("jaw mouth") and possess jaws, enamaloid teeth, paired nostrils, and, typically in fishes, paired pectoral and pelvic fins.

Two kinds of lampreys were recently unearthed from deposits dating as far back as the Late Paleozoic era, at least 325 million years ago—long antedating dinosaurs. They resembled modern lampreys but apparently lacked the oral sucker (Bardack and Zangerl 1971; Janvier and Lund 1983).

Lampreys have an antitropical distribution; that is, they occur in temperate and cooler parts of the Northern and Southern Hemispheres. About 40 living species are placed in the family Petromyzontidae by Bailey (1980), Nelson (1984), and others; some authorities place the few Southern Hemisphere species in one or two separate families (e.g., Potter 1980a). The taxonomy and nomenclature of several species have recently been the subject of spirited debate. Three genera and two parasitic and three nonparasitic species inhabit Virginia; another nonparasitic species may occur in the state.

The life histories of lampreys are complex (Hardisty and Potter 1971a, 1971b); details of many aspects of Virginia populations are poorly known. Analytic summaries of lamprey biology (the several papers by Hardisty and Potter published from 1971 through 1982; Hardisty 1979; Vladykov and Kott 1979b; Cook 1980) have kept pace with the recent flurry of specialized studies.

All species have a long larval period, which in lampreys is termed the ammocoete (i.e., "sand-bedded") stage. Ammocoetes have an oral hood over most of the mouth, sievelike cirri in the oral cavity, and poorly developed eyes and fins (Figures 15–17). They dwell in soft sediments of streams, their burrows supported by mucous-like secretions. At this stage they feed by filtering algae, protozoa, and possibly detritus, and by entrapping these materials in mucous; the mucous is produced by the gills and pharyngeal wall (Kott 1988). In many species the larval period lasts 4–6 years. During the last year of larval life, ammocoetes typically invest much of their surplus energy in body fat; consequently they change relatively little in length and may even undergo length reduction. Nonparasitic species tend to remain in the larval stage for one or two years longer than do larvae of parasitic species of the same genus.

Metamorphosis or transformation to the juvenile or adult stage begins in mid- to late summer; this nontrophic period may take more than 200 days to complete (Beamish and Medland 1988a). External changes include loss of the oral hood and cirri, development of teeth and marginal fringing on the oral disk (Figure 17), extension of the snout, eruption of eyes, modification of gill openings, enlargement of fins, and changes in pigmentation. The respiratory current changes from unidirectional to tidal owing to foregut alteration. Weight loss and length reduction may occur during transformation, but the general view is that loss of energy reserves is countered by water uptake (Beamish and Medland 1988a).

After transformation, lamprey species are sharply divisible into two biotypes—nonparasitic and parasitic. Their many differences, some of which begin developing prior to transformation, were summarized by Vladykov and Kott (1979a) and Potter (1980a). A prominent feature of lamprey evolution is that in most genera, parasitic species gave rise to one or more nonparasitic species. The former are termed stem species, the latter satellite species (Vladykov and Kott 1979a). A stem species and its satellite have long been termed paired species (Hardisty and Potter 1971c).

Nonparasitic or "brook" lampreys are small and occupy smaller streams than do parasitic species. Transformed nonparasitic lampreys do not feed; the intestine is reduced to a strap or threadlike, nonfunctional condition. In spring the dorsal fins heighten, anal finlike folds develop before and behind the genital area, the genital papilla lengthens, the gonad matures, and spawning and death occur; the postlarval life span is less than one year.

Parasitic species have longer postlarval lives, nearly two or three years depending on the species. After transformation, a brief to several-month nonfeeding period occurs, during which a functional foregut is redeveloped. In the ensuing parasitic phase, when they may be termed juveniles (Larsen 1980), they grow rapidly, attaining much larger size than nonparasitic species. They feed by attaching suctorially with the oral disk to a variety of fishes and rasping an opening on the host with the toothed laminae on the tongue. Their oral gland secretions have anticoagulant and cytolytic effects. Their food is largely blood, other body fluids, and products of cell breakdown. Hardisty and Potter (1971b) summarized reports of muscle, gills, ribs, other internal parts of fishes, fish eggs, small fishes, and a variety of bottom invertebrates also being ingested, and considered that parasitic lampreys may be predatory.

After the parasitic feeding period the body length decreases and the gut degenerates. In spring or early summer adults mature, migrate, spawn, and die. Parasitic species exhibit much the same life cycle after their predatory stage as do nonparasitic species after transformation.

Spawning areas are reached by upstream migration, from lakes or the sea for some parasitic species. Some nonparasitic species probably move only locally. Lampreys spawn in shallow parts of streams, generally in moderate or swift current in and just above riffles, on mostly sand–gravel substrates. A pit or depression nest is formed by displacing stones with the mouth or body movements. The nest may be prepared by one or both sexes, or by large groups. Some species perform courtship. In spawning, one or two males attach with the oral disk to a female and the male then tightly coils and moves the tail along her abdomen to aid in egg extrusion. Eggs adhere to the substrate and generally are buried by activity of adults. Fecundities range from 300 to 300,000; eggs are 0.8–1.4 mm diameter (Hardisty 1971).

Lampreys are most noted for their destruction of fishes, particularly in the upper four Great Lakes to which they gained access via human-made canals. However, most populations of parasitic lampreys generally are in balance with their prey; nonparasitic species are harmless and generally unnoticed. Lampreys serve as human food—considered a delicacy in some areas—and are used for bait. They are the objects of considerable research because of their primitive position in the vertebrate hierarchy, interesting and complex biology, and impact on other fish species.

Name.—Petromyzont- means "stone, to suck," from the frequent attachment of lampreys to rocks. "Lamprey" may be derived from the Greek lamperos, meaning "slimy." Lampreys have a smooth body thickly covered with mucous, and are difficult to grasp.

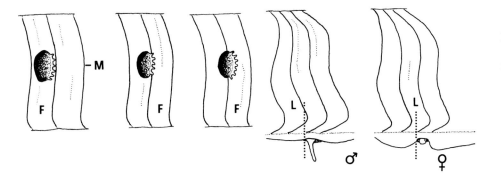

Figure 14 First (F) and last (L) trunk myomeres counted in lampreys, based on locations of myosepta (M) relative to last branchial opening and anterior end of cloacal slit. Sexual differences of adults in genital papilla and fin-folds of cloacal area shown at right.

Key to Lampreys   Petromyzontidae

Certain aspects of lamprey morphology warrant the use of special terminology and methods for identifying species. Terminology for dentition (Figure 17) is that of Hubbs and Potter (1971) and Potter (1980a). Lateral row tooth counts are made on one side beginning with the tooth just lateral or anterolateral to the supraoral teeth; the count includes the circumoral cusp(s), each counted separately, in the row. Dentition is made more obvious by blotting or drying with compressed air; strong light often is needed to examine the much-reduced dentition of nonparasitic species.

Myomeres are vertically oriented body muscle segments separated from each other by myosepta. Counts of trunk myomeres are made according to Hubbs and Trautman (1937; Figure 14): The most anterior myomere counted is the one whose posterior myoseptum passes distinctly and entirely behind the groove surrounding the base of the fringed margin of the last gill opening, so as to leave a definite (though often narrow) band of muscle between the groove and the septum. The most posterior myomere counted is that whose lower posterior angle lies in part or wholly above the anterior end of the cloacal slit (located by probing). For convenience, we first determine the last myomere and then count forward. Care must be exercised with some specimens, particularly much curved and shriveled ones, to avoid counting a myomere as more than one owing to its superficial division by a crease resembling a myoseptum. Scraping of mucous and skin often renders myosepta more distinct.

Methods of measuring are from Hubbs and Trautman (1937) and Potter (1980a). However, in measuring oral disk length, if the disk was not preserved in circular form, we forced it as nearly circular as possible. The measurement is the outer diameter, taken longitudinally, at the outside bases of the marginal fimbriae. Fin height (first and second dorsal) is taken at the point of greatest height while supporting (but not stretching) the fin vertically.

The larvae of *Ichthyomyzon bdellium* and *I. greeleyi* are not separated in the key; despite the claim by Lanteigne (1988), we are not confident that they generally are distinguishable.

Key to Genera and Species of Lampreys

1a Oral area surrounded on top and sides by an oral hood that lacks a marginal papillary fringe; mouth cavity having numerous fimbriate oral cirri; teeth and tongue absent (Figure 17A) . . . . ammocoetes larvae   2

1b Oral area lacking a hood, being round or oval, disklike (disk puckered partly closed in some specimens), the disk having a papillary fringe; oral cirri absent; teeth and tongue present (Figure 17B–E) . . . . transformed specimens   6

2a (Specimens 40 mm TL or more) Dorsal fin single (Figure 15A, B; anterior portion may be very low, but it does not rise distinctly above sag in anterior half of fin) . . . . *Ichthyomyzon*   3

2b (Specimens 40 mm TL or more) Dorsal fin double, nearly or completely divided into two parts (Figure 15F–H; anterior portion may be very low, but it rises distinctly above sag between the two fin sections) . . . . *Petromyzon* and *Lampetra*   4

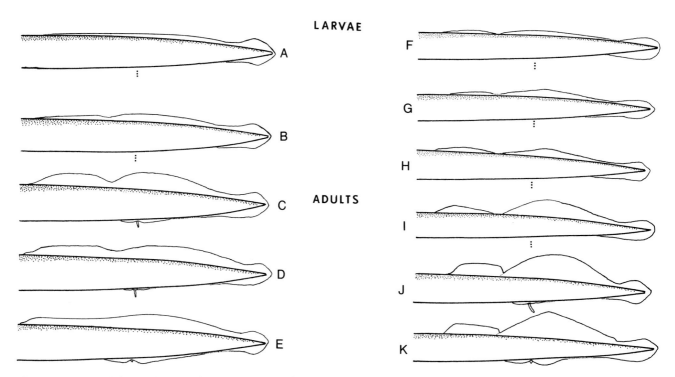

Figure 15 Dorsal fin outlines in lampreys: (A–E) Single dorsal fin in *Ichthyomyzon*. (F–K) Divided dorsal fin in (F, I) *Petromyzon*, (G, J) *Lampetra aepyptera*, and (H, K) *Lampetra appendix*. First dorsal fin overgrows origin of second dorsal in *Lampetra* adults. Dotted vertical line just below venter indicates position of cloacal slit in larvae (A, B, F–H) and parasitic juvenile (I).

3a   Myomeres (53)55–59(61); lateral line organs on upper body of 80-mm
      and larger specimens darkly pigmented, appearing dotlike ...... OHIO LAMPREY—*I. bdellium*   p. 166
      .... or MOUNTAIN BROOK LAMPREY—*I. greeleyi*   p. 170
3b   Myomeres (47)49–52(56); lateral line organs on body not darkly
      pigmented; (possibly occurs in Big Sandy drainage) ... NORTHERN BROOK LAMPREY—*I. fossor*   p. 109

4a   Myomeres (51)53–59(62) .... LEAST BROOK LAMPREY—*L. aepyptera*   p. 178
4b   Myomeres (63)65–76(80) 5

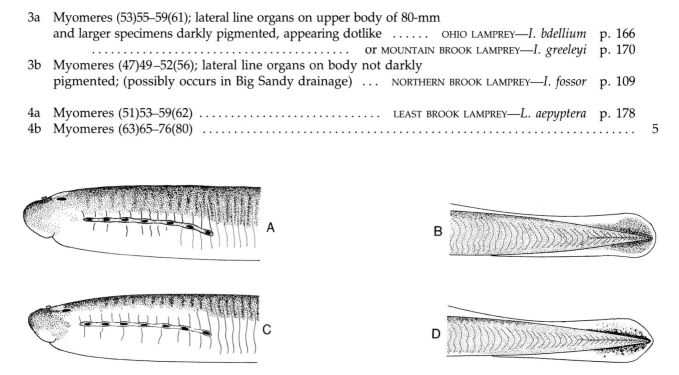

Figure 16 Head and caudal pigmentation, and caudal fin shape in lamprey larvae of 100–160 mm TL: (A, B) *Petromyzon*. (C, D) *Lampetra appendix*.

5a (Specimens 100 mm TL or more) Tail well rounded, like a beaver tail; tail pigmentation more evenly distributed and more widespread, extending nearly to fin margins; pigmentation in upper branchial region extending ventrad from middorsum nearly to branchial groove, leaving only narrow pale area above gill openings; suborbital area and lower half of lateral portion of oral hood largely pigmented (Figure 16A, B) .... SEA LAMPREY—*P. marinus*   p. 172

5b (Specimens 100 mm TL or more) Tail slightly pointed, somewhat wedgelike; tail pigmentation usually distinctly darker along edge of body, or blotchy, and more confined to base of fin along edge of musculature; pigmentation in upper branchial region extending ventrad from middorsum only about half the distance to branchial groove, leaving wide pale area above gill openings; suborbital area and lower half of lateral portion of oral hood largely unpigmented (Figure 16C, D) .... AMERICAN BROOK LAMPREY—*L. appendix*   p. 175

6a Dorsal fin single, although it may have a broad shallow notch or the anterior portion may be relatively low (Figure 15C–E) .... *Ichthyomyzon*   7

6b Dorsal fin double, sharply notched nearly or completely to body, or completely separated into 2 portions (Figure 15I–K) .... *Petromyzon* and *Lampetra*   9

7a Myomeres (47)49–52(56); lateral circumoral teeth all unicuspid; lateral line organs on body not darkly pigmented; (may occur in Big Sandy drainage) .... NORTHERN BROOK LAMPREY—*I. fossor*   p. 109

7b Myomeres (53)55–59(61); lateral circumoral teeth bicuspid (at least 4 total; Figure 17E); lateral line organs on upper body darkly pigmented, appearing dotlike 8

8a Parasitic species: juvenile retains well-developed functional intestine (with wide lumen) until TL of 175 mm or more is attained, and gonads are inconspicuous at sizes smaller than 175 mm TL; mature adult is 175 mm or more and has reduced intestine and enlarged gonads during spring .... OHIO LAMPREY—*I. bdellium*   p. 166

8b Nonparasitic species: adult has nonfunctional intestine (reduced to a strand or thread); not reaching 175 mm TL, gonads enlarged during spring .... MOUNTAIN BROOK LAMPREY—*I. greeleyi*   p. 170

9a Myomeres (51)53–59(62); (nonparasitic species with much-reduced dentition, supraoral tooth cusps well separated [Figure 17B], and TL to about 150 mm) .... LEAST BROOK LAMPREY—*L. aepyptera*   p. 178

9b Myomeres (63)65–76(80) 10

10a Supraoral tooth cusps close set, their common base narrower than throat opening (Figure 17D); parasitic species having strong dentition and TL usually much exceeding 180 mm, although transforming at about 130 mm .... SEA LAMPREY—*P. marinus*   p. 172

10b Supraoral tooth cusps widely separated, their common base equal to or greater in width than throat opening (Figure 17C); nonparasitic species having moderately reduced dentition and TL to about 180 mm .... AMERICAN BROOK LAMPREY—*L. appendix*   p. 175

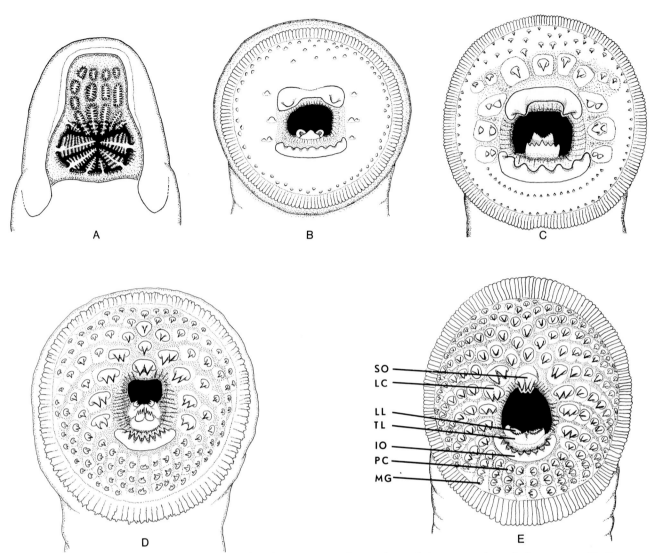

Figure 17 (A) Ammocoete larva, ventral head. Dentition of transformed (metamorphosed) lampreys: (B) *Lampetra aepyptera*. (C) *Lampetra appendix*. (D) *Petromyzon marinus*. (E) *Ichthyomyzon bdellium*. SO—supraoral; LC—lateral (bicuspid) circumoral; LL—longitudinal lingual lamina; TL—transverse lingual lamina; IO—infraoral; PC—posterior circumoral; MG—marginal (marginal fimbriae drawn schematically). (D) adapted from Vladykov and Follette (1967), (E) adapted from Hubbs and Potter (1971).

Lampreys   Genus *Ichthyomyzon* Girard

Ichthyomyzon comprises six North American freshwater species, three that are parasitic, each of which gave rise independently to a nonparasitic derivative. One of each type inhabits Virginia; another nonparasitic species may occupy the Big Sandy drainage in the state (see *Fishes of Possible Occurrence in Virginia*). The genus was the subject of a monograph by Hubbs and Trautman (1937).

Name.—*Ichthyomyzon* translates to "fish, to suck."

Ohio lamprey   *Ichthyomyzon bdellium* (Jordan)

SYSTEMATICS

The parasitic Ohio lamprey was described from Ohio by J. P. Kirtland in 1838, but under a name already used in *Ichthyomyzon*; it subsequently was renamed by Jordan in 1885. It remained confused with other lamprey species until its status and wide range in the Ohio River basin were clarified by Hubbs and Trautman (1937). They predicted that *I. bdellium* and the parasitic chestnut lamprey *I. castaneus* might

Fish 1 *Ichthyomyzon bdellium* parasitic juvenile 204 mm TL (REJ 984), VA, Scott County, Copper Creek, 16 June 1983.

intergrade where their ranges meet in the lower Ohio River. Burr (1980) had difficulty identifying specimens from that area of Kentucky because most diagnostic characteristics overlap greatly, although Starrett et al. (1960) had found these species to be distinct in the lower Ohio. The two species have been thought to differ markedly in disk size, but measurements of rounded disks greatly overlap. The shape of the transverse lingual lamina (Hubbs and Trautman 1937) and number of denticles on that lamina best separate them. In 147 upper Tennessee *I. bdellium* the range of denticles is 15–32, mean, 22.5; in 15 *I. castaneus* from the Tennessee it is 36–53, mean, 43.1.

Ichthyomyzon bdellium is most closely related to its nonparasitic derivative, *I. greeleyi*. Mature adults of both species have been collected together in Pennsylvania (Cooper 1983) and Virginia. We identified possible intergrades reported from Kentucky (Clay 1975; UL 12606) and hybrids from Pennsylvania (McBath 1968; PSU) as *I. bdellium* and *I. greeleyi*, respectively.

DESCRIPTION

Materials.—One hundred sixty-six specimens, comprising 152 parasitic juveniles and 12 maturing or mature individuals from the Clinch–Powell system of Virginia and Tennessee, and 2 juveniles from the Holston of Virginia. Color in life from 4 Virginia series.

Anatomy.—A parasitic lamprey with 1 dorsal fin and (53)56–60(61) myomeres; transformed specimens are 130–250 mm TL. General anatomy as described for family. Dorsal fin in transformed specimens is lowest anteriorly and rises smoothly to the posterior portion, or the two portions may be demarked by a slight or moderate, rounded depression. In ammocoetes, anterior portion of dorsal fin often very low, inconspicuous, and only slightly connected to the posterior portion.

Dentition.—Teeth long, curved, sharp, edges angulate, although teeth sometimes are worn down in nuptial adults. Circumoral teeth (18)20–22(23); bicuspid circumoral teeth (7)8–10(12); supraoral cusps 2–3(4); infraoral cusps (5)7–10(11); anterior row teeth (3)4–5; lateral cusps 7–9(10). Transverse lingual lamina moderately or strongly bilobed (indented anteriad), its largest denticles moderate or large, total denticles (15)18–30(32).

Measurements in % TL.—Disk diameter (3.9)4.5–6.0(7.3); snout length (7.2)7.5–9.0(9.6); eye length (1.0)1.2–1.5(1.8); branchial length (7.7)8.0–9.6(10.7), longest in ma-

turity. Tail length (24.6)26.0–30.0(31.9), longest in maturity; body depth (5.6)6.1–8.7(10.7), deepest at food satiation and maturity; first dorsal fin height (1.1)1.3–2.0(4.0), highest in mature male.

Color in Preservative.—Transformed specimens with fins, back, and side dusky to dark; belly usually pale but occasionally darkly mottled; each lateral line organ on back and side with a black dot, those on underside of branchial area are usually unpigmented in smaller parasitic specimens and usually pigmented with a prominent black dot in maturity.

Color in Life Plate 9.—Parasitic juveniles with back and side yellow-olive to gray-olive, slightly darker on back; posterior one-third of side in some specimens with brown-olive mottling and reticulation (rapidly masked by coagulation of mucus in formalin); belly pale anteriorly, remainder yellow-gold to gray-olive. Preorbital and suborbital areas the most golden part of fish; side of disk gold-olive; inner iris silvery, dusky peripherally. Spots on head and trunk olive-black; teeth dull golden. Fins yellow-olive to gray-olive, yellowest basally. Apparently mature specimens from Kentucky were bluish-gray to lead-gray, belly white, dots black (Branson 1970).

Larvae.—Ammocoetes of *I. bdellium* currently are not consistently separable from those of *I. greeleyi* (see introduction to *Key*). Vladykov (1960) indicated that in the *bdellium–greeleyi* pair, black spots may appear at lateral line organs on the body of specimens of 60 mm. In cultured *I. bdellium*, Nist (1968) found that black spots appear and increase in number and distinctness as larvae grow from 80 to 110 mm. Larger ammocoetes of the *bdellium–greeleyi* pair in Virginia have these spots.

COMPARISON

Ichthyomyzon bdellium differs from the nonparasitic *I. greeleyi* chiefly in aspects related to their contrasting postmetamorphic life histories. Parasitic phase (juvenile) *I. bdellium* differ from maturing and mature *I. greeleyi* in the following: (1) partly in total length [*bdellium* is 120–190 mm in March–May, 140–260 mm thereafter *vs.* *greeleyi* is 100–170 mm in February–May, dying by early June]; (2) intestine diameter, measured at posterior end of liver [functional, wide, 1.0–4.0% TL *vs.* nonfunctional, decreasing from 0.5% in February to threadlike, 0.1% in May]; (3) gonad, located between the paired kidneys [very small *vs.* moderate to large or spent]; (4) cloacal area [genital papilla not obviously extended from cloacal slit, and

Fish 2 Lamprey-parasitized *Etheostoma vulneratum* adult male 59 mm SL (REJ 987), VA, Scott County, Copper Creek, 17 June 1983.

anal folds poorly developed *vs.* papilla well extended, lengthy in male, and anal folds much swollen in female in April–May]; (5) anterior dorsal fin [low, 1.0–2.0% TL *vs.* moderate to high, 1.5% in February to 4.0% in May males].

Mature *I. bdellium* have secondary sexual characteristics and gonadal and intestinal development similar to those of mature *I. greeleyi*. They are best distinguished by: (6) total length [*bdellium* greater than 180 mm *vs. greeleyi* less than 170 mm]; (7) denticles on transverse lingual lamina [(15)18–30(32) *vs.* (6)8–15(18)].

BIOLOGY

Burrowing and filter-feeding of Ohio lamprey larvae in aquaria were described by Nist (1968), who found that at night they often emerged from the substrate. Nist concluded that bacteria, protozoans, decayed phytoplankton, and detritus may support satisfactory growth of *I. bdellium* larvae, in contrast with the importance generally ascribed to living algae in the diet of larval lampreys (Hardisty and Potter 1971a).

Parasitic-phase specimens from the Tennessee drainage often have a mass of dark material, apparently blood, in the gut. Hosts include paddlefish, carp, suckers, and black basses (Cope 1868b; Hubbs and Trautman 1937; Starrett et al. 1960; Trautman 1981); larger catfishes (Vladykov 1949) and other fishes presumably are also attacked. We saw a lamprey on a redhorse sucker (*Moxostoma* sp.) in the Clinch River. On 19 April in the North Fork Holston River we caught a northern hogsucker with an *I. bdellium* attached. In lower Copper Creek we found one adult each of *Noturus flavus* and *Etheostoma vulneratum* (Fish 2) that had been attacked by *I. bdellium*; these were apparently the first recorded occurrences of lamprey parasitism on these species.

Recently transformed *I. bdellium* in aquaria began to attach to suckers in late September and commenced feeding on them in late October (Nist 1968). Such early feeding may be unusual for parasitic lampreys in general; they usually delay the onset of feeding in both aquaria and nature to late winter or early spring (Hardisty and Potter 1971b). Our earliest dates of capture are 16 and 19 March; the two juveniles had incompletely keratinized teeth and had not fed recently. Later March juveniles had well-developed dentition; the gut size of some indicated that they had recently fed. Most April juveniles, including one of 119 mm TL, had fed recently. Parasitism by juveniles spans late spring and summer, and at least one of the few October juveniles (all of which had transformed the previous year) had fed recently. A maturing male taken 16 March also had fed recently.

The length of the larval period in Pennsylvania, after hatching in June, is about 4 years 1 month, including a one-year arrested growth period. Transformation begins in late July–early August (Nist 1968). Based on upper Tennessee samples (which lack recently transformed juveniles and wintering premature specimens) and Nist's study, the post-metamorphic period lasts 21 months—September through two springs later. In April–May of their last spring, they fully mature, spawn, and die; the total life span is thus about six years.

Average lengths (mm TL) of upper Tennessee parasitic-phase specimens are: March 142, April 149, May 165, June 179, July 187, August 185, September 213, October 226, including the largest specimen (253 mm) from Virginia. Maturing and fully mature specimens indicate a reduction in length from the older parasitic-phase specimens; our 12 nearly or fully mature specimens are 201–227 mm TL, mean, 211. Mc-Bath (1968) reported 240 spawners from Pennsylvania to be 185–272 mm TL, mean, 230, with no significant difference in length between the sexes. The report of a 117-mm TL spawning male (Kott et al. 1988) is obviously in error. The largest known Ohio Lamprey, a spent female that we collected in Kentucky, is 299 mm TL.

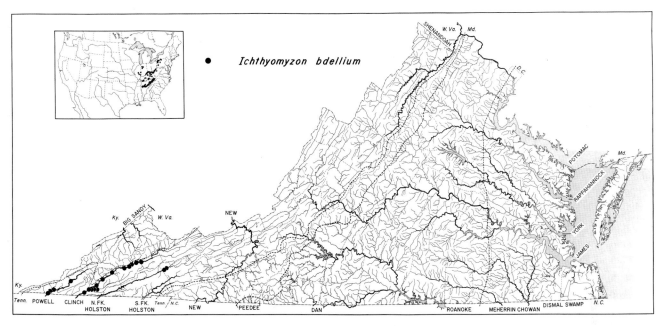

Map 13 Ohio lamprey.

Spawning occurs during late May in Pennsylvania in a manner and at a pitlike nest similar to those of other lampreys (Cooper 1983). Based on the condition of upper Tennessee specimens, spawning occurs in May and perhaps late April; the last date of capture of a mature specimen is 21 May.

HABITAT

The Ohio lamprey inhabits warm, large, main channels and the lower section of a major tributary (Copper Creek) in Virginia. It may ascend other tributaries to spawn. We took transformed specimens only in runs and riffles of clean gravel and rubble. Ammocoetes prefer slow areas with soft substrate and high detrital content (Nist 1968).

DISTRIBUTION   Map 13

Ichthyomyzon bdellium is an Ohio basin species. In Virginia, it is known recently from the Holston and Clinch–Powell systems; it probably formerly occupied the upper Big Sandy drainage. Three records are verified for the Holston; single specimens were captured in 1928 and 1981, and two in 1986, from the North Fork Holston River above Saltville. Populations below Saltville probably were decimated by pollution; this species has not reappeared despite the recent improvement of river conditions. Cope's (1868b) record may have been from a different fork of the Holston.

For the Clinch River, we verified the occurrence of *I. bdellium* up to Cleveland, a short distance above Carbo. Masnik's (1974) report from Indian Creek above Carbo is based on *I. greeleyi*. Two other records from well above Carbo remain problematic; they could be either *I. bdellium* or *I. greeleyi*: Masnik's (1974) report of *I. bdellium* from the Little River is based on an *Ichthyomyzon* ammocoete, and Wollitz's (1967a) notice of "*I. castaneus*" from the Clinch River could not be verified. Large juveniles reported farther downstream by Wollitz (1968b) as unidentified lampreys are typical *I. bdellium*.

The Ohio lamprey occurs in at least the lower 10 rkm of Copper Creek, where parasitic-phase specimens were taken in spring and summer. Some of these enter from the Clinch River, based on angler reports of lampreys attaching to migrating redhorse suckers; during spring some of the suckers ascend as far up Copper Creek as the dam at Rkm 13. Trautman (1981) considered *I. bdellium* to be migratory. Mature specimens were taken in the spring as far up as Rkm 4.5; it is unknown whether they were immigrants or residents. Presumably some larvae remain near spawning areas through the ammocoete stage and may complete their life cycle in the creek. During the 1967 fish kill below Carbo, we found dead juveniles and larvae in the Clinch River near the state line. Sources of reestablishment in the river were probably Copper Creek and the Clinch above Carbo. In the Powell River, *I. bdellium* occurs up to the North Fork mouth.

The range of *I. bdellium* in the Tennessee drainage is greatly penetrated by that of *I. castaneus* (Rohde and Lanteigne-Courchene *in* Lee et al. 1980). We found the two species to be syntopic in three tributary systems of the Tennessee—the Duck and Little Tennessee rivers and Chickamauga Creek.

Abundance.—Generally rare or uncommon; no collection with more than 10 specimens is known from Virginia.

REMARKS

The Ohio lamprey is the most primitive living freshwater vertebrate in Virginia. The life cycle of lampreys, so unlike that of most fishes, is specialized and fascinating. The Ohio lamprey apparently is an indicator of good water and substrate quality. May we long allow it to prey upon other fish species, whose survival as a species probably is not threatened by lampreys.

Name.—*Bdellium* refers to "leech," alluding to suctorial adherence to fishes, stones, and other objects, and to feeding on blood. Sometimes called "sand leech" in southwestern Virginia.

Mountain brook lamprey   *Ichthyomyzon greeleyi* Hubbs and Trautman

SYSTEMATICS

Ichthyomyzon greeleyi was described from the extreme upper Ohio basin in Pennsylvania as the nonparasitic derivative of *I. bdellium* (Hubbs and Trautman 1937). Populations later found in the middle Ohio basin in West Virginia and Kentucky were identified as *I. greeleyi.* Slightly divergent populations from the Highlands of the upper Tennessee drainage were described as *I. hubbsi* and regarded as another nonparasitic derivative of *I. bdellium* by Raney (1952a). Several times, Vladykov (e.g., 1960) and Vladykov and Kott (e.g., 1979b) stated that *I. hubbsi* was not distinguishable from *I. greeleyi,* but no support was offered. Jenkins' (unpublished) study in 1984 of virtually all then-known specimens of the *greeleyi* group led to agreement that *I. hubbsi* is conspecific with *I. greeleyi.*

DESCRIPTION

Materials.—Forty-nine premature and mature adults taken March–May from the Holston and Clinch–Powell systems, Virginia. Life color from 3 Virginia adults.

Anatomy.—A nonparasitic lamprey with 1 dorsal fin and (53)55–59 myomeres; adults are 120–160 mm TL. Dorsal fin as in *I. bdellium.*

Dentition.—Teeth short, blunt, and weakly keratinized in premature specimens, or the larger teeth long, sharp, moderately or well keratinized, but not angulate in most mature specimens. Circumoral teeth (19)21–31(33); bicuspid circumoral teeth (5)8–11(13); supraoral cusps 2–4(5); infraoral cusps (7)8–11(13); anterior row teeth (3)4–5; lateral cusps (6)7–9(11). Transverse lingual lamina moderately or well keratinized, moderately or strongly bilobed, its largest denticles minute or moderate, total denticles (6)8–15(18).

Measurements in % TL.—Disk diameter (3.6)3.8–5.2(5.4); snout length (5.6)6.0–8.0(8.8); eye length (1.1)1.2–1.5(1.6); branchial length (8.9)9.2–10.7(11.0). Tail length (28.5)30.1–33.8(34.5), averaging longest in male; body depth (6.1)7.0–9.3(9.8); first dorsal fin height (1.6)2.0–3.7(4.1), averaging lowest in prematurity, highest in mature male. Changes in proportions with growth reported by Beamish and Austin (1985).

Color in Preservative.—Fins, back, and side dusky to dark; belly pale or darkly blotched; each lateral line organ

Fish 3 *Ichthyomyzon greeleyi* adult male 130 mm TL (REJ 1096), VA, Smyth County, Middle Fork Holston River, 4 June 1984.

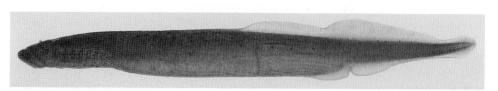

Fish 4 *Ichthyomyzon greeleyi* adult female 130 mm TL (REJ 1080), VA, Scott County, Copper Creek, 25 April 1984.

on back and side with a black dot, those on underside of branchial area usually lack the dot or rarely have a dusky one.

Color in Life   Plate 9.—A late-nuptial male with back and side of trunk heavily mottled pale and dark olive (mottling faded rapidly upon preservation), tail uniformly olive, belly mostly white; dots on head and body blackish; disk area pale orange; inner iris silvery; fins yellow-olive to pale olive. A prenuptial female was similar but with mottling confined mostly to tail and belly. A nuptial female had pronounced reticulation the length of the trunk, dark markings dark olive, interspaces silver-gray. Trautman (1981) stated that *I. greeleyi* becomes blue-black as spawning progresses.

Larvae.—Described by Beamish and Austin (1985) and Beamish and Medland (1988a); see *I. bdellium*.

COMPARISON

See *I. bdellium* account.

BIOLOGY

The diet of larval *I. greeleyi* probably is similar to that of larval *I. bdellium*. Although the dentition and disk size of transformed *I. greeleyi* often is only slightly reduced compared to that of *I. bdellium*, no evidence was found that *I. greeleyi* is parasitic or even feeds after transformation. The diameter of the anterior intestine in large ammocoetes is 1–2% TL. Regression of the gut continues during maturation; maturing February specimens had gut diameters ranging 0.3–0.5% TL, and in April–May the thread-like gut of fully mature individuals was 0.1–0.4% TL.

The larval period in North Carolina is 4.2 or 5.2 years; most of the older individuals are female. Transformation begins between early and mid-August, lasts 100–140 days, and spawning and death occur in the following May or early June (Potter and Bailey 1972; Beamish and Austin 1985; as modified by Medland and Beamish 1987; Beamish and Medland 1988a). Hence the life span is 5 or 6 years in those Highlands populations. Prespawning Virginia specimens in March have lesser development of the gonad, genital papilla, dorsal fin, and dentition than do fully mature April–May specimens.

Larger, older larvae have greater average length than adults in North Carolina; larvae beginning transformation were 111–182 mm TL, and in two populations, adult males averaged 128 and 136 mm and females were 135 and 142 mm (Beamish and Medland 1988a). Our 49 Virginia adults are 124–156 mm TL, mean, 141.6 (males 141.5 mm, females 141.9). The largest known adult is 181 mm TL from Tennessee; the next largest is 162 mm from Kentucky.

A spawning group of about 40 individuals, about equally males and females, was found in Indian Creek, a Powell River tributary in Virginia, at 1600 hours on 24 April 1971, water 15°C. They were swarming over an apparently single nest depression in a gentle, shallow run of mostly small, loose gravel, stream width 2–4 m. Earlier the same day, drifting spent adults were taken in two other Powell tributaries, water 12° and 15°C. In other years, ripe specimens were taken in Clinch River tributaries on 6 and 14 May. In the cool spring of 1984, a prenuptial female was taken in Copper Creek, a warmwater stream, on 25 April, water 14.5°C. A nuptial or postnuptial male was found in the troutwater section of the upper Middle Fork Holston River on 4 June, the latest capture date of an adult in Virginia. Reproduction occurred in mid- to late May in West Virginia, Ohio, and Pennsylvania (Schwartz 1959; Trautman 1981; Raney 1939b). Raney found nests throughout slow to moderate riffles and just above swift riffles; the peak of nest building and spawning occurred in mid-afternoon, water 18.8°C.

HABITAT

Adults of *I. greeleyi*, other than those seen spawning, were taken in strong riffles of clean gravel and rubble. Most Virginia populations occupy creeks or medium-sized streams of summer temperatures that are marginal for trout or warmer. Single adults are known from a section each of the larger (25–35 m wide) North Fork Holston and Powell rivers. Ammocoetes were found in pool sediments and muddy banks in upper Copper Creek.

DISTRIBUTION   Map 14

The mountain brook lamprey is widespread but generally localized in the Ohio basin. Records from the Kentucky drainage (Rohde and Lanteigne *in* Lee et al. 1980) are based on *I. bdellium*. In Virginia this species is known recently from the Middle and North forks of the Holston River; Copper and Indian creeks, tributaries of the Clinch River; and the Powell River and three of its tributaries—Indian, Dry, and Wallen creeks. Unidentified *Ichthyomyzon* larvae were found in the upper North Fork Holston (including Ross and Carico's [1963] specimen misidentified as a *Lampetra*) and in Big Moccasin Creek, a lower North Fork tributary. This species probably formerly occupied the upper Big Sandy drainage.

Adult *I. greeleyi* and parasitic and mature *I. bdellium*

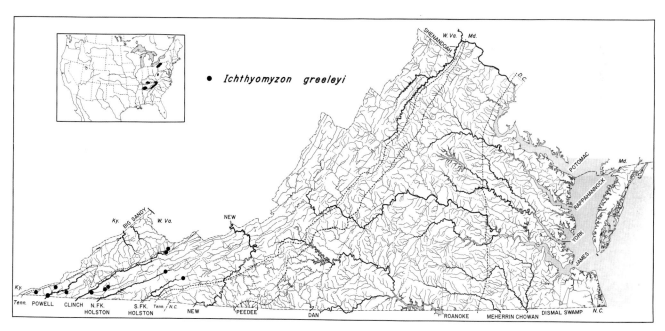

Map 14   Mountain brook lamprey.

were taken together twice in lower Copper Creek and once in the Powell River at Fletcher Ford. Mature individuals of both species were found over the same nests in Pennsylvania (Cooper 1983).

Abundance.—Excepting the spawning group, the largest number of *I. greeleyi* seen at one time in Virginia has been five adults. Its general abundance is unknown because of the secretive habits of larvae and the brief period of activity of adults.

REMARKS

This small harmless lamprey evidently was evolutionarily derived from a parasitic progenitor, *I. bdel-*

lium. Despite the difficulty inherent in detecting lamprey populations, particularly those of nonparasitic species, *I. greeleyi* appears to have a relict distribution pattern in Virginia. This stems partly from local extirpations caused by excessive siltation. Larval lampreys are known to have specific habitat requirements (Hardisty and Potter 1971a), and adults may require clean substrates for spawning. *Ichthyomyzon greeleyi* has had a general history of depletion, localization, and extirpation in other areas (Schwartz 1959; Trautman 1981). Vladykov (1973b) summarized reasons for protecting nonparasitic lampreys.

Name.—The specific name honors John R. Greeley, a fishery scientist of New York State.

Sea lampreys   Genus *Petromyzon* Linnaeus

This monotypic genus contains the sea lamprey of the North Atlantic Ocean and associated and tributary waters. It is one of the few parasitic species not known to have given rise to a nonparasitic species (Hubbs and Potter 1971).

Name.—*Petromyzon* means "stone, to suck," as described in the introduction to the family.

Sea lamprey   *Petromyzon marinus* Linnaeus

SYSTEMATICS

The parasitic sea lamprey was described from Europe in 1758. Individuals of landlocked (lake) populations typically attain smaller size than those of anadromous (sea-run) populations but are not taxonomically distinct (Bigelow and Schroeder 1948).

DESCRIPTION

Materials.—Based on Bigelow and Schroeder (1948), Vladykov (1949), Manion and Stauffer (1970), Hubbs and Potter (1971), Scott and Crossman (1973), Vladykov and Kott (1979b, 1980), Trautman (1981), and 40 Virginia specimens. Color in life from Vladykov (1949), Scott and Crossman (1973), and Youson and Potter (1979).

Fish 5 *Petromyzon marinus* adult 410 mm TL (NMC 67-819), MI, Presque Isle County, Dequeoc River, 21 July 1950.

Anatomy.—A parasitic lamprey with 2 dorsal fins and (63)65–76(80) myomeres (69–75 in 12 Virginia specimens); transformed specimens are 130–900 mm TL. Dorsal fins well separated in larger specimens, sometimes contiguous at base during maturity. The unique occurrence of rays in the anal fins of two specimens was reported (Vladykov 1973a; Vladykov and Kott 1980).

Dentition.—Teeth strongly developed, curved, sharp when not worn. Circumoral teeth usually 17–19; bicuspid circumoral teeth 8; supraoral cusps 2; infraoral cusps (6)7–9(10); anterior row teeth usually 3; posterior row teeth 3–4; lateral cusps usually 7–9. Lingual laminae strongly developed; transverse lamina pronouncedly bilobed (sharply indented anteriad), typically with 14 large denticles. Tooth development and replacement described by Manion and Piavis (1977).

Measurements in % TL.—Disk length 7.4–13.2; eye diameter 2.1–4.4, particularly large in newly transformed specimens; prebranchial length 11.3–16.8; branchial length 8.2–13.4; trunk length 42.2–56.7; tail length 23.6–33.1. Youson (1980) summarized data from late larval to early parasitic stages; Vladykov and Kott (1980) discussed proportional changes with growth and stated that males have a larger disk, eye, and tail, and a shorter trunk.

Color in Preservative.—Transformed specimens generally dark, often darkly marbled on trunk; belly pale anteriorly.

Color in Life.—Ammocoetes gray to dark brown on back and side, paler ventrally. Newly transformed specimens grayish blue to blue-black above, silvery white ventrally, violet cast on side; teeth yellow. Larger parasitic individuals dark tan or brown, usually heavily dark brown-blotched. Spawning adults blue-black.

Larvae.—Described by Gage (1928), Vladykov (1950, 1960), Manion and Stauffer (1970), Wang and Kernehan (1979), Youson and Potter (1979), Youson (1980), Vladykov and Kott (1980), and Fuiman (1982a).

COMPARISON

Juvenile and adult *P. marinus* are easily distinguished from adult *L. appendix* by using the key. The two species have similar myomere numbers; separation of their larvae is based on differences in tail shape and head and tail pigmentation. The pigment patterns change with growth such that the differences described in the key are mainly guidelines.

Specimens smaller than those illustrated (Figure 16) tend to have less-distributed head and tail melanophores; small *P. marinus* larvae often have pigment distributed more like the *L. appendix* specimen shown, and small *L. appendix* have even less-distributed pigment. The pigment differences are illustrated in size series of the two species by Vladykov (1950 [larger larvae]) and Vladykov (1960 [smaller larvae]).

BIOLOGY

A wealth of information exists on the sea lamprey, particularly for entirely freshwater populations. Potter and Beamish (1977) and Beamish (1980) reviewed and analyzed anadromous populations.

The food of larvae is mainly small algae (chiefly diatoms) and lesser amounts of protozoans; it is filtered nonselectively from water and sediments (Moore and Beamish 1973; Mallatt 1979; Moore and Mallatt 1980). Juveniles are parasitic on a wide variety of freshwater, estuarine, and marine fishes (Farmer and Beamish 1973; Farmer 1980). Mansueti (1962b) described predation on Atlantic menhaden in deeper Chesapeake Bay waters and on migrating shad in Chesapeake tributaries. Beamish (1980) listed bluefish and weakfish as hosts in the Chesapeake. A specimen from off Cape Charles, Virginia, was attached to a shark. The sea lamprey most frequently fed on catfish and crappie in Kerr Reservoir (Martin 1954), and was found on gizzard shad and chain pickerel in Lake Anna (S. R. Wells, personal communication). If host fishes are relatively large, they generally are not killed by single lamprey attacks although scars remain (Potter and Beamish 1977).

Sea lampreys are rarely preyed upon by other fishes or other vertebrates (Applegate 1950; Becker 1983). Davis (1967 *in* Beamish 1980) described a case of cannibalism in which eight small lampreys were attached together forming a chain, some individuals feeding on others.

Before the use of statoliths for determining age of lampreys, the duration of the larval phase of anadromous *P. marinus* was considered to be 6–7, possibly 8 years, with little or no growth occurring in the final 1–3 years (Potter 1980b). Statoliths from the few recently studied northern populations revealed that the larval period lasted from 4 to (usually) 5 years

(Beamish and Medland 1988b). Metamorphosis begins in July and ends during fall (Beamish and Potter 1972; Youson and Potter 1979); metamorphosing fish were 146–210 mm TL (Beamish and Medland 1988b). In Virginia, the larger ammocoetes taken on 1 November 1973 were 125–150 mm. A 160-mm specimen in stage 6 of (late) transformation was taken on 20 October 1966, far up in the freshwater reach of the Nottoway River. A 126-mm transformed specimen was taken on 28 October 1968 at the same site.

The onset of the parasitic stage is variable, ranging from soon after transforming in the fall to the following spring (Farmer 1980). Age determination of older lampreys by statoliths is less certain than for larvae; combining length–frequency and other evidence, the postmetamorphic period is about 2.5 years. With spawning and death in spring or summer, the full life span generally is approximately 8 years; a few individuals live 1 year more or less (Beamish and Medland 1988b). Mansueti (1962b) reported recently transformed (150–170 mm) individuals feeding during mid-winter in Chesapeake Bay. Juveniles commonly reach 600–900 mm, which was the approximate size range of sea lampreys spawning in a lower James drainage tributary (F. F. Snelson, in litt.). Typically smaller sizes are attained in lake populations (Farmer 1980). A sea lamprey of 1,200 mm was reported by Oliva (1953 in Vladykov and Kott 1979b).

Upstream migrations occur in Virginia and Maryland between March and June; peak spawning occurs in April and May (Beamish 1980). The sea lamprey has migrated up to 320 rkm in the Delaware and Susquehanna drainages (Bigelow and Schroeder 1948) and, based on the Cub Creek record, about 345 rkm in the Roanoke drainage. The most active migration and spawning occur at water temperatures of 10–18.5°C and 17–19°C, respectively (Beamish 1980). Manion and Hanson (1980) cited a 10–26°C spawning range. Nest construction usually is initiated by the male, but both sexes build the nest (Applegate 1950); sand–gravel bottoms in or just above riffles are favored locations. Males are territorial and the species typically is monogamous (Manion and Hanson 1980). Fecundity of anadromous specimens is the highest recorded for lamprey species, 123,900–304,830 (Beamish 1980). *Petromyzon marinus* has been experimentally hybridized with five other lamprey species (Piavis et al. 1970).

HABITAT

Ammocoetes burrow in beds of sandy silt, sometimes emerging and dispersing downstream, mainly at night (Potter 1980b). Virginia records of ammocoetes are from streams and one is from a pond (when drained) in which *L. aepyptera* also occurred. Recently transformed juveniles may overwinter in fresh water or migrate downstream to the estuarine or coastal marine environment. Beamish (1980) summarized near-shore and far-offshore records in the western Atlantic Ocean, including one from 4,099-m depth (2.5 miles) (Haedrich 1977).

DISTRIBUTION   Map 15

Anadromous sea lampreys occupy the North Atlantic Ocean, Baltic Sea, most of the Mediterranean Sea, and associated fresh waters (Hubbs and Potter 1971; Vladykov and Kott 1979b; Beamish 1980). *Petromyzon marinus* invaded Lake Erie and the upper Great Lakes during 1930–1940 via the Welland Canal, which allowed them to bypass Niagara Falls.

Spawning migrations occur in all major drainages and a Delmarva stream of Virginia (Beamish 1980; our data). Unlike the establishment of northern landlocked populations, the sea lamprey was trapped in two large Virginia impoundments but did not persist. In Kerr Reservoir, formed in 1952, fishes were parasitized by lampreys of 130–230 mm during 1953–1954 (Martin 1954). The last record above Kerr Reservoir, from "West Branch" (possibly Right Hand Fork) of Cub Creek, dates from 1935 (ammocoetes, USNM 100173). Lake Anna, created in 1972, yielded records of parasitism by, and impingement on intake screens of, *P. marinus*. One juvenile was 150 mm in 1975; the impinged specimens, the last seen, were 150–250 mm during 1978–1980 (S. R. Wells, A. C. Cooke, personal communications; our data).

Abundance.—Despite the secretive habits of larvae and the brief inland occurrence of juveniles and adults, we believe that the sea lamprey is generally localized and uncommon or rare in Virginia. Recently, ammocoetes have been frequently taken only in the middle York drainage, and then only in small numbers.

REMARKS

The sea lamprey occupies a great range of environments, including cold freshwater lakes, warm small streams, estuary shallows, and the deep ocean, among the greatest depth ranges exhibited by marine animals (Beamish 1980). Its adaptiveness was unfortunately emphasized when, upon spreading in the Great Lakes, it (along with other factors) caused rapid and massive depletion of important fish species, thus having far-reaching effects on the ecology of the lakes and the economy of the region. Attempts at lamprey

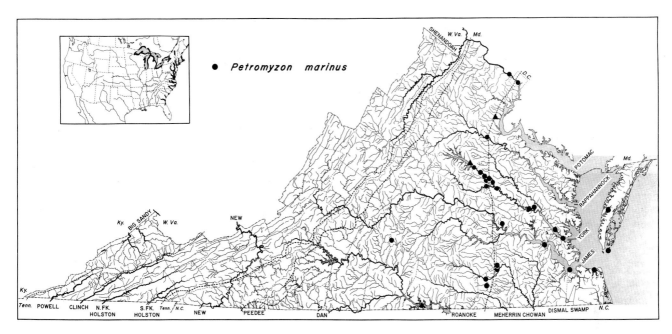

Map 15 Sea lamprey. Full extent of estuarine and oceanic range not shown.

control by chemicals, dams, and trapping are having some success.

Petromyzon marinus is esteemed a delicacy in parts of Europe and was enjoyed during colonial times in New England (Vladykov 1949; Bigelow and Schroeder 1953). Ammocoetes are often used for bait. Sea lampreys earlier were considered common in Chesapeake Bay, but have been reduced in abun-

dance by siltation, pollution, and blockage by dams of spawning areas (Hildebrand and Schroeder 1928). In recent decades they have not had any serious economic impact (Mansueti 1962b).

Name.—Marinus means "of the sea." Vladykov and Kott (1979b) proposed the common name "Atlantic sea lamprey."

Lampreys   Genus *Lampetra* Gray

In broadened concept (Hubbs and Potter 1971; Potter 1980a; Bailey 1980, 1982a), the holarctic marine and freshwater genus *Lampetra* contains about 19 species, 2 of which occur in Virginia. Since at least 1967 (Vladykov

and Follette 1967), Vladykov and coauthors have recognized most or all of the subgenera of *Lampetra* as genera.

Name.—Lampetra means "sucker of stone."

American brook lamprey

SYSTEMATICS

The nonparasitic *Lampetra appendix*, subgenus *Lethenteron*, was described from Rhode Island and New York in 1842. It is well known biologically and easily identified, but its species-level systematics has been much debated. At times, the American brook lamprey was called *aepyptera, appendix,* or *wilderi*; in a later period, it was stabilized as *L. lamottenii* (often spelled *lamottei*) (Hubbs and Trautman 1937). Bailey and Rohde (unpublished), Bailey (1982a), and Robins et al. (1980) judged *lamottenii* to be unidentifiable and reapplied the next oldest applicable name, *appendix*.

Lampetra appendix (DeKay)

In opposition, Vladykov and Kott (1982a, 1982b) recommended readoption of *wilderi* and have used it (Kott et al. 1988).

Lampetra appendix generally has been considered an eastern and central North American species, but the recently described northwestern form *L. alaskense* may be a synonym (Rohde 1979; Bailey 1980, 1982a). Rohde (1979, personal communication) recognized two subspecies in Virginia, one extending south to the James drainage, the other in the Chowan and Roanoke drainages, and westward. The names applied by Rohde predate reversion to use of *appendix*, hence they are not used here; we are uncertain of the status of the forms.

Fish 6 *Lampetra appendix* recently transformed adult 138 mm TL (RC), VA, ? York drainage.

DESCRIPTION

Materials.—Thirty-seven larvae and 45 transforming or adult specimens from eastern Virginia to New Hampshire. Measurements and some counts from Vladykov (1950), Kott (1974), Rohde et al. (1976), Vladykov and Kott (1978), and Lanteigne et al. (1981). Color in life from Vladykov (1949), Trautman (1981), and Lanteigne et al. (1981).

Anatomy.—A nonparasitic lamprey with 2 dorsal fins and myomeres numbering (63)66–71(74); adults are 120–180 mm TL. Dorsal fins are low or moderate and separate in larvae; in adults elevated and barely separate to moderately conjoined; if conjoined, having a deep notch with a line of fusion evident.

Dentition.—Teeth usually moderately or well keratinized, some moderately long, tips somewhat rounded. Marginals in one uniformly arranged series; anterior intermediate teeth 10–28; lateral intermediate teeth absent. Posterior circumorals usually minute, forming a single complete series, numbering 17–24; lateral circumoral tooth groups 3 per side, each bicuspid or, less often, two cusps completely divided at gum level. Supraoral plate with one large undivided cusp per side, rarely an additional small medial cusp; infraoral cusps 5–8. Lingual laminae denticulate or serrate; transverse lamina with 7–11 cusps, medial one enlarged.

Measurements in % TL.—Disk length 3.2–6.0; snout length 5.2–7.0; prebranchial length 10.4–13.7; eye length 1.2–2.6; branchial length 9.0–11.9. Tail length 24.0–32.3; body depth 5.2–8.7; first dorsal fin height 1.3–2.9; second dorsal fin height 2.3–6.1. Disk, snout, prebranchial, and tail lengths, and dorsal fin heights greatest in male, body depth greatest in female. See also Lanteigne et al. (1981).

Color in Preservative.—Adults have dusky to dark back and side; pale belly and fins; lateral line organs not blackened.

Color in Life.—Newly transformed adults yellow-brown on back and sides, silver-grey below. Prespawning adults dark tan to slate-brown on back and side, lighter below, fins yellow tinged. Spawning adults blue-black.

Larvae.—Described by Vladykov (1950, 1960), Manion (1972), Smith et al. (1968), Wang and Kernehan (1979), Vladykov and Kott (1980), Lanteigne et al. (1981), and Fuiman (1982a).

COMPARISON

Lampetra appendix is separated from *L. aepyptera*, the other nonparasitic Virginia species having two dorsal fins, by: (1) myomeres [63–74 in *appendix vs.* 51–62 in *aepyptera*]; (2) dentitional development [stronger *vs.* weaker]; (3) marginal teeth [1 uniformly arranged series *vs.* 1–2 irregular series]; (4) posterior circumoral teeth [a complete series present *vs.* usually absent; when present, series is usually incomplete]; (5) transverse lingual lamina [well developed, cuspidate *vs.* rudimentary, noncuspidate].

BIOLOGY

The food of the American brook lamprey is largely small algae, generally taken in proportions similar to their relative abundance in sediment and water (Moore and Beamish 1973). Adults are not known to feed.

The duration of larval life is unclear because as for other lampreys, it is difficult to recognize the older premetamorphic age-groups by length frequencies, and because of possible variation within and between populations. Seagle and Nagel (1982) thought that in Tennessee many individuals metamorphosed at 4.3 years and other individuals transformed 1–2 years later. They reviewed studies from the Great Lakes region that indicated up to 7.5 years of larval life. With age determination by statoliths, Beamish and Medland (1988b) found that the length of the larval period was 4 years for some fish and 5 years for others in a New York population, and slightly more than 5 and 6 years for an Ontario population. Seagle and Nagel (1982) found that metamorphosis began in mid-August in Tennessee; it was underway in early August in New York, where larvae as large as 221 mm TL and metamorphosing fish up to 182 mm were noted (Beamish and Medland 1988b). Adults spawn and die in the spring following metamorphosis.

Lampetra appendix is not sexually dimorphic in adult length, but the species is quite variable in body length. Ten Virginia adults are 131–143 mm, mean, 138. These are similar to Delaware populations (Rohde et al. 1976) and somewhat larger than those of New Hampshire, which may be the smallest. We measured 20 New Hampshire adults to be 102–123 mm, mean, 113; the largest probably had shrunk from the maximum (132 mm) given by Sawyer (1960). Sizes attained in the Ohio and Great Lakes basins are typically larger than on the Atlantic slope south of the

St. Lawrence drainage; see, for example, Rohde et al. (1976), Kott (1971, 1974), Vladykov and Kott (1978), and Seagle and Nagel (1982). Our one adult from the upper Tennessee drainage of Virginia was 153 mm; from the upper Tennessee of Tennessee, 116 subadults and adults were 154–218 mm, mean, 185 (Seagle and Nagel 1982). Six exceptionally large specimens, 260–317 mm TL, are known from Great Lakes tributaries in Michigan and Wisconsin; it was suggested that such sizes were attained by feeding parasitically or nonparasitically after metamorphosis (Manion and Purvis 1971; Vladykov and Kott 1980).

The aggregation of American brook lampreys at spawning sites in runs and riffles apparently is a result of local movement, not major migration (Kott 1971). Spawning occurred during mid- to late March in eastern Tennessee (Seagle and Nagel 1982), and was observed from 28 March to 4 April in Delaware (Rohde et al. 1976). The latest an adult was taken in Virginia is 16 April. Fowler's (1917b) report of lampreys spawning on 16 April in creeks of the lower Delaware drainage, although not documented by a specimen, was probably based on *L. appendix* because only this species is known from the Delaware and these creeks in particular (Rohde et al. 1975; Cooper 1983; our data). In more northerly areas spawning occurs during April to early June, and over its total range at water temperatures of 6.8–20.5°C (Rohde et al. 1976; Wang and Kernehan 1979; Seagle and Nagel 1982). It occurred most often at 15–18°C in New York (Gage 1928); the peak occurred at about 17°C in Quebec (Vladykov 1949). Trautman (1981) noted that *L. appendix* spawns later than *L. aepyptera* in Ohio. Fecundity of *L. appendix* is 1,327–3,787 ova (Vladykov 1951; Kott 1971; Rohde et al. 1976; Seagle and Nagel 1982). This species was hybridized experimentally with four other lamprey species (Piavis et al. 1970).

HABITAT

Conditions occupied by *L. appendix* over its range include those of *L. aepyptera* but have somewhat greater extremes. Inhabited streams range from low to moderate-gradient warm brooks or small rivers (rarely large rivers), to streams that are cool to cold year long and which support brook trout and slimy sculpin. Water is typically clear and substrates range from silt–sand to gravel–rubble (Vladykov 1949; Sawyer 1960; Rohde et al. 1976; Lanteigne et al. 1981; Seagle and Nagel 1982). Trautman (1981) found populations in gradients of 1.7–8.2 m/km; this range combines slow areas for ammocoetes and swifter areas for

spawning. Virginia Atlantic-slope populations typify this range of habitat occupancy, extending from lower elevations of the Blue Ridge onto the Coastal Plain; no population is known from blackwater streams. South Fork Holston-system populations are in trout water. Moore and Beamish (1973) found no evidence of habitat segregation by larvae of different sizes.

DISTRIBUTION   Map 16

The range of the widespread American brook lamprey includes the major western Chesapeake drainages from the Patuxent in Maryland southward to the James. Apparently having its southern limit on the Atlantic slope in the Chowan drainage, this species is one of the few fishes known from the Chowan but not from the Roanoke drainage. It occupies a few Virginia tributaries of the South and North forks of the Holston River, but is known only extralimitally in the Clinch and Big Sandy. In contrast to *L. aepyptera* on the Virginia Atlantic slope, its range is centered on the Piedmont and extends into montane areas.

The status of *L. appendix* in the Potomac drainage has been long confused. All original records for which specimens exist are based on *L. aepyptera*, *Petromyzon*, or *Anguilla*. The single known Potomac specimen of *L. appendix* (USNM 216443) was taken in 1948 from the Anacostia River, Maryland, near Washington, D.C. (Station 1 of Howden 1949). Based on the recent survey data from the Virginia portion of the Potomac, the American brook lamprey probably does not occur there now.

Abundance.—Rare or uncommon; the largest collection of larvae is nine specimens; of adults, four specimens.

REMARKS

The small number of, and generally wide gaps between, Virginia populations indicate that the American brook lamprey is depleted and localized in the state. Despite problems attending the detection of nonparasitic lamprey populations, we think that, given the intensity of surveys, if *L. appendix* were generally distributed in Virginia, many more populations would be known. Although it occupies a wide range of ecological conditions, one or more of its requirements are generally lacking. Some Virginia populations may be verging on extirpation. In contrast however, one population each in three separate drainages on Long Island, New York, was first no-

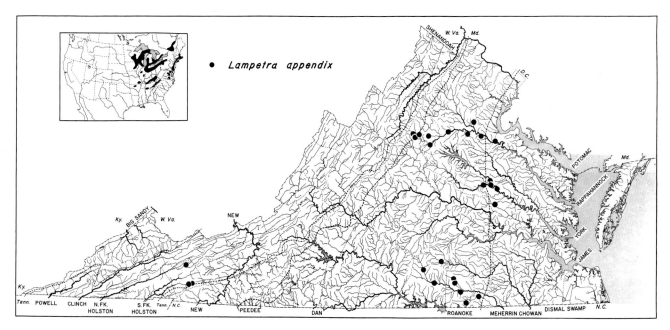

Map 16 American brook lamprey.

ticed during 1976–1984; the island had been extensively surveyed earlier (Schmidt et al. 1984). We note, though, that *L. appendix* larvae could have been taken previously on the island, but misidentified as *Petromyzon*. We do not believe that this has occurred with Virginia lampreys except perhaps for the few nonextant specimens.

Name.—*Appendix* refers to the long genital papilla of nuptial males, an "appendage" or "addition."

Least brook lamprey   *Lampetra aepyptera* (Abbott)

SYSTEMATICS

The nonparasitic *L. aepyptera* is notable for the extreme reduction of its size and dentition. It is a very distinctive species, but since its description from Ohio in 1860 it often has been confused taxonomically and nomenclaturally with *L. appendix* (Hubbs and Trautman 1937; Vladykov and Kott 1982a, 1982b). Recent disorder stemmed from the description of certain southeastern populations as a new species *Lethenteron meridionale* by Vladykov et al. (1975). They allocated *meridionale* to *Lethenteron* chiefly because it had posterior circumoral teeth (posterials). However, Bailey (1980, 1982a) and Walsh and Burr (1981) regarded their similar specimens as variant *L. aepyptera*. We concur, having noted posterials in one West Virginia and several Maryland specimens that otherwise are inseparable from typical *L. aepyptera*. We did not detect posterials in Virginia and North Carolina specimens, but F. C. Rohde (in litt.) discerned them in some from North Carolina. Kott et al. (1988) apparently did not accept the sinking of *meridionale*.

Okkelbergia was provisionally recognized by Hubbs and Potter (1971) as a genus solely for the "unpaired" *L. aepyptera*. Vladykov and Kott (1979a) postulated that the ancestor of *L. aepyptera* was a parasitic Pacific species of *Lampetra*, and placed *L. aepyptera* in that genus, subgenus *Lampetra*. We agree with Bailey (1980, 1982a) that the phylogenetic relationships of *L. aepyptera* are uncertain and tentatively recognize *Okkelbergia* as a subgenus for this species.

DESCRIPTION

Materials.—Three hundred fifteen Atlantic slope larvae and adults from the Susquehanna to the Neuse drainages on which we examined body length, myomeres, and dentition; body part measurements from Vladykov et al. (1975), Rohde et al. (1976), and Walsh and Burr (1981). Color in life from Brigham (1973), Trautman (1981), and Walsh and Burr (1981).

Anatomy.—A nonparasitic lamprey with 2 dorsal fins and myomeres numbering (51)53–59(62); adults are 80–120

Fish 7 *Lampetra aepyptera* adult male 115 mm TL (RC RGA 74-027), MD, Calvert County, tributary of Battle Creek, 12 April 1974.

mm TL. Dorsal fins low or moderate and separate in larvae; elevated, slightly conjoined, and deeply notched, with a line of fusion visible, in adults.

Dentition.—Teeth short, blunt, weakly keratinized. Marginals irregularly uni- to biserial, occasionally absent or unexposed from oral disk surface; anterior intermediate teeth 7–23; lateral intermediate teeth usually absent, 1–11 in some specimens. Posterior circumorals usually absent, 1–22 teeth in a partial or complete series in some specimens; lateral circumoral tooth groups (2)3(4) per side, each group usually unicuspid, often bicuspid, or the two cusps completely divided, none tricuspid. Supraoral plate with one large tooth per end, the teeth almost always unicuspid, rarely shallowly bicuspid; infraoral cusps 5–9(11). Lingual laminae usually rudimentary; transverse lamina usually fleshy, rarely with few rounded denticles.

Measurements in % TL.—Disk length 2.8–6.7; prebranchial length 6.9–13.4; eye length 0.9–2.6; branchial length 8.4–12.8; tail length 23.4–35.0; second dorsal fin height 2.1–7.5; disk, prebranchial length, tail length, and dorsal fin height longest in male.

Color in Preservative.—Adults have dark to dusky back and side; pale belly and fins; lateral line organs not blackened.

Color in Life.—Tan to gray-brown above belly, becoming mostly dark gray to blue-black when spawning. Nuptial color of both sexes of Kentucky specimens mottled gray-brown on dorsum; light silvery yellow ventrally; black horizontal bands on the side, through eye, and at base of first dorsal fin; dorsal fins with black-speckled marginal band; posterior margin of caudal fin darkly pigmented; gold band extending through base of caudal fin and center of dorsal fins. Some elements of this striking, rarely recorded color pattern are shown by Boschung et al. (1983).

Larvae.—Described by Vladykov (1950), Rohde et al. (1976), and Wang and Kernehan (1979).

COMPARISON

See *L. appendix* account.

BIOLOGY

Food habits of least brook lamprey larvae are unknown, but undoubtedly they feed on planktonic organisms and possibly particulate detritus. Adults do not feed.

The larval life span in Delaware is 5.4 years, the last a year of arrested growth; some ammocoetes may remain in that stage for an additional year (Rohde et al. 1976). Walsh and Burr (1981) estimated 4.5 years of larval life for a Kentucky population, but they may have had insufficient specimens to allow discernment of an additional year. Seversmith's (1953) estimate of 3 years in Maryland may have resulted from failure to distinguish one or more older age-groups; ecological conditions may influence longevity, but are not likely to effect such a short larval stage. Transformation begins in mid- to late August in Delaware (Rohde et al. 1976). Virginia specimens transformed before late October. Adults spawn and die in the next spring.

Specimens in early transformation in Delaware were 86–144 mm TL, mean, 95; adults on the Delmarva Peninsula were 75–120 mm, mean, 94 (Rohde et al. 1976). Transforming larvae in mainland Maryland were 90–130 mm, mean, 107; adults 90–120, mean, 104 (Seversmith 1953). Thirty-three Virginia adults were 91–132 mm, mean, 113. Larger sizes, usually 110–150 mm, are typical of most Kentucky populations (Walsh and Burr 1981). The maximum known length, about 180 mm TL, was reported from Ohio (Trautman 1981). The smallest adult we found is a 52-mm TL gravid female from the Patuxent drainage, Maryland (UMMZ 146639).

Spawning areas are reached with little or no migration. Reproduction occurs during mid-March to mid-April in the central and northern parts of the range, at water temperatures of 6–16°C (Seversmith 1953; Schwartz 1959; Branson 1970; Brigham 1973; Rohde et al. 1976; Wang and Kernehan 1979; Trautman 1981; Walsh and Burr 1981). Spawning was observed in the James drainage on 20 March 1972, water 8°C. Specimens collected in the Piankatank drainage, Virginia, on 28 March 1974, water 10°C, constructed a nest and spawned between 29 March and 5 April in a small aquarium with current and at room temperature; all had died by 14 April (J. A. Musick, in litt.). The latest capture date of an adult in Virginia was 14 April; the female had not yet spawned. Seversmith (1953) noted

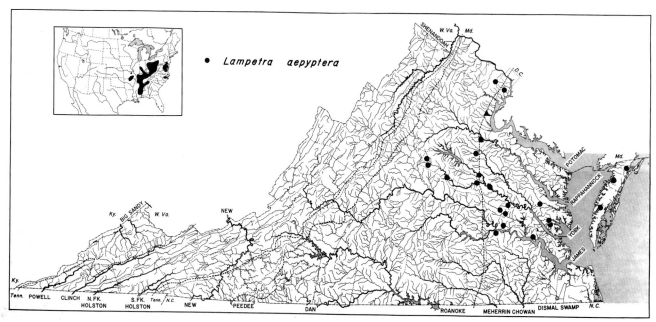

Map 17   Least brook lamprey.

that spawning extended to 10 May in central Maryland. Fowler's (1917b) report of *Lampetra* spawning during late May–early June in upper Chesapeake Bay tributaries of northern Maryland could not be verified; although it probably was based on *L. aepyptera*, the late period may be erroneous.

Spawning takes place in gentle to medium current in pool–riffle transition areas of sand and small gravel. An exceptional group spawned without apparent nest construction, over bedrock (W. C. Starnes *in* Walsh and Burr 1981). Fecundity is 572–3,816 ova (Seversmith 1953; Holbrook 1975; Rohde et al. 1976; Walsh and Burr 1981).

HABITAT

The least brook lamprey typically inhabits warm, mostly slow, predominantly sandy and silty, slightly acidic to slightly alkaline brooks and small streams. Ammocoetes were generally found in banks or sediments along runs and in pools with obvious current; transforming individuals occupied debris-ridden riffles and runs (Walsh and Burr 1981). Seversmith (1953) indicated that larvae of different ages and adults tended to segregate with regard to substrate. Larvae and subadults were taken in the upper end of a silty, sandy, small impoundment in Virginia. An exceptional stream-size record was of one *L. aepyptera* ammocoete in the large upper Pamunkey River, York drainage; it was caught with eight *L. appendix* ammocoetes, the only known case of their syntopy in Vir-

ginia. Larvae of *L. aepyptera* and *Petromyzon* are frequently taken at the same sites.

DISTRIBUTION   Map 17

Lampetra aepyptera occurs widely in the eastern United States. It extends far down the Delmarva Peninsula on the Chesapeake side and occupies all major and some minor western Chesapeake drainages. Uniquely for Delmarva, one record (PSU ELC 2241) is from an east-flowing stream, Wattsville Branch. This species is unknown from the Chowan and Roanoke drainages, which is odd because it occurs just to the south in the Tar and Neuse drainages in North Carolina. The majority of records are from the Coastal Plain, some near tidal waters. Records from about the Fall Line are not from high-gradient reaches, and the middle Piedmont sites are disjunct from the mountains that front the Blue Ridge.

Abundance.—Few collections, usually containing only a few specimens, of *L. aepyptera* are known from Virginia. Although this is a secretive animal, collecting intensity in eastern Virginia indicates that it is localized.

REMARKS

The dwarf, shy, least brook lamprey is a marked example of the evolutionary reduction undergone by nonparasitic lampreys in body length and dentition, and in the deletion of the adult feeding stage. We have documented an adult of 52 mm TL, apparently the smallest known adult of all living lamprey species. The presence of clean sand–gravel substrate in runs seems to be a requirement for reproduction; such habitat may be uncommon within the Virginia range of *L. aepyptera*. A watch should be made of known populations for possible need of their protection. This species apparently has declined in abundance and is considered threatened in North Carolina (Rohde et al. 1979).

Name.—*Aepyptera* means "high fin," alluding to the dorsal fins of nuptial specimens.

STURGEONS
Family Acipenseridae

BY JOHN A. MUSICK, ROBERT E. JENKINS, AND NOEL M. BURKHEAD

The Acipenseridae are an ancient family of bottom-feeding, anadromous and freshwater fishes of the Northern Hemisphere. They date back to the Late Cretaceous (more than 70 million years ago), and are related to another archaic family, the paddlefishes (Nelson 1984; Cavender 1986). These two families—the extant Acipenseriformes—form the sister group of all living Neopterygii (Rosen et al. 1981). The monographic study by Grande and Bemis (1991) supports a phylogeny within the order that differs radically from that of Gardiner (1984).

The Acipenseridae comprise about 23 living species within two subfamilies: Scaphirhynchinae (shovel-nose sturgeons) and Acipenserinae (typical sturgeons); only the latter are represented in Virginia. Acipenserinae has two genera, the Old World *Huso* and the circumboreal *Acipenser*. Two *Acipenser* are known from Virginia, but only the Atlantic sturgeon now occurs here.

Adult sturgeons normally range in size from 4 to 815 kg depending on the species. The Asian beluga sturgeon *Huso huso* may be the largest fish found in fresh water. The longest measured is a 5.86-m (18.9 feet) fish caught in 1940; 1,000-year old archeological material came from beluga estimated to have exceeded 6 m (19.7 feet). Weights of 1,020 and 1,228 kg (2,250 and 2,708 pounds) are known from the early 1900s, and a purported 1,361-kg (3,000 pounds) *Huso* was captured in Russia in 1827 (Gudger 1934; Berg 1948; Casteel 1976).

Sturgeons are elongate bottom-adapted fishes. Salient morphological features include a somewhat arched back and relatively flat venter; the back has one row of large bony scutes and each side has two rows of scutes, these positioned such that the body is somewhat pentagonal in cross section. The head is downsloped, the eye is small; the snout is short and broad, or much elongate, flattened, and shovel-like. The ventral surface of the snout has four pendulate barbels; the mouth is ventral, protrusile, and has thickened lips. The dorsal, pelvic, and anal fins are positioned far back on the body; the caudal fin is heterocercal; the pelvic fins are in the abdominal position and the pectoral fins are low on the body. In some species the first pectoral fin element is a horny spine; unpaired fins have fulcral scales at the leading edge; fin rays are the horny type (actinotrichia) and outnumber basal supports. A lateral line and typical scales are absent, but the skin bears many minute spiny denticles. The skeleton is cartilaginous except for ossified bones of the head; the intestine has a spiral valve.

Sturgeons are well endowed for sensing and capturing benthic prey. The ventral barbels are laden with taste buds and the mouth can extend downward at the end of a fleshy sleeve. The diet includes worms, crustaceans, insect larvae, and mollusks (Vladykov and Greeley 1964).

Sturgeons are slow-growing, late-maturing fishes. Maturation occurs between 5 and 28 years. The age of some individuals of the western North American white sturgeon may exceed 100 years (Scott and Crossman 1973); beluga sturgeon have lived 118 years (Casteel 1976). The sexes are externally indistinguishable except during the spawning season when females are swollen with roe. Adults tend to spawn at intervals of several years; the intervals appear to increase with age. Both Virginia species are anadromous, ascending from the sea or lower estuaries into rivers to spawn in the spring. Other species are strictly freshwater and all species spawn in fresh water. Eggs are 2.5 mm or greater in diameter, adhesive, and demersal.

Acipenserids have a long history of commercial importance. Large specimens may produce a few million eggs, which when ripe and cured with salt are marketed as caviar and provide the primary economic incentive for many sturgeon fisheries. In addition to the meat, which usually is smoked, and the eggs, other parts of these fishes are used. The swimbladder lining is used to make a gelatin (isinglass), which is used in food products and as glue. In the former Soviet Union, which pioneered in culture of sturgeons, the spinal cord is used to make a product called "vyaziga," and the head provides a valuable gelatin (Vladykov and Greeley 1964).

Because of slow maturation and relatively long periods between spawnings, sturgeon populations are relatively easily overfished and slow to recover. The history of sturgeon fisheries in the United States is one of unmitigated disaster for some species (Vladykov and Greeley 1964; Hoff 1980; Ryder 1890; T. Smith 1985).

Name.—*Acipenser* is the Latin name for "sturgeon."

Key to Sturgeons   Acipenseridae

Because the maximum size of the shortnose sturgeon is 1,430 mm TL, and its adults usually are smaller than 1,000 mm TL, a Virginia sturgeon greater than 1,500 mm TL is almost certainly an Atlantic sturgeon. Use caution in applying proportional diagnostic characters. The shape of the head and relative length of the snout change sharply with age; the snout becomes proportionately shorter and blunter with increasing length in both species. Consequently, the use of snout length as a proportion of total length can be misleading. Differences are obvious when comparing specimens of *A. brevirostrum* and *A. oxyrhynchus* of about equal size.

1a   Bony plates absent between anal fin and midlateral scutes; snout short, the distance from snout tip to anterior edge of upper lip about equal to or less than outer gape width (taken from outer edge of lips, Figure 18B); mouth large, inner gape width (from inside corner of lips) usually more than 65% (range 63–81%) of interorbital width; intestine dark .... SHORTNOSE STURGEON—*Acipenser brevirostrum*   p. 185

1b   Bony plates present (rarely absent) between anal fin and midlateral scutes; snout long, the distance from snout tip to anterior edge of upper lip distinctly more than outer gape width (Figure 18A); mouth small, inner gape width usually less than 60% (range 43–66%) of interorbital width; intestine pale .... ATLANTIC STURGEON—*A. oxyrhynchus*   p. 187

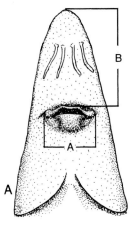
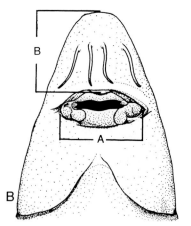

Figure 18   Ventral aspects of sturgeon, *Acipenser*, heads: (A) Distance "A" one-third to one-half of distance "B" in *A. oxyrhynchus*. (B) Distance "A" about equal to distance "B" in *A. brevirostrum*.

Sturgeons   Genus *Acipenser* Linnaeus

Acipenser is the largest genus of sturgeons, containing some 16 species of which 5 are North American (Vladykov and Greeley 1964). Two Atlantic coastal-estuarine species are known from Virginia.

Name.—See family.

Shortnose sturgeon   *Acipenser brevirostrum* Lesueur

SYSTEMATICS

The shortnose sturgeon was described from the Delaware River in 1818. Differences occur among some drainage populations but subspecies are not recognized (Dadswell et al. 1984). This species is closely related to the lake sturgeon *A. fulvescens* of inland North America (Vladykov and Greeley 1964).

DESCRIPTION

Materials.—Based on Vladykov and Greeley (1964), Gorham and McAllister (1974), and Dadswell et al. (1984). Life color from Lesueur (1818), Scott and Crossman (1973), and Dadswell et al. (1984).

Anatomy.—A sturgeon lacking bony plates on lower side posteriorly, and having a relatively short snout and a large mouth; adults are 450–900 mm TL. General anatomy as described for the family. Snout quite long and sharp in young, becoming proportionately shorter, broader, bluntly rounded or still pointed in adult; mouth large, gape width (between inner edge of lips) greater than 63% of bony interorbital width; supraanal plates absent; dorsal cephalic fontanelle closed by bone at about 160 mm TL; intestine dark; external secondary sexual differences absent.

Meristics.—Middorsal scutes 7–13; lateral scutes 21–35; ventrolateral scutes 6–11; gill rakers 22–32. Dorsal rays 38–42; anal rays 18–24.

Color in Preservative.—Dorsum dusky to dark, grading to white venter (Vladykov and Greeley 1964).

Color in Life.—Upper parts yellowish brown with green or purple cast in salt water, very dark in fresh water; lower parts yellowish or white; scutes pale; some young particularly yellowish; melanistic blotches may be present until about 600 mm TL. Fins yellowish to brown; paired fins outlined in white.

Larvae.—Described by Taubert and Dadswell (1980), Bath et al. (1981), and Dadswell et al. (1984).

BIOLOGY

Hoff (1979) presented an annotated bibliography of the biology of *A. brevirostrum*, and Dadswell et al. (1984) provided a detailed synopsis of biological data.

Shortnose sturgeon are opportunistic benthic foragers. Juveniles feed on small crustaceans and insect larvae. Adults in fresh water take mostly mollusks, benthic crustaceans, and insect larvae; in estuaries they mainly eat polychaete worms, crustaceans, and mollusks (Curran and Ries 1937; Dadswell 1979; Dadswell et al. 1984).

Acipenser brevirostrum exhibits sexual and latitudinal differences in maturation and spawning periodicity. Males and females usually mature respectively at ages 2–3 and age 6 in Georgia, ages 3–5 and ages 6–7 from South Carolina to New York, and ages 10–11 and age 13 in the St. John River, Canada (Dadswell et al. 1984). The first spawning occurs 1–16 years after maturity, and individuals generally do not breed for 1–3 years after a spawning; the hiatus in spawning

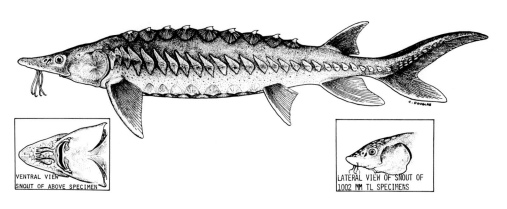

Fish 8 *Acipenser brevirostrum* 636 mm TL (NMC 67-331), NB, Kings County, Saint John River (drawing courtesy D. E. McAllister).

VENTRAL VIEW SNOUT OF ABOVE SPECIMEN

LATERAL VIEW OF SNOUT OF 1002 MM TL SPECIMENS

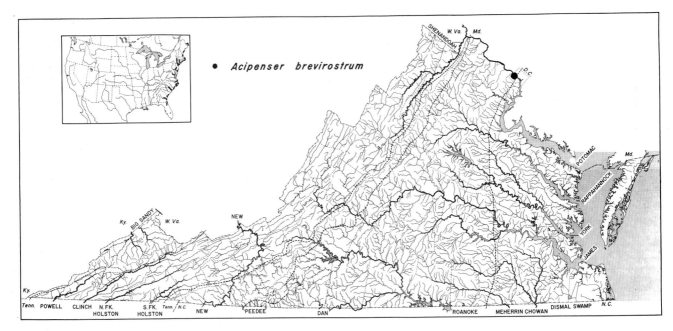

Map 18   Shortnose sturgeon.

may be more than 10 years for some fish. The oldest ages determined are 32 years for males and 67 years for females, from the St. John River (Dadswell 1979).

Lengths of both sexes at onset of maturation usually are 520–630 mm TL. Shortnose sturgeon grow faster but reach a smaller maximum size in the southern part of the range. Males and females attain respective maximum total lengths of 694 mm (586 mm FL) and 995 mm (875 mm FL) in the Altamaha River, Georgia, and 1,080 mm (970 mm FL) and 1,430 mm (1,220 mm FL) in the St. John River (Dadswell et al. 1984). The 1,430-mm TL Canadian fish is the size record for the species (Dadswell 1979).

Shortnose sturgeon are anadromous; they ascend large estuarine rivers to spawn, usually above tidal influence, as early as February in Georgia and as late as mid-May in Canada, in water of 9–12°C (Dadswell 1979; Dadswell et al. 1984). In the Delaware River, the river nearest to Virginia for which data are available, spawning occurs during the middle two weeks of April (Meehan 1910). Spawning typically occurs in swift areas of gravel or rubble bottom, such as in the Fall Zone (Dadswell et al. 1984). In some South Carolina rivers where access to the Fall Zone is barred by dams, spawning apparently occurs below the Fall Line adjacent to flooded hardwood swamps (D. E. Marchette, personal communication). Fecundity is 10,000–16,000 eggs/kg of body weight, or about 27,000–208,000 eggs per fish (Dadswell et al. 1984).

HABITAT

Shortnose sturgeon extend from fresh water to the sea, as related to the normal pattern of movement or migration of adults between spawning, feeding, and wintering areas (Dadswell et al. 1984). Upriver migrations to spawning grounds occur in spring or fall. Downstream feeding migrations in spring have spent fish joining others of the adult population. Autumnal downstream migrations are to wintering areas in lakes, lower rivers, or bays. An unknown portion of most populations may move short distances into the Atlantic Ocean. Differing patterns of movement have been found for some populations (Dadswell et al. 1984; Hastings et al. 1987). Adults normally are found in deep water (10–30 m) during winter and in shallower areas (2–10 m) in summer. Juveniles are non-migratory and typically inhabit deep swift river channels above the salt wedge (Dadswell et al. 1984).

DISTRIBUTION   Map 18

Acipenser brevirostrum occupies many of the principal riverine estuaries from the St. John River, New Brunswick, to the St. Johns River, Florida. Curiously, only one certain pre-1900 record exists for the entire Chesapeake Bay basin—a specimen from the Potomac River at Washington, D.C., in 1876 (Jenkins and Musick 1979; USNM 26273, a skin). This apparently is the basis of Potomac records by Uhler and Lugger

(1876), Smith and Bean (1899), Hildebrand and Schroeder (1928), Vladykov and Greeley (1964), Musick (1972), and Dadswell et al. (1984). McAtee and Weed (1915) stated that "two [species] of sturgeons ascend to Little Falls but no further . . ." Little Falls is the most downstream of a series of large rapids in the Potomac River Fall Zone. The record (Lee et al. 1980) for Chesapeake Bay at the mouth of the Potomac estuary stems from misinterpretation of a compilation of the 1876 record.

Based on the occurrence of *A. brevirostrum* north and south of Chesapeake Bay, it may have occupied all four major estuarine drainages of the Chesapeake in Virginia. It is improbable that this species occupied Virginia largely as a migratory component of populations which spawned elsewhere, because it has not been shown to move away from the influence of the home estuary (Dadswell et al. 1984). The closest record south of Virginia is a young specimen from the lower Chowan River (Salmon Creek) in 1881 (Vladykov and Greeley 1964; Ross et al. 1988). Undoubtedly, this species also extended into the lower Roanoke River, but not as far as Virginia. The upstream record in the Pee Dee River (Ross et al. 1988; Map 18) is below the Fall Line.

The shortnose sturgeon has recently reappeared in the Chesapeake basin in the lower Susquehanna drainage. It was first detected in 1974 (Dadswell et al. 1984); the most recent record known to us is from April 1986 (T. D. Brush, personal communication). Possibly these fish entered the upper Chesapeake from the Delaware River via the Chesapeake and Delaware Canal.

Unacceptable records of *A. brevirostrum* for Virginia are from a Norfolk fish market (DeKay 1842); the Atlantic Ocean between Cape Henry, Virginia, and Cape Fear, North Carolina (Holland and Yelverton 1973); and in 1977 from the James River (misplotted on the York) and the Rappahannock River (Dadswell et al. 1984). DeKay's record is rejected because *A. brevirostrum* was poorly known by naturalists in his time, and as C. Smith (1985) noted, DeKay tended to misidentify variants of known species. No data or specimens are known to support the cited records by

Holland and Yelverton (1973) and Dadswell et al. (1984) (Ross et al. 1988; our study).

Abundance.—Apparently extirpated from all Virginia waters. Certain other populations also are extirpated, but the shortnose sturgeon is somewhat common in some drainages.

REMARKS

Although not recorded in Virginia in more than 100 years, *A. brevirostrum* is legally endangered in the state (Burkhead and Jenkins 1991). That status is founded on possible reappearance of the species and on its federal endangered designation in 1967. The shortnose sturgeon is also endangered in Maryland and North Carolina (Lee et al. 1984; Ross et al. 1988). The reasons for widespread protective listing of this fish include its apparent extirpation from certain drainages and frequent rarity elsewhere. Pollution, dams, and over-exploitation have contributed to its decline.

Acipenser brevirostrum seems much less endangered than most other fishes in that category. It is relatively common in certain drainages; for example, the St. John, Kennebec, Hudson, Delaware, Santee, and Altamaha (Dadswell et al. 1984; Hastings et al. 1987). Early estimates of abundance generally were based on low-intensity or inefficient sampling for sturgeons; the historical record is sketchy. Current views of the abundance of *A. brevirostrum* are derived largely from sampling schemes aimed specifically for its capture. The wide distribution of the species and the existence of healthy populations led Ono et al. (1983) to suggest that it might be upgraded nationally to threatened.

Dadswell et al. (1984) recently reviewed management options for recovery of *A. brevirostrum*. Restoration might be achieved through hatchery culture and restocking. The discovery of shortnose sturgeon in the Susquehanna River holds a glimmer of hope that it may reappear in Virginia.

Name.—Brevirostrum means "short snout."

Atlantic sturgeon   *Acipenser oxyrhynchus* Mitchill

SYSTEMATICS

The Atlantic sturgeon was described from New York in 1814. Two subspecies are recognized, *A. o. oxyrhynchus* in rivers and nearshore areas of the

western North Atlantic Ocean, and *A. o. desotoi* in the northern Gulf of Mexico (Vladykov 1955; Vladykov and Greeley 1964). This species is closely related to the Old World *A. sturio* (Magnin and Beaulieu 1963).

Fish 9 *Acipenser oxyrhynchus* juvenile 422 mm TL (NMC 80-0027), NB, St. John River, January 1980.

DESCRIPTION

Materials.—Vladykov and Greeley (1964), Leim and Scott (1966), Gorham and McAllister (1974), and 5 specimens from Virginia and nearby. Life color from Vladykov and Greeley (1964) and several Chesapeake Bay specimens.

Anatomy.—A sturgeon with bony plates present on lower side posteriorly, a relatively long snout, and a small mouth; adults are 880–2,000 mm TL. Anatomy much as in *A. brevirostrum*, except: snout typically longer, more pointed; mouth smaller, gape width usually less than 60% of interorbital width; supraanal bony plates almost always present as a series immediately above or contacting anal fin base; dorsal cephalic fontanelle not closed by bone until about 900 mm TL; intestine pale.

Meristics.—Middorsal scutes 7–13; lateral scutes 24–35; ventrolateral scutes 8–11; gill rakers 15–27. Dorsal rays 30–46; anal rays 23–27.

Color in Preservative.—Dorsum dusky to dark; side and venter pale; dorsal and lateral shields much lighter than surrounding skin.

Color in Life.—Canadian specimens bluish-black dorsally, becoming paler down the side and white ventrolaterally; venter white; dorsal and lateral shields very light. Specimens from Chesapeake Bight tend brownish olive on dorsum, grading to pinkish tan on side, white ventrally; dorsal and lateral scutes always lighter than surrounding skin.

Larvae.—Described by Ryder (1890), Vladykov and Greeley (1964), Mansueti and Hardy (1967), Lippson and Moran (1974), Jones et al. (1978), and Hoff (1980).

BIOLOGY

The biology of *A. oxyrhynchus* is reviewed by Vladykov and Greeley (1964), Carlander (1969), Murawski and Pacheco (1977), Hoff (1980), Van Den Avyle (1983), and T. Smith (1985).

Atlantic sturgeon are opportunistic benthic feeders, taking worms, crustaceans, aquatic insect larvae, snails, and sand lances (Vladykov and Greeley 1964; Scott and Crossman 1973; Huff 1975).

Age at maturation varies considerably. In the Hudson River, males mature at 11–20 years and females at 20–30 years (Dovel *in* T. Smith 1985). In the St. Lawrence River, males reach maturity at 22–24 years, females at 27–28 (Scott and Crossman 1973). The maximum age recorded is apparently 60 years, from a St. Lawrence River specimen (Magnin 1964). In the Delaware River estuary, Ryder (1890) found that male Atlantic sturgeon typically were 1,830–2,130 mm TL; females averaged about 2,440 mm. Although DeKay (1842) reported an Atlantic sturgeon of 5,490 mm TL (18 feet), the largest documented is 4,270 mm TL (14 feet), caught off Canada (Vladykov and Greeley 1964).

Atlantic sturgeon are anadromous, ascending large rivers to spawn in tidal fresh water as early as February and March in northern Florida (Vladykov and Greeley 1964; Huff 1975) and in May to July in the St. Lawrence River (Scott and Crossman 1973). In Chesapeake Bay tributaries, they spawn in April and May (Hildebrand and Schroeder 1928). Spawning temperatures are 13.3–20.5°C (Borodin 1925; Huff 1975; T. Smith 1985). In South Carolina, males spawn at intervals of typically 1–5 years and females at 3–5 years (Smith et al. 1984). This species requires solid substrates upon which to lay its adhesive eggs (Vladykov and Greeley 1964; Huff 1975; T. Smith 1985). Fecundity is 800,000–3.76 million eggs (Ryder 1890; Smith 1907; Vladykov and Greeley 1964).

HABITAT

Juvenile Atlantic sturgeon may spend several years continuously in fresh water of some large rivers (Scott and Crossman 1973); in other rivers they may move downstream to brackish water when temperature drops in the fall (Dovel 1979 *in* Hoff 1980). Most Atlantic sturgeon from the Virginia portion of Chesapeake Bay were taken by trawls and gill nets from depths less than 20 m. Our captures in Atlantic coastal waters have been restricted to depths less than 20 m within 10 km of shore.

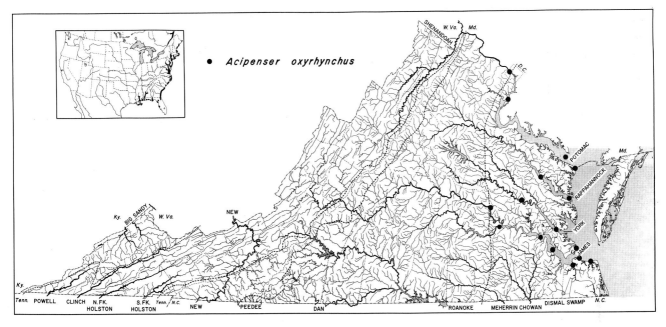

Map 19   Atlantic sturgeon. Atlantic Ocean and full Chesapeake Bay range not shown.

DISTRIBUTION   Map 19

The Atlantic sturgeon occurs along the Atlantic coast and in estuaries from Labrador to Florida and west to the Mississippi delta, and rarely to the Rio Grande (Gilbert 1992). Apparent strays were caught in Bermuda, and one purportedly was taken in northern South America more than a century ago (Vladykov and Greeley 1964; Gilbert 1978c).

Acipenser oxyrhynchus is migratory; of 4,264 Atlantic sturgeon tagged in the Hudson River, 60 tags were returned and 22 of these came from lower Chesapeake Bay (Loesch et al. 1979). This suggests that one-third of Hudson River Atlantic sturgeons may use Chesapeake Bay as a feeding area sometime during their lives. Juveniles tagged along the coast between False Cape, Virginia, and Cape Lookout, North Carolina, migrated south during November to January and then north as far as Long Island in late winter and early spring (Holland and Yelverton 1973). Juveniles tagged off South Carolina have migrated as far north as Chesapeake Bay (T. Smith 1985). Although there are a few records of Atlantic sturgeon from offshore fishing banks, most captures at sea have been very near the coast (Vladykov and Greeley 1964).

Abundance.—Severely depleted.

REMARKS

The status of Atlantic sturgeon stocks was reviewed by Hoff (1980) and T. Smith (1985). This species has been so reduced by overfishing, pollution, and dams that directed fisheries are active only in New York and Canada. Chesapeake Bay landings peaked in 1890 at 329,329 kg, after which the fishery rapidly declined. Landings fell to 73,741 kg in 1904, and to 10,386 kg in 1920 (Hildebrand and Schroeder 1928).

Currently the Atlantic sturgeon is sharply reduced in Virginia waters. Loesch et al. (1979) reported that 2,500 kg and 5,214 kg were captured and released, respectively, in 1978 and 1979 as a bycatch in the spring pound and gill-net fisheries in Virginia. All but a few of the sturgeon reported were immature; average weights were: James River 1.6 kg; York River 3.8 kg; and Rappahannock River 2.9 kg.

Although many of these juvenile sturgeon may have originated from other estuarine systems (e.g., the Hudson), recent captures of young-of-the-year Atlantic sturgeon by Virginia Institute of Marine Science trawl surveys indicate that some sturgeon still spawn in Virginia rivers. From 1964 to 1982, 36 juveniles were captured; of these, seven were less than 150 mm TL. One of these very young sturgeon was captured from the York River, the rest from the James River.

All sturgeons are fully protected in Virginia by laws pertaining to Fisheries of Tidal Waters (see also *A. brevirostrum*). The Atlantic sturgeon is ranked with special concern status in Virginia (Burkhead and Jenkins 1991). Still, our stocks may be vulnerable to fisheries elsewhere along the coast during migration.

In colder months, substantial landings of sturgeon are still reported from North Carolina; these landings likely include fish originating from Virginia and other mid-Atlantic states.

Sturgeon stocks in Virginia probably can be rehabilitated by prohibiting sturgeon landings from coastal fisheries, particularly in North Carolina, and by hatchery culture and stocking. Sturgeon culture has been used quite successfully in the former Soviet Union to aid stock recovery (Hoff 1980; T. Smith 1985).

Name.—Oxyrhynchus means "sharp snout." Gilbert (1992) noted that the valid spelling of this name is *oxyrinchus,* as originally used by Mitchill (1814b). Our recognition of the spelling change was made too late to change in text and figures.

PADDLEFISHES
Family Polyodontidae

The strange snout of the paddlefish is the basis of its common name and specific epithet. Paddlefishes, with their long oar- or spatula-shaped snout, are bizarre survivors of an ancient fish fauna. The earliest fossils date from the Late Cretaceous, about 70–75 million years ago. Five species are known, three extinct ones from western North America (Grande and Bemis 1991), *Polyodon spathula* of North America, and *Psephurus gladius* in China.

Paddlefishes can attain large size. A *Polyodon* of 2.16 m TL (7 feet, 1 inch) is known. If Nichols (1943) was correct that *Psephurus* "may reach a length of about 7,000 mm" (7 m, 23 feet), then the Chinese paddlefish would exceed in length the giant sturgeons and rank among the largest fishes of the world. However, Bailey (1975) stated that no freshwater fish ever reaches 6 m (20 feet). Nichols (1943) has been widely cited for the maximum length of *Psephurus*. He quoted it from an article written in Chinese by Ping (1931), but his translated quote is inexact; Ping gave "7 meters." L. N. Chao (in litt.) informed us that in Ping's time, the metric system may not have been that which is now used, and that Ping may have been told by fishermen that the fish reaches 7 "chi," which approximates 7 feet in the traditional Chinese system. Chenhan and Yongjun (1988) considered Ping's record to have been expressed as standard length, but Ping did not specify that; very likely it was total length including the snout appendage. In recent years, the total length of fishery-captured specimens usually was 1.5–2.5 m (4.9–8.2 feet) (W. Y. B. Chang,

in litt.). However, the largest of about 50 specimens (Chenhan and Yongjun 1988) was 1.5 m SL. The Chinese paddlefish has much declined as a result of overfishing.

The American and Chinese paddlefishes lead quite different lives. The American species is a planktivore with a nonprotrusile mouth. The Chinese species has protrusile jaws, lacks long gill rakers, and is highly predaceous on fishes and macroinvertebrates (Vasetskiy 1971; Chenhan and Yongjun 1988; Grande and Bemis 1991).

Polyodon was originally described as a shark because of the heterocercal tail and mostly cartilaginous skeleton. Several chondrichthyan fishes—goblin sharks, saw sharks, sawfishes, and longnose chimaeras—also evolved a greatly prolonged snout. Actually, polyodontids are among the most primitive, living, ray-finned fishes, and are related to the sturgeons (Dingerkus and Howell 1976; Patterson 1982; Nelson 1984; Grande and Bemis 1991). Primitive traits of paddlefishes include a spiral valve in the intestine, dermal denticles in the skin, fulcral scales on the tail, actinotrichia (horny fin rays), and a heterocercal tail.

Name.—Polyodont-, "many teeth," likely refers to the many long gill rakers. The relatively distinctly toothed, small individuals were unknown when the paddlefish was scientifically named (L. Grande, in litt.).

Paddlefishes   Genus *Polyodon* Lacepède

A monotypic genus for the North American paddlefish.

Name.—See above.

Fish 10 *Polyodon spathula* young 123 mm TL (RC), TN, Campbell County, Powell River, preserved 10 June 1981, aquarium raised.

Paddlefish   *Polyodon spathula* (Walbaum)

SYSTEMATICS

The paddlefish was described in 1792, type locality not specified. The systematics of living and extinct paddlefishes was treated by Grande and Bemis (1991).

DESCRIPTION

Materials.—Based on MacAlpin (1947), Grande and Bemis (1991), and 6 young from Tennessee and Illinois. Life color from Clay (1975), Pflieger (1975), and 1 Virginia adult.

Anatomy.—A large, often stout fish with a ventral mouth and long flattened snout rostrum; adults are 1,100–1,600 mm TL. Body elongate, slender or robust, broad, often deep; skin smooth, scales limited to a patch of rhomboid scales at base of upper caudal lobe, fulcral scales along upper edge of caudal fin, and denticles sparsely distributed over much of body. Head large; eye small; snout rostrum very long and spatulate, about 35% of TL in young, about 20% TL in adult; two minute barbels on underside of snout near mouth; mouth ventral, large; young and small juvenile with teeth on jaws, adult toothless; opercular flap fleshy, long, tapering to a point posteriorly; opercular membranes broadly conjoined, free from isthmus.

Gill rakers very long, thin, close-set, and very numerous (400–600 on outer row of first arch in adult). Head and snout covered with patches of pit sensory organs (electroreceptors); lateral line complete, with long dorsal and ventral canaliculi. Dorsal and anal fins positioned far back on body, falcate; caudal fin heterocercal, falcate; pelvic fin in abdominal position; pectoral fin placed low. Genital pore surrounded by papillae in male, area smooth in female (Vasetskiy 1971; Becker 1983); the difference may be unreliable for sexing (Russell 1986).

Color in Preservative.—Dorsum and side medium to very dusky, lower side uniform or mottled; venter pale; head and snout dusky, sensory patches dark, particularly on operculum and lower jaw. Fins dusky. Young darker than adult.

Color in Life Plate 39.—Dorsum blue-gray to olive-gray, lower side and venter silver-white to dirty-white.

Larvae.—Described by Larimore (1949), Purkett (1961), Ballard and Needham (1964), Vasetskiy (1971), Hogue et al. (1976), and Grande and Bemis (1991).

BIOLOGY

Paddlefish biology was reviewed by Vasetskiy (1971) and in the proceedings of a symposium on the species (Dillard et al. 1986).

Adult *Polyodon spathula* are indiscriminant planktivores. Feeding paddlefish cruise open water with the lower jaw dropped. The incoming water balloons the branchial cavity and is filtered across the extensive gill rakers, straining out plankton and insects (Ruelle and Hudson 1977; Carlson and Bonislawsky 1981; Becker 1983). Paddlefish feed both day and night. Prey selectivity is negligible; the percent occurrence of different plankters in the gut reflects their relative abundance in the water (Rosen and Hales 1981). The presence of bryozoans, sand, and detritus in the gut indicates that feeding sometimes occurs near or on the bottom (Bernet et al. 1977; Ruelle and Hudson 1977; Rosen and Hales 1981). Fitz (1966a) found a large juvenile to have eaten 13 threadfin shad; they probably were taken incidentally. Very small paddlefish have relatively large teeth and poorly developed gill rakers; they select and capture individual food items, chiefly microcrustaceans and small insect larvae (Rosen and Hales 1981; Russell 1986; Grande and Bemis 1991).

Paddlefish have a long juvenile phase; maturity usually is reached within ages 7 to 12; females mature latest in this range. Maturation reflects attainment of 1,100 mm TL and 6.8–9.1 kg by males, and 1,400 mm and 13.6 kg by females (Adams 1942; Carlson and Bonislawsky 1981; Russell 1986). Maximum ages of 28 and 30 have been reported (Robinson 1966; Carlander 1969) but typical life expectancy is 15 years (Adams 1942; Pasch et al. 1980). Early growth varies considerably by body of water; average lengths of age-1 paddlefish from Iowa, Oklahoma, and Tennessee were 206–958 mm TL (Houser and Bross 1959; Russell 1986). The range of averages at age 10 in 14 populations from Tennessee to Montana is 1,090–1,687 mm TL (Russell 1986).

Eleven *Polyodon* from Virginia were 12.7–47.2 kg (28–104 pounds). We examined a 29.5-kg, 1,665-mm TL specimen in the wake of the June 1967 Clinch

River fish kill; two others seen at the time by game wardens were about 18–20 kg. Masnik (1974, VPI 2803) reported a 29.5-kg specimen from the Clinch River near Dungannon in 1972. A farmer told us in 1981 that he speared three paddlefish, 17.2, 18.1, and 27.2 kg, in the Powell River during winter 1980. One each of 12.7 kg and 18.1 kg were snagged in the Clinch River at Ft. Blackmore during December 1984 by J. Gillenwater. We heard of an approximately 38-kg paddlefish from the Clinch River before the kill, and one of 47.2 kg was recently reported from the river. *Polyodon* up to 52.2 kg (115 pounds) were taken in the early 1960s from Norris Reservoir, an impoundment of the Clinch and Powell Rivers in Tennessee (Carroll et al. 1963). The heaviest paddlefish reported (Trautman 1981) is an Ohio specimen of 83.5 kg (184 pounds); maximum length is based on an Iowa fish of 2,159 mm TL (7 feet, 1 inch) (Nichols 1916).

Paddlefish may spawn from late March to late June depending on latitude and local conditions. Water temperatures near 10°C and rising water level trigger congregation and upriver migration; reservoir fish move into and up main rivers. Clean gravel substrate and water of 11–14°C seem to be spawning requirements (Purkett 1961; Pasch et al. 1980; Russell 1986).

Little is known of paddlefish spawning behavior owing to the high and turbid water in which they typically spawn. Apparent spawning activity was observed under such conditions over an inundated gravel bar in Osage River, Missouri (Purkett 1961). Spawning appeared to occur communally. A female would rush to the surface, closely followed by groups of males; gametes likely were released during the ascent. The activity occurred every few minutes from late afternoon to evening, and sounds of surface disturbance were heard after dark. Fertilized adhesive green-black eggs of 2.7–4.0 mm in diameter were found at the site when the water level receded. Fecundity ranges from 82,300 to somewhat over 1,000,000 eggs (Needham 1965; Robinson 1966; Russell 1986).

HABITAT

Polyodon is typical of warm, medium to very large rivers with long, deep, sluggish pools. Paddlefish also concentrate in other areas of reduced current; for example, below bars and in the lee of islands, and in backwaters and overflow lakes. With impoundment, major populations have persisted in some reservoirs that have a large free-flowing tributary or a significant tailwater section below an upstream dam. Paddlefish seem to prefer depths of more than 1.5 m; during late fall and winter they tend to live in deeper water. A stressed adult was found in an area of high salinity in Texas (Parker 1965).

Despite a calm-water preference, paddlefish traverse varied habitats. In addition to their often long pre- and postspawning migrations (see below), they tend to move daily during summer. Long-range movements may be required to maintain populations (Russell 1986).

DISTRIBUTION   Map 20

The paddlefish is native to the Mississippi basin and several Gulf slope drainages; few records, all old, are from the Great Lakes (Burr *in* Lee et al. 1980). In Virginia, *Polyodon* occurs only in the Clinch and Powell rivers of the Tennessee drainage. The Powell and the two lower Clinch records on Map 20 are noted under *Biology*. The other Clinch record plotted is from J. Gillenwater (personal communication) who stated that the species occurs as far upriver as Dungannon. Similar information was heard about 10 years earlier (Masnik 1974).

Paddlefish occur year-round in the Clinch River, Virginia, according to J. Gillenwater. His statement is supported by June and winter records from the Clinch or Powell rivers. Perhaps the main body of the upper Clinch–Powell population resides in Norris Reservoir, Tennessee; all paddlefish ascending into Virginia may be adult. Vagility of the species is sufficient to travel the 81 rkm from Norris Reservoir to the Virginia line and then the 43 rkm to Dungannon. Upstream spawning movements of 161–418 rkm occurred in the Missouri and Yellowstone rivers (Robinson 1966). Hubert et al. (1984) and Russell (1986) summarized migration in other waters.

Abundance.—Difficult to inventory due to the big-water habitat of the species and apparent lack of a directed fishery in the state. *Polydon* probably have been uncommon or rare through the last 50 years. None were seen during boat-shocking of many Clinch River pools during the 1960s, before the fish kill in 1967 (R. E. Wollitz, personal communication). Paddlefish returned to the lower Virginia portion of the Clinch by a few years after the kill, and according to some residents, increased there in the late 1970s and early 1980s.

REMARKS

Every now and then nature delights us with a wonderful design, a plan curious and archaic such as

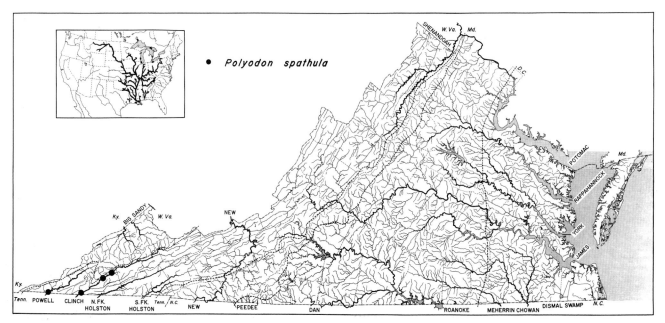

Map 20 Paddlefish.

the paddlefish. A swimming net formed by a cavernous maw and branchial sieve, the gentle river giant is a piscine Pinocchio. The snout rostrum may have dual purposes. It is covered with sensory structures (Larimore 1949) which may aid in detection of food. Its broadly flattened form may serve as a forward-positioned hydrodynamic plane, helping to counteract the downward drag of the gaping mouth when feeding. However, loss of the rostrum does not appear to overly handicap the individual; healthy fish with damaged or missing paddles have been captured. The notion that the paddle is used to stir up bottom-dwelling organisms is a myth (Rosen and Hales 1981).

Paddlefish formerly were widely abundant but many populations have declined and some peripheral ones are extirpated (Carlson and Bonislawsky 1981; Gengerke 1986). Principal reasons for decline are impoundment, channelization, siltation (particularly of spawning grounds), pollution, and overfishing. Since the late 1800s, paddlefish have been commercially harvested for caviar roe and smoked flesh; the roe are a substitute for sturgeon eggs. Paddlefish often are butchered only for the roe. The market value of roe and consequently the commercial fishing pressure have fluctuated considerably. Currently the value is up and in some areas the pressure is alarmingly high. The potential for paddlefish stock depletion is strong due to the tendency for the species to aggregate and the predictability of spawning runs and winter distribution (Pasch and Alexander 1986). Although paddlefish do not take a baited hook or lure, the sport fishery catch by snagging in many rivers and reservoirs is substantial.

Concern for paddlefish fisheries and interest in the species itself have stimulated considerable ongoing research (Dillard et al. 1986). Some states recently developed management policies. Status surveys indicate that populations of several states are still faring well and that national protective status is unwarranted (Carlson and Bonislawsky 1981; Gengerke 1986). Paddlefish are being cultured and stocked in some areas. The answer to the original question posed in the paddlefish symposium—"Is the paddlefish a threatened resource?"—appears to be "not yet" (Dillard et al. 1986).

In Virginia the paddlefish occupies only two rivers; thus, the state's population of this ancient and fascinating fish was proposed for threatened status (Burkhead and Jenkins 1991).

Name.—*Spathula*, "broad blade," refers to the snout rostrum. "Spoonbill" and "spoonbill cat" are Appalachian appellations also used elsewhere for this fish.

GARS
Family Lepisosteidae

"Gar" is an Anglo-Saxon word for spear or lance; it fits the very slender, nearly cylindrical body and pronounced snout of gar fishes. Indeed, with toothsome beak and bony armor, gars seem like swimming weapons. Gars are medium to large fishes; maximum adult sizes range from 800 mm TL for the shortnose gar *Lepisosteus platostomus* to over 3,000 mm TL for the alligator gar *Atractosteus spatula* (Lee et al. 1980).

Members of this ancient neopterygian family swam in warm shallows when giant reptiles trod the Earth. Fossils of *Atractosteus* and *Lepisosteus* date back to the Late Cretaceous; they resemble Recent gars. These lineages likely arose by the Early Jurassic, some 200 million years ago (Wiley 1976); the family may have arisen in the Permian (Late Paleozoic), more than 245 million years ago (Wiley and Schultze 1984). This family of the Lepisosteiformes contains 16 species, equally divided between the two genera, and is nearly equally composed of fossil and Recent forms.

All living gars are New World species; five occur in North America, one (plus one North American species) occurs in Central America, and one is in Cuba. Gars also occur in the fossil record of Europe, India, Africa, and purportedly South America (Wiley 1976; Cavender 1986). The distribution pattern may be related to the former connection of continents, but early gars may have dispersed through seas; a gar has been reported from a Cretaceous marine deposit (Wiley and Stewart 1977). Gars are related to another ancient surviving actinopterygian—the bowfin, family Amiidae (Patterson 1981; Nelson 1984).

Many basic morphological features of gars are primitive. The jaw mechanism is relatively simple and adapted for biting; the jaws are heavily armed with conical teeth. The skull is well ossified and has many superficial and distinctly sculptured bones; the body is covered with interlocking rhomboid bony scales whose outer layer is composed of hard acellular ganoin (sometimes called ganoid scales). Fins exhibit an advancement over sturgeons and paddlefishes; each dorsal and anal ray has a bony support and the caudal fin has the abbreviate heterocercal (hemicercal) condition. Gars have a rudimentary spiral valve in the intestine and a large, vascularized, bilobed swim bladder. The bladder is used as an accessory lung during periods of low dissolved oxygen concentration; it also provides buoyancy (Renfro and Hill 1970 *in* Moyle and Cech 1982).

Lepisosteids are basically lowland sluggish-water fishes, ranging from lakes and upland rivers to coastal swamps and brackish estuaries. Gars often lurk just beneath the surface, sometimes in small groups, or hide in vegetation. They typically ambush prey, mostly fish, by waiting for the quarry to swim close, or by slowly finning toward the intended meal. Fish are typically seized laterally with a quick sideward head snap and then maneuvered to be swallowed head first. Crustaceans such as crayfishes and crabs are plucked from the bottom. Alligator gars are known to scavenge on dead fish and refuse (Suttkus 1964; Pflieger 1975).

Spawning occurs communally with several to many males escorting females. Eggs are scattered; they are demersal, adhesive, oval, and large; those of the longnose gar are 4.0 by 2.9 to 4.5 by 3.2 mm (Simon and Wallus 1989).

Name.—Lepisoste- means "scale bone."

Gars   Genus *Lepisosteus* Lacepède

Lepisosteus was formerly the sole genus of gars, but recently the subgenus *Atractosteus*, containing the alligator gar and allies, was elevated (Wiley 1976); however, Robins et al. (1980, 1991) do not recognize this. The single Virginia gar is a true *Lepisosteus*.

Name.—See above.

Longose gar   *Lepisosteus osseus* (Linnaeus)

SYSTEMATICS

The longnose gar is the first freshwater fish named from Virginia, in 1758. The original, apparently third-handedly described specimen (Jordan and Evermann 1896) probably came from the lower James or lower York drainage. It was secured by the collector and artist Mark Catesby during his residence and travels in Virginia during 1712–1719. *Lepisosteus osseus* is closely related to the living *L. oculatus* and *L. platyrhincus* species pair, but its nearest kin appears to be the extinct *L. indicus* of India (Wiley 1976).

DESCRIPTION

Materials.—Based on Suttkus (1964), Wiley (1976), Simon and Wallus (1989), and 5 Virginia and 3 Tennessee specimens. Life color from Suttkus (1964), 1 Virginia adult, and 3 Tennessee young.

Anatomy.—An elongate fish with bony scales and a beaklike snout bearing many sharp teeth; adults are 670–1,150 mm TL. Trunk very elongate, oval or quadrate in cross section, fully covered with interlocking rhomboid scales. Head slender, many rugose cranial bones exposed; eye moderate; jaws attenuated, armed with needlelike canine teeth, upper jaw slightly occluding the lower; nares distal on upper jaw; pseudobranchae well developed; gill arches with patches of rasplike teeth. Dorsal and anal fins far back on body, rounded; caudal fin abbreviate heterocercal, rounded, dorsal leading edge with splintlike fulcral scales; pelvic fin ventral, well in advance of vent; pectoral fin ventral. Lateral line complete; cephalic lateralis moderately developed. Young with a free upper caudal filament

(fleshy extension of the distal notochord) that usually is lost between 250 and 280 mm TL.

Meristics.—Lateral line scales 57–63; predorsal scales 47–55; transverse scales between dorsal and pelvic origins 31–35. Dorsal rays 6–9; caudal rays 11–14; anal rays (7)8–10; pelvic rays 6; pectoral rays 10–13. Gill rakers short, 14–31.

Color in Preservative.—In juvenile and adult, dorsal half of body dusky; upper side and midside uniform or with scattered dark marks or blotches; lower body pale. Dorsal, caudal, and anal fins mostly pale, large oval dark spots present. Pigment pattern disruptive in young; dorsum dusky with dark middorsal stripe; midside with a dark lateral stripe; lower side with a pale stripe; venter lightly to heavily peppered with large melanophores; head dusky above, side with dark stripe through eye and across operculum, continuous with midlateral stripe; lower head peppered with large melanophores. Fins mostly pale, darkly variegated or spotted; caudal dark-margined.

Color in Life Plate 9.—Juvenile and adult pale olive-brown, brown, or green above, grading to white or silver-white on venter; side sometimes with remnants of lateral stripe in form of dark blotches or smaller marks. Distinctiveness of lateral marks and dorsal shades vary with water clarity; dorsum greenish and lateral marks obvious in clear water. Median fins cream with large black spots or marks. In young, dark marks are brown to brown-black; dorsum pale brown; lower side stripe cream.

Larvae.—Described by Mansueti and Hardy (1967), Lippson and Moran (1974), Hogue et al. (1976), Jones et al.

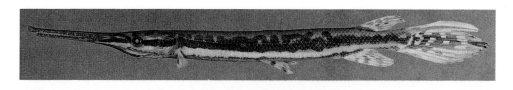

Fish 11 *Lepisosteus osseus* juvenile 179 mm TL (REJ 1154), TN, Hancock County, Clinch River, 29 June 1985.

Fish 12 *Lepisosteus osseus* juvenile 354 mm TL (REJ 929), VA, Scott County, Copper Creek, 17 June 1981.

(1978), Heufelder (1982a), Yeager and Bryant (1983), Jollie (1984), and Simon and Wallus (1989).

BIOLOGY

Larval longnose gar begin feeding at about 20 mm TL and almost immediately assume the piscivorous habit; even larvae seize larval fish laterally (Pearson et al. 1979). Microcrustaceans and immature insects are eaten more often than larval fishes during early life (Payne and Pearson 1981). A wide array of fishes dominates the diet of juvenile and adult *L. osseus*; crayfishes, crabs, insects, frogs, and a shrew have been noted as food (Cahn 1927; Lagler and Hubbs 1940; Suttkus 1964; Scott and Crossman 1973; Woolcott et al. 1974; Becker 1983).

Lepisosteus osseus exhibits sexual differences in maturation, longevity, growth rate, and maximum size. Males mature at age 3 or 4, ordinary maximum survival is age 9 or 10, and ultimate survival is age 17. Females mature at about age 6, typical maximum life expectancy is age 16 or 17, and ultimate longevity is age 22 (Netsch and Witt 1962). First-year growth of both sexes is rapid, achieving nearly half the size of maturation by averaging as much as 3.2 mm per day (Riggs and Moore 1960; Netsch and Witt 1962; Echelle and Riggs 1972). Adult males of ages 6 and 10 average 762 and 815 mm TL; adult females of ages 6 and 17 average 856 and 1,153 mm TL (Carlander 1969). We collected many adults of 700–1,000 mm TL in the Clinch system. Average weight of 27 gars from Lake Drummond was 4.1 kg (Rosebery and Bowers 1952; Brady 1969). The Virginia record is 11.4 kg (25 pounds 2 ounces). The world record, from Texas, is 1,834 mm TL (6 feet) and 22.8 kg (50 pounds) (Scott and Crossman 1973; IGFA 1985).

The longnose gar spawns during spring and early summer, ascending rivers and lower reaches of streams; it also spawns in lakes. In southwestern Virginia, spawning runs occur between mid-May and early June; according to local residents migration lasts for about two weeks. On the night of 20–21 May 1971, a gill net stretched across the mouth of Copper Creek ensnared some 40 adults attempting to enter the creek. We found adults well up the creek only during May and June. On 5 June 1984 we observed spawning at the mouth of Copper Creek; access to the creek was essentially blocked by a temporary culvert. Spawning occurred near the bank in a slow run over boulders and bedrock, depth 1–1.5 m. One female was escorted by three males. Details were not seen; snorkeling revealed adhesive eggs scattered over the bottom singly and in small clusters. Apparent spawning of *L. osseus* occurred in tidal freshwater creeks in Virginia during June (McIvor and Odum 1988).

Egg deposition also occurs in shallow weedy areas of streams and lakes, and over clay substrates (Cahn 1927; Goff 1984). Longnose gar spawned on small-mouth bass nests in Lake Erie; brood care by male bass enhanced reproductive success of the gar (Goff 1984). Haase (1969 *in* Becker 1983) observed communal spawning with up to 15 males pursuing a female. Males nudged the female with the snout; gametes were released while in an oblique head-down position, snouts near the bottom. Fecundity is 6,200–77,150 eggs (Carlander 1969). Reproductive success was low in Back Bay, Virginia, during a recent seven-year period (Norman 1981). The eggs are said to be toxic to humans (Netsch and Witt 1962). We observed *Nocomis micropogon* eating longnose gar eggs.

HABITAT

Longnose gar are found in medium-sized streams to large rivers, marshes, swamps, lakes, reservoirs, and estuaries. They are frequently associated with weedy areas and other cover in pools and backwaters. *Lepisosteus osseus* tolerates warm areas avoided by other predatory fishes in Wisconsin lakes (Becker 1983); during such warm periods gar frequently gulp air. The highest salinity record is 31‰ (Schwartz 1981b). Gar avoid lower portions of Virginia estuaries (Massmann et al. 1952; Musick 1972).

DISTRIBUTION   Map 21

The native range of *L. osseus* includes much of eastern North America. In Virginia, this species occurs in all major Atlantic slope drainages and the Tennessee drainage. It probably is more widely distributed in some Atlantic drainages than our records indicate, but it is apparently absent above the Fall Line in the Potomac, Rappahannock, and York drainages. The plot in the Piedmont of the Potomac (Lee et al. 1980) is from our misinterpretation of a record by Smith and Bean (1899) from "Little River," which actually is a side channel of the Potomac River just below the Fall Line. The single plot on the Rappahannock River represents records from unspecified sites in a 36.5-rkm section between Fredericksburg and Tappahannock (Massmann et al. 1952). A state citation gar came from the Rappahannock in 1985. The Piankatank drainage plot is from an unspecified locality in Dragon Swamp; *L. osseus* occupies much of the lower portion of the swamp (W. H. Norton, personal communication). The upper James River record is a sighting in 1986 (D. Smith, personal communica-

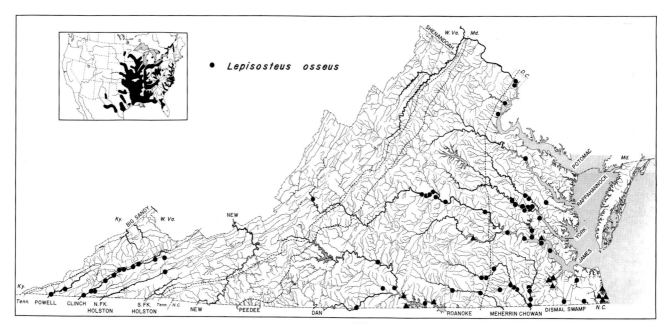

Lepisosteus osseus

Map 21 Longnose gar.

tion). The uppermost Roanoke River record is based on fish ascending from Kerr Reservoir during a recent spring (J. A. Williams, personal communication).

In the Tennessee drainage, *L. osseus* lives in the Clinch and Powell rivers, but apparently is absent now from the North Fork Holston River. The North Fork record is based on a head found in 1867 at Saltville (Cope 1868b).

Abundance.—Most often uncommon; common locally during spawning migration.

REMARKS

Larval *L. osseus* have an interesting papillose adhesive disk on the snout tip. Larvae suspend vertically from floating objects, the surface film, and vegetation, and when disturbed they free themselves and sink (Echelle and Riggs 1972).

Gars have ill repute as fish slayers in some areas, purportedly decimating fish populations. Perhaps

the well-toothed beak confers an image of great voracity. Although the sideward head-snap used to seize prey is startlingly quick, gars are rather inactive. In reality they are not more ravenous than our game species. Their numbers seem generally low in Virginia. We have observed people gathered at bridges in southwestern Virginia to shoot gars with guns during spawning runs. Killed gars usually are let drift away, a wasteful "sport."

Gloves should be worn when handling a live gar; skin can be pinched and cut between the bony scales of a writhing fish. A testimony of the toughness of the armored skin is the observation by Smith (1907) that before steel plows were available, plowshares were sometimes covered with garskin. The scales have been popular as jewelry. Although disdained in our area, gar flesh is reported to be of good quality (Smith 1907; Becker 1983).

Name.—*Osseus* means "bony," referring to the superficial head bones and ganoid scales on the head and body.

BOWFINS
Family Amiidae

The bowfin *Amia calva* is a living relict, the sole survivor in the primitive neopterygian order Amiiformes. Among Recent fishes, *Amia* is most closely related to gars, which with related extinct fishes were formerly grouped as the Holostei, as separate from the Chrondrostei (sturgeons, paddlefishes, and extinct relatives) and the Teleostei (higher bony fishes). The Amiiformes have been distinct since at least the Triassic, more than 208 million years ago, and despite their customary phylogenetic position after gars, they may have originated before gars did so (Olsen 1984; Patterson and Longbottom 1989).

The confinement of *A. calva* to eastern North American lowlands exemplifies relictive distributions that are common among archaic living fishes. Fossil *Amia* have been uncovered in western North America, Asia, and Europe; an amiid genus was recently discovered in Africa (Boreske 1974; Schultze and Wiley 1984; Patterson and Longbottom 1989). Our bowfin is a freshwater fish but some Mesozoic amiids apparently were marine (e.g., Patterson 1981; Bryant 1987). Some amiids were huge, most notably the extinct African species of 2.5–3.5 m.

Primitive anatomical features of *A. calva* include a gular plate, a nonprotrusile bite, an abbreviate heterocercal (hemicercal) tail, a heavily vascularized and subdivided airbladder (a functional lung), and a rudimentary intestinal spiral valve. The dorsal fin is very long and, as in gars, each fin ray articulates with one bony support. The bowfin lacks fulcral scales; body scales are the cycloid type but uniquely surfaced. Its larvae have an adhesive organ on the snout.

Name.—Ami-, from *Amia*, an old name for some kind of fish, possibly the bonito (Jordan and Evermann 1896). "Bowfin" derives from the long dorsal fin which undulates in ribbonlike (bowlike) waves.

Bowfins   Genus *Amia* Linnaeus

The lineage of the living bowfin has been traced by a fossil record back to the Late Cretaceous, more than 70 million years ago (Schultze and Wiley 1984; Patterson and Longbottom 1989).

Name.—See above.

Bowfin   *Amia calva* Linnaeus

SYSTEMATICS

Amia calva was described from South Carolina in 1766.

DESCRIPTION

Materials.—Based on Scott and Crossman (1973), Jones et al. (1978), and 2 Virginia subadults. Color in life from Gill (1907) and 1 Virginia subadult.

Anatomy.—A stout-bodied, cylindrical fish with a long dorsal fin and a bony (gular) plate on the underside of the lower jaw; adults are 400–600 mm TL. Body somewhat elongate, slightly compressed posteriorly; head and eye moderate; anterior nare tubular; mouth subterminal, jaws bearing small canine and peglike teeth; large gular plate present. Dorsal fin long, uniform in height; caudal fin abbreviate heterocercal, rounded, scaled at base; pelvic fin

Fish 13 *Amia calva* juvenile 239 mm SL (WHH 149), VA, Surry County, Cypress Swamp, 25 July 1983.

abdominal, pectoral fin ventral, both rounded. Body fully scaled, scales cycloid, with parallel ridges.

Meristics.—Lateral line complete, anterior scales with bifid pores, total scales 62–70. Dorsal rays 42–53; caudal rays 25–28; anal rays 9–12; pelvic rays 7; pectoral rays 16–18.

Color in Preservative.—In adult, upper half of body dusky, uniform or reticulated; lower side and venter pale; head with dark postorbital bar, oblique dark bar behind corner of mouth, and dark slash on lower jaw. Adult male retains ocellus on upper caudal base; ocellus loses pale ring or is obsolete in female. Dorsal and caudal fins dusky, darkly mottled; anal fin slightly dusky; paired fins pale. Large young and juvenile with dark chainlike pattern on body.

Color in Life.—Head, back, and upper side tan-olive with rusty tinge, reticulation dark olive; head bars dark olive. Dorsal and caudal fins pale olive with dark olive mottling; ocellus dark olive, ringed with red; lower fins pale olive. Reproductive males intensify; fins become bright green, the back bronze, and head stripes, other patterns, and the caudal spot further blacken.

Larvae.—Described by Mansueti and Hardy (1967), Jones et al. (1978), and Heufelder (1982b).

BIOLOGY

Amia calva is a predatory generalist. Young feed on microcrustaceans and insects. The diet of adults is an inventory of catchable prey; fishes predominate, followed by worms, crayfishes, insects, mollusks, and frogs (Pearse 1918; Cahn 1927; Lagler and Hubbs 1940; Lagler and Applegate 1942; Becker 1983). Bowfin are nocturnal but are most active around dawn and dusk (Gill 1907).

In comparison to paddlefish and some gars, longevity and growth are moderate. In a Canadian population, males matured at about age 4 and 450 mm TL, and females at age 4 or 5 and 600 mm (Cartier and Magnin 1967 *in* Scott and Crossman 1973 and *in* Jones et al. 1978). Maturation was noted at 380 mm TL in Ohio (Trautman 1981). Males are smaller and shorter-lived than females. Ages 7 and 9, sexes not distinguished, have been detected in wild populations (Cartier and Magnin 1967; Becker 1983), but these studies did not include very large fish. Maximum longevity in nature may much exceed 9 years; Carlander (1969) reported ages of 20, 24, and 30 years for captive fish. Adults in Canada were 450–640 mm TL, and in Ohio were 380–630 mm. Total lengths of five Dismal Swamp bowfins were 737–826 mm; average weights of Dismal Swamp and Back Bay fish were 1.2–2.0 kg (Rosebery and Bowers 1952; Brady 1969; Norman 1981). The Virginia record is 7.9 kg (17.5 pounds). The world record is 9.8 kg (21.5 pounds) from South Carolina (IGFA 1985).

An unusually satisfactory view of bowfin reproduction from early observations is summarized in Gill (1907) and Breder and Rosen (1966). Bowfin spawn during spring in water of about 16–19°C. Working chiefly at night, the male constructs a bowl-shaped nest on the bottom in shallows, among weeds, tree roots, or under logs. Vegetation is uprooted or bitten-off and placed in the nest, as is detritus. Nests may occur singly or in small groups, apparently depending on available habitat and density of spawning adults. Gametes are deposited at night after a pair courts by nudging each other and encircling the nest. Both sexes are polygamous. The male aggressively defends the eggs and young. Hatchlings remain in dense balls about the nest, but quickly drop to the bottom and disperse when disturbed. Nests contain 2,000–5,000 eggs; fecundity has been estimated as 2,765–64,000 (Jones et al. 1978). Eggs are demersal, adhesive, and covered with gelatinous filaments; diameters are 2.0–3.0 mm (Jones et al. 1978). Reproductive success was very low or nil during a recent seven-year period in Back Bay (Norman 1981).

HABITAT

The bowfin is typically associated with dark swamps and sluggish portions of open, marsh- and swamp-fringed rivers in the south. The range of habitats encompasses small streams, ditches, ponds,

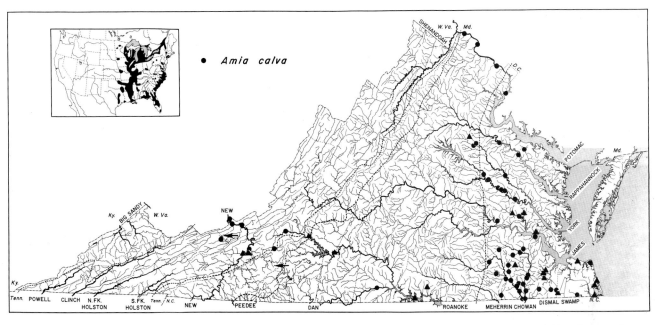

Map 22 Bowfin. Plots on Mattaponi River (York), Northwest River (Dismal Swamp), Dan River, and Kerr Reservoir are from records of the 1985 VDGIF citation program, sites unspecified. Dots on Occupacia Creek (Rappahannock) and Po and Ni rivers are also from unspecified sites (E. L. Steinkoenig, in litt.). Arrows indicate documented points of stocking in the New drainage.

lakes, and estuaries. *Amia* is usually found in shallow weedy areas and near other cover such as cut banks and stumps. Its typical habitat in Virginia may include relatively deep water; most records are from major rivers, Lake Drummond, and Back Bay. Bowfin are sedentary in a North Carolina swamp (Whitehurst 1981). Their occurrence in estuaries is occasional; one was found in an area of 5‰ salinity in North Carolina (Schwartz 1981b).

Bowfin are hardy. During warm periods they gulp surface air, and at 30°C three times more oxygen is derived from gulping than from normal gill respiration (Horn and Riggs 1973). *Amia* apparently can withstand intermittent drought periods by aestivation. A live adult was discovered in a moistened cavity beneath dried mud in a desiccated swamp (Neill 1950). Such adaptations are particularly important in swamps, which often have low oxygen content or become dry during summer.

DISTRIBUTION   Map 22

Amia calva occupies eastern North American lowlands. On the Atlantic slope it is native at least north to Maryland (Lee et al. 1981, 1984). The historical status of bowfin in Atlantic drainages south of the St. Lawrence basin in New England and New York is uncertain (C. Smith 1985). Burgess and Gilbert (*in* Lee et al. 1980) considered the records in these states to

have stemmed from introductions. Whitworth et al. (1968) doubted the authenticity of the Connecticut reports relayed by Webster (1942). A bowfin was captured around 1973 in Lake Onota, Housatonic drainage, Massachusetts (G. W. Bond, in litt.). Northeastern records may represent native relict populations, but if so, we would expect the bowfin to persist somewhere in the area between Maryland and New York.

In Virginia, bowfin are native to the Coastal Plain and perhaps the lower Piedmont, and have been introduced to the upper Roanoke and New drainages. Distributional curiosities exist in Virginia. *Amia* was considered nonnative above Great Falls of the Potomac River (Davis and Enamait 1982); it was stocked in the South Branch Potomac River, West Virginia (Stauffer et al. 1978b). We accept a Rappahannock drainage record (Cat Point Creek near Montross) based on a third-hand report from an angler, because the fish was called a bowfin and diagnostic features were described. The capture was related to us in 1971 by E. Perry, an observer of natural history when a student at Roanoke College. His father, knowing of our interest in bowfin, conferred with the angler. Our recent inquiries to game wardens and the survey by Maurakis et al. (1984) revealed no other Rappahannock record, but a canvas of anglers in 1986 indicated the presence of bowfin in Occupacia Creek and at Port Royal (E. L. Steinkoenig, in litt.). The lack of a record for the swampy Piankatank drainage is odd.

Stockings of two private fee-fishing ponds in the New drainage are known (arrows, Map 22). The pond on a branch of No Business Creek, Walker Creek system, received 500–600 adults from Michigan in 1952. Shortly after, a freshet ruptured the dam and about half the bowfin escaped, some being caught as far down the New River as Bluestone Reservoir (correspondence in 1952 by W. H. Gilpin and W. E. Martin, transmitted to E. C. Raney). Hatches Pond on Pine Creek and Pine Creek itself, Little River system, were stocked in the 1960s; the fish emanated from Canada and were advertised as pike (R. M. Cromer, W. H. Norton, D. Shanks, personal communications). Because both Walker Creek and the Little River enter the New River below Claytor Dam, the source of Claytor Lake records is unknown. Ross and Perkins (1959) listed a bowfin taken in the lake in 1953. We received occasional reports of bowfin from the lake, the last in 1984, but none were caught in many years of surveying the lake by the VDGIF (D. K. Whitehurst, in litt.).

It seems that stocking of bowfin was in vogue 20–40 years ago, as suggested by the above cases, the three upper Roanoke drainage records during 1962–1970 (Estes 1971; Jenkins and Freeman 1972), and one from the Tennessee drainage Highlands in North Carolina (Bailey et al. 1954). *Amia* persists in low numbers in the upper Roanoke; one was taken in upper Smith Mountain Lake in 1985 (D. K. Whitehurst, personal communication). The population was supplemented in 1982 when some 500 young bowfin were netted in the Santee River, South Carolina, and released in the lowermost section of a Roanoke River tributary in Salem (A. Cockrell, personal communication).

Abundance.—Uncertain in most areas due to the difficulty of seining in the Coastal Plain and the paucity of large-stream sampling by methods suited to capture of bowfin. Common in canals and Lake Drummond of Dismal Swamp (Rosebery and Bowers 1952; Brady 1969); uncommon or rare in Back Bay (Norman 1981). Large bowfin frequently are caught in the Chickahominy River and its connected Diascund Reservoir.

REMARKS

The bowfin is one of the two most advanced of the piscine living fossils in Virginia. Although it is not considered directly basal to modern teleosts, it nevertheless is an evolutionary pioneer. It provides a glimpse of the life history diversity that must have existed in ancient fish faunas. It is one of the oldest fishes that exhibits nest building and brood care, adaptive strategies so often repeated and much modified in modern fishes.

The atavistic bowfin seems to fit its dark swamp haunts. In startling contrast was the sighting in 1970 of a large individual under clear, low-water conditions in a small rocky section of the South Fork Roanoke River. That bowfin, a late survivor of a probable stocking, was holding near groups of brilliantly colored minnows spawning on *Nocomis* nests. Perhaps it had left a large downstream pool and with alimental purpose followed the upstream progression of minnow spawning.

Amia is said to be a gamefish when hooked, but even after considerable preparation, only sometimes passable as table fare. Evermann (1916) wrote that eating bowfin is like chewing cotton.

Name.—*Calva* refers to the "bare" or "bald" (scaleless) head; often called grindle or blackfish in Virginia.

FRESHWATER EELS
Family Anguillidae

The Anguillidae are a family of 15 species of true eels, all in the genus *Anguilla*, which occupy temperate and tropical portions of the Atlantic, western Pacific, and Indian oceans and their influents. The American eel *Anguilla rostrata* of the northwestern Atlantic basin is the only North American species. The species of *Anguilla* are catadromous and semelparous; they spend most of their life in fresh or brackish water and return once to oceanic spawning grounds to breed and die (Tesch 1977). The family has been traced back to the Middle Eocene, some 45 million years ago (Cavender 1986).

Although the true eels, order Anguilliformes, are represented in North American fresh waters by only one species, the group is large and diverse; 21 families and 720 species are recognized by Castle (1984). Almost all species are marine and many inhabit the deep sea. Anguilliforms have an evolutionarily advanced, serpentine body form, but in fact they are rather primitive among bony fishes. Their nearest relatives include bonefishes, tarpons, and ladyfishes—herringlike fishes with body forms typical of most fishes. Phylogenetic linkage of true eels to bonefishes and allies is based largely on the leptocephalus type of larva common to them (Greenwood et al.

1966; Castle 1984; Smith 1984). Characteristics of this larva include a highly flattened, often ribbonlike body and major reduction in size during metamorphosis.

The extremely elongate body plan of eels is highly successful. The body form is termed anguilliform, and the typical mode of traveling—by synchronous undulations of the body—is named anguilliform locomotion. Although allowing open-water swimming, this body and locomotion type is specialized for entering crevices and burrowing in soft sediments, thus permitting eel-like forms to both hunt and hide in places not normally entered by most fishes, and to back out of them by reversing the direction of the undulations. Eel-like forms typically have the paired appendages reduced in size and capability, or one or both sets of the appendages are lost. The wide success of this morphotype is evidenced by its independent evolution in other fish lineages (e.g., lampreys, hagfishes, gymnotid eels, cusk eels, and blennies), certain salamanders (e.g., sirens), glass lizards, and snakes.

Name.—Anguill-, from *Anguilla*, a Latin word for eel.

Eels   Genus *Anguilla* Shaw

A genus of about 15 eel species (Castle 1984).

Name.—See above.

American eel   *Anguilla rostrata* (Lesueur)

SYSTEMATICS

Anguilla rostrata was described from New York in 1817 but its taxonomic status has been controversial

for several recent decades. The American eel problem is actually a North Atlantic basin one, as the western Atlantic form at times has been considered conspecific with its eastern Atlantic counterpart, the Euro-

203

pean eel *Anguilla anguilla*. Morphologically the two forms differ in vertebral numbers (103–111 in *A. rostrata*; 110–119 in *A. anguilla*). Williams and Koehn (1984) regarded their strong genetic similarity to indicate only an infraspecific distinction. However, their breeding in the Sargasso Sea overlaps in both space and time, and yet they maintain morphological and life-history differences; essentially they are separate populations (Comparini and Rodino 1980; Kleckner et al. 1983). Despite the occurrence of a somewhat intermediate cohort in Iceland (Williams et al. 1984), most workers regard them as separate species.

DESCRIPTION

Materials.—Based on Hildebrand and Schroeder (1928), Scott and Crossman (1973), Tesch (1977), Hardy (1978a), and 7 Virginia lots. Color in life from Scott and Crossman (1973), Wenner and Musick (1974), Hardy (1978a), and Helfman et al. (1987).

Anatomy.—Body very elongate, round anteriorly, somewhat compressed posteriorly; dorsal and anal fins long, confluent with caudal fin; pelvic fin absent; pectoral fin positioned laterally; adults are 220–1,000 mm TL. Head short; eye moderate; mouth terminal, fairly large, jaws well toothed; nares tubular; gill opening slitlike. Skin thick, tough; scales first appear well after metamorphosis and are cycloid, oval, small, and well embedded; many groups of scale rows orient at right angles to each other, forming a tweedlike pattern. Vertebrae 103–111. Sexually maturing fish become macrophthalmic (eye becomes very large [Fish 15; Vladykov 1973c]) and the lateral line becomes prominent.

Color in Preservative.—Larva and glass eel translucent white or gray. Elver dusky or brown, much like juvenile. Juvenile (yellow stage) with top of head, back, and side dark to moderately dusky; lower head, lower side, and venter pale; dorsal and caudal fins dusky, sometimes pale margined; anal fin pale.

Color in Life.—Larva and glass eel virtually transparent. Elver brown above. Juvenile upper body olive to brown; lower body dirty pale yellow, yellow-olive, or yellow-orange, or belly white. Sexually maturing fish (silver or bronze stage) almost black dorsally, dark bronze luster to back and upper side, metallic silver sheen on lower side and venter; pectoral fin dorsally and caudal fin blackened.

Larvae.—Described by Lippson and Moran (1974), Hardy (1978a), Wang and Kernehan (1979), and Auer (1982b).

BIOLOGY

The complex life-history cycle of the American eel involves several stages and sexual dimorphisms; many biological distinctions of this species from all other North American fishes are related to catadromy. Our synopsis of the life cycle is compiled largely from Tesch (1977), Hardy (1978a), Helfman et al. (1987), and Jessop (1987).

The transparent, ribbonlike leptocephalus larvae hatch in the Sargasso Sea and passively drift westward and northward in major currents for about 1 year; they grow to as much as about 85 mm TL. Metamorphosis includes reduction in length to as little as about 50 mm and generally occurs before reaching the Continental Shelf. Now as transparent

Fish 14 *Anguilla rostrata* juvenile 178 mm TL (REJ 1014), VA, Greensville County, Fontaine Creek, 15 July 1983.

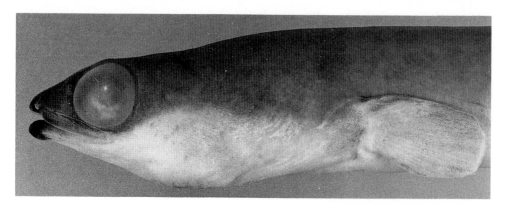

Fish 15 *Anguilla rostrata* macrophthalmic (maturing?) female 419 mm TL (REJ 1038), VA, Campbell County, Roanoke River, 12 September 1983.

glass eels, the fish are cylindrical and free-swimming. With further coastward or upriver migration, the young eels are minimally about 65 mm and darken into elvers. The juvenile (yellow) stage commences with development of full pigmentation at about 100 mm. Change to the silver (or bronze) stage and enlargement of the eye generally occur during sexual maturation. Maturing eels depart for the sea; no adult is known to have returned inshore. Unless otherwise specified, we treat only the dominant freshwater (yellow eel) stage.

Anguilla rostrata is a dietary generalist, eating live and recently dead animal matter, the diversity of which seems limited only by availability (Helfman et al. 1987). Worms, crustaceans, benthic insects, snails, clams, and fishes are widely taken (Scott and Crossman 1973; Woolcott et al. 1974; Wenner and Musick 1975). Large individuals in fresh water feed particularly on crayfishes and bottom-dwelling fishes (Ogden 1970). Foraging occurs primarily at night (Jenkins and Jenkins 1980; Helfman 1986).

The sexes differ in growth and age at maturation. Males generally are restricted to estuaries and are most abundant in the southeastern United States; these habitats have a relatively long growing season and tend to be highly productive. Males grow rapidly and mature early; as silver eels they seldom exceed 450 mm TL (usual range 220–440 mm) and are 3–10 years old (mean, 5.3 years) (Helfman et al. 1987).

Females occur throughout the less-productive freshwater and northern estuarine range of the species, and further differ from males by tending to live longer, grow larger, and mature later. Females typically mature at lengths greater than 450 mm TL (range 366–1,000 mm; mean, 525–908) and ages of 4–18 years (a southern mean, 8.6, a northern one, 12.3). Interpopulation variation of females is also evident; the largest and latest maturing individuals tend to occur in northern areas and, within a hydrographic basin, in fresh water. Some of the sexual differences may involve unusual patterns of sex determination (Helfman et al. 1987).

Anguilla rostrata populations of the Chesapeake basin and nearby seem to fit overall trends of the species (Helfman et al. 1987). From Chesapeake subestuaries, yellow females were 352–687 mm TL, silver females 418–845 mm, and silver males 339–438 (Wenner 1973; Wenner and Musick 1974). The largest known American eel seems to be a 1,524-mm TL individual from Maryland (Carlander 1969), but the largest taken in four years of extensive sampling in the Chesapeake region is 812 mm (Wenner and Musick 1974).

Maximum longevity in much of the range is about 20 years (Vladykov 1973c). American eels stocked as elvers in a Michigan lake lived 35–40 years, native *A. rostrata* of ages 42–43 are known from Nova Scotia (Jessop 1987). A captive European eel expired at the age of 88 years (Vladykov 1973c).

The fall to mid-winter migration of *A. rostrata* from Atlantic coast estuaries has long been known, but the destination has been a quest of science (Vladykov 1964). In 1922, after 20 years of exhaustive research, Johannes Schmidt (1925) concluded that the spawning area lay in the Sargasso Sea between the Bahamas and Bermuda, based on discovery there of the smallest larvae; progressively larger leptocephali were found at increasing distances from the focal area. The recent captures of the smallest known leptocephali (3.9–5.5 mm TL) in the southern Sargasso Sea have refined the location of the spawning area and identified temperature and other conditions that may cue the cessation of migration and the start of spawning. The peak of spawning occurs in February (Kleckner et al. 1983).

The depth at which adult *Anguilla* migrate and spawn is uncertain. Morphological and physiological data summarized by Kleckner et al. (1983) indicate that the American eel is adapted for migration and spawning in the upper 200 m of the ocean, but an adult *Anguilla* was photographed at the ocean bottom (2,050 m) in the Bahamas (Robins et al. 1979).

Fecundity is 400,000–2,500,000 ova based on estimates of ovarian eggs from Chesapeake fish; higher earlier estimates likely are in error. Ovarian eggs are 0.45 mm in diameter; spawned eggs are presumed to be about 1 mm in diameter and pelagic (Wenner and Musick 1974; Hardy 1978a).

HABITAT

Owing only partly to its catadromous strategy, the American eel occupies perhaps the broadest diversity of habitats of any fish species (Helfman et al. 1987). Its temperate and tropical range includes clear cold mountain streams, infertile ponds, vegetated lakes, warm reservoirs, blackwater swamps, salt marshes, open estuaries, and from upper levels to the deep floor of the ocean. In lotic habitats *A. rostrata* is usually found in pools and backwaters. Being generally nocturnal, it associates with cover during daylight, sometimes burrowing in mud and silt. *Anguilla* eels can survive some drought and low-oxygen conditions by respiratory gas exchange via the gills and skin (Hughes 1976).

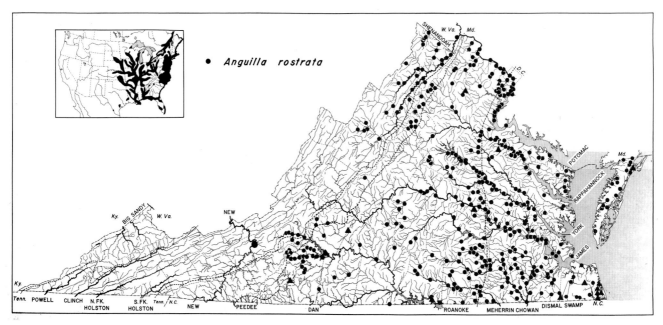

Map 23 American eel.

DISTRIBUTION Map 23

Anguilla rostrata occurs from Greenland to Venezuela, sometimes to Brazil; the range includes the Great Lakes and Mississippi basins and many oceanic islands. In Virginia it is widespread in all but one Atlantic slope drainage and it is native to the New drainage; it is unknown to extend into the upper Pee Dee drainage. It ranges particularly widely in estuaries, and inland on the Coastal Plain and Piedmont. Although it commonly occupies streams of moderate or somewhat steep gradient beyond Virginia, its only substantial inhabitations of the Valley and Ridge and the Blue Ridge provinces in the state now occur respectively in the Potomac and Rappahannock drainages.

The upper James drainage and much of the middle James have been vacated by *A. rostrata*. In the early 1900s eels were gigged at least as far upstream from the Blue Ridge as Craig County (Ingram 1987). Their extirpation is due partly to the series of low-head dams which extends from the Fall Line to the Valley and Ridge. By 1882, 23 dams averaging 4.4 m in height had been erected in conjunction with the James River and Kanawha Canal (VFC 1882; Atran et al. 1983). Eels are sometimes able to surmount such structures but the serial nature of dams acts additively; progressively fewer eels ascend each successive dam. Obstruction of upstream movement by the dams is incomplete, judging from the Piedmont records of the 1970s–1980s and the one from 1976 in the Blue Ridge.

The obstructiveness of large dams is evident also in the Roanoke drainage; the concentration of records in the upper Roanoke is a matter of history. Perhaps the first dam to stop eels is the modest (16 m high) Niagara Dam built across the Roanoke River just below Roanoke in 1906. In 1888 Jordan (1889b) found *A. rostrata* to be common above the (future) dam site; eels earlier clogged the turbine of a mill on the South Fork Roanoke River (Calhoun 1984). Despite intensive surveys above Niagara Dam during 1940–1990, the last eel report is from about 1940 (Jenkins and Freeman 1972).

The virtual, if not complete, loss of the American eel from the first three major Roanoke River tributaries below Roanoke—Back Creek, Blackwater River, and Pigg River—has resulted from more recent construction of two sets of large dams on the Roanoke River. The three dams composing the lower set were closed between 1952–1964; the succession of their reservoirs extends from the Fall Zone in North Carolina to slightly above the union of the Roanoke and Dan rivers in Virginia. The upper set of two dams, in the upper Piedmont, was completed in 1963. A few years after completion of the upper dams, *Anguilla* still was found in the Blackwater River and to a lesser extent in Back Creek (Hambrick 1973). The last known capture was in 1978 from the Pigg River (James 1979); the specimen was large (870 mm TL) and likely old.

The paucity of records of *A. rostrata* in the middle Roanoke drainage between the two sets of dams is related to scant preimpoundment survey and impedance by the lower set of dams. Perhaps some eels whose hatching postdates closure of the dams can bypass the dams; our last three records from below the upper dams are dated 1977, 1979, and 1983, 13–19 years after closure of the last dam. Alternatively, the records may be of old survivors predating impoundment; American eels have lived more than 40 years in the wild. Each record stands on one specimen; two of the specimens may no longer exist, but in collection files one of them is listed as large, the other as about 610 mm TL. The third is the 419-mm macrophthalmic, possibly maturing female depicted in Fish 15.

Kanawha Falls (8.5 m) has been a partial barrier to eels entering the New drainage; *A. rostrata* has been extremely rare above the falls for at least the last 50 years. In 1867 Cope (1868b) saw some eel skins in the lower part of the Virginia section of the drainage. We have a verbal report of an eel caught in that section, below Claytor Dam, during the mid-1950s by an angler. In the West Virginia section, Addair (1944) reported *Anguilla* from three sites and Hocutt et al. (1979) found it at one.

Abundance.—Often common or abundant in estuaries and lowland fresh waters, usually rare or uncommon in uplands and mountains of the Atlantic drainages, and very rare in the New drainage.

REMARKS

Anguilla rostrata is an awesome eel. As its story is long, so too are the coastward drift of the frail larvae, and the trek made by adults to the oceanic spawning ground. This catadromous type of migration is nearly unique among North American fishes; the only other catadromous fish in eastern North America is the mountain mullet. The complex life history of the American eel includes sexual differences, some unusual. The great geographical and ecological range of the species strains evolutionary comprehension because its breeding is panmictic—reproduction apparently occurs randomly in a single area, a strategy that prevents adaptation to local conditions (Williams and Koehn 1984). By any ecological measure the American eel is a very successful species, owing in part to generalist food habits; when in favored habitat it often is abundant (Helfman et al. 1987).

We have begun to understand the ways and whys of life of the American eel. It took extensive research to discover and confirm the oceanic spawning area. In turn, this much broadened perspectives on the biology of coastal and inland populations. It remains to be seen how well many populations fit general life history trends, and whether the American eel is a different species from the European eel.

How eels get above dams and waterfalls is not generally known. They may bypass dams by moving overland, especially on wet nights; they can survive lengthy periods out of water in moist conditions. Manooch and Raver (1984) noted that elvers have been seen "squirming" through moist grass to bypass physical barriers. Eels also may swim or literally crawl up spillways, particularly in reduced water flow. Wang and Kernehan (1979) saw young eels attempting to climb dams in Delaware. John Pancake, a writer of *The Roanoke Times and World-News* (16 Jan. 1977), asked Charles A. Wenner, a student of eels, about eels and dams. Wenner related his observation of eels ascending a 1.2-m-high dam on the York River, Virginia: "The young eels gulped in air until their cheeks seemed to puff out, . . . then moved up a damp section of the vertical dam face like inchworms." G. S. Helfman (personal communication) doubted the accuracy of this description of moving and stated that instead, small eels climb by normal body undulations (anguilliform locomotion).

The American eel is widely known beyond science. To many it is snakelike and spurned. However, the meat is firm and well flavored. The North American market for eels is small; they are more commonly regarded a delicacy in Europe and Asia. The international demand recently has resulted in an augmented eel fishery in the United States and in the transplantation of American eel elvers to Japan (Manooch and Raver 1984). *Anguilla rostrata* is a popular bait fish in coastal areas.

Name.—*Rostrata* means "snout."

HERRINGS
Family Clupeidae

BY JOSEPH C. DESFOSSE, NOEL M. BURKHEAD, AND ROBERT E. JENKINS

The Clupeidae are a cosmopolitan family of marine, freshwater, and anadromous fishes comprising some 63 genera and about 174 species (McGowan and Berry 1984; Grande 1985). The names herring and shad are given to different species in some of the same genera, and sardines and pilchards are included in the family. Four anadromous and two freshwater species occur in Virginia. Clupeids belong to the order Clupeiformes of the superorder Clupeomorpha, which contains other herringlike fishes and anchovies. Clupeomorphs are low on the piscine evolutionary ladder. The oldest known clupeomorph fossils are from the Early Cretaceous, and clupeids are richly represented in the famous Eocene Green River Formation of western North America (Grande 1985, 1989).

The size range of adults of the North American clupeids, across species, is 75–700 mm TL, the American shad being the largest (Hildebrand 1964; Lee et al. 1980). The body form of these fishes is moderate, somewhat elongate, or quite deep; in cross section, most species are moderately or very compressed; the ventral margin of the body tapers to a keel having imbricated, sharply angled, bony scutes forming a serrated "saw belly." The head is moderate in proportion; the eye is small or large and sometimes has an anterior and posterior adipose lid. The mouth is medium or large, terminal, superior or inferior, and nonprotrusile; the teeth are usually small and weak; teeth are absent in adults of some species. Pseudobranchae are present; gill rakers are long, slender, and numerous, increasing in number with age. Body scales are cycloid, serrate, or pectinate; the head is naked. The lateral line is usually absent on the body or confined to a few anterior scales, but the lateralis system is extensively branched on the head, providing increased receptivity (Stephens 1985). The dorsal fin is small or medium, and usually inserted at about midlength of the fish; the posterior dorsal rays are quite long in some species. The caudal fin is forked; the anal fin is moderately or very long; pelvic fins are abdominal and range from moderately large to small, or absent; the pectoral fins are well developed and low on the body.

Herrings are mostly silver in color, typically with a greenish or blue dorsum and upper side. This countershading—dark above, pale below—is an adaptation for concealment and occurs in many groups of fishes. When viewed from below by a predator, the silver color tends to blend with the shining mirrorlike surface of the water, whereas the green or blue back when seen from above tends to match the shade of the depths. Many species display brassy or blue iridescences dorsally; some have a dark shoulder spot, or a row of spots on the side.

Clupeids inhabit freshwater, brackish, and marine environments; some anadromous species, often called river herrings, transcend all of these. Herrings are most diverse in the tropics, but individual species tend to be more abundant in cold-temperate regions (Longhurst 1971 in McGowan and Berry 1984). Some anadromous species have naturally landlocked populations; others have been established in natural lakes and impoundments by stocking. Most herring species occur in large schools in upper levels of the water column.

Most herrings are planktivorous, swimming with the mouth agape and straining food from water with numerous long gill rakers. Herrings have large epibranchial organs in the pharynx, chambers where food particles are concentrated before swallowing (R. V. Miller 1964). Clupeids are important links in food chains, converting planktonic organisms to biomass then available for a host of predators, many of which enter the diet of humans.

Reproductive strategies within the family are varied. Marine members generally spawn in large schools near the ocean surface. Anadromous species make annual migrations into rivers and also aggregate when spawning. Many have pelagic eggs which are broadcast and subjected to currents; others spawn adhesive eggs over vegetation and other substrates. Some of the larger species are quite prolific, releasing over a half-million eggs. Egg size varies from 0.6 to 3.8 mm in diameter (Jones et al. 1978; McGowan and Berry 1984).

The spring migrations of most river herrings and shads, genus *Alosa*, in coastal and adjacent inland areas are well known. The local arrival of each species forms a chronological south to north progression, varying annually by a week or two according to prevailing temperature (Hildebrand 1964). The first species to enter the lower Chesapeake is the alewife, usually in early March. It is followed in a week or two by the American shad, and in three to four weeks by the blueback herring. Reproduction of our other *Alosa*, the hickory shad, is poorly known. The first three species have superficially similar spawning habitats and behaviors but the differences in these, in the location of sites, and in the timing of spawning prevent hybridization. Natural hybridization between our *Alosa* is unknown, and there is little possibility of it occurring (Mansueti 1962a).

Large commercial fisheries exist for many clupeids. Although bony, they are succulent and are used extensively as human food, usually when canned, salted, pickled, or smoked. Many species are processed for oil or used as fish meal for livestock feed and fertilizer. During their spawning migration, river herrings and shads are the subjects of commercial fisheries, and many are netted noncommercially. Ripe female American shad *Alosa sapidissima* are the most sought, particularly for the highly prized roe. Sport fisheries exist for some of the larger members of the family, notably the American shad, and to a lesser extent the hickory shad *A. mediocris.*

Name.—Clupe- from the Latin *Clupea*, meaning "herring."

Key to Herrings   Clupeidae

Key to Genera

1a Predorsal median line unscaled; last dorsal ray prolonged, filamentous (may be broken off) (Figure 19B); stomach thick-walled, gizzardlike. .... *Dorosoma*

1b Predorsal median line scaled; last dorsal ray not prolonged, similar in length to preceding ray (Figure 19A); stomach not thick-walled or gizzardlike. .... *Alosa*

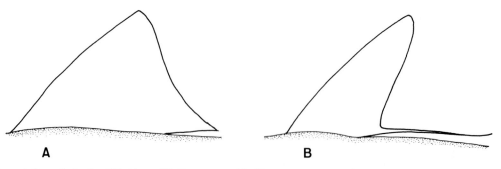

A   **B**

Figure 19 Dorsal fins of shads: (A) *Alosa.* (B) *Dorosoma* with filamentous posterior ray.

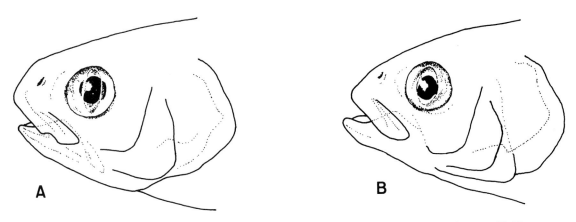

Figure 20   Heads of *Dorosoma* showing upper jaw margin and mouth position: (A) *D. cepedianum*. (B) *D. petenense*.

Key to Species of *Dorosoma*

1a   Upper jaw with notch present on ventral margin (Figure 20A);
  snout tip exceeding tip of lower jaw; anal rays (25)29–35(37) ...   GIZZARD SHAD—*D. cepedianum*   p. 212
1b   Upper jaw lacking ventral notch (Figure 20B); tip of lower jaw
  exceeding snout tip; anal rays (17)20–25(27) ....   THREADFIN SHAD—*D. petenense*   p. 215

Key to Species of *Alosa*

1a   Dorsal margin of lower jaw rising markedly, often abruptly angled
  upward (Figure 21B); eye large, its diameter usually equal to or
  longer than greatest cheek depth   2
1b   Dorsal margin of lower jaw gradually rising slightly or moderately,
  not angled upward (Figure 21A); eye moderate, its diameter
  usually less than greatest cheek depth   3

2a   Eye diameter less than or equal to snout length; peritoneum black;
  color of back bluish in life ....   BLUEBACK HERRING—*A. aestivalis*   p. 217
2b   Eye diameter greater than snout length; peritoneum pale
  (sometimes lightly peppered with melanophores, dusky); color of
  back grey-green in life ....   ALEWIFE—*A. pseudoharengus*   p. 220

3a   Gill rakers on lower limb of first gill arch 18–23 and widely spaced;
  mouth superior, anteriormost point of dorsal head profile formed
  by lower jaw; tongue having a pale area medially ....   HICKORY SHAD—*A. mediocris*   p. 223
3b   Gill rakers on lower limb of first gill arch 59–76 (26–43 in
  specimens less than 125 mm) and crowded; mouth terminal,
  anteriormost point of dorsal head profile formed by upper jaw;
  tongue not pale medially ....   AMERICAN SHAD—*A. sapidissima*   p. 225

Gizzard shads   Genus *Dorosoma* Rafinesque

Dorosoma comprises shads characterized by a distinctive muscular (gizzardlike) stomach, numerous pyloric caeca, and in most species the last dorsal fin ray prolonged as a filament (except in small young).

This North and Middle American genus has five species, two of which are found in Virginia (R. R. Miller 1950, 1960, 1964; Nelson and Rothman 1973). We place *Dorosoma* as more primitive than *Alosa*, follow-

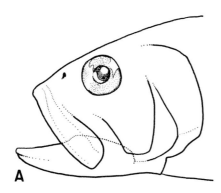 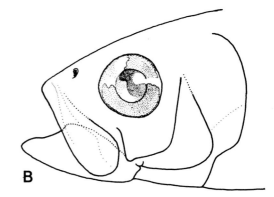

Figure 21 Mandible profiles, cheek outlines, and eye diameters in *Alosa*: (A) *A. mediocris* and *A. sapidissima*. (B) *A. aestivalis* and *A. pseudoharengus*.

ing Grande (1985) and the summary by McGowan and Berry (1984), but Stephens (1985) arranged them oppositely.

Name.—*Dorosoma* means "lanceolate-bodied."

Gizzard shad   *Dorosoma cepedianum* (Lesueur)

SYSTEMATICS

The gizzard shad was described from Delaware and Chesapeake bays in 1818. It is more closely related to species of the genus other than *D. petenense* (Miller 1960).

DESCRIPTION

Materials.—Based on Hildebrand and Schroeder (1928), Frey (1951), R. R. Miller (1960, 1964), Minckley and Krumholz (1960), and 15 Virginia lots. Life color from 3 Virginia series.

Anatomy.—A clupeid with the last dorsal fin ray very long, a small inferior mouth, a notch on the ventral margin of the maxilla, and irregularly arranged scale rows along the dorsum; adults are 175–350 mm TL. Body deep, strongly compressed; abdomen tapering ventrally to a keel bearing bony scutes. Head small; eye with adipose eyelid; snout blunt; young with a row of fine teeth on upper jaw, teeth absent in adult; gill rakers long, slender, increasing in number with age; most scales large, reduced scales extending onto caudal fin base. Dorsal fin small, its origin slightly posterior to pelvic fin origin; caudal fin deeply forked; anal fin long, margin concave; pelvic fin small; pectoral fin moderate. External sexual differences absent.

Meristics.—Lateral line essentially absent on body, scales in lateral series 52–70; prepelvic ventral scutes 17–20; postpelvic ventral scutes 10–14; total ventral scutes 27–32. Dorsal rays 10–15; anal rays 25–37; pelvic rays 7–10; pectoral rays 12–17. Gill rakers on lower limb of first arch as few as 90 in young and as many as 350 in adult.

Color in Preservative.—Head and body dusky to dark above, grading to pale ventrally; dusky shoulder spot usu-

Fish 16 *Dorosoma cepedianum* adult 120 mm SL (REJ 1036), VA, Campbell County, Roanoke River, 12 September 1983.

ally present in juvenile. Dorsal and caudal fins slightly or moderately dusky; anal fin pale, dusky-margined; pelvic fin pale; pectoral fin dusky-fringed.

Color in Life.—Dorsum and upper side bluish, olive, or brown; upper side with blue to purple iridescences, sometimes with 6–8 dark stripes or series of dark scales; shoulder spot lustrous purple to brown, equal to or slightly larger than orbit, prominent in juvenile, diffuse in adult; side silvery, often with brassy or golden reflections; abdomen milky or silver-white. Head dorsum, snout, upper jaw, and upper opercle brown to black, cheek and lower opercle silvery; iris silver and gold. Dorsal fin in adult uniformly dusky; caudal fin mostly dusky, dusky black on distal third; anal fin with distal two-thirds dark; pectoral and pelvic fins with distal half black, some specimens with pelvic fin all black; all fins grade to pale basally. In young, dorsal fin sparsely peppered with melanophores; caudal fin similar but darker; other fins almost all pale.

Larvae.—Described by Miller (1960), Bodola (1966), Mansueti and Hardy (1967), Lippson and Moran (1974), Jones et al. (1978), Wang and Kernehan (1979), and Tin (1982a).

BIOLOGY

Gizzard shad are filter feeders, using numerous fine gill rakers to strain plankton from the water column and occasionally from the bottom. The young, up to about 22 mm TL, selectively feed on certain protozoans and microcrustaceans (R. R. Miller 1960, 1964; Kutkuhn 1958; Carlander 1969; A. Smith 1971). This early feeding strategy may adversely affect survival of gamefish larvae.

Gizzard shad typically mature by ages 2 or 3 at lengths of 178–279 mm TL. Some may mature at age 1 and spawn at the end of the summer (Berry 1958; R. R. Miller 1960, 1964; Bodola 1966; Schneider 1969). Vladykov (1945 *in* R. R. Miller 1964) found females mature at 151 mm TL. Maximum longevity of *D. cepedianum* is age 10, but typical adult survival is only to ages 3 or 4 (R. R. Miller 1964; Carlander 1969).

Females grow slightly larger than males after age 2 (Berry 1958; Bodola 1966; Schneider 1969). The range of means for age-2 gizzard shad in Virginia, based mostly on reservoir populations, is 157–229 mm TL, grand mean, 191 mm (Smith and Kauffman 1982); the fastest growth occurred in Lake Anna, a large warmwater reservoir. Gizzard shad growth in Virginia averaged significantly less than other populations summarized in Carlander (1969). The largest specimen reported from Virginia is 330 mm TL (Hildebrand and Schroeder 1928); Trautman (1981) listed a 520-mm TL *D. cepedianum* from Ohio.

Gizzard shad spawn from March to August, usually between April and June in temperate latitudes (Miller 1960). Spawning occurs in freshwater sloughs, ponds, lakes, and reservoirs, usually at near-surface depths (0.3–1.6 m) but sometimes as deep as 15 m, and sometimes over vegetation or debris (Gunter 1938; Miller 1960; Shelton and Grinstead 1973; Jones et al. 1978; Wang and Kernehan 1979). Spawning has been reported to occur at midday (Miller 1960); Shelton and Grinstead (1973) detected spawning at all hours, but most intensely during 2000–0800 hours. Observations of spawning during rising temperature, from 10 to 28.9°C with most activity occurring above 18°C, indicate that daylight spawning is typical (Miller 1960; Bodola 1966). *Dorosoma cepedianum* experiences heavy postspawning mortality (Berry et al. 1956; Berry 1958).

Spawning groups swim near the surface and roll about as a mass, ejecting eggs and sperm (Miller 1960). Shelton and Grinstead (1973) reported spawning aggregations of 2–4 males and a female moving inshore along a bottom that abruptly shallowed. Eggs are demersal and adhere to algae, rocks, or other objects (R. R. Miller 1960, 1964); fecundity is 22,400–543,910 ova (Bodola 1966; Schneider 1969).

Dorosoma cepedianum is known to hybridize with *D. petenense* (Minckley and Krumholz 1960).

HABITAT

The gizzard shad is a pelagic, schooling fish that occurs in a variety of habitats. It lives in pools and runs of medium streams to rivers of low or moderate gradient, and populates reservoirs, lakes, swamps, floodwater pools, estuaries, brackish bays, and occasionally, marine waters (R. R. Miller 1960, 1964). *Dorosoma cepedianum* occurs over an array of substrates and seems tolerant of heavily silted bottoms. However, given its rarity in the Dan system, it may shun persistently turbid waters, perhaps due to depression of the plankton population. Gizzard shad also avoid the acidic dystrophic waters of interior Dismal Swamp, again probably due to low plankton productivity. Matthews (1984) detected avoidance of turbidity and decline of the population after an extended period of high turbidity in an Oklahoma reservoir. During fall and winter, *D. cepedianum* may concentrate in deep water (Jones et al. 1978). In brackish-water populations, young remain in fresh water until they reach about 70 mm TL. The highest salinity at capture in Chesapeake Bay is 20‰; occurrence in salinities up to 41.3‰ has been reported (Musick 1972; Jones et al. 1978).

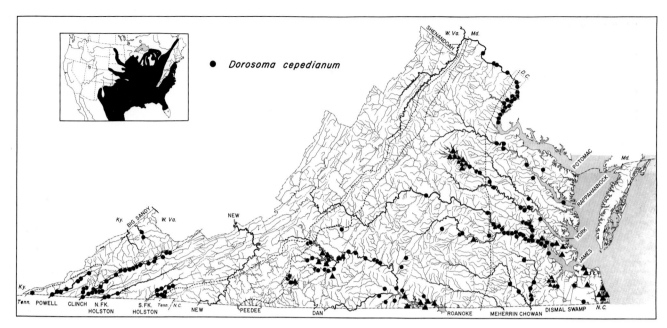

Map 24 Gizzard shad. Most main-channel Chesapeake basin records from 1978 VIMS Trawl Survey, but full estuarine distribution likely not shown.

DISTRIBUTION   Map 24

The gizzard shad is native to the Atlantic and Gulf slopes and to interior drainages of eastern and central North America. Its spread in the Great Lakes has been facilitated by canals (R. R. Miller 1957), and it has been widely stocked.

Landlocked populations occupy several Virginia reservoirs; those of the inland reservoirs stem from stockings. In Lake Anna, created in 1972, large numbers of gizzard shad began to appear in 1974. This species was not found in the North Anna River prior to impoundment, and there is no official record of it being stocked in the reservoir. However, a game warden stated that gizzard shad were present in a 1973 shipment of striped bass from the federal hatchery in Edenton, North Carolina, and that both species were released in the reservoir (Reed and Simmons 1976).

Gizzard shad may have been both trapped by dams and stocked in the impoundments of the Roanoke River that straddle the North Carolina–Virginia line. That they were stocked in Kerr Reservoir, impounded in 1952, is indicated by a note in VPI files (accession 150) that this species was first discovered there in 1962; it was thought to have been released with *D. petenense*. Farther up the Roanoke, gizzard shad were stocked by the VDGIF in Leesville Reservoir and Smith Mountain Lake during 1964–1965, shortly after impoundment (Estes 1971). Many of the records from streams of the middle Roanoke drainage may be of fish that dispersed from reservoirs. The Philpott Reservoir–upper Smith River population obviously originated from a stocking unknown to us; the reservoir was created in 1951, but the first record of *D. cepedianum* dates from 1979.

The absence of gizzard shad from the New drainage is related to blockage by Kanawha Falls, West Virginia. *Dorosoma cepedianum* is widespread in some major streams of the Tennessee drainage in Virginia. Montane conditions in the upper South and Middle forks of the Holston River likely restrict it to the lower section of each. Its confinement to lower reaches of the North Fork Holston is a pattern shown by other fishes, and may be attributable to the chronic pollution emanating from Saltville and to dams.

Abundance.—Uncommon to abundant in Chesapeake Bay tributaries throughout the year, common in the bay proper only during fall (Hildebrand and Schroeder 1928; Musick 1972). Rare to abundant in reservoirs and inland streams; most common in reservoirs.

REMARKS

Because of its direct use of phytoplankton and high reproductive capacity, the gizzard shad has been a prime candidate for introduction to waters which lack a major forage base for gamefishes. However, due to their rapid growth, gizzard shad are available to most predators for only a short time, thus they are less esteemed as forage than are threadfin shad. *Dorosoma cepedianum* is frequently cast-netted or dip-netted be-low dams and used as bait, especially for large catfish and striped bass.

Name.—*Cepedianum* is a patronym honoring Ci-toyen LaCepède, a French naturalist who described many North American fishes.

Threadfin shad   *Dorosoma petenense* (Günther)

SYSTEMATICS

The threadfin shad was described in 1867 from Lake Peten, Guatemala. Its generic group *Signalosa* is now regarded as a subgenus of *Dorosoma* (R. R. Miller 1950; Nelson and Rothman 1973).

DESCRIPTION

Materials.—Based on R. R. Miller (1964), Jones et al. (1978), and 4 Virginia series. Life color from 2 Virginia series.

Anatomy.—A shad with the last dorsal fin ray pro-longed, a terminal mouth, no notch on ventral edge of upper jaw, and regularly arranged scale rows along the dorsum anteriorly; adults are 75–175 mm TL. Basic mor-phology is similar to *D. cepedianum*.

Meristics.—Lateral line obsolete on body, scales in lateral series 41–48; prepelvic ventral scutes 15–18; postpelvic ventral scutes 8–12; total ventral scutes 23–29. Dorsal rays 11–14; anal rays 17–27; pelvic rays 7–8; pectoral rays 12–17. Gill rakers on lower limb of first arch in adults numbering up to 412.

Color in Preservative.—Head and body dusky to dark above, grading to pale ventrally, sometimes retaining silver color on side; dusky shoulder spot usually present in juvenile. Fins pale or slightly dusky.

Color in Life.—Similar to *D. cepedianum* except for fin coloration. Dorsal fin dusky, with yellowish olive tint; caudal lobes yellow medially; anal fin yellow; paired fins yellow basally.

Larvae.—Described by Taber (1969), Lippson and Moran (1974), and Jones et al. (1978).

BIOLOGY

Threadfin shad are chiefly midwater filter feeders; evidence exists that they also occasionally feed ben-thically. Food items include algae, protozoans, rotif-ers, copepods, cladocerans, invertebrate eggs, or-ganic debris, and fish larvae. Young-of-the-year and adults take the same foods (Kimsey et al. 1957; Kim-sey 1958; Haskell 1959, 1959; R. R. Miller 1964; Burns 1966; R. V. Miller 1967). Large populations of thread-fin shad may depress or alter the composition of zooplankton populations for extended periods of time, sometimes up to two years (Ziebell et al. 1986).

Threadfin shad usually mature by ages 2 or 3; some mature and spawn in the fall of their first year (Kim-sey 1958; Miller and Jorgenson 1973). Typical size range at maturation is 75–126 mm TL (Erdman 1972 *in* Jones et al. 1978). Maximum longevity appears to be age 4, though most fish do not exceed age 2 (Parsons and Kimsey 1954; R. R. Miller 1964; Johnson 1970).

Growth varies latitudinally and between estuarine and strictly freshwater populations (Johnson 1970). Threadfin shad in an Arizona reservoir grew about 25 mm TL per month during the first summer; age-1 fish were 46–86 mm (Burns 1966). Age-2 fish averaged 102 mm TL (Kimsey 1958; Schwartz 1958b; R. R. Miller 1964). Virginia specimens as large as 80–89 mm TL were reported by VIMS (1977). A maximum size of 330 mm TL and 286 g, reported from Alabama

Fish 17 *Dorosoma peten-ense* subadult 73 mm SL (REJ 729), MS, Lincoln County, Homochitto River, 24 April 1976.

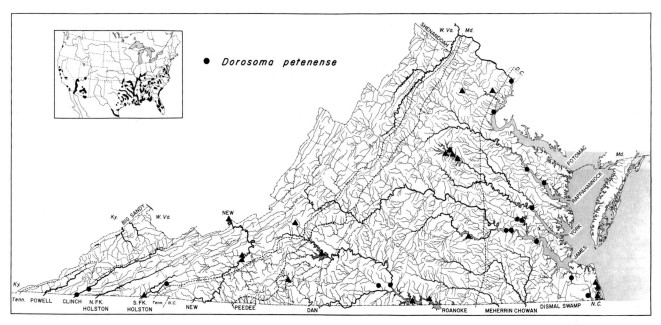

Map 25 Threadfin shad.

(Swingle 1965), likely was based on *D. cepedianum*. The record was not repeated by Burgess (*in* Lee et al. 1980), who gave maximum sizes of 178 mm TL from the United States and 220 mm TL from Guatemala.

Threadfin shad typically spawn in fresh water during April to July, at 14.4–27.2°C; conditions permitting, spawning may extend throughout the summer (Burns 1966; R. R. Miller 1964; Johnson 1971; Jones et al. 1978). Spawning usually begins at sunrise; daily activity is brief, an apparent antipredator strategy (Lambou 1965; Hanson 1970 *in* McHugh and Steinkoenig 1980; McLean et al. 1982). Large roving schools assemble; males may outnumber females 15:1. Small groups may break off toward shore, creating considerable surface disturbance (Rawstron 1964; Shelton and Grinstead 1973). Demersal adhesive eggs are often shed over submerged structures such as plant beds and brush (Berry et al. 1956; Gerdes 1961; R. R. Miller 1964; Rawstron 1964; Lambou 1965; Burns 1966). Estimated egg counts are 800–21,000 (Jones et al. 1978), but because individuals may repeatedly spawn over a season, individual egg counts may grossly underestimate fecundity.

The threadfin shad hybridizes with the gizzard shad (Minckley and Krumholz 1960).

HABITAT

Dorosoma petenense is a pelagic schooling shad of fresh and brackish water. In fresh water it lives in medium streams to rivers of low to moderate gradient; in lakes and reservoirs it usually occurs in the upper 15 m of the water column (R. R. Miller 1964; Burns 1966). Stream-dwelling *D. petenense* often congregate in turbulent zones below dams, and generally tend to associate with current more than do *D. cepedianum* (Pflieger 1975). In the Clinch River we found threadfin shad in shallow backwaters close to riffles.

Water temperature is a critical limiting factor of population success. Significant mortality of young and adults occurs below 7°C, and 5°C is the lower lethal temperature (R. R. Miller 1964; Strawn 1965). Incubation of eggs to produce viable young does not occur below 15°C (Hubbs and Bryan 1974). Threadfin shad stocked in Virginia waters are susceptible to winter mortality. During the mid- to late 1950s, threadfin shad were experimentally stocked in four Virginia impoundments. Successful reproduction took place in three of these, but severe winter temperatures eliminated the fish (Bowman et al. 1959).

Coastal Plain euryhaline populations range from fresh water to 32‰ salinity; juveniles prefer salinities below 15‰ and are most common below 5‰ (R. R. Miller 1964; Bryan and Sopher 1969; Musick 1972; Jones et al. 1978). Young remain in fresh water and undergo diel vertical migrations (Jones et al. 1978).

DISTRIBUTION Map 25

The native range of the threadfin shad extends from the lower Mississippi basin, the Gulf slope, and peninsular Florida to Guatemala and Belize (R. R.

Miller 1964). Apparently this species has only recently invaded most of the southern portion of the Ohio River basin from the lower Mississippi (Minckley and Krumholz 1960). *Dorosoma petenense* has been widely introduced as forage in lakes and reservoirs in much of the USA. After initial stocking, threadfin typically undergo population explosion and invade nearby waters. *Dorosoma petenense* spread rapidly through the lower Colorado River shortly after 1,020 individuals were stocked in Lake Havasu (Kimsey et al. 1957 *in* Johnson 1971). It has dispersed along part of the Pacific coast of California and Oregon (Krygier et al. 1973).

Dorosoma petenense probably is not native to Virginia. Its sole claim to indigenous status would rest on the records from the upper Holston and Clinch systems having stemmed from populations native elsewhere in the upper Tennessee drainage. However, although *D. petenense* apparently is native to the lower Tennessee drainage, its upriver success is related to creation of impoundments and stocking (Minckley and Krumholz 1960).

Because of the potential of *D. petenense* as a forage species, it was introduced to several small and large reservoirs and Back Bay by the VDGIF. Perhaps its first introduction to Virginia occurred in Claytor Lake during 1953 (Schwartz 1958b), a stocking not listed among Claytor introductions summarized by Hart (1981). The first known introduction to the Virginia Atlantic slope also occurred in 1953 when 250 threadfin from the Tennessee River in Tennessee were liberated in Philpott Reservoir (Martin 1953, 1954; Domrose 1963). Subsequently, *D. petenense* was introduced to all major Atlantic drainages of Virginia except the Rappahannock (Bowman et al. 1959; our data).

The threadfin shad has been only somewhat successful in Virginia, owing to extirpation by cold winters or intentional removal (E. L. Steinkoenig, D. K. Whitehurst, personal communications). The only extant lacustrine populations of which we are aware (in 1986) occur in Back Bay and Lake Anna. In the South Fork Holston system, the upper record (in 1973) may stem from escapement from a warmwater gamefish hatchery; the other record is from South Holston Reservoir, which has been stocked with threadfin by the Tennessee Wildlife Resources Agency. The two Clinch system records, one from lowermost Copper Creek, date from 1971–1972; the specimens probably had entered Virginia from Tennessee, perhaps from as far downstream as Norris Reservoir.

Abundance.—Rare to common depending on place and recent climate.

REMARKS

The widely introduced threadfin shad is better suited as a forage base for many predatory freshwater fishes than is the gizzard shad, because of its smaller size and hence greater availability. However, massive dieoffs of *D. petenense* owing to low temperatures or sudden temperature changes, its possible alteration of zooplankton communities, and its ability to invade new habitats and increase rapidly are seen as drawbacks. Some biologists believe that better gamefishing results when shad are not abundant, resulting in hungry quarry.

Name.—*Petenense* is named from its type locality, Lake Peten, Guatemala.

River herrings

A Holarctic genus, *Alosa* is represented by six species in North America, four of which occur in Virginia. *Pomolobus*, containing the first three species treated here, is now ranked as a subgenus of *Alosa*.

Genus *Alosa* Linck

Name.—*Alosa* is the Latin word for shad.

Blueback herring   *Alosa aestivalis* (Mitchill)

SYSTEMATICS

The blueback herring was described in 1814, presumably from New York. Reed (1964) found some Atlantic slope populations to be meristically distinct, but subsequent results have been less conclusive (Messieh 1977).

DESCRIPTION

Materials.—Based on Hildebrand and Schroeder (1928), Hildebrand (1964), Jones et al. (1978), and 19 Virginia lots (750 specimens counted). Life color from many Virginia specimens.

Anatomy.—A clupeid with a large eye, dorsal margin of lower jaw sloped abruptly upward, and black peritoneum;

Fish 18 *Alosa aestivalis* subadult 133 mm SL (RC), VA, Charlotte-Halifax County, Roanoke River, 26 April 1976.

adults are 150–250 mm TL. Body moderately deep and quite compressed, ventral outline more strongly convex than dorsal outline. Head and snout moderate; eye large, diameter about equal to snout length; mouth moderate, supraterminal; maxillary broad; tip of mandible not included in upper jaw and not entering into dorsal profile; upper edge of mandible strongly elevated, often with a prominent angle near midlength. Teeth on premaxillary minute in young, those on lower jaw persistent anteriorly though lacking free points in adult; tongue with permanent narrow median band of granular teeth; cheek broad, width greater than depth. Dorsal fin small, distal margin concave; caudal fin forked, lobes symmetrical; anal fin slightly longer than dorsal; pelvic fin small; pectoral fin moderate.

Meristics.—Lateral line virtually absent on body, scales in lateral series usually 46–54; longitudinal scale rows on body between bases of pelvic and dorsal fins usually 13–14; prepelvic ventral scutes (18)19–21(22); postpelvic ventral scutes (12)13–16(17); total scutes (31)33–36(37). Dorsal rays (15)16–17(19); anal rays (16)17–18(21); pelvic rays (8)9(10); pectoral rays (12)14–16(17). Gill rakers on lower limb of first arch in adults usually 41–52.

Color in Preservative.—Head and body of adult dusky to dark above, grading to pale ventrally, some retain silver on side; upper side with vague or bold dark stripes; dark shoulder spot usually present. Fins pale, or dorsal and caudal fins may be dusky. Young usually lack shoulder spot and dorsolateral stripes.

Color in Life.—Adult dark blue or bluish gray above; back and upper side with vague or distinct olive-black stripes; side silver; single black shoulder spot usually present. Fins plain, pale yellow to green. Peritoneum usually sooty, brown, or black.

Larvae.—Described by Kuntz and Radcliffe (1917), Hildebrand (1964), Mansueti and Hardy (1967), Chambers (1969), Cianci (1969), Scott and Crossman (1973), Lippson and Moran (1974), Chambers et al. (1976), Jones et al. (1978), and Wang and Kernehan (1979).

COMPARISON

It is difficult to distinguish between small *A. aestivalis* and *A. pseudoharengus*. The two most reliable characters are eye size relative to snout length, and color of the peritoneum; however, peritoneum color is sometimes unreliable. In *aestivalis* the peritoneum varies from black to, occasionally, pale gray or pearly gray (Hildebrand 1964); the gray color may approach the typically pale peritoneum of *pseudoharengus*. The use of meristics to distinguish the species has been mentioned, but this can be unreliable owing to overlapping character states (Hildebrand 1964). Methods of distinguishing the species based on scale imbrication patterns have been described (O'Neill 1980; Mac-Lellan et al. 1981). Dorsal coloration in life (blue in blueback herring, *aestivalis*; green in *pseudoharengus*) is considered to be species-specific, but ambient lighting can change the color or its perception (Bigelow and Schroeder 1953; MacLellan et al. 1981).

BIOLOGY

In fresh water, young blueback herring feed primarily on copepods and cladocerans (Burbidge 1974). Their diet in salt water consists of copepods, other plankton, pelagic shrimps, small fishes, and fish fry (Bigelow and Welsh 1925). The food of adults is similar, and during spawning migration includes insects (Creed 1985).

Maturation, age, and growth of Virginia populations have been reported by Hildebrand and Schroeder (1928), Hildebrand (1964), and Joseph and Davis (1965). In Virginia, most bluebacks mature at age 4. In Connecticut, males matured at age 3, females at age 4 (Marcy 1969). Maximum survival is 7–9 years (Netzel and Stanek 1966; Marcy 1969; Atran et al. 1983). The landlocked Kerr Reservoir population matures faster and longevity is less than in anadromous populations; adulthood is reached at age 2, and age 3 is rarely reached (Whitehurst and Carwile 1982).

In Chesapeake Bay, age-1 fish were 65–120 mm, age-2 fish were 140–184 mm, age-3 and age-4 fish were 200–250 mm SL (Hildebrand and Schroeder

1928). Growth in the first two age-classes of Kerr Reservoir fish was similar to that of Chesapeake populations. Kerr Reservoir blueback herring were 127 mm TL at age 1 and 158 mm TL at age 2; the largest individual was 178 mm TL (Whitehurst and Carwile 1982). Maximum size is 380 mm SL, locality unspecified (Burgess *in* Lee et al. 1980).

Alosa aestivalis arrives in lower Chesapeake Bay in early April, about a month later than the alewife. Spawning in lower bay tributaries begins soon after entering distinctly brackish or fresh water. Spawning in the Potomac drainage seems to occur during late April to late May (Hildebrand and Schroeder 1928; Hildebrand 1964). In Maine, water temperature at peak spawning activity was 21–24°C; spawning ceased when water exceeded 27°C (Bigelow and Welsh 1925; Loesch 1969; Edsall 1970). In Connecticut, spawning runs commenced in water as low as 4.7°C, and not until midway through the spawning period did water reach 21–24°C (Loesch and Lund 1977). Blueback herring spawn in the same general areas as alewife, but prefer sites with faster (moderate) current and associated firmer substrate (Hildebrand and Schroeder 1928; Scott and Crossman 1973; Loesch and Lund 1977). Adults return to the sea after spawning, and may return to spawn in later years; in one area of Chesapeake Bay, 44–65% of blueback herrings had spawned previously (Joseph and Davis 1965).

The landlocked Kerr Reservoir population apparently spawns in spring, but does not appreciably ascend tributaries. Most spawning presumably occurs along cove shorelines (D. K. Whitehurst, personal communication).

During spawning, a female and two or more males swim circularly at about 1 m from the surface. Swimming speed gradually increases and the group dives to the bottom, releasing gametes (Loesch and Lund 1977). The eggs settle in still water but are essentially pelagic (Kuntz and Radcliffe 1917; Lippson and Moran 1974). The eggs appear to be adhesive during the water-hardening period but become detached and suspended in the water column where sufficient turbulence occurs (Loesch and Lund 1977). Fecundity of Connecticut River blueback herring ranges 45,800–349,700 (Loesch and Lund 1977).

HABITAT

Alosa aestivalis is a typical pelagic-schooling river herring. When not migrating between spawning grounds, adults are found over the Continental Shelf, usually in water temperatures less than 13°C and depths of 27–55 m. During summer through winter, catches are virtually restricted to off New England, while in spring blueback herring range from Nova Scotia to Cape Hatteras, North Carolina, and inland (Neves 1981).

Larvae and juveniles are found in brackish and tidal fresh waters of natal streams. At about 50 mm TL they begin to move downstream; in the James River the migration is usually complete by November. Some juveniles overwinter in Chesapeake and Delaware bays (Jones et al. 1978).

DISTRIBUTION   Map 26

Blueback herring range from Cape Breton, Nova Scotia, to the St. Johns River, Florida (Hildebrand and Schroeder 1928; Bigelow and Schroeder 1953). In Virginia, bluebacks once ascended all major tributaries of Chesapeake Bay (Hildebrand and Schroeder 1928). Although many Virginia tributaries still support substantial populations, much of that range has been reduced due to overfishing, degradation of habitat, and dams. Blueback herring were introduced by the VDGIF into several Virginia reservoirs, with limited success; populations failed to become established in Occoquan Reservoir; Lakes Anna, Brittle, and Chesdin; Smith Mountain Lake, and a few small impoundments. The only clearly self-sustaining inland Virginia population developed from stocking is in Kerr Reservoir. The fish first transplanted (1958) originated from the Nottoway River (J. M. Hoffman, personal communication).

Abundance.—Usually common to abundant during spawning migrations. Commercial landings of blueback herring are usually combined with alewife under the category of river herring. As such, Virginia landings have increased after reaching an all-time low in 1981 (Loesch and Kriete 1984). Abundance in Kerr Reservoir is not known because cove sampling usually occurs when most bluebacks are in the main body of the reservoir (D. K. Whitehurst, personal communication).

REMARKS

The blueback herring population of Kerr Reservoir is the only landlocked population in Virginia and contributes greatly as forage in this heavily fished lake (Whitehurst and Carwile 1982).

Name.—*Aestivalis* means "of the summer."

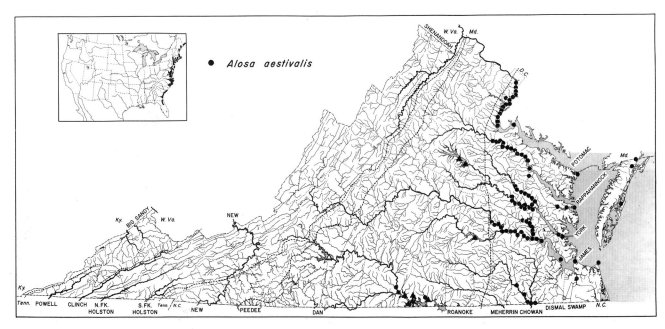

Map 26 Blueback herring. A Delmarva record is from Burgess (*in* Lee et al. 1980). Most main-channel Chesapeake basin records from 1978 VIMS Trawl Survey. Extent of distribution in the ocean, bay, and main-channel tributaries not shown. Open triangle on Smith Mountain Lake represents unverified record from a 1974 VDGIF survey.

Alewife   *Alosa pseudoharengus* (Wilson)

SYSTEMATICS

The alewife was described in 1811 from the Delaware River near Philadelphia.

DESCRIPTION

Materials.—Based on Hildebrand and Schroeder (1928), Bigelow and Schroeder (1953), R. R. Miller (1957), Hildebrand (1964), Jones et al. (1978), and 20 series (571 specimens counted) from Virginia. Life color from many Virginia specimens.

Anatomy.—A clupeid with a large eye, dorsal margin of lower jaw abruptly angled upward, and pale peritoneum; adults are 200–300 mm TL. Anatomy much as in *A. aesti-valis*; differences include a larger eye, its diameter greater than snout length.

Meristics.—Lateral line obsolete on body, scales in lateral series usually 42–54; longitudinal scale rows between bases of pelvic and dorsal fins usually 14; prepelvic ventral scutes (17)18–20(21); postpelvic ventral scutes (12)13–16(17); total scutes (31)32–35(36). Dorsal rays (15)16–18(19); anal rays (15)17–19(21); pelvic rays (7)9(10); pectoral rays (12)14–15(16). Gill rakers on lower limb of first arch in adult usually 38–46.

Color in Preservative.—Head and body of adult dusky to dark above, grading to pale ventrally, some retaining silver on side; dusky shoulder spot usually present. Fins pale or slightly dusky.

Fish 19 *Alosa pseudoharengus* subadult 83 mm SL (RC), VA, Campbell County, Roanoke River, 21 April 1976.

Color in Life.—Very similar to *A. aestivalis* except: dorsum tends grayish green; peritoneum generally pale or silvery, often with dark punctations, or pinkish gray, sometimes quite dusky.

Larvae.—Described by Ryder (1887), Prince (1907), Smith (1907), Hildebrand and Schroeder (1928), Hildebrand (1964), Mansueti and Hardy (1967), Cianci (1969), Lippson and Moran (1974), Chambers et al. (1976), Jones et al. (1978), Wang and Kernehan (1979), and Tin (1982a).

COMPARISON

See account of *A. aestivalis.*

BIOLOGY

In fresh water, young alewives feed primarily on diatoms, copepods, and ostracods. Upon entering salt water, larger fish shift their diet to include shrimps and fishes (Hildebrand and Schroeder 1928). Other prey includes squids, fish eggs, and their own larvae (Sumner et al. 1913; Bigelow and Welsh 1925). Landlocked populations feed mainly on zooplankton. They are size-selective predators that can significantly alter the size and species composition of zooplankton communities by removing larger and slower plankters (Kohler and Ney 1981). Other prey includes aquatic insects (mainly Diptera larvae and pupae) and eggs and larvae of fishes. Alewives in Claytor Lake ate larvae of several fishes, including the white and largemouth basses (Kohler 1980; Kohler and Ney 1980).

In anadromous populations, females tend to mature one year later than males; maturation of both sexes occurs in ages 3–5 (Bigelow and Welsh 1925; Cooper 1961; Havey 1961; Hildebrand 1964; Marcy 1968; Tyus 1974; Libby 1982). Maturation occurs at ages 1–3 and at smaller sizes in landlocked populations (Graham 1956; Rothschild 1966; Norden 1967; Boaze and Lackey 1974; Nigro and Ney 1982). A nonlandlocked alewife population in the lower Susquehanna River exhibited age at maturation and growth similar to landlocked populations (Foerster and Goodbred 1978). Maximum longevity is age 9 for anadromous Virginia fish (Lipton 1979; Loesch et al. 1979). Landlocked populations are shorter lived—4 years in Lake Michigan and 3 in Claytor Lake (Norden 1967; Nigro and Ney 1982).

Alewives typically are 55–109 mm TL when they leave fresh water and 65–145 mm TL at age 1 (Hildebrand 1964). Chesapeake Bay fish were 114–127 mm TL at age 1 (Bigelow and Schroeder 1953). First-year growth in Lake Michigan was 95 mm TL (Norden

1967); Claytor Lake alewives were 160 mm TL at the same age (Nigro and Ney 1982). Average length of adults in landlocked populations is 150 mm TL (Scott and Crossman 1973), whereas sea-run adults usually are 250–300 mm SL, maximally 350 mm (Burgess *in* Lee et al. 1980).

Alosa pseudoharengus spawns from March to May, earliest in the south; arrivals to Chesapeake Bay begin during late February or early March (Hildebrand 1964). Migration to spawning sites occurs under low light intensities (Cooper 1961; Kissil 1974). Water temperature during spawning ordinarily is 12.5–15.5°C (Bigelow and Schroeder 1953). Sea-run alewives spawn in sluggish tidal freshwater streams and ponds over a variety of substrates (Smith 1907; Greeley 1935 *in* Hildebrand 1964; Mansueti 1956; Rothschild 1962). Adults return to the sea after spawning; scale markings indicate that individual alewives often spawn more than once (Leim and Scott 1966).

Landlocked populations make an abbreviated spawning migration by moving to shallow areas of lakes and tributary systems. In Claytor Lake, spawning movements occurred in April when water reached 13°C (Nigro and Ney 1982); in Lake Michigan, spawning began in late June and lasted until August, in surface water of 17.5–21°C (Norden 1967).

During spawning, adults pair off and swim in upward spirals until reaching the surface with a splash (Greeley 1935 *in* Hildebrand 1964). Semidemersal eggs are scattered and eventually settle in slack water. Eggs are somewhat adhesive just after extrusion but are essentially nonadhesive afterward (Mansueti 1956). Fecundity in anadromous populations is 48,000–360,000 (Smith 1907; Belding 1921 *in* Norden 1967; Kissil 1974). Fecundity of landlocked alewife, as expected for typically smaller adults, is much less; in Lake Michigan it was 11,000–22,000 (Norden 1967) and in Claytor Lake was 13,200–49,200 (Nigro and Ney 1982).

HABITAT

Alosa pseudoharengus schools in fresh and salt water. Like the blueback herring and American shad, the alewife apparently makes diel vertical migrations, moving bottomward during daylight along with the zooplankton (Neves 1981). When not on spawning migrations, adults have about the same seasonal distribution on the Continental Shelf as do blueback herring, but tend to occur deeper, typically within 56–110 m (Neves 1981).

Young linger in natal streams, slowly moving downstream until fall when they begin to migrate seaward (Hildebrand 1964). Some alewives remain in

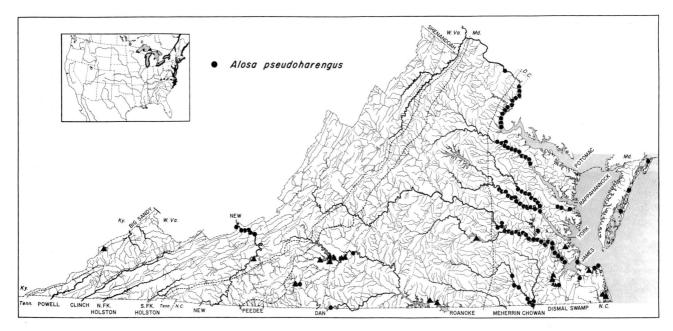

Map 27   Alewife. Delmarva records from Burgess (*in* Lee et al. 1980). Most main-river Chesapeake basin records from 1978 VIMS Trawl Survey. Extent of range in the ocean, bay, and main-river tributaries not indicated.

Chesapeake Bay through their first or second winter (Hildebrand and Schroeder 1928). There is evidence of a resident alewife population in northern Chesapeake Bay (Foerster and Goodbred 1978). Landlocked alewives inhabit open water and deep areas of lakes, moving inshore at night to feed.

DISTRIBUTION   Map 27

Anadromous alewife populations occupy the Atlantic coast from South Carolina to Newfoundland; they may have been native in the Great Lakes basin as far up as Lake Ontario. After bypassing Niagara Falls via the Welland Canal, alewives colonized the upper four Great Lakes in the last 40 years (R. R. Miller 1957; S. Smith 1970; Scott and Crossman 1973). Some smaller inland lakes and reservoirs from Virginia northward contain populations established by stocking.

In Virginia, *A. pseudoharengus* is present in all major Chesapeake Bay tributaries, but some historical spawning grounds are vacant due to dams and pollution. The alewife has been stocked by the VDGIF in several inland reservoirs; these are among the first stocked south of New Jersey. The source of the stockings of which we have information was a freshwater lake in New Jersey. The Smith Mountain Lake population started in 1965 with 3,000 alewives, which reproduced soon after. They were supplemented around 1968 by 13,500 more alewives (Anonymous

1968). Although some of these or their descendants were first found in Leesville Reservoir in 1969 (Estes 1971), the Smith Mountain population did not become large until about 1976 (Hart 1978). Claytor Lake received 110,000 alewives in 1968–1969, and that population has thrived (Boaze 1972; Boaze and Lackey 1974). Escapees from Claytor Lake apparently moved down the New River and established a population in Bluestone Reservoir, West Virginia (Lewis and Miles 1974). Alewives captured in the New River during 1971–1974 may have emanated from the Bluestone population. Lake Chesdin was stocked in 1968 (Anonymous 1968), and Flannagan Reservoir in 1969. Although *A. pseudoharengus* was caught in Flannagan in 1971 (Wollitz 1973), we are unaware of its current status in this impoundment and Lake Chesdin, nor do we know the origin of the Gaston Reservoir population.

Abundance.—Often common; locally abundant during spawning migrations. Anadromous populations in Virginia seem to be increasing after reaching an all-time low in 1981 (Loesch and Kriete 1984).

REMARKS

The closely related alewife and blueback herring are so similar in appearance that they generally are lumped under the term "river herring" by commer-

Fish 20 *Alosa mediocris* subadult 167 mm SL (UNC), NC, off Carteret County, Atlantic Ocean, 23 January 1984.

cial and other fishermen, rendering catch statistics difficult to interpret.

The oceanic haunts of the alewife and blueback herring were long unknown. The noted marine ichthyologist Samuel F. Hildebrand (1964) considered earlier notions that they live quite distant offshore from the rivers of their origin, and that their migration routes are straight toward shore. Upon analysis of data from extensive surveys since 1963 by the National Marine Fisheries Service, it became evident to Neves (1981) that, when not on spawning migration, the adults of the two species congregate over the Continental Shelf off New England.

The co-occurrence of the two species is stratified; alewives tend to live at greater depths than do bluebacks. Neves (1981) posed that the differences between the species in depth preference and dorsal coloration (green in the alewife) may be coadaptive, each species perhaps realizing reduced predation in the light/color regime of their respective depths; green light penetrates waters of the Continental Shelf

more than does blue. Too, the alewife has a slightly larger eye, another adaptation for dim light (Marshall 1965).

In inland Virginia the alewife has been considered a "small fish with a big impact" (Cochran 1982), because of its role as gamefish forage—the purpose of its transplantation to reservoirs. However, the alewife can be a mixed blessing. It tends to benefit only pelagic gamefishes such as white bass, striped bass, and walleye, not the more littoral ones such as crappies and black basses. Alewife prey on gamefish larvae (first reported from Claytor Lake) and have detrimentally altered food supplies of other fishes (S. Smith 1970; Kohler and Ney 1981; Stewart et al. 1981). At least Virginia's shorelines have not widely suffered the malodorous results of massive die-offs of alewives such as occur in the Great Lakes.

Name.—*Pseudoharengus* means "false herring." The name alewife may refer to roe-swollen female herrings, an allusion to the large belly of some beerhall maidens.

Hickory shad   *Alosa mediocris* (Mitchill)

SYSTEMATICS

The hickory shad was described in 1814, presumably from New York. This Atlantic basin species forms a species pair with the skipjack herring *A. chrysochloris* of the Gulf slope and Mississippi basin (Berry 1964).

DESCRIPTION

Materials.—Based on Hildebrand and Schroeder (1928), Mansueti (1962a), Hildebrand (1964), Jones et al. (1978), and 45 Virginia series. Life color from Hildebrand (1964).

Anatomy.—A somewhat shallow-bodied clupeid with a moderate eye, dorsal margin of lower jaw gently sloped

upward, lower jaw distinctly projecting, and relatively few gill rakers; adults are 285–450 mm TL. Body somewhat elongate, quite compressed, ventral profile more convex than dorsal. Head, snout, and eye moderate; mouth large, superior; maxillary broad; tip of mandible projecting into dorsal profile; upper margin of mandible without a prominent angle near midlength; tiny teeth present on lower jaw, palatine, and tongue; cheek depth about equal to cheek width. Dorsal fin small, distal margin straight or slightly concave; caudal fin forked, lobes symmetrical; anal fin longer than dorsal; pelvic fin small; pectoral fin moderate.

Meristics.—Lateral line absent on body, scales in lateral series usually 45–50; longitudinal scale rows on body between bases of pelvic and dorsal fins usually 16; prepelvic ventral scutes 20–21; postpelvic ventral scutes 14–16; total scutes 33–38. Dorsal rays 15–20; anal rays 19–23; pelvic rays

9; pectoral rays 15–16. Gill rakers on lower limb of first arch of adult 18–23.

Color in Preservative.—Head and body of adult dusky to dark above, grading to pale ventrally, side sometimes retaining silver color; dusky shoulder spot or row of spots usually present. Fins pale or slightly dusky.

Color in Life.—Grayish green above, shading to silver on side, white below; nape green, side of head brassy; tip of lower jaw olive-black. Dorsolateral stripes present in adult, absent in specimens less than 150 mm SL; black shoulder spot usually present, sometimes followed by several smaller ones. Dorsal and caudal fins olive-black; pelvic fin pale; pectoral fin slightly dusky. Peritoneum somewhat pale, peppered.

Larvae.—Described by Mansueti (1962a), Mansueti and Hardy (1967), Lippson and Moran (1974), Jones et al. (1978), and Wang and Kernehan (1979).

BIOLOGY

Alosa mediocris feeds mainly on fishes. Other prey includes squids, fish eggs, small crabs, and various pelagic crustaceans (Hildebrand and Schroeder 1928; Bigelow and Schroeder 1953).

Relatively little is known of the age and growth of the hickory shad. Generally they mature at 3–5 years, a few of both sexes in 2 years (Mansueti 1958c; Pate 1972). Early growth apparently is more rapid than in other east coast *Alosa*; total lengths of 140–190 mm are attained by age-1 fish. Spawning Patuxent River males were 287–414 mm TL, females were 320–452 mm (Mansueti 1962a). Average size in Chesapeake populations was 381 mm TL and 0.45 kg (1 pound), maximally 457 mm TL and 0.9 kg (2 pounds) (Hildebrand and Schroeder 1928). The maximum reported length, about 610 mm, is apparently based on a statement by Uhler and Lugger (1876) that both the hickory shad and American shad reach about 2 feet; this was repeated for *A. mediocris* by Hildebrand (1964) but not accepted by Burgess (*in* Lee et al. 1980).

Hickory shad spawn in tidal fresh water within April to early June. In Virginia they have been found in rivers as early as February and as late as May (Davis et al. 1970). Little is known of specific spawning places, times, and behavior, although there is evidence of spawning in main channels, flooded swamps, and sloughs (Mansueti 1962a; Davis et al. 1970; Pate 1972). The spawning period may be relatively long, as inferred from the large variation in size

of young fish captured the same day at one locality (Mansueti 1962a). Eggs are slightly adhesive and semidemersal; fecundity is 43,000–348,000 per female (Pate 1972).

HABITAT

Like other *Alosa*, the hickory shad is anadromous, but little is known of its specific habitat or movements. In Chesapeake Bay a definite run of adults occurs during spring and a lesser one happens in late fall; during summer only stragglers are found (Hildebrand and Schroeder 1928). The pattern may be adjusted to feeding in both the bay and the nearby ocean prior to the spawning migration (Mansueti 1958c). Young leave natal streams in early summer; some may spend the first year in Chesapeake Bay (Mansueti 1962a).

DISTRIBUTION   Map 28

Hickory shad range from Maine to Florida (Hildebrand and Schroeder 1928). Virtually all of our Virginia records are from the four major Chesapeake Bay tributaries and Delmarva, but the species is widespread in the bay.

Abundance.—*Alosa mediocris* is the least common Atlantic coast *Alosa*; it is seasonally common in many major Chesapeake Bay tributaries, the approximate center of its abundance (Musick 1972; Burgess *in* Lee et al. 1980).

REMARKS

Scientists were long split into two opinionated groups regarding the spawning location of the hickory shad. One group believed it spawned in the ocean because of the paucity of young collected in extensive freshwater and estuarine surveys. The other group correctly surmised that, similar to other *Alosa*, it spawned in fresh water. The general issue was decided when Romeo Mansueti (1962a) presented evidence of freshwater spawning. However, much remains to be learned of the biology of this, "the most enigmatic of all the estuarine clupeoids . . ." (Mansueti 1962a).

Name.—*Mediocris* means "mediocre," in reference to its food value, perhaps as compared to American shad.

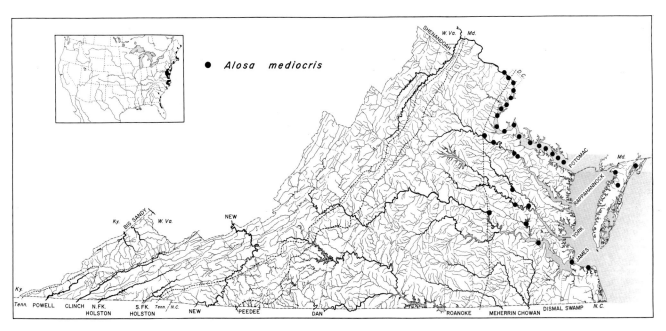

Map 28 Hickory shad. Most records from Burgess (*in* Lee et al. 1980), Atran et al. (1983), and the 1978 VIMS Trawl Survey. Full extent of range in Chesapeake basin and Atlantic Ocean not shown.

American shad   *Alosa sapidissima* (Wilson)

SYSTEMATICS

The American shad was described in 1811, probably from the Delaware River near Philadelphia. This Atlantic basin species forms a species pair with the Alabama shad *A. alabamae*, which lives in the Mississippi basin and other Gulf of Mexico tributaries (Berry 1964). Distinct populations exist in different Atlantic slope drainages (Vladykov and Wallace 1938; Warfel and Olsen 1947; Raney and Woolcott 1955; Nichols 1958, 1966; Talbot and Sykes 1958; Fischler 1959; Hill 1959; Carscadden and Leggett 1975a, 1975b; Leggett and Carscadden 1978).

DESCRIPTION

Materials.—Based on Hildebrand and Schroeder (1928), Hildebrand (1964), Scott and Crossman (1973), and 10 Virginia lots (300 specimens counted). Color in life from many Virginia specimens.

Anatomy.—A clupeid with a moderate eye, dorsal margin of lower jaw gently inclined upward, lower jaw not distinctly projecting, and numerous gill rakers; adults are 350–550 mm TL. Major anatomical features much as in *A. mediocris*; differences include: lower jaw not projecting, not entering dorsal profile; cheek deeper than wide, distinctly narrower ventrally.

Meristics.—Lateral line absent on body, scales in lateral series usually 52–64; longitudinal scale rows between bases of pelvic and dorsal fins usually 15–16; prepelvic ventral scutes (18)20–22(23); postpelvic ventral scutes (14)15–17(18); total scutes (34)35–38(39). Dorsal rays (15)16–18(19); anal rays (17)19–21(23); pelvic rays (8)9(10); pectoral rays (15)16–17(20). Gill rakers on lower limb of first arch in adults 59–76; 26–43 in specimens smaller than 125 mm.

Fish 21 *Alosa sapidissima* juvenile 137 mm SL (UNC), NC, off Carteret County, Atlantic Ocean, 23 January 1984.

Color in Preservative.—As in *A. mediocris.*

Color in Life.—Green to blue with metallic luster above, shading to silver on side, white below. Shoulder spot black, usually followed by a row of smaller spots, rarely with a second row below. Dorsal and caudal fins olive-black, tips of caudal lobes darker; paired fins pale or olive. Peritoneum pale or silver.

Larvae.—Described by Prince (1907), Leim (1924), Bigelow and Welsh (1925), Leach (1925), Mansueti (1955), Hildebrand (1964), Mansueti and Hardy (1967), Lippson and Moran (1974), Jones et al. (1978), Wang and Kernehan (1979), and Johnson (1980).

BIOLOGY

In fresh water, young *A. sapidissima* feed on small crustaceans and adult and larval insects (Leim 1924; Walburg 1956); after entering salt water, their diet shifts primarily to small shrimps (Hildebrand and Schroeder 1928). Adults are predominantly planktivorous; foods include algae, copepods, ostracods, isopods, decapod larvae, mayflies, mollusks, fish eggs, and fishes (young shad and rarely, shield darters) (Hildebrand 1964; Chittenden 1969). It was a common belief that adults did not feed during their spawning migration, but the apparent absence of feeding is due to their planktonic feeding strategy and the paucity of suitably sized food in fresh water (Atkinson 1951).

American shad typically mature by ages 3–6, some as early as age 2; males mature earlier than females (Leim 1924; LaPointe 1958; Walburg 1960; Nichols and Massmann 1963; Chittenden 1969; Leggett 1969; Carscadden and Leggett 1975a). Age at maturity increases from south to north (Leggett and Carscadden 1978). York River males matured at ages 3–4, females at ages 4–5 (Nichols and Massmann 1963). In the Delaware River, males matured at ages 3–5, females at 4–6 (Chittenden 1969). Maximum reported survival is age 11 (Cating 1953).

Growth of American shad has been extensively studied (Leim 1924; Cating 1953; Walburg 1956, 1960; LaPointe 1958; Judy 1961; Chittenden 1969; Leggett 1969). Growth differs geographically and between the sexes; females are larger at all ages (Walburg and Nichols 1967). American shad reached 5.4–6.3 kg (12–14 pounds) at the height of their abundance (McDonald 1884a; Worth 1898; Stevenson 1899). Presently, Atlantic males typically range 0.9–1.4 kg (2–3 pounds), females 1.4–1.8 kg (3–4 pounds), averaging 0.45 kg (1 pound) less than their Pacific relatives (Walburg and Nichols 1967). The maximum length of "about 600 mm (30 inches)" (Hildebrand 1964) does not equate; 30 inches equals 762 mm. Hildebrand

(1964) also cited a 660-mm (26-inch) specimen, but did not indicate SL or TL. Carlander (1969) compiled a 658-mm FL fish from New York. Burgess (*in* Lee et al. 1980) listed 584 mm as the maximum SL.

American shad spawn in tidal fresh water from March to May; they approach river mouths in Chesapeake Bay during March and April and spawn near the bay or after a long upriver migration (Hildebrand 1964). Most spawning occurs at 13–20°C (Walburg and Nichols 1967). Eggs were abundant in Virginia streams when water reached 12°C (Massmann 1952). Spawning occurs over shallow flats and in riffles (Bigelow and Welsh 1925; Massmann 1952; Barker 1965 *in* Wang and Kernehan 1979; Chittenden 1976), or anywhere in tidal fresh water at suitable temperatures. American shad seem to prefer river areas near creek mouths (Smith 1907; Mansueti and Kolb 1953). Oviposition occurs over sand, gravel, silt, muck, cobble, and boulders at water depths usually less than 3 m and currents of 15–90 cm/second (Mansueti and Kolb 1953; Walburg 1960; Barker 1965 *in* Wang and Kernehan 1979; Walburg and Nichols 1967; Marcy 1972; Leggett 1976). Daily onset of spawning has been related to decreasing light intensity, with activity taking place in the evening (Leim 1924; Walburg and Nichols 1967; Marcy 1972; Chittenden 1976). In the Pamunkey River, Massmann (1952) noted spawning at all hours, but it was more intense from noon to midnight. Spawning tends to begin earlier in turbid water (Chittenden 1976). Marcy (1972) found American shad eggs only in water with dissolved oxygen concentrations above 5 mg/liter.

American shad often spawn more than once. The percentage of repeat spawners tends to decrease with decreasing latitude (Leggett and Carscadden 1978), although previous spawners accounted for 17, 23, and 27% of the shad from the Potomac, York, and James rivers (Walburg and Sykes 1957; Nichols and Massmann 1963). Shad usually spawn once in rivers south of Cape Hatteras.

Spawning behavior has been described in detail by Medcof (1957) and Chittenden (1976). Pairs swim from the channel towards shore, releasing eggs and sperm (Atran et al. 1983). Fecundity is 116,000–659,000 eggs per female (Lehman 1953; Walburg 1960). Eggs are semidemersal and adhesive; they drift downstream until they sink and become lodged in the substrate (Chittenden 1969).

Landlocked American shad in Millerton Lake, California, exhibit higher numbers of repeat spawners and higher total lifetime fecundity than do anadromous shad (Lambert et al. 1980). Fecundity is similar to mid-Atlantic populations, but growth rate and age at maturity are lower.

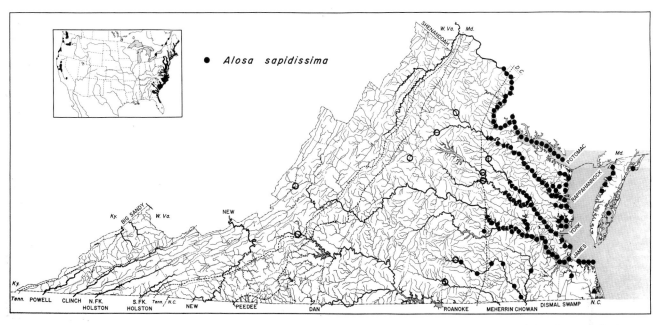

Map 29   American shad. Most records from Burgess (*in* Lee et al. 1980) and, in the Coastal Plain of the Chesapeake basin, from the 1978 VIMS Trawl Survey. Full extent of distribution in main-river tributaries, Chesapeake Bay, and the Atlantic Ocean not shown. Open circles indicate former maximum extent of migration in main rivers and certain major tributaries (see text).

HABITAT

Alosa sapidissima is a pelagic-schooling migratory species. Postspawning fish from rivers of Canada and the United States move to the Gulf of Maine in summer, to off the Mid-Atlantic states in winter, and farther south in early spring (Vladykov 1956; Talbot and Sykes 1958; Leggett and Whitney 1972; Neves and Depres 1979). Migrations are temperature induced; the best predictor of offshore distribution is bottom temperatures of 3–15°C; most shad are found between 7–13°C (Neves and Depres 1979). American shad usually enter birthplace rivers and streams from Chesapeake Bay during March and April; migration may start as early as January and may last until mid-May (Nichols and Massmann 1963). After spawning, adults return to the sea. Juveniles remain in natal streams for a brief to moderate period, and move downstream in response to currents and temperature (Chittenden 1969; Scott and Crossman 1973). Most have left Chesapeake Bay by the end of November or early December (Hildebrand and Schroeder 1928; Hildebrand 1964).

DISTRIBUTION   Map 29

American shad occur on the Atlantic coast from the St. Johns River, Florida, to Nova Scotia, rarely to Labrador (Hildebrand and Schroeder 1928; Hare and Murphy 1974). The Pacific Coast population (developed from Hudson River stock liberated in Sacramento Bay during 1871–1880) now occurs from San Diego to southern Alaska; some shad have been taken along eastern Kamchatka in the former U.S.S.R. (Svetovidov 1952; Burgess *in* Lee et al. 1980).

In Virginia, *A. sapidissima* ascends all major and some minor Chesapeake tributaries and the Nottoway River (and probably the Meherrin River) in the Chowan drainage. This species has been blocked by dams and pollution from many small independent systems and tributaries of larger rivers. Substantial loss of spawning grounds has occurred in the Rappahannock, James, and Roanoke rivers and many of their tributaries, as deduced from old records of migration to the Blue Ridge foothills or well beyond (Map 29).

Great Falls of the Potomac River, at the head of the Fall Zone, seems to have long been a natural barrier to American shad (Walburg and Nichols 1967), but this species migrated through the other fall zones in Virginia. In the Rappahannock drainage, Walburg and Nichols (1967) gave the upper limit of shad migration as Falmouth Falls in the Fall Zone. However, referring to the period before dam construction (1860), the VFC (1877a) stated that "Within the memory of persons now living, shad and herring have ascended the Rappahannock and its tributary Rapidan above the Orange and Alexandria Railroad" (Map 29). The James River was traversed to its uppermost main tributary in the Valley and Ridge Province "as high as Covington, and high up all its principal tributaries," and there was an "abundance of shad in the Rivanna above Charlottesville" (the Piedmont record in Map 29; VFC 1877a). Remains of American shad were found at an archeological site along the James River in the Valley and Ridge Province (Whyte 1989). In the Roanoke River, Stevenson (1899) and Walburg and Nichols (1967) gave the original upriver limit as the Fall Zone at Weldon, North Carolina, 401 rkm from the coast. However, the VFC (1878) noted that shad reached "nearly or quite up to Salem," an additional 400-rkm trek, comprising one of the lengthiest known for the species.

Regarding the ascent of American shad through the fairly gentle Nottoway River Fall Zone, J. R. Orgain, Jr. (personal communication) said that 2.5–5.0 cm of rain are needed weekly in March through May to allow adequate depth for passage of rocky rapids.

Alosa sapidissima was one of the first species cultured by the U.S. Fish Commission. Starting in the 1870s, billions of fry were released along the Atlantic slope, in interior drainages, and on the Pacific slope. Most Atlantic slope stockings were an attempt to augment populations that were declining due to extensive overfishing and dams (VFC 1916). Releases began in Virginia during 1873 with 40,000 fry placed in the New River, and in 1874, 100,000 were put in the Staunton (= Roanoke) River (USFC 1876, 1878). Stocking continued in the New and Roanoke, the Chowan drainage was supplied, and releases were commonly made in most major Chesapeake Bay tributaries, until 1904. United States Fish Commission records reveal that almost 500 million fry were stocked in Virginia during that period; almost half of them were returned to their Potomac River parental source. During 1927–1936, about 183.5 million more fry were stocked in Virginia (USFC 1928–1936). Improved techniques of culture and transport in the early 1900s did not stem the downtrend of the species (Mansueti and Kolb 1953).

Abundance.—Usually common, sometimes abundant during spawning migration. The center of abundance is from Connecticut to North Carolina (Gusey 1981). Populations are steadily declining as reflected in the dramatic decline in commercial landings during the 20th century.

REMARKS

American shad landings along the Atlantic coast of the United States have declined sharply since the turn of the century. From the 1896 record of 22,902 tonnes (50,500,000 pounds), annual landings had dropped to 4,000–5,000 tonnes by the 1930s and fluctuated about this range until further decline began in the 1960s (Walburg and Nichols 1967). In the 1970s, landings decreased to a low of 885 tonnes in 1979 (MacKenzie et al. 1985).

Virginia has consistently been at or near the lead in landings. The American shad fishery of the Chesapeake basin became an important seasonal industry by about 1870, and in 1897, an all-time high of 5,230 tonnes was landed in the state. Despite, and because of, continual improvement of fishing methods and increasing fishing effort, landings declined to 629 tonnes by 1960 (Walburg and Nichols 1967). Catches then fluctuated between 219 and 1,865 tonnes, and did not exceed 300 tonnes during 1985–1989 (VMRC 1985–1989). Many factors contributed to the decline in abundance of American shad, including overfishing, curtailment of spawning runs by dams, and pollution (Chittenden 1969).

Alosa sapidissima supports the largest recreational fishery of the shads. Indeed, a broad-sided shad running downstream on a light rod can be a heart stopper.

Name.—*Sapidissima* means "most delicious" or "most palatable."

PIKES
Family Esocidae

BY ROBERT E. JENKINS, RICHARD A. DIETZ, AND NOEL M. BURKHEAD

The Esocidae or pikes are a small Holarctic family of great importance to anglers. Fossils indicate that a modern esocid lineage extends back to Paleocene time, at least 58 million years ago (Wilson 1980, 1984). The five living species of the single genus *Esox* are split into two subgenera (Nelson 1972; Crossman 1978; Casselman et al. 1986), correlating nicely with the occurrence of patterned or unpatterned median fins and other characters. The subgenus *Esox* comprises the North American muskellunge *E. masquinongy*, the North American–Eurasian northern pike *E. lucius*, and the Amur pike *E. reicherti*. The latter is native to northeast Asia and has been introduced in Pennsylvania (Buss et al. 1978; Radonski et al. 1984). The eastern and central North American subgenus *Kenoza* contains the chain pickerel *E. niger* and the "little" pickerels—the redfin pickerel *E. a. americanus* and grass pickerel *E. a. vermiculatus*. All species indigenous to North America occur in Virginia; the pike and muskellunge are introduced.

Experts agree that pikes are closely related to mudminnows (family Umbridae) and that both groups are very primitive euteleosts. Traditionally, pikes plus mudminnows (the Esociformes, Esocoidei, or Esocae) have been classified in or near the same order as trouts and allies (Salmoniformes). A current trend is to consider the esociforms as more primitive than the salmoniforms, and to separate them in the phylogenetic hierarchy by the ostariophysans (minnows and allies)—see Salmonidae and inside front cover.

Whatever their higher relationships, pikes are instantly recognizable as such. The body is quite elongate and slightly to moderately compressed. Fins are soft-rayed; the single dorsal and anal fins are positioned far posterior, the tail is forked, pelvic fins are abdominal, and pectoral fins are low. In lateral view the head tapers to a point; jaws are long, somewhat duckbill-shaped, and the tip of the lower jaw is slightly outjutted. The mouth is terminal, large, and strongly toothed with canines and large patches of smaller teeth. The eye is small to medium in size. Scales are cycloid. Pikes are specialized for rapid bursts of pursuit and capture of fishes. Adults of the smaller pickerels are usually 150–200 mm long, but muskellunge reach 1,400 mm (55 inches) and exceed 31 kg (69 pounds).

Color patterns on the side of most species consist of camouflaging dark spots, bars, or chainlike markings on a paler background; the northern pike is mostly dark and bears numerous pale spots laterally. Median fins of the larger esocids are spotted or streaked; they are unmarked in pickerels. Only the redfin pickerel can be called colorful. Sexual dichromatism and obvious sexual dimorphism, other than in growth, are lacking.

All pikes occupy temperate areas; although they often are grouped as coolwater fishes, the northern pike widely populates colder waters and the pickerels are southerly disposed. Esocids inhabit lacustrine and sluggish fluvial environments, usually shallows; the larger species tend to occupy larger bodies of water and somewhat deeper areas within. Pikes generally are solitary, hovering quietly among vegetation and by logs and other cover. Ambushing a meal is the norm. A pike lurking in shade is difficult to see, but well positioned to see approaching prey (Helfman 1981).

Pikes feed largely on fishes by sight. They also eat

a variety of invertebrates (particularly young pikes), as well as frogs, snakes, ducklings, and small mammals. Like many piscivorous fishes, esocids are cannibalistic. Their early spawning time allows their young to crop the fry of later-spawning fishes (Keast 1985), resulting in rapid early growth. Old pickerels are 6–8 years of age; northern pike and muskellunge may live more than 20 years.

Spawning typically occurs in early spring, shortly after ice breakup or somewhat later in northern areas; the muskellunge is the latest spawner. In Florida, spawning of pickerels may peak in the coldest part of winter. Spawning takes place in permanently watered shallows and temporarily flooded shorelines; eggs often are broadcast over submerged vegetation and always left unguarded. A female is attended generally by one or a few males. Fecundity is 200–290,000 eggs per female and is greatest in the larger species. Eggs usually are 1.0–2.2 mm; those of most species are demersal and adhesive. Eggs of chain pickerel become nonadhesive after they water-harden and are buoyant at later stages of development (Martin 1984b). The incubation period is usually 7–14 days (Carlander 1969).

Natural and artificial hybridization among esocids has been extensively studied (Crossman and Buss 1965; Buss and Miller 1967; Buss et al. 1978). The most common natural hybrids are northern pike × muskellunge and chain pickerel × redfin pickerel. The only potential esocid crosses unknown from nature are muskellunge with all pickerels; small pickerels prob-ably would have little sexual attraction to the large muskellunge (Buss et al. 1978). From a fisheries standpoint, the most important artificially produced hybrid is the tiger muskellunge, whose parents are northern pike and muskellunge.

Chain pickerel are an underrated gamefish. The much larger northern pike and muskellunge are highly prized. Sudden strikes and tenacious fighting ability evoke the claim (Buss et al. 1978) that the family may be the most exciting of freshwater sport fishes in the world. Pikes are voracious and can exert partial control of forage populations, an ability sometimes conveying disrepute to these predators. Such attitudes probably are often based on false notions or unnatural situations. Some Virginians have even spurned the muskellunge, as it is suspected (but not shown) to have reduced some local smallmouth bass populations. However, our sighting while underwater of four large muskellunge in the dim stillness of a large pool in the Cowpasture River spelled an ultimate fishing challenge. It was accepted, but for all we know they are still there.

Esocids have flaky white meat of delicate flavor. Some captives adorn walls; others are released to live and perhaps fight again. Some fish such as the muskellunge are too valuable to be caught just once.

Name.—Esoc-, from *Esox*, Latin for "pike." Pike refers to the long pointed snout, emphasized by the elongate body. "Pickerel," a diminutive of pike, is applied to the smaller esocids.

Key to Pikes   Esocidae

The key is adapted from Casselman et al. (1986).

1a   Median fins with spots or streaks; subocular bar absent or vague; opercle about half scaled (Figure 22B); mandibular pores usually 5 or more on each side, rarely as few as 4 on one side only (Figure 22B); pelvic rays usually 10–13 . . . . larger pikes, subgenus *Esox*   2

1b   Median fins unmarked; subocular bar prominent; opercle fully scaled (Figure 23A, B); mandibular pores usually 4 on each side, rarely 3 or 5 on one side only; pelvic rays usually 8–10 . . . . pickerels, subgenus *Kenoza*   3

2a   Color pattern on side of adult is horizontal rows of pale oval spots on dark background; cheek usually fully scaled (Figure 22A); total mandibular pores 9–11, usually 5 on each side (Figure 22A) . . . .   NORTHERN PIKE—*E. lucius*   p. 232

2b   Color pattern, if present, on side of adult is dark spots, blotches, or vertical bars on paler background; cheek about half scaled (Figure 22B); total mandibular pores 12–20, usually 6–9 on each side (Figure 22B) . . . .   MUSKELLUNGE—*E. masquinongy*   p. 234

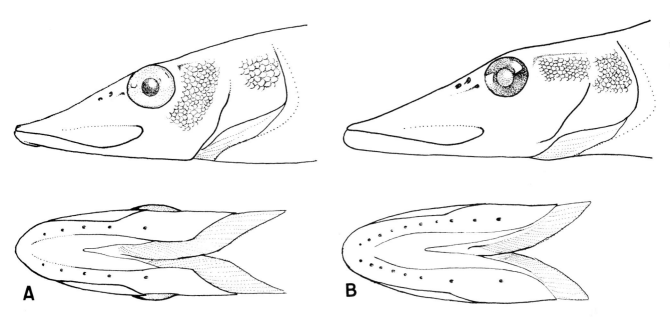

Figure 22   (A) *Esox lucius*, cheek almost completely scaled, mandibular pores (one side) usually 5. (B) *E. masquinongy*, lower half of cheek naked, mandibular pores (one side) usually 6–9.

3a   No fin red in life; adult with chainlike pattern on lower side; subocular bar vertical (Figure 23A); snout longer, distance from snout tip to center of eye greater than distance from eye center to upper end of gill opening (Figure 23A); posterior end of upper jaw not reaching behind midpoint of eye; lateral line scales usually more than 120 (114–131) .... CHAIN PICKEREL—*E. niger*   p. 239

3b   At least some fins red in life; adult with vertically barred pattern on side; subocular bar slanted posteriad (Figure 23B); snout shorter, distance from snout tip to center of eye about equal or less than distance from eye center to upper end of gill opening (Figure 23B); posterior end of upper jaw reaching behind midpoint of eye; lateral line scales usually less than 110 (94–117) .... REDFIN PICKEREL—*E. americanus*   p. 242

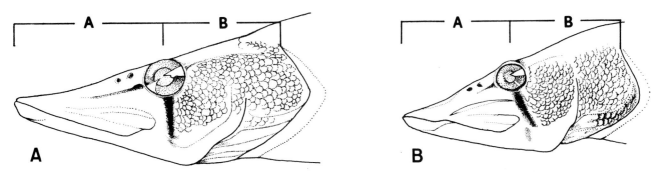

Figure 23   (A) *Esox niger*, distance "A" greater than distance "B". (B) *E. americanus*, distance "A" about equal to distance "B". Both have cheek and opercle fully or nearly fully scaled.

Pikes   Genus *Esox* Linnaeus

The single living genus of the family Esocidae.   *Name.*—See family account.

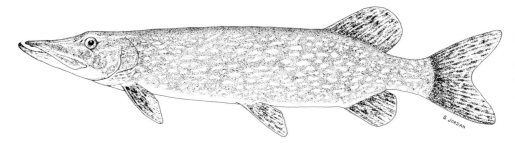

Fish 22 *Esox lucius* based on a juvenile from Illinois, with adult color pattern and form adapted from many photographs.

Northern pike   *Esox lucius* Linnaeus

SYSTEMATICS

Esox lucius was described in 1758 from Europe. This Holarctic species is highly variable but differences are insufficient for nomenclatural recognition of populations. Genetic and meristic divergence within North America may be related to isolation of stocks in separate refugia during glacial times (Morrow 1964, 1980; McPhail and Lindsey 1970; Crossman 1978; Seeb et al. 1987).

DESCRIPTION

Materials.—Based on Buss (1961), McPhail and Lindsey (1970), Scott and Crossman (1973), Becker (1983), Casselman et al. (1986), and 1 Michigan specimen. Life color based on Eddy and Surber (1947), McPhail and Lindsey (1970), Scarola (1973), Scott and Crossman (1973), Smith (1979), Trautman (1981), and Becker (1983).

Anatomy.—An esocid with pale bean-shaped markings on the side, spotted or streaked fins, cheek about fully scaled, and opercle half scaled; adults are 450–750 mm TL. Body and parts basically as described under *Family*. Body shallower and caudal fin tips more rounded than in muskellunge. A method of sexing pike by details of the vent area, and other tendencies of the sexes to differ, are described by Casselman (1974).

Meristics.—Lateral line complete, scales 105–148; principal dorsal rays 15–19; principal anal rays 12–15; pelvic rays 10–11; pectoral rays 14–17; branchiostegal rays (13)15(16); mandibular pores (3)5(6).

Color in Preservative.—Dorsum dark; side mostly dark to dusky, prominently marked with 7–9 irregular rows of pale, round or oval areas; venter pale. Ocular bars vague or absent. Dorsal, caudal, and anal fins with dark round, oval, or streaked markings; paired fins pale or with faint dusky markings. Young dark on back, with 10–15 vertical pale bars extending from upper side to venter; bars break up to form adult spotted pattern; fins somewhat spotted.

Color in Life.—Ground shade of head and body dorsally and laterally bluish or greenish gray to brownish olive; body spots white or yellow, head spots smaller, more golden; iris yellow. Venter cream to milk-white, color fingering onto lower flank. Median fins green, yellow, orange, or pale red, spotted or streaked with black; paired fins paler and may be unmarked. Silver or gray-colored mutants (silver pike), sometimes flecked with gold, are thought to occur sporadically throughout the range.

Larvae.—Described by Buss (1961), Franklin and Smith (1963), Toner and Lawler (1969), Buynak and Mohr (1979d), and Fuiman (1982b).

BIOLOGY

Esox lucius seems to eat almost any moving catchable animal of sufficient and engulfable size. Food habits and other life history aspects are summarized by Buss (1961), Carlander (1969), Toner and Lawler (1969), Inskip (1982), and Crossman and Casselman (1987). Postlarval pike eat microcrustaceans and immature aquatic insects but graduate rapidly, upon reaching about 50 mm in 4–5 weeks, to a predominantly fish diet (Scott and Crossman 1973). Adults feed heavily on game and forage fishes, as influenced largely by availability (Crossman 1962b). Optimum prey size is about one-third to one-half the length of the pike. Occasional opportunism is reflected in the variety of prey recorded from stomach analyses, including leeches, crayfishes, salamanders, frogs, ducklings, mice, and muskrats (Eddy and Surber 1947; Scott and Crossman 1973). Northern pike feed during daylight and, in suitable temperatures, remain active feeders throughout the year (Buss 1961). Their ambush style of predation requires cover such as vegetation and logs (Inskip 1982).

Sexual maturation occurs in 1–6 years, usually in the first half of this range for southerly populations; males tend to mature a year earlier than females (Toner and Lawler 1969). Females typically outlive males. Longevity is often 10–12 years, although slower-growing northern individuals may live 24–26 years (Carlander 1969).

Pike are among the most rapidly growing freshwater fishes; they generally attain 100–300 mm TL by the end of the first year. In some areas females grow more rapidly than males. Ranges of mean length at age 4 from many North American and European populations are 257–967 mm TL, and at age 8 are 452–1,041 mm (Carlander 1969; Toner and Lawler 1969; McHugh and Steinkoenig 1980). Occoquan Reservoir, Virginia, pike exhibited strong growth; 10 specimens averaged 853 mm TL at age 4 (McHugh and Steinkoenig 1980). The Virginia record catch is 12.6 kg (27 pounds 12 ounces). The angler record for North America is a 20.9-kg (46 pounds 2 ounces) New York fish. Larger pike, some mythical, have been reported from North America and Eurasia (Buss 1961; Scott and Crossman 1973).

Spawning movements begin in late winter or early spring, usually before ice breakup. Runs may be in response to increased daylight and rising waters, but spawning does not occur until water reaches about 4°C. Pike move into shallow, abundantly vegetated areas (often flooded shores) and associate in groups of one female and one to three males. The spawning act includes a period of swimming with partners positioned eye to eye, followed by inward rolling of bodies and approximated vents. Some 5–60 eggs are shed at a time and mixed and scattered by rapid body vibrations. An individual female will perform this ritual several times, generally during daylight, during a 2–5 day period (Svardson 1949; Buss 1961; Scott and Crossman 1973). Fecundity is 7,690–290,000 ova (Fuiman 1982b).

It is not known whether northern pike achieve notable reproductive success in Virginia. Northerns transported from a VDGIF hatchery and placed in a large rearing pond on a Gaston Reservoir tributary in the Elm Hill Waterfowl Refuge spawned successfully each year during 1967–1969 (Anonymous 1970). *Esox lucius* hybridizes naturally with all other native North American esocids but natural hybridization has not been recorded in Virginia. Hybrid vigor in growth and activity has been reported for the cross *E. lucius* × *E. masquinongy*, generally called the tiger musky (see *E. masquinongy, Remarks*).

HABITAT

Northern pike inhabit marshes, ponds, lakes, and pools in creeks and rivers, and prefer clear calm weedy areas (Buss 1961; Scott and Crossman 1973). Pike are considered a coolwater (mesothermal) species; they tend to occupy shallow waters during most of the year, but in warm regions retreat to deeper, cooler levels during summer. Temperature range for good growth is 10–23°C, optimally 19–21°C. Prime

growth occurs in clear mesotrophic and eutrophic waters where vegetative cover is abundant and boundary areas between vegetation and open water are extensive (Casselman 1978). Although usually sedentary, pike may travel considerable distances, particularly on spawning runs.

The pike is primarily a freshwater fish but tolerates salinities of 10‰ in the Baltic Sea and can reproduce in water of 7‰; 18‰ is lethal. It survives at extremely low dissolved oxygen concentrations, below 1 mg/liter (Casselman 1978). Self-sustaining populations can exist at pH as low as 5.0 (Inskip 1982); pH up to 9.5 has been tolerated (Scott and Crossman 1973).

DISTRIBUTION   Map 30

The northern pike has by far the broadest geographic distribution of the esocids, ranging from Arctic to north-temperate areas across Eurasia and North America. In North America it is probably indigenous as far south as northern West Virginia and central Missouri. The southern limit, as well as reduced success locally in some more northerly areas, may be related to a combination of warm temperature and virtually anoxic conditions in summer and winter (Casselman 1978; Inskip 1982). The range has been extended considerably through introductions (Carlander 1969; Crossman 1978), indicated partly on Map 30.

Esox lucius has been sparingly introduced in Virginia. About 100 "pike" were stocked in 1894 from an Illinois hatchery into the Jackson River, upper James drainage (USFC 1896a). All plotted records are from impoundments stocked by the VDGIF, except for an apparent hatchery escapee caught in the South Fork Holston River in 1987 (P. L. Angermeier, in litt.). The VGDIF stockings began in 1963 with fish obtained from the Pennsylvania Fish Commission (Gillam 1965). Mattaponi River stockings in 1965 and 1968 were unsuccessful. Northern pike are now spawned and reared in VDGIF hatcheries.

Abundance.—Usually rare or uncommon; considerably dependent on stocking density.

REMARKS

Wolf of its waters, the ecological role and value of the northern pike are sometimes controversial. It has been considered a nuisance that destroys allegedly more highly valued fish species. Conversely it has been regarded an important natural controller of forage fish. Pike were stocked in Martinsville Reservoir to reduce overpopulation by crappies, and grew to

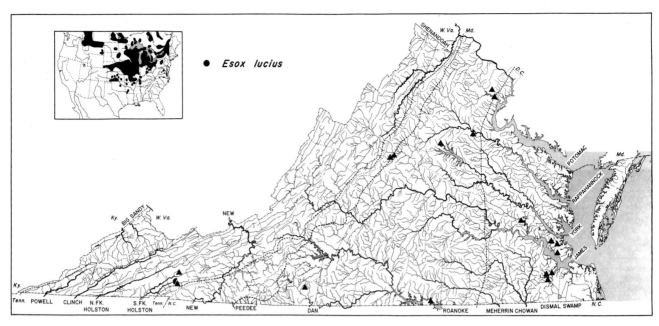

Map 30 Northern pike.

produce a former state record. Hungry Mother Lake in the upper Middle Fork Holston system has produced some of the largest northern pike in Virginia. To most anglers, the northern pike is a valued gamefish. Although lacking the greater glamour of the often larger muskellunge, the pike grows to trophy size, provides an enjoyable search, good fight, and a tasty meal of sweet, flaky white meat.

Name.—Lucius, Latin for "pike."

Muskellunge   *Esox masquinongy* Mitchill

SYSTEMATICS

Esox masquinongy was named in 1824 from Lake Erie in a magazine (Jordan and Evermann 1896; Crossman *in* Lee et al. 1980). Existence of three color patterns in the muskellunge led at times to recognition of three species, each characteristic of a different region: *E. masquinongy*, the spotted form of the Great Lakes–St. Lawrence basin; *E. ohioensis*, the barred form of the Ohio River basin; and *E. immaculatus*, a patternless or barred form, in northwestern Ontario, Wisconsin, and westward. At other times the color morphs were downgraded to subspecies or strains of *E. masquinongy*. Subspecies currently are not recognized because each color pattern is represented in different frequency in all major parts of the species' range; about as much variability exists within population groups as between; and color pattern seems to be influenced by environmental factors. Biologically important racial differences may exist, but introductions and natural and artificial hybridization confound understanding (Crossman 1978).

DESCRIPTION

*Materials.—*Based on Scott and Crossman (1973), Becker (1983), Casselman et al. (1986), 3 Virginia hatchery fish, and

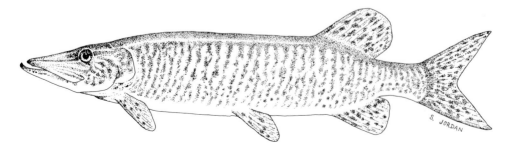

Fish 23 *Esox masquinongy* based on an adult from the Buller Fish Hatchery and an adult photographed under water in the Cowpasture River, Virginia.

1 from the Clinch River, Tennessee. Life color from Scott and Crossman (1973).

Anatomy.—An esocid with body pattern of dark bars, spots, or both on a pale background, median fins spotted or streaked, and cheek and opercle about half scaled; adults are 700–1,300 mm TL. Body and parts basically as described under *Family*. Body averages slightly deeper and caudal fin tips are more pointed than in northern pike.

Meristics.—Lateral line complete, scales (130)145–155(176); principal dorsal rays 15–19; principal anal rays 14–16; pelvic rays 11–12; pectoral rays 14–19; branchiostegal rays 16–20; mandibular pores (5)6–9(10).

Color in Preservative.—Pattern variable, basically vertically elongate, dark markings on paler ground. In three immature specimens (174–258 mm TL), head and body dorsum dusky with dark saddles and large spots; saddles continued ventrally as long and short bars, broken bars, or vertically aligned spots over dusky to pale background; venter pale. Head pale or slightly dusky laterally; preocular bar black, narrow; post- and subocular bars diffuse or absent. Median fins pale with dark spots, streaks, or both; paired fins pale. On immature fish the vertically oriented lateral body markings are widely spaced; on adults, bars and spots are more numerous, the pale interspaces reduced to less than width of dark marks.

Color in Life Plate 10.—In adult, head, back, and upper side iridescent green-gold to light brown; flank green-gold, green, brownish, gray, or silver; dark markings black, dark brown, vague, or particularly in mostly silvery fish, absent; venter cream or white; side of head pale. Fins greenish, buff, or red-brown with dark markings; fins often red from hemorrhaging during capture.

Larvae.—Described by Galat (1973), Buynak and Mohr (1979d), and Fuiman (1982b).

BIOLOGY

The voracious feeding habits of the muskellunge have earned it distinctions such as "barracuda" of fresh water (Miller and Buss 1962). Fry initially feed on microcrustaceans and insect larvae; at 4–5 weeks they switch to a diet of small fish. The adult diet is almost entirely fishes whose frequency of capture generally is directly related to availability; perch, sunfishes, catfishes, suckers, large minnows, shads, and mooneyes are commonly taken. The opportunistic muskellunge also takes a variety of other items: shrews, muskrats, grebes, ducks, salamanders, and crayfishes. There appears to be a strong predator–prey size relationship. If food of an appropriate size range is unavailable, growth and survival are jeopardized despite the abundance of smaller prey fish (Oehmcke et al. 1958; Buss 1960; Scott and Crossman

1973; Becker 1983). Additional details on the biology of the muskellunge are presented by Crossman and Goodchild (1978) and in the proceedings of a muskellunge symposium (Hall 1986).

Sexual maturity is reached in 3–5 years, usually in 3 years for males and 3–4 for females in Tennessee streams (Parsons 1959), normally 3–4 years for males and 4 years for females of Kentucky rivers (Brewer 1980, in litt.), and 3–4 years for males, 4–5 for females in West Virginia streams (Miles 1978). Females tend to outlive males. A muskellunge from Wisconsin lived more than 30 years (Oehmcke et al. 1958), but fish of age 15 are considered old. Maximum ages reported from Smith Mountain and Claytor lakes were 9 and 8 years (Hart 1978; McHugh and Steinkoenig 1980); an 18.7-kg Smith Mountain specimen was 12 years old (D. K. Whitehurst, personal communication). Although a nearly age-13 specimen was taken in Kentucky (Brewer 1980), the oldest found in other studies there (e.g., Axon 1978, 1981) and in West Virginia, North Carolina, and Tennessee were 6–8 years old.

Muskellunge are among the fastest growing and largest freshwater fishes. They typically attain 200–350 mm TL in the first year of life. Females normally exceed males in growth, particularly after 5 or 6 years. From broad geographic surveys, means of lengths at age 4 were 546–909 mm TL, and at age 8, 635–1,105 mm (Carlander 1969; Harrison and Hadley 1979; Monaghan 1985). Growth in stream populations of West Virginia, Kentucky, North Carolina, and Tennessee is within that range; age-4 fish were 605–747 mm TL (Parsons 1959; Miles 1978; Brewer 1980; Kornman 1983, 1985; Jones and Stephens 1984; Monaghan 1985; Prather 1985). Growth rate was exceptional in Smith Mountain Lake 4–14 years after impoundment; muskellunge averaged 902 mm TL at age 4 and 1,148 mm at age 8 (Hart 1978). Lake Burke fish were 864 mm at age 4 (McHugh and Steinkoenig 1980).

In some areas, growth of younger muskellunge (ages 1–3) tends to be faster in rivers than in lakes; the opposite is true for older fish (ages 7–9), perhaps because of a less abundant large-fish forage base in rivers (Harrison and Hadley 1979). However, other constraints may influence the between-habitat growth difference in North Carolina (Monaghan 1985). Carlander (1969) noted that growth often is faster in muskellunge introduced recently to streams and lakes than in established populations. Axon (1978, 1981) found accelerated growth in a newly created and stocked Kentucky reservoir.

The largest muskellunge caught in Virginia was 20.4 kg (45 pounds). The all-time angling record is 31.7 kg (69 pounds 15 ounces) from the St. Lawrence

River. Larger individuals obviously have existed, and probably do so today. However, those reported to be 45 kg (100 pounds) and slightly larger were either unauthenticated or hoaxes (Oehmcke et al. 1958; Scott and Crossman 1973).

In northern areas *E. masquinongy* spawns slightly later than northern pike, usually mid-April to late May or mid-June (Oehmcke et al. 1958; Buss 1960; Scott and Crossman 1973). Time of spawning is correlated with water temperature; temperature decrements and high water levels may interrupt spawning and reduce reproductive success. Water temperature of 12.8°C is optimal but spawning occurs at 9.5–15.5°C. Males usually precede females to spawning grounds.

Environmental conditions for spawning are similar in southern populations. In Tennessee, upstream prespawning movements begin during late March, and spawning occurs in April with water near 10°C (Parsons 1959). In Kentucky, spawning movements begin in late March when water warms to 10°C, and sometimes extend into the lower section of tributaries. Spawning normally takes place during mid-April to early May at 12.8–17.2°C (Brewer 1980). In a West Virginia river, spawning is not preceded by interpool movement, perhaps because suitable habitat is present in home pools. Spawning begins in early or mid-April, just after water averages 10°C or higher for 4–8 consecutive days; spawning appears to extend 2–3 weeks (Miles 1978).

Spawning occurs in shallows of streams and at least in northern areas, in lakes, usually over detrital accumulations or living vegetation. In northern regions, stream muskellunge spawn in slack pools and backwaters; in Kentucky and West Virginia they seem to favor areas near riffles (Brewer 1969; Miles 1978). Spawning occurs during day and night; behavior is similar to that of northern pike (Oehmcke et al. 1958; Scott and Crossman 1973; Brewer 1969; Minor and Crossman 1978). Fecundity is 10,000–250,000 ova (Fuiman 1982b).

Adult muskellunge normally are solitary and sedentary; they establish a home range in summer and winter. In Ontario, breakdown of home range during spring coincides with the onset of the spawning period. Wandering during fall occurs at water temperatures similar to those at spawning (Crossman 1977; Minor and Crossman 1978). Slight or no movement was typical in a West Virginia river, but some fish moved major distances (Miles 1978).

Esox masquinongy hybridizes in the wild with the northern pike, and that valuable cross (tiger muskellunge) is widely produced artificially.

HABITAT

The muskellunge is found in lakes, reservoirs, and slow-moving parts of rivers; it prefers cover of vegetation and structure such as brushpiles, logs, bars, and rock outcroppings. It may be more of a river species than a lake species (Crossman 1978). In the Niagara River, muskellunge use lotic areas whereas northern pike prefer more lacustrine habitats (Harrison and Hadley 1978). Streams occupied in Tennessee, North Carolina, Kentucky, and West Virginia are in rolling to montane areas and range from moderate-size (25 m in width) to large rivers. These streams have frequent deep, long pools (some of 1–2 km or more in length), have generally gravelly and rocky bottoms, are slightly acidic to slightly alkaline, and are of usually low to moderate inherent fertility (Parsons 1959; Riddle 1975; Miles 1978; Brewer 1980; Monaghan 1985).

Clear waters with temperatures of 17–25°C are optimal; water of 32°C and low oxygen content is stressfully tolerated, but feeding is reduced at about 29°C (Scott and Crossman 1973; Becker 1983). In the Barren River of Kentucky, muskellunge were found in areas of relatively deep pools influenced by spring inflow (Hoyt and Kruskamp 1982). Most muskellunge live in depths of 5 m or less, but very large ones are frequently found at greater depths.

Habitats in the primary muskellunge rivers of Virginia—the Clinch, New, and upper James—are similar to those in bordering states. The Virginia rivers are medium to large. Virginia reservoirs stocked with muskellunge vary widely in size and morphometry, and are scattered from the outer Coastal Plain to the mountains.

DISTRIBUTION   Map 31

The native range of *E. masquinongy* extends from the St. Lawrence and Hudson River valleys west through much of the Great Lakes to the upper Hudson Bay basin; it encompasses the upper Mississippi basin mostly east of that river, and includes the Ohio basin (Crossman 1978). Historical records are lacking for large segments within the range, notably almost all of Illinois and Indiana and much of Ohio. The gaps, the presence of a relict population in Iowa, fossils from Kansas and Oklahoma, and identification of a muskellunge-like fossil from Oregon (Cavender et al. 1970) indicate prehistorical fluctuation and recent constriction of its range. Because all Virginia records stem from recent stockings (*Remarks*), we are left to ponder the distributional status of the muskellunge in the state during earlier historical time.

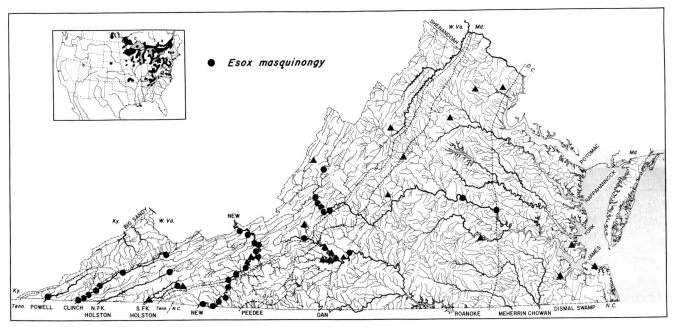

Map 31 Muskellunge. Introductions (some unsuccessful) outside native range only partly shown; see Crossman (1978).

The quest for native muskellunge in Virginia pertains only to the Ohio basin—the New, Big Sandy, and Tennessee drainages—because all Atlantic slope populations south of the Hudson River are introduced. From a New River sojourn in 1867, Cope (1868b) stated that *Esox* was unknown to fishermen; the VFC reports beginning in 1876 noted none in the drainage. There is no record of indigenous *E. masquinongy* in the three-state area drained by the Big Sandy River, nor are we aware of establishment of the species by stocking there.

Native muskellunge are localized in the extensive Tennessee drainage; the historical distribution evidently excludes Virginia. The best-documented native Tennessee drainage population occupies the Emory River watershed of the lower Clinch system, Tennessee (Parsons 1959). The Emory drains montane Appalachian (Cumberland) Plateau terrain that is similar to terrain in adjacent areas of Tennessee and Kentucky, in the Cumberland drainage and just north where native muskellunge also persist (Kuhne 1939; Brewer 1969; Riddle 1975). Similar riverine habitat exists in the Blue Ridge Province of the Tennessee drainage, but the muskellunge waned by a century ago from that portion in North Carolina (Menhinick et al. 1974; Monaghan 1985) and Tennessee. Muskellunge may not have been indigenous historically to the Georgia section of the Blue Ridge (Dahlberg and Scott 1971a, 1971b) nor to Alabama.

Native Tennessee drainage populations occupy (or occupied) hard-bottomed streams and rivers, some of

which are smaller and rockier than the typical northern habitat of well-vegetated, soft-bottomed, meandering flowages. The species had to surmount a gradient barrier (Gilbert 1980) to enter the North Carolina portion of the drainage. If the muskellunge was not a Cumberlandian resident prior to the Pleistocene, then glacial ice sheets would have forced it into the central Appalachians. Obviously it adapted, but not to a wide range of conditions.

The Virginia part of the Tennessee drainage offers a diversity of conditions similar to those of native muskellunge streams in adjacent states—cool, somewhat soft water and moderate gradient in the South Fork Holston River, and warm, hard water with lower gradient elsewhere in the Holston, Clinch, and Powell rivers. However, no muskellunge were reported here early (e.g., Cope's [1868b] interviews of rivermen in the Holston). Jim Cox, an astute watcher of the Clinch and whose ancestors were early settlers in the valley, knew of none indigenous to that river. This seems paradoxical because the rivers lacked pollution and appreciable siltation in early times. The rivers must have been in better condition than that prevalent today in most streams of adjacent states that still sustain native muskellunge.

It is difficult to hypothesize an early presence of muskellunge in Virginia based on current conditions. Some of the western Virginia rivers are suitable for survival of muskellunge today; some support growth to adulthood of stocked yearlings, but it is unknown whether stocked muskellunge are reproducing to an appreciable extent in Virginia.

We believe that long-past extirpations and only local establishment today within large watersheds are evidence that the southern Ohio basin muskellunge leads a precarious existence. Numerous "native" Cumberlandian populations exist probably because they are strongly supplemented by stocking. Perhaps the more important question is not whether the muskellunge occurred indigenously in Virginia, but why native populations survived in adjacent areas.

Muskellunge introductions began in the Virginia section of the New drainage in 1963 and have continued each year to the present (tiger musky in some plantings [Hart 1981]). North Carolina and West Virginia agencies added muskellunge to those ends of the drainage. The muskellunge was placed in the Virginia portion of the Clinch River shortly after the fish kill of 1967 (Wollitz 1972), in the other upper major branches of the Tennessee drainage about that year, and in all of these rivers in various years after. The upper South Fork Holston record is of a hatchery escapee. Dissemination of muskellunge east of the New River began in 1963—in Smith Mountain Lake as it filled. Stocking has been regular in some central and eastern Virginia rivers and reservoirs, sporadic in others (some not indicated on Map 31). Pools of the lower Cowpasture River were occupied by immigrants from James River stockings. Specimens were caught recently in the South Fork Shenandoah River, but the section is unknown to us.

Hatchery muskellunge initially were imported to Virginia from New York, Pennsylvania, West Virginia, and Tennessee (VDGIF records). The Tennessee muskellunge program began about 1960 with eggs obtained from northern states (Branham 1972). Brood stock in the other three states came largely or entirely from the Ohio basin (Buss and Miller 1967; Meseroll 1974). Since 1964, the VDGIF has maintained brood stock.

Abundance.—Generally rare, determined to a large degree by stocking density, but many factors including a suitable forage base and predation on stocked fish, are of great importance. Perhaps exceptional, Burkhead saw four large adults while diving in a Cowpasture River pool of 0.3 km length. In Kentucky rivers, legal-size muskellunge occurred on an average of one per every 4.9 to 5.7 hectares of pool habitat (Brewer 1980). However, a 2.6-km long, 6.2-hectare pool in West Virginia contained at least 15 legal-length and 12 sublegal individuals (Miles 1978).

REMARKS

Muskellunge are often said, particularly by their specialist seekers, to provide the ultimate challenge in freshwater fishing. These aquatic recluses are as evasive and stubborn as any mountain hermit and may require 100–300 hours of hunting and casting for reward. Becker (1983) noted that the average muskellunge fisher is far less successful than the average deer hunter. Some have long sought but never caught one. The unpredictability of the species is underscored by its occasional hooking by bass and panfish anglers, leading to pandemonium. Good muskellunge fishing often happens in the worst weather.

The thrill is in the fight, for when one is hooked, although often not landed, the angler has many hours of fish stories to tell. The catch frequently is a trophy; this largest esocid typically has greater girth and thus weight than northern pike of equal length. Testimony to the voracity and size of the quarry are the very large lures and baitfish, sometimes 300 mm (12 inches) long, used to engage muskellunge.

Virginia is fortunate to have had since 1963 an active program by the VDGIF of hatchery rearing and stocking of muskellunge in many rivers and reservoirs, on a put-and-grow basis. The success of stocking is dependent on many habitat characteristics and upon the forage population. Angler exploitation rates often are high in heavily fished waters. Thus many dedicated muskellunge hunters advocate release of all but the occasional true trophy, an appropriate practice due to the growing number of anglers. In 1985, 146 citation muskellunge (at least 4.5 kg, 10 pounds) were registered in Virginia.

Hope exists that populations sustained by natural reproduction will develop in Virginia. Self-sustainment, or any breeding success at all, may not be expected in southern reservoirs, but reservoir fish may use suitable tributaries for breeding. An exceptional spawning happened during 1977 in Claytor Lake or a tributary, coincidental with a spring flood that submerged areas of terrestrial grasses and shrubs (Hart 1981). More-frequent spawning is suspected to occur in the New and James rivers (D. K. Whitehurst, personal communication). However, annual releases of young hatchery fish cloud the detection of natural reproduction.

Since at least 1973, the tiger muskellunge—the muskellunge × northern pike hybrid—has been stocked (in some cases along with nonhybrid muskellunge) in several Virginia rivers and reservoirs. The comparative worth of the hybrid has been controversial, but tiger muskies usually are considered to be more sporting than the northern pike. Tiger muskies up to about 6.8 kg (15 pounds) have been caught in the Powell River.

Determination of the success of tiger muskellunge must be based on correctly identified specimens. The tiger musky is well-named; the color pattern is similar to that of barred muskellunge, but the dark bars are accentuated, the interspaces being wide and pale. The cheek is fully scaled or almost so, as in the pike (Crossman and Buss 1965; Buss and Miller 1967; Buss et al. 1978).

The tiger muskellunge is more easily cultured, has fewer disease problems, and eats commercial dry feed better than muskellunge. It was proclaimed "made to order" for successful intensive culture (Graff 1978). First-generation hybrids have excellent growth in hatcheries; consequently, larger fish may be stocked with a generally better chance of survival. They often seem to feed more actively than muskellunge, hence they may provide a greater angling return. The hybrid produced by using female muskellunge is generally considered to be sterile, but the reciprocal cross sometimes results in progeny capable of reproduction (Crossman and Buss 1965; Buss and Miller 1967; Buss et al. 1978). The tiger musky is readily accepted as a valued trophy by a growing segment of anglers in Pennsylvania (Hesser 1978). However, not all hybrid-stocking programs have been considered successful, and some states have discontinued it (D. L. Brewer, in litt.). The possibility of establishing naturally reproducing, pure muskellunge should be an impetus for continued stocking of purebreds in certain Virginia waters.

Any fan of the muskellunge will enjoy reading *The Noble Muskellunge: A Review*, by Ed Crossman (1986), who is the long-time chief scientist of the species. The article treats the scientific and angling history, and prognosis, of the muskellunge.

Name.—*Masquinongy* is variously given as from an Indian dialect through French phonetic spelling. The two most quoted derivations are mashk—deformed, and kinonge—a pike; and mas—large, kenosha—a pike (Scott and Crossman 1973). More than 50 common names or variations in spellings have been applied (Crossman 1986).

Chain pickerel   *Esox niger* Lesueur

SYSTEMATICS

Esox niger was described in 1818 from a fish obtained at a Philadelphia market. Geographic variation has been suggested to occur between northern and southern regions (Weed 1927), and among coastal and Mississippi Valley populations (Hubbs and Lagler 1958).

DESCRIPTION

Materials.—Based on Scott and Crossman (1973), Casselman et al. (1986), and 24 Virginia series. Life color from 2 samples of small Virginia adults.

Anatomy.—A chain-patterned, pale-finned, long-snouted, slender esocid with cheek and opercle fully

Fish 24 *Esox niger* young 47 mm SL (WHH 154), VA, Sussex County, Spring Creek, 26 July 1983.

Fish 25 *Esox niger* juvenile 84 mm SL (REJ 1023), VA, Amelia County, Namozine Creek, 31 August 1983.

Fish 26 *Esox niger* adult female 216 mm SL (REJ 1084), VA, Craig County, Craig Creek, 17 May 1984.

scaled; adults are 350–500 mm TL. Other characteristics are those of the family.

Meristics.—Lateral line complete, scales 114–131; principal dorsal rays 14–15; principal anal rays 11–13; pelvic rays 9–10; pectoral rays 12–15; branchiostegal rays (14)15(17); mandibular pores 4(5) per side.

Color in Preservative.—Dorsum dark; upper side often with irregular bars on dusky to pale ground; dark markings present on most of side in some fish, on all of side in others, forming a chainlike reticulate pattern over pale ground; venter pale. Pre- and subocular bars well developed; subocular bar vertical or slanted slightly anteroventrad; postocular streak usually vague or absent. Dorsal fin rays dusky or dark, membranes pale; caudal fin dusky, body pattern extending diffusely onto base; lower fins colorless. Pattern development from young to adult indicated in photographs; see also *Comparison.*

Color in Life Plate 10.—Head and body dorsum light green to brownish green; chainlike markings on side grayish green to olive; lateral pale areas mostly creamy; side often with silver and green iridescence; venter white. Ocular bars black; iris olive, inner ring gold. Dorsal and caudal fin rays olive, membranes pale; lower fins colorless. Unpatterned juveniles, dark in preservative but steel-blue in life, were taken once in a Nottoway system survey (M. D. Norman, personal communication). A mutant chain pickerel, dominantly bluish and lacking the chain pattern, was found in a New York lake (Menzel and Green 1972).

Larvae.—Described by Mansueti and Hardy (1967), Scott and Crossman (1973), Lippson and Moran (1974), Wang and Kernehan (1979), and Martin (1984b).

COMPARISON

In checking records of pickerels we encountered many misidentifications; generally, chain pickerel were called redfin pickerel *E. a. americanus.* Problems stemmed largely from not noting fin color in life and an unawareness of changes in shape and color pattern with growth. Hybridization causes problems of identification in southeastern Virginia.

In addition to the photographs, and to amplify on some characters in the *Key,* we offer: (1) fin color [not

red in *niger* vs. slightly or largely red in *americanus;* young of 20–60 mm length with red only at fin bases (Crossman 1962a)]; (2) subocular bar [vertical or, sometimes in young, slanted anteroventrad vs. oblique, slanted posteroventrad]; (3) side pattern of adult [chainlike, often with narrow, widely separated dark bars on upper side vs. entirely barred, dark bars usually wider than interspaces]; (4) principal dorsal rays [14–15 vs. 15–18].

Interspecific differences in ontogenetic development of the color patterns (Crossman 1962a, 1966) are inconsistent in Virginia fish. Often the side of large young and small juvenile redfin pickerel is distinctly barred, blotched, or both, resembling small chain pickerel. Some of the atypical fish may be hybrids.

BIOLOGY

Chain pickerel are highly predaceous and commence a piscivorous habit while quite small. Fish remains were found in about 16% of stomachs of 24 to 50-mm specimens from Georgia; small crustaceans and insects were the major dietary constituent. Frequency of fishes in the diet of *E. niger* larger than 50 mm TL increased to as much as 75%, complemented by crustaceans, insects, and incidental items. Nongamefish prey were more frequent in specimens less than 150 mm; gamefishes were found increasingly in larger specimens (Germann and Swanson 1978). Fishes composed at least 34% of the diet in Tuckahoe Creek, Virginia (Flemer and Woolcott 1966). One study identified 37 fish species taken, mainly minnows, sunfishes, and catfishes, but also redfin and chain pickerel. Frogs, snakes, and mice are also eaten (Scott and Crossman 1973). Prey size is directly proportional to predator size. Chain pickerel are active feeders in winter. The bibliography by Crossman and Lewis (1973) provides other dietary studies and extensive further information on this species.

Maturity may occur at 1–4 years of life and tends to occur earliest in the south; slow-growing fish mature at smaller sizes than do fast-growing ones. Typical life span is 3–4 years, maximally 9 years (Wich and Mullan 1958; Guillory 1979). Growth is highly variable and any regional trend is masked by fertility and other local habitat conditions. Age-4 fish from Maryland and north were 297–673 mm TL; means from Maryland, New Jersey, and Massachusetts were 594, 461, and 368 mm (Carlander 1969). The age-4 mean from Kerr Reservoir, Virginia, was about 530 mm TL (Smith and Kauffman 1982). Large pickerel are 500–750 mm TL (about 20–30 inches). The Virginia record is 3.5 kg (7.75 pounds). The largest known chain pickerel, a "lost" record, was taken in New Jersey in 1904 or 1905; it was 5.6 kg (12.25 pounds) and 991 mm (39 inches) (Smith 1953).

Chain pickerel are coldwater spawners, doing so in the north shortly after ice-out, within March to May. In Delaware, spawning was thought to occur in February and March. In Florida it took place from December through February. Spawning may last only 7–10 days in any one body of water at 2–22°C; peak spawning occurs in the middle of that range and temperatures tend to be highest in the south (Scott and Crossman 1973; Guillory 1979, 1984; Wang and Kernehan 1979). Reproductive activity occurs in lake and calm stream shallows at depths to 3 m, usually among submerged vegetation. A female and one or two males swim together for a day or two, periodically rolling inward, bringing their vents close together. Eggs and milt are shed simultaneously, and mixed and dispersed by purposeful undulations of the tail (Kendall 1917; Scott and Crossman 1973). The number of ripe eggs produced is 342–8,140 (Scott and Crossman 1973; Guillory 1979, 1984).

Esox niger hybridizes in nature with *E. lucius* and *E. americanus*; fertile offspring are produced with the latter (Raney 1957a; Crossman and Buss 1965). The number of apparent F_1 hybrids and backcrosses of chain and redfin pickerels (E. J. Crossman, in litt.) indicates that interbreeding of these species occurs relatively frequently in the Chowan and lower Roanoke drainages.

HABITAT

Chain pickerel are solitary fish found typically in clear, cool and warm, sluggish creeks, rivers, ditches, natural and artificial ponds, and lakes that are well vegetated. They generally are found in depths less than 3 m. Juveniles prefer shallows; adults tend to occupy deeper water during the day, moving into shallows at night. All ages associate with plants and logs (Scott and Crossman 1973; Guillory 1979). *Esox niger* occurs in somewhat alkaline to very acidic waters, to pH 3.8–4.0 (Scott and Crossman 1973; Hast-ings 1984). Chain pickerel sometimes move into brackish water (15‰ salinity) in winter (Scott and Crossman 1973). Several authors cite Schwartz (1964) on this species being common in salinity to 22‰, but it is improbable that the species is common at that value; most brackish water reports are of 5‰ or less. There are few estuarine records from Virginia.

The populations in montane portions of the Roanoke and James drainages occupy sparsely to abundantly vegetated pools and backwaters of small creeks to large streams. Many of the pools in the larger streams are pondlike, being lengthy and margined with lily pads.

DISTRIBUTION   Map 32

Esox niger is native to the Atlantic slope from New England to Florida, the Gulf slope, and the lower central Mississippi Valley. It dispersed through canals or was stocked in some other areas (Crossman 1978). In the Virginia Coastal Plain, *E. niger* is generally distributed in the southeastern part, but apparently occurs somewhat sparsely, although more widely than *E. americanus*, north of the Chowan drainage. It is also more diffused than *E. americanus* in most of the lower and middle Piedmont, but is largely replaced by the latter in the Potomac drainage Piedmont.

We believe the riverine populations of the montane Roanoke and James drainages to be native. The occurrence of chain pickerel in the upper James is paralleled by that of the typically lowland chubsucker *Erimyzon oblongus*, an unlikely transplant. Further, Cope (1868b) noted that "Species of this genus [*Esox*] occur in the head-waters of the Roanoke and James." The upper James population is widespread; the Roanoke population is somewhat localized, being generally distributed only in Mason (Jenkins and Freeman 1972) and Bradshaw creeks. The two reservoir records in the upper Roanoke and James likely represent dam-trapped populations. The Fairystone Reservoir, Smith River system, record is based on an angler's catch in 1984 and probably represents an introduction.

Esox niger is not native to the New River drainage. Cope (1868b) and early VFC reports stated that it was unknown to fishers. There is no basis for the statement (Ross 1959c) that it has a general distribution there. It was introduced to the West Virginia portion (F. J. Schwartz, personal communication in 1970).

Abundance.—Generally uncommon or common.

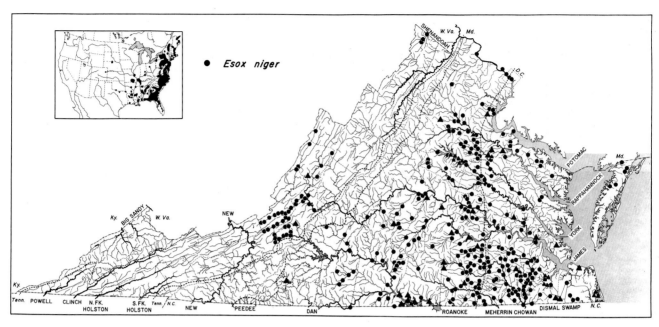

Map 32 Chain pickerel.

REMARKS

The voracious chain pickerel, disguised by color and stillness but ever ready to strike prey or lure, is the esocid or "duckbill" most frequently hooked in Virginia. It often lures anglers to unheralded but productive and picturesque waters. Small adults are scrappy on a light rod. Large ones are worthy of sustained search and provide experience for graduation to the larger pike and muskellunge. Chain pickerel are not to be ignored at a fish feast.

Name.—*Niger*, "dark" or "black," refers to juvenile coloration.

Redfin pickerel   *Esox americanus* Gmelin

SYSTEMATICS

The redfin pickerel was named as a species from New York in 1788. It is one of few North American fish subspecies with a formally recognized common name. The other subspecies of the collective "little pickerel" is the grass pickerel *E. a. vermiculatus* Lesueur. The redfin pickerel occupies the Atlantic slope, the grass pickerel largely the central Mississippi Valley and southern Great Lakes basin. The two forms were long thought to be separate species, but were found to intergrade on the Gulf slope (Crossman 1966).

DESCRIPTION

Materials.—Data on *E. a. americanus* from Crossman (1962a, 1966), Scott and Crossman (1973), Casselman et al. (1986), and 20 Virginia series. Life color from adults in 2 Chowan series.

Anatomy.—A relatively deep-bodied esocid with unspotted red fins, barred body, short snout, and cheek and opercle fully scaled; adults are 150–200 mm TL. Other characteristics are those of the family.

Meristics.—Lateral line complete, scales 94–117; principal dorsal rays 15–18; principal anal rays 13–17; pelvic rays (8)9–10; pectoral rays (13)14–15(17); branchiostegal rays (11)12–14(16); mandibular pores (3)4(5).

Color in Preservative.—Dorsum of adult uniformly dark or slightly variegated; side irregularly patterned with 20–36 straight or curved dark bars that are complete, interrupted, or branched; anterior bars often crossed by irregular pale midside stripe; venter mottled or pale. Pre-, post-, and subocular bars dark or black; subocular bar slanted posteriad; lower jaw and isthmus variably pigmented; lower jaw usually with dark bars or patches in female, diffusely pigmented in male. Dorsal fin moderately pigmented along rays, membranes dusky; caudal fin dusky or pale; lower

Fish 27 *Esox americanus* young 41 mm SL (REJ 1001), VA, Charlotte County, Little Roanoke Creek, 12 July 1983.

Fish 28 *Esox americanus* juvenile 90 mm SL (REJ 1034), VA, Charlotte County, Middle Branch Wards Fork Creek, 2 September 1983.

Fish 29 *Esox americanus* adult female 140 mm SL (REJ 1116), VA, Charlotte County, Twittys Creek, 10 July 1984.

fins slightly pigmented or colorless along rays; anal fin duskiest near base. Pattern development from young to adult indicated in photographs.

Color in Life   Plate 10.—Back and side ground shade brown to olive-black; pale predorsal stripe sometimes present; lateral bars brown to olive-black, separated by gold to white extensions of white venter. Ocular bars black; iris partly gold or brassy. Fins slightly or strongly orange-red or red, least so in dorsal and caudal, where red may be restricted to anterior ray(s), or dorsal may lack red; most or all rays of lower fins with red.

Larvae.—Described by Crossman (1962a), Mansueti and Hardy (1967), Lippson and Moran (1974), Wang and Kernehan (1979), and Fuiman (1982b).

COMPARISON

See *E. niger* account.

BIOLOGY

Young *E. americanus* feed mostly on small crustaceans and aquatic insects; at about 50 mm, fishes are added to the diet. Predominant food items of adults are crayfishes and fishes, supplemented with smaller crustaceans and insects. Centrarchids were the fishes most often eaten in North Carolina (Buss 1962; Crossman 1962a; Gatz 1979; Keast 1985).

Redfin pickerel apparently mature at ages 2 or 3 based on Crossman's (1962a) data. Maximum ages attained are 6 for redfin pickerel, 7 for grass pickerel (Carlander 1969). Females tend to live longer and grow faster and larger than males. Age-3 redfins in North Carolina were 140–205 mm FL, mean, 177 (Crossman 1962a). Our largest Virginia specimen is 201 mm FL, 212 mm TL (8.3 inches). A 483-mm TL redfin from New Jersey is suspected to have been a hybrid *E. americanus* × *E. niger* (Crossman 1966). Redfins or redfin–grass intergrades of 371 mm TL (14.6 inches) were reported from Florida by Swift et al. (1977).

Spawning occurs over a 2–4 week period in late winter or early spring at water temperatures of 4–10°C. Adults congregate in small groups in shallow, heavily vegetated areas such as flooded pond banks or stream margins to broadcast gametes

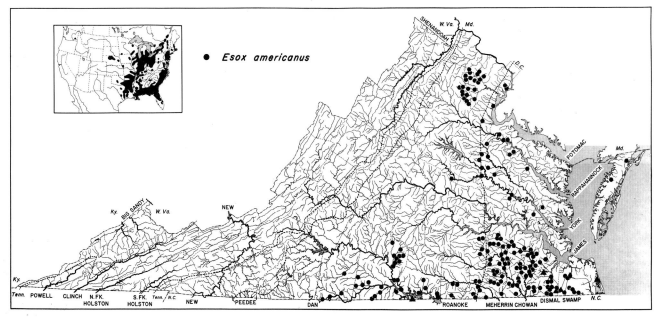

Map 33   Redfin pickerel.

(Crossman 1962a; Wang and Kernehan 1979). Primary eggs ranged 186–542 in redfin pickerel, a major difference from grass pickerel (Crossman 1962a). Natural hybridization has been documented for redfin pickerel with northern pike and chain pickerel. The redfin × chain pickerel cross in Virginia is noted under *E. niger*.

HABITAT

Redfin pickerel in Virginia typically occupy vegetated shallows of warm sloughs, drainage ditches, sluggish streams, and backwaters of faster streams. Relatively few Virginia records are from ponds and lakes. This subspecies thrives in darkly stained waters of low pH. It also does well in some reaches with sparse or no vegetation and unstained, neutral to slightly alkaline water, as in the middle Roanoke drainage. It can withstand periods of moderate turbidity but likely does best in clear water. It extends into tidal fresh water but only infrequently or rarely into brackish habitat (Crossman 1962a); Keup and Bayless (1964) reported it in 10.2‰ salinity.

DISTRIBUTION   Map 33

The total ranges of the two subspecies are given under *Systematics*; introductions elsewhere are noted by Crossman (1978). Over its range the redfin pickerel is basically a lowland species; it exhibits erratic divergences from that pattern in Virginia. It is gener-

ally distributed in much of the southeastern Coastal Plain of Virginia, extending only slightly above the Fall Line in the Chowan drainage. However, it is widely distributed in the lower and middle Piedmont of the Roanoke and Dan systems (and similarly in most drainages of North Carolina [Crossman *in* Lee et al. 1980; E. F. Menhinick, in litt.]). Conversely, it is known with certainty in the James drainage only from tributaries in the Dismal Swamp area (see below). This is puzzling as the lower James apparently has much suitable habitat. The redfin is sparsely distributed on the Coastal Plain from the York to the Potomac drainages; we confirmed the South Anna River Piedmont record. Oddly, redfin pickerel range widely in the Potomac drainage only in the upper Occoquan system. *Esox niger* is unknown in the Occoquan, a reversal of the frequent syntopy observed in much of their ranges.

We have rejected reports of *E. americanus* from the James drainage above the Dismal Swamp periphery. Cope (1868b) noted two *Esox* species in Tuckahoe Creek; this is believable from the partly swampy flowage of this tributary just above the Fall Line. However, Fowler (1945) studied Cope's material (*Esox* possibly not preserved) and admitted only *E. niger* to the James drainage fauna. Further, only *E. niger* is known from intensive survey of swampy Tuckahoe Creek (Flemer and Woolcott 1966). An estuarine report (White 1976) is based on *E. niger* (VEPCO specimen). The Johns Creek, upper James, record (Young and Maughan 1980) is virtually certain to have been founded on *E. niger*, which was not reported but is generally distributed there. The uppermost James record of *E. americanus* is from an adult from the Pagan River system in 1979 (VIMS 5543).

Abundance.—Often common.

REMARKS

The "little pickerels"—the redfin and grass pickerel subspecies—are seldom sought but often incidentally caught by anglers. They may have a significant role in the control of small-fish populations.

Name.—*Americanus*, for its homeland.

MUDMINNOWS
Family Umbridae

BY ROBERT E. JENKINS, RICHARD A. DIETZ, AND NOEL M. BURKHEAD

Mudminnows constitute a small family of freshwater, lowland, warm- to cold-adapted, Northern Hemisphere fishes. In past times the three living genera each have been recognized as separate families. *Dallia* is an Alaskan–Siberian genus of two species (Chereshnev and Balushkin 1980). *Novumbra* contains only the Olympic mudminnow *N. hubbsi* of Washington State. The remaining three species are in *Umbra*. The North American species of *Umbra* are the eastern mudminnow *U. pygmaea*, living mainly on the Atlantic slope and being the only mudminnow in Virginia, and the central mudminnnow *U. limi* of the Great Lakes and upper Mississippi basins. The European mudminnow *U. krameri* is found in eastern Europe.

Mudminnows are primitive teleosts and are most closely related to pikes; these two families form the suborder Esocoidei. Although the extinct umbrid genus *Palaeoesox* has been uncovered from deposits only as old as the Eocene (36–58 million years ago), at least one modern pike lineage had arisen by the Paleocene, indicating that the split between pikes and umbrids dates back to the Mesozoic, at least 66 million years ago (Cavender 1969; Nelson 1972).

Mudminnows and pikes share many anatomical features but are glaringly different in others and associated ways of life. Mudminnows are small fishes with a small mouth and small teeth; pikes are medium to large and slenderer, have a long snout, and the large mouth is formed of long jaws armed with large teeth. All of these fishes use cover extensively, but often for different reasons. Mudminnows (at least *Umbra*) hide by day and seek small invertebrates at night, whereas pikes are diurnal, lurking, dashing fish-eaters. Mudminnows display nuptial color and at least some are egg-guarders; the sexes of pikes look alike and their eggs are broadcast and left unattended.

Name.—Umbr-, "shade," in reference to association of these fishes with cover.

Mudminnows

The three similar species of this genus are noted above.

Genus *Umbra* Müller

Name.—See above.

Eastern mudminnow

Umbra pygmaea (DeKay)

SYSTEMATICS

Described in 1842 from New York State, *Umbra pygmaea* is most closely related to *U. limi* (e.g., Wilson and Veilleux 1982).

DESCRIPTION

Materials.—Thirteen Virginia series; counts from 14 specimens. Life color from 1 Virginia adult.

Anatomy.—A stout fish with a large, vertically elongate blotch on the caudal base, and the adult with horizontal dark and light stripes on the body; adults are 50–100 mm SL. Body somewhat elongate, broad anteriorly, deep and moderately compressed posteriorly; head moderate in length, broad; eye moderate, lateral; snout short, well rounded; mouth terminal, small; upper jaw nonprotrusile, teeth small. Scales large, cycloid; much of head scaled. Fins of moderate size, lacking spines; dorsal fin moderately posterior; caudal fin rounded; pelvic fin abdominal; pectoral fin low. Sexes similar.

Fish 30 *Umbra pygmaea* adult male 53 mm SL (HJP 64), VA, Nottoway County, Nottoway River, 19 July 1979.

Meristics.—Lateral line absent on body, lateral series scales 30–34; circumbody scales 30–36; circumpeduncle scales 19–24. Dorsal rays 13–15; branched caudal rays 9–12; total anal rays (last two elements as one) 9–10; branched anal rays 6–8; pelvic rays 6; pectoral rays 13–16.

Color in Preservative.—Dorsum dark; predorsal dark streak wide; side in young dusky to dark, uniformly so or vaguely blotched or striped; side in subadult and adult with 10–12 pale stripes alternating with dark stripes, midlateral pale stripe often widest; venter pale or dusky. Caudal base with large, vertically elongate blotch, the blotch often with a notch anteriorly that is produced by extension of midlateral pale stripe. Head dusky to dark, sometimes blotchy; postocular bar, sometimes preocular and subocular bars, present. Fins pale to dark, lower fins palest; fins lack marking pattern except caudal basally with dusky to black, slightly curved crescent produced primarily by localized darkness of most rays.

Color in Life Plate 10.—Darker areas dark olive to brown; pale areas of side cream, pale yellow, or tan; caudal marks black; green tints on head laterally; iris gold; rays of median fins olive-brown. In the spawning period males tend to be their darkest, females their palest, but these color changes vary greatly, especially during courtship (Breder and Rosen 1966).

Larvae.—Described by Mansueti and Hardy (1967), Lippson and Moran (1974), Jones et al. (1978), Wang and Kernehan (1979), and Martin (1984b).

BIOLOGY

In North Carolina and Virginia, *U. pygmaea* mainly selects midge larvae and isopod and amphipod crustaceans, and also takes ostracod crustaceans, small crayfishes, other insects and, rarely, fishes (Flemer and Woolcott 1966; Gatz 1979; G. B. Pardue and M. T. Huish, in litt.). The diet in New York, New Jersey, and Pennsylvania is much the same; it additionally includes protozoans, mosquito larvae, snails, and perhaps plant matter (Moore 1922). Moore inferred that *U. pygmaea* habitually feeds by night and conceals itself and fasts during the day.

Male *U. pygmaea* are thought to mature in 1.5 years, females in 2, but "average" sizes of the sexes at maturity, 34.8 mm TL and 37.3 mm, respectively (Jones et al. 1978), seem rather small. Scales and opercles of American *Umbra* are difficult to age. Length–frequencies of North Carolina *U. pygmaea* indicate three age-groups, 0–2 (G. B. Pardue and M. T. Huish, in litt.); most age-1 fish are 50–110 mm SL in September. Spawning females are somewhat larger than males (Breder and Rosen 1966). The largest of our few Virginia specimens is 73 mm SL, 91 mm TL. Some North Carolina fish reach the 140–149 mm TL-class (Pardue and Huish, in litt.); maximum length of about 152 mm was cited by Mansueti and Hardy (1967).

Umbra pygmaea spawns in late March and April at water temperatures of 10–15°C, in the upper Chesapeake and lower Delaware drainages (Mansueti and Hardy 1967; Wang and Kernehan 1979). Egg-laden nests were found in southern New York during 18 April–7 May (Breder and Rosen 1966). In northern North Carolina, eastern mudminnows were in reproductive condition in March and April in water of usually 12–15°C (Huish and Pardue 1978). Spawning areas are quite shallow, less than 10 cm, and perhaps typically are stream backwaters. Often the areas are reached by local movement or migration.

Males court females by flaunting spread fins; torn fins suggest intermale rivalry. Nest sites generally are reported to be cavities in algal masses (Breder and Rosen 1966; Mansueti and Hardy 1967; Wang and Kernehan 1979). Nests of one spawning association were between and under loose rocks. The spawning act was not observed but the adherence of single layers of eggs to the underside of rocks indicates an inclination or inversion for some spawnings (Breder and Rosen 1966). Other eggs were scattered, as were those in aquarium spawnings (Wang and Kernehan

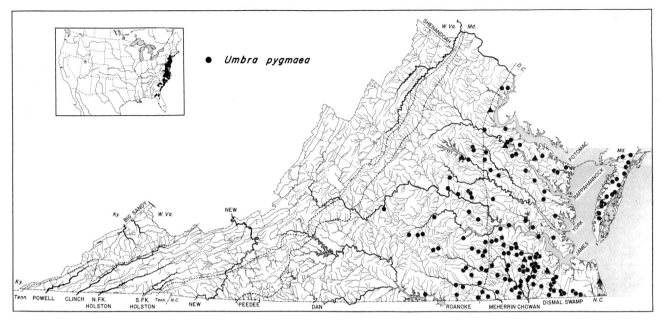

Map 34   Eastern mudminnow.

1979). Other spawning-site variations were described or cited by Breder and Rosen (1966), including the formation of depression nests in muddy or sandy bottom next to vegetative cover in still and slowly flowing areas. After spawning, both sexes frequent the nest and either may guard the eggs. Fecundity is 31–2,566 ova, mean, 342 (Jones et al. 1978).

HABITAT

The eastern mudminnow occupies varied lowland habitats including sluggish creeks to medium-sized streams, ditches, ponds, and lakes with bog, marsh, swamp, and open-water characteristics. Populations in moderate-gradient Piedmont streams are restricted to backwaters and pools. The common name refers to the typical substrate association; these fish often bury in mud and silt during the daylight period of inactivity. Profuse vegetation, bank nooks, stones, and sunken wood are also used for cover (Moore 1922). Assuredly shallows are occupied, at least for foraging, but mudminnow abundance in greater depths is not known.

Typical mudminnow waters in Virginia are clear or often somewhat turbid, slightly to darkly stained, and slightly alkaline to highly acidic. The pH at 36 capture sites in the Chowan drainage (Norman and Southwick 1985, in litt.) was 5.6–7.2 and was skewed toward the lower and middle portions of the range. *Umbra pygmaea* has been found in pH 4.0 in New Jersey (Hastings 1984). It inhabits North Carolina swamp streams with an annual pH range of 5.4–7.2 and dissolved oxygen concentration 0.6–10.0 mg/liter (Pardue et al. 1975). It occupies tidal fresh water in Virginia (Massmann 1957); apparently few records are from oligohaline zones. In Delaware, it is rare in oligohaline habitats (salinity less than 5‰) (Wang and Kernehan 1979). The highest natural salinity record is 12‰ in North Carolina (Schwartz 1981b). In a laboratory study *U. pygmaea* survived 10‰; 15‰ was lethal (Hoese 1963).

DISTRIBUTION   Map 34

Umbra pygmaea occupies the Atlantic slope from southern New York to northern Florida, just reaching the Gulf slope in Florida. It has been established in some European countries (Berra 1981). In Virginia it is found in all major and some minor Atlantic drainages, and is one of the most southerly extended of freshwater fishes on the Delmarva Peninsula, where it is generally distributed. This is chiefly a Coastal Plain fish, although it appears to be absent or rare in large areas thereof from the James drainage northward. It occurs on the lower Piedmont in the York drainage and south. The upper Piedmont record in the James is dated 1935.

Abundance.—We collected this mudminnow infrequently and in small numbers in the lower Piedmont and Coastal Plain of the James and Chowan drainages, the Chowan perhaps being its center of abundance in Virginia. Most other seined samples from Virginia are small. Although this species is among cover by day, Norman and Southwick (1985) generally obtained similar results using rotenone in the Chowan. Huish and Pardue (1978) considered *U. pygmaea* to be abundant in a swamp system of the Chowan and one in the Roanoke drainage, both in North Carolina.

REMARKS

The small eastern mudminnow is reclusive, foraging by night and hiding by day. Hence it may have relatively little value as a forage fish. It was not found to have been taken by 158 individuals of redfin pickerel (100 mm or more in length) in North Carolina (Crossman 1962a). The central mudminnow is an early spawner, thus escaping much of the predation by young grass pickerel (Keast 1985). Similar reproductive chronology probably extends partial immu-

nity from attack to *U. pygmaea*, but likely the complemental (daylight) activity pattern of many lowland piscivores is more important.

Mudminnows are useful and interesting fishes. Inhabitation of quiet shallows, and food habits of *U. pygmaea* indicate that it controls mosquito populations to at least a minor extent (Moore 1922). They are hardy fishes; they use the gas bladder as a lung to withstand the very low oxygen content that accompanies stagnation. They aestivate in mud during drought. As an aquarium fish the eastern mudminnow has had brief periods of popularity and relatively long ones of neglect (Baugh 1980). Its establishment in the wild in Europe owes partly to release by aquarists. Although tenacious and widely distributed in the populous eastern United States, our understanding of its life in nature is rather incomplete.

Name.—Pygmaea, "dwarf."

MINNOWS
Family Cyprinidae

To many persons, the term "minnows" refers to any kind of small fish, and sometimes to juveniles of larger species. True minnows, however, are defined by a combination of skeletal and other traits. Although most American minnows are small, attaining less than 150 mm TL (6 inches), the size range in the family is great. The smallest American minnow appears to be the diminutive Mexican shiner *Notropis saladonis*, whose adults are 20–30 mm SL (Hubbs and Hubbs 1958). The largest is the endangered Colorado squawfish *Ptychocheilus lucius*, formerly known to reach 1,800 mm TL (about 6 feet) and nearly 45 kg (100 pounds) weight. The largest minnow in the world may be *Catlocarpio siamensis* of southeastern Asia, which attains at least 2,500 mm TL (8.2 feet) (Smith 1945).

Minnows are widely distributed in fresh waters of North America, Europe, Asia, and Africa, and reach their greatest diversity on the latter two continents. They do not occur in Central America, South America, and Australia. The Cyprinidae are a moderately old group of bony fishes. The earliest North American cyprinid fossils, dated 31 million years ago in the Oligocene, are from the northwestern United States (Cavender 1986). Older fossils are known from the Eocene of Asia and the Paleocene of Europe (Berra 1981).

The Cyprinidae are the largest fish family in the world. There are about 2,000 species of minnows, or about 25% of all freshwater fishes and more than 9% of all fish species (Nelson 1984). The diversity of cyprinids is even more impressive in that fresh water represents only 0.0093% of all water on Earth (Berra 1981). In North America, there are about 295 described and undescribed species, 9 of which are exotic (Miller 1986; Robins et al. 1991; our data); 67 species are known from Virginia.

Cyprinids along with the many suckers, catfishes, characoids (including characins and tetras), knifeeels, and others are ostariophysan fishes. They form the superorder Ostariophysi, which dominates the freshwater fish fauna of the world. The superordinal name connotes a special adaptation common to these fishes; it translates to "small bone, bladder." Most of these fishes also are called otophysan fishes, for "ear, bladder." These terms refer to the Weberian apparatus, a structure typically composed of the often fused first four or more vertebrae, modified ribs, and three or four movable ossicles that connect the gas bladder with the inner ear (Greenwood et al. 1966; Rosen and Greenwood 1970). The ossicles function in sound transmission, analogous to the human middle-ear auditory ossicles; the gas bladder acts as an amplifier and resonator. Ostariophysans release an alarm substance (Schreckstoff) from injured skin; the substance elicits an adaptive fright reaction in members of the same species (e.g., Pfieffer 1963).

The classification within the Cyprinidae is in major revision. From comprehensive anatomical and phylogenetic analyses, Cavender and Coburn (1992) concluded that the many nominal subfamilies (-inae [formal] and -ine suffixes) should be combined into two subfamilies—Cyprininae and Leuciscinae—and that all American species are leuciscines. Both subfamilies are divisible into tribes (informal -in suffix; for example, leuciscin) or groups of genera; major subgroups of leuciscins also have the -in suffix or are termed clades (Coburn and Cavender 1992). According to their scheme for native North American leuciscines, the golden shiner *Notemigonus crysoleucas* is the only leuciscin; all others are phoxinins, which are divided into the western clade (including the *Gila* clade), the chub clade (including the exoglossin clade), and the shiner clade (including the advanced notropin clade).

The most extensive overhaul of genus-group nomenclature of American cyprinids in 40 years has resulted from studies by Mayden (1989) and Coburn and Cavender (1992). For example, according to one or both studies, the shiner genus *Notropis* has had four of its subgenera elevated to genus (including the largest, *Cyprinella*), and it gained *Ericymba* and the bigeye chub group *Hybopsis*. Some of the proposals were tentatively made but many are being accepted (Robins et al. 1991). Snelson (1991) identified disagreements in the rank, composition, or interrelations of supraspecific groups proposed by Mayden (1989) and Coburn and Cavender (1992). We may appear to have eclectically chosen classifications from the two studies, but our arrangements generally are based also on other studies including ours. With the dawning of a new synthesis of the evolutionary history of American cyprinids, the excitement and discussion currently generated among students of cyprinids would be hard to overstate (Snelson 1991).

Basic minnow characteristics include one dorsal fin, the pelvic fin in abdominal position, and the pectoral fin low on the side; an adipose fin is absent. The fins of almost all North American species are soft-rayed. The scales are cycloid. The lateral line system usually is well developed. The jaws lack teeth but the throat has stout teeth borne on the thick bony pharyngeal arch—the modified last pair of gill arches. The lips typically are thin but in some species they are specialized, enlarged and suckerlike or lobed; some species possess small barbels. A gas bladder is usually present and two-chambered. Most species have a moderate body form; some are very elongate, some quite compressed, others robust.

Sexual dimorphism and dichromatism are common in North American cyprinids. Nuptial tuberculation often is strikingly dimorphic; tubercles are conic, hard (keratinized) structures which may occur on the head, body, and fins (e.g., Figure 33). Females of some species develop tubercles, but even then the tubercles are larger and more numerous in males. Tubercles function in aggression, sexual stimulation, and maintenance of the spawning position (Wiley and Collette 1970). Males of some species also develop swollen tissues; for example, the somewhat humped nape in *Campostoma* and the striking nuptial head crest in most *Nocomis*. The genital papilla of

females often is larger and more protrusive than that of males.

Sexual dichromatism blossoms in many minnows during the spawning season. Most often only males develop nuptial coloration, but in some species, such as *Notropis chiliticus*, the female may be as brilliant. The array of patterns is diverse; hues may be deep and rich or almost translucent and may be iridescently intensified. Red is the dominant color in many species, but most colors are represented in the family. As in the darters, nuptial coloration is thought to enhance species and sex recognition, as well as to signal a state of spawning readiness.

Although most species prey on aquatic insects and microcrustaceans, minnows vary considerably in food habits and trophic morphology. Mouth position ranges from supraterminal to inferior, mouth size from small to large. Cyprinids with a large mouth (e.g., the fallfish) are often piscivorous as adults. Some species have tough pads or ridges on the jaws that allow picking or scraping food items from the substrate; others have evolved suckerlike lips. Short fleshy barbels, which usually occur in the corner of the mouth, occur in many species. Big lips, barbels, and numerous minute fleshy buds on the skin of the snout, lips, venter, and fins of some species are taste-sensory and typically are correlated with bottom feeding. Eye size and position, and the stoutness and form of the pharyngeal teeth also show a general correlation to diet. The intestine of most species is short and S-shaped, but in several genera the gut is elongated by further looping or coiling. Gut lengthening usually is associated with large amounts of algae and detritus in the diet. Peritoneum color also is generally correlated with gut morphology; this lining of the body cavity often is silvery or peppered in carnivorous species, brown or black in herbivores. The dark color is thought to block enzyme-degrading ultraviolet radiation.

Minnows are a strictly freshwater family and occur in virtually all freshwater habitats of North America—tiny creeks to big rivers, springs, swamps, sloughs, ponds, lakes, and reservoirs. As is the case with most "strictly" freshwater families, some species frequent tidal fresh and brackish water. The majority of species are warm or cool-adapted; a few are typical coldwater associates of trouts. Most species inhabit streams, particularly pools, backwaters, slow runs, and sometimes moderate riffles; some are adapted to steep gradient and strong current. Although several species are at home in both streams and lakes, most fluviatile species are intolerant of impoundments.

The reproductive strategies of American minnows are diverse. Insofar as is known, they are polygamous. Their spawning is classifiable on the basis of oviposition sites and specialized behaviors (Coburn 1986). Major categories are pelagic spawners, benthic–epibenthic spawners, egg attachers, nest-builders, and nest associates. Johnston and Page (1992) recognized other categories and considered the evolution of complex reproductive behaviors.

Pelagic spawners spawn in open water in large schools, small aggregations, or pairs. Spawning usually occurs in areas lacking appreciable current, and eggs are demersal. Benthic and epibenthic spawners spawn on or just above the bottom; spawning may occur gregariously or in pairs. Males of some species are territorial, and territorial behavior may be complex; for example, in *Rhinichthys atratulus* and *R. cataractae* (Bartnik 1970).

Egg attaching is an evolutionarily advanced behavior; there are two distinct spawning modes. Crevice spawning (characteristic of *Cyprinella*) involves placement of eggs in small crevices or fissures in rocks or logs. More advanced is egg clustering of *Pimephales*, in which eggs are placed in a single layer on the undersurface of nest cover such as stones. In both egg-attaching modes, males are territorial and the sexes are quite dimorphic and dichromatic; parental care is provided by the male.

Nest-building minnows mostly are large, chubby, sexually dimorphic species whose males purposefully transport stream substrate materials, usually gravel, by the mouth to construct nests in which eggs are buried. Eggs are deposited in cleaned loose substrate through which oxygenated water percolates; burial of eggs reduces egg predation. Among cyprinids, gravel-nest making is apparently unique to the American genera *Campostoma*, *Exoglossum*, *Nocomis*, *Semotilus*, and (V. C. Applegate, personal communication) to at least one population of *Couesius*. Nine species among the first four genera build gravel nests in Virginia, the second highest number of minnows exhibiting such behavior in any part of North America (North Carolina has 10). Nests vary from simple excavated pits, as made by *Campostoma*, to stone mounds that progress through distinct phases of construction, as erected by *Nocomis*. The *Nocomis* chubs are true architects of gravel. Jenkins (1971a) and Jenkins and Lachner (1975, 1989) argued that all gravel-nest building genera form a monophyletic group because of similarities and evolutionary trends in behavioral and morphological characters. However, based partly on phylo-

genetic relationships proposed by Coburn and Cavender (1992), Johnston and Page (1992) suggested that nest building originated independently in two or more of these genera.

The nests of many minnows attract a conglomerate of other minnow species; for example, members of *Clinostomus*, *Hybopsis*, *Luxilus*, *Lythrurus*, *Notropis*, *Phenacobius*, *Phoxinus*, and *Rhinichthys*, that predominantly or in some areas exclusively spawn over the nests. These species derive the same advantages of spawning in nests as do the nest builders and also gain protection by the presence of the nest builder (Johnston and Birkhead 1988; Wallin 1989; Johnston and Page 1992).

Total ova counts in North American cyprinids range from a few hundred to many thousands, but many estimates of annual fecundity may be inaccurate. Recent studies on the reproductive potential of minnows that spawn at intervals in a year show that one-time ova counts greatly underestimate realized fecundity (e.g., Gale and Gale 1977; Gale and Buynak 1982; Gale 1983; Heins and Rabito 1986). In the fathead minnow *Pimephales promelas*, single ova counts were 250–2,600 per female (Carlander 1969). However, Gale and Buynak (1982) determined that total ova spawned per female from May to August were 6,803–10,164, mean, 8,604. Thus, the small fathead female is relatively more fecund, by body weight, than the large common carp. The adaptive significance of producing multiple clutches is obvious—reproductive potential is greatly increased, yet the parent retains advantages of small size without cumbersome gravidness. Interestingly, the great fecundity coupled with parental care in *Cyprinella* and *Pimephales* is an exception to aspects of the r- and K-selection model.

Egg diameters of eastern North American minnows typically are 0.6–2.1 mm (Coburn 1986). Coburn found positive correlations between egg diameter and vertebral number, general habitat, and reproductive mode. Montane and upland species tend to lay larger eggs than do lowland forms, and territorial or nest-building minnows usually produce larger eggs than do fishes that are nonterritorial or do not build nests.

Minnows account for the largest percent of naturally occurring hybrids in North American freshwater fishes. By far the greatest percentage of cyprinid hybrids is produced by nest associates and nest-builders. The high frequency of hybrids is probably caused by accidental mixing of gametes of different species when spawning concurrently over nests, although breakdown in species recognition also accounts for some hybridization, especially between closely related forms (Dowling and Moore 1984, 1985a).

The worth of minnows often is overlooked. For years most fishery biologists regarded them simply as forage fishes. Certainly many cyprinids are preyed upon by game species, but the overall ecological role of minnows is far broader. Their species richness contributes to diversity and stability of aquatic ecosystems through numerous trophic specializations and complex energy cycling—the food web. Indeed, within many fish communities, the greatest range of trophic specializations occurs in the Cyprinidae. Some cyprinids that are intolerant of all but near-pristine environments serve as sensitive indicators of habitat quality.

Some of our larger native minnows are sought by fishers for sport and food. The fallfish, the largest native minnow in the eastern United States, provides good sport on light tackle and may be taken on small lures and flies. *Nocomis* chubs often are eaten by fishers. The stoneroller has a small but devoted following in the southern Appalachians. The introduced common carp ranks high among minnows as a sport and foodfish, but its popularity is well below that of typical game species. Several minnow species are propagated for bait, and many are seined at streamside for immediate use. Many cyprinids are attractive, lively, and hardy in the home aquarium.

Introduction of exotic cyprinids has been limited compared to that of some other families. By far the most successful import is the widespread common carp. Troubling to biogeographers, and potentially so to native species, are the likely extensive and undocumented releases of bait minnows in streams where they are not thought to be native.

According to the cladograms of Page and Johnston (1990b) and Coburn and Cavender (1992), the sequence of notropin shiner genera in this book would be, primitive to advanced: *Notropis, Luxilus, Lythrurus*, the extralimital *Opsopoeodus* and *Codoma*, and *Pimephales*. See also genus *Hybognathus*. We were unable to make some changes in sequence due to proximity to publication.

Name.—Cyprin-, from the ancient Greek or Latin word for carp, *Cyprinis*, in turn named for the island of Cyprus from which the common carp supposedly was introduced into Europe (Burr and Warren 1986).

Key to Minnows   Cyprinidae

Minnows tend to be the most difficult to identify of Virginia freshwater fishes because of the large number of species and the small size and close similarity of many of the species. However, most minnows are quite distinctive and readily identifiable, particularly by pigment patterns. A small marking on the body or vague lines of melanophores along fin rays may seem insignificant, but such traits often discriminate a species.

The key employs the pharyngeal tooth count as a primary diagnostic character. Although pharyngeal teeth are more difficult to study than most external characters, tooth counts tend to be less variable (invariable in some species) and thus afford greater accuracy in keying. That accuracy stems from careful removal and cleaning of the pharyngeal arch. Directions for dissecting the arch and counting teeth are given in *Anatomy and Color*. With a little practice at removing and cleaning arches, tooth counts are easily made.

The position of the dorsal fin origin is a critical character that usually has been referenced in keys only to the pelvic fin origin, often subjectively so. We express the dorsal origin relative to several points or areas (Figure 24C). To discern the position, we hold a straightedge (clear flexible plastic) on the body precisely aligned with the dorsal origin and perpendicular to the horizontal body axis; the straightedge is flexed over the curve of the body. Then the pelvic fin is spread moderately and the position where the straightedge falls relative to the pelvic base is determined.

The broad supralabial flap of *Phenacobius* is not to be confused with the small preterminal barbel in *Margariscus, Semotilus*, and *Exoglossum laurae* (Figures 25, 27, 38). In long-preserved specimens of some species of minnows, particularly shiners, the dark lateral stripe may be partly or entirely masked by retention of a silver sheen over the stripe.

Comments to aid in identifying certain newly elevated genera and in distinguishing among species of *Nocomis* precede the key to the species of those genera. Supplemental traits to help separate these and some other chub, dace, or shiner genera are also given (parenthetically) in the generic key.

Key to Genera (and to Species of Genera Monotypic in Virginia)

1a Dorsal fin with first main ray spinelike (thick and stiffened) and
serrate; dorsal rays more than 13 2
1b Dorsal fin lacking spinelike serrate ray; dorsal rays less than 13
(usually 8 in all genera) 3

2a Two barbels present on each side; lateral line scales
usually 35–39 .... COMMON CARP—*Cyprinus carpio* p. 272
2b Barbels absent; lateral line scales usually 28–32 .... GOLDFISH—*Carassius auratus* p. 275

3a Preanal distance 3 or more times as long as postanal distance
(Figure 24A); grinding surface of pharyngeal teeth with obvious
parallel rows of grooves (Figure 11C) .... GRASS CARP—*Ctenopharyngodon idella* p. 277
3b Preanal distance less than 3 times as long as postanal distance
(Figure 24B); grinding surface of pharyngeal teeth lacking obvious
parallel rows of grooves or, usually, completely lacking grooves .... native minnows 4

4a Lower jaw having a hard ridge along anterior edge (Figure 25A);
intestine in specimens larger than 40 mm very long, extremely
coiled, fully enwrapping gas bladder (Figure 26A); (mouth
subterminal or inferior; anal rays 7) .... CENTRAL STONEROLLER—*Campostoma anomalum* p. 300
4b Lower jaw lacking hard ridge along anterior edge; intestine, if
coiled, not fully enwrapping gas bladder 5

5a Lower jaw and lip unusual, having 3 divisions, the medial division
tonguelike (Figure 25C, D) .... *Exoglossum*
5b Lower jaw and lip normal (Figure 27A, B), or lips wholly suckerlike
and fleshy, and lower jaw having a short broad protuberant area
medially (Figures 25B, 38) 6

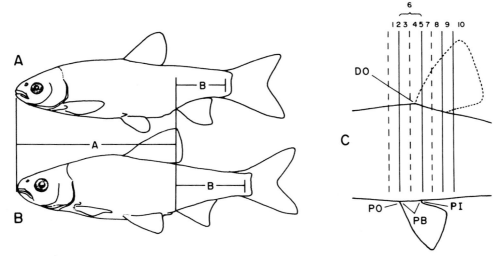

Figure 24   (A, B) Relative preanal and postanal distances: (A) *Ctenopharyngodon*, distance "A" 3 times or more greater than distance "B". (B) Native minnows, distance "A" less than 3 times greater than distance "B". (C) Position of dorsal fin origin (DO) relative to the origin (PO), base (PB), and posterior insertion (PI) of the pelvic fin; each vertical line is equidistant from adjacent ones: 1—slightly anterior to PO; 2—above PO; 3—above anterior half of PB (including PO; DO slightly posterior to PO included in this category); 4—above posterior half of PB (including PI; DO moderately posterior to PO included in this category); 5—above PI; 6—above PB; 7–10—slightly, moderately, much, or far posterior to PB. See introduction to key for using straightedge to determine position.

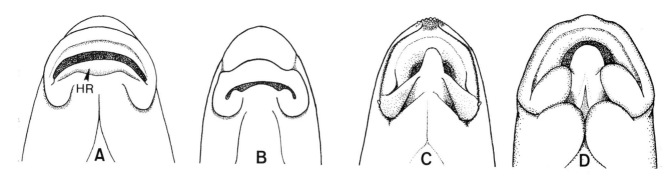

Figure 25   Modified cyprinid mouths: (A) *Campostoma* (HR—hard ridge). (B) *Phenacobius*. (C) *Exoglossum laurae*. (D) *Exoglossum maxillingua*.

6a   Barbel present at posterior end of lips (terminal position, Figure 27A), or slightly anterior to this point (preterminal position, Figure 27B) and lying partly in groove along upper lip (barbel may be tiny or, occasionally, absent) 7
6b   Barbel absent 13

7a   Barbel preterminal (Figure 27B); (barbel often absent in *Margariscus*) 8
7b   Barbel terminal (Figure 27A) 9

8a   Mouth small; body usually having numerous duskily pigmented scales producing a spotted appearance (spotting often absent in young and small juvenile); (dorsal fin lacking vaguely dusky area or dark spot just above its origin; circumbody scales (44)48–56(60); smaller species, adults usually less than 80 mm SL; Potomac drainage only) .... PEARL DACE—*Margariscus margarita*   p. 304
8b   Mouth moderate or large; body not spotted; larger species, adults usually more than 100 mm SL .... *Semotilus*

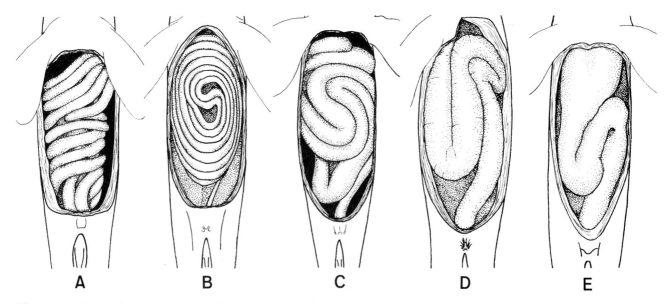

Figure 26   Cyprinid gut (intestinal) coiling and looping patterns, and peritoneal melanism: (A) *Campostoma*, highly coiled, looped around gas bladder. (B) *Hybognathus*, highly coiled in clock-spring pattern. (C) *Nocomis leptocephalus*, moderately coiled. (D) *Nocomis raneyi*, S-shaped, with anterior accessory loop. (E) most minnows, S-shaped.

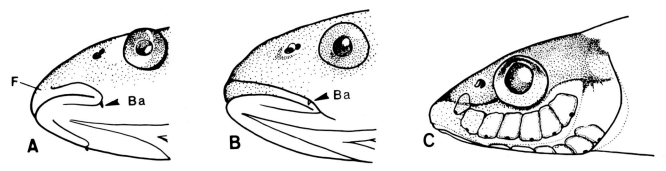

Figure 27   (A) F—frenum present, and Ba—barbel terminal, in *Rhinichthys*. (B) Frenum absent (deep crease is present between snout tip and upper lip) and barbel preterminal (subterminal) in *Margariscus* and *Semotilus*. (C) Enlarged lower cephalic lateralis canals in *Notropis buccatus*.

9a   Snout with frenum (Figure 27A) .... *Rhinichthys*
9b   Snout lacking frenum (Figure 27B) 10

10a Total radii on dorsolateral body scales usually more than 15 (Figure
      28A); larger species, often more than 100 mm SL; (body chubby;
      mouth subterminal, slightly oblique, Figures 32, 33) .... *Nocomis*
10b Total radii on dorsolateral body scales usually less than 14 (Figure
      28B); smaller fishes, rarely 100 mm SL, usually less than 80 mm;
      (*Hybopsis hypsinotus*, restricted to Pee Dee drainage, is partly
      exceptional; to separate from *Nocomis*, modally *H. hypsinotus* has 8
      anal rays [7 in *Nocomis*] and 12 circumpeduncle scales [16 or more]) 11

11a Dorsal fin with one or more membranes pigmented, the posterior
      membranes distinctly the most intensely pigmented (Figure 34A, B) .... barbeled *Cyprinella*
11b Dorsal fin membranes unpigmented (Figure 34D) or, if pigmented,
      of about equal intensity in anterior and posterior portions of the fin
      or most intense anteriorly (Figure 34C, F–I) 12

12a Anal rays modally 7 .... *Erimystax*
12b Anal rays modally 8 .... *Hybopsis*

13a Mouth inferior, lips suckerlike, enlarged, fleshy, and often coarsely
      textured (Figures 25B, 38) .... *Phenacobius*
13b Mouth and lips varied but not as above 14

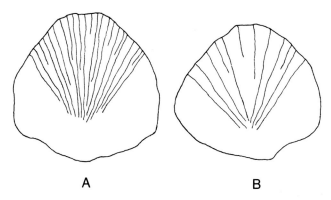

Figure 28   Radii in posterior scale field: (A) Numerous in *Nocomis*. (B) Few in *Erimystax* and *Hybopsis*.

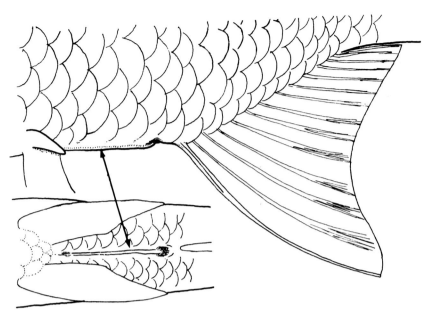

Figure 29 Ventral ridge (keel) and falcate anal fin in *Notemigonus*.

14a Midventral body between pelvic and anal fins with a largely
      nonscaled low ridge (Figure 29); (mouth medium or small, sharply
      upturned; body much compressed; dorsal fin origin moderately or
      much posterior to pelvic fin base; anal fin moderately or strongly
      falcate; pharyngeal teeth 5–5) .... GOLDEN SHINER—*Notemigonus crysoleucas* p. 280
14b Midventral ridge absent, belly moderately or broadly rounded
      between pelvic and anal fins 15

15a Lateral line scales tiny, almost always more than 62, usually many
      more; 2–3 dark lateral stripes present above anal fin origin in adult
      (lower stripe may be oblique, upper stripe may be divided into
      spots or blotches, Figure 31) .... *Phoxinus*
15b Lateral line scales medium or large, almost always less than 62,
      usually many fewer; at most, 1 dark lateral stripe above anal fin
      origin 16

16a Predorsal scales much smaller anteriorly than posteriorly, especially
      crowded just behind head, not forming regular horizontal rows
      (Figure 30A); first principal dorsal fin ray well separated from
      anterior half-ray by a moderate or wide membrane (adult only, Fish
      121); dorsal fin in subadult and adult having epibasal portion of
      anterior 1–3 principal rays distinctly darker than both basal and
      distal portions of these rays (Fish 118, 120), or this epibasal area
      having an obvious smudge or black spot (Fish 119, 121); (anal rays
      modally 7) .... *Pimephales*
16b Predorsal scales, if present, about same size anteriorly as
      posteriorly, or if smaller, forming straight or only slightly curved or
      slightly irregular horizontal rows (Figure 30B); first principal dorsal
      fin ray attached to anterior half-ray or slightly separated from it by
      a narrow membrane; dorsal fin anterobasally lacking the above
      pattern, smudge, and spot (Figures 34A–H), or if a spot is present,
      it extends to the fin base (Figure 34I) 17

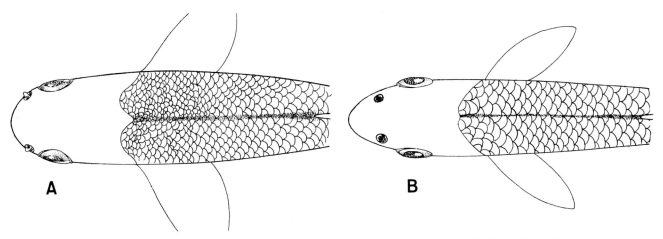

Figure 30 Predorsal squamation: (A) Scales small, crowded anteriorly in *Pimephales*. (B) Typical condition.

17a Intestine extremely long, coiled clockspringlike (Figure 26B);
(mouth small, subterminal or inferior, distinctly downcurved
posteriorly; small groove along anteroventral edge of lachrymal
extends markedly dorsad from groove that separates side of snout
from upper lip; dorsal fin origin above or slightly anterior to
anterior half of pelvic fin base; lower side well peppered;
pharyngeal teeth 4–4; anal rays modally 8; peritoneum dark;
Atlantic drainages) . . . . EASTERN SILVERY MINNOW—*Hybognathus regius*   p. 446

17b Intestine not extremely long, usually having simple, compressed
S-shaped configuration (Figure 26E)   18

18a Pharyngeal teeth usually 2,5–4,2 (Figure 11A); (mouth large,
terminal or supraterminal, oblique; body of adult moderately
compressed; lateral line distinctly downcurved on anterior body,
coursing well onto lower half of body; dorsal fin origin above
posterior half of pelvic fin base or aligned behind pelvic base; side
often darkly dappled; anal rays modally 9) . . . . ROSYSIDE DACE—*Clinostomus funduloides*   p. 290

18b Pharyngeal teeth 4–4, 1,4–4,1, or 2,4–4,2 (Figure 11B) . . . .   shiners   19

19a Dorsal fin with one or more membranes pigmented, the posterior
ones the most intensely so (Figure 34A, B); (body diamond-
patterned by rhomboidal areas formed from intersecting oblique
alignments of relatively angled, dusky or dark markings that accent
the scale submargins; dorsal fin origin over pelvic fin base;
pharyngeal teeth 4–4 or 1,4–4,1; anal rays modally 8, 9, or 10) . . . .   nonbarbeled *Cyprinella*

19b Dorsal fin membranes unpigmented (Figure 34D) or, if pigmented,
of about equal intensity in anterior and posterior portions of the fin
or most intense anteriorly (Figure 34C, F–I)   20

20a Exposed portion (lunula) of anterior lateral line scales much more
than twice as high as wide (Figure 35A); (mouth terminal, oblique;
dorsal fin origin above pelvic fin base; pharyngeal teeth 2,4–4,2;
anal rays modally 9; breast fully scaled) . . . .   *Luxilus*

20b Exposed portion of anterior lateral line scales about twice or less
than twice as high than wide (Figure 35C) (except for *Notropis
volucellus* and sawfin shiner [Figure 35B], which have 4–4 teeth and
modally 8 anal rays)   21

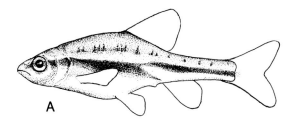
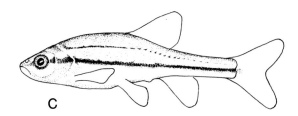
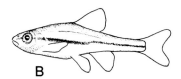

Figure 31   Lateral pigmentation in *Phoxinus*: (A) Adult and (B) young of both *P. oreas* and *P. tennesseensis* with interrupted or disaligned midlateral stripe. (C) Adult *P. erythrogaster* with uninterrupted and straight midlateral stripe (lower stripe).

21a   Anterodorsolateral scales distinctly smaller than postdorsal scales;
      (mouth terminal, oblique; body very elongate; dorsal fin origin
      moderately or much posterior to pelvic fin base; pharyngeal teeth
      2,4–4,2; anal rays usually 10–11; breast usually naked) . . . . *Lythrurus*
21b   Anterodorsolateral scales about same size as postdorsal scales . . . . *Notropis*

Key to Species of *Phoxinus*

      The characters in couplet 2 generally apply only to adults and large juveniles.

1a   Lateral stripe (if 2 stripes present, the lower) lacking interruption,
     constriction, or disalignment (Figure 31C); (may occupy Big Sandy
     drainage) . . . . SOUTHERN REDBELLY DACE—*P. erythrogaster*   p. 113
1b   Lateral stripe (if 2 stripes present, the lower) with a partial or
     complete interruption at about its midlength and a ventral
     extension toward anal fin (adult, Figure 31A), or with a slight
     constriction and disalignment (young, small juvenile, Figure 31B)   2

2a   Upper lateral stripe well developed, contiguous or slightly divided
     into spots or small blotches; (Tennessee drainage only) . .   TENNESSEE DACE—*P. tennesseensis*   p. 283
2b   Upper lateral stripe distinctly divided at least anteriorly into small
     and large blotches, or stripe absent and back having medium or
     large blotches . . . . MOUNTAIN REDBELLY DACE—*P. oreas*   p. 286

Key to Species of *Rhinichthys*

1a   Snout projecting well forward of mouth, distance from snout tip to
     most anterior point of lower lip about equal to or greater than eye
     diameter . . . . LONGNOSE DACE—*R. cataractae*   p. 293
1b   Snout scarcely projecting forward of mouth, distance from snout
     tip to most anterior point of lower lip less than eye diameter .   BLACKNOSE DACE—*R. atratulus*   p. 296

Key to Species of *Semotilus*

1a Spot just above dorsal fin origin usually vague or absent, often
moderately developed only in adult; dorsal fin origin usually above
anterior half of pelvic fin base; circumbody scales (32)33–37(39);
circumpeduncle scales (15)16(19) .... FALLFISH—*S. corporalis* p. 306
1b Spot just above dorsal fin origin prominent in adult and large
juvenile, vague in young and small juvenile; dorsal fin origin
usually slightly posterior to pelvic fin base; circumbody scales
(40)43–50(54); circumpeduncle scales 20–23(24) .... CREEK CHUB—*S. atromaculatus* p. 310

Key to Species of *Exoglossum*

1a Small preterminal barbel present in or extending from groove along
upper lip; each side of lower jaw foldlike or ridgelike (Figure 25C) ....
.... TONGUETIED MINNOW—*E. laurae* p. 313
1b Barbel absent; each side of lower jaw a large lobe (Figure 25D) ....
.... CUTLIPS MINNOW—*E. maxillingua* p. 316

Key to Species of *Nocomis*

The four Virginia species of *Nocomis* chubs are distinctive in the combinations of location, number, and size of nuptial tubercles. The key to *Nocomis* emphasizes geographic distribution (Maps 48, 49) because most Virginia drainages harbor only two species and some have only one in the state (e.g., the Pee Dee, Tennessee, and Big Sandy). Only the James drainage has three species. Distributional aspects simplify initial identification, but for certainty the specimens must be examined.

The best way to proceed in identifying specimens is to first distinguish *N. leptocephalus* from any member of the *micropogon* group that may be in a sample. This is accomplished by: (1) breast scalation [fully scaled or almost so in *leptocephalus* vs. naked or slightly scaled posteriorly in *micropogon* group (Atlantic slope populations)]; (2) intestine in specimens greater than 35 mm SL [whorled, distinctly looped toward right side of fish (Figure 26C) (whorling sometimes indicated by dark transverse marks showing through belly wall) vs. unwhorled, sections of gut all longitudinally oriented, or having a short anterior loop or kink toward left side (Figure 26D, E)]; (3) orientation of posterior edge of preopercle usually [vertical or slanted posteroventrad (specimen in Figure 33A has preopercle preserved in abnormal position) vs. slanted slightly anteroventrad]; (4) snout usually slightly [shorter, blunter vs. longer, somewhat pointed]; (5) lateral line decurvature on anterior body [more downcurved, passing through lower portion of lateral dark stripe or just below stripe vs. less curved, passing through lower portion of stripe]; (6) tubercles (and their developmental stages; see below) on front and side (lachrymal area) of snout in medium-sized juvenile to adult [absent vs. present].

Although in *Nocomis* the definitive tubercles occur only in nuptial males, the distribution of tubercle primordia can be used for species identification of nonbreeding adult males, adult females, and juveniles (Figure 33, right column). The primordia first appear as "tubercle spots" (Lachner and Jenkins 1971a)—tiny or small, round, gray spots on darker areas of the head. The spots are best discerned with the head moistened; the tiny spots of juvenile *N. raneyi* are best seen under magnification. Tubercle spots must be distinguished from cephalic lateralis pores, which are openings. An intermediate developmental stage—tubercle buds—refers to tubercle anlagen that are slightly raised but smaller than the definitive tubercle.

Spots and buds first appear in young or small juveniles (fish sizes are given in the caption to Figure 33) and are more sparsely distributed in young than in adults. However, centers of early spot and bud

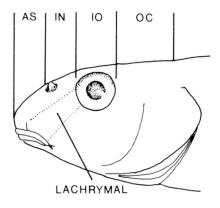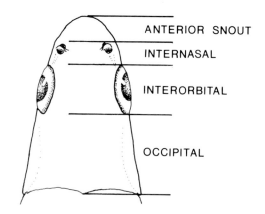

Figure 32 Areas of the head used to describe the distribution of nuptial tubercles, tubercle spots, and tubercle buds, particularly in *Nocomis*.

development are recognizable; their locations and subsequent spot and bud proliferation patterns are diagnostic. In *N. leptocephalus* (Figure 33A–C), tubercle spots first appear in the internasal and anterior interorbital areas, and with growth additional spots develop posteriorly (as well as in the former areas). In the *micropogon* group, spots also first appear in the internasal area; but soon after they also develop anterior and posterior to the internasal area and in the upper portion of the lachrymal area. In the male, the spots or buds enlarge into tubercles as the spawning period approaches.

Tubercle scars—slight depressions on the head of postnuptial males—indicate locations of lost tubercles; these scars are as diagnostic as spots, buds, and tubercles.

Hybrids of *N. leptocephalus* × *N. micropogon* are common in the many zones of co-inhabitation of the parental species on the Atlantic slope. The hybrid *N. leptocephalus* × *N. platyrhynchus* occurs occasionally in the New drainage. Both hybrids are recognizable by intermediate states of one or more diagnostic characters, particularly breast scales, intestine form, and tuberculation (characters 1, 2, and 6 above).

In the key, tubercles refer to spots, buds, tubercles, or scars on medium-sized juveniles to adults of both sexes. The snout comprises the areas anterior to the internasal area and laterally on the lachrymal bone (Figure 32).

1a Specimen from Tennessee or Big Sandy drainages; (tubercles
  present on snout, Figure 33D–F) .... RIVER CHUB—*N. micropogon*   p. 321
1b Specimen not from Tennessee or Big Sandy drainages 2

2a Specimen from New drainage 3
2b Specimen from Atlantic drainage 4

3a Circumbody scales (26)28–31(33); tubercles absent on snout
  (Figure 33A–C) .... BLUEHEAD CHUB—*N. leptocephalus*   p. 326
3b Circumbody scales (29)32–36(39); tubercles present on snout
  (Figure 33G–I) .... BIGMOUTH CHUB—*N. platyrhynchus*   p. 319

4a Breast more than 50% scaled; intestine moderately whorled in
  specimens larger than 35 mm SL (Figure 26C); tubercles absent on
  snout (Figure 33A–C) .... BLUEHEAD CHUB—*N. leptocephalus*   p. 326
4b Breast less than 40% (usually less than 20%) scaled; intestine with
  simple S-shaped configuration, or basically S-shaped but with a
  short anterior loop extending posteriorly (Figure 26D, E); tubercles
  present on snout (Figure 33D–L) 5

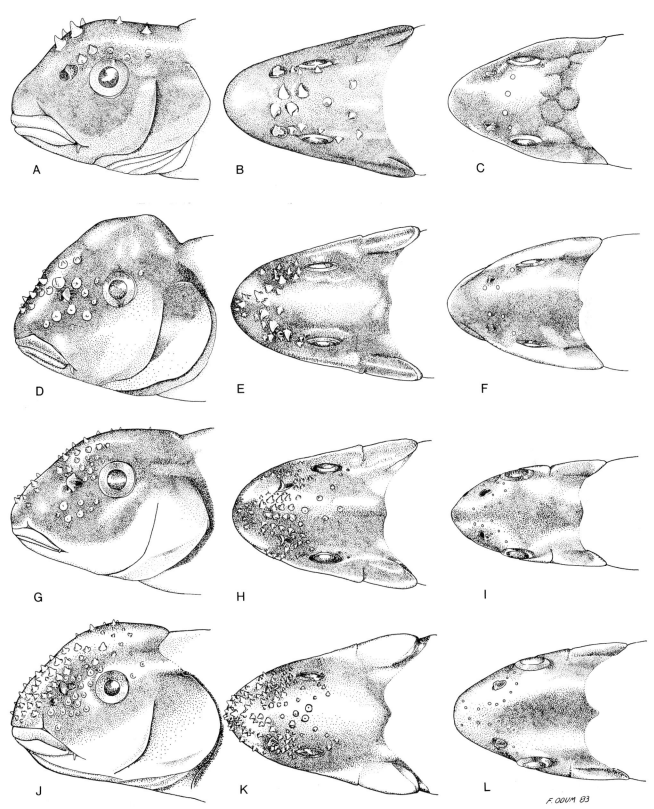

Figure 33 Tuberculation in *Nocomis*; left and center columns—nuptial crested males; right column—juveniles: (A–C) *N. l. leptocephalus*. (D–F) *N. micropogon*. (G–I) *N. platyrhynchus*. (J–L) *N. raneyi*. Definitive adult tubercle distribution shown in nuptial males. Juveniles have tubercle spots in early developmental pattern, with typical species differences in spot size shown. Tubercle spots (best studied with head moist) usually first appear at SL ranges of (in sequence of species as above): 30–40 mm; 50–70 mm; 60–80 mm; 60–90 mm.

5a   Gape width greater than interpelvic distance (between origins of
     pelvic fins); lateral line scales (37)38–40(43); tubercles absent on
     interorbital area (Figure 33D–F) .... RIVER CHUB—*N. micropogon*   p. 321
5b   Gape width equal to or slightly less than interpelvic distance;
     lateral line scales (39)40–43(45); tubercles present on interorbital
     area (Figure 33J–L) .... BULL CHUB—*N. raneyi*   p. 324

Key to Species of *Erimystax*

This genus—the slender chubs—is newly elevated from *Hybopsis*. The species have a pair of terminal barbels, a moderately or very elongate body, 4–4 pharyngeal teeth, and usually 7 anal rays. The three Virginia species occupy only the Tennessee drainage in the state. The two common species are distinctive from all other Virginia cyprinids by having a row of large spots or blotches on the side of the body.

1a   Body not spotted or blotched; middorsal stripe, if present, usually
     not subdivided into a series of dashes; circumpeduncle scales
     (11)12(14); isthmus with a group of 5–20 large papilla-like taste
     buds; (eye supralateral) .... SLENDER CHUB—*E. cahni*   p. 330
1b   Body having large spots or blotches along midside; middorsal
     stripe subdivided into a series of dashes; circumpeduncle scales
     (12)15–16(17); isthmus with numerous small or medium taste buds,
     but usually only 1–3 or none are papilla-like 2

2a   Eye lateral; midside usually with a series of large spots or rounded
     blotches (blotches sometimes interconnected to form a lateral
     stripe); lower margin of lateral pigmentation not defined by a series
     of distinct punctations (punctations if present not more obvious
     than those in scale rows just above); caudal spot about equal in
     height to last lateral blotch .... STREAMLINE CHUB—*E. dissimilis*   p. 332
2b   Eye supralateral; midside with a series of mostly square or
     rectangular blotches; lower margin of lateral pigmentation with a
     series of distinct punctations; caudal spot distinctly smaller than
     last lateral blotch .... BLOTCHED CHUB—*E. insignis*   p. 335

Key to Species of *Phenacobius*

1a   Lateral line scales 41–51; New or Big Sandy drainages 2
1b   Lateral line scales 49–68; Tennessee drainage 3

2a   Upper half of body lacking differentially darkened scales, not
     spotted; modified (axillary) scale above pelvic fin base lacking
     melanophores; Big Sandy drainage only .... SUCKERMOUTH MINNOW—*P. mirabilis*   p. 338
2b   Upper half of body in juvenile and adult with differentially
     darkened scales producing a spotted appearance; modified scale
     just above pelvic fin base peppered with melanophores; New
     drainage only .... KANAWHA MINNOW—*P. teretulus*   p. 340

3a   Tip of pelvic fin reaching just to or, usually, posterior to base of
     anal papilla; circumpeduncle scales (16)17–21(23) .... FATLIPS MINNOW—*P. crassilabrum*   p. 342

3b Tip of pelvic fin falling short of base of anal papilla or,
     occasionally, just reaching the base; circumpeduncle scales
     (13)15–17(18) . . . .   STARGAZING MINNOW—*P. uranops*   p. 343

Key to Species of *Hybopsis*

This genus—the bigeye or shinerlike chubs—recently has been combined with *Notropis* by some authors. It contains small, plain-patterned minnows having a pair of terminal barbels, 1,4–4,1 pharyngeal teeth, and modally 8 anal rays.

1a Body form of adult moderate; Tennessee and Big Sandy drainages . . . .
     . . . .   BIGEYE CHUB—*H. amblops*   p. 345
1b Body form of adult high-backed; Pee Dee drainage only . . .   HIGHBACK CHUB—*H. hypsinotus*   p. 347

Key to Species of *Cyprinella*

With the recent elevation of *Cyprinella* to a genus and its reception of certain barbeled species, separation of this group—the satinfin shiners—as a unit has become more demanding. In the generic key, *Cyprinella* is reached via two sets of couplets, one leading to barbeled species, the other to nonbarbeled species.

Most species of *Cyprinella* are recognizable at a glance as members of that group by a diamond-patterned body produced by vertically elongate, rhomboidal markings (Fish 70–77). The pattern consists of uniform cross-hatchings formed by alignments of the individual dusky or dark markings that underlie scales submarginally. There is one alignment per oblique scale row. The alignments are straight and form true rhombuses when the scale markings are angled, as is typical of juveniles. The alignments undulate slightly when the markings are distinctly curved, as often occurs in adults (notably those of barbeled species and *C. lutrensis*); these undulating alignments do not form a clear-cut diamond pattern. Although some species of certain other shiner genera have a scale-pigment pattern similar to that typical of *Cyprinella*, there remains a difficult-to-express conformity among patterns of *Cyprinella* and a distinction from those of other groups.

Cyprinella have distinctive dark pigment patterns in dorsal fin membranes, but so do some other shiners. The diagnostic trait of Virginia *Cyprinella* is the greater concentration of melanophores in the posterior 2–3 membranes compared with anterior membranes (Figure 34A, B). The pattern is obvious to the unaided eye in adult specimens (by spreading the fin), and under magnification for young. The posterior membranes in adults, particularly nuptial males, often appear black-slashed lengthwise.

Cyprinella typically have a subtle gestalt to the head—a "foxy" look effected by a somewhat pointed snout, a usually down-curved subterminal mouth, and medium or small eyes.

The name satinfin refers to the glossy or milky white of fins, generally along the fin margin. However, the color is nearly restricted to nuptial males and thus is not widely useful for group identification.

1a Barbel present at posterior end of lips   2
1b Barbel absent   3

2a Scales around back 11–13; pharyngeal teeth usually 1,4–4,1; Pee
     Dee drainage only . . . .   THICKLIP SHINER—*C. labrosa*   p. 350
2b Scales around back 15–19; pharyngeal teeth 4–4; Tennessee
     drainage only . . . .   TURQUOISE SHINER—*C. monacha*   p. 353

3a Anal rays (9)10–11; (may occupy Pee Dee drainage) . . . .   FIERYBLACK SHINER—*C. pyrrhomelas*   p. 110
3b Anal rays modally 8 or 9   4

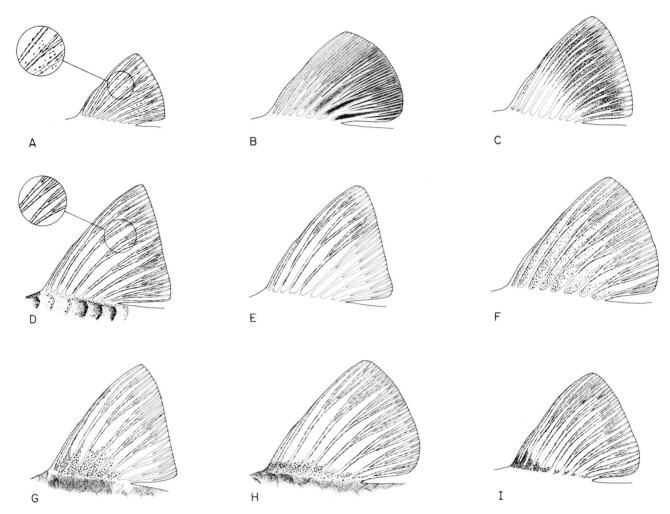

Figure 34   Melanophore pigmentation patterns in and along bases of dorsal fins of shiners: (A) Juvenile *Cyprinella galactura*, membranes pigmented, most so posteriorly and in mid-one-third of fin height. (B) Adult male *Cyprinella galactura*, maximum interradial (membranal) pigmentation, most intense posteriorly. (C) *Luxilus coccogenis*, wide band of membranal pigment centered distally to midheight of fin, membranes sparsely stippled or unpigmented basally. (D) *Notropis volucellus*, most typical pattern in shiners, with all rays finely lined with pigment, membranes unpigmented; dark-pale-dark pattern on dorsum is shown darker than typical. (E) *Notropis* sp. (sawfin shiner), only rays 1–4 or 1–5 lined with pigment; some adults have pigmented membranes; species usually has dark-pale-dark dorsum pattern. (F) *Notropis spectrunculus*, all rays pigmented; membranes well peppered, most so basally; usually has dark-pale-dark dorsum pattern. (G) *Notropis chiliticus*, basal one-fourth to one-third of membranes pigmented; last 1–2 rays usually not lined by melanophores; small pale spot on body at origin and posterior insertion of fin. (H) *Notropis rubricroceus*, membranes with pigment only near base, or membranal pigment absent; last 1–2 rays lined with pigment; pale spots and differentially dark areas absent at ends of fin and on body along base (typical of *Notropis*). (I) *Lythrurus ardens*, fin heavily pigmented anterobasally (anterobasidorsal spot).

6b Humeral bar absent or, if present, dusky and not clearly extending onto nape; dorsal fin with posterior membranes pronouncedly darker than anterior membranes; pharyngeal teeth 1,4–4,1 7

7a Lateral line scales (33)35–37(38); pectoral rays (11)13–14(16); Atlantic drainages only .... SATINFIN SHINER—*C. analostana* p. 361
7b Lateral line scales (36)37–41(43); pectoral rays (13)14–16(18); New, Tennessee, or Big Sandy drainages 8

8a Caudal fin basally (and slightly onto body) with a distinct large pale patch dorsally and ventrally, caused by absence of pigment along rays; lateral line scales (38)39–41(43) .... WHITETAIL SHINER—*C. galactura* p. 356
8b Caudal fin basally lacking distinct pale patches, moderately to well pigmented along length of rays; lateral line scales (36)37–38(40); (Clinch River, possibly also Powell River) .... STEELCOLOR SHINER—*C. whipplei* p. 359

Key to Species of *Luxilus*

Recently removed from *Notropis*, the members of this genus—the highscale shiners—are distinguishable from other shiners by the combination of primary and supplemental characters in the generic key. Adults of most Virginia species of *Luxilus* are large and deep-bodied (compared with most shiners); the anterior portion of the anterolateral body scales has a vertically elongate, dusky or dark marking (often crescentic); and scattered individual scales or patches of scales often are sharply darker than others.

The key is adapted from Gilbert (1964). Diagnostic color patterns apply mainly to large juveniles and adults. Prominent dark marks on the side refer to the sharply darker individual scales and patches of scales. The anterodorsolateral scale count (Figure 7C), a variation of the predorsal scale row count, is made in the horizontal row lying one-fourth of the distance from the middorsal line to the lateral line. It begins at the point aligned vertically with the dorsal fin origin and is made forward to the shoulder girdle.

1a Dorsal fin with medial or medial-submarginal dusky band (Figure 34C); caudal fin base pale; (Tennessee drainage only) ..... WARPAINT SHINER—*L. coccogenis* p. 367
1b Dorsal fin lacking dusky band; caudal fin base not distinctly pale 2

2a Side of body with very prominent dark marks; scales on dorsolateral body with a fine line adjacent to and paralleling posterior scale margin; dark upper half of head sharply contrasting with pale lower half, particularly in breeding male; circumpeduncle scales (12)13–15(16), usually 14; (James, Chowan, Roanoke, and New drainages) .... CRESCENT SHINER—*L. cerasinus* p. 369
2b Side of body with dark marks moderately prominent at most, or marks are very prominent but usually fewer than in *L. cerasinus*;

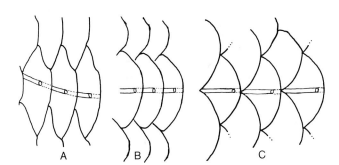

Figure 35 Height relative to width of exposed portion (lunula) of lateral line scales in shiners: (A) *Luxilus*; (B) *Notropis volucellus* and some sawfin shiners; and (C) typical of most species.

scales on dorsolateral body lacking fine line paralleling posterior scale margin; dark upper half of head not sharply contrasting with lower half; circumpeduncle scales (12)15–16(18) 3

3a   Anterior dorsolateral area on each side of body with 2–4 dark wavy parallel stripes, their unions forming distinct "V" shapes on back posterior to dorsal fin; anterodorsolateral scales (13)14–16(19); circumbody scales (23)26–29(32); (side of body usually with moderately prominent dark marks; Tennessee and Big Sandy drainages, New drainage locally) .... STRIPED SHINER—*L. chrysocephalus*   p. 378

3b   Dorsolateral area lacking wavy stripes and "V" shapes (except in large New drainage nuptial male *L. albeolus*) (some nuptial males in all populations have 3 straight dark stripes on back, 1 medial, 1 on each side dorsolaterally); anterodorsolateral scales (15)17–24(30); circumbody scales (24)26–35(39) 4

4a   Side of body usually lacking moderately prominent dark marks (in upper Roanoke and New drainages) or often having moderately prominent marks (in Chowan drainage and lower Piedmont and Coastal Plain of Roanoke drainage); anterodorsolateral scales (15)17–20(23); circumbody scales (24)26–30(33) .... WHITE SHINER—*L. albeolus*   p. 373

4b   Side of body usually with moderately prominent marks; anterodorsolateral scales (16)18–24(30); circumbody scales (26)30–35(39); (James and northerly Atlantic drainages) .... COMMON SHINER—*L. cornutus*   p. 376

Key to Species of *Lythrurus*

This group—the finescale shiners—recently was elevated from *Notropis*. The Virginia species are sufficiently diagnosed as a group in the generic key to allow their separation from other shiners.

1a   Dorsal fin origin lacking a dark spotlike concentration of melanophores; (Clinch–Powell system only) .... MOUNTAIN SHINER—*L. lirus*   p. 380

1b   Dorsal fin origin with a dark spotlike (triangular, rounded, or linear) concentration of melanophores (Figure 34I) .... ROSEFIN SHINER—*L. ardens*   p. 382

Key to Species of *Notropis*

From this genus of typical shiners the subgenera *Luxilus* and *Lythrurus* have been elevated to generic status. *Ericymba* has been added to *Notropis* (*N. buccatus*) but we have rejected the placement of *Hybopsis* in *Notropis*. The large cephalic lateralis chambers in *N. buccatus* should be revealed by a jet of compressed air or by blowing forcefully. Some species appear in key more than once.

1a   Cephalic lateralis canals on lower half of head much enlarged, forming somewhat squared chambers (Figure 27C); (small pallid species; mouth subterminal or inferior; dorsal fin origin above anterior half of pelvic fin base; anal rays modally 8) ... SILVERJAW MINNOW—*Notropis buccatus*   p. 443

1b   Cephalic lateralis canals not obviously enlarged 2

2a   Pharyngeal teeth usually 1,4–4,1 or 2,4–4,2 3

2b   Pharyngeal teeth 4–4 20

3a   Pharyngeal teeth usually 2,4–4,2 4

3b   Pharyngeal teeth usually 1,4–4,1 19

4a   Pelvic rays usually 8 5
4b   Pelvic rays usually 9 18

5a   Anal rays modally 8 or 9 6
5b   Anal rays modally 10 or 11 12

6a   Anal rays modally 8 7
6b   Anal rays modally 9 11

7a   Side distinctly pigmented below lateral line, usually to 2–3 scale
     rows below 8
7b   Side not pigmented below lateral line, or having sparse
     melanophores on first scale row below lateral line 9

8a   Dorsal fin membranes lacking pigment or with melanophores only
     near base (Figure 34H); dorsal fin origin and dorsum at posterior
     end of dorsal fin base entirely dusky; midlateral stripe developed
     from tail to head (sometimes less intense anteriorly); upper side not
     speckled .... SAFFRON SHINER—*N. rubricroceus*   p. 391
8b   Dorsal fin membranes well pigmented basally, melanophores
     present through basal 1/4 of one or more membranes (Figure 34G);
     dorsal fin origin and dorsum at posterior end of dorsal fin base
     each with a small pale area; lateral pigmentation includes a
     posteriorly developed midlateral stripe (which anteriorly fades
     completely); upper side often with many relatively darkened scales
     which produce a speckled appearance .... REDLIP SHINER—*N. chiliticus*   p. 395

9a   Anterior tip of dorsal fin, when depressed, just reaching to or
     extending only slightly past posterior tip of fin; (New drainage
     only) .... NEW RIVER SHINER—*N. scabriceps*   p. 413
9b   Anterior tip of dorsal fin, when depressed, extending well past
     posterior tip of fin 10

10a Lateral stripe best developed posteriorly, usually weak anteriorly;
     snout not encircled by bold dark band; lower lip and chin not
     pigmented (except lower lip pigmented in some young) ... SPOTTAIL SHINER—*N. hudsonius*   p. 410
10b Lateral stripe well developed from tail to head; snout encircled
     by bold dark band; lower lip and chin well pigmented
     (Figure 36D) .... IRONCOLOR SHINER—*N. chalybaeus*   p. 437

11a Mouth subterminal; peritoneum silvery, melanophores small,
     sparse; New drainage only .... NEW RIVER SHINER—*N. scabriceps*   p. 413
11b Mouth terminal; peritoneum black, dark, or at least 50% covered
     ventrally with medium or large melanophores; Tennessee drainage
     only .... POPEYE SHINER—*N. ariommus*   p. 405

12a Dorsal profile distinctly elevated to dorsal fin origin; lateral line
     usually incomplete .... HIGHFIN SHINER—*N. altipinnis*   p. 440
12b Dorsal profile nearly horizontal in contour, lacking distinct
     elevation to dorsal fin origin; lateral line usually complete 13

13a Dorsal fin origin usually moderately or much posterior to pelvic fin
     base 14
13b Dorsal fin origin above or slightly posterior to pelvic fin base 17

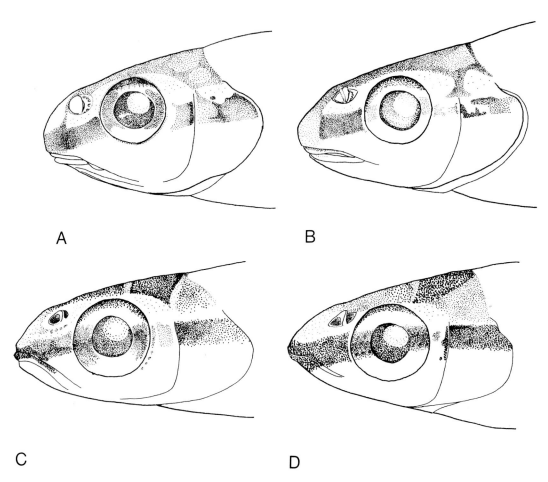

A   B

C   D

Figure 36 Diagnostic snout and lip pigmentation patterns in *Notropis*: (A) *N. alborus*. (B) *N. procne*. (C) *N. bifrenatus*. (D) *N. chalybaeus*.

14a   Anterior body below lateral line peppered with fine melanophores,
         often to 3 scale rows below; (James drainage only) . . . . ROUGHHEAD SHINER—*N. semperasper* p. 403
14b   Anterior body below lateral line immaculate or with a few
         melanophores, usually extending no more than 1 scale row below 15

15a   Anterior portion of lateral body stripe very diffuse; anterior lateral
         line pores not distinctly outlined by pigment (not distinctly stitched);
         predorsal stripe weakly developed, barely evident . . . . EMERALD SHINER—*N. atherinoides* p. 397
15b   Anterior portion of lateral body stripe distinct (although less
         intense than posterior portion); anterior lateral line pores outlined
         above and below by melanophores (stitched); predorsal stripe
         moderately well developed, distinct 16

16a   Chin pigment forming an elongate triangular patch (Figure 37A);
         anal rays modally 11; scales around back usually 15–17; anterior tip
         of dorsal fin, when depressed, extending past posterior tip of fin;
         anal fin margin slightly falcate . . . . COMELY SHINER—*N. amoenus* p. 399
16b   Chin pigment forming a rectangular or irregular patch (Figure 37B);
         anal rays modally 10; scales around back usually 13–15; anterior tip
         of dorsal fin, when depressed, about reaching posterior tip of fin;
         anal fin margin straight . . . . ROSYFACE SHINER—*N. rubellus* p. 386

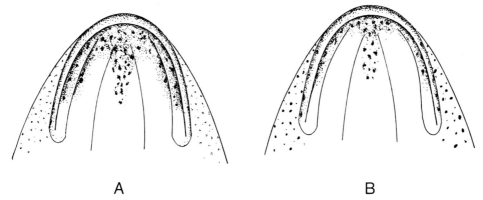

Figure 37 Chin pigmentation in *Notropis*: (A) *N. amoenus*. (B) *N. rubellus*.

17a Predorsal and anterior dorsolateral scales distinctly irregular in size,
shape, and/or orientation; anterior dorsolateral scale rows slightly
downcurved; circumbody scales (19)20–24(25); Tennessee, New,
and James drainages .... TELESCOPE SHINER—*N. telescopus* p. 408
17b Predorsal and anterior dorsolateral scales nearly uniform in
size; anterior dorsolateral scale rows horizontal, not downcurved;
circumbody scales (25)26–27(29); (may occupy Pee Dee
drainage) .... SANDBAR SHINER—*N. scepticus* p. 110

18a Mouth terminal; dorsal fin origin above posterior half of pelvic fin
base or slightly posterior; anal rays (9)10–11(13) .... SILVER SHINER—*N. photogenis* p. 401
18b Mouth subterminal or inferior; dorsal fin origin above anterior half
of pelvic fin base or slightly anterior; anal rays (7)8(9) ..... SPOTTAIL SHINER—*N. hudsonius* p. 410

19a Mouth terminal or slightly subterminal; caudal spot usually
rectangular; prominent pale stripe present just above posterior half
of dark midlateral stripe in adult; lower lip lined with
melanophores; Tennessee drainage (possibly also New drainage
near North Carolina) .... TENNESSEE SHINER—*N. leuciodus* p. 389
19b Mouth distinctly subterminal or slightly inferior; caudal spot, if
present, usually round, oval, or triangular; prominent pale stripe
absent above posterior half of dark midlateral stripe in adult; lower
lip usually lacking melanophores (except in small specimens);
Atlantic and New drainages .... SPOTTAIL SHINER—*N. hudsonius* p. 410

20a Anal rays modally 8 or 9 21
20b Anal rays modally 7 23

21a Dorsal fin with only the first 4–5 rays finely outlined
with melanophores (Figure 34E); (dorsal fin in adult often
with melanophores in first 4–5 membranes; Tennessee
drainage only) .... SAWFIN SHINER—*Notropis* undescribed species p. 419
21b Dorsal fin with all rays finely outlined with melanophores (Figure
34D, F) 22

22a Dorsal fin membranes lacking melanophores (Figure 34D) ..... MIMIC SHINER—*N. volucellus* p. 416
22b Dorsal fin membranes, especially anterior ones, in adult and large
juvenile slightly to heavily peppered with melanophores (Figure
34F); (Tennessee drainage only) .... MIRROR SHINER—*N. spectrunculus* p. 422

Key to Species of *Pimephales*

True carps   Genus *Cyprinus* Linnaeus

Cyprinus is the monotypic genus for the common carp. In recognizing two subfamilies of the Cyprinidae, Cavender and Coburn (1992) considered the African–Eurasian subfamily Cyprininae to include certain major carps such as barbins and labeonins, as well as *Cyprinus*.

Name.—See above.

Common carp   *Cyprinus carpio* Linnaeus

SYSTEMATICS

The common carp was described in 1758 from Europe. It is a tetraploid species (Buth 1984). Several squamation varieties infrequently occur in wild populations—the mirror carp with very large, irregular lateral scales, and the nearly naked leather carp. Other varieties have been cultured but are rare in nature in North America. Koi carp are colorful mutants often kept in garden ponds. Israeli carp are also *C. carpio*.

DESCRIPTION

Materials.—Based on Scott and Crossman (1973 [for counts]) and 5 Virginia specimens. Color in life from 3 Virginia specimens.

Anatomy.—A stout, high-backed minnow with 2 pairs of pendulate barbels and a large spinelike ray at front of dorsal and anal fins; adults are 350–700 mm TL. Body deep, somewhat compressed or cylindrical, dorsal profile much elevated; dorsal fin long-based, its origin above or anterior to pelvic fin origin. Head moderate or large, downsloped;

Fish 31 *Cyprinus carpio* juvenile 176 mm SL (REJ 1002), VA, Charlotte County, Twittys Creek, 13 July 1983.

eye small or moderate, lateral; snout narrowly rounded; frenum absent. Mouth small or moderate, subterminal; a medium-sized barbel arises from side of snout and a large barbel hangs from angle of mouth. Dorsal fin concave anteriorly; dorsal and anal spinelike rays serrate posteriorly. Breast and belly fully scaled. Tubercles of nuptial male fine, occurring on head and pectoral fin.

Meristics.—Pharyngeal teeth 1,1,3–3,1,1, teeth in main row molariform; lateral line complete, scales usually 35–39. Dorsal spine 1, rays (15)18–20(23); anal spine 1, rays (4)5(6); pelvic rays 8–9; pectoral rays (14)15–16(17).

Color in Preservative.—Ground shade light or moderately dusky; head dorsum and back moderately dusky to dark; scales on side with dark basal spot or crescent, margins medium dusky or dark; venter pale. All fins moderately dusky.

Color in Life.—Juvenile and nonnuptial adult brassy olive; scale bases dark olive, venter silver-brassy. Dorsal fin gray-olive; caudal fin olive with red wash in lobes, best developed in lower lobe; anal and pelvic fins with red wash; pectoral fin medium olive. Nuptial adult similar except venter pale yellow, and red in lower caudal lobe and anal fin more intense.

Larvae.—Described by Mansueti and Hardy (1967), Taber (1969), Lippson and Moran (1974), Jones et al. (1978), Kindschi et al. (1979), Loos et al. (1979), Heufelder and Fuiman (1982), and Gerlach (1983).

BIOLOGY

The common carp is an omnivore; the diet includes aquatic and terrestrial invertebrates, small fishes, plants, and organic refuse (Scott and Crossman 1973; Eder and Carlson 1977; Becker 1983). Several authors reported the gathering of common carp below sewage outfalls, and purportedly they can be sustained on stockyard feces. Carp often root in soft bottoms,

ejecting silt while retaining edible items, and sometimes sip at the surface, eating algae and other floating organisms (Scott and Crossman 1973). Brain morphology indicates relatively high development of areas associated with taste feeding (Satô 1941; Evans 1952). The molariform teeth aid in crushing a variety of items including small clams, seeds, and fibrous plants.

Some rapidly growing males may mature at age 1, but in temperate climates most males mature at ages 2–4; females generally mature at ages 3 or 4 (Carlander 1969). The usual longevity of carp is 9–15 years (Becker 1983). Common carp seldom exceed 20 years in North America; the sometimes reported age of 150 years obviously is imaginative (Scott and Crossman 1973). Growth in North American populations is fairly uniform considering the range of occupied latitudes; adults at age 5 typically are 350–500 mm TL, extremes being 130–874 mm (Carlander 1969). The VDGIF historical (1970) angling record is 27.2 kg (60 pounds), exceeding the accepted world record of 26.2 kg, also from Virginia (IGFA 1985). The largest common carp on record appears to be a 37.4-kg (82.5-pound) fish from South Africa (Carlander 1969).

Spawning in North America occurs from late March to August and possibly September, at water temperatures of 9–32°C; activity usually begins at 14–18°C and terminates at 28°C (Jones et al. 1978). Wang and Kernehan (1979) reported spawning in Delaware to last from early May through early July, mostly in May and June, at 16–22°C. We noted spawning in late May and early June in the James River, and on 30 May in the Little River (Floyd County) at 21.5–24°C; Surber (1970) implied a similar period in the Shenandoah system. Spawning generally occurs in shallow backwaters and sloughs, and along shorelines of impoundments; it occurred throughout the tail and mid-

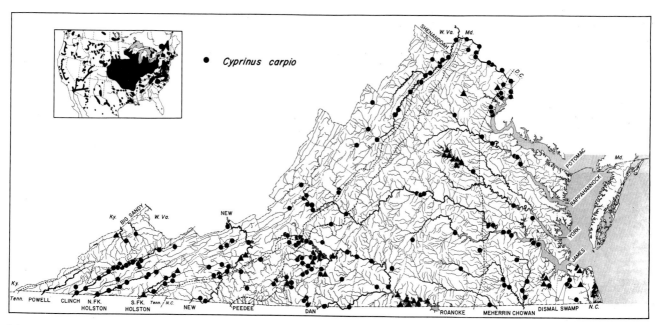

Map 35   Common carp.

dle of a pool in the Little River. In the absence of vegetation, common carp may spawn over tree roots or open bottom. Typically several males closely surround and nudge a female with the snout; the mating act often includes considerable surface commotion. Eggs are adhesive and demersal. Carp are among the most fecund of North American fishes; ovaries of large females may contain over 2 million eggs (Carlander 1969). The naturally occurring hybrid common carp × goldfish has been reported from North America (Schwartz 1981a).

HABITAT

The adaptable carp occurs in about every type of inland aquatic habitat, generally excepting high-gradient, small, coldwater mountain streams, alpine lakes, hot springs, and very low-pH waters. In streams the common carp typically is found in sluggish pools and backwaters over soft bottom. It associates with vegetation or occurs in open settings. Carp sometimes rove in schools. Vagility is variable; extreme distances of 1,000 rkm or more have been traversed during spring spawning migrations, but most carp do not appear to move much (Carlander 1969; Becker 1983). Ponds, lakes, and reservoirs are also occupied, rarely below depths of 30 m (Becker 1983).

Cyprinus is very tolerant of environmental conditions unfavorable to most fishes. It can accommodate persistent turbidity, low dissolved oxygen (it may gulp atmospheric air in anoxic conditions), relatively high temperatures (up to 35°C), and heavily polluted water (Carlander 1969; Jones et al. 1978; Becker 1983). It enters tidal fresh and brackish water (to 17.6‰ salinity) in Chesapeake Bay tributaries (Schwartz 1964), and purportedly enters sea water in Russia (Jones et al. 1978).

DISTRIBUTION   Map 35

Indigenous to Asia, the common carp was cultured in Europe by the 13th century, and by the 19th century wild populations occurred throughout temperate Eurasia (Peterson and Drews 1957; Courtenay et al. 1984). The exact native-range boundaries may never be known because transfers began as early as Roman times (Courtenay et al. 1984).

Cyprinus was first imported to North America in 1831 and liberated in the Hudson River, New York (Courtenay et al. 1984). However, the carp craze did not sweep the country until the late 1870s, at which time its propagation was undertaken by newly created state and federal hatchery systems, and the common carp was quickly disseminated across the country, including Virginia. It rapidly became established; by the early 1900s large commercial catches were being reported, particularly in the upper Mississippi basin (Forbes and Richardson 1920; Hildebrand and Schroeder 1928).

The earliest introduction of the common carp in Virginia known to us was in 1880 (VFC 1882). Much earlier in the region the name carp was applied to carpsuckers, genus *Carpiodes*. *Cyprinus* now occurs in all major drainages of Virginia and probably is continuously distributed through main river channels.

Abundance.—Usually uncommon or common.

REMARKS

Early promoters of the common carp perceived it as a swimming panacea, particularly for the south, a region that S. F. Baird believed to need a popular equivalent to the trouts of northern states (Hildebrand and Schroeder 1928). The common carp quickly gained political backing by congressmen, who found it easy to fulfill constituents' requests for the newly imported fish (Regier 1976). Perhaps the notion of a carp in every pond preceded a chicken in every pot. However, the carp quickly declined in public esteem, and by the mid-1890s its introduction was considered by many to be a serious mistake. Some states have costly carp eradication programs; generally they do not work well, sometimes harm ecosystems, and must be continued to approach intended results.

The common carp's fall from grace apparently was precipitated by several factors. Like all cyprinids its meat is laden with small intramuscular bones, reducing ease of preparation and effecting a spiky meal. Adams and Hankinson (1928) lamented that if the public would only learn to prepare the fish correctly, it would not be so maligned. However, fastidious preparation may include keeping the fish alive in fresh clean water for a period of time prior to cleaning, a facility and habit most Americans lack.

The common carp became a scapegoat. Concurrent with its rapid proliferation was the decline of favored native game and commercial fishes. The carp became labeled a "spawneater" and a rogue. It was said, and is still held, to cause excessive turbidity by its rooting and spawning activities. Hildebrand and Schroeder (1928) correctly warned that the decline of native fishes generally was not attributable to the carp, but rather to the result of general degradation of aquatic ecosystems.

It is slowly being conceded that the common carp is not the villain it was long labeled, nor is it by any stretch of the imagination the popular equivalent of trout. Although it has a plebeian palate, it can be wary of a baited hook; often it stages a whale of a fight when hooked. Interestingly, common carp can lock-in on a taste "search image." We heard of carp congregating below fruiting mulberry trees, and they could only be caught with a hook threaded with a ripe mulberry. Sometimes it is the quarry of bow-and-arrow fishermen. In zealous defense of the carp, Peterson and Drews (1957) suggested it as a possible food source in a nuclear holocaust.

Name.—*Carpio*, Latin name for carp.

Crucian carps   Genus *Carassius* Nilsson

Carassius is a Eurasian genus of the subfamily Cyprininae; it contains two species, the goldfish *C. auratus*, and the Crucian carp *C. carassius*.

Name.—*Carassius*, from karass or karausche, European vernacular names for the Crucian carp.

Goldfish   *Carassius auratus* (Linnaeus)

SYSTEMATICS

Carassius auratus, described in 1758 from China and Japan, is considered a tetraploid derivative of *C. carassius* (Raicu et al. 1981; Buth 1984). The goldfish has a great variety of anatomical and color mutants.

DESCRIPTION

Materials.—Based on Taylor and Mahon (1977), Raicu et al. (1981), and our 2 specimens. Life color from Jones et al. (1978).

Anatomy.—A stocky minnow with a long-based dorsal fin and a large, posteriorly serrate spine in front of dorsal and anal fins; adults are 130–400 mm TL. Body stout, deep and compressed; caudal peduncle short; dorsal fin origin above or anterior to pelvic fin origin. Head and eye moderate, eye lateral; snout blunt; frenum absent; mouth small or moderate, terminal. Nuptial male with fine tubercles on opercle, dorsum, and pectoral fin; paired fins longest in male.

Meristics.—Pharyngeal teeth 4–4; lateral line complete, scales 28–32. Dorsal spines 2–3 (1 large one), rays (14)15–18; anal spines 2–3 (1 large), rays 5–6; pelvic rays 8–10; pectoral rays 14–17.

Color in Preservative.—Juveniles that were golden in life are pale, except dark visceral mass evident through abdominal wall.

Fish 32 *Carassius auratus* juvenile 44 mm SL, aquarium specimen.

Color in Life.—Highly variable. Naturalized fish are olive-brown or gray-olive with bronze sheens. Mutants are uniform or variegated silver, white, gray-yellow, gold, or orange, sometimes with black marks or blotches.

Larvae.—Described by Battle (1940), Mansueti and Hardy (1967), Lippson and Moran (1974), Jones et al. (1978), Loos et al. (1979), Snyder (1979), Wang and Kernehan (1979), Heufelder and Fuiman (1982), and Gerlach (1983).

BIOLOGY

Goldfish are omnivores. Although not well documented in the United States, the diet consists of phytoplankton, macrophytes, aquatic insects, and small fishes (Dobie et al. 1956; Carlander 1969; Seaman 1979).

Age and size at maturation are variable, apparently relating to feedback from an intrinsic growth substance (Carlander 1969). Maturation may occur at age 1; longevity of wild fish is usually 6 or 7 years. Age-3 fish in Wisconsin are 170–200 mm TL (Becker 1983); adults in Ohio typically are 250–400 mm TL (Trautman 1981). Goldfish tend to become stunted in dense populations.

The spawning season is long, lasting from late March to mid-August in Lake Erie, and February to November in Alabama, at a temperature range of 16–29°C (Battle 1940; Carlander 1969). Spawning occurs in June and July in Delaware, and begins in late April or early May and extends into the summer in the Potomac drainage (Lippson and Moran 1974; Wang and Kernehan 1979). Spawning takes place in coves and backwaters over aquatic macrophytes and tree roots. One or more males court and chase a female; adhesive eggs are shed in open water (Breder and Rosen 1966). Spawning occurs intermittently; females may lay 2,000–4,000 eggs per spawning (Dobie et al. 1956). Estimates of up to 400,000 eggs, presumably ovarian counts, have been reported (Jones et al. 1978). Common carp × goldfish natural hybrids have been reported in North America (Schwartz 1981a); Taylor and Mahon (1977) provide a detailed analysis of this cross in a Canadian population.

HABITAT

Goldfish are usually associated with vegetated areas of sluggish pools and backwaters in low-gradient warm streams. They also occur in ponds, lakes, and reservoirs. We found a few specimens in rocky pools of moderate-gradient streams. *Carassius* is a hardy minnow with a very high temperature tolerance, up to 41°C (Carlander 1969). It occasionally enters brackish water; maximum reported salinity is 17‰ (Schwartz 1964).

DISTRIBUTION   Map 36

Native to Asia and eastern Europe, the goldfish has been introduced worldwide in temperate latitudes. It was the first exotic fish introduced to North America, arriving in the late 1600s (Courtenay et al. 1984). Goldfish were maintained at a hatchery in Lexington, Virginia, during 1875–1877, and were intended for distribution the following year (VFC 1877a). They were propagated on a moderate scale in Washington, D.C., and Wytheville, Virginia, during the late 1800s by the USFC. Populations in the Potomac River probably are descendants of fish reared by the USFC, and may be the only established riverine populations in Virginia. Our Virginia records are few and scattered and do not reflect the extent of goldfish held in park ponds or those orphaned into the wild from aquaria.

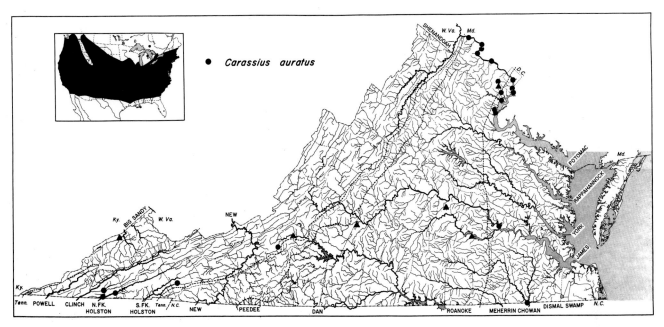

Map 36 Goldfish. Shaded part of inset too inclusive; goldfish absent from many sections of mountain chains.

Abundance.—Generally rare in the wild; sometimes numerous in ponds.

REMARKS

In its many mutant varieties, the goldfish is one of the most revered ornamental fishes. Because of its hardiness it is cultured for bait, and sometimes called a "Baltimore." *Carassius auratus* also has been used as a bioassay organism, a biasing practice because it is more tolerant of some environmental factors than are many native fishes.

Name.—*Auratus* means "golden."

Grass carps   Genus *Ctenopharyngodon* Steindachner

The monotypic genus *Ctenopharyngodon* is a member of the Eurasian xenocyprin group which Howes (1981) classified in the subfamily Cyprininae, but which was placed in the Leuciscinae by Cavender and Coburn (1992).

Name.—*Ctenopharyngodon*, "comb throat teeth," refers to the striated crown of the pharyngeal teeth.

Grass carp   *Ctenopharyngodon idella* (Valenciennes)

SYSTEMATICS

The grass carp was described from China in 1844. It reproduces naturally as a diploid (48 chromosomes), but most fish introduced to Virginia are supposedly sterile triploids (72 chromosomes).

DESCRIPTION

Materials.—Based on Nichols (1943), Minckley (1973), Shireman and Smith (1983), Crossman et al. (1987), and 5 fish from a Loanoke, Arkansas, hatchery. Color in life from Pflieger (1975).

Anatomy.—A stout-bodied minnow with a short caudal peduncle, broad head, and grooved pharyngeal teeth; adults are 500–900 mm TL. Body moderate or somewhat elongate in profile, cylindrical or slightly compressed; caudal peduncle short, relatively deep; dorsal fin origin somewhat anterior to pelvic fin origin. Head somewhat short; eye moderate, lateral; snout narrowly rounded or pointed, lacking frenum; mouth terminal, size moderate. Nuptial male with tubercles on head, upper caudal peduncle, leading edge of dorsal fin, and both pectoral fin surfaces; pectoral longest in male.

Meristics.—Pharyngeal teeth variable, usually 2,4–4,2, crowns of teeth in major row striately grooved (Figure 11C);

Fish 33 *Ctenopharyngodon idella* subadult male 218 mm SL, AR, Lonoke Hatchery, Arkansas, August 1984.

lateral line complete, scales 35–42. Dorsal rays 8–9; anal rays 8–10; pelvic rays 8–9; pectoral rays 19–22.

Color in Preservative.—Head and body dorsum slightly dusky to dark; side pale or silvery, scales darkly outlined; venter pale. Fins pale or moderately dusky.

Color in Life.—Back olive-brown, side silver, venter white.

Larvae.—Described by Conner et al. (1980) and Shireman and Smith (1983).

BIOLOGY

The life history of the grass carp is summarized by Shireman and Smith (1983); other reviews are cited by Guillory (*in* Lee et al. 1980). The *Transactions of the American Fisheries Society* devoted about half of a 1978 issue to reports on the distribution and ecology of grass carp.

Grass carp are herbivores. Young eat plankton, but by about 20 mm TL they begin switching to aquatic macrophytes; by 45–86 mm TL macrophytes dominate the diet. Epiphytic microcrustaceans and aquatic insects are incidentally ingested with macrophytes, and when vegetation is unavailable, insects and small fishes may be eaten. The grass carp is selective; unpalatable plants usually are eaten only after preferred ones are cropped. The grooved pharyngeal teeth are well suited for shredding vegetation.

Maturation, growth, and longevity are highly variable. Age at maturation is 1–11 years in wild Eurasian populations. Males tend to mature earlier and at smaller size than females. The usual range in size of maturing males in wild populations is 510–600 mm SL, females 580–670 mm. Adult *C. idella* in the Amur River typically are 5–11 years old; maximum known longevity is 21 years. Early growth in nutrient-rich environments is rapid. Some fish exhibit average weight gains of 1 kg per month in the first year, but such growth in wild populations apparently is un-

common. Age-6 fish from several populations in the Amur basin are 498–544 mm SL. A 10-kg specimen was removed from a Virginia pond (J. W. Kauffman, personal communication). A likely reliable maximum length of 1,100 mm TL and weight of 59 kg have been noted, and rather incredible weights of 120–180 kg (about 265–397 pounds) have entered the literature.

Wild populations in temperate latitudes spawn in May and June; several spawning peaks may occur. The grass carp begins movement to spawning areas when water temperature reaches 15–17°C; spawning occurs at 18–23°C. Initiation of spawning movements appears strongly tied to rising water levels. Migrations of up to 1,000 rkm have been reported. Reproduction occurs in large rivers and canals with moderate to strong current; grass carp do not spawn in ponds or lakes. Mating occurs communally, several males following a female; rolling at the surface and jumping often occur. Egg numbers range 10,000–1,276,000. The semipelagic eggs drift downstream and hatch in current; hatchlings sequester in vegetated backwaters.

HABITAT

Ctenopharyngodon idella is a vagile minnow adapted to warm large rivers with a moderate diversity of current-defined habitats. Grass carp typically occur in vegetated pools, backwaters, and coves during warm months and retreat to the bottom of deeper sections in winter. They readily adapt to pond culture. This hardy fish can live in moderate to high turbidity, accommodates a pH range of 5.0–9.0 and near-anoxic water (dissolved oxygen as low as 0.5 mg/liter), and occasionally enters salinities of 7–12‰.

DISTRIBUTION   Map 37

Native to eastern Asia, the grass carp has a long history of aquaculture dating to the Chinese T'ang Dynasty (618–917 AD), and has been introduced

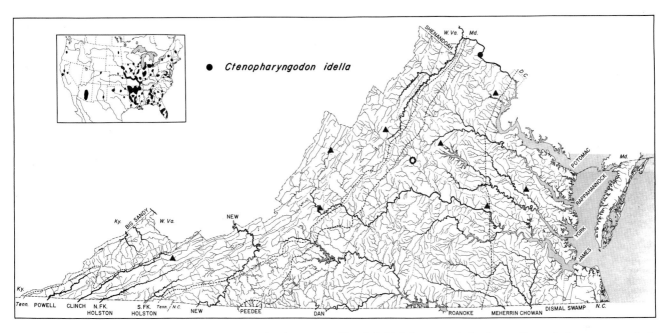

Map 37 Grass carp. Closed symbols are records of purportedly triploid fish; open circle shows the only known record of diploid fish; other diploids may be introduced.

worldwide. It was first brought to the USA in 1963 from Malaysia and Taiwan to be raised in experimental ponds in Alabama and Arkansas (Guillory and Gasaway 1978). The purpose of introduction was to explore *C. idella*'s possible use as a biological controller of densely growing or otherwise undesirable aquatic plants, especially exotic species such as water hyacinth, Eurasian watermilfoil, and hydrilla (Shireman 1984).

Following its introduction to the USA, *Ctenopharyngodon* was released or escaped and subsequently has naturally immigrated or been transported to waters of at least 35 states (Guillory and Gasaway 1978). It reached Canadian waters of Lake Erie by 1985 (Crossman et al. 1987). Although Pflieger (1978) could not document reproduction in Missouri streams, the very rapid dispersal of grass carp suggested natural reproduction (or massive releases). Reproduction of *Ctenopharyngodon* was verified by the capture of larvae in the Mississippi River of Arkansas and Louisiana (Conner et al. 1980). Considering its great reproductive potential and peregrine nature, the grass carp can be expected to invade much of the Mississippi basin by the year 2000.

Grass carp have been sparingly imported to Virginia. The VDGIF provides permits for purchase of only the certified sterile triploid. The distribution map indicates a small fraction of the liberated, presumably triploid populations. During 1983–1987, 125 permits for importation of triploids from approved

Arkansas hatcheries were granted, and the application rate appears to be rising (T. P. Gunter, in litt.). The VDGIF has stocked triploids in Lakes Burke, Orange, and Shenandoah, and in the spring pond at Coursey Springs Fish Hatchery. These fish originated from a fish farm in Loanoke, Arkansas, and were maintained in Virginia at the Stevensville Fish Hatchery prior to dispersal. The only stream record known to date from in or along Virginia is a single fish captured in the Potomac River, probably a pond escapee (Enamait and Davis 1982).

Importation of potentially reproductive diploid grass carp is illegal in Virginia. A diploid population discovered in a pond just north of Charlottesville was removed with rotenone by the VDGIF (J. W. Kauffman, personal communication).

Abundance.—Presently rare; introductions have been limited but are increasing.

REMARKS

The grass carp is obviously here to stay. The stocking of presumably sterile triploid fish in closed and open waters was approved by the U.S. Fish and Wildlife Service in 1985 (Radonski 1986), but most states have banned their use (Allen et al. 1986; Allen and Wattendorf 1987). Unfortunately, it seems probable that reproductive diploid fish from the Mississippi basin will eventually invade and naturalize in other basins and drainages. Although there are abundant data concerning the effects of grass carp on pond and lake ecosystems, scant information exists regarding its potential influence on our riverine ecosystems.

Triploids are produced by physically shocking eggs—immersing them in cold or warm water, or using hydrostatic pressure—to stimulate retention of a set of chromosomes normally expelled during gamete development (Clugston and Shireman 1987). Triploid female grass carp are sterile but triploid males may have a remote chance of reproducing with diploid females (Allen et al. 1986; Allen and Wattendorf 1987).

If diploid grass carp become established in large rivers of Virginia, the overall effect would be negative, probably resulting in reduced habitat diversity. Aquatic macrophytes serve as nurseries and refugia for invertebrates and fishes and also stabilize river bottoms (Hynes 1970). The effect of macrophyte cropping may be greatest in the lower Piedmont and Coastal Plain, where habitat diversity may be provided more by vegetation than by rocky bottom. Other possible effects are increased turbidity and alteration of food webs and nutrient cycles. Several studies have demonstrated that relatively high grass carp densities can lead to extensive cropping of vegetation, which in turn may lead to eutrophication and algal blooms (Taylor et al. 1984).

In general, our experience with exotic species has been overwhelmingly negative; very few species are arguably beneficial. Unfortunately, the lesson of hindsight seems to be repeatedly ignored. Although sterile grass carp seem an attractive means of control of aquatic macrophytes, their use may prove environmentally expensive. Diploids have escaped from well-intentioned aquaculturists, and worse, certain state agencies with cavalier attitudes have released reproductive fish.

Name.—*Idella* means "distinct." Grass carp sometimes are called "white Amur," for the Amur River where they are native.

Golden shiners   Genus *Notemigonus* Rafinesque

Phylogenetically and biogeographically, the monotypic genus *Notemigonus* is one of the more interesting native North American minnows. Several early and recent workers have indicated that it probably is most closely related to golden shinerlike Eurasian genera of the nominal subfamily Abramidinae (e.g., Coad 1975; Gosline 1978). Similarities among *Notemigonus* and the Eurasian genera include a fleshy ventral ridge (Figure 29), a deep and compressed body with a much decurved lateral line, and a falcate, long-based anal fin. Howes' (1981) osteological study did not support such a relationship.

Cavender and Coburn (1992) concluded from bone, scale, and earlier-used characters that *Notemigonus* is the only American member of the subfamily Leuciscinae that is not a phoxinin, and that its kinship is with Eurasian leuciscins (="abramidins"). Loos et al. (1979) found that the early development of *Notemigonus* is distinct from that of other eastern American minnows. We note that the nuptial tubercle pattern of *Notemigonus* is quite different from that of other American minnows. The golden shiner was successfully hybridized with a Eurasian leuciscin, the rudd *Scardinius erythrophthalmus*, which has been introduced to North America.

Name.—*Notemigonus*, "back, angled," in reference to the narrow back.

Golden shiner   *Notemigonus crysoleucas* (Mitchill)

SYSTEMATICS

The golden shiner was described from New York in 1814. It is a geographically plastic species; variation is described by Schultz (1926), Gosline (1948), Hart (1952), and Scott and Crossman (1973).

DESCRIPTION

Materials.—Counts from Frey (1951), Scott and Crossman (1973), and Coad (1975); other characteristics from 16 Virginia lots (tuberculation from CU 14369). Color in life from Hildebrand and Schroeder (1928), Coad (1975), and 2 Virginia adults.

Anatomy.—A deep-bodied compressed minnow with a much upturned mouth, fleshy ridge between pelvic fin and anus, and falcate anal fin; adults are 70–200 mm TL. Body moderate or deep in profile and moderately or strongly compressed, most so in adult; venter between pelvic fin base and anus with partly unscaled ridge, best developed in adult; dorsal fin origin moderately or much posterior to pelvic fin base. Head moderate or small; eye moderate or large, lateral; snout pointed or somewhat rounded; frenum absent; mouth medium or small, terminal or supraterminal, sharply upturned. Belly and breast fully scaled. Nuptial male with mostly tiny tubercles on head, body, and all fins, including the ventral surfaces of paired fins.

Fish 34 *Notemigonus crysoleucas* adult male 74 mm SL (REJ 1018), VA, Southampton County, Tarrara Swamp, 15 July 1983.

Fish 35 *Notemigonus crysoleucas* juvenile 28 mm SL (REJ 1015), VA, Greensville County, Cattail Creek, 15 July 1983.

Meristics.—Pharyngeal teeth 5-5; lateral line complete, markedly downcurved, scales (39)44–56(57); scales above lateral line 8–11; scales below lateral line 2–4; circumpeduncle scales 14–16. Dorsal rays (7)8(9); anal rays quite variable, (8)12–15(19); pelvic rays (8)9; pectoral rays 16–17(18).

Color in Preservative.—In medium to large adult, head dorsum and back moderately dusky; lateral scales sometimes darkly outlined and with dark bases, or pattern vague when silver color retained; venter pale; cheek and opercle pale or silvery. Fins usually pale except caudal dusky. Juvenile and small adult similar to large adult except back with dark predorsal and postdorsal stripe; midlateral stripe present until about 110–120 mm TL, darkest in young and small juvenile.

Color in Life Plate 11.—Body silvery to brassy, sometimes with blue sheens dorsally; midlateral stripe in juvenile olive-black. Fins of breeding adult pale to bright yellow, paired fins sometimes crimson; anal fin sometimes red and with dark margin.

Larvae.—Described by Mansueti and Hardy (1967), Lippson and Moran (1974), Snyder et al. (1977), Snyder (1979), Jones et al. (1978), Loos et al. (1979), Wang and Kernehan (1979), Buynak and Mohr (1980b), and Heufelder and Fuiman (1982).

COMPARISON

The golden shiner is quite similar to the recently introduced rudd *Scardinius erythrophthalmus*. Both species should be identified in the same couplet in the *Key*. A distinguishing character is given in *Fishes of Possible Occurrence*.

BIOLOGY

The golden shiner is primarily a midwater to surface planktivore (Keast and Webb 1966; Gatz 1979; Hall et al. 1979). Principal prey include microcrustaceans and terrestrial and aquatic insects. Benthic insects, snails, and algae are occasionally eaten; Keast and Webb (1966) found increased ingestion of algae in late summer. The gut has a well-developed accessory loop (Coad 1975), deviating from the S-shaped gut of most carnivorous minnows. Movements in lakes parallel plankton migrations (Hall et al. 1979). Brain morphology is indicative of sight feeding (Evans 1952); Hall et al. (1979) noted that the eye is most sensitive to twilight wavelengths.

Maturation of both sexes in Michigan occurs at ages 1–3; most fish mature at age 2. Maturation is size-dependent; minimum size range of maturing fish is 50–70 mm SL in Michigan and New York. Maximum survival is 9 years (Cooper 1936; Forney 1957). Females tend to grow faster and live longer than males. Age-3 males in Michigan are 85–117 mm SL, females are 88–120 mm. In Ohio, age-3 fish of both sexes are 137–210 mm TL, about 108–166 mm SL (Hart 1952). Our largest Virginia adult is 181 mm SL, 231 mm TL.

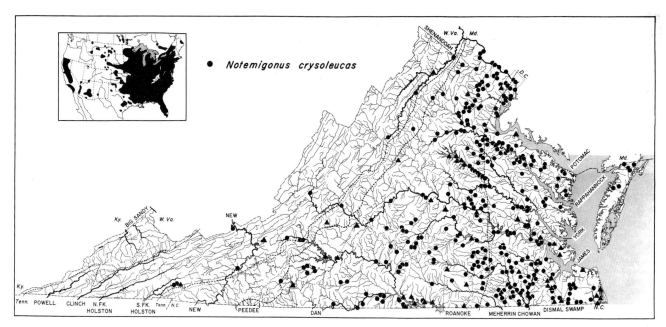

Map 38   Golden shiner.

A 267-mm TL specimen is from Ohio (Trautman 1981).

Spawning may occur from April into August (Carlander 1969; Jones et al. 1978); in the Potomac drainage it may extend into October (Lippson and Moran 1974). Golden shiners in a North Carolina swamp were gravid from mid-April to early August, water 15–21°C (Whitehurst 1981). In culture ponds spawning occurred between 21 and 26° and ceased above 26° (Dobie et al. 1956). Spawning shiners are gregarious; one or more males pursue a female in open water. Adhesive eggs are shed over vegetation, gravel, and sometimes nests of black bass and bluegill (Webster 1942; Kramer and Smith 1960; Loos et al. 1979; De-Mont 1982). Fecundity has been estimated as up to 200,000 eggs per female, but given the duration of the spawning season, cumulative egg production by an individual may be much higher.

Because of the suspected close affinity of *N. crysoleucas* to certain Eurasian minnows, more than usual interest would attend its hybridization with an American minnow. The hybrid *Notemigonus* × *Notropis chrysocephalus* was listed from an Illinois Lake by Tranquilli et al. (1981), but it is not confirmable. J. A. Tranquilli (in litt.) informed us that the identification was made by L. M. Page of the Illinois Natural History Survey. However, Page (in litt.) did not recall seeing the specimens and they are not at the INHS. Schwartz (1972) cited Hubbs (1970) concerning artificial hybridization of *Notemigonus* with a cyprinodontid but the embryos did not develop. The citation of intrafamilial *Notemigonus* hybrids by Schwartz

(1981a), credited to McAllister and Coad (1978), concerns only hypothetical crosses. Male *Notemigonus* will readily hybridize with female *Scardinus erythrophthalmus* in the laboratory (Burkhead and Williams 1991).

HABITAT

The golden shiner is a warmwater species occurring in a wide spectrum of lacustrine habitats and slack water of creeks, streams, and rivers. It typically is found in medium to large streams of low to moderate gradient, and in swamps, ditches, sloughs, ponds, lakes, and reservoirs. It sometimes schools in the open and along edges of weedy areas. In lakes, Hall et al. (1979) found it to occur in shallow inshore areas among vegetation during the day and to move into open water at dusk, coincident with plankton migrations.

Notemigonus is tolerant of persistent turbidity and high temperature. It has one of the highest lethal temperature tolerances of any indigenous North American fish, near 40°C (Alpaugh 1972). Norman and Southwick (1985) found it in moderately acidic waters (pH 5.5) of the Chowan drainage; it has been found in New Jersey lakes at pH 4.2 (Graham 1989). The golden shiner enters tidal freshwater sections of rivers and occasionally brackish areas. In the tidal Pamunkey River it is more common in vegetated coves than in the main channel (Raney and Massmann 1953). The maximum reported salinity association is 27‰ (Schwartz 1981b).

DISTRIBUTION   Map 38

Notemigonus is extensively distributed in eastern North America, but exhibits an aversion to montane and many upland areas. It is widely introduced. In Virginia the golden shiner is widespread east of the Blue Ridge and is found on the Delmarva Peninsula. It probably is more prevalent than shown, as our data base includes few samples from farm ponds, to which it is often introduced. Most records from the Blue Ridge and Valley and Ridge probably are of introductions. The golden shiner is the most common bait minnow in our area; many introductions undoubtedly are the result of bait release. It has been sparingly introduced to the New drainage (earliest records: North Carolina 1949; Virginia 1971; West Virginia 1970) and upper Tennessee drainage (earliest Virginia record 1966, near a hatchery using this species as forage).

Abundance.—Uncommon to abundant in Piedmont and Coastal Plain; rare in uplands.

REMARKS

Propagation of the golden shiner has been intensively studied; culture methods are described by Dobie et al. (1948, 1956) and Forney (1957). It is an excellent forage fish for introduction to ponds with largemouth bass. Large golden shiners are often caught by bait- and flyfishermen.

Name.—*Crysoleucas* means "golden white," in reference to body color. The name originally should have been spelled *chrysoleucas*; international rules of nomenclature require retention of the spelling in the first valid description.

Redbelly daces   Genus *Phoxinus* Rafinesque

The genus *Phoxinus* contains fine-scaled, ornately colorful, small minnows which occupy creeks and northerly bogs and lakes; two of the six North American species inhabit Virginia. The six species composed the genus *Chrosomus*, but were combined with the Eurasian genus *Moroco* into *Phoxinus* by Banarescu (1964), who gave no reason for the merger. Banarescu was followed by most North American ichthyologists, often only because the move was accepted by the Committee on Names of Fishes (Bailey et al. 1970). Thus *Phoxinus* was rendered the only genus of the family Cyprinidae that is native to both Eurasia and North America.

Quite divergent views on generic and specific status were espoused in two largely osteological studies, as exemplified by the treatment of a Virginia species. Mahy (1975) included the American redbelly daces in *Phoxinus* and considered *P. oreas* to be a subspecies of *P. erythrogaster*; he did not treat *Moroco*. Gasowska (1979) recognized *Phoxinus*, *Moroco*, and *Chrosomus* as genera and proposed *Parchrosomus* as a new genus solely for *P. oreas*.

Nuptial color and tuberculation, particularly the pearly silver-white spot at fin origins and the comb-like breast tubercles, indicate that the Eurasian *P. phoxinus* (the type species of *Phoxinus*) and the six American *Phoxinus* form a monophyletic group (Jenkins and Starnes 1981; Starnes and Jenkins 1988). In a primarily osteological study, Howes (1985) also stressed breast tuberculation to congenerically link these species; he tentatively retained in *Phoxinus* three or four nominal Asian forms that apparently are closely related to *P. phoxinus*. The Eurasian genus *Lagowskiella* (including *Moroco*) and related Eurasian genera were excluded from *Phoxinus* by Jenkins and Starnes (1981) and Howes (1985). *Phoxinus* (including *Chrosomus*) and related Eurasian genera are relatively primitive members of the chub clade of the phoxinin group of the subfamily Leucisinae (Cavender and Coburn 1992; Coburn and Cavender 1992).

Name.—*Phoxinus* is Greek for a minnow; it also means pointed or tapering and may refer to the snout. Banarescu (1964) is the first reviser in selecting *Phoxinus* over *Chrosomus* ("colored body"); both names date from Rafinesque (1820).

Tennessee dace   *Phoxinus tennesseensis* Starnes and Jenkins

SYSTEMATICS

This species was long confounded with, or regarded a subspecies of *P. oreas*, until described by Starnes and Jenkins (1988) from the Holston system of Virginia and elsewhere in the upper Tennessee drainage of Tennessee.

DESCRIPTION

Materials.—From over the range of the species (Starnes and Jenkins 1988). Color in life from 3 Virginia series.

Anatomy.—A fine-scaled minnow with two dark lateral stripes, the lower stripe at about its midlength being partly or entirely disaligned and having, in adult, a deflection

Fish 36A *Phoxinus tennesseensis* adult male 51 mm SL (REJ 1236), VA, Smyth County, Bear Creek, 20 May 1990.

Fish 36B *Phoxinus tennesseensis* adult female 47 mm SL (REJ 1236), VA, Smyth County, Bear Creek, 20 May 1990.

toward the anal fin; adults are 40–55 mm SL. Body form moderate, occasionally somewhat robust; dorsal fin origin slightly or moderately posterior to pelvic fin base. Head moderate; eye moderate or small, lateral; snout pointed or narrowly rounded; frenum absent; mouth small, subterminal, nearly horizontal; breast fully scaled. Intestine long, whorled; peritoneum dark.

Tubercles of male small or tiny, present over much of head, body, and most fins; tubercles elaborated as a patch on each of upper and lower operculum, comblike rows on breast, and encrustations on lower caudal peduncle.

Meristics.—Pharyngeal teeth 5–5; lateral line incomplete, midlateral scales (64)66–78(81); horizontal scale rows (diagonally from dorsal fin origin to anus) (27)28–33(34). Dorsal rays 8; principal caudal rays 19; anal rays (7)8(9); pelvic rays (6)8(9); pectoral rays (13)14–16(17).

Color in Preservative.—Young and small juvenile dusky above, pale below; dusky middorsal stripe present. Upper body unmarked or with few to numerous vague spots and irregular flecks, smaller than eye, markings best developed in larger fish. Two dusky or dark lateral stripes present in adult; lower stripe first developing in small young, upper stripe first appearing in large young or small juvenile and becoming prominent in large juvenile or adult. Upper lateral stripe usually more narrow and pale than lower stripe, usually uninterrupted on anterior half of body, tapering and often subdivided into speckles posteriorly, usually disappearing well short of caudal fin. Lower lateral stripe very slightly narrowed or disaligned or both at about its

midlength in young; with growth in juvenile and adult the disalignment increases, the two sections of the stripe may disconnect, and the posterior portion of the anterior section may lengthen and deflect obliquely toward the anal fin.

All fins largely or fully pale, pelvic and anal fins palest; dorsal fin often having dark streak epibasally; small vague caudal spot usually present at end of lower lateral stripe.

Nuptial male body stripes, spots, and blotches dark or black; lips, underside of head, and breast sooty or black. Nuptial female markings usually dusky or moderately dark.

Color in Life.—Young and juvenile olive above, side silver except lateral stripes dusky, belly white. Nuptial male with ground shade of dorsum tan or olive; dark marks and areas dusky or dark, or in peak the head ventrally and breast are jet black. Lower side and belly suffuse red to, in peak, intense scarlet; red also on tip and lower side of snout, upper and lower operculum, body just posterior to upper edge of operculum and bordering the opercular opening, along base of dorsal fin, and diffusely in caudal fin midbasally. Stripe just above lower lateral black stripe flat to shiny silver or gray-mustard (gold stripe not seen in Virginia). Silver-white below eye and along upper and lower edges of operculum; iris silver or yellow-gold where not black.

Lower fins moderate to bright lemon yellow; dorsal and caudal fins pale dusky or pale yellow, occasionally lemon; area of lower procurrent caudal rays lemon. Pearly silver-white area encircles pectoral fin base and is present at origin of all fins, or absent at dorsal, caudal, or anal fin origins.

Nuptial female subdued, with little or no red, silver, or gold, less often red moderately developed; dark areas dusky to diffusely black except chin pale as far as known; fins yellowed as in male, but usually paler or yellow absent; white spots and streaks usually smaller, less obvious than in male, or absent.

COMPARISON

Phoxinus daces are readily separable from most other minnows by the size of the scales, which are so small that they are not individually discernible by the unaided eye.

Large juvenile and adult *P. tennesseensis* and *P. oreas* are unmistakably distinguished from other eastern minnows by their color patterns, most notably in both the prominent interruption and ventral deflection of the lower dark lateral stripe (Figure 31A). Although young, juveniles, and some adult females of these two species lack some adult markings, their lower lateral stripe is slightly narrowed and disaligned where the interruption and deflection later develop beneath the dorsal fin (Figure 31B).

Use the following to distinguish *P. tennesseensis* from *P. oreas*: (1) upper lateral stripe and upper body pattern [stripe moderately or well developed on anterior half of body, spots and blotches absent above stripe or, if present, smaller than the eye in *tennesseensis* vs. stripe weak or absent, replaced dorsolaterally (and on dorsum) by large spots and blotches which often are larger than the eye in *oreas*]; (2) body form of adult usually [moderate vs. somewhat robust]; (3) color in life of nuptial male, on posterior half of body below lower lateral black stripe [red, developed from edge of black stripe to venter vs. silver or gold horizontal stripe below black stripe, then red to venter]; (4) color in life of nuptial male, between disconnected ends of lower lateral black stripe [largely or entirely red vs. entirely silver or gold].

BIOLOGY

The long whorled gut of the Tennessee dace indicates that this species feeds primarily on living and decaying plants; such materials were consumed by the few specimens examined (Starnes and Jenkins 1988). Having similar adult sizes, the four advanced species of *Phoxinus* may have similar patterns of maturation, growth, and longevity (Starnes and Jenkins 1988). *Phoxinus cumberlandensis* and *P. erythrogaster* lived 2–3 years; however, they matured in 1 year (Settles and Hoyt 1976, 1978; Starnes and Starnes 1981), whereas many specimens of *P. tennesseensis*

were immature yearlings. Our reproductive adults were 8 males of 46–51 mm SL, mean, 49, and 16 females 42–54 mm, mean, 48. The largest Virginia specimen is 58 mm SL; the largest known is 60 mm SL from Tennessee (Starnes and Jenkins 1988).

The Tennessee dace breeds in May, as determined in middle Bear Creek, a Middle Fork Holston River tributary. On 20 May 1990, water 16°C, small groups of nuptial *P. tennesseensis* and *Notropis rubricroceus* occupied spawning pits being dug in gravel in pool tails and runs by *Campostoma anomalum* and *Luxilus chrysocephalus*. The Tennessee dace may also spawn communally on unmodified beds of clean gravel, as known for some other species of *Phoxinus*. We caught peak nuptial Tennessee dace in a gravel run in middle Bear Creek on 20 May 1974, water 16.5°C. They were associated with highly colored *L. chrysocephalus* and *N. rubricroceus*, which spawn on gravel beds in the absence of nest-building stonerollers and chubs; no nests were noted at the site. A similar observation of *P. tennesseensis* was made in Tennessee in mid-May (Starnes and Jenkins 1988).

HABITAT

The Tennessee dace is essentially restricted to cool and cold, clear, small creeks. It typically dwells in rocky, gravelly, and silty pools in moderate-gradient wooded reaches, although the largest Virginia series is from a pasture reach.

DISTRIBUTION   Map 39

Phoxinus tennesseensis is endemic to and sharply localized within the Valley and Ridge and a few montane fringes of this province in the upper Tennessee drainage of Tennessee and Virginia (Starnes and Jenkins 1988). Only two small populations are known in Virginia, in headwater tributaries of the North or Middle forks of Holston River.

In the North Fork system, the population occupies the Bland County portion of Lick Creek; it may extend into the Smyth County section of the creek, where *P. oreas* is known (in lowermost Lynn Camp Creek). All records from the Middle Fork system, Smyth County, are from Bear Creek except for a specimen reported as *Phoxinus* sp. by Feeman (1980) from the mainstem Middle Fork just above the Bear Creek mouth. The unretained specimen of *P. "oreas"* taken in 1986 from Walker Creek (Saylor et al. 1988), a tributary of the Middle Fork midsection, may have been *P. tennesseensis*. The Tennessee dace occurs near Damascus, Virginia, in upper Beaverdam Creek, Tennessee, a tributary of Whitetop Laurel Creek of the

South Fork Holston system. *Phoxinus oreas* is recorded from two upstream sites in Whitetop Laurel Creek, Virginia.

Abundance.—Generally rare or uncommon; not found in many springs and cool creeks sampled by the Virginia Trout Survey and us.

REMARKS

The spawning male Tennessee dace—a true "red-belly dace"—displays the same dazzling variety of colors as the mountain redbelly dace *P. oreas*, although it lacks the prominent black blotches that adorn the back of the latter. The two species differ sharply in success. The relictive *P. tennesseensis* is very localized and often rare or uncommon in a region seemingly having extensive suitable habitat. *Phoxinus oreas* is generally distributed and usually common or abundant over much of the montane portion of its range, and it does well in many Piedmont streams. The Tennessee dace seems tied to small creeks including extreme headwaters but is absent in many trout streams. *Phoxinus oreas* populates lengthier reaches and, in mountains, is typically associated with trout as well as with warmwater faunas.

Phoxinus tennesseensis may be imperiled (Starnes and Jenkins 1988). Even with several populations in Tennessee, it has special concern status there (Starnes and Etnier 1980). With only two, perhaps three, small populations detected in Virginia, it is endangered there (Burkhead and Jenkins 1991). Threats to the Tennessee dace include impoundment, siltation, stream desiccation, disturbance of streambeds by floods and channelization, and introduction of *P. oreas*.

Name.—*Tennesseensis*, for the drainage to which the dace is confined.

Mountain redbelly dace

SYSTEMATICS

The mountain redbelly dace was first noticed by Cope (1868b) from a tributary of the North Fork Roanoke River, Virginia. This species of the central Atlantic slope and New drainage is the most advanced member of *Phoxinus* and forms a species pair with *P. tennesseensis* of the upper Tennessee drainage. The pair is the sister group of *P. cumberlandensis* in the upper Cumberland drainage (Starnes and Starnes 1978; Starnes and Jenkins 1988).

DESCRIPTION

Materials.—From the entire range of the species, based on Starnes and Jenkins (1988) and 25 more lots from Virginia. Color in life from Raney (1947b) and 9 series.

Anatomy.—A fine-scaled, blotch-backed minnow with one dark lateral stripe, the stripe partly or entirely disaligned at midlength and having an extension directed ventroposteriad toward the anal fin; adults are 40–55 mm SL. Morphology essentially as in *P. tennesseensis* but tending slightly stockier; other differences are treated by Starnes and Jenkins (1988).

Meristics.—Pharyngeal teeth usually 5–5; lateral line incomplete, midlateral scales (64)68–78(81); horizontal scale rows (27)28–33(34). Dorsal rays 8; principal caudal rays 19; anal rays 8(9); pelvic rays (7)8(9); pectoral rays (13)14–16(17).

Phoxinus oreas (Cope)

Color in Preservative.—As in *P. tennesseensis* except: in large juvenile or not until adult, entire upper lateral stripe is replaced by dorsolateral spots or blotches or both; blotches tend largest anteriorly; often some blotches fuse with midback blotches, which are derived from subdivided middorsal stripe; head dorsum blotched; blotches jet black in peak-colored male.

Color in Life Plate 11.—As in *P. tennesseensis* except as noted in *Comparison* under that species; also, in nuptial male *P. oreas* the area just below anterior portion of black lateral stripe usually is partly silver or gold; back yellow-gold between black blotches in peak phase (not seen in the few nuptial male *P. tennesseensis* available); stripe above lower lateral black stripe silver or gray-mustard, or in peak, bright yellow-gold (only silver and gray-mustard seen in *P. tennesseensis* in Virginia); and snout dorsolaterally with yellow V-shaped area (perhaps absent in *P. tennesseensis*).

A few nuptial females are as blackened, red-bellied, and yellow-finned as the typical nuptial male; many females have bright yellow paired fins but lack black and red.

Larvae.—Described by Loos et al. (1979).

COMPARISON

Distinguished from *P. tennesseensis* and other minnows in the account of that species.

BIOLOGY

The long gut adapts the mountain redbelly dace to an herbivore–detritivore mode of nutrition. In two

Fish 37A *Phoxinus oreas* adult male 49 mm SL (REJ 1235), VA, Roanoke County, Catawba Creek, 9 May 1990.

Fish 37B *Phoxinus oreas* adult female 58 mm SL (REJ 1235), VA, Roanoke County, Catawba Creek, 9 May 1990.

Virginia populations this species fed exclusively on algae and detritus (Flemer and Woolcott 1966; W. J. Matthews, in litt.); these items and aquatic insects were found in the diet of North Carolina fish (Gatz 1979). Age and growth probably are similar to those of other advanced *Phoxinus* species, but most yearling *P. oreas* are immature. Females were considered to average slightly larger than males (Cope 1868b; Raney 1947b), but S. B. Harvey (in litt.) found no length difference; his breeding adults from Virginia were 173 males of 37–64 mm SL, mean, 48, and 43 females of 40–57 mm, mean, 47. The largest known specimen, 66 mm SL, is from Virginia.

Phoxinus oreas spawns from mid-spring into early summer on gravel nests of other minnows. Of the 30 days during 11 years through 1990 in which we or S. B. Harvey (in litt.) recorded reproductive aggregations of this dace on *Nocomis leptocephalus* nests in central Virginia, all but one day occurred during 28 April–21 June. Raney (1947b) found *P. oreas* spawning on a *Nocomis* nest during 21–22 June in central Virginia. On our exceptional date, 9 July 1989, nuptial dace were on the nest of a late-breeding *N. leptocephalus*. Daytime water temperatures taken on 26 dates when breeding groups were observed on *Nocomis* nests spanned 14.5–25.3°C, mean, 19.4.

Nuptial mountain redbelly dace assembled on

nests of *Semotilus atromaculatus* in a rivulet at Roanoke College during 23 March–15 May in 1987–1990, water 12.5–22°C, mean, 15.3. The 9 July dace aggregation also occurred here. In 1990 the onset of dace spawning was asynchronous with that of *Semotilus* nesting, which began on 12 March; *P. oreas* first gathered over nests on 23 March. Breeding may also occur in gravel runs in the absence of nest-builders, but we found no evidence of this; the upstream limits of dace and nest-building chubs are about the same. *Phoxinus oreas* has not been found to aggregate on the nest of the two species of *Exoglossum*, which breed concurrently with *Nocomis* but their nests generally are smaller, have smaller pebbles, and occur in slower current.

The mountain redbelly dace is a communal spawner; typically 15–50 males jockey low over a chub nest. Females entering the nest are swarmed by usually 2–10 males and spawning often occurs en masse (Raney 1947b; S. B. Harvey, in litt.; our observations). Often in apparent attempts to court, one to several males chase females that are away from a nest.

Hybridization occurs with the nest builder *Nocomis leptocephalus* and its nest associates *Clinostomus funduloides* (Norman and Southwick 1985; RC), *Luxilus cerasinus* (Raney and Lachner 1946c; Hambrick 1977),

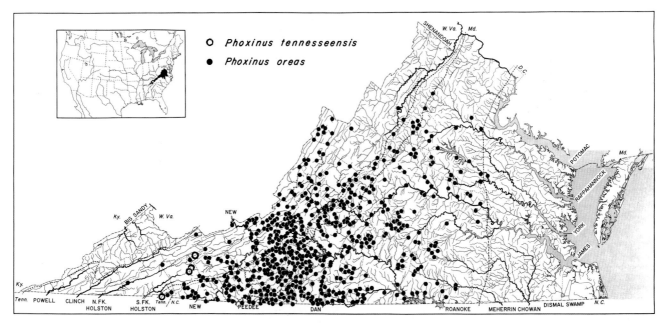

Map 39 Tennessee dace and mountain redbelly dace. Tumbling Creek and upper Whitetop Laurel Creek records of *P. oreas* in the Holston are uncertain; see *Distribution* under *P. oreas*. The portion of the range in the state of Tennessee is occupied by *P. tennesseensis*.

L. cornutus (Raney 1950; RC), probably *L. albeolus* (RC), and possibly *Campostoma anomalum* (RC).

HABITAT

Like many dace species, *P. oreas* is characteristic of creeks and small streams up to about 15 m wide, in montane and upland regions. It occasionally occurs as sparse populations in medium-sized streams. The mountain redbelly dace occurs primarily in pools, often in slow runs, and occasionally in riffles. Jenkins and Freeman (1972) did not report it from riffles because it was very rare in that habitat; occupied riffles usually were short. Matthews (1990) reported varying, sometimes high-percentage catches of *P. oreas* from riffles and noted that adults were much more abundant in pools. This species inhabits sandy, gravelly, and rocky areas. Moderate turbidity and siltation are tolerated, judging from its occupation of much of the upper and middle Piedmont.

DISTRIBUTION   Map 39

Phoxinus oreas occurs on the Atlantic slope from the Potomac to the Neuse drainage and occupies the Pee Dee, New, and Tennessee drainages (Starnes and Starnes *in* Lee et al. 1980; Starnes and Jenkins 1988). Its status (i.e., native or introduced), in 4 of the 11 drainages is questionable. Its availability to bait sein-

ers and spectacular coloration enhance its being moved about in buckets. Multiple introductions to a drainage seem possible. Several of the cases parallel those of *Nocomis leptocephalus* or *Thoburnia rhothoeca*.

Two systems of the Potomac drainage are populated, both likely via transplantation. *Phoxinus oreas* is known in Strait Creek, South Branch system, at two adjacent sites sampled in 1975. The area is considerably trafficked by trout fishermen. In the South Fork Shenandoah system this species is widespread but localized; the earliest capture was in 1956. Raney (1950) erred in ascribing to Miller (1946) an earlier Potomac record; Miller's new records were for the New drainage.

In the Rappahannock drainage the earliest record dates to 1951, from the South River of the Rapidan system in the Blue Ridge. The Blue Ridge portion of the drainage had been moderately well surveyed before 1951. The South River heads against the James drainage, a likely source for *P. oreas*. All subsequent records date since 1971; the first record for the upper Rappahannock system proper is from 1974. If *P. oreas* is native to the drainage, the Blue Ridge and upper Piedmont tributaries would be expected to be more widely inhabited. Recent downstream dispersal and further colonizations following release in the Rapidan may have caused the distribution pattern; perhaps the upper Rappahannock proper records represent an additional introduction.

In the York drainage the first record is from 1946 in a tributary next to the James; all other records date since 1958. The distribution pattern is wide and somewhat localized, as expected in a middle and lower Piedmont area, and contrasts with the Rappahannock pattern. We therefore consider *P. oreas* as probably native to the York.

The first capture of *P. oreas* in the Pee Dee drainage was during 1970 in North Carolina (Bortone 1972). Bortone thought the population to have stemmed from bait introduction. We agree because this species was not found in the extensive survey of the drainage during 1960–1961 by the North Carolina Wildlife Resources Agency, nor earlier or later in North Carolina by many others. Bortone's site is just across the divide from the Dan system, Roanoke drainage, where the dace is common. There are eight records of *P. oreas*, all from 1983–1984, in the small Virginia portion of the Pee Dee.

The New drainage population has distributional oddities, as occurs commonly with fishes of the drainage. The distribution pattern is general in much of the Virginia portion of the New, but the dace is localized or absent in a group of eastern tributaries below Claytor Lake and in several northwestern tributaries. Much of the North Carolina section is unpopulated; most records are near Virginia (E. F. Menhinick, in litt.; NCSM 4020 [apparently reported as *Rhinichthys atratulus* by Richardson and Carnes 1964]). The West Virginia population is considerably disjunct from Virginia; it apparently occupies only the Greenbrier system (Hocutt et al. 1978; MCZ uncataloged, tributary Knapp Creek; probably Addair's [1944] specimens of *P. "erythrogaster"*).

Perhaps the best evidence of native status in the New is McDonald's specimen (USNM 131368) taken near Wytheville in 1885; it predates the 1938 series on which the first report from the drainage (Miller 1946) is based. The range of *P. oreas* in the New is sufficiently wide above and below Claytor Dam that it is unlikely that all subpopulations stemmed from multiple introductions. Further, the population connects those of *P. oreas* on the Atlantic slope with its close kin in the Tennessee drainage, *P. tennesseensis*.

Three records in the upper Holston system are listed by Starnes and Jenkins (1988); they span 1966–1983. The adult (REJ 980) constituting one of these, the lower of the two for Whitetop Laurel Creek on Map 39, could not be located for restudy, but it undoubtedly was *P. oreas*. Three records mapped here are not plotted by Starnes and Jenkins (1988). Concerning two of these, *P. oreas* was reportedly taken farther up Whitetop Laurel Creek and in Tumbling Creek during the Virginia Trout Survey in 1978. Although the specimens were not saved, likely they were introduced *P. oreas*. The specimens for the third record (the farthest down the Holston, in 1955) are lost, but Ross and Carico (1963) stated that they clearly were not the fish now known as *P. tennesseensis*.

Abundance.—Often common or abundant from New drainage east to central Piedmont; usually rare or uncommon, sporadically common in lower Piedmont; rare in Tennessee drainage.

REMARKS

The nuptial male mountain redbelly dace is a harlequin of silver, gold, yellow, red, olive, and black. Edward C. Raney (1947b) proclaimed it one of the most brilliantly colored vertebrates. Its discoverer Edward Drinker Cope apparently was impressed by the dace and mentioned it in a letter to his father. Its ornate color pattern is the most complex in *Phoxinus*, a genus replete with gaudiness.

Fish enthusiasts on collecting tours in Virginia anticipate seeing this dace and often make a special effort to find it. However, many are disappointed upon netting them in only subdued or silvery colors, often the case even during the breeding season. What could be expected of a small fish among piscine and other predators, but to show its colors only when they count most—over the nest. We have seen *P. oreas* "fire up" upon gathering to spawn. When one of these gems is captured for a photograph, the picture should be taken quickly because the red and black can diminish quickly with lack of sexual stimuli or natural setting.

Phoxinus oreas is a quite successful herbivore in the central half of Virginia. It is one of the most headward inhabitants, tolerating the abrupt changes in physical-chemical conditions which occur in intermittent streams (Matthews and Styron 1981). Males would seem vulnerable to overhead predators when over nests in shallow water, but in fact the dace is well disguised; the reds are not visible in dorsal view and the blotchy back effects camouflage. It is mainly the silver-white spots that give them away to the observer, from the side.

The mountain redbelly dace is a strong candidate for designation as the "state fish" of Virginia, owing to its regal colors and the great success of many populations; most of its range is in Virginia.

Name.—Oreas, "of the mountains."

Redside daces　　Genus *Clinostomus* Girard

Clinostomus contains two colorful eastern American species, one of which occurs in Virginia. It has a checkered history of lumping and splitting with the western genera *Richardsonius* and *Gila* (Bailey 1956; Uyeno 1961; Buhan 1969). Mayden (1989) allied *Clinostomus* with *Richardsonius*; Coburn and Cavender (1992) ranked them as the most primitive sister group in the shiner clade.

Name.—*Clinostomus* translates as "inclined mouth," referring to the markedly oblique mouth.

Rosyside dace　　*Clinostomus funduloides* Girard

SYSTEMATICS

The rosyside dace was described by Girard (1856) from the Potomac River, Washington, D.C. Of the three subspecies (Deubler 1955), *C. f. funduloides* occurs in Virginia. Nomenclature was clarified and the long-used name *vandoisulus* was rejected by Lachner and Deubler (1960). Masnik (1971) described patterns of intraspecific variation that support the occurrence of stream captures between the Roanoke and New drainages.

DESCRIPTION

Materials.—Based on Lachner and Deubler (1960), Masnik (1971), and 41 Virginia lots. Color in life based mainly on 3 Virginia adults.

Anatomy.—A moderately compressed minnow with dark dappling on the side and a large mouth; adults are 50–80 mm SL. Body form moderate, slightly or moderately compressed; dorsal fin origin above posterior half of pelvic fin base or, usually, slightly or moderately posterior to base. Head moderate; eye lateral, medium or large; snout pointed or narrowly rounded, frenum absent; mouth large, terminal or slightly supraterminal, oblique. Belly fully scaled, breast nearly fully scaled. Peritoneum silver.

Nuptial male extremely tuberculate, head with small to medium-sized tubercles, body coarsely tuberculate all over, and in peak male all fins with tubercles. Female with scattered head tubercles; genital papilla of reproductive female about twice the size of male papilla and with a prominent fleshy ventral ridge.

Meristics.—Pharyngeal teeth usually 2,5–4,2; lateral line complete, scales (44)47–54(58); circumbody scales (30)33–38(41); circumpeduncle scales (16)17–21(23). Dorsal rays (7)8(9); principal caudal rays (16)19(21); anal rays (8)9(10); pelvic rays (6)8(10); pectoral rays (13)15–16(17).

Color in Preservative.—Large juvenile and adult with dorsum dusky to dark, with darker middorsal stripe; upper body scales faintly or distinctly duskily outlined; midside with wide dusky stripe, most intense posteriorly; lower side pale, sometimes weakly peppered; entire side with few to many dark crescents (dark margins of regenerated scales). Head dorsum, snout, and upper opercle dusky, cheek and chin pale. All fins pale. Young and small juvenile slightly dusky dorsally; dark midlateral stripe is diffuse (but still obvious) and often splits into two stripes anteriorly.

Breeding adult often distinctly bicolored, upper body dusky to quite dark; anterodorsolateral scale pattern sometimes effecting several narrow dark stripes; body tubercles of male appear as linear series of tiny pale spots; venter pale except for scattered dark crescents. Dorsal and caudal fin rays dusky-margined; caudal base sometimes with small dark spot; lower fins pale except for leading edge of pectoral.

Color in Life Plate 11.—Juvenile olive dorsally; often with slight rosy tinge on side, most intense as a bar just behind head. Nonbreeding adult same or, often, moderately rosy laterally. Breeding male olive to olive-black dorsally, shading to lime or lime-gold dorsolaterally; gold stripe along most of upper edge of dusky midside stripe, and gold also along posterior half of lower edge of dusky stripe; mid- and lower side of anterior two-thirds of body rosy to rosy-orange, deepest just above pectoral fin base; venter silver. Head dorsum, snout, and upper opercle olive-black; cheek, lower opercle, and chin silver. Dorsal and caudal fins olive-yellow, pale-margined; anal and pelvic fins pale; leading edge of pectoral fin dusky olive. Large females often rosy.

Larvae.—Described by Hogue et al. (1976), Loos et al. (1979), and Snyder (1979).

COMPARISON

The rosyside dace is common in much of Virginia and resembles several often encountered shiners. This dace is separated in the *Key* from most genera of shiners by the pharyngeal tooth count (major row teeth almost always 5–4 *vs.* 4–4). The following features allow quick sorting of *C. funduloides* without having to dissect teeth: (1) mouth large, terminal, quite downsloped posteriorly; (2) dorsal fin origin usually posterior to pelvic fin origin; (3) scales moderately small and, in larger juvenile and adult, often differentially darkened and effecting a dappled body; (4) in large young and small juvenile, the midlateral stripe posteriorly is moderately wide and somewhat

Fish 38 *Clinostomus funduloides* adult male 60 mm SL (REJ 971), VA, Grayson County, Big Chestnut Creek, 9 June 1983.

Fish 39 *Clinostomus funduloides* young 27 mm SL (REJ 971), VA, Grayson County, Big Chestnut Creek, 9 June 1983.

diffuse; at about midlength of the body the stripe often splits and is divided to the shoulder area, the narrow upper division usually curved slightly dorsad, the wider lower division usually bowed ventrad; (5) in small young, the midlateral stripe usually is undivided, straight, moderate in width, and of about equal intensity throughout; (6) a rosy or orange suffusion on the flank, most intense above the pectoral fin base, is often present in large juveniles and adults; it tends to intensify in preservative (and later fades).

BIOLOGY

Clinostomus funduloides is a drift seeker, patrolling middle and upper levels of the water column. The diet consists primarily of aquatic and terrestrial insects, and much lesser amounts of worms, arachnids, crayfishes, snails, algae, and detritus (Breder and Crawford 1922; Flemer and Woolcott 1966; Gatz 1979).

Maturation, age, and growth were studied in a Potomac drainage, Maryland and Pennsylvania, population by R. Davis (1972). Brief comments on a population near Washington, D.C. were made by Breder (1920a, 1920b). Davis found nearly half of the age-1 fish to be mature by spring (minimum size 53 mm TL), and maximum age to be 4 years. Mean lengths at ages 2 and 3 were 73 and 85 mm TL. Age-2 adults from the Smith River, Virginia, were 44–54 mm SL, averaging 49 mm. Davis did not detect a growth

difference between the sexes; most of our largest adults are females. The largest Virginia specimen we examined is 92 mm SL, 115 mm TL. Lachner and Deubler (1960) reported a 93-mm SL fish.

Spawning occurs in spring and early summer. We collected tuberculate, well-colored males and gravid females between early April and late June, water 12.7–25.2°C. R. Davis (1972) concluded on the basis of ovarian conditions that spawning occurs from early or mid-May to late June. The rosyside dace is a nest associate of the nest-building minnows *Nocomis* and *Semotilus*. Spawning sites are unknown for dace populations allotopic to nest builders. We observed aggregations of *C. funduloides* over *Nocomis leptocephalus* nests, and it likely spawns over nests of *N. micropogon*, based on collection of a hybrid. Loos et al. (1979) reported association with *Semotilus atromaculatus* nests; the hybrid with *S. corporalis* connotes spawning on the latter's nest. Mature and maturing ova range 121–997 (R. Davis 1972).

The spawning of *C. funduloides* on nests of other minnows and among many nest associates has led to hybridization. Rosyside dace have crossed with the nest-building minnows *Nocomis leptocephalus* (Gilbert 1978a), *N. micropogon* (RC), *Semotilus atromaculatus* (TU 25313), and *S. corporalis* (USNM 195951). Hybrids with nest associates involve *Luxilus cornutus* (Raney 1950; TU 25837; RC), *Luxilus* sp. (either *L. albeolus* or *L. cerasinus*; RC), *Notropis rubellus* (Tsai and Zeisel 1969), and *Phoxinus oreas* (Norman and Southwick 1985; RC).

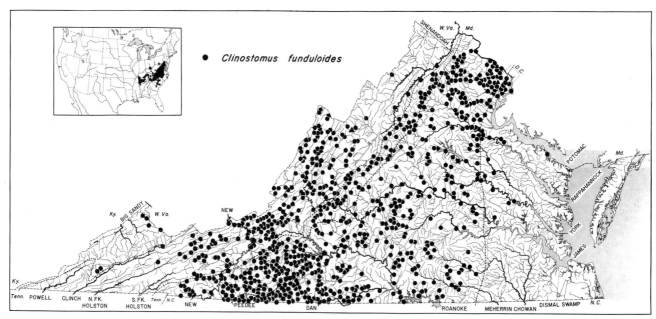

Map 40   Rosyside dace.

HABITAT

The rosyside dace typically occurs in low and high-gradient creeks, occasionally in medium-sized streams, and rarely in rivers. Neves and Pardue (1983) found it only in the middle and lower section of an order-2 mountain stream. This dace extends from mountain trout streams to warm, sluggish, lower Piedmont waters. Many of its Piedmont streams are often turbid. It avoids major impoundments and rarely occurs in small impoundments and natural ponds. *Clinostomus funduloides* is not particularly gregarious, but occasionally is found in small groups. A pool species, adults roam in open water or along margins near cover. Rosyside dace occur over a variety of substrates including sand and slightly silted bottoms, but given its near absence from the Virginia portion of the Big Sandy drainage, it may be intolerant of heavy siltation. Neves and Pardue (1983) found it at pH 6.3 in the Blue Ridge and Norman and Southwick (1985) captured it in Chowan drainage waters of pH 6.5–7.0. Maximum movement of marked individuals averaged only 13.4 m (Hill and Grossman 1984).

DISTRIBUTION   Map 40

Clinostomus funduloides occurs in Atlantic slope drainages from the lower Delaware to the Savannah, and in the middle and lower Ohio basin. It apparently is indigenous to all major Virginia drainages but peculiarities of distribution exist.

Absence of *C. funduloides* from the heavily sampled mainchannel Roanoke River above Smith Mountain Lake is notable because the species is found in other large upland Roanoke drainage tributaries. Ross (1972a) erred in stating that it had disappeared from the North and South forks of Roanoke River; it generally occupies much of their lengths. The basis for localization in much of the Shenandoah system is not evident. The upper Tennessee drainage contains a few scattered populations of *C. f. funduloides*, most of them in cool and cold streams.

The rosyside dace occurs sporadically on the Coastal Plain from the James drainage northward. Some of these populations may be relics of a past era of wider lowland distribution; a wide Coastal Plain distribution pattern would have been fragmented by postglacial formation of the Chesapeake Bay estuary system. Several other typically upland species exhibit similar distributions (Lee et al. 1975; Franz and Lee 1976; Lee and Norden 1976).

Abundance.—Uncommon or common, often abundant, in much of its range; common at the two westernmost Virginia sites. Allowing for different sampling intensities in the Piedmont and mountains (Maps 1–5), *C. funduloides* is about equally abundant in both areas.

REMARKS

The rosyside dace is characteristic of our montane and Piedmont creeks. It trophically complements another upland creek resident, the mountain redbelly dace *Phoxinus oreas* which is principally a herbivore–detritivore. *Clinostomus funduloides* is quite unusual in that nonnuptial adults develop a vivid rosy-orange flank color after preservation (Breder 1972). We have specimens preserved for as long as five years that still retained color.

Name.—*Funduloides* means "*Fundulus*-like." Girard considered this dace to be similar to the topminnow genus *Fundulus*, probably owing to the posterior position of the dorsal fin, slightly supraterminal mouth, and small size.

Daces   Genus *Rhinichthys* Agassiz

Rhinichthys contains at least seven species, five of which inhabit only western North America; it includes the loach minnow, formerly the monotypic genus *Tiaroga* (Peden and Hughes 1988; Coburn and Cavender 1992). The other two species occupy Virginia. The genus is one of the most advanced of the western cyprinid clade (Coburn and Cavender 1992). Most *Rhinichthys* are fine-scaled and have a frenum, a ventral mouth, and a barbel at the corner of the mouth.

Name.—*Rhinichthys*—"snout fish"—alludes to the prominent snout.

Longnose dace   *Rhinichthys cataractae* (Valenciennes)

SYSTEMATICS

The longnose dace, described from New York in 1842, has three or four subspecies, the eastern one being *R. c. cataractae* (Bailey and Allum 1962; Peden and Hughes 1988; Renaud and McAllister 1988). *Rhinichthys cataractae* is closely related to the western *R. evermanni* (Bisson and Reimers 1977).

DESCRIPTION

Materials.—Based on Scott and Crossman (1973), Bisson and Reimers (1977), Becker (1983), and 19 Virginia lots. Color in life based on 3 Virginia series.

Anatomy.—A sleek minnow with tiny scales, a long snout with a frenum, and a ventral mouth with a barbel at each corner; adults are 60–85 mm SL. Body somewhat elongate, anteriorly robust, caudal peduncle deep; dorsal fin origin above posterior half of pelvic fin base or aligned behind base. Head moderate; eye small, slightly supralateral; snout markedly downsloped, long, the tip much in advance of mouth, broad padlike frenum present; mouth moderate-sized, distinctly inferior, horizontal; lips fleshy, with a small terminal barbel at each corner.

Nuptial male with small densely spaced tubercles on head; tiny tubercles on body except breast; pectoral fin with thickened leading ray and moderate-sized recurved tubercles; other lower fins with tiny tubercles. Female lacks tubercles. Genital papilla of male small, triangular; papilla of gravid female relatively large and fleshy.

Meristics.—Pharyngeal teeth usually 2,4–4,2; lateral line complete, scales 61–75; circumpeduncle scales 25–30. Dorsal rays 8; anal rays 7; pelvic rays (7)8; pectoral rays (12)13–15(17).

Color in Preservative.—In juvenile, dorsum dusky or dark; dark predorsal stripe often present; side slightly paler than dorsum; midlateral stripe usually well developed head to tail, often ending posteriorly in a large oval mark; lower side pale or moderately dusky; occasionally, much of side with scattered dark scales or irregular blotches; venter pale. Head dorsum dusky or dark; side of snout often with narrow preocular bar; lips, cheek, and lower opercle pale. Fins pale, except dorsal fin with slight but uniform basal duskiness, and caudal fin with a dusky or dark, often wedge-shaped spot.

Adult dusky or quite dark dorsally; predorsal stripe usually obscure or absent; side as in juvenile or quite dark; midlateral stripe often not evident; belly and breast pale. Head dusky or dark dorsally and laterally; preocular bar obscure; upper lip sometimes dusky anteriorly; lower lip and ventral head pale. Fins duskier than in juvenile, relatively darker dorsal fin base retained; caudal fin spot large and dark or diffuse, or absent.

Color in Life   Plate 11.—Juvenile and small adult pale olive to dark olive dorsally and on much of side, pale below; dorsal and caudal fins pale or reddish, lower fins pale. Nuptial male with dark olive or olive-black dorsum and upper side; side light olive, sometimes with bronze iridescence; much of side mottled with scattered black scales or blotches; lower side straw-olive, sometimes with a bronze cast or pale green iridescence; caudal peduncle sometimes with pale red cast; breast and belly whitish, remainder of venter dusky with olive-black pigment. Head dorsum, snout, and cheek olive-black, cheek sometimes iridescently green-flecked; lower lip and gular area white. Dorsal and caudal fins dull red to deeply dark red in membranes, rays light to dark olive; caudal spot black; anal and pelvic fins with pale red cast; pectoral fin dark red in membranes, rays olive-black.

Fish 40 *Rhinichthys cataractae* adult female 86 mm SL (REJ 1093), VA, Carroll County, Big Reed Island Creek, 3 June 1984.

Fish 41 *Rhinichthys cataractae* juvenile 39 mm SL (REJ 1042), VA, Augusta County, Middle River, 22 September 1983.

Larvae.—Described by Fuiman and Loos (1977), Buynak and Mohr (1979c), Loos et al. (1979), Snyder (1979, 1981), Cooper (1980), and Heufelder and Fuiman (1982).

COMPARISON

Large, relatively longnosed specimens of *R. atratulus* somewhat resemble *R. cataractae* and often have been misidentified as the latter. Use the key carefully.

BIOLOGY

The longnose dace primarily eats aquatic insects, particularly midge larvae, and occasionally worms, small crustaceans, mites, algae, and other plant material (Reed 1959; Gee and Northcote 1963; Gerald 1966; Becker 1983). Based on brain morphology, Evans (1952) considered *R. cataractae* to be a "skin taster," a view supported by well-developed taste buds on the snout, lips, lower head, and membranes of lower fins.

The longnose dace matures in 2 years and maximally lives 5 years (Reed 1959; Gee and Machniak 1972; Reed and Moulton 1973; Becker 1983). Age-2 fish were 64–86 mm TL, mean, 76, in Pennsylvania; 68–96 mm TL in Wisconsin; and in Minnesota and Massachusetts averaged 62 and 70 mm TL (Reed 1959; Reed and Moulton 1973; Becker 1983). Females tended to be larger than males by age 3 and only females achieved age 5. The largest Virginia specimen is 116 mm SL (139 mm TL). The largest specimens reported, "seven-inch adults" (178 mm, presumably

TL), from Lake Superior, were attributed by Scott and Crossman (1973) and Becker (1983) to Hubbs and Lagler (1949), but we are unable to verify this. A 157-mm (presumably TL) ("6.2-inches") specimen was reported from Montana (Brown 1971).

Rhinichthys cataractae spawns from early April to mid-June in Wisconsin, water 11.1–23.3°C, mean, 17.2 (Becker 1983). Gonadal development and tuberculation of Virginia adults indicated that most spawning occurs during April and May; the majority of June adults were spent. In streams, spawning occurs in relatively shallow areas over fine to coarse substrates where the current is greater than 5 cm/second (Greeley and Bishop 1933; Bartnik 1970). The longnose dace sometimes uses *Nocomis* nests for spawning (E. A. Lachner, personal communication). Bartnik (1972) discovered that *R. c. cataractae* principally spawns during daylight, whereas a western form spawns at night.

Males are territorial and aggressively defend small depressions on the bottom. However, these depressions may not constitute true nests in the sense of purposeful substrate manipulation (see *R. atratulus*). Aggressive behavior consists primarily of chasing and biting (Bartnik 1970). Spawning occurs on the bottom with one or more males in lateral contact with a female. Females may deposit 200–1,200 eggs (McPhail and Lindsey 1970); total ova range 1,400–2,800 (Becker 1983).

Hybrids parented by *R. cataractae* with the following have been reported: *Campostoma anomalum* (Bailey

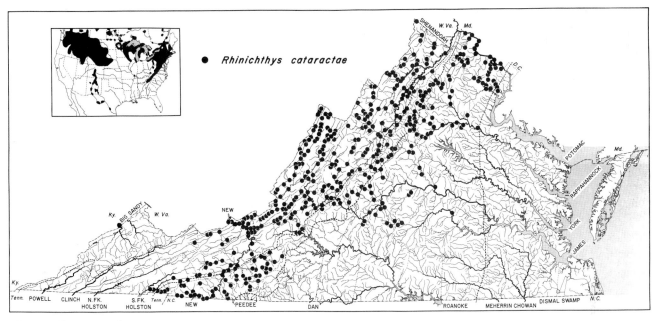

Map 41 Longnose dace.

and Allum 1962; Ross and Cavender 1977), *Nocomis micropogon* (Raney 1940e; Stauffer et al. 1979b; see also *N. micropogon* account), *N. platyrhynchus* (USNM 108215), *Semotilus atromaculatus*, and *Luxilus cornutus* (Ross and Cavender 1977).

HABITAT

Rhinichthys cataractae lives in moderate and high-gradient streams of widely varied size and temperature. In Virginia it typically is a fast-water fish, associating with rubble, boulder, and bedrock bottoms in the swifter reaches. Its congener the blacknose dace also inhabits swift water, but is often found in gentle current. The preference for swift currents by *R. cataractae* develops early in life (Gee and Northcote 1963). The home range is small; average maximum movement was 13.4 m in a Georgia stream (Hill and Grossman 1984).

In northern parts of its range the longnose dace occurs widely in lakes as well as in streams. In a Canadian lake population, offshore longnose dace were believed to inhabit current-swept channels; the greatest inshore density occurred in rocky areas when large waves were breaking (Gee and Machniak 1972).

DISTRIBUTION Map 41

The longnose dace is the most broadly distributed species of *Rhinichthys*, extending from northern Canada to northern Mexico and, in the northern United

States, from coast to coast. It avoids much of the silty plains, and it does not occupy many seemingly hospitable regions of mid- and lower latitudes of the United States.

In Virginia, *R. cataractae* is native to the Potomac, Rappahannock, James, New, and Tennessee drainages, its range being chiefly montane and upper Piedmont regions. Oddly, the longnose dace is sporadic or absent in most of the western tributaries in the Valley and Ridge Province of the New drainage. The report of *R. cataractae* in the York drainage (Jenkins et al. 1972) is based on specimens (UR 2781–2805) that probably were taken in the Rappahannock drainage (W. S. Woolcott, in litt.).

In the Tennessee drainage of Virginia, only the South Fork Holston system is inhabited; the population there forms the northern terminus of a pattern of restriction to the Blue Ridge section of the drainage. It seems strange that the longnose dace does not also occupy the other branches of the Holston system and any of the Clinch system in Virginia. The confinement of *R. cataractae* in the Tennessee drainage may reflect narrow adaptation to relatively cool, high-gradient streams. Perhaps *R. cataractae* gained access to the upper Tennessee via stream capture with the New; this would also explain its absence from most of the lower and middle Ohio basin.

The listing of *R. cataractae* from the Big Sandy drainage by Jenkins et al. (1972) is from the Russell Fork system (F. J. Schwartz, in litt.). We have not verified the record and no earlier one exists for the drainage.

Recently, however, the longnose dace was found in the Russell Fork of Kentucky, at 1.2 km below the Virginia line (Stephens and Prather 1985); bait bucket introduction is suspected. Minor range extensions have been detected in Ohio and West Virginia, close to long-known populations (Barnes et al. 1985). The middle Cumberland drainage, Tennessee, record (Lee et al. 1980) apparently is based on *R. atratulus* (D. A. Etnier, personal communication).

Rhinichthys cataractae apparently has been introduced to, and is spreading in, the upper Roanoke drainage. We first found it in Tinker Creek in 1974, but not elsewhere in the drainage in the 1970s. First records for the Roanoke River, near the mouth of Tinker Creek, are 1981, and in 1986 the dace was captured in Tinker tributaries. We reject Fowler's (1923) earlier Tinker system record; it could not be tied to an ANSP specimen, and Fowler (1945) did not list *R. cataractae* from the Roanoke drainage.

Abundance.—Usually uncommon or common.

REMARKS

The longnose dace is a marvel of form and function. Its streamlined body and downsloped pointed snout manifest an ability to buck strong current. As further adaptation to torrents, adults have a rudimentary gas bladder (Bailey and Allum 1962), reducing the energy needed to hold in lesser velocity at the bottom. When snorkeling in a chute, one is obliged to find firm purchase on the bottom, and there among the surges of bubbles and the buffeting currents, one can admire the seeming ease with which this minnow moves about its home.

Name.—*Cataractae*, "of cataracts," befits the habitat of this species in many regions, and also refers to its type locality, Niagara Falls.

Blacknose dace   *Rhinichthys atratulus* (Hermann)

SYSTEMATICS

The widespread common blacknose dace, described from "North America" in 1804, constitutes a distinctive subgroup of *Rhinichthys*. Three subspecies generally have been recognized in the last 50 years: *R. a. atratulus* primarily on the Atlantic slope, *R. a. obtusus* Agassiz occupying mainly the southern portion of the Ohio River basin, and *R. a. meleagris* Agassiz in north-central and western parts of the species range (Hubbs 1936; Matthews et al. 1982). *Rhinichthys a. atratulus* and *R. a. obtusus* commonly interbred in Meadow Creek, a James drainage tributary (Map 42); thus they were retained as subspecies by Matthews et al. (1982), who suggested that *R. a. obtusus* and *R. a. meleagris* are consubspecific.

Rhinichthys a. meleagris was elevated to species status by C. Smith (1985), based on its occurrence with *R. a. atratulus* in the Lake Ontario drainage, New York (Hubbs and Brown 1929; Hubbs and Lagler 1958). Here the geographic ranges of the forms "overlap little, if any," and the forms exhibit "little evidence" of intergradation (C. Smith 1985). However, the exact nature and extent of their distributional relationship and reproductive interaction is undetermined (Jenkins 1988). Smith's (1985) elevation of *R. a. meleagris* affects the systematics of *R. a. obtusus*, which he did not formally treat. Because *obtusus* and *meleagris* are sister taxa (Matthews et al. 1982), if only one of these is recognized as a species or subspecies, the name *obtusus* should be applied based on first revisorship of Jordan and Gilbert (1883:208, not 885–886).

Our understanding of the systematics of the *atratulus* group should be markedly improved by studies focused on zones of possible contact between taxa in Virginia, West Virginia (Matthews et al. 1982; Adkins et al. 1985), and the Lake Ontario drainage.

DESCRIPTION

Materials.—Based on Schontz (1962), Matthews et al. (1982), and 112 Virginia lots. Life color from Matthews et al. (1982) and many Virginia lots.

Anatomy.—A robust minnow with small scales, a frenum, and a ventral mouth with a barbel at each corner; adults are 40–70 mm SL. Body moderate in profile, somewhat stocky; dorsal fin origin moderately posterior to pelvic fin origin, sometimes slightly posterior to pelvic base. Head moderate; eye small, lateral or slightly supralateral; snout moderate or, in large adult, somewhat long, pointed or slightly rounded; frenum wide; mouth medium-sized, subterminal or slightly inferior, with fleshy lips and a barbel at each corner. Breast and belly fully scaled.

Nuptial male with small tubercles often densely distributed on head dorsum, snout, and upper operculum; body with tiny to small tubercles; pectoral fin with thickened pads on dorsal surface of rays; pelvic fin tuberculate. Male genital papilla not obvious; female papilla protruding with anal papilla. Large nuptial female with back somewhat humped predorsally.

Meristics.—Pharyngeal teeth in *R. a. atratulus* usually 2,4–4,2; lateral line complete, scales (46)51–58(63) [in *R. a. obtusus*, (56)57–64(70)]; scales across back (23)24–26 [(26)29–32(33)]; caudal peduncle scales above lateral line (11)12–

Fish 42 *Rhinichthys a. atratulus* adult female 47 mm SL (REJ 966), VA, Patrick County, Dan River, 7 June 1983.

Fish 43 *Rhinichthys a. obtusus* adult male 75 mm SL (WHH 108), VA, Wise County, Dotson Fork, 29 June 1983.

13(14) [(13)14–15(16)]. Dorsal rays (7)8; anal rays (6)7(8); pectoral rays (12)13–15(16).

Color in Preservative.—Dorsum dusky; vague middorsal stripe sometimes present; back and upper side with scattered tiny dark specks and dark scales; narrow supramidlateral pale stripe sometimes present; dark midlateral stripe well developed along entire side. In *R. a. atratulus,* lower side usually pale or with few dark scales (except side often strongly spotted or mottled in Rappahannock drainage, resembling next form); in *R. a. obtusus,* side usually with many dark specks and dark scales, these often forming rows or broadly grouped, effecting mottling and irregular blotches, obscuring midlateral stripe. In both forms head dorsum dusky; lateral snout with dark preocular bar, contiguous with a narrow dark band encircling snout tip; lips, chin, cheek, and lower opercle pale. Fins pale, except dorsal distinctly dusky along most of base, paling at anterior 2 rays and last ray; caudal fin with a basal dark spot.

Color in Life Plate 11.—Juvenile, adult female, and nonbreeding adult male olive above; side stripe black, brown, or reddish; ventrally white or silver-white. Most fins pale; pectoral fin yellow-olive or reddish, depending on subspecies.

Nuptial male *R. a. atratulus* with dorsum medium or dark olive, and with scattered black scales and flecks of bronze and green iridescence; supramidlateral stripe tan, bronze, or bronze-rust; midlateral stripe rust-orange or orange-brown, sometimes with scattered black scales or dusky black pigment; lower side and venter silver-white or with yellow to yellow-gold luster. Head dorsum dusky olive; preocular bar and band that encircle snout are black; horizontal iris bar and upper opercular mark black; cheek and lower opercle silver-white or yellow to yellow-gold. Dorsal, caudal, and anal fins with pale amber-yellow wash; caudal spot black; pelvic fin pale orange or orange-red; pectoral fin bright orange-red.

Nuptial male *R. a. obtusus* principally differ from *R. a. atratulus* by having a greater number of scattered black scales or black splotching on back and side; midlateral stripe, when present, black and overlaid with rust-orange; cheek, lower opercle, and lower side of body translucent bright orange; venter silver-white to translucent pale orange. Fin colors similar to *R. a. atratulus* except pectoral usually dusky olive or amber, sometimes pale orange.

Larvae.—Described by Fuiman and Loos (1977), Buynak and Mohr (1979c), Loos et al. (1979), Snyder (1979), Wang and Kernehan (1979), and Heufelder and Fuiman (1982).

COMPARISON

See *Rhinichthys cataractae.*

BIOLOGY

A synthesis of biological data on the blacknose dace was compiled by Trial et al. (1983). This fish eats a variety of small organisms, principally aquatic insects. Other items entering the diet include worms, spiders, mites, terrestrial insects, larval fishes, algae, and detritus (Breder and Crawford 1922; Schontz 1962; Tarter 1970; Rollwagen and Stainken 1980; Johnson 1982).

Rhinichthys atratulus usually matures at age 2 and maximum longevity is slightly longer than 3 years (Noble 1965; Tarter 1968; Reed and Moulton 1973). Age-2 fish were 40–60 mm SL in Iowa, 40–72 mm SL in Nebraska, and 61–76 mm SL in Minnesota (Noble 1965; Bragg and Stasiak 1978; Becker 1983). Age-2 fish averaged 54 mm TL in Massachusetts (Reed and Moulton 1973). Adult females tend to be larger than adult males. *Rhinichthys a. obtusus* commonly reaches larger sizes than *R. a. atratulus* in Virginia. The largest Virginia *R. a. atratulus* reported is 74 mm SL (Schontz 1962); the biggest Virginia *R. a. obtusus* examined by us is 85 mm SL, 102 mm TL. The size record is a *R. a. obtusus* of 115 mm TL from Kentucky (Tarter 1968: Figure 6).

Rhinichthys atratulus is reported to spawn from early May through July in water 15.6–22°C (Schwartz 1958a; Noble 1965); in Virginia we saw spawning between 5 April and 10 July in this temperature range. Typical spawning sites are shallow, gravelly and sand–gravel pool tails and slow to moderate runs that are open or sheltered (Traver 1929; Raney 1940b; Bartnik 1970). Such habitats are preferred breeding sites by other fishes, and the blacknose dace has been observed spawning on fallfish nests and white sucker redds (Reed 1971; Ross and Reed 1978; Loos et al. 1979). We saw reproductively active blacknose dace loosely associated with creek chub nests; they generally occurred there when chubs were hiding.

Differences in breeding behavior among the three subspecies of *R. atratulus* were summarized by Raney (1940b) and Schwartz (1958a). Observations by Bartnik (1970) and Matthews et al. (1982), and subsequently by R. E. Jenkins, indicate that the differences may only reflect individual variations, some influenced by habitat. The blacknose dace is a territorial substrate spawner. The spawning act occurs as just-formed pairs align parallel, or the male curves the body and places his urosome over the female, holding her to the bottom.

Localized swimming, territorial bouts, and body quivering that accompanies gamete extrusion often result in small silt-cleared areas or shallow depressions. Such areas are not "nests" (Schwartz 1958a) in the sense of purposeful movement of bottom materials (Woolcott and Maurakis 1988). However, the blacknose dace does move pebbles with the snout—the female pushes gravel as a sign of spawning readiness, and both sexes root for eggs when not spawning (Traver 1929; Raney 1940b; Schwartz 1958a; Bartnik 1970; Jenkins' observations). Bartnik (1970)

noted that blacknose dace bury their eggs, but didn't state how. Burial apparently occurs by substrate disturbance during spawning (e.g., Loos et al. 1979). Earlier references to stone and debris carrying by *R. atratulus* apparently are based on other minnow genera (Schontz 1962).

Mature or near-mature eggs range 166–741 per female; total ova range 375–9,142 (Traver 1929; Schontz 1962; Noble 1965; Tarter 1969).

The *atratulus* group is interesting in that no natural intergroup crosses have been documented (Bartnik 1970; Ross and Cavender 1977; Matthews et al. 1982). The listing of hybrids with *R. cataractae* and *Nocomis micropogon* by Trautman (1981) needs verification. R. E. Jenkins observed nuptial male *Phoxinus oreas* attempting to spawn with adult female *R. atratulus* several times in a 15-minute period. The latter were rooting in the pit of a *Semotilus atromaculatus* nest while the chub was hiding. Male *Phoxinus*, one or two at a time, quivered the body against the *Rhinichthys*, but the latter continued foraging.

HABITAT

The blacknose dace occupies tiny to medium-sized streams of gentle to steep gradient. This eurythermal dace is most common in gentle riffles and runs, and backwaters and pools near current ecotones. Bartnik (1970) observed the greatest densities of blacknose dace in currents less than 45 cm/second. Montane Virginia populations typically are associated with hard bottom; on the Piedmont and Coastal Plain, *R. atratulus* also inhabits sandy and softer bottoms. In northern regions the blacknose dace inhabits ponds and lakes as well as streams. A detailed study of its habitat characteristics is by Trial et al. (1983).

DISTRIBUTION   Map 42

Rhinichthys atratulus is native to much of the eastern United States and extends into southern Canada; subspecies ranges are noted in *Systematics*. In Virginia, where it occupies all principal drainages, it is distributed throughout montane provinces and outlying areas. Major population groups occur in the lower Piedmont of the Potomac and Rappahannock drainages; most other drainages have scattered Piedmont populations. The absence of the blacknose dace in nearly all of the Piedmont of the Roanoke drainage is surprising. The only lower Piedmont, Roanoke record is from our

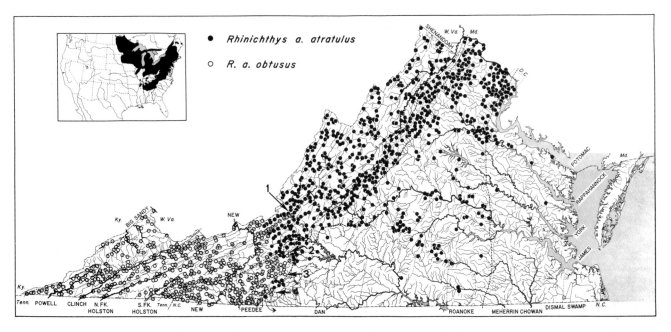

Map 42 Eastern and western blacknose daces. Arrows to open circles indicate: 1—intergradation area in lower Meadow Creek, James drainage, Craig Co; 2—two sites for *R. a. obtusus* in upper Lick Fork system of upper Roanoke drainage proper, Floyd Co; 3—One site for *obtusus*-like population in upper Shooting Creek, upper Smith branch of Dan system, Roanoke drainage, Franklin Co; 4—Four sites of *R. a. obtusus* in upper Dan system within and above gorge, Patrick Co.

collection in a small spring-fed stream. A few relict populations also exist in the outer Coastal Plain of Virginia, including the Piankatank drainage, and on the Delmarva Peninsula of Maryland.

Abundance.—Often common or abundant in montane and upland areas; usually rare, sometimes common in lowlands.

REMARKS

In cold mountain streams the blacknose dace is a typical associate of the brook trout, and even has a streamer fly named after it. The dace is also ubiquitous in warm mountain creeks.

Name.—*Atratulus*, "dressed in black," refers to the stripe on the body and around the snout.

Stonerollers   Genus *Campostoma* Agassiz

The distinctive eastern and central North American genus *Campostoma* contains four species, one of which inhabits Virginia. The genus is notable for the hard (keratinoid?) ridge on the lower jaw and the very long, coiled intestine looped around the gas bladder (Figures 25A, 26A). A tough jaw ridge or long coiled gut occur in several other minnows, but the extreme length of the alimentary canal in *Campostoma* reflects a pinnacle of herbivorous adaptation in North American minnows.

Within the exoglossin clade of the chub clade, *Campostoma* is considered to be the sister group of *Dionda* (Mayden 1989; Coburn and Cavender 1992). Coburn and Cavender regard these genera along with *Hybog-*

nathus to form a monophyletic lineage of herbivores. *Dionda* and *Hybognathus* do not make nests. From its pit-nesting and cheek and breast keratinizations, *Campostoma* was aligned with the ridge- or mound-nest builders *Semotilus*, *Exoglossum*, and *Nocomis* by Jenkins (1971b) and Jenkins and Lachner (1975, 1989), and it was so linked by Maurakis and Woolcott (1989). Maurakis and Woolcott no longer place *Campostoma* in this group because it does not overtly transport stones when nesting, and for anatomical reasons (W. S. Woolcott, personal communication).

Name.—*Campostoma* means "curved mouth."

Central stoneroller   *Campostoma anomalum* (Rafinesque)

SYSTEMATICS

Described in 1820 from Kentucky, *C. anomalum* presents complex systematic problems whose study has led so far to recognition of a former subspecies as a species, *C. oligolepis* (Pflieger 1971; Burr 1976; Burr and Smith 1976), and description of a new species, *C. pauciradii* (Burr and Cashner 1983). The taxonomic and geographic limits of the three subspecies of *C. anomalum*—*C. a. anomalum*, *C. a. pullum* (Agassiz), and *C. a. michauxi* Fowler—remain uncertain.

Campostoma a. anomalum occurs in much of the Ohio basin, occupying Virginia in the Big Sandy and Potomac drainages (Ross 1952, 1958a, 1958b; Masnik and Knollenberg 1972). Populations in the upper James, Roanoke, and New drainages were considered undescribed subspecies (Ross 1952, 1958b; Davis 1953), but later, along with the upper Tennessee drainage population, were identified with *C. a. michauxi* described by Fowler (1945) from the Santee drainage (Ross and Carico 1963; Ross and Masnik 1971). Jenkins et al. (1972) followed the later designations, and we tentatively continue to do so.

Buth and Burr (1978) recognized the Roanoke and New populations as an undescribed subspecies and considered Tennessee drainage fish to be *C. a. anomalum*; they did not analyze the James population.

However, Buth (1984) stated that re-encoding and reanalysis of Buth and Burr's (1978) data are needed. Burr and Cashner (1983) regarded *C. oligolepis* to be the stoneroller in much of the lower and middle Tennessee, and found that a form widespread in the upper Tennessee including Virginia exhibits tuberculation of *C. a. pullum* (i.e., *C. anomalum* in general).

DESCRIPTION

Materials.—Scale counts from Ross (1952, 1958b) and Ross and M. T. Masnik (in litt.); counts of fin rays and pharyngeal teeth from 38 Virginia specimens; other traits from 49 Virginia lots. Color in life based on many juveniles and adult females, and 5 nuptial males, from Virginia.

Anatomy.—A chublike minnow with a ventral mouth, lower jaw with a hard ridge, and the intestine very long and looped about the gas bladder; adults are 60–150 mm SL. Body moderate in profile, stocky; dorsal fin origin above pelvic fin base. Head and eye moderate, eye lateral; snout rounded, lacking frenum; mouth ventral, lower jaw with hard ridge along its edge. Breast and belly fully scaled. Gut very long, with extended coils looped around gas bladder; peritoneum black.

Nuptial male with medium to large tubercles on head dorsum including just above nares (internasal tubercles reduced or absent in some parts of upper Tennessee drain-

Fish 44 *Campostoma anomalum* adult male 94 mm SL (REJ 970), VA, Carroll County, Pauls Creek, 9 June 1983.

Fish 45 *Campostoma anomalum* adult female 86 mm SL (REJ 991), VA, Russell County, Little River, 21 June 1983.

age); lower edge of cheek and branchiostegals roughened with tubercle-like structures; lower side of snout just anterior to lachrymal with patch of apparently keratinized tissue; flaplike extension from corner of lips present; upper body with many medium-sized tubercles; breast scales with rough edges; nape and head dorsum sometimes swollen; all fins tuberculate in some specimens, caudal tubercles on leading edge(s) only. Male genital papilla moderate-sized, recessed in swollen mound; female papilla larger, more exposed.

Meristics.—Pharyngeal teeth 1,4–4,1 in all Virginia drainages except perhaps the James, in which a 4–4 count may be common; lateral line complete, scales (43)47–55(58); circumbody scales (37)41–54(56); circumpeduncle scales 18–25(26). Dorsal rays 8; principal caudal rays 19; anal rays 7, rarely 6; pelvic rays 8; pectoral rays (16)17–19. Potomac drainage scale counts: lateral line (41)44–47(51); circumbody (33)36–39(42); circumpeduncle 19–20(21).

Color in Preservative.—Adult upper body dusky to dark; faint midlateral dark stripe sometimes present posteriorly; scattered dark (regenerated) scales on side and dorsum; venter pale. Dorsal fin pale or slightly dusky, often with faint submedial dark band; caudal base often with distinct dark spot; caudal fin sometimes dusky basally, often forming a blotch, otherwise pale; lower fins pale overall or dusky medially. Juvenile similar to adult except midlateral stripe more pronounced and fins less marked or unmarked. Breeding male moderately to very dusky dorsally and laterally; lateral snout pad and lips pale; dorsal fin with dark medial to submedial band; caudal spot absent, medial rays dusky or dark basally; lower fins usually with dusky or dark medial streaks.

Color in Life Plate 12.—Dorsum and upper side olive to brown-olive with brassy sheen, regenerated scales on back and side dark olive; venter silver or white; fins olive or pale. Breeding male brown, dark olive, or black-olive dorsally; side brassy to brassy-orange, grading to pale brassy ventrally; breast silvery white; head dark olive dorsally; posterior edge of opercle and axilla of pectoral fin black, opercle sometimes with faint pink blush; cheek pale brassy-orange; lateral snout pad and fleshy lip flap white. Dorsal fin pale yellow distally, medial band black, anterobasally iridescent orange; caudal fin blotch blackened, remainder of fin dusky olive; anal fin similar to dorsal but usually less blackened; pelvic and pectoral fins pale to moderate yellow-orange, with dusky or black medial streaks.

Larvae.—Described by Reed (1958), Hogue et al. (1976), Loos et al. (1979), Perry and Menzel (1979), Buynak and Mohr (1980a), and Heufelder and Fuiman (1982).

BIOLOGY

Campostoma anomalum is a grazing minnow which uses the tough ridge on the lower jaw to scrape algae from rocks and other hard substrates (Fowler and Taber 1985). In some settings the diet may consist largely of detritus (Kraatz 1923; Starrett 1950b; Burkhead 1980; Felley and Hill 1983), in others mostly living algae (Minckley 1963; Power and Matthews 1983). This species generally feeds in schools and can substantially reduce standing crops of algae (Power and Matthews 1983). Its intestine is the longest of any American minnow, up to 7.9 times the body length (Kraatz 1924); such length is adapted for digesting detritus and algae. The central stoneroller is also opportunistic, rarely eating aquatic insects, and takes a worm-baited hook during the spawning season. Scale-eating was reported from aquarium observations and a stream-dwelling specimen (Burkhead 1980).

Age at maturation varies considerably. In eastern Tennessee some individuals of both sexes matured in 1 year (Burkhead 1980), but 2 years was typical. In nearby Great Smoky Mountains National Park, no 2-year-olds had matured, the majority of females matured in 3 years, and most males became adult in 4 or 5 years (Lennon and Parker 1960). A 54-mm SL Virginia male was mature, and adult females as small as 51 mm TL were found in Ohio (Trautman 1981). Typical adult survivorship appears to be 3 or 4 years (Gunning and Lewis 1956; Burkhead 1980; Becker 1983; McAllister 1987); some Great Smokies fish were 6 years old (Lennon and Parker 1960). Males grow faster than females. Age-3 stonerollers are 100–160 mm SL (Burkhead 1980); in Lennon and Parker's (1960) study age-3 fish were 125–190 mm TL. Our largest Virginia stoneroller is 165 mm SL, 200 mm TL; a record 287-mm TL specimen was reported from Tennessee (Lennon and Parker 1960).

Nesting occurs in the spring at water temperatures of 10.8–26.8°C (Hankinson 1919; Smith 1935). Peak activity occurs in Virginia during April and May, water 13–25°C. Large postnuptial males have been found in Virginia as early as late April. Spawning usually takes place on gravel in runs and pool tails. Activity resembling reproductive behavior, including stone carrying, often occurs on nests of *Nocomis* and *Semotilus* chubs. Reighard (1943) saw *Campostoma* spawning on *Nocomis* nests, but we and R. J. Miller (1964) did not, and Cooper (1980) found no *Campostoma* eggs in *Nocomis* nests. Stonerollers also nest on trout redds (*Remarks*). Perhaps stonerollers often "root" for eggs in nests of other species. Breeding common, striped, and saffron shiners and Tennessee dace associate with stoneroller pits; occasionally a stoneroller pit is reworked by a nuptial male creek chub (Miller 1962a; our data).

Spawning behavior has been described by Hankinson (1919), Smith (1935), R. J. Miller (1962a, 1964),

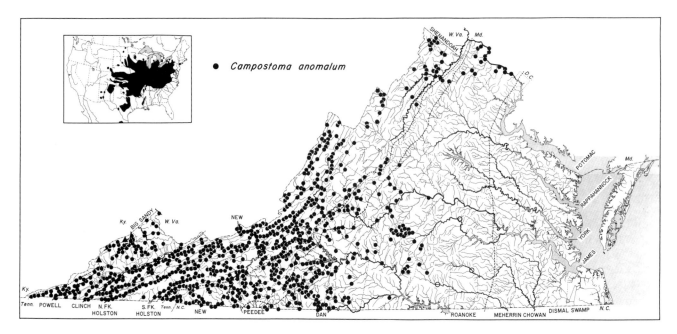

Map 43   Central stoneroller. Open circles indicate questionable records.

and Burkhead (1980). Within the general spawning congregation, females usually hold at the periphery of the nesting area, sometimes in deeper water by cover. Males excavate shallow pits by picking up or pushing stones. Pits are aggressively defended against intruding conspecifics but frequently are shared with or yielded to other species. More than one male may excavate an individual pit, and pit fidelity is low. When a female enters a pit to spawn, nearby males rush the pit in a mating frenzy. Fecundity is 150–4,800 ova (Burkhead 1980; Heufelder and Fuiman 1982; Becker 1983).

Campostoma anomalum hybridizes with *Luxilus cornutus* (Menzel 1978), *Nocomis leptocephalus* (Raney 1947b), *N. micropogon*, *N. platyrhynchus* (CU), *Rhinichthys cataractae* (Bailey and Allum 1962; Ross and Cavender 1977), *Semotilus atromaculatus* (Cross and Minckley 1960; Ross and Cavender 1977), and possibly *Phoxinus oreas* (RC).

HABITAT

The central stoneroller occupies usually clear streams of varying size and temperature that have moderate or high gradient. In Virginia it occurs commonly in slow parts of pools but is most prevalent in hard-bottom runs and riffles. In Oklahoma, *C. anomalum* was usually captured in depths less than 1 m and was not associated with cover during warmer months (Felley and Hill 1983). Winter collecting and snorkeling in the Roanoke River found it to be one of very few fishes in riffles and runs. The central stone-

roller is generally intolerant of impoundment; Becker (1983) noted that it was uncommon in Wisconsin lakes. In an eastern Tennessee stream, *C. anomalum* declined sharply in abundance immediately following channelization (Beets 1979).

DISTRIBUTION   Map 43

The central stoneroller is widespread in the southern Great Lakes and upper and middle Mississippi basins, the western Gulf slope, and the central Atlantic slope. Some peripheral records represent recession of populations, others introductions. This species is present in all major Virginia drainages except the Rappahannock and York. Among populations in the Blue Ridge and west, those in the Shenandoah system are peculiarly disjunct.

In the James and Roanoke drainages, *C. anomalum* declines markedly from the middle Piedmont eastward. It may have been more common on the Piedmont prior to extensive deforestation and ensuing siltation. The isolated headwater record in the Rivanna system of the James proper is valid (MPM 8263). The cluster of records in the uppermost Appomattox system of the James is not surprising; upland habitat is common there. The lowermost record (open circle) in the Appomattox system is unverified. It is listed in the University of Richmond catalog (UR 841), but is not recorded in W. S. Woolcott's field notes nor was a specimen located (W. S. Woolcott, in litt.). *Campostoma* is listed for a lower Dan system site collected in 1962 (VPI 1781), but it was not found there in an intensive collection in 1978 nor in nearby streams during an extensive 1977 survey.

Upper Meherrin system, Chowan drainage records represent an outpost population, but here again, suitable habitat is present. *Campostoma* was taken four times at the North Meherrin River site during 1962–1983, and in Owl Creek farther upstream in 1979. Specimens from the Meherrin River site (VPI 1035; open circle) have not been sought for confirmation. The only record for the Nottoway system is based on an apparently faultily labeled collection which likely came from the upper Roanoke. The collection (VPI 991 = AMNH 61945) also contained the only Nottoway records of *Luxilus cerasinus*, *Pimephales notatus*, and *Moxostoma erythrurum* (discussed in *L. cerasinus* account).

The Pee Dee drainage population may have been introduced, perhaps twice. The two records are widely separated, surprising for a Blue Ridge frontal area if the species is native. One record is from Wilkes County, North Carolina, taken in 1960 by J. R. Bailey (DU JRB 60-20; Menhinick et al. 1974). However, the extensive survey of the North Carolina portion of the drainage during 1960–1961 by the North Carolina Wildlife Resources Commission revealed no other stonerollers. The Virginia record is from Pauls Creek in 1983 (REJ 970), where another species suspected of introduction (*Phoxinus oreas*) also was taken. Abbott's (1959) report from the Virginia Pee Dee is invalid; also listed or subsequently identified from the collection are three species (*Nocomis platyrhynchus*, *Luxilus albeolus*, *Notropis photogenis*) that indicate the collection came from the New drainage. R. D. Ross (in litt.) concurred with this interpretation.

The central stoneroller is widespread in the New, Tennessee, and Big Sandy drainages. This may seem anomalous for the Big Sandy, because the drainage is about as heavily silted as is the Piedmont; however, riffles may be better defined in the Big Sandy.

Abundance.—Often common to ubiquitous; generally common in most drainages from the Blue Ridge westward; common in some upper and middle Piedmont areas.

REMARKS

The stoneroller is one of the most trophically specialized American minnows by virtue of the hard jaw ridge and extreme gut elongation. Ecologically it is a "creek cow," converting the energy of algae and detritus to biomass useable by carnivores. It is also one of the most tuberculate minnows; peak nuptial males are virtual swimming rasps. Postnuptial males often are found battered, dying and dead, with fungused wounds, and are testimony to the effectiveness of their sexual armor.

For those who explore streams, the tuberculate stoneroller is a harbinger of spring. To one gentleman in southwestern Virginia, its disappearance in early summer is a mystery of nature. He asked if we knew where the "hornyhead" went. We informed him that they don't go anywhere, that males are always present, but after spawning some die and others shed their "horns" just as a buck deer loses antlers. He shook his head and said, "That's not right."

The fascination with stonerollers appears endemic to the southern Appalachians, where during spring, fishermen gather along creeks and harvest hundreds for the table. In the vicinity of Great Smoky Mountains National Park, the stoneroller is so prized by some fishermen that only they are creeled; trout are released (Lennon and Parker 1960). The collective enthusiasm of "hornyhead" or "knottyhead" fishermen in eastern Tennessee was sufficient to successfully lobby the Tennessee Wildlife Resources Agency for a study of the stoneroller fishery (Beets 1979; Burkhead 1980). The stoneroller is also an important bait fish in some areas.

In Great Smoky Mountains National Park, *C. anomalum* often spawns at redds of rainbow trout, after the trout have spawned but usually before trout eggs hatch. Where the stoneroller is abundant, trout reproduction is sharply reduced by destruction of the redds (Lennon and Parker 1960). This interaction may be viewed in a positive light; introduced, naturalized rainbow trout have been extensively displacing native brook trout in the park.

Name.—*Anomalum* means "abnormal" or "different," referring to the ridge on the lower jaw. *Michauxi* is for André Michaux, a Frenchman who botanically explored the Carolinas and elsewhere in North America during the early 1800s. "Stoneroller" is derived from the behavior of nest-digging males or feeding fish.

Pearl daces   Genus *Margariscus* Cockerell

The pearl dace had shuttled between recognition as the monotypic genus *Margariscus* and placement in *Clinostomus*, *Gila*, or *Richardsonius*, until Hubbs (1955) allocated it to *Semotilus*. The merger was affirmed by Bailey and Allum (1962) and widely followed, despite Legendre's (1970) proposal that the pearl dace be transferred to *Phoxinus*. The pearl dace fit in *Semotilus* because it shared with those species a small preterminal barbel, and secondarily the 2,5–4,2 pharyngeal tooth count and other features.

Because the pearl dace is unknown to construct a nest and the true species of *Semotilus* are gravel-nest builders, and from other lines of evidence (e.g., Wells 1978), Jenkins and Lachner (1971, 1989) considered that the pearl dace is most closely related to the northern lake chub genus *Couesius*. Coburn and Cav-ender's (1992) elevation of *Margariscus* to generic rank was accepted by Johnston and Ramsey (1990). As a member of the chub clade, *Margariscus* is the sister group of the lineage whose most primitive members are *Couesius*, *Semotilus*, and the southeastern *Hemitremia*.

*Name.—Margariscus—*pearly.

Pearl dace   *Margariscus margarita* (Cope)

SYSTEMATICS

Margariscus margarita was described from Pennsylvania in 1868. Two subspecies are recognized, the eastern one being *M. m. margarita* (Bailey and Allum 1962; McPhail and Lindsey 1970; Scott and Crossman 1973).

DESCRIPTION

*Materials.—*Eight Virginia series including counts from 26 specimens. Life color from a spring and a fall Virginia series.

*Anatomy.—*A small-scaled, faintly spotted minnow with a preterminal barbel; adults are 45–80 mm SL. Body somewhat elongate, oval anteriorly, more compressed posteriorly; dorsal fin origin above posterior half of pelvic fin base or slightly posterior to base, rarely moderately posterior to base. Head and eye moderate-sized, eye lateral; snout well rounded; frenum absent; mouth terminal, small, oblique; small, preterminal, flat barbel usually present, often absent. Breast mostly or fully scaled. Breeding male with small tubercles on head, scale margins, and most fins; tubercles of female smaller, restricted in distribution (Fava and Tsai 1976). Skin on body and fins thickened in breeding adults.

*Meristics.—*Pharyngeal teeth usually 2,5–4,2; lateral line complete, scales (46)50–56(60); scales above lateral line 23–26(27); scales below lateral line (20)22–27(28); circumbody scales (44)48–56; circumpeduncle scales (20)21–24(25). Dorsal fin rays 8(9); principal caudal rays 19(20); anal rays (7)8(9); pelvic rays (7)8(9); pectoral rays 13–15(16). Gill rakers 4–8.

*Color in Preservative.—*Dorsum and upper side dusky; middorsal stripe usually boldly dark; dark lateral stripe best developed posteriorly, occasionally diffuse or absent anteriorly; body usually distinctly paler along upper edge of lateral stripe. Side spotted or diffusely splotched, caused by irregularly spaced, single or small groups of dark (regenerated) scales; these markings best developed in adult, often absent in young and small juvenile. Lower side usually pale, or with scattered dark scales and fine melanophores outlining scale pockets 1–2 rows below lateral line; postocular area with dark smudge. Fins slightly dusky; caudal spot small, often triangular.

Color in Life Plate 12.—Juvenile dorsum medium olive; side silver, dark spotting and lateral stripe sometimes evident; dorsal, caudal, and pectoral fins pale olive. Adult female has green and gold sheen laterally, pale body areas iridescent pearl; inner edge of iris gold; fins yellow-olive. Prenuptial male has pale pink wash on lower side, slightly intensified at pectoral base, fainter along upper edge of dark lateral stripe; rosy in small area on upper operculum and side of snout of some specimens. Slightly rosy on lower side of some fall-collected males. Rosy (or pinkish orange) probably intensifies on flank of nuptial male, as it is known to do north of Virginia.

*Larvae.—*Detailed description lacking; see Snyder (1979) and Heufelder and Fuiman (1982).

Fish 46 *Margariscus margarita* adult male 53 mm SL (REJ 1044), VA, Augusta County, Mossy Creek, 22 September 1983.

BIOLOGY

The pearl dace feeds principally on microcrustaceans and immature insects; the diet includes fingernail clams, snails, small fishes, and plant matter. The presence in intestines of sand, detritus, and winged insects indicates both benthic and pelagic feeding (McPhail and Lindsey 1970; Lalancette 1977; Stasiak 1978).

Margariscus margarita matures in 1 year; maximum survival is about 4 years (Fava and Tsai 1974; Chadwick 1976; Lalancette 1977; Stasiak 1978). In these studies, females consistently grew faster and lived longer than males; only females reached age 4. Age-2 males and females in Maryland were 48 and 51 mm SL (Fava and Tsai 1974), and were slower growing than age-2 fish from Quebec (Lalancette 1977) and Nebraska (Stasiak 1978). The largest Virginia specimen is 82 mm SL, 105 mm TL; the largest known is from British Columbia, 158 mm TL (McPhail and Lindsey 1970).

Spawning takes place in the spring. In Virginia it likely begins in mid-April and extends to early May; our females were heavily gravid in early April, water 10°C. Spawning occurred in early May in Quebec (Lalancette 1977). Although the pearl dace is widespread, its spawning behavior has been observed but once, in Michigan during mid-June in water of 17.2–18.3°C (Langlois 1929). Males defended a small territory over a sand–gravel stream bottom; intruding males were escorted away via parallel swimming. Spawning occurred in the defended territory; a male clasped a female by positioning his caudal peduncle over the female's posterior body and his pectoral fin under her anterior body, and the two fish quivered together. The pearl dace produces sounds when courting (Winn and Stout 1960). Maryland females of ages 1 and 3 averaged 900 and 2,140 total ova (Fava and Tsai 1974).

HABITAT

In Virginia the pearl dace is typically found in large spring runs and small, moderate-gradient, spring-fed streams. Apparently it occupies medium-sized streams only in the vicinity of major spring inflow. These waters vary from mostly hard bottomed to extensively silted. The dace most commonly inhabits pools and often is associated with submersed aquatic vegetation. Habitat characteristics in the Potomac drainage are summarized by Tsai and Fava (1982). Lakes and bogs, as well as lotic habitats, are populated in northern parts of the range.

Average summer temperature of pearl dace waters in the Potomac drainage was 18.1°C (Tsai and Fava 1982). Citing laboratory determination of high-temperature tolerance (to 31.1°C) of pearl dace, Tsai and Fava suggested that summer temperature was unimportant but that maturation may depend on stable, relatively high winter temperature as occurs in springs. However, during winter this species occupies very cold water in many northern areas and probably also in many central Appalachian streams. Stauffer et al. (1984) determined that in central Pennsylvania *M. margarita* prefers water of 16.0°C, lower than the preferenda of the two *Semotilus* species studied. The indication that *M. margarita* has a higher temperature tolerance than *Cottus cognatus*, a species frequently syntopic with *M. margarita* in Virginia, agrees with the larger number of pearl dace populations in the Potomac drainage.

DISTRIBUTION   Map 44

Margariscus margarita is a boreal and north-temperate fish, ranging widely in Canada and the northern United States. Its distribution extends down the Appalachians to a southern limit in the Valley and Ridge Province of the Potomac drainage, where it is quite localized.

In Virginia, 30 records were verified from 18 spring runs and other streams; all major divisions of the Shenandoah and upper Potomac systems are represented. Tsai and Fava (1982) reported pearl dace at two additional Shenandoah sites; one of these was said to be in Augusta County but both were plotted in Rockingham County. Their "Adams" Creek is Abrams Creek.

The site of a South Fork Shenandoah River record of one pearl dace (Jordan 1889b; USNM 40249) may be in error (Map 44, open circle). The river is much larger than at documented Virginia localities; the site is in an otherwise wide hiatus in the species range; Jordan reported that the water was 25.6°C. The specimen may have come from Jordan's Waynesboro locality on the stream now named the South River. Jordan found large springs (20.6°C) feeding the South River; he did not list the pearl dace from the South River, but it has been found there by others. The New drainage record of pearl dace (Jordan 1889b; Jordan and Evermann 1896) is founded on young *Exoglossum laurae* (UMMZ [IU 7936]; USNM 40205).

Abundance.—Generally uncommon.

REMARKS

The pearl dace in Virginia, like the slimy sculpin, has a relict distribution that probably results from

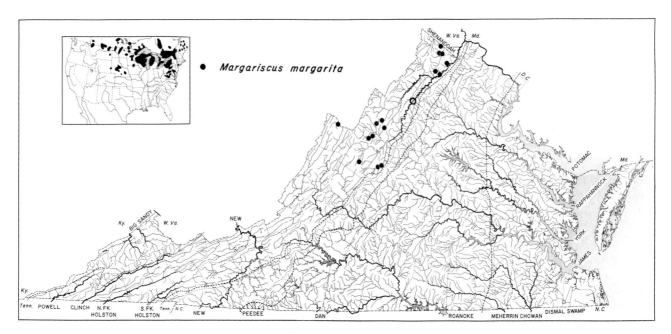

Map 44   Pearl dace. Open circle indicates possibly erroneous locality data.

natural warming of streams after glacial times and by removal of streamside shade. Because both species occur as few, scattered populations, they were proposed by Jenkins and Musick (1979) for special concern status in the state. We regard the subsequently discovered populations to negate that proposal.

Name.—Margarita is Greek for "pearl."

Chubs   Genus *Semotilus* Rafinesque

Semotilus now comprises four species, two of which inhabit Virginia; the pearl dace *Margariscus margarita* has just been extracted from the genus. In addition to their preterminal barbel and 2,5–4,2 teeth, the species of *Semotilus* are medium or large minnows with a spot or smudge in the dorsal fin anterobasally, and they construct mound-pit or ridge-pit nests. The genus was positioned in the chub clade as the sister group of *Hemitremia* (Coburn and Cavender 1992).

Name.—Semotilus means "banner (i.e., fin), spotted," signifying the distinctive dark spot in the dorsal fin of the type species *S. atromaculatus* (Jordan and Gilbert 1883).

Fallfish   *Semotilus corporalis* (Mitchill)

SYSTEMATICS

The fallfish was described from New York in 1817. Geographic variation in meristic and morphometric characters is not evident in small samples of drainage or areal populations from Quebec to the James drainage.

DESCRIPTION

Materials.—Thirteen Virginia lots and many others from elsewhere over the range; counts from 133 specimens. Life color from many juveniles and adults from Ontario and New York, many juveniles from Virginia, and color plate in Raney (1969a).

Anatomy.—A minnow with a preterminal barbel and lateral mosaic pattern of dark scale margins; adults are 150–300 mm SL. Body form moderate, slightly or moderately compressed; dorsal fin origin usually above anterior half of pelvic fin base, occasionally slightly anterior to pelvic origin or above posterior half of pelvic base. Head and eye moderate in size, eye lateral; snout moderately rounded; frenum absent; mouth moderate or large, slightly subterminal, slightly oblique; barbel small, preterminal, rarely absent. Breast nearly fully or fully scaled. Breeding male with medium-sized tubercles on front and side of snout and over eye; small to minute tubercles on lower operculum, caudal peduncle, and most fins.

Meristics.—Pharyngeal teeth usually 2,5–4,2; lateral line complete, scales (43)44–47(50); circumbody scales (32)33–

Fish 47 *Semotilus corporalis* adult male 185 mm SL (REJ 1044), VA, Augusta County, Mossy Creek, 22 September 1983.

Fish 48 *Semotilus corporalis* juvenile 43 mm SL (WHH 179), CT, Litchfield County, Housatonic River, 2 September 1983.

37(39); circumpeduncle scales (15)16(19). Dorsal fin rays 8(9); principal caudal rays 19; anal rays (7)8; pelvic rays (7)8(9); pectoral rays (15)17–18(19). Gill rakers 7–10(11).

Color in Preservative.—Young to medium-sized juvenile with dark middorsal stripe; back and upper side dusky, becoming abruptly (in young) to gradually (juvenile) paler near midside, effecting a pale stripe along dorsal edge of black or dusky midlateral stripe. Midlateral stripe widest on anterior half of body, tapering on caudal peduncle, then enlarging to an oval or round spot or smudge on caudal base; lower side pale or slightly dusky. Fins pale or slightly dusky.

In large juvenile and adult the lateral stripes are lost; the mosaic pattern of dark scale margins, particularly the mark at scale bases, becomes the dominant body pattern, extending distinctly onto lower side; much of median area of each scale often remains silvery; humeral (shoulder) bar dark or black. Fins become duskier, dorsal and caudal darkening distally; dorsal fin dusky along base, and a diffuse spot, or separate intensifications that effect a smudge, develop anterobasally. Nuptial male duskier overall than female; side of head quite dark in some males.

Color in Life Plate 12.—Juvenile, nonbreeding adult, and nuptial female dominantly olive above, silver-sided, fins pale or sooty; rosy tinge proximally in paired fins of larger fish. Breeding male dorsum silvery olive or brassy olive to dark olive; side mostly silvery, brassy, or bronze, dark scale bases olive-black; lower side with pink flush; venter white; side of dark head suffused with pink-violet or blue iridescence; iris silver-gold; humeral bar steel blue, pectoral axilla rosy. Dorsal and caudal fins yellow-olive or sooty gray; lower fins pale to deep rosy, rosy usually best developed in pectoral; lower fins sometimes with pale leading edge.

Larvae.—Described by Mansueti and Hardy (1967), Reed (1971), Jones et al. (1978), Buynak and Mohr (1979e, 1980a), Loos et al. (1979), Snyder (1979), and Heufelder and Fuiman (1982).

BIOLOGY

Young *S. corporalis* feed on phytoplankton, zooplankton, and insects. Juveniles and adults are generalized predators; they favor insects, particularly terrestrial forms during warm months, but also take crayfishes and fishes. They sometimes ingest large volumes of algae and detritus (Breder and Crawford 1922; Reed 1971). The dietary significance of algae and detritus is unknown; perhaps they are consumed incidentally. In Maine lakes fallfish often eat smelt (Cooper 1940).

The fallfish is a long-lived large minnow that grows at a fairly even rate. It first spawns typically at age 2 or 3 based on adjustment of Reed's (1971) and Ross' (1983, in litt.) data according to Victor and Brothers' (1982) study of daily otolith increments. Mature yearlings are rare; Fowler's (1912) 76-mm TL ("three inches long") female with fully developed ova likely was a deviant yearling. Maximum longevity is 9 years. According to Reed (1971), males grow faster than females after 3 years, but Victor and Brothers (1982) found no significant sexual difference in growth in three populations.

From eight populations of Pennsylvania to New Brunswick, averages of total length at age 4 were 161–245 mm (Reed 1971); in three New York streams they were 179–230 mm (Victor and Brothers 1982). The New York samples were from a small area but revealed nearly the same growth variability as did Reed's geographically broad samples. The New York study also indicated that fallfish population density was inversely related to stream size, and that the combination of low fallfish density and large stream size (or warmer water) seemed related to faster growth. Our adults of varied age collected from April to early July from over the species range comprised 31 males of 134–340 mm SL, mean, 226, and 19 females 112–317 mm, mean, 235.

A maximum size range of 457–508 mm TL ("18–20 inches") usually is cited for *S. corporalis*. We found no literature reference with a precise measurement greater than the average of 462 mm TL (18.2 inches) from two Massachusetts fish (Reed 1971). A male of 393 mm SL, 476 mm TL (18.7 inches) from the upper James drainage in Virginia is the largest we verified. A 360-mm TL fallfish weighed 0.9 kg (2 pounds) (Webster 1942). Judging from the documented fish and perhaps the size of some nests, this species may rarely reach the 1.4–1.8 kg ("three or four pounds") reported long ago (Bell 1897).

North of Virginia, spawning begins in late April or early May and extends into June in water of 14.4–19°C (Reed 1971; Ross and Reed 1978; Jenkins' data). A nest can be built in one day but the nesting period may be substantially interrupted by coolness and, likely, high water. The earliest a fully tuberculate male was caught in Virginia was 12 April. In Virginia, Jenkins observed a nest in late construction stage on 18 May, water 18°C, and Maurakis et al. (1990) found active nests during 7–16 May, mean temperature 15.0°C.

Nests are built in gravel–rubble runs and glides above riffles, in the open or along banks beneath overhanging cover, and in the middle of gently flowing pools. They may be solitary or spaced by only a few meters. The largest nests seen in Virginia were in open portions of pools, usually one to a pool. Nests may also occur on gravel shoals of lakes (Webster 1942).

Completed fallfish nest mounds usually are domelike and occasionally have a pit at the downstream edge. Typical nests are 0.5–1.0 m in diameter, 0.1–0.3 m in height. Maurakis et al. (1990) implied that all 12 mounds they observed had a pit below them. Some of the largest mounds reported, from New York, were 1.8 m × 0.9 m (Raney 1940c); mounds near that

size are built in Virginia. Slightly wider but much higher nests, to 1.5 m height, were photographed in Canada and described by Wilson (1907). Most stones are gravel-sized (Maurakis et al. 1990); fallfish carry them as far as 5 m to the nest. Nests often are topped with small rubble.

Nest construction and spawning of *S. corporalis* were described from Massachusetts by Ross and Reed (1978) and Ross (1983). Each nest is built by one male; flattened nests may be rebuilt by another male. A depression is made by removing and carrying stones with the mouth; then the pit usually is filled, first with smaller stones, and a mound is begun. Spawning occurs on a low or high mound, is cued by stone-dropping of the nest builder, and involves one or usually more females; no spawning embrace occurs. One to several sneaker or satellite males may rush the nest, resulting in a riot of gamete release. A spawning episode is consummated in a few seconds or acts may be repeated in rapid succession, after which stones are added to the nest.

At a nest in New York, the nest maker spawned 21 times with one or the other female present; the three fish were joined by an intruding male on two other spawnings. Typical spawning acts began as a short downstream drift to above the pit, followed by a semihyperbolic (downward to upward) swim that ascended over the mound; the adults were parallel and no overt quivering was detected (Jenkins' observations). Contrary to that implied by Maurakis et al. (1990), communal spawning anywhere on the downstream slope of the mound does not preclude subsequent burial of eggs by the host male.

Nuptial male *S. corporalis* often are aggressive; their agonistic acts include parallel swimming, butting, and chasing. Indeed, this minnow may hold a record for duration and distance covered by parallel swimming. Jenkins watched two fallfish parallel-swim 9 times, 0.5–10 minutes per swim (mean, 3.0), in varying directions over 3–44 m (mean, 16). Only a small fraction of males construct nests in a given year, usually those age 6 and older and about 280 mm TL and larger. Fecundity is 2,000–12,000 eggs (Reed 1971).

Fallfish rarely hybridize. One *Clinostomus funduloides* × *S. corporalis* (USNM 195951) was identified from Virginia. *Luxilus cornutus* × *S. corporalis* was reported from three other states (Bailey 1938b; Greeley 1938; Davis and Enamait 1982). Nest associates include the *Clinostomus* and *Luxilus*, *Lythrurus ardens*, *Notropis rubellus*, and *Phoxinus oreas*.

HABITAT

Fallfish occupy typically clear, cool and warm, sandy to hard-bottomed creeks, streams, and rivers

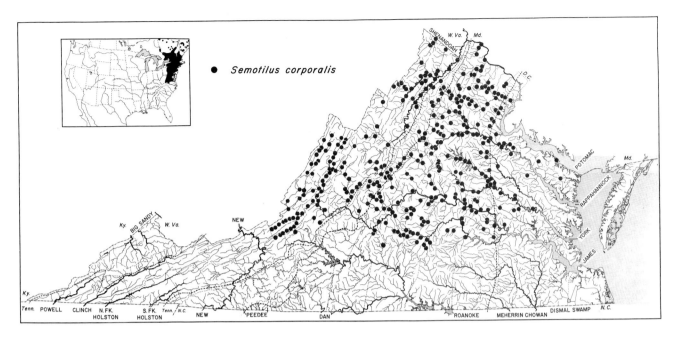

Map 45 Fallfish.

of moderate, sometimes low gradient (e.g., Trail et al. 1983). Adults prefer areas at least 0.5 m deep and 8 m wide. All life stages are found in pools and slow runs; normally only adults roam the deeper parts of large pools and, occasionally, swift water. Tidal freshwater streams also are occupied (Raney and Massmann 1953). There is only one reservoir record in Virginia but fallfish commonly are found in ponds and lakes in the northeast. In Connecticut lakes, young occur in shallows in mixed schools with other minnows and killifishes, and schooling adults range from beaches to deep water (Webster 1942). The final preferred temperature of the fallfish is 22.3°C (Stauffer et al. 1984).

DISTRIBUTION   Map 45

An eastern species, *S. corporalis* occurs indigenously in the James Bay, Lake Ontario, and St. Lawrence basins, and from New Brunswick south to the James drainage, Virginia; it has been introduced in the Roanoke drainage. The Lake Superior drainage record is erroneous; recent establishment in the Lake Erie drainage of New York most likely resulted from introduction (Scott and Crossman 1973; Hadley and Clulow 1979). In Virginia the fallfish is found in all physiographic provinces of the Atlantic slope, but sparingly on the Coastal Plain. In individual Virginia streams, its distributional relationship with *S. atromaculatus* is largely complementary, *S. corporalis* occurring downstream.

The Roanoke drainage population was discovered in 1987 by the capture of some 40 specimens including adults in the upper Falling River, Campbell County (P. L. Angermeier, personal communication). We strongly suspect that it started with fish introduced from the adjacent James drainage.

Abundance.—Generally uncommon or common, much more common above the Fall Line. Its abundance in most large main channels has not been estimated; fallfish generally are rare or uncommon in the upper James River.

REMARKS

Semotilus corporalis is the largest native minnow east of the Rockies and constructs the largest stone mound nests known among fishes. It is quite wary during nest-building, more so than *Nocomis* chubs. We perceive the fallfish as a "silver ghost" because often only a fleeting image rewards a patient stalk of the nest. The dusky dorsal and caudal fin margins of the fallfish stand out in life, serving as excellent markers for distinguishing it from *Nocomis* chubs while underwater and from streambank vantage.

Perhaps with an explorer's exuberance, Bell (1897) stated that material of a fallfish nest in Canada weighed up to 4 or 5 tons, and individual stones weighed up to 0.4 kg ("about one pound"). We do not accept the total weight of the Canadian nests. Possibly some nest stones were about the estimated weight but likely they were pushed rather than lifted.

Large size and game nature have earned fallfish some popularity among anglers (Kopp 1955; Bratton

1978). Fallfish often readily take bait, artificial flies, and lures, an attribute which sometimes lands them in disfavor. In marginal trout water, fallfish may outnumber trout and are proficient at taking a fly before the more-desired quarry. Still, we find that fallfish often require careful enticement to strike.

The palatability of fallfish is in dispute. Like all minnows, they are bony. Thoreau is often quoted that ". . . it tastes like brown paper, salted." Atkins (1905), a fish culturist, gave them as high a billing as he did brook trout. Many recent authors considered the meat to be firm and sweet. Regardless of its worth as food, we regard large fallfish to be an interesting and undersought gamefish.

Name.—*Corporalis* means "bodily." In 1817 Mitchill coined the epithet from the vernacular corporal, corpalum, or corporalen applied by Dutch settlers perhaps in reference to the military rank, possibly alluding to aggressive behavior (Bicknell and Dresslar 1885; C. Smith 1985). Fallfish derives from occurrence in splash basins beneath falls (Fowler 1905). Often they are called silver chub in Virginia and elsewhere.

Creek chub   *Semotilus atromaculatus* (Mitchill)

SYSTEMATICS

The creek chub, described from New York in 1818, and the recently described or resurrected southeastern species *S. lumbee* and *S. thoreauianus* (Snelson and Suttkus 1978; Johnston and Ramsey 1990) compose the *atromaculatus* group.

DESCRIPTION

Materials.—Twenty-nine Virginia lots plus counts from 44 specimens from the northeastern Atlantic slope, Roanoke drainage, and Ohio basin. Color in life from several Virginia series including 6 breeding males.

Anatomy.—A chubby minnow with a preterminal barbel and dark basidorsal fin spot; adults are 80–200 mm TL. Body moderate to somewhat elongate, stout; dorsal fin origin usually slightly posterior to pelvic fin base, occasionally moderately posterior to base or above posterior half of base. Head and eye moderate, eye lateral; snout rounded, lacking frenum; mouth large, terminal, oblique; jaws with firm, narrow, plicate pad behind lips; preterminal barbel usually present. Tuberculate male with usually 3–7 large recurved tubercles per side distributed from prenarial to supraorbital areas; encrustment of tiny tubercles often present on opercle and subopercle; file of tubercles on margins of body scales, best developed on caudal peduncle dorsally; all fins may have tubercles, best developed on pectoral.

Meristics.—Pharyngeal teeth usually 2,5–4,2; lateral line complete, scales (49)52–58(62); circumbody scales (40)43–50(54); circumpeduncle scales 20–23(24). Dorsal and anal rays 8; principal caudal rays 19; pelvic rays (7)8(9); pectoral rays (14)15–18(20). Gill rakers 8–11.

Color in Preservative.—Dorsum dark to dusky; dark predorsal stripe well developed in small fish, indistinct or absent in large ones; dorsolaterally dark to dusky, except often a pale stripe along dark midlateral stripe; scales darkly margined, usually forming diamond-hatched pattern; lower side slightly dusky or pale, some scales darkly margined; small adults and smaller fish have midlateral stripe and caudal spot, but stripe and spot faint or lost in large adult; head dorsum dark to dusky, cheek and lower opercle pale, opercle bordered by dark humeral bar. (Creek chubs frequently are infested with cutaneous black-spot parasites; these should not be confused with normal pigmentation spots.) Dorsal fin mostly pale or slightly dusky, medially streaked in some adult males; dark spot on dorsal fin anterobasally is obvious in juvenile and adult, incipient in young; caudal fin pale or dusky, sometimes with medial smudge; lower fins pale.

Color in Life Plate 12.—Juvenile and adult female olive above; side pale olive with silver and sometimes violet or brassy iridescence; lateral stripe leaden; venter white. Fins pale or slightly olive except for olive to black dorsal spot. In young and small juvenile, area of incipient dorsal fin spot is pale reddish. Breeding male olive dorsally; side

Fish 49 *Semotilus atromaculatus* subadult 78 mm SL (WHH 101), VA, Buchanan County, Home Creek, 27 June 1983.

brassy olive with diffuse olive midlateral stripe overcast with violet iridescence; rosy cast on lower body, cheek, and opercle; dorsal fin having olive-black spot and submedial red wash bordering the medial interradial black streaking; caudal fin dusky olive; lower fins with rosy wash.

Larvae.—Described by Lippson and Moran (1974), Buynak and Mohr (1979e, 1980a), Kranz et al. (1979), Snyder (1979, 1981), Wang and Kernehan (1979), and Heufelder and Fuiman (1982).

BIOLOGY

The creek chub is a large-mouthed general carnivore or omnivore. Young favor zooplankton and insects. Adults take these items too, but a major shift to feeding on small fishes occurs at about age 2, and the ration of fishes increases to 70% around age 4 (Keast 1985). The dietary breadth includes crayfishes, mollusks, and, rarely, frogs. Terrestrial insects are common summer and fall foods. Plants including berries sometimes are eaten (Dinsmore 1962; Keast 1966; Barber and Minckley 1971; Moshenko and Gee 1973; Angermeier 1982, 1985; Felley and Hill 1983). Brain morphology indicates that *S. atromaculatus* is principally a sight feeder (Evans 1952).

In northern parts of the range males usually mature at slightly smaller size (60 mm TL) than do females (65 mm); both sexes may mature in 1 year but 2 or more years is typical (Greeley 1930; Scott and Crossman 1973; Powles et al. 1977). Maximum longevity is 7 years but life expectancy in some populations is only 3 or 4 years. Males grow faster than females after age 2 (Powles et al. 1977). In a wide geographic sample, the range of means at age 3 was 97–198 mm TL (Carlander 1969; Becker 1983). The largest Virginia specimen is a 208-mm TL male; Becker (1983) cited a 330-mm TL male from North Dakota. The 300-mm maximum SL given by Johnston and Ramsey (1990; C. E. Johnston, personal communication) is based on Trautman (1981), who apparently reported only TL.

The reproductive period of the nest-building creek chub includes March through May; in northern Ontario it may extend into June (Powles et al. 1977). Water temperatures at the onset of the period are 12–18°C (Moshenko and Gee 1973; Ross 1977a). Active spawning occurs at about 15–17°C, but nesting subsides in high turbidity and when the temperature drops below 11°C (McMahon 1982). In eastern Virginia, spawning was observed on seven occasions during 14 April–13 May, water 13.3–16.7°C (E. G. Maurakis, in litt.). In a rivulet on the Roanoke College campus during 1987–1990, *S. atromaculatus* initiated nesting no later than (by year) 19, 5, and 12 April and 12 March; the latest date for an active nest was 15 May 1987. Males worked in daytime water temperatures ranging from 12.5° to 19.5°C; the two observed spawning episodes occurred at 18–19.5°C. Nesting interrupted by high, turbid water restarted before normal level and clarity were restored.

Semotilus atromaculatus constructs nests typically in gravel and sand–gravel runs and pool tails. Males dig a pit, depositing excavated stones immediately upstream to form a mound or ridge. Stones are transported by the mouth and, occasionally, by pushing with the snout. Usually a single male constructs a nest, but several males may work a nest in the early stages. Nests may be closely spaced (within 0.5 m of each other) or quite dispersed. Intermale aggression includes swinging laterally with the tuberculate head, chasing, and parallel swimming. The amount of time spent off the nest in aggressive behavior correlates negatively with spawning success. Nesting males are not overtly hostile to groups of mountain redbelly dace spawning at chub nests; only occasionally are dace swiped at.

Usually a single female enters the nest at a time, most often tail first from upstream. She often is driven off by the male, mainly when she seemingly is improperly positioned to start the mating act or behaves like an intruding male. When spawning the female usually is oriented vertically, the male horizontally curved about her. After spawning she may momentarily list belly-up, and then is driven away. The vertical clasp of the female tends not to occur when her size about equals the male's (E. G. Maurakis, in litt.). Eggs are deposited in the pit and covered with stones after each spawning session.

Nest mounds are progressively extended downstream by taking stones from the lower end of the pit and dropping them at the upper end of the pit. Thus nest mounds become elongate and ridgelike after several spawning episodes; the pit is at the lower end of a buried trench. In one such case the nest was about 5 m long. The description of nest construction, territoriality, and spawning is based on accounts by Reighard (1910), R. J. Miller (1964, 1967), and Ross (1976, 1977a, 1977b), and from observations by R. E. Jenkins; nest dimensions and habitat were analyzed by Maurakis et al. (1990). Ross' studies examined the behavior of nest-satellite males and showed that, unlike the fallfish, the creek chub is not a communal spawner. Unique observations of group spawning without building a nest were reported by Sisk (1966). However, Sisk later told M. R. Ross (in litt.) that he no longer was convinced that the assemblage had been spawning. Fecundity is 1,115–7,539 mature ova (Moshenko and Gee 1973; Schemske 1974). About

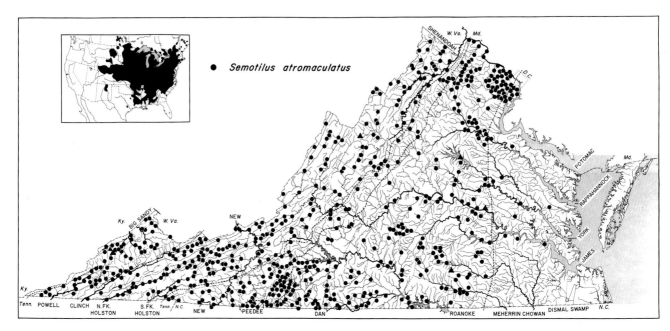

Map 46   Creek chub.

half the ova mature in a year and are spawned over a 2–3 week period (Powles et al. 1977).

Hybridization of *S. atromaculatus* seems rare, partly reflecting the low species richness typical of creeks. A hybrid involving *Clinostomus funduloides* was found in Virginia (TU 25313); E. G. Maurakis (in litt.) saw that species spawning on a creek chub nest in Virginia. Other crosses, with Virginia species, that were collected outside the state involve *Campostoma anomalum* (Cross and Minckley 1960; Ross and Cavender 1977), *Luxilus cornutus* (six states; Greeley 1938; Bailey and Oliver 1939; Koster 1939; Taylor 1954; Cross and Minckley 1960; Baxter and Simon 1970; Trautman 1981), and *Rhinichthys cataractae* (Ross and Cavender 1977; Trautman 1981). Natural hybrids with entirely extralimital species are known (Greene 1935; Greeley 1938; Koster 1939; Cross and Minckley 1960; Trautman 1981); others have been produced experimentally (Ross and Cavender 1981).

HABITAT

The common name creek chub connotes its typical habitat—creeks optimally 2–7 m wide (McMahon 1982; Felley and Hill 1983; Meffe and Sheldon 1988). Large-stream records in Virginia are based on one or few specimens, possibly stragglers from tributaries. The virtual restriction of the creek chub in Virginia to very small (4 m or less width), permanent and intermittent streams differs from Jenkins' experience in western New York, where the creek chub zone extends distinctly farther downstream. Inhabited Virginia streams generally have moderate to somewhat

low gradient and cool or warm water. The final temperature preferendum in Pennsylvania is 26.4°C (Stauffer et al. 1984).

All life stages usually occupy scantily or unvegetated pools, backwaters, and slow runs in Virginia; larger fish are relatively prevalent in pools (Finger 1982a). Occurrence in fast and slow water, typically near vegetation and other cover, was found in Oklahoma (Felley and Hill 1983). The creek chub rarely inhabits ponds or lakes. It is rather silt-tolerant (Branson et al. 1984), as demonstrated by its wide occurrence in the Big Sandy drainage. Although accommodating pH as low as 5.4 (McMahon 1982), the combination of low gradient and insufficient gravel for nesting probably render swampy Coastal Plain streams inhospitable. *Semotilus atromaculatus* was reported, apparently as a rare stray, from the oligohaline zone of James River (White 1976).

DISTRIBUTION   Map 46

Semotilus atromaculatus is widespread in eastern and central North America. Its southeastern distribution was clarified by Johnston and Ramsey (1990). The creek chub occurs in all upland and montane Virginia drainages, being generally distributed in most areas from the Fall Line westward. It probably occurs more widely in the Piedmont than our records indicate. Populations outlying the Fall Line generally are localized; it is absent from the Chowan Coastal Plain.

Abundance.—Usually uncommon.

REMARKS

The creek chub seems an adaptable fish, yet it is restricted to rather small streams. They are sometimes taken by fishermen and generally regarded as one of the "hornyheads." Becker (1983) noted that they have fine flavor. They also are excellent bait; although propagated in some areas (Washburn 1945), they have not gained commercial importance in Virginia.

The creek chub is one of the easier fishes to watch for the interesting progression of nest building and spawning, interspersed with bouts among kin and unrelated intruders. A classic presentation on its breeding habits earned Jacob Reighard (1910) of the University of Michigan a prize of $100 in gold (C. Smith 1985). Many more details of the creek chub's sexual and social life have since been learned, but physiological ecology of chub nests is an untouched topic.

Name.—Atromaculatus—"black spot"—pertains to the prominent dorsal fin mark.

Cutlips minnows   Genus *Exoglossum* Rafinesque

The two species of *Exoglossum* occur in Virginia. The common name of this eastern genus of chub-bodied minnows refers to the peculiar oral structures. In both species the lower jaw is tonguelike but bony medially and lacks a definitive lip; the upper lip is hoodlike (Figure 25C, D). The common names of the species reflect their primary differences. In the cutlips minnow *E. maxillingua* the tissue at each side of the lower jaw is lobed, thick and fleshy, each lobe resembling a cushion "cut" from lip tissue; this species lacks a barbel. In the tonguetied minnow *E. laurae* the sides of the lower jaw are bridged to the upper lip by a flap derived from the lower lip, hence the upper lip is "tied to the tongue"; a preterminal barbel is present. Convergently, similar modifications occur in the Asian cyprinid genus *Sarcocheilichthys* (Yonezawa 1958; Banarescu and Nalbant 1967).

The genus *Parexoglossum* was erected by Hubbs (1931) for *E. laurae* so as to stress the oral differences from *E. maxillingua*. The genus was synonymized with *Exoglossum* by Bailey et al. (1970) and Jenkins and Lachner (1971). Gilbert and Bailey (1972) regarded the differences to be adequately valued at the species level. In lateral view and in many life history aspects the two species are alike, but in oral morphology *Parexoglossum* is subgenerically distinct from and less advanced than *Exoglossum* (Jenkins et al. *in* Lee et al. 1980).

Exoglossum was regarded to be phylogenetically linked to certain genera such as *Semotilus* and *Nocomis* partly because these fishes build nests by transporting gravel in the mouth (Jenkins 1971a; Jenkins and Lachner 1975, 1989). The hypothesized alignment of *Exoglossum* with *Phenacobius* is discussed under genus *Phenacobius*.

Name.—Exoglossum—"outside tongue"—refers to the superficial resemblance of the anteromedial portion of the lower jaw to a tongue.

Tonguetied minnow   *Exoglossum laurae* (Hubbs)

SYSTEMATICS

Exoglossum laurae was named from the New drainage of Virginia and West Virginia by Hubbs (1931). Trautman (1931) described *Parexoglossum hubbsi* from Ohio but later (1957, 1981) synonymized it with *E. laurae*; he noted that the forms may be inseparable but retained *hubbsi* as a subspecies. An unfinished study of variation in this species by Jenkins indicates that at least most of the differences listed by Trautman (1931) are nonexistent. Electrophoresis of blood from an Ohio and a New drainage population revealed no significant difference (M. Pressick, according to S. H. Taub, in litt.).

DESCRIPTION

Materials.—Based on Hubbs (1931), Trautman (1931), 20 lots from Virginia, and 13 from elsewhere over the range; original counts from 63 specimens. Life color from Trautman (1981) and 3 Virginia lots.

Anatomy.—A robust minnow with lower jaw lacking a definitive lip, each side of lower jaw with a flap of skin and preterminal barbel; adults are 70–135 mm SL. Body moderate in profile, broad anteriorly; dorsal fin origin above or slightly posterior to pelvic fin origin. Head broad, lateral profile moderate; eye moderate, lateral; snout broadly rounded or slightly pointed. Mouth subterminal or inferior, moderate in size; upper jaw nonprotrusile, frenum narrow; snout tip and medial portion or most of upper lip papillose; upper lip (Figure 25C) moderate or thick, thickest laterally, outer edges nearly triangular or forming four sides of hexagon; lower jaw lacking normal lip, posteriorly bridged to hind portion of upper lip by wide flap; barbel small, preterminal, 1 per side, occasionally absent. Breast (10)50–90(100)% scaled. Peritoneum silver; gut S-shaped. Nuptial tubercles in male only, the small tubercles occurring only on dorsal surface of pectoral and pelvic rays 2 through 3–6.

Fish 50 *Exoglossum laurae* adult male 120 mm SL (REJ 978), VA, Wythe County, South Fork Reed Creek, 14 June 1983.

Fish 51 *Exoglossum laurae* subadult male 86 mm SL (REJ 1046), VA, Craig County, Sinking Creek, 26 September 1983.

Meristics.—Pharyngeal teeth 1,4–4,1, arch small; lateral line complete, scales (47)48–52(54); circumbody scales (37)38–43(44); circumpeduncle scales 16–20(21). Dorsal rays 8(9); principal caudal rays 19(21); anal rays 7(8); pelvic rays 8(9); pectoral rays (15)16–17(18). Gill rakers (2)4–6.

Color in Preservative.—Dorsally dark or dusky, scale margins darkest, grading to pale ventrally; dark middorsal and midlateral stripes and caudal spot usually weak or lost in adult; fins slightly or moderately dusky, or, in young and juvenile, lower fins pale. Nuptial male generally darker overall, head and back darkest; underside of head moderately dusky; belly slightly dusky; in some fish, scattered upper body scales slightly darker than others; some large females quite dark too.

Color in Life Plate 12.—Dorsum to midside olive or olive-brown, flank dusky, ventrally pale; upper side and much of urosome often with violet sheen; anterior flank silver; fins pale or rays yellow-olive to dusky olive; dorsal and caudal rays dull red-brown in some. Large nuptial male, and some large males at other than breeding period, blackish on dorsum and side; side with violet iridescence; fins quite dusky.

BIOLOGY

The life history of the tonguetied minnow is largely unknown. Greeley (1927) noted that this species feeds on small crustaceans and insect larvae. Yearlings and some 2-year-olds are immature (our data); age-4 fish are the oldest known (S. H. Taub, in litt.). Adult males are larger than adult females; 11 tuberculate males from Virginia, Pennsylvania, and New York are 85–134 mm SL, mean, 102; 14 females are 67–137 mm, mean, 95. Our largest Virginia specimen is 137 mm SL, 163 mm TL, apparently the largest known for the species.

Exoglossum laurae prepares pebble-mound nests during May in Ohio, water about 14–18°C (S. H. Taub, in litt.). Trautman (1981) noted that in Ohio the period of most active spawning is usually mid-May when water approaches 16°C. In Pennsylvania Raney (1939c) found active tonguetied minnow nests on 10 and 15 June, water 20.5–21.0°C. In Sinking Creek, Virginia, Maurakis et al. (1991) saw spawning on 26 and 29 May 1989, water 15°C. We found apparently uncompleted nests in Sinking Creek on 15 May 1973; in mid-afternoon of 20 June 1973, water 20°C, spawning was observed there by R. E. Jenkins and E. A. Lachner. The approach of the female to the nest from downstream and the spawning posture were the same as in the cutlips minnow.

Nests typically are located under or against banks, logs, and large rocks in typically slow, sometimes

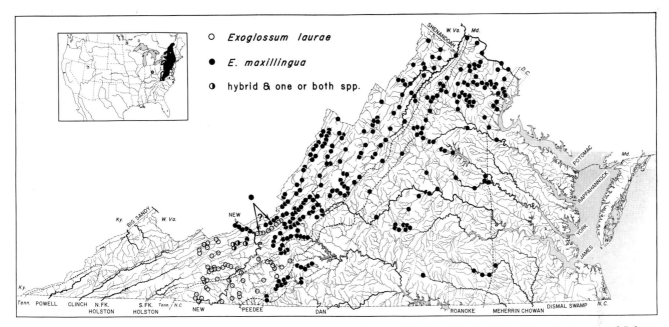

Map 47 Tonguetied minnow and cutlips minnow. Plot arrowed toward Sinking Creek of the New drainage and Johns Creek on the James drainage represents Cope's specimens labeled as from the former but probably from the latter.

moderate current at depths of 0.2–0.5 m. A single male constructs a nest although other males sometimes intrude. Pit excavation does not precede or accompany nest building (S. H. Taub, *in litt.*; our observations). Nests are round or oval, 0.3–1.0 m in greatest dimension. A consistent characteristic is the nearly uniform size of nest pebbles; the average pebble size is smaller than that in nests built by *Nocomis leptocephalus* of equal length.

A nuptial male *Luxilus albeolus* appeared briefly several times at an active Sinking Creek nest, but the tonguetied minnow always drove it off. Fecundity is about 1,800 eggs per female (S. H. Taub, *in litt.*).

Natural hybridization has frequently occurred between *E. laurae* and *E. maxillingua* in parts of the Walker Creek system of the New drainage (Map 47), to which *E. maxillingua* probably was introduced. Four lots with hybrids were taken in Big Walker, Little Walker, and Dismal creeks during 1956–1957 and reported as *E. laurae* by Ross and Perkins (1959); one lot was collected in Big Walker Creek in 1963.

HABITAT

The tonguetied minnow occurs in medium-sized creeks to small rivers that are gravelly and rocky and have about equal frequencies of pools and riffles. In Ohio this minnow generally is most numerous in waters that are seldom turbid, have little siltation, and have low fish-species diversity and biomass; *Nocomis* is typically rare or absent in these streams

(Trautman 1981). The tonguetied minnow zone was below that of the creek chub (Brown 1960). Taub (*in* Trautman 1981) supported Trautman's conclusions and added that *E. laurae* is a coolwater fish, maximum summer temperature at capture being 21°C. These conditions generally seem to apply to Virginia populations, although somewhat warmer water is also occupied. In Ohio waters *E. laurae* inhabits moderately flowing riffles and pools (Trautman 1981). Its abode in Virginia is pools and runs with substrate structure for shelter.

DISTRIBUTION   Map 47

Exoglossum laurae exists as three well-separated population groups: (1) in the upper Allegheny and Genesee drainages, Pennsylvania and New York; (2) in the Great Miami and Little Miami drainages, southwestern Ohio; and (3) in the New drainage, West Virginia, Virginia, and North Carolina (Jenkins et al. *in* Lee et al. 1980). The only record (CU 32639) for the Monongahela drainage, near the New, is from an unspecified site in Leading Creek, Randolph County, West Virginia, in 1951. The locality data were questioned by Jenkins et al. (*in* Lee et al. 1980) but F. J. Schwartz (in litt.) supported the data.

The distribution pattern in the New drainage of Virginia and West Virginia appears to be general. However, strong populations seem localized; there is only one record for the New River in Virginia, and none for the river in West Virginia.

Abundance.—Generally uncommon.

REMARKS

The tonguetied minnow should be watched for decline. Some populations in the New drainage of Virginia and West Virginia are low or extirpated. Major range contraction has occurred in Ohio (Trautman 1981), in the Monongahela and lower Allegheny drainages, and elsewhere as indicated by the large gaps among the three population groups. Although much of this waning may be related to natural factors, *E. laurae* is sensitive to stream and bank alteration (Taub *in* Trautman 1981).

Hybridization between the two *Exoglossum* in the Walker Creek system is a good study topic. The system has been scarcely sampled since hybridization was detected in 1963.

Name.—The specific epithet is for the late Laura C. Hubbs, wife and companion in the field and laboratory of the late Carl L. Hubbs.

Cutlips minnow   *Exoglossum maxillingua* (Lesueur)

SYSTEMATICS

Exoglossum maxillingua was described from Maryland in 1817. Counts of small samples from the New, Roanoke, Chowan, James, Delaware, and St. Lawrence drainages fail to show any obvious geographic variation in meristic characters. Body form and color pattern are essentially the same over the studied range.

DESCRIPTION

Materials.—Twenty-nine collections from Virginia, 10 elsewhere; counts from 46 specimens from the above-indicated drainages. Life color from Van Duzer (1939), 5 Virginia lots, and fish observed on nests in New York and Ontario.

Anatomy.—A chubby minnow with a narrow bony lower jaw bordered on each side by a large fleshy oval lobe; adults are 65–130 mm SL. Morphology essentially as in *E. laurae*, except for oral structures (Figure 25D): Upper lip tends to be more semicircular; lower jaw appears 3-lobed, the actual jaw narrow, tonguelike but hard, bordered on each side by a large soft oval lobe; barbel absent; obvious papillae usually absent from snout tip.

Meristics.—Pharyngeal teeth 1,4–4,1, arch small; lateral line complete, scales (48)49–56(57); circumbody scales (41)42–47(50); circumpeduncle scales 16–21. Dorsal rays 8, principal caudal rays (18)19; anal rays 7; pelvic rays 8(9); pectoral rays 15–17. Gill rakers 4–8.

Color in Preservative.—Same as in *E. laurae*.

Color in Life Plate 12.—Same as in *E. laurae* except some adult males also brassy on upper side.

Larvae.—Described in Fuiman and Loos (1978), Loos et al. (1979), Snyder (1979), and Buynak and Mohr (1980a).

BIOLOGY

The cutlips minnow has a strange lower jaw, but its diet is typical of many other benthopelagic minnows. In Maryland to New York this species primarily eats aquatic insect larvae. Small individuals feed particularly on midges; adults prey most commonly on caddisflies. Worms, crayfishes, mites, snails, fingernail clams, fish eggs, and lamprey larvae are occasionally or rarely eaten. Plant material and detritus are scantily ingested (Breder and Crawford 1922; Adams and Hankinson 1928; Rimsky-Korsakoff 1930; Haase and Haase 1975; Johnson 1981; Pappantoniou et al. 1984a, 1984b; Vadas 1990). We observed *E. maxillingua* feeding in nature from surfaces of flat rocks; it also en-

Fish 52 *Exoglossum maxillingua* adult male 109 mm SL (REJ 1044), VA, Augusta County, Mossy Creek, 22 September 1983.

gulfs and spits out sand, probably retaining the contained food, and takes midwater drift. In an aquarium, food was sought in small crevices, and descending food was taken (Breder and Crawford 1922).

The typical maximum life span in Pennsylvania and New York is slightly more than 4 years (Haase and Haase 1975; Pappantoniou et al. 1984a, 1984b); age-5 fish were found by Saga (1973 in Haase and Haase 1975). Yearlings and some age-2 fish are immature. Of adults from Virginia, Pennsylvania, and New York, 26 males are 71–131 mm SL, mean, 93, and 21 females are 62–128 mm, mean, 85. Our largest specimen is a male of 132 mm SL, 157 mm TL (6.2 inches) from the peripheral Chowan drainage, Virginia, population. That this species reaches 8 inches (Whitworth et al. 1968) is unverified.

The male cutlips minnow is a mound-nest maker. In New York the nesting period typically is late May to early July in water of 16.1–21.5°C (Greeley 1927; Van Duzer 1939; R. J. Miller 1964; R. E. Jenkins' observations). An extreme early nesting for central New York occurred on 8–9 May, water 13.9°C (Hankinson 1922). In the late-warming upper St. Lawrence River, spawning dates are 24 June–8 July, when water temperature is 16.1–18.9°C (Jenkins and Jenkins 1980, and later observations). Mid-May through mid-June, perhaps earlier, are nesting times in Virginia at water temperature of 18–20°C (Maurakis et al. 1991).

Nests are typically built in slower current than the average Nocomis chub nest; sites include slow runs, pools, and backwaters with appreciable water exchange. Dence (1937) recorded nesting in a New York lake. Generally the nest is under or against a bank, boulder, or log. Nests are notable for the rather uniform size of pebbles; one nest was partly topped with many dead snail shells. Most nests are 0.2–0.5 m wide; no pits have been noted. Some cutlips make an "afternest," smaller and close to the original one (Van Duzer 1939). Nest building and spawning are performed during daylight.

Spawning takes place on the upstream slope of the mound, where the current is reduced (Maurakis et al. 1991). With the male waiting quietly, the female approaches from downstream and positions ventrolateral to the male. They curve their bodies together, female on the inside, and the male's caudal peduncle is held over that of the female. In this position, probably the male's tuberculate upper surfaces of the paired fins aid in maintaining the embrace. They then move a short distance upstream, tremoring and releasing gametes on the nest. These acts sometimes are repeated in rapid succession. The eggs are then covered with pebbles. Fecundity is 345–1,177 eggs (Fuiman and Loos 1978).

Other breeding cyprinids generally are drawn only to the cutlips minnow nests located in the faster currents of the nest-habitat range. The associates include Luxilus cornutus and (rarely) N. rubellus in New York (Van Duzer 1939; R. J. Miller 1964; R. E. Jenkins' observations). The few active nests seen in Virginia lacked other species. Hybridization with Exoglossum laurae is indicated under that species and on Map 47.

HABITAT

Cutlips minnows occupy cool and warm, moderate-gradient streams of varied size; occasionally they populate large rivers, but avoid small creeks. Gravelly and rocky, typically clear waters are favored. In Virginia, many of the peripheral records are from streams with outlying populations of clear-water species. Some of the Nottoway system records are from slightly stained water. Some northern lakes are inhabited, at times only near tributary mouths (Adams and Hankinson 1928). In Virginia, E. maxillingua typically dwells in pools and runs; juveniles and adults occasionally occupy riffles. It was widely distributed among habitats and was particularly abundant in runs in a New York stream (Finger 1982a). This species generally is associated with cover. In winter it was often found under rocks with margined madtoms (Van Duzer 1939).

DISTRIBUTION   Map 47

The cutlips minnow is the Atlantic slope counterpart of the tonguetied minnow. It ranges from the Lake Ontario–St. Lawrence basin and the Housatonic drainage, Connecticut, south to the Roanoke drainage, Virginia and barely North Carolina; a probably introduced population occupies the New drainage. Its occurrence in the Passaic drainage, New Jersey, may be due to dispersal via a canal (E. Smith 1905).

On the Virginia Atlantic slope, the cutlips minnow is generally distributed in the Valley and Ridge Province but not in the Blue Ridge. Most Piedmont populations south of the Potomac drainage are localized, often in headwaters, and most outlying populations occur in and near the Fall Zone. In the upper Roanoke drainage, E. maxillingua joins Noturus gilberti and Percina rex in occupying the upper Roanoke and Pigg rivers and being apparently absent in the interjacent Back Creek and Blackwater River.

The New drainage population of E. maxillingua is interesting for its hybridization with E. laurae and the questionable status as native or introduced. The apparent first records of E. maxillingua (and hybrids) are from the Walker Creek system in 1956. Beginning in 1971, E. maxillingua was found in the New River from the mouth of Big Walker Creek to the head of Bluestone Reservoir at the West Virginia line (Hambrick et al. 1973; Hocutt et al. 1973). It is unknown below Bluestone Reservoir (e.g., Hess 1983; Lobb 1986), thus the range is quite small.

With one exception, early records of E. maxillingua in the New (Cope 1868b [Walker Creek]; Jordan 1889b; Fowler 1923, 1924) are based entirely on E. laurae (Hubbs 1931; Jenkins' study). The exceptional record is problematic. Cope's collection in 1867 of E. "maxillingua" from Sinking Creek of the New drainage (questioned record on Map 47) comprises 46 E. laurae, 6 E. maxillingua, and 2 Campostoma anomalum; all were in one jar when studied by Jenkins in 1966 (ANSP 1615-68; paratypes of E. laurae). If these species actually had been taken together in Sinking Creek during Cope's time, E. maxillingua would firmly be regarded native (Jenkins et al. 1972). However, we now believe it highly probable that the two Exoglossum species were combined from collections made in Sinking Creek (laurae) and the James drainage (maxillingua).

Sinking Creek is one of the most intensively sampled New River tributaries, but efforts since 1937 by Burton and Odum (1945), Ross and Perkins (1959), E. C. Raney, and several others have not found E. maxillingua there. In sum, we believe that this species probably was introduced to the New drainage. The data indicate an introduction to the Walker Creek system; these waters are well known for gamefishing, and E. maxillingua likely is a bait fish in the region.

Abundance.—Usually uncommon.

REMARKS

The cutlips minnow knocks the eyes out of fishes by a single sudden glancing blow. Sometimes the attacked fish is killed and sometimes the eye is eaten. The eye-gouging behavior seems to be brought on by crowding (e.g., in a bucket, aquarium, or natural low water) and may be a territorial response (Dymond 1937; Johnson and Johnson 1982; Schmidt 1985; C. Smith 1985). The narrow bony portion of the lower jaw probably hits under the eye. The frontally broader lower jaw of the tonguetied minnow seems less able to accomplish this weird behavior; eye-attacking is not known for this species.

To what, then, are the specialized jaws of *Exoglossum* adapted? Cope (1869) and Adams and Hankinson (1928) suggested that the "tongue" (lower jaw) may be used like a shovel to dislodge snails and insect larvae from surfaces, and to crush mollusk shells against the roof of the mouth. Such behavior could add encased, substrate-adherent caddisfly larvae to the diet. Cope (1869) related the strong oropharyngeal muscles of the cutlips minnow to crushing its food, which seems plausible, considering the form of the oral bones (Buhan 1969) and the smallness of the tooth arch. The large soft lateral jaw lobes of E. maxillingua may serve as "bumpers" to center food items toward the medial portion of the lower jaw. Sensory structures on the lobes may help to detect food.

The strikingly uniform and small size of pebbles in the mound nests of *Exoglossum* may be related to the structure and size of the mouth. These fishes have a somewhat lesser stone-grasping ability than do other stone-toting chubs. Coupled with nesting in relatively slow water (for chubs), there may be a minimum stone size that allows adequate percolation of water through the nest for respiration of embryos. *Exoglossum* may be selecting stones as large as they can handle, instead of picking up variable-sized stones as *Nocomis* do.

The cutlips minnow is generally distributed in northern Virginia and north, thus its fragmented range in much of southern Virginia is notable. In the Roanoke drainage it is an indicator of good-quality upland habitat, the minnow being largely restricted to the same streams as the jeopardized Roanoke logperch and orangefin madtom.

Name.—Maxillingua, "jawbone tongue."

Chubs   Genus *Nocomis* Girard

The eastern and central North American genus *Nocomis* contains seven species, four of which occupy Virginia. The species have a small terminal barbel, 4–4 or 1,4–4,1 pharyngeal teeth, and a stout body (Figures 9–11, 27A). Nuptial males develop medium to very large tubercles and, in two species groups, swollen crests on the head (Figure 33). Males of all species construct a gravel nest by digging a pit, then filling and covering it with a mound. Spawning occurs at intervals in a trough excavated on the early or late mound and filled after each episode (E. A. Lachner, personal communication). Behavioral details are given under *N. micropogon*.

Reinstatement of *Nocomis* as a genus from a subgenus in the *Hybopsis* generic assemblage was proposed by Lachner and Jenkins (1967), defended by Jenkins and Lachner (1971), and is fully accepted. We consider *Nocomis* to be most closely related to the other gravel-nest builders of the genera *Semotilus* and *Exoglossum* (see family introduction and genus *Campostoma*). Coburn and Cavender (1992) placed *Nocomis* near *Exoglossum* in an advanced but unresolved trichotomy of the exoglossin clade, and in the encompassing chub clade, distant from *Semotilus*.

Nocomis is divisible into three species groups: the extralimital, primitive *biguttatus* group (Lachner and Jenkins 1967, 1971b); the *micropogon* group (Lachner and Jenkins 1971a); and the advanced *leptocephalus* group (Lachner and Wiley 1971). For a long period all *Nocomis* were considered a single wide-ranging species, *N. kentuckiensis*; that name is now regarded a *nomen dubium* (unidentifiable). Hubbs (1926) recognized three species; each now typifies a different species group containing three species or, in the *leptocephalus* group, one species with three subspecies.

Virginia has been a focus for systematic study of *Nocomis*. In the total range of the genus, only the James drainage has three species living in the same tributary.

Name.—Jordan (1929) noted that *Nocomis* is an Indian name for "daughter of the moon," indicating a feminine derivation from Nokomis in Longfellow's *Song of Hiawatha*. However, species epithets in *Nocomis* have been masculine since Girard authored the genus, derivation unstated, in 1856 (except when species of *Nocomis* were placed in *Hybopsis*). We retain the masculine as listed by Eschmeyer and Bailey (1990) and requested by the International Code of Zoological Nomenclature (ICZN 1985: Art. 30d) for genus-group names of uncertain gender but with an originally associated masculine species-group name (*Nocomis bellicus* Girard 1856).

Bigmouth chub   *Nocomis platyrhynchus* Lachner and Jenkins

SYSTEMATICS

Nocomis platyrhynchus was described from the New drainage of North Carolina, Virginia, and West Virginia by Lachner and Jenkins (1971a). Morphologically it is the most primitive form of the *micropogon* species group—the river chub group.

Nocomis platyrhynchus is so similar to *N. micropogon* that the decision to rank it a species was made arbitrarily by Lachner and Jenkins. In most of the few differences the forms overlap broadly. Essentially in all but one of the differences, *N. platyrhynchus* is approximately intermediate between *N. micropogon* and *N. raneyi*, the other member of the species group. In the exceptional character, circumbody scales, *N. platyrhynchus* resembles *N. raneyi*. *Nocomis platyrhynchus* has the greatest posterior extension of dorsal head tubercles in the group, but its typical pattern and tubercle numbers tend to be intermediate between *N. micropogon* and *N. raneyi*.

Assessment of the status of *N. platyrhynchus* using reproductive criteria in nature is precluded; being endemic to the New drainage, it is allopatric to *N. micropogon*. Evidence of long-past gene interchange between *N. platyrhynchus* and populations of *N. micropogon* in the Monongahela and Potomac drainages, which were interconnected with the New via stream captures, was interpreted from tuberculation (Lachner and Jenkins 1971a). However, the character states involved are primitive; they have little or no phylogenetic value.

A genetic study by Esmond et al. (1981) detected no difference between *N. platyrhynchus* and *N. micro-*

pogon, leading Hocutt et al. (1986) to downgrade *platyrhynchus* to a subspecies of *micropogon*. Esmond et al. (1981) included no outgroup in their genetic study and thus had no firm basis for comparison. R. P. Morgan II (in litt.), C. H. Hocutt, J. R. Stauffer, Jr., and J. M. Quattro broadened the genetic study to include three outgroup species of *Nocomis*. In this still unpublished work, they found a few but minor differences between *N. platyrhynchus* and *N. micropogon*, and they too held these taxa to be synonymous. We, however, rank *N. platyrhynchus* as a species based on its morphology; it is an evolutionary species.

DESCRIPTION

Materials.—Based on Lachner and Jenkins (1971a) and 6 more Virginia series. Color in life from Lachner and Jenkins (1971a) and 1 additional series including 3 prenuptial males.

Anatomy.—A chub with a small terminal barbel, medium to large tubercles on snout tip, lachrymal, and often on head dorsum posterior to eyes, mouth large, circumbody scales usually 32–36, and gut nonwhorled; adults are 90–200 mm SL. Body moderate in profile, terete or slightly compressed; dorsal fin origin above or very slightly posterior to pelvic fin origin. Head moderate; eye medium or small, lateral; snout somewhat pointed, except well rounded in nuptial male; frenum absent; mouth large, subterminal, horizontal; barbel small, terminal. Breast usually 40–70% scaled. Caudal fin fairly small, upper lobe nearly pointed, usually slightly longer than rounded lower lobe. Peritoneum all dark or (often) partly silver; intestine usually S-shaped, occasionally with a very short anterior accessory loop.

Fish 53 *Nocomis platy-rhynchus* juvenile 67 mm SL (REJ 640), VA, Floyd County, Little River, 6 May 1973.

Tubercles in male only; present from tip of snout and lachrymal onto head dorsum, posteriorly to anterior interorbital area or as far back as posterior occipital area; hiatus present or absent between anterior snout and internasal tubercles; head tubercles medium to large; small tubercles present on dorsal surface of pectoral rays; small nuptial male with head dorsum little or not at all swollen, large male with prominent cephalic crest. Anal and genital papillae largest in female.

Meristics.—Pharyngeal teeth 4–4, generally hooked or pointed, these and arch of moderate stoutness; lateral line complete, scales (38)39–41(43); circumbody scales (29)32–36(39); circumpeduncle scales 16–18(20). Dorsal rays 8; principal caudal rays 19; anal rays 7; pelvic rays 8; pectoral rays 16–18. Gill rakers 4–8.

Color in Preservative.—Shaded dark or dusky dorsally to pale ventrally; dark middorsal stripe present in small fish and some adults; scales from dorsum to upper flank dark-margined, margins averaging very slightly wider in female; dark or dusky midlateral stripe well developed or, in some adult males, almost completely absent; dark scapular bar present. Fins pale, or dorsal, caudal, and pectoral rays dusky; caudal spot dark, small, often absent in large male.

Color in Life.—Body dorsum olive-brown or olive; middorsal stripe iridescent gold or yellow-olive; side mostly silver, brassy, or yellow-olive, often with green and violet reflections; belly white; lateral stripe green or leaden. Head dorsally olive-black or olive; laterally olive to yellow-olive, often with iridescent silver, gold, or green; iris dusky to gold, narrowly bordered at pupil by iridescent yellow, gold, or orange, all of these colors sometimes absent. Dorsal and caudal fins orange or red distally, remainder olive to yellow-olive, or fins virtually all yellow-olive; anal fin white, pale yellow, or bright yellow; paired fins mostly pale, or bright yellow or yellow-olive; anal and pelvic rays 1–3 partly satiny white or yellow-white. Nuptial (non-peak) male pink to rosy over lower head and body except breast; scapular bar iridescent pale blue.

COMPARISON

See discussion preceding the *Key to Nocomis* species.

BIOLOGY

The life history of the bigmouth chub is scantily known. It feeds on immature mayflies, caddisflies, midges, and blackflies (Hess 1983), and probably consumes other invertebrates and occasional fishes, as do other *Nocomis* chubs. Benthic and drift items are included in the diet (Lobb and Orth 1988).

Age-1 and age-2 fish are immature. Males tend to attain much larger size than females. Twenty-two males judged to be adult by tubercles or tubercle scars are 139–222 mm SL, mean, 179; 15 gravid or spent females are 81–140 mm, mean, 110. The largest Virginia specimen is 200 mm SL, exceeded by the 222-mm fish from West Virginia.

Spawning occurs during late April to early June in the New River in West Virginia; active nests were found in water of 15–25°C. The gravel mounds are located in riffles, runs, and tails of pools, at depths to 0.75 m; most mounds are built within 10 m of a bank (Lobb and Orth 1988). Jenkins' observation, in the Little River of Floyd County on 30 May, water 22–24°C, indicates that the male nesting behavior seen (mounding, digging a spawning trough, and quivering in the trough before spawning) is like that of other *Nocomis*.

Nocomis platyrhynchus hybridizes with *Campostoma anomalum, Luxilus albeolus, L. chrysocephalus, Nocomis leptocephalus,* and *Rhinichthys cataractae* (Lachner and Jenkins 1971a; Hocutt et al. 1978; Stauffer et al. 1975, 1979b, 1979c; Goodfellow et al. 1984; RC).

HABITAT

The bigmouth chub acts like the other members of the river chub group in preferring warm, typically clear, gravelly and rocky, moderate-gradient, medium-sized streams to large rivers. In the large New River, *N. platyrhynchus* prefers runs and riffles of varied bottom type, often bedrock (Lobb and Orth 1988). In tributaries it occupies the same habitats and occasionally is found in pools. No record from an impoundment is known to us.

DISTRIBUTION   Map 48

Nocomis platyrhynchus is endemic to and widely distributed in the New River drainage of North Carolina, Virginia, and West Virginia. Records of *N. micropogon* and some of those of *N. leptocephalus* from the drainage are actually of *N. platyrhynchus* (Lachner and Jenkins 1971a).

Abundance.—Generally uncommon based on most tributary collections; in the New River, common at several stations between North Carolina and Claytor Lake (Benfield and Cairns 1974), rare or uncommon somewhat below Claytor Dam (Ross 1973; our obser-

vations), and uncommon or common in the lowermost Virginia section (Hocutt et al. 1973).

REMARKS

The New River above Kanawha Falls, West Virginia, is one of the most ancient watercourses on Earth. Endemic to this drainage, *N. platyrhynchus* is the most primitive member of the river chub group as judged from morphology. With the New drainage as a hub, *N. platyrhynchus*-like stocks probably gave rise to *N. micropogon* in the Ohio basin below Kanawha Falls, and to *N. raneyi* after reaching the Atlantic slope via stream capture (Lachner and Jenkins 1971a).

Name.—*Platyrhynchus*—"wide snout"—refers to the broad snout and large mouth.

River chub   *Nocomis micropogon* (Cope)

SYSTEMATICS

The river chub was named from Pennsylvania in 1865 from a hybrid *Luxilus cornutus* × *Nocomis micropogon*. Lachner and Jenkins (1971a) restricted the name *micropogon* to that parental species of the type specimen. The closest relative of *N. micropogon* is *N. platyrhynchus*.

DESCRIPTION

Materials.—Based on Lachner and Jenkins (1971a) and 33 additional Virginia lots. Color in life from Lachner and Jenkins (1971a) and 6 more Virginia lots.

Anatomy.—A chub with a small terminal barbel, medium to large tubercles on snout tip, lachrymal, and as far back on head as posterior internasal area, circumbody scales usually 30–33, and intestine unwhorled; adults are 90–180 mm SL. The body, its parts, and sexual dimorphism essentially as in *N. platyrhynchus* except: breast almost always naked or very slightly scaled (0–20%) in Atlantic slope

populations, usually moderately to nearly fully scaled (30–80%) in the Tennessee drainage, and gape averages slightly wider. In tuberculation the most posterior tubercles (or spots, buds, scars) rarely occur posterior to internasal area, and when in interorbital area the tubercles are in the anterior one-third; hiatus usually present between anterior snout and internasal tubercles.

Meristics.—Pharyngeal teeth 4–4, teeth and arch of moderate stoutness; lateral line complete, scales (37)38–40(43); circumbody scales (28)30–33(36); circumpeduncle scales (14)16–17(19). Dorsal rays 8(9); principal caudal rays (18)19; anal rays 7(8); pelvic rays 8; pectoral rays (15)17–18(19). Gill rakers (6)7–9(10).

Color in Preservative.—As in *N. platyrhynchus*.

Color in Life Plate 13.—Virginia populations essentially as in *N. platyrhynchus* except dorsal and caudal fins perhaps always pale orange or red-orange distally; paired fins possibly slightly less yellow on average. Peak color of large nuptial male a pink or rosy flush from venter to upper

Fish 54 *Nocomis micropogon* subadult 138 mm SL (REJ 980), VA, Washington County, Whitetop Laurel Creek, 15 June 1983.

side; dorsal and lower fins edged satiny white or yellow-white. The lateral stripe of nuptial males can change rapidly between blackish and pale green. Such changes seem to be correlated with agonistic behavior at nests; lack of the band apparently signifies dominance.

Larvae.—Described in Loos et al. (1979), Snyder (1979), Buynak and Mohr (1980a), Cooper (1980), and Heufelder and Fuiman (1982).

COMPARISON

See comparative diagnosis heading the *Key* to species of *Nocomis*.

BIOLOGY

The river chub forages on and just above the bottom, and feeds opportunistically on drift (Jenkins and Burkhead 1984). The diet is primarily immature aquatic insects; much less important are worms, crustaceans, water mites, mollusks, and fishes. Algal and vascular plant material is often consumed in major amounts (Lachner 1950b; Hickman and Fitz 1978). Considerable food probably is taken by sight feeding; the small barbels likely are not of great utility in feeding (Davis and Miller 1967).

Some males are capable of spawning when 2 years old; all males of age 3 and at least 130 mm SL are mature. Age-3 females are adult. Very few river chubs live 4 years; the oldest known was age 5 (Lachner 1952; Scott and Crossman 1973). The faster growth of males becomes obvious by the end of the first year. At the end of the third summer, males from Virginia and New York were 124–150 mm SL, mean, 138, females 99–125 mm, mean, 111 (Lachner 1952). Age-3 river chubs were 104–116 mm SL in Ontario (Scott and Crossman 1973). Of adult river chubs from Virginia and extralimital portions of the upper Tennessee drainage, 72 males were 121–219 mm SL, mean, 160; 17 females were 83–150 mm, mean, 108.

Although *N. micropogon* is big for an eastern minnow, it is the smallest species of the river chub group. The largest specimens recently caught or observed in Virginia and elsewhere are 180–189 mm SL, one of these from Virginia being 227 mm TL. A 287-mm TL specimen is known from Ohio (Trautman 1981). Three other specimens taken long ago also were larger than recently caught individuals: one of 219 mm SL was taken during 1883 in Virginia; one of 233 mm SL, 280 mm TL was caught around 1870 in Michigan; one about 270 mm SL, 320 mm TL, is of unknown provenance (Lachner and Jenkins 1971a). Whether these three specimens were curios selec-

tively preserved for their large size, or were typical-size adults for their time and place, is unknown.

Mid-spring to early summer is nest-making time in runs and tails of pools. In Michigan, over four years, nests were built during 20 April–28 May in water of 15–20.5°C (Reighard 1943). In Catatonk Creek, New York, R. J. Miller (1964) found a deserted fresh nest on 1 May 1960 but additional nests were not noted in that year until 3 June. In 1959 and 1961, nests were begun on 4 June and 30 May. Water temperatures in Catatonk Creek in 1959, 1960, and 1961 at the start of nesting were 20.0, 18.9, and 12.2°C. In 1961, nesting ended on about 19 June. Miller noted upstream migration into the study section. Jenkins observed active nests in the same section of Catatonk Creek between 22 May and 11 June, 1965–1968; over 10 of the days the water was 15.6–20.6°C, mean, 18.0. An extreme date and temperature of spawning—9 July and 28.3°C—were recorded in New York by Greeley (1929).

In four upper Tennessee drainage streams of Virginia over seven years, dates of nesting activity were 21 May–30 June, water 17–26.7°C, mean, 21.2. The Virginia average probably is skewed toward the latter part of the breeding period. In any one stream section, most nesting probably occurs in a week; a cold spell or high water can interrupt nesting.

Typical gravel mounds of the river chub are 33–102 cm in diameter and 3–33 cm in height (R. J. Miller 1964). The nests take 20–30 hours to complete, that time generally spread during daylight over 2–4 days. A fairly large nest was found by Reighard (1943) to have a pit plus mound volume of 67 liters, and was composed of some 7,050 stones. Reighard estimated that the single male swam a total of 25.7 km within the nest area to gather materials. As known for other mound-building minnows, the largest nests tend to be constructed earliest and by the largest, presumably oldest males (R. J. Miller 1964). Nest-building apparently occurs only during daylight.

When ready to spawn, the male tosses or carries stones a few centimeters to the side, fashioning a spawning trough or pit on the upstream half of the nest; more than one trough may be made at a nest. Trough-making often involves fairly deep digging for stones. Sideways expelling of stones usually alternates with directly forward stone drops, made after the male swims about half a body length upstream while tremoring the posterior body and spreading the colorful lower fins over the trough. The tremoring and forward stone-dropping are apparent signs of readiness to spawn; tremoring also serves to clean the stones.

The female initiates spawning by entering the

trough and taking a position at the male's flank or under him. The male holds his body nearly straight and parallel to the female; he may hold the female with his posterior body over her, and with a tuberculate pectoral fin under her. Spawning acts last about one second, and often occur several times in rapid succession; 41 occurred in a three-minute period. Spawning episodes often involve more than one female. The male seems to terminate episodes; he chases females from the trough, fills it, and progresses with mounding (Reighard 1943; R. J. Miller 1964; R. E. Jenkins' observations). Fecundity of small females is 460–725 eggs (Lachner 1952).

Most natural hybrids of *N. micropogon* involve the typical nest associates *Campostoma anomalum*, *Clinostomus funduloides*, *Luxilus chrysocephalus*, and *L. cornutus* (E. A. Lachner and R. E. Jenkins, unpublished data). The river chub rarely hybridizes with *Nocomis raneyi*, but very frequently with *N. leptocephalus* (Lachner and Jenkins 1971a). The origin and status of the "Cheat minnow," "*Rhinichthys bowersi*"—a hybrid of *Nocomis micropogon* × *Rhinichthys cataractae*—are under debate; this form is either a continuously produced hybrid not deserving taxonomic status, or a species of hybrid origin (Raney 1940e; Stauffer et al. 1979b; Cooper 1980; Goodfellow et al. 1984; Morgan et al. 1984).

HABITAT

Although the river chub and the two other members of the *micropogon* group extend up into 10-m wide sections of some tributaries, truly they are the riverine chubs of the genus. *Nocomis micropogon* typically is found in medium and large tributaries and mainstreams (Lachner and Jenkins 1971a). Its frequency of capture in the Ohio River (Pearson and Krumholz 1984) indicates that it is not a stray there. It typically occupies clear, gravelly and rocky streams of moderate to somewhat high gradient, and extends from warm sections up into the lower end of wild-trout waters. Typical Coastal Plain habitat is unsuitable. Juveniles and adults commonly inhabit pools, runs, and riffles; adults are least often found in riffles.

DISTRIBUTION Map 48

Nocomis micropogon occurs from the eastern Lake Michigan drainage to the Lake Ontario drainage, south on the Atlantic slope from the Susquehanna to the James drainage, and in many parts of the Ohio basin. Peripheral populations in eastern Ontario (Goodchild and Tilt 1976) and the Delaware (Cooper

1983), Santee (UNCC 33), Savannah (Lachner and Jenkins 1971a), and Mobile drainages (Suttkus and Ramsey 1967) probably are introduced.

The distributional relationship of *N. micropogon* and *N. raneyi* in the James drainage is noted in the *N. raneyi* account. The record of *N. micropogon* in upper Johns Creek (upper James) by Young and Maughan (1980) is not accepted; the collections were discarded. The record probably is based on *N. leptocephalus*, which is common in that reach but not reported in their study. The lower James River record of *N. micropogon* (Lachner and Jenkins 1971a) is based on specimens identified as *N. leptocephalus* by Massmann (1957), but which we now regard as unidentifiable.

Abundance.—Usually uncommon or common; only one specimen has been taken recently in the Big Sandy drainage; the others were collected in 1937.

REMARKS

Nocomis chubs are often common and probably serve as important forage to gamefishes. They are often used as bait. They are of great interest because of their nest-building activities.

Many fascinating behaviors occur at nests of *N. micropogon* and kin. The nest-building process and spawning of the resident male alone bear watching. Many colorful minnow species spawn on chub nests. The male chub generally seems to pay no attention to these associates; only occasionally does he swipe at them with his tubercle-studded head. Frequently the male butts and chases away egg-foraging predators such as suckers.

The most intensive and prolonged ritualized battles occur when a nuptial male river chub the size of the resident male intrudes at the nest. Slow and often lengthy parallel swims with strong tail beating, punctuated by head swinging at each other, often result. The swollen soft nuptial crest (Figure 33) cushions some blows to the head, but the battered, fungused males found during the breeding period attest to the effectiveness of tubercles as weapons. General debilitation from battle as well as the energy drain from nest building must also result in the relatively high number of dying and dead large males seen around the end of the spawning period.

"Accessory" or "supernumerary" male river chubs are often observed on nests (Reighard 1943; Jenkins' observations), as occurs in other species of *Nocomis* (E. A. Lachner, personal communication). These males have a dark lateral stripe, lack nuptial color and tubercles or have weakly developed tubercles, but are near or within the size range of highly tuberculate nest-making males. Because they resemble females, we have wondered whether accessories are satellite or sneaker males seeking to spawn. However, all of 10 medium-sized (88–140 mm SL) nontuberculate river chub males captured with tuberculate males had small testes. Reighard (1943) saw some accessories engage in limited nest building, but never saw one

spawn. Reighard also noted a large "female" excavate a spawning trough; possibly this was a nontuberculate male. More observations are needed to understand sociobiology of *Nocomis* nests.

Name.—*Micropogon*, meaning "small beard," is based on the very small barbels in Cope's hybrid type specimen.

Bull chub   *Nocomis raneyi* Lachner and Jenkins

SYSTEMATICS

Nocomis raneyi was described from many streams in Virginia and North Carolina by Lachner and Jenkins (1971a). It is the sister species of the lineage comprising *N. micropogon* and *N. platyrhynchus*. The atypical traits of *N. raneyi* in the upper James River and lower reaches of certain of its tributaries were suspected to have been induced during ontogenetic development by chemically polluted water (Lachner and Jenkins 1971a). Later study supports that hypothesis; the pollution source apparently is the paper mill on the lower Jackson River at Covington.

DESCRIPTION

Materials.—From Lachner and Jenkins (1971a) and 80 other Virginia lots; counts given for Virginia specimens only. Life color from Lachner and Jenkins (1971a) and 5 additional lots including 11 nuptial males.

Anatomy.—A chub with a small terminal barbel, numerous crowded small to medium tubercles present from snout tip and lachrymal onto head dorsum to usually posterior interorbital area, breast usually naked, circumbody scales usually 32–35, and intestine unwhorled; adults are 100–240 mm SL. *Nocomis raneyi* is quite similar to *N. micropogon* and *N. platyrhynchus*, differing on the average in: body deeper and more compressed in adult male; head and snout shorter, snout slightly sharper; mouth smaller; tail larger. Breast usually naked, rarely scaled as much as 30%. Tubercles extend well into interorbital area, sometimes occipital

area, in medium-sized juvenile to adult; hiatus lacking between anterior snout and internasal tubercles.

Meristics.—Pharyngeal teeth 4–4, stout, crowns often rounded, arch heavy; lateral line complete, scales (39)40–43(45); circumbody scales (31)32–35(37); circumpeduncle scales (15)16–17(18). Dorsal rays 8(9); principal caudal rays 19; anal rays (6)7; pelvic rays (7)8(9); pectoral rays (15)16–18(19). Gill rakers (6)7–10(11).

Color in Preservative.—Same as in the other members of the river chub group, except dark scale margination tends to be narrower; dark lateral stripe faint or absent in large juvenile and adult.

Color in Life Plate 13.—Essentially as in the other members of the river chub group. Two large nuptial male *N. raneyi* had rosy flush from venter to dorsum and into dorsal and anal fins; satiny yellow-white margin in all fins (in tail of only one fish); this is the peak development seen in the species group.

Larvae.—A description supposedly of *N. raneyi* from Elliott Creek was given by Potter et al. (1980), but almost certainly it is based on *N. leptocephalus*. The adults whose gametes produced the larvae were discarded (W. A. Potter, in litt.). Fuiman et al. (1983) misinterpreted information from Jenkins, who had stated that *N. raneyi* was unknown from Elliott Creek and had not been taken nearby in many years.

Fish 55 *Nocomis raneyi* subadult 137 mm SL (REJ 1010), VA, Halifax County, Banister River, 14 July 1983.

COMPARISON

See discussion preceding the *Key* to the species of *Nocomis*.

BIOLOGY

The bull chub feeds on benthic and drifting insects, snails, and occasionally on crayfishes and fishes. The strong pharyngeal arch and broad rounded teeth adapt it for crushing mollusks. Large amounts of filamentous algae are sometimes taken, perhaps incidentally while searching for animal food (Jenkins and Lachner *in* Lee et al. 1980). Based on brain morphology, *N. raneyi* is a sight-feeder (Reno 1969b).

Nocomis raneyi of five years age are known (Lachner and Jenkins 1971a; our data). Males grow larger than females; of adults from Virginia, 35 males are 177–242 mm SL, mean, 220, and 58 females are 96–198 mm, mean, 135. The largest measured Virginia specimen is exceeded by a 266-mm SL male from North Carolina, but we observed still larger bull chubs in Virginia.

Nest building was recorded during 4 May–3 June in the upper James and Roanoke drainages; the observations were made on 11 days over six years. Water temperatures during daylight periods were 18–23.3°C, mean, 20.9. Some larger juvenile *N. raneyi* may be nest accessories (*N. micropogon*, Remarks). The 27 larger nontuberculate males taken in or near spawning periods are 144–227 mm SL, mean, 176; only one has slightly enlarged testes. Two of these males, 193 and 197 mm SL taken on 18 April, have small testes but had a faint pink flank, the color perhaps a prenuptial stage. Their obvious but flat tubercle spots may have later developed tubercles.

The bull chub rarely hybridizes with *N. leptocephalus* and *N. micropogon* (Lachner and Jenkins 1971a, unpublished data). A tentatively identified cross is *Luxilus albeolus* × *N. raneyi*.

HABITAT

The bull chub typically occupies major rivers and their larger tributaries; populations in smaller (8–12 m wide) streams sometimes also are strong. The patchy distribution pattern on the Piedmont of the Chowan and Roanoke drainages probably is related more to heavy siltation than to collecting intensity. In the Fall Zone of the Nottoway River, *N. raneyi* was more common in gravelly and rocky sections than in sandy areas. Old-timers told us that this species inhabited the Roanoke River Fall Zone in North Carolina before impoundment. Apparently the bull chub finds isolated areas of gravel to its liking on the Coastal Plain. This species occupies both fast and slow water; large individuals are most often found in pools, small ones in riffles, runs, and well-flowing parts of pools.

DISTRIBUTION   Map 48

The bull chub occurs in the James, Chowan, Roanoke, Tar, and Neuse drainages, Virginia and North Carolina. In Virginia it is widely distributed in the Valley and Ridge and upper Piedmont provinces; in the Chowan and Roanoke drainages it may be generally sporadic in the lower Piedmont and upper Coastal Plain. Very recent records (not plotted) from the James River and lower reaches of its larger Piedmont tributaries indicate a contiguous range there.

The original distributional status of *N. raneyi* in the James drainage has been uncertain. This species was believed to have entered the James from the Roanoke drainage via stream capture, hence it has been considered native (Robins and Raney 1956; Lachner and Jenkins 1971a). The capture hypothesis was based on suggested localization of the bull chub in the James to an area including Craig Creek that is adjacent to the Roanoke. Localization was attributed partly to ecological interference from *N. micropogon*, whose range is largely complementary to that of *N. raneyi*. Native status of *N. raneyi* in the drainage is corroborated by three bones from two late-prehistoric archeological sites (Thompson 1989; Whyte 1988, 1989). Fossil pharyngeal arches reported by Guilday et al. (1977) as *N. cf. raneyi* (CM 29689 in part) from the upper James are not stout enough to belong to this species.

The possibility of introduction to the James was discussed by Lachner and Jenkins (1971a) and Jenkins et al. (1972). The later basis for doubting native status (Stauffer et al. 1982; Hocutt et al. 1986) included the discovery that *N. raneyi* has a much wider range in the drainage—from the lower Jackson River well into the Coastal Plain. The first major range extensions were from the lower Piedmont in 1966 (verified in 1971) and the Coastal Plain in 1973. Given the 1951 date of the first James drainage record, dispersal and progressive colonization after introduction could account for the developing distribution pattern. Similar scenarios in the James are argued for other species (e.g., *Scartomyzon cervinus*; *Noturus gilberti*; Biogeography). In contrast, the bull chub case involves the apparent disappearance of a close relative (*N. micropogon*) from much of the drainage in the 1970s–1980s and its replacement by *N. raneyi*.

Both the native and introduction hypotheses suffer from the scarcity of pre-1970 collections from the James River and lower reaches of most of its larger

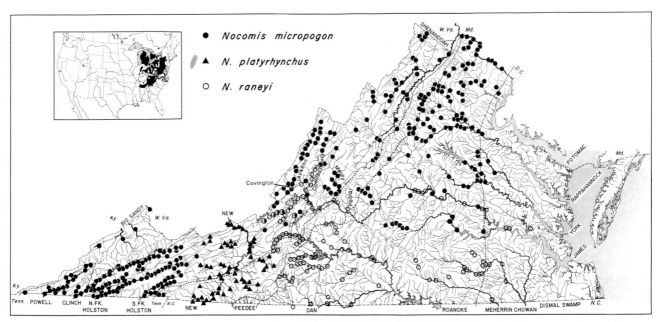

Map 48 River chub, bigmouth chub, and bull chub. Right-half-shaded circles in Craig–Johns Creek system of upper James drainage represent occurrence, but not necessarily synchrony, of *N. micropogon*, *N. raneyi*, and/or their hybrids. Large right-half-shaded circle in middle Catawba Creek represents a hybrid *N. micropogon* × *N. raneyi*. Solid dot just east of latter is for a hybrid *N. leptocephalus* × *N. micropogon*.

tributaries. Both are viable hypotheses unless the prehistoric remains of *N. raneyi* are correctly identified.

Abundance.—Usually uncommon or common.

REMARKS

Large size, a swollen head with horns (tubercles), and aggressive disposition render the nesting male *N. raneyi* a bullish chub. It rivals the fallfish for the title of largest native eastern American minnow. Commensurate with its size, it builds the largest nests among *Nocomis* species; some mounds are 110 cm in diameter and 35 cm high. The stones are carried in the mouth by the male, often for 2–4 m or more. Some of the flat nest stones are so large—at least 10 cm—that it is difficult to believe a chub moved them, but we have seen such stones pushed or tugged along the bottom.

The interaction of *N. raneyi* and *N. micropogon* in the James drainage is one of the many fascinating facets of the systematics of the river chub group. For a long time these fish were considered the same species because the diagnostic nuptial male of *N. raneyi* was unknown. Lachner and Jenkins found that one of the best and most enjoyable ways to catch adults was by angling. With adequate nuptial males finally at hand, they traced diagnostic features through adult females, juveniles, and large young, allowing species identification at all these ages, thus setting the stage for ecological and behavioral studies.

Name.—For the late Edward C. Raney of Cornell University, renowned ichthyologist and major professor to a large number of students, including the describers of the species.

Bluehead chub   *Nocomis leptocephalus* (Girard)

SYSTEMATICS

The bluehead chub was described from North Carolina in 1856. Three subspecies were recognized by Lachner and Wiley (1971), *N. l. leptocephalus* being the one in Virginia. The subspecies are based on nuptial tuberculation, but the species actually is divisible into four population groups based on tubercles. The species is divisible differently on the basis of

two distinctly different nuptial-male color patterns whose geographic distributions are discordant with tubercle differences. Virginia has one of the tuberculation forms and both color forms. The nearly all-blue form occurs in the Pee Dee drainage; the other form is orange-striped on the body and occupies all other Virginia drainages populated by the species (presumably including the York and Rappahannock, from which we have not seen a nuptial male).

Fish 56 *Nocomis leptocephalus* juvenile male 118 mm SL (REJ 1002), VA, Charlotte County, Twittys Creek, 13 July 1983.

DESCRIPTION

Materials.—From Lachner and Jenkins (1971a), Lachner and Wiley (1971), and 78 other Virginia lots; tubercle distribution and meristics from populations of Virginia drainages only. Life color from 14 lots of the orange-striped form including 16 nuptial males, and 1 male of the blue form each from Pauls Creek, Virginia, and Back Creek, Mecklenburg County, North Carolina.

Anatomy.—A chub with a small terminal barbel, head tubercles very large and on dorsum only, circumbody scales usually 28–31, and gut whorled; adults are 70–160 mm SL. Body moderate or quite stocky, terete or slightly compressed; dorsal fin origin above or slightly behind pelvic fin origin. Head moderate or short, fairly broad; eye moderate or small, lateral; snout moderately or well rounded; frenum absent; mouth large, subterminal; barbel small, terminal. Breast (60)70–100% scaled. Caudal fin moderate in size, lobes usually well rounded. Peritoneum dusky or dark; intestine whorled in anterior body cavity.

Tubercles in male only; head tubercles large to very large, present in internasal, interorbital, and often occipital areas; small tubercles on dorsal surface of pectoral rays; small nuptial male with slight head swelling centered internasally; large male tends to have large dorsal cephalic crest. Anal and genital papillae largest in adult female.

Meristics.—Pharyngeal teeth usually 4–4, generally hooked or pointed, these and arch of moderate stoutness; lateral line complete, scales (37)38–41(43); circumbody scales (26)28–31(33); circumpeduncle scales 16(18). Dorsal rays 8(9); principal caudal rays (17)19(21); anal rays 7; pelvic rays (7)8; pectoral rays (15)16–18(19). Gill rakers (4)5–9.

Color in Preservative.—Essentially as in the members of *micropogon* group, described under *N. platyrhynchus*, except: dark posterior scale margins tend to be wider and dark anterior margins (scale pockets) narrower, the side appearing less cross-hatched; dark lateral stripe usually absent in medium to large nuptial male; nuptial male of blue form in Pee Dee drainage tends to have rays of all fins moderately to quite dusky, as opposed to rays of lower fins pale or slightly dusky in other Virginia populations.

Color in Life Plate 13.—Dorsum tan or olive; middorsal stripe gold or yellow-olive; upper and midside grading olive to yellow, generally with some silver and brass sheen; fish from turbid water often dominantly dusky white or silver; lower side and venter silver-white. Iris with inner half usually brilliant orange-red. Dorsal and caudal fins faint orange or bright orange-red; lower fins typically pale orange or yellow, pectoral the most orange, anal the least colored, sometimes white; satiny yellow or yellow-white along anterior anal and pelvic rays.

Nuptial male in most Virginia drainages adds blue over head laterally and on snout frontally, and yellow-orange to orange midlateral stripe on anterior half of body. In life the blue is often pale or powder blue; in postnuptial male in life, and in all males in preservative, the blue darkens, frequently to slate blue. Wide bright red-orange iris ring also fades quickly.

Nuptial male in Pee Dee drainage has blue head but lacks orange stripe; body develops pale blue cast from head posteriorly as far as area above anal fin base, from midhorizontal level to lower side; paler blue on belly, breast white; blue deepest on posterior scale margins; lower half caudal peduncle iridescent brass; upper side scale medians iridescent copper (less yellow than lower caudal peduncle), posterior scale margins olive. Inner iris ring silver in Virginia specimen. Caudal fin dull pale orange; other fins with rays dark blue, membranes pale blue. All the blue except on head is ephemeral in preservative.

Larvae.—Described by Loos et al. (1979), Fuiman et al. (1983), and apparently Potter et al. (1980); see *N. raneyi*.

COMPARISON

See the preface to the *Key*.

BIOLOGY

The bluehead chub is an omnivore, feeding on a wide variety of aquatic insects and plant material, particularly algae. In a North Carolina study the principal food was insects, but in a lower Piedmont stream in Virginia, plants were taken in the greatest amount (Flemer and Woolcott 1966; Gatz 1979). This species may be more reliant on cutaneous taste buds than are other *Nocomis* chubs (Davis and Miller 1967).

Nocomis leptocephalus matures within 3 years. Maximum longevity detected by Lachner (1952) was 3 years and a few months, but large males were not included in his samples from Virginia and North Carolina. Males grow the fastest; of 2-year-olds in two Virginia samples, males were 59–104 mm SL, mean, 77, and females were 50–80 mm, mean, 62 mm. As in all other *Nocomis*, the sexes of adult bluehead chubs differ sharply in size. Of adults from Virginia, 51 males were 94–165 mm SL, mean, 134, and 69 females were 62–118 mm, mean, 83. The 105 larger immature males in these collections were 56–137 mm, mean, 85; 13 immature females were 55–90 mm, mean, 69. The largest Virginia specimen is 165 mm SL; the largest known of the species, 10 males ranging 192–214 mm SL, are from North Carolina (Lachner and Jenkins 1971a).

The bluehead chub constructs gravel-mound nests generally during May and early June in Virginia; extreme dates from 13 years of data are 28 April and 14 July, the latter in a lower Piedmont stream. Water temperatures of nesting from 35 site observations are 12.5–25.3°C, mean, 20.2; the second lowest value is 15°C. In the upper Coastal Plain of South Carolina, nesting was observed during 15 June–4 July, water 19–21°C (Wallin 1989). The gravel mounds typically are built in runs, pocket areas of riffles, and tails of pools, generally next to a boulder, log, or bank (e.g., Lachner and Wiley 1971). In *Nocomis* (and other mound nesters), nest size is related to the size of its builder; the average bluehead chub nest built by one male is similar to that of *N. micropogon* and usually smaller than that of *N. raneyi*. The bluehead chub may be extreme in the genus for the high frequency of nests built by and spawned upon by more than one male; Wallin (1989) noted up to five males (mean, 2.6) adding stones to a mound. Typical-sized females produce 710–800 eggs (Lachner 1952).

Nocomis leptocephalus was found more frequently with *N. raneyi* in Virginia than with the other two members of the river chub group, but the former two rarely hybridize. The frequency of hybridization of *N. leptocephalus* with *N. platyrhynchus* and *N. micropogon* is moderate to high, particularly with the latter (Lachner and Jenkins 1971a). *Nocomis leptocephalus* hybridizes accidentally with *Campostoma anomalum*, *Clinostomus funduloides*, *Luxilus albeolus*, *L. cerasinus*, *L. coccogenis*, *L. cornutus*, and *Phoxinus oreas* (Raney 1947b; Gilbert 1978a; Cashner et al. 1979; Lachner and Jenkins, original data).

HABITAT

The stream zones occupied by the bluehead chub are centered further upstream than those of the members of the river chub group. Blueheads generally extend from headwaters into streams 20–30 m wide, and rarely occupy or occur in small numbers in large rivers. Strong populations occur in cool brook trout creeks (Neves and Pardue 1983; our observations) as well as in warm sections. Often-turbid streams support this chub but populations in typically clear streams generally are more dense. Pools, runs, and riffles, and sand to boulder and bedrock substrates are occupied, but *N. leptocephalus* is not often found over silt beds.

DISTRIBUTION   Map 49

The bluehead chub is a southeastern species; it ranges from the Potomac drainage south on the Atlantic slope to Georgia, and west on the Gulf slope to lower Mississippi River tributaries. In the Ohio basin, it is moderately widespread in the New drainage and localized (extralimitally) in the Tennessee drainage (Jenkins and Lachner *in* Lee et al. 1980). This species is extensively distributed in mountains and the Piedmont; its eastern limit generally corresponds with the Fall Line in Virginia and North Carolina, but in most southerly drainages it extends far into the Coastal Plain (Lachner and Wiley 1971).

The original distributional status of *N. leptocephalus* in the Potomac, Rappahannock, and York drainages has been questioned. Two divisions of the Potomac are populated. The two records from Strait Creek of the upper drainage proper are dated 1975. That stream in particular is much trafficked by bait fishermen; an introduction is probable. The other Potomac populations are widely scattered in the South Fork Shenandoah system; the earliest record we verified is from 1956. The pattern is strange for a species so generally distributed in the adjacent James drainage, but not unlike that of several species native in the Shenandoah. Therefore, and also because this is the northern (perhaps climatically determined) boundary of the species range, we differ from Jenkins et al. (1972) and later authors by considering the Shenandoah population to be native rather than introduced.

The first Rappahannock record is from the upper Rapidan system, adjacent to the James drainage, in 1947. Subsequent captures indicate downstream spread into the lower Rappahannock (below the Rapidan mouth, first record in 1972) and upper Rappahannock proper (1974; extreme upper tributaries in 1982). The pattern is somewhat similar to that in the Shenandoah but we see no strong basis for considering the Rappahannock population native. If native, it should have been found in earlier collections made all along the Blue Ridge and outlying areas. The York population is probably native owing to its more general distribution and four records dating to 1935–1938.

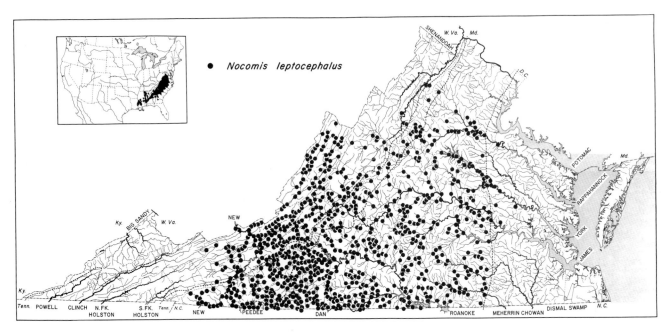

Map 49 Bluehead chub.

The New drainage population is considered native because of records at least as early as 1885 and 1888 (Cope's [1868b] collections need study), and from its wide dispersion. Peculiarly, *N. leptocephalus* is absent from nearly all of the drainage in West Virginia; it is known there only in the East River (Stauffer et al. 1975) and Indian Creek (P. S. Hambrick, in litt.), a Bluestone Reservoir tributary. These records are slightly farther down the drainage than noted by Lachner and Jenkins (1971a). *Nocomis leptocephalus* was believed to have a limited range in the New drainage of North Carolina (Lachner and Jenkins 1971a), but from confirmation of some of the bluehead chubs reported by Richardson and Carnes (1964) and later collections, it appears to be widespread. *Nocomis leptocephalus* is relatively localized in some western tributaries of the New River.

Abundance.—Generally common or abundant in the mountains and upper Piedmont except in the Potomac drainage, where it is usually rare or uncommon. Typically common or uncommon in the lower Piedmont.

REMARKS

The gravel-mound nests of the bluehead chub are common in many Virginia streams during spring and early summer. Fishermen and landowners have told us that the gravel piles probably are made by children or crayfish. Cope (1868b) guessed that the nests were made by suckers, but this was corrected by Raney (1947b). Raney, however, missed seeing the male chub at the nest first credited to *N. leptocephalus*. Nesting males of all *Nocomis* generally are wary; upon disturbance they are the first fish to flee and usually the last to reappear. However, they can be oblivious to observers during episodes of repeated spawning and intense aggression. Obviously Raney (1947b) saw a nest that still had a male *Nocomis* affiliated, because other cyprinid species were spawning on it.

It is typical that nest associates—mostly daces and shiners—use fresh nests; such nests have the cleanest gravel, thus enhancing survival of eggs and larvae. We never saw a chub nest with spawning cyprinids that had been permanently vacated by its maker. The upstream progression of peak spawning of the chub-nest association coincides with increasing water temperature. There is no evidence of substantial upstream migration of these fishes in Virginia; spawning of the associates seems tuned to that of locally resident chubs.

Nests of *Nocomis leptocephalus* host the largest number of cyprinid associates in central Virginia. We have found up to six species in addition to the chub at individual nests; overall in the state, at least 13 species clearly reproduce on bluehead chub nests. The diversity is related to richness of the southeastern ichthyofauna; also, many of the nest associates match *N. leptocephalus* in preferring somewhat small streams. A coevolutionary process is evident; the nests probably favor the survival of all of the users' embryos. Truly, many aspects of the future ecology of streams are determined at chub nests.

Name.—*Leptocephalus*—"small head."

Slender chubs   Genus *Erimystax* Jordan

The eastern and central North American genus *Erimystax* was recently elevated from *Hybopsis* by Mayden (1989) and Coburn and Cavender (1992). In the exoglossin clade of the more inclusive chub clade, *Erimystax* was ranked as the sister group of *Macrhybopsis* (*M. aestivalis* and allies) by Coburn and Cavender, but Mayden (1989) and we consider *Erimystax* to be most closely related to *Phenacobius*.

The slender chubs have an elongate rounded body, an inferior mouth, a pair of terminal barbels, 4–4 teeth, and 7 anal rays. The species are speckled, or have a subdivided lateral stripe, or have a row of large spots or blotches on the side. Three of the five species inhabit Virginia.

Name.—*Erimystax*—"very moustached" (barbeled).

Slender chub   *Erimystax cahni* (Hubbs and Crowe)

SYSTEMATICS

Erimystax cahni was described from Tennessee in 1956. It is the sister to the advanced group containing the species having a blotched body (Mayden 1989; our data).

DESCRIPTION

Materials.—One Virginia and 15 Tennessee series; counts from 54 specimens (Harris 1986; our data). Life color from 3 series.

Anatomy.—A minnow with a very long snout, inferior mouth, terminal barbel, and the lateral stripe often subdivided into chevrons; adults are 50–80 mm SL. Body moderately elongate, terete; dorsal fin origin above anterior half of pelvic fin base or occasionally slightly anterior to pelvic origin. Head moderate, dorsal profile evenly, gently downsloping through very long snout; eye large, supralateral; snout tip slightly rounded or pointed; frenum absent; mouth small, inferior, horizontal; lips moderate, medial portion little expanded or not expanded anteriad; one small or medium barbel at each end of and distinct from the lips; numerous papillate taste buds at isthmus. Breast naked.

Tubercles in male tiny, densely distributed on top and side of head; wider spaced on dorsal and lateral body; present on pectoral and pelvic fins. Nuptial male with friction pad on lower cheek.

Meristics.—Pharyngeal teeth 4–4; lateral line complete, scales (39)40–45(49); scales around back 11–13; scales around belly (12)13–15(17); circumbody scales (25)27–30(32); circumpeduncle scales (11)12(14); predorsal scale rows (15)16–18(19). Dorsal rays (7)8; principal caudal rays 19(20); anal rays (6)7(8); pelvic rays (7)8(9); pectoral rays (13)14–16(18).

Color in Preservative.—Dusky above, nonspeckled; each scale with curved, dusky or dark mark; pre- and post-dorsal stripe narrow, sometimes interrupted. Midside stripe darkest posteriorly, narrowing and then widening just anterior to caudal spot; on posterior half of body, stripe often slightly interrupted at each scale, forming longitudinal pattern of alternating pale and dark V-marks or chevrons that point anteriad; V-marks sometimes masked by leaden silvery overlay; stripe often diffuse on anterior body, revealing pair of punctations (stitching) on each lateral line scale; slight scale margin pigmentation extending to lower side anteriorly.

Fins plain except for caudal pattern: small dark spot at end of midlateral stripe, the spot diffusing distad through medial rays of fin; base of upper and lower 2–3 rays dark, diffusing distad; pale area between each pair of the three darkly streaked areas. Dorsal fin base darkest posteriorly, except small pale spot on body at base of last ray.

Color in Life Plate 14.—Head and body yellowish tan to brown dorsally; midback with a longitudinal series of short narrow gold lines; lateral stripe and sometimes area slightly above are iridescent pale green; lower side and belly silvery white; in some lighting, side with violet iridescence, upper body mostly silver. Iris silver to brassy yellow. Caudal fin base pattern evident; medial caudal spot often

Fish 57 *Erimystax cahni* adult female 57 mm SL (REJ 935), TN, Hancock County, Clinch River, 6 July 1981.

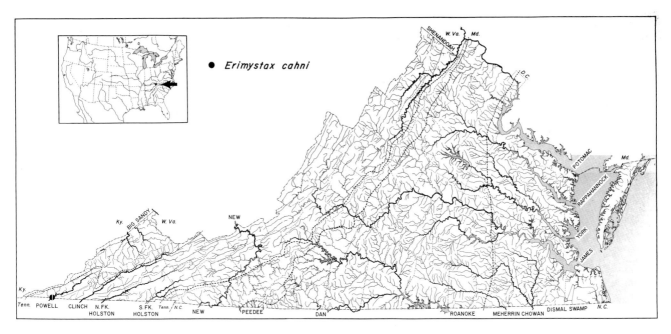

● *Erimystax cahni*

Map 50 Slender chub.

masked by silver; fins otherwise pale. Sexual dichromatism unknown.

BIOLOGY

A limited life history study by Jenkins (1975a) was the basis for summaries by Jenkins et al. (*in* Lee et al. 1980), Parker and Dixon (1980), White (1982), and the USFWS (1983). Of 14 young to adult fish, 12 consumed mostly or entirely insect larvae, chiefly mayflies, caddisflies, and midges. Three had taken large numbers of tiny snails, and two had ingested one minute Asiatic clam *Corbicula*. The slender chub may be a more visual feeder than other species of *Erimystax* (Davis and Miller 1967; Reno 1969b).

The statement that *E. cahni* lives about 4 years (Jenkins et al. *in* Lee et al. 1980) is emended. A young specimen of 25 mm SL in mid-July and four young of 31–32 mm SL in late June, combined with length frequency data for other specimens (102), indicate rapid growth in the first year and a maximum age of 2 years and a few months. Mature fish are ages 1 and 2. No difference between the sexes in growth was noted. Fish in spawning condition were 17 males, 53–71 mm SL, mean, 60, and 9 females, 54–65 mm, mean, 59. The largest known slender chubs are two females of 81 mm SL from Tennessee.

Spawning occurs in late April–early May, based on fully gravid females caught on 23 April 1971, and largely and fully spent females on 2 May 1975, in the Clinch River in Tennessee. Reproductive habitat likely is that typically occupied by adults during warmer parts of the year; that is where nuptial specimens were found. Spawning behavior probably is similar to that of *E. insignis*.

HABITAT

Erimystax cahni is a fish of the open, moderately to swiftly flowing, shallow flats and shoals of warm, usually clear, moderate-gradient, large streams and rivers (30–125 m wide). Frequently the slender chub is taken as shallow as 0.3 m, rarely 0.1 m. Occasionally it inhabits slow runs, but we never found it in a backwater or pool. Young occupy the same habitat as adults. A specific habitat requirement appears to be the presence of major areas (greater than 25 m²) of clean, small (pea-sized) to medium gravel. Usually the chub is found on pea gravel, infrequently on sand–gravel mix and large gravel. Its winter habitat may be pools (Starnes and Etnier 1980).

DISTRIBUTION   Map 50

Erimystax cahni has one of the smallest ranges among North American riverine fishes; it is known only from the upper Tennessee River drainage in Tennessee and Virginia. The area of the two Powell River sites in Lee County, Virginia (Fletcher Ford and island at Fletcher Cliff, Rkm 188.7 and 189.7 [Feeman 1987]), may be the upper limit of *E. cahni*; this species has never been taken in a reach of lesser river width. The next upstream site sampled, 4.3 rkm above Fletcher Cliff, was sampled four times during 1979–1980 but yielded no slender chubs, nor did all of the many efforts above there.

The range of the slender chub has been receding. It was found in the Holston River of Tennessee in 1941, just before impoundment (Etnier et al. 1979), and occurred widely in the Clinch and Powell rivers of Tennessee. It has lost populations in the Clinch and Powell owing to impoundment and pollution; in the early 1980s its range extremes spanned a total of 111.9 rkm in these two rivers. Within these limits the slender chub is discontinuously distributed; the rivers have frequent long, inhospitable pools and many swift areas lack suitable substrate. The chub is known recently from only nine sites (Burkhead and Jenkins 1982a).

Erimystax cahni probably inhabited the Clinch River in Virginia but would have been wiped out during the 1967 fish kill. Although the Kyles Ford population (that nearest to Virginia, 21 rkm below the state line) sometimes has been strong, there is no evidence that the species has dispersed upriver. In contrast, *Etheostoma tippecanoe* has recovered in the Clinch River between Kyles Ford and the Virginia line (and above).

Abundance.—Rare to uncommon at the two Powell River sites in Virginia during 1979–1981; of the 12 total samples for which we have complete data (9 or 10 reported by Feeman [1987]), the slender chub was taken in 7, yielding a sum of 19 specimens from 6 samples (number unknown in the other). At record sites in the Clinch and Powell rivers in Tennessee, the chub has fluctuated from apparently absent to common; generally its abundance has been low and rarely was it the most abundant minnow on the swift flats. In the Frost Ford–Brooks Island reach of the Clinch River in Tennessee, *E. cahni* was uncommon or common in our three samples taken at normal flow during 1975–1981 (Burkhead and Jenkins 1982a) and was uncommon at Frost Ford in 1985. This species has been

absent or rare at this and several other record sites in the late 1980s (J. N. Stoeckel, personal communication).

REMARKS

The slender chub was federally designated as threatened in 1977, with critical habitat defined as extending from Tennessee to include in Virginia the Powell River of Lee County and the Clinch River of Scott County (USFWS 1983). Critical habitat was designated in Virginia initially to protect Tennessee populations and to enhance dispersal into Virginia. The population in the Powell of Virginia, at 2.7 and 3.7 rkm above Tennessee, was discovered in 1979 by TVA biologists (Feeman 1987). The slender chub is officially listed as endangered in Virginia.

The prospects of *E. cahni* establishing itself appreciably farther upriver in the Powell and entering the Clinch of Virginia are low; ample beds of pea gravel may be absent or too far apart. The continued existence of this species at any locality depends on reduction of chemical pollution and silt sedimentation, and preservation of gravel bars. Removal of gravel could instantaneously deplete local populations; removal of gravel upstream could curtail chub recovery by reducing the natural replacement of gravel swept downstream during spates.

Name.—For Alvin R. Cahn, whose contributions include preimpoundment surveys for the Tennessee Valley Authority (Cahn 1938a, 1938b). Cahn had the foresight to recognize the value and irreplaceability of natural history collections and sought their deposition at museums. Unduplicatable distribution records and many new species of fishes secured by Cahn and his staff were entered in the ledgers of the University of Michigan Museum of Zoology under the direction of Carl L. Hubbs. The correspondence file at the UMMZ between these men is a veritable gold mine of ichthyological history. Cahn found the slender chub at the foot of Norris Dam virtually as the dam was closed in 1936, condemning the lower Clinch population to oblivion.

Streamline chub   *Erimystax dissimilis* (Kirtland)

SYSTEMATICS

Erimystax dissimilis was described from Ohio in 1840 and is a member of the group of *Erimystax* chubs having a blotched body. It is the sister of the recently elevated *E. harryi* (Harris 1986), which was described as a subspecies of *E. dissimilis* by Hubbs and Crowe (1956).

DESCRIPTION

Materials.—Thirty-one Virginia series plus counts by Harris (1986) from 92 specimens from the Holston, Clinch, and Powell systems. Color in life from 5 Virginia series of adults.

Anatomy.—A very elongate minnow with an inferior mouth, a barbel, and usually a row of large spots or blotches on the side; adults are 60–100 mm SL. Body very

Fish 58 *Erimystax dissimilis* adult male 93 mm SL (REJ 994), VA, Washington County, North Fork Holston River, 22 June 1983.

elongate, terete; dorsal fin origin slightly anterior to pelvic fin origin or occasionally above anterior half of pelvic fin base. Head and snout of moderate length; eye moderate or somewhat large, lateral or very slightly supralateral; snout broadly rounded or almost pointed; frenum absent; mouth, lips, and barbel as in *E. cahni*; papillate taste buds usually absent from isthmus, sometimes 1–2 present. Breast naked. Nuptial features as in *E. cahni*.

Meristics.—Pharyngeal teeth 4–4; lateral line complete, scales (42)44–48(50); circumbody scales (28)30–33(36); circumpeduncle scales (12)15–16(17); predorsal scales rows 18–21(23). Dorsal rays 8; principal caudal rays 19; anal rays (6)7; pelvic rays (7)8–9; pectoral rays (16)17–19.

Color in Preservative.—Dusky above, speckled with few or more commonly, many small dark spots and X-marks; each normally pigmented scale with a curved dusky or dark mark; predorsal stripe narrow, subdivided into a series of short dashes; postdorsal stripe developed as predorsal stripe or represented by a series of small spots. Midside with a row of large dusky or black spots or blotches that usually are round, sometimes oval or rectangular, longest axis usually horizontal; these marks or intensifications of the midlateral stripe number (excluding caudal spot) (3)6–10(12), rarely 0–2. Midlateral marks sometimes masked by dark midlateral stripe. Midlateral stripe occasionally slightly dusky, revealing stitching on some lateral line scales; stripe occasionally silvery; stripe not notably narrowed or broadened posteriorly; upper and lower edges of stripe lack row of distinct dark punctations. Body below lateral stripe immaculate.

Fins plain except pattern of longitudinal caudal streaks present as in *E. cahni*; caudal spot usually round or square, large, prominent, similar in height to posterior midlateral body spots. Dorsal fin base darkest posteriorly, except small pale spot present on body at base of last ray.

Color in Life Plate 14.—Back and upper side pale olive, overcast with iridescent silver or pale violet or both. Midlateral stripe iridescent silver or pale green, sometimes with pale gold glints; midlateral spots and blotches pale violet, blue, or black; some fish with blue and violet general sheen on midside. Lower side and belly silvery white. Head dorsum olive; side gold, silver, and violet; iris dusky, silver, or gold.

BIOLOGY

Streamline chubs were observed picking food from the upper surface of stones in Tennessee and Virginia (Harris *in* Lee et al. 1980; Jenkins and Burkhead 1984). Their food comprises an array of benthic insect larvae and other invertebrates; the larvae are primarily mayflies, caddisflies, and midges. This species also takes major amounts of microscopic and larger plant material (Harris 1986). Often it forms bottom-feeding aggregations, in many instances among or adjacent to *Phenacobius uranops*. From snorkeling we gained the impression that these aggregations are fairly compact and roving.

Erimystax dissimilis matures in 1 year, based on the many virtual 1-year-olds among 114 Virginia specimens taken during late April to mid-June. Two other fish, of uncertain maturity status, included an apparently senile, very large, unsexable specimen. Except perhaps for the latter specimen, the oldest fish were 2 years and a few months of age. Harris (1986) recorded specimens, mostly females, of age 3. Eight young taken in Tennessee on 29 June were 29–41 mm SL, mean, 35. The 114 clearly mature chubs were 61 males of 63–95 mm SL, mean, 76, and 43 females of 57–103 mm, mean, 76. Length–frequency data indicate that the sexes have very similar or equal growth rates. Trautman's (1981) data indicate that growth may be slightly slower in Ohio. The largest Virginia specimen is a 114-mm SL female, perhaps the largest known.

Spawning apparently occurs mostly from late April to late May in Virginia. A single April male was in reproductive condition on 25 April, most females taken on 2 May were partly spent, and almost all those from late May were spent or nearly so. Harris (1986) determined the same spawning time in western Tennessee after reanalyzing data for his earlier statement (*in* Lee et al. 1980). Harris (*in* Lee et al. 1980) found that average fecundity is 400 eggs. The streamline chub hybridizes with *Erimystax x-punctata* (Trautman 1981).

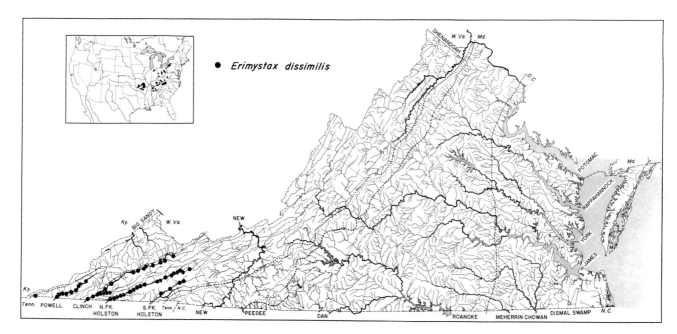

Map 51 Streamline chub. The range west of the Mississippi River is that of the recently elevated Ozark chub *Erimystax harryi*.

HABITAT

The streamline chub inhabits warm, moderate-gradient, typically clear, medium and large-sized streams and rivers. It is found in riffles, but is most characteristic of moderate and slow runs and well-flowing portions of pools with clean gravel and gravel–rubble mix. It also occupies areas of mostly rubble and boulder. Trautman (1981) noted disappearance of *E. dissimilis* from a riffle that became silted.

Erimystax dissimilis often is found at the same sites as *E. cahni* and *E. insignis*, but they differ in ecological distribution. *Erimystax cahni* appears to prefer smaller gravel and perhaps generally shallower runs, *E. dissimilis* occupies a variety of hard substrates and commonly inhabits deeper runs and pools, and *H. insignis* is more closely associated with swift shallow, often rubbly riffles. *Erimystax cahni* is exclusively riverine, *E. dissimilis* extends into only the lower reaches of larger tributaries, and *E. insignis* ascends higher (e.g., in the South Fork Holston River and Copper Creek) and drops out of the Clinch River fauna somewhat below Virginia.

DISTRIBUTION   Map 51

The streamline chub has a wide but generally disjunctive range in the Ohio basin. In the upper Tennessee drainage of Virginia, it is essentially a riverine species. All Holston system records are from the main channel of the Middle and North forks. In the

Clinch–Powell system it extends into lower Copper, Indian, and Wallen creeks, and the Little River.

A single record exists of *E. dissimilis* in the New River drainage (UMMZ 119265); four young were taken in 1935 from the New River at Prince, West Virginia, by Addair (1944). The specimens are in very poor condition, but our identification agrees with those made by C. L. Hubbs and W. R. Crowe in 1940 and 1949. It is difficult to accept that the streamline chub was extirpated from the New, but this may be one of the number of strange natural distributions in the drainage. Instead, the specimens may have been taken in the adjacent Kanawha drainage.

Records of the streamline chub exist for the Big Sandy drainage of Kentucky (Clay 1975), but this species probably succumbed to siltation in the Virginia portion.

Abundance.—Generally uncommon or common.

REMARKS

Erimystax dissimilis is one of several chubs whose body form departs from the typical concept of a chub. Its elongation approaches the extreme of some suckermouth minnows, genus *Phenacobius*.

A feature that phylogenetically unites *E. dissimilis*, the four other species of *Erimystax*, certain other minnows formerly placed in *Hybopsis*, and the genus *Phenacobius* is the nuptial or friction pad on the lower cheek of breeding males. The fine structure of the pad, as revealed by light and scanning electron microscopy, includes a rough-textured surface (data of R. L. Mayden and R. E. Jenkins). This structure apparently functions during spawning. When we rubbed the cheek pad of a male against the mucoid surface of a female, marked resistance to slippage was felt. The pad probably aids the male to hold the female; it may also help the male to retain purchase on the substrate in the spawning area. Although *E. dissimilis* has not been observed spawning, the location of the pad indicates that the spawning behavior of *E. dissimilis* may be similar to that of *E. harryi* and *E. insignis* observed by Harris (1986).

Name.—*Dissimilis* means "not similar" (i.e., to certain shiners in whose genus it was placed when first described).

Blotched chub   *Erimystax insignis* Hubbs and Crowe

SYSTEMATICS

The blotched chub, described from Kentucky in 1956, is an advanced member of *Erimystax* (Mayden 1989). Two subspecies are recognized: *E. i. insignis* from the Cumberland and middle and lower Tennessee drainages, and *E. i. eristigma* Hubbs and Crowe from mainly the Blue Ridge portion of the Tennessee. Populations of the Holston, Clinch, and Powell systems, Tennessee and Virginia, are intergrades (Hubbs and Crowe 1956; Harris 1986).

DESCRIPTION

Materials.—Nineteen Virginia series; meristic data from 84 specimens from the Holston, Clinch, and Powell Rivers (Harris 1986). Life color from 3 Virginia lots.

Anatomy.—A blotch-sided, bulbous-snouted minnow with a nublike barbel and supralateral eye; adults are 50–75 mm SL. Body form moderate or slightly elongate, slightly compressed; dorsal fin origin slightly anterior to pelvic fin origin or occasionally above anterior half of pelvic fin base. Head length moderate; eye large, supralateral; snout somewhat short, broadly rounded; frenum absent; mouth moderate in size, inferior, horizontal; lips moderately thick, medial portion much expanded anteriad; barbel essentially absent or a nubbin on posterior end of lip; underside of head densely covered with moderate-sized taste buds, rarely 1–2 papillate buds present at isthmus. Breast naked or almost so. Nuptial features as in *E. cahni* except tubercles slightly larger on average.

Meristics.—Pharyngeal teeth 4–4; lateral line complete, scales (37)39–42(45); circumbody scales (26)28–30(33); circumpeduncle scales (13)15–16(17); predorsal scale rows (14)16–18(19). Dorsal rays 8; principal caudal rays 19; anal rays (6)7; pelvic rays (5)7–8(9); pectoral rays (13)15–17.

Color in Preservative.—Basic pigmentation and speckling same as *E. dissimilis* except: midside with a row of (5)6–9(10) large, dark or black spots and blotches; these marks on anterior body tend to be rectangular, longest axis vertical; marks often square or round on posterior body. Prominent small specks or X-marks tend to form horizontal rows on midside, 1–2 rows passing through lower portion of large marks, another row (less often developed) aligned with upper edge of large marks. Caudal spot vague or prominent, almost always much smaller than adjacent midside blotch.

Color in Life   Plate 14.—Same as *E. dissimilis*.

BIOLOGY

The blotched chub eats a variety of immature insects, mainly midge and blackfly larvae, a few other invertebrates, and large amounts of microscopic plants and detritus (Harris 1986). Sometimes it searches along plant stems for food. Based on the cephalic lateralis and taste bud systems, Reno (1969b) suggested that *E. insignis* uses these structures to a greater degree, relative to vision, than do *E. cahni* and *E. dissimilis*.

Fish 59 *Erimystax insignis* adult male 58 mm SL (REJ 984), VA, Scott County, Copper Creek, 16 June 1983.

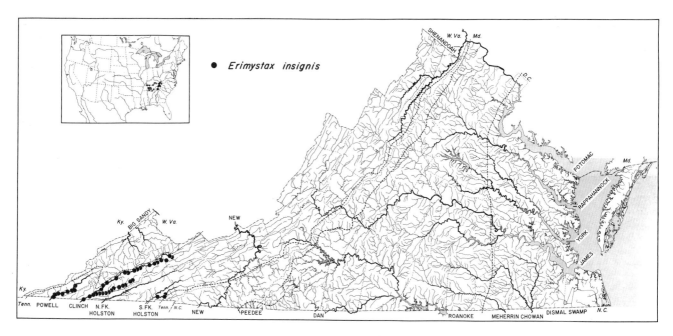

Map 52 Blotched chub.

Most individuals mature in 1 year; all are adult by 2 years. The smallest immature fish taken during the breeding period was 41 mm SL; the largest was 56 mm. The oldest specimens found were slightly over 2 years old. Young were 23–39 mm SL in late July; in early August they were 34–42 mm, mean, 38. The sexes apparently grew at similar rates; of mature fish collected during 17 March–21 June, 44 males were 47–77 mm SL, mean, 59, and 51 females were 47–80 mm, mean, 59. Most of our specimens were from Virginia; Harris (1986) found similar maturation and growth patterns in a Tennessee population. The largest Virginia specimen is a female of 80 mm SL. An 86-mm SL female is from Tennessee (Harris 1986).

The blotched chub has a late spring to early summer spawning period. A female from Tennessee on 14 April was fully gravid; those from Virginia during 14–21 May were mostly or fully gravid. Most of the early to mid-June Virginia fish were partly or essentially fully spent. Some Tennessee females on 12 June, water 25°C, had eggs freely flowing. Spawning was observed in Tennessee on the afternoons of 28–29 May, water 15°C, by Harris (1986). Females rested in depressions between or behind rocks; the male approached from the side or downstream and eventually contacted the female cheek to cheek and vent to vent; they spawned by quivering and then the male departed.

HABITAT

Erimystax insignis typically occupies moderate to high-gradient, usually clear, cool and warm, medium to large streams, and sometimes rivers. Large young, juveniles, and adults inhabit moderate to swift runs and riffles of unsilted gravel and rubble substrates. Young first occupy shallow areas with little or no current, and move into typical adult habitat later in the summer (Harris 1986). During winter a group of blotched chubs was found under a boulder in a pool.

DISTRIBUTION Map 52

The blotched chub is confined to the Cumberland and Tennessee drainages, where it has a wide but often disjunctive distribution (Harris *in* Lee et al. 1980); Virginia populations show the greatest degree of contiguity. The major Virginia populations are in the Powell and Clinch rivers and Copper Creek. Other tributaries inhabited include Wallen Creek (just above its mouth in the Powell River), Castle Run, Cove and Stony creeks (just above their mouths), and the lower Little River in the Clinch system. A small population occurs in the South Fork Holston River; the absence of *E. insignis* from the Middle and North Forks of the Holston River is unexplained.

Abundance.—Usually uncommon or common in the Clinch–Powell system, rare in the South Fork Holston River.

REMARKS

The color pattern of the blotched chub renders it one of the most easily identifiable Virginia minnows, making it a ready subject for novice observers of small fishes to obtain meaningful observations.

Name.—*Insignis*, meaning "notable" or "distinguished," refers to the square and rectangular lateral blotches, a unique, advanced feature among American cyprinids.

Suckermouth minnows   Genus *Phenacobius* Cope

BY ROBERT E. JENKINS AND STEPHEN P. McININCH

The western Virginia ichthyofauna has a relative wealth of the remarkable bottom-living suckermouth minnows; four of the genus' five species occur in that part of the state. These small minnows are convergent with suckers by having very thick, fleshy, papillose, and sometimes plicate lips (Figures 25B, 38). Most species are elongate; the stargazing minnow *P. uranops* is extreme among American cyprinids in slenderness.

Suckermouth minnows exhibit other adaptations for living on the bottom in swift water; for example, a reduced gas bladder, small anal fin, supralateral eyes, and proliferation of external taste buds. All species have a well-developed pelvic axillary process (an elongate flesh-covered scale at the pelvic fin base) and an anteriorly positioned dorsal fin; some have markedly unequal caudal lobes (the upper being longer and more pointed). As a consequence of attenuation of the body, the anal fin origin is much posterior to the vent.

Phenacobius species have a tough pad or plate on the jaws just behind the lips. The pads were thought by Cope (1867, 1868b) to be cartilaginous, but they seem to be keratinoid or collagenous. The pads of *P.*

crassilabrum are unique for an American minnow, often being prominently multiridged and toothlike (Figure 38). Four of the five species often have a well-developed supralabial flap of tissue, usually concealed in the groove above the side of the upper lip when the mouth is closed (Gilbert and Bailey 1972). Sometimes the flap has a small protuberance or barbel-like papilla pendant from its edge (Figure 38).

Nuptial tuberculation and coloration are not elaborate; a sexual difference in color may occur only in *P. crassilabrum*. The pectoral fin of adult males is longer than that of adult females. Nuptial males have a frictional (unculous) pad on the cheek.

Intergeneric relationships of highly distinctive, specialized organisms often are disputed; *Phenacobius* is no exception. In the first description of a suckermouth minnow, *P. mirabilis* was placed in the cutlips minnow genus *Exoglossum* by Girard (1856). Citing an early edition of Moore (1968), Minckley and Craddock (1962) considered that *Phenacobius* was most closely related to *Exoglossum*, although they noted its striking resemblance to some *Hybopsis*, which then included *Erimystax*. Coburn and Cavender (1992) regarded *Phenacobius* and *Exoglossum* to be sister groups

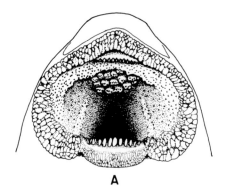   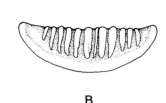   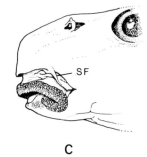

A   **B**   **C**

Figure 38 Labial and oral adaptations of suckermouth minnows, *Phenacobius*: (A) *P. crassilabrum* (mouth widely open) with papillose lips, ridged plate on both jaws, and taste buds on oral cavity surfaces. (B) Ridged plate from lower jaw of *P. crassilabrum*. (C) *P. uranops* with smooth jaw plate and supralabial flap (SF) bearing a barbel-like protuberance on its edge.

and coupled them, within the chub clade, as the most advanced lineage of the exoglossin clade (which also contains *Erimystax*).

We regard *Phenacobius* to be the sister group of *Erimystax*, an alignment perhaps traceable to Cope (1867), who considered *Phenacobius* to be allied with barbeled minnows then placed in *Hybopsis*. Jenkins and Lachner (1971) and Jenkins and Burkhead (1984) believed *Phenacobius* to be phylogenetically close to *Erimystax* and certain other former members of "*Hybopsis*." The nuptial cheek pad, several hydrodynam-

ic-benthic adaptations, and the basic biology of *Phenacobius* apparently are homologously shared with *Erimystax* rather than *Exoglossum*. Mayden (1989) concluded that *Phenacobius* and *Erimystax* constitute a monophyletic group.

Name.—*Phenacobius* means "deceptive life." Cope recognized these fishes to be minnows but was so struck by their resemblance to suckers that he mailed the original description of the genus from his field quarters.

Suckermouth minnow　　*Phenacobius mirabilis* (Girard)

SYSTEMATICS

Phenacobius mirabilis was described from Arkansas in 1856. The recognition of one taxon for this species was affirmed by Hubbs and Ortenburger (1929b). *Phenacobius mirabilis* probably is the most primitive species of *Phenacobius* in that its lips, scale size, body form, eye position, and perhaps the gas bladder are the least divergent of the genus from American cyprinids in general. Mayden (1989) gave it the same rank from osteological evidence.

DESCRIPTION

Materials.—From Cross (1967), Pflieger (1975), Becker (1983), and 12 lots including 1 Virginia specimen. Life color from Ellis (1914), Forbes and Richardson (1920), Cross (1967), Eddy and Underhill (1974), Bauer and Branson (1979), and Trautman (1981).

Anatomy.—A suckermouth minnow of moderate or somewhat elongate body form and moderate scale size; adults are 40–80 mm SL. Body form terete; dorsal fin origin slightly or moderately anterior to pelvic fin origin. Head moderate; eye small, round, lateral; snout broadly rounded or blunt; frenum absent. Mouth and lips as described under the genus; supralabial flap absent or weakly developed, protuberances absent; jaw pads weak, not ridged. Breast and part of belly naked. Caudal lobes equal or subequal.

Nuptial male with small tubercles scattered on head, anterior body, and most fins; friction pad present on lower cheek.

Meristics.—Pharyngeal teeth 4–4, lateral line complete, scales 41–51; scales around back 13–16; scales around belly 19–21; circumpeduncle scales usually 16. Dorsal and pelvic rays 8; anal rays (6)7; pectoral rays 13–16.

Color in Preservative.—Upper body dusky, predorsal and usually postdorsal stripes present; upper body pattern of curved dark mark on each scale; dark lateral stripe present; lower body pale. Dorsal, caudal, and pectoral fins very slightly dusky; dorsal fin base unpatterned; lowermost caudal ray pale; caudal spot usually prominent, round in small fish, rectangular or horizontally elongate in adult; anal and pelvic fins pale.

Color in Life.—Upper head and body yellowish to dark olive; lateral stripe dusky, overlaid with iridescent sheens of silver, gold, green, and blue; yellow line along body just above lateral stripe; lower body silvery white. Dorsal, caudal, and pectoral fins slightly dusky; other fins transparent or whitish; caudal spot black. Breeding male with iridescent blue and silver on body; lower caudal rays with yellow-orange flush; likely no pronounced difference between sexes nor between breeding and nonbreeding fish.

Larvae.—See Fuiman et al. (1983).

Fish 60 *Phenacobius mirabilis* adult female 67 mm SL (SIUC 5963), KS, Lyon County, Neosho River, 13 November 1982.

BIOLOGY

The suckermouth minnow feeds largely on insect larvae, mainly midges and caddisflies, and perhaps detritus; it also takes worms and snails (Ellis 1914; Forbes and Richardson 1920; Starrett 1950b; Stegman 1959). The taste-sensitive snout and lips are used to root in sand and gravel (Forbes and Richardson 1920; Pflieger 1975). *Phenacobius mirabilis* matured by age 2 (73–87 mm TL) during summer of that age in Wisconsin; age-3 fish were reported (Becker 1983). Adults were 64–100 mm TL in Ohio (Trautman 1981). Our Virginia specimen is 66 mm TL; the largest known is about 120 mm TL from Ohio (Trautman 1981).

The protracted spawning period, sometimes involving migration, extends from April to August; geographic variation in timing is apparent. Males probably remain reproductively active throughout the breeding season and females may spawn two or more times in that period. Specimens in breeding condition were found in water of 14–25°C (Cross 1950, 1967; Starrett 1951). Spawning is believed to occur on gravel in riffles. Mature ova from two specimens numbered 830 and 1,640 (Becker 1983).

HABITAT

Phenacobius mirabilis occurs in clear to heavily turbid, warm, moderate-gradient streams and rivers (Cross 1967; Becker 1983) which have sufficient permanent flow and gradient to prevent silt accumulation locally (Cross 1967; Trautman 1981). This species is usually found in runs and riffles over sand and gravel, and has been taken in pools with mud and sludge bottoms (Cross 1950, 1967). Starrett (1950a) noted that it preferred rubble and moved into shallower water in the evening; a similar movement was detected by Deacon (1961). Young usually are found in backwaters (Minckley 1959). In winter this fish often is one of the predominant species remaining in riffles (Smith 1979).

DISTRIBUTION   Map 53

The suckermouth minnow is widespread in the Plains region of the Mississippi basin and eastward into Ohio and West Virginia; it also inhabits the western Lake Erie drainage and certain western Gulf slope drainages. In Virginia the suckermouth minnow is known only from two sites in the Big Sandy drainage—Knox Creek (Tug Fork system) and Levisa Fork in Buchanan County. The records are dated 1982–1983. Apparently *P. mirabilis* recently extended into Virginia via the Kentucky–West Virginia portion of the drainage. It was first found in the upper section of the Kentucky–West Virginia portion in 1956 and has spread there (Turner 1961; Evenhuis 1973; Clay 1975; Robinson and Branson 1980). Most of the few Big Sandy records for Kentucky are from the Russell Fork branch of Levisa Fork, thus *P. mirabilis* may be expected to occupy that branch in Virginia. However, the Big Sandy population in Virginia is one of the few of this species living in mountains; thus it may remain localized.

Abundance.—Rare; each of the two Virginia collections are of one specimen. It is expected to increase.

REMARKS

Primarily a Plains fish, the suckermouth minnow is one of the few fishes to recently enter the Big Sandy drainage of Virginia. It is a fish on the move (Burr et al. 1980). Its eastward range expansion, from Illinois to eastern Ohio and from western Kentucky to western West Virginia (Burr and Page 1986; Burr and Warren 1986), has been credited to expansion of its habitat. As eastern virgin prairie and forest were converted into farmland, turbidity and siltation of streams increased, and *P. mirabilis* invaded (Zahuranec 1962).

Suckermouth minnow populations have been reported to increase rapidly after invasion and then decline, perhaps because of competition with other riffle species (Cross 1967; Trautman 1981). Smith's (1979) seemingly paradoxic suggestion, that siltation causes decimation of *P. mirabilis*, accords with the species' preference for current-swept substrates and streams below silt-settling basins (Gilbert 1980). It may be that *P. mirabilis* has a higher tolerance of siltation than most riffle inhabitants and can succeed after depletion of the latter. Its subsequent replacement may then occur with the decline of siltation and return of other fishes. Several authors have noted that *P. mirabilis* is most successful in nondiverse fish communities. The drastic reduction or extirpation of many species in the Big Sandy should favor the suckermouth minnow there.

Name.—Mirabilis—"strange." Girard described the suckermouth minnow in the genus *Exoglossum*, which he (1856) regarded to be "The most curious genus" of American cyprinoids.

Kanawha minnow   *Phenacobius teretulus* Cope

SYSTEMATICS

The Kanawha minnow was described by Cope (1867) from the New River of Virginia. It probably is more closely related to the three fine-scaled species of *Phenacobius* than to *P. mirabilis* (Minckley and Craddock 1962; Mayden 1989).

DESCRIPTION

Materials.—Eighteen series from Virginia, 4 from North Carolina, and 1 from West Virginia; counts from 16 specimens. Color in life from one Virginia series.

Anatomy.—A moderate or moderately elongate, spotted suckermouth minnow with medium-sized scales; adults are 55–85 mm SL. Body form terete; dorsal fin origin varies from moderately anterior to pelvic fin origin to being above anterior half of pelvic fin base. Head moderate; eye moderate, round or slightly oval, lateral or slightly supralateral; snout somewhat long, well rounded; frenum absent. Mouth and lips as described for genus; supralabial flap usually moderately developed, occasionally absent, lacking protuberances; jaw pads moderately developed, not ridged. Breast and part of belly naked. Caudal lobes often markedly unequal, upper lobe longer and more pointed. Tubercles and cheek pad as in *P. mirabilis*.

Meristics.—Pharyngeal teeth 4–4; lateral line complete, scales 43–48(49); scale around back 13–14(15); scales around belly (15)17–19; circumbody scales (30)32–35; circumpeduncle scales (15)16(19); predorsal scale rows (16)17–20(21). Dorsal rays 8; principal caudal rays 19; anal rays 7(8); pelvic rays (7)8(9); pectoral rays (14)15–16.

Color in Preservative.—Dusky above; dark predorsal stripe present, postdorsal stripe usually present; side slightly paler along dorsal edge of the diffuse to dark midlateral stripe; lower side slightly spotted, evenly dusky, or pale; underside pale. Curved dark mark on posterior edge of upper and midbody scales; spotted appearance of upper and midbody rendered by some scales being more fully or entirely darkened, the dark scales isolated or occurring in groups, in the latter case forming blotches; small fish tend to have few or no spots, some adults mostly spotted and blotched. Dorsal, caudal, and pectoral fins usually slightly dusky; dorsal fin base not distinctly patterned; caudal spot small, usually moderately dark, sometimes absent; anal and pelvic fins pale. Among large nuptial fish, male tends to have slightly more fin pigmentation than female.

Color in Life Plate 14.—Dorsum olive; middorsal stripe iridescent gold; spotting on side olive-black. Midlateral stripe with anterior half iridescent violet, some scales more violet than others, rendering a dappled effect; posterior half iridescent pale green and, in some fish, with a few violet scales; an iridescent brassy line present along upper edge of stripe. Lower side with a few dark scales, mostly creamy white to iridescent silver. Head olive above, some gold and green glints on side, silver below. Caudal fin olive; other fins orange, the shade very faint in dorsal and anal, slight in pelvic, pectoral the most intense orange but still pale, deepest basally; male tends to have deeper-toned orange than female but shades overlap. Description is of exceptionally large nuptial adults from Big Reed Island Creek; it is uncertain whether nuptial, year-round, or size-influenced colors were observed; see Deacon et al. (1979) for a photograph of a less colorful male.

BIOLOGY

Juvenile and adult Kanawha minnows feed mainly on immature mayflies, caddisflies, and dipterans; other items include worms and snails (Hambrick et al. 1975). Based on length–frequency data from 79 specimens, all apparent age-2 and some age-1 fish taken during late April–late June were mature. Two large, scale-aged adults were 2 years old. There was no evidence of older fish nor a sexual difference in growth. Thirty tuberculate males were 52–90 mm SL, mean, 69, and 25 prespawning to spent females were 50–90 mm, mean, 71. The largest specimen of each sex was 110 mm TL; they are from Big Reed Island Creek, Virginia, and are the largest known of the species. Spawning occurs in late April–early June based on examination of ovaries. Spawning was in progress in Big Reed Island Creek on or about 3 June 1984, water 19.4°C. The adults occupied runs of 0.3–1 m depth and mostly large gravel substrate.

Fish 61 *Phenacobius teretulus* adult female 90 mm SL (REJ 1093), VA, Carroll County, Big Reed Island Creek, 3 June 1984.

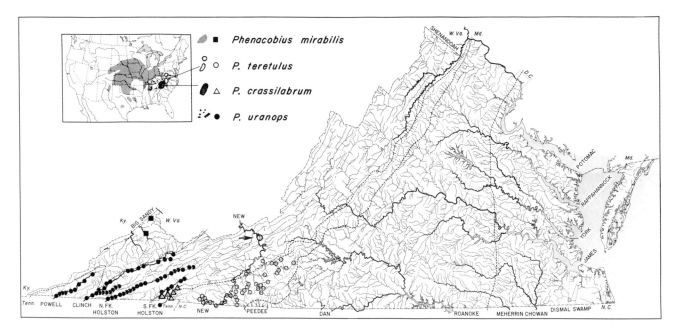

Map 53 Suckermouth minnow, Kanawha minnow, fatlips minnow, and stargazing minnow. Arrow to New River points at 1867 record (type locality) of Kanawha minnow; arrow from dot in Tennessee to South Fork Holston River denotes syntopy of fatlips minnow and stargazing minnow.

HABITAT

Juveniles and adults typically occupy clear, moderate-gradient streams and the upper New River; their habitat extends from cold native brook trout creeks to warm rivers. A preference for soft water is exhibited (Ross and Perkins 1959). Large juveniles and adults inhabit runs and riffles chiefly of clean gravel and rubble. Young captured in a pool indicate a tendency for that stage to occupy gentler currents (Hambrick et al. 1975).

DISTRIBUTION   Map 53

Phenacobius teretulus is endemic to the New (upper Kanawha) drainage of North Carolina, Virginia, and West Virginia. It is generally distributed only in the upper section of the drainage, within the Blue Ridge Province. Populations outlying the fringe of the Blue Ridge live in conditions typical of that province. Two of the three West Virginia tributary populations are in or near the Appalachian Plateau (Hambrick et al. 1975; Hocutt et al. 1978, 1979) in habitats similar to those of the Blue Ridge. A few specimens were taken in the New River in the center of the Valley and Ridge Province during 1867 by Cope. One or more localities of his other specimens are uncertain (Hambrick et al. 1975). Because the present distribution pattern of *P. teretulus* is identifiable with Blue Ridge habitat, and

because it is unlikely that this species would have been completely extirpated from the Valley and Ridge, Cope's specimens taken in the Valley and Ridge may have been stragglers.

Abundance.—Generally rare or uncommon throughout its range.

REMARKS

The spotted body pattern of *P. teretulus* is related to loss and regeneration of scales, as happens in some other minnows (e.g., stonerollers and pearl dace). The skin associated with regenerated scales is darker than at scales showing no sign of loss. Increase of pigment may have a light-shielding function while the rapidly growing scale is filling its locus.

The Kanawha minnow was listed as threatened in North Carolina (Bailey 1977). That status was based largely on a now defunct proposal for two large impoundments. The species now is doing fairly well in Virginia despite natural constraints on its distribution (Jenkins and Musick 1979), but it is localized and rare in West Virginia (Hocutt et al. 1978, 1979).

Name.—Teretulus is a diminutive of "terete" body form. *Teretulus* also is a generic name used at times by Cope for certain suckers, hence an allusion to the suckerlike features of *Phenacobius.*

Fatlips minnow *Phenacobius crassilabrum* Minckley and Craddock

SYSTEMATICS

Described from North Carolina and Tennessee in 1962, *P. crassilabrum* is the cognate of *P. uranops*; these species compose the most advanced lineage of *Phenacobius* (Mayden 1989).

DESCRIPTION

Materials.—From Minckley and Craddock (1962) and 11 Virginia, 3 Tennessee, 5 North Carolina, and 1 Georgia series; counts from 20 specimens except 30 for circumpeduncle scales. Life color from 3 Virginia series.

Anatomy.—A suckermouth minnow with quite small scales and usually 17–21 circumpeduncle scales; adults are 55–85 mm SL. Body form moderate or distinctly elongate, terete; dorsal fin origin above anterior half of pelvic fin base, occasionally slightly anterior to pelvic origin. Head length moderate; eye quite small, round, lateral or very slightly supralateral; snout somewhat long, well rounded; frenum absent. Mouth and lips as described for genus; supralabial flap usually well developed, without protuberances; jaw pads well developed and, in adult, often strongly ridged (Figure 38). Breast naked to nearly fully scaled; caudal lobes equal or subequal, upper lobe usually longer and more pointed. Tuberculation and cheek pad essentially as in *P. mirabilis*.

Meristics.—Pharyngeal teeth 4–4; lateral line complete, scales (54)56–65(68); scales around back (16)17–20(22); scales around belly 21–25(27); circumbody scales (39)40–47(48); circumpeduncle scales (16)17–21(23), typically 19–20; predorsal scale rows (24)25–29(30). Dorsal rays 8; principal caudal rays (18)19; anal rays 7; pelvic rays 8(9); pectoral rays 14–16.

Color in Preservative.—Dusky above; dark pre- and postdorsal stripe present; zone along upper edge of midlateral stripe generally same shade or very slightly paler than upper side. Individual upper body scales uniformly dusky or almost so, not prominently dark-edged. Dark lateral stripe present; lower side and belly pale; pelvic axillary scale usually slightly peppered. Dorsal, caudal, and pectoral fins dusky; dorsal fin base unpatterned; caudal spot medium or small; area just above and below spot depigmented; anal and pelvic fins pale. Pectoral fin tends to be more dusky in nuptial male.

Color in Life Plate 14.—Head and body dorsum olive, tan, or brown, sometimes with iridescent gold and violet glints. Middorsal stripe and line just above midlateral stripe iridescent gold; midlateral stripe iridescent pale gold and green; violet glints on side of winter fish. Lower body silvery white, often with gold glints; caudal base with pale tan area just above and below spot. Head with gold and pale green tints laterally; iris partly coppery. Dorsal, caudal, and pectoral fins pale olive; anal and pelvic fins white.

Nuptial male has pale rusty iridescent tint in middorsal and midlateral stripes, side of head, and upper lip. Dull rusty suffusion in fins, pectoral the most rusty, particularly basally; caudal the least, essentially pale olive. Male also slightly duskier than female.

COMPARISON

The two species of suckermouth minnows in the Tennessee drainage of Virginia—*P. crassilabrum* and *P. uranops*—are distinguished by characters in addition to those in the *Key*: (1) dorsolateral pigment pattern, each scale [uniformly pigmented or nearly so *vs.* usually a distinct, curved or angular dark mark on posterior half of each scale]; (2) eye position and shape [lateral or very slightly supralateral, round *vs.* distinctly supralateral, usually oval]; (3) body form (moderate or distinctly elongate but caudal peduncle somewhat stout *vs.* extremely elongate, caudal peduncle quite slender); (4) jaw pads, particularly lower pad [usually ridged (Figure 38) *vs.* nonridged]; (5) eye size, horizontal length of orbit [very small, usually 5.2% SL or less *vs.* moderate, usually 5.3% SL or larger].

BIOLOGY

The bulk of the diet of *P. crassilabrum*, based on 16 adults from Virginia, North Carolina, and Tennessee, comprises larvae of midges and the cranefly *Antocha*. Immature caddisflies and beetles are taken in smaller numbers (V. L. Webb, in litt.).

Fish 62 *Phenacobius crassilabrum* adult female 82 mm SL (REJ 981), VA, Washington County, South Fork Holston River, 15 June 1983.

Length–frequency, gonads, and tubercles of 145 specimens, a few of these scale-aged, from much of the range indicate that some yearlings of both sexes are immature (the largest was 62 mm SL), all age-2 fish can spawn, and that few if any fish survive the third winter (i.e., 2.8 years). There is no clear indication of any sexual difference in growth. Thirty-seven tuberculate males are 53–84 mm SL, mean, 70, and 25 prespawning to recently spent females are 59–87 mm, mean, 73. The two largest specimens are a male and a female each 91 mm SL (112 TL) from Virginia.

Spawning apparently occurs during May and June, possibly also April. Males were strongly tuberculate from 3 April to 27 June. The two females taken on 18 May 1981 in the Nolichucky River in Tennessee were fully spent. Of nine females found on 18 May 1971 in the South Fork Holston River, Virginia, water 18°C, only one had begun to spawn. On 15 June 1983 in that river, all of the six adult females were spent or partly so. The reproductive fish taken in Virginia were in habitat typical of the species. In the only description of spawning behavior of any species of suckermouth minnow, Johnston (1990) noted male *P. crassilabrum* defending territories on nests of *Nocomis micropogon*. Spawning, by a male clasping a female, or by two males and one female, occurred during 30 May–3 June at 15–17°C in North Carolina.

HABITAT

The fatlips minnow occupies typically clear, moderate to high-gradient streams and rivers. Juveniles and adults inhabit runs and riffles of clean gravel, rubble, and boulder. Adults were found in the same habitat during winter, water 0–2°C, about as commonly as they were found there in other seasons.

DISTRIBUTION   Map 53

Phenacobius crassilabrum is endemic to the Blue Ridge and its fringes in the upper Tennessee drainage of Virginia, North Carolina, Tennessee, and Georgia.

The range spans major systems from the South Fork Holston to the Little Tennessee; notably the fatlips minnow is unknown from the Hiwassee system in the southern end of the Blue Ridge. In Virginia, *P. crassilabrum* occupies the lower, unimpounded 32-rkm reach of the South Fork Holston River and was found once (1973) in a major South Fork tributary, Laurel Creek, just above Damascus. These stream sections are cool, marginal trout water.

Phenacobius crassilabrum and *P. uranops* have a largely complementary distributional relationship. The former tends to occupy cooler, higher-gradient streams as in the Blue Ridge; *P. uranops* is characteristic of warm, moderate-gradient Valley and Ridge waters. They are known to occur syntopically only in the Nolichucky system of Tennessee and the South Fork Holston system of Tennessee (before impoundment) and Virginia. The lower South Fork population of *P. crassilabrum* (in Virginia) probably is favored by the cooling effect of Laurel Creek.

Abundance.—Usually uncommon or common.

REMARKS

Finding that the fatlips minnow spawns territorially on chub nests was more predictable than for other *Phenacobius*, because it seems to be the most (perhaps only) sexually dichromatic species of the genus. In nest-associating minnows, the males generally are more colorful than females.

Phenacobius crassilabrum extends into Virginia via only one stream system. Its zonation there relative to the stargazing minnow *P. uranops* and to physical and possibly chemical factors is similar to that observed southward. Experimental and other studies are needed to support or reject the explanations we imply for the distribution pattern. *Phenacobius crassilabrum* is considered to have special concern status in Virginia because it occupies only two contiguous streams.

Name.—Crassilabrum, "thick lip" or "fat lip."

Stargazing minnow   *Phenacobius uranops* Cope

SYSTEMATICS

Described from the North Fork Holston River of Virginia (Cope 1867), the stargazing minnow is one of the two most advanced species of *Phenacobius* (Mayden 1989).

DESCRIPTION

Materials.—From Minckley and Craddock (1962), 37 lots from Virginia, and 11 from Tennessee; counts from 69 specimens. Color in life from 6 lots.

Anatomy.—An extremely elongate suckermouth minnow with usually 15–17 circumpeduncle scales; adults are 60–95 mm SL. Body very shallow throughout, nearly cylindrical; dorsal fin origin above or slightly anterior to pelvic fin origin. Head moderate; eye distinctly supralateral, moderate in size, usually oval; snout elongate, rounded or blunt; frenum absent. Mouth and lips as described for genus; supralabial flap usually moderately developed, occasionally barbel-like or terminating in single or multiple papillae; jaw pads moderate, not ridged. Breast naked. Caudal fin lobes usually equal, occasionally subequal, up-

Fish 63 *Phenacobius uranops* adult female 71 mm SL (REJ 1080), VA, Scott County, Copper Creek, 25 April 1984.

per lobe more pointed. Tubercles and cheek pad as in *P. mirabilis*.

Meristics.—Pharyngeal teeth 4–4; lateral line complete, scales (49)51–59(61); scales around back (13)14–15(17); scales around belly (18)19–22(24); circumbody scales (34)35–39(42); circumpeduncle scales (13)15–17(18); predorsal scale rows (20)21–25(27). Dorsal rays 8(9); principal caudal rays 19(20); anal rays (6)7; pelvic rays 7–8(9); pectoral rays 15–17(18).

Color in Preservative.—Dusky above; dark predorsal and postdorsal stripe present or postdorsal stripe occasionally absent; each scale on upper half of body distinctly darker posteriorly, effected by a curved or, occasionally on posterior body, angular mark; longitudinal pale stripe located just above midlateral stripe moderately developed or absent; midlateral stripe dark or black; lower body essentially immaculate. Dorsal, caudal, and pectoral fins slightly dusky; dorsal base lacking distinctive pattern; dark caudal spot small or medium, occasionally absent; anal and pelvic fins pale.

Color in Life Plate 14.—Dorsum pale olive to olive; middorsal stripe iridescent brassy, gold, and greenish, interrupted at intervals; prominent midlateral stripe with sheens of silver, green, blue-violet, and steel blue; gold longitudinal stripe above midlateral stripe; lower side silver-white. Dorsal, caudal, and pectoral fins light olive; pelvic and anal fins very pale yellow-olive to white. Sexual difference not discerned.

BIOLOGY

Juvenile and adult stargazing minnows feed on an array of benthic insects, chiefly midge and caddisfly larvae; small amounts of detritus were found in all guts examined. This species often feeds as mobile groups of 10–20 adults among or near streamline chubs. It is a daylight, gleaning feeder, using sensitive lips to locate food at the top and sides of substrate particles. Its feeding extends into winter.

Virtually all specimens taken during the reproductive period were mature, these being ages 1 and 2. The exception was an apparent age-1 runt of 45 mm SL in mid-June. No age-2 fish was found after the spawning period, based on length frequency (and sometimes scale-aging) of many large specimens. No growth difference between the sexes was noted. North Fork Holston River adults averaged about 10 mm greater in length than Clinch River fish. Two young, 18–20 mm SL, were taken on 19 June. Reproductive fish were 74 males of 56–94 mm SL, mean, 76, and 79 females, 57–101 mm, mean, 72. The largest known specimen is the latter female, 119 mm TL, from Virginia. Spawning occurs during May and June, possibly also in late April. During that period the species occupies its typical habitat.

HABITAT

Phenacobius uranops is found in generally clear, moderate-gradient streams and small rivers. It inhabits riffles and, more commonly, runs of 15–50 cm depth. Adults and juveniles are nearly always found over clean or very slightly silted gravel and small to medium rubble. Adults were taken in this habitat during mid-winter about as frequently as in warmer times. The two small young were caught in a calm shallow area at a bar of sand, gravel, and small pieces of coal. The stargazing minnow prefers warm water, as indicated by its absence from the strongly spring-influenced upper Little River of the Clinch system. Its localization in the South Fork Holston River may be related to avoidance of cool water and competitive interaction with *P. crassilabrum*.

DISTRIBUTION   Map 53

Phenacobius uranops occurs in the Tennessee, Cumberland, and Green River drainages. Within the Tennessee drainage of Virginia, it is contiguously distributed or nearly so in main stems in the Valley and Ridge Province and avoids the adjacent Blue Ridge and Appalachian Plateau.

Abundance.—Usually uncommon.

REMARKS

When browsing treatises on fishes of foreign lands, we are struck that in fast waters of southwestern Virginia there is a minnow about as remarkable as any—the stargazing minnow with suckerlike lips, upward-oriented eyes, and a pencil-like body.

Name.—Uranops—"sky eye" or sky-watcher—alludes to the supralateral position of the eye.

Bigeye chubs   Genus *Hybopsis* Agassiz

The formerly heterotypic *Hybopsis* has a continuing history of taxonomic instability. Criteria for allocation of species to the genus included their having a terminal barbel and 4–4 major-row pharyngeal teeth, and their lack of a frenum and specializations that mark other genera. About 34 described and undescribed, mostly small, benthic species were included (Reno 1969a; Clemmer 1971; Lachner and Jenkins 1971a). When recognized in broad sense, *Hybopsis* was subdivided into monotypic or larger groups, or formal subgenera. At other times the groups were ranked as separate genera, sometimes with one or a few species placed congenerically with shiners. Bailey (1951) ended a period of generic segregation by lumping nine barbeled genera under *Hybopsis*, an arrangement that stood for 16 to 40 years depending on the group.

As fundamental intrageneric differences were substantiated and phylogenetic realignments were warranted, *Hybopsis* s.l. (i.e., in broad sense) was progressively dismembered. Recognized as genera were *Nocomis* (Lachner and Jenkins 1967), *Couesius* and *Platygobio* (McPhail and Lindsey 1970), *Oregonichthys* (Hubbs et al. 1974), *Yuriria* (Smith et al. 1975), and *Erimystax, Extrarius,* and *Macrhybopsis* (Mayden 1989). Certain species were transferred among these genera and some were placed in still other genera; for example, *H. boucardi* and *H. harperi* were added to *Notropis* (Gilbert and Bailey 1972). Hence the species were scattered through the western, chub, and shiner clades of the phoxinin lineage. The final cut occurred with the referral of the *amblops* group to *Notropis* by Coburn and Cavender (1992), rendering *Hybopsis* nonexistent as a genus, as accepted by Robins et al. (1991).

The *amblops* group is a monophyletic lineage composed of *Hybopsis amblops* (the type species of *Hybopsis*) and five or six other eastern North American species (Clemmer 1971; Mayden 1989; Coburn and Cavender 1992). In form, color, and benthic habit, these fishes resemble several species of *Notropis* shiners, some of which had been inserted in *Hybopsis* by Mayden (1989). If not a genus, then *Hybopsis* s.s. (strict sense) is recognizable within *Notropis* as a subgenus or simply as the *amblops* group. Coburn and Cavender (1992) indicated insecurity of the berth of *Hybopsis* s.s. in *Notropis* by stating that *Hybopsis* (and *Ericymba*) "... may, and probably will, reemerge as genera enlarged by species now placed mostly in *Alburnops.*" *Alburnops* has long been a (nondelineated) subgenus of *Notropis*.

We retain *Hybopsis* as a genus for the *amblops* group; some other workers are doing so. This stance has merit partly because of the projected reelevation of the genus.

Name.—Hybopsis means "round-faced" or "protuberant-faced"; it refers to the prominent snout of *H. amblops*.

Bigeye chub   *Hybopsis amblops* (Rafinesque)

SYSTEMATICS

Named from Kentucky in 1820, *Hybopsis amblops* is now considered monotypic (Clemmer 1971; Clemmer and Suttkus 1971). It is most closely related to *H. lineapunctata* (Wiley and Mayden 1985).

DESCRIPTION

Materials.—From Clemmer (1971), Clemmer and Suttkus (1971), and 25 Virginia series. Life color from 3 Virginia lots of nuptial fish.

Anatomy.—A shinerlike chub with a terminal barbel and black lateral stripe; adults are 45–65 mm SL. Body form moderate, slightly compressed; dorsal fin origin above anterior half of pelvic fin base. Head moderate; eye large, slightly oval, slightly supralateral; snout somewhat short, broadly rounded; frenum absent; mouth small, inferior, horizontal; lips moderate; barbel small, terminal. Breast naked. Tubercles in male tiny or small, best developed on head dorsum, anterodorsal body, and pectoral fin. Genital pore area of nuptial female moderately enlarged.

Meristics.—Pharyngeal teeth typically 1,4–4,1; lateral line complete, scales (34)35–37(38); scales around back 9–11(12); scales around belly (9)11(13); circumbody scales

Fish 64 *Hybopsis amblops* adult male 54 mm SL (REJ 991), VA, Russell County, Little River, 21 June 1983.

(20))22–24(27); circumpeduncle scales 12(13); predorsal scale rows (11)12–14(15). Dorsal rays 8; principal caudal rays (18)19(20); anal rays (7)8(10); pelvic rays (7)8(9); pectoral rays (13)14–16(17).

Color in Preservative.—Upper body pattern of curved dusky markings along or near scale margins; predorsal stripe vague or bold; postdorsal stripe vague or absent; in some specimens a slightly dusky horizontal line courses between each upper body scale row; midlateral stripe moderate or bold, bordered ventrally on anterior half of body by pairs of specks (stitching) at lateral line pores; side just below lateral line immaculate or scale margins slightly pigmented. Lateral stripe continued onto opercle, diffuse or lacking on preopercle; subnasal area dark. Fins unpatterned except dorsal fin base slightly darker posteriorly than anteriorly; small, often triangular caudal spot usually connected to midlateral stripe; pale area present just above and below caudal spot.

Color in Life Plate 15.—Upper body pale olive to straw; side silver, dark stripe and caudal spot sometimes obvious; venter silver-white. Fins pale; most of pectoral fin and its base have a yellow tinge in some males.

BIOLOGY

Two summer adults fed on microcrustaceans and midge larvae. The majority of bigeye chubs may mature by age 1; only two males and one female were immature of 112 specimens taken during 25 April–21 June in Virginia. Males tend to attain larger size than females. The breeding fish were 60 males, 43–70 mm SL, mean, 54, and 49 females, 41–66 mm, mean, 50; growth was similar to that in Missouri and Ohio (Pflieger 1975; Trautman 1981). The largest Virginia specimen is the 70-mm SL, 88-mm TL male. Trautman reported a 99-mm TL bigeye chub from Ohio. Swingle's (1965) fish in the 5-inch TL class (127–152 mm) likely was a silver chub *Macrhybopsis storeriana*.

Hybopsis amblops is in spawning condition in Virginia from possibly late April, clearly from May, through June. Six young of 12–20 mm SL, mean, 16, were taken on 19 June. Early July fish were postnup-

tial. Spawning during June was suggested for Illinois and Missouri (Forbes and Richardson 1920; Pflieger 1975). As a general statement, Cross (1967) gave the period as between late April and early June. Clemmer (1971) noted that spawning occurs in late spring to early summer in the southern part of the range.

HABITAT

The bigeye chub populates typically clear, cool and warm, moderate-gradient creeks, streams, and rivers about as frequently as in creeks. It occupies pools, backwaters, and slow runs, and is often found along water willow beds. It commonly associates with vegetation in Illinois (Smith 1979), but Clemmer (1971) and we found that plants are not required habitat in some other parts of the range. Trautman (1981) noted its preference for clean sand and fine gravel; Smith (1979) stated that these substrates and extremely clear water are necessary. In the Tennessee drainage of Virginia, where beds of sand and fine gravel are rare, we found this species most frequently over gravel, less often rubble; substrates generally were slightly silted at most. In late December torpid bigeye chubs were found under a large rock.

DISTRIBUTION Map 54

Hybopsis amblops ranges from southern Great Lakes tributaries to the lower Ohio basin and Ozarks. It is widely and generally distributed in the Tennessee drainage of Virginia. Apparently it has expired in our portion of the Big Sandy drainage, where it was recorded only in 1937.

Abundance.—Often common.

REMARKS

The bigeye chub is doing well in the upper Tennessee drainage. It repopulated the formerly chemically devastated section of the Clinch River, and is

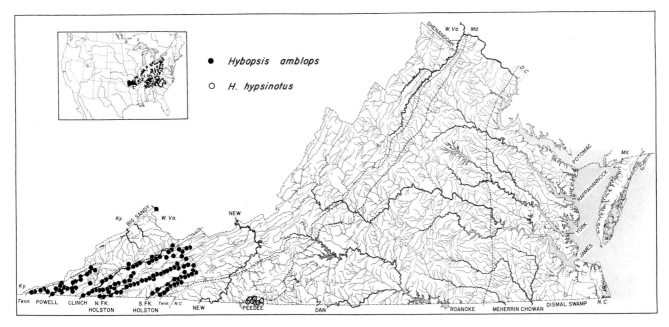

Map 54 Bigeye chub and highback chub.

widespread in the North Fork Holston River below previous pollution outfalls at Saltville. It apparently has been eradicated from the upper Big Sandy drainage, probably because of siltation resulting from coal mining. Authors throughout its range have noted that the bigeye chub prefers clear water and unsilted or little-silted bottom. Siltation is also thought to be a culprit in the dwindling or extirpation of this species in Kansas, Illinois, Michigan, and Ohio (Zahuranec 1962; Cross 1967; Smith 1979; Smith et al. 1981; Trautman 1981).

Name.—*Amblops*, "blunt face," denotes the form of the snout. The name instead may have been coined as "stupid eye," referring to the look imparted by the dorsally directed eyes (C. Smith 1985).

Highback chub   *Hybopsis hypsinotus* (Cope)

SYSTEMATICS

Hybopsis hypsinotus was described from North Carolina in 1870; the type locality was restricted to the Pee Dee drainage by Jenkins and Lachner (*in* Gilbert 1978b). An unpublished study over the full range of the species by R. E. Jenkins and E. A. Lachner showed the Pee Dee and Santee drainage populations to differ meristically, subspecifically at most.

The highback chub probably is most closely related to *H. rubrifrons* owing to the occurrence in both of red color and unculous patches in nuptial males, and spawning on *Nocomis* nests. This sister-taxa relationship is supported by osteological characters (Wiley and Mayden 1985). *Hybopsis hypsinotus* is the more advanced species based on extreme redness, tonal darkness, and antrorse head tubercles of nuptial males, and on the elevated adult body form (Burkhead et al. 1985).

DESCRIPTION

Materials.—Thirty-seven lots from the Carolinas and 8 from Virginia. Life color based on one lot each of prespawning and spawning fish from Virginia.

Anatomy.—A high-backed, barbeled, shinerlike chub; adults are 40–60 mm SL. Body form of juvenile moderate; adult high-backed, deep-bellied, moderately to well compressed; dorsal fin origin usually above anterior half of pelvic fin origin, sometimes over posterior half; elevation of back causes a notable obliqueness in dorsal fin base. Head moderate in length, vaulted posteriorly, depressed, broad dorsally; eye moderate in size, round, lateral; snout moderate or short, moderately or broadly rounded; frenum absent; mouth small, inferior, horizontal; lips moderate; barbel small, terminal, rarely absent. Breast naked to fully scaled.

Nuptial tubercles on head dorsum of male moderate in size, many antrorse, forming a triangular patch from occiput to anterior interorbital area, then a V-shaped hiatus surrounding supraorbital, circumnarial, and snout tubercles; body tubercles best developed anterodorsally, many

Fish 65 *Hybopsis hypsinotus* adult male 50 mm SL (REJ 970), VA, Carroll County, Pauls Creek, 9 June 1983.

antrorse on nape; pectoral and dorsal fins are the most tuberculate. Unculous padlike tissue developed particularly on snout, ventrolateral and ventral areas of head, lower body scales, and some fin rays. Females with few or no head dorsum tubercles and reduced or no unculous tissue. Genital pore area of spawning female much swollen.

Meristics.—Pharyngeal teeth 1,4–4,1; lateral line complete, scales (34)35–37(38); scales around back 11–14(15); scales around belly (9)10–13(14); circumbody scales (22)23–29(30); circumpeduncle scales (10)12–13(15); predorsal scale rows (13)14–17. Dorsal rays 8; principal caudal rays 19; anal rays (7)8(9); pelvic rays (7)8(9); pectoral rays (12)14–16. Gill rakers (4)5–8(10).

Color in Preservative.—Essentially as in *H. amblops* except pigmentation below lateral line usually slightly duskier and extending more ventrad, to base of lower fins; lateral stripe and caudal spot usually slightly paler; dorsal fin base essentially uniformly stippled. Species is dichromatic, nuptial male body duskier than female, some fin membranes slightly, evenly dusky, most so in all dorsal membranes.

Color in Life Plate 15.—Adult female upper body olive to straw; lateral stripe dusky or black; lower side dusky or silver-white; belly silver-white or white; iris partly silver or pale gold; lower body, cheek, and lips with pale red tinge in some fish. Fins pale, all lacking red in some fish; other fish pale red or medium red in dorsal, caudal, and less often the anal fin.

Prenuptial, small nuptial, and some large spawning males much like large females, but generally more dusky; belly, head ventrolaterally, and snout dorsum pale red; lips moderate red, the upper most so; iris pale red, mostly silver. All fins moderate carmine red from base to almost the margin, red deepest in dorsal on rays and membranes, least in paired fins, mostly on rays; fin margins clear, no hint of white.

Large peak males with upper body dark olive to nearly black; lateral stripe masked; midside with coppery glints in some fish; lower side very dusky and with very ephemeral purple iridescence; belly pale carmine; head areas noted

above are more intense carmine, pale red suffused more dorsad and ventrad. Fins moderate to intense carmine, margins clear. Jordan and Brayton (1878) noted violet body luster, rosy head, and red fins of Santee drainage fish. A slide (courtesy W. N. Roston) of a tuberculate male in natural habitat in the Santee shows iridescent gold line along dorsal fin base and just above lateral stripe.

BIOLOGY

The highback chub feeds mainly on microcrustaceans and aquatic and terrestrial insects (Gatz 1979). This species typically may not reproduce until age 2; a mid-June collection contained several immature fish which were much smaller than breeding fish. Males averaged larger than females among adults taken during 8–23 June in Virginia. The 22 males were 41–61 mm SL, mean, 53, and 16 females were 42–53 mm, mean, 48. The largest male is surpassed by one of 68 mm SL, 84 mm TL from North Carolina.

The reproductive period includes late May and June; strongly tuberculate or gravid fish also were noted from mid-April to late July. We witnessed spawning in Pauls Creek, Virginia, on 20 June 1984, water slightly turbid and 20.6°C in early evening. At the same site on 9 June 1983, water clear and the same temperature in late morning, highback chubs were prenuptial or in an interlude from spawning. Nuptial *H. hypsinotus* were found only on two active nests built by *Nocomis leptocephalus*; none were taken by seining the 60 m between the nests. The nests were in slow to moderate runs close to bank or boulder cover. Of the nest-spawning associates, including *Clinostomus funduloides*, *Notropis chiliticus*, and *Phoxinus oreas*, only the highback chubs seemed oblivious to observers.

Three dark male highback chubs were continually active, appearing frenzied over the one nest we observed for about 10 minutes. Generally they rapidly head-butted, circled, and chased each other. Often two males parallel-swam for short distances of erratic direction, and returned quickly to the nest, sometimes repeating this activity in unbroken cycles. A dusky male briefly appeared a few times and was embattled. Females entered the nest one at a time and stayed for up to 30 seconds; their movements were less rapid, appearing unaggressive. Virtually every time a female reached the nest, a male departed battle and usually spawned or attempted such quickly, without courting. Spawning occurred on or just above the nest, the sexes parallel for about one second, after which the male dashed toward other males (if they had not already distracted the spawning male from spawning).

Nuptial male highback chubs gathered over a *Nocomis leptocephalus* nest in northern North Carolina on 26 May, water 11–17°C (Johnston 1989b, in litt.) W. N. Roston informed us that *H. hypsinotus* spawned among an aggregation of *Notropis lutipinnis* at a *N. leptocephalus* nest in the Santee drainage. Aggregation of *H. rubrifrons*, the cognate of *H. hypsinotus*, over *Nocomis* nests was reported by Maurakis and Loos (1986).

HABITAT

Over its range *H. hypsinotus* occupies cool and warm, clear and somewhat turbid, small creeks to medium rivers from the Blue Ridge to about the Fall Line. The largest series we took in Virginia were from Pauls Creek, a small stream with varied substrate including much bedrock and sand; moderate amounts of silt were also present. Elsewhere in the state, both generally turbid, silty streams, and clear, largely hard-bottomed ones yielded few chubs. Nonspawning adults were taken in Pauls Creek only from flowing backwaters and gentle to moderate runs, depth 30–80 cm, and only from or very near cover of undercut banks and logs; usually but one or two adults were caught at each spot. Single specimens were occasionally found in pools.

In the Carolinas the highback chub was more abundant in streams of 4–5 m width than in those of 12–15 m. It was found most frequently in slow and moderately flowing pools with bottoms of mud, sand, gravel, and rubble, and usually was not taken in riffles (E. G. Maurakis, in litt.).

DISTRIBUTION Map 54

Hybopsis hypsinotus is widespread in the Pee Dee and Santee drainages from Virginia to South Carolina. A record (CHM CF17) for the Savannah drainage, Aiken County, South Carolina, needs duplication for acceptance. The 11 Virginia records (10 sites) are well distributed in most of the small portion of the Pee Dee in the state. A record is lacking for the two westernmost tributaries, which are trout water.

Abundance.—Generally rare or uncommon.

REMARKS

Based on tuberculation and a brief century-old notice of nuptial color, we suspected that reproduction of the highback chub involved an interesting repertoire. However, we were somewhat surprised to find it spawning on *Nocomis* nests, and were amazed at the energy the fish expended in aggressive behavior. It is questionable that an individual male could maintain such pace, and avoid debilitating injury and infection from tubercle scathing, through many days of the suggested spawning period. Perhaps our "prenuptial" fish were in an interlude of rest between spawning episodes.

The highback chub was considered by Jenkins and Musick (1979) to be of special concern status in Virginia. We retract that recommendation because we subsequently found it of wider occurrence in the state. However, the population should be watched; its range is quite small and its tolerance limits to turbidity and siltation are unknown.

Name.—Hypsinotus, "high-backed."

Satinfin shiners Genus *Cyprinella* Girard

Cyprinella was extracted from *Notropis* by Mayden (1989) and Coburn and Cavender (1992), a move considered warranted by many others and foreseen by Jenkins (*in* Gilbert 1978b). Containing 26 nonbarbeled and 3 barbeled species, *Cyprinella* is the second largest American cyprinid genus (after *Notropis*). The nonbarbeled species are divided into two clades, each

comprising three or four species groups and one having a phylogenetically isolated species (Mayden 1989). The barbeled species form two separate lineages of uncertain relationship to each other and to nonbarbeled species. The genus ranges from southern Canada through the eastern and central United States into Mexico; six species are known from Virginia and three more may occur here. Diagnoses or full descriptions of *Cyprinella* are given by Gibbs (1955, 1957), Jenkins and Burkhead (1984), and Mayden (1989); some obvious features of Virginia species are noted at the head of the *Key to Cyprinella*.

The instability in the early generic history of nonbarbeled *Cyprinella* is similar to that of several other groups of American minnows; old groupings often bear little resemblance to those currently recognized. Concepts of the generic level were in flux; the composition of genera changed as poorly known species were studied and others were discovered. Before 1885, *Cyprinella* generally was ranked a genus but many of its nonbarbeled species were spread among one to five other genera or subgenera. Nearly uninterruptedly since 1885, *Cyprinella* has been a division or subgenus of *Notropis* (Gibbs 1955, 1957). All of its described nonbarbeled members finally were joined under *Cyprinella*, as a subgenus of *Notropis*, by Bailey and Gibbs (1956), who identified Jordan (1929) as the first reviser for selection of the generic name.

The naturalness (monophyly) of nonbarbeled *Cyprinella* does not appear to be questioned. The only tentatively included member has been the divergent Mexican species called *Cyprinella ornata* (Mayden 1989; Coburn and Cavender 1992) or, as we follow, *Codoma ornata* (Miller 1976, 1978, 1986; Hendrickson et al. 1980; Minckley and Vives 1990; Page and Johnston 1990b). *Notropis* s.l. (including *Cyprinella*) was considered monophyletic by R. M. Bailey (*in* Mendelson 1975), but Mayden (1989) and Coburn and Cavender (1992) dispelled this and concluded that on phylogenetic grounds, *Cyprinella* should be elevated. Allocation of the barbeled species to

Cyprinella is addressed in their accounts (*C. labrosa*, *C. monacha*). In the notropin clade of the phoxinin lineage, *Cyprinella* is the least-derived member of the advanced group that includes *Codoma* and *Pimephales* (Page and Johnston 1990b; Coburn and Cavender 1992).

Crevice-spawning is a taxonomic trait uniting *Cyprinella* and allies as the *Pimephales* clade, the most advanced lineage within the notropin clade (Page and Johnston 1990b; Coburn and Cavender 1992). It occurs in all 16 species whose behavior is known (e.g., Hendrickson et al. 1980; Wallace and Ramsey 1981; Rabito and Heins 1985; Ferguson 1989; Richter 1989; Heins 1990), including three species for which observations are not published: *C. chloristia* (D. G. Cloutman, personal communication), *C. nivea*, and *C. pyrrhomelas* (E. G. Maurakis, in litt.).

Another reproductive behavior may be diagnostic of *Cyprinella* as a whole or some of its lineages—solo mock spawning (the solo run). In this act (known for 10 species) the nuptial male quivers while swimming along the breeding crevice; he appears to be milting, displaying, or both. The behavior occurs during spawning sessions, often before and well after individual spawning acts. The solo run occurs in diverse *Cyprinella* including *C. monacha* and was not reported in *Codoma ornata* by Minckley and Vives (1990). Fractional spawning—production and spawning of multiple egg clutches during each reproductive year (Heins and Rabito 1986)—may also be a norm in *Cyprinella*.

Name.—*Cyprinella* means "small carp" (i.e., small cyprinid).

Thicklip shiner   *Cyprinella labrosa* (Cope)

SYSTEMATICS

The thicklip shiner was described by Cope (1870) from a North Carolina series composed of that species and the Santee shiner. The name *labrosa* was fixed to the thicklip shiner by the lectotype designation of Jenkins and Lachner (*in* Gilbert 1978b). Concurrently the name *zanema* Jordan and Brayton, 1878 was resurrected for the Santee shiner.

The two barbeled species *C. labrosa* and *C. zanema* had long resided in the same barbeled minnow genus with *Hybopsis* s.s. They are removed to *Cyprinella* based on several suites of characters (Coburn and Cavender 1992; our data), some aspects of which were interpreted differently by Mayden (1989) who retained the two species in *Hybopsis*. Robins et al. (1991) favored allocation to *Cyprinella*.

Cyprinella labrosa and *C. zanema* compose the *labrosa* group; the undescribed thinlip chub is tentatively considered a subspecies of *C. zanema* (Jenkins and Lachner *in* Lee et al. 1980). *Cyprinella labrosa* and *C. zanema* differ more from each other than do the members of most pairs of closely related species of *Cyprinella*. They do not appear to be closely linked to the other barbeled species of *Cyprinella*, *C. monacha*. Their closest relatives may be certain southeastern species that also have an inferior mouth, notably *C. nivea* and *C. leedsi*.

DESCRIPTION

Materials.—Twenty-one series from over the species' range. Life color from Pee Dee and Santee drainages (Jordan 1889b; field notes of J. S. Ramsey and E. C. Raney;

Fish 66 *Cyprinella labrosa* adult male 53 mm SL (NCSM 5410), NC, Burke County, Johns River, 15 May 1969.

Fish 67 *Cyprinella labrosa* adult female 45 mm SL (NCSM 5410), NC, Burke County, Johns River, 15 May 1969.

slides by R. F. Denoncourt and W. R. Roston; thicklip chub photo in Deacon et al. [1979] is of *C. zanema*).

Anatomy.—A long-barbeled shiner with a dark-streaked dorsal fin; adults are 40–55 mm SL. Body profile moderate, well compressed; dorsal fin origin above pelvic fin base. Head and snout length moderate; eye medium or small, round or slightly oval, positioned lateral; snout somewhat rounded or nearly pointed; frenum absent; mouth moderate-sized, inferior, horizontal; lips thick; barbel terminal, long. Breast naked. Distinct membrane present between last preprincipal and first principal dorsal rays.

Nuptial tubercles of male large, antrorse, and arranged in 2 uneven rows on head dorsum; tubercles usually absent on snout tip and preorbital, or if present, as many as 3 on each area; tubercles on body are best-developed, medium-sized, and antrorse on nape and lower urosome, 1 per scale on urosome; pelvic and anal fins have largest fin tubercles. Female with few weak tubercles on head dorsum, or none; genital papilla sometimes bulbous.

Meristics.—Pharyngeal teeth usually 1,4–4,1; lateral line complete, scales (35)36–38(39); scales around back 11–13; scales around belly (9)10–11(12); circumbody scales (22)23–26(27); circumpeduncle scales (11)12(13); predorsal scale rows (14)15–17(18). Dorsal rays 8(9); principal caudal rays 19; anal rays (7)8; pelvic rays 8; pectoral rays (13)14–15. Gill rakers (5)7–9(10).

Color in Preservative.—Middorsal stripe usually vague or absent; basic pattern on back and side formed by a curved, nearly rhombus-shaped marking at each scale; in-dividual scales or variably sized groups of scales darker than others, forming random spotting or blotchiness on side as far ventral as about 1 scale row below lateral line; lower side slightly dusky; lateral stripe dusky or dark posteriorly, diffuse or, usually, absent anteriorly; anterior lateral line scales often stitched.

Dorsal fin with posterior membranes dusky- or black-streaked medially to subdistally, pale basally; other membranes less intensely, more uniformly dusky; preprincipal membrane with little or no pigment; dorsal base darkest posteriorly, except body at base of last dorsal ray has a small pale spot, the spot best developed in nuptial male. Caudal fin dusky epibasally, duskiness somewhat crescentic; caudal darkest midhorizontally, subtending two pale basal areas; caudal spot small or absent. Lower fins with anterior 1–2(5) membranes dusky. All fins pale distally. Nuptial male has darkest fins. Young and small juvenile have little or no fin membrane pigment, body vaguely spotted or uniformly patterned.

Color in Life.—Juvenile and adult female olive above, side silver, lateral stripe bluish posteriorly, bordered above by brass; dark scale marks distinct at some angles of light; fins pale. Nuptial male steel blue on back and side of body, particularly posteriorly, with silver sheen and dark marks obvious at some angles; venter silver-white. Head dorsum partly brown; snout tip orange to red-brown; side including eye silver and gold. All fins milky-edged and orange to red-brown, latter best developed in membranes; colors best developed in dorsal and anal fins, particularly anteriorly; paired fins reddish anteriorly.

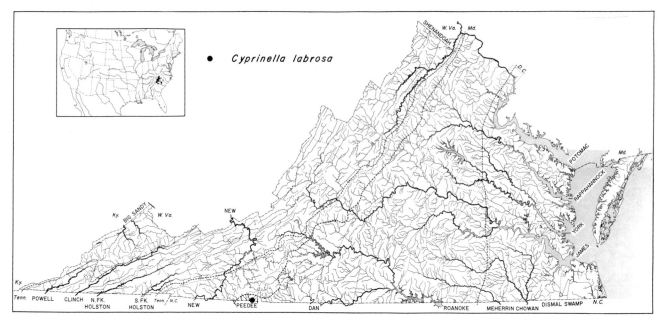

Map 55 Thicklip shiner.

BIOLOGY

Eighteen juvenile and adult thicklip chubs fed in decreasing importance on water mites and larvae of midges, blackflies, mayflies, stoneflies, and beetles; one ate a snail (M. G. Pfleger, in litt.). Maturation occurs at ages 1 or 2, usually age 2; most fish of 26–40 mm SL, apparently age 1, were not in reproductive condition during the spawning period. A few fish of 35–40 mm appeared to be entering breeding condition at that time. The sexes are similar in size; of adults taken during 15 May–18 August from over the species range, 46 males were 41–55 mm SL, mean, 47, and 30 females were, 37–59 mm, mean, 46. The latter specimen is the largest known, 73 mm TL, from North Carolina; the largest from Virginia is 48 mm SL.

The spawning period is lengthy, possibly mid-May to late August, judging from gonad and tubercle development. As with other *Cyprinella* species, individual *C. labrosa* may spawn fractionally over the period. Females with mature ova rarely are plump, suggesting that a relatively small complement of eggs is mature at any one time. Peak-tuberculate males typically have small testes, suggesting relatively sporadic spawning rather than servicing many females in a short period.

HABITAT

Cyprinella labrosa is primarily a resident of warm, clear to often turbid, Blue Ridge foothill and upper Piedmont streams and rivers. Adults occupy runs and riffles over sand and gravel; rubble and usually boulder and bedrock also characterize sample sites. Thicklip chubs often are caught in the same seine haul as *C. zanema* (D. G. Cloutman, J. S. Ramsey, E. C. Raney, in litt.).

DISTRIBUTION   Map 55

Cyprinella labrosa lives in the Pee Dee and Santee drainages, North and South Carolina. The single Virginia record of three adults (USNM 105075) was taken in the Ararat River at Pedigos Mill in 1933. We could not locate the site; the map plot is at Pedigos Cemetery. Our fruitless searches in Virginia for the thicklip shiner were made in small and medium-sized streams at and near the state line; other workers recently sampled headwater and intermediate sections.

Abundance.—Probably extirpated in Virginia; usually uncommon in the Carolinas.

REMARKS

The phylogenetic position and generic status of *C. labrosa* have been in question. Discovery of its spawning site and behavior would allow critical systematic interpretation relative to the crevice-spawning norm of *Cyprinella*. Unfortunately such a find may no longer be possible in Virginia.

Name.—*Labrosa*, for its thick "lips." We apply the common name shiner, instead of chub, to this species.

Turquoise shiner   *Cyprinella monacha* (Cope)

SYSTEMATICS

The barbeled shinerlike *Cyprinella monacha* was described from the North Fork Holston River, Virginia, by Cope (1868b), who recognized some of its similarities to *Cyprinella* but placed it generically with barbeled minnows. Jordan (1924) emphasized its distinctiveness by creating for it a monotypic genus *Erimonax*, but subsequently it was grouped with *Erimystax* chubs both when these were submerged in *Hybopsis* or ranked as a genus. Jenkins and Burkhead (*in* Lee et al. 1980; 1984) and Burkhead et al. (1985) regarded the turquoise shiner to be most closely related to *Cyprinella*, and Dimmick (1988) considered its discord with *Erimystax*. Our finding that this species spawns in, and performs solo runs along crevices, and Coburn and Cavender's (1992) substantiation of its shared heritage with *Cyprinella* based on osteology and scale morphology, resulted in formal allocation to that genus. Mayden (1989) had kept the turquoise shiner in *Erimystax* but now agrees (personal communication) that it belongs in *Cyprinella*.

Cyprinella monacha may be linked to *C. galactura*. In particular, these two shiners are advanced, *C. monacha* most so, in aspects of the pale and dark zones on the anterior body of nuptial males. They are similar in the reduction of urosomal tuberculation and its replacement by (keratinized?) ridges on scales. These features occur weakly in *C. camura*, considered by Gibbs (1961) and us to be the closest relative of *C.* *galactura*, and in *C. whipplei*. The single known hybrid of *C. monacha* has *C. galactura* as the other parent (Burkhead and Bauer 1983). D. G. Cloutman (in litt.) found the same undescribed species of gill parasite *Dactylogyrus* only on *C. monacha* and *C. galactura* among 18 cyprinid species examined from the Tennessee drainage. He has additional parasite data indicating close phylogenetic relationships of these and other *Cyprinella* hosts.

DESCRIPTION

Materials.—From Jenkins and Burkhead (1984) and an additional 10 Virginia and 2 Tennessee series. Color in life from Jenkins and Burkhead (1984) and 12 other series or observations that include 13 nuptial males.

Anatomy.—A minnow with an inferior mouth, terminal barbel, large caudal spot, and blackened posterior dorsal fin membranes; adults are 55–90 mm SL. Body moderately elongate, subterete; adult male deeper and more compressed than adult female; dorsal fin origin above pelvic fin base. Head length moderate; eye small, lateral; snout somewhat long, rounded or blunt; frenum absent; mouth small, inferior, often sharply downcurved posteriorly; lips moderate, medial portion of upper lip much expanded anteriad; one small barbel at each corner of lips, barbel sometimes absent; medium-sized taste buds well developed on ventral head. Breast nearly naked to fully scaled, usually about half scaled.

Tubercles of nuptial male small to medium-sized, mod-

Fish 68 *Cyprinella monacha* adult male 73 mm SL (REJ 995), VA, Washington County, North Fork Holston River, 22 June 1983.

Fish 69 *Cyprinella monacha* juvenile 41 mm SL (REJ 982), VA, Washington County, North Fork Holston River, 16 June 1983.

erate or numerous, many antrorse, on head dorsum and tip and side of snout; preinternarial hiatus present or absent; body tubercles sparse, usually minute; tubercles present on pectoral and pelvic fins. A few nuptial males have a friction pad on lower cheek and operculum; male often has small firm ridges on urosome scales.

Meristics.—Pharyngeal teeth 4–4; lateral line complete, scales (52)55–60(62); scales around back (15)16–18(19); scales around belly 13–15(17); circumbody scales (30)32–36(38); circumpeduncle scales (15)16–18(20); predorsal scale rows 24–27(28). Dorsal rays 8; principal caudal rays 19; anal rays (7)8; pelvic rays (7)8(9); pectoral rays 13–15(16).

Color in Preservative.—Dusky to dark above, scales darkly submargined but not rhomboid-patterned; pale below. Small fish with dark pre- and postdorsal stripe; dark lateral stripe often well developed only posteriorly; usually many lateral line scales stitched; caudal spot medium or large, sometimes slightly subdivided vertically; dorsal fin with sparse melanophores in posterior membranes. Most of these features are retained in adult female and juvenile male; darkening of dorsal membranes increases with age; dorsal fin base about uniformly pigmented or darkest posteriorly, and often with a small pale spot on body at base of last ray. Nuptial male moderately or very dark above, scale submargination usually indistinct; caudal spot not subdivided but often quite large and bold, and posterior dorsal fin membranes much blackened.

Color in Life Plate 40.—Young and juvenile gray dorsally, gray or silver laterally; narrow middorsal and dorsolateral stripe iridescent green, sometimes gold-suffused; midlateral stripe dusky; fins pale; caudal spot dark. Adult female and non-nuptial adult male tan, gray, or olive-green dorsally, rest of body bright silver, often masking lateral stripe and caudal spot; fins pale except larger fish have partly dark dorsal fin.

Nuptial male has upper side of body pronouncedly iridescent turquoise to cobalt blue; peak male with blue wash extending from midside to lower side and onto caudal base ventrally; blue glints on postpectoral bar and upper side of head. Color changes and fades rapidly in formalin, greenish tone lost first, then upper side becomes steel blue, then dark. Some small mature males have little or no blue on body during part or all of breeding season. Dorsum olive or tan with some green or gold glints; midside to belly silvery cream. Head dorsum same as body dorsum; side silver; iris silver or gold. All fins with satiny turquoise, most so in dorsal; some fins with gold glints; upon placement in formalin turquoise disappears, leaving an also ephemeral satiny white distally.

Blue nuptial male has two large, sharply demarked, whitish zones on anterior half of body side, each bounded by a dark zone slightly darker than posterior body; pale zones wider ventrally than dorsally. This obvious pattern is rapidly lost in stressed fish before preservation. A hint of the pattern remains in some long-preserved fish, the posterior pale zone becoming inobvious or lost.

BIOLOGY

Life history aspects of the turquoise shiner are described from Jenkins and Burkhead (1984) and later observations in the North Fork Holston River of Virginia and in the Emory River of Tennessee. Young, juveniles, and adults are benthic insectivores, taking 90% immature midge and blackfly larvae; much of the remainder is mayfly nymphs. The virtually uniform minuteness of their food is notable.

Most males and females mature in 2 years; some may spawn at 1 year. The oldest fish detected, based on the few fish aged with certainty, is age 3; the sexes appear to have similar longevity. Adult males average larger than adult females; 42 tuberculate males were 60–89 mm SL, mean, 74, and 12 gravid females were 53–77 mm, mean, 68. The largest known specimen is a male 92 mm SL from North Carolina.

Cyprinella monacha probably has an extended breeding period. Spawning was observed during afternoons on 6 June 1984 in the North Fork Holston River in Virginia, and on 8 July 1983 in the Emory River in Tennessee, water 26.1° and 27.2°C. Gravid females and highly colored tuberculate males were found from mid-May to mid-August. *Cyprinella monacha* is a crevice-spawner, ovipositing in narrow slots and fissures on sides of unanchored stones and elevated bedrock, and in a corner formed by a rock lying on another. The depth of one slot was nearly that of the body of the male; he and one or more females (one at a time) inserted much or all of the body into the slot while turned on the side. This species is polygamous but individual males used only one site, along which they made characteristic milting or displaying swims (solo runs) before and after spawnings. One breeding site had three actively spawning males each at a different spot within 5 m of the others. Breeding sites were located in moderate current of shallow portions of runs, some at the head and others at about the midlength. The sites were strewn with large rubble and boulder; substrates were unsilted.

Mature ova per female numbered 157–791; these counts may greatly underestimate fecundity if this species spawns fractionally. On 28 June 1985, under stream conditions similar to those when spawning was observed in other years, the turquoise shiner was found in breeding color but reproductive behavior was not seen, indicating a hiatus in spawning.

The single known hybrid specimen involving *C. monacha* was produced with *C. galactura* (Burkhead and Bauer 1983). In the North Fork Holston River we saw a male *C. galactura*, 10–20 mm longer than male *C. monacha*, usurp two spawning crevices of *C. mo-*

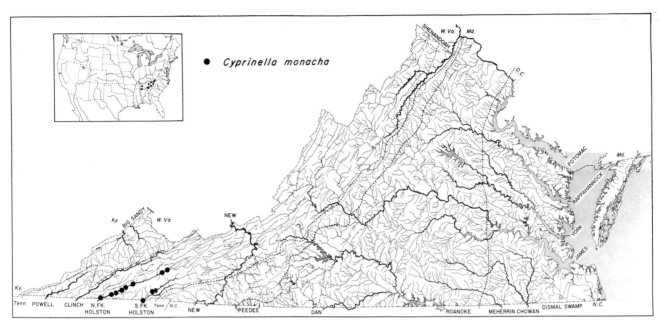

Map 56   Turquoise shiner.

nacha for about 10 minutes. During this and briefer periods, the *C. galactura* repeatedly made spawning movements (solo runs) in the portion of the crevice where *C. monacha* had just spawned intermittently. In the Emory River, nuptial *C. galactura* and *C. spiloptera* frequented *C. monacha* spawning areas.

HABITAT

Cyprinella monacha typically occupies warm, usually clear, medium streams to medium rivers of moderate gradient. It favors moderate to swift currents and ranges over gravel to bedrock, rarely occurring on sand and apparently always avoiding appreciably silted areas. Jenkins and Burkhead (1984) thought that in the North Fork Holston this species preferred small gravel, but subsequently it was found commonly over large gravel, rubble, bedrock, and among boulders. The Middle Fork Holston population is also associated with large substrate materials and bedrock. Habitat characteristics are discussed by Jenkins and Burkhead (1984).

DISTRIBUTION   Map 56

The turquoise shiner is endemic to the Tennessee River drainage; the former and current ranges are documented by Jenkins and Burkhead (1984) except for later discoveries in Virginia. The Virginia populations are in the North and Middle forks of the Hol-

ston River. In the upper North Fork Holston, above Saltville, the turquoise shiner was last seen in 1954. It seems to be recovering in the North Fork in Washington County, the first county below Saltville, perhaps owing to pollution abatement at Saltville. It was first observed at the five western Washington County sites (two dots on map) during 1981–1983, and found at these sites in all later efforts. The upper two Washington County sites (one dot) yielded the fish first in 1983, and on both visits during 1984–1985. In Scott County, *C. monacha* is known from five sites (three dots), but the subpopulations in at least the central and western part of the county were low through 1984. Holston Mill in central Scott County did not yield a specimen on 3 of its last 4 samplings.

The South Fork Holston River records in Tennessee predate impoundment. The discovery of *C. monacha* in a short section of the Middle Fork during 1984 (Haxo and Neves 1984) suggests that it may exist in the Virginia portion of the South Fork, although the latter has been moderately well surveyed. The turquoise shiner inhabited the Clinch and Powell rivers in Tennessee, but it was last seen there in 1893. It may also have lived in the lower main stems of the Clinch and Powell in Virginia.

Abundance.—Rare or uncommon, as indicated also for the late 1800s (Cope 1868b; Jordan 1889b). Feeding and breeding groups often are found sharply localized to a small part of any riffle–run sequence.

REMARKS

Some structural and color features of the turquoise shiner resembled those of satinfin shiners but the nuptial male of this species was long undescribed. The tuberculation and color of the male caught for us in 1968 by D. A. Etnier and C. R. Gilbert further keyed its linkage with *Cyprinella*, and this was substantiated by scale anatomy, bones, and breeding behavior.

Cyprinella monacha seems a fragile species. It does not appear to forage as opportunistically as some associated minnows. The brilliance of the turquoise and dark-zoned nuptial male must be attractive to finned predators, as is the burnished-silver female. We saw smallmouth bass slash through an area with three spawning males, but the shiners may have been unseen behind boulders. Adaptively, the blue upper side is not detectable from directly above, hence predation by overhead predators such as kingfishers may be abeyed. However, the male's exposure by tilting to the spawning crevice constitutes a hazardous tradeoff—fertilization, flight, or feasted upon.

A group of turquoise shiners persisted to breed when harassed by three face-masked observers, one flashing strobe lights. They resumed spawning after being sought by smallmouth bass and following intrusion and possible hybridization by *C. galactura*. After activity in the area settled and as we were contemplating the fortune and significance of our observations, a tractor forded the river, its tires rising over the bedrock slab housing a clutch of turquoise shiner eggs. The eggs were safely tucked in a side crevice.

The turquoise shiner has fared poorly in the last 120 years. Although found only in the Tennessee drainage, it occurred widely in mountains and uplands. The disjunctive distribution pattern (Map 56) may instead have been nearly contiguous before extensive deforestation and impoundment. Only five systems are now known to be occupied, two or more of them tenuously. As many as seven human-caused factors eradicated populations; some of these affect extant ones (Jenkins and Burkhead 1984). *Cyprinella monacha* has been federally designated as threatened since 1977; it is endangered in Virginia (Burkhead and Jenkins 1991).

Until pollution from Saltville was reduced, the North Fork Holston River population may have been approaching extirpation. The shiner now seems to be spreading in the river, and a federal recovery plan has been drafted for its protection and enhancement (Boles 1983). Clearly a watch is needed; the North Fork population is dependent on that single river. The recently discovered Middle Fork Holston population is enclosed by a reservoir just below it and by a dam about 10 rkm upstream.

Name.—*Monacha*—"monk" or "monastic"—was applied by Cope for its suspected solitary habits and "isolated [unique combination of] characters."

For about 50 years *C. monacha* has been called the spotfin chub. With its allocation to the shiner genus *Cyprinella*, we proposed to colleagues that it be renamed the turquoise shiner. The name shiner is generic; substantively it applies to *C. monacha* better than does chub. We believe that species reclassified generically are valid candidates for alteration of their common name as well as the scientific name. Intuitively, we do not accept *a priori* that common names should be more stable than scientific names, particularly for species that have been poorly known.

In specific sense, we employ turquoise shiner for *C. monacha*, in deference to the enduring application of spotfin shiner to *C. spiloptera*. The name turquoise shiner is used in some major publications on endangered species (Williams et al. 1989; Burkhead and Jenkins 1991).

Whitetail shiner   *Cyprinella galactura* (Cope)

SYSTEMATICS

The whitetail shiner was described from Holston River tributaries in Virginia (Cope 1868a). Gibbs (1957, 1961) aligned *C. galactura* with *C. camura*. We note the possible close relationship of *C. galactura* also to *C. monacha* (see that account). Mayden (1989) considered *C. galactura* to be the sister of *C. venusta*.

DESCRIPTION

Materials.—Twenty Virginia lots; counts from Tennessee drainage specimens (Gibbs 1961). Color in life from about 25 Virginia adults, and color plates in Pflieger (1975) and Boschung et al. (1983).

Anatomy.—A satinfin shiner with a depigmented patch at the upper and lower caudal base; adults are 50–100 mm SL. Body moderate or somewhat deep in profile, moderately or strongly compressed; dorsal fin origin above pelvic fin base. Head moderate; eye medium or small, lateral; snout pointed or slightly rounded; frenum absent; mouth moderate-sized, subterminal, somewhat oblique. Belly completely scaled; breast usually fully scaled.

Nuptial male with many scattered, small to medium, mostly antrorse tubercles on head dorsum and tip and side of snout; no hiatus between tubercles on snout tip and

Fish 70 *Cyprinella galactura* adult male 107 mm SL (REJ 995), VA, Washington County, North Fork Holston River, 22 June 1983.

Fish 71 *Cyprinella galactura* juvenile 47 mm SL (REJ 982), VA, Washington County, North Fork Holston River, 16 June 1983.

internasal area; several tubercles on chin; nape tubercles much smaller than head dorsum tubercles; body weakly tuberculate; small firm ridges developed on lower urosome scales in largest males; tubercles small on pectoral fin, minute or absent on other fins. In adult male, dorsal fin somewhat elongate, margin distinctly rounded; snout tip more pronounced, mouth more subterminal; body deeper, more compressed.

Meristics.—Pharyngeal teeth 1,4–4,1; lateral line complete, scales (38)39–41(43); scales around back (11)13(15); scales around belly usually 11; circumbody scales usually 26; circumpeduncle scales usually 14. Dorsal rays 8; anal rays (8)9(10); pectoral rays (14)15–16(18).

Color in Preservative.—Ground shade slightly to moderately dusky, middorsal stripe present; back and side diamond-patterned; midlateral or submidlateral stripe usually vaguely dusky, sometimes enlarged and rounded posteriorly; head dorsum, snout, and opercle dusky. Dorsal fin with anterior membranes unpeppered or slightly peppered (Figure 34A), with dusky streak in middle membranes, and last 2–4 membranes with dark medial streak; dorsal membranes also pigmented between forks of some rays (Figure 34B). Caudal fin pale or slightly dusky, upper and lower portions of base depigmented, lacking melanophores along rays in pale patches; caudal spot usually absent; lower fins pale or pectoral dusky.

Breeding male duskier on upper body than female; midlateral stripe often wide, vague or moderate posteriorly. Narrow humeral bar and wide zone posterior to and well separated from the bar are duskier than remainder of mid-

and lower side, and the area between these marks usually is slightly paler than posterior midside, effecting a dark- and pale-zoned anterior side. Dorsal fin with all membranes moderately to heavily pigmented, posterior lengthwise streaks black (Figure 34B).

Color in Life Plate 15.—Juvenile of both sexes and adult female olive above, side with silvery overlay, belly white. Peak breeding male with turquoise sheen on dorsum; upper side with pale blue, purple, and rosy iridescences, entire side with delicate to distinct rosy cast; anterior side with a wide silvery zone bordered anteriorly and posteriorly, respectively, by a somewhat steely blue humeral bar and a dusky zone ("dark- and pale-zoned"); lower side milky or silvery white; venter silver-white; cheek and opercle rosy, iris sometimes slightly orange.

Dorsal fin of nuptial male slightly dusky olive, sometimes with pale rosy cast; iridescent orange streak in first membrane, satin white streaks about anterior ray, posterior rays, and along margin; bold black streaks in last 2–4 membranes. Caudal base with upper and lower portions white, lobes tipped satin white, elsewhere fin olive. Anal fin milky white about first and last rays, margin, and base. Pelvic fin satin white along margin, sometimes with salmon pink streak on anterior rays. Pectoral fin suffused with salmon pink-orange, margin milky white.

COMPARISON

In the Tennessee drainage the whitetail shiner generally occurs with the superficially similar warpaint shiner *Luxilus coccogenis*. Both have a depigmented caudal base, a prominent mark which may confuse identification. They are easily separated by a suite of characters; the first three are readily recognizable underwater: (1) dorsal fin pigmentation of adult (Figure 34B, C) [posterior membranes with black lengthwise streak, widest basally, in *galactura vs.* wide dusky or black band across width of fin, band centered in distal half of fin, in *coccogenis*]; (2) caudal pigmentation [depigmented base subdivided abruptly into upper and lower pale patches; fin lacking submarginal dusky or black band *vs.* depigmented basal area not subdivided; dusky or black submarginal band present]; (3) humeral bar [absent or vague *vs.* distinct, very dusky or black]; (4) mouth position, size [subterminal, moderate *vs.* terminal, large]; (5) anal fin margin [essentially straight *vs.* distinctly concave]; (6) dorsal fin pigmentation in young [membranes medially lightly peppered with melanophores in posterior half of fin *vs.* membranes lacking pigment, rays more distinctly outlined with melanophores where submarginal band later develops].

BIOLOGY

Life history aspects of *C. galactura* were reported by Outten (1958) largely from the upper Tennessee drainage in North Carolina. The diet is diverse allochthonous and benthic organisms including worms, mites, insects, larval fishes, and plant material. The whitetail shiner feeds on both drift and substrate items (Jenkins and Burkhead 1984). Its active nature and quick response to drift indicate that prey detection is visual.

Both sexes mature by age 2; Outten (1958) seemed to imply that some fish mature in 1 year. Most of Outten's age-3 fish were females as was the only one of age 4. Males consistently averaged larger than females in age 2; of those taken during February–July, males were 46–101 mm SL, mean, 69, females were 37–84 mm, mean, 59 (Outten 1958). Our many very large specimens are males; the largest from Virginia is 121 mm SL, 148 mm TL, a record or near-record size (*Remarks*).

Spawning occurred between 25 May and 28 June, water 24–28°C, in North Carolina (Outten 1958). We took nuptial males in Virginia, North Carolina, and Tennessee 20 May–16 August. Spawning occurs in shallow moderate-current runs and pool sections adjacent to appreciable current. Eggs typically are deposited above the bottom in crevices or on undersurfaces of boulders, sticks, or trash. Males are territorial, chasing or escorting intruders from the nest. Ovarian eggs ranged 404–1,815; eggs in clutches numbered 127–382 (Outten 1958). As reported for other *Cyprinella*, females probably are polygamous fractional spawners; fecundity over a spawning season would greatly exceed single ovarian egg counts.

Putative hybrids of *C. galactura* × *C. spiloptera* were noted by Gibbs (1961); we collected specimens apparently of this hybrid in Copper Creek. One specimen of *C. galactura* × *C. monacha* is known from Tennessee (Burkhead and Bauer 1983). Behavioral potential for hybridization is described under *C. monacha*. Schwartz (1981a) misinterpreted a statement by Menhinick et al. (1974), based on comments by Gibbs (1963) regarding "intergrades" between *C. analostana* and *C. chloristia*, and erroneously reported hybridization between *C. analostana* and *C. galactura*.

HABITAT

The whitetail shiner occupies cool and warm, moderate gradient, typically clear, lotic waters ranging from large creeks to rivers. It occurs over a variety of substrates in runs and sections of pools and eddies near faster current. In riffles and other strong currents, *C. galactura* is sometimes found in pockets in the lee of boulders; generally it is rare in open swift water. Based on its success in part of the Big Sandy drainage, it appears to be somewhat tolerant of siltation.

DISTRIBUTION   Map 57

Cyprinella galactura is native to the Tennessee and Cumberland drainages and part of the southern Ozarks. It is considered native (but possibly introduced) to the Savannah and Santee drainages on the Atlantic slope (Hocutt et al. 1986; Swift et al. 1986). The range pattern comprises two upland–montane population centers cleaved by central Mississippi Valley lowlands. The pattern may be a remnant of a contiguous pre-Pleistocene range whose north-central, formerly upland area was altered by Pleistocene glaciations (Wiley and Mayden 1985).

In Virginia the whitetail shiner is native to and generally distributed in the Tennessee drainage. It occupies the Big Sandy and New drainages but we now doubt earlier conclusions (Jenkins et al. 1972; Stauffer et al. 1982; Hocutt et al. 1986) that it is indigenous to these drainages.

Native status in the Big Sandy was proposed by Jenkins et al. (1972) based on one record in 1937 (USNM 104157). The Virginia portion of the Big Sandy was scantily inventoried until the early 1970s, when the whitetail shiner was found widespread in, but restricted to, the Russell Fork system. This species is known also from four localities in that system in Pike County, Kentucky (Warren 1981; Burr and

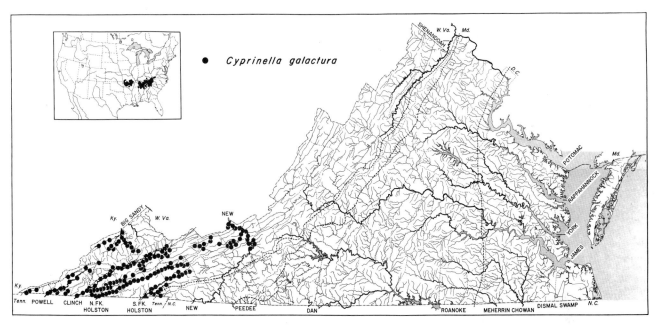

Map 57 Whitetail shiner.

Warren 1986). If native to the drainage, at least relict populations should have been discovered in other upper branches. Warren (1981) also considered the whitetail shiner as most likely introduced to the Big Sandy.

Introduction of *C. galactura* to the New drainage is interpreted from a suggested sequence of absence, recent local appearance, and spread. The shiner was not found in the drainage until 1954, when it was taken in Wolf Creek by R. D. Ross. Ross and Carico (1963) hypothesized that the New population was founded when Wolf Creek captured a North Fork Holston tributary. The apparently post-1955 dispersal of *C. galactura* in the New drainage below Claytor Dam, coupled with its absence above the dam, indicate recent introduction. Lack of a record for some areas or entire tributaries below the dam is attributable to unsuitable habitat, physical barriers, or inadequate sampling. Considering the good success of the whitetail shiner in other montane drainages (even the degraded Russell Fork system), occupation of the New above Claytor Lake would be expected had it entered the drainage via stream capture. Based on records by Hess (1983), the whitetail shiner has spread down the drainage into West Virginia; however, Lobb (1986) did not report it there. Its absence in the Little River, the first major tributary below Claytor Dam, probably is temporary.

Abundance.—Usually uncommon or common.

REMARKS

The nuptial male whitetail shiner is a very attractive minnow by virtue of its subtle iridescences and svelte form. For a novice fish-watcher or collector, it is one of the easiest minnows to identify—after the warpaint shiner is also learned. *Cyprinella galactura* may be the largest species of its genus. The blacktail shiner *C. venusta* was stated to reach 152 mm standard length (Gilbert and Burgess *in* Lee et al. 1980), but this seems to trace to Swingle (1965) who gave inch-class total-length data. A *C. venusta* of 126 mm SL, 150 mm TL (C. R. Gilbert, personal communication) may be exceeded by *C. galactura* in Missouri, where the latter reaches "about 6 inches" (152 mm) TL (Pflieger 1975).

Name.—*Galactura*—"milky tail."

Steelcolor shiner   *Cyprinella whipplei* Girard

SYSTEMATICS

The steelcolor shiner, named in 1856 from Arkansas, is closely related to *C. analostana* and *C. camura* (Gibbs 1963; Mayden 1989).

DESCRIPTION

Materials.—Counts from Gibbs (1963); other traits from 10 lots, 1 from Virginia. Life color from 2 Clinch River lots, 2 from the Arkansas drainage, and 1 each from the Cumberland, White, and Ouachita drainages.

Fish 72 *Cyprinella whipplei* adult male 84 mm SL (SIUC 8949), KY, Marshall County, West Fork Clarks River, 16 June 1979.

Fish 73 *Cyprinella whipplei* juvenile 41 mm SL (SIUC 8948), KY, Marshall County, West Fork Clarks River, 16 June 1979.

Anatomy.—A satinfin shiner with a fairly deep body, dorsal fin distinctly convex-margined in adult male, and typically 9 anal rays; adults are 60–115 mm TL. Form and sexual dimorphism as in *C. galactura* except: body tends to be deeper; hiatus is almost always present between tubercles on snout tip and internasal area.

Meristics.—Pharyngeal teeth usually 1,4–4,1; lateral line complete, scales (36)37–38(40); scales around back (11)13–15; scales around belly usually 11; circumbody scales usually 26; circumpeduncle scales usually 14. Dorsal rays 8; anal rays (8)9(10); pectoral rays (13)14–16(17), usually 15.

Color in Preservative.—Very similar to *C. galactura* except: caudal base lacks abruptly depigmented patches; anterior dorsal fin membranes more heavily peppered in juvenile; dark and pale zones usually absent on side of nuptial male, faint at most.

Color in Life Plate 15.—Juvenile of both sexes and adult female as in *C. galactura* except whitened caudal base patches absent. Nuptial male dorsum steel blue with violet to rose sheens; side and venter silvery white, side sometimes also with pale rosy tint; cheek and opercle slightly purplish; snout with slight red cast. All fins with pale yellow tone, most intense in anal, least in pectoral; all fins white on anterior tip or white-edged.

COMPARISON

Cyprinella whipplei is easily confounded with *C. spiloptera*. In Virginia they occur together only in the Clinch River. Distinctions include: (1) anal rays usually [9 in *whipplei* vs. 8 in *spiloptera*]; (2) pectoral rays usually [15 vs. 14]; (3) dorsal fin of adult male [elongate, distal margin distinctly rounded vs. not elongate, distal margin virtually straight]; (4) body depth [24–28% SL vs. 22–25%]; (5) melanophore peppering of anterior dorsal fin membranes (Figure 34A) [slight or moderate vs. absent or slight]; (6) nape tubercles compared to head dorsum tubercles [much smaller on nape vs. slightly smaller on nape].

BIOLOGY

The life history of the steelcolor shiner has not been much studied. Most of the so-identified specimens analyzed by Lewis and Gunning (1959) were *C. lutrensis* (Gibbs 1963). Pflieger (1975) considered the steelcolor shiner to be primarily a drift-feeder which fed mostly on terrestrial and aquatic insects, occasionally on worms, mites, and small crustaceans. He surmised that prey detection was visual.

Some individuals mature by age 1, most by age 2; the smallest size at maturation for males was 49 mm SL, for females 38 mm (Pflieger 1965). Young and juveniles are 25–64 mm TL; adults are 63–114 mm (Pflieger 1975; Trautman 1981). Of the correctly identified *C. whipplei* from Indiana studied by Lewis and Gunning (1959), 15 averaged 53 mm SL at age 2 and ranged 67–82 mm at capture. The largest specimens tend to be males. A Clinch River, Tennessee, specimen is 94 mm SL; fish of such size undoubtedly occupy Virginia. Maximum lengths of 134–140 mm TL were reported by Pflieger (1975) and Trautman (1981); a Missouri specimen (SIUC uncataloged) is 115 mm SL, 141 mm TL.

Reproductive behavior was studied in Ohio (Pflieger 1965). Spawning occurs during early June to mid-August, usually near riffles. Eggs are deposited in crevices or furrows on logs and among tree roots; the sites are above the bottom. Aggregated males defend small territories at the sites while females generally hold close by. Activity is intense; Pflieger noted that at times 20 males were actively displaying, chasing, and spawning at each site. Egg counts by Lewis and Gunning (1959) are actually from *C. lutrensis*. *Cyprinella whipplei* hybridized with *C. spiloptera* in aquaria but no natural hybrids have been noted (Pflieger 1965).

HABITAT

Cyprinella whipplei occupies warm, moderate to somewhat low-gradient, large streams to medium-sized rivers. It occurs in runs, pools, and backwaters over a variety of substrates. In Oklahoma, Felley and Hill (1983) found it over mud, sand, and gravel in slow currents in shallows. Pflieger (1975) considered it to be a schooling minnow and noted that it was less tolerant of turbidity than was the spotfin shiner. It occupies unvegetated rivers (Gilbert and Burgess *in* Lee et al. 1980), but in the Clinch River we generally found it in backwaters partially floored with *Elodea* and fringed with *Justicia*.

DISTRIBUTION   Map 58

The steelcolor shiner is indigenous to much of the Mississippi basin, avoiding central base-leveled areas, and occupies a small part of the Mobile drainage. In Virginia it is found in the widest section of the Clinch River. It may not enter the Virginia reach of the Powell River due to stream-size limitation.

The several reports of *C. whipplei* (or *C. analostana* or some combination of these and other names) from the New drainage are either based on *C. spiloptera* or the specimens apparently do not exist; we regard all of the reports to have been of *C. spiloptera*, the only *Cyprinella* we verified from the New other than the distinctive *C. galactura*. The reports include: Cope (1868b [4 ANSP lots]); Goldsborough and Clark (1908 [8 USNM lots]); Fowler (1910 [Cope's specimens], 1923 [ANSP 81973]); Addair (1944 [UMMZ 119299]); Rosebery (1950a, 1950b [nonextant]); Ross and Perkins (1959 [VPI 485 nonextant; VPI 823 at CU; VPI 858 at AMNH]); Gibbs (1963 [UMMZ 118765, 1 spm. with 9 anal rays but otherwise typical of *C. spiloptera*]); and Richardson and Carnes (1964 [NCSM 2726]).

Abundance.—Rare; 5 records, 17 specimens taken since 1954.

REMARKS

The steelcolor shiner is a big-stream species in Virginia, being restricted to the lower portion of the Clinch River. Based on its limited range and rarity in the state, this species has been recommended for threatened status in Virginia (Burkhead and Jenkins 1991).

Name.—Whipplei honors Lt. A. W. Whipple, who led an early survey in the Southwest, returning with many fishes to be described by Girard.

Satinfin shiner   *Cyprinella analostana* **Girard**

SYSTEMATICS

Cyprinella analostana was described from Rock Creek, a Potomac River tributary in Washington, D.C. (Girard 1859). Its closest relative is *C. chloristia*, which was downgraded to a subspecies by Gibbs (1963) because of suggested intergradation in the Pee Dee drainage of North Carolina. Bailey et al. (1970), Gilbert (1978b), and Mayden (1989) favored species status for both.

DESCRIPTION

Materials.—Thirty-eight Virginia lots; counts from Gibbs (1963). Life color from about 30 Virginia adults.

Anatomy.—A satinfin shiner with a somewhat deep body, dorsal fin margin straight or very slightly convex, and usually 9 anal rays; adults are 45–70 mm SL. Body form, fins, and sexual and other features as in *C. galactura* except body tends to be deeper; preinternarial hiatus in

Fish 74 *Cyprinella analostana* adult male 61 mm SL (REJ 1000), VA, Bedford County, Goose Creek, 12 July 1983.

Fish 75 *Cyprinella analostana* juvenile 33 mm SL (REJ 1000), VA, Bedford County, Goose Creek, 12 July 1983.

tuberculation almost always present; dorsal fin margin straight or very slightly convex, the fin not long.

Meristics.—Pharyngeal teeth usually 1,4–4,1; lateral line complete, scales (33)35–37(38); scales around back 11–13(15); scales around belly usually 11; circumbody scales usually 24–26; circumpeduncle scales usually 14. Dorsal rays 8; anal rays (7)9(10); pectoral rays (11)13–14(16).

Color in Preservative.—Similar to *C. galactura* except lateral stripe posteriorly more distinctly centered just below midlateral level; anterior dorsal fin membranes tend to be duskier; caudal base lacks abruptly depigmented patches; in very large fish, all lower fins somewhat dusky, the anal darkest, medially.

Color in Life Plate 15.—Similar to *C. whipplei* except side and venter possibly more milky white than silvery; snout not reddish; lower fins, sometimes all fins, lack yellow; dark and pale zones absent on side of nuptial male.

Larvae.—Described by Mansueti and Hardy (1967), Lippson and Moran (1974), Jones et al. (1978), Snyder (1979), and Wang and Kernehan (1979).

COMPARISON

The satinfin shiner often is confused with the very similar spotfin shiner *C. spiloptera*; in Virginia they occur together widely in the Potomac drainage and limitedly in the Roanoke. Differences include: (1) anal rays usually [9 in *analostana* vs. 8 in *spiloptera*]; (2) lateral line scales usually [35–37 vs. 37–39]; (3) body depth [24–27% SL vs. 22–25%]; (4) pigmentation of anterior dorsal fin membranes [moderately or very dusky vs. absent or only slightly dusky, except in nuptial male].

BIOLOGY

An opportunistic feeder particularly on drifting items, *C. analostana*'s diet consists principally of microcrustaceans, terrestrial and aquatic insects, and algae (Flemer and Woolcott 1966; Gatz 1979). Considerable amounts of algae are taken during mid-fall to early spring in the James River (Woolcott et al. 1974).

Age at maturation, longevity, and growth rate are known from western New York populations (Stone 1940 in Carlander 1969). Maturation occurred in 1 or 2 years; the smallest mature male was 53 mm TL, the smallest mature female was 47 mm. Age 4 was attained only by females. Males grew more rapidly than females. Of age-2 fish, males were 54–81[?] mm TL, mean, 72, females 54–71 mm, mean, 63. In Virginia streams the largest fish tend to be males; the largest known from the state (and apparently the total range) is 77 mm SL, 96 mm TL.

Satinfin shiners spawn during daytime from late May to mid-August in water of 18–30°C in New York

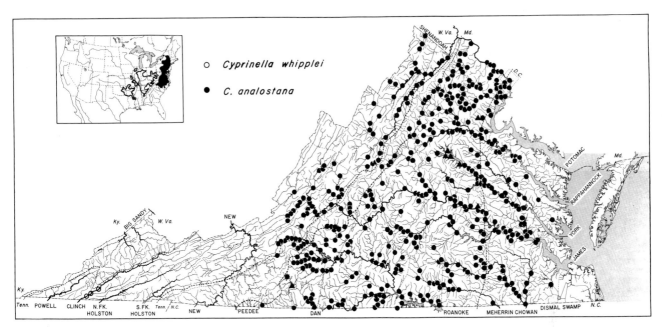

Map 58   Steelcolor shiner and satinfin shiner.

and Maryland; most spawning apparently occurs in early June to mid-July (Stone 1940 *in* Carlander 1969; Winn and Stout 1960; Stout 1975). Our males with peak-developed nuptial color and tubercles were taken largely in early June to mid-July. Males are territorial. Stout (1975) showed that sound— "knocks" and "purrs" produced by males—plays a role in territorial encounters and courting. Spawning behavior is typical of *Cyprinella*; eggs are deposited in crevices on wood and artificial substrates (Stout 1975; Gale and Buynak 1978). Females spawn fractionally during as many as 11 sessions averaging about eight days apart over a reproductive season (Gale and Buynak 1978). Total individual fecundity was 381–3,628 spawned eggs, up to four times the largest number of ovarian eggs counted by Stone (Gale and Buynak 1978).

The listing of the hybrid *C. analostana* × *C. spiloptera* by Loos et al. (1972) could be based on one or more nonhybrid specimens with atypical anal ray counts. Introgressive hybridization of these species in a New York lake was postulated by Gibbs (1963). Although these species exhibit nearly identical spawning behaviors and have broadly overlapping breeding periods, no spawning occurred when pairs composed of both species were held in artificial pools (Gale and Buynak 1978).

HABITAT

The satinfin shiner generally occupies warm medium-sized streams to major rivers of moderate to low gradient. Populations persist in streams that become heavily turbid from rains. This species occurs in pools, backwaters, and runs of shallow to moderate depth over a variety of substrates. From winter to late April, *C. analostana* inhabits pools of 1.0–1.3 m depth with sand or mud bottom and is associated with brush and other debris; from early May to late August, it occurs in shallower water or open pools with moderate current (Stout 1975). Typically a midwater to subsurface minnow, *C. analostana* occurs singly or in small schools. It commonly occupies tidal fresh water and has been found in 2‰ salinity (Mansueti and Hardy 1967). Although it inhabits darkly stained Coastal Plain streams, our lowest pH record is 6.4 (Norman and Southwick 1985). A few Virginia impoundments are occupied.

DISTRIBUTION   Map 58

Cyprinella analostana ranges on the Atlantic slope from the Lake Ontario and Hudson drainages south to the Pee Dee drainage. In Virginia it is widespread in all major Atlantic slope drainages from mountains to lowlands, and populates certain minor coastal drainages between the Rappahannock and York. Records of *C. nivea* from Virginia (Jordan 1889b; Jackson and Henderson 1942) are based on *C. analostana*; reports of *C. analostana* in the New drainage are founded on *C. spiloptera* (*C. whipplei* account).

Abundance.—Usually uncommon or common.

REMARKS

The satinfin shiner is the most widespread *Cyprinella* in Virginia. It is a fine aquarium fish as it readily accepts dried food and is active. Large males often retain a semblance of nuptial color for several months after tubercles have dropped off. As indicated by Stout's (1975) study, broader analysis of the biology and systematics of sound production in *Cyprinella* would be most worthy.

Name.—*Analostana* was coined from Analostan Island (renamed Theodore Roosevelt Island) in the Potomac River near the type locality.

Spotfin shiner   *Cyprinella spiloptera* (Cope)

SYSTEMATICS

Cyprinella spiloptera was described from Michigan in 1868. Gibbs (1957) hypothesized that it is most closely related to the *C. lutrensis* clade; Mayden (1989) placed it basally in the *whipplei* clade, hence near the *lutrensis* clade. The spotfin shiner was partitioned into an eastern and a western subspecies by Gibbs (1958). Based on the reanalysis by Schaefer and Cavender (1986), we do not recognize subspecies. Schaefer and Cavender disclosed a large anatomical overlap between eastern and western populations, and found discordant patterns of variation in a suite of characters, including those considered diagnostic by Gibbs (1958).

DESCRIPTION

Materials.—Twenty lots, 12 from Virginia; counts from Gibbs (1958). Life color based on 2 series from the Cumberland drainage, 1 from the upper Tennessee, and 2 from the upper Roanoke.

Anatomy.—A satinfin shiner with usually 8 anal rays; adults are 40–70 mm SL. Form and sexual dimorphism similar to *C. galactura* except hiatus almost always present between tubercles on snout tip and internasal area; dorsal fin margin of nuptial male is straight.

Meristics.—Pharyngeal teeth usually 1,4–4,1; lateral line complete, scales (36)37–39(41); scales around back (11)13–15; circumbody scales usually 26–28; circumpeduncle scales

Fish 76 *Cyprinella spiloptera* adult male 74 mm SL (REJ 1114), VA, Bedford County, Beaverdam Creek, 9 July 1984.

Fish 77 *Cyprinella spiloptera* juvenile 35 mm SL (REJ 986), VA, Scott County, Clinch River, 17 June 1983.

usually 14. Dorsal rays 8; anal rays (7)8(9); pectoral rays (12)13–15(16), usually 14.

Color in Preservative.—Very similar to *C. galactura* except caudal fin base lacks abruptly pale patches; melanophores absent or sparse in anterior dorsal fin membranes at all life stages, except melanophores often moderately concentrated in nuptial male.

Color in Life Plate 15.—Nonbreeding fish basically similar to *C. galactura* except lacking caudal depigmented patches. Nuptial male body silver-white, upper parts with blue and violet iridescence; all fins of peak male mostly pale yellow and with white on anterior tip or fully along margin; smaller breeding male usually with pale yellow only in caudal fin, some fins with white.

Larvae.—Described by Snyder et al. (1977), Snyder (1979), Loos et al. (1979), and Heufelder and Fuiman (1982).

COMPARISON

See accounts of *C. whipplei* and *C. analostana*.

BIOLOGY

The spotfin shiner is an active middepth feeder on drift and to a lesser degree on bottom organisms. The diet is predominantly terrestrial and aquatic insects; microcrustaceans, decapods, water mites, plant material including seeds, and detritus are also eaten (Starrett 1950b; Minckley 1963; Mendelson 1975; Hess 1983; Angermeier 1985; Vadas 1990).

Most individuals in New York matured at age 1, some not until age 2; most spawners in Ohio were age 3 (Stone 1940 *in* Carlander 1969; Pflieger 1965). The smallest mature individuals of both sexes were 38 mm SL, about 47 mm TL (Pflieger 1965). Maximum longevity is age 5. Age-2 spotfin shiners from New York, Iowa, and Wisconsin were 59–98 mm, 43–69 mm, and 55–67 mm, all TL (Carlander 1969; Becker 1983). Our largest Virginia spotfin is 80 mm SL, 100 mm TL; perhaps the largest overall is 120 mm TL from Ohio (Trautman 1981).

Spawning occurs from about mid-June to mid-August. Eggs are deposited in crevices formed by loose bark on fallen trees and stumps (Hankinson 1930; Pflieger 1965; Trautman 1981). Spotfin shiners also use artificial spawning structures, preferring crevices 1.5 or 3.0 mm wide (Gale and Gale 1976). Males are highly territorial; they bite, butt, and chase each other to establish dominance at crevices. Gale and Gale (1977) observed a male grasp an intruder by the pelvic fin and pull him some 30 cm from the territory. Most spawning occurs in the morning.

Cyprinella spiloptera is a fractional spawner, a strategy that greatly increases reproductive potential. In a wading pool, a pair spawned 12 times at intervals of 1–7 days during 16 June–10 August, releasing 169–945 eggs per spawning episode, totaling 7,474 eggs (Gale and Gale 1977). This total is about 6.5 times higher than the highest number of ovarian eggs counted by Stone (1940). Gale and Gale (1977) noted that hatching times closely corresponded to modal intervals of spawning, indicating efficient use of available crevice sites. Hybridization is noted under *C. galactura*, *C. whipplei*, and *C. analostana*.

HABITAT

The spotfin shiner occurs in generally clear streams of moderate gradient and in reservoirs and lakes. It is a warmwater species and is most characteristic of medium to large streams and rivers. In running water, it typically occurs in runs, well-moving pools, and backwaters adjacent to appreciable current. The spotfin shiner generally is a midwater species and sometimes forms small schools that occasionally are mixed with other minnows (Mendelson 1975). It is found over a variety of substrates; in Wisconsin it is most frequently taken over sand, mud, and gravel (Becker 1983). In lakes the spotfin shiner occupies shallows.

DISTRIBUTION   Map 59

Cyprinella spiloptera is widespread in the middle and upper Mississippi basin, the Great Lakes–St. Lawrence basin, and the Atlantic slope from the Hudson to the Potomac drainage; it also inhabits the Roanoke drainage. In Virginia it is indigenous to the Potomac, New, Tennessee, and Big Sandy; the Roanoke population apparently is introduced.

Curiously, *C. spiloptera* was not reported in early Potomac surveys; perhaps it was mistaken for *C. analostana*. Our first record for the Potomac is 1951. A Potomac record of *C. "whipplei"* by Crawford (1921) may have been based on *C. spiloptera*, but the description is not diagnostic and the drawing does not appear to depict a *Cyprinella*.

Like several other Potomac species, the distribution of *C. spiloptera* in the Shenandoah system is strange; the basis for its virtual restriction to the lower portion is not known. In a report on the Potomac, Ross (1959a) misidentified as *C. analostana* the *C. spiloptera* he collected at some sites. For other sites where he took *Cyprinella* he failed to list either species; our maps reflect corrections. The record of *C. spiloptera* from the North River of the Shenandoah system (VPI 706) is suspiciously disjunct from others. The She-

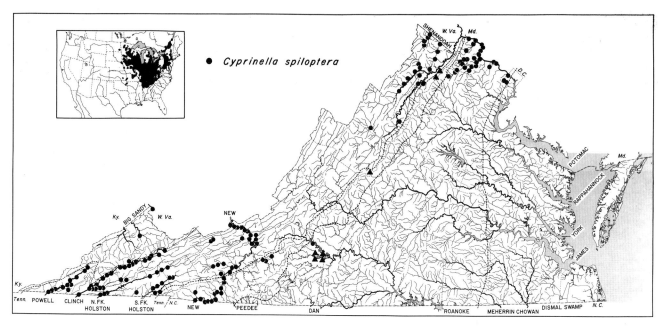

Map 59   Spotfin shiner.

rando Lake record (RC) in the extreme upper South Fork Shenandoah system is regarded as stemming from an introduction; it is dated 1973.

We discovered *Cyprinella spiloptera* in Smith Mountain Lake of the Roanoke drainage in 1980. The report (Hart 1978) of *C. analostana* being abundant in Smith Mountain Lake at an unspecified time during 1973–1976 may have been founded on *C. spiloptera*. This well-established reservoir population of the spotfin shiner apparently is introduced, most likely from the nearby New drainage. Perhaps spotfins were transferred with white bass from Claytor Lake.

In the New drainage the spotfin shiner is widespread in the New River. It extends far up some tributaries, rendering peculiar its apparent absence from others. Records of *C. whipplei* and *C. analostana* in the New are actually of *C. spiloptera* (see *C. whipplei*). The spotfin shiner is generally distributed in the Clinch and Powell rivers, but is infrequently taken in the Holston system. The large hiatus in its range in the mid-reach of the North Fork Holston River is paralleled by several other fishes and may be related to chronic pollution from Saltville.

Abundance.—Rare to common; generally rare in the Holston system and Big Sandy drainage.

REMARKS

Like its cousin the satinfin shiner, the spotfin shiner is a good native fish for aquaria. The spotfin has spawned in captivity. It uses sounds in territorial encounters and probably when courting (Winn and Stout 1960). *Cyprinella spiloptera* may be an important new forage minnow in Smith Mountain Lake; we found it in coves in the upper and lower reservoir. Some of the coves are distant from major feeders, hence the shiner may reproduce in the reservoir.

Name.—*Spiloptera*, "spot fin," refers to the dark streaks in the dorsal fin.

Highscale shiners   Genus *Luxilus* Rafinesque

The genus *Luxilus* of eastern and central North America comprises nine species (Mayden 1988b), five of which inhabit Virginia; a monograph on the group is by Gilbert (1964). *Luxilus* had long been judged one of the most distinctive subgenera of *Notropis*; supported by cladistic analysis, it was elevated by Mayden (1989) and Coburn and Cavender (1992). Its generic rank was adopted by Robins et al. (1991) but is controversial (Snelson 1991). In the notropin clade, *Luxilus* is positioned between *Notropis* s.l. and the more advanced *Lythrurus*; these genera are primitive to the *Pimephales* clade including *Cyprinella* (Coburn and Cavender 1992).

We propose the generic vernacular highscale shiners for *Luxilus*, in reference to the highly elevated anteromidlateral scales (height of lunula much more than twice the width; Figure 35A). The members are medium or large for shiners and have a compressed body, the dorsal fin origin above the pelvic fin base, a medium or large terminal mouth, 2,4–4,2 teeth, and typically 9 anal rays; sexual dichromatism is pronounced. The species commonly or exclusively are nest associates of gravel nest-building minnows; some species dig rudimentary spawning pits.

Luxilus is divisible into an Interior Highlands *zonatus* group, a southeastern *coccogenis* group, and a widespread *cornutus* group (Gilbert 1964; Mayden 1988b). Virginia is a meeting ground for the four species of the *cornutus* group—the common shiners; when adult, these species are deep-bodied and have blackened crescents or blotches laterally.

Name.—Luxilus—"little, light"—connotes a small silvery fish.

Warpaint shiner   *Luxilus coccogenis* (Cope)

SYSTEMATICS

Cope (1868a and *in* Günther 1868) described the warpaint shiner from the upper Holston system in Virginia. It is most closely related to the southeastern *L. zonistius* (Gilbert 1964).

DESCRIPTION

Materials.—From Gilbert (1964) and 15 Virginia lots. Life color based mainly on 5 Virginia adults.

Anatomy.—A shiner with a dark submarginal band in dorsal and caudal fins, depigmented caudal fin base, dark humeral bar, and large oblique mouth; adults are 65–95 mm SL. Body somewhat elongate or moderately deep, slightly or moderately compressed; dorsal fin origin above pelvic fin base, often above the posterior half. Head moderate; eye large, lateral; snout moderately rounded or somewhat pointed; mouth large, terminal, oblique, tip of lower jaw sometimes slightly projecting. Anterolateral scales much

higher than wide, particularly along lateral line (Figure 35A); breast and belly fully scaled.

Nuptial male with medium-sized tubercles on snout, above eye, and on chin; pectoral fin well tuberculate; small to minute tubercles on other fins except none on caudal; female with few small tubercles on snout and chin. Genital papilla of male small, recessed in pit; female papilla swollen, apparently not creased or bilobed posteriorly.

Meristics.—Pharyngeal teeth 2,4–4,2; lateral line complete, scales (39)40–42(43); circumbody scales (25)26–28(30); circumpeduncle scales (14)15(16); anterodorsolateral scales (15)16–18(19). Dorsal rays 8; anal rays (8)9(10); pectoral rays 14–16(17).

Color in Preservative.—Upper body moderately dusky; back with dark pre- and postdorsal stripe; dorsolateral scales vaguely to distinctly dark margined. Midlateral stripe vague or dark, darkest posteriorly; side often with few to numerous dark crescents; dark humeral bar present; lower side and venter pale. Head dark or dusky dorsally, ventral

Fish 78 *Luxilus coccogenis* adult male 86 mm SL (REJ 987), VA, Scott County, Copper Creek, 17 June 1983.

Fish 79 *Luxilus coccogenis* juvenile 47 mm SL (REJ 984), VA, Scott County, Copper Creek, 16 June 1983.

half pale. Dorsal fin with wide dusky or dark medial to submarginal band (Figure 34C); caudal fin with basal half depigmented, then a medial to submarginal dusky or dark band, margin pale; caudal spot absent or very small and vague; other fins pale.

Breeding male as above except humeral bar, lateral crescents, and dark fin bands bolder; anal fin sometimes with short dark streaks.

Color in Life   Plate 16.—Body mostly silver; when not obscured by silver, upper body olive-gray; humeral bar black; lateral scales sometimes brassy, darker scale margins olive-black; opercle anteriorly with faint or distinct vertical orange-red bar, remainder of opercle and cheek silver. Dorsal and caudal fin bands dusky black.

Nuptial male as above except major dark markings jet black in peak development; side sometimes with rosy cast; opercular bar and upper lip bright red-orange. Dorsal fin anterobasally orange-red; upper and lower margins of caudal depigmented area with faint orange streaks; pectoral fin axilla with orange-red mark. Large adult retains slight or moderate color all year, except rosy absent on side.

COMPARISON

See *Cyprinella galactura*.

BIOLOGY

The life history of *Luxilus coccogenis* is known almost entirely from North Carolina populations studied by Outten (1957). The warpaint shiner feeds on aquatic and terrestrial insects in the middle and upper water column. Terrestrial insects are particularly important in the summer and fall diet. We have seen *L. coccogenis* leap from the water when feeding. Worms and spiders are minor food items.

Most *L. coccogenis* mature at age 2; maximum longevity is four years but very few survive to age 3. Males grow faster than females. Age-2 males collected at various times of the year were 50–89 mm SL, females were 53–88 mm. Our largest Virginia specimen is 116 mm SL, 143 mm TL, equaling the largest reported by Fowler (1936), the maximum SL accepted by Gilbert (1964).

The warpaint shiner is a spawning associate of the nest-building chubs *Nocomis micropogon* and (based on a hybrid) *Nocomis leptocephalus*. Spawning on other than chub nests has not been reported. We have never seen warpaint shiner males massed over nests. We observed nuptial *L. coccogenis* over river chub nests in Virginia on six occasions in five years between 21 May and 21 June, water 18.9–23.8°C, mean, 20.7. Outten (1957) saw nest associations in North Carolina during 8 June–17 July, water 19.7–27.5°C, but witnessed spawning only on 11–12 June, water

20–23.8°C. We observed spawning in the North Fork Holston River during the afternoon of 21 May 1974, water 19°C.

Nuptial male *L. coccogenis* exhibit the frontal attack and parallel swim aggressive behaviors described for other *Luxilus* (Outten 1957; our observations). Jousting occurs between males attempting to establish or maintain territories over the nest. Females may inadvertently elicit a frontal attack by approaching a male from the front; successful spawning occurred only when the female approached the male from the rear flank. No tilt display was seen with the six spawning acts we observed, nor was tilting described by Outten. A sigmoidal spawning clasp occurred in each act that we saw, but a clasp was not mentioned by Outten. Numbers of mature ova were 300–750 (Outten 1957).

Although *L. coccogenis* commonly spawns on chub nests when 1–3 other species of shiners are breeding, hybrids of the former are rare. Apparently the only record of an intrageneric hybrid is a large adult male *L. c. chrysocephalus* × *L. coccogenis*, 112 mm SL (RC SCS 23), taken in a Clinch River tributary in Virginia. The only other cross known to us is with *Nocomis leptocephalus*, one specimen from North Carolina.

HABITAT

The warpaint shiner occurs in typically clear creeks, streams, and rivers of moderate to high gradient; it seems to avoid cold headwaters. It is found, sometimes in small schools, in pools, slow runs, and calm margins of riffles.

DISTRIBUTION   Map 60

Luxilus coccogenis is indigenous to the middle and upper Tennessee drainage; its center of abundance is in the Blue Ridge and the Valley and Ridge provinces. Native or introduced populations exist in the upper New, Santee, and Savannah drainages. In Virginia its distribution is general except that it avoids Appalachian Plateau waters.

The warpaint shiner is established, probably by introduction, in the New drainage of North Carolina. It was first taken there in 1941, then in 1949, 1970, 1977, and 1986. Most records are from the South Fork of the New; E. F. Menhinick (in litt.) plotted a record on the North Fork of the New.

Abundance.—Usually uncommon or common; one of the most frequently collected shiners in the Tennessee drainage.

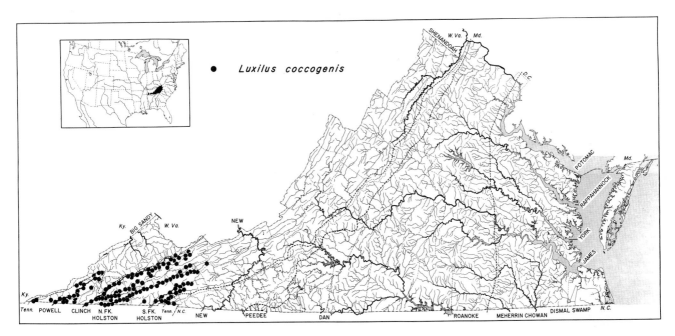

Map 60 Warpaint shiner.

REMARKS

The warpaint shiner owns one of the best descriptive common names among North American fishes. The nuptial male, with a red-orange slash on the cheek and upper lip and sharp tubercles on the snout and chin, certainly appears dressed for bat-tle. This species is one of the easiest shiners for the beginner to recognize, but we caution of possible confusion with *Cyprinella galactura* (see *Comparison*).

Name.—*Coccogenis* translates as "red cheek"—the distinctive mark on the side of the head.

Crescent shiner   *Luxilus cerasinus* (Cope)

SYSTEMATICS

Luxilus cerasinus was described by Cope (1868a) from the upper Roanoke drainage in Montgomery County, Virginia; the type locality apparently is in the North Fork Roanoke system. It was placed in the *cornutus* group by Gilbert (1964), where we retain it based on body form, color pattern, and other traits. Genetic data have been interpreted as indicating that *L. cerasinus* is most closely related to the *coccogenis* group (Rainboth and Whitt 1974; Menzel 1976; Buth 1979b, Wiley and Mayden 1985), but the data either were not treated phylogenetically or character coding warrants reanalysis (Buth 1984). Relative to the other members of the *cornutus* group, distinctions of the crescent shiner include relatively small size, fuchsia shade of nuptial males, dark horizontal eye bar not connected to body stripe in nuptial males, and antrorse tubercles. Future consideration of interrelations should include aspects of reproductive behav-ior, notably the tilt display and sigmoidal spawning clasp (e.g., R. J. Miller 1967).

DESCRIPTION

Materials.—Based on Raney (1947b), Gilbert (1964), and 48 Virginia lots. Life color from 8 freshly preserved Virginia adults and observation of many individuals over nests.

Anatomy.—A deep-bodied shiner with a rounded snout and several or many boldly dark crescents on side; adults are 50–75 mm SL. Body slightly or quite deep, compressed, particularly deep in nuptial male; dorsal fin origin above anterior half of pelvic fin base, often over the pelvic origin. Head deep; eye medium or large, lateral; snout rounded; mouth moderate-sized, terminal, oblique. Anterior midlateral scales very high (Figure 35A); breast and belly fully scaled.

Nuptial male with medium-sized tubercles densely distributed over head dorsum and side of snout; a row of medium tubercles along side of lower jaw; medium to small tubercles numerous on nape; small to tiny tubercles on

Fish 80 *Luxilus cerasinus* adult male 77 mm SL (REJ 1005), VA, Charlotte County, Horsepen Creek, 13 July 1983.

Fish 81 *Luxilus cerasinus* juvenile 47 mm SL (REJ 1005), VA, Charlotte County, Horsepen Creek, 13 July 1983.

leading edges of dorsal fin and upper caudal lobe, and on anterior rays of pectoral fin except first ray; in large male, upper body including urosome with small to tiny tubercles along submarginal or marginal portion of scales; many tubercles on head dorsum and larger ones on nape are distinctly antrorse; female with few small tubercles on head. Male genital papilla small, somewhat recessed in a pit; female papilla large, often slightly bilobed or with a medial crease posteriorly.

Meristics.—Pharyngeal teeth 2,4–4,2; lateral line complete, scales (38)39–40(41); circumbody scales (CBS) (23)25–28(30); circumpeduncle scales (12)13–15(16); anterodorsolateral scales (ADS) (14)15–19(22); scale index ADS+CBS (37)41–46(51). Dorsal rays 8; anal rays (8)9.

Color in Preservative.—Upper body slightly or moderately dusky; dark predorsal and postdorsal stripe present; dorsolateral scales duskily outlined, sometimes forming narrow dusky stripes. Midside with dusky or dark stripe, sometimes evident only posteriorly; several or many lateral scales with a dark or black, vertical or crescentic mark, these usually occurring in patches; the darkest portion of the marks underlie the exposed mid-portion of scales, and the posterior edge of the mark usually is intensified as a fine line. Lower side and venter pale. Head dusky dorsally, cheek and chin pale. Dorsal, caudal, and anal fins slightly dusky along rays, otherwise pale; caudal spot absent or very small and vague; paired fins pale.

Breeding adult similar except crescents and dark humeral bar bolder, and dark midlateral stripe often absent; large males have dark area either or both preorbitally and postorbitally, and if the latter, it does not extend to the body.

Color in Life Plate 16.—Dorsum of body and head olive to olive-gray; side of body, cheek, and venter silver; side sometimes with pale purple-red sheen; lateral crescents olive-black or black. Dorsal, caudal, and anal fins of juvenile and adult often with wide, pale red submarginal band; pelvic fin pale; anterior half of pectoral fin amber-orange.

Peak nuptial male with much of dorsum olive or olive-black; middorsum with yellow-gold or yellow-green iridescent stripe, the stripe best developed posteriorly, often covering much of dorsum; narrower stripe of same hues and slightly less brightness is present dorsolaterally; vague pale stripe often present between middorsal and dorsolateral stripes; all stripes straight or slightly and evenly curved. Side and venter deep crimson or fuchsia-red, crescents jet black, narrow humeral bar black; head dorsum blue-gray or olive-black, cheek and opercle crimson, upper lip deep red. Dorsal and caudal fins with wide submarginal red band; lower fins red except narrow pale margin.

Larvae.—Described by Loos and Fuiman (1978).

COMPARISON

Luxilus cerasinus and *L. albeolus* often co-occur in large numbers in the Roanoke drainage. They are readily separable without counting scales. In specimens of similar size, *L. cerasinus* has more numerous and slightly bolder crescents on the side and has a slightly deeper body. Crescent development in *L. cerasinus* starts on the anterior body when specimens reach 30–40 mm TL, but in *L. albeolus* not until (if at all) a distinctly greater body length is attained. The same differences occur between these species in the Chowan and New drainages, and to a slightly lesser extent for *L. cerasinus* and *L. cornutus* in the James drainage.

BIOLOGY

The crescent shiner generally feeds in the lower levels of the water column. The diet consists principally of aquatic insects, but at times includes many terrestrial insects. Worms, zooplankton, snails, larval fishes, and plant material are eaten in small amounts (Schwartz and Dutcher 1962; Gatz 1979; Mauney 1979; Surat et al. 1982). Mauney (1979) found that terrestrial insects were predominantly eaten in early summer whereas Surat et al. (1982) detected no seasonal variation in the diet. A microbial intestinal flora was described by Hershey and Clarke (1980).

Both sexes generally mature by age 2, a few individuals by age 1. Minimum size for mature males is about 60 mm SL, 40 mm for mature females (Stagner 1959). The longest survival is age 4. Males grow faster and tend to live slightly longer than females. Of age-2 fish in a South Fork Roanoke River population, males were 43–88 mm SL, females were 41–65 mm (Stagner 1959). The record size is from Virginia, a 105-mm SL male (Schwartz and Dutcher 1962).

In late March, eruption of tubercles and increased color development signal the forthcoming spawning season. We observed spawning aggregations in eight years in Virginia, on 13 occasions between 19 May–11 July, mostly in late May–early June; 11 water temperatures then recorded were 17.8–25.3°C, mean, 21.8.

Spawning behavior of *L. cerasinus* is typical of the other members of the *cornutus* group. This shiner is a spawning associate of the nest-building chubs *Nocomis leptocephalus*, *N. raneyi*, and perhaps other nest builders. Groups of brightly colored crescent shiner males assemble over gravel nests; the larger males jockey for spaces near the upstream end (Raney 1947b; our observations). Agonistic behavior includes the frontal attack and parallel swim. Males court or signal receptivity by listing the dorsum—the tilt display—toward females that approach from the side or rear. The spawning act involves a very rapid and characteristic embrace—the sigmoid clasp. Here the female is maneuvered head-up by the male, who laterally wraps around her in a "C" configuration; the tail usually is curved outward, completing the sigmoid curve (Raney 1940a).

Luxilus cerasinus hybridizes with *Luxilus cornutus*, *Lythrurus ardens*, *Nocomis leptocephalus*, and *Phoxinus oreas* (Raney and Lachner 1946c; Hambrick 1977; RC). Menzel (1976, 1977) discussed crossing of *L. cerasinus* and *L. cornutus* as a basis for the hybrid origin of *L. albeolus*. *Luxilus cerasinus* and *L. albeolus* often spawn concurrently on the same chub nests. We would be surprised if they do not hybridize, but are unsure that hybrids would be easily identified by anatomy and color.

HABITAT

Luxilus cerasinus abounds in creeks, streams, and small rivers of moderate to somewhat high gradient in the Piedmont and mountains. It does not appear to be a major element of the fauna of the main lower Roanoke and Dan rivers, nor of cold streams, but it persists in some frequently turbid streams. Typically a pool shiner, large juveniles and adults frequently occur also in moderate runs and riffles (Jenkins and Freeman 1972; Surat et al. 1982); it may be a transient in riffles (Matthews 1990). This species is found over an array of substrates ranging from silted to hard. It is a schooling minnow; moderately large schools have been observed in pools near current ecotones. During colder periods of winter, *L. cerasinus* as well as other minnows retreat to deeper pools (Surat et al. 1982; our data). This shiner disfavors abrupt decreases in temperature and dissolved oxygen (Matthews and Styron 1981).

DISTRIBUTION   Map 61

The crescent shiner occupies the James, Chowan, Roanoke, Cape Fear, and New drainages of Virginia and North Carolina. It is widespread only in the Roanoke; its original distributional status—native or introduced—in the other drainages is arguable.

The James drainage has five apparently established populations—four in tributaries of the James system,

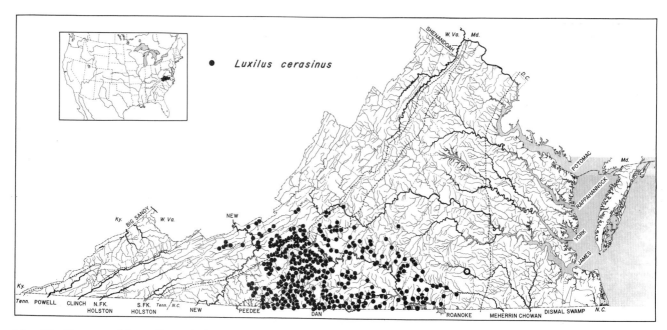

Map 61   Crescent shiner. Open circle on Nottoway indicates unaccepted record.

one in the Appomattox system. The lower three James system populations may be interconnected by breeding cohorts in the James River and intervening tributaries, thus there may be only three separate population groups. Disjunction between the James and Appomattox system populations and the recency of first notice of all populations are evidence of more than one introduction. Most of the populations are in popular gamefishing streams; *L. cerasinus* is readily available to bait seiners in the adjacent Roanoke drainage. Menzel (1977) also gave evidence of introduction.

The streams and years of first capture in the James proper are, progressing upriver: Ivy Creek system, 1971; Rocky Row Run, 1972; Jennings Creek system, 1965; and lower Barbours Creek and adjacent Craig Creek, 1967 and 1972 respectively. *Luxilus cerasinus* is doing well in lower Barbours Creek, but apparently has spread little in Craig Creek. At the lower record site on Craig Creek, it was taken during 1972 but not in later efforts. In the upper Appomattox system, the crescent shiner was found in Holiday Creek, just below a state-maintained fishing impoundment and park, in 1976 (Abbott et al. 1977) and 1979.

The New drainage is notorious for aberrant distribution patterns of apparently native fishes. *Luxilus cerasinus* has such a pattern and was accepted as native as recently as Hocutt et al. (1986). However, we now believe that this species probably was introduced, perhaps more than once. The pattern is one of near restriction to a block of eastern tributaries below

Claytor Dam; this species also occupies the western Walker Creek system and, above Claytor Lake, the upper Big Reed Island Creek system. All records are recent, 1951 the earliest, and many are in streams previously surveyed adequately for minnows.

The record of *L. cerasinus* from Fox Creek in the New drainage near North Carolina (Lachner and Jenkins 1971a) is apparently based on a faultily labeled series (originally VPI 1591, renumbered 1594). The Fox Creek system has been well surveyed since 1967 but has not yielded *L. cerasinus*.

The apparent absence of *L. cerasinus* in the Nottoway system of the Chowan drainage is queer because this species is fairly successful in the upper Meherrin system of the Chowan and in the adjacent lower Piedmont portion of the Roanoke drainage. A record for the Nottoway (VPI 991 = AMNH 61944) is doubtful; the collection also contains the only Nottoway records of *Campostoma anomalum*, *Pimephales notatus*, and *Moxostoma erythrurum*. The probability of establishing four unique system records with one collection is low. *Luxilus cerasinus* may not be native to the Meherrin; the earliest record is dated 1958

Records for the Cape Fear drainage, North Carolina, date from 1968 and later (Hendrickson and Becker 1975). We add one from the upper Haw River in 1959 (CU BBC 564).

Abundance.—Often common or abundant; one of the most ubiquitous minnows in the middle and upper Roanoke drainage.

REMARKS

The brilliant crimson colors of nuptial crescent shiners and other minnows prompted Cope (1868a) to compare them with the bright birds of the forest and the flowers in the field. Warbler migrations draw flocks of birders to the woods, and spring wildflower pilgrimages are tradition in the southern Appalachians. However, few walk clear streams to seek the tell-tale stone mounds swarming with cherry red minnows fulfilling their yearly ritual. Therein is a treat.

Name.—*Cerasinus* translates as "cherry red."

White shiner   *Luxilus albeolus* Jordan

SYSTEMATICS

Luxilus albeolus was named from the upper Roanoke River, Virginia, by Jordan (1889b). It is a member of the *cornutus* group and most resembles *L. cornutus* (Gilbert 1964); in fact, it had long been regarded a subspecies of *L. cornutus*. It replaces *L. cornutus* south of the James drainage, and in the northern portion of its range it occurs with *L. cerasinus*.

Finding that *L. albeolus* has blood protein and other traits that are intermediate between *L. cerasinus* and *L. cornutus*, Menzel (1976, 1977) hypothesized that *L. albeolus* originated from widespread introgressive hybridization of ancestral stocks of the other two species. Buth (1979b) supported this hypothesis.

Two races of *L. albeolus* were described by Gilbert (1964). The chiefly upland–montane (northern) race, initially recognized from the upper Roanoke and New drainages, has a shallower body and fewer or no dark lateral crescents when compared with the mostly Piedmont (southern) form, which occupies the Tar, Neuse, and Cape Fear drainages. Of the two forms, the northern one least resembles *L. cerasinus*. The racial differences probably reflect character displacement (Menzel 1976), whereby the northern form diverged in morphology and color as a response to sharing that portion of its range with *L. cerasinus*. *Luxilus albeolus* in the lower Roanoke and Chowan drainages, where it occurs with *L. cerasinus* and lives in Piedmont conditions, resembles upland populations.

In the New drainage, *L. albeolus* tends to resemble *L. chrysocephalus* in color pattern, indicating a formerly unnoticed taxonomic problem.

DESCRIPTION

Materials.—From Gilbert (1964) and 42 Virginia lots. Color in life mainly from 10 freshly preserved adults and observations of about 20 nuptial males over nests.

Anatomy.—A plain or slightly crescented *Luxilus* shiner; adults are 65–90 SL. Body somewhat elongate or moderately deep, slightly or well compressed; other aspects of morphology similar to *L. cerasinus*.

Nuptial male head tuberculation much as in *L. cerasinus* except dorsum tubercles less densely distributed, more concentrated anteriorly, and most of them erect, a few being slightly antrorse; body with small tubercles on nape, tubercles absent elsewhere on body; some males with tiny tubercles on leading edge of dorsal fin; female lacking tubercles. Genital morphology similar to *L. cerasinus*.

Meristics.—Pharyngeal teeth 2,4–4,2; lateral line complete, scales 37–40(41); circumbody scales (CBS) (24)26–30(33); circumpeduncle scales (13)15–16(17); anterodorsolateral scales (ADS) (15)17–20(23); scale index ADS+CBS (41)44–50(55). Dorsal rays 8; anal rays 9(11).

Color in Preservative.—Dorsum dusky, dark middorsal stripe present; dorsolateral and lateral scales duskily outlined; dorsolateral area with dusky stripe in some large adults from Atlantic slope; New drainage adult males tend to have 2–3 dusky wavy dorsolateral stripes as in *L. chrysocephalus*; dusky midlateral stripe widest and boldest posteriorly; side of large adult sometimes with few dark crescents, otherwise not prominently marked; lower side and venter pale. Head and fins as in *L. cerasinus*.

Color in Life Plate 16.—Juvenile, adult female, and nonbreeding male with dorsum olive, side and venter mostly silver. Nuptial male dorsum mostly blue-gray to olive; middorsum and dorsolateral area each with an iridescent yellow or gold stripe; vague pale stripe sometimes present between middorsal and dorsolateral stripes (stripes seen in nesting males in Roanoke drainage and the one male observed on a nest in the Little River of the New drainage). Side partly silver, upper side when held at certain angles has blue, green, and purple iridescences; mid- and lower side with rosy wash in large male; midlateral scales with dark olive base. Head dorsum, upper cheek, and upper and posterior opercle blue-gray; head dorsum sometimes with suffuse red; lower cheek, lower opercle, and snout pale rosy. Dorsal, caudal, and anal fins with submarginal red band; pelvic fin with rosy base and faint rosy streaks; pectoral fin gray along leading edge, a rosy wash posteriorly; paired fins pale along distal margin.

COMPARISON

See *L. cerasinus* for comparison with that species.

Difficulty may occur in separating *L. albeolus* and *L. chrysocephalus* collected in the New drainage, particu-

Fish 82 *Luxilus albeolus* adult male 119 mm SL (REJ 1011), VA, Mecklenburg County, Allens Creek, 14 July 1983.

Fish 83 *Luxilus albeolus* juvenile 56 mm SL (REJ 1037), VA, Campbell County, Roanoke River, 12 September 1983.

larly near the West Virginia line where the species overlap and might hybridize (Map 62). Medium-sized and larger juveniles should be preliminarily identified by the number of differentially dark crescentic marks on the side: few or none in *albeolus vs.* several to, in large specimens, many in *chrysocephalus.* Regarding the apparently best meristic difference, Gilbert (1964) gave the anterodorsolateral scale count as usually 17–20 in *albeolus vs.* usually 14–16 in *chrysocephalus* populations of our region. However, Gilbert's meristic data from the New are combined with those of the Roanoke drainage; the New population of *L. albeolus* could be more similar to *L. chrysocephalus.*

BIOLOGY

Aquatic and terrestrial insects are the principal diet of the white shiner (Surat et al. 1982; Hess 1983). It primarily feeds in midwater levels and most activity occurs during afternoon (Surat et al. 1982).

In North Carolina Piedmont populations, 20% of the males matured in 1 year, 50% in 2, and all by 3 years. Of females, 66% matured at age 1 and all matured by age 2 (Stagner 1959). Minimum size at maturation of males was 73 mm SL, for females 48 mm. The oldest individuals of both sexes were age 3.

Males grow faster than females; age-2 males were 41–97 mm SL and females were 33–75 mm (Stagner 1959). Gilbert (1964) listed maximum size as about 130 mm SL; our largest specimen, from Virginia, is 131 mm SL, 162 mm TL.

Nuptial male white shiners were observed over *Nocomis leptocephalus* nests between 4 May and 14 July; water temperatures on six observations were 17.5–24°C, mean, 19.9. Spawning periods of *L. albeolus* and *L. cerasinus* greatly overlap and both species frequently occur concurrently on nests. Reproductive activities of *L. albeolus* appear typical of the *cornutus* group as described for *L. cerasinus*; however, we saw actual spawning by only one *L. albeolus*. In particular, the male tilted the dorsum toward a female just before spawning, the nuptial embrace was sigmoidal, and he pushed mid-nest gravel a few centimeters upstream by head-down-to-forward movements.

Luxilus albeolus hybridizes in nature with *Nocomis leptocephalus*, *N. platyrhynchus*, *Notropis rubellus*, and *N. rubricroceus*. Menzel (1978) reported the hybrid *L. albeolus* × *Lythrurus ardens*; he suggested that the possible cross *L. albeolus* × *Notropis amoenus* discussed by Snelson (1968) was more likely *L. albeolus* × *L. ardens*. We have a *Nocomis* (probably *N. raneyi*) × *L. albeolus* hybrid, and one of *Luxilus* (probably *albeolus*) × *Phoxinus oreas*. See also *Systematics* and *N. cerasinus, Biology.*

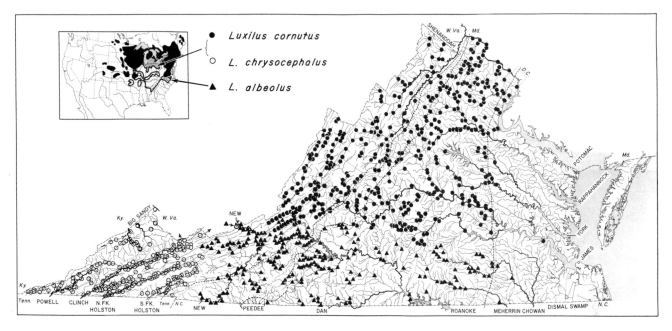

Map 62 Common shiner, striped shiner, and white shiner. Inset: range of *L. albeolus* is shown by dotted shading; northern area of overlap of *L. cornutus* and *L. chrysocephalus* is depicted by oblique shading; other, much smaller areas of overlap are not indicated.

HABITAT

Luxilus albeolus is principally a pool inhabitant in cool and warm streams of moderate gradient; it occurs less frequently in fast water than does *L. cerasinus* (Surat et al. 1982; Matthews 1990). Its longitudinal zonation nearly matches that of *L. cerasinus*; it does not typically populate streams as small as does *L. cerasinus* (our data). *Luxilus albeolus* occurs most often in midcolumn, whereas *L. cerasinus* is more epibenthic (Surat et al. 1982). The white shiner is fairly intolerant of abrupt drops in temperature and dissolved oxygen (Matthews and Styron 1981). During winter it gathers with other minnows in deeper sections of pools.

The white shiner is found over firm and soft bottoms including moderately silted ones. Gilbert (1964) suggested that the southern race is more tolerant of turbidity than is the northern race; of this we are unsure. The northern race fares well in the silty lower Piedmont of the Chowan drainage, but not so in the lower Roanoke and Dan systems. The greater success of *L. cerasinus* in the lower Roanoke and Dan seems related to its tendency to inhabit smaller, higher-gradient, less silted reaches.

DISTRIBUTION Map 62

The white shiner is indigenous to the drainages from the Chowan south to the Cape Fear, and in the New. It ranges from mountains to the Fall Line; few populations occur on the upper Coastal Plain.

The distribution pattern of *L. albeolus* in the New drainage is strange. It barely extends into North Carolina. In Virginia it occurs widely in the main channel and many well-separated tributary systems, but is apparently absent or localized in several others. Some of the latter have unsuitable habitat, such as the cold, high-gradient Little and Big Stony creeks in the northeastern sector, but such conditions do not prevail in other tributaries; for example, western Reed Creek, which has yielded only one record well above the mouth. (Gilbert's [1964] statement that *L. albeolus* is plentiful in Reed Creek is based on a collection near the mouth.) The distribution in West Virginia is also wide but sporadic (Addair 1944; Gilbert 1964; Hocutt et al. 1978, 1979; Hess 1983; Lobb 1986; *L. chrysocephalus, Distribution*).

Gilbert (1964) thought that *L. albeolus* had been introduced to the New, and that its range has been expanding. We are unsure that expansion has occurred (beyond perhaps local population increases) and we accept it to be native, owing to a specimen (ANSP 4044) taken during 1867 in Walker Creek, Virginia, by Cope (1868b). Although Cope (p. 229, 240) noted that *L. albeolus* (identified as *L. cornutus*) was common in all streams examined, his comments on p. 245 indicate that was not always the case in the New.

A "New drainage" record of *L. "albeolus"* requires comment. Goldsborough and Clark (1908) reported *L. cornutus* from Horsepen Creek, Big Sandy drainage, Virginia. Hubbs and Raney (1944) believed Horsepen Creek to be in the New drainage and considered the record to be of *L. albeolus*. C. R. Gilbert reidentified the Horsepen Creek specimens (USNM 56492, 56669) as *L. chrysocephalus* in 1959 (J. T. Williams, personal communication), but Gilbert (1964) listed them in the synonymy of *L. albeolus*, perhaps on the basis of their supposedly being from the New.

The record of *L. albeolus* for the Pee Dee drainage (Bortone 1972) is based on *Notropis chiliticus* (UNC 5650).

Abundance.—Usually uncommon or common.

REMARKS

The white shiner is notable from its proposed mode of origin—the long-past hybridization of stocks of *L. cerasinus* and *L. cornutus*. That phenomenon probably occurred at least largely in the Roanoke drainage, based on what we know of native distributions. Interestingly, *L. albeolus*-like fish are now appearing in the James drainage because *L. cerasinus*, apparently established by recent introduction, is hybridizing with native *L. cornutus*. Some 23% of the specimens of the common shiner group studied from Jennings Creek are hybrid, and part of the genome of *L. cerasinus* is being introgressed to *L. cornutus* (Menzel 1977).

Name.—*Albeolus*, diminutive for "white," refers to the pallidness of all but nuptial males.

Common shiner   *Luxilus cornutus* (Mitchill)

SYSTEMATICS

Described in 1817 from New York, the common shiner is a typical species of the *cornutus* group. Its closest relatives are *L. albeolus* and *L. chrysocephalus* (Gilbert 1964; Menzel 1976; Buth 1979b).

The relationship between *L. cornutus* and *L. chrysocephalus* has been considerably studied and debated. Before Gilbert's (1961a, 1964) anatomical and color analysis, *L. chrysocephalus* was regarded a subspecies of *L. cornutus*. Gilbert argued that the two forms merited species status even though they freely hybridized in some areas. R. J. Miller (1968) critiqued Gilbert's argument and considered *L. chrysocephalus* a subspecies. Genetic studies demonstrated low-level differentiation between *L. cornutus* and *L. chrysocephalus* (Rainboth and Whitt 1974; Menzel 1976), but Buth (1979b) did not detect any fixed allelic differences. Buth (1984) concluded that the taxa might best be considered "semispecies" (i.e., in an intermediate stage of genomic isolation).

Subsequent genetic, morphological, behavioral, and ecological analyses revealed fixed allelic differences and evidence of selection against hybrids (Dowling and Moore 1984, 1985a, 1985b; Dowling et al. 1989; Gleason 1985). The divergence time between the taxa, 1.9–2.5 million years, estimated by Dowling and Moore (1985b) corresponds to the Late Pliocence separation hypothesized by Gilbert (1964). *Luxilus cornutus* and *L. chrysocephalus* seem to have differentiated, albeit imperfectly, beyond the semispecies phase; with selection against hybrids they act as biological species—perhaps the ultimate apomorphy.

DESCRIPTION

Materials.—From Gilbert (1964) and 15 Virginia lots. Life color from 3 Virginia lots and observations of many males on nests in Virginia.

Anatomy.—A *Luxilus* shiner with a deep body, few to many dark lateral crescents, and one wide dark dorsolateral stripe per side in nuptial male; adults are 65–100 mm SL. Basic morphology mostly similar to *L. cerasinus*. Nuptial

Fish 84 *Luxilus cornutus* adult male 106 mm SL (WHH 178), CT, Litchfield County, East Aspetuck River, 28 August 1983.

male tuberculation as in *L. albeolus* except that lateral body scales have small tubercles in a marginal or submarginal row. Genital morphology similar to that of *L. cerasinus*.

Meristics.—Pharyngeal teeth 2,4–4,2; lateral line complete, scales (36)38–40(43); circumbody scales (CBS) (26)30–35(39); circumpeduncle scales (13)15–16(18); anterodorsolateral scales (ADS) (16)18–24(30); scale index ADS+CBS (42)48–59(67). Dorsal rays 8; anal rays (8)9(10).

Color in Preservative.—Similar to the crescent shiner except having fewer dark crescents on average and, in nuptial male, presence of a wide dark stripe on dorsolateral body.

Color in Life Plate 16.—Dorsum of juvenile and adult olive, side and belly silver; crescents black-olive; fins pale. Nuptial male dorsum largely olive-gray, blue-gray, or olive-black; middorsal stripe and the wider, nonwavy, main dorsolateral stripe iridescent silver, yellow, gold, or green; the stripes fade immediately upon death. Raney's (1940a) photographs of nesting males show an additional vague pale stripe anteriorly between the prominent middorsal and dorsolateral stripes. Side silver, slightly bronze, rosy, or moderately red; lateral crescents olive-black; humeral bar black. Head dorsum dark blue-gray or olive-black, cheek and opercle slate-blue or gray-black with a ventral red wash; gular area and lips reddish. Dorsal fin dusky gray-black with red submargin and sometimes basal rosy wash; caudal fin dusky gray with red submargin; anal and pelvic fins pale with submarginal reddish band; pectoral fin dusky gray-black with posterior rosy wash; all fins have narrow pale distal margin.

Larvae.—Described by Loos and Fuiman (1978), Loos et al. (1979), Perry and Menzel (1979), Snyder (1979), Buynak and Mohr (1980d), and Heufelder and Fuiman (1982).

COMPARISON

See *L. cerasinus*.

BIOLOGY

Luxilus cornutus feeds opportunistically in all levels of the water column. The diet consists largely of aquatic and terrestrial insects, and includes worms, microcrustaceans, spiders, small fishes, algae, vascular plants, and detritus (Breder and Crawford 1922; Starrett 1950b; Flemer and Woolcott 1966; Keast 1966; Moyle 1973; Vadas 1990). Fee (1965) noted greater ingestion of algae and vascular plants during periods of increased turbidity.

Both sexes mature in 2 years; some fish survive 5 years (Carlander 1969). Van Oosten (1932 *in* Becker 1983) reported a questionable longevity of 9 years.

Minimum size at maturation in a New York population was 40 mm SL for males, 37 mm for females. Males tend to grow faster than do females (Fee 1965; Carlander 1969). Age-2 males in New York were 35–56 mm SL, females were 30–45 mm (Carlander 1969). Age-2 fish were 71–92 mm TL in Wisconsin and 61–73 mm SL in Ontario (Hart 1952; Becker 1983). Our largest Virginia specimen is 117 mm SL, 151 mm TL; Trautman (1981) reported a maximum size of 208 mm TL from Ohio.

Spawning occurs in spring and early summer. In New York, R. J. Miller (1964) observed reproductive activities primarily during late May and early June, water 14.4–25.6°C. Spawning generally occurred at 17°C and higher and usually ceased with a distinct temperature drop. An Iowa population possibly spawned into late July (Fee 1965). In Virginia, reproductive males were seen on nests of *Nocomis leptocephalus*, *N. raneyi*, or *Semotilus corporalis* on nine times between 11 May–7 June during six years; water temperatures on six days were 17.5–23.9°C, mean, 20.2. The common shiner also spawns on nests of other species of *Nocomis*, *S. atromaculatus*, *Exoglossum*, and *Campostoma* (R. J. Miller 1964).

Spawning behavior of *L. cornutus* is detailed by Raney (1940a), R. J. Miller (1964), and others, and is similar to that of *L. cerasinus*. Hankinson (1932) saw *L. cornutus* and *L. chrysocephalus* spawning closely adjacent to each other and Gleason (1985) found both species breeding on the same *Nocomis* nests. *Luxilus cornutus* dislodges spawning substrate pebbles with the snout but rarely picks them up with the mouth (Raney 1940a; R. J. Miller 1964; C. A. Gleason, in litt.). Eggs number 400–1,950 (Fee 1965).

Many hybrids involving *N. cornutus* have been described, including those with the Virginia species *Campostoma anomalum*, *Clinostomus funduloides*, *Luxilus cerasinus*, *Lythrurus ardens*, *Nocomis leptocephalus*, *N. micropogon*, *Notropis rubellus*, *Phoxinus oreas*, *Rhinichthys cataractae*, *Semotilus atromaculatus*, and *S. corporalis* (Gilbert 1964; Menzel 1976, 1977, 1978; Ross and Cavender 1977; RC). Morphology and spawning behavior of one of the most common cyprinid hybrids in eastern North American streams, *L. cornutus* × *N. rubellus*, were described by Raney (1940d) and R. J. Miller (1962b, 1963).

HABITAT

The common shiner occurs in typically clear, cool and warm creeks, streams, and rivers of moderate gradient. It also lives in lakes and may spawn on lake shoals (Becker 1983). It is primarily a pool dweller but is frequently found at current ecotones and occasionally in fast water. We observed many common shiners feeding with *Notropis rubellus* in midwater of a moderate run. *Luxilus cornutus* occurs in open water and at cover, and over firm and soft bottoms. In a Minnesota lake, young and juveniles occurred in shallow areas, and adults schooled in 1–4 m depth above aquatic macrophytes (Moyle 1973).

DISTRIBUTION   Map 62

Luxilus cornutus is native to the Atlantic slope and the Great Lakes–St. Lawrence, upper Mississippi, and southern Hudson Bay basins. In Virginia the common shiner is found on the Atlantic slope from the Potomac to the James drainage. It is nearly evenly distributed from the mountains to the Fall Zone, and some populations extend into the extreme upper Coastal Plain. The record (White 1976) from the James River oligohaline zone is arbitrarily accepted; the specimens apparently are lost. Reports of *L. cornutus* from the Ohio basin of Virginia stem from misidentification of *L. chrysocephalus* or they are related to the former synonymy of the two species.

Abundance.—Usually uncommon or common.

REMARKS

"Common" shiner is a good name for *L. cornutus* and the other three species of the *cornutus* group. The name pertains particularly well to this group in Virginia, for they are often common to abundant.

The interactive relationship between *L. cornutus* and its sibling *L. chrysocephalus* has served, and will continue to serve, as a forum on species-level systematic biology. Investigations cited under *Systematics* reveal the dynamic nature of the speciation process and our understanding of it.

Name.—*Cornutus*, "horned," refers to the tubercles on the head of nuptial males.

Striped shiner   *Luxilus chrysocephalus* (Rafinesque)

SYSTEMATICS

Luxilus chrysocephalus was described from Kentucky in 1820 and is a member of the *cornutus* group (Gilbert 1964). Its taxonomic status is discussed under *L. cornutus*. The Virginia subspecies of the striped shiner is *L. c. chrysocephalus*.

DESCRIPTION

Materials.—From Gilbert (1964) and 16 Virginia lots. Life color from 5 Virginia series and many males on nests in Virginia.

Anatomy.—A *Luxilus* shiner with a deep body, few to many dark crescents on the side, and 2–4 wavy dark dorsolateral stripes per side; adults are 65–100 mm SL. Basic body, scale, and genital morphology similar to that of *L. cerasinus* except back often highly arched anteriorly in large nuptial male. Nuptial tuberculation as in *L. albeolus* except tubercles more evenly distributed and not antrorse on head dorsum.

Meristics.—Pharyngeal teeth 2,4–4,2; lateral line complete, scales (36)37–39(42); circumbody scales (CBS) (23)26–29(32); circumpeduncle scales (12)15–16(17); anterodorsolateral scales (ADS) (13)14–16(19); scale index ADS+CBS (38)40–45(48). Dorsal rays 8; anal rays (8)9(10).

Color in Preservative.—Similar to *L. cerasinus* except the side averages fewer dark lateral marks or crescents; upper side with 2–4 narrow wavy or zig-zag stripes which converge dorsally behind dorsal fin, the stripes often distinctly bowed upward just behind the head.

Color in Life   Plate 16.—Dorsum green-olive or straw-olive; middorsal and dorsolateral stripes dark olive or olive-black; side silver, lateral crescents dark olive; venter silver-white.

Nuptial male dorsum green-olive; middorsal and the one main dorsolateral stripe (per side) iridescent yellow or gold; wavy lines not iridescent. Iridescent stripes not noted in Ozarkian fish (Pflieger 1975; underwater video by W. R. Roston). Side mostly white and with either or both yellow and rosy wash anteriorly; crescents numerous, black or olive-black; venter silver-white or with vague rosy wash; head dorsum and cheek lead-gray. Dorsal and caudal fins dusky olive with submarginal red band and narrow clear margin; anal fin white with submarginal red band; pelvic fin with yellow cast and submarginal red band; pectoral fin dusky olive with submarginal red band.

Larvae.—Described by Yeager (1979) and Heufelder and Fuiman (1982).

COMPARISON

See *Luxilus albeolus* and *Notropis ariommus*.

BIOLOGY

Aquatic and terrestrial insects, the dominant food items of the striped shiner, are taken from the bottom, surface, and mid-water. Other foods include

Fish 85 *Luxilus chryso-cephalus* adult male 122 mm SL (REJ 990), VA, Tazewell County, Mud Fork, 21 June 1983.

Fish 86 *Luxilus chryso-cephalus* juvenile 45 mm SL (REJ 991), VA, Russell County, Little River, 21 June 1983.

small crayfishes, fish eggs, small fishes, algae, and detritus (Gillen and Hart 1980; Angermeier 1985).

From an Ohio population, Ball (1937 *in* Marshall 1939) suggested that males mature between 65–76 mm SL and females between 60–74 mm; these data fall within the age-2 size ranges provided by Marshall (1939). Maximum survival appears to be age 6 (Carlander 1969). Age-2 fish from Ohio and Tennessee were, respectively, 53–105 mm SL, mean, 83, and 61–74 mm SL, mean, 69 (Marshall 1939; Hart 1952). Males attain much larger size than females. The largest Virginia example examined by us is 143 mm SL, 178 mm TL. Trautman (1981) gave a maximum size of 240 mm TL from Ohio.

Reproductive activities of *L. chrysocephalus* were observed over *Nocomis micropogon* nests on four days and at *Campostoma anomalum* pits on one day (two sites) in Virginia. On two other days we collected apparently spawning fish in clean gravel runs along with hordes of brilliantly colored *Notropis rubricroceus*; no chub nests were in the immediate area. These seven occasions occurred during 20 May–14 June, each day in a different year; water temperature was 16.0–26.7°C, mean, 19.6. *Luxilus chrysocephalus* was seen spawning on *Nocomis effusus* nests in Tennessee during three years (2–12 June, 17.8–25.6°C).

Spawning behavior is typical of the *cornutus* group (Hankinson 1932). In Ohio *L. chrysocephalus* some-times picks up stones from and drops them on the spawning site (C. A. Gleason, in litt.). We saw similar behavior in Virginia. Whether this behavior constitutes rudimentary nest building, egg burial, or substrate-cleaning behavior, is unknown. The striped shiner may also make depressions in gravel by swimming and spawning movements. Egg counts from two specimens are 900 and 1,150, but it is unclear whether the data are from *L. chrysocephalus* or *L. cornutus* (Ball 1937 *in* Carlander 1969).

Many hybrids involving *L. chrysocephalus* have been reported, including those with the following species with which it is or may be sympatric in Virginia: *Luxilus coccogenis, Nocomis micropogon, N. platyrhynchus, Notropis leuciodus, N. photogenis* (but see that species), and *N. rubellus* (Gilbert 1964; Stauffer et al. 1979a, 1979c; our data). Hybridization between *L. chrysocephalus* and *L. cornutus* is well known northwest of Virginia (see *L. cornutus, Systematics*), but the two species are allopatric in Virginia. See the *Notemigonus crysoleucas* account regarding an unverified hybrid.

HABITAT

The striped shiner inhabits creeks, streams, and rivers that typically are clear or slightly turbid, cool or warm, and have moderate gradient. It also is found in lakes and reservoirs near tributary mouths, but is not known to spawn in lacustrine environments. It principally occupies pools and backwaters with hard and soft bottoms.

DISTRIBUTION   Map 62

Luxilus chrysocephalus is widespread in the southern Great Lakes and Mississippi basins and on the Gulf slope. In Virginia it occurs widely in the Tennessee drainage and in part of the Big Sandy drainage, but is localized in the New drainage.

Luxilus chrysocephalus and *L. albeolus* have an interesting distributional relationship in the New drainage, in which hybridization should be looked for. *Luxilus chrysocephalus* sporadically occupies the lower portion, almost entirely in West Virginia; *L. albeolus* is also scattered in West Virginia but widespread in Virginia. Both inhabit the Gauley, Greenbrier, and East River systems in West Virginia and the lower New River just into Virginia (Gilbert 1964; Stauffer et al. 1975, 1976; Hocutt et al. 1978, 1979; Hess 1983; Lobb 1986). Both also occupy the West Virginia portion of the Bluestone system (Gilbert *in* Lee et al. 1980; J. R. Stauffer, in litt.); we took an adult *L. chrysocephalus* from Mud Fork, a Bluestone tributary in Virginia. Gilbert (1964) considered *L. chrysocephalus* to be introduced to the drainage, and other workers

(e.g., Hocutt et al. 1986) agreed. Although an early record is lacking for the New, as opposed to *L. albeolus*, the case otherwise is similar to that of *L. albeolus* and we prefer to regard *L. chrysocephalus* as probably native.

Abundance.—Usually uncommon or common.

REMARKS

Luxilus chrysocephalus is the largest notropin shiner. Because of marked anatomical and color variation according to size and sex, more than one student has erred in a laboratory exam, when presented with a series of the striped shiner and asked: "How many species are present?"

All four species of *Luxilus* in the New drainage have distributional peculiarities, such that native status for part or all of their ranges in the drainage can be questioned. Perhaps the peculiarities will someday be correlated with entirely natural factors.

Name.—*Chrysocephalus* translates as "golden head." Rafinesque probably based the description on an adult female or a juvenile with gold iridescence dorsally.

Smallscale shiners   Genus *Lythrurus* Jordan

Lythrurus is another eastern and central North American group that was just resurrected from *Notropis* by Mayden (1989) and Coburn and Cavender (1992). This move also has been accepted by Robins et al. (1991) and is debatable (Snelson 1991). The phylogenetic position of *Lythrurus* hypothesized by Coburn and Cavender is noted under genus *Luxilus*. In a monographic study of *Lythrurus*, Snelson (1972) considered this group to be closely related to typical members of the subgenus *Notropis*. He recognized four species groups; intrageneric relations were addressed by Wiley and Mayden (1985) and Mayden (1989).

Lythrurus shiners, for which we suggest the common name smallscale shiners, comprise eight species, two of which occupy Virginia. They have a slender to somewhat deep body, the dorsal fin origin posterior to the pelvic fin base, mouth moderately large and terminal, scales (especially predorsal scales) fairly small, pharyngeal teeth 2,4–4,2, anal rays usually 10–12, and the female urogenital papilla is large for shiners (Snelson 1972). The species are sexually dichromatic and some associate with nests of other species.

Name.—*Lythrurus*—"blood (red) tail."

Mountain shiner   *Lythrurus lirus* (Jordan)

SYSTEMATICS

The mountain shiner was described from Georgia in 1877. Snelson (1972, 1980) placed it with *L. ardens* in the *ardens* group. Wiley and Mayden (1985) considered *L. ardens* and *L. umbratilus* to be sister species, and Mayden (1989) excluded *L. lirus* from the *ardens*

group. Based on their yellow or gold nuptial color, *L. lirus* and *L. fumeus* may be sister species.

DESCRIPTION

Materials.—From Snelson (1980) and 10 Virginia series. Life color from 8 Virginia series.

Fish 87 *Lythrurus lirus* adult male 48 mm SL (REJ 992), VA, Russell County, Copper Creek, 21 June 1983.

Anatomy.—An elongate *Lythrurus* shiner that has moderately small scales and is mostly pallid; adults are 40–50 mm SL. Body slender, somewhat compressed; dorsal fin origin moderately or much posterior to pelvic fin base. Head moderate; eye moderate, lateral; snout somewhat pointed or bluntly rounded; mouth medium or large, terminal, oblique. Breast usually naked; belly about 70% naked.

Nuptial male with medium to large, close-set antrorse tubercles on head dorsum; one to few tubercles often on chin; small tubercles on anterior half of body, occasionally including belly; pectoral fin tuberculate. Female rarely with tubercles on head, then tiny. Male genital papilla small, recessed in pit; female papilla large, bulbous.

Meristics.—Pharyngeal teeth usually 2,4–4,2; lateral line complete or, often, incomplete; midlateral scales (36)40–45(49); circumbody scales (23)25–30(34); circumpeduncle scales (10)12–13(17); anterior dorsolateral scale rows (19)21–26(29). Dorsal rays 8(9); caudal rays (18)19(20); anal rays (9)10–11(12); pelvic rays (7)8(9); pectoral rays (12)13–14(15).

Color in Preservative.—Upper body slightly dusky, scales usually faintly outlined with fine melanophores; pre- and postdorsal stripe narrow, usually faint. Midlateral stripe narrow, moderately or boldly developed on posterior half of body; stripe widening and its ventral portion diffuse or not expressed on anterior half of body; melanophores rarely extending below lateral line; scapular bar absent. Head dorsum dusky; dark stripe on body often continued across operculum and on snout; lower side of head pale; lips darkly outlined, chin (except for tip) and remainder of underside of head unpigmented. All fins pale; distinct caudal spot usually absent, although notable duskiness often extends from lateral stripe onto caudal fin.

Color in Life   Plate 17.—Adult female with pale green back; narrow iridescent yellow-gold middorsal stripe and dorsolateral stripe; silver side grading to white venter; fins pale. Nuptial male with straw, gold-olive, or lime back, often iridescent; narrow iridescent stripes (located as in female) wholly or mixed gold, green, or blue; wide midlateral stripe iridescent silver to pale or medium green. Often the iris and cheek, and less frequently the upper operculum, pale yellowish gold, gold, or coppery gold; head dorsum (where tuberculate) off-white or pale powder blue. Fins uncolored or caudal and, less often, pectoral somewhat yellow. Possible peak development, seen in a very large Clinch River male, is head laterally yellow-gold, body side with silvery yellow sheen (body side not golden, *contra* Snelson 1980). Some nonbreeding fish with gold iris and cheek.

COMPARISON

See *Notropis rubellus* account for comparison with that species.

Lythrurus lirus is similar to *L. ardens*, and they may occur together in a small part of the Clinch system. They are readily separated by: (1) dark spot or linear mark at dorsal fin origin [absent in *lirus* vs. present in *ardens* (Figure 34I)]; (2) gular pigment [absent or present only at extreme tip of chin (just posterior to midpoint of lower lip) vs. present, developed in one-third to one-half of the distance from anterior midpoint of lower lip to posterior end of lower lip].

BIOLOGY

Many gaps exist in the knowledge of the mountain shiner. Sexual dimorphism in adult size is absent (Snelson 1980). Of nuptial adults taken in Virginia during May–July, 32 males were 39–54 mm SL, mean, 46, and 34 females were 37–53 mm, mean, 45. The largest known specimen, 58 mm SL, is from Virginia (F. F. Snelson, in litt.).

The period of peak breeding activity appears to be May and June based on tubercle and gonadal development (Snelson *in* Lee et al. 1980). Fully nuptial specimens were collected in Virginia from early May through early July. We saw small loose groups in nuptial condition (although apparently not spawning) in pools and slow runs, but never over *Nocomis micropogon* nests then active in the same stream reaches. The mountain shiner has not been recorded over nests in other states, thus it probably does not spawn over chub nests.

HABITAT

Lythrurus lirus lives in moderate-gradient, generally clear, cool and warm, large creeks and streams; occa-

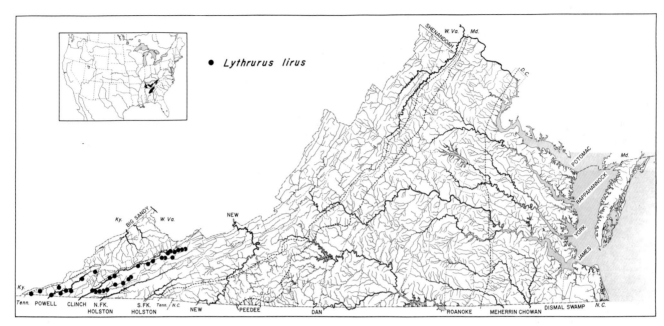

Map 63   Mountain shiner.

sionally a few specimens are taken in wider sections of the Clinch and Powell rivers. It is generally found in sluggish and moderately flowing parts of pools and backwaters, rarely in runs. During warmer months it usually occupies mid- and higher depths over a variety of soft and hard substrates. Open water and bank areas with cover are inhabited; this shiner seems to occupy open areas more often at night than during daylight.

DISTRIBUTION   Map 63

The mountain shiner is indigenous to the Mobile and Tennessee drainages and reaches its northern limit in Virginia; our records are from 10 tributaries of the Clinch or Powell rivers plus those rivers, all in the Valley and Ridge Province. Its apparent absence from the entire Holston system, also largely in the Valley and Ridge Province of Tennessee and Virginia, is odd.

Abundance.—Usually rare or uncommon, occasionally common.

REMARKS

Biologically the mountain shiner is one of the most poorly known notropin shiners. Contrary to the connotation of the common name, it avoids high-gradient montane streams.

Name.—*Lirus*, "pale like a lily," fits this pallid shiner.

Rosefin shiner   *Lythrurus ardens* (Cope)

SYSTEMATICS

Lythrurus ardens was named by Cope (1868b and *in* Günther 1868) from a Roanoke River tributary, apparently in the North Fork system of Virginia. Its phylogenetic position is uncertain (Snelson 1990; *Lythrurus lirus* account). Two subspecies of *L. ardens* were defined by Snelson (1990): *L. a. ardens* on the central Atlantic slope and in the New drainage, and *L. a. fasciolaris* (Gilbert) in the remainder of the species range in the Ohio basin; both inhabit Virginia. *Lythrurus a. fasciolaris* at times was incorrectly called *N. a.* *lythrurus*, as clarified by Snelson and Pflieger (1975) and Gilbert (1978b). *Lythrurus matutinus* of the Tar and Neuse drainages in North Carolina was regarded a synonym of *L. a. ardens* by (Snelson (1990). Its distinctive nuptial color was depicted by Page and Burr (1991), who considered it a species.

DESCRIPTION

Materials.—From Snelson (1990) and our 44 Virginia lots. Life color from many James and Roanoke drainage series.

Fish 88 *Lythrurus ardens* adult male 59 mm SL (REJ 964), VA, Franklin County, Otter Creek, 7 June 1983.

Fish 89 *Lythrurus ardens* juvenile 33 mm SL (NMB 746), VA, Floyd County, Little River, 1 May 1983.

Anatomy.—A slender *Lythrurus* shiner with a dark spot at the anterior base of the dorsal fin and small crowded nape scales; adults are 45–65 mm SL. Body moderately or quite elongate, slightly or moderately compressed (body deepest and nape more elevated in nuptial male *fasciolaris*); dorsal fin origin moderately or much posterior to pelvic fin base. Head moderate; eye moderate, lateral; snout subacute or narrowly rounded, sometimes squared at tip; mouth large, terminal, oblique. Breast usually naked; belly about 60% naked.

Nuptial male with medium to large, densely arranged, antrorse tubercles on nape, head dorsum to snout tip, and tip and side of lower jaw; anterior half of body side with small tubercles, tubercles reduced on lower side where skin is much thickened; pectoral fin tuberculate; dorsal fin with leading ray tuberculate proximally. Adult female often with a few tiny tubercles on head and nape. Male genital papilla small, recessed in pit; female papilla large, bulbous.

Meristics.—Pharyngeal teeth usually 2,4–4,2; lateral line complete, scales (41)42–48(53); circumbody scales (28)31–35(41); circumpeduncle scales (12)13–16(18); predorsal scales (25)26–31(35); predorsal scale rows (20)22–27(31). Dorsal rays (7)8(9); anal rays (9)10–11(14), usually 10 in Tennessee drainage, usually 11 in New drainage and on Atlantic slope; pectoral rays (12)13–14(16).

Color in Preservative.—Dorsum dusky or dark, dorsolateral scales dark edged; pre- and postdorsal stripe narrow, faint or moderately bold, unless obscured by dark back; midlateral stripe usually moderately dusky or black posteriorly, paler or absent anteriorly; side with melanophores extending 1–2 scale rows below lateral line; scapular bar diffuse or dark. Head dorsum and snout dusky to dark; most of cheek and operculum pale; lips dark, anterior one-third to one-half of gular area stippled. Dorsal fin anterobasally with a dark or black spot or distinctive triangular intensification of melanophores (Figure 34I); the dorsal fin

mark is vague, tending linear, but still diagnostic in small specimens; distinct caudal spot usually absent, dark lateral stripe extended through caudal base and suffused posteriad; lower fins pale except leading edge of pectoral dusky. Nuptial male tends to be darker than other adults and often has 10–14 dusky bars on upper body.

Color in Life Plate 17.—Juvenile and adult other than nuptial male with olive back, silver side, and silver to white belly; large nonbreeding male often with eye and part of median fins reddish. Nuptial male with upper body olive or purplish-black toned, overlaid with one or all of silver, blue, and green iridescence. Nuptial color, a translucent red that may be slightly purplish (Raney 1947b), lilac, or orange tinged, develops on body side (mainly anterior half), iris, cheek, along preopercle-opercle suture, on opercular membrane, snout, lips, and gular area. In fins, except for pale margin, reddish occurs in distal half of dorsal, distal one-third of caudal, anterodistally in anal, and anteriorly in pectoral and pelvic; dorsal fin spot black. Brightest red are the iris and dorsal and anal fins; red usually diffuse, often absent on body.

Larvae.—Described by Loos and Fuiman (1978) and Fuiman et al. (1983).

COMPARISON

See accounts of *Lythrurus lirus* and *Notropis semperasper*.

BIOLOGY

In warmer times of the year, *L. ardens* often feeds on terrestrial insects (Meredith and Schwartz 1959; Lotrich 1973; Small 1975). Surface feeding during lulls from spawning has been observed (Raney 1947b). The rosefin shiner also eats benthic aquatic insects, algae, and detritus (Surat et al. 1982), and probably takes considerable mid-water insect drift.

Some individuals apparently mature in 1 year; maximum longevity is between 2 and 3 years (Meredith and Schwartz 1959; Jenkins and Burkhead 1975a). Adult males average larger than adult females; of Virginia adults collected during May and June, 20 males were 42–72 mm SL, mean, 63, and 25 females were 40–62 mm, mean, 53. The largest Virginia specimen we examined is the 72-mm SL, 87-mm TL specimen; Trautman (1981) listed an 89-mm TL fish from Ohio.

Spawning may extend from late April to mid-or late June; in Virginia most activity occurs from mid-May to early June. In 25 observations (22 in Virginia, 3 in Tennessee) of rosefin shiners spawning over chub nests during 5 May–12 June, water temperatures were 12.5–25.6°C, mean, 19.6. Lythrurus ardens is one of the more common spawning associates of nesting Nocomis chubs in the central third of Virginia; we have observed it over nests of N. effusus, N. leptocephalus, N. micropogon, and N. raneyi. We also saw it spawning once on a fallfish nest and have never seen it spawning on other than a nest.

Breeding males congregate slightly to well above the nest surface and its periphery. They attempt to maintain small territories by jockeying, circle-chasing, and occasional parallel swimming; larger males tend to hold the area over the upstream end of the nest. Interaction with other species of nest associates occurs relatively infrequently (Raney 1947b). Females keep to the nest periphery, swimming over the nest only to spawn. Spawning is quite brief and apparently includes lateral contact between the sexes slightly above the nest surface. Raney (1947b) noted that during nuptial activity the rosefin shiner is "fearless," being undaunted by a seine swept over the nest. We find that L. ardens when spawning is one of the species least disturbed by an observer, but generally it scatters from slight commotion even then.

Lythrurus ardens hybridizes in Virginia with Luxilus albeolus, L. cerasinus, and L. cornutus (Menzel 1978; RC).

HABITAT

The rosefin shiner lives in warm large creeks to rivers of moderate gradient. Its typical absence from small headwaters is related to its reduced adaptation to abrupt physicochemical changes (Matthews and Styron 1981). It lives in clear and frequently turbid streams. Generally it is found in mid- and higher depths over soft and hard bottoms. Barclay (1984)

determined the home range to be about 30 m in pools lacking predators and about 20 m when predators were present. The single Virginia reservoir record is of young shiners from the head of a cove fed only by a small brook; L. ardens is nowhere considered a typical reservoir fish.

Lythrurus ardens was characterized as predominantly a pool dweller by Jenkins and Freeman (1972) and Surat et al. (1982); commonly it also inhabits backwaters near appreciable flow. However, Raney (1950) commented that the usual abode of L. ardens was moderately fast water, and Leonard et al. (1986) characterized young and adults as run inhabitants. We observed a mixed group of L. ardens and Luxilus cornutus feeding on drift in the upper strata of a rapid run in current estimated at 0.8–1.0 m/second.

DISTRIBUTION   Map 64

Lythrurus ardens (arbitrarily including the matutinus form) occurs on the Atlantic slope from the York drainage to the Cape Fear drainage, and in several drainages of the Ohio basin, including in Virginia the New and a small part of the Tennessee. It is widespread from the mountains to the Fall Line in the James, Chowan, and Roanoke drainages.

The probable introduction of L. ardens into the York drainage from the adjacent James drainage is indicated by the collecting chronology of the Deep Creek site, upper South Anna system, that yielded the first drainage record. This species was not found in 1962 but was taken in 1968 or 1969, and again in 1972. It was not recorded in a preimpoundment survey of the North Anna system during the late 1960s and early 1970s, but began appearing there in 1979, likely owing to spread from the South Anna.

The rosefin shiner has a peculiar distribution in the New drainage; it is nearly restricted to the Virginia portion. In West Virginia it occupies the East River (Hambrick et al. 1973; Stauffer et al. 1975) and two streams in Monroe County (P. S. Hambrick, J. R. Stauffer, in litt.), all near Virginia. Of the 12 records of L. ardens from the Blue Ridge in North Carolina by Richardson and Carnes (1964), 10 are based on Notropis rubellus and one on N. leuciodus (NCSM); a specimen for the other record could not be found.

The range in the New drainage lies chiefly in the Valley and Ridge Province. Although several records exist for the Blue Ridge, there is none from any major tributary system entirely in that province and only one from the New River therein, at the province fringe. Ross and Perkins (1959) thought that L. ardens exhibited a preference for hardwater streams, which largely issue in the Valley and Ridge, but records in upper softer-water sections of Blue Ridge (and Pied-

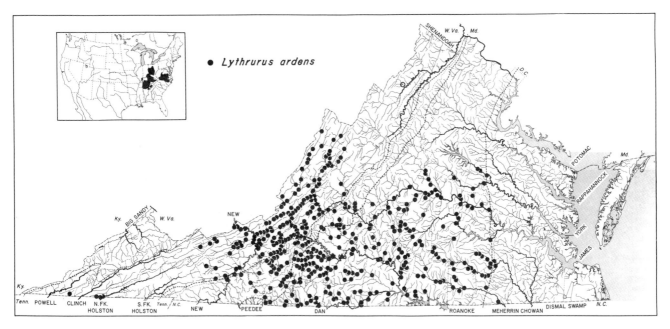

Lythrurus ardens

Map 64 Rosefin shiner.

mont) streams indicate wider adaptation. Still, the abundance and continuity of distribution of this shiner in both provinces seem erratic.

The somewhat restricted nature of the range of *L. ardens* in the New could indicate recent introduction to the drainage. Moreover, it was not reported from the 1939–early 1940s survey throughout Sinking Creek by Burton and Odum (1945), but now is widely distributed in the lower half of the creek. We regard the New population as probably native because it was discovered relatively early (first in 1922 [Fowler 1923: ANSP 81974, 81976]); it easily could have been missed earlier, and it occurs above and below Claytor Lake which was impounded in 1939.

The sharply localized rosefin shiner populations in Possum Creek of the North Fork Holston system and Blackwater Creek of the Clinch system in Virginia are either native relicts or introduced. The records are dated 1967–1971. We tentatively support the native option because in Tennessee there are at least two localized populations in the Clinch system and this species is spottily distributed in the Holston (Snelson *in* Lee et al. 1980; Feeman 1986).

The only evidence of the rosefin shiner having occupied the Potomac drainage (Ross 1959a, 1969) is weakened by the disappearance of the single speci-

men. The record was sufficiently questionable to Snelson (*in* Lee et al. 1980) to prohibit plotting. Further, Ross did not report the *Notropis rubellus* (CU 52900 series) taken in the same collection; he may have confused the two species. If the record is valid, likely it represents an introduction, as concluded by Ross (1969), Jenkins et al. (1972), and Hocutt et al. (1986). The report of *L. ardens* from the Big Sandy drainage (Stauffer et al. 1982; Hocutt et al. 1986) is erroneous (Snelson 1990).

Abundance.—Usually uncommon or common, frequently abundant.

REMARKS

The rosefin shiner is a confidence builder for the student just learning to recognize species of shiners. The black spot at the anterior end of the dorsal fin base betrays the identity of what otherwise looks like many other silvery shiners.

Name.—*Ardens*, "burning" or "glowing," refers to the reddish, sometimes fiery shade of nuptial males. *Fasciolaris*, "band, small," refers to the lateral bars of nuptial males.

True shiners   Genus *Notropis* Rafinesque

Notropis contains about 93 living, described or undescribed species (Gilbert 1978b; our data) and ranges from Canada to Mexico. Formerly the largest genus of

North American freshwater fishes, recent net subtraction of 45 species (by elevation of *Cyprinella*, *Codoma*, *Opsopoeodus*, *Luxilus*, and *Lythrurus*, and by synonymizing *Ericymba*) leaves *Notropis* with fewer species than the darter genus *Etheostoma* (about 112 species). Twenty-two *Notropis* shiners, one undescribed, inhabit Virginia; another may extend into the state from North Carolina.

Species of *Notropis* are small and have 4–4 major-row pharyngeal teeth; all species lack a frenum and nearly all lack a barbel. Silver color is dominant; breeding males of many species have bright colors (chiefly red) and some are boldly black-patterned. Much variation occurs across the genus in morphology, color, and biology. Douglas and Avise (1982) suggested that *Notropis* diversified rapidly, but that is not clear.

The limits of *Notropis* and its phylogeny are uncertain, despite the efforts to discern them (e.g., Loos and Fuiman 1978; Mayden 1989; Coburn and Cavender 1992). We arbitrarily exclude from *Notropis* the *amblops* group (genus *Hybopsis* here), include *Ericymba* and *Pteronotropis* as subgenera, and retain the *boucardi* group in the genus. Many of Mayden's (1989) proposals regarding the position of individual species or small groups are not adopted. In reviewing Mayden's paper, Snelson (1991) indicated that conservatism is desirable for some of the issues.

Most divisions of *Notropis* are unclearly identified. There appear to be 10–12 (or more) subgenera, species groups, or series of species; 10–20 species are unplaced. Affiliations of Virginia species are noted in species accounts. The arrangement and numbers of Virginia species are: subgenus *Hydrophlox* 3 or 4 (*N. rubellus* may belong in next); subgenus *Notropis* 6; *N. hudsonius*; *N. scabriceps*; *volucellus* group 1; *spectrunculus* group 2; *procne* group 3; *Chirope* 1; *texanus* group 1; *N. altipinnis*; subgenus *Ericymba* 1.

Name.—*Notropis* translates to "back keel." It probably was based on a specimen whose back was ridged owing to shrinkage (Bailey and Miller 1954).

Rosyface shiner   *Notropis rubellus* (Agassiz)

SYSTEMATICS

Notropis rubellus was described in 1850 from Lake Superior. Its placement in the subgenus *Hydrophlox* as the sole member of the *rubellus* group is due mainly to its red breeding color and pectoral fin tuberculation (Snelson 1968; Swift 1970). Mayden and Matson (1988) thought that *N. rubellus* is more closely related to species of the subgenus *Notropis*, which do not redden but with which *N. rubellus* shares many anatomical similarities including (Coburn and Cavender 1992) scale morphology. An intensification of red along the lateral line in some *N. rubellus* or an undescribed form (photographs: Phillips et al. 1982; Boschung et al. 1983) is typical of the other Virginia species of *Hydrophlox*; the pattern was not seen in Virginia *N. rubellus*.

Two subspecies are recognized. The large range of *N. r. rubellus* includes Virginia drainages from the Potomac to the James, the New, and the Big Sandy. The vaguely defined *N. r. micropteryx* (Cope), described from the Holston system of Virginia by Cope (1868b), inhabits the Tennessee and Cumberland drainages. A mitochondrial DNA study did not resolve relationships among four populations including both these taxa (Dowling and Brown 1989). The form in the Red River drainage may be a separate subspecies or species (Gilbert 1978b; Humphries et al. 1988).

DESCRIPTION

Materials.—From Snelson (1968), counts from 22 adults probably from the New drainage of Virginia (F. F. Snelson, in litt.), and 37 Virginia lots. Color in life based on 8 series of adults from the Potomac, James, New, Tennessee, and Cumberland drainages of Virginia and Kentucky.

Anatomy.—A slender shiner with a somewhat pointed snout, moderate eye, and rather posteriorly positioned dorsal fin; adults are 50–70 mm SL. Body elongate; dorsal fin

Fish 90 *Notropis rubellus* adult female 61 mm SL (WHH 98), VA, Buchanan County, Tug Fork, 27 June 1983.

origin moderately or much posterior to pelvic fin base. Head and eye moderate in size, eye lateral; snout somewhat pointed, rarely acutely so; mouth moderate in size, terminal, slightly oblique. Breast and belly fully scaled.

Peak nuptial male with small tubercles on head; those on body minute, moderately dense-set; first pectoral ray lacking tubercles, other rays with relatively large, recurved tubercles; other fins with sparse minute tubercles. Nuptial female with small head tubercles and tiny tubercles on nape and anterior midside. Genital papilla a small triangular flap, sometimes fused with the anal papilla; no sexual difference in external genital configuration.

Meristics.—Pharyngeal teeth usually 2,4–4,2; lateral line complete, scales (38)39–41; scales above lateral line 6–7; scales below lateral line 3–4; circumbody scales (25)26–29(31); circumpeduncle scales (13)14(16); predorsal scales (21)22–26(30); anterodorsolateral scales (19)20–21(23). Dorsal rays 8; anal rays (9)10(11); pelvic rays 8; pectoral rays 13–14.

Color in Preservative.—Dorsum ground shade slightly dusky, back with dark pre- and postdorsal stripe; dorsolateral scales duskily outlined, scale centers well peppered with melanophores. Dark midlateral stripe diffuse and wide anteriorly, bolder and narrower posteriorly, terminating in an oval or square mark; anterior portion of lateral line dipping below stripe, pores with dark stitch marks; lower side and venter pale, usually immaculate, sometimes with a few melanophores below lateral line anteriorly. Head dorsum and snout dusky, cheek pale; chin with melanophores along jaw and extending medially onto gular, but usually not forming a "V" (Figure 37B). All fins pale; caudal fin lacks a spot (except for dark mark at base, fully connected to and of same width and intensity as lateral stripe).

Color in Life Plate 17.—Dorsum of female and nonbreeding male gray, straw-olive, or olive; midside silver; lower side and venter silver-white; fins pale. Nuptial male in Tennessee and Cumberland drainages similar to former except head dorsum, snout, cheek, and fin bases reddish; peak male with red wash just behind opercle and along lower posterior half of body. Peak male in James drainage similar to that in upper Susquehanna drainage in having considerable red on anterior half of body.

Larvae.—Described by Reed (1958), Loos and Fuiman (1978), Loos et al. (1979), Snyder (1979), Heufelder and Fuiman (1982), and Fuiman et al. (1983).

COMPARISON

The rosyface shiner may be confused with the comely, emerald, and roughhead shiners, all of which are slender and have a quite posteriorly positioned dorsal fin. The rosyface shiner is distinguished from these by fin shape; specimens with untattered fin margins are thus desirable and fin shapes are best seen with specimens in fluid. *Notropis rubellus* is sep-

arated from the other three by: (1) anterior tip of dorsal fin when pressed against back [about reaching tip of posterior rays in *rubellus vs.* extending obviously posterior to tip of posterior rays in *amoenus, atherinoides,* and *semperasper*]; (2) anal fin margin [straight or very slightly concave *vs.* distinctly concave or falcate]. *Notropis rubellus* is further distinguished from *N. semperasper* by melanophore pigmentation below the stitched portion of the lateral line [absent or a few specks just behind head *vs.* scattered but numerous specks from head to pelvic fin base, some farther posteriad].

Notropis rubellus may also be confused with the slender *N. lirus*; they are separated by: (1) predorsal squamation [normally formed scales same size as lateral body scales, scales obvious in *rubellus vs.* scales small, often not obvious in *lirus*]; (2) breast squamation [fully scaled *vs.* nearly or completely naked]; (3) gular pigmentation [scattered or densely arranged melanophores present *vs.* lacking].

BIOLOGY

Notropis rubellus feeds throughout the water column, opportunistically seizing drift and benthic organisms. The diet is dominated by aquatic and terrestrial insects; small quantities of spiders, fish eggs, fishes (presumably larvae), and algae also are taken (Pfeiffer 1955; Reed 1957b; Flemer and Woolcott 1966). Hess (1983) found about one-third of the diet in New River fish to be blackflies.

Maturation occurs in 1 or 2 years; maximum survival is about 3 years (Pfeiffer 1955; Reed 1957b; Becker 1983). Age-3 females tend to attain slightly greater lengths than males. Age-2 males in New York ranged 58–69 mm SL, mean, 63, females 56–70 mm, mean, 64 (Pfeiffer 1955). Pennsylvania age-2 males were 50–68 mm SL, mean, 59, females 52–68 mm, mean, 60 (Reed 1957b). Generally *N. r. micropteryx* does not grow as large as *N. r. rubellus* typically does in the east. Our largest Virginia specimens are, respectively, 62 mm SL and 75 mm SL, the latter 92 mm TL. The largest rosyface shiner reported is 76 mm SL, from Pennsylvania (Reed 1957b).

The rosyface shiner spawns during May and June, sometimes early July, in water 20.0–28.8°C (Pfeiffer 1955; Reed 1957a; R. J. Miller 1964). In New York, R. J. Miller (1964) reported aggregations over *Nocomis* nests in water of 20°C, but he did not observe spawning at temperatures less than 21°C. Becker (1983) speculated that in Minnesota, spawning extended into August, based on the September capture of a 20-mm fish. Spawning takes place in Virginia from late May to mid-June, based on captures of ripe fe-

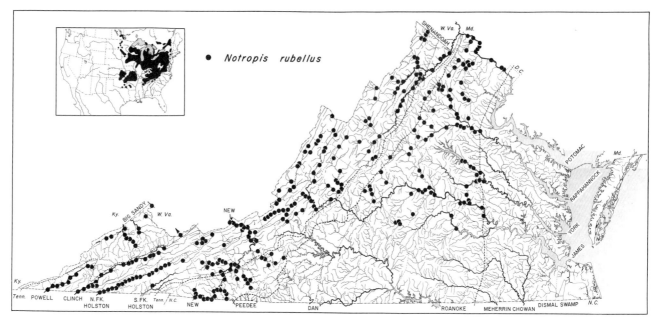

Map 65   Rosyface shiner.

males and colored milting males; the water during our one Virginia observation of *N. rubellus* over a *Nocomis* nest was 21.5–24°C.

Spawning occurs in shallow runs and riffles, either on unmodified gravel substrate or over minnow nests, sucker redds, and longnose gar spawning sites (Hankinson 1932; Pfeiffer 1955; Reed 1957a; R. J. Miller 1964; Pflieger 1975). In Virginia we saw *N. rubellus* spawning only on a *Nocomis leptocephalus* nest; but most of our observations of chub nests in Virginia were made above the upstream limits of *N. rubellus*; undoubtedly it uses nests of the other three *Nocomis* species and *Semotilus corporalis*. Spawning groups of usually 15–25 individuals hover about the spawning area; males vie for preferred sites, sometimes the spawning trough of the chub. *Notropis rubellus* exhibits the characteristic cyprinid frontal blows and parallel swims, the swims covering from a few centimeters to 2 m (R. J. Miller 1964). Spawning occurs on or just above the substrate and consists of side-by-side contact and quivering. Egg counts range 450–1,482 (Pfeiffer 1955; Becker 1983).

Notropis rubellus hybridizes with the Virginia species *Clinostomus funduloides* (Tsai and Zeisel 1969), *Luxilus albeolus* (Gilbert 1964; CU 52228; RC), *L. chrysocephalus* (Gilbert 1964), *L. cornutus* (Raney 1940d; R. J. Miller 1962b, 1963), *Notropis rubricroceus* (RC), and *N. volucellus* (Bailey and Gilbert 1960). Spawning behavior, morphology, and hermaphroditism of the *L. cornutus* × *N. rubellus* hybrid are discussed by Raney (1940d) and Miller (1962b, 1963). Snelson (1968) tentatively identified the cross *N. amoenus* × *N. rubellus*.

HABITAT

Notropis rubellus occupies warm, typically clear streams and rivers of moderate gradient. Adults favor swifter current than do most shiners. It is unknown from impoundments in Virginia but in some areas it lives in natural lakes in the vicinity of stream mouths (Becker 1983). In Oklahoma the rosyface shiner is most common over sand, gravel, and rubble; during winter it occupies pools (Felley and Hill 1983). Retreat to sluggish water for winter occurs also in Pennsylvania (Reed 1957b). In Virginia the rosyface shiner occurs most commonly in runs and in pools at current ecotones, and is found over firm and soft substrates. It is a schooling species; we observed it feeding in midwater in a large school mixed with *Luxilus cornutus*. Trautman (1981) noted that it was intolerant of turbidity and siltation in Ohio.

DISTRIBUTION   Map 65

Notropis rubellus occurs from the Red River of the North drainage and the Great Lakes–St. Lawrence basin south through much of the Mississippi basin, and south on the Atlantic slope to the James drainage. The population recently reported in the Delaware drainage (Cooper 1983) may be introduced. Subspecies ranges are noted under *Systematics*.

In addition to much of the Atlantic slope in Virginia, *N. rubellus* is native to the New, Big Sandy, and Tennessee drainages. It is evenly distributed in large streams insofar as sampling has been adequate. Such a general pattern is unusual for the Shenandoah system because many Potomac drainage species are localized or inexplicably absent there. The most downstream populations abruptly terminate at the Fall Line, exhibiting a classic pattern of Coastal Plain avoidance.

The single record in the Middle Fork Holston River and the lack of any from the South Fork Holston system are curious; the streams have been well surveyed and *N. rubellus* is widespread in the North Fork Holston, Clinch, and Powell rivers. The Middle Fork record is dated 1937 (USNM *ex* 104082). We do not accept the Middle Fork record of Ross and Carico (1963) because *N. rubellus* is not listed in the VPI catalog entry for the collection. Specimens labeled from the Middle Fork (CU 41840-7 series) probably were taken in Pennsylvania (R. Schoknecht, personal communication).

Abundance.—Usually uncommon or common.

REMARKS

Like so many northeastern United States fishes, the rosyface shiner is relatively well studied in the northern half of its range, but little knowledge exists on southerly populations. We do not know how many species or subspecies are currently cloaked under its name.

Name.—*Rubellus* is a diminutive of "red," alluding to a small fish in rosy nuptial dress.

Tennessee shiner   *Notropis leuciodus* (Cope)

SYSTEMATICS

Notropis leuciodus was named from the Holston system of Virginia by Cope (1868a) and is a member of the *leuciodus* group (or *nubilus* group) of the subgenus *Hydrophlox* (Swift 1970; Wiley and Mayden 1985). *Hydrophlox* shiners comprise an upland–montane group of eight or nine described species which typically have a moderate or elongate body form, the dorsal fin origin positioned well posterior to the pelvic fin origin, 8–10 anal rays, and are moderately or brilliantly colored when spawning.

DESCRIPTION

Materials.—From Ramsey (1965), counts from 10 Tennessee and 2 New drainage adults, and other traits in 20 Virginia lots. Life color from many breeding fish examined in hand or observed closely over nests, and from underwater photos of a spawning group, all in the Tennessee drainage; 2 lots from the Cumberland drainage (F. F. Snelson, in litt.; our data).

Anatomy.—A slender shiner with a slightly rounded snout and a prominent midlateral stripe terminating in a dark rectangular caudal spot; adults are 40–60 mm SL. Body somewhat elongate; dorsal fin origin usually above posterior half of pelvic fin base, occasionally above anterior half or slightly posterior to base. Head and eye moderate, eye lateral; snout slightly rounded; mouth moderate in size, terminal or very slightly subterminal, moderately oblique. Breast mostly scaled; belly fully scaled.

Nuptial male with densely distributed small head tubercles; small tubercles, some retrorse, on body; all fins, sometimes including dorsal surface of first pectoral ray, with small tubercles; sometimes ventral surface of pectoral with small tubercles. Female with tiny cephalic tubercles. Genital papilla triangular when free, sometimes fused with anal papilla; no sexual difference.

Meristics.—Pharyngeal teeth usually 2,4–4,2 (Swift 1970) but 1,4–4,1 in 10 specimens from the Holston and Clinch systems and as reported by Ramsey (1965). Lateral line complete, scales (36)38–40(41); circumbody scales (20)22–24(26); circumpeduncle scales 12(14); predorsal scale

Fish 91 *Notropis leuciodus* adult male 45 mm SL (REJ 992), VA, Russell County, Copper Creek, 21 June 1983.

rows (12)14–15(21). Anal rays (7)8–9, usually 8; pectoral rays (13)14–16(18).

Color in Preservative.—Dorsum ground shade slightly or moderately dusky; dark pre- and postdorsal stripe present; dorsolateral scales distinctly dark-margined. Just above dark midlateral stripe is a pale stripe that is best developed posteriorly, usually obscured by duskiness anteriorly; midlateral stripe dark or black posteriorly, less intense and usually slightly wider anteriorly, or anteriorly it is masked by silver color; lateral line stitched anteriorly; lateral line posteriorly ascends into dark midlateral stripe; lower side and venter pale. Head dorsum and snout dusky, cheek and chin pale. Dorsal and caudal fins slightly dusky along rays; caudal with dark rectangular basal spot that is slightly darker (black) than posterior end of midlateral stripe; caudal spot connected to or vaguely separate from lateral stripe; pale mark present above and below caudal spot; other fins pale.

Color in Life   Plate 17.—In juvenile and nonbreeding adult, dorsum pale olive; side silver, lateral line stitching black; lower side and venter silvery white; fins pale except black caudal mark. Peak nuptial male mostly fiery red on body; upper side with silver to lime iridescent stripe; broad midlateral silver stripe most evident posteriorly; silver flank stripe seen only in Tennessee drainage fish. Head dorsum and venter bright red; side of head silver or suffused with red; iris typically all silver, but slightly to moderately suffused with red in some fish. All fins with red, sometimes only slightly red suffused, best developed proximally; pectoral fin the most, caudal the least colored; pectoral fin origin silver, masked with red in some fish. Some spawning males are reddened (diffusely) only on anterior half of body. Nuptial female same as nonbreeding adult or with pale red.

Larvae.—Described by Loos and Fuiman (1978) and Fuiman et al. (1983).

COMPARISON

Notropis leuciodus commonly occurs with and is sometimes mistaken for *N. telescopus* and *N. rubricroceus*. *Notropis leuciodus* is separated from *N. telescopus* by: (1) caudal spot [intensely dark, rectangular in *leuciodus vs.* a vague smudge in *telescopus*]; (2) dorsolateral scale pattern [horizontal rows nearly straight, scales of uniform size and shape *vs.* one or two rows distinctly downbowed, scales usually distinctly varied in size and shape]; (3) anal rays usually [8–9 *vs.* 10–11]; (4) tips of leading dorsal fin rays when fin depressed [just reaching tips of posterior rays *vs.* exceeding tips of posterior rays]; (5) eye size [medium *vs.* large]; (6) nuptial color [present, red *vs.* absent, always silver-sided].

Notropis leuciodus and *N. rubricroceus* have similar-shaped caudal spots but are distinguished partly by: (1) pigmentation below lateral line on anterior half of body [almost always immaculate, sometimes with scattered slight pigmentation in *leuciodus vs.* well pigmented, scales darkly margined 1–3 scale rows below lateral line in *rubricroceus*]; (2) stitching along anterior half of lateral line [present *vs.* absent]; (3) mouth [terminal or very slightly subterminal *vs.* distinctly subterminal]; (4) body form [slender *vs.* slightly deeper].

BIOLOGY

The life history of the Tennessee shiner is poorly known. Some fish do not mature until age 2. Of specimens captured in late May and early June, the smallest clearly mature male was 38 mm SL; the smallest mature female was 37 mm. Although the testes of some small (38–42 mm SL) males are thick, white, and may have produced sperm, the fish are nontuberculate. Females tend to grow slightly larger than males. Of adults, 20 males were 38–60 mm SL, mean, 47, and 20 females were 37–65 mm, mean, 50. Our largest Virginia specimen is the 65-mm female; Gilbert and Burgess (*in* Lee et al. 1980) reported a maximum size of 68 mm SL.

Reproductive activity occurs in spring and early summer. Outten (1962) observed spawning aggregations in North Carolina from mid-May to early June, water 18.3–25°C. We saw reproductive activity on six occasions in Virginia and three in Tennessee during 19 May–30 June, water 17–25.6°C, mean, 20.6. *Notropis leuciodus* is a spawning associate of the nest builders *Nocomis micropogon* and *N. effusus*; groups of about 25–50 nuptial males occur over single chub nests. It also spawns in shallow gravel runs without nests (W. R. Roston, underwater video). Males usually hold positions close to the substrate. Spawning involves the lateral pairing of a male and female, sometimes 4–8 fish in a writhing group. Other nuptial cyprinids gathering over nests at the same time are *Campostoma anomalum*, *Lythrurus ardens*, *Luxilus chrysocephalus*, *L. coccogenis*, and *Notropis rubricroceus*.

Gilbert (1964) listed the hybrid *Luxilus chrysocephalus × N. leuciodus*, a cross we have collected in Virginia. We also report the combination *N. leuciodus × N. rubricroceus* (RC); three were collected from chub nests with many of the parental species.

HABITAT

The Tennessee shiner lives in typically clear, cool and warm, large creeks to rivers of moderate gradient. It generally occurs in midwater of gentle riffles, runs, and pool sections adjacent to moderate and swift current. It is a schooling shiner and has been observed mixed with rosyface and telescope shiners. During winter when riffles and open parts of pools were largely

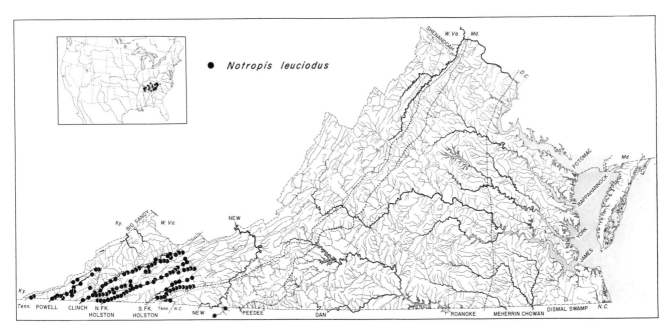

Map 66   Tennessee shiner.

vacated by fishes, *N. leuciodus* was found beneath boulders with *Hybopsis amblops* and *Erimystax insignis*.

DISTRIBUTION   Map 66

Notropis leuciodus is native to the Tennessee, Cumberland, Green, and Savannah drainages (Ramsey 1965; Gilbert and Burgess *in* Lee et al. 1980). The Virginia population is generally distributed in the Tennessee. Likely through introduction, the Tennessee shiner occurs in the New drainage of North Carolina, perhaps Virginia also. Two specimens (NCSM 2240) were taken during 1963 in the Little River, which joins the New River in Virginia; they were misidentified as *Notropis ardens* by Richardson and Carnes (1964). In 1986 a specimen was collected in Crab Creek, a Little River tributary close to Virginia (D. A. Etnier, in litt.).

Abundance.—Usually uncommon or common; one of the most frequently encountered shiners in the Tennessee drainage.

REMARKS

The Tennessee shiner is one of the many regionally common *Notropis* about whose life history we know little. It has a complex pattern of genetic variation (Matson and Mayden 1988). Its iridescent silver flank stripe should be considered in future phylogenetic analysis of *Hydrophlox*. The stripe is about one scale wide and follows the curved ventrolateral body contour of nuptial males, sometimes females. Its distribution among taxa is discordant with the species groups recognized by Swift (1970). It occurs in *N. leuciodus* of the upper Holston and Clinch systems (and perhaps certain other populations), *N. chrosomus*, and *N. rubricroceus*, but apparently not in *N. chiliticus*, *N. lutipinnis*, *N. chlorocephalus*, *N. nubilus*, and *N. rubellus*, nor is it reported in *N. baileyi*.

Name.—Leuciodus, "white appearing," was coined because the silver (and tints of red) of summer fish reminded Cope of the shining hues of mussel nacre.

Saffron shiner   *Notropis rubricroceus* (Cope)

SYSTEMATICS

The saffron shiner was discovered near the mouth of Tumbling Creek, a tributary of the North Fork Holston River, by Cope (1868b). It is a member of the subgenus *Hydrophlox*, and with *N. chiliticus* and three other southeastern upland–montane species whose nuptial males have yellow or white fins, it forms the *rubricroceus* group (Swift 1970).

DESCRIPTION

Materials.—Twenty-one Virginia series including counts of 40 specimens from the New and Tennessee drain-

Fish 92 *Notropis rubricroceus* adult male 44 mm SL (REJ 976), VA, Pulaski County, Pine Run, 14 June 1983.

Fish 93 *Notropis rubricroceus* juvenile 31 mm SL (REJ 976), VA, Pulaski County, Pine Run, 14 June 1983.

ages. Color in life from 6 Virginia lots and an underwater photo by W. R. Roston.

Anatomy.—A shiner with a narrowly rounded snout, dark lateral stripe posteriorly, somewhat elongate caudal spot, and much pigment below lateral line; adults are 40–60 mm SL. Body moderate or somewhat deep; dorsal fin origin usually above posterior half, occasionally above anterior half, of pelvic fin base. Head and eye moderate in size, eye lateral; snout slightly rounded or subacute, tip slightly more pronounced on average in nuptial male; mouth moderate in size, subterminal, somewhat oblique. Breast usually 0–30% scaled; belly usually fully scaled.

Nuptial male quite tuberculate; tiny tubercles occur densely on head; small tubercles on body including breast and belly; many head and body dorsum tubercles retrorse; pectoral fin with medium-sized tubercles, on both surfaces in some fish; dorsal, caudal, and anal fins often with tiny tubercles. Female with tiny head tubercles; minute tubercles on upper body and sometimes lower side; pectoral and dorsal fins sometimes with few minute tubercles. Genital papilla tubular, fused to anal papilla, similar in the sexes.

Meristics.—Pharyngeal teeth usually 2,4–4,2; lateral line complete, scales (36)37–40(42); circumbody scales (25)26–29(31); circumpeduncle scales (12)14–15; predorsal scales (16)18–21(24); predorsal scale rows (15)16–19(20). Anal rays (7)8(9); pectoral rays (13)14–15. Cephalic lateralis pores, IO (9)10–11(13); SO 7–9(10); POM (8)9–10(12); ST 2(4) on each side of interruption, rarely uninterrupted.

Color in Preservative.—Dorsum moderately dusky, dorsolateral scales darkly outlined; dark middorsal stripe present; upper side with pale stripe just above dark mid-lateral stripe, stripes most contrasting posteriorly, sometimes present only posteriorly; lateral line pores lack stitching; side well pigmented 1–3 scale rows below lateral line, effected by dark scale margins; venter pale. Head dorsum and snout dusky, venter pale. Fins slightly dusky along rays; dorsal membranes occasionally slightly peppered basally (Figure 34H); caudal spot a square, rectangular, or elongate continuation of midlateral stripe, fully joined to and of same intensity as the stripe.

Color in Life Plate 17.—Juvenile and nonbreeding adult olive dorsally, mostly silver or white elsewhere, fins pale; adult often with pale red suffusion on snout and lips. Nuptial female as just described, some with pale yellow fins.

Nuptial male dorsum dark red; largest peak-colored males with powder blue middorsal stripe, 1–2 scales wide, on nape and sometimes urosome. Upper side with iridescent gold-yellow stripe from tail to head, the stripes joined across occiput by a large, somewhat flat-toned, lime-yellow or gold-yellow patch. Midside variable, mostly gold or, in the apparent peak, red; lateral line scale row always red, and red more intense in that row than elsewhere on body side; red following lateral line where line passes through midside stripe; black lateral stripe often evident posteriorly. Flank with silver stripe from pectoral fin base almost to tail; some fish with isolated mirrorlike silver scales just above flank stripe, on midside, and around pectoral fin origin (latter sometimes gold); venter pale red to deep red.

Head red from interorbital area to snout tip, on lips, and underside particularly bright; occipital area lime-yellow or gold-yellow; deep red in a streak or wide area from over eye to red lateral line on body; much of operculum iridescent gold-yellow, shading to silver dorsally in most fish; iris mostly silver, or mostly red with silver inner ring. Fins olive-yellow to orange-yellow (saffron), brightest yellow proximally, margins tending pale, caudal fin the palest.

Larvae.—Described by Loos and Fuiman (1978) and Fuiman et al. (1983).

COMPARISON

Characters separating *N. rubricroceus* from *N. leuciodus* are in the latter's account.

BIOLOGY

Diet and age–growth data for *N. rubricroceus* are from Outten's (1958) study conducted primarily in North Carolina. The saffron shiner primarily eats aquatic and terrestrial insects, and also takes worms, millipedes, spiders, algae, and vascular plants. The presence of sand and terrestrial arthropods in the gut suggests that the entire water column is hunted for prey.

Both sexes mature by age 2 although some fast-growing individuals may spawn as yearlings. Outten (1958) reported maximum longevity of males to be age 3, females age 5; the latter is surprising for a small shiner. Age-2 males were 39–59 mm SL, mean, 50; age-2 females were 36–61 mm, mean, 49. Our largest saffron shiner from Virginia is a 65-mm SL male; Outten's largest, a female, is 67 mm SL. A maximum size of about 70 mm SL is reported by Gilbert (*in* Lee et al. 1980).

The saffron shiner typically spawns in spring and early summer. Outten (1958) observed its spawning at *Nocomis micropogon* nests in North Carolina during 12 May–21 July, water 16.1–30°C. In Virginia, spawning groups were seen on five occasions over nests of *N. micropogon* or *N. leptocephalus*, and once at pits being dug by *Campostoma anomalum* and *Luxilus chrysocephalus*. On two other instances peak-colored males and ripe females were taken in runs of pea-sized gravel; they may have been spawning despite the absence of chub nests. Dates and water temperatures of the Virginia observations were 20 May–30 June, 15–21.1°C, mean, 17.7.

Males assemble near the substrate in groups of 20–60 individuals at a nest and compete for preferred positions (Outten 1958). Females tend to remain at the periphery of the male group and enter the spawning arena singly or a few at a time. The female is joined by one or more males; the brief vibratory spawning act attracts adjacent males to the site. Spawning is most frequent in mid-morning and early afternoon. Egg counts were 445–1,174 (Outten 1958).

We collected the hybrids *Luxilus albeolus* × *N. rubricroceus* and *N. leuciodus* × *N. rubricroceus*, the latter from chub nests. The former probably were produced on nests also, as we observed the two species on a *N. leptocephalus* nest.

HABITAT

The saffron shiner is characteristic of clear creeks to medium-sized streams of moderate to high gradient. A requirement appears to be relatively low temperature. Most populations are in high-gradient creeks, but the shiner extends downstream in much larger and slower waters which are fed by high-volume springs. This species is a pool-and-run dweller, usually associated with stony bottoms; it often also occupies pockets among large rocks in riffles.

DISTRIBUTION   Map 67

Notropis rubricroceus is native to the upper Tennessee drainage of North Carolina, Tennessee, and Virginia. Its presence in headwaters of the Savannah and Santee drainages may be best explained by stream capture (Ramsey 1965), but the New drainage population apparently stemmed from recent introduction. In the Virginia section of the Tennessee, the saffron shiner is widespread only in the Holston system. The few populations in the Clinch system are in tributaries with voluminous springs. Masnik's (1974) record from warm Copper Creek is based on three other species (UNC 7404). The upper Powell River record is dated 1938; the species may be extirpated from that system.

In the New drainage, *N. rubricroceus* was first found in 1963; soon after it was widespread. The track seems to embark from a Virginia tributary near the North Carolina line. It extends through the main channel into other Virginia and a few North Carolina tributaries in the Blue Ridge, and down (northward) into the Valley and Ridge Province. Now the shiner is a dominant minnow where found in Virginia tributaries. Although the pattern can be interpreted as recent expansion of formerly localized, natural populations, this hypothesis is outweighed by the evidence favoring introduction.

As of 1986, the saffron shiner inhabited at least 11 tributary systems of the New River. A widespread ecological change that would have provoked marked population expansion in, and emigration from these is unknown. The tributary populations are interconnected through the large warm New River; small numbers were taken in about half of the major rotenone collections in the upper New River during 1972–

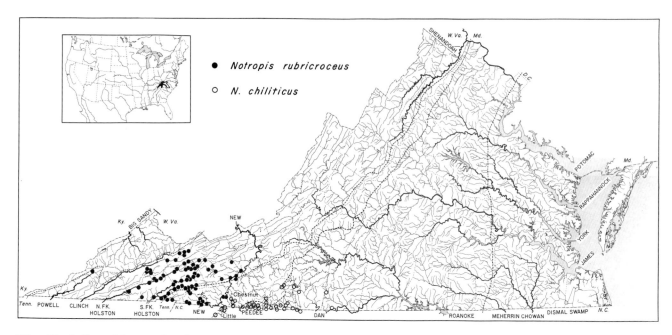

Map 67   Saffron shiner and redlip shiner.

1974 (Benfield and Cairns 1974; AMNH 69305, 69312). Thus the New River serves as a marginal conduit for intertributary dispersal of the saffron shiner.

Notropis rubricroceus probably was not present in the New drainage much before 1963; it was not noted in major surveys during 1957 in Virginia and 1963 in North Carolina (Ross and Perkins 1959; Richardson and Carnes 1964). Earlier efforts, including those of Breder and Breder (1923) and Raney (1941), also did not find the fish. Many streams in the upper New are popular for angling; bait pails could easily be stocked with saffron shiners just west of the New. R. D. Ross (personal communication) told us that a game warden considered it feasible for shiners to have been stocked with bass (or trout) from a hatchery in the upper Holston system. *Notropis rubricroceus* is plentiful in the streams flowing along both upper Holston gamefish hatcheries.

The geochronology of records indicates that *N. rubricroceus* was first established within the New in the Fox Creek system, Virginia, near the North Carolina line (Map 67). Six collections made there during 1957 did not include the shiner (Ross and Perkins 1959), but it was common to abundant in Big Fox Creek well above the mouth and in lower Middle Fox Creek during 1963. At the same time it was not found in lowermost Big Fox, that is, at the mouth of Little Fox Creek (*contra* Ross 1969), but it has been ubiquitous there in the several samplings since 1967. The data indicate that *N. rubricroceus* progressed downstream

in Fox Creek, probably from the heavily trout-fished upper reaches.

First tributary records of *N. rubricroceus* above Fox Creek, in geographic sequence, are: Big Wilson Creek in 1971, North Fork New River 1969, and Helton Creek 1969. The range of the shiner is much greater in streams below Fox Creek, suggesting current-enhanced dispersal: Elk Creek in 1969, Cripple Creek 1978, Mill Creek 1975, Shorts Creek 1971, Reed Creek 1976, Pine Creek 1983, and Peak Creek 1978. The population in a Peak Creek headwater indicates dispersal through part of Claytor Lake (similar to the apparent movement of other small species through Bluestone Reservoir on the lower New River). Most systems between Fox Creek and Claytor Lake that lack records have not been adequately surveyed recently.

The New drainage distribution of *N. rubricroceus* is of further interest, by being complementary to that of a close relative, the redlip shiner *Notropis chiliticus* (Map 67). The presence of *N. chiliticus* in the New, also probably due to introduction, may provide a test of their species status—will they interbreed freely when living together? Currently they are unknown to cohabit any tributary system, but the ranges interdigitate; *N. chiliticus* occupies at least two tributary systems. Perhaps both fishes synchronously dispersed in the New River, avoided significant interbreeding, and have adjusted into separate tributaries. Thus they would be acting as biological species. Further shiner dispersal and further study should be illuminating.

Abundance.—Often common or abundant.

REMARKS

The red, yellow, and silver nuptial male saffron shiner is a harlequin. The yokelike pattern on the top of the head, formed by the union of the bright golden yellow stripe from each side of the body and looking like an elongate "U", is unique among the *Hydrophlox* shiners. It is a trenchant field character for recognizing the species over nests.

A chub nest covered by a batch of spawning saffron shiners is a fiery spot in a stream, an aquatic pot-of-color. The shiners sometimes behave as a school, moving in colored waves punctuated by other brightly dressed minnows. At other moments the harmony of movement disrupts into territorial battles among competing males, and the tempo over the nest pitches to pandemonium when an egg-burdened female appears.

Name.—*Rubricroceus*, "red saffron," from the dominant colors of the body and fins, respectively, of nuptial males.

Redlip shiner   *Notropis chiliticus* (Cope)

SYSTEMATICS

Described in 1870 from North Carolina, the redlip shiner is a member of the *rubricroceus* group of the subgenus *Hydrophlox* (Swift 1970).

DESCRIPTION

Materials.—Sixteen Virginia lots including counts from 33 specimens. Life color from 7 lots, 3 of spawning fish.

Anatomy.—A shiner with a small pale spot at each end of dorsal fin base, dorsal fin dusky proximally, and side of body often vaguely spotted; adults are 40–55 mm SL. Basic morphology, sexual ornamentation, and most other features similar to *N. rubricroceus* except: dorsal fin margin usually slightly posterior to pelvic fin base or sometimes above posterior pelvic insertion; peak male lacks tubercles on breast and belly. Genital papilla of male tubular, fused with anal papilla; female papilla flat, triangular, free from anal papilla. Breast usually naked; belly 70–100% scaled.

Fish 94 *Notropis chiliticus* adult male 47 mm SL (REJ 971), VA, Grayson County, Big Chestnut Creek, 9 June 1983.

Fish 95 *Notropis chiliticus* juvenile 30 mm SL (REJ 966), VA, Patrick County, Dan River, 7 June 1983.

Meristics.—Pharyngeal teeth usually 2,4–4,2; lateral line complete, scales 36–37(39); circumbody scales (24)25–28(30); circumpeduncle scales (12)13–14; predorsal scales (14)16–19(21); predorsal scale rows (14)15–18(19). Anal rays 8(9); pectoral rays (13)14–15. Cephalic lateralis pores, IO (9)10–11(12); SO (6)7–9(10); POM (7)9–10(12); ST 2(4) on each side of interruption, rarely uninterrupted.

Color in Preservative.—Similar to *N. rubricroceus* except: upper side and midside often with scattered single or small patches of wholly dusky or dark regenerated scales; anterior portion of lateral line occasionally stitched; dorsal fin with marked peppering of membranes extending well above base, the fin base and immediately adjacent portion of back particularly dark except at each end of fin; ends of dorsal base pale, paleness extending onto immediately adjacent areas of back, effecting a pale spot at each end of fin (Figure 34G).

Color in Life Plate 17.—Juvenile and nonbreeding adult with back straw or olive; side silver; venter silver-white; snout, lips, and chin red-suffused; dorsal and caudal fins with red suffusion or distinct slashes anterobasally.

Nuptial male with wide iridescent lime-gold middorsal stripe; dorsolaterally olive suffused with red, appearing carmine; wide iridescent gold-yellow stripe on each side extending from midlateral level on caudal peduncle to upper side anteriorly; in subpeak male these stripes may be silver or lime-gold; scattered dark scales, if present in lateral stripe, black; lower side and venter slightly red-suffused to, in peak condition, bright red; red most intense along anterior portion of lateral line, red following the line into the posterior section of the midlateral gold-yellow stripe; occasional specimens with a few slightly silvered scales just above anal fin, silver flank stripe absent.

Head dorsum to snout tip flat-toned lime-gold or, in peak, gold; side of head in less-colored fish largely silver, snout tip and lips red, iris silver; in peak state, side of head and chin mostly iridescent gold-yellow, red reduced on snout and lips, iris mostly brilliant red. Fins pale yellow, brightest proximally, dorsal and anal distinctly red anterobasally; in maximum state, fins bright yellow or orange-yellow, caudal the least so, red slightly reduced or almost absent in dorsal and anal fins; iridescent silver patch on breast next to pectoral base.

Breeding female as described for nonbreeding adult or, in peak phase, with same pattern and nearly as colorful as brightest male.

BIOLOGY

The life history of *N. chiliticus* is poorly known. The diet, based on 20 adults from North Carolina and Virginia, consists mostly of varied aquatic and terrestrial insects; occasionally a worm, centipede, plant material, detritus, or sand are taken (L. A. Goodwin, in litt.). Results of the study agree with those of Gatz (1979). The breadth of the diet suggests bottom-to-surface feeding. Some age-1 fish are immature. The

smallest mature male found was 39 mm SL, the smallest female was 36 mm. Of thirteen adults each, males ranged 39–52 mm SL, mean, 46, females 36–60 mm, mean, 51. The 60-mm SL female, from Virginia, is the largest known to us.

We found spawning groups of *N. chiliticus* on nests of *Nocomis leptocephalus* in Virginia on 24 May 1977 and 4 and 20 June 1984, water 17.8, 18.9, and 20.6°C. A loose aggregation of highly colored males seen in Virginia on 24 April 1985, water 23.3°C, may have been spawning in the absence of a nest (R. E. Watson, in litt.), as known for other *Hydrophlox*. Other breeding cyprinids found with *N. chiliticus* over chub nests in Virginia are *Campostoma anomalum*, *Clinostomus funduloides*, *Hybopsis hypsinotus*, and *Phoxinus oreas*. Johnston (1989b and in litt.) observed *N. chiliticus* spawning on *N. leptocephalus* nests in North Carolina on 26 May at 11–17°C; their positions on the nests and behavior were similar to those of *N. rubricroceus*.

HABITAT

The redlip shiner characteristically lives in usually clear creeks and streams of high to moderate gradient. It occupies warm and cold waters, some of which contain native brook trout. It typically lives in pools and runs with bottoms ranging from moderately silted sand to bedrock.

DISTRIBUTION   Map 67

Notropis chiliticus, a Piedmont–Blue Ridge species, is extensively distributed in the Pee Dee drainage, occupies a major portion of the Dan system of the Roanoke drainage, and is localized in the Cape Fear and New drainages; one record is from the Santee drainage (Menhinick et al. 1974). The range is largely in North Carolina; south-central Virginia and, barely, South Carolina (Cloutman and Olmsted 1979) are included.

The redlip shiner has been considered native to the Dan system (e.g., Hocutt et al. 1986), but it may have been introduced. There are no old records, the earliest being 1952 in the Dan system proper and 1977 in the Smith River subsystem. Its disjunctive distribution in the middle Dan and throughout the Smith, and its apparent absence in the lower Dan, may stem from separate introductions in upper portions of the system. The range pattern contrasts with the nearly uniform spread of the species in the adjacent Pee Dee drainage. However, the Dan system was scantily sampled prior to the 1950s; the range in the Dan can be deemed as relictive (native). Pee Dee–Dan stream capture would have allowed dispersal to the Dan

(*Biogeography*). We side with native status for the Dan population.

The redlip shiner was discovered about 1985 in the Deep River system of the Cape Fear drainage in Moore and Randolph counties, North Carolina (G. B. Pottern, in litt.). The population likely is introduced.

The upper New drainage has two tributary populations of *N. chiliticus* that are considered to be introduced, perhaps separately. The populations are complementary to those of the apparently introduced *N. rubricroceus*. The redlip shiner is flourishing in upper Big Chestnut Creek and its tributaries in Virginia, where it was discovered in 1976. It is now abundant at the site inventoried in 1957 where it was not reported by Ross and Perkins (1959), and it was not found in middle Big Chestnut Creek in 1941 by E. C. Raney. We did not capture it at two sites in Galax, lower Big Chestnut, in 1983; that section is polluted but the redlip shiner may disperse through it.

The other New drainage population is well established in the North Carolina portion of the Little River system, which enters the New River in Virginia at 35.4 rkm above Big Chestnut Creek. In reporting the first samples (NCSM) of redlip shiner taken in the system in 1963, Richardson and Carnes (1964) speculated that this species probably was introduced by bait fishermen. The record of *N. chiliticus* from a tributary of the South Fork New River (Gilbert and Burgess *in* Lee et al. 1980) is based on six *N. rubellus*

(NCSM 1695) initially reported as *Lythrurus ardens* by Richardson and Carnes (1964).

Abundance.—Usually uncommon or common in the New and Pee Dee drainages and the Dan system proper; generally rare in the Smith watershed of the Dan.

REMARKS

The breeding male redlip shiner is a sparkling red and yellow fish. In peak nuptial condition the redness of the lips, evident in nonbreeding individuals, is reduced or lost. Surprisingly, in formalin many nonbreeding adults become redder about the mouth, and red develops on the body. Breder (1972) stated that the rosyside dace *Clinostomus funduloides* was the only fish known to him that intensified chromatic coloration after preservation.

All four Virginia species of the subgenus *Hydrophlox* inhabit the New drainage; we judge three of them to be introduced. The situation is similar to that of the genus *Luxilus*. The main difference is that the introduced *Hydrophlox* are primarily headwater species and are concentrated in the upper part of the New, where only one of the introduced *Luxilus* occurs.

Name.—*Chiliticus*, "pertaining to lips," alludes to the distinctive red lips.

Emerald shiner *Notropis atherinoides* Rafinesque

SYSTEMATICS

Described from Lake Erie in 1818, the emerald shiner is the type species of the subgenus *Notropis* and thus is also the type species of the genus *Notropis*. The subgenus is typified by an elongate body, a dorsal fin origin much posterior to the pelvic fin origin, a terminal mouth, 10–11 anal rays, 2,4–4,2 pharyngeal teeth, and no chromatic nuptial coloration.

Notropis atherinoides is closely related to *N. amoenus* (Snelson 1968). Two subspecies of *N. atherinoides* were recognized by Hubbs and Lagler (1958); the nominate form occurs in Virginia. Despite geographic variation, recognition of subspecies may be unwarranted (Hubbs 1922; Bailey and Allum 1962; Scott and Crossman 1973; Resh et al. 1976).

DESCRIPTION

Materials.—From Snelson (1968), Campbell and Mac-Crimmon (1970), Scott and Crossman (1973), Clay (1975),

Mayhew (1983), and 3 lots from the Clinch or Powell rivers, Virginia and Tennessee. Life color from Raney (1969b), Pflieger (1975), and Phillips et al. (1982).

Anatomy.—A slender, generally pallid shiner with a faint midlateral stripe; adults are 55–70 mm SL. Body quite elongate, slightly or moderately compressed; dorsal fin origin moderately or much posterior to pelvic fin base. Head and eye moderate, eye lateral; snout slightly pointed or distinctly rounded; mouth terminal, moderate in size, slightly oblique. Breast about 90% scaled; belly fully scaled. Anal fin margin distinctly concave or falcate. Nuptial male with tiny tubercles on head and sometimes body; small tubercles on pectoral fin; some females have well-developed pectoral fin tubercles.

Meristics.—Pharyngeal teeth usually 2,4–4,2; lateral line complete, scales 35–43; circumbody scales (21)23–25(28); circumpeduncle scales 12–14(15). Dorsal rays 8; anal rays (9)10–11(13); pelvic rays 8(9); pectoral rays (13)14–16(17).

Color in Preservative.—Ground shade pale or slightly dusky; middorsal stripe faint; dorsolateral scales weakly

Fish 96 *Notropis atherinoides* adult male 50 mm SL (SIUC 6296), IL, Jackson County, Mississippi River, 12 November 1981.

margined by melanophores; side with diffuse midlateral stripe, best developed posteriorly, often obscured by silver pigment; anterior lateral line pores lack dark stitching, midside immaculate or with few melanophores anteriorly; lower side and venter pale. Head dorsum dusky; lips and chin with scattered melanophores; cheek and opercle pale. Fins pale; caudal spot absent or vague smudge present.

Color in Life.—Dorsum translucent straw-green to green; side with iridescent silver or green stripe; lower side and venter silver-white. Fins pale. Nuptial color lacking.

Larvae.—Described by Hogue et al. (1976), Loos and Fuiman (1978), Loos et al. (1979), Snyder (1979), Heufelder and Fuiman (1982), and Fuiman et al. (1983).

COMPARISON

Characters distinguishing *N. atherinoides* from *N. rubellus* are found in that account. *Notropis atherinoides* is separated from *N. photogenis* by: (1) pelvic rays usually [8–8 in *atherinoides* vs. 9–9 in *photogenis*]; (2) middorsal stripe usually [faint vs. bold]; (3) internarial pigmentation usually [uniform vs. two distinctly dark crescents present].

BIOLOGY

In streams the emerald shiner feeds in the mid- and upper water column, mostly on drifting terrestrial and aquatic insects; benthic insects are also taken (Minckley 1963; Mendelson 1975). Lake-dwelling individuals eat microcrustaceans, other plankton, and insects (Cahn 1927; Fuchs 1967; Campbell and MacCrimmon 1970). *Notropis atherinoides* possesses relatively long, slender gill rakers, an adaptation for planktivory.

Few *N. atherinoides* are mature as yearlings; most first spawn at age 2 (Campbell and MacCrimmon 1970). Maximum longevity is age 4 (Flittner 1964 *in* Becker 1983). Females grow faster and larger than males. Age-2 males from Lake Erie were 46–65 mm SL and females were 50–75 mm (Carlander 1969). In a Canadian lake, age-2 males were 64–69 mm SL,

females 67–73 mm (Campbell and MacCrimmon 1970). The largest Virginia specimen we examined is 70 mm SL; Becker (1983) reported a 97-mm SL (124 mm TL) specimen from Wisconsin.

Northern populations of the emerald shiner spawn as early as late May and sometimes continue into early August; most activity occurs in June and July (Adams and Hankinson 1928; Campbell and MacCrimmon 1970; Becker 1983). The onset of reproduction occurs at 20–23°C (Flittner 1964 *in* Becker 1983; Campbell and MacCrimmon 1970). Spawning occurs over various substrates, but typically over gravel. In lakes, pelagic spawning occurs offshore at night in 2–6 m depth; fish in breeding schools may number in the millions in a given area (Dobie et al. 1956; Flittner 1964 *in* Becker 1983; Campbell and MacCrimmon 1970). Egg counts range 888–5,443 per female (Heufelder and Fuiman 1982).

Notropis atherinoides has hybridized with *N. volucellus* (Mayhew 1983). Snelson (1968) tentatively identified a hybrid *N. amoenus* × *N. atherinoides*.

HABITAT

The emerald shiner lives in lakes and in slow runs, backwaters, and pools of large streams to big rivers that have moderate or low gradient. It often forms large schools in upper water levels. Although seemingly tolerant of turbidity in the Plains, it avoids turbid streams in Ohio (Metcalf 1966; Trautman 1981).

DISTRIBUTION   Map 68

The emerald shiner has one of the largest distributions of North American minnows. It occurs from the Gulf slope through the Mississippi and Great Lakes–St. Lawrence basins to the upper Mackenzie River drainage, Canada, and occupies the upper Susquehanna drainage. In Virginia, *N. atherinoides* is known only from the main channels of the Clinch and Powell rivers. An upper Powell record (Masnik 1974) is actually of *N. telescopus* (USNM 104113). The emerald shiner has been taken more frequently in the Tennessee portion of the upper Clinch and Powell than in Virginia (Masnik 1974; our data). Its absence from the South and Middle forks of Holston River may be related to relatively high gradient and small stream size. The lack of a record for the North Fork Holston may be due to insufficient stream size or formerly heavy pollution. Jordan's (1889b) *N. "atherinoides"* from the Holston system is a mix of *N. photogenis* and *N. rubellus* (UMMZ IU 8066; F. F. Snelson, in litt.)

The record from the New drainage by Goldsborough and Clark (1908) is assumed to be a misidentification of *N. photogenis* or *N. rubellus* (Stauffer et al. 1976); we were unable to locate the specimens.

Abundance.—Very rare. The three specimens known from the Clinch River are dated 1969 and 1981 (VPI 2350; C. F. Saylor, in litt.). At the one upper Powell River site, 254 specimens were reported from a 1968 collection by the TVA (1970). The four specimens sent to us from that collection are *N. atherinoides*, but many or all of the other specimens may have been *N. rubellus* or *N. photogenis*; these two species are widespread in the Powell and the latter was not reported at the site by the TVA.

REMARKS

Notropis atherinoides merits threatened status in Virginia because of its restriction to and rarity in the Clinch and Powell rivers (Burkhead and Jenkins 1991). The populations may be depressed by pollution and sedimentation; their apparent big-river requirements are not well met in the state.

Pickled emerald shiners originating from the Great Lakes region are often sold as bait in Virginia under the name "Great Lakes shiner."

Name.—Atherin- means "smelt," which are fishes of the family Osmeridae and which have a silver stripe on the side. Fishes of the family Atherinidae are called silversides. Both smelts and atherinids are elongate and usually small. The suffix *-oides* confers "like a" to the prefix. Thus *atherinoides* appropriately refers to a small slender silver-sided fish.

Comely shiner   *Notropis amoenus* (Abbott)

SYSTEMATICS

Described from New Jersey in 1874, *N. amoenus* is placed in the subgenus *Notropis* and is closely related to *N. atherinoides* (Snelson 1968). Coburn (1983) placed it in the *photogenis* group of the subgenus and excluded *N. atherinoides* from that group.

DESCRIPTION

Materials.—From Snelson (1968) and 21 Virginia lots. Life color from Snelson (1968).

Anatomy.—A slender shiner with a somewhat pointed snout, dorsal fin quite posteriorly placed, strongly concave anal fin margin, and distinctive gular pigmentation; adults are 55–75 mm SL. Form of body and parts essentially as in *N. atherinoides* except snout typically more acute. Breast and belly fully scaled.

Nuptial male with small tubercles on head; body with tiny tubercles, best developed on nape and upper side; pectoral fin densely tuberculate; dorsal and anal fins with scattered minute tubercles. Female usually lacks tubercles, rarely with minute ones on head and nape. Genital papilla of male small, recessed in slitlike pit; that of female protruding from pit, fused to anal papilla.

Meristics.—Pharyngeal teeth usually 2,4–4,2; lateral line complete, scales (35)37–40(47); circumbody scales (25)27–31(36); circumpeduncle scales (12)14–15(18); predorsal scales (18)22–27(34). Dorsal rays (7)8(9); anal rays (9)10–12; pelvic rays (7)8(9).

Color in Preservative.—Ground shade variable, pale to moderately dusky. Pallid specimens lack obvious melano-

Fish 97 *Notropis amoenus* adult male 60 mm SL (REJ 1024), VA, Amelia County, Deep Creek, 31 August 1983.

phore expression except for a vague midlateral stripe. Moderately pigmented fish usually have a faintly dusky mid-dorsal stripe; scales on back and upper side duskily outlined, centers usually pale; upper side sometimes with pale stripe posteriorly along dorsal border of dark midlateral stripe; midlateral stripe diffuse anteriorly, intense posteriorly, upper border sharply margined; anterior lateral line pores usually lack stitching; lower side and venter immaculate. Head dorsum and snout dusky; lips dark; chin with a dusky, elongated, triangular (V-like) patch of melanophores (Figure 37A). All fins pale; caudal spot absent.

Color in Life.—Dorsum pale olive; upper side with brassy stripe; mid- and lower side silver; fins pale. Chromatic nuptial coloration absent.

Larvae.—Described by Mansueti and Hardy (1967), Jones et al. (1978), Loos and Fuiman (1978), Loos et al. (1979), Buynak and Mohr (1980b), and Fuiman et al. (1983).

COMPARISON

See *N. rubellus.*

BIOLOGY

Little has been published on the life history of the comely shiner. Gonads and tuberculation of fish collected in April through August reveal that both sexes mature at about 50 mm SL; our smallest mature specimens are a male, 52 mm SL, and a female, 51 mm. Females appear to grow larger than males. Twelve adult males were 52–70 mm SL, mean, 60, and 13 females 51–84, mean, 65 mm. Our largest Virginia specimen is the 84-mm SL female; Snelson (1968) reported an 86-mm SL specimen.

Tuberculate adults were found from early April (in North Carolina) to late August (Snelson 1968). Virginia females captured in late April were not fully gravid; ripe and spent ones were taken together between late June and late August. Spawning has not been observed. Two tuberculate *N. amoenus* were caught with several reproductive *Lythrurus ardens* at an active (late-stage) *Nocomis raneyi* nest in Virginia on 23 May 1964, water 24.4°C. The comely shiners may have been feeding on eggs (Snelson 1968), or perhaps were spawning. Loos et al. (1979) and Buynak and Mohr (1980b) reported *N. amoenus* breeding over completed *Nocomis micropogon* nests in the Susquehanna River. J. J. Loos (personal communication) suggested that *N. amoenus* may crepuscularly or nocturnally spawn over chub nests, an intriguing notion because a close relative, *N. atherinoides*, is a night-spawner.

All putative hybrids involving *N. amoenus* are questionably identified or clearly misidentified (Snelson 1968; Menzel 1978).

HABITAT

The comely shiner typically occupies warm, medium streams to large rivers of moderate to low gradient. It inhabits smaller streams most frequently in the northern part of its range (Snelson 1968). It occurs over a variety of substrates and is usually associated with slow runs and pool sections adjacent to moderate current. Large adults occasionally have been taken from swift riffles. We never collected a large series of the comely shiner, thus it may not typically assemble in large schools. Although present in the Nottoway and Blackwater systems, which include dystrophic streams, *N. amoenus* was taken there only in waters of pH 6.8–7.0 (Norman and Southwick 1985). No population is known to have persisted in a river section after its impoundment.

DISTRIBUTION   Map 68

Notropis amoenus ranges on the Atlantic slope from the Hudson to the Pee Dee drainage and is known long ago from a Finger Lakes tributary (Snelson 1968). It occurs in all major eastern drainages of Virginia and in the small Piankatank drainage, just south of the Rappahannock. In most of the drainages whose larger waters have been adequately sampled, *N. amoenus* is generally distributed in large tributaries and main rivers. Exceptional is the Piedmont portion of the Roanoke system proper, where this species was found at few sites. The record of *N. amoenus* from Shingle Creek (Jordan 1889b; USNM 40192), the only one from the Dismal Swamp area, is likely an error (*Biogeography*).

The only Pee Dee drainage record known to us is of six adults (NCSM) from Rocky Creek, Montgomery County, North Carolina in 1973. Hocutt et al. (1986) surmised that the population is introduced based on the uniqueness and recency of the capture.

Abundance.—Usually rare or uncommon; particularly rare in the Roanoke system.

REMARKS

The possible night-time use of chub nests by the comely shiner would add another dimension to the importance of these nests.

Name.—*Amoenus* means "pleasing" or "lovely." Abbott may have been impressed by the streamlined body.

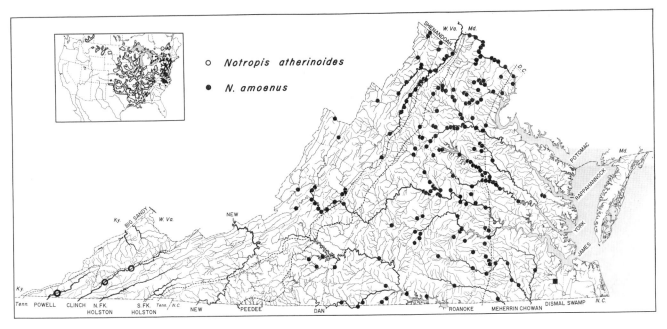

Map 68   Emerald shiner and comely shiner. Solid square on Shingle Creek denotes record with questionable locality data.

Silver shiner   *Notropis photogenis* (Cope)

SYSTEMATICS

The silver shiner, described in 1865 from Pennsylvania (Gilbert 1971), is a member of the subgenus *Notropis* (Snelson 1968). Coburn (1983) placed it and certain other shiners in the *photogenis* group of the subgenus.

DESCRIPTION

Materials.—From Gruchy et al. (1973), Stauffer et al. (1979a), Trautman (1981), and 21 Virginia lots, including anal, pelvic, and dorsal ray counts from 21 specimens. Life color from 5 Virginia adults.

Anatomy.—An elongate shiner with 9 pelvic rays and dark internarial crescents; adults are 65–95 mm SL. Body very elongate, somewhat compressed; dorsal fin origin above or slightly posterior to the posterior insertion of the pelvic fin. Head moderate; eye large, lateral; snout long, somewhat pointed or slightly rounded; mouth large, terminal, somewhat oblique, lower jaw sometimes slightly projecting. Anal fin margin distinctly concave. Breast and belly fully scaled.

Nuptial male with small, densely distributed head tubercles, tiny tubercles on body, small dense patches of tubercles on pectoral fin, and tiny scattered tubercles on dorsal and pelvic fins. Male genital papilla small, recessed in pit; female papilla slightly larger, protruding, fused with anal papilla.

Meristics.—Pharyngeal teeth usually 2,4–4,2; lateral line complete, scales (36)39–41; scale rows above lateral line 5; predorsal scales less than 22. Dorsal rays 8; anal rays (9)10–11(13); pelvic rays (8)9(10); pectoral rays 15–17.

Color in Preservative.—Dorsum mostly slightly dusky; dark middorsal stripe bold; upper body scales weakly or sharply outlined; dark midlateral stripe well developed, but sometimes obscured by silver pigment; anterior lateral line

Fish 98 *Notropis photogenis* adult male 97 mm SL (TVA), TN, Lincoln County?, Elk River, 28 April 1981.

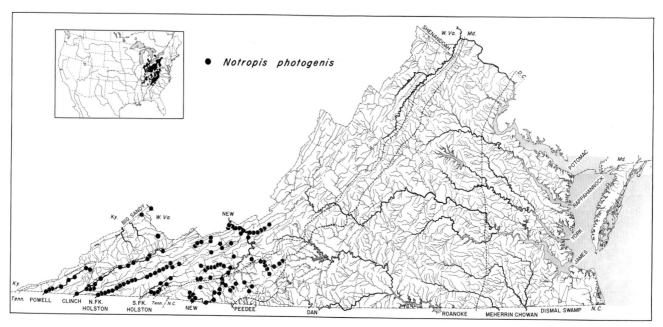

Map 69   Silver shiner.

pores usually stitched; lower side pale or with few scattered melanophores. Head dorsum and snout dusky; each naris almost always bordered medially by a dark curved marking (internarial crescent); lips dark, chin with scattered melanophores. Fins pale; caudal spot absent, midlateral stripe terminating in a vague oval mark over caudal base.

Color in Life   Plate 18.—Dorsum gray, middorsal line iridescent gold, sometimes bluish; an iridescent gold or blue dorsolateral stripe sometimes present; side and venter silver; occiput with golden iridescence, remainder (dorsal and dorsolateral areas) of head and snout dusky gray. Fins pale.

COMPARISON

See *N. atherinoides*.

BIOLOGY

Notropis photogenis feeds to a major extent at the surface on terrestrial insects; it also eats aquatic insect larvae, microcrustaceans, worms, and algae, some probably from the substrate (Gruchy et al. 1973; Smith et al. 1981; Hess 1983; Parker and McKee 1984a). Trautman (1981) observed silver shiners to leap from the surface to take flying insects.

The silver shiner matures in 1 or 2 years, usually between 55–60 mm SL in Canada (Parker and McKee 1984a). The smallest mature fish examined from Virginia are a 61-mm SL male and a 67-mm female. Maximum longevity is about 3 years. Age-2 silver shiners were 87–98 mm SL in Canada and 80–90 mm

SL in Michigan (Smith et al. 1981; Parker and McKee 1984a). Of Virginia adults, 18 males were 61–117 mm SL, mean, 89; 15 females were 61–109, mean, 86 mm. The 117-mm SL (142 mm TL) male appears to be the largest known.

Spawning-ready adults are found from early May to mid-June in Virginia. Canada populations apparently spawn in mid- to late June, water 17–23°C (Parker and McKee 1984a). Spawning has not been observed; perhaps it occurs at dusk or night as known for *N. atherinoides* of the same subgenus.

Hybridization between *N. photogenis* and *Luxilus chrysocephalus* is reported by Stauffer et al. (1979a). This cross would be difficult to distinguish from the common hybrid *L. chrysocephalus* × *N. rubellus*; although Jenkins was involved with that study, we are not now convinced of the identification.

HABITAT

The silver shiner is found in warm streams and rivers of moderate gradient. It is essentially a main-channel fish in the Tennessee drainage of Virginia. The only population in any tributary of the five branches of the drainage in Virginia is in lower Copper Creek, where this species is confined to the largest pools and is rare. In the New drainage and, judging from few records, in the Big Sandy drainage the silver shiner extends into small streams. Occupation of small streams appears to occur also in Ohio based on Trautman's (1981) range map.

Although typically associated with clear water and little-silted bottoms, *N. photogenis* may not be closely associated with the substrate; it usually patrols mid- and upper reaches of the water column. In Virginia it is usually found as schools or small groups in pools and large backwaters near ample current. In other areas it may frequently occupy swift current (Smith et al. 1981; Trautman 1981; Parker and McKee 1984a).

DISTRIBUTION Map 69

Notropis photogenis ranges from the Lake Erie drainage south through most of the Ohio basin. It is widely distributed in the New and Tennessee drainages of Virginia but verges on extirpation in the upper Big Sandy drainage; only three records (1983–1989) are known from the Big Sandy in Virginia.

Abundance.—Generally uncommon.

REMARKS

The silver shiner is a sleek *Notropis*, well adapted for cruising the near-surface zone. As a potential meal for predators, it counters with alertness and speed. Large silver shiners look good enough to be fried like smelt and eaten.

Name.—*Photogenis*, "light cheek," refers to silveriness of that part (and much of the fish).

Roughhead shiner   *Notropis semperasper* Gilbert

SYSTEMATICS

Notropis semperasper was described in 1961 from Potts and Dunlap creeks, tributaries of the Jackson River, upper James drainage, Virginia (Gilbert 1961b). It is a member of the subgenus *Notropis* (Snelson 1968; Jenkins and Burkhead 1975a) and is placed in the *ariommus* group with *N. scepticus*, *N. ariommus*, and *N. telescopus* (Coburn 1983).

As an endemic species of the upper James drainage, *Notropis semperasper* is notable in having no apparent close relative that is historically native to an adjacent drainage. Gilbert (1961b) suggested that it has affinity with *N. scepticus* of the south Atlantic slope. If these two species are derived from a common stock, they probably evolved independently in well-separated drainages (Hocutt et al. 1986). *Notropis scabriceps* of the New drainage was suggested as a close relative of *N. semperasper* by Jenkins et al. (1972), but further study (Jenkins and Burkhead 1975a) dispelled this.

DESCRIPTION

Materials.—From Gilbert (1961b), Jenkins and Burkhead (1975a), and 34 Virginia series. Life color mainly from several May-collected adults.

Anatomy.—A shiner with a somewhat rounded snout, large eye, and much pigment below the lateral line anteriorly; adults are 45–65 mm SL. Body moderately elongate, somewhat compressed; dorsal fin origin usually slightly posterior to pelvic fin base, occasionally above or moderately posterior to the posterior insertion of pelvic fin. Head moderate; eye large, essentially lateral; snout slightly acute to, more often, moderately rounded; mouth large, terminal, oblique. Anal fin margin concave. Breast nearly naked; belly fully or almost fully scaled.

Both sexes and all age-groups bear tubercles. Nuptial male with small, densely set tubercles on head, tiny tubercles on body except on breast and urosome; pectoral fin with dense patches of small tubercles; tiny scattered tubercles on other fins. Nuptial female similar except tubercles smaller and fins rarely tuberculate. Tubercles retained over most of the year, best developed during breeding season, lost by winter. Juvenile tuberculation similar in location to adult but typically less dense. A young specimen 17 mm SL has relatively few but proportionately large tubercles on snout and lower jaw. Genital papilla of both sexes fused to anal papilla; nuptial male papilla tubular, slightly protruding from recessed pit; female papilla flat, protruding from swollen anal mound.

Meristics.—Pharyngeal teeth usually 2,4–4,2; lateral line complete, scales (37)39–41(43); circumbody scales 26–29(31); circumpeduncle scales (11)13–14(15); predorsal scale rows

Fish 99 *Notropis semperasper* adult male 55 mm SL (operculum abnormal) (REJ 1200), VA, Craig County, Craig Creek, 21 September 1987.

(18)20–23(27). Dorsal rays 8; branched caudal rays 17; anal rays (9)10–11(12); pelvic rays 8; pectoral rays 15–16(17).

Color in Preservative.—Dorsum slightly or moderately dusky, dark middorsal stripe present; dorsolateral scales duskily outlined, scale centers usually peppered; midlateral stripe diffuse or dark anteriorly, darkest posteriorly, sometimes obscured by silver; anterior lateral line pores darkly stitched; many scattered melanophores or crosshatchings present below lateral line anteriorly, sometimes on entire lower side in adult, but often sparse or absent in juvenile; venter pale. Head dorsum and snout dusky; lips dark, chin with scattered dark pigment; cheek and lower opercle pale. Fins pale; caudal spot absent.

Color in Life.—Dorsum green to olive, side silver, venter silver or silver-white; chromatic nuptial coloration absent.

COMPARISON

Characters distinguishing *N. semperasper* from *N. rubellus* are in that account.

Notropis semperasper is discerned from *Lythrurus ardens* by: dark spot at dorsal fin origin [absent in *semperasper* vs. present in *ardens* (Figure 34I)].

Notropis semperasper is separated from *N. telescopus*, which apparently was recently introduced to the upper James drainage, by: (1) predorsal scale rows [(18)20–23(27) in *semperasper* vs. (12)13–15(16) in *telescopus*]; (2) anterior dorsolateral scales [more uniform in shape and size, and paler edged vs. few to several scales irregularly shaped or distinctly unequal in size, and darker edged, the upper and lower margins forming distinct horizontal zig-zag stripes].

BIOLOGY

The diet of 20 adult roughhead shiners was almost exclusively immature aquatic insects. Small amounts of sand and detritus in the gut indicate that some feeding occurs on the bottom (S. W. Hipple, in litt.). Both sexes mature in 2 years; the life span appears to be 3 years, perhaps rarely 4. Growth of the sexes is essentially alike; age-2 fish were about 31–61 mm SL (Jenkins and Burkhead 1975a). A 79-mm SL female is the largest known specimen.

Based on gonadal development and time of peak tuberculation, most spawning occurs from early or mid-May to early June, and may continue into July and perhaps August (Jenkins and Burkhead 1975a). The reproductive habitat and behavior are unknown. Loos et al. (1972) suggested that *N. semperasper* spawns over *Nocomis* nests. Maurakis et al. (1991) observed an intruding roughhead shiner drive a resident male *Exoglossum maxillingua* from its nest.

HABITAT

The roughhead shiner occupies warm, usually clear, medium streams to small rivers having moderate gradient. It is usually associated with runs of moderate current and sections of pools near appreciable flow (Jenkins and Burkhead 1975a). Gilbert (1961b) reported taking *N. semperasper* in riffles. We rarely collected it in riffles and occasionally observed it in swift runs. It occurs over a variety of substrates, most often slightly silted or unsilted bottoms. Nearly all of the occupied streams are of high quality.

DISTRIBUTION　Map 70

Notropis semperasper is endemic to the Valley and Ridge Province of the upper James drainage, Virginia; its range is the smallest of the three fishes endemic to the James drainage (the others being *Percina notogramma montuosa* and *Etheostoma longimanum*). It is one of the few upper James fishes unknown from the Blue Ridge and unknown to normally populate or straggle onto the Piedmont. The others are *Notropis volucellus, N. telescopus, Noturus gilberti,* and *Ameiurus platycephalus,* none of which may be native to the drainage. The contiguity within subpopulations and the sharpness of their range limits indicate that high gradient, small stream size, turbidity, and siltation combine to produce the tight distribution of the roughhead shiner (Jenkins and Burkhead 1975a).

Abundance.—Rare to common, generally uncommon.

REMARKS

The roughhead shiner warrants special concern status. It is limited to relatively pristine Valley and Ridge streams. It may have occupied streams near the lower boundary of the Valley and Ridge, but may have been extirpated by the increase of sediment during historical time. Jenkins and Burkhead (1975a) estimated that 432 rkm of streams were occupied in the upper James, about 35 rkm of which were lost recently by the creation of Lake Moomaw. We are apprehensive that the apparently introduced, rapidly spreading telescope shiner *N. telescopus* may competitively jeopardize the roughhead shiner.

Name.—*Semperasper* means "always rough," referring to the development of tubercles by young-of-the-year and juveniles, and to the retention (at least by adults) of tubercles through much of the year.

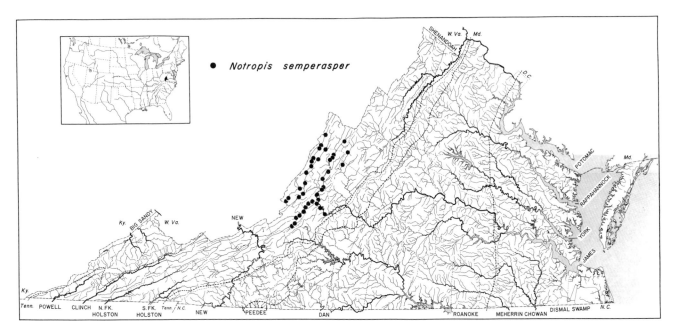

Map 70 Roughhead shiner.

Popeye shiner   *Notropis ariommus* (Cope)

SYSTEMATICS

Named from Indiana in 1868, the popeye shiner was infrequently captured but sufficiently known prior to 1900 to allow its recognition as a species; thereafter it was rarely seen until the 1960s. In 1939 the similar telescope shiner *N. telescopus* was reduced to a subspecies of *N. ariommus* in Kuhne (1939), apparently on the word of C. L. Hubbs (e.g., 1941b); other ichthyologists followed the move. Gilbert (1969) reaffirmed their species-level distinctness.

Notropis ariommus is a member of the subgenus *Notropis* (Snelson 1968; Gilbert 1969). Coburn (1983) recognized in the subgenus an *ariommus* group containing also *N. telescopus*, *N. semperasper*, and *N. scepticus*. Gilbert (1969) stated that *N. ariommus* most closely resembles *N. scepticus*.

DESCRIPTION

Materials.—From Gilbert (1969) and 24 Virginia lots. Life color from 3 Virginia adults.

Anatomy.—A shiner with a huge eye, nearly straight dorsolateral scale rows, and usually 9 anal rays; adults are 55–80 mm SL. Body moderate or somewhat elongate, slightly or moderately compressed; dorsal fin origin above pelvic fin base, usually mid-base. Head moderate; eye very large, essentially lateral; snout rounded or slightly pointed; mouth large, terminal, oblique. Breast about 80% scaled.

Nuptial male with densely distributed small tubercles on head, small to tiny tubercles on body except breast and urosome; pectoral fin with dense patches of tiny tubercles, other fins with scattered minute tubercles; female with tiny tubercles on snout. Male genital papilla small, tubular, recessed in pit; female genital papilla flat, fused with protruding anal papilla.

Fish 100 *Notropis ariommus* adult male 66 mm SL (TVA), TN, Maury County, Duck River, 6 May 1981.

Meristics.—Pharyngeal teeth usually 2,4–4,2; lateral line complete, scales (35)36–39; circumbody scales (22)23–25(28); circumpeduncle scales 12(14); predorsal scales (14)15–17(18). Dorsal rays 8; anal rays (8)9(10); pectoral rays (13)14–15.

Color in Preservative.—Dorsum dusky, dark middorsal stripe present; dorsolateral scales aligned in relatively straight horizontal rows, dark margined, and usually with slightly dusky centers; dark midlateral stripe often divided lengthwise into narrow upper line and wider lower stripe; anterior lateral line pores not stitched or vaguely stitched; lower side and venter immaculate. Head dorsum and snout dusky to dark; side of snout with cloudy spongy tissue in large specimens; lips dark, chin with dark broad-based "V" pigment pattern in about 70% of adults, otherwise a dark smudge; cheek and lower opercle pale. Fins pale; caudal spot absent, posterior end of midlateral stripe diffuse, rounded.

Color in Life Plate 18.—Dorsum pale olive to green-brown, middorsal stripe iridescent gold; dorsolateral scale margins dark olive or black; dorsolateral iridescent stripe gold, rosy, or bluish; side and venter silver. Side of snout, cheek, and opercle silver to slightly brassy. In nuptial male, rays of dorsal and caudal fins distinctly dark outlined, fin margins clear; anal and pelvic fins pale; pectoral fin pale straw; reproductive female lacks sharp outlining of dorsal and caudal rays, lower fins pale.

COMPARISON

Notropis ariommus is distinguished from *N. telescopus* (see also that species) by: (1) anal rays usually [9 in *ariommus* vs. 10 in *telescopus*]; (2) anterodorsolateral horizontal scale rows [nearly straight vs. distinctly down-curved]; (3) pigmentation bounding anterior lateral line pores [punctations vague or absent vs. dark-stitched]; (4) chin pigmentation [usually a dark broad-based "V" vs. melanophores scattered, "V" absent]; (5) circumbody scales [23–26 vs. 20–23]; (6) predorsal scales [15–18 vs. 13–15].

Notropis ariommus can be separated from somewhat similar juvenile *Luxilus chrysocephalus* by: (1) shape of anterior lateral line scales [normally shaped in *ariommus* (Figure 35C) vs. much higher than wide in *chrysocephalus* (Figure 35A)]; (2) eye size [very large vs. moderate]; (3) dorsolateral dark stripes [absent vs. usually 2–4 vague or dark stripes converging behind dorsal fin].

BIOLOGY

The life history of the popeye shiner is poorly known. The smallest mature individuals from Virginia are a 53-mm SL male and a 49-mm female. A 46-mm SL male is tuberculate (Gilbert 1969). Of Vir-

ginia adults, 18 males were 53–81 mm SL, mean, 67, and 18 females were 49–85 mm, mean, 66; both sexes form two size modes. The 85-mm SL female appears to be the size record for the species. Based on tubercle and gonadal development, spawning occurs from late May to late June. In early July, females had reduced ovaries with atretic ova, and males had lost most tubercles. We are unable to identify a few large specimens from the North Fork Holston River; they may be hybrids, *N. ariommus* × *N. telescopus* (NMB 155; REJ 926).

HABITAT

The popeye shiner inhabits warm, moderate-gradient, small to medium rivers that usually are clear. Rarely does it occupy small streams (e.g., Rice et al. 1983). The only Virginia record from a main-river tributary is from lowermost Copper Creek in late May. It is a current-loving minnow, usually occurring in runs and the heads of pools, seldom in riffles. Generally we found it associated with clean-swept gravel and small rubble; Gilbert (1969, 1980 *in* Lee et al. 1980) also described a gravel-substrate association. It often assembles in small schools in depths ranging about 0.5–1.5 m, and fares well at sites with diverse habitat such as braided channels, backwaters, and edges of water willow beds.

DISTRIBUTION   Map 71

Notropis ariommus is indigenous to most of the principal drainages of the Ohio basin and formerly occupied the western Lake Erie drainage. The historical range is wide, but populations north of the Ohio River are extirpated and those to the south generally are localized and widely disjunct (Gilbert 1969, 1980 *in* Lee et al. 1980; Trautman 1981; Warren and Cicerello 1983). In Virginia the popeye shiner occurs in the North Fork Holston, Clinch, and Powell rivers.

The popeye shiner has been thought to have declined in most of its range during 1894–1948 and to have subsequently rebounded well in some southern rivers (Gilbert 1969). Its capture at only three sites in the whole range during 1894–1948 (Etnier et al. 1979) is partial evidence of decline. Although it is extirpated north of the Ohio River, we are unsure that it declined in much of the area south.

As Gilbert (1969) pointed out, *N. ariommus* was not found during 1894–1948 at several sites south of the Ohio River where it previously had been taken. However, this 56-year span includes a period of general inactivity in surveying for eastern North American freshwater fishes. Further, *N. ariommus* typically is a

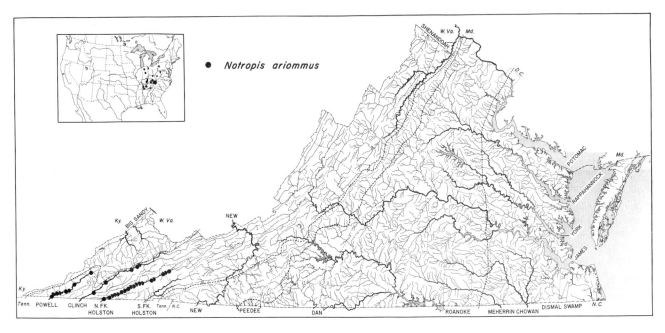

Map 71   Popeye shiner.

river inhabitant; such waters generally had been the least sampled. Thus Gilbert's general scenario of decline and increase may not apply to several southern populations.

The varied success of *N. ariommus* in Virginia partly supports Gilbert's hypothesis. It was first found in the North Fork Holston River in 1970, and by 1980 it was widely distributed and sometimes common. The population may have been suppressed by pollution since the early 1900s; it was not detected in 1928 by H. R. Becker nor during the 1950s by R. D. Ross, based on our study of Ross and Carico's (1963) specimens reported as *N. ariommus telescopus*. The population may have been depressed even before 1900, possibly by siltation; Cope and Jordan did not find the species in the Holston of Virginia during 1867 and 1888 respectively.

The early status of *N. ariommus* in the upper Clinch River is uncertain; the stream was scantily collected until the 1960s. Much of the Clinch population in Virginia presumably was eliminated in the 1967 fish kill. Tributary mouths likely were refugia during the kill and for a brief period after. Of the five popeye shiner records, the upper three were made during 1969–1970 near and on either side of the pollutant outfall in Russell County. The next downstream record, from Pendleton Island, Scott County, in 1984 (C. F. Saylor, in litt.), indicates that the popeye shiner has reinfiltrated the center of the killed zone. The lower record (10 adults) from lowermost Copper Creek in 1971 is the only one for this intensively

sampled section, suggesting that the fish immigrated from the Clinch River. Surprisingly, the large area of suitable habitat in the Clinch River at Speers Ferry, 0.4 rkm below Copper Creek, has not yielded *N. ariommus* despite considerable sampling from July 1967 to 1984.

The Powell River, Virginia, population of *N. ariommus* is doing well. Its early history is unknown because the lower main channel was essentially unsurveyed before 1968, the year of the first capture (TVA 1970).

Abundance.—Usually rare or uncommon, occasionally common.

REMARKS

The popeye shiner has been recommended for special concern status in Virginia because of its limited distribution—restriction to three main-river channels—and an affinity for clean gravel substrate. Its healthy status in the North Fork Holston is an encouraging example of recovery upon abatement of habitat degradation.

The rarity or patchy distribution of *N. ariommus* in the upper Clinch is only partly attributable to the fish kill. It may result from normal population fluctuation, as exhibited by the other rare or localized gravel-run inhabitants in the upper Clinch: *Erimyatax cahni*, *Ammocrypta clara*, and *Etheostoma tippecanoe*.

The hugeness of the eye of *N. ariommus* is related to

retention of that relative size from an early developmental stage. In most other minnows the eye exhibits negative allometric growth; that is, its proportion of the body length decreases with increase of the body length. The eye of *N. ariommus* indicates that vision is important to this species for detecting prey.

Name.—Ariommus means "large eye."

Telescope shiner   *Notropis telescopus* (Cope)

SYSTEMATICS

Named in 1868 from the Holston system, Virginia (Cope 1868a), *N. telescopus* is a member of the *ariommus* group of the subgenus *Notropis* (Coburn 1983). During 1939–1968 it was considered a subspecies of the popeye shiner (see *N. ariommus*).

DESCRIPTION

Materials.—From Gilbert (1969) and 21 Virginia lots; predorsal scale row and anal ray counts from 28 James drainage specimens are included. Life color from Pflieger (1975) and 2 Virginia adults.

Anatomy.—A shiner with a large eye, ventrally dipping horizontal anterior dorsolateral scale rows, and usually 10 anal rays; adults are 45–60 mm SL. Body moderate or somewhat elongate in profile, slightly compressed; dorsal fin origin above pelvic fin base, usually mid-base. Head moderate; eye large, lateral; snout slightly acute or somewhat rounded; mouth large, terminal, oblique. Breast and belly fully scaled.

Nuptial male with densely spaced small tubercles on head, small to tiny tubercles on body except absent on urosome; pectoral fin with dense patches of tiny tubercles, other fins with minute scattered tubercles. Female with small tubercles on head, body, and, rarely, pectoral fin. Male genital papilla small, tubular, recessed in pit; that of female slightly larger, protruding from pit.

Meristics.—Pharyngeal teeth usually 2,4–4,2; lateral line complete, scales (35)36–39: circumbody scales (19)20–24(25); circumpeduncle scales (11)12(13); predorsal scales (12)13–15(17); predorsal scale rows (12)13–15(16). Dorsal rays 8; anal rays (9)10–11(12) [often 9, usually 10 in James drainage]; pelvic rays 8; pectoral rays 14–16.

Color in Preservative.—Dorsum slightly or moderately dusky, dark middorsal stripe present; dorsolateral scales usually dark margined and anteriorly forming 2–3 downcurving dark zig-zag lines, the lines formed by apposition of the lower ends of scale-margin markings with the upper ends of the margins in the scale row just below; caudal peduncle with short pale stripe dorsolaterally; dark midlateral stripe usually very diffuse anteriorly, intense posteriorly; anterior or all lateral line pores dark stitched; lower side and venter pale. Head dorsum and snout moderately dusky; lips dark; chin with scattered melanophores; cheek and lower opercle pale. Fins pale; caudal spot absent, vague, or dark.

Color in Life Plate 18.—Back dark olive, middorsal stripe and scale margins black; side silver; venter silver-white; fins pale. Chromatic nuptial color absent.

Larvae.—Described by Loos and Fuiman (1978) and Fuiman et al. (1983).

COMPARISON

A primary mark of this species is the large nape and anterior dorsolateral scales; usually a few to several of these are distinctly irregular in shape and markedly unequal in size. These traits often are rendered obvious by the rather dark scale margins, which in part form zig-zag stripes along the back. See accounts of *N. leuciodus*, *N. ariommus*, and *N. semperasper* for comparison with those species.

BIOLOGY

Little has been published on the life history of the telescope shiner. Insects were eaten by Missouri fish,

Fish 101 *Notropis telescopus* adult female 50 mm SL (REJ 1103), VA, Washington County, North Fork Holston River, 6 June 1984.

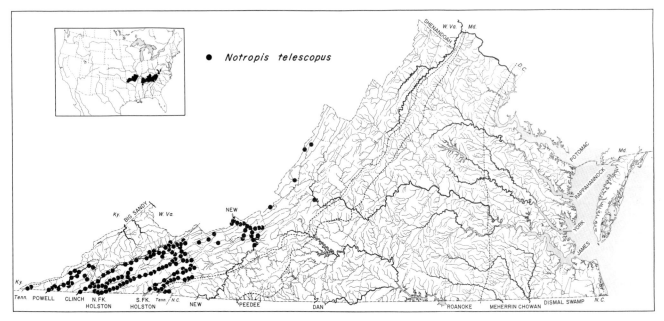

Map 72 Telescope shiner.

and the diet of New River specimens was dominated by blackflies and midges (Pflieger 1975; Hess 1983). Twenty fish from the Clinch and Holston rivers consumed immature benthic insects and adult midges, the latter indicating surface feeding (K. M. Sullivan, in litt.).

Among our Virginia samples the smallest mature fish are a male 43 mm SL and a female 45 mm. Sixteen adult males were 43–55 mm SL, mean, 49; 19 females were 45–69 mm, mean, 54. Our largest Virginia adult is a 72-mm SL female; Gilbert (*in* Lee et al. 1980) reported a maximum of 78 mm SL.

Spawning apparently occurs in May and June, based on gonadal development and tuberculation. Females freely exuded ova in mid-May and were in postspawning condition in late June. The possible hybrid *N. ariommus* × *N. telescopus* is noted under *N. ariommus*.

HABITAT

Notropis telescopus occupies typically clear, cool and warm, moderate-gradient streams. It is one of the most upstream-extending shiners; it ranges into lower headwaters, perhaps owing to a rather low temperature preference of 20°C (Cherry et al. 1977). It also flourishes in large rivers of the upper Tennessee drainage. The telescope shiner usually occurs in backwaters, flowing pools, and runs that have hard or silty substrates. It is a schooling shiner and often mixes with other *Notropis*. The home range is about

30 m in large pools and up to 50 m in pools lacking predators (Barclay 1984).

DISTRIBUTION   Map 72

The telescope shiner exhibits a distribution pattern similar to that of *Cyprinella galactura*. The two large upland population centers—in the Appalachians and Ozarks—are divided by Mississippi Valley lowlands. The eastern center encompasses the Cumberland and Tennessee drainages. A small population in the upper Green drainage may be native (Warren and Cicerello 1983). The populations in the New and James drainages obviously are introduced.

In Virginia the range of *N. telescopus* spans from all major trunks of the Tennessee drainage into the headwaters of moderate-gradient tributaries. The range limits coincide with edges of the Valley and Ridge Province. High stream gradients may prevent significant populating of the Blue Ridge and Appalachian Plateau, for the shiner largely avoids streams in the higher mountains of the Valley and Ridge.

In the New drainage, *N. telescopus* apparently was introduced in the Virginia section below Claytor Dam and has literally swept through that part of the drainage, colonized the West Virginia part, and established itself in the Kanawha River. Gilbert (1969) and Ross (1969, as *N. ariommus*) regarded the New drainage population to be introduced, but they had scant data. The data now available from many sources support its introduced status and, furthermore, suggest rapid dispersal.

All captures of *N. telescopus* in the New drainage before 1972 were in Virginia; the first two occurred in 1958 in lower Big Walker Creek (UR 427, 430; Map 72). In 1962 it was taken nearby in lowermost Little Walker Creek. Above Big Walker Creek, it was found in lower Spruce Run and at two places in lower Sinking Creek in 1961. Below Walker Creek, it was in the midsection of the Wolf Creek system by 1971. Obviously the telescope shiner was dispersing through the New River, in much of which (below Claytor Dam) it was caught during 1971–1972 (e.g., Hocutt et al. 1973; Ross 1973).

The pattern of these and subsequent records indicates that the shiner was established in the Virginia portion of the New drainage in the mid- or late 1950s. It was not taken in surveys during 1938–1957, most notably those by G. W. Burton (Burton and Odum 1945), E. C. Raney, and R. D. Ross (Ross and Perkins 1959). The range of *N. telescopus* in the Virginia portion of the New drainage is now wide and apparently contiguous. Below Claytor Dam, most Virginia streams or major sections thereof that lack a record have been sampled scantily or not at all in recent years.

Notropis telescopus almost certainly was transplanted from the Tennessee drainage to the New, but we are uncertain in which stream the New drainage population was founded. We believe it to be in the middle third of the Virginia section below Claytor Dam, based on the sites of the several earliest records and because the fish seems to have spread in both directions from there. If so, then downstream dispersal has occurred faster and farther than upstream dispersal.

The telescope shiner has room to expand farther upstream. It occurs near but is unknown from the Little River system, the first major tributary below Claytor Dam. The two Little River records in Lee et al. (1980) are based on shiners other than *N. telescopus* (C. R. Gilbert, in litt.; UR 1561, 1947), but this was not realized at the time Jenkins submitted the records for plotting.

In the West Virginia portion of the New drainage, the telescope shiner was recorded during 1972–1974 in the lower portion of the East River and the Greenbrier system (Hambrick et al. 1973; Stauffer et al. 1975; Hocutt et al. 1978). It is one of the most abundant fishes in the New River from Bluestone Dam (just above the Greenbrier mouth) to about 16 rkm downstream (Hess 1983; Lobb 1986). It now extends into the lower Gauley system of the New drainage and below Kanawha Falls into the upper Kanawha River (Hocutt et al. 1979; Gilbert *in* Lee et al. 1980).

In the extreme upper James drainage, *N. telescopus* was first captured during 1983–1986 in four tributaries: Back Creek, Little Back Creek, Dunlap Creek, and, according to D. A. Cincotta (personal communication), the West Virginia portion of Potts Creek. All of these streams were extensively sampled during 1955–1973. A single introduction is likely; it probably predated closure in 1980 of Gathright Dam on the Jackson River, because the dam and its Lake Moomaw split the populations. In 1987 the shiner was found well below these streams in lowermost Catawba Creek, whereas it was absent in two collections made in the creek during 1964–1965.

Abundance.—Uncommon to abundant; one of the more abundant *Notropis* in the Tennessee drainage and in the New drainage below Claytor Lake. It was common in our Catawba Creek collection.

REMARKS

Rates of dispersal generally are poorly known for North American freshwater fishes. Introduced species afford opportunities to monitor their success or lack thereof. The spread of the telescope shiner in the New drainage has been fairly rapid, greater than that of the Roanoke darter in the lower New, and similar to that of the saffron shiner in the upper New. It will be interesting to chart the expected further invasion of *N. telescopus* in the James drainage, where varying extents of dispersal have been noted for the probably introduced black jumprock, orangefin madtom, and Roanoke darter.

Name.—*Telescopus* means "far seeing," in reference to the large eye.

Spottail shiner   *Notropis hudsonius* (Clinton)

SYSTEMATICS

The spottail shiner was described from New York in 1824 by the inventor DeWitt Clinton. Its phylogenetic position is uncertain. We arbitrarily place it after most of the shiner subgenera that typically have a 2,4–4,2 dental formula. In external anatomy and color it strongly resembles *Hybopsis amblops*, the type species of the *amblops* group, a lineage of shinerlike "chubs." Mayden (1989) found *N. hudsonius* to have a skeletal trait nearly unique to the *amblops* group. *Notropis hudsonius* lacks the small barbel typical of the *amblops* group but so does one member of that group.

Notropis hudsonius ranges and varies widely; it has been divided into four subspecies, two of which occur in Virginia (Hubbs and Lagler 1958). Seaman (1968) considered the subspecies to be invalid because of clinal gradations in morphology and irregular patterns of variation in color. Tooth counts are highly variable; of 20 different phenotypes in Minnesota, the dominant formula was expressed in only about 50% of the specimens (Eastman and Underhill 1973).

DESCRIPTION

Materials.—From central Atlantic slope populations (Seaman 1968; our 36 Virginia lots). Life color from several Virginia adults.

Anatomy.—A somewhat slim shiner with a large eye, rounded snout, subterminal or inferior mouth, usually a caudal spot, and pelvic rays often 9; adults are 60–90 mm SL. Body moderately elongate, somewhat compressed; dorsal fin origin usually above anterior half of pelvic fin base, occasionally slightly anterior to pelvic origin. Head moderate; eye large, supralateral, pupil often slightly wider vertically; snout well rounded; mouth moderate, distinctly subterminal or slightly inferior. Breast and belly usually fully scaled.

Nuptial male with tiny tubercles on much of head; minute tubercles on anterior body; files of tiny tubercles on pectoral fin; other fins with tubercles few, minute, or absent. Gravid female with minute tubercles on head and nape only. Seaman (1968) found greater tubercle development. Genital papilla small in both sexes.

Meristics.—Pharyngeal teeth usually 2,4–4,2, 2,4–4,1, 1,4–4,2, or 1,4–4,1; rarely the minor row tooth is absent on one or both sides; lateral line complete, scales (34)35–38(40); scales above lateral line 11–13(14); scales below lateral line (11)12–13(14); circumbody scales (24)26–28(30); predorsal scales (12)13–15(17). Anal rays (7)8(9); pelvic rays (7)8–9(10); pectoral rays 13–16(17).

Color in Preservative.—Large juvenile and adult with slightly or moderately dusky dorsum and upper side, scales dark edged, alignment of edging occasionally effecting dusky narrow horizontal zig-zag lines; pre- and postdorsal stripe narrow, faint or moderately bold, rarely absent. Mid-lateral stripe narrow to moderate in width, faint to bold, darkest posteriorly, diffusing anteriorly and underlined there by dark-stitched lateral line pores; melanophores usually faintly extending for about one scale row below lateral line; lower side and venter pale. Head dorsum, snout, and upper lip dusky to dark; lower lip, lower side, and underside of head pale. Dorsal fin pale; caudal spot usually present, variable in intensity, size, and shape, and disconnected from or confluent with lateral stripe; basal portion of most upper and lower caudal rays somewhat pigmented, diffusing distally; lower fins pale.

Some juvenile and adult spottail shiners are quite pallid overall, lateral stripe vague, caudal spot absent. Young and

Fish 102 *Notropis hudsonius* adult male 56 mm SL (REJ 1045), VA, Craig County, Craig Creek, 26 September 1983.

Fish 103 *Notropis hudsonius* adult male 65 mm SL (REJ 968), VA, Patrick County, Ararat River, 8 June 1983.

small juvenile typically have narrow dark lateral stripe and relatively large, round or oval caudal spot.

Color in Life.—Dorsum pale olive; side silver, sometimes with gold or brassy sheen; venter white. Nuptial adult apparently same color as nonbreeding adult.

Larvae.—Described by Mansueti and Hardy (1967), Lippson and Moran (1974), Jones et al. (1978), Loos and Fuiman (1978), Loos et al. (1979), Snyder (1979), Heufelder and Fuiman (1982), and Fuiman et al. (1983), who noted the possible misidentification of specimens illustrated in first three references.

BIOLOGY

Life history aspects of the spottail shiner have been well analyzed in the Great Lakes and other northern areas, and several contributions to its biology are from eastern populations; a bibliography is by Shapiro (1975). In northern areas this species ate microcrustaceans, aquatic and terrestrial insects, fingernail clams, young shiners, fish eggs, and plant material (Forbes and Richardson 1920; Cahn 1927; Edsall 1964; Carlander 1969; Vadas 1990). In the New River it took a greater percentage (84%) of immature blackflies than did the other 25 fish species sampled (Hess 1983). In the James River estuary, *N. hudsonius* fed mostly on microcrustaceans, insects, mollusks (particularly the Asiatic clam), and plant material including seeds (VIMS 1977).

Age at maturation varies with growth rate; rapidly growing fish mature by age 1 or 2, slower growing ones mature by age 2 or 3. Threshold size for maturation is about 55 mm SL; maximum life span is 5 years. Females live longer and reach larger size than males (Peer 1966; Wells and House 1974; Becker 1983). Age-2 fish from northern populations were 58–102 mm TL (Carlander 1969). In the James River estuary age-2 individuals averaged 90 mm TL (VIMS 1977). A Virginia specimen of about 135 mm TL was reported by White (1976); the largest known spottail shiner seems to be about 147 mm TL from Ohio (Trautman 1981).

Spawning time is dependent on temperature. In Lake Michigan it may start in late June and extend into early September (Wells and House 1974). In Virginia, breeding appears to occur during mid-April to mid-June. Females were gravid in the James River estuary during April (VIMS 1977); late June adults were spent and July fish had shrunken gonads. Larvae were captured in late May and early June in the Potomac River (Loos et al. 1979).

In Lake Michigan spawning occurred at variable depths (up to 4.6 m) over sandy bottom and in patches of filamentous algae (Wells and House 1974). In the Potomac River and elsewhere, eggs were found attached to sand and gravel in shallow riffles (Loos et al. 1979). Reproduction also takes place in tidal waters. Spawning occurs as large aggregations and in groups of two to five individuals (Wang and Kernehan 1979). Fecundity is 100–8,898 ova (Wells and House 1974; Jones et al. 1978).

HABITAT

Notropis hudsonius lives in an array of lotic habitats, ranging from typically clear, mostly rocky, moderate-gradient streams to often turbid, sandy, muddy, silty, and sluggish water. Although it stably populates some medium-sized mountain streams, it seems more at home in upland large rivers and estuaries. It occupies pools, backwaters, runs, and, rarely, riffles. It is known from only two Virginia reservoirs but in northern regions it typically inhabits (in addition to rivers) shallow and offshore portions of lakes, sometimes to considerable depth (Wells and House 1974). The spottail shiner commonly occupies tidal fresh and brackish water, in salinities as high as 10.7‰ (Jones et al. 1978), and also occupies inundated marshes (Rozas and Odum 1987a, 1987b). In estuaries it is more abundant in open areas than among submerged vegetation (Rozas and Odum 1987c). It is a warmwater fish in Virginia but occupies year-round cool and cold northern waters; temperature preference data are summarized by Coutant (1977).

DISTRIBUTION   Map 73

Notropis hudsonius, one of the widest ranging North American minnows, occurs from about the Mackenzie River mouth in northern Canada through the upper and middle Mississippi basin, the Great Lakes region, and on the Atlantic slope from the St. Lawrence to the Altamaha drainage, Georgia.

In Virginia the spottail shiner is native to all major Atlantic slope drainages. Of minor drainages, it is definitely known only from the Piankatank (Merriner et al. 1976). The record at the Dismal Swamp periphery is from Jordan's (1889b) report; his list from the site has been questioned for other species (*Biogeography*). The contiguous distribution in estuarine rivers and somewhat higher-elevation portions of Chesapeake drainages is well documented; the paucity of records from the Piedmont reaches of the James, Roanoke, and Dan rivers is related to scant collecting effort. We are baffled by the apparent scarcity or localization of the species in the Appomattox River and main stems of the Chowan drainage.

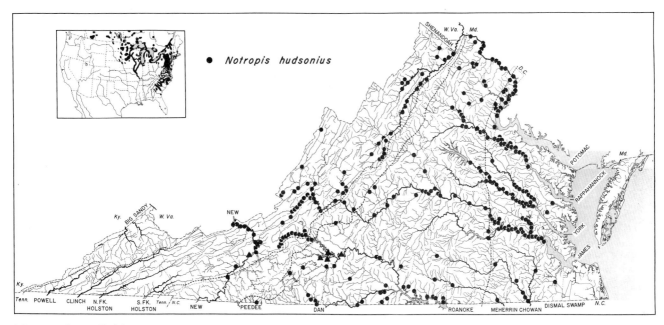

Map 73   Spottail shiner.

The spottail shiner probably was introduced to the New drainage, probably in Claytor Lake as bait, purposely (for forage), or inadvertently along with game-fish stockings. The first capture in the New drainage was from Claytor Lake during 1948–1949 (Rosebery 1950b); the reservoir had been created in 1939 and heavily stocked thereafter. *Notropis hudsonius* still populates Claytor Lake (Boaze 1972). Because of its virtual restriction below Claytor Dam to the main channel and the near absence of collecting therein before 1971, *N. hudsonius* was taken in the New River only once during 1950–1970—in 1961 well below Claytor Lake. During 1971–1974 it was collected widely in the New River below Claytor Lake (Hocutt et al. 1973; Ross 1973). The first West Virginia record is dated 1972, from the lower East River near the Virginia line (Hambrick et al. 1973; Stauffer et al. 1975). The spottail apparently spread through Bluestone Reservoir, West Virginia, and now occupies the New River somewhat below Bluestone Dam (Hess 1983; Lobb 1986). It has moved above Claytor Lake, the uppermost record being from a 1973 collection (Benfield and Cairns 1974).

We have not seen the specimen(s) reported as *N. hudsonius* from "Holston River" by Fowler (1923), and would not accept the locality data if the specimen is this species; the spottail shiner is absent from the Ohio basin except for the introduced population noted above.

Abundance.—Generally rare or uncommon, locally common, in medium-sized mountain and Piedmont streams; usually uncommon or common on the Coastal Plain, chiefly in large rivers and estuaries.

REMARKS

The spottail shiner is important forage to gamefishes in northern lakes and rivers; the same likely is true in Virginia.

Name.—*Hudsonius*, "of the Hudson," the river from which it was described.

New River shiner   *Notropis scabriceps* (Cope)

SYSTEMATICS

Notropis scabriceps was described from Virginia tributaries of the New drainage by Cope (1868a). Its subgeneric affinities are not clear. Jenkins (*in* Lee et al. 1980 and *in* Hocutt et al. 1986) noted its formerly reputed allies and suggested that this endemic species of the New drainage is closely related to the Ozarkian endemic species *N. greenei*, also of uncertain affinity.

DESCRIPTION

Materials.—Sixteen Virginia and 3 North Carolina lots; counts from 35 specimens. Color in life from 3 nuptial or near-nuptial adults.

Fish 104 *Notropis scabriceps* adult female 68 mm SL (NMB 868), VA, Floyd County, Little River, 27 April 1984.

Anatomy.—A shiner with a subterminal mouth, large supralateral eye, small caudal spot often present, and the head of nuptial male heavily tuberculate; adults are 45–65 mm SL. Body build moderate overall, somewhat stocky anteriorly, slightly compressed; dorsal fin origin above pelvic fin base, usually the posterior half of the base. Head moderate in length, somewhat broad; eye large, supralateral; mouth moderate, subterminal, slightly oblique. Breast 80–100% scaled; belly full scaled.

Nuptial male heavily tuberculate, small to medium dense-set tubercles on most of head; body tuberculation best developed anteriorly, tiny tubercles on most body scales including breast and anterior belly of peak male; pectoral fin with multiple rows of tiny tubercles on all anterior rays; pelvic and anal fins with few minute tubercles only in peak male. Female head and body tuberculation much reduced compared with equal-sized male; fins lack tubercles. Our early September adults lack tubercles; tubercles on November specimens (Shingleton 1985) may be old decapped tubercle cores. Genital papilla small, recessed in pit in male; slightly larger, slightly protruding in nuptial female.

Meristics.—Pharyngeal teeth usually 2,4–4,2, often 2,4–4,1 or 1,4–4,2, rarely 1,4–4,1; lateral line complete, scales 36–37(38); circumbody scales (23)25–27(29); circumpeduncle scales 12–13(16); predorsal scale rows (14)15–18(19). Dorsal rays 8; principal caudal rays 19(20); anal rays 8(9); pelvic rays 8(9); pectoral rays (14)15–16. Gill rakers 5–7; post-Weberian vertebrae 33–34.

Color in Preservative.—Dorsum slightly dusky; middorsal stripe very narrow, faint, or absent; upper body scales duskily or darkly submargined, medians slightly or moderately dusky. Midlateral stripe narrow to moderate in width, darkest posteriorly, diffuse or absent anteriorly; anterior lateral line pores weakly or darkly stitched; scales duskily submargined to about one scale row below lateral line; lower side and venter pale. Head dorsum, snout, and lips dusky; chin, cheek, and lower opercle pale.

Fins completely or essentially pale; dorsal fin base area usually with dark-pale-dark pattern, anterior one-third–one-half of fin base paler than adjacent predorsal midline and posterior portion of base (Figure 34D); caudal spot small, variably shaped, often triangular, or spot often absent.

Color in Life Plate 18.—Upper body straw or medium olive with silver and lime iridescence; midbody silver, lateral stripe leaden or masked by brilliant silver that sometimes has pale lime and lavender reflections; lower side anteriorly and belly silver-white, lower side posteriorly white with scattered silver scales. Head dorsum and snout olive to dusky black; iris silver, inner rim gold or brass tinted; cheek and lower opercle bright silver. Fins pale except pectoral with pale olive wash anteriorly. Reproductive color change apparently absent.

COMPARISON

The New River shiner is superficially quite similar to, and often collected with, the mimic shiner *N. volucellus*. They are distinguished by: (1) pharyngeal teeth [1,4–4,1 to, usually, 2,4–4,2 in *scabriceps vs.* 4–4 in *volucellus*]; (2) circumbody scales usually [25–27 *vs.* 19–22]; (3) height relative to width of the exposed portion of anterior lateral line scales [height about 2 times more than width (Figure 35C) *vs.* height clearly greater than 2 times width (Figure 35B)]; (4) eye size; position [usually larger; distinctly supralateral *vs.* usually smaller; lateral or very slightly supralateral]; (5) nuptial male tuberculation on cheek just below eye compared with that on lower part of cheek [about equally developed (a rather uniformly rough-headed fish, most head tubercles small to medium) *vs.* poorly developed or absent (tubercles well developed mainly on snout and lower cheek, most head tubercles tiny to small]. Do not confuse neuromasts—pit-like sensory structures—with tubercles. Neuromasts are best and extensively developed in *volucellus*; see *Comparison* under that species.

BIOLOGY

The diet of *N. scabriceps* is largely unknown. A few adults from a Virginia collection had eaten caddisfly larvae and leeches. These items and the subterminal mouth indicate bottom-oriented feeding.

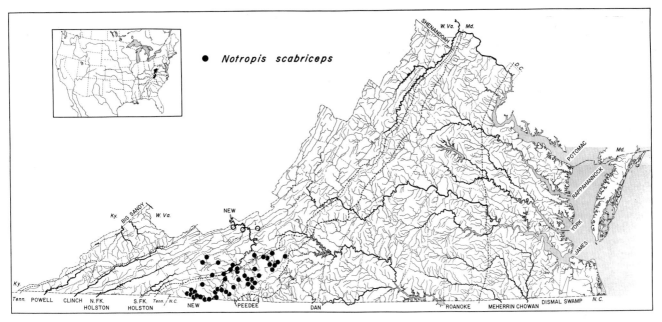

Map 74 New River shiner. Open circles denote pre-1900 Valley and Ridge Province records.

Shingleton (1985) found age-2 fish to be adult and noted that some age-1 individuals mature in late summer in the Greenbrier River, West Virginia; we determined the same for Virginia and North Carolina. Maximum longevity is about 3 years. No growth difference occurred between the sexes in West Virginia, where age-2 adults average 58 mm TL. Of adults taken in Virginia and North Carolina from early May to mid-August, 36 males were 41–65 mm SL, mean, 52, and 41 females were 41–69 mm, mean, 52. The largest Virginia specimen is 72 mm SL, 90 mm TL, apparently the largest known.

Spawning may start in late May, peak during June, and may extend well into August in West Virginia, based on ovarian development (Shingleton 1985); our data indicate the same for Virginia and North Carolina. Shingleton's mature ova counts of 362–1,930 likely underestimate fecundity; he found evidence that females spawn more than once a year.

HABITAT

Notropis scabriceps occupies small and large, normally clear tributaries of somewhat high to moderate gradient, and inhabits the large upper main channel of the New River. It occurs in pools and backwaters, often near swift water, and avoids heavily silted areas. The New River shiner is cool-adapted; its final preferred temperature of 19.3°C (Shingleton et al. 1981) is lower than that of 12 of the 15 New drainage fish species (all but the trouts) tested by Cherry et al.

(1977). In Virginia it commonly populates lower reaches of trout creeks as well as somewhat warm streams. It may prefer soft water such as occurs in most Blue Ridge Province streams; the only post-1957 record from the calcareous Valley and Ridge Province is from North Fork Reed Creek in 1976.

DISTRIBUTION   Map 74

The vernacular name connotes the restriction of this species to the New drainage. Its strongholds are the Blue Ridge of North Carolina and Virginia and the Greenbrier system in the Valley and Ridge Province of West Virginia. There are three notable departures from a general distribution over the total range (Jenkins *in* Lee et al. 1980): localization in the Appalachian Plateau of West Virginia; natural absence or recent human-caused extirpation in parts of the Valley and Ridge of Virginia; and absence from the New River in West Virginia and much of Virginia.

The general scarcity of *N. scabriceps* in the Appalachian Plateau, contrasted with its abundance in the upper Greenbrier (Hocutt et al. 1978, 1979; Shingleton 1985) and the Blue Ridge, may be related to watershed damage from coal mining and logging.

The New River shiner seems to have receded from much of the Valley and Ridge Province. The three verified records (open circles) in the northern half of the province in Virginia stem from the late 1800s. The middle Wolf Creek record of 1885 (Jenkins *in* Lee et al. 1980) actually is near the mouth; not plotted is a dubious record for upper Spruce Run by Ross and Perkins (1959). The waning of *N. scabriceps* from the Valley and Ridge in Virginia may be associated with warming of streams by removal of riparian vegetation; the low-temperature preference of the species is corollary.

In the New River, *N. scabriceps* is now virtually restricted to the Blue Ridge portion. Cope (1868b) implied that it occupied the New River well within the Valley and Ridge, but none of his specimens are from the river (Gilbert 1978b). The only acceptable record from well below the Blue Ridge is from West Virginia (Addair 1944). Although impoundment by Bluestone Reservoir and Claytor Lake may have caused extirpation from the inundated reaches, the two tailwaters likely offer acceptable temperatures. Perhaps then, *N. scabriceps* avoids the larger river reaches.

Abundance.—Usually rare or uncommon in the Valley and Ridge, typically uncommon or common in the Blue Ridge.

REMARKS

The New River shiner is isolated to a single drainage. It was considered to be threatened in North Carolina, largely in response to a now withdrawn proposal for major impoundment, and has been regarded as imperiled in West Virginia (Bailey 1977; Hocutt et al. 1979). Although not jeopardized in much of the known range in Virginia (Jenkins and Musick 1979), the loss of some populations indicates a lability to decline. On another time scale, if indeed *N. scabriceps* is closely related to the Ozarkian *N. greenei*, extensive extirpation of their ancestral form occurred prehistorically.

Name.—*Scabriceps* means "rough head"; the head of reproductive males has more abrasive tubercle armament than that of the roughhead shiner *N. semperasper*.

Mimic shiner   *Notropis volucellus* (Cope)

SYSTEMATICS

Described in 1865 from Michigan, the mimic shiner is the name bearer of the *volucellus* group. The group is unified partly by markedly elevated anterior lateral line scales and pectoral fin tuberculation—medium-sized uniserial tubercles, those on the first ray (at least in *N. volucellus*) slightly larger than those on the second. The latter is one of the traits linking the *volucellus* group to the *spectrunculus* group (see next species).

The *volucellus* group is part of an array of small, largely pallid shiners, most of them having 7 or 8 anal rays, 4–4 pharyngeal teeth, and a subterminal or inferior mouth. With varied constituency including the next five species in this book, the array sometimes has been united with other shiners in the subgenus *Alburnops*. The typical members of *Alburnops*, such as *N. blennius*, do not occur in Virginia. Specialists tend to subdivide *Alburnops* or extract from it highly distinctive species and well-defined monophyletic groups (Swift 1970; Snelson 1971; Loos and Fuiman 1978; Burr and Mayden 1981; Chernoff et al. 1982; Mayden 1989; Coburn and Cavender 1992).

The *volucellus* group itself remains poorly understood systematically. It includes *N. volucellus*, *N. cahabae*, *N. buchanani*, perhaps *N. saladonis*, at least one undescribed species, and the recently elevated *N. wickliffi* addressed by Ramsey (1975), Gilbert (1978b), Trautman (1981), Bauer (*in* Trautman 1981), Starnes and Etnier (1986), and Mayden and Kuhajda (1989).

DESCRIPTION

Materials.—Forty Virginia lots; counts from 54 specimens from the James, Chowan, Roanoke, New, and Tennessee drainages. Life color from Cross (1967) and Trautman (1981).

Anatomy.—A shiner with a subterminal or inferior mouth, strongly elevated anterior lateral scales, dorsal fin with all rays lined by pigment but membranes unpigmented, and a small caudal spot; adults are 35–55 mm SL. Body form moderate, slightly compressed; dorsal fin origin above pelvic fin base, usually the posterior half. Head moderate; eye medium or large, lateral or slightly supralateral; snout slightly or moderately rounded; mouth small or moderate, subterminal or slightly inferior, slightly oblique. Anterior lateral line scales markedly elevated; breast (0)20–100% scaled; belly (70)100% scaled.

Nuptial male with tiny or small tubercles on head, tubercles dense-set in peak male on tip and upper side of snout; tubercles moderately developed on lower cheek, chin, and lower jaw rami, and scattered on head dorsum; body often lacking tubercles, and when tubercles present, they are minute along scale margins, best developed dorsolaterally. Pectoral fin with medium-sized (for fins) tubercles in mostly one row on rays 1–5 or more, usually 2 tubercles per ray segment, and tubercles on first ray tending slightly larger than those on second ray. Female apparently lacks tubercles. Male genital papilla small, recessed in pit, the pit sometimes largely covered by scales; female papilla often slightly larger, sometimes bulbous.

Meristics.—Pharyngeal teeth 4–4; lateral line complete, scales (34)35–38(39); circumbody scales (18)19–22(24); cir-

Fish 105 *Notropis volucellus* adult female 48 mm SL (WHH 270), TN, Greene County, Nolichucky River, 19 June 1984.

cumpeduncle scales (10)12; predorsal scales 13–16(17); predorsal scale rows 13–15(16). Anal rays (7)8(9), almost always 8; pectoral rays (12)13–15. Cephalic lateralis, IO usually uninterrupted, pores (9)11–12(14); SO (7)8–9(10); POM (7)8–11(12); ST usually interrupted, (1)2–3(4) per side.

Color in Preservative.—Upper body slightly to moderately dusky; middorsal stripe narrow, moderately distinct or absent; upper body scales duskily or darkly submargined, scale medians pale or dusky. Midlateral stripe narrow to moderate in width, darkest posteriorly, diffuse or, usually, absent anteriorly; anterior lateral line pores weakly or boldly dark stitched; melanophores usually extending the width of one scale row below lateral line on anterior half of body; lower side and venter pale. Head dorsum and snout dusky; upper lip usually well stippled with melanophores, lower lip usually unpigmented or with few melanophores, very rarely well marked; chin, cheek (except at orbit), and lower opercle unpigmented.

Fins pale; all dorsal rays finely lined by melanophores for at least much of the length (Figure 34D); dorsal fin base usually dusky or dark along posterior half, relatively pale anteriorly, and midback just anterior to dorsal fin slightly darker than adjacent back (darker areas usually not as dark as in Figure 34D); caudal spot usually present, tiny or small, dusky or dark, variably shaped but often triangular. Some specimens quite pallid overall; our photo (Fish 105) shows an unusually dark one.

Color in Life.—Upper body greenish-, bluish-, or olive-straw, or gray, overlaid with silver; side silver; ventrally silver or milk-white. No special breeding color known.

Larvae.—Described by Snyder (1979) and Heufelder and Fuiman (1982).

COMPARISON

For mimic shinerlike specimens from the New drainage, see *Comparison* under *N. scabriceps*.

A primary diagnostic trait of *N. volucellus* is the markedly elevated anterior lateral line scales, best seen in the 3rd to 7th scales from the head. The character, quantified by Snelson (1971), refers to the height compared with the horizontal width of the exposed portion of scales (Figure 35B). Some specimens of *N. volucellus* have scales that are relatively higher (or narrower horizontally) than shown. Among Virginia shiners, markedly high scales also occur in species of the genus *Luxilus* and the sawfin shiner.

Another feature of *N. volucellus* that aids in sorting it from many other shiners except the sawfin shiner and *N. spectrunculus* is the extensive development of neuromasts—tiny pitlike sensory structures. Neuromasts are best developed on the anterior half of the head dorsum, snout, subnasal area, around the orbit, particularly on the cheek, and on the anterior portion of lateral line scales.

Primary characters for distinguishing among *N. volucellus*, the sawfin shiner, and *N. spectrunculus* include details of dorsal fin pigmentation (Key couplets 21–22; Figure 34D–F). Other differences are given in the following two species accounts.

BIOLOGY

Most life history data of the mimic shiner are derived from northern lake populations. Microcrustaceans and aquatic and terrestrial insects are principal prey; other foods include water mites, algae, vascular plants, and detritus (Black 1945; Moyle 1973). New River fish ate mostly midges (Hess 1983).

In an Indiana lake both sexes matured in 1 year; 2-year-olds occurred in relatively low numbers. Adults were mostly 40–60 mm TL; females grew the fastest (Black 1945). A 3-year-old female was found in Wisconsin. Age-2 fish of a Wisconsin river population were 52–65 mm TL, and at the second annulus averaged 50 mm (Becker 1983). A 66-mm SL, 77-mm TL female from the North Fork Holston River, Virginia, is the largest known to us.

Notropis volucellus is considered to be a summer spawner in the northern part of its range (Black 1945).

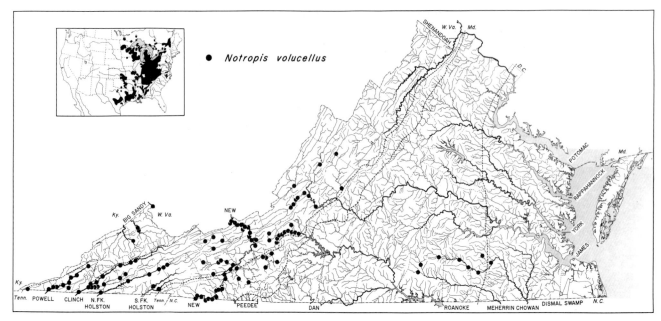

Map 75   Mimic shiner.

In Virginia, breeding may begin in May and extend into August, based on tubercle and gonadal development. In Kansas, Cross (1967) found evidence of spawning during late June to August in shallow riffles. From his lack of success in an extensive attempt to observe spawning in a lake, Black (1945) thought that *N. volucellus* probably spawned in deeper water at night. Counts of mature ova number 67–960 (Black 1945; Becker 1983).

Hybridization is known with *N. atherinoides* and *N. rubellus* (Bailey and Gilbert 1960; Mayhew 1983).

HABITAT

In Virginia latitudes the mimic shiner customarily lives in warm streams of low to moderate gradient. In Virginia drainages it is most regularly encountered in large tributaries and the main channel, but it occasionally is found in small streams. This species occurs primarily in pools and backwaters with gravel, sand, and silt bottoms. It is not particularly silt tolerant in Ohio (Trautman 1981); the same seems to be true in Virginia. The mimic shiner thrives in many northern lakes, often among stands of rooted plants, but it is unknown from any Virginia reservoir. In lakes (and perhaps rivers) it has been found to school inshore during daylight and to disband into small groups at night and enter deep water (Black 1945; Moyle 1973). A reverse diel pattern, inshore movement at night, in a Minnesota lake was attributed to a rich predator fauna (Hanych et al. 1983).

DISTRIBUTION   Map 75

A very wide-ranging minnow, *N. volucellus* extends from the Red River of the North drainage and the Great Lakes–St. Lawrence basin, south in much of the Mississippi basin, and occurs in many Gulf slope drainages. On the central Atlantic slope it occupies the Susquehanna, James, Chowan, Roanoke, Tar, and Neuse drainages.

Most Atlantic slope populations of Virginia and North Carolina are localized; they form two widely, physiographically separate population groups (map inset). In the James and, with one exception, the Roanoke drainage, *N. volucellus* is known only from the Valley and Ridge Province. In the Roanoke it was also taken in the lower Piedmont, in Little Grassy Creek, Halifax County, North Carolina, during 1953 (UMMZ 177032). The lower Roanoke population may be extirpated; much of the lower Piedmont portion of the drainage, including lower Grassy Creek, was impounded beginning in 1953. Six records (Carnes 1965) from the lower Coastal Plain of the Roanoke drainage are unverified.

The Chowan, Tar, and Neuse populations are on the lower Piedmont and upper Coastal Plain; they are barred from the upper Piedmont by the location of the drainages. In the James and Roanoke, however, *N. volucellus* prehistorically was not blocked by structural barriers from dispersing eastward to the Piedmont.

The wide separation of the montane and lowland

population groups may have resulted from two chronologically separate invasions of the Atlantic slope by montane-adapted fish that left the New drainage via stream capture. This hypothesis requires the first-founded population to have dispersed, adapted to, and survived only in relatively lowland areas. Later entrants would have remained adapted to the upper James and upper Roanoke.

Although some of the Virginia Atlantic slope populations were recently discovered and occupy a small range, we do not believe them to be introduced, contrary to our conclusion on the Susquehanna population documented by Malick (1978). The James population was discovered in 1957, that of the Chowan in 1968, but the inhabited stream sections were spottily surveyed before then, and the mimic shiner generally is localized and rare there. We identified *N. volucellus* in the first collection from the Roanoke, Cope's in 1867 (ANSP 4123–25). This small shiner is quite frail (Black 1945) and thus not likely to be successfully introduced.

Notropis volucellus is widely distributed in the Virginia portion of the Ohio basin. Fewer departures from a general distribution in larger streams occur in the New drainage than in the Tennessee drainage. The lesser success of this species in the North Fork Holston (Feeman 1986) and Clinch rivers may be related to slow recovery from long-term pollution and fish kills. The apparent demise of the mimic shiner in

the Middle and South forks of the Holston River—it was taken only once in each during 1947 and 1937, respectively—may be linked with the demise of close relatives; the sawfin and mirror shiners also are unknown recently from these rivers. In the Big Sandy drainage, *N. volucellus* was not found in any of the branches until 1982–1983; it may be localized owing to heavy siltation and acidic pollution.

Abundance.—Usually rare or uncommon. Although numbers of museum specimens and our subjective abundance estimates made in the field often may not indicate the true abundance of small benthic pool-dwelling fishes, we never encountered a major concentration of mimic shiners in Virginia.

REMARKS

The relatively nondescript appearance of *N. volucellus* can be confusing to the identifier, but it serves as a clue to species identification. As with many other small organisms, a close careful look reveals a unique combination of traits that marks the species.

Name.—*Volucellus* is the diminutive of the Latin *volucer*, meaning "winged" or "swift." The common name is based on the vexing similarity to numerous other shiners.

Sawfin shiner   *Notropis* sp. (undescribed species)

SYSTEMATICS

Formerly confounded with *N. volucellus* and *N. spectrunculus*, the sawfin shiner was recognized as an undescribed species in the early 1960s by John S. Ramsey. Its species status is based on anatomical and color distinctions, its complementary (rarely syntopic) relationship with *N. spectrunculus*, and on common syntopy with *N. volucellus*.

The sawfin shiner plus *N. spectrunculus* and *N. ozarcanus* form the *spectrunculus* group, founded partly on very large, serrately rowed tubercles on the first pectoral ray, and on melanophore fin patterns; the two Virginia species have most fins reddened. The *spectrunculus* group is linked to the *volucellus* group by well-elevated anterior line scales, notable neuromast development on these scales and extensively on the head, pectoral fin tuberculation (see *N. volucellus*), and many other basic similarities (Ramsey 1965; Swift 1970; Mayden 1989; our data).

DESCRIPTION

Materials.—Fourteen Virginia and 6 Tennessee lots; counts from 16 Virginia and (Branson 1983) 100 Kentucky specimens. Life color mainly from 5 Virginia series.

Anatomy.—A shiner with a subterminal or slightly inferior mouth, well-elevated anterior lateral line scales, dorsal fin with only the first 4–5 rays lined by melanophores, and usually a small caudal spot; adults are 40–55 mm SL. Morphology much as in *N. volucellus*; exceptions include: dorsal fin origin above the posterior half of pelvic fin base, or often slightly behind the pelvic base; anterior dorsal rays are shorter relative to the posterior tip of the fin. Anterior lateral line scales moderately to much elevated; nape and belly fully scaled; breast (40)80–90% scaled.

Nuptial male lacking tubercles on head or, usually, with a few tiny tubercles along lower edge of snout; occasionally a few tiny tubercles also on midfront of snout, below nares, above orbital rim, on lower cheek, and on lower jaw. Pectoral fin distinctively tuberculate, tubercles in one file on rays 2–4, 2–5, or 2–6; tubercles two-rowed on ray 1; the anterior row is on the leading edge and its tubercles are the

Fish 106 *Notropis* sp., sawfin shiner, adult male 50 mm SL (NMB 779), VA, Washington County, North Fork Holston River, 6 July 1983.

largest on the fish, and very large for fin tubercles; ray 1 tubercles have tip hooked mesially; tubercles absent on other fins and body or, rarely, first pelvic ray has few tiny tubercles basally. Female lacks tubercles. Skin of nuptial male slightly thickened, mainly on anterior body. Female genital papilla moderate-sized, often domed, pore on short pointed central projection.

Meristics.—Pharyngeal teeth 4–4; lateral line complete, scales (34)35–38(39); circumbody scales (19)20–22(23); circumpeduncle scales 12; predorsal scales (13)14–15(17). Anal and pelvic rays (7)8(9), almost always 8; pectoral rays (12)13–15(16).

Color in Preservative.—Head and body patterned essentially as in *N. volucellus*, except: overall the pigmentation tends slightly darker, the body pattern more distinct; in darkest fish, melanophores extend 1.5–2 scale rows below lateral line on anterior body; lower lip and anterior half of chin usually pigmented.

Dorsal fin with only rays 1–4(5) finely bordered by melanophores (Figure 34E), and often the membranes between these rays (and not posterior membranes) are peppered, most so basally; some adult females and perhaps some smaller adult males lack melanophores in all dorsal fin membranes; basidorsal dark-pale-dark pattern usually present, generally less contrastive than in Figure 34D. Caudal spot usually slightly bolder and larger than in *N. volucellus*, medium-sized at most. Lower fins with rays 1–3 or 4 and associated membranes lightly peppered or dusky, most so basally and medially in anal and pelvic, for most of length in pectoral; membranes of lower fins not pigmented in small fish.

Nuptial male, compared with female, often with body pattern slightly less distinct, apparently due to thickened skin; chin and fin patterns tend to be duskier.

Color in Life Plate 19.—Back pale gray or pale olive-gray, silvery dorsolaterally at some angles; head dorsum olive; side and venter of head and body silver, side sometimes with pale violet iridescent tint. Nuptial male with red fins; red of dorsal fin somewhat dark; caudal fin pale red or red absent; lower fins bright medium red or orangish brick-red, generally best developed in membranes; red develops primarily in areas where membranes have melanophores, thus anterobasally except adjacent to base; red persistent for several days in preservative; nonreddened parts of fins clear or somewhat opaque, not distinctly white. Red noted in September specimen. Nuptial female largely unstudied; one had faint red in dorsal and lower fins.

COMPARISON

See *Comparison* under *N. volucellus* and *Description* under *N. spectrunculus*. The best way to separate the sawfin shiner from these two species is by carefully viewing under magnification the pigmentation along the edge of the dorsal rays (Key couplets 21–22; Figure 34D–F): Only rays 1–4 or 5 are lined with melanophores in the sawfin shiner whereas rays 1–7 or all 8 rays are bordered by melanophores in *spectrunculus* and *volucellus*. The caudal spot differences are only average ones; they did not distinguish the sawfin shiner from *N. spectrunculus* in our syntopic collection (REJ 1195).

BIOLOGY

Twenty adult sawfin shiners from the upper Tennessee drainage had fed on immature aquatic insects, mostly midges and caddisflies; mayflies and a beetle were also taken. Most fish contained detritus; a roundworm was found in one gut (C. M. Stephens, in litt.). We observed groups of sawfin shiners feeding on the bottom and in midwater.

Of adults taken during late April to early July, 29 males were 37–53 mm SL, mean, 44, and 33 females were 39–59 mm, mean, 47. The larger average size of females is evident in most series. The 59-mm SL female, from Virginia, is the largest sawfin of which we are aware.

Spawning probably spans mid-May to at least early July in the upper Tennessee. Ripe females occurred with fully nuptial males on 13 May, water 19°C. Partly or completely spent females were taken with fully gravid ones during mid- and late June. In early July some females had shrunken ovaries with atretic

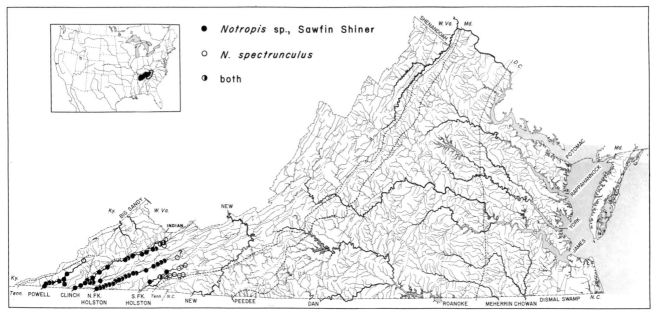

Map 76 Sawfin shiner and mirror shiner. Queried open circle denotes questionable record by Ross and Carico (1963).

ova; others were fully gravid. August adults were in postspawning condition.

HABITAT

The sawfin shiner typically lives in warm, usually clear, large streams and rivers of moderate gradient. It occupies well-moving pools, backwaters adjacent to appreciable current, and gentle and moderate runs. It is commonly associated with clean gravel and rubble as well as somewhat silted substrates. Sometimes it forms moderate-sized schools.

DISTRIBUTION   Map 76

The sawfin shiner is endemic to and widespread in uplands of the Tennessee and Cumberland drainages of Alabama, Tennessee, Virginia, and Kentucky. Its range complements that of *N. spectrunculus*; the sawfin is an upland and intermontane valley inhabitant and *N. spectrunculus* is typically a montane fish.

In Virginia the sawfin shiner is contiguously distributed or nearly so in the medium to wide sections of the North Fork Holston, Clinch, and Powell rivers, it stably populates lower Copper Creek and the lower Little River of the Clinch, and occasionally is found in lower sections of small tributaries. It is not known from the South Fork Holston system in Virginia, which may be too cool or high-gradient.

The sawfin seems to have disappeared from the

Middle Fork Holston River. It was collected there three times, in 1888 (with *N. spectrunculus*), 1937, and 1951. The uppermost segment of the population could have been affected by pollution from Marion (Saylor et al. 1988); however, the sawfin has rebounded from heavier pollution and large fish kills in the North Fork Holston and Clinch rivers. Spillway dams in the Middle Fork would have impeded upstream recruitment. The impoundment of the South Holston River may have extirpated any recruitment source for the lowermost Middle Fork.

Because the sawfin shiner presently is widely distributed in the North Fork Holston River, we are puzzled that it was not reported from an extensive 1950s survey of that system by Ross and Carico (1963). This species could have been identified as some other *Notropis* but we found no sawfin shiner from that period in Ross' collections. The sawfin shiner may not have been notably depressed in the 1950s by pollution from Saltville. It was collected about as frequently during 1970–1985 as it was by early collectors (Jordan in 1888, Becker in 1928). It was also taken during 1954 in all three samples by personnel of the Academy of Natural Sciences, Philadelphia; one of the sites was above, and two well below Saltville (Patrick 1961, as *N. spectrunculus*; UMMZ). Ross may simply have lost specimens; a similar situation exists for *Notropis ariommus*, *Percina evides*, and *Etheostoma zonale* in the Holston.

The sawfin shiner and *N. spectrunculus* were collected together in three Virginia streams. One collection is from the Middle Fork Holston River in 1888 (USNM 40560, 40615, 203249). Another is from the Clinch River at Cedar Bluff in 1978 (OSM 42113, 42115; J. S. Ramsey, in litt.). The third site is in Indian Creek, which enters the Clinch at Cedar Bluff and is smaller than streams typically occupied by the sawfin. Only *N. spectrunculus* was reported by Masnik (1974) from the four lower to middle Indian Creek sites (two plots on Map 76) that he sampled during 1971–1973. However, his specimens from this stream and nearby Pounding Mill Creek have not been critically studied. At one of Masnik's lower Indian Creek sites (Mouth of Laurel), we took 4 adult sawfin shiners and 17 adult *N. spectrunculus* in 1987 (REJ 1195).

Abundance.—Often common, occasionally abundant in the North Fork Holston, Clinch, and Powell rivers, usually rare or uncommon in their tributaries; possibly extirpated in the Middle Fork Holston.

REMARKS

Red-finned, silvery sawfin shiners are pretty. Although this species is well known among southeastern ichthyologists, it is cryptic when not in breeding color, much resembling the mirror shiner, mimic shiner, and others. Its distinctiveness eluded even the keen eye of Carl L. Hubbs, a 20th century giant in North American fish systematics. Hubbs, however, may have been unable to compare nuptial colors. When John S. Ramsey found an obscure trait—fine bordering by melanophores of only the anterior rays of the dorsal fin, other differences became apparent, and it was soon learned that the sawfin and mirror shiners were fundamentally, ecologically distinct as well.

Name.—The common name "sawfin shiner," coined by J. S. Ramsey, refers to the prominent serrately rowed tubercles on the first pectoral fin ray.

Mirror shiner   *Notropis spectrunculus* (Cope)

SYSTEMATICS

The mirror shiner was described from Bear Creek, a Middle Fork Holston River tributary in Virginia (Cope 1868b). Its species-group affiliation is treated under its close ally the undescribed sawfin shiner. Ramsey (1965) studied variation but did not report on the Holston and Clinch populations in Virginia which exhibit slight divergence.

DESCRIPTION

Materials.—Four Virginia and 4 North Carolina lots; counts from 33 Virginia specimens. Life color from 4 large nuptial males (REJ 1096), 3 adult females from the Middle Fork Holston River, and 1 lot from Indian Creek of the Clinch system.

Anatomy.—A shiner with a low mouth, dorsal fin with melanophores bordering all rays and peppering membranes, and a prominent wedge-shaped caudal spot; adults are 40–55 mm SL. Morphology much like *N. volucellus* and the sawfin shiner, differing on the average from both in: body more elongate and more cylindrical in large adult; dorsal fin origin slightly more posterior, usually above posterior end of pelvic fin base or slightly behind; head somewhat broader in large adult; snout somewhat blunt in large nuptial male. Anterior dorsal fin ray length, tuberculation, and genital papilla as in sawfin shiner. Anterior lateral line scales slightly elevated or height about normal (Figure 35C); nape fully scaled; breast 0–90% scaled; belly 80–100% scaled.

Skin thickening of large nuptial male better developed on body than in sawfin shiner; skin much thickened (keratin-ized or unculous) on lower fins, particularly distal half of anal and pelvic rays where it forms a large whitish padlike area.

Meristics.—Pharyngeal teeth 4–4; lateral line complete or nearly so, scales 35–39; circumbody scales (20)24–26, highest counts tending to occur in Holston; circumpeduncle scales 12(13); predorsal scales (12)16–21. Anal rays (7)8–9 [9 in 10 of 16 Middle Fork Holston fish, 9 in 2 of 17 Clinch specimens]; pectoral rays (13)14–15.

Color in Preservative.—Head and body as in sawfin shiner except: upper body pattern of dark scale submargining often slightly less distinct; dark stitching of anterior lateral line scales often paler or absent, or obscured by dark scale submargining; on anterior lower side, melanophores usually extend 2–3 scale rows below lateral line, to near belly; chin peppered on anterior one-third to two-thirds; lower edge of preopercle and anterior breast sometimes peppered.

Differences in fins from the sawfin shiner are: dorsal fin (Figure 34F) has all rays (or the first 7 of 8 rays) bordered, often very faintly, by melanophores; all dorsal membranes stippled, melanophores usually extend to near distal margin. Caudal spot typically larger than in sawfin, medium to somewhat large; usually bold, distinctly darker than posterior portion of lateral stripe; usually triangular. Lower fins with larger dusky area than in sawfin, in darker specimens extending to near distal margin anteriorly and present in basal portion of posterior rays; anal fin with concave distal edge to dusky area, least pigmented on ray 6, and in paler specimens the basal portion of middle rays are unpigmented, but that of last ray has one to few specks of pigment just above base.

Fish 107 *Notropis spectrunculus* adult male 59 mm SL (REJ 1069), VA, Smyth County, Middle Fork Holston River, 4 June 1984.

Fish 108 *Notropis spectrunculus* adult female 40 mm SL (REJ 979), VA, Smyth County, Middle Fork Holston River, 14 June 1983.

Nuptial male body, chin, and fins slightly to distinctly duskier than in female.

Color in Life Plate 19.—Nuptial female with upper body ground shade straw to light olive, scale submargins dark olive; head dorsum dark olive; side silver; belly white with silver reflections; fins clear, caudal spot black.

Nuptial males from Middle Fork Holston with pale olive upper body; most of side with bluish lavender iridescence; lower side and venter silver; head dusky dorsally and about snout; iris silver with faint bronze cast; cheek and opercle silver and with pale bronze line along preopercle–opercle suture. All fins pale carmine in large area, where membranes and forks of rays bear melanophores, hence in almost all of dorsal and caudal, and approximately basal half of lower fins; non-carmine distal margin of dorsal and caudal fins clear or slightly opaque white, that of anal and pelvic fins (with thick skin pads) heavily white, not clear nor satiny; caudal spot black. Carmine fin color very ephemeral; carmine areas turned dusky carmine within 2–3 minutes after death, and carmine had virtually disappeared when specimens were photographed in next 2–5 minutes.

Smaller, less colorful nuptial males from Indian Creek with tan-olive back; middorsal stripe iridescent gold-tan; narrow dorsolateral stripe iridescent gold-red; dorsal fin dull red except for pale margin; caudal as dorsal, reddest submarginally; lower fins with wide, slightly whitish distal and posterior margins (best developed in anal and pelvic fins), remainder dull red, reddest anterobasally.

COMPARISON

In addition to the above description comparing the sawfin shiner, see *Comparison* under *N. volucellus*.

BIOLOGY

As is true for so many small fishes, the distribution and general habitat are well known but little information exists on life history. Sixteen adult males from Virginia were 38–59 mm SL, mean, 45, and 17 adult females were 38–56 mm, mean, 47. The 59-mm male is the largest we have seen from Virginia. The largest mirror shiner known to us is 68 mm SL, from North Carolina.

Spawning probably occurs during late spring and early summer in Virginia. Prenuptial specimens were taken on 22 April; a very gravid female was found with non-peak nuptial males on 1 May, and fully nuptial fish were taken on 4 and 14 June. Males were well tuberculate in an 11 June series but the females, all with medium to large ovaries but no heavily yolked ova, may have been in an interlude from spawning. Some late-August females from North Carolina were fully gravid.

HABITAT

The mirror shiner lives in generally clear, cool or cold, large creeks to medium-sized streams of moderate to high gradient. Adults occupy the head and relatively sluggish parts of pools, backwaters near well-moving current, slow runs, and occasionally riffles. We observed them over bottoms of rubble, boulder, and bedrock. This species is not particularly gregarious in Virginia, perhaps owing to low abundance.

DISTRIBUTION   Map 76

Notropis spectrunculus occupies the upper Tennessee, Savannah, and Santee drainages (Ramsey 1965). Its complementary distribution with the sawfin shiner is described under that species. The confinement of *N. spectrunculus* to the Blue Ridge, its fringes, and a few ecologically similar areas indicates a restrictive adaptation to cool, typically high-gradient streams (e.g., Gilbert and Seaman 1973; Gilbert 1980). This species is not known in the Tennessee drainage from below an elevation of 457 m (1,500 feet) (Ramsey 1965). New records for Virginia are in agreement; the lowest Virginia record is 463 m in the Powell River. The much lower altitude (and likely the lowest gradient) given by Masnik (1974), from a Powell River tributary in Tennessee, is based on nonextant specimens collected and reidentified as the sawfin shiner by D. A. Etnier (personal communication).

The Virginia populations of the mirror shiner form a relict pattern; localization tends to increase and persistence tends to decrease with increasing distance from the Blue Ridge. The longest stream reach occupied is along the Blue Ridge base, in the upper South Fork Holston River. The currently populated, upper portion of the Middle Fork Holston is fed by several large springs. This species has occupied the lowermost part of two upper Middle Fork tributaries (Bear and Nicks creeks); the last record is from 1958. The lower Middle Fork population probably is extirpated; the one record is dated 1888. The habitat there is atypical for the species.

It is not clear that *N. spectrunculus* has occupied the North Fork Holston system during historical time. Patrick's (1961) North Fork record of the mirror shiner was founded on the sawfin shiner (UMMZ). Neves and Widlak's (1988) specimen was dissected and not relocated (R. J. Neves, in litt.); it was from a North Fork site occupied by the sawfin shiner. Ross and Carico's (1963) record from a lower North Fork tributary was based on *N. leuciodus* (Feeman 1986). The open circle on the upper North Fork Holston River (Map 76) is based on Ross and Carico (1963); a voucher specimen could not be located. Subsequent sampling in the upper North Fork and Lick Creek failed to find *N. spectrunculus*.

The Clinch population is sharply localized, its main body probably restricted to a few tributaries (Indian and Pounding Mill creeks as far as is known); only one specimen is known from the main river. The Powell population may have died out; the only record of *N. spectrunculus* is dated 1938, from a center of subsequent extensive coal mining.

Abundance.—Usually rare or uncommon.

REMARKS

The nuptial male mirror shiner had long eluded us. When finally seeing it in gallant breeding dress, differences from the sawfin shiner were as evident as were the basic similarities. It now seems that the mirror shiner fits a common evolutionary trend in fishes. In species in which only the males exhibit prominent sexual structures or colors, the sexes as adults tend to be equal-sized or males are larger.

It seems peculiar that in Virginia *N. spectrunculus* is known from only four main-river tributaries. Many unoccupied streams are clean and course through the Blue Ridge, Appalachian Plateau, or backbone mountains of the Valley and Ridge Province; perhaps most of them are too small or too warm. A notable apparently uninhabited stream is Whitetop Laurel Creek, the largest Blue Ridge tributary of the South Fork Holston and a fine trout stream. Also strange is the virtual absence of the mirror shiner in the Watauga system, the large southern branch of the South Fork Holston arising in the North Carolina Blue Ridge.

The mirror shiner merits special concern status in Virginia because of its small, recently constricted distribution and narrow habitat range.

Name.—*Spectrunculus* was regarded by Jordan and Evermann (1896) to mean a diminutive of "spectrum," an image. However, Cope likely derived the name from *specca*, meaning "speck," and *trunculus*, diminutive for "stem," in reference to the distinctive spot at the end of the caudal peduncle.

Sand shiner   *Notropis stramineus* (Cope)

SYSTEMATICS

The sand shiner was described as *stramineus* in 1865 from Michigan by Cope, and has been known by that name since the partial untanglement of its nomenclature by Suttkus (1958). Mayden and Gilbert (1989) found that it had been described earlier as *ludibundus* in 1856 from Kansas by Girard. Although that name has not been used since its proposal, Mayden and Gilbert regarded it to replace *stramineus*. Robins et al. (1991) have petitioned the ICZN to conserve the name *stramineus*. Two subspecies of the sand shiner

Fish 109 *Notropis stramineus* adult female 50 mm SL (WHH 103), VA, Buchanan County, Lester Fork, 28 June 1983.

are recognized, of which *N. s. stramineus* occurs in Virginia (Bailey and Allum 1962; Tanyolac 1973).

Notropis stramineus, N. alborus, N. chihuahua, N. heterolepis, N. mekistocholas, N. procne, N. rupestris, N. uranoscopus, and the undescribed palezone shiner have been stated or implied to form the *procne* group (Snelson 1971; Loos and Fuiman 1978; Burr and Mayden 1981; Page and Beckham 1987; Jenkins' study). These species have 7 or 8 anal rays, 4–4 pharyngeal teeth, and a shagreen-like layer of tiny tubercles on pectoral fin rays. Some of these species at times have been loosely combined with several other small, largely pale shiners in a broadened subgenus *Alburnops* (see *N. volucellus*).

DESCRIPTION

Materials.—Twenty-nine lots collected in Kansas, Kentucky, Illinois, New York, Tennessee, West Virginia, and Virginia, including counts from 12 specimens from the Big Sandy drainage, Virginia. Life color from Cross (1967), Raney (1969b), Scott and Crossman (1973), and Trautman (1981).

Anatomy.—A shiner with a subterminal or slightly inferior mouth, 7 anal rays, and small triangular caudal spot; adults are 30–45 mm SL. Body form moderate; dorsal fin origin usually above the anterior half of the pelvic fin base, occasionally above the posterior half. Head length moderate; eye medium-sized, lateral or very slightly supralateral; snout slightly pointed or somewhat rounded; mouth medium-sized, subterminal or slightly inferior, horizontal or slightly oblique. Breast 0–50% scaled; belly usually 100% scaled.

Nuptial male with small, moderately to closely spaced tubercles on head; body with tiny tubercles submarginally on scales of nape and anterior upper side; pectoral fin with shagreen of tubercles; female apparently lacks tubercles or has much reduced tuberculation. Male genital papilla small, inobvious; female papilla slightly larger, protruding with anal papilla.

Meristics.—Pharyngeal teeth 4–4; lateral line complete, scales 35–37; circumbody scales 23–24; circumpeduncle scales 12; predorsal scales 14–16(17); predorsal scale rows 13–15(16). Anal rays 7; pectoral rays (12)14–15.

Color in Preservative.—Dorsum slightly dusky, middorsal stripe weakly or moderately developed; dorsolateral scales darkly submargined, anterior fields usually pale; midlateral stripe narrow, usually restricted to posterior body, sometimes bordered dorsally (at least posteriorly) by pale zone; anterior lateral line pores weakly to prominently dark stitched; lower side and venter essentially immaculate, except for dusky midventral stripe behind anal fin. Head dorsum and snout dusky; lips usually slightly or moderately dusky; chin slightly dusky or unpigmented; cheek and opercle pale.

Dorsal fin with melanophores along all rays except occasionally the last; dorsal base usually with dark-pale-dark pattern, anterior one-third–one-half of base relatively pale, remainder of base and midline immediately anterior to dorsal origin slightly darker than adjacent areas (Figure 34D). Caudal fin typically with small, usually wedge-shaped spot; anal fin pigmented along base; pelvic fin pale; anterior pectoral rays dusky. Sexes apparently alike.

Color in Life.—Dorsum straw to straw-olive, dark scale outlining evident; side silver with green and lavender sheens, black stitching on anterior lateral line pores obvious; venter silver-white. Head dorsum and snout olive; cheek and opercle silvery. Dorsal and caudal fins with straw cast; black caudal spot sometimes inobvious; anal and pelvic fins pale; pectoral fin dusky on leading rays. Chromatic nuptial color absent or straw shade intensified.

Larvae.—Treated by Perry and Menzel (1979), Heufelder and Fuiman (1982), and Fuiman et al. (1983).

COMPARISON

Notropis stramineus and *N. procne* may occur together in the New drainage of Virginia, where the former is rare (or extirpated) and *N. procne* recently has become established (Map 77). Both are small, mostly pale shiners with a subterminal or inferior mouth, 7 anal rays, and anterior lateral line scales not notably higher than wide. They differ on average in: (1) body form [slightly higher-backed and deeper in *stramineus vs.* more slender, dorsum and venter more parallel in *procne*]; (2) pigmentation of lateral snout (over lachrymal bone) relative to dorsal snout [about equally dusky *vs.* usually distinctly darker (Figure 36B)]; (3) anterior continuation of midlateral body stripe [usually absent *vs.* usually present, narrow]; (4) dark stitching of lateral line pores [weak to bold on anterior half of body, occasionally present but weak posteriorly *vs.* most or all pores usually evidently stitched, although partly obscured posteriorly by lateral stripe]; (5) pigmentation of scales bordering mid-dorsal stripe [scales usually only darkly outlined, other exposed areas pale or with few melanophores *vs.* usually the posterior one-third–one-half of scales pigmented, scales pale only anteriorly]. Differences in tuberculation of nuptial males are: (6) number of tubercle rows on upper orbital rim [usually 1–2, sometimes 3 *vs.* 0–1]; (7) tuberculation of lachrymal and cheek [moderate to dense *vs.* bare or with few tubercles].

BIOLOGY

During warm months the sand shiner eats drifting aquatic and terrestrial insects; benthic insects are the primary prey during colder times. Other items taken include leaf material, algae, and detritus (Stegman 1959; Mendelson 1975; Gillen and Hart 1980).

Sand shiners mature in 1 year at about 28–30 mm SL; maximum longevity is 3 years. The sexes grow at equal rates; individuals in the third year were 35–55 mm SL in Iowa and Kansas (Starrett 1951; Summerfelt and Minckley 1969; Tanyolac 1973). The largest Virginia specimen we saw was 48 mm SL; Tanyolac (1973) gave maximum size as 64 mm SL, from Colorado.

Notropis stramineus spawns in water of 27–37°C, intermittently from late May through June in southern Illinois, late June through late September in Kansas, and late August through September in Iowa (Starrett 1951; Summerfelt and Minckley 1969; Tanyolac 1973). Fish from the Big Sandy drainage of Virginia were partly spent in early to mid-June, and one female had ova resorbing. In addition to typical fluviatile habitats, spawning occurs in lakes at sandy shallows and creek mouths (Hubbs and Cooper 1936). Egg counts per female were 250–2,660 (Starrett 1951; Summerfelt and Minckley 1969; Tanyolac 1973).

HABITAT

The sand shiner occupies pools with appreciable flow and slow runs in warm streams of moderate to low gradient and varied size and turbidity. In the upland southeastern portion of the range it tends to populate only, or is dependent at some stage on, moderately large streams (Etnier et al. 1979). In the northern United States the sand shiner commonly lives in lakes as well as streams. It associates chiefly with relatively clean sand and gravel substrates, and appears quite warm-adapted as evidenced by high spawning temperatures (Summerfelt and Minckley 1969). It is an epibenthic schooling minnow and tends to group with other cyprinids. Cahn (1927) reported it to occur in schools as large as 5,000.

DISTRIBUTION   Map 77

Notropis stramineus is widely distributed in the Great Lakes–St. Lawrence basin and the upper half of the Mississippi basin, and is localized in the Cumberland and Tennessee drainages. It is widely distributed in the Plains and areas of similar habitat, and is rare in upland areas (Gilbert *in* Lee et al. 1980). Etnier et al. (1979) documented a wide distribution in the Tennessee portion of the Clinch and Holston systems before impoundment. The only record of *N. stramineus* in the Tennessee drainage of Virginia (Ross and Carico 1963) is not supported by a specimen; we deem it a misidentification.

In Virginia, *N. stramineus* occurs in the Big Sandy drainage and is known from the New drainage. Its ample range in Big Sandy main stems seems due to recent immigration or substantial population increase. The sand shiner was not taken in surveys of the Virginia section during the late 1930s by L. P. Schultz nor in 1972 by us; the first capture was in 1982. The Kentucky portion of the Big Sandy, where this fish is widespread (Burr and Warren 1986), would have been the recruitment source.

In the New drainage, *N. stramineus* has been spottily distributed in West Virginia since at least 1933 (Addair 1944). The one Virginia specimen was taken in the lowermost East River, at Glen Lyn near the West Virginia line, in May 1973 (Stauffer et al. 1975). Intensive sampling of the site and others nearby during the next 19 months yielded no other specimen (Stauffer et al. 1976), nor had the many collections from the New River at Glen Lyn and somewhat above during 1971–1972 (Hocutt et al. 1973). The New drainage in Virginia lacks expanses of sand and fine gravel substrate, hence a significant increase of the shiner is not expected. Fowler's (1923) record of *N. deliciosus* (as the sand shiner was long erroneously known) from Brush Creek of the New is based on *N. volucellus* (ANSP 109540).

Abundance.—Generally rare or uncommon, apparently increasing in the Big Sandy.

Swallowtail shiner

SYSTEMATICS

The swallowtail shiner, named from Pennsylvania in 1865, typifies a clan of small, pale or "blackline" shiners comprising the *procne* group (see *N. stramineus*). Snelson (1971) regarded *N. procne* to be an Atlantic slope derivative of *N. stramineus*, but Jenkins and Sorenson (*in* Lee et al. 1980) considered its closest relative to be the undescribed rare palezone shiner of the Tennessee and Cumberland drainages.

Two subspecies were recognized by Raney (1947a), *N. p. procne* ranging from the James drainage north, and *N. p. longiceps* (Cope) extending from the Roanoke drainage south. The interjacent Chowan population presumably was included in *longiceps*. Although Raney gave a suite of differences, they were average ones and were presented summarily without reference to variation. Thus the distinctiveness of the subspecies was questioned (Ross 1969; Snelson 1971), and in some cases subspecies were not recognized (Jenkins and Freeman 1972; Gilbert 1978; Hocutt et al. 1986). We arbitrarily allow subspecies owing to the large number of putative differences; a comprehensive study is needed.

DESCRIPTION

Materials.—From Hubbs and Raney (1947), Snelson (1971), and 61 Virginia lots; counts from 73 Virginia speci-

REMARKS

The pallid sand shiner is well adapted for living on sandy bottom. This stands it well in the aptly named Big Sandy drainage, where relatively few upland–montane fishes flourish. Its current success there parallels two other arenicolous fishes, the silverjaw minnow and the suckermouth minnow.

Name.—*Stramineus* means "of straw"—straw colored.

Notropis procne (Cope)

mens. Life color from 9 lots of adults taken during spring and summer from the Roanoke and Chowan drainages.

Anatomy.—A somewhat slender shiner with a subterminal or slightly inferior mouth and a well-developed narrow midlateral stripe with most lateral line pores darkly stitched; adults are 40–55 mm SL. Body somewhat elongate, low-backed; dorsal fin origin above pelvic fin base, usually the posterior half; otherwise anatomy is much like that of *N. stramineus*. Breast usually naked; belly 80–100% scaled.

Nuptial male with small well-spaced tubercles on head dorsum; lateral snout, cheek, and opercle with few or no tubercles (sensory structures may appear as tubercles); body with small tubercles submarginally on scales of nape and anterolaterally, occasionally on posterior scales; pectoral fin with shagreen of tiny tubercles; other fins with sparse minute tubercles or tubercles absent, most frequently absent on caudal; female with much reduced tuberculation.

Meristics.—Pharyngeal teeth 4–4; lateral line usually complete, scales (33)34–37; circumbody scales (21)22–25(26); circumpeduncle scales 12(13); predorsal scales 13–17(22); predorsal scale rows 13–16(17). Dorsal rays 8; anal rays 7(8); pectoral rays (12)13–15. Cephalic lateralis pores, IO (9)10–12(14); SO (6)7–9(10); POM (7)8–11(12); ST (1)2(3) on each side of interruption.

Fish 110 *Notropis procne* adult female 42 mm SL (REJ 1003), VA, Charlotte County, Twittys Creek, 13 July 1983.

Color in Preservative.—Basic pattern much like *N. stramineus*; differences given in *Comparison* under that species. Sexes very similar.

Color in Life   Plate 19.—Dorsum translucent straw or pale yellow, dorsolateral scales darkly outlined; mid- and lower side mostly silver, black-stitched lateral line pores evident; midlateral stripe leaden with steel blue cast; venter silver-white. Head dorsum and snout straw to brownish; preocular mark black, sometimes partly obscured by silver; cheek and opercle silver; side of head sometimes with yellow tint.

Dorsal fin faint straw or yellow, yellow most intense along anterior half of base; caudal fin pale, caudal spot black; anal fin pale; pelvic fin pale or with slight yellow to yellow-orange wash basally; pectoral fin and body about its base pale yellow to yellow-orange, brightest basally. Sexual dichromatism lacking; Raney's (1947a) statement that males are darker than females when in water may apply to melanophore pattern.

From cursory observations of James drainage specimens, we can not affirm Raney's (1947a) contention that nuptial *N. p. longiceps* are more yellowed than *N. p. procne*; moreover, none of our Virginia specimens, nor Snelson's (1971) and our North Carolina fish, were widely yellow.

Larvae.—Described by Loos and Fuiman (1978), Loos et al. (1979), and Fuiman et al. (1983).

COMPARISON

See the account of *N. stramineus* for distinguishing that species, and that of *N. bifrenatus* for segregating *N. procne*, *N. alborus*, and *N. bifrenatus* as a group from *N. chalybaeus* and *N. altipinnis*.

Notropis procne is separable from the similar and syntopic *N. alborus* by: (1) predorsal stripe [present in *procne vs.* absent in *alborus*]; (2) snout tip pigmentation relative to preocular area (Figure 36) [distinctly paler *vs.* moderately dark or black, intensity about that of preocular area]; (3) upper lip pigmentation [slightly or moderately peppered *vs.* melanophores absent]; (4) breast squamation, usual % scaled [0–10 *vs.* 50–100].

Notropis bifrenatus is also similar to *N. procne* and they often are found together. Separate them by: (1) body form typically [more elongate in *procne vs.* higher-backed in *bifrenatus*]; (2) mouth (Figure 36) [horizontal or slightly oblique *vs.* moderately or quite oblique]; (3) snout tip and upper lip pigmentation (Figure 36) [about equally dusky, paler than dark preocular area (over lachrymal bone) *vs.* blackened medially, about same as preocular area]; (4) caudal spot usually [smaller, somewhat triangular, disconnected from lateral stripe *vs.* larger, round, oval, or rectangular, confluent with lateral stripe].

BIOLOGY

The swallowtail shiner feeds on worms, mites, microcrustaceans, aquatic and terrestrial insects, diatoms, and filamentous algae; insects dominate the animal fraction of the adult diet. The appreciable sand in guts indicated a propensity to feed on the bottom, but most aquarium specimens kept well above the bottom (Breder and Crawford 1922; Gatz 1979). Vadas (1990) noted that a considerable amount of detritus was eaten.

Length–frequency data from 311 Smith River (Roanoke drainage) specimens collected in June revealed that most age-2 fish had matured; the smallest adult of each sex was 39 mm SL. From elsewhere in southern Virginia, the smallest mature fish were a male 37 mm SL and a female 38 mm, but the appearance of gonads of some fish as small as 33 mm taken in mid-May indicated that they would have ripened soon. Maximum longevity in the Smith River population was 3 years. From the Rappahannock drainage, Raney (1947a) reported yearling adults as small as 33 mm SL and that some fish lived 3 years. Although the largest of Raney's and our specimens were females, average adult sizes of the sexes were similar. Of Smith River adults, 117 males were 39–58 mm SL, mean, 47, and 94 females were 39–65 mm, mean, 48. Means for the Rappahannock were both 44. The 65-mm SL specimen seems to be the largest reported for the species.

Notropis procne apparently spawns within mid-May to late July in Virginia, based on gonadal and tubercle development. One fully gravid female was taken with spent ones on 25 August. In the Rappahannock drainage, Raney (1947a) observed spawning on sand and fine gravel in an area of moderate current as shallow as 10 cm, on 18 June in water of 25.6°C. The grouped males attempted to maintain individual territories, whereas females generally held quietly near the spawning site. Spawning occurred with the sexes side by side, the male with his pectoral fin under and the caudal peduncle over the female. The brevity of the spawning embrace indicated that multiple acts were needed to exhaust an egg complement.

The swallowtail shiner may diverge from its close relatives by spawning on nests of other fishes. Although the data are scanty, this species seems to use both cyprinid and centrarchid nests, thus differing from the many minnow species that typically spawn on nests of only other minnows. In the Potomac drainage, eggs of *N. procne* were found attached to pebbles in nests of the redbreast sunfish *Lepomis auritus* (Loos et al. 1979).

While snorkeling at a *Nocomis* gravel-mound nest in

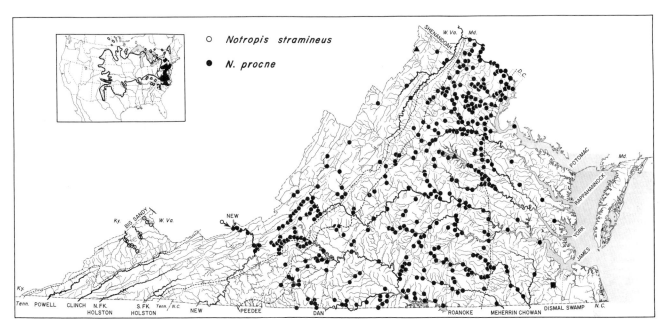

Map 77   Sand shiner and swallowtail shiner. Solid square on Shingle Creek represents record with questionable locality data.

the upper Roanoke River, we observed 4–5 adult *N. procne* actively swimming to hold position at the nest; the moderately swift current was unusual habitat for the shiner. The shiners often made frontal attacks and chased each other; other swallowtail shiners entering the nest area were chased by those there. Twice a nest visitation resulted in two shiners aligning parallel and quivering on the surface of the nest, apparently spawning. On the 18 May 1974 date the water was about 21°C.

On 29 May 1974 in the lower South Fork Roanoke River, three adult *N. procne* were collected from another *Nocomis* nest. Both nests had spawning white, crescent, and rosefin shiners; *N. procne* may have been feeding on the eggs of those species. The swallowtail shiner was not noticed over many other *Nocomis* nests studied in the upper Roanoke and James drainages by E. A. Lachner and R. E. Jenkins. However, its presence among aggregations of nest associates could have been missed.

HABITAT

Notropis procne occupies warm, clear and turbid, large creeks to large rivers of moderate to low gradient. It is a pool shiner, usually found near the head and tail of pools over areas of soft and firm bottom, and is sometimes associated with plants. It is quite rare in Virginia impoundments and generally uncommon in lakes northward (Raney 1969b). Winter day-

time observations found *N. procne* active in pools and riffle ecotones when water was 7.5°C, but at 2°C it and many other species occurred under rocks and leaf detritus. When uncovered the swallowtail shiner quickly sought new shelter.

DISTRIBUTION   Map 77

The swallowtail shiner occurs on the Atlantic slope from the upper Delaware and Susquehanna drainages, New York, to the Santee drainage, South Carolina; in the Ohio basin it occupies the New drainage of Virginia. An old record for a Finger Lakes tributary in New York was compiled by Jenkins and Sorensen (*in* Lee et al. 1980), who also gave a 1951 record for southern Lake Ontario. Subsequent surveys indicate that *N. procne* no longer exists in these northerly waters (e.g., C. Smith 1985).

On the Virginia Atlantic slope, the swallowtail shiner inhabits all major drainages, the Piankatank drainage, and a Mobjack Bay tributary. Most Coastal Plain populations appear to be localized; the long extension in the Nottoway River parallels that of several other upland species. Jordan's (1889b) record from the Blackwater River of the Chowan was repeated at the same and closely adjacent sites in 1984 by M. D. Norman and R. Southwick. However, Jordan's report from Shingle Creek at the Dismal Swamp periphery remains questionable (*Biogeogra-*

phy). *Notropis procne* is extensively distributed in the Piedmont, but oddly it is absent or rare in several moderately or well-surveyed tributary systems; for example, Tuckahoe Creek near the James Fall Zone, and the Falling and Pigg rivers and Goose Creek of the middle Roanoke drainage. In the Blue Ridge it avoids tumbling streams, doing well apparently only in sandy Back Creek of the Roanoke. In the Valley and Ridge Province it is generally distributed in the Roanoke drainage and certain James River tributaries, but is localized in the Shenandoah system.

The New drainage population probably is introduced, judging by the 1971 date of the first valid record (Hocutt et al. 1973; Ross 1973) and confinement of the shiner to the section bounded by Bluestone Reservoir and Claytor Dam. Essential restriction of *N. procne* to the main river indicates insufficient time (or sampling) or improper habitat for its extension well into tributaries. Of the two tributary records below Claytor Dam, that from the lowermost East River at the state line (Stauffer et al. 1975) is expected. The other record is from the upper Little River in the Blue Ridge during 1976, an unlikely dispersal considering the distance, habitat, and time for a small fish presumably introduced during the 1960s. Likely the single specimen was taken on the Atlantic slope and added to the Little River collection by a student when a multidrainage series of collections was being sorted at Virginia Commonwealth University.

A specimen of *N. procne* (VPI 762) labeled as being from Big Reed Island Creek (above Claytor Dam) was not included in the original species list for the collection, nor in the report (Ross and Perkins 1959) on the collection; hence we reject the locality data. The record of *N. procne* from the North Carolina part of the New (Richardson and Carnes 1964) is based on *Pimephales notatus* (NCSM 5160).

Abundance.—Usually uncommon or common.

REMARKS

The swallowtail shiner is a graceful and delicate-appearing minnow that does well in aquaria. The dark-yellow-dark pattern at the dorsal fin base of this and certain other shiners (Figure 34D) seems to have phylogenetic significance, and to other shiners may enhance species recognition.

Name.—*Procne* is from the Greek Prokne, a daughter of Pandion who was transformed into a swallow by the gods (C. Smith 1985). *Longiceps* means "long head"; a relatively long snout is supposedly diagnostic of *N. p. longiceps*.

Whitemouth shiner   *Notropis alborus* Hubbs and Raney

SYSTEMATICS

The whitemouth shiner was described from North Carolina and the lower Roanoke drainage of Virginia by Hubbs and Raney (1947). It is quite similar to *N. procne* and certain other members of the *procne* group (see *N. stramineus*). Snelson (1971) considered its closest affinity in the group to lie with *N. heterolepis*. Page and Beckham (1987) gave evidence that *N. alborus*, *N. heterolepis*, and *N. rupestris* form a monophyletic lineage. Relatively greater evolutionary distance between *N. alborus* and *N. procne* is indicated by their frequent syntopy. We do not follow Mayden's (1989) allocation of *N. alborus* to *Hybopsis*.

DESCRIPTION

Materials.—From Hubbs and Raney (1947), Snelson (1971), and 4 Virginia and 2 North Carolina lots. Life color from 13 adults, 12 from Virginia, 1 from North Carolina.

Anatomy.—A shiner with a well-rounded or blunt snout encircled frontally by a dark band, and the midlateral stripe prominent and fully confluent with the caudal spot; adults are 40–50 mm SL. Body profile moderate or somewhat elongate, dorsal contour often distinctly elevated; dorsal fin origin above or, usually, slightly anterior to pelvic fin origin. Head moderate; eye medium-sized, lateral; snout well rounded or blunt; mouth small, subterminal or slightly inferior, nearly horizontal. Breast 50–90% scaled; belly fully scaled.

Tuberculation of nuptial male perhaps incompletely known; tiny tubercles scattered on top and side of head; tubercles possibly absent on body; pectoral fin with shagreen of minute tubercles.

Meristics.—Pharyngeal teeth 4–4; lateral line complete, scales (31)32–34(35); circumbody scales 23–24; circumpeduncle scales 11–12; predorsal scales (13)14–17(21); predorsal scale rows 12–13(16). Dorsal rays 8; anal rays 7; pelvic rays 8; pectoral rays (13)14–15(16).

Color in Preservative.—Dorsum slightly dusky, middorsal stripe essentially absent, occasionally a vague hint of a stripe present; upper body scales duskily outlined; relatively wide pale zone present above midlateral stripe; midlateral stripe moderate or bold, about uniform in darkness and width from head to tail; lateral line pore areas darkened, the small marks often oval or crescentic rather than stitchlike; lower side and venter pale or, occasionally, with sparse melanophores, most so on urosome, dusky midventral postanal line absent. Head dark dorsally; snout tip encircled by a very dusky or black band, width equal to or slightly less than that of connected preocular bar (Figure 36A); pale crescentic area just above snout band; exposed portion of upper lip (when mouth closed) wholly unpigmented, or with very few melanophores medially along edge of snout. (Six large adults composing a series from the Pee Dee drainage, North Carolina [UNCC 78-48] have upper lip conspicuously dark frontally.) Lower lip, chin, cheek, and lower opercle pale; bold postocular bar usually present, confluent with midlateral body stripe.

Fins pale; dorsal fin base area lacking dusky-pale-dusky pattern, the base usually slightly darker posteriorly than adjacent dorsum, but gradually paling, not contrastive as compared with Figure 34D; caudal spot black, conjoined and about equal in width to midlateral stripe, spot usually subrectangular; anal fin base pigmented. No sexual difference noted.

Color in Life.—Dorsum pale straw, sometimes olive tinted; lateral stripe black with steely blue-violet iridescence; silver sometimes present just above and below stripe; lower side and venter white with hint of violet iridescence; lateral head stripe black; iris straw where not blackened. Pectoral fin with yellow wash proximally, most intense at base; other fins pale; caudal spot black.

COMPARISON

See account of *N. procne* for distinguishing that species. *Notropis alborus*, *N. procne*, and *N. bifrenatus* are separated from *N. chalybaeus* and *N. altipinnis* in the account of *N. bifrenatus*.

BIOLOGY

The natural history of the whitemouth shiner is scantily known. The diet consists of microcrusta-ceans, mites, diatoms, and detritus (Gatz 1979; R. K. Law, in litt.). Of Virginia adults, 11 males are 36–48 mm, mean, 43, and 8 females are 34–47, mean, 41; the 48-mm male is the largest *N. alborus* known from the state. The specimens in the above-noted Pee Dee drainage, North Carolina, series are 48–54 mm SL; the latter is the largest known of the species. *Notropis alborus* likely spawns in late spring and early summer; mid- and late March Virginia specimens are decidedly prenuptial.

HABITAT

A middle and lower Piedmont species, *N. alborus* lives in warm small creeks to medium-sized streams typified by long pools with varied soft and hard substrates. In Kettles and Mines creeks, Virginia, we found the shiner in shallow small pools and in deep and shallow portions of long pools having clay, silt, sand, gravel, and bedrock substrates.

In North Carolina, *N. alborus* seemed to occupy a slightly different habitat from *N. procne* and *N. mekistocholas* (Snelson 1971). Although characteristics were not specified, Snelson infrequently collected *N. alborus* with the two other species, which tended to occupy well-flowing parts of pools, and in the case of *N. mekistocholas*, also slow runs (Snelson 1971). Menhinick et al. (1974) stated that *N. alborus* was common in riffles and swift currents of small and medium streams of the Roanoke, Cape Fear, and Pee Dee drainages. We question that Menhinick et al. distinguished *N. alborus* from *N. procne* in the field.

The water at our four Virginia or North Carolina sites was clear and colorless at two, stained slightly brownish at one, and turbid at the other. The whitemouth shiner is unknown to associate with higher submersed vegetation. This species tends to move upstream more than downstream during spring months (Hall 1972).

Fish 111 *Notropis alborus* adult male 45 mm SL (REJ 1145), VA, Mecklenburg County, Mines Creek, 12 March 1985.

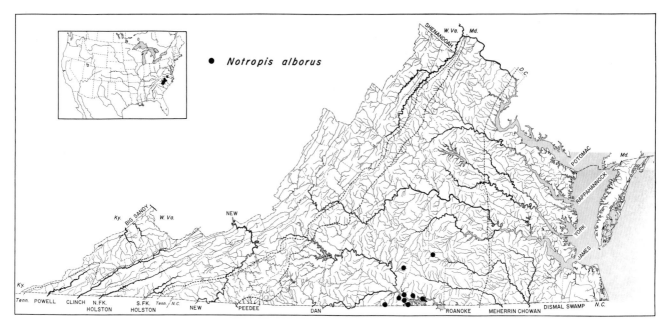

Map 78 Whitemouth shiner.

DISTRIBUTION   Map 78

The whitemouth shiner is known from the Chowan, Roanoke, Cape Fear, Pee Dee, and Santee drainages, Virginia and North Carolina. Its absence from the interjacent Tar and Neuse drainages is notable. Its listing from the Neuse (Jenkins et al. 1972) is based on specimens initially identified by a colleague, but later reidentified as *N. procne* by E. F. Menhinick (in litt.). Gilbert (*in* Lee et al. 1980) stated the southern limit of *N. alborus* to be the Pee Dee drainage, but plotted its occurrence in the Santee drainage. The plot is founded on two series (Menhinick et al. 1974; UNCC 6, 53) from Mecklenburg County, North Carolina, taken in 1966 and verified by Jenkins. Questioning of native status in the Santee (Hocutt et al. 1986) is due to the localization of the population; one of the capture sites is a heavily bait-fished, main-river impoundment. The Santee, South Carolina report of *N. alborus* by Freeman (1952) is based on six specimens; we located two of these specimens and reidentified them as *Hybopsis hypsinotus* (CHM 6748–49).

The range of *N. alborus* in Virginia is quite small and has been dwindling. The only Chowan record is of two specimens (RC) from the upper Nottoway River, taken in 1968 by T. Zorach. Because the Chowan of Virginia subsequently was extensively collected (e.g., Norman and Southwick 1985 and in litt.), and we unsuccessfully sought *N. alborus* at the record site in 1983, the shiner may have perished in this drainage.

In the Roanoke drainage, *N. alborus* appears to

have vanished from the Roanoke Creek system, which in 1947 yielded the uppermost Virginia record (CU 17005). In 1983 we searched unsuccessfully for it at nine sites in the system. This species was reported in the first publication stemming from the 1974–1976 Roanoke Creek study (Ney and Mauney 1981), but after we questioned the identification of the nonextant specimens, *N. procne* was substituted for *N. alborus* by Mauney and Maughan (1986).

One of the three known whitemouth shiner populations persisting in Virginia occupies middle Mines Creek, a tributary of Allen Creek of Gaston Reservoir; it was found regularly there during 1984–1985. Just below Mines Creek, middle Kettles Creek yielded specimens in 1991. Kerr Reservoir tributaries produced five records during 1938–1949 before impoundment (1952–1953), but none in surveys during 1977–1984 in the Virginia portion of the Kerr watershed. The 1938–1949 record sites are inundated, flowing but adversely affected by Clarksville, or perhaps too small to support a stable population. Surviving Kerr watershed populations are in Aarons Creek of the Dan River arm, Virginia (1987 collection, examined courtesy of P. L. Angermeier), and Grassy Creek, North Carolina (1978, RC). *Notropis alborus* may occur in other North Carolina tributaries in the lower Dan–Kerr–Gaston area, but according to the intensive Dan survey of 1977 by E. D. Frankensteen and our work since 1977, it certainly is not generally distributed.

Abundance.—Uncommon in Mines and Kettles creeks; abundance in Aarons Creek unknown. None of Hubbs and Raney's (1947) series from various parts of the range were notably large, and Snelson (1971) stated that *N. alborus* was much less common in the Cape Fear than its close relatives.

REMARKS

The whitemouth shiner is a plain-colored but attractively gracile and interesting minnow. Some of the interest involves its protection. Based on data available for the 1978 symposium on Virginia's endangered biota, the status of *N. alborus* was undetermined (Jenkins and Musick 1979); its small-stream environment had been insufficiently surveyed. With the now strong evidence that the range of *N. alborus* in Virginia has been sharply curtailed and is quite small, we proposed it for threatened status in Virginia (Burkhead and Jenkins 1991). It may suffer from even slight habitat perturbations. Channelization and construction of small impoundments in the Roanoke Creek system generally had little effect on the total fish population (Ney and Mauney 1981; Mauney and Maughan 1986), but may have contributed to the reduction or extirpation of the whitemouth shiner.

Name.—*Alborus* means "white mouth"—the unpigmented lips and oral cavity.

Bridle shiner   *Notropis bifrenatus* (Cope)

SYSTEMATICS

Described from Pennsylvania in 1869, *N. bifrenatus* is one of numerous blackline (or blackstripe), typically lowland-dwelling shiners. It is the type species of the genus-group *Chirope* Jordan (Gilbert 1978b), a name never in common use. Based partly on a pilot study by Swift (1975), Loos and Fuiman (1978) recognized *Chirope* as a subgenus of *Notropis*, and following Jordan and Evermann (1896), included three other small black-lined shiners in the subgenus. One of these, *N. heterodon*, was suggested as the closest relative of *N. bifrenatus* by Gilbert (*in* Lee et al. 1980). The others are *N. anogenus* and *N. maculatus* (and *N. atrocaudalis*, regarded as a subspecies by Jordan and Evermann). However, it is uncertain that *Chirope* is a natural group. Mayden (1989) proposed placing *N. bifrenatus* in the genus *Hybopsis*.

Geographic variation was not detected in *N. bifrenatus* in a limited study by Jenkins and Zorach (1970). Oddly for a *Notropis*, the left-side pharyngeal tooth count was 5 in 2 of 7 specimens from the recently discovered Santee drainage population; otherwise the population appeared typical of the species.

DESCRIPTION

Materials.—From Jenkins and Zorach (1970) plus 14 more Virginia lots; counts from 75 Virginia specimens. Life color of nonbreeding adults from 10 Virginia specimens; nuptial color according to Harrington (1947b) and Scarola (1973).

Anatomy.—A shiner with the snout and front of upper lip encircled by an anteriorly constricted dark band, and midlateral stripe usually prominent and confluent with bold caudal spot; adults are 28–40 mm SL. Body form usually moderate, predorsal contour distinctly elevating toward dorsal fin or, occasionally, the form somewhat slim and not heightened; large adults, particularly gravid females, often somewhat deep bodied; dorsal fin origin above the pelvic fin base, usually the anterior half. Head moderate; eye large, lateral; snout somewhat pointed or moderately rounded; mouth medium-sized, slightly subterminal,

Fish 112 *Notropis bifrenatus* adult male 32 mm SL (REJ 1023), VA, Amelia County, Namozine Creek, 31 August 1983.

distinctly oblique. Breast usually 90–100% scaled; belly fully scaled.

Nuptial male with minute tubercles on head and nape; pectoral fin with shagreen of tubercles, first ray bowed anteroventrad; female nontuberculate. Genital papilla small in both sexes.

Meristics.—Pharyngeal teeth 4–4; lateral line incomplete in small adults, usually nearly complete or complete in large adults, midlateral scales (31)33–36(37); circumbody scales (20)23–25(27); circumpeduncle scales (10)11–12(15); predorsal scales (11)13–15(17); predorsal scale rows (11)12–15. Dorsal rays 8; principal caudal rays 19; anal rays 7 (very rarely 8); pelvic rays 8; pectoral rays (11)12–13(14). Cephalic lateralis canals often interrupted, pores: IO(8)10–14(17); SO 7–10(13); POM (4)8–11(12); ST (0)4–6(8).

Color in Preservative.—Dorsum slightly or moderately dusky, middorsal stripe narrow and faint, or absent; dorsolateral scales duskily to dark edged; upper side with wide pale stripe along dark midlateral stripe; midlateral dusky or dark stripe narrow to moderate in width, lateral line pores usually dark stitched; lower side and venter pale except for dusky line of pigment along anal fin base and caudal peduncle midventrally. Head dorsum dusky; side of snout (over lachrymal bone) quite dusky or black, darkness constricting as it encircles snout tip; upper lip also pigmented, particularly frontally; muzzle thus appears "moustached" or "bridled" (Figure 36C); lower lip, chin, cheek, and lower opercle devoid of melanophores or, very rarely, a file of melanophores along side of lower lip; mouth (inside) not pigmented.

Fins pale; dorsal fin base uniformly pigmented or, rarely, slightly darker posteriorly and evenly paling anteriad, not darkened just anterior to dorsal origin. Caudal spot usually confluent with, bolder, and wider than posterior end of midlateral stripe, the spot round, oval, or somewhat rectangular. Relatively pale specimens often have the dusky lateral stripe ending just short of, or in contact with the anterior point of a triangular or diffuse caudal spot.

Nuptial male, compared with female, darker pigmented on margins of upper body scales and on anterior pectoral rays.

Color in Life.—Dorsum straw colored, dorsolateral scales black-olive edged; supramidlateral stripe straw; midlateral stripe black with green-blue iridescence; lower side and venter pale straw with scattered silver reflections. Head dorsum and snout dusky brown; snout band and horizontal upper opercular bar black; cheek and lower opercle pale. Fins pale; basicaudal spot black, caudal base with yellow-orange wash. Nuptial male light yellow to bright yellow-gold on lower side of body; nuptial male and female with dorsal, caudal, and anal rays faint yellow.

Larvae.—Described by Harrington (1947a), Mansueti and Hardy (1967), Jones et al. (1978), Loos and Fuiman (1978), Snyder (1979), and Wang and Kernehan (1979).

COMPARISON

The other small, blackline or blackstripe shiners of the Atlantic slope which live in or near the Virginia range of *N. bifrenatus* are *N. procne*, *N. alborus*, *N. chalybaeus*, and *N. altipinnis*. As many as four of these species have been found at a single locality, three of them concurrently (Stony Creek of the Chowan drainage). The first three species are segregated as a group from the latter two by: (1) anal rays almost always [7 *vs.* 8 or more]; (2) pharyngeal tooth count [4–4 *vs.* 2,4–4,2, occasionally only 1 minor row tooth]; (3) chin pigmentation (Figure 36) [absent or, occasionally in *N. procne*, slightly dusky *vs.* usually well pigmented anteriorly]; (4) mouth pigmentation, internally [absent *vs.* dusky, sprinkled with large melanophores, particularly the roof anteriorly].

Notropis bifrenatus is distinguished from *N. procne* in that account and is paired in the *Key* with *N. alborus*. Many keys ascribe an incomplete lateral line to *N. bifrenatus*, but this condition generally does not hold for adults 40 mm SL and greater, from Delaware and south (Jenkins and Zorach 1970; this study).

BIOLOGY

The biology of the bridle shiner is well known chiefly from R. W. Harrington's studies in New Hampshire and New York. This apparently sight-feeding species feeds on an array of microcrustaceans and aquatic insects; detritus and living plant material sometimes are taken. *Notropis bifrenatus* has been observed foraging from sunfish nests in the absence and presence of the male sunfish (Bailey 1938b; Webster 1942; Harrington 1948b).

The bridle shiner matures in 1 year; males tend to mature slightly earlier than females in the first breeding season. Maximum longevity is 2 years and a few months; no specimens had passed more than two winters (Harrington 1948a). The smallest adult male found by Harrington (1947a, 1948a), and by us in Virginia, was 25 mm SL, but Harrington (1947b) reported a 24-mm male with nuptial color. Females as small as 30 mm produced fertile eggs (Harrington 1947a; 1948a). Males tend to grow slightly faster than females in the first year, but the difference is reversed in the second year. Age-2 males were 35–45 mm SL, mean, 39, females 35–43 mm, mean, 40 (Harrington 1948a). Of nearly mature and mature Virginia specimens collected during April to July, 18 males were 25–48 mm SL, mean, 35, and 37 females were 24–49 mm, mean, 37. The largest specimen known from Virginia is the 49-mm SL female; maximum size is 50 mm SL, from Delaware (Jenkins and Zorach 1970).

Specimens 45 mm and larger are more common in Delaware, Maryland, and Virginia than in New York and New England.

In New Hampshire the bridle shiner spawned from 7 to 30 June; the height of activity occurred in the latter part of the period. Associated reproductive behavior began in late May and persisted into mid-July. All these activities occurred in water of 14.4–26.7°C (Harrington 1947a, 1947b, 1948a). Webster (1942) noted *N. bifrenatus* to breed during June and part of July in Connecticut, although spawning was not observed. The reproductive period in Virginia broadly overlaps that in New Hampshire; mid-April specimens were prenuptial; late May fish were in reproductive condition; late June through July females, except for one gravid individual in mid-July, were partly to entirely spent; males retained tubercles through mid-July.

Spawning occurs in localized areas within calm pools, just below the surface and above beds of submergent macrophytes. Occasionally a male drives away another male from the spawning arena. Males "nose" females, and usually 1–3 males swiftly pursue a typically larger female. The spawning act culminates the pursuit of a female and occurs rapidly, with 1–2 males closely flanking and quivering with the female. Six to slightly more than 15 eggs are shed per spawning (Harrington 1947b, 1951). Harrington (1948a) estimated that 1,062–2,110 ova are produced in a year, but he (1951) thought that this may not accurately estimate total fecundity. It is uncertain that the adhesive eggs stick to plants, but the larvae apparently have cement glands which allow adherence to plants (Loos and Fuiman 1978).

HABITAT

Notropis bifrenatus is a gregarious warmwater fish which usually occurs in slack areas of sluggish creeks, streams, and rivers, in natural ponds and lakes, and in impoundments. It occupies nearshore areas, typically associating with soft bottom and moderate to abundant submersed aquatic vegetation (Adams and Hankinson 1928; Bailey 1938b; Harrington 1947a; Horwitz *in* Cooper 1985). Many records are from large marshes or marsh-fringed shores; in such areas the bridle shiner's specific affiliation may be with submersed vegetation. Some records are from beaches (Jenkins and Zorach 1970; later collections). Most writers indicate that *N. bifrenatus* has a propensity for clear water.

The bridle shiner seems not particularly acid tolerant, judging from its general avoidance of the New Jersey Pine Barrens (Hastings 1979) and highly acidic areas of the Virginia and other Coastal Plain areas. The pH was 7.0 at the North Carolina Coastal Plain locality (Bayless and Smith 1962) and 8.0 at the Jolly Pond outlet (VIMS 2394) in a calcareous area of the Chickahominy system in Virginia.

Notropis bifrenatus is a freshwater oligohaline fish (Jenkins and Zorach 1970). It seems unlikely that it actually occupied the maximum salinity of 11.8‰ noted by Hildebrand and Schroeder (1928). In the lower Delaware River area, few specimens were found in tidal fresh water; the remainder were in impoundments and, more abundantly, in freshwater streams (Wang and Kernehan 1979).

Notropis bifrenatus occupies a wide range of biotopes in Virginia, although it has not been found in truly standing water. In Appomattox River tributaries we found this fish in slow current near moderate flow, in sluggish pools and backwaters, and in a barely flowing beaver pond. Some Appomattox specimens were taken among and near submersed vegetation, but no higher plants existed at one site. Substrates were sand, silt, mud, and detritus. The water ranged from colorless to moderately stained; it was clear but probably becomes considerably turbid after substantial rainfall. Some areas at one station had an oily surface slick. Records in the James River and Chickahominy River estuaries are from marshes and beaches, where salinity generally was less than 2‰ (VIMS 1977; Rozas and Odum 1987a, 1987b; McIvor and Odum 1988).

DISTRIBUTION   Map 79

Notropis bifrenatus ranges from the Lake Ontario–St. Lawrence basin and southern Maine south to the Santee drainage of South Carolina. However, in the five major drainages between the Chowan and Santee, it is known only from one collection in a Neuse drainage tributary in North Carolina (Jenkins and Zorach 1970). The Neuse population probably is extirpated (Rohde et al. 1979). The existence of the Santee population was recognized in 1981 through capture of several series in Lake Marion; a series from that impoundment in 1954 and one from Lake Moultrie also are verified (Coleman *in* Braswell 1991; our data). The Santee population is unlikely to have been introduced by bait fishermen. The shiner is quite small and delicate, and has been unavailable near South Carolina.

The Virginia populations of the bridle shiner have been localized and some are extirpated or nearly so. All confirmed Potomac drainage records are from 1935 or earlier. We did not plot two old USNM records from the Potomac with hazy locality data, nor

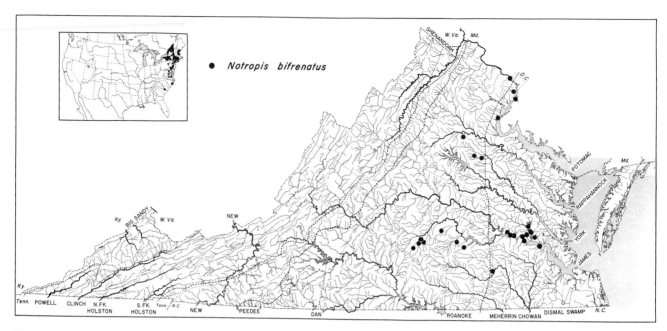

Map 79   Bridle shiner.

unverified records from a Coastal Plain area of the Potomac River surveyed by the Virginia Power Company during 1971–1976.

The Rappahannock drainage population may be extirpated; the only record is from a Flat Creek site in 1933. Recently the drainage was extensively surveyed and that site was sampled (Maurakis et al. 1987). In the York drainage the bridle shiner has been found, sporadically and as recent as 1983, only in the upper Mattaponi system.

The James drainage is occupied by the most successful Virginia populations. In the Piedmont of the Appomattox system during 1983 we found the bridle shiner at the lowermost, middle, and uppermost sites; the earliest of the other five records (four sites) is 1970. However, the shiner is not generally distributed in the Appomattox system. The Coastal Plain records are from the lower Chickahominy River and tributaries during 1949–1986; Herring Creek in 1975; and James River marsh and "beach seine" areas during 1968–1976 (including verification of one of the records from White [1976], the lowermost plotted here).

The Chowan population is known only from Stony Creek in the vicinity of the Route 301 bridge. *Notropis bifrenatus* was taken in four of six collections made during 1967–1968, but not in four made during 1971–1984. Moderate surveys elsewhere in the Stony Creek system and extensive canvasing of the Virginia part of the Chowan drainage during 1967–1986 failed to reveal the bridle shiner. Considering its localization

in the Chowan and the Carolinas, the apparent absence of the bridle shiner in the Roanoke drainage is not surprising.

Abundance.—Rare or uncommon.

REMARKS

Notropis bifrenatus is a frail, generally slow-swimming fish; where common, it serves as important forage of pickerel and other calm-water predators. Although not qualifying as a "miniature" fish, when compared with many South American freshwater species not exceeding 26 mm SL (Weitzman and Vari 1988), it is one of the smallest shiners. Its diminution is paralleled by reductive development of the laterosensory canal system on the head and body, as shown in one of the more detailed descriptions of the skull of a fish species (Harrington 1955). Reduction of lateral line canals and proliferation of skin-surface neuromasts, also traits of *N. bifrenatus* (Jenkins and Zorach 1970), seem to occur commonly in shiners characteristic of calm, weedy waters (Swift 1970).

Much is known of the bridle shiner's life history, and until recently this species was thought to be faring well in most of its ample historical range. With the wide variety of habitat conditions it normally occupies, one might think that this fish would broadly populate the lower Piedmont and Coastal Plain. However, it is absent from many areas within its general range and declining alarmingly in others.

In Virginia the bridle shiner is successful, perhaps limitedly, in only the James drainage, and it may be extirpated from four other drainages (including the Roanoke for which there is no record). The downward trend appears real; we do not believe that many populations remain undiscovered in the state. This shiner is easy to collect by seine, and much of the Virginia range recently was moderately to well sampled, the Chowan drainage extensively by ichthyocide. We carefully looked for the bridle shiner when in its territory, and searched collections of blacklined shiners (*N. procne*, *N. alborus*, *N. altipinnis*, and *N. chalybaeus*) made by other workers for possible inclusion of *N. bifrenatus*—to no avail. In contrast, the shiner has been found somewhat regularly, although in small numbers, in suitable habitat during the last 40 years in the James drainage.

Beyond Virginia, *N. bifrenatus* seems to be holding up well in New York, but has sharply receded in Massachusetts, New Jersey, Pennsylvania, and Maryland (e.g., Horwitz *in* Cooper 1985; C. Smith 1985; K. E. Hartel, in litt.). Extensive extirpation in the Carolinas is predicated partly on the existence (and presumed native status) of the Santee drainage population.

Habitat alteration appears to be the general factor afflicting *N. bifrenatus*. The chief common denomina-tor may be turbidity sufficient to impair the food-sighting ability of the fish and the growth of submerged plants. The bridle shiner depends on vegetated areas for feeding, breeding, and hiding. Submerged aquatic vegetation is important to the fish and macroinvertebrate fauna of a tidal freshwater marsh in the Chickahominy system occupied (sparingly) by *N. bifrenatus* (Rozas and Odum 1987b).

It may be more than spurious that our last validated Potomac record of the bridle shiner, dated 1935, corresponds with the virtually complete disappearance of submerged aquatic macrophytes from the tidal freshwater Potomac River and tributaries, owing to increased turbidity and consequent light reduction. Recently, vegetation has dramatically increased in the lower Potomac (Carter and Rybicki 1986), but recruitment populations of the bridle shiner may not exist.

We conservatively recommended that the bridle shiner be granted special concern status in Virginia (Burkhead and Jenkins 1991); its status should be ascertained in other states.

Name.—*Bifrenatus* means "two bridled," referring to the black preocular bars that unite across the snout.

Ironcolor shiner   *Notropis chalybaeus* (Cope)

SYSTEMATICS

Named from Pennsylvania in 1869, *N. chalybaeus* is allocated to the *texanus* group (Swift 1970; Mayden 1989). This assemblage, composed of "blackline" or "blackstripe" Piedmont and lowland shiners with 2,4–4,2 teeth, has been associated at times with the subgenus *Alburnops* of *Notropis* (see *N. volucellus*).

DESCRIPTION

Materials.—From Swift (1970) and 11 Virginia lots; meristic data from populations in Maryland and the Chowan and Roanoke drainages (Swift 1970), and from 32 specimens from the Piankatank, James, Chowan, and Roanoke drainages. Life color from Marshall (1947), Swift (1970), Pflieger (1975), and C. Smith (1985).

Anatomy.—A shiner with a dark lateral stripe confluent with a usually equally intense caudal spot, and the snout tip, lips, anterior chin, and mouth dusky to dark; adults are 24–40 mm SL. Body form moderate or deep, moderately or well compressed, extreme specimens being quite deep, slabsided (Fish 113); predorsal contour slightly or distinctly elevated toward dorsal fin origin; dorsal fin origin above pelvic fin base, usually the posterior half. Head moderate; eye large, lateral; snout somewhat pointed; mouth some-

Fish 113 *Notropis chalybeaus* adult female 37 mm SL (body deeper than typical) (REJ 1015), VA, Greensville County, Cattail Creek, 15 July 1983.

what small or medium, terminal or slightly subterminal, distinctly oblique. Breast 0–20(40)% scaled, usually 1 scale anterior to each pectoral fin origin; belly completely scaled.

Nuptial male with medium-large tubercles on chin, lower jaw rami, and lower edge of snout, chin appearing rasplike and upper lip overhung by pendant snout tip tubercles; small tubercles on side of snout and cheek, tiny tubercles over eye and occasionally elsewhere on head dorsum; body with few minute tubercles on nape, slightly larger ones on anterior midside; pectoral fin rays with shagreen of tubercles, first ray occasionally bowed anteroventrad. Female occasionally with few small tubercles on lower jaw. Male genital papilla concealed behind recessed anal papilla; female genital papilla inobvious, anal papilla distinctly protruding.

Meristics.—Pharyngeal teeth usually 2,4–4,2; lateral line incomplete or complete, midlateral scales 32–34(36); circumbody scales (24)25–27(28); circumpeduncle scales (10)12; predorsal scales 14–19(21). Dorsal rays (7)8; principal caudal rays 19; anal rays 8; pelvic rays 7–8(9); pectoral rays 11–13.

Color in Preservative.—Dorsum slightly or moderately dusky, middorsal stripe faint or absent; dorsolateral scales distinctly darker marginally or about uniformly pigmented; pale supramidlateral stripe present; midlateral stripe diffusely dark or black, moderately wide, tending slightly wider on anterior body; lower side and venter pale except midventrally, where double row of melanophores extends from tail to usually around front of anus, sometimes ending just posterior to anus or as far forward as interpelvic area.

Head dorsum dusky or dark; side and tip of snout, both lips, and anterior chin pigmented moderately or much darker than adjacent areas of snout dorsum; intensity of pigment at snout tip (along edge immediately above upper lip) equal to or slightly paler than that of upper lip, in the latter case the snout tip not notably blackened, *contra* Figure 36D; lower lip and anterior chin pigmentation coupled to form dusky to dark area that is crescentic or straight-edged posteriorly. Inside of mouth, particularly oral valves and roof, sprinkled with large melanophores; gular area, cheek, and lower opercle pale.

Dorsal fin with pigment along rays, base lacking dark-pale-dark pattern; caudal "spot" usually a continuation of midlateral stripe, equal in intensity and height to, and fully confluent with the stripe; posterior edge of spot not rounded, not notably diffusing posteriad along medial caudal rays; otherwise spot slighter darker and narrower than end of stripe, and diffused posteriad; lower fins pigmented along rays.

Color in Life.—Dorsum straw-olive to dark olive; supramidlateral stripe straw; snout markings, midlateral stripe, and caudal spot dark; lower side and venter silver-white; fins pale. Nuptial male dorsum yellow-olive or with reddish brown added to olive cast; supramidlateral stripe dull yellow or bright orange; head and body below dark lateral stripe silvery with orange or rosy wash, the orange or rosy shade more obvious on lower caudal peduncle. Iris orange

above black bar, white below. Caudal fin with orange window above and below spot, and orange or rosy cast sometimes extending into all fins. Nuptial color varies with staining of water, more orange in dark red-brown conditions, rosier in clearer water. Breeding female paler than bright male; yellow stripe above dark lateral stripe, cream or white below stripe; yellow above iris bar.

Larvae.—Described by Marshall (1947), Mansueti and Hardy (1967), Jones et al. (1978), Loos and Fuiman (1978), Wang and Kernehan (1979), and Heufelder and Fuiman (1982).

COMPARISON

Notropis chalybaeus and *N. altipinnis* are distinguished as a group from other Atlantic slope blackline or blackstripe shiners—*N. procne*, *N. alborus*, and *N. bifrenatus*—in the account of the latter.

Notropis chalybaeus and *N. altipinnis* can be differentiated by: (1) anal rays usually [8 in *chalybaeus* vs. 10 in *altipinnis*]; (2) breast scalation, % scaled [0–20(40) vs. 100]; (3) scale size dorsolaterally, as indicated by Fish 113 and 114, and reflected by predorsal count [larger, 14–19(21) vs. smaller, (19)21–26(28)]; (4) mouth size [moderately small vs. moderately large]. Many pigmentary differences exist (see *Descriptions*).

BIOLOGY

The adult life history of the ironcolor shiner is known chiefly from Marshall's (1947) study in Florida. He found masticated small animals and considerable fragments of vegetation in the gut; the plant material apparently was not being digested. Presumably its animal prey typically includes insects; Cope (1869) noted that a specimen had devoured minute insect larvae. This fish locates food by sight.

In Wisconsin a male ironcolor shiner matured apparently in 1 year, and a Missouri fish of 52 mm TL was 2 years old; age-1 Wisconsin fish averaged 29 mm TL (Becker 1983). The average of 39 mm SL from a North Carolina lake (Frey 1951) probably reflects selection of large specimens for morphological study. Of 41 Virginia specimens collected during 5 May–10 September, most putative yearlings had matured; only four—females 26–29 mm SL and showing some ova enlargement by mid-July—possibly were immature. From the length–frequency data, the largest Virginia specimens were judged to be 2 years old. Marshall (1947) reported females to average slightly larger than males. Our adults were 22 males of 24–40 mm SL, mean, 33, and 15 females of 29–37 mm, mean, 33. The 40-mm SL male is the largest Virginia specimen;

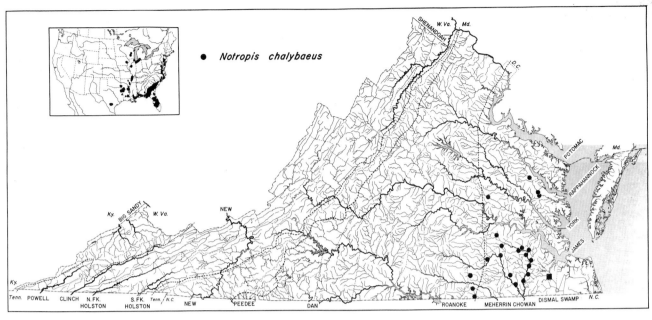

Map 80   Ironcolor shiner. Solid square on Single Creek represents record with questionable locality data.

this species reaches 55 mm SL but rarely exceeds 45 mm (Swift 1970 and *in* Lee et al. 1980).

The spawning season in subtropical Florida extends from mid-April through late September, in water of 15–25°C (Marshall 1947). In Maryland and Delaware, spawning is thought to occur during mid- and late spring (Wang and Kernehan 1979). Our few early May females seemed prenuptial; a late-May male was highly tuberculate. Early-June to late-July specimens were in reproductive condition, although many females were partly spent. Late-August and early-September males had vestiges of tubercles, and the August female was postnuptial.

Spawning takes place in sluggish sandy pools, where males chase females, seeking those in reproductive readiness. Signaling such, the female stops fleeing, then the pair makes a quick side-by-side dash with the ventral surfaces appressed. Eggs apparently sink and stick to sand and other bottom materials (Marshall 1947). A gravid female held 246 mature ova (Becker 1983).

HABITAT

Notropis chalybaeus is a slackwater shiner of warm, low-gradient, usually clear creeks, streams, and swamps. As is generally true elsewhere, it is essentially a Coastal Plain species in Virginia; the habitat at three outer Piedmont or Fall Zone record sites resembled those eastward. The Basherkill River, New York, population is isolated in an intermontane area; the stream is low-gradient and heavily vegetated. The ironcolor shiner loosely aggregates over detritus, mud, silt, and sand, and in open water and weedy areas (e.g., Meffe and Sheldon 1988). It is rarely seen in lakes and other standing waters, and then usually near the inlet or outlet (Swift 1970).

The ironcolor shiner occupies tannin-stained water and has been found in water as acidic as pH 4.2, but normally it may avoid excessively acidic conditions (Smith 1953; Hastings 1979, 1984; Graham 1989). In Arkansas it occurs in pH 6.2–6.7 (Robison 1977); the one determination for Virginia was pH 6.9. *Notropis chalybaeus* enters tidal fresh water in Florida, North Carolina, and Delaware, but is much more abundant in nontidal conditions (Bailey et al. 1954; Keup and Bayless 1964; Wang and Kernehan 1979). We have no verified record of it living in tidal water Virginia.

DISTRIBUTION   Map 80

The ironcolor shiner exhibits a classic (U-shaped) lowland distribution pattern, ranging from the lower Hudson drainage south to Florida, west along the Gulf slope, and up the central Mississippi basin into the southern Great Lakes region. Except in the southeast, many populations are disjunct.

The Virginia distribution has peculiarities. Like certain other characteristically Coastal Plain inhabitants (e.g., two *Enneacanthus* sunfishes), *N. chalybaeus* apparently is absent from much of the Chesapeake basin in Maryland and Virginia. However, it is a member of the depauperate freshwater ichthyofauna of the Piankatank drainage, isolated between the Rappahannock and York drainages; the five records (three sites) span 1961–1976. The single James drainage record (UR 3567) is from Beaverdam Creek, a Chickahominy River tributary, in 1976. The validity of the locality data for Jordan's (1889b) Shingle Creek, Dismal Swamp periphery, specimen (SU 614) is questionable (*Biogeography*).

In the Chowan drainage *N. chalybaeus* is well dispersed in the Blackwater system; 3 of 11 records (9 sites) are from the 1980s. It is localized in the Nottoway system; 6 of the 7 records (6 sites) are from 1969–1979. The other record is of one specimen from the extensive recent Nottoway survey by Norman and Southwick (1985, later collections); it was taken in 1984 at Station 49 but was not identified until 1989. The two captures in the Meherrin system are dated 1979 and 1983. In North Carolina several records exist for the Chowan but only one or two for the Roanoke

drainage (Smith 1963; Carnes 1965; Swift 1970; Menhinick et al. 1974; E. F. Menhinick, in litt.).

Abundance.—Generally rare or uncommon.

REMARKS

The ironcolor shiner and bridle shiner are the most diminutive of Virginia shiners, and they are similar in morphology, color, habitat, and life history. The poor success of the ironcolor shiner in Virginia parallels that of the bridle shiner, and it too may be a candidate for protective status in the state. On a full-range basis though, *N. chalybaeus* is considerably more widespread and has not suffered a general decline recently.

Name.—*Chalybaeus* means of iron or steel; it refers to the shining dark lateral stripe.

Highfin shiner   *Notropis altipinnis* (Cope)

SYSTEMATICS

Notropis altipinnis was described from North Carolina in 1870. The relationships of this distinctive south Atlantic slope lowlands "blackstripe" shiner are uncertain. Hubbs (1941b) compared it with a species of the subgenus *Notropis*, but Snelson (1968) argued its disparity from that group. Its close resemblance to *N. cummingsae*, also of the south Atlantic Coastal Plain, was noted by Hubbs and Raney (1951) and Gilbert and Burgess (*in* Lee 1980). *Notropis altipinnis* was included in the *texanus* species group (see *N. chalybaeus*) by Mayden (1989), who did not treat *N. cummingsae*. Swift (1970) noted that juvenile *N. altipinnis*, *N. cummingsae*, and *N. welaka* often have a pale longitudinal middorsal streak on the head, but we were unable to recognize even a short streak in our specimens of *N. altipinnis*.

Hubbs and Raney (1948) separated the highfin

shiner into six subspecies, a different one in each major drainage where the species was then known. Generally, these were based on few samples and have not been regarded as valid (Gilbert 1978b; Gilbert and Burgess *in* Lee et al. 1980). We do not recognize subspecies, but suggest that geographic variation merits reanalysis with modern techniques.

DESCRIPTION

Materials.—Thirteen Virginia lots, including our counts of 38 Chowan or Roanoke drainage specimens, and counts from 79 Chowan specimens studied by Hubbs (1941b) and Hubbs and Raney (1948). Life color from nuptial and postnuptial Chowan drainage fish.

Anatomy.—A blackstripe shiner with modally 10 anal rays, lips and anterior chin dark, and caudal fin with a small spot; adults are 30–45 mm SL. Body form moderate

Fish 114 *Notropis altipinnis* adult female 46 mm SL (REJ 1015), VA, Greensville County, Cattail Creek, 15 July 1983.

or somewhat elongate, slightly or moderately compressed; dorsal fin origin usually slightly posterior to pelvic fin origin, occasionally above posterior one-third of pelvic base. Head moderate; eye large, lateral; snout somewhat pointed or moderately rounded; mouth somewhat large, terminal or very slightly subterminal, distinctly oblique. Breast and belly 100% scaled.

Larger nuptial males have minute tubercles crowded on head dorsum, some on snout and chin, and rowed on lower jaw rami; chin tubercles the largest on head; minute tubercles on anterior nape; pectoral fin tubercles the largest on the fish, but still tiny, bi- to triserial (not shagreen-like); pectoral rays stronger than in female, first ray often bowed anteroventrad; some large males and most smaller nuptial males have only the pectoral fin tuberculate. Larger females have tubercles rowed on lower jaw rami and scattered on snout; jaw tubercles tend larger than in males; largest females have minute tubercles on pectoral rays. Smallest nuptial females bear few to several minute tubercles along lower jaw rami. Larger immature males and females have tiny (though distinct, pointed) chin tubercles during breeding season. Male genital papilla inobvious; female papilla somewhat protruding with bulbous anal papilla.

Meristics.—Pharyngeal teeth 2,4–4,2; lateral line incomplete or complete, midlateral scales (34)35–37(38); circumbody scales (24)25–27(8); circumpeduncle scales 12–13(16); predorsal scales (19)21–26(28); predorsal scale rows 16–18. Dorsal rays 8; principal caudal rays 19; anal rays (9)10(11); pelvic rays 8; pectoral rays 14–16.

Color in Preservative.—Dorsum moderately dusky, middorsal stripe moderate or obsolete; dorsolateral scales distinctly darker marginally or nearly uniformly pigmented, not obviously bicolored; pale supramidlateral stripe present. Midlateral stripe about equally intense over full length, varying among specimens from diffusely dark to black, usually moderately dark, moderately wide, and distinctly wider anteriorly; midlateral stripe usually edged dorsally (on mid-third of body) or traversed (on posterior third) by fine black line along horizontal myoseptum; lateral line pores sometimes stitched where line curves below lateral stripe; lower side and venter pale except midventrally, where darkened by double row of melanophores usually from tail to about anus.

Head dorsum dusky or dark; side of snout, both lips, and anterior chin pigmented moderately or strongly, darker than tip and dorsum of snout; when viewed ventrally, pigmentation of lips and closely adjacent portion of lower jaw forms somewhat semicircular dark chin area, from which stippling usually extends slightly posteriad only at midline of chin. Circumnarial pigmentation darkest dorsally (more intense than middorsal internarial area), sparse or absent elsewhere. Inside of mouth, particularly oral valves and roof, sprinkled with large melanophores; gular area posteriorly, cheek, and lower opercle pale.

Dorsal fin pigmented along rays, base lacking dark-pale-dark pattern; caudal spot usually triangular, usually slightly darker than posterior portion of midlateral stripe, but its triangular shape usually obscured by melanophores broadly interconnecting spot and stripe, hence spot and stripe virtually a continuation; caudal spot diffusing posteriad, medial caudal rays darker proximally than those adjacent; lower fins usually pigmented along some or all rays. Nuptial male with pectoral rays more darkly lined than female.

Color in Life.—Dorsum straw-olive or olive; supramidlateral stripe iridescent gold; midlateral stripe, side of snout, and caudal spot black; venter white; fins pale. We never noted particularly colorful highfin shiners. Snelson (1968) stated that *N. altipinnis* apparently develops chromatic breeding colors, based on North Carolina specimens described (Jordan 1889b; Hubbs 1941b) as having a yellowish or orange-yellow snout and the dorsal, caudal, and anal (or all) fins amber or faintly reddish.

COMPARISON

See *N. bifrenatus* for distinguishing that species plus *N. procne* and *N. alborus* as a group from *N. altipinnis* and *N. chalybaeus*. *Notropis altipinnis* and *N. chalybaeus* are compared in the account of the latter.

BIOLOGY

The natural history of the highfin shiner is scantily known. The diet in North Carolina consisted mostly of terrestrial insects and lesser amounts of filamentous algae (Gatz 1979). Twenty-nine Virginia specimens, mostly adults, took almost entirely microcrustaceans and terrestrial insects; some aquatic insects were ingested (A. H. Campbell, in litt.).

Length–frequency data from 202 Chowan drainage specimens taken during 12 May–29 August indicated that about half the yearlings and all age-2 fish of both sexes were mature; age-2 fish were relatively uncommon. The largest immature fish were a male 37 mm SL and a female 34 mm. The 46 adult males were 31–46 mm, mean, 37, and 90 females were 28–48 mm, mean, 38. Our largest Virginia specimen is the 48-mm female; individuals as large as 51 mm SL are known from North Carolina (Hubbs and Raney 1948).

Notropis altipinnis in apparent spawning condition were collected during 18 March–3 June in North Carolina (Hubbs and Raney 1948), but the breeding period may span mid-spring to late summer. In our Chowan samples, the adults taken on 12 May were in prenuptial or nuptial condition. Those taken on 23 May were in breeding condition, although some females appeared partly spent, and both females caught on 26 June were partly spent. On 15 July most females were largely spent but some were quite gravid. All four large males taken on 29 August had retained tubercles and one of five females had many ripe ova; the other females were partly or fully spent.

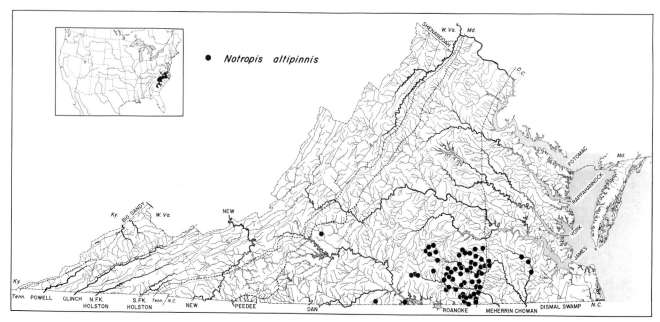

Map 81 Highfin shiner.

HABITAT

In Virginia *N. altipinnis* is characteristic of the outer Piedmont. It typically lives in creeks to medium-sized streams; all records are from tributaries and upper reaches of main-stem rivers. These streams have somewhat low gradient and generally are not swampy or marshy; their warm water is colorless to moderately stained, and clear to intermittently turbid. At 19 capture sites in the Nottoway system and two in the Blackwater system, the pH was 6.3–7.0, usually 6.6–6.9 (Norman and Southwick 1985, in litt.). The highfin shiner aggregates in pools and backwaters, often in the lee of modest current, and is found over a variety of soft and hard substrates. Its habitat in the Carolinas seems essentially the same based on Hubbs and Raney (1948). No association with plants has been noticed. This species tends to move upstream more frequently than down during spring months (Hall 1972).

DISTRIBUTION   Map 81

Indigenous to the south Atlantic slope, the highfin shiner occurs from the Chowan drainage of Virginia to the Savannah drainage in South Carolina. It is chiefly a mid- and lower Piedmont fish in much of its range. In Virginia it is nearly restricted to that area; plotted records include those from Norman and Southwick's (1985) collections made during 1982 and 1984, plus their extensive survey of 1985–1986. The

basis of the highfin shiner's abrupt termination about the Fall Line in the Nottoway and Meherrin systems of the Chowan may be an avoidance of low gradient and large streams.

The Coastal Plain population is localized in the middle Blackwater system; it was discovered by Jordan (1889b) and extant in the 1980s. Jordan's record and two of three recent ones are from the Blackwater River; the other is from lowermost Terrapin Swamp. The middle Blackwater River has more current than its headwater swamps and swampy tributaries and is smaller than the unoccupied Piedmont and Coastal Plain reaches of the Nottoway and Meherrin rivers.

Unlike the generality of occurrence of *N. altipinnis* in the Piedmont section of the Nottoway and half of the Meherrin, this species is localized in some streams and apparently absent from most others in the upper, Lunenburg County section of the Meherrin. Of the 23 sampled sites in that section, all sampled since 1958 (mostly in the 1980s), the shiner was caught at four. Most notably, *N. altipinnis* was not found in seven samples from the lower North Meherrin River, where one site yielded 30 species to us. It was present in three of four collections from the South Meherrin River and the one from the lowermost Middle Meherrin River.

The lower two Roanoke drainage records represent isolated populations at the native upper limit. Much unimpounded water remains in the Virginia part of the Gaston–Kerr Reservoir area, but *N. altipinnis* is generally absent, paralleling the situation in the adjacent upper Meherrin. The record from the lower site predates impoundment; the other is from 1983.

The surprising middle Roanoke drainage record is the kind whose validity we would sharply question, had we not collected the specimen. It was taken in 1981 from Elk Creek, a small, typical upper Piedmont stream in the Goose Creek system. Apparently it represents an introduction, perhaps concurrent with intentional stocking of mosquitofish in the area (see *Gambusia holbrooki*).

Abundance.—Usually uncommon, occasionally abundant.

REMARKS

Notropis altipinnis parallels the whitemouth shiner *Notropis alborus* and Carolina darter *Etheostoma collis* by centering in smaller streams on the outer Pied-

mont, and in being little researched. The latter two species are much the less abundant. The highfin shiner probably serves as important forage for pickerels and sunfishes.

Although the highfin shiner is not a well-tuberculated species, it exhibits unusual tuberculation traits that in combination may be unique among fishes. Least unusual is the development of tubercles by females. Juvenile males and females bear chin tubercles, a condition that held down to the smallest fish (24 mm SL) among the 66 judged by gonads as clearly immature; chin tubercles tend to be larger in females than in males. Larger reproductive females develop pectoral fin tubercles, and some larger nuptial males have only pectoral fin tubercles. We add *N. altipinnis* to the short list of black-mouthed *Notropis* (Suttkus and Bailey 1990).

Name.—*Altipinnis* translates to "high fin."

Silverjaw minnow

SYSTEMATICS

The silverjaw minnow is a small eastern North American shiner named from Pennsylvania in 1865. It long stood as the monotypic genus *Ericymba*, based on the marked enlargement of the cephalic lateral line canal on the cheek (infraorbital canal) and lower jaw (preopercular-mandibular canal) (Figure 27C). These canals are subdivided into quadrate chambers and their sensory cells are large (Reno 1971; Hoyt 1972).

Mayden (1989) allied *Ericymba* with several species of *Notropis* and placed them in a *Hybopsis* clade. In adding *Ericymba* to *Notropis*, Coburn and Cavender (1992) suggested that the silverjaw minnow is most closely related to certain species of the subgenus *Alburnops*. They considered that *Ericymba* later may be reinstated and enlarged with some species currently allocated mostly to *Alburnops*.

The shagreen-like pectoral fin tuberculation (Wal-

Notropis buccatus Cope

lace 1973b; D. Ross 1974) and distinctive downward flexure of the first pectoral ray of nuptial male *N. buccatus* may aid in phylogenetic placement. These traits occur also in the *Notropis procne* group and certain other shiners (e.g., Jenkins and Zorach 1970; herein).

DESCRIPTION

Materials.—Ten series from the Big Sandy and 1 from the Rappahannock; counts from 25 Virginia specimens. Color in life from Clay (1975).

Anatomy.—A shiner with large supralateral eyes and enlarged lateralis system canals on cheek and jaw; adults are 35–65 mm SL. Body nearly fusiform, somewhat compressed, back slightly or moderately elevated; dorsal fin origin above anterior half of pelvic fin base. Head moderate; eye large, supralateral; snout slightly or moderately

Fish 115 *Notropis buccatus* adult female 50 mm SL (WHH 104), VA, Buchanan County, Knox Creek, 28 June 1983.

rounded; frenum absent; mouth moderate, subterminal or slightly inferior; cephalic lateralis canals on cheek and lower jaw greatly enlarged, subdivided into chambers. Belly fully scaled; breast usually nearly fully scaled. Peritoneum silver.

Nuptial tubercles on pectoral rays 2 through 5, 6, or 7, tubercles tiny, forming shagreen-like layer; large peak males add tiny head and nape tubercles, and have leading pectoral ray bowed distinctly downward.

Meristics.—Pharyngeal teeth usually 1,4–4,1 (1,4-[in 4 fish]; 0,4-[1]; 1,5-[1]); lateral line complete, scales (30)32–33(34); circumbody scales (20)22–24(26); circumpeduncle scales (11)12; predorsal scales (12)14–15(18); predorsal scale rows (12)13–14. Dorsal rays 8; anal rays (7)8; pelvic rays 8; pectoral rays 14–16.

Color in Preservative.—Ground shade pale or slightly dusky; upper body scales faintly or moderately outlined with melanophores; narrow dark middorsal stripe present; midside with narrow faint or moderately dusky stripe, most intense posteriorly; lower side sometimes slightly dusky, most so anteriorly; venter pale. Head dorsum and snout slightly dusky; cheek, chin, and lower opercle pale. All fins pale; caudal base sometimes with small dark spot.

Color in Life.—Dorsum pale olive with silver sheen; upper side straw; midlateral stripe faint; lower side and venter silver white; cheek and opercle silver. *Notropis buccatus* does not develop nuptial coloration.

Larvae.—See Hoyt (1971b), Loos et al. (1979), Snyder (1979), and Heufelder and Fuiman (1982).

BIOLOGY

The silverjaw minnow is a benthic feeder; the diet includes worms, microcrustaceans, insects, fingernail clams, snails, tiny crayfishes, algae, and detritus (Hoyt 1970; Lotrich 1973; Wallace 1976). Midge larvae are consistently important in the diet. It feeds throughout the day, relying mostly on taste and tactile senses to locate food.

Maturation, age, and growth in Kentucky were analyzed by Hoyt (1971a, 1971b) and in Indiana by Wallace (1971b, 1973b). Some members of both sexes mature by midsummer of age 1; all are mature by age 2. The oldest individuals typically are age 3; few survive to age 4. Older males exhibit a slight tendency to increase in length faster than older females. *Notropis buccatus* of ages 1 and 3 averaged 47 and 76 mm TL in Kentucky; in Indiana the averages were 30 and 57 mm TL. Wallace (1971b) detected possible compensatory growth in fish which had experienced slow growth during an unusually cool growing season. The largest Virginia specimen is 69 mm SL, 76 mm TL; the largest listed by Trautman (1981) for Ohio is 97 mm TL.

Based on gonadal development and tuberculation, spawning occurs between March and late July (Hankinson 1919; Hoyt 1971a; Wallace 1973b). Some females may spawn more than once in a year. Large age-1 fish probably spawn late in the period. Spawning may occur in groups on sand and gravel (Hankinson 1919; Hoyt 1971a; D. Ross 1974). Numbers of mature ova are 150–1,350 (Hoyt 1971a; Wallace 1973b).

HABITAT

Notropis buccatus is a bottom-oriented minnow which occurs principally in warm streams of moderate to low gradient. It appears to prefer creeks, but extends into rivers. The silverjaw minnow inhabits open shallow runs and pools over a variety of substrates but is most common in areas of clean-swept sand or sand–gravel mixtures (D. Wallace 1972). This well describes its habitat in western Virginia, but in eastern Virginia streams with sparse sand, it is found over rubble, gravel, and isolated sand patches (J. J. Loos, E. G. Maurakis, personal communications). *Notropis buccatus* is a gregarious minnow, feeding as small aggregations and moderate-sized schools, and is often mixed with other minnows.

The silverjaw minnow is moderately tolerant of turbidity and is successful in some areas degraded by coal mine pollution, but it appears to be intolerant of silted bottoms in Indiana and Ohio (D. Wallace 1972; Trautman 1981). It appears tolerant of silt in the Virginia portion of the Big Sandy drainage, an area heavily impacted by soil sedimentation. Burr et al. (1980) indicated that *N. buccatus* may be expanding its range in Kentucky in response to effects of channelization.

DISTRIBUTION   Map 82

The silverjaw minnow has one of the more anomalous distribution patterns of North American freshwater fishes; its total range has a hiatus about as large as each of the two major population groups. The northern group encompasses southern parts of the Great Lakes basin, northern parts of the Ohio basin, a small outlying area of the middle Mississippi basin, and an eastern finger on the Atlantic slope comprising the Rappahannock, Potomac, and lower Susquehanna drainages. The southern population group is on the eastern Gulf slope. The hiatus includes most of the Green, Cumberland, and Tennessee drainages.

The peculiar range of *N. buccatus* within Virginia and in the extralimital portions of Virginia drainages partly reflects the pattern of the total range. The Big

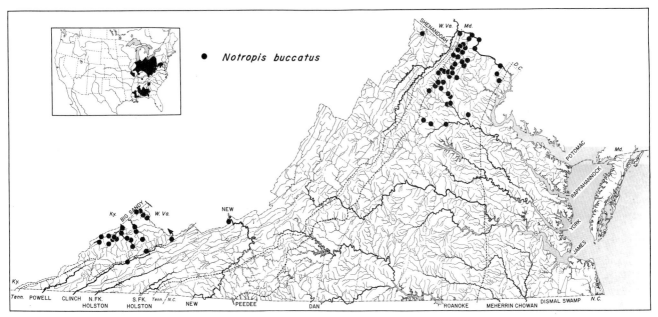

Map 82 Silverjaw minnow.

Sandy population is widespread and contiguous with those in the remainder of that drainage. Its Virginia segment may have been founded quite recently by natural upstream dispersal; the first record is from 1972. The species is expanding its range elsewhere in the Ohio basin (Smith 1979; Trautman 1981; Burr et al. 1980). The records in the East River of the New drainage (Stauffer et al. 1975, 1976) are not unexpected as the species sporadically inhabits the West Virginia portion of the drainage.

The Tennessee drainage records from Virginia, although rejected by Starnes and Etnier (1986), are the only valid ones for the drainage; they are from the Clinch River and a tributary in 1972 (Masnik 1974; our verification). They probably represent one or more introductions from the Big Sandy. Sand-dwelling fishes have fared poorly in the middle and upper Tennessee, although a sand darter *Ammocrypta clara* has persisted (Etnier et al. 1979; Gilbert 1980; Starnes and Etnier 1986).

On the Atlantic slope, the exclusive sharing of *N. buccatus* by the Rappahannock, Potomac, and lower Susquehanna drainages is a unique pattern, accreditable to stream captures (Ross 1952; Jenkins et al. 1972; Hocutt et al. 1986). However, this species may have entered the Susquehanna via bait buckets (Denoncourt et al. 1975), and it has been considered "probably introduced" to the Potomac through (apparently undocumented) stocking by the U.S. Bureau of Fisheries (Bean and Weed 1911). Its apparent absence from the Shenandoah system is puzzling, but

not unlike that of several other Potomac fishes. Introduced status in the Potomac would indicate that the fish was introduced to the Rappahannock also, for which the first record is 1962.

Abundance.—Rare to common, sometimes abundant.

REMARKS

The large head canals of the silverjaw minnow are unique among American cyprinids, but are paralleled by the trout-perch, pirate perch, and others. The canal chambers may enhance resonation and, hence, detection of vibrations produced by movement of prey (see *Percopsis omiscomaycus*, *Remarks*). Moore et al. (1950) found the cellular structure of the eye in *N. buccatus* to be well suited for living over bright sandy bottoms, where sunlight can be especially dazzling.

Why is there a large range gap in the southern Ohio basin? Unsuccessful invasions and extirpations have been postulated (Wallace 1973a; Gilbert 1980; Starnes and Etnier 1986), but the answer is not at hand. Middle Cumberland drainage records (Wallace 1973a; Burr et al. 1980; Cicerello and Butler 1985) suggest extirpations as an explanation. The gap may even be naturally larger; one or more of the Cumberland drainage populations could be introduced.

Name.—*Buccatus* means "cavity" or "cheek," referring to the modified head canals and an area in which they occur.

Silvery minnows   Genus *Hybognathus* Agassiz

Hybognathus comprises plain-colored minnows that have a very long, coiled intestine (Figure 26B), a long nonhooked grinding surface on the 4–4 pharyngeal teeth, an elaborate pharyngeal filtering apparatus (Hlohowskyj et al. 1989), and a subterminal or inferior mouth. Seven species currently are recognized in this eastern and central North American genus, one of which inhabits Virginia. Mayden (1989) positioned *Hybognathus* in an assemblage of the chub clade com- prising *Campostoma*, *Dionda*, *Exoglossum*, and *Nocomis*. Coburn and Cavender (1992) grouped *Hybognathus* with *Campostoma* and *Dionda* as a herbivorous clade within the exoglossin clade of the more inclusive chub clade.

Name.—*Hybognathus* means "humped jaw," in reference to a slight ventral protrusion sometimes present on the lower jaw frontally.

Eastern silvery minnow   *Hybognathus regius* Girard

SYSTEMATICS

Hybognathus regius was described by Girard (1856) apparently from the Potomac River in Washington, D.C. and vicinity, and other waters of Maryland. Because of purported intergradation, Hubbs and Lagler (1941, 1958) regarded the eastern silvery minnow to be an Atlantic slope subspecies of *H. nuchalis*, which inhabits the Mississippi basin and Gulf slope. Bailey (1954) determined the two forms to be widely allopatric, precluding gene exchange. Pflieger's (1971) elevation of *H. regius* to a species was substantiated by Hlohowskyj et al. (1989).

DESCRIPTION

Materials.—Eleven Virginia lots; counts of 30 specimens from the James and Chowan drainages; tuberculation from Raney (1939a). Nuptial color in life based on Raney (1939a, 1942); other data from 5 Virginia adults.

Anatomy.—A minnow with a deep lachrymal groove, medium or large, laterally positioned eye, and pigmentation well below the lateral line anteriorly; adults are 60–90 mm SL. Body fusiform, moderate to somewhat deep and compressed; dorsal fin origin above anterior half of pelvic fin base or slightly anterior. Head moderate; eye medium or large, lateral; snout somewhat pointed or well rounded; frenum absent; mouth small, subterminal or inferior, lips downsloped posteriorly. Belly fully scaled, breast partly naked. Gut very long, spirally coiled, peritoneum black

(Figure 26B). Nuptial tubercles very small, densely covering head and anterior body; all fins finely tuberculate; genital papilla of nonbreeding adult female large and plicate.

Meristics.—Pharyngeal teeth 4–4; lateral line complete, scales (32)34–37(38); dorsal and anal rays 8; pelvic rays (7)8; pectoral rays (14)15(16).

Color in Preservative.—Ground shade pale; dorsum dusky, scale margins somewhat darker than bases; middorsal stripe well developed; duskiness of upper side usually uniform down to midlateral stripe, sometimes distinctly paler just above stripe; dark midlateral stripe moderate or wide, widest and most intense posteriorly; lateral stripe often obscured by silvery pigment; anterior lower side well peppered with melanophores, often outlining scale pockets and effecting a cross-hatched pattern; posterior lower side and venter pale. Head dorsum and snout moderately dusky; cheek, opercle, and chin pale. Dorsal and caudal rays outlined with fine melanophores; caudal spot occasionally present, triangular; lower fins pale.

Color in Life.—Dorsum pale olive; side and venter silver, sometimes brassy. Dorsal, caudal, and leading edge of pectoral fin with slight brown wash. Breeding male distinctly darker dorsally than female, with pale yellow sides and fins and silver venter.

Larvae.—Apparently the only descriptions solely based on *H. regius* are those of Raney (1939a) and Wang and Kernehan (1979). The following include data based on *H. nuchalis*: Mansueti and Hardy (1967), Lippson and Moran

Fish 116 *Hybognathus regius* adult male 51 mm SL (REJ 1022), VA, Amelia County, Appomattox River, 31 August 1983.

(1974), Jones et al. (1978), and Heufelder and Fuiman (1982). See also Fuiman et al. (1983).

BIOLOGY

The life history of the eastern silvery minnow has received scant attention. Raney (1939a) reported consumption of ooze, diatoms, and other algae, which likely reflect the principal diet. The tasting and food-sorting ability conferred by the specialized pharyngeal apparatus (Hlohowskyj et al. 1989), and the lengthy digestive time afforded by the long gut, are adaptations for feeding on algae and detritus. Because of its silty slow-water habitat, *H. regius* may consume more detritus than lithic aufwuchs.

Eastern silvery minnows typically mature by 2 years, in 1 year when growth is rapid; maximum longevity is 3 years in New York (Raney 1942; Forney 1957). Hastings and Good (1977) found two size-class modes in New Jersey, the larger group possibly comprising fish of ages 1 and 2. Of 2-year-olds in a hatchery pond, males were 76–87 mm TL, mean, 82; females were 78–96 mm TL, mean, 88 (Raney 1942). Twenty-five adults collected in July and November from Virginia, all possibly age 1, were 66–84 mm SL, mean, 74. Specimens in the 120–129 mm TL size-class were found in the lower James River (White 1976). The largest Virginia specimen we found is 108 mm SL, 133 mm TL, taken in 1888. The largest verified specimen appears to be 157 mm TL from upper Chesapeake Bay (Hildebrand and Schroeder 1928). Fowler (1909) repeated hearsay of *H. regius* reaching 229 mm TL (9 inches), which we do not accept.

Spawning occurs in New York during late April to mid-May, water 13–20°C (Raney 1939a, 1942; Forney 1957). In Delaware spawning apparently takes place during April and May, water 10–20°C (Wang and Kernehan 1979). Large schools migrate into and spawn in shallows of backwaters, coves, and tidal creeks; successful reproduction also occurs in ponds. Eggs are shed on or above silted detrital areas that are unvegetated or have sprouting plants, and apparently also in sand and gravel areas (Raney 1939a; Wang and Kernehan 1979). Spawning occurs during daylight and is communal. Males swarm about a female, jockeying for position (Raney 1939a). Hildebrand and Schroeder (1928) and Raney (1939a) reported females to be gravid with yolked ova in early winter, a condition also found in November-collected Virginia females. Fecundity is 2,000–6,600 mature eggs (Raney 1939a).

HABITAT

In Virginia, *H. regius* chiefly occupies large streams and rivers of moderate to low gradient; its occurrence in smaller streams and creeks is geographically erratic. This schooling species typically inhabits pools and other slackwater areas and generally is associated with detritus, mud, silt, and sand bottoms. It seems to tolerate intermittent moderate turbidity. The eastern silvery minnow frequently occurs in tidal fresh and slightly brackish water and occasionally enters the mesohaline zone, occupying salinities up to 14.0‰ (Raney and Massmann 1953; Musick 1972). It is found in slightly acidic streams (pH 6.8; Norman and Southwick 1985), but apparently avoids moderately acidic situations. It also occurs in alkaline streams draining carbonate strata. This species seems intolerant of impoundments in Virginia; northward it populates natural lakes and also reproduces in artificial ponds.

DISTRIBUTION   Map 83

Hybognathus regius is native to the Atlantic slope from the Lake Ontario–St. Lawrence basin south to the Altamaha drainage of Georgia. In Virginia it occurs in all major drainages, mainly from the middle Piedmont into the middle Coastal Plain.

The population in the upper Shenandoah system is relictive; two of the four records (three sites) are old. Each of the three sites is in a different branch of the South Fork Shenandoah system—the North, Middle, and South rivers. In the former, McDonald took specimens (USNM 132284) in Muddy Creek during 1885. The North River subsystem has been moderately well sampled since the 1950s. The Middle River record is dated 1956 (Ross 1959a; specimen verified). The site was worked four times during 1971–1983; the subsystem has been moderately sampled elsewhere although sparsely in the lower Middle River. In the South River at Waynesboro, Jordan's (1889b) record is verified (USNM 40147) and one specimen of *H. regius* was taken there in 1989 (P. L. Angermeier, in litt.). Apparently this species has been rare in the South River during the last four decades (e.g., Ross 1959a, 1972b; Seagle and Hendricks 1979). Pollution from Waynesboro (Cairns and Dickson 1972) may depress the population.

In the upper James drainage, Jordan (1889b) reported *Hybognathus* from a James River reach that subsequently has been sparsely sampled but long degraded by paper mill effluent from Covington. Acceptance of the record is based on his correct identification of other *Hybognathus* specimens. A second sample of *H. regius* (USNM 39533) taken by McDonald in 1885 and labeled only Virginia apparently is from the upper James or Shenandoah drainages. Possibly it is from the lowermost base-leveled section of Mill or Sinking creeks of the upper James. The lot was cataloged right after McDonald's specimens of an-

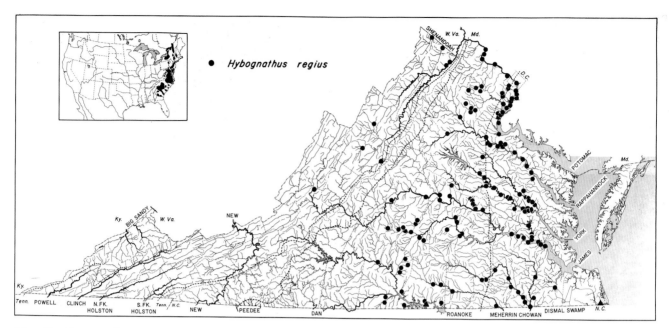

Map 83   Eastern silvery minnow.

other species from Mill and Sinking creeks at "Gold-water" (= Gala, sometimes called Gala Water).

The extirpation or depletion of *H. regius* at two of the four record sites in the upper Shenandoah and James drainages can be attributed to pollution. Because many uninhabited streams there are healthy, localization of the peripheral Valley and Ridge Province populations may be related to marginal ecological conditions, in which slight changes caused the demise of populations. The crucial changes may have occurred largely in main rivers upon which many tributary populations were dependent. Major population losses of riverine species of *Hybognathus* have occurred elsewhere (P. Smith 1971; Etnier et al. 1979; Krumholz 1981).

Recent records of *Hybognathus* from the upper Roanoke drainage are considered invalid (Jenkins and Freeman 1972). Fowler's (1923, 1924) reports from "Kanawha Creek" of the New drainage are discounted. They would be based on material collected by Cope (1868b); Fowler applied that (unidentifiable) stream name only to some of Cope's samples from the New. Cope did not report *Hybognathus* from Virginia and the specimens were not relocated.

Abundance.—Usually uncommon or common, sometimes abundant.

REMARKS

Species of *Hybognathus* are some of the more nondescript small minnows; the general blandness of *H. regius* is an initial clue for field identification. This species has a distinctive "dumb" look, afforded by the underslung, posteriorly downcurved mouth. It sometimes is locally popular as a bait minnow and is suited for pond culture (Raney 1942; Forney 1957). It is an ooze-eater that fulfills an important trophic link as a forage species—transferring energy in detritus to piscivores. Perhaps humans should be included, as Schwartz (1963) noted that silvery minnows are esteemed by some when deep-fried.

Name.—*Regius* means "royal." Girard (1856) considered it a large and beautiful species.

Bluntnose minnows   Genus *Pimephales* Rafinesque

Pimephales is an eastern and central North American genus of four species, three of which occupy Virginia. They are distinguished from most shiners by their small, crowded, irregularly arranged predorsal scales (Figure 30). Epibasally the dorsal fin of large juveniles and adults has a dark spot or blotch anteri-

orly (sometimes posteriorly also), or the rays in that area are smudged. The last short anterior ("rudimentary") dorsal fin ray is distinctly separated from the first principal (unbranched) ray by a membrane, a condition best developed in breeding males. Other advanced traits include reduced dentition (4–4) and in nuptial males, a dark head, cushionlike nape pad, low numbers of large snout tubercles, and in some species, reduced pectoral fin tubercles (supplanted by ridgelike pads on membranes). Nest territoriality and cluster-spawning on the ceiling of a cavity also are derived features.

Customarily, *Pimephales* has been evolutionarily ranked as highly advanced among American minnows, and at times was recognized as a subfamily Pimephalinae (Hubbs and Black 1947; Cross 1953). Based mainly on osteology and reproductive behavior, *Pimephales* is now placed as the sister group of *Codoma* in the advanced lineage of the notropin clade that includes the less derived *Opsopoeodus* and *Cyprinella* (Page and Ceas 1989; Page and Johnston

1990b; Minckley and Vives 1990; Coburn and Cavender 1992). Following the phylogeny proposed by these authors, the sequence of Virginia notropin genera should be the relatively primitive broadcast spawners—*Notropis* (and *Hybopsis*?), *Luxilus*, and *Lythrurus*—and then the egg-attachers—*Cyprinella* and *Pimephales*.

Name.—*Pimephales* means "fat head," in reference to the blunt snout and thick skin on the head of breeding males. We apply the common name bluntnose minnows to the genus, from the best-known species *P. notatus*. Another vernacular name could be blackheaded minnows, in reference to that color phase of nuptial males.

Fathead minnow   *Pimephales promelas* Rafinesque

SYSTEMATICS

Pimephales promelas was described in 1820 from Kentucky. Although three subspecies have been recognized north of Mexico (Hubbs and Black 1947; Hubbs and Lagler 1949, 1958), clinal and discordant character variation indicates that recognition of subspecies is inappropriate (Taylor 1954; Vandermeer 1966).

DESCRIPTION

Materials.—From Cross (1967), Scott and Crossman (1973), and 8 Virginia adults. Color in life from Harlan and Speaker (1956), Cross (1967), Scott and Crossman (1973), Pflieger (1975), and Boschung et al. (1983).

Anatomy.—A minnow with a short and often blunt snout, small oblique mouth, and dark midlateral stripe with fine dark lines extending retrodorsad; adults are 40–60 mm TL. Body somewhat deep and compressed; dorsal fin origin above or slightly posterior to the pelvic fin origin. Head and eye moderate in size; eye lateral; snout short, broadly rounded or blunt; frenum absent; mouth small, terminal or slightly subterminal, oblique. Predorsal scales much reduced in size, irregularly arranged; breast naked, belly sparsely to fully scaled. Peritoneum black; gut long and whorled, or shorter, having only an elongate right loop and medial kink.

Adults quite sexually dimorphic; nuptial male with snout abruptly blunt; large tubercles on snout and chin; small tubercles on pectoral fin in a single unbranched file on rays 2–5, 6, or 7; nape with prominent pad of spongy rugose tissue; rudimentary leading ray of dorsal fin thickened, sometimes with a small distal knob; caudal lobes short, very rounded; lower fins large.

Meristics.—Pharyngeal teeth 4–4; lateral line typically incomplete, midlateral scales 41–54; scales above lateral line

9–10; scales below lateral line 9–11. Dorsal rays 8; anal rays 7; pelvic rays 8; pectoral rays (14)15–16(18).

Color in Preservative.—Ground shade pale; upper body scales duskily submargined; dark middorsal and midlateral stripes present; upper side with fine oblique dark lines (subcutaneous blood vessels) arising at midlateral stripe; lower side and venter pale, or lower urosome slightly dusky. Head dorsum dark, snout dusky, chin and cheek pale. Dorsal fin slightly dusky, with a small spot or smudge anteriorly above origin in adult; caudal fin slightly dusky; caudal spot small, vague to intense, usually dash-shaped, or spot absent; caudal base sometimes with a narrow vertical dark bar; lower fins pale.

Breeding male with sooty or black head; nape pad gray or whitish; side with alternating pale and dark zones, first pale zone directly behind head and encircling breast, the second below dorsal fin; males in zoned color phase not noted in some areas. Dorsal fin mostly dark, decreasing in intensity to pale margin; caudal fin often with medial dark blotch grading into weak medial band, lobes pale; anal base black, fin streaked posteriorly; pelvic fin with dark streaks; pectoral fin mostly pale, leading edge black.

Color in Life.—Upper body straw-olive to pale brown; side pallid or silver, sometimes with purplish or brassy cast; midlateral dusky stripe sometimes evident; venter silver-white; cheek and opercle with gold and lime iridescence. Pale zones of nuptial male sometimes yellowish.

Larvae.—Described by Hogue et al. (1976), Snyder et al. (1977), Buynak and Mohr (1979f), Kindschi et al. (1979), Perry and Menzel (1979), Snyder (1979, 1981), and Heufelder and Fuiman (1982).

BIOLOGY

Adult *P. promelas* are omnivores. Of three populations, one ate mostly insects, another only algae, and the third entirely detritus (Cahn 1927; Coyle 1930 *in*

Scott and Crossman 1973; Starrett 1950b). Several Wisconsin specimens consumed microcrustaceans, insects, algae, and detritus (Pearse 1918). The moderately long coiled gut is intermediate between the short S-shaped gut characteristic of carnivores and the quite long and coiled one typical of many algae and detritus feeders.

Fathead minnows mature rapidly and are short-lived. In Iowa ponds both sexes matured in 1 year; some even reproduced in late summer of the year they hatched (Markus 1934). They did not spawn in the first year in New York ponds (Forney 1957). In Iowa rivers age 2 was commonly achieved and an age-3 fish was detected; smallest size at maturation was 40 mm TL for females and 48 mm for males (Carlson 1967). Males grow faster than females; adults are usually 40–60 mm TL. Our largest Virginia specimen is 58 mm TL; an 89-mm TL fathead is known from Ohio (Trautman 1981), and one of 102 mm TL has been reported (Lee and Shute *in* Lee et al. 1980).

Spawning occurs in May through August in water of 15–32°C (Markus 1934; Forney 1957; Carlander 1969). Young appear over a seven-week period in Ontario (Keast 1985). Spawning takes place in calm shallows of streams and along shore in ponds and lakes. The male selects a site at lily pads, stones,

boards, logs, or other suitable objects. He cleans the undersurface, where eggs are to be laid, by rubbing with the spongy nape pad and dorsal fin (Markus 1934; McMillan 1972; Smith and Murphy 1974). The specialized pad contains mucous-secreting cells and taste buds. It apparently allows marking the spawning site, facilitates chemosensory assessment of eggs (Smith and Murphy 1974), and may have fungicidal properties.

The male pugnaciously defends the nest site, confronting intruders and allowing only persistent females to enter and spawn (McMillan 1972; McMillan and Smith 1974). Male aggressiveness towards females may be an adaptation to counteract mimicry of females by deceptive male cuckolders. Both sexes are polygamous and spawning behavior is similar to that of *P. vigilax* (e.g., McMillan and Smith 1974). Eggs are laid mostly in a single layer maintained by the male (Wynne-Edwards 1932; Markus 1934). Females spawn fractionally; Markus (1934) counted 12 spawnings by a female during a 69-day period. Gale and Buynak (1982) noted five females each to spawn 16–26 times at intervals of 2–16 days within a 93-day period. Totals of 6,803–10,164 eggs were produced—the equivalent of 1.7–4.0 million eggs per kg of fish.

The fathead minnow hybridizes with *P. notatus* (Trautman 1981).

Fish 117 *Pimephales promelas* adult male 48 mm SL (RC), VA, Loudoun County, tributary Catoctin Creek, 13 June 1983.

Fish 118 *Pimephales promelas* adult female 42 mm SL (REJ 986), VA, Scott County, Clinch River, 17 June 1983.

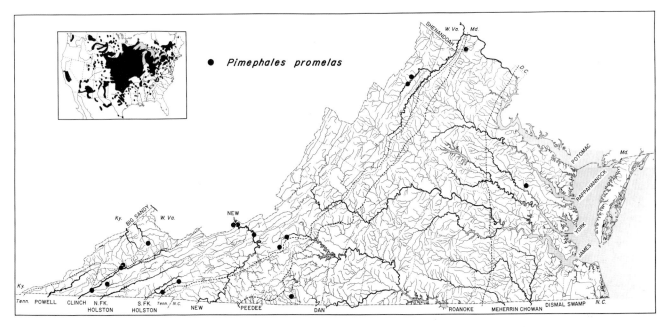

Map 84 Fathead minnow. Open triangle on Smith Mountain Lake represents unverified record.

HABITAT

Pimephales promelas is typically found in pools and backwaters in warmwater creeks of moderate to low gradient and occasionally in large streams. Adults of all three Virginia species of *Pimephales* have been found in the same backwater of the Clinch River at Speers Ferry. The fathead also occupies ponds and lakes, generally near the shoreline. It is frequently associated with weedy cover. It tolerates unstable environments and certain inhospitable conditions such as desiccating, typically muddy streams and high-alkalinity waters (e.g., pH to 9.8 and total alkalinity to 29,000 mg/liter) (Minckley 1959; Carlander 1969). However, it is apparently intolerant of competition from other fishes, generally being common only in low-diversity communities (Hubbs and Cooper 1936; Starrett 1950a).

DISTRIBUTION   Map 84

A widespread minnow, *P. promelas* is apparently native to the northwestern Gulf slope, the Mississippi, Great Lakes–St. Lawrence, Hudson Bay, and MacKenzie basins, and the north-central Atlantic slope. It has been widely introduced within these limits and elsewhere.

Although it is native to the Tennessee and Big Sandy drainages, we consider all populations in Virginia as well as those in extralimital parts of the New drainage to have been introduced. The earliest record of capture in the state is 1950. The fathead minnow is

one of the most popular and widely disseminated bait minnows, and the Virginia populations likely are the result of bait-bucket release or hatchery escapement. The York drainage record may represent an escape from the Stevensville Hatchery. The likely source of the South Fork Holston records is the esocid ponds at Buller Hatchery.

It is unknown how many records (if any) represent stable populations. This species probably exists in numerous reservoirs and farm ponds. Hart (1978) reported it abundant in Smith Mountain Lake; this more likely pertains to *P. notatus*. The record from the Dan River system is based on Conner and Maughan (1984). Two records from the Virginia portion of the Powell River (TVA 1970) and one from the Tennessee part (Masnik 1974) probably are based on *P. notatus*, which is common there but was not reported in the three collections.

Abundance.—Rare.

REMARKS

The hardy fathead minnow is, in a sense, preadapted to bait-bucket conditions by its ability to thrive in environments unfavorable for many fishes. It is widely used to assay the effects of chemicals. It is commercially raised to meet the demand of the bait market. Methods of pond culture are described by Hasler et al. (1946), Dobie et al. (1956), and Forney (1957). The fathead is also an excellent candidate for classroom study. It is obtainable from many fishing tackle stores, requires minimal care, and will spawn in aquaria.

The fathead minnow was considered by Cross (1967) and others to be by nature a pioneer of unstable streams, ditches, and ponds in the Plains region. It hardly seems to have gained foothold in the generally less variable waters of Virginia, perhaps because of the diversity of the native fauna. A case in point is the capture of four fathead minnows at two sites in the upper Roanoke drainage in 1975; intensive subsequent sampling throughout the section revealed no more.

Name.—*Promelas* combines the prefix pro, meaning "before" or "in front of," and melas, "black." The name refers to the black head of breeding males.

Bullhead minnow   *Pimephales vigilax* (Baird and Girard)

SYSTEMATICS

Pimephales vigilax was named in 1853 from Oklahoma. Hubbs and Black (1947) divided it into two allopatric species but shortly after, these were considered subspecies (Hubbs 1951; Cross 1953; Hampton 1954). *Pimephales v. perspicuus* (Girard) is the form in Virginia.

DESCRIPTION

Materials.—From Hubbs and Black (1947) and 10 lots including 1 from Virginia. Life color from Cross (1967) and Pflieger (1975).

Anatomy.—A blunt-snouted minnow with a dusky midlateral stripe, small intense caudal spot, and silver peritoneum; adults are 50–75 mm TL. Body moderate in profile, stocky anteriorly, slightly compressed posteriorly; dorsal fin origin above or slightly posterior to pelvic fin origin. Head moderate in profile, broad; eye moderate, lateral; snout short, well rounded or blunt; frenum absent; mouth small, slightly subterminal, nearly horizontal. Anterior pre-dorsal scales reduced in size, crowded, rowed pattern somewhat obscure; breast naked; belly partly or fully scaled. Peritoneum silver; gut simple, S-shaped.

Sexual dimorphism marked in adults; nuptial male with head and anterior body broad; snout very blunt, usually with 2 rows of large tubercles; pectoral fin said to bear obsolescent tubercles (we found no definitive tubercles); nape with finely rugose spongy pad; rudimentary dorsal fin ray thickened, dorsal fin low, rays somewhat longer posteriorly than anteriorly; caudal lobes broadly rounded.

Meristics.—Pharyngeal teeth 4–4; lateral line complete, scales (37)38–42(44); scales above lateral line (6)7–8; scales below lateral line (4)5(6). Dorsal rays 8; anal rays 7; pelvic rays 8; pectoral rays usually 15–16.

Color in Preservative.—Ground shade pale; middorsal stripe obscure or, usually, absent; upper body scales vaguely or moderately duskily submargined, their scale bases typically dusky, sometimes pale; side with midlateral dusky or dark stripe, lateral line pores dark-stitched; lower side and venter pale. Head dorsum and snout dusky; cheek and chin pale; side of snout below nostril, just above upper

Fish 119 *Pimephales vigilax* adult male 69 mm SL (SIUC 8637), KY, Hickman County, 19 March 1982.

Fish 120 *Pimephales vigilax* juvenile male 49 mm SL (RC), TN, Marshall County, Duck River, 29 April 1980.

lip, usually with a dashlike or crescentic mark or smudge. Dorsal fin mostly pale, small dark spot near midheight of anterior rays; this spot often lacking in young and usually represented in juvenile by only a slight intensification on rays; caudal spot small or medium, usually round or oval, usually bold, often crossed by a dusky vertical line; lower fins pale.

Nuptial male with sooty or black head; body dusky gray-black, lacking pale zones; general darkening often masks scale and other markings; nape pad gray-white. Dorsal fin with black anterior and posterior blotches, midsection with black streaks (base may completely darken during breeding); caudal fin with black submarginal band, darkest medially; anal and pelvic fins pale; pectoral fin with black leading edge.

Color in Life.—Dorsum yellow-olive to tan, scales usually lacking distinct dark outline; side silver-white, dusky midlateral stripe usually faint; venter silver. Fins pale, black spot in anterior dorsal fin faint.

Larvae.—Described by Taber (1969), Snyder (1979), and Heufelder and Fuiman (1982).

COMPARISON

Pimephales vigilax is sometimes confused with *P. notatus*. Differences between breeding males include: (1) snout tubercles, numbers of horizontal rows and individual tubercles [usually 2 rows, less than 10 tubercles in *vigilax* vs. 3 rows, about 16 tubercles in *notatus*]; (2) barbel at corner of lips [absent vs. a small stubby protuberance present].

In addition to characters in the *Key*, generally consistent but slight differences between subadult, adult female, and nonbreeding adult male *vigilax* and *notatus* are: (3) mouth position [slightly subterminal vs. distinctly subterminal to slightly inferior]; (4) dorsolateral pigmentation [scales not sharply outlined with melanophores, scale bases often dusky vs. scales sharply dark submargined, bases usually pale]; (5) dorsal fin origin relative to pelvic fin base [above anterior half of base vs. above posterior half or slightly behind]; (6) anterior body [slightly deeper and broader vs. relatively streamlined].

BIOLOGY

Pimephales vigilax feeds on bottom ooze, diatoms and other plant material, worms, tiny crustaceans, aquatic insects, fingernail clams, and snails (Cahn 1927; Starrett 1950b; Parker 1964; Eddy and Underhill 1974). Starrett found that bullhead minnows ate mostly plant material and worms during high-water periods.

Like other *Pimephales*, *P. vigilax* is fast-maturing and short-lived. All age-1 fish over 50 mm TL in a Wisconsin population were mature; the oldest fish were age 2 (Becker 1983). Males grew faster than females; adults were 50–79 mm TL. We lack an adult from Virginia; Trautman (1981) reported a maximum size of 94 mm TL.

Spawning occurs between late May and September (Forbes and Richardson 1920; Starrett 1951; Carlander 1969). It takes place in pool shallows beneath stones or debris; when natural cavities are lacking, sometimes the male burrows through silt to create a space beneath an object (Parker 1964). The male cleans the cavity roof and defends the nest. The complex ovipositioning behavior was described by Page and Ceas (1989). The male and female press together, the male under the female, as they turn on their sides in the nest cavity and swim in a circle. The male then presses against the female while she undulates and attaches one or more eggs to the ceiling. Becker (1983) reported 320–390 mature eggs from two females. Females probably are fractional spawners, and counts of ovarian eggs would underestimate total fecundity.

Pimephales vigilax hybridizes with the bluntnose minnow (Trautman 1981).

HABITAT

The bullhead minnow typically occupies shallow backwaters and pool margins of clear and muddy, medium and large rivers of moderate to low gradient. It occurs on firm bottoms, appears tolerant of moderate but not extensive siltation, and often forms groups around plants, rocks, logs, or floating debris (Parker 1964). Forbes and Richardson (1920) considered *P. vigilax* the fifth most abundant big-river fish in Illinois. P. Smith (1971) noted the loss of populations in medium-sized streams owing to desiccation. Bullhead minnows also occur in natural lakes and impoundments.

DISTRIBUTION   Map 85

Pimephales vigilax is native to the Mississippi basin and the Gulf slope, and has been sparingly introduced elsewhere. In Virginia it is known only recently from three main branches of the Tennessee drainage, the first years of capture being 1979 in the Powell River, 1980 in the Clinch River, and 1981 in the North Fork Holston River. The lack of earlier records probably is related to the following. The Virginia sections of the Powell and Clinch were little surveyed until the late 1960s; in much of the 1900s the Powell and North Fork Holston were chronically degraded by pollution, and the Clinch River had a devastating fish kill in 1967. *Pimephales vigilax* probably

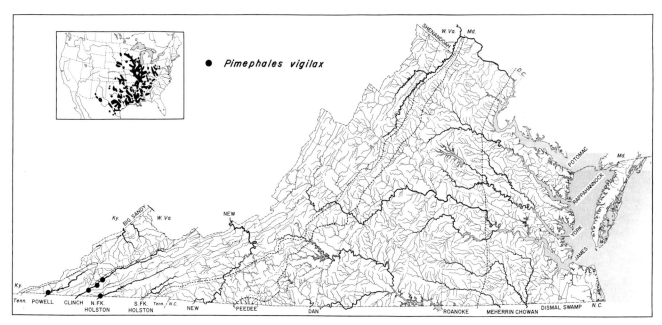

Map 85 Bullhead minnow.

occupied Virginia near the Tennessee line before degradation. Pollution levels recently have been reduced and the occurrence of *P. vigilax* in Virginia reaches of these streams probably represents natural repopulation.

We doubt that the recent bullhead minnow records in Virginia are of bait bucket releases; *P. vigilax* is indigenous to the upper Tennessee drainage and typically is not a commercial bait minnow. Further, it is unlikely that released fish would have established populations within the same brief period in the three rivers.

Abundance.—Rare: altogether, 22 specimens were taken in six collections, and the species was "rare" in

the other Virginia collection (J. C. Feeman, in litt.); it was not taken at most of the six sites after the first record (the Powell River plot represents two sites).

REMARKS

The bullhead minnow is a large-river fish that may never have penetrated much above the present population sites in Virginia.

Name.—*Vigilax* means "alert" or "watchful," perhaps in reference to the vigil of the nest-guarding male.

Bluntnose minnow   *Pimephales notatus* (Rafinesque)

SYSTEMATICS

Pimephales notatus was described from the Ohio River in 1820. Geographic variation of this widely ranging minnow has not been analyzed, although Hubbs and Black (1947) suggested that significant variation occurs. Lateral line scale counts from three Virginia drainages are low, nearly distinct from those presumably from Canada (Scott and Crossman 1973).

DESCRIPTION

Materials.—From Scott and Crossman (1973) and 21 Virginia lots; lateral line scale counts from 36 specimens from the Roanoke, Tennessee, and Big Sandy drainages of Vir-

ginia. Color in life from Scott and Crossman (1973), Pflieger (1975), and Phillips et al. (1982).

Anatomy.—A blunt-snouted minnow with a streamlined body, dusky midlateral stripe terminating in a small intense caudal spot, and black peritoneum; adults are 45–90 mm SL. Basic morphology as in *P. vigilax*; several differences are given in the *Comparison* section under *P. vigilax* and in the *Key*. Gut length and looping pattern variable, not particularly long, with an elongate right loop and a medial kink; peritoneum dark. Sexual dimorphism similar to *P. vigilax* except pectoral fin rays 3–5, 6, or 7 tuberculate.

Meristics.—Pharyngeal teeth 4–4; lateral line complete, scales (37)38–42(43); dorsal rays 8; anal rays 7(8); pelvic rays 8; pectoral rays (14)15–16(17).

Fish 121 *Pimephales notatus* adult male 80 mm SL (WHH 234), VA, Rockingham County, War Creek, 12 May 1984.

Fish 122 *Pimephales notatus* nonbreeding male 63 mm SL (SIUC 8947), IL, Johnson County, Dutchman Creek, 1 November 1983.

Color in Preservative.—Similar to *P. vigilax* except dark crescent or smudge lacking from lower side of snout; scale submargins dorsolaterally tend more sharply outlined and bases paler, conveying a rhomboid pattern.

Color in Life.—Nonbreeding and breeding adults similar to *P. vigilax* except scale pattern and lateral stripe tend slightly more obvious, the stripe sometimes with a slight purplish cast.

Larvae.—Described by Buynak and Mohr (1979f), Loos et al. (1979), Perry and Menzel (1979), Snyder (1979), and Heufelder and Fuiman (1982).

COMPARISON

See *P. vigilax.*

BIOLOGY

Pimephales notatus was characterized as primarily herbivorous by Felley and Hill (1983), as detritivorous by Angermeier (1985), and as omnivorous (in some habitat settings) by Vadas (1990). The diet includes microcrustaceans, aquatic insects, worms, and fish eggs (Kraatz 1928; Starrett 1950b; Keast 1970; Moyle 1973; Hess 1983).

Maturation and longevity data are from Van Cleave and Markus (1929), Westman (1938), and Gale (1983); a ratio of 1.24 SL:TL was used to convert Gale's data to SL. Females mature in 1 year and are 42–57 mm SL when adult; males mature in 2 years and are 58–90 mm SL when adult. Van Cleave and Markus (1929) detected that 51% of males in the size range of tuberculate males were nontuberculate; such fish may be nest cuckolders, or perhaps simply are slow-maturing. The largest Virginia specimen is a tuberculate male of 89 mm SL, 106 mm TL. A possible maximum size of 110 mm TL was reported from Ohio (Trautman 1981).

The duration of the reproductive period is similar to that of *P. promelas* and *P. vigilax.* In the northern half of the range, spawning may occur from May into August (Hankinson 1908; Hubbs and Cooper 1936; Gale 1983). Reproductive activity lasted only about seven weeks in western New York (Westman 1938), and in an Ontario area young appeared during a five-week period (Keast 1985). In Missouri the peak of spawning is in late May and June (Pflieger 1975). Tuberculate males have been detected only in May and June in Virginia. Spawning occurs in water of 19–31°C (Westman 1938; Gale 1983).

Tuberculate males defend nest cavities beneath stones, cans, boards, and paper (Hankinson 1908; Hubbs and Cooper 1936; Westman 1938; Gale 1983). Most spawning occurs at night. Both sexes are polygamous. Spawning behavior is like that of *P. vigilax* (Page and Ceas 1989; Page and Johnston 1990b); adhesive eggs are attached to the cavity roof in single-layered groups, rarely in clumps. Females are fractional spawners, mating 7–19 times at average intervals of five days; the mean number of eggs per clutch was 212. Fecundity per mated pair was 1,112–4,195 (Gale 1983).

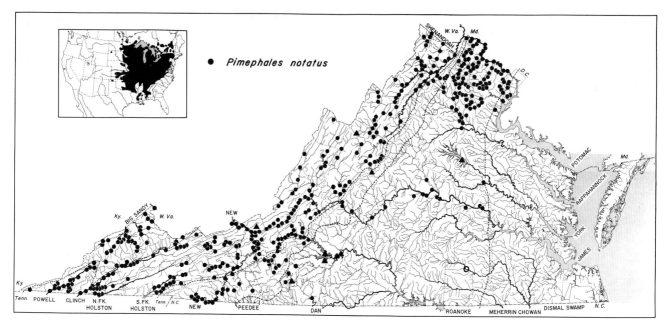

Map 86 Bluntnose minnow. Open circle represents record with probably faulty locality data; record likely from upper Roanoke drainage.

Pimephales notatus has hybridized with *P. promelas* and *P. vigilax* (Trautman 1981).

HABITAT

Of the three Virginia *Pimephales*, the bluntnose minnow exhibits the greatest habitat plasticity. It ranges from small creeks to large, usually clear rivers of moderate to low gradient; it occupies pools and backwaters. It is a gregarious minnow, often found adjacent to cover, particularly water willow beds, but sometimes is more abundant in open areas (Larimore et al. 1952). Bluntnose minnows occur over substrates ranging from soft silted bottoms, particularly sand–silt mixtures, to boulder and bedrock (D. Wallace 1972). Winter snorkeling and collecting (water 0–2°C) located groups beneath boulders in the Roanoke River. In one instance a group of bluntnose minnows and swallowtail shiners shared a refuge with a torpid smallmouth bass of about 1 kg. *Pimephales notatus* rarely enters tidal fresh water (Hastings and Good 1977). In ponds, lakes, and reservoirs, it is usually found near shorelines (Moyle 1973) and appears to avoid heavily weeded areas (Scott and Crossman 1973).

DISTRIBUTION Map 86

Pimephales notatus is native and widespread in the Mississippi and Great Lakes–St. Lawrence basins,

and native also to the Red River of the North drainage and the central Gulf slope. It occurs widely on the central Atlantic slope, and has been considered native from the Hudson to the James drainage by Hubbs and Lagler (1958). However, the indigenous status in some Atlantic drainages is doubtful. The distribution of the bluntnose minnow is erratic and enigmatic in much of Virginia. Many of its peculiarities indicate establishment by introductions, a hypothesis supported by its high esteem and availability as bait and often by the recency of first capture in drainages. We have noted a progressive recent spread of the species in certain drainages.

The status of *P. notatus* in the Susquehanna and Delaware drainages bears on questions in Virginia, because the Susquehanna and the other drainages of the Chesapeake basin, south to the James, were interconnected during glacial times (*Biogeography*). This minnow is extensively distributed in the Susquehanna and hence would seem native. However, it was not reported from the lower Susquehanna until the early 1900s (Fowler 1906). Native status in the Susquehanna is supported by the native status accorded to this species (with debate) in the adjacent, relatively isolated Delaware by Mihursky (1962).

The current distribution and abundance of the bluntnose minnow in the Potomac drainage probably resulted from stockings, naturalization, and rapid spread. Uhler and Lugger (1876) did not report this species from the drainage. The first known Virginia record is from a lower Shenandoah River tributary in 1897 (USNM 103401 series). Shortly after, it was considered common to abundant in the lower Potomac and tributaries by Bean and Weed (1911, correcting an omission of the species by Smith and Bean [1899]), McAtee and Weed (1915), and Radcliffe and Welsh (1916). It may have been used as forage in bass and sunfish culture ponds operated in Washington, D.C. by the former U.S. Fish Commission, and the minnows may have been disseminated with centrarchids.

The Rappahannock drainage population evidently is introduced. The first record—1972—is from the main river at several rkm above its largest feeder, the Rapidan River. The next record—1975—is from a headwater tributary of the Rappahannock River. All 14 subsequent records are between or near those sites in the upper Rappahannock system proper, except for the lower Rapidan River capture in 1981. If *P. notatus* were native to the drainage, it should be as widely distributed in the Rapidan system as in the Rappahannock proper.

The two York drainage records suggest two introductions. A specimen was found in the South Anna River in 1979 (Reed 1980), and two (examined by us) were impinged on the intake screen of the North Anna Nuclear Plant in 1981.

The bluntnose minnow probably was introduced to the James drainage. It is widely distributed above the Blue Ridge (first recorded in 1928) and extends through the main valley to the Fall Line (earliest found in 1949 on the middle Piedmont). Its absence in many prior collections above the Blue Ridge, from most tributaries arising on the Blue Ridge, and from the entire Appomattox system, indicates initial establishment above the Blue Ridge and subsequent dispersal downstream. It may have been introduced with shipments of centrarchids.

There is one Chowan drainage record, from 1958 (VPI 991 = AMNH 61945), but the locality data are questionable (see *Luxilus cerasinus* and *Biogeography*); we believe that the sample is from the upper Roanoke drainage.

We interpret the distribution pattern in the Roanoke proper and Dan systems of the Roanoke drainage to stem from at least two introductions. Most Piedmont records are associated with heavily fished reservoirs. *Pimephales notatus* seems well adapted to Piedmont conditions judging from its strong success in the Potomac; if native to the Roanoke drainage, it should be widespread on the upper Piedmont. The earliest record in the Roanoke proper is dated 1947, in the Dan 1951. The isolated record in the upper Pigg River is from 1990. Specimens collected during 1940–1941 in the Roanoke

River and reported by Jackson and Henderson (1942) as *Chrosomus* (= *Phoxinus*) *oreas* may have been *P. notatus*. Both have a whorled gut; *P. oreas* is an exceedingly rare straggler in the section comprising the four sites from which it was listed. Specimens that Fowler (1923) identified as the bluntnose minnow from the South Fork Roanoke River are missing; we assume them to have been reidentified.

The New drainage has a host of fishes known or contended to be introduced, but *P. notatus* appears to be indigenous. It was captured by Cope (1868b), A. R. Crandall in about 1871 (MCZ), and Jordan (1889b); the first two times predate known centrarchid stockings. Native status in the New is more likely than in Atlantic slope drainages because *P. notatus* is an Ohio basin species.

Correspondingly, one may presume that populations of the upper Tennessee and Big Sandy drainages are native. The number and spread of records in the Big Sandy support the presumption for this drainage, but certain aspects in the Tennessee, including the section in northeastern Tennessee, are curious. The only pre-1900 report is from the Powell River in Tennessee (Woolman 1892; Evermann 1918). Cope (1868b), Jordan (1889b), and others did not find the bluntnose minnow in presently occupied streams. The earliest capture in Virginia was in 1937 from the Middle Fork Holston River. Also, there is a lengthy range hiatus in the North Fork Holston which is not fully attributable to pollution from Saltville. The unoccupied reach presently has a diverse fish fauna comprising some sensitive species. The upper two *P. notatus* records are at least 15 rkm above Saltville.

Abundance.—Usually uncommon to abundant; often one of the more common pool and backwater minnows.

REMARKS

As with all *Pimephales*, the blackened nuptial male bluntnose minnow, with a ram of snout tubercles and aggressive disposition, must appear formidable to small fishes venturing too near its nest. Schmidt (1983) suggested that the short stubby "barbel" of breeding male *P. notatus* has a pheromonal function; Dimmick (1988) found this structure to lack taste buds. The bluntnose minnow is one of the most important forage fishes in northern lake communities. It is hardy and reared for commercial bait sale (Hasler et al. 1946; Dobie et al. 1956).

Name.—*Notatus* means "mark," probably referring originally to the caudal fin spot, as Rafinesque did not mention the dorsal fin spot in his description.

SUCKERS
Family Catostomidae

Suckers comprise a moderate-sized group of fishes that are strongly adapted for feeding on bottom organisms. Many of the larger species such as redhorses, northern hogsucker, and white sucker are familiar to fishermen and stream watchers. The largest American suckers, the buffalofishes, reach about 1 m long (3.3 feet) and weigh up to 15 kg (33 pounds). Generally unnoticed are the small, striped or blotchy jumprock suckers, torrent suckers, and the Roanoke hogsucker that are hidden among rocks in rapids.

The catostomid family is widespread in fresh waters of North America, from the Arctic Circle (one species) well into Mexico. Beyond that, *Myxocyprinus asiaticus* is relictively confined to some rivers in China, and the longnose sucker *Catostomus catostomus* ranges across northern North America to northeastern Siberia. The greatest diversity is in the southeastern United States. Virginia is endowed with a large sucker fauna; of the some 75 species in the family (including as many as 9 that are undescribed), 18 are native to the state.

Catostomids are classified in the highly successful superorder Ostariophysi, which comprises fishes having a Weberian apparatus and certain other adaptations (see *Family Cyprinidae*). Within the order Cypriniformes, suckers usually are positioned after minnows owing partly to their further trophic specialization (Greenwood et al. 1966). Although suckers most resemble minnows among North American fishes, their closest kinship may lie with the loaches, a Eurasian group of cyprinoids (Siebert 1984). Suckers settled North America long ago; suckerlike fossils found in Paleocene deposits of Alberta are about 62 million years old (Wilson 1980).

The family has undergone substantial diversification including convergent courses of some lineages.

Its proposed phylogenies have varied by the types of characters studied and the methods applied (Miller 1959; Jenkins 1970; Bussjaeger and Briggs 1978; Buth 1978; Siebert 1982; Fuiman 1985; Smith *in* Bookstein et al. 1985; Smith 1992). We follow Smith's (1992) phylogenetic classification and consequent nomenclature, which according to Robins et al. (1991) were unavailable in time for evaluation for the 1991 names list of the American Fisheries Society. Most or all of Smith's generic alterations were foreshadowed or proposed also by Bailey (1959a), Jenkins (1970), or Buth (1978, 1979c), as well as in some much earlier classifications. Differing from those efforts, Smith studied nearly all extant and some extinct species in the family. He (personal communication) considered that the phylogenetic logic backing the changes is convincing, even though the sociology of new name changes may be discomforting.

Of the three subfamilies, the Ictiobinae and Cycleptinae contain primitive genera having a long-based dorsal fin (23–35 rays in living species). The ictiobines are five buffalofishes (*Ictiobus*), three carpsuckers (*Carpiodes*), and the extinct genera *Amyzon* and (in northern Asia) *Vasnetzovia*. The blue sucker *Cycleptus elongatus* and the Chinese sucker *Myxocyprinus asiaticus* are the only cycleptines. Virginia's sole ictiobine is a carpsucker; the blue sucker may extend into the southwestern edge of the state.

The genera with a short-based dorsal fin (9–17 rays) comprise the subfamily Catostominae, which is divided into two tribes. In the tribe Catostomini, *Catostomus* is quite diverse in western North America and three allied, small or monotypic genera occur there; only one species of *Catostomus* occupies Virginia. Among the tribe Moxostomatini, two of the three chubsuckers (*Erimyzon*) inhabit Virginia; their

459

ally the spotted sucker *Minytrema melanops* is extralimital.

Completing the family, the *Moxostoma* group contributes the greatest diversity of suckers to the Virginia fauna—14 species, the most of any state. It encompasses hogsuckers (*Hypentelium*), torrent suckers (*Thoburnia*), jumprocks (most species of *Scartomyzon*), and redhorses (*Moxostoma* in part). The extinct harelip sucker—formerly the monotypic genus *Lagochila*—has just been added to *Moxostoma*. Accompanying that reranking, *Thoburnia* and *Scartomyzon* are newly elevated from subgeneric status, leaving *Moxostoma* with two subgenera, *Moxostoma* and *Megapharynx*. We term the redhorses of these subgenera "typical" redhorses, to demarcate them from redhorses in *Scartomyzon*.

Genetically, suckers are tetraploid fishes; that is, they have double the usual number of chromosomes. This apparently has been a factor in the evolution of the family, although many of the duplicate gene expressions have been silenced—they are functionally diploid (Uyeno and Smith 1972; Buth 1979d).

Structurally, suckers are sleek, chunky, or compressed and deep-bodied; all have cycloid scales; the dorsal fin is inserted well in advance of the pelvic fin; the pelvic fins are in abdominal position; and the pectoral fins are placed low. They lack fin spines, an adipose fin, and barbels. Most notable is their modification for bottom-oriented feeding; in almost all species the mouth is inferior—opening ventrally—and is bordered by protractile, thick, fleshy, highly sensitive lips. Jaw teeth are absent but the last (5th) pharyngeal arch has many long, fine teeth in one comblike row.

Color patterns of suckers usually are dusky or drab in preservative; few species have distinctive markings. In life many have a brassy or coppery gloss over the side, with subtle gold, green, or purple sheens at scale bases, and orange or red fins. Several have nuptial color consisting mainly of a dark or rosy lateral stripe. Young and small juveniles tend to have a characteristic blotch-saddle pattern which adults may assume at night.

Nuptial tubercles of males of the Catostominae are well developed on the anal fin and lower lobe of the tail, such that maintaining the spawning embrace is aided. Small to minute tubercles roughen most other parts of the fish, mainly in males (Branson 1961; Jenkins 1970; Wiley and Collette 1970). Males of a few species have medium to large snout tubercles; those of chubsuckers may be the largest among all fishes. Catostomine adult males generally are recognizable by a longer anal fin, and by inner pelvic rays which are longer than outer ones (Spoor 1935; Jenkins 1970; Phillips and Underhill 1971).

Catostomids populate essentially the full range of fluvial and lacustrine freshwater habitats; a few species extend into low-salinity estuaries. Most of the larger species inhabit lakes and backwaters, pools, and gentle and moderate runs of rivers. Most of the normally slow-water dwellers spawn in runs. When in calm water, the larger suckers often rest in open, benthic or near-bottom areas; the infrequency of their use of structural cover may be related to reduced predation owing to the body size. Many species avoid substantially silted areas—a contradiction of the often held notion that suckers in general are mud-loving.

Ecologically contrasted to the large, calm-water dwellers are most of the southern Appalachian jumprocks, torrent suckers, and hogsuckers, and the western mountain suckers of the subgenus *Pantosteus* of *Catostomus*. These are strongly adapted to rapids by: streamlining of the body; diminution in size (allowing occupation of pockets of slower current); enlarged paired fins (appressed to the bottom by current); and reduced gas-bladder volume (less buoyancy). The underside of the paired fins in swift-water moxostomatins has ridges with an emery-paper feel (Jenkins 1970), similar to the unculiferous roughened areas recently found in other ostariophysans (Roberts 1982). The ridges may be friction pads that aid position maintenance on the bottom in swift water, as found in some cyprinoids of Himalayan mountain torrents (Hora 1922, 1952).

The cleanliness of the habitat occupied by swift-water and some other suckers helps dispel the idea that suckers in general are quite tolerant of turbidity, siltation, and low oxygen. Their bottom-feeding specializations result in an inability to feed on drifting organisms that are important to so many other fishes; most suckers must feed on clean bottoms. During periods of oxygen depletion suckers are disadvantaged structurally and behaviorally for using surface-layer oxygen (Lowe et al. 1967).

Distribution patterns of suckers reflect general habitat preferences. Most ictiobines are successful in low-gradient large rivers and calm oxbows, thus they may dominate sucker faunas in central Mississippi Valley lowlands. Many other species, typified by redhorses, prefer medium to large streams and rivers of moderate gradient. Most of these avoid lowlands; their distribution patterns arc north of the lower Mississippi Valley. Jumprocks, torrent suckers, and hogsuckers generally are restricted to upland and montane areas and are characteristic of medium to small streams.

Three other distributional features occur in Virginia. No moxostomatin except *Hypentelium nigricans* may have been native to the New drainage in historical time. (The native status in the New of *Thoburnia rhothoeca*, *Scartomyzon cervinus*, and *Moxostoma erythrurum*, each known from one or two streams, is debatable.) Second, five *Moxostoma* species (plus *Carpiodes cyprinus*) which inhabit the Kentucky part of the Big Sandy drainage are absent from the Virginia portion of the drainage, apparently owing to siltation and perhaps chemical pollution from coal mining. Finally, no member of the *Moxostoma* group is clearly known from the entirely Coastal Plain Blackwater system of the Chowan drainage. Redhorses were reported from the Blackwater River by Corning (1967a); if present, they must be rare. The river has been badly polluted, but its acidic tributaries (and nearby Dismal Swamp) also seem naturally inhospitable to redhorses.

Suckers have presented relatively few problems in determining the original distributional status—native or introduced—of populations in Virginia drainages. Inadvertent and purposeful transplantations probably have been rare. Suckers are infrequently used as bait as compared with minnows, hence are less liable to be introduced. Two stockings were made in the 1870s: probably the quillback from the Roanoke to the James drainage, and one or more redhorse species from the Roanoke River to the New River (VFC 1879). Exceptional difficulties exist in determining the natural distribution of the torrent sucker *Thoburnia rhothoeca*.

The usual foods of suckers are small. Some species are primarily midwater planktivores, but most take food directly from the bottom; for example, insect larvae, sediment zooplankton, other invertebrates, and plant material. Three suckers—the extinct harelip sucker *Moxostoma lacerum* and the redhorses *Moxostoma carinatum* and *M. hubbsi*—are specialized in different ways for feeding on mollusks. The two redhorses have molariform pharyngeal teeth and their other masticatory structures are enlarged; although their principal food is mussels and snails, they often eat soft invertebrates. Substantial numbers of shelled mollusks are taken in some situations by suckers other than these three (Baker 1916, 1918). The harelip sucker, whose frail pharyngeal apparatus could not crush shells, may have been the only true mollusk specialist in the family.

Many suckers swallow detritus along with living animals and algae, lending the family a reputation as trophic generalists. Moyle and Li (1979) stated that most suckers belong to the detritus and algae-feeding guild. This may characterize some suckers, but many are chiefly invertebrate feeders. In the first experimental study of this question—a field and laboratory study of the white sucker *Catostomus commersoni*—Ahlgren (1988) found that detritus was consumed voluntarily, but that the intake of detritus decreased proportionately with increasing availability of benthic invertebrates. Suckers are able to sort and eject unwanted material via the mouth and opercular openings. Some materials are sensed by the taste-bud-laden lips; judging from gut contents, often only desired food is engulfed.

Many suckers are thought to feed most actively at night (Moyle 1976), although this has not been confirmed for most species. The lips, other taste sensory systems, and some brain lobes are differentially developed in accordance with habitat and feeding behavior of the species (Miller and Evans 1965). Protrusile lips (Edwards 1926) coupled with a head-down foraging stance (Eastman 1980) allow suckers to feed on the bottom while swimming above it. The numerous comblike teeth in the throat are capable of chewing and perhaps straining and manipulating food (Eastman 1977). The long coiled gut of many suckers (Weisel 1962; Jenkins 1970) probably increases digestion time, important to obtaining nutrition from detritus and living plant material.

Shortly after hatching, suckers resemble many minnows in having a terminal mouth and in feeding on invertebrates at or near the surface (Stewart 1926; Fuiman 1982c). We have seen postlarval *Hypentelium* and *Thoburnia rhothoeca* feeding near the surface, well above the bottom. Young suckers soon become bottom-oriented as the mouth changes to the inferior position. Suckers often feed gregariously. Minnows and sunfishes occasionally follow suckers, apparently feeding on stirred-up food.

The medium and larger suckers tend to be moderately long-lived, 8–15 years. Maximum validated longevities are 28 to 41 years in the western lake-dwelling cui-ui (Scopettone et al. 1986). In most species, adult females have larger average size than adult males.

Reproductive behavior of suckers was summarized by Page and Johnston (1990a). Suckers typically spawn during spring but some continue into early summer. They often migrate considerable distances in rivers and streams, although some species or certain populations may reach spawning grounds by only local movement. Some of the questions concerning the extent of sucker migration are probed by Smith (1977) and Curry and Spacie (1979, 1984). Most suckers spawn on clean gravel beds in streams and rivers; some reproduce in calm pools, ponds, and lakes, on or well above the bottom.

Most species of catostomines generally spawn as a tremoring trio, a female tightly flanked on each side by a male. Spawning acts involving more than two males may be a norm in *Hypentelium*; in the creek chubsucker *Erimyzon oblongus*, spawning usually occurs with a female paired with only one male (Page and Johnston 1990a). Males of a few species, perhaps only some of those with large head tubercles, are overtly aggressive. The river redhorse *Moxostoma carinatum* is the only sucker known to construct a definitive redd (a depression) and to perform ritualized courtship display. For most catostomines, silt often is removed from oviposition sites by disturbance of substrate associated with spawning activities, and some eggs are buried during the spawning act. No sucker is known to guard eggs. Moderate to large numbers of demersal, adhesive or nonadhesive eggs of 1.5–3.5 mm diameter are laid (Fuiman 1982c).

Hybridization is unknown or rare in most eastern suckers (Hubbs 1955; Hubbs et al. 1943a; Jenkins 1970). In the east, it apparently occurs most frequently in *Erimyzon*. *Catostomus* and allies often hybridize in the west. Barriers to hybridization among the *Moxostoma* species that spawn in the same streams include differences in spawning periods, temperatures, and habitat use. Sequential timetables of spawning are becoming apparent (e.g., Meyer 1962; Jenkins 1970; Pflieger 1975; Becker 1983; Curry and Spacie 1984), although some populations may not follow the schedule (Smith 1977).

The worth of suckers is high. They are admirable for successful specialization. Although often labeled as rough, coarse, or trash fish, they are better termed forage and food species. Suckers often dominate the fish biomass of aquatic communities, are important in the food web, and are often eaten by humans. Larimore et al. (1952) noted that a strong smallmouth bass population seemed to be associated with a high percentage of suckers and low percentage of minnows. Similar findings concerning suckers and smallmouth bass were made by Brown (1960). Suckers do not appear to depress community diversity. Rather, they are integral parts of communities; the most diverse fish faunas in Virginia include 5–11 species of suckers.

Why have suckers been maligned? In some cases this simply stems from ignorance, partly because they are not bass, trout, or other "name" fishes. At times, perhaps the name "sucker" is the sole reason. They are accused of eating eggs and fry of more-valued fishes, and of competing for food with other species. Few such cases have withstood scientific inquiry; the benefits of suckers outweigh possible (or imagined) minuses (Moyle 1977b; Holey et al. 1979). Most deplorable are sucker eradication programs, particularly by poisoning, that cause great harm to an entire ecosystem as well as to target species.

In many areas suckers are fished commercially and recreationally in much of the year. Opportunities to harvest large numbers during spawning runs are heralded widely in some regions, only locally in others. We participated in sucker fries in Kentucky and North Carolina, and can attest to their good-tasting although bony flesh. The flesh is firmest when fish are taken in cool and cold water. Small suckers make good bait.

The sporting qualities of large suckers should not be dismissed. Those that are snagged, noosed, speared, or gigged provide a hunt as well as food. On a light rod a sucker can be quite tenacious. A purported silver redhorse was embattled for two hours in Ontario (Scott and Crossman 1973). In the St. Lawrence River, a 3.2-kg (7 pounds) greater redhorse *Moxostoma valenciennesi* landed by Jenkins made long runs and frequent leaps, such that a fully loaded tourboat passing by was almost swamped as viewers dashed to one side to watch the ruckus.

Suckers generally are underfished, and should be used to a greater extent as food (Galloway and Kevern 1976). The opposite may be true in areas where they are popular. The Duck River system, western Tennessee, has supported a major fishery for five species of redhorses. During 1952–1968 two hatcheries were operated there by redhorse clubs to raise and stock these fishes (J. M. Stubbs, in litt.).

Name.—Catostom- means "under mouth"—the inferior position of the mouth.

Key to Suckers   Catostomidae

Many persons have dreaded trying to identify eastern suckers, particularly the redhorses and allies of the tribe Moxostomatini. Problems owing to formerly inadequate knowledge of species limits and diagnostic characters of these fishes have been rectified largely by Robins and Raney (1956) and Jenkins (1970). Difficulties are further reduced when relatively few species need to be considered on a regional or state basis. With care and experience, one can confidently identify preserved moxostomatins at least as small as 40 mm. Living adults and large juveniles of the Virginia species can be identified instream.

We emphasize shapes and surface texture of the lips. Figure 42 shows typical lips drawn from adults and large juveniles. Observation of textural details is best made with lips blotted, under strong light, and except for large specimens, with magnification. Character states of lip surfacing include: *plicate* (Figure 42I, K, L)—lip longitudinally grooved or pleated, appearing folded; *papillose* (Figure 42A, D, H)—with small round papillae or pimplelike structures; papillae may be slightly elevated, the lip appearing pebbled (Figure 42A, H), or papillae may be well elevated and resemble villi (Figure 42D); *subplicate* (lower lip, Figure 42J)—plicae of a portion of a lip are deeply, transversely or obliquely subdivided; subdivisions are not distinctly separated, and many of them are elongate; *plicate–papillose* (Figure 42E, F)—lip with a mixture of plicae and separated papillae; *semipapillose* (Figure 42G)—nearly all plicae or ridges are subdivided into oblong or oval, nonelevated papilla-like elements.

Intraspecific variations of lips occur but the critical invariable or least variable traits are indicated in the *Key*. Generally, young and small juveniles have slightly smoother, less dissected lip surfaces than do adults. Large adults tend to have more posteriorly developed, fuller lips than smaller fish. Large adults of species with plicate lips tend to have the largest amount of branching of plicae (the plicae remaining longitudinally oriented) and greater superficial (shallow) transverse creasing (producing a corrugated appearance to the lip surface, Figure 42K). In such cases the lips are still recognizable as plicate. The angle formed by the posterior edge of the halves of the lower lip varies to such an extent that this character is generally not diagnostic for species with plicate lips (Figure 42I–L).

Accurate determination of the position of the caudal base—to measure standard length and to end the lateral line scale count—is particularly important. Flexing the tail to determine the endpoint (Figure 7) can lead to error, notably for species with heavy urosomal musculature and large thick scales. Our data and key are based on Jenkins' (1970) method: remove one or two scales from just below the midlateral portion of the caudal fin base and probe forward with a fine-pointed tool to detect the posterior end of a hypural bone. That point is then projected vertically to midheight of the lateral line scale—where the scale is transected by the lateral line. The transection point is the standard length endpoint and is used to determine the last lateral line scale counted. Criteria for including or excluding the scale on which the point falls are given in *Anatomy and Color*. The count-termination scale is best identified first; then the lateral line count is made forward.

Head length measurements exclude the opercular membrane.

Circumpeduncle scale counts are very important for separating groups of suckers. These are the least circumpeduncle counts (Figure 7). A scale is excluded if the scale immediately above and the one immediately below, in the same oblique scale row, overlap each other to the slightest degree at their exposed edges, thus cutting off the middle-positioned scale from externally visible contact with any scale in the oblique row just anterior.

A difficult couplet (3) concerns recognition of *Moxostoma carinatum* on the basis of its thick pharyngeal arch and molariform teeth (Figure 11E). Dissection of the arch can be time-consuming (see *Anatomy and Color*). However, the stoutness of the arch can be determined quickly, without dissection, by probing with a fine-pointed tool into the gill chamber anteromediad from the inner edge of the cleithrum (Figures 9, 10). In *M. carinatum* the lateral edge of the arch is very close to the cleithrum; in other species the lateral edge of the arch is well inward from the anterior edge of the cleithrum. The difference holds for large young.

"Dark scale bases" refers to the anterior margin (crescentic or straight-edged scale pockets) of the exposed portion of scales being sharply darker than the central area of the scales (Figure 45A). This trait is best seen on the anterodorsolateral body in adults. Young and small juveniles have the incipient pattern, particularly when compared to species which lack the pattern or have it poorly developed.

Key to Genera (and to Species of Genera Monotypic in Virginia)

1a Dorsal fin rays 24 or more .... QUILLBACK—*Carpiodes cyprinus* p. 469
1b Dorsal fin rays 18 or less 2

2a Lateral line absent on body .... *Erimyzon*
2b Lateral line well developed, complete on body 3

3a Lateral line scales 55 or more, those on anterior body distinctly smaller than those on caudal peduncle .... WHITE SUCKER—*Catostomus commersoni* p. 524
3b Lateral line scales 50 or less, all about equal in size .... tribe Moxostomatini 4

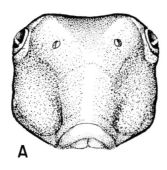
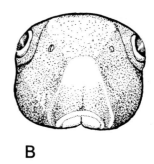

A   B

Figure 39   Head dorsum: (A) Concave, *Hypentelium nigricans*. (B) Convex, *Scartomyzon cervinus*.

4a   Head flat or slightly to moderately concave between eyes (Figure
      39A); (lower lip as in Figure 42A, B; caudal fin base usually with 2
      [sometimes fused] pale areas, Figure 40; circumpeduncle scales
      usually 16; gas bladder 2-chambered, Figure 41A) .... *Hypentelium*
4b   Head slightly or moderately convex between eyes (Figure 39B,
      except *Scartomyzon ariommus* similar to *Hypentelium*); (lower lip
      varied; caudal fin base with or, including *S. ariommus*, lacking pale
      area; circumpeduncle scales modally 12, 15, or 16; gas bladder 2-,
      3-, or 4-chambered) 5

5a   Circumpeduncle scales modally 12; (radii absent in lateral scale
      fields, Figure 43A) .... *Moxostoma*
5b   Circumpeduncle scales modally 15 or 16 6

6a   Caudal fin base with 2 large pale or slightly dusky areas that are
      highlighted by longitudinal black streaks on adjacent portion of
      caudal rays (Figure 40); dorsal rays (9)10(11); lower lip plicate-
      papillose (Figure 42E, F); radii present, usually several, in lateral
      scale fields (Figure 43C); gas bladder 2-chambered and much
      reduced, total length 5–20% SL; peritoneum black (Figure 41B) .... *Thoburnia*
6b   Caudal fin base lacking 2 pale areas, the base not highlighted by
      prominent black streaks on adjacent portion of caudal rays; dorsal
      rays (9)11–12(13); lower lip papillose or plicate (Figure 42D, I); radii
      absent or few in lateral scale fields (Figure 43A, B); gas bladder 3-
      or 4-chambered and moderately reduced at most, total length more
      than 20% SL; peritoneum fully silvery or lightly dappled with
      melanophores (Figure 41C–E) .... *Scartomyzon*

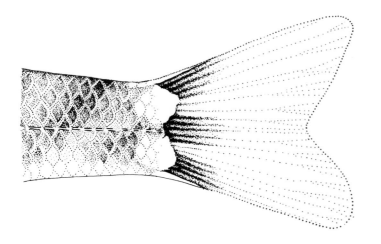

Figure 40   Caudal base depigmentation and ray intensification: *Hypentelium* and *Thoburnia*.

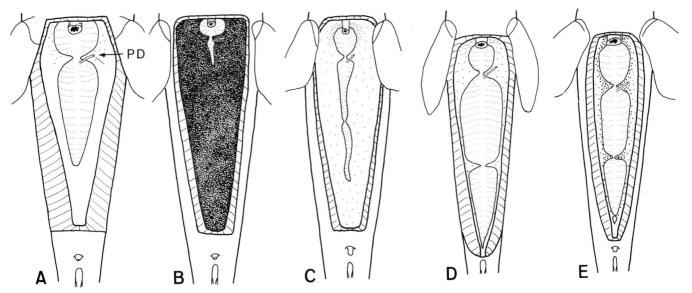

Figure 41 Gas bladders (2-, 3-, or 4-chambered) and degree of peritoneal melanism: (A) *Hypentelium nigricans*. (B) *Thoburnia*. (C) *Scartomyzon cervinus*. (D) *Moxostoma macrolepidotum*. (E) *Scartomyzon ariommus*. PD—pneumatic duct, its connection to gut omitted.

Key to Species of *Erimyzon*

1a	Midlateral scales 34–38 .... LAKE CHUBSUCKER—*E. sucetta*	p. 472
1b	Midlateral scales 40–46 .... CREEK CHUBSUCKER—*E. oblongus*	p. 475

Key to Species of *Hypentelium*

1a Lips papillose (Figure 42A) (upper lip rarely subplicate anteriorly); lateral line scales (44)45–48(50); dark saddle between head and dorsal fin usually moderately developed; widespread ..... NORTHERN HOGSUCKER—*H. nigricans* p. 478

1b Lips papillose on outer surfaces, subplicate or plicate on inner surfaces (Figure 42B); lateral line scales (38)40–43(44); saddle between head and dorsal fin usually vague or absent; Roanoke drainage only .... ROANOKE HOGSUCKER—*H. roanokense* p. 482

Key to Species of *Thoburnia*

1a Lower lip with relatively fewer round papillae compared with oblong papillae and plicae (Figure 42F); lower lip usually extending less posteriorly, and the halves tending more triangular in form; Roanoke system of Roanoke drainage and north on Atlantic slope and New drainage .... TORRENT SUCKER—*T. rhothoeca* p. 485

1b Lower lip with a relatively greater number of round papillae compared with oblong papillae and plicae (Figure 42E); lower lip usually extending more posteriorly, and the halves tending more truncate or broadly rounded posteriorly; restricted to upper Dan system of Roanoke drainage .... RUSTYSIDE SUCKER—*T. hamiltoni* p. 489

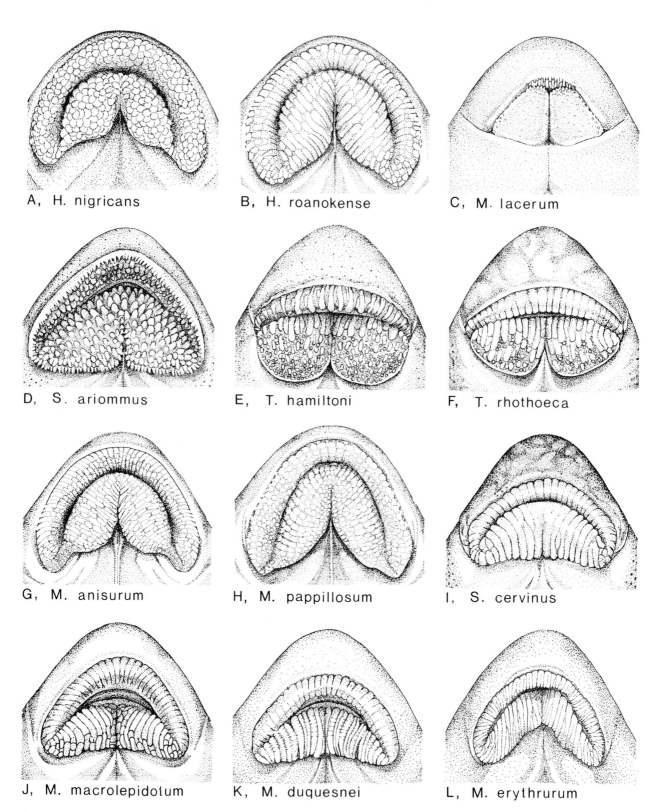

A, H. nigricans B, H. roanokense C, M. lacerum

D, S. ariommus E, T. hamiltoni F, T. rhothoeca

G, M. anisurum H, M. pappillosum I, S. cervinus

J, M. macrolepidotum K, M. duquesnei L, M. erythrurum

Figure 42 Lips in moxostomatin suckers: Types of lip surfaces (definitions precede key): Papillose—A, D, H. Semipapillose—G. Plicate-papillose—B, E, F. Subplicate—lower lip of J. Plicate—I, K, L (lower lip of K being corrugate; lower lip of *M. erythrurum* shown with sharper posterior angle than typical of species).

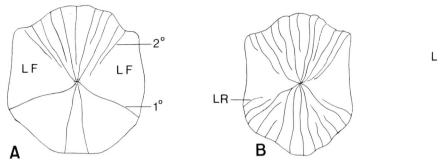
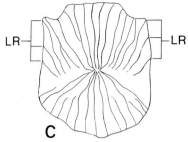

Figure 43 Scale radii in lateral fields—LF (positional dorsal and ventral fields); 1°—primary radius (extends from margin to focus); 2°—secondary radius (not reaching focus). (A) Lateral radii absent in *Moxostoma*. (B) 1 secondary lateral radius in *Scartomyzon cervinus*. (C) 6 secondary lateral radii in *Thoburnia rhothoeca*.

Key to Species of *Scartomyzon*

1a Lips entirely papillose, flattened, anterior and lateral edges
     sometimes flared downward (Figure 42D); head dorsum flat or
     slightly concave; eye large; Roanoke drainage only .... BIGEYE JUMPROCK—*S. ariommus*   p. 496

1b Lips plicate or sublicate, thick, nonflared (Figure 42I); head dorsum
     slightly or moderately convex; eye small or moderate 2

2a Caudal and dorsal fin tips not notably darker than elsewhere on
     these fins; circumbody scales (33)36–37(39); Pee Dee drainage only ....
     .... SMALLFIN REDHORSE—*S. robustus*   p. 491

2b Caudal and dorsal fin tips black or distinctly duskier than
     elsewhere on these fins (Figure 44); circumbody scales (29)31–34(35);
     Roanoke, Chowan, James, and New drainages .... BLACK JUMPROCK—*S. cervinus*   p. 493

Key to Species of *Moxostoma*

1a Upper lip nonprotractile, bound directly to snout; halves of lower
     lip completely separated into 2 round or subtriangular lobes (Figure
     42C) .... HARELIP SUCKER—*M. lacerum*   p. 519

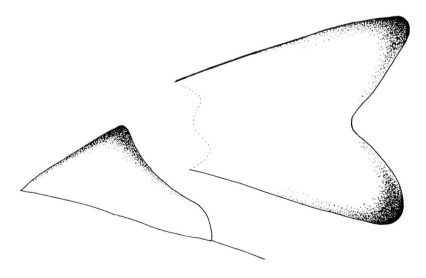

Figure 44 Dorsal and caudal fin tip pigmentation in *Scartomyzon cervinus*.

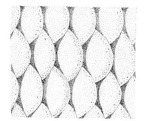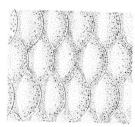

Figure 45 Dorsolateral scale pigmentation patterns in *Moxostoma*: (A) *M. macrolepidotum*. (B) *M. duquesnei*. (C) *M. erythrurum*.

1b   Upper lip protractile, separated from snout by deep groove; halves
of lower lip moderately or broadly fused 2

2a   Upper and lower lips basically plicate (Figure 42K, L) or upper lip
plicate and lower lip subplicate (Figure 42J); posterior margin of
lower lip forming slightly acute (about 80°) to very obtuse (almost
180°) angle (Figure 42J–L) 3

2b   Upper and lower lips fully or nearly fully papillose or
semipapillose; posterior margin of lower lip forming moderate or
very acute angle (i.e., V-lipped) (Figure 42G, H) 6

3a   Pharyngeal arch thick, lower teeth large, molariform, 6–9 teeth on
lower half of tooth row (Figure 11E); (lips plicate, Figure 42K, L;
head moderate or large, length usually 24–25% SL; lateral line
scales (41)42–44(46); scale bases moderately or markedly darker
than central portion of scales (Figure 45A); tail reddish in life;
Tennessee drainage, possibly also Big Sandy drainage) ....   RIVER REDHORSE—*M. carinatum*   p. 509

3b   Pharyngeal arch moderate, lower teeth smaller, comblike, 12–30
teeth on lower half of tooth row (Figure 11D) 4

4a   Lower lip subplicate posteriorly or wholly (Figure 42J); head small
and short, length usually 19.5–22.5% SL in adult and large juvenile;
scale bases moderately or quite darker than posterior portion of
scales (Figure 45A); tail usually reddish in life ...   SHORTHEAD REDHORSE—*M. macrolepidotum*   p. 503

4b   Lower lip plicate (Figure 42K, L); head moderate or large, length
usually 21–26% SL; scales not markedly darker at their base than at
posterior margin (Figure 45B, C); tail dusky in life 5

5a   Lateral line scales (43)44–47(48); circumbody scales (31)32–36(38);
pelvic fin rays modally 10–10 (left–right sides) in Clinch, Powell,
and Big Sandy drainages, modally 9–9 in Holston; caudal peduncle
somewhat elongate and shallow, length usually 13.0–15.5% SL,
depth usually 8.5–10.0% SL; anterior dorsolateral scales fairly
uniformly dusky or dark (Figure 45B) ....   BLACK REDHORSE—*M. duquesnei*   p. 500

5b   Lateral line scales (39)40–43(45); circumbody scales (29)30–33(36);
pelvic rays modally 9–9; caudal peduncle generally stout, length
usually 12.0–14.0% SL, depth usually 9.5–11.5% SL; anterior
dorsolateral scales with posterior portion obviously darker
than median, pigment shades somewhat demarcated
(Figure 45C) ....   GOLDEN REDHORSE—*M. erythrurum*   p. 506

6a Lower lip semipapillose, its fine ridges (plicae) deeply, transversely, and somewhat irregularly dissected, resultant papillae somewhat irregularly arranged and unequal in size; front of upper lip generally smooth, lacking papillae; lower lip usually abruptly thinned posterolaterally, to its juncture with upper lip (Figure 42G); dorsal fin margin usually very slightly concave or straight, occasionally slightly convex; dorsal rays (12)14–15(17); caudal peduncle depth usually 10.5–12.0% SL .... SILVER REDHORSE—*M. anisurum*   p. 513

6b Lower lip papillose, papillae usually round, regularly arranged, small, and generally subequal or equal in size; front of upper lip papillose; lower lip usually not abruptly thinned posterolaterally (Figure 42H); dorsal fin margin almost always falcate or moderately concave, rarely slightly concave; dorsal rays (11)12–13(15); caudal peduncle depth usually 9.0–10.5% SL .... V-LIP REDHORSE—*M. pappillosum*   p. 516

Carpsuckers   Genus *Carpiodes* Rafinesque

This primitive genus contains silvery suckers with a deep body and a long-based dorsal fin. It is currently construed to have three species, one in Virginia. Mississippi basin populations of carpsuckers have a troubled taxonomic history; the status of most populations was clarified by Hubbs (1930a), Hubbs and Black (1940a), and Trautman (1956), but a comprehensive analysis remains warranted. The south Atlantic and eastern Gulf slope populations carry names of Mississippi basin species but their exact status is unknown.

Name.—*Carpiodes* means "carplike," based on similarity to the common carp *Cyprinus carpio*.

Quillback   *Carpiodes cyprinus* (Lesueur)

SYSTEMATICS

The quillback was described from tributaries of upper Chesapeake Bay in 1817. The status of certain western Mississippi basin populations—*C. "forbesi"*—seems unresolved (Bailey and Allum 1962; Starrett and Fritz 1965; Cornelius 1966; Metcalf 1966; Pflieger 1975; Trautman 1981). Central Atlantic slope populations south to the Roanoke drainage align with the subspecies *C. c. cyprinus*; those in the Ohio basin are *C. c. hinei* (Trautman 1956, 1981; Hubbs and Lagler 1958). We recognize *C. cyprinus* and *C. velifer* to occur on the Atlantic slope south of Virginia, based particularly on their similarity in nuptial tuberculation with Mississippi basin populations described by Huntsman (1967).

DESCRIPTION

Materials.—By drainage, the numbers of mostly adult specimens studied are: Potomac 2, James 2, Roanoke 9, Pee Dee 2, Santee 8, and Savannah 8. Color in life based on 5 adults from the Roanoke drainage and 1 young from the Appomattox River.

Anatomy.—A silvery deep-bodied sucker with a long-based dorsal fin; adults are 250–400 mm SL. Body moderately or very deep, high-backed, compressed; dorsal fin base long. Dorsal fin margin falcate anteriorly, the tip moderately or much extended and tapering to a point; anterior dorsal fin height 25–40% SL, 50–100% of base length of the fin; caudal fin well forked. Head deep and short; eye moderate or large.

Mouth subterminal or inferior; lips moderate or thin, lower lips meeting at about a 90° angle, lacking a nipple at their juncture, surfaces semipapillose. Teeth comblike. Gas bladder 2-chambered.

Nuptial tubercles in male tiny to moderate over most of head, largest on cheek and operculum; nape, midside, and lower side tuberculate in larger specimens; all fins of larger males with tubercles, few and tiny on most fins, moderately developed on pectoral. Female tubercle pattern essentially as in male but less developed.

Meristics.—Lateral line scales 35–39; circumbody scales 31–38; circumpeduncle scales (17)18(19). Dorsal rays 26–32; anal rays 8–9; pelvic rays 8–10; pectoral rays 15–16.

Color in Preservative.—Dusky above, pale below; scale pockets forming dark crescents, posterior margin of scales

Fish 123 *Carpiodes cyprinus* young 59 mm SL (SIUC 5575), KY, Fulton County, Mississippi River, 6 August 1982.

with fine black line. All fins uniformly pale or dusky or, in adult, lower fins dark centrally, broadly pale-margined. Some young with alternating pale and dusky horizontal stripes above lateral line.

Color in Life.—Back olive to brown with some brassy; side silvery, some fish with general golden yellow iridescence and scales bases with green tint; iris largely silvery. Fins medium to dark gray, or lower fins in adult white-bordered.

Larvae.—Described by Mansueti and Hardy (1967), Lippson and Moran (1974), Jones et al. (1978), Loos et al. (1979), Buynak and Mohr (1980c), Fuiman (1979b, 1982c), and Snyder (1979).

BIOLOGY

Considered a generalist feeder on fine-grained particles (Beecher 1980), this carpsucker takes insects, small mollusks, other invertebrates, plant material, and usually large amounts of flocculent detritus, along with much sand (Cahn 1927; Harlan and Speaker 1956; Beecher 1979; Becker 1983).

At least some age-4 fish are mature; the oldest known is 11 years (Woodward and Wissing 1976). In Ohio, males tend to grow faster than females; age-5 males averaged 287 mm TL, females 277 mm (Woodward and Wissing 1976). Iowa fish of age 5 ranged 221–345 mm TL (Vanicek 1961). Of reproductive migrants in Indiana, females averaged larger, 373 mm TL, range 281–444 mm, compared with 352 mm, 305–385 mm for males (Curry and Spacie 1984). In Nebraska, mature females were 356–578 mm TL, males 239–537 mm (Madsen 1971). (June's [1977] *C. "cyprinus"* were *C. carpio*.) The largest quillback, 660 mm TL, was reported from Ohio by Trautman (1981), who noted that dwarfing occurs in some populations. A 483-mm TL specimen is the largest known to us from Virginia (Neal 1967).

Spawning occurs from mid-April through much of June, perhaps slightly later, in water of 11–25°C (Gale and Mohr 1976; Smith 1977; Curry and Spacie 1984). Fuiman (1979b) found quillback eggs on 20 May in a James River tributary. Ripe fish were taken through September in Ohio (Woodward and Wissing 1976). Upstream spawning migrations, with entry of medium and small streams, have been noted for some populations (Madsen 1971; Smith 1977; Trautman 1981).

In lower and middle Back Creek, a tributary of Smith Mountain Lake, immigration of quillback increased during 4–30 April 1971; large concentrations were in pools and deep runs on 30 April but spawning was not observed. A resident of the Back Creek vicinity said that quillback spawn in early May during day and night. We were told that quillback move into the lower several rkm of Copper Creek in spring. All Virginia records from tributaries of the largest rivers are of adults in spring or young in summer and fall, indicating that the young retreat from tributaries, juveniles dwell mainly in large rivers, and adults leave the rivers only to spawn.

Quillback have been reported to spawn in riffles, in calm parts of streams, and in overflow bayous, with eggs laid on gravel, sand, mud, and organic matter (Harlan and Speaker 1956; Smith 1977; Loos et al. 1979). Gale and Mohr (1976) considered the quillback to be the least discriminating of spawning habitat among 16 species of Susquehanna River fishes. Fecundity is 15,235–63,779 ova (Woodward and Wissing 1976). A hybrid *C. cyprinus × C. velifer* was reported from Wisconsin (Becker 1983).

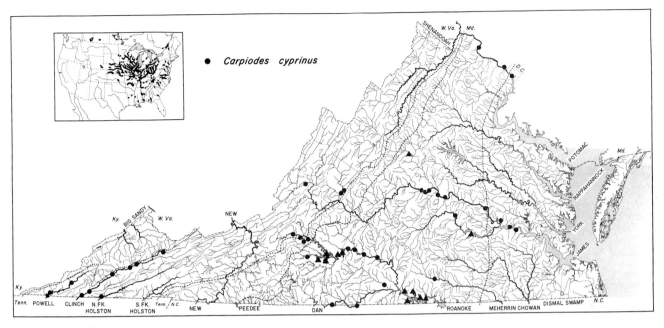

Map 87 Quillback.

HABITAT

Carpiodes cyprinus is found in warm lakes, reservoirs, and low to moderate-gradient rivers; it sometimes occurs in small streams and ditches in central and western portions of its range. In Virginia it remains in reservoirs and rivers except around the spawning period, when it enters medium-sized streams. In rivers the quillback generally occurs in calm water over varied substrates but seldom over mud; during low water it shifts to swifter and sometimes deeper water (Vanicek 1961; Beecher 1980). It inhabits turbid silted conditions of central and prairie waters and the Dan River, Virginia, but seems less tolerant of such conditions than is the river carpsucker *C. carpio* (Harlan and Speaker 1956; Pflieger 1975; Trautman 1981). This species typically is not an estuarine fish; Musick (1972) reported it from 10.7‰ salinity.

DISTRIBUTION   Map 87

This carpsucker ranges from the upper Hudson Bay basin to the Gulf slope. The Delaware drainage population may have been founded by individuals which traversed the Chesapeake–Delaware Canal (Mihursky 1962). *Carpiodes cyprinus* extends erratically in major Atlantic drainages from the Susquehanna to the Altamaha. It skips the Rappahannock and York, and in North Carolina, the Tar, Neuse, and Cape Fear. The only Chowan record is from 1985 (M. D. Norman, personal communication). Quillback may also occupy the Big Sandy drainage in the state, at least during migration.

The VFC (1877b) noted transferral of "buffalo" to Catawba Creek of the James. Probably the fish were quillback and the source was the adjacent Roanoke drainage. The VFC stated that the fish was previously unknown from the James. However, we doubt that sampling had been sufficient to indicate it was absent; even today this main-channel fish is rarely taken. The establishment by stocking of *Carpiodes* in a drainage is improbable unless heavily stocked, which would have been quite unlikely in those times. Evidence that *Carpiodes* is native to the James is a diary entry (deciphered by McDonald 1887) by a commercial fisherman well above Richmond: in 1769, he wrote "caught 2 fine carp in our traps." This obviously referred to a carpsucker; the common carp *Cyprinus carpio* was not brought into the country until 1831. "Carp" apparently was also applied to *Carpiodes* by early English settlers of North Carolina (our interpretation of Lawson 1709).

Abundance.—Probably generally uncommon; rare in the Meherrin River; not easily inventoried because of its preference for large deep waters. Locally abundant when migrating and spawning.

REMARKS

Mint silver and golden sides render the quillback a handsome sucker. Its occurrence in river reaches may be unnoticed until its influx to tributaries for spawning. Sometimes this species is taken by snagging during the run.

Name.—*Cyprinus* refers to the generic name of the common carp, to which carpsuckers are similar in morphology and habits.

Chubsuckers   Genus *Erimyzon* Jordan

The three species of this genus, two in Virginia, are well-named from their body form. They lack a lateral line on the body, have a short-based dorsal fin, and nuptial males develop very large tubercles on the side of the snout. They are typical of low-gradient waters.

Name.—*Eri*, intensive particle, "very"; *myzo*, "to suck."

Lake chubsucker   *Erimyzon sucetta* (Lacepède)

SYSTEMATICS

Erimyzon sucetta was made known in 1803 from South Carolina, but was not clearly separated from the other chubsuckers until Hubbs' (1930a) study. Hubbs discerned an eastern and a western subspecies but Bailey et al. (1954) considered the differences insufficient for taxonomic recognition.

DESCRIPTION

Materials.—Ten lots totaling 24 specimens from Virginia.

Anatomy.—A chunky large-scaled sucker; adults are 100–300 mm SL. Body moderately deep, moderately compressed; profile of back sharply declining posteriad along dorsal fin base; young more elongate, contours smoother.

Fish 124 *Erimyzon sucetta* adult male 170 mm SL (NCSM 9701), NC, Craven County, Lake Ellis Simon, 23 July 1980.

Fish 125 *Erimyzon sucetta* juvenile 65 mm SL (WHH 148), VA, Surry County, Otterdam Swamp, 25 July 1983.

Dorsal fin base short, dorsal fin margin slightly concave or, in adult, well rounded. Head and orbit length moderate; snout prominent.

Mouth subterminal, oblique; halves of lower lip forming an angle of 60–120°, widest in adults; lips plicate. Gas bladder 2-chambered.

Sexual dimorphism marked in shape of anal fin and tuberculation. Anal fin of male bilobed, membranes of posterior lobe often much incised, hence rays distally free; female anal fin normal. Cephalic tubercles only on side of snout, very large, recurved, 3–4 per side, or somewhat smaller and more numerous; elsewhere, well-developed tubercles only on anal fin and lower urosome; female lacks or has very reduced tuberculation (Frey 1951; Jenkins 1970). Our tuberculate Virginia male, 107 mm SL, has tubercles only on anal fin, probably owing to the small size of the fish.

Meristics.—Lateral line absent, midlateral scales (to caudal base) (34)35–37(38); circumbody scales (30)32–35(36); circumpeduncle scales (16)17–18(19). Dorsal rays 11–12(13); anal rays 7(8); pelvic rays 9(10); pectoral rays 14–15(16).

Color in Preservative.—Young *Erimyzon* are very distinctive, with a black lateral stripe the length of the body, the stripe encircling snout, and enlarged into a caudal spot; pale stripe present above midlateral stripe and extending around snout, setting off dark markings above and below (head appearing muzzled); head and body dorsum dark except for middorsal pale stripe that is widest on head; dorsal fin black anterodistally.

During juvenile stage, head and fin patterns lost, midlateral stripe usually less intense, body more generally dusky, fins uniformly pale or dusky or lower fins duskiest distally; midlateral stripe sometimes subdivided into 6–9 dusky blotches that extend ventrad and dorsad and align, connected or not, with vague saddles; blotch-saddles V-shaped, apex anterior.

Color in Life.—Young with orange caudal and dorsal fins and snout dorsum (based on notes by T. Zorach from Dismal Swamp specimens—specimens apparently were in preservative for several days, thus the colors probably were reddish in life). Two juveniles and one subadult from Coppahaunk Swamp with back olive, grading to silvery olive on lower side; dorsolaterally with gold, green, and brassy iridescence; midlateral stripe sooty; iris brown or orange-brown; dorsal and caudal fins pale olive to straw-olive; other fins pale olive to colorless; red absent.

Larvae.—Described by Shaklee et al. (1974) and Fuiman (1979a, 1982c).

COMPARISON

Erimyzon sucetta and *E. oblongus* vary geographically such that certain characters used to separate them in some regions do not work in Virginia, and some populations may vary more than previously known. The following is based on Virginia specimens: (1) scales along midbody to caudal base [34–38 in *sucetta* vs. 40–46 in *oblongus*]; (2) circumbody scales [30–36 vs. 35–45]. Relative scale size of large juveniles and adults can be discerned without counting, after gaining a concept of the differences by study of comparative material. In juveniles and subadults taken concurrently from Coppahaunk Swamp, *sucetta* was the chunkiest and lacked red in all fins; *oblongus* had, depending on the fin, a tinge or distinct red in all fins. These body-form and fin-color states need further study, particularly in young and adults, to substantiate the differences.

BIOLOGY

The lake chubsucker feeds on microcrustaceans, aquatic insects, mollusks, algae, and detritus (Cahn 1927; Ewers and Boesel 1935 *in* Carlander 1969; Shireman et al. 1978; Winter 1983).

In a study apparently conducted in Florida, maturity was believed to be reached in the third year of life (Shireman et al. 1978). Cooper (1935) stated that in Michigan both sexes mature in the third summer (age 2). Most age-1 fish were mature in Nebraska; only 2 of 1,669 specimens attained age 4 (Winter 1983). *Erimyzon sucetta* is known to reach age 8 in New York (Carlander 1969). Cooper's (1935) statement indicates that in Michigan, *E. sucetta* reaches about 170 mm TL at age 4. At the same age, Indiana fish were 216–254 mm TL; in North Carolina the means from five lakes had a range of 224–244 mm TL (Carlander 1969).

Large lake chubsuckers, 300 mm TL and more, occupy southern regions; Carlander's (1969) listing of a large specimen from Connecticut is based on *E. oblongus* (Webster 1942). Particularly large fish are from North Carolina and Florida, and the largest, 432 mm TL, is from Louisiana (Frey 1951; Carlander 1969; Shireman et al. 1978). The biggest of the few we have seen from Virginia is 151 mm SL. Our 107-mm SL tuberculate male indicates that *E. sucetta* may not get large in Virginia.

Spawning begins in late March or early April and continues well into June in Illinois (Bennett and Childers 1966), and occurs in late April to late May, water 16–23°C, in Nebraska (Winter 1983). Cooper (1935) stated that the spawning period lasts about two weeks and may extend into early July in Michigan. Evidence of spawning during March to mid-April in Florida was found by Swift et al. (1977). In Virginia, reproduction probably occurs within late March to May. Eggs are scattered on vegetation in ponds (Cooper 1935), and spawning undoubtedly occurs also in calm parts of streams. Fecundity is 1,000–

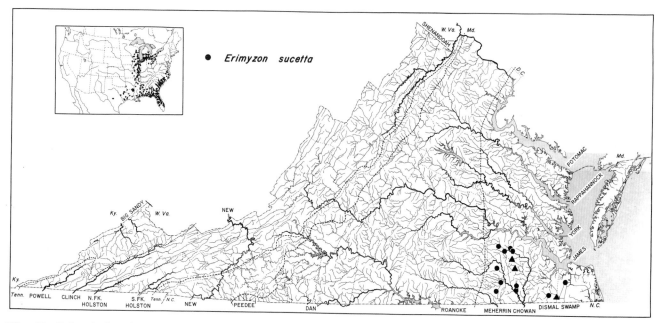

Map 88   Lake chubsucker (introduced range in Nebraska not shown).

20,000 eggs (Cooper 1935; Shireman et al. 1978; Becker 1983; Winter 1983).

Hybrids and backcrosses of *E. oblongus* × *E. sucetta* were found in North Carolina, mostly in disturbed situations such as drainage ditches (Hanley 1977). Shute et al. (1981) also found evidence of hybridization by these species in North Carolina.

HABITAT

Over its range, *E. sucetta* occupies lowland warmwater ponds, lakes, ditches, and calm parts of streams, and occurs over mud, silt, sand, and, apparently rarely, fine gravel. It is usually associated with dense submersed vegetation and clear but stained water. Trautman (1981) regarded it to be highly intolerant of turbidity and siltation, but siltation may not be a general limiting factor. Pflieger (1975) stated that habitat requirements of *E. sucetta* and *E. oblongus* are similar, and that their largely complementary distribution in Missouri may result from competition.

Analysis of the 13 of 14 accepted records of *E. sucetta* at separate Virginia sites reveals that nine sites are swampy streams or flowages of 1–9 m, mostly 1–2 m width; two are ponds; and, in or near Dismal Swamp, one is a ditch and one a canal. Vegetation was sparse to profuse at six sites and was absent at three (no data on others). The range of pH from four sites was 5.6–6.8. Apparently the lake chubsucker species does not tolerate highly acidic waters in much of Dismal Swamp. *Erimyzon sucetta* was reported from 1.86‰ salinity in North Carolina (Keup and Bayless 1964).

DISTRIBUTION   Map 88

The lake chubsucker occupies lowlands of the southern Great Lakes, the central Mississippi Valley, and the Coastal Plain of the Gulf and Atlantic slopes, north to the Dismal Swamp and Chowan drainage of Virginia. Statements of occurrence farther north on the Atlantic slope apparently are based on former taxonomic confusion with, or misidentification of, *E. oblongus*. The paucity of records of *E. sucetta* in northeastern North Carolina is partly related to rejection of identifications made in the 1960s surveys by the North Carolina Wildlife Resources Commission (Wall and Gilbert *in* Lee et al. 1980; E. F. Menhinick, in litt.). No support was found for the report (Jordan and Brayton 1878) of *Erimyzon* in the Clinch River, Tennessee.

Abundance.—Generally rare, eight specimens being the most known in a collection.

REMARKS

Young of both chubsuckers often school above the bottom, and in body form, color, and gracefulness they resemble black-striped shiners; the pigment pattern of their head is unmistakable. Juveniles and adults may rest with only the tips of lower fins contacting the substrate. The lake chubsucker is considered a culturable forage fish in ponds (Cooper 1935; Bennett and Childers 1966; Shireman et al. 1978; Winter 1983).

Name.—*Sucetta* is a Latinization of the French "sucet," for "sucker."

Creek chubsucker   *Erimyzon oblongus* (Mitchill)

SYSTEMATICS

Erimyzon oblongus was described from New York in 1814 but was long considered a subspecies of *E. sucetta*. Hubbs (1930a) elevated *E. oblongus* and recognized three subspecies: the eastern *E. o. oblongus* south to Virginia; the western *E. o. claviformis*; and *E. o. connectans*, an intermediate form in Georgia. However, Hubbs had scant material, none from the Carolinas. Frey (1951) identified *E. o. connectans* from southeastern North Carolina. Bailey et al. (1954) considered *E. o. oblongus* and *E. o. claviformis* to be well-marked subspecies, and stated that *E. o. connectans* of Georgia probably is best treated as an intergrade. Further systematic study is deserved.

DESCRIPTION

Materials.—Twenty-nine Virginia lots including counts from 48 specimens from Delmarva and all major Atlantic drainages except the Rappahannock. Color in life based on 25 specimens from the upper James, middle Roanoke, and Chowan.

Anatomy.—A robust, moderately large-scaled sucker; adults are 90–250 mm SL. Body somewhat elongate, well rounded or somewhat compressed, back moderately elevated; other features as in *E. sucetta* except snout tubercles 3, rarely 4 per side, and no tuberculate female found (Carnes 1958; Wagner and Cooper 1963; our observations).

Meristics.—Lateral line absent, midlateral scales (40)41–43(46); circumbody scales (35)38–43(45); circumpeduncle scales 17–19(21). Dorsal rays 11–13; anal rays (6)7; pelvic rays (7)9(10); pectoral rays (14)15–16(17).

Color in Preservative.—As in *E. sucetta* except juvenile and adult *E. oblongus* possibly more frequently in lateral blotch-dorsal saddle phase. However, only a few *E. sucetta* were examined and the ability of living *E. oblongus* to replace the dark midlateral stripe with the blotch-saddle pattern (Bean 1903) probably extends to *E. sucetta*.

Color in Life Plate 20.—Body and fin colors change from young to adult stages. Young with back dusky olive; dorsolateral stripe yellow-olive; midlateral stripe black; lower side and belly silvery white. Juvenile and adult with back green-olive to dark olive; side iridescent golden green, some brassy, scale margins dark olive; lower side and belly silvery white; midlateral stripe blackish or absent; blotch-saddles slightly darker than ground color or absent; iris silver, orange, or orange-brown, usually with dusky areas.

In young, dorsal and caudal fins pale to medium red,

Fish 126 *Erimyzon oblongus* adult male 127 mm SL (REJ 1035), VA, Charlotte County, East Branch Wards Fork Creek, 2 September 1983.

Fish 127 *Erimyzon oblongus* young 40 mm SL (REJ 1015), VA, Greensville County, Cattail Creek, 15 July 1983.

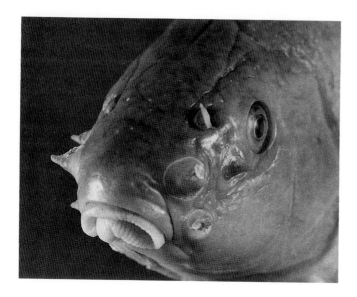

Fish 128   Snout tubercles of *Erimyzon oblongus*.

brightest basally; lower fins pale. In large juvenile and small adult, dorsal and caudal fins mostly olive, tinge of red persisting distally in some specimens; anal fin pale or olive, acquiring red tinge mostly distally in rays; paired-fin membranes become orange-red to carmine, most so in pectoral, rays clear or pale olive. Large nuptial males with dorsal, caudal, and anal fins dusky, paired fins yellow-olive; fins of our large nuptial males lacked red.

Larvae.—Described by Carnes (1958), Mansueti and Hardy (1967), Lippson and Moran (1974), Jones et al. (1978), Fuiman (1979b, 1982c), Snyder (1979), and Wang and Kernehan (1979).

COMPARISON

See account of *E. sucetta.*

BIOLOGY

The kinds of foods eaten by *E. oblongus* appear to be much the same as those of *E. sucetta,* based on Adams and Hankinson (1928), Flemer and Woolcott (1966), and Gatz (1979). In a marsh area of the James River estuary, the creek chubsucker fed almost entirely on planktonic crustaceans, many of which occur in and around submersed plants (VIMS 1977). The subterminal mouth of chubsuckers indicates they feed less on the bottom than most other suckers (Pflieger 1975).

Some creek chubsuckers mature by age 2, no males older than age 5 were found, and some females reached age 7. Males exceed females in growth until the fourth year, when sizes equalize, after which females grow faster. We studied tuberculate males as small as 140–150 mm SL. At age 4 the size range,

sexes combined, from North Carolina was 305–384 mm TL, mean, 351 (Carnes 1958). In Pennsylvania, weighted means at age 4 for two year-classes were males 332 mm TL, females 309 mm (Wagner and Cooper 1963). Apparently the eastern subspecies attains much larger sizes than does the western one (e.g., Hubbs 1930a). A Virginia specimen of 311 mm TL was reported by VIMS (1977). Carnes (1958) reported fish up to 411 mm TL in North Carolina. Mansueti (1957 *in* Mansueti and Hardy 1967) gave maximum size as about 457 mm, presumably TL and from Maryland, but Elser (1961) gave the Maryland record as 419 mm TL.

The spawning period of a North Carolina population of *E. oblongus* was estimated to last 20–30 days within late March to late April; the upstream migration began when water had reached 11°C for two weeks (Carnes 1958). Whitehurst (1981) found specimens in reproductive condition in another North Carolina stream during March through May, water 11.5–17°C. From Delaware to New York, the creek chubsucker spawns during April and May in 14.4–22°C (Adams and Hankinson 1928; Fuiman 1979b; Wang and Kernehan 1979). In Indiana and Illinois, breeding took place during mid-April to mid-May at 15–24°C (Hankinson 1919; Stegman 1959; Curry and Spacie 1984; Page and Johnston 1990a). Webster (1942) gave late April for Connecticut; the northernmost population, in Maine, continues spawning into early June (Everhart 1966).

Creek chubsuckers were ripening in Virginia during mid-March, some were gravid and some spent in mid-April, and a large postnuptial male with a fungused head was found dying on 30 April. However, collections taken during 18–22 May contain highly tuberculate males, and the females appear only partly spent.

Most indications of spawning were of fish in pools or moderate current of small streams, on sand and gravel in 0.5–1.2 m depth. Page and Johnston (1990a) observed spawning in runs in human-made ditches averaging about 1 m wide and 0.2 m deep; the oviposition sites had sand–gravel substrate and included breeding pits of minnows. Fuiman (1979b) observed a male and female spawning near shore in a hatchery pond, at the base of a submergent macrophyte on a mud bottom, depth 0.3–0.5 m.

The very large snout tubercles of male *Erimyzon*, resembling curved thorns, are formidable weaponry and indicate the possibility of an interesting agonistic ritual associated with spawning. The deep grooves on the cephalic skin of some males indicate aggressive encounters. The snout (and fin) tubercles would also help to maintain spawning position. Observations have been sketchy but in sum they indicate variable behavior, probably correlating with the number and proximity of males present, and with the appearance of females at spawning sites.

Hankinson (1919) saw two tuberculate males "pulling at the stones" on a gravel shoal; once they flanked a female and spawned. The stone-pulling likely was displacement activity; harmful aggressive contact between males may be deferred sometimes by tinkering with the substrate. Wang and Kernehan (1979) found much splashing and excited swimming associated with spawning; gravel at the site was cleaned but eggs were randomly distributed. A spawning group in the lower Susquehanna drainage of Pennsylvania was in an area of cleared substrate (C. R. Robins, in litt.). Curry and Spacie (1984) stated that gravel was uncovered from sand by spawning activity, and that males actively defended small cleared depressions.

Recently, a superior description has appeared of the advanced reproductive behavior of *E. oblongus* in Illinois (Page and Johnston 1990a). This species does not construct a nest but males move stones in minnow nests with the snout. Males defend territories by butting other males with their heads; they aggressively parallel-swam, sometimes while pushing each other with the head and apparently interlocking the snout tubercles. Males periodically court and attempt to lead females to the territories. Females dig in gravel with the snout apparently in order to signal readiness to spawn. In 22 consummated spawnings, the female was attended by one male in 18 and by two males in 4.

Fecundity is 7,500–83,000 ova (Carnes 1958; Wagner and Cooper 1963). Natural hybrids of *E. oblongus* × *E. sucetta* were noted in the *E. sucetta* account.

HABITAT

The creek chubsucker is an occupant of ditches, creeks to rivers, and natural and artificial ponds and lakes. In Virginia it most often inhabits creeks of low or moderate gradient. It is found on soft and firm bottoms and may be less associated with submersed vegetation in some regions than *E. sucetta*. Hastings (1984) considered *E. oblongus* to be independent of sheltered habitats such as weed beds and Gerking (1945) found it relatively rarely in weedy situations, but Brown (1960) stated it was distinctly associated with submerged plants.

In Virginia, *E. oblongus* was most often found in vegetated areas; schooling young frequently were encountered in calm shallows, adults were in deep pools. This species is typical of lowlands, and although Pflieger (1975) found it largely replaced by *E. sucetta* in the Missouri Coastal Plain, it is clearly the dominant chubsucker in well-flowing and swampy habitats in the Virginia Coastal Plain. The best populations in Ohio were found in clear waters with little siltation (Trautman 1981), but this species tolerates some turbidity (Gerking 1945; Wang and Kernehan 1979; Smith et al. 1981; our observations).

The somewhat isolated Valley and Ridge population of the upper James drainage lives mostly in warm streams. Major stretches are characterized by long pools and occasional sloughs, both often vegetated. At other extremes of the range, this species seems to avoid the highly acidic waters of Dismal Swamp, although it is widespread in the New Jersey Pine Barrens (Hastings 1979, 1984). It extends into tidal fresh water and has been recorded in salinities of 2.1–2.17‰ north and south of Virginia (Keup and Bayless 1964; Wang and Kernehan 1979) and in an area of 9‰ in North Carolina (Schwartz 1981b).

DISTRIBUTION Map 89

The lowland range pattern of *E. oblongus* generally conforms with that of *E. sucetta*; differences include occurrence of *E. oblongus* well above the Coastal Plain, its skirting of Florida (Gilbert and Wall 1985), and the extension far north of Virginia. In Virginia the creek chubsucker has penetrated far south on Delmarva and occurs in all major and many minor Atlantic drainages but not the Pee Dee. The single Shenandoah record is from 1897; records elsewhere

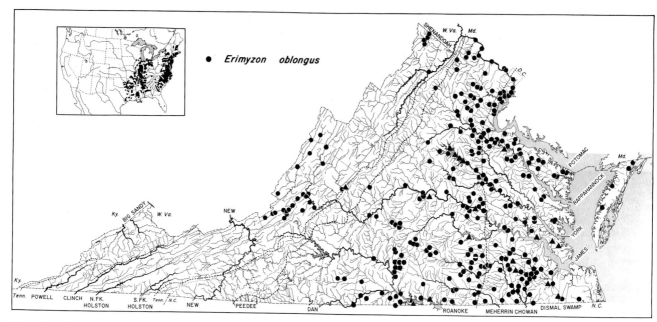

Map 89 Creek chubsucker.

in the Valley and Ridge Province are recent. A specimen of *E. oblongus* (ANSP 6898) apparently was inadvertently added to Cope's collection of *Moxostoma* from the Holston. Except for an apparently introduced population in North Carolina (Bailey et al. 1954), *Erimyzon* is absent in the upper Tennessee drainage.

Abundance.—Generally uncommon.

REMARKS

In the New Jersey Pine Barrens the creek chubsucker is an open-water free-swimming fish and serves as a food source for chain pickerel. Although abundant in some New Jersey lakes, in Pine Barrens lakes it rarely is eaten by pickerel when other forage fishes are present (Hastings 1979).

Name.—Refers to the "oblong" body shape.

Hogsuckers Genus *Hypentelium* Rafinesque

Hogsuckers are somewhat strange looking, with the large, forward-protruding lips, the head squared or concave dorsally, and a slender caudal peduncle. They are recognizable also by the prominently blotched and saddled body and the large scales. The genus is highly specialized for living on the bottom in swift current, and is most closely related to torrent suckers. Two of the three species of *Hypentelium* inhabit Virginia.

Name.—*Hypentelium* translates to "below, five lobes." Rafinesque (1820) stated that the name expresses the form of the lower lip. However, that and other points of the description (lips very small, very minute scales) do not fit hogsuckers.

Northern hogsucker *Hypentelium nigricans* (Lesueur)

SYSTEMATICS

Described from Lake Erie in 1817, *H. nigricans* was long confused with *H. etowanum* until the latter was elevated by Hubbs (1930a), and was confounded with *H. roanokense* until the latter was described by Raney and Lachner (1947). Hubbs (1930a) noted that *H. nigricans* seems to be fairly consistent in characters over

its wide range, although he, Raney and Lachner (1947), and Buth (1977b, 1980) noted geographic variation.

DESCRIPTION

Materials.—From Raney and Lachner (1947), Jenkins (1970), and 29 Virginia series, including our counts from 28 specimens. Color in life from 10 Virginia juveniles or adults.

Fish 129 *Hypentelium nigricans* adult male 155 mm SL (REJ 964), VA, Franklin County, Otter Creek, 7 June 1983.

Anatomy.—A saddled, elongate, concave-headed, papillose-lipped sucker; adults are 125–300 mm SL. Body elongate, well rounded, caudal peduncle elongate, slender. Dorsal fin short, margin straight or slightly concave; upper caudal lobe somewhat pointed, lower lobe less so, notch rounded. Head somewhat square in cross section, flattened ventrally, slightly or markedly concave dorsally, concavity best developed interorbitally and most pronounced in adult; eye dorsolateral, moderate in size.

Mouth inferior, upper lip rarely in advance of snout tip when mouth closed; lips thick, halves of lower lip appressed anteriorly, posterior to which they form usually acute angle; lip surfaces usually entirely papillose, papillae small to medium; front of upper lip subplicate in some specimens. Gas bladder 2-chambered. Nuptial tubercles of male best developed on anal fin, lower caudal lobe, and caudal peduncle ventrally, tubercles scattered and minute elsewhere; tuberculation of female much reduced.

Meristics.—Lateral line complete, scales (44)45–48(50); scales across back (14)15–17; scales across belly (20)22–25(28); circumbody scales (37)38–43(47); circumpeduncle scales (14)16(17). Dorsal rays (9)11(12); caudal rays 18; anal rays (6)7(8); pelvic rays 9(10); pectoral rays (16)17–19.

Color in Preservative.—Dominant pattern usually 5 lateral blotches extending obliquely posterodorsad to form saddles; first (on nape) and third (just behind dorsal fin) saddles often poorly developed, sometimes obsolete; body generally darkly speckled below and between blotch-saddles; body dorsolaterally often with alternating series of vaguely contrasting dark and pale stripes, each pale stripe following a horizontal scale row. Head dark, often speckled, except lower cheek and venter pale.

Dorsal, caudal, pelvic, and pectoral fins speckled, streaked, or both, paired fins usually the least marked; anal fin usually all pale. Caudal base scales generally depigmented, the pale area highlighted by dark streaking on caudal rays basally; darkening often medially subdivides pale area into 2 pale patches.

Color in Life.—Back and side with base shade tan to pale olive; dark markings medium to dark olive or brownish; rusty areas sometimes on body; back and side with silvery, yellow, gold, copper, or green iridescence; snout and front of upper lip sometimes orange-tinged in small juvenile; iris golden to coppery; venter pearl.

Dorsal and caudal fins mostly pale yellow or olive; anal fin white or pale yellow; paired fins pale yellow-olive to pale orange. A few very large adults mostly golden and coppery on side and back, lacking obvious blotch-saddles. Nuptial color and sexual dichromatism absent.

Larvae.—Described by Buynak and Mohr (1978a, 1980c), Snyder (1979), and Fuiman (1979b, 1982c).

COMPARISON

In addition to characters in the *Key*, *H. nigricans* is distinguished from the syntopic Roanoke drainage endemic *H. roanokense* by several other means; the color differences often allow species identification in the field. Fish of 50 mm TL and larger can be sorted by using: (1) body form [more elongate in *nigricans* vs. stockier anteriorly, foreshortened in *roanokense*]; (2) lateral snout pigmentation usually [more uniformly dark vs. dark but black-speckled pattern more evident]; (3) dark and light horizontal stripes usually [absent or faint vs. moderately developed]; (4) adult size, mm SL [usually 125 mm or much larger vs. almost always less than 120 mm]. Raney and Lachner (1947) listed additional differences.

BIOLOGY

Young northern hogsuckers feed mostly on immature aquatic insects and microcrustaceans, occasionally on algae (Forbes 1903; Greeley 1927). Larger fish show the same tendencies and also take small amounts of small mollusks, rarely fish eggs (Forbes and Richardson 1920; Hickman and Fitz 1978; Becker 1983; Hess 1983). This sucker has been characterized as an aggressive feeder, stirring up the bottom and even overturning stones while foraging (Reighard 1920; Pflieger 1975). We saw similar behavior in riffles, runs, and pools. Adults pushed and overturned gravel with the snout and lips by moving slowly forward, and in one case a large adult bisected a fresh *Nocomis* nest in apparent search for eggs. However, overt uptilting and overthrusting of stones, as occurs in logperches, were not detected.

Maturity sets in by age 2 for some males; nearly all are mature at age 3. Most females mature at age 3, some not until age 4. The northern hogsucker is known to reach age 10 (Raney and Lachner 1946a). Reproductive adults in Indiana were 3–8 years old, mean, 5.4 (Curry and Spacie 1984). The sexes grow at about equal rates in the first five years, after which females grow faster than males (Raney and Lachner 1946a). Adult females were larger than adult males in Minnesota and Indiana (Eddy and Underhill 1974; Curry and Spacie 1984).

Age-4 fish of both sexes in two New York streams were 180–291 mm TL, mean, 233 (Raney and Lachner 1946a). Wisconsin fish of age 4 were 266–283 mm TL (Becker 1983). Age-4 Missouri fish averaged 300 mm TL; faster growth tended to occur in larger streams (Purkett 1958), as also was suggested for Indiana (Curry and Spacie 1984). Rather large age-4 fish, 356–376 mm TL, mean, 358, were reported from Oklahoma populations (summary by Carlander 1969). In Ohio, adults are 180–360 mm TL but dwarfing is common in small streams; some males breed when only 100 mm TL (Trautman 1981). The smallest reproductive *H. nigricans* we encountered in Virginia were a 155-mm TL male and a 290-mm TL female. Our largest specimen, not measured, was about 450 mm TL (about 18 inches) from Big Walker Creek. Wollitz (1968a) reported fish of that size from Big Walker and Reed creeks. Maximum size of the species may be 610 mm TL based on word of commercial fishermen on Ohio rivers and lakes (Trautman 1981).

Hypentelium nigricans spawns during April and May, in water of 11–23°C, in much of its range (Hankinson 1919; Reighard 1920; Raney and Lachner 1946a; Pflieger 1975; Smith 1977; Fuiman 1979b, 1982c; Curry and Spacie 1984). Trautman (1981) reported a late March–early June range. In Virginia during various years, females were running ripe on 30 March, 18 and 22 April, and 1 May; reproductive behavior was seen on 17 and 22 April, and on 15 and 24 May; water temperatures on six of these dates were 11.5–21.5, mean, 15.9°C; spent females were recorded as early as 18 April.

Spawning in Virginia on 24 May coincided with that of immigrant golden redhorses, which were not present during the 15 May hogsucker spawning at the same site. In Ohio and Indiana, northern hogsucker spawning preceded that of golden redhorse (Smith 1977; Curry and Spacie 1984). Trautman (1981) stated that *H. nigricans* is highly migratory, ascending streams to reproduce; Gerking (1953), Minckley (1963), and we found no evidence of movement coincident with spawning, and Curry and Spacie (1984) did not clearly indicate any migration.

The typical spawning habitat is reportedly gravelly tails of pools; sometimes shallow sides of pools are used (Raney and Lachner 1946a). Curry and Spacie (1984) noted spawning on medium gravel of riffles 35–45 cm deep, current 0.4–0.6 m/second. Our four observations were made in slow to swift runs. Depth was about 10 cm at one site and the backs of some males broke the surface.

The northern hogsucker has an interesting reproductive repertoire which contrasts with that of other sucker genera. A female enters and intermittently swims slowly about the general spawning area. She attracts 3–11 males that form a mobile troupe. We saw troupes of 3–6 males, each troupe with a single female distinctly larger than the attendants. The males follow her closely, and when she stops they jockey and stack about her flanks and back, all heading upstream when in spawning stance. The males stack such that their genital area is approximately next to or above that of the female. The group seems to spend considerable time in spawning position without the act occurring. Spawning seems to be initiated by quivering of the female. Similar behavior was reported by Raney and Lachner (1946a). Reighard (1920) illustrated individuals in spawning position.

No *H. nigricans* × *H. roanokense* hybrids were noted by Raney and Lachner (1947), but the overlap in habitat and spawning time of these species could lead to hybridization. We handled a much larger number of hogsuckers from the Roanoke drainage than did Raney and Lachner, identifying most by concordance among coloration, body length, form of body, fins, and lips, and lip surfaces. Such an approach, without counting scales and rays, could fail to discern some hybrids. We noted three possible hybrids (CU 52192; REJ 311, 525), two of which identifications were supported by meristic counts. However, these specimens may only represent extreme variants in certain characters.

HABITAT

Hypentelium nigricans is a familiar fish of clean, cool and warm, gravelly and rocky, upland and montane, large creeks to small rivers; it occasionally is found in large rivers. It has been reported most often from runs and riffles, possibly owing to relative ease of capture there. Adults in a Kentucky spring run exhibited a marked preference for deeper pools (Minckley 1963).

In Virginia we caught or observed juvenile and adult northern hogsuckers about equally frequently

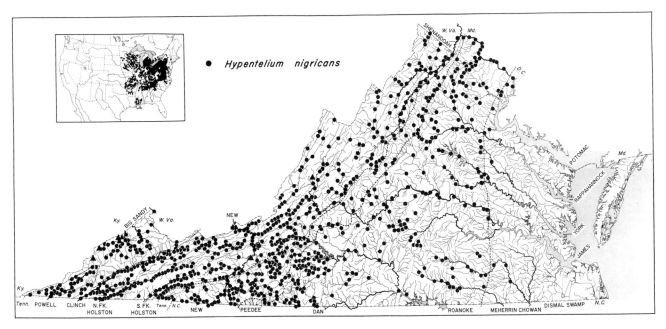

Map 90   Northern hogsucker.

in slow, moderate, and fast currents. This species typically occupies hard substrates in the state, and becomes localized to such bottoms in sandy or moderately silted streams. It has been regarded as intolerant of pollution, siltation, and channel modification (Smith 1979; Trautman 1981), although Eddy and Underhill (1974) found it to be numerous in waters moderately enriched by agriculture. Its use of a wide range of stream habitats is documented by Leonard et al. (1986).

In lacustrine habitats in Illinois, the northern hogsucker occurs in impoundments only as stragglers and is absent from natural lakes and sloughs (Smith 1979). In Ohio, small populations occupy larger Ohio impoundments; those in small impoundments and Lake Erie have been regarded as strays (Trautman 1981). In New York, *H. nigricans* occasionally inhabits lakes, usually near stream mouths, and seems to grow relatively rapidly in such areas (Raney and Lachner 1946a). A few Virginia records are from impoundments. This species avoids darkly stained, acidic waters. It was reported once from brackish water of Tangier Sound, eastern Chesapeake Bay (Musick 1972), a record that seems to warrant substantiation; the closest population is across the bay (Lee et al. 1981).

DISTRIBUTION   Map 90

Hypentelium nigricans is widespread in much of the Great Lakes, upper Mississippi, and Ohio basins, and in the Ozarks and its upland outliers. On the eastern Gulf and south Atlantic slopes it is present only in certain drainages and only in their upper reaches; an isolated population group occurs in the lower Mississippi–central Gulf slope region. On the central Atlantic slope it occurs widely in most upland and montane regions from the Neuse drainage to New York. It is questionably native in the Delaware drainage (Mihursky 1962).

In Virginia, the northern hogsucker is widely distributed in much of the major drainages; it dwindles eastward through the Piedmont and barely enters the Coastal Plain. Paralleling several other species in the Chowan drainage, the farthest downslope extension is in the Nottoway River. *Hypentelium nigricans* is unknown from the Virginia section of the Pee Dee drainage and is localized in the North Carolina part (E. F. Menhinick, in litt.). Compared to many members of the fauna of the heavily silted Big Sandy drainage, *H. nigricans* is relatively widespread there, perhaps owing to an affinity for current-swept substrates.

Abundance.—Usually uncommon or common, most numerous in upper Piedmont and westward. Notably less abundant in Fairfax County than the white sucker.

REMARKS

The boxlike head, vacuumlike mouth, slender posterior body, and prominent saddles render hogsuckers unmistakable. The head concavity and expansive paired fins probably serve as hydrofoils, and coupled with a reduced gas bladder, strongly adapt these fishes for life on the bottom in swift waters. We have seen them maintain position on the riffle floor without moving. Trautman (1981) noted that if properly positioned, recently killed specimens would remain in place.

Camouflaged to blend with varicolored stones, hogsuckers are the woe of the stealthy angler, for when almost trod upon they dash to cover, alerting gamefishes. Strong hogsucker populations signal potentially good bass-fishing streams (Larimore et al. 1952). The fascinating breeding behavior of hogsuckers merits more attention than the few literary glimpses. The observer should be alert during spring for tight groups of hogsuckers, as normally they are not gregarious.

Name.—*Nigricans* means "blackish."

Roanoke hogsucker　　*Hypentelium roanokense* Raney and Lachner

SYSTEMATICS

One of the fruits of Raney and Lachner's spring forays to the upper Roanoke drainage was the capture of an endemic hogsucker. At first it appeared that they had discovered dwarfed mature *H. nigricans*, but laboratory study soon revealed that two specifically distinct hogsuckers—a small one and a large one—lived side by side in many streams. The new species was dubbed *H. roanokense* (Raney and Lachner 1947). Earlier collectors failed to recognize it partly because they lacked specimens in breeding condition.

Hypentelium roanokense has a mosaic of primitive and advanced anatomical and color traits (Jenkins 1970). Smith (1992) placed it as the sister species of *H. nigricans*, both more advanced than *H. etowanum*. Genetically it is the most divergent, advanced hogsucker (Buth 1980).

DESCRIPTION

Materials.—From Raney and Lachner (1947), Jenkins (1970), and 36 Virginia lots; our counts from 23 specimens. Life color from notes or slides of 17 specimens.

Anatomy.—A chunky hogsucker with subplicate lips; adults are 60–100 mm SL. Morphology as in *H. nigricans* except for the following. Anterior body foreshortened, stouter. Lips large, often protruding before snout tip, rarely fully retracted within general snout contour when preserved; lip surfaces papillose or plicate on front of upper lip, coarsely papillose or subplicate on posterior portion of lower lip, plicate or subplicate on inner surface of both lips, plicae best developed on inner portion of upper lip.

Meristics.—Lateral line complete, scales (38)40–43(44); scales across back (12)13–15; scales across belly 19–23; circumbody scales (33)34–38(39); circumpeduncle scales (15)16(17). Dorsal rays (10)11(12); caudal rays (17)18; anal rays 7(8); pelvic rays (8)9(10); pectoral rays 15–16(17).

Color in Preservative.—As described for *H. nigricans* with the following exceptions. First (predorsal) saddle usually vague or represented by dark speckles, occasionally wholly absent, very rarely well developed; dorsolateral stripes usually obvious; lateral snout with speckling or reticulation usually sharply darker than dusky ground.

Color in Life Plate 20.—Much as in *H. nigricans*, except many fish have a more tan or rusty ground color; dark markings blacker; iridescences largely silvery; occasional adults with a broad orange wash on side, or an orangebrown stripe along part or all of midside; paired fins tend brighter orange. Nuptial color change and sexual dichromatism apparently absent.

Fish 130 *Hypentelium roanokense* adult male 75 mm SL (REJ 1039), VA, Montgomery County, South Fork Roanoke River, 16 September 1983.

COMPARISON

See *H. nigricans*.

BIOLOGY

The diet of Roanoke hogsuckers comprises insect larvae (mostly Diptera), algae, and detritus (W. J. Matthews et al., in litt.). Some males are mature by age 1; apparently the remainder become mature by age 2. Raney and Lachner (1947) stated that females mature and spawn when 3 years old. Some of our reproductive females appear to be age 2 based on length comparisons with those aged by Raney and Lachner. These authors found a 1-year-old male with tubercles but immature gonads. We collected several apparent immature fish during spring, males maximally 80 mm TL, females 106 mm, with weak tubercles on the anal fin. (Our standard lengths were converted to TL using Raney and Lachner's factor of 1.23.) Raney and Lachner suggested a differential mortality rate; many more females than males reached age 4, and only females were in age 5.

Males grew faster than females in their first year, but in age 2 and thereafter females were larger. However, as occurs with other age and growth studies by Raney and Lachner, intersexual and interspecific differences, although probably real, generally were based on specimens taken in various times of different years; lengths were not back-calculated to a standard reference point (i.e., an annulus). Age-2 males were 66–105 mm TL, mean, 80, females 75–120 mm, mean, 88; these were outgrown by the few Roanoke specimens of *H. nigricans* studied (Raney and Lachner 1947). Our reproductive adults, taken during March–May throughout the upper Roanoke drainage, were, in TL: 40 males 66–119 mm, mean, 94; 34 females 91–134 mm, mean, 112. The largest reported Roanoke hogsucker apparently is a female 117 mm SL, 140 mm TL (Raney and Lachner 1947: 8, 10 [not 125 mm TL, p. 5]).

Reproduction of *H. roanokense* is unwitnessed. Female gonadal conditions indicate a spawning period beginning with but perhaps not as long as that of *H. nigricans* in the same region. Fully gravid fish were taken 12 March–22 April; partly spent fish in 17 March–22 April; all from 24–31 May were fully spent. A running-ripe female was found on 12 April and one on 12 May, water 14.4 and 20°C. Possible hybrids *H. nigricans* × *H. roanokense* are noted under *H. nigricans*.

HABITAT

Hypentelium roanokense is characteristic of cool and warm, moderate to high-gradient creeks and streams.

It commonly populates rocky, gravelly, sandy, and moderately silted streams, and it may be as abundant on sand and sand–gravel mix as it is on gravel and rubble (Raney and Lachner 1947; our observations). In heavily silted streams, this species occupies the firmer substrates.

The pattern of ecological distribution of *H. roanokense* in many streams of the Roanoke drainage is much the same as that of *H. nigricans*. The two are frequently syntopic, judging from collections of 10 or more hogsuckers. Both were caught in about equal frequency in riffles, runs, and pools; often they were caught in the same net haul. Their tendencies to differ are the farther upstream penetration or greater abundance of *H. roanokense* in creeks (width less than 10 m), whereas *H. nigricans* usually is the dominant or only hogsucker in medium-sized waters (20–30 m width) (Raney and Lachner 1947; Hambrick 1973; James 1979; our observations).

DISTRIBUTION   Map 91

The Roanoke hogsucker is confined to and widespread in the upper and middle Roanoke drainage, Virginia and North Carolina; its range terminates short of the junction of the Roanoke and Dan rivers. Most North Carolina records were verified by Jenkins (*in* Lee et al. 1980). Both species of *Hypentelium* populate all major tributary systems in mountains and the upper Piedmont, but *H. roanokense* appears to be the slightly more widespread of the two in the middle Piedmont. Exceptions for *H. nigricans* include the greater number of records in the Banister watershed (lower Dan system) and its occurrence near the Dan River mouth. We do not accept Hart's (1978) record of *H. roanokense* in Smith Mountain Reservoir; although it may have been taken as a stray, no specimens were available for verification.

Hypentelium roanokense is one of few fishes typical of the upper Roanoke but unknown from the Chowan drainage. Although there are two records from the Chowan, one is clearly based on *H. nigricans* (VPI 995 = CU 48027); the unlocated specimens for the other record (AMNH accession list for VPI 987) are assumed to be *H. nigricans*. Enigmatically, *H. nigricans* is the only hogsucker present in the Tar and Neuse drainages, North Carolina. Because *H. roanokense* is an offshoot of *nigricans*-like stock, in succeeding that stock in the Roanoke it could have used routes of egress to the Chowan, Tar, and Neuse. Apparently it did not; if it had, it probably would have survived peripheral to the Roanoke as did *H. nigricans* in the Chowan, Tar, and Neuse.

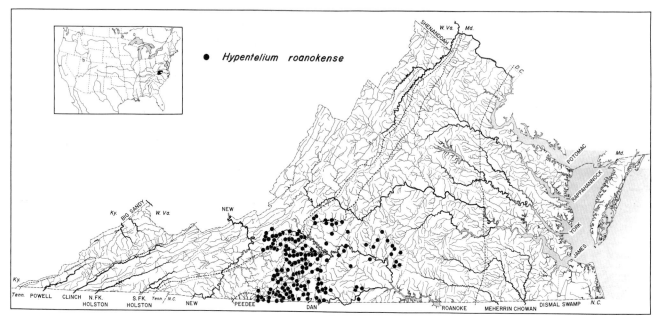

Map 91 Roanoke hogsucker.

Abundance.—Usually uncommon or common in mountains and upper Piedmont, generally rare on middle Piedmont. Rare in the Roanoke River above Glenvar (about 3 rkm above Salem), apparently absent below Glenvar (Jenkins 1979a).

REMARKS

The Roanoke hogsucker may be the most diminutive sucker. We found a mature male of 54 mm SL (66 mm TL) among less than 100 adults. The initial recognition of *H. roanokense*—from ripe fish—as a dwarf species distinct from *H. nigricans* underscores the importance of observing and collecting fishes early in the year, when often the least is known of their lives.

Name.—*Roanokense*, for the drainage to which it is restricted.

Torrent suckers   Genus *Thoburnia* Jordan and Snyder

Two of the three species of *Thoburnia*—the torrent sucker *T. rhothoeca* and the rustyside sucker *T. hamiltoni*—are endemic or nearly so to Virginia. We designate them the rustyside group (as a subgroup of the *Moxostoma* group) because of the orange or red-orange lateral stripe of adults. The remaining species is the somewhat distantly related and relatively primitive blackfin sucker *T. atripinnis*, a localized relict in Kentucky and Tennessee; it lacks the rusty stripe. Together the three species may be termed the torrent suckers, although based on the habitat of *T. atripinnis* (Timmons et al. 1983), that name also is best restricted to the rustyside group. The need for a collective common name to unite the three species may be only temporary (see *Scartomyzon ariommus*).

Thoburnia has varied in taxonomic rank, starting with the original description of the first known species, the torrent sucker. Thoburn described that species in Jordan and Evermann (1896), who grouped it with hogsuckers as a subgenus *Hypentelium* of *Catostomus*. Jordan and Snyder (*in* Jordan 1917) described *Thoburnia* as a monotypic genus for *T. rhothoeca*, which Hubbs (1930a) deemed to be so divergent that he erected a new tribe, Thoburniini. *Thoburnia hamiltoni* was added to the genus when described by Raney and Lachner (1946c).

When Bailey (1959a) described *T. atripinnis*, he downgraded *Thoburnia* to a subgenus of *Moxostoma* because in some traits that species narrowed the anatomical gap between the rustyside group and *Scartomyzon*. Partly because *Scartomyzon* then was a subgenus of *Moxostoma*, *Thoburnia* was given the same status. Some discontent with the lumping arose, as summarized by Jenkins (1970) and Buth (1979c), but Bailey's arrangement generally was followed.

Jointly the studies by Nelson (1948), Miller and

Evans (1965), Jenkins (1970), and Buth (1978, 1979c) strongly indicate that the closest relatives of *Thoburnia* are the hogsuckers. Their genealogical relationship is cued particularly by the caudal base depigmentation pattern, which is exclusively shared among catostomids by *Hypentelium* and the rustyside group. Phylogenetically then, *Thoburnia* warranted extraction from *Moxostoma*; it could be ranked as a subgenus of *Hypentelium* or a separate genus. Buth (1979c) tentatively recognized it (including *T. atripinnis*) as a genus, as had Miller and Evans (1965) during the period of a conceptually broad

Moxostoma. Smith's (1992) analysis combining former and new data corroborates the elevation of *Thoburnia*, which he too proposed.

The evolution of *Thoburnia* has paralleled in several ways that of the small, swift-water western mountain suckers, subgenus *Pantosteus* of *Catostomus*, treated by Smith (1966, 1992), Minckley (1973), and Minckley et al. (1986).

Name.—For Wilbur Wilson Thoburn, author of the first-described species and professor of bionomics at Stanford University.

Torrent sucker   *Thoburnia rhothoeca* (Thoburn)

SYSTEMATICS

The torrent sucker was described by Thoburn (*in* Jordan and Evermann 1896) from six specimens taken at an uncertain locality, supposedly "some point in eastern Tennessee or southwestern Virginia, thought to be from the French Broad River at Wolf Creek, Tennessee." The Wolf Creek site is in the Tennessee drainage, from which *T. rhothoeca* has not since been reported; its occurrence there in historical time is doubtful. Hubbs (1930a) and Raney and Lachner (1946c) believed that the types probably came from Virginia, most likely the James drainage; Böhlke (1953) agreed when designating the lectotype. We exhaustively researched the question of the type locality, found it to be apparently unresolvable, and arbitrarily affirm that most likely it is in the upper James drainage of Virginia.

Thoburnia rhothoeca and *T. hamiltoni* are coadapted to swift water and intimately related. They are so similar in morphology, color, habitat preference, and known life history aspects that their separate species status has been questioned by Ross (1969) and informally by others. We counted and measured selected characters on 21–22 specimens of each form and studied lips and coloration of more than 200 of each,

finding that they differ distinctly, but with slight overlap, in relative extent of papillosity and form of the lips. The differences that Miller and Evans (1965) discerned in brain morphology require substantiation from larger samples.

Genetic divergence between *T. rhothoeca* and *T. hamiltoni* was determined electrophoretically by Buth (1977a, 1979c). Based on his (1978) data, the level of divergence is about that of many pairs of obviously good species of moxostomatins. Hence these forms qualify as evolutionary, sibling species.

DESCRIPTION

Materials.—From Raney and Lachner (1946c), Bailey (1959a), Jenkins (1970), and 39 series from the Roanoke, Chowan, James, or Rappahannock, including counts and measurements from 21 specimens. Color in life based on slides of 10 adults and notes from 12 collections.

Anatomy.—A blotched sucker with a torpedo-shaped body, short head, and plicate-papillose lips; adults are 85–150 mm SL. Body elongate, round; caudal peduncle stout. Dorsal fin short-based, dorsal fin margin straight or very slightly concave; caudal fin small, notch shallow and rounded, upper lobe slightly rounded, lower lobe usually

Fish 131 *Thoburnia rhothoeca* adult male 106 mm SL (REJ 1039), VA, Montgomery County, South Fork Roanoke River, 16 September 1983.

well rounded. Head small, slightly convex dorsally; snout broadly rounded, often bulbous; eye small, lateral.

Mouth distinctly inferior; upper lip a low narrow crescent when intruded, surface rounded, bearing closely to well-spaced plicae. Lower lip flattened, extending well posteriad medially, posterolateral margins usually slanting obliquely toward corner of mouth, often well-notched between halves of lips. Lower lip surface mostly plicate anteriorly, grading posteriad into usually few or moderate numbers of mostly oblong papillae, often with many round papillae and a few plicae intermixed. Edge of upper and lower jaws with ridge of tough tissue. Gas bladder 2-chambered, much reduced or obsolete. Nuptial tubercles in male well developed on anal fin and lower caudal lobe; small or minute tubercles on other fins, head, and body; female tuberculation very reduced.

Meristics.—Lateral line complete, scales (43)45–48(51); scales across back 13–15; scales across belly (21)22–23(24); circumbody scales (36)37–40; circumpeduncle scales (14)16–18(20). Dorsal rays (9)10; caudal rays 18; anal rays 7; pelvic rays (8)9(10); pectoral rays (14)15–17.

Color in Preservative.—Head and body dark from back ventrad to just below midbody, then usually sharply paler below, even when dusky or speckled ventrolaterally; side with 4–5 solid or diffuse blotches, 2–4 of these often extending obliquely posterodorsad to form saddles, markings best developed in young; horizontal dark and light stripes moderately or vaguely developed on side, vague or absent on back. Lower front of snout evenly peppered or, often, slightly mottled.

Caudal base with a pair of large depigmented areas, set off by blackened basal portion of fin rays; elsewhere caudal and other fins pale to dusky, darkest along rays, unmottled except occasionally pectoral slightly mottled.

Color in Life Plate 20.—Paler parts of upper head and body yellowish tan to olive, dark markings olive-brown to black; iris silver to gold. Midlateral stripe about two scales wide, pale orange to bright red-orange in prenuptial and nuptial males; usually orange-brown, occasionally fully orange in nuptial female; stripe of postnuptial fish eventually dulls, often absent.

Depigmented areas of caudal base creamy or pale orange; caudal fin dark olive or blackened along base, distally pale yellow or orange on rays; other fins same as caudal except where blackened.

BIOLOGY

The torrent sucker feeds heavily on algae, other plant material, and detritus; generally much lesser amounts of insect larvae, mainly midges, are taken (Flemer and Woolcott 1966; W. J. Matthews et al., in litt.). Opportunism is indicated by an adult with the digestive tract crammed with midge larvae (Jenkins 1970).

Most males are mature at age 2 and all spawn at age 3; females first spawn when age 3. Females tend to survive longer than males, the oldest males being age 5, females age 7. Males of age 2 averaged longer than females, but this was reversed by age 3 in which males were about 80–125 mm TL, mean, 102, females 85–130 mm, mean, 112. Growth slowed only slightly through age 5 (Raney and Lachner 1946b). Five age-classes were found in one tributary by Neves and Pardue (1983). The largest specimen is a Virginia female 163 mm SL, 192 mm TL. Apparently this species does not spawn at sizes as small as some Roanoke hogsuckers; our smallest tuberculate male torrent sucker is 78 mm SL, 94 mm TL.

The breeding behavior and habitat of *T. rhothoeca* are unknown, but owing to its preference for swift water, undoubtedly it uses riffles. The spawning period probably is during mid-spring. Raney and Lachner (1946b) found ripe females in late March and early April, water 13–16°C. We encountered ripe females on 16, 18, and 20 April, water 17°C on the 16th. Milt was pressed from males in late February and was freely running in late May, but milting probably is not a good indicator of actual spawning time for suckers. Egg counts of 742–1,749 were reported by Raney and Lachner (1946b).

HABITAT

The torrent sucker is typical of cold to warm, moderate to high-gradient, small creeks to medium-sized streams. It is found occasionally or rarely in large rivers such as the midsection of the South Fork Shenandoah and James rivers. This species is well named; of the 500 large juveniles and adults we netted, more than 99% came from moderately or very fast water—riffles and runs as shallow as 15 cm, including the strongest in which we could stand or snorkel. Matthews (1990) also ranked juvenile and adult *T. rhothoeca* as typical riffle fish. This species chiefly occupies clean gravel, rubble, and boulder, and sometimes considerably sandy sections. We observed very small young swimming near the surface, and small young holding deeper but off the bottom in a pool.

Although *T. rhothoeca* populates some moderately and heavily silted streams, in these it generally is localized in extreme headwaters and other oases of relatively clean bottom. We found this pattern in the upper and lower Appomattox system and the lowermost two tributaries occupied in the James drainage, as did Flemer and Woolcott (1966) for one of them. The pattern generally holds for the Chowan drainage (field notes of M. D. Norman and T. Zorach).

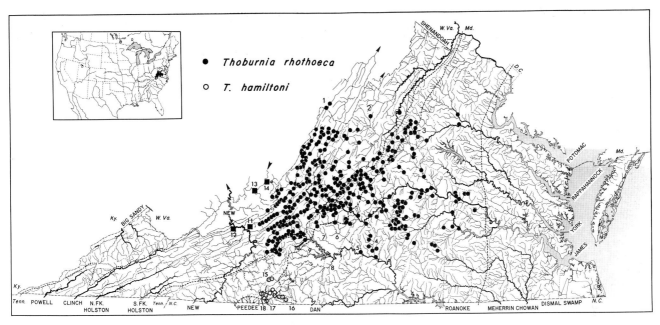

Map 92 Torrent sucker and rustyside sucker. Squares represent the four New drainage records of *T. rhothoeca*; these are questioned or rejected in the *Distribution* section. Numbers refer to: 1—North Fork of South Branch Potomac River; 2—War Branch; 3—Conway River site (in Rapidan system) of first Rappahannock drainage record; 4—Falling River; 5—Seneca Creek; 6—Otter Creek; 7—Goose Creek; 8—Pigg River; 9—Blackwater River; 10—Back Creek; 11—Little Stony Creek; 12—Wolf Creek; 13—Greenbrier River at mouth of Second Creek; 14—Howard Creek (open square at White Sulphur Springs); 15—Smith River; 16—South Mayo River; 17—Little Dan River; 18—Dan River.

DISTRIBUTION   Map 92

The small range of the torrent sucker is largely central Virginia, in mountains and uplands of the Potomac, Rappahannock, James, Chowan, and Roanoke drainages. Small portions of the upper James drainage and Potomac system proper in West Virginia are also populated. Records exist for the New drainage of Virginia and West Virginia, but this species apparently does not live there now. (However, see *Epilogue* under *New Drainage Fauna* in *Biogeography* section.) The native range of *T. rhothoeca* is uncertain.

Thoburnia rhothoeca is widespread and common in the upper James, the Blue Ridge section of Piedmont tributaries, in much of the Piedmont Foothills subprovince (Map 7), and the upper Appomattox system. Eastward it extends generally sporadically to near the Fall Line; the smaller number of records there is related to lesser collecting intensity and lower-gradient silted conditions. The James population is native based on the wide distribution that lacks peculiarities, and because Cope, Jordan, and other early collectors took the species.

The Potomac drainage has two population groups of the torrent sucker. That in the upper South Fork Shenandoah system is regarded as probably native,

owing partly to an 1885 record (USNM 132071) by M. McDonald. However, McDonald's other record (USNM 131125) is problematic, and the 16 subsequent captures are dated no earlier than 1952. The status of the population is questioned also because of absence of the species in much of the system and owing to its localization and general rarity in the section occupied. This contrasts with the wide distribution and strong abundance of the species in the adjacent James. Also, the lowermost record is the most recent (1990), indicating the possibility of spreading from an upstream area of introduction. However, a number of other species show a similar geographic pattern in, or are unexpectedly apparently absent from, the Shenandoah (*Biogeography*).

The population of *T. rhothoeca* in the upper Potomac system proper, West Virginia, is known only within 12 rkm comprising the upper North Fork of South Branch Potomac River and the lower portion of its tributary Laurel Fork (J. R. Stauffer, in litt; possibly reported as the spotted sucker *Minytrema melanops* by Ross and Lewis 1969, according to Stauffer et al. 1978a). The population probably is introduced based on the recency of all verified records (1973–1976), its localization (it was not found in 17 collections from the South Branch system of Virginia during 1956–

1977), ready availability of the torrent sucker as bait from the nearby James, and considerable fishing pressure in the area. It may, however, be a relict population (Stauffer et al. 1978a, 1978b).

The Rappahannock drainage population is regarded as probably introduced. It has a pattern indicating release of fish into, and spreading from, the upper Rapidan system. Rappahannock headwaters have been extensively sampled beginning in the 1940s, but the first capture of *T. rhothoeca* (UR 344) was not until 1958, and the outlying Rapphannock River record is from 1972.

The Chowan drainage population is known only from the upper Little Nottoway River and two of its tributaries, Mallorys and Whetstone creeks. The first record is from 1968, the other three from 1984. The population is arbitrarily regarded as native. It may be a relict that gained entry to the Chowan from the Roanoke drainage, the Appomattox system, or both. It is a bit surprising that *T. rhothoeca* is not more widespread in the upper Chowan; several streams have habitat similar to those typically occupied in other drainages.

In the Roanoke drainage, the torrent sucker populates six major tributary systems of the middle and upper Roanoke system proper, in sequence beginning downstream (and by years of records): Falling River (widely, records since 1974); Seneca Creek (sampled once, 1979); Otter River (one North Fork site, 1980, 1983); Goose Creek (mainstream and Day Creek, 1978, 1979); Back Creek (lowermost, 1972); Roanoke River and virtually all tributaries (1867 and 1948–present). The geographic–chronologic pattern probably represents combinations of relict and introduced populations.

Cope's specimens taken in 1867 from the North Fork Roanoke system were the basis on which Jenkins et al. (1972) considered *T. rhothoeca* to be native in the Roanoke drainage. The three specimens (ANSP 6916–18) were found with 12 *Scartomyzon cervinus* and had been misidentified as *T. hamiltoni* by Robins and Raney (1956). Being in the same jar with *S. cervinus* (a native of the Roanoke but presumably introduced to the James) would indicate that all 15 specimens came from the upper Roanoke, hence that *T. rhothoeca* was present early and thus native to the drainage. However, there are cases of apparent mislabeling of other species taken by Cope. Moreover, Jordan should have found it in the Valley and Ridge Province in 1888, and so too should have Raney and others in their early efforts. After Cope's record, the oldest is from 1948 (CU 11545); *T. rhothoeca* has been widespread and common above Salem since about 1965.

The New drainage often has been invoked as the area from which *Thoburnia* gained access to the central Atlantic slope. However, if the rustyside group does not share a close ancestor with the geographically distant *T. atripinnis* (see *Scartomyzon ariommus*), that hypothesis loses some support. The potentially valid four records of *T. rhothoeca* (sites 11–14 on Map) have been given intense scrutiny, most of whose details cannot be given here.

The specimen for the 1952 record from Little Stony Creek (Site 11; CU 24966) probably came from the James drainage, but was misplaced in a New drainage collection by a student at the Mountain Lake Biological Station. Three adult *T. rhothoeca* cataloged as from Wolf Creek, Giles County, Virginia (Site 12; USNM 39529) were taken by M. McDonald in 1885. They were reported by Miller (1946) and Raney and Lachner (1946c), and have been a primary basis for believing *T. rhothoeca* to be native to the New. The collection data seem in order but discrepancies and omissions of data for some of McDonald's other Virginia collections render the Wolf Creek record questionable.

A specimen of *T. rhothoeca* (Site 13; CU 4957) labeled from the "Greenbrier River and Second Creek" (presumably at their confluence), Greenbrier County, West Virginia, was taken by A. H. Wright in 1931. Hubbs and Raney (1944) and Raney and Lachner (1946c) considered the record doubtful but we believe that the record is not clearly rejectable. One specimen of *T. rhothoeca* (Site 14; MCZ 35704) was supposedly collected "near White Sulphur Springs, West Virginia" in about 1871 by A. R. Crandall. The town is on Howard Creek, a Greenbrier tributary near Second Creek. Hubbs (1930a) rejected the record partly because of vague data and lack of success in finding the species within and near White Sulphur Springs during 1928.

In conclusion, we grudgingly agree that *T. rhothoeca* is probably native to the New drainage; three of the four records may be valid, that in Wolf Creek the most likely so. The long history of extensive collecting in the drainage and the small number of specimens of *T. rhothoeca* would indicate that it was localized, rare, and disappearing from the drainage in the early 1900s.

In sum, we regard the torrent sucker to be certainly native to the James, probably native to the Shenandoah, Chowan, Roanoke, and New, and probably introduced to the Potomac proper and Rappahannock. The different drainage populations of this species (and *T. hamiltoni*) exhibit sharply varied success.

Abundance.—Often common or abundant in many mountain and Piedmont streams where substrate is largely swept free of silt, rare in other streams of those areas.

REMARKS

The torrent sucker was considered by Hubbs (1941a) to be one of the most completely adapted of North American fishes to swift current. The fusiform body, expansive paired fins, thick heavy skull, and obsolete gas bladder allow it to swim or hold position in such waters with seemingly little effort. The body size, small for a sucker, permits occupation of cavities and other microhabitats of reduced current within riffles. The tough tissue over its jaws enhances scraping of attached algae and insects from stones. The bright orange or red-orange stripe is a nuptial adornment unusual in the *Moxostoma* group. This species often dominates the fish biomass of riffles. Small *T. rhothoeca* formed the bulk of food of adult brown trout in an upper Roanoke tributary (Garman and Nielsen 1982), and we found one in the stomach of one of the few smallmouth bass that we sampled. Zoogeographically this species presents a morass to determining its native range, perhaps the most challenging among Virginia fishes.

Name.—*Rhothoeca*—"torrent, to inhabit."

Rustyside sucker   *Thoburnia hamiltoni* Raney and Lachner

SYSTEMATICS

Thoburnia hamiltoni is endemic to the upper Dan River system, Roanoke drainage, Virginia, from whose South Mayo branch it was described by Raney and Lachner (1946c). It and *T. rhothoeca* form the rustyside group of the genus *Thoburnia*. The species status of these allopatric siblings is discussed under *T. rhothoeca*. *Thoburnia hamiltoni* is the more advanced based on its greater degree of lip papillosity (Jenkins 1970) and genetic criteria (Buth 1979c).

DESCRIPTION

Materials.—From Raney and Lachner (1946c), Jenkins (1970), and 18 more series; meristic and morphometric data from 22 specimens. Color in life based on 7 series comprising some 180 specimens.

Anatomy.—A streamlined, blotched, faintly striped sucker with plicate-papillose lips; adults are 75–125 mm SL. Morphometry essentially as in *T. rhothoeca* except *T. hamiltoni* differs, with overlap, by its smaller eye and the lower lips being longer overall, wider posteriorly, and having shorter plicae and greater numbers of round papillae.

Meristics.—Lateral line complete, scales (43)44–47; scales across back 13–15; scales across belly (20)21–24(25); circumbody scales 36–41; circumpeduncle scales (15)16–17(18). Dorsal rays (9)10(11); caudal rays 18; anal rays (6)7; pelvic rays (8)9(10); pectoral rays 13–16.

Color in Preservative.—As in *T. rhothoeca* except horizontal dark and light striping on upper half of body usually slightly better developed (but also often vague or absent on back).

Color in Life.—As in *T. rhothoeca* including the varying shades of the lateral stripe—orange or red-orange in nuptial and other males, brown or rusty in nuptial females.

BIOLOGY

Life history data of *T. hamiltoni* (Jenkins 1978) indicate considerable similarity to *T. rhothoeca*. Alimentary tracts of *T. hamiltoni* contained large amounts of flocculent organic matter, probably mostly detritus. Small numbers of mayfly, caddisfly, and truefly larvae were also taken.

The onset of maturity is directly related to the rate

Fish 132 *Thoburnia hamiltoni* adult female 102 mm SL (REJ 965), VA, Patrick County, South Mayo River, 7 June 1983.

of growth. In rapid-growth populations, no age-1 fish were obviously reproductive but all age-2 males and all age-3 females were mature, whereas in populations of slow-growers, maturity was clearly exhibited only by age-3 and older males, and by only 67% of age-3 females. Age-4 fish, the oldest detected, composed 14.5% of the 220 scale-aged specimens; 41% of the age-4 fish were male.

Females consistently averaged larger than males after age 2. Growth was slowest in Rich Creek, the coolest and smallest stream from which a good sample was obtained; age-3 males were 83–107 mm TL, mean, 92, females 87–120 mm, mean, 102. In other populations at the same age and time, males were 110–130 mm, mean, 119, females 115–150 mm, mean, 129. The smallest mature fish was a male 68 mm SL, 81 mm TL. The largest specimen was a female 153 mm SL, 187 mm TL. The conversion formulas are TL = SL × 1.185 and SL = TL × 0.844.

The breeding period of the rustyside sucker undoubtedly is in April and may include late March and early May, based on gonadal and tubercle conditions. A late March female was fully gravid; most or all of many mid-May and late May fish were in postnuptial phase.

HABITAT

Most streams occupied by the rustyside sucker are small, moderate or high gradient, usually clear, have scant or no higher vegetation, and are in the Blue Ridge and prominent outlying mountains. Cold spring runs and warm streams are inhabited. Elevations of record sites are 277–567 m (Jenkins 1978). We subsequently found this species in the two largest streams (12 m wide) from which it is known. Large juveniles and adults are virtually restricted to swift and moderate currents of riffles, runs, and the head of pools having clean or very slightly silted gravel, rubble, boulder, and bedrock. Small juveniles often are found in such areas and in the body of small pools, rarely if at all in calm soft-bottomed backwaters.

DISTRIBUTION   Map 92

Thoburnia hamiltoni is known only from the upper Dan River system, Roanoke drainage, Patrick County, Virginia. It may extend just into North Carolina. There are three well-separated populations (numbered on Map): (15) uppermost Rockcastle creek and one of its tributaries, Smith River subsystem; (16) South Mayo River and seven tributaries; and (17, 18) Dan River proper, Little Dan River, and two Little

Dan tributaries. The 25 record sites known in 1978 are shown in a detailed map by Jenkins (*in* Lee et al. 1980). Occupation of five more sites is indicated herein.

The rustyside sucker is extremely localized in the Smith subsystem, which was extensively sampled during 1977–1981, and in the portion above Philpott Reservoir resurveyed in 1984. The population in Rockcastle Creek is restricted to headwaters including Little Creek. An unverified report of a "rustysided sucker" came recently from Shooting Creek, a different branch of the Smith above the reservoir (W. H. Norton, personal communication). The remainder of the Dan also has been extensively investigated. *Thoburnia hamiltoni* is sporadic in the Mayo River subsystem; it is widespread in the upper South Mayo, but is unknown from the North Mayo, despite seemingly suitable habitat. In 1983 we extended the range of *T. hamiltoni* in the South Mayo River to just below the industrialized corridor of Stuart, where it occurred in fair numbers. Until 1983 all captures in the Dan system proper were from the Little Dan River and its tributaries. In that year the Dan River yielded one specimen of *T. hamiltoni*.

Reports of *T. hamiltoni* in the upper Roanoke proper (Robins and Raney 1956; Bailey 1959a; Ross 1969; Cairns et al. 1971; and others) are based on *T. rhothoeca* (Jenkins 1970 and later; Buth 1977a, 1979c).

Abundance.—Usually uncommon or common; quite rare in the upper Dan River.

REMARKS

The relict rustyside sucker has helped to guide inquiry into some ancient drainage patterns of central Appalachia and on the dispersal and evolution of regional fishes. In appearance this species is a twin of the torrent sucker. They are coadapted to a rigorous, much-fluctuating environment—swift, small streams—but the rustyside sucker does not succeed in Piedmont-type streams as does the torrent sucker.

Thoburnia hamiltoni is one of Virginia's most localized fishes. Jenkins (*in* Miller 1972) considered it to be in jeopardy because it seemed to have declined recently. Although it remains unclear that population levels had actually changed, Jenkins' (1978) survey for *T. hamiltoni* found it doing well in most streams where it was formerly known, and it was discovered in others. Burkhead and Jenkins (1991) consider the rustyside sucker to merit special concern status because of its limited total range and an indicated sensitivity to siltation.

Name.—After William J. Hamilton, Jr., vertebrate zoologist of Cornell University.

Jumprock suckers   Genus *Scartomyzon* Fowler

Originally described in 1913 as a subgenus of *Moxostoma*, *Scartomyzon* is freshly ranked as a genus by Smith (1992). That status derives from the closer phylogenetic affinity of *Scartomyzon* to *Thoburnia* and *Hypentelium* than to the typical redhorses, subgenera *Moxostoma* and *Megapharynx*.

Scartomyzon currently contains 8–10 species of which 2 are undescribed (Robins and Raney 1956, 1957; Buth 1978; Jenkins *in* Lee et al. 1980; Miller and Smith 1986). Inclusion of *S. ariommus* in the genus may be temporary. Most of the species are called jumprocks, which tend to be small, often striped or blotchy, and to inhabit fast water; two of the redhorses are larger and occupy slower current.

The genus ranges on the Atlantic slope from Virginia southwestward just into the eastern Gulf slope of Alabama. Beyond a large range gap on the Gulf slope, it then extends from central Texas and southern New Mexico deeply south into Mexico, onto the Pacific slope.

Name.—*Scarto*, nimble, quick; and *myzo*, to suck; hence agile suckers. The name fits jumprocks, some species of which are known to jump or break the surface in the spawning period. Both sexes of some redhorses (including *Moxostoma*) also practice the behavior.

Smallfin redhorse   *Scartomyzon robustus* (Cope)*

SYSTEMATICS

Described from the Pee Dee drainage, North Carolina, by Cope (1870), the specific name indicates a stout body form. However, Cope may have identified elongate specimens of *S. robustus* as *Moxostoma erythrurum*. Subsequently, *S. robustus* was confused with other jumprocks and redhorses until it was largely untangled by Robins and Raney (1956); they too considered it a typically robust species. We broaden the concept of *S. robustus* to include elongated fish, the usual adult body form among our material from the Pee Dee, Santee, and Savannah drainages. Two series of elongate fish from the Santee were tentatively and erroneously identified as the slender species *S. rupiscartes* by Jenkins (1970). Dahlberg and Scott (1971a) also noted problems in identifying *S. robustus*.

Scartomyzon robustus was considered by Robins and Raney (1956) and Jenkins (1970) to be a relatively primitive member of *Scartomyzon*, closest to the species of *Scartomyzon* in Texas and Mexico. *Scartomyzon*

rupiscartes was linked to these species by Buth (1978). Smith (1992) grouped *S. robustus* with the Texan–Mexican species and considered this lineage to be advanced with *Scartomyzon*.*

DESCRIPTION

Materials.—All drainage populations (Robins and Raney 1956); our counts are from 48 Pee Dee specimens in 13 North Carolina or 6 Virginia lots.

Anatomy.—A jumprock sucker of moderate or slender build, with plicate or subplicate lips; adults are 200–360 mm SL. Body form moderate or elongate, nearly round, particularly elongate in adult, in which the ventral contour is straight or nearly so and the back is slightly elevated. Dorsal fin margin slightly concave; caudal upper lobe slightly rounded or pointed, lower lobe and notch moderately rounded. Head and eye moderate in size, head dorsum distinctly convex, eye lateral.

Lips moderate or large; upper lip plicate; halves of lower lip posteriorly straight or forming wide crescent, surface plicate, often a few plicae branched, plicae sometimes transversely subdivided (subplicate) in adult. Gas bladder large, 3-chambered in two specimens; another with a nipplelike fourth chamber.

Nuptial tubercles strongly developed in male only on anal and lower caudal rays, much reduced elsewhere.

Meristics.—Lateral line complete, scales (44)45–48; scales across back (14)15–16; scales across belly (17)19–20(21); circumbody scales (33)36–37(39); circumpeduncle scales (15)16. Dorsal rays 11–12(13); caudal rays 18; anal rays 7; pelvic rays 9; pectoral rays (15)17–18; gill rakers (27)28–34(37).

---

*In 1992, R. E. Jenkins determined that the "smallfin redhorse *Scartomyzon robustus* (Cope)" is a species of *Scartomyzon* that never was validly named. He will describe it with the common name brassy jumprock. The species described as *robustus* by Cope in 1870 actually is the large molar-toothed redhorse on the south Atlantic slope that is mentioned under *Systematics* in the account of the river redhorse *Moxostoma carinatum*. Its proper name is robust redhorse *Moxostoma robustum* (Cope). Cope's specimen of *robustus* has long been lost. Rediscovered after 110 years, the robust redhorse has been found in the Pee Dee, Savannah, and Oconee rivers of the Carolinas and Georgia since 1980.

Fish 133 *Scartomyzon robustus* adult male 223 mm SL (REJ 970), VA, Carroll County, Pauls Creek, 9 June 1983.

Fish 134 *Scartomyzon robustus* juvenile 102 mm SL (REJ 970), VA, Carroll County, Pauls Creek, 9 June 1983.

Color in Preservative.—Young and small juvenile horizontally dark-and-light striped on body from dorsum to lower side, dark stripes distinctly the narrowest; side often with 4 blotches, back with 3 or 4 saddles. With growth the blotch-saddle pattern is lost first; adult bears little or no striping, the dark stripes slightly narrower or equal in width to pale stripes, and scales darken along their margins, particularly along the base (scale pocket). Head grading from dark above to pale below, unmottled. Fins plain, pale in young and small juvenile; in adult, dorsal and caudal membranes slightly to very dusky, lower fins pale or slightly dusky.

Color in Life.—Two Virginia adults with olive dorsum; side with brassy, silvery olive, and greenish iridescence and lacking golden sheen; venter pearly; iris largely silvery. Dorsal and caudal fin rays olive, membranes dusky or black; anal rays dusky, membranes partly with pale yellow cast; paired fins pale orange. Cope (1870) and Robins and Raney (1956 [apparently based on prenuptial adults, CU 11982]) described a golden cast on body; some of the reddish they noted in certain fins may have been blood vessels.

Small juveniles from the Pee Dee drainage of Virginia and North Carolina with yellowish or olive dorsum; body side with alternating light olive (dark in preservative) and silvery yellow stripes; snout and side of head yellowish. Dorsal and caudal fins translucent white or pale red, other fins translucent white or pale orange. Robins and Raney (1956) noted upper lip red-orange.

BIOLOGY

Aquatic insects and sand were noted in the gut of a few smallfin redhorse (Gatz 1979). Based on sensory morphology, Miller and Evans (1965) predicted that this species fed in slower waters and ingested more detritus than did some jumprock suckers.

Adult females average larger than males based on specimens taken over the geographic range during late March–early June. Fifteen males were 217–285 mm SL, mean, 252; 7 females were 237–291 mm, mean, 271. Forty-one specimens from Lake Norman, North Carolina, were 160–440 mm TL, mean, 383 (D. G. Cloutman, in litt.). The largest Virginia specimen is 248 mm SL; a 463-mm TL female of 1.06 kg (2.3 pounds), the largest of which we are aware, came from Lake Norman. Cope (1870) mentioned a Pee Dee specimen of 6 pounds and an *"erythrurus"* from the Santee of 7 pounds; these may have been the undescribed form of river redhorse.

Spawning probably occurs during mid-spring and late spring. Of North Carolina males, those taken on 22 March 1948 had incompletely developed tubercles; those caught on 5 April 1940 and 30 April 1966 had tubercles in peak development. Fish captured on 16 May 1966, at the same site as the 30 April fish, were in postnuptial condition, as was a 2 June 1961 male. Two Virginia adults had maximum tubercle development on 8–9 June 1983. *Scartomyzon robustus* apparently makes an upstream migration to spawn (Hall 1972).

HABITAT

Most smallfin redhorse studied by Robins and Raney (1956) were from medium-sized streams. This species extends from cool large creeks to warm large rivers, and it is known from reservoirs in at least three of the five drainages inhabited. In the minor segment of the Pee Dee drainage in Virginia, *S. robustus* occurred in sometimes rather turbid, moderate-gradient creeks of 5–10 m width. Substrates were varied at our five record sites; gravel and rubble were common, boulder and bedrock uncommon. Some sites had considerable sand and silt, others were mostly of clean, hard bottom. Large juveniles and adults were found in pools and gentle runs; small juveniles occurred in backwaters.

DISTRIBUTION   Map 93

Scartomyzon robustus is found in five major drainages from the Cape Fear in North Carolina to the Altamaha in Georgia. This encompasses the Pee Dee drainage, where, in Virginia the smallfin redhorse extends into the extreme upper Piedmont of Patrick and Carroll counties. The eight records are from five streams, almost all sites being at or near the state line.

Abundance.—Generally uncommon.

REMARKS

This poorly known sucker is peripheral in Virginia. Some of the clearer streams in the Pee Dee drainage of Virginia, such as Pauls and Johnson creeks, would be good places to observe its habits. Jenkins and Musick (1979) had one record of *S. robustus* for Virginia, and proposed the species for state special concern status. However, as with the highback chub and Piedmont darter, also confined to the Pee Dee in Virginia but now known from additional streams there, we do not believe that this status is currently warranted.

Name.—*Robustus* refers to the body form of some of the first-described specimens, but is a misnomer for the species as a whole.

Black jumprock   *Scartomyzon cervinus* (Cope)

SYSTEMATICS

Cope (1868b) described the distinctive black jumprock from the upper Roanoke drainage. From his color plate and certain Roanoke drainage specimens, Cope clearly had this species in hand but did not distinguish it from *Thoburnia rhothoeca*; features of both species were included in the description of *S. cervinus* (Hubbs 1930a; Raney and Lachner 1946c; Robins and Raney 1956; Lachner and Jenkins 1971a). The lectotype designation of *S. cervinus* (Robins and Raney 1956) affixes that name to the Roanoke drainage population. We judge the type locality to be in the North Fork Roanoke system.

Populations of the James, Chowan, and Roanoke drainages were considered by Robins and Raney (1956) to differ on a racial level from those of the Tar and Neuse drainages by being slightly finer scaled, less blotched on the lower side, and lacking a black-tipped anal fin. They had only one Chowan specimen and eight from the Tar and Neuse. With more Chowan specimens, we found that the population aligns meristically with those of the James and Roanoke. In these three populations the lower side of the head and body occasionally is blotched and the anal fin rarely is black-tipped.

Jenkins (1970) regarded *S. cervinus* to be the most primitive of the Atlantic slope species of *Scartomyzon* that typically inhabit swift water, but more advanced than the group comprising *S. robustus* and the species of Texas and Mexico. Buth (1978) also assigned *S. cervinus* a somewhat primitive position, and Smith (1992) placed it basally in the *Scartomyzon* lineage.

DESCRIPTION

Materials.—From Robins and Raney (1956), Jenkins (1970), and 55 additional Virginia series including counts from 12 Chowan and 27 Roanoke specimens. Color in life from 13 specimens.

Anatomy.—An elongate, blotchy and striped sucker with black-tipped or black-edged dorsal and caudal fins and plicate lips; adults are 85–155 mm SL. Body elongate, nearly round. Dorsal fin margin straight or slightly convex; caudal upper lobe pointed or slightly rounded, lower lobe moderately rounded, notch moderately deep and slightly rounded. Head and eye moderate in size; head dorsum very slightly or distinctly convex; eye lateral.

Lips small for a sucker; posterior edge of lower lip cres-

Fish 135 *Scartomyzon cervinus* adult male 95 mm SL (REJ 965), VA, Patrick County, South Mayo River, June 1983.

centic; surfaces entirely plicate. Gas bladder somewhat reduced, 3-chambered, rarely 2-chambered. Scale radii described below.

Nuptial tubercles strongly developed in male on anal and lower caudal rays and on lower caudal peduncle, minute and widely scattered elsewhere on fins and body; female with much reduced tuberculation, although skin over scales on lower caudal peduncle may be much thickened.

Meristics.—Lateral line complete, scales (40)41–44(45); scales across back 13–14(15); scales across belly (14)16–18(20); circumbody scales (29)31–34(35); circumpeduncle scales (12)15–16. Dorsal rays (10)11(12); caudal rays 18; anal rays (6)7; pelvic rays (8)9; pectoral rays 14–16.

Color in Preservative.—Dusky to dark above, pale on lower side and belly or pale only on belly; pattern usually dominated by diffuse lateral blotches and saddles, as many as 6 and 5 respectively, and alternating dark and light stripes on midside and upper side; dark and light stripes about equal in width in young, dark stripes widest in adult. Snout tip and side of head often blotchy or mottled; sometimes, perhaps depending on quality of preservation, blotching and striping are inobvious.

Chief diagnostic feature in juvenile and adult is black tip of dorsal fin and both lobes of caudal; black often extends diminishingly to last dorsal ray and caudal notch; anal fin rarely black-tipped. Some young exhibit incipient black tips; that is, dorsal and caudal fins are slightly duskier at tips than subdistally. All fins of adult occasionally dark-streaked or blotchy, most so in caudal and pectoral.

Color in Life Plate 20.—Dark markings dark olive or black; paler areas with silver, yellow, or brassy iridescence or all these glosses; lateral body often overlaid with violet hue; upper lip sometimes pale orange. Except for black tips, fins vary from slightly dusky to yellow-olive to orange, the orange usually best developed in the caudal fin, but sometimes only the paired fins are pale orange, others dusky white. Sexual dichromatism and nuptial coloration apparently absent.

COMPARISON

The black jumprock is easily distinguished from other suckers by its combination of black-tipped dorsal and caudal fins, entirely plicate lips, typically 15–16 circumpeduncle scales, and lack of caudal base depigmentation.

Along with other species of *Scartomyzon*, *S. cervinus* is separated in the *Key* from the torrent suckers *Thoburnia* partly by its lack of lateral field radii on scales and by having a 3-chambered gas bladder. These are the usual traits of *S. cervinus*. However, in 24 nonregenerated scales (3 each from 8 specimens) from *S. cervinus*, 20 lacked lateral radii, 1 had 1 primary lateral radius, 1 had 1 secondary lateral radius, and 1 had 2 secondary lateral radii; even so, *Thoburnia* typically has more lateral radii. (Figure 43 shows 1 secondary lateral radius in *S. cervinus* and 6 in *T. rhothoeca*.) The gas bladder was 3-chambered in 18 *S. cervinus*, 2-chambered in 1 specimen; in the latter specimen it did not approach the obsolete condition of *Thoburnia* (Figure 41).

BIOLOGY

The food of the black jumprock is insect larvae (chiefly midges), water mites, and small amounts of algae and detritus (W. J. Matthews, in litt.). On several occasions we watched fairly tight groups of 5–12 adults gleaning food from surfaces of loose rocks and bedrock, the fish often becoming vertical or nearly inverted when following contours of rocks.

Some but apparently not all individuals spawn at age 2. Adult females average larger than adult males. Of mature fish taken during December to July, 58 males were 69–136 mm SL, mean, 107; 52 females were 87–163 mm, mean, 123. The smallest of these males is 83 mm TL; the largest known specimen is a female 164 mm SL, 195 mm TL.

Scartomyzon cervinus apparently spawns in mid- and late spring. Females seem to vary in their time of ripening. The gonads and genital papillae of females taken on 16 and 17 April indicated that spawning was in progress. A running-ripe female was recorded as late as 13 June; many taken in late May and early June

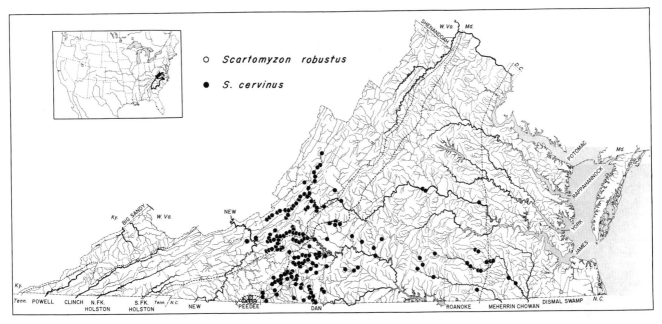

Map 93 Smallfin redhorse and black jumprock.

appeared yet to spawn. Mostly-spent females were found as early as late May, and late June and July females appeared to have completed spawning, although some early July males remained fully tuberculate. Normal water temperatures during the spawning period are 14–23°C; spawning likely occurs in swift water.

HABITAT

Large juveniles and adults of this small sucker favor well-flowing to rather swift current in warm, moderate-gradient, large creeks to small rivers. They typically occupy clean rubble, boulder, and bedrock, and are collected or observed about equally in shallow (0.3 m) and deeper areas (to about 1.5 m). Much of their foraging occurs in open areas; they exhibit little or no preference for cover beyond general association with coarse substrate (Leonard et al. 1986; our observations). Young and small juveniles, however, usually are found in sluggish pool shallows and deeper backwaters, often on silted and detritus-laden bottoms. The black jumprock avoids much of the heavily silted waters of the Piedmont. It was numerous at a Fall Zone site in the Nottoway River; strays or small established populations occur farther down the river.

DISTRIBUTION   Map 93

Scartomyzon cervinus occurs in the New, James, Chowan, and Roanoke drainages in Virginia, the Dan system of the Roanoke in North Carolina, and in the Tar and Neuse drainages of North Carolina. It is clearly native to the Chowan, Roanoke, Tar, and Neuse; we believe that it probably was introduced to the James and New.

This sucker was first found in the James drainage in 1951, in Johns Creek at Newcastle, just above the mouth in Craig Creek. Its presence was accredited to stream capture involving the Roanoke drainage (Robins and Raney 1956). Natural dispersal to the James was supported by Lachner and Jenkins (1971a), but they and later authors, to Hocutt et al. (1986), questioned its native status. Introduction was indicated by the putative rapid, post-1950 spread of the fish in and from Craig Creek. An alternate hypothesis of recent spread from a localized native population lacks obvious support because ecological conditions have been relatively stable in the drainage since 1950.

Cope's and Jordan's extant specimens of "*cervinus*" from the James drainage are *Thoburnia rhothoeca* (Lachner and Jenkins 1971a). Although Burton and Odum's (1945) sampling in Craig and Johns creeks may not have been intensive at each site, it was sufficiently extensive to have yielded *S. cervinus* if this species was native. After its discovery at Newcastle in 1951, the sucker has been found widespread in Craig and Johns creeks well above Newcastle since at least 1964, and was found during that year in lowermost Craig.

First records in the drainage above Craig Creek are from the lower Cowpasture River in 1972, the middle Cowpasture in 1984, and the lower Jackson River in

1973. In the Valley and Ridge Province below Craig Creek, the upper James River first yielded specimens in 1962, Catawba Creek in 1964, Jennings Creek in 1965, and Buffalo Creek of the Maury River in 1961. In the Blue Ridge, lower Rocky Row Run produced *S. cervinus* in 1974. It was caught in the midsection of the James River during 1972–1973 (White et al. 1977), and at the head of the Fall Zone in 1979. As in the Craig system, in nearly all these streams the first record postdates sampling that likely would have detected the fish had it been present. Although middle James tributaries lack a jumprock record, they have been sparsely collected since the suggested recent outbreak of the species; *S. cervinus* likely has moved into many of them.

The two New drainage records are from the lower portion of two closely adjacent New River tributaries. Juveniles and adults were found in Back Creek in 1987, and one adult was caught in Toms Creek during 1988 (P. L. Angermeier, personal communication; Back Creek specimens verified by Jenkins). Back Creek had not been sampled previously, hence *S. cervinus* could have long resided there undetected. However, Back Creek is unlikely to have sustained a relict jumprock population; Ross and Perkins (1959) stated that it has little surface flow because of underground solution. *Scartomyzon cervinus* apparently is a new arrival also in Toms Creek; it was not found there in seven collections during 1951–1982.

The New drainage population probably originated from bait-bucket transfer from the Roanoke or James drainages. Had *S. cervinus* been native to the New, it is unlikely that two relict populations would be so closely situated. Either Back Creek or Toms Creek could have been the initial receptor of released black jumprocks; they are bait-fished for warmwater species, and Toms Creek has a stocked-trout fishery. Bait fishing occurs throughout the drainage; *S. cervinus* could have been introduced in the New River or some other tributary. This species apparently is established; likely it will be on the move because the sucker fauna of the New drainage is depauperate.

Abundance.—Usually uncommon or common in mountains and adjacent uplands, generally uncommon or rare eastward.

REMARKS

Scartomyzon cervinus is one of several small rheophilic suckers that enrich the faunas of central Atlantic slope rivers, most notably the Appalachians of Virginia. This is a handsome sucker, having varihued iridescences the year around and being marked by black-tipped dorsal and caudal fins. Its aggressive and agile feeding behavior is interesting to watch.

Name.—*Cervinus,* "tawny," like a fawn, which we attribute to the lateral stripe of the *T. rhothoeca* specimens confounded with the black jumprock in the original description.

Bigeye jumprock   *Scartomyzon ariommus* (Robins and Raney)

SYSTEMATICS

The bizarre bigeye jumprock was described by Robins and Raney (1956) from the upper Roanoke and Dan systems of the Roanoke drainage. When first collected by the describers, it was immediately recognized as a highly divergent species. Likely it would have been described by its earlier captors had it not been for the chaotic taxonomic state of Atlantic slope jumprocks and redhorses perpetrated by Cope (1870) and Fowler (1913).

The bigeye jumprock was placed in *Scartomyzon* by Robins and Raney (1956), who judged that it "... indeed, would seem almost worthy of generic recognition." They concluded that it represents an intermediate stage of evolution between *Scartomyzon* and *Thoburnia;* this was echoed by Bailey (1959a). Jenkins (1970) aligned *S. ariommus* with *Thoburnia atripinnis* and noted that *T. atripinnis* diverges sharply from the rustyside group of *Thoburnia.* Buth (1978) found that *S. ariommus* is advanced and extremely distinctive genetically, but held that it falls within *Scartomyzon.*

Smith (1992) placed *S. ariommus* basally in the *Thoburnia–Hypentelium* lineage, hence as more advanced than *Scartomyzon.* Substantiation of those relationships would lead to the description of a new genus for *S. ariommus,* which in turn would render *Scartomyzon* a monophyletic lineage (Smith 1992, personal communication). The new genus may include *T. atripinnis.*

DESCRIPTION

Materials.—Seventy lots from Virginia and 1 from North Carolina, including those studied by Jenkins (1970); meristic data from 80 specimens. Life color from 26 Virginia specimens.

Anatomy.—A large-eyed sucker with thin, flattened, markedly papillose lips; adults are 100–190 mm SL. Body

Fish 136 *Scartomyzon ariommus* adult male 131 mm SL (REJ 1126), VA, Montgomery County, South Fork Roanoke River, 24 September 1984.

elongate, anteriorly about as wide as deep, round or nearly square in cross section; caudal peduncle somewhat deep, compressed; back often with shallow depression just behind dorsal fin, nape sometimes slightly concave anteriorly in very robust specimens. Dorsal fin margin straight or very slightly concave; caudal fin rather large compared with shallow body, lobes well rounded or almost pointed, lower lobe roundest, notch round and moderately shallow. Head short, particularly postorbitally; dorsum flat or slightly concave; eye oval, supralateral, large (6.9–8.4% SL, mean, 7.7 in 21 specimens 35–69 mm SL; 6.0–7.9% SL, mean, 6.8 in 43 of 70–180 mm).

Lips thin, flattened, flared, with pendant papillae forming fringed edges; when mouth closed, most of upper lip curves posteriad, hoodlike, over its base and part of lower lip; halves of lower lip separated by deep notch, forming wide angle posteriorly; when mouth fully open, lips form nearly circular sucking disk; most papillae large, well separated, symmetrically rowed. Medial portion of upper and lower jaws covered with pad of firm tissue. Gas bladder large, 3-chambered in 11 specimens, 4-chambered in 17, 4th chamber small, narrow or bulbous. Lateral fields of scales on upper half of midbody usually lacking radii, occasionally with 1–3 secondary radii, rarely 1–2 primary radii.

Nuptial tubercles of male strongly developed on anal and lower caudal rays, sometimes on caudal peduncle; other fins, head, and body with small to minute tubercles, best developed and retrorse along scale margins. Female with reduced tuberculation, although scale-margin tubercles often as on male, and lower caudal peduncle scales of large specimens having much-thickened skin.

Meristics.—Lateral line complete, scales (42)43–46(47); scales across back 12–13(15); scales across belly (15)16–18; circumbody scales (29)31–33(34); circumpeduncle scales (13)15–16. Dorsal rays (9)11(12); caudal rays 18; anal rays 7; pelvic rays 8–9; pectoral rays (14)15–17(18).

Color in Preservative.—Dusky to dark above; usually pale, occasionally slightly dusky below; scales darkest submarginally; alternating dark and light stripes usually absent on upper body, vague when present, dark stripes widest. Young to adult occasionally with 4 lateral blotches, all except sometimes last blotch confluent with a saddle, last saddle when present usually narrow; young and small juvenile with distinct or vague midlateral dark stripe, somewhat intensified through blotches. Head and fins lacking mottling and reticulation. Fins pale or with slightly dusky rays. Dorsal fin often distinctly dusky at anterior tip or along anterior half of distal margin; rarely a large dark anterodistal blotch present, best developed in adult. Many specimens have apparent black-spot parasites forming rows of punctations on body.

Unique, possibly nuptial color indicated in both sexes; reproductive fish with side of head and body distinctly darker than in most other specimens; head particularly blackened ventrolaterally, sharply demarked from pale venter. Pattern retained to a lesser extent in some fish long after spawning; pattern present in some small, possibly mature specimens.

Color in Life Plate 21.—Nonblackened juvenile and adult with back leaden to olive-gray; side green-gray to olive, usually with violet iridescent hue, sometimes with dull bronze reflections; lower side and venter pearly; upper operculum sometimes iridescent green; iris black or silvery or both; anterior surface of upper lip pale orange in some young and juveniles. All fins pale, dusky, or dull yellow-olive to dull red; fins rarely bright when colored, anal and caudal usually reddened, paired fins tending orange.

BIOLOGY

Life history aspects of the bigeye jumprock were reported (in litt.) by Roanoke College seniors from research directed by Jenkins. P. H. Lahrmann and E. G. Coggin treated food habits, and N. A. Mudrick studied age, growth, maturation, and ovarian development. Based on 27 specimens, this species feeds on immature mayflies and caddisflies, and particularly on midges, blackflies, the cranefly *Antocha*, and detritus. It takes lesser amounts of stonefly and moth (*Parargyractis*) larvae and water mites.

Maturation of some age-2 and all age-3 fish of both sexes occurred as early as September; spawning may first occur at age 3 or 4. A few age-2 females of 97–101 mm SL, taken late in the spawning period or just

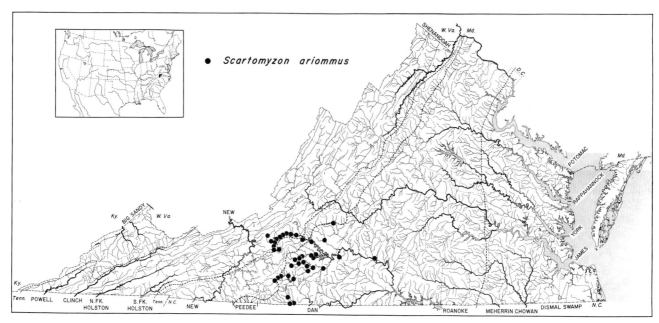

Map 94   Bigeye jumprock.

after, had tuberculation and dark nuptial-like coloration. They were questionably adult; their small ovaries were either immature or fully spent. Two males
and three females reached age 6 and a female was 7.5
years old. Clearly mature fish collected during September–April include 56 males of 104–153 mm SL,
mean, 134, and 58 females of 105–188 mm, mean, 149.
From 72 scale-aged specimens, males averaged larger
than females at age 1 and the converse was true for
ages 2–6. Through ages 2–6 the differences between
the sexes in mean length increased progressively
from 1.6 to 12.8 mm. At age 4, males averaged 136
mm SL, females 142 mm. The largest known specimen is the age-7 female, 188 mm SL, 226 mm TL.

Scartomyzon ariommus apparently is the earliest-
spawning sucker in Virginia. Based on gonadal and
tubercle development, Jenkins and Lahrmann (*in* Lee
et al. 1980) predicted that it spawned in March, but
they lacked February specimens. These criteria applied to subsequently acquired specimens indicate
that spawning occurs mainly in February and early
March. Most late-March females and all but one of
many April females were fully spent. Water temperatures during February–March are 2–17°C. Maturing
and mature ova in a February and a March female
were 1.0–1.2 mm.

HABITAT

The bigeye jumprock is characteristic of montane
and upper Piedmont warm streams of moderate gradient that vary in clarity and are slightly to heavily
silted. It typically occupies streams of 10–25 m width
and is rarely found in creeks 3–5 m wide. Large
juveniles and adults generally are localized in deep
runs and well-flowing parts of pools floored with
relatively unsilted rubble, boulder, and jagged outcrop; they rarely are found in shallow riffles of gravel
and small rubble. Young and small juveniles usually
inhabit shallow slow sections of runs and pools having sand or sand–gravel bottoms; occasionally they
are taken in rubble riffles. Many more adults have
been taken than small fish, indicating that small fish
may prefer areas as deep as do adults. *Scartomyzon
ariommus* has not been found in the cold and cool
tailwater sections of the upper Smith and Dan rivers,
which otherwise have excellent habitat.

DISTRIBUTION   Map 94

Scartomyzon ariommus is endemic to the upper and
middle Roanoke drainage in Virginia and North
Carolina. All records predating July 1979 from both
states were plotted by Jenkins and Lahrmann (*in* Lee
et al. 1980), including the current easternmost record
from the lower Falling River, Virginia, in 1979. Two
other efforts at that locality during 1977–1983 failed
to find the species. New records include first capture in
certain other systems on the Virginia Piedmont:
North Fork Otter River, Goose Creek, and Beaverdam Creek. The data indicate that the bigeye jump-

rock occurs more widely in the Roanoke system proper than in the Dan system.

The record for the Chowan drainage (Jenkins et al. 1975) was determined (Jenkins and Musick 1979) to have faulty locality data; the specimens probably came from the upper Roanoke. Hence *S. ariommus* is one of the few fishes characteristic of the upper Roanoke that does not occur in the Chowan.

Abundance.—Generally uncommon in the mountains and upper Piedmont, rare in middle Piedmont; most abundant in the least-silted streams. Owing to its strong tendency to occur only in localized areas of preferred habitat, major portions of each riffle–run–pool sequence may be void of this species. However, 5–10 adults are sometimes collected in one or a few passes through high-quality habitat.

REMARKS

The remarkable bigeye jumprock is one of the most sought and difficult-to-catch fish in the upper Roanoke. Its distribution and typical habitat have been discerned only recently, largely by using electrofishing equipment. It may not venture far from cover. One of our most memorable sights while snorkeling was finding several adult *S. ariommus* deep in a crevice beneath a large boulder, all in a row, peering out with large eyes.

Scartomyzon ariommus is highly divergent from other moxostomatins in several aspects of lip and body form, frequent presence of a 4th gas-bladder chamber, retrorse scale-margin tubercles, and dark-headed nuptial coloration. Robins and Raney (1956) considered this species to be apparently adapted to swift water. This is tenable regarding body form, but the large gas bladder indicates that its typical habitat has less current. We usually find the adults in pools and parts of runs protected by rocks from swift current.

Based on brain and lip morphology, notably the densest concentration of taste buds on lip papillae known in a sucker, Miller and Evans (1965) hypothesized that the bigeye jumprock feeds primarily by rooting between and under stones for a limited variety of food organisms. The large facial lobe and small vagal lobes of the brain indicate that *S. ariommus* recognizes food chiefly by taste buds on the lips, hence that it is a "skin taster." Our observations of a young specimen in an aquarium serve as evidence that it is not strictly a lip taster. This fish fed on the bottom and ejected considerable amounts of sand via the opercular openings, rather than by rejection through the mouth, indicating taste-sorting of food in the oropharyngeal cavity.

Is the eye particularly large in the bigeye jumprock? The short head of this species could lend the impression of a very large eye. As is typical of most fishes including suckers (Jenkins 1970), the eye is large in young *S. ariommus* and becomes proportionately smaller with increase in fish length (*Description*). Still, the eye of *S. ariommus* is distinctly larger than in other species of jumprocks, the torrent suckers, and some redhorses; it remains relatively large through adulthood.

What is the adaptive significance of the large eye? Partly because the aquarium specimen of *S. ariommus* did not appear to recognize chopped earthworms as food when dropped directly within view, Jenkins (1970) suggested that the large eye serves to enhance detection of predators. The supralateral position of the eye on a benthic fish would increase the overhead field of view where most predators would occur. Owing to its stronger association with slower or deeper water than other small suckers in the upper Roanoke, *S. ariommus* might be subject to greater predation pressure than those species. A major predator would be the native Roanoke bass, which lurks in habitats like those favored by the bigeye jumprock.

Scartomyzon ariommus has been considered a relict survivor of an ancestral stock of wider range in the Appalachians (Robins and Raney 1956; Robins 1961). It appears to have not fared well in historical times. Siltation probably has caused extirpation of some populations, resulting in the fragmented distribution pattern on the Piedmont. The best populations, with continuous distribution, occupy the Roanoke River and its forks above Roanoke and the upper Smith River above Philpott Reservoir.

Impoundments have ousted the population in some river reaches, but surprisingly this species seems to have survived, likely unaided by recruitment, in some small tributaries of reservoirs. Examples are Old Woman Creek of lower Leesville Reservoir (1970 record), Beaverdam Creek of upper Smith Mountain Lake (1983), and Nicholas Creek of Philpott Reservoir (1977). The bigeye jumprock also persists in Town Creek, which joins the cold tailwater of Philpott Reservoir (1958–1986).

The bigeye jumprock has been considered rare over its range and has special concern status in North Carolina (J. R. Bailey 1977). Jenkins and Musick (1979) indicated that it did not warrant protective status in Virginia because, owing to more-effective collecting methods, it was found to be doing well in certain streams and was newly discovered in others. We caution, however, that this species should be watched for continuation of its suggested decline. It is a fascinating fish that merits further ecological, behavioral, and systematic study.

Name.—Ariommus is derived from *ari*, a strengthening prefix, and *omma*, "eye"; hence "big eye."

Redhorse suckers   Genus *Moxostoma* Rafinesque

Being sheared of the former subgenera *Thoburnia* and *Scartomyzon* (Smith 1992), *Moxostoma* now has 10 or 11 species (1 or 2 undescribed) of typical redhorses and also the harelip sucker *M. lacerum* (formerly *Lagochila lacera*). The genus is a primitive relative to the *Scartomyzon*, *Thoburnia*, and *Hypentelium* lineages (Smith 1992). The typical redhorses have been divided into the subgenera *Megapharynx* (two species) and *Moxostoma* (Robins and Raney 1956). Phylogenetic uncertainties remain that are independent of inclusion or exclusion of *M. lacerum* (Smith 1992),

hence our recognition of the subgenera is chiefly for convenience.

Most species of *Moxostoma* are widely distributed; six populate Virginia and the extinct harelip sucker did so. The two *Megapharynx* have northerly ranges.

Name.—Moxostoma is Rafinesque's misspelling of *Myzostoma*—"sucking mouth." Formal rules of nomenclature dictate that here the original spelling must be retained. "Redhorse" refers to the red fins (often orange, usually the lower fins) of most species and to large body size.

Black redhorse   *Moxostoma duquesnei* (Lesueur)

SYSTEMATICS

Described from the Ohio River in 1817, *M. duquesnei* was confounded with other redhorses, particularly *M. erythrurum*, and paraded under a multiplicity of names until it was clearly distinguished by Hubbs (1930a). Its taxonomic history was further clarified by Jenkins (1970), who intends to designate a neotype. *Moxostoma duquesnei* is divisible into two races, one in the Mobile drainage, the other in the remainder of the

range (Jenkins 1970). Geographic variation occurs within the races; for example, the Holston and Clinch populations differ in one of the main characters used to identify the species, pelvic ray number (*Comparison*).

The black redhorse is a somewhat primitive member of the subgenus *Moxostoma* (Jenkins 1970; Buth 1978). Smith (1992) placed it in a group of shortheaded redhorses (see *M. lacerum*).

Fish 137 *Moxostoma duquesnei* juvenile 107 mm SL (REJ 982), VA, Washington County, North Fork Holston River, 16 June 1983.

Fish 138 *Moxostoma duquesnei* juvenile 50 mm SL (REJ 622), VA, Scott County, Big Moccasin Creek, 10 January 1973.

DESCRIPTION

Materials.—From Jenkins (1970) and 26 later collected lots; counts given from Holston, Clinch, and Big Sandy populations. Life color chiefly from Jenkins (1970).

Anatomy.—A slender redhorse with plicate lips, upper body dusky, lateral line scales usually 44–47, and pelvic rays often 10; adults are 180–300 mm SL. Body elongate, round or slightly compressed, dorsal profile low, caudal peduncle moderate in juvenile, somewhat slender in adult. Dorsal fin margin usually slightly concave; caudal lobes about equal, tips pointed or lower tip slightly rounded, notch shallow or moderately deep. Head somewhat small in adult, convex dorsally; snout somewhat blunt in most fish, occasionally broadly rounded, appearing bulbous in adult; eye moderate or small, lateral.

Lips medium or large; posterior angle usually 110–170°, tending widest in adult; surfaces deeply plicate. Pharyngeal arch moderate, teeth comblike, nonmolariform. Gas bladder 3-chambered.

Nuptial tuberculation of male well developed, largest tubercles (medium-sized) occur on rays of anal fin and lower caudal lobe; very small to minute tubercles elsewhere on fins, body, and head. Female lacks tubercles; lower urosome skin quite thick.

Meristics.—Lateral line complete, scales (43)44–47(48); circumbody scales (31)32–36(38); circumpeduncle scales 12–14(16), usually 12; predorsal scale rows (14)16–19(20). Dorsal rays 12–14; caudal rays (17)18(19); anal rays 7(8); pelvic rays (8)9–10, usually 9 in Holston, 10 in Clinch; pectoral rays 16–18(19).

Color in Preservative.—Body and head dark to dusky above, grading to pale ventrally; dark and pale stripes occasionally present, vague on upper side; side of young and small juvenile usually with cross-hatched pattern, but in large juvenile and adult, scales of upper half of body uniformly pigmented or margin only slightly darker than median; posteriormost scales over caudal rays usually not outlined by dark pigment; young and occasionally juvenile with 4 lateral blotches, 3 saddles. Dorsal and caudal fins dusky or dark, often very slightly darker along margin; lower fins pale or pelvic and pectoral dusky.

Color in Life.—Large juvenile and adult with back olive, sometimes with gray or tan cast; side silvery yellow or golden yellow, sometimes with gray or bronze cast, and pale green iridescence often on scale bases. In young and small juvenile, side tends largely silvery. Dorsal and caudal fins dusky or dark, but sometimes with faint red tinge in small fish; all lower fins orange or red-orange, or in small fish, anal is white.

Spawning males in central Missouri had light pinkish midlateral band on body, above and below which the fish were uniform metallic greenish black (Bowman 1970). In southern Ohio, males on a spawning bed had a strikingly different pattern—essentially the same as in *M. erythrurum*

(Smith 1977, later observation [personal communication]). A nuptial stripe was not reported for breeding males in Illinois by Page and Johnston (1990a), who did record it for *M. erythrurum*. Black redhorse males on a spawning shoal in Virginia were not noted to differ in color from nonnuptial adults but they were not actively spawning or notably aggressive.

Larvae.—See Snyder (1979) and Fuiman (1982c).

COMPARISON

Moxostoma duquesnei and *M. erythrurum* often are common in their mostly mutual ranges and are among the most difficult species of redhorses to distinguish from each other. Scale count differences separate more than 90% of specimens (*Key*). The pelvic ray count is useful on a geographic basis. Generally in *duquesnei* of the Clinch system (and in the Big Sandy drainage near Virginia), one or both pelvics have 10 rays; *erythrurum* typically has 9 rays throughout its range. However, *duquesnei* typically has 9 rays in the Holston system. *Moxostoma duquesnei* lacks medium and large tubercles on the snout; they are present in nuptial male *erythrurum*.

Shapes are useful for separating large juveniles and adults, but it helps to have both species at hand to recognize the differences. In addition to differences in the caudal peduncle (*Key*), these include: (1) snout [often more prominently exceeding front of upper lip, sometimes bulbous in *duquesnei* vs. usually only slightly exceeding upper lip, not obviously bulbous in *erythrurum*]; (2) posterior angle of lower lips usually [more obtuse, 110–170° vs. less obtuse, 90–135° (Figure 42L shows narrower angle than typical)].

The slight pigmentary difference described in the *Key* is helpful in preliminary sorting of the species (Figure 45; Jenkins 1970; Kott et al. 1979); it is best discerned on the anterodorsolateral body. It is useful for fish of 50 mm SL and larger, but because both species vary somewhat within and between size groups, the differences are best discerned with similar-sized specimens of both species at hand.

BIOLOGY

Comprehensive studies of black redhorse biology are by Bowman (1970) in Missouri and Smith (1977) in Ohio. This species feeds principally on aquatic insects, other invertebrates, algae, and detritus (Bowman 1970; Smith 1977). Groups often traverse pools in a regular pattern, feeding intermittently but most actively during low light intensity (Smith 1977). We saw adults feeding in a run.

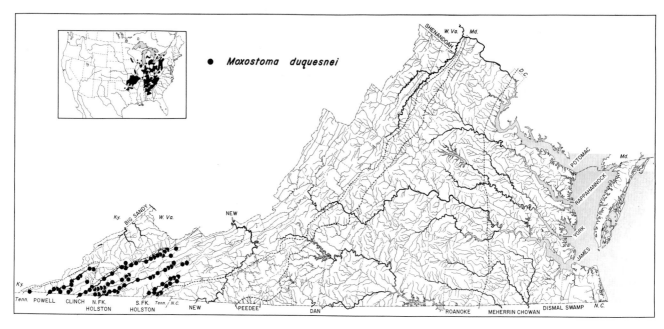

Map 95   Black redhorse.

Some *M. duquesnei* mature in 2 years, all by 4–6 years; maximum life span is 10 years. Females grow faster than males in some but not all populations (Bowman 1970; Smith 1977). Mean lengths at age 5 of several populations from Oklahoma to Ontario are 244–480 mm TL; relatively rapidly growing fish tend to live in large streams and impoundments (Purkett 1958; Carlander 1969; Bowman 1970; Smith 1977; Curry and Spacie 1984; McAllister et al. 1985). Large adults in Virginia are about 400 mm TL. A 686-mm TL, 2.4-kg (5.3 pounds) black redhorse was listed from the Nolichucky River in Tennessee by Ward (1960); however, this may have been the river redhorse *M. carinatum*. The heaviest black redhorse may be a Missouri fish of 658 mm TL (25.9 inches), 3.2 kg (7 pounds) reported by Pflieger (1975).

Spawning occurs in April, May, or both months, over most of the geographic range, into early June in Ontario, in water of 9–23°C, mean, 16.4 (Cross 1967; Bowman 1970; Smith 1977; Curry and Spacie 1984; McAllister et al. 1985; Page and Johnston 1990a). In Missouri, movements from deeper pools begin in March or early April; some fish migrate 9 rkm upstream. The start of spawning varies as much as two weeks between years but the period lasts only four days (Bowman 1970). In some areas black redhorse live year-round near breeding sites (Smith 1977; Curry and Spacie 1984).

Spawning takes place on beds of gravel and small rubble in runs and riffles. Few of the apparently suitable sites in a stream section are used in a year. In Virginia, spawning aggregations occurred in the South Fork Holston River and Copper Creek in the afternoon on 23 April 1977 and 25 April 1971, water 14.5° and 12–14°C. Behavior is unspecialized; territorial behavior has been described as present and absent (Bowman 1970; Page and Johnston 1990a). Fecundity is 1,357–17,252 ova (Bowman 1970; Smith 1977; Curry and Spacie 1979; Becker 1983; McAllister et al. 1985).

HABITAT

Moxostoma duquesnei occupies cool and warm, large creeks to large rivers of moderate gradient. The largest populations develop in streams that typically are clear and little silted (Bowman 1970). Some individuals dwell in reservoirs. This species tends to be more abundant than *M. erythrurum* in cool, swift, rocky streams, and declines when excessive siltation occurs. Adults generally inhabit sluggish and well-flowing pools, sometimes moderately silted ones; in small streams they are localized in deeper pools. Young often are found in calm shallows.

DISTRIBUTION   Map 95

The black redhorse is found in the southern Great Lakes, upper Mississippi, and Ohio basins, the Ozark and Ouachita mountains and their outliers, and in the upper Mobile drainage. As is true of most other Mississippi basin redhorses, this species is arrayed west, north, and east of the lower Mississippi Valley lowlands, avoiding most of that corridor. In Virginia the black redhorse is widely distributed in the Tennessee drainage. It lives in the Kentucky part of the Big Sandy drainage but apparently it is extirpated from the Virginia section.

Abundance.—Usually uncommon or common.

Shorthead redhorse   *Moxostoma macrolepidotum* (Lesueur)

SYSTEMATICS

The shorthead redhorse was named in 1817 from the Delaware River, but it is uncertain that it actually occurred there (Jenkins 1970). Lachner (1967) and Jenkins (1970) broadened the use of the name *macrolepidotum* to comprise all forms of shorthead redhorse. For a long period many populations of this species were called *M. aureolum*, but that name and *macrolepidotum* also were applied at times to other redhorses (Jenkins 1970).

The shorthead redhorse is the most widespread and perhaps most polytypic redhorse. Three subspecies are recognized: *M. m. macrolepidotum* in most of the range including the Virginia Atlantic slope; *M. m. breviceps* (Cope) in the Ohio basin including southwestern Virginia; and *M. m. pisolabrum* Trautman and Martin primarily in the Ozarks. *Moxostoma m. breviceps* had long been recognized as a species; Jenkins (1970) believed it to intergrade but this was not substantiated in a preliminary biochemical study by Buth (1979a).

The relationships hypothesized for *M. macrolepidotum* have varied. Jenkins (1970) placed it intermediate in the subgenus *Moxostoma* but could not directly link it to another species. Buth (1978) allied it with *M.*

REMARKS

The black redhorse is fairly sensitive to siltation and other forms of pollution (e.g., Trautman 1981), as evidenced in the upper Big Sandy, but it holds strongly in the Virginia portion of the Tennessee drainage. We attest that this redhorse is flavorful but, as with the rest of its group, bony.

Name.—For the type locality, Fort Duquesne, now Pittsburgh.

carinatum, but Smith (1992) grouped it with shortheaded species (see *M. lacerum*). Clearly the *breviceps* and *pisolabrum* forms are advanced within the species.

DESCRIPTION

Materials.—From over the species range (Jenkins 1970) including 48 recently studied Virginia samples. Life color from Jenkins (1970) and 6 subsequent Virginia or eastern Tennessee samples.

Anatomy.—A short-headed, high-backed redhorse with dark scale bases and relatively small lips, the lower lip plicae deeply subdivided posteriorly; adults are 200–350 mm SL. Body form moderate, nearly round, or in some adults, moderately compressed; caudal peduncle moderate. Dorsal fin margin concave; caudal fin tips pointed, notch moderate or deep; in *breviceps,* dorsal falcate and upper caudal lobe usually markedly longer than lower lobe. Head short (particularly in adult), convex dorsally; snout somewhat blunt, rounded, or conic, dorsal contour sharply and smoothly rising through nape to dorsal fin origin; eye moderate, lateral.

Mouth and lips somewhat small for a redhorse, particularly small in *breviceps;* upper lip plicate; lower lip straight-edged or slightly concave posteriorly, surfaces plicate in small young; with growth, lower-lip plicae quickly become

Fish 139 *Moxostoma m. macrolepidotum* adult male 282 mm SL (REJ 1038), VA, Campbell County, Roanoke River, 12 September 1983.

progressively subdivided, beginning in corners and posteriorly, by deep transverse grooves, resulting in subplicate condition; thus divided plicae appear as round or longitudinally elongate papillae. Pharyngeal arch moderate, teeth comblike. Gas bladder 3-chambered. Tuberculation much as in *M. duquesnei*; thickened lower urosome scales ridgelike in some females.

Meristics.—Lateral line complete, scales (39)42–44(46); circumbody scales (28)30–33(37); circumpeduncle scales (11)12–13(16), usually 12; predorsal scale rows (12)15–17(20). Dorsal rays (10)12–13(15), usually 13 in subspecies *macrolepidotum*, 12 in *breviceps*; caudal rays (17)18(19); anal rays 7(8); pelvic rays (8)9–10(11), usually 9 in *macrolepidotum*, 10 in *breviceps*; pectoral rays (14)16–17(19).

Color in Preservative.—As in *M. duquesnei* except scale bases (scale pockets) sharply darker than scale medians; dorsal and caudal fins not duskier along margin.

Color in Life.—Body dark olive to tan-olive dorsally, often with silver or gray overtone; side silvery, yellow, golden, or coppery, scale bases dark and with subtle green iridescence; venter white with silver reflections. Dorsal fin entirely sooty or slightly or moderately red distally and anteriorly. Caudal fin deep red, particularly distally and along upper and lower few rays, or with only a trace of red in these areas, or red apparently absent, fin slate-toned. Anal fin reddish, pale orange, or white; paired fins pale red or pale orange. Subspecies *breviceps* tends to have the most intensely reddened fins.

Nuptial color apparently not different from nonspawning adult color. Spawning males appeared slightly more intensely colored than females in Illinois (Burr and Morris 1977), but we have not found this in subspecies *macrolepidotum* in Virginia, nor in color photographs of Tennessee *breviceps*.

Larvae.—Described by Buynak and Mohr (1979a, 1980c), Fuiman (1979b, 1982c), Fuiman and Witman (1979), and Snyder (1979).

COMPARISON

A rather small head that is markedly downsloped to the snout tip, and the dark scale bases anterodorsolaterally (Figure 45A) are prominent diagnostic features of the shorthead redhorse. The subplicate condition of the lower lips (Figure 42J) is unique in *Moxostoma* to this species, but specimens should be carefully examined for this detail, best seen by drying the lips and, for small specimens, with magnification. The relatively small lower lips, their posterior edges forming a straight or broadly concave line, should also be looked for.

BIOLOGY

Life history aspects of the shorthead redhorse were examined in Iowa by Meyer (1962) and in Illinois by

Sule and Skelly (1985). This species feeds on aquatic insects, small crustaceans, mollusks, algae, and detritus (Meyer 1962; Minckley 1963; summary in Jenkins 1970; Becker 1983; Sule and Skelly 1985). Feeding behavior is varied: *M. m. breviceps* was observed flicking fins rapidly and pushing between small stones and gravel with the snout; *M. m. pisolabrum* rolled these materials (Minckley 1963); *M. m. macrolepidotum* in Back Creek, upper Roanoke drainage, mouthed on the bottom, not obviously moving stones and rarely flicking fins (Jenkins' observations).

Maturation occurs in 3 years in some males and females (Meyer 1962), but most reports give age 5 for the first spawning (Burr and Morris 1977; Curry and Spacie 1979, 1984; Sule and Skelly 1985). Fish living 12–14 years in Canada are the oldest reported (Scott and Crossman 1973). No pronounced sexual difference in growth rate was noted by Meyer (1962), but Sule and Skelly (1985) found that females grew faster after age 3. Age-5 fish of one or more populations of the three subspecies have mean lengths spanning 310–420 mm TL (Purkett 1958; Meyer 1962; Baker 1966; Becker 1983; Curry and Spacie 1984; Sule and Skelly 1985). Large adults in Virginia are about 400 mm TL. Among the largest reported are fish of 2.7 kg (6 pounds) from Ohio and Wisconsin; a 619-mm TL specimen from Ohio was 1.9 kg (4 pounds 2 ounces) (Trautman 1981; Becker 1983). Larger fish—655 mm TL, 3.1 kg (6.7 pounds), and 3.6–4.5 kg (8–10 pounds)—have been reported from Iowa and Minnesota (Meyer 1962; Eddy and Surber 1947), but these may have been *M. carinatum* or *M. valenciennesi* (Jenkins 1970).

The breeding period of *M. macrolepidotum* occurs within early April to early July, varying by region, local conditions, and seasonal climate. Water temperatures reported for spawning are 11–21°C, mean, 14.7 (Meyer 1962; Jenkins 1970; Pflieger 1975; Burr and Morris 1977; June 1977; Trautman 1981; Curry and Spacie 1984; Sule and Skelly 1985; P. A. Hackney, in litt.). Most reports are of spawning on largely gravel and small rubble; Jones et al. (1978) cited spawning on sand. Spawning congregations in Back Creek, Virginia, used slow and moderate runs and pool tails having mainly a large-gravel substrate. These and other spawning groups in Virginia were located in streams that were sparsely or unoccupied by shorthead redhorse adults except around breeding time. Groups were observed during late morning to late afternoon on 17 May 1969 (two sites) and 12 and 26 May 1971, water 17–21.5°C, mean, 19.8. Behavior was typical of that described by Burr and Morris (1977).

Fecundity ranges 9,262–44,000 eggs (Moore and Cross 1950; Meyer 1962; Curry and Spacie 1979;

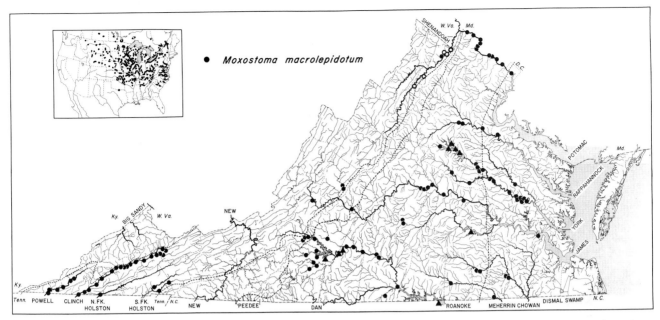

Map 96 Shorthead redhorse. Open circles on Shenandoah River represent unallocatable records of "redhorse sucker" (see *M. erythrurum, Distribution*).

Becker 1983; Sule and Skelly 1985). A specimen from the James River, Virginia, appears to be a hybrid *M. erythrurum* × *M. macrolepidotum* (VISR VGC 48).

HABITAT

The shorthead redhorse is prevalent in warm, moderate-gradient, large streams and rivers. Over much of its range it is also found in shallows of natural and artificial lakes (Sule and Skelly 1985). Most individuals observed in Virginia were holding or feeding in deeper pools of silted and clean sand, gravel, rubble, and bedrock. Individuals and groups often foraged into shallow, moderately swift runs floored with clean gravel and rubble. Some young and small juveniles were taken in shallow backwaters. This species populates most or all major reservoirs within its altitudinal range in Virginia. It occupies freshwater zones of estuaries; Schwartz (1981b) reported it in or near 8‰ salinity in North Carolina.

DISTRIBUTION Map 96

The most broadly distributed of the redhorses, *M. macrolepidotum* occupies the Hudson Bay, Great Lakes–St. Lawrence, and Mississippi basins, and the Atlantic slope from the Hudson drainage to the San-

tee drainage, perhaps excepting the Delaware. Subspecies distributions are noted under *Systematics*. The single North Fork Holston River record is from 1974; the shorthead redhorse may have been formerly extirpated by pollution from Saltville, and have been unable to regain foothold because of the dam at Holston Mill, Scott County. This species has strongly repopulated the long Clinch River reach that was affected by the 1967 fish kill. It may enter the Big Sandy drainage in Virginia from Kentucky.

Abundance.—Probably uncommon or common in preferred habitat, but generally collected in small numbers owing to its mobility and occupation of large deep waters. It congregates in some medium-sized streams during spawning migration.

REMARKS

This sleek redhorse is regarded by many as the best eating of suckers (Becker 1983). The shorthead is sensitive to and easily killed by excessive siltation and other forms of pollution (Sule and Skelly 1985). Perhaps surprisingly, spawning occurred in a heavily polluted reach of the Susquehanna River (Gale and Mohr 1976).

Name.—*Macrolepidotum,* "large-scaled"; *breviceps,* "short head."

Golden redhorse   *Moxostoma erythrurum* (Rafinesque)

SYSTEMATICS

The golden redhorse was described in 1818 from the Ohio River and three tributary drainages. The tortuous taxonomic and nomenclatural history of this member of the subgenus *Moxostoma* was unraveled by Hubbs (1930a) and Jenkins (1970); Jenkins intends to designate a neotype. Two races were recognized by Jenkins (1970), one in the Tallapoosa system of the Mobile drainage, the other in the remainder of the range.

Moxostoma erythrurum was considered by Jenkins (1970) to be advanced and most closely related to *M. carinatum*, based mainly on the large head tubercles and dusky-stripe nuptial color in both. Smith's (1992) arrangement is the same. Buth (1978) placed *M. erythrurum* closest to *M. anisurum* and distant from *M. carinatum*.

DESCRIPTION

Materials.—From Jenkins (1970) and 43 more collections; counts given only from populations of Virginia and extralimital portions of systems heading in Virginia. Life color based on 22 Virginia or eastern Tennessee specimens.

Anatomy.—A redhorse with lateral line scales usually 40–43, pelvic rays typically 9, bicolored upper body scales, and plicate lips; adults are 200–375 mm SL. Body form moderate, slightly compressed, dorsal profile low or moderate; caudal peduncle moderate or short and deep. Dorsal fin margin concave; caudal lobes about equal, usually pointed, notch shallow or moderately deep. Head moderate, convex dorsally; snout blunt or slightly rounded, tip little in advance of upper lip; eye moderate or large, lateral.

Lips medium or large; posterior angle usually 90–130°, tending widest in adult; surfaces deeply plicate. Pharyngeal arch moderate, teeth comblike. Gas bladder 3-chambered. Tuberculation of body and fins basically as in *M. duquesnei*;

strikingly different in having medium and large tubercles on snout, cheek, and often elsewhere on head of male.

Meristics.—Lateral line complete, scales (39)40–43(45); circumbody scales (29)30–33(36); circumpeduncle scales (11)12(14), almost always 12; predorsal scale rows (12)14–17(19). Dorsal rays (11)13–14(15); caudal rays (16)18(19), almost always 18; anal rays 7; pelvic rays (8)9–10, usually 9; pectoral rays (15)16–18(19).

Color in Preservative.—As in *M. duquesnei* except body slightly paler overall, scale medians distinctly paler than dusky margins, thus scales appear bicolored, marginated.

Color in Life Plate 21.—Very similar in variability to *M. duquesnei*, except back usually more tan, copper, or bronze, side tending more yellow-gold or brassy; some large juveniles basically silvery at least in certain lights.

Spawning fish have dusky or dark markings: midlateral stripe from snout to caudal base; a narrower and often interrupted, horizontal stripe dorsolaterally, this stripe on each side of body connected across anterior nape; and dorsal saddles. Gold stripe between dark stripes and extending across occiput. Occurrence and intensity of pattern in male and female correlate directly with peaks of spawning and agonistic behavior; pattern extremely ephemeral, lost upon capture of specimens. Pattern observed in Back Creek of Roanoke drainage and the Powell River.

Some aspects of the nuptial pattern were reported from Michigan, Illinois, and Ohio (Reighard 1920; Smith 1977; Page and Johnston 1990a); Reighard and Smith also noted bright orange or white blotches or elongate spots on body of some fish. Spawning males in Missouri have broad yellowish stripe along upper side, stripe absent in females (Pflieger 1975, in litt., Moreau River). Some spawning males in Missouri had a slightly dusky stripe, others a dark one (W. N. Roston, photographs); other dark marks would be obscured owing to the posture of the fish.

Larvae.—Some counts in Snyder (1979); described by Fuiman and Witman (1979) and Fuiman (1982c).

Fish 140 *Moxostoma erythrurum* juvenile 163 mm SL (REJ 1039), VA, Montgomery County, South Fork Roanoke River, 16 September 1983.

COMPARISON

See *M. duquesnei*.

BIOLOGY

Natural history aspects were studied most intensively in Iowa (Meyer 1962) and Ohio (Smith 1977). The golden redhorse eats aquatic insects, other invertebrates, and detritus; small amounts of algae are taken (Meyer 1962; Minckley 1963; Smith 1977; Gatz 1979; Becker 1983). Diel activity is similar to that of black and silver redhorses. Aggregations repeatedly course the length of a pool during day and apparently at night, intensifying feeding activity at daybreak and dusk (Smith 1977). We observed a single adult, and another time a small group, feeding and being followed by a juvenile smallmouth bass, which apparently was seeking invertebrates stirred up by the suckers.

Depending on the population, some individuals first spawn at age 3, 4, or 5; maximum longevity is 11 years. Adult females tend to grow faster than adult males. Average lengths at age 5 of numerous populations west and north of Virginia range 254–551 mm TL (Jackson 1956; Purkett 1958; Meyer 1962; Baker 1966; Carlander 1969; Becker 1983; Curry and Spacie 1984). Faster growth tended to occur in reservoirs. The largest Virginia specimen is 400 mm SL (about 500 mm TL). The largest reported is 660 mm TL, 2.0 kg (4.5 pounds) from Ohio (Trautman 1981).

Golden redhorse are mid-spring to late spring spawners. In some years in Missouri, spawning begins in the third week of April, and in other years it continues into early June there and in Minnesota; these periods bracket those reported for other states. Reproduction at any one site may last only about five days. Spawning temperatures range 10–22.5°C, mean, 17.9; the mean may be low because two authors reported only minimum temperature (Hankinson 1932; Cross 1967; Eddy and Underhill 1974; Pflieger 1975; Burr and Morris 1977; Smith 1977; Trautman 1981; Becker 1983; Curry and Spacie 1984; Page and Johnston 1990a). Spawning was observed in Virginia during day and night on 23–24 April 1971, water 13°C, and 24 May 1969, 19.5–21.5°C.

No spawning migration was found by Gerking (1953) and Curry and Spacie (1984), and many fish tagged by Smith (1977) had not migrated. In some areas spawning is preceded by upstream migration (e.g., Pflieger 1975; our observations in small streams). Spawning sites are gravel beds in often very shallow runs and riffles. A trio of two males and one female consummate the typical spawning act, as in most suckers, but other breeding activities are specialized. Males are highly aggressive, defending spawning sites or individual distances usually by forceful butting with the ram of snout tubercles.

Repeated localized spawning sometimes results in a shallow substrate depression (Reighard 1920 [as *M. "aureolum"*]; Eddy and Underhill 1974; Smith 1977; E. A. Lachner [personal communication] in James drainage; Jenkins' observations in Roanoke and Tennessee drainages). M. B. Trautman (personal communication in 1968) observed *M. erythrurum* spawning more often than any other sucker in Ohio, most frequently at night. Often he saw males make a depression in gravel by orienting at an angle to the bottom and moving stones with the snout. He also viewed bottom materials moved by a male "flopping" on its sides, as salmonids construct a redd. No purposeful redd construction was seen in extensive observations in Ohio by Smith (1977, personal communication).

Fecundity is 5,041–25,350 eggs (Meyer 1962; Smith 1977; Curry and Spacie 1979; Becker 1983). A Virginia specimen appears to be a hybrid golden × shorthead redhorse.

HABITAT

Moxostoma erythrurum occupies about the broadest spectrum of warmwater habitats of any redhorse; for example, large creeks, big rivers, natural lakes, and impoundments, in montane to somewhat lowland areas (Jenkins 1970). Tolerance of moderate turbidity and siltation is indicated by the species ranging into lower-gradient situations than does *M. duquesnei*, but *M. erythrurum* avoids or is rare in cooler higher-gradient areas populated by *M. duquesnei*. The golden redhorse is most abundant in moderately clear, unpolluted streams with large permanent pools and well-defined rocky riffles (Pflieger 1975; Trautman 1981). In streams it is essentially restricted to pools (except in the spawning period), occurring over silt, sand, gravel, rubble, and bedrock. Young and small juveniles are found more frequently in shallower areas, often small backwaters, than are adults. Inshore areas are occupied in lakes.

DISTRIBUTION   Map 97

The golden redhorse is widespread in the southern Great Lakes basin, the Mississippi basin, and the Mobile drainage; it is localized in the upper Hudson Bay basin, isolated in a few eastern lower Mississippi River tributaries, and occupies the Atlantic slope in

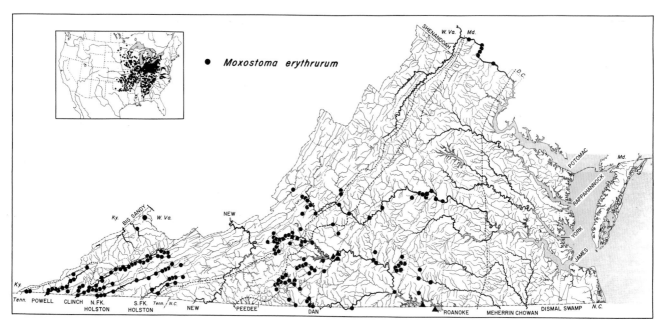

Map 97   Golden redhorse. Open circle on Nottoway River represents rejected record.

the Potomac, James, Chowan, and Roanoke drainages.

Although widely distributed in the James and Roanoke, *M. erythrurum* is sporadic or absent in many of the encompassed systems. In the Chowan it is localized in the upper Meherrin system and not verified from the Nottoway system, despite extensive recent sampling in the latter. The Nottoway River plot (VPI 991 = CU 47993) is based on a specimen probably from the upper Roanoke drainage (see *Luxilus cerasinus*).

The Potomac drainage population of *M. erythrurum* has a peculiar distribution that is probably a result of introduction. The apparent first records from Lunice and Mill creeks, tributaries of the South Branch Potomac River in Grant County, West Virginia, are represented by three specimens (CU 32355, 32357) collected in 1953 by Sullivan (1956). Jenkins (1970), unaware of Sullivan's report and due to the uniqueness of the records, regarded them to be mislabeled and not from the Potomac. However, a series taken in 1971 (NLU 18930) from the South Fork of South Branch Potomac River in Hardy County, West Virginia, influenced Jenkins (*in* Stauffer et al. 1982; *in* Hocutt et al. 1986) to consider the golden redhorse to be present and probably introduced to the Potomac.

Moxostoma erythrurum seems to have spread recently and far in the Potomac drainage from a small

area; it now spans the northern arc of the Potomac River along West Virginia, Maryland, and Virginia (Jenkins *in* Lee et al. 1980), based on collections in 1975–1977 (Davis and Enamait 1982 [some series verified by Jenkins, later used as comparative material by Davis and Enamait]), and on a later survey (E. G. Maurakis, *in* litt.). The golden redhorse also was reported from a tributary in Maryland (Matthews et al. 1978). Open circles plotted on the Shenandoah River (Map 96) are based on samples taken during 1965–1971 and identified as "redhorse sucker" (Surber 1970, 1972); they may represent *M. erythrurum*.

Moxostoma erythrurum is the only redhorse known from the New drainage. It was found in one stream of the Gauley system, West Virginia, in 1976 (Hocutt et al. 1979). It has been considered introduced or native (respectively, Stauffer et al. 1982; Hocutt et al. 1986); we side with introduced.

It appears that the tolerance of *M. erythrurum* to siltation and other kinds of pollution may be exceeded in the Virginia section of the Big Sandy drainage. The Levisa Fork record is dated 1937, that in Knox Creek 1988.

Abundance.—Generally uncommon or common in the Tennessee drainage and in mountains and upper Piedmont of the Roanoke drainage; apparently rare in the Blackwater River of the upper Roanoke drainage and in the upper James, Chowan, and Big Sandy drainages.

REMARKS

The golden redhorse is one of the most common redhorses. It often invades small streams to spawn, then disappears downstream until the next spring. Its breeding behavior is fun to watch for the males are quite aggressive. One male often butts another sideways toward a third male, who returns the hammering; a three-fish shoving match may ensue. The large head tubercles definitely come into play in bouts and often as an aid in clasping the female when spawning.

Name.—*Erythrurum* means "red tail," a misnomer except for some young and small juveniles.

River redhorse   *Moxostoma carinatum* (Cope)

SYSTEMATICS

Cope (1870) named the river redhorse a new genus and species *Placopharynx carinatus*, from Indiana. Based on its large molariform pharyngeal teeth and associated trophic modifications, *Placopharynx* was recognized as a monotypic genus until synonymized with *Moxostoma* by Bailey (1951). Robins and Raney (1956) and Jenkins (1970) allocated the river redhorse to the subgenus *Moxostoma*, owing partly to the still larger pharyngeal arch and teeth of *Moxostoma hubbsi*, a member of the subgenus *Megapharynx* whose other member has a normal arch and teeth; trophic modifications were not decisive for classification. Jenkins (1970) and Smith (1992) considered *M. carinatum* to be most closely related to *M. erythrurum*, but more advanced based on its redd-building and courtship display. Buth (1978) aligned *M. carinatum* with *M. macrolepidotum*.

Moxostoma carinatum has been long known to have a wide distribution but never had been recorded on the Atlantic slope south of the St. Lawrence drainage. Thus it was startling to learn that a population exists in each of the Savannah and Pee Dee rivers (Map 98). Only two specimens are known; one was captured in 1980 by P. E. Stacey, the other in 1985 by M. Humphreys. They are judged to be *carinatum*-like based on the heavy pharyngeal arch, stout molariform teeth, plicate lips, large body size, and other characters. However, they differ notably from each other and from *M. carinatum* elsewhere over the range. More specimens are required to determine the status of this apparently rare south Atlantic slope form. Any fish suspected of such identity should have life colors recorded, living tissue samples fast-frozen, and be preserved carefully with the body straight. (This south Atlantic slope form has recently been identified as the robust redhorse *Moxostoma robustum* [Cope]. See the note in the account of the misnamed "smallfin redhorse *Scartomyzon robustus*," page 491.)

More surprising is the notice from central Mexico of fossil bones of an undescribed species that may be more closely related to *M. carinatum* than to any living sucker in Mexico (Miller and Smith 1986).

DESCRIPTION

Materials.—From Jenkins (1970) and 23 additional series; counts from over the species range except the south Atlantic slope.

Anatomy.—A redhorse with dark scale bases, plicate lips, and a stout pharyngeal arch bearing molariform teeth; adults are 350–550 mm SL. Body moderate in profile, back

Fish 141 *Moxostoma carinatum* juvenile 70 mm SL (REJ 986), VA, Scott County, Clinch River, 17 June 1983.

little elevated, body nearly round or, in adult male, quite compressed; caudal peduncle moderate. Dorsal fin margin usually concave, occasionally straight; caudal with upper lobe pointed and usually longer than lower lobe, the lower lobe usually rounded, notch moderate or deep. Head moderate, convex dorsally; snout blunt or slightly rounded, the tip slightly in advance of upper lip; eye moderate, lateral.

Lips medium or large; posterior angle usually 110–150°; surfaces deeply plicate. Pharyngeal arch very stout; lower teeth quite enlarged, molariform, the broad, convexly rounded crown of freshly replaced teeth becoming flat or concave with wear; uppermost teeth comblike. Gas bladder 3-chambered. Tuberculation much as in *M. erythrurum*, featuring medium and large tubercles on snout, cheek, and elsewhere on head, except body usually lacks tubercles.

Meristics.—Lateral line complete, scales (41)42–44(46); circumbody scales (30)32–35(37); circumpeduncle scales 12–13(15), usually 12; predorsal scale rows (13)15–17(18). Dorsal rays (12)13–14(15); caudal rays 18; anal rays 7; pelvic rays (8)9(10); pectoral rays (15)16–18(19).

Color in Preservative.—Essentially as stated for *M. macrolepidotum*, except in medium-sized juvenile to adult the scales in posteriormost vertical row on caudal base often darkly outlined posteriorly, forming a fine zig-zag line.

Color in Life.—Back olive or tan with brass or copper reflections; side yellow, brassy, or coppery, becoming silver on flank, scale bases with subtle yellow and green iridescence; venter white. Small fish tend to be dominantly silvery. Caudal and dorsal fins wholly or only distally red, often bright crimson, red most intense in adult; lower fins orange to orange-red (Jenkins 1970; Gilbert 1978c: cover plate).

Nuptial male with dark midlateral stripe from snout tip to above anal area, head appearing dark-masked underwater (Cahaba River, Alabama fish, P. A. Hackney, in litt.; G. H. Clemmer, personal communication). In Wisconsin, spawning male dark olive, female rich gold, on side (Becker 1983). Lack of mention of distinct dark stripe in Wisconsin males may be related to its ephemeral nature, as found in Alabama and as occurs in *M. erythrurum*.

Larvae.—Some counts in Snyder (1979); some aspects indicated by Hackney et al. (1968); described by Fuiman (1982c).

COMPARISON

A primary feature of *M. carinatum* is the heavy pharyngeal arch bearing molariform lower teeth (Figure 11E). Removal of the arch may be difficult. A quick method for discerning relative arch size without dissection is described just above the *Key. Moxostoma carinatum* is also recognizable from the combination of a moderate-sized head, entirely plicate lips, and dark scale bases.

A helpful character for preliminary identification of small *M. carinatum* is the usual presence of a bold black spot (melanophore) at the base of the gill rakers on the midhalf of the first gill arch. Medium-sized juveniles often have several spots along the basal portion of rakers; some small young (less than 40 mm SL) lack spots; spots were not found in adults. This trait appears occasionally in some other redhorses, but it is developed most frequently and intensely in *M. carinatum*.

BIOLOGY

Life history data are primarily from studies conducted in Alabama by Hackney et al. (1968) and Tatum and Hackney (1970), in Ontario by Parker and McKee (1984b), and from reviews by Jenkins (1970) and McAllister et al. (1985). The enlarged pharyngeal masticatory apparatus of the river redhorse is adapted for crushing shells of mussels, snails, and crayfishes. Mollusks, including the introduced Asiatic clam *Corbicula*, often are eaten in high frequency, particularly by adults, but immature aquatic insects also are important forage (Forbes and Richardson 1920; Hackney et al. 1968; Eastman 1977; Parker and McKee 1984b). Mollusks formed only 19% of the gut contents of 12 Quebec specimens, the rest largely being amphipod crustaceans and, particularly, mayfly larvae (Mongeau et al. 1986). Detritus occasionally forms a small percentage of gut contents. Evidence exists of feeding by sight (McAllister et al. 1985).

Both sexes were thought by Tatum and Hackney (1970) to mature in 3 years, but they had difficulty in aging specimens by scales. The river redhorse scale depicted by Tatum and Hackney (1970: Figure 2) was restudied by P. A. Hackney (in litt.): two annuli were repositioned, one annulus was reidentified as a check (false annulus), and the outer check was regarded as an annulus. The scale was stated by Tatum and Hackney (1970) to be from an age-3 specimen but we believe it could be age 5. Length frequencies of small wild-caught specimens (Jenkins 1970) indicate slower early growth than that concluded by Tatum and Hackney; the ages that they determined may be underestimates.

The smallest mature male was 380 mm TL, female 411 mm (Tatum and Hackney 1970; P. A. Hackney, in litt.). The oldest known *M. carinatum* are 14 years (Parker and McKee 1984b) and 16 years (J. M. Stubbs, in litt.). Means of lengths at age 5 were 246–424 mm TL (Purkett 1958; Becker 1983; McAllister et al. 1985). Other growth data are by Elkin (1956), Jackson (1956), Ward (1960), and Baker (1966); see also Carlander (1969). The slowest growth occurred in Ontario. Growth in Ozark streams is slower than for other redhorses during the first few years of life, but eventually the river redhorse surpasses the others (Pflieger 1975). Perhaps faster growth is associated with a shift to heavier feeding on mollusks.

Moxostoma carinatum attains fairly large size in Virginia; a small sample of anglers reported it to reach about 2.7 kg ("6 pounds"). One of 610 mm TL (24 inches) was taken in the South Fork Holston River in 1973 (J. C. Feeman, in litt.). Specimens over 600 mm TL (23.6 inches) have been widely reported (Swingle 1965; Phillips and Underhill 1971; Pflieger 1975; Smith 1979; Becker 1983; Parker and McKee 1984b; Yoder and Beaumier 1986). From Ohio, Trautman (1981) reported a 737-mm TL (29 inches), 4.8-kg (10.5 pounds) fish, and stated that 6.4 kg (14 pounds) is the maximum known to rivermen. Phillips et al. (1982) noted that in Minnesota the species reaches 914 mm ("3 feet") and 6.8 kg ("15 pounds"); but Eddy and Underhill (1974) cited perhaps lesser length ("over 2 feet") for Minnesota fish weighing "up to 15 pounds." A 768-mm TL (30.25 inches), 5.47-kg (12 pounds 1 ounce) specimen, and one of 6.12 kg (13.5 pounds, length unknown) were reported from the Duck River, Tennessee, in 1965 (J. M. Stubbs, in litt.). The heaviest apparent river redhorse reported was 7.26 kg ("16 pounds") from the Flint River, Alabama (Tatum and Hackney 1970).

The upstream spawning run, or perhaps in some cases local movement, brings river redhorse to shoals in mid-April in central Alabama, two to four weeks later than the black redhorse; the breeding period lasts about one week (Hackney et al. 1968; P. A. Hackney, in litt.). In Tennessee, spawning generally occurs within mid-April to early May (J. M. Stubbs, in litt.). In the Ozarks the river redhorse is said to spawn slightly earlier than the black redhorse (Pflieger 1975). Reproduction in Wisconsin apparently occurs during mid-May; *M. erythrurum* spawns then too but in shallower water (Becker 1983). Spawning temperatures range 18–24.3°C. Spawning takes place in gravel and gravel–rubble shoals or runs at depths of 0.2–1.2 m and currents of 0.6–1.0 m/second. Milt or eggs flow freely only from fish that have lost much of the mucous covering.

The reproductive behavior is fascinating for a sucker and for fishes in general. It was observed in the Cahaba River, Alabama, from the vantage of stepladders in the spawning "shoals"—usually shallow areas at the head of gravel-bottomed riffles (Hackney et al. 1968; P. A. Hackney, in litt.). Males precede females to the shoals. Each male excavates a redd by sweeping with the tail, working with the lips, and pushing and rolling with the head and body. Completed redds are large, 1.2–2.4 m across including the

spoil ridge, 1.5–3.0 m long, and 0.2–0.3 m deep. At least eight redds were found in each spawning colony.

The resident male holds the redd; another male often joins. Intermale aggression by butting with the large head tubercles is infrequent. Upon approach by a female, the resident male swims rapidly, rhythmically back and forth across the redd, and is joined by another male in synchronized motion for a few seconds. Then the female takes position between the males and joins the dance. Movement shortly becomes subdued, the trio aligns more tightly, and spawning occurs in typical sucker fashion.

Fecundity is 6,078–23,085 eggs of 3–4 mm diameter (Hackney et al. 1968). A specimen from Missouri appears to be a hybrid involving *M. carinatum* and either *M. erythrurum* or *M. macrolepidotum* (Jenkins 1970).

HABITAT

The river redhorse is aptly named, for it essentially populates only large streams and rivers. Some medium-sized streams are ascended on the spawning run; during most of the year, generally the only *M. carinatum* found in such waters are young and small juveniles. Pflieger (1975) stated that this species seems less tolerant of turbidity and siltation than the other four redhorses in Missouri. The same conclusion was reached in other regional studies and from discerning reductions of the historical range of the species (Jenkins 1970).

Moxostoma carinatum tends to be most numerous in well-flowing portions of pools and moderate and swift runs having minimally silted substrates of gravel, rubble, and boulder (Parker and McKee 1984b; Yoder and Beaumier 1986; our data). Individuals also may be distributed throughout pools. Adults apparently avoid shallow portions of pools at least during daylight, at which time young and small juveniles often are found there and in backwaters. Several records exist for natural lakes and impoundments in much of the range; *M. carinatum* is fairly abundant in Fontana Reservoir, North Carolina (Baker 1966).

DISTRIBUTION   Map 98

The river redhorse inhabits intermontane, upland, and rolling regions of the southern Great Lakes–St. Lawrence basin, the Mississippi basin, and the Gulf slope drainages from the Pearl to the Escambia. A form occupies the Atlantic slope in the Savannah and Pee Dee drainages. *Moxostoma carinatum* has been

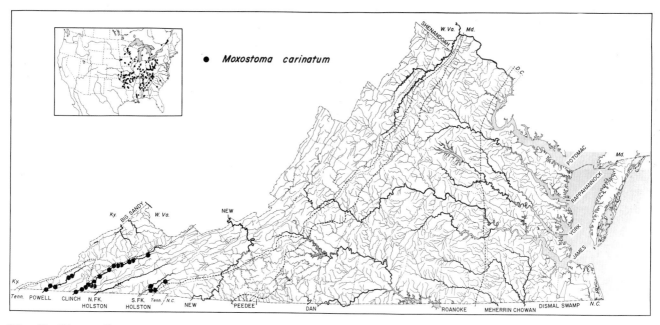

Map 98   River redhorse.

extirpated from much of its range, particularly in the Plains (Jenkins 1970 *in* Lee et al. 1980). However, owing mainly to proper sampling techniques, recent surveys have rediscovered a few populations and found a few new ones (Phillips and Underhill 1967; Trautman 1981; Parker and McKee 1984b; Yoder and Beaumier 1986; see also *Systematics*).

In Virginia the river redhorse occupies 4 of the 5 main trunks of the Tennessee drainage. Lower Copper Creek is the only tributary of which we are aware that is ascended by spawning migrants, which swim as far as 13 rkm to Spivey Mill Dam.

Copper Creek evidently served as a refuge for *M. carinatum* during the late June 1967 fish kill in the Clinch River. Recruitment to the river occurred rapidly; several young were taken in late July and early August 1967 from the Clinch at 1 rkm below Copper Creek. The river redhorse now strongly populates much or all of the affected section; reestablishment undoubtedly stemmed also from the river above Carbo, from Tennessee, and perhaps from tributaries other than Copper Creek.

Extirpation of the river redhorse from the North Fork Holston River is presumed, based on the extensive pollution by industrial effluents from Saltville. Reentry to most of the river would have been barred by Holston Mill Dam in middle Scott County. A recruitment population may not have existed; the main Holston River has been degraded by pollution from Kingsport, at the North Fork–South Fork junction. The only Holston River record is from far down-

stream, below Cherokee Dam, Tennessee, in 1941 (D. A. Etnier, in litt.). The South Fork Holston population in Virginia and Tennessee has been reduced by impoundments and pollution.

As with the other four redhorses in the southern Ohio basin, fairly recent records of *M. carinatum* exist for the Kentucky portion of the Big Sandy drainage near the Virginia line (Jenkins 1970; Howell 1981), but most of these species apparently have been extirpated in the Virginia part. There is only one Big Sandy, Virginia record of a redhorse (*M. erythrurum*) after 1937.

The presence of the *carinatum*-like form in the Savannah and Pee Dee drainages indicates that it inhabits (or is extirpated from) the interjacent Santee drainage. Clearly it is a big-river inhabitant, hence easily missed by seiners. Redhorses of 6–7 pounds reported from the Santee and Pee Dee as *M. erythrurum* or *Scartomyzon robustus* by Cope (1870) likely were this form (see *Systematics*).

Abundance.—A good estimate of the general abundance of *M. carinatum* is lacking for Virginia because of the mobility of the species and the difficulty in adequately sampling its big-water habitat. Based on the number of times that it was captured in the Clinch and Powell rivers (at least 26), from the frequency of seining small specimens therein, and from reports by local persons, likely it is uncommon or common in these rivers. It was common in the Clinch River in western Scott County judging from the number of carcasses during the 1967 fish kill. Probably it is uncommon or rare in the Middle and South forks of Holston River.

REMARKS

The river redhorse is one of the largest, least numerous, and trophically and behaviorally most divergent species of *Moxostoma*; thus it is one of the most fascinating. The tubercle-armored and black-flushed nuptial male is magnificent. *Moxostoma carinatum* is mysterious for its long undetected residence in some rivers, most notably the distinctive populations discovered on the south Atlantic slope in 1980–1985.

The heavy pharyngeal arch and molariform teeth of *M. carinatum* have been stressed as a means of species identification, but also hidden internally are further adaptations for crushing snails and mussels. Compared to other redhorses, the muscles that work the tooth arches are enlarged, skull bones on which the muscles originate are strengthened and more firmly sutured, and the chewing pad (and its bony support) on the underside of the skull is large and tough (Jenkins 1970; Eastman 1977).

The unique behavioral repertoire of redd-building and the three-fish courtship "dance" has been studied only in an Alabama river. It would be interesting to determine the geographic extent of the pattern. Persistence and perhaps luck will be involved in finding spawning fish in clear water from a vantage that permits observation of details. Our few attempts in Virginia have failed.

The river redhorse, including its south Atlantic slope form, has fared poorly over the last 100 years, being depleted or extirpated in much of its homeland (Jenkins 1970). Chiefly to blame are impoundments, siltation, and pollution. Its anatomical specializations would seem advantageous for feeding on mollusks that are rarely or never eaten by other suckers and most regional fishes in general. However, in many North American river basins the molluscan fauna has also suffered. The only other sucker with molariform teeth—*Moxostoma hubbsi* living in a small portion of the St. Lawrence drainage—is endangered. Trophic specialization can be a liability.

To many people in western Virginia, *M. carinatum* is *the* redhorse, owing to its large size, palatability, and gameness at the end of a line. It is often baitfished in the state; here and elsewhere during spawning time it is noosed and snagged by gangs of hooks (e.g., Hackney and Tatum 1966). Virginia has had a controversial law allowing suckers to be shot by rifles during the spawning period in the Clinch River of Scott County and the South Fork Holston River in Washington County. The quarry of many "hunters" is the river redhorse. Judging from the numbers of gunners present on highway and low suspension bridges during springtime when rivers are clear, their impact on the population could be substantial. The bridges often are located at fords or shoals which are potential spawning grounds.

The river redhorse apparently has been extirpated from the North Fork Holston and upper Big Sandy drainages. Only four populations exist in Virginia; an entire population could be lost with one catastrophic event. Hence we regard this species to have special concern status in the state. The Atlantic slope form is considered to warrant threatened status in its full range: North Carolina, South Carolina, and Georgia (Williams et al. 1989).

Name.—*Carinatum* means "keeled," in reference to very low ridges on the dorsal aspect of the skull. The undescribed form was dubbed bighead redhorse by Williams et al. (1989); however, one of the two specimens has a small head.

Silver redhorse   *Moxostoma anisurum* (Rafinesque)

SYSTEMATICS

The silver redhorse, subgenus *Moxostoma*, was described in 1820 from the Ohio River and large tributaries by Rafinesque, who did not preserve type specimens. Because the description indicates that Rafinesque had more than one species at hand, Jenkins intends to designate a neotype to affix the name *anisurum* to the silver redhorse.

The Atlantic slope populations from Virginia to Georgia were recognized as a species, *M. collapsum*, by Robins and Raney (1956). Jenkins (1970) downgraded this form to a race of *M. anisurum*, and Buth (1978) concurred. However, it may differ on a higher level based on the more elongate body form and smaller head parts (and perhaps its tendency to occupy smaller streams) than in the Mississippi basin populations.

Although *M. anisurum* and *M. pappillosum* are the only *Moxostoma* with a V-shaped lower lip, they differ in lip texture and several other ways; Jenkins (1970) and Buth (1978) did not regard them as intimately related. However, the urohyal bone of the two species indicates that they are more closely related to each other than to other *Moxostoma* (W. C. Dickinson,

Fish 142 *Moxostoma anisurum* juvenile 135 mm SL (REJ 1039), VA, Montgomery County, South Fork Roanoke River, 16 September 1983.

in litt.). That relationship is reflected in Smith's (1992) cladogram, which shows the two species as the most primitive *Moxostoma*.

DESCRIPTION

Materials.—From Jenkins (1970) plus 30 more lots comprising populations over the species range. Color in life from Jenkins (1970) and 8 more Virginia samples.

Anatomy.—A redhorse of moderate or high-backed form, with a V-shaped lower lip, lip surfaces semipapillose, dorsal rays usually 14–15, dorsal fin margin usually very slightly concave or straight, and scale bases typically pale; adults are 300–450 mm SL. Profile moderate or slightly high-backed on south Atlantic slope, back prominently elevated elsewhere; body slightly or moderately compressed; caudal peduncle moderate or short and deep. Dorsal fin margin usually straight or very slightly concave, occasionally slightly convex; straight or convex margin occurs most frequently in adult; upper caudal fin tip usually pointed, lower tip usually slightly rounded, lobes equal in length or upper longer, notch moderate or deep. Head moderate or large, convex dorsally; snout blunt or slightly rounded, tip usually little exceeding upper lip; eye moderate or large, lateral.

Lips V-shaped, medial portion of posterior margin of lower lip forming acute angle; lateral portion usually abruptly narrowed toward end; lips often pendant in large juvenile and adult; ventral surface of upper and lower lips with fine plicae that are transversely grooved to form papilla-like subdivisions, these being low and generally oblong (semipapillose condition); front of upper lip smooth or shallowly plicate, not papillose. Pharyngeal arch moderate, teeth comblike. Gas bladder 3-chambered. Tuberculation basically as in *M. duquesnei*.

Meristics.—Lateral line complete, scales (38)40–42(46); circumbody scales (28)32–35(39); circumpeduncle scales 12(15); predorsal scale rows (12)13–15(18). Dorsal rays (12)14–15(17); caudal rays (17)18(19); anal rays 7; pelvic rays (8)9(10); pectoral rays (16)17–19(20).

Color in Preservative.—Basically as in *M. erythrurum*.

Color in Life.—Dorsum tan, brown, or olive; side mostly shining silver, yellow, gold, copper, or brassy, or mixtures of these, and yellow and pale green iridescence on scale bases; young and juvenile are the most silvery. Hackney et al. (1971) described brassy color on body of nuptial Alabama fish, whereas Smith (1977) noted bright metallic silver on reproductive specimens in Ohio. Virginia fish exhibit about the same body color during the spawning run as in the rest of the year. Dorsal and caudal fins olive, dusky, or slate in most fish; some small fish with vague red in part of dorsal and caudal; lower fins pale orange or orange-red.

Larvae.—Some counts in Snyder (1979); small young described by Fuiman (1982c).

COMPARISON

Collectively, *Moxostoma anisurum* and *M. pappillosum* are sorted from other redhorses by the V-shaped lips and by subdivision of the ventral surfaces of the lips into round or oblong, papilla-like elements (Figure 42). Interspecific differences additional to those in the *Key* include: (1) body form usually [higher backed in *anisurum vs.* more elongate in *pappillosum*]; (2) scale bases anterodorsolaterally usually [pale *vs.* dark]; (3) caudal fin of adult in life usually [olive, dusky, or slate *vs.* reddish at least distally or along upper and lower edges].

BIOLOGY

The most intensive study of silver redhorse biology was conducted in Iowa (Meyer 1962). This species feeds on insect larvae, microcrustaceans, crayfishes, mollusks, algae, and detritus, and has taken fry of shiners (Meyer 1962; Smith 1977; Gatz 1979; Becker 1983). Individuals were present in pools in the upper Roanoke drainage but were not seen feeding in runs, unlike the other redhorse species present.

Silver redhorse males and females first spawn at ages of 5, 6, or 7; very rarely do they live 12–14 years

(Meyer 1962; Hackney et al. 1971; Smith 1977; Becker 1983). Meyer (1962) noted no pronounced differences in growth rates between the sexes, but Hackney et al. (1971) found that after age 6, growth rates of females exceeded those of males. Average lengths at age 5 in eight populations from Alabama to Wisconsin were 261–503 mm TL (above authors; Purkett 1958). The largest specimen known from close to Virginia is 469 mm SL (535 TL, converted from Carlander 1969) from the North Carolina portion of Gaston Reservoir. Maximum sizes are 711 mm TL (28 inches), 4.3 kg (9.5 pounds) from Alabama (Hackney et al. 1971), and 4.5 kg (10 pounds) reported by rivermen in Ohio (Trautman 1981).

Moxostoma anisurum is one of the earliest-spawning redhorses (Greeley 1929). In Alabama it spawned during 21–25 March 1967, on 1 April 1969, and on 8 April 1970 (Hackney et al. 1971; P. A. Hackney, in litt.). In Tennessee it is often called "March horse" as the run often starts then (J. M. Stubbs, in litt.). Generally the spawning period in southern and mid-latitudes of its interior range is given as April and early May; water temperatures are 11–15°C, mean, 13.5 (Meyer 1962; Pflieger 1975; Smith 1977; Curry and Spacie 1984). Breeding time of the south Atlantic slope race appears similar; upstream migrants in nuptial condition, some possibly spawning, were found in Virginia during 31 March–29 April of various years. Migration of silver redhorse was studied by Hall (1972, as *M. collapsum*).

Spawning occurs in shallow riffles over gravel and rubble (Meyer 1962; Hackney et al. 1971; Pflieger 1975). Scott (1967) stated that a pair of large adults were observed spawning in the Chippewa River, Ontario, on 9 June 1954, at a depth of about 1.5 m. This would be deeper than that known for most redhorses, and would render the fish difficult to identify without capture. The presence of only two fish (if they were actually spawning) would be unusual; spawning redhorses almost always congregate in greater numbers and spawn as a trio. Fecundity is 14,910–36,340 eggs (Meyer 1962; Becker 1983).

HABITAT

In the Mississippi basin and north, the silver redhorse typically inhabits large streams and, apparently more frequently, small to big rivers. It occupies such waters on the south Atlantic slope, but at least in the Roanoke and Neuse drainages, juveniles and adults tend to occur in medium-sized streams more frequently than west of the slope. Natural and artificial lakes are inhabited in many areas (Jenkins 1970). In north Alabama young silver redhorse move down-stream to Wheeler Reservoir and remain there until they mature (Hackney et al. 1971).

Within streams, *M. anisurum* is a pool dweller. In Missouri it prefers larger, deeper pools with moderately clear water and gravel bottom (Pflieger 1975). In Illinois it associates mainly with firm-bottomed pools (Smith 1977). In Ohio and Wisconsin its typical riverine habitat is said to be of low or base gradient and to have minimal siltation (Trautman 1981; Becker 1983), but Smith (1977) found this species in pools over sand and silt and not gravel in Ohio. In Virginia, medium and large silver redhorse occupy the deeper portions of pools in moderate-gradient streams; they occur in about equal frequency over silt, sand, gravel, and rocky areas. Young and small juveniles often are taken in small pools and fairly shallow backwaters. Only migrating adults are observed in runs and riffles.

DISTRIBUTION   Map 99

The silver redhorse is widespread in the Hudson Bay, Great Lakes–St. Lawrence, and upper and central Mississippi basins, and in south Atlantic slope drainages from the Altamaha to the Chowan. Four small *M. anisurum* (USNM 40603, UMMZ [IU 7918]) from Shingle Creek of the Nansemond system, a tributary of the James River estuary, had been long identified as *M. pappillosum*, following Jordan (1889b). The identification was corrected by Jenkins (1970) but the locality data probably are faulty (*Biogeography*).

The only Virginia record in the Powell River is of 10 specimens (one young verified by Jenkins) taken in 1968 (TVA 1970). The two Clinch River records are from sampling in 1965 by Wollitz (1967a). *Moxostoma anisurum* was rare in the Clinch River before and after the 1967 kill. We found none among 72 redhorses between Copper Creek and the state line in the wake of the kill. None were among at least 90 *Moxostoma* taken by rotenone at the state line in 1972 (Masnik 1974). *Moxostoma anisurum* occupies the Clinch River in Tennessee above Norris Reservoir based on one adult (REJ 503) taken at 30 rkm below the Virginia line in 1971.

As with other *Moxostoma*, the silver redhorse may temporarily enter Virginia tributaries of the Big Sandy drainage from Kentucky.

Abundance.—Usually uncommon or common in the Chowan and Roanoke drainages; extremely rare in the Tennessee drainage.

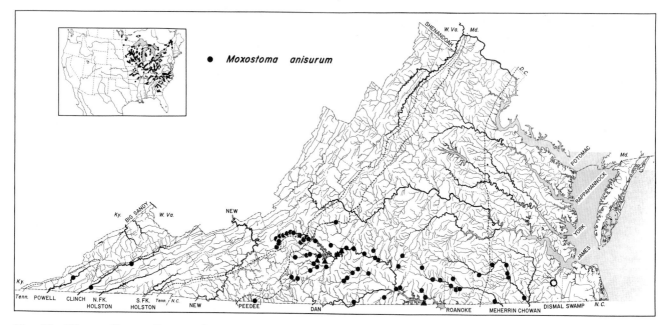

Map 99   Silver redhorse. Open circle at Dismal Swamp fringe represents a collection with problematic locality data.

REMARKS

The riverine habitude of the silver redhorse in the Mississippi basin contrasts sharply with its typical extension into medium-sized streams on the Atlantic slope of Virginia and at least northern North Carolina. A biogeographic enigma, presented also by other redhorses, is the lack of a population in the New drainage between the major population groups of the Atlantic slope and Mississippi basin.

Name.—*Anisurum*, "unequal tail," from the upper lobe of the tail often being longer than the lower lobe.

V-lip redhorse   *Moxostoma pappillosum* (Cope)

SYSTEMATICS

Moxostoma pappillosum is the only redhorse now recognized as a species among the eight nominal forms of the subgenus *Moxostoma* that were described by Cope (1870) from North Carolina. Because Cope's specimens of *M. pappillosum* no longer exist and the description applies partly to *M. anisurum*, Jenkins (1970) intends to designate a neotype.

The V-lip redhorse was believed by Robins and Raney (1956) to be basically related to *M. carinatum*. Buth (1978) regarded it as the most primitive species in the subgenus *Moxostoma*, clustering closest to *M. macrolepidotum* and *M. carinatum*. Current thought is that *M. pappillosum* and *M. anisurum* are sister species and primitive in the genus; see silver redhorse.

DESCRIPTION

Materials.—From Jenkins (1970) plus 26 later series comprising all populations. Color in life from Jenkins (1970) and 8 more Virginia series.

Anatomy.—A redhorse of rather shallow form, with V-shaped lower lip, lip surfaces finely papillose, dorsal rays usually 12–13, dorsal fin margin moderately concave or distinctly falcate, and scale bases dark; adults are 230–325 mm SL. Body profile elongate, little or not at all elevated toward dorsal fin; body nearly round or slightly compressed; caudal peduncle length moderate, depth shallow. Dorsal fin margin falcate (hooked anteriorly), moderately concave or, occasionally and most frequently in small fish, slightly concave; caudal lobes pointed, equal in length or almost so, notch moderate or deep. Head moderately long, particularly through a prominent snout, convex dorsally; snout truncate or broadly rounded, tip generally slightly exceeding upper lip; eye moderate or large.

Lips V-shaped, posterior edge of halves of lower lip forming acute angle; lower lip generally mostly full, usually not abruptly narrowed posterolaterally but evenly tapered to corners; entire exposed surface (when mouth in normal closed position) with slightly oval to round papillae, papillae generally small. Pharyngeal arch moderate, teeth comblike. Gas bladder 3-chambered. Tuberculation much as in *M. duquesnei*.

Meristics.—Lateral line complete, scales (39)42–44(46); circumbody scales (29)30–33(36); circumpeduncle scales

Fish 143 *Moxostoma pappillosum* juvenile 128 mm SL (REJ 1000), VA, Bedford County, Goose Creek, 12 July 1983.

(11)12; predorsal scale rows (13)14–17(18). Dorsal rays (11)12–13(15); caudal rays (16)18; anal rays 7(8); pelvic rays (8)9(10); pectoral rays (15)17–18(20).

Color in Preservative.—Essentially as in *M. macrolepidotum*, except dorsal fin margin often duskiest along margin, and dusky caudal spot or blotch often present in small young.

Color in Life Plate 21.—Back tan-olive, often with silver sheen; side silver, gold, or brassy, scale bases dark with green and brassy reflections. Dorsal fin olive or dusky, occasionally faint red anteriorly. Caudal fin olive or dusky, generally with faint red distally about median rays, slightly deeper red through lobes, but often red restricted to edge of lobes or absent. Anal fin medium or pale orange, orangered, or white. Paired fins orange or pale red. Sexual dichromatism and distinctive nuptial color unknown.

COMPARISON

See account of *M. anisurum*.

BIOLOGY

The V-lip redhorse has received little attention from fishery biologists and ichthyologists. Ostracods, vascular plants, and silt were ingested by a few specimens (Gatz 1979); aquatic insects almost certainly are consumed. Based on lip and brain morphology, *M. pappillosum* seems capable of greater taste discrimination than most other redhorses (Miller and Evans 1965). On five occasions, up to 25 juveniles and adults were observed feeding during mid-day in Back Creek and the upper Roanoke River. Foraging occurred in pool shallows and slow runs, occasionally swift runs, and over sand, gravel, and rubble. The body was held above the bottom and the pectoral fins were spread; each pectoral fin was alternately lifted and placed on the bottom in a scooping or flicking movement. Stones frequently were moved when feeding. All V-lip redhorses fed similarly and in a manner different from other redhorses at the same site.

The V-lip redhorse is one of the smaller species of redhorse. Cope (1870) stated that it reaches 300 mm ("one foot") and does not exceed 0.45 kg ("one pound"). Sixteen tuberculate males were 215–337 mm SL, mean, 269, and 6 adult females were 250–363 mm, mean, 286. The largest Virginia specimen is 271 mm SL; the 363-mm SL specimen, the largest known, is from the North Carolina side of Gaston Reservoir. We aged a 273-mm SL female as at least 6 years.

Based on tuberculation and gonad development, *M. pappillosum* apparently is the latest-spawning *Moxostoma* in Virginia. Tubercles attain moderate development in northern North Carolina and Virginia during late April and early May, and remain strongly developed in some males into early July in Virginia. Milting males were taken on 1 June in North Carolina (F. F. Snelson, in litt.) and as late as 11 July in Virginia. A partly gravid female was caught on 25 June and a spent one on 11 July, both in Virginia. Further evidence of late spawning is the small size (compared to syntopic redhorses) of young *M. pappillosum* during fall in the upper Roanoke drainage: 26 taken on 27 September 1971 or 4 October 1982 are 24–38 mm SL, mean, 31.

On 13 June an angler in the upper Blackwater River of the upper Roanoke drainage told us that it was a bit early for the redhorse run to reach the section. We apply the statement to *M. pappillosum* because that species is fairly common through the stream, *M. erythrurum* is very rare, *M. anisurum* is an early spawner, and *M. macrolepidotum*, a fairly early spawner, is unknown that far upstream.

HABITAT

Moxostoma pappillosum favors warm, medium-sized streams to medium rivers of moderate or gentle gradient. Occasionally it is taken in large creeks on the middle and outer Piedmont. It inhabits streams that typically are clear and some that most often are slightly or moderately turbid and moderately silted.

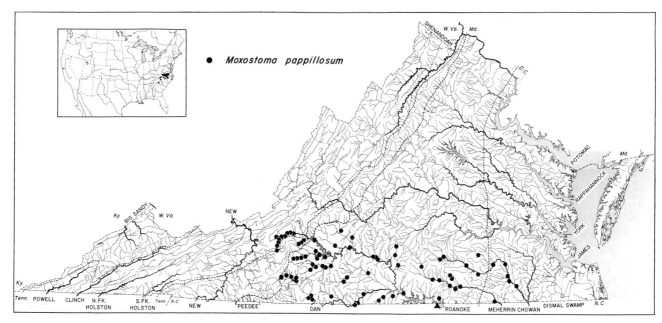

Moxostoma pappillosum

Map 100   V-lip redhorse.

Large juveniles and adults occur in pools, foraging there and into runs; young and small juveniles often are found in calm shallows. All stages occur over a variety of soft and hard bottoms. Gaston Reservoir and probably other impoundments are occupied but *M. pappillosum* seems to populate such waters less than does *M. anisurum* and *M. macrolepidotum*.

DISTRIBUTION   Map 100

Moxostoma pappillosum occupies the major Atlantic slope drainages from the Chowan and Roanoke south to the Santee in South Carolina. The record from the Dismal Swamp periphery, some from the Carolinas, and those south of the Santee are erroneous (Jenkins 1970; Rohde et al. 1979; *M. anisurum* account). Records from Pee Dee and Santee drainage reservoirs, North Carolina (Menhinick et al. 1974) need verification.

The V-lip redhorse is generally distributed in the upper Roanoke drainage, becoming sporadic on the middle Piedmont and eastward. It extends into the Coastal Plain in the Chowan drainage, but like the other Virginia redhorses, it is unknown from the swampy Blackwater system of the Chowan. It may ascend into the Virginia portion of the Pee Dee drainage.

Abundance.—When found in Virginia the V-lip redhorse is usually uncommon or common compared to redhorses in general, but is rare or absent in several well-sampled stream sections near centers of abundance. It is rare in the southern portion of its range in the Carolinas.

REMARKS

Ecologically and phylogenetically, the V-lip redhorse is one of the poorest known of its group. The time is right for a solid life history study. Cope (1870) stated that *M. pappillosum* was quite abundant in parts of the Pee Dee and Santee drainages where he observed net and trap fisheries. It was highly valued as the best of food among suckers. Unless Cope was misinformed or he misidentified many suckers as *M. pappillosum*, the abundance of the species has declined in the southern rivers. At the rate suckers were being harvested, Cope questioned that they could sustain their populations.

Name.—*Pappillosum* refers to the papillose (i.e., pimplelike) surface of the lips. The common name V-lip redhorse had been used for *M. collapsum*, but was buried when that form was synonymized with *M. anisurum* (Jenkins 1970). *Moxostoma pappillosum* has been called the suckermouth redhorse, but all redhorses have such a mouth. Because neither common name has been entrenched, we apply the diagnostic "V-lip" to *M. pappillosum*, a move accepted by Robins et al. (1991).

Harelip sucker   *Moxostoma lacerum* (Jordan and Brayton)

BY ROBERT E. JENKINS

SYSTEMATICS

The now-extinct *Lagochila lacera* was presented as a new species, genus, and subfamily (Lagochilinae) from Georgia and Tennessee by Jordan and Brayton (1877). The subfamily was rarely recognized but *Lagochila* held monotypic rank until recently. Its non-protractile upper jaw, uniquely cleft lower lip, and delicate pharyngeal teeth were the early basis for that stature. Its additional suite of trophic and other specializations was noted by Jenkins (1970, later study), and he and G. R. Smith (*in* Bookstein et al. 1985; Smith 1992) detected extensive modification of skull bones. The harelip sucker is a very distinctive catostomid, hence determining its phylogenetic relationships has been quite challenging.

Lagochila was compared with and considered to be related to *Moxostoma* by Jordan and Brayton (1877). Based on their sharing the circumpeduncle scale count of 12, Bailey (1959a) considered *Lagochila* to be derived from the subgenus *Moxostoma*, a relationship corroborated by several other characters (Jenkins 1970). Partly because the closest ally of *Lagochila* was not evident, Jenkins (1970) regarded it to be the terminal, advanced offshoot of the *Moxostoma* lineage. In merging *Lagochila* with *Moxostoma*, Smith (1992) placed the harelip sucker as an advanced member in a group of short-headed redhorses comprising *M. duquesnei*, *M. macrolepidotum*, and *M. poecilurum*.

If one accepts Smith's hypotheses that *Lagochila* belongs in the short-headed group and that the group stemmed transitionally *within* the genealogy of the subgenus *Moxostoma*, then retaining *Lagochila* as a monotypic genus renders *Moxostoma* an unnatural (paraphyletic) group. Two nomenclatural alternatives exist for producing a natural (monophyletic) group. (1) The short-headed group including the harelip sucker could be removed from *Moxostoma* and recognized as a separate genus (resurrection of the name *Teretulus*, Rafinesque 1820, founded on *M. macrolepidotum*, would apply—it is older than the name *Lagochila*). At least one additional generic name change would be warranted for species not placed in the short-headed group. Or, (2) *Lagochila* could be added to *Moxostoma*.

Bailey (1959a) questioned maintaining the genus *Lagochila*, but he followed Hubbs (1930a) and Trautman (1957) in wrongly believing that the harelip sucker differed from redhorses only in lip anatomy. Robins et al. (1991) retained *Lagochila* as a genus, possibly to avert changing its name and others in the *Moxostoma* group when the whole phylogeny was not known. Unlike other pending corrections of classification in the group, Smith (1992) and I believe that sufficient evidence exists for placing *Lagochila* in *Moxostoma* now. The great divergence of the harelip sucker lineage from typical redhorses may have occurred on a relatively rapid (macroevolutionary?) scale (Smith 1992, personal communication).

DESCRIPTION

Materials.—All 33 extant nonfossil specimens deposited in 10 museums (Jenkins 1970, later study). The specimens represent records from 14, 15, or 16 of the 19 or 20 site records. (Specimens for two of the records apparently were kept by fishermen.) Color in life based on Jordan and Brayton (1877) and Jordan (1882, 1889b).

Anatomy.—A sucker with upper jaw nonprotractile, upper lip hoodlike, and lower lip cleft into two lobes; adults reached at least 313 mm SL. Body form moderate, somewhat compressed. Dorsal fin margin slightly concave or falcate; caudal fin tips pointed, notch fairly deep. Head short, convex dorsally; snout well rounded in juvenile, proclivous to tip in adult; eye moderate or large, lateral.

Upper lip and snout contiguous, no groove between

Fish 144 *Moxostoma lacerum* juvenile 90 mm SL (CAS-SU 3785, shown with museum tag), AL, Florence County, Cypress Creek, 5 June 1884.

them, and forming hoodlike front (Figure 42C); lower lip cleft to jaw bone, consisting of 2 ovoid or subtriangular lobes; upper and lower lip separated at corners by deep fissure; inner surfaces of lips partly, finely plicate, finely papillate, or having both fine plicae and papillae. Pharyngeal arch very small, frail, the teeth comblike, very delicate. Gas bladder 4-chambered, 4th chamber quite small. Nuptial tubercles unknown, but probably well developed on lower caudal lobe and anal fin as in all other *Moxostoma* and related genera.

Meristics.—Lateral line complete, scales 42–46; circumbody scales 31–34; circumpeduncle scales 12; predorsal scale rows 15–18. Dorsal rays (11)12; caudal rays 18; anal rays 7; pelvic rays (8)9; pectoral rays 15–17.

Color in Preservative.—Dusky dorsally, shading to pale ventrally; old faded specimens hint that bases and margins of scales were somewhat darker than scale medians, and that juvenile had 4 lateral blotches and 3 saddles. Fins plain, pale.

Color in Life.—Dorsally olive to steel-blue, side and belly silvery; dorsal and caudal fins creamy, dusky-edged; lower fins creamy or faint orange.

BIOLOGY

Extinct species such as the harelip sucker present a challenge to decipher life history aspects, behavior, and habitat. Tenable hypotheses arise largely from study of functional anatomy and comparison to close relatives whose biology is known—in this case, redhorses. The extant harelip sucker specimens, particularly the lone adult, were examined for data bearing on life history (Jenkins 1970, later study), which were linked with the study by Miller and Evans (1965) on brain anatomy and other sensory adaptations of suckers.

Except for the lips, *M. lacerum* externally resembles redhorses; however, it is marked by trophic specializations throughout the alimentary tract. Some of the specializations are unique among suckers; the lips are different from all other fishes. The alimentary tract of 9 of 10 specimens contained food, the adult being the exception. All nine had snail operculae (shell lids) in few to large numbers (4–114, mean, 27). Some of the operculae were identified to the genus *Campeloma*, others as *Goniobasis* (B. A. Branson, H. Van Der Schalie, in litt.). Some harelip sucker guts had soft parts and radulae (bands of teeth) of snails. Two specimens had eaten one or two limpets (noncoiled snails). Midge larvae (1–13) were taken by four specimens. Other items found in small numbers in a few specimens were copepod and cladoceran microcrustaceans, a water mite, mayfly and caddisfly larvae, and fingernail clams. Mollusks numerically com-

posed about 90% of the diet. Most specimens had a few sand grains in the gut and some had a trace of algal filaments or vascular plant fragments.

The relative size of brain lobes, fairly large eye, and the few labial taste buds of *M. lacerum* indicate that it was a sight feeder, a major contrast with other suckers (Miller and Evans 1965). These authors concluded "It is probable that *Lagochila* fed on larger organisms or particles, first locating them visually and then manipulating them with the lips." Labial manipulation may have been restricted to grasping food because the upper lip is nonprotractile and the lower lip lobes lack direct muscular attachment.

Other anatomical aspects are correlated with sight feeding, carnivory, or both. The short intestine is typical of carnivores. The low number of cephalic lateral line pores may indicate that food detection occurred chiefly by vision, as opposed to sensing vibrations of prey movement with the lateral line canal receptors. Eyes certainly could be more important than the lateral line "ears" for recognizing mollusks; mollusks move too slowly to be perceived by the latter. The few short gill rakers indicate a reduced ability for straining food items from unwanted material. The few bits of abiotic material in the gut indicate that essentially only food was plucked from the stream bottom.

Moxostoma lacerum is similar to two other species of redhorse suckers, *M. carinatum* and *M. hubbsi*, in taking numbers of shelled mollusks, but the resemblance ends here. The pharyngeal apparatus of these living redhorses is adapted for crushing shells; that of *M. lacerum* is so small and frail that the teeth would have broken with the first bite, particularly on the heavy-shelled snails. Thus the harelip sucker probably ingested whole mollusks, then digested soft parts from the shell. It seemed enigmatic that no mollusk shells were found in *M. lacerum*, but malacologists assured me that shells could have been dissolved in preservative; the specimens certainly had been long preserved.

As a sight-feeder, the harelip sucker probably fed during daylight. The characteristic foraging posture of many *Moxostoma*—head often inclined downward—likely was assumed by *M. lacerum*, based on similar external and internal tail structure (Eastman 1980).

The only clearly mature specimen is a female of 313 mm SL, 401 TL (15.8 inches), and 528 g (1.2 pounds) eviscerated weight, from Tennessee. Based on the scales, it is at least 6 and possibly 8 years old. Klippart (1878) sent an Ohio specimen weighing "several pounds" to Jordan. Jordan (1882) mentioned this "fine large" specimen and gave the length of the species as 1–1.5 feet. The specimen no longer exists (Trautman 1981); it probably weighed about 2 pounds

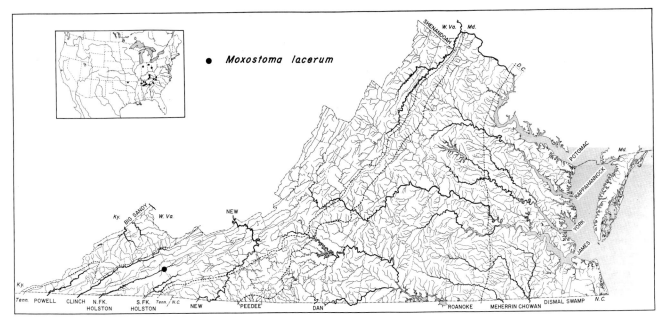

Map 101 Harelip sucker. On inset, archeological sites are included.

based on the maximum length given by Jordan and weights of equally long *Moxostoma* reported by Carlander (1969) and others. Evidence that the harelip sucker often attained one pound is from its value as a foodfish (Jordan and Brayton 1877; Klippart 1878; Jordan 1882).

The harelip sucker migrated and spawned in spring, as do most suckers. Klippart told Jordan (1878) that in May it ascends the Scioto River in central Ohio; fishermen called it the "May sucker." The capture date and exact reproductive state of the extant adult female are unknown. The ovaries are somewhat enlarged, total weight 14.4 g; the gonadosomatic index of 28.5 is too low for a fully gravid redhorse. Larger ova are about 1.5 mm diameter, small for ripe ova of redhorses. The female apparently was captured with a spear, tempting thought that it had been on a shallow spawning bed; probably it had not been spawning when taken.

HABITAT

All records of *M. lacerum* are from streams or rivers (about 10–70 m width) having moderate gradient and which course through rolling, upland, or intermontane terrain. There is a weak indication that small harelip suckers were taken most frequently in the smaller streams, adults in the larger ones. Substrates at most sites were mainly gravel and rocks; typically the water was clear and, except in one case, unvegetated. Six summer temperatures originally associated with captures range from 17.2° to about 25°C, mean, about 21.7 (Jenkins 1970).

The harelip sucker probably was mainly a pool inhabitant and foraged into slow runs, as do many *Moxostoma*. Jordan and Brayton (1877) stated that it "frequents rather deep waters"; their information may have come from fishermen and been based on adults. That *M. lacerum* usually occupied gentle current is indicated by the small size of the cerebellum, a brain part associated with balance and posture. By contrast, suckers with a large cerebellum tend to occupy swift water (Miller and Evans 1965).

Other adaptations of *M. lacerum* to slow water are the moderate body physiognomy, moderate size and form of the fins, a well-developed gas bladder, and a large opening (fontanelle) in the skull roof. Riffle-dwelling moxostomatins tend to be elongated (more streamlined) and have expansive paired fins (hydrofoils), a reduced gas bladder (antibuoyant), and the opening of the skull roof reduced or closed (benthic position aided by greater density).

DISTRIBUTION   Map 101

The 19 or 20 records of capture of the harelip sucker indicate that historically it was widespread but localized; its range included the lower and middle Ohio basin, the White drainage of the Ozarks, and the Maumee system of the Lake Erie drainage (Jenkins *in* Lee et al. 1980). Most sites (11) are in the Cumberland and Tennessee drainages. The Virginia record is "a few" specimens (three preserved) from the North Fork Holston River in or just above Saltville in 1888 (Jordan 1889b); Cope (1868b) did not take *M. lacerum* there in 1867. Post-Pleistocene fossil specimens have been uncovered from three archeological digs in the Tennessee drainage of Tennessee (Bogan and Bogan 1985; A. E. Bogan, in litt.; W. C. Dickinson, personal communication).

The records are from eight states; at least two other states certainly were occupied (Illinois, Missouri), perhaps even three more (Mississippi, Pennsylvania, West Virginia). The distribution pattern is fragmentary, but based on the habitat of *M. lacerum* and the typical patterns of *Moxostoma*, the harelip sucker probably avoided Mississippi Valley lowlands below the Ohio River mouth and perhaps the Blue Ridge section of the Tennessee drainage.

Abundance.—Extinct. Conflicting reports of former abundance are further confounded by concurrent waning of the species. The harelip sucker was believed to be common in the southern bend region of the Tennessee River in Tennessee, Alabama, and Georgia, and very abundant in the Scioto River of central Ohio during the 1870s, but both reports were initially by fishermen and may have been based on localized spawning aggregations.

Capture data hint that in the late 1800s, harelip sucker populations generally were less dense than those of each of the five sympatric redhorse species that are widespread in the Mississippi basin. Most collections of *M. lacerum* by ichthyologists contain one or a few specimens. From the numbers of site records during the late 1800s, this species was taken much less frequently than *M. duquesnei* and *M. erythrurum* in the shared portions of their ranges; similar to the harelip sucker, *M. duquesnei* and *M. erythrurum* normally occupy medium-sized streams to major rivers. Relative to the three more-restrictedly riverine *Moxostoma*—*M. anisurum*, *M. carinatum*, and *M. macrolepidotum*—and discounting stream size, *M. lacerum* was found about equally or slightly more often in most of the general, overlapping portions of their ranges. However, the latter comparison is spurious; by inhabiting medium-sized streams, the harelip sucker was more vulnerable to capture than the three riverine species.

REMARKS

The first known specimen of the harelip sucker was taken in 1859 and had long reposed unreported in a museum; it had been in a jar with redhorses. The early published captures east and west of the Mississippi River and in the Great Lakes basin span the 17-year period 1877–1893. *Moxostoma lacerum* is the first and most widespread fish known to have become extinct in the United States during modern times (Williams 1977).

The harelip sucker's specialized adaptations for feeding are remarkable. Observations of its behavior are precluded, but snippets of information from old literature coupled with recent morphological analyses yield a fair concept of its lifestyle. The availability of 33 specimens divided among 10 institutions emphasizes the importance of the sometimes mundane curatorial duties of carefully preserving, labeling, storing, and maintaining specimens. For this, a debt is owed to our predecessors and colleagues at institutional museums.

The big question remains, why is the harelip sucker extinct? To answer this, the distribution and abundance of the species and chronology of its demise warrant elaboration. Despite the few early claims of its being common or abundant (and recent emphasis on them), *M. lacerum* seems to have been disjunctly distributed and generally uncommon or rare by no later than the 1880s. Supposedly in 1884 it was "Not rare" at one or two upper White drainage sites in the Ozarks of Arkansas (Jordan and Gilbert 1886), but that is the only capture west of the Mississippi River. Thus there is no basis for the claim by Jordan and Evermann (1896) that it is "abundant only in the Ozark Mountains."

Substantiating generally low abundance of the harelip sucker, it apparently was not taken in the earliest fish collections from the Ohio basin, most notably those made about 1850 in the southern bend region of the Tennessee River (Agassiz 1854) and in Ohio by Kirtland during about 1838–1849 (Trautman 1981). Surely Rafinesque would have described it had he encountered it on his ventures in the middle Ohio basin during 1818–1820 (Pearson and Krumholz 1984). Further, bones of *M. lacerum* are very rare at an intensively studied archeological site on the lower Little Tennessee River that is dated about 900 AD (Bogan and Bogan 1985).

From the evidence here and under *Abundance*, it is inappropriate to term the harelip sucker the "Passenger Pigeon of the fish world" (Williams 1977), for that extinct bird formed incredibly large flocks. We don't know that the harelip sucker ever was truly abundant or generally distributed.

Apprised that the harelip sucker was well known to fishermen in the southern bend region of the Tennessee River and in the Scioto River, Jordan (1882) judged it remarkable that so distinctive a fish should have long eluded ichthyologists in the Ohio River basin. I agree that *M. lacerum* would have been readily identified; the few captures in Jordan's time imply that it was well down the road to extinction even then. There is little wonder that its waning went long undetected. Ichthyologically, the period 1850–1900 featured broad but unintensive exploration of North American drainages. Collecting sites rarely were resurveyed soon after because there was so much water to cover; emphasis was on the undescribed species continually discovered.

Continual drop-out of the harelip sucker is indicated by no later than the 1850s. All record sites except that in Virginia yielded the harelip sucker on the first sampling; all of its captures by ichthyologists are the last for each site. The single record each for the Ozarks and the Kentucky and Scioto drainages, and the two for the Maumee drainage are the only ones for the region or drainages.

The last notice of the harelip sucker was in 1893, when in northwestern Ohio Kirsch (1895) found a juvenile at one site and "many" smaller ones at another. The captures probably were no surprise; Kirsch had taken *M. lacerum* at four sites in Kentucky, Tennessee, or Alabama in 1889–1891. Few sampling forays occurred during 1901–1925; extinction of the harelip sucker became evident much later. Jordan et al. (1930) stated that this species is nowhere very common. Kuhne (1939) noted that there are no recent records. Lachner (1956) pronounced it probably extinct and the ichthyological community agreed (Robins et al. 1980).

Habitat alterations appear to be major culprits in the extinction of the harelip sucker (Trautman 1957, 1981; Jenkins 1970 *in* Lee et al. 1980; Williams and Finley 1977; Gilbert 1980; Ono et al. 1983; Williams and Nowak 1986; Miller et al. 1989). From tantalizing bits of habitat data by collectors of *M. lacerum* and the current good quality of some record sites relative to the general stream conditions in its former range, the emergent pattern indicates that this species persisted only in the clearer and least silted, warm streams. Very few streams, perhaps none, that are warm and of much size remain in pristine condition in the East.

The general increase in turbidity and sedimentation associated with the widespread deforestation that occurred through the 1800s probably contributed substantially to the demise of the harelip sucker. A direct suffocating effect by turbidity on *M. lacerum*

was hypothesized by Trautman (1957, 1981), but Jenkins (1970) argued against this being the critical factor. Sedimentation may have decreased the abundance of its molluscan prey, but the general kinds of mollusks and other foods that the harelip sucker ate are still present in numbers.

Silt deposits result from suspended silt, and as *M. lacerum* apparently was a sight-feeder, perhaps it couldn't see sufficient amounts of food at least intermittently—long enough for population after population to fade. As noted under *Moxostoma carinatum* and by Miller and Smith (1981), trophically specialized suckers have fared poorly; *M. lacerum* is a prime example. Interspecific competition for food may not have been a factor because few other fishes in the range of the harelip sucker are mollusk specialists. Deterioration of water quality by industrial and municipal wastes probably afflicted some populations.

Possibly devastative to the harelip sucker were dams, not the immense ones whose construction in the Ohio basin began mainly in the mid-1930s, but the many mill and other dams on large and small streams that fragment populations of migratory fishes. The reproductive biology of this species is poorly known. *Moxostoma lacerum* may have had specific spawning-bed preferences and traveled long distances to find them. Successful reproduction may have relied on large groups of spawners, perhaps with a social structure disrupted by dwindling numbers.

What are the lessons of the harelip sucker? Among several, that widespread species—a strongly divergent lineage in this case—can decline and vanish almost undetected in our midst. Long before its discovery, *M. lacerum* likely was in precarious balance with its environment. The scales were tipped against it by modification of forests and streams; the fish was too specialized to adapt. The extinction of the harelip sucker is particularly regrettable for lost opportunities to understand its unique adaptations. It would have been a neat fish to know.

Name.—*Lacerum* refers to the lacerated or "torn" (cleft) lower lip. One may mourn the burial in *Moxostoma* of the splendid generic name *Lagochila*—"hare lip," also alluding to the lower lip.

Finescale suckers Genus *Catostomus* Lesueur

This group, including the mountain suckers of the former subgenus *Pantosteus* (Smith 1992), comprises some 28 species (about 5 undescribed), all of which live in western North America. Two species extend into the east, one into Virginia. They are elongate and

have papillose lips and small scales; in many species the scale size grades larger toward the posterior body.

Name.—*Catostomus* means "under mouth," in reference to the inferior position of the lips and mouth.

White sucker   *Catostomus commersoni* (Lacepède)

SYSTEMATICS

The white sucker was described in 1803, type locality unknown. This extensively distributed species was considered by Scott and Crossman (1973) to vary rather widely from area to area. Bailey and Allum (1962) did not recognize subspecies largely for lack of a thorough analysis. Metcalf (1966) found geographic variation that indicated differentiation of the species into three major population groups. Dwarf white suckers of the Northeast, which often occur with larger members of the species, are not taxonomically distinct (Beamish and Crossman 1977) but nonetheless are interesting. These fish inspired biosystematic studies that determined dwarfs to be mainly early maturing individuals which did not grow much or live long thereafter. *Catostomus commersoni* apparently is the most primitive species of the genus (Smith 1992).

DESCRIPTION

Materials.—From Cross (1967), J. Nelson (1968a), Scott and Crossman (1973), Beamish and Crossman (1977), McElman and Balon (1980), and 24 Virginia series. Color in life from many Virginia series and an apparently spawning large male from the James drainage.

Anatomy.—An elongate, fine-scaled, papillose-lipped sucker; adults are 180–400 mm SL. Body elongate, nearly round in cross section; head dorsum slightly rounded; eye size moderate, eye lateral. Dorsal fin short-based, margin straight or slightly concave; caudal fin tips pointed or somewhat rounded. Lips thick, lower lip with obtuse angle posteriorly, surfaces fully and coarsely papillose. Pharyngeal teeth comblike. Gas bladder 2-chambered. Scale size grading from small anteriorly to large posteriorly. Nuptial tubercles of male well developed on anal and lower caudal rays and scales of lower urosome; tiny tubercles on other fins, head, and body.

Meristics.—Lateral line complete, scales 53–74; circumpeduncle scales 17–24; dorsal rays 10–14; anal rays 6–8; pelvic rays 9–11; pectoral rays 15–18.

Color in Preservative.—Back and side dark to dusky, scales dark margined, venter pale; often 5–10 narrow dusky stripes on upper half of body; head and body slightly or heavily speckled and irregularly blotched in young, sometimes in small adult; young and small juvenile with 3 round or oval blotches along body midside. Dorsal, caudal, and pectoral fins pale or dusky; anal and pelvic fins pale.

Color in Life.—Back and midside brown to olive, side sometimes yellow-olive or orange-olive and often with brassy iridescence; lower side yellow-gold to pearly. Dorsal

Fish 145 *Catostomus commersoni* adult male 161 mm SL (WHH 108), VA, Wise County, Dotson Fork, 29 June 1983.

Fish 146 *Catostomus commersoni* juvenile 58 mm SL (WHH 162), VA, Lunenburg County, Cruppers Run, 27 July 1983.

and caudal fins olive, or caudal sometimes orange or red-tinged distally; lower fins white, yellow, or orange, paired fins brightest.

Nuptial male with two broad dark stripes, one dorsolateral and one lateral; lateral stripe suffused with rose; pale between stripes and at occiput; nuptial color very ephemeral.

Larvae.—Described by Stewart (1926), Mansueti and Hardy (1967), Lippson and Moran (1974), Long and Ballard (1976), Buynak and Mohr (1978c, 1980c), Jones et al. (1978), Fuiman (1979b, 1982c), Fuiman and Witman (1979), Snyder (1979), Wang and Kernehan (1979), McElman and Balon (1980), and McElman (1983).

BIOLOGY

Owing to its considerable abundance and wide distribution, the white sucker is one of the most studied nongamefishes in North America; most information is from populations north of Virginia. This species often feeds chiefly on midge larvae and small crustaceans; lesser amounts of other aquatic insects and other arthropods, snails, fingernail clams, other invertebrates, and fish eggs are taken (Keast 1966; Beamish 1974; Woolcott et al. 1974; Eder and Carlson 1977; Gatz 1979; Barton 1980). Terrestrial insects that had probably drowned were noted in the diet in some of the above studies. Algae, other plants, and detritus are also consumed (Smith 1977; others above). Keast (1966) suggested that the high volume of detritus in the guts of some fish resulted from deliberate selection. Reviews of earlier studies on food habits are by Stewart (1926) and Adams and Hankinson (1928).

In some northeastern populations, some fish mature at age 2 and first spawn at age 3, whereas other fish in the same and other populations spawn first at age 5 (Beamish 1973; Beamish and Crossman 1977; Quinn and Ross 1985). Barton (1980) stated that in Alberta the minimum age of spawning was 5 for males and 6 for females; curiously, he noted that the sexes were mature or approached maturity at ages 2 and 3 respectively. Geen et al. (1966) found that many spawners in British Columbia were 10–15 years old, and indicated that not all mature fish spawn each year. In Massachusetts, males generally were three times as likely to spawn in a given year as were females, although the adult sex ratio approximated 1:1 (Quinn and Ross 1985). Maximum age is 17 years (Beamish 1973).

Marked variation in growth was observed in different parts of the same area by Raney and Webster (1942); Beamish (1973) indicated that wide ranges in growth occurred throughout the species range. In several Ontario populations, mean lengths at age 5

were 150–425 mm FL. Carlander (1969) listed a range at age 5 of 140–660 mm TL. Upon maturing, females grow faster than males. One of the largest verified white suckers was 560 mm SL, 635 mm TL from Connecticut (Webster 1942). Trautman noted commercial fishermen's reports of larger fish from Ohio. We have seen specimens of about 400 mm TL from Virginia; our smallest nuptial male is 170 mm SL, but truly dwarf adults have not been found in the state.

The upstream migration and spawning of white suckers precedes that of local redhorse species (Gale and Mohr 1976; Smith 1977; Jenkins and Jenkins 1980; Curry and Spacie 1984). The run begins in late March in some southern parts of the range, and spawning may extend into July in northern areas (Pflieger 1975; Galloway and Kevern 1976; Jones et al. 1978). The onset of the run may be triggered by an increase in temperature (4–12°C) and stream level (Stewart 1926; Raney and Webster 1942; Geen et al. 1966; Barton 1980; Montgomery et al. 1983). The spawning period may last 50 days in a single area, but individual fish probably are reproductively active during only part of the period (Barton 1980). Spawning may continue in water of 15–23°C (Trautman 1981; Curry and Spacie 1984), sometimes peaking in the lower part of this range (Raney 1943). In Virginia, we caught males in nuptial color on 14 and 29 March and observed reproductive behavior (but not actual spawning) on 4 April.

The typical spawning habitat is riffles of largely gravel in large creeks to large rivers. Spawning occurred in a sluggish pool during low water when riffles were very shallow (Raney 1943); it occurs rarely or occasionally in lake shallows (McElman and Balon 1980). Mating behavior described by Reighard (1920) is similar to that of most suckers. Fecundity is 20,000–139,000 ova (Raney and Webster 1942; Scott and Crossman 1973). Natural hybridization is known only with other species of the tribe Catostomini, none of which occur in Virginia (Hubbs et al. 1943a; J. Nelson 1968a).

HABITAT

Catostomus commersoni is considered to be very generalized in habitat requirements. It populates a wide range of gradients and substrates that are clean to heavily silted. It occupies waters that range from clear to rather turbid, unvegetated to heavily vegetated, and oligotrophic to nutrient-laden (e.g., Trautman 1981). It inhabits small creeks to large rivers, ponds, lakes, and reservoirs.

In Virginia from the New drainage eastward, the white sucker is characteristic of moderate and high-

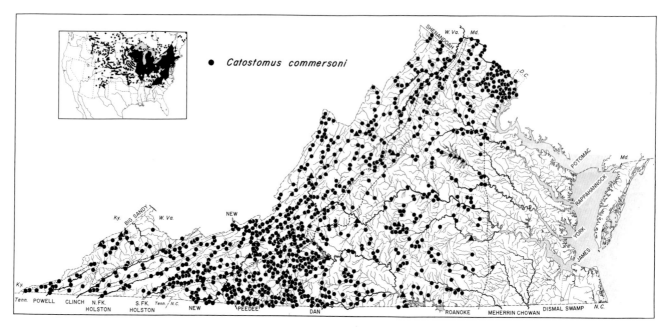

Catostomus commersoni

Map 102   White sucker.

gradient, unsilted and heavily silted creeks and streams. Large juveniles and adults occupy pools that are fairly deep or that have structural shelter. Small white suckers are also taken in these situations and in open shallow areas. West of the New drainage, the white sucker is nearly restricted to small and medium creeks. The maximum salinity record is 1.53‰ from Maryland (Hildebrand and Schroeder 1928).

DISTRIBUTION   Map 102

The white sucker occurs from Arctic basins south into upper reaches of certain Gulf slope drainages. It is widespread in all major drainages of Virginia but generally shuns the Coastal Plain.

Although present in the lower Piedmont of the Roanoke drainage in Virginia and widespread in the neighboring upper Tar drainage of North Carolina, only questionable records are reported (Menhinick et al. 1974) from the adjacent Neuse drainage, North Carolina. The listing of *C. commersoni* for the Neuse (Jenkins et al. 1972, et seq.) is based on young taken in 1963 from Alderidge Creek in the upper drainage (VPI 1580).

Abundance.—Usually uncommon or common; about as common in creeks in extreme western Virginia as it is in small and medium-sized streams of easterly montane and upland areas. Rare in two of the three branches of the Big Sandy drainage.

REMARKS

The ubiquitous white sucker is typical of many fishes by being amply studied in areas north and west of Virginia, but its biology and ecological role in the state are little known. It is often used as bait in northern areas and is suitable for culture (Forney 1957). The white sucker is the favored bait of anglers seeking the illusive muskellunge in the New and James drainages.

Name.—After Phelebert Commerson, a French naturalist and noted collector of fishes who never saw a white sucker (Jordan 1929).

BULLHEAD CATFISHES
Family Ictaluridae

The family Ictaluridae contains some of Virginia's most familiar fishes. It comprises the large forktail catfishes (genus *Ictalurus*) and the large flathead catfish *Pylodictis olivaris*, the mostly medium-sized bullheads (*Ameiurus*), the small cryptic madtoms (*Noturus*), and three blind subterranean genera of Texas or Mexico. The great size range among the species spans from the pygmy madtom of less than 40 mm SL to the blue catfish which attains at least 1,650 mm TL (65 inches) and 68 kg (150 pounds). The vernacular "catfish" derives from the similarity of the facial barbels of these fishes to cat whiskers.

The Ictaluridae are the largest freshwater fish family entirely indigenous to North America; all fossil and living species are known only here. The family belongs to the "old fauna" group (Miller 1965). Fossils have been unearthed from Paleocene deposits of 58–66 million years ago; two living species are represented by fossils from divisions of the Miocene about 11–21 million years old (Lundberg 1975; Cavender 1986). However, many extant species probably are much younger. About 46 living species are in the family; Virginia hosts 15 species. Due partly to introductions, the Roanoke drainage has a greater number of species (8) of medium- and large-sized catfishes than occurs in the Mississippi basin (Burkhead et al. 1980).

Ictalurids are ostariophysan fishes—they have a bony Weberian apparatus specialized for hearing (see *Family Cyprinidae*). Ictalurids lack scales; the mouth usually is inferior, occasionally terminal, and the upper jaw is nonprotractile; the jaws have small teeth densely grouped as patches (cardiform); there are 8 barbels (Figure 4), 2 dorsally (nasal position), 1 arising at each corner of the mouth (maxillary), and 4 on the chin (mental). The first main supporting element of the dorsal and pectoral fins is a stout spine which bears prominent serrae (sawlike teeth) in some species. All species have an adipose fin and a single dorsal fin; the pelvic fins are positioned abdominally and the pectorals are low on the side. Coloration in the family is generally drab; patterns when present are usually spots, mottling, or dark saddles. Intensity of pigment patterns can vary by habitat and time of day (Rasquin 1949).

Secondary sexual dimorphism may be limited to breeding adults. Males often have swollen dorsal head (epicranial) and nape muscles, associated tissues, and lips. In some species slight differences in the genital papillae occur between the sexes. Sexual dichromatism is almost entirely lacking.

Ictalurids are notorious for the "sting" inflicted by their pectoral and dorsal fin spines. Glands located at the base of these spines release a toxin which flows along the spines, and may enter a puncture wound caused by a spine. The most virulent stings, similar to a bee sting, are credited to madtoms (Birkhead 1972).

Bullheads have a well-developed chemical communication system enabling the development of social systems, including pecking orders (Todd 1971). The sensory mediators of chemical stimuli are numerous cutaneous "taste buds" present on the body and particularly on the barbels. Much interesting work remains to be done regarding catfish social behavior. Social systems are unknown in madtoms, but they do possess the cutaneous sensory system. Todd (1971) noted that bullheads do not locate food by smell but rather by means of taste sensors on the skin. Sharks have been described as "swimming noses"; catfishes may be considered "finned tongues."

Ictalurids exhibit a variety of habits and habitat preferences. Most species are diurnally and nocturnally active, more often nocturnal. During daylight all types of shelter are sought. Some of the medium and large species demonstrate great habitat plasticity, occurring in pools and riffles of clear to heavily turbid creeks and rivers, and from montane areas to tidal fresh water. Ponds, lakes, and reservoirs are also inhabited. Some species extend into mesohaline zones but no ictalurid is known to spawn in salinity greater than 2.0‰ (Perry 1973). Other species, particularly some madtoms, exhibit habitat specificity, living almost entirely in pools or only in riffles of clear streams within one or two physiographic provinces. Most madtoms are slow-water dwellers (Starnes and Starnes 1985). The specialized species often are the most intolerant of habitat perturbation.

Most ictalurids are carnivores; some appear to be omnivores. The life span of most madtoms is 4–6 years; larger catfishes may live more than 15 years. Nest construction and spawning usually occur in the typically occupied habitat; nests are generally sheltered. Spawning behavior of larger ictalurids appears fairly uniform. During courting or spawning, the male and female often align side-by-side and head-to-tail, sometimes head-to-head. In the only observation of spawning by a madtom, the brindled madtom, the pair was oriented side-by-side and head-to-head (Fitzpatrick *in* Mayden 1983).

Both monogamy and polygamy in a single breeding season are known among ictalurids. Parental care apparently is the rule and may vary by sex; duties include nest-site preparation, chasing intruders, manipulating the egg mass orally, and fanning eggs and larvae. The male usually is the principal care-giver, but two care-givers tend to be more successful than one (Blumer 1985a, 1985b, 1986). Eggs are self-adhesive, demersal, and about 2–6 mm in diameter; fecundity is moderate to low. Young black-colored bullheads sometimes form densely packed groups or "balls."

Artificial hybridization within or between the genera *Ictalurus*, *Ameiurus*, and *Pylodictis* has produced 25 different hybrid crosses, some of commercial importance (Yant et al. 1976). Natural hybridization within the family apparently occurs quite rarely. Reasons for the rarity may include pair bonding, territoriality, and spawning in well-defined, often secluded areas. Excellent species-recognition abilities may prevail (Taylor 1969; Menzel and Raney 1973). Taylor consid-

ered that natural hybrids may result mainly from the occasional breakdown of psychological barriers to intermating, and not from ecological accidents. However, some hybridization may be attributed to submarginal or disturbed ecological situations and to crowding (Trautman 1948, 1981; Menzel and Raney 1973).

Economically the Ictaluridae are one of the most important North American freshwater families. Catfishes are sought by recreational and commercial fishermen (Menzel 1945) and have been widely stocked in natural waters and farm ponds. Channel catfish are extensively cultured in artificial ponds for commercial distribution. Madtoms are favored bait for bass fishing and are gaining popularity among aquarists specializing in native fishes.

Detailed maps that discern total native and introduced ranges are lacking for several species of catfishes (Lee et al. 1980). Identifications to only the generic level and misidentifications of species pervade the database; for example, Hubbs (1945) stated that bullheads have been "sadly confused." Suspected undocumented introductions have also compromised zoogeographic study, as exemplified in Virginia by half of its ictalurid species. In compiling total-range maps of *Ictalurus* and *Ameiurus*, we found that the distributions of some species have wide, apparently natural gaps, whereas they are indicated by some authors to be essentially continuous. We attempted to portray the gaps in our maps, which include introduced populations, and we emended range limits in some regions for congruence with better known limits in adjacent areas.

Collecting ictalurids often requires specific methods. Seining is the least effective for catching catfishes. Ichthyocides, gill nets, trap nets, and electrofishing generally yield better results. Corcoran (1979) reported that the weak signal produced by a magneto-powered field telephone was more efficient than typical backpack shockers for collecting bullheads. Seining and backpack electrofishing are generally effective for sampling madtoms, except the pool-dwelling *Noturus flavipinnis*. Capture success for some pool inhabitants greatly increases by sampling at night.

Name.—Ictalur-, from the type genus *Ictalurus*, meaning "fish cat."

Key to Bullhead Catfishes   Ictaluridae

Anal fin ray counts, particularly important in *Ictalurus* and *Ameiurus*, include the smallest splintlike anterior rudimentary rays, which often are surrounded by fatty subcutaneous tissue and are not externally obvious. The rays are exposed by slitting and peeling away the skin along the fin base; substage microscope lighting aids in detection of fin rays. These and some other rays are minute in *Noturus*;

Figure 46 Adipose fin types: (A) Adnexed. (B) Adnate.

they are best counted from soft X-ray radiographs, although ray counts are not used in our key to madtoms.

Gill raker counts are critical for identifying some bullheads. All rakers on the first arch are counted including the smallest, clearly formed elements. To detect anterior rakers, often it is necessary to cut opercular muscles and forcefully rotate the operculum outward. Not considered in the key is that small (25–40 mm SL) specimens of *Ictalurus* and *Ameiurus* have about two fewer rakers than do larger fish (Menhinick 1989).

Important comments on intraspecific variation in the degree of forking of the tail are given under *Comparison* in the account of *Ameiurus catus*.

Intensity of pigment expression tends to vary with shade of the substrate and whether specimens are collected during day or night. The diagnostic dark basal blotch in the dorsal fin of *A. platycephalus* and *A. brunneus* is occasionally obscure in life but becomes evident after preservation.

Diagnoses of alevins (small young) of *Ictalurus*, *Ameiurus*, and *Pylodictis* are found in Cloutman (1979).

There are four species of madtoms not included in the key but which may occur in the Tennessee or Big Sandy drainages of Virginia; see *Fishes of Possible Occurrence*.

Key to Genera (and to Species of Genera Monotypic in Virginia)

1a Adipose fin adnexed (free from caudal fin, Figures 46A, 48); larger catfishes 2
1b Adipose fin adnate (attached to caudal fin, although juncture sometimes notched, Figure 46B); small catfishes .... MADTOMS—*Noturus*

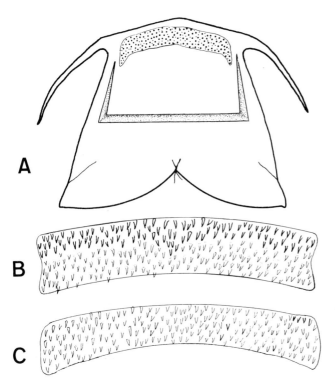

Figure 47 Premaxillary tooth patches of: (A) *Pylodictis olivaris* and *Noturus flavus*. (B) *Ameiurus brunneus*. (C) *Ameiurus platycephalus*.

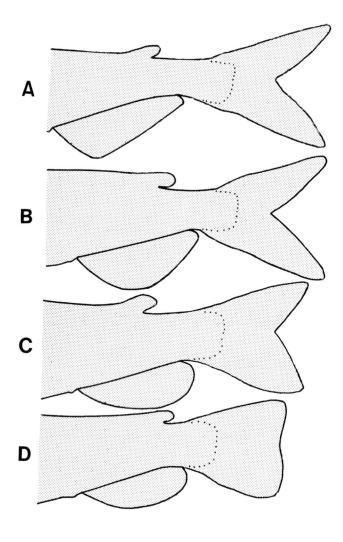

Figure 48 Caudal and anal fin shapes in the medium and large catfishes: (A) *Ictalurus furcatus*. (B) *Ictalurus punctatus*. (C) *Ameiurus catus*. (D) Most *Ameiurus* bullheads.

2a Premaxillary tooth patch with distinct posterolateral extensions (Figure 47A); upper caudal fin lobe partly pale (varies in adult) .... FLATHEAD CATFISH—*Pylodictis olivaris* p. 567
2b Premaxillary tooth patch lacking distinct posterolateral extensions (Figure 47B, C); upper caudal fin lobe not partly pale 3

3a Caudal fin deeply forked (Figure 48A, B) .... FORKTAIL CATFISHES—*Ictalurus*
3b Caudal fin moderately forked or emarginate (Figure 48C, D) .... BULLHEAD CATFISHES—*Ameiurus*

Key to Species of *Ictalurus*

1a Anal fin margin straight (Figure 48A); anal rays (27)30–36(38); never spotted .... BLUE CATFISH—*I. furcatus* p. 533
1b Anal fin margin rounded (Figure 48B); anal rays (23)25–30(32); young to small adult usually with few to many dark spots ... CHANNEL CATFISH—*I. punctatus* p. 535

Key to Species of *Ameiurus*

1a Caudal fin moderately forked (Figure 48C); (anal rays 22–25) ..... WHITE CATFISH—*A. catus* p. 538
1b Caudal fin emarginate (Figure 48D) 2

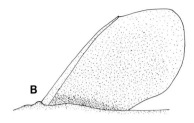

Figure 49 Pigmentation of dorsal fin in *Ameiurus*: (A) Blotchfin bullheads. (B) Other bullheads.

2a Dorsal fin with dark basal blotch (Figure 49A); eye size moderate .... BLOTCHFIN BULLHEADS 3
2b Dorsal fin lacking dark basal blotch (Figure 49B); eye size small .... SMALLEYE BULLHEADS 4

3a Mental (chin) barbels usually lacking pigment (pigment may be present in large specimens on lateral mental barbels, rarely on medial mental barbels); maxillary barbel bicolored, leading edge pale and posterior edge dusky or dark; premaxillary tooth patch in large juvenile and adult narrower medially, lateral ends not indented, and teeth uniform-sized (Figure 47C); anal rays (19)22–24(26); gill rakers (10)11–13(17) .... FLAT BULLHEAD—*A. platycephalus* p. 541
3b Mental barbels usually profusely pigmented (occasionally pigment developed only basally in small specimens); maxillary barbel uniformly dark; premaxillary tooth patch in large juvenile and adult uniformly wide, lateral ends indented, and in adult, anterior teeth larger than posterior teeth (Figure 47B); anal rays (13)17–20(22); gill rakers (11)12–16(18) .... SNAIL BULLHEAD—*A. brunneus* p. 543

4a Mental (chin) barbels pale; anal rays 24–27(28) .... YELLOW BULLHEAD—*A. natalis* p. 545
4b Mental barbels dark; anal rays (18)20–24(25) 5

5a Gill rakers (12)13–15(16); caudal fin base uniformly dusky or dark in large juvenile and adult .... BROWN BULLHEAD—*A. nebulosus* p. 547
5b Gill rakers (15)17–19(21); caudal fin base with rectangular, slightly depigmented area often present in large juvenile and adult .... BLACK BULLHEAD—*A. melas* p. 550

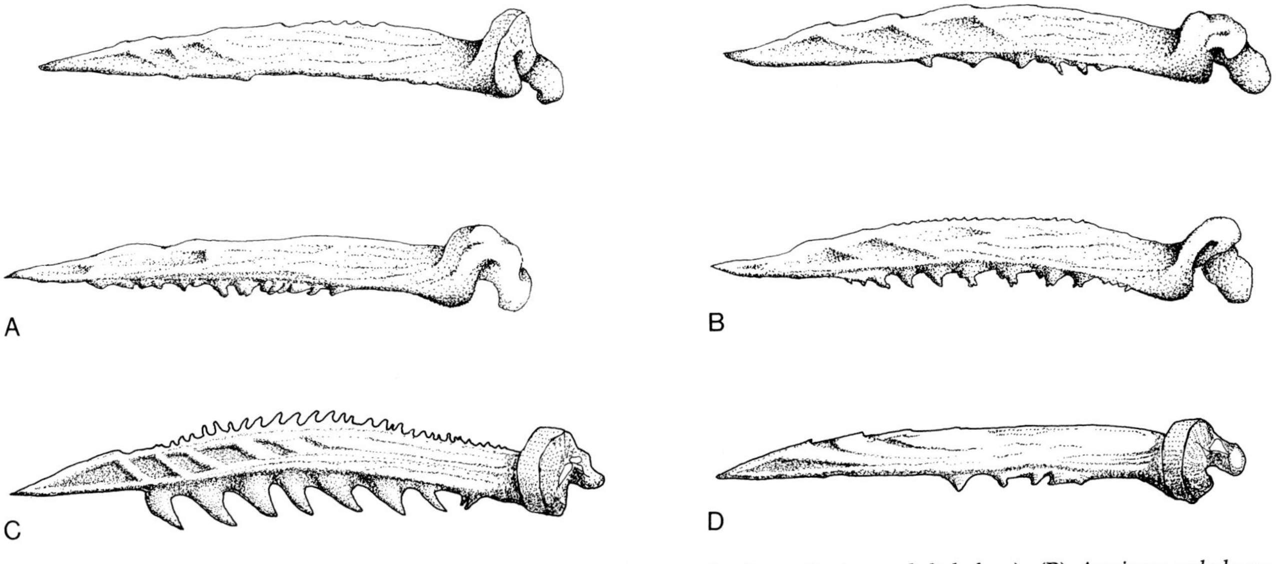

Figure 50 Pectoral spines (anterior edge at top): (A) *Ameiurus melas* (juvenile top, adult below). (B) *Ameiurus nebulosus* (juvenile top, adult below). (C) *Noturus* subgenus *Rabida*. (D) *Noturus* subgenus *Noturus* (redrawn in part from Taylor 1969).

Key to Species of *Noturus*

1a Dorsum lacking saddles, nearly uniformly pigmented; pectoral spine nearly straight, lacking anterior serrae, posterior serrae small and not curved (Figure 50D) .... subgenus *Noturus*   2
1b Dorsum saddled; pectoral spine distinctly curved and having anterior and posterior serrae, several posterior serrae large and curved (Figure 50C) .... subgenus *Rabida*   5

2a Premaxillary tooth patch with distinct posterolateral extensions (Figure 47A); pale crescent present on nape, and a small pale mark present on dorsum just behind dorsal fin .... STONECAT—*N. flavus*   p. 552
2b Premaxillary tooth patch lacking posterolateral extensions; dorsal color pattern not as above 3

3a Mouth terminal or very slightly subterminal; prominent narrow dark midlateral streak present; body chunky; rudimentary caudal rays notably high (caudal fin quite broad) .... TADPOLE MADTOM—*N. gyrinus*   p. 560
3b Mouth distinctly subterminal or inferior; midlateral streak absent or, if present, not prominent; body not chunky; rudimentary caudal rays not notably high (caudal fin not notably broad) 4

4a Caudal fin margin pale, the pale portion slightly to distinctly wider on upper lobe (often forming a somewhat triangular pale area) than on lower lobe; caudal fin submarginally is distinctly darker on lower lobe than upper lobe .... ORANGEFIN MADTOM—*N. gilberti*   p. 554
4b Caudal fin margin dusky or black, or if margin is pale, the pale portion is narrow and equal in width on upper and lower lobes; caudal fin with dusky or black color equally developed on both lobes .... MARGINED MADTOM—*N. insignis*   p. 557

5a Saddle at adipose fin extending dorsad nearly or completely to fin margin; caudal fin base completely encircled with dark band (Figure 51A) .... YELLOWFIN MADTOM—*N. flavipinnis*   p. 562
5b Saddle at adipose fin, if present, usually extending no farther dorsad than midheight of fin, fin margin pale; caudal fin base usually not encircled by dark band, but if encircled, pigment not uniform (Figure 51B) .... MOUNTAIN MADTOM—*N. eleutherus*   p. 565

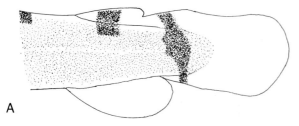
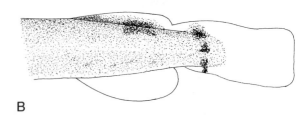

A

B

Figure 51 Caudal peduncle and adipose fin pigmentation (pattern on other fins omitted): (A) *Noturus flavipinnis*. (B) *Noturus eleutherus*.

Forktail catfishes   Genus *Ictalurus* Rafinesque

Ictalurus contains large catfishes including the largest member of the family, the blue catfish. Two species are found in the eastern United States, both in Virginia; most *Ictalurus* species occur in the southwestern United States and Mexico. The generic common name refers to the deeply forked caudal fin (which has pointed or slightly rounded lobes), but some Mexican species have a weakly forked caudal. The genus is divisible into a *furcatus* group and a *punctatus* group (Lundberg 1975).

Name.—*Ictalurus* translates to "fish cat."

Blue catfish   *Ictalurus furcatus* (Lesueur)

SYSTEMATICS

Ictalurus furcatus, described in 1840 from New Orleans, is the type species of the *furcatus* group. Its closest living relative is *I. balsanus* of Mexico (Lundberg 1975).

DESCRIPTION

Materials.—From Clay (1975), 4 small specimens each from Kentucky and Virginia; anal ray counts also from Cloutman (1979), Lundberg (1982), and B. M. Burr (in litt.); gill raker counts from D. A. Etnier (in litt.). Color in life based on Cross (1967) and Clay (1975).

Anatomy.—A catfish with a deeply forked tail and a long straight-margined anal fin; adults are 500–900 mm TL. Body slender in juvenile and small adult, stout and robust in large adult; body round anteriorly, slightly compressed posteriorly. Head depressed, lateral profile of head dorsum straight in juvenile, slightly convex in adult; eye small or moderate; mouth subterminal or inferior. Pectoral spine straight or slightly curved; anterior margin roughened; posterior serrae large, curved. Sexual dimorphism unknown.

Meristics.—Dorsal fin with 1 spine, 6 rays; branched caudal rays 15; anal rays (27)30–36(38); pelvic rays 8; pectoral with 1 spine, 8–9 rays; gill rakers 14–21.

Color in Preservative.—Dorsum and side of juvenile slightly to moderately dusky, lacking spots; venter pale; all fins except pectoral with dusky margin, bases pale; mental barbels pale, others dusky.

Color in Life.—Dorsum gray to blue-gray; side silver to white; venter white.

Larvae.—Alevin keyed and illustrated in Hogue et al. (1976) and Cloutman (1979).

COMPARISON

Problems in distinguishing the blue catfish from the similar channel catfish *I. punctatus* have led to erroneous records (Bailey and Allum 1962; Burkhead et al. 1980). Anglers often confuse the two species because the name blue catfish is descriptive of some dark unspotted adult channel catfish (and of some white catfish).

A diagnostic character generally found in the literature is number of anal fin rays; the ranges often have been stated as 30–35 in *furcatus* vs. 24–29 in *punctatus*. Different and overlapping ranges have been reported respectively: 27–34 (usually 29 or more) vs. 23–29 (usually 27 or less) (Clay 1975); and 29–38 (most often 35) vs. 25–32 (most often 29) (Lundberg 1982). Lundberg's counts were made in an osteological study and include all rudimentary rays, but it is uncertain that Clay consistently detected all rays. Our counts are

Fish 147 *Ictalurus furcatus* juvenile 100 mm SL (SIUC 5667), KY, Ballard County, Ohio River, 6 August 1982.

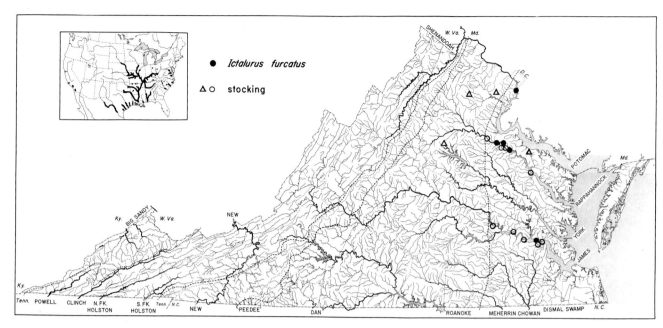

Map 103   Blue catfish.

33–35 *vs.* 27–30, from Virginia or the upper Tennessee drainage in Tennessee.

We emphasize the use of anal fin shape to separate the species. In *I. furcatus* it is relatively straight along the distal margin, whereas in *I. punctatus* it is distinctly rounded. This difference is evident in both early young (Hogue et al. 1976: Figure 8.1, 8.2) and adults. Some *I. furcatus* may have the anal margin rounded because of abrasion. A difference in the gas bladder is illustrated in Pflieger (1975): 2-chambered (having a submedial constriction) in *furcatus* *vs.* 1-chambered in *punctatus*.

BIOLOGY

Small invertebrates are the staple of young and small juveniles. Blue catfish larger than 200–300 mm consume an array of invertebrates, fishes, and occasionally frogs (Harlan and Speaker 1956; Pflieger 1975). The occurrence of mollusks in the diet, including the introduced Asiatic clam (*Corbicula* sp.), was one of the points favoring the introduction of this catfish to California (Pelzman 1971).

Weight at maturation of cultured fish was reported as approximately 2.3 kg (Ray 1971 *in* Pelzman 1971); such fish would be about 400–600 mm TL (Carlander 1969). Blue catfish of ages 4–8 are 400–700 mm TL (Carlander 1969). Pflieger (1975) reported that a 1,397-mm TL (55 inches) specimen from Missouri weighing 40.9 kg (90 pounds) was about 21 years old. Pre-1900 records of blue catfish weighing up to 143 kg (315 pounds) are intriguing but lack verification

(Cross 1967; Pflieger 1975). A 68-kg (150 pounds) specimen of *I. furcatus* sent to the Smithsonian Institution in 1879 was described as *Ameiurus ponderosus* (Cross 1967). Lengths of the 68-kg and larger fish were not reported, but Cross examined a specimen of 1,651 mm TL (65 inches) weighing 45.7 kg (100.5 pounds). Specimens weighing up to 18 kg are still taken frequently in Missouri (Pflieger 1975), but the average in all areas is much smaller. The Virginia record is 25.7 kg (56 pounds 12 ounces); the IGFA (1985) record is 44 kg (97 pounds) from South Dakota.

Blue catfish breed when water temperature reaches 21–24°C, in April and May in Louisiana (Jordan and Evermann 1920) and June to early July in Iowa (Harlan and Speaker 1956). Clemens (1968) stated that they spawn at the same time and temperature as channel catfish, and in similar nests (Harlan and Speaker 1956). The nests are sheltered and both sexes share in brooding (Jones 1965 *in* McClane 1974). About 2,000 eggs are laid per pound (0.45 kg) of female (Ray 1971 *in* Pelzman 1971).

HABITAT

A large-river species, *I. furcatus* typically inhabits deep swift channels and well-flowing pools. It enters sloughs and backwaters in spring, and also occupies reservoirs. It occurs in estuaries downstream to 11.4‰ salinity (Perry 1968 *in* Pelzman 1971), but is rare in brackish water in North Carolina (Schwartz 1981b).

DISTRIBUTION   Map 103

Ictalurus furcatus is native to the Mississippi basin and Gulf slope, and has been stocked on the Atlantic slope and in California. We verified it in Virginia from the Rappahannock and James river estuaries. Young fish from a Texas hatchery were introduced by the VDGIF into these waters: 97,800 fish in the Rappahannock, 64,100 in the James. The earliest years of stockings, some contrary to Burkhead et al. (1980), are 1974, 1975, and 1977 for the Rappahannock and 1975 for the James (J. J. McHugh, in litt.; C. A. Sledd, personal communication). Four impoundments in eastern Virginia were stocked during 1981–1983 (E. L. Steinkoenig, in litt.).

Invalid old and recent reports for the Potomac and New drainages, for which we have not found a clear stocking record, are discussed by Burkhead et al. (1980). A blue catfish was caught in the Potomac River just below Washington, D.C., in 1987; the identification was affirmed by L. K. Knapp, an ichthyologist of the Smithsonian Institution (A. W. Norden, personal communication). How the fish got into the Potomac is unknown; perhaps it dispersed from the Rappahannock via Chesapeake Bay during a high influx of fresh water.

The blue catfish is indigenous to the Tennessee drainage but unknown from the Virginia section. The record from the North Fork Holston River (Milligan and Ruane 1978) is actually of *I. punctatus* (J. C. Feeman, personal communication).

Abundance.—Unknown. Apparently *I. furcatus* has been established in Virginia by stocking and the population is building; commercial fishermen took small and large specimens in the Rappahannock and James rivers in the 1980s (C. A. Sledd, E. L. Steinkoenig, personal communication).

REMARKS

The blue catfish provides a new and popular fishery in the large estuaries of the James and Rappahannock rivers. It ranks as one of Virginia's largest freshwater or anadromous fishes, currently outweighed perhaps only by the Atlantic sturgeon, paddlefish, common carp, and striped bass. During the 1980s, the state angling record for the blue catfish steadily climbed to 20.6 kg (45 pounds 8 ounces) in 1989; most records came from the Rappahannock. In late 1991, the record jumped to 25.7 kg (56 pounds 12 ounces) for a fish from the James, just exceeding the state record flathead catfish.

Name.—*Furcatus* means "forked," referring to the deeply forked tail.

Channel catfish   *Ictalurus punctatus* (Rafinesque)

SYSTEMATICS

Described from the Ohio River in 1818, the channel catfish was named anew as many as 22 more times (Corcoran 1981), but currently not even subspecies are recognized (Bailey et al. 1954). Lundberg (1975) regarded it to have been morphologically stable since a stage of the Miocene about 17–21 million years ago. *Ictalurus punctatus* is closely related to *I. lupus* of Texas and New Mexico (Yates et al. 1984).

DESCRIPTION

Materials.—Fifteen series, including 13 Roanoke and 7 Tennessee drainage fish for anal ray and gill raker counts; counts also from Taylor (1969), Scott and Crossman (1973), Clay (1975), and Lundberg (1982). Color in life from Trautman (1981) and 3 Virginia adults.

Anatomy.—A catfish with the body usually spotted, tail deeply forked, and anal fin margin rounded; adults are 300–700 mm TL. Body somewhat elongate, rotund anteriorly in large adult, compressed posteriorly. Head depressed, profile of head dorsum and nape straight; eye small or medium; mouth subterminal or inferior. Pectoral spine nearly straight; slightly dentate on anterior margin; well-developed curved serrae on posterior margin. Male genital papilla small, flat, and turgid when breeding (Clemens and Sneed 1957); papilla incorporates urinary pore, hence it has a urogenital pore. Papilla present or absent in female, genital pore centered in fleshy mound, genital pore separate from urinary pore (Moen 1959; Norton et al. 1976).

Meristics.—Dorsal fin with 1 spine, 6 rays; branched caudal rays 15; anal rays (23)25–30(32); pelvic rays 8; pectoral with 1 spine, 8–9 rays; gill rakers 13–15(18).

Color in Preservative.—Dorsum and upper side moderately dusky to dark; side with few to many dark spots in small and some large specimens, adult often lacking spots; venter pale; fins dusky, sometimes with slightly dark margin; barbels usually pigmented; peritoneum silver.

Color in Life.—Dorsum and upper side gray to slate blue, sometimes olive with yellow sheen; spots gray to black; lower side and venter white to silver; fins dusky gray. Breeding male with blue-black head and body dorsum, silver-white belly. Albinos were reported from the York drainage (Menzel 1944).

Fish 148 *Ictalurus punctatus* juvenile 147 mm SL (REJ 1028), VA, Amelia County, Appomattox River, 1 September 1983.

Fish 149 *Ictalurus punctatus* subadult female 243 mm SL (REJ 1010), VA, Halifax County, Banister River, 14 July 1983.

Larvae.—Described by Mansueti and Hardy (1967), Lippson and Moran (1974), Wang and Kernehan (1979), and Tin (1982b); alevin diagnosed by Cloutman (1979).

COMPARISON

See *I. furcatus* and *Ameiurus catus.*

BIOLOGY

Like other medium- and large-sized catfishes, *I. punctatus* is an omnivore and exhibits an ontogenetic dietary shift (Sule et al. 1981). Young depend primarily on plankton and aquatic insect larvae, whereas juveniles and adults apparently eat almost any available aquatic invertebrate, fishes, other vertebrates, and some plants (Bailey and Harrison 1948; Menzel 1945; Woolcott et al. 1974; VIMS 1977).

Maturation occurs at 4–6 years and 330–560 TL in many areas; Carlander (1969) cited reports of maturity at age 2. A Virginia specimen was maturing at 160–179 mm TL; some females were mature at 230–260 mm TL (Menzel 1945; VIMS 1977). Maximum longevity is about 22 years, but age 15 is rarely reached (Carlander 1969). Growth varies latitudinally

and is usually fastest in southern populations. Individuals attain about 320–450 mm TL by age 5 in Virginia and in similar latitudes elsewhere (Carlander 1969; Wollitz 1972; Davis and Enamait 1982). The Virginia record channel catfish is 14.5 kg (32 pounds); the IGFA (1985) record is 26.3 kg (58 pounds) from South Carolina.

Spawning begins in late May and peaks in late June–early July in the James River (Menzel 1945). Spawning occurs at 21–30°C. Nests are constructed in sheltered areas by the male or by both sexes (Clemens and Sneed 1957). Immediately before and during spawning, both sexes orient head to tail and envelop each other's snout with their caudal fin. The male cares for the eggs (Clemens and Sneed 1957; Clemens 1968). Average-sized James River females produce 4,200–10,600 eggs per year (Menzel 1945). Clemens and Sneed (1957) determined fecundity to be 3,000–4,000 eggs per pound (0.45 kg) of female.

Four specimens from an Illinois river "seem" to be hybrid *I. punctatus* × *Pylodictis olivaris* (O'Donnell 1935). Taylor (1969) did not accept the identification for lack of morphological data and specimens, as well as the distant relationship of the genera. It is unlikely

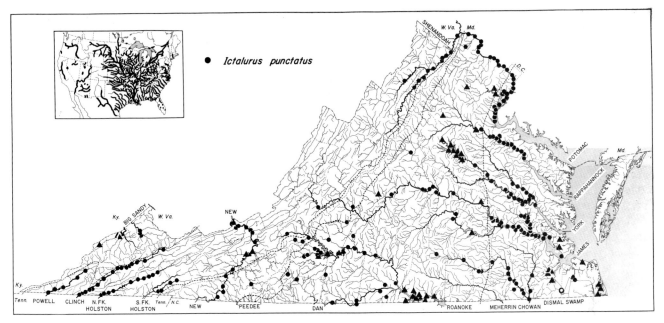

Map 104 Channel catfish. Open circle indicates questionable record.

that four hybrids would have been taken in one river, and the cross not have been reported elsewhere.

HABITAT

The channel catfish typically inhabits warm large streams, big rivers, ponds, lakes, and reservoirs. In running water, *I. punctatus* usually is associated with pools but is also found in moderate current; it occupies a variety of substrates. It is adapted to clear and turbid upland and lowland streams. Although it occurs in darkly stained freshwater main channels on the Coastal Plain, apparently it is intolerant of moderately to highly acidic waters of smaller swampy Coastal Plain tributaries and interior Dismal Swamp. It typically populates upper sections of estuaries (Perry 1973), having salinity as high as 15.1‰ in Virginia (Musick 1972).

DISTRIBUTION   Map 104

The natural range of the channel catfish includes the Hudson Bay, Great Lakes–St. Lawrence, and Mississippi basins, and the Gulf slope. This species has been widely introduced westward and in some northeastern states. Its status on the south Atlantic slope is unclear; it is possibly introduced in Georgia (Dahlberg and Scott 1971b) and probably so in North Carolina (Smith 1907) and South Carolina. It is found in all major Virginia drainages, but is clearly native to only the Big Sandy and Tennessee drainages, and apparently native to the New drainage. Native status in the New is based on the record by Cope in 1867 (Burkhead et al. 1980) and by McDonald in 1885. The absence of *I. punctatus* in 1892 from the lower Chowan and Roanoke drainages and other tributaries of Albemarle Sound, North Carolina (Smith 1893), indicates that it has been introduced there. The failure to find bones of *I. punctatus* at a 250–800-year-old Indian settlement along the upper James River corroborates an introduced status in the drainage (Whyte 1989).

Introduction of channel catfish to the Potomac drainage is discussed by Burkhead et al. (1980). The Central and Wytheville rearing stations released fish, some or all from Missouri and Illinois, into the Potomac (during 1889–1905), upper James (1893–1894), upper Roanoke (1904), and New and Clinch (both 1917–1921) drainages (USFC 1893–1928; Smith and Bean 1899; Fearnow 1929). *Ictalurus punctatus* is unknown in the Meherrin system of Virginia but probably is present because it occupies the North Carolina portion (E. F. Menhinick, in litt.).

The single *I. punctatus* specimen from Lake Drummond, Dismal Swamp, in 1952 (VIMS 74) was either introduced or the locality data are incorrect. It was collected by W. H. Massmann but was not listed by Andrews (1971), who used Massmann's data. Channel catfish were stocked in Lake Drummond around 1969 by a fish farmer, but have not been found in later surveys (M. D. Norman, in litt.; our data).

Abundance.—Usually uncommon or common.

REMARKS

The channel catfish perhaps is the most familiar and popular catfish in North America. It is prized as game and food by many anglers and is widely raised in hatcheries and distributed commercially. Holmes et al. (1974) described its culture in Virginia ponds.

Name.—*Punctatus*, "spotted," is based on body markings.

Bullhead catfishes   Genus *Ameiurus* Rafinesque

This genus contains medium-sized catfishes that collectively are called bullheads, so named for the large head and "bullish" disposition of breeding males. Six of the seven species of *Ameiurus* occur in Virginia.

The status of *Ameiurus* has vacillated from that of a genus to that of a strict synonym of *Ictalurus*. Taylor (1954) ended a lengthy period of generic ranking of *Ameiurus* by lumping it with *Ictalurus*. Taylor (1954, 1969) did not recognize subgenera in *Ictalurus*; he regarded the combined assemblage to form a continuous (albeit heterogeneous) lineage within which the white catfish *Ameiurus catus* was said to bridge a main morphological gap.

Ameiurus was recognized as a subgenus of *Ictalurus* by Lundberg (1975, 1982) based on a suite of osteological characters of fossil and living species. He concluded that *Ameiurus* and *Ictalurus* have evolved separately since at least the Oligocene, 24–36 million years ago—much earlier than the evolutionary branching indicated by Taylor (1969). The data indicate that bullheads are more closely allied genealogically to *Noturus*, *Pylodictis*, and specialized cave-dwelling genera. Except for its moderately forked tail, an apparent evolutionary reversal, *A. catus* shares advanced traits with *Ameiurus* and not *Ictalurus*; it is a "... perfectly good bullhead, osteologically ..." (Lundberg 1970 *in* LeGrande 1981).

Lundberg's critical analyses reopened the issue of the status of *Ameiurus*, although in 1982 he "opted for inertia" by maintaining its subgeneric rank until completion of study. Lundberg (1992) reinstated *Ameiurus* as a genus, as anticipated by Burr and Warren (1986), Miller (1986), Bailey and Robins (1988a, 1988b), and us; Robins et al. (1991) have concurred.

Ameiurus is divisible into two species groups, the *natalis* group and the *catus* group (Lundberg 1975). The *natalis* group consists of the typical bullheads— our "smalleye" bullheads, all having a small eye (Burkhead et al. 1980), relatively rounded head dorsum (sometimes only slightly; rarely it is flat), and an emarginate caudal fin. Its three species, *A. natalis*, *A. nebulosus*, and *A. melas*, occur in Virginia.

Of the four species in the *catus* group, three are "flat-headed" bullheads (Yerger and Relyea 1968): *A. platycephalus*, *A. brunneus*, and the Floridean spotted bullhead *A. serracanthus*. The three have a (usually) flattened head, relatively large (medium-sized) eye, emarginate tail, and a large dark blotch in the basal portion of the dorsal fin. We prefer to call them "blotchfin" bullheads because of that prominent trait and because they overlap in head shape with the smalleye bullheads. *Ameiurus catus*, which occurs in Virginia, also has a relatively large eye, but has a more convex head, lacks the dorsal fin blotch, and is somewhat intermediate between *Ictalurus* and the bullheads in having a moderately forked tail.

Name.—*Ameiurus*, "privative, curtailed," refers to the lack of a deep notch in the caudal fin; that is, having the emarginate condition (in most species) (Burr and Warren 1986). The genus has been spelled *Amiurus* but *Ameiurus* is correct (R. R. Miller 1986: errata; Bailey and Robins 1988a, 1988b). Thus we note this additional exception to the spelling rule that "i goes before e except after c"—and in *Ameiurus*.

White catfish   *Ameiurus catus* (Linnaeus)

SYSTEMATICS

Described from the "northern part of America" in 1758, *A. catus* is one of the most distinctive bullheads.

DESCRIPTION

Materials.—From Taylor (1969), Scott and Crossman (1973), Burkhead et al. (1980), and 23 additional Virginia specimens. Color in life from Clay (1975), Trautman (1981), and 5 Virginia adults.

Anatomy.—A bullhead with a moderately forked tail; the largest *Ameiurus*, adults are 200–450 mm TL. Body stout; trunk nearly round in cross section anteriorly, compressed posteriorly. Head depressed, sloping markedly to snout in juvenile, less so in adult; dorsal head profile straight or slightly convex; eye fairly large in young, mod-

Fish 150 *Ameiurus catus* adult male 146 mm SL (REJ 1036), VA, Campbell County, Roanoke River, 12 September 1983.

erate in adult; mouth slightly inferior. Pectoral spine nearly straight; anterior surface roughened; posterior margin weakly serrate. Male genital papilla elongate, conical, terminal pore enveloped by flattened processes; papilla essentially absent in female, pore centered in villate mound. Epicranial and cheek muscles slightly or moderately bulging in two late-July adult males, not pronounced in gravid females taken then.

Meristics.—Dorsal fin with 1 spine, 5–7 rays; branched caudal rays 15; anal rays 22–24(25); pelvic rays 8; pectoral with 1 spine, 8–9 rays; gill rakers 18–21(23).

Color in Preservative.—Dorsum and upper side of adult dusky to dark; lower side pale, sometimes slightly mottled along midside; venter pale; young uniformly dusky on dorsum and side. All fins of adult slightly or moderately dusky, lacking a distinctly dark margin; fins of young with pale base, all but pectoral and pelvic have dark margins. Nasal barbel dark; maxillary barbel with pale leading edge in large adult, completely dark in smaller fish; mental barbels pale. Peritoneum pale in juvenile and small adult, dusky brown in large adult.

Color in Life Plate 22.—Dorsum gray or blue-gray; upper side gray, grading to white ventrally, occasionally mottled laterally; dorsum and upper side sometimes with gold and pale green tints; median fins dusky gray; paired fins white or slightly dusky gray. Dorsum dark gray in breeding male.

Larvae.—Described by Mansueti and Hardy (1967), Lippson and Moran (1974), and Wang and Kernehan (1979); alevin diagnosed by Cloutman (1979).

COMPARISON

Although the channel catfish *I. punctatus* typically has a spotted body and a deeply forked tail, its adults often lack spots and some large adults have the tail only moderately forked, hence resembling *A. catus*. Some young and small juvenile *A. catus* have a well-forked tail, as is typical of *I. punctatus*. Thus unless an identification of these species is obvious, we recommend using: (1) gill rakers [18–21(23) in *catus* vs. 13–15(18) in *punctatus*]; (2) anal rays [22–24(25) vs. (23)25–28(30)].

BIOLOGY

Young and juveniles predominantly eat aquatic insects. Adults are omnivorous, consuming a variety of aquatic invertebrates, fishes, and plants (Menzel 1945; Carlander 1969).

For a somewhat long-lived species, white catfish mature quite early under some conditions. Under culture conditions, some 2-year-old males are mature and females may mature in 1 year (Sneed and Clemens 1963). Menzel's (1945) data applied to Miller's (1966) summary suggest that maturity is attained at 3–4 years in some Virginia rivers. Maximum known longevity is 14 years (Schwartz and Jachowski 1965). White catfish are usually 250–450 mm TL by age 6 (Carlander 1969). Brady (1969) found only small thin specimens in Lake Drummond, suggesting stunting; the white catfish was the fourth most common species. Our largest Virginia specimen of *A. catus* is only 330 mm TL, but the species probably reaches 500 mm in the state; it attains 590 mm TL in South Carolina (Carlander 1969). Menzel stated that in Virginia estuaries white catfish rarely exceed 2.3 kg. The state record is 2.1 kg (4 pounds 11 ounces).

Spawning probably occurs from late May into July in Virginia, depending on seasonal conditions. Females were gravid in late July in Leesville Reservoir. Minimum spawning temperature is about 21°C. Both sexes prepare the sizeable nest, 0.8–0.9 m in diameter and 0.3–0.5 m in depth, in sand or gravel. The spawning act involves a lateral head-to-tail orientation with the male curving his caudal fin around the

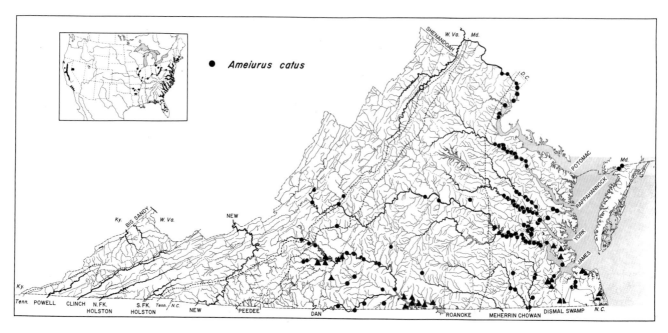

Map 105   White catfish. The South Fork Shenandoah River record (open circle) is not acceptable.

head of the female. Eggs are guarded and fanned by one or both sexes (Gill 1907; Fowler 1917a; Breder and Rosen 1966). Clutch size was reported as 1,400–1,500 eggs (Fowler 1917a); two prespawning females contained 3,200–3,500 eggs (Menzel 1945).

HABITAT

White catfish occupy warm ponds, reservoirs, medium and large rivers, rarely small streams, and extend into brackish water. Extreme salinity records are 14.5‰ in Maryland and 27‰ in North Carolina (Schwartz and Jachowski 1965; Schwartz 1981b). This species is found in the highly acidic waters of Lake Drummond, but is rare in associated ditches and tributaries. Trautman (1981) suggested that it favors conditions intermediate to the relatively swifter currents and firmer substrates preferred by channel catfish and the sluggish silty situations in which some other species of *Ameiurus* abound. In the Roanoke River we found white and channel catfishes associated with cover in long pools and deep slow runs.

DISTRIBUTION   Map 105

Ameiurus catus is native to the major Atlantic slope drainages from the Delaware drainage (Mihursky 1962) south to Florida and on the eastern Gulf slope (Swift et al. 1986). It has been established by introductions in other regions. In the Potomac, Rappahannock, and York drainages it is largely or entirely

restricted to the Coastal Plain, but in the James and Roanoke it extends into the Valley and Ridge Province, and in North Carolina to about the Blue Ridge foothills (E. F. Menhinick, in litt.). The four uppermost James records are from Jordan (1889b) and our recent creel checks and angling.

The record from the South Fork Shenandoah River is questionable. *Ameiurus catus* is one of the species reported from a collection by Ross (1959a: VPI 726), but the accession page for the collection includes *I. punctatus*, which was not reported. The *A. "catus"* were eaten in the field at night; likely they were misidentified *I. punctatus*.

As is usual with atypical and problematic records, the Shenandoah record inspired further inquiry into the range of *A. catus* in the Potomac drainage. Surprisingly, this species is unknown from the many collections and creel surveys made in the main-stem Shenandoah and its forks during 1964–1971 (Surber 1970, 1972) and later (J. W. Kauffman, personal communication). We know of only four records from the drainage above Washington, D.C. Three are old records from the Fall Zone (McAtee and Weed 1915; two dots on Map 105 for the main channel, Chesapeake and Ohio Canal, and extreme lower section of a tributary). The fourth record, a specimen from the lower North Branch Potomac River, Maryland, is thought to have originated from stocking (Davis and Enamait 1982). Because the Potomac River above the Fall Line has been extensively surveyed (e.g., Cairns and Kaesler 1971; Davis and Enamait 1982), we conclude that the white catfish is not clearly established above Great Falls, and may never have been.

Abundance.—Generally uncommon or common.

REMARKS

This sizeable catfish is widely taken by anglers and commercial fishermen in Virginia (Menzel 1945). Cle-

mens (1968) considered it the easiest of all catfishes to culture; it grew rapidly in an Alabama pond (Elrod 1971). Its flavor is comparable to that of channel catfish. Virginia and Maryland populations have been sources for stocking other areas (Nelson and Gerking 1968; Clay 1975; Trautman 1981; Pearson and Krumholz 1984).

Name.—*Catus* means "cat."

Flat bullhead   *Ameiurus platycephalus* (Girard)

SYSTEMATICS

Ameiurus platycephalus was described from South Carolina in 1859. Its systematics were clarified by Yerger and Relyea (1968) and its variation was documented also by Corcoran (1981). Further diagnosis of the Virginia population was made by Burkhead et al. (1980). The flat bullhead is placed in the *catus* species group and is most closely related to *A. brunneus* (Lundberg 1975, 1982, 1992).

DESCRIPTION

Materials.—From Yerger and Relyea (1968), Burkhead et al. (1980), Corcoran (1981), and 3 additional specimens; new ray counts (except anal) from 5 specimens. Color in life based on 6 juveniles and adults from Virginia.

Anatomy.—A bullhead with an emarginate tail, dark blotch in dorsal fin basally, and bicolored maxillary barbels; adults are 150–220 mm SL. Body stout, depressed anteriorly, compressed posteriorly. Head profile straight or slightly convex dorsally; eye moderate in young to adult; mouth moderately inferior; premaxillary tooth patch lacking lateral indentations (being rounded), narrowed medially, teeth of uniform size in juvenile and adult. Pectoral spine nearly straight; anterior margin roughened; posterior serrae small, numerous. Two early-June males exhibit slight to moderate epicranial swelling; their genital papilla relatively large, slightly flattened, tip with large fleshy pa-

pillae in one, ventrally bilobed in the other. A single early-June gravid female lacks definitive papilla; genital pore surrounded by large fleshy papillae.

Meristics.—Dorsal fin with 1 spine, 6 rays; branched caudal rays 15; anal rays (19)22–24(26); pelvic rays 8; pectoral with 1 spine, 8–9 rays; gill rakers (10)11–13(17).

Color in Preservative.—Dorsum dusky or dark, usually uniform; side slightly or heavily mottled; venter pale. Median fins usually with narrow dark margin; pectoral and occasionally pelvic fins lack dark margin, although pectoral spine frequently covered with dark skin. Basal dark blotch in dorsal fin evident in juvenile and adult, often so in young. Nasal barbel dark; maxillary barbel bicolored, leading edge pale. Mental barbels usually pale; lateral mental barbels may be pigmented in large adult, but medial pair usually pale, and if pigmented, only basally. Peritoneum silver.

Color in Life Plate 22.—Dorsum olive to medium brown; upper side with pale yellow-green wash; lower side cream to white; lateral mottling olive-brown or olive-black, sometimes extending onto caudal and anal fins; venter cream or white. Dark margin of median fins black, basidorsal blotch olive-brown or black, sometimes evident only upon preservation; all fins with slight yellow or yellow-green wash.

Larvae.—Alevin diagnosed by Cloutman (1979).

Fish 151 *Ameiurus platycephalus* adult female 161 mm SL (REJ 1002), VA, Charlotte County, Twittys Creek, 13 July 1983.

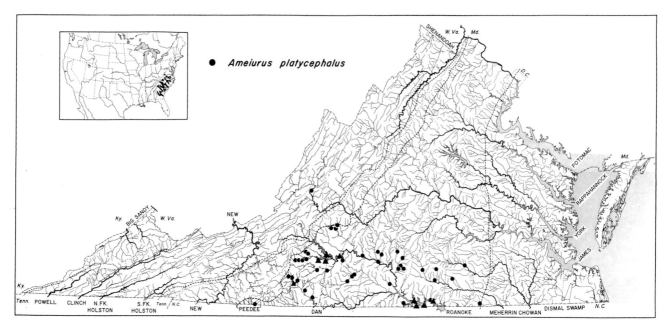

Map 106   Flat bullhead.

BIOLOGY

The life history of a North Carolina reservoir population was studied by Olmsted and Cloutman (1979). *Ameiurus platycephalus* is an omnivore although plants are not as important as animal food. A wide range of predominantly aquatic invertebrates and fishes are eaten; one specimen contained a mouse.

Females mature in their third year; age at maturation of males is unknown. Males may normally outlive females; age 7 is known for males, age 5 for females. Growth is similar in the sexes to age 3; females grow at slower rates thereafter. Average size at age 4 is 225 mm TL for males, 217 mm for females. Olmsted and Cloutman's largest specimen is at least 286 mm TL. The largest Virginia specimen is 250 mm SL. We know little of the larger sizes attained by *Ameiurus* species in Virginia; except for the white catfish, the species are not included in the record or citation programs of the VDGIF, and most species are rarely distinguished by anglers.

Spawning occurs in June and July in North Carolina, at water temperatures of about 21–24°C. Fecundity is 207–1,742 mature ova. Spawning behavior has not been reported.

HABITAT

In Virginia the flat bullhead occupies warm, medium and large tributaries and main stems of drainages from the Blue Ridge foothills to the lower Piedmont. Occasionally it inhabits large creeks.

Southward it extends well into Coastal Plain habitat (Yerger and Relyea 1968; Corcoran 1981). *Ameiurus platycephalus* associates with cover in pools and backwaters, sometimes near swift current. It is known also from nearshore areas of all major reservoirs in the Virginia part of the Roanoke drainage. Corcoran (1981) indicated that *A. platycephalus* reaches its greatest abundance in rocky pool and riffle habitats on the Piedmont, but we have never collected it in a rocky riffle or run in Virginia.

DISTRIBUTION   Map 106

Ameiurus platycephalus ranges on the Atlantic slope from Virginia to Georgia. In Virginia it occurs widely in the Roanoke drainage, is localized in the Chowan, and barely extends into the state's section of the Pee Dee. A surprising first drainage record is of two adult flat bullheads from the upper James River just below Glen Wilton, Botetourt County, by Burkhead's angling in 1984. Until recently the James River above the Fall Zone had been scantily surveyed; it is possible that some yellow bullhead records (specimens not seen by us) may actually be *A. platycephalus*. The flat bullhead was not identified in the 1987–1990 survey of the James River (G. C. Garman, in litt.). We tentatively regard it as native to the James; the specimens may have been stocked and escaped from a farm pond.

Abundance.—Seemingly generally uncommon in the Roanoke, rare in the Meherrin, and only one record (Norman and Southwick 1985) is from the Nottoway. Only one or few adult flat bullheads have been taken in any single Virginia collection. Its apparent low abundance may be related to territoriality, to the peripheral nature of the populations, or to the difficulty of catching the species.

REMARKS

Yerger and Relyea (1968) noted a local preference in Georgia for the flat bullhead as table fare, and we enjoyed this fish at a Gaston Reservoir fish fry. The specimens for the unique upper James drainage record were on a stringer and were devoured by a turtle(s) at night.

Name.—*Platycephalus* means "flat head." We have heard this species called "shoehead" in the Gaston Reservoir area.

Snail bullhead   *Ameiurus brunneus* (Jordan)

SYSTEMATICS

Ameiurus brunneus was described from Georgia by Jordan in 1877, but the next time Jordan collected it, he synonymized it with *A. platycephalus* (Jordan 1889b; Jordan and Evermann 1896). *Ameiurus brunneus* was resurrected and rediagnosed by Yerger and Relyea (1968). Its variation was further studied by Corcoran (1981); the Virginia population was treated by Burkhead et al. (1980). It is placed in the *catus* species group by Lundberg (1975, 1982, 1992), closest to *A. platycephalus*. Corcoran (1981) considered *A. brunneus* to be more advanced than *A. platycephalus* based on chromosomal numbers.

DESCRIPTION

Materials.—Yerger and Relyea (1968), Burkhead et al. (1980), Corcoran (1981), and our 7 adults; new ray counts (except anal) from 3 specimens. Life color from Jordan (1877a), Yerger and Relyea (1968), and 2 Virginia juveniles.

Anatomy.—A bullhead with an emarginate tail, dark basidorsal blotch, and wholly dark maxillary barbel; adults are 120–170 mm SL. Body stout, slightly depressed anteriorly, compressed posteriorly. Head profile straight or slightly convex above; eye moderate in young to adult; mouth moderately or strongly inferior; premaxillary tooth patch laterally indented and uniformly wide, having two sizes of cardiform teeth in adult. Pectoral spine essentially as in *A. platycephalus*. Genital papilla of reproductive male large, conical, not bilobed; that of female small, sometimes inconspicuous, recessed in a pit, surrounded by large fleshy papillae. Epicranial swelling not evident in immediately pre- and postspawning adults.

Meristics.—Dorsal fin with 1 spine, 6 rays; branched caudal rays 15; anal rays (13)17–20(22); pelvic rays 8; pectoral with 1 spine, 9 rays; gill rakers (11)12–16(18).

Color in Preservative.—Dorsum and side uniformly shading dark to dusky, or darkly to duskily mottled; venter pale or slightly dusky. Most of fins typically paler than body; dorsal fin usually with a large dark blotch (blotch may be less frequently present and less distinct on the average than in *A. platycephalus*); narrow dark margin usually present on fins of adult. All barbels profusely pigmented in juvenile and adult, maxillary barbel darkest; mental barbels may appear pale in small juvenile, but melanophores are usually discernible under magnification. Peritoneum silver.

Color in Life.—Dorsum and side pale olive-brown to gray-brown, mottled with same shades; venter white. Dorsal fin blotch blackish (sometimes evident only upon preservation).

Larvae.—Alevin described by Cloutman (1979).

BIOLOGY

Essentially unstudied; life history aspects are probably similar to those reported for *A. platycephalus*. A

Fish 152 *Ameiurus brunneus* juvenile 86 mm SL (REJ 918), NC, Rockingham County, Smith River, 3 June 1981.

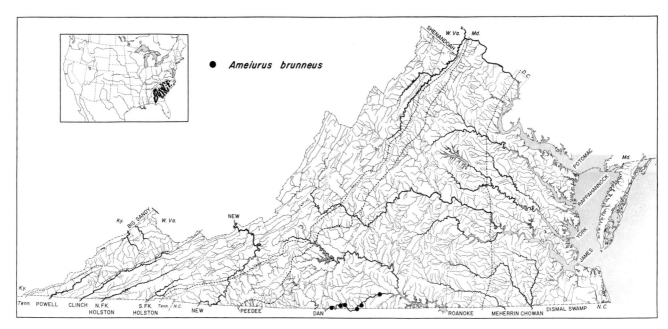

Map 107   Snail bullhead.

sketch of the diet by Yerger and Relyea (1968) indicates omnivory; insect larvae, snails, shiners, filamentous algae, and aquatic macrophytes are eaten. The largest reported specimen is 320 mm SL (Corcoran 1981); the largest Virginia specimen is 181 mm SL. Adults from the Dan system were in prespawning and postspawning condition in April and June respectively, suggesting a May to early June spawning period.

HABITAT

The snail bullhead occupies warm, medium to large streams and rivers. It is thought by Yerger and Relyea (1968) to favor higher-gradient rocky sections, and to inhabit well-flowing pools and riffles. In the outer Coastal Plain south of Virginia, Corcoran (1981) found it common in rivers having a soft organic substrate. In the lower Smith River we took juveniles in slow and moderate runs among rubble and boulders and found an adult in a backwater. It is unknown from any Virginia reservoir.

DISTRIBUTION   Map 107

The range of this southern Atlantic and eastern Gulf slope bullhead has its northern terminus in the Roanoke drainage. Discovered in 1976, the Roanoke population is known only from the Piedmont of the Dan River system above Kerr Reservoir. In 1981 we found it in the North Carolina section of the Smith

River, a Dan tributary. Within the Dan system, *A. brunneus* is restricted to the main stem and larger tributaries, being absent from higher-gradient streams arising on Blue Ridge foothills. To the south, *A. brunneus* commonly penetrates high-gradient headwater areas (Yerger and Relyea 1968; Bryant et al. 1979), frequently those upstream from reaches occupied by *A. platycephalus*. Both species also occur sympatrically, occasionally syntopically. The wide distribution of *A. platycephalus* in uplands of the Roanoke proper and Dan systems, and the recency of discovery and restriction of *A. brunneus* to the middle and lower Dan—a switch of typical distributional interrelationships—indicate that *A. brunneus* was introduced to the Roanoke drainage (Burkhead et al. 1980).

Abundance.—Rare or uncommon.

REMARKS

Bullheads usually are considered to be good eating. Although anglers generally do not distinguish the snail bullhead from other bullheads, many undoubtedly have made fine meals. Monitoring of *A. brunneus* in the Dan system would have zoogeographic relevance. If headwater penetration occurs, then the hypothesis that this species has been introduced to the Roanoke drainage would be supported.

Name.—*Brunneus* means "brown."

Yellow bullhead   *Ameiurus natalis* (Lesueur)

SYSTEMATICS

Described in 1819 from an unknown locality, *A. natalis* belongs to the *natalis* species group (Lundberg 1975, 1982, 1992), our "smalleye bullheads." Two nominal subspecies, *A. n. natalis* and *A. n. erebennus*, have been listed by many authors. Taylor (1954) found no significant differences between populations in three widely separated areas; Bailey et al. (1954) concluded that information was insufficient for recognition of subspecies.

DESCRIPTION

Materials.—From Taylor (1969), Scott and Crossman (1973), Burkhead et al. (1980), and 25 additional Virginia specimens. Life color from Scott and Crossman (1973) and 1 Virginia adult.

Anatomy.—A bullhead with an emarginate tail and pale chin barbels; adults are 120–300 mm SL. Body stout, compressed posteriorly. Head depressed, profile of head dorsum straight or slightly convex in juvenile and adult, moderately convex in nuptial male; eye small; mouth slightly or moderately inferior. Pectoral spine nearly straight; anterior serrae few, best developed distally; posterior serrae 5–8, moderate or large. Two males from June and July had pronounced swelling of dorsal head and nape musculature; genital papilla elongate, conical, flattened at base.

Meristics.—Dorsal fin with 1 spine, 6 rays; branched caudal rays 16; anal rays 24–27(28); pelvic rays 8; pectoral with 1 spine, 7–8 rays; gill rakers (12)13–16(18).

Color in Preservative.—Dorsum and side uniformly grading moderately dark to dusky; venter pale; fins usually uniformly dusky or dark, but narrowly dark-margined in some specimens. Nasal and maxillary barbels dark; mental barbels pale, usually immaculate.

Color in Life.—Dorsum olive-brown; side olive-brown to gold; venter yellow to white; fins dusky brown or olive-brown. Young dark brown on dorsum and side, venter white.

Larvae.—Described by Mansueti and Hardy (1967), Lippson and Moran (1974), Wang and Kernehan (1979), and Tin (1982b); alevin diagnosed by Cloutman (1979).

BIOLOGY

Young yellow bullheads feed primarily on microcrustaceans and insect larvae; adults are omnivorous but mainly eat various aquatic invertebrates and fishes (Flemer and Woolcott 1966; Russell 1976; Becker 1983). Females probably mature by age 2, based on the size of gravid fish reported by Scott and Crossman (1973) and Becker (1983). Age-3 fish, about half the life span, average 226 mm TL in Wisconsin and 371 mm TL in Tennessee (Carlander 1969). Brady (1969) reported a 355-mm TL specimen from Dismal Swamp, Virginia. A yellow bullhead from Ohio was 465 mm TL (18.3 inches) and 1.6 kg (3 pounds 10 ounces) (Trautman 1981).

Reproduction occurs during spring to mid-summer in Wisconsin and Canada (Scott and Crossman 1973; Becker 1983), and probably from late April through June in Virginia. Spawning habitat and behavior of *A. natalis* are typical of smalleye bullheads (Cahn 1927; C. Wallace 1972). Spawning occurs in shallow circular nests excavated near cover or in open settings, in calm water. The spawning pair assumes a head-to-tail posture, often with the caudal fin of one or both curved about the snout of the other; nest guarding and egg fanning are performed by the male. Wallace noted that a pair of yellow bullheads excavated a nest in a site too small for spawning. The eggs were deposited outside the nest, but the male guarded only the nest; this suggests that the nest was the releasor

Fish 153 *Ameiurus natalis* adult male 114 mm SL (REJ 1019), VA, Southampton County, Mill Swamp, 15 July 1983.

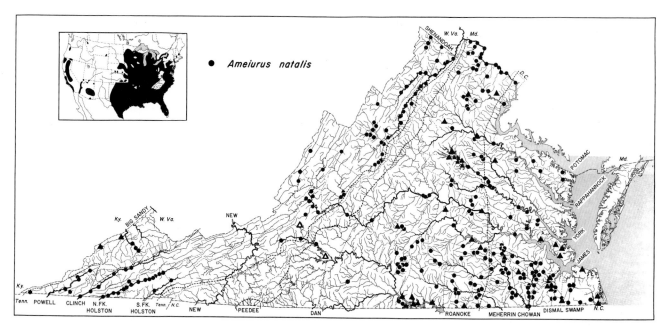

Map 108 Yellow bullhead. Open triangles signify unverified records.

of guarding behavior. Some 200–700 eggs are laid (C. Wallace 1972; Scott and Crossman 1973).

HABITAT

A warmwater species, *A. natalis* is found in pools and backwaters of lotic habitats and in ponds, lakes, and reservoirs. In running water, it spans the range from moderate-gradient intermontane situations, where it extends from medium-sized streams to rivers, to sluggish lower Piedmont and Coastal Plain waters, including creeks. The yellow bullhead associates with cover, often dense vegetation (Hastings 1979). It is tolerant of high acidity and is the most abundant fish in interior Dismal Swamp (Brady 1969). The yellow bullhead is more tolerant of acid water than the brown bullhead, and the latter is the more tolerant of polluted water (Hastings 1979). Although Kendall and Schwartz (1968) cited an occurrence at 15‰ salinity in Florida, Schwartz (1981b) reported the yellow bullhead to be rare in salinity greater than 5‰ in North Carolina. Judging from Map 108 and Musick (1972), *A. natalis* is not an estuary inhabitant in Virginia. In Florida it enters caves and may reproduce there (Relyea and Sutton 1973).

DISTRIBUTION   Map 108

Native to eastern and central North America, *A. natalis* has been widely introduced elsewhere. In Virginia it is considered indigenous to all major Atlantic

slope drainages and to the Tennessee and Big Sandy drainages; however, its occurrence in the upper Big Sandy may be due to introduction. This species is unknown from the New drainage in Virginia but was found recently in the West Virginia portion (Hocutt et al. 1979; Hess 1983), where it may have been introduced.

The peculiar range of *A. natalis* in the upper Roanoke and Dan systems is typical of problems that beset zoogeographic analysis: unlikely localization, misidentification of specimens, and undocumented but probable introductions. The four stream plots in the upper Roanoke and lower Dan represent our six collections of *A. natalis*. However, it was not until Hambrick (1973) and we rejected several records (clearly or probably of *A. platycephalus*) that *A. natalis* appeared to be absent from nearly all of the Roanoke and Dan above their junction. External characters for their easy separation were unclear until Burkhead et al. (1980) emphasized the blotched dorsal fin and larger eye of *A. platycephalus*. We therefore doubt the two reservoir records, neither of which are represented by a specimen: Carvins Cove Reservoir in 1960 (VPI 209), Smith Mountain Reservoir (Hart 1978). Localization of *A. natalis* in the upper Roanoke indicates that it was introduced, but we are reluctant to accept this because the verified Dan system (Banister River) record may indicate normal (but limited) extension upriver from lowland centers of abundance. However, the Dan population also may have been introduced.

Abundance.—Generally rare in western Virginia and intermontane streams of Atlantic slope drainages, usually uncommon or common eastward.

REMARKS

Based on its distribution and abundance, the yellow bullhead is one of the most commonly caught catfishes in Virginia. Bullheads are catfishes for kids, for they require little skill to angle and to a six-year-old they seem quite formidable.

Name.—*Natalis* refers to "nates" (buttocks); it probably alludes to the swollen and medially furrowed dorsal head and nape muscles of breeding males.

Brown bullhead   *Ameiurus nebulosus* (Lesueur)

SYSTEMATICS

Ameiurus nebulosus was described in 1819 from the Delaware River. It is placed in the *natalis* species group and is closely allied to *A. melas* (Lundberg 1975, 1982, 1992). The two nominal subspecies, *A. n. nebulosus* (purportedly the form in Virginia) and *A. n. marmoratus* (Hubbs 1940; Hart 1952), are of dubious status and need study (Bailey et al. 1954).

DESCRIPTION

Materials.—From Taylor (1969), Scott and Crossman (1973), data and specimens of Burkhead et al. (1980), and 7 more Virginia specimens. Color in life from Scott and Crossman (1973) and 4 Virginia specimens.

Anatomy.—A bullhead with an emarginate tail, dark chin barbels, and usually 13–15 gill rakers; adults are 140–340 mm SL. Body chubby, compressed posteriorly. Head depressed, profile of dorsum straight in juvenile to distinctly convex in some adults; eye small; mouth slightly subterminal. Pectoral spine described under *Comparison*. Male genital papilla elongate, conical; female lacks papilla, genital pore a slit bordered by papillae; external differences at anal–genital area same as described by Moen (1959) for *Ictalurus punctatus* (Blumer 1985a). Epicranial tissues and nape musculature swollen in nuptial male; head width greatest in male (Blumer 1985a).

Meristics.—Dorsal fin with 1 spine, 6(7) rays; branched caudal rays 15(16); anal rays (18)20–24; pelvic rays 8; pectoral with 1 spine, (7)8(9) rays; gill rakers (12)13–15(16).

Color in Preservative.—Dorsum uniformly dusky or black; side slightly or heavily mottled; venter pale; some fish mostly black. Fins variable, nearly uniformly slightly dusky, moderately dusky, or black; the pale basicaudal bar described for *A. melas* is also present on some young *A. nebulosus*. All barbels pigmented, profusely so in large juvenile and adult.

Color in Life Plate 22.—Dorsum and side gray, brown, or black, sometimes with green or olive-gold cast, mottling evident or not so; venter dirty white to yellow; fins usually olive-brown, sometimes black.

Larvae.—Described by Mansueti and Hardy (1967), Lippson and Moran (1974), Wang and Kernehan (1979), and Tin (1982b); alevin diagnosed by Cloutman (1979).

COMPARISON

Ameiurus nebulosus and *A. melas* are often difficult to distinguish. Wheeler (1978) discussed the problem relative to introduced European populations, and used anal ray count and fin color differences employed by Scott and Crossman (1973) to distinguish

Fish 154 *Ameiurus nebulosus* adult female 175 mm SO (REJ 1036), VA, Campbell County, Roanoke River, 12 September 1983.

these species in Canada. However, the ray count difference does not apply to the Virginia populations or the few others in the eastern United States that we have studied; anal rays usually number 20–24 in both species. We also found that body and fin coloration have no consistent discriminatory value because of ontogenetic and putative habitat-related variability in both species. Geographic variation of both species needs critical study (Burr and Warren 1986); it may explain the differences reported by Scott and Crossman (1973).

In a key to the catfishes of Pennsylvania, Cooper (1983) stated that Burkhead et al. (1980) added confusion to the literature by employing gill raker counts for the separation of *A. nebulosus* and *A. melas*, and by not using the degree of serration of the posterior edge of the pectoral fin spine. Serration is usually described as moderate in *nebulosus* vs. weak or absent in *melas*. Actually the number and size of serrae increase with age in *A. melas* (Paloumpis 1963); this may be a general pattern in both *Ameiurus* and *Ictalurus* (Hubbs and Hibbard 1951).

The states of pectoral spine serrae change with age. (1) In young fish (about 30–50 mm SL), 2–3 weak anterior serrae, and 2–4 small and sharp posterior serrae occur in *nebulosus* vs. serrae absent or a few weak notches present in *melas*. (2) In juveniles (about 50–140 mm SL; Figure 50), anterior serrae are absent or weak, posterior serrae moderate in *nebulosus* vs. anterior serrae absent or weak, posterior serrae weak or moderate in *melas*. (3) In adults (larger than about 140 mm SL; Figure 50), anterior serrae are absent or weak, posterior serrae usually moderate in *nebulosus* vs. anterior serrae usually absent, posterior serrae weak or moderate in *melas*. Because of intraspecific variation related to fish size, and owing to interspecific overlap among specimens of similar size, errors in identifying *A. nebulosus* and *A. melas* are likely to result from sole reliance on pectoral serrae. Spines of alevin *A. nebulosus* and *A. melas* are illustrated by Cloutman (1979); we have not seen serrae as proportionately large in larger young and older fish of either species as those he depicted.

The utility of gill raker counts (usually 13–15 in *nebulosus* vs. usually 17–19 for *melas*) was suggested to Burkhead et al. (1980) by W. R. Taylor and was supported by Menhinick (1989). Because gill rakers are incompletely developed in the young of both bullheads, pectoral spine serrae may be a better character for identifying specimens of that stage.

An interesting difference between *A. nebulosus* and *A. melas* is the length of the pored lateral line (measured from first to last body pores, including any interrupted sections), expressed as % SL. In *A. nebu-* *losus* this character tends to be isometric, whereas in *A. melas* it exhibits positive allometry (i.e., pored canal length increases faster than fish length). In *A. nebulosus* the pored lateral line ranged 44–70% SL, mean, 59.2 (14 specimens) vs. 13–50% SL, mean, 31.2 (13) in *melas*. The only overlap occurred with three putative *A. nebulosus* from Gaston and Kerr reservoir tributaries, the area harboring the only Atlantic slope population of *A. melas* in Virginia. One of the three exhibited other anomalous character states (see *Biology*). The lateral line character needs further study; in Virginia the difference may be confounded by the possible presence of two forms of *A. nebulosus* in the Roanoke drainage (Hubbs and Lagler 1958).

BIOLOGY

The brown bullhead is omnivorous. Young eat a variety of microcrustaceans; adults eat algae, a broad spectrum of aquatic invertebrates, and fishes (Carlander 1969). Gatz (1979) found that filamentous algae and aquatic insects were equally important in the diet in North Carolina; Gunn et al. (1977) reported apparent digestion of algae.

Age-3 brown bullheads are mature (Harlan and Speaker 1956; Blumer 1985a), and maximum longevity is about 9 years (Rubec and Qadri 1982). Adult males tend to be longer than adult females. *Ameiurus nebulosus* averages 180–259 mm TL at age 4 in various Canadian and United States populations (Rubec and Qadri 1982). The largest Virginia specimen at hand is 222 mm SL. A brown bullhead of 478 mm TL (18.8 inches) weighing 1.8 kg (3 pounds 14 ounces) is reported from Ohio (Trautman 1981).

Reproduction of *A. nebulosus* was summarized from the literature and studied in Munro Lake, Michigan, by Blumer (1985a, 1985b, 1986). In the southern United States spawning begins in April and may continue to late summer. In northern states, adults attending young have been observed from late June to early July. In Munro Lake, newly spawned eggs were found during a limited period (10–24 days) each year. Water temperatures during the reproductive period were 14–29°C (Tin 1982b; Blumer 1985a). Nesting occurs in shallows, in the open, in natural shelters such as under logs and in burrows, and in litter such as cans. In lakes and in pools and backwaters of streams, the typical spawning substrate is firm sand that is cleared of silt by one or both parents.

Courtship and spawning sometimes includes the typical ictalurid head-to-tail spawning posture (Breder 1935:173, Figure 15). Both sexes or either sex alone perform egg-maintenance and nest-guarding responsibilities. Michigan females produced 1,500–

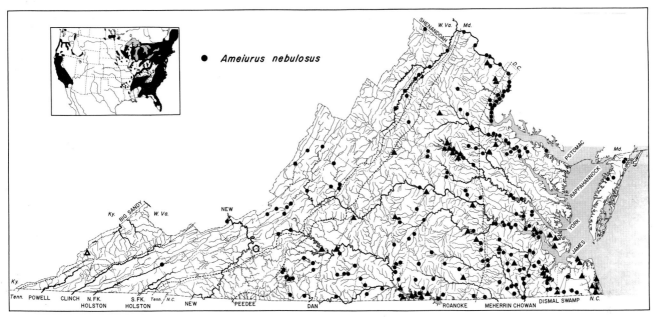

Map 109   Brown bullhead. Open symbols are for rejected, doubtful, or important but unverified records.

2,600 mature ova, to be spawned in single clutches. Broods of 610 and 778 fry were reported by Scott and Crossman (1973); broods of several hundred young each were observed by Blumer (1986).

The hybrid *A. melas* × *A. nebulosus* was reported from Ohio by Trautman (1957), and apparently was noted by Hubbs (1955), but Taylor (1969) did not include it in his critical review of ictalurid hybrids. However, Trautman (1981) listed it from (apparently) Pennsylvania, and again, as hybrid swarms in some parts of Ohio. This hybrid was also identified in Wisconsin (Becker 1983). An odd, possibly hybrid specimen (102 mm SL, WHH 159) from Little Poplar Creek, a Gaston Reservoir tributary in Virginia, has atypical, broadly coalesced gill rakers on both first arches. The moderately mottled side and pectoral serration are typical of *A. nebulosus*, but the pored lateral line length is suggestive of *A. melas*.

HABITAT

The brown bullhead is a warmwater fish characteristic of backwaters and pools of moderate-gradient and sluggish large creeks, streams, and rivers, and of ponds, lakes, and reservoirs. Trautman (1981) indicated that it was not particularly tolerant of turbidity. In Virginia it ranges into areas of low pH, including Dismal Swamp, apparently to a greater extent than it does in the New Jersey Pine Barrens (Hastings 1979). It extends into estuaries to 8‰ salinity in Virginia

(Musick 1972). The record from 27‰ salinity in North Carolina (Schwartz 1981b) may be due to entrapment of the fish after runoff of less-saline water.

DISTRIBUTION   Map 109

Ameiurus nebulosus is native to the Atlantic and Gulf slopes and to the Mississippi and Great Lakes basins; it has been widely transplanted in North America and Europe. It is found in all major Atlantic slope drainages of Virginia and on the lower Delmarva Peninsula.

The brown bullhead probably was introduced to the New drainage; only three widely separate records are known below Claytor Lake, including one from West Virginia (Hocutt et al. 1979; Burkhead et al. 1980). The Meadow Creek, Virginia, record is now rejected because the collection also contained *Etheostoma nigrum*, a darter otherwise not known from this section of the New. The specimens were used in class laboratory exercises and could easily have been transposed from other collections (J. R. Reed, in litt.). Neither species was taken subsequently at the same site by Reed or us.

A collection in 1981 from the North Fork Holston River produced the first validated record of *A. nebulosus* for the Tennessee drainage of Virginia; two specimens had been listed as *A. melas* by Widlak (1982). The one specimen (VPIFU) examined by us was found to be *A. nebulosus*, and the identification of both was changed to that species by Neves and Widlak (1988). Likely the record stems from stocking. Two unverified records of *A. nebulosus* were reported (Peltz and Maughan 1979) from closely adjacent small impoundments in the Powell system. They may have been based on *A. melas*, but if correctly identified, then stocking is implicated; at least one other species taken apparently was introduced. Surprisingly, *A. nebulosus* is unknown from the Big Sandy drainage of Virginia and Kentucky (Burr and Warren 1986; see *A. melas*).

Abundance.—Rare or uncommon in western Virginia, often common or abundant in the middle Piedmont and Coastal Plain.

REMARKS

The brown bullhead is easily angled, widely stocked in farm ponds, and provides good table fare.

Name.—*Nebulosus*, "cloudy," alludes to body mottling.

Black bullhead   *Ameiurus melas* (Rafinesque)

SYSTEMATICS

Described in 1820 from the Ohio River or environs, *A. melas* is a member of the *natalis* species group; among living species it is most closely related to *A. nebulosus* (Lundberg 1975, 1982). The two nominal subspecies *A. m. melas* and *A. m. catulus*, the former purportedly the native Virginia form, are only briefly characterized by Hubbs and Ortenburger (1929a) and lack detailed analysis.

DESCRIPTION

Materials.—From Taylor (1969), Scott and Crossman (1973), Burkhead et al. (1980), 6 specimens from Illinois, and 1 from Kentucky. Color in life from Scott and Crossman (1973) and 1 Virginia adult.

Anatomy.—A bullhead with an emarginate tail, dark chin barbels, and usually 17–19 gill rakers; adults are 140–300 mm SL. Body robust, compressed posteriorly. Head depressed, lateral profile of dorsum straight in juvenile to distinctly convex in some adults; eye small; mouth slightly subterminal. Pectoral spine straight or slightly curved, posterior serrae variable (Figure 50; *Comparison* under *A. nebulosus*).

Meristics.—Dorsal fin with 1 spine, 6 rays; branched caudal rays 15; anal rays (19)20–24(25); pelvic rays 8; pectoral with 1 spine, 8 rays; gill rakers (15)17–19(21).

Color in Preservative.—Dorsum moderately dusky or black, darkest in breeding adult; side usually grading from black or moderately dusky to slightly dusky, occasionally mottled; venter pale. Fins moderately dusky or black; caudal base usually with pale, often barely discernible vertical bar in juvenile and adult. Barbels dusky or black. Peritoneum pale brown or dusky brown.

Color in Life.—Dorsum and upper side olive, brown, or black; lower side green-gold, yellow, or white; boundary of upper and lower side pattern sometimes mottled; venter yellow or white; fins brown or black. In breeding male, dorsum and upper side black, venter bright yellow to milky white.

Larvae.—Described by Tin (1982b); alevin distinguished by Cloutman (1979).

COMPARISON

See *A. nebulosus*.

Fish 155 *Ameiurus melas* juvenile 79 mm SL (SIUC), KY, Webster County, Knoblick Creek, 8 October 1978.

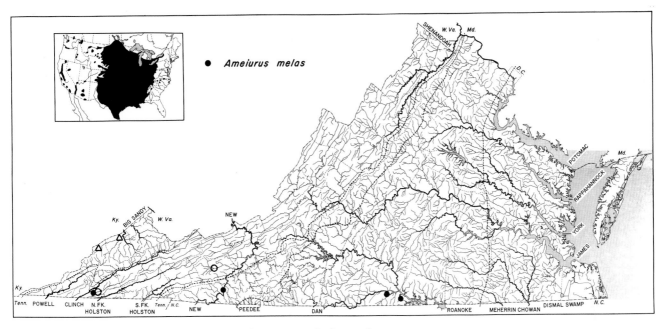

Map 110   Black bullhead. Open symbols indicate unverified records.

BIOLOGY

The life history of the black bullhead is well known from the summary by Carlander (1969) and studies in Iowa and Kentucky (Forney 1955; Campbell and Branson 1978). Young feed primarily on microcrustaceans; juveniles and adults eat a variety of invertebrates and fishes. Plants are ingested but may not be important in the diet. Maturity occurs by age 2 or 3; maximum longevity is 9 years. Black bullheads typically are 150–300 mm TL by age 4. Stunting is common in small ponds. The largest Virginia specimen is 158 mm SL. A black bullhead of 427 mm TL (16.8 inches) and 1.2 kg (2 pounds 12 ounces) is listed from Ohio by Trautman (1981).

Ameiurus melas probably spawns during late May and June in Virginia, the most frequent period reported in other states. Water temperatures at spawning are 21–30°C (Scott and Crossman 1973; Campbell and Branson 1978). The following description of spawning is condensed from Cahn (1927), Harlan and Speaker (1956), and Wallace (1967). Spawning occurs over sand in backwaters. The female excavates a shallow nest by fin fanning and pushing the substrate with the snout. Spawning adults assume a lateral head-to-tail position, the male embracing the female by wrapping his caudal fin about her snout. Nest guarding is done by both sexes. Typical fecundity is 2,550–3,850 ova (Campbell and Branson 1978).

Ameiurus melas is known to hybridize with *A. nebulosus* (see that account).

HABITAT

The black bullhead is a warmwater fish found in pools and backwaters of creeks, streams, and rivers, and in ponds, lakes, and reservoirs. It tolerates extreme environmental conditions, including high temperature, low dissolved oxygen, and considerable turbidity, that are limiting to many other fishes (Campbell and Branson 1978; Trautman 1981).

DISTRIBUTION   Map 110

Ameiurus melas is indigenous to central North America from southern Canada to northern Mexico and has been widely introduced. In Virginia it may have been native only to the Big Sandy drainage, but we were unable to verify any in-state record from this drainage. Big Sandy records that we plotted are from Flannagan and North Fork Pound reservoirs (Wollitz 1972, 1973, 1975a, 1975b), but no specimens were saved. Wollitz's samples from Pound Reservoir were reported as *A. nebulosus* but were likely *A. melas*. *Ameiurus melas* has been reported from several sites in the Kentucky part of the Big Sandy (Howell 1981), and *A. nebulosus* is unknown from the drainage (Burr and Warren 1986; Hocutt et al. 1986). Howell (1981) indicated that Big Sandy records of many species, including *A. nebulosus*, were supported by "extant museum collection reports or specimens," but in many cases these reports are not supported by preserved specimens and remain questionable. Adding to the uncertainty, *A. melas* may be native in the Big Sandy only to areas outside Virginia; it generally is absent from montane areas and all putative Virginia records are from impoundments managed for sport fishes.

Only one specimen is documented from the Virginia section of the Tennessee drainage, an adult from Copper Creek in 1969. Taylor et al. (1971) considered it a possible introduction. Wollitz (1967b) reported *A. melas* from a millpond near the Copper Creek site. The second specimen of *A. "melas"* reported from the North Fork Holston River by Widlak (1982) has not been relocated; the record is rejected (see *A. nebulosus*). Burkhead et al. (1980) regarded *A. melas* as probably introduced and not established in the New; there is one verified record from 1939 (USNM 109467) and one questionable report (Wollitz 1968a).

On the Virginia Atlantic slope, we took juvenile *A. melas* in 1979 from two Kerr Reservoir tributaries, Roanoke drainage. This species apparently has been introduced and established in the North Carolina portions of the Dan system of the Roanoke and the Pee Dee drainage. The Pee Dee perhaps is the source of the Roanoke population (Burkhead et al. 1980). We do not accept several reports from the Roanoke and northward (Burkhead et al. 1980); records from the North Carolina section of the Roanoke River (Hassler et al. 1981) also are questionable.

Abundance.—Rare; represented by one or few specimens when found.

REMARKS

Although delectable when fried, the low abundance of the black bullhead in Virginia indicates that it rarely becomes table fare in the state.

Name.—*Melas* means "black." Smalleye bullheads such as *A. melas* are frequently referred to as "mudcats" by anglers.

Madtoms   Genus *Noturus* Rafinesque

Madtoms are small catfishes with an adnate adipose fin—the posterior margin of the adipose fin is attached to the caudal fin—a trait absent in other ictalurid genera of Virginia. *Noturus* is the most speciose ictalurid genus, comprising 27 species (2 undescribed), including 6 in Virginia.

In his monograph, Taylor (1969) recognized three subgenera. The subgenus *Noturus* contained only the stonecat *N. flavus*; the other madtoms were divided between the subgenera *Schilbeodes* and *Rabida*. However, based mainly on chromosome morphology, LeGrande (1981) suggested subgeneric consolidation of *Schilbeodes* with *Noturus*. *Noturus* is the first described and hence has priority for usage. Mayden (1983) and we accept this arrangement, although madtom phylogeny and classification remain under active study. Recently, Grady and LeGrande (1992), using allozyme, morphological, and chromosomal characters in multiple cladistic analyses, recognized the three subgenera of *Noturus*. We became aware of their study too late to revise these accounts accordingly. Pigmentation patterns in the subgenus *Noturus* are mostly plain; in *Rabida* the back typically has bold saddles, the side may be mottled, and some fins are banded or blotched.

Much of the knowledge of madtom biology stems from very recent research. Mayden (1983) and Mayden and Walsh (1984) review systematics, ecology, and life history of the genus.

Name.—*Noturus* translates as "back tail," in reference to the confluent adipose and caudal fins. The name madtom was given as "Mad-Tom" by Jordan (1889b). The name apparently alludes to their seemingly inane swimming behavior when startled (Ono et al. 1983). Madtoms often are called "catminnows" in Virginia.

Stonecat   *Noturus flavus* Rafinesque

SYSTEMATICS

Noturus flavus, described in 1818 from the Ohio River, is the type species of the recently enlarged subgenus *Noturus*. Near relatives include *N. gilberti*, *N. exilis*, and *N. insignis* (Taylor 1969; LeGrande 1981). Exact placement of *N. flavus* within *Noturus* is problematic (LeGrande 1981); we arbitrarily place it basally. The upper Tennessee drainage population of the stonecat is chromosomally distinctive (LeGrande and Cavender 1980).

DESCRIPTION

Materials.—From Taylor (1969) and five Virginia specimens.

Fish 156 *Noturus flavus* subadult male 59 mm SL (REJ 1080), VA, Scott County, Copper Creek, 25 April 1985.

Anatomy.—A madtom with an unscrawled body, pale-margined tail, and posterior extensions of the tooth patch on the upper jaw; adults are 70–150 mm SL. Body slender, compressed posteriorly; head broad, depressed; eye small or moderate; mouth subterminal. Pectoral spine straight; surface usually only roughened, lacking prominent serrae. A mature male of 101 mm SL has enlarged epicranial swelling; genital papilla conical, apically notched.

Meristics.—Dorsal fin with 1 spine, (5)6 rays; upper caudal rays (27)29–33(36); lower caudal rays (26)27–31(33); anal rays 15–18(19); pelvic rays (8)9–10; pectoral with 1 spine, 9–11 rays.

Color in Preservative.—Dorsum of head and body moderately dusky or dark, except nape demarked anteriorly by a pale crescent, and a smaller, more distinct pale spot occurs at posterior end of dorsal fin base; side grading moderately dusky to pale. Dorsal and adipose fins each with dark basal blotch, pale distally; caudal fin pale-margined, upper lobe with subtriangular pale area, rest of fin dusky, darkest submarginally; anal, pelvic, and pectoral fins essentially pale. Barbels pale or slightly dusky.

Color in Life Plate 22.—Back and side gray, olive, or brown, often with yellow cast; postdorsal spot yellow; fins with pale yellow cast, blotches gray to blackish.

Larvae.—Described by Tin (1982b) and Walsh and Burr (1985).

BIOLOGY

The life history of Illinois and Missouri populations and literature on *N. flavus* were analyzed by Walsh and Burr (1985). Stonecats feed on many aquatic invertebrates, chiefly immature insects, and infrequently on fishes; adults often take crayfishes. Four Virginia and Tennessee specimens had eaten mayfly, caddisfly, and midge larvae. The stonecat is the latest-maturing (3–4 years), longest-lived (9 years), and largest madtom (Walsh and Burr 1985). In Ohio stream populations and Lake Erie, age-4 fish averaged 104 and 181 mm SL, respectively (Gilbert 1953 *in* Carlander 1969). The record size for the species (and

genus) is 312 mm TL (12.3 inches), 0.5 kg (1 pound 1 ounce) from Lake Erie (Trautman 1981), a size that apparently is not approached in streams (Walsh and Burr 1985). The largest Virginia specimen is 126 mm SL.

Nesting occurs during June to, in Ohio, August beneath large rocks in riffles, runs, and lake shallows when water exceeds about 25°C. The male guards the nest. Gravid females in stream populations generate 189–570 mature ova. The male broods the embryos, of which 50–500 have been counted in different clutches (Greeley 1929; Gilbert 1953 *in* Carlander 1969; Walsh and Burr 1985).

HABITAT

Stonecats inhabit warm streams and rivers of moderate or moderately low gradient. Medium and large streams seem to be favored in Virginia. This species typically lives under rocks in runs and riffles. Rocky and sandy lake shores with wave-induced currents are occupied by some northern populations, but *N. flavus* is not known to persist in impoundments (Taylor 1969).

DISTRIBUTION Map 111

Noturus flavus is one of the most widespread and northerly inclined madtoms, being native to the Mississippi, Great Lakes–St. Lawrence, and Hudson Bay basins. In Virginia it is known only in the Tennessee drainage, from one lower and one upper major tributary of the Clinch River (Copper Creek, Little River), similarly in the North Fork Holston River (Big Moccasin Creek, Laurel Creek), and from the lower South Fork Holston River. The population in the South Holston of Virginia, known from a specimen taken in 1959, may be extirpated because of impoundment (Burkhead and Jenkins 1991). The apparent absence of the stonecat in the North Fork Holston and Clinch rivers may be related to fish kills in the 1960s and earlier. However, the lack of a record from the Clinch River at the recently well-collected first major run–riffle area below Copper Creek may result from an avoidance of large rivers by the upper Tennessee population. Otherwise, recruitment from Copper Creek would have been expected to occur, following rapid recovery of the Clinch River from the 1969 fish kill.

The stonecat probably was extirpated, without record, from the Virginia part of the Big Sandy drainage. It is known in the New drainage at two West Virginia sites, earliest taken in 1951; the population may be introduced (Hocutt et al. 1979, 1986).

Abundance.—The stonecat is rare in the entire Tennessee drainage, which is surprising due to the abundance of apparently suitable habitat. We know of only 23 specimens in 14 collections from Virginia; 7 specimens from Big Moccasin Creek are the most taken at a time. Nine records are from Copper Creek, in whose extreme lower section the species apparently has increased recently, based on the comparison of a few samples taken during 1983–1984 with those of the intensive survey in 1967–1973.

REMARKS

Because of their small size, madtoms rarely are table fare. The stonecat, which attains relatively large size in Lake Erie, reportedly is good eating (Greeley 1929). An adult from Copper Creek in 1983 furnished the first evidence of attack on a madtom by a parasitic lamprey, in this case *Ichthyomyzon bdellium*.

We regard *N. flavus* to merit special concern status in Virginia became of its rarity there and elsewhere in the Tennessee drainage, and because the upper Tennessee population appears to be taxonomically distinct (T. M. Cavender, in litt.).

Name.—*Flavus,* "yellow," refers to the tint of some specimens.

Orangefin madtom   *Noturus gilberti* Jordan and Evermann

SYSTEMATICS

The orangefin madtom was made known by Jordan and Evermann (*in* Jordan 1889a) from the upper Roanoke River and its South Fork in Virginia. It was positioned basally in the subgenus *Schilbeodes* and considered to be rather specialized by Taylor (1969), and was regarded as primitive in the broadened subgenus *Noturus* by LeGrande (1981).

DESCRIPTION

Materials.—From Taylor (1969) and 50 series from the Roanoke and James drainages. Living color from many Roanoke and James drainage fish.

Anatomy.—A madtom with a pale area on the upper caudal lobe, body lacking scrawling and saddles, and posterior extensions absent from the tooth patch on the upper jaw; adults are 60–80 mm SL. Body moderately or quite elongate, well compressed posteriorly. Head somewhat narrow, depressed; eye small; mouth subterminal or inferior; barbels short. Pectoral fin and its spine quite short, spine one-third to one-half the length of longest ray and with few small posterior serrae. Reproductive male with swollen anterodorsal muscles, swelling absent in gravid female; male genital papilla about twice as long as female papilla; papilla centered in swollen villate mound. Cutaneous taste buds on head, particularly ventrally, and on body of both sexes enlarged during breeding season.

Meristics.—Dorsal fin with 1 spine, (5)6 rays; upper caudal rays (22)24–26(27); lower caudal rays (23)24–27; anal rays 14–16(18); pelvic rays 9–10; pectoral with 1 spine, 9–10 rays.

Color in Preservative.—Dorsum and upper side dusky or dark, lacking saddles; a narrow dusky streak often present along lateral line; venter pale. Dorsal fin with large dark blotch basally, elsewhere usually pale, sometimes slightly dusky. Adipose, anal, and pelvic fins usually mostly pale, dusky basally. Pectoral fin pale or dusky. Caudal fin pale-margined, the pale edge slightly or, usu-

Fish 157 *Noturus gilberti* adult male 69 mm SL (REJ 1039), VA, Montgomery County, South Fork Roanoke River, 16 September 1983.

ally, much wider on upper half of fin, often forming a somewhat triangular pale area; adjacent to pale margin the caudal is slightly to quite dusky, distinctly darkest in lower half of fin. Nasal barbel dusky, other barbels pale.

Color in Life   Plate 23.—Upper half of head and body pale gray to medium brown, often with slight yellow-olive cast; mid- and lower side very pale gray to yellow-olive, sometimes with slight pink vascular cast; venter whitish, slight pink cast in some specimens. Pale areas in all fins colorless or, usually, with very slight to moderate yellow wash, most intense in pectoral, never bright orange (except when fins are folded); basal blotch in dorsal fin and sub-marginal dusky area in lower caudal lobe light to medium brown with slight yellow-olive cast; nasal barbel dusky brown.

BIOLOGY

The orangefin madtom feeds almost entirely on immature aquatic insects, particularly mayflies, hy-dropsychid caddisflies, and midges; at least some of its foraging occurs at night. Both sexes mature by age 2; some individuals may spawn at age 1. The life span is 3 years or less. Females attain slightly larger size than males; most adult males are 60–75 mm SL, fe-males 70–80 mm (Jenkins 1977a; Burkhead 1983). The largest specimen is 85 mm SL, from Virginia (Taylor 1969).

Spawning has not been observed, but based on gonadal conditions, it apparently occurs from late April through May in cool and warm sections of the upper Roanoke River, and probably into June in cool Dan River tailwaters. Temperatures of inhabited wa-ters in the upper Roanoke during this period of 1982 were 10–17°C; the Dan River was 17°C where a gravid female was found on 1 June 1977. Spawning appears to peak at about 19–20°C (Simonson and Neves 1986). Breeding sites probably are beneath rubble, the typ-ical habitat of the madtom at these times. Fecundity is quite low; mature ova number 32–70 (Jenkins 1977a; Burkhead 1983).

HABITAT

Orangefin madtoms exhibit a rather narrow range of habitat selection. They occur only in small to large, moderate-gradient, intermontane and upper Pied-mont streams; cool and warm waters are inhabited. The most successful populations—in Craig Creek, the Roanoke drainage above Salem, and the Dan River—occupy generally clear waters; others are in more frequently turbid streams. The madtom inhabits moderate to strong runs and riffles having little or virtually no silt. It appears to be an obligate intersti-cine dweller; during daytime snorkeling and day and night collecting it was found only in or near cavities formed by rubble and boulders. The relatively narrow head and small fins are adaptive to small cavities. *Noturus gilberti* is not known from an impoundment (Jenkins 1977a; Burkhead 1983; Simonson and Neves 1986).

DISTRIBUTION   Map 111

Noturus gilberti is a relict species native to the upper Roanoke drainage in Virginia and North Carolina; five isolated populations inhabit the drainage. It is endemic to the Roanoke if the population in the up-per James drainage stemmed from an introduction.

In the upper Roanoke system proper, *N. gilberti* occurs contiguously in suitable habitat of the Roanoke River from Salem upstream, through the South Fork, and into lower Bottom and Goose creeks; the range extremes span 59 rkm. In the Pigg River system, it populates much of the lower 25 rkm of Big Chestnut Creek, up to an impoundment, and in 1986 a specimen was found in the Pigg River at 4 rkm above Chestnut Creek. In the Dan system, the mad-tom occurs within about 54 rkm of the Dan River from about Danbury, North Carolina, into Virginia, ending at the gorge in the Blue Ridge. This stretch is below three impoundments which serve as silt traps. *Notu-rus gilberti* was taken in the lower North Fork of South Mayo River in 1952, and rediscovered there and found in the South Mayo River in 1985; all sites are within or just above Stuart, 7 rkm total (Jenkins 1977a; Burkhead 1983; Simonson and Neves 1986).

Other Roanoke drainage populations or subpopu-lations have vanished or almost so. *Noturus gilberti* was found in the lower 7 rkm of the North Fork Roanoke River during 1968–1981, but not in nine collections during 1985 (Jenkins 1977a; Burkhead 1983; Simonson and Neves 1986). The upper Smith River, Dan system, yielded 1 specimen in a 1985 survey, but none were caught at 26 sites there nor at 16 sites in a major tributary, Rockcastle Creek, during 1985–1986. One specimen was taken in the Little Dan River in 1952 (verified in 1984), but none were found in one collection during 1977 nor in 14 collections during 1985.

We accord probably-introduced status to the James drainage population principally because of an appar-ent range expansion determined from surveys made specifically for *N. gilberti* in 1972 and 1977 (Jenkins 1977a) and 1984–1986 (Simonson and Neves 1986). Central to the issue is the intensively surveyed Craig Creek system. The lower portion of other upper James tributaries—waters of size and quality similar

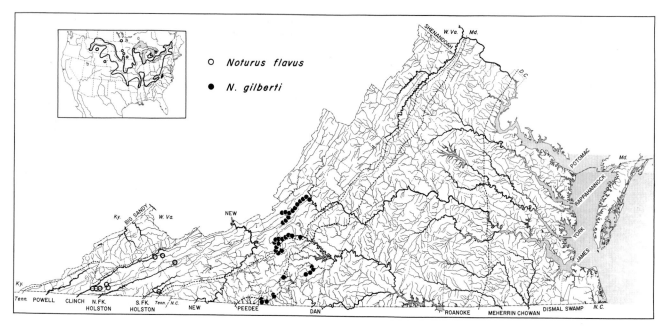

Map 111 Stonecat and orangefin madtom.

to Craig Creek—and the upper James River itself have been moderately or well surveyed.

Noturus gilberti was first found in the James drainage in Johns Creek, the largest Craig Creek tributary, just above the mouth at Newcastle in 1951 (Robins and Raney 1956). It was also taken in Johns Creek at Newcastle in 1952 but not again in the stream until 1984, when it was found at and well above Newcastle (Simonson and Neves 1986). Collectors in lower Johns Creek before 1951 could easily have missed the madtom, but some of those working during 1953–1983 would likely have found it, had it been abundant. We judge that during 1951–1983 the madtom dispersed upstream; the population may have reached a readily detectable level only during the later part of the period.

In Craig Creek, *N. gilberti* was found near Newcastle in 1963, and since then it has generally been taken in that area. The chronology of many other records indicates progressive dispersal in Craig Creek to well above and below Newcastle, down to the mouth by 1984. Between the ends of the range, some 124 rkm are occupied in the Craig system. Beyond the Craig system, the madtom was not found in inventories during 1956–1975 nor during the 1984–1986 search. Most notably, it was not caught in lower Catawba Creek, the first major James River tributary below Craig Creek, during the surveys in 1984 by Simonson and Neves (1986) and in 1987 by Jenkins.

Noturus gilberti probably was introduced to the Craig system, because of: the suggested recent spread of the species; its apparent absence from ex-

tensive good habitat elsewhere in the James; the popularity of madtoms as bait; the moderate sport-fishing pressure on the Craig system; the proximity of the upper Roanoke Valley, from which many anglers embark; and the Roanoke River being an ample source of *N. gilberti* for bait. Burkhead (1983) indicated that madtoms are seined and sold (often illegally) in the Roanoke Valley, and Simonson and Neves (1986) summarized VDGIF reports indicating that madtom use by area fishermen is extensive; see also *N. insignis, Remarks*.

The introduction hypothesis is supported by the identification of 163 pectoral spines of *Noturus insignis* and none of *N. gilberti* from an excavated Indian village, the Bessemer site located at the mouth of Craig Creek (Whyte 1989). Use of the site by Indians is radiocarbon-dated as 250–800 years before present.

Abundance.—Although several orangefin madtoms may be found by normal sampling efforts in Craig Creek and the Roanoke drainage above Salem, this species generally is rare or uncommon. Whereas Jordan (1889b) stated that about 40% of the madtoms taken in the Roanoke River in Roanoke and Salem during 1888 were *N. gilberti*, now it appears to be extirpated in Roanoke and its population density in Salem is much reduced.

REMARKS

The orangefin madtom was regarded as threatened in North Carolina and Virginia (Bailey 1977; Jenkins and Musick 1979)—hence in its whole range. It is under consideration by the U.S. Fish and Wildlife Service for federal protective status, as recommended by Jenkins (1977a) and petitioned by Burkhead following his 1983 report. From a third status survey, Simonson and Neves (1986) did not recommend protective status, which compelled reconsideration of our earlier stand.

In 1983 we knew five populations to have occupied, within the previous 35 years, suitable habitat between range extremes totaling about 128 rkm. The length was more than doubled, to 269 rkm, chiefly by Simonson and Neves' inventory in 1984–1986. They found the South Mayo population to be extant; they determined that a major reach of Big Chestnut Creek and a Pigg River site were inhabited; the range in the Craig Creek system was greatly extended; and the Smith River population was first reported. Simonson and Neves' range estimate of 269 rkm was based on ends of inhabited reaches; they mathematically determined *N. gilberti* to actually inhabit about 144 rkm.

Of the 144 rkm, the orangefin madtom is very rare in Salem and the populations or subpopulations in the North Fork Roanoke, Smith, and Little Dan rivers are minuscule or extirpated. The inhabited reaches of Big Chestnut Creek and the Pigg River are moderately to heavily silted. The South Mayo population is restricted to the impacted area of Stuart. Outside the 144 rkm, *N. gilberti* has long been absent from the Roanoke River below Salem. These data and the highly fragmented nature of the range in the Roanoke drainage indicate a history of decline. The one major range extension occurred in the James drainage—in 1975 the ends of the range were known to span about 19 rkm; by 1985 they were at least 124 rkm apart.

In reconsidering the question of protective status for *N. gilberti*, one must now weigh more heavily the detrimental effect of the recently recognized common use of native madtoms as bait in the upper Roanoke and James drainages. Little or no concern is given to discerning between rare and common species when stocking the bait tank.

We again conclude that *N. gilberti* merits threatened status (Burkhead and Jenkins 1991). Although some Roanoke drainage populations are faring better than earlier thought, some of these and others have declined or could disappear because of slight increases in siltation or chemical pollution. The probably-introduced Craig system population is doing quite well and could spread from those relatively pristine waters. However, if transplanted populations carry reduced weight in status assessment, then the orangefin could be placed in the same category—endangered—that is federally designated for its compatriot the Roanoke logperch.

Name.—*Gilberti* is a patronym of the eminent ichthyologist Charles H. Gilbert, a colleague of Jordan and Evermann.

Margined madtom   *Noturus insignis* (Richardson)

SYSTEMATICS

Noturus insignis, subgenus *Noturus*, was described in 1836 from the Philadelphia area. Taylor (1969) allied it with *N. nocturnus* whereas LeGrande (1981) considered it most closely related to *N. exilis*.

Two subspecies were recognized by Hubbs and Raney (1944), the nominate form in Atlantic slope drainages excluding the Roanoke, and *N. i. atrorus* of the Roanoke and New drainages. Taylor (1969) synonymized the two subspecies; he considered blackened fin margins, diagnostic of *N. i. atrorus*, to be geographically incongruent or to exhibit environmental variation, and that otherwise the forms differed little. The problem may need additional study.

A distinctive spotted form of *N. insignis*, discovered in 1977 in the upper Dan River, Patrick County, Virginia, merits subspecific recognition (Matthews and Jenkins 1979; W. J. Matthews, in litt.).

DESCRIPTION

Materials.—From Taylor (1969) and 80 Virginia series. Color in life from 10 Virginia specimens including 5 of the spotted form.

Anatomy.—A madtom with a nonblotched body and some median fins usually dark-edged; adults are 90–120 mm SL. Body moderately elongate, compressed posteriorly. Head moderate or broad, very depressed; eye large; mouth inferior. Pectoral spine straight; anterior serrae absent; posterior serrae moderate in size, few to many. Reproductive male has slight or moderate epicranial swelling; genital papilla long, conical. Female lacks head swelling; genital papilla about half as long as in male, flattened, subtriangular.

Meristics.—Dorsal fin with 1 spine, (5)6 rays; upper caudal rays (27)29–33(35); lower caudal rays (26)28–31(33); anal rays (15)17–19(21); pelvic rays (8)9–10; pectoral with 1 spine, (7)8–9(10) rays.

Fish 158 *Noturus insignis* (upland form) adult male 102 mm SL (REJ 1036), VA, Campbell County, Roanoke River, 12 September 1983.

Fish 159 *Noturus insignis* (spotted form) adult male 91 mm SL (REJ 967), VA, Patrick County, Dan River, 8 June 1983.

Fish 160 *Noturus insignis* (lowland form) adult male 89 mm SL (REJ 1028), VA, Amelia County, Appomattox River, 1 September 1983.

Color in Preservative.—Head and body dorsum dark to moderately dusky, not saddled; side moderately to slightly dusky, often with a narrow dark midaxial streak; venter pale. Mental barbels pale, others variously dusky. Pectoral, pelvic, and adipose fins dusky or pale, adipose and leading edge of pectoral darkest; basal one-third to one-half of dorsal fin often dark.

Marked variation occurs in dorsal, caudal, and anal fin pattern, from broadly black-margined to narrowly dusky-margined to nearly uniformly dusky. The blackest-margined populations occupy generally clear streams in montane–upland portions of the James, Roanoke, New, and Tennessee drainages. Some specimens in lowlands of the James and Roanoke, and some in uplands of other central Atlantic slope drainages, also have dark fin margins. In some specimens of all Virginia populations, the dorsal, caudal, and anal fins (whether partly black or dusky, but seemingly more frequent when dusky) have a uniformly narrow, pale margin.

In its extreme of spotting, the upper Dan River form has spots on head, body, all fins, and some barbels.

An adult albino was found in the Chowan drainage (Southwick and Norman 1987).

Color in Life Plate 23.—Head and body dorsum dark to medium brown with olive or pale yellow cast; side medium to pale brown with olive or yellow tint; venter white. Pale fin areas light yellow with slight olive cast; dark areas dusky pale brown in Coastal Plain populations to black in some upland populations. Mental barbels white, others dusky brown.

The Dan River spotted form exhibits similar body and fin coloration; spots are medium to dark brown-black.

Larvae.—Described by Bowman (1936) and Mansueti and Hardy (1967).

BIOLOGY

Noturus insignis eats a variety of aquatic invertebrates, mostly aquatic insect larvae; fishes and terrestrial insects are occasionally taken (Bowman 1932, 1936; Flemer and Woolcott 1966). In Pennsylvania most males mature in 2 years, some apparently in 1 year; mature females are at least 2 years old. Four-

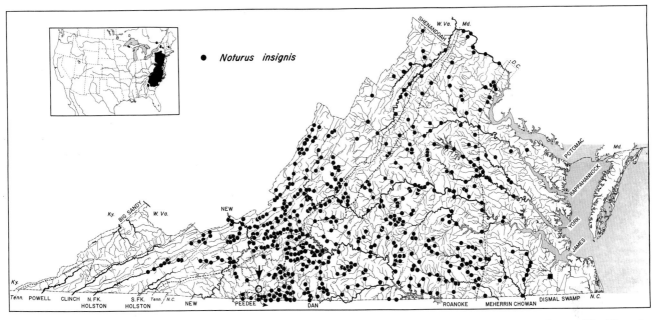

Map 112 Margined madtom. Arrow points to open circle for undescribed spotted form in Dan River Gorge. The Dismal Swamp record (square; Jordan 1889b) is questionable.

year-old margined madtoms are known. Adults are 90–120 mm TL at 24–30 months (Clugston and Cooper 1960). The largest known specimen is 150 mm SL, 179 mm TL, from Virginia.

Females have mature ova during May and June in, respectively, lowland and montane populations of Virginia. Nests are sited beneath flat rocks in gentle runs and in slow water above and below riffles (Fowler 1917a; Bowman 1936; Greeley 1936). Fecundity is 53–223 mature ova per female; eggs number 54–200 per clutch and are attended by a single guardian male (Bowman 1932).

HABITAT

The margined madtom is found in low and moderate-gradient sections of large creeks to large rivers; it occupies soft and hard bottoms of pools, runs, and riffles. During daylight it is generally associated with substrate cover; at night it is often in open areas. Except for a possible stray, there is no record of *N. insignis* from an impoundment in Virginia, although this species is known in lakes elsewhere. In the Coastal Plain the margined madtom is most commonly found in the larger streams and rivers; it usually avoids swampy streams. Schwartz (1981b) found it in oligohaline zones to 5‰ salinity. Cool and warm waters are occupied; the spotted form is in a cool reach.

DISTRIBUTION Map 112

Noturus insignis is indigenous in the New drainage and on the Atlantic slope in drainages from the Altamaha, Georgia, north to at least the lower Hudson, New York. The populations in the Finger Lakes (extirpated?), Mohawk, and St. Lawrence drainages, New York (Taylor 1969; C. Smith 1985) likely are introduced. Virtually certain to have originated via transplantation are the populations in Michigan (extirpated?), New Hampshire, and near Ottawa (Taylor 1969; Coad 1986). The Monongahela drainage population, Maryland, Pennsylvania, and West Virginia (Taylor 1969), also could be nonnative; *N. insignis* is considered unsuccessfully introduced in the Youghiogheny branch of the Monongahela (Hendricks et al. 1983). Recent range extensions and the use of madtoms as bait (*Remarks*) calls to question the distributional status of *N. insignis* in the New and Tennessee drainages.

The margined madtom was considered native in the New drainage by Jenkins et al. (1972), based partly on its capture by Cope in 1867. We retain that status despite an erratic distribution which indicates that one or more subpopulations may have stemmed from transplantation. This species is largely restricted to the lower (northern) half of the Virginia portion of the drainage—in the Valley and Ridge Province; it is absent from most of the Blue Ridge in Virginia and all of the North Carolina and West Virginia portions. The report by Ross and Perkins (1959) from Big Wilson Creek of the New, adjacent to the North Carolina line, probably is in error. The site is well above the nearest population, the species was not accessioned for the collection at Virginia Tech, nor were specimens found by us.

Ross and Perkins (1959) indicated that *N. insignis* prefers hardwater streams in the New, but present knowledge shows partial discordance for that drainage (and others). The madtom is unknown from Cripple Creek, a hardwater Valley and Ridge stream fringing the Blue Ridge, but does occur in the softwater section of Little Reed Island Creek in the Blue Ridge. We took it in Big Reed Island Creek in 1984, the first verified record for that much sport-fished Blue Ridge stream. Madtoms were reported from a 1976 survey of Laurel Fork, a Big Reed Island Creek tributary; they were discarded but probably were *N. insignis*.

The margined madtom probably was introduced to the North Fork Holston River (Taylor 1969) based on localization and recency of the records. The first records are from 1951 and 1954 (Ross and Carico 1963), the three sites being above Saltville. The spread of this species below Saltville was retarded by pollution that emanated heavily from there through the 1960s. Now it also occurs below Saltville and in the lower sections of three upper North Fork tributaries. The population in the Watauga River branch of the Holston, North Carolina, also likely is introduced.

The spotted form is extremely localized, being known only in and slightly below the gorge cut into the Blue Ridge escarpment by the upper Dan River. It may intergrade with typical *N. insignis* above and below the gorge.

Abundance.—The typical form is often common; it is the most common madtom, and probably the most abundant ictalurid in Virginia. The spotted form is rare or uncommon.

REMARKS

Evidence that Indians ate the margined madtom was found in the zooarcheological investigation of an upper James drainage site (Whyte 1989). The pattern of burning on the bones indicates that the fish were roasted.

Madtoms are excellent bait for smallmouth bass; *N. insignis* is the species most frequently used in the New drainage and eastward. Anglers claim that smallmouth bass strike madtoms from any angle, but always swallow them head first to avoid stings from the venomous spines.

The trafficking and release of madtoms acquired for bait apparently has started new drainage populations, and likely has added alien fish to native populations. Such transplantations almost always are undocumented, but considerable evidence of their occurrence has mounted. In referring to the origin of an Ontario population of *N. insignis*, Coad (1986) noted that Pennsylvania anglers often take madtoms north. Our inquiry to five fishing tackle shops in the upper Roanoke Valley in August 1988 revealed that four sold madtoms but none were in the liveries. The madtoms are supplied by persons who seine the surrounding drainages. The retail price is $1.00–$1.50 per head; the local demand exceeds the supply. Introduction of madtoms is also considered under *N. gilberti*.

The spotted form of *N. insignis* merits consideration for endangered status if it is taxonomically recognized (Burkhead and Jenkins 1991). It is jeopardized by a hydroelectric facility on the upper Dan River that dewaters 5 rkm below the lower dam and causes marked fluctuation in the succeeding reach below the powerhouse.

Name.—*Insignis*, "remarkable" or "extraordinary," perhaps refers to fin pigmentation or the long adipose fin.

Tadpole madtom   *Noturus gyrinus* (Mitchill)

SYSTEMATICS

The tadpole madtom, described in 1817 from New York, is one of the most advanced members of the subgenus *Noturus* and is closely related to *N. lachneri* (Taylor 1969; LeGrande 1981).

DESCRIPTION

Materials.—From Taylor (1969) and 20 Virginia specimens. Color in life from 1 Virginia adult.

Anatomy.—A stubby madtom with a broad tail and a dark line on the side; adults are 50–85 mm SL. Head and anterior trunk nearly round in cross section, belly rotund; body compressed posteriorly; eye small; mouth terminal; caudal fin broad. Pectoral spine small, nearly straight, lacking serrae or weakly notched. Breeding male with swollen lips, enlarged cephalic epaxial muscles, and large bulbous genital papilla; female papilla with deep median groove ending in a small bump (Whiteside and Burr 1986).

Meristics.—Dorsal fin with 1 spine, (5)6 rays; upper caudal rays (27)28–34(36); lower caudal rays (22) 24–29(32);

Fish 161 *Noturus gyrinus* adult female 56 mm SL (REJ 1019), VA, Southampton County, Mill Swamp, 15 July 1983.

anal rays (12)14–17(18); pelvic rays (5)8–9(10); pectoral with 1 spine, (5)7–8(10) rays.

Color in Preservative.—Head and body dark or dusky dorsally; side moderately to slightly dusky, and with an obvious linear midlateral dark stripe; belly pale. Fins of adult uniformly dusky or dark, or the dorsal with a dark base, adipose pale-margined, or caudal with a barely evident dark margin.

Color in Life.—Head and body dark gold-brown dorsally; pale gold-brown to moderate gold-brown laterally, midlateral stripe dark brown; venter gold. Fins dusky gold.

Larvae.—Described by Mansueti and Hardy (1967), Wang and Kernehan (1979), and Tin (1982b).

BIOLOGY

The life history of *N. gyrinus* in Illinois was documented and data on this species from other areas were collated by Whiteside and Burr (1986). The tadpole madtom preys mainly on crustaceans (particularly isopods) and immature aquatic insects (chiefly midges) (Todd 1973; Whiteside and Burr 1986). Maturity is usually achieved by age 2, sometimes age 1, and few fish reach age 3. Adults are usually 50–85 mm SL (Hooper 1949; Mahon 1977; Whiteside and Burr 1986). The largest Virginia specimen at hand is 63 mm SL; a specimen of 112 mm TL is known from Ohio (Trautman 1981).

A Virginia female each from April and May contained well-yolked ova, suggesting a partly earlier spawning time than the May–August period of northern populations (Hankinson 1908; Cahn 1927; Bailey 1938b; Mahon 1977; Whiteside and Burr 1986). Egg clutches found in trash; for example, in cans and crockery (Adams and Hankinson 1928; Bailey 1938b), indicate that spawning sites include shelter. Egg clutches have been found under guard by a male and a female, others by the male alone (Whiteside and Burr 1986). Numbers of mature ova per female range 43–323 (Mahon 1977; Whiteside and Burr 1986).

Noturus gyrinus hybridizes with *N. miurus* (Trautman 1948; Menzel and Raney 1973).

HABITAT

Tadpole madtoms populate warm creeks, streams, and rivers; they inhabit cover in backwaters and other sluggish areas. Only two records are from Virginia impoundments, but outside of Virginia they commonly inhabit ponds, lakes, and reservoirs. In the New Jersey Pine Barrens *N. gyrinus* is characteristic of dense beds of submerged aquatic vegetation and avoids excessively acidic waters (Hastings 1979, 1984). In most Chowan drainage record sites, cover such as logs and debris was extensive, but submerged vegetation was sparse at many sites and absent at several others; pH at 14 sites was 6.3–6.9 (Norman and Southwick 1985). The tadpole madtom is rare in oligohaline zones, to 5‰ salinity, in North Carolina (Schwartz 1981b).

DISTRIBUTION   Map 113

Noturus gyrinus is widely distributed in lowlands of eastern and central North America, skirting the Appalachian uplands and mountains. In Virginia it is found in the lower Piedmont or Coastal Plain of all major Atlantic slope drainages, but is unknown from the Virginia section of the Delmarva Peninsula and Dismal Swamp proper.

Abundance.—Generally rare or uncommon.

REMARKS

The pectoral spine sting of *N. gyrinus* is one of the most toxic assayed by Birkhead (1972).

Name.—Gyrinus, Greek for "tadpole," refers to the distinctive body form of the species.

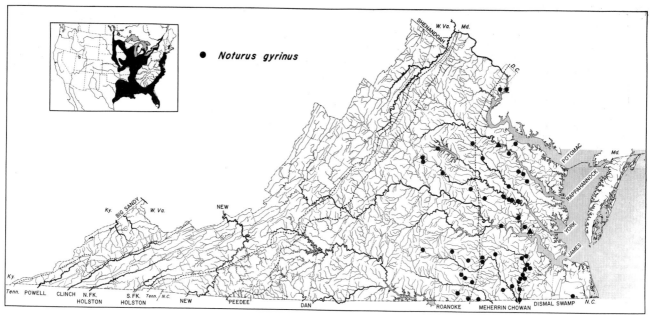

Map 113 Tadpole madtom.

Yellowfin madtom   *Noturus flavipinnis* Taylor

SYSTEMATICS

Noturus flavipinnis was described by Taylor (1969) from the upper Tennessee drainage of Georgia and Tennessee, and the North Fork Holston River in Virginia. It is a member of the subgenus *Rabida* and is closely related to *N. miurus* (Taylor 1969; LeGrande 1981).

DESCRIPTION

Materials.—From Taylor (1969), Taylor et al. (1971), P. Shute (1984), and 26 Virginia specimens. Life color from Taylor et al. (1971) and 2 more Virginia specimens.

Anatomy.—A saddled, blotch-finned madtom; adults are 70–110 mm SL. Body stocky anteriorly, compressed posteriorly. Head broad, depressed; eye large; mouth inferior. Pectoral spine slightly curved and bearing several anterior and posterior serrae, some of the latter large and curved. Adipose fin with a slight or well-developed notch at juncture with caudal fin. Reproductive male with epicranial swelling; no swelling in female. Genital papilla of a large October male broad, triangular, about twice as long as conical papillae of two mature May females.

Meristics.—Dorsal fin with 1 spine, (5)6 rays; upper caudal rays (29)31–34(35); lower caudal rays 25–27(28); anal rays 14–15(16); pelvic rays 8–9, pectoral with 1 spine, (7)8(9) rays.

Fish 162 *Noturus flavipinnis* adult female 55 mm SL (NMB 611), VA, Scott County, Copper Creek, 13 August 1981.

Color in Preservative.—Dorsum and side mostly moderately dusky or pale, venter immaculate. Body with 4–5 dark saddles, 1 each at occiput (often absent), dorsal fin origin (often vague), just posterior to dorsal fin, at adipose fin (extended onto fin), and at caudal fin base (extended to encircle base of fin). Saddle at dorsal origin often interrupted medially by 1 large or 2 small pale areas. Dorsal, anal, and pectoral fins with pigment about midlength of rays effecting short streaks or a bar, distally pale, somewhat dusky at base and on spines and adjacent areas. Caudal fin duskily or darkly mottled or streaked, markings tending to form 1–3 crescentic dark bars, the posteriormost being widest. Pelvic fin usually pale. Mental barbels pale or the lateral pair slightly dusky; maxillary barbel dusky. Day-collected specimens tend to have darker bodies overall than night-collected specimens, in which saddles tend to be more contrastive (Fish 162).

Color in Life   Plate 23.—Head and body mostly pale yellow-brown to yellow-gray, slight pink cast midlaterally; first two saddles medium or dark brown-gray, other saddles brown-black. All fins except pelvic usually very pale yellow along base; pelvic fin translucent white with pink cast; fin markings dark gray or black. Retinal reflection (eye shine) at night bright pink (P. Shute 1984; our observation).

Larvae.—Described by P. Shute (1984).

COMPARISON

Noturus flavipinnis and *N. eleutherus* appear fairly similar and co-inhabit the Tennessee drainage; pigmentary differences in the *Key* merit amplification (Figure 51): (1) adipose fin [a prominent dark saddle extends from the body through the fin, usually to the distal margin in *flavipinnis* vs. basally the fin typically is uniformly dusky or dark, or has a horizontally elongate blotch (confluent with saddle), and the pale margin usually is wide, horizontally elongate, and continuous in *eleutherus*]; (2) caudal fin base [completely encircled by a usually well-demarked crescentic dark band *vs.* usually not completely encircled by dark band, the dorsal and ventral marks usually interrupted medially and often lacking distinct margins, or large dark marks absent]. Other differences include: (3) preopercular-mandibular pores (Figure 8) modally [11 *vs.* 10]; (4) upper caudal rays usually [31–34 *vs.* 22–25]. No interspecific overlap occurs in caudal rays but extreme care is required in counting rudimentary rays.

BIOLOGY

The life history of the yellowfin madtom was studied in Copper Creek, Virginia, and Citico Creek, Tennessee (Jenkins 1975b; P. Shute 1984). This species almost exclusively eats immature forms of all major groups of benthic aquatic insects. Intact stomach contents indicate day and night feeding. Sexual maturity is usually attained in 2 years and many adults are 3 years old; maximum longevity may be 5 years. Adult males are 74–114 mm SL, adult females are 65–112; most of the larger fish are males. The largest Virginia specimen is 99 mm SL; the 114-mm SL specimen reported from Tennessee by Shute is the largest known.

Nesting occurs within about mid-May to mid-July, and is triggered by water temperatures rising to 20–23°C. Eggs are deposited in cavities beneath flat rubble in pools usually less than 1 m deep. Females produce 121–278 mature ova; clutch sizes are about half the average fecundity (P. Shute 1984).

HABITAT

Noturus flavipinnis occupies typically clear, moderate-gradient, small streams to medium or large rivers. Two of the extant populations occur in warm water, the other in a cool–warm transition area (middle Citico Creek). In Copper Creek the yellowfin madtom prefers calm water, usually pools and occasionally backwaters beside runs and riffles; slow runs are rarely occupied. During day and night this species generally lives near shore in slightly or moderately silted areas; at night it can be found in open areas having little-silted gravel and rocks. Its cover includes sticks, logs, leaf litter, undercut banks, rocks, and trash (Jenkins 1975b; Burkhead and Jenkins 1982b). Jordan (1889b) found the yellowfin madtom among weeds in the North Fork Holston River. This species apparently has low vagility (P. Shute 1984).

DISTRIBUTION   Map 114

Noturus flavipinnis is endemic to the Valley and Ridge Province of the upper Tennessee drainage; only six populations are clearly documented. Three of these—in the North Fork Holston River of Virginia, Hines Creek in Tennessee, and Chickamauga Creek of Georgia—are extirpated (Taylor 1969). The extant, widely disjunct populations occupy Copper Creek in Virginia and the Powell River and Citico Creek in Tennessee. Approximately 94 rkm are bracketed by recent records, but *N. flavipinnis* is highly localized in the Powell and Citico Creek. One pre-1900 record each from the Clinch and Tennessee rivers in Tennessee (Taylor 1969) may actually be of *N. eleutherus* (Burkhead and Jenkins 1982b).

In Copper Creek, coursing 98 rkm in Scott and Russell counties, *N. flavipinnis* has been found widely

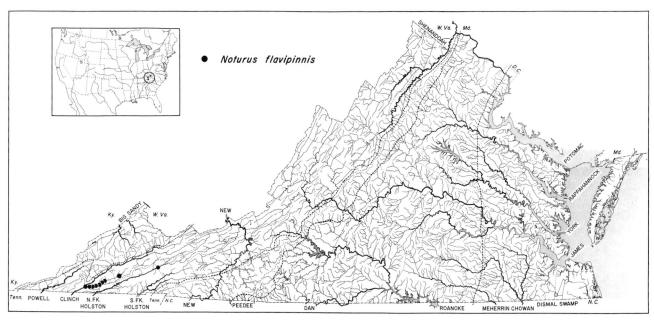

Map 114 Yellowfin madtom.

in the lower 47 rkm (at 13 of 14 sites, in 26 of 91 collecting or snorkeling efforts), and was taken in 1 of 2 collections made at Rkm 78. It was not taken in 14 collections made within Rkm 57–75, 4 within Rkm 83–96, nor in the 8 tributaries sampled. This species may have moved from Copper Creek into the Clinch River after the 1967 river kill, but it was not detected at the recently well-collected site 1 rkm below the creek.

The Powell River population is known from three specimens taken in 1968–1983 at two sites (Rkm 160, 172) in Tennessee (Feeman 1987). Because the upper site is 27 rkm below Virginia, it is possible that the madtom occupies the Powell in Virginia. However, the river has been extensively sampled (although mostly during the day) by experienced TVA personnel using a variety of collecting techniques suited to capturing cryptobenthic species (Feeman 1987). Further, the Powell has been degraded by coal mining operations located primarily in Virginia. The Powell records may be related to straying from unknown tributary populations (P. Shute 1984).

The North Fork Holston River population is known from specimens captured just above Saltville in 1888 by Jordan (1889b: as *N. miurus*). Its demise is odd because the site was not affected by the pollution that long emanated from Saltville. The presence of the madtom above Saltville may not have resulted from recruitment from downstream; Cope (1868b) did not collect it about Saltville in 1867, nor apparently did Jordan below the record site. The population above

Saltville may have succumbed to siltation (Jenkins and Burkhead 1984). Taylor (1969) suggested that *N. flavipinnis* may be unable to coexist with *N. insignis* in the North Fork Holston. However, these species differ in habitat use, and *N. flavipinnis* probably was gone from the North Fork by the time *N. insignis* became established.

Abundance.—Probably rare or uncommon, but difficult to inventory, particularly elusive during daylight. Burkhead and Jenkins (1982b) thought that *N. flavipinnis* may have declined recently in middle Copper Creek (Rkm 28–78); it had been taken at 4 of 8 sites during 1965–1972, but not at any of these sites during 1979–1985. We also considered a possible decline in lower Copper Creek (Rkm 0–23); it had been taken at 8 of 10 sites during 1965–1972, but later at only 6 sites and seemingly less frequently per unit of effort.

We early recognized that seining at night was more effective for sampling the yellowfin madtom than were seining or electrofishing during daylight; the largest numbers taken during 1969–1972 were caught at night—single collections of 17, 11, and 8 specimens. Electrofishing during the day may stun this species only deep within cover, where it will remain undetected. However, only very recently have we become greatly impressed with the improved efficiency of night collecting. In the lower 78 rkm of the creek during 1965–1985, 32 specimens were taken in 92 daytime collections, about half of the specimens by manic efforts; 70 specimens were caught in 19 night-time collections. This forced reconsideration of our view (Burkhead and Jenkins 1982b) of the madtom's abundance.

The data shed doubt that *N. flavipinnis* has declined in Copper Creek—most of the more recent sampling efforts were in daytime. However, some results still raise concern regarding the abundance of the madtom. For example, although the two largest early collections (11, 17 specimens; Taylor et al. 1971) were made at night, the efforts were hard and long (2.5, 3.5 hours). Since 1975, the site that had yielded the 17 specimens has yielded none in 5 day collections and only 1 in a night collection (when open areas of a pool were prebaited with diced chicken livers). Perhaps the 1969 collection depleted the population, and recruitment was very low. Intensive efforts at other sites in the lower and middle creek where habitat apparently was suitable yielded no specimens; if the madtom was common we should have found it.

Thus we regard *N. flavipinnis* as rare or uncommon in Copper Creek. It may be localized within short reaches; the basis for any localization is obscure because backwaters and short and long pools with abundant cover are typical throughout the creek.

REMARKS

The yellowfin madtom was thought to be extinct when it was described in 1969, from specimens captured during 1884–1893; it was rediscovered in Copper Creek in 1969. The six verified populations are remnants of a much fuller distribution in the upper Tennessee drainage. This species was listed in 1977 as federally threatened (Anonymous 1977). The later discovery of a small population in Citico Creek, Tennessee (Bauer et al. 1983; P. Shute 1984) should not affect that status. *Noturus flavipinnis* is legally ranked as threatened in Virginia, but a recommendation for state endangered status is to be considered (Burkhead and Jenkins 1991). The Copper Creek population appears to be the best of the species; it should be well protected.

Name.—*Flavipinnis* means "yellow fin," a curious name selection by Taylor (1969), who had seen only old faded specimens.

Mountain madtom   *Noturus eleutherus* Jordan

SYSTEMATICS

While collecting in the upper Tennessee drainage of Tennessee, D. S. Jordan plucked a mountain madtom from the jaws of a water snake and described it as a new species (Jordan 1877a). *Noturus eleutherus* is an advanced member of the subgenus *Rabida* (Taylor 1969; LeGrande 1981).

DESCRIPTION

Materials.—From Taylor (1969) and 18 series from the upper Tennessee drainage, Virginia and Tennessee. Life color from 1 Virginia adult.

Anatomy.—An often splotchy madtom usually with a wide pale margin on the adipose fin; adults are 40–60 mm SL. Body stout anteriorly, compressed posteriorly. Head moderately depressed; eye moderately large; mouth inferior. Pectoral spine slightly or moderately curved, bearing small anterior serrae and large curved posterior serrae.

Meristics.—Dorsal fin with 1 spine, (5)6 rays; upper caudal rays (21)22–25(27); lower caudal rays (20)21–24(26); anal rays (12)13–15(16); pelvic rays (8)9(10); pectoral with 1 spine, (7)8–9 rays.

Color in Preservative.—Dorsum mostly moderately dusky or dark; 2–3 dark dorsal saddles present, at dorsal fin

Fish 163 *Noturus eleutherus* adult male 49 mm SL (REJ 986), VA, Scott County, Clinch River, 17 June 1983.

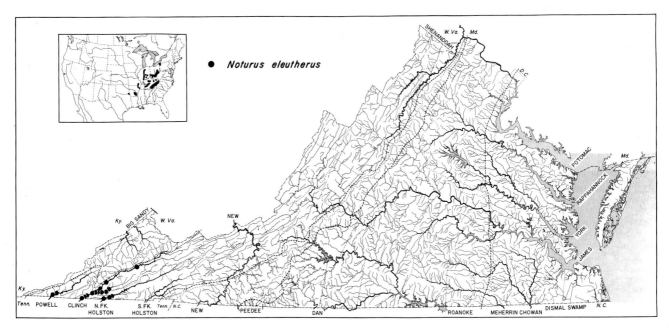

Map 115   Mountain madtom.

origin, posterior dorsal fin insertion, and adipose fin (where often absent); adipose saddle usually not extending dorsad to fin margin, leaving a wide pale distal area (Figure 51). Side varied, nearly uniformly slightly dusky or moderately mottled and dark; venter usually pale. A crescentic bar often present at caudal fin base, usually interrupted medially. Dorsal, anal, and pectoral fins darkly mottled or streaked, or pale; caudal fin streaks sometimes forming 2–3 irregular crescentic bands, margin usually pale; pelvic fin pale.

Color in Life   Plate 23.—Head dorsum and saddles dark brown; side medium brown; lateral mottling mostly dark brown; fin mottling pale to dark brown; bar at caudal base medium to dark brown; lower cheek and pectoral fin base with pink cast; venter pale with pink cast.

Larvae.—Described by Starnes and Starnes (1985).

COMPARISON

See *N. flavipinnis.*

BIOLOGY

Life history aspects of upper Tennessee drainage, Tennessee, populations of the mountain madtom were studied by Starnes and Starnes (1985). This species is a nocturnal predator of immature aquatic insects. The life span is 4–5 years. The sexes grow at similar rates, but males tend to live longer and attain greater length. Fish of age 24–35 months are 37–47 mm SL. The largest Virginia specimen is 63 mm SL; a 66-mm SL male is reported from Tennessee. Spawning occurs during June and July on gravel in cavities beneath flat rubble in gently flowing pools. On 2 July a male was found guarding a clutch of 70 eggs beneath a rock in an area of clean gravel in a pool. Mature eggs per female range 55–115.

HABITAT

Noturus eleutherus generally is found among gravel, rubble, and plants in riffles and runs of typically clear, warm, medium to large streams and rivers. It is not known to occupy impoundments.

DISTRIBUTION   Map 115

The mountain madtom occurs widely but disjunctly in the Ohio basin and limitedly in uplands west of the lower Mississippi River. In Virginia it occupies the Tennessee drainage, where it is restricted to the North Fork Holston, Clinch, and Powell rivers and lower Copper Creek.

Noturus eleutherus was a victim of the chemical spill that began at Carbo (Map 11) and swept the lower 106 rkm of Clinch River in Virginia (and beyond) on 10–14 June 1967. It probably occupied suitable habitat in all that reach, based on captures at 8 rkm above Carbo in 1971–1973, its recovery pattern in the Clinch, and its distribution elsewhere.

Repopulation of the Clinch River began quickly; the resident population of Copper Creek probably was only a local source. At Speers Ferry 1 rkm below Copper Creek, a specimen was taken on 25 July 1967 and a few others were caught later that year. *Noturus eleutherus* apparently did not become common at Speers Ferry until the early 1980s. It was rare at 8 rkm below Copper Creek in 1970, but was abundant at the state line another 8 rkm downstream in 1973. At Craft Mill 12 rkm above Copper Creek, it was not taken in 1969, but was found there consistently during 1979–1980. In 1981–1984 the mountain madtom was taken at the Pendleton Island–Fort Blackmore area 11–13 rkm above Craft Mill. The 65-rkm range gap from Fort Blackmore to Carbo is not known to have been sampled after 1974 (*Biogeography*). Much of the river probably was repopulated by spawn of madtoms that had taken refuge at the mouths of small tributaries during the kill.

In the North Fork Holston River, the chronic and sometimes severe pollution that formerly originated at Saltville (Map 11) apparently has had a lasting effect on *N. eleutherus*. Habitat physically suited to this species is common in the long reach below Saltville, but only the lowermost portion is known to be occupied.

Abundance.—Usually uncommon.

REMARKS

The mountain madtom is the most common small catfish in southwestern Virginia, where in most streams any madtom is an interesting catch.

Name.—*Eleutherus* means "free," in reference to the partial (notched) division of the adipose and caudal fins.

Flathead catfishes   Genus *Pylodictis* Rafinesque

This is a monotypic genus for the flathead catfish.

Name.—*Pylodictis* means "mud fish."

Flathead catfish   *Pylodictis olivaris* (Rafinesque)

SYSTEMATICS

Described in 1818 from the Ohio River or environs, *P. olivaris* is indistinguishable today from Middle Miocene (11–15 million-year-old) fossils of the lineage (Lundberg 1975, 1982). Its closest relative is the small albino widemouth blindcat *Satan eurystomus* which inhabits deep artesian wells in Texas (Hubbs and Bailey 1947; Suttkus 1961; Lundberg 1982).

DESCRIPTION

Materials.—From Taylor (1969), Scott and Crossman (1973), and 4 small Virginia specimens. Color in life from Trautman (1981).

Anatomy.—A catfish with posterior extensions of the tooth plate on the upper jaw, and in juveniles the upper tip of the tail usually pale; the second largest ictalurid, adults are 400–900 mm TL. Body somewhat slender or bulky, depressed anteriorly, round or slightly compressed posteriorly. Head broad and flat; eye small or moderate; mouth terminal. Pectoral spine nearly straight, roughened anteriorly, posterior serrae numerous.

Meristics.—Dorsal fin with 1 spine, 6 rays; branched caudal rays 15; anal rays 14–17; pelvic rays (9)10; pectoral with 1 spine, 10–11 rays.

Color in Preservative.—Dorsum, side, and fins of juvenile and adult dusky, with moderate to heavy dark mottling or blotching; upper caudal lobe pale in young, juvenile, and some adults; venter pale or blotched; barbels pale or dusky.

Color in Life.—Young dark brown to black; adult dorsum, side, and fins yellow, olive, or brown, mottled with medium to dark brown; venter yellow to yellow-white. Upper caudal tip white in young, paler than lower lobe in juvenile and some adults.

Fish 164 *Pylodictis olivaris* juvenile 138 mm SL (NMB 154), VA, Scott County, North Fork Holston River, 28 August 1973.

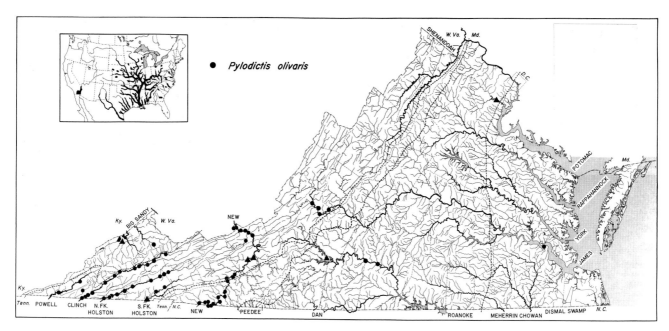

Map 116 Flathead catfish.

Larvae.—Described by Tin (1982b); alevin diagnosed by Cloutman (1979).

BIOLOGY

Pylodictis exhibits a dietary shift similar to other catfishes. Young depend on microcrustaceans and insect larvae; adults feed on crayfishes, clams, and particularly, fishes (Minckley and Deacon 1959; Guier et al. 1984). Males mature in 3–4 years, females 4–5; the darkening of the upper caudal lobe may indicate attainment of sexual maturity (Minckley and Deacon 1959). Age 19 has been reached by this species (Carlander 1969). *Pylodictis* grows faster in shallow turbid waters than in clear waters (Carlander 1969; Minckley and Deacon 1959). Adults attain 600–800 mm TL at ages 8–9 (Carlander 1969; Guier et al. 1984). Flathead catfish are known to exceed 1,000 mm TL and weigh over 31 kg (Carroll and Hall 1964), and have been thought to reach 45 kg (100 pounds). The size record for flathead catfish in Virginia is 25.9 kg (57 pounds) from South Holston Reservoir in 1972; a 25.4-kg (56 pounds) flathead was taken in 1988 from Occoquan Reservoir.

Spawning likely peaks in June and July in Virginia, based on data from similar latitudes elsewhere (Carlander 1969). The nest is a cleaned substrate near cover or in a cavity (Deacon 1961). The caudal embrace characteristic of some *Ictalurus* and *Ameiurus* species also occurs in *Pylodictis* (Fontaine 1944). Females contained 6,900–11,300 total ova (Minckley and Deacon 1959). Dubious natural hybrids are noted under *I. punctatus*.

HABITAT

The flathead catfish inhabits warm large streams, big rivers, lakes, and reservoirs. In streams young and juveniles are usually associated with riffles; larger fish favor moderate to deep pools. Trautman (1981) reported feeding (apparently by adults) in shallow riffles at night. Minckley and Deacon (1959) found adults strongly associated with cover. This species tolerates heavy turbidity but is usually found over hard or only slightly silted bottoms (Trautman 1981).

DISTRIBUTION Map 116

Pylodictis olivaris is native to the southern Great Lakes and Mississippi basins and most Gulf slope drainages, and is introduced on the Atlantic slope and in California. In Virginia it is indigenous to the New, Tennessee, and Big Sandy drainages, and introduced to the Potomac, James, and Roanoke drainages.

In Virginia the distribution of the flathead catfish in the New River and most main branches of the Tennessee drainage is general. The indicated absence of the species from the South Fork Holston River probably is related to cool temperature or a higher than suitable gradient. There is only one stream record from the Big Sandy drainage in Virginia, a young specimen from Levisa Fork—oddly in the headwater. Native status in the New drainage is based partly on specimens taken in 1867 (Cope 1868b; ANSP 8359-61).

The establishment of the flathead catfish on the Atlantic slope in Virginia stemmed from releases of apparently few individuals, as in a successful introduction in North Carolina (Guier et al. 1984). The population in Occoquan Reservoir, a main-tributary impoundment in the lower Potomac drainage, developed from stocking of 12 fish from the New River in 1965 (E. L. Steinkoenig, personal communication). Introductions to the lower James and middle Roanoke rivers, including Smith Mountain Reservoir, via accidental and intentional releases during 1965–1977, were discussed by Burkhead et al. (1980). By 1985 substantial numbers of flatheads were being angled in the Roanoke River (D. K. Whitehurst, personal communication).

Pylodictis olivaris mysteriously appeared recently in the Botetourt County reach of the upper James River. Two adults were caught in 1983 (D. K. Whitehurst, personal communication) and one was seen by Burkhead while snorkeling in 1985. During 1987–early 1988, flathead catfish were caught only at the upper 2 of 8 James River sites, which were located in the Valley and Ridge, Piedmont, or Fall Zone and which were repetitively sampled by boat electroshocker and explosives (G. C. Garman, personal communication). Garman's captures are the upper and lower of the four upper James records on Map 116.

It is difficult to believe that *P. olivaris* reached the upper James River from the introduction site in the James estuary; in addition to the distance, it would have had to bypass numerous dams. The recency of records, species localization, and presence of dams indicate an upper James introduction. Native status in the James is improbable; this large distinctive catfish would have been noticed long ago if it were native.

The flathead catfish is expected to spread widely in the James and Roanoke rivers. Although it was classed as only semimobile by Funk (1955), following establishment it dispersed rapidly and widely in the Cape Fear River, North Carolina (Guier et al. 1984).

Abundance.—We lack good data on the abundance of the flathead catfish in large bodies of water in Virginia. Based on our capture of very few young and juveniles in runs and riffles of rivers, it may be generally rare or uncommon.

REMARKS

Good flavor and large size have made the flathead catfish popular among anglers. Sport fisheries have developed for the introduced populations on the Atlantic slope. The flathead became the dominant mainstream predator within 15 years after introduction to the Cape Fear River, North Carolina. However, an associated severe decline in other fish species, particularly catfishes, also occurred (Guier et al. 1984).

A local method of capturing catfishes—grabbling, tickling, or noodling—is done by feeling under banks, ledges, and other cover, and grabbing the fish by the lower jaw or gill cover. As Manooch and Raver (1984) noted, scarred hands can attest to successful fishing. The large size of some flathead catfish, magnified underwater, has disquieted aquatic rescue and recovery crews in Virginia.

Name.—*Olivaris* means "olive colored."

TROUTS
Family Salmonidae

The Salmonidae include some of the most familiar sport and foodfishes in the Northern Hemisphere, and because of successful introductions, some species are well known in many regions of the Southern Hemisphere. The family includes chars, trouts, salmons, graylings, whitefishes, and others. The brook, brown, and rainbow trouts occupy Virginia.

The family traces back to at least the Middle Eocene (about 50 million years ago), based on the undoubted salmonid *Eosalmo* unearthed in British Columbia (Wilson 1977). Miller (1965) placed the Salmonidae in the "old fauna" and Cavender (1980, 1986) indicated that the family may have had a marine Cretaceous origin (more than 70 million years ago). The genus *Hucho* was identified from the younger Miocene of Idaho (Smith and Miller 1985).

Most classifications place the Salmonidae in a very primitive position among euteleosts, near the mudminnows and pikes of the order Esociformes. We follow the hypothesis that salmonids are more advanced and place the order Salmoniformes in higher phylogenetic rank than the Esociformes and ostariophysans (minnows and allies) (Fink and Weitzman 1982; Lauder and Liem 1983; Fink 1984; Martin 1984b; *Cladogram*). Debate on the composition and relationships of the Salmoniformes will continue (Kendall and Behnke 1984; Rosen 1985a; Smith 1988).

There are about 65 living species of salmonids divided among three groups. At times these groups have been considered separate families, but currently they generally are recognized as subfamilies: Coregoninae—whitefishes and ciscoes; Thymallinae—graylings; Salmoninae—trouts, salmons, chars, and others (Cavender 1970; Kendall and Behnke 1984; Behnke 1990).

On the species-group level, many of these fishes still present major systematic problems stemming from marked adaptability or plasticity in life history and morphology. Divergent taxonomic views often result when two similar but distinctive forms live together, generally maintaining separate identities but still possessing the potential to interbreed. The forms may be regarded as species by some workers and as subspecies, races, or strains by others. Original analyses and keys to earlier literature are by Behnke (1980), Todd and Smith (1980), and Todd et al. (1981).

Salmonids exhibit a wide range in adult size. The pygmy whitefish of 280 mm TL is dwarfed by the largest living salmonid, the chinook salmon, which reaches 1,490 mm TL (4.9 feet) and 57.2 kg (126 pounds) (Scott and Crossman 1973). As with many vertebrate lineages, the largest salmonids are extinct. *Smilodonichthys* was a giant salmonlike fish of the western United States that may have reached 1,900 mm SL (at least 7 feet TL). The breeding male had two huge teeth at the front of the upper jaw, thus inspiring the use of *Smilodon*—after the extinct sabretoothed cats (Cavender and Miller 1972).

Basic salmonid morphology is so characteristic that the term troutlike often is applied to fishes of similar form. Salmonids are terete, streamlined, slightly to strongly compressed, and usually have a stout caudal peduncle. The head and eye typically are of moderate size; the mouth is nonprotrusile, terminal or nearly so, medium to large, and has small to fairly large conical teeth. Fins lack spines; the dorsal fin is placed about midlength on the fish; the adipose fin, a prominent salmonid feature, is well developed; the caudal fin is broad, forked or truncate. The lower fins are moderate-sized, the pelvic in abdominal position, the pectoral low. Scales are cycloid, typically small or minute on the body, and absent on the head.

Sexual dimorphism and dichromatism are dramatically developed in some salmonine species, moderately expressed in graylings, and reduced in whitefishes. Breeding males of some of the Pacific salmons (*Oncorhynchus*) develop a large hump on the nape and the most extreme kypes—a pronounced elongation and inward-hooking of the jaws distally. Kypes bear irregularly hooked teeth used in territorial aggression. Kypes in trouts of the genera *Oncorhynchus*, *Salmo*, and *Salvelinus* occur on the lower jaw, and are often reduced or absent in some of the species (Vladykov 1963; Morton 1965). Breeding tubercles develop in some whitefishes and one salmonine, the lake trout (Wiley and Collette 1970; Collette 1977).

Spawning colorations range from the sooty black of the chum salmon to the fire-bellied brilliance of the brook trout and Arctic char. Between these examples occur all shades of yellow and orange, iridescent greens and blues, and in rainbow trout the famous crimson-pink side stripe. In some of the more colorful species the patterns occur year-round in both sexes, although males are brighter during spawning. Except in most whitefishes, the young are patterned on the side with a series of large oval or round blotches called parr marks. Despite their bright colors, trouts blend well with their surroundings, particularly from an overhead view.

Salmonids are coldwater stenotherms; they generally occur only in waters with maximum summer temperatures of about 21°C or less, and many are most active at 10–15°C. Thermal requirements for self-sustaining trout populations are complex; for example, the entire annual temperature cycle determines the natural occurrence of brook trout (Hokanson et al. 1973). Different thermal tolerance limits may characterize spawning, early development, maturation, and general viability of adults. Trout may survive adversely warm periods by taking refuge in direct spring inflows (although they may then be limited by crowding and resultant competition). Winter produces a different set of hardships, including ice scouring, on stream-dwelling trout and many of their foods.

Virtually all thermally suitable habitats are exploited by salmonids. They occur in mountain rivulets, large rivers, dark-stained beaver ponds, clear deep oligotrophic lakes, estuaries, and far-offshore areas of oceans. The evolution of anadromous life styles by most salmonid genera has greatly diversified the range of habitats used.

Most trouts eat essentially all appropriate-sized animals that live in or fall into water. Dietary shifts are typical of many species. Young first eat minute arthropods, then graduate to larger and larger prey, and as adults often favor large crustaceans and fishes. Continued feeding on tiny insects by some large trout exemplifies the visual acuity of the group. Owing to the varying availability of foods in different microhabitats, individual trout in the same stream section may chiefly feed on different prey. For example, a trout with a home range (or hydrodynamically determined feeding lair) by a tree-covered bank may feed more on terrestrial insects than will trout in midstream (Bachman 1984, 1985). Being opportunists, trout often switch to a prey species that has just become abundant; for example, a particular mayfly during its emergence ("hatch") from the larval stage. Prey-switching does not occur uniformly in a population (Bryan and Larkin 1972). Some salmonids, particularly the cisco type of whitefishes, are planktivores and use long gill rakers to strain food.

Reproductive patterns vary from egg scattering in some whitefishes to nest construction and stereotyped ritual in most salmonines. Salmon and trout exhibit prespawning movements, usually upstream. The distance varies from 100 m or less in some nonanadromous stream-dwelling trout to nearly 1,500 rkm for some steelhead populations and up to 7,400 km, including oceanic travel, for Pacific salmon. Timing of the spawning migration also varies. Most *Salmo* and *Salvelinus* migrate and spawn within late summer to midwinter, western trouts (*Oncorhynchus*) midwinter to early summer.

One of the more fascinating aspects of anadromy is the high degree of fidelity (up to 95%) in homing to birthplace streams (Hasler et al. 1978). The ability to return to natal streams results from olfactory imprinting of young fish, probably on stable organic compounds unique to a stream.

Spawning sites generally are just above and below riffles, in shallows with gravel substrate. The female selects the site and constructs the nest, termed a redd. Redd construction is accomplished by a process sometimes referred to as cutting. Oriented upstream, the female rolls on her side, appresses the tail onto the substrate, and forcefully undulates the tail and body, dislodging and raising substrate materials. Heavier stones settle quickly while finer materials trail downstream. Repeated cutting results in an elliptical redd with a downstream mound (Briggs 1953; Needham 1961; Webster 1981).

During redd construction a dominant male usually pairs with the female; both may chase away intruders and swimmers-by. Once the redd is completed, the female rests in it and is soon joined by the male. During gamete release both sexes, side by side, typically arch the back, gape, and quiver. After each spawning the female reworks the redd by cutting just upstream, dislodging gravel that settles over the just fertilized eggs. Redds tend to be elongated and contain eggs from a succession of spawnings by a female. When spawning is complete, the eggs are protected by burial within loosely piled gravel, through which oxygenated water freely percolates. Both sexes are polygamous and may survive to spawn in additional years, except for Pacific salmons which die after spawning.

Small mature males that lack obvious secondary sexual features occur in some Pacific salmons. These "jacks" migrate, spawn as "sneakers" with a female that is mating with a larger male, and die after spawning. Similar patterns have been detected in Atlantic salmon, brown trout, and Arctic char, and may be widespread in the subfamily. This alternative life history strategy involving sneaker males has only recently been well researched (Gross 1984, 1985).

Eggs of salmonids are typically 2–7 mm (Kendall and Behnke 1984). Fecundity ranges from about 80 mature ova in very small trouts to over 150,000 in some whitefishes. Eggs initially are adhesive; upon water hardening they become semibuoyant and can be moved within redd cavities by current. Incubation times vary inversely with temperature. In salmonines the larvae generally remain in the redd until the yoke sac is nearly absorbed. The time from spawning to emergence may range from 1–2 months in Virginia to 9 months in far-northern waters. Springtime-spawning salmonids tend to have shorter incubation periods because reproduction occurs in rising temperatures.

Hybridization often occurs in nature between trouts of the genus *Oncorhynchus*, commonly as a result of the introduction of rainbow trout (e.g., Behnke 1992). Rarely do other trouts crossbreed in the wild. Artificial hybridizations have been made with the aim of supplementing fisheries, but due to hybrid sterility, little success has been realized (Buss 1959; Buss and Wright 1956, 1958). The "splake" noted in the brook trout account is an exception.

The wide acclaim of trout is underscored by the introduction of many species into waters far outside their original historical ranges. A zeal for enhancing fisheries by introducing exotic trouts developed in the late 1800s in North America. Brown trout were shipped from Europe, brook trout were sent west, rainbow trout were carried back east, and salmon were put just about anywhere people thought they ought to be. Rainbow and brown trout have become naturalized in Virginia but the success here of transplanted northern strains of brook trout seems in

doubt. Six other salmonids have been liberated in the state during the past 110 years; some vanished without trace, others were caught by fishermen for a brief period (*Introduced Fishes*).

Alien species often adversely affect natives, as the rainbow has affected brook trout. Owing to introductions (and many other factors), genetically distinct native forms (whether taxonomically recognized or not) with unique potential for fisheries management have been modified by hybridization or lost through competition (Behnke and Zarn 1976). As Behnke (1979) remarked, no single genetic stock of native trout will be the "trout for all seasons." Perpetuation of widely varied fishing opportunities relies on sustained genetic diversity in the form of pure gene pools.

The wild-trout resource of Virginia was estimated in 1975 as about 200 streams totaling 965 rkm. Gratifyingly, the intensive 1976–1979 statewide survey by the VDGIF identified 446 streams comprising 3,265 rkm with wild trout; that is, trout produced by spawning in natural streams. Of these, 2,198 rkm (67%) harbor pure native brook trout, more than in the other southeastern states combined. Wild rainbow trout occupy 20% of Virginia's trout streams; the remainder have naturalized populations of brown trout or combinations of the three species (Mohn and Bugas 1980; Bugas and Mohn 1981).

Trout management in Virginia is determined by stream type and secondarily by the bent of anglers. Streams supporting substantial natural reproduction generally are not stocked. Many of these are small in size and are closely guarded secrets. Many streams, particularly those incapable of, or only marginally supporting reproduction, are stocked on a put-and-grow basis. Some of these have a strong holdover of trout to successive years. Put-and-take stocking is practiced in country and city streams that are too warm for trout during summer or otherwise are temporarily inhospitable, but which can furnish recreation briefly. Some of Virginia's reservoirs are managed as two-story fisheries—trout in deeper cooler water, bass and other warmwater fishes in lesser depths. In all, 167 Virginia waters were slated to receive announced stocking during 1991.

Blue-ribbon waters of the Old Dominion include the tumbling brook trout streams along the Blue Ridge, many in Shenandoah National Park such as the Rapidan River; the Smith River tailwater section—a Piedmont fishery for large, wild, selectively feeding brown trout; the limestone-meadowed Mossy Creek with its weeded currents and fine browns; and the many scenic wild-rainbow streams in the southern sector of the Blue Ridge. State and federal management agencies have implemented modern practices of special fishing regulations for several Virginia streams.

The amount of trout water in Virginia must have been much greater in prehistoric times than 100–300 years ago when the state was being extensively deforested. In the last few decades the health of some trout populations probably improved by the alleviation of direct threats to stream quality. A grave matter now is the increasing acidity of streams owing to acid deposition, principally via precipitation, whose effects extend throughout watersheds (Kahn 1985). Of particular concern are the wild-trout waters in the Blue Ridge and the higher slopes of the Valley and Ridge Province (Camuto 1991).

The mean acidity of precipitation in Virginia is about pH 4.2—nearly 10 times greater than the preindustrial levels of ≥5.0 (Buikema et al. 1985 in Webb et al. 1990). Shenandoah National Park receives the highest rate of acid-forming sulfate deposition among U.S. national parks (Webb et al. 1990). Generally the soils on Virginia's mountains have relatively little natural buffering capacity (Webb et al. 1989; Cosby et al. 1991). That capacity has been substantially depleted by acid deposition; only 7% of 341 trout streams sampled in the Blue Ridge and the Valley and Ridge provinces during 1987 were adequately buffered (Webb et al. 1990). The median pH for these streams was 6.7, well above a biologically critical threshold of 6.0. In the future, about 40% are expected to have a pH below 4.7 (Webb et al. 1990). The worst prognosis is for the mountains in the Valley and Ridge, which tend to have lower alkalinity than Blue Ridge streams (Webb et al. 1989). Substantial ecological change including loss of fisheries is expected.

Name.—Salmon-, from *Salmo*, the Latin name for the salmon of the Atlantic; derived from *salio*, meaning "to leap." "Trout" is from the Latin *trutta*, meaning trout.

Key to Trout   Salmonidae

The juveniles and adults of the three Virginia species are easily distinguished by characters provided in the key; see Martinez (1984) for diagnostic characters of young specimens. The counting of branched fin rays is aided by passing strong light through the fin from the underside; the last two obvious ray branches are counted as one ray. Total dorsal and anal fin ray counts in species accounts include the minute anterior rudiments, best seen by peeling away a small flap of skin along the base of fins.

1a   Dorsum vermiculated (having a wormlike pattern), side with pale
spots, dark spots absent; shaft of vomer (elongate posterior
portion) lacking teeth (Figure 52B) . . . . BROOK TROUT—*Salvelinus fontinalis*   p. 575
1b   Dorsum and side dark-spotted, pale spots absent; shaft of vomer
with 1–2 rows of teeth (Figure 52A)   2

2a   Caudal fin usually not spotted, occasionally with spots on lobes
only; spots on head medium-sized, few, and absent from snout
anterior to nares; side with red spots, but rosy blush, blotches, and
stripe absent, in life; adipose fin pale-edged or slightly, vaguely
spotted, and in life partly orange; branched anal rays (7)8(9) . .   BROWN TROUT—*Salmo trutta*   p. 580
2b   Caudal fin widely spotted; spots on head small, usually numerous,
and occurring from occiput to snout tip; side with pinkish blush,
blotches, or stripe, but red spots absent, in life; adipose fin at least
mostly black-edged, and in life not orange; branched anal rays
(8)9–10 . . . . RAINBOW TROUT—*Oncorhynchus mykiss*   p. 584

Chars   Genus *Salvelinus* Richardson

Virginia's native brook trout is one of the 7–10 species recognized among the three subgenera of *Salvelinus* (Behnke 1980; Cavender 1980; Kendall and Behnke 1984). The genus may contain as many as 15–16 species (Behnke 1990). Chars lack black spots on the body, but in some species the side is red-

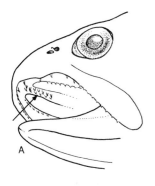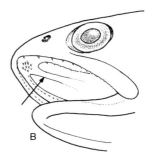

Figure 52 Vomerine teeth: (A) *Salmo trutta* and *Oncorhynchus mykiss*. (B) *Salvelinus fontinalis* (redrawn from McPhail and Lindsey 1970).

dappled; breeding males have a flamboyant crimson belly and red-, black-, and white-marked lower fins.

Name.—*Salvelinus* is derived from salvelin, an old (Germanic?) name for chars. The name char is de-

rived from chare, an old Anglo-Saxon name for these fishes, possibly rooted in Gaelic (from caera meaning red or blood-colored), or French (from cear meaning blood) (Morton 1980); these allude to the red belly of breeding males.

Brook trout   *Salvelinus fontinalis* (Mitchill)

SYSTEMATICS

The brook trout was described in 1814 from the vicinity of New York City. Its closest relative is the extinct silver char *S. agassizi* known only from New Hampshire. The two species constitute the subgenus *Baione* (Behnke 1972, 1980; Jenkins *in* Lee et al. 1980).

Salvelinus fontinalis exhibits relatively little geographic variation in structure and color compared with other widespread trouts (Behnke 1980). Populations in Great Smoky Mountains National Park (GSMNP) in North Carolina and Tennessee, and other southern Appalachian areas have been suggested to be subspecifically distinct from northern populations based on apparent differences in morphology, color, and life history (Lennon 1967). Recent morphological and biochemical studies of southern brook trout populations have contrasting conclusions. Estes and White (1985) and Harris (1985) did

not find subspecific differentiation, whereas Stoneking et al. (1981) reported variation between the GSMNP and northern (Pennsylvania and New York) populations comparable with subspecific differences in other groups. Stoneking et al. (1981) did not examine geographically intermediate populations, hence differences could reflect clinal variation.

DESCRIPTION

Materials.—From Rounsefell (1962), Scott and Crossman (1973), Power (1980), and 21 Virginia series; dorsal and anal fin counts from 18 specimens. Color in life from Kendall (1914), Scott and Crossman (1973), and 1 Virginia lot.

Anatomy.—A char with pale spots on the side and a vermiculate dorsum; adults are 130–250 mm TL. Body moderate in profile, slightly or moderately compressed; mouth terminal, large; jaws long, jaw angle well behind eye. Dor-

Fish 165 *Salvelinus fontinalis* adult male 183 mm SL (REJ 1048), VA, Floyd County, Shooting Creek, 7 October 1983.

sal fin moderate-sized, on about mid-length of body; adipose fin small; caudal fin broad, forked, emarginate, or truncate; lower fins moderate-sized. Large breeding male develops small kype on lower jaw.

Meristics.—Pored lateral line scales 109–130, total midlateral scales 195–243; total dorsal rays (12)13–15, branched rays 8–9(10); total anal rays 12–14, branched rays (6)7–8(9); pelvic rays 7–10; pectoral rays 10–15; gill rakers 13–22; pyloric caeca (20)33–45(55).

Color in Preservative.—Back and upper side vermiculate (dark and pale areas irregular, longer ones wormlike); side with numerous pale spots of varied size and shape; venter pale except dusky ventrolaterally and around genital opening, particularly dark in those areas in nuptial male. Head dorsum vermiculate or duskily spotted; side mostly dusky; lower margin of lower jaw pale in nuptial male; gular area dusky or dark along jaw margin. Parr marks remain somewhat evident in many small adults.

Dorsal fin spotted and marbled with black; adipose fin with dusky marks; caudal fin with leading edges pale, bordered with dark streaks, remainder of fin irregularly duskily tessellated or marbled; lower fins with pale anterior margin, then bordered by black streak, remainder of each fin weakly marked or pale.

Color in Life Plate 24.—Breeding male with ground color from dorsum to midside a medium to dark olive; pale vermiculations and spots olive, yellow-olive, or yellow; small red spots, haloed with pale blue, scattered on side, less numerous than other pale marks; parr marks of small male olive-gray, dorsal margin of marks merges with shade of dorsum; lower side grading olive-yellow to orange to orange-red, bordered by black at ventrolateral margin; venter and lower jaw milky white.

Dorsal fin pale olive-yellow with black bars or marks. Adipose fin yellow-olive; caudal fin yellow-olive with black marks, lower leading margin milky white and paralleled just above by black streak; lower fins with anterior margin milky white, bordered by black streak, elsewhere orange-red.

Dorsum of nonbreeding adult similar to breeding fish; side silvery with pale olive tones and blue-green and golden iridescences; pale spots reduced in contrast; red spots usually paler or inevident; milky white and dark marks in fins similar to breeding adults; ventrolateral red hues reduced or absent.

Larvae.—Early development described in detail by Balon (1980a, 1980b); descriptions and comparisons in Scott and Crossman (1964, 1973), Auer (1982c), and Martinez (1984).

BIOLOGY

Brook trout populations differ substantially in some life history aspects, often on a north–south and coastal–inland basis. Extensive reviews and analyses of its biology are by Power (1980) and Raleigh (1982). Brook trout begin feeding on microcrustaceans about 20–30 days after hatching. Adults forage primarily on aquatic and terrestrial insects, and also typically feed on fishes; unusual prey such as meadow mice are sometimes taken (Kendall 1914; Brown and Buck 1939; Bridges and Mullan 1958; McAfee 1966b; Carlander 1969; Scott and Crossman 1973; LaRoche 1979; Power 1980). Brook trout were observed feeding on rosyside dace and crayfish in Virginia (W. Roston, personal communication). Kendall (1914) wryly noted that a list of stomach contents of *S. fontinalis* would fill a book.

Age at maturation varies from 1 or typically 2 years in southern populations to 3–4 years in northern populations. Longevity is 3–4 years in southern populations and often 6–7 years in the north. Remarkable exceptions are slow-growing, age-15 fish in a California lake (McAfee 1966b). Population analyses of 26 Virginia streams found that brook trout of ages 1 and 4 averaged 146 and 321 mm TL; age 3 (254 mm) was the maximum age detected in most streams (Mohn and Bugas 1980). These lengths are comparable to some Wisconsin and Canadian populations with good growth (McFadden 1961; Scott and Crossman 1973), and when compared to adjacent states, Virginia brook trout show excellent growth (Mohn and Bugas 1980).

Brook trout tend to grow larger in larger bodies of water. In many big lakes and rivers in the Northeast, a number of 2.3–2.7 kg (5–6 pounds) fish are caught annually (Scott and Crossman 1973). Anadromous fish average larger per equal age than, but do not exceed maximum sizes of, strictly freshwater fish. Most large brook trout caught in Virginia are stocked brood fish; for example, the state record specimen of 2 kg (5 pounds 10 ounces) and similar-sized fish caught in 1987–1990. In 1985 a 1.8-kg (4 pounds) stream-raised brook trout was landed in the North River near the mouth of year-round cold Mossy Creek (L. O. Mohn, in litt.). The long-standing world record is 6.6 kg (14.5 pounds) from Ontario.

Salvelinus fontinalis is an autumnal spawner; the onset of spawning is tuned to decreasing day-length and temperature. In Virginia, egg-laying spans late October and November (Lennon 1961; Mohn and Bugas 1980); in earlier-cooling northern areas spawning occurs in August and September. Typical water temperatures at spawning are 3–10°C (Carlander 1969; Hokanson et al. 1973; Power 1980). In streams, redds nearly always are cut in gravel but sand bottoms with upwelling water are sometimes used. Spawning may also occur in upwelling and non-upwelling areas of lakes; well-oxygenated water and gravel substrate would seem of particular importance in the latter.

Females construct redds that at first are defended by both sexes, later only by the female. Females sometimes spawn with different males in the same year. After each spawning, the female brushes the eggs into crevices, then reworks the redd by excavating a new egg pit. The redd is abandoned when spawning is completed (Needham 1961; Power 1980). Fecundity varies from about 100 to, in very large females, 5,000 eggs. Incubation period varies with temperature, averaging 129 days at 3°C and 60 days at 8°C (Power 1980).

The hybrid brook trout × brown trout is called the tiger trout because of its bold pattern of large vermiculations and aggressive disposition. It is rarely produced in nature (Witzel 1983); several that apparently were naturally produced are known from Shenandoah National Park (L. O. Mohn, in litt.). The brook trout × lake trout hybrid—the splake—is fertile, reproduces naturally, exhibits many desirable traits, and is stocked in several Canadian lakes (Scott 1956; Berst et al. 1980).

HABITAT

Appalachian brook trout are typically associated with rocky, tumbling, mountain creeks and small streams that have permanent cool or cold flow or occasionally are intermittent. They also occupy open streams of moderate gradient where temperature and other conditions are adequate. Brook trout often penetrate into extreme headwaters, usually extending higher than blacknose dace and sculpins in Virginia. No distinct upper altitude limited the distribution of brook trout in Colorado (Vincent and Miller 1969). Northern populations naturally occur in ponds, lakes, brooks, and rivers; some coastal populations are anadromous (Bridges and Mullan 1958; Power 1980).

Bodies of water with various natural substrates, including extensive areas of sand, silt, mud, and detritus, are occupied by brook trout. A few moderately silted, sandy streams in Virginia harbor wild brook trout as large as 400 mm TL; suitable spawning substrate is available in their headwaters. However, moderate loading of streams by fine particles can sharply reduce standing crops of trout food and can impair or prevent reproduction by trout (Cordone and Kelley 1961; Saunders and Smith 1965; Burns 1970). Populations in reaches with unproductive bottoms can be sustained in part by drifting invertebrates, crayfishes, and forage fishes, or by food organisms associated with aquatic and terrestrial vegetation.

Brook trout can be vigorous in water temperatures of 5–19°C; adults prefer 14–16°C. Spawning is virtually restricted to water of 15°C and lower; a mean below 9°C is required for optimal developmental and hatching success. The upper lethal limit of hatchlings is 20°C, and for juveniles and adults it is about 25°C (MacCrimmon and Campbell 1969; Hokanson et al. 1973; Power 1980). Brook trout frequently occur in Virginia streams with summer temperatures up to 21°C; these streams cool at night. Limiting temperatures cause brook trout to seek direct spring inflow. Reduced success in waters of marginal temperature is related partly to competition with more heat-tolerant species (Mohn and Bugas 1980), which are numerous in some drainages of Virginia.

Moderate precipitation of somewhat regular frequency is an important environmental criterion. Intermittent mountain streams with permanent pools contain brook trout in Virginia (Mohn and Bugas 1980). However, droughts in Shenandoah National Park during spawning seasons, as well as flood scouring, strongly depressed populations in the early 1950s (Lennon 1961). Severe summer drought followed by a very cold winter reduced standing stocks by 85–93% in two James drainage tributaries (LaRoche 1979).

Although brook trout have been reported to occur in a wide pH range, 4.1–9.5 (Creaser 1930), the lower limit of survival, especially for embryos and hatchlings, appears to be pH 4.5 (Power 1980; Baker 1984). The pH range observed during the 1975–1978 survey of Virginia trout streams was 6.8–8.5 (Mohn and Bugas 1980).

DISTRIBUTION   Map 117

The native range of the brook trout extends from the Hudson Bay basin and northeastern Canada south through much of the Great Lakes basin, a small part of the upper Mississippi drainage proper, east to the coast from Maine to New Jersey, and down the Appalachian chain to northern Georgia. Through introductions, the brook trout has become extensively distributed in North America and is established on all continents except Australia and Antarctica, although its world distribution is less than that of the rainbow and brown trouts (MacCrimmon and Campbell 1969; MacCrimmon et al. 1971).

Salvelinus fontinalis is the only salmonid native to Virginia and is the only trout species in an estimated 2,198 rkm of streams, 67% of the total trout water in the state (Mohn and Bugas 1980). Here the brook trout is tied to montane areas—essentially the Blue

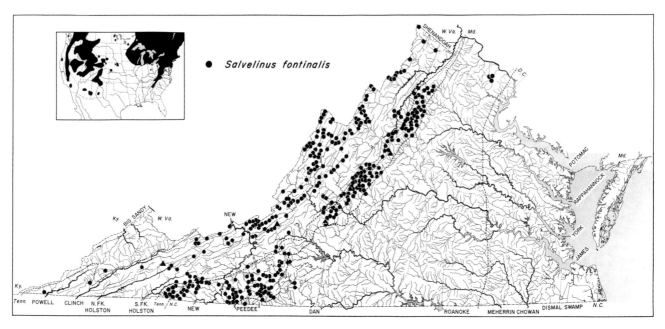

Map 117   Brook trout.

Ridge and the Valley and Ridge provinces. It presently occurs in all Virginia drainages heading in mountains except perhaps the Big Sandy; the York, Chowan, and minor eastern drainages are excluded. The headwaters of the York, the closest of these to the Blue Ridge, arise at about elevation 245 m, much less than the approximate low-elevation limit of 600 m suggested by MacCrimmon and Campbell (1969) for brook trout in the region. Most Virginia populations occur at elevations higher than 460 m (Webb et al. 1989, 1990).

The determination of the historical native range of brook trout in Virginia is uncertain because the picture is clouded by extirpation and stocking. Population losses are largely attributable to warming and siltation of streams owing to deforestation. Introductions began in 1876; the VFC (1877a) stated that "The streams on both sides of the Blue Ridge throughout its extent, are admirably adapted to trout, and once abounded with them." However, brook trout probably are not native to the Pee Dee drainage. Although no early sampling efforts are known from the very small Virginia portion of the Pee Dee, the remainder of its montane section (in North Carolina) was excluded from the range of the brook trout by Smith (1907).

Conflicting comments concern its status in the Big Sandy drainage. The VFC (1877a) noted that "The tributaries of the Sandy . . . abound in trout." However, *S. fontinalis* was not listed in a literature survey

of the ichthyofauna of the entire drainage (Howell 1981), and Hess et al. (1985) stated that no native trout fisheries exist there. With the environmental havoc wrought by coal mining in the Big Sandy watershed, it is possible that the brook trout was native but extirpated. Its native status in the Roanoke drainage is also questionable. An early record in the upper Roanoke system proper (hearsay in 1888 to Jordan [1889b]) postdates early stocking of that part of the drainage (VFC 1877b). Some populations in the upper Dan River system may be native.

Specific statements amply indicate that brook trout are indigenous to the Potomac, Rappahannock, James, New, and Tennessee drainages (Cope 1868b; VFC 1877a). This species was restricted to the Blue Ridge in the Rappahannock but the extent of its original distribution is unclear in the other drainages. Based partly on recent records from unstocked streams, the range in the Shenandoah, James, and New included the Blue Ridge and higher slopes in the Valley and Ridge Province. During glacial times, the range almost certainly included streams fed by large springs in broad valleys of the Valley and Ridge. Many of these populations probably perished with deforestation, as indicated by the large range hiatus through the agricultural Great Valley in northern to southwestern Virginia (Map 117).

It is not clear that brook trout were widespread in the upper Tennessee drainage of Virginia. Apparently they are native to the South Fork Holston system (Cope 1868b), the only Virginia portion originating in the Blue Ridge. Jordan (1889b) also noted their presence in the South Fork. The records in the Middle Fork and North Fork systems of the Holston and in the Clinch–Powell systems are recent and from stocked waters. With the number of cold montane and valley streams lying north of the South Fork Holston, it would seem that some populations, if native, would have endured, but we are unaware of any. The verbal report to Woolman (1892) of brook trout in the Powell River several rkm below the Virginia line is questionable and may postdate stocking of the area.

Culture and stocking of brook trout was begun in 1876 to replenish populations ravaged by "murderers" (VFC 1877a). The 1882 VFC report stated that the agency was unable to raise and stock sufficient quantities to compensate for the depletion by unlawful fisheries. Hatcheries established at Virginia Tech and Virginia Military Institute initially raised brook trout shipped as eggs from Troutdale, New Jersey (VFC 1877a). Local fish were also captured to establish brood stocks (VFC 1877b). Tributaries of the Shenandoah, James, and Roanoke were stocked in 1876–1877; these predate the "earliest" USFC stocking in 1887 reported for Virginia by MacCrimmon et al. (1971). The Wytheville federal hatchery began operation in 1882 and received its first consignment of brook trout eggs from Michigan in 1885 (USFC 1885). It also used wild fish from Virginia waters, plus hatchery stocks from Maine, New Hampshire, Massachusetts, Connecticut, and Tennessee. Wytheville fish were dispersed across the state (USFC 1889, 1899, 1900, 1931, 1934).

A surprising Piedmont population of brook trout exists in Difficult Run and some of its tributaries, a small Potomac River tributary system near Washington, D.C. Smith and Bean (1899) stated that "In former years this fish inhabited Difficult Run . . . but was supposed to have been long since exterminated. Recently, however, a few have been taken in this stream." McAtee and Weed (1915) did not find brook trout in Difficult Run, but they had sampled only the lower part. The population was thriving in the 1940s (L. O. Mohn, in litt.), and was studied recently (Lovich 1984). Jenkins and Musick (1979) regarded the population as probably native. Although brook trout were liberated in Difficult Run and tributaries during 1902–1904 and 1917–1921 (USFC 1904, 1905a 1905b; Fearnow 1929), Lovich (1984) and we did not find a

stocking record to predate Smith and Bean's (1899) report.

Abundance.—Often common in undisturbed or slightly disturbed, forested and pasture streams with ample flow and cool or cold water. Considering the number of individual tributary populations, it is the most common trout in Virginia.

REMARKS

The brook trout ". . . recedes from civilization . . .; does not relish much sunshine, and abhors muddy water . . ." (VFC 1877a). This old observation still characterizes wild brook trout, although they may persist in modified waters as long as sufficient cover, food, cool water, and for spawning, gravel substrate are available. The brook trout symbolizes the wildness of the eastern mountains, so much of which has been adversely changed. Deforestation and consequent warming and siltation of streams share culpability with various kinds of pollution including acid precipitation (Power 1980; Baker 1984).

In many areas brook trout have been encroached upon by the introduced rainbow and brown trouts. The rainbow has caused extensive reduction of brook trout in Great Smoky Mountains National Park (King 1937; Jones 1978; Kelly et al. 1979), but in Virginia, brook trout have been relatively resistant to invasion. Takeover by wild rainbow trout occurred mostly in the Mount Rogers highland area, adjacent to the corners of North Carolina and Tennessee (Mohn and Bugas 1980). Brook trout do not warrant protective status in Virginia other than by water-quality and fishing regulations (Jenkins and Musick 1979).

It is fitting that spawning brook trout and the deciduous mountain forest mutually celebrate autumn with glorious displays of yellow, orange, and red hues. Upon seeing a male brookie in full nuptial regalia, surely anglers have marveled at the beauty and perfection of this small predator.

Name.—*Fontinalis* means "living in springs," an appropriate name for a fish which has cooler temperature requirements than the brown and rainbow trouts. It was called a trout by early North American settlers familiar with brown trout of their homeland, and to this day that appellation remains stubbornly associated. *Salvelinus fontinalis* should be called the brook char. Common Appalachian colloquialisms are native trout and speckled trout.

Atlantic trouts and salmons

Eight or nine species divided among four subgenera constitute this primarily Eurasian genus (Kendall and Behnke 1984); two of the subgenera may be elevated (Behnke 1990). Only the Atlantic salmon is native also to North America. Only the widely introduced brown trout currently is known in Virginia. The European Ohrid trout *Salmo letnica* has been introduced to Tennessee and may extend into Virginia (*Species of Possible Occurrence*). The removal of Pacific trouts from *Salmo* is discussed under the genus *Oncorhynchus*.

Genus *Salmo* Linnaeus

Most members of *Salmo* are silvery or drab and darkly spotted; the brown trout typically is red-spotted and often has rich yellow and orange body tones and red in some fins. Other members of the genus have red spots when young and during spawning (Vladykov 1963).

Name.—See Family account for scientific name; see generic account of *Oncorhynchus* for common name.

Brown trout   *Salmo trutta* Linnaeus

SYSTEMATICS

The brown trout was described from Europe in 1758. It is placed in the subgenus *Salmo* with *S. salar* (Atlantic salmon) and three other Eurasian species (Behnke 1968). Many forms of the *S. trutta* complex in Eurasia have been recognized as races, subspecies, or species; for example, 16 subspecies by Blanc et al. (1971). The most widely mentioned subspecific epithets often are coupled with divergent ways of life. These are *S. t. trutta*, sea-run European trout; *S. t. fario* Linnaeus, resident stream, German, or Von Behr trout; and *S. t. levenensis* Günther, Loch Leven trout, particularly of lakes in the British Isles. Sea-run fish tend to be silvery; Loch Leven trout tend to be dark, lacking yellow and most or all of the orange-red of the resident stream form. Each of these biotypes occurs widely in many of the same regions of Eurasia.

Extensive studies of morphology, biochemistry, and chromosomes indicate that the three life history forms have *S. trutta* as their common ancestor, and that geographically separate populations of each form adapted independently to the same ecological conditions. For example, the sea, stream, and lake forms of the British Isles are more closely related to each other phylogenetically than to similar life history forms of

other regions, such as the Baltic Sea basin (Behnke 1986).

A tenet in systematics is that for designation of a subspecies, all of its populations should have descended from the same immediate ancestral stock; that is, constitute a single evolutionary lineage. Collective recognition of one life history type (e.g., all lake forms of brown trout in Eurasia) as one subspecies violates this tenet. Allocation of separate subspecific status to each distinctive population throughout Eurasia would overburden the nomenclatural scheme. Additional problems stem from mixing of forms in hatcheries and by stocking. Thus the trend is to not formally recognize subspecific taxa in *S. trutta*.

DESCRIPTION

Materials.—From Rounsefell (1962), Behnke (1968), Scott and Crossman (1973), and 2 adults and 12 lots of young and juveniles from Virginia; dorsal and anal ray counts from 6 specimens. Color in life based mainly on 3 adults from streams; many other stream fish were examined.

Anatomy.—A dark- and red-spotted trout; adults are 160–630 mm TL. Body moderate in profile, somewhat com-

Fish 166 *Salmo trutta* adult male 294 mm SL (REJ 1044), VA, Augusta County, Mossy Creek, 22 September 1983.

pressed; mouth terminal, moderate or large, jaw angle somewhat behind eye. Dorsal fin moderate-sized, origin at about midlength of body; adipose fin small; caudal fin broad, forked, emarginate, or truncate; lower fins moderate, pelvic axillary process prominent. Large breeding males develop a prominent kype on lower jaw; anal fin margin throughout year tends to be rounded (convex) in male, concave or notched in female (Gruchy and Vladykov 1968).

Meristics.—Pored lateral line scales 100–130; total dorsal rays 14–16, branched rays 10–12; total anal rays 10–13, branched rays 7–9; pelvic rays 9–10; pectoral rays 12–15; gill rakers 14–22; pyloric caeca 25–60.

Color in Preservative.—In adult, dorsum dark or dusky, side paler, venter slightly dusky or pale; side including operculum with many small to large dark spots, many of which are pale-ringed; pale spots also present. Dorsal fin with dark spots or streaks, sometimes pale-tipped; adipose fin and upper and lower caudal lobes with few or no spots or streaks, adipose slightly or not at all dusky-edged; lower fins pale or dusky; pelvic and anal fins often with pale leading edge bordered posteriorly by dark streak the length of the fins.

Color in Life Plate 24.—Dorsum tawny to olivebrown, often with brassy overtone; ground shade of side tan to yellow, sometimes brassy; back and side with olivebrown to black spots, side with orange to red spots (pale in preservative); some spots on side haloed dirty white or pale blue; venter and lower head dirty white to pearl. Dorsal fin amber to olive, marks brown to black; adipose fin yellowolive with orange-red areas; caudal fin olive, sometimes streaked orange-red; anal and pelvic fins with dirty white leading edge, then dark, remainder olive to slightly orangeolive or amber; pectoral fin olive to orange-olive. Lake residents often largely silvery, markings reduced.

Larvae.—Described by Scott and Crossman (1964, 1973), Auer (1982c), and Martinez (1984).

BIOLOGY

Food habits of *S. trutta* vary with habitat, fish size, and sometimes sex (Jonsson and Gravem 1985). Young begin feeding on invertebrates at 27–31 days after hatching (Brown and Buck 1939). Juveniles and adults eat a wide range of prey of aquatic and terrestrial origin, mostly insects (Carlander 1969; Bachman 1984). Brown trout in limestone streams often gorge on isopod and amphipod crustaceans. Larger fish seek larger food items and are often dominantly piscivorous. In a Virginia stream, brown trout larger than 280 mm TL exhibited the shift to fishes, taking a variety of species including many torrent suckers (Garman and Nielsen 1982). We found a 500-mm TL brown trout that had suffocated by engulfing a

330-mm brown; the head of the latter extended into the stomach, and the anterior body filled the gill cavity of its captor. Brown trout are opportunistic, often consuming crayfishes, much less often mollusks, salamanders, frogs, and rodents (Scott and Crossman 1973).

Individual brown trout exhibit food preferences, including switching to different prey, that may be attributable to greater availability of prey type or to individual bias; for example, for certain taste or tactile stimuli (Ringler 1985). Large brown trout are believed to feed mainly nocturnally, but the evidence is conflicting (Willers 1981).

As in many species living under a variety of conditions, the age and size at maturation of brown trout are variable. McFadden et al. (1965) compared these aspects in fertile and infertile Pennsylvania streams. Maturation occurred in 1–4 years, usually 1–2 years in fertile streams and 2–3 years in infertile ones. Larger fish tended to mature earlier than small ones in both stream types. Typical maximum longevity is ages 8–10; an age-18 fish is known from Europe (Carlander 1969).

Of age-1 and age-3 *S. trutta* in New Hampshire, New York, and Pennsylvania streams, 50% were 147–188 and 259–292 mm TL (Carlander 1969). In a New River tributary in Virginia, 16 fish averaged 81 and 253 mm TL at ages 1 and 3 (P. E. Bugas, in litt.). In a late October sample from the Smith River (D. K. Whitehurst, in litt.), 25 brown trout of age 1 were 180–275 mm TL, mean, 205, and four of age 3 were 295–355 mm, mean, 328. Nearly half of the annual growth in a Pennsylvania limestone stream occurred from April through June (Beyerle and Cooper 1960).

The largest brown trout caught in Virginia was 8.5 kg (18 pounds 11 ounces). The American record should be the 17.9 kg (39 pounds 9 ounces) fish caught in Arkansas in 1988. Slightly smaller, formerly record brown trout were debated by Sapir (1979) and Schwiebert (1983). An anadromous form of brown trout in the Caspian Sea weighed up to 51 kg (112.5 pounds) (Berg 1948). Behnke (1979, 1986) considered that size unverified but accepted the average weight of 14.9 kg (32.9 pounds) attained in 1935.

Spawning in northern states and Canada may span October to February, but generally it is finished by December. It usually occurs in water of 6.7–8.9°C (Scott and Crossman 1973; Auer 1982c). Several anglers noted spawning in November in Virginia, and we observed it in late October. Two hatchery strains in Virginia spawn during November and December (Kincaid 1981). Redds generally are excavated in shallow, gravelly pool–riffle transition areas. Larger females tend to spawn in deeper, swifter areas and

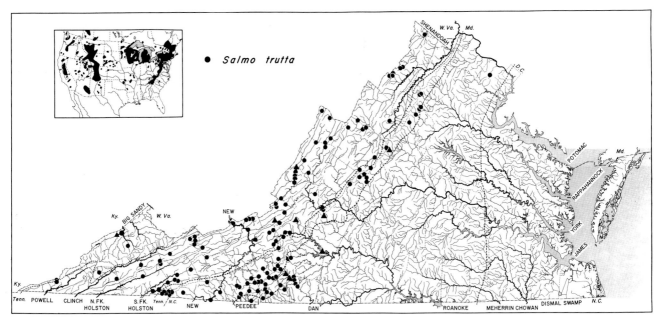

Map 118   Brown trout.

bury eggs deeper within redds than do smaller fish (Ottaway et al. 1981). Spawning is similar to that of brook trout except that the brown trout does not sweep eggs into gravel crevices after spawning (Webster 1981). Fecundity is 100–2,400 eggs; incubation is 148 days at 1.9°C and 33–36 days at 11.1–11.2°C (Auer 1982c). The hybrid tiger trout—of brook trout × brown trout parentage—is rare in nature (Witzel 1983).

HABITAT

Brown trout occupy cool and cold creeks, streams, rivers, and natural and artificial ponds and lakes. They succeed in streams of high and low gradient and hard and soft bottom. In soft-bottomed habitats, food sources typically are vegetation-associated invertebrates and forage fish. Areas of clean gravel and ample current are needed for natural reproduction. In six Virginia streams, *S. trutta* biomass was positively correlated with alkalinity, hardness, amount of canopy, and percent of gravel and rubble substrate (Keklak and Neves 1981).

The use of habitat components varies among and within streams (Marchant and Reimherr 1985). In a Pennsylvania limestone stream, brown trout feeding stations were rigidly located at hydrodynamic points which allowed low energy expenditure by the fish; cover was relatively unimportant (Bachman 1984, 1985). In a western stream the salient feature of a dominant fish's territory was the close proximity of

cover (Jenkins 1969). Brown trout adapt to fluctuating water and temperature levels in many reservoir tailwaters.

Brown trout tolerate warmer temperature regimes than do brook trout. Upper lethal limits are 25–29°C, the preferred range is 12.4–17.6°C, and the optimum range is 18–24°C (MacCrimmon and Marshall 1968; Carlander 1969; Coutant 1977). MacCrimmon and Marshall (1968) noted that unlike many species, brown trout exhibit peak metabolism in temperatures approaching the upper incipient lethal temperature. However, 15°C and higher cause excessive mortality of eggs.

DISTRIBUTION   Map 118

The native range of the brown trout is Iceland, Europe, western Asia, and northwestern Africa (MacCrimmon and Marshall 1968; MacCrimmon et al. 1970). Brown trout have been extensively introduced; naturalized populations occur on all continents except Antarctica. Its entrance to the New World was in the form of fertilized eggs shipped in 1882 from England to Massachusetts; the three fish that matured were not bred. In 1883, fertilized eggs were shipped from Germany by Baron von Behr to Fred Mather, a pioneer fish culturist in New York, and hatched in New York and Michigan (Schwiebert 1983; Behnke 1986). Behnke noted that von Behr's original shipment contained eggs of two distinct brown trout forms. Other shipments and forms followed, and were cultured and dispersed. For decades brown trout have been widely established in North America.

The Wytheville, Virginia, hatchery was among the earliest of North American facilities to receive brown trout eggs from Germany, in 1885 (McDonald 1886). Rearing success of these eggs and of eggs and fry received in 1887 was negligible, typical of artificial brown trout propagation in Virginia until the 20th century. Apparently the only early disbursement to Virginia streams was of 230 adults in 1890–1891 (sites unknown) and 85 fish in 1893–1894 (to a Potomac drainage tributary [USFC 1893, 1896a]). The next liberation in Virginia that we noted was during 1927–1930 when 41,500 "Loch Leven" browns were distributed (USFC 1928–1931). In ensuing years *S. trutta* slipped into disfavor with some fish culturists and segments of the angling public, primarily because of relatively low susceptibility to angling and competitive reduction of native brook trout. However, cases of the latter tend to occur only in lower reaches of the brook trout zone.

The VDGIF stocked brown trout in the Roanoke River in 1958, and 15 streams were supplied in 1961 (Hoffman 1961; Martin 1961); releases have continued to the present. Brown trout are stocked in many fewer streams than brook and rainbow trouts, as the general strategy for browns is to establish wild populations. Most naturalized populations in the state were derived from post-1960 introductions.

Naturalized Virginia populations are concentrated in the southern sector of the Blue Ridge Province, and occur in scattered streams elsewhere within and west of the Blue Ridge. The best self-sustained population is in the upper 20 rkm of the Smith River below Philpott Reservoir, on the upper Piedmont. The small wild population in Difficult Run and tributaries on the Potomac drainage Piedmont is noted by Lovich (1984); the plot on Map 118 is not specific.

Abundance.—Generally rare or uncommon, but common in several streams harboring reproducing populations and those regularly stocked and having good-quality habitat for hold-over to successive years. Because of relatively low susceptibility to angling, brown trout are noted for persisting as strong populations in waters considered "fished out."

REMARKS

The overall effect of many alien fish species has been negative. Some native species have been displaced or eliminated and natural habitats have been altered. The brown trout, considered the most valu-

able exotic fish introduced to North America (Lachner et al. 1970), is a prime exception.

The wild brown trout is the fox of streams, wily and old-growing in its countenance of selectivity. Perhaps programmed into its behavioral repertoire are many centuries of selection from the old contest, angler *vs.* trout. Perhaps the brown trout simply is more intelligent, learning better than other trouts, or it is inherently warier (R. B. Miller 1957). Who is to say which is the predator? The trout preys on skill, self-confidence, and patience, sending many an angler home weary and dull-eyed. Wild browns in heavily fished waters respond to fishing pressure by becoming more discriminating, erring only (but not every time) after the perfect cast and drag-free drift of a realistic artificial fly. On the other hand, brown trout will attack lures that look nothing like food. In this small system, the angler and trout coevolve, each responding and improving to the demands of the other. But even with the recent major advances in tackle technology and fishing methods, some lunkers remain seemingly untouchable.

In describing how the "historic" (1979) Virginia record brown trout engulfed his lure in the Smith River, Bill Nease exclaimed "It made a suck-hole as big as a car hood!" (W. N. Cochran, personal communication). That fish, of 8.5 kg (18 pounds 11 ounces) was one of a number of very large browns, 4.4–7.7 kg (10–17 pounds), caught in the Philpott Dam tailwater section of the Smith River during the mid- and late 1970s. Smith River still produces large brown trout, but not at the same rate or upper size range as in the 1970s. The 1970s fish waxed on alewife shot through Philpott Dam during power generation. Philpott Lake subsequently gained a different forage base (gizzard shad) and a new predator (walleye); the distribution and abundance of forage fish near the dam, and hence their availability to trout below, may have changed.

Lake Moomaw has supplanted the Smith River as the premier producer of large brown trout in Virginia. It was created in 1980 on the Jackson River of the upper James drainage and has an alewife forage base. From January through November 1987, 484 state-citation—1.4 kg (3 pounds) and larger—browns were registered from Moomaw. The 1988 rate is beating that, and some fish are topping 4.5 kg (10 pounds), causing the VDGIF to raise the minimum size for a citation to 1.8 kg (4 pounds). The long and large tailwater of the Jackson River has a highly promising trout fishery being developed by the VDGIF.

Name.—*Trutta* is Latin for trout.

Pacific trouts and salmons

Until recently *Oncorhynchus* had comprised only the six species of North Pacific basin salmon. It has been broadened to include the six species of North Pacific basin trout (including the rainbow trout) because these trouts are more closely related to Pacific salmons than to the true *Salmo* of the North Atlantic basin, with which they had been placed generically. *Salmo*, the oldest of the two generic names, is retained by the Atlantic group because its type species is the Atlantic salmon. These phylogenetic concepts were developed chiefly from anatomical studies conducted by a number of workers over a wide time span. Detailed analysis of fossil and living species (Smith and Stearley 1989; Stearley 1992; Stearley and Smith 1993) indicates that the time has come for nomenclatural change—to make classification reflect phylogeny. Further, it makes good biogeographic sense to generically separate the Atlantic and Pacific basin groups. The change is accepted by Robins et al. (1991).

A suggestion by Kendall and Behnke (1984), based partly on Vladykov (1963) and Vladykov and Gruchy (1972), to recognize a genus *Parasalmo* for only western trouts, has been stayed by reevaluation of extinct

Genus *Oncorhynchus* Suckley

western North American trouts formerly placed in *Rhabdofario*, now *Oncorhynchus* (Smith and Stearley 1989; Stearley 1992; Stearley and Smith 1993). The extinct genus *Smilodonichthys* falls into *Oncorhynchus* too.

The western North American trouts of the genus *Oncorhynchus* are diverse in color, anatomy, ecology, and other characteristics. They comprise four evolutionary lineages of species, subspecies, or races labeled the rainbow, redband, golden, and cutthroat series. One or both of the first two are represented in Virginia. Most forms are black-spotted or otherwise darkly patterned and display a rosy or golden blush or stripe on the side, or a red slash (cutthroat mark) along the lower jaw.

Name.—*Oncorhynchus* means "hooked snout," in reference to the kype of the upper or lower jaw of mature males. The common name—Pacific trouts and salmons—collectively refers to the North American species, their eastern USSR populations, and a possibly extinct, poorly known species on Taiwan (Behnke et al. 1962).

Rainbow trout   *Oncorhynchus mykiss* (Walbaum)

SYSTEMATICS

The rainbow trout was first described in 1792 from the Kamchatka Peninsula in far eastern USSR as *Salmo mykiss*. It was again described "as new" in 1836 from the Columbia River, Washington, as *S. gairdneri* Richardson. Strong evidence indicating that *gairdneri* and *mykiss* are conspecific has accrued.

The Kamchatkan trout had generally been considered a strictly Far Eastern species. Until recently it was misunderstood by American ichthyologists owing largely to inadequate material, and Asian workers long had an incomplete concept of it and its American counterpart. Behnke (1966) reviewed the taxonomic history of *mykiss* and found that *gairdneri* possibly was only subspecifically distinct, but recognized them as species based on different vertebral numbers. Unfortunately, X-ray films of (probably) the Eurasian salmonid genus *Brachymystax* were confused for those of *mykiss*, and the reported vertebral difference was in error (Behnke 1992). Recent genetic studies demonstrate that the divergence of Kamchatkan and American populations is within the range of intraspecific variation; in fact, it is quite small (Mednikov and Akhundov 1975 *in* Behnke 1992; Okazaki 1984). In Okazaki's (1984) study the populations were consid-

ered conspecific and merged under *mykiss*. Substitution of the name *mykiss* for *gairdneri* in North America—once they were regarded as clearly the same species—was required by the international rules of nomenclature; *mykiss* is the first described.

The rainbow trout as a species is taxonomically and biologically diverse (Behnke 1992). For example, the coastal subspecies (*irideus* in North America, *mykiss* in Kamchatka) and an interior North American "redband" subspecies (*gairdneri*) have both anadromous (steelhead or coastal) and nonanadromous (resident freshwater) stocks, which often occur in the same drainages; although differing dramatically, they may interbreed when natural barriers are mitigated. The redband trout group contains other subspecies, including the golden trouts of California (Behnke 1992).

The "rainbow" trout long stocked in Virginia originated at least largely from the McCloud River system of the Sacramento River drainage in California. Its exact heritage, however, is uncertain. It could be the true coastal rainbow trout (one of the steelheads), or a nonanadromous stock of redband trout, or more likely a hatchery-hybridized mixture of the two (Behnke 1992, in litt.). Intensifying the overall problem have been transplantations of varied genetic stocks and their hybridization in nature and in hatcheries over many years.

DESCRIPTION

Materials.—From Rounsefell (1962), Scott and Crossman (1973), and 8 Virginia series of juveniles and adults; dorsal and anal ray counts from 25 specimens. Color in life based particularly on 5 small Virginia adults; many others examined.

Anatomy.—A black-spotted, rosy-sided trout; adults are 150–400 mm TL in Virginia, often 800 mm in many other areas. Body moderate in profile, slightly or moderately compressed; mouth terminal, moderate or large in size, jaw angle somewhat behind eye. Dorsal fin moderate-sized, centered on body; adipose fin small; caudal fin broad, forked or emarginate; lower fins moderate; pelvic axillary process large. Large breeding males develop a prominent kype.

Meristics.—Pored lateral line scales 100–150; total dorsal rays (13)15–17, branched rays (8)10–11(12); total anal rays (12)14–16, branched rays (8)9–10; pectoral rays 11–17; gill rakers 16–22; pyloric caeca 27–80.

Color in Preservative.—Dorsum dark to dusky, grading to slightly dusky or pale ventrally; dorsum and side of head and body black-spotted. Dorsal and caudal fins black-marked, their spots often grading to streaks distally; adipose fin spotted, mostly or entirely black-margined; lower fins pale, sometimes spotted in large adults.

Color in Life   Plate 24.—Dorsum brassy olive, flecked with green and purple iridescence; side with dark olive to black spots; midside with wide pink, red, or purple band or blush, forming blotches or a continuous stripe; lower side dirty white. Dorsal, adipose, and caudal fins pale olive to amber or purplish gray with black spots; lower fins pale, or orange-red, red, or purplish gray, spots when present black; tips of anal and pelvic fins often white in large juvenile and small adult. Lake fish often are dominantly silvery, lacking a pink stripe. "Golden trout" stocked occasionally in Virginia are mutants selectively bred in hatcheries for recessive coloration alleles.

Larvae.—Described by Scott and Crossman (1964, 1973), Auer (1982c), and Martinez (1984).

BIOLOGY

The biology of anadromous steelhead trouts differs in many ways from resident freshwater rainbows. As Virginia lacks sea-going populations, only brief mention is made of steelheads. Popular reviews of the biology of rainbow trout forms are by Behnke (1984) and in many books on fishing; detailed studies are cited by Scott and Crossman (1973), Raleigh et al. (1984), and Behnke (1992).

Rainbow trout begin feeding 16–20 days after hatching (Brown and Buck 1939). The predatory appetite early becomes tuned to small crustaceans and insects; mostly crustaceans, insects, and fishes are taken by adults (McAfee 1966a; Scott and Crossman 1973). A stocked rainbow in the Roanoke River ate a Roanoke darter. Oceanic steelheads grow fast on squids and fishes, and fish diets promote attainment of large size by resident freshwater rainbows (Morrow 1980).

Longevity and growth are variable. In Virginia, naturalized *O. mykiss* generally mature at age 1 and survive to ages 3 or 4 (Mohn and Bugas 1980; Brayton 1981; Neves et al. 1985). Canadian fish usually mature around ages 3–5 (Scott and Crossman 1973). Maximum longevity is age 11; age-7 fish are typically the oldest in many populations (Carlander 1969). *Oncorhynchus mykiss* in 11 Virginia streams averaged 113 and 206 mm TL at ages 1 and 3, and two age-4 trout averaged 257 mm TL (Mohn and Bugas 1980). A migrant apparently from Philpott Reservoir was 414 mm TL at age 4 (W. H. Norton, in litt.). Some steelhead and lacustrine rainbows exceed 1 m TL. Scott

Fish 167 *Oncorhynchus mykiss* subadult 162 mm SL (REJ 1048), VA, Floyd County, Shooting Creek, 7 October 1983.

and Crossman (1973) cited a 23.6-kg (52 pounds) Kamloops "rainbow" from British Columbia. The Virginia record is 5.7 kg (12 pounds 9 ounces). The IGFA all-tackle world record is 19.1 kg (42 pounds 2 ounces) from Alaska, apparently a steelhead.

Wild populations of rainbow trout typically spawn in spring, when water temperature is between 10 and 15°C (e.g., Scott and Crossman 1973). Eggs exposed to long periods of 0–4°C suffer abnormalities and high mortality (Raleigh et al. 1984). Increasing day length, water flow, and water temperature are stimuli for migration and spawning. The Virginia hatchery brood stock has been genetically selected for early egg-taking; that is, July through September (Kincaid 1981). Evidence exists that naturalized rainbows in Virginia tend to revert to late-winter and spring spawning. In three streams *O. mykiss* spawned between February and early May; most activity occurred in March and April (Brayton 1981; Neves and Brayton 1985). Morrison and Smith (1986) demonstrated in Montana that a domestic strain that spawns in early winter in a hatchery environment can revert to spring spawning when exposed to temperatures experienced in the wild.

Rainbows migrate upstream to spawning grounds; males usually arrive first. Upstream movement begins in December in some tributaries of the upper Smith River; some fish probably emanate from Philpott Reservoir (W. H. Norton, in litt.). Populations in small streams may move little or not at all. Redds generally are cut in gravel runs; spawning behavior is similar to that of brown trout (Webster 1981). Fecundity generally is 200–9,000 eggs per female. In three Virginia streams the range was 85–1,143 ova for fish of 157–318 mm TL (Brayton 1981). Incubation periods are 101 days at 3.2°C and 44 days at 7.5°C.

Oncorhynchus mykiss hybridizes naturally with *O. aguabonita* (golden trout), *O. clarki* (cutthroat trout), and the redband trout (McAfee 1966a; Behnke 1992).

HABITAT

Rainbow trout inhabit creeks, streams, rivers, ponds, and lakes. Most wild rainbow populations in Virginia occur in forested small rocky streams. Rainbow trout associate with a wide variety of substrates, and in streams they are at home in calm pools and in pockets within swift riffles. Prime requisites for optimal feeding stations appear to be low current velocity and access to a plentiful food supply. Depth is not clearly defined as a site-selection factor and canopy cover is preferred but not essential. Escape cover, however, must be nearby (Raleigh et al. 1984). Steelhead may spend as much as 36 months in the open

ocean. Steelhead introduced to the Great Lakes gain most of their growth in the lakes and ascend tributaries to spawn.

The preferred temperature range of *O. mykiss* is 12–19°C; 15°C is considered most favorable for food consumption, and feeding is negligible below about 5°C and above 25°C (Garside and Tait 1958; Coutant 1977; Raleigh et al. 1984). Many waters supporting viable fisheries often are 15–20°C for prolonged periods each year. Self-sustaining populations do not become established if water temperatures do not fall below 13°C seasonally (MacCrimmon 1971). A redband trout of the Owyhee basin, Nevada, is adapted to desiccated mountain streams, and has been observed to be quite lively during many-day periods of 28°C daily maxima; however, nighttime cooling appears important to its viability (Behnke 1992).

DISTRIBUTION   Map 119

The North American native range of *O. mykiss* includes Pacific drainages from northern Mexico to Alaska and a small part of the upper Mackenzie drainage of Canada; the range extends far inland in some drainages. In northeastern Asia the freshwater distribution is centered in the Kamchatka Peninsula and extends south to the mouth of the Amur River. Steelheads widely roam the North Pacific Ocean, often 1,600 km from land; the stocks return to North American and Asian rivers to spawn (MacCrimmon 1971; Behnke 1992; Okazaki 1984).

The rainbow trout is perhaps the most widely successful of the introduced salmonids. It has been established on all continents except Antarctica (MacCrimmon 1971; Behnke 1992), and probably is the most frequently stocked trout. This species was first cultured in 1874 in California. It was introduced to Virginia at the Wytheville hatchery sometime during 1880–early 1882 (VFC 1885; MacCrimmon 1971); it proved to be the most successful of the trouts cultured there. The McCloud stock(s) from the Baird Station, California, spawned at Wytheville in winter of 1883–1884, and in 1886–1887 the first generation of hatchery-produced eggs was obtained from the former year-class (McDonald 1889). *Oncorhynchus mykiss* hence was spread across the state in both suitable and inhospitable waters.

Currently, rainbow trout are naturalized in many streams draining the Blue Ridge and the Valley and Ridge provinces, but the total inhabited stream length in Virginia is considerably less than that of native brook trout. About 13% of typical order-1 and order-2 brook trout streams are co-inhabited by other trout (Mohn and Bugas 1980), mostly rainbows. Most

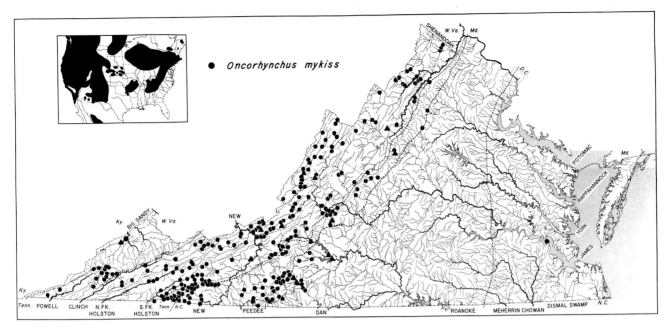

Map 119 Rainbow trout.

Piedmont records are of stocked fish; reproduction apparently occurs to a very limited extent in the upper Piedmont tailwater section of the Smith River, where brown trout spawning is so successful. In Virginia the majority of trout currently stocked to provide put-and-take fisheries are rainbows. The odd record in the lower James River is of two adults with eroded fins, probable escapees from the Harrison Lake National Fish Hatchery 55 rkm upstream (White 1976).

Abundance.—Often common in naturalized populations; stocked fish generally are rapidly depleted.

REMARKS

The rainbow trout may be the most widely known of the trouts in the world. It ranks among the top five most-sought gamefishes in North America. Although a recently stocked rainbow may not be as desirable a quarry as a wild brook trout, the naturalized rainbows in numerous Virginia streams possess a striking palette of colors and can be as demanding of a careful approach and delicate cast as any trout.

An attempt to establish a steelhead-like rainbow, the McConaughy strain, in Lake Moomaw and its feeders (Jackson River and Back Creek of the upper James drainage) has been made by the VDGIF. This strain also is being added to the one present in the Philpott Reservoir–upper Smith River system. The McConaughy strain adapts to lake environments (Dwyer and Piper 1984) and provides a spectacular fishery in Nebraska during its long-distance spawning migration from Lake McConaughy. It developed there from introductions of a steelhead-like rainbow probably made before the virtual domestication of hatchery strains (Van Velson 1978; Behnke 1979).

Name.—*Mykiss* is a vernacular of the trout in Kamchatka (Jordan and Evermann 1896).

TROUT-PERCHES
Family Percopsidae

The Percopsidae are a family of small fishes endemic to North America. The two living species are the eastern trout-perch *Percopsis omiscomaycus* and the western sand roller *P. transmontanus*. Three extinct percopsid or near-percopsid genera date from the Eocene, and an unnamed relative occurs in 62-million-year-old Paleocene beds (Wilson 1979, 1980).

All living members of the order Percopsiformes are freshwater residents, but the group may have had a marine origin (Rosen and Patterson 1969). This order comprising trout-perches, pirate perches, and cavefishes actually is an unnatural group; the latter two families form a sister group but there is no strong evidence that they are closely linked to trout-perches (Rosen 1985a). All of these fishes are basal members of the superorder Paracanthopterygii, which includes cods and allies (Patterson and Rosen 1989).

Percopsids are among the most primitive of the extant "percopsiforms" (Patterson 1981; Nelson 1984) and are evolutionarily intermediate among bony fishes. They have an adipose fin and the head is scaleless, conditions prevalent in several less advanced families (e.g., trouts). Fin spines and ctenoid scales, common in many higher groups typified by perches, occur in percopsids. Fin spines are weak in extant percopsids; the positions of their paired fins are intermediate between those of lower and higher fishes.

Name.—Percops-, "perchlike." The common name denotes combined features of trouts and perchlike fishes.

Trout-perches — Genus *Percopsis* Agassiz

This genus consists of the widely ranging *P. omiscomaycus*, and *P. transmontanus* of the Columbia River drainage, Pacific Northwest.

Name.—See above.

Trout-perch — *Percopsis omiscomaycus* (Walbaum)

SYSTEMATICS

The trout-perch was described in 1792 from Hudson Bay, Canada. Its geographic variation appears to be minimal (McPhail and Lindsey 1970; Scott and Crossman 1973).

DESCRIPTION

Materials.—From McPhail and Lindsey (1970), Scott and Crossman (1973), Becker (1983), and 22 Kentucky specimens. Color in life from McPhail and Lindsey (1970), Pflieger (1975), Smith (1979), and Phillips et al. (1982).

Anatomy.—A fish with supralateral eyes, well-developed adipose fin, and a lateral row of dark spots; adults are 80–110 mm TL. Body somewhat elongate, slightly compressed. Head and supralateral eye moderate or large; snout moderate; frenum present; mouth small or moderate, subterminal, jaws and throat bearing small cardiform and villiform teeth. Anterior cephalic lateralis canals enlarged, with quadrate chambers; lower side of head and lower jaw with many small papillae; branchiostegal membranes separate. Scales finely ctenoid; head and anterior part of nape and breast naked. Dorsal fin single, its origin approximately above the pelvic fin origin; adipose fin moderate; caudal fin forked, lobes subacute; anal and pelvic fins

Fish 168 *Percopsis omiscomaycus* adult female 82 mm SL (SIUC 7253), KY, Carter County, Tygarts Creek, 2 July 1981.

small, pelvic subthoracic; pectoral fin long, narrow, positioned submidlaterally.

Meristics.—Lateral line complete, scales 43–60; dorsal spines (1)2(3), dorsal rays (9)10–11; 1 anal spine, anal rays (5)6–7(8); 1 pelvic spine, pelvic rays 8–9; pectoral rays (12)13–14(15).

Color in Preservative.—Ground shade pale; upper body duskily flecked primarily as scale outlines; three series of dusky spots or small blotches, one middorsal, one dorsolateral, and one midlateral; lower side peppered with fine melanophores. Head dorsum and snout dusky, opercle with horizontal dark bar. All fins pale, rays of dorsal, caudal, and anal fins finely pigmented.

Color in Life.—Flesh translucent; dorsum with a straw, pale green, or leaden cast, sometimes with silver and purple iridescences; dorsal and lateral markings gray-black; anterior mid- and lower side silver (from silver peritoneum); opercle with green and gold iridescences; iris largely silver. Fins transparent, dorsal, caudal, and anal fins slightly dusky gray.

Larvae.—Described by Magnuson and Smith (1963) and Auer (1982e).

BIOLOGY

The diet of *Percopsis* consists of algae, small crustaceans, insects, mollusks, and an occasional small fish (Clemens et al. 1923; Kinney 1950 *in* Carlander 1969; McPhail and Lindsey 1970; Morrow 1980). Emery (1973) observed trout-perch feeding at or just above the bottom in Ontario lakes; feeding groups moved to shallows during dusk and dark. Benthopelagic feeding is probably characteristic as indicated by the papillae (likely external taste buds) on the lower jaw and head, and the subterminal mouth. The supralaterally positioned eye, typical of benthic-oriented fishes, may be more functional in predator detection than in sighting of food.

Maturation, longevity, and growth differ between the sexes. In Lake Michigan, 84% of males and 50% of females matured at age 2. Minimum size at maturity

was 60 mm TL for males and 75 mm for females; all individuals were mature at 84 and 89 mm TL, respectively (House and Wells 1973). Similar differences were found in Minnesota lakes (Magnuson and Smith 1963). In a Kentucky stream, females matured between 59–65 mm TL and were probably age 1 (Muth and Tarter 1975). In Michigan, males and females survived to ages 7 and 8, but only to ages 3 and 4 in Minnesota and West Virginia (Magnuson and Smith 1963; House and Wells 1973; Watkins 1974). Age-3 males from Michigan averaged 103 mm TL, females 107 mm; nearly identical differences were observed in Minnesota. Maximum size has been given as 200 mm TL (McPhail and Lindsey 1970; Eddy and Underhill 1974; Morrow 1980), but the largest documented specimen may be one of 152 mm TL from Lake Michigan (House and Wells 1973; Becker 1983).

Trout-perch in a Kentucky stream spawned in late April and May at 15°C (Muth and Tarter 1975). In northern lake populations, several spawning peaks occurred between May and September (Magnuson and Smith 1963; House and Wells 1973). Lake-dwelling adults generally spawn in the cooler waters of tributaries during summer. Spawning in streams occurs in rocky riffles; in lakes it takes place in shallow areas over sand or gravel. Spawning occurs nocturnally and communally; two or more males of the group cluster about a female just beneath the surface (Magnuson and Smith 1963). Massive die-offs in lake populations, mostly of older males, are evident after spawning (Magnuson and Smith 1963; House and Wells 1973). Fecundity is 126–1,329 yolked eggs; mature eggs are yellow and 1.2–1.6 mm diameter (Magnuson and Smith 1963; Muth and Tarter 1975).

HABITAT

Percopsis omiscomaycus is found in cold and warm lakes and moderate to low-gradient, large streams and rivers. It occurs in turbid and clear water over muck, sand, and rocky bottoms. Trout-perch were considered intolerant of silt and turbidity by Clay

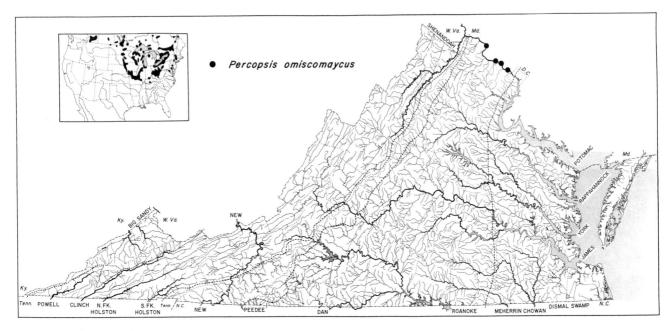

Map 120 Trout-perch.

(1975) and Trautman (1981), but McPhail and Lindsey (1970) and Scott and Crossman (1973) found them to be tolerant, even adapted to these conditions in Canada. Except during nocturnal feeding runs into shallows, trout-perch are found in relatively deep areas of streams, associated with bottom detritus, undercut banks, and logs, and offshore in lakes (Magnuson and Smith 1963; Emery 1973). Becker (1983) reported capture down to 90 m depth in lakes.

DISTRIBUTION   Map 120

The trout-perch is extensively distributed from Alaska to eastern Canada and south in the upper half of the Mississippi basin. Because of its tolerance of cold turbid water, it probably was in the forefront of reinvading species following glacial retreat. Small disjunct populations occurred on the Atlantic slope as far south as the Susquehanna and Potomac drainages.

In the Potomac drainage, *P. omiscomaycus* was recorded only from or near the main channel between the Fall Line and the Blue Ridge. Uhler and Lugger (1876) first reported it from the Potomac and Susquehanna rivers. Smith and Bean (1899) listed it as not abundant in two Potomac tributaries; Radcliffe and Welsh (1916) found it very abundant at a Chesapeake and Ohio Canal site in 1911. The latter is the last documented record for the Potomac drainage (Lee et al. 1984; our data). A possible subsequent capture is noted among E. C. Raney's records of Virginia fishes,

apparently written during a museum visit. Two adult *Percopsis* were taken in a brook one mile above Great Falls, between the Chesapeake and Ohio Canal and the town of Potomac, Maryland. They were indicated to have been collected on 29 July 1948, but Raney also dated his note as that year. Possibly a misapplication of that year to the collection occurred, which we cannot resolve because the deposition of the specimens is not indicated. In any event, extensive recent surveys of the Potomac River, particularly by Davis and Enamait (1982), leave no doubt that *Percopsis* is gone from the drainage. The same is true for the Susquehanna (Lee et al. 1984).

Reasons for the demise of the trout-perch in the Potomac and Susquehanna drainages are unclear. Lee et al. (1976) suggested that the early records represented introduced populations of brief tenure. We consider this unlikely (see *Percina caprodes*); most early stockings were of game species, and governmental agencies in charge were infant when the trout-perch was first reported from these drainages (Milner 1874).

Early stockings of predatory gamefishes may have contributed to the extirpation of *P. omiscomaycus*. Before the transplanting of smallmouth bass to the Potomac drainage in 1854, the principal piscivores above Great Falls were the American eel and redbreast sunfish. The Potomac became predator-enriched in a relatively short period. Channel catfish and the rock, smallmouth, and largemouth basses were established prior to 1900 (Smith and Bean 1899);

the walleye was added shortly after (McAtee and Weed 1915). The spate of predation pressure could have initiated a trend of decline, which may have been intensified by abiotic factors. The latter probably include warm temperature, judging by the Potomac being a southern range limit.

Percopsis may eventually be found in the Big Sandy drainage of Virginia; a major upstream range extension has been documented in the Levisa Fork system of Floyd County, Kentucky (Rice et al. 1983).

Abundance.—Extirpated.

REMARKS

In areas of its abundance, the trout-perch serves as a major prey item of several gamefishes, particularly walleye. That role may have sealed its fate in Virginia.

The unusual enlargement in the trout-perch of cephalic lateralis canals into chambers also occurs in the silverjaw minnow *Notropis buccatus* and the pirate perch *Aphredoderus sayanus*. The three species are typically associated with slackwater habitats. The membranous covering of canal chambers may be a more sensitive transmitter or amplifier of vibration stimuli than would canal pores (Moore and Burris 1956; Reno 1971). In contrast, the general absence of cephalic canal expansion in current-loving species likely is related to the great amount of vibration "noise" in riffles.

Name.—*Omiscomaycus* is attributed to an Algonkian Indian name that includes the root for the word "trout" (McPhail and Lindsey 1970).

PIRATE PERCHES
Family Aphredoderidae

The pirate perch *Aphredoderus sayanus* of eastern and central North America is the only living species of this family. An extinct genus is known from western North American deposits as old as the Oligocene or Late Eocene (Cavender 1986). Aphredoderids and cavefishes form a monophyletic group provisionally placed in the order Percopsiformes (Rosen 1962; Patterson and Rosen 1989), which is positioned intermediately between lower and higher bony fishes. Prominent features shared by pirate perches and cavefishes include exposed cephalic neuromasts occurring in ridge configurations and a forward (jugular) position of the vent (anus and urogenital pore). The vent is in conventional location in larval pirate perch; it shifts anteriad to attain the jugular position by the late juvenile or early adult stage (Mansueti 1963).

Name.—Aphredoder- means "excrement throat"—the anus is located just behind the head. The pirate perch was so named by Abbott because it ate only fishes in his aquarium, and from its perchlike semblance.

Pirate perches   Genus *Aphredoderus* Lesueur

A monotypic genus.

Name.—See above.

Pirate perch   *Aphredoderus sayanus* (Gilliams)

SYSTEMATICS

The pirate perch was described from Pennsylvania in 1824. Two subspecies are recognized, the nominate one occurring on the Atlantic slope (Boltz and Stauffer 1993).

DESCRIPTION

Materials.—Twenty-three Virginia series; counts from 46 specimens. Life color from 4 lots of juveniles and adults from the Chowan drainage; nuptial color from Brill (1977).

Anatomy.—A drab, dark, and stout-bodied fish with a jugular vent; adults are 45–90 mm SL. Body moderate in profile, compressed, back arched. Head and eye moderate; snout rounded, anterior naris enclosed in a short tube; frenum present; mouth large, terminal or supraterminal, oblique; jaws bearing patches of cardiform teeth. Head with ridges of exposed neuromasts; canals of cephalic lateralis enlarged; gill rakers few, mostly short; branchiostegal membranes narrowly conjoined; a large round protuberance at isthmus in adult. Scales ctenoid; cheek and opercle scaled; breast 80–100% scaled. Dorsal fin single; caudal fin usually very slightly emarginate, tips rounded; anal fin margin rounded; pelvic fin subthoracic; pectoral fin lateral.

Meristics.—Lateral line incomplete or complete, midlateral scales (38)39–42(47); scales above lateral line (7)8–10(11); scales below lateral line (9)10–13(15). Dorsal spines 3–4(5), first spine quite small, rays (9)10–11(12); principal caudal rays (16)18(19); anal spines (2)3, rays (5)6(7); pelvic rays (6)7(8); pectoral rays (10)11–12.

Color in Preservative.—Head and body dusky, dorsal half moderately so to dark, ventral half moderately to slightly dusky; lower side often with a dark posteriorly tapering stripe; upper side occasionally with a vague stripe;

Fish 169 *Aphredoderus sayanus* adult male 52 mm SL (REJ 1015), VA, Greensville County, Cattail Creek, 15 July 1983.

basicaudal area with a dusky or dark bar, sometimes represented by two smudges. Pre-, post-, and subocular bars variously expressed; side of head with pale, exposed neuromast ridges sometimes creating an angular vermiculate pattern. Dorsal and anal fins moderately dusky or dark, often narrowly pale-margined; caudal fin mostly dark, most of edge pale; paired fins pale or slightly dusky.

Color in Life   Plate 24.—Head dorsum, back, and most of side brown-black to olive, sides sometimes with violet to purple cast; lower-side stripe black; anterior lower side straw or tan with dense melanophore peppering; iris copper; black ocular bars generally vague; cheek, lower operculum, and prepectoral area iridescent silver-blue. Nuptial male mostly velvety black, venter dark, anal and pelvic fins dusky or black; female less darkened overall, abdominal area pale, anal and pelvic fins clear or slightly dusky.

Larvae.—Described by Mansueti (1963), Martin and Hubbs (1973), Hardy (1978b), Wang and Kernehan (1979), and Auer (1982d).

BIOLOGY

Adult pirate perch are primarily insectivorous but often eat small crustaceans, other invertebrates, and small fishes (Forbes and Richardson 1920; Flemer and Woolcott 1966; Huish and Shepherd 1975; Gatz 1979). Mostly grass shrimp were taken in southeastern Virginia (E. O. Murdy, in litt.). Feeding mainly occurs during dim periods or at night (Parker and Simco 1975; Hastings 1979). Abbott (1862) considered *A. sayanus* to be strictly nocturnal.

Maturation occurs at 35 mm for females in Florida and 55 mm for males in the Chesapeake region (Hardy 1978b). Maximum longevity is age 4; age-2 fish are 82–110 mm TL in Oklahoma (Hall and Jenkins 1954). In North Carolina both sexes survive to age 3 and females grow faster than males (Huish and Shepherd 1975). Pirate perch reach 144 mm TL (Lee *in* Lee et al.

1980). The largest Virginia specimen of which we are aware is 101 mm SL, 123 mm TL (R. Southwick, in litt.).

Spawning time varies latitudinally. Gravid females were found in January and February in Florida (Swift et al. 1977); spawning occurred on 1 May in Illinois (Forbes and Richardson 1920). Some pirate perch were ripe in North Carolina during January through March (Huish and Shepherd 1975); likely only males were ripe in the early part of that period (Murdy and Wortham 1980). Spawning occurred during the first two weeks of April in southeastern Virginia (Murdy and Wortham 1980). A South Anna River, Virginia, female had very large gonads on 15 March. Movements perhaps associated with the spawning period were noted in North Carolina (Hall 1972; Whitehurst 1981).

Fecundity is 129–160 eggs (Hardy 1978b). Mature ova from Texas *Aphredoderus* were 1.0 mm in diameter (Martin and Hubbs 1973). Mature or maturing ova from a Virginia female were almost 1 mm in diameter (Murdy and Wortham 1980). However, 10 mature ova of our gravid Virginia female were 1.5–1.7 mm, and Brill (1977) reported that eggs spawned in New Jersey were 2 mm.

Some reproductive aspects of *A. sayanus* have been observed and others speculated upon, but behavioral knowledge remains fragmentary and perhaps unnaturally skewed by aquarium observations. Most reports indicate that the pirate perch is a nester or practices other forms of parental care. Abbott (1862) did not observe spawning but stated that the pirate perch probably guards eggs as do sunfishes, suggesting a nest. He noted that young swim in pods guarded by adults, as do bullhead catfishes. Similar comments by Eddy and Surber (1947) seem to have been taken from Abbott. Forbes and Richardson (1920) noted that the pirate perch spawned in a hatch-

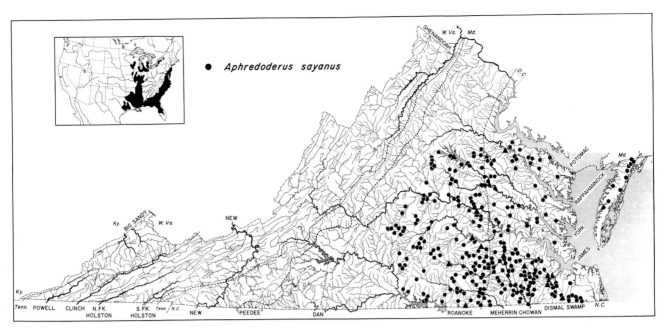

Aphredoderus sayanus

Map 121 Pirate perch.

ery trough. Katula (1973) observed adults leading young in an aquarium; Katula (1987) recounted certain details of the spawning.

In an aquarium spawning, some eggs were scattered but most were concentrated, although not in the depression that apparently had been fanned out in gravel substrate by one or more adults (Brill 1977). Other spawnings by the same female occurred three and four weeks later. None of the spawnings were actually witnessed, and Brill considered the possibility that all eggs initially were concentrated. Each spawning was preceded during a 24-hour period by episodic activity of swimming up and down and vigorous splashing at the surface by a male. Brill (1977) regarded the spawnings as possibly abortive due to the unnatural setting; he (personal communication) did not find evidence of branchial or oral egg retention. Similar rapid prespawning or spawning behavior was seen by Katula (1987), who also considered this to be a marked departure from the usual sluggishness of the species. About that time a circular depression was noticed in the sand bottom, and several days later there were some 125 eggs in or near the depression.

Insufficient knowledge of reproductive behavior of the pirate perch led to speculation that eggs are incubated in the branchial cavity. This stems from the close phylogenetic relationship between the pirate perch and cavefish families and from the position of the urogenital opening near or under the branchiostegal membranes in both families (Pflieger 1975). Mar-

tin and Hubbs (1973) suggested branchial breeding; they found that eggs expressed from female pirate perch tended to move along a groove into the gill chamber. The urogenital pore is directed forward, lying just posterior to a large knoblike protuberance on the isthmus. The protuberance may serve as a "deflector," dividing the eggs into two streams directed laterally into the branchial cavities, via the pair of groovelike depressions noted by Martin and Hubbs.

Because of the scanty evidence for branchial breeding, we believe that if it occurs in pirate perch, it is not the norm. Temporary retrieval of eggs into the orobranchial cavity may be prompted by egg predators, or for cleaning or to move eggs. A preserved gravid female pirate perch, found with three eggs in one branchial cavity, was considered by Boltz and Stauffer (1986) as evidence of branchial brooding. However, the eggs were not explicitly identified to species nor was any embryonic development mentioned. The "pirate perch" eggs and those of other species in the collection should be compared. Weakening the evidence for branchial brooding is that this behavior is known in only one of six cavefish species; it may have originated in cavefishes.

HABITAT

Aphredoderus inhabits warm, low to moderate-gradient creeks, streams, and rivers, as well as swamps, ponds, lakes, and reservoirs. It occupies calm water and usually is associated with vegetation and other cover. In Illinois, adults moved between a river and a floodplain pool; the floodplain was an important nursery area (Kwak 1988). In Virginia, pirate perch range from slightly alkaline and neutral Piedmont streams to the more acidic, dystrophic portions of the Dismal Swamp. In the New Jersey Pine Barrens, *Aphredoderus* is associated with a set of fishes generally restricted to acidic water, all known from pH as low as 4.0 (Hastings 1984). It largely avoids estuaries in Virginia, but has been reported from salinities up to 10.15‰ (Keup and Bayless 1964). During winter pirate perch partially bury in sand (Abbott 1862).

DISTRIBUTION   Map 121

Aphredoderus ranges widely in waters draining flat and rolling terrain on the Atlantic slope from Long Island to Florida, the Gulf slope west to Texas, through the central Mississippi Valley, and occupies southern portions of the Great Lakes basin. In Virginia it occurs in all major Atlantic slope drainages, some minor ones, and on the Delmarva Peninsula. It is found far above the Fall Line but short of outlying mountains on the upper Piedmont. Its near absence from the Virginia portion of the Potomac drainage (four recent records) and lack of records for the Piedmont of the Rappahannock are peculiar.

Abundance.—Usually uncommon or common in our samplings of the Chowan drainage.

REMARKS

The pirate perch is one of many drab or darkly colored Coastal Plain–lower Piedmont species. In color and quiescent manner it is well adapted to darkly stained or vegetated, shaded waters. Actually this species is not all that unattractive in appearance, as some individuals exhibit iridescence; it is popular with many aquarists. It presents a potentially rewarding challenge to observe reproductive behavior in nature or under as-close-to-natural conditions as possible in aquaria. Care and feeding are described by Quinn (1976) and Brill (1977); Brill was able to maintain fish in reproductive condition on live and frozen foods.

Name.—*Sayanus* is a patronym in honor of Thomas Say, an early 19th century entomologist.

CAVEFISHES
Family Amblyopsidae

The name cavefish suggests that most species of this small percopsiform family are adapted for subterranean existence. The members of the family exhibit an array of specializations which allow them to feed in the dark, but not all live in caves. Amblyopsids are endemic to eastern and central North America. Five of the six species occupy waters of limestone belts east and west of the Mississippi River between the southern limit of glaciation and the northern edge of the Cretaceous Mississippi Embayment; none of the five extend east to Virginia (Map 122). Only the single Virginia species, the swampfish *Chologaster cornuta*, occurs on the Atlantic slope (Woods and Inger 1957; Hill 1969; Willis and Brown 1985). Hypotheses on the basis of the large range gap are given in *Biogeography*. Amblyopsids are unknown in the fossil record, although the related pirate perches (Aphredoderidae) date back to the Oligocene or Late Eocene.

The six amblyopsid species form an evolutionary series, from adaptation to darkly stained surface waters to living in caves. The swampfish is strictly a surface-water dweller (epigean); the springfish *Chologaster agassizi* is a facultative head-spring and cave occupant (troglophile); and four species in the three genera *Amblyopsis*, *Typhlichthys*, and *Speoplatyrhinus* are obligate cave dwellers (troglobites).

Amblyopsids are small; adults are 23–85 mm SL (Lee et al. 1980). The species are similar in physiognomy and in many specialized attributes. The body is somewhat elongate, broad anteriorly, compressed posteriorly; the head is medium or large, slightly or moderately depressed; the mouth is terminal or supraterminal; nasal openings are enclosed in tubes or bordered by flaps; the branchiostegal membranes are narrowly or widely conjoined; the anal and urogenital openings (vent) migrate to a jugular position by a body length of 15–25 mm; scales are cycloid, tiny, and embedded; the skin has exposed neuromasts (sense organs) occurring in ridge configurations that look like stitches. The single dorsal fin is small and has inconspicuous spines, or lacks spines; the caudal fin is rounded or spatulate; the anal fin is small; the pelvic fin is absent except abdominally positioned in one species; the pectoral fin is moderate or long, and lateral.

Certain morphological features, particularly those relating to sensory compensation for darkness, demonstrate the adaptive transition from the epigean *C. cornuta* to the troglobitic species. In *C. cornuta* the body is pigmented with relatively large melanophores *vs.* in troglobites the melanophores are minute and sparse, the fish appearing pigmentless; eyes small, optic nerve and optic lobe somewhat reduced *vs.* eyes virtually lost, nerve and lobe atrophied; neuromasts and tactile skin receptors (organs of environmental perception) moderately developed *vs.* hypertrophied, occurring in prominent ridges; semicircular canals and otoliths (organs of equilibrium) relatively small *vs.* hypertrophied (Poulson 1963).

The Coastal Plain swamp habitat of *C. cornuta* is distinct from the transitional spring and cave habitat occupied by *C. agassizi* and the cave streams of troglobites. Cave aquifers have relatively constant temperatures (about 10–15°C across temperate latitudes), exhibit a relatively narrow range of pH (6.8–8.0), and are nutrient poor. Degradation of generally scarce organic drift from terrestrial sources is the principal energy source; food is thus the principal limiting factor for troglobites, and life histories are modified accordingly. Indeed, the entire faunal biomass of deep cave streams is only 1–2,500 g per hectare (Poulson and White 1969).

Lateral line receptors of cavefishes aid in locating sparse living and moving prey, which are primarily small arthropods (particularly crustaceans), an occasional small salamander (Clay 1975; Pflieger 1975), or even other cavefish (Poulson 1963). Metabolic rates are reduced and the evolution of efficient foraging behaviors promotes detection and capture of prey (Poulson 1963; Poulson and White 1969).

Troglobitic cavefishes exhibit delayed maturation, slower growth, and greater longevity than *Chologaster*. Amblyopsid fecundity is low; cave species are the least fecund but have the largest eggs. Numbers of mature ova average 98 in *C. cornuta* and 23 in *Amblyopsis rosae* and maximum ovum diameters for the same species are 1.2 and 2.2 mm (Poulson 1963).

Reproduction occurs in spring and early summer, coinciding with influx of nutrients during rainy periods (Poulson and White 1969). No details of spawning behavior are known for the family. Females of *A. spelaea* carry fertilized eggs in the gill cavities (branchial incubation). This type of parental care, rare in North American fishes, may occur throughout the family (Woods and Inger 1957), but for the other five species, circumstantial evidence is conflicting or direct support is lacking.

Several interesting similarities between the related pirate perch *Aphredoderus sayanus* and *C. cornuta* suggest that swamps may have been the arena for evolution of characters pivotal to the troglobitic life mode. *Aphredoderus sayanus* and *C. cornuta* are small, nocturnally active swamp dwellers with hypertrophied sensory structures other than eyes (Woods and Inger 1957). Adoption of a night-time period of peak activity may be a predator-avoidance response, particularly for small fishes living in a predator-rich environment. Although amblyopsids lack a fossil history, their close ancestors may have been small, based on the size of extinct and living percopsiforms (Rosen and Patterson 1969).

Cavefishes lack commercial and bait value, though some populations have been exploited for the local aquarium trade. They are fascinating subjects for evolutionary and ecological study. Some aspects of the subterranean environment are similar to deep seafloor habitats (Poulson 1971).

Name.—Amblyops- means "dim-sighted," in reference to reduced or degenerate eyes.

Swamp and spring fishes

Chologaster contains two species, one of which occurs in Virginia, that have small but functional eyes and normal skin pigmentation.

Name.—*Chologaster* means "lame belly" and "maimed belly," in reference to the absence of pelvic

Genus *Chologaster* Agassiz

fins (Smith and Welch 1978) and perhaps to the dark slashlike line along the lower side of *C. cornuta*, the type species.

Swampfish   *Chologaster cornuta* Agassiz

SYSTEMATICS

The swampfish was described from South Carolina in 1853.

DESCRIPTION

Materials.—From Woods and Inger (1957) and 5 North Carolina and 8 Virginia series. Life color from 2 Chowan drainage series (S. P. McIninch, in litt.; our data).

Anatomy.—A bicolored and lined fish with tiny eyes and no pelvic fins; adults are 25–50 mm SL. Body somewhat elongate, round anteriorly, compressed posteriorly. Head depressed; eye very small; anterior naris tubal, posterior naris with large flap; frenum well developed; mouth supraterminal, fleshy lower lip occluding upper lip. Neuromasts or papillae in short rows on head, body, and caudal fin; gill rakers absent; branchiostegal membranes broadly conjoined, usually covering jugular vent. Scales tiny, cycloid, embedded. Both sexes with cylindrical genital papilla; snout tip of male with a unique Y-shaped fleshy appendage, that of female with two fleshy bumps. Dorsal fin short, rounded; caudal fin spatulate; anal fin rounded; pelvic fin absent; pectoral fin moderate, rounded; all fins with incised margin, dorsal and pectoral with fatty bases.

Meristics.—Lateral line canal absent on body; dorsal rays (8)11(12); branched caudal rays 9–11; anal rays (8)9(10); pectoral rays (9)10(11).

Color in Preservative.—Sharply bicolored, dorsal half shading from very to slightly dusky, ventral half pale; predorsal stripe best developed anteriorly, sometimes narrowly bifurcate; side with three dark stripes or lines, one dorsolateral, one along midside demarking body bicolora-

Fish 170 *Chologaster cornuta* adult male 36 mm SL (NCSM 9012), NC, Pitt County, Kitten Creek, 7 January 1980.

tion, stripe on lower side wide anteriorly, tapering posteriorly to fine line or series of spots. Dorsal fin dark basally, often with a few dark marks medially and distally; caudal fin mottled, streaked, or dark, tending pale basally and along margin; lower fins pale.

Color in Life Plate 24.—Back brown; upper side brown to tan; lower side and venter pale straw with slight rosy cast; stripes black; head sometimes with slight orange or yellow cast. Fins mostly or entirely transparent, dark marks brown-black.

BIOLOGY

Principal foods of the swampfish include midge larvae, amphipods, and cladocerans (Rohde and Ross 1986). Midge larvae were the item taken most frequently in a North Carolina stream (G. B. Pardue and M. T. Huish, in litt.). Poulson (1963) suggested that *C. cornuta* fed mostly at night, ambushing or stalking prey; it foraged on the substrate and took small crustaceans in aquaria.

Chologaster cornuta is basically an annual fish; the maximum longevity of 14–15 months reported by Poulson just exceeds the spawning period of yearlings. A few age-2 fish were found by Rohde and Ross (1986). Adults are 23–57 mm SL (Poulson 1963); adult males average 41 mm SL, females 48 mm (Rohde and Ross 1986). The largest Virginia specimen we examined is 56 mm SL.

According to Poulson (1963), spawning occurs in early April and fecundity averages 98 mature ova of 0.9–1.2 mm diameter. In North Carolina, reproduction occurs from early March to mid-April in water of 13–19°C; mature ova number 10–98, mean, 27; mean ovum diameter is 1.48 mm (Rohde and Ross 1986).

Spawning behavior is unreported. Poulson and White (1969) indicated that *C. cornuta* is a branchial incubator; they inferred that larvae are 3 mm long at hatching and would leave the gill cavity in one month when 8 mm. Rohde and Ross (in litt.) collected one free-living specimen each of 9 and 10 mm on 14 May. However, Poulson and White's assertion that *C. cornuta* is a branchial incubator is based on the docu-

mented occurrence of that habit only in *A. spelaea* among amblyopsids (T. L. Poulson, personal communication; Breder and Rosen 1966). F. C. Rohde (in litt.) studied specimens alive in jars in the field and later when preserved, and searched the residue of collection jars for eggs, but found no evidence of branchial incubation.

Our data from *C. cornuta* differ from some of the above. Of specimens taken during 29 January–20 February in the Tar drainage, North Carolina (NCSM 9118, 9225), the females were fully gravid, indicating that reproduction may begin in early March. Their fecundity was relatively high; two typical specimens of 42 and 45 mm SL had 339 and 426 mature ova of 1.1–1.5 mm diameter, mean, 1.28. The ovaries contained a volume of mature ova far exceeding the capacity of the branchial cavity.

HABITAT

Swampfish occur in lowland swampy creeks to rivers, ditches, ponds, and lakes that typically are acidic and dark-stained. At seven record sites in the Blackwater system, pH was 5.7–6.8 (M. D. Norman, in litt.). This species lives benthically in close association with cover. Swampfish were not found in a lower Chowan drainage stream that was altered by channelization (Huish and Pardue 1978). In North Carolina it was found rarely in brackish water in salinities up to 5‰ (Schwartz 1981b).

DISTRIBUTION   Map 122

Chologaster cornuta occurs on the Coastal Plain from southeastern Virginia to Georgia. Almost all Virginia records are from the Nottoway and Blackwater systems and the Dismal Swamp. Swampfish seem more localized in the Nottoway, which was extensively surveyed with rotenone by Norman and Southwick (1985), than in the much less surveyed Blackwater. The disjunct 1984 record from Seashore State Park (C. A. Pague, in litt.) indicates that swampfish may occur more widely east of Dismal Swamp than shown.

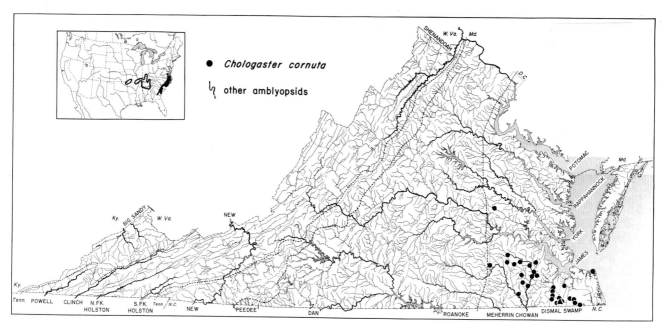

Map 122   Swampfish.

The range extension to the Chickahominy system of the James drainage is based on a 1983 collection from lower Sledds Creek (J. M. Mudre, in litt.). Prior recognition of the James as the northern range limit (e.g., Raney 1950) is based on records from swamps or distributary canals at the north periphery of the Dismal Swamp. These flowages originally joined the Elizabeth or Nansemond systems of the lower James estuary, but their linkages with the Dismal Swamp may have been entirely human-made, thus Jenkins et al. (1972) did not regard *C. cornuta* to be native to the James.

Abundance.—Generally rare or uncommon. The swampfish is particularly rare in the Chickahominy system; it was taken once by electrofishing and not found at the site nor others in that and several nearby streams when electrofished four times previously at six-month intervals (J. M. Mudre, in litt.). Our abundance assessment may be biased; it is based largely on sampling during daylight, but *C. cornuta* is nocturnal, cryptic by day, and difficult to inventory by seining (Poulson 1963). The largest Virginia series were taken in the Blackwater system by a nonselective ichthyocide.

REMARKS

Chologaster cornuta is a living model of preadaptation to caves. Although it differs dramatically in habitat use from other amblyopsids, it occupies dark waters which rapidly quench light, it is secretive, and it leads a nocturnal life. Details of spawning behavior are wanting for the entire family. The swampfish would seem a good candidate for shedding light on the reproductive behavior of cavefishes. However, attempts to observe such behavior in aquaria have failed (T. L. Poulson, F. C. Rohde, in litt.), as did those for *C. agassizi* (e.g., Smith and Welch 1978). Perhaps an aquarist with a "wet thumb" and luck will make the breakthrough. The genital pore of *C. cornuta* usually is covered by the branchiostegal membranes, hence egg release could be directly into the branchial cavity. The bizarre snout appendage of males is suggestive of moth antennae and may serve as a pheromonal chemoreceptive or emissive organ, although Poulson (1961) believed it to be a contact-stimulatory organ.

Name.—*Cornuta* means "horn," referring to the protuberant anterior narial tubes.

SILVERSIDES
Family Atherinidae

Silversides derive their vernacular name from the shiny stripe on the side. Atherinids are generally small fishes, usually 50–150 mm TL, but some species reach 700 mm TL (Berra 1981). This largely inshore marine family ranges world-wide in temperate and tropical latitudes. Fossil silversides are known back to the Eocene (Scott and Crossman 1973), between 36 and 58 million years ago. The family contains about 160 species of which one freshwater and three euryhaline species inhabit Virginia. The higher classification of silversides and other atherinomorph groups such as killifishes and needlefishes is in a state of flux (Parenti 1981; Rosen and Parenti 1981; B. White et al. 1984).

Atherinids are elongate, slender, and compressed; the head is small or moderate, eye moderate or large, mouth terminal, jaws often long, protrusile, with small to medium teeth; lateral line absent or almost so on body; scales cycloid. Silversides usually have two dorsal fins, the first being spinous and sometimes inconspicuous; caudal fin forked; anal fin long, falcate; pelvic fins small, in abdominal position; pectoral fins high on side. Males typically are smaller than females (Breder and Rosen 1966).

Silversides are surface and near-surface schooling fishes found in open water and along shores of streams, lakes, estuaries, and inshore oceanic habitats. The principal diet of most species is small crustaceans. Spawning behavior and habitats are diverse; spawning typically occurs in open water or on vegetation. The California grunion *Leuresthes tenuis* has the novel strategy of spawning on sand beaches during periods of particularly high tides; fry return to the ocean during the next series of high tides (Walker 1952; Fitch and Lavenberg 1971). Eggs typically bear filaments and are 0.5–2.5 mm in diameter (B. White et al. 1984).

Silversides have been considered layers of eggs for external fertilization. Surprisingly, a population of the brook silverside was recently announced to practice internal fertilization, laying fertilized eggs (Grier et al. 1990). The small, nonelaborate genital papilla of the male would not suggest internal fertilization. (A highly developed intromittent [copulatory] organ is shown in Fish 181, a male mosquitofish.)

Some atherinids, such as the grunion, are highly valued as food. Silversides are important forage fishes, and although fragile, they are used as bait.

Name.—Atherin-, "spike or arrow," alludes to the elongate body and fin shapes.

Brook silversides   Genus *Labidesthes* Cope

This genus occurs almost entirely within the United States; currently one species is recognized.

Name.—*Labidesthes* translates to "a pair of forceps, to eat," in reference to the elongate jaws.

Brook silverside   *Labidesthes sicculus* (Cope)

SYSTEMATICS

Labidesthes sicculus was described from Michigan in 1865. Two subspecies are sometimes recognized but intraspecific variation is poorly known (Hubbs and Allen 1943; Bailey et al. 1954; Lee *in* Lee et al. 1980). Geographic variation of early life stages was discussed by Rasmussen (1980).

DESCRIPTION

Materials.—From J. S. Nelson (1968b), Scott and Crossman (1973), Smith (1979), Becker (1983), 1 series from Illinois, and 4 from Tennessee. Life color from 1 Arkansas specimen.

Anatomy.—A silver-striped, slender fish with beaklike jaws; adults are 65–90 mm SL. Body elongate, compressed; head short; eye large; snout long; mouth protrusile, terminal; jaws elongate, downcurved posteriorly, with medium-sized, sharp, conical teeth. Second dorsal and anal fins concave, anal fin long; caudal fin forked; pelvic fin small; pectoral fin pointed. Genital papilla (palp) of breeding male short; genital papilla absent in female (Grier et al. 1990); Becker (1983) apparently described the anal area as the genital papilla.

Meristics.—Lateral line often with a few pored scales, midlateral scales 74–95; first dorsal spines 3–6; second dorsal 1 spine, 9–13 rays; anal 1 spine, 20–27 rays; pelvic 1 spine, 5 rays; pectoral rays 12–13.

Color in Preservative.—Body pallid, side with dark stripe, most pronounced posteriorly, tapering anteriorly; dark stripe often overlaid with silver; upper side and dorsum dusted with fine melanophores, often outlining scale margins; predorsal stripe weak; upper and lower jaws moderately dusky; iris silver. Fin membranes pale, all but pelvic outlined with fine melanophores. First dorsal fin of male black-tipped, but only lightly pigmented in female.

Color in Life Plate 40.—Body translucent; dorsum pale straw, dorsal scales faintly dark-outlined; midlateral stripe and peritoneum silver with lime-green to pale blue iridescence; lower jaw and opercle metallic blue; gular area and venter silver to pale straw. Fins transparent.

Larvae.—Described by Hogue et al. (1976), Frietsche et al. (1979), Rasmussen (1980), Tin (1982c), and Grier et al. (1990).

BIOLOGY

Young brook silverside are microphagous, eating mainly planktonic microcrustaceans; larger fish also ingest aquatic and terrestrial insects (Cahn 1927; Keast 1965, 1970; Keast and Webb 1966; Mullan et al. 1968; Hess 1983). The dietary shift is associated with inshore movement. Brook silverside occasionally leap from the water to seize flying insects (Hubbs 1921; Cahn 1927).

Labidesthes is short-lived and rapidly growing relative to many species of its size. Maximum longevity is 21–23 months; typical survival appears to be just over one year (Cahn 1927; J. S. Nelson 1968b). In Wisconsin, adult size was achieved by the first fall (mean SL, 66 mm in late October); some growth was exhibited in the next year (mean SL, 76 mm in August–September; Cahn 1927). In Indiana some 3-month-olds reached the modal size of 12-month fish. Individuals may spawn only once, as yearlings. Adults were unavailable from Virginia; we took them as large as 56 mm SL in the Clinch River near Virginia. Maximum reported length is 112 mm SL (Lee *in* Lee et al. 1980), but this probably is based on Pflieger (1975), who gave 112 mm ("about 4.4 inches") and expressed this in TL. J. S. Nelson (1968b) reported a 109-mm FL fish from Indiana.

Spawning in the north-central states spans May to August; most activity occurs in May and June at 17–23°C (Hubbs 1921; Cahn 1927; J. S. Nelson 1968b). Females approach males that are in surface territories or groups; eventually a pair glides obliquely downward (Hubbs 1921; Cahn 1927; Breder and Rosen 1966). Apparently it is during the descent, when the abdominal surfaces often are in contact, that the male can use the short genital papilla as an intromittent organ. Grier et al. (1990) clearly showed that in a Florida population, eggs are fertilized internally and

Fish 171 *Labidesthes sicculus* adult male 75 mm SL (SIUC), IL, Alexander County, Horseshoe Lake spillway, 6 March 1982.

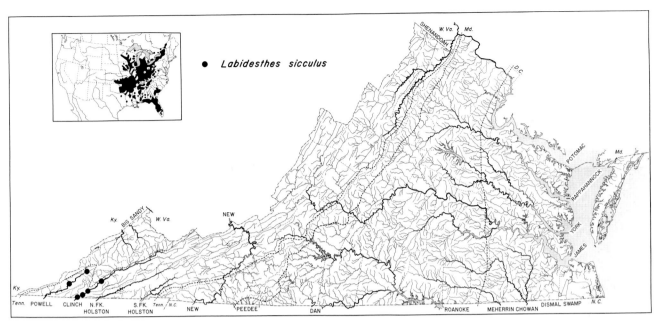

Map 123   Brook silverside.

embryonic development commences within the ovary. For a Wisconsin population, Cahn (1927) stated that eggs are extruded during the mating descent and slowly settle toward the bottom. Eggs attach to floating objects, vegetation, and the bottom by 1–3 long filaments (Hubbs 1921, 1928; Cahn 1927; J. S. Nelson 1968b; Rasmussen 1980). Becker (1983) found 450 and 785 mature or maturing eggs in two females.

HABITAT

Brook silverside often is a misnomer; in many areas this species is more typical of lakes and large rivers (Cahn 1927; Greene 1935; Smith 1979; Phillips et al. 1982). It also occurs in sloughs and reservoirs as well as creeks. It inhabits cool and warm waters of low to moderate gradient and highly varied substrates; vegetation may or may not be present. Gerking (1945) stated that turbidity had not affected its distribution in Indiana, but Trautman (1981) noted its decline with increased turbidity, and most authors suggested that it prefers clear water. In lakes during the first summer the brook silverside occurs in schools at or near the surface over deep water, sometimes moving inshore at night; later in the year it remains in shallows (Hubbs 1921, 1928; Cahn 1927).

In the Clinch and Powell rivers of Virginia and Tennessee, *L. sicculus* has been found only in large sections; minimum width at our sites was 25 m. Broad backwaters, narrow and relatively sluggish ar-eas adjacent to runs, and a sloughlike cutoff channel were inhabited; schools were not encountered.

DISTRIBUTION   Map 123

Labidesthes sicculus is native to the Great Lakes–St. Lawrence and Mississippi basins and the Gulf and southeastern Atlantic slopes. It extends into Virginia in the Clinch and Powell rivers of the Tennessee drainage. Its absence from the North Fork Holston River may be related to former chemical pollution. It has been introduced in West Virginia to the Potomac and New drainages (Lewis and Miles 1974; Stauffer et al. 1978a, 1978b). Its status in the Potomac is unknown to us, but it appears to be established in the New River below Bluestone Dam, based on captures during 1982 and 1984 (Hess 1983; Lobb 1986).

Abundance.—Seemingly rare in the Clinch and Powell rivers of Virginia and Tennessee. Known in Virginia from 9 collections totaling about 30 specimens. Perhaps more abundant than suggested because open surface waters of large pools in these rivers rarely are sampled for small fishes.

REMARKS

Because the brook silverside is the only strictly freshwater atherinid in Virginia and it is rare in the state, its capture here is always interesting. Its localization and rarity have earned it special concern status in Virginia (Burkhead and Jenkins 1991). Schooling *L. sicculus* are known to occasionally leap en masse from the water, a habit reminiscent of their distant cousins, the flyingfishes. Despite such potential predator-escape behavior and the protection gained from schooling, the brook silverside seems vulnerable at the surface. One is reminded though, that few predators occur at near-surface levels in the open, and that the nearly transparent silverside body reduces detectability.

Name.—*Sicculus* means "dried," in reference to its capture in drying river-edge pools (Pflieger 1975).

KILLIFISHES
Family Fundulidae

The killifishes and topminnows that make up the family Fundulidae were recently extracted from the Cyprinodontidae (Parenti 1981), a move followed by some (e.g., Able 1984; Cavender 1986; Wiley 1986) but not all (Robins et al. 1991). Most fundulids are small; adults range from 15 mm SL for the pygmy killifish *Leptolucania ommata* to about 180 mm SL in *Fundulus grandissimus*. The family comprises about 38 species in four or five genera; the greatest diversity is in lowlands of eastern and central North America. The family extends southward to Yucatan and occurs on Bermuda, Cuba, and the Pacific coast of California and Mexico. The oldest fossil dates to the Miocene (Smith 1981), 5–24 million years ago. Nine species of fundulids occupy Virginia; three occur strictly in fresh water, the others are euryhaline.

Most killifishes have a moderate or chunky body that broadens anteriorly and planes to a flattened head dorsum. The mouth is protrusile, more typically terminal than superior, and has a characteristic angled appearance. Jaws bear medium-sized teeth; the throat has well-developed teeth attached to pharyngeal bones. Fins lack spines; the dorsal fin is single and usually inserted posteriorly; the caudal fin is truncate or rounded; the pelvic fins are in the abdominal position and the pectoral fins are inserted laterally. The cephalic lateralis system is well developed but a lateral line usually is absent on the body. Scales are cycloid; the head dorsum has large platelike scales arranged in specific patterns.

Most species exhibit prominent sexual dimorphism. The dorsal and anal fins of males are usually larger than in females, and males of some species bear tiny tubercle- or spinelike contact organs (Fowler 1916; Wiley and Collette 1970; Collette 1977). In some species the sexes differ in average size, and sexual dichromatism occurs in breeding and nonbreeding coloration. The breeding dress of the male northern studfish *Fundulus catenatus* is dazzling.

Fundulids typically inhabit calm margins of freshwater and estuarine creeks, rivers, marshes, swamps, ponds, and lakes; marine species occur inshore. Most are warmwater fishes. Some species tend to school whereas individuals of others occur as small groups or are scattered. Some frequent dense weed beds or dispersed plant cover; others roam open water. Griffith (1974) found that under laboratory conditions, euryhaline species of *Fundulus* tolerate salt concentrations over 70‰, whereas strictly freshwater killifishes perish at levels less than half that; all of the species studied by Griffith tolerate salinities much higher than those found in their typical habitats. He postulated that *Fundulus* initially was a brackish-marine group that invaded fresh water.

The small mouth of most killifishes restricts the size range of food items. Fundulids are typically carnivorous, occasionally piscivorous, and some species appear to be omnivorous. Some species seem proficient at feeding throughout the water column; others tend to have restrictive modes.

Spawning generally occurs in shallow areas, often in weeds. Extended spawning periods during warm times of the year appear to be the norm. Fecundity tends to be low but many species may be fractional spawners. Ova are small to medium and have surface adornments including filaments. Egg diameters range from 1.0 mm for *L. ommata* to 3.5 mm for *F. catenatus* (Fisher 1981; Able 1984).

Some species are commonly used for bait; their schooling habits in shallow water render them highly vulnerable to capture. Killifishes and topminnows of the Fundulidae and allied families are considered important for mosquito control (Rosen 1973). They have a strong following among aquarium enthusiasts, and have a journal devoted to their care and study—the *Journal of the American Killifish Association*. Emphasis has been on tropical killies but much enjoyment and new information have been derived from observations by aquarists of North American species.

Name.—Fundus, "bottom," and ulus, "little," refer to the sometime habitat or size of the first-described species *F. heteroclitus*. Killifishes were called "killivisch" by early Dutch settlers of New York, in reference to living in "kills," a Dutch word for canals or streams (Fowler 1916; Rosen 1973). "Topminnow" comes from surface dwelling and small size. Topminnows and allies are often called "toothcarps" to distinguish them from true minnows or carps, which lack jaw teeth.

Key to Killifishes *Fundulus*

Virginia killifishes and topminnows are easily distinguished by using the photographs and, generally, the key. Regarding the position of the dorsal fin origin relative to that of the anal fin origin (couplet 2), in adult females the fold of skin enveloping the anal fin base anteriorly may obscure the anal fin origin. Probe to determine where the leading anal ray inserts on the body. We count the last two elements of the dorsal and anal fins as one ray; data from some publications are adjusted accordingly. The count of scales in the midlateral series ends posteriorly at the caudal fin base (Figure 7), just as if the scales had lateral line pores. Of the five species in the key, only *F. diaphanus* and *F. heteroclitus* occur sympatrically, in estuaries, hence the capture site indicates the identity of specimens found inland.

1a   Dorsal rays 8 or less; (Chowan drainage only) . . . . .   LINED TOPMINNOW—*Fundulus lineolatus*   p. 614
1b   Dorsal rays 9 or more   2

2a   Side barred, sometimes only posteriorly; dorsal fin origin usually
       distinctly anterior to anal fin origin   3
2b   Side not barred, instead with diamond-patterned scale markings,
       narrow stripes, or flecks; dorsal fin origin usually above or
       posterior to anal fin origin   4

3a   Gill rakers (9)10–12(13); scales in midlateral series (31)30–36(38);
       (estuaries only) . . . .   MUMMICHOG—*F. heteroclitus*   p. 607
3b   Gill rakers (4)5–6(7); scales in midlateral series (35)39–44(50);
       (estuaries, uplands of James drainage and north) . . . .   BANDED KILLIFISH—*F. diaphanus*   p. 608

4a   Side with diamond-shaped hatchmarkings (male), irregularly
       arranged dark spotlike flecks (female), or both; anal rays
       (10)11–12; scales in midlateral series (34)35–37(40); Roanoke
       drainage only . . . .   SPECKLED KILLIFISH—*F. rathbuni*   p. 610
4b   Side with alternating dark and pale stripes (male), or several series
       of dashes or broken lines (female); anal rays (13)14–15(16); scales in
       midlateral series (41)43–49(51); Tennessee drainage only .   NORTHERN STUDFISH—*F. catenatus*   p. 612

Killifishes   Genus *Fundulus* Lacepède

This North American genus, the largest in the family, contains about 33 species, most of which occur in eastern and central North America. Evolutionary relationships are treated by Wiley (1986).

Name.—Fundulus means "little one of the bottom."

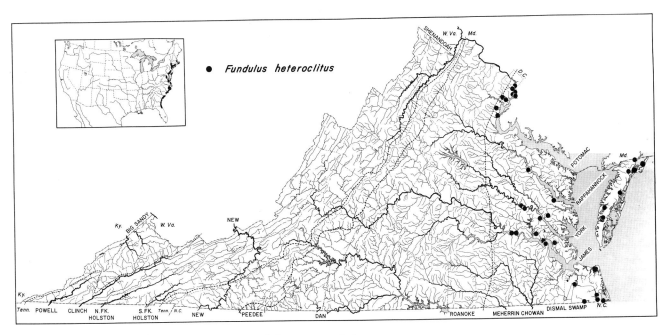

Map 124   Mummichog. Full estuarine extent of the range not shown.

Mummichog   *Fundulus heteroclitus* (Linnaeus)

The mummichog, the type species of the subgenus *Fundulus*, is a typical resident of estuaries, particularly the mesohaline zone, and extends into 32‰ salinity (Musick 1972; Fritz and Garside 1974). It rarely or only seasonally ventures into tidal fresh water in our area. Map 124 shows only record sites that we encountered when seeking records of fresh-water fishes, thus it does not portray the full estuarine range of *F. heteroclitus*. This species is usually common, sometimes abundant, in shallow areas of creeks and rivers; it occurs among weedy cover or on open mudflats. Reviews of its biology are by Rosen (1973), Scott and Crossman (1973), Fritz and Garside (1975), Hardy (1978a), and Wang and Kernehan

Fish 172 *Fundulus heteroclitus* adult male 55 mm SL (UNCW), NC, Hanover County, Bradley Creek, 19 October 1983.

Fish 173 *Fundulus heteroclitus* adult female 51 mm SL (UNCW), NC, Hanover County, Bradley Creek, 19 October 1983.

(1979); subspecies are defined by Relyea (1983). Most of Volume 26, Number 1 of the *American Zoologist* of 1986 concerns the history of study and new research results on the mummichog.

The other killifish candidate for freshwater status in Virginia is the spotfin killifish *Fundulus luciae* (Baird), which ranges from Connecticut to Georgia. It occurs in upper shallow portions of tidal marshes where brackish water often is diluted by freshwater inflow to less than 1‰, and it extends into salinity of 30‰, rarely 40‰ (Richards and Bailey 1967; Griffith 1974; Byrne 1978; Shields and Mayes 1983). The spotfin killifish and mummichog are in the halophilic group of *Fundulus*, having high salinity tolerance (106 to 120‰) under experimental conditions (Griffith 1974).

Banded killifish   *Fundulus diaphanus* (Lesueur)

SYSTEMATICS

The banded killifish was described from New York in 1817. Two widely ranging subspecies are recognized, *F. d. diaphanus* on the Atlantic slope and *F. d. menona* (Jordan and Copeland) of the upper Mississippi and Great Lakes–St. Lawrence basins (Shapiro 1947, as mapped by Gilbert and Shute *in* Lee et al. 1980). *Fundulus diaphanus* is placed in the subgenus *Fontinus* (J. L. Brown 1957; Rosen 1973; Wiley 1986).

DESCRIPTION

Materials.—From Scott and Crossman (1973), Hardy (1978a), and 7 Virginia lots; counts from 13 specimens. Life color from 10 juveniles to adults secured in early spring from the Shenandoah system; nuptial male color from Richardson (1939) and Schwartz (1969).

Anatomy.—A narrow-barred killifish; adults are 50–75 mm SL. Body elongate, slightly compressed; head dorsum flat; mouth terminal, small, protrusile. Dorsal fin origin distinctly anterior to anal fin origin; caudal fin truncate or slightly rounded; paired fins small.

Nuptial male with dorsal and anal fins larger than in female. Male with tubercles on dorsal, anal, pelvic, and uppermost pectoral rays, fin tubercles best developed distally; tubercles present on margins of midlateral scales between pelvic fin origin and posterior insertion of anal fin; spinules present on margins of cheek, opercle, and occasionally predorsal scales of peak males. Male genital papilla small, protruding from or hidden by small flat sheath of skin; genital opening of female enclosed by large thick sheath of skin enveloping anterobasal portion of anal fin. Sexes of summer adults are readily distinguishable without magnification by genital characters.

Meristics.—Midlateral scales (35)39–44(50). Dorsal rays (10)13–14(15); anal rays (9)10–11(13); pelvic rays 6; pectoral rays (14)16–17(19); gill rakers (4)5–6(7).

Color in Preservative.—Dorsum slightly or moderately dusky, sometimes irregularly darkly flecked; side partly pale and having 15–20 narrow dusky bars in male, 8–15 bars in female; partial or complete faint midlateral stripe in some adults; venter pale. Fins pale or slightly dusky. Adult male usually slightly duskier than female, side bars usually wider, fins darker, dorsal and anal fins often vaguely spotted or flecked.

Color in Life   Plate 25.—Dorsum straw-olive; midside silver with pink and bluish sheens; lower side straw to pale olive; venter silvery white; lateral bars dusky olive; cheek silver with blue iridescence; iris with coppery glint. Fins yellow-olive to pale olive. Spawning males rapidly brighten, background brilliant bluish green, bars and fin markings pronounced; bars may be iridescent blue.

Larvae.—Described by Foster (1974), Hardy (1978a), Wang and Kernehan (1979), and Jude (1982).

BIOLOGY

The diverse diet of *F. diaphanus* indicates that it gleans small organisms from the bottom, water col-

Fish 174 *Fundulus diaphanus* adult male 49 mm SL (WHH 234), VA, Rockingham County, War Creek, 21 May 1984.

umn, and surface. It feeds mostly on midge larvae and microcrustaceans but takes many other aquatic invertebrates and terrestrial insects, and occasionally plants (Moore 1922; Adams and Hankinson 1928; Keast 1966, 1970; Vadas 1990). Plant material may be taken incidentally while foraging on attached animals.

Maturation has been reported to occur at 64 mm TL (Carlander 1969), but it begins at about 40 mm TL and age 1 in Nova Scotia (Fritz and Garside 1975). Length–frequencies from a New Jersey tidal freshwater population (Hastings and Good 1977) indicate that reproductive age-1 fish are 50–75 mm SL during June–August. Some individuals in a Wisconsin lake population achieved age 3; averages of 37 and 66 mm TL were reached at ages 1 and 3 (Becker 1983). Four age-classes were found in Nova Scotia; age-3 fish were 67–80 mm TL (Fritz and Garside 1975). Our largest upland specimen is an 89-mm TL female. A banded killifish of about 105 mm TL was taken from the James River estuary, but the remainder reported by White (1976) were 85 mm or less. Specimens of 114 mm TL were reported from New York and Canada (Adams and Hankinson 1928; Scott and Crossman 1973).

Gravid females occurred from April to September in the Chesapeake basin (Hildebrand and Schroeder 1928). Spawning was observed from early May through August in Delaware (Wang and Kernehan 1979), but usually for briefer periods elsewhere, in water of 21–32°C (Hardy 1978a). Males are territorial, defending a space among vegetation or a sandy depression in shallows; they chase and court females. Richardson (1939) observed that during preliminary pursuit, females in an aquarium released a single egg which dangled from them on a thread, possibly as a "come hither" stimulus. The male then commenced more vigorous pursuit, driving a female to a spawning site against weeds. The eggs bear filaments and may adhere to surroundings. Fecundity is 32–252 mature ova (Scott and Crossman 1973; Fritz and Garside 1975; Hardy 1978a; Wang and Kernehan 1979; Becker 1983).

The natural cross *F. diaphanus* × *F. heteroclitus* was considered rare by Hubbs et al. (1943b). We have not seen the analysis of this hybridization by Fritz (1973 *in* Fritz and Garside 1975).

HABITAT

The banded killifish exhibits a sharp dichotomy of habitat occupation in Virginia—estuarine areas and the upper Piedmont and mountains. In estuaries this species inhabits freshwater and oligohaline zones of large rivers, creeks, and marshes, generally avoiding adjacent inland areas of low pH as it does in New Jersey (Hastings 1979, 1984). Most lowland Virginia records (Map 125) are in or near main estuaries, but these habitats may be overrepresented in our data because of sampling bias. In Delaware, *F. diaphanus* is most abundant in freshwater sections of tidal creeks (Wang and Kernehan 1979). This species grows faster, is more fecund, is under less physiological stress, and is more abundant in brackish than in fresh water in Nova Scotia, but paradoxically it has a strong preference for fresh water (Fritz and Garside 1974, 1975). Although found rarely in salinity as high as 20‰ (Musick 1972), its experimental upper limit is 73.4‰ (Griffith 1974). *Fundulus diaphanus* often schools in sparsely vegetated and open sandy areas (Raney and Massmann 1953; Hardy 1978a). Colgan (1974) described a rapid burying behavior into sand, obviously for predator avoidance.

In contrast to lowland populations, the banded killifish also inhabits cold and warm, upland and montane creeks, streams, and rivers having silted or hard bottoms. There it frequents pool margins with and without vegetation and usually occurs in small scattered groups. It seems to favor limestone streams and spring runs of the Valley and Ridge Province. Perhaps the hard water of these streams is a physiological link with brackish water. Inland north of Virginia, *F. diaphanus* inhabits ponds and lakes as well as running water.

DISTRIBUTION   Map 125

Fundulus diaphanus occurs on or near the coast, and in some Atlantic slope areas well inland, from South Carolina to Newfoundland, and extends westward through the St. Lawrence–Great Lakes and upper Mississippi basins into the Red River of the North drainage. In Virginia its inland extent varies by drainage. In the James and York it does not appear to reach the Fall Line, but occurs far above there in the Rappahannock and Potomac–Shenandoah.

The two upper James records, from the years 1933 and 1952, may represent introductions based on the lack of recent records and proximity to Shenandoah populations. However, we consider them more likely to be remnant native populations that may have died out; this species is widely but not generally distributed in Virginia above the Fall Line. The long distance of the two record sites from estuarine James populations indicates that dispersal to the upper James may have occurred via surface captures or underground transfers of water from the upper Shenandoah. The record (triangle) on Kerr Creek of the Maury River system is from pondlike Big Spring, one of the largest limestone springs in the James drainage.

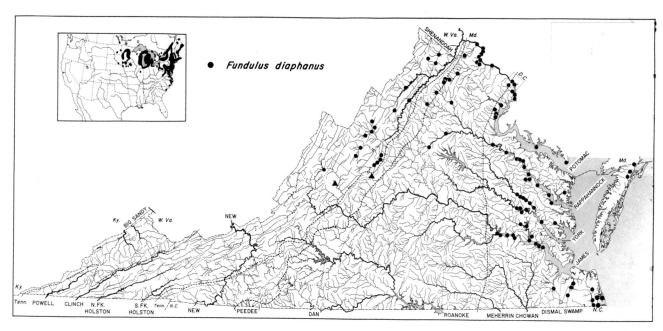

Fundulus diaphanus

Map 125 Banded killifish.

Abundance.—Often common or abundant in estuaries, usually uncommon in uplands.

REMARKS

The banded killifish is frequently used as bait because of its general abundance and hardy nature. It is raised for this purpose in some northern states. Scott and Crossman (1973) noted its purported ability to survive several days in wet leaves.

Name.—*Diaphanus* means "transparent," likely in reference to the slight translucency of the body.

Speckled killifish   *Fundulus rathbuni* Jordan and Meek

SYSTEMATICS

Fundulus rathbuni was described in 1889 from North Carolina. It is placed in the subgenus *Xenisma*, an upland clear-water group that includes studfishes such as *F. catenatus* (Williams and Etnier 1982; Wiley 1986; Rogers and Cashner 1987; Cashner et al. 1988). For its small geographic range, the speckled killifish exhibits ample meristic variation (Brown 1955).

DESCRIPTION

Materials.—From Brown (1955), Williams and Etnier (1982), and 8 Virginia and 2 North Carolina lots. Life color from 7 Virginia nuptial adults.

Anatomy.—A flecked or diamond-patterned killifish; adults are 40–70 mm SL. Body elongate, compressed posteriorly; head dorsum flat; mouth small, terminal, protrusile. Dorsal fin origin above or very slightly anterior or posterior to anal fin origin; caudal fin truncate or slightly rounded; anal and dorsal fin sizes about equal; pelvic and pectoral fins somewhat small.

Breeding male with dorsal and anal fins elongate posteriorly, dorsal mostly so; those of female rounded. Male with tubercles distally on rays of dorsal, anal, and pelvic fins, and on scale margins midlaterally between midlength of pelvic fin (when adducted) to midbase of anal fin; minute spinules on cheek and opercle scales. We did not detect breast tubercles, although Williams and Etnier (1982) did; perhaps these are restricted to largest males. Sexual differences in genital opening are similar to those in *F. diaphanus*.

Meristics.—Scales in midlateral series (34)35–37(40); circumbody scales (23)25–28(30); circumpeduncle scales (16)19–20(21). Dorsal rays 10–11(13); caudal rays (13)14–16(17); anal rays (10)11–12; pectoral rays (14)16–17(18).

Color in Preservative.—Adult male with dorsum dusky; predorsal stripe vague or moderate; side with diamond- or hexagonally hatched pattern caused by scale pocket pigmentation; spots sometimes present on anterior side near pectoral fin; faint dusky lateral stripe sometimes present; venter pale. Cheek, opercle, and chin have dark flecks and spots; eye rimmed posteriorly and ventrally with a dark line extending ventrad toward corner of jaw. Dorsal fin dusky, sometimes spotted basally, posteriorly, or both; caudal fin

Fish 175 *Fundulus rathbuni* adult male 60 mm SL (REJ 1009), VA, Halifax County, Powells Creek, 14 July 1983.

Fish 176 *Fundulus rathbuni* adult female 61 mm SL (REJ 1009), VA, Halifax County, Powells Creek, 14 July 1983.

dusky, pale margined; anal fin pale or dusky, sometimes with dark streaks or spots; paired fins pale or slightly dusky. Adult female generally similar but paler overall, entire side strongly flecked, scale-margin pattern on side less distinct, fins unmarked except dorsal sometimes slightly streaked. Subadult male has body flecks undergoing loss and the fins darkening.

Color in Life Plate 25.—Nuptial male with dorsum olive; middorsal stripe slightly paler; small round iridescent gold spot present at dorsal fin origin. Upper side olive with pale blue sheen; mid- and lower side silver with pale blue, sometimes pale greenish-blue sheen, blue best developed midlaterally; venter silver; side of head silver with faint green-blue tinge, spots dark olive. Dorsal and caudal fins with yellow-orange margin, widest and best developed in caudal; anal fin with marginal yellow-orange tinge, silver at base, spotting dark. A male from the Pee Dee drainage, North Carolina, was basically similar but had a faint iridescent gold stripe on the midlateral body. The male shown in color by Williams and Etnier (1982) was from the same North Carolina stream as ours, but was not depicted in full breeding dress. Nuptial female silvery olive, flecks dark, not noted with blue body or yellow fins.

BIOLOGY

Snippets of the life history of *F. rathbuni* are known. Five Virginia adults had eaten several midge larvae; one had taken a caddisfly skin. All five had sand in the gut, indicating that midges were gleaned from the bottom. Midge pupae, other aquatic insects, and a small shiner were eaten by North Carolina fish (Lee *in* Lee et al. 1980).

Possibly all males and clearly most females first spawn at age 1, based on study of gonads, tuberculation, and length–frequencies of Virginia specimens taken during late June through late July. The largest immature fish was a 39-mm SL female. Both sexes reached age 2 and their growth was similar. Of obviously nuptial fish, 18 males were 41–62 mm SL, mean, 50; 35 females were 38–69 mm, mean, 48. The 69-mm female is Virginia's largest; an 80-mm SL fish was reported from North Carolina (Lee *in* Lee et al. 1980).

Spawning extends from about mid-May through July in North Carolina; young were found on 1 August (Lee *in* Lee et al. 1980). Our North Carolina females were postnuptial in mid-August. Virginia females were gravid in June to mid-July; a 21-mm SL young was caught on 14 July. About 300 eggs in three size groups were counted from individual females by Lee.

HABITAT

Fundulus rathbuni occupies pools, backwaters, and slow runs in gentle-gradient sections of generally shallow creeks that have sandy and silty substrate. Macrophytes and concentrations of algae were absent in pools at our record sites in Virginia and North Carolina. Speckled killifish quickly retreated to cover

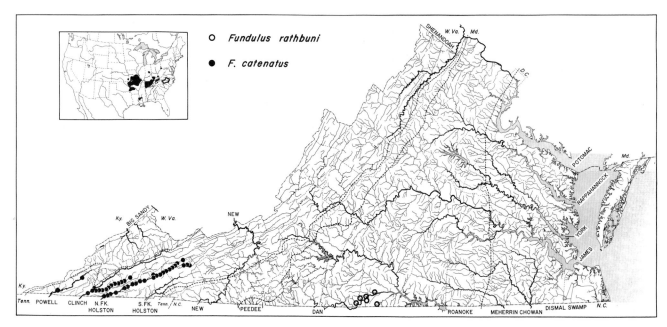

Map 126 Speckled killifish and northern studfish.

when disturbed. Apparently this species is nonmigratory (Hall 1972).

DISTRIBUTION   Map 126

Fundulus rathbuni is essentially a North Carolina Piedmont species, ranging from the Santee to the Roanoke drainage, except that it is absent from the Tar drainage. It barely enters Virginia, being known only from the lower Dan system of the Roanoke in five direct Dan River tributaries and one Hyco River tributary. It is similarly restricted in the Dan system of North Carolina.

Abundance.—Generally uncommon or locally common.

REMARKS

The speckled killifish lacks the gaudiness of its studfish kin but has a subdued attractiveness. Little is known of its biology and it is a good candidate for aquarium study of spawning behavior. This species is recommended for special concern status in Virginia (Burkhead and Jenkins 1991).

Name.—*Rathbuni* is a patronym honoring Richard Rathbun of the former U.S. Fish Commission.

Northern studfish   *Fundulus catenatus* (Storer)

SYSTEMATICS

The northern studfish was described in 1846 from Alabama. The largest and perhaps gaudiest of the subgenus *Xenisma*, *F. catenatus* is most closely allied to the southern studfish *F. stellifer* (Thomerson 1969; Wiley 1986; Rogers and Cashner 1987).

DESCRIPTION

Materials.—Nine Virginia series and Thomerson's (1969) counts from Virginia specimens. Color in life mainly from 2 Virginia adults.

Anatomy.—A horizontally striped or dashed killifish; adults are 60–95 mm SL. Body elongate, broad or slightly

compressed anteriorly, moderately compressed posteriorly; dorsal profile of head flat or slightly convex; mouth terminal, protrusile. Dorsal fin origin above or slightly behind anal origin; caudal fin subtruncate or truncate; dorsal and anal fins moderate or large, both fins elongate posteriorly in adult male; paired fins small. Tuberculation similar to that of *F. rathbuni*.

Meristics.—Midlateral scales (41)43–49(51). Dorsal rays 12–13(14); anal rays (13)14–15(16); pectoral rays 15–16(17).

Color in Preservative.—Adult male dusky dorsally, dorsal fin preceded by dark dash; side with 4–7 pairs of pale and dusky stripes, most evident along mid- and lower side; venter pale. Cheek pale or slightly dusky, rarely faintly flecked; line along posterior and ventral portions of orbital

Fish 177 *Fundulus catenatus* adult male 74 mm SL (REJ 992), VA, Russell County, Copper Creek, 21 June 1983.

Fish 178 *Fundulus catenatus* adult female 78 mm SL (REJ 992), VA, Russell County, Copper Creek, 21 June 1983.

rim vague or, usually, absent. Dorsal fin dusky basally to pale distally; pale interradial spots present basally; submarginal dark streaks or flecks rarely present. Caudal fin with proximal four-fifths dusky and usually with small dark spots or streaks; subdistally darkest, occasionally black-banded; distally pale. Anal and pelvic fins pale; pectoral fin slightly dusky, rarely dark-tipped. Dominant female pattern dotted or horizontally scrawled dorsally; side with 6–9 series of horizontally elongate punctations and dashes effecting interrupted lines; head as in male except usually paler; fins pale, spotting vague or, usually, absent; distal half of caudal fin unpatterned.

Color in Life Plate 25.—Spawning male spectacular; dorsum copper and olive; predorsal dash iridescent gold; body side iridescent pale to deep blue, and with 8–10 orange-red to red lines or series of spots and dashes (red areas become pale areas in preservative); venter and prepectoral area silver, red-spotted. Preocular patch, cheek, opercle, and branchiostegals iridescent lime-gold to yellow in spawning-peak males; latter three areas mostly silver and pale blue in other males; head red-spotted laterally. Caudal fin spots grading from red basally to dark, then dusky to black band, distally pale yellow or orange. Other fins red-spotted basally, pale yellow or medium yellow distally. Nonbreeding male much subdued; female with olive shades on back and side.

BIOLOGY

Northern studfish eat an array of aquatic and terrestrial insects, microcrustaceans, and other invertebrates. The change in food habits with growth is expressed by adults taking larger items, particularly insects. Young and juveniles usually feed in backwaters; adults search there and in open pools and runs, particularly during morning and late afternoon. Most feeding is from the bottom and water column (McCaskill et al. 1972; Fisher 1981). Pflieger (1975) noted that this species ate a surprising variety of bottom life, including small crayfishes.

In Kentucky streams some females matured at age 1, males at age 2; maximum life span was 5 years (Fisher 1981). The largest males were generally larger than associated females (Thomerson 1969; Pflieger 1975; Fisher 1981; our data), but Fisher determined that growth rates of the sexes generally were not significantly different. The former size differential may result from differences in age distribution; Fisher found twice as many age-4 males as females and his single age-5 fish was a male. Age-3 males were 88 mm TL, females 84 mm (Fisher 1981). The Virginia record studfish, 114 mm SL (140 mm, 5.5 inches TL), equals that of Tennessee (D. A. Etnier, personal communication). Pflieger (1975) suggested that this species reaches 6 inches or more in Missouri. The much larger size given by Shute (*in* Lee et al. 1980) is in error (J. R. Shute, personal communication).

Spawning occurs from mid-May to early August in Missouri. Males guard small territories in calm shallows near shore; no nest is prepared. Eggs are laid on clean gravel; an occurrence of egg deposition in a longear sunfish nest has been noted (Pflieger 1975). In Kentucky, females with ripening ova were found from late April until July (Fisher 1981). In Virginia, ovarian development and male color and tuberculation indicated spawning between mid-May to at least mid-July, at 13–23°C. We saw males courting on 19 May. Counts of maturing ova were 28–245 (Fisher 1981); mature ova are covered with filaments.

HABITAT

Fundulus catenatus is an occupant of cutoff pools, backwaters, and sluggish margins of runs in clear, warm, moderate-gradient creeks to rivers. Adults occasionally venture into gentle runs. This species generally occurs as well-separated small groups in areas lacking vegetation; sometimes it occupies beds of submersed plants and margins of water willow stands. It associates with bottoms of sand to rock; Pflieger (1975) indicated that it avoids silted areas but we did not find this clearly indicated in Virginia.

DISTRIBUTION   Map 126

The main northern studfish populations are centered in uplands of the lower Ohio basin and the Ozark and Ouachita mountains. Peripheral populations, some of them possibly introduced, have been discovered in southern Mississippi, Kentucky, and northern West Virginia (Bart and Cashner 1980; Burr and Warren 1986; Hocutt et al. 1986).

Fundulus catenatus has an anomalous distribution pattern in the upper Tennessee drainage, particularly in Virginia. The only generalization is that it occupies the Valley and Ridge Province. In the Holston system the studfish is generally distributed (although usually rare or uncommon) in the main stem North Fork and occupies lower portions of several North Fork tributaries. Its absence from the South Fork may be attributable to higher gradient or cooler temperature, but

that would not account for its absence in the lower Middle Fork.

In the Clinch system *F. catenatus* occurs virtually throughout Copper Creek, but occurs only sporadically in the Clinch River near the mouth of Copper Creek and at a few sites in Tennessee. The Clinch pattern indicates a preference for small to medium-sized streams, but this would not explain either its apparent absence from most Clinch tributaries in Virginia or its relative success in the large North Fork Holston River.

The northern studfish seems to barely persist in the Powell River in Virginia. The only recent Powell River record is from Hall Ford in 1987 (P. L. Angermeier, in litt.). The upper Powell River record, one specimen (USNM 104043), is dated 1937; conflictive map plotting (Thomerson 1969; Masnik 1974; herein) stems from unspecific original locality data. *Fundulus catenatus* occurs sparingly in the Tennessee section of the Powell. Although the Powell system has sedimentation problems, the fish fauna of the main stem generally is healthy. The wide range gap in the middle Tennessee drainage is also strange, probably caused in part by impoundment.

Abundance.—Generally uncommon; it typically is localized within stream sections.

REMARKS

The nuptial male *F. catenatus* is one of the largest killifishes. It is the dandy of backwaters, dressed in an electric blue suit with red pinstripes and yellow, red-dappled fins. "Studfish" is an appropriate appellation. As a frequent near-surface dweller, the studfish's very large anal fin is probably more important in courting displays than is the dorsal fin. The gold predorsal dash and preocular patch are quite evident when searching for these fish from stream banks.

Name.—*Catenatus* means "chained," in reference to the lateral color pattern.

Lined topminnow   *Fundulus lineolatus* (Agassiz)

SYSTEMATICS

Following its description in 1854 from Georgia, the lined topminnow generally was confused with other members of the *notti* group, whose five lowland forms constitute a section of the subgenus *Zygonectes* (Wiley 1986). We follow Wiley (1977) in regarding the forms as species. Brown (1958) considered the lined topminnow to be an allopatric subspecies of *F. notti*. Rivas (1966) considered it a species owing to sympa-

try in Florida with the member of the *notti* group later described by Wiley (1977) as *F. escambiae*. Co-occupation of two drainages by *F. lineolatus* and *F. escambiae* was indicated by Wiley and Hall (1975), Swift et al. (1977), and Wiley (*in* Lee et al. 1980).

DESCRIPTION

Materials.—From Frey (1951), Brown (1958), Wiley (1977), and 4 Virginia lots including counts from 15 speci-

Fish 179 *Fundulus lineolatus* adult male 40 mm SL (WHH 152), VA, Sussex County, Coppahaunk Swamp, 26 July 1983.

Fish 180 *Fundulus lineolatus* adult female 40 mm SL (WHH 152), VA, Sussex County, Coppahaunk Swamp, 26 July 1983.

mens; dorsal and anal ray counts have been adjusted (last two elements counted as one ray), as for all *Fundulus* species. Life color from 2 Virginia lots.

Anatomy.—A narrow-barred or lined, black-cheeked killifish; adults are 30–45 mm SL. Body moderate, nearly quadrate anteriorly, compressed posteriorly; dorsal profile of head flat or slightly concave; mouth superior, terminal, protrusile. Dorsal fin origin above or just behind anal fin origin; caudal fin long, spatulate; paired fins small. Tubercles and spinules absent; dorsal and anal fins larger, more elongate in male. Genital differences similar to those of *F. diaphanus.*

Meristics.—Midlateral scales (32)34–36(38); circumbody scales (21)23–26(28); circumpeduncle scales (15)16(19). Dorsal rays (5)7(8); anal rays (8)9(10); pelvic rays (5)6(7); pectoral rays 12–13(14).

Color in Preservative.—Male body dorsum dusky, head dorsum dark; upper side of larger adults with 1–3 rows of faint to dark spots; side mostly dusky to pale, and with usually 10–13 long narrow dark bars, sometimes additional short ones; venter pale; cheek very dusky or black (i.e., teardrop broad). Dorsal fin pale or slightly dusky, membranes sometimes weakly tessellated basally; caudal fin pale; anal fin pale or slightly dusky, membrane tessellations often obvious; paired fins pale. Female similar to male except side with only hint of barring and, creating the dominant pattern, 6–8 narrow horizontal dark lines; all fins pale. Frey (1951) noted that specimens from dark water were more melanistic.

Color in Life Plate 25.—Nuptial male head and body dorsum yellowish olive, distinctly yellow on side of snout;

occiput with longitudinal gold streak; side bars olive-black to black; much of side with copper sheen, best developed anteriorly; pectoral fin base iridescent silver to pale blue, continued as conspicuous narrow stripe along lower side to caudal base, sometimes extending dorsad on latter. Much of opercle iridescent greenish blue to blue, ventrally more silver; opercular membrane yellow; paler areas of iris copper; subocular area black with scattered blue glints. Fins yellow-olive to pale yellow, best developed in rays; dark parts of tessellated areas dark olive to black. Adult female similar except dorsal head and body, side of snout, and opercular membrane olive; ventrolateral stripe more silver; some with red tinge pre- and postorbitally; fins with little or no yellow. Adults are easily recognized in water by a pale star-shaped blotch on head dorsum. Young lack blue and yellow, but have prominent red blush pre- and postorbitally.

BIOLOGY

A glimpse of the natural history of the lined topminnow was provided by specimens collected during July in Virginia. Stomach contents of six adults indicate omnivory; all contained some insects, one had only insects, two were packed with algae, and two had taken many seeds. Aquatic and terrestrial insects including damselfly larvae, a beetle, a hymenopteran, and midges were eaten.

Males matured at 35 mm SL, females at 30 mm. Fifteen adult males were 35–47 mm SL, mean, 39; 23 females were 30–49 mm, mean, 37. Our largest specimen is a female 49 mm SL; Frey (1951) reported a 63-mm SL fish from North Carolina. A 16 July collec-

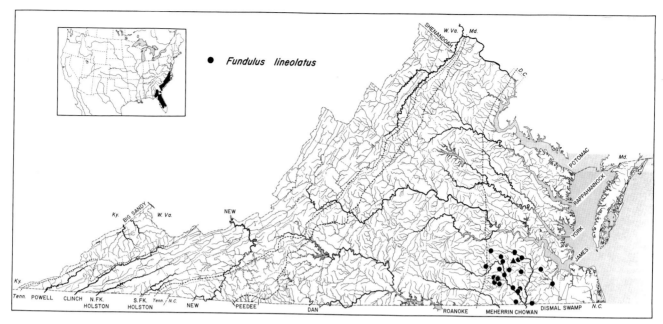

Map 127   Lined topminnow.

tion contained many young of 13–22 mm SL. All mid- to late July samples contained gravid females. The number of mature ova present at one time is low, about 25 in a 34-mm female. If spawning is pro- tracted, as suggested by different size groups of young, *F. lineolatus* may be a fractional spawner. Dif- ferent ovum developmental stages were present in ovaries; several mature ova were 2.0–2.2 mm in di- ameter and were covered with filaments.

HABITAT

Lined topminnows generally are found in margins and backwaters of swamps and creeks, forming small groups in upper water strata among submersed plants. The single Virginia lacustrine record was from near the outflow of a heavily weeded pond. This species may typically inhabit ponds and lakes else- where (Frey 1951; Swift et al. 1977). *Fundulus lineola- tus* occurs in moderately acidic dark waters, avoid- ing the very acidic interior Dismal Swamp; pH at four record sites was 5.5–6.7. Although a strictly freshwater inhabitant, its experimental upper salin- ity tolerance was 27.8‰ (Griffith 1974, as *F. swampi- nus*).

DISTRIBUTION   Map 127

Fundulus lineolatus is a Coastal Plain species ranging from southeastern Virginia to southern Florida and the Ocklockonee drainage in the Florida panhandle. In the Chowan drainage of Virginia it is widespread in the Nottoway system and somewhat localized in the Blackwater system. Of the three records (two sites) for the Nansemond system of the James drain- age (including the periphery of Dismal Swamp), the last dates from 1971. The lined topminnow probably occurs in the poorly surveyed Virginia portion of the lower Meherrin system. Localization of this species may be related to the occurrence of suitable vegeta- tion.

Abundance.—Most often uncommon.

REMARKS

This small, pretty killifish stands out as one of the few colorful species among our Coastal Plain ichthy- ofauna. It is an excellent candidate for spawning studies in aquaria.

Name.—*Lineolatus* means "lined," the pattern of fe- males.

LIVEBEARERS
Family Poeciliidae

As the common name implies, most poeciliids are viviparous or ovoviviparous—they bear live young. Livebearers are small, the adult size range in the family is about 15–180 mm TL; most species are less than 50 mm (Berra 1981; Nelson 1984). The Poeciliidae generally have been restricted to species found in the temperate and tropical Americas. Parenti (1981) expanded their scope by including many species of Africa and Madagascar and a phylogenetically isolated South American species, some 300 in all. Poeciliids are in the order Cyprinodontiformes, which includes killifishes, topminnows, and their allies (Parenti 1981). If Parenti's arrangement stands, then livebearing may have evolved independently at least four times in the order.

Poeciliids have an elongate or stubby body form, and the head often is flat dorsally. The mouth is typically small, terminal or supraterminal, usually protrusile; jaws have small teeth or a few piscivorous species have larger conical teeth. The dorsal fin is short-based, often small, and is positioned at about midlength of the body or more posteriorly; the caudal fin is rounded or truncate; the anal fin is placed more anterior than usual in fishes and is much modified in males (see below); pelvic fins are small, subthoracic; pectoral fins are high-set. The head dorsum and body typically are fully covered with cycloid scales.

Adult livebearers exhibit pronounced sexual dimorphism. Females are typically larger and more robust anteriorly than males in the subfamily Poeciliinae (including *Gambusia*); males are larger than females in other subfamilies (Parenti 1981). The anal fin of the male is modified into an intromittent organ—the gonopodium—that functions in internal fertilization. The highly modified rays of this structure support distinctive spines and hooks; gonopodial morphology is of great taxonomic utility. The caudal and pectoral fins are dimorphic in some species. The sexes are slightly to dramatically dichromatic; coloration in some species is polymorphic. In the Poeciliinae, males are drab to elaborately colorful; females typically are drab.

The biology and systematics of poeciliids are treated extensively in Meffe and Snelson (1989). Livebearers occur in a diverse range of freshwater habitats, but are generally absent from high-gradient montane settings; many reside in brackish water. Most poeciliids occur in shallows with little or no current and are often associated with vegetation. The ecological plasticity of certain species of mosquitofishes (*Gambusia*) has enabled their establishment in many parts of the world. Most species are opportunistic insectivores or omnivores. Prey detection is apparently visual; the adeptness of the mosquitofish at capturing its namesake has earned it great popularity as a natural mosquito-control agent.

Reproduction is a fascinating aspect of poeciliid biology, summaries of which are found in Breder and Rosen (1966), Thibault and Schultz (1978), and Keenleyside (1979). Most species are lecithotrophic (ovoviviparous); the developing embryos derive nourishment from yolk (Wourms 1981). Fertilization is internal and usually involves copulation or placement of spermatozeugmata (bundles of sperm) at the genital opening of the female. Sperm storage by the female enables fertilization of successively developing clutches of ova from a single copulation. More elaborate reproductive strategies occur in several unisexual species. Gynogenetic females may use sperm from other poeciliid species only to stimulate egg development. Hybridogenetic females use sperm of other species to produce hybrids, but in subsequent crosses only the maternal genes are passed through the egg, thus perpetuating the unisexual hybrid.

Courtship ranges from persistent chases to moderately elaborate displays. Mating often occurs while the female is swimming, and it is thought that the function of the display is to slow the female down, allowing copulation. The degree of courtship varies inversely with gonopodial length. Males with long gonopodia display less; apparently they are able to see the intromittent organ in their hind visual field and thus are more accurate in thrusting. Males sometimes use the pectoral fin to steady the gonopodium, and several *Gambusia* have a notch in the pectoral fin to facilitate this function (Warburton et al. 1957). Peden (1973) demonstrated that the dark mark ("gravid spot") on the posterior abdomen of females serves as a thrusting target for males; this mark increases in size as ova mature.

Fecundity varies considerably within a species. Females typically produce several broods each year, and the number of young generally increases as females get larger (older). Based on relatively few species, egg diameter is 0.8–3.6 mm (Thibault and Schultz 1978; Turner and Snelson 1984).

Livebearers have long been favored aquarium fishes because of their small size, attractive coloration, adaptability, and interesting modes of reproduction. The ever-popular guppy *Poecilia reticulata* is one of the most widely known nongame species in the world. It is responsible for the childhood fascination with fishes of some ichthyologists. The diminutive least killifish *Heterandria formosa* of the southeastern United States may be the smallest vertebrate to bear live young (Berra 1981).

Name.—Poecili- means "variegated," in reference to color pattern.

Gambusias   Genus *Gambusia* Poey

A genus of some 45 species in temperate and tropical America, of which 10 occur in the United States, and one occurs in Virginia. Most U.S. species live in the Southwest; four of these are depleted and two apparently are extinct. These rare endemic species are associated with fragile spring habitats in arid environments. In contrast, the Virginia species—the eastern mosquitofish—is very adaptable and widespread.

Name.—*Gambusia* is derived from the Cuban vernacular term gambusino signifying "nothing," with the idea of a joke or farce. To fish for gambusino means to catch nothing (Jordan and Evermann 1896).

Eastern mosquitofish   *Gambusia holbrooki* Girard

SYSTEMATICS

Gambusia holbrooki, described from Florida in 1859, is placed in the subgenus *Arthrophallus* (Rivas 1963). It had long been recognized as a subspecies of *G. affinis* (Hubbs 1961; Rosen and Bailey 1963), until the genetic study by Wooten et al. (1988). *Gambusia holbrooki* is an Atlantic slope species, ranging south through Florida; *G. affinis* extends west and south from Alabama and up the Mississippi Valley into the southern Great Lakes basin. Exact range limits of the species in Alabama are yet to be defined. "Mosquitofish" as used in some cases herein refers to both species and sometimes to the genus *Gambusia* in general.

DESCRIPTION

Materials.—Eleven Virginia lots; counts from 33 adults. Life color from 3 Chowan series.

Anatomy.—A livebearer with a supraterminal mouth, delicate reticulate pattern on side and back, and posteriorly placed dorsal fin; adults are 20–40 mm TL. Body moderate or deep, somewhat compressed; dorsal fin inserted posteriorly on body, behind pelvic fin origin; head short, dorsal surface flat, snout broad; mouth supraterminal, lacking frenum, jaws bearing small teeth. Adults sexually dimorphic; anal fin of male with anterior rays elongate, modified into intromittent organ (gonodopodium); male pectoral fin curved at leading edge distally; female larger in size.

Meristics.—Lateral line absent, midlateral scales (26)29–30(31); circumpeduncle scales (14)15–16. Dorsal rays 7; anal rays 8(9); pelvic rays (5)6; pectoral rays 12–13(14).

Color in Preservative.—Ground shade dusky, back and side with delicate diamond-shaped scale pattern, occasionally with scattered dark flecks; back with narrow predorsal dark stripe; side occasionally with faint narrow midlateral dark stripe or series of small spots; venter pale. Head dark dorsally, snout dusky; subocular bar absent or present, wide, dusky to black; opercle with diffuse dusky area. Dorsal and caudal fins mostly pale, with few to many fine dark spots, these sometimes aligned; other fins pale. Adult female with a small or large dark mark (gravid spot) on lower side above vent.

Fish 181 *Gambusia holbrooki* adult male 26 mm SL (WHH 163), VA, Halifax County, Hyco River, 28 July 1983.

Fish 182 *Gambusia holbrooki* adult female 40 mm SL (WHH 163), VA, Halifax County, Hyco River, 28 July 1983.

Color in Life.—Body pale to medium olive with green and purple glints; head pale olive, iris with purple sheen, subocular mark blue-black, opercle with blue-purple iridescence; dorsal and caudal fins dusky light tan; gravid spot bluish purple.

Larvae.—Described by Foster (1974), Hardy (1978a), Wang and Kernehan (1979), and Conrow and Zale (1985).

BIOLOGY

Mosquitofish hover just beneath the surface, seizing small prey from near or at the surface; they also graze on the surfaces of plants and other objects. As the common name implies, they prey on larval and pupal mosquitos, but their diet is diverse and includes worms, microcrustaceans, mites, terrestrial and other aquatic insects, snails, and algae (Hildebrand and Schroeder 1928; Krumholz 1948; Harrington and Harrington 1961; Gatz 1979).

Gambusia species can greatly reduce mosquito populations in ponds (Krumholz 1948); they are significant predators of mosquitos in salt marshes (Harrington and Harrington 1961). In the latter study, *G. holbrooki* quickly switched to other prey when mosquito populations declined. Moyle (1976) discussed studies indicating that introduction of mosquitofishes can upset the balance of native predators of mosquitos, or that too low a stocking rate of *Gambusia* actually may lead to an increase of mosquito populations.

These livebearing fishes mature rapidly and may reproduce 4–6 weeks after birth. Fish achieving maturity in early summer generally die before winter. Usually only fish born later in the reproductive season survive to the following spring, and few of these survive to 15 months (Krumholz 1948). Both sexes mature near 20 mm TL, males at a slightly smaller size than females (Krumholz 1948; Trendall 1982). Male growth slows after gonopodium differentiation; adult males usually are 22–33 mm TL. Females average larger, adults attain 20–45 mm TL (Krumholz 1948). Our largest Virginia fish are a 32-mm TL male and a 53-mm female. The largest female reported by Krumholz is 63 mm TL, from Michigan.

Reproduction of *G. holbrooki* occurs between mid-April and September in Virginia (Hildebrand and Schroeder 1928). Krumholz (1948) considered all overwintering females in an Illinois study to be virgin. Martin (1975) observed sexual activity during winter in Florida. In latitudes with well-defined seasons, the onset of copulation appears closely related to increasing temperature and light (Sawara 1974 *in* Hughes 1985). Minimum reproductive threshold temperatures of 15.5 and 20°C have been reported; cessation of sexual activity occurred when water temperature dropped below 18°C (Medlen 1951; Hardy 1978a).

Adults are polygamous and promiscuous. Martin (1975) detected an apparent density-dependent effect; that is, significantly fewer aggressive interactions and lower mating frequency in the field than in aquaria.

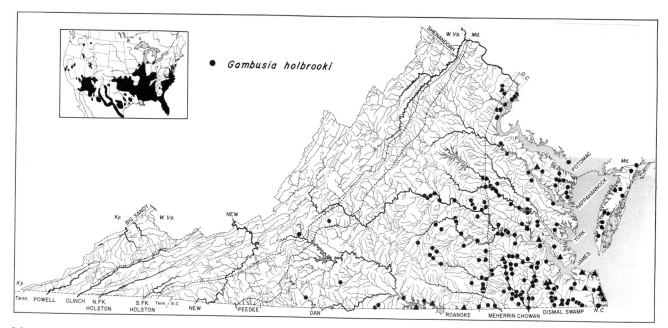

Map 128   Eastern mosquitofish. Inset shows combined continental United States range of *G. holbrooki* and *G. affinis*.

In nature, females typically outnumber males in the total population; males may be the most locally abundant sex during times of courtship. Male-to-male encounters may result in brief gonopodial swaggering displays; the gonopodium is also used in displays to females. The dark abdominal gravid spot of females is a releasing stimulus, it identifies receptive individuals, and also serves as a thrusting target (Peden 1973). A single copulation may fertilize several successive broods.

The gestation period is about 3–4 weeks (Krumholz 1948; Maglio and Rosen 1969). The number of broods varies with size and age of females and fertility of water (Krumholz 1948; Goodyear et al. 1972; Hughes 1985). Typically, 3–4 broods are produced, but 2–8 broods per season have been noted (Hardy 1978a). The number of young per brood is variable; Bonham (1946) found 1–354 young per brood. Early mortality is high, an estimated 98% in a pond population (Maglio and Rosen 1969).

HABITAT

The eastern mosquitofish is an adaptable lowland slackwater fish. Near-surface groups are generally found in shallow, vegetated and unvegetated areas of creeks, ditches, swamps, and marshes, and in pools and backwaters of streams. It also occurs along shorelines of ponds, lakes, and reservoirs. *Gambusia holbrooki* usually is found over muddy or sandy substrates. Females near parturition (giving birth)

generally occur over pale sandy bottoms, whereas females in early pregnancy prefer dark substrates. Mosquitofishes avoid bottoms that contrast to the substrate shade to which they are currently acclimated (Maglio and Rosen 1969).

Gambusia holbrooki tolerates inhospitable settings such as warm and sulphur springs, muddy and polluted water, rather acidic to quite alkaline conditions, and even near-anaerobic environments where dissolved oxygen is less than 1 mg/liter (Hardy 1978a). It occurs in tidal estuaries; maximum reported salinities are 18‰ in Virginia (Musick 1972) and 22‰ in North Carolina (Schwartz 1981b). At least one mosquitofish species can acclimate to full seawater and higher salt concentrations (Chervinski 1983). Maglio and Rosen (1969) reported that diurnal movements in a pond were related to temperature preference; adults sought the highest temperature below 33°C. Temperature preference data are summarized by Coutant (1977). Krumholz (1944) noted that mosquitofish overwinter on the bottom of ice-covered ponds.

DISTRIBUTION   Map 128

The eastern mosquitofish is native on the Atlantic slope from the Delaware drainage south to the tip of Peninsula Florida and west into at least eastern Alabama. It (and/or *G. affinis*) has been extensively introduced in the western United States and temperate and tropical areas worldwide, primarily for mosquito control. As a result, the mosquitofish has one of the largest distributions among freshwater fishes. *Gambusia* was even introduced by the U.S. Army to South Pacific islands during World War II. Krumholz (1948) and Hardy (1978a) provide a partial chronology of introductions and a list of regions receiving *Gambusia*.

In Virginia the eastern mosquitofish apparently is native to all major Atlantic slope drainages and occurs on Delmarva. The uppermost four records in the Roanoke drainage are either known or presumed to represent introduced populations. The record from the Lick Run branch of Tinker Creek, an upper Roanoke River tributary, is from 1986; the specimens may be waifs from an adjacent pond. The Smith River site (NMB 587 in 1981) is a short distance below Martinsville Reservoir; mosquitofish collected there probably were escapees from the reservoir, where they may have been introduced along with crappies. The upper Banister system record (CU 16872 in 1947) is relatively disjunct from others and may have stemmed from an introduction. A landowner informed us of successful transfer in 1976 of *Gambusia* from Okefenokee Swamp in Georgia to a small artificial swamp in the upper Big Otter River system. We have had inquiries regarding stocking of ponds, hence *G. holbrooki* may appear elsewhere in Virginia outside its normal range.

Abundance.—Often common or abundant below the Fall Line, generally rare or uncommon above.

REMARKS

The eastern mosquitofish is a hardy species in many respects, including the ability to survive stagnant, low-oxygen conditions. Its small size, flat head, and supraterminal mouth enable it to obtain oxygen from the surface layer. Adaptability, prolific nature, and opportunistic feeding habits make *G. holbrooki* a potential mosquito-control agent. However, negative results from mosquitofish introduction have also been observed. *Gambusia* introductions are at least partly responsible for the decline or displacement of several southwestern endemic poeciliids (Miller 1961; Minckley and Deacon 1968; Ono et al. 1983), and have had similar effects on foreign faunas (Myers 1965 *in* Moyle 1976).

Name.—*Holbrooki* honors John E. Holbrook, a 19th century naturalist of North America.

STICKLEBACKS
Family Gasterosteidae

Threespine stickleback   *Gasterosteus aculeatus* Linnaeus

The threespine stickleback has a southern limit in Virginia estuaries (Map 129). It has an extensive range northward, on the Pacific coast, and in Europe. This small fish is easily recognized by the dorsal spines being few in number and not connected to each other; the pelvic fin is represented by a large spine; by having bony plates on the side of the body; and by having a very slender caudal peduncle.

Fish 183 *Gasterosteus aculeatus* adult female 56 mm SL (VIMS), VA, York County, York River, 22 February 1984.

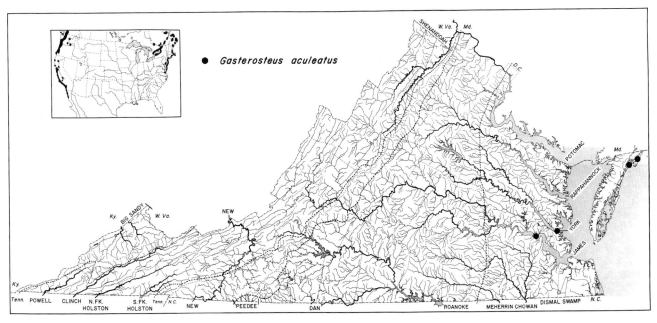

Map 129   Threespine stickleback.

In different parts of its range the threespine stickleback thrives in both fresh and salt water. In Virginia it is anadromous or semianadromous, spawning in fresh or slightly brackish water during spring. It is locally common during winter and spring in small tributaries of the James and York estuaries, and is generally rare or absent at other times (Musick 1972). It occurs more widely than indicated by our few records, which are derived largely from freshwater collecting efforts. It is one of the most-studied nongamefishes; reviews of its biology are by Scott and Crossman (1973), Wootton (1976), Coad (1981), Allen and Wootton (1982), and Heufelder (1982c).

SCULPINS
Family Cottidae

The sculpin family Cottidae of the order Scorpaeniformes (scorpionfishes and allies) is widely distributed in salt and fresh waters of north temperate to Arctic regions; a few marine species live in the Southern Hemisphere. Freshwater sculpins often are called muddlers; they modeled for the famous series of hand-tied fishing flies of that name (Gapen 1983). Sometimes they are called millers' thumb, from the somewhat flattened head. At first glance many consider them ugly or weird-looking, for they appear quite different from most freshwater fishes. Nonetheless they are fascinating and ecologically important animals.

As many as 17 families have been considered to be true cottids (Washington et al. 1984a, 1984b). Most of the 225–300 species of Cottidae are marine (Nelson 1984). Fossil cottids are known from deposits as old as the Oligocene in Belgium (Berra 1981), 25–36 million years ago. Extinct and living freshwater genera including *Cottus* are known from the North American Miocene (Kimmel 1975; Smith 1975, 1981), 11–25 million years ago. In our sequencing, we follow Greenwood et al. (1966) and Nelson (1984) in placing cottids (Scorpaeniformes) before the Perciformes.

Cottus, by far the largest cottid genus (and the sole subject of this section hereafter), contains about 42 freshwater species; 28 occur only in North America, 13 are exclusively Eurasian, and 1 (the slimy sculpin *C. cognatus*) lives in both North America and northeast Asia. The Eurasian *C. gobio* is considered a complex by Robins (1961). Eight species are recognized in Virginia; they constitute the most diverse *Cottus* fauna in the East. Three are undescribed and the status of certain others is in question. West Virginia ranks next in the East, with five species. Some western United States *Cottus* faunas are speciose: 8 species in California (Moyle 1976), 10 in Washington (Wydoski and Whitney 1979), and 13 in Oregon (Bond 1961).

Cottus are small bottom-dwelling fishes with a large broad head and large terminal mouth. The upper jaw is protrusile and lacks a frenum (except in an albino specimen from a cave in West Virginia); patches of small teeth occur on the jaws and roof of the mouth. The eye is placed high; the preopercle bears spines. The anteriorly rounded body tapers to a somewhat compressed caudal peduncle; scales are reduced to prickles or are absent; the body often is heavily coated with mucous. Fin spines are flexible; the first dorsal fin is short-based, the second long-based, and these are slightly separate or united; the caudal fin is broad, rounded or truncate; the anal fin is long-based, the pelvic fin small and thoracic, the pectoral fin large, fanlike, and lateral on the body.

In coloration, freshwater sculpins have followed the general trend in scorpaeniform fishes—they form a "motley" group (Breder 1972). Most *Cottus* match the shade of the substrate. The typical pattern consists of dark saddles extending onto the side; the body also is blotched, scrawled, mottled, or spotted, and often has slight iridescent sheens. Fins usually are tessellated, banded, or marbled; the first dorsal fin often is edged with orange or red. Sexual dichromatism is displayed in many species; nuptial males generally are darker or black and the first dorsal fin margin is redder than in females. Large males of some species tend to be more "bull-headed" and have some fins higher than do females.

Sculpins often are abundant in cool swift water in Virginia. They inhabit spring runs, creeks, and streams that typically are clear year-round and cold to cool in summer; that is, good to marginal trout water.

Some species populate warmer waters, sometimes large rivers, but even their strongest populations appear to occur in cooler, smaller biotopes. Juveniles and adults of most species occupy stony bottoms of runs and riffles, hiding under rocks and other cover during much of daylight. Of the Virginia species, the banded sculpin *C. carolinae* and the Potomac sculpin *C. girardi* show the strongest predilection in certain (perhaps competitive) situations for slow but distinctly flowing water. *Cottus carolinae* was found to inhabit interstices of gravel in an area of cool subsurface percolation when the streambed surface was dry (Stegman and Minckley 1959).

Sometimes large sculpin populations are found in silted, heavily vegetated areas, particularly in spring runs; the plants provide refuge for both sculpins and their food. Sculpins occupy lakes, often to considerable depths, well north of Virginia and in the west. Typical members of the *carolinae* group have been found in caves in Virginia and elsewhere; a possibly undescribed West Virginia species of this group has strongly adapted to cave life (Williams and Howell 1979). Most *Cottus* are sedentary, but some populations of the prickly sculpin *C. asper* migrate downstream to spawn in Pacific estuaries.

Sculpins eat a variety of benthic invertebrates and fishes. The large mouth admits relatively large prey including crayfishes and, as noted for *C. carolinae*, salamanders. Their voracity is shown by the observation of a sculpin engulfing a sculpin that was swallowing a sculpin (W. N. Roston, personal communication), but the prey generally is small crustaceans and insect larvae. Sculpins are often regarded as opportunistic feeders. In a natural stream we handfed crayfish to *C. carolinae*. However, selective feeding of *C. bairdi* and *C. cognatus* has been demonstrated (Anderson 1975; Gilson and Benson 1979; Newman and Waters 1984).

Sculpins lie on the bottom and ambush approaching prey. Some species feed during daylight or in both day and night, relying heavily on sight to capture prey during the day. Night-feeding and occupation during darkness of open areas or the top of rocks seems typical of some species (e.g., *C. bairdi*, *C. cognatus*, and *C. carolinae*). Sculpins can locate moving organisms by seismosensory receptors of the lateral line system (Hoekstra and Janssen 1986). In northern Europe two *Cottus* species shift from night activity in autumn to day activity in winter; the shift is triggered by changing light conditions, and apparently is under genetic control (Andreasson 1973).

Cottus have received bad press owing to their predation on salmonid eggs and fry, and as potential competitors for food with these valuable fishes. However, Moyle's (1977a, 1977b) broad review and analysis indicate that sculpins can severely limit salmonid populations only under exceptional or artificial conditions which are found chiefly in the Pacific Northwest, and that beneficial interactions exist—salmonids and other fishes commonly prey on sculpins. Fishes or fish eggs were found rarely in the diet of some *Cottus* species in Virginia.

Several species of *Cottus* first spawn at the end of the second year of life (age 2). In other species, maturation occurs at age 1, 3, or 4 (e.g., Williams 1968; Patten 1971). Typical maximum longevity in temperate regions appears to be 3–4 years. A *C. cognatus* and a coast-range sculpin *C. aleuticus* reached 7 and 8 years, respectively, in northwestern North America (Mason and Machidori 1976), and a *C. gobio* attained age 9 in England (Fox 1978). In several species males grow more rapidly than females. The largest *Cottus* in the East is *C. carolinae*; a Virginia specimen of 144 mm SL, 185 mm TL (7.3 inches) is the largest documented. It appears to be exceeded in America only by the Pacific slope *C. asper*. Although the latter has been stated to reach 300 mm TL, Scott and Crossman (1973) considered that dubious; the largest *C. asper* reported by Kresja (1967) was 192 mm TL, and Mason and Machidori (1976) found none near that length.

Sculpins generally spawn once a year in winter, spring, or cool boreal summer (e.g., Patten 1971). The female lays all ripe ova in one episode. Spawning at any single locality may last two or three days (Hann 1927; Koster 1936) or up to one month (Nagel 1980). Some individuals of a Japanese species apparently spawn twice in one breeding season, and females in a productive stream in England reproduce up to four times in a 2–3 month spawning period (Fox 1978; Goto 1987). The pygmy sculpin *C. pygmaeus*, confined to a single Alabama spring, may spawn during most of the year (Williams 1968).

Nest sites are small cavities under rocks, logs, and diverse other structures that are selected and guarded by the male. The sexes invert to deposit gametes on the cavity ceiling, the eggs being clumped into several tiers. The male, who may spawn with more than 10 females, remains with the nest, fanning and protecting eggs and young for up to eight weeks (Downhower and Brown 1980). Reproductive behavior, including some exceptional aspects, is described in the account of the Clinch sculpin. The well-researched *C. bairdi* exhibits sexual selection, in which most females mate preferentially with large males, which are better nest-defenders. However, small females generally avoid the largest males as mates because they may be cannibalized (Downhower et al. 1983).

Fecundity generally is low to moderate, 30–7,410

ova, but 10,000 have been estimated for the largest specimen of *C. asper* (Kresja 1967; Williams 1968; Patten 1971). Eggs are adhesive and large—2–3 mm diameter—and incubate for 2.5–5 weeks (Heufelder 1982d; Washington et al. 1984b).

Hybridization seems to occur rarely among *Cottus* species in nature. In most cases it has been only tentatively identified (Wydoski and Whitney 1979; Strauss 1986); possible widespread hybridization in the Great Lakes between *C. bairdi* and *C. cognatus* is only suspected (Godkin et al. 1982). The cross *C. bairdi* × *C. cognatus* is documented from a single Pennsylvania stream (Strauss 1986), and we describe the one hybrid specimen recognized in Virginia, *C. baileyi* × *C. carolinae*. However, the close similarity and ample variability of many sculpin species render detection of hybrids difficult at best by traditional methods; Strauss' (1986) "known" hybrids were discovered electrophoretically.

Different spawning periods are barriers to hybridization among some syntopic *Cottus* species; other restraints to interbreeding are unidentified. Although behavioral isolating mechanisms may exist, the bulk of the rather fragmentary data indicates general similarity in breeding behavior of *Cottus*.

We unintentionally created an experiment in species discrimination during March–April 1987. Placed together and well fed in the same 38-liter aquarium were two heavily gravid female black sculpins *C. baileyi*, three large dark nuptial males of what we thought to be the black sculpin, and a few other black sculpins, all of which had just been collected at a Little River site in Tazewell County, Virginia. The males defended nest cavities and acted seemingly just as five male Clinch sculpins did to spawn successfully with eight female Clinch sculpins under the same conditions in three other aquaria. However, the "black sculpins" did not spawn in three weeks; upon preserving them and examining their morphology, the nuptial males were found to be Clinch sculpins. In addition to demonstrating that (despite considerable experience) one is not infallible at field and aquarium identification of *Cottus*, this indicates that at least one of the species is well able to discern nonconspecific mates and that discrimination against them can occur even under forced reproductive conditions.

In both eastern and western North America, some species of *Cottus* have extensive ranges and others are sharply localized. Widespread species pervaded major regions of the continent by routes opened before or during the melting of glaciers. Localization generally is related to speciation of populations isolated by stream capture in montane areas, and to retraction of species into pockets—both streams and lakes—of cool water during climatic warming. Some sculpins may have dispersed via subterranean aquifers (see *C. baileyi* and *C. girardi*).

The distribution of *Cottus* in Virginia does not appear to be corrupted by bait-bucket introductions. The case of *Cottus girardi* is a possible exception. Although sculpins are touted as bait in some regions, we are unaware that they are so used in Virginia.

General patterns of sculpin distribution in Virginia are dictated largely by montane habitat and drainage divides (Maps 130–133). The York and Chowan drainages and the Appomattox system lack mountains and *Cottus*; the genus apparently lacked a route to the montane upper Pee Dee drainage. Each species and species group has a distinctive pattern. Only *C. bairdi* and *C. girardi* extend somewhat east of the Blue Ridge; the eastern populations are connected to montane ones or are localized in outlying areas of hills and springs. Other than the Piedmont population of *C. girardi*, that species and *C. carolinae* (the *carolinae* group) are confined to the strip of limestone drainages in the Valley and Ridge Province. The *C. bairdi-baileyi* pair widely populates the Valley and Ridge Province and softer waters of the Blue Ridge and Appalachian Plateau. *Cottus bairdi*, in extending eastward from the Valley and Ridge of the New drainage, is more generally distributed than are members of the *carolinae* group. The relict pattern of *C. cognatus* stems from close ties to scattered high-volume cold springs in the Potomac drainage. Similarly, the three species of broadband sculpins are restricted to cold or cool water in western Virginia, although one population may be warm-adapted.

The abundance of *Cottus* in Virginia streams is as variable as in most fish groups. Widespread and localized species alike vary from rare to abundant at different sites. Localized species seem to persist chiefly in disjunct patches of prime habitat.

Allopatry of closely related forms is the rule in Virginia. Either no such pair of species occupies the same drainage, or if they do, they are segregated into different systems. Although competition between less-related *Cottus* species is possible, the extent to which it has shaped the ranges and influenced patterns of abundance is unknown. *Cottus bairdi* is the only sculpin in the Rappahannock, Roanoke, and Big Sandy drainages, and *C. carolinae* is the only one in the Powell system. In the New drainage, the Bluestone sculpin apparently dwells by itself in the Bluestone system. This is the only case in Virginia of full intradrainage allopatry; three other sculpins occur elsewhere in the New drainage. Two species are sympatric (and syntopic) in the North Fork Holston system and the New drainage, three in the Potomac drainage and in the South Fork Holston, Middle Fork Holston, and Clinch systems.

The degree of association of species in specific sites or mesohabitats is noted in species accounts. Variations in syntopy may be due to competitive interaction. The frequent occurrence of members of the *carolinae* group in stream margins, slow runs, and pools may result from their displacement from faster current by other species. Other circumstances, such as the sole occupation and great abundance of *C. cognatus* in certain cold spring runs, may be related to different habitat preferences of potential competitors. We are only beginning to uncover ecological relationships among *Cottus* (Andreasson 1969, 1972; Matheson 1979; Finger 1982b; Matheson and Brooks 1983; Anderson 1985). Virginia is a ripe field for their study.

Name.—Cott-, from the Greek kottos (Jordan 1876) or kotta (Brown 1956), meaning "head," in reference to that notably large part. "Sculpin" seems to be a corruption of the ancient Greek name *Scorpaena* (Moyle 1976) given to a genus of the order Scorpaeniformes (scorpionfishes and allies, including *Cottus*).

Sculpins   Genus *Cottus* Linnaeus

A large genus of freshwater sculpins that is characterized, species enumerated, and whose name is explained above.

and in Pacific slope drainages (e.g., Wydoski and Whitney 1979; Peden et al. 1989).

IDENTIFICATION, CHARACTERS, AND GROUPS OF VIRGINIA *COTTUS*

The genus *Cottus* provides systematic biologists with many challenging problems, encapsulated by Bailey and Dimick (1949): "Among its many forms convergent and divergent evolution is rife, geographic variation is often extreme, and individual variation may be great. The parallel evolution of almost all characters in diverse phyletic lines renders difficult the recognition of natural affinities. *Cottus* appears to be a plastic group . . ." Robins (1954, 1961) clarified many systematic problems in the East, and provided a synthesis of species groups. Jenkins learned how to identify eastern species groups by studying specimens that Robins had identified at Cornell University.

We recognize eight species in Virginia, one with two subspecies. The percentage of forms that are undescribed or of uncertain status is easily the highest of any family in the state. The three species of broadband sculpins are undescribed. An undescribed putative subspecies of *C. carolinae*, the Kanawha sculpin, may be a species. The species status of *C. girardi*, although substantiated here, merits reconsideration when its close relatives are better understood; the species status of *C. baileyi* is dubious. The population of *C. cognatus* has been regarded by another researcher to constitute an undescribed species.

Unsolved sculpin problems are not endemic to Virginia. They also occur in the Tennessee drainage Highlands, the Mobile drainage of Alabama and Georgia (J. D. Williams, personal communication),

Identification

Many workers consider the process of identifying sculpins to be among the most difficult encountered among North American freshwater fish groups. Misidentifications have compromised major aspects of studies (e.g., see introduction to broadband sculpins, and *Systematics* under *C. girardi*). Of all groups that we have studied, *Cottus* are the most demanding of an "eye" for characters and a "feel" for their variation, by size, sex, habitat, and drainage.

Keys to species of *Cottus* often lead to misidentifications. Some species vary so greatly, particularly between drainages, that the utility of keys is much diminished. Frequently even the best diagnostic characters, including those subdividing species into groups, are highly variable, and couplets which describe the range of variation become cumbersome. We wrote a key and distributed it; our colleagues found the accompanying comparison tables more useful. We therefore eliminated the key and expanded the tables.

Steps in Identification.—Proposed steps of identifying Virginia *Cottus* are:

(1) Determine the species known in the drainage from which the unidentified specimens were collected (Table 7, 8). Thus several species, occasionally all but one, may quickly be eliminated from further consideration. Inspect distribution maps (Maps 130–133) because species frequently are differently distributed in a drainage. Geographic ranges are sufficiently known that few surprises (deviant records) are expected.

Table 7 Comparison of typical character states (in at least 75% of adults) and geographic ranges of Virginia populations of *Cottus*. The three species of broadband sculpins are compared in Table 8. See *Description* and *Comparison* in species accounts and the *Identification* section for further data on character states below and other characters.

Character	*b. bairdi*	*baileyi*	*cognatus*	broadband sculpins	*c. carolinae* Holston	*c. carolinae* Clinch–Powell	*carolinae* subsp. Kanawha sculpin	*girardi*
Chin mottling	Absent	Absent	Absent	Absent or slight	Moderate or strong	Absent to moderate	Slight or moderate	Moderate or strong
Saddle width	Moderate or wide	Moderate or wide	Moderate	Moderate or wide	Narrow or moderate	Narrow or moderate	Narrow or moderate	Narrow or moderate
Adult size, mm SL	50–80	45–75	35–65	50–80	75–110	75–110	70–110	45–95
Lateral line Pores	Incomplete 20–25	Incomplete 23–30	Incomplete 21–25	Complete 31–34	Complete 31–34	Complete 31–34	Incomplete 26–33	Incomplete 20–25
Pectoral rays	14–15	15	13–14	14–16	16–17	15–17	16–17	15
Pelvic rays	4; 3–4 in New	4	3	4	4	4	4	4
Palatine tooth patch	Small or moderate	Absent or small	Small or moderate	Small to large	Large	Large	Large	Large
Preopercular spines	Reduced	Reduced	Reduced	Strong or reduced	Strong	Strong	Strong	Strong
Median chin pores	Separate	Separate	United	Separate	Separate	Separate	Separate	United
Range Widespread in:	Potomac, Rappahannock, James, New	Holston	—	South and Middle Fork Holston	Holston	Clinch, Powell	Valley and Ridge of New	Potomac–Shenandoah
Localized in:	Roanoke, Big Sandy	Upper Clinch	Potomac–Shenandoah	Upper Clinch, Bluestone of New	—	—	—	Cowpasture of James

(2) Use the illustrations (Plates 26 and 27; Fish 184–200; Figures 53–63). Illustrated fish were selected to portray as many typical features as possible. In matching unidentified specimens and illustrations, emphasize illustrations other than those of blackened nuptial males; such males are the least frequently captured. Color states should be determined from well-preserved specimens. Those physiologically stressed (e.g., overcrowded in a bucket) or that died prior to preservation generally will be unusually pallid or will have other unnatural patterns.

(3) Consult comparative Tables 7 and 8 and two-species comparisons (in species accounts) to determine that the characters used to align specimens with illustrations are diagnostic. Descriptions in species accounts provide a checklist of traits and variations with which correctly identified speci-

mens should agree. Tables and comparisons may also reveal other characters for consideration.

(4) Comparative material already housed in fish collections, if correctly identified, is of great benefit as a check of identifications.

Characters

The sequence of character groups is coloration, morphometry and certain other structural aspects, meristics, reproduction and size of species, and distribution. Other characters are described in the *Glossary*. Some characters are described by the species groups, whose members are listed in the last part of this section.

Coloration.—Variation of pattern and intensity is an adaptive ability of sculpins; some changes occur

Table 8 Comparison of typical character states or dominant tendencies of the three undescribed species of broadband sculpins. Details in text. D2—second dorsal fin.

Character	Holston sculpin	Clinch sculpin	Bluestone sculpin
Life color of pale upper and midbody areas	More tan-olive or brown-olive	More pearl-olive or pearl-gray	More gray-olive or brown-olive
Chin mottling	Absent or slight	Absent	Absent or slight
Saddle width; edging in life	Wide; normal	Wide; pale-edged	Moderate; normal
Lateral band 3	More slanted, wider ventrally	More vertical, about equal width throughout	More slanted, wider ventrally
First dorsal fin pattern: rays; membranes	Uniform or moderately tessellated; unpatterned, pale	Uniform; unpatterned, pale or dusky, or slashed	Fin marbled or mottled
Second dorsal fin	Tessellated	Unpatterned	Marbled
Caudal fin pattern; intensity	Tessellated; equal to D_2	Unpatterned; equal to D_2	Marbled; darker than D_2
Body form	More robust	More robust	More elongate
Eye size	Moderate	Moderate or large	Small or moderate
Palatine tooth patch	Moderate	Small or moderate	Large
Preopercular spine 3	Short or absent	Short or absent	Long
Prickling, postpectoral	Moderate	Slight	Absent
Dorsal fin height	Moderate or high	Moderate or high	Low or moderate
Dorsal fin connection	Slight	Slight	Unconnected
Caudal fin shape	Subtruncate or truncate	Subtruncate or round	Subtruncate or truncate
Pectoral rays, mean	16.0	15.0	15.7
Spawning period	Late November to mid-January	February–March	January–February

within a few minutes. Individuals become relatively plain on a uniform substrate, more variegated over multihued background. The darker the bottom or cavity, the darker the fish, to a point. Nuptial females and small nuptial males do not darken to the degree of large nuptial males in species with partly or wholly black males. Nuptial males can rapidly change from uniformly blackened to mostly pale with prominent body markings.

Wydoski and Whitney (1979) found that some sculpins darkened in water containing an anesthetic, and we found the same for certain fish, particularly nuptial males. *Cottus* held alive in a bucket of water often become paler overall, the patterns less contrasting, than when they were captured, but typically they rapidly redarken when placed in formalin. Shades of red and orange in our color photos consistently seem slightly paler than in life, even though the specimens were photographed within five min-

utes after death and the color had not faded. Our descriptions are of color in life.

Chin Pattern Figure 53.—This character refers to the distribution of melanophore pigment in the hemispherical area bounded by and excluding the lower lip. The "uniform" pattern refers to equally or subequally spaced pigment. "Mottling" results from distinctly unequal distribution of pigment, forming dusky to dark chains or reticulate dark patches on an otherwise paler chin. Masnik (1974) designated a reference series of six specimens expressing the range of degrees of mottling. Mottling generally becomes apparent when specimens reach 30–40 mm SL. Sparsely distributed large melanophores, which often occur in small specimens of all groups, should not be construed as mottling. Mottling can be masked by general darkening of nuptial males.

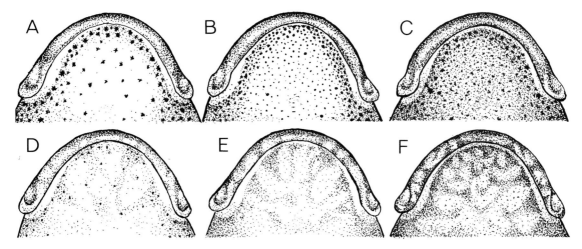

Figure 53 Chin pigmentation of sculpins, *Cottus* (see definitions in text). (A–C) *bairdi* group, chin usually unmottled: (A) pale, (B) moderate, (C) dark. (D–E) *carolinae* group, chin usually mottled: (D) slightly, (E) moderately, (F) strongly (heavily).

Saddle-Bands Figures 54, 62.—These are the large dark dorsal-to-lateral markings that disrupt the overall pattern. "Saddle" refers to the dorsal portion, "band" to the lateral extension. Four primary saddle-bands are described by Williams and Robins (1970) and shown in Figure 62. All may be diffuse; saddle-band 1 often is absent. Occasionally a hint of an additional saddle occurs between saddles 2 and 3 (Figure 56B, D).

Caudal Notch Figure 57.—The notch is an indentation at midheight of the posterior edge of the caudal-base band (band 4), not an irregularity above or below midside.

Fins Figures 55, 56.—Patterns on the fins are fundamental characters in *Cottus* but their terminology has been inconsistent. We discerned primary patterns and their ontogeny from small juveniles to adults, and have applied standard terms.

Markings range from tessellations through mottling to marbling. Tessellation colors are given in the following format: darker mark first, then a slash, then the pale area (e.g., olive/yellow). The three states may form a developmental series. The series would be incomplete in most species; marbling is rare in all but the Bluestone sculpin. When it occurs in *C. bairdi* and *C. baileyi*, marbling generally is poorly developed (pale areas dusky) and apparently is a stage leading to a uniformly dusky or black fin. When paler areas are notably irregular, as in the *bairdi–baileyi* pair, "windowed" is applied (Figure 56C).

"Banded" (Plate 27) refers to a caudal fin with one or two crescentic marks on the distal half. Bands are caused by intensification or fusion of dark tessellation-marks. They frequently occur in the *bairdi–baileyi* pair. "Banded" also applies to a single, horizontal, subdistal–medial dark area through the first dorsal (Figure 55E). It develops from the "2-spotted" (Figure 55A) condition most characteristic of *C. cognatus*, or, as in *C. girardi*, it arises by fusion and intensification of mottling. The peak nuptial male expression in these species is the dark to black fin (Figure 55C, F).

A "slashed" fin has an elongate dusky or dark mark, more intense than the surrounding area, in one

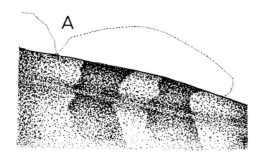

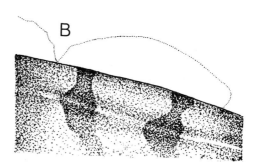

Figure 54 Saddle width in sculpins, *Cottus*: (A) Broad. (B) Narrow.

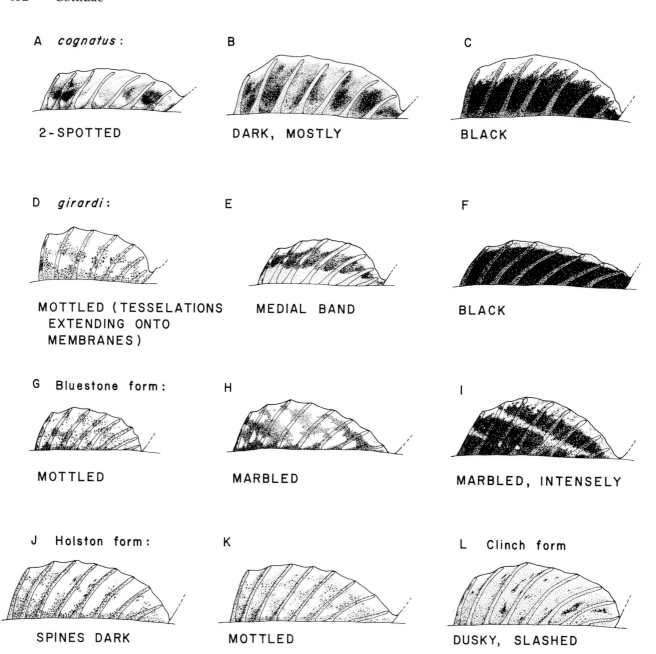

Figure 55   First dorsal fin patterns and intensities in sculpins, *Cottus*. (A–C) *bairdi* group as shown by *C. cognatus*: (A) adult female, (B) nonpeak nuptial male, (C) peak nuptial male. (D–F) *carolinae* group as shown by *C. girardi*: (D) juvenile, (E) small nuptial male, (F) large nuptial male. (G–L) Broadband sculpins, *Cottus* spp. (G–I) Bluestone sculpin: (G) juvenile, (H) adult female, (I) adult male. (J–K) Holston sculpin: (J) adult female, (K) adult male, (L) Clinch sculpin, adult male.

or a few of the membranes of the first dorsal fin (Figure 55L).

The "flecked" state occurs in postnuptial males of the *bairdi* group and *C. girardi* (Figure 56D; Fish 199). Apparently it is caused by localized retention of melanophore aggregations in formerly wholly blackened fins. Other states and relative darkness are indicated in Figures 55 and 56.

First Dorsal Fin Margin in Life.—According to the literature, the first dorsal fin in the *bairdi* group gen-

erally has a wide, bright red-orange or red distal margin, particularly in nuptial males. The fin margin of the *carolinae* group has been considered narrow and pale orange. Although an average difference exists between the groups, in the *bairdi* group the margin often is narrow and pale orange or virtually entirely creamy.

Darkness of Nuptial Males.—The presence, absence, or intensity and extent of blackening are of systematic significance. Blackness sometimes is a flash phase and sometimes it has a long duration. The degree of

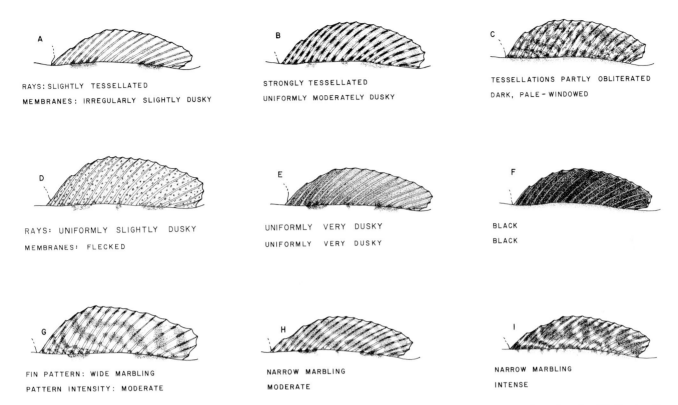

Figure 56 Second dorsal fin patterns and intensities in adults of sculpins, *Cottus*: (A) Holston sculpin female. (B) *C. girardi* female. (C) *C. baileyi* male. (D) *C. girardi* male. (E) *C. bairdi* male. (F) *C. baileyi* male. (G) *C. c. carolinae* female. (H, I) Bluestone sculpin: (H) Female. (I) Male.

darkening is related to proximity to spawning, aggression, and size of males; larger males tend to be darker than smaller males.

Morphometry in General.—Proportions of body and fin parts are sufficiently variable within species and overlapping between species to disallow their use as a convenient and consistent means of species identification; the differences in shape between two nuptial male *C. cognatus* (Plate 26; Fish 188) exemplify typical variation. Measurement methods and specimen preservation often differ enough to preclude repeatable results. Generally only near-extreme and extreme proportions of specimens yield clues to species identity; for example, the occasional pronounced robustness of the head and anterior body coupled with a slender caudal peduncle in the *carolinae* group.

Apart from use of measurements purely for species identification, Daniels and Moyle (1984) delimited subspecies of *Cottus klamathensis*, Godkin et al. (1982) separated *C. bairdi* and *C. cognatus*, and Strauss (1980) segregated species into groups by rigorous mathematical procedures. The newer methods of shape analysis by truss network, used for *Cottus* by Strauss and Bookstein (1982) and Bookstein et al. (1985), merit application to samples encompassing the range of species.

Dorsal Fin Union.—The extent to which the dorsal fins are conjoined or separate varies within and between species. The following states were recognized (see panels in Figure 55): distinctly separate (H); slightly separate; unseparated and unjoined (G, I); very slightly joined (E, J); slightly joined (B, C, K); moderately joined (D, F, L); widely joined (A).

Caudal Fin Shape Figure 57.—Three subjectively scored states are recognized; almost all individuals of a given species fall within two of them. In most species, large specimens tend to have a rounder tail than small ones. In no species group do all species have the same typical shape.

Thickness of Spines and Rays.—Differences in this character merit quantification. The *bairdi–baileyi* pair tends to have the thickest fin support elements (Figure 55B), broadband sculpins the frailest (Figure 55K).

Prickling Figure 58.—When present on the body, prickles usually are confined to the anterior portion, mostly below the lateral line (postpectoral area). Prickling is best seen by drying the skin with an air stream or stroking anteriad with a pointed tool. We

Figure 57 Caudal fin shapes of sculpins, *Cottus*; notch in caudal base band shown in truncate example.

TRUNCATE   SUBTRUNCATE   ROUNDED

did not study head prickling, nor stain prickles or examine their shape; for such analyses see McAllister and Lindsey (1961) and McAllister (1964). Older fish tend to have proportionately smaller or more embedded prickles, or lose them (Maughan 1978). Koli (1969) discusses variation in prickling.

Prickling is a vexing character; some species are virtually consistent in its absence, or presence and degree of development, whereas others are quite variable. Robins and Miller (1957) stated that prickling tends to be reduced in populations of mountain brooks and best developed in lake fish. A weak trend was detected in Virginia. Some spring- or coolwater species that occupy runs and riffles (*C. baileyi*, *C. cognatus*, and the Clinch and Bluestone sculpins) have little or no prickling, whereas *C. c. carolinae*, frequently a warm-river, gentle-current tenant, usually has well-developed prickling.

Palatine Teeth Figure 59.—Medium and large patches of palatine teeth are readily discerned by drying or probing. Detection of small patches (1–7 teeth) and the absence of teeth require careful observation, often by removal of epithelial tissue. The jaws may be cut by scissors at one or both angles to better expose the roof of the oral cavity. Damage from cutting often is less than that from strongly forcing the mouth open, and the teeth can be studied more carefully. Palatine teeth are obscure or lacking in small specimens, and seem to increase in number with growth. Our data are from large juveniles and adults. Robins (1954) and Strauss (1980) noted species differences in the vomerine patch.

Preopercular Armature Figure 60.—Armature or spination can be discerned by probing the edge of the preopercle, but is best studied by skin incision and

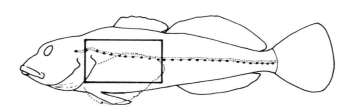

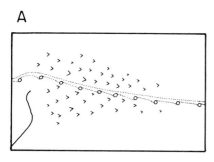 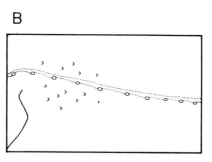 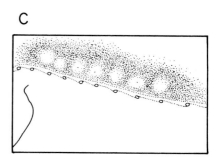

A   B   C

Figure 58 Prickling of postpectoral area in sculpins, *Cottus* (whole fish with postpectoral area defined by rectangle, pectoral fin outlined): (A) *C. carolinae*, prickling well developed, characteristic of numerous populations. (B) Clinch sculpin, typical slight prickling. (C) Bluestone sculpin, prickling essentially absent, instead with small pale areas, some with a minute rounded nub.

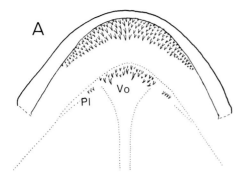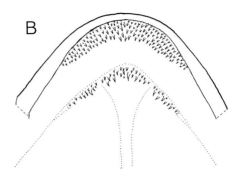

Figure 59 Roof of mouth showing palatine tooth patches of sculpins, *Cottus*: (A) Slightly developed. (B) Moderately developed. Pl—palatine teeth; Vo—vomerine teeth.

removal of connective tissue. Right-side spines were examined to avoid damaging the potentially photographable left side. Development of each spine was scored relative to strong development of the same spine; *C. carolinae* was the template for strong spines (Figure 60 legend).

Species characterized as having strong armature are the most consistently so and tend to have the cross-sectionally roundest spines. Spines are relatively longer, more slender, and sharper in the young of a population than in adults, in fish from Piedmont streams compared with fish from swift mountain streams, and in lake versus stream specimens (Robins 1954).

Meristics in General.—Species and subspecies differences among *Cottus* are no less marked than in many genera of closely related species. Many differences are slight and convergent trends are common, but the small differences often can be correlated with other characters.

Cephalic Lateralis System Figure 60.—Detailed illustrations of the cephalic lateral line canals and pores are given by Robins and Miller (1957). Virginia sculpins are similar in canal configurations and typical pore counts, except for the anterior portion of the preopercular-mandibular canals on the chin (POM or PM, Figure 61; McAllister 1968). These chin canals are separate or united; if united, a single median pore exists. Partially fused median pores, a rarity, were considered united.

Lateral Line Canal on Body Figure 62; Tables 7, 8.—The development of the lateral line on the body is an extremely useful character in *Cottus*. Its completeness and incompleteness are reflected by endpoint areas and, usually, pore counts. Methods of counting canal pores and terminology are partly indicated in Figure

62. Counts were begun at the posterior end (at the caudal fin base), to apprise the variable end first. Doubled pores (closely adjacent pores on an uninterrupted segment of the lateral line) were counted as one; doubling is rare and usually involves the occurrence of one of the pores on a canaliculus (side branch). The number of canal interruptions was counted. Numerous interruptions significantly increase the pore count but do not affect scoring of the posterior extension of the line. Thus a fish with a high pore count may have a distinctly incomplete canal. A complete lateral line canal usually has 31–34 pores and no interruption. The lateral line canal reaches its full development when individuals are 30–40 mm SL; our counts were made on specimens at least 40 mm. An incomplete lateral line may be functionally extended by a series of external neuromasts (Sideleva 1979).

Fin Spines and Rays Tables 7, 8.—Methods of counting followed Robins and Miller (1957). The last two (very rarely three) dorsal and anal ray elements were counted as one ray when they stem from a single pterygiophore. This is the "doubled" or "branched" condition, and is almost always found in Virginia sculpins. Accurate counts generally result by counting the last two elements as two only when their lower ends are well separated externally. The pelvic fin of *Cottus* has a hidden anterior splintlike spine attached directly to the first ray; the spine is not counted. The fourth pelvic ray is smaller than and sometimes slightly medial to the third; it is counted even if rudimentary.

Reproductive Characters.—In sexing *Cottus* the entire abdominal cavity of unripe fish usually was opened by cutting along both flanks and transversely anterior to the pelvic fins. The saclike urinary bladder, usually on the right side, and the dorsally located, enlarged

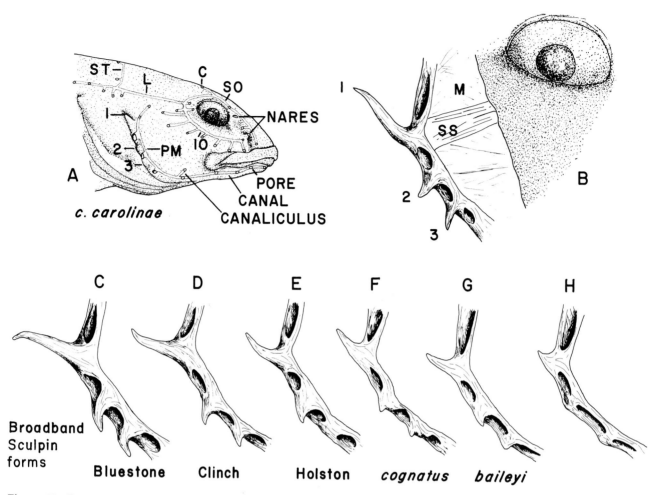

Figure 60 Preopercular armature and cephalic lateralis system of sculpins, *Cottus*; specimens 59–76 mm SL: (A) Location of spines (1–3), beneath skin, relative to pores of preopercular-mandibular canal. Lateralis canals or pores (adapted from Robins and Miller 1957): C—coronal pore; IO—infraorbital; L—lateral; PM—preopercular-mandibular; SO—supraorbital; ST—supratemporal. (B) Preopercular spines exposed by dissection; M—muscle; SS—suborbital stay bone. (C) Ventroflexion of tip of spine 1 is atypical. Spine development states are: Strong (well developed)—all spines in B, C; spine 1 in D. Moderately developed—spine 1 in E, F; spine 2 in D, E, G. Weak (slight)—spine 1 in G, H; spines 2 and 3 in F. Spine 3 is absent in E and spines 2 and 3 are absent in H.

kidneys should not be confused with gonads. Ovaries are fused for about half their length; testes are largely separate.

Maturity, adult size, and spawning period. Craddock (1965) stated that it was difficult to judge maturity of males from the appearance of testes, and impossible to tell if an individual was spent. However, we found that mature males have much-enlarged, cream-colored testes within one or two months before spawning and a few weeks after; immature males have small gray testes. Often it is difficult to press milt from reproductive males, but they exude a fine stream of milt for a few minutes upon being placed in formalin. Prenuptial and nuptial females are readily recognized as mature by their enlarged

ova. We seem generally unable to distinguish spent females from immature females by gross examination of ovaries, because the former generally spawned all ripe ova. Adult sizes cited are based on prenuptial and nuptial fish, and on a few others judged to be clearly adult based on large size.

Determination of the spawning period generally is based on ovarian condition. Females with greatly enlarged ovaries are considered imminent spawners. Savage (1963) stated that when the genital pore area became swollen (Figure 63C, E), the female spawned within a few hours. We found ova in the genital papilla of some fish, indicating that they were spawning. The extent of the spawning period was estimated from percentages of gravid and apparently spent fe-

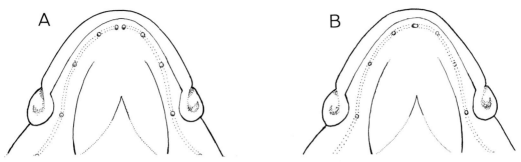

Figure 61 Underside of head of sculpins, *Cottus*, showing mandibular portion of preopercular-mandibular canals; anteriormost pores: (A) Unfused, 2 pores. (B) Fused, 1 median pore.

males (equal in length or larger than all but the smaller gravid fish) taken in and near the indicated or known period. The spawning period at an individual site may occur during only a small portion of the general breeding period; at some localities all adult females spawn in less than a week.

Genital papilla   Figure 63. This structure was indicated by Robins (1954) to differ between the *bairdi* and *carolinae* groups: long, flattened, and triangular only in males of the former; a simple rounded protuberance in both sexes of the *carolinae* group. However, Robins (1961) found as we did that the papilla is sexually dimorphic in *C. girardi*. We found (and note in the accounts) much greater variation within species than noted by Robins.

Distribution   Maps 130–133.—Patterns of geographical and ecological distribution are summarized in the

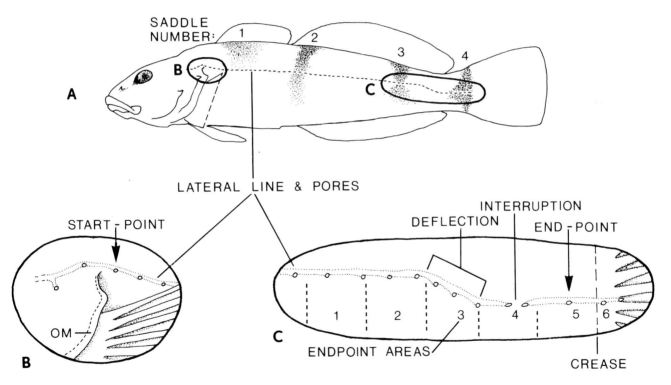

Figure 62 Sculpins, *Cottus*: (A) Saddles numbered; areas of startpoint and endpoint for lateral line pore count on body are indicated. (B) Start of pore count (arrow) is with first pore partly or entirely posterior to attachment of opercular membrane—OM. (C) Last pore counted (arrow) is on or just anterior to crease produced by flexing caudal fin toward observer. Canal shown is complete (i.e., to caudal fin base) and has one interruption. On specimens with an incomplete canal, a pale line (superficially suggesting completeness) extends posteriad from last pore. Pore count endpoint areas: 1 and 2 each are the length of the deflection (area 3, measured along oblique axis); 4 and 5 each are half the length from the deflection to the caudal base crease; 6 is posterior to the caudal base (i.e., on caudal fin). A canal is "complete" when ending in area 6 or the posterior half of 5; "incomplete" when ending anterior to the posterior half of 5.

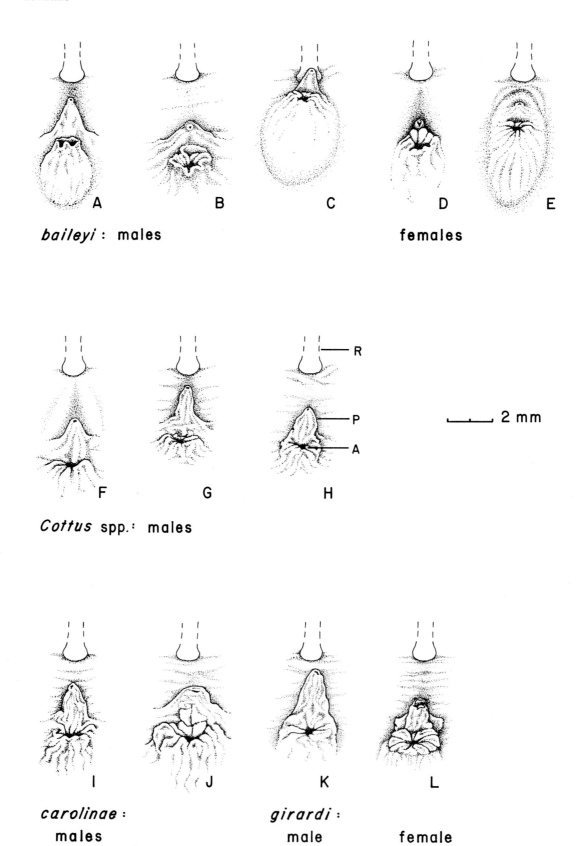

Figure 63   Genital papillae of nuptial or nearly nuptial sculpins, *Cottus*; full range of variation not shown. Broadband sculpins, *Cottus* spp.: (F) Bluestone sculpin, (G) Clinch sculpin, (H) Holston sculpin. A—anus, R—base of first anal ray, P—papilla.

family introduction. Specimens for nearly all plots were verified by Jenkins, or Robins' identifications were accepted, or they were from Masnik's (1974) study involving repeated conferral on *Cottus* with Jenkins. Exceptions to the verification procedure chiefly concern records of *C. carolinae* in the Tennessee drainage by TVA personnel; however, descriptions of diagnostic characters were forwarded to those persons and the many lots subsequently checked were found to be correctly identified. All geographically and ecologically atypical records were verified, or in event of missing specimens, rejected; very few cases of the latter arose.

Species-Groups and Interrelationships

The *Cottus* of Virginia have been divided between two species groups—*bairdi* and *carolinae* (Bailey and Dimick 1949; Robins 1954); we recognize a third—broadband sculpins. Each group has three forms in Virginia: (1) the *bairdi* group consisting of *C. bairdi*, *C. baileyi*, and *C. cognatus*; (2) the *carolinae* group with *C. carolinae*, Kanawha sculpin (tentatively a subspecies of *C. carolinae*), and *C. girardi*; and (3) the broadband group comprising the undescribed Holston, Clinch, and Bluestone sculpins. The *bairdi* group has an extensive range in eastern and western North America, comprising at least 10 species (Bailey and Bond 1963; our study). The *carolinae* group is widespread in the central and southern Appalachians, the Ozarks, and outliers; it includes the West Virginia cave sculpin and possibly *C. rhotheus* of the Pacific Northwest.

A major surprise of our study was discovery of three undescribed forms, which we recognize as species and collectively term the broadband sculpins. This assemblage is endemic to western Virginia and immediately adjacent waters. The group apparently is not monophyletic, but we cannot confidently allocate any of the forms to the *bairdi* or *carolinae* groups. They may be relicts, as postulated for *C. girardi* by Robins (1954, 1961), although the literature gives no indication of close kinship with western sculpins.

Intragroup relationships of Virginia *Cottus* are discussed under *Systematics* in species accounts. We seem far from a comprehensive understanding of interrelationships of American *Cottus* and of these to

Eurasian species. It was hoped that this study would elucidate the direction of evolutionary change of characters, but characters generally were found to be too variable or to exhibit a greater number of a parallelisms or convergences than formerly known. Robins (1954) recognized the polarity of a number of character states in the *carolinae* group, but the correctness of some of these and their application outside that group are in doubt.

Despite uncertainties, we support the zoogeographically logical separation of a *bairdi* group and a *carolinae* group in the East. Although we found greater overlap of the groups (e.g., in genital papillae, nuptial color), their eastern taxa vary around distinctive modes for the groups in certain pigmentation patterns, general morphometry and adult size, palatine teeth, and preopercular armature. Closely related species, such as those of a species group or species pair, tend to be geographically isolated from each other or ecologically incompatible; distantly related taxa generally can share a habitat. Thus one or more members of a group typically are widely syntopic with taxa of another group in Virginia, but sympatry of two members of the same group is rare. Exceptions are *C. cognatus* and *C. bairdi*, perhaps the cave and Kanawha sculpins, and perhaps the Kanawha sculpin and *C. c. carolinae* in the lower Holston system. Each group appears to have a separate but similar history of dispersal or fractionation.

There is little wonder that so much intergroup character overlap occurs. Sculpins have a bent to diverge in isolated areas of profuse cool water, and both groups have populations isolated in and adapted to many of the same areas. Recognition of the *bairdi* and *carolinae* groups serves as a working hypothesis for understanding sculpin biology.

Conclusions on interrelationships from an extensive morphological and electrophoretic study of eastern *Cottus* by Strauss (1980) differ sharply from the above. Some taxa of the *bairdi* group are moved to the *carolinae* group and vice versa. Strauss' interpretation of the morphological data agreed well with relationships proposed by Robins and accepted by us, but interpretations stemming from the genetic data did not; Strauss stressed the genetic data.

Mottled sculpin   *Cottus bairdi* (Girard)

SYSTEMATICS

The systematics of the widespread mottled sculpin, named from Ohio in 1850, are not completely understood. Four subspecies often are recognized. *Cottus b.*

bairdi occurs in Virginia and widely north and west; Robins (1954) clarified the status of most of its eastern populations. Unresolved problems concerning the southeastern "smoky sculpin" form of *C. bairdi* and the black sculpin *C. baileyi* are addressed under the latter species and *Distribution* of the Holston sculpin.

Several authors, including Scott and Crossman (1973), and Bailey and Smith (1981), did not recognize subspecies in *C. bairdi* in eastern North America. This may have resulted partly from reduced confidence in some of Robins' conclusions owing to the synonymizing of *C. girardi* with *C. bairdi* by Savage (1962), shortly after Robins described *C. girardi*. That lumping was wrong (see *C. girardi*). Robins (1954) substantiated the status of the Great Lakes form *C. bairdi kumlieni*. In nuptial coloration and blotching it more closely resembles *C. cognatus* (Koster 1936; Robins 1954). Godkin et al. (1982) seemed to suggest that *kumlieni* may be the product of hybridization between *C. bairdi* and *C. cognatus*.

Within *C. b. bairdi*, Robins (1954) recognized on the basis of variation in pectoral ray count, a Blue Ridge race on the central Atlantic slope from the Patapsco drainage, Maryland, to the Roanoke drainage. We found that character to generally agree with the absence of a notch in the caudal base band in populations from the Roanoke to the Potomac drainage.

A wide distributional gap exists in central North America (Map 130). Robins (1954) considered the upper Missouri drainage population to be the subspecies *C. b. bairdi*, but we question that it is even that species. Two subspecies are recognized west of the continental divide: *C. b. semiscaber* in the Columbia drainage adjacent to the upper Missouri, and *C. b. punctulatus* of the upper Colorado drainage (Bailey and Dimick 1949; Robins and Miller 1957). They may not be well understood taxonomically, and redefinition of the species limits of *C. bairdi* is warranted (Bisson and Bond 1971; Peden et al. 1989).

DESCRIPTION

Materials.—From Robins (1954; counts included here are only for specimens from Atlantic slope drainages of Virginia and all parts of the New drainage) and the following number of series from Virginia or as specified (in parentheses are numbers of specimens on which selected characters were counted): Potomac 35(62), Rappahannock 15(15), James 22(162), Roanoke 19, New 27 (38 from West Virginia), and Big Sandy 5. Life color data from: Potomac drainage 4 series; James 2; Roanoke 3; New 5.

Anatomy.—A *Cottus* with an unmottled chin, first dorsal fin often blackened, and an incomplete lateral line; adults are 50–80 mm SL. Body form moderate or robust, large nuptial male particularly bull-headed; snout short; eye moderate. Dorsal and anal fin height moderate or high; dorsal fins usually slightly connected; caudal fin subtruncate or rounded; dorsal spines and rays moderate or thick.

Palatine tooth patch slightly to strongly developed, usually moderately developed. Preopercular spine 1 usually moderate; spine 2 moderate or slight; spine 3 moderate,

Fish 184 *Cottus b. bairdi* adult male 56 mm SL (REJ 1063), VA, Augusta County, Whisky Creek, 3 April 1984.

Fish 185 *Cottus b. bairdi* adult female 61 mm SL (REJ 1176), VA, Wythe County, South Fork Reed Creek, 11 March 1986.

slight, or (usually) absent. Prickling postpectorally moderate to absent. Male genital papilla very broad-based, tip broadly rounded or pointed, not prolonged beyond general outline of papilla.

Meristics.—Lateral line incomplete, pores (15)20–25(27). Dorsal spines (6)7–8(9); dorsal rays (15)16–18(19), last branched; anal rays (11)12–13(14), last branched; pelvic rays almost always 4 (exceptions are 3 rays in 4.6% of 326 sides of James drainage specimens; 3 in 13.6% of 272 counts from New drainage); pectoral rays (13)14–15(16). Cephalic lateralis pores typically: ST 3; LAT 5; SO 4, apparently including COR pore; IO 9; PM 11, sides said to be separate (Robins 1954). We found varied tendencies for PM canals to unite medially, as indicated under *C. cognatus* and *Comparison* below; also united in 32.4% of 37 fish from the New drainage, West Virginia.

Color in Preservative.—Body ground shade usually slightly or moderately dusky; back and side usually markedly mottled, scrawled, or reticulated with slightly darker shade; black-spotting usually absent or sparse, occasionally moderate, heavily spotted fish seen only from South Fork Reed Creek; saddles usually moderately bold or intense except saddle 1 often diffuse; hint of saddle occasionally present at midlength of second dorsal fin base. Saddles 2 and 3 usually moderate or narrow, much less often broad; saddle-bands 2 and 3 short or long, vertical or slanted anteroventrad. Lower side often blotched, blotches usually interconnected and/or vague. Caudal base band with lower portion variably extended anteriorly, markedly or barely encircling dorsal and ventral caudal base; posterior edge usually straight, sometimes slightly convex or concave in Potomac, Rappahannock, James, and Roanoke drainages; almost always notched or concave medially in New and Big Sandy.

Chin almost always unmottled, melanophores very small. Head dorsum dusky or dark; side usually mottled, occasionally with 1–2 cheek bars or spots.

First dorsal fin distally with narrow or wide pale band; spines tessellated in small fish; membranes within mid-third of fin height slightly dusky or, often, with 2-spot pattern; becoming wholly dusky or black through the horizontal length of fin (except distal margin) and basally in large fish, membranes darker than spines. Second dorsal, caudal, anal, and pelvic fins usually tessellated, dark marks longest; anal and pelvic the least or not at all tessellated, occasionally all fins untessellated; second dorsal and caudal occasionally flecked or windowed, rarely marbled; caudal tessellations often fused, widest and boldest submarginally, effecting 1–2 wide bands. Pectoral fin usually moderately tessellated; base occasionally darker, rarely with distinct blotch.

Nuptial male head dark sooty or blackish (not jet black); body moderately sooty or normal, saddle-bands and smaller marks remain distinct, although often less obvious than in nonbreeding male. Fins of medium and large dark males darkly peppered or uniformly dusky or dark, except first dorsal pale-edged and then black nearly or fully to base; membranes darker than rays in all fins.

Color in Life Plate 26.—Head and body dorsum and side with tan or pale to medium olive ground shade, overlaid with dusky olive to olive-brown mottling and scrawling and, often, russet reticulation; small spots when present olive-black; saddle-bands olive-black to brown-black; palest areas of lower side gold-olive to pale olive; venter off-white to pale gray; iris partly brassy.

First dorsal fin margin creamy yellow-orange, pale orange, or bright orange-red, often interrupted at intervals; spines tessellated rusty/pale olive, or all olive except orange tinge distally; membranes below margin are pale to black, tending olive basally. Second dorsal, caudal, and pectoral ray tessellations olive, usually russet, pink, or tomato red/pale olive or yellow-olive; or rays uniformly olive or reddish, pectoral the least reddish; membranes pale to dusky, often with reddish extending from rays partly through membranes. Anal and pelvic rays tessellated gray/yellow-olive or white, or rays all white; membranes pale or dusky.

Nuptial male head, body, and fins darker than in female, some males with dusky blue tint to chin and belly; russet on body often masked by duskiness; first dorsal fin margin usually partly creamy, usually with red component brighter than on body, still always with orange tinge, color band best developed (complete or slightly interrupted) in largest males; both dorsal, caudal, and pectoral fins with russet remaining unmasked in some fish. See account of *C. baileyi* for additional comments on nuptial color.

Geographic variation in coloration was not noted; intrapopulation variation is substantial.

Larvae.—Described by Koster (1936), Bailey (1952), Ludwig and Norden (1969), Nagel (1980), and Heufelder (1982d).

COMPARISON

Cottus bairdi is distinguished from *C. cognatus* of the Potomac drainage and the Bluestone sculpin of the New drainage in those accounts. Differences from *C. baileyi* of the Tennessee drainage are treated in that account.

Cottus girardi of the Potomac drainage and Cowpasture system of the James drainage is separated from *C. bairdi* of those drainages by: (1) caudal base band, posterior edge, medially [usually unnotched (i.e., entire posterior edge vertically straight, slightly convex, or slightly concave) in *bairdi* (in 80–90% of fish, Matheson 1979) vs. virtually always notched, usually deeply, in *girardi*]; (2) median chin pores [united in only 8% of Potomac, 34% of James fish vs. united in 77% and 81%, respectively, in Virginia (51% in Maryland and Pennsylvania)]; (3) chin pattern [almost always unmottled, rarely slightly mottled vs. usually slightly to strongly mottled, often unmottled]; (4) preopercular spines 2 and 3 and palatine tooth patches usually [reduced vs. well developed]; (5) for living fish and those in preservative up to about one week, color of second dorsal and caudal fins [partly or entirely a reddish shade, at least on markings of rays *vs.* reddish never present]; (6) first dorsal fin pattern [fish with 2 spots would be *bairdi* (if not *cognatus*) *vs.* never 2 spots in *girardi* (although it shares several other patterns with *C. bairdi*); (7) adult size [rarely exceeds 80 mm SL *vs.* often larger].

The New drainage form of *C. carolinae*, the undescribed Kanawha sculpin, is discerned by applying to it character states 3–7 above of *C. girardi*. Also use: (8) lateral line pores in fish greater than 40 mm SL (line incomplete in both forms) usually [20–25 in *bairdi vs.* 26–33 in *carolinae*]; (9) pectoral rays almost always [14–15 *vs.* 16–17].

Sorting of *C. bairdi* from *C. carolinae* and *C. girardi*, particularly juveniles, is often speeded by the generally overall darker, less contrastingly patterned body of *C. bairdi*.

The utility of the caudal band notch (character 1, above) is reduced by geographic variation. *Cottus bairdi* almost always has a notch in the New drainage, whereas the notch is seldom present in Potomac and James *C. bairdi*, opposite the condition of *C. girardi* in the Potomac and James. In New drainage *C. carolinae*, the notch is often present in some Virginia subpopulations; it was absent in all 15 specimens of 5 series from the West Virginia section.

BIOLOGY

Cottus bairdi is predominantly an insectivore in many waters; it also feeds heavily on isopod and amphipod crustaceans and other invertebrates when available, but rarely on fishes (Koster 1937; Bailey 1952; Dineen 1951; Matheson 1979; Rohde and Arndt 1981). It will prey selectively on isopods and amphipods, sometimes mainly on a particular size range of these items (Anderson 1975; Gilson and Benson 1979). Mottled sculpins feed largely at night (Anderson 1985; Hoekstra and Janssen 1985).

Sexual maturation usually occurs in 2 years; the fish are ready to spawn during the second spring after hatching (Hann 1927; Koster 1936; Ludwig and Lange 1975; Nagel 1980; Anderson 1985; Reagan and West 1985). Most Virginia yearlings are immature. Maturation occurs in 1 year for the small short-lived fish of the Delaware Coastal Plain (Rohde and Arndt 1981). Maximum longevity is 6 years (Reagan and West 1985). Males grow faster than females except for *C. b. kumlieni* (Koster 1936). Four age-classes were found in a Virginia stream (Neves and Pardue 1983). The size of fish in Virginia populations is similar to most other eastern ones. In collections of spawning adults from the Roanoke and New drainages, 22

males were 54–79 mm SL, mean, 61, and 44 females 47–67 mm, mean, 55. Size differences between breeding males and females were more pronounced in Ohio (Downhower and Brown 1979).

The largest Virginia specimen is a male 91 mm SL, 113 mm TL (4.4 inches), distinctly larger than any other seen in the state. *Cottus b. bairdi* of about that size have been reported from several other states (Robins 1954; Eddy and Underhill 1974), and to 103 mm SL in Wisconsin and 113 mm SL in Michigan (Hann 1927; Ludwig and Norden 1969). A 132-mm TL mottled sculpin was listed from Lake Superior, in the geographic range of *C. b. kumlieni* (Scott and Crossman 1973). Large fish appear to be more frequent in the West, to 140 mm TL (Bailey 1952; considered *C. b. bairdi* by Robins [1954]) or 145 mm TL (Brown 1971) in Montana. Fish greater than 177 mm were noted in Colorado (Woodling 1985).

Cottus bairdi typically spawns in mid-March and April in the southern Appalachians (Robins 1954; Nagel 1980; Reagan and West 1985) and in late April, May, or June in northern areas (Smith 1922; Hann 1927; Koster 1936; Ludwig and Norden 1969; Godkin et al. 1982), in water of 5–16°C. Eggs were brooded as late as July in a New York lake (Adams and Hankinson 1928). The Delaware Coastal Plain population spawns during late February and March at temperatures similar to those of higher elevation or latitude (Rohde and Arndt 1981). Egg-guarding during November–February in Missouri was ascribed to *C. bairdi* by Pflieger (1975), but it apparently is based on the subsequently described *C. hypselurus* (Rohde and Arndt 1981; Robins and Robison 1985; our data).

In Virginia, two New drainage series indicate that spawning began in 1972 a day or two before 16–17 April. Fish ready to spawn were taken in the Roanoke drainage on 12 March 1982; two egg masses were found on 1 April 1952 (VPI 434). Egg masses were discovered on 19 March and 16 April 1977 in the Shenandoah system (Matheson 1979).

Nest sites typically are cavities cleared under stones, but eggs are placed in or under a wide range of other sites or materials. These include logs, planks, tiles, concrete blocks, bricks, crockery, cans, bottles, and even a dog skull (Koster 1936; Downhower and Brown 1977; Rohde and Arndt 1981), to which Ludwig and Norden (1969) added plants, tunnels in firmly packed loam, and crevices among large gravel. Larger males select larger spawning cavities, defend them better, and tend to breed earlier, longer, and with more females than do smaller males. Female mate choice is cued to size of males, larger ones being preferred (Downhower and Brown 1977, 1980; Downhower and Yost 1977; Brown 1981). As many as 13 females spawn with one male; 2–4 females with each male is suggested as average. Reproductive behavior reported by Savage (1963) is based on *C. girardi*.

Mature ova per female range 35–406; eggs per nest mass tally 54–2,874 (Smith 1922; Koster 1936; Bailey 1952; Ludwig and Norden 1969; Patten 1971; Brown 1981; Rohde and Arndt 1981; Anderson 1985). Fecundity is lower and ova size greater (mean, 3.0–3.3 mm) in the smoky sculpin form of *C. bairdi* (Nagel 1980; Reagan and West 1985).

Hybridization of *C. bairdi* with *C. cognatus* in Lake Ontario and Pennsylvania was noted by Godkin et al. (1982) and Strauss (1986).

HABITAT

Mottled sculpins typically occupy cool, clear, moderate and high-gradient creeks, streams, and small rivers. They commonly populate stony shallows of lakes in the northern United States and Canada. This is one of the most headward-penetrating species in Virginia; it often occurs with brook trout. In contrast to obligate coldwater fishes, it frequently populates streams with warmwater faunas. Overall it seems best regarded as a coolwater fish. Summer water temperatures at Iowa sites were 16–22°C, mean, 20 (Johnson 1972); in Ontario the mean was 16.6°C (Hallam 1959). In the lower Tennessee drainage, *C. bairdi* primarily occupies the coldest springs (Armstrong and Williams 1971). Thermal restriction may occur in the upper Roanoke River, where over many years this species has not been found in warm water below the Roanoke forks, although the substrate is suitable (Map 130; records seemingly below the forks are from tributaries).

Confinement of *C. bairdi* in Virginia largely to relatively cool montane areas may be related to intolerance of heavy siltation on the Piedmont. Trautman (1981), Smith et al. (1981), and others regarded this species to be most common in clear streams with riffles. It spans alkaline to somewhat acidic environments, to pH 6.3 in Virginia (Neves and Pardue 1983) and 5.7 in Delaware (Rohde and Arndt 1981).

Large juveniles and adults generally occupy runs and riffles of gravel, rubble, and boulder; they occasionally inhabit plant beds. In pools they usually are located in well-flowing parts. Differences in microhabitat use within *C. bairdi*—adult males tending to live in somewhat slower water than adult females and immatures—and the possibility of interactive segregation from *C. girardi* were discerned by Matheson and Brooks (1983). Mottled sculpins seem to distribute themselves in streams according to substrate particle size; larger sculpins occupy rubble, smaller ones finer materials (G. Smith *in* Downhower and Brown 1979).

DISTRIBUTION   Map 130

Cottus bairdi occurs from the Hudson Bay basin, Labrador, and Quebec south (although absent from most of New England) to the lower Ohio basin and down the Appalachian chain. Isolated populations or population groups occupy the Delmarva Coastal Plain (Franz and Lee 1976; Rohde and Arndt 1981), middle and lower Cumberland (UMMZ 125698; Burr and Warren 1986) and Tennessee drainages (Robins 1954; Armstrong and Williams 1971; UT), and the northern Ozarks (Robins and Robison 1985). The range of the smoky sculpin is considered under *C. baileyi* and the Holston sculpin; problems of delimiting the western range of *C. bairdi* are noted under *Systematics*.

In Virginia, *C. bairdi* is largely restricted to the Blue Ridge and west, being absent only in the Pee Dee among Atlantic slope drainages heading in mountains. Somewhat disjunct populations occur in a moderate-gradient area in the Piedmont of the James drainage. The more distant isolation of the population group in the Rappahannock drainage just above the Fall Line is discussed in *Biogeography*. This species appears to be absent from the Piedmont portion of the Potomac drainage in Virginia; records from Washington, D.C., and vicinity in Maryland (Dietemann 1975) need verification. Oddly, *C. bairdi* is lacking in many montane tributaries of the upper Roanoke system, being found only in the North and South forks and other tributaries above Salem. In the Dan system it occupies the upper Smith and Dan-proper watersheds, but not the Mayo.

In the New drainage, the mottled sculpin is generally distributed in the Blue Ridge and the Valley and Ridge provinces in North Carolina and Virginia. It is less successful in the Valley and Ridge and Appalachian Plateau of West Virginia, but is not as limited as is *C. carolinae*.

Abundance and Syntopy.—Generally uncommon or common; common or abundant at some of the Big Sandy drainage sites. Syntopic in the Potomac drainage with *C. cognatus* and *C. girardi*, and in the New drainage with *C. carolinae*; see those accounts.

REMARKS

The status of the mottled sculpin as the most abundant *Cottus* in the United States is related to its use of

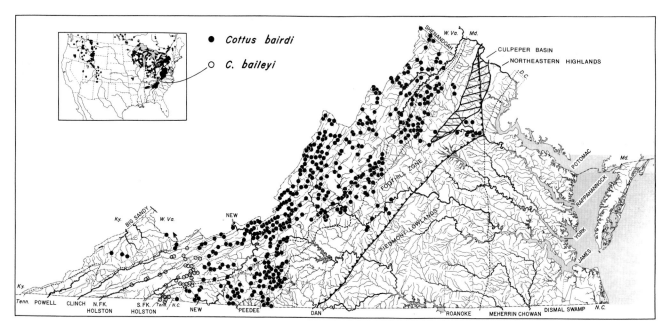

Map 130   Mottled sculpin and black sculpin. Total range of *C. baileyi* shown, except for the Watauga system, Tennessee, where populations of the typical form and possible intergrades with the smoky sculpin may occur. Piedmont subprovinces are described under *Drainages* (Map 7).

a great variety of natural and trash nest cover as spawning sites, to its cleaning and guarding of the sites, and to its upstream penetration into high gradients that offer relatively unsedimented nest sites. The tenacity of *C. bairdi* in the Virginia portion of the Big Sandy drainage, where many benthic fishes have been extirpated, seems remarkable, but is explainable partly by the above habits.

Name.—For Spencer F. Baird, vertebrate zoologist, first U.S. Fish Commissioner, and a Secretary of the Smithsonian Institution.

Black sculpin   *Cottus baileyi* (Robins)

SYSTEMATICS

This form in the extreme upper Tennessee drainage was described by Robins (1961) from headwaters of the three forks of the Holston River, Tennessee and (largely) Virginia. Masnik (1973) discovered it in two tributaries of the uppermost Clinch system. Robins (1961) considered it clearly a member of the *bairdi* group. Phylogenetically and geographically, its closest relatives are *C. b. bairdi*, which occupies the lower Tennessee drainage and is widely arrayed to the west, north, and east of the Tennessee, and the smoky sculpin, an undescribed form which extends in the Tennessee south from the southern edge of the range of *C. baileyi* (Map 130) fully down the Appalachian Highlands and occupies the Blue Ridge of two south Atlantic and two Gulf slope drainages.

The status of *C. baileyi* as a species is debatable. It was ranked a species by Robins (1961) largely on the basis of his erroneous conclusion that the smoky sculpin intergraded with the "broadband sculpin." Because he regarded the smoky sculpin to be a subspecies of *C. bairdi*, the broadband sculpin thus also was conspecifically linked to *C. bairdi*. As a further corollary, because the broadband and *C. baileyi* co-occupy the extreme upper Tennessee and obviously are specifically distinct, the broadband was held to represent *C. bairdi* therein. Thus *C. baileyi* was unpaired and given species status.

We believe that *C. baileyi* is much more variable than formerly thought, and that it grades morphologically toward the smoky sculpin. We would be inclined to consider these conspecific except for unclear situations in the Watauga branch of the South Fork Holston in Tennessee, where the black and smoky sculpins may meet. Further, Strauss (1980) found genetic distinctions of (and within) *C. baileyi*. Species status of *C. baileyi* would be corroborated by the determination that it is more distantly related to *C. bairdi* than is the Clinch sculpin.

DESCRIPTION

Materials.—By systems, the following number of series (and numbers of specimens counted): Clinch 4(34); North Fork Holston 6(34); Middle Fork Holston 20(22); upper South Fork Holston 8(44); Whitetop Laurel Creek 4(23); Tennessee Laurel Creek 4(11); Beaverdam Creek 2(14). Color in life based on 11 series total from the Clinch and Middle and South forks of the Holston.

Anatomy.—A sculpin with an unmottled chin, first dorsal fin often blackened, lateral line usually incomplete, palatine tooth patch usually absent or very small, and pectoral rays usually 15; adults are 45–75 mm SL. Body and fins as described for *C. bairdi.*

Palatine tooth patches absent or, when present, almost always small; the percentages of sides with teeth: Clinch 0, North Fork 44, Middle Fork 11, upper South Fork 16, Whitetop Laurel 46, Tennessee Laurel 0, and Beaverdam Creek 50. Preopercular spines same as in *C. bairdi* except spine 2 often absent. Prickling almost always absent, very rarely slightly developed postpectorally in adult. Male genital papilla quite variable, flaplike and broadly triangular as in *C. bairdi,* or with a narrow tip much extended from a moderate or broad base, or nearly entirely elongate, narrow.

Meristics.—Lateral line development variable, usually incomplete in Clinch to upper South Fork Holston, pores (20)23–30(34), means 25.2–27.7 depending on population, endpoint usually area 4 or shorter, occasionally area 5, rarely 6, frequency of interruption 15–86% of specimens depending on the population; usually complete or almost so in remainder of South Fork system, pores (26)28–34(36), means 31.1–32.3, endpoint area usually 5 or 6, usually interrupted (71–91% of fish). Dorsal spines (6)7–8(9), usually 8 only in Clinch; dorsal rays (15)16–17(18), last ray very rarely unbranched; branched caudal rays (7)9(10); anal rays 12–13(14), last always branched; pelvic rays 4, but usually 3 in North Fork, rarely 3 in others; pectoral rays (13)15(16), often 14 in North Fork and 16 in upper South Fork. Cephalic lateralis pores: ST 3(4); LAT (4)5(6); SO (2)3(4); COR (0)1; IO (8)9–10(11); PM 10–11(12), median pores all are separate only in Middle Fork, united in 4–72% of other populations, overall united in 27% of 175 specimens.

Color in Preservative.—As described for *C. bairdi* except nuptial male usually somewhat darker overall, sometimes virtually all black, which was seen by us and Robins (1961) only in Middle Fork fish. Caudal base band notched posteriorly in about 20% of fish in all populations.

Color in Life Plate 26.—Essentially as in *C. bairdi* except as noted just above for nuptial male; a few large prespawning males from the Clinch had a fully red band on first dorsal fin margin.

Fish 186 *Cottus baileyi* adult male 68 mm SL (REJ 1054), VA, Smyth County, Middle Fork Holston River, 17 March 1984.

Fish 187 *Cottus baileyi* adult female 57 mm SL (REJ 1178), VA, Tazewell County, Little River, 11 March 1986.

COMPARISON

The black sculpin is distinguished from the Holston sculpin under the latter species. Black sculpins with small palatine tooth patches tend to have been misidentified as the Holston sculpin or *C. bairdi*.

Cottus baileyi is distinguished from *C. carolinae* by: (1) lateral line [incomplete or, if complete, usually interrupted posteriorly in *baileyi* vs. usually complete and uninterrupted in *carolinae*]; (2) pectoral rays usually [15 vs. 16–17]; (3) chin mottling [absent vs. usually moderate or strong]; (4) saddle width usually [moderate or wide vs. moderate or narrow, particularly narrow in Holston system]; (5) palatine tooth patch [absent or tiny vs. medium or large]; (6) preopercular spine 3 [slightly developed or absent vs. moderate or strong]; (7) adult size [usually less than 75 mm SL vs. generally larger].

BIOLOGY

During summer in the upper South Fork Holston, *C. baileyi* fed throughout daylight hours on whatever insect larvae it could catch. The bulk of these were mayflies, midges, blackflies, and craneflies. Crustaceans, water mites, and fishes were rarely taken (Novak and Estes 1974). The black sculpin hosted larvae of a unionid mussel (Neves et al. 1985).

Age at attainment of maturity, overall growth pattern, and sexual differences are probably similar to those of most eastern populations of *C. bairdi*. Most yearlings are immature. In samples with 10 or more specimens, a male was largest in 10, a female largest in 1, and sexes were of equal size in 1. Although considered a small species by Robins (1961), moderate size typifies adults of many populations. Adults taken during 17 February–24 April comprised 103 males of 45–78 mm SL, mean, 61, and 119 females 41–83 mm, mean, 55. The 83-mm female, the largest known specimen of the species, is 101 mm TL; it and most other specimens greater than 70 mm SL are from the Little River system of the Clinch.

Spawning occurs in late winter to mid-spring. In the Little River system, all females were in prespawning condition on 17 February 1985, 22 February 1987, and 11 March 1986, at 7.8°, 8.3°, and 14°C. Spawning had been in progress on or before 26 March 1987, at 7.2°C, based on the capture of gravid and spent females. Gravid females were taken from the end of March to mid-April in the South Fork Clinch River (Masnik 1974).

In the Middle Fork Holston at Marion during 1984, spawning may have just begun on 19 February, at the end of a warm spell (temperature not taken); females were bulging with ova and some had ova in the genital papilla. However, on 17 March at 1 rkm upstream, water 6.7°C, all females captured still appeared ready to spawn. On 24 April at the head of the Middle Fork, water 7.2°C, females were spent but some black, probably nest-guarding males were found (the only time we saw truly black males). On 22 April 1972 in lower Nicks Creek, a Middle Fork tributary, *C. baileyi* was associated with egg clusters. In the Middle Fork at the Nicks Creek mouth, gravid and spent females were taken on 1 April 1940, 8.3°C (Robins 1961; E. C. Raney's field notes).

Nest sites were under stones in shallow riffles. Mature ova in two females numbered 77 and 78 and averaged 3.4 mm in diameter (Robins 1961), about the size of the relatively large eggs produced by the smoky sculpin.

A hybrid *C. baileyi* × *C. carolinae* is described under the latter species.

HABITAT

Cottus baileyi is a fish of cool to cold spring runs, creeks, and streams of the Blue Ridge and the Valley and Ridge provinces. It occupies typically clear, moderate- and high-gradient waters. It was taken in order 2 and 3 sections of a North Fork Holston tributary (Garman et al. 1982); its lowest occurrence in the Clinch system is at an order 5 site in the Little River (Masnik 1974). In the upper South Fork Holston system, it occurred in the main channel, larger tributaries, and in a headwater spring (Novak and Estes 1974). In the Middle Fork Holston system, it was uncommon or rare in a spring-fed tributary (just above Marion) but was always common in the adjacent main river. Records from streams wider than about 15 m are rare and are of one or few individuals.

A primary restraint on the success of the black sculpin appears to be warm water; virtually all black sculpin records are from trout waters or those having such potential. In this respect, *C. baileyi* apparently differs on average from *C. bairdi*. Large juvenile and adult black sculpins inhabit runs and riffles of gravel to boulder and occasionally well-flowing parts of pools. The adults tend to be most common in shallow, swift riffles. Young and small juveniles frequently occupy stream margins and slow runs.

DISTRIBUTION   Map 130

The black sculpin is endemic to the extreme upper Tennessee drainage in western Virginia and just into northeastern Tennessee. It was identified from Doe Creek of the upper Watauga branch of the South Fork Holston in Tennessee (Robins 1961), but our samples from Doe Creek and its receiver (Roan Creek) resemble the smoky sculpin.

The most localized population occupies two major areas of springs in the Clinch system—the Little River watershed (described under Clinch sculpin) and the South Fork Clinch River. Masnik (1973) suggested that *C. baileyi* reached the Clinch from the Holston via subterranean drainage. Valley portions of the area have considerable large underground aquifers, many in caves, but crossflow may not have occurred under the main dividing ridge. In addition to stream capture, another possibility is that during glacial times *C. baileyi* was widespread in elevations lower than those now inhabited, and extended its range down the Holston and up the Clinch.

Abundance and Syntopy.—Often common or abundant. Often lives in fast water with the Holston sculpin or Clinch sculpin; usually in such cases either one of these forms or *C. baileyi* is scarce. *Cottus carolinae* almost always occurs with *C. baileyi*, but tends to occupy slower water.

REMARKS

Truly black-colored sculpins seem generally elusive or illusive in the upper Tennessee drainage. Better knowledge of the frequency and chronology of this color expression will contribute to determining the taxonomic status of *C. baileyi* and the smoky sculpin.

Name.—In recognition of the many contributions to North American ichthyology by Reeve M. Bailey, University of Michigan.

Slimy sculpin   *Cottus cognatus* (Richardson)

SYSTEMATICS

The slimy sculpin was described in 1836 from northern Canada. Its closest kin among eastern *Cottus* probably is *C. bairdi*. Two subspecies have been recognized in the northern sector of its range, *C. c. cognatus* and *C. c. gracilis* Heckel; the latter also extends southward into the central and eastern United States (McAllister and Lindsey 1961). Although these and a third, western, form have zoogeographic significance, McPhail and Lindsey (1970) believed the distinctions marginal, and that pending further study, subspecific names should be omitted. Other treatments of its variation in northern regions are by McAllister (1964), Scott and Crossman (1973), and Wells (1977).

The population in the Potomac drainage, which we regard as the southernmost of the slimy sculpin, presents an interesting systematic problem. Robins (1961) considered it to be an undescribed form which seemed to be related to *C. cognatus*. Strauss (1980) stated that it has been confused with *C. cognatus* and is most similar in morphometry to *C. bairdi*, but from genetic data he concluded that it was a separate species derived from *C. girardi*. The problem concerns five isolated subpopulations or population groups in the Potomac. We did not detect differences in morphology and color among the three Virginia subpopulations and one in West Virginia. Strauss had studied only a series of the northern Potomac subpopulation from Maryland. His and our morphological data indicate that the issue concerns a single Potomac form.

We regard the immediate ancestry of the Potomac form to be with typical *C. cognatus* for the following reasons. It agrees with *C. cognatus* and differs from *C. bairdi* or *C. girardi* or both by having: (1) 3 pelvic rays and usually 13–14 pectoral rays, both derived features of *C. cognatus*; (2) a relatively non-robust head; (3) a long series of dark blotches on the lower body, blotches tending to be separate from more dorsally located saddle-bands; (4) an unmottled chin; (5) first dorsal fin with pale margin (usually red-orange in life) moderate to wide; (6) developmental pattern of blackness beginning anteriorly and posteriorly in first dorsal fin, the "2-spotted" pattern; (7) small maximum size; and particularly, (8) a marked affinity for the coldest waters available. Potomac slimy sculpins are similar to *C. cognatus* in preopercular spine development, prickling, and shape of the genital papilla and caudal fin. Based on frequent syntopy of the three species in the Potomac, their phylogenetic affinities are relatively distant for eastern *Cottus*.

Distinctions of the Potomac slimy sculpin population from others of *C. cognatus* are: (1) mandibular canals united, 1 median chin pore; (2) palatine tooth patch almost always present, usually moderately developed; (3) last dorsal and anal rays almost always branched (doubled); and (4) genetic (Strauss 1980). The significance of the latter will be unclear until more than one Potomac subpopulation is analyzed genetically and character states are polarized. In *C.*

cognatus elsewhere, mandibular canals are separate, palatine teeth usually or always are absent, and, except in northwestern North America, the last dorsal and anal rays generally are unbranched (McAllister and Lindsey 1961; McAllister 1964).

The union of mandibular canals, generally a derived condition, is unusual in *Cottus*. In *C. cognatus* it is uniquely fixed in juveniles and adults of the Potomac population (*Description*). However, the other sculpins in the Potomac and some nearby drainages exhibit parallel divergence. Canal union is typical of *C. girardi* in the Potomac and James drainages (80% of 177 Virginia specimens), but rare or absent in all other taxa of the *carolinae* group. Union occurs occasionally in *C. bairdi* of the Potomac (8% of 146 specimens) and Rappahannock (13% of 15) and more often in the James (34% of 173). The geographically more distant *C. baileyi* also exhibits marked variation. Although mandibular canal characters frequently are useful at the species level in cottids (McAllister 1968), the variation noted here suggests localized lability and convergence among species.

The Potomac population of the slimy sculpin probably is the most distinctive of the species. The closely adjacent population, in the lower Susquehanna drainage of Pennsylvania (Letort Spring Run, Conodoguinet Creek), is similar to those northward except for frequent doubling of the last dorsal ray. We have not studied the subpopulation reported by Matthews et al. (1978) in the Conochocheague system of the northern Potomac, southern Pennsylvania, which is geographically closest to the lower Susquehanna; it could be quite instructive.

Strauss (1980) considered that whatever the evolutionary history of the Potomac form, it seems best served by recognition as a separate species. Because of its strong similarity to, and the variability elsewhere of, *C. cognatus* (particularly in derived states of the species), we apply that name to the Potomac form. It may, however, be recognizable as a separate subspecies.

[*Editor's note*: Based on current intensive study led by Richard L. Raesly at Frostburg State University, the authors now agree that the Potomac drainage population is a species distinct from *Cottus cognatus*. Jenkins has suggested its common name be checkered sculpin.]

DESCRIPTION

Materials.—Nineteen Potomac lots, 17 from Virginia, 2 from West Virginia; 49 specimens usually counted. Life color from 4 lots from the South Fork Shenandoah system.

Anatomy.—A sculpin with distinct blotches along lower body and 3 pelvic rays; adults are 35–65 mm SL. Form slender or moderately stocky; head small or moderate; caudal peduncle shallow or deep. Dorsal fins slightly or moderately conjoined; caudal fin rounded, truncate, or usually subtruncate.

Palatine tooth patch usually slightly or moderately developed, occasionally strong, rarely absent (2 of 73 specimens). Preopercular spine 1 moderate; spine 2 moderate, weak, or occasionally absent; spine 3 absent or often weak. Prickling absent or weak postpectorally. Male genital papilla flaplike, triangular, or occasionally narrow, tubular.

Meristics.—Lateral line markedly incomplete, endpoint area 1 or 2, rarely 3; pores (19)21–25(27), 1 specimen each had 3 and 5 interruptions and 30 and 33 pores. Dorsal spines 7–8; dorsal rays 16–17(18), last ray branched (unbranched in 1 of 49 fish); branched caudal rays 9; anal rays 11–13(14), last ray branched in only 1 fish; pelvic rays 3 (148 sides); pectoral rays 13–14(15). Cephalic lateralis pores: ST 3(5); LAT (4)5(7); SO 3(5); COR 1; IO (7)8–9(11); PM 10–11, median pores united in 272 fish including several young, partly divided in 2 young, fully divided in 5 young.

Color in Preservative.—Juvenile, adult female, and nonbreeding male with pale to moderately dusky ground shade, dark marks usually prominent. Saddles 1–3 moder-

Fish 188 *Cottus cognatus* adult male 51 mm SL (REJ 1064), VA, Augusta County, Mossy Creek, 3 April 1984.

Fish 189 *Cottus cognatus* adult female 46 mm SL (REJ 1065), VA, Augusta County, Mossy Creek, 3 April 1984.

ate in width; small saddle often present under first dorsal fin posteriorly; saddle 1 usually ends at lateral line, saddles 2 and 3 there or slightly below. Upper side between saddles usually not prominently marked, occasionally with fine reticulation, vague scrawling, or a few distinct small spots. Lower side appearing checkered by a series of (4)6–8(10) dark or black, small to large blotches, best developed on urosome; most blotches separate from or narrowly connected to bold midside marks; blotches round, square, rectangular, or irregular; blotches tend to be most distinctive in small fish; smaller vague marks or peppering often present between blotches. Caudal base band usually notched posteriorly.

Chin usually uniformly pigmented, occasionally slightly mottled anteriorly owing to darkening at mandibular pores. Side of head with 1–4 spots, blotches, or lines radiating from lower half of orbit.

First dorsal fin darkened anteriorly and posteriorly, sometimes weakly tessellated. Other fins usually distinctly tessellated, occasionally all fins weakly so, or often only the anal and pelvic nontessellated. Pectoral base generally with large dark spot.

Nuptial male body black anteriorly, dark sooty posteriorly, markings nearly masked, belly gray. Fins black, excepting a moderate to wide pale first dorsal fin margin. Some large apparently egg-brooding males with dark or black head have body markings only slightly obscured and all fins dusky, except for partly blackened first dorsal. Dark sooty or black males are known north to Alaska (Koster 1936; Miller and Kennedy 1946; Morrow 1980).

Color in Life Plate 26.—Juvenile, adult female, and nonbreeding male with pale ground shade of upper head and body being yellow-olive to pale olive; darker marks tan to pale olive; darkest marks dark olive, dark brown, or olive-black. Lower body dark marks as above, tending slightly paler; these interspersed with creamy pale yellow, pale lime, or very faintly blue-tinged spots and scrawls. First dorsal fin margin pale or medium yellow or orange, brightest in larger specimens. Spines of first dorsal and rays of other fins, when tessellated, pale olive to olive-black/pale yellow; membranes colorless or pale yellow wash.

Nuptial male essentially as described under preservation; blackness of head and anterior body in peak development with velvet tone. Paler males with body ground pale to medium olive; fins retain yellow to olive marks. First

dorsal marginal band moderate or wide, creamy only, yellow, or bright orange.

Larvae.—Described by Koster (1936) and Heufelder (1982d).

COMPARISON

In Virginia, *C. cognatus* warrants separation from the Potomac drainage populations of *C. bairdi* and *C. girardi*. Rough-sorting of collections by the blotching pattern on the lower side can enable a high percentage of correct recognition of *C. cognatus*, sometimes 100% after a concept of the differences is gained. In *C. cognatus* the lower blotches generally are bold, and most are largely or entirely separated from midside blotches. In *C. bairdi* the lower side is usually mottled or scrawled; if blotched, the blotches are interconnected to each other or to those at midheight of the body. *Cottus girardi* is intermediate, but its high degree of interconnection of lower side blotches to those above generally distinguishes it.

Additional means of quick-sorting *C. cognatus* from Potomac *C. bairdi* are: (1) notch at midheight of posterior margin of caudal base band [usually present in *cognatus vs.* absent in *bairdi*]; (2) dark marks of fin tessellations [finer, more numerous, particularly on caudal where 5–7 marks develop on median rays *vs.* wider, fewer, usually 3–5 on caudal (tessellation may be absent in pale specimens and adult males of both species)]; (3) reddish in caudal fin [not seen in *cognatus vs.* present, unless masked in dark adults].

To further aid in separating *C. bairdi*, we recommend (Table 7): (4) pelvic rays [3 in *cognatus vs.* 4 in about 90% of *bairdi*]; (5) median chin pores [1 in all but some young *vs.* 2 in about 90% of *bairdi*]. Certain other proposed methods for distinguishing these species (Hubbs and Lagler 1949) are of little or no use in Virginia. McAllister's (1964) ratio of caudal peduncle and postorbital lengths separated 82% of Virginia specimens (60 fish), but his and our methods of measurement may not be exactly alike; other problems exist with the character (Godkin et al. 1982).

For distinguishing *C. cognatus* from *C. girardi*, in addition to using the lower side pattern (see above), try: (1) pelvic rays [3 in *cognatus vs.* 4 in *girardi*]; (2) pectoral rays usually [13–14 *vs.* 15]; (3) chin pigmentation [almost always uniform, occasionally darkened at mandibular pores *vs.* often moderately or strongly mottled posterior to pores, occasionally uniform]; (4) first dorsal fin membrane pigmentation (character not applicable to adult males having the black median band) [2-spotted, conspicuously blacker anteriorly and posteriorly, much more so than in midlength (Figure 55A) *vs.* pale anteriorly and posteriorly, or darker anteriorly than posteriorly, or uniformly mottled (Figure 55D)]; (5) preopercular spine 3 [absent or weak (Figures 60E, F, H) *vs.* usually moderate (Figure 60D), occasionally weak or (Figure 60B) strong]; (6) size, SL [rarely larger than 65 mm *vs.* adults often larger than 65 mm].

BIOLOGY

Cottus cognatus feeds mainly on insect larvae, particularly midges, and takes worms, small crustaceans, clams, and snails. It feeds heavily on isopods and amphipods in spring runs and other habitats where these crustaceans often are abundant. Fishes and fish eggs are seldom taken. Small slimy sculpins tend to rely on microcrustaceans (Koster 1937; Petrosky and Waters 1975; Craig and Wells 1976; Morrow 1980; Becker 1983). Feeding occurs during both day and night (B. D. Snyder and R. F. Denoncourt, in litt.), but apparently mostly at night in some waters (Newman and Waters 1984).

Maturity was first attained by most fish at age 2, rarely age 1 or 3, in New York, Michigan, and Minnesota (Koster 1936; Petrosky and Waters 1975; Anderson 1985). In Saskatchewan and Alaska, maturation generally was delayed until age 4, and closely corresponded to a minimum size of 67–75 mm TL (Craig and Wells 1976). Most of our apparent yearlings were immature during spring. An age-7 fish was reported by Craig and Wells (1976).

Average lengths of age-3 specimens from two Michigan sites were 72 and 90 mm TL (Becker 1983); males tend to grow faster than females there (Anderson 1985). Age-3 Alaskan fish were 54–79 mm TL, mean, 65 (Craig and Wells 1976). From New York populations, Koster (1936) gave lengths of mature males as 43–100 mm SL, mean, 69, females 39–85 mm, mean, 54. Virginia slimy sculpins typically are smaller and the size disparity between the sexes is

not as great. Our 98 obviously mature (April) males were 43–66 mm SL, mean, 50, and 101 females 35–65 mm, mean, 46. In 12 collections with 10 or more specimens, a male was the largest in 8, female in 2, sizes equal in 2. The largest Virginia specimen is a 74-mm SL, 92-mm TL male. The largest reported *C. cognatus*, apparently from Saskatchewan, was 127 or 121 mm TL (Van Vliet 1964 *in*, respectively, Craig and Wells 1976 and Morrow 1980).

Cottus cognatus spawned in New York during 27 March–3 May, water 4.5–10°C (Koster 1936). In Minnesota, spawning occurred in late April (Petrosky and Waters 1975), and northward to Alaska it extended into June; water ranged 3–11.5°C, 6°C or less being optimal (Craig and Wells 1976; Heufelder 1982d). In Lake Ontario, spawning occurred during 11–25 May at 4–6°C (Godkin et al. 1982). Breeding was in progress in Mossy and Whisky creeks, Virginia, on 3 April 1984, at 8.9–10°C; egg clutches and many gravid females were found. Gravid and spent females were taken on 18 April 1972 in the Middle River, Virginia. Nest sites and spawning of *C. cognatus* are typical of the genus (Koster 1936). We found breeding fish in a temporarily watered, heavily silted section of upper Mossy Creek. This species also spawns in somewhat deep areas of lakes (Foltz 1976; Heufelder 1982d). Fecundity ranges 42–1,420, typical nests have 150–600 eggs, and 10 clutches may be in a nest (Morrow 1980; Heufelder 1982d). A nest in Mossy Creek contained about 8 clutches.

Hybridization with *C. bairdi* was found in a Pennsylvania stream (Strauss 1986) and may occur extensively in Lake Ontario (Godkin et al. 1982).

HABITAT

The wide range of habitat populated by the slimy sculpin includes small rocky brooks, silted vegetated spring runs, large rivers, and shallows and depths of oligotrophic lakes; it also has been found in brackish tide pools in northern Canada. Large juveniles and adults typically occupy runs and riffles; young and often older fish are found in slow runs and pools. Individuals of these life stages occur on hard substrates, sand, and silt; small fish often live among plants.

Cottus cognatus is an obligate coldwater species. Its preferred temperature and upper lethal limits are 13° and 25°C in New Brunswick (Symons et al. 1976). For Lake Michigan fish, the preferred range is 9–12°C and the ultimate upper lethal temperature is 26.5°C (Otto and Rice 1977). Summer temperatures at collection sites in Iowa were 11–17°C, mean, 14, 6°C lower than those of *C. bairdi* (Johnson 1972). In Wisconsin the

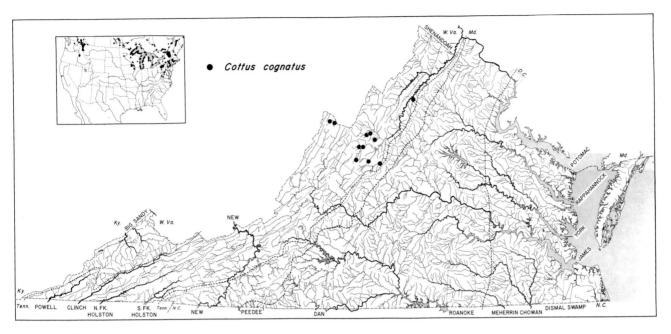

Map 131   Slimy sculpin.

summer average was 13.8°C (Becker 1983). It was not found in New York except in waters capable of supporting brook trout (Greeley 1928).

The maximum water temperature record for *C. cognatus* in Virginia is 20°C, on 22 May; summer temperature-associated records are unavailable. In Virginia, this species is restricted or almost so to high-volume spring runs and more-typical streams just below major springs. Most records are from 2–5 m wide watercourses, exceptions being upper Mossy Creek (0.6–2 m wide above its main source) and the Middle River (10–12 m). These alkaline Valley and Ridge Province waters issue from limestone aquifers; most traverse pastures and appear to be rather fertile. They vary from rocky to almost entirely silted; aquatic macrophytes range from absent to profuse there. Normally they are clear but most or all become turbid from rainstorms.

The extreme localization of *C. cognatus* in Virginia (Map 131) is obvious relative to the general distribution of *C. bairdi* in the Valley and Ridge and Blue Ridge provinces of the Potomac–Shenandoah (Map 130). Stable, low, water temperature apparently is crucial. Cold springs of Virginia usually emerge at 9–13°C and vary but 1–3°C, whereas typical surface streams probably fluctuate 17–22°C over a year (Collins et al. 1930). The absence of *C. cognatus* from many valley and montane trout streams indicates that their summer temperatures periodically are too high or that *C. bairdi* is more successful at moderate temperatures.

DISTRIBUTION   Map 131

The cold-adapted slimy sculpin ranges from Siberia across the northern and much of the southern extent of Canada (Walters 1955; McAllister and Lindsey 1961), fingering down the Rockies into Idaho, the upper Mississippi basin to Iowa, the southern Great Lakes, and from New England down the Appalachians to the Potomac drainage in Virginia, where it has a very disjunctive distribution.

Five subpopulations or population groups are recognizable on a geographic basis in the Potomac: (1) tributaries of Conochocheague Creek and the Monocacy River, northern Potomac system proper, Pennsylvania and Maryland (Matthews et al. 1978; Strauss 1980); (2) three streams, four sites in Berkeley and Jefferson counties, West Virginia, tributaries of the Potomac River just above the Shenandoah River mouth (Cincotta et al. 1986a); (3) the South Branch Potomac River and its tributary, Strait Creek, Highland County, Virginia (the first stream was erroneously termed South Fork by Jenkins and Musick 1979, and their Laurel Fork record is based on an atypical specimen of *C. bairdi*); also possibly in the West Virginia section of the South Branch Potomac (Cincotta et al. 1986a); (4) Lower Pass Run of Hawksbill Creek, a South Fork Shenandoah River tributary, Page County, Virginia; and (5) the upper South Fork Shenandoah River system, Augusta County, Virginia—Naked Creek and Mossy Creek of the North River, the upper Middle River and two of its tributaries, Christians and Back creeks, and Baker Spring of the South River.

The persistence of *C. cognatus* in the Potomac drainage is related to cold water. The Maryland population is in a high-volume spring that feeds a trout hatchery (Strauss 1980; Lee et al. 1984). One of the two Pennsylvania populations is in Falling Spring Creek (Matthews et al. 1978), a famous limestone trout stream. Cooling of lower Strait Creek, also supporting a trout farm, by a large spring was discussed by Ross (1959a); the surrounding area of the South Branch Potomac has several major springs (Collins et al. 1930). Lower Pass Run has a wild-trout fishery maintained by springs, above which the stream partly dries in summer. The prime trout water of Mossy Creek is a narrow and deep spring run of about 12 rkm length, beginning with the main spring at Mt. Solon and fed by numerous seepages. Baker Spring, the single largest spring listed for the Potomac–Shenandoah of Virginia by Collins et al. (1930), flows at 20 m³/minute. The largest stream site supporting *C. cognatus*, in the Middle River at the Route 250 bridge, is chilled by springs within a few rkm above (L. O. Mohn, personal communication). This species was taken there in all five collections during 1956–1983; we did not find it among Ross' (1959a) three collections from lower Middle River.

Although populations of *C. cognatus* may exist elsewhere in the Shenandoah system, it is odd that none have been found in the North Fork watershed, and only one is known from the South Fork below its main branches. Most of the North Fork and middle and lower South Fork watersheds have geology and groundwater potential similar to the upper South Fork (VDCED 1968).

Records of *C. cognatus* in Virginia south of the Potomac are erroneous. That plotted in the York drainage (McAllister et al. *in* Lee et al. 1980) is from a stray transfer-dot (D. S. Lee, in litt.); errant records in other regions are noted by Bailey (1982b). The often-cited James drainage record (Raney 1950) is based on five specimens (CU 10126; UMMZ), most of which agree with typical *C. cognatus* as to pelvic ray count and palatine teeth. In the latter character and their unfused mandibular canals, they differ from Potomac *C. cognatus*. Although faded, they still suggest the color pattern of *C. bairdi*. Robins (1954) and we identified them as *C. bairdi*.

Abundance and Syntopy.—This species is common or abundant in upper and middle Mossy Creek, upper Naked Creek, and upper Middle River. Numbers of specimens preserved by others indicate similar population levels in upper Back Creek and Pass Run.

Among 6 of the 10 Virginia populations of *C. cognatus*, *C. bairdi* generally is common or abundant. *Cottus girardi* was found with *C. cognatus* in four streams and generally was rare. *Cottus cognatus* is the only sculpin known in Mossy and Naked creeks; no other sculpin species was taken by other collectors in Back Creek or Baker Spring.

REMARKS

The slimy sculpin in Virginia is a relict of colder climate that prevailed during Pleistocene glacial times. With interglacial warming, its populations contracted into the year-round coldest waters. Its presumably local differentiation in the Potomac drainage probably predated the last glaciation; the similarity among the subpopulations would have stemmed from range expansion and interbreeding during a glaciation. The pearl dace *Margariscus margarita* has had a parallel distributional history in the Potomac, but it persists in many more streams than *C. cognatus*.

We are unable to identify factors other than temperature that critically limit *C. cognatus*. High gradient such as in Blue Ridge streams seems relatively unimportant, because *C. cognatus* populates strong riffles. Most *C. cognatus* streams of Virginia are rather alkaline (Collins et al. 1930); this species occupies such conditions elsewhere but also lives in acidic waters (e.g., Koster 1936). Siltation does not appear to be a major general limiting factor. Heavy siltation of Mossy Creek may have caused the demise of its native brook trout population, but *C. cognatus* flourishes there; persistence of the sculpin may be due to its habit of cleaning and spawning on the underside of objects and to the dense population of arthropod foods among lotic vegetation. An unusual turbidity and silt load apparently caused a low year-class of *C. cognatus* in Minnesota; the population rebounded by increased growth and decreased mortality of older fish (Petrosky and Waters 1975).

Cottus cognatus was nominated for special concern status in Virginia by Jenkins and Musick (1979). However, from its later discovery in 3 streams, now 10 in all, and recognition of its silt tolerance, we do not believe that it clearly merits protective status in the state. We caution however, that siltation probably contributed to its demise in streams with insufficient flow to prevent heavy sedimentation throughout. Removal of riparian vegetative cover probably allowed water temperatures to elevate beyond tolerance in previously marginal streams.

The single identified Maryland *C. cognatus* population is considered threatened (Lee et al. 1984). Restudy of *C. "bairdi"* may reveal more populations there. The status of *C. cognatus* in West Virginia is similar to that in Maryland (Cincotta et al. 1986a).

Name.—cognatus, "kindred," was applied by Sir John Richardson because of the slimy sculpin's similarity to a European sculpin.

Broadband sculpins   *Cottus* spp.

Three undescribed forms of *Cottus* are here given a common name for the river system to which each is endemic—Holston sculpin, Clinch sculpin, and Bluestone sculpin (Map 132). Partly for convenience they are collectively dubbed "broadband sculpins," translated from the unpublished scientific name proposed by Robins (1954) in reference to wide saddles. They constitute a sharply localized assemblage; one form is confined to southwestern Virginia, the others nearly so. They are big-spring and cool-stream isolates. Their characteristics are given in Tables 7 and 8.

With a grouped concept of broadband sculpins, the broadband was regarded a subspecies of *C. bairdi* by Robins (1954:141) "entirely" on the basis of its supposed intergradation in the middle Clinch system with the Tennessee drainage Highlands form of *C. bairdi*, the undescribed smoky sculpin. The site, in Little Sycamore Creek, Tennessee, is distant from the nearest populations of both forms—not unreasonable, as some sculpins occur as relicts in coldwater oases. Robins concluded that the broadband sculpin, not *C. baileyi* (which occurs in much the same area as the broadband—Map 130), best represented the *bairdi* group in the extreme upper Tennessee. He noted, however, that the middle Clinch population needed more study.

The stated basis for subspecific status of the broadband sculpin became irrelevant when we found the single putative intergrade sample (UMMZ 154585) to be *C. carolinae*. The specimens agree with *C. carolinae* particularly in color pattern and preopercular spination. Their low lateral line pore and pectoral ray counts could indicate a broadband intergrade. However, we interpret these data as extending the wide zone of intergradation of *C. c. carolinae* and *C. c. zopherus* slightly farther up the drainage into the middle Clinch system. We found similar *C. carolinae* in the nearby lower Powell system (i.e., another range extension).

Thus broadband sculpins are partly divorced from *C. bairdi*. Two of the forms act as biological species in syntopy with *C. carolinae* and *C. baileyi*, one of the reasons Jenkins (1976) recognized broadband sculpins as a species. *Cottus baileyi* actually is the replacement of *C. bairdi* in the extreme upper Tennessee.

Questions now posed concern the number and status of taxa of broadband sculpins. Robins (1954) recognized one subspecies based on the Holston and Bluestone populations. Masnik (1974) first identified the broadband (as *C. bairdi* subspecies) from the Clinch, and noted some differences of that population from the Holston population. We find that each population represents a separate taxon.

Determination of the status of the three forms based on reproductive criteria in nature is not currently possible; although their small ranges are closely adjacent, they are allopatric (Map 132). The Bluestone form is isolated in the New drainage. The Clinch and Holston forms are only two ridges apart in the upper Tennessee drainage but are separated by 730 rkm (from Stony Creek of the Clinch to the junction of the North and South forks of Holston River); no population is known in the intervening North Fork Holston.

Despite close geographic proximity and living in somewhat similar ecological settings, they have been isolated and have diverged (Table 8). The differences are about as substantial as among most eastern sculpin species. In particular the forms look different in life, based on close study of many specimens in the field and in aquaria. They do not appear to form a monophyletic group; no obviously advanced characteristic has been identified to unite them. None of the three are alignable with certainty to either the *bairdi* group or *carolinae* group (although possible allocations to these are considered in species accounts). They qualify as evolutionary species; they are separate lineages. We consider them species also for convenience in future study; separate descriptions avoid confusion caused by data lumping.

If any of the three forms are to be regarded as conspecific, we would restrict that status to the Holston and Clinch forms, and recognize them as separate subspecies under the vernacular broadband sculpin. The Bluestone sculpin could retain its appellation as a separate species. The Holston and Clinch forms are more similar to each other in morphology and color than to the Bluestone sculpin. However, the indicated breeding times of the Holston and Clinch forms are at opposite extremes for the group, with little or no overlap (Table 8).

REMARKS

Broadband sculpins exemplify the cyclic frustration and progress in identification and understanding of *Cottus*. Considerable study was needed during several field trips and in the laboratory before we could accurately identify sculpins in some Tennessee and New drainage streams. Although we made minor breakthroughs, subsequent forays continued to reveal new problems. Finally it dawned that the "broadband sculpin" was a complex of three forms. For too long we had tried unsuccessfully to make them fit concepts of other species or each other. Upon gaining some comfort in our knowledge of Virginia populations, questions of species identity cropped up nearby in the Tennessee drainage and were only partly settled. We wonder what new problems await farther down the drainage.

Holston sculpin   *Cottus* sp.

SYSTEMATICS

The Holston sculpin is recognized from the South Fork and Middle Fork Holston systems of the upper Tennessee drainage, Virginia and Tennessee. No difference was found between the populations of the two systems.

The intended holotype of the broadband sculpin, as a subspecies of *C. bairdi*, was a Holston sculpin, but the unpublished description (Robins 1954) gave about equal weight to two series of the Bluestone sculpin. The Holston sculpin is most similar to the Clinch sculpin, but we lack a compelling reason to unite them taxonomically.

The Holston sculpin may be allocatable to the *bairdi* group based on the moderate or reduced state of its preopercular armature, palatine tooth patches, and body prickling. In average body form it seems somewhat intermediate between the *bairdi* and *carolinae* groups. Its typical caudal fin shape is like that of the *carolinae* group. Its complete lateral line is typical of *C. carolinae* in the Tennessee drainage, differing from the distinctly incomplete line of most *C. bairdi* and *C. baileyi*. However, regional representatives of both the *bairdi* and *carolinae* groups have a lateral-line condition that is atypical of their group.

In coloration the Holston sculpin has a mixture of or intermediacy between character states of the two groups in chin pattern, saddle width, lateral band orientation, and first dorsal fin margin. It has no indication of the 2-spot dorsal fin pattern of the *bairdi* group, but the full extent of that feature in the *bairdi* group needs study, as does the peak nuptial male Holston sculpin.

The Holston sculpin acts as a stable biological species in the midst of *C. baileyi* and *C. carolinae*; the three species live together plentifully. The Holston sculpin may be an early derivative of the *bairdi* lineage. Its present form may have arisen through long-past hybridization of a population each of the *bairdi* and *carolinae* groups.

DESCRIPTION

Materials.—Thirty-five Virginia series including counts from 77 specimens. Life color from 8 lots of large juveniles and adults.

Anatomy.—A broad-saddled sculpin with most fins slightly or moderately tessellated, and the chin slightly mottled or unmottled; adults are 65–80 mm SL. Form of head and body moderate or somewhat robust; eye moderate, usually 6.3–7.5% SL. Dorsal and anal fin height moderate or high; dorsal fins usually slightly connected, never separated by a gap; caudal fin subtruncate or truncate, very rarely rounded; dorsal spines and rays moderate or thin.

Palatine tooth patch moderately or well developed, occasionally slightly developed, rarely absent (in 3 of 108 sides). Preopercular spine 1 strong; spines 2 and 3 moderate or weak, occasionally absent. Prickling moderately developed as a postpectoral patch. Male genital papilla usually moderate in length and width, flat or oval, usually well-rounded distally, sometimes elongate and narrow.

Meristics.—Lateral line almost always complete, endpoint area 6, rarely anterior part of area 5, pores (31)32–34(36). Dorsal spines 7–8(9); dorsal rays 16–18, last occasionally single; branched caudal rays (8)9; anal rays (12)13–14, last always branched; pelvic rays 4; pectoral rays (15)16(17). Cephalic lateralis pores: ST 3(5); LAT 5; SO 3; COR 1(2); IO (8)9; PM 11(12), median pores united in 19% of 72 fish.

Color in Preservative.—Upper body ground shade moderately dusky to dark, darker scrawling and mottling usually sparse or absent; upper body often considerably black-spotted; saddles moderately intense or bold except saddle 1 often absent. Saddles 2 and 3 moderate or very wide; edges of saddle-bands usually moderately defined, often irregular; anterior edge of saddles usually concave, overall usually markedly extended anteroventrad; bands 2 and 3 variably slanted or, often, largely absent; lower portion of band 3, when band short, generally not represented by distinctive spot or small blotch on flank. Lower side usually mottled, sometimes with one or few small irregular diffuse blotches. Caudal base band usually markedly extended anteroventrad; barely or not ringing base of upper and lower caudal rays; posterior edge vertical or convex and unnotched.

Fish 190 *Cottus* sp., Holston sculpin, adult male 99 mm SL (REJ 1169), VA, Washington County, Middle Fork Holston River, 6 January 1986.

Fish 191 *Cottus* sp., Holston sculpin, adult male 81 mm SL (REJ 1079), VA, Washington County, South Fork Holston River, 24 April 1984.

Chin unmottled or, equally frequently, slightly mottled anteriorly, rarely moderately mottled. Head dorsum dark to dusky; side usually mostly mottled; spot, smudge, or short oblique bar usually present on cheek; operculum usually darkest posteriorly.

First dorsal fin with narrow pale margin, margin not sharply defined; spines usually grading uniformly dusky to dark, sometimes vaguely tessellated; membranes usually slightly and uniformly dusky, occasionally mottled. Second dorsal and caudal rays slightly or moderately tessellated, dark marks distinctly the longest; membranes usually vaguely mottled, occasionally vaguely marbled. Anal and pectoral rays usually well tessellated; membranes of anal pale, of pectoral dusky. Pelvic fin usually pale, rays occasionally slightly tessellated. Pectoral base generally dark or vaguely mottled, very rarely with a large blotch.

Nuptial color and sexual dichromatism unknown. The largest known male (Fish 190) was taken in reproductive condition and has a darker (but not black) head and chin than most fish seen in other seasons. Its anterior parts are not much darker than posterior ones; the darkness may be related to the size of the fish or to living under dark rocks. Three smaller reproductive males taken with the dark one have typical shades, the same as females.

Color in Life   Plate 26.—Upper head and body ground shade tan-olive to true olive, rarely olive-gray, sometimes with mustard tinge; mottling and reticulation olive-brown, occasionally russet; saddle-bands dark olive, olive-black, or dark brown; lower side pale areas pale yellow, creamy gold, or yellow-green; venter off-white; iris brassy around inner edge.

First dorsal fin margin tinged pale orange about spine tips, orange often absent midway between spine tips. Robins (1954) noted a wide bright orange margin on the first dorsal fin, but his color photo may be lost (J. Homa, in litt.); the fish may have been *C. baileyi*. We saw no such margin in our eight extensively studied samples or in many other carefully examined samples. First dorsal spines uniformly olive or olive-black, or tessellated olive-black/olive; membranes very pale olive or colorless.

Second dorsal rays tessellated olive to black, occasionally russet/yellow-olive to pale; membranes colorless, faint yellow, or, when marbled, dark areas sometimes pale orange or russet. Caudal fin as in second dorsal, plus pale tessellations and distal margin occasionally yellow or pale orange. Anal rays tessellated dark gray/pale yellow; membranes off-white. Pelvic fin all white or tessellated pale gray/white. Pectoral fin as caudal, except basally often pale orange. Color same year-round; no sexual dichromatism detected except that largest males may exhibit darker head.

COMPARISON

The Holston sculpin is distinguished from other broadband sculpins in Table 8.

Separated from *C. baileyi* by: (1) lateral line [almost always complete, uninterrupted, usually 32–34 pores in Holston sculpin *vs.* usually incomplete and interrupted, usually 31 or fewer pores in *baileyi*]; (2) palatine tooth patch [moderately or well developed *vs.* absent or occasionally slightly developed]; (3) prickling postpectorally [moderate *vs.* almost always absent, rarely slight]; (4) chin mottling [absent or slight, melanophores often moderate sized *vs.* almost always absent, melanophores minute].

Distinguished from *C. c. carolinae* by: (1) saddle width [moderate or wide in Holston sculpin *vs.* narrow in South and Middle Fork Holston populations of *carolinae*]; (2) chin mottling [absent or slight *vs.* moderate or strong].

BIOLOGY

Holston sculpins prey on a variety of benthic immature aquatic insects; 1 of 14 consumed a crayfish (H. J. Rolfs, in litt.). Most individuals in a series from the lower South Fork Holston River on 11 November 1972 apparently matured as almost 2-year-olds. Thirty-two immature fish, apparently almost 1 year old, were 37–48 mm SL, mean, 44. All but two of the remaining specimens in the series were clearly mature, those mature being 21 males, 68–80 mm SL, mean, 75, and 26 females, 63–84 mm, mean, 72. The exceptions were two males, 68 and 76 mm, with small testes. The largest known specimen is a male 99 mm SL, 117 mm TL from Virginia.

A November–December spawning period was indicated by the South Fork Holston fish taken on 11 November 1972; their gonads were fully ripe or almost so. Less apparent were the maturity status of many fish and the spawning time in the Middle Fork Holston below and just above Marion on 17 December 1985. At the lower site, near the mouth of Walker Creek, water 5°C, a male of 66 mm SL and three females 57, 62, and 68 mm had large gonads; however, 17 other adult-sized fish (55–66 mm) were either spent or immature. At 16 rkm upstream, in the main channel and in an adjacent short spring run at Mt. Carmel, water 5.5° and 12°C respectively, all Holston sculpins appeared immature; six were 64–76 mm. Spent or immature females of 68–84 mm and a milting male of 71 mm were taken at the Mt. Carmel site on 27 January 1985, water 1° and 11°C in the channel and spring run. Reproduction may continue into January. On 6 January 1986, water 2°C, four milting males, 65–99 mm SL, were caught in the lower Middle Fork among slab rubble. On the same date and temperature in the lower South Fork, both females found, 72 and 82 mm, were gravid.

HABITAT

The Holston sculpin lives in typically clear streams of moderate to high gradient and varying tempera-

tures. It extends from the lower portions of the South and Middle forks of the Holston into their headwaters, lower sections of some major tributaries, and short spring runs. The variety of habitats is about that occupied by the Clinch sculpin. The Middle Fork has aspects of a limestone stream; its lower portion is warm. Much of the lower South Fork is cool freestone water, although generally alkaline (Novak 1968; Wolitz 1972; Jenkins and Burkhead 1975b). Large juveniles and adults favor runs and riffles of unsilted gravel, rubble, and boulder, and generally reside under rubble.

DISTRIBUTION   Map 132

The Holston sculpin is known with certainty only from the upper Holston system of the upper Tennessee drainage. Its range in Virginia is contiguous in the South and Middle forks, down to South Holston Reservoir. Its apparent absence from the North Fork Holston may be related to higher summer water temperature, which reaches 26°C in much of the length. Although it occupies small cold springs in the South and Middle forks (and could do so in the North Fork system), such occurrences may be occasional and nonreproductive. Records of *C. bairdi*, as the Holston sculpin often has been identified, from the North Fork by Feeman (1980) are based on *C. baileyi* or discarded specimens probably of the latter.

The range of the Holston sculpin becomes unclear below Virginia, partly due to impoundments. This species was found in the South Fork just below the Virginia line prior to impoundment, and much farther downstream during 1972 in the tailwater at Riverside. It may simply drop out of the upper Tennessee fauna just below the Watauga system, the largest South Fork Holston tributary in Tennessee. Robins (1954) listed a series (CU 25953) from Doe River of the Watauga; we agree that it is of typical Holston sculpins. A problematic sample (UMMZ 157428) from another Watauga tributary, Elk River, was identified by Robins as the broadband sculpin, but he considered it to resemble in some ways the smoky sculpin form of *C. bairdi*. We think it is the smoky sculpin, and so identified several other Watauga series.

Abundance and Syntopy.—Generally uncommon in the South and Middle forks of Holston River. Abundant in a riffle–run of the lower South Fork in 1972 (Jenkins and Burkhead 1975b) and 1983, but not found there in January 1986. Occurs in all sections with *C. c. carolinae*, although the latter tends to occupy slower current. Lives with and is usually numerically dominated by *C. baileyi* in the upper South and Middle forks, in most of Smyth County in the South Fork, down into Marion in the Middle Fork.

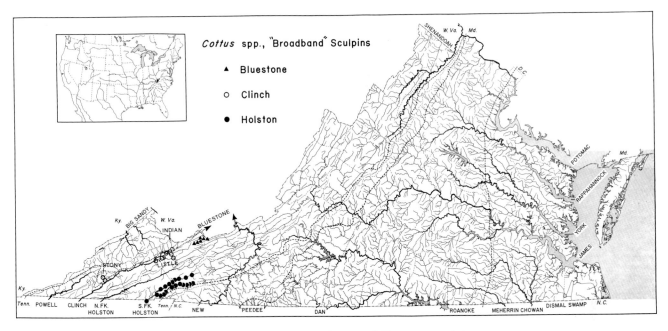

Map 132 Broadband sculpins: Holston sculpin, Clinch sculpin, and Bluestone sculpin.

REMARKS

Initially the Holston sculpin was the best known of the three broadband sculpins, because it occurred along major highways traveled by most fish collectors. However, with the recent recognition of the other two forms as distinct, and the ease in capturing them in numbers, they were focused upon. It was not until winter 1985–1986 that we finally studied in the field Holston sculpins that were spawning or about to. Still, the taxonomically important nuptial male Holston sculpin awaits discovery—unless future-captured specimens reveal that we already have examined males in peak breeding condition. The *Cottus* of the Watauga and Tennessee River tributaries farther south also deserve study during winter and spring breeding times to clarify the ranges of the Holston, smoky, and black sculpins.

Clinch sculpin   *Cottus* sp.

SYSTEMATICS

This broadband sculpin form is known only from three small parts of the upper Clinch River system in Virginia. Few, slight differences occur among the three populations (termed the Stony Creek, Little River, and Clinch River–Indian Creek populations).

Among broadband sculpins, the Clinch sculpin is most similar to the Holston sculpin. It is not an intermediate form, being extreme for the group in vagueness of fin patterns, the often rounded caudal fin, smaller palatine tooth patch, stockiness of large nuptial males, and, as far as is known, blackening of nuptial males.

The Clinch sculpin may belong to the *bairdi* group, based on the robust form of large nuptial males; reduced preopercular spination, palatine tooth patch size, body prickling, and chin mottling; rounded caudal fin; and low pectoral ray count. The darkened patches or slashes occasionally present in the first dorsal fin of the Clinch sculpin may be a transformation state of the 2-spot pattern common in the *bairdi* group. The generally complete lateral line of the Clinch sculpin is dissimilar from the typical *C. bairdi* condition, but completeness is common in some *bairdi*-group populations of the upper Tennessee drainage (e.g., the smoky sculpin and South Fork Holston *C. baileyi*). Ecologically the Clinch sculpin fits into the *bairdi* group, particularly through the latter two forms; at least two of its three populations are largely restricted to cool or cold water.

DESCRIPTION

Materials.—Sixteen samples; counts from 83 specimens. Color in life from 10 lots.

Anatomy.—A broad-saddled sculpin with the anterior edge of the 2nd and 3rd lateral body bands usually oriented vertically (and the anteroventral portion of the 3rd band

Fish 192 *Cottus* sp., Clinch sculpin, adult male 66 mm SL (REJ 1184), VA, Tazewell County, Little River, 27 March 1987.

Fish 193 *Cottus* sp., Clinch sculpin, adult female 75 mm SL (REJ 1163), VA, Scott County, Stony Creek, 21 September 1985.

disjunct), fins typically plainly pigmented, and chin generally unmottled; adults are 50–80 mm SL. Head and body form usually moderate, occasionally quite robust, particularly in large nuptial male; eye moderate, usually 6.5–7.3% SL. Dorsal and anal fin heights moderate to high; dorsal fins usually slightly confluent or unconnected, rarely slightly separated; caudal fin subtruncate or rounded; dorsal spines and rays moderate or very thin.

Palatine tooth patch usually slightly developed, occasionally moderately, rarely strongly developed. Preopercular spine 1 strong; spine 2 moderate or slight, rarely absent; spine 3 usually weak, occasionally lacking. Prickling postpectorally moderate or, usually, slight, represented by few, very short but distinctly excised, pointed nubs; prickles occasionally absent in Clinch–Indian population. Male genital papilla elongate, wholly narrow, oval.

Meristics.—Lateral line in Stony and Little populations always complete, uninterrupted, endpoint almost always area 6, rarely posterior part of area 5, pores 31–34(35); in Clinch–Indian population, lateral line frequently slightly incomplete (27% of specimens), endpoint 5.0–5.5, and usually interrupted subterminally (55%), pores 30–34(35). Dorsal spines (6)7–8; dorsal rays 16–17(18), last occasionally single; branched caudal rays 8–9(10); anal rays (11)12–13(14), last always double; pelvic rays 4; pectoral rays (13)14–16, mean, 15.2 in Stony, 14.9 in Little, and 14.8 in Clinch–Indian. Cephalic lateralis pores: ST 3; LAT (4)5(6); SO 3; COR 1; IO (7)9(10); PM 11, median pores united in 9% of 74 fish.

Color in Preservative.—Ground shade paler, plainer overall, less scrawled and mottled than on the other two broadbands, but saddle-bands bolder on average. In adult other than large nuptial male, upper body background slightly to moderately dusky, mottling usually vague or absent; rarely black-spotted, few spots at most; saddles moderate to bold, except saddle 1 usually absent. Saddles 2 and 3 wide, occasionally moderate; edges of saddle-bands moderately or well-defined, often straight, usually vertical overall; band 3 often short, anterior edge usually vertical or slanted posteroventrad, anteroventral extension usually absent or, often, represented by distinctive spot, smudge, or blotch on flank between bands 2 and 3; posteroventral edge of band 3 widely separate from band 4. Lower side moderately or vaguely mottled, or unmottled. Caudal base band as in Holston sculpin except usually not markedly extended anteriad.

Chin unmottled or, rarely, slightly mottled anteriorly. Head basically as in Holston sculpin; spot on cheek usually more prominent in Clinch sculpin, due to generally paler head.

Fin patterns as in Holston sculpin except as follows. Spines or rays of all fins usually untessellated, sometimes vaguely tessellated; membranes usually slightly pigmented and unpatterned, mottling and marbling vague at most; first dorsal fin membranes occasionally slightly and evenly darker in posterior portion of fin, or one or two posterior membranes often duskily or darkly slashed; occasionally one or two anterior membranes are also slashed or only these are slashed.

Nuptial male somewhat duskier overall on head, body (saddle-bands still obvious), and fins than female. Maximally, head and body blackened, except belly dusky, saddle-bands largely or entirely obscured; all fins except pelvic very dusky to black, first dorsal darkest, membranes darker than spines; pale first dorsal margin more demarked. Reproductive males can rapidly change between wholly blackened and paler, well patterned.

Color in Life   Plate 26.—Upper head and body ground shade pale tan-olive to pale olive-gray, sometimes with russet reticulation; saddle-bands dark olive-gray to black; back and side between saddle-bands with many small spots and flecks of pale gray, pearly, or powdery blue-green, these often highlighting edges of saddle-bands and producing very bold saddle-bands; highlighting effect best developed in Little River population (pale spots and flecks rapidly turn pale yellow to dusky in preservative); venter off-white; iris partly brassy; upper lip pale red in some fish. Fins much as in Holston sculpin, except first dorsal margin of nuptial male with creamy color added (creamy pink in some fish); pale orange, rust, or red-brown often on rays and/or membranes; pelvic sometimes pale red distally; pectoral less often pale orange.

COMPARISON

The Clinch sculpin is diagnosed from other broadband sculpins in Table 8 and is separated from *C. baileyi* in the same manner as is the Holston sculpin (see that account).

To distinguish from *C. carolinae* of the Clinch system, use the combination of: (1) saddle width [moderate to wide in Clinch sculpin *vs.* narrow or moderate, rarely wide in *carolinae*]; (2) anterior edge of saddle-band 3 usually [vertical or nearly so *vs.* slanted distinctly anteroventrad, when developed ventrally]; (3) chin mottling [absent or, rarely, slight *vs.* usually slight or moderate, rarely absent or strong]; (4) postpectoral prickling usually [slight *vs.* well developed]; (5) preopercular spines 2 and 3 [absent to moderate *vs.* strong]; (6) palatine tooth patch size [usually small or medium *vs.* large].

BIOLOGY

The Clinch sculpin feeds chiefly on aquatic insect larvae. Nine specimens from Stony Creek ate mayflies and caddisflies; a few dipterans and a worm also were taken (K. A. Cronin, in litt.).

Maturation, age, length, and reproduction of the Little River population were studied by S. R. Crockett III and R. E. Jenkins (unpublished data). Most males and females mature by 2 years. Of the 68 specimens captured during 22 February–19 April and aged by otoliths, all 13 of age 1, and a 48-mm SL male and two

47-mm females among the 20 age-2 individuals were juvenile. The smallest mature fish were a 56-mm male and a 45-mm female; all age-3 Clinch sculpins were adult. Age 4 was attained by three males and four females, and two females lived 5 years.

Males averaged slightly larger than females in most of ages 1–4, but the differences were slight (and samples small). Nine age-3 males ranged 64–75 mm SL and 13 females 61–77; means of both sexes were 70 mm. Of all adults collected during mid-February to mid-April, 32 males were 56–80 mm SL, mean, 68, and 50 females 45–84 mm, mean, 64. The largest specimen is a 108-mm SL, 129-mm TL female from upper Stony Creek. Of the five other Clinch sculpins taken with the largest one (in 1973) three were larger than those in all other collections. Specimens taken at the site and below in Stony Creek during 1985 were of typical size.

Spawning occurs in February and March, based on the annual cycle of gonadal development and partly confirmed by aquarium observations. The range of temperatures of Little River on five visits to our sampling site (0.6–1.0 rkm below the mouth of Maiden Spring) in February or March 1985–1987 was 7.8–14.4°C. All reproductive and spent adults were found in runs and riffles chiefly of gravel, rubble, and boulder.

Little River fish captured on 22 February 1987 spawned in three aquaria (38 or 77 liters) beginning 17 days later, during 11–21 March. Water was initially kept at 8–9°C; starting six days before the first spawning it was maintained at 13–14°C. All eight of the females spawned. Males are polygynous; five of the six spawned, one with three females, one with two, and three with one.

Characteristic of *Cottus*, males enlarged cavities beneath rocks by sweeping gravel with fins, pushing and rolling with the snout and body, and transporting materials in the mouth. Males were highly territorial; they defended the nest cavity and vicinity against other males by elevation of fins and gill covers, nodding, shaking, performing acts that resemble yawning and barking, and jaw fighting—two males grasping each other's jaw and tugging and twisting. Generally the dominant males were the darkest. The dominant male of three males in a 77-liter tank spawned with two females; the subdominant male spawned with one, and the peon not at all.

The passive females were given much the same treatment by males as occurred between males, likely partly as courtship or perhaps to aid in sex recognition, but male–female encounters never involved jaw fighting. Males seemed to court also by assuming a nearly or fully inverted posture in the cavity. When a female was in the cavity, the male frequently quivered against her with the body and beat her with a pectoral fin. In the one spawning act witnessed, both sexes were inverted during egg extrusion, which occurred within 45 seconds (following a many-hour period of inversion in the spawning position). The female made many apparently forceful body contortions just before and during oviposition. The eggs, adhering to the roof of the cavity and some drooping in small masses about the female, were then packed into a several-tiered mass by the male using his tail area; eggs possibly were fertilized then also. Then the female was forced from the nest. The eggs were fanned and guarded by the male.

The spawning inversion of the Clinch sculpin may be the longest recorded among all fishes. The longest inversion for an egg-clustering darter (duskytail darter) seems to be somewhat over five hours (Layman 1984a). Inversion times for six female Clinch sculpins were 4.3–36.7 hours, mean, 16.0 hours. During these periods, the female, occasionally and briefly, and the male, usually, were upright.

Fecundity of the Clinch sculpin is 73–312, mean, 184 ripe ova, based on 33 females 45–76 mm SL, mean, 62. The diameter of mature ova was 2.3–2.9 mm, mean, 2.5, in the female with the largest ova. Like other *Cottus*, this species spawns all or nearly all ripe ova. Of the aquarium spawners, the spent gonads of six lacked residual ova, and one had two ova (the other female could not be studied). Most other spent females lacked large ova; numbers of large, mostly atretic ova in seven specimens were 1–24, mean, 5.7. Eggs hatched after 29–36 days of incubation in water 13–14°C.

HABITAT

Like most other Virginia *Cottus*, large juvenile and adult Clinch sculpins occupy runs and riffles, less frequently well-flowing portions of pools. They are most common among unsilted large gravel, rubble, and boulder, and avoid deeply silted areas. This species occupies moderate to somewhat high-gradient sections of typically clear spring runs to large streams, having in common loose rocks and in most of them, lengthy sections of cool to cold water.

In Stony Creek the Clinch sculpin occurs in the main channel well below and to at least 4 rkm above Brickey Spring. The lower channel averages about 10 m in width; at the upper record site the width is usually 3 m. The sculpin extends into the 1–3-m wide lowermost section of Straight Fork, whose mouth is between the lower and upper sites.

Stony Creek, a freestone stream in Scott County,

largely drains the front of the Appalachian Plateau. Its substrate is dominated by unsilted rounded rubble and boulder; on our three visits the water was crystal clear and colorless. Some of the lower stream, in the Valley and Ridge Province, has been channelized; despite greater sun exposure, rainbow trout occur at least as far down as 3 rkm from the mouth during early summer. The lower section has at least one medium-sized spring and is cooled by large Brickey Spring, which provides at least 20% of the flow of lower Stony Creek during low water. Stony Creek at 0.7 rkm below Brickey Spring was 17°C during a 27°C summer afternoon and low water. Upper Stony Creek and tributaries are also cool.

In the Little River the Clinch sculpin is known wherever the stream was sampled—from the foot of a mill dam at 0.6 rkm below Maiden Spring down to the mouth. The stream is 15–25 m wide throughout. In 1985 the lower section was not notably silted, but immediately below the dam the stream was heavily sedimented. The dam was partially broken in about 1984, allowing silt that had accumulated upstream to imbed much of the substrate within 0.5 rkm downstream. By March 1986 most of the silt had been swept farther downstream.

The limestone-based Little River system, Russell and Tazewell counties, courses the Valley and Ridge Province and characteristically has angular rocks. On 10 visits the river was slightly turbid as often as it was clear, and was green-tinted when clear. Its water has high alkalinity (total alkalinity 118 mg/liter near the origin, 132 mg/liter near the mouth) and pH (7.9–8.4) (Wollitz 1968b). The basin has many caves, from two of which issue large spring runs. Maiden Spring, supposedly the largest in the Clinch system of Virginia (Collins et al. 1930), joins Maiden Spring Creek to form the Little River. Maiden Spring Creek is a lengthy stream whose lower portion is fed by two large springs. One of these, contributing most of the volume of lower Liberty Creek (see *C. baileyi* account), has about the volume of Maiden Spring. The springs cause marked cooling of the Little River. At 0.6 rkm below the mouth of Maiden Spring, Little River was 20.6°C on a hot summer evening; more than 10 rkm downstream it was 19.4°C on a warm summer afternoon. Lower Little River is warmwater.

In the Clinch River, the Clinch sculpin occurs at the west and east limits of Cedar Bluff and at the next upstream locality sampled, Pounding Mill, 12 rkm above. In Indian Creek, joining the Clinch at Cedar Bluff, the sculpin was found in the lower portion, and in lowermost Lowe Branch, an open roadside spring-run tributary of the mid-section; it was not found in Indian Creek at the mouth of Lowe Branch. All record sites are in the Valley and Ridge Province, except that Lowe Branch fringes the Appalachian Plateau in Tazewell County.

The Clinch–Indian population occupies a range of stream widths, from 15–20 m in Clinch River to 2–4 m in Lowe Branch. Substrate, turbidity, water color, and, likely, water chemistry are similar to the Little River. Segments of this population seems to inhabit warmer water than do the other populations. The Clinch River was 20°C and Lowe Branch 23°C on a June afternoon with air 24–25°C; the temperature at our Lowe Branch site was 24°C on a hot May day (VPI 2779). The Clinch River at Cedar Bluff has a typical warmwater fish fauna; however, Indian Creek and Pounding Mill Creek have coolwater isolates in addition to the Clinch sculpins.

DISTRIBUTION   Map 132

The Clinch sculpin is endemic to the upper Clinch River system, Tennessee drainage, Virginia. The range of the three known tributary system populations—in Stony and Indian creeks and the Little River—and that of the Clinch River population are discussed under *Habitat*. The mouths of Stony Creek and the Little River are separated by 115.5 rkm of the Clinch River, and the occupied part of the Clinch River (at Cedar Bluff) and the Indian Creek mouth are 37 rkm above the Little River mouth.

The extension of the Clinch sculpin well up into a cool narrow section of Stony Creek, compared with its apparent absence in cool and somewhat larger Maiden Spring Creek and Liberty Creek, is enigmatic. Liberty Creek spring run supports a robust population of *C. carolinae*, including the largest sculpins known in the East, indicating prime sculpin conditions. The *C. carolinae* population would not seem to competitively bar the Clinch sculpin from these streams, based on their wide syntopy elsewhere. Thus perhaps *C. baileyi* is a significant competitor of the Clinch sculpin in the Little River system; its range there is nearly complementary to (upstream from) that of the Clinch sculpin.

Abundance and Syntopy.—In Stony Creek, abundant at the lower site, uncommon at the upper site. In Little River, common just below the dam, uncommon in the lower part. Common in Clinch River at Cedar Bluff and lower Indian Creek, rare (1 specimen known) in Lowe Branch of middle Indian Creek. *Cottus carolinae* was uncommon to common in lower Stony Creek and much of Little River, was absent or rare at the Clinch River sites (VPI 2538, identified as *C. carolinae* by Masnik 1974, is the Clinch sculpin), and rare or uncommon in Indian Creek. *Cottus baileyi* was uncommon just below the dam and not found elsewhere in Little River, nor was it taken in the other streams.

REMARKS

A nuptial male Clinch sculpin once exhibited "cave man" behavior toward a just previously inverted, unspawned female. The female had dashed from the nest cavity to take a piece of chopped earthworm; the male rushed out, grabbed her by the pectoral fin with his jaws, and rapidly swam back to the cavity. He released her, then clamped her snout in his jaws, shook and dropped her, and then he shook his head and quivered his body. The female promptly reinverted, upon which the male ate the piece of worm, and reattended her. Elements of this behavior were exhibited by other pairs, whereby a male grasped a female but did not carry her, or took her only near the nest. Some intermale aggressive behavior also was similar.

Confinement of the Clinch sculpin to three small areas might render it a candidate for conservation status. However, the populations are doing well, and most of the occupied tributaries are protected by having trout-water status.

Bluestone sculpin   *Cottus* sp.

SYSTEMATICS

This species of the broadband sculpin group is an isolate in the upper Bluestone system of the New drainage in Virginia and West Virginia. The Virginia subpopulations are contiguous; no difference was detected among them.

The Bluestone sculpin is the most distinctive of the three broadbands. It is marked especially by distinctly marbled dorsal and caudal fins, incorrectly attributed also to the Holston form by Robins (1954). Its morphology and color indicate that it stemmed from a different stock than did the broadband sculpins in the Tennessee drainage.

The Bluestone sculpin probably is most closely related to *C. carolinae*. Both have a distinctly anteroventral slant to the anterior edge of saddle-band 3, strong preopercular spination, large palatine tooth patches, a typically truncate caudal fin, and the first dorsal fin faintly edged with orange. The marbled first dorsal fin pattern of the Bluestone sculpin (mottled in young fish) likely is derived from the mottled pattern typical of *C. carolinae*. Also, the lateral line is complete in the Bluestone sculpin and most populations of *C. carolinae*. The Bluestone sculpin is similar to the population of *C. carolinae* in the adjacent upper Clinch system, in characters by which the latter variably tends to differ from "typical" *C. carolinae*: fins occasionally somewhat marbled; chin mottling often reduced; saddles commonly moderate in width; and lateral bands often diffuse, irregularly edged.

Alignment of the Bluestone sculpin with the *carolinae* group has biogeographic support. In Virginia, the three forms of this group are virtually restricted to the Valley and Ridge Province; their range limits nearly mirror the edges of the province (Map 133). The Bluestone sculpin also is endemic to the Valley and Ridge Province and its range fits a gap in that of the New drainage form of *C. carolinae*.

Differences between the Bluestone sculpin and typical *C. carolinae* are collectively substantial. The Bluestone sculpin is smaller; it essentially lacks body prickling; chin mottling almost always is absent or poorly developed; the dorsal fins typically are wider apart; pectoral rays usually number 15–16 (usually 16–17 in *C. carolinae* of the upper Tennessee); fine pale spotting is lacking on the flank (often present in *C. carolinae*); and the dorsal and caudal fins are marbled (rare in *C. carolinae* overall, about as frequent as in most other regional *Cottus*).

With a grouped concept of the broadband sculpin, Robins and Robison (1985) considered that in fin marbling it approached their new Ozarkian species, *C. hypselurus*. However, the Bluestone sculpin typically has both dorsal fins and the caudal fin marbled, whereas the first dorsal of *C. hypselurus* has basically the 2-spot and banded patterns, and its usual caudal pattern may be described as tessellated or mottled (by our definitions). When the caudal is marbled in *C. hypselurus*, it is unlike that of the Bluestone sculpin. From these and numerous other differences, we conclude that the Bluestone sculpin and *C. hypselurus* have quite distant affinity. We agree with Robins and Robison (1985) that *C. hypselurus* belongs in the *bairdi* group.

DESCRIPTION

Materials.—Twelve series; most counts from 55 specimens. Life color from 7 series.

Anatomy.—A sculpin with saddles of moderate width, marbled dorsal and caudal fins, and an unmottled or slightly mottled chin; adults are 60–80 mm SL. Head and body form moderate or elongate; eye small or moderate, usually 5.9–6.6% SL. Dorsal and anal fin heights low or

Fish 194 *Cottus* sp., Bluestone sculpin, adult male 70 mm SL (REJ 1060), VA, Tazewell County, Wrights Valley Creek, 1 April 1984.

Fish 195 *Cottus* sp., Bluestone sculpin, adult female 60 mm SL (REJ 1135), VA, Tazewell County, Bluestone River, 27 January 1985.

moderate; dorsal fins usually separate, with no gap or about equally frequently a slight or distinct gap between, rarely slightly connected; caudal fin subtruncate or truncate; dorsal spines and rays moderate or thin.

Palatine tooth patch usually strongly, occasionally moderately developed. Preopercular spines strong, occasionally only spine 3 moderate. Prickling usually absent even in young and juvenile; prickling usually represented by a few pale, slightly raised spots postpectorally just above the lateral line, sometimes a few also just below lateral line, fewer than above; occasionally the spots have a tiny blunt nub; occasionally one or a few nubs on a specimen have a minute point. Male genital papilla usually elongate, narrow, oval, occasionally moderately broad-based.

Meristics.—Lateral line always complete or essentially so, usually terminating in endpoint area 6, occasionally area 5, pores (31)32–34(35). Dorsal spines 7–8; dorsal rays 16–17(18), last occasionally single; branched caudal rays 9(10); anal rays (12)13–14, last always branched; pelvic rays 4; pectoral rays (14)15–16(17). Cephalic laterialis pores: ST 3; LAT 5; SO 3–4; COR 1; IO 9; PM 10(11), median pores separate in all 58 specimens.

Color in Preservative.—Body ground shade slightly to heavily dusky, scrawling and mottling usually slightly darker, diffuse; a few black spots occasionally on upper body; saddles usually moderately pronounced, often diffuse, except saddle 1 often absent or, middorsally, barely hinted. Saddles 2 and 3 usually moderate in width, occasionally wide or somewhat narrow; edges of saddle-bands generally slightly or moderately defined, irregular, anterior edge overall slanted sharply anteroventrad; lower portion of band 3 usually extending well below lateral line, the anterior end extended far anteriad and interconnected with flank markings, never represented by an isolated distinctive mark, the posterior end often joined or nearly so with band 4. Lower side usually diffusely mottled. Caudal base band as in Holston sculpin, or if notched the notch is not medial.

Chin usually unmottled, occasionally slightly mottled, rarely moderately mottled. Head otherwise as in Holston sculpin.

First dorsal fin with narrow pale margin. Both dorsal fins and caudal fin typically moderately to strongly, narrowly marbled; first dorsal the least frequently marbled but usually marbled; second dorsal and caudal almost always marbled; caudal almost always the darkest of the three; dark components of marbling usually longer than pale marks in the three fins, particularly the caudal. First dorsal fin usually obliquely crossed by 2–3 pale lines; if dark bands through membranes are incomplete, fin is distinctly mottled. Second dorsal fin marbling has slightly dusky to black, usually moderately dusky background, traversed by oblique pale lines that course straight or curve posteroventrad and fuse or nearly so with the less oblique or horizontal pale epibasal or basal line(s). Caudal fin marbling irregular, usually with 1–2 long, zig-zag, overall vertical pale lines, shorter pale lines, and pale margin. Anal rays slightly or moderately tessellated, membranes usually pale. Pelvic fin slightly pigmented or pale. Pectoral rays moderately or strongly tessellated or marbled, membranes about evenly dusky.

Pre- and postnuptial adults of same shades as those in spring and summer; sexual dichromatism not detected.

Color in Life Plate 27.—Although the fins are distinctly marked, this is a drably hued sculpin having essentially the same range of color variation as the Holston sculpin, except that the body tends to be more olive-gray than olive-brown. Juvenile, more often than adult, frequently with russet reticulation on upper body and pale orange-red in second dorsal and caudal fins.

COMPARISON

The Bluestone sculpin is distinguished from other broadband sculpins in Table 8. It is not known to occur with any other cottid, but it may occur with *C. b. bairdi* and the New drainage form of *C. carolinae*. The latter two forms have an incomplete lateral line; the line is complete in the Bluestone sculpin. Other differences are indicated in Table 7.

BIOLOGY

The Bluestone sculpin feeds on various immature benthic insects, particularly mayflies and caddisflies, and to a lesser degree on stoneflies and dipterans. Isopods and amphipods also were important foods in 17 specimens (K. A. Cronin; H. J. Rolfs, in litt.). Heavy feeding on the two crustacean items, which were not found among stomach contents of the other broadband sculpins, is related to their abundance (particularly among vegetation) in spring-run feeders and the main channel of the Bluestone River.

The Bluestone sculpin lives at least 2 years; most or all yearlings are immature. Mature fish taken during 27 January–31 March included 26 males of 58–82 mm SL, mean, 70, and 45 females of 54–90 mm, mean, 68. Several large males taken during that period had small gonads and genital papillae. The 90-mm SL, 107-mm TL female is the largest specimen of the species seen.

The breeding period seems to occur between those of the two other broadband sculpins. On 27 January 1985 (water 6.7–8.9°C), 17 of 20 adult females were fully gravid, 1 was partly spent, and 2 were fully spent. On 17 February 1985 (water 4.4°C), all 4 adult females found were spent, as were 15 taken on 11 March 1986 (11°C), and 17 on 16 March 1984 (10–11.1°C). Young of 18–24 mm SL were collected on 21 June 1983.

HABITAT

The environment of the Bluestone sculpin in Virginia is strongly flowing limestone spring runs, comprising the upper Bluestone River, its main and small tributaries, and high-volume springs. Stream widths are 1–10 m. Substrates are dominated by gravel and rubble; lengthy slow portions of the main channel and some springs are heavily silted. Watercress, moss, and emergent plants are common in some stretches. The waters are cool to cold; the highest of four summer water temperatures was 17°C, during 33°C air temperature. Juveniles and adults are most frequently found in runs and riffles of boulder and rubble. Juveniles are common on gravel and sometimes among plants, uncommon or rare in silted slack water.

DISTRIBUTION   Map 132

The Bluestone sculpin is known only from the extreme upper Bluestone River system of the New drainage, and it is the only *Cottus* in Virginia that does not occur with a congener. It is generally distributed in a segment of the system draining the Valley and Ridge Province in Tazewell County, Virginia, from headwaters to just within the city of Bluefield and in Wrights Valley Creek. It was found here in every sampling, except not in a once-sampled, heavily disturbed tributary along a shopping center. Below Bluefield, the Bluestone River receives two major tributaries from Virginia: Mud Fork, which fringes the Appalachian Plateau, and Laurel Fork, which is in that province. Neither fork yielded *Cottus* at the one site sampled in each during 1983 and 1991.

In the Bluestone River, the success of the Bluestone sculpin changes abruptly in the populous Bluefield area, which straddles the Virginia–West Virginia line. The river here has been badly degraded; dissolved oxygen concentrations have approached zero for extended summer periods (VBCED 1970). When seined in 1985 at 2 rkm below the lower Bluefield sewage treatment plant in Virginia, the river water and bottom had a grayish cast typical of organically polluted water; fishes were rare and *Cottus* was not found. Similar findings were recorded in about 1958 by R. D. Ross (fieldnote).

In West Virginia below Bluefield, only one specimen of *Cottus*, a juvenile Bluestone sculpin, is known from 20 or more samples made during 1900–1985 in the Bluestone system. It was found during 1985 in the Bluestone River at Bramwell, about 15 rkm below the lower Bluefield sewage treatment plant. The West Virginia part of the stream is almost entirely within the Appalachian Plateau in an extensively coal-mined area.

The East River, a New River tributary which heads in Bluefield and courses the Valley and Ridge mostly in West Virginia, was suspected to harbor the Bluestone sculpin. Although it too has water quality problems, Stauffer et al. (1975) reported *C. carolinae* from the lower four stations. We verified *C. carolinae* from three sites; *C. b. bairdi* was the species at the upper site.

Abundance.—Uncommon to abundant, generally common, dominating runs and riffles.

REMARKS

Thousands of years ago the present watershed of the upper Bluestone River probably was drained westward by the Clinch River, but was captured by "Old Bluestone River" (Ross 1972a). The present divide in this cave- and sink-riddled region is gentle. Perhaps these opposed systems had more than one contact and interchange of aquatic biota. This is suggested by differential distinctiveness of the Bluestone sculpin and the snubnose darter *Etheostoma simoterum*. The darter is widespread in the Tennessee and Cumberland drainages, but in the New drainage occupies only the Bluestone and adjacent Wolf Creek; the New population represents the same form as in the Clinch (D. A. Etnier, in litt.). Divergence of the sculpin may indicate longer residency.

The Bluestone River headwaters are a brief drive west along a heavily traveled four-lane highway from Bluefield. This small part of the system is generally paralleled by roads, bridged many times, and courses through expanding commercial and residential areas for much of its length. Hence it would seem that the endemic sculpin is imperiled by potential disaster such as chemical truck spills, and general progress. However, its occurrence in numerous spring runs and longer tributaries, including Wrights Valley Creek in an adjacent rural valley, would furnish ample survivors and recruitment sources for the Virginia population. The Bluestone sculpin is nearly extirpated from West Virginia. In 1908, Goldsborough and Clark stated that the ichthyofauna of the Bluestone River there was greatly reduced by effects of mining. Bluestone tributary watersheds in West Virginia also have been extensively mined.

Banded sculpin   *Cottus carolinae* (Gill)

SYSTEMATICS

Cottus carolinae was described from Kentucky by Gill (1861). The original description and Gill's (1876) redescription and figure clearly are of this species, but the type locality is in dispute. A putative type specimen of *C. carolinae* (MCZ 33438) is labeled Maysville, Kentucky (Williams and Robins 1970), and Gill (1861, 1876) also gave Maysville as the type locality. However, Maysville is on the Ohio River in northeastern Kentucky, well beyond the range of *C. carolinae* (Burr and Warren 1986). Our analysis of the history of the types led to the conclusion that the type locality is Russellville, southwestern Kentucky, in the Green River drainage range of *C. carolinae*. This is based on cotypes (USNM 2859) that apparently are not extant (Robins 1954; K. E. Hartel, in litt; S. L. Jewett and W. C. Starnes, personal communications).

Cottus carolinae is a rather variable species, particularly in Virginia. Five subspecies have been recognized and *C. c. carolinae* is divisible into five races (Robins 1954; Williams and Robins 1970). Those in Virginia are the midlands race of *C. c. carolinae* in the Tennessee drainage, and the undescribed subspecies in the New drainage that has been termed the Kanawha banded sculpin or simply Kanawha sculpin (*C. carolinae* subsp. on Map 133). The Virginia forms are not well understood; they are more variable than indicated by Robins (1954).

The *C. c. carolinae* population of the South and Middle forks of the Holston River has a strongly mottled chin; the saddle-bands are extremely narrow dorsally, mostly solid, and have well-defined edges laterally. In the upper Clinch–Powell system, the chin often is only slightly mottled or unmottled, saddles frequently are moderate in width, and lateral bands tend to be diffuse throughout. Some North Fork Holston subpopulations tend to be intermediate in these characters. In lateral line pore and pectoral ray counts, fish from the lower and middle Clinch and the lower Powell in Tennessee are similar to populations of the upper Tennessee River corridor that were identified (Robins 1954) as intergrades of *C. c. carolinae* × *C. c. zopherus* (see introduction to broadband sculpins). These counts tend to increase progressing upstream in the Clinch and Powell Rivers, into Virginia headwaters. Only in the upper Clinch–Powell do subpopulation means agree with that of the Holston, except that pectoral ray counts remain low in the upper Powell. The Clinch population was poorly known by Robins, and he lacked a Powell sample.

The Kanawha sculpin may prove to be a key in determining the taxonomic status of forms in the *carolinae* group, but its status also needs to be reassessed. It is widespread in the New drainage but reported elsewhere only in the Mossy Creek system of the lower Holston, Jefferson County, Tennessee. From our study of Robins' series and UT BHB 287 from Mossy Creek, we agree that the population is quite similar to that of the New. However, the differences from *C. c. carolinae* (lateral line typically incomplete, chin mottling reduced, saddle-bands relatively diffuse) are in trends that occur, seemingly independently, in other populations of the *carolinae* group. The Mossy Creek population could be only a local variant of *C. c. carolinae*, or the composite Kanawha sculpin may be a species, its Mossy Creek population persisting as a relict in sympatry with *C. c. carolinae*.

Much more distinctive is an albino sculpin known from a cave in the Greenbrier system of the New drainage, West Virginia. Although provisionally regarded as consubspecific with the Kanawha sculpin by Williams and Howell (1979), this specimen (the only one known) diverges in several ways in addition to color. For example, uniquely among *Cottus* it has a frenum. We regard it to be a different species. Spelunkers should be on the lookout for it or a similar form in Virginia; Culver et al. (1973) noted that subterranean waters of a small part of the Greenbrier karst area flow into the James drainage.

The relationship between *C. carolinae* and *C. girardi* is probed in the account of the latter. The closest relative of *C. carolinae* beyond the east-central United States has been thought to be *C. rhotheus* of the Pacific Northwest (McAllister and Lindsey 1961; Bailey and Dimick 1949; Wydoski and Whitney 1979: color photo; Robins and Robison 1985). That proposal may be as "far out" as the large geographical distance between the species. Similarities between *C. carolinae* and *C. ricei*, of the Great Lakes and northwestward, were noted by Scott and Crossman (1973).

DESCRIPTION

Materials.—From data by Robins (1954) from the Holston and Clinch populations of *C. c. carolinae* and the New population of the Kanawha sculpin, plus the following numbers of series (and number of specimens counted for mainly lateral line pores and pectoral rays): *C. c. carolinae*—Holston 26(5), Clinch 26(115), Powell 5(25); Kanawha sculpin—Virginia 18(12), West Virginia 6(16). Extensive meristic and morphometric data, including ontogenetic variation, are given for a Kentucky population by Craddock (1965). Life color from 15 Virginia lots of *C. c. carolinae* and 3 lots of the Kanawha sculpin.

Fish 196 *Cottus c. carolinae* adult female 78 mm SL (REJ 994), VA, Washington County, North Fork Holston River, 22 June 1983.

Fish 197 *Cottus carolinae* subspecies, adult male 82 mm SL (REJ 1073), VA, Bland County, Laurel Creek, 9 April 1984.

Fish 198 Hybrid, *Cottus baileyi* × *C. c. carolinae* adult male 74 mm SL (NMB 935), VA, Tazewell County, Liberty Creek, 29 March 1985.

Anatomy.—A sculpin typically having the first dorsal fin and chin mottled, saddles narrow, and the preopercular spines and palatine tooth patches strongly developed; adults are 75–110 mm SL. Body moderately elongate or very robust, high-backed; head short or long; snout profile somewhat angulate or broadly rounded. Dorsal and anal fin heights usually moderate; dorsal fins usually slightly connected or separate, rarely a gap between; caudal fin truncate or subtruncate; dorsal spines and rays moderate or thin.

Palatine tooth patch large, occasionally moderate. Preopercular spines strong. Prickling usually well developed postpectorally in the Tennessee drainage, usually slight or absent in the Kanawha sculpin. Male genital papilla usually moderate in base width and length, broadly rounded distally, occasionally long and slender.

Meristics.—Lateral line in Tennessee drainage fish almost always complete, endpoint rarely in anterior portion of area 5 or 4, pores (28)31–34(35); lateral line in Kanawha sculpin usually incomplete, often ending in area 2 or 3, occasionally complete, particularly in the East River, pores (24)26–29(35). Dorsal spines (6)7–8(9); dorsal rays (15)16–17(18), last branched; branched caudal rays (8)9; anal rays (10)12–13(15), often 14 in the Clinch, last branched; pelvic rays (3)4, virtually always 4. Pectoral rays (15)16–17(18) in Holston, extreme upper Clinch, and all of New; usually 15–16, modally 16, occasionally 17 in lower half of Virginia section of Clinch and Powell. Cephalic lateralis pores, in Tennessee drainage: ST 3(6); LAT 5(6); SO 3(4); COR 1(2); IO 9–10; PM (10)11, canals fused anteriorly in 1 of 45 fish.

Color in Preservative.—Body ground shade usually slightly or moderately dusky, often finely mottled and scrawled slightly darker, lower side often finely reticulated (interspaces being small pale spots); body rarely with numerous small black spots. Saddles in South and Middle forks of the Holston very narrow, saddle 4 "pinched," and edges of saddle-bands usually sharply defined; in other rivers saddles narrow or moderate, rarely wide, and edges of saddle-bands often irregular or diffuse; saddles usually continued well below lateral line, anterior edge slanted distinctly anteroventrad. Caudal base band usually narrowly or moderately encircling upper and lower edge of caudal fin; posterior edge convex, vertical or, least frequently, notched.

Chin moderately or strongly mottled in Holston; elsewhere usually slightly or moderately mottled, occasionally strongly mottled, and occasionally unmottled. Head usually mottled laterally, often with irregular lines or bars radiating below eye.

First dorsal fin distally pale; remainder usually tessellated or mottled, darkest basally; rarely marbled. Other fins except pelvic usually tessellated, dark and pale areas about equal in length at least on dorsal and anal; moderately marbled dorsal and caudal fins (marbling wide) were found only in Clinch fish, rarely. Pelvic fin almost always slightly tessellated or unpatterned. Kanawha sculpins tend to have rather vaguely patterned fins. Pectoral fin base in Tennessee and Kanawha forms often with small, rarely prominent blotch.

Spawning males darker than females (Wallus and Grannemann 1979). This appears to be the only record of nuptial color. However, in a series (UAIC 4875.06) of reproductive fish from one of Wallus and Grannemann's sites, males had the typical year-round shade, about that of associated females. In Virginia, dark males were found occasionally through the year, as frequently as dark females; most of these probably were from relatively low-illuminated cavities under dark rocks. On the few times in which fish in reproductive condition were taken, average shade of the sexes was equal. Our darkest specimens are very dark anteriorly but not black; chin mottling and body markings remain evident.

Color in Life Plate 27.—Highly variable, drab to colorful, often at the same sites. In *C. c. carolinae*, upper body ground shade and mottling olive-brown, olive-gray, tan, copper, or bright rust; lower side paler, more lustrous, of interspersed shades of two or more of the above colors plus cream, yellow, gold, or pale green; saddle-bands dark olive, brown, or black. Head dorsally and laterally like upper body; pale areas of chin often pale yellow or pearly; inner ring or wider portion of iris often brassy.

First dorsal fin margin pale yellow or pale orange, the color usually discontinuous; spines tessellated dark olive or black/olive or yellow-olive; membranes colorless or pale yellow wash. Second dorsal, caudal, and pectoral fins tessellated as first dorsal, or often pale orange to pale russet added; membranes pale yellow or pale orange in some fish; caudal sometimes orange-margined. Anal and pelvic rays tessellated olive or gray/yellow-olive or white, or all white; membranes pale.

Nuptial male possibly slightly darker than female. Our darkest large reproductive male (REJ 1169) retained olive tone on head and body; fins were of normal shades.

Kanawha sculpin as above except distinctly coppery and rusty fish not seen, body ground shade often pale tan or straw; fish with vague or no fin tessellations have rays mostly yellow olive or straw.

Larvae.—Described by Craddock (1965), Hogue et al. (1976), and Wallus and Grannemann (1979).

COMPARISON

For specimens from the Tennessee drainage, see *Comparison* under *C. baileyi* and Holston and Clinch sculpins; for New drainage, see *C. bairdi* and Bluestone sculpin.

BIOLOGY

The banded sculpin is primarily a nighttime predator; a surge of feeding is exhibited from evening to midnight (Minckley et al. 1963). It takes mainly small crustaceans and insects; large sculpins subsist more on crayfishes and fishes than do small ones (Minckley 1963; Minckley et al. 1963; Craddock 1965; Small 1975; Hickman and Fitz 1978; Starnes and Starnes 1985). A 93-mm SL *C. c. carolinae* consumed a dusky salamander *Desmognathus fuscus* of 83 mm TL in Virginia.

Cottus carolinae generally first spawn when 2 years old; at least for females, few mature in 1 year (Craddock 1965). Small (1975) thought that age-1 fish contributed most of the spawn; however, the aging may have been incorrect. Few fish survive beyond 3 years. Early growth was studied by Wallus and Grannemann (1979); they noted that spawning males were larger than females. Craddock (1965) found that growth rates of the sexes were about equal; 2-year-old fish averaged 120–135 mm TL depending on the station in a Kentucky spring stream; the smallest reproductive fish were 90 mm TL. Among many medium to large *C. c. carolinae* from Virginia during November–March, those clearly adult were 8 males of 79–102 mm SL, mean, 92, and 7 females 74–111 mm, mean, 89. Adult Kanawha sculpins sampled in September–April included 15 males of 75–111 mm SL, mean, 92, and 14 females of 70–115 mm, mean, 89. Small reproductive adults were found in Shorts Creek, near the upstream end of the range of the Kanawha form; these were a male of 63 mm SL and a female, 60 mm.

The banded sculpin is the largest *Cottus* in eastern and central North America. The largest known specimen, a female of 144 mm SL, 185 mm TL (7.3 inches), is from Liberty Creek, a spring-run stream in the upper Clinch system, Virginia. When shown the specimen, anglers told of larger sculpins in the creek. Specimens nearly this size have been reported from many parts of the species range. The much greater size reported by Blankenship and Resh (1971) is due to omission of the decimal point when citing Craddock (1965:66).

The reproductive period of *C. c. carolinae* in northern Alabama was January–February in 14°C (Wallus and Grannemann 1979). Female *C. carolinae infernatis* were ripe in central Alabama during late January–early February at 9–13°C (Williams and Robins 1970). In a spring stream of northern Kentucky, spawning was deduced to occur during January though March, possibly also in April (Craddock 1965). Reports of spawning in May (Minckley 1963; Pflieger 1975) lack a sound basis. In the Tennessee drainage of Virginia, two gravid females were found on 17 December 1985 (in a spring run of 12°C), a partly spent one was caught on 10 January 1973, and a fully spent one on 27 January 1985. All of the many females taken in February and March were fully spent. In Sinking Creek of the New drainage, females were spent on 12 February 1972 and from mid-March to mid-April of other years; one from Shorts Creek was fully gravid on 28 February 1971.

Spawning occurs on the underside of rocks and logs in slow and swift current of spring runs and creeks (*Remarks*). Usually only one cluster of 100–300 eggs was found in nests (Wallus and Grannemann 1979). Spawning apparently took place in a cave near the entrance (Craddock 1965). Counts of 123 and 150 mature or maturing ova were from *C. carolinae infernatis* (Williams and Robins 1970). The 60-mm-SL Shorts Creek Kanawha sculpin had 68 mature ova of 1.5–2.3 mm diameter, mean, 1.8. Ova or egg diameters reported in the three above studies all averaged larger than in the Shorts Creek specimen.

A hybrid *C. baileyi* × *C. carolinae* (Fish 198) was taken in Liberty Creek of the upper Clinch on 29 March 1985 (NMB 935). The adult male, 74 mm SL, exuded milt when preserved. *Cottus carolinae* apparently had finished spawning at the site before 17 February in that year, but *C. baileyi* was in its spawning period on 29 March. Both species strongly populate the generally shallow spring run, and co-inhabit its riffles. The hybrid exhibits states of *baileyi* in fin pigmentation (but the dark first dorsal band is reduced for the size of the fish) and pectoral ray count (14). It resembles *carolinae* in body form (for its size and sex), narrow saddles, lower side reticulation, chin (but only slightly mottled), palatine teeth, and prickling. The lateral line is incomplete (pores 30), like *baileyi*, but interrupted to an extent not seen in any other *Cottus* specimen. The terminal segment (in

endpoint area 5) is quite disjunct from the remainder of the line (endpoint 2), suggesting partial, late ontogenetic expression of *carolinae*.

Two puzzling specimens are from the Hiwassee system of Georgia (UT 129.40; Hitch and Etnier 1974). Other than the above hybrid, they are the only specimens of at least partial *C. carolinae* parentage that we have seen with a dark-banded first dorsal fin.

HABITAT

Cottus carolinae occupies typically clear, moderate-gradient creeks and streams, and is generally thought to be the eastern sculpin most tolerant of warm riverine conditions (e.g., Robins 1954; Hitch and Etnier 1974; Pflieger 1975; Cashner and Brown 1977). This is substantiated for both subspecies in Map 133. However, strong populations form rarely in the larger and warmer Virginia rivers; the densest populations and largest fish tend to occur in cool to cold small streams and spring runs. Both Virginia forms enter and sometimes occur well into caves, such as Maiden Spring Cave (Robins 1954; Williams and Howell 1979).

Large juveniles and adults inhabit riffles, runs, slow margins, and pools; when they are in pools, they generally are near the upper and lower ends. Banded sculpins seem to occupy slow current more frequently in streams whose rapid areas are dominated by other sculpins, but an interaction has not been quantitatively documented. Substrates are gravel, boulder, and, most frequently, rubble. This species lives under cover by day and is stationed on tops of rocks at night (Greenberg and Holtzman 1987; Greenberg 1991). Young populate calm backwaters of silt and detritus (Minckley 1963) and swifter, hard-bottomed areas. The banded sculpin is sedentary, having a small home range (Small 1975; L. A. Greenberg, in litt.).

DISTRIBUTION   Map 133

The *carolinae* group is widespread in uplands of the southern Appalachians, Ozarks, and outlying areas. In Virginia the banded sculpin is generally distributed in the Valley and Ridge Province of the Tennessee and New drainages, but is absent from the Blue Ridge and Appalachian Plateau provinces. The pattern is basically continued southward along the western fringe of the Blue Ridge (generally about the North Carolina–Tennessee line), and is duplicated in its northeastern extension by *C. girardi*. Notably, that species occurs in a small section of the upper Piedmont but is not present in the Blue Ridge.

The range of the Kanawha sculpin in the West

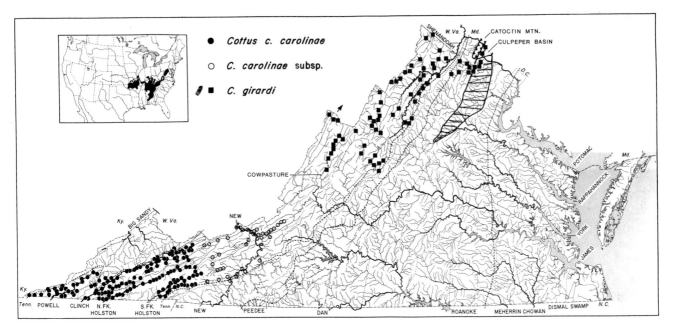

Map 133 Banded sculpin and Potomac sculpin.

Virginia portion of the New drainage has been obscured by erroneous records, mapped subsequently by Lee et al. (1980) and Burr and Page (1986). We have reidentified as *C. bairdi* 3 of the 4 series reported by Hocutt et al. (1979) as *C. carolinae* from the Gauley system in the Appalachian Plateau. Their "*carolinae*" from Gauley Station 11 has not been found, but we assume it to be *C. bairdi*. The Kanawha sculpin is present in the lower Greenbrier system, but is not found as widely in the system as is indicated by records of Hocutt et al. (1978). All of their relocated specimens from the upper half of the system are *C. bairdi*; we did not see specimens of "*carolinae*" from Stations 4, 11, 14, 28, and 29.

Constraints on penetrance of the Blue Ridge and Appalachian Plateau may be soft water and high gradient, factors invoked by Gilbert (1980) to explain similar patterns of other species along the western edge of the Blue Ridge in the Tennessee drainage. The absence of *C. carolinae* from upper and middle Big Stony Creek of the New drainage, Virginia, in the Valley and Ridge along the West Virginia line, would seem an exception, but this is mostly a tumbling soft-water stream. The apparent absence of this sculpin from lower Big Stony probably is related to effects from an industry.

Difficulties with the hypothesis that water chemistry and gradient are barriers stem from the occupation by *C. carolinae* of riffles in the Valley and Ridge and the likelihood that soft-water zones generally do not end as sharply at the edge of the Appalachian Plateau as do the upstream limits of this species. Perhaps these factors operate synergistically. Interspecific competition does not seem to be a major factor limiting upstream extension, because *C. carolinae* is usually syntopic with other sculpins, and no *Cottus* inhabit the Appalachian Plateau of the upper Clinch and Powell systems (except both *C. carolinae* and the Clinch sculpin, barely, in middle Stony Creek).

Abundance and Syntopy.—Usually uncommon, sometimes abundant. *Cottus c. carolinae* is syntopic with all three other *Cottus* (black, Holston, and Clinch sculpins) in the Tennessee drainage of Virginia, but usually is less numerous than these at least in swift shallow water. The same relationship exists between the Kanawha form and *C. bairdi* in the New drainage.

REMARKS

Until recently, the time and mode of spawning of the banded sculpin had been a mystery, owing to the paucity of fieldwork during its winter spawning period. Reproductive timing was first deduced from gonadal condition of adults and dates of capture of young fish (Robins 1954; Craddock 1965; Small 1975). However, intensive year-round study by the latter two workers found no nests, supporting Robins' (1954; *in* Williams and Robins 1970) contention that eggs were broadcast instead of being laid in nests.

Secretiveness of breeding fish was indicated partly by evidence of spawning in a cave (Craddock 1965). Finally, Wallus and Grannemann (1979) discovered *C. carolinae* breeding in typical *Cottus* fashion, by clustering eggs on the ceiling of cavities. Their observations were made in small streams whose deeper waters were accessible. To round-out understanding of this species, winter diving needs to be done in larger streams—in dry-suits!

Name.—Dedicated to Caroline Henry, a friend of the author of the species, Theodore N. Gill.

Potomac sculpin

Cottus girardi Robins

SYSTEMATICS

The Potomac sculpin had a one-year initial stand as a species; its lumping was improper and the ensuing taxonomic confusion pervaded life history and behavioral studies. *Cottus girardi* was described by Robins (1961) from the Potomac drainage of Virginia, West Virginia, Maryland, and Pennsylvania. Stemming from an aquarium study of reproductive behavior during 1959–1960, Savage could not distinguish *C. girardi* from the mottled sculpin *C. bairdi*. Following with primarily morphological analysis, Savage (1962) synonymized *C. girardi* with, and (1963) ascribed its reproductive behavior to, *C. bairdi*.

Savage (1962) had both species in the morphological study. Of his 17 USNM lots from 14 sites, 9 contain a total of 16 specimens of *C. girardi*; a greater number of, or only *C. bairdi* (559 specimens) is contained in 16 of the lots. In the remaining lot (USNM 192993), all 33 specimens are *C. girardi*, some of which Savage (1963) used in his behavioral study. Our resolution of quirks in the catalog and Savage's (1962, 1963) data leads us to believe that his behavioral observations were *only* of *C. girardi*.

General acceptance of Savage's synonymy of *C. girardi* was immediate, but Robins (in litt.) continued to hold that it was a separate species. In the early 1970s we found two readily separable color forms in a James drainage tributary that aligned with Robins' concepts of *C. girardi* and *C. bairdi*. Next we encountered a mixed series from a Potomac drainage tributary in which specimens resembling *C. girardi* were spent but *C. bairdi* had yet to spawn. Further study led to the announcement (Jenkins 1976) that *C. girardi* warranted removal from the synonymy of *C. bairdi*; this was confirmed by morphological and genetic analyses (Strauss 1980; Matthews 1980).

The question remains, what is the status of the Potomac sculpin relative to its actual close relatives—other forms of the *carolinae* group? Six diagnostic features of *C. girardi* were noted by Robins (1961): an incomplete lateral line (usually 20–25 pores), low pectoral ray count (usually 15), sexually dimorphic genital papilla, reduction in chin mottling, saddle-bands often diffuse, and anterior mandibular (chin) pores usually united. However, all but the last are shared as the typical condition of some populations of *C. carolinae*; among the first five characters, *C. girardi* is extreme only in reduction of the lateral line. The importance of chin pore union is questioned owing to parallel trends in the other species of *Cottus* in the Potomac and certain other drainages. Pore union is rare in *C. carolinae*, but 18% of specimens at a Kentucky site have united pores (Craddock 1965).

Cottus girardi actually is quite distinctive. Based on one breeding male, Robins (1961) suggested that *C. girardi* may have prominent nuptial coloration; our and Savage's materials substantiate this. Unique to *C. girardi* among members of its group is the development by small (age-1) nuptial males of a black band in the first dorsal fin. The mature status of age-1 male *C. girardi* also seems to differ from many populations of *C. carolinae*. Our maturation data are from a population of *C. girardi* in which growth appears typical of the species. The difference between the sexes in growth rate (males faster), may also be distinctive in the species group. The dorsal fins of *C. girardi* usually have a wider connection than in *C. carolinae*.

The closest relative of *C. girardi*, at least geographically, is the New drainage form of *C. carolinae*—the Kanawha sculpin. They exhibit similar trends in lateral line reduction and non-nuptial color, but owing to the ample variability of the species group overall, those resemblances may be spurious. Final judgment on the taxonomic status of *C. girardi* is deferred until the nature of species limits in the group is firmly founded.

No difference was found in morphology and color between populations of *C. girardi* in the Potomac and James drainages except for a slight shift in average pectoral ray number (but see *Description*).

DESCRIPTION

Materials.—From Robins (1961) and 29 lots (24 specimens counted) from the Potomac drainage, 9 (51) from the James; chin pores counted on more specimens. Life color from 4 Potomac lots and 1 James lot.

Anatomy.—A *Cottus* typically with a mottled or black-banded first dorsal fin, mottled chin, narrow or moderate

Fish 199 *Cottus girardi* adult male 82 mm SL (WHH 242), VA, Rockingham County, Dry River, 23 May 1984.

Fish 200 *Cottus girardi* adult female 59 mm SL (REJ 1042), VA, Augusta County, Middle River, 22 September 1983.

saddles, and well-developed preopercular spines and palatine tooth patches; adults are 45–95 mm SL. Characteristics are as in *C. carolinae*, with the following exceptions and qualifications. Dorsal fins moderately or broadly united more frequently than they are slightly united; they are never separated by a gap. Caudal fin occasionally rounded in large nuptial males. Prickling postpectorally strong to, often, absent. Male genital papilla, including that of small mature fish, usually long, the distal half slender.

Meristics.—Lateral line markedly incomplete, endpoint in area 2 or anteriorly, occasionally area 3, pores (17)20–25(29). Dorsal spines (6)7–8(9); dorsal rays 16–17(18), last rarely unbranched; branched caudal rays (7)8–9; anal rays (10)12–13(14), last branched; pelvic rays 4; pectoral rays (14)15(16), 7% of Potomac drainage and 29% of James drainage specimens with 14 rays. Cephalic lateralis pores: ST 3; LAT 5; SO 3; COR 1; IO (8)9; PM 11, median pores united in 81% of 115 Potomac, Virginia, and 77% of 62 James specimens, but united in only 51% of 39 specimens from the Potomac of Maryland and Pennsylvania.

Color in Preservative.—Range and frequency of variation essentially as in *C. carolinae*, except for the following differences and qualifications. Saddles usually narrow, occasionally moderate. Lower side of small fish often blotched in checkered pattern. Caudal base band virtually always notched posteriorly, usually deeply so (Matheson 1979; our data). Chin unmottled to strongly mottled, often strongly mottled in small fish and large females; reduction in mottling partly associated with increased nuptial darkening, producing a uniformly dusky or black chin in large nuptial males.

Large nuptial males (in aquaria) darkened or blackened overall except for a pale first dorsal fin margin; head darkest, body heavily sooty, markings sometimes barely discernible, belly gray; fin-blackening more intense in membranes than rays in all fins except the caudal. First dorsal fin with black medial band appearing in small mature males, developing from mottled pattern (not from 2-spotted pattern often seen in members of *bairdi* group). Small mature male retains juvenile male and adult female pattern of dark and light contrasts on body and most fins.

Confusion exists concerning certain published drawings of *Cottus*: (1) labeled *C. girardi* (Lee 1976); (2) labeled *C. girardi* (Lee et al. 1980); (3) labeled *C. bairdi* (Lee et al. 1980); and (4) unidentified species on the cover of Lee et al. (1980). The specimen in drawing 1 has not been relocated for identification; it is believed to be a composite drawing of two or more specimens (D. S. Lee, personal communication). We think that the drawing was partly based on a species other than *C. girardi*, owing to the pelvic ray count of 3 and lack of a notch on the caudal base band. Drawings 2–4 are of the same specimen but not that (those) of drawing 1; the specimen also has not been relocated, and likely is not *C. girardi*.

Color in Life Plate 27.—As in *C. c. carolinae* except as follows. General base tone usually yellow-olive to olive; pale spotting usually extensive, best developed on lower

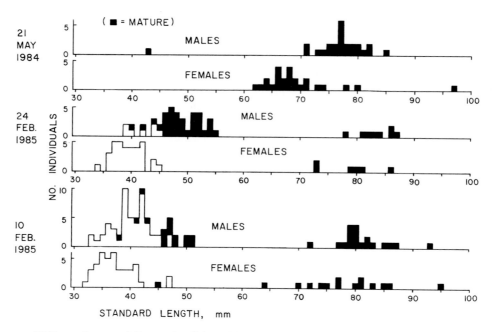

Length–frequency of 223 specimens of *Cottus girardi* from War Branch, Rockingham County, Virginia, at the County Route 613 bridge (the 21 May and 10 February samples are from just above the bridge, the other just below, all by backpack electroshocker). Most age-1 fish apparently were not saved in 1984. The 1985 samples were made to assess all age-groups. The numbers of mature fish are not cumulative with immature fish of the same length.

side of head and body, often yellow-olive to creamy olive; lower side often with pale green or coppery tints or both, but no pronouncedly coppery or rusty fish seen; none observed with an orange-margined caudal fin.

Large nuptial males blackened as described above; saddle-bands obvious in some; fine spotting of lower side pale gray to dark olive; distal band of first dorsal fin averaged slightly more orange than in adult female, but still creamy; distal band narrower than in small fish; first dorsal fin olive basally.

Spawning males in Savage's (1963) photos range from generally dusky (much darker than female) to black, the latter as in our blackest males; only the dusky phase is exhibited by Savage's preserved specimens. Savage noted that changes in shade occurred rapidly. He also described males that turned partly jet black, but the body paled, during spawning and agonistic encounters of nest-guarding.

COMPARISON

For *Cottus* from the Potomac drainage, see *C. bairdi* and *C. cognatus*; for those from the James drainage, also see *C. bairdi*.

BIOLOGY

Food habits of *C. girardi* are typical of freshwater sculpins. The bulk of the diet in Naked Creek, Virginia, is benthic insect larvae, mostly mayflies, caddisflies, and midges. Amphipods, crayfishes, snails,

other invertebrates, and fantail darters are taken rarely (Matheson 1979).

Most or all males mature by the end of the first year of life, based on 233 specimens (of all ages) from War Branch in Virginia, that were aged by length–frequency analysis (bar graph). Of age-1 males taken on 10 February 1985, 24% were mature. Two weeks later spawning was still imminent, and 83% of the yearlings were mature; these again were mostly the larger yearlings. Mature yearlings (38–55 mm SL, mean, 44) had a well-developed genital papilla; the several fish observed when placed in formalin released milt. Immature yearling males were 33–47 mm. Small, apparent age-1 males from Maryland also were mature. Based on studies of *C. bairdi*, small "sport" males of *C. girardi* probably do not spawn as frequently as do large males. Only one age-1 female (45 mm SL) showed a slight sign of adulthood in February 1985; immature females were 32–46 mm. All age-2 fish were mature. The largest male and the two largest females probably were 3 years old.

Growth of War Branch Potomac sculpins occurred at about equal rates in each of the first two years for the 1983 and 1984 year-classes (fish taken in February 1985). Their faster growth than the 1982 year-class (sampled in May 1984) may be related to the mildness of the 1984–1985 winter and to removal of some of the 1982 year-class. Matheson (1979) found no difference between the sexes in growth, but his sample was small and mostly of young. War Branch males were consistently larger than females at ages 1 and 2. The jump in percent maturation of age-1 males in 1985 was accompanied by an apparent growth spurt; in two weeks males increased by an average of 5.7 mm and females increased by 2.7. The size of large adults in War Branch was similar to that in many other streams; of age-2 War Branch fish, 49 males were 71–87 mm SL, mean 79, and 45 females were 62–86 mm, mean 74. The largest known specimen is a female of 111 mm SL, 137 mm TL from Virginia.

Spawning apparently occurs in late winter and early spring. All of the adults from War Branch on 10 and 24 February 1985, water 3.3 and 11.1°C, were in prespawning condition. One gravid female was found in the Middle River system on 3 April 1984, water 8.9°C; another was taken on 17 April 1971. Spent fish were taken on 21 April 1958 in Naked Creek. From the 24 February sample, four large males and five large females were kept in a 116-liter aquarium at 11–14°C. Four spawnings occurred during 5–11 March; two egg clusters adhered on a glass side of the tank, two others adhered to the underside of a stone forming the roof of a nest cavity. Clusters of 100–300 eggs had up to six tiers; one male guarded those in the nest cavity. Many eggs died or were eaten by sculpins; some hatched during 3–8 April.

Eggs, probably all spawned by *C. girardi*, were found in Maryland by Savage (1963) on 11 March in 1959 and 1960, water 6–7°C. Temperatures ranged 6–16°C during the breeding season. We counted 134 mature ova in one of his females, 55 mm SL; ovum diameter was 1.6–2.3 mm, mean, 2.0.

HABITAT

The eurythermal Potomac sculpin occupies much the same habitat as does *C. carolinae*—usually clear, moderate-gradient creeks, streams, and small rivers. Only a few specimens are known from the well-sampled large Potomac River (Davis and Enamait 1982). Most large channels of the drainage in Virginia have not been sampled sufficiently to reveal the true abundance of sculpins. Our records support statements (Robins 1961; Matheson and Brooks 1983) that *C. girardi* is tolerant of warm water. Its general absence or rarity in high-volume cold spring runs may be related to competitive interaction with *C. bairdi* and *C. cognatus*.

Cottus girardi dominated the benthic fish fauna in a rocky, pastured stretch of War Branch, a creek. Juveniles and adults occupied all habitats in February, concentrating much more in swift currents than in

sluggish, silty parts of pools. Large fish were found more frequently beneath larger stones and in deeper runs than were small fish. In Naked Creek, *C. girardi* tended to inhabit slower, deeper runs than did *C. bairdi*. Immature and adult male *C. girardi* occupied slower current and silty bottom or plant beds more frequently than did adult female *C. girardi* (Matheson and Brooks 1983).

DISTRIBUTION   Map 133

Cottus girardi occupies all major hydrographic subdivisions of the Potomac drainage except those on the lower Piedmont and Coastal Plain. It avoids the Blue Ridge, to which it has ready access. This Valley and Ridge distributional pattern is discussed under *C. carolinae*. The population of the Goose Creek system on the upper Piedmont occupies warm, sandy, and gravelly streams in hilly, mostly noncalcareous terrain (Ross 1959a; *Biogeography*). The erroneous Virginia Piedmont record (Jenkins et al. *in* Lee et al. 1980) east of the presently known limit was based on vague locality data that had been misinterpreted.

When first described, the Potomac sculpin was known widely but only from that drainage. In the James drainage, it was found during 1971 in both main branches of the Cowpasture River; a Cowpasture series taken in 1958 was reidentified by us as this species. Strauss (1980) found *C. girardi* in Conodoguinet Creek of the lower Susquehanna drainage, Pennsylvania, in 1979.

The recency of first capture and localization of *C. girardi* in the James and Susquehanna suggest the possibility of introductions, but it is more likely that the populations are native. The Cowpasture River drains a limestone area noted for caves; egress from the Potomac drainage may have occurred via a subterranean aquifer, if not by surface stream capture. Of Virginia sculpins, *C. girardi* and *C. carolinae* are the best candidates to have used an underground route. Because *C. girardi* is an Atlantic slope isolate of Mississippi basin stock, and the James drainage is partly adjacent to that basin, the James population may be the oldest of the species. If that is true, its present restriction to one tributary system of the James is even stranger. We believe that *C. girardi* stock probably first reached the Atlantic slope in the Potomac by stream capture involving the developing New drainage, as suggested by Hocutt et al. (1986). Further evidence of a New-to-Potomac route is the absence of the *carolinae* group from the Roanoke drainage, which shares many fishes with the New and James.

Abundance and Syntopy.—Often uncommon or common; abundant in the part of War Branch recently sampled thrice. Nearly always found with *C. bairdi*, which, however, was rare in War Branch and was not found in all 21 collections of *C. girardi* from the direct Potomac River tributary systems in Virginia just north and south of the main Shenandoah River. Both species were recorded in 71% of the 83 other Virginia collections of *C. girardi*. *Cottus girardi* and *C. cognatus* rarely are taken together.

REMARKS

In blackened nuptial color and faster growth of males than females, the Potomac sculpin apparently bridges gaps between the *carolinae* and *bairdi* groups, the major constituents of the eastern *Cottus* fauna. Robins (1954, 1961) considered *C. girardi* to be primitive in the *carolinae* group, but some of the traits on which that assessment was based are now known to be shared with *C. carolinae*. Male nuptial features currently provide little help in determination of phylogenetic position within the *C. carolinae* group.

It is ironic that, despite the former taxonomic confusion of *C. girardi* and *C. bairdi*, the two species are readily distinguishable even in the field when alive.

Name.—A tribute to Charles F. Girard, an early student of sculpins and who described many kinds of fishes secured by explorers of the western frontier.

STRIPED BASSES
Family Moronidae

The Moronidae are a small family of freshwater and anadromous estuarine and marine percoids, represented by the genera *Morone* with four North American species and *Dicentrarchus* with two European–North African species (Johnson 1984). The latter two species were placed in *Morone* by Waldman (1986). Johnson cleaved this group from the temperate bass family Percichthyidae because evidence is lacking that the group has a close affinity with that family (or with any other percoid group). This action is a refinement of Gosline's (1966) removal of percichthyids from the catch-all sea bass family Serranidae. Such shifts are symptomatic of the difficulties in discerning relationships among the many generalized, largely marine percoids.

The common name of the family—striped basses (Jenkins 1988)—is based on the three boldly striped North American species and on the name bass given to five of the six species, including the widely known striped bass *M. saxatilis*. In recognizing Moronidae as a family, the North American species were collectively called river basses (Jordan 1929) or white basses (Jordan et al. 1930), names that are not in general use.

The paleontological record of North American moronids dates only to the Early Pleistocene, about 1.5 million years ago, based on fossils determined to be white bass (Smith and Lundberg 1972; Smith 1981). The four extant North American *Morone* are divisible into two species groups, one with *M. saxatilis* and *M. chrysops*, the other of *M. americana* and *M. mississippiensis* (the yellow bass, which does not occur in Virginia). Each pair has a euryhaline and a strictly freshwater representative (Woolcott 1957; Bowen and Chapman 1985). Two of the three *Morone* in Virginia are indigenous to the state, the other (white bass) possibly so.

General features of these typical percoids include medium or large size; body moderately elongate or deep, terete or compressed; mouth moderate or large, terminal, lower jaw often jutting slightly before snout; teeth small, in patches; opercle with 2 pointed or rounded spines; pseudobranchium well developed, not covered by a membrane; body completely scaled, scales ctenoid; lateral line complete, extending well onto caudal fin. Fin spines stout; dorsal fins slightly separate or slightly conjoined, second dorsal fin with 1 anterior spine; caudal fin emarginate or forked; pelvic fin thoracic; pectoral fins positioned high on side. Several of the external features adapt these fishes to chase and out-swim prey (Gosline 1985). Moronids of both sexes are dominantly silvery with dusky or bold lateral stripes.

The Moronidae occupy a wide range of habitats—the inshore ocean, estuaries, lowland and upland rivers, and lakes. When in rivers, adults are generally found in large ones; young and juveniles of some species occupy smaller streams. Some species naturally populate lakes; many populations have been established in impoundments.

All *Morone* frequently feed in roaming voracious schools, often or typically on fishes. Their vertical distribution in lakes may coincide strongly with the depth of abundant prey, usually shad. Foraging schools often are crepuscularly and nocturnally active. Prey detection probably is visual for all species.

Reproduction of *Morone* occurs in the spring when schools migrate and spawn in shoal areas and channels. Spawning grounds of Chesapeake striped bass are in the principal estuarine rivers of the basin. Spawning typically occurs in aggregations at or near the surface, with males outnumbering females. *Morone* species are very fecund; large females will release many thousands to a few million eggs that, depending on the species, are buoyant, semibuoyant, or demersal. Mature unfertilized eggs are tiny to moderate in size; the averages for species or populations range from 0.7 mm (white perch) to about 1.3 mm (striped bass) in diameter. Fertilized striped bass eggs often are 2–3 mm, maximally 4.6 mm (Hardy 1978b; Johnson 1984). Natural hybridization has been limited to cases where one species (e.g., *M. mississippiensis*) has invaded areas populated by another (e.g., *M. chrysops*); it is increasing due to stocking and natural dispersal. The technology of artificial crossing has produced many intrafamilial combinations. The hybrid white bass × striped bass has a major role in the development of sport fisheries (Stevens 1984; Axon and Whitehurst 1985).

Recreationally and economically, the Moronidae may be the most important small family of freshwater fishes in North America. All species are widely sought by anglers. The striped bass, the largest of *Morone*, has the most avid following. The colonists marveled at its abundance and palatability. The striped bass is the commercially most important member of the family, but has been declining drastically.

Name.—Gill (1898) stated that the derivation of the word *Morone* is unknown; the ichthyological sense, if any, of the stem (moron?) escapes us. In describing the genus, Mitchell (1814a *in* Gill 1898) placed in it the white perch, the yellow perch (Percidae), and a centrarchid.

Key to Striped Basses *Morone*

The three Virginia species are easily distinguished by the key. Identification of the hybrid *M. chrysops* × *M. saxatilis* can be difficult; see Table 9 and the account of *M. saxatilis*. See Waldman (1986) for variations in tongue dentition.

1a   Dorsal fins distinctly conjoined by a membrane; median tooth patch absent on tongue (Figure 64A); longest anal spine usually ¾ or more of the height of the fin .... WHITE PERCH—*M. americana*   p. 677
1b   Dorsal fins slightly separate or, if bases in contact, not connected by a membrane; median tooth patch present on tongue (Figure 64B, C); longest anal spine usually ½ to ¾ of the height of the fin 2

2a   Median tooth patches on tongue somewhat elongate, clearly divided (Figure 64C); lateral line scales (53)57–63(65); soft rays in second dorsal fin (10)11–12(14) .... STRIPED BASS—*M. saxatilis*   p. 679
2b   Median tooth patch on tongue oval, single (occasionally having narrow medial division, Figure 64B); lateral line scales (52)54–58(60); soft rays in second dorsal fin (12)13(14) .... WHITE BASS—*M. chrysops*   p. 686

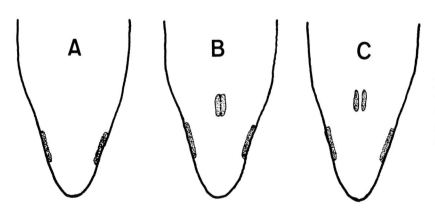

Figure 64 Typical form of cardiform tooth patches on medial portion of tongue (basihyal bone) in *Morone*: (A) *M. americana* (medial teeth absent); (B) *M. chrysops*; (C) *M. saxatilis*.

Striped Basses   Genus *Morone* Mitchill

This genus has four North American species, three of which occur in Virginia, and perhaps two Afro-European species. At times each of the North American species has been placed in a genus by itself (Jordan 1929); at other times, some or all have been placed in the genus *Roccus*. Whitehead and Wheeler (1966 *in* Bailey et al. 1970) demonstrated the priority of *Morone* over *Roccus*, unfortunately resulting in suppression of the latter esteemed, formerly entrenched name.

Name.—See the family account.

White perch   *Morone americana* (Gmelin)

SYSTEMATICS

The white perch was described in 1789 from New York. Woolcott (1962) found slight differences in morphology of populations north of the Delaware River from those south; the Delaware River population was intermediate. Within the northern and southern population groups, certain subpopulations exhibited lower levels of distinction. Mansueti (1961b) considered the James River population to be the most distinctive morphologically in the Chesapeake basin. Variation in mitochondrial DNA indicates the existence of three subgroups or stocks in the Chesapeake basin (Mulligan and Chapman 1989).

DESCRIPTION

Materials.—From Mansueti (1961b), Woolcott (1962), 3 Virginia, 6 Maryland, and 10 Delaware specimens. Life color from Scott and Christie (1963), Scarola (1973), and Scott and Crossman (1973).

Anatomy.—A plain or faintly striped and deep-bodied, perchlike fish; adults are 125–250 mm TL. Body moderately compressed and deep, back prominently arched; head and eye moderate; mouth moderate, terminal, tips of jaws about equal; tongue with two narrow tooth patches on anterolateral margin, none medially. Dorsal fins deeply emarginate, slightly conjoined by membrane; first dorsal much elevated and very stout spined; caudal fin moderately forked or emarginate, lobes subacute; anal fin concave; pectoral fin subacute. Anal spines quite stout, not graduated in length; spine 1 much shorter than spines 2 and 3; spines 2 and 3 subequal, the longest 75% or more of the height of the fin.

Meristics.—Lateral line scales (44)46–49(52); scales above lateral line (6)8–9(10); scales below lateral line (9)10–12(14); circumpeduncle scales (17)20–22(24). First dorsal spines (8)9(11); second dorsal 1 spine, (10)11–12(13) rays; anal spines 3 (2 in small young [Mansueti 1964]); anal rays (8)9–10; pectoral rays (10)14–17(18).

Color in Preservative.—Head and body dusky or dark above, grading to pale ventrally; side of body usually with several series of darkened scales forming vague, interrupted horizontal stripes. Median and pelvic fins nearly uniformly dusky; pectoral fin pale.

Color in Life.—Upper body silvery, golden or brassy gray, or olive, sometimes dark brown or almost black;

Fish 201 *Morone americana* female 107 mm SL (RCHJP 59), VA, Southampton County, Nottoway River, 3 July 1979. (Most of the dorsal fin membranes are torn.)

lower side pale olive to silver-green; venter silvery white. Chin sometimes pink to purple, this and other head parts have a blue luster when breeding. Median fins and pelvic fin dusky; anal and pelvic fins sometimes with rosy tint; pectoral fin pale.

Larvae.—Described by Mansueti (1964), Lippson and Moran (1974), Hardy (1978b), and Wang and Kernehan (1979).

BIOLOGY

Because of its euryhaline nature, the diet of *M. americana* is diverse. In estuaries it feeds on worms, shrimps, microcrustaceans, young squids, and fishes. In freshwater environments it particularly takes microcrustaceans, grass shrimp, crayfishes, insect larvae, and fishes (Hildebrand and Schroeder 1928; Cooper 1941 *in* Thoits 1958; Webster 1942; Reid 1972; Schaeffer and Margraf 1986). Larger adults were primarily piscivorous in the James River estuary (VIMS 1977). Raney (1965) noted that adults sometimes rise to take mayfly adults.

Maturation, longevity, and growth have been studied in the Delaware, Patuxent, York, and James estuaries (Mansueti 1961b; Wallace 1971a; St. Pierre and Davis 1972; VIMS 1977). A broad summary of northern United States and Canada populations was presented by Thoits (1958) and of these and other populations by Hardy (1978b). Maturation was related to size and age; no fish were mature at less than 90 mm SL nor at age 1. Most age-2 and all older males were mature; some females were mature at age 2, all were mature at age 4 and above (Mansueti 1961b). Females tend to outlive males, although Wallace (1971a) detected the opposite. Typical upper longevity was 4–7 years; maximum age observed was 17 years in Maine.

Females generally grew slightly faster than males but the rates approximately equalized in the fifth or sixth year. However, Mansueti (1961b) found that differential growth was maintained throughout life. Similar growth occurs in most of the species' range; populations from North Carolina to Maine had a range of means at age 4 of 200–265 mm TL (Mansueti 1961b; St. Pierre and Davis 1972; Norman 1973; VIMS 1977). The Virginia record is 1.0 kg (2 pounds 4 ounces). Carlander (1953 *in* Scott and Crossman 1973) reported a 483-mm TL fish from Maine weighing 2.2 kg (4 pounds 12 ounces).

Morone americana is a semianadromous species which moves upstream from lower and mid-estuary zones of Chesapeake rivers to spawn from late March to May, occasionally into early June. Most spawning

takes place over 1–2 weeks when water is 10–16°C. Breeding aggregations occur in tidal fresh and slightly brackish water in usually sandy or rocky shoal areas of large rivers and small tributaries (Mansueti 1961b, 1964). Fecundity is 20,000–150,000 ova (Hardy 1978b). Eggs are markedly adhesive and demersal. Natural hybridization of white perch and white bass has occurred in Lake Erie owing to the recent invasion by the white perch (Todd and Tomcko 1985; Todd 1986).

HABITAT

White perch are characteristic inhabitants of creek-like, riverine, and embayed portions of estuaries; the largest populations occur in salinities of 5–13‰. They do well in fresh water, particularly ponds and lakes in many east-central and northeastern areas, and rarely enter the ocean (Mansueti 1964). White perch are not typical of Chesapeake Bay proper; fish captured there may have been "flushed" from rivers during floods (Mulligan and Chapman 1989). During most of the year this species is found in shallow and moderate depths; it occupies deep water in winter (Mansueti 1961b).

DISTRIBUTION   Map 134

The estuarine native range of *M. americana* is from Nova Scotia to South Carolina. This species became established in many freshwater ponds and lakes, some well inland, after being stocked or landlocked by dams. Its spread in the lower Great Lakes and St. Lawrence River via shipping channels, initiated around 1950, has been documented by Scott and Christie (1963), Scott and Crossman (1973), Trautman (1981) and Todd (1986).

In Virginia the white perch is indigenous to all coastal drainages and Back Bay. The Fall Line appears to be a natural upstream barrier in rivers where this zone is precipitous. The population above the Potomac River Fall Line (Mansueti 1961b) likely was derived through stocking or by movement through the Chesapeake and Ohio Canal in Maryland; all other Virginia populations above the Fall Line are considered introduced. The Smith Mountain Lake record is based on one adult (RC) collected in 1977; its origin is unknown, as this species has not been reared at the Brookneal Striped Bass Hatchery (D. K. Whitehurst, personal communication). The restriction of *M. americana* in the Blackwater system to its lower section may reflect intolerance of acidic conditions and a pollution barrier emanating at Franklin; the former

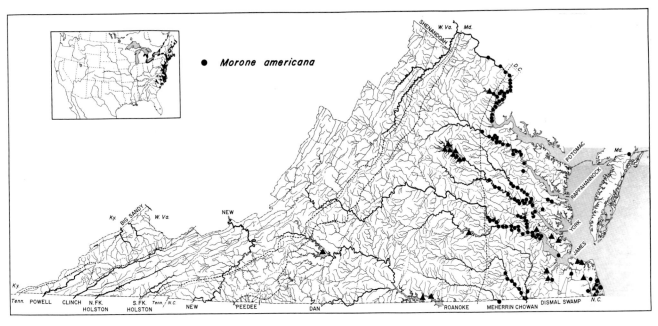

Map 134 White perch. Species present in additional Chesapeake and coastal estuaries.

would also explain its absence from the interior Dismal Swamp. White perch occur in the North Carolina section of the Meherrin system (E. F. Menhinick, in litt.); the lack of a record for the Virginia part probably reflects low collecting intensity. White perch were propagated and heavily stocked in estuaries of the Chesapeake region during a 55-year period beginning about 1882, without tangible results (Mansueti 1964).

Abundance.—Uncommon to abundant in estuaries; the Chesapeake basin is a major center of abundance. Generally uncommon in Virginia lakes.

REMARKS

The white perch can be considered a brackish-water substitute for sunfishes. This silvery panfish often is taken in good numbers and is sporty and flavorful. It has supported important commercial fisheries. During 1971–1974 the James River population was nearly eliminated by a massive kill of unknown cause (St. Pierre and Hoagman 1975). A major kill also occurred in the Potomac River during 1963.

Name.—*Americana* was so named as it was one of the first fishes to be described from the "new land."

Striped bass *Morone saxatilis* (Walbaum)

SYSTEMATICS

The striped bass was described in 1792 from New York State. Although not notably variable when compared to most species with well-founded subspecies, some 11 races or populations have been recognized within its native Atlantic and Gulf estuarine–coastal range (e.g., Raney 1952b, 1957b; Barkuloo 1970; Berggren and Lieberman 1978; Setzler et al. 1980; Chapman 1989). The races are based on slight dissimilarities among populations associated with major hydrographic areas; for example, the Chesapeake basin population differs from that of Albemarle Sound–Roanoke River, North Carolina. In turn, some popu-

lations are composed of slightly differentiated subpopulations, some of which are associated with a single major drainage.

All Virginia drainages and certain Maryland ones which contribute to the Chesapeake population have been recognized to harbor different striped bass subpopulations (e.g., Morgan et al. 1973). However, questions remain concerning the distinctiveness and geographic extent of some subpopulations. Some of the differences of opinion are related to the varied character sets analyzed (meristic, morphometric, genetic, migration pattern) and to the slight but complex variation within the species.

Fish 202 *Morone saxatilis* male 284 mm SL (NMB 520), VA, Franklin County, Smith Mountain Lake, 26 August 1980.

DESCRIPTION

Materials.—From many published illustrations and 5 Virginia specimens. Meristics are given only from Chesapeake and Albemarle–Roanoke–Kerr populations (Raney and de Sylva 1953; Raney 1957b; Beitch 1963); Setzler et al. (1980) summarize these and other populations. Color in life from Scott and Crossman (1973) and Hardy (1978b).

Anatomy.—A streamlined bass with bold dark stripes; adults are 300–900 mm TL. Body terete, profile moderate, back little elevated; head and eye moderate; mouth somewhat large, terminal; tongue with two narrow tooth patches on anterolateral margin, and two distinct medial patches. Dorsal fins slightly separate; caudal fin moderately or weakly forked, lobes pointed; anal fin concave; pectoral fin subacute. Anal spines of moderate stoutness, graduated in length; longest spine about 40–60% of the fin height.

Meristics.—Lateral line scales (53)57–63(65); scales above lateral line 9–11(13); scales below lateral line (13)14–16; circumpeduncle scales 25–30. First dorsal spines (8)9–10(11); second dorsal 1 anterior spine, (10)11–12(14) rays; anal spines 3 (2 in small young [Mansueti 1958b]); anal rays (9)10–11(12); pectoral rays (13)14–16(17).

Color in Preservative.—Dorsal half of head and body dark or dusky; ventral half dusky to pale; side with 7–8 dark stripes, usually none interrupted. Median fins dusky; second dorsal, caudal, and anal fins with pale bases; pelvic fin pale; pectoral fin slightly dusky.

Color in Life.—Dorsum dark olive to steel-blue; side and venter silver with brassy sheens; lateral stripes dark olive to black. Median fins pale green or dusky green or black; pelvic fin white or dusky; pectoral fin greenish.

Larvae.—Described by Mansueti (1958a, 1958b), Lippson and Moran (1974), Morgan (1975), Sidell et al. (1978), Hardy (1978b), Fritzche and Johnson (1979), Wang and Kernehan (1979), and Olney et al. (1983).

BIOLOGY

The detailed synopsis of biological data on *M. saxatilis* by Setzler et al. (1980) is a rich source of infor-mation, as are the proceedings of a symposium that broadly address environmental problems of this species (Coutant 1985a). The striped bass is a predaceous generalist, usually becoming piscivorous after the early juvenile stage. Young feed on a variety of worms, small crustaceans, insects, and fishes (Hildebrand and Schroeder 1928; Raney 1952b; Harrell et al. 1977). Adults take fishes, squids, clams, lobsters, crabs, shrimps, and other invertebrates (Smith 1907). At least 26 fish species are eaten by Chesapeake stripers (Hollis 1952). Blue crabs *Callinectes sapidus* constitute a major dietary item during spring in Albemarle Sound (Manooch 1973). Open-water fishes such as clupeids (shads, alewife, and herrings), much less so littoral species (black basses and crappies), are principal prey in freshwater impoundments such as Kerr Reservoir (Neal 1967, 1971). Striped bass feed heavily during spawning migration, fasting for only a brief period just before and during spawning (Trent and Hassler 1966).

Male *M. saxatilis* usually are mature at age 2. Females typically first spawn at age 4 or 5; some older fish do not spawn each year. Maximum longevity is about age 10, most fish 11 years of age and older are female, and a 29- to 31-year-old fish is the oldest reported (Neal 1976; Setzler et al. 1980; Kohlenstein 1981).

Growth of the sexes in the upper Chesapeake and Kerr Reservoir populations is similar until age 3, after which females grow faster (Raney 1952b; Mansueti 1961a; Neal 1976). The middle Roanoke drainage produces striped bass ranking near or at the top in growth rate among contemporary populations compiled by Setzler et al. (1980). Large numbers of age-6 fish creeled in the middle Roanoke and lower Dan rivers during 1965–1974 averaged 770 mm TL overall; annual averages varied little from this size (Neal 1971, 1976). Averages of age-6 fish from reservoir nettings were: Kerr 787 mm, Smith Mountain 856 mm, and Claytor 693 mm (Hart 1978, 1981; Smith and Kauffman 1982; Whitehurst and Carwile 1982). Age-6 anadromous fish in upper Chesapeake averaged 690 mm (converted from Mansueti 1961a). Fish of the same age averaged 724 mm in Santee–Cooper Reservoir, South Carolina (Stevens 1958 in Setzler et al. 1980).

The largest striped bass reported from the Maryland portion of the Chesapeake by Mansueti (1961a) was 1,136 mm TL, 22.4 kg (49 pounds 6 ounces); during 1975–1980 fish weighing 48 kg (106 pounds) and 48.5 kg (107 pounds) were taken in studies by G. E. Krantz (personal communication). Total lengths of the largest stripers netted in some Virginia reservoirs were: Kerr 991 mm; Smith Mountain 1,054 mm; Claytor 853 mm. The Virginia landlocked striped bass record is 19.2 kg (42 pounds 6 ounces) taken in Smith Mountain Lake during 1988. The all-time record landlocked fish is 27.1 kg (59 pounds 12 ounces) from Arizona in 1977. The angling-record anadromous fish is 35.6 kg (78 pounds 8 ounces) from New Jersey in 1982; it was 22 or 23 years old (H. J. Spear, in litt.). The greatest length of M. saxatilis (from California) is about 1,829 mm ("about 6 feet"—Scofield and Bryant 1926 in Hardy 1978b). One-hundred-pound stripers would be about that length (Goode 1884); colonists commonly reported fish of that weight along the Atlantic coast.

The largest reported stripers, 56.7 kg (125 pounds) from Albemarle Sound, have been widely attributed to Smith (1907:271) but originally (1893) he did not report them to be that large. Smith could have erred on the weight as he did on the year of capture; he stated (1907:271) that these fish were caught in 1891 during his Albemarle survey, but the survey was made in 1892 (Smith 1893:185, 192; 1907:422). Apparently he saw some very large bass, "some weighing over 100 pounds" (Smith 1893); later (1907) he stated that "the writer saw several striped bass . . . each of which weighed 125 pounds." It is curious that the several largest were the same categorical weight. Further, it is surprising that such weights were not reported from the Albemarle–lower Roanoke fishery in many years of study by S. G. Worth (in Raney 1952b). The heaviest striper on record instead appears to be a 50.8-kg (112 pounds) fish from Massachusetts (Goode 1884, 1887).

Anadromous Virginia stripers typically spawn in the lower 40–120 rkm of tidal and nontidal sections of large rivers, in salinities less than 10‰, usually less than 1‰ (Tresselt 1952; Sheridan et al. 1960; Atran et al. 1983). Males tend to ascend rivers before females (Trent and Hassler 1968). The tendency to spawn in rock-strewn areas in some rivers, such as the Fall Zone of the Roanoke (Raney 1952b), may reflect a preference for spawning in strong current. Upriver migration and spawning of the Chesapeake populations occur between April and early June; spawning occurs at 10.5–23.6°C and peaks at 13.9–19.0°C (Tresselt 1952; Johnson and Koo 1975; Setzler et al. 1980). Lower Roanoke River stripers begin to ascend the river in mid-March and spawn mainly during May; optimum temperature for successful hatching and survival is about 17–18°C (Hassler et al. 1981). Middle Roanoke drainage fish mostly spawn in April to early June at 14–24°C, optimum, 16–21°C. Some spawning peaks occurred a few weeks apart in the Roanoke, coinciding with rising water temperature (Neal 1967, 1968, 1976), but the spawning period often is more concentrated (Setzler et al. 1980). Migration and spawning may also be triggered by an increase in river flow (e.g., Fish and McCoy 1959); increased discharge from Leesville Dam is a stimulant to middle Roanoke ascendents.

Morone saxatilis spawns in roving surface and near-surface congregations (Smith 1907; Hildebrand and Schroeder 1928; Raney 1952b). Eggs are semibuoyant or buoyant and nonadhesive; they are broadcast in moderate to strong current. Chesapeake fish yield 15,000–4,000,000 mature ova (Jackson and Tiller 1952; Setzler et al. 1980). Eggs usually require 2–3 days to hatch and 4–10 days for larvae to become free swimming and feed (Hardy 1978a).

After hatching, the movements of striped bass vary by sex, age, size, and population (e.g., Vladykov and Wallace 1952; Raney et al. 1954; Massmann and Pacheco 1961; Berggren and Lieberman 1978; Kohlenstein 1981; Van Winkle et al. 1984). In the Chesapeake basin, both sexes stay for at least two years in nurseries in lower portions of birthplace rivers or in the bay proper. Exodus to the Virginia coast begins in early spring; postspawning adults follow later. When they first leave the bay, most stripers are age 3 or 4; nearly 90% of the emigrants are female. The largest fish tend to travel farthest north, some reaching Maine. Coastal fish head generally southward in fall, overwintering off New Jersey to Cape Hatteras. Coastal (oceanic) migrations may be feeding migrations, the fish following movements of prey species; migrations may also represent tracking of the adult coolwater niche (Coutant 1985b). Large numbers, not necessarily of the fall coastal cohort, winter in the bay and its tributaries. The resident Chesapeake population consists mainly of juvenile and adult males and immature females. The Albemarle Sound–Roanoke River anadromous population, the principal one spawning in North Carolina, also makes coastal movements but contributes little to northern Atlantic areas (Berggren and Lieberman 1978; Van Winkle et al. 1979; Hassler et al. 1981). Populations in the ex-

Table 9 Characters of the hybrid *Morone chrysops* male × *M. saxatilis* female and the parental species. Data for the hybrid are from Bayless (1968, 1972), H. Williams (1976), and Kerby (1979); data for the parental species are from accounts herein and preceding references. Measurements are from subadult and adult fish.

Character	*chrysops*	Hybrid	*saxatilis*
Lateral stripes	Faint or moderate, often broken	Bold, often broken	Bold, occasionally broken
Median tongue teeth	1 patch, occasionally weakly divided	1, usually 2 patches	2 distinct patches
Arch of back	Pronounced	Pronounced	Slight
Fork length:body depth ratio Mean	3.0–4.0 3.48	3.1–4.0 3.47	4.0–5.3 4.44
Body depth:head length ratio Mean	1.0–1.5 1.20	1.0–1.3 1.16	0.7–1.0 0.89
Lateral line scales	(52)54–58(60)	54–63	(53)57–63(65)
Scales above lateral line	(7)8(9)[a] (10)11[b] 9–10[c]	10–12	9–11(13)
Scales below lateral line	(15)16(17) 13–14[c]	15–18	(13)14–16
Dorsal soft rays	(12)13(14)	11–13	(10)11–12(14)
Anal rays	(11)12(13)	10–12	(9)10–11(12)
Pectoral rays	(15)16(17)	15–17	(13)14–16(17)

[a]Bayless (1968).
[b]Kerby (1979).
[c]Our counts.

tremes of the Atlantic range, including those south of Cape Hatteras, and in Gulf of Mexico tributaries, rarely undertake coastal migrations.

Spawning striped bass have been thought to home to birthplace waters, but the evidence for homing is generally weak and controversial (Morgan et al. 1973; Coutant 1985b). No inter-river shift was noted in North Carolina (Chapoton and Sykes 1961). Although males showed some homing tendency in the middle Roanoke drainage, no strong evidence was found (Whitehurst and Carwile 1982); the modification of Roanoke River flow and temperature by Leesville Dam may override homing instincts. In the Chesapeake basin, males have little fidelity to natal breeding grounds; females have a stronger homing instinct (Chapman 1989). Upper Chesapeake stripers, blocked from Susquehanna River spawning grounds by a dam, have been reproducing in the Chesapeake and Delaware Canal (Johnson and Koo 1975).

Hybridization.—Artificial hybridization of *Morone* was achieved in 1965 with the production of *M. chrysops* (white bass) × *M. saxatilis* (striped bass) fry by South Carolina biologists and subsequent survival of the hybrids in a Tennessee impoundment (Stevens 1965). Since then, *M. saxatilis* has been crossed with the other species of *Morone* (Bayless 1968, 1972; Bonn et al. 1976; Kerby 1979). The white bass × striped bass (WB × SB) cross exhibits faster growth and attains larger size than does the white bass; an 11-kg (24 pounds 3 ounces) hybrid from Leesville Reservoir in Virginia is the world record. The WB × SB hybrid also has a higher rate of larval survival and often grows faster in the first 1.5–2 years than do striped bass.

Starting in 1966, stockings of WB × SB have occurred in several Virginia impoundments (Kerby et al. 1971; Hart 1981; Southwick 1986). Apparent escapees turned up in the Rappahannock estuary during 1968–1969 (Kerby et al. 1971). They occupied water with salinities up to 17‰, and outgrew the stripers at least for the first 2.5–3 years. The hybrid stocked in Virginia and most other areas is a product of crossing male white bass with female stripers (e.g., Freeze 1984).

Identification of the hybrid can be difficult; it tends to closely resemble either parental species depending on the character. Identification should rely on a suite of characters, notably striping, tongue tooth patch, and body form; see Table 9, Southwick (1986), Waldman (1986), and Quinn (1989). The possible occurrence of backcrossing would complicate the problem;

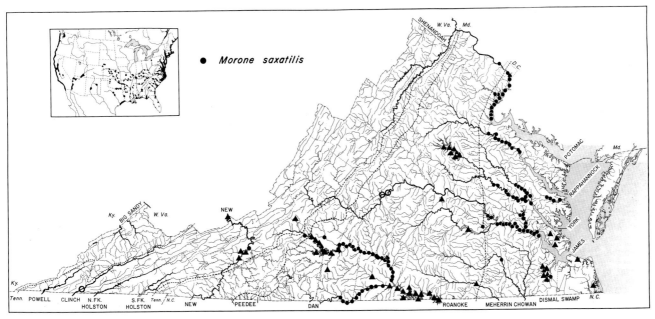

Map 135 Striped bass. The species is also distributed throughout Chesapeake region and along coast. Open circles on the James River represent sections fished by the Cabells during 1743–1795. Open circle on the Clinch River denotes unverified anglers' records from uncertain site(s) in the western Scott County portion of that river.

backcrosses have been produced in hatcheries. The reciprocal cross WB female × SB male (developed in Florida but not stocked in Virginia) more closely resembles the white bass (Ware 1975).

HABITAT

Striped bass are anadromous schooling fish that live in large freshwater rivers, small and large estuaries, and the ocean. Most oceangoing fish travel near the surf but some range 6–8 km offshore and waifs have been reported up to 113 km from land (Raney 1952b; Bigelow and Schroeder 1953). Ordinarily, stripers roam sandy, gravelly, and rocky areas of shallow and moderate depths. They sometimes encounter heavy turbidity, particularly on spawning runs in the Roanoke and Dan rivers. Stripers favor alkaline water and do not populate very acidic water.

Morone saxatilis is physiologically adapted for life-long residence in fresh water; this has allowed the development of fisheries in many inland reservoirs. The failure of self-sustaining populations to develop from nearly all of these fisheries is related to inhospitable conditions in feeder rivers; for example, shallow depth, inadequate current to prevent eggs and larvae from settling and smothering in soft sediments, and insufficient riverine distance from reservoirs, where eggs would also settle.

Some reservoir populations experience summer mortality at rates of concern to fishery managers (Matthews 1985a). Distributional shifts related to unfavorable conditions and fish size have been detected. As water warmed, adults became less mobile and tended to localize in cooler (less than 25 or 26°C) and better oxygenated areas (dissolved oxygen higher than 3 or 4 mg/liter) (Cheek et al. 1985). In effect, striped bass may be "squeezed" into the zone between a too-warm upper layer and an oxygen-deficient deeper one (Coutant 1985b; Matthews et al. 1989).

DISTRIBUTION Map 135

Morone saxatilis is native to the Atlantic slope from the St. Lawrence River, Canada, to the St. Johns River, Florida, and on the Gulf slope between the Suwannee River, Florida, and eastern Texas (Waldman 1986). It was introduced to the Pacific slope in 1879; self-sustaining anadromous populations occur between British Columbia and northern Mexico, and migrations extend 315 rkm in the Sacramento River. This species also has been introduced to Eurasia (Setzler et al. 1980).

Many inland United States impoundments have put-and-grow fisheries but only two in the East have self-sustaining populations—Kerr Reservoir in Virginia and North Carolina, and Santee–Cooper Reservoir in South Carolina. A few additional fluvial reservoir systems, mostly in the central and western states, have some natural reproduction (Stevens 1984; Matthews et al. 1989). Nearly all major and many moderate-size Virginia reservoirs have been stocked with stripers reared at the Brookneal Hatchery from middle Roanoke River stock.

In the Chesapeake basin of Virginia, indigenous populations currently are restricted to below the Fall Line. The extent of each nursery is shown by Loesch et al. (1982). We found no indication in the early literature of striped bass completely spanning the Fall Zone except in the James River. The few *M. saxatilis* taken in the early 1900s from the Potomac River between Little Falls and Great Falls (McAtee and Weed 1915) are the only ones of which we are aware from above the foot of the Fall Line in that river; they may have bypassed Little Falls via the Chesapeake and Ohio Canal. The old dam on the Fall Line of the Rappahannock River would stop migrants, but they were not so obstructed from the Piedmont in the York drainage. The unique Nottoway River record is of a 51-mm (probably SL) specimen taken in August 1967; likely it is a product of limited spawning in the river.

An interesting former extension of striped bass to the upper Piedmont in the James River is revealed by the diary of a net and trap fishery operated by Col. William Cabell and his son during 1743–1795. Their fishery was located at two island groups between the mouths of the Rockfish and Tye rivers, 158 and 167 rkm above the Fall Line (Map 135). McDonald (1887) deciphered the difficult hand of the diary containing catch records during 1769–1795; the VFC (1877b) report provides background. The diary supports assertions that stripers ascended to Balcony Falls (VFC 1877a) at the foot of the Blue Ridge, but does not support the VFC (1877b) report of extension to Covington, far into the Valley and Ridge Province. J. White et al. (1984) determined that the Cabell section yielded adult stripers only during fall, thus agreeing with the VFC (1877b). Adults of at least 7.3 kg (16 pounds) were taken but most apparently were much smaller. Although this species was able to surmount the James Fall Line, that feat and American shad migrations were halted by damming. J. White et al. (1984) concluded that stripers, in contrast to shad, did not migrate to the Cabell section during the spring spawning period, and therefore that the cohort was not a prime candidate for restoration by construction of fishways.

The presence of adult stripers during fall in the upper Piedmont of the James deviates from the known residency and movement patterns of stocks elsewhere in the Chesapeake basin, although a similar pattern was suggested for the Delaware River (VFC 1877a, 1877b; Chittenden 1971). We agree that spawning of stripers in the Cabell section was unlikely, but stripers could have spawned in the lengthy Piedmont reach below; at least, the James Piedmont cohort was valued.

The Albemarle Sound–lower Roanoke anadromous population occupies an extensive freshwater and brackish embayment behind the North Carolina Outer Banks. Its spawning migration formerly extended some 320 rkm up the Roanoke River to at least Clarksville, Virginia, where "rock fish" were abundant around 1790 (VFC 1877a). A large striped bass was taken in or near the Blue Ridge section of the Roanoke River, 275 rkm above Clarksville, in about 1900 (W. N. Cochran, in litt.). The VFC (1877a) report indicated that numbers reaching Virginia had declined by 1840. Migrants were being heavily harvested in much of the lower river, especially the Roanoke Rapids area in North Carolina (VFC 1878), which is the present upper limit of anadromous stripers in the Roanoke (Trent and Hassler 1968). The 130-rkm stretch from Roanoke Rapids to above Clarksville is now inundated by three reservoirs.

The population in the upper, first-created of these reservoirs, Kerr, supports a valuable fishery that during spring migration extends 148 rkm up the middle Roanoke (Staunton) River, to Leesville Dam, and 60 rkm in the Dan River to a dam in Danville (Neal 1968; Whitehurst and Carwile 1982; Rogier et al. 1985). Migrants rarely turn into tributaries of these rivers, and then only during high water. The Kerr population was founded by entrapment, stocking, or both. Naturally occurring stripers may have been landlocked by the closure of Kerr Dam in 1953 (Beitch 1963); D. K. Whitehurst (in litt.) considers this strongly probable. From 1953 to 1955, 3 million fry of Albemarle origin were liberated in Kerr Reservoir by the North Carolina Wildlife Resources Commission (Surber 1958). Reservoir anglers caught a few stripers in 1954; yearlings were caught in 1957 and 1958, a glimmer of impending establishment (Neal 1971).

Striped bass, and perhaps the white bass × striped bass hybrid, ascend the Clinch River from Norris Reservoir in Tennessee, and may reach the Virginia line (81 rkm upstream) in high water during spring of some years (R. D. Bishop and R. E. Wollitz, personal communications). We have an angler report of a 16-kg (about 35 pounds) specimen caught in the Clinch of Virginia around 1981, and one of a 5-kg (11 pounds) "stripe" from the river at Ft. Blackmore 42 rkm above the state line.

Abundance.—Locally rare to common, often depending on movements of spawning and feeding groups. Anadromous populations have fluctuated over the past 150 years; landlocked populations fluctuate according to stocking density and environmental conditions.

REMARKS

Few fish have so aroused the interest of sport and commercial fishermen. Striped bass attract a flotilla of anglers to the Roanoke and Dan rivers during spring. The sudden surface explosions of predaceous schools at dawn and dusk in many of Virginia's larger reservoirs are electrifying. Striper migrations in Chesapeake Bay and along the coast are a complex wonder, and these fish have a loyal following too.

The striped bass was praised by early colonists for its flavor and great abundance, and was compared to the Atlantic salmon, a fish of royalty in the mother country (Jordan and Evermann 1920). It was responsible for the first legislation in our country to protect a fish, when in Massachusetts during 1639 its use as fertilizer was banned, and in 1670 a tax levied on the fishery was used to help establish the first public schools in the New World (Setzler et al. 1980). In its early years the VFC (1877a) stated that, next to shad and herring, the striped bass was the most abundant and valued fish in Virginia waters.

Despite great demands on striped bass, until about 1885 it seemed to have held up well except for major local decreases (Raney 1952b). Although still abundant around the turn of the century, its decline was increasingly apparent (Jordan and Evermann 1920). The trend was buffered by exceptionally strong year-classes, a phenomenon linked to sporadic or supposedly cyclic years of very favorable conditions which allowed high reproductive success. Dominant year-classes and increased abundance of striped bass in coastal waters from Maine to Cape Hatteras have been widely attributed to reproductive success and subsequent migration of Chesapeake stocks (Kriete et al. 1979; Kohlenstein 1981). The Chesapeake basin produced 91% of the stripers found on the Atlantic coast in 1975, reflecting the extremely strong 1970 Chesapeake year-class (Berggren and Lieberman 1978). Relative contributions from different estuarine sources to coastal populations can vary substantially depending on year-class success, sex, differential fishing mortality, and method of estimation (Van Winkle and Kumar 1982; Van Winkle et al. 1984).

From an analysis of commercial striped bass landings on the entire east coast during 1930–1966, Koo (1970) discerned a 6-year cycle of dominant year-classes. However, no cycle was apparent in Virginia during the same period (Grant 1974), and the rigorous analysis by Van Winkle et al. (1979) yielded no support for such cycles. Koo (1970) stated that the increased landings during 1930–1966 were due mainly to increases in abundance, and that the species was not in danger of overexploitation. However, the often high rate of tag returns by Chesapeake commercial fishermen in recent years (Moore and Burton 1975) challenges the latter statement.

Until very recently, the last strong Chesapeake year-class, the largest on record, was produced in 1970 (Atran et al. 1983); the overall catch declined after its depletion (Setzler et al. 1980). From a 1973 high, Virginia's commercial landings have dropped precipitously; landings in 1981 were the smallest since 1934 and the fourth smallest on record (Atran et al. 1983). The downward trend in landings from Virginia to Maine continued into at least 1983; that of North Carolina stocks was similar (Boreman and Austin 1985). The decline in recreational catch of Atlantic stripers has been equally sharp, falling 90% in the last decade (Boyle 1984a, 1984b).

Factors reducing striped bass stocks over the decades include nutrient enrichment and chemical contamination of nursery areas, overharvest, and damming of spawning areas; natural variables such as water temperature and flow exert control in some years (e.g., Mansueti 1961c; Chittenden 1971; Loesch et al. 1982; Hall 1984; Hall et al. 1984, 1989; Coutant 1985b; Price et al. 1985; Goodyear 1985). Boyle (1984a, 1984b) and Hall et al. (1985) considered acidity to contribute to the decimation of *M. saxatilis* in the Chesapeake. This may be a simplistic view; the effect may be localized in those eastern bay tributaries lacking sufficient natural buffering.

The Chesapeake (and mid- and northern Atlantic) striped bass is not threatened or endangered in an official sense, but it is beleaguered (Coutant 1985a). Its reduction is symptomatic of societal disregard for aquatic environments. Repair of the problem, if possible, will require considerable funding and cooperation among commercial and sport fishery interests, and diverse state, interstate, and federal agencies. Management responses are being channeled partly through the Atlantic States Marine Fisheries Commission, which has developed the Interstate Striped Bass Management Plan, and the federally created Atlantic Striped Bass Conservation Act.

The most stringent regulation to date has been the politically courageous action in 1985 by Maryland, followed by Delaware, of imposing a moratorium on harvest of striped bass. Although this reduced the take of Chesapeake stripers, the lack of equal action by Virginia allowed a major shift of the catch to come from its waters. In 1988, a two-year harvest ban was federally imposed on Virginia. Moratoria invoke hardship to many concerns economically dependent on the striped bass, but restoration of anadromous stocks to acceptable levels would generate great economic benefit (Radonski 1985). As a temporary close to the chapter, striped bass just made a dramatic comeback in Chesapeake Bay, and the ban was lifted in late 1990; still, the recreational and commercial harvests are closely regulated.

Recovery of the striped bass would progress by improvement of spawning and nursery habitat and continued catch reduction. Stocking may also aid, if native populations do not become adversely blurred genetically. The VDGIF released 180,000 stripers of Kerr Reservoir stock to the James River in 1985. In 1986 the USFWS, VDGIF, and VIMS jointly embarked on a program to capture and spawn estuarine fish and return fingerlings to home waters.

Though anadromous stocks have been in deep trouble, striped bass have prospered inland during the last three decades. Many reservoirs have been stocked with striped bass (and its hybrids) to provide recreational fisheries; the trend will continue. This species is popular particularly because it reaches large size. Ecologically, it fills a predatory niche by feeding on large clupeid fishes such as gizzard shad that often glut reservoirs, tying up much productivity in biomass unused by humans (Coutant 1985b).

The initial impetus for creation of reservoir fisheries arose because of the natural spawning success and remarkable growth of striped bass following their entrapment by dams in the Santee–Cooper River system, on the South Carolina Coastal Plain (Surber 1958; Stevens 1958, 1984). Establishment by the early 1960s of a self-perpetuating striped bass population in Kerr Reservoir produced a bonanza fishery extending some 200 rkm up the middle Roanoke (Staunton) and Dan rivers during the spawning run. The population has a precarious existence. The middle

Roanoke has been under substantial control by the Smith Mountain–Leesville hydroelectric facility since its dams were closed in 1963. Reduced and erratic discharge and cold temperatures in the tailwater suppress striper migration and spawning. Four successive years (1963–1966) of reproductive failure occurred in the Roanoke; although partly offset by increased spawning in the Dan River, the Kerr population dangerously declined. An amended cooperative agreement in 1969 between the power authority and the VDGIF concerning the discharge schedule (including "attraction" flows) from Leesville Dam resulted in reversal of the trend (Neal 1971, 1976). Proposals for additional impoundments on the middle Roanoke were stopped by its designation in 1978 as a Virginia Scenic River, an act supported by a strong striped bass lobby.

The Brookneal Hatchery, established by the VDGIF in 1963 on the bank of middle Roanoke striper spawning grounds, has little or no role in sustaining that population, but is critical for many others. In some years a portion of the yield is liberated in Kerr Reservoir, but it goes chiefly to many of the larger impoundments (Map 135). Smith Mountain and Leesville reservoirs receive a major share of the young fish and produce many of the big stripers caught in inland Virginia. Philpott Reservoir is not stocked in order to avoid endangering its trout population.

Virginia's hatchery-reared stripers yield further returns to the overall fishery program. Often they have been exchanged by the VDGIF for other game species, including muskellunge, northern pike, and walleye, produced in other states. In essence, the striped bass can be called Virginia's "money fish."

Name.—*Saxatilis* means "rock dweller," somewhat a misnomer for this pelagic schooling species. It is frequently called rock, rockfish, and striper.

White bass   *Morone chrysops* (Rafinesque)

SYSTEMATICS

The white bass was described in 1820 from the "Falls of Ohio," on the Ohio River at Louisville. It is closely related to the striped bass *Morone saxatilis* (Woolcott 1957). Wright and Hasler (1967) found that in several Wisconsin lakes *M. chrysops* occurred as biochemically distinct subpopulations. Divergence probably resulted from isolation by distance and from homing of subpopulations to different spawning grounds.

DESCRIPTION

Materials.—From Bayless (1968), Cross (1967), Scott and Crossman (1973), Kerby (1979), 1 West Virginia adult, and 10 Tennessee young. Color in life from Scott and Crossman (1973), Pflieger (1975), and Trautman (1981).

Anatomy.—A deep-bodied fish with faint to moderate, often broken lateral stripes; adults are 230–410 mm TL. Body moderately compressed, deep; back prominently arched; head small or moderate; eye moderate; mouth moderate, terminal, lower jaw slightly protruding; tongue

Fish 203 *Morone chrysops* male 119 mm SL (RC), WV, Kanawha River, 25 September 1978.

with two narrow tooth patches on anterolateral margin, and a single median patch (occasionally weakly subdivided). Dorsal fins not conjoined, slight or no gap between; first dorsal fin markedly convex; caudal fin forked, lobes often pointed; anal fin concave; pectoral fin pointed. Anal spines moderately stout, somewhat graduated in length, longest spine 50–75% of the height of the fin. Sigler (1948) described urogenital differences between the adult sexes; most obvious are the swollen postanal papilla-like folds of the female, folds absent or scarcely evident in males.

Meristics.—Lateral line scales (52)54–58(60); scales above lateral line (7)8–11; scales below lateral line (15)16(17) [our counts 13–14]. First dorsal spines 9; second dorsal 1 spine, (12)13(14) rays; anal spines 3; anal rays (11)12(13); pectoral rays (15)16(17).

Color in Preservative.—Dorsum dark to dusky, diminishing gradually to pale venter; side with 5–9 faint or moderately obvious narrow stripes, 2 or more stripes often interrupted, broken sections occurring between main stripes. Median and pectoral fins dusky; pelvic fin pale.

Color in Life Plate 40.—Dorsum bluish, dark green, or gray; side and venter silver; body with blue to gold iridescence; lateral stripes gray-olive to dark olive. Median fins with pale bases, dusky gray-blue distally; paired fins pale to milky white.

Larvae.—Described by Taber (1969), Yellayi and Kilambi (1970), Dorsa and Fritzche (1979) and Fuiman (1982d).

BIOLOGY

Young *M. chrysops* eat zooplankton, insects, and larval fishes. Adults are predominantly piscivores, forming predaceous schools whose peaks of feeding often occur at dawn and dusk (Webb and Moss 1968; Pflieger 1975). Adults primarily take alewife, black crappie, and crayfishes in Claytor Lake (Boaze 1972;

Kohler 1980). Feeding centers on large mayflies during heavy hatches in this lake (Hart 1981).

Most white bass are mature at age 2; typical longevity is 4–6 years. Claytor Lake produced an 8-year-old fish (Hart 1981); age-9 fish were noted in New York (Forney and Taylor 1963 *in* Webb and Moss 1968). Females grow faster than males at all ages in Tennessee waters and Claytor Lake (Webb and Moss 1968; Boaze 1972). Good growth occurs in four major Virginia reservoirs; means of total length in mm at age 4 are: Claytor 351, Leesville 371, Smith Mountain 406, Flannagan 409 (Boaze 1972; Hart 1981; Smith and Kauffman 1982). The Virginia record of 3.09 kg (6 pounds 13 ounces) is the world record (*Remarks*).

Spawning runs commence in late April or early May in Virginia and Kentucky at 15–17°C; distances traveled vary from 3 to 241 rkm (Chadwick et al. 1966). Spawning may occur in a series of peaks (Cochran 1971; Kindschi et al. 1979). Males precede females to spawning shoals at the heads of reservoirs and in rivers. Spawning occurs at the surface where males outnumber females; the female swims in a circle, twisting violently while tended by several males (Webb and Moss 1968). Females bear 140,000–994,000 total ova (summary in Fuiman 1982d). The eggs are demersal and adhesive, and attach to the substrate.

Natural hybrids of *M. americana* × *M. chrysops* are documented by Todd and Tomcko (1985) and Todd (1986). *Morone chrysops* and *M. mississippiensis* are suspected to crossbreed in nature (Helm 1958 *in* Fuiman 1982d; Becker 1983). The cross *M. chrysops* × *M. saxatilis* had been known only from artificial propagation (Bonn et al. 1976), but natural hybridization appears to be occurring in some Virginia lakes and elsewhere (D. K. Whitehurst, personal communication). A prac-

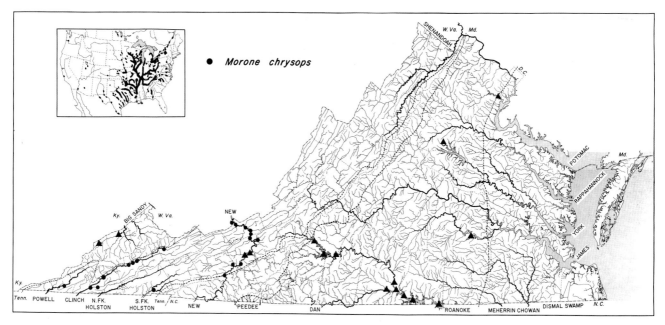

Map 136 White bass. Records on Leesville, Kerr, and Gaston reservoirs are unspecific.

tical problem is distinguishing potential record *M. chrysops* from the hybrid (Table 9; *M. saxatilis* account).

HABITAT

The white bass is associated with lakes, reservoirs, and pools in large streams and rivers. In Claytor Lake it ranges from the surface to 14 m depth, frequently following alewife schools (Boaze 1972). Its preference for clear water (Pflieger 1975; Trautman 1981) is related to dependence on sight feeding (Greene 1962 *in* Scott and Crossman 1973).

DISTRIBUTION   Map 136

White bass are indigenous to the Great Lakes–St. Lawrence and Mississippi basins and western Gulf slope drainages. They have been moderately introduced in the southeastern United States, sparingly in the West.

White bass are native to the main-stem and large tributaries of the Tennessee drainage, but perhaps did not extend into Virginia until the development of reservoir populations. In the South Fork Holston River they normally ascend only one or two pools above the reservoir to spawn (R. E. Wollitz, personal communication). White bass in the lower-gradient Clinch and Powell rivers of Virginia may have migrated from Norris Reservoir, Tennessee, or are progeny of those that did so. The few Clinch River and

Copper Creek records plotted are from 1964–1984 (Wollitz 1965; C. F. Saylor, personal communication). In 1985 we were told by residents of the Pendleton Island area of Clinch River, Scott County, that large numbers of white bass or "stripes" of 0.7–0.9 kg ascend the river during spring floods; some remain year-round. The name stripe is commonly applied to *M. chrysops* in southwestern Virginia. We saw the Powell River specimen when landed in August 1972.

Our earliest capture records of *M. chrysops* in drainages where it clearly was introduced are: New in 1959, Big Sandy 1966, Roanoke 1969, James 1976, and Potomac 1977. The 99 *M. chrysops* placed in Claytor Lake established the thriving population there, and this species may have escaped to the river below Claytor Dam. Some of the lower New River fish probably emanated from Bluestone Reservoir, West Virginia. Because white bass were not stocked in the Roanoke drainage by the VDGIF until 1970 (Hart 1978), the specimens netted from Smith Mountain Lake in 1969 probably came from unauthorized stocking by anglers; these fish purportedly came from Claytor Lake (Cochran 1969). The species is now established in most major impoundments of the Roanoke drainage.

Abundance.—*Morone chrysops* is common in Leesville, Claytor, and South Holston reservoirs. It may be locally abundant as feeding aggregations and during spawning runs, but is generally uncommon or rare in other reservoirs and rivers.

REMARKS

The gregarious habits, scrappy nature, and tasty firm meat of the white bass make it a favorite of many anglers. It is particularly sought during spawning runs in upper arms of reservoirs and their feeders, and year-round in Claytor Lake. In upper Claytor Lake during June and July, when the burrowing mayfly *Hexagenia* hatches in large numbers, a small cohort of fly-rodders seeks rampaging schools of white bass.

The state and world record white bass (*Biology*) was caught in 1989 in Lake Orange, a modest-sized head-water impoundment in the North Anna River system (York drainage), north-central Virginia. To determine that it was not a hybrid, it was carefully examined by VDGIF biologists, studied anatomically at the Smithsonian Institution, and was certified genetically as a white bass by experts at the Chesapeake Bay Institute. The origin of this fish remains a mystery; Lake Orange is unknown to have been stocked with white bass, striped bass, or their hybrids. Again, an angler may have introduced this species.

Name.—Chrysops means "gold eye."

SUNFISHES
Family Centrarchidae

The Centrarchidae comprise sunfishes, black basses, rock basses, crappies, and lesser known species. The family is one of the most important groups of North American freshwater fishes, owing to the highly esteemed sporting and food qualities of many of the species. The wide native range of many species has been augmented by stocking. Much interest is centered on black basses, genus *Micropterus*, but most genera contain important gamefishes. Centrarchids are small to medium-sized percoid fishes. The smallest species compose the banded sunfish genus *Enneacanthus*, whose adults range about 30–70 mm SL. The largemouth bass *Micropterus salmoides* is the largest, historically reaching over 900 mm TL (about 3 feet) and 10 kg (22 pounds).

The Centrarchidae are the second largest freshwater fish family indigenous to North America. (The bullhead catfishes, Ictaluridae, are the largest.) There are 30 living species (including one undescribed black bass) representing 8 genera; 19 species inhabit Virginia. Recently excluded from the family are the pygmy sunfishes, genus *Elassoma* (Johnson 1984; see *Fishes of Possible Occurrence*). The Centrarchidae are included in Miller's (1965) "old fauna"; fossil records go back to the Eocene, some 36–58 million years ago (Cavender 1986). Phylogenies have been proposed by Bailey (1938a), Smith and Bailey (1961), Branson and Moore (1962), Avise et al. (1977), and Mabee (1988).

The native limits of all but one extant centrarchid are within the region east of the Rocky Mountains from southern Canada to northern Mexico; the Sacramento perch *Archoplites interruptus* lives in California. The geographic range of sunfish fossils exceeds the historical native range; the northernmost record is from Alaska and the southernmost is from southern

Mexico (Uyeno and Miller 1963; Smith et al. 1975; Cavender 1986).

The basic morphology of centrarchids is much like that of many other percoid families. Sunfishes have a moderately elongate or suboval body that is moderately or very compressed, often discoid; a medium or large head; mouth small to spacious, terminal or supraterminal, with the upper jaw protrusile; small teeth on jaws and some oral cavity bones; the lower pharyngeal arches bear conical or molariform teeth; eye medium or large; lateral line usually complete; body fully scaled, scales ctenoid except in *Acantharchus*. The spines and rays of the dorsal fin are united, usually broadly, by a membrane; caudal fin usually emarginate; anal fin spinous anteriorly; pelvic fins in thoracic position, typically with 1 spine and 5 rays, and bound to the body by a membrane; pectoral fins are set high on the body.

The typical centrarchid morph parallels the form and function evolved in many marine percoid families (Gosline 1971, 1985). It includes a deep, moderately or very compressed torso; contiguous dorsal fins, the soft-rayed portion often enlarged; enlarged soft anal fin; size of the caudal fin reduced relative to the dorsal and anal fins; and a relatively small mouth in some species. Functional traits associated with this morphology are an inability to attain rapid swimming speeds, a general adaptation to lake environments, and most feeding behavior dominated by nipping, plucking, or gleaning.

Black basses (*Micropterus*) represent an adaptive extreme of centrarchids. They have an elongate subcompressed body; a relatively small dorsal and anal fin; a relatively large, more emarginate caudal fin; a large mouth; greater association with current; and a tendency to chase prey. A different, compressed-bod-

Fish 204 *Ambloplites rupestris* 31 mm SL.

Fish 205 *Ambloplites cavifrons* 31 mm SL.

Fish 206 *Acantharchus pomotis* 37 mm SL.

Fish 207 *Centrarchus macropterus* 19 mm SL.

Fish 208 *Pomoxis nigromaculatus* 40 mm SL.

Fish 209 *Pomoxis annularis* 40 mm SL.

Fish 210 *Micropterus dolomieu* 42 mm SL.

Fish 211 *Micropterus punctulatus* 50 mm SL.

Fish 212 *Micropterus salmoides* 44 mm SL.

Fish 204–212 Young centrarchids.

ied extreme is exemplified by crappies (*Pomoxis*) and especially the flier (*Centrarchus*); these have large, nearly symmetrical dorsal and anal fins.

Coloration within the family ranges from drab to brightly multihued. Many species have dark spots, speckles, blotches, bars, or stripes contrasting with silver, green, olive, or brown ground shades. Sexual dichromatism often constitutes heightened contrast between dark or bright marks and the ground color. *Lepomis* sunfishes exhibit striking sexual dichromatism, especially during the breeding season; males display brilliant hues of red to yellow and green to blue, often set off by iridescent sheens. Melanistic patterns of centrarchids can vary by time of day (bold marks or blotches characteristic of night coloration), mood (rapid darkening or paling), or life-cycle stage.

Most sunfishes and basses typically live in lakes, ponds, and in pools and backwaters of streams. Most species are typical of the Coastal Plain and other lowland areas. Among notable exceptions is the run- and rapids-dwelling shoal bass, an undescribed species of *Micropterus* that is endemic to the Apalachicola drainage in the southeastern United States (Ramsey 1975). The family occupies diverse waters, finding suitable habitat ranging from montane streams to lowland swamps. Some centrarchids enter tidal fresh water and infrequently stray into the mesohaline zone of estuaries. Most species typically associate with cover such as logs and weed beds.

Centrarchids are generalized sight-feeding carnivores, typically taking crustaceans, insects, and fishes. The large mouth of many species allows capture of a wide size range of prey fishes; the larger black basses are particularly piscivorous. Adult Roanoke bass *Ambloplites cavifrons* feed mainly on crayfishes. The redear sunfish *Lepomis microlophus* may be a true prey specialist; it feeds heavily on snails and small clams, crushing them with molariform pharyngeal teeth (Lauder 1983).

The reproductive behavior of basses and sunfishes is one of the most interesting and often watched aspects of their biology. In the basic centrarchid spawning plan, the male excavates a shallow, generally circular nest. The diameter of the nest depends on substrate composition and the body size and extent of movement of the male; usually it is two to three times the male's length (Keenleyside 1979). In nest-making the male assumes a nearly vertical position and vigorously fans the substrate with the tail, suspending and removing silt and small debris. Some

Fish 213   *Enneacanthus obesus* 22 mm SL.

Fish 214   *Enneacanthus chaetodon* 20 mm SL.

Fish 215   *Lepomis gulosus* 33 mm SL.

Fish 216   *Lepomis cyanellus* 34 mm SL.

Fish 217   *Lepomis auritus* 30 mm SL.

Fish 218   *Lepomis megalotis* 29 mm SL.

Fish 219   *Lepomis macrochirus* 39 mm SL.

Fish 220   *Lepomis gibbosus* 37 mm SL.

Fish 221   *Lepomis microlophus* 31 mm SL.

Fish 213–222   Young centrarchids.

species also use the mouth to push or grasp larger particles for transport to the nest periphery. When brooding eggs, generally the male departs the nest only to defend his territory or to engage in courtship. Species of *Enneacanthus* are known to make nest cavities within vegetation as well as to form depressions on the bottom.

Nests occur singly, in small groups, or in crowded colonies. Although located most often in shallows, nesting may occur deeper than 2 m, especially in reservoirs with steeply sloped margins. Virtually all species spawn strictly in fresh water; a notable exception is Richmond's (1940) observation of the redbreast sunfish *Lepomis auritus* nesting in slightly brackish water. Nesting occurs during mid-spring to early summer for most species. Breeding periods often are lengthy; most spawning occurs early in the period or as several peaks over the season.

The characteristic spawning act involves a listing sideways by the female, during which both sexes orient head to head and ventrally contact each other, often while moving circularly over the nest. The male guards the nest at least until the eggs hatch; sometimes species of *Micropterus* herd schools of fry.

The recent discoveries of alternative patterns of male reproduction in some sunfish species are intriguing (Gross 1982, 1984; Dominey 1988). For example, in the bluegill *Lepomis macrochirus*, in addition to the larger nesting or parental males which construct and defend nests, there are two kinds of cuckolder males. Small, relatively young "sneakers" fertilize eggs by darting from cover to join an ovipositing pair. Intermediate-sized "satellites" or "female mimics" deceptively gain proximity to parental male–female pairings by exhibiting female behavior or color.

Centrarchid eggs range in size from 0.8 mm (pumpkinseed, white crappie) to 2.5 mm (smallmouth bass) (Hardy 1978b). Many estimates of fecundity are probably unreliable because of problems in accurately estimating large numbers of ova, varied criteria of analysis (enumerating total ova versus mature ova), and in particular because females may spawn several times in a given year.

Intrageneric hybridization occurs in all polytypic genera and is relatively common in *Lepomis* sunfishes.

It tends to occur most frequently when spawning sites are limited or disturbed, when one species greatly outnumbers another, and with introduced species (Hubbs 1955). Artificial hybridization has produced a much larger number of intra- and intergeneric crosses than are known in nature. Hatching success and growth of the hybrid progeny have been used in phylogenetic analyses (West and Hester 1966; Hester 1970; West 1970).

The propensity of *Lepomis* to hybridize interspecifically in nature seems peculiar, as all species are sexually dichromatic and the males of each species differ in nuptial coloration from those of all other species. However, Noble's (1938) demonstration that sexual dichromatism alone does not always effect sex recognition in the pumpkinseed may indicate occasional failure of sunfishes to identify conspecific mates. The breakdown of species-isolating mechanisms may extend to behavioral and habitat attributes. *Lepomis* has a relatively recent evolutionary history; hybridization may have played an important role in its speciation, much as considered for *Micropterus* by Hubbs and Bailey (1940) and Hubbs (1955).

The hybrid vigor of some crosses has characteristics desired in sport fishes—rapid growth, larger maximum size, and more rod-fighting power (Childers 1967, 1975). Unfortunately, hybridization resulting from the introduction of nonindigenous species and subspecies apparently has had adverse effects, such as extirpation of the Roanoke bass from a portion of its native range by introduced rock bass, and possible reduction of genomic fitness of certain largemouth bass populations by mixing of the northern and Florida subspecies.

The chief resource use of centrarchids is recreational fishing. The avid interest in sunfishes and basses led to their wide dissemination by governmental agencies and private individuals; many species are naturalized beyond native limits, some overseas. Revenues generated by black bass angling, which often is highly competitive, amount to millions of dollars annually. Native-fish aquarists have long kept several members of the family; the small *Enneacanthus* species are especially popular.

Range-mapping of many centrarchids is problematic. Most species are moderately wide ranging, but there has been an excessive tendency in mapping to indicate contiguous distributions. In our map insets we have attempted to portray gaps evidenced in the dot-distribution maps of Lee et al. (1980) and other literature. We also strove to determine the native range limits for all species within and near Virginia. Many of these, particularly the black basses, have a twisting trail of distributional literature that defies resolution. Some distribution patterns in Virginia reflect general rarity and habitat specificity (*Enneacanthus chaetodon*), are based on paucity of sampling in certain areas, or remain curious and unexplained (e.g., the hiatus of *Lepomis gibbosus* in the middle New drainage).

Name.—Centrarch- means "spine anus," referring to the prominent anal spines of all species. The common name is from the most speciose genus, *Lepomis*, the sunfishes.

Key to Sunfishes   Centrarchidae

The key is chiefly for adults and large juveniles. Because of ontogenetic variation in color patterns, photographs of young specimens are included (Fish 204–221). Table 10 compares small specimens of *Micropterus*. For small fish of all species, we recommend studying size series to determine developmental changes in pigment patterns and body proportions. Lateral line scale counts in the key include unpored scales anterior to the caudal base.

Of particular importance in *Lepomis* are the size, shape, and pigment of the "earflap" (opercular flap). The earflap varies markedly, being inobvious in small young of all species, and much prolonged or deepened in large adults of some. The pale margin characteristic of several species becomes obvious only in large juveniles and adults. In the field, inspect the earflap margin for the species-specific presence or absence of redness that fades in preservative.

Key to Genera (and to Species of Genera Monotypic in Virginia)

1a	Anal spines (4)5–7(8)	2
1b	Anal spines (2)3(4)	5
2a	Gill rakers 15 or fewer	3
2b	Gill rakers 20 or more	4

3a Caudal fin emarginate; scales ctenoid (Figure 6) .... *Ambloplites*
3b Caudal fin rounded; scales cycloid (scale shape typical of percoids—truncate
    and scalloped anteriorly—but lacking ctenii) .... MUD SUNFISH—*Acantharchus pomotis* p. 708

4a Dorsal spines 11–13 .... FLIER—*Centrarchus macropterus* p. 711
4b Dorsal spines 5–8 .... *Pomoxis*

5a Body elongate, basslike, greatest body depth usually less than ⅓ of
    standard length; lateral line scales 55 or more .... *Micropterus*
5b Body deep and strongly compressed, sunfishlike, greatest body
    depth usually more than ⅓ of standard length; lateral line scales
    less than 55 6

6a Caudal fin rounded (Figure 5; sometimes truncate or very slightly
    emarginate in *E. chaetodon*); lateral line scales (23)25–32(35) .... *Enneacanthus*
6b Caudal fin emarginate; lateral line scales (36)37–50(54) .... *Lepomis*

Key to Species of *Ambloplites*

1a Cheek fully scaled, the scales medium-sized and slightly or moderately
    embedded, the posterior margins obvious; body lacking distinct round
    pale spots, although vague pale areas may be present; anal fin of adult
    dark-margined; lateral line scales (35)38–43(45); scales above lateral line
    (to first dorsal fin origin) (6)7–8(9); breast scales between ventral ends
    of pectoral fin bases (19)21–25(27) .... ROCK BASS—*A. rupestris* p. 699
1b Cheek naked or partly scaled, the scales tiny or small and much embedded;
    body often with distinct round pale spots; anal fin of adult not dark-margined;
    lateral line scales (38)41–47(49); scales above lateral line (8)9–11(12); breast
    scales (26)28–34(36); (Roanoke and Chowan drainages only) .... ROANOKE BASS—*A. cavifrons* p. 703

Key to Species of *Pomoxis*

1a Dorsal spines (6)7–8; length of dorsal fin base equal to or greater
    than distance from first dorsal spine to eye (Figure 65A); side with
    irregularly arranged dark flecks or small blotches .... BLACK CRAPPIE—*P. nigromaculatus* p. 713
1b Dorsal spines 5–6(7); length of dorsal fin base less than distance
    from first dorsal spine to eye (Figure 65B); side with dark flecks
    tending to form vertical bars .... WHITE CRAPPIE—*P. annularis* p. 715

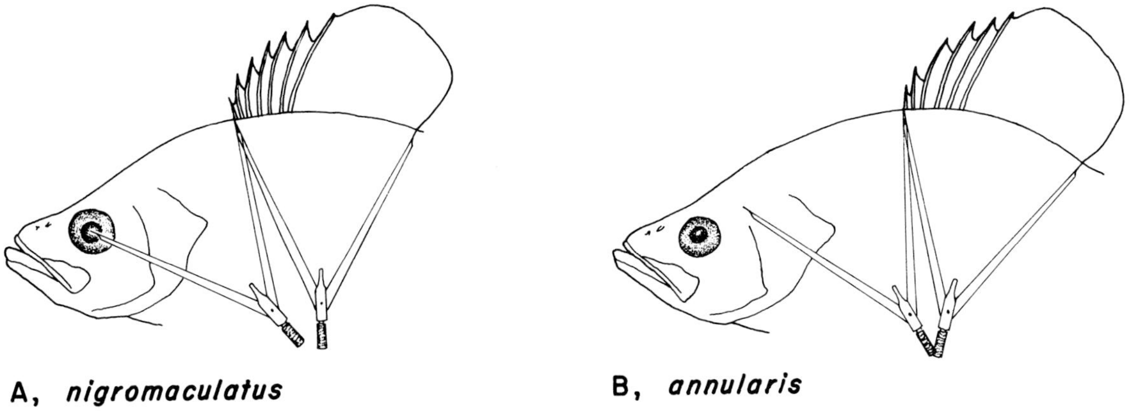

A, *nigromaculatus*   **B, *annularis***

Figure 65 Relationship of dorsal fin base length to distance from dorsal fin origin to eye in *Pomoxis*: (A) Base length reaches eye in *P. nigromaculatus*. (B) Base length falls short of eye in *P. annularis*.

Key to Species of *Enneacanthus*

1a   Dorsal fin deeply emarginate (deep notch near juncture of spinous
      and soft-rayed portions); dorsal fin with only first 2–3 interspinous
      membranes distinctly darkened, rest of fin much paler, sometimes
      tessellated but not spotted; (Chowan drainage only) .... BLACKBANDED SUNFISH—*E. chaetodon* p. 723
1b   Dorsal fin not deeply emarginate near juncture of spinous and soft-
      rayed portions; all dorsal fin membranes mostly uniformly duskily
      or darkly pigmented, with rows of pale spots particularly in soft-
      rayed portion 2

2a   Circumpeduncle scales (least count) (17)19–22(24); body side
      pattern of adult male dominated by dark bars .... BANDED SUNFISH—*E. obesus* p. 717
2b   Circumpeduncle scales (14)16–18(20); body side pattern of adult
      male dominated by pale spots .... BLUESPOTTED SUNFISH—*E. gloriosus* p. 721

Key to Species of *Micropterus* (see also Table 10)

Young and small juveniles (about 25–100 mm TL)

1a   Lateral pigmentation consisting of weakly to well-developed
      narrow bars; caudal spot weakly developed or absent .... SMALLMOUTH BASS—*M. dolomieu* p. 726
1b   Lateral pigmentation consisting of a bold irregular midlateral stripe;
      caudal spot well developed 2

2a   Tongue with narrow medial patch of small teeth (may be felt with
      a fine point on small fish); widest vertical expansions of anterior
      portion of midlateral stripe developed in 4–7 horizontal scale rows ....
      .... SPOTTED BASS—*M. punctulatus* p. 730
2b   Tongue lacking teeth; widest vertical expansions of anterior portion of
      midlateral stripe developed in 2–4 horizontal scale rows .... LARGEMOUTH BASS—*M. salmoides* p. 732

Larger juveniles and adults (greater than about 100 mm TL)

1a   Posterior end of upper jaw extending posterior to eye; first dorsal
      fin markedly convex, shortest posterior spine less than ½ the
      length of longest spine; anal and second dorsal fin membranes
      unscaled above basal sheath of fin .... LARGEMOUTH BASS—*M. salmoides* p. 732
1b   Posterior end of upper jaw not extending posterior to eye; first
      dorsal fin not markedly convex, shortest posterior spine more than
      ½ the length of longest spine; anal and second dorsal fin
      membranes with splintlike scales on membranes above basal sheath
      of fin 2

2a   Side plain, mottled, or barred; scales above lateral line (11)12–13;
      circumpeduncle scales 29–31(32); lateral line scales (68)71–77(81) ....
      .... SMALLMOUTH BASS—*M. dolomieu* p. 726
2b   Side with wide, irregularly margined, dark midlateral stripe; scales
      above lateral line (7)8–9; circumpeduncle scales (22)23–27; lateral
      line scales (55)60–68(72) .... SPOTTED BASS—*M. punctulatus* p. 730

Table 10 Comparison of typical character states of Virginia black basses, genus *Micropterus*. Pigment patterns of young are partly from Ramsey and Smitherman (1972).

	Species		
Stage	*dolomieu*	*punctulatus*	*salmoides*
Young (25–60 mm TL)			
Lateral pigmentation	Narrow bars	Narrow midlateral stripe or series of blotches	Narrow midlateral stripe or series of blotches
Caudal fin band	Bold, uniform across fin	Bold, uniform across fin	Weak, darkest on lobes
Juvenile and adult			
Bold irregular midlateral stripe	Absent	Present	Present
Frequency of occurrence of medial tongue tooth patch	About 50%	100%	0%
Pyloric caeca	Simple	Simple	Forked
Squamation of basal portion of membranes of 2nd dorsal and anal fins[a]	Splintlike scales present	Splintlike scales present	Splintlike scales absent
Posterior end of upper jaw relative to posterior rim of orbit	End of jaw not reaching rim (mouth relatively small)	End of jaw even with rim	End of jaw extends posterior to rim (mouth relatively large)

[a]Basal sheath of typical (not splintlike) scales not included. To detect splintlike scales in small fish, probe fin membranes with a pointed tool under magnification.

Key to Species of *Lepomis*

1a Tongue with small median tooth patch; mouth large, upper jaw extending to point below middle of eye; dark lines radiating from or under eye are usually wide and straight (Figure 66A); fins usually boldly marbled and mottled .... WARMOUTH—*L. gulosus*   p. 737

1b Tongue lacking teeth (teeth rarely present in *L. cyanellus*); mouth small (except in *L. cyanellus*), upper jaw not extending to below middle of eye; lines radiating from or under eye are absent or narrow, mostly irregular, and dusky, rarely very dark (Figure 66B); fins plain or only moderately mottled 2

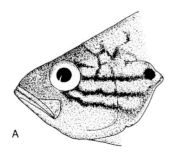

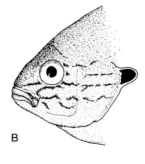

Figure 66 Head color patterns in *Lepomis*: (A) *L. gulosus*. (B) *L. megalotis*.

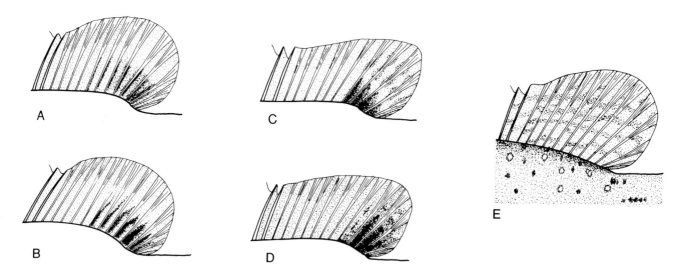

Figure 67   Second dorsal fin color patterns in *Lepomis*: (A) Juvenile *L. macrochirus*. (B) Adult *L. macrochirus*. (C) Juvenile *L. cyanellus*. (D) Adult *L. cyanellus*. (E) Adult *L. gibbosus*.

2a   Posteroventral area of second dorsal fin with markings (streaks, blotches, spots, or 1 spot) distinctly darker than any pattern that may be in anterior part of second dorsal (Figure 67A–D) 3
2b   Posteroventral area of second dorsal fin lacking distinct dark markings, or markings about same intensity as in anterior part of second dorsal (Figure 67E) 4

3a   Mouth large, upper jaw length greater than eye diameter; pectoral fin rounded and short, its tip not reaching dorsal margin of body when oriented perpendicular to body axis; opercular flap pale- or dusky-margined, the margin always paler than black central portion (Figure 68G, H) .... GREEN SUNFISH—*L. cyanellus*   p. 739
3b   Mouth small, upper jaw length about equal to eye diameter; pectoral fin pointed and long, its tip extending to or beyond dorsal margin of body when oriented perpendicular to body axis; opercular flap black to distal margin (Figure 68C) .... BLUEGILL—*L. macrochirus*   p. 747

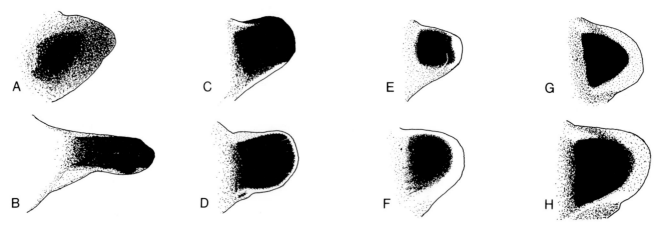

Figure 68   Opercular flap (earflap) color patterns in *Lepomis*: (A) Juvenile *L. auritus*. (B) Adult *L. auritus*. (C) *L. macrochirus*. (D) *L. megalotis*. (E) *L. gibbosus*. (F) *L. microlophus*. (G) Juvenile *L. cyanellus*. (H) Adult *L. cyanellus*.

Rock basses   Genus *Ambloplites* Rafinesque

Two of the four species of *Ambloplites* live in Virginia (Cashner and Suttkus 1977; Cashner and Jenkins 1982). The genus has either a basal position in centrarchid phylogeny (Branson and Moore 1962), or it is moderately advanced (Smith and Bailey 1961; Mabee 1988).

Name.—*Ambloplites* means "blunt armature," coined for the wide flat opercular spine. "Rock basses" refers to the frequent use of rocks as cover by most species. The species often are called redeye; the large eye typically is bright red.

Rock bass   *Ambloplites rupestris* (Rafinesque)

SYSTEMATICS

The rock bass was described in 1817 from lakes of New York, Vermont, and Canada. Its close relationship to the Roanoke bass *A. cavifrons* is discussed under that species.

DESCRIPTION

Materials.—From Cashner and Jenkins (1982) and 30 more Virginia specimens. Life color based on 10 Virginia specimens; nuptial color from Gross and Nowell (1980), Noltie (1985), and our observations.

Anatomy.—A large-mouthed centrarchid with obvious cheek scales, usually 5 anal spines, and a dark-margined anal fin; adults are 110–200 mm TL. Body moderately compressed, stocky; lateral profile of head dorsum convex; mouth large, terminal or supraterminal; eye large; cheek scales medium to large, evident; pectoral fin rounded; caudal fin emarginate. Differences between the sexes of spawning adults are described by Noltie (1985).

Meristics.—Lateral line scales (35)38–43(45); scales above lateral line (6)7–8(9); scales below lateral line (11)12–14(15); circumpeduncle scales 18–22. Dorsal spines (10)11(12); dorsal rays (10)11–12; anal spines 5–6, usually 5; anal rays 10–11; pectoral rays (12)14–15.

Color in Preservative.—Overall appearance dusky to dark, variegated, blotched, or striped. Side and top of head and nape uniformly dusky to dark; back dark; dorsolaterally often with irregular pale marks but rarely distinctly spotted; side below lateral line with dark stripes; venter uniformly dusky, slightly mottled, or dark. Median fins mostly slightly dusky to very dark, pale spots in membranes (best developed basally); second dorsal and caudal fins sometimes with narrow dark margin; medium to large juvenile and adult with dark to black margin on anal fin and sometimes pelvic fin, dark margin absent or slightly developed in young and small juvenile. Side in young and small juvenile often with large dark blotches or zones; same pattern may occur in adult, particularly female.

Color in Life Plate 28.—Head dorsum and nape pale olive to olive-brown; pale lateral areas silvery, yellowish, or brassy; dark lateral stripes olive-black; venter silvery to

Fish 222 *Ambloplites rupestris* adult male 145 mm SL (REJ 1046), VA, Craig County, Sinking Creek, 26 September 1983.

Fish 223 *Ambloplites rupestris* adult female 103 mm SL (REJ 1041), VA, Botetourt County, Craig Creek, 21 September 1983.

brassy with olive-black peppering; iris partly or fully bright red. Median fins olive-brown to black with pale olive to yellow-olive membrane spots; second dorsal and caudal fins with hint of black margin; anal fin margin in juvenile and adult black (most so in large male), boldly contrasted or at least distinctly darker than remainder of fin; pelvic fin occasionally with leading ray and hind edge dark, otherwise pelvic and always the pectoral fin uniform pale yellow to olive. Spawning male becomes moderately to very dark over entire body; female may be quite blotched.

Larvae.—Described by Buynak and Mohr (1979b) and Tin (1982d).

COMPARISON

Some characters in the *Key*, as well as body contours, that distinguish the rock bass from the Roanoke bass merit elaboration: (1) anal fin margin, darkness and contrast [moderately dusky or black in juvenile and adult, the edge distinctly contrasting with rest of fin in *rupestris* vs. dark margin usually absent, rarely slightly developed, never distinctly contrasting in *cavifrons*]; (2) pale spotting on upper body and side of head in adult [spots often absent on body or, when present, usually irregularly shaped, less obvious; head never spotted vs. spots usually present on body, rounder, more distinct; head often spotted]; (3) adult predorsal body contour in lateral view usually [more convex, more bull-headed and hump-backed vs. more evenly sloped to the mouth, occiput sometimes slightly concave].

BIOLOGY

A generalist predator, the large-mouthed rock bass eats a variety of microcrustaceans, insects, and other invertebrates when young; with growth, it shifts to larger prey (Keast and Webb 1966). Adults also feed on insects and other invertebrates including terrestrial forms, and add fishes and, particularly, crayfishes to the diet (Probst et al. 1984; Vadas 1990).

Age and growth have been widely studied; summaries are by Scott (1949), Brown (1960), and Carlander (1977). Sexual maturation generally occurs by age 3 and ages greater than 6 are uncommonly attained; a 13-year-old was taken in a Wisconsin Lake. Differences in growth rate between the sexes were reported for some areas but not others. In northern lakes the range of means of total length at age 4 was 83–181 mm, unweighted grand mean 124; comparable data for 15 streams or lakes in Ohio, Indiana, Illinois, Kentucky, North Carolina, and Oklahoma are 147–203, mean, 175. (The mean of 244 mm TL from a Tennessee stream is excluded due to small sample size.) A combined sample of age-4 fish from streams of several Virginia drainages averaged 147 mm TL (Petrimoulx 1983). From 14 stream populations of the New and upper Tennessee drainages the range of means at age 4 was 117–168 mm TL, unweighted mean 132 (Wollitz 1972). In the Potomac River, the age-4 mean was 182 mm TL (Davis and Enamait 1982).

Rock bass larger than 250 mm TL (10 inches) are rarely encountered. We have a reliable angler's report of a 330-mm TL (13 inches) rock bass from the upper James drainage. The Virginia record weight of 1 kg (2 pounds 2 ounces) is from a different fish caught in the upper James, and one from the Tennessee drainage. From over the species range, apparently the greatest lengths reported are 340 mm TL (13.4 inches) and 373 mm TL (14.7 inches), the former questionably from Canada, the latter from Ohio (Scott and Crossman 1973; Trautman 1981). The former fish weighed 1.64 kg (3 pounds 10 ounces), the Ohio fish 0.88 kg (1 pound 15 ounces). A 1.5-kg (3 pounds 5 ounces) specimen came from Michigan (Becker 1983). The IGFA (1985) angling record is 1.36 kg (3 pounds) from Ontario. The often cited maximum size of rock bass was based on a Roanoke bass (see account).

Spawning occurs during April to July; the exact timing depends on location and weather. Nesting was reported from late April to early June in the Shenandoah system (Surber 1970); we observed a pair of A. rupestris spawning in the Little River of Floyd County on 30 May, water 22°C. Females remained ripe into late June in a high-elevation section of the New drainage (Tyus 1970). The range of water temperature during spawning is 15.6–26°C (Scott and Crossman 1973; Carlander 1977; Jenkins and Jenkins

1980); the peak of spawning occurs in the low 20s°C (Gross and Nowell 1980).

Males fan out circular nests in shallows having coarse sand to large gravel substrate and pugnaciously defend them against intruders. Each may spawn with several females, and a female may spawn with several males. Almost half the males in an Ontario river nested more than once in a single breeding season, but few males raised more than one brood as far as the larval stage. Flooding, predation, and fouling of nests by algae were major causes of brood failure (Noltie and Keenleyside 1986). Fecundity is 2,000–11,000, the average female lays about 5,000 eggs, and fry per nest average about 800 (Becker 1983).

Ambloplites rupestris hybridizes in nature with A. cavifrons (Cashner and Jenkins 1982; Jenkins and Cashner 1983) and other Ambloplites (Cashner and Suttkus 1977). It has been experimentally crossed with various centrarchid genera (Tyus 1973).

HABITAT

Rock bass occupy clear, moderate-gradient, cool and warm creeks, streams, and rivers; they inhabit pools and backwaters, and strongly associate with shelter. Their preferences are very similar to smallmouth bass (Probst et al. 1984) and Roanoke bass, but they tend to occupy lesser currents. Rock bass apparently avoid areas of moderate to heavy siltation and turbidity in Virginia. They prosper in vegetated and unvegetated areas of lakes and reservoirs northward, but occur in few Virginia impoundments.

DISTRIBUTION   Map 137

Ambloplites rupestris is native to the Mississippi, Great Lakes–St. Lawrence, and southern Hudson Bay basins, and was introduced in many other areas. In Virginia, it is indigenous only to the Tennessee and Big Sandy drainages, and has been introduced to the New and all major Atlantic slope drainages.

Until recently the rock bass was generally considered native to the New drainage. Cashner and Jenkins (1982) contested that status based partly on their interpretation of statements by Cope (1868b). Their conclusion is corroborated by an early comment (VFC 1877a) that the New lacked gamefishes except for catfishes. Our analysis of stocking records reveals earlier and wider dissemination than indicated by Cashner and Jenkins (1982); it is based on stocking records for 1875–1935 (VFC 1877a–1882; USFC 1876–1936; McDonald 1886). Generally only first records for a system are noted below; Map 137 shows additional

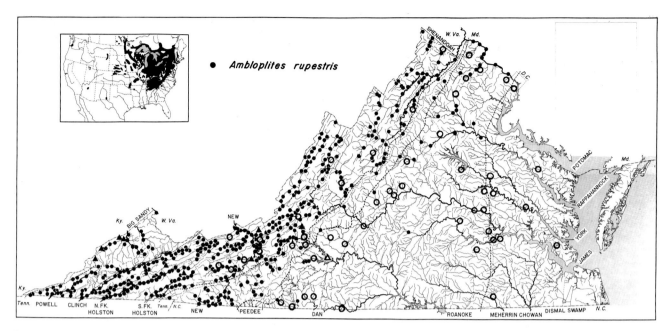

Map 137 Rock bass. Open circles show sites, several only approximately located, stocked during 1875–1921; we were unable to even approximately place the sites of several other early stockings. The many instances in which early "applicants" were supplied rock bass for stocking lack locality designations. Transplants west of New drainage not shown. Open triangle on Smith Mountain Lake is an unverified record from an unspecified site in the reservoir (Hart 1978); possibly it is based on the Roanoke bass.

records. An analysis of stocking cannot be complete because the many applicants that were early supplied with fish lack geographic placement.

The first stockings in the New drainage were transfers in 1875 of adults from a pond near Saltville, apparently in the North Fork Holston system, to Toms Creek of the lower New and three sites in the middle James drainage. In 1879, fish of unstated origin, probably the Holston, were carried from a breeding pond in the upper James to an upper James tributary.

Ambloplites rupestris rapidly became established in the New; by 1889 the Wytheville Hatchery was supplied by seining Reed, Peak, and Wolf creeks of the drainage. The Central Station Hatchery also had received rock bass by 1889 and served as another dissemination point. From one or both hatcheries, the drainages that received fish were (in geographic sequence): lower Potomac 1887, upper Potomac 1898, Shenandoah 1887, lower Rappahannock 1902, upper Rappahannock 1898, Rapidan 1904, York 1887, lower James 1900, Appomattox 1902, Nottoway 1895, Meherrin 1921, middle and upper Roanoke proper 1902, and Dan 1893.

Stockings continued into recent years in Virginia (Cashner and Jenkins 1982); the later releases may have founded some populations. However, owing to the paucity of surveying before the 1940s, it is impos-

sible to determine when most Virginia rock bass populations actually were established. First years of verified capture of *A. rupestris* in Atlantic slope drainages within Virginia are: Potomac 1911, Rappahannock 1944, James 1928, Roanoke proper 1952, and Dan 1941.

Many stockings failed, notably those in silted outer Piedmont and Coastal Plain streams and ponds. All introduction sites that we located in the York drainage were ponds; rock bass are now absent from the York. The Blackwater River (upper Roanoke) population persisted until about 1963, and rock bass also died out from streams and ponds of the upper Dan before about 1970 (Jenkins and Cashner 1983).

The lack of a record of rock bass in the middle James River and downstream through the Fall Zone is odd, particularly in view of the strong population there of the ecologically similar smallmouth bass. The smallmouth population is self-sustaining, but its wider establishment may be related to the apparently heavier and wider stocking of this species in the middle James. Most or all stockings of rock bass in and near the James Fall Zone were made in ponds, from which this species may not have escaped. Some transplants to middle James tributaries may have failed because of siltation (Jenkins and Burkhead 1975a). In time, rock bass likely will disperse into the middle main-stem James River and establish through the Fall Zone.

Abundance.—Often common in montane provinces, generally rare on the Piedmont. Where established by introduction, the rock bass often becomes one of the most common centrarchids.

REMARKS

The fighting tenacity of the rock bass on a fishing rod matches its ability to establish and proliferate in suitable areas. These are desirable attributes of most intentionally stocked species, but the introduction of this competitive, prolific sunfish apparently contributed to the demise of the Roanoke bass in the upper Roanoke drainage (Cashner and Jenkins 1982; Jenkins and Cashner 1983; herein). Rock bass caused the decline of the much-valued brook trout fishery in Laurel Bed Lake. The lake was then drained to remove rock bass, only to have well-intentioned anglers restock them.

Name.—Rupestris means "living among rocks." This species and the cognate Roanoke bass frequently are called redeye.

Roanoke bass   *Ambloplites cavifrons* Cope

SYSTEMATICS

Cope (1868b) described *A. cavifrons* from the "head waters of the Roanoke River, Montgomery County, Virginia." Based on reconstruction of his itinerary of exploration in 1867, the type locality is the North Fork Roanoke River or one of its tributaries, not the South Fork considered by Cashner and Jenkins (1982).

At various times the Roanoke bass was considered a species or a subspecies of the rock bass *A. rupestris.* Ross (1969) suggested that the Roanoke bass was extirpated from the upper Roanoke River due to introgressive hybridization with rock bass. Cashner and Jenkins (1982) and Jenkins and Cashner (1983) documented hybridization between the two taxa and regarded *A. cavifrons* to be a species. A limited electrophoretic study supported species status (Garman 1988).

DESCRIPTION

Materials.—From Cashner and Jenkins (1982), 24 wild Virginia adults, and 14 young from a hatchery. Life color from Petrimoulx and Jenkins (1979), Petrimoulx (1984), and 6 adults and 1 young from Virginia.

Anatomy.—A large-mouthed centrarchid with few or no cheek scales, usually 6 anal spines, a pale-spotted body, and an undarkened or noncontrasting anal fin margin; adults are 150–235 mm SL. Body compressed and robust; lateral profile of head dorsum nearly straight, often slightly concave over eye; mouth large, terminal or supraterminal; eye large; cheek scales apparently absent, or few, small, deeply imbedded, and inobvious; pectoral fin rounded; caudal fin emarginate.

Meristics.—Lateral line scales (38)41–47(49); scales above lateral line (8)9–11(12); scales below lateral line 14–15(16); circumpeduncle scales 20–22. Dorsal spines 11–12; dorsal rays 11–12; anal spines (5)6(7); anal rays 10–11(12); pectoral rays (14)15(16).

Color in Preservative.—Body moderately dusky to very dark; large juvenile and adult with few to many, vague to sharply demarked, pale spots on upper body; spots sometimes also on lower body and side of head; spots generally absent in young and small juvenile. Side often with vague to bold dark stripes effected by paler dorsal and ventral fields of scales. Head uniformly dusky or dark (except for spots), or small fish often with wide dark area on cheek; opercular spot dark, edge often slightly paler. Dorsal fins and basal half of caudal and anal fins with few to many pale spots in membranes; anal fin not dark-margined, or if margin dark, then not notably darker than adjacent part of fin; pelvic and pectoral fins uniformly dusky. Young (about 30 mm SL) with dusky banding and mottling over pale body; irregular lateral stripes few, developing; dorsal, caudal, and anal fins slightly dusky, lightly mottled; pelvic and pectoral fins pale.

Color in Life   Plate 28.—Head and body dorsum medium to dark olive-brown or mostly olive; cheek and opercle olive-brown to brassy olive; cheek spots, if present, iridescent whitish, brassy, or gold-green; iris mostly bright red; opercle spot dark olive or black; body spots and lateral pale stripes silvery, brassy, pale lime-green, or gold-green; venter white or pale yellow-green or olive-black. In some specimens the side of the head and the body from back to belly are heavily spotted (in preservative the spots become less contrastive or are indistinct). Fins pale olive to olive-black; basal fin mottling, when present, olive-brown to black; pale fin spots white to yellow; pelvic rays white to yellow-olive. Spawning male very dark in body and fins, increasing the contrast with pale spots; nuptial female remains mostly olive, relatively pale. In young the dorsal mottling and banding brown-olive; dorsal and lateral pale areas white with slight pink-green cast; venter opalescent; iris pale orange-red; dark pigment in fins brown-black.

COMPARISON

See *A. rupestris.*

Fish 224   *Ambloplites cavifrons* adult male 217 mm SL (REJ 921), VA, Henry County, Smith River, 10 June 1981.

Fish 225   *Ambloplites cavifrons* subadult male 158 mm SL (REJ 1032), VA, Lunenburg County, North Meherrin River, 2 September 1983.

BIOLOGY

Life history data for Virginia populations are from Petrimoulx (1983, 1984) and Garman (1988). The species also has been studied in North Carolina (W. Smith 1970, 1971; McBride et al. 1982). Young chiefly eat small crustaceans and insects; juveniles and adults take fishes, insects, and particularly crayfishes. The high frequency of river weed *Podostemum* in stomachs of Roanoke bass indicates that foraging is concentrated in areas of appreciable current (McBride et al. 1982).

Both sexes mature in age-class 2 or 3; few fish live past 6 years, a 9-year-old being the oldest reported. The sexes grow at about equal rates. At age 4 in Virginia, nine fish from Town Creek averaged 201 mm TL, and 19 specimens from six streams including Town Creek were 179–262 mm TL, mean, 216 (Petrimoulx 1983; Garman 1988). Growth was similar in North Carolina; among large samples from the Tar River, age-4 fish ranged 186–239 mm TL, mean, 208,

and from the Eno River of the Neuse drainage, 217–250 mm, mean, 219 (McBride et al. 1982). McBride et al. considered that W. Smith's (1970, 1971) growth data may not be comparable owing to differing methods of analysis. The largest specimen captured in these studies was about 305 mm TL.

Ambloplites cavifrons is the largest species of the genus, but sizes attained have been uncertain owing to misidentifications or failure to attempt identifications. Based on place of capture and secondarily on large size, we regard the following records to have been of Roanoke bass. The often-cited largest *A. "rupestris"* of 1.7 kg (3.75 pounds) traces to Bean (1903), then back to Dr. W. Overton (*in* Bean 1903), who had referred to "rock bass" from the vicinity of Stony Creek in the Chowan drainage, Virginia, where *A. cavifrons* is native. The VFC (1877a) noted that "red-eye" were said to reach 3 pounds in the Chowan and Roanoke drainages. The "James drainage" specimen of *A. cavifrons* caught in 1883 and considered the largest of the species—355 mm "SL"—by Cashner and Jenkins (1982:USNM 32631) is actually 290 mm SL, 355 mm TL. This specimen, reported as 355.6 mm ("14 inches") by Bean (1903), has a further interesting history (*Distribution*).

Martin (1953) listed a "rock bass" in the 15-inch class (381–403 mm TL) from Philpott Reservoir, on the Smith River, shortly after its filling, and indicated that 17% of those creeled exceeded 300 mm TL. During 1980–1990 a number of specimens around 0.9 kg (2 pounds) were landed in Virginia. The largest "rock bass" formally accepted by the VDGIF is the state historic record of 1.11 kg (2 pounds 7 ounces) caught in 1976 (*Remarks*). This fish was about 370 mm TL (282 mm SL) according to Petrimoulx's (1983) length–weight relationship equation and our conversion by SL = 0.794 TL. W. Smith (1970) noted an angler's report of a 1.93-kg (4.25 pounds) specimen from North Carolina.

The best statement concerning maximum size of *A. cavifrons* in Virginia is in a 1958 letter from R. G. Martin, then Fish Division Chief of the VDGIF, to E. C. Raney: "We have many authentic accounts . . . of two and three pound rock bass [sic] being caught from the Roanoke and Smith rivers and an occasional report of a four pound [1.81 kg] fish being creeled. . . . The last report that I recall was of a three pound four ounce rock bass caught in the Smith River about five miles below Bassett, Virginia in 1953."

Spawning observations of Roanoke bass in streams have not been reported. *Ambloplites cavifrons* may nest in faster water than does *A. rupestris* because it occupies such currents during the reproductive season (and other times) more frequently than does *A. rupestris*. In North Carolina hatchery ponds, spawning began when water reached 20–22°C and occurred from mid-May to mid-June (W. Smith 1971). Petrimoulx (1984) observed spawning in a Buller Hatchery pond (Virginia) in mid-June, at 20°C. Males construct circular nests in clay and gravel near banks. Nesting males court any approaching female. Both sexes are polygamous; males occasionally mate simultaneously with two females. The male guards the nest and attends the larvae. Fecundity is 3,000–11,500 mature (or maturing) ova.

Ambloplites cavifrons hybridized, perhaps introgressively, with *A. rupestris* in the upper Roanoke drainage; the population of *A. rupestris* had been established by introduction (Cashner and Jenkins 1982; Jenkins and Cashner 1983).

HABITAT

Roanoke bass occur in warm large creeks, streams, and small rivers of moderate to moderately low gra-

dient and typically clear (but often turbid) water. The range of habitat includes darkly stained, swamp-margined upper Coastal Plain rivers. In the upper Piedmont, large juveniles and adults inhabit sheltered areas of deep runs, the current-swept heads of pools, and, less often, the sluggish parts of pools. In Virginia, these life stages associate with rocky, gravelly, and well-silted bottoms, the latter particularly in the lower Piedmont and upper Coastal Plain (G. C. Garman, in litt.).

Despite this species' occurrence in appreciably silted sections, "Roanoke bass habitat" was identified by Petrimoulx (1983) as firm substrate among boulders and bedrock in moderate to swift current. In the North Carolina Piedmont and Coastal Plain, *A. cavifrons* was collected only in sections with perceptible flow and bottoms composed chiefly of rock, gravel, and sand (W. Smith 1970). Habitat characteristics of juveniles and adults are quantified by Petrimoulx (1980) and Garman (1988). The habitat of the young is unknown; they seem quite secretive (Jenkins and Cashner 1983; Petrimoulx 1983, 1984) and likely occur well under cover in calm water.

The occurrence of the Roanoke bass in impoundments is considered below.

DISTRIBUTION   Map 138

Ambloplites cavifrons inhabits the Chowan and Roanoke drainages of Virginia and the Tar and Neuse drainages of North Carolina (W. Smith 1971; Cashner and Jenkins 1982; Jenkins and Cashner 1983). In Virginia the range extends disjunctively from the Valley and Ridge Province and fringes of the Blue Ridge into the upper Coastal Plain.

The Roanoke bass apparently is extirpated from the extreme upper Roanoke system from Roanoke upstream, in the Valley and Ridge. Extensive surveying of the main river and its forks during 1968–1991 yielded no *A. cavifrons*. A specimen taken in 1949 from Mason Creek, an upper Roanoke River tributary, is the only *A. cavifrons* known from that subsequently well-sampled creek; it had been erroneously reported, based on the museum-ledger entry, as *A. rupestris* by Jenkins and Freeman (1972). The Roanoke bass likely last occurred in this area in Bradshaw Creek, a North Fork Roanoke tributary. It was caught there, with rock bass and hybrids, in 1978, but not found by Petrimoulx (1980) in 1979, by us in 1984, nor by Garman (1988) in 1987.

The Roanoke bass remains widespread in unimpounded sections of the Blackwater and Pigg rivers, both on the upper Piedmont, but it is generally rare or uncommon. The two other populations verified in the Piedmont of the Roanoke system are in the North

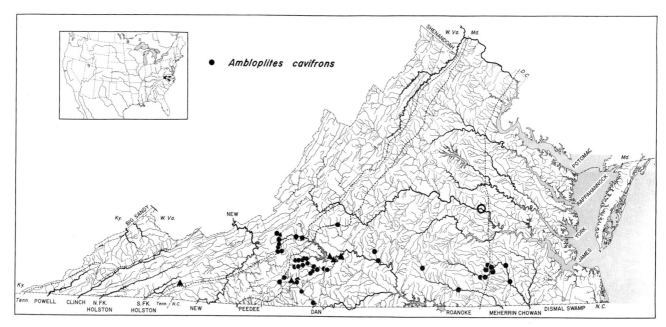

Map 138 Roanoke bass. Open circle denotes area of capture of an apparently stocked specimen. Westernmost triangle locates the Buller Fish Hatchery population.

Fork Otter and Falling rivers. A few *Ambloplites* specimens, probably *A. cavifrons*, have been reported by anglers from the middle Roanoke River near Brookneal; they may have strayed from a tributary. The main-stem middle Roanoke River is generally inhospitable to *Ambloplites*; it is mostly sand and silt laden, often turbid, and its volume fluctuates greatly according to releases from Leesville Dam.

In the Dan system, small populations occur in the Smith River above Philpott Reservoir, in the lower Smith River well below the tailwater trout zone (one recent record), and in Town Creek, a middle Smith tributary (Jenkins 1981; Garman 1988). Not until 1983 was the "rock bass" above Philpott Reservoir confirmed to be *A. cavifrons*; the population is very sparse. "Rock bass" were reported from Philpott collections and creel surveys up to about three years after filling of the reservoir (Martin 1953, 1954). Our queries indicate that *Ambloplites* has been unknown from the reservoir in recent years. A specimen of *A. cavifrons*, the only one known from the North Carolina portion of the Roanoke drainage, was found in the Dan River just below the Smith River mouth in September 1987. It may have been moved from the Smith River by the heavy flood earlier that month; that section of the Dan River had been well sampled in the previous several years (D. G. Cloutman, personal communication). Before the 1900s, the Roanoke bass probably occupied much of the Dan River and major tributaries in addition to the Smith River and Town Creek.

The Chowan drainage populations occupy the two main rivers, the Nottoway and Meherrin, that arise on the Piedmont, and one tributary system of each river. The Nottoway River from the Fall Zone to well downstream consistently yielded citation-sized specimens during 1970–1990. The Stony Creek (Nottoway system) population is known since the late 1800s, but it is localized in the lower section and is small. Roanoke bass also occupy lower Sappony Creek, the major lower Stony Creek tributary, based on an angler's report and one specimen taken in 1986 (M. D. Norman, in litt.); none were found in Sappony Creek by Petrimoulx (1980) and Garman (1988). The Meherrin River record is from 1977. The North Meherrin River population, known from 1958 to the present, has a restricted range.

The large specimen of *A. cavifrons* taken in 1883 at "Manchester"—the south side of the James River in Richmond—was discredited as a valid record for the James drainage by Cashner and Jenkins (1982), who implied that the specimen probably came from the Chowan drainage. We still think that specimen came from the Chowan, but now believe that the fish was later caught in the James. After Cashner and Jenkins' study, we learned that in 1877 an unspecified number of adult "red-eye perch" were stocked in the James River above Richmond, the source being "Stony Creek" (VFC 1878, 1882). There are at least 12 so-named streams in Virginia, but circumstances point to the one in the middle Nottoway system of the Chowan. It is near Richmond and has a long-known Roanoke bass population; specimens taken there in 1887 were given to the USNM by Dr. Overton. It is interesting that the James specimen, stocked as an adult, was caught six years later. It is not surprising that Roanoke bass did not become established in the James. The river is large; it is (and was then) subdivided within the Fall Zone at Richmond by dams and islands—deterrents to a fish seeking a mate. The stocking probably was of few fish.

Other stockings, without lasting effect, of apparent *A. cavifrons* are of an unknown number from the upper Roanoke to Catawba Creek of the upper James (VFC 1877b), and of two adults from the Roanoke at Salem to the New River near Radford (VFC 1879). Details of recent stockings of the Pigg River and Town Creek with Roanoke bass from the Buller Hatchery are noted by Jenkins and Cashner (1983).

Few records of *A. cavifrons* are from impoundments. The tandem Smith Mountain Lake and Leesville Reservoir, which have inundated an upper Piedmont section of the Roanoke River since 1963, each are fed by a stream containing *A. cavifrons* and not *A. rupestris*. We identified a specimen as a Roanoke bass that was taken from lower Smith Mountain Lake in 1974, and a 1.08-kg "rock bass" was landed there in 1988. Also in 1988, Leesville Reservoir yielded several large *Ambloplites*, many of them to a fishing guide who had fished it for more than 20 years but had not previously seen *Ambloplites* there (Cochran 1988). Stocking of Roanoke bass in North Carolina impoundments (and streams) did not result in their establishment other than in hatchery ponds (W. B. Smith, in litt.).

Abundance.—Relative to most other centrarchids, Roanoke bass are generally rare in Virginia. Most collections contain only one or two specimens; with normal collecting efforts, and even in lengthy searches of stream sections populated by Roanoke bass, capture of five or more specimens occurs rarely. The density of most Roanoke bass populations normally may be lower than typical of *A. rupestris*, or most Roanoke bass populations are living in marginal conditions. The rarity of capture of young may reflect generally poor reproductive success.

REMARKS

The Roanoke bass has one of the smallest native ranges of North American gamefishes, and the range has decreased, becoming disjunctive apparently in historical time. Although *A. cavifrons* has occupied four physiographic provinces and still lives in a wide variety of habitats, many populations may be existing at tolerance limits. It is gone from the Valley and Ridge section of the Roanoke drainage. Elsewhere in Virginia it generally is localized, having been depleted or exterminated by impoundment, pollution, and, likely, siltation. Siltation was wrought by extensive deforestation during Caucasian settlement; new sediment continues to overload most Piedmont and many Coastal Plain streams. The value of *A. cavifrons* as a sport fish has been underestimated. Thus we regard it to have special concern status in Virginia (Burkhead and Jenkins 1991); it has the same status in North Carolina (Bailey 1977).

The Nottoway River population is enigmatic; it occupies a considerably silted reach from the lower Piedmont to the upper Coastal Plain. The smallmouth bass, Roanoke logperch, and a few other upland–montane species—most of them swift-water dwellers—exhibit a similar pattern. Recent captures of several adult Roanoke bass in long, heavily silted Nottoway pools (M. D. Norman, in litt.) may indicate general adaptation to such conditions. However, the Chowan population as a whole is not strong. The other three species of *Ambloplites*, including the lowland-inhabiting *A. ariommus* and the Ozarkian *A. constellatus*, also avoid heavily silted biotopes (Cashner *in* Lee et al. 1980).

The loss of the native Roanoke bass population from the extreme upper Roanoke drainage may be ultimately attributed to competitive interaction, particularly during reproduction, with the alien rock bass. Although circumstantial, the evidence is substantial: the demise of the population coincides with the attainment of numerical dominance by rock bass during about 1945–1965; the rock bass has been generally distributed above Roanoke since 1965. The two species have quite similar habits. Certainly they interacted reproductively—they hybridized, supporting Ross' hypothesis of extirpation of the Roanoke bass by introgressive hybridization. Further, Petrimoulx's (1984) observation of a juvenile *A. rupestris* repeatedly challenging a nesting male *A. cavifrons*, when Roanoke bass did not bother nesting conspecifics, may indicate a disadvantage to Roanoke bass within a rock bass population.

Habitat degradation probably contributed to the decline of the upper Roanoke population. However, probably only the main-river population segment from Salem to somewhat below Roanoke would have been eradicated by the pollution that was prevalent during 1920–1970. Although the Roanoke River and its major tributaries above Salem have not been pristine in the 20th century, they still appear suited to Roanoke bass. In type and quality of habitat, these streams much resemble Town Creek on the upper

Piedmont, which supports the densest Roanoke bass population known to us in Virginia (and which lacks rock bass). The upper Roanoke offers better upland habitat than most Piedmont streams (other than perhaps Town Creek).

The sport fishery for Roanoke bass often is specialized. In North Carolina, this fish is ardently sought by the few anglers knowing where and how to catch it (W. Smith 1970); the same applies in Virginia. However, most landings probably are made when seeking centrarchids (or other species) in general. We have not tasted a much more palatable fish than Roanoke bass.

It is unfortunate that the words of early fishery workers, in reference to the "red-eye" (*A. cavifrons*) of the Chowan and Roanoke, did not become deeds. This species had high repute as a panfish and afforded good sport. "It is worthy of wider diffusion" (VFC 1877b), and "We propose next spring to distribute this fish to all our rivers" (VFC 1877a). However, the true rock bass of far southwestern Virginia, which was not distinguished from the Roanoke bass, served for nearly all in-state stockings.

With the sport and food values, regional uniqueness, and decline of *A. cavifrons*, carefully planned attempts to establish new populations by stocking are merited. The York drainage would be a good choice; its entirely Piedmont and Coastal Plain habitats are not occupied by rock bass and unlikely to support them. Piedmont sections of the Rappahannock and James drainages would also be strong candidates for stocking. Petrimoulx (1980) evaluated the potential of some of these and other streams to support Roanoke bass. However, a likely competitor, the spotted bass, recently was established in some of these drainages (and the middle Roanoke).

Attempts to reestablish populations of Roanoke bass in heavily silted streams in its native range may be a wastage of fish. Recent stockings of the Pigg River and Town Creek did not produce a sustained increase of the populations (James 1979; Jenkins and Cashner 1983). North Carolina biologists had no apparent success in establishing Roanoke bass (McBride et al. 1982).

World record Roanoke bass probably lurk in Virginia. The Virginia historic record "rock bass" of 1.11 kg (2 pounds 7 ounces), caught in Nottoway River (in 1976) and thus certainly a Roanoke bass, is just shy of the current angling mark of 1.13 kg (2 pounds 8 ounces) from North Carolina. It was only in 1989 that the Roanoke bass category was added to the VDGIF state record program; *Ambloplites* species remain undistinguished in the citation program. Petrimoulx and Jenkins (1979) considered that based on localities of capture, approximately 64% of the Virginia citation "rock bass" (1 pound or 0.45 kg) recorded during 1964–1977 were Roanoke bass. Of the 76 citations in 1983, 66 almost certainly were Roanoke bass.

The reigning disorder in distinguishing the Virginia species of *Ambloplites* was ironically accented when we found that the mounted cast of a former state record from the Smith River, hence almost certainly *A. cavifrons*, was painted by the taxidermist to resemble *A. rupestris*. We submit that most anglers could identify the species if afforded information depicting the key color and anatomical differences that are discernable in the field. Confidence in species identification would enhance fishing for, and further the diffusion of knowledge on, the Roanoke bass.

Name.—*Cavifrons* is interpreted as "depressed front," in reference to the smooth, sometimes slightly depressed, "caved" profile of the head dorsum. It is generally called rock bass and redeye by anglers.

Mud sunfishes   Genus *Acantharchus* Gill

Acantharchus is the monotypic genus for the mud sunfish, a moderately primitive lineage within the Centrarchidae.

Name.—*Acantharchus* means "thorn (spine) anus," in reference to well-developed anal spines.

Mud sunfish   *Acantharchus pomotis* (Baird)

SYSTEMATICS

Acantharchus pomotis was described from New Jersey and New York in 1855. It has complex clinal variation but subspecies are not recognized (Cashner et al. 1989).

DESCRIPTION

Materials.—From Cashner et al. (1989) and 1 North Carolina and 8 Virginia specimens. Life color from 7 Virginia adults, a New Jersey specimen described by Gebhardt (1986), and young described by Swift et al. (1977).

Fish 226 *Acantharchus pomotis* adult female 88 mm SL (REJ 1018), VA, Southampton County, Tarrara Swamp, 15 July 1983.

Anatomy.—A chunky, mottled or striped sunfish with cycloid scales; adults are 100–170 mm SL. Body slightly compressed, overall form stocky; mouth terminal, large; eye large; pectoral and caudal fins rounded; scales lack ctenii although scale shape resembles that of many percoid fishes (i.e., anterior margin truncate, scalloped).

Meristics.—Lateral line scales (on Atlantic slope) (34)37–43(45); diagonal scale rows on body (16)17–22(23); circumpeduncle scales (20)23–28(30). Dorsal spines (10)11(12); dorsal rays (9)10–12(13); anal spines (4)5(6); anal rays (9)10(11); pectoral rays 14–15.

Color in Preservative.—Dorsum and upper side dusky or dark; 2–3 dark horizontal bars on cheek; opercular spot mostly very dark or black, posterior margin lighter; middle and lower side mostly dusky with darker scales forming mottling or irregular stripes; some fish with irregular stripes on most of side; venter slightly or moderately dusky. Dorsal and caudal fins uniformly dusky or very dark; anal fin slightly dark-margined on spinous portion; pelvic fin pale-margined anteriorly; pectoral fin pale.

Color in Life Plate 28.—Dorsum medium or dark brown to olive-black; iris dull red; opercular spot brown-black; dark horizontal bars on cheek brown to olive-black, pale areas on cheek and upper side golden olive; lateral dark mottling and stripes olive-brown; lower side and venter brassy; fins olive. A fall-collected New Jersey specimen had a quite dark back, lower body brilliant iridescent yellow, and fins tinted yellow. Young mostly pale olive.

Larvae.—Not studied; Hardy (1978b) and Wang and Kernehan (1979) described young and juveniles.

BIOLOGY

Stomach contents of 101 North Carolina specimens were chiefly crustaceans (particularly amphipods) and insects; 4% of them had eaten fishes (G. B. Pardue and M. T. Huish, in litt.). Maximum longevity is 8 years (Mansueti and Elser 1953). Age-4 fish averaged 83 mm SL in New York and 105 mm SL in Maryland (Breder and Redmond 1929; Mansueti and Elser 1953). A Virginia specimen reached 152 mm TL (M. D. Norman, in litt.). One of the smaller centrarchids, the largest specimen recorded was 170 mm SL and apparently 206 mm TL (Mansueti and Elser 1953; Elser 1961); the same maximum SL was reported by Cashner et al. (1989). The spawning period in Virginia is unknown; an adult female was spent in mid-July. In New Jersey, nesting occurs during early June on soft bottom among vegetation (Breder 1936).

HABITAT

Acantharchus pomotis reportedly is mud-loving, nocturnal, secretive (Abbott 1870, 1894), and sedentary (Whitehurst 1981). In streams it prefers sluggish pools, and it commonly occupies swamps and ponds. We found it associated with plants and other cover. It tolerates the highly acidic waters of Dismal Swamp. It is considered to be a strictly freshwater species (Musick 1972). An apparent waif (VIMS 2372) was captured by bottom trawl (depth 20 m) from the Rappahannock River just above its mouth in 1973. This is the only record for the river in 25 years of the VIMS trawl survey (T. A. Munroe, in litt.). Salinity at the site normally is 14–20‰ (Brehmer 1972).

DISTRIBUTION   Map 139

Acantharchus pomotis is widely distributed in the Atlantic Coastal Plain from northern New Jersey

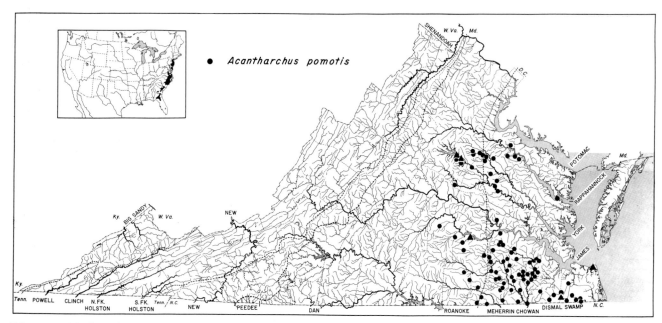

Map 139 Mud sunfish.

southward, and may be extirpated in southern New York. It also occupies the extreme eastern Gulf slope in Georgia and Florida.

On the Virginia Coastal Plain, the mud sunfish appears to be generally distributed only in the Chowan drainage and interior Dismal Swamp. Records from the James to the Rappahannock drainages are arrayed about equally above and below the Fall Zone. Puzzling is the absence of records from many middle and outer Coastal Plain streams in these drainages, notably the Chickahominy River of the James. The extension of *A. pomotis* into the lower Piedmont in Virginia is atypical of the species elsewhere. The largest gap in its range comprises western Chesapeake Bay tributaries from the Potomac drainage in Virginia and Maryland to the Susquehanna drainage of Maryland.

We reject two records for the Potomac drainage of Virginia. The one by Cashner (*in* Lee et al. 1980), Stauffer et al. (1982), and Hocutt et al. (1986) is based on a collector's report submitted by a vertebrate zoologist to the VDGIF. The record was added to

Cashner's map by Jenkins; subsequently we found the specimen (LC 71-12) to be *Lepomis gulosus*. The other Potomac record, recently from Lake Fairfax, is also from a collector's report to the VDGIF. However, the two adult-sized specimens were bioassayed and the identification can not be verified. Extensive collecting in the lower Potomac of Virginia and Maryland has not yielded a verified specimen.

Abundance.—Usually uncommon.

REMARKS

While the book was in press, and too late for summary here, various aspects of the life history and ecology of the mud sunfish were published by Pardue (1993).

Name.—*Poma* seems to mean "lid" or "gill cover" (see genus *Lepomis*), and *ot* refers to "ear," hence the whole operculum, its opercle, or just the opercular flap or "earflap."

Fliers   Genus *Centrarchus* Cuvier and Valenciennes

Close affinity of the monotypic genus *Centrarchus* with *Pomoxis* was indicated from morphological studies by Bailey (1938a), Smith and Bailey (1961), and Branson and Moore (1962). Also based on anatomy, the sister taxon of *Centrarchus* has been hypothesized to be *Archoplites*, and *Pomoxis* is the other lineage of their advanced clade (Mabee 1988). Avise et al. (1977)

grouped *Centrarchus* with *Ambloplites* and *Enneacanthus* based on one biochemical character, an arrangement that we do not follow.

Name.—*Centrarchus*, "spine anus," connotes the relatively numerous anal spines.

Flier   *Centrarchus macropterus* (Lacepède)

SYSTEMATICS

The apparently monotypic flier was described in 1801 from South Carolina.

DESCRIPTION

Materials.—Eight Virginia series including counts from 20 specimens from the Rappahannock drainage and southward; dorsal spine counts also by E. F. Menhinick (in litt.). Color in life from 4 Virginia adults.

Anatomy.—A relatively pallid, black-spotted very compressed sunfish, adults are 70–190 mm TL. Body extremely compressed; snout slightly upturned; mouth oblique, supraterminal, and moderate in size; eye large; caudal fin emarginate; pectoral fin long, pointed.

Meristics.—Lateral line scales (36)37–41(42); scales above lateral line 6–7; scales below lateral line (11)13–14(15). Dorsal spines (11)12(13); dorsal rays (12)13–14; anal spines 7–8; anal rays (14)15–16(17); pectoral rays (11)13–14.

Color in Preservative.—Head and body grading from dark or dusky dorsally to slightly dusky or pale ventrally; side with many dark spots (on scale centers) arranged in several interrupted linear series, and with faint dusky streaks interconnecting spots; subocular bar or blotch dark; opercular spot small, dark. Median fins uniformly dusky or with many pale spots and basal pale streaks; second dorsal, caudal, and anal fins sometimes with narrow dark margin; pelvic fin pale or dusky; pectoral fin pale. Young and juvenile (to about 75 mm SL) with an ocellus in second dorsal fin (Fish 207). Young with 4–5 dark vertical bars.

Color in Life.—Head and body dorsum olive-brown; side brassy yellow to brassy olive; lateral spots olive-black; cheek and opercle with blue-green sheen; subocular mark black; iris copper with vertical black bar; opercular spot black. Median fins dusky olive, pale spots and streaks pale yellow-olive; pelvic fin dusky olive; pectoral fin amber.

Larvae.—Described by Conner (1979).

BIOLOGY

The diet of *C. macropterus* is diverse. In a Virginia Piedmont stream, fliers took arachnids, minute crustaceans, and insects, particularly water boatman (Flemer and Woolcott 1966). In Lake Drummond of Dismal Swamp, they ate microcrustaceans, aquatic and terrestrial insects, small fishes, and algae (Russell 1976).

Females have matured when as small as 70–75 mm TL; some fliers have lived 8 years. Mean total length at age 4 was 155 mm in Airfield Pond, and 168 mm in Lake Drummond (Rosebery and Bowers 1952; Carlander 1977; Smith and Kauffman 1982). Fliers as large as 250 mm TL have been taken in a Maryland pond (Enamait and Davis 1982). The largest Virginia specimen is 245 mm TL (194 mm SL). Data with this specimen (USNM 174947), hooked in a pond on the Fort A. P. Hill Military Reservation, indicate that an

Fish 227 *Centrarchus macropterus* adult male 97 mm SL (REJ 1015), VA, Greensville County, Cattail Creek, 15 July 1983.

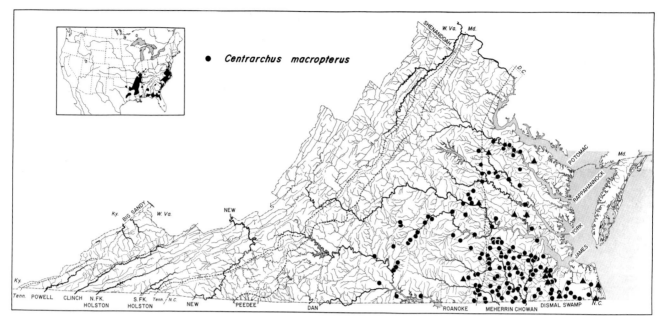

Centrarchus macropterus

Map 140 Flier.

approximately 356-mm TL (about 14 inches) flier was also caught.

Reproduction is summarized in Carlander (1977). An early spawner, adults congregate and nest usually within March to May when water is 14–17°C. Females carry 1,900–37,500 eggs. The only report of natural hybridization is with the white crappie (Burr 1974).

HABITAT

Centrarchus populates sluggish channels, backwaters, and pools in streams, as well as swamps, ponds, and lakes. It has adapted to the low-pH waters of the Coastal Plain, and has been found in an upper mesohaline zone in salinity as high as 7‰ (Musick 1972).

DISTRIBUTION   Map 140

The flier ranges in lowlands from Maryland to Florida, along the Gulf slope, and up the central Mississippi Valley. In Virginia it extends from the outer Coastal Plain onto the Piedmont, reaching farthest inland in the southern part of the state. It is consid-

ered indigenous to the Rappahannock drainage and south. It was discovered recently in a farm pond in the lower Potomac drainage of Maryland (Lee et al. 1981; Enamait and Davis 1982). If it were native to the Potomac, it should have been found in the Virginia portion.

Abundance.—Often common, sometimes locally abundant; quite numerous in Lake Drummond (Russell 1976).

REMARKS

Although smaller and less meaty than many other sunfishes, the flier is reputed to have excellent flavor and to be a delight on the end of a light fly rod. When small fliers are viewed laterally by potential predators, the eyelike spot—an ocellus—in the hind portion of the dorsal fin (Fish 207), coupled with the true eye, may cause predators to perceive a larger fish and desist from attack.

Name.—*Macropterus* translates to "large fin."

Crappies   Genus *Pomoxis* Rafinesque

Pomoxis contains the two crappies, both of which occur in Virginia.

Name.—*Pomoxis* means "opercle, sharp"; it refers to the posterior end of the opercle, which is not notably sharp in *Pomoxis*. The common name crappie (often pronounced croppie) apparently was derived

from the French Canadian word Crapet, the etymology of which is unclear (Smith 1903). Crapet may have been derived from crapoud, which means toad, or it may have been applied to fish with a large head and mouth. Crapet sometimes is used in Canada for *Pomoxis* and certain other sunfishes (Legendre 1954; Scott and Crossman 1973).

Black crappie   *Pomoxis nigromaculatus* (Lesueur)

SYSTEMATICS

The black crappie was described from Ohio in 1829.

DESCRIPTION

Materials.—Four Virginia and 1 Illinois series; counts from Scott and Crossman (1973) and Trautman (1981). Life color from 1 Virginia adult and Scott and Crossman (1973).

Anatomy.—A speckled, very compressed centrarchid; adults are 100–400 mm TL. Body strongly compressed; head somewhat long; snout slightly upturned; mouth supraterminal, oblique, large; eye large. Anal and dorsal fins nearly equal in base length; caudal fin shallowly or moderately forked; pectoral fin rounded.

Meristics.—Lateral line scales 36–44; dorsal spines 7–8 (rarely 6); dorsal rays 14–16; anal spines 6–7; anal rays 16–18; pectoral rays 13–15.

Color in Preservative.—Ground shade of body pale; head dorsum, cheek, and opercle dusky, latter parts occasionally speckled or blotched; side darkly variegated, most so dorsolaterally, and lacking definitive bars; venter pale. Median fins dusky or dark, with many clear spots and streaks producing a vermiculated pattern; pelvic fin slightly dusky medially; pectoral fin pale. Young have narrow bars on side; median fins mostly dusky, clear windows developing at 40 mm SL.

Color in Life Plate 28.—Ground color of side of head and body silver; dark lateral marks olive to black; dorsum usually olive-brown; dorsolateral head and body with brassy green sheens; venter silver. Median fins dusky black, pale membrane spots white, spines yellow-olive. Breeding male with intensified dark pigments and sheens.

Larvae.—See Anjard (1974), Hardy (1978b), Conner (1979), Wang and Kernehan (1979), and Tin (1982d).

BIOLOGY

Young black crappies prey on microcrustaceans, insects, and larval fishes. Adults are piscivorous, but also eat a variety of aquatic organisms and terrestrial insects (Hanson and Quadri 1979; Kohler 1980).

Both sexes usually mature by age 2 and often survive 6–7 years, maximally 13 years. No consistent difference in growth rate occurs between the sexes (Carlander 1977). From 53 populations of rivers, ponds, or reservoirs in Virginia, the range of means of length at age 3 is 132–270 mm TL, unweighted grand mean 203 (Wollitz 1972; Norman 1973, 1981; Hart 1978, 1981; Shuber and Sledd 1981; Sledd and Shuber 1981; Davis and Enamait 1982; Smith and Kauffman 1982). The indicated growth rates are typical of the species elsewhere in the eastern and central United States (Carlander 1977). An age-8 black crappie from Kerr Reservoir was 395 mm TL (15.6 inches) (LaRoche 1985). The rod-and-reel world record recognized by the IGFA (1985) is a 2.05-kg (4.5 pounds) specimen from Kerr Reservoir in Virginia. From a South Carolina study, Carlander (1977) compiled a *P. nigromaculatus* of 472 mm TL weighing 2.18 kg (4.8 pounds).

The black crappie is an early spawner, congregating and constructing nests in some part of the period from March to July, earliest in the South, in water of about 15–20°C. It probably spawns mostly during April in Virginia. Nests are excavated in shallow to moderately deep water (to 6 m), may be quite crowded, and are usually associated with vegetation.

Fish 228 *Pomoxis nigromaculatus* adult male 117 mm SL (REJ 997), VA, Bedford County, Beaverdam Creek, 11 July 1983.

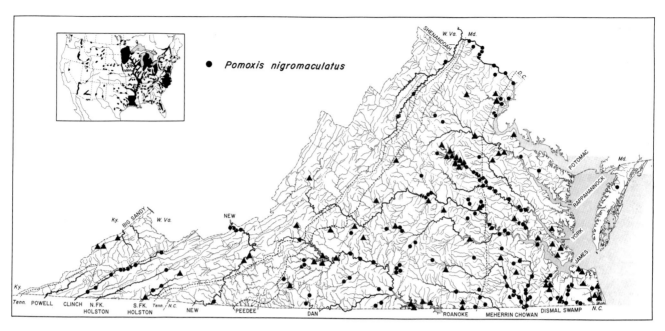

Map 141   Black crappie.

Females are highly fecund, bearing 11,000–188,000 small eggs, mean diameter 0.93 mm (Breder 1936; Hansen 1951; June 1977; Carlander 1977).

The black crappie apparently rarely hybridizes in nature with the white crappie (Bailey and Lagler 1938; Bailey and Allum 1962; Trautman 1981).

HABITAT

Black crappies are found in swamps, ponds, lakes, reservoirs, and slack water of low to moderate-gradient creeks to rivers. They usually associate with aquatic vegetation, fallen trees, stumps, and other structure. Fallen trees are often placed along drawdown zones in reservoirs to serve as "crappie attractors." *Pomoxis nigromaculatus* tolerates acidic waters of interior Dismal Swamp and occasionally enters tidal fresh water.

DISTRIBUTION   Map 141

Pomoxis nigromaculatus is native in the Great Lakes–St. Lawrence and Mississippi basins, on the Gulf slope, and along the south Atlantic slope north to probably the James drainage. It has been widely transplanted in these and other regions.

Indigenous status in the James drainage is indicated by Cope's (1868b) report of "*Pomoxys* sp." apparently from Tuckahoe Creek near its mouth just above Richmond. Fowler (1907) identified the specimen(s) as *P. sparoides*, a synonym of *P. nigromacula-*

tus. Early records support native status just south of the James. Jordan (1889b) reported *P. sparoides* from Dismal Swamp in Virginia, and Smith (1893) found it in the lower Chowan and Roanoke drainages of North Carolina. However, judgments on the prehistorical distribution of many species on the central Atlantic slope are arbitrary. Undocumented transplants of the black crappie from the Carolinas may have occurred in the early 1800s, analogous to the case of the largemouth bass.

The original status of the black crappie in the Potomac, Rappahannock, and York drainages is problematic. Uhler and Lugger (1876) stated that *P. nigromaculatus* (as *Centrarchus hexacanthus*) "probably" occurred in some tributaries of the lower Potomac, that it was "said to occur" near the mouth of the Chester River (eastern Chesapeake basin, Maryland), and that it was sold in Baltimore markets. The vague references and the context of the account indicate that Uhler and Lugger may have seen market specimens, and that the localities possibly were heard from fishmongers, who may have been peddling shipped-in fish under the guise of locally caught (fresh) specimens.

We treat black crappie populations north of the James as introduced, because currently this species occurs sporadically north of the James, nearly half of the Rappahannock records are from (possibly stocked) ponds, and excluding the Potomac, all records are relatively recent (the earliest for the Rappahannock is 1959, the York 1949). The first documented stocking of *Pomoxis* in this area occurred in

1894; both species of crappie were liberated in the middle Potomac by the USFC, and by 1898 they had become common (Smith and Bean 1899).

Pomoxis nigromaculatus probably is not indigenous to the upper portion in Virginia of the James, Roanoke, Pee Dee (no Virginia record), Tennessee, and Big Sandy drainages, nor to any of the New drainage, based on the lack of early records and avoidance by the species of montane streams.

Abundance.—Often common in small and large reservoirs, Lake Drummond, and Back Bay; sporadically common in streams.

REMARKS

The black crappie is one of the most popular pan fishes in Virginia. Large ones can give a strong sustained fight on a light rod. With the right conditions and techniques, enough specimens have been taken by individual anglers on single days in Virginia to fill coolers. However, it seems prudent that the VDGIF recently limited the daily one-person take of crappies to 25 (both species summed) in nearly all state waters.

Name.—*Nigromaculatus* means "black spotted."

White crappie   *Pomoxis annularis* Rafinesque

SYSTEMATICS

The white crappie was described from the Ohio River in 1818.

DESCRIPTION

Materials.—Four Virginia adults and several young from Iowa; counts from Scott and Crossman (1973) and Trautman (1981). Life color from Hansen (1951) and Pflieger (1975).

Anatomy.—A vaguely barred, very compressed centrarchid; adults are 120–400 mm TL. Head and body strongly compressed; snout slightly upturned; mouth large, supraterminal, oblique; eye large. Dorsal and anal fins of similar length, nearly symmetrical; caudal fin emarginate or shallowly forked; pectoral fin rounded.

Meristics.—Lateral line scales usually 34–44; dorsal spines 5–6(7), rarely 7; dorsal rays (13)14–15; anal spines 6–7; anal rays 16–18; pectoral rays usually 13.

Color in Preservative.—Ground shade pale; dorsum slightly or moderately dusky; side with many scale-sized spots forming narrow, often irregular, and often interrupted bars, the bars narrowest and most interrupted ventrally; venter pale. Median fins vermiculated, irregular pale windows contrasting with dusky areas; pectoral and pelvic fins unpatterned.

Color in Life.—Dorsum dark olive with emerald and purple sheens; side silvery white; lateral blotches and bars brown or black; dusky areas in median fins black. Breeding male darker and more boldly marked than female.

Larvae.—Described by Anjard (1974), Hardy (1978b), Conner (1979), Wang and Kernehan (1979), and Tin (1982d).

Fish 229 *Pomoxis annularis* adult male 122 mm SL (REJ 1011), VA, Mecklenburg County, Allens Creek, 14 July 1983.

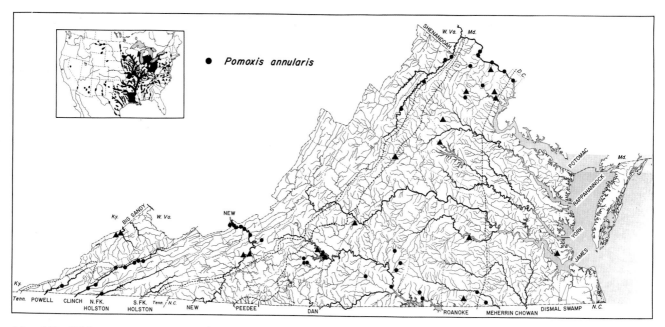

Map 142   White crappie.

BIOLOGY

Young and juvenile white crappies feed on micro-crustaceans and insects. Adults eat a variety of fishes, insects, and other aquatic invertebrates including plankton (Hansen 1951; Mathur 1972; Kohler 1980).

Both sexes mature by age 2 or 3, many survive to age 7, and the maximum known life span is 9 years. The sexes do not consistently differ in average growth rate (Carlander 1977). From 11 Virginia impoundments, the range of mean lengths at age 3 was 144–292, unweighted grand mean 215 (Prosser 1973; Hart 1978, 1981; LaRoche 1985; Smith and Kauffman 1982). The great difference between the slowest and fastest growth rates is typical of many regions (Carlander 1977). The longest Virginia specimen of which we know was 344 mm TL (LaRoche 1985). Maximum size is considered under *Remarks*.

Spawning occurs sometime within March to July over the species range, most likely April in Virginia, when water is 16–20°C. As with other centrarchids, male white crappies fan out nests and guard eggs. Spawning occurs on firm or soft bottom, in open areas or under banks and other cover, at depths of 0.1–6 m. Eggs may be deposited on the substrate or on algae, macrophyte leaves, and tree roots (Hansen 1943, 1951; Carlander 1977). *Pomoxis annularis* may be one of the most fecund centrarchids; counts of the mature eggs (0.8–0.9 mm in diameter) are 2,900–213,000 per female, and total eggs number 13,000–

326,000 (Carlander 1977). Hansen (1951) noted that only a portion of the eggs in ripe females may be laid.

Pomoxis annularis hybridizes rarely in nature with *P. nigromaculatus* (Bailey and Lagler 1938; Bailey and Allum 1962; Trautman 1981), and with *Centrarchus macropterus* (Burr 1974).

HABITAT

The white crappie is a warmwater fish that resides in ponds, lakes, reservoirs, and pools of low to moderate-gradient streams and rivers. It often associates with aquatic vegetation and other cover. Hubbs and Lagler (1958) and Pflieger (1975) noted it to be more tolerant of turbidity than is the black crappie, but Hansen (1951) did not find this to be true in Illinois. An indication that the white crappie fares better in turbid conditions was detected in Claytor Lake (Hart 1981). The white crappie apparently shuns acidic waters in the New Jersey Pine Barrens (Hastings 1979); the same is indicated in Virginia by its virtual absence from the Coastal Plain.

DISTRIBUTION   Map 142

The white crappie is native to the southern Great Lakes region, the Mississippi basin, and many Gulf slope drainages. Its original status on the south Atlantic slope is hazy. For lack of an early record and owing to wide stocking, we consider it introduced to the Virginia portion of the Atlantic slope. Also, Smith (1907) reexamined an old record and concluded that *P. annularis* was not known early in any part of North Carolina. Based partly on introductions in Georgia (Dahlberg and Scott 1971a, 1971b), Lee et al. (1980) questioned whether it was native anywhere on the Atlantic slope. Because it avoids montane streams, it probably was not indigenous to the upper Tennessee and Big Sandy drainages of Virginia nor the entire New drainage.

Abundance.—Generally rare or uncommon in streams; common in some impoundments.

REMARKS

The white crappie tends to average slightly larger than the black crappie. Virginia boasts the IGFA angling record for black crappie, and it may well have produced the largest white crappie. The largest "crappie" registered with the VDGIF, a 2.38-kg (5 pounds 4 ounces) fish caught in a private pond in 1985, was slightly larger than the IGFA (1985) white crappie record of 2.35 kg (5 pounds 3 ounces) from Mississippi. The Virginia specimen probably was a white crappie, but unfortunately the VDGIF generally has not distinguished species of *Pomoxis* for the record and citation programs.

Banded sunfishes Genus *Enneacanthus* Gill

All three species of *Enneacanthus* occur in Virginia. The genus has been considered to have close affinities with *Lepomis* and *Micropterus* (Smith and Bailey 1961; Branson and Moore 1962). In Mabee's (1988) phylogeny, *Enneacanthus* is the sister group of *Lepomis* and the two taxa constitute a near-basal lineage among the Centrarchidae.

The species of *Enneacanthus* are well adapted to lowland calm-water habitats (Sweeney 1972). Their small size, compressed body, and quiet hovering suit them for hiding in vegetation, the principal cover. The lateral barring disrupts the body outline, enhanc-

ing concealment. The rounded tail provides rapid acceleration into cover for escaping predators and to capture nearby prey. Physiologically the three species acclimate to highly acidic conditions, and at least one species tolerates brief periods of very low oxygen level.

Name.—*Enneacanthus* means "nine spines," the modal dorsal spine number for two species. We tender the name banded sunfishes for this genus, in reference to the barring present on the side of all species.

Banded sunfish *Enneacanthus obesus* (Girard)

SYSTEMATICS

Enneacanthus obesus, described from Massachusetts in 1854, often is difficult to distinguish from its sympatric and close relative the bluespotted sunfish *E. gloriosus*. Adults of the two species are very similar; their juveniles resemble one another more than they resemble their own adults (Graham 1985). We find that some of the characters used by Sweeney (1972) to distinguish the species are too variable or insufficiently diagnostic. Many of our adults present a persistent challenge to identify, a problem that includes an odd variation pattern whose basis may be hybridization.

The frequency distribution of pored lateral line scale counts from our typical and putative *E. obesus* is bimodal, the two divisions of the range being separate: (15)18–23(25), typical of *E. obesus*; and (26)28–32(34), atypical of *E. obesus* and congruent with *E. gloriosus*. About 40% of our *E. obesus* specimens effect the higher division of the range; about 50% of them

are from Dismal Swamp, Virginia and North Carolina.

The similarity in pored lateral line scale counts of our atypical (or hybrid) *E. "obesus"* with *E. gloriosus* is opposite the situation prevalent among New Jersey populations of introgressed hybrids of these species. Although Graham and Felley (1985) regarded the four New Jersey hybrid means to be intermediate between those of the parental species, three of them are very close to those of typical *E. obesus*.

DESCRIPTION

Materials.—From Bailey (1938a), Sweeney (1972), and our counts of certain characters from 134 specimens (92 from Virginia, 42 from Dismal Swamp of North Carolina). Life color from photographs in Scarola (1973) and Baugh (1980), and accounts by Harrington (1956) and Cohen (1977).

Anatomy.—A chubby dark-banded sunfish lacking a deep notch between the dorsal fins; adults are 40–70 mm

Fish 230 *Enneacanthus obesus* adult female 59 mm SL (REJ 1019), VA, Southampton County, Mill Swamp, 15 July 1983.

SL. Body deep, much compressed or somewhat thick; head dorsum usually slightly or moderately convex in profile in juvenile and adult; mouth supraterminal, oblique, moderate-sized; eye moderate; pectoral and caudal fins rounded. Second dorsal and anal fins of breeding male enlarged, extending posteriorly to nearly midlength of caudal fin, and longest pelvic rays distally filamentous; second dorsal and anal fins of nuptial female barely reach caudal fin base, and pelvic fin lacks filamentous extensions.

Meristics.—Midlateral scales (27)30–32(35); pored lateral line scales (15)18–23(25) [see *Systematics*]; scales above lateral line (4)5–6; scales below lateral line (10)11–12(13); circumpeduncle scales (17)19–22(24). Dorsal spines (7)8–9(11); dorsal rays (9)11–12(13); anal spines 3; anal rays (9)10–11(14); pectoral rays (10)11–13.

Color in Preservative.—Body ground shade of adult mostly slightly to moderately dusky; entire dorsum dark; subocular bar usually present; opercular spot dark; dark postocular smudge or bar occasionally present. Usually 4–6 dark lateral bars in adult male; lateral bars often weakly developed in juvenile, subadult male, and adult female. Side usually not spotted; when spots present, they are usually few and lack distinct margins; lateral scales often have pale centers and slightly dusky dorsal and ventral scale fields, forming narrow, low-contrast stripes. Median fins dusky with few pale membranal spots in young, many uniserial spots in adult; pelvic fin lengthwise dark on anterior or medial rays, entire fin dark in breeding male; pectoral fin pale.

Reproductive adult darker overall on body and fins; male with almost completely dark head and body, bars prominent, 2–4 scales wide; female similar except with pale or slightly dusky cheek and gular area, and body slightly paler between bars than in male.

Color in Life.—Ground color olive to green-olive; lateral bars olive-black or black; side with many iridescent whitish, coppery, or brassy flecks; cheek with iridescent flecks or wavy lines, lower opercle with bluish iridescence; opercular spot black, bordered with iridescent gold-green margin; iris orange-red. Median fins dusky olive to olive-brown, spots white to blue; pelvic fin dusky olive; pectoral fin pale. Nuptial male and, to lesser extent, nuptial female, with gold-green or blue specks on head, body, and median fins; fin spines glowing white.

Larvae.—Not studied; Wang and Kernehan (1979) described young.

COMPARISON

Problems of separating *E. obesus* from *E. gloriosus* in Virginia occur particularly with juveniles and adult females, as well as with atypical, possibly hybrid fish (see *Systematics*). Some southerly *Enneacanthus* populations also are difficult to identify to species (Peterson and Ross 1987). Based on Graham and Felley (1985), comments by other colleagues, and our study, it is notable that Sweeney (1972) did not indicate a significant problem in consistently distinguishing the two species.

We separate the species by a combination of: (1) circumpeduncle scales (least count; see *Key to Suckers*) [(17)19–22(24) in *obesus* vs. (14)16–18(20) in *gloriosus*] (interspecific overlap is about 10%); (2) lateral bars and pale spotting on body of nuptial male [bars usually boldly dark; spots sometimes present as crescentic flecks vs. bars usually absent; spots always present, very distinct, rounded]; (3) anterodorsal profile and body thickness [profile usually more convexly rounded, body chubbier through middle *vs.* profile straighter, body thinner]; (4) pored lateral line [incomplete, usually terminating anterior to the posterior end of the anal fin base in typical *obesus* vs. complete or extending well posterior to the anal fin base in *gloriosus*; (5) pored lateral line scales [(15)18–23(25) in typical *obesus* vs. (20)28–32(35) in *gloriosus*].

Life color differences in New Jersey are indicated by J. H. Graham (in litt.). The general cast of *obesus* is more olive-green, whereas *gloriosus* often has a golden-purple sheen (golden especially below pectoral fin, purple particularly on abdomen). Among reproductive males, in *obesus* the bright markings are mostly gold-green crescentic flecks, and this species never appears bluish, whereas in *gloriosus* the markings are greenish yellow or gold, broadly oval spots, and the body often is mostly dark olive-blue, almost black. After the breeding season, in *obesus* the flecks and spots fade and the sexes become indistinguishable.

Two reputed diagnostic characters failed to regularly distinguish our specimens: opercular spot length relative to pupil diameter (equal to or greater than pupil diameter in *obesus*, less in *gloriosus*; both species often have the other character state); bony notch on posterior end of maxilla (supposedly only in *obesus*, but often occurs in *gloriosus*).

BIOLOGY

Microcrustaceans and insects (particularly midge larvae) are the major foods of the banded sunfish in a Connecticut reservoir (Cohen 1977), where the bluespotted sunfish is absent. Other than virtual restriction to feeding on small animals, Cohen suggested that banded sunfish may feed nonpreferentially. However, he noted that this species most often occurred in and around bottom vegetation during daytime. In New Jersey the banded sunfish and bluespotted sunfish exhibit much dietary overlap, but *E. obesus* gleans invertebrates from surfaces of submersed plants to a greater extent than does *E. gloriosus* (Graham 1989).

Some females spawn as yearlings; maximum longevity is 6 years. Males tend to live longer and grow slightly faster than females; age-3 fish of both sexes are typically 50–60 mm TL (Cohen 1977). A Virginia specimen of 74.5 mm SL and a Connecticut fish of 89 mm TL (Cohen 1977) may be the largest known.

Females were gravid and males were in nuptial color during April through July in Virginia. A late spring through summer spawning period has been deduced for Delaware, based on capture of small young in summer and early fall (Wang and Kernehan 1979). Breeding takes place during early spring in New Jersey (Graham 1985). In Connecticut the banded sunfish reproduces in June and July; the strongest indications of spawning occur when surface water is 23–27°C (Cohen 1977).

Males defended territories and excavated nests in gravel in aquaria (Harrington 1956; Wang and Kernehan 1979). In other aquaria, dominant reproductive males made nestlike depressions in sand with the mouth but the depressions were not maintained (Cohen 1977). Cohen found that in a Connecticut reservoir, males exhibited breeding behavior while occurring closer to shore than usual and away from aquatic vegetation; they associated with sandy areas and rock ledges. Mean fecundity ranges from 802 eggs in yearlings to 1,400 in 6-year-olds (Cohen 1977).

Hybrids of the banded and bluespotted sunfishes are reported from New Jersey (Graham and Felley 1985) and may occur in Virginia and northeastern North Carolina (see *Systematics*).

HABITAT

Enneacanthus obesus occupies lakes, ponds, swamps, and calm parts of open streams, and is nearly restricted to blackwaters. In northern Florida it seems to be restricted to small streams and standing water in swamps (Swift et al. 1977). The banded sunfish inhabits shallows (to about 2 m) and is closely associated with dense aquatic vegetation that is rooted in or suspended over detritus-laden, silty, muddy, or sandy bottoms. In New Jersey it strongly affiliates with water of pH lower than 6.0, and has been observed in bog water of pH 3.7, near the lethal threshold for all fishes. It also occurs in slightly alkaline situations (Graham and Hastings 1984; Graham 1989). The ecologic settings of *E. obesus* in Virginia resemble those over most of the species range.

DISTRIBUTION   Map 143

The banded sunfish ranges in lowlands from New Hampshire to Alabama (Ramsey 1984; AU 5663), and has been transplanted along with *E. gloriosus* to ponds in western Mississippi (Peterson and Ross 1987). In Virginia it is restricted to the Coastal Plain, highly localized in the York and James drainages, and sporadic in the Chowan drainage; it may have a general distribution in Dismal Swamp.

Both verified York drainage records (UMMZ 102337, RC) are from the Maracossic Creek system—

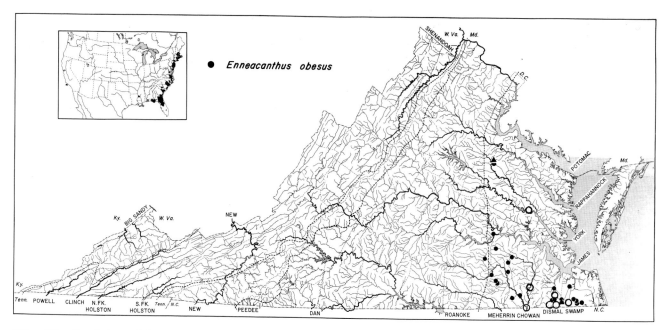

Map 143   Banded sunfish. Closed circles indicate verified records, open circles unverified.

Maracossic Creek or one of its tributaries and Smoots Pond; they are dated 1934 and 1973. The population may have been introduced along with largemouth bass from south of Virginia. We were unable to locate a specimen for the record (Raney and Massmann 1953) from the lower Pamunkey system (creek mouth at Sweet Hall Landing), nor for the record (Sweeney 1972) farther up the York (site uncertain). Both sites are mapped in Lee et al. (1980).

Our James drainage record (UCS 5896) is from Ashtons Creek below Ruffins Pond in the lower Appomattox system, in 1971. The report (Cope 1868b) of *E. guttatus* from Tuckahoe Creek, a low-gradient James tributary just above the Fall Zone, was accepted as *E. obesus* by Raney (1950), but Fowler (1907) apparently had identified Cope's specimens as *E. gloriosus*. Although the name *guttatus* had been identified with *E. obesus* by Bailey (1938a), and *E. obesus* is included in the type series of *guttatus* from Philadelphia, *guttatus* is fixed as a synonym of *E. gloriosus* by type designation (Böhlke 1984). We consider Cope's Tuckahoe Creek *Enneacanthus* (ANSP 12894-5) to be *E. gloriosus*; although the specimens are discolored and missing some circumpeduncle scales, the scales are large and the lateral line is completely pored.

Potomac drainage records are considered invalid or unconfirmed. The record by Lee et al. (1980) and Hocutt et al. (1986) is based on our determination that both *E. obesus* and *E. gloriosus* were in one collection (UCS 6217, 6812). Later we identified all of these specimens as *E. gloriosus*. Specimens for Sweeney's (1972) Potomac record have not been located; they could have been small *E. gloriosus*. Because Sweeney's unverified Susquehanna drainage record may also be erroneous, we believe that *E. obesus* is absent in western Chesapeake drainages from the Rappahannock to the Susquehanna. The Chesapeake range hiatus is nearly as wide as that of *E. chaetodon*.

Abundance.—Generally rare or uncommon, perhaps faring best in Dismal Swamp.

REMARKS

The three species of *Enneacanthus* are fine aquarium fishes and are often sought by native-fish enthusiasts. As with other centrarchids, adult males are territorial and should not be crowded in a tank. The species can fare well in a vegetated tank; the plants provide shelter and serve to compartmentalize territories. Live food is much preferred. Meriting study in nature is whether the species typically spawn in a nest excavated on the bottom, or create hollows in vegetation, and how the nest normally is prepared.

Name.—*Obesus*, meaning "fat," refers to the somewhat chubby appearance, particularly of adult males.

Bluespotted sunfish   *Enneacanthus gloriosus* (Holbrook)

SYSTEMATICS

The bluespotted sunfish was described from South Carolina in 1855. Systematic problems of *E. gloriosus* are discussed under *E. obesus*.

DESCRIPTION

Materials.—From Bailey (1938a), Sweeney (1972), and our counts of selected characters from 125 Virginia specimens. Life color from 4 Virginia adults.

Anatomy.—A pale-spotted sunfish lacking a deep indentation in the dorsal fin; adults are 40–70 mm SL. Body deep, much compressed; head dorsum profile straight or slightly convex; mouth terminal or supraterminal, small or moderate in size; eye moderate; pectoral and caudal fins rounded. Breeding male with enlarged second dorsal and anal fins; female lacks enlarged fins.

Meristics.—Midlateral scales (25)30–32(35); pored lateral line scales (20)28–32(35); scales above lateral line 4–5(7); scales below lateral line (10)11(13); circumpeduncle scales (14)16–18(20). Dorsal spines (7)8–9(11); dorsal rays (9)10–12(13); anal spines (2)3(4); anal rays (8)9–10(13); pectoral rays (9)12–13.

Color in Preservative.—Dorsum and upper side moderately to very dusky; cheek slightly dusky with variously developed subocular bar or smudge; opercle dusky; opercular spot dark, sometimes with pale medial crescent. Side moderately to very dusky, with numerous pale spots scattered or in interrupted horizontal series; lateral bars usually absent in adult male, bars usually present in young and juvenile of both sexes and occasionally in adult female; venter pale or slightly dusky. Median fin membranes dusky, with uniserial clear spots; spots best developed basally in adult; anterior half of pelvic fin longitudinally dark; pectoral fin pale.

Color in Life   Plate 28.—Dorsum and upper side dark olive-brown; cheek, opercle, and side of body with numerous iridescent silver, gold, green, or blue spots; opercle and cheek suffused with gold-green sheen; iris dull red; opercular spot black except for medial blue-green crescentic mark; venter brassy. Pale spots in median fins whitish; remainder of dorsal and caudal fins olive-brown; anal fin suffused with brown-red; anterior half (lengthwise) of pelvic fin olive-brown, posterior half pale; pectoral fin pale. Breder and Redmond (1929) noted that when alarmed, *E. gloriosus* darkens and its pale spots become more evident. Breeding male also darkens, spots glow.

Larvae.—Described by Breder and Redmond (1929), Anjard (1974), and Wang and Kernehan (1979).

COMPARISON

See *E. obesus*.

BIOLOGY

The bluespotted sunfish obtains small food items, chiefly insects and other small invertebrates, from the

Fish 231 *Enneacanthus gloriosus* adult male 65 mm SL (WHH 151), VA, Sussex County, Assamoosic Swamp, 26 July 1983.

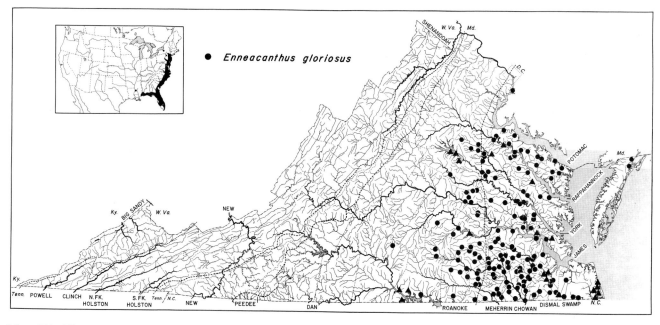

Map 144   Bluespotted sunfish.

entire water column and vegetation (Moore 1922; Breder and Redmond 1929; Gatz 1979). It takes free-swimming and benthic invertebrates more often than does the banded sunfish; the difference in foraging habits is most prevalent among young (Graham 1989).

Females mature in 2 years; adults are 30–50 mm SL at age 3. Breder and Redmond (1929) and Werner (1972) determined some individuals to have lived 5 years. The largest Virginia specimen at hand is 72 mm SL; maximum length in Hardy's (1978b) compilation is 80 mm SL or TL.

Gravid females were found from July to September in New Jersey (Breder and Redmond 1929), but Graham (1985) stated that *E. gloriosus* spawns there in early spring. A late spring through early fall breeding period is indicated in the lower Delaware River area (Wang and Kernehan 1979). We found gravid females from May to September in Virginia.

Enneacanthus gloriosus seems to spawn both on the bottom and in plants. North of Virginia it nests in very shallow spots by excavating a small dish-shaped depression in sand, sometimes beneath plants, and by making a cavity in a bed of plants (Breder and Redmond 1929; Breder and Rosen 1966; Wang and Kernehan 1979). Fecundity is about 600 eggs (Occhiogrosso and Goodbred 1981). Recently hatched larvae rise to the surface and hang from the surface film (Breder and Redmond 1929).

HABITAT

Enneacanthus gloriosus occupies the general range of low-gradient habitats in Virginia. It is characteristic of thickly vegetated, slightly to darkly stained, small and medium-sized swamps, ponds, and small impoundments. It also inhabits pools and backwaters of sluggish and moderately flowing creeks, streams, and medium-sized rivers in the state. Our westernmost record is from a moderate-gradient headwater with regularly alternating pools and runs and occasional patches of submersed plants. At another moderate-gradient site lacking substantial aquatic macrophytes, a specimen was found among tree roots.

Most Virginia records are from circumneutral or slightly more acidic water; the highly acidic Dismal Swamp is also populated. On the New Jersey Coastal Plain the bluespotted sunfish spans pH 4.1 to 7.0, but it typically resides in those more basic than pH 6.0 (Graham and Hastings 1984; Graham 1989). It occupies slightly brackish water to at least a limited extent in North Carolina (Schwartz 1981b) and Virginia; the maximum salinity record is 12.9‰ (Hildebrand and Schroeder 1928). Although found in tidal (and nontidal) fresh water in Delaware, none were taken in brackish water (Wang and Kernehan 1979).

DISTRIBUTION   Map 144

The bluespotted sunfish occupies the Coastal Plain and lower and middle Piedmont, and ranges indigenously from the lower Hudson drainage of New York through Florida and westward to the Biloxi Bay system of Mississippi. It has been established via introduction in small parts of the Finger Lakes drainage in New York, and the lower Mississippi basin in Mississippi (Werner 1972; Peterson and Ross 1987). Its range in Virginia includes some minor coastal drainages, and it is the only *Enneacanthus* that extends south to the Virginia portion of the Delmarva Peninsula. It reaches farthest into the Virginia Piedmont in the southern half of the state; it also has populated well into the Piedmont in Pennsylvania and New York.

The uppermost record in the Roanoke drainage was obtained from the Roanoke Creek system in 1983. No *E. gloriosus* were taken in many other collections made since 1935 at the same site or in lower gradient, more vegetated portions of the system. We accept the three Kerr Reservoir records (Neal 1967) because of the record from higher elevation above the reservoir, because of another record from just below the reservoir, and because *E. obesus* is unknown to ascend the Fall Line in Virginia.

Abundance.—Generally uncommon or common, most numerous in the Coastal Plain; the bluespotted sunfish is by far the most abundant *Enneacanthus* in Virginia.

REMARKS

The reflective spots of this bantam sunfish render it a jewel of dark waters.

Name.—*Gloriosus*, "glorious," is bestowed from the long, spotted fins and iridescent silver to blue body spots contrasting with dark and other hues.

Blackbanded sunfish   *Enneacanthus chaetodon* (Baird)

SYSTEMATICS

The blackbanded sunfish was named from New Jersey in 1855. The sharp distinction of *E. chaetodon* from the other two species of *Enneacanthus* served as the basis for long recognition of a genus *Mesogonistius* solely for the former. *Mesogonistius* was lumped with *Enneacanthus* without explanation by Eddy (1957); the merger was supported by Branson and Moore (1962) and Sweeney (1972), and is generally accepted. Bailey (1941) recognized two subspecies, but Sweeney (1972) deemed the differences insufficient for subspecific recognition.

DESCRIPTION

Materials.—From Bailey (1938a, 1941), Schwartz (1961), Sweeney (1972), and 2 Virginia and 2 North Carolina lots. Life color from 1 Virginia lot.

Anatomy.—A sunfish with bold black bars and a markedly notched dorsal fin; adults are 30–60 mm SL. Body deep, much compressed; lateral profile of head dorsum straight or slightly convex; eye medium or large; mouth small, terminal. Dorsal fin strongly emarginate near juncture of spinous and soft portions; pectoral fin narrow, somewhat pointed; caudal fin rounded or slightly truncate in young and juvenile, becoming truncate or slightly emarginate in adult. Second dorsal and anal fins not enlarged in breeding male.

Meristics.—Midlateral scales (23)25–29(32); scales above lateral line (4)5(6); scales below lateral line (9)10–12(13); circumpeduncle scales 16–22. Dorsal spines (8)10(11); dorsal rays (10)11–12(13); anal spines 3(4); anal rays (10)11–12(14); pectoral rays (8)9–11(12).

Color in Preservative.—Body ground shade pale; dorsum slightly to moderately dusky; upper side slightly dusky, variegated; lower side pale. Side with 5–6 complete (dorsum to venter) bold dark bars, first bar on head passes through eye, the third extends through anterior portion of dorsal fin and medial portion of pelvic fin, forming a bar longer than body depth; a total of 3–4 incomplete (medially interrupted) bars often occur between complete bars. Opercular spot dark with pale medial crescent; median fins tessellated to slightly variegated; pectoral fin pale.

Color in Life Plate 29.—Body ground color mostly opalescent white, with brassy sheen; dorsum medium olive-brown except for bars; iris orange-copper; olive-brown variegations on upper half of body; opercular spot and lateral bars, including fin components of bars, black. Pelvic spine and leading pelvic ray orange-copper; third membrane of first dorsal fin with pale copper sheen (red in some specimens [Sweeney 1972]); median fin tessellations olive-brown. Citing an early report of nuptial color, Breder and Rosen (1966) indicated that females embolden the color pattern and males become pale, but Seal (1914) stated that the pattern and shade of nuptial fish of both sexes vary similarly.

Larvae.—Described by Hardy (1978b).

BIOLOGY

The diet of the blackbanded sunfish in Maryland and Delaware comprises an array of small inverte-

Fish 232 *Enneacanthus chaetodon* adult female 48 mm SL (WHH 152), VA, Sussex County, Coppahaunk Swamp, 26 July 1983.

brates associated with aquatic macrophytes (Seal 1914; Schwartz 1961; Wujtewicz 1982). Maryland fish survived 3–4 years, and were about 30–60 mm SL in the second and third years (Schwartz 1961). In Delaware, some females were 20 mm longer than males; females had survived to age 3 but the studied males had reached only age 1 (Wujtewicz 1982). Age 3 is attained in nature by both sexes in Virginia; aquarium specimens have lived at least 8 years (Sternburg 1986). The largest of the few Virginia specimens of *E. chaetodon* that we studied is 50 mm SL; perhaps the largest known is 70 mm SL, from Delaware (Wujtewicz 1982).

Spawning occurs during March in North Carolina (Smith 1907). In Delaware, females were gravid from early May to late June, water 21–28°C (Wujtewicz 1982). Mid- to late spring and water temperatures of 20–23° appear to be the norm for breeding according to the following references.

The variable nests and reproductive behavior are described largely from aquarium observations by Seal (1914), Breder (1936), Breder and Rosen (1966), Sternburg (1986), and Quinn (1988). Nests range from small cleared areas and saucer-shaped depressions formed in sand or gravel substrate beneath vegetation or where the male removes vegetation, to hollows made among plant roots or in masses of plants such as filamentous algae, water milfoil, and tape grass. In nature the nests are in shallows usually about 30 cm deep. Movement of bottom materials has

been attributed to using the mouth, body, tail, or just "finning." Males are territorial and females are driven from nests shortly after spawning, but in one case the male and female attended eggs and free-swimming fry (Quinn 1988). Fecundity is 233–920 mature ova based on preserved specimens (Wujtewicz 1982), but a female laid only about 50 eggs (Quinn 1988).

HABITAT

The blackbanded sunfish inhabits thickly vegetated ponds, swamps, and pools of creeks to rivers. The three Virginia record sites—two small impoundments and their immediate outlets, and a swamp—have in common lush beds of submersed plants. *Enneacanthus chaetodon* is weakly associated with acidic (pH 4.1–6.6) dystrophic habitats in New Jersey (Graham and Hastings 1984). Graham and Hastings (1984) summarized reports from New Jersey and Maryland of its occurrence in neutral and slightly alkaline situations, and of reproduction in neutral water. The pH at two Virginia sites was 6.4 and 6.6. *Enneacanthus gloriosus* is present and *E. obesus* is unknown at the three Virginia sites.

DISTRIBUTION Map 145

The blackbanded sunfish is sporadically distributed in the Coastal Plain from New Jersey to Florida. Explanations for its distributional gaps (including the

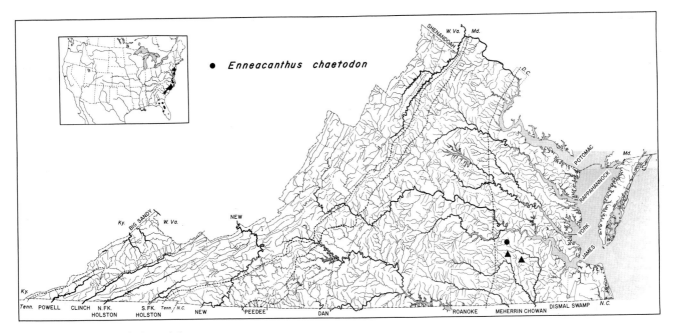

Map 145 Blackbanded sunfish.

entire western Chesapeake basin), localizations, and frequent rarity include drainage modifications associated with glaciation, lack of plant cover, naturally inhospitable water chemistry, and habitat degradation (Jenkins et al. 1975; Burgess et al. 1977; Graham and Hastings 1984). In Virginia, *E. chaetodon* is known only at three sites in the Blackwater or Nottoway systems of the Chowan drainage. In North Carolina, two records exist for the Chowan and one for the lowermost Roanoke drainage (Jenkins et al. 1975; E. F. Menhinick, in litt.). At individual localities this species tends to occupy very circumscribed areas (Smith 1907).

Abundance.—Common at one Virginia locality; few taken but abundance unknown at the others.

REMARKS

Until recent decades *E. chaetodon* was most familiar to aquarists in parts of Europe and southeast Asia; it had been kept in Germany by 1897. Even in recent years commercial breeders have mailed live fish from Asia to their land of ancestry (Quinn 1988). The blackbanded sunfish has been sold recently under the name "banded sunfish" in pet stores in the Norfolk–Virginia Beach area. If the sources of specimens sold in Virginia are native populations, the practice is illegal in view of the endangered status granted the species by the VDGIF in 1987.

Enneacanthus chaetodon was regarded to merit special concern status in Virginia by Jenkins and Musick (1979). It was then known from only two sites, but that relatively uncritical status was preferred because of the possible existence of additional populations. We now recommend (Burkhead and Jenkins 1991) its status in Virginia to be threatened. Although only one more population was discovered in extensive surveys during the 1980s, this species likely populates other waters in the state.

Name.—*Chaetodon* means "hair (or fine, narrow) toothed," a characteristic of the marine butterflyfish genus *Chaetodon*, to some species of which the blackbanded sunfish bears an outward resemblance.

Black basses   Genus *Micropterus* Lacepède

The largest centrarchids are black basses, genus *Micropterus*. This second-most speciose genus of centrarchids contains seven living species (one undescribed); three species inhabit Virginia. *Micropterus* has a basal position in the family (Mabee 1988). The large Mexican fossil species *M. relictus* represents the southernmost record of the family (Smith et al. 1975).

For more than a century only two species of *Micropterus* were recognized—the smallmouth bass and largemouth bass—and undescribed forms were variously confused with them. Hubbs (1927) recognized the spotted bass, other species were described (Hubbs and Bailey 1940; Bailey and Hubbs 1949), and the Guadalupe bass was elevated from the subspecific level (Hubbs 1954b).

Name.—*Micropterus* means "small fin"; it is based on a smallmouth bass with a damaged dorsal fin.

Early naturalists applied the common name black bass to the smallmouth bass because of its superficial similarity to the marine tautog *Tautoga onitis*, sometimes called the blackfish (Webster 1980). Webster considered that the word "bass" was derived from the Dutch "basse," corresponding to perch. Henshall (1939) suggested its derivation from the Old English "barse," the German "baarsh," or the Dutch "baarse," meaning "perch."

Smallmouth bass   *Micropterus dolomieu* Lacepède

SYSTEMATICS

The smallmouth bass was described in 1802 from an unstated type locality. It is a member of the subgenus *Micropterus*. Two subspecies were recognized by Hubbs and Bailey (1940): *M. d. dolomieu*, the widespread form native to and transplanted within Virginia; and *M. d. velox*, endemic to the middle Arkansas River drainage. However, Bailey (1956 *in* Pflieger 1971) later considered the subspecies to be invalid because of weak meristic definition and possible clinal intergradation (Ramsey 1975). Still, Ramsey noted that examples of *M. d. dolomieu* and *M. d. velox* appear different and that genetic disunity exists. Whether these forms are nameworthy seems debatable. Unfortunately, future resolution of the problem may be exacerbated by possible mixing of the forms over decades of stocking. Both forms may have been mixed in Virginia.

DESCRIPTION

Materials.—From Hubbs and Bailey (1940) and 40 Virginia specimens. Life color from 10 Virginia specimens.

Anatomy.—A relatively streamlined centrarchid with a mostly dark side that often is barred, dorsal fin not deeply notched; adults are 200–430 mm TL. Body moderately elongate or somewhat stocky, somewhat compressed; dorsal profile of head slightly or moderately convex; mouth large, terminal or slightly supraterminal (lower jaw slightly exceeding snout tip), posterior end of maxilla not extending past posterior rim of eye (in specimens greater than 200 mm TL). Dorsal fin slightly or moderately emarginate at juncture of spinous and soft portions; caudal fin moderately forked; pectoral fin rounded. Small tooth patch sometimes present on tongue.

Meristics.—Lateral line scales (68)71–77(81); scales above lateral line (11)12–13; scales below lateral line (19)21–23; circumpeduncle scales 29–31(32). Dorsal spines (9)10(11); dorsal rays (12)14(15); anal spines (2)3; anal rays (9)11(12); pectoral rays (15)16–17(18).

Color in Preservative.—Dorsum dark; cheek usually with 3 dark horizontal or oblique bars; opercular spot dark, triangular; side plain, variegated, or with many narrow dark bars; venter slightly dusky or speckled. First dorsal fin uniformly dusky; second dorsal, caudal, and anal fins sometimes slightly mottled, margins pale or suffusedly dark; pelvic fin with medial dusky streaks, leading edge pale; pectoral fin uniformly pale.

Color in Life   Plate 29.—Dorsum medium to dark olive or bronze; cheek bars dark olive; iris dull red or bright red; opercular spot brown or black; lateral barring and variegations olive-brown; lower side brassy-olive, olive, or whitish. Dorsal, caudal, and anal fins with olive-brown mottling (when mottled), otherwise pale olive; pelvic and pectoral fins sometimes with pale orange wash.

Fish 233 *Micropterus dolomieu* adult male 149 mm SL (REJ 1039), VA, Montgomery County, South Fork Roanoke River, 16 September 1983.

Larvae.—Described by Anjard (1974), Hardy (1978b), and Tin (1982d).

BIOLOGY

Fingerling smallmouth bass exhibit the carnivorous appetite of adults, eating microcrustaceans, insects, and small fishes (Lachner 1950a). Juveniles and adults graduate to crayfishes and fishes as the principal diet and also take insects (Woolcott et al. 1974; Coble 1975; Carlander 1977; Miner 1978; Pavol and Davis 1982; Probst et al. 1984).

Both sexes usually mature in 3–4 years, extremes being 2 and 9 years (Emig 1966a); maximum age is 15 years (White 1970 *in* Scott and Crossman 1973). Smallmouth bass in northern populations normally live longer than those in southern ones. Although growth rates vary substantially among bodies of water within limited areas, adult sizes tend to be similar in the north and south (Rosebery 1950a; Brown 1960; Scott and Crossman 1973; Carlander 1977). From 14 lotic populations of Virginia and three sections of the Potomac River in Maryland, means at age 4 were 211–320 mm TL, unweighted mean 252 (Sanderson 1958; Wollitz 1972; Kauffman 1975; Davis and Enamait 1982; Smith and Kauffman 1982). River populations tended to have faster growth rates than those of streams.

Growth at age 4 generally was much faster in Virginia reservoirs than in rivers. In Claytor Lake the means were 345 (in 1948–1949) and 310 mm TL (1976–1978); in Philpott Reservoir the mean was 399 mm, and in Smith Mountain Lake 422 mm (Rosebery 1950a; Hart 1978, 1981; Smith and Kauffman 1982). The unweighted grand mean from reservoirs is 369 mm. The largest smallmouth bass known from Virginia was 3.6 kg (8 pounds); the all-time record, from Kentucky, was 5.4 kg (11 pounds 15 ounces).

Spawning generally occurred during 1–15 May, water 16–22°C, in the Shenandoah system (Surber 1970). We observed nests with free-swimming larvae in the James River on 19 May 1984. In streams males construct nests near shore in 30–60 cm depth, on firm bottoms in slow currents and often adjacent to cover. Details of courtship and spawning behavior are described by Ridgway et al. (1989). Males vigorously defend nests having eggs and remain aggressive for several days after the eggs hatch (Pflieger 1966). Nest counts in the Shenandoah annually ranged 6–141 per mile during 1965–1969 (Surber 1970). Hubert (1976) estimated numbers of mature ova to be 2,601–27,716 for Alabama females of 305–521 mm TL. Counts of eggs on nests in Missouri averaged 2,517 (Pflieger 1966). An average of 3,943 fry rose off nests in a Maine lake (Neves 1975).

The smallmouth bass naturally hybridizes with the spotted bass in a few areas (Hubbs and Bailey 1940; Pflieger and Fajen 1975). Only one case is known of hybridization in the wild with the largemouth bass—in a recently constructed Texas reservoir (Whitmore and Hellier 1988). Natural hybrids between the smallmouth and bluegill are reported from a reservoir in Hawaii (Childers 1975). First- and second-generation progeny of artificially crossed male smallmouth bass × female largemouth bass can be fast growing and very aggressive, and have attacked swimmers and pets (Childers 1975). This hybrid has been dubbed the "meanmouth."

HABITAT

Smallmouth bass inhabit cool and warm, generally clear, large creeks, streams, and rivers with gravelly and rocky substrates and a frequent succession of riffles, runs, and pools. Typically they occupy runs and pools (Leonard et al. 1986). Often they become a dominant species in reservoirs that impound streams with the above attributes, and are prolific in many natural northern lakes. Smallmouth bass generally do not proliferate in soft-bottomed ponds and lowland reservoirs. In Virginia, *M. dolomieu* occasionally disperses to, or may be resident in, tidal freshwater sections of the Rappahannock and James rivers, and is reported to occur in such conditions elsewhere (Pavol and Davis 1982). During winter, stream-dwelling smallmouth seek cover in pools. A winter-diving observation in a Roanoke River pool, water 0°C, found a few adult smallmouth bass sharing space beneath a boulder with quiescent groups of crescent shiners and bluntnose minnows.

The populations of smallmouth bass in the Piedmont and Coastal Plain of the Chowan drainage are notable owing to the absence of the species from nearly all of the much-silted Appomattox, lower Roanoke, and Dan systems. The Meherrin system population is known only from one site in the North Meherrin River, but it was present during the three samplings made in 1958–1983. The substrate is largely sand, but riffles have gravel and rubble, and pools have outcroppings. The Nottoway system populations above and in the Fall Zone have rocky habitat available, but most of the bottom of the pools is silted sand. The Coastal Plain Nottoway population is in seemingly marginal habitat; small breeding groups may be present but the lowermost records probably are of waifs.

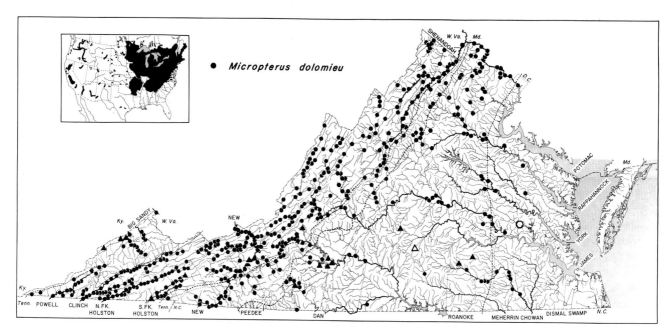

Map 146   Smallmouth bass. Open symbols signify unverified records.

DISTRIBUTION   Map 146

The native range of *M. dolomieu* encompasses the Great Lakes–St. Lawrence and upper Mississippi basins, southward in the Ohio basin to Georgia and Alabama, and westward to the Red drainage of eastern Oklahoma; central Mississippi Valley lowlands are avoided. Smallmouth bass have been widely introduced in North America and elsewhere (Hubbs and Bailey 1938; Robbins and MacCrimmon 1974).

Difficulties in determining the native distribution and stocking history of smallmouth bass and largemouth bass *M. salmoides* are magnified by early nomenclatural vagaries that include interchanges of specific epithets (Henshall 1939). The smallmouth bass often was called *salmoides* or *fasciatus* and was frequently dubbed "black bass." The largemouth bass sometimes was referenced as *nigricans*, "Carolina chub," and "James River chub." We allocated the literature on *Micropterus* in Virginia and vicinity to species based chiefly on accompanying descriptions of morphology or habitat occurrence, or both lines of evidence.

In Virginia the smallmouth bass is native to the Big Sandy and Tennessee drainages and is nonnative to the New and all major Atlantic slope drainages. In a shaded distribution map, Hubbs and Bailey (1938) indicated that the New drainage population was indigenous. However, Cope (1868b) did not report the smallmouth bass from his extended stay on the New during 1867, and the VFC (1877a) stated that the New

"has in its main stream little else [gamefishes] than the cat fish."

Early statements indicating native status of smallmouth bass in the Roanoke and James drainages are erroneous. Fowler (1907) reported that a specimen(s) collected by Cope in 1867 came from the upper Roanoke, which would predate known stockings, but Cope (1868b) did not list it from there. Cope (1868b: 216, as *M. fasciatus*) had reported the smallmouth from the Tennessee drainage, but this record was omitted by Fowler (1907). Jordan (1889b) believed the smallmouth to be indigenous to the upper James based on his collecting in 1888, but the James had been stocked by 1871. No *Micropterus* bones were found at a fossil site and an archeological site in the upper James (Guilday et al. 1977; Whyte 1989).

The initial introduction of smallmouth bass to the James drainage occurred much later than interpreted by Robbins and MacCrimmon (1974:70–71). They indicated that Milner (1874:525) related that smallmouth bass were planted in a pond near Richmond in the James drainage in the early 1800s. However, Milner (1874) had based his report on Norris (1864:461), who stated that *Grystes salmoides*, the "James River chub," was transferred *from* the James to ponds north of the drainage. Further, Norris' statement is actually based on largemouth bass (see that account).

Apparently the first known successful introduction of smallmouth bass to a Virginia drainage—the Potomac—is the well-documented transfer in 1854 by William Shriver of about 20 adults from Wheeling, West Virginia (Ohio basin) to the Chesapeake and Ohio Canal at Cumberland, Maryland (Eoff 1855). Other transfers probably occurred in the 1860s, according to Milner (1874). Smallmouth were stocked in Maryland and Pennsylvania tributaries of the Potomac in 1873 by commissions of those states (Milner 1874). By 1876, the smallmouth bass was widespread in the upper Potomac of Maryland (Uhler and Lugger 1876). Davis and Enamait (1982) stated that by 1870 it had diffused throughout the Potomac River watershed, but the claim may not have applied to Virginia.

Descendents of smallmouth bass liberated in 1854 and soon after undoubtedly spread into the Virginia portion of the Potomac drainage. Stockings within Virginia are unknown until 1871, when smallmouth bass were placed at various points in the upper and middle James drainage between Covington and the Tye River mouth (VFC 1877a). By 1877, *M. dolomieu* extended down the James to Richmond (VFC 1877b). State personnel apparently made the 1871 stockings, although the Virginia Fish Commission was not created until 1875 (VFC 1877a). During 1875–1876, smallmouth bass were stocked in most major upland Virginia streams east of the Tennessee drainage (VFC 1877a). The source of fish for the 1871–1876 Virginia stockings is uncertain; the fish may have originated from the Potomac population, or may have been native Holston system fish.

The VFC (1878) noted that "nearly all of our principal streams have been already stocked with [smallmouth] bass . . . ," and that 179 large specimens from the Holston were liberated in New River tributaries. Within-James and James-to-upper South Fork Shenandoah transfers had just been made but other routes are uncertain. The year 1879 was the last of intensive intra- and interdrainage transfers (VFC 1879). Smallmouth bass again were moved within the James and from the James to the upper South Fork Shenandoah; fish also went from the Holston, Roanoke, and James to the New drainage. By 1882, smallmouth fishing in the Shenandoah, James, Rappahannock, and New was a chief attraction to summer visitors (VFC 1882).

In 1887 the Wytheville hatchery procured *M. dolomieu* from the New drainage, and in 1891 the Central Station brood ponds (Washington, D.C.) received 1,900 black basses from the Neosho Hatchery in Missouri (USFC 1894). The Neosho transfer probably contained the nominal subspecies *M. d. velox* (see *Systematics*) and perhaps the spotted bass *M. punctulatus*. The Neosho fish were dispersed to unknown places, possibly not Virginia. The success of culturing smallmouth bass at these stations was much less than

that achieved with largemouth bass; stockings apparently occurred less frequently than during the 1870s. By the 1920s the culture of smallmouth was much refined and many thousands were reared and stocked. The Wytheville brood stock was augmented by 60 adults from Lake Erie in 1927 (USFC 1928).

The smallmouth bass was early stocked in many lower Piedmont and Coastal Plain streams and ponds of Virginia. Although most efforts apparently failed to establish the species, some of the scattered lowland records may represent relicts of these introductions.

An interesting pattern of establishment occurred in the lower North and South Anna rivers and the upper Pamunkey River of the York drainage. Despite early stockings near the Fall Line in the North and South Anna, smallmouth bass have prospered only since impoundment of the North Anna in 1972. Lake Anna ameliorated acid mine pollution from Contrary Creek and retained silt from its watershed, resulting in habitat enhancement in the tailwater. Some of the smallmouth that had persisted in the lower South Anna then dispersed and established populations in the lower North Anna and upper Pamunkey (VEPCO 1982; Massie 1984).

Abundance.—Smallmouth bass are uncommon to common in montane portions of Virginia except for some main rivers; they decrease in abundance on the Piedmont and Coastal Plain. Distributional gaps in Piedmont sections of the Rappahannock and James rivers may reflect limited sampling rather than absence or rarity of *M. dolomieu*. Smallmouth bass are virtually absent in the moderately to heavily silted middle and lower Dan system and are unknown from a major Dan tributary, the Banister River.

REMARKS

The smallmouth bass is one of the most valued and studied fishes in North America. Although it was historically popular within its native range and was the early subject of governmental and private stocking programs, the advocacy of the smallmouth by J. A. Henshall truly endeared it to the American angler. Before the turn of the century Henshall captured the imagination with his often quoted phrase "inch for inch and pound for pound the gamest fish that swims." A magazine dedicated to this species and titled *Smallmouth* was recently started. Patrons of the smallmouth bass will find a gold mine of information in Robbins and MacCrimmon (1974) and Stroud and Clepper (1975).

Name.—*Dolomieu* is a patronym honoring M. Dolomieu, a French mineralologist and associate of Lacepède, and for whom the rock type dolomite is also named (C. Smith 1985). The specific epithet is changed from the genitive (*dolomieui*) according to the new International Code of Zoological Nomenclature (ICZN 1985). The reversion to Lacepède's original spelling (*dolomieu*) was recommended by Bailey and Robins (1988a).

Spotted bass   *Micropterus punctulatus* (Rafinesque)

SYSTEMATICS

The identity of the spotted bass, a member of the subgenus *Micropterus*, was confounded from the start. It was described by Rafinesque from the Ohio River in 1819 and probably twice more in 1820, possibly from a mix of spotted bass and smallmouth bass (Hubbs and Bailey 1940). Subsequently the spotted bass was generally unrecognized by ichthyologists and anglers for more than a century. This owes to its resemblance to other black basses in commonly used diagnostic characters—to the smallmouth in upper jaw length and several other features and to the largemouth in some aspects of color, notably the dark lateral stripe. However, Trautman (1981) noted that commercial fishermen of the Ohio River had long believed the spotted bass to be a distinct species.

Micropterus punctulatus was found to possess a unique set of characters and was recognized as a species by Hubbs (1927), but he gave it a new scientific name because he regarded none of the 21 prior names of black basses to have been founded on the spotted bass. Hubbs and Bailey (1940) reexamined Rafinesque's original description of *punctulatus* and applied that name to the spotted bass. They also recognized three subspecies; *M. p. punctulatus* is the form in Virginia. Systematics of *M. punctulatus* were also studied by R. Gilbert (1978).

DESCRIPTION

Materials.—Twenty-one specimens from Virginia and Tennessee, and counts from Hubbs and Bailey (1940); all data from *M. p. punctulatus.* Life color from plate in Pflieger (1975); Virginia specimens are typical.

Anatomy.—A blotched, speckled, and usually stripe-sided bass with a low first dorsal fin; adults are 250–380 mm SL. Body somewhat elongate or slightly stocky, moderately compressed; dorsal profile of head nearly straight or moderately convex; mouth terminal or slightly supraterminal, large, the posterior end of maxilla usually even with posterior rim of eye. Dorsal fin not deeply emarginate at juncture of spinous and soft portions; caudal fin moderately forked; pectoral fin rounded. Small patch of tiny teeth present on tongue.

Meristics.—Lateral line scales (55)60–68(72); scales above lateral line (7)8–9; scales below lateral line (14)15–17(18); circumpeduncle scales (22)23–27. Dorsal spines 9–10(11); dorsal rays 11–13(14); anal spines (2)3(4); anal rays (9)10(11); pectoral rays (14)15–16(17).

Color in Preservative.—Body with a midlateral series of narrowly to broadly conjoined dark blotches, generally effecting a wide stripe, terminating as a caudal spot in some specimens; dorsolateral area unmarked or slightly mottled; ventrolateral area with longitudinal rows of dark spots or speckles; venter pale. Head dorsum dark; cheek with 3 horizontal or oblique dark bars, upper bar extending onto opercle, fusing with dark triangular-shaped opercular spot in some specimens. First dorsal fin dusky; second dorsal fin mottled basally, uniform distally; caudal fin uniformly dusky, rays dark; anal fin mottled basally, otherwise uniformly dusky; pectoral and pelvic fins pale.

Color in Life.—Ground shade of dorsum pale olive to dark olive or green; dorsolateral mottling dark olive; dor-

Fish 234 *Micropterus punctulatus* subadult male 121 mm SL (REJ 1038), VA, Campbell County, Roanoke River, 12 September 1983.

solateral scale centers whitish, forming longitudinal rows; midlateral blotches or stripe olive-brown or olive-black; ground color of lower side and venter whitish, ventrolateral spots olive-black; cheek bars dark olive, opercular spot black. First dorsal fin pale olive; second dorsal fin mostly pale olive, basal mottling olive-brown; caudal fin olive with yellow wash; anal and pelvic fins whitish; pectoral fin pale.

Larvae.—Described by Conner (1979); Pflieger (1975) provided a general account of hatching times and coloration.

BIOLOGY

Prey preference and the size-related dietary shift of the spotted bass are similar to those of the smallmouth bass. Young and small juveniles feed on microcrustaceans and small insects; with growth, they progress to larger insects, crayfishes, and fishes (Vogele 1975; Hess 1983).

Some *M. punctulatus* mature as yearlings, some not until 4 years. The maximum known age is 7 years (Vogele 1975). Spotted bass generally grow faster in reservoirs than in running water (Vogele 1975). Claytor Lake fish at age 4 averaged 340 mm TL in 1948–1949, but were 290 mm in 1976–1978 (Rosebery 1950a; Hart 1981). In the Clinch and New rivers the age-4 means were 274 and 226 mm TL (Wollitz 1972). A 2.7-kg (5 pounds 12 ounces) spotted bass was caught in Claytor Lake (Hart 1981); the world record is 3.9 kg (8 pounds 10.5 ounces), from Arkansas.

Spawning usually begins when water temperature reaches 15–19°C, probably late April to mid-May in Virginia. Nests in reservoirs are usually constructed on firm and sometimes soft bottoms in 1.5–6.7 m depth (Vogele 1975). In streams, nests are located in pool margins similar to those used by smallmouth bass (Pflieger 1975). In an Arkansas reservoir, mature ova were 3,806–30,586 per female; 87–3,820 larvae were counted on 15 nests (Vogele 1975).

In some areas spotted bass hybridize in nature with smallmouth bass, but we have not detected this in Virginia. Pflieger and Fajen (1975) found a high frequency of hybridization in Missouri streams where the spotted bass was introduced.

HABITAT

Spotted bass are intermediate between smallmouth bass and largemouth bass in habitat requirements. In Virginia, *M. punctulatus* commonly is found in warm, clear to moderately turbid, moderate-gradient streams and rivers. Trautman (1981) stated that it appeared to be more tolerant of turbidity and siltation than were the smallmouth or largemouth basses. In many areas, particularly west of the Mississippi River, spotted bass typically extend into large creeks; some populations are augmented by upstream immigrants during spring (Pflieger and Fajen 1975; Vogele 1975). *Micropterus punctulatus* becomes established in reservoirs; it does not occupy swampy situations in which largemouth bass often flourish.

DISTRIBUTION   Map 147

The spotted bass is native to the Mississippi basin and Gulf slope. It has been introduced beyond but not to the extent of the smallmouth and largemouth basses. In Virginia it is native only to the Tennessee and Big Sandy drainages.

We regard *M. punctulatus* as introduced to the New drainage for lack of an early record. Cope (1868b) reported black bass to be "absent or rare" there; we construe that he did not see a specimen. Goldsborough and Clark (1908) and Breder and Breder (1923) did not capture *M. punctulatus* in the New drainage of West Virginia and North Carolina, nor did Hubbs (1927) indicate any records. The chronology, points of stocking, and source of *M. punctulatus* introduced to the New drainage are unknown. Although the 19th and early 20th century reports of the VFC and USFC did not distinguish the spotted bass, it is improbable that this species was introduced to Virginia in that period (see smallmouth bass, *Distribution*). The first spotted bass specimen known from the Virginia section (and apparently the entire New drainage) was collected by Hubbs in 1928. Hubbs and Bailey (1940) depicted this species as well spread in the New River and to occupy lower reaches of some tributaries.

On the Atlantic slope, spotted bass were stocked by the VDGIF in the Appomattox system of the James drainage and in the Falling River of the Roanoke drainage during 1976–1977, and in the South Anna River of the York drainage in 1979. This species apparently has become established in the three streams. Stockings in the Appomattox were made in the upper portion, from which we took specimens in 1979 and heard of good catches in 1984 (A. L. LaRoche, personal communication). We caught young in a lower Appomattox tributary in 1984; farther down the Appomattox, upper Lake Chesdin yielded adults in 1986 (B. E. Ingram, personal communication). In the Falling River, several *M. punctulatus* were hooked, even blind-snagged (suggesting abundance), by anglers just below the lowermost dam during spring 1983. In 1984 we caught an adult in the Roanoke River at the Falling River mouth. From the South Anna, we verified a juvenile spotted bass taken in 1979, and C. A. Sledd (personal communication) indicated that this

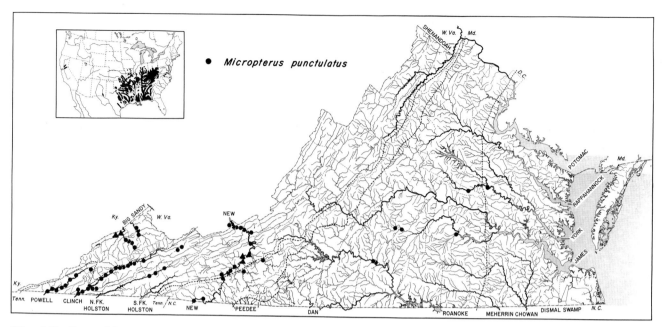

Map 147 Spotted bass.

species is established down into the upper Pamunkey River. Although it is spawning in the South Anna (D. J. Shuber, personal communication), apparently it has not followed the smallmouth bass in colonizing the North Anna River. A stocking during 1977 of *M. punctulatus* in the Pedlar River, in the Blue Ridge of the James drainage, apparently failed; smallmouth bass were recently found to be common there (D. K. Whitehurst, personal communication).

Abundance.—Generally rare or uncommon. In the North Fork Holston River the spotted bass is known only from the Saltville area. Its apparent absence in the lower North Fork may reflect the pollution history of that stream. The absence of spotted bass in the South Fork Holston may be due to high gradient, but its absence in the Middle Fork Holston is curious. It is

uncommon to common in Claytor Lake and Flannagan Reservoir. The introduced population in the Appomattox system appears to be thriving (A. L. La-Roche, personal communication).

REMARKS

The spotted bass provides anglers with sport and tasty eating in some areas of Virginia that are not well suited to the smallmouth or largemouth basses. The spotted bass is often misidentified; specimens should be carefully keyed and checked against Table 10, descriptions, and photographs of all black basses.

Name.—*Punctulatus* means "with small spots." Often this fish is called "Kentucky bass," a misnomer considering its wide native range.

Largemouth bass   *Micropterus salmoides* (Lacepède)

SYSTEMATICS

The largemouth bass was described in 1802 from South Carolina. It was retained in the monotypic genus *Huro* by Hubbs and Bailey (1940) because of the large mouth, deeply emarginate dorsal fin, absence of splintlike scales basally on the soft dorsal and anal fins, and forked pyloric caeca. Bailey and Hubbs (1949) later placed the largemouth bass in the genus

Micropterus with the other black basses and ranked *Huro* as a subgenus. Recognition of subgenera is supported by Smith et al. (1975).

Two subspecies are recognized: *M. s. salmoides* (northern largemouth bass), the widespread form possibly indigenous to western Virginia; and *M. s. floridanus* (Florida largemouth bass), which in typical form was confined essentially to the Florida peninsula. Bailey and Hubbs (1949) detected their intergra-

Fish 235 *Micropterus salmoides* adult male 137 mm SL (REJ 1004), VA, Charlotte County, Horsepen Creek, 13 July 1983.

dation north to southern South Carolina and west to Alabama. Both subspecies and their intergrades have been introduced in Virginia and far beyond their native ranges, resulting in a much wider range of intergradation (Chew 1975; Philipp et al. 1983).

DESCRIPTION

Materials.—From Hubbs and Bailey (1940), Chew (1975), and 30 Virginia specimens. Life color from 2 small Virginia adults.

Anatomy.—A stripe-sided, robust, very large-mouthed bass with a deeply notched dorsal fin; adults are 230–650 mm TL. Body somewhat elongate or distinctly stocky, slightly or moderately compressed, large adults often with deep belly; dorsal profile of head slightly or moderately convex; mouth terminal or supraterminal, large (posterior end of upper jaw extending past posterior rim of eye in specimens greater than about 140 mm TL). Dorsal fin deeply emarginate at junction of spinous and soft portions; caudal fin moderately forked; pectoral fin rounded. Teeth absent on tongue. Genital pore pear-shaped in mature male, round in female (Parker 1971).

Meristics.—Lateral line scales (58)61–65(69); scales above lateral line 7–8(9); scales below lateral line (14)15–17; circumpeduncle scales (24)26–28(30). Dorsal spines (9)10(11); dorsal rays (11)12–13(14); anal spines (2)3; anal rays (10)11(12); pectoral rays (13)14–15(17). *M. s. floridanus* has higher average meristic values: lateral line scales (65)69–73(77); scales above lateral line (7)8–9(10); scales below lateral line (16)17–18; circumpeduncle scales (27)28–31(32).

Color in Preservative.—Midside with a prominent series of closely spaced bars or blotches, these usually coalesced to form a wavy-edged stripe; dorsum uniform or mottled; lower side speckled, venter pale; cheek with 2 dark oblique bars; opercular spot dark, often triangular. Spinous and soft dorsal fins dusky, latter slightly mottled; caudal fin moderately dusky or dark, sometimes weakly mottled, anal, pelvic, and pectoral fins pale.

Color in Life Plate 29.—Midlateral stripe or blotches olive or olive-black; dorsum olive with brassy and green sheens, mottling dark olive; lower side and venter dirty opalescent white; cheek bars olive; opercular spot black. Dorsal and caudal fins pale olive to medium olive, mottling olive-brown; anal and pelvic fins off-white; pectoral fin pale orange-olive. Heidinger (1975) noted that spawning adults undergo vivid color changes.

Larvae.—Described by Taber (1969), Anjard (1974), Hardy (1978b), Conner (1979), Wang and Kernehan (1979), and Tin (1982d). Development of *M. s. floridanus* is described by Chew (1974).

BIOLOGY

The largemouth bass preys on a wide array of aquatic animals. Young mainly feed on plankton, small insects, and small fishes; adults chiefly take larger insects, larger fishes, and crayfishes (Keast 1965; Miner 1978; Kohler 1980; Davies 1981; Sule 1981; Sule et al. 1981). Adults are more piscivorous than are smallmouth or spotted basses.

Maturation of largemouth bass is correlated with length of the growing season; in southern latitudes maturity often is attained by age 1, in northern areas not until age 3 or 4 (Carlander 1977). Typical survival in Virginia latitudes is 8–10 years; an age-16 specimen is known from Indiana (Carlander 1977).

Growth varies considerably by locale. From 50 populations in reservoirs throughout Virginia and Back Bay, the range of mean lengths at age 4 was 251–475 mm TL, unweighted mean 371 (Smith and Kauffman 1982). From Claytor Lake the means were 404 mm in 1948–1949 and 361 mm in 1976–1978 (Rosebery 1950a; Hart 1981). From five sections of the Potomac or Shenandoah rivers, Virginia or Maryland, the age-4 means were 279–345 mm TL, mean, 318 (Sanderson 1958; Surber 1972; Davis and Enamait 1982). The tidal Rappahannock River produced fast growth; age-4

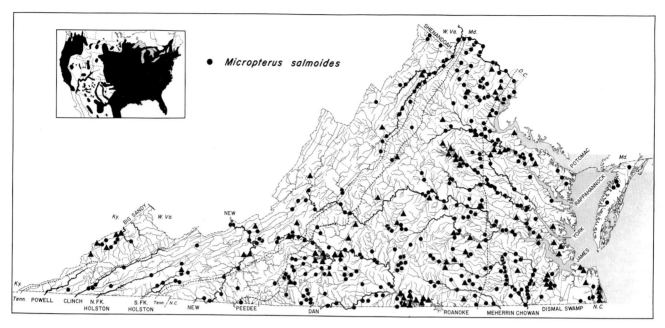

Map 148　Largemouth bass.

fish averaged 419 mm TL (Smith and Kauffman 1982). The largest largemouth bass caught in Virginia weighed 7.5 kg (16 pounds 10 ounces); the world record is 10.1 kg (22 pounds 4 ounces) from Georgia.

Spawning occurs in the spring when water approaches 16–18°C and can continue to 24°C (Carlander 1977). The normal spawning period in Virginia probably spans May and June. Estes (1971) found gravid fish in June through July in Leesville Reservoir, a pumped-storage impoundment with greatly fluctuating water levels. Several authors have reported two or three distinct spawning peaks in a year (summary, Hardy 1978b). The male fans out a nest and guards it against intruders; sometimes spawning occurs on unprepared bottom. Nests are made on a variety of substrates in pools and backwaters of streams and along shores of ponds and reservoirs in depths of 0.3–0.6 m, but sometimes as deep as 8.2 m (Carlander 1977). Nests may be found in open settings or in association with ledges, logs, or aquatic macrophytes, and may be well spaced or crowded. In Maine, adults of ages 4 and 6 averaged 17,501 and 21,751 total ova (Kelly 1962).

Many experimental hybrid crosses involving largemouth bass have been produced. The only known case of natural hybridization occurred in a newly created Texas reservoir, where the other parental species, smallmouth bass, is not native (Whitmore and Hellier 1988).

HABITAT

Micropterus salmoides inhabits marshes, swamps, ponds, lakes, reservoirs, and creeks to large rivers. In lotic situations it occupies pools and backwaters. It prefers warm, generally clear water, and is less tolerant of turbidity than is the spotted bass (Trautman 1981). Largemouth bass are found in the slightly acidic portions of the Chowan drainage and the periphery of Dismal Swamp. In the New Jersey Pine Barrens they are well established in all but the most acidic lakes. Calabrese (1969 *in* Hastings 1979) reported tolerance of pH 4.0, but that largemouth bass apparently were unable to reproduce in low-pH waters. Largemouth bass populate estuaries, being known from salinity as high as 12.9‰ in Virginia (Musick 1972).

DISTRIBUTION　Map 148

Micropterus salmoides is native to the Great Lakes–St. Lawrence and Mississippi basins and the Gulf and south Atlantic slopes; both subspecies have been widely transplanted in North America and beyond (Robbins and MacCrimmon 1974). We regard the largemouth bass as introduced to the Atlantic and New drainages in Virginia, and tentatively as native to the Virginia portion of the Tennessee and Big Sandy drainages. A case for introduced status in the far western drainages could be made from the relative recency of our first records—Tennessee 1952, Big Sandy 1966. However, a long time gap often separates the first stockings made long ago and the earliest records from scientific collecting. No zooarcheological evidence exists for native occurrence of *M. salmoides* anywhere in Virginia (T. R. Whyte, in litt.).

The northern native limit of the largemouth bass on the Atlantic slope is uncertain. Hubbs and Bailey (1940) regarded the largemouth bass to be native on the Atlantic slope from Florida to Virginia, whereas Hubbs and Lagler (1958) stated "... to North Carolina and possibly farther [north] ..., introduced elsewhere extensively." The more important question —to which drainages are the species native—often has not been addressed. A major aspect of the issue concerns the lower James drainage; some decisions on distributional status in southerly drainages have been premised on that in the James. Our progress in elucidating the matter stems partly from untangling names formerly applied to black basses (see smallmouth bass, *Distribution*).

Norris' (1864:461) comments indicate that the largemouth bass is native in the James: "From my boyhood [1820s] I have known ponds stocked with large fish which were not native to such waters. One instance was the transfer of what was called the 'James River Chub,' the magnificent fresh-water Bass, *Grystes salmoides*. They were taken *from* [our emphasis] the James River and placed in mill-ponds fed by small brooks a hundred miles north of Richmond." From an incomplete literature survey but based mainly on Cope's (1868b) capture in 1867 of *M. salmoides* from Tuckahoe Creek, a lower James River tributary, Jenkins (most recently *in* Hocutt et al. 1986) regarded this species as native north to the James.

To the contrary, Whig (1876) stated that largemouth bass were brought to Virginia from farther south. Noting Whig, Robbins and MacCrimmon (1974) speculated that the transfer(s) occurred in the early 1800s; however, they indicated native status in the James, Dismal Swamp, Chowan, and Roanoke drainages on their distribution map. Comments in the earliest VFC reports (1876, 1877a) support Whig's statement and an early 1800s transfer(s). The 1876 VFC report states: "The popular name of the pond bass—southern chub—betrays its origin. It was brought to this State from South Carolina about the beginning of this century. It now abounds in all the mill-ponds in Eastern Virginia in which it has been placed, and is found in large quantities in the quiet coves of the James, Rappahannock and other tidal waters." The source of Whig's (1876) and the VFC (1876) comments is unknown; perhaps the knowledge was general.

The transfer in the early 1800s to ponds "a hundred miles north" of the James River (Norris 1864) implies that the Potomac drainage was stocked long before the earliest Potomac record, dated 1876 (Bean and Weed 1911). However, the above quoted VFC (1876) statement indicates that some or all of the northerly ponds were in the Rappahannock drainage. Further, Uhler and Lugger (1876) did not report largemouth bass from the Potomac drainage of Maryland, and Davis and Enamait (1982) stated that the year of introduction to the Potomac was most likely after 1874. Thus the 1876 specimen (or its parents) probably was stocked not long before then. If so, this case deviates from the usual long duration between early stockings and first verified captures in Virginia drainages. Other first-specimen records for drainages are (from north to south): Rappahannock 1951; York 1897; James, Dismal Swamp, and Chowan 1888; Roanoke 1935; Pee Dee 1983; New 1928.

From the early popularity of the largemouth bass, the propensity of people to move them around, and the statements by Whig (1876) and the VFC (1876, 1877a), we conclude that this species was introduced to the James (and interconnected Dismal Swamp), and from there it was transferred elsewhere in Virginia prior to stockings documented by the VFC and USFC. Thus we believe also that the largemouth bass is not native to the Chowan and its prehistorical connection, the Roanoke. Interdrainage transfer was the principal early mode of introducing or replenishing fish stocks, and the Chowan and Roanoke are adjacent to the James. It would have been easier to carry largemouth bass to the James across one divide—had it been native in the Chowan or Roanoke to start with—than from South (and North) Carolina.

Micropterus salmoides clearly is native to North Carolina but its prehistorical northern limit there is unknown. John Lawson (1709), an early Carolinian explorer and naturalist, listed an array of freshwater fishes including the largemouth bass (as "Brown Pearch" or "Welch-men"). He stated that this species abounded in all creeks and ponds. Although he did not give specific sites, the detail of his descriptions (many places identifiable) and the lack of fanciful observations indicate that he meant that the largemouth occurred in the areas he surveyed. Lawson's some 1,000-mile journey proceeded up the lower Santee drainage in South Carolina, thence across North Carolina Piedmont sections of the Pee Dee, Cape Fear, and Neuse drainages, and then through the lower Tar River country. Based on Lawson's fish descriptions, itinerary, and residence, and owing to the proximity and great similarity of the Tar and Neuse ichthyofaunas, we offer that the northern native limit of *M. salmoides* is the Tar drainage, the first major drainage south of the Roanoke and Chowan.

The period of extensive largemouth bass dissemination in Virginia began in the late 1870s, blossomed in the 1890s, and continued long after. The VFC (1877b) noted shipments (possibly from south of Virginia) to interior ponds. The USFC was the most active agency of largemouth bass dispersion. In the 1890s largemouth were reared at the Wytheville, Virginia, and Washington, D.C., fish-culture stations, and were scattered in much of the state but sparingly in the Blue Ridge.

Recently the VDGIF has stocked largemouth bass only in new impoundments. "Largemouth" and "Florida largemouth" were planted in Lake Anna during 1972–1977 (Sledd and Shuber 1981); the genetic heritage of the population was later identified as nearly 50:50 northern and Florida largemouths. The genome in Kerr Reservoir is mostly the northern form, and in Lake Prince it is chiefly the Florida form (Philipp et al. 1983). Lake Conner apparently has a mixed population (see below). Briery Creek Lake was stocked with Florida bass in 1986–1987.

Abundance.—Generally uncommon or common in streams and reservoirs on the Piedmont and Coastal Plain, and in impoundments in montane areas. As with the smallmouth bass, scarcity of records in the middle James drainage may reflect limited sampling. Absence of largemouth bass from interior Dismal Swamp may be related to acidity. Largemouth have been common to abundant in Back Bay after periods of little or no storm- or human-caused saltwater intrusion (Norman 1981).

REMARKS

The allure of catching largemouth bass generates millions of dollars annually. It is the most important species of black bass in 42 states of the United States, and the most important gamefish in 11 of them (Robbins and MacCrimmon 1974). It is the most widespread of the *Micropterus*, reflecting the interest in its fighting power and table-fare quality. It probably was the first fish to be raised in culture ponds in North America. However, the fish raised in 1765 by John Dayeas near Charleston, South Carolina, were used for fertilizer in rice fields (Robbins and MacCrimmon 1974). In addition to introductions beyond its native range in North America, it has been stocked in Cuba, Puerto Rico, Central and South America, Africa, Europe, and the USSR. Not only is the largemouth bass one of the most valued (and studied) fishes in North America, it is certainly one of the most sought vertebrates in the world.

The Florida largemouth bass has a reputation for faster growth than the northern form, a primary reason for transplanting it. Lake Conner, Halifax County, recently yielded some of the largest largemouth bass known from Virginia; they are suspected to be the Florida form, which was stocked in small numbers, or they are intergrades (W. E. Neal, personal communication). However, the growth difference between the subspecies is inconsistently expressed, and the Florida form may be less catchable than the northern one (Zolczynski and Davies 1976). There are indications that the growth potential of Florida bass in the new Briery Creek Lake will not be realized unless the number and size of fish taken are carefully managed.

In reference to qualities of Florida bass, Philipp et al. (1983) cautioned that conclusions of many former studies are open to question because the genetic purity of the subject fish was not confirmed. Philipp et al. and Whitmore and Hellier (1988) further warned that propagation and dispersal of nonnative stocks may genetically contaminate and reduce overall fitness of established bass, an effect that may be irreversible.

Name.—*Salmoides* means "salmonlike"; it is derived from the appellation "lake trout" or "trout" used long ago in South Carolina.

Lepomis sunfishes   Genus *Lepomis* Rafinesque

Lepomis is the largest genus of the Centrarchidae; 7 of the 11 species live in Virginia. Its closest relative appears to be *Enneacanthus* (Mabee 1988). The *Lepomis* (or "typical") sunfishes confronted early naturalists with generally similar morphologies, an array of color patterns, and a propensity to hybridize; hybridization generally was not recognized or understood then. Coupled with an uncritical tendency of some early workers, it is easy to understand how such a large number of generic (15) and specific (75) synonyms was proposed for only 11 species. The resulting nomenclatural tangle was particularly clarified by Bailey (1938a), who reduced the genera (except *Chaenobryttus*) to subgenera of *Lepomis* and allocated synonyms to species. Bailey's intrageneric classification is largely followed despite indications of different affiliations for some species in genetic studies by Avise and Smith (1974b, 1977) and Avise et al. (1977).

Name.—*Lepomis* is derived from *lepis* (scale), and *omis* (shoulder) or *pomis* (cover or lid—the gill cover, operculum). Rafinesque poorly formed several names of taxa. After several years of debate on the gender of *Lepomis* (Brown 1954; Bailey and Robins 1988a; Etnier and Warren 1990), the name was fixed as masculine by the International Commission on Zoological No-menclature (ICZN 1992). This decision is consistent with established usage.

The common name "sunfish" alludes to the deep and rounded lateral profile, to the yellow, orange, and red colors of many species, and to the propensity of some species to hover in open water, "sunning."

Warmouth   *Lepomis gulosus* (Cuvier)

SYSTEMATICS

The warmouth was described in 1829 from Lake Pontchartrain, New Orleans. It long constituted the monotypic genus *Chaenobryttus* until Bailey et al. (1970) relegated *Chaenobryttus* to a subgenus of *Lepomis*. They noted that the degree of anatomical difference between *L. gulosus* and *L. cyanellus* was no more than that between *L. cyanellus* and other members of *Lepomis*. The generic merger was supported by discovery of a natural hybrid population, warmouth × bluegill (Birdsong and Yerger 1967). Smith and Lundberg (1972) preferred retention of *Chaenobryttus* as a genus, finding in *L. gulosus* and a new fossil species a unique osteological character; they argued that hybridization was not a sound criterion for congeneric status. Mayden et al. (1992) on the authority of Wainwright and Lauder (1992), also recognize *Chaenobryttus* as a genus distinct from *Lepomis*. Genetic analyses by Avise and Smith (1974b, 1977) did not resolve the question.

DESCRIPTION

Materials.—From Bailey (1938a), Frey (1951), Birdsong and Yerger (1967), and 15 Virginia series. Life color from 3 Virginia adults.

Anatomy.—A large-mouthed, stripe-cheeked, mottled sunfish; adults are 85–200 mm TL. Body robust, compressed, and deep; dorsal profile of head convex, indented over eye; mouth large, terminal, moderately oblique; eye large. Dorsal fin shallowly emarginate at junction of spinous and soft portions; caudal fin emarginate, lobes rounded; pectoral fin rounded. Tongue with a patch of tiny teeth.

Meristics.—Lateral line scales (38)41–45(48); scales above lateral line (6)7–8(9); scales below lateral line (12)13–14(15); circumpeduncle scales (20)21–22(23). Dorsal spines (9)10(11); dorsal rays (9)10(11); anal spines 3; anal rays 9–10; pectoral rays (12)14.

Color in Preservative.—Dorsum uniformly dark or mottled; side mottled, variegated, or both, many scales with dark portions contrasting with pale to dusky portions; pale scales sometimes outlining 6–7 poorly defined bars; venter dusky; cheek with 3 horizontal or oblique dark stripes; opercular spot dark, pale or dusky margined. Dorsal, caudal, and anal fins mottled, with many interradial pale spots; pelvic fin with dark streaks; pectoral fin pale.

Color in Life Plate 29.—Dorsum medium or dark brown; dark lateral areas brassy brown to olive-brown; pale

Fish 236 *Lepomis gulosus* adult male 83 mm SL (WHH 151), VA, Sussex County, Assamoosic Swamp, 26 July 1983.

lateral areas brassy white with green iridescence; venter golden brassy with pale green iridescence; dark areas of head brown, pale areas brassy with pale blue iridescence; iris red and black; opercular spot black. Spots in first dorsal fin yellow-olive, those in second dorsal and caudal fins with pale blue-green iridescence; base of second dorsal just anterior to its posterior insertion, and the back at that point, with a tomato-red spot in large reproductive males; anal fin spots yellow-olive; pelvic fin streaks olive-brown; pectoral fin pale. Larimore (1957) noted that spawning adults exhibit vivid color changes.

Larvae.—Described by Larimore (1957), Hardy (1978b), Conner (1979), and Tin (1982d).

BIOLOGY

The food of young and small juvenile warmouth is primarily plankton and small insects. Large juveniles and adults eat insects, snails, crayfishes, and fishes; sometimes the latter two items dominate the diet (Larimore 1957; Flemer and Woolcott 1966; Gatz 1979).

Maturation usually is achieved by fish of 75–100 mm TL and ages 1 or 2 (Larimore 1957). Maximum reported survival is age 8. In a wide geographic sample, typical age-3 warmouth ranged 100–180 mm TL (Carlander 1977). Age-3 fish averaged 130 mm TL in a central eastern Virginia impoundment (Smith and Kauffman 1982). Several *L. gulosus* within 203–226 mm TL were reported from southeastern Virginia impoundments by Norman (1973). An Ohio specimen of 284 mm TL (11.2 inches) and 0.5 kg (1 pound) was listed by Trautman (1981), and a 287-mm TL specimen from Oregon was compiled by Carlander (1977).

The breeding period spans mid-spring into summer, sometimes into early fall in some areas (Carlander 1977). The period in Virginia is unknown. Spawning began in Illinois when water reached 21°C (Larimore 1957). Males nest at cover, which is apparently more important than substrate firmness in nest-site selection; nests are at depths of 0.05–1.5 m (Carlander 1977). Nests usually were not in close proximity in Illinois (Larimore 1957), but in Florida, nesting fish were gregarious (Carr 1940 *in* Larimore 1957). Courtship and spawning were described by Larimore (1957). Eggs per female were 4,500–63,200 (Larimore 1957).

Lepomis gulosus is known to hybridize in nature with *L. cyanellus*, *L. gibbosus*, *L. macrochirus*, and *L. microlophus* (Bailey 1938b; Birdsong and Yerger 1967; Childers 1967). Compilations of the cross *L. auritus* × *L. gulosus* are traceable to the general comment by McAtee and Weed (1915) that "*gulosus* . . . seems to

hybridize with all," referring to *L. gibbosus*, *L. cyanellus*, and *L. auritus*.

HABITAT

Warmouth inhabit pools and backwaters of low-gradient creeks, streams, and rivers, as well as swamps and natural and artificial ponds and lakes. They frequently associate with aquatic macrophytes and other cover. Highly acidic sections of the Dismal Swamp interior are inhabited by this species. *Lepomis gulosus* is considered a strictly freshwater fish, almost always occupying salinities less than 1.5‰; the maximum reported occurrence is 17.4‰ (Swingle 1971 *in* Hardy 1978b; Musick 1972).

DISTRIBUTION   Map 149

The warmouth is native to the southern Great Lakes region (Bailey and Smith 1981), the Mississippi basin, the Gulf slope, and the south and central Atlantic slope; its northern limit on the latter is uncertain (Hubbs and Lagler 1958). It has been transplanted within parts of this general range; for example, southern Ohio (Trautman 1981). Apparently it is colonizing the Ontario shore of Lake Erie (Crossman and Simpson 1984).

For Virginia, we regard all of the few records from the Tennessee, New, and upper parts of the Roanoke, James, and Shenandoah drainages to be based on nonindigenous populations. The records are from impoundments or near resorts that offered fishing. Warmouth from Illinois were at the Central Station Hatchery by 1893, and at least the Shenandoah River proper and two streams in the upper James drainage were then stocked (USFC 1895). At least three sites in the middle James drainage were stocked around 1901 (USFC 1902). The lower Potomac drainage was stocked in about 1895; shortly after, the warmouth apparently became common locally (Smith and Bean 1899).

The stocking records, although probably incomplete (and not nearly as numerous as for *Ambloplites* and *Micropterus*), do not preclude native occurrence of the warmouth on the Atlantic slope of central and northern Virginia. Lee et al. (1976, 1981, 1984) and Hocutt et al. (1986) treated *L. gulosus* as native (but possibly introduced) north to the Potomac and Susquehanna. However, we consider it native only as far north as the James. Native status in the lower Roanoke, Chowan, and Dismal Swamp is based on the general distribution of the species. In the James it is founded on the 1867 record from Tuckahoe Creek, just above the Fall Zone (Cope 1868b, as *L. gillii*;

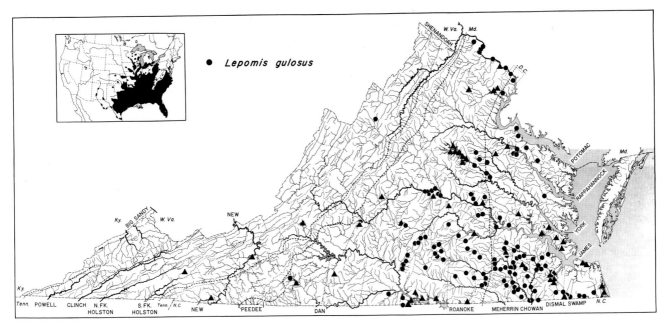

Map 149 Warmouth.

Fowler 1907). That status is tenuous; warmouth could have been added to the James in the early 1800s along with largemouth bass from South Carolina. We arbitrarily regard the warmouth as introduced to the York and Rappahannock drainages based on its apparent absence from much of the lower Piedmont and Coastal Plain sections, where it should be widespread if native. The first York record dates from 1934, near a probably stocked pond (see *Enneacanthus obesus*); the next oldest record is 1973. The earliest Rappahannock record is 1968. The Potomac was stocked (see above), and we treat all records as derived from such.

Abundance.—Generally uncommon; locally common in portions of the Chowan drainage and Dismal Swamp.

REMARKS

Because of its distribution the warmouth is familiar to anglers essentially only on the lower Piedmont and Coastal Plain. This species takes a wide variety of natural bait, lures, and flies. The early angling writer James Henshall ranked it just below black basses in its vigor at the end of a line. Larimore (1957) wrote that most people consider it an excellent table fish. At times it has a "muddy" flavor that generally is blamed on association with silt bottom and turbid water, but Larimore gave evidence that this is caused by food organisms in its diet. Warmouth he caught off silt bottom usually had excellent flavor and texture.

Name.—*Gulosus* means "gluttonous."

Green sunfish   *Lepomis cyanellus* Rafinesque

SYSTEMATICS

Lepomis cyanellus was described in 1819 from the Ohio River. With a broad generic concept of *Lepomis* sunfishes, Bailey (1938a) recognized *Apomotis* as a monotypic subgenus for *L. cyanellus*. As with some other sunfishes, the nomenclatural history of *L. cyanellus* is studded with binomens. Bailey listed 35 names that had been applied to hybrids between *L. cyanellus* and three other *Lepomis*. The green sunfish is closely related to *L. gulosus* and *L. symmetricus* (Bailey 1938a; Branson and Moore 1962).

DESCRIPTION

Materials.—From Bailey (1938a) and 28 Virginia lots. Life color from 2 Virginia adults.

Anatomy.—A large-mouthed sunfish with a wide pale margin on the earflap; adults are 70–180 mm TL. Body

Fish 237 *Lepomis cyanellus* adult male 132 mm SL (REJ 1034), VA, Charlotte County, Middle Branch Wards Fork Creek, 2 September 1983.

deep, somewhat compressed, slightly or rather stocky; dorsal profile of head slightly convex, straight, or slightly concave: mouth large, terminal, slightly oblique; eye large; earflap about equal in length and deep. Dorsal fin moderately emarginate at junction of spinous and soft portions in juvenile and small adult, nearly straight at juncture in large adult; caudal fin emarginate, lobes rounded; longest pelvic ray in some adults with short filamentous extension; pectoral fin rounded. Gill rakers long; small patch of teeth occasionally present on tongue.

Meristics.—Lateral line scales (43)46–50(53); scales above lateral line 8–9(10); scales below lateral line (16)17–18(19); circumpeduncle scales 23–25. Dorsal spines (9)10(12); dorsal rays 10–11(12); anal spines 3; anal rays (8)9–10; pectoral rays 13–14(15).

Color in Preservative.—Lateral body a mosaic of dusky to dark scale margins and pale scale centers, dark margins often united to form many narrow stripes; vague lateral bars sometimes present on small adult; small black flecks often present dorsolaterally, less frequently midlaterally, in juvenile and adult; venter dusky. Head uniformly dusky or sometimes with dark marks or wavy lines on cheek; opercular spot large and with relatively wide, pale posterior margin. Both dorsal fins usually moderately dusky; second dorsal with a dusky or black basiposterior smudge or spot, which sometimes has spikelike projections of pigment radiating distad on membranes; caudal fin uniformly dusky or slightly mottled, except margin pale; anal fin pale-margined, moderately dusky or dark basally with streaks in membranes radiating to margin, particularly in posterior part of fin; basiposterior anal fin spot distinct or weakly defined.

Color in Life Plate 29.—Body side with iridescent pale blue stripes alternating with brown, gold, or brassy stripes; blue stripes sometimes broken into short segments or a series of spots, almost always broken on flank and caudal peduncle; dorsum olive-brown; venter golden with scattered iridescent white scales. Head ground shade medium

to dark olive with iridescent pale blue spots and wavy lines on upper lip, cheek, and opercle; opercular spot mostly black, posterior margin with purple-gold iridescence. Dorsal fin mostly olive, mottling dark olive-brown; second dorsal with pale orange margin and, basiposteriorly, a black smudge or spot; caudal fin olive with pale streaks, both lobes with pale orange margin; anal fin mostly yellow-olive with olive-black interradial streaks, submarginally orange, marginally white on anterior half of fin, basiposterior spot black; pelvic fin orange medially, margin orange-white; pectoral fin clear except rays narrowly bordered with dusky or black.

Larvae.—Described by Hardy (1978b), Conner (1979), and Tin (1982d). Childers (1967) described larvae of three hybrids.

BIOLOGY

The typical switching with growth by centrarchids to larger prey items is exhibited by *L. cyanellus*. Adults feed mostly on benthic insects, but their diet is a smorgasbord of aquatic organisms and terrestrial insects (Minckley 1963; Etnier 1971; Sadzikowski and Wallace 1976). The green sunfish possesses a large mouth suited for piscivory, but fish accounted for a small percent of the diet in the above studies. However, this species fed heavily on small fishes that were concentrated in a drying pond (Greenfield and Deckert 1973), and Forbes and Richardson (1920) found that fishes made up one-third of the diet in Illinois. Predation by introduced populations of green sunfish in small North Carolina streams greatly suppressed native fish populations (Lemly 1985).

Maturation occurs earlier in areas with longer growing seasons; for example, at age 1 in Missouri compared with age 3 in Michigan. The oldest members of many populations are age 6 or 7; maximum

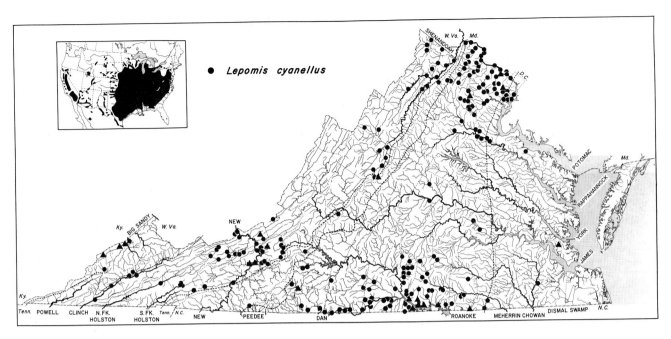

Map 150 Green sunfish.

known survival is 10 years. In a geographically broad compilation, age-3 green sunfish were 80–200 mm TL (Carlander 1977). Age-3 fish in a Virginia impoundment averaged 173 mm TL (Smith and Kauffman 1982), larger than the about 40 adults we saw in the state. A 279-mm TL specimen reported from Utah (Carlander 1977) may be the record.

Spawning times of *L. cyanellus* in Virginia have not been reported, but protracted spawning periods have been observed elsewhere (Cahn 1927; Childers 1967; Pflieger 1975). Based on those reports the reproductive period in Virginia probably is late May through July and may extend into August. Males construct nests in pools and backwaters, often near vegetation. Hunter (1963 *in* Scott and Crossman 1973) observed colonial nesting in depths of 4–35 cm, but Pflieger (1975) reported that gregarious nesting was unusual. The territorial males produce a grunting sound during courtship and spawning (Gerald 1971). Females are moderately fecund, bearing 2,000–10,000 ova (Beckman 1952). Some species of shiners have been observed as nest-spawning associates (Hunter and Wisby 1961; Pflieger 1975).

Lepomis cyanellus hybridizes naturally with *L. auritus*, *L. gibbosus*, *L. gulosus*, *L. macrochirus*, *L. megalotis*, and *L. microlophus*. We found the *L. cyanellus* × *L. macrochirus* cross in Virginia.

HABITAT

The green sunfish is an occupant of slow pools and backwaters of moderate-gradient, clear and turbid creeks, streams, and rivers, and of ponds, lakes, and reservoirs. It is a strictly freshwater fish (Musick 1972) and seemingly is generally intolerant of low pH; it is rare below the Fall Line. A detailed summary of habitat characteristics is by Stuber et al. (1982).

DISTRIBUTION Map 150

The green sunfish is native to the Great Lakes and Mississippi basins and the Gulf slope, and has been widely introduced elsewhere. In Virginia it is probably native to the Tennessee, Big Sandy, and New drainages, and has been introduced on the Atlantic slope. We regard it as native to the Virginia portion of the Tennessee and Big Sandy because of that status elsewhere in these drainages. However, it is rare and sporadic in the Virginia portions and we suspect that many or all of the records ultimately stemmed from stocking.

Lepomis cyanellus is considered indigenous to the New drainage, contrary to Jenkins et al. (1972), because we now recognize that Cope (1868b, as *L. mineopas*) took it in 1867 at two well-separated sites and McDonald found it during 1885 in Wolf Creek. Cope's records almost certainly predate stocking. Surprisingly, *L. cyanellus* appears to be the only centrarchid native to the New. Its distribution there is peculiar. The plots indicate a preference for Valley and Ridge waters, but this species is virtually absent in a major portion of the province in Wythe County. One Wythe County record is by Cope (at his approximately located "Austinville" site). The other, from upper Cripple Creek, probably resulted from escapees from several fee-fishing ponds beside the collecting station (England and Cumming 1972).

Times of introduction of the green sunfish to the Atlantic slope are unknown; the USFC generally did not distinguish species of *Lepomis* in its reports. The earliest records for Virginia parts of Atlantic slope drainages are: Potomac 1900; Rappahannock 1941; James 1947 (but taken in 1931 in Potts Creek, West Virginia [CU 4906]); Roanoke 1951; Chowan 1960. The Pee Dee record, in 1976, is unverified; we accept it because *L. cyanellus* occupies the North Carolina portion of the drainage (E. F. Menhinick, in litt.).

Abundance.—Generally rare or uncommon in most of Virginia; found most abundantly, sometimes common locally, in the Potomac, lower Roanoke proper, and middle and lower Dan systems. Its wide distribution in parts of the Dan reflects tolerance of the often turbid conditions there.

REMARKS

The green sunfish is the species most frequently brought or described to us by anglers wishing to know what "strange sunfish" they have caught. Unusual prey consumed by green sunfish include a shrew and a bat (Huish 1947; Jones and Hettler 1959 *in* Carlander 1977).

Name.—*Cyanellus* means "blue."

Redbreast sunfish   *Lepomis auritus* (Linnaeus)

SYSTEMATICS

The redbreast sunfish was described in 1758 from Philadelphia. Bailey (1938a) placed it in the monotypic subgenus *Lepomis*; he, and Branson and Moore (1962) allied it with *L. megalotis*. Genetically, *L. auritus* clustered closest to *L. punctatus* (Avise and Smith 1974b).

DESCRIPTION

Materials.—From Bailey (1938a) and 48 Virginia lots. Color in life from Davis (1972) and 7 Virginia adults.

Anatomy.—A plain-sided sunfish with a long, entirely dark earflap; adults are 90–185 mm TL. Body deep, very compressed; predorsal profile markedly convex overall, slightly depressed at occiput; mouth moderate in size, terminal, oblique; eye large; earflap short or slightly elongate in juvenile, becoming quite long in adult. Dorsal fin slightly or moderately emarginate at junction of spinous and soft portions; caudal fin emarginate, lobes rounded or slightly acute; pelvic fin with small filamentous projection of longest ray; pectoral fin rounded or subacute. Gill raker length short to medium.

Meristics.—Lateral line scales (39)42–46(54); scales above lateral line 7–8(9); scales below lateral line 14–15(16); circumpeduncle scales 21–23. Dorsal spines (9)10(11); dorsal rays 11–12; anal spines 3; anal rays (8)9–10; pectoral rays (13)14–15.

Fish 238 *Lepomis auritus* adult male 123 mm SL (REJ 994), VA, Washington County, North Fork Holston River, 22 June 1983.

Color in Preservative.—General appearance is uniform duskiness; side sometimes with scattered dark scales; head and cheek uniformly dusky, cheek sometimes with dark wavy lines; earflap black, dark margined. Dorsal fin mostly dusky, often darker posterobasally; caudal fin usually uniformly dusky, sometimes mottled basally or with submarginal dark fringe; anal fin nearly uniform, margin paler posteriorly than anteriorly; pelvic fin dusky, usually dark in breeding fish; pectoral fin pale.

Color in Life Plate 30.—Dorsum usually olive or olive-brown, sometimes scales have pale blue iridescent marks; side and ventrolateral caudal peduncle pale blue, with orange or yellow-orange spots, the spots sometimes forming poorly defined yellow or orange bars; breast and abdomen range from bright orange-yellow (typical of adult female) to deep red-orange (typical of large nuptial male). Head olive or olive-brown, sometimes yellow to orange wash on opercle; iridescent blue wavy lines on cheek and upper lip, cheek sometimes wholly pale blue. Dorsal fin medium olive, entire fin may be pale margined, or second dorsal with pale yellow to orange wash that occasionally is pronounced marginally; caudal fin olive to olive-brown, and with yellow to orange wash; caudal lobes may be bright yellow or brick red, particularly in nuptial male; anal fin medially olive, base and margin olive or pale blue; pelvic fin dusky black in breeding adult; pectoral fin pale olive or amber. Webster (1942) reported the spawning female to be considerably darker than the male and to have distinct bars.

Larvae.—Described by Anjard (1974), Buynak and Mohr (1978b), Hardy (1978b), and Wang and Kernehan (1979).

BIOLOGY

A generalist predator, *L. auritus* eats insects, crayfishes, other arthropods, mollusks, and occasionally fishes. Aquatic insects are its dietary staple (Webster 1942; Flemer and Woolcott 1966; J. Davis 1972; Woolcott et al. 1974; Gatz 1979; Hess 1983).

Maturity was reached in 2 years by some North Carolina females (J. Davis 1972). Most older members of the species are 4–5 years; maximum survival is 8 years (Carlander 1977). Adult males grew faster than adult females in the James River (Saecker and Woolcott 1988). In Virginia the range of means of length at age 3 from 11 stream and reservoir populations, plus a sample combined from several rivers, was 119–173 mm TL, unweighted mean 140 (Wollitz 1972; Shuber and Sledd 1981; Petrimoulx 1983; Smith and Kauffman 1982). Growth is about the same in streams and reservoirs; growth rates in Virginia are similar to those summarized for North Carolina and the Potomac River in Maryland (Carlander 1977; Davis and Enamait 1982). The largest redbreast sunfish of which we are aware from Virginia is 205 mm TL (Petrimoulx 1983); one of 241 mm TL is known from Maryland

(Elser 1961). This species does not attain nearly the considerable weights, for sunfish, reached by bluegill and redear sunfish in some ponds and lakes.

Before entering shallow waters for nest construction, *L. auritus* clusters in quiescent schools or hiberniums, which dissolve when water reaches 10°C (Breder and Rosen 1966). In Virginia we observed redbreasts guarding nests on various dates during 31 May–13 July; Richmond (1940) observed active nests from June to early August. Studies summarized by J. Davis (1972) and Hardy (1978b) noted water temperatures during the breeding period of 16–28°C, with peak spawning occurring within 20–28°C. Nests are constructed by males over usually silt-free or lightly silted sand and gravel, often in association with cover. Nests may be closely spaced, occasionally touching (Breder 1936; Richmond 1940; J. Davis 1972; our observation). Nests are typically located in calm pool margins in less than 1 m depth, but may be constructed in the lee of large rocks near swift current (Breder 1936; Buynak and Mohr 1978b). Richmond (1940) described nesting in a tidal freshwater section of the Chickahominy River, Virginia, where nests were exposed but remained water-filled at low tide; the river was slightly brackish during low-water periods. *Lepomis auritus* did not produce sounds during courtship or spawning (Gerald 1971). Numbers of ova averaged 963 in age-2 females and 8,250 in age-6 fish (J. Davis 1972).

Lepomis auritus naturally hybridizes with *L. cyanellus*, *L. gibbosus*, *L. macrochirus*, and *L. microlophus* (Bailey 1938a). See the account of *L. gulosus* regarding the putative hybrid with that species. We caught several *L. auritus* × *L. macrochirus* in Virginia.

HABITAT

The redbreast sunfish is typically found in pools and backwaters of warm, usually clear but occasionally turbid creeks, streams, and rivers of low or moderate gradient. We often caught it by angling near slow runs. It also occurs in ponds and reservoirs. Generally it avoids swamps; based on its distribution, it seems intolerant of the highly acidic waters of interior Dismal Swamp. *Lepomis auritus* is one of few fishes found in elevated water temperatures, to 39°C, just below a power plant in the James River (Saecker and Woolcott 1988). Richmond (1940) reported nesting in slightly brackish water, and Schwartz (1981b) gave a salinity record of 7.0‰. However, these observations are of extreme conditions or waifs; this sunfish is a freshwater species (Musick 1972).

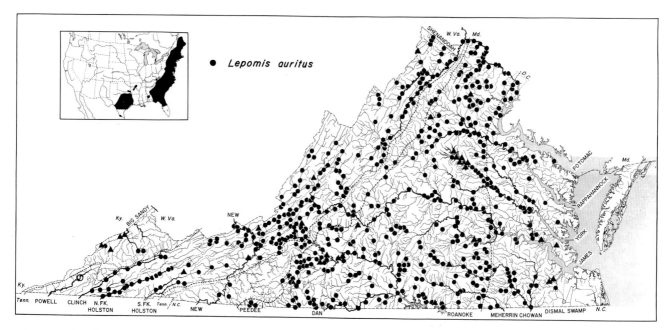

Map 151 Redbreast sunfish. Open circle indicates unverified record.

DISTRIBUTION   Map 151

The redbreast sunfish is native to the Atlantic slope probably from New Brunswick to central Florida, and west on the Gulf slope to the Apalachicola drainage. The extent of its introduced range indicated by Lee et al. (1980), and largely copied here, may be too inclusive. For example, in Kentucky *L. auritus* was stocked in several areas but is established only in the extreme southeastern portion (Burr 1980; Bell et al. 1985).

In Virginia the redbreast sunfish has been transplanted to all drainages west of the Atlantic slope. In the New drainage it was first stocked in Claytor Lake in 1939 (Rosebery 1950b) and is well established downstream; its first capture below Claytor was in 1952. There are scattered records above Claytor, possibly reflecting separate releases, as *L. auritus* generally avoids the Blue Ridge.

The times and sites of introduction to most branches of the Tennessee drainage are unknown. About 19,000 redbreast sunfish were stocked in the Clinch River in 1969, after the fish kill of 1967 (Wollitz 1970). The single (unretained) Powell River specimen was taken by the TVA in 1976. First records for the Holston system are: North Fork 1954; Middle Fork 1951; South Fork 1966. Fitz (1966b) reported the first

capture in the Tennessee portion of the South Fork Holston, from Boone Reservoir, in 1956. The late 1920s–early 1930s were active periods of "sunfish" dispersal by the USFC, and may be the times of earliest introduction of *L. auritus* to the Holston system. This species is also introduced to the Big Sandy; our first record of capture is from 1966.

Abundance.—Often common in mountain, Piedmont, and upper Coastal Plain waters.

REMARKS

The redbreast sunfish is the most commonly caught centrarchid in many upland Virginia streams, but compared with the bluegill it does not seem to generally thrive in ponds. On light tackle it provides good sport; many persons favor its flavor over the black basses. Adult males exhibit a splendid mix of red, orange, yellow, and various shades of blue, whose iridescence is difficult to capture on film.

Name.—*Auritus* means "eared," in reference to the long opercular flap of adults. Virginia anglers commonly call the species sunperch, yellowbelly perch, and robin.

Longear sunfish   *Lepomis megalotis* (Rafinesque)

SYSTEMATICS

Named in 1820 from Kentucky, *L. megalotis* is classified with *L. marginatus* in the subgenus *Icthelis* (Bailey 1938a), a relationship that is genetically supported (Avise and Smith 1974b, 1977). Of the possibly five subspecies of longear sunfish (Bailey 1938a), *L. m. megalotis* is the form in Virginia (B. H. Bauer, in litt.).

DESCRIPTION

Materials.—From Bailey (1938a) and 11 Virginia lots. Life color based mostly on 1 nuptial male from the upper Clinch system and from a color plate in Boschung et al. (1983).

Anatomy.—A sunfish with a large pale-margined earflap and prominent wavy marks on side of head; adults are 75–150 mm TL. Body much compressed, deep, nearly round in lateral profile; dorsal head mostly quite convex, emarginate at occiput; mouth small, terminal, oblique; earflap large, long and wide in adult. Dorsal fin shallowly or markedly emarginate at juncture of spinous and soft portions; caudal fin emarginate, lobes rounded; pelvic fin in adult with filamentous extension of longest ray; pectoral fin rounded. Gill rakers short.

Meristics.—Lateral line scales (36)38–44(46); scales above lateral line (6)7(8); scales below lateral line (13)14–15(16); circumpeduncle scales (18)19–21(22). Dorsal spines (9)10(11); dorsal rays (10)11(12); anal spines 3; anal rays 9–10; pectoral rays 13–14(15).

Color in Preservative.—Body slightly to moderately dusky; side with many dark crescents or marks (pigmented posterior scale fields), marks sometimes aligned horizontally to form interrupted stripes or vertically aligned to form narrow bars; venter slightly dusky; head uniformly dusky except side with 3–5 sometimes broken, wavy dark lines; earflap mostly black, with a distinctly pale margin of variable width. Dorsal, caudal, and anal fins uniformly dusky, anal dark in breeding male; pelvic fin moderately dusky or black; pectoral fin pale.

Color in Life Plate 30.—Nuptial male with ground shade of dorsum and side of body orange-brown and that of venter, cheek, and opercle bright orange; dorsum and side also having a mosaic of pale blue to bright blue spots, the blue scales often with black posterior margin; blue marks on venter reduced to flecks; cheek and opercle with pale blue wavy lines (some specimens with head nearly all blue); lips blue; iris red and black; earflap black with white to pale blue margin. Dorsal fin membranes dusky olive, spines and rays iridescent pale blue; caudal and anal fins same as dorsal except anal with narrow black margin on spines; pelvic fin dusky black; pectoral fin pale. Juvenile and adult female subdued overall; earflap margin partly orange.

Larvae.—Described by Taber (1969), Conner (1979), Tin (1982d), and Yeager (1981).

BIOLOGY

The longear sunfish eats a variety of aquatic invertebrates and terrestrial insects (Minckley 1963;

Fish 239 *Lepomis megalotis* adult male 91 mm SL (REJ 992), VA, Russell County, Copper Creek, 21 June 1983.

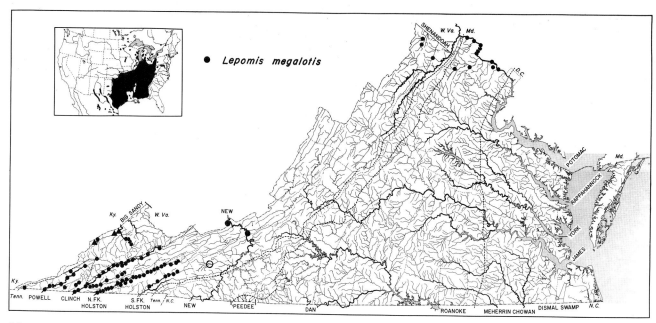

Map 152   Longear sunfish. Open circle is unverified record.

Whitaker et al. 1973; Carlander 1977; Laughlin and Werner 1980). It has been observed feeding on benthic material raised by feeding hogsuckers (Huck and Gunning 1967), and gleaning ectoparasites from catfishes in an aquarium (Spall 1970).

Maturation occurs in about 2 years; longevity of 9 years is reported but the oldest members of most populations are typically 5 or 6 years old (Carlander 1977). Average total length of age-3 fish from the Clinch River was 107 mm and from the Potomac River was 108 mm (Wollitz 1972; Enamait and Davis 1982). Our largest Virginia specimen is 132 mm TL. From Carlander's summary, the largest longear sunfishes are from Alabama and within the 178–203-mm (7-inch) TL class.

The reproductive period of *L. megalotis* probably spans from late May to early July in Virginia. We observed nesting in mid- and late June, in water up to 25°C. Nesting occurred between late May and late July in Ontario, and peak spawning was observed in Louisiana in late June, water 29–31°C (Keenleyside 1978). Males are territorial when nesting; nests often occur as crowded colonies on gravel bottoms in depths of 0.2–3.4 m (Carlander 1977; Keenleyside 1978). Males emit grunting sounds during courtship and spawning (Gerald 1971). Ovarian ova from females of ages 2 and 3 ranged 236–940, and stripped mature ova ranged 177–717 (Boyer 1969 *in* Carlander 1977). Scott and Crossman (1973) reported total ova ranges of 2,360–22,119.

Natural hybridization has occurred with *L. cyanel-*

lus, L. gibbosus, and *L. macrochirus* (Bailey 1938a; Childers 1967).

HABITAT

The longear sunfish occupies warmwater ponds, reservoirs, and pools and backwaters of streams and rivers. It avoids the higher-gradient streams of both the Blue Ridge and the Valley and Ridge provinces. Longear sunfish did not associate with aquatic plants in Michigan lakes (Laughlin and Werner 1980), but showed a distinct preference for densely vegetated areas of large streams in New York (C. Smith 1985). *Lepomis megalotis* avoids silt in New York (Raney 1965), but in Virginia it tolerates substantial siltation. It seems to have little tolerance of brackish water (Bailey et al. 1954).

DISTRIBUTION   Map 152

Lepomis megalotis is native to portions of the Great Lakes–St. Lawrence and Mississippi basins and the Gulf slope. It has been sparingly introduced outside the native range.

In Virginia the longear sunfish is native to the Big Sandy and Tennessee drainages and apparently has been introduced to the New and Potomac drainages. The times and sources of the introductions are unknown. The three records for the Virginia part of the New may represent more than one introduction. The first record is dated 1928; the two specimens (UMMZ

95249) were seined from the East River near the state line by C. L. Hubbs, in the same year he collected *L. megalotis* in the Gauley system of the New in West Virginia. The second record is from 1961; the young specimens (R. D. Suttkus, personal communication) were seined in the New River at the Spruce Run mouth. The other record, from Reed Creek in 1966 (Wollitz 1968a), is unverified but probably valid. Rosebery (1950a) listed *L. megalotis* as stocked in Claytor Lake, but later he (1950b) changed the identification to *L. auritus*. *Lepomis megalotis* may have died out from the Virginia portion of the New; it persists in the West Virginia section (Lobb 1986). It is established in the Potomac drainage; our first record is from the West Virginia portion in 1953 (CU 32354).

Abundance.—Generally uncommon or common.

REMARKS

The breeding male longear sunfish is one of the most brilliantly colored of Virginia sunfishes.

Name.—*Megalotis*, "large ear," refers to the opercular flap, which is very large in adult males.

Bluegill *Lepomis macrochirus* Rafinesque

SYSTEMATICS

The bluegill, described in 1819 from the Ohio River, is placed by itself in the subgenus *Helioperca* (Bailey 1938a; Branson and Moore 1962). The subspecies *L. m. macrochirus* is native to Virginia (Hubbs and Lagler 1958; Felley 1980). Mixing of *L. m. macrochirus* and *L. m. purpurescens* via stocking has been detected in some states (Avise and Smith 1974a) and may have occurred in Virginia.

DESCRIPTION

Materials.—From Bailey (1938a), Frey (1951), Felley (1980), and 34 Virginia lots. Life color largely from 3 Virginia nuptial males and color plate in Childers (1967).

Anatomy.—A barred or plain-sided sunfish with a short dark-margined earflap and black spot in rear of second dorsal fin; adults are 80–220 mm TL. Body deep, very compressed; dorsal profile of head straight or slightly convex, nape bulging in large males; mouth small, terminal, oblique; eye large; earflap round or oval, not notably longer than wide. Dorsal fin slightly or moderately emarginate at junction of spinous and soft portions; caudal fin emarginate, lobes rounded; pelvic fin with filamentous extension of longest ray in adult male; pectoral fin elongate, pointed. Gill rakers long.

Meristics.—Lateral line scales (38)41–46(50); scales above lateral line 7–8(9); scales below lateral line (14)15–16(17); circumpeduncle scales (18)19–20(21). Dorsal spines (9)10(12); dorsal rays (9)10–11(13); anal spines 3; anal rays (9)11–12; pectoral rays (12)13–14(15).

Fish 240 *Lepomis macrochirus* adult male 148 mm SL (REJ 1047), VA, Franklin County, Ferrum College Pond, 7 October 1983.

Color in Preservative.—Young to small adult with several narrow, moderately dusky or dark bars on side that contrast with pale to moderately dusky ground shade; bars lost in adult, body a mosaic of dusky scale margins and paler centers; venter pale or dusky. Head uniformly dusky; earflap entirely black in large adult, but sometimes in juvenile and small adult there is a pale or slightly dusky submarginal area. Dorsal fin mostly uniformly dusky and, in juvenile and adult, with a dark blotch in second dorsal posterobasally; dorsal fin blotch distinct or only hinted by interradial peppering or streaks in small fish; caudal and anal fins uniformly dusky or with interradial dark streaks, except anal sometimes with hint of a posterobasal blotch; pelvic fin pale or dark in adult; pectoral fin pale.

Color in Life Plate 30.—Nuptial male with dorsum and upper side pale blue, blue-olive, or blue-green, some fish with violet luster; bars when present are medium to dark olive; lower side and venter about same shade as dorsum, or brassy to russet; head medium to dark olive; cheek and opercle with lime-green to blue iridescence; lower jaw and ventral margin of operculum pale blue to turquoise; iris copper to red; earflap black. Median fins medium to dark olive, blotches or streaks black; pelvic fin dusky or black; pectoral fin pale yellow-olive. Adult female and juvenile largely olive, and with purple and yellow sheens on body.

Larvae.—Described by Taber (1969), Anjard (1974), Hardy (1978b), Conner (1979), Wang and Kernehan (1979), and Tin (1982b). Childers (1967) described larvae of three hybrids.

BIOLOGY

Young and juvenile bluegills are planktivores; adults typically eat small aquatic and terrestrial insects (Rosebery 1950a; Flemer and Woolcott 1966; Sadzikowski and Wallace 1976; Sule et al. 1981). Small prey size is associated with the small mouth size of *L. macrochirus* (Keast and Webb 1966; Gatz 1979). A relatively high volume of plants was eaten by bluegills in Michigan (Ball 1948). Etnier (1971) and Sadzikowski and Wallace (1976) correlated plant ingestion with the use of plants as a substrate by aquatic insect prey. Bluegills have been observed cleaning (removing external parasites from) a few fish species, and nipping (probably feeding) from surfaces of turtles and manatees (Powell 1984).

Bluegills mature at age 1 or 2; longevity of 11 years is known, but the oldest members of many populations are 4–6 years (Carlander 1977). Growth in Virginia varies by body of water much like that elsewhere in mid-latitudes of the range. The range of average lengths at age 3 from 69 Virginia populations, mostly in impoundments, is 96–180 mm TL, unweighted mean 140 (Rosebery 1950a; Martin 1955; Wollitz 1973; Hart 1978, 1981; McHugh and Steinkoenig 1980; Sledd and Shuber 1981; Smith and Kauffman 1982). *Lepomis macrochirus* commonly responds to limited food and crowding by exhibiting retarded growth; farm-pond populations often are largely composed of stunted fish. The Virginia record of 2.04 kg (4 pounds 8 ounces) is near the world record of 2.15 kg (4 pounds 12 ounces) from Alabama.

Spawning may occur in most of the growing season. Spawning occurred from February to October in Florida, and from May to August in Wisconsin (Carlander 1977). The reproductive season in Virginia likely spans May to August or September. Males construct nests usually in shallows on sand or gravel; nests frequently occur in colonies (Coggeshall 1924; Crowe 1959; Gross and MacMillan 1981). Estes (1949 *in* Carlander 1977) reported that females of 120 mm TL averaged five spawnings and produced about 80,000 eggs per year.

Lepomis macrochirus hybridizes naturally with all other Virginia species of *Lepomis* (Childers 1967); we recorded crosses with *L. auritus*, *L. cyanellus*, and *L. gibbosus* in the state.

HABITAT

Bluegills are found in pools and backwaters of low to moderate-gradient creeks, streams, and rivers, and in all types of lacustrine habitats in Virginia. This warmwater species occupies clear and turbid waters, hard and silted substrates, exhibits a moderate tolerance of low pH and darkly stained waters (Graham and Hastings 1984), and occurs in oligo- and mesohaline zones, to 18‰ (Musick 1972).

DISTRIBUTION   Map 153

The bluegill is native to the Great Lakes–St. Lawrence and Mississippi basins, the Atlantic slope probably from North Carolina southward, and the Gulf slope west to Texas. It is the most widely introduced species of *Lepomis*.

In Virginia the native range of *L. macrochirus* encompasses the Tennessee and Big Sandy drainages, and possibly the Pee Dee drainage. It has been introduced in all other drainages and Delmarva. The distribution map would be greatly filled with dots if many farm-pond populations, of which we have few records, were plotted.

Times and points of initial introduction to Virginia

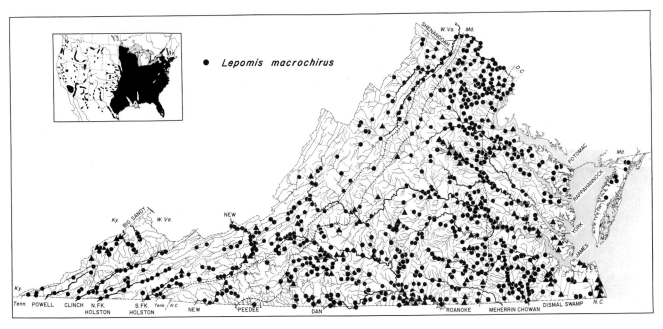

Map 153   Bluegill.

drainages are unknown; likely they were made after those of the smallmouth and largemouth basses. Apparently bluegills were stocked at many points and times in all drainages; they continue to be liberated in new ponds and reservoirs. Our first drainage records are: Potomac 1916; Rappahannock 1938; York 1938; James 1945; Dismal Swamp 1941; Chowan 1938; Roanoke 1947; Pee Dee 1983; New 1936.

Abundance.—One of the most common sunfishes in Virginia, bluegills probably are the most abundant centrarchid in ponds and lakes. They are absent or rare in cool high-gradient trout water and thus do not occur in most small streams in the Blue Ridge and the Valley and Ridge provinces.

REMARKS

The angling experience of many children begins with the prolific and scrappy bluegill. A testimony of its popularity and wide dissemination is that a colleague, on his initial collecting trip to South Africa, was amused when one of the first fishes he captured in this exotic land was the bluegill (J. R. Stauffer, personal communication). The state record of 2.04 kg (4.5 pounds) from a pond is indicative of the growth potential of this species; some waters regularly yield giants. However, many underfished pond populations are crowded with runts.

Name.—*Macrochirus* means "large hand," probably alluding to body shape.

Pumpkinseed   *Lepomis gibbosus* (Linnaeus)

SYSTEMATICS

Described in 1758 from the Carolinas, *L. gibbosus* is placed with *L. microlophus* in the subgenus *Eupomotis* (Bailey 1938a), a sister-species relationship supported by Branson and Moore (1962) and Lauder (1983). However, Avise and Smith (1974b, 1977) allied *L. gibbosus* with *L. punctatus* and *L. auritus*, and grouped *L. microlophus* with *L. megalotis* and *L. marginatus*. From the strong similarity of *L. gibbosus* and *L. microlophus* in morphology and color, we side with Bailey's

arrangement. Slight geographic variation was noted in the pumpkinseed by Scott and Crossman (1973); Bailey (1938a) did not recognize subspecies.

DESCRIPTION

Materials.—From Bailey (1938a) and 35 Virginia lots including circumpeduncle scale counts from 27 specimens. Life color from 7 Virginia subadult to adult specimens.

Anatomy.—A chubby sunfish with an orange mark on the earflap margin and a blue and yellow-spotted or or-

Fish 241 *Lepomis gibbosus* adult female 109 mm SL (REJ 1029), VA, Amelia County, Flat Creek, 1 September 1983.

ange-spotted body; adults are 70–160 mm TL. Body compressed, suboval, stocky, particularly in large adult. Dorsal profile of head nearly straight in young to markedly convex in adult; mouth small, terminal, oblique; eye large; earflap small or medium in size, not elongate. Dorsal fin margin straight or slightly emarginate at junction of spinous and soft portions; caudal fin emarginate, lobes rounded or subacute; pelvic fin with filamentous extension of longest ray; pectoral fin long, pointed. Gill raker length short or moderate.

Meristics.—Lateral line scales (36)37–44(47); scales above lateral line 6–7(8); scales below lateral line (12)14–15; circumpeduncle scales (17)18–20(21). Dorsal spines (9)10(12); dorsal rays (10)11–12(13); anal spines (3)4; anal rays (8)9–10(12); pectoral rays (11)12–13(14).

Color in Preservative.—Side of young, juvenile, and small adult darkly speckled and barred; most adults lack distinct bars; upper side with few to many pale spots or pale small vertical areas on otherwise darkened scales; lower side and venter speckled or slightly dusky. Head mostly dusky; cheek and opercle with 4–8 dark wavy lines; earflap black, except posterior margin or entire free margin pale, the posterior pale area widest and sometimes crescentic anteriorly. First dorsal fin uniformly dusky; second dorsal, caudal, and sometimes anal fins mottled basally, elsewhere dusky; pelvic fin pale or dark; pectoral fin pale.

Color in Life Plate 30.—Dorsum olive; upper side with reticulate pattern of iridescent blue lines or otherwise largely darkened scales; few to many scales with yellow to bright orange center; lower side, breast, and belly yellow, gold, or brassy orange, with iridescent pale blue wavy lines and flecks. Head dorsum olive; cheek and opercle lemon yellow to brassy gold with wavy iridescent blue lines and marks; iris copper. Earflap mostly black, dorsal and ventral

margins (if pale) opalescent to light blue, midposterior spot pale orange to bright orange-red. Dorsal fin mostly dusky olive; second dorsal fin basally mottled dark olive-brown, yellow interradial streaks in medial portion; caudal fin yellow-olive with olive-brown mottling or streaks; anal fin suffused with yellow-olive wash, and mottled or streaked dark olive basally; pelvic fin dusky yellow or dusky black in breeding male; pectoral fin amber.

Larvae.—Described by Anjard (1974), Wang and Kernehan (1979), Hardy (1978b), and Tin (1982d).

COMPARISON

Lepomis gibbosus can easily be confused with *L. microlophus*. Distinguishing features of preserved specimens include: (1) lateral body scales [several with pale centers (yellow or orange in life), appearing spotted or speckled, especially dorsolaterally, in *gibbosus* (Figure 67E) *vs.* uniformly pigmented, unspotted in *microlophus*]; (2) cheek pattern [several dark wavy lines (blue in life) (Figure 66B) *vs.* uniformly pigmented, unpatterned]; (3) dorsal and sometimes anal fins [mottled basally (Figure 67E) *vs.* uniformly pigmented or with membranal streaks]; (4) body form typically [chubby *vs.* less deep, thinner (except for large adult)]; (5) dorsal head profile [usually moderately or very convex *vs.* nearly straight or moderately convex].

The extent of red or orange on the earflap margin in living and freshly preserved specimens, and later in preservative the width of the pale area that was orange or red in life, often are solely used to identify the two species (Figure 68E, F; Plate 30). However, these characters are variable and exhibit only average differences. In both species, large fish tend to have larger and brighter red margins and wider pale margins. Generally, in *gibbosus* the red or orange is confined to the posterior portion of the earflap; the pale margin typically is distinctly wider and paler posteriorly than ventrally. In *microlophus* the red or orange is restricted as in *gibbosus* or it occurs widely along the margin; the pale margin usually is about uniform in width and paleness posteriorly and ventrally.

BIOLOGY

Young and juvenile *L. gibbosus* feed on microcrustaceans and small aquatic insects and progress to larger prey with growth. Pumpkinseeds have molariform pharyngeal teeth and, like the redear sunfish, they feed extensively on snails and small clams in some environments (Sadzikowski and Wallace 1976; Laughlin and Werner 1980; Mittelbach 1984). *Lepomis gibbosus* also ingests an assortment of aquatic and terrestrial insects, other small arthropods, occasionally small fishes, and incidental plant material (Flemer and Woolcott 1966; Keast 1966; Etnier 1971).

Pumpkinseeds mature in 1–3 years; in nature they rarely survive 8 years, but a captive lived 12 (Carlander 1977). Virginia pumpkinseeds show average to strong growth compared with that summarized by Carlander (1977). From 24 impoundments, Back Bay, and the Shenandoah River in Virginia, the range of means of length at age 3 was 102–168 mm TL, unweighted mean 137 (Norman 1973; Prosser 1973; Kauffman 1975; McHugh and Steinkoenig 1980; Smith and Kauffman 1982). From Minnesota, Carlander (1977) listed a pumpkinseed of about 400 mm TL (15-inch class), that obviously was underweight, 0.45 kg (1 pound). The IGFA (1985) accepted a Virginia pumpkinseed of 0.51 kg (1 pound 2 ounces) as the world record.

The reproductive season of *L. gibbosus* in Virginia begins in early May, perhaps April, and may extend into August. Surber (1970) found nests with eggs in the Shenandoah system on 3 May, water 16°C, and Whitehurst (1981) reported spawning activity during May to August in a North Carolina swamp of 17–21°C. Similar seasonal extremes were summarized by Breder (1936). Nesting usually occurs colonially in open shallow areas on sand and small gravel (H. Miller 1963; Clark and Keenleyside 1967; Surber 1970). Indiana females developed 1,034–2,436 eggs (Ulrey et al. 1938 *in* Carlander 1977).

Lepomis gibbosus hybridizes naturally with *L. auritus*, *L. cyanellus*, *L. gulosus*, *L. macrochirus*, and *L.*

megalotis (Childers 1967). We captured specimens of *L. gibbosus* × *L. macrochirus* in Virginia.

HABITAT

Pumpkinseeds are calm-water fish, inhabiting pools and backwaters of creeks, streams, and rivers. They also proliferate in ponds and reservoirs. They occur over soft and firm bottoms and often are associated with macrophytes and other cover. *Lepomis gibbosus* is tolerant of darkly stained waters of pH as low as 4.1 (Graham and Hastings 1984). It sometimes occupies slightly brackish water, and has been recorded in salinity as high as 18.2‰ (Hildebrand and Schroeder 1928).

DISTRIBUTION   Map 154

Lepomis gibbosus is native to the Great Lakes–St. Lawrence and upper Mississippi basins and on the Atlantic slope from South Carolina, but possibly from the Savannah drainage in Georgia (Dahlberg and Scott 1971a), northward. It has been modestly introduced beyond its indigenous range and extensively transplanted within.

Although native to all Atlantic slope drainages of Virginia, surprisingly we lack records for the Otter and Goose Creek systems of the middle Roanoke system, and, in their Virginia portions, most of the upper Dan system and all of the Pee Dee drainage. *Lepomis gibbosus* appears to be very rare, possibly introduced, in the upper Pee Dee of North Carolina.

The presence of the pumpkinseed in the New and Tennessee drainages is undoubtedly due to introductions at unknown times and sites. This species probably was introduced to the New in the vicinity of the Wytheville hatchery (upper Reed Creek system), an early center of centrarchid dispersal (especially for *Lepomis*) during 1917–1921. Its distribution in the New is somewhat localized, suggesting multiple introduction, but the New is notable for peculiar distribution patterns of many fishes. The earliest collector's record for the New is probably from the 1940s, based on Rosebery's (1950a) statement that the pumpkinseed was common in Claytor Lake.

The Middle and South Fork Holston populations also likely originated from the Wytheville hatchery; our first record for both systems is dated 1951. The pumpkinseed first reported from South Holston Reservoir in Tennessee was caught in 1962 (Fitz 1966b); dams on the South Fork Holston River may have barred *L. gibbosus* from reaching the North Fork Holston system. The Powell system specimen, which we verified, was collected in 1974. The Big Sandy drain-

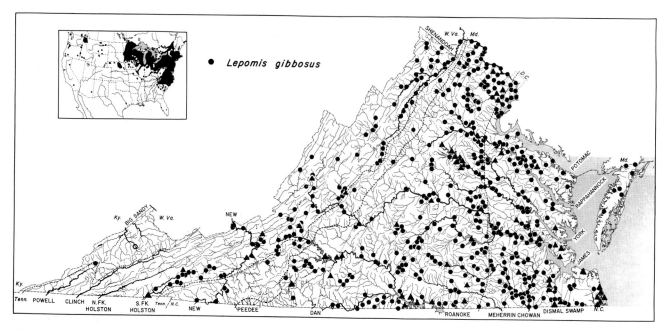

Map 154 Pumpkinseed. Open circle in Big Sandy denotes unconfirmed record.

age record, from 1982, is unconfirmed; it may have been based on *L. microlophus*, which has been stocked in the drainage.

Abundance.—One of the most abundant *Lepomis* in Virginia; usually uncommon or common on the Coastal Plain and lower Piedmont, generally uncommon or rare in the Blue Ridge and the Valley and Ridge.

REMARKS

David Starr Jordan was quite taken with the attractiveness and symmetry of the pumpkinseed, regarding it "A very beautiful and compact fish, perfect in all its parts, looking like a brilliant coin fresh from the mint." It rivals the longear sunfish in beauty, and because of its greater distribution in the state, it is seen by many more Virginians. It has made many a child's first fish catch not the last.

Name.—*Gibbosus* means "humpbacked," in particular reference to large males. Smith (1903) provided an extensive list of common names applied to sunfishes and basses. For *L. gibbosus* he quoted "Frank Forrester" (a pseudonym) as remarking ". . . the numerous spots on its body have procured for it the absurd name of pumpkin-seed in many States." We think the name is diagnostic and a delightful departure from the norm of common appellations.

Redear sunfish   *Lepomis microlophus* (Günther)

SYSTEMATICS

Described from Florida in 1859, *L. microlophus* is placed in the subgenus *Eupomotis* with *L. gibbosus*. Two subspecies were recognized by Bailey (1938a); one is still undescribed. We are unaware of the subspecific identity of the introduced form(s) in Virginia.

DESCRIPTION

Materials.—From Bailey (1938a) and 6 Virginia and 24 Georgia specimens. Life color from 8 Virginia adults.

Anatomy.—A speckle-sided sunfish with a usually red-margined earflap; adults are 130–240 mm TL. Body moderately or very deep, very compressed, although some large adults chubby; dorsal profile of head nearly straight or moderately convex; mouth small, terminal, oblique; eye large; earflap small or medium in size, not elongate. Spinous and soft portions of dorsal fin moderately emarginate at their confluence; caudal fin emarginate, lobes rounded; pelvic fin possibly lacking filamentous extension; pectoral fin long, pointed. Gill raker length short or medium.

Meristics.—Lateral line scales (40)41–44(47); scales above lateral line (6)7–8; scales below lateral line 14–15; circumpeduncle scales (19)20–21(22). Dorsal spines 10(11);

Fish 242 *Lepomis microlophus* adult male 116 mm SL (REJ 1047), VA, Franklin County, Ferrum College Pond, 7 October 1983.

dorsal rays (10)11–12; anal spines 3; anal rays (9)10–11; pectoral rays 13–15(16).

Color in Preservative.—Ground shade slightly to moderately dusky; side with many dark scales producing a speckled pattern; venter uniformly pale or very dusky. Head unpatterned, mostly dusky; cheek and gular area pale; earflap mostly black, margin partly pale and partly dusky. Median fins uniformly dusky or membranes of second dorsal, caudal, and anal with dark streaks, caudal sometimes mottled basally; pelvic fin pale or dusky; pectoral fin pale.

Color in Life Plate 30.—Head and body dorsum olive with iridescent green sheen; body side silver to iridescent pale blue, some fish with many poorly defined spotlike areas grading from olive on posterior body to pale yellow or pale orange anteriorly, orange best developed at pectoral fin base; belly and breast with pale yellow or orange wash. Head dorsum and snout olive, laterally silver to pale blue (lacking stripes), some fish with many pale orange spots laterally; iris dusky olive, silver, copper, or red, or a mixture of these. Earflap largely black, variously rimmed with white or pale orange to bright red; non-black margin about uniform in width posteriorly and ventrally; small fish often have very little red on earflap, and when only slight red is present, it is generally restricted to posterior margin; large adults, particularly males, tend to have flap nearly or completely red-margined. Median fins dusky or olive, markings dark; pelvic fin white, yellow-olive, peppered, or dusky; pectoral fin pale olive.

Larvae.—Described by Conner (1979).

COMPARISON

See *Lepomis gibbosus* account.

BIOLOGY

Redear sunfish generally select small prey. Adults have large molariform pharyngeal teeth well suited for crushing snails and small mussels, important dietary items to many populations. Carothers and Allison (1968 *in* Carlander 1977) reported that redear sunfish nearly eliminated snails from a pond. An array of aquatic insects including midges and occasionally fishes are also eaten (Emig 1966b; Wilbur 1969).

Some redear sunfish in the deep South mature at age 1; those in the middle and northern parts of the range first spawn at age 2. Maximum reported survival is age 8, but the oldest fish in many populations are 5 or 6 years of age (Carlander 1977). The range of average lengths at age 3 for redear sunfish from 10 Virginia impoundments is 135–216 mm TL, unweighted mean 182 (Smith and Kauffman 1982), a typical growth range for the species (Carlander 1977). The Virginia record of 2.15 kg (4 pounds 12 ounces) is surpassed by a 2.18-kg (4 pounds 13 ounces) redear from Florida.

The onset of spawning varies by latitude, generally occurring in the spring when water approaches 20–21°C. Spawning normally ends by mid-summer, but extends into October in some southern states (Wilbur 1969; Carlander 1977). Wilbur (1969) reported synchrony of spawning with full or new moons in Florida. Nests usually are in water shallower than 2 m; often they occur near vegetation and in colonies. Males make a grunting sound during courtship (Gerald 1971). Estimates of mature ova per female are 15,001–30,144 (Wilbur 1969).

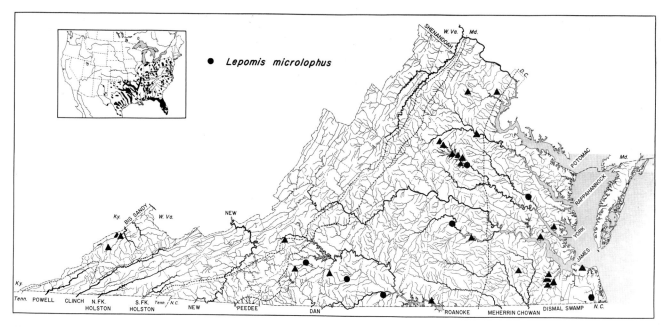

Map 155   Redear sunfish.

Lepomis microlophus hybridizes in nature with *L. auritus*, *L. cyanellus*, *L. gulosus*, and *L. macrochirus* (Bailey 1938a; Childers 1967). Hybridization probably occurs in Virginia.

HABITAT

Predominantly a lacustrine species, *L. microlophus* inhabits generally clear, vegetated ponds and lakes. It occurs widely in pools and backwaters of streams with the same attributes. Carver (1967 *in* Carlander 1977) reported tolerance of turbidity in Louisiana. Kilby (1955) found redear sunfish in areas of salt marshes with salinities of 5.3–12.3‰, but most fish occurred in less than 5‰.

DISTRIBUTION   Map 155

The redear sunfish is native to the middle and lower Mississippi basin, the Atlantic slope from Florida to perhaps no farther north than Georgia, and the Gulf slope west into Texas (Bailey 1938a). All Virginia populations have been recently established by introduction. Many Virginia farm ponds likely contain this species, but our records include scant data from ponds. Most stream records probably are of escapees from stocked ponds or lakes. The first years of collection or stocking records by drainage are: Potomac ca. 1958; Rappahannock ca. 1977; York ca. 1971;

James 1967; extreme southeastern Virginia 1977; Chowan 1977; Roanoke 1971; Big Sandy 1972.

Jordan's (1889b) Dismal Swamp specimens of *L. "holbrooki,"* which he distinguished from *L. gibbosus*, actually are *gibbosus* (Bailey 1938a). The record by Raleigh et al. (1978) from the Clinch River is rejected. The unretained specimens were first identified by Raleigh et al. as *Lepomis punctatus* (Masnik 1974), also unknown from the Clinch.

Abundance.—We are unaware of the general abundance of redear sunfish in ponds and lakes of Virginia; it probably varies considerably according to local conditions. We rarely found it in streams, and generally then near stocked ponds and in small numbers.

REMARKS

Because of its greater growth potential compared with most *Lepomis* sunfishes, the redear sunfish has become popular among pond and lake anglers in Virginia. Purportedly it is warier and more difficult to catch than the bluegill.

Name.—*Microlophus* means "small crest" or "mane." Pflieger (1975) interpreted this as "small nape," whereas Moyle (1976) thought "small crest" alluded to the ear flap. The common southern vernacular "shellcracker" comes from the habit of eating snails and clams by crunching the shells.

PERCHES
Family Percidae

BY ROBERT E. JENKINS, WILLIAM H. HAXO, AND NOEL M. BURKHEAD

The Percidae are a moderately large freshwater family that contains several widely known fishes such as yellow perch and walleye. Most of its members—the diverse darters—are seldom noticed, but many are of exceptional beauty. Percids vary widely in size from the fountain darter *Etheostoma fonticola*, whose adults reach 35 mm SL (40 mm TL) and about 0.5 g (Page and Burr 1979), to the Eurasian pikeperch *Stizostedion lucioperca*, which can reach 1,300 mm TL and 15 kg (Popova and Sytina 1977).

There are about 176 species of percids, of which 162 occur in North America and 14 in Eurasia. The uncertainty of the total reflects the undetermined status of several nominal or undescribed darters. Virginia harbors 45 percid species. The family is divisible into two subfamilies, concepts of which differ among authorities (Collette 1963; Hubbs 1971; Collette and Banarescu 1977; Page 1985). Nine or 10 genera are recognized; 4 of them are entirely Eurasian. Two genera containing medium or large species are shared by Eurasia and North America: *Perca*—perches in the strictest sense—with one North American species, the yellow perch; and *Stizostedion*—pikeperches—having the walleye and sauger in North America.

Darters are small fishes composing the exclusively North American tribe Etheostomatini; all species occur east of the continental divide and one Mexican species also lives on the Pacific slope. Three or four genera are recognized: *Percina* with about 40 species, *Ammocrypta* having 7 (its subgenus *Crystallaria* may be elevated), and *Etheostoma* containing about 112. The status and composition of some darter subgenera are in flux (e.g., Page 1981, 1983; Bailey and Etnier 1988; Simons 1992).

The early fossil record of the Percidae is problematic (Cavender 1986). The record of the speciose darters has the greatest void, being limited to the Pleistocene. The roots of the family apparently are deep in time; the family probably originated from an anadromous sea basslike stock on the Eurasian landmass during the early Cenozoic. Ancestors of modern darters may have invaded North America via the North Atlantic land bridge in pre-Eocene or Early Eocene time, at least 45 million years ago, long before true perch and pikeperch stocks colonized the continent (Collette and Banarescu 1977; Patterson 1981).

Generalized percids represent a basic anatomical plan exhibited by many basal members of the great series of perciform fishes, most of which are marine. Salient features of American percids include: body form moderate or elongate, cylindrical or well compressed; mouth and teeth usually small or moderate-sized, but a large mouth and canine teeth occur in piscivorous pikeperches; and opercle with 1 posterior spine. The two dorsal fins are separate or slightly united, the first spinous, the second supported mostly or entirely by rays; caudal fin rounded or emarginate, well forked only in larger species; anal fin with 1 or 2 spines; pelvic fins in thoracic position and having 1 spine; and pectoral fins set high on the side. Cephalic lateralis canals are well developed; the lateral line is usually complete, extending onto the tail in pikeperches and some species of *Percina*; scales are ctenoid.

Sexual dimorphism tends to be least developed in *Perca* and *Stizostedion*, although females of these genera tend to outgrow males. Most darters are dimorphic and markedly dichromatic; males often are

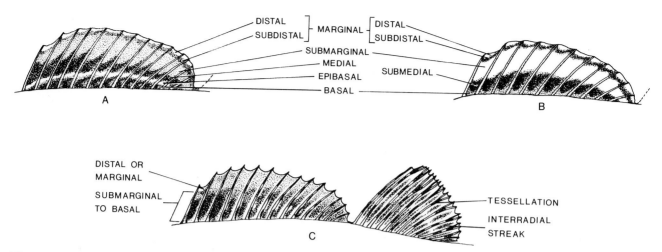

Figure 69   Bands, zones, or areas of color patterns in fins of adult darters; width and intensity of bands may vary by sex or life stage: (A) First dorsal of male *Etheostoma blennioides*. (B) First dorsal of male *Percina roanoka*. (C) First and second dorsal of female *P. notogramma*.

larger and have some fins proportionately larger than females. Thickened body tissues, ridges or knobs on fin spines and rays, or breeding tubercles develop in many species, most often in males. Ctenii of the enlarged midventral scales become particularly spine-like and down-pointing in males of some *Percina*. The genital papilla usually is largest in the female; the variety of papilla configurations generally is correlated with modes of egg deposition (see below and Figure 70).

The coloration of many darters, particularly in *Etheostoma*, is spectacular. Males undergo a vernal chromatic transformation, becoming virtual aquatic butterflies. These living jewels display hues of red, orange, gold, yellow, green, and blue, often enhanced by metallic sheens and set off by black markings. Males in particular tend to have intricate dorsal fin patterns (Figure 69). Indeed, darters are among the most attractive vertebrates, yet their splendor often is ephemeral; nuptial coloration develops shortly before the spawning season and usually diminishes soon after. Males of many species are colorful year-long, although less so than in nuptial expression, whereas others simply blacken during the breeding period, sometimes only briefly. Development of breeding coloration in females is minimal or lacking. Many of the more drab species live in darkly stained swamps or spawn in dark cavities. The translucent flesh of sand darters confers camouflage when on that substrate, in which they often bury.

The varied biology of percids has been summarized in PERCIS (1977), Kendall (1978), Kuehne and Barbour (1983), and Page (1983, 1985). The range of habitats occupied by American percids covers nearly the full spectrum of freshwater environments; a few species extend into low-salinity estuaries. Most species are warmwater eurytherms; a few prefer cool water. Most species are nonmigratory.

The larger percids differ from the darters in habitat preferences and certain anatomical traits. The yellow perch and pikeperches typically occupy lakes and sluggish parts of rivers, inhabiting shallows and moderate depths. In adaptation to living above the bottom, they have a well-developed gas bladder, a forked tail, and the paired fins are moderate in size. In contrast, most darters are rheophilic and shallow-dwelling. Nearly all darters are cryptobenthic; their size (usually less than 80 mm SL) allows use of abundant hiding places between and under stones, plants, and other cover. In most darters, the gas bladder is rudimentary or absent, the tail is rounded or slightly emarginate, and the pectoral fins are large (Page and Swofford 1984).

Pikeperches typically are fish-eaters; the yellow perch feeds more on invertebrates. Darters feed on small aquatic invertebrates, particularly immature aquatic insects; the Chironomidae (midges) and the Hydropsychidae (caddisflies) are major dietary constituents. Vision plays an important role in prey detection; darters make lateral head movements to help find prey. Most percids are diurnally active; having extremely sensitive eyes, the walleye and sauger typically are more active at night.

The diversity of color patterns and reproductive morphology mirrors the varied reproductive repertoire of percids, especially darters. Most percids spawn during spring, but reproduction may begin as early as December in southern latitudes. The onset of

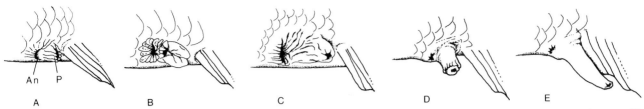

Figure 70 Genital papillae and spawning modes in female darters: (A) *Etheostoma rufilineatum* 55 mm SL, egg-burier. (B) *Etheostoma podostemone* 56 mm SL, egg-clusterer. (C) *Percina burtoni* 126 mm SL, mode unknown. (D) *Etheostoma simoterum* 44 mm SL, egg-attacher. (E) *Etheostoma swannanoa* 47 mm SL, egg-burier. An—anus; P—papilla.

spawning is controlled by photoperiod and may be modified by water temperature; continuation and termination of spawning are regulated by temperature (Hubbs 1985).

Six reproductive guilds of percids, based on modes of egg deposition, are recognized; in phylogenetic sequence they are: broadcasters, stranders, buriers, attachers, clumpers, and clusterers (Page 1985). To the list of 84 species already so classified (Page 1985; Page and Simon 1988; Voiers 1988; Carney and Burr 1989; Johnston 1989a; Keevin et al. 1989; Fisher 1990), we add six: *Percina rex*, *P. roanoka*, and *Etheostoma swannanoa* are buriers; *E. cinereum* and *E. collis* are attachers; *E. podostemone* is a clusterer.

Broadcasters, as represented by most *Stizostedion* and the European *Percarina demidoffi*, scatter many thousands of eggs over an unprepared bottom. *Stizostedion lucioperca* spawns over a pit that is formed, fanned, and guarded by the male. A derivation of broadcasting occurs in the stranding guild, which includes two species of *Perca* and one *Gymnocephalus*; thousands of eggs are encased in gelatinous mucous within the female and remain in a strand after spawning. Broadcasters and stranders tend to be r-selected species, characterized by small eggs, high fecundity, no parental care, and a tendency for females to complete spawning in one episode.

The other guilds are composed of darters. Egg-burying is derived from broadcasting; eggs typically are released into the substrate and overt parental care is absent. Some egg-burying females partly entrench themselves in the substrate, but on firm substrate the eggs may be ejected into interstices. Some buriers have a long, thick genital papilla which is placed on or in the substrate (Figure 70). All *Percina* and *Ammocrypta* (where known), and many *Etheostoma* belong to this guild. A modification of egg-burying is attaching, in which adhesive eggs are placed, often one at a time, on plants, sticks, or rocks. The papilla of attachers often is long and narrow. Parental care, by virtue of selective egg placement, is passive.

An advanced variation of egg-burying is clumping. Here the male selects the spawning site, usually a cavity beneath a stone, and defends the site after spawning. The female enters the nest and wedges the eggs between the stone and the bottom. Clumping is known only in advanced members of the subgenus *Nothonotus* of *Etheostoma*. Clusterers resemble clumpers in behavior in that eggs are deposited in a compact group beneath cover and the male selects and guards the nest, but differ in that both sexes invert during spawning and eggs are usually laid in a single tier on the underside of the cover. Three subtypes of clustering are recognized (Page 1985).

Darter guilds demonstrate a shift toward K-selected strategy. Fecundity is reduced and parental care progresses from passive (nonrandom placement of eggs) to active (nest guarding). The guilds correlate only generally with percid phylogeny; certain egg-deposition modes evolved independently in some groups, such as clustering in the subgenera *Boleosoma* and *Catonotus* of *Etheostoma* (Collette and Banarescu 1977; Page 1985). The burying and attaching guilds each encompass a heterogeneous assemblage of species (Page 1981, 1985).

Relatively little is known about reproductive social interaction in darters. It is possible that detailed knowledge of spawning behaviors will refine the reproductive guilds defined by Page (1985) and perhaps shed new light on phylogenetic relationships (Warren et al. 1986a). Discoveries of fascinating behaviors, such as fertilization-sneaking cuckolder males, may await the student (Voiers 1988; Fisher 1990; see *Etheostoma collis*). It was only recently discovered that dominant males of the tessellated darter *Etheostoma olmstedi* fertilize eggs and often leave the nest, which then is cleaned and defended by subordinate males (Constantz 1979, 1985). This surrogate (alloparental) care-giving apparently is unique among fishes.

Reflecting different behavioral modes and selection strategies, the fecundities of American *Perca* and *Stizostedion* are 2,000–615,000, and egg diameters are 1.0–1.5 mm (Hardy 1978b), whereas darters produce 70–4,000 ova of 0.7–2.5 mm diameter (Page 1983). Most darters probably are fractional spawners, ovipositing several times during the general reproductive period (Gale and Deutsch 1985). Thus many fecundities cited here would be underestimates. Percid eggs are demersal and adhesive. Natural hybridization is known to occur within *Stizostedion* and between and within *Percina* and *Etheostoma* (e.g., Page 1976b). Considerable experimental hybridization of percids has been performed by Clark Hubbs and collaborators (e.g., Hubbs 1971, 1986).

Percids are economically and environmentally important fishes. Pikeperches and the yellow perch have long been sought by commercial fishermen and anglers. Darters generally thrive only in environments of good quality and thus are indicators of aquatic health. They are links in aquatic systems and some furnish forage for gamefishes. Because darters are so diverse, they provide clues for inferring ancient river-drainage patterns.

Aquarists, snorkelers, and photographers have developed keen interest in the fascinating darters. The best series of color photographs of darters in their natural habitat was just published (*in* Quinn 1991) by William N. Roston, a dentist. The books by Kuehne and Barbour (1983) and Page (1983) contain color photos of nearly all darters and summaries of the natural history of each. Page opened his treatise with a quote from D. S. Jordan, the father of North American ichthyology: "These [darters] we found to be the most fascinating, vivacious, and individual of all river fishes."

Name.—Perc-, from *Perca*, meaning "perch." When resting on the bottom, these fishes often are propped (perched) by the pelvic fins.

Key to Perches   Percidae

Caution is needed in identifying darter genera. The flesh of *Ammocrypta* (and to a lesser degree *Etheostoma vitreum*) is translucent only in life; when placed in preservative the body quickly becomes opaque. The modified midventral scales (scutes) in *Percina* number from one or a few in the interpelvic area (more typical of females) to a complete series extending from the breast to the anus (Page 1976a; Figure 73). If modified scales are not obvious on the ventral midline, then carefully examine the interpelvic area. In young and juveniles, these scales can be distinguished from normal belly scales by their fewer and larger ctenii. For identifying Atlantic slope species of the subgenus *Alvordius*, see *Comparison* in the account of *Percina notogramma* concerning variation of the dark gular bar.

Key to Genera (and to Species of Genera Monotypic in Virginia)

1a Posterior margin of preopercle moderately or strongly serrate (Figure 71); branchiostegal rays usually 7, rarely 8; adult of panfish or gamefish size .... pikeperches, perch 2

1b Posterior margin of preopercle smooth or occasionally weakly, rarely moderately serrate (Figure 83); branchiostegal rays usually 6, rarely 7; small fishes .... darters 3

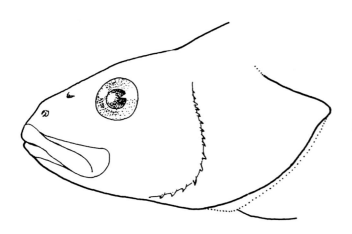

Figure 71 Serrate preopercle in *Perca.*

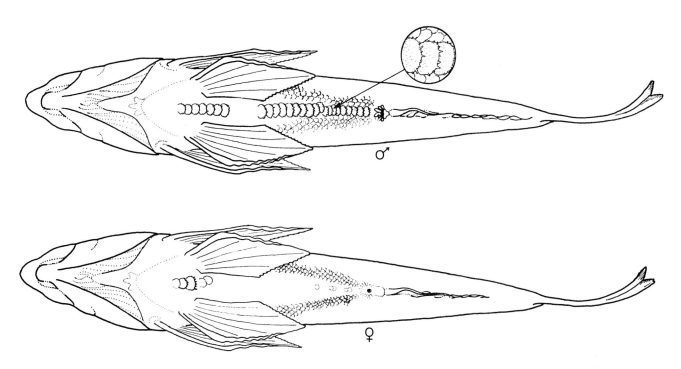

Figure 72 Modified midventral scales in *Percina*; top, male; bottom, female: Shown are logperches, subgenus *Percina*; in other groups of *Percina*, modified midventral scales may differ in position, number, and overall size, and in number and size of their spines (ctenii).

2a Side uniform, mottled, or blotched in adult, or small fish with vague interrupted bars; prominent canine teeth present on both jaws; anal rays 11–14 .... *Stizostedion*

2b Side with 5–9 moderate or long, bold bars; prominent canine teeth absent; anal rays 6–9 .... YELLOW PERCH—*Perca flavescens*   p. 775

3a Body extremely elongate, its greatest depth contained 7–9 times in standard length; body pallid except for a narrow midlateral stripe and a series of small middorsal blotches; body translucent in life; (Clinch and Powell rivers only) .... WESTERN SAND DARTER—*Ammocrypta clara*   p. 815

3b Body not extremely elongate, its greatest depth contained less than 7 times in standard length; body usually well pigmented 4

4a Belly and interpelvic area with 1 or more highly modified (enlarged, often strong-spined) scales (Figure 72) (except in *P. aurantiaca*; see below); (lateral line always complete; premaxillary frenum present, Figure 73A, except in *P. copelandi*) .... *Percina*

4b Belly and interpelvic area lacking modified scales (*Percina aurantiaca* fits here; distinguished from *Etheostoma* by its high lateral line scale count of 84–99); (lateral line complete or incomplete; frenum present or absent) .... *Etheostoma*

Key to Species of *Stizostedion*

1a Lower lobe of caudal fin white-tipped; first dorsal fin not boldly spotted or streaked, but the last 1–2 membranes nearly all black .... WALLEYE—*S. vitreum*   p. 768

1b Lower lobe of caudal fin not white-tipped; first dorsal fin with many dark spots or streaks, the last 1–2 membranes not all black; (Tennessee and possibly Big Sandy drainages only) .... SAUGER—*S. canadense*   p. 772

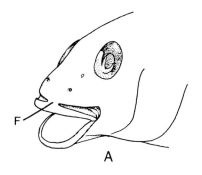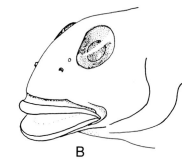

Figure 73 (A) F—frenum present. (B) Frenum absent, upper jaw protracted.

Key to Species of *Percina*

1a Premaxillary frenum absent (Figure 73B) or weakly developed;
(snout moderate or blunt, Figure 74; lateral line scales 48–57;
midlateral body with a row of dark smudges intermixed with
smaller dark markings; dorsolateral body with small flecks and
X-like markings; dorsal saddles absent or not bold; single median
caudal spot usually present; Clinch and Powell rivers, possibly also
New and Big Sandy drainages) .... CHANNEL DARTER—*P. copelandi* p. 812
1b Premaxillary frenum always present (Figure 73A), usually well
developed 2

2a Midventral scales weakly modified or not modified; dorsolateral
area of juvenile and adult with a horizontal row of irregularly
spaced spots; (midlateral pattern a series of conjoined blotches;
lateral line scales (84)86–93(99); snout profile usually moderate,
Figure 74C; large darter; Tennessee drainage only) ...... TANGERINE DARTER—*P. aurantiaca* p. 810
2b One or more highly modified midventral scales almost always
present (Figure 72); dorsolateral row of spots absent 3

3a Snout long, relatively pointed or bulbous in profile (Figure 74D, E) 4
3b Snout short or moderate, relatively blunt or moderate in profile
(Figure 74B, C) 9

4a Snout tip not projecting beyond upper jaw (Figure 74D);
interorbital width less than maximum width between pelvic fin
origins; total dorsal fin elements usually less than 29 5
4b Snout tip projecting distinctly beyond upper jaw (Figure 74E);
interorbital width about equal to maximum width between pelvic
fin origins; total dorsal fin elements usually more than 28 .... logperches, subgenus *Percina* 7

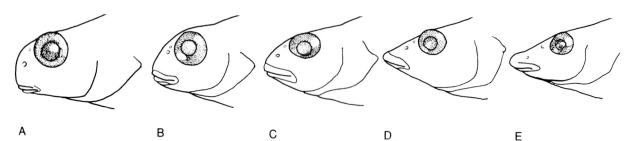

A   B   C   D   E

Figure 74 Snout shapes in darters: (A) Very blunt. (B) Blunt. (C) Moderate (moderately rounded). (D) Sharp. (E) Bulbous.

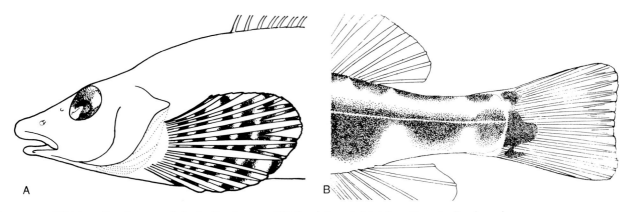

Figure 75   (A) Tessellated pectoral fin in *Percina rex*. (B) Caudal spot–blotch pattern in *Percina sciera*.

5a   Lateral pattern consisting of large, broadly conjoined blotches
(often forming a wide lateral stripe with undulating dorsal and
ventral margins); subocular bar usually present; small dark spot
often at origin of second dorsal fin; scales above lateral line (6)7–
8(9); (Tennessee drainage only) . . . . LONGHEAD DARTER—*P. macrocephala*   p. 791
5b   Lateral pattern consisting of a series of small, separate or slightly
conjoined blotches; subocular bar absent or, rarely, vague; no spot
at origin of second dorsal fin; scales above lateral line (8)9–16(18) 6

6a   Breast unscaled or slightly scaled; New and Big Sandy drainages
only . . . . SHARPNOSE DARTER—*P. oxyrhynchus*   p. 779
6b   Breast nearly fully or fully scaled; (may occupy South Fork Holston
River) . . . . OLIVE DARTER—*P. squamata*   p. 112

7a   Pectoral fin distinctly tessellated (Figure 75A); lateral blotches
usually vertically elongate, sometimes each blotch represented by a
large spot; Chowan and Roanoke drainages only; (nape 90–100%
scaled) . . . . ROANOKE LOGPERCH—*P. rex*   p. 785
7b   Pectoral fin weakly tessellated or not tessellated; lateral pattern
consisting of narrow bars or round or oval blotches; absent from
Chowan and Roanoke drainages 8

8a   Lateral pattern consisting of wide round or oval blotches; nape
(0)10–70(100)% scaled . . . . BLOTCHSIDE LOGPERCH—*P. burtoni*   p. 781
8b   Lateral pattern zebralike, consisting of narrow bars; nape (40)90–
100% scaled in New drainage and west . . . . LOGPERCH—*P. caprodes*   p. 788

9a   Restricted to Tennessee or Big Sandy drainages 10
9b   Absent from Tennessee and Big Sandy drainages 13

10a Subocular bar usually absent; caudal fin base usually with 3 dark
spots, the lower 2 often fused and forming an irregular blotch
(Figure 75B); (lateral pattern consisting of separate or slightly
conjoined blotches) . . . . DUSKY DARTER—*P. sciera*   p. 777
10b Subocular bar almost always present, occasionally faint; caudal fin
base with 1 dark spot, sometimes indistinct 11

11a   Upper body usually uniformly pigmented, lacking distinct saddles
    or horizontal wavy lines; lateral blotches broadly conjoined
    (Tennessee drainage only) .... LONGHEAD DARTER—*P. macrocephala* p. 791
11b   Upper body with distinct saddles or wavy lines; lateral blotches
    separate or narrowly or moderately conjoined 12

12a   Upper body with horizontal dark wavy lines, many of which are
    disconnected from saddles; lateral blotches not blending dorsally to
    near, nor confluent with, the saddles .... BLACKSIDE DARTER—*P. maculata* p. 793
12b   Upper body lacking horizontal dark wavy lines, or if dark lines are
    present, they almost always connect to saddles; adult specimens
    with dark lateral blotches blending dorsally to near, or confluent
    with, the saddles .... GILT DARTER—*P. evides* p. 807

13a   New drainage specimens 14
13b   Atlantic drainage specimens 15

14a   Lateral line scales 56–72; circumpeduncle scales 19–25 ....
    .... APPALACHIA DARTER—*P. gymnocephala* p. 798
14b   Lateral line scales 38–54; circumpeduncle scales 14–18 ...... ROANOKE DARTER—*P. roanoka* p. 804

15a   Melanophores on underside of head absent or distributed
    uniformly or nearly so on gular area, lower jaw rami, and anterior
    portion of lower lip 16
15b   Melanophores on underside of head, when present (which is
    typical of adult), distinctly more concentrated on gular area, often
    forming a dusky or dark midlongitudinal gular bar that is distinctly
    darker than (when pigmented) the lower jaw rami and lower lip 17

16a   Scales above lateral line (5)6–7(9); circumpeduncle scales (18)20–
    22(24); dorsal spines (11)13–15(17); lateral blotches mostly oval and
    their ventral margins usually well defined; first dorsal fin in life
    lacking submarginal yellow or orange band, and in preservative the
    fin lacking distinct horizontal banding .... STRIPEBACK DARTER—*P. notogramma* p. 795
16b   Scales above lateral line 4–5(6); circumpeduncle scales (14)15–17(18);
    dorsal spines (9)10–11(12); lateral blotches vertically elongate, often
    with their ventral margins diffusing onto abdomen; first dorsal fin
    in life with submarginal yellow or orange band, and in preservative
    the fin with distinct horizontal banding .... ROANOKE DARTER—*P. roanoka* p. 804

17a   Lateral line scales (48)53–61(66); lateral blotches square or
    rectangular; Roanoke drainage and north .... SHIELD DARTER—*P. peltata* p. 800

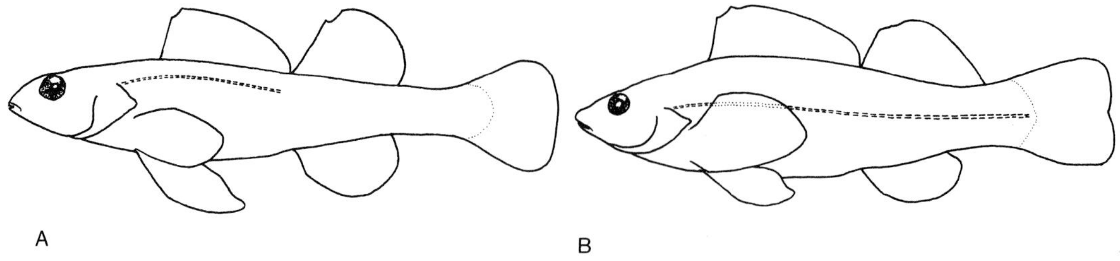

Figure 76 Lateral line in darters: (A) Arched (high on body), incomplete in subgenus *Hololepis* of *Etheostoma*. (B) Nonarched (midlateral), complete in most species of other groups.

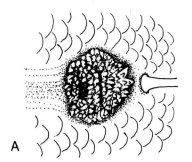
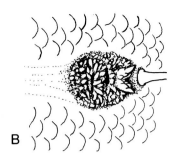
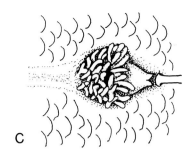

Figure 77 *Etheostoma vitreum* with villi in anal–urogenital area, and bifurcate (or more branched) genital papilla: (A) Nonbreeding female. (B) Breeding female. (C) Breeding male.

17b   Lateral line scales (44)47–52(58); lateral blotches mostly oval; Pee
Dee drainage only . . . .   PIEDMONT DARTER—*P. crassa*   p. 802

Key to Species of *Etheostoma*

1a   Lateral line slightly arched or straight anteriorly, positioned
midlaterally or just above (Figure 76B)   2
1b   Lateral line distinctly bowed upward anteriorly, reaching level of ¼
of body depth from middorsum (Figure 76A); (lateral line
incomplete)   26

2a   Anus surrounded by numerous villi (Figure 77); (snout long,
somewhat pointed, lips produced; frenum absent; branchiostegal
membranes narrowly conjoined; dorsolateral body speckled,
midside with scrawlings or small blotches; Piedmont and Coastal
Plain of Atlantic drainages) . . . .   GLASSY DARTER—*E. vitreum*   p. 852
2b   Anus not surrounded by numerous villi, although a few skin folds
or fleshy extensions may occur in anal–urogenital area (Figure 70)   3

3a   Branchiostegal rays (Figure 78) usually 5; (counting the superficial
folds or grooves of branchiostegal membrane may yield higher
count than actual number)   4
3b   Branchiostegal rays usually 6   5

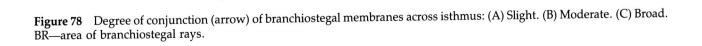

Figure 78 Degree of conjunction (arrow) of branchiostegal membranes across isthmus: (A) Slight. (B) Moderate. (C) Broad. BR—area of branchiostegal rays.

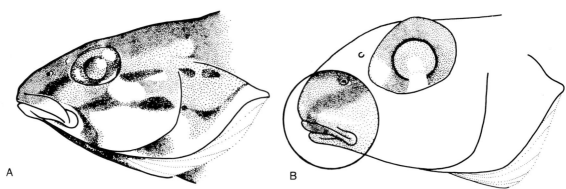

Figure 79 (A) Head pigmentation in *Etheostoma rufilineatum*. (B) Maxilla bound to snout in *Etheostoma blennioides*.

4a Snout blunt or moderate (Figure 74B, C); lateral body with
scrawling, irregularly shaped blotches, V-shaped marks, and (or)
bars, the posterior marks in adult nearly or completely encircling
venter; dorsolateral and most lateral marks about equally dark;
saddles 6(7–8); vomerine teeth present . . . . BANDED DARTER—*E. zonale*   p. 832
4b Snout very blunt (Figure 74A); lateral body with mostly solid,
rounded blotches, the posterior blotches not nearly encircling the
ventral body; lateral marks much darker than dorsolateral marks
(except saddles); saddles 7–9(10); vomerine teeth absent . . . . SNUBNOSE DARTER—*E. simoterum*   p. 835

5a Gill rakers on first arch absent or very small protuberances;
(Tennessee drainage only) . . . . ASHY DARTER—*E. cinereum*   p. 817
5b Gill rakers on first arch moderately or well developed, often small
but not all are very small protuberances 6

6a Lateral line complete or nearly so, 7 or fewer unpored scales 7
6b Lateral line incomplete, almost always 10 or more unpored scales 22

7a Frenum usually well developed (Figure 73A) 8
7b Frenum usually weakly developed or absent (Figure 73B) 18

8a Nape at least partly scaled, usually more than 50% so 9
8b Nape naked 14

9a Side of upper lip (maxilla) bound to side of snout by fleshy
nongrooved bridge of tissue (Figure 79B); lateral blotches usually
U-shaped . . . . GREENSIDE DARTER—*E. blennioides*   p. 830
9b Side of upper lip (maxilla) not bound to side of snout by a fleshy
bridge of tissue, instead a long groove dividing them (Figure 79A);
lateral blotches not U-shaped 10

10a Pectoral fin not tessellated; saddles often constricted medially
(hourglass-shaped); (Tennessee drainage only) . . . . SPECKLED DARTER—*E. stigmaeum*   p. 838
10b Pectoral fin tessellated; saddles usually uniform in width 11

11a Big Sandy drainage only . . . . VARIEGATE DARTER—*E. variatum*   p. 823
11b New or Tennessee drainage only 12

12a Tennessee drainage only . . . . SWANNANOA DARTER—*E. swannanoa*   p. 819
12b New drainage only 13

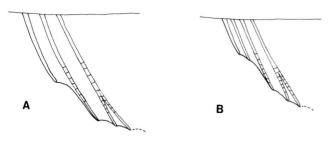

Figure 80 Anterior supporting elements of the anal fin in darters: (A) *Etheostoma nigrum*, 1 spine. (B) *Etheostoma podostemone*, 2 spines. Spine(s) may be very thin; they are unsegmented. First ray is almost always unbranched in darters and may resemble a thin spine. Identity as a ray is discerned by distal segmentation, rendered more visible by careful scraping of skin and strong light.

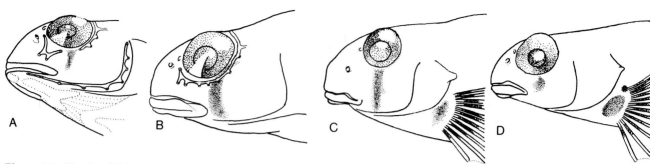

Figure 81 Heads of *Etheostoma* subgenus *Boleosoma*: (A) *E. nigrum* with interrupted infraorbital canal (IO) of 4+3 pores and preopercular-mandibular canal with 9 pores. (B) *E. olmstedi* with uninterrupted IO of 8 pores. (C) *E. podostemone* with linear subocular bar. (D) *E. longimanum* with ovoid subocular smudge or blotch.

21a Infraorbital canal almost always interrupted (Figure 81A); James and Roanoke drainages (mainly mountains to Fall Line) and New and Big Sandy drainages [see *E. nigrum* account for problematic populations in Appomattox system and upper Chowan and lower Roanoke drainages] .... JOHNNY DARTER—*E. nigrum* p. 846

21b Infraorbital canal almost always uninterrupted (Figure 81B); all Atlantic drainages, but only below Fall Line in James system proper [see 21a] .... TESSELLATED DARTER—*E. olmstedi* p. 849

22a Opercle at least partly scaled; lateral pattern barred, blotched, or flecked 23

22b Opercle naked; lateral pattern usually barred 25

23a Larger gill rakers short and stubby, width about equal to length; frenum absent or, if present, narrow or moderately developed; (Tennessee drainage only) .... SPECKLED DARTER—*E. stigmaeum* p. 838

23b Larger gill rakers long and thin, width much less than length; frenum always well developed, moderate or wide 24

24a Dorsal spines 12–14; rarely larger than 30 mm SL, 35 mm maximum; (Clinch River and Copper Creek only) .... TIPPECANOE DARTER—*E. tippecanoe* p. 862

24b Dorsal spines 8–11; adult usually larger than 30 mm SL ... RAINBOW DARTER—*E. caeruleum* p. 871

25a Lateral line scales (pored plus unpored) (38)40–45(48); total dorsal fin elements (17)18–19(21); pectoral fin rays peppered or lined with melanophores only distally (Figure 82A); Clinch system of Tennessee drainage only .... DUSKYTAIL DARTER—*E. percnurum* p. 877

25b Lateral line scales (pored plus unpored, in populations of Tennessee drainage in Virginia) (44)46–54(59); total dorsal fin elements (18)20–22(23); pectoral fin rays peppered or lined with melanophores for most of their length (Figure 82B); widespread .... FANTAIL DARTER—*E. flabellare* p. 873

26a Caudal fin base usually with 4 vertically aligned dark spots, the medial 2 quite bold; infraorbital canal uninterrupted (Figure 83A); preopercle margin fully, moderately serrate (Figure 83A); (Chowan drainage and east only) .... SAWCHEEK DARTER—*E. serrifer* p. 882

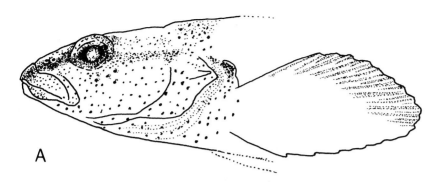

A

Figure 82 Lateral head and pectoral fin pigmentation in subgenus *Catonotus*; fin pigmentation is along rays, which are not shown: (A) *Etheostoma percnurum* "freckle-headed" subadult. (B) *Etheostoma flabellare* subadult with typical head pigmentation; pectoral melanophores may form tessellation pattern in some specimens.

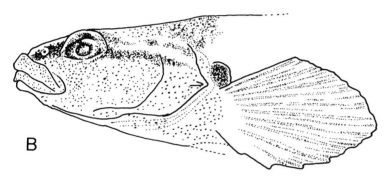

B

26b Caudal fin base usually with 3 vertically aligned dark spots, or if 4 spots are present, 1 or both of the medial 2 are not notably bolder than the other 2; infraorbital canal interrupted (Figure 83B); preopercle margin usually entire, occasionally partly, weakly serrate (Figure 83B) 27

27a Breast 100% scaled; anal spines 2; infraorbital pores usually 3+2 (3 anterior and 2 posterior pores, Figure 83B) .... SWAMP DARTER—*E. fusiforme* p. 884

27b Breast 0–80% scaled; anal spines 1, rarely 2; infraorbital pores usually 4+1; (Roanoke drainage only) .... CAROLINA DARTER—*E. collis* p. 886

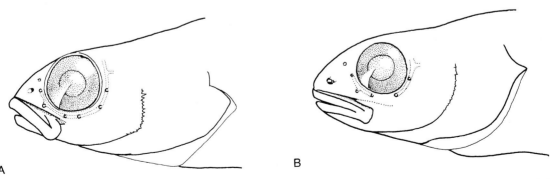

A   B

Figure 83 Infraorbital canal (IO) and preopercle margin in darters: (A) *Etheostoma serrifer*, IO uninterrupted (6 pores, usually), preopercle moderately serrate. (B) *Etheostoma fusiforme*, IO interrupted (3+2 pores), preopercle weakly serrate (serrae usually absent, margin entire).

Pikeperches   Genus *Stizostedion* Rafinesque

The combination "pikeperch" connotes the similarity of these fishes in piscivorous habits to true pikes (Esocidae) and from membership in the true perch family. Except for their canine teeth and elongate body, pikeperches are very different in appearance from pikes. *Stizostedion* contains the largest members of the Percidae. This Holarctic genus comprises three Eurasian and two North American species; the latter two occur in Virginia. Four are primarily freshwater species; *S. marinum* lives in brackish zones of the Black and Caspian seas and rarely enters rivers (Collette and Banarescu 1977).

Name.—*Stizostedion* means "pungent throat"—the sharp canine teeth on the roof of the mouth.

Walleye   *Stizostedion vitreum* (Mitchill)

SYSTEMATICS

The walleye was described from New York in 1818. Two subspecies have been recognized, the widespread yellow walleye *S. v. vitreum* and the blue pike *S. v. glaucum* (Regier et al. 1969; Trautman 1981). The latter, endemic to Lakes Erie and Ontario, is now considered to be extinct (Collette and Banarescu 1977; Bailey and Smith 1981). The population in the Mobile drainage appears to be genetically unique (Murphy 1990).

DESCRIPTION

Materials.—From Scott and Crossman (1973), Colby et al. (1979), and 7 Virginia specimens. Color in life from Trautman (1981), Becker (1983), and 2 Virginia adults.

Anatomy.—An elongate fish with prominent canine teeth, a dark blotch in rear of first dorsal fin, and pale-tipped lower caudal lobe; adults are 300–780 mm TL. Body elongate, nearly round, tapering to a slender peduncle; head moderate in length, slightly depressed; eye large, supralateral; frenum absent; mouth terminal, large; jaws with canine teeth; branchiostegal membranes separate. Dorsal fins well separated; first dorsal margin convex; second dorsal and anal margins straight or slightly concave; caudal fin forked, lobes rounded or subacute; pelvic fin larger than pectoral fin. Cheek variable, usually sparsely scaled; opercle, nape, breast, and belly well scaled.

Meristics.—Lateral line complete, scales (80)86–92(108); first dorsal spines (12)13–14(16); second dorsal spines 1(2), rays (18)19–21(22); anal spines 2, usually weak; anal rays (11)12–13(14); pelvic spine 1, rays 5; pectoral rays 13–15(16).

Color in Preservative.—Ground shade dusky; side and back with uniform heavily dusky mottling; upper side sometimes with several vertical or slightly oblique vague bars and blotches, some of these connected over back to form saddles; venter pale. Head mottled and blotched, underside pale. First dorsal fin mostly dusky or with dusky interspinous streaks and marks, last 2–3 membranes very dark or black, forming a blotch; second dorsal fin with narrow tessellations; caudal fin tessellated, lower lobe pale-tipped; anal and pelvic fins pale; pectoral fin weakly tessellated, usually with a dark basal blotch.

Color in Life.—Ground color pale yellow; mottling and blotches gray, olive-brown, or brown; side often with brassy sheen or overall golden; venter white to pale yellow. Posterior 2–3 first dorsal fin membranes black; second dorsal and caudal fins with brown tessellations; lower caudal lobe and tip of anal fin white; pectoral fin pale olive.

Larvae.—Described by Deason (1934 *in* Becker 1983), Norden (1961), Mansueti (1964), W. Nelson (1968b), Hardy (1978b), Colby et al. (1979), and Auer (1982f).

BIOLOGY

Overviews of walleye biology are by Collette et al. (1977) and Ney (1978); Colby et al. (1979) provided an

Fish 243 *Stizostedion vitreum* adult male 328 mm SL (REJ 1038), VA, Campbell County, Roanoke River, 12 September 1983.

extensive synthesis of the literature. The diet of young walleyes mirrors the adult preference for fish, but also includes roundworms, leeches, microcrustaceans, other zooplankton, crayfishes, insects, mollusks, and frogs (Raney and Lachner 1942; Eschmeyer 1950). The voracious young sometimes are cannibalistic. Cahn (1927) noted seven recently hatched walleyes in a "string"; each had swallowed the posterior of the preceding fish. Walleyes in Claytor Lake are principal predators of alewives (Boaze 1972; Kohler 1980); before establishment of the alewife they ate mainly sunfishes (Rosebery 1950a). Walleyes are largely visual predators; the large, very sensitive eyes are adapted for detection of prey during the typical evening, night, and early morning feeding forays (Ali and Anctil 1977; Collette et al. 1977). Other senses such as hearing and smell must be involved in prey detection to some extent (Regier et al. 1969). Feeding usually occurs at or near the bottom; walleye often move inshore to feeding grounds as light intensity diminishes (Colby et al. 1979).

Virginia walleyes exhibit about half the longevity of those in the northern United States and Canada but reach similar sizes (Colby et al. 1979). Both sexes mature at age 2 in many southeastern populations; in Canada, males typically mature at ages 2–4 and females at ages 3–6 (Scott and Crossman 1973; Hackney and Holbrook 1978). Oldest members of many Virginia populations are of ages 4–6 (Smith and Kauffman 1982); maximum longevity known from the state is age 8 (Rosebery 1950a). Fish reaching age 15 have been reported from Canada (Scott and Crossman 1973); one remarkable age-29 fish is documented from New York (Culligan 1985).

In a Canadian population of long-lived walleyes, females grew faster than males after age 7 (Rawson 1957). Walleyes larger than 4 kg invariably are females (Hackney and Holbrook 1978). The ranges of average lengths for ages 2 and 4 from nine Virginia lakes were 323–437 and 455–554 mm TL (Smith and Kauffman 1982). The Virginia historical record specimen was identified as a walleye (R. E. Wollitz, personal communication) but its weight of 10.2 kg (22 pounds 8 ounces) has been questioned (W. E. Neal, personal communication). The accepted Virginia record is 5.9 kg (12 pounds 15.9 ounces); the world record is 11.3 kg (25 pounds) from Tennessee.

The walleye is an early spawner; migration begins soon after ice-out in northern regions. Spawning occurs within one to three weeks during March to June depending on the region, in water of 2.2–15.6°C; most activity takes place in 5.6–10°C (Hokanson 1977). Spawning usually occurs in March and early April in Virginia (D. K. Whitehurst, in litt.). Walleyes congregate before spawning, sometimes in large numbers, and usually migrate short distances to spawning grounds (Eschmeyer 1950; Rawson 1957). Spawning occurs at dusk and night, usually over gravel or rock substrate in shallow areas of lakes and rivers. Walleyes rarely spawn over vegetation in flooded areas (Regier et al. 1969). In rivers, spawning seems to be most frequent in runs and reservoir tailwaters, but it also occurs in riffles (Eschmeyer 1950). Mansueti (1964) reported spawning in the freshwater section of upper Chesapeake Bay.

Males arrive at spawning grounds first and usually outnumber females until the peak of spawning. Spawning occurs communally and nonterritorially; males and females in intermittently segregated subgroups exhibit brief simple courtship just preceding the spawning act (Ellis and Giles 1965; Colby et al. 1979). Eggs are broadcast over the bottom; eventually most eggs drop into crevices where they may be protected from predators, but are in danger of being smothered by sediment. Fecundity is 23,000–615,000 (Hardy 1978b).

Walleyes rarely hybridize in nature with saugers (Stroud 1948; Clayton et al. 1973). Regier et al. (1969) speculated that introgression between *Stizostedion* species may have occurred in western Lake Erie. Artificial hybridization of sauger and walleye was summarized by Colby et al. (1979); the hybrid was described also by W. Nelson (1968b).

HABITAT

Stizostedion vitreum occupies a broad spectrum of habitats in rivers, lakes, and impoundments. Concerning rivers, it distinctly favors those of medium to large size, low to moderate gradient, and with clear to somewhat turbid water. These range from moderately alkaline to moderately acidic and include tidal freshwater reaches. Walleyes infrequently enter brackish water (Scott and Crossman 1973; Hardy 1978b). Bottom types occupied include detritus, shifting sand, gravel, rubble, and boulder; clean hard bottoms are preferred. In rivers, walleye are associated with pools, backwaters, and deep runs above and below riffles. Suitable lakes generally are larger than 400 hectares (about 1,000 acres) in area. Cover is sought during daylight, although walleyes may be active during that time under turbid conditions. Subadults and adults often form groups (Colby et al. 1979).

The walleye is generally classified as a coolwater fish, but it prospers in an appreciable range of thermal conditions. During summer in warm lakes, walleyes generally congregate well below the surface; in

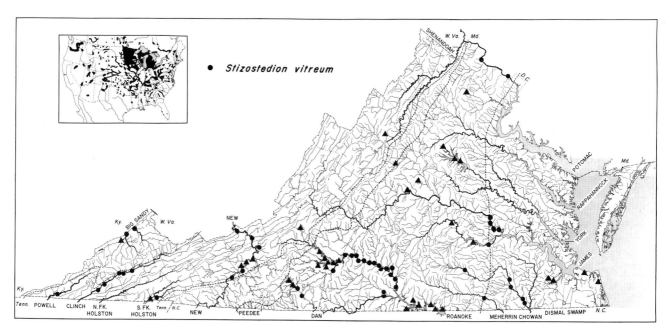

Map 156 Walleye.

Norris Reservoir, Tennessee, they occurred down to 15 m depth (Dendy 1945, 1946a, 1946b). Preferred summer temperatures were 23.2°C in Norris Reservoir, Tennessee, and 20.6°C in a Wisconsin lake (Coutant 1977; Fitz and Holbrook 1978). Regier et al. (1969) reported walleyes to be most successful in mesotrophic lakes with minimum visibility of 1.2–3 m, although heavy turbidity is tolerated (Colby et al. 1979). Movements are short, often only a few kilometers, but exceptional individuals have been recaptured up to 322 km from the point of release (Eschmeyer 1950; Rawson 1957).

DISTRIBUTION   Map 156

The native range of *S. vitreum* extends from the Mackenzie River drainage of northern Canada and the southern half of the Hudson Bay basin south through the Great Lakes–St. Lawrence basin and most of the Mississippi basin. The walleye has been widely introduced beyond its indigenous range, but the southern limits of that range are uncertain. Some populations on the western Gulf slope probably are introduced (Barila *in* Lee et al. 1980), but those in the eastern portion may be native (Swift et al. 1986). The Mobile drainage population was considered native by Hubbs and Lagler (1958) and Regier et al. (1969); that status was supported by Murphy (1990).

The populations on the Atlantic slope south of the St. Lawrence probably are introduced. Hubbs and Lagler (1958) were uncertain about the original distri-

butional status on the central and south Atlantic slope, and Rostlund (1952) doubted that the walleye was indigenous there. Statements by Hackney and Holbrook (1978) on native occurrence in the Southeast do not reflect the older literature.

In Virginia the walleye apparently is native only to the Tennessee and Big Sandy drainages. Most Clinch River records predate the first known stocking of 1968; the Powell River record does not antedate that river's 1968 stocking. The Flannagan Reservoir (Big Sandy drainage) records are of stocked fish. Prior to extensive impacts from coal mining in the Big Sandy, walleye barely extended into Virginia via the Levisa and Russell forks (R. E. Wollitz, personal communication). South Holston Reservoir has been stocked in Tennessee; Virginia records from the reservoir and the river just above may stem from that source. The walleye is assumed to have been native to, but extirpated from, the North Fork Holston River owing to pollution.

In several other Virginia drainages the walleye was stocked early; only recently have we become aware of the extent. Prior treatments suggested that *S. vitreum* was native (but possibly introduced) to the New drainage (Jenkins et al. 1972; Stauffer et al. 1982). Our reanalysis (in part, Hocutt et al. 1986) indicates that it was introduced to the New. It was not reported by anglers to Cope (1868b). The VFC (1877a) stated that New River "has in its main stream little else [of game-fishes] than the cat fish." Apparently the first stocking was in 1921 with fish hatched in Virginia from eggs obtained from a Lake Champlain, Vermont, hatchery (USFC 1922). Rosebery (1950a, 1950b), Boaze (1972), Hart (1981), Murphy (1981), and White-hurst (1985) summarized subsequent intensive stock-ings made in Claytor Lake since its impoundment in 1939; these appear traceable to Lake Erie and Hudson Bay stocks via agencies of four states beyond Vir-ginia.

We regard the central Atlantic slope populations of walleye to have been introduced. Uhler and Lugger (1876) stated that *S. vitreum* occurred in the mountain regions and was "scarcely if at all brought to the Baltimore markets." Apparently their first statement referred to the Youghiogheny drainage of the Ohio basin in western Maryland, where the walleye was regarded as native by Hendricks et al. (1983). The Potomac drainage was first stocked with walleye be-tween 1901 and 1904 (USFC 1905a; Bean and Weed 1911); later stockings are listed in Manville (1968), Davis et al. (1982), and Davis and Enamait (1982). The York drainage was first stocked in 1975 in Lake Anna (Sledd and Shuber 1981). The Rappahannock drain-age apparently lacks walleye.

The populations of the James and Roanoke (and Chowan) drainages were considered native but pos-sibly introduced by Jenkins et al. (1972) and Stauffer et al. (1982). We now believe that they were intro-duced. The James River has supported considerable net fisheries but there is no mention in Cabell's diary (late 1700s, see *Morone saxatilis*), early VFC reports, or other reports of "pike" or other common names for the walleye in the drainage. *Stizostedion vitreum* was held in high esteem in other areas, and certainly would have been mentioned. Our earliest James record—1977—is from the Lake Chesdin impound-ment of the lower Appomattox River. These fish probably came from stockings in Amelia Lake farther up the Appomattox system (D. K. Whitehurst, in litt.). In the 1980s the VDGIF developed a walleye fishery in the Appomattox River below Lake Ches-din.

Walleyes formerly were considered probably native to the Chowan and Roanoke drainages owing to their capture in the lower portion of these drainages and elsewhere in the Albemarle Sound region of North Carolina during a survey in 1892 by Smith (1893). Jenkins was also influenced by Cope's (1870) sketchy statement that *Stizostedion* occurred in the Neuse drainage of North Carolina. However, Smith (1907) gave conflicting evidence of native status in the Chowan–Roanoke, noting that some persons thought it to be nonnative; Smith's earliest record was from 1878. Nonnative status in these freshwater-connected Albemarle tributaries is indicated by a clear statement

in the Virginia Fish Commissioner's report for the year 1877 (VFC 1877b). In a paragraph titled "A New Fish," an unidentified species was described that could have been only the walleye; it was said to have ". . . appeared in the Nottoway [Chowan drainage] within the last year or two."

The sequence of these observations indicates that walleyes were stocked in the Chowan or Roanoke or both drainages in the early 1870s, but the source(s) is unknown. M. D. Norman (in litt.) related anglers' reports that walleyes were released from railroad tank cars at bridges in southeastern Virginia many years ago. The Meherrin River was stocked with 830,000 fry in 1904 (USFC 1905b). The VDGIF intro-duced 164,000 walleyes to the Nottoway River during 1980–1982. Since 1981, this species has been caught in the Nottoway and Meherrin rivers and as far away as in Currituck Sound, a northern connection of Albe-marle Sound in North Carolina (M. D. Norman, in litt.).

Colonization by walleye of the lower Roanoke drainage may have led to its rapid dispersal upstream through much of the main channel on the Piedmont. Smith (1893) reported *S. vitreum* at the Fall Line of the Roanoke River in North Carolina. Before formation of Kerr Reservoir, spawning runs extended into the Dan River and other tributaries (Martin 1954). Walleyes were common during filling of Leesville Reservoir and Smith Mountain Lake in 1963; around that time it made spawning runs into the Pigg River but declined in abundance about five years later (W. E. Neal, L. G. Hart, personal communications). Walleyes subse-quently were stocked for a period with little success, but they are now well established in these reservoirs and in the Roanoke River between Leesville and Kerr reservoirs. Recent stocking programs involve Gaston, Carvin Cove, and Philpott reservoirs in the Roanoke drainage. Records from the Smith River are of appar-ent escapees from Philpott. The Banister River, Dan River tributary, record is of a young specimen seined in 1983.

Abundance.—Usually uncommon or common; de-pendent in many waters on stocking levels.

REMARKS

The walleye is Virginia's largest percid and is often said to be the finest freshwater foodfish in North America; we heard it called "freshwater lobster." Pri-marily thought of as a midwestern and northern fish, the walleye is much a newcomer to the state. With stocking in several reservoirs in Virginia, the species is gaining in popularity, particularly as anglers learn the specific sites, depths, and methods to catch them. Catches tend to be greatest at dusk and dawn, when the fish are moving and feeding (Colby et al. 1979).

Although walleye fisheries exist in some Virginia rivers, the management focus is on reservoir populations. Attempts at development and effective management by the VDGIF of walleye populations in reservoirs have had varied success, as has been the general trend in North America (Laarman 1978). Southern river populations in other states typically declined with impoundment and were revived in reservoirs only by stocking programs (Hackney and Holbrook 1978). *Stizostedion vitreum* undergoes large fluctuations in year-class strength, often independent of numbers stocked (Koonce et al. 1977). Discrete intralacustrine subpopulations in Claytor Lake and other areas (Murphy 1981) may further complicate management.

Several montane to lowland Virginia impoundments have been stocked entirely on a put-and-grow basis, but the strategy for others is to establish or supplement self-sustaining fisheries. To this end, many nonnative cohorts, from sources including Lake Champlain, Lake Erie, and the Hudson Bay basin, have been introduced. Walleyes from Georgia were placed in Flannagan Reservoir in 1965; these probably also had a northern origin (Hackney and Holbrook 1978).

Conditions in several Virginia reservoirs seem favorable for walleye reproduction, but possibly only Claytor Lake has developed a self-sustaining population of substantial size. Success in Claytor may be related to cool water in relatively high altitude (563 m), and to substantial spawning habitat in this narrow riverine impoundment. However, even there, annual reproduction is erratic and must frequently be supplemented by stocking to bolster recruitment. Reproduction occurs in Smith Mountain Lake and the Roanoke River below Leesville Reservoir (J. J. Ney, D. K. Whitehurst, in litt.). Some reproduction may also be occurring in Philpott Reservoir and in the New, Clinch, and Powell rivers.

Name.—*Vitreum* means "glassy," referring to the clarity of the large cornea of living fish. Mitchill (1818) stated that the eyes were "like semiglobes of glass." Walleyes have long been called that, and also their eyes have been described as milky or opaque. Such interpretations partly stem from the intense reflectivity of the eye as viewed with a light beam at night.

Sauger   *Stizostedion canadense* (Smith)

SYSTEMATICS

The sauger was described from Canada in 1834. No subspecies currently are recognized; variation within populations may be about equal to that between populations (Scott and Crossman 1973; Smith 1979).

DESCRIPTION

Materials.—From Scott and Crossman (1973), Becker (1983), and 6 specimens (2 from Virginia). Life color from above references, Smith (1979), and the 2 Virginia adults.

Anatomy.—An elongate percid with prominent canine teeth, oblique bold blotches on body, and multi-spotted first dorsal fin; adults are 250–460 mm TL. Form of body and parts as in the walleye; cheek well scaled.

Meristics.—Lateral line complete, scales (79)87–95(100); first dorsal spines (10)12–13(15); second dorsal spines 1(2), rays (16)17–19(22); anal spines 2, usually weak; anal rays 12–13; pelvic spine 1, rays 5; pectoral rays 14–16.

Color in Preservative.—Ground shade dusky; side with 3–4 large dark lateral blotches, some or all united into a saddle; first lateral blotch usually extending posteroventrad, fusing with second blotch; other blotches usually markedly oblique; area between blotches and saddles heavily peppered and scrawled, sometimes with small dark blotches; venter pale except breast peppered. Head

Fish 244 *Stizostedion canadense* adult male 238 mm SL (NCSM 5688), NC, Madison County, Big Laurel River, 15 August 1972.

Fish 245 *Stizostedion canadense* juvenile 100 mm SL (INHS 79691), MN, Goodhue County, Lake Pepin, 17 August 1966.

blotched and scrawled dorsally and laterally, paler below. First dorsal fin with a series of usually 2–4 medium or large spots, sometimes also streaks, on each membrane; second dorsal fin tessellated; caudal rays tessellated, marks coalesced at base; anal fin pale or anteriorly slightly peppered; pelvic fin with short dark streaks along rays; pectoral fin weakly tessellated, often with basal dark blotch. Juvenile body and fin markings similar to adult but much reduced.

Color in Life.—Ground color yellowish-olive to dull brown; angular blotches, saddles, and other marks dark brown; venter milky to dirty white; eye silvery and highly reflective.

Larvae.—Described by W. Nelson (1968b) and Auer (1982f).

BIOLOGY

Larval *S. canadense* first feed on microcrustaceans, thereafter on fish fry and an occasional aquatic insect (W. Nelson 1968a; Becker 1983). Adults are almost exclusively piscivorous, even eating lampreys, but may supplement the diet with leeches, crustaceans, and insects (Dendy 1946b; Scott and Crossman 1973; Wahl 1982; McBride and Tarter 1983). Saugers are sight feeders, adapted to low-light and night activity. In clear waters they are most active in early morning and evening, but in turbid situations the feeding period is longer (Scott and Crossman 1973; Becker 1983). They may feed continuously during the reduced light intensity of winter (Wahl 1982). Swenson (1977) found relatively high food consumption rates in early and late summer. McBride and Tarter (1983) related greater autumnal food intake to increased activity in cooler periods.

Southern populations are shorter lived but faster growing than those of northern United States and Canada (Scott and Crossman 1973; Becker 1983). Males in northern populations mature at ages 2–3 and females at ages 4–6. In Virginia latitudes both sexes mature at ages 2–3. The oldest Clinch River sauger reported by Wollitz (1972) was age 4, the typical maximum age reached in many Tennessee reservoirs

(Hackney and Holbrook 1978). Scott and Crossman (1973) cited longevity of age 13 in a Canadian lake. Females grow slightly faster and reach slightly larger sizes than males (Hassler 1956; Becker 1983). Clinch River saugers of ages 2 and 4 averaged 310 and 452 mm TL (Wollitz 1972); similar data were noted for Tennessee reservoirs (Hackney and Holbrook 1978). The Virginia record is 2.5 kg (5.5 pounds) from South Holston Reservoir; the world record is 3.9 kg (12 pounds 9 ounces) from North Dakota (IGFA 1985).

The reproductive season extends from mid-March in Alabama to late June in North Dakota, locally lasting about two weeks (W. Nelson 1968a; Scott and Crossman 1973; Hokanson 1977; June 1977; Becker 1983). Males apparently precede females to the spawning ground (W. Nelson 1968a). Spawning occurs nocturnally in water of 4°C in North Dakota to 14°C in Tennessee (Hokanson 1977). In lakes, spawning occurs along sandy or rocky shores and over rocky reefs in depths of 0.6–3.6 m. In rivers, spawning occurs in deep rocky runs. A female is attended by one or more males; the semibuoyant eggs are scattered and settle among rocks. Fecundity is 9,000–152,000 (Auer 1982f).

Natural hybridization occurs with the walleye (Stroud 1948; Clayton et al. 1973). Scott and Crossman (1973) suggested that a former record-sized sauger may have been a hybrid sauger × walleye.

HABITAT

Stizostedion canadense inhabits large streams, rivers, and lakes. The northern native limits of this "coolwater" species appear to be correlated with the 15.5°C July isotherm (Ryder et al. 1964). Preferred summer temperature ranges of 22.3–27.7°C (Wabash River—Gammon 1971) and 16.7–21.7°C (Norris Reservoir—Dendy 1946a) have been reported, but saugers have been found in heated effluents up to 33.6°C (Becker 1983). Saugers were taken as deep as 23 m in Norris Reservoir, but were more common above 15 m (Dendy 1946a, 1946b). Canadian populations are as-

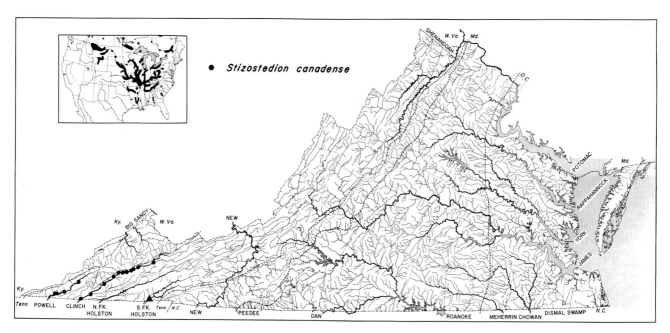

Map 157　Sauger.

sociated with turbid rivers and shallow lakes; in one bay, the sauger attained dominance over the walleye after the bay became turbid (Scott and Crossman 1973). Southern populations frequently occur in clear water. In rivers, saugers are reported to prefer deep swift runs as well as slower currents and deep backwaters where walleyes are typically found (Pflieger 1975; Becker 1983). On rare occasions saugers enter the brackish zone of the St. Lawrence River (Scott and Crossman 1973).

DISTRIBUTION　Map 157

The sauger is native to the Hudson Bay, Great Lakes–St. Lawrence, and upper and middle Mississippi basins. It has been introduced to the lower Mississippi basin and a few drainages on the Gulf and southeastern Atlantic slopes (Barila *in* Lee et al. 1980). In Virginia it is apparently native to the upper Tennessee drainage, perhaps also to the Big Sandy drainage. Recent records are from the Clinch and Powell rivers and South Holston Reservoir. It probably occupied the North Fork Holston River before the extensive pollution that originated at Saltville. *Stizostedion canadense* may infrequently enter the lowermost section of the South Fork Holston River above the reservoir.

Abundance.—Uncommon or rare. We took only 2 specimens, boat-shocking by Wollitz (1972) produced

only 11, and the sauger did not seem well known to anglers in southwestern Virginia. Saugers were numerous in the Clinch and Powell rivers and then virtually disappeared, but since about 1980 have been making a good comeback (J. W. Heironimus, personal communication).

REMARKS

The eye of the sauger is remarkably adapted for prey detection at night and in turbid water; it is even more sensitive than that of the walleye (Ali and Anctil 1977; Collette et al. 1977). Vertical migration of the sauger is partly the result of avoidance of high light intensities. This species is the most migratory of pikeperches; individuals in one study traveled up to 380 rkm at minimal average swimming speeds of 19.7 km/day upstream and 21.1 km/day downstream (Collette et al. 1977).

Although smaller than the walleye, the sauger provides a good-sized fillet and shares with the walleye the reputation of being excellent table fare.

We recommend that the sauger be granted special concern status in Virginia. There are only three populations; those of the Clinch and Powell rivers each are vulnerable to a single catastrophic chemical spill.

Name.—*Canadense*, "of Canada," referring to the provenance of the first-described specimens.

Perches   Genus *Perca* Linnaeus

Of the three species of *Perca*, the North American yellow perch and the Eurasian perch *P. fluviatilis* are the most familiar members of the Percidae. The other *Perca* is confined to highlands of eastern Russia (Collette and Banarescu 1977).

Name.—*Perca*, the old Latin word for "perch."

Yellow perch   *Perca flavescens* (Mitchill)

SYSTEMATICS

The yellow perch was described from New York in 1814. At times over the past 150 years it has been held that *P. flavescens* is morphologically and biologically indistinguishable from its Eurasian counterpart *P. fluviatilis* (e.g., Svetovidov and Dorofeeva 1963; Thorpe 1977). However, Collette and Banarescu (1977) supported the retention of these two taxa as species.

DESCRIPTION

Materials.—From Frey (1951), Scott and Crossman (1973), and 8 Virginia lots. Life color from 3 Virginia adults.

Anatomy.—A percid having moderate body form, separate dorsal fins, and bold vertical lateral bars; adults are 130–300 mm TL. Anterior body elevated, tapering posteriorly to a slender peduncle; head moderate; eye medium or large; snout rounded or subacute; frenum absent; mouth medium-sized, terminal, jaws with small teeth; preopercle margin serrate, opercle spine prominent; branchiostegal membranes separate. Dorsal fins slightly or moderately separated, first dorsal convex, second dorsal straight-margined; caudal fin somewhat small, forked; anal fin small; pelvic fin larger than pectoral. Genital opening of female becomes greatly enlarged and distended during spawning (Parker 1942). Opercle partly scaled; nape, breast, and belly fully scaled.

Meristics.—Lateral line complete, scales (50)55–64(70); scales above lateral line 6–8(10); scales below lateral line (12)13–15(18); first dorsal spines (11)12–14(15); second dorsal spines 1–2(3), rays (12)13–15(16); anal spines 2; anal rays (6)7–8(9); pelvic 1 spine, 5 rays; pectoral rays 13–15.

Color in Preservative.—Ground shade slightly dusky; side with 5–9 ventrally tapered dark bars, these usually bilaterally symmetrical and united across dorsum, but sometimes alternating, forming a small blotch on side opposite complete bar; dorsum flecked with small dark marks between bars; venter pale. Head dorsum and opercle dusky or dark, cheek dusky. First dorsal fin mostly dusky, last 2–3 membranes darkened; second dorsal fin dusky distally; caudal fin dusky; anal fin slightly dusky; pelvic and pectoral fins pale.

Color in Life   Plate 31.—Paler areas of lateral body green to gold with brassy iridescence; lateral bars and head dorsum dark olive; venter silver-white. First dorsal fin dusky gray-black, last 2–3 membranes nearly solid black; second dorsal fin dusky gray distally; caudal fin yellow-olive basally, dusky gray distally; anal fin orange-red on leading margin, remainder of fin pale; nearly all of pelvic fin orange-red; pectoral fin amber.

Larvae.—Described by Norden (1961), Mansueti (1964), Rohde (1974), Hardy (1978b), Wang and Kernehan (1979), and Auer (1982f).

Fish 246 *Perca flavescens* adult male 109 mm SL (REJ 1018), VA, Southampton County, Tarrara Swamp, 15 July 1983.

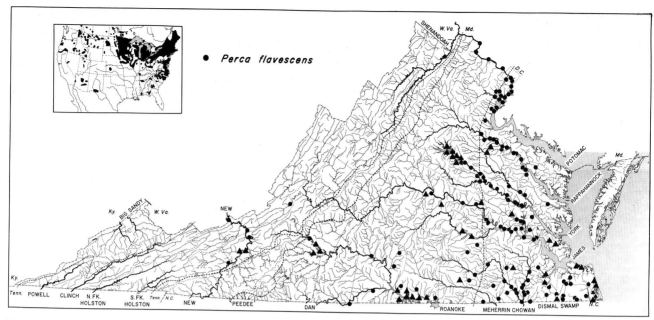

Map 158   Yellow perch.

BIOLOGY

Larval and young *Perca* feed on algae and plankton (Noble 1975). Dietary diversity begins expanding when young exceed 30 mm TL (Ney and Smith 1975), culminating in an assortment of prey including worms, crustaceans, insects, mollusks, and fishes (Muncy 1962; Keast 1965, 1970; Russell 1976; Thorpe 1977; Gatz 1979). In a Canadian lake, *P. flavescens* over 150 mm TL primarily eat crayfishes and fishes (Keast and Webb 1966). This species is considered a secondary piscivore; young fishes compose 30–40% of the adult diet (Keast 1985). Yellow perch actively feed during winter (Moffett and Hunt 1943). They are sight feeders primarily adapted to daylight activity (Ali et al. 1977).

Males mature earlier but do not live as long or grow as fast as do females (Scott and Crossman 1973). In Maryland many age-1 males of 115 mm TL were mature, but females were not mature until age 3 and 170 mm TL (Muncy 1962). All age-2 males greater than 130 mm TL and all age-3 females greater than 145 mm TL were mature in a South Carolina reservoir (Clugston et al. 1978). Few yellow perch in Claytor Lake survived past age 4; maximum longevity was age 7 (Hart 1981). Miller and Buss (1962) reported longevity of 13 years in Pennsylvania.

Growth varies considerably among water bodies, especially in the first year, and fish in dense populations frequently exhibit stunting (Ney 1978). Age-3 adults from the New River and Claytor Lake aver-

aged 241 and 201 mm TL (Wollitz 1972; Smith and Kauffman 1982). Growth in these Virginia populations was slightly greater than for most northern populations summarized in Clugston et al. (1978) and Ney (1978). The Virginia record is 1.0 kg (2 pounds 5 ounces), which is nearly doubled by the world record specimen of 1.9 kg (4 pounds 3 ounces), caught in 1865 in New Jersey.

Spawning can occur in late winter (Maryland) to early summer (Minnesota) over a temperature range of 2.0 to 18.6°C (Hokanson 1977). Peak spawning activity lasted for about three days in Maryland at 8.5–10°C, a range almost identical to the temperature range of greatest gamete viability (Tsai and Gibson 1971; Hokanson 1977). Spawning typically occurs at night in shallow areas over vegetation, submerged trees, and sandy to rocky bottoms. Coastal Plain populations spawn in nontidal and tidal water up to 2.5‰ salinity (Muncy 1962; Mansueti 1964). Spawning occurs communally with up to 25 males pursuing a female (Harrington 1947c). The female has a single ovary which produces a gelatinous accordion-like ribbon of densely packed eggs, a gamete configuration unique among North American fishes. The strands of eggs have an internal passage which may aid aeration, and are up to 2.4 m long (Hardy 1978b). Single eggs are immediately recognizable by the many attachment discs. Fecundity is 2,000–157,600 eggs (Brazo et al. 1975; Hardy 1978b).

HABITAT

Yellow perch occur in a wide range of cool- and warmwater habitats. They are found in creeks, streams, and rivers of low to moderate gradient, where they prefer pools and backwaters; they also are characteristic of ponds and lakes. They occupy waters which vary considerably in color, turbidity, pH, and productivity. Occurrence at pH 4.4 has been recorded from a bog lake (Rahel 1982 in Hastings 1984). Yellow perch extend into brackish zones of rivers down to salinities of 12.9‰ (Hildebrand and Schroeder 1928). They are gregarious; schools or small groups roam in shallow areas among vegetation and other cover during warm months; in winter they retreat to deeper, more open areas.

DISTRIBUTION   Map 158

Perca flavescens is native from the middle Mackenzie drainage in Canada southeast through lower Hudson Bay to the Great Lakes–St. Lawrence and upper Mississippi basins, and on the Atlantic slope possibly to South Carolina (Lee *in* Lee et al. 1980). It has been extensively introduced outside its native range.

In Virginia the yellow perch has a Coastal Plain–lower Piedmont predilection. It is native to the Atlantic slope and has been introduced to the New drainage. Previous studies questioned its native status on the Virginia Atlantic slope (Andrews 1971; Jenkins et al. 1972; Stauffer et al. 1982). This uncertainty was based partly on the lack of capture by Jordan (1889b) and on the early active stocking by the USFC and VFC. However, Lawson's (1709) listing from eastern North Carolina of the "First Pearch," which he considered to be the "same sort of Pearch as are in England" (i.e., *Perca fluviatilis*), could refer only to *P. flavescens*. The latter was also listed by Uhler and Lugger (1876) from Maryland. The disjunct record in Craig Creek of the upper James drainage is dated 1971; the specimen likely escaped from a fee-fishing pond in the upper Craig system.

The earliest dates of introduction of yellow perch to the New drainage in Virginia appear to be 1917–1921 (Fearnow 1929), when it was released at several places in Reed Creek. Claytor Lake was never stocked with *P. flavescens* (Hart 1981); the population probably is derived from perch previously established in the New River.

Abundance.—Rare to common; sometimes abundant below the Fall Line.

REMARKS

Fun and easy to catch and a joy to eat, the yellow perch is a basic panfish. It is many a youngster's "first fish." Locations of good populations of large perch often are guarded secrets, for the fillet is as valued as that of its walleye kin. It is an important commercial foodfish in the Great Lakes region.

Name.—*Flavescens*, "yellowish," describes a dominant base color. Often called raccoon or ringed perch in our region, from the barred color pattern.

Darters and Logperches

This genus of darters contains about 40 species including at least 5 that are undescribed; 15 species occur in Virginia. *Percina* species are distinguished from other darters by a row of enlarged, often spinous-edged scales along the midline of the breast and belly; these features are best developed in males and may be absent in some females. Most *Percina* have a row of dark blotches along the side; in some species these are modified into narrow bars or united into a broad midlateral stripe. A few species have diverse bright chromatic colors. The largest darters are in *Percina*, although many are as small as is typical in *Etheostoma*.

Genus *Percina* Haldeman

Name.—*Percina*, diminutive for *Perca*, means "little perch."

Dusky darter   *Percina sciera* (Swain)

SYSTEMATICS

The dusky darter was described from Indiana in 1883. It is the only Virginia member of the subgenus *Hadropterus*, a southern group treated by Richards and Knapp (1964) and Suttkus and Ramsey (1967).

Two subspecies are recognized, of which *P. s. sciera* is the Virginia form (Hubbs 1954a).

DESCRIPTION

Materials.—Mississippi basin populations: Hubbs (1954a), Richards and Knapp (1964), Page (1983), 8

Fish 247 *Percina sciera* adult male 84 mm SL (REJ 349), VA, Scott County, Copper Creek, 11 October 1969.

Fish 248 *Percina sciera* juvenile 38 mm SL (SIUC 8998), KY, Graves County, unnamed tributary, 13 November 1983.

series from the central Mississippi basin, and 6 from the upper Clinch system. Life color from Page and P. Smith (1970), Kuehne and Barbour (1983), Page (1983), and 1 Clinch River adult.

Anatomy.—A blotched or wholly dark darter with usually 3 caudal spots; adults are 50–100 mm SL. Form of body and snout moderate; frenum well developed; branchiostegal membranes moderately conjoined; caudal fin emarginate. Nuptial male with a low keratinized ridge along anal rays. Female genital papilla short, ridged, tip fimbriate.

Cheek, opercle, nape, belly, prepectoral, and most of breast scaled. Modified midventral scales in male, 0(2) on midbreast, 2–3 interpelvic, belly with nearly complete row, spines slightly elevated or not elevated when breeding; female with 2–3 slightly modified interpelvic scales.

Meristics.—Lateral line complete, scales (56)59–68(71); scales above lateral line 7–10; scales below lateral line 12–16; circumpeduncle scales 21–28. Dorsal spines (10)11–13(14); dorsal rays 11–12(13); anal spines 2; anal rays (7)8–9(10); pectoral rays (12)13–15.

Color in Preservative.—Lateral body with 8–12 large dark blotches, interconnected with smaller dusky to dark areas. Back with 8–10 saddles, which are occasionally obscured by general duskiness in males. Dorsolateral area with irregular dark marks, often connected to lateral blotches, occasionally to saddles. Lower side and belly pale, dusky, or darkly blotched. Preocular bars conjoined at snout tip; postocular bar distinct; subocular bar often absent. Adult male usually darker overall, patterns less distinct than in female.

First dorsal fin almost uniformly light dusky or lightly tessellated, darker basally in male. Second dorsal and anal fin tessellated, basally dusky. Caudal fin tessellated; caudal base with 3 vertically aligned spots, lower 2 often fused and combined with last lateral blotch. Pelvic and pectoral fins uniformly pale or moderately tessellated. In nuptial male, fins dusky to dark and body very dark, lateral blotching often obscured.

Color in Life   Plate 31.—Adult ground color olive dorsally, yellow to yellow-brown laterally, yellow to white ventrally; markings dark brown to black. Large breeding male dark brown-black; black vertical bars extending dorsally over back; upper body with blue-green iridescence. First dorsal fin dusky olive-brown, sometimes with faint yellow-orange band distally.

Larvae.—Described by Page and P. Smith (1970).

BIOLOGY

The dusky darter's diet is mainly midge and blackfly larvae, seasonally supplemented by caddisfly and mayfly larvae (Page and P. Smith 1970; Miller 1983). Most individuals mature by age 1; maximum life span is 4.5 years. Males grow more rapidly than females, averaging 73 mm SL (females 62 mm) in the second year. Maximum length is 110 mm SL (Page 1983); the largest Virginia specimen is 84 mm SL.

Reproduction has been described for an Illinois population (Page and P. Smith 1970). Spawning occurs in May to early July in gravel riffles; males apparently are territorial. It is likely that *P. sciera* buries its eggs. Fecundity is 80–196 mature eggs. Natural hybridization is known with *P. caprodes* (Hubbs and

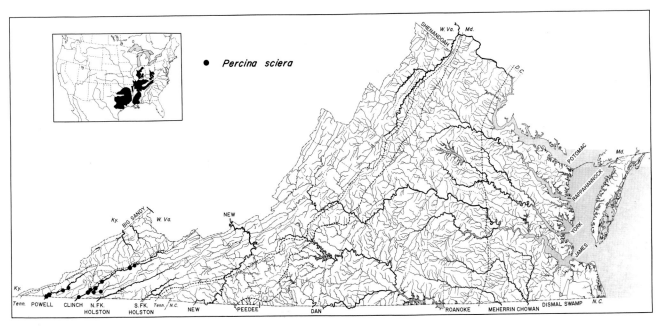

Map 159   Dusky darter.

Laritz 1961) and *P. nigrofasciata* (Suttkus and Ramsey 1967).

HABITAT

Over its range the dusky darter typically inhabits warm, low to moderate-gradient streams and rivers with ample areas of clean gravel bottom. It prefers runs and riffles of moderate depth in northern areas (Page and P. Smith 1970; Trautman 1981). In Virginia and eastern Tennessee it is nearly restricted to rivers and lower reaches of larger tributaries, and is virtually always found in margins of gentle runs and pools.

DISTRIBUTION   Map 159

Percina sciera is widespread in the middle and lower Mississippi basin and on the central and western Gulf slope. In Virginia it is confined to the Clinch and Powell rivers and lower Copper Creek. Feeman (1980) listed *P. sciera* from two North Fork Holston River localities, an error apparently repeated in part by Lee et al. (1980); see *P. macrocephala*. The dusky darter is known from the upper Big Sandy drainage in Kentucky, just below the Virginia line.

Abundance.—Rare, taken in small numbers in only 22 collections.

REMARKS

Although widespread and often common in parts of its range, the dusky darter is an obscure species in Virginia.

Name.—*Sciera* means "dusky."

Sharpnose darter   *Percina oxyrhynchus* (Hubbs and Raney)

SYSTEMATICS

The sharpnose darter was described from West Virginia and the New River of Virginia by Hubbs and Raney (1939). It is placed in the subgenus *Swainia* together with four other Mississippi basin species including its sister species *P. squamata* (Page 1974; Mayden 1985a; Wiley and Mayden 1985). Systematics of *Swainia* are treated in detail by Thompson (1977).

DESCRIPTION

Materials.—From Page (1977, 1983), Thompson (1977), and 17 Virginia lots (10 from the New drainage, 7 from the Big Sandy). Life color from 15 Virginia adults.

Anatomy.—An elongate darter with a long sharp snout; adults are 55–90 mm SL. Body elongate, slightly compressed; snout particularly elongate, slender, sharp-tipped; frenum wide; branchiostegal membranes moderately or

Fish 249 *Percina oxyrhynchus* adult male 69 mm SL (REJ 972), VA, Grayson County, Big Fox Creek, 10 June 1983.

Fish 250 *Percina oxyrhynchus* subadult 58 mm SL (WHH 107), VA, Dickenson County, Russell Fork, 29 June 1983.

broadly united; caudal fin slightly emarginate; lower fins moderate or short. Breeding male with keratinized ridge on anal and pelvic fin rays. Female genital papilla moderate in length, broad, flattened, ridged, sometimes subdivided distally.

Cheek sometimes fully scaled, upper half usually covered with embedded cycloid scales; opercle, nape, and belly completely scaled; breast naked or as much as half-scaled; prepectoral area often scaled. Modified midventral scales present in both sexes, 1–3 on midbreast, 1–2 interpelvic, complete or nearly complete row on belly, scales less modified in female; spines usually erect.

Meristics.—Lateral line complete, scales (66)70–79(82); scales above lateral line 9–12(13); scales below lateral line (13)14–15(16); circumpeduncle scales 24–31. Dorsal spines (12)13–14; dorsal rays (11)13(14); anal spines 2; anal rays 8–9; pectoral rays (13)14(15).

Color in Preservative.—Lateral body with 9–12 vague or distinct dark blotches connected by narrow, faintly dusky areas; blotches vaguely extend slightly more dorsad and ventrad in some breeding males than in females; back with 10–12 saddles. Dorsolateral area with variable dark markings; lower side and belly pale or dusky. Preocular bars conjoined at snout tip; postocular bar well developed; subocular bar rarely present, then vague.

First dorsal fin banded, narrow clear distal edge, dark subdistally, submarginally a broad pale band, medially to basally dark to dusky. Second dorsal, anal, and pelvic membranes dusky basally, fading distally; second dorsal and caudal rays usually tessellated, occasionally uniformly dark. Caudal base with small dark spot. Pectoral fin pigmented on rays only. Spawning male becomes distinctly more dusky on the body, obscuring color patterns, and fins darken, masking tessellations; female patterns remain distinct.

Color in Life Plate 31.—Adult dark olive to brown-black dorsally, olive dorsolaterally, olive to yellow laterally and ventrally; markings dark olive to brown; opercle and anterior pectoral base with blue-green iridescence. First dorsal fin bands: narrow clear edge; dusky or black subdistally; orange submarginally; basal half dusky or black; orange brighter and dusky areas darker in nuptial male. Second dorsal membranes dusky to black, rays olive and suffused with orange, most intense on leading ray. Other fins generally pale or olive. Dorsal and ventral areas of caudal fin with orange tint.

BIOLOGY

The biology of *P. oxyrhynchus* is largely unknown but probably is similar to that of *P. phoxocephala*, a species of the subgenus *Swainia* studied by Page and Smith (1971). Three sharpnose darters ate mostly mayfly and caddisfly larvae; midge and blackfly larvae were also taken (Hess 1983). The largest known specimen is 97 mm SL and from Virginia (Thompson 1977). Thompson deduced the spawning period to be centered in May, possibly extending from April to early June. Our 27 April female was gravid; a 14 June sample appears to have been taken near the height of spawning; a 28 June female was spent. *Percina oxyrhyncus* probably is an egg-burier, as known for *P. phoxocephala* (Page and Simon 1988). Natural hybridization with *P. roanoka* is discussed by Hocutt and Hambrick (1973).

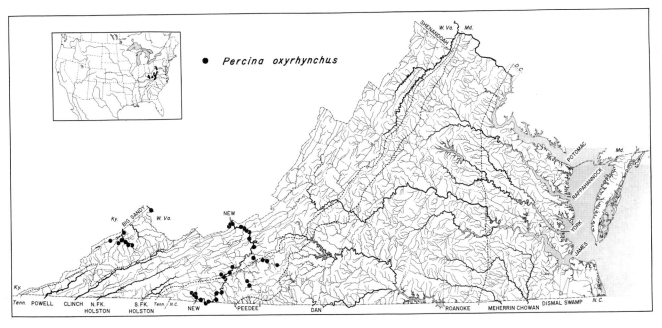

Map 160   Sharpnose darter.

HABITAT

Percina oxyrhynchus occupies moderate-gradient streams and rivers (Denoncourt et al. 1977a; Thompson 1977). Adults are typically found among unsilted gravel, rubble, and boulders in runs and riffles; juveniles are more frequently taken over sand in lesser current. The sharpnose darter fares better than most darters in the generally silty Russell Fork system of the Big Sandy drainage. It inhabits cool and warm streams, and frequently occurred in a heated discharge of 35°C in the New River (Stauffer et al. 1976).

DISTRIBUTION   Map 160

The sharpnose darter is found in drainages entering the upper and middle Ohio River from the south,

including the New and Big Sandy of Virginia. Its distinctly varied success in the main branches of the Big Sandy is puzzling.

Abundance.—Generally uncommon or rare.

REMARKS

The long sharp snout of *P. oxyrhynchus* may be an adaptation for grasping cryptic food items from small crevices among stones, as suggested by the photograph of a foraging *P. phoxocephala* (Page 1983).

Name.—*Oxyrhynchus* means "sharp nose." The *-us* ending is an emendation from *-a* by Robins et al. (1991).

Blotchside logperch   *Percina burtoni* Fowler

SYSTEMATICS

Percina burtoni is a member of the subgenus *Percina*—the logperches, a group of large darters that use their distinctive snout to overturn stones while foraging. It had long been held that there were only one or two species of logperches, but the subgenus contains 12 forms including at least 9 species, some undescribed (Jenkins 1976; Jenkins et al. 1977; Thompson 1978, 1985 *in* Lee et al. 1980; Morris and Page 1981). Page (1974) ranked the subgenus *Percina* as the most advanced of the genus, phyletically dis-

tant from the subgenus *Swaina*. Thompson (1977) and we place the subgenus *Percina* closest to *Swaina*.

Cope (1868b) and Jordan (1889b) caught the blotchside logperch in the North Fork Holston River and considered it to be a "marked variety" of *P. caprodes*. In a pioneer study of geographic and ontogenetic variation in fishes, specifically of logperches, Moenkhaus (1894) also recognized the distinctness of the blotchside logperch. With Cope's specimens and one from North Carolina, Fowler (1945) described the blotchside logperch as a subspecies of *P. caprodes*.

Morphology and color of *P. burtoni* and its frequent syntopy and lack of interbreeding with *P. c. caprodes* led R. E. Jenkins and T. Zorach to recommend it for species rank to the American Fisheries Society's Names Committee (Bailey et al. 1970); that status has been unanimously accepted. *Percina burtoni* is most closely related to certain logperches, such as *P. rex*, having an orange band in the first dorsal fin and blotched sides.

DESCRIPTION

Materials.—Sixty-six lots from throughout the species' range. Color in life from 14 Virginia specimens including 4 nuptial males.

Anatomy.—A blotch-sided, scrawl-backed darter with a long, conic or piglike snout; adults are 85–130 mm SL. Body form moderate or robust; snout long, broad, tip declivous, much exceeding upper jaw, hence mouth inferior; snout tip in young and juvenile sharp, slightly rounded, or blunt; snout tip in adult bulbous or blunt, often callous anteriorly and dorsally, dorsal surface transversely grooved. Frenum wide; branchiostegal membranes slightly conjoined; both dorsal fins highest in adult male; caudal fin slightly emarginate, truncate, or very slightly rounded, lower lobe often slightly longer in adult male. Female genital papilla short,

flat or moundlike, triangular, broadly rounded or truncate, smooth or ridged, tip often with one to several lobules (Figure 70); male papilla usually slightly shorter, smooth or pitted, otherwise similar to female. Nuptial male with tubercles on lower body scales; pelvic and anal rays and lower rays of caudal and pectoral fins each with a keratinized ridge.

Cheek and opercle 80–100% scaled; nape (0)10–70(100)% scaled; belly 60–100% scaled; breast 10–20% scaled; prepectoral area with 0–9(19) scales. Modified midventral scales of male a complete or nearly complete row on belly and a patch in interpelvic area, sometimes also on midbreast; spines retrorse to erect when breeding; female with few, less-modified scales, these often only in interpelvic area.

Meristics.—Lateral line complete, scales (86)87–94; scales above lateral line (9)12–16(18); scales below lateral line (16)18–23(26); circumpeduncle scales (32)33–39(40). Dorsal spines (15)16–17(18); dorsal rays (13)14–16; anal spines 2; anal rays (10)11–12; pectoral rays 14–15(16); gill rakers 17–20. Cephalic lateralis canals uninterrupted, pores: IO 9–10; SO 4; LC (anterior to ST) 2–3; POM 9–11; ST 3.

Color in Preservative.—Female and nonbreeding male with back and upper side vertically scrawled, 8–11 of these marks forming narrow saddles, many scrawls connected with large lateral blotches; the 7–9 blotches round or oval, often higher than wide, and often diffusing ventrad. Head

Fish 251 *Percina burtoni* adult male 107 mm SL (REJ 1182), VA, Smyth County, North Fork Holston River, 19 April 1986.

Fish 252 *Percina burtoni* adult female 94 mm SL (REJ 1182), VA, Smyth County, North Fork Holston River, 19 April 1986.

dorsum uniformly dark or vermiculated; subocular bar diffuse or moderately distinct, wide; other head marks diffuse to prominent; chin and gular area pale or dusky, more notably dusky along lower jaw; prepectoral area lightly or moderately peppered, no spot or blotch.

First dorsal fin with narrow dusky to dark distal margin along posterior one-third–one-fifth; margin pale (clear or opaque) elsewhere as is submarginal band; remainder of fin duskily to darkly mottled or streaked; spines lightly to moderately tessellated. Second dorsal membranes slightly mottled to streaked, rays slightly to moderately tessellated. Caudal fin as second dorsal except membranes pale. Caudal spot intense, round, medial, and distinct, or in larger specimens, diffuse, elongated ventrad, submedial, connected to last blotch. Lower fins pale or pectoral rays uniformly dusky or weakly tessellated.

Nuptial male slightly duskier overall, particularly the underside; breast sooty or dark; scrawling and other body and head marks, except main saddles and lateral blotches, reduced. First dorsal fin distally and subdistally pale except for narrow black edge along posterior one-third–one-fifth; remainder of membranes uniformly dusky except sometimes spotted basally; spines nontessellated. Second dorsal membranes with dusky or dark streak from base to margin, intensified distally to form dusky or black margin. Caudal membranes mostly pale, margin pale or dark; rays weakly to nontessellated. Anal fin usually slightly duskier distally and basally than subdistally. Pelvic fin moderately dusky or black. Pectoral membranes pale or moderately dusky; rays nontessellated.

Color in Life Plate 31.—Juvenile and adult, except nuptial male, with body ground shade straw to pale olive dorsally, pale to yellow-olive on lower side, belly white; markings dark olive to black; gold, green, or blue iridescence on side of head, prepectoral area, and lateral blotches; iris silver, pale copper, and dusky. Fin marks olive-brown to brown-black; except for marks, rays pale to yellow-olive; first dorsal membranes submarginally lack color in small specimens, pale orange in larger ones.

Nuptial male as adult female except head and body tone dusky olive, anterior underside dusky or sooty black; first dorsal fin bright red-orange submarginally, narrow clear margin along most of fin, black-edged posteriorly; streaks in both dorsal fins tan-orange except brown-black basally in second dorsal; second dorsal and caudal margins blackish; pelvic fin quite sooty or black. Darkening of general body and, particularly, the breast, pelvic fin, and margins of second dorsal and caudal fins seen only in April–June males; intensification of orange in dorsal fins may be restricted to that period.

BIOLOGY

The specific foods taken by *P. burtoni* have not been determined, but undoubtedly are largely benthic insects similar to those eaten by *P. rex* and *P. caprodes*. Beginning when young, logperches use their snout to push or, usually, overturn stones, shells, and sticks in search of insects beneath. The long, broad, conic or piglike snout and large (for darters) body size of logperches adapts them to this manner of feeding. Often the moved stones are one-third the size of the fish; we saw a *P. burtoni* overturn a stone that was slightly longer than itself. Three juveniles actively turned stones, averaging 9.3 flips/minute/fish, during 8 minutes in Copper Creek; similar behavior was observed in the Little River, Tennessee. Less frequently, food was gleaned from the general surface of the substrate. However, Greenberg (1991) recorded only 25% of the feeding bites of *P. burtoni* to occur at flipped stones; he found that this species fed only from gravel and rubble. W. C. Starnes and N. M. Burkhead filmed a blotchside logperch which used the snout to smash a caddisfly stone case attached to a rock and then ate the exposed larva.

Yearlings are immature; longevity is at least 4 years. Males probably grow faster than do females. Five reproductive males from Virginia and Tennessee were 115–138 mm SL, mean, 127, and five such females were 82–126 mm, mean, 102. The largest known specimen of each sex is included in these ranges and is from Virginia; the largest male was 160 mm TL.

Spawning apparently starts in April and probably extends into June. A female taken on 10 April had a mature egg within the tip of the genital papilla. Three late-April females were fully gravid. One female each taken on 16 and 30 June appeared to have been still capable of spawning. A 10 June male was shedding fin ridges and interconnecting keratinized tissue in strips; apparently this tissue is normally deciduous postnuptially.

Spawning habitat probably is clean loose gravel in moderate to strong flow. Twice at the head of pools, in the same or consecutive net hauls, we caught a fully gravid female with a peak-colored nuptial male. These likely were spawning or imminently spawning pairs; no other adults were found in intensive sampling of the sites. These instances occurred in Copper Creek on 25 April 1971 and the North Fork Holston River on 19 April 1986; water was 19°C in the Holston site.

HABITAT

Percina burtoni mainly populates medium to large streams and small rivers having moderate gradient, warm and typically clear water, and largely unsilted substrates of mostly gravel and rubble. In Virginia, young frequented slow runs and pools; larger juveniles and adults occupied riffles, runs, and occasionally pools. In eastern Tennessee, this species occu-

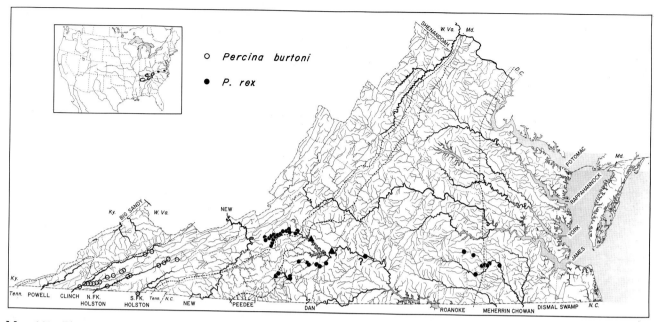

Map 161 Blotchside logperch and Roanoke logperch. Middle Roanoke River record of *P. rex* is unverifiable.

pied runs and pools, spending about 25% of the time above the bottom (Greenberg 1991).

DISTRIBUTION   Map 161

The blotchside logperch has been found in uplands and mountains of the middle Cumberland drainage and most major subdivisions of the Tennessee drainage. It may be extirpated in the Cumberland and occurs disjunctly in the Tennessee. In Virginia it occupies the North Fork Holston River, the lower section of a major upper North Fork tributary (Laurel Creek), the Clinch River within 8 rkm of two major tributaries (Copper Creek and Little River), and both of these Clinch tributaries. Only in Copper Creek has *P. burtoni* been found to extend into the lower headwaters. It was taken in the South Fork Holston River of Tennessee near the Virginia line just before impoundment. Recent extensive surveying indicates it to be absent from the entire South and Middle forks of the Holston and from the Powell River.

Percina burtoni appears to have recently expanded its range or locally increased its population density in the North Fork Holston. During 1867–1980 it was known only from Saltville and upstream in Smyth County; it has persisted there. We found it at Holston Mill, Scott County, on only the two latest visits, 1981 and 1984; the site had been sampled seven times during 1954–1975. We also found *P. burtoni* at two sites in middle Washington County—Buffalo Ford and about 2 rkm upstream—in 1984; it was found at neither in 1983. None were seen at many apparently suitable sites in Scott and Washington counties during 1970–1984.

Abundance.—Uncommon or rare in all extant populations throughout the range (e.g., Greenberg 1991). Most collections contain one or two specimens; the most taken in any sample during the 1900s was six specimens. Snorkeling through prime habitat in lower Copper Creek in 1973 revealed 1–4 fish in some run–pool sites, and none in others. In 1984 a few groups each of 10–20 juveniles were seen in Copper Creek at its mouth, and one small group was found in the North Fork Holston River. *Percina burtoni* at the mouth of Copper Creek were impeded from entering the creek because the entire flow was funneled at high velocity through a large culvert placed there temporarily during bridge construction. They were intermixed with juveniles of other blotched darters, *P. aurantiaca* and *P. evides*.

REMARKS

The stately blotchside logperch is one of Virginia's largest darters. Its foraging by flipping stones is fascinating to watch. Overturning stones opens a food source largely unexploited by fishes, and this species also feeds by normal means. Paradoxically, *P. burtoni* generally is localized and uncommon or rare. It may not find enough nonembedded stones for foraging in quiet water, but the typically higher density of aquatic insects in runs and riffles suggests that food is not a limiting resource. Hence, this species may naturally occur in low densities. A similar case exists for the Roanoke logperch.

The blotchside logperch is considered of special concern in Virginia (Burkhead and Jenkins 1991). Nearly all extant populations, most of which are localized, are in Virginia and Tennessee. It is apparently extirpated from Kentucky, possibly so from North Carolina, and barely persists in Alabama. Its recent apparent increase in the North Fork Holston River is encouraging, but this species is close to being threatened nationally.

Name.—For E. Milby Burton, former Director of the Charleston Museum, who caught the holotype.

Roanoke logperch   *Percina rex* (Jordan and Evermann)

SYSTEMATICS

Percina rex, subgenus *Percina*, was described from the upper Roanoke River by Jordan and Evermann (*in* Jordan 1889a). Fowler (1945) considered it a subspecies of *P. caprodes* but was not followed. An unpublished study by R. E. Jenkins and T. Zorach determined that the Roanoke logperch clearly merited species standing. *Percina rex* probably is most closely related to the geographically disjunct *P. burtoni*.

DESCRIPTION

Materials.—One hundred twelve lots representing all known populations. Color in life from 15 photographed specimens, 15 others in aquaria, some 30 feeding, and 3 spawning instream.

Anatomy.—A large darter with round or vertically elongate lateral blotches, back much scrawled, most fins strongly patterned, and snout moderate or long, conic or piglike; adults are 80–115 mm SL. Morphology essentially as described for *P. burtoni* except: body slightly less robust; snout moderate or long; branchiostegal membranes slightly or moderately conjoined; anal fin higher in adult male than in female; caudal fin slightly emarginate or truncate.

Cheek and opercle usually 80–100% scaled; nape 90–100% scaled; belly 70–80% scaled; breast 5–10% scaled, very rarely an unmodified scale centrally; prepectoral area with 0–4 scales. Modified midventral scales absent from central portion of breast in both sexes; belly row usually 70–80% complete in male, 30% in female; interpelvic area with patch of scales in both sexes; all scales less modified in female; spines retrorse or erect in nuptial male.

Meristics.—Lateral line complete or one unpored scale present posteriorly, scales 83–89(90); scales above lateral line (8)10–13; scales below lateral line 14–19; circumpeduncle scales (30)31–33(35). Dorsal spines (13)15–17; dorsal rays (14)15–16; anal spines 2; anal rays 10–12; pectoral rays 13–15; gill rakers 16–17(19). Cephalic lateralis canals uninterrupted, pores: IO (7)8–9(10); SO 4(5); LC (anterior to ST) 2–3; POM 9–11; ST 3(4).

Fish 253 *Percina rex* adult male 103 mm SL (REJ 1039), VA, Montgomery County, South Fork Roanoke River, 16 September 1983.

Fish 254 *Percina rex* adult female 90 mm SL (REJ 1039), VA, Montgomery County, South Fork Roanoke River, 16 September 1983.

Color in Preservative.—Mostly similar to *P. burtoni* in basic pattern, ontogenetic changes, and sexual dichromatism, but sharp differences exist: lateral blotches 8–11, oblong (longer vertically) or round, and centered well below lateral line, more frequently unconnected to dorsal marks, and in nuptial male, lower ends relatively distinct. Subocular bar prominent; oblique dark streak usually present postorbitally and one on cheek posteroventrally; prepectoral area usually with 1–2 large spots, or bar, or blotch, or wholly dark; chin often with a dark spot or bar medially, as well as a bar along lower jaw.

First dorsal fin with complete dusky or black margin, clear or opaque band entirely submarginal, basal half black-tessellated, black-streaked, or both; in nuptial male, basal half a wide black band. Second dorsal and caudal fins strongly black-tessellated, second dorsal membranes sometimes also streaked basally; membranes with margin or submargin (or both) dusky or black, equally or less intense than basally, and parts of margins often clear. Caudal spot not extended ventrad. Anal fin slightly tessellated or nontessellated, membranes slightly dusky basally and marginally. Pelvic fin typically pale; pectoral moderately or strongly tessellated.

In nuptial male, pelvic fin slightly or moderately dusky, uniformly so or slightly tessellated, never black; breast slightly dusky.

Color in Life Plate 31.—Much as in *P. burtoni* except for the following (most differences in types of melanophore patterns, their locations, and shades of darkness are noted above): marks on dorsal, caudal, and often the pectoral fins black; orange to red-orange band of first dorsal fin entirely bordered above by dusky or black. Nuptial male ground color becomes slightly duskier overall, fin marks blacker, and perhaps the red-orange of the first dorsal fin more brilliant; pelvic fin usually slightly or moderately dusky; breast slightly dusky at most.

BIOLOGY

Life history studies by Jenkins (1977b), Jenkins et al. (*in* Lee et al. 1980), and Burkhead (1983) provide the basis for this synopsis. The Roanoke logperch feeds benthically on a wide variety of immature insects. Young and juveniles prey heavily on midges, adults mainly on caddisflies and midges. A primary foraging tactic is overturning gravel and small rocks to locate food. Juveniles and adults flipped an average 2.3 stones per minute during 51 5-minute instream observation periods; young (observed only in aquaria) also turned stones. Food also was often sought from unturned substrate. Drifting invertebrates were not observed to be taken in nature, but aquarium specimens fed above the bottom as well as on it.

Males mature in 2 years, a few females may mature by age 2, and all females are mature by age 3. The oldest male and female both lived about 6.5 years.

Males may slightly exceed females in growth rate; age-3 males were 82–114 mm SL, mean, 90, and females 80–112 mm, mean, 88. The largest male was 122 mm SL, the largest female 116 mm.

Spawning probably occurs in mid-April to early May and may not extend into June (Burkhead 1983), contrary to Jenkins (1977b) and summaries of the latter by Jenkins and Musick (1979) and Jenkins et al. (*in* Lee et al. 1980). Four spawnings were witnessed during 0945–1130 hours on 20 April 1982 in the upper Roanoke River, water 12–14°C. Three or four males and one or two females were present in a swift, deep run floored with gravel and small rubble. Males acted aggressively toward each other; one or two at a time followed a female, apparently soliciting her by erecting the dorsal fins, while she roamed slowly about and sometimes fed. Just before some spawning acts, the male nudged the female with the snout. Spawning occurred with a male mounted on the female in typical *Percina* fashion; mounting and quivering lasted 2–5 seconds. During quivering the female was prevented from burying by the hard bottom. Mature ova counts are 180–640; eggs are adhesive and demersal.

HABITAT

Percina rex inhabits medium and large, warm, usually clear streams and small rivers of moderate and somewhat low gradient; two records are from impoundments. In streams, all life stages avoid moderately and heavily silted areas except during winter periods of inactivity. Most young and small juveniles were found in sandy areas of slow runs and pools. During most of the mild and warm months, adults commonly inhabit the main body of pools, runs, and riffles, and typically associate with gravel and rubble (Jenkins 1977b; Burkhead 1983; Simonson and Neves 1986). In Stony Creek, a largely sandy, silty, and slightly stained tributary of the Nottoway River, we found adult *P. rex* only on gravel patches. In the similar midsection of the Nottoway River the darter associates mainly with gravelly and rocky Fall Zone habitat and gravelly areas above and below the zone (Norman and Southwick 1985). Adults segregate before and during much of the spawning period—males in riffles, females in deeper runs. When water temperature drops below 8°C, *P. rex* goes under rocks and becomes quiescent (Burkhead 1983).

DISTRIBUTION Map 161

The Roanoke logperch is confined to the Roanoke and Chowan drainages of Virginia; the populations are small and separated by wide river gaps or large impoundments. In the Valley and Ridge Province, *P. rex* is contiguously distributed in the upper Roanoke River and its lower North and South forks, and is known from lower Mason and Tinker creeks. On the Piedmont, the Pigg River and the lowest reach of one of its tributaries—Big Chestnut Creek—are sparsely inhabited; 15 specimens are known since 1967 (Burkhead 1983; Simonson and Neves 1986). The record of an electrostunned but not captured "logperch" in the mid- or late 1970s in the middle Roanoke River is from a rocky swift section (L. G. Hart, personal communication). A search of the approximate locality in 1986 yielded no logperch (Simonson and Neves 1986).

Only two streams in the Dan system—the upper Smith River and one of its tributaries, lower Town Creek—are known to harbor *P. rex*. Our three upper Smith River records, totaling six specimens from two sites, are dated 1985–1986. The river was extensively sampled by electroshocking and two sites were rotenoned (Petrimoulx 1980; Simonson and Neves 1986; W. Adams, personal communication). The lower 1 rkm of Town Creek produced one specimen in the single collection made during 1977 and two in the collection made during 1991 (Jenkins 1977b; our data), and none in single samples made during 1979 and 1985. At about 4 rkm upstream (Route 606 bridge just below Henry), one Roanoke logperch was taken in each of the three collections made during 1986–1987 (Garman 1988, in litt.). None were found during 1979 in the section spanning 2 rkm below the upper site.

The outlying Chowan drainage population occupies a portion of the Nottoway system centered in and extending well above and below the Fall Zone. Recent records are from the Nottoway River, its tributary Stony Creek, and Butterwood Creek, an upper Stony Creek tributary (Jenkins et al. *in* Lee et al. 1980; Norman and Southwick 1985; Simonson and Neves 1986). Sappony Creek, a lower Stony Creek tributary, yielded three specimens in 1949 but none in 10 collections during 1978–1987.

The two impoundment records are curious; both reservoirs have been well surveyed. The adult taken in Smith Mountain Lake by electrofishing during 1981 in the upper end of the Beaverdam Creek arm probably strayed from the upper Roanoke River. We found no *P. rex* during 1983–1984 in the lowermost flowing section of Beaverdam Creek, a small silty creek. The other record is of two adults taken by rotenone during 1989 in a cove of Leesville Reservoir near its dam (M. C. Duvall, personal communication). The cove had been sampled in 1986 and perhaps earlier. The logperches likely came from the Pigg River, whose mouth is about 20 rkm above the cove.

Abundance.—Almost always rare or uncommon, never abundant; the largest population occupies the upper Roanoke River from Roanoke city into the lower reach of its main forks.

REMARKS

The Roanoke logperch is a relict survivor of logperch stock that dispersed to the Roanoke drainage from the Ohio basin. Its now-extinct ancestral stock must have occupied the New drainage.

David Starr Jordan (1889b) considered the Roanoke logperch to be a superb darter. Its maximum age of about 6.5 years is the oldest known among darters. Its stone-flipping foraging behavior is unusual among fishes; color paintings of *P. rex* in a stance to flip stones are in Anonymous (1974) and Ono et al. (1983). An exceptional record from a movement study concerns an adult found 2.3 rkm below the site where it had been marked 10 months earlier; the fish was on a fisherman's stringer with five other Roanoke logperch (Burkhead 1983).

Percina rex is an indicator of higher-quality streams in uplands of the Roanoke drainage; it has not fared well because such waters have been much reduced. Judging from its fragmented range, many Piedmont populations must have existed; most of them probably perished in the last 150 years. The continued existence of the population in the Pigg system probably is tenuous owing to low numbers of the species and siltation of the system. This is further indicated by the absence of *P. rex* from the neighboring Blackwater River and Back Creek, which have slightly better logperch habitat than the Pigg.

The sparse upper Smith River subpopulation is cut off from recruitment by Philpott Reservoir and jeopardized by chemical effluents and the proposed Charity Dam. The tiny Town Creek subpopulation is thermally isolated by the cold Smith River tailwater below Philpott Dam. Little hope would exist for expansion of the hypothetical middle Roanoke population; the tailwater river usually is turbid and its flow fluctuates markedly. The Chowan drainage population apparently is confined to two or three streams. The uppermost Roanoke drainage population, perhaps the only strong one, occupies a small area that is continually encroached upon by industrial, residential, and agricultural development (Burkhead 1983). Segments of the population currently are jeopardized by a proposed water-supply impoundment and a channelization project (Moser 1989, 1991).

The Roanoke logperch has been a prime candidate for protective status owing to its small total range, the disjunction and low population density of the essentially four populations, and the immediate threats to the best (upper Roanoke) population. The populations in the Pigg, Smith, and Nottoway systems could perish with minor habitat degradation. Simonson and Neves (1986) determined that the stream lengths within the ranges of the populations total 235.2 rkm. However, they estimated that in these reaches there are only 34.2 rkm of habitat occupied by or suited to *P. rex*.

Threatened status nationally was recommended for the Roanoke logperch based on extensive studies by Jenkins (1977b) and Burkhead (1983). Coupling these studies with the wider sampling and analysis by Simonson and Neves (1986), and recognizing the ongoing and projected development of the upper Roanoke watershed, the USFWS listed *P. rex* as federally endangered in August 1989 (Moser 1989).

Name.—Jordan and Evermann crowned this darter *rex*—"king."

Logperch   *Percina caprodes* (Rafinesque)

SYSTEMATICS

The logperch, a member of the subgenus *Percina*, was described from the Ohio River in 1818. Moenkhaus (1894) discerned several infraspecific varieties; some of these and other forms are now recognized as distinct subspecies or species (see *P. burtoni*). Morris and Page (1981) defined subspecies of *P. caprodes*; the two in Virginia are the Ohio logperch *P. c. caprodes* and the northern logperch *P. c. semifasciata* (DeKay).

DESCRIPTION

Materials.—Ninety-five series of *P. c. caprodes* from throughout the Tennessee drainage and 18 series of *P. c. semifasciata* from the Potomac and Susquehanna drainages and two other upper Chesapeake Bay tributaries. The description pertains to *P. c. caprodes* unless otherwise indicated. Color in life mainly from 6 specimens from the upper Tennessee.

Anatomy.—A zebra-barred darter with a logperch type of snout and an elongate body; adults are 70–120 mm SL. Morphology as in *P. burtoni* except body more slender; snout shorter; anal fin longest in male (Reighard 1913); caudal fin slightly emarginate.

Cheek and opercle 90–100% scaled; nape (40)90–100% scaled; breast naked except for modified scales; belly partly scaled; prepectoral area naked. Modified midventral scales absent from midbreast; 0–6 interpelvic scales in both sexes; belly midline 80–100% scaled in male, modified scales absent in female; spines retrorse or erect in nuptial male.

Meristics.—Lateral line complete, scales (82)85–91(94); scales above lateral line (8)9–12(13); scales below lateral line (13)15–19(21); circumpeduncle scales (28)31–34(36). Dorsal spines (13)14–16(17); dorsal rays (13)15–17(18); anal spines 2; anal rays (9)10–11(13); pectoral rays 14–15(16); gill rakers 15–18. Cephalic lateralis canals uninterrupted, pores: IO 8–9(10); SO 4; LC (from ST anteriorly) 2–3; POM 9–10; ST 3(4).

Percina c. semifasciata is slightly less elongate; has larger scales, for example, lateral line (68)70–80(81); spine and ray counts modally lower; nape naked or nearly so.

Color in Preservative.—The basic body pattern of *P. c. caprodes* is one of dark, narrow, straight or slightly curved bars extending from midback ventrad; the (11)14–19(23) bars (9 primary ones) cross the lateral line and most continue onto the lower side, none markedly broadened or forming a blotch (see *Remarks*). Head dorsum uniform, occasionally vermiculate; head bars including subocular diffuse or absent; prepectoral spot and blotch absent.

First dorsal fin membranes slightly peppered basally, adult developing a dark streak in each that may extend to margin, least so in anterior membranes (which tend to have an oblique clear window submarginally); second dorsal membranes with dusky streak in basal half and dusky marginally. Dorsal and caudal fins with spines or rays tessellated. Basicaudal spot distinct, round, medial. Lower fins pale, slightly dusky, or pectoral vaguely tessellated. Nuptial male slightly darker than female (Reighard 1913; Winn 1958b), but fins never as boldly patterned as nuptial *P. rex*.

Percina c. semifasciata has fewer bars, usually 8–15 (8 primary ones) extending well below the lateral line; these tend slightly shorter and wider than in *P. c. caprodes*.

Fish 255 *Percina caprodes* adult male 87 mm SL (REJ 981), VA, Washington County, South Fork Holston River, 15 June 1983.

Color in Life Plate 31.—The differences of both sexes of *P. caprodes* from female and nonbreeding male *P. burtoni*, in addition to those indicated above for melanophore patterns, are: pale areas of midside iridescent pale green; lower side iridescent pale gold, green, or blue. Yellow or orange wash or band never seen in first dorsal fin of the many upper Tennessee fish examined, although spines and rays may be yellowish between dark tessellations.

Larvae.—Treated by Taber (1969), Cooper (1978), Grizzle and Curd (1978), Hardy (1978b), and Auer (1982f).

BIOLOGY

Larval and young logperch feed on microcrustaceans (Taber 1969); juveniles and adults take a wide variety of insects, other invertebrates, and occasionally fish eggs (Turner 1921; Cahn 1927; Keast and Webb 1966; Mullan et al. 1968; Thomas 1970; Hickman and Fitz 1978). In the juvenile stage, *P. caprodes* has an inflated swim bladder and may travel well above the bottom in calm water, but feeding occurs benthically (Dobbin 1941; Emery 1973; Grizzle and Curd 1978). Logperch also seek prey in lakes and streams by overturning stones (Keast and Webb 1966; Pflieger 1975; Greenberg 1991; observation by N. M. Burkhead in the Caddo River, Arkansas).

Logperch live about 4 years, rarely maturing by age 1. The sexes grow at equal rates, averaging 95–110 mm TL at age 2 in Illinois and Wisconsin (Thomas 1970; Lutterbie 1979). The largest fish, 155–160 mm SL, are from Arkansas (B. A. Thompson, in litt.). The largest from Virginia is 140 mm SL, one of the few *P. c. caprodes* from that part of the New drainage. *Percina c. semifasciata* reached at least 120 mm SL in the Potomac River.

Spawning occurs on sand or gravel in swift current of streams and near shores of lakes, from mid-March to mid-July depending on the location (Taber 1969; Page 1983). Hubbs and Strawn (1963) stated that reproduction is initiated by water temperatures of 10–15°C. Although based largely or entirely on logperch forms not occurring in Virginia, these temperatures probably apply to Virginia; spawning probably extends into the low 20°sC. We found *P. caprodes* in reproductive condition in the upper Tennessee drainage during 1 April–20 May. Unlike most darters, *P. caprodes* is not a territorial spawner; it often forms spawning groups, and one or more males attempt to supplant a male spawning with a single female. Eggs are buried by the spawning act; if not covered they are eaten by logperches and suckers (Reighard 1913; Ellis and Roe 1917; Winn 1958a, 1958b). Fecundity is 100–3,100 ova (Winn 1958b, whose counts probably include immature ova; Nance 1978 *in* Page 1983).

Percina caprodes has hybridized naturally with *P. sciera* (Hubbs and Laritz 1961), *P. phoxocephala* (Thompson 1977; Trautman 1981), *P. shumardi* (Carlander 1941; Hubbs 1945), and *P. maculata* (Hubbs and Brown 1929; Page 1976b; Thomas 1970). The cross *P. caprodes* × *P. copelandi* (Hubbs 1926) seems unlikely, and although relisted by Hubbs (1955), it was identified before Hubbs and colleagues clearly distinguished *P. copelandi* from another *Percina* species (Hubbs 1930b). Winn (1953, 1958b) observed *P. caprodes* in the spawning territory of *P. copelandi* but indicated that they bred at different times.

HABITAT

The logperch inhabits warm streams to large rivers of moderate gradient. It often populates lakes and reservoirs and was taken once in uppermost Claytor Lake. We found juvenile and adult *P. c. caprodes* frequently in riffles, runs, and pools of mostly gravel and rubble. In the Chesapeake region, *P. c. semifasciata* occupied mid-sized streams to large rivers. Smith and Bean (1899) stated that it was not uncommon in gravelly streams; most or all extant Potomac drainage specimens are from the Potomac River. It extended into tidal areas; Smith and Bean reported it taken by fishermen at Washington, D.C. wharves, and Mansueti (1964) took it in tidal freshwater in Maryland.

DISTRIBUTION   Map 162

Percina c. caprodes occurs throughout the Ohio basin and in the White, Ouachita, and Red drainages of the southwestern Mississippi basin. In the upper Tennessee drainage it is widely distributed in the Valley and Ridge Province but largely avoids the Blue Ridge. In Virginia its general range in the Clinch system is much like that of its close relative *P. burtoni*, although it is more a main-river inhabitant. It is repopulating the long reach of the Clinch River that was affected by the 1967 alkaline spill. It is widespread in the Powell River, from which *P. burtoni* is apparently absent; it extends farther up the South Fork Holston River than did *P. burtoni*. *Percina caprodes* appears to have been rare historically in the North Fork Holston River and remains rare; apparently it has not rebounded after pollution abatement to the extent that *P. burtoni* has—only one specimen is from below Saltville, in 1976. In the Big Sandy drainage of Virginia it is known only from Levisa Fork (one record in 1937, four in 1982) and Knox Creek (one record in 1988).

The first capture of the logperch in the New drainage in 1971 indicates recent introduction, but more

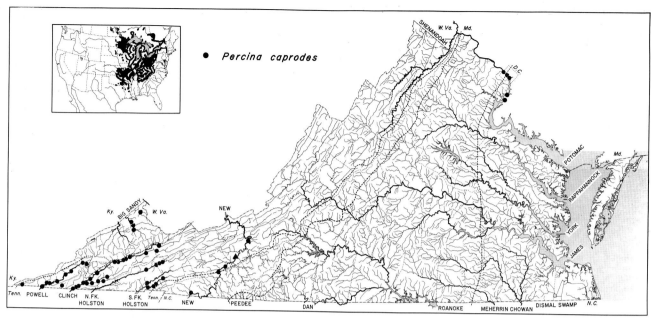

Map 162   Logperch.

likely the species is native, rare (as elsewhere in the Blue Ridge), and largely confined to the (previously poorly) sampled main channel. The now 19 records span from North Carolina (E. F. Menhinick, personal communication) to the lower Gauley River in West Virginia (Hocutt et al. 1979; Hess 1983). Our search to substantiate the report of *P. c. caprodes* in the Potomac drainage (Jenkins et al. 1972) has been fruitless and we no longer accept the record.

Percina c. semifasciata is widely distributed in the Hudson Bay, Great Lakes–St. Lawrence, and upper Mississippi basins; it intergrades along central parts of its southern fringe (Thompson *in* Lee et al. 1980; Morris and Page 1981; Trautman 1981). It is extirpated from the Potomac drainage, its southeastern limit. Six records, eight specimens (USNM) dated 1855–1910 are from the Potomac River within Washington, D.C., in and just below the Fall Line. It was also reported apparently from that area by Bean (1880) and Smith and Bean (1899). It occurred in the upper Potomac estuary proper or its tributaries, based on two specimens from Bryan Point in 1912 (USNM 85399–85400) and the record from Pomonkey Creek (Uhler and Lugger 1876), both places in Maryland. The last Potomac drainage record is from 1938 (Lee et al. 1981). The northern logperch persists in the lower Susquehanna River in Maryland and Pennsylvania, and in two of its tributaries in Lancaster and York counties, Pennsylvania. Concerning two upper Chesapeake tributaries, it is extirpated from Winters Run (A. W. Norden, in litt.) and has uncertain status in the Northeast River, where it was taken in 1950.

Lee et al. (1981) considered that, judging from localization, the Chesapeake basin populations may have been accidentally introduced. The earliest dates of capture in the Potomac—1855—and Susquehanna—1842 (Haldeman 1842)—bear against introduction.

Abundance.—Rare or uncommon.

REMARKS

The logperch is the first-described darter. The name *caprodes*—piglike, coined for the snout, is also applicable to the novel feeding behavior of this and other logperches (Moyle 1976; Burkhead and Jenkins 1977; Starnes and Etnier 1980). The snout is used to gain purchase on the underside of stones for pushing and overturning them, a deed involving considerable body-muscular effort. Uncovered substrate is then inspected for food.

At night logperch seek cover and become quiescent (Emery 1973). Trautman (1981) reported that during sunny days they hide under rocks or bury in sand with only the eyes exposed. Smith (1979) considered the name "logperch" to derive from its habit of hiding in brush and log jams. Emery (1973) did not find coloration of *P. c. semifasciata* at night to differ from that of daytime. However, at night we took adults of *P. c. caprodes* which had four of the saddles and the nine primary lateral bars much expanded; these marks and the side of head were much darker at night than during the day.

When fried, logperch are as desirable a foodfish as yellow perch and sunfishes (Eddy and Surber 1947).

The logperch has declined or disappeared owing to habitat perturbation in many areas beyond Virginia (Kuehne and Barbour 1983). It probably succumbed to extensive siltation in much of the upper Big Sandy drainage and was depleted in the North Fork Holston River owing to pollution from Saltville. Unlike *P. burtoni*, it has not clearly reestablished residence below Saltville. The Potomac drainage population apparently was extirpated by pollution and sedimentation (Lee 1977; Lee et al. 1984).

Name.—*Caprodes* means "like a pig," from the prominent snout that often is fleshy, upturned, and blunt. *Semifasciata* translates to "half-banded," referring to the fewer, shorter lateral bars of that subspecies.

Longhead darter   *Percina macrocephala* (Cope)

SYSTEMATICS

Percina macrocephala was described from Pennsylvania in 1869. Page (1978) found significant geographic variation in this species—at least three distinct population groups—but did not describe subspecies. Page (1974, 1978) considered *P. macrocephala* to be the most primitive member of the subgenus *Alvordius*, which comprises eight described species, seven of which occur in Virginia.

Among Virginia *Percina*, the maximum extent of elongation and elevation of ctenii on scales along the lower caudal peduncle and caudal base occurs in *P. macrocephala*. This condition grades toward that in the Kentuckian–Ozarkian subgenus *Odontopholis*, whose two species develop a highly spinose caudal keel and have pronounced ctenii on lower body scales (Collette 1965; Page 1976a). Peduncular spination may be interpreted as evidence for a close relationship between *P. macrocephala* and *Odontopholis*, and would be congruent with their strong resemblance in color pattern. If this hypothesis is accepted, then the relatively reduced ventral scales of *Odontopholis* would be an advanced trait, the function of the scales being supplanted by the caudal keel and anal fin.

DESCRIPTION

Materials.—Page's (1978, 1983) meristic data from the upper Tennessee drainage, and 1 West Virginia and 7 Virginia collections. Color in life from Page (1978, 1983) and 3 large adult females.

Anatomy.—A darter with broadly conjoined lateral blotches and a fairly long, subconic snout; adults are 65–90 mm SL. Body form moderately elongate; head long; snout long, somewhat sharp; frenum well developed; branchiostegal membranes separate; caudal fin slightly emarginate. Keratinized ridges absent or only slightly developed on anal rays of nuptial male. Female genital papilla short, broad, flat, and grooved ventrally and distally.

Cheek and opercle usually naked; nape scaled posteriorly except on midline; belly with normal scales posteriorly except on midline; breast usually naked, occasionally with a few embedded scales. Modified midventral scales in male, none on midbreast, 1–3 in interpelvic area, 9–18 on belly; female with a row of less-modified scales on belly. In nuptial male, modified scales with long, retrorse to antrorse spines, and scales along anal fin base and ventral caudal peduncle densely spinulose (INHS 27154).

Meristics.—Lateral line complete, scales 70–81(82); scales above lateral line (6)7–8(9); scales below lateral line (10)11–13(14); circumpeduncle scales 24–26(28). Dorsal spines (11)13–15(16); dorsal rays (11)12–13(14); anal spines 2; anal rays 8–10(11); pectoral rays (12)13–14.

Color in Preservative.—Lateral body with 8–14 broadly conjoined dark blotches, usually forming a dark stripe with undulate margins; in many specimens a narrow pale stripe accents the upper edge of most blotches; dorsolaterally usually uniformly dusky (upper Tennessee form normally

Fish 256 *Percina macrocephala* adult female 90 mm SL (REJ 1182), VA, Smyth County, North Fork Holston River, 19 April 1986.

lacks dorsal saddles); middorsally a dark stripe from occiput to posterior end of second dorsal fin; area on back between dorsal fins often darker than remainder of fin base, often producing a dark spot, particularly in juvenile and pale specimens. Lower side and venter pale, but somewhat dusky in spawning male; occasionally lower side with irregular dark patches. Preocular bar extends to upper lip, sometimes conjoined with bar on opposite side; subocular bar variable, fully developed and curving posteriad to underside of head, or interrupted, or absent; postocular bar wide, connecting with midlateral stripe; irregular dark patches occasionally on chin and gular area.

First dorsal fin banded, distally clear, subdistally black, submarginally clear, epibasally dark, basally clear. Other fins with rays tessellated, membranes clear in all but second dorsal, whose membranes in male have a dusky streak. Caudal fin base with dark round spot having a dusky or black bar connected ventrally.

Color in Life.—Dorsum and upper side olive, tan, or brown; markings brown to black; narrow straw or yellow stripe just above lateral blotches; lower side and venter yellow or white. Pale band of first dorsal fin lacks bright orange; other fins commonly pale yellow to olive. Three large adult females (collected 19 April or 3 May) lacked color in submargin of first dorsal fin; tessellated spines and rays with dark segments dusky to black, pale segments pale yellow; lateral blotches pale green when specimen electroshocked, darkening later.

COMPARISON

Although the longhead darter is very distinctive, many of its key characters tend to overlap with one or more other Virginia *Percina*. A character for quick separation of many *P. macrocephala* is the general presence of a distinct small dark area or spot on the back between the dorsal fins.

BIOLOGY

The scant life history data are mostly from Kentucky fish (Page 1978). Foods include mayfly larvae and crayfishes. In Tennessee, feeding occurred on most types of hard bottom, but not on sand or silt (Greenberg 1991). The life span is 3–4 years; yearlings are immature and are 50–66 mm SL in May. The maximum length reported is 102 mm SL from Kentucky; the largest Virginia specimen is 90 mm SL. Spawning probably occurs within March to May.

HABITAT

The longhead darter inhabits warm, clear streams and rivers of moderate gradient. In much of its range it occupies well-flowing pools, runs, and deep riffles with substrates ranging from weed beds to bedrock;

apparently the bottom usually is rocky (Lachner et al. 1950; Page 1978; Trautman 1981; Cooper 1983; Kuehne and Barbour 1983). In the upper Tennessee drainage of Tennessee, Greenberg (1991) found *P. macrocephala* in low current velocities and commonly in silted areas. Of the 12 species of darters that he studied, the longhead darter had the lowest residency rate and spent the most time (61%) in the water column.

In Virginia, all 12 juveniles and adults that we collected were in backwaters and pools that were well flowing or, more frequently, sluggish; some of these fish were in parts of long pools distant from riffles. These fish were taken close to stream banks during day and night, generally from slightly to heavily silted substrates which had detritus and sticks projecting above the substrate. This darter may use sunken brush and other material to keep itself above silt.

DISTRIBUTION   Map 163

Percina macrocephala has a spotty distribution throughout the Ohio basin. In Virginia it is known from two tributaries—Copper Creek and Little River—of the Clinch River and in the North and Middle forks of the Holston River. The actual site where the Little River specimen was taken in 1967 is unknown (R. E. Wollitz, in litt.).

Since 1970, the longhead darter has been verified only in lower Copper Creek and the North Fork Holston above Saltville. Feeman (1980) listed *P. sciera* from the North Fork at two sites: one near the state line, one above Saltville. Later he (1986) considered both records to have been *P. macrocephala*, but no specimens exist (J. C. Feeman, in litt.). We verified Feeman's (1986) second record of *P. macrocephala* from above Saltville, and also found this species there. The longhead darter was taken in the Middle Fork Holston River only during 1888 and 1937. It may have occupied the South Fork Holston River in Virginia; it was last taken in the river just below the Virginia line in 1947, shortly before impoundment.

Abundance.—Quite rare, only 29 specimens in 17 collections have been verified from Virginia. Although the Virginia habitat described above is sampled relatively infrequently in the upper Tennessee drainage, we have long recognized the longhead darter's association with it and frequently have sampled that habitat heavily in Copper Creek, generally without finding the darter. In 1986 we carefully sampled both sides of a long pool in the North Fork

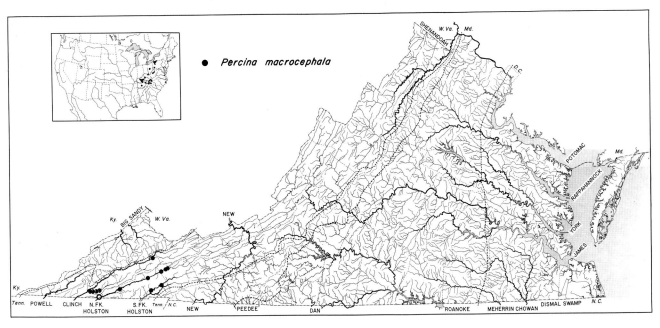

Percina macrocephala

Map 163 Longhead darter. Unverified record shown by open circle.

Holston River above Saltville, but found only one specimen.

REMARKS

Although the longhead darter lacks bright colors, it is a majestic species. Its frequency of eating cray-fishes, higher than that known for other darters, is related to its relatively large body and mouth size (Page 1978). It is threatened in Virginia because of its rarity and apparently shrinking distribution (Burkhead and Jenkins 1991).

Name.—*Macrocephala* means "big head."

Blackside darter   *Percina maculata* (Girard)

SYSTEMATICS

The blackside darter was described from Michigan in 1859. This member of the subgenus *Alvordius* is widespread in the Mississippi basin and elsewhere, contrasting with the complex of five *Alvordius* centered in the New and adjacent Atlantic slope drainages of Virginia. *Percina maculata* is closely related to *P. notogramma* of the central Atlantic slope.

DESCRIPTION

Materials.—From Beckham (1980, 1986), Page (1983), 3 series from Illinois, and 1 series from Tennessee. Life color from Petravicz (1938), Winn (1958b), and Page (1983).

Anatomy.—A laterally blotched and dorsolaterally variegated darter; adults are 40–70 mm SL. Body form moderate; snout moderate; frenum present; branchiostegal mem-

Fish 257 *Percina maculata* adult female 53 mm SL (SIUC 7446), IL, Effingham County, Little Wabash River, 26 February 1983.

branes separate or slightly united; caudal fin slightly emarginate. Nuptial male with keratinized ridge on anal rays and underside of pelvic rays. Female genital papilla moderate in length, broad, tip fimbriate.

Cheek nearly fully scaled; opercle fully scaled; nape moderately scaled; belly scaled except anteriorly in male and midventrally in female; breast usually naked. Midbelly of male with an incomplete row of 7–13 large modified scales, spines retrorse to erect when breeding; modified scales absent in female.

Meristics.—Lateral line complete, scales (53)60–75(81); scales above lateral line 7–11; scales below lateral line 10–13; circumpeduncle scales (18)20–26(29). Dorsal spines (12)13–15(17); dorsal rays (10)12–13(16); anal spines (1)2(3); anal rays (7)8–9(13); pectoral rays (11)13–14(16).

Color in Preservative.—Body side with 6–9 dark, horizontally elongate blotches, slightly or moderately interconnected by dusky to dark areas. Dorsum with 8–9 bilaterally symmetrical or asymmetrical brown saddles; predorsal saddle forked posteriorly, usually not contacting dorsal fin. Dorsolateral area with irregular brown marks, sometimes connected to saddles or lateral blotches, sometimes interconnected to form a wavy horizontal stripe. Ventrolateral area and venter pale. Preocular bar well developed, occasionally diffusing into darkened head color, stippling extending onto upper lip; postocular bar evident, sometimes interrupted, occasionally blending into lateral pigmentation; subocular bar usually well defined.

First dorsal fin partly or entirely dark to black basally, darkest anteriorly; pigmentation diffusing into subdistal level, sometimes darkening there, most so posteriorly; distal edge between each spine partly or entirely clear; membranes usually clear basally, clear areas extend distally along spines, interrupting dark areas; spines often tessellated except in large nuptial male. Second dorsal fin slightly dusky basally, fading toward margin, occasionally tessellated. Caudal rays tessellated, membranes clear; basicaudal spot medial. Lower fins generally clear or dusky, pectoral most often tessellated. Breeding male tends duskier than female.

Color in Life.—Ground color of adult yellow-olive to olive dorsally and laterally; venter white to yellow; markings light brown to black. Breeding male with iridescence on opercle and cheek becoming dusky emerald green; dark brown iris becomes brilliant gold. Also in breeding male, the dorsal design, lateral blotching, and ventral paleness may change into green or yellow-gold, overlaid by 6–7 wide slate-silver vertical bars, a color phase reported only by Petravicz (1938). Female retains subdued color throughout the year except that a mild overall duskiness develops during spawning. The intensity of the melanophore pattern can vary widely.

Larvae.—Described by Petravicz (1938) and Auer (1982f).

COMPARISON

Percina maculata was contrasted to *P. gymnocephala* by Beckham (1980, 1986). Slight modal differences were found in some external meristic characters; some head proportions differed sharply but the measured sample was small and needs supplementation.

Percina maculata is separable geographically from *P. gymnocephala*, a species endemic to the New drainage. The two are physically distinguishable by: (1) basicaudal spot [medial in *maculata* vs. centered submedially in juvenile, indistinct or absent (fused with last lateral blotch) in adult *gymnocephala*]; (2) first dorsal fin [shade gradually changing from dark near base to slightly paler submarginally, usually lacking distinct dark subdistal band, and narrow edge usually incompletely clear vs. distinctly paler submarginally than basal half, distinct dark band present subdistally, and the entire margin with a narrow clear band]; (3) opercle squamation [fully scaled vs. usually 20–60% scaled]; (4) modified midventral scales in female [absent vs. present].

BIOLOGY

Blackside darter young feed mainly on microcrustaceans; adults feed predominantly on insects (Forbes 1878; Turner 1921; Karr 1963; Thomas 1970; Page 1983). Trautman (1957) observed a high frequency of surface feeding by *P. maculata*, with occasional jumping for flying insects. Smart and Gee (1979) found that *P. maculata* often fed above the bottom and took more diverse food items than did a syntopic darter.

The larger females probably spawn at age 1; smaller ones probably first spawn in the second spring (Thomas 1970). Winn (1958b) concluded that yearlings were rarely mature. Maximum life span is slightly over 4 years (Thomas 1970). Apparently both sexes grow equally fast and reach similar maximum lengths. Fish of ages 2 and 3 averaged 66–80 mm TL (Karr 1963; Thomas 1970; Lutterbie 1979). The largest Virginia specimen is 57 mm SL; Beckham (1986) gave maximum length as 95 mm SL.

Reproductive data were reported by Petravicz (1938), Winn (1958a, 1958b), and Thomas (1970) from Illinois and Michigan. This darter migrates upstream to its spawning ground in March or April and probably spawns into mid-May. Petravicz observed spawning on 3 May at 16.5°C over sand and gravel in moderate current at a depth of about 30 cm. Hankinson (1932) witnessed *P. maculata* spawning on a *Nocomis* nest. It is considered an egg-burier, spawning as it burrows partially into sand or by forcing eggs into gravel interstices. Fecundity is 1,000–1,758 total ova (Winn 1958b). Natural hybridization has been documented with *P. caprodes* (see that species) and two extralimital darters.

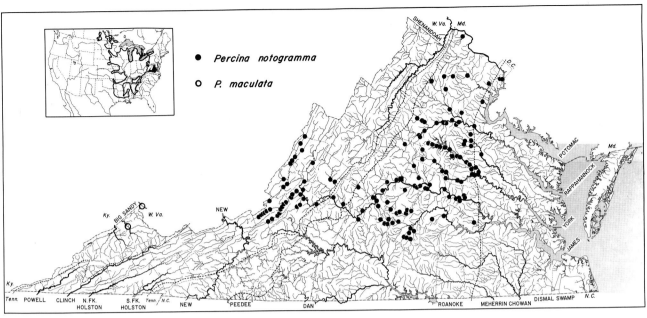

Map 164   Stripeback darter and blackside darter. Square on James River indicates Scottsville.

HABITAT

The blackside darter inhabits clean, cool and warm streams and rivers of moderate gradient. It can be found in the diverse currents of pools and riffles and over substrates varying from silt to rubble (Thomas 1970).

DISTRIBUTION   Map 164

Percina maculata is widely distributed in the Great Lakes–St. Lawrence and Mississippi basins and on the Gulf slope. In Virginia it is known from two streams in the Big Sandy drainage; both records are from 1937.

The record from the North Fork Holston River above Saltville stems from a 1928 collection by H. R. Becker (UMMZ 119678; Moore and Reeves 1955; Page 1983). We believe that the specimens are not from Virginia. In correspondence (UMMZ file) to Becker regarding his collections, the curator wrote that "The assistant this summer seems to have mixed up some of the labels . . ." *Percina maculata* is not otherwise known from the Tennessee drainage of Virginia. Another apparent locality error appears for *Etheostoma spectabile* in the same collection; this species is unknown from Virginia.

Abundance.—Apparently extirpated.

REMARKS

The blackside darter is widespread and common in much of its range. It probably was restricted in Virginia to the Big Sandy drainage where it may have been common; L. P. Schultz took it in 2 of 4 collections in 1937. Because no other records were found, Jenkins and Musick (1979) considered its status to be undetermined, possibly extirpated. The large number of collections since 1980, all lacking *P. maculata*, indicates that it is gone from the state.

Name.—*Maculata* means "spotted."

Stripeback darter   *Percina notogramma* (Raney and Hubbs)

SYSTEMATICS

The stripeback darter, subgenus *Alvordius*, was described from Maryland in 1859 by Girard. Its original name is preoccupied in the genus by the blackside darter, hence Raney and Hubbs (1948) provided a new name (Collette and Knapp 1967). Two subspecies are recognized: *P. n. montuosa* Hogarth and Woolcott is endemic to the upper and middle James drainage; *P. n. notogramma* occupies the remainder of the range (Hogarth and Woolcott 1966). *Percina notogramma* is closely related to *P. maculata*.

DESCRIPTION

Materials.—From Raney and Hubbs (1948), Hogarth and Woolcott (1966), Loos and Woolcott (1969), and 28

Fish 258 *Percina noto-gramma* adult female 60 mm SL (REJ 1041), VA, Botetourt County, Craig Creek, 21 September 1983.

Fish 259 *Percina noto-gramma* juvenile 36 mm SL (RC), VA, Louisa County, North Anna River, 28 August 1970.

Virginia series. Life color from Raney and Hubbs (1948) and 11 adults.

Anatomy.—A laterally blotched and dorsolaterally striped darter; adults are 45–65 mm SL. Body and snout form moderate; frenum present; branchiostegal membranes separate or slightly conjoined; caudal fin slightly emarginate. Anal fin rays and underside of pelvic rays with keratinized ridge, and skin over lower body scales much thickened in nuptial male. Female genital papilla a semi-rectangular flap with small subdivisions distally.

Cheek partly scaled; opercle fully scaled; nape partly scaled or naked; breast nearly naked, with some small scales, or with 2–3 modified scales; belly of female naked; belly of male naked anteriorly, but posteriorly with modified scales, spines elevated in nuptial male.

Meristics.—Lateral line complete, scales (49)52–63(67); scales above lateral line (5)6–7(9); scales below lateral line (8)9–10(12); circumpeduncle scales (18)20–22(24). Dorsal spines (11)13–15(17); dorsal rays 11–12(14); anal spines 2; anal rays (8)9–10(11); pectoral rays 13–14(15). *Percina n. montuosa* is a smaller-scaled form; for example, lateral line scales (58)59–64(67) *vs.* (49)53–60(64) in *P. n. notogramma*.

Color in Preservative.—Midlateral body with 6–8 dark or black ovoid blotches (occasionally 1–2 square), slightly or moderately interconnected; brown dorsolateral stripe usually present, undulating or very irregular, continuous or interrupted; saddles dusky, brown, or black, usually bilaterally asymmetrical, infrequently connected to adjacent saddles, often connected by a dash to one or a few points of the dorsolateral dark stripe; predorsal saddle often forked posteriorly, not contacting dorsal fin. Lower side and venter pale or rarely with pigmented patches, but uniformly dusky in breeding specimens. Preocular bar wide; postocular bar of varying intensity; subocular bar distinct, dipping onto underside of head; square supraocular bar evident; gular area often immaculate but may be slightly or moderately dusky, rarely dark. Chin and (anteriorly or fully) the lower jaw rami and lower lip about equally pigmented as gular area, hence median gular area not demarcated from adjacent area; breast occasionally diffusely dusky.

First dorsal fin (Figure 69C) with melanophores sparsely or densely distributed throughout membranes except for partial or complete, narrow clear distal margin (no subdistal or submarginal black or pale band); fin darkest anterobasally, where membranes black in nuptial male; spines clear or slightly tessellated. Second dorsal membranes dusky or black-streaked, darkest basally; rays tessellated or, in nuptial male, black-edged. Caudal membranes clear to dusky in nuptial fish; rays well tessellated, sometimes forming distinct bands; caudal base with 2 vertically aligned pale areas; basicaudal spot dark, medial. Other fins with membranes clear or dusky, rays sometimes slightly tessellated. Nuptial male is slightly darker than the female.

Color in Life Plate 32.—Upper body ground shade straw, tan, or pale olive; saddles olive or olive-black; dorsolateral stripe dark olive or brown; lateral blotches blackish olive or black (but pale green in two spring males); lower opercle and prepectoral iridescent gold, green, and blue;

lower body side in two ripe females dull pale yellow, shading to iridescent yellow-gold with some pale blue tints posteriorly; venter tan to cream.

COMPARISON

The *Key to Percina* (couplet 15) uses gular pigmentation to divide the four Virginia Atlantic slope species of the subgenus *Alvordius* into two groups (*P. notogramma* and *P. roanoka* as one; *P. peltata* and *P. crassa* as the other). The character applies mainly to adults and is variable; it can be successfully used by careful application of the couplet. In addition to using meristic characters in the key and descriptions (and often geography), juveniles can be separated by comparing their lateral, dorsal, and fin color patterns with those of identified adults. Some aspects of adult patterns are incompletely developed in juveniles (e.g., Fish 258 and 259).

Percina notogramma is frequently captured near *P. peltata*; in addition to the gular pigment character, they are distinguished by: (1) lateral blotches [most or all oval in *notogramma vs.* most or all square or rectangular, or broadly confluent in *peltata*]; (2) dorsolateral pattern [usually an irregular dark stripe with a pale stripe above and below the dark stripe *vs.* no distinct stripes (except for interconnections of saddles)]; (3) dorsal pattern [saddles often asymmetrical, usually not interconnected *vs.* saddles usually symmetrical, interconnected at each corner by a short dark line, forming a chainlike pattern]; (4) predorsal saddle [usually Y-shaped posteriorly, the fork separated from the dorsal fin by a pale area *vs.* saddle square or hourglass-shaped, contacting the dorsal fin origin]; (5) first dorsal fin, distal half [nearly uniformly dusky (Figure 69C) *vs.* banded (Fish 261, 262)]; (6) basicaudal spot [medial, usually distinct *vs.* submedial, usually diffuse]; (7) caudal fin [slightly emarginate *vs.* emarginate, obviously forked]; (8) opercle [fully scaled *vs.* unscaled or with few scales].

BIOLOGY

Stoneflies were eaten by 3 of 4 fish (Flemer and Woolcott 1966); undoubtedly other insects and other invertebrates serve as food. The yearlings we examined were immature. This species lives 3 years. The sexes do not differ in growth rate; age-2 fish attained 46–71 mm SL, mean, 58 (Link 1971). The 71-mm specimen, from Virginia, is the largest known.

Females in eastern and central Virginia were ripe from 25 March to 15 April, water 7–16°C (Loos and Woolcott 1969). We found females in apparent reproductive condition on 16 May in eastern Virginia and on 17 May (water 14.5°C) in the upper James drainage; an upper James male was spent on 3 June. Loos and Woolcott (1969) assumed that spawning occurs in gravel riffles, and observed *P. notogramma* to be an egg-burier in aquaria. Natural hybridization is known with *P. peltata* in the James and York drainages, with introgression occurring in the York (Loos and Woolcott 1969).

HABITAT

The preferred habitat of the stripeback darter is warm, moderate-gradient, usually clear streams and rivers. Raney and Hubbs (1948) stated that it occupies riffles, pools near riffles, and sometimes weedbeds; their observations were largely or entirely of *P. n. notogramma*. Hogarth and Woolcott (1966) thought that *P. n. montuosa* differed from *P. n. notogramma* by inhabiting the faster parts of riffles. Our records from 10 spring to fall collections, 8 of *P. n. montuosa*, and our other observations indicate that both subspecies clearly favor sluggish current. We caught or observed *P. n. montuosa* among gravel, rubble, and boulder substrates that were clean, silted, or cloaked with detritus. The only occasion in which we took specimens in fast current was during high water in a normally dry area.

DISTRIBUTION Map 164

Percina notogramma is endemic to the Atlantic slope from the Patuxent drainage in Maryland to the James drainage of Virginia and West Virginia. Its apparent absence from the Shenandoah system of Virginia is peculiar, but paralleled by several other fishes. The subspecies' ranges in the James drainage were separated (Hogarth and Woolcott 1966) near Scottsville; *P. n. montuosa* was considered to be restricted to montane areas including Blue Ridge outliers, and *P. n. notogramma* to be a Piedmont inhabitant. Hogarth and Woolcott plotted two records of *P. n. montuosa* from the Hardware River system, a northern tributary just below Scottsville; the specimens were not listed among their materials and we did not find them. In the lower Slate River, a southern tributary of the James on the Piedmont just below Scottsville, we took two small-scaled specimens (CU 50640) resembling *P. n. montuosa*. A few specimens (RC) from upper Slate River tributaries are more similar to the nominate subspecies.

Abundance.—Generally uncommon.

REMARKS

The stripeback darter differs in habitat preference from *P. peltata*, a widely sympatric relative in the subgenus *Alvordius*. *Percina notogramma* usually occupies pools; *P. peltata* occurs in runs and riffles.

Percina notogramma may represent an early stock of *Alvordius* on the central Atlantic slope (Robins 1961). The New drainage now constitutes a geographic gap between the ranges of *P. notogramma* and its intimate relative in the Ohio basin, *P. maculata*, although that gap may be filled by *P. gymnocephala*. The divergence of *P. notogramma* into two subspecies within a single drainage would be curious. Perhaps the upstream small-scaled form evolved in the James drainage from a stock of *P. maculata*, and after dispersal via stream capture or an extended river it gave rise in a northerly drainage to a large-scaled form which subsequently invaded the James.

The status of the subspecies merits more study. Hogarth and Woolcott (1966) found them living in proximity (Map 164); they did not identify intergrades and found two populations in the range of *P. n. notogramma* that resembled *P. n. montuosa* in certain meristic characters.

Percina notogramma is faring well in the Rappahannock, York, and James drainages, but it is rare in the Virginia portion of the lower Potomac drainage and has not been found in Maryland since 1944 (Lee et al. 1981).

Name.—*Notogramma* means "back line"—the dorsolateral stripe; *montuosa* denotes "of the mountains."

Appalachia darter   *Percina gymnocephala* Beckham

SYSTEMATICS

The Appalachia darter, subgenus *Alvordius*, was described from the New drainage of North Carolina, Virginia (Fox Creek), and West Virginia by Beckham (1980). Although *P. gymnocephala* is allopatric to closely related species, the nuptial coloration reported here supports its species rank. This species was previously considered a population of *P. maculata*, but Beckham (1980) regarded its closest relative to be *P. peltata*. We believe that *P. gymnocephala* is more closely allied to *P. peltata* and *P. crassa* than to other *Alvordius*.

DESCRIPTION

Materials.—From Beckham (1980), Page (1983), and 6 Virginia lots. Color in life from 8 nonbreeding adults, 6 breeding males, and 3 breeding females from Virginia.

Anatomy.—A laterally blotched darter with a naked or slightly scaled head; adults are 45–70 mm SL. Body form moderate; length and form of snout moderate; frenum present; branchiostegal membranes separate or slightly conjoined; caudal fin slightly emarginate. Nuptial male with keratinized ridge on anal fin rays. Female genital papilla moderate in length, broad, fimbriate distally.

Cheek, opercle, and nape naked or slightly scaled; breast usually naked except for a modified scale; belly usually 40–80% scaled. Both sexes with 1 modified scale each on breast and interpelvic areas; male with 7–14 modified scales along belly midline, spines erect during breeding; female with 0–9 less-modified belly scales.

Meristics.—Lateral line complete, scales (56)61–68(72), rarely 1 unpored; scales above lateral line (6)7(8); scales below lateral line 9–12; circumpeduncle scales (19)21–24(25). Dorsal spines (12)13–15(16); dorsal rays (10)11(13); anal spines (1)2; anal rays (7)8–9(10); pectoral rays (13)14–15(16).

Color in Preservative.—Body side with 6–9 oval, square, or rectangular blotches, interconnected by dusky or dark areas; dorsum with 7–8 square, rectangular, or irregular, brown or blackish saddles, sometimes interconnected to form a chainlike pattern; predorsal saddle does not contact dorsal fin. Dorsolateral area typically with irregular scrawling, scrawls often connected to blotches or saddles; scrawls more numerous and finer in female; no dorsolateral stripe.

Fish 260 *Percina gymnocephala* adult female 59 mm SL (REJ 973), VA, Grayson County, Big Fox Creek, 10 June 1983.

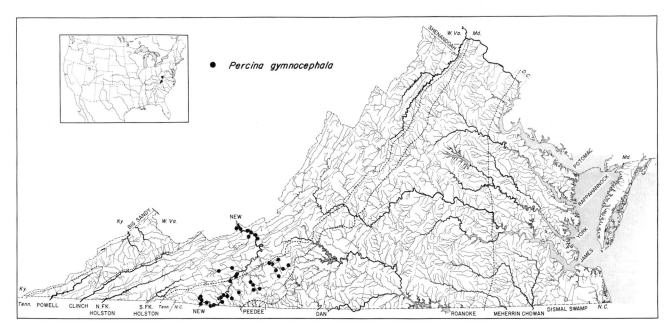

Map 165   Appalachia darter.

Head dorsum and upper lip dark; preocular bar wide; supraocular bar short; dark stripe follows orbit posteroventrally; subocular bar prominent in adult and usually in juvenile. Upper cheek with oval or crescentic dark area; upper opercle with irregular blotch; dusky or dark median chin bar usually present; venter of head elsewhere and breast with generalized stippling or irregular dusky patches. Both sexes can become dusky during spawning.

First dorsal fin with a distal narrow clear band, subdistally a dark or black band, submarginally slightly or moderately dusky, medially to basally dark or black and with clear streaks. Second dorsal rays and membranes slightly tessellated or fully pigmented except for clear areas along rays; female tends to be more tessellated. Caudal rays tessellated or in nuptial male largely dark, membranes clear; caudal base with submedial spot in juvenile, distinct spot absent in adult but there is a diffuse dark area that blends into last lateral blotch, often below the lateral line; 2 vertically aligned pale areas at caudal base. Other fins clear, dusky, or tessellated.

Color in Life   Plate 32.—Nonbreeding adult with ground color of back and side olive to tan; venter cream to yellow; markings brown or black. Nuptial male with iridescence of cheek, opercle, and prepectoral area silvery blue to lime; iris and immediate postpectoral area copper; dorsum tan or olive, marks blackish; lateral blotches distinctly blue-green, interspaces pale blue-green; area immediately ventral to lateral blotches golden yellow, most intense above anal fin. In both sexes, lowermost side dull orange to brassy. In nuptial male, first dorsal fin submarginal band ephemerally silky golden green; caudal base with 2 yellow spots; pelvic and pectoral fins with yellow wash; pelvic fin brassy basally.

Beckham (1980) stated that *P. gymnocephala* lacks bright colors and sexual dichromatism. We found males to have varied, sometimes bright hues; females were somewhat subdued. Beckham (in litt.) actually had observed essentially the same colors in nonbreeding North Carolina adults as we did in nuptial Virginia fish.

COMPARISON

See *P. maculata*.

BIOLOGY

Little is known about the life history of the Appalachia darter. Our few yearlings were immature. Six nuptial males were 57–72 mm SL, 4 nuptial females were 59–69 mm. Beckham (1980) reported a maximum length of 80 mm SL; our biggest from Virginia is 73 mm SL. Of females taken on 27 April, one was fully gravid and one was partly spent; from 10 June of different years, one female was partly spent and one fully spent. Males taken on 3 June were apparently in full nuptial color. Thus the spawning period in Virginia includes late April–early June.

HABITAT

Percina gymnocephala occupies cool and warm, usually clear streams and rivers of upland gradient. It is taken in gravelly and rocky runs and riffles during spring and summer and in deeper slower water during fall.

DISTRIBUTION   Map 165

The Appalachia darter is endemic to the New drainage, in which it occurs from North Carolina to West Virginia. In Virginia it is generally distributed in the Blue Ridge Province; in the Valley and Ridge it occupies the New River and only a few tributaries.

Abundance.—Generally uncommon.

REMARKS

The Appalachia darter is one of the last fishes described as new from Virginia and is now recognized to be one of the more colorful species of the subgenus *Alvordius*. It merits life history study.

Name.—*Gymnocephala* means "naked (unscaled) head."

Shield darter   *Percina peltata* (Stauffer)

SYSTEMATICS

This member of the subgenus *Alvordius* was described from Pennsylvania in 1864. Three subspecies were recognized by Raney and Suttkus (1948): *P. p. peltata* from the James drainage northward; an undescribed subspecies endemic to the upper Roanoke drainage; and *P. p. nevisense* (Cope) in the Tar, Neuse, and possibly the Chowan drainages. Mayden and Page (1979) did not consider subspecies, but showed that in some characters the Chowan population is closest to that of the upper Roanoke. In an unpublished study of geographic variation, J. T. Goodin and W. S. Woolcott concluded that *nevisense* is the only form in the Chowan, Roanoke, Tar, and Neuse, and that it should be ranked a species. However, we continue to recognize *nevisense* as a subspecies pending wider review of the manuscript.

We regard *P. peltata* to be allied to *P. gymnocephala* based on similar first dorsal fin pattern, form and location of basicaudal marking, and other features. These species do differ sharply in nuptial color and other characters; Mayden and Page (1979) indicated that the nearest relative of *P. peltata* probably is *P. crassa*.

DESCRIPTION

Materials.—From Hogarth and Woolcott (1966), Loos and Woolcott (1969), Mayden and Page (1979), Page (1983), and 47 Virginia series. Color in life from Taylor (1982, 1983) and 11 specimens from the Roanoke, Chowan, and Appomattox drainages.

Anatomy.—A square- or rectangular-blotched and chain-backed darter; adults are 40–70 mm SL. Body form

Fish 261 *Percina peltata* (northern form) adult female 74 mm SL (REJ 1028), VA, Amelia County, Appomattox River, 1 September 1983.

Fish 262 *Percina peltata* (southern form) adult male 69 mm SL (REJ 998), VA, Bedford County, North Fork Otter Creek, 12 July 1983.

moderate or elongate; snout moderate; frenum wide; branchiostegal membranes scarcely connected; caudal fin moderately emarginate or well forked. Nuptial male with keratinized ridge on anal rays and ventral surface of pelvic rays. Female genital papilla moderate in length, broad, flat, often multilobulate distally.

Cheek usually naked in specimens from the James drainage and north, partly scaled in those from the Roanoke and south; opercle naked or with few scales; nape naked or partly scaled; breast naked except for modified scales; belly naked anteriorly. Modified midventral scales in male, 1 midbreast, 1(2) interpelvic, (3)4–6(7) on belly, spines retrorse or erect when breeding; scales less modified in female, 1 midbreast, 0(1) interpelvic, rarely 1 on posterior belly.

Meristics.—Lateral line complete, scales (48)53–61(66); scales above lateral line (5)6–7(9); scales below lateral line (6)8–11(12); circumpeduncle scales (16)18–22(23). Dorsal spines (10)12–14(15); dorsal rays (11)12–13(14); anal spines 2; anal rays (8)9(11); pectoral rays 13–15.

Color in Preservative.—Body side with 6–9 square or elongate rectangular dark blotches, these usually interconnected by narrower dark areas; blotches and interconnections sometimes all of equal height, forming a dark lateral stripe. Dorsum with 7–9 dark, usually symmetrical, often hourglass-shaped saddles interconnected by dark semicircles, forming a chain along dorsum; predorsal saddle contacting dorsal fin. Just below the chain are a few irregular marks, sometimes connected to the chain but more often to lateral blotches. Lower side and venter pale, rarely with irregular pigmentation. Preocular bar wide, extending onto upper lip and occasionally blending into dark head pigmentation; postocular pigmentation diffuse or distinct, occasionally bar-shaped; sub- and supraocular bars usually well defined. Medial gular bar quite variable, intense to absent; breast occasionally moderately pigmented.

First dorsal fin bands: distal clear; subdistal dusky or dark; submarginal usually clear, sometimes partly obscured by slight duskiness; medial with dark or black elongate areas, blackest in nuptial male; basal usually clear, occasionally dusky; spines tessellated or all clear. Other fins tessellated or pale, rarely with distinct interradial pigment patches in second dorsal. Caudal base with 2 vertically aligned pale spots and a submedial dark blotch, the blotch more spotlike in young and juvenile. Nuptial male slightly duskier overall on body and with blacker fin markings than female.

Color in Life Plate 32.—Dorsum ground shade pale olive; markings olive-brown or olive-black; lateral blotches dark olive or black. Iridescent parts of cheek, postocular slash, lower opercle, and pectoral fin base silver to blue-green; between side blotches and ventrolaterally, the body is silver, gold, or blue-green, sometimes with a slight brassy tint. Fins lack chromatic color.

COMPARISON

See *P. notogramma.*

BIOLOGY

The shield darter probably feeds mainly on insects. Some males mature as yearlings; females generally first ripen by age 2. Maximum age is 3; the sexes grow at equal rates, attaining 55–71 mm SL, mean, 62, in the second year (Link 1971). Page (1983) reported a maximum length of 75 mm SL; our largest specimen from Virginia is 74 mm SL.

Reproductive behavior was studied by New (1966) and Loos and Woolcott (1969). Spawning occurs from mid-April through May in New York. Virginia females were ripe on 29 March, water 12°C, and males were ripe through 1 June, to 16°C. The female selects a spawning site of sand and fine gravel mix in areas of rubble and boulder at the head of, or in riffles. *Percina peltata* is an egg-burier; each spawning act yields 15–25 eggs. Natural hybridization occurs with *P. notogramma* (Loos and Woolcott 1969).

HABITAT

The shield darter inhabits warm streams and rivers of low to moderate gradient and varied substrates; it avoids moderately and heavily silted areas. It occupies beds of submersed vegetation that may develop in riffles during the summer (New 1966; Loos and Woolcott 1969). In the James drainage and northward it usually occupies gravel and rubble in swift water. In the Chowan and Roanoke drainages, the shield darter typically inhabits pools and slow runs of sandy substrate, less often faster water and coarser substrate types. In the Blackwater system of the Chowan it was taken only in areas of clean-swept sand in the main channel, in swamp-margined dark water, pH 6.5.

DISTRIBUTION Map 166

Percina peltata is an Atlantic slope darter which occurs in drainages from the Hudson to the Neuse, including all major Atlantic drainages of Virginia. It was taken in the Blackwater River at Zuni in 1888 (Jordan 1889b, as *E. aspro,* UMMZ [IU 4818 in part]) and also in 1984 at this and two nearby sites, but not in Blackwater tributaries. We believe that the USNM specimen, verified by us as *P. peltata* and reported from Dismal Swamp by Jordan (1889b), has faulty locality data (*Biogeography*). It is strange that *P. peltata* (and *P. notogramma*) is not recorded from the Shenandoah system of Virginia.

Abundance.—Generally uncommon, usually more numerous in the Piedmont than in the mountains. *Percina peltata* seems to have declined in the Roanoke drainage above the city of Roanoke; it was taken sporadically in small numbers until 1976, but not in more recent surveys. Its probable depletion in Craig Creek of the upper James drainage, perhaps related to the invasion by *P. roanoka,* is noted under the latter.

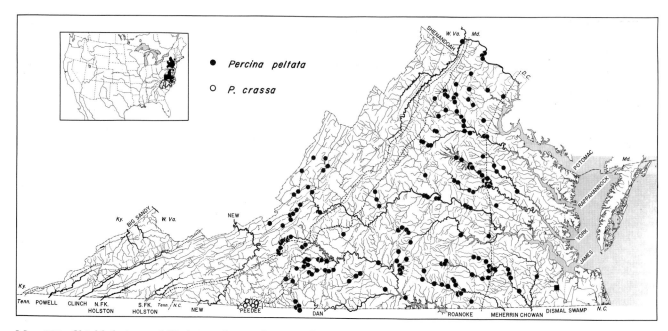

Map 166 Shield darter and Piedmont darter. Square refers to record of *P. peltata* with probably erroneous locality data.

REMARKS

The shield darter is one of the most widespread species of *Percina* on the Atlantic slope.

Name.—*Peltata*, meaning "shield," is probably based on the lateral blotches or the large modified belly scales. *Nevisense* translates to "birthmark," in allusion to the blotches.

Piedmont darter   *Percina crassa* (Jordan and Brayton)

SYSTEMATICS

The Piedmont darter, subgenus *Alvordius*, was described from South Carolina in 1878. It was synonymized under *P. peltata* by Jordan (1889b). Raney and Suttkus (1948) excluded it from that species, and it was formally resurrected by Bailey and Gosline (1955). We agree with Mayden and Page (1979) that *P. crassa* is intermediate evolutionarily between *P. peltata* and *P. roanoka*. Mayden (*in* Lee et al. 1980) interpreted *P. crassa* to be more closely linked to *P. peltata*.

DESCRIPTION

Materials.—From Mayden and Page (1979), 3 lots from North Carolina, and 4 from Virginia. Color in life from Mayden and Page (1979), 2 Virginia adult females, and 1 lot of North Carolina adults.

Anatomy.—A laterally blotched darter with a clear or dusky submarginal band in the first dorsal fin; adults are 50–65 mm SL. Body moderate or robust; snout length and form moderate; frenum wide; branchiostegal membranes separate or slightly conjoined; caudal fin moderately emar-

Fish 263 *Percina crassa* adult male 56 mm SL (REJ 969), VA, Patrick County, Johnson Creek, 8 June 1983.

Fish 264 *Percina crassa* adult female 57 mm SL (REJ 970), VA, Carroll County, Pauls Creek, 9 June 1983.

ginate. Rays of anal fin and underside of pelvic fin with a keratinized ridge in breeding male. Female genital papilla small or moderate in size, broad, flat, with short subdivisions distally.

Breast (except for modified scales) and cheek naked; opercle naked or dorsally scaled; nape naked or posteriorly scaled; belly midline usually naked in female, naked anteriorly and followed with usually 4–8 modified scales in male; midbreast and interpelvic area each with usually 1 modified scale in both sexes; spines retrorse or erect in male.

Meristics.—Lateral line complete, scales (44)47–52(58); scales above lateral line (4)5–6(7); scales below lateral line (6)7–8(10); circumpeduncle scales 15–20. Dorsal spines (10)11–12(13); dorsal rays 11–12(13); anal spines (1)2; anal rays (7)8–9(10); pectoral rays (12)13–14(15).

Color in Preservative.—Midlateral body with 7–9 dark, round, oval, or vertically elongate, moderately interconnected blotches; dorsum with 8–10 bilaterally symmetrical or slightly asymmetrical dark saddles, these usually interconnected in chainlike fashion by dusky or dark U-shaped markings which appear as a wavy dorsolateral stripe; predorsal saddle squared or irregularly shaped posteriorly, contacting or not contacting dorsal fin. Lower side and venter pale, becoming somewhat dusky in adult male. Preocular bar wide, sometimes diffusing into upper head color and upper lip; postocular slash bold or dispersed; subocular bar distinct, extending onto underside of head; supraocular bar short, well defined; gular bar slightly or very intense; dusky breast patch present, more evident in male, or absent.

First dorsal fin bands: distal clear; subdistal dusky; submarginal clear or slightly dusky, sometimes largely dusky from extensions of adjacent dark bands; medial to basal dark; spines generally clear or slightly tessellated. Second dorsal membranes distally clear or pale, basal third dusky to dark; rays tessellated. Caudal membranes generally clear; rays tessellated; base with 2 vertically aligned pale spots between which is a dark medial spot that often extends ventrally. Other fins with rays tessellated, membranes usually clear except anal and pelvic fins slightly peppered basally. Nuptial male duskier overall than female.

Color in Life.—Nonbreeding male and female similar, with no bright colors; dorsal marks dark brown; lateral blotches dark green; venter white to yellow; caudal base spots pale yellow; pelvic and pectoral fins faintly yellow. In breeding male, first dorsal fin with a bright yellow submarginal band (Mayden and Page 1979); prespawning Cape Fear drainage males had pale yellow submarginal band; lateral blotches greenish; darkly pigmented areas become more intense and background increases in duskiness in nuptial male.

COMPARISON

See *P. notogramma*.

BIOLOGY

The life history of *P. crassa* is largely unknown. Based on the few specimens studied, this species eats aquatic insects (Gatz 1979). Female yearlings (about 40 mm SL) were immature but a yearling male (44 mm SL) appeared capable of spawning. Maximum length is 75 mm SL (Page 1983); our largest from Virginia is 57 mm SL.

The spawning period probably is mid- to late spring. Females were gravid on 15 May in a North Carolina mountain stream. A female from cool Pauls Creek was gravid on 9 June; one taken a day earlier from the warmer Ararat River seemed spent. Reproductive behavior probably is similar to that of *P. peltata*.

HABITAT

The Piedmont darter occupies cool and warm, moderate-gradient creeks, streams, and rivers. It is commonly associated with rubble and gravel riffles and runs; our gravid female was taken in a backwater.

DISTRIBUTION Map 166

Percina crassa is known from the Cape Fear, Pee Dee, and Santee drainages; in Virginia it lives only in the Blue Ridge foothills of the Pee Dee.

Abundance.—Rare; our 7 records are from 6 sites in 4 streams; a total of only 7 specimens is known from 5 of the collections, the number of specimens is unknown for the remainder.

REMARKS

Percina crassa was considered of special concern in Virginia by Jenkins and Musick (1979), who knew it from only two streams. Although the Pee Dee drains a minor portion of the state and *P. crassa* is rare there, its more recent discovery in two other streams obviates a recommendation of protective status (Burkhead and Jenkins 1991).

Name.—*Crassa* connotes the "thick" body form.

Roanoke darter   *Percina roanoka* (Jordan and Jenkins)

SYSTEMATICS

Percina roanoka was described from the upper Roanoke drainage of Virginia by Jordan and Jenkins (*in* Jordan 1889a). In the late 1940s it was considered to be a subspecies of *P. crassa* by E. C. Raney (Collette and Knapp 1967; Raney, personal communication), and was formally downgraded by Bailey and Gosline (1955). It was elevated to species status by Page (1974); its variation was studied by Mayden and Page (1979). Two population groups are recognized, one in the Neuse, Tar, and Chowan drainages, the other in higher altitudes of the Roanoke, James, and New drainages. *Percina roanoka* is considered to be the most advanced member of the subgenus *Alvordius* owing to its low meristic values and bright colors. It is most closely related to *P. crassa* (Mayden and Page 1979).

DESCRIPTION

Materials.—From Mayden and Page (1979) and 80 Virginia lots. Life color from photos of 5 males and 1 female, and notes and observations of many other Virginia specimens.

Anatomy.—A darter with vertically elongate lateral blotches and a strongly banded first dorsal fin; adults are 35–55 mm SL. Body moderate or robust; snout slightly rounded or moderately blunt; frenum present; branchiostegal membranes slightly or moderately conjoined; caudal fin

Fish 265 *Percina roanoka* adult male 51 mm SL (REJ 1039), VA, Montgomery County, South Fork Roanoke River, 16 September 1983.

Fish 266 *Percina roanoka* adult female 43 mm SL (REJ 1039), VA, Montgomery County, South Fork Roanoke River, 16 September 1983. (Wide separation between the dorsal fins is unusual.)

slightly emarginate. Breeding male with keratinized ridge on rays of anal fin, underside of pelvic fin, and pectoral fin ventrally. Female genital papilla short or moderate in length, somewhat flattened, rectangular or broadly triangular, lobulate at tip.

Cheek and breast unscaled (except for breast scute); opercle scaled or unscaled; nape usually scaled except anteriorly or medially; belly of female nearly naked, that of male usually well scaled except anteriorly; modified scales of male usually 6–10 on belly, 1 each on midbreast and interpelvic area, spines somewhat elevated; female with smaller scutes, usually 1–2 on posterior belly, 1 each on anterior areas.

Meristics.—Lateral line complete, scales (38)42–50(54); scales above lateral line 4–5(6); scales below lateral line (5)6–7(8); circumpeduncle scales (14)15–17(18). Dorsal spines (9)10–11(12); dorsal rays (9)10–11(12); anal spines (1)2(3); anal rays (7)8–9(10); pectoral rays (12)13–14(15).

Color in Preservative.—Lateral body with 8–14 dark, vertically elongate or oval blotches (or bars) that often extend to venter, particularly on anterior two-thirds of body; blotches are most elongate in large adult; most or all blotches are oval in young and juveniles; blotches moderately interconnected midlaterally by smaller dark areas. Dorsolateral area pale to dusky, sometimes with small flecks, sometimes with a pale stripe above blotches. Dorsum with 6–9 generally square dark saddles, sometimes interconnected by short lines; predorsal saddle connected or not so to dorsal fin. Belly pale, uniformly dusky, or blotchy; breast and underside of head pale, dusky, or dark; gular bar not demarcated. Preocular bar extends onto upper lip; subocular bar present, usually somewhat diffuse; postocular bar often divided by pale streak; supraocular mark present or absent; prepectoral area mostly dusky or with a dark blotch.

First dorsal fin bands (Figure 69B): distal pale; subdistal dark or black; submarginal pale; submedial to basal dark or black, or often with clear or dusky windows at base; spines tessellated or uniformly dusky or dark. Second dorsal membranes dusky to dark-streaked throughout; rays tessellated or uniformly dusky. Caudal membranes pale or slightly dusky; rays tessellated or uniformly dark; caudal base with 2 vertically aligned pale spots, the lower usually smaller, rarely absent; pale spots separated by a medial or submedial dark spot, smudge, or blotch that usually fuses with the adjacent body blotch. Anal, pelvic, and pectoral membranes pale, or anal and pelvic membranes slightly dusky or dark, pelvic darkest; rays uniformly pale, tessellated, or dark. Breeding male often very dark overall, most markings obscured, submarginal first dorsal fin band nearly so, pectoral and caudal membranes pale or slightly dusky.

Color in Life Plate 32.—Female dorsal markings dark brown or dark olive; dorsolateral stripe tan or orange; cheek and opercle with tint of brassy and pale lime iridescence; ventrolateral area from anus onto pectoral base pale, light yellow, or brassy orange; Hobson (1979) meant flank dull

yellow, not full yellow; first dorsal fin with yellow or pale orange submarginal band; upper and lower caudal spots pale orange.

Breeding male dorsum dark olive or black; dorsolateral stripe yellow-orange; head mostly dark olive, sometimes with dirty gold tint; iris partly coppery; lateral body turquoise or sky blue, largely obscuring sooty bars; lower side and venter olive-orange posteriorly to burnt orange anteriorly. Submarginal first dorsal fin band bright orange; pale caudal spots dusky to bright orange; first anal spine tinted olive to orange.

COMPARISON

See *P. notogramma.*

BIOLOGY

Throughout the year, *P. roanoka* feeds chiefly on mayfly, blackfly, and midge larvae (Hobson 1979; Matthews et al. 1982; Hess 1983). Some yearlings appear mature; maximum life span is 3 years. Hobson found no sexual difference in size among adults; those in the third year of life were 40–56 mm SL, mean, 49. The largest Virginia specimen is 65 mm SL, the maximum known for the species.

Spawning was observed in the upper Roanoke River on 23 April 1982, water 12°C, in a deep riffle on a sand–gravel substrate among large rubble and small boulders. The male mounted the female in a manner similar to that of other egg-buriers. In Craig Creek during 1977, spawning had started before 22 April. Hobson (1979) deduced from the condition of gonads that the spawning period in the Virginia mountains was late May to early June, but he lacked sufficient specimens collected before this interval. Spawning probably starts in early April on the Coastal Plain and extends to early June in the mountains. Natural hybridization occurs with *P. oxyrhyncha* (Hocutt and Hambrick 1973).

HABITAT

The Roanoke darter lives in warm, typically moderate-gradient, generally clear large creeks, streams, and rivers. In mountain and Piedmont areas adults mainly occupy gravel, rubble, and boulder runs and riffles; young and juveniles are more common in pools, slow runs, and riffle margins. Adults inhabit gentle currents and sand and gravel bottoms on the Coastal Plain. Adult *P. roanoka* are well adapted morphologically to fast water (Matthews 1985b); 92% of specimens taken during five sampling periods in the upper Roanoke drainage were captured in riffles (Matthews et al. 1982; Matthews 1990). However, the

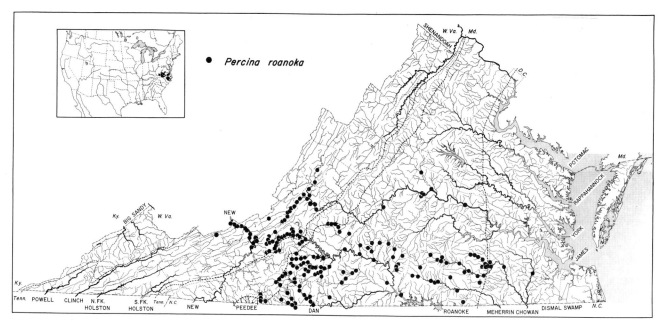

Map 167   Roanoke darter.

collecting method used in pools may have underestimated this species (Matthews 1990). The Roanoke darter had relatively low survival in water of low dissolved oxygen content (Matthews and Styron 1981).

DISTRIBUTION   Map 167

Percina roanoka is widespread in the James to the Neuse drainages and the lower New drainage, North Carolina, Virginia, and barely West Virginia. The easternmost Virginia record (Jordan 1889b, as *E. aspro*) from the Blackwater River is verified (USNM 40391, UMMZ [IU 4818 in part]), and this species persists there under marginal conditions (M. D. Norman, in litt.). The populations of the James and New drainages are probably introduced.

The James population was regarded as probably native by Lachner and Jenkins (1971a), but owing to its subsequent range expansion, we now consider it to be introduced. Craig Creek, Craig County, is identified as the area of establishment and focus of dissemination. The first record, from upper Craig Creek at about Rkm 15 (distance above the mouth of Johns Creek, Newcastle) is dated 1958 (VPI 1006), not 1964 as suggested by Ross (1969). The darter had not been taken at Rkm 4 in 1957, but during 1963–1964 it was found at that site and up to Rkm 20.

In the early 1960s *P. roanoka* appeared in Craig Creek below Johns Creek. It had not been found within 2–4 rkm below the mouth of Johns Creek in 1957 and 1960, but during 1963 it was well established at three sites in that reach. It was abundant at Rkm 15

(above the James River) in 1967 and probably reached the mouth of Craig Creek about that time. The Roanoke darter dispersed above and below Craig Creek and entered some tributaries, but the picture is sketchy due to generally scant collecting in the middle James drainage during the late 1960s to mid-1980s. The first records above Craig Creek are from the James and lower Cowpasture rivers in 1972–1973. *Percina roanoka* was absent from the James River at the Catawba Creek mouth (first major tributary below Craig Creek) and from lowermost Catawba Creek in 1964 and 1965, but present in lower Catawba Creek when next sampled, in 1987. The James River record below and nearest Craig Creek is from 1972–1973, but by that time the darter occupied the middle James River (White et al. 1977), about 240 rkm below Craig Creek, and by 1975 it populated the middle Rivanna River in Fluvanna County. It was first found in the James River of eastern Powhatan County in 1984; it probably has colonized the Fall Zone.

In the New drainage the Roanoke darter was first found during 1963 (Ross 1969; Hocutt and Hambrick 1973) or 1964 (CU 48037), not 1965 as suggested by Ross (1973). The site was the New River at about the center of the section from Claytor Dam to the head of Bluestone Reservoir. The next records, from 1968–1972 (Hocutt et al. 1973; Ross 1973), indicate that *P. roanoka* virtually spanned this section and flourished at some sites. In 1970 it was taken in West Virginia at the Greenbrier River mouth, just below Bluestone Dam (Hocutt and Hambrick 1973), and now it is the most abundant darter in the New River from the dam to some 20 rkm below (Hess 1983; Lobb and Orth 1986). *Percina roanoka* appears to be extending into New River tributaries—Toms Creek (first record in 1981 or 1982), Wolf Creek (1987), and Big Walker Creek (1991).

The New drainage population was considered to be probably introduced by Hocutt and Hambrick (1973); we agree based on the recency of its discovery, population explosion, subsequent range expansion, and its absence above Claytor Lake. Although unknown from lakes, the dispersal of *P. roanoka* was not greatly impeded by Bluestone Reservoir, a run-of-the-river impoundment.

Abundance.—Common or abundant in many montane and upper Piedmont streams; numbers decrease toward the Coastal Plain.

REMARKS

The Roanoke darter, one of the most beautiful *Percina*, helps to trace the upper Roanoke site(s) that

E. D. Cope, the first fish collector of the area, sampled in 1867. Obviously he did not see this species, for he would have recognized it as new and described it; it is thus likely that he sampled only quite small streams, which the species avoids.

The waxing distribution of *P. roanoka* in the James and New drainages is attributable to opportunism. The pioneering of this darter indicates potential for competitive interaction with native species. *Percina peltata* may have been displaced by *P. roanoka* from part of the James; we have not taken *P. peltata* in Craig Creek in a number of years, whereas *P. roanoka* is now abundant. The two population diffusions of the Roanoke darter are remarkable in light of perhaps a typically low vagility of the species. A radioactively tagged adult stayed under or near its "home rock" for the 10 months it was tracked (Lee and Ashton 1981).

Name.—*Roanoka* refers to the Roanoke River, from which it was described.

Gilt darter   *Percina evides* (Jordan and Copeland)

SYSTEMATICS

The gilt darter, described from Indiana in 1877, and the southern *P. palmaris* compose the subgenus *Ericosma*. Of the three subspecies of the gilt darter, *P. e. evides* occurs in Virginia. The other two can be regarded as formally described by Denoncourt (1969b). Systematics were studied comprehensively by Denoncourt (1969a) and evolutionary relationships were treated by Page (1974, 1981).

DESCRIPTION

Materials.—From Denoncourt (1969a) and 19 Virginia lots; meristic data are from only *P. e. evides* of the upper Tennessee drainage. Life color from Denoncourt (1969a) and 10 Virginia specimens.

Anatomy.—A darter with lateral blotches often confluent with saddles; adults are 50–60 mm SL. Body form moderate; snout somewhat short, rounded or moderately blunt; frenum wide; branchiostegal membranes separate or slightly conjoined; caudal fin slightly emarginate. Breeding tubercles of male located on lower caudal rays, most or all anal and pelvic rays, and lower body scales posterior to pelvic fin; small tubercles on lower head in some specimens. Anal and pelvic fin tubercles form on keratinized ridges; ridge also present on anal spines. Modified midbelly scales with up to 3 tubercles each, *P. evides* being the only *Percina* with greater than 1 tubercle per scute. Some females have small tubercles on anal and pelvic fins (Collette 1965; Wiley and Collette 1970). Female genital papilla moderate in length, triangular or broad, fimbriate distally.

Cheek partly scaled; opercle partly or completely scaled; nape usually scaled medially; breast with central modified

Fish 267 *Percina evides* adult male 55 mm SL (REJ 982), VA, Washington County, North Fork Holston River, 16 June 1983.

Fish 268 *Percina evides* adult female 44 mm SL (REJ 984), VA, Scott County, Copper Creek, 16 June 1983.

scale surrounded by 1–5 smaller scales; 1 interpelvic scute; belly midline usually naked in female, male with incomplete row of 7–13 modified scales, most spines slightly elevated when breeding.

Meristics.—Lateral line complete (53)57–67(76); scales above lateral line 7–9(10); scales below lateral line (8)9–11(13); circumpeduncle scales (20)22–25(27). Dorsal spines 11–13(14); dorsal rays (10)11–13; anal spines 2; anal rays (6)8–9(10); pectoral rays (12)13–15(16).

Color in Preservative.—Midlateral body with 7–9 dusky or dark blotches that usually are narrowly or moderately interconnected; 7–9 saddles present, these usually slightly paler than and often confluent with blotches; juvenile and female dorsolateral area with crosshatchings. Lower side and venter of female pale; male moderately or heavily peppered, producing a gray shade. Tip of upper lip with narrow pale notch; post-, sub-, and supraocular bars distinct or, often in breeding male, obscured by overall darkening of head.

First dorsal fin distally clear; subdistally to base pale to dark, but virtually all dark or black in nuptial male (some males have clear basal windows); spines clear or pigmented in association with membrane pattern; last membrane with increased pigmentation often forming a spot. Second dorsal membranes slightly peppered in juvenile and female, dark or black in nuptial male, most intense basally; rays clear or tessellated. Caudal membranes generally pale, but in some males slightly or moderately dusky, particularly subdistally; rays vaguely tessellated or entirely pigmented; caudal base usually with 2 vertically aligned pale spots (sometimes masked in breeding male). Caudal spot fully fused with last lateral blotch, thus appearing absent; last blotch often with a posteroventral extension on caudal base. Pelvic and anal membranes and rays generally pale, rarely slightly pigmented in female, dark or black in nuptial male; pectoral membranes and rays pale in female, dusky or dark in male.

Color in Life Plate 33.—Male coloration is the most variable of all Virginia darters; individuals may rapidly change aspects of pattern and color. Males during spawning period usually have patches of blue-green iridescence on cheek and opercle; lateral body may change from iridescent blue-green to orange-gold luster; lateral blotches metallic slate gray, green-black, or black. Ground shade, including lower side and belly, brilliant gilt, orange-red, or dark burnt orange; breast may be darker.

First dorsal fin subdistally to base burnt orange, occasionally with a reddish shade. Second dorsal and anal fins with orange streaks. Caudal base spots yellow to gold. Pectoral base having brassy streaks. Female occasionally with slight reddish lower body, having some red specks in pectoral, but more often pale.

BIOLOGY

Principal items of the gilt darter's diet are immature mayflies, caddisflies, blackflies, and midges (Hickman and Fitz 1978; Becker 1983; Hatch 1983). In Minnesota sexual maturity is reached at 11–13 months by males, and 22–23 months by females; in both sexes, size at maturity is about 50 mm SL (Hatch 1983). A 48-mm male and a 42-mm female from Virginia were mature. Maximum life span is 4 years (Lutterbie 1979). During the first three months of life, growth rates of both sexes are equal, but by six months males become significantly larger (Denoncourt 1969a). The disparity in size between the sexes further increases with age (Hatch 1983). The average length of age-2 Wisconsin fish is 69 mm TL (Lutterbie 1979). The largest specimen known is 80 mm SL from Kentucky (Denoncourt 1969a); the largest Virginia specimen is 67 mm SL.

Percina evides spawned in Copper Creek in May, water 17–20°C (Denoncourt 1969a), and in Tennessee on 2 and 17 June and 9 July, water 17–20°C (Page et al. 1982). Spawning in Tennessee occurred over sand and gravel interspersed with cobble and boulder, in upper parts of riffles 30–60 cm deep. In Minnesota Hatch (1983) found that spawning occurred in cobble raceways from June to mid-July in water of 17–23°C. The gilt darter is an egg-burier (Page et al. 1982). Females produce 132–347 mature ova (Hatch 1983).

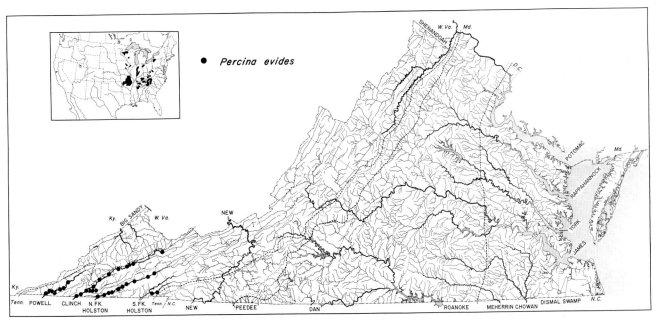

Map 168   Gilt darter.

HABITAT

Percina evides inhabits clean, cool and warm streams and rivers of moderate gradient. It is a main-stem species in Virginia; lower Copper Creek is the only tributary section with a resident population. In Virginia and the Clinch–Powell system of Tennessee, adults seem to prefer riffles and runs with loose large gravel and small rubble; juveniles are more often associated with slower current and smaller gravel. In the Little River of eastern Tennessee, *P. evides* occupies essentially the same range of habitats as in Virginia (Greenberg 1991). In Minnesota, it is found most frequently in rubble riffles and cobble or boulder raceways (Hatch 1986). Gilt darters sometimes form groups with other blotch-sided darters.

DISTRIBUTION   Map 168

Percina evides had a wide range within the western Lake Erie, Ohio, and upper Mississippi basins and in the Ozarks. In Virginia it is generally distributed in the Powell, Clinch, and North Fork Holston rivers, and is localized in the lower South Fork Holston River. Only two North Fork Holston records predate 1970—from 1953 and 1955 in the lower half of the river. These collections (VPI 522, 630) were not recognized to contain *P. evides* until after the report by

Ross and Carico (1963). The indicated former rarity or localization of *P. evides* in the North Fork Holston may have resulted from industrial pollution from Saltville, which has been curtailed since 1972; recently, this species has been widespread in the river. The gilt darter also appears to have made a good recovery in the Clinch River after the 1967 fish kill. The two records from the New drainage in North Carolina (Richardson and Carnes 1964) are based on *P. gymnocephala* (NCSM 4009, 4187).

Abundance.—Usually uncommon or common; rare in the South Fork Holston River.

REMARKS

Percina evides is a chameleon among darters; males can go through markedly different color phases, all dazzling, in less than a minute. Its contemporary distribution within the general range boundary is quite spotty, and it is extirpated from at least three northern states (Harlan and Speaker 1956; Denoncourt 1969a; Smith 1979; Trautman 1981). It appears to be highly intolerant of siltation (Hatch 1986). Although it is doing well in three Virginia rivers, a major disturbance could wipe out the population of a system.

Name.—*Evides* means "comely."

Tangerine darter   *Percina aurantiaca* (Cope)

SYSTEMATICS

Percina aurantiaca was described from the North Fork Holston River at Saltville, Virginia, by Cope (1868b). It is the sole member of the subgenus *Hypohomus* and is not closely related to any other living *Percina* (Thompson 1973b; Page 1974). Although the tangerine darter has primitive characteristics (e.g., relatively large body size and high meristic values), its exquisite nuptial coloration is advanced for the genus (Thompson 1977).

DESCRIPTION

Materials.—From Thompson (1977) and 27 lots from Virginia and Tennessee. Life color from Howell (1971), Thompson (1977), and 15 Virginia specimens.

Anatomy.—A darter with broadly conjoined lateral blotches which usually form a stripe; adults are 90–130 mm SL. Body moderately elongate; snout moderately short, moderate in shape; frenum well developed; branchiostegal membranes separate or slightly conjoined; caudal fin slightly emarginate. Breeding male with keratinized ridge on spines and rays of anal and pelvic fins, larger specimens with ridge on lower 4 rays of pectoral fin. An apparently unique feature is a pad formed by epidermal thickening on the dorsal portion of the caudal peduncle of large nuptial males. Female genital papilla moderately short, bulbous, rugose, with terminal fingerlike projections.

Cheek, opercle, nape, and belly fully scaled; breast partly or fully scaled; midventral scales of male weakly modified on interpelvic area and belly, some ctenii slightly to well erected; female with usually few, barely modified interpelvic scales.

Meristics.—Lateral line complete, scales (84)86–93(99); scales above lateral line 11–16; scales below lateral line 15–21; circumpeduncle scales (31)32–37(38). Dorsal spines (13)14–15(16); dorsal rays (12)13–14(15); anal spines 2; anal rays (9)10–11(12); pectoral rays (13)14–15(16).

Color in Preservative.—Lateral body with 8–11 dark or black, moderately or broadly fused blotches that usually form a continuous stripe; blotches tend to suffuse ventrally on breeding male. Dorsum with a dark line along fin bases and 10–12 small saddles that usually are bilaterally symmetrical, or, particularly in nuptial male, the dorsum is nearly uniformly dark. Dorsolateral area slightly or quite dusky, with a longitudinal row of spots from head to second dorsal fin. Lower side and venter of female pale, male pale or dusky, but sooty on breast and around pectoral base. Pre- and postocular bars present or these areas all dark; subocular bar absent.

First dorsal fin bands: distal edge pale or slightly dusky; if dusky, the distal–subdistal band remains narrow, darkest posteriorly; submarginal clear or pale; medial wide, dusky, most intense posteriorly and basally; basal narrow, pale, except in adults in which it is crossed on each membrane by a dusky streak extending into the medial band. Dorsal spine pigmentation follows the membrane banding pat-

Fish 269 *Percina aurantiaca* adult male 130 mm SL (REJ 994), VA, Washington County, North Fork Holston River, 22 June 1983.

Fish 270 *Percina aurantiaca* juvenile 71 mm SL (REJ 982), VA, Washington County, North Fork Holston River, 16 June 1983.

tern, or spines entirely dark. Second dorsal fin pale or dusky, darkest basally, dusky-margined in some nuptial males. Other fins nearly uniformly pale or dusky except most of anal and all of pelvic dark or black in nuptial male. Nuptial male is darker overall than female but body patterns are usually retained.

Color in Life Plate 33.—Juvenile and adult female light olive on dorsum; markings brown to black; lower side and venter of small juvenile creamy, adult female pale to moderate yellow; juvenile may have pale yellow gular area. Adult female opercle with yellow luster; first dorsal submarginal band pale orange; distal two-thirds of second dorsal rays and all of caudal rays yellow-olive.

Large nuptial male in peak color with dorsal and lateral blotches dark olive or black; areas between and below blotches with blue-green iridescence, accentuating the blotches; lower side and venter bright tangerine; breast black; gular area brilliant orange-red; lower side of head shading yellow to red; pectoral base silky sky blue. First dorsal fin submarginal band bright burnt orange, medial band orangish olive or black. Second dorsal fin basally olive, grading to rusty orange distally; distal half of caudal fin olive-orange; pelvic and anal membranes silky sky blue over black. Small, apparently mature males have subdued expression of bright and black coloration and large males have moderate development of orange coloration through much of the year except winter.

BIOLOGY

Primary food items are immature midges and mayflies for juveniles, caddisflies and mayflies for adults. Howell (1971) and Greenberg (1991) observed *P. aurantiaca* rolling small gravel and snail shells to feed on exposed prey. Movement of substrate may not be the same behavior as the overt stone-flipping performed by logperches with their specialized snout.

Some males may mature in one year; most or all age-2 females are mature (Howell 1971). Maximum life span is slightly over 4 years. Howell's limited data indicate that the sexes grow at equal rates; age-3 fish were 90–115 mm SL. However, Howell's and our largest specimens are males; perhaps males grow faster than females after age 3 or live longer. The largest reported specimen is a 152 mm SL (175 mm TL) male from Tennessee (Hitch and Etnier 1974); Virginia's largest is a 130 mm SL male.

Spawning was observed by us on 21 May 1974 in the North Fork Holston River of Virginia, water 21°C; and by D. A. Etnier and R. A. Stiles (in litt.) on 26 June 1973 at 23°C in the Little Pigeon River of Tennessee. Spawning occurred in shallows of moderate to swift current; substrate at one site was mostly gravel with some intermixed sand and the other was a sandy patch. The spawning act was typical of egg-burying species of *Percina*. No parental care or terri-

toriality was noted. Howell (1971) saw spawning on 18 July in an artificial raceway constructed in a cool (14.5°C) spring run. The late date and low temperature of spawning, site preparation by the female, and territoriality by the male noted by Howell may be artifacts associated with the unnatural environs. The number of mature ova was 120–578 in May specimens; eggs apparently mature periodically as the breeding season progresses (Howell 1971).

HABITAT

Percina aurantiaca inhabits clear, cool and warm streams and rivers of moderate gradient. In Virginia, juveniles and adults generally occupy pools and slow runs of gravel, rubble, boulder, and bedrock, and are occasionally found in swifter, shallower sections. Commonly, they rove near the bottom in open water; often they perch on large boulders and logs in pools as deep as 2.5 m. Occupation of the gravel–sand breeding habitat may occur only during the spawning season, and for much of that period only by nuptial males. Howell (1971) stated that large males occupy riffles during summer and fall in Tennessee, and Thompson (1977) found that in spring, adults, particularly males, occur in swift runs and riffles. During summer in the Little River of Tennessee, Greenberg (1991) found *P. aurantiaca* in deeper water than 12 other darter species; it occurred in riffles, runs, and most frequently in pools. It was often associated with silty substrate but spent 25% of the time above the bottom and typically fed on rocky substrate.

DISTRIBUTION   Map 169

The tangerine darter is endemic to montane sections of the upper Tennessee drainage. Of Virginia main stems, it inhabits the South and North forks of the Holston River and the Clinch and Powell rivers. The single South Fork record is from 1970. It has been taken in three Virginia tributaries: the now degraded Guest River of the Clinch in 1947; Copper Creek of the Clinch, which has a stable population below Spivey Mill Dam; and lowermost Big Moccasin Creek, a tributary of the North Fork Holston River.

Abundance.—Generally uncommon; apparently rare in the South Fork Holston River. As with other large darters, the more successful populations appear to be of low density compared with many smaller darter species. By snorkeling, Greenberg (1991) and we found *P. aurantiaca* to be much more abundant than the other large syntopic *Percina*—*P. burtoni, P. caprodes,* and *P. macrocephala.*

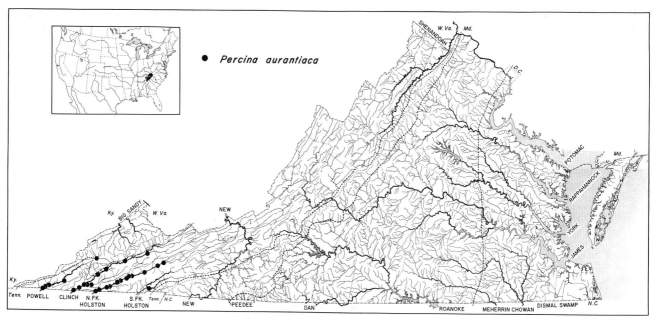

Map 169 Tangerine darter.

REMARKS

Percina aurantiaca is probably the most spectacular of the darters based on its combination of large size and bright contrasting colors. The male shown in color (Plate 33) was a lucky catch. After intensive but unsuccessful attempts on several days to capture a large nuptial male, and while setting collecting strategy for the next day, one of us recalled that we had taken this species in lower Big Moccasin Creek 14 years earlier. Considering all options with much debate, and Big Moccasin with doubt, we worked the stream hard the next morning, and on the last net haul took a brilliant lone male. Upon return to the lab, records revealed that its capture was a first for the species in that stream.

Name.—Aurantiaca, "orange-colored."

Channel darter   *Percina copelandi* **(Jordan)**

SYSTEMATICS

The channel darter was described from Indiana in 1877. It is the only described species of the subgenus *Cottogaster*, which has one or more undescribed forms on the Gulf slope. Its systematics were treated by Winn (1953) and Page (1974, 1981, 1983).

DESCRIPTION

Materials.—From Denoncourt (1976), Page (1983), and 13 series from the Clinch–Powell system of Tennessee and Virginia. Life color from Winn (1953) and 2 Virginia specimens.

Anatomy.—A slender darter with a series of small, usually separate lateral blotches; adults are 35–50 mm SL. Body

Fish 271 *Percina copelandi* adult male 42 mm SL (RC), VA, Lee County, Powell River, 14 May 1980.

Fish 272 *Percina copelandi* adult female 37 mm SL (REJ 986), VA, Scott County, Clinch River, 17 June 1983.

slender; snout moderate or blunt; frenum usually absent, occasionally weakly developed; branchiostegal membranes separate or slightly conjoined; caudal fin slightly emarginate. Breeding male with keratinized ridge on anal and pelvic spines and rays; tubercles on ventral aspect of pelvic rays 3–4 of peak nuptial males, the tubercles appearing as subdivisions of a ridge. Female genital papilla bulbous or pear-shaped with short distal fimbriae.

Cheek scaled or naked; opercle scaled; nape scaled posteriorly; breast naked except a central modified scute present; belly of female naked or with 1–4 modified scales posteriorly; belly of male lacks normal scales anteriorly and has a nearly complete medial row of 6–11 modified scales; spines variably elevated, short.

Meristics.—Lateral line complete, scales 48–57; scales above lateral line 4–6; scales below lateral line 6–8; circumpeduncle scales 16–18. Dorsal spines (9)10–11(12); dorsal rays (10)11–12(14); anal spines 2; anal rays (7)8–9(10); pectoral rays 13–15.

Color in Preservative.—Midside with 10–14 dark speckles and horizontally elongate small smudgelike blotches, these marks rarely interconnecting to form a stripe; midside markings often appearing XW-like. Back and upper side with small flecks and X-like marks; saddles vague when present. Lower side and venter pale, becoming dusky in nuptial male. Preocular bar present; subocular bar absent, faint, or distinct, often only a small spot.

First dorsal fin bands: marginal dark; submarginal clear; basal dark; bands most contrastive in nuptial male; membranes clear in female; spines tessellated in both sexes. Second dorsal membranes of male streaked or moderately pigmented; in female, clear or slightly stippled basally; rays tessellated in both sexes. Caudal membranes clear, rays tessellated in both sexes. Caudal base usually with a dark medial spot and a pale area above and below. Other fins of female clear except pectoral rays tessellated. In male, anal fin slightly peppered; pelvic fin darkly pigmented in breeding season; pectoral membranes clear, rays wholly pigmented.

Color in Life Plate 33.—Male and female life colors very similar except that male is more heavily pigmented. Body markings medium to dark brown; side of head and lateral body silvery with a hint of blue-green iridescence, blue-green slightly more intense in nuptial male.

BIOLOGY

The life history of *P. copelandi* is not well known. Foods include midge and mayfly larvae and micro-crustaceans (Turner 1921; Winn 1953; Cross 1967). Three females of 34–36 mm SL were mature at age 1 (Winn 1958b). Scott and Crossman (1973) stated that males grow larger than females. Page (1983) reported a maximum length of 60 mm SL; the largest Virginia specimen is 50 mm SL.

The channel darter spawns during April and May in Kansas and in June and July in Michigan (Winn 1953, 1958a, 1958b; Cross and Collins 1975). Spawning time in Virginia is most likely in April and May. This species is an egg-burier; it spawns in swift current between small rocks and in fine gravel behind large rocks, in water 20–21°C. Parental care is not practiced. Age-1 females bore 357–415 eggs and age-2 fish averaged 715 eggs (Page 1983). A doubtful record of hybridization with *P. caprodes* is noted under that species.

HABITAT

Over its range the channel darter inhabits warm, low- and moderate-gradient rivers; in northern parts of its range it also lives in lake shallows. In Virginia and eastern Tennessee, it is associated with moderate and swift riffles and runs having mixed small gravel to medium rubble substrate.

DISTRIBUTION   Map 170

The channel darter occurs widely but disjunctly in the Great Lakes–St. Lawrence, Ohio, and lower Mississippi basins; populations on the Gulf slope shown in the map inset represent one or more undescribed forms. In Virginia, it is restricted to the Clinch and Powell rivers; the populations are contiguous with those in the Tennessee portion of the rivers. The lesser ascendance of the Clinch by *P. copelandi*, compared with the much smaller Powell, may be a result of the depletion of the species during the 1967 fish kill. All records from the Clinch postdate the kill; those at the upper three sites are from 1979–1984. This species may extend into the Virginia portion of the Big Sandy because it occurs in Kentucky within a few rkm of the state line (Burr and Warren 1986).

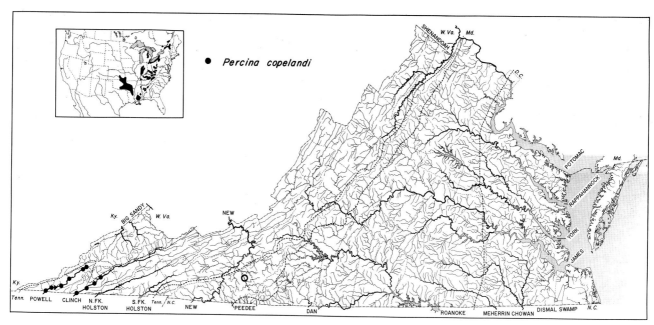

• *Percina copelandi*

Map 170   Channel darter. Open circle represents the dubious New drainage record.

A lone specimen of *P. copelandi* (UMMZ 204118) was in a jar with four *P. gymnocephala* (UMMZ 95372) taken by C. L. Hubbs from Big Reed Island Creek of the New drainage in 1931 (E. C. Beckham, R. R. Miller, in litt.). We found the specimen to be a typical *P. copelandi*, but believe that it came from a drainage other than the New. It could have been transposed to the jar of *P. gymnocephala* after Hubbs identified the Big Reed Island collection. Hubbs had a keen eye, and by 1931 he knew the distinctive *P. copelandi* (Hubbs 1930b), but he never reported it from the New. Therefore, we regard the presence of *P. copelandi* in the jar with *P. gymnocephala* (known only from the New) as a curatorial error, and we reject this record.

Abundance.—Rare or uncommon.

REMARKS

The small channel darter resembles the johnny darter and is quite distinct from other *Percina* species. It is one of the few darters in the upper Tennessee drainage that is strictly riverine and not known to move into tributaries. The channel darter was recommended for special concern status in Virginia, owing to its restriction in the state to the Clinch and Powell rivers (Burkhead and Jenkins 1991). The Clinch–Powell population is one of only two known in the Tennessee drainage; the other is based on a record from the lowermost section of the drainage in western Kentucky.

Name.—Copelandi refers to Herbert E. Copeland, who discovered the species.

Sand darters   Genus *Ammocrypta* Jordan

Ammocrypta comprises six or seven species including one that lives in Virginia. A second species occurs adjacently in Kentucky and may inhabit Virginia. With a very elongate, pallid, and translucent body, sand darters are well adapted to their typical habitat of shifting sand and sand–gravel substrates.

Ammocrypta has been long recognized as a genus. Its subgenus *Ammocrypta* was revised by Williams (1975). Simons (1992) proposed the merging of this subgenus into the subgenus *Boleosoma* of *Etheostoma*. However, we continue to recognize *Ammocrypta* as a

genus because it appears that the sister group of *Ammocrypta* has not been clearly identified (see *Etheostoma vitreum*).

The other subgenus of *Ammocrypta*—*Crystallaria*—contains only the crystal darter *A. asprella*; it was elevated to genus by Simons (1991). The lumping of *Ammocrypta* and the resurrection of *Crystallaria* were accepted by Page and Burr (1991) but not Robins et al. (1991).

Name.—Ammocrypta means "hidden in sand."

Western sand darter   *Ammocrypta clara* Jordan and Meek

SYSTEMATICS

The western sand darter was described from Iowa in 1885. It is the most primitive species of *Ammocrypta* (Simons 1992). The Powell River population has distinctively high scale counts (Starnes et al. 1977).

DESCRIPTION

Materials.—From Williams (1975), Starnes et al. (1977), and 15 specimens from the Clinch and Powell rivers in Virginia and Tennessee. Life color from 1 adult female from the Clinch River, Virginia.

Anatomy.—A pallid, very elongate darter; adults are 35–55 mm SL. Snout moderately long and sharp; frenum absent; eye supralateral; branchiostegal membranes slightly or moderately conjoined; opercular spine well developed; caudal fin slightly emarginate. Nuptial male develops breeding tubercles on pelvic, anal, and caudal fin rays. Male and female genital papilla short, tubular, sometimes slightly ridged. Cheek and opercle partly scaled; body dorsum, as far posterior as the end of second dorsal fin, usually naked or with a few isolated scales; caudal peduncle variably scaled, completely in some specimens; belly and breast naked.

Meristics.—Lateral line complete, scales (71)77–81(84); dorsal spines (10)11(12); dorsal rays (10)11; anal spines 1; anal rays 8–10; pectoral rays (12)13.

Color in Preservative.—Very pale overall; body opaque. Lateral body with a fine dark longitudinal stripe; 11–15 small spots or smudges occur along the lateral stripe; both the stripe and spots are best developed posteriorly. Dorsum with 18–24 small dark blotches; dorsolateral area lightly stippled, not spotted or flecked; lower side and belly pale except stippled along caudal peduncle midventrally. Head dorsum dark posteriorly; snout with irregular pattern; upper lip usually with 2 spots near tip. Fins lightly pigmented, on or along spines and rays, except sometimes pelvic unpigmented.

Color in Life.—Body quite translucent (rapidly becomes opaque upon preservation), grayish; cheek and opercle with subtle blue-green iridescence; blue-green iridescence less evident along midlateral body. Faint iridescent blue on opercle may be breeding color (Feeman 1987).

BIOLOGY

The western sand darter eats mainly aquatic insects (Forbes and Richardson 1920; Miller and Robison 1973). Wisconsin fish live 3 years and attain 51–66 mm TL in age 2 (Lutterbie 1979). Females usually are larger than males; maximum length is 59 mm SL (Williams 1975). The largest Virginia specimen is 50 mm SL.

Ammocrypta clara breeds apparently during late June to early August in Iowa and Wisconsin (Starrett 1950a; Lutterbie 1979). Williams (1975) indicated that most spawning occurs in July and early August; the bulk of his data may have been from the northern half of the species range. He suggested a prolonged spawning period based on the presence of large ova in late August specimens. Feeman (1987) suggested that in the upper Tennessee drainage, *A. clara* moves into shallow riffles to spawn during June, perhaps late May; young were taken on 16 June in the Powell River (J. C. Feeman, in litt.). In our upper Tennessee specimens, tubercles had begun developing by late May; a 17 June female appeared to be spent; and late June males had well-developed tubercles.

HABITAT

Over its range, the western sand darter inhabits warm, low and moderate-gradient, medium and large rivers; it typically occupies sand and sand–gravel substrates (Williams 1975). In Virginia it lives in the largest sections of the Clinch and Powell rivers and seemingly occupies atypical substrate for sand darters. In the Clinch at Speers Ferry we took two adults in a large riffle–run area, surface current about 0.5 m/second; the substrate chiefly was large gravel mixed with small and medium rubble. Small patches of sand were in the lee of some of the few boulders in the run, but the darters were taken at least 10 m from the sand. Judging from the rarity of the species, the habitat probably is marginal. We did not capture *A. clara* at the Powell site in Virginia, but noted some sandy areas, with small particles of coal intermixed, in slight to moderate current. Overall in the Clinch and Powell of Virginia and Tennessee, sizeable areas of sand are rare.

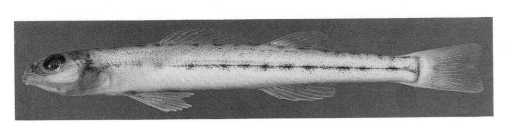

Fish 273 *Ammocrypta clara* adult female 44 mm SL (REJ 986), VA, Scott County, Clinch River, 17 June 1983.

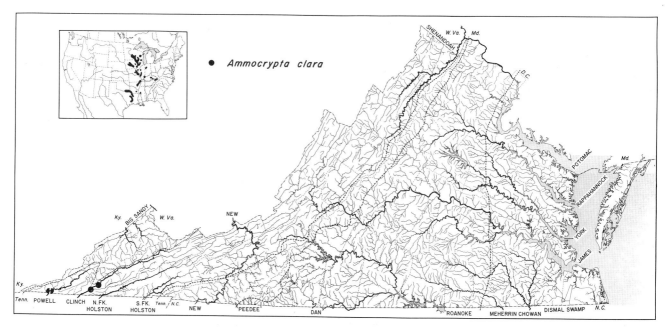

Map 171   Western sand darter.

DISTRIBUTION   Map 171

Ammocrypta clara ranges widely in the central Mississippi basin and an adjacent portion of the Gulf slope, but its distribution is spotty, particularly in the lower Ohio basin. The Virginia record sites mark the upper limits of the population of the Clinch–Powell system, the only population known in the Tennessee drainage. All records are from the Clinch and Powell rivers above Norris Reservoir. The sites span 137 rkm (37 rkm in Virginia) but the darter is discontinuously distributed.

The Clinch–Powell population was rediscovered (*Remarks*) in Tennessee during 1976 (Starnes et al. 1977). Feeman (1987) implied that *A. clara* was first recorded in Virginia in 1980 or 1981, but a specimen was caught there in 1979. We believe that *A. clara* was extirpated from the Clinch River in Virginia by the June 1967 fish kill, and that it reestablished itself either from Tennessee, from mouths of Virginia tributaries, or from both sources.

Abundance.—The western sand darter was rare at the three Virginia record sites; only 17 specimens are known. In the Clinch–Powell during 1950–1985, it was not taken in several samples at the record sites, nor at many others within or near the inhabited reaches. Most of the sites had healthy fish faunas in nearly all of that period. It may be difficult to estimate the population size of *A. clara* in the upper Tennessee (Starnes et al. 1977; Feeman 1987), but we believe that it can be readily caught when common.

REMARKS

The very pellucid, nearly colorless body of sand darters serves as camouflage on the pale sandy bottoms with which they typically associate. These species also rest and hide in sand with only the eyes and snout exposed. We have not observed burying behavior of *A. clara*, but *A. pellucida* plunges headfirst into sand. Burying may be energetically economical, by reducing the energy cost of otherwise maintaining position on the top of the substrate in current (Daniels 1989).

The first recent capture of a sand darter in the upper Tennessee drainage was actually a rediscovery. Woolman (1892) reported a sand darter to be the most abundant darter at a Powell River site in Tennessee during 1890. A second species of sand darter was discovered in the lower Tennessee in 1976 (Starnes et al. 1977). We do not foresee many new discoveries of *Ammocrypta* in the drainage because its relict distribution there is related to extensive main-river impoundment.

We consider the western sand darter to be threatened in Virginia because of its relict occurrence, indicated low density, the paucity of largely sandy habitat, and morphological differentiation of the stock. Apparently this species has been recovering in the Clinch and Powell rivers, but the long hiatus in its capture indicates that it easily could be set back.

Name.—*Clara* means "clear"—the translucency of the body.

Darters   Genus *Etheostoma* Rafinesque

Virginia has a generous share of the small, often dazzlingly colored *Etheostoma* darters. Of the more than 112 species (102 described, 10 or more undescribed), 26 inhabit the state. *Etheostoma* is the largest genus of North American freshwater fishes.

Name.—*Etheostoma*, meaning "various mouth," was coined for differences in mouth size and position among the few species known to Rafinesque (Jordan and Evermann 1896; Page and Swofford 1984).

Ashy darter   *Etheostoma cinereum* Storer

SYSTEMATICS

The ashy darter was described from Alabama in 1845. Its variation was analyzed by Shepard and Burr (1984). It constitutes the primitive monotypic subgenus *Allohistium* (Bailey and Gosline 1955; Page 1977; Bailey and Etnier 1988). The very distinctive *E. cinereum* was positioned between the subgenera *Litocara* and *Etheostoma* by Page (1981). Based on tuberculation and aspects of coloration, Bailey and Etnier (1988) and we suggest that *Litocara* is most closely linked to the *variatum* group of *Etheostoma*; it is relatively advanced in snout form and caudal color pattern. Hence the stem group of *E. cinereum* is unidentified.

DESCRIPTION

Materials.—From Shepard and Burr (1984) and 3 Kentucky and 21 Tennessee specimens. Life color from 2 nuptial males and associated specimens from the Little River in Tennessee.

Anatomy.—A spotted and obliquely barred darter; adults are 55–80 mm SL. Body moderate or somewhat elongate, slightly compressed; snout moderately long, sharp; lips prominent, papillose; frenum wide; branchiostegal membranes separate or slightly conjoined; second dorsal fin very high in large adult, most so in male; caudal fin truncate, occasionally slightly emarginate. Large breeding male with tubercles on pelvic and anal rays. Female genital papilla a long conical tube. Cheek, opercle, and belly always scaled, scales usually small and embedded on cheek;

Fish 274 *Etheostoma cinereum* adult male 52 mm SL (NMB 835), TN, Blount County, Little River, 18 February 1984. (Concavity of anal fin margin is an abnormality.)

Fish 275 *Etheostoma cinereum* adult female 62 mm SL (NMB 835), TN, Blount County, Little River, 18 February 1984.

nape usually naked, sometimes slightly scaled; breast naked. Gill rakers rudimentary on first arch.

Meristics.—Lateral line complete, scales (50)53–60(63); scales above lateral line 6–8(10); scales below lateral line (9)10–13(14); circumpeduncle scales (20)22–25(26). Dorsal spines (10)11–13(14); dorsal rays (11)12–13(14); anal spines (1)2; anal rays 7(8–9); pectoral rays 14–15(16).

Color in Preservative.—Midside with 10–13 round or rectangular dark spots; most spots connect to a faint or moderately dark bar which slants posteroventrad and diffuses onto lower side; bars best developed in adult. Dorsolateral area heavily freckled, many of the small spots aligned into undulating rows. Dorsum with 5–8 generally vague saddles. Pre- and postocular bars well developed; preocular bars meet on snout tip to form a V. Overall ground shade pale to moderately dusky, darkest in large nuptial male.

First dorsal fin with dark marginal band; membranes from submargin to base heavily spotted, rays tessellated or all dusky. Second dorsal membranes spotted, or spots coalesced to form a dark streak in each membrane; rays tessellated or all dark. Caudal fin variably dusky, rays generally tessellated; caudal spot medial or submedial, usually irregularly shaped, vague. Lower fins in juvenile and adult female pale, rays sometimes pigmented; in adult male, anal and pelvic fins dusky or very dark, pectoral fin slightly dusky.

Color in Life   Plate 34.—Juvenile and adult female dorsum to midside tan to tan-olive, markings brown; side and venter of juvenile creamy, and with faint oblique bars; female similar, but with increased duskiness in bars. First dorsal fin with bright red marginal band; distal half of second dorsal and caudal membranes bright red.

Breeding male dorsal and lateral markings brown to black; lateral body sometimes with bronze iridescence; ground pattern a series of fine oblique lines, one per scale row, of blue-green iridescence over dark olive. Lips, lower head, breast, posteroventral caudal peduncle, and lower few caudal rays pale blue to dark blue. Pelvic and anal fins intense aqua blue, margin and some membranes subdistally black. First dorsal fin distal band bright to dark red; from submargin toward base, spots grade from red or brown to black; anteromedially a blue spot present in some fish, blue suffused posteriorly in one male. Second dorsal fin with most membrane spots and streaks bright to dark red, lower spots red to brown; rays reddish. A small spawning male markedly changed overall body shade rapidly (1–3 seconds) and frequently; shades varied from moderately dusky to very dark, usually darkening when courting and spawning.

BIOLOGY

The life history of *E. cinereum* is known chiefly from the study by Shepard and Burr (1984). Major food items are midge and burrowing mayfly larvae and oligochaete worms; large adults ingest many fewer midges than do smaller fish. The papillose lips of this darter probably are a specialization for detecting food.

Most yearling males and females are mature; maximum life span is 52 months. Shepard and Burr (1984) found no significant difference in growth between the sexes; means for 2-year-old males and females were 74 mm and 71 mm SL. Maximum size is 100 mm SL from Tennessee; the one Virginia specimen is 50 mm SL.

We observed spawning in an aquarium by fish taken from the Little River of Tennessee on 18 February 1984, water 9°C. Spawning by a single pair occurred on 9 March, water 20°C. Courting by both sexes, the male more solicitous, usually lead to mounting of the female and spawning. Oviposition, usually one egg per spawning act, occurred on the vertical side of a clear plastic box filter. Judging from gonad and tubercle development, this species probably spawns in late February to mid-April (Shepard and Burr 1984; our data). In the Little River, the ashy darter migrated upstream during spring (Greenberg 1991).

HABITAT

Etheostoma cinereum inhabits typically clear, cool and warm streams and rivers of moderate gradient. It is generally found in sluggish pool margins among rubble and boulders (Shepard and Burr 1984). In the Little River, most adults were found in a slow backwater, to 1 m depth, where stones had a slight silt overlay.

DISTRIBUTION   Map 172

The ashy darter is widespread but very localized in the Tennessee and Cumberland drainages (Shepard and Burr 1984). In 1970, Jenkins found the single Virginia specimen (VPI 2153) in a jar with four *Percina sciera*, all labeled *P. maculata*. The sample was taken in 1964 by R. E. Wollitz, but originally had only "Clinch River, Virginia" as data. Wollitz (personal communication) recounted in 1971 that the site was between Speers Ferry (just below Copper Creek mouth, Scott County) and Cleveland (Russell County), a reach of 99 rkm.

Two records of *E. cinereum*, based on the above specimen, are plotted for Virginia in compilations by Lee et al. (1980) and Page (1983)—at Speers Ferry and Cleveland. Apparently Masnik's (1974) Speers Ferry location of the record was copied by Lee et al. and Page. Wollitz's data furnished to Lee et al. by Jenkins led to the Cleveland record in both compilations. We

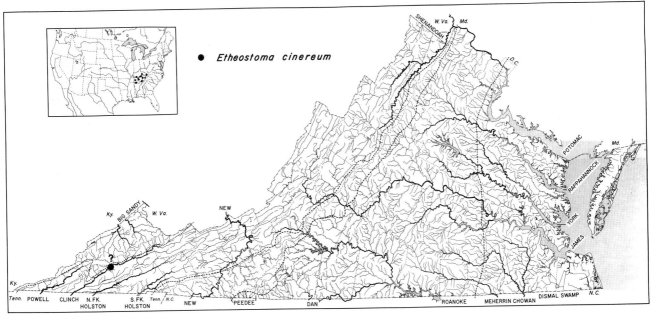

Map 172 Ashy darter. The Clinch River record is valid but the collection site is unspecific.

arbitrarily place the record at the Scott–Russell County line.

Abundance.—*Etheostoma cinereum* was listed as common in the Clinch River by Wollitz (1965), who noted that identification of certain species was tentative. From his list of darters combined from 15 stations and the sampling method he used (electrofishing from a boat), we doubt that he took many *E. cinereum*. The VPI specimen is the only one we found in his collections. Throughout its range *E. cinereum* is rare or uncommon; seldom are more than five individuals taken per collection. However, this species is hard to collect by routine seining methods.

REMARKS

The 1967 Clinch River kill starting at Carbo wiped out virtually all fishes in the main channel downstream to the Tennessee line (*Biogeography*). The extremely toxic discharge was so large, and the river was so low, that some wastewater was forced about 0.8 rkm upstream, to 7.5 rkm below Cleveland. Cleveland is the uppermost possible site of Virginia's *E. cinereum* specimen. If the ashy darter had lived only below Carbo, it may be gone from Virginia. The section above Carbo was fairly well sampled during 1969–1972 (Masnik 1974). The darter is unknown from the Holston, Clinch, and Powell rivers of Tennessee (Shepard and Burr 1984), hence none of these would be a recruitment source. Based on its habitat preference, the ashy darter is unlikely to have occupied a Clinch River tributary before the kill. The most plausible refuge, lower Copper Creek, is smaller than streams typically occupied by *E. cinereum* and has been intensively sampled.

The ashy darter is of special concern nationally (Williams et al. 1989); only 7 of the 15 tributary-system populations are known to have been extant during the past 25 years (Shepard and Burr 1984).

Name.—*Cinereum* means "ashy gray."

Swannanoa darter	*Etheostoma swannanoa* **Jordan and Evermann**

SYSTEMATICS

Etheostoma swannanoa was described by Jordan and Evermann (*in* Jordan 1889a) from the South Fork Swannanoa River of North Carolina and the Middle and South forks of the Holston River of Virginia. Within the subgenus *Etheostoma*, the Swannanoa darter is placed in the *thalassinum* species group, which contains two south Atlantic slope species (*E. thalassinum, E. inscriptum*) and the Tennessee drainage endemic species *E. blennius* (Richards 1966; Thompson 1973a; Burr 1979; Page 1981). Burr (1979) and Bailey and Etnier (1988) indicated that *E. swannanoa* and *E. blennius* are sister species. Bailey and

Etnier (1988) and we disagree with the inclusion of *E. blennius* in the *variatum* species group by Wiley and Mayden (1985) and Mayden (1987a, 1987b). The two traits used for that linkage also are shared with at least *E. swannanoa* and *E. thalassinum*.

DESCRIPTION

Materials.—From Collette (1965), Richards (1966), Wiley and Collette (1970), Page (1981), 1 Tennessee, 3 North Carolina, and 11 Virginia series; meristic data exclusively from Richards (1966). Life color from 8 Virginia series; brilliant green fish from the Little River.

Anatomy.—A barred or blotched darter with rows of orange spots laterally; adults are 50–75 mm SL. Body moderate or robust in profile, slightly or moderately compressed; snout short and blunt; frenum well developed; branchiostegal membranes broadly conjoined; caudal fin slightly emarginate or truncate. Breeding male with tubercles on lower body scales in the form of thickened pads that often are elevated and pointed; ridges present on rays of lower fins; female nontuberculate (except see *Remarks*). Female genital papilla tubular, thick, very long, the longest among darters (Figure 70). Cheek, opercle, and breast naked; nape and belly usually fully scaled.

Meristics.—Lateral line complete, scales (46)48–58(62); scales above lateral line 6–8(9); scales below lateral line (5)6–7(8); circumpeduncle scales (15)17–22(23). Dorsal spines (10)11–13; dorsal rays (11)12–13(14); anal spines 2; anal rays (7)8–9; pectoral rays (14)15–16(17).

Color in Preservative.—Midside with 8–11 large dark marks, more barlike and slightly oblique anteriorly, more blotchlike posteriorly. Dorsolateral area light to dark, usually spotted, blotched, or scrawled. Adult male with scale centers dark, forming longitudinal rows of spots from upper to lower side, occasionally onto belly. Dorsum with usually 6 saddles, often only 3 or 4 present, 1 each at nape, posterior insertion of both dorsal fins, and caudal peduncle. Lower side and belly pale or dusky. Head dusky or dark, patterns vague, subocular bar occasionally present. Some large nuptial males very dusky to dark overall, marks largely masked.

First dorsal fin spine tips pale; distal band dark; submarginally to submedially slightly to heavily peppered, sometimes a dark streak evident in each membrane or a dark medial band is formed; epibasally to basally pale to dark;

Fish 276 *Etheostoma swannanoa* adult male 69 mm SL (REJ 1149), VA, Tazewell County, Little River, 31 March 1985.

Fish 277 *Etheostoma swannanoa* adult female 54 mm SL (REJ 1079), VA, Washington County, South Fork Holston River, 24 April 1984.

spines evenly pigmented (except for tips). Second dorsal membranes pale or dark, streaked if dark, streaks most evident in spawning male; rays tessellated or all dark. Caudal membranes dusky; rays tessellated or evenly pigmented; caudal base with dark median spot or suffusion vertically flanked by 2 pale areas. Anal, pelvic, and pectoral fins in male usually evenly pigmented, rays appear pale due to epidermal thickening; in female and juvenile, membranes clear, rays slightly pigmented.

Color in Life Plate 34.—Adult female upper body pale to dark olive; lateral marks darker olive; lower side pale yellow or satiny cream; venter cream. Rows of dusky orange-red spots present on upper side and midside of large female. Lower head, breast, and basal half of genital papilla turquoise in some specimens, wholly pale in others. First dorsal fin distal and basal bands and pectoral base pale orange. Several ventral rays of caudal fin, basal half of anal fin, and pelvic fin base light turquoise in some specimens.

Prenuptial and most nuptial males with ground color of upper head and body tan to tan-olive, side of body grading from creamy olive dorsolaterally to satiny white ventrally; spots forming longitudinal rows rusty orange or brown; bars grading from dark olive to pale olive, some with a hint of turquoise diffusing ventrad; lower head and breast varying shades of turquoise; iris dusky coppery to bright orange.

First dorsal spine tips white; distal band yellow-orange to orange-red; submarginal to submedial streaks red-brown to, proximally, blackish olive; epibasally often a row of dusky orange to bright golden orange short streaks or spots; black basally along much of the fin. Second dorsal membrane streaks largely orange-red to red-brown; rays yellow-olive to olive-brown. Caudal membranes brown or orange distally in some specimens, upper base and lower portion of fin turquoise, elsewhere membranes and rays olive; upper and lower areas of caudal base also pale tan. Anal and pelvic fins turquoise, pale orange distally in some fish; pectoral fin base bronze, rays olive dorsally to salmon ventrally. Small adult males have lesser development of turquoise, orange, and red.

In largest nuptial males, turquoise was more intense and in some areas was replaced by emerald green; also, bright green occurred on entire underside of head and body and almost all of caudal fin. These fish rapidly developed and lost reddish hues in the second dorsal and caudal fins, altered the body ground shade from creamy to dusky, and varied the intensity of the lateral bars. These peak colors were present when fish were collected and during aggression, spawning, and some rest periods in an aquarium.

BIOLOGY

The Swannanoa darter is a typical swift-water benthic insectivore; 15 adults from North Carolina and Virginia fed chiefly on immature mayflies, caddisflies, and midges (R. L. Steele, in litt.). Based on lengths or scale-aging of 96 Virginia specimens, most males and females first spawn at age 2. A few age-1

fish may have matured late in the spawning period. Age-3 males and females survived into early fall; one April male was age 4. Males tend to exceed females in size; of Virginia adults captured during 17 February–22 June, 35 were males of 53–84 mm SL, mean, 66, and 35 were females, 47–69 mm, mean, 58. An 85-mm SL male from Tennessee is the largest known (Page 1983: Plate 12G ["75 mm SL" given as maximum size on p. 65 is in error, according to L. M. Page]).

The spawning period was suggested by Richards (1966) to be April and May, based on the presence of tubercles on males from late March through early June. Richards took apparent spawning pairs in the Middle Fork Holston River on 2 April, water 7.5°C; the habitat was rubble and small gravel in riffles 30–45 cm deep. Most fish in the Middle Fork on 22 April 1972, and in the South Fork Holston River on 24 April 1984 (water 8°C), seemed prenuptial or in an interlude from spawning.

Adults from the Little River on 17 February 1985 (7.8°C) appeared to be prenuptial. At the same site on 31 March 1985 (14.4°C), males were in peak nuptial color, and a pair spawned two days later in an aquarium. At that site in 1986, on 11 March (10°C), males were in peak color and females almost fully gravid; on 19 April (15°C), males were brilliant, females were fully gravid, and one female released ripe ova when pressed. Males and females taken during mid- to late June in Virginia and North Carolina appeared to be in spawning condition. A spawning period of late March through June, perhaps involving more than one peak, is indicated.

When the Little River fish were placed in an aquarium, two males sometimes laterally displayed with fins erect and chased each other in tight circles. One male spawned several times with one of the five ripe females. The female buried herself partially in fine to pea-size gravel, and then was mounted by the male. Diameters of six stripped ripe ova were 1.9–2.2 mm.

HABITAT

The swannanoa darter inhabits cool, moderate and high-gradient, clear streams (up to 30 m width in Virginia). It occupies riffles of mostly rubble and scattered areas of gravel and boulder. In the South Fork Holston River, juveniles and gravid females were taken with equal frequency in slower shallower areas and the swifter deeper portions, to 60 cm depth; the largest males most commonly occurred in the latter. In the Little River nearly all of the prenuptial and spawning fish were found in predominantly rubble,

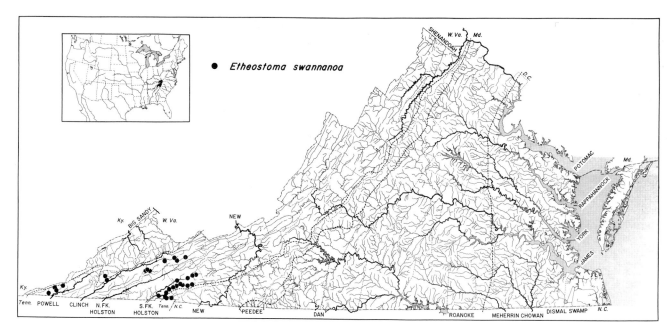

Map 173   Swannanoa darter.

gentle to swift riffles of 30–50 cm depth. Much of the stretch was slightly to moderately silted due to recent draining of a pond; *E. swannanoa* tended to localize in the least silted areas. Habitats occupied by *E. swannanoa* in the Little River and Stony Creek, two Clinch River tributaries with contrasting habitat, are described under the Clinch sculpin. Because the Swannanoa darter apparently is absent from several streams within its general range that have suitable clarity and gradient, cool water may be an important habitat characteristic for this species.

DISTRIBUTION   Map 173

Etheostoma swannanoa is endemic to the upper Tennessee drainage. It occupies much of the southern Blue Ridge Province, barely extending into the Virginia part of that province in Whitetop Laurel Creek, a trout stream. The largest Virginia population occupies the portion of the South Fork Holston River within the Valley and Ridge Province near the Blue Ridge; most of these fish are in trout water or sections fed by such. Elsewhere in the Valley and Ridge, this species disjunctly inhabits the upper Middle Fork Holston River and a few tributaries of the Clinch and Powell rivers; many of the sites are in reaches fed by large limestone springs. The largest specimens known from Virginia are from the Little River just below Maiden Spring, the largest spring in the region.

The generally warmer North Fork Holston system is unoccupied by the Swannanoa darter. Page's record (1983; UMMZ 187521) there is based on specimens that apparently have been mislabeled (R. M. Bailey, in litt.). They were collected by Jordan (1889b), who reported *E. swannanoa* only from the South and Middle forks of the Holston and from the Swannanoa River. Jordan noted that "It is evidently a species of the cold, clear waters"; he gave 23.9°C as the North Fork temperature.

Abundance.—Generally uncommon.

REMARKS

The gloriously hued Swannanoa darter is the darter most restricted to cool streams in Virginia.

Future students of the darter relationships mentioned in *Systematics* should consider that *E. swannanoa* exhibits a trend toward the *variatum* group in nuptial tuberculation. All four large female Swannanoa darters in one series (Middle Fork Holston, REJ 538) have moderate development of acute tubercles on the lower body. Tubercles are absent from large nuptial females in six other series, as also determined by other investigators from many more specimens.

Name.—*Swannanoa* was named after the Swannanoa River in the Blue Ridge of North Carolina.

Variegate darter   *Etheostoma variatum* Kirtland

SYSTEMATICS

The variegate darter, a member of the subgenus *Etheostoma*, was described from Ohio in 1838. With two Ozarkian species (*E. euzonum*; *E. tetrazonum*) and two New drainage endemic species (*E. kanawhae*, *E. osburni*), it forms the *variatum* species group (Hubbs and Black 1940b; Richards 1966; Tsai 1967; Burr 1979; Page 1981; Page and Cordes 1983; McKeown et al. 1984). The enigmatic Maryland darter *E. sellare* may also be in this group (e.g., Knapp 1976; Wiley and Mayden 1985). *Etheostoma variatum* is the sister species of the *E. kanawhae–E. osburni* species pair (McKeown et al. 1984; Wiley and Mayden 1985; Mayden 1987a, 1987b).

DESCRIPTION

Materials.—From Hubbs and Black (1940b), Raney (1941), Collette (1965), Trautman (1981), Page (1983), 1 collection each from New York, West Virginia, and Kentucky, and 2 Virginia adults; our circumpeduncle scale counts from 16 specimens. Color in life from Trautman (1957, 1981), Kuehne and Barbour (1983), and Page (1983).

Anatomy.—A speckled or barred darter with 4 saddles; adults are 50–75 mm SL. Body form moderate or somewhat robust; snout moderate, frenated; branchiostegal membranes broadly united; caudal fin truncate. Breeding tubercles on lower body in both sexes. Female genital papilla stout, moderately long, rounded or somewhat compressed, tip slightly indented. Cheek naked; opercle naked or partly scaled; nape and belly scaled; breast usually scaled posteriorly.

Meristics.—Lateral line complete, scales (48)50–56(60); scales above lateral line 6–7(8); scales below lateral line (7)8–9(10); circumpeduncle scale rows (18)20–22(25). Dorsal spines (11)12–13; dorsal rays (12)13–14(16); anal spines 2; anal rays (8)9–10; pectoral rays (14)15(16).

Color in Preservative.—Back with 4, rarely 5 saddles (sometimes 6—Trautman 1981), these often separate from lateral bars in female, generally confluent with some bars in male. Side usually speckled or evenly dusky anteriorly, generally with 1 dark bar just behind the head and usually 6 bars on posterior body including the caudal base; bars are vertical and, notably in female, may develop only as blotches below the lateral line, large marks being absent. Subocular bar vertical or sloped anteroventrad, wide, often vague; prepectoral area usually with dark mark. Some males very dark, obliterating some body markings.

First dorsal fin of adult female with six bands, sequentially: pale distally, dusky, clear, broad blackish, narrow clear, and basally black; male first dorsal fin similar but bands more highly defined. Second dorsal fin somewhat tessellated in female; mostly dusky with darker margin and base in male. Caudal and pectoral fins somewhat tessellated in both sexes, duskier in male; anal and pelvic fins plain in female, dusky in male.

Fish 278 *Etheostoma variatum* adult male 77 mm SL (WHH 104), VA, Buchanan County, Knox Creek, 28 June 1983.

Fish 279 *Etheostoma variatum* adult female 64 mm SL (SIUC 7989), KY, Wolfe County, Red River, 25 October 1978.

Color in Life.—Adult male with dorsum olive, belly light green, breast white or blue-tinted. Lateral bars green to blue-green (dark in preservative); interspaces yellow, each with 1 or more orange or orange-red spots or a similarly colored bar. Flank anteriorly with a reddish blush or a wide, bright red-orange or red stripe.

First dorsal fin bands (sequence as above): clear, orange-red, clear, blue-black, clear, red-brown. Second dorsal fin mostly dusky olive-green; orange-red speckling tending to form rows along membranes; dusky blue margin. Caudal fin margin and base dusky blue-black, centrally orange-green with red spots. Anal and pelvic fins dusky green; tips of spines and anterior rays whitish; pectoral fin olive with rows of reddish or brown spots.

In nuptial male, blue-green, orange, and red colors are intensified (orange between dark body bars may be somewhat masked in blackish males); colors in female are subdued or largely olive.

Larvae.—Described by May (1969).

BIOLOGY

The diet of the variegate darter is midge larvae, other immature insects, and mites (Turner 1921; Wehnes 1973 *in* Page 1983; Nemecek 1978). This species first spawns at age 2 and lives 3 years. Males grow more rapidly than females; average lengths of Pennsylvania fish at the end of the third summer (age 2) are males 67 mm SL and females 62 mm (Lachner et al. 1950). The largest Virginia specimen is 77 mm SL; maximum size is 90 mm SL (Page 1983) .

Individuals of an Ohio population moved downstream during winter, occupied pools, and migrated back into spawning riffles in the spring. Spawning occurs during April and May in natural waters of Ohio, and it occurred in an aquarium in late March, water 10–15.5°C (May 1969). Spawning was completed by the first week of June in (presumably) the upper Ohio basin (Nemecek 1978).

HABITAT

Etheostoma variatum occupies warm streams and rivers and tends to localize in riffles of gravel, rubble, boulder, some sand, and little siltation. The two recent Virginia records are from small streams, one of which has been stocked with trout and thus presumably is cool.

DISTRIBUTION   Map 174

The variegate darter is widespread in most of the upper and middle Ohio River basin, but is absent from the New drainage; it occurs sparingly in Virginia in the Big Sandy drainage. It apparently has been extirpated from much of the Big Sandy of Virginia. Two records are from Levisa Fork and Long Branch in 1937; only two other collections were made in the upper drainage in that year. Wide surveying of the upper Big Sandy began in 1970 and yielded only one record each from Dismal and Knox creeks.

The record of *E. variatum* by Evermann and Hildebrand (1916) for Indian Creek, a Powell River tributary near Cumberland Gap, was erroneously placed in the Cumberland drainage by Hubbs and Trautman (1932) and Hubbs and Black (1940b). These authors, Masnik (1974), and we could not locate the specimen, which probably was misidentified (see *E. caeruleum*). *Etheostoma variatum* actually is unknown from the Tennessee and Cumberland drainages.

Abundance.—Often common in parts of its range, but only 10 specimens are known from Virginia (8 taken in 1937, 2 in 1979–1983).

REMARKS

The rarity and localization of the variegate darter in Virginia is an apparent result of extensive siltation caused largely by coal mining. Jenkins and Musick (1979) considered the conservation status of *E. variatum* in Virginia to be undetermined, possibly extirpated. This opinion predated much of the recent sampling, which in some major streams has been intensive. The darter's Virginia status should be endangered (Burkhead and Jenkins 1991). This species can be considered a "canary" of the health of rivers of the coal region.

Name.—*Variatum* stands for "variegated" coloration.

Kanawha darter   *Etheostoma kanawhae* (Raney)

SYSTEMATICS

Etheostoma kanawhae was described in 1941 from the upper and middle New River drainage of Virginia and North Carolina. It and *E. osburni*, both advanced members of the *variatum* group of the subgenus *Etheostoma*, form a species pair that is endemic to the New drainage.

DESCRIPTION

Materials.—From Raney (1941), Page (1983), and 12 Virginia series; our counts from 24 specimens. Color in life from 5 Virginia series.

Anatomy.—A speckled or barred darter with 5–6 saddles and 47–58 lateral line scales; adults are 50–65 mm SL.

Fish 280 *Etheostoma kanawhae* adult male 66 mm SL (NMB 869), VA, Floyd County, West Fork Little River, 27 April 1984.

Fish 281 *Etheostoma kanawhae* adult female 54 mm SL (REJ 973), VA, Grayson County, Big Fox Creek, 10 June 1983.

Body form and snout moderate; frenum present; branchiostegal membranes broadly united; caudal fin truncate or slightly emarginate. Breeding tubercles and genital papilla as in *E. variatum*. Cheek and opercle naked; nape and belly fully scaled; breast (0)10–20(40)% scaled.

Meristics.—Lateral line complete, scales (47)50–58; scales above lateral line 6–7(8); scales below lateral line 7–8(10); circumpeduncle scales 18–21. Dorsal spines (11)12–13(14); dorsal rays 12–13(14); anal spines 2; anal rays 8–9(10); pectoral rays (14)15(16).

Color in Preservative.—Essentially as in *E. variatum*, except that the back has 5–6 saddles and the side has (8)9–10(11) dark zones, bars, or blotches. As in *E. variatum*, the lateral dark areas are less obvious or shorter anteriorly, and some specimens, most frequently females, have the side only speckled or plain. We have not seen *E. kanawhae* as dark as some *E. variatum*.

Color in Life Plate 34.—Virtually as in *E. variatum*, except that adult males usually have 9–10 red-spotted or red-barred areas along body. In our color plate of a 66-mm SL prespawning or spawning male (the most colorful we studied) and in several other reproductive males (including photos—Deacon et al. 1979; Kuehne and Barbour 1983; Page 1983), there is considerable tan to olive on the body including borders of red marks; at most, the red marks on the side form interrupted or short bars; and the cheek has a yellow-orange cast. Raney's (1941) description of the largest known male (72 mm SL) indicates that in peak development some red bars are long.

Nuptial female slightly more subdued than small nuptial male; slightly blue-tinged at most; areas that are red in male typically are yellow- or orange-spotted, or distinct chromatic marks are absent.

COMPARISON

Etheostoma kanawhae is distinguished from *E. osburni* by its larger scales: (1) lateral line scales [(47)50–58 in *kanawhae* vs. (58)59–66(71) in *osburni*]; (2) scales above lateral line [6–7(8) vs. (7)8–9]; (3) scales below lateral line [7–8(10) vs. 9–11]; (4) circumpeduncle scales [18–21 vs. (22)23–24(26)].

Differing also is the location of the posteriormost pore of the anterior section of the infraorbital canal—generally pore 4. In *kanawhae* it occurs at the end of a short or medium-length caniculus that extends upward, or it occasionally opens on the main canal or on a short ventrally extending caniculus. In *osburni* the pore occurs at the end of a long caniculus that extends upward almost to the eye.

Life colors of males differ on average but this may be related to fish size. Compared with *kanawhae*, the larger *osburni* are more ornate, with the cheek orange-red and additional small red marks present on head and breast; blue-green more widespread on body; more bars present on body; red bars on body larger, more pronounced, most or all of the anterior bars connected to red flank stripe; most red bars set off from blue-green by white border; 1–2 red spots develop within certain blue-green bars in some males; all fins except the first dorsal have more red; clear

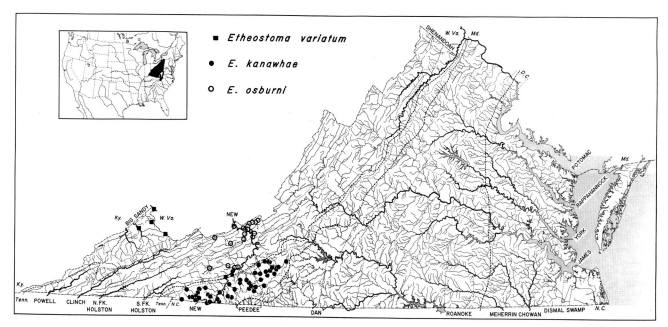

Map 174   Variegate darter, Kanawha darter, and candy darter. The total range (inset) of variegate darter is the dark area west and north of white area (candy darter).

bands in first dorsal fin are narrowed or obliterated by a wider medial bluish band.

BIOLOGY

Fifteen Kanawha darters had fed on immature insects, mainly mayflies, caddisflies, midges, and blackflies (R. C. Bumgarner, in litt.). Based on gonadal and length–frequency data from 53 specimens, many of them scale-aged, some males are mature at age 1 and all fish of both sexes spawn at age 2. Both sexes attained age 3, the oldest being an October male. The largest immature fish sampled during 27 April–10 June were a 45-mm SL male and a 42-mm female. Of adults from this period, 14 males were 43–69 mm SL and 15 females were 48–63 mm, both means 57. Although not indicated by the mean lengths, males tend to reach larger size than females. The largest Virginia female was 63 mm SL; seven males were larger. The largest specimen is a male 72 mm SL from North Carolina (Raney 1941).

Spawning occurs in mid- to late spring. Peak nuptial color occurred in early April to early June fish. Ovarian condition of Raney's (1941) early April specimens indicated that spawning was imminent in the warmwater forks of the New River in North Carolina. Ovarian and tubercle development of females taken on 4 June 1984, most of them captured together with a highly colored male, indicated that spawning was in progress. These fish were in a Virginia brook trout stream, in riffles of mixed sand, gravel, and rubble,

depths 0.3–0.7 m; the water was 18.9°C. Fish from a warmer stream on 10 June of 1976 and 1983 were largely or fully gravid. The Kanawha darter may be territorial, based on the high frequency of large males with mutilated fins.

HABITAT

The Kanawha darter occupies runs and riffles with hard substrate in cold and warm, generally clear creeks and streams, and it extends into the large New River.

DISTRIBUTION   Map 174

Etheostoma kanawhae is endemic to the upper and middle New River drainage of Virginia and North Carolina, where it is virtually restricted to, and generally distributed in the Blue Ridge Province. Its range is complementary (parapatric) to that of its close relative *E. osburni*.

The lowermost system occupied by *E. kanawhae* is the Little River, which is mostly in the Blue Ridge and joins the New River in the Valley and Ridge Province just below Claytor Dam. In the Little River system, this species is widespread in the Blue Ridge but is unknown from the Valley and Ridge. The Little River population is isolated; the range gap (of both *E. kanawhae* and *E. osburni*) in the New River may have resulted from extirpation owing partly to creation of Claytor Lake. Closest to the head of the lake, the

Kanawha darter is present in the New River and lower Shorts Creek just within the Valley and Ridge, and it is widespread in the Blue Ridge portion of the Big Reed Island Creek system. Records of *E. kanawhae* (and *E. osburni*) are notably lacking from Cripple Creek, the uppermost western Valley and Ridge tributary. Above Cripple Creek, *E. kanawhae* is widely distributed into the headwaters of the New.

Our present concept of the complementary ranges of *E. kanawhae* and *E. osburni* derives from reidentification of many specimens. All of Ross and Perkins' (1959) records of *E. osburni* from the Little River system and above, except those from Reed Creek, are of *E. kanawhae*. Below the Little River, Ross and Perkins' (1959: VPI 890 [= AMNH 61637]) specimen of *E. osburni* from Dismal Creek (Walker Creek system) was faultily regarded as *E. kanawhae* by Jenkins and Musick (1979), based on an error by a colleague. The record of *E. kanawhae* from the lower New River in Virginia had been accepted by Jenkins and Musick (1979) from a catalog and was compiled by Hocutt et al. (*in* Lee et al. 1980), Page (1983), and Wiley and Mayden (1985); we redetermined the four specimens (CU 24950) to be *E. osburni*. We reidentified as *E. flabellare* the poorly preserved specimen on which the 1885 record (Jenkins and Musick 1979: USNM 131549) of *E. kanawhae* from the upper Reed Creek system was based. The record of *E. kanawhae* in the New River between the Little River and Reed Creek, and that of

E. osburni in upper Sinking Creek (Hocutt et al. *in* Lee et al. 1980) are misplots of records from typical parts of their ranges.

Abundance.—Rare to abundant, usually uncommon or common.

REMARKS

The nuptial male Kanawha darter is a splendidly colorful fish, only slightly less so than its compatriot in the New drainage, the candy darter.

Etheostoma kanawhae was ranked as threatened in North Carolina and Virginia because of proposed large impoundments on the upper New River (Bailey 1977; Deacon et al. 1979; Williams 1981; Williams et al. 1989). However, because the project plans have been shelved and because this species is generally distributed in the Blue Ridge Province, including many protected headwater trout streams, Jenkins and Musick (1979) and Burkhead and Jenkins (1991) concluded that it did not merit protective status. Much of the upper New River was recently designated a National Scenic River.

Name.—*Kanawhae* is based on the Kanawha River, the lower continuation of the New River in West Virginia.

Candy darter   *Etheostoma osburni* (Hubbs and Trautman)

SYSTEMATICS

Etheostoma osburni was described from the middle and lower New River drainage of Virginia and West Virginia by Hubbs and Trautman (1932), whose "variant" specimens were reidentified as *E. kanawhae* by Raney (1941). These cognate endemic species of the New drainage are advanced members of the *variatum* group of the subgenus *Etheostoma*.

DESCRIPTION

Materials.—From Hubbs and Trautman (1932), Raney (1941), Page (1983), 15 series from Virginia, and 2 from West Virginia; our counts from 36 specimens. Color in life from 3 Virginia samples.

Anatomy.—A speckled or barred darter with 5–6 saddles and 58–71 lateral line scales; adults are 55–80 mm SL. Body moderate or somewhat elongate; snout moderate; frenum present; branchiostegal membranes broadly conjoined. Breeding tubercles and female genital papilla as in

E. variatum. Cheek and opercle naked; nape and belly fully scaled; breast 0–20(35)% scaled.

Meristics.—Lateral line complete, scales (58)59–66(71); scales above lateral line (7)8–9; scales below lateral line 9–11; circumpeduncle scales (22)23–24(26). Dorsal spines (10)12–13(14); dorsal rays (12)13–14(16); anal spines 2; anal rays (8)9–10(11); pectoral rays (14)15.

Color in Preservative.—Essentially as in *E. kanawhae*, except that dark lateral bars or blotches tend to be more numerous, 10–11(12); melanistic specimens not seen.

Color in Life Plate 34.—The "candy-striped" nuptial male is brilliantly ornate. Coloration of large, highly colored specimens is much the same as described for *E. kanawhae*; differences are noted under *Comparison* for that species. In juvenile and small nuptial male, red bars are relatively narrow or interrupted; some anterior red bars are connected to the red flank stripe; bars between red bars are mostly green (more blue in large adult male), most prominent below lateral line; fin colors subdued. Blue-green apparently had largely faded before the specimen (probably a large male) in Kuehne and Barbour (1983) was photo-

Fish 282 *Etheostoma osburni* adult male 86 mm SL (REJ 1082), VA, Giles County, Big Stony Creek, 26 April 1984.

Fish 283 *Etheostoma osburni* adult female 70 mm SL (REJ 988), VA, Giles County, Big Stony Creek, 20 June 1983.

graphed. Adult female as described for *E. kanawhae* or slightly more blue-tinged and red-orange marked; slightly less colorful than small adult male *E. osburni*.

Kuehne and Barbour (1983) stated that nuptial color of the candy darter persists longer than in most darters; the comment apparently is based on only one observation of this species in Big Stony Creek during June. Spawning probably extends into June in that stream. Our prenuptial to postnuptial males taken during late April, mid-June, and early July in Big Stony Creek had essentially the same hues and brightness.

COMPARISON

See *E. kanawhae*.

BIOLOGY

The natural history of *E. osburni* is probably similar to that of the two other Virginia members of the *variatum* group, *E. variatum* and *E. kanawhae*. Fourteen specimens ate larvae of mayflies, caddisflies, and true flies, particularly midges; one had taken a water mite (T. E. Inman, in litt.). Sixty-seven specimens indicated a pattern of maturation and longevity, and a sexual difference in size that are common in darters. Maturation occurred within 2 years. Males and females lived 3 years but none of that age were found after July. The largest immature fish taken during 9

April–6 July were a 58-mm SL male and a 53-mm female. Males attained larger size than females; of adults taken in that period, 10 were males of 66–86 mm SL, mean, 76, and 24 were females of 51–71 mm, mean, 64. The largest of each sex is from Virginia; the male is the largest specimen known.

Spawning occurs in mid- to late spring. In Big Stony Creek, probable prenuptial specimens were taken on 27 April 1984, water 11°C. Apparent prespawning and spawning fish were found on 26 April 1985 at 15.5°C. On 20 June 1983, water 18°C, adults had retained tubercles and females contained mature ova. On 6 July 1963, water 17°C, adults lacked tubercles and were spent. All adults were taken among rubble and boulder in runs and riffles at depths of 0.4–1 m; very few small patches of sand were present. Kuehne and Barbour (1983) took apparent postnuptial specimens in Big Stony Creek in June, but did not give a date. Postnuptial specimens were taken in the warm New River on 19 June. Based on the high frequency of large males with damaged fins, these fish may be territorially aggressive.

HABITAT

The candy darter populates rocky, typically clear, cold creeks and warm streams, and extends into the large New River; adults occupy runs, riffles, and swift pockets.

DISTRIBUTION   Map 174

Etheostoma osburni is endemic to the New drainage; a report from the Kanawha drainage proper is rejected (Hocutt et al. 1979, 1986). It occupies the Valley and Ridge Province of Virginia and West Virginia and the Appalachian Plateau of West Virginia. Its complementary distributional relationship with *E. kanawhae* is discussed under that species. The candy darter is well distributed in certain West Virginia streams (Hocutt et al. 1978, 1979) and in Big Stony Creek of Virginia, a mostly cold, tumbling, boulder-strewn softwater (Ross and Perkins 1959) stream near the West Virginia line. Elsewhere in Virginia its range appears to have been reduced in the last 40 years; some tributary populations may be extirpated.

In the Wolf Creek system, three specimens were taken in trout water in the lower 1 rkm of Laurel Creek in 1951; we caught a total of five juveniles in lowermost Laurel Creek on two visits in 1984. The upper Wolf system has been well surveyed, but the main stem below Laurel Creek has been scantily sampled for darters. In lower Big Walker Creek, *E. osburni* was taken during 1957–1963 from two sites, one specimen at each; we sought it unsuccessfully in Big Walker during 1991. One specimen was taken in 1957 from Dismal Creek, a troutwater tributary in the Walker system. In both Sinking Creek and Spruce Run, *E. osburni* was reported (Burton and Odum 1945) only at the lowest station. The records are supported by UMMZ 137578, one candy darter labeled "Sinking Creek and Spruce Run." Subsequently Sinking Creek was extensively sampled and lower Spruce Run was moderately worked, without finding *E. osburni*.

Four New River sites in Giles County yielded nine *E. osburni* during 1952–1974 (Hocutt et al. 1973; Stauffer et al. 1976; CU 24950, 25360). The sites are at or within 3 rkm of the mouths of the East River, Big Stony Creek, or Little Stony Creek. Segments of the New River population may be resident or derived by waifing from tributaries. The range gap below Claytor Dam may be related to tailwater conditions including pollution from a munitions plant (Ross 1973). *Etheostoma osburni* was not found by intensive sampling in the tailwater of Bluestone Dam in West Virginia during 1984 (Lobb 1986).

A disjunct population of *E. osburni* is known from two western New River tributaries—Reed Creek and Pine Run—in the Valley and Ridge Province near the Blue Ridge Province. This population is situated between those of *E. kanawhae* in Big Reed Island Creek and the upper New River. In lower Reed Creek, 12 candy darters were taken during 1931–1957 but none by us in 1983 and 1991. From Reed Creek or its South Fork, Hubbs and Trautman (1932) and we identified as *E. osburni* a specimen taken in 1885 (USNM 39542, plotted on the South Fork), but we did not find this species in lower and middle South Fork Reed Creek during 1983–1986. One *E. osburni* was found in lower Pine Run in 1954 but none by us in 1983.

Because *E. osburni* appears to be most successful in Virginia in high-gradient, soft, cool, Blue Ridge-type waters, it is odd that most records from typical Valley and Ridge tributaries are from the lower reaches. If this species was more common in the upper (Blue Ridge-like) reaches, it should have been detected more widely by the greater intensity of collecting exerted there. The lack of a record of *E. osburni* (and *E. kanawhae*) from several tributary systems in the Valley and Ridge of the New is notable. The largest of these systems—Peak Creek—has had major pollution.

Abundance.—The candy darter generally is rare in Virginia; at best, we found it to be uncommon in Big Stony Creek. Kuehne and Barbour (1983) indicated great difficulty in capturing this species in Big Stony, probably because of seine-obstructive boulders and strong currents. We have always taken it there at several sites above the gypsum plant, most successfully by electroshocker.

REMARKS

The candy darter's pattern of red, white, and blue-green hues makes it one of the most exquisitely colored North American freshwater fishes (Kuehne and Barbour 1983; Page and Burr 1991).

Etheostoma osburni and *E. kanawhae* probably originated in the lower and upper New drainage respectively from an *E. variatum*-like ancestor (*Biogeography*). Their intimate phylogenetic relationship is shown by strong similarities in coloration, morphology, biotopes, life history aspects, and indeed, their genomes. Competitive former adjustment of their complementary ranges is indicated by the occurrence of the Little River population of *E. kanawhae* within a hiatus in the range of *E. osburni*. Hence it could be coincidental that their shared range boundary is a physiographic boundary.

The candy darter was listed as threatened in Virginia and West Virginia by Deacon et al. (1979), Williams (1981), and Williams et al. (1989). Burkhead and Jenkins (1991) may have underrated the jeopardy of the candy darter in Virginia by recommending it for only special concern status. This species may be threatened or endangered in Virginia owing to local-ization or extirpation of most populations there.

Kuehne and Barbour (1983) indicated that trout stocking may adversely affect *E. osburni*; trout can prey on darters. We believe that wading by anglers may reduce some darter populations. Anglers tend to avoid slick boulders by stepping on sandy patches in their lee. Patches of sand, which may be spawning sites of the candy darter, are scarce in the swift wa-ter of most Virginia trout streams. However, trout streams such as Big Stony Creek are better protected legally than most others.

Name.—After Raymond C. Osburn, an ichthyolo-gist of Ohio State University. We proposed and Rob-ins et al. (1991) accepted the common name "candy darter" to replace the cumbersome "finescale saddled darter." The term candy-stripe has been applied (Richards 1966) to the pattern of *E. osburni* and certain other members of the *variatum* group.

Greenside darter   *Etheostoma blennioides* Rafinesque

SYSTEMATICS

The greenside darter was described in 1819 from the Ohio River. It is a constituent of the five-member *blennioides* species group of the subgenus *Etheostoma* (Collette 1965; Richards 1966; R. V. Miller 1968; Bailey and Etnier 1988). Miller (1968) recognized four sub-species; two occur in Virginia—*E. b. blennioides* in the Big Sandy, New, and Potomac drainages, and *E. b. newmanii* (Agassiz) in the Tennessee drainage.

DESCRIPTION

Materials.—From Lachner et al. (1950), Fahy (1954), Col-lette (1965), R. V. Miller (1968), 24 collections from the upper Tennessee, 2 from the New, 2 from the Big Sandy, and 1 from the Cumberland drainages. Color in life from 4 lots of nuptial male *E. b. newmanii* and 1 of *E. b. blennioides*; the description is principally from *E. b newmanii*; some differences from *E. b. blennioides* are noted.

Anatomy.—A darter with a lateral series of U- or V-shaped marks; adults are 60–90 mm SL. Body elongate, slightly compressed; snout somewhat short, moderate or blunt, often bulbous, and may slightly overhang tip of upper lip; side of upper lip uniquely bound to side of snout by skin (Figure 79B); frenum present, sometimes concealed by a small knob at front of upper lip, sometimes poorly developed; branchiostegal membranes broadly conjoined; caudal fin emarginate. Breeding male occasionally with tu-bercles like those of *E. swannanoa*. Female genital papilla becomes long and tubular during winter and shrinks soon

Fish 284 *Etheostoma blennioides newmanii* adult male 104 mm SL (REJ 981), VA, Washington County, South Fork Holston River, 15 June 1983.

Fish 285 *Etheostoma b. blennioides* adult female 53 mm SL (REJ 977), VA, Wythe County Reed Creek, 14 June 1983.

after spawning. Cheek, opercle, nape, and belly scaled; breast naked or partly scaled.

Meristics.—Lateral line complete, scales (59)66–80(86); circumpeduncle scales (21)24–30(32). Dorsal spines (11)13–14(16); dorsal rays (11)12–14(16); anal spines 2; anal rays (6)7–9(10); pectoral rays (13)14–15(16).

Etheostoma b. blennioides differs from *E. b. newmanii* by having lower scale, dorsal spine, and dorsal ray counts; a small naked area often on anterior belly; and a less-developed knob on lip tip.

Color in Preservative.—Midside with 5–8 dark U- or V-shaped marks; with dark interspaces, the marks occasionally form a sinuous line; in breeding male, marks diffuse onto lower side and occasionally into saddles as distinct bands, sometimes obliterating the U-design. Dorsolateral area irregularly patterned; dorsum with usually 6–7 saddles. Ocular bars distinct or obscured by general darkening of head; subocular bar curved ventroposteriad; preocular bars often interconnected to form a "moustache" on snout tip; snout and cheek sometimes with additional wavy marks; prepectoral bar usually well developed. Male is duskier overall than female, especially during spawning.

First dorsal fin usually as in Figure 69A, with a narrow clear distal band; subdistal and submarginal areas pale to dark, subdistal darkest; medially dark; epibasally pale or clear; basally moderately dusky to dark; rays uniform or tessellated. Second dorsal membranes streaked, fading distally, rays uniform or tessellated. Lower fins variably pigmented, the pectoral the most often tessellated, the anal the most frequently uniformly pale. Fins darkest in large male, banding and tessellation usually obscured.

Color in Life Plate 35.—Small breeding male *E. b. newmanii* with head and body mostly pale olive to medium olive, lateral bars dark green; in large male, head and body intensify in darkness, green bars nearly obscured. In *E. b. blennioides*, lateral bars bright green, quite distinct from general duskiness. In both subspecies, first dorsal fin edge white; subdistal and submarginal bluish green; medial black (submedially sometimes clear); epibasal pale or orange; basal black. Second dorsal fin with black-streaked membranes; posteriorly, basal half with bluish green areas; basally also pale orange and black; rays straw-olive. Caudal fin distally straw-olive, elsewhere bluish green including distinctly brighter dorsal and ventral areas which extend onto caudal peduncle. Anal and pelvic fins mostly bluish green; white on distal edge most prominent on knobs of leading spine or rays. Pectoral fin dark olive. Female paler overall, mostly yellowish green to olive.

Larvae.—Described by Fahy (1954), Baker (1979), and Auer (1982f).

BIOLOGY

The life history of *E. b. blennioides* in New York was described by Fahy (1954). Young and juveniles mainly eat minute crustaceans and blackfly larvae; older fish chiefly take various insect larvae (Turner 1921; Fahy 1954; Wynes and Wissing 1982; Hess 1983; Starnes and Starnes 1985). Large individuals may feed at night (Greenberg 1991). Katula (1986) reported that greenside darters eat snails by cupping them in the mouth and sucking the flesh out; this likely was an aquarium observation. Katula did not report this for other darters. In some other studies cited above, snails formed a small portion of the greenside darter's diet, but in the others snails were not noted.

Maturity may be reached in age 1, but usually not until age 2 (Lachner et al. 1950; Fahy 1954). The giant specimen noted below is the oldest known, age 5. Studies in New York (Fahy 1954), Pennsylvania (Lachner et al. 1950), and Kentucky (Wolfe et al. 1978) showed that males generally grow faster and attain larger sizes than females. Age-2 fish showed variable growth in those states; the range of means was 58–74 mm SL for males and 54–72 mm for females. Our largest Virginia specimen is 104 mm SL. The largest known specimen of any species of *Etheostoma* is a male *E. b. newmanii* of 140 mm SL, 166 mm TL, from the middle Cumberland drainage of Tennessee (REJ 559).

Spawning occurs in late February to late March in Arkansas (Hubbs 1985) and it ends in mid-June in New York (Fahy 1954); it occurs at 11–23°C (Winn 1958a). Based on latitude and development of nuptial color, *E. blennioides* probably spawns from late March to early May in Virginia. In some areas the eggs are attached among vegetation growing on rocks (Lachner et al. 1950; Fahy 1954; Winn 1958b; Pflieger 1975). Schwartz (1965b) reported spawning over fine sand in the lee of boulders; although odd for an egg-attacher, this may also occur in Virginia, where the greenside darter is not often associated with vegetation. The average number of small and large ova per female is 784 (Winn 1958b); the range of numbers of ova to be spawned in one season is 404–1,832 (Fahy 1954).

HABITAT

In Virginia, *E. blennioides* inhabits cool and warm, typically clear streams and rivers of moderate gradient. Juveniles and adults are usually associated with riffles and runs of rubble and boulder. The species tends to associate with vegetation (McCormick and Aspinwall 1983); Greenberg (1991) notes the association to be slight.

DISTRIBUTION   Map 175

The greenside darter is widespread in the lower Great Lakes basin, the Ohio basin, and the Ozark and

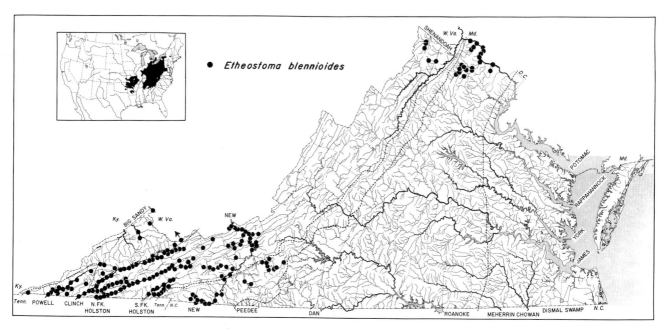

Map 175   Greenside darter.

adjacent uplands (R. V. Miller 1968); on the Atlantic Slope it occupies the Susquehanna (Denoncourt et al. 1977b) and Potomac drainages. In Virginia its distribution in sizeable streams of the Tennessee drainage is broad. In the New drainage, it occurs erratically in the Valley and Ridge and the Blue Ridge provinces. Its localization and rarity in the Big Sandy indicates an intolerance of heavy siltation.

The Potomac drainage population of *E. b. blennioides* has been considered native by authors from Schwartz (1965b) to Hocutt et al. (1986), but its major extent and rapid rate of recent range expansion indicates introduction. It was first detected in the drainage in Maryland and West Virginia during the late 1950s and in a Virginia tributary in 1964. It later was found widely in all suitable areas of Maryland and Pennsylvania (Denoncourt *in* Lee et al. 1980; Davis and Enamait 1982; Cooper 1983); Schwartz (1965b) lacked records for many of these areas. The amount of collecting in the four-state area of the drainage during 1900–1950 leaves little doubt that if native, the greenside darter would have been found earlier. It is difficult to explain its pattern of range extension as a reaction to pervasive changes in the ecology of the

drainage. Hence we regard the greenside darter as probably introduced in the Potomac. It will be interesting to see if *E. blennioides* invades the Shenandoah system, which is shunned by all Potomac darters except the fantail darter.

Abundance.—Usually uncommon or common.

REMARKS

The greenside darter is the largest member of the speciose genus *Etheostoma*. We were impressed with the differences in body color between the subspecies in the Tennessee and New drainages, notably the brilliant green bars in the New, although R. V. Miller (1968) stated that the patterns are basically the same. The unique binding of the side of the upper jaw to the side of the snout in the greenside darter should be investigated relative to the reputed snail-sucking ability of this fish.

Name.—*Blennioides* means "blenny-like," referring to the similarity in form to many of the small marine blennies.

Banded darter   *Etheostoma zonale* (Cope)

SYSTEMATICS

The banded darter was described by Cope (1868b) from the North Fork Holston River in Virginia. For much of its taxonomic history, it has had stable resi-

dence in the subgenus *Etheostoma*, generally as a member of the *blennioides* group (e.g., Bailey and Gosline 1955; Collette 1965; Richards 1966; Tsai and Raney 1974). Page (1981) considered *E. zonale* to be more closely allied with the snubnose darters, subgenus *Ulocentra*, and used the older name *Nanostoma* for the subgenus comprising *E. zonale* and the snubnose darters. We follow Bailey and Etnier (1988), who corrected some of Page's data, gave new evidence that *E. zonale* should remain in the *blennioides* group of *Etheostoma*, and retained *Ulocentra* for snubnose darters.

Two subspecies of *E. zonale* were recognized by Tsai and Raney (1974); the southern one was elevated to *E. lynceum* by Etnier and Starnes (1986). Three races of the banded darter in Virginia were defined by Tsai and Raney (1974).

DESCRIPTION

Materials.—From Tsai and Raney (1974), Page (1983), 1 Tennessee, 1 North Carolina, and 25 Virginia series; squamation and meristic data (Tsai and Raney 1974) represent the Ohio, South Fork Holston, and Tennessee river races. Color in life from 4 males and 1 female from Virginia.

Anatomy.—A barred, blotched, or V-marked darter with 1–2 medial or submedial caudal spots; adults are 40–55 mm SL. Body form moderate; snout short and blunt; frenum well developed; branchiostegal membranes broadly conjoined; caudal fin slightly emarginate or truncate. Tubercles absent; female genital papilla moderate in length, conic or tubular. Cheek naked to fully scaled; opercle and nape fully scaled; breast naked or very slightly scaled posteriorly; belly naked to half-scaled.

Meristics.—Lateral line complete, occasionally slightly incomplete, scales (39)43–56(63); scales above lateral line (3)5–6(8); scales below lateral line (6)7–9(11); circumpeduncle scales (15)17–21(22). Dorsal spines (8)11(12); dorsal rays (9)11–13(14); anal spines 2; anal rays (6)7–8(9); pectoral rays (12)13–15(16).

Color in Preservative.—Midside with 8–13 dark primary marks which are solid and blotchlike, or have a pale center, or are V-shaped; in adult, a diffuse to dark bar may extend ventrad from or between each primary mark and often girdles the venter; bars occasionally extend to the dorsum; primary marks often connected midlaterally by spots or a dark line; primary marks often have a separate spot between or just below them. Dorsolateral area variably scrawled or blotched; dorsum with 6(7–8) saddles. Head dusky overall; postocular and sometimes other spots present; subocular bar well defined; preocular bar distinct, occasionally meeting on snout tip with its counterpart. Lower side and venter pale or dusky; cheek, chin, and body venter sometimes spotted. Large breeding male dark overall.

First dorsal fin of adult male essentially as in Figure 69A and described under *E. blennioides*. Other fins of both sexes similar to those of *E. blennioides*. Caudal base with 4 vertically aligned spots, the medial or submedial 2 sometimes fused.

Color in Life Plate 35.—Adult male and female with dark olive body marks; ground shade cream to straw; body bars light and dark shades of green. Breeding male underside of head light to dark green. First dorsal fin distally clear or white; subdistally and submarginally black to light green, darkest subdistally, anteriorly sometimes tinted turquoise; medial band blackened; epibasally with clear windows and reddish, becoming dark basally. Second dorsal fin rusty basally. Caudal fin with leading rays turquoise. Anal and pelvic fins with turquoise wash, sometimes more intense anteriorly and posteriorly in anal, basally in pelvic.

Fish 286 *Etheostoma zonale* adult male 59 mm SL (REJ 982), VA, Washington County, North Fork Holston River, 16 June 1983.

Fish 287 *Etheostoma zonale* adult female 36 mm SL (REJ 982), VA, Washington County, North Fork Holston River, 16 June 1983.

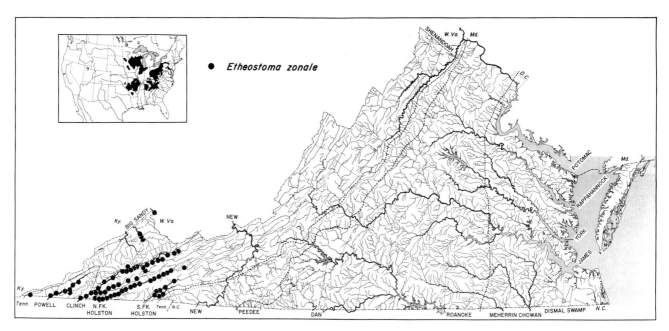

Map 176 Banded darter.

In highest-colored males, much of distinctive colors obliterated by overall darkening.

Larvae.—Described by Auer (1982f).

BIOLOGY

The diet of *E. zonale* consists mainly of midge and blackfly larvae (Forbes 1878; Adamson and Wissing 1977; Erickson 1977; Hickman and Fitz 1978; Nemecek 1978; Cordes and Page 1980; Wynes and Wissing 1982). Spawning first occurs at age 1 or 2; an age-4 specimen is the oldest known (Lachner et al. 1950; Erickson 1977; Lutterbie 1979). Males average larger than females by the end of the second growing season in Minnesota (Erickson 1977); in Pennsylvania, respective mean lengths in age 2 were 49 and 43 mm SL (Lachner et al. 1950). Mean lengths at age 2, sexes pooled, from three areas of Wisconsin were 45–50 mm TL (Lutterbie 1979). Page (1983) reported a maximum size of 65 mm SL; the largest Virginia specimen is 59 mm SL.

Spawning may occur from mid-March to early June in Arkansas (Hubbs 1985), during April and May, and sometimes into June in more northern areas (Forbes and Richardson 1920; Lachner et al. 1950; Schwartz 1965a; Cross 1967; Miller and Robison 1973; Pflieger 1975; Lutterbie 1979). Females still contained eggs on 20 July in Kentucky (Burr and Mayden 1979). A Virginia female flowed eggs on 19 April; ovarian conditions indicated that spawning occurs into at

least mid-June in Virginia. *Etheostoma zonale* spawns in riffles of depths less than 60 cm and typically attaches its eggs to vegetation (Trautman 1957; Pflieger 1975; Nemecek 1978). Fecundity is 80–262 mature ova (Erickson 1977). Hybridization was reported to occur with *E. caeruleum* (Trautman 1957).

HABITAT

The banded darter typically populates warm, moderate-gradient streams and rivers in Virginia. It is generally found in moderate and swift currents among gravel, rubble, and boulder, often near submersed vegetation. Occasionally it inhabits pools with slightly silted substrate. McCormick and Aspinwall (1983) noted that it prefers to live among plants, from which it gleans insects (Greenberg 1991).

DISTRIBUTION   Map 176

Etheostoma zonale occurs in a few areas of the Great Lakes basin and is widespread in the upper Mississippi basin, the Ohio basin, and the Ozarks and vicinity (Page 1983). On the Atlantic slope it apparently has been introduced to the Susquehanna and Savannah drainages (Tsai and Raney 1974; Denoncourt and Stauffer 1976). In Virginia it is generally distributed in the main stems and the lower portion of large tributaries of the Tennessee drainage, and is localized in the Big Sandy drainage.

Abundance.—Usually uncommon in all branches of the Tennessee drainage, rare in the Big Sandy. Tsai and Raney (1974) suggested that the banded darter was rare in the North Fork Holston River during the mid-1900s. It was taken in the North Fork near Saltville during the 1800s by Cope and Jordan, and in 1928 by H. R. Becker. Tsai and Raney found only one record from the 59 North Fork collections made during the 1950s and reported by Ross and Carico (1963). Actually, Ross took it at least twice in the North Fork (and once in the Middle Fork), but did not report it. Although *E. zonale* may have been reduced by pollution from Saltville, it was taken in several collections by others during the 1950s. TVA personnel and we found it regularly in the North Fork Holston at the start of surveying, which began in the early 1970s, before industrial shut-down at Saltville.

REMARKS

The banded darter is one of several darter species whose small nuptial males often are more colorful than the much-darkened large males. Long-distance movement of *E. zonale* was indicated by its downstream extension of over 400 rkm through the Susquehanna drainage in apparently three years (Denoncourt and Stauffer 1976). This may have been aided by the record flooding from Hurricane Agnes in 1972 (Denoncourt et al. 1975; Hocutt et al. 1986).

Name.—*Zonale* means "banded."

Snubnose darter   *Etheostoma simoterum* (Cope)

SYSTEMATICS

This species of the subgenus *Ulocentra* was described by Cope (1868b) from the "Holston River and its tributaries" in Virginia. He probably caught it in the Middle and North Fork systems of the Holston. Recognition of *Ulocentra* as the subgenus for snubnose darters, excluding *E. zonale*, is discussed under *E. zonale*. *Ulocentra* is a southeastern group of about 15 colorful species, some of which are undescribed. The nominate subspecies *E. s. simoterum* lives in Virginia (Page and Mayden 1981; D. A. Etnier and R. W. Bouchard, in litt.).

DESCRIPTION

Materials.—From Bouchard (1977), Page (1983), and 23 series from Virginia; meristic counts from *E. s. simoterum*. Life color from 12 nuptial males representing all Virginia drainage populations.

Anatomy.—A snub-nosed, blotched darter; adults are 40–55 mm SL. Body moderate or robust, elevated and rather compressed in large males; snout short, slightly rounded to very blunt, bluntest in large males; frenum narrow, sometimes obscured by a crease; branchiostegal membranes widely conjoined; caudal fin slightly emarginate or truncate. Tubercles absent; female genital papilla moderately long, tubular (Figure 70). Cheek, opercle, and nape fully scaled, scales usually embedded on cheek; belly naked anteriorly or fully scaled; breast usually naked.

Meristics.—Lateral line complete, scales (42)48–53(58); scales above lateral line (4)5–6; scales below lateral line 6–8; circumpeduncle scales 17–20. Dorsal spines (10)11(13); dorsal rays (10)11(13); anal spines 2; anal rays (6)7(8); pectoral rays (13)14(15).

Color in Preservative.—Midside with 7–9 blotches, most or all vaguely or conspicuously connected by a narrow or broad dark area; blotches and interconnections sometimes form a dark lateral stripe with undulating margins. Dorso-

Fish 288 *Etheostoma simoterum* adult male 49 mm SL (WHH 111), VA, Dickenson County, Roaring Fork, 29 June 1983.

Fish 289 *Etheostoma simoterum* adult female 44 mm SL (WHH 111), VA, Dickenson County, Roaring Fork, 29 June 1983.

lateral area usually with a cross-hatched design, occasionally speckled. Dorsum with 7–9(10) saddles; those on nape and at posterior end of first dorsal fin often pronounced; saddles tend to fuse in large males. Pre- and subocular bars well developed, preocular bars sometimes form a nexus on snout tip; other marks often present on cheek, opercle, and prepectoral area.

First dorsal fin with approximately the distal half pale to dark, with 1 or more clear or pale windows in breeding male; epibasally dark or black; basally clear or pale, except blackened in some large males. Second dorsal membranes darkly spotted or streaked; in nuptial male, black streaks are pale centrally, the fin basally black, rays pale; female with pale areas more extensive and rays tessellated. Other fins uniformly pale, moderately speckled, or almost fully dark or black, darkest in male; caudal base with 0–4 vertically aligned dark spots.

Color in Life   Plate 35.—Breeding male with midlateral stripe black or occasionally the black reduced and stripe suffused with blue-green; dorsolateral and ventrolateral areas with undulating rows of orange spots on a gold or tan base, or these areas nearly fully orange; dorsal saddles black. Head black and blue-green, the latter best developed on snout, lips, and venter; breast black. Fins, where not black or clear: first dorsal orange-red, anterodistally sometimes with blue-green tint; second dorsal orange-red; caudal turquoise, sometimes only on leading rays; anal and pelvic turquoise, brightest on the least-blackened anal. Juvenile and adult female with hints of orange but much paler than in male.

BIOLOGY

The food of *E. simoterum* in Tennessee is midge larvae supplemented by other aquatic insect larvae, microcrustaceans, water mites, and snails (Page and Mayden 1981; L. A. Greenberg, in litt.). Gut contents of 102 fish, mostly adults, from Virginia also included small numbers of amphipods and fingernail clams (J. K. Novak, in litt.).

Both sexes spawned as yearlings and rarely survived a second winter in Tennessee; the oldest specimen was 23–24 months old (Page and Mayden 1981). At four sites in the Little River of Tennessee, growth of young increased nearly threefold from the highest elevation to the lowest (Greenberg and Brothers 1991). Males grew the fastest; at age 1, males were 49 mm and females were 44 mm SL (Page and Mayden 1981). Maximum size is 70–72 mm SL (Greenberg and Brothers 1991); the largest from Virginia is 61 mm SL.

Snubnose darters from a Tennessee stream on 16 April (water 19°C) spawned two days later in an aquarium at 25–27°C. Eggs were attached to sides and tops of stones, less often buried in gravel; they were not guarded (Page and Mayden 1981). Page and Mayden believed that *E. simoterum* spawned in April and perhaps early May in Tennessee. In the upper Middle Fork Holston River (20 May 1990; water 13°C), we observed spawning on the vertical face of a concrete bridge pillar in moderate current; eggs were laid in a mat of filamentous algae. We took spent females on 2 June 1981 in Copper Creek, but on 29 June 1983 in the Big Sandy drainage of Virginia, females were gravid and males were in peak color. Fecundity is 110–240 mature ova (Page and Mayden 1981).

HABITAT

The snubnose darter occupies typically clear, cool and warm, moderate-gradient waters; it often extends from lower headwaters to main rivers. It generally is associated with slow runs, backwaters, and the shallows and body of well-flowing pools which have relatively clean gravel, rubble, boulder, and bedrock. We took it from heavily silted sections of both the main channel and, during winter, a major feeder spring of the Bluestone River.

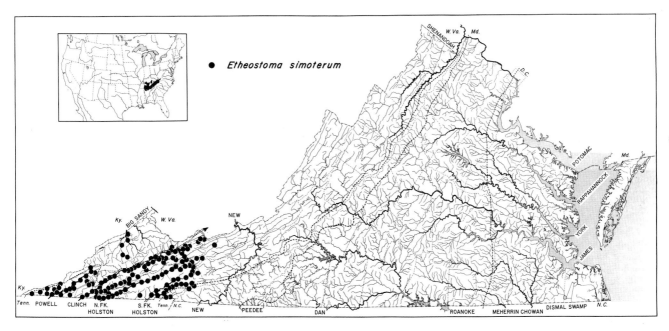

Map 177   Snubnose darter.

DISTRIBUTION   Map 177

Etheostoma simoterum is widespread in the Tennessee and Cumberland drainages and is highly localized in the New and Big Sandy drainages. In Virginia it is generally distributed in all systems of the Tennessee except for high-gradient streams of the Blue Ridge, Appalachian Plateau, and many of those on higher mountains of the Valley and Ridge Province. Its avoidance of high gradient is especially notable in North Carolina; it is absent from the Blue Ridge (Gilbert 1980). The recency of discovery and the localization of *E. simoterum* in the New and Big Sandy indicate that the species has been introduced there. It was considered probably introduced to the New and probably native to the Big Sandy by Hocutt et al. (1986), but we argue for native status in both.

The New drainage populations are in the upper Bluestone system (including the small main river, Wrights Valley Creek, and a short spring run) and upper Wolf Creek. Both populations are in the Valley and Ridge Province. In the Bluestone system the first record is from the Bluestone River in 1976; the upper river had been sampled only three times before 1976. At least one of the two sites sampled in 1951 was above the known limit of the species; the other 1951 sample was taken under difficult conditions (C. R. Robins, in litt.); and the 1972 collection was aimed primarily at riffle fishes. The other record sites in the system were not sampled until 1984. Hence *E. simo-*

terum may have existed in the Bluestone system long before 1976, but was easily missed.

The snubnose darter may not extend into the larger West Virginia section of the Bluestone in the Appalachian Plateau. Searches for it around Bluefield and below in the mid-1980s were unsuccessful (J. R. Stauffer, personal communication). Virtually the same is true for the endemic Bluestone sculpin. Appalachian Plateau habitat may be unsuited for these species; avoidance of the plateau may be related to pollution and siltation from urbanization and coal mining in the Plateau.

The other New drainage population of *E. simoterum* was discovered in Wolf Creek at Hicksville in 1987 by P. L. Angermeier. The upper Wolf system had been intensively surveyed during the 1950s (Ross and Perkins 1959), and collections were made earlier and later, but none within 5 rkm of the record site.

The distinct geographic separation and localization of the Bluestone and Wolf populations can be attributed to two introductions, or can be interpreted as a native, relict pattern. Erratic distribution patterns are common among fish species that clearly are native to the New.

All Big Sandy drainage records of *E. simoterum* are from the Russell Fork system in Virginia since 1972. None of the four streams that yielded a record had been sampled prior to the first record for each. Aquatic habitats in the drainage have been much abused, a factor in the localization of *E. simoterum* (and many other species).

Abundance.—Generally uncommon or common in the Tennessee drainage and Bluestone system. Uncommon or rare in the Big Sandy; data for 4 of the 5 collections reveal 17 snubnose darters taken.

REMARKS

This slackwater darter is particularly recognizable, as are most species of the subgenus *Ulocentra*, by its blunt snout, which in large males resembles that of the bull sperm whale. *Etheostoma simoterum* and the redline darter *E. rufilineatum* are among the most col-

orful and most common darters in the Tennessee drainage. Both feed benthically by day but partition food resources by occupying different current speeds and foraging sites—the redline under rocks, the snubnose darter perched more on the sides and top of stones (e.g., Greenberg 1991). The bright color and relatively open habitat of the male snubnose indicate an interesting trade-off. The colors may be obvious to predators, but attractive to female snubnoses.

Name.—*Simoterum* means "snubnose." With recognition of the Cumberland drainage form as a subspecies of *E. simoterum*, "Tennessee" is dropped from the common name; as now constituted, the species occurs in seven states.

Speckled darter   *Etheostoma stigmaeum* (Jordan)

SYSTEMATICS

The speckled darter, described from Georgia in 1877, is a member of the subgenus *Doration* (Cole 1967), which has been linked with the *Boleosoma* group of subgenera (e.g., Bailey and Gosline 1955). Bailey and Etnier (1988) noted instead that *Doration* may be aligned with the subgenus *Oligocephalus*.

Doration comprises five intimately related forms; of these, the three described forms may be the same species. The two undescribed forms are endemic to the Cumberland drainage (Howell 1968, in litt.). Both nominal forms that are endemic to the Tennessee drainage occupy Virginia—*E. jessiae* (Jordan and Brayton), and *E. meadiae* (Jordan and Evermann). Typical *E. stigmaeum* is widespread, but inhabits only the lower portion of the Tennessee drainage (Howell *in* Lee et al. 1980; Page 1983).

In his first analysis of *Doration*, Howell (1968) recognized *jessiae* as a subspecies of *stigmaeum*; the populations in the Clinch and Powell systems, from which *meadiae* had been described, were considered to be intergrades of *stigmaeum* and *jessiae*. Later, How-

ell (*in* Lee et al. 1980) elevated the three Tennessee drainage forms to species. Page (1981, 1983) and Robins et al. (1991) ranked only *stigmaeum* and *jessiae* as species. Partly from discussions of variation in this group with D. A. Etnier and W. C. Starnes (in litt.), for Virginia we arbitrarily recognize only one species with two subspecies—*E. stigmaeum meadiae* in the Clinch and Powell systems and *E. stigmaeum jessiae* in the Holston system.

DESCRIPTION

Materials.—From Howell and Boschung (1966), Howell (1968, in litt.), Page (1983), 11 lots from Tennessee, and 14 from Virginia. Tuberculation from Cross and Minckley (1958), Winn (1958a, 1958b), Collette (1965), and Virginia specimens. Meristic data are for *meadiae* from the Clinch–Powell and (in brackets) *jessiae* from throughout its range in the Tennessee. Life color from 3 Virginia lots of *meadiae*.

Anatomy.—A VX-marked, blotched, or barred darter with hourglass-shaped saddles; adults are 35–50 mm SL. Body moderate or somewhat elongate, slightly com-

Fish 290 *Etheostoma stigmaeum* adult male 49 mm SL (REJ 1056), VA, Scott County, Copper Creek, 17 March 1984.

Fish 291 *Etheostoma stigmaeum* adult male 42 mm SL (REJ 987), VA, Scott County, Copper Creek, 17 June 1983.

pressed; snout moderate or somewhat pointed, lips moderately prominent; frenum absent or moderately well developed; branchiostegal membranes separate or slightly conjoined; caudal fin slightly emarginate or truncate. Breeding male with tubercles and keratinized ridges on anal and pelvic rays and tubercles on belly scales. Breast usually naked, and belly naked to fully scaled in both forms; cheek 0–10% scaled [(0)10–30(50)% in *jessiae*]; opercle 70% or more scaled in both; nape 50–90% scaled [(60)90–100%].

Meristics.—Lateral line incomplete or complete, pored scales 38–47 in *meadiae* [(25)34–48(55) in *jessiae*]; total midlateral scales 45–53 [(44)47–56(59)]; transverse scales (rows from origin of second dorsal fin to anal fin base) 9–12 [(9)10–12(14)]; circumpeduncle scales 15–17 [(11)16–19(21)]. Dorsal spines 11–13 [11–13(14)]; dorsal rays 10–12 [11–13]; anal spines 2 in both forms; anal rays (7)8–9(10) [8–9(10)]; pectoral rays, sum of both sides 28–30 [(27)28–30(32)].

Color in Preservative.—Midside with 7–11 dark marks, each consisting of 1–3 VX-shaped marks; 1–4 spots or dashes usually present between or below areas of VX-marks; in adult, midside marks often suffused or obliterated by duskiness, forming blotches or, in nuptial male, bars that extend onto lower side. Dorsolateral area crosshatched, often lightly flecked; dorsum usually with 6 vague or moderately obvious saddles that usually are constricted medially (hourglass-shaped). Pre- and subocular bars well developed, the former rarely meeting on snout tip; postocular spot or smudge evident.

First dorsal fin of adult male with clear distal band; subdistal area dusky or moderately dark; submarginal pale to dusky; medial pale; epibasal dark; basal dark with clear windows. Second dorsal fin basally dark, fading distally to dusky. Caudal rays tessellated or wholly pigmented, membranes dusky distally; caudal spot absent or present, usually submedial. Anal and pelvic rays clear, membranes dusky or dark; pectoral fin with only rays pigmented, uniformly so. Both dorsal fins and caudal fin of juvenile and adult female generally with clear membranes and nontessellated rays; anal and pelvic fins not pigmented.

Color in Life Plate 36.—Juvenile and nonbreeding adult (of *mediae*) olive dorsally, straw-yellow laterally, cream ventrally. Adult male has hint of nuptial coloration out of breeding season. Adult female generally subdued,

some with hints of blue and yellow-orange in same areas as male.

Breeding male with deep metallic (electric) blue lateral bars; ground pattern of side a series of fine oblique white to pale blue lines, one line per scale row; between lines the scales are olive-orange or burnt orange, becoming more yellow on caudal peduncle; dorsum olive; breast and gular area black, remainder of venter dusky gray. Lips, cheek, and opercle deep metallic blue; remainder of head dark olive.

First dorsal fin of nuptial male with distal band deep blue; subdistal white; submarginal orange; medial narrow, pale white; epibasal deep blue which extends basally at midlength of fin; basal mostly dusky black to clear. Second dorsal fin with black base fading to dusky margin; medially and submedially on anterior few membranes is a deep blue irregular area; anterior rays, distal to the latter anterior area and extending to posterior membranes, subtle yellow or orange. Caudal fin basally deep blue; anal fin basally with a large area of deep blue, distal to which is a clear or dusky area and sometimes a blackened area that has a hint of iridescent yellow; pelvic fin black, rays distally with hint of iridescent yellow; pectoral base iridescent blue-green, rays basally iridescent bronze.

BIOLOGY

The life history of the speckled darter is largely unknown. The largest specimen is 58 mm SL from Virginia. In much of its range, *E. stigmaeum* spawns from late March to perhaps late May (Hubbs 1985). We found brilliantly colored males from late March to late April in the gentle flow of pool shallows and in moderate runs over areas of gravel or gravel and sand. Nuptial males are territorial; the female is an egg-burier (Winn 1958a, 1958b, as *E. saxatile*).

HABITAT

In Virginia, *Etheostoma stigmaeum* occupies clear, warm, moderate-gradient streams and rivers. It is commonly associated with sand and gravel in slow to moderately flowing margins of pools and runs. In the Little River of Tennessee, the *jessiae* form occurred in

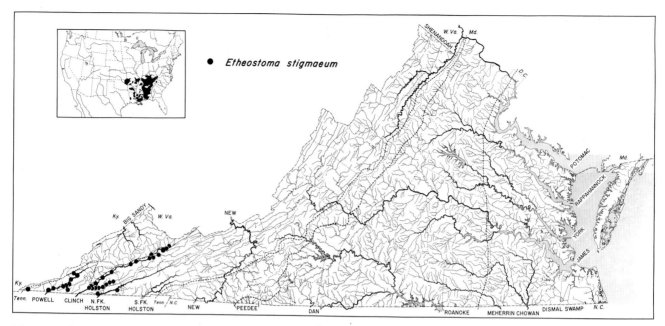

Etheostoma stigmaeum

Map 178   Speckled darter. The two records on North Fork Holston tributaries are of *E. stigmaeum jessiae*. Clinch–Powell records are of the *meadiae* form of *E. stigmaeum*.

very slow shallows at areas of mostly sand and large amounts of silt (Greenberg 1991).

DISTRIBUTION   Map 178

The speckled darter is found in the lower Ohio and Mississippi basins and adjacent Gulf Slope drainages; in Virginia it occupies the Tennessee drainage. The *meadiae* form is widespread in the Clinch and Powell systems. *Etheostoma s. jessiae* is broadly distributed in the Tennessee drainage but known in Virginia only from two tributaries of the North Fork Holston River in Scott County. One specimen (CU 68500) was found in Possum Creek in 1970, but none were found in five other samples from the creek during 1954–1982; it was identified as *E. jessiae* by W. M. Howell (M. Hopiak, in litt.). The other Virginia specimen of *jessiae* (UMMZ 130756) is from Cove Creek in 1937, which apparently has been sampled only one other time, in 1954; we identified it as probably *E. s. jessiae*. We have been unable to verify Page's (1983) record from the upper North Fork Holston River.

Abundance.—Usually rare or uncommon, occasionally common in the Clinch and Powell systems; rare (or extirpated) in the Holston system.

REMARKS

The metallic blue of the breeding male speckled darter is brilliant, and coupled with its yellow and orange, the fish's appearance is electrifying. *Etheostoma stigmaeum jessiae* (as *E. jessiae*) was listed as endangered in Virginia by the VDGIF (1987). Because it may no longer inhabit the state, Burkhead and Jenkins (1991) recommended undetermined status.

Name.—*Stigmaeum* means "speckled"; *jessiae* honors Jessie D. Brayton, the wife of one of the describers; *meadiae* is for Meadie H. Evermann, wife of one of the authors of the taxon. The name blueside darter has been applied to *E. jessiae* when recognized as a species.

Longfin darter   *Etheostoma longimanum* Jordan

SYSTEMATICS

Etheostoma longimanum was described from the upper James drainage by Jordan (1888). It most closely resembles *E. podostemone* but they are distinct genet-

ically (J. Shute 1984) and in morphology and color. Within the five-member subgenus *Boleosoma*—the johnny darter group—these two species uniquely share the combination of 2 anal spines, well-united branchiostegal membranes, development of orange and blue or turquoise body colors in nuptial males, and (Page 1981; J. Shute 1984) several other features. The two species have been considered sister species owing to their basic similarity and geographic adjacency—*E. longimanum* is endemic to the James drainage, *E. podostemone* to the Roanoke drainage. However, the sister species of *E. longimanum* may be *E. (Ioa) vitreum* (see that account).

DESCRIPTION

Materials.—From Miles (1964), Cole (1957, 1972), and 22 series, from which 35 specimens were counted for meristic data. Color in life from 50 adults from Catawba Creek.

Anatomy.—A laterally XW-marked or blotched darter; adults are 35–60 mm SL. Body form moderate or elongate; snout moderate or blunt; frenum absent; branchiostegal membranes moderately or broadly conjoined; caudal fin slightly or moderately emarginate; both dorsal fins high; membranes between first three dorsal spines often notably wide; pectoral fin quite long. Tips of some pectoral, pelvic, anal, and first dorsal fin elements with a small whitish thickening in some nuptial males; tubercles absent. Genital papilla short, low, bilobed in female. Opercle 40–90% scaled; belly 50–70% scaled; cheek, nape, and breast naked.

Meristics.—Lateral line complete, scales (39)42–46(51); scales above lateral line 4–5(6); scales below lateral line (5)6–8(9); circumpeduncle scales (16)17–19(21). Dorsal spines (8)9–10(11); dorsal rays (10)11–12(13); anal spines 2, rarely 1; anal rays (5)6–7(8); pectoral rays (12)13(14); gill rakers (7)8–11(12). IO uninterrupted, pores (7)8(9); POM pores (9)10; ST uninterrupted.

Color in Preservative.—Upper body flecked, speckled, spotted, and with 6 saddles, the smaller marks not forming straight horizontal rows. Midlateral body with 8–12 smudges or dark blotches underlying dark XW-marks, often obliterating them. Subocular mark round or oval, smudgelike, diffuse or intense; prepectoral area usually with 1–2 spots or blotches. Nuptial male head and body wholly slightly dusky to, in peak condition, heavily blackened, except lower lip distinctly paler medially.

Dorsal fin membranes in adult pale, or dusky with darker spots or a streak in each membrane; spines and rays tessellated. Caudal membranes pale or slightly dusky; rays slightly tessellated or uniformly dusky, lower rays sometimes darker than upper rays; caudal spot medial or submedial. Lower fins pale, tessellated, or slightly dusky. Fins blacken in peak nuptial male, anal and pelvic fins and anterior membranes of first dorsal fin the darkest; fin marks obliterated, except that in some of both sexes a narrow black edge occurs on second dorsal, and thickenings on tips of spines and rays are paler than adjacent areas.

Fish 292 *Etheostoma longimanum* adult male 58 mm SL (REJ 1040), VA, Roanoke County, Catawba Creek, 21 September 1983.

Fish 293 *Etheostoma longimanum* adult female 51 mm SL (REJ 1040), VA, Roanoke County, Catawba Creek, 21 September 1983.

Color in Life Plate 36.—Juvenile with brown-black marks on whitish to pale olive ground; lower opercular and prepectoral areas with gold to green iridescence, as in non-blackened adult. Adult female and nonbreeding male blackish-marked on an olive, yellow-olive, or yellow-orange ground; some nuptial females with a hint of iridescent turquoise on base of upper body scales. Dorsal fins with lightly orange-spotted membranes in some males; other fins pale.

Nuptial male with posterior portion of most scales from dorsum to midside flat burnt orange, anterior portion of each of these scales iridescent turquoise; lower body scales mostly dusky burnt orange, posterior margin black; some scales of lower side also with slight turquoise; black lateral blotches and dorsal saddles distinct or fusing to form vertical bars. Head dusky to black, iris mostly gold, lower lip pale medially. In some males the body becomes quite dusky, most so ventrally and ventrolaterally; in peak male the head and body are virtually wholly blackened, the marks obscured, orange color absent, and turquoise occurs mainly or only on upper body; lower lip still paler than chin.

Dorsal fins of nuptial male with membranes (except anterior blackened area of first dorsal) yellow-olive or yellow and having a series of spots or a streak that is bright to burnt orange. Other fins dusky or black, pelvic and anal darkest.

When spawning or nest guarding in aquaria, some large males rapidly changed between dusky and black. The male pictured by Kuehne and Barbour (1983) obviously was in peak nuptial color when alive, but apparent artifacts of the photo are the blueness of the caudal fin (likely owing to the black background) and the lack of iridescent turquoise on the body (probably lost in preservative).

COMPARISON

Etheostoma longimanum differs from the syntopic member of *Boleosoma*, *E. nigrum* (and the problematic upper Appomattox *E. nigrum*-like population), in: (1) infraorbital canal [uninterrupted in *longimanum vs.* usually interrupted in *nigrum*]; (2) union of branchiostegal membranes [broad or, usually, moderate *vs.* rarely moderate, usually slight]; (3) anal spines almost always [2 *vs.* 1]; (4) lateral line scales usually [42–46 *vs.* 37–40 in James drainage *nigrum*]; (5) subocular mark [rounded, smudgelike, often diffuse *vs.* a vertical bar, usually well-defined]; (6) midlateral XW marks [blackish, smudged, blotchlike *vs.* tending brownish, distinctly XW-shaped]; (7) upper side ground shade of juvenile in life [white to pale olive *vs.* straw or tan]; (8) nuptial male color [blackish with turquoise and orange on body, orange in dorsal fins *vs.* dusky to blackish only].

BIOLOGY

Based on four adults, the longfin darter eats mayfly, caddisfly, and truefly (mostly midge) larvae, and water mites. Sexual maturity is reached in 1 or 2 years; maximum longevity is about 4 years. Males grow faster and attain greater length than females. Two-year-old males average 55 mm SL, females 46 mm (Raney and Lachner 1943). Maximum size is 74 mm SL.

Spawning pairs were found in upper James drainage tributaries during 15 April–15 May of three years, water 16–23°C (W. D. Voiers, in litt.). A nest of 600 eggs was found on 23 May in Craig Creek; most females appeared to have already spawned (Page et al. 1981). Some longfin darters were in breeding condition during early June in Barbours Creek (Kuehne and Barbour 1983; R. A. Kuehne, personal communication); the late date seems related to the coolness of the stream. This species typically inverts to spawn on undersides of stones in riffles and runs. Adhesive eggs are laid in single-layered clusters, each tended by a territorial male (Page et al. 1981; W. D. Voiers, in litt.). Eggs hatch in 5–6 days at 20°C (W. D. Voiers, in litt.).

We observed spawnings in aquaria of longfin darters from Catawba Creek. A male taken on 8 April 1984 (stream 10°C) spawned on 15 April (aquarium 25°C) and, with a different female, on 21 April (17°C). A male and female caught on 26 April 1984 (stream 13°C) spawned two days later (aquarium 17°C). Individual females laid 60–120 eggs which were guarded and occasionally fanned by the male.

In Catawba Creek on 26 March 1990, we found most adult females to be gravid, others spent; males were in low and moderate nuptial color. A large single-tiered cluster of eggs, apparently of this species, was found on the underside of a piece of cement block in a run. Two days later in an aquarium at 19.7°C, one of the males spawned with two females (the three synchronously in one spawning) in an unusual fashion for an inverting spawner—only on top of a sloping small flat rock. The cavity under the rock and two other available cavities were not used. For at least four days after the spawnings, generally the male idled on the rock or chased minnows and other longfin darters from it. Males were in peak nuptial color in Catawba Creek on 9 May 1990 and 15 May 1991.

HABITAT

Etheostoma longimanum typically inhabits cool and warm, moderate to somewhat high-gradient creeks,

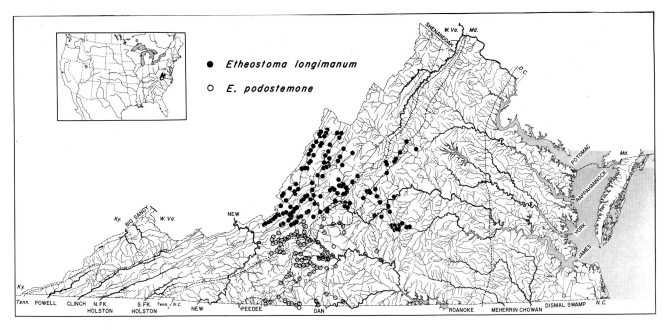

Map 179   Longfin darter and riverweed darter.

streams, and small rivers; it was captured at one site in the larger upper James River. Adults generally occupy moderate and swift runs and riffles having clean gravel, rubble, or boulder. Fall sampling during low water found adults common also in silty pools. Young and small juveniles tend to occur most frequently in reduced current at margins of fast water and in pools.

DISTRIBUTION   Map 179

The longfin darter is endemic to the upper and middle James drainage of Virginia and (in Potts Creek) West Virginia. It is generally distributed in the upper James. In the middle James proper it is restricted to the Blue Ridge Province and outlying montane tributaries. It is one of the few upper James fishes not found in the Bremo Bluff area of the middle James River by White et al. (1977). The localized population in the upper Appomattox system occupies a Piedmont upland area with frequent clean riffles.

A specimen of *E. longimanum* (ANSP 13861) taken by Cope and labeled as from Sinking Creek of the New drainage apparently has faulty locality data. Although Cope's tabulation for the New drainage (1868b:240) lists *E. olmstedi* (another species of *Boleosoma*), he stated (p. 213–214) that he found no *Boleosoma* in the New. Fowler (1907) reported the specimen as *E. nigrum*. *Boleosoma* otherwise is unreported from Sinking Creek and surrounding tributaries of

the New; the area has been extensively sampled. The specimen probably came from Johns Creek, Cope's upper James drainage site.

Abundance.—Often common in mountains and, on the middle Piedmont, in the extreme upper Appomattox system.

REMARKS

Breeding male longfin darters are strikingly handsome, with a turquoise, orange, and black body accentuated by expansive orange-dappled dorsal fins. Behavioral flexibility of the species is shown by spawnings involving one or two females at a time, and by eggs being laid on both the top and underside of rocks.

As adults, *E. longimanum* and *E. nigrum*, both members of the subgenus *Boleosoma*, largely segregate in stream habitats of the James drainage. The former generally occupies the swifter, harder-bottomed places, *E. nigrum* the intervening slower, more sandy and silty situations. In the Roanoke drainage, another species of *Boleosoma*, *E. podostemone*, has the same habitat relationship with *E. nigrum* as does *E. longimanum*.

Name.—*Longimanum* refers to "long hand"—the pectoral fin length.

Riverweed darter   *Etheostoma podostemone* (Jordan and Jenkins)

SYSTEMATICS

Etheostoma podostemone, a member of the subgenus *Bolesoma*, was described from the upper Roanoke drainage by Jordan and Jenkins (*in* Jordan 1889a). Its phylogenetic relationships are noted under *E. longimanum*.

DESCRIPTION

Materials.—From Miles (1964), Cole (1957, 1972), and our 29 series from which 32 specimens were meristically counted. Life color from 6 Virginia series.

Anatomy.—A laterally XW-marked or evenly spotted darter; adults are 30–55 mm SL. Body elongate or somewhat moderate; snout blunt; frenum absent; branchiostegal membranes moderately or broadly united; caudal fin truncate or rounded; dorsal fins high and caudal very rounded in adult male. Tips of some pectoral, pelvic, and first dorsal fin elements have a small whitish rounded thickening in nuptial male. Largest males in peak nuptial condition with small and medium-sized tubercles, tips rounded or subconic, on front of snout. Female genital papilla short, low, bilobed (Figure 70). Opercle usually 50–80% scaled; belly usually 50–60% scaled; cheek, nape, and breast naked.

Meristics.—Lateral line complete, scales (35)37–40(41); scales above lateral line (2)3–4(5); scales below lateral line (4)5–7(8); circumpeduncle scales (13)15–16(18). Dorsal spines 8–10(11); dorsal rays (11)12–13(15); anal spines 2, rarely 1; anal rays (5)6–7(8); pectoral rays (10)12–13; gill rakers (8)9–11. IO uninterrupted, (7)8(9) pores; POM pores 8–10(11); ST uninterrupted.

Color in Preservative.—Upper body flecked, speckled, spotted, and with 6 saddles. Midside with 7–10 XW marks, these best developed in juvenile and often smudged by dark pigment in adult; in adult male, some or all dorsolateral to ventrolateral marks are replaced by straight horizontal rows of spots, one spot per scale, spotting best developed on posterior half of body. Subocular mark well developed, linear or rectangular, vertical; 1–2 spots or blotches in prepectoral area; other dark marks often on lower head and paired fin bases. Nuptial male with head and body dusky, most marks remaining distinct; lower lip similar shade as chin.

Dorsal, caudal, and pectoral fin supports, and sometimes the first dorsal membranes are tessellated. Caudal base often with a medial or submedial black spot. Pelvic and anal fins with slight or no tessellation. Fins darken in nuptial male, obscuring or obliterating tessellations; first dorsal fin darkest in anterior membranes; dorsal fins and caudal fin with a narrow dark margin. In peak male, anal and pelvic fins black, much darker than other fins; thickenings on tips of spines and rays paler than adjacent areas.

Color in Life Plate 36.—Juvenile with blackish marks on a white or pale olive ground. Adult female body with pale olive base shade and dark olive to black marks; first dorsal fin with orange-brown distally and lightly orange-spotted membranes; second dorsal and caudal membranes lightly orange-spotted; all fins with pale yellow wash.

Fish 294 *Etheostoma podostemone* adult male 57 mm SL (REJ 1058), VA, Franklin County, Blackwater River, 20 March 1984.

Fish 295 *Etheostoma podostemone* adult female 45 mm SL (REJ 1039), VA, Montgomery County, South Fork Roanoke River, 16 September 1983.

Nuptial male body ground color iridescent gold to orange, lower side anteriorly flat orange, mid- and upper side sometimes with pale blue tint; center of some scales on anterior body dark orange, those on posterior body with a blue-black spot; saddles blue-black; midside with a series of deep-lying dark blue blotches, representing juvenile XW marks. Head dusky to black, darker ventrally; lips about same shade as chin; iris slightly golden in some fish.

Dorsal fins and caudal fin of nuptial male with pale to orange rays, anterior membranes of first dorsal blackened, other membranes yellow-olive to pale orange and with a series of spots or a streak that is bright to burnt orange. Pelvic and anal rays pale or dusky, anal membranes silky pale blue in peak make; pelvic membranes possibly only blackened. Pectoral fin rays tessellated or all black, membranes clear. A male spawned in an aquarium in the golden phase, head and fins unblackened.

COMPARISON

Etheostoma podostemone differs from the syntopic *E. nigrum* in: (1) IO canal [uninterrupted in *podostemone* vs. usually interrupted in *nigrum*]; (2) branchiostegal membranes conjoined usually [broadly vs. slightly]; (3) anal spines usually [2 vs. 1]; (4) lateral line scales usually [37–40 vs. 41–44 in Roanoke drainage *nigrum*]; (5) lateral XW marks [blackish, often smudged in female, replaced by a series of large spots or blotches in male vs. brownish, unmodified in female and nonbreeding male, replaced by dusky or dark bars in nuptial male]; (6) body ground color of upper side of juvenile in life [white or pale olive vs. straw or tan]; (7) bluish and orange in nuptial male [present vs. absent].

BIOLOGY

The riverweed darter feeds almost entirely on immature benthic insects. Its main food during most of the year is midge larvae; increased feeding on caddisfly larvae occurs in the fall. Immature mayflies, beetles, other dipterans, and rarely, water mites, snails, and fish eggs are also eaten. Feeding activity is greatest during daylight (Matthews et al. 1982; Haxo et al. 1985).

Sexual maturity is reached in 1 or 2 years; maximum longevity is 4 years. Males grow faster than females in the first year and are larger as adults. Age-2 males average 40 mm SL, females 38 mm; the largest specimen is a 70-mm SL male (Haxo et al. 1985).

Riverweed darters from the upper Roanoke drainage spawned in aquaria within 31 March to late May, in different periods in the three years of observations; water was 17–20°C. Spawning pairs inverted on the underside of stones; the adhesive eggs were laid in single-tiered clusters and guarded by the territorial male. Eggs hatched in about 13 days at 17°C. Mature ova were 123–345 in 13 preserved specimens (Haxo et al. 1985).

HABITAT

The riverweed darter occupies cool and warm, moderate-gradient creeks, streams, and rivers (Matthews and Styron 1981; Matthews et al. 1982; Haxo et al. 1985). Although it lives in streams that often are turbid, populations in clearer streams tend to be larger. Adults generally inhabit moderate and swift runs and riffles during most of the year (Matthews 1990), and sometimes shift to slower runs and pools in winter. During the spawning period, adults were found most often at the head of riffles. Young tend to occupy slow areas near swift areas. Adult riverweed darters typically associate with clean loose medium gravel, rubble, and small boulders; young associate with these substrates and often with sand and slightly silted areas.

DISTRIBUTION   Map 179

The riverweed darter is confined to the upper and middle Roanoke drainage; nearly limited to Virginia, it extends into North Carolina in the Dan system. It is contiguously distributed in the Valley and Ridge Province and in several streams in the Blue Ridge and upper Piedmont. Populations on the middle Piedmont are localized, indicating an intolerance of heavy siltation. *Etheostoma podostemone* is the only darter native to the upper Roanoke drainage that is not shared with the Chowan drainage.

Abundance.—Generally uncommon or common in mountains and the upper Piedmont, becoming scarcer on the middle Piedmont.

REMARKS

The elegant nuptial male riverweed darter sports a mosaic of varied subtle and bright hues. Only this species among members of the subgenus *Boleosoma* develops breeding tubercles; the location of the tubercles on the frontal snout is unique among percids. The presence of tubercles in perhaps only the largest nuptial males accents the value of such specimens for determining the full range of occurrence of secondary sexual characters.

Name.—*Podostemone* is derived from *Podostemum*, a genus of riverweed, a filamentous vascular aquatic plant with which it occasionally associates.

Johnny darter   *Etheostoma nigrum* Rafinesque

SYSTEMATICS

Etheostoma nigrum, described in 1820 from Kentucky, often had the tessellated darter *E. olmstedi* synonomized under it; both are in the subgenus *Boleosoma*. We collectively refer to these sibling, largely allopatric taxa as "johnny darters" owing to their intimate relationship and mutual distinctions from *E. longimanum* and *E. podostemone*. Recognition of *E. nigrum* and *E. olmstedi* as separate biological species is based mainly on studies in zones of sympatry in the Lake Ontario–St. Lawrence drainage (Stone 1947; Cole 1965; McAllister et al. 1972; Chapleau and Pageau 1985). The case is controversial (e.g., Scott and Crossman 1973).

The occurrence of *E. nigrum* and *E. olmstedi* in some Virginia and North Carolina drainages was documented by Cole (1957, 1967, 1972); he did not note problems in identifying them but had few specimens from critical areas. Studies of James drainage populations (Clark 1978; Falls 1982) and our meristic data (704 specimens) from the James, Chowan, and Roanoke drainages indicate that the taxa have substantially interbred or evolutionarily converged in parts of these drainages. Meristically, the "problematic" populations (Map 180) are variably intermediate or interjacent between typical populations; specimens from downstream areas of problematic populations tend to be more *olmstedi*-like, upstream ones more *nigrum*-like.

Etheostoma n. nigrum is the subspecies in Virginia and North Carolina; racial differentiation has occurred among its James, Roanoke, and Tar–Neuse drainage populations (Cole 1957, 1972). Another subspecies, *E. nigrum susanae* (Jordan and Swain), is endemic to the upper Cumberland drainage near Virginia (Starnes and Starnes 1979; Warren 1981). Variation within *E. nigrum* still presents taxonomic problems (Lagler and Bailey 1947; Bailey and Allum 1962; Underhill 1963; Cole 1972; McAllister et al. 1972; Kott and Humphreys 1978; Starnes and Starnes 1979; J. Shute 1984).

DESCRIPTION

Materials.—From typical populations of the James and Roanoke drainages—Cole (1957, 1972), and our 48 lots from which 227 specimens were counted meristically. Color in life from 6 Virginia lots.

Anatomy.—An XW-marked darter with an interrupted infraorbital canal; adults are 30–40 mm SL. Body form moderate or elongate; snout moderate or blunt; frenum absent; branchiostegal membranes slightly (rarely moderately) connected; caudal fin truncate or rounded; first dorsal fin of adults quite high. Tips of some pectoral, pelvic,

Fish 296 *Etheostoma nigrum* adult male 35 mm SL (REJ 990), VA, Tazewell County, Mud Fork, 21 June 1983.

Fish 297 *Etheostoma nigrum* adult male 47 mm SL (REJ 1040), VA, Roanoke County, Catawba Creek, 21 September 1983.

anal, and first dorsal fin supports with a whitish well-developed knob or a slight thickening in nuptial male (Bart and Page 1991); tubercles absent. Genital papilla short, low, bilobed in female. Squamation (% of area scaled): cheek 0–30(90), opercle (10)50–100, nape 0–40(90), breast 0(100), belly 0–100.

Meristics.—Lateral line complete, scales (35)37–44(49), usually 37–40 in the James, 41–44 in the Roanoke; scales above lateral line 3–5(6); scales below lateral line (4)5–8(9); circumpeduncle scales (13)14–16(17). Dorsal spines (7)8–9(10); dorsal rays (10)11–12(13); anal spines 1, very rarely 2; anal rays 6–8(9); pectoral rays (10)11–12(13); gill rakers (7)8–9(10). IO canal almost always interrupted, pores (5)6–8(9), modally 7 on Atlantic slope, 6 in Ohio basin; POM pores (8)9–10(11); ST canal usually uninterrupted.

Color in Preservative.—Upper body flecked, speckled, spotted, and usually with (4)6(7) vague quadrate saddles; midside with (7)8–11(12) XW-shaped marks and additional smaller marks. Preocular bar unbroken; subocular mark usually linear, vertical, rarely spotlike; prepectoral spot very rarely present. Both dorsals, the caudal, and pectoral fins tessellated; (3)4–7(8) bars on caudal fin; basicaudal spot usually present, weak; lower fins pale. Nuptial male with generally dusky head and body, marks obscured or obliterated, or with diffuse dusky bars; fins dusky or black.

Color in Life Plate 36.—Ground shade straw or pale tan dorsally and laterally, dark marks brown to brown-black; gold-green iridescence on lower opercular and prepectoral areas. Nuptial male mostly dusky to blackish, lacking bright colors.

Larvae.—Described by Auer (1982f).

COMPARISON

Etheostoma nigrum is distinguished from *E. longimanum* and *E. podostemone* in those accounts.

Several characters are purported to distinguish *E. nigrum* and *E. olmstedi* (Cole 1967; McAllister et al. 1972; Page 1983), but most vary within and between populations to such extents that they are of little consistent discriminatory value. The most useful characters for identifying Virginia fish are: (1) IO canal (Figure 81) almost always [interrupted in *nigrum* vs. uninterrupted in *olmstedi*]; (2) IO pores modally [7 vs. 8]; (3) POM pores modally [9 in the Roanoke drainage, 10 in the James vs. 10 or 11]; (4) second dorsal rays modally [11 vs. 13 or 14 (except 11 in *E. o. vexillare* of the Rappahannock drainage)]; (5) in Virginia, *E. nigrum* normally is smaller than *E. o. olmstedi* and *E. o. atromaculatum* [maximally 40 mm SL in *nigrum* vs. commonly 45–55 mm (and larger)].

A prominent distinction in male nuptial coloration appears in Virginia specimens. In *nigrum* the dusky or blackened second dorsal and caudal fins have little or no pattern. In *olmstedi* the dark marks (including tessellations) in these fins contrast with the paler areas (often more so than in Fish 298), forming spots, scrawls, streaks, and marbling. We have not seen in *olmstedi* the dark lateral bars that occur in some nuptial *nigrum*.

BIOLOGY

The major food of *E. nigrum* is midge larvae; other small insect larvae, microcrustaceans, and other invertebrates are eaten, but the ingestion of algae and detritus probably is incidental (Forbes 1878; Hankinson 1908; Turner 1921; Karr 1963; Flemer and Woolcott 1966; Smart and Gee 1979; Paine et al. 1982; Martin 1984a). Feeding is more frequent during daytime than at night (Emery 1973). The johnny darter is highly adapted morphologically for benthic feeding (Smart and Gee 1979; Paine et al. 1982).

Yearlings are mature (Speare 1965) but such males have relatively low reproductive success (Grant and Colgan 1983). *Etheostoma nigrum* commonly lives 2 years, rarely 4 (Lutterbie 1979). It is sexually dimorphic in size (Winn 1958b); age-2 males averaged 49 mm, females 46 mm SL in Michigan (Speare 1960). In Virginia, adults are 30–40 mm SL and the largest Virginia specimen is a 50-mm SL, 60-mm TL female. The largest reported specimen is 64 mm SL, 77 mm TL from Wisconsin (Lutterbie 1979).

Spawning occurs in mid-March to mid-May in Mississippi and from mid-April to mid-June north of Virginia (e.g., Parrish et al. 1991). Specimens near or in breeding condition were taken in Virginia during 18 April–21 June. Spawning does not occur frequently until water reaches 10°C (Grant and Colgan 1983), or it begins at 15–18°C (Speare 1965); it may continue up to 25°C (Hankinson 1919). Spawning occurs in shallow parts of streams in slow to moderate current and in margins of ponds and lakes in some regions.

Nest cover includes shelving stones, wood, tiles and cans, and plates set for experimental purposes. The male and female typically invert to attach and fertilize a single layer of eggs on the underside of the nest cover; the male territorially attends the nest (Hankinson 1908, 1919, 1932; Winn 1958a, 1958b; Speare 1965). Spawning sites and behavior are similar to those of *E. olmstedi* and *E. (Boleosoma) perlongum* (Shute et al. 1982), except that *E. nigrum* apparently does not create a depression under its cover (Lindquist et al. 1981) and, differing from *E. olmstedi*, the nesting male is not known to tend eggs fertilized

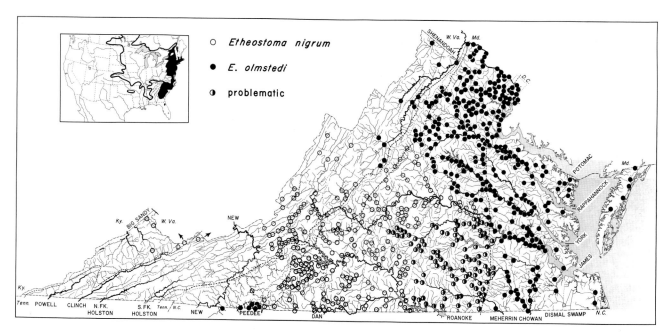

Map 180 Johnny darter and tessellated darter. Problematic populations (in Falling River of the James drainage just above the Fall Line, and the Appomattox, Nottoway, and Meherrin systems, and the Roanoke drainage) are of intergraded, hybrid, and/or differentiated fish; see *Systematics*.

by other males (Grant and Colgan 1983). Pairs of *E. nigrum* spawned on top of aquarium substrate without inverting (Forbes and Richardson 1920)—a reversion to a primitive mode of spawning in the absence of suitable nest cover (Page 1983). Potential clutch size per spawning, determined from mature and mature-ripening ovaries of Mississippi fish, was 54–192 oocytes; results of some earlier fecundity studies are questionable (Parrish et al. 1991).

The hybrid *E. nigrum* × *E. olmstedi* was reported by McAllister et al. (1972); Falls (1982) contested the interpretation. Chapleau and Pageau (1985) regarded their few intermediate specimens as nonhybrids; Cole (1965) reported introgressive hybridization in New York; and Clark (1978) and we believe that ancestry may be mixed in some of the problematic Virginia populations.

HABITAT

In Virginia, *E. nigrum* inhabits warm, moderate-gradient creeks, streams, and rivers; it rarely occurs in lacustrine biotopes. It occupies pools and slow runs having rubble substrate but more typically gravel, sand, silt, and detritus. Elsewhere its habitat is similar to that in Virginia (e.g., Englert and Seghers 1983a) and includes vegetated areas (Paine et al. 1982). The johnny darter extended into stony riffles in a low-diversity situation in Manitoba (Smart and Gee

1979). This species prefers warm water (Ingersoll and Claussen 1984).

DISTRIBUTION   Map 180

Etheostoma nigrum occupies much of the Hudson Bay, Great Lakes, Mississippi, and Mobile basins; on the central Atlantic slope it occurs in the James, Roanoke, Tar, and Neuse drainages of Virginia and North Carolina.

In the James system proper, the johnny darter extends from mountains to tributaries just above the Fall Line; in the Roanoke drainage, it widely populates the upper and middle sections. Its lower limit in the Roanoke and its occurrence in the Appomattox system and the Chowan drainage are uncertain owing to taxonomic problems involving *E. olmstedi*. The johnny darter is highly localized in the New and Big Sandy drainages of Virginia.

In the New drainage, *E. nigrum* occupies a few streams in the lower part of the West Virginia section, where it is believed to be native (Addair 1944; Hocutt et al. 1979). Two disjunct, questionably native populations were discovered in Virginia during 1983–1984, in Mud Fork of the Bluestone system near West Virginia, and in Big Reed Island Creek within the Blue Ridge Province. The Mud Fork record is from the only fish collection known from the stream. The Big Reed Island Creek system has been well sampled but yielded only one record; the site and nearby tributaries are heavily sport-fished, hence subject to bait-bucket introductions.

Two records for the Virginia portion of the New drainage are considered erroneous. The specimen reported by Fowler (1923) from Laurel Creek of the Little River system was not found. The record for lower Meadow Creek of the same system is treated under *Ameiurus nebulosus*. The four records (Richardson and Carnes 1964) from the New in North Carolina are unacceptable. One is based on *E. blennioides* (NCSM); the others are confusingly reported or based on nonextant specimens, some or all of which may have been *E. kanawhae*, whose young and small juveniles are similar in pattern to *E. nigrum*. Two specimens of *E. nigrum* (ANSP 13971–72) taken by Cope in 1867 and labeled Holston River obviously have faulty locality data, a case similar to one treated under *E. longimanum*.

The record of *E. olmstedi* in a middle Piedmont reach of the James River (White et al. 1977) probably is based on *E. nigrum*; we reidentified some of the specimens as *E. nigrum* but did not find the others. Specimens reported as *E. nigrum* from the South Fork Shenandoah system (Ross 1959a) are *E. olmstedi*; the same is presumed for *E. nigrum* recorded there by Potter et al. (1981). The listing of *E. nigrum* in the York drainage (Jenkins et al. 1972) is founded on *E. olmstedi* (Hocutt et al. 1986).

Abundance.—The johnny darter often is common in much of its Virginia range.

REMARKS

The dainty johnny darter is a common component of many Virginia stream ecosystems. It probably functions in the food chain as an important converter of invertebrates, and may serve as forage for gamefishes (Scott and Crossman 1973; Englert and Seghers 1983b). As a potential antipredation fright response, when the johnny darter is exposed to the skin extract of conspecific fish, it "freezes" and afterward exhibits reduced activity (Smith 1982). Trautman (1981) remarked that among the darters in Ohio, *E. nigrum* occupied the greatest diversity of natural conditions and was the most tolerant of pollution. The same is not clearly indicated for Virginia; its tolerance of silt may be generally exceeded in the Big Sandy drainage.

Name.—Rafinesque apparently had studied a nuptial male when he named *E. nigrum* as "black." A "johnny" is a fine fellow, in this case a fine little fish (Jordan and Evermann 1896).

Tessellated darter   *Etheostoma olmstedi* Storer

SYSTEMATICS

Etheostoma olmstedi, subgenus *Boleosoma*, was described from Connecticut in 1842. Its relationships and species-level systematic problems are considered under *E. nigrum*. All four subspecies of the tessellated darter occur in Virginia (Cole 1967): *E. o. olmstedi* Storer, *E. o. atromaculatum* Girard, *E. o. vexillare* Jordan, and *E. o. maculaticeps* Cope. Cole's decisions on the status of the first three hinged partly or entirely on their interactions in Virginia; his criteria for judging that of *E. o. maculaticeps* included an uncertain aspect of drainage history (Hocutt et al. 1986).

The validity of subspecies in *E. olmstedi* was questioned by Zorach (1971), Falls (1982), J. R. Shute (1984), and Chapleau and Pageau (1985), but not by Clark (1978) for the James drainage. R. E. Watson (in litt.) found infraspecific differentiation in the Potomac drainage to differ from Cole's (1967) notion of the two subspecies there. We recognize subspecies in *E. olmstedi* partly to facilitate describing their diverse morphology and habitat-use patterns. The rife evidence of mosaic, parallel, or convergent evolution in "johnny darters" calls for determining their phylogeny before the subspecific taxa can be firmly accepted as monophyletic units.

DESCRIPTION

Materials.—From typical Virginia populations of the four subspecies—Cole (1957, 1967), Clark (1978), and our 18 series from which 189 specimens were counted meristically. Life color from 5 Virginia series.

Anatomy.—A speckled and XW-marked darter with an uninterrupted infraorbital canal; adults are 35–55 mm SL, but are usually less than 45 mm in *E. o. vexillare*. Body form moderate or elongate; snout moderate or blunt; frenum absent; branchiostegal membranes usually slightly, occasionally moderately conjoined; caudal fin truncate or rounded; first dorsal fin quite high in adult. In nuptial male, tips of some pectoral and pelvic fin rays or spines with a well-developed whitish knob, and some fish also with a slight thickening on some supports of the first and second dorsal and anal fins (Gale and Deutsch 1985; Page and Bart 1989; Bart and Page 1991); tubercles absent. Genital papilla short, low, bilobed in female. Squamation: subspecies *vexillare* and *maculaticeps* have cheek, nape, and breast naked, belly weakly or moderately scaled; *o. olmstedi*

Fish 298 *Etheostoma olmstedi* adult male 46 mm SL (REJ 969), VA, Patrick County, Johnson Creek, 8 June 1983.

Fish 299 *Etheostoma olmstedi* adult male 46 mm SL (REJ 1028), VA, Amelia County, Appomattox River, 1 September 1983.

usually has nape and breast naked, cheek and belly much varied; *atromaculatum* usually has all areas fully scaled.

Meristics.—The ranges of scale and fin-element counts are composites for the species in Virginia. Lateral line complete, scales (34)36–58(64), usually 36–40 in subspecies *vexillare*, 42–48 in *o. olmstedi* and *maculaticeps*, and 48–58 in *atromaculatum*; scales above lateral line (3)4–6(7); scales below lateral line (5)6–9(11); circumpeduncle scales (13)17–20(22). Dorsal spines (7)8–9(11); dorsal rays (10)12–14(17) but usually 11–12 in *vexillare*; anal spines (0)1(2), but usually 2 in *maculaticeps*; anal rays (5)7–9(10), but usually 6–7 in *vexillare* and *maculaticeps*, 7–8 in *o. olmstedi*, and 8–9 in *atromaculatum*; pectoral rays (10)12–13(15); gill rakers (7)8–9(10). IO canal uninterrupted, pores (6)8–9(10); POM pores (7)10–11(13); ST canal almost always uninterrupted.

Color.—Same as *E. nigrum* except XW marks on midside number (7)8–11(12) and caudal fin bars (4)5–8(9); because these counts average higher in larger specimens, the interspecific differences may stem from the larger size of *E. olmstedi*. These species also differ in nuptial color (*Comparison* in *E. nigrum* account).

Larvae.—See Rohde (1974), Hardy (1978b), Wang and Kernehan (1979), and Auer (1982f).

COMPARISON

See *E. nigrum* account.

BIOLOGY

The tessellated darter eats immature insects and other small invertebrates; midge larvae are the most frequently taken items (Baker 1916; Hildebrand and Schroeder 1928; Layzer and Reed 1978). It feeds throughout the day, most actively between 0600–1200 hours (Layzer and Reed 1978) and detects prey mainly by vision, responding particularly to movement (Roberts and Winn 1962).

Maturity is attained in 1 year (Tsai 1972); 2 years of age is commonly attained, but 4 years is rare (Raney and Lachner 1943; Tsai 1972; Layzer and Reed 1978). In all five Connecticut populations studied, males averaged larger than females but the differences were not significant (Layzer and Reed 1978); in all seven Massachusetts, New York, and Maryland populations examined, growth differences between the sexes were statistically significant (Raney and Lachner 1943; Tsai 1972). In Connecticut populations, means of length at age 2 ranged 53–70 mm TL for males and 51–61 mm for females. For New York fish in their second year, means were 51 mm SL for males and 43 mm for females. In a Maryland population in a cold tailwater and one in a warmer sewage-polluted stream, means at age 2 were 50 and 48 mm SL for males; females averaged 47 mm in both. Three of the subspecies commonly reach 60 mm SL but *E. o. vexillare* does not exceed 48 mm SL (Cole 1967). Our largest Virginia specimen (subspecies uncertain) is 66 mm SL. Raney and Lachner (1943) reported an 88-mm SL male from Massachusetts.

Reproduction occurs from late March through June, mainly during a 6–7 week period (Adams and Hankinson 1928; Hildebrand and Schroeder 1928; Raney and Lachner 1943; Wang and Kernehan 1979; Gale and Deutsch 1985). In Maryland the breeding season is May and June and may start in late April (Tsai 1972). In Virginia, dark males were taken during 25 April–23 May in the Fall Zone and lower Piedmont of the Nottoway system, and on 8 June in the Blue Ridge foothills of the Pee Dee drainage. Wang and Kernehan (1979) cited spawning temperatures of 10–15°C; Tsai (1972) found ranges of 12.5–14.5°C in a cold tailwater and 16.0–18.5°C in a warmer stream. No evidence of movement was found in the lower Delaware River area (B. Smith 1971 in Wang and Kernehan 1979), but movement would occur when departing brackish reaches to spawn in fresh water (Wang and Kernehan 1979).

Nest sites and behavior are similar to those of *E. nigrum* except that *E. olmstedi* fans a depression under its nest cover (Adams and Hankinson 1928; Atz 1940; Constantz 1979; Lindquist et al. 1981). Also, *E. olmstedi* is unique in that subordinate males regularly clean and defend egg clutches that have been fertilized and abandoned by a dominant male; males may roam and spawn in more than one nest (Constantz 1979, 1985). Fecundity is 54–668 ova based on single counts per female (Hildebrand and Schroeder 1928; Tsai 1972; Hardy 1978b), but like many darters, *E. olmstedi* is a fractional spawner. Females spawned 2–8 clutches producing 97–1,435 eggs, mean 727, in a season (Gale and Deutsch 1985). Hybridization is noted under *E. nigrum*.

HABITAT

The tessellated darter occupies creeks, streams, rivers, swampy flowages, and estuaries under a variety of temperature and water-clarity conditions. It usually occurs in pools and slow runs, and is found on substrates ranging from silt, mud, and detritus to clean gravel and larger stones. It is known to bury in sand until only its eyes are exposed (Nash 1908 in Adams and Hankinson 1928). Very few Virginia records are from ponds or reservoirs; ponds and lakes are occupied more frequently farther north.

Most Virginia Coastal Plain records are in or near main rivers which are chemically influenced by the Piedmont. This and the absence of *E. olmstedi* from Dismal Swamp proper indicate that it avoids blackwaters of very low pH. In the New Jersey Pine Bar-

rens, the tessellated darter is restricted to main-stem tidal waters and tributaries with reduced acidity (Hastings 1979, 1984). This species was markedly reduced or extirpated below outfalls of chlorinated sewage (Tsai 1968, 1972).

The "downstream" subspecies *E. o. atromaculatum* commonly extends into tidal fresh water and has been considered unique among darters by its presence in brackish water. Salinity records (‰) in the Chesapeake Bay or Delaware River basins are: 2.23 (Hildebrand and Schroeder 1928), 2.41 (Cole 1967), 4 (B. Smith 1971), up to 5.2 (Hoener 1969), about 6.0 (White et al. 1972), 6.8 (Massmann et al. 1952), 8.0 (Wang and Kernehan 1979), and 13 (Musick 1972). The tessellated darter occupied low salinity (to 6‰) in North Carolina estuaries that are subject to periodic floodwater runoff (Schwartz 1981b). Cole (1957, 1967) noted that because local sharp salinity gradients often occur, precise association of specimens and water samples is needed to determine the salinity distribution of organisms. He suggested that darters may retreat into pockets of fresh water along shore as main flows become slightly brackish.

DISTRIBUTION   Map 180

Etheostoma olmstedi is widespread on the Atlantic slope from southern Canada to southern Georgia; an isolated population occurs in northern Florida (Cole 1967; Burgess et al. 1977) and one in the upper New drainage. Its subspecies form a complex distribution pattern in which the intergrade zones are narrow to wide (e.g., Cole 1967; Zorach 1971). *Etheostoma o. olmstedi* and *E. o. atromaculatum* (or intergrades) extend from North Carolina to New England and Canada; typically the former inhabits uplands, the latter lowlands. In nonintergraded form, *E. o. vexillare* populates only uplands of the Rappahannock drainage. *Etheostoma o. maculaticeps* occupies the Pee Dee drainage of Virginia and is widespread in uplands and lowlands southward.

In Virginia, *E. olmstedi* is widely distributed in the Coastal Plain; the range includes some minor Chesapeake drainages and extends amply down the Delmarva Peninsula. In the Piedmont, it pervades in the Potomac, Rappahannock, and York drainages, but is represented in the Appomattox system, the Chowan drainage, and part of the Roanoke drainage (and perhaps the Tar and Neuse drainages of North Carolina) by taxonomically problematic populations (*Systematics* under *E. nigrum*). The tessellated darter is localized in the Valley and Ridge Province of the Potomac. The probably introduced population in the New drainage was discovered during 1986 in the

Little River system of North Carolina, just south of the Virginia line (J. R. Shute, personal communication).

Abundance.—The tessellated darter is one of the most common darters in Virginia; its general rarity in the Shenandoah system seems exceptional.

REMARKS

D. S. Jordan (1925) noted that the tessellated darter (and johnny darter) is among the smallest and most plainly colored of darters, "yet in the delicacy, wariness and quaintness of motion they are among the most interesting, especially in the aquarium." The care of nests by males that did not fertilize the eggs (alloparental care) is a fascinating attribute of this species. *Etheostoma olmstedi* is important forage of some gamefishes in lakes (Raney and Lachner 1942, 1943), and from its commonness, this may be so in Virginia streams.

The success of *E. olmstedi* in upland–montane biotopes is varied; in some drainages this accords with the degree of morphological similarity of the population to the regionally upland-disposed *E. nigrum*. *Etheostoma o. vexillare*, the form perhaps most similar to *E. nigrum*, thrives in uplands of the Rappahannock drainage. *Etheostoma o. maculaticeps* also exhibits trends toward *E. nigrum*, such that Cole (1957) first considered it a subspecies of *E. nigrum*; it too is successful in uplands. In contrast, the localization and rarity of *E. o. olmstedi* in the upper Potomac drainage of Virginia may be related to retarding of adaptation to uplands by genetic influx from the lowland-inhabiting *E. o. atromaculatum*.

Name.—For its discoverer, the naturalist Charles Olmstead. Subspecific epithets include: *atromaculatum*—"black spotted"; *maculaticeps*—"spotted head"; and *vexillare*—"flag," perhaps coined for the patterned fins.

Glassy darter   *Etheostoma vitreum* (Cope)

SYSTEMATICS

Described from North Carolina in 1870, the distinctive glassy darter is the monotype of the subgenus *Ioa*. Bailey and Etnier (1988) placed it in the *Boleosoma* group of subgenera, in which it is most closely related to the subgenus *Boleosoma* (Winn and Picciolo 1960; Jenkins 1971b; Page 1981, 1985). Some of its specializations for perching on and burying in sand have been regarded as evolutionarily convergent with those of sand darters, genus *Ammocrypta* (Hubbs 1941a; Page and Swofford 1984). In contrast, Simons (1992) concluded that *Ammocrypta* is the sister group of *Ioa*; his phylogeny places *Ammocrypta* in *Etheostoma*. He was followed by Page and Burr (1991) but not by Robins et al. (1991). We do not accept Simons' arrangement for the following reasons.

Distinctions of *E. vitreum* from *Ammocrypta* include the presence in *E. vitreum* of: (1) basic body pigmentary pattern of dark spots, speckles, and flecks, the midlateral flecks sometimes forming modified X- or W-shaped marks; (2) tessellated fins; (3) a thickening or knob well developed at tip of pelvic spine and rays of some nuptial fish; (4) genital papilla bifurcate; (5) nuptial shade of head and body blackened; (6) anal–urogenital area with a cluster of villilike papillae (here termed villi, as distinct from the larger urogenital papilla); (7) nuptial tubercles present in both sexes, best developed on the pectoral fin; (8) ctenii well-elevated on cheek and body scales of nuptial fish; (9)

pectoral fin very long, pointed; (10) communal spawning; and (11) early spawning period. Further, *E. vitreum* is less translucent than *Ammocrypta* (Page 1983; our observations).

States 1–5 collectively indicate direct kinship of *E. vitreum* with *Boleosoma*; the degree of translucence is corroboratory. States 6–11 are unique or transformed (autapomorphous) in *E. vitreum*. Some of the states are defined or distributed among taxa differently than considered by Simons (1992); others are newly evaluated here.

Etheostoma vitreum and *E. (Boleosoma) longimanum* may be sister species. The very long pectoral fin of *E. vitreum* may be an elaboration (for sand-dwelling) of the lengthy pectoral of *E. longimanum*. Resembling *E. vitreum* and differing from other *Boleosoma*, *E. longimanum* has an emarginate tail and in dark males the lower lip remains relatively pale. It may have phylogenetic bearing that the glassy darter is endemic to the central Atlantic slope, where *Boleosoma* is most diverse.

The egg-attaching behavior of *E. vitreum* likely was derived from that of the subgenus *Boleosoma* (Winn and Picciolo 1960). This hypothesis is beset by the communal spawning of *E. vitreum* in upright posture on top of rocks; *Boleosoma* species typically spawn as pairs while inverted in cavities. However, *E. vitreum* also lays eggs on the sides of structures and while inverted in cavities. Further, and supporting an *E.*

longimanum–E. vitreum sister-group relationship, *E. longimanum* has the plasticity to oviposit on the top of structures and with two females at a time (our data).

Most of the character states used by Simons (1992) to directly support monophyletic grouping of *Ioa* and *Ammocrypta* are osteological; they may be nongenealogically shared as adaptations for penetrating, moving, or respiratory water exchange in sand. Our stand is based on states from four or more separate character complexes. Resolution of the conflicting phylogenetic hypotheses will involve study of additional character sets (Johnston 1989a). Therefore, we hold that *Ioa* is most closely related to *Boleosoma*, and believe that the position and hence status of *Ammocrypta* are uncertain.

DESCRIPTION

Materials.—From Jenkins (1971b), Page (1983), and 40 other Virginia series. Life color from Taylor (1983), Quinn (1991), and 7 Virginia lots.

Anatomy.—A somewhat translucent, quite elongate, fat-lipped darter with very long pectoral fins and villate anal–urogenital area; adults are 35–55 mm SL. Body moderately or quite elongate, cylindrical; eye supralateral, interorbital width narrow; snout moderate or long, broad dorsally, the tip rounded or sharp; frenum absent. Mouth medium-sized, terminal; lips thick, their front usually well in advance of snout tip, the fish appearing shovel-nosed; branchiostegal membranes usually slightly conjoined; pectoral and pelvic fins long, pointed; caudal fin very slightly emarginate or truncate.

Nuptial structures developed in both sexes, most so in male. Tubercles often present on branchiostegal, pectoral, and less often, pelvic rays. Spines and rays of lower fins, occasionally all fins, with much-thickened skin, most so on pelvic; pelvic spine and anterior rays thickest distally, thickenings rarely knoblike, membranes usually not notably incised; skin thickenings may replace tubercles. Ctenoid edges of scales distinctly elevated on head laterally and ventrolaterally and on much of body, particularly lower half, forming very rough surface; ctenoid edges elevated by a padlike thickening of skin under the nonimbricated part (lunula) of scales; outer surface of scales padded except for tips of ctenii.

Uniquely among darters, anus surrounded by a compact cluster of villi (Figure 77). Genital papilla moderate-sized, typically bifurcate in both sexes, usually conical or slightly flattened, occasionally pear-shaped with a tubular tip. In breeding fish of both sexes, anal villi tend to be longer than in nonbreeding male; anal–urogenital area swollen, moundlike, particularly in female; in female the genital papilla is surrounded and often obscured by villi, and the tip of the papilla often is villately subdivided.

Cheek and opercle fully scaled; nape partly scaled; belly fully scaled to almost naked; breast naked.

Meristics.—Lateral line complete, scales 50–65; scales above lateral line 5–8; scales below lateral line 7–9; circumpeduncle scales 18–22. Dorsal spines 8–9; dorsal rays 13–14; anal spines 1–2; anal rays 8–10; pectoral rays (12)13(14).

Color in Preservative.—Midside with a series of dark marks of varied number and size, usually small; the marks are spots, speckles, flecks, X- or W-shaped, or horizontally elongate. Dorsum with 6–8 dark saddles or concentrations of flecks; dorsum and side usually with scattered small dark spots and flecks; preocular dark dash or spot(s) present;

Fish 300 *Etheostoma vitreum* adult male 42 mm SL (JRR 264), VA, Louisa County, South Anna River, 15 March 1974.

Fish 301 *Etheostoma vitreum* adult female 55 mm SL (REJ 1017), VA, Southampton-Greensville County, Meherrin River, 15 July 1983.

dark marks brown or black, tending darkest laterally. Fins clear; dorsal, caudal, and pectoral rays tessellated; caudal spot small, medial, black; lower 2–3 branched caudal rays often uniformly dusky proximally.

Except during the breeding season, this species is moderately or quite pallid, as is true of small nuptial female. During interludes in spawning, large nuptial female and small and large nuptial male are slightly to moderately dusky, male tending darkest. Peak nuptial male sooty to black on head and body, darkest on lower half; lips remain pale or dusky; fins (except for tessellations), much of underside of head, anal–urogenital area, and lateral line remain pale.

Color in Life   Plate 36.—Body somewhat translucent, dorsally to midlaterally dark tan to pale straw where not darkly marked; flesh rapidly becomes opaque in preservative; body of breeding fish that is slightly dusky when alive becomes medium straw to pale olive when freshly preserved. Dark marks pale brown to black, tending darkest laterally. Side of head, spaces between dark midside marks, and some upper body flecks iridescent silver, gold, or gold-green. According to Winn and Picciolo (1960), males become totally black during particularly intense spawning activities; however, in our preserved males with a sooty or blackened body, the fins and pale parts noted above remained pallid.

Often considered to be notably translucent, nonnuptial *E. vitreum* vary from slightly more to slightly less translucent than other fairly pale darters, e. g., nonbreeding adult *E. nigrum* and juvenile *E. longimanum* and *E. podostemone*. Prespawning, slightly dusky *E. vitreum* are not translucent.

Larvae.—Described by Rohde (1974) and Hardy (1978b).

BIOLOGY

Etheostoma vitreum probably is chiefly an insectivore; gut contents of four Virginia adults, each from a different river, were entirely midge larvae. This species is most active at dusk and dawn, normally remaining buried in sand with only the eyes exposed unless it is disturbed or seeking food (Lee and Ashton 1979, 1981). It may also forage while buried, detecting food by lateral line sense organs.

Some age-1 and all age-2 *E. vitreum* from Virginia were mature; the largest immature fish was 35 mm SL. Of adults taken during 21 February–28 March, 39 males were 31–59 mm SL, mean, 43; 47 females were 30–51 mm SL, mean, 42. The 59-mm SL male was scale-aged as probably 3 years old. The largest known specimen is a male of 60 mm SL from Virginia.

An early spawner, the glassy darter spawns during mid-March to mid-April, water 10–19°C, in Maryland (Winn and Picciolo 1960). In Virginia, based on collections taken during 1941–1984 from much of the species range, spawning began in late February in some years and in cooler years it may have ended as late as early April. The earliest date a spent female was recorded was 21 February, and most or all females taken in mid- to late March were postnuptial; the latest date for a gravid female was 28 March (Jenkins 1971b; our data). In the mild winters of 1989–1990 and 1990–1991, the glassy darter spawned early and quickly in the Blackwater and Pigg rivers on the upper Piedmont; water was 5–8°C. In 1990, all fish were prenuptial on 1 February and spent on 18 February; the same was true for 10 and 23 February 1991 except that a ripe female was found on 23 February (M. A. Hartman and G. M. Keenum, in litt.)

Etheostoma vitreum is a communal breeder—a reproductive mode that is unique or nearly so among darters. Winn and Picciolo (1960) observed spawning activities in a Maryland stream and aquaria. Intermale aggression was mild; 1–10 males attended a spawning female. Oviposition sites were rocks, a concrete spillway, and a log, comprising cavities and open surfaces ranging from horizontal to vertical; all were in strong current near shifting sand. Some spawning occurred while fish were inverted, judging from comments and Figure 2 of Winn and Picciolo (1960). Eggs were laid singly, generally on surfaces directly facing the current, and sometimes were distributed from the top to the underside of structures. One rock was used by 50 or more spawning fish and had 30,000–50,000 eggs. Egg clusters were depicted as having 1–2 (or more) tiers.

Maryland females laid 68–223 adhesive eggs, averaging about 100 in a spawning season (Winn and Picciolo 1960). Maturing or mature ova numbered 136–496, mean 335, in Virginia females of 40–57 mm SL (M. A. Hartman and G. M. Keenum, in litt.). Females produce one clutch per year, judging by the brevity of the spawning period and the extremely reduced ovaries of all spent fish. The testes of imminently spawning males were exceptionally large for darters; those of specimens taken two weeks later were greatly reduced, and later-caught fish also were spent.

HABITAT

The glassy darter inhabits warm, low- and moderate-gradient creeks, streams, and rivers. Some populations occupy usually clear streams, others live in often turbid conditions. In North Carolina, *E. vitreum* was confined to unsilted shifting sand (Lee and Ashton 1979). In several upper Piedmont streams of Virginia we found adults in riffles, fast and slow runs, and well-flowing sections of pools and backwaters; they always were associated with sand bars or sand

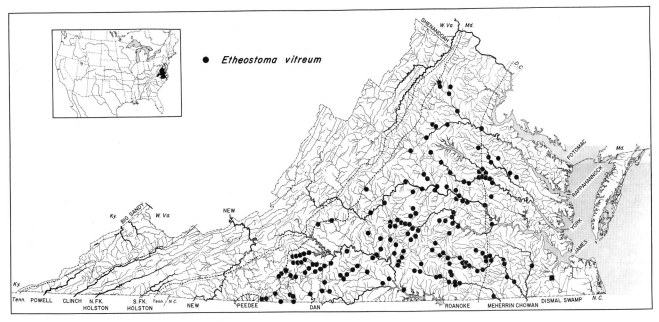

Map 181 Glassy darter. The record (square) at the Dismal Swamp periphery has questionable locality data.

flats. In the Nottoway system the greatest abundance was at sand bars (Norman and Southwick 1985, in litt.)

In an autumn sampling at a Blackwater River site (upper Roanoke drainage) 25 adults were found; all were associated with sand. None were sighted before they were disturbed, thus most of them had been buried. Most occupied moderate runs; a few were in the main body of pools, slow runs, and mostly rocky riffles. Wide expanses of shifting sand yielded fewer specimens than smaller areas of sand; silted-over sand apparently was not populated. In riffles, glassy darters were at strips of sand at least 0.5 m wide and 1.5 m long and in the lee of boulders. Captures occurred in depths of 0.4–1.2 m. In all habitats the darters were found no closer than about 1 m from each other.

Current speeds inhabited by adult *E. vitreum* are intermediate on average among those of syntopic *Boleosoma* adults; *E. nigrum* occupies slower areas, *E. longimanum* and *E. podostemone* swifter water.

DISTRIBUTION   Map 181

Etheostoma vitreum occurs on the Atlantic slope from a western tributary of upper Chesapeake Bay in Maryland south to the Neuse drainage of North Carolina (Lee et al. *in* Lee et al. 1980). It is unknown in the Virginia portion of the Potomac, but has been found in the Anacostia system of the Potomac in Maryland, near Washington, D.C. The heartland for this species

in Virginia is the Piedmont, but there is no record for many well-surveyed streams in this province that have seemingly suitable habitat. Most records from the Coastal Plain of Virginia are in main rivers having strong Piedmont influence. In the drainages heading in mountains, the glassy darter extends up to but stops at the foot of the Blue Ridge. Persistent localization is demonstrated at the only record site in the Blackwater River of the Chowan drainage, on the Coastal Plain: the glassy darter was taken at Zuni in 1888 and 1984 (Jordan 1889b; M. D. Norman, in litt.). We doubt the validity of the locality data for Jordan's (1889b) report from Shingle Creek on the periphery of Dismal Swamp (*Biogeography*).

Abundance.—In about equal frequency, *E. vitreum* is rare, uncommon, or common in the upper Piedmont and upper Coastal Plain; it is often common or abundant in the lower Piedmont.

REMARKS

The glassy darter is highly specialized for living on and in the sand environment. Its shovel-like snout affords an entering wedge to the substrate; burrowing is little impeded by the slender body. The long pectoral fins may aid in covering itself with sand; they may also serve as hydrofoils for anchorage when resting on top of sand. The pallid flesh with touches of dark flecking blends with the substrate.

Daily and seasonal movements of *E. vitreum* were

monitored after injecting specimens with a tiny piece of radioactive wire (Lee and Ashton 1979, 1981). Among interesting observations, it was learned that during cold water and flood periods the darters commonly buried themselves as deeply as 3 cm into sand. One fish acted like a mole, making its way for some 80 cm through sand while buried about 1 cm.

The distinctive spawning style of the glassy darter—communal egg-attaching—and other reproductive attributes is well adapted. The attachment of eggs above the bottom on solid structures precludes or reduces the smothering of eggs by shifting sand. The ability of the glassy darter to stay on a rock or to maintain spawning position in fast current is enhanced by tubercles, thickened fin supports, and padded scales with elevated ctenii (Jenkins 1971b). The bloom of villi around the urogenital papilla may aid in pressing eggs to the substrate. Communality

may accrue from localization of suitable spawning sites, from attraction of additional adults to a spawning group, and from the necessity of involving numerous males to ensure fertilization in swift current.

Although glassy darter eggs may be unattended and most are exposed, Winn and Picciolo (1960) regarded egg predation to be low owing to the lesser activity of other fishes during the cold- to coolwater spawning period, because of the avoidance of swift water by many predators, and by shrouding of eggs in turbidity.

Although there is no immediate threat to the continued existence of *E. vitreum* in Virginia and North Carolina, it merits threatened status in Maryland (Lee et al. 1984).

Name.—Vitreum means "glassy."

Bluebreast darter   *Etheostoma camurum* (Cope)

SYSTEMATICS

Etheostoma camurum, described from Tennessee in 1870, is a member of the subgenus *Nothonotus*—the bluebreast darters, one of the most diverse subgenera of darters (Etnier and Williams 1989). Six of the 16 species occupy Virginia; as many as four inhabit the same riffle–run areas of the Clinch River. *Etheostoma camurum* is intimately related to *E. chlorobranchium* (Zorach 1967, 1968, 1972; Etnier and Williams 1989). They are evolutionary species; their parapatric distribution in the Tennessee drainage may allow evaluating them as possible biological species.

DESCRIPTION

*Materials.—*From Zorach (1972) and 23 series from the upper Tennessee drainage: 13 from Virginia, 10 from Ten-

nessee; the meristic data given are from the upper Tennessee. Life color from 5 Virginia series.

*Anatomy.—*A lined, checkered, and faintly barred darter with black and pale banding on the margin of the second dorsal, caudal, and anal fins, and the head not boldly marked; adults are 35–60 mm SL. Body moderate in profile, compressed; snout moderately short and blunt; frenum well developed; branchiostegal membranes separate or slightly conjoined; caudal fin truncate or rounded. Female genital papilla short, flattened or globose; tubercles absent. Cheek, nape, and breast naked; opercle and belly scaled.

*Meristics.—*Lateral line complete or with a few unpored scales, midlateral scales (52)54–62(66); scales above lateral line (5)6–8(9); transverse scales (14)15–18(20); circumpeduncle scales (19)20–23(26). Dorsal spines 10–12; dorsal rays (11)12–13(14); anal spines 2; anal rays (6)7–8(9); pectoral rays 13–15.

Fish 302 *Etheostoma camurum* adult male 47 mm SL (REJ 986), VA, Scott County, Clinch River, 17 June 1983.

Fish 303 *Etheostoma camurum* adult female 44 mm SL (REJ 984), VA, Scott County, Copper Creek, 16 June 1983.

Color in Preservative.—Side with small blotches forming vague or prominent checkered pattern; vague vertical or slightly oblique bars sometimes present; multiple horizontal dark lines, each pair outlining a scale row, best developed on posterior body; both sexes may have bars; female usually checkered and faintly lined, male distinctly lined. Side of adult male with irregularly arranged small pale spots (reddish in life). Humeral spot black, from which dark line extends along posterior base of pectoral fin. Dorsum dusky or dark, saddles vague, appearing as extensions of lateral bars; venter pale or dusky. Head marks generally vague; pre-, sub-, and postocular bars occasionally moderately developed, the latter 2 often spotlike.

In male, first dorsal fin with incomplete narrow dark edge in most fish, occasionally a distal area pale; most of fin dusky, basally darker, anterior membranes darkest. Second dorsal, caudal, and anal fins with a distal dark band; subdistally clear; remainder dusky or dark. Pelvic fin dark basally, fading distally; pectoral membranes clear, rays generally dusky or darkly pigmented. Fin patterns in female similar but lighter, both dorsal fins and anal fin sometimes slightly tessellated. Caudal base in both sexes often with 2 submedian dark spots (sometimes fused) and a dark spot at each of upper and lower edge of body.

Color in Life   Plate 37.—Nuptial male with lines, bars, and saddles dark olive or black; side paler olive or olive-gray; head olive to tan; breast blue, dark gray, or olive; belly gray; flank anterior to anus often with an orange flush. Body laterally on urosome and anteriad, occasionally to shoulder, with scattered orange-red or blood red spots, each the size of one scale, between dark lines; spots red-brown on female; spots sometimes absent in both sexes.

First dorsal fin margin of nuptial male faint orange to brick red, remainder olive-gray to olive-tan. Second dorsal, caudal, and anal fins distally black; subdistally creamy white or pale yellow; submarginally amber, mahogany, orange-red, or brick red, the band often widest and brightest in the anal; remainder of these fins olive to gray; fins occasionally dull olive submarginally. Pelvic fin margin amber to brick red, remainder black. Pectoral rays red-brown or blackish olive.

COMPARISON

Etheostoma camurum and *E. chlorobranchium* differ in typical life colors of the larger nuptial males: (1) second dorsal, caudal, and anal fins submarginally [amber, brown, or reddish in *camurum vs.* green or blue-green in *chlorobranchium*]; (2) lateral body base tone [olive *vs.* blue-green]; (3) breast [blue, gray, or olive *vs.* blue-green]; (4) adult males differ in size [rarely attaining 65 mm SL *vs.* often exceeding 70 mm]. Females of both species are smaller. Meristic values tend lower in *E. camurum*, but their utility is limited by geographic variation in both species (e.g., Schmidt 1980).

BIOLOGY

Etheostoma camurum feeds mainly on dipteran larvae; mayfly and other insect larvae are also eaten (Stiles 1972; Bryant 1979). Males average larger than females. The largest specimen reported is 70 mm SL (Page 1983); that from Virginia is 67 mm SL.

Reproduction peaks in Ohio from mid-May to early June, water 21–24°C, and is completed by the end of June (Mount 1959). In the Little River of Tennessee, spawning extends from late May until late July or early August (Stiles 1972). The spawning period is typical for *Nothonotus* but its late extension is unusual for most darters. Females selected spawning sites at the head of riffles; they buried in sand or fine gravel in the lee of boulders and were mounted by the male. Burial usually lasted 20–30 minutes; females emerged and reburrowed several times during the period. On one occasion, about 100 eggs were laid in an irregularly shaped cluster. Males were territorial, guarding a site sometimes for two hours or more after females had been driven away (Mount 1959; Stiles 1972). Hybridization with *E. tippecanoe* has occurred (Zorach 1967).

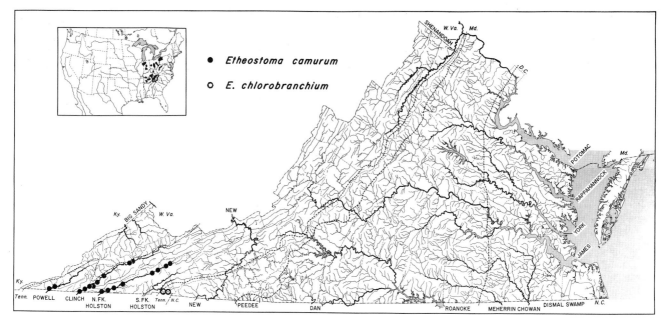

Map 182 Bluebreast darter and greenfin darter.

HABITAT

The bluebreast darter inhabits typically clear or slightly turbid, warm, moderate-gradient, large streams and rivers. Adults generally occupy silt-free runs and riffles having large gravel, rubble, and boulders. In Virginia, this species was captured much less commonly in areas of large slab rocks and in shallow runs of gravel than in the above habitats. Habitat characteristics are considered in detail by Stiles (1972) and Greenberg (1991).

DISTRIBUTION   Map 182

Etheostoma camurum is widespread but sporadically distributed in the Ohio River basin. It occupies the Valley and Ridge Province in the upper Tennessee drainage, hence it is parapatric to *E. chlorobranchium* in the Blue Ridge Province. The total-range map reflects clarification of some erroneous or ambiguous aspects of these ranges in the Tennessee that persisted beyond Zorach's (1972) study.

In the Virginia portion of the Tennessee drainage, the bluebreast darter inhabits the North Fork Holston, Clinch, and Powell rivers, Laurel Creek just above its mouth in the North Fork, and the lower 8 rkm of Copper Creek in the Clinch system.

Recently there has been a gap in the range of *E. camurum* in both the North Fork Holston and Clinch rivers. The records in these rivers are concentrated near the Tennessee state line and above the sites of major industries whose effluents have stressed the rivers—Saltville on the Holston and Carbo on the Clinch (Map 11). A recent return or increase of *E. camurum* in part of the afflicted sections is indicated. In the Holston this species was found just below Saltville during 1973–1976 and near the Scott–Washington County line in 1981. In the Clinch it was taken just below Carbo in 1969–1972, at Pendleton Island in 1984, and at Craft Mill in 1980, as well as below Copper Creek since 1967.

The apparent absence of *E. camurum* from the lower South and Middle forks of Holston River in Virginia may have been caused by the creation of South Holston Reservoir, and in the Middle Fork, by pollution. This species may not have occupied the reach of the South Fork above the reservoir owing to the coolness of the water.

Abundance.—Generally uncommon.

REMARKS

The bluebreast darter is considered to be of special concern in Virginia because it is nearly restricted to three main-river channels that have been adversely impacted, and because this species seemingly does not tolerate even moderate degrees of siltation (Burkhead and Jenkins 1991).

Name.—*Camurum* means "blunt-headed."

Greenfin darter   *Etheostoma chlorobranchium* Zorach

SYSTEMATICS

The greenfin darter, subgenus *Nothonotus*, was described from North Carolina and Tennessee in 1972. Its relationships are noted under *E. camurum*.

DESCRIPTION

Materials.—From Zorach (1972), 2 specimens from Virginia, 1 series from Tennessee, and 10 series from North Carolina; most meristic data from the Watauga branch of the South Fork Holston system. Color in life from 4 Virginia adults: a large male (REJ 980); photos of a male in an aquarium by R. W. Standage; and photos of 2 freshly preserved adults, at least one a male, by M. E. Seehorn.

Anatomy.—As in *E. camurum* except green or blue-green toned and adults typically larger, 45–70 mm SL; *E. chlorobranchium* is the largest species of *Nothonotus*.

Meristics.—Lateral line complete or nearly so, midlateral scales (61)63–70(72), 61 and 68 in two Virginia specimens; scales above lateral line (16)17–20(21); circumpeduncle scales 22–25(27). Dorsal spines (11)12(13); dorsal rays (12)13–14; anal spines 2; anal rays (7)8–9; pectoral rays (13)14(15).

Color in Preservative.—Similar to *E. camurum* except that the side and sometimes one or more fins have increased melanistic blotching in some populations; the general body tone of large male *E. chlorobranchium* tends darker.

Color in Life.—As in *E. camurum* except as noted in *Comparison* under that species. The four Virginia adults seem atypically variable. Three were drab compared with typical North Carolina specimens; they were mostly olive to yellow-olive; breast pale blue in at least one specimen; red spots present on body; pelvic and pectoral fins pale yellow or orange distally. Median fins of two large males were olive or pale yellow-green proximal to the submarginal bands; one male also had a very slight red-orange tint submarginally in the anal fin. Only the specimen photographed in an aquarium had bright green median fins typical of the species, and its pelvic fins were slightly green. One specimen was quite melanistic on the body, as in *E. chlorobranchium* of the Watauga system.

COMPARISON

See *E. camurum*.

BIOLOGY

The natural history of the greenfin darter is largely unknown, but probably similar to that of *E. camurum*. Of breeding adults from the Nolichucky River system in North Carolina, 37 males are 45–85 mm SL, mean, 63, and 20 females are 47–66 mm, mean, 54. The largest known specimen is 86 mm SL from Tennessee (Zorach 1967); the largest from Virginia is about 75 mm SL. Hybridization occurs with *E. rufilineatum* (Zorach 1967; R. A. Stiles, in litt.).

HABITAT

Etheostoma chlorobranchium inhabits clear, cool and warm, moderate- and high-gradient rocky streams (Zorach 1972). In Virginia it was captured from riffles of boulder and loose rubble in a wild-trout stream.

DISTRIBUTION   Map 182

The greenfin darter is endemic to the upper Tennessee drainage, where it is nearly or fully confined to the Blue Ridge Province in Georgia, North Carolina, Tennessee, and Virginia. Its parapatric relationship with *E. camurum* is noted in that account.

Fish 304 *Etheostoma chlorobranchium* adult male 68 mm SL (REJ 980), VA, Washington County, Whitetop Laurel Creek, 15 June 1983.

In Virginia, *E. chlorobranchium* is known only from the lower 9 rkm of Whitetop Laurel Creek, a tributary to Laurel Creek of the South Fork Holston system. Capture sites are just above the mouth (immediately above Damascus; R. W. Standage, in litt.), at the mouth of Straight Branch (M. E. Seehorn, in litt.), and at Taylors Valley.

Abundance.—Rare; known in Virginia from 6–8 specimens: 2 or 3 taken in 1970, 1 each in 1976 and 1983, and 2 or 3 in 1987. Our three efforts at Taylors Valley, almost entirely with an electroshocker for a combined 3.5 hours, yielded two of the specimens.

REMARKS

The Virginia population of the greenfin darter is the northernmost of the species. This species is one of the most localized Virginia fishes. Despite that its home water in Virginia is a protected high-quality trout stream that arises in the Mount Rogers National Recreation Area, *E. chlorobranchium* is threatened (Jenkins and Musick 1979; Burkhead and Jenkins 1991) or endangered (VDGIF 1987) in the state.

Name.—*Chlorobranchium*—"green-arm"—refers to the green fins of adult males.

Redline darter *Etheostoma rufilineatum* (Cope)

SYSTEMATICS

Described from North Carolina in 1870, *Etheostoma rufilineatum* has an intermediate evolutionary position within the subgenus *Nothonotus*, more advanced than that of *E. camurum* and *E. chlorobranchium* (Etnier and Williams 1989). Zorach (1970) stated that geographic variation in *E. rufilineatum* was insufficient for recognition of subspecies.

DESCRIPTION

Materials.—From Zorach (1970), Page (1983), 5 Tennessee, and 25 Virginia series; meristic data from Virginia systems of the Tennessee drainage. Life color from many breeding males and females from Virginia.

Anatomy.—A barred or checkered darter, the head with dark dashes and large spots; adults are 45–70 mm SL. Body

Fish 305 *Etheostoma rufilineatum* adult male 64 mm SL (REJ 981), VA, Washington County, South Fork Holston River, 15 June 1983.

Fish 306 *Etheostoma rufilineatum* adult female 59 mm SL (REJ 981), VA, Washington County, South Fork Holston River, 15 June 1983.

moderate or moderately deep and compressed; snout sharp, moderate in length; frenum present; branchiostegal membranes separate or narrowly conjoined; caudal fin subtruncate or rounded. Female genital papilla short, conical (Figure 70); tubercles absent. Nape, cheek, and breast naked; opercle and belly scaled.

Meristics.—Lateral line complete or nearly so, midlateral scales (47)49–57(62); scales above lateral line (4)5–7(8); scales below lateral line (5)6–8(9); circumpeduncle scales (17)18–22(23). Dorsal spines (10)11–12(13); dorsal rays (10)11–12(13); anal spines 2; anal rays (6)7–8(9); pectoral rays (11)13–14(15).

Color in Preservative.—Lateral body with narrow dark horizontal lines, more intense posteriorly, and 8–11 bars which usually are broken into 2–4 segments, the lines and bars producing a checkered appearance; many interlinear pale spots present; dorsum with 8–10 saddles; head ventrally pale or partly or fully dusky or black, belly pale or dusky. Preocular bars widely separated or, if connected, only by pigmentation on upper lip; subocular bar usually partly or completely divided into two, each portion often horizontally elongate, dashlike; postocular bar usually distinct; cheek and opercle with 2–3 spots or dashes (Figure 79A).

First dorsal fin of male marginally pale, becoming dusky to dark basally, occasionally with the anterior few membrane bases darker. Second dorsal and anal fins distally dark, submarginally or much of fin pale, basally dusky to dark. Caudal fin distally dark, wide submarginal pale area, oblong or round dark medial area, base pale and often depicting an hourglass shape. Pelvic fin distally pale, basally dusky; pectoral fin pale. Female with all fins tessellated or slashed with black; caudal base with hourglass-shaped pale area. In both sexes, caudal base with 2 medial dark spots, sometimes fused to form a dark vertical slash, and often with a dark spot at upper and lower edges of fin.

Color in Life Plate 37.—Breeding male with dark brown or black checks and lines on body. Between the lines are numerous orange or red spots (when isolated on 1 scale) or blocks (extending 2–4 scales); areas between the lines are creamy or tan when not orange or red. Venter creamy tan or orange; the intermediate stage is orange mottling on a tan base. Lips, cheek, and opercle often with varying number of orange or red spots and dashes. Breast and pectoral fin base blue-green, blue, or blue-gray.

First dorsal fin distally clear, subdistally orange-red, submarginally pale, gradually darkening to base; rays with a hint of green in some specimens. Second dorsal fin distally dark green or black, subdistally clear, submarginally orange-red, medially olive-yellow and often continuing down rays to base between black membranes. Caudal fin similar to second dorsal but with orange-red band continuing around and connecting to hourglass-shaped area at base; dorsal and ventral bulb of hourglass paler orange, similar to venter. Anal fin similar to second dorsal but basally lighter and often with a hint of blue-green. Pelvic fin margin clear, submargin orange-red, median yellow-olive, base similar to

anal base. Pectoral fin similar to pelvic but lacking basal darkening, membranes generally pale.

Breeding female lacks bright colors, although some have a yellow wash in all fins.

Larvae.—Described by Simon et al. (1987).

BIOLOGY

The redline darter's most important food items are truefly larvae, particularly midges; other insects and invertebrates are taken, sometimes in major amounts (Stiles 1972; Hickman and Fitz 1978; Bryant 1979; Widlak 1982; Starnes and Starnes 1985; Widlak and Neves 1985; Fisher and Pearson 1987). The redline darter lives under rocks and is a diurnal feeder (Greenberg 1991).

Most yearlings are mature; maximum longevity is 4 years. Males exceed females in growth rate; age-2 males were 51–69 mm TL, mean, 58, females were 43–65 mm, mean, 55 (Widlak and Neves 1985). *Etheostoma rufilineatum* reaches 76 mm SL (Etnier *in* Lee et al. 1980); the largest Virginia specimen is 67 mm SL.

Spawning was witnessed by Stiles (1972) in the Little River of Tennessee between 21 May and 7 August. Ripe females were found in Virginia as early as 3 May and as late as 18 August; peak development of ovaries occurred in mid-July (Widlak and Neves 1985). This species is an egg-burier whose reproductive behavior is similar to that of *E. camurum* (Stiles 1972). Stiles noted multiple burials of females, as many as three one on top of another, all guarded by one male. Numbers of maturing and ripe ova were 23–131 and total potential egg complements were 50–331; some of the fish examined might have spawned (Widlak and Neves 1985). Hybridization occurs with *E. chlorobranchium* (Zorach 1967; R. A. Stiles, in litt.).

HABITAT

Etheostoma rufilineatum typically occupies clear and warm creeks, streams, and rivers of moderate gradient. Adults are generally associated with shallow to moderately deep runs and riffles of gravel, rubble, and small boulders; they also occupy fast chutes. Young tend to occupy slow current. Details of habitat use are given by Stiles (1972), Widlak and Neves (1985), Fisher and Pearson (1987), and Greenberg (1991). Owing to an intolerance to hypoxia, the redline darter is physiologically prediotally to swift water (Ultsch et al. 1978).

DISTRIBUTION Map 183

The redline darter is confined to and occurs in most of the Tennessee and Cumberland drainages (Zorach

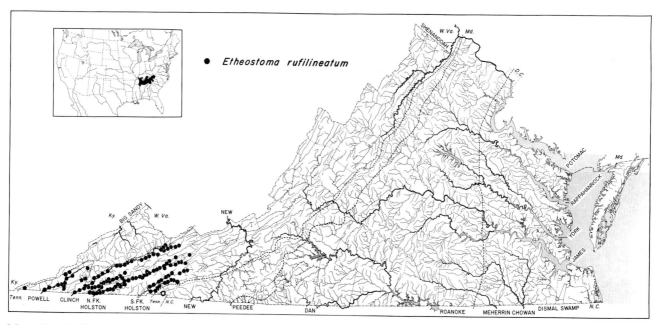

Etheostoma rufilineatum

Map 183   Redline darter. Open circle on Whitetop Laurel Creek represents unaccepted record.

1970). It occupies all major divisions of the upper Tennessee in Virginia; it is generally distributed in the Valley and Ridge Province and avoids the Blue Ridge and Appalachian Plateau. We suspect that the report from a Virginia trout survey of a "redline darter" from Whitetop Laurel Creek, within the Blue Ridge, was based on the superficially similar *E. chlorobranchium*, which occurs very near the capture site. Our intensive efforts near the site and sampling by M. E. Seehorn have failed to find *E. rufilineatum* in this stream.

The apparent absence of *E. rufilineatum* in Whitetop Laurel and two largely springfed, major Clinch River tributaries—Big Cedar Creek and upper Little River—indicate that it is limited by cool water. The records from trout-water sections of the upper South and Middle forks of Holston River appear to oppose that hypothesis, but this species generally is uncommon or rare there.

Abundance.—Usually common or abundant, one of the most abundant darters in the Tennessee drainage of Virginia.

REMARKS

The male redline darter maintains varied bright colors throughout the year; they become intensified during the breeding season. The most harlequined specimens we have seen are large fish from the robust population of the lower South Fork Holston River. Ramsey (1984) considered that *E. rufilineatum* "qualifies as one of the world's most beautiful vertebrates." Although spectacularly hued, it is no more colorful than many other darters, sunfishes, and nuptial minnows. It is so common in many streams that we tend to overlook its attractiveness.

Name.—Rufilineatum—"red-lined."

Tippecanoe darter   *Etheostoma tippecanoe* Jordan and Evermann

SYSTEMATICS

Described from Indiana in 1890, the Tippecanoe darter diverges from the norm in its subgenus *Nothonotus* (Zorach 1969; Page 1981). Many of its features are advanced; considering its habit of clumping eggs in the substrate, it may be phylogenetically close to the above-bottom, egg-clumping species of *Nothonotus* such as *E. maculatum* (Warren et al. 1986a).

The Clinch River population of *E. tippecanoe* is dis-

tinctive in coloration, squamation, and the position of a cephalic lateralis pore (Zorach 1969). Our specimens from the Duck River in the lower Tennessee drainage conform to those from the Clinch. Zorach (1969) declined to name this form, but it could be a separate species.

DESCRIPTION

Materials.—From Zorach (1969), Page (1983), and 11 series from the Clinch River (4 from Virginia, 7 from Ten-

Fish 307 *Etheostoma tippecanoe* adult male 28 mm SL (REJ 1099), VA, Scott County, Clinch River, 5 June 1984.

Fish 308 *Etheostoma tippecanoe* adult female 23 mm SL (REJ 1099), VA, Scott County, Clinch River, 5 June 1984.

nessee); meristic data only from the Clinch. Life color from 4 Clinch River series.

Anatomy.—A flecked or barred darter with a dark band around the caudal base; adults are 20–30 mm SL. Body moderate in profile, compressed; snout moderate or moderately sharp; frenum moderate; branchiostegal membranes slightly or moderately conjoined; caudal fin truncate. Female genital papilla small, flattened or bulbous; tubercles absent. Cheek naked or with 1–4 postorbital scales; opercle scaled; nape and breast naked; belly scaled posteriorly.

Meristics.—Lateral line incomplete, midlateral scales (44)46–48(52), unpored scales 13–17; scales above lateral line 3–4(5); scales below lateral line 5–8; circumpeduncle scales (19)20–21(22). Dorsal spines 12–13(14); dorsal rays 11–12(13); anal spines 2; anal rays (7)8–9; pectoral rays (11)12.

Color in Preservative.—Side with vague or dark bars, 10–11 when all present, sometimes each connected to a saddle; bars best developed on posterior half of body; posteriormost bar generally the most prominent, encircling the caudal base, sometimes incomplete midlaterally; anteriormost bar often vague, but usually expanded and intensified dorsally as a yokelike saddle; in some males and females only the yoke and caudal bar are present. Ground shade of upper body dusky, ventrally usually pale; female tends more flecked and less barred than male; often several flecks or X-like marks are darker than the general scale pattern-

ing. Pre-, post-, and subocular bars present, the former rarely meeting on the snout. Head and breast mostly blackened in some nuptial males.

Male first dorsal fin distally dark, most so posteriorly; subdistally pale; submarginally to base dusky to dark; anterior few membranes dark, sometimes forming a diffuse spot. Second dorsal fin similar but slightly paler and without anterior spot. Caudal membranes mostly pale or slightly dusky; distally slightly dusky; subdistally pale; rays mostly dusky to dark; base with 2 large pale patches, often separated by 2 dark spots which may fuse. Other fins generally pale with occasional basal duskiness; pelvic fin darkly streaked in male. Female first dorsal fin dusky throughout; other fins with pale membranes and, in large specimens, tessellated rays.

Color in Life Plate 37.—Breeding male with bars and breast blue or black, breast the most frequently blue. Upper body gold or gold-olive; side olive-yellow, bright yellow, or moderately orange; belly gold-yellow, sometimes with a pale blue wash. Opercle and gular area gold or deep red-orange; lips yellow-orange. Caudal base with 2 yellow-gold patches. First dorsal fin subdistally gold or red-orange, remainder of fin olive-brown to tan. Second dorsal fin distally olive, basally olive-brown to tan. Caudal fin with membranes, much of a few upper and lower rays, and distal one-third of other rays olive, occasionally deep red-orange; rays dark blue or black basally. Other fins gold to yellow with slight black peppering; anal fin may have a deep red-orange hue.

In spawning male the orange intensifies on the body,

obscuring most bars (Warren et al. 1986a). In all of our Clinch River collections we saw no male as dark as that depicted (artifactually) by Kuehne and Barbour (1983). Female subdued, generally mottled olive-brown, and may have a faint gold cast (Zorach 1969).

Larvae.—Described by Simon et al. (1987); length of hatchlings given by Warren et al. (1986a).

BIOLOGY

The Tippecanoe darter's diet, based on 16 specimens from the Clinch and Big South Fork Cumberland rivers in Virginia and Tennessee, consists of mayfly, caddisfly, and midge larvae. Midges dominated numerically; volumetrically mayflies appeared to be the most important item (A. R. Clarke, in litt.).

Etheostoma tippecanoe may be an annual species; all 29 nuptial fish from Kentucky were 12 months old (Warren et al. 1986a) and our largest male was about that age. Warren et al. also took small, apparently immature males and females at the same time (late July) that they took the nuptial fish. The largest fish in our collections are males; the adult males studied by Warren et al. were 22–31 mm SL, mean, 28; females were 21–27 mm, mean, 26. The largest reported specimen is 35 mm SL (Zorach 1969); the largest from Virginia is 31 mm SL.

Typical of its subgenus, *E. tippecanoe* is a relatively late spawner. Females from the Clinch and Big South Fork Cumberland rivers taken in mid-May to early July were very gravid; a female from the Clinch on 4 August had eggs freely flowing. Many males in peak breeding condition were found during July in Tennessee (Feeman 1987). Kentucky fish taken on 21 July, water 26°C, spawned six days later in an aquarium at 25–27.5°C (Warren et al. 1986a). Kentucky females were spent in mid-August (Kuehne and Barbour 1983). Jenkins and Musick's (1979) note that this species apparently spawns during the spring was based on a 14 April sample of fish that were thin and thought to be spent; we now believe that these had not yet ripened.

Spawning occurs in runs and riffles of gravel or sand–gravel. In Ohio, spawning areas were in current that was gentle but sufficient to remove silt (Trautman 1981). In a spawning or near-spawning group in Kentucky, the largest males occupied the deepest, fastest current available and were segregated from females (Warren et al. 1986a). Apparently-breeding fish in Tennessee were numerous in shallow swift areas (Feeman 1987). From aquarium observations, Warren et al. (1986a) found that males are territorial and apparently select the spawning site. Females

are egg-buriers and have a sustained period of complete body burial; withdrawal from gravel and reburial also occurs. More than one female at a time were attended by a single male. Trautman (1981) also observed male territoriality. Fecundity is quite low—as many as 58 (mean, 30) mature ova and up to 72 more (mean, 23) potentially mature ova are generated (Warren et al. 1986a). Hybridization with *E. camurum* was reported by Trautman (1957) and confirmed by Zorach (1967).

HABITAT

Etheostoma tippecanoe inhabits warm, moderate-gradient, large streams and rivers. Adults occupy shallow to deep, moderate to swift runs and riffles having little or no silt. They retire to deeper, slower water in winter (Trautman 1981). This species typically is associated with major areas of pea-sized loose gravel. In the Clinch River at Horton Island we found it only on a small strip of pea gravel within a broad area of mostly large gravel and rubble. However, at Speers Ferry on the Clinch this species is generally distributed in a run–riffle of mostly large gravel to medium rubble.

DISTRIBUTION   Map 184

The Tippecanoe darter occupies most major drainages of the Ohio basin but its populations generally are quite isolated (Zorach 1969; Hocutt *in* Lee et al. 1980; Page 1983). It was first collected in the upper Tennessee drainage from the Clinch River in Tennessee in 1963; during 1975–1983 it was discovered in the Sequatchie River of the middle Tennessee and in the Duck and Buffalo rivers of the lower Tennessee (Anonymous 1983; Feeman 1987). In Virginia it occupies the Clinch River and it inhabited Copper Creek, a Clinch tributary.

The discovery of *E. tippecanoe* in the Clinch system of Virginia was closely followed by the species' demise in most of the system due to a massive fish kill in the Clinch River during 10–14 June 1967. In the lower 1 rkm of Copper Creek during 1967, we took one adult in May and Denoncourt (1969a) caught five each in July and August. Their capture in the spring and summer indicates that the species reproduced in the creek. The Copper Creek population probably was marginal and small; the fish were found only near the mouth, and the creek there is narrower than most or all other streams inhabited by *E. tippecanoe*. Intensive sampling during November 1967 to 1985 yielded no more Tippecanoe darters. Thus, it is likely

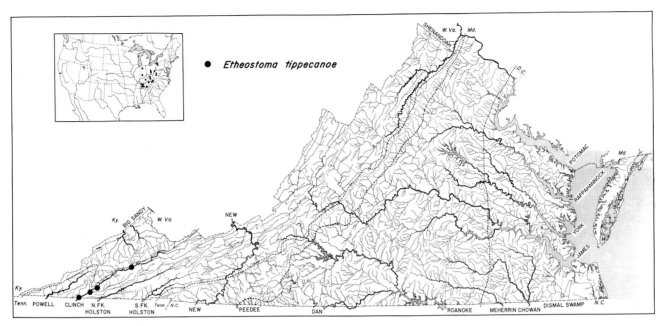

Map 184 Tippecanoe darter.

that the Copper Creek population had been sustained by recruitment from the Clinch River, which would accord with the species' one-year life span.

We believe that recovery of the darter in the nearby section of the Clinch River was initiated by young of the 1967 Copper Creek year-class (whose parents presumably died soon after spawning). It would have taken several generations for this low-fecundity species to rebuild its population in the large Clinch River. In three collections made specifically for darters during July–November 1967, the Clinch at Speers Ferry (1 rkm below Copper Creek) did not yield *E. tippecanoe*, nor did the river across from the creek mouth in 1973. The next (1979) collection at Speers Ferry included 1 *E. tippecanoe*; 17 were taken in three collections in 1980. In 1983–1984 and 1991, the darter was uncommon or common at Speers Ferry; its return to Copper Creek is anticipated.

Wider recovery of *E. tippecanoe* has occurred in the Clinch River of Virginia. A capture of this species at the state line (15 rkm below Speers Ferry) occurred in 1972 (Masnik 1974). We did not find it during 1970 at a site with suitable habitat between the state line and Speers Ferry. Nor did we take it in 1969 at Craft Mill (13 rkm above Speers Ferry), but it was found there consistently during 1979–1980. Recovery at Craft Mill could have stemmed from Speers Ferry, tributary mouths, and Carbo (91 rkm above Speers Ferry). *Etheostoma tippecanoe* was found at Carbo in 1971 (Masnik 1974) but not in 18 other collections made between Carbo and Craft Mill during 1970–1985. Its

occurrence at Carbo (and probably somewhat above) obviously predates the kill.

Abundance.—Uncommon or common at Speers Ferry in 1983–1984 and 1991; abundance unknown elsewhere in the Virginia portion of the Clinch River. *Etheostoma tippecanoe* is noted for fluctuations in abundance. For example, the population at Frost Ford of the Clinch River in Tennessee fluctuated between low numbers in 1970–1971 and 1975 and high numbers in 1973, 1982, and 1985. Variation in capture rate in that section of the Clinch was noted also by Feeman (1987). Large annual fluctuations in numbers occur in Ohio (Trautman 1981). Due to the small size of the fish, some specimens pass through standard-size net mesh; this may lead to underestimation of abundance.

REMARKS

The tiny golden male Tippecanoe darter, embellished with orange, red, and blue, is a veritable jewel of Clinch River rapids. It is Virginia's smallest darter and the second smallest of its clan (Page and Burr 1979).

Threatened status was recommended for *Etheostoma tippecanoe* in Virginia by Jenkins and Musick (1979) and Burkhead and Jenkins (1991); the VDGIF (1987) listed it as endangered. This species currently occupies only one main river of Virginia and is tied to clean riffles, often only those of pea-sized gravel. Its desertion of spawning territory due to siltation was noted by Trautman (1981). Its one-year life span and low fecundity contribute to the wide population fluctuations seen in the Tennessee portion of the Clinch River and noted elsewhere (e.g., Warren et al. 1986a). Because suitable gravel shoals exist in the Powell River—the twin of the Clinch in Tennessee and Virginia, we believe that the Tippecanoe darter formerly occurred there, but is extirpated.

Name.—*Tippecanoe* is the name of the river in Indiana from which the darter was described.

Sharphead darter   *Etheostoma acuticeps* Bailey

SYSTEMATICS

The sharphead darter, described from Tennessee in 1959, is a primitive or moderately advanced member of the subgenus *Nothonotus* (Zorach 1972; Etnier and Williams 1989).

DESCRIPTION

Materials.—From Bailey (1959b), Zorach and Raney (1967), Jenkins and Burkhead (1975b), Page (1981, 1983), 2 additional specimens from Virginia, and 6 series from Tennessee. Life color from 2 Virginia males and many nuptial fish from the Nolichucky River of Tennessee.

Anatomy.—A barred, sharp-snouted darter; adults are 35–60 mm SL. Body form moderate in lateral profile, compressed; snout the narrowest and sharpest in the subgenus; frenum well developed; branchiostegal membranes separate or narrowly conjoined; caudal fin subtruncate or slightly rounded. Female genital papilla small, flattened or bulbous; tubercles absent. Cheek, opercle, nape, and breast naked; belly fully scaled.

Meristics.—Lateral line complete or almost so, midlateral scales 54–65, unpored scales 0–9; scales above lateral line (3)4–6(7); scales below lateral line 8–9; circumpeduncle scales 22–27. Dorsal spines 11–13; dorsal rays 11–13; anal spines (1)2; anal rays 7–9; pectoral rays 12–14.

Color in Preservative.—Side with 11–16 dusky or dark, vertical or slightly oblique bars; juveniles tend to have midlateral blotching; multiple narrow horizontal lines most prominent on posterior body. Saddles generally small, vague, often connected to lateral bars. Dorsum and upper side dusky to dark; venter dusky to pale. Preocular bar distinct or masked by general darkness; subocular bar vague or masked; postocular slash usually present.

Fins not mottled or tessellated. First dorsal fin dusky to dark, darkest anteriorly and basally; slightly darkened along distal edge except spine tips often slightly paler. Other fins pale or dusky, second dorsal darkest, its membranes and those of anal sometimes notably darkened. Caudal base with 2 submedial dark spots, sometimes fused; upper and lower portion of caudal base often with a dark spot; often a pale vertical bar behind latter spots.

Color in Life Plate 37.—Nuptial male dorsum dark olive; venter tan; side occasionally with a turquoise tinge; cheek and opercle olive-brown; branchiostegals suffused pale orange; breast blue-green. First dorsal fin distally with suffused turquoise, remainder dark olive. Other fins brighter turquoise, anal the most so, pectoral usually the least. Male photographed by Bryant (*in* Deacon et al. 1979) has more highly developed nuptial color than we have seen but the lower fins seem too true blue.

Adult female and nonbreeding male with head and body mostly straw-olive to brown-olive, venter slightly yellow-tinged. Fin rays olive-yellow to straw-yellow.

Larvae.—Described by Bryant (1979) and Simon et al. (1987).

BIOLOGY

The sharphead darter eats mainly mayfly, midge, and blackfly larvae; caddisfly and other larvae are also taken. Both sexes mature as 1-year-olds and

Fish 309 *Etheostoma acuticeps* adult male 44 mm SL (REJ 981), VA, Washington County, South Fork Holston River, 15 June 1983.

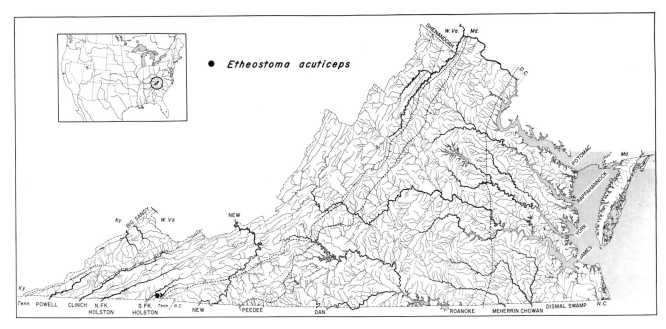

Map 185 Sharphead darter.

some individuals live 3 years. Males attain larger size than females; the largest specimen known is a 70-mm SL male from Tennessee, and Virginia's largest is 52 mm SL (Jenkins and Burkhead 1975b; Bryant 1979).

Sharphead darters in breeding condition were found between late June and mid-August in the Nolichucky River of Tennessee (Bryant 1979); this agrees with our observations in that river and indications of the same spawning period in the South Fork Holston River (Bailey 1959b; Jenkins and Burkhead 1975b). Spawning has not been witnessed; apparently it occurs in areas of swift current. Bryant (1979) and we failed in attempts to have nuptial fish spawn in aquaria. Bryant (1979) and Simon et al. (1987) presented indirect evidence that *E. acuticeps* is an egg-burier; details would be enlightening relative to the behavioral differences among darters employing this mode of oviposition (Warren et al. 1986a). Bryant noted aggressive tail-biting in aquaria and found many wild-caught males with apparent caudal-bite wounds during the breeding season; we frequently noted wounds. Stiles (1972) rarely observed biting in three other *Nothonotus* species. Fecundity is 100–484 mature and maturing ova (Jenkins and Burkhead 1975b; Bryant 1979).

HABITAT

Etheostoma acuticeps inhabits cool and warm, typically clear or slightly turbid, moderate-gradient, large streams and rivers (Jenkins and Burkhead 1975b; Bry-

ant 1979; Haxo and Neves 1984). Where common, particularly in the Nolichucky River, the sharphead darter usually occupies moderate and swift runs and riffles of rubble and boulder and often occurs among lush growths of riverweed (*Podostemum*). It has an affinity for swifter chutelike water in the South Fork Holston River.

DISTRIBUTION   Map 185

The sharphead darter is endemic to the upper Tennessee drainage, being known only from the Nolichucky River in North Carolina and Tennessee, two Nolichucky tributaries in North Carolina, and the South Fork Holston River in Tennessee and Virginia. From over 100 collections made in the South and Middle forks of the Holston River in Virginia since 1888, only five *E. acuticeps* altogether were taken at two localities of the South Fork, all within 5.1 rkm above the head of South Holston Reservoir (Jenkins and Burkhead 1975b; Haxo and Neves 1984).

Abundance.—Extremely rare in Virginia.

REMARKS

With its sharp snout, *E. acuticeps* would be efficient at picking small insects from crevices among stones. Its diet or microhabitat differs distinctly from syntopic species of darters including other *Nothonotus* (Bryant

1979). The turquoise-colored peak nuptial male is spectacular.

At the time of its description in 1959, the only known site of *E. acuticeps* had just been inundated by South Holston Reservoir, Tennessee. Specimens of this species, but not so identified originally, had been taken in 1930 farther down the South Fork Holston River and in the upper North Toe River of the upper Nolichucky system in North Carolina (Zorach and Raney 1967; Zorach 1972; Jenkins and Burkhead 1975b). By the late 1960s the species was thought, apparently correctly, to no longer exist in the free-flowing stretch of the lower South Fork Holston due to the cold discharge from the dam. Searches during that decade in the mica-laden North and South Toe had failed. Thus by 1970 the sharphead darter appeared to be extinct.

Persistent efforts in the South Fork Holston of Virginia led to the rediscovery of the species in 1972 (Jenkins and Burkhead 1975b). We then considered it endangered on the national level because of its extreme localization and rarity. We chose not to sample the Nolichucky owing to reports of adverse habitat and negative collecting results by others (e.g., Ward 1960).

It was surprising good news that during 1975–1977, *E. acuticeps* was found in the lower Nolichucky River of Tennessee and in one of its major North Carolina tributaries, Cane River (Saylor and Etnier 1976; Bry-

ant et al. 1979). Its much wider occurrence and strong populations in both rivers, plus the discovery of a population in the lowermost North Toe River were documented by Haxo and Neves (1984). Based particularly on its presence in four rivers and the strength of the Nolichucky River populations, Haxo and Neves concluded that the species did not warrant federal protective status.

Although the future of the sharphead darter is brighter than earlier thought, the few populations are not without risk. This species is considered threatened in Tennessee and North Carolina (Starnes and Etnier 1980; Braswell 1991).

The South Fork Holston, Virginia, population was regarded as endangered by Jenkins and Musick (1979), VDGIF (1987), and Burkhead and Jenkins (1991). Localization and rarity of the darter there were supported by Haxo and Neves' (1984) and our post-1980 surveys. Some of the pollution problems in the South Fork system noted by Jenkins and Burkhead (1975b) have been relieved, but other potential pollution problems exist. Also living in the midst of the South Fork population are very robust populations of *E. rufilineatum* and sculpins, which may be competitors (and the sculpins predators) of *E. acuticeps*. The sharphead darter seems to be "hanging by a thread" in Virginia.

Name.—Acuticeps means "sharp head."

Wounded darter　　*Etheostoma vulneratum* (Cope)

SYSTEMATICS

The wounded darter is a member of the *maculatum* group, the most advanced major clade of the subgenus *Nothonotus* (Etnier and Williams 1989). Cope (1870) described *E. vulneratum* from the Tennessee drainage of North Carolina, in the same paper with the original description of the bleeding darter *E. sanguifluum*, which occupies the adjacent Cumberland drainage. Later the two taxa were considered conspecific with the spotted darter *E. maculatum*, which inhabits northerly drainages of the Ohio basin.

Etheostoma vulneratum and *E. sanguifluum* were resurrected as subspecies of *E. maculatum* by Zorach and Raney (1967) and Williams and Etnier (1978), all of whom noted that the three allopatric forms might properly be regarded as species. *Etheostoma sanguifluum* was elevated to that status, with *E. vulneratum* its subspecies, by Page (1985). With the description of the boulder darter *E. wapiti* from the lower Tennessee drainage, the wounded darter is recognized as a spe-

cies endemic to the upper Tennessee (Etnier and Williams 1989).

DESCRIPTION

Materials.—From Zorach and Raney (1967), Page (1983), Etnier and Williams (1989), 22 series from Virginia, and 3 from Tennessee. Color in life from about 30 Virginia adults.

Anatomy.—A lined, checkered, or faintly barred darter with a narrow dark margin on the tail; adults are 35–65 mm SL. Body moderate in profile, moderately compressed; snout moderate or short, sharp; frenum narrow; branchiostegal membranes separate or narrowly conjoined; caudal fin subtruncate or rounded. Female genital papilla very small, flattened or bulbous; tubercles absent. Cheek partly scaled behind eye or naked; opercle and belly scaled; nape and breast naked.

Meristics.—Lateral line complete or nearly so, midlateral scales (51)54–62(66); scales above lateral line (4)5–7(8); scales below lateral line 8–12; circumpeduncle scales (19)20–24. Dorsal spines (11)12–13(15); dorsal rays (11)12–

Fish 310 *Etheostoma vulneratum* adult male 66 mm SL (REJ 981), VA, Washington County, South Fork Holston River, 15 June 1983.

Fish 311 *Etheostoma vulneratum* adult female 51 mm SL (REJ 991), VA, Russell County, Little River, 21 June 1983.

13; anal spines 2; anal rays 7–9(10); pectoral rays (12)13–14(15).

Color in Preservative.—Side with many small blotches forming vague or prominent checkered pattern, or with vague vertical or slightly oblique bars, and with multiple series of horizontal dark lines, the lines best developed on posterior body; female usually checkered and faintly lined, male distinctly lined, both sexes may have bars. Adult male side with irregularly arranged, small pale spots from caudal base to anterior third of body, occasionally to head (spots red in life). Humeral spot black, from which a dark line extends along posterior base of pectoral fin. Dorsum dusky or dark; venter pale or dark. Head markings generally vague; subocular bar occasionally well developed.

Fin patterns in male: first dorsal fin with incomplete narrow black edge in most fish; in others the distal and subdistal areas pale; medially dusky except for usually a few (1 to many) pale spots, each in an interspinous area (spots red in life); basally dark to black, usually darkest anteriorly. Second dorsal, caudal, and anal fins with a narrow dark margin varying from prominent to absent, the margin best developed on the caudal; distally or, if black-margined, subdistally pale; remainder of these fins dusky to dark. Pelvic fin dusky to dark; pectoral fin pale or with dusky rays. In female, fin margination as in male but dark and pale edgings reduced; first dorsal and anal fins mostly dusky to dark, sometimes slightly mottled; second dorsal and caudal fins dominantly tessellated; pelvic and pectoral fins similar to male but paler. In both sexes, caudal base

with 2 vague or distinct medial dark spots and 1 spot usually present at each of upper and lower caudal insertions. Dark margination of median fins is best developed in Holston system fish and generally weakly developed, sometimes absent in the Clinch–Powell population.

Color in Life Plate 37.—Nuptial male dorsum dark olive; side paler olive or olive-gray; horizontal lines black; breast and belly gray or breast very rarely faint dusky green. Lateral body with scattered small blood red spots on posterior two-thirds of body, occasionally anteriorly. Marginal pale areas of both dorsal and caudal fins cream to pale peach; blood red spots in median of first dorsal best developed in Clinch River specimens, spots often absent in Holston populations; some spots surrounded with blue-green in some Clinch males. Caudal fin with upper and lower 1–3 principal rays red-streaked; lower rudimentary rays tinted blue-green. Anal fin and less so the pelvic fin suffused with blue-green. Adult female rarely has a few pale red spots on first dorsal fin and body; fin margins not creamy; a few specimens with an ephemeral pale mottled stripe on head dorsum and nape.

Larvae.—Described by Simon et al. (1987).

BIOLOGY

The bulk of the wounded darter's diet in Tennessee is midge larvae supplemented by other insect larvae

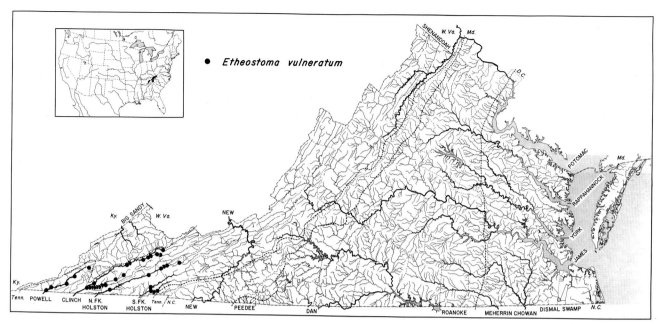

Map 186   Wounded darter.

and other invertebrates (Stiles 1972; Bryant 1979). Maturation, growth, and longevity are similar to those of the intimately related spotted darter *E. maculatum* studied by Raney and Lachner (1939). In that species, both sexes mature by age 2. Spotted darter males tend to outgrow females; average standard lengths of age-2 fish were 48 mm for males and 44 mm for females. The largest specimens of *E. vulneratum* of which we are aware are males of 73 mm SL from the Clinch system and 70 mm from the Holston system in Virginia.

The reproductive period in Tennessee was thought to begin sometime between the last two weeks of May and early June, and was generally finished by the last week of July; water was 16–20°C (Stiles 1972). Wounded darters typically spawn in moderate current of runs, sometimes in the body of riffles. Eggs are deposited as multitiered masses on the underside of rocks, often wedged into a corner formed by one rock resting on another. In some cases, egg-clumping apparently involved inversion by both sexes. Males and females defended clutches of 17–166 eggs (Stiles 1972).

HABITAT

Etheostoma vulneratum inhabits warm, moderate-gradient streams and rivers (Zorach and Raney 1967; Stiles 1972; Greenberg 1991). In Virginia, adults are characteristic of gentle to moderate runs with little or no siltation, and are strongly associated with loose slab rubble. Occasionally they occur in well-flowing pools, generally at the tail end. We found adults in a strong riffle in the North Fork Holston River. Juveniles are commonly taken among gravel and rubble.

DISTRIBUTION   Map 186

The wounded darter is endemic to the upper Tennessee drainage of North Carolina, Tennessee, and Virginia; upper Tennessee records that formerly applied to *E. maculatum* are referred to *E. vulneratum* (*Systematics*). In Virginia it is found in the main stem of all major branches of the Tennessee within the Valley and Ridge Province; it is known to extend into lower headwaters only in Copper Creek. *Etheostoma vulneratum* apparently has not amply rebounded in the North Fork Holston River below Saltville after major reduction of pollution there, but has reappeared in part of the heavily stressed zone of the Clinch River below Carbo.

Abundance.—Generally uncommon.

REMARKS

The name wounded darter appropriately coincides with the first-noticed parasitism by any lamprey on any darter—the Ohio lamprey on an adult *E. vulneratum* from Copper Creek (Fish 2).

Name.—Vulneratum—"wounded"—is an analogy of the red spots on the body and fins to droplets of blood.

Rainbow darter   *Etheostoma caeruleum* Storer

SYSTEMATICS

The rainbow darter, described from Illinois in 1845, is the only Virginia representative of *Oligocephalus*, one of the largest subgenera of *Etheostoma*. Knapp (1964) recognized three subspecies; the population in the Big Sandy drainage and likely that in the New drainage (Esmond and Stauffer 1983) is the widespread *E. c. caeruleum*. The Powell system population may consist of intergrades, which occur elsewhere in the Tennessee drainage.

DESCRIPTION

Materials.—From Collette (1965), Page (1983), Grady and Bart (1984), and 5 series from the Big Sandy drainage of Virginia. Color in life from 1 lot from the Big Sandy.

Anatomy.—A well-barred or mottled darter; adults are 35–50 mm SL. Body moderate or robust, slightly or well compressed; snout moderate; frenum present; branchiostegal membranes narrowly or, usually, moderately conjoined; caudal fin subtruncate or rounded. Breeding tubercles present in male on scales of posterior half of belly, mainly just above anal fin base and on lower caudal peduncle. Female genital papilla short, wide, flat, or tubular. Cheek and breast naked; nape scaled or naked; opercle and belly scaled.

Meristics.—Lateral line incomplete, midlateral scales (36)41–50(57), pored scales (16)26–32(39); scales above lateral line (4)5–6(7); scales below lateral line (6)7–8(10); circumpeduncle scales (16)18–20(23). Dorsal spines (8)10(11); dorsal rays (10)12–14(15); anal spines 2; anal rays 6–7; pectoral rays (10)13(15).

Color in Preservative.—Side with 9–14 dark, slightly oblique bars which usually are darkest on posterior half of body; bars most prominent on and usually encircle caudal peduncle in male; in female, bars often end above venter. Dorsum with 6–10 saddles, several usually vague. Ground shade of male dusky or dark dorsally, fading toward venter; female generally paler but having more numerous dark flecks and, often, interrupted rows of spots. Pre- and postocular bars generally well defined, subocular bar highly variable or absent. Caudal base with 0–3 vertically aligned spots or dashes of variable intensity.

First dorsal fin in male distally clear; subdistal dusky or dark; submarginal clear or pale; medial dusky or dark; epibasal pale; basal dusky or dark. Second dorsal fin margin dark; most of fin pale to dusky, rays darkest; membranes dark basally. Caudal fin margin dusky or dark; rays evenly dusky or dark; membranes (proximal to margin) pale or dusky. Anal fin margin dusky or dark; remainder mostly pale or dusky; basal dusky or dark. Pelvic fin similar to anal but lacking marginal band. Pectoral fin membranes clear, rays evenly peppered. First dorsal of female similar to male; second dorsal also similar but tessellated throughout.

Fish 312 *Etheostoma caeruleum* adult male 48 mm SL (WHH 104), VA, Buchanan County, Knox Creek, 28 June 1983.

Fish 313 *Etheostoma caeruleum* adult female 40 mm SL (WHH 104), VA, Buchanan County, Knox Creek, 28 June 1983.

Caudal membranes clear, rays well tessellated. Anal fin generally clear, occasionally with basal spotting. Pelvic and pectoral fins clear except that pectoral has tessellated rays.

Color in Life.—Nuptial male dorsal and lateral markings, excluding bars, brown to black on light green ground. Bars turquoise, between which are areas of red-orange, both most evident posteriorly. Dorsolateral area with orange spots. Cheek with turquoise area, becoming iridescent green on opercle; gular and branchiostegal areas yellow to orange. Caudal base with two orange spots.

First dorsal fin of nuptial male with margin and submargin light turquoise; proximally yellow-orange; a small red-orange spot near posterior end of fin in some specimens. Second dorsal fin margin turquoise, much of fin orange-streaked, base turquoise. Caudal fin margin turquoise; membranes orange-streaked; leading edges turquoise. Anal spines, rays, and marginal band turquoise; remainder of membranes orange. Pelvic fin turquoise with white knob on tips of rays. Pectoral fin margin clear, much of fin orange.

Female with brown to black body markings. First dorsal fin margin turquoise; submarginal narrow clear band; medial red; remainder tessellated brown to black. Second dorsal fin with hint of red medially. Anal fin with small area of turquoise anteriorly; small median area posteriorly in membranes is orange.

Larvae.—Described by Cooper (1979) and Auer (1982f).

BIOLOGY

In many areas the major food of *E. caeruleum* is midge larvae, supplemented by caddisfly, mayfly, other insect larvae, and other invertebrates (Turner 1921; Lotrich 1973; Nemecek 1978; Paine et al. 1982; Wynes and Wissing 1982; Hess 1983; Grady and Bart 1984; Martin 1984a; Fisher and Pearson 1987). Caddisfly larvae were the most important item in an Ohio study (Adamson and Wissing 1977). Wynes and Wissing (1982) reported consumption of midges to be most prevalent in April and May and that an increase in consumption of mayflies and caddisflies occurred in July and August.

Differences in foraging strategies and associated morphology occur between the rainbow and fantail darters. In Illinois *E. caeruleum* used its subterminal mouth to feed from exposed surfaces of rocks, whereas *E. flabellare*, having a terminal mouth and more flexible body, searched crevices (Schlosser and Toth 1984). Although these authors found no evidence that the two species partition food resources, Fisher and Pearson (1987) detected such in Kentucky.

Yearling rainbow darters are capable of reproducing; maximum longevity is 3 years in the lower Mississippi basin and 4 years in Wisconsin. The sexes do not differ in growth rate; 2-year-olds usually are 35–50 mm SL (Lutterbie 1979; Grady and Bart 1984). The largest specimen reported is 64 mm SL (Page 1983); the largest from Virginia is 53 mm SL.

Spawning begins as early as late February in Arkansas and extends to mid-June in Wisconsin, lasting two or three months in most areas (Schwartz 1965a; Grady and Bart 1984; Hubbs 1985). Males establish small roving territories in runs and riffles (Winn 1958a, 1958b; Grady and Bart 1984). When females enter a spawning ground they are pursued and courted by one or more males, who may establish a moving territory around females. When ready to spawn, the female buries the ventral half of the body, the male mounts her back, and both commence quivering; 3–7 eggs are released during each act. Females may spawn with more than one male. Up to 125 mature ova were found in a single female (Grady and Bart 1984). Age-2 fish lay an average of 880 eggs (Winn 1958b). Hybridization is known to occur with *E. zonale* (Trautman 1981).

HABITAT

Etheostoma caeruleum inhabits warm, moderate-gradient creeks, streams, and rivers. In Virginia it typically occupies runs and riffles of sand, gravel, and rubble, and is occasionally found in pools. The rainbow darter is the most common swift-water species in part of Ontario; adult females occupy runs and riffles, males occupy only riffles (Englert and Seghers 1983a). Juveniles tend to occur in slower shallower areas than do adults (Fisher and Pearson 1987). Rainbow darters are rarely found on gravel patches overlying soft sand (Grady and Bart 1984). This species tolerates quite low oxygen levels during summer—as low as 1.65 mg/liter (Hlohowskyj and Wissing 1984).

DISTRIBUTION   Map 187

The rainbow darter is widely distributed in the lower Great Lakes and in the upper and middle Mississippi basins; isolated populations occur in the lower Mississippi basin and, in West Virginia only, in the upper Potomac drainage. Esmond and Stauffer (1983) argued that the Potomac population is native, but as in many similar cases of extreme localization (such as *Thoburnia rhothoeca* in the same area), it may have been introduced.

Etheostoma caeruleum has been found within Virginia in three drainages. The Big Sandy population, known in the state from 19 collections in 6 streams, is obviously native; its fragmentation probably is related to extensive siltation. The Powell system record is from Indian Creek in 1973 (Masnik 1974); the pop-

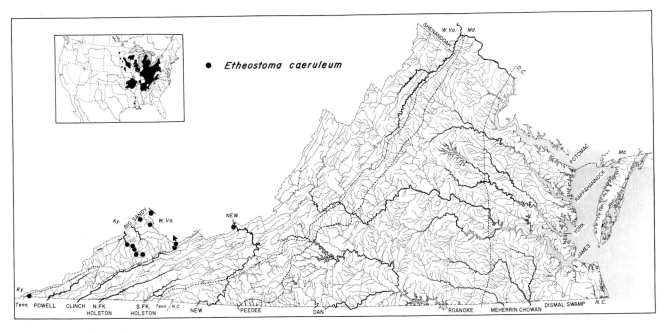

Map 187   Rainbow darter.

ulation is far separated from those in lower Clinch River tributaries. Evermann and Hildebrand's (1916) record of *E. variatum* from Indian Creek may have been *E. caeruleum*.

In the New drainage, the rainbow darter is known from the New River in the vicinity of the Virginia–West Virginia line since 1972 (Hocutt et al. 1973; Stauffer et al. 1976), and somewhat below there since 1982 (Hess 1983; Lobb 1986). It is also known from a small area in each of two New River tributaries: lower East River near the Virginia–West Virginia line since 1972, where it has been rare (Hambrick et al. 1973; Stauffer et al. 1975); and in the extreme lower Gauley system of West Virginia since 1976, where it is sometimes common (Hocutt et al. 1979). The data indicate at least two recent introductions—in the vicinity of the East River mouth and in the lower Gauley—with subsequent spreading from the East River downstream in the New. Filling of the range gap in the lower New River seems to be happening; the darter was rare above the state line in 1972, but became more abundant below by 1982. However, because of the many distributional peculiarities of native fishes in the New, it is possible that the rainbow darter is native to at least one portion of the New. This species also has a patchy range in the middle and upper Tennessee drainage. The record (Fowler 1945) of *E. caeruleum* from the Little River system of the New in Virginia are based on *E. flabellare* (ANSP 74841–42).

Abundance.—Rare in the New drainage and Powell system, uncommon in the Big Sandy drainage.

REMARKS

The aptly named rainbow darter is a peripheral species in Virginia. It will be interesting to see if it can resist extirpation in the New drainage in the face of the explosive spread of the apparently introduced Roanoke darter *Percina roanoka*.

Name.—*Caerulum* means blue or shades thereof.

Fantail darter   *Etheostoma flabellare* Rafinesque

SYSTEMATICS

Etheostoma flabellare was described in 1819 from the "Ohio River"; the type locality probably was in a tributary in northern Kentucky (McGeehan 1985). Its phylogenetic relationships within the subgenus *Catonotus* are noted under *E. percnurum*.

The fantail darter is by far the most widespread and polytypic member of *Catonotus*, which comprises 18 species (Braasch and Mayden 1985; Ceas et al. 1991). Four of the five subspecies recognized by McGeehan (1985) occur in Virginia: *E. f. flabellare* in the Big Sandy drainage; *E. f. humerale* (Girard) in the Potomac, James, Chowan, and Roanoke drainages; *E. f.*

brevispina (Coker) in the Pee Dee drainage; and an undescribed subspecies in the New and Tennessee drainages.

DESCRIPTION

Materials.—Our 292 series from Virginia, North Carolina, and eastern Tennessee, including meristic data from 210 specimens largely from the upper Tennessee drainage. Other meristic data from the three-state area (Ross 1958b, 1962; Buhan 1966; Stutz 1968); counts from *E. f. brevispina* are excluded. Life color from 10 Virginia lots.

Anatomy.—A darter with a low first dorsal fin, the side typically barred, and a rounded and prominently tessellated or marbled tail; adults are 35–60 mm SL. Body somewhat elongate, the depth nearly uniform throughout; snout moderately short, slightly pointed or rounded; frenum present; mouth usually terminal, horizontal or slightly oblique; large nuptial male pugfaced, lower jaw sometimes exceeding upper jaw and distinctly oblique; branchiostegal membranes moderately or broadly conjoined. Both dorsal fins and anal fin low, first dorsal particularly low; caudal fin rounded.

Nuptial male with small or large knob on tip of dorsal fin spines; anal and pelvic spines and lower pectoral rays ridged with thickened skin. Also in male, scales of the lower side with smoothly thickened or ridged skin; in large male in peak development, all body scales heavily rugose, some rugae present on lower cheek; head dorsum and nape rarely rugose; skin usually thickest on anterior and medial exposed portions of scales. Female genital papilla a grooved, broad, flat or bulbous pad; some large females

with slight knobbing on dorsal spine tips, and slightly thickened, smooth-surfaced skin on lower body scales.

Cheek and opercle naked; nape usually naked, often 10–40% scaled, rarely 70–90% scaled; belly usually 100% scaled, often 60–90% scaled, rarely 0–50% scaled; breast naked or very rarely with a few scales.

Meristics.—Lateral line incomplete, midlateral scales (40)46–54(60), pored scales (14)26–38(45); scales above lateral line, to origin of second dorsal fin, (6)7–9(10); scales below lateral line (6)8–11(13); circumpeduncle scales (19)22–26(30). Dorsal spines (5)7–8(9); dorsal rays (10)13–14(15); anal spines (1)2(3); anal rays (6)7–9(10); pectoral rays 11–13(14).

Color in Preservative.—Lateral body vertically barred; bars often short, not extending onto lower side; bars tending boldest and longest and extending onto dorsum in large male; bars of female and juvenile often vague, short, blotch- or spotlike; bars tend to be particularly reduced or absent in lower Dan system and Chowan drainage specimens, and in these fish (occasionally in other drainages too) each upper body scale often has a chevron, crescent, or spotlike dark mark, the upper body appearing crosshatched or having rows of distinct spots. Bars usually number 6–12, highest in the Potomac, James, Chowan, and lower Roanoke drainages and the Clinch system, lowest in the Holston system and upper portions of the New, Pee Dee, and Roanoke drainages.

Dorsum with (6)7–8(10) saddles, these occasionally connected in a chainlike design; between saddles and in dorsolateral area, body often duskily flecked in small and medium-sized fish, plain in large males; dorsum rarely wholly

Fish 314 *Etheostoma flabellare* adult male 62 mm SL (REJ 988), VA, Giles County, Big Stony Creek, 20 June 1983.

Fish 315 *Etheostoma flabellare* juvenile 33 mm SL (WHH 158), VA, Brunswick County, Pea Hill Creek, 27 July 1983.

pale. Large black humeral spot present above pectoral fin base. Head usually pale or dusky laterally, melanophores generally numerous, small to minute; pre-, sub-, and post-ocular stripe or bar usually present except in very dark-headed specimens; subocular bar the least frequently present and usually the shortest.

First dorsal fin medially pale; each membrane distally to subdistally with a ventrally rounded, dusky area (partly where knobs develop), forming a generally vague, ventrally undulating subdistal band that is interrupted at and just before each spine; fin basally dusky or dark. Second dorsal and caudal fins usually moderately or strongly tessellated, mottled, or marbled (Figures 55, 56); dark and pale areas generally aligned in an irregularly undulating pattern; dark marks best developed immediately adjacent to rays; second dorsal fin often slightly dusky basally. Anal and pelvic fins pale; pectoral fin pale, or for much or all its length uniformly dusky (Figure 82B) or vaguely tessellated. Caudal fin base with 2 vertically aligned spots, 1 spot or blotch, or no mark.

In nuptial male, the head and the rounded dusky areas on first dorsal fin darken; the head sometimes becomes black; first dorsal fin with sharply defined black basal band; pattern of second dorsal and caudal fins intensifies; second dorsal fin dusky or dark basally, duskiness often extending distally, mottled pattern sometimes obscured; caudal fin becomes the most intensely marbled; anal and pelvic fins slightly dusky, sooty, or nearly black, evenly so or slightly darker basally.

Color in Life   Plate 38.—Generally drab; ground shade of back and side tan to brown, sometimes yellow- or orange-toned; marks dark olive or black; venter pale gray to white. Where not darkened, fins often pale yellow-tinged, rarely all fins lemon yellow; dorsal fin knobs yellow, gold, or orange. Blackness of head in nuptial male can pale rapidly.

Larvae.—Described by Lake (1936), Cooper (1979), Auer (1982f), and Paine (1984).

BIOLOGY

The fantail darter feeds principally on mayfly, caddisfly, and midge larvae (Karr 1964; Lotrich 1973; Small 1975; Adamson and Wissing 1977; Baker 1978; Mauney 1979; Matthews et al. 1982; Becker 1983; Martin 1984a; Vadas 1990). The size of some of its food was impressive to Turner (1921); frequently the stomach was filled by one large larva which sometimes was nearly as long as the fish. A tendency to take large prey was noted also by Matthews et al. (1982) and Fisher and Pearson (1987). *Etheostoma flabellare* forages in crevices between and under stones, enabled by its terminal mouth and shallow flexible body (Paine et al. 1982; Schlosser and Toth 1984). It feeds at night as well as actively during the day (Matthews et al. 1982).

Maturation occurs by age 1 in at least some fish (Lake 1936); all 18 Virginia specimens aged as 2-year-olds were mature. Males tend to live longer, maximum longevity being 5 years, and grow faster than females (Lake 1936; Karr 1964; Lutterbie 1979; Becker 1983). Baker (1978) suggested that Karr (1964) erroneously added a year to the age. Growth varies within areas such that no overall geographic trend is evident. Averages at age 2 are 45–64 mm TL in areas west and north of Virginia (Karr 1964; Lotrich 1973; Small 1975; Lutterbie 1979), and 52 mm SL in Kentucky (Baker 1978). Age-2 Smith River, Virginia, fish taken in June were 32–47 mm SL, mean, 41. New drainage fish tend to be biggest; our largest from the New (and all of Virginia) was 74 mm SL. The largest fantail reported by McGeehan, from the New (state unspecified), is 78 mm SL.

Spawning occurs from April into June in much of the range, as found in certain studies cited above and summaries by Page (1983) and Hubbs (1985). Small (1975) implied that spawning began in mid-March in a Kentucky stream. Schwartz's (1965a) comment on spawning extending into July in western Pennsylvania is unclear; he (1967) reported that breeding occurs in late June and early July in a montane area of West Virginia. Based on gravidness and nuptial color, spawning takes place largely during April and May in Virginia; a fantail nest was found on 20 May. Temperatures at spawning are 15–24°C. The spawning habitat is runs and slow riffles including shallows (Lake 1936; Winn 1958b; Schwartz 1965a; Baker 1978; Trautman 1981).

Suitable breeding sites are stones with a space beneath, for *E. flabellare* is an egg-clusterer. The male selects and defends the nest. Adhesive eggs are laid and fertilized by inverting to the underside of the stone. Several females may spawn, one at a time, with a single male. Lake (1936) found an average of 169 eggs, maximum 562, in nests and thought that females laid an average of 34 eggs during a spawning episode. Winn (1958a) counted 62–298 eggs in six clusters. Apparently the fantail darter is a fractional spawner; females spawn about five times in a year (Lake 1936). Single ovarian egg counts per female range from 40 to 586 (Lake 1936; Karr 1964; Winn 1958b; Small 1975).

HABITAT

The fantail darter is ubiquitous over much of its range in cool and warm, gravelly and rocky brooks and medium-sized streams; to a lesser extent it occurs in large streams and rivers. In northern areas it inhabits shore areas of lakes (Hubbs and Lagler 1958;

Trautman 1981), where it may breed at wave-washed sites. The fantail darter thrives in clear, unsilted and slightly silted streams. Judging from its abundance in much of the Virginia Piedmont, it tolerates frequent slight to moderate turbidity. Populations tend to be denser in warmer open streams than in cool forested ones in Virginia. This species has been found among weed beds (Trautman 1981; Paine et al. 1982) but is not typically associated with vegetation.

Etheostoma flabellare is characteristic of riffles in northern areas which have few swift-water fish species (e.g., Greene 1935; Karr 1964; Englert and Seghers 1983a; Mundahl and Ingersoll 1983). The same is true in the more diverse faunas of the upper Ohio basin, the Ozarks, and the southern Appalachians (e.g., Schwartz 1965a; Pflieger 1975; Matthews 1990). In Michigan, Winn (1958b) noted that *E. flabellare* moved to larger riffles after breeding. In New York (Lake 1936) and Ohio (Trautman 1981), most fantail darters went to larger, deeper, and sometimes swifter sections after spawning, where they wintered. In an Ohio stream, Mundahl and Ingersoll (1983) found that although this species exhibited a slight tendency to move upstream in early fall, they stayed in riffles. In the Allegheny drainage, Schwartz (1965a) noted that it remained relatively immobile through summer in riffles.

Some habitat shifts may be related to reduced stream levels in summer (Winn 1958b). In Illinois, however, *E. flabellare* emigrated less from riffles than did another darter species (Schlosser and Toth 1984); in Kentucky, it was the last darter species to depart riffles during low water (Lotrich 1973). Stegman and Minckley (1959) observed it living within a streambed in Illinois whose surface was dry; the substrate was large loose gravel and had strong percolation of water.

Larger fish tend to locate in deeper, swifter current (Winn 1958b; Schwartz 1965a; Matthews 1985b; Fisher and Pearson 1987). This is true in much of Virginia, where young fish tend to occupy shallows in margins of riffles, runs, and pools (e.g., Jenkins and Freeman 1972).

In most of Virginia, adult fantail darters tend to concentrate in shallow sections of riffles. This species is less equipped morphologically for very strong currents than are two other upper Roanoke darters (Matthews 1985b). The only deviation from riffle inhabitation that we found in Virginia occurs in Copper Creek, where (except in headwaters) all life stages are nearly restricted to slow runs, backwaters, and pools. It is tempting to attribute this habitat shift to competitive displacement in a darter-rich fauna. Evidence exists that *E. rufilineatum* caused depression of the *E.*

flabellare population in a Kentucky stream (Fisher and Pearson 1987). Copper Creek harbors 15 darter species including *E. rufilineatum*; adults of about half the species prefer slow runs or slack water. The fantail darter may also be at an interactive disadvantage relative to its close kin in the creek, the duskytail darter (*E. percnurum* account).

DISTRIBUTION   Maps 188, 189

Etheostoma flabellare is widely distributed in the southern Great Lakes–St. Lawrence basin and south in the Mississippi basin through the Ozarks, southern Appalachians, and certain adjacent uplands. On the Atlantic slope, it occurs in most major drainages from the Santee north to the lower Susquehanna, and is present in the upper Susquehanna and Hudson drainages. Its absence from the York and Rappahannock drainages is striking (*Biogeography*).

An upland–montane species in Virginia, the fantail darter becomes sporadic in occurrence in the lower Piedmont and its range ends at or near the Fall Line. The populations in the upper Tennessee drainage of Virginia tend to be discontinuous compared with the general pattern in the New drainage and in other montane and upland areas eastward. Sharply contrasting is the localization of *Etheostoma flabellare* in the Big Sandy drainage.

Abundance.—Often common or abundant from the New drainage east through the middle Piedmont. In the Blue Ridge Province, it is less abundant in tumbling streams within the northern sector of the escarpment (Map 7) than in gentler streams in the plateau portion of the New drainage. Usually rare or uncommon in the lower Piedmont and west of the New. Populations in the Fall Zone generally are sparse.

REMARKS

The fantail was considered the "darter of darters" by D. S. Jordan and H. E. Copeland (*in* Jordan and Evermann 1896). It is a highly successful, abundant fish in many parts of its extensive range. Undoubtedly this is partly due to its specialized mode of spawning and related adaptations. Its attachment of eggs to the ceiling of a small cavity reduces the chances of egg siltation or predation. Nests are defended aggressively by males. The male generally is drab, enhancing his concealment and that of the nest.

Body-surface tissues of nuptial male *E. flabellare* may coat eggs with a bactericide and fungicide during the nesting period. The thickened and ridged,

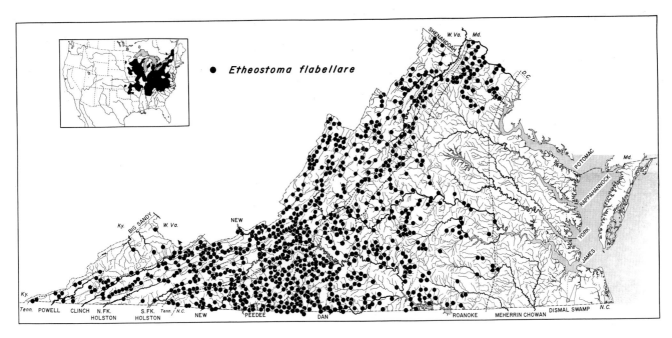

Map 188   Fantail darter.

nonkeratinized skin on the lower body may have a secretory or stimulatory function (Cross 1967; Mayden 1985b). Some males have a great proliferation of this tissue and are particularly slimy, unlike the effect of conic tubercles that roughen body and fin surfaces of other species. The soft-surfaced golden knobs located atop dorsal spines of nuptial males protect eggs from puncture; may serve to clean the nest roof and the eggs; and may mimic eggs, thereby attracting females to spawn (Page 1975; Layman 1984b; Page and Swofford 1984; Page and Bart 1989; Bart and Page 1991). Egg-mimicking has been supported experimentally (Knapp and Sargent 1989).

The fantail darter has other adaptations working for it, judging from its extensive zonal distribution—headwaters to main rivers. It is a trophic generalist compared with other darters in a montane fauna (Matthews et al. 1982). It is territorial, aggressively holding a living space (Seifert 1963). Within the subgenus *Catonotus*, it is unique in occupying gravel and rubble in moderate to swift currents (Page and Schemske 1978; Braasch and Mayden 1985), yet it is not as restricted physiologically to highly oxygenated water as are some other darters (Ultsch et al. 1978). In some areas, *E. flabellare* shifts habitat due to seasonal or water-level changes, but some populations may not emigrate from riffles even with strong cause—Lotrich (1973) virtually dug fantails from nearly dry riffles, and Stegman and Minckley (1959) found them down in dry-surfaced riffles.

Among darters, *E. flabellare* is relatively tolerant of adverse habitat changes (Trautman 1981). However, its localization in the Big Sandy drainage indicates that its tolerance limits are exceeded in that extensively coal-mined region. Reduction of a fantail darter population also occurred in a similarly affected area of Kentucky (Lotrich 1973).

Name.—*Flabellare*, "fanlike," applies to the rounded, expansive, strongly patterned tail of adult males. *Humerale*, "of the shoulder," is from the large black mark in that position. *Brevispina* refers to "short spines" of the first dorsal fin. The scientific name of the subspecies found mainly in the New and upper Tennessee drainages, to be published by McGeehan, will be coined from the robust head.

Duskytail darter   *Etheostoma percnurum* Jenkins (New Species)

SYSTEMATICS

Etheostoma percnurum is here described formally as a new species, by R. E. Jenkins alone, as a member of the subgenus *Catonotus* from Copper Creek and the Clinch River in Virginia and from five streams in Tennessee. In the *flabellare* group of *Catonotus*, this cryptic species is most closely related to the fantail darter *E. flabellare*. The stripetail darter *E. kennicotti* is the other member of the *flabellare* group. The Virginia

Fish 316 *Etheostoma percnurum* adult male 38 mm SL (REJ 471), VA, Scott County, Copper Creek, 19 May 1971. Holotype—UMMZ 220237.

Fish 317 *Etheostoma percnurum* adult female 38 mm SL (REJ 471), VA, Scott County, Copper Creek, 19 May 1971. Paratype—UMMZ 220238.

population of *E. percnurum* differs significantly from other populations in the color pattern of certain fins and some aspects of squamation. A separate, more detailed paper is to be published on the systematics of the *flabellare* group.

DESCRIPTION

Materials.—From the entire range of the species; meristic data from 161 specimens. Life color mainly from Copper Creek fish; certain aspects of Little River, Tennessee, fish from Layman (1984a, 1984b, 1991). Holotype—UMMZ 220237, nuptial male, 37.6 mm SL. Type locality—Virginia, Scott County, Copper Creek just below mouth of Obeys Creek, 5.1 air km NNE of center of Gate City, 19 May 1971, N. M. Burkhead, R. E. Jenkins, M. A. Kuhl. Paratypes taken with holotype—UMMZ 220238, 55 specimens, 23–45 mm SL.

Anatomy.—A narrow-barred darter with a distally dusky pectoral fin, the second dorsal and caudal fins finely tessellated or nontessellated, and the first saddle often yokelike; adults are 28–45 mm SL. Body somewhat elongate, depth little tapered, caudal peduncle deep; snout somewhat short, pointed or well rounded; frenum present; mouth terminal, horizontal, slightly oblique in large fish; branchiostegal membranes usually moderately conjoined. Dorsal fins and anal fin moderately low; fin-support elements frail. Nuptial fin knobs, skin surfacing, and genital papilla as in *E. flabellare*; these features are less developed in *E. percnurum* only when compared to larger specimens of the fantail. Cheek, opercle, nape, and breast naked; belly almost always 0–20% scaled in Copper Creek and Cumberland drainage fish, (40)50–80(100)% scaled in Little River fish.

Meristics.—Lateral line incomplete, midlateral scales (38)40–45(48), pored scales (16)18–28(31); scales above lateral line, to second dorsal fin origin, (5)6–7(8); scales below lateral line (7)8–9(11); circumpeduncle scales (21)22–25(28). Dorsal spines (6)7(8); dorsal rays (10)11–12(13); anal spines (1)2(3), almost always 2; anal rays (6)7–8; pectoral rays 12–13(14).

Color in Preservative.—Lateral body typically with vertical narrow bars, these numbering (10)11–14(15), often 2–3 bars fork from a saddle; bars often vague in all life stages; upper portion of bars occasionally absent; bars often slightly widened at midheight of body. Body ground pattern on upper side and midside uniformly vaguely flecked or cross-hatched, no hint of horizontal lines; flank melanophores usually in vertical files. Dorsum with (6)7(9) saddles, first saddle often boldest, widest, and confluent with large black humeral spot, nape appearing yoked.

Head dark above; lower half with usually well-spaced melanophores, these often medium or very large in young, juvenile, and small adult, the fish freckle-headed (relatively small melanophores are shown in Fish 316 and 317 and Figure 82A); breast and prepectoral area often freckled. Preocular and postocular stripe or dash present, subocular mark absent.

First dorsal fin as in *E. flabellare*. Second dorsal fin usually vaguely tessellated or mottled, basally dusky; membranes slightly duskier distally than at midheight. Caudal fin usually finely and vaguely tessellated, most intensely basally, least patterned distally, the distal portion often uniformly vaguely dusky. Caudal fin base lacks spot or has 2 vague, vertically aligned submedial spots. Anal and pelvic fins unpigmented or with a wide slightly dusky marginal area; if latter, pigment slight or absent elsewhere; pelvic best pigmented in Copper Creek fish. Pectoral fin unpigmented except dusky along rays distally, often forming a curved band (Figure 82A).

Large nuptial male modified from the above, the head varying from slightly dusky in some fish to nearly black in others. First dorsal fin with round dusky areas (associated with spine-tip knobs) becoming duskier; basally a narrow black band. Second dorsal fin duskiest basally and distally, a vague band formed through each area; rays tend to lose pattern and membranes tend to become uniformly dusky in Copper Creek fish; rays are more prominently marbled in Little River fish. Caudal fin loses pattern, except that the dusky margin is accentuated, in Copper Creek specimens; tessellations more intense in Little River fish. Anal, pectoral, and sometimes pelvic fins blacken along rays from margin to submargin, proximal edge of blackened areas sharply defined.

Color in Life.—Dull overall; in both sexes, ground shade of back and side straw to brown-olive or gray-olive, sometimes with pale yellow wash that is best developed posteriorly; saddles, bars, and head dorsum medium or dark olive; belly dingy white to pale gray. Where fins are not darkened, dorsals and caudal white or pale yellow; first dorsal membranes each with a distal–subdistal patch of yellow to orange; paired fins white or pectoral yellow-tinted. In nuptial male, iris golden; fin knobs pale gold; anal fin creamy white proximally, sharply contrasting with black margin; darkenings described above.

Larvae.—Described by Layman (1991).

BIOLOGY

Etheostoma percnurum is a benthic invertivore; small individuals feed most frequently on small crustaceans and midge larvae. As darter size increases, so does size and variety of prey consumed. Large duskytails take a wide range of taxa, primarily midge, mayfly, and caddisfly larvae (Layman 1991).

In the Little River of Tennessee, some 1-year-olds are sexually mature; the smallest nest-guarding male was 39 mm SL and the smallest gravid female was 28 mm (Layman 1991). From Copper Creek during several breeding seasons encompassing 14 April–11 June, the smallest obviously mature male was 35 mm SL, the smallest mature female 26 mm; the largest immature fish were a 38-mm male and a 26-mm female. Apparently many fish do not spawn as yearlings in Copper Creek. Known longevity is 2 years; some individuals may live a few more months (Layman 1991).

Males grow faster than females; at age 1 in the Little River, males averaged 40 mm SL, females 35

mm (Layman 1991). Our data from Copper Creek, combining age-1 and apparent age-2 fish taken during 14 April–11 June, are: 21 immature males of 26–38 mm SL, mean, 30 mm; 11 adult males 35–47 mm, mean, 40; 11 immature females 24–26 mm, mean, 25; and 55 adult females 26–45 mm, mean, 31. Maximum known sizes, both from males, are 48 mm SL from Virginia and 53 mm from Tennessee (Layman 1991).

The spawning season in the Little River is late April or early May through June, at water temperatures of 17.5–24°C. Aquarium spawnings occurred at 13–24°C; the earliest spawning was on 6 April (Layman 1991). In Copper Creek we caught a ready-to-spawn female on 25 April; most spawning apparently takes place in May, water 18–21°C. The few females we took in June were either in an interlude between spawnings or had finished spawning. Cumberland drainage females were gravid on 20 May.

Spawning habitat in the Little River is that occupied during nonbreeding times—shallow pools or moderate-velocity runs of largely rubble and boulders (Layman 1991). However, at a Copper Creek site on 19 May 1971 we found nuptial fish, particularly males, concentrated in a gravel–rubble run of moderate current, and a male was in a swift run. At that time juveniles generally remained in slower margins of runs and pools. The adult duskytail habitat was more typical of that of small adults of *E. rufilineatum*, which uniquely was less common than the duskytail at the time. The eight other darter species at the site were rare or uncommon; adult duskytails may have shifted to this habitat owing to low populations of other species.

The duskytail darter is an egg-clusterer; a single tier of eggs is spawned during a long period of inversion under slab-shaped cobbles in depths of 55 to 85 cm or more. The male cleans and aggressively protects the nest cavity. Counts of mature ova per female were 19–44, mean, 27; the numbers of eggs per cluster laid in single spawning episodes were 12–40, mean, 27. This species spawns fractionally; a female spawned six times in an aquarium at intervals of 4–8 days. Both sexes are polygamous; clusters had 23–200 eggs (Layman 1984b, 1991).

HABITAT

The biotope of *E. percnurum* is generally clear, warm, moderate-gradient, intermontane streams and rivers. Populations occur in stream widths of 10–80 m; Copper Creek is the narrowest typically occupied, usually 10–15 m wide in the inhabited reach. Individuals occur in near-shore shallows, in moderate midstream depths, and perhaps in deep water.

In the Little River, adults occur predominantly in pools, less frequently in moderately swift runs, and are associated with relatively clean gravel, rubble, and boulders. Young and juveniles also seem to prefer pools but are more abundant than adults in swift runs. Because duskytails generally remain under cover, small individuals could use the interstices among gravel in swift water more so than do adults. During summer, *E. percnurum* occurred in areas with dense growth of riverweed (*Podostemum*) (Layman 1991).

Habitats occupied in Copper Creek much resemble those populated in the Little River; the range of habitat includes slack water, detritus, slightly silted stones, and bedrock. In Copper Creek we did not find young or juveniles to be more abundant in faster current than were adults. An exceptional concentration of apparently breeding adults occupied a moderate-velocity run (*Biology*).

Physiographically, the duskytail darter occurs in the little-buffered Cumberland Plateau (Big South Fork Cumberland River) and the calcareous Valley and Ridge (the other streams). The occupied reach of two Valley and Ridge streams (Abrams and Citico creeks) fringes the Blue Ridge.

DISTRIBUTION   Map 189

Etheostoma percnurum is endemic to the upper Tennessee and middle Cumberland drainages. Six relict populations are known: one in Copper Creek, Virginia, and five in Tennessee—Citico Creek, Abrams Creek, the Little River, the South Fork Holston River, and the Big South Fork Cumberland River. The State of Tennessee populations are known either from one or few sites, or (Abrams Creek, South Fork Holston) are extirpated.

The Copper Creek population extends from the mouth upstream for about 29 rkm in this 98-rkm long, order-5 stream. Also, one duskytail was taken during 1980 in the Clinch River at Speers Ferry, 1 rkm below the mouth of Copper Creek. Whether it strayed from the creek or represented a population reestablished after the 1967 fish kill is unknown. If reestablished in the Clinch, the population would be small based on ample survey of the Speers Ferry site since 1979.

Etheostoma percnurum and *E. flabellare* have complementary ranges in Copper Creek—the duskytail occupies the lower main channel, the fantail occurs in the middle and upper portions and major tributaries. They have been taken syntopically in three areas of the creek, a few times in the same net haul; the fantail (adults included) is the rarer species in the overlap zone (Map 189). Their ecological relationship may be "intense competitive" (Jenkins and Musick 1979),

based on their essentially separate zonations in Copper Creek and their great similarities in habitat use and life history. Most other species of *Catonotus* exhibit patterns which indicate interspecific competition (Page and Smith 1976; Page and Schemske 1978; Braasch and Mayden 1985).

Other hypotheses exist to explain the Copper Creek pattern. Because Copper Creek in Areas 7–11 (Map 189) is the narrowest stream typically occupied by *E. percnurum*, the upstream limit of this species may be affected by stream size. (Countering that is its indicated greater abundance at the upper two areas than at all those below.) Within the speciose fish fauna of the upper Tennessee drainage, *E. flabellare* mainly inhabits small streams and often occurs in lower abundance compared with nearby areas east and west. Hence the downstream limit of the fantail in Copper Creek may be related to influences other than the duskytail. Elsewhere in or near duskytail populations, the fantail is known only from the Abrams Creek system (only well above the duskytail) and the South Fork Holston River (one *E. percnurum* was captured with two *E. flabellare*). Because both species are absent from several major parts of the upper or middle Tennessee and Cumberland drainages, factors other than their interaction obviously limited them there.

Abundance.—Generally rare or uncommon in Copper Creek (Map 189); rare in the Clinch River at Speers Ferry. From Copper Creek, the largest collections by far, in which the duskytail darter was somewhat common, were of 56 fish (mostly breeding adults) mainly from a single pool-run, and 46 specimens (chiefly young) taken by a three-hour effort. All medium and large series from Copper Creek were taken in 1970–1971, after we learned that kick-hauling is much more effective for collecting *E. percnurum* than are kick-seining in riffles and seine-sweeping in pools (see *The Study of Fishes*). During 1981–1985 the duskytail darter was rare or uncommon (often not taken) at the six sites that were well-sampled within Areas 1–10 (Map 189).

REMARKS

Etheostoma percnurum is a species of superlatives. It is the most drab darter in Virginia. It occupies two large drainages, yet is extremely localized; it is the rarest and has the most fragmented range of the species of the *flabellare* group. It is unique within the large subgenus *Catonotus* by its restriction to larger streams and major rivers.

The duskytail darter is in serious trouble. Of the six

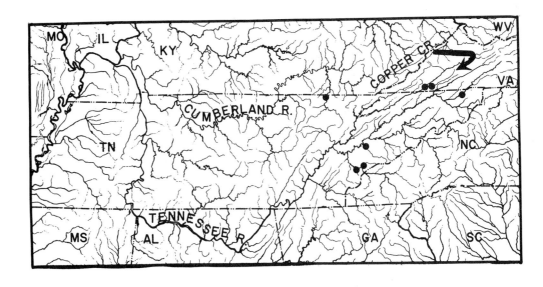

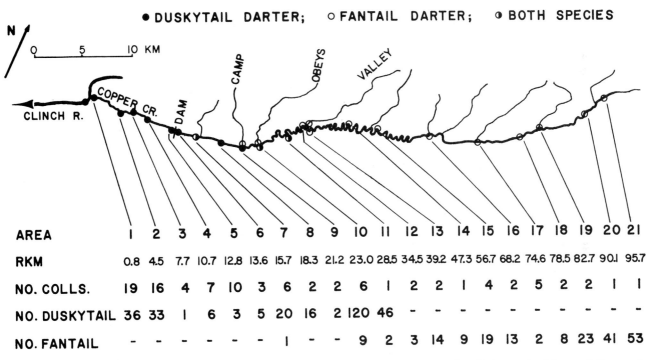

AREA	1	2	3	4	5	6	7	8	9	10	11	12	13	14	15	16	17	18	19	20	21
RKM	0.8	4.5	7.7	10.7	12.8	13.6	15.7	18.3	21.2	23.0	28.5	34.5	39.2	47.3	56.7	68.2	74.6	78.5	82.7	90.1	95.7
NO. COLLS.	19	16	4	7	10	3	6	2	2	6	1	2	2	1	4	2	5	2	2	1	1
NO. DUSKYTAIL	36	33	1	6	3	5	20	16	2	120	46	-	-	-	-	-	-	-	-	-	-
NO. FANTAIL	-	-	-	-	-	-	1	-	-	9	2	3	14	9	19	13	2	8	23	41	53

Map 189 Duskytail darter and fantail darter. Upper: Total known range of the duskytail darter; 4 of 6 populations are extant. Lower: Distribution of two species of *Catonotus* in the Copper Creek system, Scott and Russell counties, Virginia. "Areas" are in the main channel; many are lengthy stream sections; the center of each area is given in river kilometers. Number of collections from each area includes those in which *Catonotus* was not taken. The 98 collections constitute only those in which darters were sought and for which we have complete species lists (in 1986).

known populations, two are extirpated and the others are sharply localized. Many populations must have perished to produce this relict pattern. Impoundment, siltation, and pollution apparently are chief causes. This species is considered threatened in Tennessee and endangered in Virginia (Starnes and Etnier 1980; Burkhead and Jenkins 1991), and merits

federal protection under one of these categories. (It was federally designated as endangered in 1993.)

Name.—*Percnurum*—"dusky tail"—alludes to the reduced barring on the tail, which contrasts markedly with the patterns of the other members of the *flabellare* group—the fantail and stripetail darters.

Sawcheek darter   *Etheostoma serrifer* (Hubbs and Cannon)

SYSTEMATICS

The sawcheek darter, described from North Carolina in 1935, is primitive compared to its close relatives and it exhibits clinal and local variations (Collette 1962). *Etheostoma serrifer*, *E. fusiforme*, *E. collis*, and three extralimital species have constituted the subgenus *Hololepis*, a close-knit group called swamp darters (Hubbs and Cannon 1935; Collette 1962). These drab species have a pale, distinctly incomplete lateral line that courses high on the body.

Page (1981) formed a subgenus *Boleichthys* by merging *Hololepis* with the three species of the subgenus *Microperca* plus *Etheostoma* (*Oligocephalus*) *exile*. We are disposed against this arrangement. *Microperca* has a set of advanced distinctions not shared with *Hololepis* (Burr 1978). Page (1981) cited Burr (1978) regarding intermediacy of *E. collis* and *E. saludae* between *Hololepis* and *Microperca*. However, Burr had noted intermediacy in only certain meristic features; *E. collis* and *E. saludae* are typical (and advanced) *Hololepis*. Until a firmer basis arises for considering the three genus groups to form a monophyletic group, we recognize the natural lineages *Hololepis* and *Microperca* as subgenera, as favored by Collette (1962), Burr (1978), and Bailey and Etnier (1988).

DESCRIPTION

Materials.—From Hubbs and Cannon (1935), Collette (1962), and 26 Virginia series from which 41 specimens were counted meristically. Color in life from Collette (1962) and 3 Virginia adults.

Anatomy.—A laterally checkered, multi-blotched, or dark-striped darter with a short pale lateral line high on the body, usually 4 caudal spots, and moderately serrate preopercle; adults are 35–50 mm SL. Body somewhat elongate, slightly compressed; snout short, rounded; frenum present; branchiostegal membranes narrowly conjoined; preopercle margin fully and moderately serrate; caudal fin rounded or subtruncate. Breeding tubercles in male on anal rays and lower surface of pelvic rays. Female genital papilla moderately long, tubular, tip flattened and bilobed. Cheek, opercle, posterior head dorsum, nape, breast, and belly scaled.

Meristics.—Lateral line high on body, incomplete, midlateral scales (44)50–58(66), pored scales (20)28–40(45); scales above lateral line (3)4–5; scales below lateral line (10)11–13(15); circumpeduncle scales 23–27 (Page 1983). Dorsal spines (9)10–12(13); dorsal rays (11)12–13(14) (our data); anal spines 2; anal rays (4)5–6(7) (our data); pectoral rays (11)12(13). Infraorbital canal uninterrupted, usually 6 pores (Figure 83A); interorbital pores usually 2.

Color in Preservative.—Midside with 11–15 irregular, usually separate or slightly connected blotches and smaller marks, these sometimes fused into a wide, dark or black lateral stripe; upper side dusky, often lightly speckled, and on the body at least anteriorly there is a pale, slightly arched narrow line that includes the lateral line; dorsum dusky or dark, usually with irregular saddles. Lower side pale, slightly stippled, or speckled. Subocular bar or spot present or absent; preocular and postocular bars dark; lower side of head often freckled.

Fin membranes usually clear except that both dorsal fins and anal fin sometimes pigmented basally, or first dorsal also with a concentration of melanophores along posterior edge of spines. Dorsal and caudal rays tessellated; other fin rays clear or tessellated. Caudal base with 4 vertically aligned spots, the 2 (very rarely 1) medial ones large, quite bold, the upper and lower ones small, vague or distinct, round or elongate.

Sexual dichromatism present, male is duskier on body and particularly in dorsal, anal, and pelvic fin membranes; one possibly atypical male had a submedial black band in the first dorsal fin.

Color in Life Plate 38.—Lateral marks dark brown or black; upper body tan or olive, lateral line pale tan; nape with slight bluish cast; head laterally and breast with bluish gold iridescence; belly pale olive. Caudal base bright orange between black medial spots; all fin rays brick red. Jordan (1889b, as *E. quiescens*) noted red in the body.

Fish 318 *Etheostoma serrifer* adult male 44 mm SL (WHH 157), VA, Brunswick County, Rattlesnake Creek, 27 July 1983.

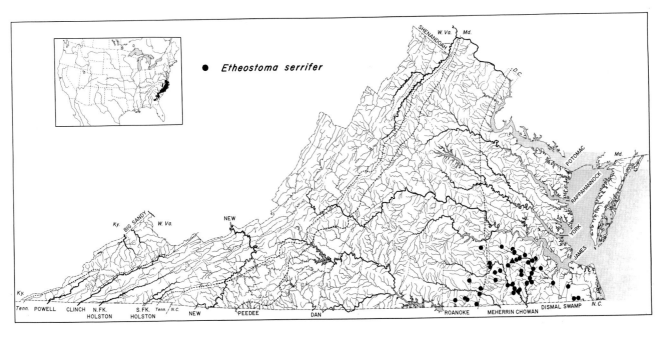

Map 190 Sawcheek darter.

BIOLOGY

Etheostoma serrifer appears to feed on an array of invertebrates. Twenty Virginia specimens took amphipods (31% of total items) and isopods (5%); stonefly (1%), mayfly (22%), beetle (7%), and midge (31%) larvae; and snails (3%) (K. A. Tyler, in litt.). Aquarium specimens ate worms (Collette 1962). Females grow the largest. A 57-mm SL female from South Carolina is the largest known specimen (Collette 1962); the largest from Virginia is a 52 mm SL female. The presence of breeding tubercles during late March in Georgia and South Carolina (Collette 1962) indicates that this species reproduces around early April in Virginia. Our single specimen taken during spring (12 April) in Virginia is a highly tuberculate male.

HABITAT

The sawcheek darter occupies warm slow streams, swamps, and ponds. It is generally associated with typically amber or darkly stained Coastal Plain waters and bottoms of sand, mud, and detritus that are often littered with sticks and stumps. Most Virginia records are from margins of swamps and all parts of small streams; it was taken twice in a large stream—the lower Nottoway River. Only 1 of our 46 site records was in a pond, from near the outflow when it was being drained. We commonly found the sawcheek darter in both heavily vegetated and open areas. The pH at 12 record sites was usually 6.4–6.7, extremes were 5.7 and 6.8.

Compared with most species of *Hololepis*, *E. serrifer* prefers slightly more open, better oxygenated, and less sluggish waters (Collette 1962). Collette noted that when present at the same site, *E. serrifer* was usually in weeds in midstream and *E. fusiforme* typically occurred in backwaters. However, at the few Virginia sites where we found both species in good numbers, they were intermixed in weedy shallows. From our other Coastal Plain collections of one or both species, we could not discern a general habitat difference between them. Among all Virginia collections, *E. serrifer* was absent from the quiet waters of interior Dismal Swamp, whereas 4 of the 82 records of *E. fusiforme* are from Lake Drummond of interior Dismal Swamp and 4 are from other lakes or ponds. Only *E. fusiforme* extends well into the Piedmont, in almost moderate-gradient streams, although it still lives in calm water there.

DISTRIBUTION   Map 190

Etheostoma serrifer ranges from the Altamaha drainage in Georgia north to the Chowan drainage and to the Nansemond River and Elizabeth River systems of the lower James River estuary of Virginia. It likely has native status in the James; in 1973 it was taken in a Nansemond headwater distant from canal connections with Dismal Swamp. The large majority of Virginia records are from below the Fall Line; those on the lower Piedmont are from low gradients.

Abundance.—Rare to common.

REMARKS

The sawcheek darter and the two other "swamp darters" of Virginia are relatively drab in comparison to most of our other darters, probably an adaptation for concealment in dim environments.

Name.—*Serrifer* means "saw-bearing," from the serrate edge of the preopercle. The original spelling is restored; the recently used *serriferum* is an unjustified emendation (Robins et al. 1991).

Swamp darter   *Etheostoma fusiforme* (Girard)

SYSTEMATICS

The swamp darter, subgenus *Hololepis*, was described from Massachusetts in 1854. Apparently it is most closely related to *E. collis*. Two subspecies are recognized; *E. f. fusiforme* is the Virginia form (Collette 1962).

DESCRIPTION

Materials.—Meristic data on *E. f. fusiforme* from Collette (1962); other data from 34 Virginia lots. Color in life from Collette (1962) and 7 Virginia females.

Anatomy.—A laterally blotched, speckled, or blotched and speckled darter with a short pale lateral line high on the body, fully scaled breast, and 2 anal spines; adults are 25–40 mm SL. Body elongate, moderately compressed; snout short, rounded; frenum present; branchiostegal membranes narrowly conjoined; preopercle usually entire, occasionally partly and weakly serrate; caudal fin subtruncate or rounded. Breeding tubercles in male on anal rays and underside of pelvic rays. Female genital papilla a moderately elongate tapering tube, tip unnotched, pointed or broadly rounded, with a long slitlike opening. Cheek, opercle, nape, belly, and breast fully scaled; posterior head dorsum variably scaled.

Meristics.—Lateral line high on body, incomplete, midlateral scales (40)46–50(62), pored scales (0)6–20(26); scales above lateral line 2–3(5); scales below lateral line (6)7–9(12); circumpeduncle scales 18–22 (Page 1983). Dorsal spines (8)9–11(13); dorsal rays (8)9–10(11) (our 22 counts); anal spines 2; anal rays (5)6–8(9); pectoral rays (12)13(15). Infraorbital canal interrupted, usually 3+2 pores (Figure 83B); no interorbital pores.

Color in Preservative.—Similar to *E. serrifer* but with the following differences. Dark lateral blotches or medium-sized irregular marks usually fewer, often less than 12, and often only slightly more intense than dorsolateral marks, and may evenly grade in intensity toward dorsolateral marks. Body more speckled and scrawled overall, often with a cross-hatched pattern. Fins of adult male possibly generally darker than in female; first dorsal membranes darker anteriorly than posteriorly, and darker submedially than basally. Caudal base almost always with 3 vertically aligned small spots or flecks, 1 of these medial; rarely there are 4 spots, and if so, the medial 2 usually are not markedly bolder than the other 2.

Color in Life.—Lateral blotches dark brown; anterior half of body with slight greenish iridescence; dorsum olive-brown; abdomen pale tan-olive. Dorsal and caudal fin rays sometimes with slight brick red cast.

BIOLOGY

The swamp darter feeds mostly on microcrustaceans and aquatic insect larvae, particularly on midges (Flemer and Woolcott 1966; Gatz 1979; Schmidt and Whitworth 1979). In aquaria they readily eat small animals that move (Collette 1962). An annual species, yearlings are mature and few, if any, fish survive a second autumn (Schmidt and Whitworth 1979; Clemmons and Lindquist 1983). Females reach larger size than males; the largest known is 49 mm SL from New York (Collette 1962), the largest from Virginia 43 mm SL.

Breeding occurs during late March through mid-May in New Jersey, in late April in New York, and

Fish 319 *Etheostoma fusiforme* adult female 37 mm SL (WHH 148), VA, Surry County, Otterdam Swamp, 25 July 1983.

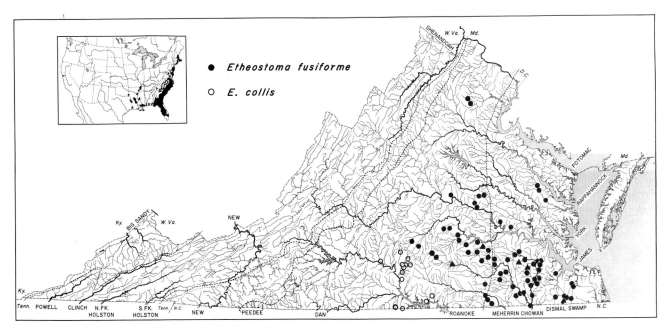

Map 191   Swamp darter and Carolina darter.

during May and June in Connecticut (Collette 1962; Schmidt and Whitworth 1979). In Lake Waccamaw, North Carolina, spawning occurs from late winter to September (Clemmons and Lindquist 1983). The swamp darter is an egg-attacher (Fletcher 1957; Collette 1962) whose reproductive behavior appears generally similar to *E. collis*. Collette's (1962) reference to the male beating the female with his pelvic fins concerns behavior after the male mounted the female (B. B. Collette, in litt.). Judging from Fletcher's (1957) photograph, pectoral beating by the male, characteristic of *E. collis*, is also practiced by *E. fusiforme*.

HABITAT

The swamp darter typically occupies warm ponds, swamps, and sluggish creeks, streams, and rivers. It inhabits open and stick- and stump-cluttered bottoms of sand, mud, and detritus and often dwells in thick vegetation. In most areas it rarely occurs in obviously flowing water (Collette 1962). In Connecticut it is more numerous in ponds than in streams, but is found occasionally in rocky riffles (Schmidt and Whitworth 1979).

Most Virginia populations occur in streams. Of Piedmont populations, the habitats of some are similar to those in much of the Coastal Plain; others live in typical Piedmont streams, but there too in slow water. Over its range, habitat descriptors include waters that are colorless to darkly stained; clear or, much less often, turbid; slightly alkaline to generally acidic (to pH 3.7 [Smith 1953]); and fresh, rarely brackish

(salinity to 5‰ [Schwartz 1981b]). The pH at 18 Virginia record sites was usually 6.2–6.8; extremes were 5.7–7.2. Comparisons of the habitat of *E. fusiforme* with those of *E. serrifer* and *E. collis* are given in the accounts of those species.

DISTRIBUTION   Map 191

Etheostoma fusiforme essentially is a Coastal Plain species, ranging from Maine to Florida, west along the Gulf slope, and up the lower central Mississippi Valley (Collette 1962). It has been taken south on the Delmarva Peninsula almost to Virginia. Apparently it was introduced to a few montane ponds in North Carolina (Bailey et al. 1954).

The swamp darter has three distributional peculiarities in Virginia: its allopatry with *E. collis* (see that species); the existence of populations as far west as the middle Piedmont in the Potomac (Coastal Plain populations only in Maryland), James, and Chowan drainages (to headwaters in the Chowan); and its absence from the Rappahannock and York drainages. The latter two aspects are difficult to explain, particularly in combination. The high sea levels, higher than at present, caused by melting of some continental glaciers may have eliminated Coastal Plain populations of the Rappahannock, York, and Potomac (in Virginia) drainages, and may be the factor that caused dispersal to the middle Piedmont in other drainages. However, the Piankatank drainage population, on the outer Coastal Plain between the Rappahannock and York, was not erased although the

Piankatank lacks elevations as high as those of some Coastal Plain Rappahannock and York tributaries. Upland dispersal apparently did not occur in the latter two drainages. The possibility that *E. fusiforme* occurs locally and rarely in the Rappahannock and York drainages only slightly reduces the level of the enigmas. Certain other Coastal Plain species (e.g., *Enneacanthus chaetodon* and *E. obesus*) present similar zoogeographic questions.

Abundance.—Rare to common.

REMARKS

The swamp darter is easy to care for in aquaria, interesting to watch, and one of the easiest of darter species to transport, possibly because of a low oxygen requirement (Collette 1962). Among the five darters studied experimentally by Ultsch et al. (1978), *E. fusiforme* was in a class by itself as a stillwater form that is tolerant of low oxygen concentration. Its critical oxygen tension is 2.1 mg/liter at 20°C. However, Ultsch et al. (1978) noted that this value is not especially low and that some other factor (e.g., temperature tolerance) may allow this species to persist in stagnant water during the summer.

Name.—Fusiforme—"spindle-shaped"—refers to its body form.

Carolina darter   *Etheostoma collis* (Hubbs and Cannon)

SYSTEMATICS

Etheostoma collis, subgenus *Hololepis*, was described from South Carolina in 1935. It probably is most closely related to, and more advanced than, *E. fusiforme*.

Three allopatric taxa compose the *collis* group of the Carolinas and Virginia (Collette 1962): *E. collis lepidinion* Collette in the Roanoke, Neuse, and Cape Fear drainages; *E. c. collis* in the Pee Dee drainage and the Catawba system of the Santee drainage; and *E. saludae* in the Saluda system of the Santee drainage. Collette (1962) had some doubt of their status; he stated that three species, three subspecies, or some combination of these were tenable. Collette noted that *E. saludae* was intermediate in some morphological characters between the subspecies of *E. collis*; he tentatively identified as *E. c. lepidinion* the one specimen then known from the Cape Fear drainage, adjacent to the range of *E. c. collis*. Morphology of the Cape Fear specimens collected later (6 lots; NCSM) and the recently discovered Tar drainage population (15 lots; NCSM), combined with Collette's data, allow resolution of the questions.

Only two characters were held to distinguish both forms of *E. collis* from *E. saludae* (Collette 1962; Page 1983): interorbital pores almost always 0 in *collis* vs. 2 in *saludae*; and anal spines always 1 vs. usually 2. Of our 13 Cape Fear specimens, 8 have 2 interorbital pores, 2 have 1 pore, and 3 have none, for a mean of 1.4; all have 1 anal spine. Thus they approach *E. saludae* in interorbital pores but resemble *E. collis* in anal spines. In other differential characters of the *collis* group, the Cape Fear fish align with *E. c. lepidinion*, and to a lesser extent with *E. saludae*, in infraorbital pores (4+1 in 12 specimens); they align with *E.*

c. collis and *E. saludae* in breast squamation (all naked); and they are intermediate between *E. c. collis* and *E. saludae* on one extreme and *E. c. lepidinion* in nape squamation (5–100% scaled, mean 41.2).

The Tar drainage population, within the geographic range of *E. c. lepidinion*, has nape squamation variably intermediate (0–100% scaled, mean 41.7; 22 specimens) between that of *E. c. collis* and *E. saludae* (usually 0–30% scaled, means 2.8 and 15.2) on one extreme and *E. c. lepidinion* (70–100%, mean 96.4).

Variation in the *collis* group is discordantly mosaic; no nominal taxon nor individual drainage population is sufficiently distinctive from all others in any character for taxonomic recognition. Hence we regard *E. collis* and *E. saludae* to be conspecific and do not recognize subspecies. *Etheostoma collis* and *E. saludae* were originally described in the same publication (Hubbs and Cannon 1935), *E. saludae* the first in page sequence. As first revisers, we choose the name *collis* for the broadened species. *Collis* translates to hill, hence alludes to the exclusively Piedmont range of the species; the name *saludae* has too restrictive a geographic connotation. Robins et al. (1991) followed our decision.

DESCRIPTION

Materials.—From Hubbs and Cannon (1935), Collette (1962), our 7 series (24 specimens counted) from Virginia, and 15 series (22 specimens) from the Tar drainage, North Carolina; meristics from populations of the Roanoke, Tar, and Neuse drainages. Color in life from 14 spawning adults from Virginia.

Anatomy.—A laterally blotched, speckled, or blotched and speckled darter with a short pale lateral line high on the body and 1 anal spine; adults are 25–40 mm SL. Body

Fish 320 *Etheostoma collis* adult male 33 mm SL (REJ 1145), VA, Mecklenburg County, Mines Creek, 12 March 1985.

Fish 321 *Etheostoma collis* adult female 35 mm SL (REJ 1001), VA, Charlotte County, Little Roanoke Creek, 12 July 1983.

elongate, slightly or moderately compressed; snout short, rounded; frenum present; branchiostegal membranes narrowly conjoined; preopercle margin smooth, occasionally partly and weakly serrate; caudal fin rounded or subtruncate. Breeding tubercles of male and genital papilla of female similar to those of *E. fusiforme*; male with well-developed papilla. Head dorsum naked posteriorly; nape (0)30–100% scaled; belly scaled or unscaled along midline; breast (0)10–60(80)% scaled.

Meristics.—Lateral line high on body, incomplete, midlateral scales (35)36–47, pored scales (10)13–18(22); scales above lateral line (2)3(4); scales below lateral line (7)8–10(11); circumpeduncle scales 18–22 (Page 1983). Dorsal spines 8–10; dorsal rays 11–12(13); anal spines 1(2); anal rays (6)7–8(9); pectoral rays (11)12(13). Infraorbital canal interrupted, pores usually 4+1, occasionally 3+1 or 3+0; interorbital pores almost always absent, rarely 1.

Color in Preservative.—Essentially as in *E. fusiforme*.

Color in Life Plate 40.—Spawning male moderately dark with lateral marks brown- or black-olive; dorsum ground shade pale olive, its marks medium or blackish olive. Lower head and pectoral base with greenish iridescence; iris partly coppery. Nuptial male can rapidly become paler or darker, and when darkest the breast and belly are black, lateral marks black on sooty ground, and fins black-patterned or wholly sooty. Peak darkness was seen only occasionally in some spawning males.

Paler spawning males and all spawning females with lateral and dorsal marks olive; dorsum ground shade straw. Some fish with lower head and pectoral base having yellow and green iridescence, belly with a light gold wash. First dorsal fin distally with rusty wash; on tessellated second

dorsal and caudal rays, dark marks occasionally rusty, interspaces pale yellow; lower fins clear or very pale yellow.

BIOLOGY

The biology of the Carolina darter in nature is little known. Fourteen specimens fed on microcrustaceans (copepods, ostracods, cladocerans), true flies (mostly midge, rarely blackfly larvae), and occasionally mayfly larvae (E. H. Knicely, in litt.). Both sexes of breeding adults taken in Mines Creek, Mecklenburg County, Virginia, included 1- and 2-year-old fish; the 35 males were 26–41 mm SL, mean, 31, the 38 females 25–37 mm, mean, 31. The 41-mm male is the largest Virginia specimen; Lee et al. (1980) and Page (1983) noted a 50-mm SL male from North Carolina.

Eight male and six female Carolina darters caught in Mines Creek on 12 March 1985, water 13.3°C, spawned extensively upon being placed in a 110-liter aquarium at 19–20.5°C on 13 March, continuing until they were preserved on 15 March. Their spawning may have been early for *E. collis* because spring 1985 had an early start. In North Carolina, this species may usually breed at the end of March and early April (Collette 1962).

Nuptial males, less so the females, generally roamed all bottom areas of the aquarium; dark males threatened or chased away other dark males. Male courtship included erection of the dorsal fins, tapping the female anteriorly with the snout, and beating her with pectoral fins. If receptive, she usually seemed to signal so by a downward flexion of the head. To spawn, the male mounted the female's back, erected his median fins, and spread the pelvic fins along her sides (Plate 40). Subsequent apparent stimulatory behavior by the male included rubbing his head on the female's dorsum and rapidly beating her with the pectoral fins. Spawning involved intense quivering and slight advance of the pair. Usually one egg, but sometimes as many as three, was released with each act; eggs adhered immediately to the substrate. About 95% of the spawnings occurred on gravel; others were on leaves, within moss, against the aquarium glass, and (once) on a stick.

Most spawning acts involved a dark male and a pale female. Of great interest were spawnings by pale males, which resemble females and may be called sneakers or satellites, terms applied to bluegills by Gross (1982, 1984; *Glossary*). Pale males rarely were chased away by dark males; usually they spawned after a short swim to a female being courted by a dark male, joining them just before or during the spawning act.

Eggs were opaque white when deposited; they became transparent in two minutes. Ten water-hardened eggs, some slightly oval, were 0.9–1.2 mm, mean 1.05, in length. Most hatching occurred in 9–11 days at 19–20.5°C; hatchlings were 3–4 mm TL. During daylight the larvae (approximately 500) stayed at or just below the water surface; many gathered along tank walls. At night they huddled among gravel. By four weeks after hatching, they had begun to consistently act like adult darters by remaining on or near the bottom.

HABITAT

Etheostoma collis differs from the swamp darter norm by inhabiting hilly regions on the lower and middle Piedmont. It occupies rivulets and creeks with infrequent short riffles in wooded and pasture areas. Juveniles and adults reside in pools and very slow runs, usually occurring on sand, gravel, and detritus in open and stick-littered areas. Likely they also dwell among vegetation.

The year-round and apparent breeding habitat of the only strong Virginia population we found, in Mines Creek, was gentle runs and shallow and occasionally deep pools; stream width was usually 2.5 m, range 1–6 m. The substrate was sand, gravel, and small rubble—mostly gravel—with slight amounts of silt and detritus. Water was clear and stained light amber, and the habitat contained a few small patches

of bushy aquatic moss. The Carolina darter was generally distributed through areas of open and wooded banks but was not taken in riffles. It was found regularly in a tricklelike branch of Mines Creek. The pH of the two streams was 6.8 and 6.4 (S. P. McIninch, in litt.).

Unusual occurrences of *E. collis* were in a swampy section of Roanoke Creek (where flow, strong in places, braided through bushes and trees) and in the medium-sized lower Falling River (the one specimen was in a short, narrow, mostly swift side channel below a dam).

DISTRIBUTION   Map 191

The Carolina darter occurs as localized populations on the Piedmont from the Roanoke drainage in Virginia to the Santee drainage of South Carolina. The population in the extreme upper Tar drainage of North Carolina was discovered in 1980 (A. L. Braswell, personal communication); in the Cape Fear drainage this species occupies the Deep and Haw river systems.

The preference of the Carolina darter for creeks that are unattractive to most collectors could mean that this species is not localized, just undersurveyed. However, the intensity of collecting in the lower and middle Roanoke drainage of Virginia, often with capture of *E. collis* in mind, indicates that its range is disjunctive and that some populations have declined.

In the Roanoke Creek system (cluster of records, Map 191), *E. collis* was taken in all three collections made during 1935–1959 at a site in Middle Branch of Wards Ford Creek. However, L. M. Page failed to find it there in 1975, and we did not find it there or at three other sites in the Wards Fork watershed during 1979–1983, although these sites had apparently suitable habitat. Mauney (1979) and Ney and Mauney (1981) found *E. collis* to be rare in four other branches (six sites) of Roanoke Creek. (A specimen of Mauney's [1979] *E. "fusiforme"* was reidentified as *E. collis* [INHS 74111], and we believe that the other, apparently discarded specimens were *E. collis*.) However, we took no *E. collis* in 1983 at six localities in Mauney's survey area, including some of his sites. Only a main-channel Roanoke Creek site yielded *E. collis* in 1983. The holotype series of the nominal *E. c. lepidinion*, taken in 1956, was thought to have been from a tributary of Horsepen Creek of the Roanoke Creek system (Collette 1962), but it was from a nearby separate Roanoke River tributary, Sandy Creek, where we did not find *E. collis* in 1983.

The uppermost record in the Roanoke drainage,

from lower Falling River in 1983, is as odd as the habitat (see above). Falling River is separated by a major gap from the other record sites; *E. collis* was not taken there in 1977 and 1979.

The ranges of *E. collis* and *E. fusiforme* are mutually exclusive, possibly owing to different adaptations (Collette 1962) or to ecological incompatibility of these closely related species. Evidence of incompatibility is the (atypical) occurrence of *E. fusiforme* in the Piedmont of the Chowan, James, and Potomac drainages. There the habitat of *E. fusiforme* is similar to that of *E. collis*, indicating that it could live in the Piedmont of the Roanoke if *E. collis* were absent. This is countered, however, by the apparent absence of both species from the Piedmont of the Meherrin system and by the gap between their ranges in the Roanoke of North Carolina.

Abundance.—Generally rare or uncommon; common or abundant in Mines Creek.

REMARKS

The Carolina darter joins the growing list of animals (Gross 1984; Weldon and Burghardt 1984) in which some males—sneakers or satellites—deceive other males of their species by mimicking juveniles or females in order to gain reproductive access to females.

Etheostoma collis and the similarly distributed whitemouth shiner *Notropis alborus* were considered for protective status in Virginia, but were listed as status undetermined owing to scant recent survey efforts in their territory (Jenkins and Musick 1979). Subsequent surveys indicate that the state population of *E. collis* warrants special concern status (or threatened as for *N. alborus*), but probably not that of endangered as so designated by the VDGIF (Burkhead and Jenkins 1991).

Name.—*Collis,* ''hill,'' for living in the Piedmont.

DRUMS
Family Sciaenidae

The Sciaenidae are a family of perchlike fishes that occur worldwide in estuaries and continental fringes of tropical and temperate seas. Few of the 245 species in 56 genera are freshwater fishes; the only one in North America is the freshwater drum *Aplodinotus grunniens*. The family dates back to the Upper Cretaceous, at least 70 million years ago (Berra 1981).

Sciaenids are medium to large spiny-rayed fishes whose lateral line extends to the outer edge of the tail. Their swim bladder serves as a resonating chamber; the vibration of special muscles against it produces a drumming or croaking sound (H. Smith 1905; Fremling 1978). The underwater sounds were a source of confusion to naval sonar operators until their origins were identified.

Many species, such as sea trouts, weakfishes, drums, croakers, and kingfishes, are important sport and commercial fish. Small sciaenids have been considered saltwater counterparts of the sunfishes due to the ease of their capture and to their palatability (Becker 1983). The otoliths or earstones are rather large and, as with most fishes, can be used to determine the age of a specimen. Otoliths have also been used as money and jewelry.

Name.—Sciaen-, from the Greek *skiaina* for a perch-like marine fish.

Drums   Genus *Aplodinotus* Rafinesque

A monotypic genus of North and Central America (Chao 1978). Only the male is capable of drumming.

Name.—*Aplodinotus*—"simple back" or "single back," in reference to the conjoined dorsal fins.

Freshwater drum   *Aplodinotus grunniens* Rafinesque

SYSTEMATICS

The freshwater drum was described from the Ohio River in 1819. As with many large-river fishes, *A. grunniens* exhibits little or no geographic variation in much of its range (Dymond and Hart 1927; Krumholz and Cavanah 1968; Scott and Crossman 1973).

DESCRIPTION

Materials.—From Dymond and Hart (1927), Krumholz and Cavanah (1968), Scott and Crossman (1973), Fremling (1978), and 1 Illinois and 9 Tennessee specimens. Life color from Scott and Crossman (1973) and Pflieger (1975).

Anatomy.—A silvery, compressed and high-backed, spiny-rayed fish with a subterminal mouth; adults are 250–650 mm TL. Head short, strongly declined to snout; snout blunt; mouth medium-sized, subterminal; frenum absent; upper lip with a small central pore flanked by 2 slits; pharyngeal teeth molariform, in sizeable patches; chin with 5 pits medially; branchiostegal membranes free from isthmus. The two dorsal fins partly conjoined; first dorsal arched, stout-spined; second dorsal long-based; caudal fin rounded or triangular distally; pelvic fin with distal filament. Scales ctenoid, caudal fin partly scaled. Male with single urogenital opening behind anus; female has separate urinary and genital orifices (Moen 1959).

Meristics.—Lateral line scales 48–53, all pored; additional pored scales continue to end of caudal fin; dorsal spines 8–9; second dorsal with 1 leading spine, rays 25–33; anal spines 2, second spine very strong; anal rays 7–8; pectoral rays usually 17.

Fish 322 *Aplodinotus grunniens* adult male 193 mm SL (SIUC 8946), IL, Jackson County, Big Muddy River, 11 November 1983.

Color in Preservative.—Back dark or dusky, side dusky, belly pale. Dorsal, caudal, and anal fins dusky or dark; pelvic and pectoral fins dusky or pale.

Color in Life.—Back gray, dark green, or olive-brown; body overall silver with subtle blue and purple reflections; pelvic fin often orange-tinged.

Larvae.—Described by Hogue et al. (1976) and Fuiman (1982e).

BIOLOGY

The freshwater drum is predominantly a benthic feeder. Young and small juveniles eat mostly microcrustaceans and midge larvae; larger immature aquatic insects become important food items as growth continues. Mayfly larvae and small crustaceans are significant food through most of life; adults complement the diet with crayfishes and small fishes. The pharyngeal teeth are adapted for crushing snails and mussels but mollusks constitute a relatively small part of the diet. This may be due to a decreased availability of certain mollusks in recent times, a result of increased siltation of waterways (Daiber 1953a; Scott and Crossman 1973; Sule et al. 1981).

Males mature at least one year before females, usually starting at age 3; all males are mature by age 6; virtually all females are mature by age 7 (Daiber 1953b; Wrenn 1969; Nelson 1974). Maximum recorded age is 17 years (Becker 1983). In the Clinch River, *A. grunniens* averaged 310 and 439 mm TL at ages 4 and 7 (Wollitz 1968a), comparing well with growth in other populations summarized by Wrenn (1969) and Becker (1983). Freshwater drum of 1.2 m (4 feet) and 27 kg (60 pounds) were reported by Jordan and Evermann (1898). Based partly on otoliths from aboriginal Indian sites in five states, Witt (1960) estimated that no fish he studied weighed over 11.6 kg

(25.5 pounds). The angling record is 27.7 kg (54 pounds 8 ounces) from Tennessee. The largest Virginia drum known to us, 4.8 kg (10 pounds 8 ounces), is shown in a photograph in the July 1965 issue of *Virginia Wildlife.*

Spawning typically occurs from early May through July, depending on latitude, and may extend into September; water of 18.9–22.2°C brings on spawning (Daiber 1953b; Butler 1965; Nord 1967 *in* Becker 1983; Wrenn 1969; June 1977). With the onset of the spawning season, males begin to produce a drumming sound, likely an attractant to females. Drum spawn pelagically in open water. Schools of spawning drum have been observed milling slowly at a lake surface, often breaking the water with their backs (Wirth 1958 *in* Becker 1983). Fecundity is 27,000–508,000 eggs (Daiber 1953a; Goeman 1983). Eggs are about 1 mm in diameter; they and early larvae float in the surface film (Daiber 1953a; Scott and Crossman 1973).

HABITAT

Aplodinotus grunniens inhabits lakes, reservoirs, and pools in low to moderate-gradient rivers. It occupies clear and turbid water although it seems to prefer turbidity and mud bottom (Scott and Crossman 1973; Pflieger 1975; Becker 1983). Matthews (1984) found that with increased turbidity in a reservoir, larval drum were distributed throughout the water column, contrasting with their normal concentration near the bottom. Drum occur from the shallows to depths of 12–18 m in the Great Lakes (Becker 1983).

DISTRIBUTION   Map 192

The freshwater drum has the greatest latitudinal distribution of any native North American freshwa-

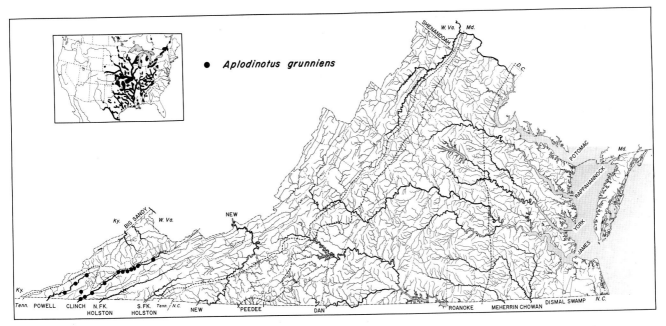

Aplodinotus grunniens

Map 192 Freshwater drum.

ter fish. It extends from the lower Hudson Bay basin and lower St. Lawrence River, widely through the Mississippi basin and along the Gulf slope, and south to Guatemala. In Virginia it is found only in the Clinch and Powell systems and is nearly confined to their main channels. We heard two reports of its occurrence in lower Copper Creek of the Clinch. Wollitz (1968b) found it in the North Fork Clinch River.

Abundance.—Unknown due to its deep-water preference; we heard of only occasional catches and saw very few on anglers' stringers.

REMARKS

Although the freshwater drum is important commercially in parts of its range, in Virginia it apparently is most frequently taken by anglers bait-fishing the bottom for catfishes and suckers. The flesh may not generally be regarded of choice taste and texture, but it is quite worthy of the table. Small fish of 0.5–1 kg (1–2 pounds) usually are more palatable than large ones (Becker 1983).

Name.—*Grunniens*—"grunting," for sounds made most intensely during the spawning season and often when caught.

References

REFERENCES

Abbott, B. J. 1959. A preliminary report on an occurrence of *Campostoma anomalum* (Rafinesque) in the Yadkin River drainage system. Virginia Journal of Science 10:177–180.

Abbott, C. C. 1862. Notes on the habits of *Aphredoderus sayanus*. Proceedings of the Academy of Natural Sciences of Philadelphia 1861:95–96.

Abbott, C. C. 1870. Mud-loving fishes. American Naturalist 4:385–391.

Abbott, C. C. 1894. A naturalist's rambles about home, 2nd edition, revised. D. Appleton, New York.

Abbott, T. M., K. L. Dickson, and W. A. Potter. 1977. *Notropis cerasinus* (Cope) record from the Appomattox River drainage. Virginia Journal of Science 28:167–168.

Able, K. 1984. Cyprinodontiformes: development. Pages 362–368 *in* Moser et al. (1984).

ACE (Army Corps of Engineers). 1943. Kanawha River Huntington District high-water profiles. Sheet 4. U.S. Army Corps of Engineers, Huntington, West Virginia.

Adams, C. C. 1901. Baseleveling and its faunal significance, with illustrations from the southeastern United States. American Naturalist 35:839–852.

Adams, C. C. 1915. The variations and ecological distribution of the snails of the genus *Io*. Memoirs of the National Academy of Science 12 (Part 2).

Adams, C. C., and T. L. Hankinson. 1928. The ecology and economics of Oneida Lake fish. Bulletin of the New York State College of Forestry at Syracuse University 1:235–548. (Also: Roosevelt Wild Life Annals 1[3–4].)

Adams, L. A. 1942. Age determination and rate of growth in *Polyodon spathula*, by means of the growth rings of the otoliths and dentary bone. American Midland Naturalist 28:617–630.

Adamson, S. W., and T. E. Wissing. 1977. Food habits and feeding periodicity of the rainbow, fantail, and banded darters in Four Mile Creek. Ohio Journal of Science 77:164–169.

Addair, J. 1944. The fishes of the Kanawha River system in West Virginia and some factors which influence their distribution. Doctoral dissertation. Ohio State University, Columbus.

Adkins, M. D., M. L. Little, J. Meadows, D. C. Tarter, R. D. Taylor, and B. Wyant. 1985. Electrophoretic analysis of blacknose dace, *Rhinicthys* [sic] *atratulus*, in two streams in West Virginia. ASB (Association of Southeastern Biologists) Bulletin 32:60.

Agassiz, L. 1854. Notice of a collection of fishes from the southern bend of the Tennessee River, Alabama. American Journal of Science and Arts 17 (Series 2):297–308, 353–365.

Ahlgren, M. O. 1988. Diet selection and the seasonal contribution of detritus to the diet of the juvenile white sucker (*Catostomus commersoni*). Page 57 *in* Abstracts of the 68th Annual Meeting of the American Society of Ichthyologists and Herpetologists.

Ali, M. A., and M. Anctil. 1977. Retinal structure and function in the walleye (*Stizostedion vitreum vitreum*) and sauger (*S. canadense*). Journal of the Fisheries Research Board of Canada 34:1467–1474.

Ali, M. A., R. A. Ryder, and M. Anctil. 1977. Photoreceptors and visual pigments as related to behavioral responses and preferred habitats of perches (*Perca* spp.) and pikeperches (*Stizostedion* spp.). Journal of the Fisheries Research Board of Canada 34:1475–1480.

Allen, J. R. M., and R. J. Wootton. 1982. Age, growth and rate of food consumption in an upland population of the three-spined stickleback, *Gasterosteus aculeatus* L. Journal of Fish Biology 21:95–105.

Allen, S. K., R. G. Thiery, and N. T. Hagstrom. 1986. Cytological evaluation of the likelihood that triploid grass carp will reproduce. Transactions of the American Fisheries Society 115:841–848.

Allen, S. K., and R. J. Wattendorf. 1987. Triploid grass carp: status and management implications. Fisheries (Bethesda) 12(4):20–24.

Alpaugh, W. C. 1972. High lethal temperatures of golden shiners (*Notemigonus crysoleucas*). Copeia 1972:185.

Alt, D. 1974. Arid climatic control of Miocene sedimentation and origin of modern drainage, southeastern United States. Pages 21–29 *in* R. Q. Oaks and J. R. DuBar, editors. Post-Miocene stratigraphy, central and southern Atlantic Coastal Plain. Utah State University Press, Logan.

American Geological Institute. 1962. Dictionary of geological terms. Doubleday, Garden City, New York.

Anderson, C. S. 1985. The structure of sculpin populations along a stream size gradient. Environmental Biology of Fishes 13:93–102.

Anderson, R. V. 1975. Selective feeding of the mottled sculpin, *Cottus bairdi* Girard, in Illinois. Transactions of the Illinois State Academy of Science 68:118–121.

Andreasson, S. 1969. Interrelations between *Cottus poecilopus* Heckel and *C. gobio* L. (Pisces) in a regulated north Swedish river. Oikos 20:540–546.

Andreasson, S. 1972. Distribution of *Cottus poecilopus* Heckel and *C. gobio* L. (Pisces) in Scandinavia. Zoologica Scripta 1:69–78.

Andreasson, S. 1973. Seasonal changes in diel activity of *Cottus poecilopus* and *C. gobio* (Pisces) at the Arctic Circle. Oikos 24:16–23.

Andrews, J. 1979. The present ice age: Cenozoic. Pages 173–218 *in* B. S. John, editor. The winters of the world: earth under the ice ages. John Wiley and Sons, New York.

Andrews, J. D. 1971. Fish for beauty in Dismal Swamp! (One man's view of the swamp). Virginia Journal of Science 22:5–13.

Angermeier, P. L. 1982. Resource seasonality and fish diets in an Illinois stream. Environmental Biology of Fishes 7:251–264.

Angermeier, P. L. 1985. Spatio-temporal patterns of foraging success for fishes in an Illinois stream. American Midland Naturalist 114:342–359.

Anjard, C. A. 1974. Centrarchidae—sunfishes. Pages 178–193 *in* A. J. Lippson and R. L. Moran, editors. Manual for identification of early developmental stages of fish of the Potomac River estuary. Maryland Department of Natural Resources, Power Plant Siting Program, Miscellaneous Publication 13, Annapolis.

Anonymous. 1955. North Fork of the Holston River, Virginia, June 28–July 4, 1954, stream survey report for the Commonwealth of Virginia State Water Control Board. Academy of Natural Sciences of Philadelphia, Philadelphia.

Anonymous. 1964. The Tennessee River navigation system: history, development, and operation. Tennessee Valley Authority, Knoxville, Tennessee.

Anonymous. 1968. [Stocking records]. Virginia Wildlife 29(7):13.

Anonymous. 1970. Conservationgram. Virginia Wildlife 31(6):13.

Anonymous. 1973. Reader's Digest scenic wonders of America. Reader's Digest Association, Pleasantville, New York.

Anonymous. 1974. Endangered vertebrates of Virginia. Virginia Wildlife 35(9):13–15, 18.

Anonymous. 1977. Threatened and endangered plants and animals. Federal Register 42 (9 September 1977): 45527–45529.

Anonymous. [1983]. Snail darter survey—July, August, and October 1983. U.S. Fish and Wildlife Service, Endangered Species Field Office, Asheville, North Carolina.

Anonymous. 1984. Obituary, Edward C. Raney. Fisheries (Bethesda) 9(4):28–29.

Anonymous. 1986. Carp to embark on a new career in

Craig County. Virginia Water Resources Research Center, Water News 17(3):3. (Virginia Polytechnic Institute and State University, Blacksburg.)

Anonymous. 1989a. Endangered and threatened wildlife and plants, subpart B—lists. U.S. Fish and Wildlife Service. Code of Federal Regulations 50 CFR 17.11 & 17.12, January 1, 1989.

Anonymous. 1989b. Endangered and threatened wildlife and plants; animal notice of review. Federal Register 54 (6 January 1989):554–579.

Anonymous. 1989c. Regional news: region 6. U.S. Fish and Wildlife Service Endangered Species Technical Bulletin 14(1–2):15.

Anonymous. 1990. Fishing guide. Virginia Wildlife 51(4): 19–34.

Applegate, V. C. 1950. Natural history of the sea lamprey (*Petromyzon marinus*) in Michigan. U.S. Fish and Wildlife Service, Special Scientific Report—Fisheries 55.

Arber, E., and A. G. Bradley, editors. 1910. Travel and works of Captain John Smith. John Grant, Edinburgh, UK.

Armstrong, J. G., and J. D. Williams. 1971. Cave and spring fishes of the southern bend of the Tennessee River. Journal of the Tennessee Academy of Science 46:107–115.

Atkins, C. G. 1905. Culture of the fallfish or chub. American Fish Culturist 2:189.

Atkinson, C. E. 1951. Feeding habits of shad (*Alosa sapidissima*) in fresh water. Ecology 32:556–557.

Atran, S. M., J. G. Loesch, W. H. Kriete, and B. Rizzo. 1983. Feasibility study of fish passage facilities in the James River, Richmond, Virginia. Virginia Institute of Marine Science Applied Marine Science and Ocean Engineering Special Report 269 to Virginia Department of Game and Inland Fisheries (Federal Aid in Sport Fish Restoration Project F-39-P Study V, Job 5, Completion Report) Richmond, Virginia.

Atz, J. W. 1940. Reproductive behavior in the eastern johnny darter, *Boleosoma nigrum olmstedi* (Storer). Copeia 1940:100–106.

Auer, N. A., editor. 1982a. Identification of larval fishes of the Great Lakes basin with emphasis on the Lake Michigan drainage. Great Lakes Fishery Commission Special Publication 82-3, Ann Arbor, Michigan.

Auer, N. A. 1982b. Family Anguillidae, freshwater eels. Page 63 *in* Auer (1982a).

Auer, N. A. 1982c. Family Salmonidae, trouts. Pages 80–145 *in* Auer (1982a).

Auer, N. A. 1982d. Family Aphredoderidae, pirate perch. Pages 458–463 *in* Auer (1982a).

Auer, N. A. 1982e. Family Percopsidae, trout-perches. Pages 464–469 *in* Auer (1982a).

Auer, N. A. 1982f. Family Percidae, perches, Pages 581–648 *in* Auer (1982a).

Avise, J. C., and M. H. Smith. 1974a. Biochemical genetics of sunfish. I. Geographic variation and subspecific intergradation in the bluegill, *Lepomis macrochirus*. Evolution 28:42–56.

Avise, J. C., and M. H. Smith. 1974b. Biochemical genetics of sunfish. II. Genic similarity between hybridizing species. American Naturalist 108:458–472.

Avise, J. C., and M. H. Smith. 1977. Gene frequency comparisons between sunfish (Centrarchidae) populations at various stages of evolutionary divergence. Systematic Zoology 26:319–335.

Avise, J. C., D. O. Straney, and M. H. Smith. 1977. Biochemical genetics of sunfish. IV. Relationships of centrarchid genera. Copeia 1977:250–258.

Axelrod, H. R. 1970. Photography for aquarists. Tropical Fish Hobbyist Publications, Neptune City, New Jersey.

Axon, J. R. 1978. An evaluation of the muskellunge fishery in Cave Run Lake, Kentucky. American Fisheries Society Special Publication 11:328–333.

Axon, J. R. 1981. Development of the muskellunge fishery at Cave Run Lake in 1974–1979. Kentucky Department of Fish and Wildlife Resources, Federal Aid in Sport Fish Restoration, Project F-39(2–5), F-40(1–2), Final Report, Frankfort.

Axon, J. R., and D. K. Whitehurst. 1985. Striped bass management in lakes with emphasis on management problems. Transactions of the American Fisheries Society 114:8–11.

Bachman, R. A. 1984. Foraging behavior of free-ranging wild and hatchery brown trout in a stream. Transactions of the American Fisheries Society 113:1–32.

Bachman, R. A. 1985. How trout feed. Trout 26(1):10–16.

Bailey, D. S. 1974. The occurrence of mercury in the fish and sediment of the North Fork of the Holston River 1970–1972. Virginia State Water Control Board, Basic Data Bulletin 41, Richmond.

Bailey, J. E. 1952. Life history and ecology of the sculpin *Cottus bairdi punctulatus* in southwestern Montana. Copeia 1952:243–255.

Bailey, J. R. 1977. Freshwater fishes. Pages 265–298 *in* J. E. Cooper, S. S. Robinson, and J. B. Funderberg, editors. Endangered and threatened plants and animals of North Carolina. North Carolina State Museum of Natural History, Raleigh.

Bailey, J. R., and J. A. Oliver. 1939. The fishes of the Connecticut watershed. Pages 150–189 *in* Biological survey of the Connecticut watershed. New Hampshire Fish and Game Department Survey Report 4, Concord.

Bailey, R. M. 1938a. A systematic revision of the centrarchid fishes, with a discussion of their distribution, variations, and probable interrelationships. Doctoral dissertation. University of Michigan, Ann Arbor.

Bailey, R. M. 1938b. The fishes of the Merrimack watershed. Pages 149–185 *in* Biological survey of the Merrimack watershed. New Hampshire Fish and Game Department Survey Report 3, Concord.

Bailey, R. M. 1941. Geographic variation in *Mesogonistius chaetodon* (Baird), with a description of a new subspecies from Georgia and Florida. Occasional Papers of the Museum of Zoology University of Michigan 454.

Bailey, R. M. 1945. Review of "Some considerations on the distribution of fishes in Ontario" by I. Radforth. Copeia 1945:125–126.

Bailey, R. M. 1948. Status, relationships, and characters of the percid fish, *Poecilichthys sagitta* Jordan and Swain. Copeia 1948:77–85.

Bailey, R. M. 1951. A checklist of the fishes of Iowa with keys for identification. Pages 187–238 *in* J. R. Harlan and E. B. Speaker, editors. Iowa fish and fishing. Iowa State Conservation Commission, Des Moines.

Bailey, R. M. 1954. Distribution of the American cyprinid fish *Hybognathus hankinsoni* with comments on its original description. Copeia 1954:289–291.

Bailey, R. M. 1956. A revised list of the fishes of Iowa, with keys for identification. Pages 327–374 *in* J. R. Harlan and E. B. Speaker, editors. Iowa fish and fishing. Iowa State Conservation Commission. Des Moines.

Bailey, R. M. 1959a. A new catostomid fish, *Moxostoma* (*Thoburnia*) *atripinne*, from the Green River drainage, Kentucky and Tennessee. Occasional Papers of the Museum of Zoology University of Michigan 599.

Bailey, R. M. 1959b. *Etheostoma acuticeps*, a new darter from the Tennessee River system, with remarks on the subgenus *Nothonotus*. Occasional Papers of the Museum of Zoology University of Michigan 603.

Bailey, R. M. 1975. Review of "Freshwater fishes of Canada" by W. B. Scott and E. J. Crossman. Transactions of the American Fisheries Society 104:161–162.

Bailey, R. M. 1980. Comments on the classification and nomenclature of lampreys—an alternative view. Canadian Journal of Fisheries and Aquatic Sciences 37:1626–1629.

Bailey, R. M. 1982a. Comment on Reeve M. Bailey's view of lampry systematics: Reply. Canadian Journal of Fisheries and Aquatic Sciences 39:1217–1220.

Bailey, R. M. 1982b. Review of "Atlas of North American freshwater fishes" by D. S. Lee, C. R. Gilbert, C. H. Hocutt, R. E. Jenkins, D. E. McAllister, and J. R. Stauffer. Copeia 1982:983–985.

Bailey, R. M., and M. O. Allum. 1962. Fishes of South Dakota. Miscellaneous Publications Museum of Zoology University of Michigan 119.

Bailey, R. M., and C. E. Bond. 1963. Four new species of freshwater sculpins, genus *Cottus*, from western North America. Occasional Papers of the Museum of Zoology University of Michigan 634.

Bailey, R. M., and M. F. Dimick. 1949. *Cottus hubbsi*, a new cottid fish from the Columbia River system in Washington and Idaho. Occasional Papers of the Museum of Zoology University of Michigan 513.

Bailey, R. M., and D. A. Etnier. 1988. Comments on the subgenera of darters (Percidae) with descriptions of two new species of *Etheostoma* (*Ulocentra*) from southeastern United States. Miscellaneous Publications Museum of Zoology, University of Michigan 175.

Bailey, R. M., and R. H. Gibbs. 1956. *Notropis callitaenia*, a new cyprinid fish from Alabama, Florida, and Georgia. Occasional Papers of the Museum of Zoology University of Michigan 576.

Bailey, R. M., and C. R. Gilbert. 1960. The American cyprinid fish *Notropis kanawha* identified as an interspecific hybrid. Copeia 1960:354–357.

Bailey, R. M., and W. A. Gosline. 1955. Variation and systematic significance of vertebral counts in the American fishes of the family Percidae. Miscellaneous Publications Museum of Zoology University of Michigan 93.

Bailey, R. M., and H. M. Harrison. 1948. Food habits of

the southern channel catfish (*Ictalurus lacustris puncta-tus*) in the Des Moines River, Iowa. Transactions of the American Fisheries Society 75:110–138.

Bailey, R. M., and C. L. Hubbs. 1949. The black basses (*Micropterus*) of Florida, with description of a new species. Occasional Papers of the Museum of Zoology University of Michigan 516.

Bailey, R. M., and K. F. Lagler. 1938. An analysis of hybridization in a population of stunted sunfishes in New York. Papers of the Michigan Academy of Science, Arts and Letters 23:577–606.

Bailey, R. M., and R. R. Miller. 1954. Request that the generic name "Notropis" Rafinesque, 1818 (class Osteichthyes, order Cyprinida, family Cyprinidae) be placed on the "Official list of generic names in zoology": question of possible use of the Commission's plenary powers to determine the gender of this generic name. Bulletin of Zoological Nomenclature 9 (9):272–274.

Bailey, R. M., and C. R. Robins. 1988a. Changes in North American fish names, especially as related to the International Code of Zoological Nomenclature, 1985. Bulletin of Zoological Nomenclature 45(2):92–103.

Bailey, R. M., and C. R. Robins. 1988b. *Ameiurus* Rafinesque, 1820 (Osteichthyes, Siluriformes): proposed designation of *Silurus lividus* Rafinesque, 1820 (= *Pimelodus natalis* Lesueur, 1819) as the type species. Bulletin of Zoological Nomenclature 45(2):135–137.

Bailey, R. M., and G. R. Smith. 1981. Origin and geography of the fish fauna of the Laurentian Great Lakes basin. Canadian Journal of Fisheries and Aquatic Sciences 38:1539–1561.

Bailey, R. M., H. E. Winn, and C. L. Smith. 1954. Fishes from the Escambia River Alabama and Florida, with ecologic and taxonomic notes. Proceedings of the Academy of Natural Sciences of Philadelphia 106:109–164.

Bailey, R. M., and six coauthors. 1970. A list of common and scientific names of fishes from the United States and Canada. American Fisheries Society Special Publication 6.

Baker, F. C. 1916. The relation of mollusks to fish in Oneida Lake. New York State College of Forestry at Syracuse University 16 (Technical Publication 4):1–365.

Baker, F. C. 1918. The relation of shellfish to fish in Oneida Lake, New York. New York State College of Forestry at Syracuse University 17 (Circular 21):1–47.

Baker, J. M. 1979. Larval development of the greenside darter, *Etheostoma blennioides newmanii* (Agassiz). Pages 70–91 *in* R. D. Hoyt, editor. Proceedings, 3rd symposium on larval fish. Western Kentucky University, Bowling Green.

Baker, J. P. 1984. Fish. Pages 5–74 to 5–129 *in* A. P. Altshuller and R. A. Linthurst, editors. The acidic deposition phenomenon and its effects: critical assessment review papers, volume 2. U.S. Environmental Protection Agency, Report EPA-600/8-83-016BF, Washington, D.C.

Baker, J. R. 1978. The fantail darter *Etheostoma flabellare* in the Salt River drainage, Kentucky. Transactions of the Kentucky Academy of Science 39:150–159.

Baker, W. D. 1966. Power Reservoir investigations. North Carolina Wildlife Resources Commission, Federal Aid in Sport Fish Restoration, Project F-16-R, Jobs IIIA–C, Final Report, Raleigh.

Ball, R. C. 1937. A seasonal study of the food habits of the common shiner [*Notropis cornutus* (Mitchill)]. Master's thesis. Ohio State University, Columbus. (Not seen; cited in Marshall 1939; Carlander 1969.)

Ball, R. C. 1948. Relationship between available fish food, feeding habits of fish and total fish production in a Michigan lake. Michigan Agricultural Experiment Station Technical Bulletin 206, Michigan State College, East Lansing.

Ballard, W. W., and R. G. Needham. 1964. Normal embryonic stage of *Polyodon spathula*. Journal of Morphology 114:465–477.

Balon, E. K. 1980a. Early ontogeny of the brook charr, *Salvelinus* (*Baione*) *fontinalis*. Pages 631–666 *in* E. K. Balon, editor. Charrs: salmonid fishes of the genus *Salvelinus*. Dr. W. Junk, The Hague, Netherlands.

Balon, E. K. 1980b. Comparative ontogeny of charrs. Pages 703–720 *in* E. K. Balon, editor. Charrs: salmonid fishes of the genus *Salvelinus*. Dr. W. Junk, The Hague, Netherlands.

Banarescu, P. 1964. Fauna republicii populare Romine, volume 13, Pisces—Osteichthyes. Editura Academiei Republicii Populare Romine, Bucharest, Romania.

Banarescu, P., and T. T. Nalbant. 1967. Revision of the genus *Sarcocheilichthys* (Pisces, Cyprinidae). Vestnik Ceskoslovenske Spolecnosti Zoologicke 31:293–312.

Barber, W. E., and W. L. Minckley. 1971. Summer foods of the cyprinid fish *Semotilus atromaculatus*. Transactions of the American Fisheries Society 100:283–289.

Barbour, C. D., and J. H. Brown. 1974. Fish species diversity in lakes. American Naturalist 108:473–489.

Barclay, L. A. 1984. Summer home ranges of five cyprinid fishes in an upper Cumberland Plateau stream, and effects of predation on home range size. ASB (Association of Southeastern Biologists) Bulletin 31:48.

Bardack, D., and R. Zangerl. 1971. Lampreys in the fossil record. Pages 67–84 *in* M. W. Hardisty and I. C. Potter, editors. The biology of lampreys, volume 1. Academic Press, New York.

Barker, J. 1965. Observations on some areas of the Delaware River between Belvidere and Scudders Falls, New Jersey in respect to their utilization by American shad, *Alosa sapidissima* (Wilson), for spawning purposes in 1963 and 1964. Bureau of Fisheries Laboratory, Miscellaneous Report 28, New Jersey Department of Conservation and Economic Development, Trenton. (Not seen; cited in Marcy 1972.)

Barkuloo, J. M. 1970. Taxonomic status and reproduction of striped bass (*Morone saxatilis*) in Florida. U.S. Bureau of Sport Fisheries and Wildlife Technical Papers 44.

Barnes, M. D., D. L. Rice, and T. E. Linkous. 1985. New locality records of the longnose dace, *Rhinichthys cataractae* (Cyprinidae), in the upper Ohio River Valley. Ohio Journal of Science 85:135–136.

Barry, R. G. 1983. Late-Pleistocene climatology. Pages 390–407 *in* H. E. Wright and S. C. Porter, editors.

Late-Quaternary environments of the United States, volume 1. University of Minnesota Press, Minneapolis.

Bart, H. L., and R. C. Cashner. 1980. New records for the northern studfish, *Fundulus catenatus*, in the lower Mississippi and Gulf coastal drainages. Proceedings of the Southeastern Fishes Council 3(2):1–4.

Bart, H. L., and L. M. Page. 1991. Morphology and adaptive significance of fin knobs in egg-clustering darters. Copeia 1991:80–86.

Bartnik, V. G. 1970. Reproductive isolation between two sympatric dace, *Rhinichthys atratulus* and *R. cataractae*, in Manitoba. Journal of the Fisheries Research Board of Canada 27:2125–2141.

Bartnik, V. G. 1972. Comparison of the breeding habits of two subspecies of longnose dace, *Rhinichthys cataractae*. Canadian Journal of Zoology 50:83–86.

Barton, B. A. 1980. Spawning migrations, age and growth, and summer feeding of white and longnose suckers in an irrigation reservoir. Canadian Field-Naturalist 94:300–304.

Bath, D. W., J. M. O'Conner, J. B. Alber, and L. G. Arvidson. 1981. Development and identification of larval Atlantic sturgeon (*Acipenser oxyrhynchus*) and shortnose sturgeon (*A. brevirostrum*) from the Hudson River estuary, New York. Copeia 1981:711–717.

Battle, H. I. 1940. The embryology and larval development of the goldfish (*Carassius auratus* L.) from Lake Erie. Ohio Journal of Science 40:82–93.

Bauer, B. H., and B. A. Branson. 1979. Distributional records for and additions to the ichthyofauna of Kentucky. Transactions of the Kentucky Academy of Science 40:53–55.

Bauer, B. H., G. R. Dinkins, and D. A. Etnier. 1983. Discovery of *Noturus baileyi* and *N. flavipinnis* in Citico Creek, Little Tennessee River system. Copeia 1983:558–560.

Baugh, T. 1980. A net full of natives: some North American fishes. R/C Modeler, Sierra Madre, California.

Baxter, G. T., and J. R. Simon. 1970. Wyoming fishes. Wyoming Game and Fish Department Bulletin 4.

Bayless, J. D. 1968. Striped bass hatching and hybridization experiments. Proceedings of the Annual Conference Southeastern Association of Game and Fish Commissioners 21(1967):233–244.

Bayless, J. D. 1972. Artificial propagation and hybridization of striped bass, *Morone saxatilis* (Walbaum). South Carolina Wildlife and Marine Resources Department, Columbia.

Bayless, J. D., and W. B. Smith. 1962. Survey and classification of the Neuse River and tributaries, North Carolina (with Appendix). North Carolina Wildlife Resources Commission, Federal Aid in Sport Fish Restoration, Project F-14-R, Job I-A, Final Report, Raleigh.

Beamish, F. W. H. 1980. Biology of the North American anadromous sea lamprey, *Petromyzon marinus*. Canadian Journal of Fisheries and Aquatic Sciences 37:1924–1943.

Beamish, F. W. H., and L. S. Austin. 1985. Growth of the mountain brook lamprey, *Ichthyomyzon greeleyi* Hubbs and Trautman. Copeia 1985:881–890.

Beamish, F. W. H., and T. E. Medland. 1988a. Metamorphosis of the mountain brook lamprey, *Ichthyomyzon greeleyi*. Environmental Biology of Fishes 23:45–54.

Beamish, F. W. H., and T. E. Medland. 1988b. Age determination of lampreys. Transactions of the American Fisheries Society 117:63–71.

Beamish, F. W. H., and I. C. Potter. 1972. Timing of changes in the blood, morphology, and behavior of *Petromyzon marinus* during metamorphosis. Journal of the Fisheries Research Board of Canada 29:1277–1282.

Beamish, R. J. 1973. Determination of age and growth of populations of the white sucker (*Catostomus commersoni*) exhibiting a wide range of size at maturity. Journal of the Fisheries Research Board of Canada 30:607–616.

Beamish, R. J. 1974. Growth and survival of white suckers (*Catostomus commersoni*) in an acidified lake. Journal of the Fisheries Research Board of Canada 31:49–54.

Beamish, R. J., and E. J. Crossman. 1977. Validity of the subspecies designation for the dwarf white sucker (*Catostomus commersoni utawana*). Journal of the Fisheries Research Board of Canada 34:371–378.

Bean, B. A., and A. C. Weed. 1911. Recent additions to the fish fauna of the District of Columbia. Proceedings of the Biological Society of Washington 24:171–174.

Bean, T. H. 1880. Check-list of duplicates of North American fishes distributed by the Smithsonian Institution in behalf of the United States National Museum, 1877–1880. Proceedings of the United States National Museum 3:75–116.

Bean, T. H. 1903. The food and game fishes of New York. New York Forest Fish and Game Commission Report 7:247–460.

Beck, B. 1971. The many miles of Dan River. Virginia Wildlife 32(5):7–9, 22.

Becker, G. C. 1983. Fishes of Wisconsin. University of Wisconsin Press, Madison.

Beckham, E. C. 1980. *Percina gymnocephala*, a new percid fish of the subgenus *Alvordius*, from the New River in North Carolina, Virginia, and West Virginia. Occasional Papers of the Museum of Zoology Louisiana State University 57.

Beckham, E. C. 1986. Systematics and redescription of the blackside darter, *Percina maculata* (Girard), (Pisces: Percidae). Occasional Papers of the Museum of Zoology Louisiana State University 62.

Beckman, W. C. 1952. Guide to the fishes of Colorado. University of Colorado Museum, Boulder.

Beecher, H. A. 1979. Comparative functional morphology and ecological isolating mechanisms in sympatric fishes of the genus *Carpiodes* in northwestern Florida. Doctoral dissertation. Florida State University, Tallahassee.

Beecher, H. A. 1980. Habitat segregation of Florida carpsuckers (Osteichthyes: Catostomidae: *Carpiodes*). Florida Scientist 43:92–97.

Beets, J. P. 1979. Population dynamics of the stoneroller minnow, *Campostoma anomalum anomalum* (Rafinesque), in streams of a five-county area in upper east Tennessee. Master's thesis. University of Tennessee, Knoxville.

Behnke, R. J. 1962. Review of "The Balkan Lake Ohrid and its living world" by S. Stankovic. Copeia 1962:478–479.

Behnke, R. J. 1966. Relationships of the far eastern trout, *Salmo mykiss* Walbaum. Copeia 1966:346–348.

Behnke, R. J. 1968. A new subgenus and species of trout, *Salmo (Platysalmo) platycephalus*, from southcentral Turkey, with comments on the classification of the subfamily Salmoninae. Mitteilungen aus dem Hamburgischen Zoologischen Museum und Institut 66:1–15.

Behnke, R. J. 1972. The systematics of salmonid fishes of recently glaciated lakes. Journal of the Fisheries Research Board of Canada 29:639–671.

Behnke, R. J. 1979. Monograph of the native trouts of the genus *Salmo* of western North America. Report to U.S. Fish and Wildlife Service, Rocky Mountain Regional Office, Denver.

Behnke, R. J. 1980. A systematic review of the genus *Salvelinus*. Pages 441–480 *in* E. K. Balon, editor. Charrs: salmonid fishes of the genus *Salvelinus*. Dr. W. Junk, The Hague, Netherlands.

Behnke, R. J. 1984. Steelhead trout. Trout 25(1):43–48.

Behnke, R. J. 1986. Brown trout. Trout 27(1):42–47.

Behnke, R. J. 1990. About trout: how many species? Trout 31(3):63, 66–69.

Behnke, R. J. 1992. Native trout of western North America. American Fisheries Society Monograph 6.

Behnke, R. J., T. P. Koh, and P. R. Needham. 1962. Status of the landlocked salmonid fishes of Formosa with a review of *Oncorhynchus masou* (Brevoort). Copeia 1962:400–407.

Behnke, R. J., and M. Zarn. 1976. Biology and management of threatened and endangered western trouts. U.S. Forest Service General Technical Report RM-28.

Beitch, E. 1963. Striped bass histo-morphological study. Virginia Commission of Game and Inland Fisheries, Federal Aid in Sport Fish Restoration, Project F-5-R-8, Job 11, September 26, 1960–February 28, 1962. Final Report, Richmond.

Belding, D. L. 1921. A report upon the alewife fisheries of Massachusetts. Massachusetts Department of Conservation, Division of Fisheries and Game. (Not seen; cited in Norden 1967.)

Bell, D. E., A. R. Jones, and K. W. Prather. 1985. Evaluation of redbreast sunfish stockings in Kentucky streams. Kentucky Department of Fish and Wildlife Resources, Fisheries Bulletin 75, Frankfort.

Bell, R. 1897. Recent explorations to the south of Hudson Bay. Geographical Journal 10:1–18.

Benfield, E. F., and J. Cairns. 1974. A three-year report: pre-impoundment ecological reconnaissance of the New River in the area of the proposed Appalachian Power Company's Blue Ridge Project. Center for Environmental Studies, Virginia Polytechnic Institute and State University, Blacksburg.

Bennett, G. W., and W. F. Childers. 1966. The lake chubsucker as a forage species. Progressive Fish-Culturist 28:89–92.

Berg, L. S. 1948. Freshwater fishes of the U.S.S.R. and adjacent countries, volume I, 4th edition. Zoologicheskii Institut Akademii Nauk SSSR, Guide to the Fauna of the USSR 27. (Translated from Russian: Israel Program for Scientific Translations for the National Science Foundation, Washington, D.C., 1962.)

Berggren, T. J., and J. T. Lieberman. 1978. Relative contributions of Hudson, Chesapeake, and Roanoke striped bass, *Morone saxatilis*, stocks to the Atlantic coast fishery. U.S. National Marine Fisheries Service Fishery Bulletin 76:335–345.

Berggren, W. A., and J. A. Van Couvering. 1974. The Late Neogene biostratigraphy, geochronology, and paleoclimatology of the last 15 m.y. Palaeogeography, Palaeoclimatology, Palaeoecology 16:1–216.

Berggren, W. A., and J. A. Van Couvering. 1978. Biochronology. American Association of Petroleum Geologists Studies in Geology 6:39–56.

Berkman, H. E., and C. F. Rabeni. 1987. Effect of siltation on stream fish communities. Environmental Biology of Fishes 18:285–294.

Bernet, C. K., Y. J. McGaha, and C. M. Cooper. 1977. Observations on the growth rate of young paddlefish. Journal of the Mississippi Academy of Sciences 22.

Berra, T. M. 1981. An atlas of distribution of the freshwater fish families of the world. University of Nebraska Press, Lincoln.

Berry, F. H. 1958. Age and growth of gizzard shad in Lake Newman, Florida. Proceedings of the Annual Conference Southeastern Association of Game and Fish Commissioners 11(1957):318–331.

Berry, F. H. 1964. Review and emendation of "Family Clupeidae" by S. F. Hildebrand. Copeia 1964:720–730.

Berry, F. H., M. T. Huish, and H. Moody. 1956. Spawning mortality of the threadfin shad, *Dorosoma petenense* (Günther), in Florida. Copeia 1956:192.

Berst, A. H., P. E. Ihssen, G. R. Spangler, G. B. Ayles, and G. W. Martin. 1980. The splake, a hybrid charr *Salvelinus namaycush* × *S. fontinalis*. Pages 841–887 *in* E. K. Balon, editor. Charrs: salmonid fishes of the genus *Salvelinus*. Dr. W. Junk, The Hague, Netherlands.

Beyerle, G. B., and E. L. Cooper. 1960. Growth of brown trout in selected Pennsylvania streams. Transactions of the American Fisheries Society 89:255–262.

Bicknell, E. P., and F. B. Dresslar. 1885. A review of the species of the genus *Semotilus*. Proceedings of the Academy of Natural Sciences of Philadelphia 37:14–18.

Bigelow, H. B., and W. C. Schroeder. 1948. Cyclostomes. Pages 29–58 *in* J. Tee-Van, editor. Fishes of the western North Atlantic, part 1. Sears Foundation for Marine Research, Yale University, New Haven, Connecticut.

Bigelow, H. B., and W. C. Schroeder. 1953. Fishes of the Gulf of Maine. U.S. Fish and Wildlife Service Fishery Bulletin 53. (Reprinted 1964, Museum of Comparative Zoology, Harvard University, Cambridge, Massachusetts.)

Bigelow, H. B., and W. C. Schroeder. 1964. Family Osmeridae. Pages 553–597 *in* Fishes of the western North Atlantic, part 3. Sears Foundation for Marine Research, Yale University, New Haven, Connecticut.

Bigelow, H. B., and W. W. Welsh. 1925. Fishes of the Gulf of Maine. U.S. Bureau of Fisheries Bulletin 40.

Biggins, R. 1989. Coal mining and the decline of freshwater mussels. U.S. Fish and Wildlife Service Endangered Species Technical Bulletin 14(5):5.

Biggs, T. H. 1974. Geographic and cultural names in Virginia. Virginia Division of Mineral Resources, Information Circular 20, Charlottesville.

Bird, S. O. 1985. Eden in peril: the troubled waters of the Chesapeake Bay. Virginia Division of Mineral Resources, Publication 56, Charlottesville.

Birdsong, R. S., and R. W. Yerger. 1967. A natural population of hybrid sunfishes: *Lepomis macrochirus* × *Chaenobryttus gulosus*. Copeia 1967:62–71.

Birkhead, W. S. 1972. Toxicity of stings of ariid and ictalurid catfishes. Copeia 1972:790–807.

Bisson, P. A., and C. E. Bond. 1971. Origin and distribution of the fishes of Harney Basin, Oregon. Copeia. 1971:268–281.

Bisson, P. A., and P. E. Reimers. 1977. Geographic variation among Pacific Northwest populations of longnose dace, *Rhinichthys cataractae*. Copeia 1977:518–522.

Black, J. D. 1945. Natural history of the northern mimic shiner, *Notropis volucellus volucellus* Cope. Investigations of Indiana Lakes and Streams 2:449–469.

Blanc, M., P. Banarescu, J.-L. Gaudet, and J.-C. Hureau. 1971. European inland water fish: a multilingual catalogue. Fishing News (Books), London.

Blankenship, S., and V. H. Resh. 1971. An unusual record of feeding in *Cottus carolinae*. Transactions of the Kentucky Academy of Science 32:10–11.

Bloom, A. L. 1983a. Sea level and coastal morphology of the United States through the Late Wisconsin glacial maximum. Pages 215–229 *in* H. E. Wright and S. C. Porter, editors. Late-Quaternary environments of the United States, volume 1. University of Minnesota Press, Minneapolis.

Bloom, A. L. 1983b. Sea level and coastal changes. Pages 42–51 *in* H. E. Wright, editor. Late-Quaternary environments of the United States, volume 2. University of Minnesota Press, Minneapolis.

Blumer, L. S. 1982. A bibliography and categorization of bony fishes exhibiting parental care. Zoological Journal of the Linnean Society 76:1–22.

Blumer, L. S. 1985a. Reproductive natural history of the brown bullhead *Ictalurus nebulosus* in Michigan. American Midland Naturalist 114:318–330.

Blumer, L. S. 1985b. The significance of biparental care in the brown bullhead, *Ictalurus nebulosus*. Environmental Biology of Fishes 12:231–236.

Blumer, L. S. 1986. The function of parental care in the brown bullhead *Ictalurus nebulosus*. American Midland Naturalist 115:234–238.

Boaze, J. L. 1972. Effects of landlocked alewife introduction on white bass and walleye populations, Claytor Lake, Virginia. Master's thesis. Virginia Polytechnic Institute and State University, Blacksburg.

Boaze, J. L., and R. T. Lackey. 1974. Age, growth and utilization of landlocked alewives in Claytor Lake Virginia. Progressive Fish-Culturist 36:163–164.

Bodola, A. 1966. Life history of the gizzard shad, *Dorosoma cepedianum* (Lesueur), in western Lake Erie. U.S. Fish and Wildlife Service Fishery Bulletin 65:391–425.

Bogan, A. E., and C. M. Bogan. 1985. Faunal remains. Pages 369–410 *in* G. F. Schroedl, R. P. S. Davis, and C. C. Boyd, editors. Archeological contexts and assemblages at Martin Farm. University of Tennessee Department of Anthropology, Report of Investigations 39, Knoxville. (Also: Tennessee Valley Authority Publications in Anthropology 37, Knoxville.)

Böhlke, E. B. 1984. Catalog of type specimens in the ichthyological collection of the Academy of Natural Sciences of Philadelphia. Special Publication Academy of Natural Sciences of Philadelphia 14.

Böhlke, J. E. 1953. A catalogue of the type specimens of recent fishes in the Natural History Museum of Stanford University. Stanford Ichthyological Bulletin 5:1–168.

Boles, H. 1983. Recovery plan for spotfin chub *Hybopsis monacha*. U.S. Fish and Wildlife Service, Atlanta.

Boltz, J. M., and J. R. Stauffer. 1986. Branchial brooding in the pirate perch, *Aphredoderus sayanus* (Gilliams). Copeia 1986:1030–1031.

Boltz, J. M., and J. R. Stauffer. 1993. Systematics of *Aphredoderus sayanus* (Teleostei: Aphredoderidae). Copeia 1993:81–98.

Bond, C. E. 1961. Keys to Oregon freshwater fishes. Oregon Agricultural Experiment Station Technical Bulletin 58.

Bond, C. E. 1979. Biology of fishes. W. B. Saunders, Philadelphia.

Bonham, K. 1946. Management of a small farm pond in Texas. Journal of Wildlife Management 10:1–4.

Bonn, E. W., W. M. Bailey, J. D. Bayless, K. E. Erickson, and R. E. Stevens, editors. 1976. Guidelines for striped bass culture. American Fisheries Society, Southern Division, Striped Bass Committee, Bethesda, Maryland.

Bookstein, F. L., B. Chernoff, R. L. Elder, J. M. Humphries, G. R. Smith, and R. E. Strauss. 1985. Morphometrics in evolutionary biology. Special Publication Academy Natural Sciences of Philadelphia 15.

Boreman, J., and H. M. Austin. 1985. Production and harvest of anadromous striped bass stocks along the Atlantic Coast. Transactions of the American Fisheries Society 114:3–7.

Boreske, J. R. 1974. A review of the North American fossil amiid fishes. Bulletin of the Museum of Comparative Zoology 146:1–87.

Borodin, N. 1925. Biological observations on the Atlantic sturgeon *Acipenser sturio*. Transactions of the American Fisheries Society 55:184–190.

Bortone, S. A. 1972. Recent capture of *Phoxinus oreas* (Pisces:Cyprinidae) from the Yadkin–Pee Dee River drainage, North Carolina. Journal of the Elisha Mitchell Scientific Society 88:28–29.

Boschung, H. T. 1989. Atlas of fishes of the upper Tombigbee River system, Alabama–Mississippi. Proceedings of the Southeastern Fishes Council 19:1–104.

Boschung, H. T., J. D. Williams, D. W. Gotshall, D. K. Caldwell, and M. C. Caldwell. 1983. The Audubon Society field guide to North American fishes, whales, and dolphins. Knopf, New York.

Bouchard, R. W. 1977. *Etheostoma etnieri*, a new percid fish from the Caney Fork (Cumberland) River System, Tennessee, with a redescription of the subgenus *Ulocentra*. Tulane Studies in Zoology and Botany 19:105–130.

Bowen, B. W., and R. W. Chapman. 1985. Phylogenetic relations in the genus *Morone* as inferred by mitochondrial DNA analyses. Page 44 *in* Abstracts of the 65th Annual Meeting of the American Society of Ichthyologists and Herpetologists.

Bowen, D. Q. 1978. Quaternary geology: a stratigraphic framework for multidisciplinary work. Pergamon Press, New York.

Bowman, H. B. 1932. A description and ecologic study of the margined madtom, *Rabida insignis* (Richardson). Master's thesis. Cornell University, Ithaca, New York.

Bowman, H. B. 1936. Further notes on the margined madtom, *Rabida insignis* (Richardson), and notes on a kindred species, *Noturus flavus* (Rafinesque). Doctoral dissertation. Cornell University, Ithaca, New York.

Bowman, M. L. 1970. Life history of the black redhorse, *Moxostoma duquesnei* (Lesueur), in Missouri. Transactions of the American Fisheries Society 99:546–559.

Bowman, N. R., J. R. Sheridan, and R. E. Wollitz. 1959. Fisheries management investigations of impoundments. Virginia Commission of Game and Inland Fisheries, Federal Aid in Sport Fish Restoration, Project F-5-R-5, July 1, 1958–June 30, 1959. Annual Report, Richmond.

Boyer, R. L. 1969. Aspects of the behavior of the longear sunfish, *Lepomis megalotis* (Rafinesque) in two Arkansas reservoirs. Master's thesis. Oklahoma State University, Stillwater. (Not seen; cited in Carlander 1977.)

Boyle, R. H. 1984a. A rain of death on the striper? Sports Illustrated 60(17):40–54.

Boyle, R. H. 1984b. A bass ackwards attempt to save the striper. Sports Illustrated 61(20):19.

Braasch, M. E., and R. L. Mayden. 1985. Review of the subgenus *Catonotus* (Percidae) with descriptions of two new darters of the *Etheostoma squamiceps* species group. Occasional Papers of the Museum of Natural History University of Kansas 119.

Brady, P. M. 1969. The sport fishery of Lake Drummond in the Dismal Swamp of Virginia. Master's thesis. Virginia Polytechnic Institute and State University, Blacksburg.

Bragg, R. J., and R. H. Stasiak. 1978. An ecological study of the blacknose dace, *Rhinichthys atratulus*, in Nebraska. Proceedings of the Nebraska Academy of Sciences and Affiliated Societies 88:8.

Brandt, T. M., and C. B. Schreck. 1975. Effects of harvesting aquatic bait species from a small West Virginia stream. Transactions of the American Fisheries Society 104:446–453.

Branham, L. 1972. Muskies down in Dixie. Field and Stream 77(1):54,84,88.

Branson, B. A. 1961. Observations on the distribution of nuptial tubercles in some catostomid fishes. Transactions of the Kentucky Academy of Science 64:360–372.

Branson, B. A. 1970. Measurements, counts, and observations on four lamprey species from Kentucky (*Ichthyomyzon, Lampetra, Entosphenus*). American Midland Naturalist 84:243–247.

Branson, B. A. 1983. Observations on the palezone and sawfin shiners, two undescribed cyprinid fishes from Kentucky. Transactions of the Kentucky Academy of Science 44:103–106.

Branson, B. A., D. C. Batch, and W. A. Curtis. 1984. Small-stream recovery following surface mining in east-central Kentucky. Transactions of the Kentucky Academy of Science 45:55–72.

Branson, B. A., and G. A. Moore. 1962. The lateralis components of the acoustico-lateralis system in the sunfish family Centrarchidae. Copeia 1962:1–108.

Branson, E. B. 1912. A Mississippian delta. Bulletin Geological Society of America 23:447–456.

Braswell, A. L., chairman. 1991. Scientific council report on the conservation status of North Carolina freshwater fishes. Submitted to the Nongame Advisory Committee of the North Carolina Wildlife Resources Commission, North Carolina State Museum of Natural Sciences, Raleigh.

Bratton, P. H. 1978. Tale of a minnow. Virginia Wildlife 39(9):10–11.

Braun, E. L. 1950. Deciduous forests of eastern North America. Hafner Press, New York. (Reprinted 1974.)

Brayton, S. L. 1981. Reproductive biology, energy content of tissues, and annual production of rainbow trout (*Salmo gairdneri*) in the South Fork of the Holston River, Virginia. Master's thesis. Virginia Polytechnic Institute and State University, Blacksburg.

Brazo, D. C., P. I. Tack, and C. R. Liston. 1975. Age, growth, and fecundity of yellow perch, *Perca flavescens*, in Lake Michigan near Ludington, Michigan. Transactions of the American Fisheries Society 104:726–730.

Breder, C. M. 1920a. Some notes on *Leuciscus vandoisulus* (Cuv. and Val.). Copeia 82:35–38.

Breder, C. M. 1920b. Further notes on *Leuciscus vandoisulus* (Cuv. and Val.). Copeia 87:87–90.

Breder, C. M. 1935. The reproductive habits of the common catfish, *Ameiurus nebulosus* (Le Sueur), with a discussion of their significance in ontogeny and phylogeny. Zoologica (New York) 19:143–185.

Breder, C. M. 1936. The reproductive habits of North American sunfishes (family Centrarchidae). Zoologica (New York) 21:1–48.

Breder, C. M. 1972. On the relationship of teleost scales to pigment patterns. Contributions from the Mote Marine Laboratory 1:1–79. (Sarasota, Florida.)

Breder, C. M., and R. B. Breder. 1923. A list of fishes, amphibians and reptiles collected in Ashe County, North Carolina. Zoologica (New York) 4:1–23.

Breder, C. M., and D. R. Crawford. 1922. The food of certain minnows. Zoologica (New York) 2:287–327.

Breder, C. M., and A. C. Redmond. 1929. The blue-spotted sunfish: a contribution to the life history and habits of *Enneacanthus* with notes on other Lepominae. Zoologica (New York) 9:379–401.

Breder, C. M., and D. E. Rosen. 1966. Modes of reproduction in fishes. Natural History Press, Garden City, New York.

Brehmer, M. L. 1972. Biological and chemical study of Virginia's estuaries. Virginia Polytechnic Institute and State University Water Resources Research Center Bulletin 45.

Brewer, D. L. 1969. Musky studies. Federal Aid in Sport

Fish Restoration, Progress Report, Project F-31-R-2, Jobs II-B to II-E, April 1, 1968–March 31, 1969. Kentucky Department of Fish and Wildlife Resources, Frankfort.

Brewer, D. L. 1980. A study of native muskellunge populations in eastern Kentucky streams. Kentucky Department of Fish and Wildlife Resources, Fisheries Bulletin 64, Frankfort.

Bridges, C. H., and J. W. Mullan. 1958. A compendium of the life history of the eastern brook trout *Salvelinus fontinalis* (Mitchill). Massachusetts Division of Fisheries and Game, Fisheries Bulletin 23, Boston.

Briggs, J. C. 1953. The behavior and reproduction of salmonid fishes in a small coastal stream. California Department of Fish and Game, Fish Bulletin 94.

Brigham, W. U. 1973. Nest construction of the lamprey, *Lampetra aepyptera*. Copeia 1973:135–136.

Brill, J. S. 1977. Notes on abortive spawning of the pirate perch, *Aphredoderus sayanus*, with comments on sexual distinctions. American Currents 5(4):10–16.

Brown, C. J. D. 1971. Fishes of Montana. Big Sky Books, Montana State University, Bozeman.

Brown, C. J. D, and C. Buck. 1939. When do trout and grayling fry begin to take food? Journal of Wildlife Management 3:134–140.

Brown, E. H. 1960. Little Miami River headwater-stream investigations. Ohio Department of Natural Resources, Federal Aid in Sport Fish Restoration, Project F-1-R. Final Report, Columbus.

Brown, J. L. 1955. Local variation and relationships of the cyprinodont fish, *Fundulus rathbuni* Jordan and Meek. Journal of the Elisha Mitchell Scientific Society 71:207–213.

Brown, J. L. 1957. A key to the species and subspecies of the cyprinodont genus *Fundulus* in the United States and Canada east of the Continental Divide. Journal of the Washington Academy of Sciences 47:69–77.

Brown, J. L. 1958. Geographic variation in southeastern populations of the cyprinodont fish *Fundulus notti* (Agassiz). American Midland Naturalist 59:477–488.

Brown, L. 1981. Patterns of female choice in mottled sculpins (Cottidae, Teleostei). Animal Behaviour 29:375–382.

Brown, M. E., editor. 1957. The physiology of fishes, volumes 1 and 2. Academic Press, New York.

Brown, P. M., J. A. Miller, and F. M. Swain. 1972. Structural and stratigraphic framework, and spatial distribution of permeability of the Atlantic Coastal Plain, North Carolina to New York. U.S. Geological Survey Professional Paper 796.

Brown, R. W. 1954. Composition of scientific words. Published by the author, Baltimore, Maryland. (Not seen; cited in Bailey and Robins 1988a.)

Brown, R. W. 1956. Composition of scientific words, revised edition. Random House, New York.

Bryan, C. F., and T. R. Sopher. 1969. New northern record for the thread fin shad, *Dorosoma petenense* (Günther), in coastal waters of California. California Fish and Game 55:155–156.

Bryan, J. E., and P. A. Larkin. 1972. Food specialization by individual trout. Journal of the Fisheries Research Board of Canada 29:1615–1624.

Bryant, L. J. 1987. A new genus and species of Amiidae (Holostei: Osteichthyes) from the Late Cretaceous of North America, with comments on the phylogeny of the Amiidae. Journal of Vertebrate Paleontology 7:349–361.

Bryant, R. T. 1979. The life history and comparative ecology of the sharphead darter, *Etheostoma acuticeps*. Tennessee Wildlife Resources Agency Technical Report 79-50, Nashville. (Also: Master's thesis. University of Tennessee, Knoxville.)

Bryant, R. T., J. P. Beets, and M. G. Ryon. 1979. Rediscovery of the sharphead darter, *Etheostoma acuticeps*, in North Carolina (Pisces: Percidae). Brimleyana 2:137–140.

Bugas, P. H., and L. O. Mohn. 1981. Silver in our streams: Virginia offers more troutwaters than you might have imagined. Virginia Wildlife 62(5):23–25, 29.

Buhan, P. J. 1966. Two races of *Etheostoma flabellare flabellare* Rafinesque from the Roanoke River of Virginia and the Neuse River of North Carolina. Master's thesis. Virginia Polytechnic Institute and State University, Blacksburg.

Buhan, P. J. 1969. The comparative osteology and taxonomy of the North American cyprinid genera, *Richardsonius*, *Clinostomus* and *Semotilus*, with notes on other minnows. Doctoral dissertation. Virginia Polytechnic Institute and State University, Blacksburg.

Buikema, A. L., and nine coauthors. 1985. Virginia acid precipitation network summary report: 1982–1984. Virginia Air Pollution Control Board, Richmond. (Not seen; cited in Webb et al. 1990.)

Burbidge, R. G. 1974. Distribution, growth, selective feeding, and energy transformations of young-of-the-year blueback herring, *Alosa aestivalis* (Mitchill), in the James River, Virginia. Transactions of the American Fisheries Society 103:297–311.

Burgess, G. H., C. R. Gilbert, V. Guillory, and D. C. Taphorn. 1977. Distributional notes on some north Florida freshwater fishes. Florida Scientist 40:33–41.

Burkhead, N. M. 1980. The life history of the stoneroller minnow *Campostoma a. anomalum* (Rafinesque) in five streams in east Tennessee. Tennessee Wildlife Resources Agency Technical Report 80-50, Nashville. (Also: Master's thesis. University of Tennessee, Knoxville.)

Burkhead, N. M. 1983. Ecological studies of two potentially threatened fishes (the orangefin madtom, *Noturus gilberti*, and the Roanoke logperch, *Percina rex*) endemic to the Roanoke River drainage. Report to U.S. Army Corps of Engineers, Wilmington District, Wilmington, North Carolina.

Burkhead, N. M., and B. H. Bauer. 1983. An intergeneric cyprinid hybrid, *Hybopsis monacha* × *Notropis galacturus*, from the Tennessee River drainage. Copeia 1983:1074–1077.

Burkhead, N. M., and R. E. Jenkins. 1977. Preliminary studies of stone flipping behavior in the subgenus *Percina* (Percidae, Etheostomatini). *In* Abstracts of the

57th Annual Meeting of the American Society of Ichthyologists and Herpetologists.

Burkhead, N. M., and R. E. Jenkins. 1982a. Five-year status review of the slender chub, *Hybopsis cahni*, a threatened cyprinid fish of the upper Tennessee drainage. Report to U.S. Fish and Wildlife Service, Newton Corner, Massachusetts.

Burkhead, N. M., and R. E. Jenkins. 1982b. Five-year status review of the yellowfin madtom, *Noturus flavipinnis*, a threatened ictalurid catfish of the Tennessee drainage. Report to U.S. Fish and Wildlife Service, Newton Corner, Massachusetts.

Burkhead, N. M., and R. E. Jenkins. 1991. Fishes. Pages 321–409 *In* K. A. Terwilliger, coordinator. Virginia's endangered species. McDonald and Woodward, Blacksburg, Virginia.

Burkhead, N. M., R. E. Jenkins, W. H. Haxo, and S. P. McIninch. 1985. Spawning behavior and sexual dimorphism of the minnows *Hybopsis* (? *Notropis* (*Cyprinella*)) *monacha* and *H. hypsinotus*: phylogenetic implications. Page 47 *in* Abstracts of the 65th Annual Meeting of the American Society of Ichthyologists and Herpetologists.

Burkhead, N. M., R. E. Jenkins, and E. G. Maurakis. 1980. New records, distribution and diagnostic characters of Virginia ictalurid catfishes with an adnexed adipose fin. Brimleyana 4:75–93.

Burkhead, N. M., and J. D. Williams. 1991. An intergeneric hybrid of a native minnow, the golden shiner, and an exotic minnow, the rudd. Transactions of the American Fisheries Society 120:781–795.

Burns, J. W. 1966. Threadfin shad. Pages 481–487 *in* Calhoun (1966).

Burns, J. W. 1970. Spawning bed sedimentation studies in northern California streams. California Fish and Game 56:253–270.

Burr, B. M. 1974. A new intergeneric hybrid combination in nature: *Pomoxis annularis* × *Centrarchus macropterus*. Copeia 1974:269–271.

Burr, B. M. 1976. Distribution and taxonomic status of the stoneroller, *Campostoma anomalum*, in Illinois. Natural History Miscellanea (Chicago) 194.

Burr, B. M. 1978. Systematics of the percid fishes of the subgenus *Microperca*, genus *Etheostoma*. Bulletin Alabama Museum of Natural History 4.

Burr, B. M. 1979. Systematics and life history aspects of the percid fish *Etheostoma blennius* with description of a new subspecies from Sequatchie River, Tennessee. Copeia 1979:191–203.

Burr, B. M. 1980. A distributional checklist of the fishes of Kentucky. Brimleyana 3:53–84.

Burr, B. M., and R. C. Cashner. 1983. *Campostoma pauciradii*, a new cyprinid fish from southeastern United States, with a review of related forms. Copeia 1983:101–116.

Burr, B. M., and R. L. Mayden. 1979. Records of fishes in western Kentucky with additions to the known fauna. Transactions of the Kentucky Academy of Science 40:58–67.

Burr, B. M., and R. L. Mayden. 1981. Systematics, distri-

bution and life history notes on *Notropis chihuahua* (Pisces: Cyprinidae). Copeia 1981:255–265.

Burr, B. M., and M. A. Morris. 1977. Spawning behavior of the shorthead redhorse, *Moxostoma macrolepidotum*, in Big Rock Creek, Illinois. Transactions of the American Fisheries Society 106:80–82.

Burr, B. M., and L. M. Page. 1986. Zoogeography of fishes of the lower Ohio–upper Mississippi basin. Pages 287–324 *in* Hocutt and Wiley (1986).

Burr, B. M., and L. M. Page. 1987. Philip Wayne Smith 1921–1986. Copeia 1987:839–840.

Burr, B. M., M. E. Retzer, and R. L. Mayden. 1980. A reassessment of the distributional status of five Kentucky cyprinids. Transactions of the Kentucky Academy of Science 41:48–54.

Burr, B. M., and P. W. Smith. 1976. Status of the largescale stoneroller, *Campostoma oligolepis*. Copeia 1976:521–531.

Burr, B. M., and M. L. Warren. 1986. A distributional atlas of Kentucky fishes. Kentucky Nature Preserves Commission, Scientific and Technical Series 4, Frankfort.

Burton, G. W., and E. P. Odum. 1945. The distribution of stream fish in the vicinity of Mountain Lake, Virginia. Ecology 26:182–194.

Buss, K. 1959. Trout and trout hatcheries of the future. Transactions of the American Fisheries Society 88:75–80.

Buss, K. 1960. A literature survey of the life history and culture of the muskellunge. Pennsylvania Fish Commission, Benner Spring Fish Research Station Special Purpose Report, Bellefonte.

Buss, K. 1961. A literature survey of the life history and culture of the northern pike. Pennsylvania Fish Commission, Benner Spring Fish Research Station Special Purpose Report, Bellefont.

Buss, K. 1962. A literature survey of the life history of the redfin and grass pickerels. Pennsylvania Fish Commission, Benner Spring Fish Research Station, Bellefonte.

Buss, K., J. Meade, and D. R. Graff. 1978. Reviewing the esocid hybrids. American Fisheries Society Special Publication 11:210–216.

Buss, K., and J. Miller. 1967. Interspecific hybridization of esocids: hatching success, pattern development, and fertility of some F$_1$ hybrids. Technical Papers of the U.S. Bureau of Sport Fisheries and Wildlife 14.

Buss, K., and J. E. Wright. 1956. Results of species hybridization within the family Salmonidae. Progressive Fish-Culturist 18:149–158.

Buss, K., and J. E. Wright. 1958. Appearance and fertility of trout hybrids. Transactions of the American Fisheries Society 87:172–181.

Bussjaeger, C., and T. Briggs. 1978. Phylogenetic implications of bile salts in some catostomid fishes. Copeia 1978:533–535.

Buth, D. G. 1977a. Biochemical identification of *Moxostoma rhothoecum* and *M. hamiltoni*. Biochemical Systematics and Ecology 5:57–60.

Buth, D. G. 1977b. Alcohol dehydrogenase variability in *Hypentelium nigricans*. Biochemical Systematics and Ecology 5:61–63.

Buth, D. G. 1978. Biochemical systematics of the Moxostomatini. Doctoral dissertation. University of Illinois, Urbana–Champaign.

Buth, D. G. 1979a. Creatine kinase variability in *Moxostoma macrolepidotum* (Cypriniformes; Catostomidae). Copeia 1979:152–154.

Buth, D. G. 1979b. Biochemical systematics of the cyprinid genus *Notropis*—1, the subgenus *Luxilus*. Biochemical Systematics and Ecology 7:69–79.

Buth, D. G. 1979c. Genetic relationships among the torrent suckers, genus *Thoburnia*. Biochemical Systematics and Ecology 7:311–316.

Buth, D. G. 1979d. Duplicate gene expression in tetraploid fishes of the tribe Moxostomatini (Cypriniformes, Catostomidae). Comparative Biochemistry and Physiology 63B:7–12.

Buth, D. G. 1980. Evolutionary genetics and systematic relationships in the catostomid genus *Hypentelium*. Copeia 1980:280–290.

Buth, D. G. 1984. Allozymes of the cyprinid fishes. Pages 561–590 *in* B. J. Turner, editor. Evolutionary genetics of fishes. Plenum, New York.

Buth, D. G., and B. M. Burr. 1978. Isozyme variability in the cyprinid genus *Campostoma*. Copeia 1978:298–311.

Butler, R. L. 1965. Freshwater drum, *Aplodinotus grunniens*, in the navigational impoundments of the upper Mississippi River. Transactions of the American Fisheries Society 94:339–349.

Butts, C. 1940. Geology of the Appalachian Valley in Virginia, Part I—geologic text and illustrations. Virginia Geological Survey Bulletin 52.

Buynak, G. L., and H. W. Mohr. 1978a. Larval development of the northern hog sucker (*Hypentelium nigricans*), from the Susquehanna River. Transactions of the American Fisheries Society 107:595–599.

Buynak, G. L., and H. W. Mohr. 1978b. Larval development of the redbreast sunfish (*Lepomis auritus*) from the Susquehanna River. Transactions of the American Fisheries Society 107:600–604.

Buynak, G. L., and H. W. Mohr. 1978c. Larval development of the white sucker (*Catostomus commersoni*) from the Susquehanna River. Proceedings of the Pennsylvania Academy of Science 52:143–145.

Buynak, G. L., and H. W. Mohr. 1979a. Larval development of the shorthead redhorse (*Moxostoma macrolepidotum*) from the Susquehanna River. Transactions of the American Fisheries Society 108:161–165.

Buynak, G. L., and H. W. Mohr. 1979b. Larval development of rock bass from the Susquehanna River. Progressive Fish-Culturist 41:39–42.

Buynak, G. L., and H. W. Mohr. 1979c. Larval development of the blacknose dace (*Rhinichthys atratulus*) and longnose dace (*Rhinichthys cataractae*) from a Susquehanna River tributary. Proceedings of the Pennsylvania Academy of Science 53:56–60.

Buynak, G. L., and H. W. Mohr. 1979d. Larval development of the northern pike (*Esox lucius*) and muskellunge (*Esox masquinongy*) from northeast Pennsylvania. Proceedings of the Pennsylvania Academy of Science 53:69–73.

Buynak, G. L., and H. W. Mohr. 1979e. Larval development of creek chub and fallfish from two Susquehanna

River tributaries. Progressive Fish-Culturist 41:124–129.

Buynak, G. L., and H. W. Mohr. 1979f. Larval development of the bluntnose minnow (*Pimephales notatus*) and fathead minnow (*Pimephales promelas*) from northeast Pennsylvania. Proceedings of the Pennsylvania Academy of Science 53:172–176.

Buynak, G. L., and H. W. Mohr. 1980a. Larval development of stoneroller, cutlips minnow, and river chub with diagnostic keys, including four additional cyprinids. Progressive Fish-Culturist 42:127–135.

Buynak, G. L., and H. W. Mohr. 1980b. Larval development of golden shiner and comely shiner from northeastern Pennsylvania. Progressive Fish-Culturist 42:206–211.

Buynak, G. L., and H. W. Mohr. 1980c. Key to the identification of sucker larvae in the Susquehanna River near Berwick, Pennsylvania. Proceedings of the Pennsylvania Academy of Science 54:161–164.

Buynak, G. L., and H. W. Mohr. 1980d. Larval development of the common shiner (*Notropis cornutus*) from northeast Pennsylvania. Proceedings of the Pennsylvania Academy of Science 54:165–168.

Byrne, D. M. 1978. Life history of the spotfin killifish, *Fundulus luciae* (Pisces: Cyprinodontidae), in Fox Creek Marsh, Virginia. Estuaries 1:211–227.

Cady, R. C. 1938. Ground-water resources of northern Virginia. Virginia Geological Survey Bulletin 50.

Cahn, A. R. 1927. An ecological study of southern Wisconsin fishes: the brook silversides (*Labidesthes sicculus*) and the cisco (*Leucichthys artedi*) in their relations to the region. Illinois Biological Monographs 11:1–151.

Cahn, A. R. 1938a. The work of the TVA in relation to the wildlife resources of the Tennessee Valley. Journal of the Tennessee Academy of Science 13:174–179.

Cahn, A. R. 1938b. Progress report of the fisheries investigations of the Tennessee Valley Authority. Transactions of the American Fisheries Society 68:61–66.

Cailliet, G. M., M. S. Love, and A. W. Ebeling. 1986. Fishes: a field and laboratory manual on their structure, identification, and natural history. Wadsworth, Belmont, California.

Cairns, J., J. S. Crossman, K. L. Dickson, and E. E. Herricks. 1971. The recovery of damaged streams. ASB (Association of Southeastern Biologists) Bulletin 18:79–106.

Cairns, J., and K. L. Dickson. 1972. An ecosystematic study of the South River, Virginia. Virginia Polytechnic Institute and State University, Water Resources Research Center Bulletin 54, Blacksburg.

Cairns, J., and R. L. Kaesler. 1971. Cluster analysis of fish in a portion of the upper Potomac River. Transactions of the American Fisheries Society 100:750–756.

Calabrese, A. 1969. Effect of acids and alkalies on survival of bluegills and largemouth bass. Technical Papers of the U.S. Bureau of Sport Fisheries and Wildlife 42. (Not seen; cited in Hastings 1979.)

Calhoun, A., editor. 1966. Inland fisheries management. California Department of Fish and Game, Sacramento.

Calhoun, P. 1984. Big Spring Mill: a legacy of the past. Salem Times-Register (19 January):C1.

Campbell, J. S., and H. R. MacCrimmon. 1970. Biology of the emerald shiner *Notropis atherinoides* Rafinesque in Lake Simcoe, Canada. Journal of Fish Biology 2:259–273.

Campbell, R. D., and B. A. Branson. 1978. Ecology and population dynamics of the black bullhead, *Ictalurus melas* (Rafinesque), in central Kentucky. Tulane Studies in Zoology and Botany 20:99–136.

Camuto, C. 1991. Dropping acid in the southern Appalachians: a wild trout resource at considerable risk. Trout 32(1):16–23, 26–23, 36.

Carlander, K. D. 1941. The darters (Etheostominae) of Minnesota. Proceedings of the Minnesota Academy of Science 9:41–48.

Carlander, K. D. 1953. Handbook of freshwater fishery biology with the first supplement. Brown, Dubuque, Iowa. (Not seen; cited in Scott and Crossman 1973.)

Carlander, K. D. 1969. Handbook of freshwater fishery biology, volume 1. Iowa State University Press, Ames.

Carlander, K. D. 1977. Handbook of freshwater fishery biology, volume 2. Iowa State University Press, Ames.

Carlson, D. M., and P. S. Bonislawsky. 1981. The paddlefish (*Polyodon spathula*) fisheries of the midwestern United States. Fisheries (Bethesda) 6(2):17–27.

Carlson, D. R. 1967. Fathead minnow, *Pimephales promelas* Rafinesque, in the Des Moines River, Boone County, Iowa, and the Skunk River drainage, Hamilton and Story counties, Iowa. Iowa State Journal of Science 41:363–374.

Carnes, W. C. 1958. Contributions to the biology of the eastern creek chubsucker, *Erimyzon oblongus oblongus* (Mitchill). Master's thesis. North Carolina State University, Raleigh.

Carnes, W. C. 1965. Survey and classification of the Roanoke River and tributaries, North Carolina (with Appendix). North Carolina Wildlife Resources Commission, Federal Aid in Sport Fish Restoration, Project F-14-R, Job I–Q, Final Report, Raleigh.

Carney, D. A., and B. M. Burr. 1989. Life histories of the bandfin darter, *Etheostoma zonistium*, and the firebelly darter, *Etheostoma pyrrhogaster*, in western Kentucky. Illinois Natural History Survey Biological Notes 134.

Carothers, J. L., and R. Allison. 1968. Control of snails by the redear (shellcracker) sunfish. FAO (Food and Agriculture Organization of the United Nations) Fisheries Reports 44:399–406. (Not seen; cited in Carlander 1977.)

Carr, A. F. 1940. Notes on breeding habits of the warmouth bass. Florida Academy of Sciences Proceedings 4:108–112. (Not seen; cited in Larimore 1957.)

Carrier, L. 1975. Agriculture in Virginia, 1607–1699. Virginia 350th Anniversary Celebration Corporation, Historical Booklet 14, Williamsburg.

Carroll, B. B., and G. E. Hall. 1964. Growth of catfishes in Norris Reservoir, Tennessee. Journal of the Tennessee Academy of Science 39:86–91.

Carroll, B. B., G. E. Hall, and R. D. Bishop. 1963. Three seasons of rough fish removal at Norris Reservoir, Tennessee. Transactions of the American Fisheries Society 92:356–364.

Carscadden, J. E., and W. C. Leggett. 1975a. Meristic differences in spawning populations of American shad, *Alosa sapidissima*: evidence for homing to tributaries in the St. John River, New Brunswick. Journal of the Fisheries Research Board of Canada 32:653–660.

Carscadden, J. E., and W. C. Leggett. 1975b. Life history variations in populations of American shad, *Alosa sapidissima* (Wilson), spawning in tributaries of the St. John River, New Brunswick. Journal of Fish Biology 7:595–609.

Carter, L. J. 1977. Chemical plants leave unexpected legacy for two Virginia rivers. Science 198:1015–1020.

Carter, V., and N. Rybicki. 1986. Resurgence of submerged aquatic macrophytes in the tidal Potomac River, Maryland, Virginia, and the District of Columbia. Estuaries 9:368–375.

Cartier, D., and É. Magnin. 1967. La croissance en longueur et en poids des *Amia calva* L. de la région de Montréal. Canadian Journal of Zoology 45:797–804. (Not seen; cited in Scott and Crossman 1973.)

Carver, D. C. 1967. Distribution and abundance of the centrarchids in the recent delta of the Mississippi River. Proceedings of the Annual Conference Southeastern Association of Game and Fish Commissioners 20(1966):390–404. (Not seen; cited in Carlander 1977.)

Case, E. C. 1940. Cope—the man. Copeia 1940:61–65.

Cashner, R. C., and J. D. Brown. 1977. Longitudinal distribution of the fishes of the Buffalo River in northwestern Arkansas. Tulane Studies in Zoology and Botany 19:37–46.

Cashner, R. C., B. M. Burr, and J. S. Rogers. 1989. Geographic variation of the mud sunfish, *Acantharchus pomotis* (Family Centrarchidae). Copeia 1989:129–141.

Cashner, R. C., and R. E. Jenkins. 1982. Systematics of the Roanoke Bass, *Ambloplites cavifrons*. Copeia 1982:581–594.

Cashner, R. C., F. L. Pezold, and J. M. Grady. 1979. A preliminary list of the fishes of Clark Creek in western Mississippi with a new record for the southern redbelly dace, *Phoxinus erythrogaster*. ASB (Association of Southeastern Biologists) Bulletin 26:67.

Cashner, R. C., J. S. Rogers, and J. M. Grady. 1988. *Fundulus bifax*, a new species of the subgenus *Xenisma* from the Tallapoosa and Coosa River systems of Alabama and Georgia. Copeia 1988:674–683.

Cashner, R. C., and R. D. Suttkus. 1977. *Ambloplites constellatus*, a new species of rock bass from the Ozark Upland of Arkansas and Missouri with a review of western rock bass populations. American Midland Naturalist 98:147–161.

Casselman, J. M. 1974. External sex determination of northern pike, *Esox lucius* Linnaeus. Transactions of the American Fisheries Society 103:343–347.

Casselman, J. M. 1978. Effects of environmental factors on growth, survival, activity, and exploitation of northern pike. American Fisheries Society Special Publication 11:114–128.

Casselman, J. M., E. J. Crossman, P. E. Ihssen, J. D. Reist, and H. E. Brooke. 1986. Identification of muskellunge, northern pike, and their hybrids. American Fisheries Society Special Publication 15:14–46.

Casteel, R. W. 1976. Fish remains in archeology. Academic Press, New York.

Castle, P. H. J. 1984. Notacanthiformes and Anguilliformes: development. Pages 62–93 *in* Moser et al. (1984).

Cating, J. P. 1953. Determining age of Atlantic shad from their scales. U.S. Fish and Wildlife Service Fishery Bulletin 54:187–199.

Cavender, T. M. 1969. An Oligocene mudminnow (Family Umbridae) from Oregon, with remarks on relationships within the Esocoidei. Occasional Papers of the Museum of Zoology University of Michigan 660.

Cavender, T. M. 1970. A comparison of coregonines and other salmonids with the earliest known teleostean fishes. Pages 1–32 *in* C. C. Lindsey and C. S. Woods, editors. Biology of coregonid fishes. University of Manitoba Press, Winnipeg.

Cavender, T. M. 1980. Systematics of *Salvelinus* from the North Pacific. Pages 295–322 *in* E. K. Balon, editor. Charrs: salmonid fishes of the genus *Salvelinus*. Dr. W. Junk, The Hague, Netherlands.

Cavender, T. M. 1986. Review of the fossil history of North American freshwater fishes. Pages 699–724 *in* Hocutt and Wiley (1986).

Cavender, T. M., and M. M. Coburn. 1992. Phylogenetic relationships of North American Cyprinidae. Pages 293–327 *in* Mayden (1992).

Cavender, T. M., J. G. Lundberg, and R. L. Wilson. 1970. Two new fossil records of the genus *Esox* (Teleostei, Salmoniformes) in North America. Northwest Science 44:176–183.

Cavender, T. M., and R. R. Miller. 1972. *Smilodonichthys rastrosus*, a new Pliocene salmonid fish from western United States. Museum of Natural History Bulletin 18, University of Oregon, Eugene.

Ceas, P. A., L. M. Page, D. L. Swofford, and D. G. Buth. 1991. Evolutionary relationships within the *Etheostoma squamiceps* complex (Percidae; subgenus *Catonotus*) with descriptions of five new species. *In* Abstracts of the 71st Annual Meeting of the American Society of Ichthyologists and Herpetologists.

Chadwick, E. M. P. 1976. Ecological fish production in a small Precambrian Shield lake. Environmental Biology of Fishes 1:13–60.

Chadwick, H. K., C. E. von Geldern, and M. L. Johnson. 1966. White bass. Pages 412–422 *in* Calhoun (1966).

Chambers, J. R. 1969. Methods of distinguishing larval alewife (*Alosa pseudoharengus*) from larval blueback herring (*A. aestivalis*). Master's thesis. College of William and Mary, Williamsburg, Virginia.

Chambers, J. R., J. A. Musick, and J. Davis. 1976. Methods of distinguishing larval alewife from larval blueback herring. Chesapeake Science 17:93–100.

Chao, L. N. 1978. A basis for classifying western Atlantic Sciaenidae (Teleostei: Perciformes). NOAA (National Oceanic and Atmospheric Administration) Technical Report, NMFS (National Marine Fisheries Service) Circular 415.

Chapleau, F., and G. Pageau. 1985. Morphological differentiation of *Etheostoma olmstedi* and *E. nigrum* (Pisces: Percidae) in Canada. Copeia 1985:855–865.

Chapman, J., H. R. Delcourt, and P. A. Delcourt. 1989. Strawberry fields, almost forever. Natural History 9/89:50–59.

Chapman, R. W. 1989. Spatial and temporal variation of mitochondrial DNA haplotype frequencies in the striped bass (*Morone saxatilis*) 1982 year class. Copeia 1989:344–348.

Chapoton, R. B., and J. E. Sykes. 1961. Atlantic coast migration of large striped bass as evidenced by fisheries and tagging. Transactions of the American Fisheries Society 90:13–20.

Cheek, T. E., M. J. Van Den Avyle, and C. C. Coutant. 1985. Influences of water quality on distribution of striped bass in a Tennessee River impoundment. Transactions of the American Fisheries Society 114:67–76.

Chenhan, L., and Z. Yongjun. 1988. Notes on the Chinese paddlefish, *Psephurus gladius* (Martens). Copeia 1988:482–484.

Chereshnev, I. A., and A. V. Balushkin. 1980. A new species of blackfish, *Dallia admirabilis* sp. n. (Umbridae, Esociformes) from the Amguema River basin (Arctic Chukotka). Journal of Ichthyology 20(6):25–30.

Chernoff, B., R. R. Miller, and C. R. Gilbert. 1982. *Notropis orca* and *Notropis simus*, cyprinid fishes from the American Southwest, with description of a new subspecies. Occasional Papers of the Museum of Zoology University of Michigan 698.

Cherry, D. S., K. L. Dickson, J. Cairns, and J. R. Stauffer. 1977. Preferred, avoided, and lethal temperatures of fish during rising temperature conditions. Journal of the Fisheries Research Board of Canada 34:239–246.

Chervinski, J. 1983. Salinity tolerance of the mosquito fish, *Gambusia affinis* (Baird and Girard). Journal of Fish Biology 22:9–11.

Chew, R. L. 1974. Early life history of the Florida largemouth bass. Florida Game and Fresh Water Fish Commission, Fishery Bulletin 7, Tallahassee.

Chew, R. L. 1975. The Florida largemouth bass. Pages 450–458 *in* R. H. Stroud and H. Clepper, editors. Black bass biology and management. Sport Fishing Institute, Washington, D.C.

Childers, W. F. 1967. Hybridization of four species of sunfishes (Centrarchidae). Illinois Natural History Survey Bulletin 29:159–214.

Childers, W. F. 1975. Bass genetics as applied to culture and management. Pages 362–372 *in* R. H. Stroud and H. Clepper, editors. Black bass biology and management. Sport Fishing Institute, Washington, D.C.

Chittenden, M. E. 1969. Life history and ecology of the American shad, *Alosa sapidissima*, in the Delaware River. Doctoral dissertation. Rutgers University, New Brunswick, New Jersey.

Chittenden, M. E. 1971. Status of the striped bass, *Morone saxatilis*, in the Delaware River. Chesapeake Science 12:131–136.

Chittenden, M. E. 1976. Present and historical spawning grounds and nurseries of American shad, *Alosa sapidissima*, in the Delaware River. U.S. National Marine Fisheries Service Fishery Bulletin 74:343–352.

Cianci, J. M. 1969. Larval development of the alewife,

Alosa pseudoharengus (Wilson), and the glut herring, *Alosa aestivalis* (Mitchill). Master's thesis. University of Connecticut, Storrs.

Cicerello, R. R., and R. S. Butler. 1985. Fishes of Buck Creek, Cumberland River drainage, Kentucky. Brimleyana 11:133–159.

Cincotta, D. A. 1978. Literature review and plan of study for instream flow needs for fish and aquatic life on selected streams within the Kanawha River basin in West Virginia. Report from West Virginia Department of Natural Resources, Elkins, to Ohio River Basin Commission, Cincinnati, Ohio.

Cincotta, D. A., K. L. Dull, S. L. Markham, and R. D. Williams. 1986a. Ichthyofaunal checklist and comparison of two North Branch Potomac River tributaries where alleged Ohio–Potomac River stream captures occurred. Proceedings of the Pennsylvania Academy of Science 60:129–134.

Cincotta, D. A., R. L. Miles, M. E. Hoeft, and G. E. Lewis. 1986b. Discovery of *Noturus eleutherus, Noturus stigmosus,* and *Percina peltata* in West Virginia, with discussions of other additions and records of fishes. Brimleyana 12:101–121.

Clark, F. W., and M. H. Keenleyside. 1967. Reproductive isolation between the sunfish *Lepomis gibbosus* and *L. macrochirus.* Journal of the Fisheries Research Board of Canada 24:495–514.

Clark, J. A. 1981. Comment [on Late Wisconsin and Holocene tectonic stability of the United States mid-Atlantic coastal region]. Geology 9:438.

Clark, J. A., and C. S. Lingle. 1979. Predicted relative sea-level changes (18,000 years B.P. to present) caused by late-glacial retreat of the Antarctic ice sheet. Quaternary Research 11:279–298.

Clark, J. E. 1978. Distribution of *Etheostoma nigrum* Rafinesque, *Etheostoma olmstedi* Storer, and their introgressive hybrid populations in the James River drainage. Master's thesis. University of Richmond, Richmond, Virginia.

Clark, W. B., and B. L. Miller. 1912. The physiography and geology of the Coastal Plain province in Virginia. Virginia Geological Survey Bulletin 4:13–222.

Clay, W. M. 1975. The fishes of Kentucky. Kentucky Department of Fish and Wildlife Resources, Frankfort.

Clayton, J. W., R. E. K. Harris, and P. N. Tretiak. 1973. Identification of supernatant and mitochondrial isozymes of malate dehydrogenase on electropherograms applied to the taxonomic discrimination of walleye (*Stizostedion vitreum vitreum*), sauger (*S. canadense*), and suspected interspecific hybrid fishes. Journal of the Fisheries Research Board of Canada 30:927–938.

Clemens, H. P. 1968. A review of selection and breeding in the culture of warm-water food fishes in North America. FAO (Food and Agriculture Organization of the United Nations) Fisheries Reports 44:67–80.

Clemens, H. P., and K. E. Sneed. 1957. The spawning behavior of the channel catfish *Ictalurus punctatus.* U.S. Fish and Wildlife Service Special Scientific Report—Fisheries 219.

Clemens, W. A., J. R. Dymond, N. K. Bigelow, F. B. Adamstone, and W. J. K. Harkness. 1923. The food of

Lake Nipigon fishes. University of Toronto Studies 22. (Also: Publications of the Ontario Fisheries Research Laboratory 16.)

Clemmer, G. H. 1971. The systematics and biology of the *Hybopsis amblops* complex. Doctoral dissertation. Tulane University, New Orleans.

Clemmer, G. H., and R. D. Suttkus. 1971. *Hybopsis lineapunctata,* a new cyprinid fish from the upper Alabama River system. Tulane Studies in Zoology and Botany 17:21–30.

Clemmons, M. M., and D. G. Lindquist. 1983. Reproductive biology of the swamp darter in Lake Waccamaw, North Carolina. Page 12 *in* Abstracts of the 63rd Annual Meeting of the American Society of Ichthyologists and Herpetologists.

CLIMAP (Climate Long-Range Investigation Mapping and Prediction) project members. 1976. The surface of the ice-age Earth. Science 191:1131–1137.

Cloutman, D. G. 1979. Identification of catfish alevins of the Piedmont Carolinas. Pages 176–185 *in* R. Wallus and C. W. Voigtlander, editors. Proceedings of a workshop on freshwater larval fishes. Tennessee Valley Authority, Division of Forestry, Fisheries, and Wildlife Development, Norris, Tennessee.

Cloutman, D. G., and L. L. Olmsted. 1979. First record and status of the redlip shiner, *Notropis chiliticus* (Cope), from South Carolina. Page 130 *in* D. M. Forsythe and W. B. Ezell, editors. Proceedings of the first South Carolina endangered species symposium. South Carolina Wildlife and Marine Resources Department, Charleston.

Cloutman, D. G., and L. L. Olmsted. 1983. Vernacular names of freshwater fishes of the southeastern United States. Fisheries (Bethesda) 8:7–11.

Clugston, J. P., and E. L. Cooper. 1960. Growth of the common eastern madtom, *Noturus insignis* in central Pennsylvania. Copeia 1960:9–16.

Clugston, J. P., J. L. Oliver, and R. Ruelle. 1978. Reproduction, growth, and standing crops of yellow perch in southern reservoirs. American Fisheries Society Special Publication 11:89–99.

Clugston, J. P., and J. V. Shireman. 1987. Triploid grass carp for aquatic plant control. U.S. Fish and Wildlife Service Fish and Wildlife Fishery Leaflet 8.

Coad, B. W. 1975. On the intergeneric relationships of North American and certain Eurasian cyprinid fishes (Cypriniformes, Cyprinidae). Doctoral dissertation. University of Ottawa, Canada.

Coad, B. W. 1981. A bibliography of the sticklebacks (Gasterosteidae: Osteichthyes). Syllogeus 35.

Coad, B. W. 1986. The margined madtom (*Noturus insignis*) in Canada. Trail and Landscape 20:102–108.

Coad, B. W. 1987. Absent records of fishes in the Ottawa District. Trail & Landscape 21:249–254.

Coble, D. W. 1975. Smallmouth bass. Pages 21–33 *in* R. H. Stroud and H. Clepper, editors. Black bass biology and management. Sport Fishing Institute, Washington, D.C.

Coburn, M. M. 1983. Anatomy and relationships of *Notropis atherinoides.* Dissertation Abstracts International 43(8) (unpaginated reprint.)

Coburn, M. M. 1986. Egg diameter variation in eastern North American minnows (Pisces: Cyprinidae): correlation with vertebral number, habitat, and spawning behavior. Ohio Journal of Science 86:110–120.

Coburn, M. M., and T. M. Cavender. 1992. Interrelationships of North American cyprinid fishes. Pages 328–373 in Mayden (1992).

Cochran, B. 1969. State finds white bass in Smith Lake. Roanoke Times (30 November):C9.

Cochran, B. 1971. Spring white bass. Virginia Wildlife 32(3):14–15.

Cochran, B. 1982. Alewife: small fish with big impact. Roanoke Times & World-News (16 May).

Cochran, B. 1987. Jaws: fish caught in Roanoke River resembles tough cousin but is harmless. Roanoke Times & World-News (3 October):B1.

Cochran, B. 1988. Jumbo-sized rock bass reeled in. Roanoke Times & World-News (1 December):C4.

Coggeshall, L. T. 1924. A study of the productivity and breeding habits of the bluegill, Lepomis pallidus (Mitch.). Proceedings of Indiana Academy of Science 33:315–320.

Cohen, A. B. 1977. Life history of the banded sunfish (Enneacanthus obesus) in Green Falls Reservoir, Connecticut. Master's thesis. University of Connecticut, Storrs.

Cohen, D. M. 1969. Names of fishes. Commercial Fisheries Review 31(5):18–20.

Cohen, D. M. 1984. Ontogeny, systematics, and phylogeny. Pages 7–11 in Moser et al. (1984).

Cohen, S. 1981. Historic springs of the Virginias: a pictorial history. Pictorial Histories Publishing Company, Charleston, West Virginia.

Colby, P. J., R. E. McNicol, and R. A. Ryder. 1979. Synopsis of biological data on the walleye Stizostedion v. vitreum (Mitchill 1818). FAO (Food and Agriculture Organization of the United Nations) Fisheries Synopsis 119.

Cole, C. F. 1957. The taxonomy of the percid fishes of the genus Etheostoma, subgenus Boleosoma, of eastern United States. Doctoral dissertation. Cornell University, Ithaca, New York.

Cole, C. F. 1965. Additional evidence for separation of Etheostoma olmstedi Storer from Etheostoma nigrum Rafinesque. Copeia 1965:8–13.

Cole, C. F. 1967. A study of the eastern johnny darter, Etheostoma olmstedi Storer (Teleostei, Percidae). Chesapeake Science 8:28–51.

Cole, C. F. 1972. Status of the darters, Etheostoma nigrum, E. longimanum and E. podostemone in Atlantic drainages (Teleostei, Percidae, subgenus Boleosoma). Virginia Polytechnic Institute and State University Research Division Monograph 4:119–138.

Colgan, P. 1974. Burying experiments with the banded killifish, Fundulus diaphanus. Copeia 1974:258–259.

Collette, B. B. 1962. The swamp darters of the subgenus Hololepis (Pisces, Percidae). Tulane Studies in Zoology 9:115–211.

Collette, B. B. 1963. The subfamilies, tribes, and genera of the Percidae (Teleostei). Copeia 1963:615–623.

Collette, B. B. 1965. Systematic significance of breeding tubercles in fishes of the family Percidae. Proceedings of the United States National Museum 117(3518):567–614.

Collette, B. B. 1967. The taxonomic history of the darters (Percidae: Etheostomatini). Copeia 1967:814–819.

Collette, B. B. 1977. Epidermal breeding tubercles and bony contact organs in fishes. Symposia of the Zoological Society of London 39:225–268.

Collette, B. B., and P. Banarescu. 1977. Systematics and zoogeography of the fishes of the family Percidae. Journal of the Fisheries Research Board of Canada 34:1450–1463.

Collette, B. B., and L. K. Knapp. 1967. Catalog of type specimens of the darters (Pisces, Percidae, Etheostomatini). Proceedings of the United States National Museum 119:1–88.

Collette, B. B., and seven coauthors. 1977. Biology of the percids. Journal of the Fisheries Research Board of Canada 34:1890–1899.

Colliers Encyclopedia. 1984. Macmillan Education, New York.

Collins, W. D., M. D. Foster, F. Reeves, and R. P. Meacham. 1930. Springs of Virginia. A report on the discharge, temperature, and chemical character of springs in the southern part of the Great Valley. Virginia Commission on Conservation and Development, Division of Water Resources and Power Bulletin 1, Richmond.

Colquhoun, D. J., and H. S. Johnson. 1968. Tertiary sea-level fluctuation in South Carolina. Palaeography, Palaeoclimatology, Palaeoecology 5:105–126.

Comparini, A., and E. Rodino. 1980. Electrophoretic evidence for two species of Anguilla leptocephali in the Sargasso Sea. Nature 287:435–437.

Conley, J. F. 1978. Geology of the Piedmont of Virginia—interpretations and problems. Virginia Division of Mineral Resources, Publication 7:115–149, Charlottesville.

Conner, J. V. 1979. Identification of larval sunfishes (Centrarchidae, Elassomatidae) from southern Louisiana. Pages 17–52 in R. D. Hoyt, editor. Proceedings of the 3rd symposium on larval fish. Western Kentucky University, Bowling Green.

Conner, J. V., R. P. Gallagher, and M. F. Chatry. 1980. Larval evidence for natural reproduction of the grass carp (Ctenopharyngodon idella) in the lower Mississippi River. U.S. Fish and Wildlife Service Biological Services Program FWS-OBS-80/43:1–19.

Conner, J. V., and R. D. Suttkus. 1986. Zoogeography of freshwater fishes of the western Gulf slope of North America. Pages 413–456 in Hocutt and Wiley (1986).

Conner, L. L., and O. E. Maughan. 1984. Changes in invertebrate and fish populations, and water chemistry in a small stream above and below two impoundments. Virginia Journal of Science 35:242–247.

Conners, J. A. 1986. Quaternary geomorphic processes in Virginia. Pages 1–22 in J. N. McDonald and S. O. Bird, editors. The Quaternary of Virginia—a symposium volume. Virginia Division of Mineral Resources, Publication 75, Charlottesville.

Conrow, R., and A. V. Zale. 1985. Early life history stages of fishes of Orange Lake, Florida: an illustrated identification manual. Florida Cooperative Fish and Wildlife Research Unit, School of Forest Resources and Conservation, Technical Report 15, Gainesville.

Constantz, G. D. 1979. Social dynamics and parental care in the tessellated darter (Pisces: Percidae). Proceedings of the Academy of Natural Sciences of Philadelphia 131:131–138.

Constantz, G. D. 1985. Alloparental care in the tessellated darter, *Etheostoma olmstedi* (Pisces: Percidae). Environmental Biology of Fishes 14:175–183.

Cook, D. G., editor. 1980. Proceedings of the sea lamprey international symposium. Canadian Journal of Fisheries and Aquatic Sciences 37:1585–2214.

Cook, F. A., D. A. Albaugh, L. D. Brown, S. Kaufman, J. E. Oliver, and R. D. Hatcher. 1979. Thin-skinned tectonics in the crystalline southern appalachians; COCORP seismic-reflection profiling of the Blue Ridge and Piedmont. Geology 7:563–567.

Cooper, B. N. 1966. Geology of the salt and gypsum deposits in the Saltville area, Smyth and Washington counties, Virginia. Pages 11–34 *in* J. L. Rau, editor. Second symposium on salt, volume 1. Northern Ohio Geological Survey. (Not seen; cited in McDonald 1984.)

Cooper, E. L. 1983. Fishes of Pennsylvania and the northeastern United States. Pennsylvania State University Press, University Park.

Cooper, E. L. 1985. Fishes. Carnegie Museum of Natural History Special Publication 11:167–256.

Cooper, G. P. 1935. Some results of forage fish investigations in Michigan. Transactions of the American Fisheries Society 65:132–142.

Cooper, G. P. 1936. Age and growth of the golden shiner (*Notemigonus crysoleucas auratus*) and its suitability for propagation. Papers of the Michigan Academy of Science, Arts and Letters 21:587–597.

Cooper, G. P. 1940. A biological survey of the Rangeley Lakes, with special emphasis to the trout and salmon. Maine Department of Inland Fisheries and Game Fish, Survey Report 3, Augusta.

Cooper, G. P. 1941. A biological survey of lakes and ponds of the Androscoggin and Kennebec River drainage systems of Maine. Maine Department of Inland Fisheries and Game Fish, Survey Report 4, Augusta. (Not seen; cited in Thoits 1958.)

Cooper, J. E. 1978. Eggs and larvae of the logperch, *Percina caprodes* (Rafinesque). American Midland Naturalist 99:257–269.

Cooper, J. E. 1979. Description of eggs and larvae of fantail darter (*Etheostoma flabellare*) and rainbow (*E. caeruleum*) darters from Lake Erie tributaries. Transactions of the American Fisheries Society 108:46–56.

Cooper, J. E. 1980. Egg, larval and juvenile development of longnose dace, *Rhinichthys cataractae*, and river chub, *Nocomis micropogon*, with notes on their hybridization. Copeia 1980:469–478.

Cooper, R. A. 1961. Early life history and spawning migration of the alewife, *Alosa pseudoharengus*. Master's thesis. University of Rhode Island, Kingston.

Cope, E. D. 1867. [Description of a new genus of cyprinoid fishes from Virginia.] Proceedings of the Academy of Natural Sciences of Philadelphia 19:95–97.

Cope, E. D. 1868a. On the genera of fresh-water fishes *Hypsilepis* Baird and *Photogenis* Cope, their species and distribution. Proceedings of the Academy of Natural Sciences of Philadelphia 19 (1867):156–166.

Cope, E. D. 1868b. [Year according to Gilbert 1971]. On the distribution of fresh-water fishes in the Allegheny region of southwestern Virginia. Journal of the Academy of Natural Sciences of Philadelphia, Series 2, 6, Part 3, Article 5 (1869):207–247.

Cope, E. D. 1869. Synopsis of the Cyprinidae of Pennsylvania. Transactions of the American Philosophical Society, New Series, 13, Part 3, Article 13:351–399.

Cope, E. D. 1870. A partial synopsis of the fishes of the fresh waters of North Carolina. Proceedings of the American Philosophical Society 11:448–495.

Corcoran, M. F. 1979. Electrofishing for catfish: use of low-frequency pulsed direct current. Progressive Fish-Culturist 41:200–201.

Corcoran, M. F. 1981. Geographic variation and evolutionary relationships of two species of bullhead catfishes (Siluriformes: Ictaluridae) in the southeastern United States. Doctoral dissertation. Duke University, Durham, North Carolina.

Cordes, L. E., and L. M. Page. 1980. Feeding chronology and diet composition of two darters (Percidae) in the Iroquois River system, Illinois. American Midland Naturalist 104:202–206.

Cordone, A. J., and D. W. Kelley. 1961. The influences of inorganic sediment on the aquatic life of streams. California Fish and Game 47:189–228.

Cornelius, R. R. 1966. A morphological study of three Iowa carpsuckers. Proceedings of the Iowa Academy of Science 73:177–179.

Corning, R. V. 1967a. Warmwater fisheries management investigations [Blackwater system]. Virginia Commission of Game and Inland Fisheries, Federal Aid in Sport Fish Restoration, Project F-5-R-11, Job 9—General survey, January 1, 1965–June 30, 1966. Job Completion Report, Richmond.

Corning, R. V. 1967b. Warmwater fisheries management investigations [Mattaponi system]. Virginia Commission of Game and Inland Fisheries, Federal Aid in Sport Fish Restoration, Project F-5-R-12, Job 9—General survey, July 1, 1966–June 30, 1967. Job Completion Report, Richmond.

Corning, R. V., and N. S. Prosser. 1969. Warmwater fisheries management investigations [Blackwater to Rappahannock drainages]. Virginia Commission of Game and Inland Fisheries, Federal Aid in Sport Fish Restoration, Project F-5-R-14, Job 9—General survey, July 1, 1959–June 30, 1968. Job Completion Report, Richmond.

Cosby, B. J., P. F. Ryan, J. R. Webb, G. M. Hornberger, and J. N. Galloway. 1991. Mountains of western Virginia. Pages 297–318 *in* D. F. Charles, editor. Acid deposition and aquatic ecosystems: regional case studies. Springer-Verlag, New York.

Courtenay, W. R., D. A. Hensley, J. N. Taylor, and J. A. McCann. 1984. Distribution of exotic fishes in the continental United States. Pages 41–77 *in* W. R. Courtenay and J. R. Stauffer, editors. Distribution, biology, and management of exotic fishes. Johns Hopkins University Press, Baltimore, Maryland.

Courtenay, W. R., and J. R. Stauffer, editors. 1984. Distribution, biology, and management of exotic fishes. Johns Hopkins University Press, Baltimore, Maryland.

Courtenay, W. R., and J. N. Taylor. 1984. The exotic ichthyofauna of the contiguous United States with preliminary observations on intracontinental transplants. EIFAC (European Inland Fisheries Advisory Commission) Technical Paper 42(2):466–487.

Coutant, C. C. 1977. Compilation of temperature preference data. Journal of the Fisheries Research Board of Canada 34:739–745.

Coutant, C. C. 1985a. Striped bass: environmental risks in fresh and salt water. Transactions of the American Fisheries Society 114:1–2.

Coutant, C. C. 1985b. Striped bass, temperature, and dissolved oxygen: a speculative hypothesis for environmental risk. Transactions of the American Fisheries Society 114:31–61.

Cox, W. E. 1988. Guide to the papers of George Sprague Myers, *circa* 1903–1986, and undated. Guides to Collections, Archives and Special Collections of the Smithsonian Institution, Number 8, Washington, D.C.

Coyle, E. E. 1930. The algal food of *Pimephales promelas* (fathead minnow). Ohio Journal of Science 30:23–35. (Not seen; cited in Scott and Crossman 1973.)

Craddock, J. E. 1965. Some aspects of the life history of the banded sculpin, *Cottus carolinae carolinae*, in Doe Run, Meade County, Kentucky. Doctoral dissertation. University of Louisville, Kentucky.

Craig, A. J. 1970. Vegetational history of the Shenandoah Valley, Virginia. Geological Society of America Special Paper (Regional Studies) 123:283–296.

Craig, P. C., and J. Wells. 1976. Life history notes for a population of slimy sculpin (*Cottus cognatus*) in an Alaska stream. Journal of the Fisheries Research Board of Canada 33:1639–1642.

Crawford, D. R. 1921. A record of *Notropis whipplei* from the District of Columbia. Copeia 101:87–89.

Creaser, C. W. 1930. Relative importance of hydrogen-ion concentration, temperature, dissolved oxygen, and carbon-dioxide tension, on habitat selection by brook trout. Ecology 11:246–262.

Creed, R. P. 1985. Feeding, diet, and repeat spawning of blueback herring, *Alosa aestivalis*, from the Chowan River, North Carolina. U.S. Fish and Wildlife Service Fishery Bulletin 83:711–716.

Cross, F. B. 1950. Effects of sewage and of a headwaters impoundment on the fishes of Stillwater Creek in Payne County, Oklahoma. American Midland Naturalist 43:128–145.

Cross, F. B. 1953. Nomenclature in the Pimephalinae, with special reference to the bullhead minnow, *Pimephales vigilax perspicuus* (Girard). Transactions of the Kansas Academy of Science 56:92–96.

Cross, F. B. 1967. Handbook of fishes of Kansas. University of Kansas Museum of Natural History Miscellaneous Publication 45.

Cross, F. B., and J. T. Collins. 1975. Fishes in Kansas.

University of Kansas, Museum of Natural History, Public Education Series 3, Lawrence.

Cross, F. B., R. L. Mayden, and J. D. Stewart. 1986. Fishes in the western Mississippi drainage. Pages 363–412 *in* Hocutt and Wiley (1986).

Cross, F. B., and W. L. Minckley. 1958. New records of four fishes from Kansas. Transactions of the Kansas Academy of Science 61:104–108.

Cross, F. B., and W. L. Minckley. 1960. Five natural hybrid combinations in minnows (Cyprinidae). University of Kansas Publications of the Museum of Natural History 13:1–18.

Crossman, E. J. 1962a. The redfin pickerel, *Esox a. americanus* in North Carolina. Copeia 1962:114–123.

Crossman, E. J. 1962b. Predator–prey relationships in pikes (Esocidae). Journal of the Fisheries Research Board of Canada 19:979–980.

Crossman, E. J. 1966. A taxonomic study of *Esox americanus* and its subspecies in eastern North America. Copeia 1966:1–20.

Crossman, E. J. 1977. Displacement, and home range movements of muskellunge determined by ultrasonic tracking. Environmental Biology of Fishes 1:145–158.

Crossman, E. J. 1978. Taxonomy and distribution of North American esocids. American Fisheries Society Special Publication 11:13–26.

Crossman, E. J. 1980. The role of reference collections in the biomonitoring of fishes. Pages 357–378 *in* C. H. Hocutt and J. R. Stauffer, editors. Biological monitoring of fish. D. C. Heath and Co., Lexington, Massachusetts.

Crossman, E. J. 1986. The noble muskellunge: a review. American Fisheries Society Special Publication 15:1–13.

Crossman, E. J., and K. Buss. 1965. Hybridization in the family Esocidae. Journal of the Fisheries Research Board of Canada 22:1261–1292.

Crossman, E. J., and J. M. Casselman. 1987. An annotated bibliography of the pike, *Esox lucius* (Osteichthyes: Salmoniformes). Royal Ontario Museum Life Sciences Miscellaneous Publication.

Crossman, E. J., and C. D. Goodchild. 1978. An annotated bibliography of the muskellunge, *Esox masquinongy* (Osteichthys: Salmoniformes). Royal Ontario Museum Life Sciences Miscellaneous Publication.

Crossman, E. J., and G. E. Lewis. 1973. An annotated bibliography of the chain pickerel, *Esox niger* (Osteichthyes: Salmoniformes). Royal Ontario Museum Life Sciences Miscellaneous Publication.

Crossman, E. J., S. J. Nepszy, and P. Krause. 1987. The first record of grass carp, *Ctenopharyngodon idella*, in Canadian waters. Canadian Field-Naturalist 101:584–586.

Crossman, E. J., and R. C. Simpson. 1984. Warmouth, *Lepomis gulosus*, a freshwater fish new to Canada. Canadian Field-Naturalist 98:496–498.

Crossman, J. S., J. Cairns, and R. L. Kaesler. 1973. Aquatic invertebrate recovery in the Clinch River following hazardous spills and floods. Virginia Polytechnic Institute and State University Water Resources Research Center Bulletin 63.

Crowe, W. R. 1959. The bluegill in Michigan. Michigan

Department of Conservation Fish Division Pamphlet 31.

Culligan, W. J. 1985. Special features. New York State Conservationist 40(3):55.

Culver, D., J. R. Holsinger, and R. Baroody. 1973. Toward a predictive cave biogeography: the Greenbrier Valley as a case study. Evolution 27:689–695.

Cummins, K. W., and G. H. Lauff. 1969. The influence of substrate particle size on the microdistribution of stream macrobenthos. Hydrobiologia 34:145–181.

Curran, H. W., and D. T. Ries. 1937. Fisheries investigations in the lower Hudson River. Pages 124–145 in A biological survey of the lower Hudson watershed. Supplemental to the 26th Annual Report of the New York State Conservation Department, Albany.

Curray, J. R. 1965. Late Quaternary history, continental shelves of the United States. Pages 723–735 in H. E. Wright and D. G. Frey, editors. The Quaternary of the United States. Princeton University Press, Princeton, New Jersey.

Curry, K. D., and A. Spacie. 1979. The importance of tributary streams to the reproduction of catostomids and sauger. Purdue University, Water Resources Research Center, Technical Report 126, West Lafayette, Indiana.

Curry, K. D., and A. Spacie. 1984. Differential use of stream habitat by spawning catostomids. American Midland Naturalist 111:267–279.

Dabney, V. 1971. Virginia the new dominion. Doubleday and Company, Garden City, New York.

Dadswell, M. J. 1979. Biology and population characteristics of the shortnose sturgeon, *Acipenser brevirostrum* Lesueur 1818 (Osteichthyes: Acipenseridae), in the Saint John River Estuary, New Brunswick, Canada. Canadian Journal of Zoology 57:2186–2210.

Dadswell, M. J., B. D. Taubert, T. S. Squiers, D. Marchette, and J. Buckley. 1984. Synopsis of biological data on shortnose sturgeon, *Acipenser brevirostrum* Lesueur 1818. NOAA (National Oceanic and Atmospheric Administration) Technical Report NMFS (National Marine Fisheries Service) 14. (Also: FAO [Food and Agriculture Organization of the United Nations] Fisheries Synopsis 140.)

Dahlberg, M. D., and D. C. Scott. 1971a. The freshwater fishes of Georgia. Bulletin of the Georgia Academy of Science 29:1–64.

Dahlberg, M. D., and D. C. Scott. 1971b. Introductions of freshwater fishes in Georgia. Bulletin of the Georgia Academy of Science 29:245–252.

Daiber, F. C. 1953a. The life history and ecology of the sheepshead, *Aplodinotus grunniens* Rafinesque, in western Lake Erie. Abstracts of Doctoral Dissertations 64:131–136. (Ohio State University Press, Columbus.)

Daiber, F. C. 1953b. Notes on the spawning population of the freshwater drum (*Aplodinotus grunniens* Rafinesque) in western Lake Erie. American Midland Naturalist 50:159–171.

Daniels, R. A. 1989. Significance of burying in *Ammocrypta pellucida*. Copeia 1989:29–34.

Daniels, R. A., and P. B. Moyle. 1984. Geographic variation and a taxonomic reappraisal of the marbled sculpin, *Cottus klamathensis*. Copeia 1984:949–959.

Davies, J. H. 1981. Food habits of largemouth bass in two coastal streams of North Carolina. Pages 346–350 in L. A. Krumholz, editor. The warmwater streams symposium. American Fisheries Society, Southern Division, Bethesda, Maryland.

Davis, B. J., and R. J. Miller. 1967. Brain patterns in minnows of the genus *Hybopsis* in relation to feeding habits and habitat. Copeia 1967:1–39.

Davis, J., J. P. Miller, and W. L. Wilson. 1970. Biology and utilization of anadromous alosids. Completion Report 1967–1970 (U.S. National Marine Fisheries Service Project VA AFC-1) to Virginia Institute of Marine Science, Gloucester Point, Virginia.

Davis, J. R. 1972. The spawning behavior, fecundity rates, and food habits of the redbreast sunfish in southeastern North Carolina. Proceedings of the Annual Conference Southeastern Association of Game and Fish Commissioners 25(1971):556–560.

Davis, R. M. 1972. Age, growth, and fecundity of the rosyside dace, *Clinostomus funduloides* Girard. Chesapeake Science 13:63–66.

Davis, R. M., and E. C. Enamait. 1982. Distribution and abundance of fishes and benthic macroinvertebrates in the upper Potomac River, 1975–1979. Maryland Department of Natural Resources, Federal Aid in Sport Fish Restoration, Project F-29-R, Study I, Final Report, Annapolis.

Davis, R. M., E. C. Enamait, and L. Fewlass. 1982. Statewide fisheries survey and management. Maryland Department of Natural Resources, Federal Aid in Sport Fish Restoration, Project F-29-R-6, Study VI, Job Progress Report, Annapolis.

Davis, W. M. 1903. The stream contest along the Blue Ridge. Geographical Society of Philadelphia Bulletin 3:213–224.

Davis, W. S. 1953. *Campostoma anomalum roanokense*, a new subspecies of the stoneroller minnow in the James and Roanoke rivers. Master's thesis. Virginia Polytechnic Institute and State University, Blacksburg.

Deacon, J. E. 1961. Fish populations, following a drought, in the Neosho and Marias des Cygnes rivers of Kansas. University of Kansas Publications of the Museum of Natural History 13:359–427.

Deacon, J. E., G. Kobetich, J. D. Williams, and S. Contreras. 1979. Fishes of North America endangered, threatened, or of special concern: 1979. Fisheries (Bethesda) 4(2):29–44.

Deason, H. J. 1934. The development of fishes, tracing the natural developments from eggs to fry. The Fisherman 3(11):1, 3. (Not seen; cited in Becker 1983.)

Dees, L. T. 1961. Rains of fishes. U.S. Fish and Wildlife Service Fishery Leaflet 513.

Deevey, E. S., and R. F. Flint. 1957. Postglacial Hypsithermal Interval. Science 125:182–184.

DeKay, J. E. 1842. Zoology of New York, or the New York fauna; part IV, fishes. W. and A. White and J. Visscher, Albany, New York.

Delcourt, P. A., and H. R. Delcourt. 1984. Late Quaternary paleoclimates and biotic responses in eastern North America and the western North Atlantic Ocean.

Palaeogeography, Palaeoclimatology, Palaeoecology 48:263–284.

DeMont, D. J. 1982. Use of *Lepomis macrochirus* Rafinesque nests by spawning *Notemigonus crysoleucas* (Mitchill) (Pisces: Centrarchidae and Cyprinidae). Brimleyana 8:61–63.

Dence, W. A. 1937. Preliminary reconnaissance of the waters of the Archer and Anna Huntington Wild Life Forest Station and their fish inhabitants. Bulletin of the New York State College of Forestry at Syracuse University 10:610–672. (Also: Roosevelt Wild Life Bulletin 6[4].)

Dendy, J. S. 1945. Predicting depth distribution of fish in three TVA storage-type reservoirs. Transactions of the American Fisheries Society 75:65–71.

Dendy, J. S. 1946a. Further studies of depth distribution of fish, Norris Reservoir, Tennessee. Journal of the Tennessee Academy of Science 21:94–104.

Dendy, J. S. 1946b. Food of several species of fish, Norris Reservoir, Tennessee. Journal of the Tennessee Academy of Science 21:105–127.

Dennis, S. D. 1981. Mussel fauna of the Powell River, Tennessee and Virginia. Sterkiana 71:1–7.

Dennis, S. D. 1985. Distributional analysis of the freshwater mussel fauna of the Tennessee River system, with special reference to possible limiting effects of siltation. Doctoral dissertation. Virginia Polytechnic Institute and State University, Blacksburg. (Also: Tennessee Wildlife Resources Agency, Technical Report 85-2, Nashville.)

Denoncourt, R. F. 1969a. A systematic study of the gilt darter *Percina evides* (Jordan and Copeland) (Pisces, Percidae). Doctoral dissertation. Cornell University, Ithaca, New York.

Denoncourt, R. F. 1969b. A systematic study of the gilt darter *Percina evides* (Jordan and Copeland) (Pisces, Percidae). Dissertation Abstracts International 30:1408.

Denoncourt, R. F. 1976. Sexual dimorphism and geographic variation in the bronze darter, *Percina palmaris* (Pisces: Percidae). Copeia 1976:54–59.

Denoncourt, R. F., C. H. Hocutt, and J. R. Stauffer. 1975. Extensions of the known ranges of *Ericymba buccata* Cope and *Etheostoma zonale* (Cope) in the Susquehanna River drainage. Proceedings of the Pennsylvania Academy of Science 49:45–46.

Denoncourt, R. F., C. H. Hocutt, and J. R. Stauffer. 1977a. Notes on the habitat, description and distribution of the sharpnose darter, *Percina oxyrhyncha*. Copeia 1977:168–171.

Denoncourt, R. F., W. A. Potter, and J. R. Stauffer. 1977b. Records of the greenside darter, *Etheostoma blennioides*, from the Susquehanna River drainage in Pennsylvania. Ohio Journal of Science 77:38–42.

Denoncourt, R. F., and J. R. Stauffer. 1976. A taxonomic study of recently introduced populations of the banded darter, *Etheostoma zonale* (Cope), in the Susquehanna River. Chesapeake Science 17:303–304.

Deubler, E. E. 1955. A taxonomic study of the cyprinid fish *Clinostomus vandoisulus* (Valenciennes) in the eastern United States. Doctoral dissertation. Cornell University, Ithaca, New York.

Dietemann, A. J. 1975. A provisional inventory of the fishes of Rock Creek, Little Falls Branch, Cabin John Creek, and Rock Run, Montgomery County, Maryland. Maryland–National Capital Park and Planning Commission, Environmental Planning Document, Hyattsville, Maryland.

Dietrich, R. V. 1954. Geology of the Pilot Mountain area, Virginia. Bulletin of the Virginia Polytechnic Institute Engineering Experiment Station Series 91, 47(4):1–32.

Dietrich, R. V. 1959. Geology and mineral resources of Floyd County of the Blue Ridge Upland, southwestern Virginia. Bulletin of the Virginia Polytechnic Institute Engineering Experiment Station Series 134, 52(12):1–160.

Dietrich, R. V. 1970a. Geology and Virginia. University Press of Virginia, Charlottesville.

Dietrich, R. V. 1970b. V = f(S . . .). Virginia Polytechnic Institute and State University Research Division Monograph 2:67–99.

Dillard, J. G., K. L. Graham, and T. R. Russell, editors. 1986. The paddlefish: status, management and propagation. American Fisheries Society, North Central Division Special Publication 7, Bethesda, Maryland.

Dimmick, W. W. 1988. Ultrastructure of North America cyprinid maxillary barbels. Copeia 1988:72–80.

Dineen, C. F. 1951. A comparative study of the food habits of *Cottus bairdii* and associated species of Salmonidae. American Midland Naturalist 46:640–645.

Dingerkus, G., and W. M. Howell. 1976. Karyotypic analysis and evidence of tetraploidy in the North American paddlefish, *Polyodon spathula*. Science 194:842–844.

Dinsmore, J. J. 1962. Life history of the creek chub, with emphasis on growth. Proceedings of the Iowa Academy of Science 69:296–301.

Distler, D. A. 1968. Distribution and variation of *Etheostoma spectabile* (Agassiz) (Percidae, Teleostei). University of Kansas Science Bulletin 5:143–208.

Dobbin, C. N. 1941. A comparative study of the gross anatomy of the air-bladders of ten families of fishes of New York and other eastern states. Journal of Morphology 68:1–29.

Dobie, J. R., O. L. Meehan, S. F. Snieszko, and G. N. Washburn. 1956. Raising bait fishes. U.S. Fish and Wildlife Service Circular 35.

Dobie, J. R., O. L. Meehan, and G. N. Washburn. 1948. Propagation of minnows and other bait species. U.S. Fish and Wildlife Service Circular 12.

Dodd, C. K., G. E. Drewry, R. M. Nowak, J. M. Sheppard, and J. D. Williams. 1985. Endangered and threatened wildlife and plants; review of vertebrate wildlife; notice of review. Federal Register 50 (18 September 1985):37958–37967.

Dominey, W. J. 1988. Mating tactics in bluegill sunfish. ASB (Association of Southeast Biologists) Bulletin 35:61.

Domrose, R. J. 1963. Evaluation of the threadfin shad introductions. Virginia Commission of Game and Inland Fisheries, Federal Aid in Sport Fish Restoration, Project F-5-R-8, July 1, 1961–December 31, 1962. Job Completion Report, Richmond.

Dorsa, W. J., and R. A. Fritzsche. 1979. Characters of

newly hatched larvae of *Morone chrysops* (Pisces, Perci-chthyidae), from Yocona River, Mississippi. Journal of the Mississippi Academy of Sciences 24:37–41.

Dott, R. H., and R. L. Batten. 1981. Evolution of the earth, 2nd edition. McGraw-Hill, New York.

Douglas, H. H. 1964. Caves of Virginia. Econo Print, Falls Church, Virginia.

Douglas, M. E., and J. C. Avise. 1982. Speciation rates and morphological divergence in fishes: tests of gradual versus rectangular modes of evolutionary change. Evolution 36:224–232.

Douglas, M. E., W. L. Minckley, and H. M. Tyus. 1989. Qualitative characters, identification of Colorado River chubs (Cyprinidae: genus *Gila*) and the "art of seeing well." Copeia 1989:653–662.

Dowling, T. E., and W. M. Brown. 1989. Allozymes, mitochondrial DNA, and levels of phylogenetic resolution among four minnow species (*Notropis*: Cyprinidae). Systematic Zoology 38:126–143.

Dowling, T. E., and W. S. Moore. 1984. Level of reproductive isolation between two cyprinid fishes, *Notropis cornutus* and *N. chrysocephalus*. Copeia 1984:617–628.

Dowling, T. E., and W. S. Moore. 1985a. Evidence for selection against hybrids in the family Cyprinidae (genus *Notropis*). Evolution 39:152–158.

Dowling, T. E., and W. S. Moore. 1985b. Genetic variation and divergence of the sibling pair of cyprinid fishes, *Notropis cornutus* and *N. chrysocephalus*. Biochemical Systematics and Ecology 13:471–476.

Dowling, T. E., G. R. Smith, and W. M. Brown. 1989. Reproductive isolation and introgression between *Notropis cornutus* and *N. chrysocephalus* (family Cyprinidae): comparisons of morphology, allozymes, and mitochondrial DNA. Evolution 43:620–634.

Downhower, J. F., and L. Brown. 1977. A sampling technique for benthic fish populations. Copeia 1977:403–406.

Downhower, J. F., and L. Brown. 1979. Seasonal changes in the social structure of a population of mottled sculpins, *Cottus bairdi*. Animal Behaviour 27:451–458.

Downhower, J. F., and L. Brown. 1980. Mate preferences of female mottled sculpins, *Cottus bairdi*. Animal Behaviour 28:728–734.

Downhower, J. F., L. Brown, R. Pederson, and G. Staples. 1983. Sexual selection and sexual dimorphism in mottled sculpins. Evolution 37:96–103.

Downhower, J. F., and R. J. Yost. 1977. The significance of male parental care in the mottled sculpin, *Cottus bairdi*. American Zoologist 17:936.

Dwyer, W. P., and R. G. Piper. 1984. Three-year hatchery and field evaluation of four strains of rainbow trout. North American Journal of Fisheries Management 4:216–221.

Dymond, J. R. 1937. New records of Ontario fishes. Copeia 1937:59.

Dymond, J. R., and J. L. Hart. 1927. The fishes of Lake Abitibi (Ontario) and adjacent waters. University of Toronto Studies Biological Series, Publications of the Ontario Fisheries Research Laboratory 28.

Eastman, J. T. 1977. The pharyngeal bones and teeth of catostomid fishes. American Midland Naturalist 97:68–88.

Eastman, J. T. 1980. The caudal skeletons of catostomid fishes. American Midland Naturalist 103:133–148.

Eastman, J. T., and J. C. Underhill. 1973. Intraspecific variation in pharyngeal tooth formulae of some cyprinid fishes. Copeia 1973:45–53.

Echelle, A. A., and C. D. Riggs. 1972. Aspects of the early life history of gars (*Lepisosteus*) in Lake Texoma. Transactions of the American Fisheries Society 101:106–112.

Eddy, S. 1957. How to know the freshwater fishes. W. C. Brown Company, Dubuque, Iowa.

Eddy, S., and T. Surber. 1947. Northern fishes with special reference to the upper Mississippi Valley. C. T. Branford Company, Newton Centre, Massachusetts.

Eddy, S., and J. C. Underhill. 1974. Northern fishes with special reference to the upper Mississippi Valley. University of Minnesota Press, Minneapolis.

Eder, S., and C. A. Carlson. 1977. Food habits of carp and white suckers in the South Platte and St. Vrain rivers and Goosequill Pond, Weld County, Colorado. Transactions of the American Fisheries Society 106:339–346.

Edmunds, G. F., S. L. Jensen, and L. Berner. 1976. The mayflies of North and Central America. University of Minnesota Press, Minneapolis.

Edsall, T. A. 1964. Feeding by three species of fishes on the eggs of spawning alewives. Copeia 1964:226–227.

Edsall, T. A. 1970. The effects of temperature on the rate of development and survival of alewife eggs and larvae. Transactions of the American Fisheries Society 99:376–380.

Edwards, L. F. 1926. The protractile apparatus of the mouth of the catastomid fishes. Anatomical Record 33:257–270.

Eldredge, N., and S. M. Stanley, editors. 1984. Living fossils. Springer-Verlag, New York.

Elkin, R. E. 1956. The fish population of two cut-off pools in Salt Creek, Osage County, Oklahoma. Proceedings of the Oklahoma Academy of Science 35:25–29.

Ellis, D. V., and M. A. Giles. 1965. The spawning behavior of the walleye, *Stizostedion vitreum* (Mitchill). Transactions of the American Fisheries Society 94:358–362.

Ellis, M. M. 1914. Fishes of Colorado. University of Colorado Studies 11:5–136.

Ellis, M. M., and G. C. Roe. 1917. Destruction of log perch eggs by suckers. Copeia 47:69–71.

Elrod, J. H. 1971. Dynamics of fishes in an Alabama pond subjected to intensive fishing. Transactions of the American Fisheries Society 100:757–768.

Elser, H. J. 1961. These are the champs: record Maryland fishes. Maryland Conservationist 38(2):15–17.

EMC (Elkem Metals Company). 1984. Application for a new license for the Hawks Nest-Glen Ferris Project, Project 2512. Submitted to U.S. Federal Energy Regulatory Commission (FERC). FERC, Washington, D.C.

Emery, A. R. 1973. Preliminary comparisons of day and night habits of freshwater fish in Ontario lakes. Journal of the Fisheries Research Board of Canada 30:761–774.

Emery, A. R., and R. Winterbottom. 1980. A technique for fish specimen photography in the field. Canadian Journal of Zoology 58:2158–2162.

Emery, K. O., and L. E. Garrison. 1967. Sea levels 7,000 to 20,000 years ago. Science 157:684–687.

Emig, J. W. 1966a. Smallmouth bass. Pages 354–366 in Calhoun (1966).

Emig, J. W. 1966b. Red-ear sunfish. Pages 392–399 in Calhoun (1966).

Emiliani, C., and N. J. Shackleton. 1974. The Brunhes epoch: isotopic paleotemperatures and geochronolgy. Science 183:511–514.

Enamait, E. C., and R. M. Davis. 1982. Biological surveys of lakes, ponds, and impoundments. Maryland Department of Natural Resources, Federal Aid in Sport Fish Restoration, Project F-29-R-6, Jobs 1–2, January 1–December 31, 1981. Progress Report, Annapolis.

Encyclopedia Americana. 1986. Grolier Inc., Danbury, Connecticut.

England, R. H., and K. B. Cumming. 1972. Stream damage from manganese strip-mining. Proceedings of the Annual Conference Southeastern Association of Game and Fish Commissioners 25(1971):399–418.

Englert, J., and B. H. Seghers. 1983a. Habitat segregation by stream darters (Pisces: Percidae) in the Thames River watershed of southwestern Ontario. Canadian Field-Naturalist 97:177–180.

Englert, J., and B. H. Seghers. 1983b. Predation by fish and common mergansers on darters (Pisces: Percidae) in the Thames River watershed of southwestern Ontario. Canadian Field-Naturalist 97:218–219.

Eoff, J. 1855. On the habits of the black bass of the Ohio (Grystes fasciatus). Pages 289–290 in 9th Annual Report of the Board of Regents, Smithsonian Institution, Washington, D.C.

Erdman, D. S. 1972. Inland game fishes of Puerto Rico, 2nd edition. Journal of the Department of Agriculture of Puerto Rico 4:1–96. (Not seen; cited in Jones et al. 1978.)

Erickson, J. E. 1977. The life history of the banded darter, Etheostoma zonale zonale (Cope), in the Cannon River, Minnesota. Dissertation Abstracts International (Section B) 38:2569.

Eschmeyer, P. H. 1950. The life history of the walleye, Stizostedion vitreum vitreum (Mitchill), in Michigan. Michigan Department of Conservation, Bulletin of the Institute of Fisheries Research 3.

Eschmeyer, W. N., and R. M. Bailey. 1990. Genera of recent fishes. Pages 7–433 in W. N. Eschmeyer. Catalog of the genera of Recent fishes. California Academy of Sciences, San Francisco.

Esmond, E. F., C. H. Hocutt, R. P. Morgan, and J. R. Stauffer. 1981. Taxonomic status of two sibling cyprinid species, Nocomis micropogon and N. platyrhynchus. In Abstracts of the 61st Annual Meeting of the American Society of Ichthyologists and Herpetologists.

Esmond, E. F., and J. R. Stauffer. 1983. Taxometric comparison of the Atlantic slope and Ohio River populations of Etheostoma caeruleum Storer. American Midland Naturalist 109:390–397.

Estes, C. M. 1949. The fecundity of the bluegill (Lepomis macrochirus) in certain small east Texas reservoirs. Master's thesis. North Texas State College, Denton. (Not seen; cited in Carlander 1977.)

Estes, R. D. 1971. The effects of the Smith Mountain Pump Storage Project on the fishery in the lower reservoir, Leesville, Virginia. Doctoral dissertation. Virginia Polytechnic Institute and State University, Blacksburg.

Estes, R. D., and D. Y. White. 1985. Systematics of the brook trout, Salvelinus fontinalis (Mitchill) in the Great Smoky Mountains National Park. 1. meristic and morphometric analysis. Page 60 in Abstracts of the 65th Annual Meeting of the American Society of Ichthyologists and Herpetologists.

Etnier, D. A. 1971. Food of three species of sunfishes (Lepomis, Centrarchidae) and their hybrids in three Minnesota Lakes. Transactions of the American Fisheries Society 100:124–128.

Etnier, D. A., and R. E. Jenkins. 1980. Noturus stanauli, a new madtom catfish (Ictaluridae) from the Clinch and Duck rivers, Tennessee. Bulletin Alabama Museum of Natural History 5:17–22.

Etnier, D. A., and W. C. Starnes. 1986. Etheostoma lynceum removed from the synonymy of E. zonale (Pisces, Percidae). Copeia 1986:832–836.

Etnier, D. A., W. C. Starnes, and B. H. Bauer. 1979. Whatever happened to the silvery minnow (Hybognathus nuchalis) in the Tennessee River? Proceedings of the Southeastern Fishes Council 2(3):1–3.

Etnier, D. A, and M. L. Warren. 1990. Lepomis Rafinesque, 1819 (Osteichthyes, Perciformes): proposed fixation of masculine gender for the name. Bulletin of Zoological Nomenclature 47:280–282.

Etnier, D. A., and J. D. Williams. 1989. Etheostoma (Nothonotus) wapiti (Osteichthyes: Percidae), a new darter from the southern bend of the Tennessee River system in Alabama and Tennessee. Proceedings of the Biological Society of Washington 102:987–1000.

Evans, H. E. 1952. The correlation of brain pattern and feeding habits in four species of cyprinid fishes. Journal of Comparative Neurology 97:133–142.

Evenhuis, B. L. 1973. Inventory and classification of streams in the Big Sandy River drainage. Kentucky Department of Fish and Wildlife Resources, Fisheries Bulletin 57, Frankfort.

Everhart, W. H. 1966. Fishes of Maine. Maine Department of Inland Fisheries and Game, Augusta.

Evermann, B. W. 1916. Notes on the fishes of the Lumber River. Copeia 1916:77–80.

Evermann, B. W. 1918. The fishes of Kentucky and Tennessee: a distributional catalogue of the known species. U.S. Bureau of Fisheries Bulletin 35:293–368.

Evermann, B. W., and S. F. Hildebrand. 1910. On a collection of fishes from the lower Potomac, the entrance of Chesapeake Bay, and from streams flowing into these waters. Proceedings of the Biological Society of Washington 23:157–163.

Evermann, B. W., and S. F. Hildebrand. 1916. Notes on the fishes of east Tennessee. U.S. Bureau of Fisheries Bulletin 34:431–451.

Ewan, J., and N. Ewan. 1970. John Banister and his natural history of Virginia 1678–1692. University of Illinois Press, Urbana.

Ewers, L. A., and M. W. Boesel. 1935. The food of some

Buckeye Lake fishes. Transactions of the American Fisheries Society 65:57–70.

Fahy, W. E. 1954. The life history of the northern greenside darter, *Etheostoma blennioides blennioides* Rafinesque. Journal of the Elisha Mitchell Scientific Society 70:139–205.

Falls, R. K. 1982. An electrophoretic comparison of gene loci in *Etheostoma nigrum* and *Etheostoma olmstedi* from the James River drainage, Virginia. Master's thesis. University of Richmond, Richmond, Virginia.

Farmer, G. J. 1980. Biology and physiology of feeding in adult lampreys. Canadian Journal of Fisheries and Aquatic Sciences 37:1751–1761.

Farmer, G. J., and F. W. H. Beamish. 1973. Sea lamprey (*Petromyzon marinus*) predation on freshwater teleosts. Journal of the Fisheries Research Board of Canada 30:601–605.

Farringer, R. T., A. A. Echelle, and S. F. Lehtinen. 1979. Reproductive cycle of the red shiner, *Notropis lutrensis*, in central Texas and south central Oklahoma. Transactions of the American Fisheries Society 108:271–276.

Fava, J. A., and C. Tsai. 1974. The life history of the pearl dace, *Semotilus margarita*, in Maryland. Chesapeake Science 15:159–162.

Fava, J. A., and C. Tsai. 1976. Tuberculation of the pearl dace, *Semotilus margarita* (Pisces: Cyprinidae). Copeia 1976:370–374.

Fearnow, E. C. 1929. Results of game-fish plantings by the United States Bureau of Fisheries. U.S. Bureau of Fisheries Economic Circular 67.

Fee, E. 1965. Life history of the northern common shiner, *Notropis cornutus frontalis*, in Boone County, Iowa. Proceedings of the Iowa Academy of Science 72:272–281.

Feeman, J. C. 1980. A quantitative survey of fish and macroinvertebrates of the Holston River basin: August–September 1973. Tennessee Valley Authority, Report WR(70)-40-4-80.1, Norris, Tennessee.

Feeman, J. C. 1986. Fishes of the North Fork Holston River system, Virginia and Tennessee. Proceedings of the Southeastern Fishes Council 4(4):4–10.

Feeman, J. C. 1987. Results of fish surveys in the Tennessee River drainage, 1979–1981. Brimleyana 13:99–121.

Felley, J. D. 1980. Analysis of morphology and asymmetry in bluegill sunfish (*Lepomis macrochirus*) in the southeastern United States. Copeia 1980:18–19.

Felley, J. D., and L. G. Hill. 1983. Multivariate assessment of environment preferences of cyprinid fishes of the Illinois River, Oklahoma. American Midland Naturalist 109:209–221.

Fenneman, N. M. 1938. Physiography of eastern United States. McGraw-Hill, New York.

Ferguson, M. T. 1989. Crevice spawning behavior of *Cyprinella trichroistia*, *C. gibbsi*, and *C. callistia*. ASB (Association of Southeastern Biologists) Bulletin 36:66.

Finger, T. R. 1982a. Fish community–habitat relations in a central New York stream. Journal of Freshwater Ecology 1:343–352.

Finger, T. R. 1982b. Interactive segregation among three species of sculpins (*Cottus*). Copeia 1982:680–694.

Fink, W. L. 1984. Salmoniforms: introduction, and basal

euteleosts: relationships. Pages 139 and 202–206 *in* Moser et al. (1984).

Fink, W. L., and S. H. Weitzman. 1982. Relationships of the stomiiform fishes (Teleostei), with a description of *Diplophos*. Bulletin of the Museum of Comparative Zoology 150:31–93.

Fischler, K. J. 1959. Contributions of Hudson and Connecticut rivers to New York–New Jersey shad catch of 1956. U.S. Fish and Wildlife Service Fishery Bulletin 60:161–174.

Fish, F. F., and E. G. McCoy. 1959. The river discharges required for effective spawning by striped bass in the rapids of the Roanoke River of North Carolina. North Carolina Wildlife Resources Commission, Raleigh.

Fisher, J. W. 1981. Ecology of *Fundulus catenatus* in three interconnected stream orders. American Midland Naturalist 106:372–378.

Fisher, W. L. 1990. Life history and ecology of the orangefin darter *Etheostoma bellum* (Pisces: Percidae). American Midland Naturalist 123:268–281.

Fisher, W. L., and W. D. Pearson. 1987. Patterns of resource utilization among four species of darters in three central Kentucky streams. Pages 69–76 *in* W. J. Matthews and D. C. Heins, editors. Community and evolutionary ecology of North American stream fishes. University of Oklahoma Press, Norman.

Fitch, J. E., and R. J. Lavenberg. 1971. Marine food and game fishes of California. University of California Press, Berkeley.

Fitz, R. B. 1966a. Unusual food of a paddlefish (*Polyodon spathula*) in Tennessee. Copeia 1966:356.

Fitz, R. B. 1966b. Distribution of the pumpkinseed (*Lepomis gibbosus*) and redbreast sunfish (*Lepomis auritus*) in Tennessee. Journal of the Tennessee Academy of Science (July):98.

Fitz, R. B., and J. A. Holbrook II. 1978. Sauger and walleye in Norris Reservoir, Tennessee. American Fisheries Society Special Publication 11:82–88.

Fitzpatrick, J. F. 1986. The pre-Pliocene Tennessee River and its bearing on crawfish distribution (Decapoda: Cambaridae). Brimleyana 12:123–146.

Flemer, D. A., and W. S. Woolcott. 1966. Food habits and distribution of the fishes of Tuckahoe Creek, Virginia, with special emphasis on the bluegill, *Lepomis m. macrochirus* Rafinesque. Chesapeake Science 7:75–89.

Flescher, D. D. 1983. Fish photography. Fisheries (Bethesda) 8(4):2–6.

Fletcher, A. M. 1957. A rare darter-spawning. The Aquarium (June):202–203.

Flint, R. F. 1957. Glacial and Pleistocene geology. John Wiley and Sons, New York.

Flittner, G. A. 1964. Morphology and life history of the emerald shiner *Notropis atherinoides*. Doctoral dissertation. University of Michigan, Ann Arbor. (Not seen; cited in Becker 1983.)

Foerster, J. W., and S. L. Goodbred. 1978. Evidence for a resident alewife population in the northern Chesapeake Bay. Estuarine and Coastal Marine Science 7:437–444.

Foltz, J. W. 1976. Fecundity of the slimy sculpin, *Cottus cognatus*, in Lake Michigan. Copeia 1976:802–804.

Fontaine, P. A. 1944. Notes on the spawning of the shovelhead catfish, *Pylodictis olivaris* (Rafinesque). Copeia 1944:50–51.

Forbes, S. A. 1878. The food of Illinois fishes. Bulletin of the Illinois State Laboratory of Natural History 1(2):71–89.

Forbes, S. A. 1903. On the food of young fishes, 2nd edition. Reprint and emendment of Bulletin of the Illinois State Laboratory of Natural History 1(3):71–85.

Forbes, S. A., and R. E. Richardson. 1920. The fishes of Illinois, 2nd edition. Illinois Natural History Survey, Urbana.

Forney, J. L. 1955. Life history of the black bullhead, *Ameiurus melas* (Rafinesque), of Clear Lake, Iowa. Iowa State College Journal of Science 30:145–162.

Forney, J. L. 1957. Bait fish production in New York ponds. New York Fish and Game Journal 4:150–194.

Forney, J. L., and C. B. Taylor. 1963. Age and growth of white bass in Oneida Lake, New York. New York Fish and Game Journal 10:194–200. (Not seen; cited in Webb and Moss 1967.)

Foster, N. R. 1974. Order Atheriniformes (Belonidae, Cyprinodontidae, Poeciliidae). Pages 115–151 *in* A. J. Lippson and R. L. Moran, editors. Manual for identification of early developmental stages of fishes of the Potomac River estuary. Maryland Department of Natural Resources, Power Plant Siting Program, Miscellaneous Publication 13, Annapolis.

Fowler, H. W. 1905. The fishes of New Jersey. Pages 41–477 *in* Annual Report of the New Jersey State Museum (1905), Trenton.

Fowler, H. W. 1906. *Pimephales notatus* in the lower Susquehanna. American Naturalist 40:743.

Fowler, H. W. 1907. Some new and little-known percoid fishes. Proceedings of the Academy of Natural Sciences of Philadelphia 58:510–528.

Fowler, H. W. 1909. A synopsis of the Cyprinidae of Pennsylvania. Proceedings of the Academy of Natural Sciences of Philadelphia 60:517–553.

Fowler, H. W. 1910. Notes on the variation of some species of the genus *Notropis*. Proceedings of the Academy of Natural Sciences of Philadelphia 62:273–293.

Fowler, H. W. 1912. Some features of ornamentation in fresh-water fishes. American Naturalist 46:470–476.

Fowler, H. W. 1913. Notes on catostomid fishes. Proceedings of the Academy of Natural Sciences of Philadelphia 65:45–60.

Fowler, H. W. 1916. Some features of ornamentation in the killifishes or toothed minnows. American Naturalist 50:743–750.

Fowler, H. W. 1917a. Some notes on the breeding habits of local catfishes. Copeia 42:32–36.

Fowler, H. W. 1917b. Notes on the spawning habits of our lampreys. Aquarium Notes News 4:28–32.

Fowler, H. W. 1918. Fishes from the middle Atlantic states and Virginia. Occasional Papers of the Museum of Zoology University of Michigan 56.

Fowler, H. W. 1922. Records of fishes for the eastern and southern United States. Proceedings of the Academy of Natural Sciences of Philadelphia 74:1–27.

Fowler, H. W. 1923. Records of fishes for the southern states. Proceedings of the Biological Society of Washington 36:7–34.

Fowler, H. W. 1924. Notes on North American cyprinoid fishes. Proceedings of the Academy of Natural Sciences of Philadelphia 76:389–416.

Fowler, H. W. 1936. Fresh-water fishes obtained in North Carolina in 1930 and 1934. The Fish Culturist 15:192–194.

Fowler, H. W. 1945. A study of the fishes of the southern Piedmont and Coastal Plain. Monographs of the Academy of Natural Sciences of Philadelphia 7.

Fowler, J. F., and C. A. Taber. 1985. Food habits and feeding periodicity in two sympatric stonerollers (Cyprinidae). American Midland Naturalist 113:217–224.

Fox, P. J. 1978. Preliminary observations on different reproduction strategies in the bullhead (*Cottus gobio* L.) in northern and southern England. Journal of Fish Biology 12:5–11.

Franklin, D. R., and L. L. Smith. 1963. Early life history of the northern pike, *Esox lucius* L., with special reference to the factors influencing the numerical strength of year classes. Transactions of the American Fisheries Society 92:91–110.

Franz, R., and D. S. Lee. 1976. A relict population of the mottled sculpin, *Cottus bairdi*, from the Maryland Coastal Plain. Chesapeake Science 17:301–302.

Frazer, P. 1900. The life and letters of Edward Drinker Cope. American Geologist 26:67–128.

Freeman, H. W. 1952. Fishes of Richland County, South Carolina. University of South Carolina Publications, Series III, Biology 1:28–41, Columbia.

Freeze, M. 1984. Life history and biology of the striped bass and striped bass hybrids. Pages 17–27 *in* J. P. McCraren, editor. The aquaculture of striped bass, a proceedings. University of Maryland, Sea Grant Publication UM-SG-MAP-84-01, College Park.

Fremling, C. R. 1978. Biology and functional anatomy of the freshwater drum *Aplodinotus grunniens*. Nasco, Fort Atkinson, Wisconsin.

Frey, D. G. 1951. The fishes of North Carolina's Bay Lakes and their intraspecific variation. Journal of the Elisha Mitchell Scientific Society 67:1–44.

Frick, G. F., and R. P. Stearns. 1961. Mark Catesby, the colonial Audubon. University of Illinois Press, Urbana.

Fridley, H. M. 1950. The geomorphic history of the New–Kanawha River system. West Virginia Geological and Economic Survey, Reports of Investigations 7, Charleston.

Frietsche, R. A., R. D. Miracle, and R. W. McFarlane. 1979. Larvae and juveniles of the brook silverside, *Labidesthes sicculus*. Pages 187–197 *in* R. Wallus and C. W. Voigtlander, editors. Proceedings of a workshop on freshwater larval fishes. Tennessee Valley Authority, Norris, Tennessee.

Frissell, C. A., W. J. Liss, C. E. Warren, and M. D. Hurley. 1986. A hierarchical framework for stream habitat classification: viewing streams in a watershed context. Environmental Management 10:199–214.

Fritz, E. S. 1973. Hybridization and isolating mechanisms between sympatric populations of *Fundulus heteroclitus* and *F. diaphanus* (Pisces: Cyprinodontidae). Doctoral dissertation. Dalh usie University, Halifax, Nova Scotia. (Not seen; cited in Fritz and Garside 1975.)

Fritz, E. S., and E. T. Garside. 1974. Salinity preferences of *Fundulus heteroclitus* and *F. diaphanus* (Pisces: Cyprinodontidae): their role in geographic distribution. Canadian Journal of Zoology 52:997–1003.

Fritz, E. S., and E. T. Garside. 1975. Comparison of age composition, growth, and fecundity between two populations each of *Fundulus heteroclitus* and *F. diaphanus* (Pisces: Cyprinodontidae). Canadian Journal of Zoology 53:361–369.

Fritzche, R. A. 1978. Development of fishes of the Mid-Atlantic Bight. An atlas of egg, larval and juvenile stages, volume 5. U.S. Fish and Wildlife Service Biological Services Program FWS-OBS-78/12.

Fritzche, R. A., and G. D. Johnson. 1979. Striped bass vs. white perch: application of a new morphological approach to ichthyoplankton taxonomy. Pages 19–29 *in* R. Wallus and C. W. Voigtlander, editors. Proceedings of a workshop on freshwater larval fishes. Tennessee Valley Authority, Norris, Tennessee.

Fuchs, E. H. 1967. Life history of the emerald shiner, *Notropis atherinoides*, in Lewis and Clark Lake, South Dakota. Transactions of the American Fisheries Society 96:247–256.

Fuiman, L. A. 1979a. Materials for a description of lake chubsucker (*Erimyzon sucetta*), larvae. Pages 92–99 *in* R. D. Hoyt, editor. Proceedings of the 3rd symposium on larval fish. Western Kentucky University, Bowling Green.

Fuiman, L. A. 1979b. Descriptions and comparisons of catostomid fish larvae: northern Atlantic drainage species. Transactions of the American Fisheries Society 108:560–603.

Fuiman, L. A. 1982a. Family Petromyzontidae, lampreys. Pages 23–37 *in* Auer (1982a).

Fuiman, L. A. 1982b. Family Esocidae, pikes. Pages 155–173 *in* Auer (1982a).

Fuiman, L. A. 1982c. Family Catostomidae, suckers. Pages 345–435 *in* Auer (1982a).

Fuiman, L. A. 1982d. Family Percichthyidae, temperate basses. Pages 510–523 *in* Auer (1982a).

Fuiman, L. A. 1982e. Family Sciaenidae, drums. Pages 649–655 *in* Auer (1982a).

Fuiman, L. A. 1985. Contributions of developmental characters to a phylogeny of catostomid fishes, with comments on heterochrony. Copeia 1985:833–846.

Fuiman, L. A., J. V. Conner, B. F. Lathrop, G. L. Buynak, D. E. Snyder, and J. J. Loos. 1983. State of the art of identification for cyprinid fish larvae from eastern North America. Transactions of the American Fisheries Society 112:319–332.

Fuiman, L. A., and J. J. Loos. 1977. Identifying characters of the early development of the daces *Rhinichthys atratulus* and *R. cataractae* (Osteichthyes: Cyprinidae). Proceedings of the Academy of Natural Sciences of Philadelphia 129:23–32.

Fuiman, L. A., and J. J. Loos. 1978. Morphological changes during the larval development of the cutlips minnow, *Exoglossum maxillingua*. Transactions of the American Fisheries Society 107:605–612.

Fuiman, L. A., and D. C. Witman. 1979. Descriptions and comparisons of catostomid fish larvae: *Catostomus catostomus* and *Moxostoma erythrurum*. Transactions of the American Fisheries Society 108:604–619.

Funk, J. L. 1955. Movement of stream fishes in Missouri. Transactions of the American Fisheries Society 85:39–57.

Funk, V. A., and D. R. Brooks. 1990. Phylogenetic systematics as the basis of comparative biology. Smithsonian Contributions to Botany 73.

Furcron, A. S. 1939. Geology and mineral resources of the Warrenton Quadrangle, Virginia. Virginia Geological Survey Bulletin 54.

Gage, S. H. 1928. The lampreys of New York State—life history and economics. Pages 157–191 *in* A biological survey of the Oswego River system. Supplemental to 17th Annual Report (1927) of the New York State Conservation Department, Albany.

Galat, D. L. 1973. Normal embryonic development of the muskellunge (*Esox masquinongy*). Transactions of the American Fisheries Society 102:384–391.

Gale, W. F. 1983. Fecundity and spawning frequency of caged bluntnose minnows—fractional spawners. Transactions of the American Fisheries Society 112:398–402.

Gale, W. F., and G. L. Buynak. 1978. Spawning frequency and fecundity of satinfin shiner (*Notropis analostanus*)—a fractional crevice spawner. Transactions of the American Fisheries Society 107:460–463.

Gale, W. F., and G. L. Buynak. 1982. Fecundity and spawning frequency of the fathead minnow—a fractional spawner. Transactions of the American Fisheries Society 111:35–40.

Gale, W. F., and W. G. Deutsch. 1985. Fecundity and spawning behavior of captive tessellated darters—fractional spawners. Transactions of the American Fisheries Society 114:220–229.

Gale, W. F., and C. A. Gale. 1976. Selection of artificial spawning sites by the spotfin shiner (*Notropis spilopterus*). Journal of the Fisheries Research Board of Canada 33:1906–1933.

Gale, W. F., and C. A. Gale. 1977. Spawning habits of spotfin shiner (*Notropis spilopterus*)—a fractional, crevice spawner. Transactions of the American Fisheries Society 106:170–177.

Gale, W. F., and H. W. Mohr. 1976. Fish spawning in a large Pennsylvania River receiving mine effluents. Proceedings of the Pennsylvania Academy of Science 50:160–162.

Galloway, J. E., and N. R. Kevern. 1976. Michigan suckers, their life histories, abundance and potential for harvest. Michigan State University, Sea Grant Program Technical Report 53, East Lansing.

Gammon, J. R. 1971. The response of fish populations in the Wabash River to heated effluents. 3rd National Symposium on Radioecology, Oak Ridge, Tennessee.

Gapen, D. D. 1983. Muddler. Trout 24(1):34–41.

Gardiner, B. G. 1984. Sturgeons as living fossils. Pages 148–152 *in* N. Eldredge and S. M. Stanley, editors. Living fossils. Springer-Verlag, New York.

Garman, G. C. 1988. Habitat analysis of the Roanoke bass

(*Ambloplites cavifrons*). Virginia Commission of Game and Inland Fisheries, Federal Aid in Sport Fish Restoration, Project F-67-R, September 1, 1986–December 31, 1987, Project Completion Report, Richmond.

Garman, G. C., and L. A. Nielsen. 1982. Piscivority by stocked brown trout (*Salmo trutta*) and its impact on the nongame fish community of Bottom Creek, Virginia. Canadian Journal of Fisheries and Aquatic Sciences 39:862–869.

Garman, G. C., and L. A. Nielsen. 1992. Medium-sized rivers of the Atlantic Coastal Plain. Pages 315–349 *in* C. T. Hackney, S. M. Adams, and W. H. Martin, editors. Biodiversity of the southeastern United States: Aquatic communities. Wiley, New York.

Garman, G. C., T. L. Thorn, and L. A. Nielsen. 1982. Longitudinal variation in the fish community of Brumley Creek, Virginia, and implications for sampling. Proceedings of the Annual Conference Southeastern Association of Game and Fish Commissioners 36(1982):386–393.

Garrett, W. E., and K. Garrett. 1987. George Washington's Patowmack Canal. National Geographic 171:716–753.

Garside, E. T., and J. S. Tait. 1958. Preferred temperature of rainbow trout (*Salmo gairdneri* Richardson) and its unusual relationship to acclimation temperature. Canadian Journal of Zoology 36:564–567.

Gasowska, M. 1979. Osteological revision of the genus *Phoxinus* Raf., sensu Banarescu 1964, with description of a new genus, *Parchrosomus* gen. n. (Pisces, Cyprinidae). Annales Zoologici (Warsaw) 34:371–413.

Gatz, A. J. 1979. Ecological morphology of freshwater stream fishes. Tulane Studies in Zoology and Botany 21:91–124.

Gebhardt, B. 1986. Magnificent mudder. American Currents (October):6.

Gee, J. H., and K. Machniak. 1972. Ecological notes on a lake-dwelling population of longnose dace (*Rhinichthys cataractae*). Journal of the Fisheries Research Board of Canada 29:330–332.

Gee, J. H., and T. G. Northcote. 1963. Comparative ecology of two sympatric species of dace (*Rhinichthys*) in the Fraser River system, British Columbia. Journal of the Fisheries Research Board of Canada 20:105–118.

Geen, G. H., T. G. Northcote, G. F. Hartman, and C. C. Lindsey. 1966. Life histories of two species of catostomid fishes in Sixteenmile Lake, British Columbia, with particular reference to inlet stream spawning. Journal of the Fisheries Research Board of Canada 23:1761–1788.

Gengerke, T. W. 1986. Distribution and abundance of paddlefish in the United States. Pages 22–35 *in* J. G. Dillard, L. K. Graham, and T. R. Russell, editors. The paddlefish: status, management and propagation. American Fisheries Society, North Central Division, Special Publication 7, Bethesda, Maryland.

Gerald, J. W. 1966. Food habits of the longnose dace, *Rhinichthys cataractae*. Copeia 1966:478–485.

Gerald, J. W. 1971. Sound production during courtship in six species of sunfish (Centrarchidae). Evolution 25:75–87.

Gerdes, J. H. 1961. The role of the threadfin shad, *Dor-osoma petenense*, in the food web of a small, new impoundment. Master's thesis. University of Arizona, Tucson. (Not seen; cited in Jones et al. 1978.)

Gerking, S. D. 1945. The distribution of the fishes of Indiana. Investigations of Indiana Lakes and Streams 3:1–137.

Gerking, S. D. 1953. Evidence for the concepts of home range and territory in stream fishes. Ecology 34:347–365.

Gerlach, J. M. 1983. Characters for distinguishing larvae of carp, *Cyprinus carpio*, and goldfish, *Carassius auratus*. Copeia 1983:116–121.

Germann, J. F., and C. D. Swanson. 1978. Food habits of chain pickerel in the Suwannee River, Georgia. Georgia Journal of Science 36:153–158.

Gibbs, R. H. 1955. A systematic study of the cyprinid fishes belonging to the subgenus *Cyprinella* of the genus *Notropis*. Doctoral dissertation. Cornell University, Ithaca, New York.

Gibbs, R. H. 1957. Cyprinid fishes of the subgenus *Cyprinella* of *Notropis*. I. Systematic status of the subgenus *Cyprinella*, with a key to the species exclusive of the *lutrensis–ornatus* complex. Copeia 1957:185–195.

Gibbs, R. H. 1958. Cyprinid fishes of the subgenus *Cyprinella* of *Notropis*, II, distribution and variation of *Notropis spiloterus*, with the description of a new subspecies. Lloydia 20(1957):186–221.

Gibbs, R. H. 1961. Cyprinid fishes of the subgenus *Cyprinella* of *Notropis*. IV the *Notropis galacturus—camurus* complex. American Midland Naturalist 66:337–354.

Gibbs, R. H. 1963. Cyprinid fishes of the subgenus *Cyprinella* of *Notropis*. The *Notropis whipplei–analostanus–chloristius* complex. Copeia 1963:511–528.

Gilbert, C. R. 1953. Age and growth of the yellow stone catfish, *Noturus flavus* (Rafinesque). Master's thesis. Ohio State University, Columbus. (Not seen; cited in Carlander 1969.)

Gilbert, C. R. 1961a. Hybridization versus intergradation: an inquiry into the relationship of two cyprinid fishes. Copeia 1961:181–192.

Gilbert, C. R. 1961b. *Notropis semperasper*, a new cyprinid fish from the upper James River system, Virginia. Copeia 1961:450–456.

Gilbert, C. R. 1964. The American cyprinid fishes of the subgenus *Luxilus* (genus *Notropis*). Bulletin of the Florida State Museum Biological Sciences 8:95–194.

Gilbert, C. R. 1969. Systematics and distribution of the American cyprinid fishes *Notropis ariommus* and *Notropis telescopus*. Copeia 1969:474–492.

Gilbert, C. R. 1971. Emended publication dates for certain fish species described by E. D. Cope, with notes on the type material of *Notropis photogenis* (Cope). Copeia 1971:474–479.

Gilbert, C. R. 1976. Composition and derivation of the North American freshwater fish fauna. Florida Scientist 39:102–111.

Gilbert, C. R. 1978a. The nominal North American cyprinid fish *Notropis henryi* interpreted as an intergeneric hybrid, *Clinostomus funduloides* × *Nocomis leptocephalus*. Copeia 1978:177–181.

Gilbert, C. R. 1978b. Type catalogue of the North American cyprinid fish genus *Notropis*. Bulletin of the Florida State Museum Biological Sciences 23:1–104.

Gilbert, C. R., editor. 1978c. Fishes, volume 4. University Presses of Florida, Gainesville, and Florida Game and Fresh Water Fish Commission, Tallahassee.

Gilbert, C. R. 1980. Zoogeographic factors in relation to biological monitoring of fish. Pages 309–355 *in* C. H. Hocutt and J. R. Stauffer, editors. Biological monitoring of fish. D. C. Heath and Company, Lexington, Massachusetts.

Gilbert, C. R. 1987. Zoogeography of the freshwater fish fauna of southern Georgia and Peninsula Florida. Brimleyana 13:25–54.

Gilbert, C. R. 1992. Atlantic sturgeon, *Acipenser oxyrinchus*. Pages 31–39 *in* C. R. Gilbert, editor. Rare and endangered biota of Florida, volume II. Fishes. University Press of Florida, Gainesville.

Gilbert, C. R., and R. M. Bailey. 1972. Systematics and zoogeography of the American cyprinid fish *Notropis* (*Opsopoeodus*) *emiliae*. Occasional Papers of the Museum of Zoology University of Michigan 664.

Gilbert, C. R., and W. Seaman. 1973. The effect of stream gradient on distribution of fishes in the Tennessee River system of Tennessee and North Carolina. ASB (Association of Southeastern Biologists) Bulletin 20:55.

Gilbert, C. R., and B. R. Wall. 1985. Status of the catostomid fish *Erimyzon oblongus* from eastern Gulf slope drainages in Florida and Alabama. Florida Scientist 48:202–207.

Gilbert, R. J. 1978. Status of the spotted bass, (*Micropterus punctulatus*) (Centrarchidae), in the eastern United States. ASB (Association of Southeastern Biologists) Bulletin 25:57.

Gill, T. 1861. Observations on the genus *Cottus*, and descriptions of two new species (abridged from the forthcoming report of Capt. J. H. Simpson). Proceedings of the Boston Society of Natural History 8:40–42.

Gill, T. 1876. Report on ichthyology, appendix L. Pages 383–431 *in* Report of explorations across the Great Basin of the Territory of Utah for a direct wagon-route from Camp Floyd to Genoa, in Carson Valley, in 1859. Engineer Department, U.S. Army, Washington, D.C.

Gill, T. 1897. Address in memory of Edward Drinker Cope. Herpetological and ichthyological contributions. American Philosophical Society Memorial Volume 1:1–23 [pagination of reprint].

Gill, T., editor. 1898. Report in part of Samuel L. Mitchill, M. D., Professor of natural history, etc., on the fishes of New York. Printed for the author, Washington, D.C.

Gill, T. 1907. Parental care among fresh-water fishes. Smithsonian Institution Annual Report 1905:403–531.

Gillam, H. L. 1965. Pike–muskie rearing operation expands. Virginia Wildlife 26(8):9, 20–21.

Gillen, A. L., and T. Hart. 1980. Feeding interrelationships between the sand shiner and the striped shiner. Ohio Journal of Science 80:71–76.

Gilson, R. F., and A. Benson. 1979. Prey preference and size-selective predation by the mottled sculpin (*Cottus bairdi bairdi*). Proceedings of the Pennsylvania Academy of Science 53:135–138.

Ginther, H. 1968. Captain Staunton's River. Dietz Press, Richmond, Virginia.

Girard, C. 1856. Researches upon the cyprinoid fishes inhabiting the fresh waters of the United States, west of the Mississippi Valley, from specimens in the museum of the Smithsonian Institution. Proceedings of the Academy of Natural Sciences of Philadelphia 8:165–213.

Girard, C. 1859. Ichthyological notes. Proceedings of the Academy of Natural Sciences of Philadelphia 11(4–6):56–68.

Givens, P. G. 1983. The New River early settlement. Edmonds Printing, Pulaski, Virginia.

Gleason, C. A. 1985. Reproductive isolation of *Notropis cornutus* and *N. chrysocephalus* in Cedar Fork Creek, Ohio. Page 66 *in* Abstracts of the 65th Annual Meeting of the American Society of Ichthyologists and Herpetologists.

Godkin, C. M., W. J. Christie, and D. E. McAllister. 1982. Problems of species identity in the Lake Ontario sculpins *Cottus bairdi* and *C. cognatus*. Canadian Journal of Fisheries and Aquatic Sciences 39:1373–1382.

Goeman, T. J. 1983. Freshwater drum spawning and fecundity in the upper Mississippi River. Proceedings of the Iowa Academy of Science 90:132–133.

Goff, G. P. 1984. Brood care of longnose gar (*Lepisosteus osseus*) by smallmouth bass (*Micropterus dolomieui*). Copeia: 1984:149–152.

Goldsborough, E. L., and H. W. Clark. 1908. Fishes of West Virginia. U.S. Bureau of Fisheries Bulletin 27:29–39.

Goldstein, R. M. 1978. Quantitative comparison of seining and underwater observation for stream fishery surveys. Progressive Fish-Culturist 40:108–111.

Goodchild, G. A., and J. C. Tilt. 1976. A range extension of *Nocomis micropogon*, the river chub, into eastern Ontario. Canadian Field-Naturalist 90:491–492.

Goode, G. B. 1884. The fisheries and fishery industries of the United States, section I, natural history of useful aquatic animals. U.S. Commission of Fish and Fisheries, Report of the Commissioner of Fisheries, Washington, D.C.

Goode, G. B. 1884–1886. The beginnings of natural history in America. Proceedings of the Biological Society of Washington 3:35–105. (Reprinted 1901. Pages 355–406 *in* Annual report of the U.S. National Museum for year ending June 30, 1897, Part II, Washington, D.C.)

Goode, G. B. 1887. American fishes: a popular treatise upon the game and food fishes of North America. L. C. Page & Company, Boston.

Goode, G. B. 1901a. Museum-history and museums of history. Pages 65–81 *in* Annual report of the U.S. National Museum for year ending June 30, 1897, Part II, Washington, D.C.

Goode, G. B. 1901b. The genesis of the United States National Museum. Pages 83–191 *in* Annual report of the U.S. National Museum, for year ending June 30, 1897, Part II, Washington, D.C.

Goodfellow, W. L., C. H. Hocutt, R. P. Morgan, and J. R. Stauffer. 1984. Biochemical assessment of the taxonomic status of "*Rhinichthys bowersi*" (Pisces: Cyprinidae). Copeia 1984:652–659.

Goodin, J. T., editor. 1985. Virginia's endangered species. Virginia Commission of Game and Inland Fisheries, Richmond.

Goodyear, C. P. 1985. Toxic materials, fishing, and environmental variation: simulated effects on striped bass population trends. Transactions of the American Fisheries Society 114:107–113.

Goodyear, C. P., C. E. Boyd, and R. J. Beyers. 1972. Relationships between primary productivity and mosquitofish (*Gambusia affinis*) production in large microcosms. Limnology and Oceanography 17:445–450.

Gorham, S. W., and D. E. McAllister. 1974. The shortnose sturgeon, *Acipenser brevirostrum*, in the Saint John River, New Brunswick, Canada, a rare and possibly endangered species. Syllogeus 5.

Gosline, W. A. 1948. Some possible uses of X-rays in ichthyology and fishery research. Copeia 1948:58–61.

Gosline, W. A. 1966. The limits of the fish family Serranidae, with notes on other lower percoids. Proceedings of the California Academy of Sciences 33:91–112.

Gosline, W. A. 1971. Functional morphology and classification of teleostean fishes. University Press of Hawaii, Honolulu.

Gosline, W. A. 1978. Unbranched dorsal-fin rays and subfamily classification in the fish family Cyprinidae. Occasional Papers of the Museum of Zoology University of Michigan 684.

Gosline, W. A. 1985. Relationships among some relatively deep-bodied percoid fish groups. Japanese Journal of Ichthyology 31:351–357.

Goto, A. 1987. Polygyny in the river sculpin, *Cottus hangiongensis* (Pisces: Cottidae), with special reference to male mating success. Copeia 1987:32–40.

Gowing, M. C. 1974. Virginia beyond the Blue Ridge. A pictorial survey of western Virginia. Commonwealth Press, Radford, Virginia.

Grady, J. M., and H. L. Bart. 1984. Life history of *Etheostoma caeruleum* (Pisces: Percidae) in Bayou Sara, Louisiana and Mississippi. Pages 71–81 *in* D. G. Lindquist and L. M. Page, editors. Environmental biology of darters. Kluwer Boston, Hingham, Massachusetts.

Grady, J. M., and W. H. LeGrande. 1992. Phylogenetic relationships, modes of speciation, and historical biogeography of the madtom catfishes, genus *Noturus* Rafinesque (Siluriformes: Ictaluridae). Pages 747–777 *in* Mayden (1992).

Graff, D. R. 1978. Intensive culture of esocids: The current state of the art. American Fisheries Society Special Publication 11:195–201.

Graham, J. H. 1985. Niche ontogeny and progressive deviation in two congeneric sunfishes. Page 68 *in* Abstracts of the 65th Annual Meeting of the American Society of Ichthyologists and Herpetologists.

Graham, J. H. 1989. Foraging by sunfishes in a bog lake. DOE (U.S. Department of Energy) Symposium Series 61:517–527.

Graham, J. H., and J. D. Felley. 1985. Genomic coadaptation and developmental stability within introgressed populations of *Enneacanthus gloriosus* and *E. obesus* (Pisces: Centrarchidae). Evolution 39:104–114.

Graham, J. H., and R. W. Hastings. 1984. Distributional patterns of sunfishes on the New Jersey Coastal Plain. Environmental Biology of Fishes 10:137–148.

Graham, J. J. 1956. Observations on the alewife, *Pomolobus pseudoharengus* (Wilson), in freshwater. University of Toronto Studies Biological Series 62, Publications of the Ontario Fisheries Research Laboratory 74:1–43.

Grande, L. 1985. Recent and fossil clupeomorph fishes with materials for revision of the subgroups of clupeoids. Bulletin of the American Museum of Natural History 181:231–372.

Grande, L. 1989. The Eocene Green River lake system, Fossil Lake, and the history of the North American fish fauna. Pages 18–28 *in* J. Flynn, editor. Mesozoic/Cenozoic vertebrate paleontology: classic localities, contemporary approaches. 28th International Geological Congress fieldtrip guidebook T322, American Geophysical Union, Washington, D.C.

Grande, L., and W. E. Bemis. 1991. Osteology and phylogenetic relationships of fossil and Recent paddlefishes (Polyodontidae) with comments on the interrelationships of Acipenseriformes. Journal of Vertebrate Paleontology 11 (1, supplement):1–121.

Grant, G. C. 1974. The age composition of striped bass catches in Virginia rivers, 1967–1971, and a description of the fishery. U.S. National Marine Fisheries Service Fishery Bulletin 72:193–199.

Grant, J. W. A., and P. W. Colgan. 1983. Reproductive success and mate choice in the johnny darter, *Etheostoma nigrum* (Pisces: Percidae) Canadian Journal of Zoology 61:437–446.

Greeley, J. R. 1927. Fishes of the Genesee region with annotated list. Pages 47–66 *in* A biological survey of the Genesee River system. Supplemental to 16th Annual Report of the New York State Conservation Department, Albany.

Greeley, J. R. 1928. Fishes of the Oswego watershed. Pages 84–107 *in* A biological survey of the Oswego River system. Supplemental to 17th Annual Report of the New York State Conservation Department, Albany.

Greeley, J. R. 1929. Fishes of the Erie–Niagara watershed. Pages 150–179 *in* A biological survey of the Erie–Niagara system. Supplemental to 18th Annual Report of the New York State Conservation Department, Albany.

Greeley, J. R. 1930. A contribution to the biology of the horned dace, *Semotilus atromaculatus* (Mitchill). Doctoral dissertation. Cornell University, Ithaca, New York.

Greeley, J. R. 1935. Fishes of the watershed, with annotated list. Pages 63–101 *in* A biological survey of the Mohawk–Hudson watershed. Supplemental to 24th Annual Report of the New York State Conservation Department, Albany. (Not seen; cited in Hildebrand 1964.)

Greeley, J. R. 1936. Fishes of the area with annotated list. Pages 45–88 *in* A biological survey of the Delaware and Susquehanna watersheds. Supplemental to 25th Annual Report of the New York State Conservation Department, Albany.

Greeley, J. R. 1938. Fishes of the area with annotated list. Pages 48–73 *in* A biological survey of the Allegheny and Chemung watersheds. Supplemental to 27th Annual Report of the New York State Conservation Department, Albany.

Greeley, J. R., and S. C. Bishop. 1933. Fishes of the upper Hudson watershed with annotated list. Pages 64–101 *in* A biological survey of the upper Hudson watershed. Supplemental to 22nd Annual Report of the New York State Conservation Department, Albany.

Greenberg, L. A. 1991. Habitat use and feeding behavior of thirteen species of benthic stream fishes. Environmental Biology of Fishes 31:389–401.

Greenberg, L. A., and E. B. Brothers. 1991. Intrastream variation in growth rates and time of first otolith increment formation for young-of-the-year *Etheostoma simoterum* (Cope) (Percidae). Journal of Fish Biology 38:237–242.

Greenberg, L. A., and D. A. Holtzman. 1987. Microhabitat utilization, feeding periodicity, home range and population size of the banded sculpin, *Cottus carolinae*. Copeia 1987:19–25.

Greene, C. W. 1935. The distribution of Wisconsin fishes. Wisconsin State Conservation Commission, Madison.

Greene, G. N. 1962. White bass feeding: scent or sight. Transactions of the American Fisheries Society 91:326.

Greenfield, D. W., and G. D. Deckert. 1973. Introgressive hybridization between *Gila orcutti* and *Hesperoleucus symmetricus* (Pisces: Cyprinidae) in the Cuyama River basin, California. II. Ecological aspects. Copeia 1973:417–427.

Greenwood, P. H., D. E. Rosen, S. H. Weitzman, and G. S. Myers. 1966. Phyletic studies of teleostean fishes, with a provisional classification of living forms. Bulletin of the American Museum of Natural History 131:339–456.

Gregory-Phillips, C., and H. G. Marshall. 1990. Phytoplankton composition and seasonal growth patterns in Lake Drummond, Dismal Swamp, Virginia. Virginia Journal of Science 42:65.

Grier, H. J., D. P. Moody, and B. C. Cowell. 1990. Internal fertilization and sperm morphology in the brook silverside, *Labidesthes sicculus* (Cope). Copeia 1990:221–226.

Griffith, J. S. 1983. Snorkel and scuba. U.S. Forest Service General Technical Report INT-138:34–36.

Griffith, R. W. 1974. Environment and salinity tolerance in the genus *Fundulus*. Copeia 1974:319–331.

Grizzle, J. M., and M. R. Curd. 1978. Posthatching histological development of the digestive system and swim bladder of logperch, *Percina caprodes*. Copeia 1978:448–455.

Grizzle, J. M., and W. A. Rogers. 1976. Anatomy and histology of the channel catfish. Alabama Agricultural Experiment Station, Auburn University, Auburn.

Gross, M. R. 1982. Sneakers, satellites and parentals: polymorphic mating strategies in North American sunfishes. Zeitschrift fuer Tierpsychologie 60:1–26.

Gross, M. R. 1984. Sunfish, salmon, and the evolution of alternative reproductive strategies and tactics in fishes.

Pages 55–75 *in* G. Potts and R. Wootton, editors. Fish reproduction: strategies and tactics. Academic Press, New York.

Gross, M. R. 1985. Disruptive selection for alternative life histories in salmon. Nature (London) 313:47–48.

Gross, M. R., and A. M. MacMillan. 1981. Predation and the evolution of colonial nesting in bluegill sunfish (*Lepomis macrochirus*). Behavioral Ecology and Sociobiology 8:167–174.

Gross, M. R., and W. A. Nowell. 1980. The reproductive biology of rock bass, *Ambloplites rupestris* (Centrarchidae), in Lake Opinicon, Ontario. Copeia 1980:482–494.

Grosvenor, M. B. 1965. Wondrous world of fishes. National Geographic Society, Washington, D.C.

Gruchy, C. G., R. H. Bowen, and I. M. Gruchy. 1973. First records of the silver shiner, *Notropis photogenis*, from Canada. Journal of the Fisheries Research Board of Canada 30:1379–1382.

Gruchy, C. G., and V. D. Vladykov. 1968. Sexual dimorphism in anal fin of brown trout, *Salmo trutta*, and close relatives. Journal of the Fisheries Research Board of Canada 25(4):813–815.

Gudger, E. W. 1934. The largest fresh-water fishes: the giant sturgeons of the world. Journal of the American Museum of Natural History 34:282–286.

Guier, C. R., L. E. Nichols, and R. T. Rachels. 1984. Biological investigations of flathead catfish in the Cape Fear River. Proceedings of the Annual Conference Southeastern Association of Fish and Wildlife Agencies 35(1981):607–621.

Guilday, J. E., P. W. Parmalee, and H. W. Hamilton. 1977. The Clark's Cave bone deposit and the Late Pleistocene paleoecology of the central Appalachian Mountains of Virginia. Bulletin of the Carnegie Museum of Natural History 2.

Guillory, V. 1979. Life history of chain pickerel in a central Florida lake. Florida Game and Fresh Water Fish Commission, Fishery Bulletin 8, Tallahassee.

Guillory, V. 1984. Reproductive biology of chain pickerel in Lake Conway, Florida. Proceedings of the Annual Conference Southeastern Association of Fish and Wildlife Agencies 35(1981):585–591.

Guillory, V., and R. D. Gasaway. 1978. Zoogeography of the grass carp in the United States. Transactions of the American Fisheries Society 107:105–112.

Gunn, J. M., S. V. Quadri, and D. C. Mortimer. 1977. Filamentous algae as a food source for the brown bullhead (*Ictalurus nebulosus*). Journal of the Fisheries Research Board of Canada 34:396–401.

Gunning, G. E., and W. M. Lewis. 1956. Age and growth of two important bait species in a cold-water stream in southern Illinois. American Midland Naturalist 55:118–120.

Gunter, G. S. 1938. Seasonal variation in abundance of certain estuarine and marine fishes with particular reference to life histories. Ecological Monographs 8:313–346.

Günther, A. 1868. Catalogue of the fishes in the British Museum. Catalogue of the Physostomi, containing the families Heteropygii . . . [through] . . . Halosauridae, in the British Museum, volume 7. Taylor and Francis, London.

Gusey, W. F. 1981. The fish and wildlife resources of the south Atlantic coast. Environmental Affairs 6:58–60. (Shell Oil Company, Houston.)

Haase, B. L. 1969. An ecological life history of the longnose gar, *Lepisosteus osseus* (Linnaeus), in Lake Mendota and in several other lakes of southern Wisconsin. Doctoral dissertation. University of Wisconsin, Madison. (Not seen; cited in Becker 1983.)

Haase, R., and B. L. Haase. 1975. Feeding ecology of the cutlips minnow, *Exoglossum maxillingua*, in the Delaware River at Bushkill, Pennsylvania. Proceedings of the Pennsylvania Academy of Science 49:67–72.

Hack, J. T. 1957. Submerged river system of Chesapeake Bay. Geological Society of America Bulletin 68:817–830.

Hack, J. T. 1965. Geomorphology of the Shenandoah Valley, Virginia and West Virginia, and origin of the residual ore deposits. U.S. Geological Survey Professional Paper 484.

Hack, J. T. 1969. The area, its geology: Cenozoic development of the southern Appalachians. Virginia Polytechnic Institute and State University Research Division Monograph 1:1–17.

Hack, J. T. 1980. Rock control and tectonism—their importance in shaping the Appalachian Highlands. U.S. Geological Survey, Professional Papers 1126B:B1–B17.

Hack, J. T. 1982. Physiographic division and differential uplift in the Piedmont and Blue Ridge. U.S. Geological Survey Professional Papers 1265.

Hackney, P. A., and J. A. Holbrook. 1978. Sauger, walleye, and yellow perch in the southeastern United States. American Fisheries Society Special Publication 11:74–81.

Hackney, P. A., G. R. Hooper, and J. F. Webb. 1971. Spawning behavior, age and growth, and sport fishery for the silver redhorse, *Moxostoma anisurum* (Rafinesque), in the Flint River, Alabama. Proceedings of the Annual Conference Southeastern Association of Game and Fish Commissioners 24(1970):569–576.

Hackney, P. A., and W. M. Tatum. 1966. "Redhorse are shoaling" cry calls fishermen to Cahaba. Alabama Conservation 36(6):21–24.

Hackney, P. A., W. M. Tatum, and S. L. Spencer. 1968. Life history of the river redhorse, *Moxostoma carinatum* (Cope), in the Cahaba River, Alabama, with notes on the species as a sport fish. Proceedings of the Annual Conference Southeastern Association of Game and Fish Commissioners 21(1967):324–332.

Hadley, W. F., and K. Clulow. 1979. First records of the fallfish from the Lake Erie drainage of New York. New York Fish and Game Journal 26:192–193.

Haedrich, R. L. 1977. A sea lamprey from the deep ocean. Copeia 1977:767–768.

Haldeman, S. S. 1842. Descriptions of two new species of the genus *Percina*, from the Susquehanna River. Journal of the Academy of Natural Sciences of Philadelphia 8:330.

Hall, C. A. S. 1972. Migration and metabolism in a temperate stream ecosystem. Ecology 53:585–604.

Hall, D. J., and seven coauthors. 1979. Diel foraging behavior and prey selection in the golden shiner (*Notemigonus crysoleucas*). Journal of the Fisheries Research Board of Canada 36:1029–1039.

Hall, G. E., editor. 1986. Managing muskies. American Fisheries Society Special Publication 15.

Hall, G. E., editor. 1987. Age and growth of fish. Iowa State University Press, Ames.

Hall, G. E., and R. M. Jenkins. 1954. Notes on the age and growth of the pirateperch, *Aphredoderus sayanus*, in Oklahoma. Copeia 1954:69.

Hall, L. W. 1984. Field assessment of striped bass, *Morone saxatilis*, larval survival as related to contaminants and changes in water quality parameter: final report. Applied Physics Laboratory, Johns Hopkins University, Laurel, Maryland.

Hall, L. W., L. O. Horseman, and S. Zeger. 1984. Effects of organic and inorganic chemical contaminants on fertilization, hatching success, and prolarval survival of striped bass. Archives of Environmental Contamination and Toxicology 13:723–729.

Hall, L. W., A. E. Pinkney, L. O. Horseman, and S. E. Finger. 1985. Mortality of striped bass larvae in relation to contaminants and water quality in a Chesapeake Bay tributary. Transactions of the American Fisheries Society 114:861–868.

Hall, L. W., M. C. Ziegenfuss, S. J. Bushong, M. A. Unger, and R. L. Herman. 1989. Studies of contaminant and water quality effects on striped bass prolarvae and yearlings in the Potomac River and upper Chesapeake Bay in 1988. Transactions of the American Fisheries Society 118:619–629.

Hallam, J. C. 1959. Habitat and associated fauna of four species of fish in Ontario streams. Journal of the Fisheries Research Board of Canada 16:147–173.

Halstead, L. B. 1982. Evolutionary trends and the phylogeny of the Agnatha. Pages 159–196 *in* K. A. Joysey and A. E. Friday, editors. Problems of phylogenetic reconstruction. Academic Press, New York.

Hambrick, P. S. 1973. Composition, longitudinal distribution and zoogeography of the fish fauna of Back Creek, Blackwater River and Pigg River, tributaries of the Roanoke River in south-central Virginia. Master's thesis. Virginia Polytechnic Institute and State University, Blacksburg.

Hambrick, P. S. 1977. The intergeneric hybrid, *Notropis cerasinus* × *Phoxinus oreas* (Pisces: Cyprinidae), in the upper Roanoke River drainage, Virginia. American Midland Naturalist 98:238–243.

Hambrick, P. S., C. H. Hocutt, M. T. Masnik, and J. H. Wilson. 1973. Additions to the West Virginia ichthyofauna, with comments on the distribution of other species. Proceedings of the West Virginia Academy of Science 45:58–60.

Hambrick, P. S., R. E. Jenkins, and J. H. Wilson. 1975. Distribution, habitat and food of the cyprinid fish *Phenacobius teretulus*, a New River endemic. Copeia 1975:172–176.

Hampton, R. 1954. Intergradation of the bullhead minnow. Transactions of the Kansas Academy of Science 57:480–481.

Hankinson, T. L. 1908. Fish of Walnut Lake. Pages 198–

216 *in* A biological survey of Walnut Lake, Michigan. Biological Survey of the State of Michigan, State Board of Geological Survey Report (1907), Lansing.

Hankinson, T. L. 1919. Notes on life-histories of Illinois fishes. Transactions of the Illinois State Academy of Science 12:132–150.

Hankinson, T. L. 1922. Nest of the cut-lips minnow *Exoglossum maxillingua* (Lesueur). Copeia 1922:1–3.

Hankinson, T. L. 1930. Breeding behavior of the silverfin minnow, *Notropis whipplii spilopterus* (Cope). Copeia 1930:73–74.

Hankinson, T. L. 1932. Observations on the breeding behavior and habitats of fishes in southern Michigan. Papers of the Michigan Academy of Science, Arts and Letters 15:411–425.

Hanley, R. W. 1977. Hybridization between the chubsuckers *Erimyzon oblongus* and *E. sucetta* in North Carolina. *In* Abstracts of the 57th Annual Meeting of the American Society of Ichthyologists and Herpetologists.

Hann, H. W. 1927. The history of the germ cells of *Cottus bairdii* Girard. Journal of Morphology and Physiology 43:427–497.

Hansen, D. F. 1943. On nesting of the white crappie, *Pomoxis annularis*. Copeia 1943:259–260.

Hansen, D. F. 1951. Biology of the white crappie in Illinois. Illinois Natural History Survey Bulletin 25:209–265.

Hanson, J. M., and S. U. Quadri. 1979. Seasonal growth, food, and feeding habits of young-of-the-year black crappie in Ottawa River. Canadian Field-Naturalist 93:232–238.

Hanson, W. D. 1970. Acclimatization and utilization of threadfin shad. Missouri Department of Conservation, Federal Aid in Sport Fish Restoration, Project F-11R-19, Work Plan J, Job 2, Jefferson City. (Not seen; cited in McHugh and Steinkoenig 1980.)

Hanych, D. A., M. R. Ross, R. E. Magnien, and A. L. Suggars. 1983. Nocturnal inshore movement of the mimic shiner (*Notropis volucellus*): a possible predator avoidance behavior. Canadian Journal of Fisheries and Aquatic Sciences 40:888–894.

Haq, B. U., W. Berggren, and J. Van Couvering. 1977. Corrected age of the Pliocene/Pleistocene boundary. Nature (London) 269:483–488.

Hardisty, M. W. 1971. Gonadogenesis, sex differentiation and gametogenesis. Pages 295–359 *in* M. W. Hardisty and I. C. Potter, editors. The biology of lampreys, volume 1. Academic Press, New York.

Hardisty, M. W. 1979. Biology of the cyclostomes. Chapman and Hall, London.

Hardisty, M. W., and I. C. Potter, editors. 1971–1982. The biology of lampreys, volumes 1 through 4b. Academic Press, New York.

Hardisty, M. W., and I. C. Potter. 1971a. The behaviour, ecology and growth of larval lampreys. Pages 85–125 *in* M. W. Hardisty and I. C. Potter, editors. The biology of lampreys, volume 1. Academic Press, New York.

Hardisty, M. W., and I. C. Potter. 1971b. The general biology of adult lampreys. Pages 127–206 *in* M. W. Hardisty and I. C. Potter, editors. The biology of lampreys, volume 1. Academic Press, New York.

Hardisty, M. W., and I. C. Potter. 1971c. Paired species. Pages 249–277 *in* M. W. Hardisty and I. C. Potter, editors. The biology of lampreys, volume 1. Academic Press, New York.

Hardy, J. D. 1978a. Development of fishes of the Mid-Atlantic Bight. An atlas of egg, larval and juvenile stages, volume 2. U.S. Fish and Wildlife Service Biological Services Program FWS-OBS-78/12.

Hardy, J. D. 1978b. Development of fishes of the Mid-Atlantic Bight. An atlas of egg, larval and juveniles stages, volume 3. U.S. Fish and Wildlife Service Biological Services Program FWS-OBS-78/12.

Hare, G. M., and H. P. Murphy. 1974. First record of the American shad (*Alosa sapidissima*) from Labrador waters. Journal of the Fisheries Research Board of Canada 31:1536–1537.

Harlan, J. R., and E. B. Speaker, editors. 1956. Iowa fish and fishing, 3rd edition. Iowa State Conservation Commission, Des Moines.

Harrell, R. D., and D. G. Cloutman. 1978. Distribution and life history of the sandbar shiner, *Notropis scepticus* (Pisces: Cyprinidae). Copeia 1978:443–447.

Harrell, R. M., H. A. Loyacano, and J. D. Bayless. 1977. Zooplankton availability and feeding selectivity of fingerling striped bass. Georgia Journal of Science 35:129–135.

Harrington, R. W. 1947a. The early life history of the bridled shiner, *Notropis bifrenatus* (Cope). Copeia 1947:97–102.

Harrington, R. W. 1947b. The breeding behavior of the bridled shiner, *Notropis bifrenatus* (Cope). Copeia 1947:186–192.

Harrington, R. W. 1947c. Observations on the breeding habits of the yellow perch, *Perca flavescens* (Mitchill). Copeia 1947:199–200.

Harrington, R. W. 1948a. The life cycle of the bridled shiner, *Notropis bifrenatus* (Cope). American Midland Naturalist 39:83–92.

Harrington, R. W. 1948b. The food of the bridled shiner, *Notropis bifrenatus* (Cope). American Midland Naturalist 40:353–361.

Harrington, R. W. 1951. Notes on spawning in an aquarium by the bridled shiner, *Notropis bifrenatus*, with counts of the eggs deposited. Copeia 1951:85–86.

Harrington, R. W. 1955. The osteocranium of the American cyprinid fish, *Notropis bifrenatus*, with an annotated synonymy of teleost skull bones. Copeia 1955:267–290.

Harrington, R. W. 1956. An experiment on the effects of contrasting daily photoperiods on gametogenesis and reproduction in the centrarchid fish, *Enneacanthus obesus* (Girard). Journal of Experimental Zoology 131:203–223.

Harrington, R. W., and E. S. Harrington. 1961. Food selection among fishes invading a high subtropical salt marsh: from onset of flooding through the progress of a mosquito brood. Ecology 42:646–666.

Harris, J. L. 1986. Systematics, distribution, and biology of fishes currently allocated to *Erimystax* (Jordan), a subgenus of *Hybopsis* (Cyprinidae). Doctoral dissertation. University of Tennessee, Knoxville.

Harris, J. W. 1985. Systematics of the brook trout, *Salveli-*

nus fontinalis (Mitchill) in the Great Smoky Mountains National Park. II. Electrophoresis. Page 74 *in* Abstracts of the 65th Annual Meeting of the American Society of Ichthyologists and Herpetologists.

Harrison, E. J., and W. F. Hadley. 1978. Ecological separation of sympatric muskellunge and northern pike. American Fisheries Society Special Publication 11:129–134.

Harrison, E. J., and W. F. Hadley. 1979. Biology of the muskellunge (*Esox masquinongy*) in the upper Niagara River. Transactions of the American Fisheries Society 108:441–451.

Harrison, H. C., and R. G. Martin. 1960. A list of the fishes of Virginia. Virginia Wildlife 21(9):16–19.

Harrison, W., R. J. Malloy, G. A. Rusnak, and J. Terasmae. 1965. Possible Late Pleistocene uplift Chesapeake Bay entrance. Journal of Geology 73:201–229.

Hart, J. S. 1952. Geographic variations of some physiological and morphological characters in certain freshwater fish. University of Toronto Biological Series 60. (Also: Publications of the Ontario Fisheries Research Laboratory 72.)

Hart, L. G. 1978. Smith Mountain Reservoir research study. Virginia Commission of Game and Inland Fisheries, Federal Aid in Sport Fish Restoration, Project F-30-R, April 16, 1973–April 15, 1976, Project Completion Report, Richmond.

Hart, L. G. 1981. Claytor Lake fish population study. Virginia Commission of Game and Inland Fisheries, Federal Aid in Sport Fish Restoration, Project F-35-R, April 1, 1976–March 31, 1980, Project Completion Report, Richmond.

Haskell, W. L. 1959. Diet of the Mississippi threadfin shad, *Dorosoma petenense atchafalayae*, in Arizona. Copeia 1959:298–302.

Hasler, A. D., A. T. Scholz, and R. M. Horrall. 1978. Olfactory imprinting and homing in salmon. American Scientist 66:347–355.

Hasler, A. D., H. P. Thomsen, and J. C. Neess. 1946. Facts and comments on raising two common bait minnows. Wisconsin Conservation Bulletin 210-A-46.

Hassler, W. W. 1956. The influence of certain environmental factors on growth of Norris Reservoir sauger (*Stizostedion canadense canadense* (Smith)). Proceedings of the Annual Conference Southeastern Association of Game and Fish Commissioners 9(1955):111–119. (Not seen; cited in Fitz and Holbrook 1978.)

Hassler, W. W., N. L. Hill, and J. T. Brown. 1981. The status and abundance of striped bass, *Morone saxatilis*, in the Roanoke River and Albemarle Sound, North Carolina, 1956–1980. North Carolina Department of Natural Resources and Community Development, Division of Marine Fisheries, Special Scientific Report 38, Raleigh.

Hastings, R. W. 1979. Fish of the Pine Barrens. Pages 489–504 *in* R. T. T. Forman, editor. Pine Barrens: ecosystem and landscape. Academic Press, New York.

Hastings, R. W. 1984. The fishes of the Mullica River, a naturally acid river system of the New Jersey Pine Barrens. Bulletin of the New Jersey Academy of Science 29:9–23.

Hastings, R. W., and R. E. Good. 1977. Population analysis of the fishes of a freshwater tidal tributary of the lower Delaware River. Bulletin of the New Jersey Academy of Science 22:13–20.

Hastings, R. W., J. C. O'Herron III, K. Schick, and M. A. Lazzari. 1987. Occurrence and distribution of shortnose sturgeon, *Acipenser brevirostrum*, in the upper tidal Delaware River. Estuaries 10:337–341.

Hatch, J. T. 1983. Life history of the gilt darter, *Percina evides* (Jordan and Copeland), in the Sunrise River, Minnesota. Dissertation Abstracts International 43(11).

Hatch, J. T. 1986. Distribution, habitat, and status of the gilt darter (*Percina evides*) in Minnesota. Journal of the Minnesota Academy of Science 51:11–16.

Hatcher, R. D. 1972. Developmental model for the southern Appalachians. Geological Society of America Bulletin 83:2735–2760.

Hatcher, R. D. 1978. Tectonics of the western Piedmont and Blue Ridge, southern Appalachians: review and speculation. American Journal of Science 278:276–304.

Havey, K. A. 1961. Restoration of anadromous alewives at Long Pond, Maine. Transactions of the American Fisheries Society 90:281–286.

Haxo, W. H., N. M. Burkhead, and R. E. Jenkins. 1985. Life history aspects of *Etheostoma podostemone*. Page 74 *in* Abstracts of the 65th Annual Meeting of the American Society of Ichthyologists and Herpetologists.

Haxo, W. H., and R. J. Neves. 1984. A status survey of the sharphead darter (*Etheostoma acuticeps*). Status Report to U.S. Fish and Wildlife Service, Endangered Species Field Office, Asheville, North Carolina.

Heidinger, R. C. 1975. Life history and biology of the largemouth bass. Pages 11–20 *in* R. H. Stroud and H. Clepper, editors. Black bass biology and management. Sport Fishing Institute, Washington, D.C.

Heidinger, R. C., D. R. Helms, T. I. Hiebert, and P. H. Howe. 1983. Operational comparison of three electrofishing systems. North American Journal of Fisheries Management 3:254–257.

Heins, D. C. 1990. Mating behaviors of the blacktail shiner, *Cyprinella venusta*, from southern Mississippi. Proceedings of the Southeastern Fishes Council 21:5–7.

Heins, D. C., and F. G. Rabito. 1986. Spawning performance in North American minnows: direct evidence of multiple clutches in the genus *Notropis*. Journal of Fish Biology 28:343–357.

Helfman, G. S. 1981. The advantages to fishes of hovering in shade. Copeia 1981:392–400.

Helfman, G. S. 1986. Diel distribution and activity of American eels (*Anguilla rostrata*) in a cave-spring. Canadian Journal of Fisheries and Aquatic Sciences 43:1595–1605.

Helfman, G. S., D. E. Facey, L. S. Hales, and E. L. Bozeman. 1987. Reproductive ecology of the American eel. American Fisheries Society Symposium 1:42–56.

Helfrich, L. A., D. L. Weigmann, R. J. Neves, and P. T. Bromley. 1986. The Clinch, Powell, and Holston rivers of Virginia and Tennessee: wildlife and water quality. Virginia Cooperative Extension Service, Publication 460-110, Virginia Polytechnic Institute and State University, Blacksburg.

Helfrich, L. A., D. L. Weigmann, K. W. Nutt, and R. M. Sterrett. 1990. Springs of Virginia revisited: a comparative analysis of the current and historical water-quality data. Virginia Journal of Science 41:14–27.

Helm, W. T. 1958. Notes on the ecology of panfish in Lake Wingra with special reference to the yellow bass. Doctoral dissertation. University of Wisconsin, Madison. (Not seen; cited in Fuiman 1982d.)

Hendricks, M. L., J. R. Stauffer, and C. H. Hocutt. 1983. The zoogeography of the fishes of the Youghiogheny River system, Pennsylvania, Maryland and West Virginia. American Midland Naturalist 110:145–164.

Hendrickson, D. A., W. L. Minckley, R. R. Miller, D. J. Siebert, and P. H. Minckley. 1980. Fishes of the Río Yaqui basin, México and United States. Journal of the Arizona–Nevada Academy of Science 15:65–106.

Hendrickson, H. T., and K. L. Becker. 1975. Distributional notes on cyprinid fishes from Guilford County, North Carolina. Journal of the Elisha Mitchell Scientific Society 91:230–232.

Henshall, J. A. 1939. Book of the black bass. D. Appleton-Century, New York.

Herald, E. S. 1961. Living fishes of the world. Doubleday, Garden City, New York.

Herbold, B., and P. B. Moyle. 1986. Introduced species and vacant niches. American Naturalist 128:751–760.

Hershey, J. H., and G. A. Clarke. 1980. The intestinal flora of *Notropis cerasinus*. Virginia Journal of Science 31:9–12.

Hess, L. 1983. Preliminary analysis of the food habits of some New River fishes with emphasis on black fly utilization. Pages 15–21 *in* Proceedings New River Symposium, April 14–16, 1983, Blacksburg, Virginia. National Park Service, New River Gorge National River, Glen Jean, West Virginia.

Hess, L., J. Woodrum, and R. Menendez. Circa 1985. Fishery resources of the Big Sandy River, Levisa Fork and Tug Fork, West Virginia and Kentucky. Report to U.S. Army Corps of Engineers, Huntington, West Virginia.

Hesser, R. B. 1978. Management implications of hybrid esocids in Pennsylvania. American Fisheries Society Special Publication 11:302–307.

Hester, F. E. 1970. Phylogenetic relationships of sunfishes as demonstrated by hybridization. Transactions of the American Fisheries Society 99:100–103.

Heufelder, G. R. 1982a. Family Lepisosteidae, gars. Pages 45–56 *in* Auer (1982a).

Heufelder, G. R. 1982b. Family Amiidae, bowfin. Pages 56–62 *in* Auer (1982a).

Heufelder, G. R. 1982c. Family Gasterosteidae, sticklebacks. Pages 494–509 *in* Auer (1982a).

Heufelder, G. R. 1982d. Family Cottidae, sculpins. Pages 656–676 *in* Auer (1982a).

Heufelder, G. R., and L. A. Fuiman. 1982. Family Cyprinidae, carps and minnows. Pages 174–344 *in* Auer (1982a).

Hickman, G. D., and R. B. Fitz. 1978. A report on the ecology and conservation of the snail darter (*Percina tanasi* Etnier) 1975–1977. Tennessee Valley Authority, Technical Note B28, Norris, Tennessee.

Hildebrand, S. F. 1964. Family Clupeidae. Pages 257–385, 397–442, 452–454 *in* Fishes of the western North Atlantic, part 3. Sears Foundation for Marine Research, Yale University, New Haven, Connecticut.

Hildebrand, S. F., and W. C. Schroeder. 1928. Fishes of Chesapeake Bay. U.S. Bureau of Fisheries Bulletin 43. (Reprinted 1972. Tropical Fish Hobbyist Publications, Neptune City, New Jersey.)

Hill, D. M., E. A. Taylor, and C. F. Saylor. 1975. Status of faunal recovery in the North Fork Holston River, Tennessee and Virginia. Proceedings of the Annual Conference Southeastern Association of Game and Fish Commissioners 28(1974):398–413.

Hill, D. R. 1959. Some uses of statistical analysis in classifying races of American shad (*Alosa sapidissima*). U.S. Fish and Wildlife Service Fishery Bulletin 59:269–286.

Hill, J., and G. D. Grossman. 1984. Home range estimates for several stream fishes. Page 130 *in* Abstracts of the 64th Annual Meeting of the American Society of Ichthyologists and Herpetologists.

Hill, L. G. 1969. Distributional and populational isolation of the spring cavefish, *Chologaster agassizi* (Pisces: Amblyopsidae). Proceedings of the Oklahoma Academy of Science 48:32–36.

Hitch, R. K., and D. A. Etnier. 1974. Fishes of the Hiwassee River system—ecological and taxonomic considerations. Journal of the Tennessee Academy of Science 49:81–87.

Hlohowskyj, C. P., M. M. Coburn, and T. M. Cavender. 1989. Comparison of a pharyngeal filtering apparatus in seven species of the herbivorous cyprinid genus, *Hybognathus* (Pisces: Cyprinidae). Copeia 1989:172–183.

Hlohowskyj, I., and T. E. Wissing. 1984. Seasonal differences in the tolerances of *Etheostoma blennioides*, *E. flabellare*, and *E. caeruleum* to decreasing oxygen levels. Page 130 *in* Abstracts of the 64th Annual Meeting of the American Society of Ichthyologists and Herpetologists.

Hobson, J. F. 1979. Life history aspects of a percid fish, *Percina crassa roanoka*, the piedmont darter. Bios 3:148–157.

Hocutt, C. H. 1979a. Drainage evolution and fish dispersal in the central Appalachians: summary. Geological Society of America Bulletin 90(Part I):129–130.

Hocutt, C. H. 1979b. Drainage evolution and fish dispersal in the central Appalachians. Geological Society of America Bulletin 90(Part II):197–234.

Hocutt, C. H., R. F. Denoncourt, and J. R. Stauffer. 1978. Fishes of the Greenbrier River, West Virginia, with drainage history of the central Appalachians. Journal of Biogeography 5:59–80.

Hocutt, C. H., R. F. Denoncourt, and J. R. Stauffer. 1979. Fishes of the Gauley River, West Virginia. Brimleyana 1:47–80.

Hocutt, C. H., and P. S. Hambrick. 1973. Hybridization between the darter *Percina crassa roanoka* and *Percina oxyrhyncha* (Percidae, Etheostomatini), with comments on the distribution of *Percina crassa roanoka* in New River. American Midland Naturalist 90:397–405.

Hocutt, C. H., P. S. Hambrick, and M. T. Masnik. 1973. Rotenone methods in a large river system. Archiv fuer Hydrobiologie 72:245–252.

Hocutt, C. H., R. E. Jenkins, and J. R. Stauffer. 1986. Zoogeography of the fishes of the central Appalachians and central Atlantic Coastal Plain. Pages 161–211 in Hocutt and Wiley (1986).

Hocutt, C. H., and E. O. Wiley, editors. 1986. The zoogeography of North American freshwater fishes. John Wiley and Sons, New York.

Hoekstra, D., and J. Janssen. 1985. Non-visual foraging behavior of the mottled sculpin, *Cottus bairdi*, in Lake Michigan. Environmental Biology of Fishes 12:111–117.

Hoekstra, D., and J. Janssen. 1986. Lateral line receptivity in the mottled sculpin (*Cottus bairdi*). Copeia 1986:91–96.

Hoener, F. K. 1969. The relationship of the distribution of freshwater fish to salinity in the James, York, and Rappahannock River estuaries. Virginia Institute of Marine Science, NSF Undergraduate Research Program Report, Gloucester Point.

Hoese, H. D. 1963. Salt tolerance of the eastern mudminnow, *Umbra pygmaea*. Copeia 1963:165–166.

Hoff, J. G. 1979. Annotated bibliography and subject index on the shortnose sturgeon, *Acipenser brevirostrum*. NOAA (National Oceanic and Atmospheric Administration) Technical Report NMFS (National Marine Fisheries Service) SSRF (Special Scientific Report Fisheries) 731.

Hoff, J. G. 1980. Review of the present status of the stocks of the Atlantic sturgeon *Acipenser oxyrhynchus* Mitchill. Report to U.S. National Marine Fisheries Service Northeast Region, Gloucester, Massachusetts.

Hoffman, J. M. 1960. Survey of trout and smallmouth bass streams: Shenandoah River Study. Virginia Commission of Game and Inland Fisheries, Federal Aid in Sport Fish Restoration, Project F-8-R-5, Job 3, June 1, 1959–March 31, 1960, Progress Report, Richmond.

Hoffman, J. M. 1961. Virginia's 1961 trout program. Virginia Wildlife 22(4):16–17.

Hoffman, R. L. 1969. The biotic regions of Virginia. Virginia Polytechnic Institute and State University Research Division Bulletin 48:23–62.

Hogarth, W. T., and W. S. Woolcott. 1966. The mountain stripeback darter, *Percina notogramma montuosa*, n. ssp. from upper James River, Virginia. Chesapeake Science 7:101–109.

Hogue, J. J., R. Wallus, and L. K. Kay. 1976. Preliminary guide to the identification of larval fishes in the Tennessee River. Tennessee Valley Authority Technical Note B19, Norris, Tennessee.

Hokanson, K. E. F. 1977. Temperature requirements of some percids and adaptations to the seasonal temperature cycle. Journal of the Fisheries Research Board of Canada 34:1524–1550.

Hokanson, K. E. F., J. H. McCormick, B. R. Jones, and J. H. Tucker. 1973. Thermal requirements for maturation, spawning, and embryo survival of the brook trout, *Salvelinus fontinalis*. Journal of the Fisheries Research Board of Canada 30:975–984.

Holbrook, W. P. 1975. Fecundity and sex ratio in the least brook lamprey, *Lampetra aepyptera* (Abbott) in Lynn Creek, Wayne County, West Virginia. Proceedings of the West Virginia Academy of Science 57:150–153.

Holey, M., and six coauthors. 1979. "Never give a sucker an even break." Fisheries (Bethesda) 4(1):2–6.

Holland, B. F., and G. F. Yelverton. 1973. Distribution and biological studies of anadromous fishes offshore North Carolina. North Carolina Department of Natural and Economic Resources, Special Scientific Report 24, Raleigh.

Hollis, E. H. 1952. Variations in the feeding habits of the striped bass, *Roccus saxatilis* (Walbaum), in Chesapeake Bay. Bulletin of the Bingham Oceanographic Collection, Yale University 14:111–133.

Holmes, D. W., V. M. Douglass, and R. T. Lackey. 1974. Pond and cage culture of channel catfish in Virginia. Journal of the Tennessee Academy of Science 49:74–78.

Holsinger, J. R. 1964. The biology of Virginia caves. Pages 57–74 in H. H. Douglas, editor. Caves of Virginia. Econo Print, Falls Church, Virginia.

Holsinger, J. R. 1975. Descriptions of Virginia caves. Virginia Division of Mineral Resources Bulletin 85, Charlottesville.

Holsinger, J. R., and D. C. Culver. 1988. The invertebrate cave fauna of Virginia and a part of eastern Tennessee: zoogeography and ecology. Brimleyana 14:1–164.

Hooper, F. F. 1949. Age analysis of a population of the ameiurid fish *Schilbeodes mollis* (Hermann). Copeia 1949:34–38.

Hora, S. L. 1922. Structural modifications in the fish of mountain torrents. Records of the Indian Museum (Calcutta) 24:31–61.

Hora, S. L. 1952. Functional divergence, structural convergence and pre-adaptation exhibited by the fishes of the cyprinoid family Psilorhynchidae Hora. Journal of the Bombay Natural History Society 50:880–884.

Horn, M. H., and C. D. Riggs. 1973. Effects of temperature and light on the rate of air breathing of the bowfin, *Amia calva*. Copeia 1973:653–657.

House, R., and L. Wells. 1973. Age, growth, spawning season, and fecundity of the troutperch (*Percopsis omiscomaycus*) in southeastern Lake Michigan. Journal of the Fisheries Research Board of Canada 30:1221–1225.

Houser, A., and M. G. Bross. 1959. Observations on growth and reproduction of the paddlefish. Transactions of the American Fisheries Society 88:50–52.

Howden, H. F. 1949. An ecological study of the distribution of the fish in the Anacostia River tributaries in Maryland. Master's thesis. University of Maryland, College Park.

Howell, J. F. 1971. The life history and ecology of *Percina aurantiaca* (Cope). Doctoral dissertation. University of Tennessee, Knoxville.

Howell, J. F. 1981. The ichthyofauna of the Big Sandy River basin, with special emphasis on the Levisa Fork drainage. Appalachian Development Center Research Report 2, Morehead State University, Morehead, Kentucky.

Howell, W. M. 1968. Taxonomy and distribution of the percid fish, *Etheostoma stigmaeum* (Jordan), with the validation and redescription of *Etheostoma davisoni* Hay. Doctoral dissertation. University of Alabama, Tuscaloosa.

Howell, W. M., and H. T. Boschung. 1966. A natural hybrid darter, *Etheostoma whipplii artesiae* × *Etheostoma stigmaeum* (Pisces, Percidae). American Midland Naturalist 76:510–514.

Howes, G. J. 1981. Anatomy and phylogeny of the Chinese major carps *Ctenopharyngodon* Steind., 1866 and *Hypophthalmichthys* Blkr., 1860. Bulletin of the British Museum (Natural History) Zoology 41:1–52.

Howes, G. J. 1985. A revised synonymy of the minnow genus *Phoxinus* Rafinesque, 1820 (Teleostei: Cyprinidae) with comments on its relationships and distribution. Bulletin of the British Museum (Natural History) Zoology 48:57–74.

Hoyt, R. D. 1970. Food habits of the silverjaw minnow, *Ericymba buccata* Cope, in an intermittent stream in Kentucky. American Midland Naturalist 84:226–236.

Hoyt, R. D. 1971a. The reproductive biology of the silverjaw minnow, *Ericymba buccata* Cope, in Kentucky. Transactions of the American Fisheries Society 100:510–519.

Hoyt, R. D. 1971b. Age and growth of the silverjaw minnow, *Ericymba buccata* Cope, in Kentucky. American Midland Naturalist 86:257–275.

Hoyt, R. D. 1972. Anatomy and osteology of the cephalic lateral-line system of the silverjaw minnow, *Ericymba buccata* (Pisces: Cyprinidae). Copeia 1972:812–816.

Hoyt, R. D., and W. H. Kruskamp. 1982. Seasonal occurrences and movement patterns of fish in the Barren River, Kentucky. Transactions of the Kentucky Academy of Science 43:168–175.

Hubbs, C. 1954a. A new Texas subspecies, *apristis*, of the darter *Hadropterus scierus*, with a discussion of variation within the species. American Midland Naturalist 52:211–220.

Hubbs, C. 1954b. Corrected distributional records for Texas fresh-water fishes. Texas Journal of Science 6:277–291.

Hubbs, C. 1956. Relative variability of hybrids between the minnows, *Notropis lepidus* and *N. proserpinus*. Texas Journal of Science 8:463–469.

Hubbs, C. 1961. Isolating mechanisms in the speciation of fishes. Pages 5–23 *in* W. F. Blair, editor. Vertebrate speciation. University of Texas Press, Austin.

Hubbs, C. 1967. Analysis of phylogenetic relationships using hybridization techniques. Bulletin of the National Institute of Sciences of India 34:48–59.

Hubbs, C. 1970. Teleost hybridization studies. Proceedings of the California Academy of Sciences 38:289–298.

Hubbs, C. 1971. Survival of intergroup percid hybrids. Japanese Journal of Ichthyology 18:65–75.

Hubbs, C. 1985. Darter reproductive seasons. Copeia 1985:56–68.

Hubbs, C. 1986. Darter hybrids for home aquaria. American Currents November 1985:7–10.

Hubbs, C., and C. Bryan. 1974. Maximum incubation temperature of the threadfin shad, *Dorosoma petenense*. Transactions of the American Fisheries Society 103:369–371.

Hubbs, C., and C. M. Laritz. 1961. Natural hybridization between *Hadropterus scierus* and *Percina caprodes*. Southwestern Naturalist 6:188–192.

Hubbs, C., and K. Strawn. 1963. Differences in the developmental temperature tolerance of central Texas and more northern stocks of *Percina caprodes* (Percidae: Osteichthyes). Southwestern Naturalist 8:43–45.

Hubbs, C. L. 1921. An ecological study of the life-history of the fresh-water atherine fish *Labidesthes sicculus*. Ecology 2:262–276.

Hubbs, C. L. 1922. Variations in the number of vertebrae and other meristic characters of fishes correlated with the temperature of water during development. American Naturalist 56:360–372.

Hubbs, C. L. 1926. A check-list of the fishes of the Great Lakes and tributary waters, with nomenclatorial notes and analytical keys. Miscellaneous Publications Museum of Zoology University of Michigan 15.

Hubbs, C. L. 1927. *Micropterus pseudaplites*, a new species of black bass. Occasional Papers of the Museum of Zoology University of Michigan 184.

Hubbs, C. L. 1928. Ecological studies of southern Wisconsin fishes. Ecology 9:249–252.

Hubbs, C. L. 1930a. Materials for a revision of the catostomid fishes of eastern North America. Miscellaneous Publications Museum of Zoology, University of Michigan 20.

Hubbs, C. L. 1930b. Further additions and corrections to the list of the fishes of the Great Lakes and tributary waters. Papers of the Michigan Academy of Science, Arts and Letters 11:425–436.

Hubbs, C. L. 1931. *Parexoglossum laurae*, a new cyprinid fish from the upper Kanawha River system. Occasional Papers of the Museum of Zoology University of Michigan 234.

Hubbs, C. L. 1936. An older name for the black-nosed dace. Copeia 1936:124–125.

Hubbs, C. L. 1940. Speciation of fishes. American Naturalist 74:198–211.

Hubbs, C. L. 1941a. The relation of hydrological conditions to speciation in fishes. Pages 182–195 *in* A symposium on hydrobiology. University of Wisconsin Press, Madison.

Hubbs, C. L. 1941b. A systematic study of two Carolinean minnows, *Notropis scepticus* and *Notropis altipinnis*. Copeia 1941:165–174.

Hubbs, C. L. 1945. Corrected distributional records for Minnesota fishes. Copeia 1945:13–22.

Hubbs, C. L. 1951. *Notropis amnis*, a new cyprinid fish of the Mississippi fauna, with two subspecies. Occasional Papers of the Museum of Zoology University of Michigan 530.

Hubbs, C. L. 1955. Hybridization between fish species in nature. Systematic Zoology 4:1–20.

Hubbs, C. L. 1964a. History of ichthyology in the United States after 1850. Copeia 1964:42–60.

Hubbs, C. L. 1964b. David Starr Jordan. Systematic Zoology 13:195–200.

Hubbs, C. L., and E. R. Allen. 1943. Fishes of Silver Springs, Florida. Proceedings of the Florida Academy of Sciences 6:110–130.

Hubbs, C. L., and R. M. Bailey. 1938. The small-mouthed bass. Cranbrook Institute of Science Bulletin 10.

Hubbs, C. L., and R. M. Bailey. 1940. A revision of the black basses (*Micropterus* and *Huro*) with descriptions of four new forms. Miscellaneous Publications Museum of Zoology University of Michigan 48.

Hubbs, C. L., and R. M. Bailey. 1947. Blind catfishes from artesian waters of Texas. Occasional Papers of the Museum of Zoology University of Michigan 499.

Hubbs, C. L., and J. D. Black. 1940a. Status of the catostomid fish, *Carpiodes elongatus* Meek. Copeia 1940: 226–230.

Hubbs, C. L., and J. D. Black. 1940b. Percid fishes related to *Poecilichthys variatus*, with descriptions of three new forms. Occasional Papers of the Museum of Zoology University of Michigan 416.

Hubbs, C. L., and J. D. Black. 1947. Revision of *Ceratichthys*, a genus of American cyprinid fishes. Miscellaneous Publications Museum of Zoology University of Michigan 66.

Hubbs, C. L., and D. E. S. Brown. 1929. Materials for a distributional study of Ontario fishes. Transactions of the Royal Canadian Institute 17(Part 1):1–56.

Hubbs, C. L., and M. D. Cannon. 1935. The darters of the genera *Hololepis* and *Villora*. Miscellaneous Publications Museum of Zoology University of Michigan 30.

Hubbs, C. L., and G. P. Cooper. 1936. Minnows of Michigan. Cranbrook Institute of Science Bulletin 8.

Hubbs, C. L., and W. R. Crowe. 1956. Preliminary analysis of the American cyprinid fishes, seven new, referred to the genus *Hybopsis*, subgenus *Erimystax*. Occasional Papers of the Museum of Zoology University of Michigan 578.

Hubbs, C. L., and C. W. Hibbard. 1951. *Ictalurus lambda*, a new catfish, based on a pectoral spine from the Lower Pliocene of Kansas. Copeia 1951:8–14.

Hubbs, C. L., and C. Hubbs. 1958. *Notropis saladonis*, a new cyprinid fish endemic in the Río Salado of northeastern México. Copeia 1958:297–307.

Hubbs, C. L., L. C. Hubbs, and R. E. Johnson. 1943a. Hybridization in nature between species of catostomid fishes. Contributions from the Laboratory of Vertebrate Biology of the University of Michigan 22.

Hubbs, C. L., and K. F. Lagler. 1941. Guide to the fishes of the Great Lakes and tributary waters. Cranbrook Institute of Science Bulletin 18.

Hubbs, C. L., and K. F. Lagler. 1949. Fishes of Isle Royale, Lake Superior, Michigan. Papers of the Michigan Academy of Science, Arts and Letters 33:73–133.

Hubbs, C. L., and K. F. Lagler. 1958. Fishes of the Great Lakes region. Cranbrook Institute of Science Bulletin 26.

Hubbs, C. L., R. R. Miller, and L. C. Hubbs. 1974. Hydrographic history and relict fishes of the north-central Great Basin. California Academy of Sciences Memoirs 7.

Hubbs, C. L., and A. I. Ortenburger. 1929a. Further notes on the fishes of Oklahoma with descriptions of new species of Cyprinidae. University of Oklahoma Bulletin New Series 434, Publications of the University of Oklahoma Biological Survey 1:15–43. (Norman, Oklahoma.)

Hubbs, C. L., and A. I. Ortenburger. 1929b. Fishes collected in Oklahoma and Arkansas in 1927. University of Oklahoma Bulletin New Series 434, Publications of the University of Oklahoma Biological Survey 1:47–112. (Norman, Oklahoma.)

Hubbs, C. L., and I. C. Potter. 1971. Distribution, phylogeny and taxonomy. Pages 1–65 *in* M. W. Hardisty and I. C. Potter, editors. The biology of lampreys, volume 1. Academic Press, New York.

Hubbs, C. L., and E. C. Raney. 1939. *Hadropterus oxyrhynchus*, a new percid fish from Virginia and West Virginia. Occasional Papers of the Museum of Zoology University of Michigan 396.

Hubbs, C. L., and E. C. Raney. 1944. Systematic notes on North American siluroid fishes of the genus *Schilbeodes*. Occasional Papers of the Museum of Zoology University of Michigan 487.

Hubbs, C. L., and E. C. Raney. 1947. *Notropis alborus*, a new cyprinid fish from North Carolina and Virginia. Occasional Papers of the Museum of Zoology University of Michigan 498.

Hubbs, C. L., and E. C. Raney. 1948. Subspecies of *Notropis altipinnis*, a cyprinid fish of the eastern United States. Occasional Papers of the Museum of Zoology University of Michigan 506.

Hubbs, C. L., and E. C. Raney. 1951. Status, subspecies, and variations of *Notropis cummingsae*, a cyprinid fish of the southeastern United States. Occasional Papers of the Museum of Zoology University of Michigan 535.

Hubbs, C. L., and M. B. Trautman. 1932. *Poecilichthys osburni*, a new darter from the upper Kanawha River system in Virginia and West Virginia. Ohio Journal of Science 32:31–38.

Hubbs, C. L., and M. B. Trautman. 1937. A revision of the lamprey genus *Ichthyomyzon*. Miscellaneous Publications Museum of Zoology, University of Michigan 35.

Hubbs, C. L., B. W. Walker, and R. E. Johnson. 1943b. Hybridization in nature between species of American cyprinodont fishes. Contributions from the Laboratory of Vertebrate Biology of the University of Michigan 23.

Hubert, W. A. 1976. Estimation of the fecundity of smallmouth bass, *Micropterus dolomieui* Lacepede, found in the Wilson Dam tailwaters, Alabama. Journal of the Tennessee Academy of Science 51:142–144.

Hubert, W. A., S. H. Anderson, P. D. Southall, and J. H. Crance. 1984. Habitat suitability index models and instream flow suitability curves: paddlefish. U.S. Fish and Wildlife Service Division of Biological Services FWS-OBS-82/10.80.

Huck, L. L., and G. E. Gunning. 1967. Behavior of the longear sunfish, *Lepomis megalotis* (Rafinesque). Tulane Studies in Zoology 14:121–131.

Huff, J. A. 1975. Life history of Gulf of Mexico sturgeon, *Acipenser oxyrhynchus desotoi* in Suwannee River, Florida. Florida Marine Research Publications 16.

Hughes, A. L. 1985. Seasonal changes in fecundity and size at first reproduction in an Indiana population of the mosquitofish *Gambusia affinis*. American Midland Naturalist 114:30–36.

Hughes, G. M., editor. 1976. Respiration of amphibious vertebrates. Academic Press, New York.

Huish, M. T. 1947. The short-tailed shrew (*Blarina*) as a source of food for the green sunfish. Copeia 1947:198.

Huish, M. T., and G. B. Pardue. 1978. Ecological studies

of one channelized and two unchannelized wooded coastal swamp streams in North Carolina. U.S. Fish and Wildlife Service Biological Services Program FWS-OBS-78/85.

Huish, M. T., and M. E. Shepherd. 1975. Life history and ecology of the pirate perch, *Aphredoderus sayanus* (Gilliams). Journal of the Elisha Mitchell Scientific Society 91:76.

Humphries, C. J., and L. R. Parenti. 1986. Cladistic biogeography. Oxford University Press, New York.

Humphries, J. M., R. C. Cashner, and W. J. Matthews. 1988. Systematics of the rosyface shiner, *Notropis rubellus*. Page 113 *in* Abstracts of the 68th Annual Meeting of the American Society of Ichthyologists and Herpetologists.

Hunt, C. B. 1974. Natural regions of the United States and Canada. W. H. Freeman and Company, San Francisco.

Hunter, J. R. 1963. The reproductive behavior of the green sunfish, *Lepomis cyanellus*. Zoologica (New York) 48:13–24. (Not seen; cited in Scott and Crossman 1973.)

Hunter, J. R., and W. J. Wisby. 1961. Utilization of the nests of green sunfish (*Lepomis cyanellus*) by the redfin shiner (*Notropis umbratilis cyanocephalus*). Copeia 1961:113–115.

Huntsman, G. R. 1967. Nuptial tubercles in carpsuckers (*Carpiodes*). Copeia 1967:457–458.

Hynes, H. B. N. 1970. The ecology of running waters. University of Toronto Press, Toronto.

ICZN (International Commission on Zoological Nomenclature). 1985. International code of zoological nomenclature, 3rd edition. W. D. L. Ride, C. W. Sabrosky, G. Bernardi, and R. V. Melville, editors. University of California Press, Berkeley.

ICZN (International Commission on Zoological Nomenclature). 1992. Opinion 1684 *Lepomis* Rafinesque, 1819 (Osteichthyes, Perciformes): gender fixed as masculine. Bulletin of Zoological Nomenclature 49(2):169–170.

IGFA (International Game Fish Association). 1985. World record game fishes. Ft. Lauderdale, Florida.

Imbrie, J., A. McIntyre, and T. C. Moore. 1983. The ocean around North America at the last glacial maximum. Pages 230–236 *in* H. E. Wright and S. C. Porter, editors. Late-Quaternary environments of the United States, volume 1. University of Minnesota Press, Minneapolis.

Ingersoll, C. G., and D. L. Claussen. 1984. Temperature selection and critical thermal maxima of the fantail darter, *Etheostoma flabellare*, and johnny darter, *E. nigrum*, related to habitat and season. Pages 95–102 *in* D. G. Lindquist and L. M. Page, editors. Environmental biology of darters. Kluwer Boston, Hingham, Massachusetts. (Also: Environmental Biology of Fishes 11:131–138.)

Ingram, B. 1987. A sporting history: Craig County. Virginia Wildlife 48(2):26–29.

Inskip, P. D. 1982. Habitat suitability index models: northern pike. U.S. Fish and Wildlife Service Biological Services Program Report FWS-OBS-82/10.17.

Jackson, H. W., and C. Henderson. 1942. A study of the stream pollution problem in the Roanoke, Virginia,

metropolitan district, part II, macroscopic invertebrate and vertebrate faunae; the toxicity of viscose wastes to fishes. Bulletin of the Virginia Polytechnic Institute, Engineering Experiment Station Series 51:91–120.

Jackson, H. W., and R. E. Tiller. 1952. Preliminary observations on spawning potential in the striped bass (*Roccus saxatilis* Walbaum). Chesapeake Biological Laboratory Publication 93, Solomons, Maryland.

Jackson, S. W. 1956. Rotenone survey of Black Hollow on Lower Spavinaw Lake, November, 1953. Proceedings of the Oklahoma Academy of Science 35:10–14.

Jaco, B. D. 1967. Fish kill—Clinch River—June 10–15, 1967. Memorandum to supervisor of fish investigations, Fish and Wildlife Branch, Tennessee Valley Authority, Norris, Tennessee.

James, D. L. 1979. Ecological studies of the fishes of the Pigg River system, south-central Virginia, with special reference to threatened species. Master's thesis. Virginia Commonwealth University, Richmond.

Janssen, R. E. 1953. The Teays River, ancient precursor of the East. Scientific Monthly 77:306–314.

Janvier, P. 1981. The phylogeny of the Craniata, with particular reference to the significance of fossil "agnathans." Journal of Vertebrate Paleontology 1:121–159.

Janvier, P., and R. Lund. 1983. *Hardistiella montanensis* n. gen. et sp. (Petromyzontida) from the Lower Carboniferous of Montana, with remarks on the affinities of the lampreys. Journal of Vertebrate Paleontology 2:407–413.

Jenkins, R. E. 1970. Systematic studies of the catostomid fish tribe Moxostomatini. Doctoral dissertation. Cornell University, Ithaca, New York.

Jenkins, R. E. 1971a. Behavioral and morphological evidence of monophyly of nest-building cyprinid fishes. ASB (Association of Southeastern Biologists) Bulletin 18:40.

Jenkins, R. E. 1971b. Nuptial tuberculation and its systematic significance in the percid fish *Etheostoma (Ioa) vitreum*. Copeia 1971:735–738.

Jenkins, R. E. 1975a. *Hybopsis cahni* Hubbs and Crowe 1956, slender chub. Status Report to the Office of Endangered Species, U.S. Fish and Wildlife Service, Washington, D.C.

Jenkins, R. E. 1975b. *Noturus flavipinnis* Taylor 1969, yellowfin madtom. Status Report to the Office of Endangered Species, U.S. Fish and Wildlife Service, Washington, D.C.

Jenkins, R. E. 1976. A list of undescribed freshwater fish species of continental United States and Canada, with additions to the 1970 checklist. Copeia 1976:642–644.

Jenkins, R. E. 1977a. Orangefin madtom, *Noturus gilberti* Jordan and Evermann 1889. Status Report to the Office of Endangered Species, U.S. Fish and Wildlife Service, Washington, D.C.

Jenkins, R. E. 1977b. Roanoke logperch, *Percina rex* (Jordan and Evermann) 1889. Status Report to the Office of Endangered Species, U.S. Fish and Wildlife Service, Washington, D.C.

Jenkins, R. E. 1978. Rustyside sucker, *Moxostoma hamiltoni* (Raney and Lachner) 1946. Status Report to the Office of Endangered Species, U.S. Fish and Wildlife Service, Washington, D.C.

Jenkins, R. E. 1979a. Assessment of fish diversity of the upper Roanoke River basin. Pages A1–A131 *in* K. L. Dickson, editor. Aquatic ecological classification and evaluation of streams and stream reaches in the upper Roanoke River basin, Virginia. Institute of Applied Sciences, North Texas State University, Denton, and Wilmington District Corps of Engineers (Contract DACW54-78-C-0053), Wilmington, North Carolina.

Jenkins, R. E. 1979b. A classification system for streams in the upper Roanoke River basin. Pages G1–G6 *in* K. L. Dickson, editor. Aquatic ecological classification and evaluation of streams and stream reaches in the upper Roanoke River basin, Virginia. Institute of Applied Sciences, North Texas State University, Denton, and Wilmington District Corps of Engineers (Contract DACW54-78-C-0053), Wilmington, North Carolina.

Jenkins, R. E. 1981. Aquatic study of the Smith River— proposed Ridgeway Hydroelectric Project area, Henry County, Virginia and Rockingham County, North Carolina, June–July 1981. R. W. Beck and Associates, Seattle.

Jenkins, R. E. 1987. Introduced fishes in Virginia drainages, with special reference to cryptic introductions and biogeographic study. Page 57 *in* Abstracts of the 67th Annual Meeting of the American Society of Ichthyologists and Herpetologists.

Jenkins, R. E. 1988. Review of "The inland fishes of New York State" by C. L. Smith. Copeia 1988:263–265.

Jenkins, R. E., and N. M. Burkhead. 1973. Distribution and habitat of the fishes in Copper Creek, a Clinch River tributary, Virginia. ASB (Association of Southeastern Biologists) Bulletin 20:61.

Jenkins, R. E., and N. M. Burkhead. 1975a. Distribution and aspects of life history and morphology of the cyprinid fish *Notropis semperasper* endemic to the upper James River drainage, Virginia. Chesapeake Science 16:178–191.

Jenkins, R. E., and N. M. Burkhead. 1975b. Recent capture and analysis of the sharphead darter, *Etheostoma acuticeps*, an endangered percid fish of the upper Tennessee River drainage. Copeia 1975:731–740.

Jenkins, R. E., and N. M. Burkhead. 1984. Description, biology and distribution of the spotfin chub, *Hybopsis monacha*, a threatened cyprinid fish of the Tennessee River drainage. Bulletin Alabama Museum of Natural History 8:1–30.

Jenkins, R. E., and R. C. Cashner. 1983. Records and distributional relationships of the Roanoke bass, *Ambloplites cavifrons*, in the Roanoke River drainage, Virginia. Ohio Journal of Science 83:146–155.

Jenkins, R. E., and C. A. Freeman. 1972. Longitudinal distribution and habitat of the fishes of Mason Creek, an upper Roanoke River drainage tributary, Virginia. Virginia Journal of Science 23:194–202.

Jenkins, R. E., and P. S. Hambrick. 1972. Distribution of the fishes of the New (upper Kanawha) River drainage, North Carolina, Virginia and West Virginia. ASB (Association of Southeastern Biologists) Bulletin 20:61.

Jenkins, R. E, and D. J. Jenkins. 1980. Reproductive be-

havior of the greater redhorse, *Moxostoma valenciennesi*, in the Thousand Islands Region. Canadian Field-Naturalist 94:426–430.

Jenkins, R. E., and E. A. Lachner. 1971. Criteria for analysis and interpretation of the American fish genera *Nocomis* Girard and *Hybopsis* Agassiz. Smithsonian Contributions to Zoology 90.

Jenkins, R. E., and E. A. Lachner. 1975. Relationships of several cyprinid groups: nestbuilders and lineages of *Hybopsis*. Pages 95–96 *in* Abstracts of the 55th Annual Meeting of the American Society of Ichthyologists and Herpetologists.

Jenkins, R. E., and E. A. Lachner. 1989. Are gravel-nest-building minnows monophyletic? Page 103 *in* Abstracts of the 69th Annual Meeting of the American Society of Ichthyologists and Herpetologists.

Jenkins, R. E., E. A. Lachner, and F. J. Schwartz. 1972. Fishes of the central Appalachian drainages: their distribution and dispersal. Virginia Polytechnic Institute and State University Research Division Monograph 4:43–117. [Publication erroneously stamped 1971.]

Jenkins, R. E., and J. A. Musick. 1979. Freshwater and marine fishes. Pages 319–373 *in* D. W. Linzey, editor. Endangered and threatened plants and animals of Virginia. Virginia Polytechnic Institute and State University, Sea Grant Program, Publication VPI-SG-79-13, Blacksburg.

Jenkins, R. E., L. A. Revelle, and T. Zorach. 1975. Records of the blackbanded sunfish, *Enneacanthus chaetodon*, and comments on the southeastern Virginia freshwater ichthyofauna. Virginia Journal of Science 26:128–134.

Jenkins, R. E., and W. C. Starnes. 1981. Systematics of the Holarctic dace genus *Phoxinus* (Cyprinidae). *In* Abstracts of the 61st Annual Meeting of the American Society of Ichthyologists and Herpetologists.

Jenkins, R. E., B. A. Thompson, and T. Zorach. 1977. Review and systematic problems of the logperch darter subgenus *Percina*, fish family Percidae. *In* Abstracts of the 57th Annual Meeting of the American Society of Ichthyologists and Herpetologists.

Jenkins, R. E., and T. Zorach. 1970. Zoogeography and characters of the American cyprinid fish *Notropis bifrenatus*. Chesapeake Science 11:174–182.

Jenkins, T. M. 1969. Social structure, position choice and microdistribution of two trout species (*Salmo trutta* and *Salmo gairdneri*) resident in mountain streams. Animal Behavior Monographs 2:57–123.

Jessop, B. M. 1987. Migrating American eels in Nova Scotia. Transactions of the American Fisheries Society 116:161–170.

John, B. S., editor. 1979. The winters of the world: earth under the ice ages. John Wiley and Sons, New York.

Johnson, D. W. 1905. The distribution of fresh-water faunas as an evidence of drainage modifications. Science 21:588–592.

Johnson, G. D. 1978. Development of fishes of the Mid-Atlantic Bight. An atlas of egg, larval and juvenile stages, volume 4. U.S. Fish and Wildlife Service Biological Services Program FWS-OBS-78/12.

Johnson, G. D. 1984. Percoidei: development and relationships. Pages 464–498 *in* Moser et al. (1984).

Johnson, J. E. 1970. Age, growth, and population dynamics of threadfin shad, *Dorosoma petenense* (Günther), in central Arizona reservoirs. Transactions of the American Fisheries Society 99:739–753.

Johnson, J. E. 1971. Maturity and fecundity of threadfin shad, *Dorosoma petenense* (Günther), in central Arizona reservoirs. Transactions of the American Fisheries Society 100:74–85.

Johnson, J. H. 1981. The summer diet of the cutlips minnow, *Exoglossum maxillingua*, in a central New York stream. Copeia 1981:484–487.

Johnson, J. H. 1982. Summer feeding ecology of the blacknose dace, *Rhinichthys atratulus* in a tributary of Lake Ontario. Canadian Field-Naturalist 96:282–286.

Johnson, J. H., and E. Z. Johnson. 1982. Observations on the eye-picking behavior of the cutlips minnow, *Exoglossum maxillingua*. Copeia 1982:711–712.

Johnson, J. R. 1980. Morphology and development of hatchery cultured American shad (*Alosa sapidissima* Wilson), with a comparison between field sampled and cultured specimens. Master's thesis. College of William and Mary, Williamsburg, Virginia.

Johnson, M. 1972. Distribution of sculpins (Pisces: Cottidae) in Iowa. Proceedings of the Iowa Academy of Science 78:79–80.

Johnson, P. G. 1983. The New River early settlement. Edmonds Printing Company, Pulaski, Virginia.

Johnson, R. K., and T. S. Y. Koo. 1975. Production and distribution of striped bass (*Morone saxatilis*) eggs in the Chesapeake and Delaware Canal. Chesapeake Science 16:39–55.

Johnston, C. E. 1989a. Spawning in the eastern sand darter, *Ammocrypta pellucida* (Pisces: Percidae), with comments on the phylogeny of *Ammocrypta* and related taxa. Transactions of the Illinois Academy of Science 82:163–168.

Johnston, C. E. 1989b. Spawning activities of *Notropis chlorocephalus*, *N. chiliticus*, and *Hybopsis hypsinotus*, three nest associates of *Nocomis leptocephalus* in the southeastern United States. ASB (Association of Southeastern Biologists) Bulletin 36:67.

Johnston, C. E. 1990. Spawning observations of *Phenacobius crassilabrum* (Cyprinidae), a poorly known minnow of the upper Tennessee River drainage. Page 105 *in* Abstracts of the 70th Annual Meeting of the American Society of Ichthyologists and Herpetologists.

Johnston, C. E., and W. S. Birkhead. 1988. Spawning in the bandfin shiner, *Notropis zonistius* (Pisces: Cyprinidae). Journal of the Alabama Academy of Science 59:30–33.

Johnston, C. E., and L. M. Page. 1992. The evolution of complex reproductive strategies in North American minnows (Cyprinidae). Pages 600–621 *in* Mayden (1992).

Johnston, C. E., and J. S. Ramsey. 1990. Redescription of *Semotilus thoreauianus* Jordan, 1877, a cyprinid fish of the southeastern United States. Copeia 1990:119–130.

Jollie, M. 1984. Development of cranial and pectoral girdle bones of *Lepisosteus* with a note on scales. Copeia 1984:476–502.

Jones, A. R., and D. E. Stephens. 1984. Muskellunge streams investigation in the South Fork Kentucky River drainage. Kentucky Department of Fish and Wildlife Resources, Fisheries Bulletin 71, Frankfort.

Jones, P. W., F. D. Martin, and J. D. Hardy. 1978. Development of fishes of the Mid-Atlantic Bight. An atlas of egg, larval and juvenile stages, volume 1. U.S. Fish and Wildlife Service Biological Services Program FWS-OBS-78/12.

Jones, R. A. 1965. Blue catfish, *Ictalurus furcatus*. Page 121 *in* A. J. McClane, editor. McClane's standard fishing encyclopedia. Holt, Rinehart and Winston, New York.

Jones, R. D. 1978. Regional trends of the trout resource. Pages 1–27 *in* T. J. Harshbarger, editor. Southeastern trout resource: ecology and management symposium proceedings. U.S. Forest Service, Southeastern Forest and Range Experiment Station, Asheville, North Carolina.

Jones, R. S., and W. F. Hettler. 1959. Bat feeding by green sunfish. Texas Journal of Science 11:48. (Not seen; cited in Carlander 1977.)

Jonsson, B., and F. R. Gravem. 1985. Use of space and food by resident and migrant brown trout, *Salmo trutta*. Environmental Biology of Fishes 14:281–293.

Jordan, D. S. 1876. Manual of the vertebrates of the northern United States. Jansen, McClurg and Company, Chicago.

Jordan, D. S. 1877a. A partial synopsis of the fishes of upper Georgia; with supplementary papers on fishes of Tennessee, Kentucky, and Indiana. Annals of the New York Lyceum of Natural History 11:307–377.

Jordan, D. S. 1877b. On the distribution of freshwater fishes. American Naturalist 1877:607–613.

Jordan, D. S. 1878. A synopsis of the family Catostomidae. Bulletin of the United States National Museum 12:97–230.

Jordan, D. S. 1882. Report on the fishes of Ohio. Report of the Geological Survey of Ohio 4(Part I):737–1002, Columbus.

Jordan, D. S. 1888. Description of a new species of *Etheostoma* (*E. longimana*) from James River, Virginia. Proceedings of the Academy of Natural Sciences of Philadelphia 40:179.

Jordan, D. S. 1889a. Descriptions of fourteen species of fresh-water fishes collected by the U.S. Fish Commission in the summer of 1888. Proceedings of the United States National Museum 11:351–362.

Jordan, D. S. 1889b. Report of explorations made during the summer and autumn 1888, in the Alleghany region of Virginia, North Carolina and Tennessee, and in western Indiana, with an account of the fishes found in each of the river basins of those regions. U.S. Fish Commission Bulletin 8(1888):97–173.

Jordan, D. S. 1902. The fish fauna of Japan, with observations on the geographical distribution of fishes. Proceedings of the American Association for the Advancement of Science 14:545–567.

Jordan, D. S. 1905. The origin of species through isolation. Science 22:545–562.

Jordan, D. S. 1908. The law of geminate species. American Naturalist 42:73–80.

Jordan, D. S. 1917. Changes in names of American fishes. Copeia 1917:85–89.

Jordan, D. S. 1922. The days of a man, being memories of a naturalist, teacher and minor prophet of democracy. World Book, Yonkers-on-Hudson, New York.

Jordan, D. S. 1924. Concerning the genus *Hybopsis* of Agassiz. Copeia 1924:51–52.

Jordan, D. S. 1925. Fishes. D. Appleton, New York.

Jordan, D. S. 1928. The distribution of fresh-water fishes. Smithsonian Institution Annual Report 1927:355–385.

Jordan, D. S. 1929. Manual of the vertebrate animals of the northeastern United States, inclusive of marine species, 13th edition. World Book, Yonkers-on-Hudson, New York.

Jordan, D. S., and A. W. Brayton. 1877. On *Lagochila*, a new genus of catostomid fishes. Proceedings of the Academy of Natural Sciences of Philadelphia 29:280–283.

Jordan, D. S., and A. W. Brayton. 1878. On the distribution of the fishes of the Alleghany region of South Carolina, Georgia, and Tennessee, with descriptions of new or little known species. Bulletin of the United States National Museum 12:3–95.

Jordan, D. S., and B. W. Evermann. 1896–1900. The fishes of North and Middle America: A descriptive catalogue of the species of fish-like vertebrates found in waters of North America, north of the isthmus of Panama. Bulletin of the United States National Museum 47(Parts 1–4):1–3313.

Jordan, D. S., and B. W. Evermann. 1920. American food and game fishes. Doubleday, Page, and Company, Garden City, New York.

Jordan, D. S., B. W. Evermann, and H. W. Clark. 1930. Check list of the fishes and fishlike vertebrates of North and Middle America north of the northern boundary of Venezuela and Columbia. U.S. Commission of Fish and Fisheries, Report of the U.S. Commissioner of Fisheries for 1928, Appendix X, Washington, D.C.

Jordan, D. S., and C. H. Gilbert. 1883. Synopsis of the fishes of North America. Bulletin of the United States National Museum 16.

Jordan, D. S., and C. H. Gilbert. 1886. List of fishes collected in Arkansas, Indian Territory, and Texas, in September, 1884, with notes and descriptions. Proceedings of the United States National Museum 9:1–25.

Jordan, R. R. 1974. Pleistocene deposits of Delaware. Pages 30–52 in R. Q. Oaks and J. R. DuBar, editors. Post-Miocene stratigraphy, central and southern Atlantic Coastal Plain. Utah State University Press, Logan.

Joseph, E. B., and J. Davis. 1965. A preliminary assessment of the river herring stocks of lower Chesapeake Bay. Virginia Institute of Marine Science Special Scientific Report 51.

Jude, D. J. 1982. Family Cyprinodontidae. Pages 477–486 in N. A. Auer, editor. Identification of larval fishes of the Great Lakes basin with emphasis on the Lake Michigan drainage. Great Lakes Fishery Commission Special Publication 82-3, Ann Arbor, Michigan.

Judson, S. 1975. Evolution of Appalachian topography. Pages 29–44 in W. N. Melhorn and R. C. Flemal, editors. Theories of landform development. Publications in Geomorphology, Binghamton, New York.

Judy, M. H. 1961. Validity of age determinations from scales of marked American shad. U.S. Fish and Wildlife Service Fishery Bulletin 61:161–170.

June, F. C. 1977. Reproductive patterns in seventeen species of warmwater fishes in a Missouri River reservoir. Environmental Biology of Fishes 2:285–296.

Kahn, J. H. 1985. Acid rain in Virginia: Its yearly damage amounts to millions of dollars. Virginia Polytechnic Institute and State University, Water Resources Research Center Special Report 21.

Karr, J. R. 1963. Age, growth, and food habits of johnny, slenderhead and blacksided darters of Boone County, Iowa. Proceedings of the Iowa Academy of Science 70:228–236.

Karr, J. R. 1964. Age, growth, fecundity and food habits of fantail darters in Boone County, Iowa. Proceedings of the Iowa Academy of Science 71:274–280.

Katula, R. S. 1973. [On pirate perch breeding]. American Currents 1(2):17 [Not seen; 3-paragraph note read by telephone by W. J. Fisk to Jenkins].

Katula, R. S. 1986. Greenside gourmet. American Currents (October):6.

Katula, R. S. 1987. Spawning of the pirate perch recollected. American Currents (June/July–August/September):19–20.

Kauffman, J. 1975. Shenandoah Valley fisheries investigation. Virginia Commission of Game and Inland Fisheries, Federal Aid in Sport Fish Restoration, Project F-29-2, May 3, 1974–May 1, 1975, Progress Report, Richmond.

Kauffman, J. 1980. Effect of a new mercury-induced consumption ban on angling pressure: South Fork of the Shenandoah River, Virginia. Fisheries (Bethesda) 5(1):10–12.

Keast, A. 1965. Resource subdivision amongst cohabiting species in a bay, Lake Opinicon, Ontario. Great Lakes Research Division Publication 13, University of Michigan, Ann Arbor.

Keast, A. 1966. Trophic interrelationships in the fish fauna of a small stream. Pages 51–79 in Great Lakes Research Division Publication 15, University of Michigan, Ann Arbor.

Keast, A. 1970. Food specializations and bioenergetic interrelations in the fish faunas of some small Ontario waterways. Pages 377–411 in J. H. Steele, editor. Marine food chains. Oliver and Boyd, Edinburgh, UK.

Keast, A. 1985. The piscivore feeding guild of fishes in small freshwater ecosystems. Environmental Biology of Fishes 12:119–129.

Keast, A., and D. Webb. 1966. Mouth and body form relative to feeding ecology in the fish fauna of a small lake, Lake Opinicon, Ontario. Journal of the Fisheries Research Board of Canada 23:1845–1874.

Keenleyside, M. H. A. 1978. Reproductive isolation between pumpkinseed (*Lepomis gibbosus*) and longear sunfish (*L. megalotis*) (Centrarchidae) in the Thames River, southwestern Ontario. Journal of the Fisheries Research Board of Canada 35:131–135.

Keenleyside, M. H. A. 1979. Diversity and adaptation in fish behaviour. Springer-Verlag, New York.

Keevin, T. M., L. M. Page, and C. E. Johnston. 1989. The spawning behavior of the saffron darter. Transactions of the Kentucky Academy of Science 50:55–58.

Keklak, T. A., and R. J. Neves. 1981. An evaluation of environmental variables in brown trout streams of Virginia. Virginia Journal of Science 32:94.

Kelly, G. A., J. S. Griffith, and R. D. Jones. 1979. Changes in the distribution of trout within the Great Smoky Mountains National Park since 1900. In R. D. Estes, T. Harshbarger, and G. B. Pardue, editors. Brook trout workshop (abstracts). U.S. Forest Service, Southeastern Forest and Range Experiment Station, Asheville, North Carolina.

Kelly, J. W. 1962. Sexual maturity and fecundity of the largemouth bass, Micropterus salmoides (Lacepède), in Maine. Transactions of the American Fisheries Society 91:23–28 (Not seen; cited in Carlander 1977.)

Kelso, D. P., and C. F. Bright. 1976. Preliminary studies on the distribution of the ichthyofauna of Fairfax County, Virginia. Virginia Journal of Science 27:46.

Kendall, A. W., E. H. Ahlstrom, and H. G. Moser. 1984. Early life history stages of fishes and their characters. Pages 11–22 in Moser et al. (1984).

Kendall, A. W., and R. J. Behnke. 1984. Salmonidae: development and relationships, Pages 142–149 in Moser et al. (1984).

Kendall, A. W., and F. J. Schwartz. 1968. Lethal temperature and salinity tolerances of the white catfish, Ictalurus catus, from the Patuxent River, Maryland. Chesapeake Science 9:103–108.

Kendall, R. L., editor. 1978. Selected coolwater fishes of North America. American Fisheries Society Special Publication 11.

Kendall, W. C. 1914. The fishes of New England: the salmon family, part 1—The trout or charrs. Memoirs of the Boston Society of Natural History 8:1–103.

Kendall, W. C. 1917. The pikes: their geographical distribution, habits, culture and commercial importance. U.S. Bureau of Fisheries Document 853.

Kendall, W. C. 1927. The smelts. U.S. Bureau of Fisheries Bulletin 42:217–375.

Kennett, J. P. 1982. Marine geology. Prentice-Hall, Englewood Cliffs, New Jersey.

Kerby, J. H. 1979. Meristic characters of two Morone hybrids. Copeia 1979:513–518.

Kerby, J. H., V. G. Burrell, and C. E. Richards. 1971. Occurrence and growth of striped × white bass hybrids in the Rappahannock River, Virginia. Transactions of the American Fisheries Society 100:787–790.

Keup, L., and J. Bayless. 1964. Fish distribution at varying salinities in Neuse River basin, North Carolina. Chesapeake Science 5:119–123.

Kilby, J. D. 1955. The fishes of two Gulf coastal marsh areas of Florida. Tulane Studies in Zoology 2:175–247.

Kimmel, P. G. 1975. Fishes of the Miocene–Pliocene Deer Butte Formation, southeast Oregon. University of Michigan Museum of Paleontology Papers on Paleontology 14:69–87.

Kimsey, J. B. 1958. Possible effects of introducing thread-fin shad (Dorosoma petenense) into the Sacramento–San Joaquin Delta. California Department of Fish and Game, Inland Fisheries Administrative Report 58-16, Sacramento. (Not seen; cited in Burns 1966; Miller 1967.)

Kimsey, J. B., R. H. Hagy, and G. W. McGammon. 1957. Progress report of the Mississippi threadfin shad, Dorosoma petenensis atchafalayae, in the Colorado River for 1956. California Department of Fish and Game, Inland Fisheries Administrative Report 57-23, Sacramento. (Not seen; cited in Johnson 1971.)

Kincaid, H. L. 1981. Trout strain registry. U.S. Fish and Wildlife Service, National Fisheries Center–Leetown FWS-NFC-L/81-1. Kearneysville, West Virginia.

Kindschi, G. A., R. D. Hoyt, and G. J. Overmann. 1979. Some aspects of the ecology of larval fishes in Rough River Lake, Kentucky. Pages 139–166 in R. D. Hoyt, editor. Proceedings of the 3rd symposium on larval fish. Western Kentucky University, Bowling Green.

King, P. B. 1975. United States—Appalachian region. Pages 522–531 in R. W. Fairbridge, editor. The encyclopedia of world regional geology, part 1: Western Hemisphere (including Antarctica and Australia). Dowden, Hutchinson & Ross, Stroudsburg, Pennsylvania.

King, W. 1937. Notes on distribution of native speckled trout and rainbow trout in the streams of the Great Smoky Mountains National Park. Journal of the Tennessee Academy of Science 12:351–361.

Kinney, E. C. 1950. The life history of the trout-perch, Percopsis omiscomaycus (Walbaum), in western Lake Erie. Master's thesis. Ohio State University, Columbus (Not seen; cited in Carlander 1969; Scott and Crossman 1973; Muth and Tarter 1975.)

Kirk, P. W., editor. 1979. The Great Dismal Swamp. University Press of Virginia, Charlottesville.

Kirkwood, J. B. 1957. A brief study of the Levisa Fork and Russell Fork of the Big Sandy River. Kentucky Department of Fish and Wildlife Resources, Fisheries Bulletin 21, Frankfort.

Kirsch, P. H. 1895. Report upon investigations in the Maumee River basin during the summer of 1893. U.S. Fish Commission Bulletin (1894):315–337.

Kissil, G. W. 1974. Spawning of the anadromous alewife, Alosa pseudoharengus, in Bride Lake, Connecticut. Transactions of the American Fisheries Society 103:312–317.

Kleckner, R. C., J. D. McCleave, and G. S. Whippelhauser. 1983. Spawning of American eel, Anguilla rostrata, relative to thermal fronts in the Sargasso Sea. Environmental Biology of Fishes 9:289–293.

Klippart, J. H. 1878. Descriptions of Ohio fishes, arranged from manuscript notes of Professor D. S. Jordan, by his assistant, Ernest R. Copeland. Pages 83–116 in 2nd Annual Report of the Ohio State Fish Commission (1877), Columbus.

Knapp, L. W. 1964. Systematic studies of the rainbow darter, Etheostoma caeruleum (Storer), and the subgenus Hadropterus (Pisces, Percidae). Dissertation Abstracts International 25(3) [unpaginated reprint].

Knapp, L. W. 1976. Redescription, relationships and status of the Maryland darter, *Etheostoma sellare* (Radcliffe and Welsh), an endangered species. Proceedings of the Biological Society of Washington 89:99–118.

Knapp, R. A., and R. C. Sargent. 1989. Egg-mimicry as a mating strategy in the fantail darter, *Etheostoma flabellare*: females prefer males with eggs. Behavioral Ecology and Sociobiology 25:321–326.

Kohlenstein, L. C. 1981. On the proportion of the Chesapeake Bay stock of striped bass that migrates into the coastal fishery. Transactions of the American Fisheries Society 110:168–179.

Kohler, C. C. 1980. Trophic ecology of an introduced, land-locked alewife (*Alosa pseudoharengus*) population and assessment of alewife impact on resident sportfish and crustacean zooplankton communities in Claytor Lake, Virginia. Doctoral dissertation. Virginia Polytechnic Institute and State University, Blacksburg.

Kohler, C. C., and J. J. Ney. 1980. Piscivority in a land-locked population of alewife, *Alosa pseudoharengus*. Canadian Journal of Fisheries and Aquatic Sciences 37:1314–1317.

Kohler, C. C., and J. J. Ney. 1981. Consequences of an alewife die-off to fish and zooplankton in a reservoir. Transactions of the American Fisheries Society 110:360–369.

Koli, L. 1969. Geographical variation of *Cottus gobio* L. (Pisces, Cottidae) in northern Europe. Annales Zoologici Fennici 6:353–390.

Koo, T. S. Y. 1970. The striped bass fishery in the Atlantic states. Chesapeake Science 11:73–93.

Koonce, J. F., T. B. Bagenal, R. F. Carline, K. E. F. Hokanson, and M. Nagiec. 1977. Factors influencing year-class strength of percids: a summary and a model of temperature effects. Journal of the Fisheries Research Board of Canada 34:1900–1909.

Kopp, L. J. 1955. Try fallfish. Pennsylvania Angler 24(5):20, 32.

Kornman, L. E. 1983. Muskellunge streams investigation at Kinniconick and Tygarts creeks. Kentucky Department of Fish and Wildlife Resources, Fisheries Bulletin 68, Frankfort.

Kornman, L. E. 1985. Muskellunge streams investigation in Red River, Station Camp Creek, and Sturgeon Creek. Kentucky Department of Fish and Wildlife Resources, Fisheries Bulletin 77, Frankfort.

Koster, W. J. 1936. The life-history and ecology of the sculpins (Cottidae) of central New York. Abstract of Doctoral dissertation. Cornell University, Ithaca, New York.

Koster, W. J. 1937. The food of sculpins (Cottidae) in central New York. Transactions of the American Fisheries Society 66:374–382.

Koster, W. J. 1939. Some phases of the life history and relationships of the cyprinid, *Clinostomus elongatus* (Kirtland). Copeia 1939:201–208.

Kott, E. 1971. Characteristics of pre-spawning American brook lampreys from Big Creek, Ontario. Canadian Field-Naturalist 85:235–240.

Kott, E. 1974. A morphometric and meristic study of a population of the American brook lamprey, *Lethenteron*

lamottei (Lesueur), from Ontario. Canadian Journal of Zoology 52:1047–1055.

Kott, E. 1988. European lampreys update. Environmental Biology of Fishes 23:155–157.

Kott, E., and G. Humphreys. 1978. A comparison between two populations of the johnny darter, *Etheostoma nigrum nigrum* (Percidae), from Ontario, with notes on other populations. Canadian Journal of Zoology 56:1043–1051.

Kott, E., R. E. Jenkins, and G. Humphreys. 1979. Recent collections of the black redhorse, *Moxostoma duquesnei*, from Ontario. Canadian Field-Naturalist 93:63–66.

Kott, E., C. B. Renaud, and V. D. Vladykov. 1988. The urogenital papilla in the Holarctic lamprey (Petromyzontidae). Environmental Biology of Fishes 23:37–43.

Kraatz, W. C. 1923. A study of the food of the minnow *Campostoma anomalum*. Ohio Journal of Science 23:265–283.

Kraatz, W. C. 1924. The intestine of the minnow *Campostoma anomalum* (Rafinesque), with special reference to the development of its coiling. Ohio Journal of Science 24:265–298.

Kraatz, W. C. 1928. Study of the food of the blunt-nosed minnow, *Pimephales notatus*. Ohio Journal of Science 28:86–98.

Kraft, J. C., and D. F. Belknap. 1986. Holocene epoch coastal geomorphologies based on local relative sea-level data and stratigraphic interpretations of paralic sediments. Journal of Coastal Research Special Issue 1:53–59.

Kramer, R. H., and L. L. Smith. 1960. Utilization of nests of largemouth bass, *Micropterus salmoides*, by golden shiners, *Notemigonus crysoleucas*. Copeia 1960:73–74.

Kranz, V. R., K. N. Mueller, and S. C. Douglas. 1979. Development of the young of the creek chub, *Semotilus atromaculatus*. Pages 100–120 *in* R. D. Hoyt, editor. Proceedings of the 3rd symposium on larval fish. Western Kentucky University, Bowling Green.

Kresja, R. J. 1967. The systematics of the prickly sculpin, *Cottus asper* Richardson, a polytypic species. Part II. Studies on the life history, with especial reference to migration. Pacific Science 21:414–422.

Kriete, W. H., J. V. Merriner, and H. M. Austin. 1979. Movement of 1970 yearclass striped bass between Virginia, New York, and New England. Proceedings of the Annual Conference Southeastern Association of Fish and Wildlife Agencies 32 (1978):692–696.

Krumholz, L. A. 1944. Northward acclimatization of the western mosquitofish, *Gambusia affinis affinis*. Copeia 1944:82–85.

Krumholz, L. A. 1948. Reproduction in the western mosquito fish, *Gambusia affinis affinis* (Baird and Girard), and its use in mosquito control. Ecological Monographs 18:1–43.

Krumholz, L. A. 1981. Observations on changes in the fish population of the Ohio River from Rafinesque to 1980. Transactions of the Kentucky Academy of Science 42:1–15.

Krumholz, L. A., and H. S. Cavanah. 1968. Comparative morphometry of freshwater drum from two mid-western localities. Transactions of the American Fisheries Society 97:429–441.

Krygier, E. E., W. C. Johnson, and C. E. Bond. 1973. Records of the California tonguefish, threadfin shad and smooth alligatorfish from Yaquina Bay, Oregon. California Fish and Game 59:140–142.

Kuehne, R. A., and R. M. Bailey. 1961. Stream capture and the distribution of the percid fish *Etheostoma sagitta*, with geologic and taxonomic considerations. Copeia 1961:1–8.

Kuehne, R. A., and R. W. Barbour. 1983. The American darters. University of Kentucky Press, Lexington.

Kuhne, E. R. 1939. A guide to the fishes of Tennessee and the mid-south. Tennessee Department of Conservation, Division of Game and Fish, Nashville.

Kuntz, A., and L. Radcliffe. 1917. Notes on the embryology and larval development of twelve species of teleostean fishes. U.S. Bureau of Fisheries Bulletin 35:87–134.

Kutkuhn, J. H. 1958. Utilization of plankton by juvenile gizzard shad in a shallow prairie lake. Transactions of the American Fisheries Society 87:80–103.

Kwak, T. J. 1988. Lateral movement and use of floodplain habitat by fishes of the Kankakee River, Illinois. American Midland Naturalist 120:241–249.

Laarman, P. W. 1978. Case histories of stocking walleyes in inland lakes, impoundments, and the Great Lakes—100 years with walleyes. American Fisheries Society Special Publication 11:254–260.

Lachner, E. A. 1950a. Food, growth and habits of fingerling northern smallmouth bass, *Micropterus dolomieu dolomieu* Lacepède, in trout waters of western New York. Journal of Wildlife Management 14:50–56.

Lachner, E. A. 1950b. The comparative food habits of the cyprinid fishes *Nocomis biguttatus* and *Nocomis micropogon* in western New York. Journal of the Washington Academy of Sciences 40:229–236.

Lachner, E. A. 1952. Studies of the biology of the cyprinid fishes of the chub genus *Nocomis* of northeastern United States. American Midland Naturalist 48:433–466.

Lachner, E. A. 1956. The changing fish fauna of the upper Ohio basin. Pages 64–78 *in* Man and the waters of the upper Ohio basin. University of Pittsburgh, Pymatuning Laboratory of Ecology, Special Publication 1, Pittsburgh, Pennsylvania.

Lachner, E. A. 1967. Status of the catostomid fish name *Catostomus aureolus* Lesueur. Copeia 1967:455–457.

Lachner, E. A., and E. E. Deubler. 1960. *Clinostomus funduloides* Girard to replace *Clinostomus vandoisulus* (Valenciennes) as the name of the rosyside dace of eastern North America. Copeia 1960:358–360.

Lachner, E. A., and R. E. Jenkins. 1967. Systematics, distribution, and evolution of the chub genus *Nocomis* (Cyprinidae) in the southwestern Ohio River basin, with the description of a new species. Copeia 1967:557–580.

Lachner, E. A., and R. E. Jenkins. 1971a. Systematics, distribution, and evolution of the chub genus *Nocomis* Girard (Pisces, Cyprinidae) of eastern United States, with descriptions of new species. Smithsonian Contributions to Zoology 85.

Lachner, E. A., and R. E. Jenkins. 1971b. Systematics, distribution, and evolution of the *Nocomis biguttatus* species group (family Cyprinidae: Pisces) with a description of a new species from the Ozark upland. Smithsonian Contributions to Zoology 91.

Lachner, E. A., C. R. Robins, and W. R. Courtenay. 1970. Exotic fishes and other aquatic organisms introduced into North America. Smithsonian Contributions to Zoology 59.

Lachner, E. A., E. F. Westlake, and P. S. Handwerk. 1950. Studies on the biology of some percid fishes from western Pennsylvania. American Midland Naturalist 43:92–111.

Lachner, E. A., and M. L. Wiley. 1971. Populations of the polytypic species *Nocomis leptocephalus* (Girard) with a description of a new subspecies. Smithsonian Contributions to Zoology 92.

Lady, L. 1983. Bluestone Lake—past, present, and future. Pages 183–201 *in* Proceedings New River Symposium, April 14–16, 1983, Blacksburg, Virginia. National Park Service, New River Gorge National River, Glen Jean, West Virginia.

Laerm, J., and B. J. Freeman. 1986. Fishes of the Okefenokee Swamp. University of Georgia Press, Athens.

Lagler, K. F. 1956. Freshwater fishery biology. Brown, Dubuque, Iowa.

Lagler, K. F., and V. C. Applegate. 1942. Further studies of the food of the bowfin (*Amia calva*) in southern Michigan, with notes on the inadvisability of using trapped fish in food analysis. Copeia 1942:190–191.

Lagler, K. F., and R. M. Bailey. 1947. The genetic fixity of differential characters in subspecies of the percid fish, *Boleosoma nigrum*. Copeia 1947:50–59.

Lagler, K. F., J. E. Bardach, R. R. Miller, and D. R. M. Passino. 1977. Ichthyology, 2nd edition. Wiley, New York.

Lagler, K. F., and F. V. Hubbs. 1940. Food of the long-nosed gar (*Lepisosteus osseus oxyurus*) and the bowfin (*Amia calva*) in southern Michigan. Copeia 1940:239–241.

Lake, C. T. 1936. The life history of the fan-tailed darter *Catonotus flabellaris flabellaris* (Rafinesque). American Midland Naturalist 17:816–830.

Lalancette, L.-M. 1977. Croissance, reproduction et régime alimentaire du mulet perlé, *Semotilus margarita*, du Lac Gamelin, Quebéc. Naturaliste Canadien 104:493–500.

Lambert, T. R., C. L. Toole, J. M. Handley, M. A. Koeneke, D. F. Mitchell, and J. C. S. Wang. 1980. Environmental conditions associated with spawning of a landlocked American shad, *Alosa sapidissima*, population. American Zoologist 20:813.

Lambou, V. W. 1965. Observations on size distribution and spawning behavior of threadfin shad. Transactions of the American Fisheries Society 94:385–386.

Langlois, T. H. 1929. Breeding habits of the northern dace. Ecology 10:161–163.

Lanteigne, J. 1988. Identification of lamprey larvae of the

genus *Ichthyomyzon* (Petromyzontidae). Environmental Biology of Fishes 23:55–63.

Lanteigne, J., J. M. Hanson, and S. U. Quadri. 1981. Occurrence and growth patterns of the American brook lamprey, *Lethenteron lamottenii*, in the Ottawa River. Canadian Field-Naturalist 95:261–265.

LaPointe, D. F. 1958. Age and growth of the American shad, from three Atlantic coast rivers. Transactions of the American Fisheries Society 87:139–150.

Larimore, R. W. 1949. Changes in the cranial nerves of the paddlefish, *Polyodon spathula*, accompanying development of the rostrum. Copeia 1949:204–212.

Larimore, R. W. 1957. Ecological life history of the warmouth (Centrarchidae). Illinois Natural History Survey Bulletin 27:1–83.

Larimore, R. W., Q. H. Pickering, and L. Durham. 1952. An inventory of the fishes of Jordan Creek, Vermilion County, Illinois. Illinois Natural History Survey Biological Notes 29.

Larkin, G. R., and M. Nagy. 1983. Recreational use of Bluestone Lake and environs. Pages 179–181 *in* Proceedings New River Symposium, April 14–16, 1983, Blacksburg, Virginia. National Park Service, New River Gorge National River, Glen Jean, West Virginia.

LaRoche, A. L. 1979. The impacts of stocking hatchery reared trout on the native brook trout populations of two streams in central Virginia. Master's thesis. Virginia Polytechnic Institute and State University, Blacksburg.

LaRoche, A. L. 1985. Reservoir investigation—Kerr Reservoir. Virginia Commission of Game and Inland Fisheries, Federal Aid in Sport Fish Restoration, Project F-39, Richmond.

Larsen, L. O. 1980. Physiology of adult lampreys, with special regard to natural starvation, reproduction, and death after spawning. Canadian Journal of Fisheries and Aquatic Sciences 37:1762–1779.

Lauder, G. V. 1983. Neuromuscular pattern and the origin of trophic specialization in fishes. Science 219:1235–1237.

Lauder, G. V., and K. F. Liem. 1983. The evolution and interrelationships of the actinopterygian fishes. Bulletin of the Museum of Comparative Zoology 150:95–197.

Lauder, W. R. 1968. Stream capture, piracy. Pages 1054–1057 *in* R. W. Fairbridge, editor. The encyclopedia of geomorphology. Reinhold, New York.

Lauff, G. H., editor. 1967. Estuaries. American Association for the Advancement of Science Publication 83.

Laughlin, D. R., and E. E. Werner. 1980. Resource partitioning in two co-existing sunfish: pumpkinseed (*Lepomis gibbosus*) and northern longear sunfish (*Lepomis megalotis peltastes*). Canadian Journal of Fisheries and Aquatic Sciences 37:1411–1420.

Laurenson, L. B. J., and C. H. Hocutt. 1986. Colonisation theory and invasive biota: the Great Fish River, a case study. Environmental Monitoring and Assessment 6:71–90.

Lawrence, H. L. 1976. Yugoslavia's Ohrid trout comes to America. Fishing World 23(2):58–60,64,66.

Lawson, J. 1709. A new voyage to Carolina; containing the exact description and natural history of that country: together with the present state thereof. And a journal of a thousand miles, travel'd thro' several nations of Indians. Giving a particular account of their customs, manners, etc. London (Reprinted 1967. H. T. Lefler, editor. University of North Carolina Press, Chapel Hill.)

Layman, S. R. 1984a. The life history and ecology of the duskytail darter, *Etheostoma* (*Catonotus*) species, in Tennessee's Little River. Master's thesis. University of Tennessee, Knoxville.

Layman, S. R. 1984b. The duskytail darter, *Etheostoma* (*Catonotus*) sp., confirmed as an egg-clusterer. Copeia 1984:992–994.

Layman, S. R. 1991. Life history of the relict, duskytail darter, *Etheostoma* (*Catonotus*) sp., in Little River, Tennessee. Copeia 1991:471–485.

Layzer, J. B., and R. J. Reed. 1978. Food, age and growth of the tessellated darter, *Etheostoma olmstedi*, in Massachusetts. American Midland Naturalist 100:459–462.

Leach, G. C. 1925. Artificial propagation of shad. Pages 459–486 *in* Appendix 8, U.S. Commission of Fish and Fisheries, Report of the U.S. Commissioner of Fisheries for 1924, Washington, D.C.

Leary, R. F., F. W. Allendorf, and K. L. Knudson. 1985. Developmental instability and high meristic counts in interspecific hybrids of salmonid fishes. Evolution 39:1318–1326.

Lee, D. S. 1976. Aquatic zoogeography of Maryland. Atlantic Naturalist 31:147–158.

Lee, D. S. 1977. The darters of Maryland. Maryland Conservationist 53(4):18–23.

Lee, D. S. 1987. The star-nosed mole on the Delmarva Peninsula: zoogeographic and systematic problems of a boreal species in the south. Maryland Naturalist 31:44–57.

Lee, D. S., and R. E. Ashton. 1979. Seasonal and daily activity patterns of the glassy darter, *Etheostoma vitreum* (Percidae). ASB (Association of Southeastern Biologists) Bulletin 26:36.

Lee, D. S., and R. E. Ashton. 1981. Use of ^{60}Co tags to determine activity patterns of freshwater fishes. Copeia 1981:709–711.

Lee, D. S., C. R. Gilbert, C. H. Hocutt, R. E. Jenkins, D. E. McAllister, and J. R. Stauffer. 1980. Atlas of North American freshwater fishes. North Carolina State Museum of Natural History, Raleigh.

Lee, D. S., and A. W. Norden. 1976. The blacknose dace in the Delmarva Peninsula. Atlantic Naturalist 31(1):38–39.

Lee, D. S., A. W. Norden, and C. R. Gilbert. 1976. A list of the fishes of Maryland and Delaware. Chesapeake Science 17:205–211.

Lee, D. S., A. W. Norden, and C. R. Gilbert. 1984. Endangered, threatened, and extirpated freshwater fishes of Maryland. Pages 287–328 *in* A. W. Norden, D. C. Forester, and G. H. Fenwick, editors. Threatened and endangered plants and animals of Maryland. Maryland Department of Natural Resources, Natural Heritage Program Special Publication 84-1, Annapolis.

Lee, D. S., A. W. Norden, C. R. Gilbert, and R. Franz. 1975. Upland fish faunas of the Delmarva Peninsula.

Page 100 *in* Abstracts of the 55th Annual Meeting of the American Society of Ichthyologists and Herpetologists.

Lee, D. S., S. P. Platania, C. R. Gilbert, R. Franz, and A. Norden. 1981. A revised list of the freshwater fishes of Maryland and Delaware. Proceedings of the Southeastern Fishes Council 3(3):1–10.

Lefler, H. T. 1967. Introduction, notes, and editing. *In* John Lawson. 1709. A new voyage to Carolina. 1967 reprint, University of North Carolina Press, Chapel Hill.

Lefler, H. T., and A. R. Newsome. 1954. North Carolina, the history of a southern state. University of North Carolina Press, Chapel Hill.

Legendre, P. 1970. The bearing of *Phoxinus* (Cyprinidae) hybridity on the classification of its North American species. Canadian Journal of Zoology 48:1167–1177.

Legendre, V. 1954. Key to the game and commercial fishes of the province of Quebec. Volume 1. The freshwater fishes. Société Canadienne d'écologie, and Game and Fisheries Department, Montréal.

Leggett, W. C. 1969. Studies on the reproductive ecology of the American shad (*Alosa sapidissima* Wilson). A comparison of populations from four rivers of the Atlantic seaboard. Doctoral dissertation. McGill University, Montreal.

Leggett, W. C. 1976. The American shad (*Alosa sapidissima*), with special reference to its migration and population dynamics in the Connecticut River. American Fisheries Society Monograph 1:169–225.

Leggett, W. C., and J. E. Carscadden. 1978. Latitudinal variation in reproductive characteristics of American shad (*Alosa sapidissima*): evidence for population specific life history strategies in fish. Journal of the Fisheries Research Board of Canada 35:1469–1478.

Leggett, W. C., and R. R. Whitney. 1972. Water temperature and the migrations of American shad. U.S. National Marine Fisheries Service Fishery Bulletin 70:659–670.

LeGrande, W. H. 1981. Chromosomal evolution in North American catfishes (Siluriformes: Ictaluridae) with particular emphasis on the madtoms, *Noturus*. Copeia 1981:33–52.

LeGrande, W. H., and T. M. Cavender. 1980. The chromosome complement of the stonecat madtom, *Noturus flavus* (Siluriformes: Ictaluridae), with evidence for the existence of a possible chromosomal race. Copeia 1980:341–344.

Lehman, B. A. 1953. Fecundity of Hudson River shad. U.S. Fish and Wildlife Service Research Report 33:1–8.

Leim, A. H. 1924. The life history of the shad, *Alosa sapidissima* (Wilson) with special reference to factors limiting its abundance. Contributions to Canadian Biology, New Series 2:163–284.

Leim, A. H., and W. B. Scott. 1966. Fishes of the Atlantic Coast of Canada. Fisheries Research Board of Canada Bulletin 155.

Lemly, A. D. 1985. Suppression of native fish populations by green sunfish in first-order streams of Piedmont North Carolina. Transactions of the American Fisheries Society 114:705–712.

Lennon, R. E. 1961. The trout fishery in Shenandoah National Park. U.S. Fish and Wildlife Service Special Scientific Report—Fisheries 395.

Lennon, R. E. 1967. Brook trout of Great Smoky Mountains National Park. U.S. Fish and Wildlife Service Technical Paper 15.

Lennon, R. E., and P. S. Parker. 1960. The stoneroller, *Campostoma anomalum* (Rafinesque), in Great Smoky Mountains National Park. Transactions of the American Fisheries Society 89:263–270.

Leonard, P. M., and D. J. Orth. 1983. Biotic integrity of fish communities and cultural pollution problems of the tributaries of the New River Gorge National River. Pages 123–135 *in* Proceedings New River Symposium, April 14–16, 1983, Blacksburg, Virginia. National Park Service, New River Gorge National River, Glen Jean, West Virginia.

Leonard, P. M., D. J. Orth, and C. J. Goudreau. 1986. Development of a method for recommending instream flows for fishes in the upper James River, Virginia. Virginia Polytechnic Institute and State University, Water Resources Research Center Bulletin 54.

Leopold, L. B., M. G. Wolman, and J. P. Miller. 1964. Fluvial processes in geomorphology. Freeman, San Francisco.

Lesueur, C. A. 1818. Description of several species of chondropterigious fishes, of North America, with their varieties. Transactions of the American Philosophical Society 1:383–394.

Leviton, A. E., R. H. Gibbs, E. Heal, and C. E. Dawson. 1985. Standards in herpetology and ichthyology: Part I, standard symbolic codes for institutional resource collections in herpetology and ichthyology. Copeia 1985:802–832.

Lewis, G., and B. Miles. 1974. Forage introductions. Job 3-1, stream and lake survey. West Virginia Department of Natural Resources, Bureau of Sport Fisheries and Wildlife, Federal Aid in Sport Fish Restoration, Project F-10-R-(7-15), July 1, 1964–June 30, 1973, Final Report, Charleston.

Lewis, W. M., and G. E. Gunning. 1959. Notes on the life history of the steelcolor shiner, *Notropis whipplei* (Girard). Transactions of the Illinois State Academy of Science 52:59–64.

Libby, D. A. 1982. Decrease in length at predominant ages during a spawning migration of the alewife, *Alosa pseudoharengus*. U.S. National Marine Fisheries Service Fishery Bulletin 80:902–905.

Lichtler, W. F., and P. N. Walker. 1979. Hydrology of the Dismal Swamp, Virginia–North Carolina. Pages 140–168 *in* P. W. Kirk, editor. The Great Dismal Swamp. University Press of Virginia, Charlottesville.

Lindquist, D. G., J. R. Shute, and P. W. Shute. 1981. Spawning and nesting behavior of the Waccamaw darter, *Etheostoma perlongum*. Environmental Biology of Fishes 6:177–191.

Link, G. W. 1971. Comparative age and growth of two darters, *Percina peltata* (Stauffer) and *Percina notogramma* (Raney and Hubbs), in Virginia. Master's thesis. University of Richmond, Richmond, Virginia.

Linzey, D. W., editor. 1979. Proceedings of the symposium on endangered and threatened plants and animals of Virginia. Virginia Polytechnic Institute and State University, Sea Grant Program Publication VPI-SG-79-13, Blacksburg.

Lippson, A. J., editor. 1973. The Chesapeake Bay in Maryland. An atlas of natural resources. John Hopkins University Press, Baltimore.

Lippson, A. J., and R. L. Lippson. 1984. Life in the Chesapeake Bay. Johns Hopkins University Press, Baltimore.

Lippson, A. J., and R. L. Moran, editors. 1974. Manual for identification of early developmental stages of fishes of the Potomac River estuary. Maryland Department of Natural Resources, Power Plant Siting Program, Miscellaneous Publication 13, Annapolis.

Lipton, D. W. 1979. Comparison of scales and otoliths for determining age and growth of the alewife (*Alosa pseudoharengus*, Wilson). Master's thesis. College of William and Mary, Williamsburg, Virginia.

Lobb, M. D., III. 1986. Habitat use by the fishes of the New River, West Virginia. Master's thesis. Virginia Polytechnic Institute and State University, Blacksburg.

Lobb, M. D., III, and D. J. Orth. 1988. Microhabitat use by the bigmouth chub *Nocomis platyrhynchus* in the New River, West Virginia. American Midland Naturalist 120:32–40.

Loesch, J. G. 1969. A study of the blueback herring, *Alosa aestivalis* (Mitchill), in Connecticut waters. Doctoral dissertation. University of Connecticut, Storrs.

Loesch, J. G., R. J. Huggett, and E. J. Foell. 1982. Kepone concentration in juvenile anadromous fishes. Estuaries 5:175–181.

Loesch, J. G., and W. H. Kriete. 1984. Study of *Alosa* stock composition and year-class strength in Virginia. Virginia Institute of Marine Science, Annual Report Anadromous Fish Project, Gloucester Point.

Loesch, J. G., W. H. Kriete, J. C. Travelstead, E. J. Foell, and M. A. Hennigar. 1979. Biology and management of mid-Atlantic anadromous fishes under extended jurisdiction, part II: Virginia. Virginia Institute of Marine Science Special Report 236.

Loesch, J. G., and W. A. Lund. 1977. A contribution to the life history of the blueback herring, *Alosa aestivalis*. Transactions of the American Fisheries Society 106:583–589.

Loiselle, P. V., and G. W. Barlow. 1978. Do fishes lek like birds? Pages 31–79 in E. S. Reese and F. J. Lighter, editors. Contrasts in behavior. Wiley, New York.

Long, W. L., and W. W. Ballard. 1976. Normal embryonic stages of the white sucker, *Catostomus commersoni*. Copeia 1976:342–351.

Longhurst, A. R. 1971. The clupeoid resources of tropical seas. Oceanography and Marine Biology: an Annual Review 9:349–386. (Not seen; cited in McGowan and Berry 1984.)

Loos, J. J., and L. A. Fuiman. [1978]. Subordinate taxa of the genus *Notropis*: a preliminary comparative survey of their developmental traits. Pages 1–50 in L. L. Olmsted, editor. Proceedings of the first symposium on freshwater larval fish. Duke Power Company, Huntersville, North Carolina.

Loos, J. J., L. A. Fuiman, N. R. Foster, and E. K. Jankowski.

1979. Notes on early life histories of cyprinoid fishes of the upper Potomac River. Pages 93–139 in R. Wallus and C. W. Voigtlander, editors. Proceedings of a workshop on freshwater larval fishes. Tennessee Valley Authority, Norris, Tennessee.

Loos, J. J., and W. S. Woolcott. 1969. Hybridization and behavior in two species of *Percina* (Percidae). Copeia 1969:374–385.

Loos, J. J., W. S. Woolcott, and N. R. Foster. 1972. An ecologist's guide to the minnows of the freshwater drainage systems of the Chesapeake Bay area. ASB (Association of Southeastern Biologists) Bulletin 19:126–138.

Lotrich, V. A. 1973. Growth, production, and community composition of fishes inhabiting a first-, second-, and third-order stream of eastern Kentucky. Ecological Monographs 43:377–397.

Lovich, J. 1984. Capitol trout. Virginia Wildlife 45(2):20–23.

Lowe, C. H., D. S. Hinds, and E. A. Halpern. 1967. Experimental catastrophic selection and tolerances to low oxygen concentration in native Arizona freshwater fishes. Ecology 48:1013–1017.

Ludwig, G. M., and E. L. Lange. 1975. The relationship of length, age, and age-length interaction to the fecundity of the northern mottled sculpin, *Cottus b. bairdi*. Transactions of the American Fisheries Society 104:64–67.

Ludwig, G. M., and C. R. Norden. 1969. Age, growth and reproduction of the northern mottled sculpin (*Cottus bairdi bairdi*) in Mt. Vernon Creek, Wisconsin. Milwaukee Public Museum Occasional Papers Natural History 2.

Lundberg, J. G. 1970. The evolutionary history of North American catfishes, family Ictaluridae. Doctoral dissertation. University of Michigan, Ann Arbor. (Not seen; cited in LeGrande 1981.)

Lundberg, J. G. 1975. The fossil catfishes of North America. University of Michigan Museum of Paleontology Papers on Paleontology 11.

Lundberg, J. G. 1982. The comparative anatomy of the toothless blindcat, *Trogloglanis pattersoni* Eigenmann, with a phylogenetic analysis of ictalurid catfishes. Miscellaneous Publications, Museum of Zoology, University of Michigan 163.

Lundberg, J. G. 1992. The phylogeny of ictalurid catfishes: a synthesis of recent work. Pages 392–420 in Mayden (1992).

Lutterbie, G. W. 1979. Reproduction and age and growth in Wisconsin darters. Museum of Natural History, Reports on the Fauna and Flora of Wisconsin 15, University of Wisconsin–Stevens Point.

Lynch, D. D., E. H. Nuckels, and C. Zenone. 1987. Low-flow characteristics and chemical quality of streams in the Culpeper geologic basin, Virginia and Maryland. U.S. Geological Survey, Miscellaneous Investigations Series, Map I-1313-H (Sheets 1, 2), Reston, Virginia.

Lyons, J. 1989. Correspondence between the distribution of fish assemblages in Wisconsin streams and Omernik's ecoregions. American Midland Naturalist 122:163–182.

Mabee, P. M. 1988. Supraneural and predorsal bones in

fishes: development and homologies. Copeia 1988:827–838.

MacAlpin, A. 1947. *Paleopsephurus wilsoni*, new polyodontid fish from the Upper Cretaceous of Montana, with a discussion of allied fish, living and fossil. Contributions from the Museum of Paleontology, University of Michigan 6:167–234.

MacCrimmon, H. R. 1971. World distribution of the rainbow trout. Journal of the Fisheries Research Board of Canada 28:663–704.

MacCrimmon, H. R., and J. S. Campbell. 1969. World distribution of brook trout, *Salvelinus fontinalis*. Journal of the Fisheries Research Board of Canada 26:1699–1725.

MacCrimmon, H. R., B. L. Gots, and J. S. Campbell. 1971. World distribution of brook trout, *Salvelinus fontinalis*: further observations. Journal of the Fisheries Research Board of Canada 28:452–456.

MacCrimmon, H. R., and T. L. Marshall. 1968. World distribution of brown trout, *Salmo trutta*. Journal of the Fisheries Research Board of Canada 25:2527–2548.

MacCrimmon, H. R., T. L. Marshall, and B. L. Gots. 1970. World distribution of brown trout, *Salmo trutta*: further observations. Journal of the Fisheries Research Board of Canada 27:811–818.

MacKenzie, C., L. S. Weiss-Glanz, and J. R. Moring. 1985. Species profiles: life histories and environmental requirements of coastal fishes and invertebrates (Mid-Atlantic)—American shad. U.S. Fish and Wildlife Service Biological Report 82 (11.37) TR EL-82-4.

MacLellan, P., G. E. Newsome, and P. A. Dill. 1981. Discrimination by external features between alewife and blueback herring. Canadian Journal of Fisheries and Aquatic Sciences 38:544–546.

Madsen, M. L. 1971. The presence of nuptial tubercles on female quillback (*Carpiodes cyprinus*). Transactions of the American Fisheries Society 100:132–134.

Maglio, V. J., and D. E. Rosen. 1969. Changing preference for substrate color by reproductively active mosquitofish, *Gambusia affinis* (Baird and Girard) (Poeciliidae, Atheriniformes). American Museum Novitates 2397.

Magnin, É. 1964. Croissance en longeur de trois esturgeons d'Amerique du Nord: *Acipenser oxyrhynchus* Mitchill, *Acipenser fulvescens* Rafinesque, et *Acipenser brevirostris* Lesueur. Internationale Vereinigung für theoretische und angewandte Limnologie Verhandlungen 15:968–974.

Magnin, É., and G. Beaulieu. 1963. Étude morphométrique comparée de l'*Acipenser oxyrhynchus* Mitchill du Saint-Laurent et de l'*Acipenser sturio* Linné de la Gironde. Naturaliste Canadien 90:5–38.

Magnuson, J. J., and L. L. Smith. 1963. Some phases of the life history of the trout-perch. Ecology 44:83–95.

Mahon, R. 1977. Age and fecundity of the tadpole madtom, *Noturus gyrinus*, on Long Point, Lake Erie. Canadian Field-Naturalist 91:292–294.

Mahy, G. 1975. Ostéologie comparée et phylogénie des poissons cyprinoïdes. III. Ostéologie comparée de *C. erythrogaster* Rafinesque, *C. eos* Cope, *C. oreas* Cope, *C. neogaeus* (Cope), et *P. phoxinus* (Linné) et phylogénie du genre *Chrosomus*. Naturaliste Canadien 102:617–642.

Malick, R. W. 1978. The mimic shiner, *Notropis volucellus* (Cope), in the Susquehanna River drainage of Pennsylvania. Proceedings of the Pennsylvania Academy of Science 52:199–200.

Mallatt, J. 1979. Surface morphology and functions of pharyngeal structures in the larval lamprey *Petromyzon marinus*. Journal of Morphology 162:249–273.

Manion, P. J. 1972. Variations in melanophores among lampreys in the upper Great Lakes. Transactions of the American Fisheries Society 101:662–666.

Manion, P. J., and L. H. Hanson. 1980. Spawning behavior and fecundity of lampreys from the upper three Great Lakes. Canadian Journal of Fisheries and Aquatic Sciences 37:1635–1640.

Manion, P. J., and G. W. Piavis. 1977. Dentition throughout the life history of the landlocked sea lamprey, *Petromyzon marinus*. Copeia 1977:762–766.

Manion, P. J., and H. A. Purvis. 1971. Giant American brook lampreys, *Lampetra lamottei*, in the upper Great Lakes. Journal of the Fisheries Research Board of Canada 28:616–620.

Manion, P. J., and T. M. Stauffer. 1970. Metamorphosis of the landlocked sea lamprey, *Petromyzon marinus*. Journal of the Fisheries Research Board of Canada 27:1735–1746.

Manooch, C. S., III. 1973. Food habits of yearling and adult striped bass, *Morone saxatilis* (Walbaum), from Albemarle Sound, North Carolina. Chesapeake Science 14:73–86.

Manooch, C. S., and D. Raver. 1984. Fisherman's guide: fishes of the southeastern United States. North Carolina State Museum of Natural History, Raleigh.

Mansueti, A. J. 1963. Some changes in morphology during ontogeny in the pirate perch, *Aphredoderus s. sayanus*. Copeia 1963:546–557.

Mansueti, A. J., and J. D. Hardy. 1967. Development of fishes of the Chesapeake Bay region: an atlas of egg, larval, and juvenile stages, part 1. University of Maryland, Natural Resources Institute, College Park.

Mansueti, R. J. 1955. Natural history of the American shad in Maryland waters. Maryland Tidewater News 11 (Supplement 4):1–2.

Mansueti, R. J. 1956. Alewife herring eggs and larvae reared successfully in lab. Maryland Tidewater News 13(1):2–3.

Mansueti, R. J. 1957. Tentative key to the adult freshwater fishes and fishlike vertebrates of Maryland and the District of Columbia. University of Maryland, Department of Zoology, College Park. (Not seen; cited in Mansueti and Hardy 1967.)

Mansueti, R. J. 1958a. Eggs, larvae and young of the striped bass, *Roccus saxatilis*. Maryland Department of Research and Education, Chesapeake Biological Laboratory, Contribution 112, Solomons.

Mansueti, R. J. 1958b. The development of anal spines and soft-rays in young striped bass, *Roccus saxatilis*. Maryland Department of Research and Education, Chesapeake Biological Laboratory, Contribution 113, Solomons.

Mansueti, R. J. 1958c. The hickory shad unmasked. Nature Magazine 51:351–354, 386.

Mansueti, R. J. 1961a. Age, growth and movements of striped bass, *Roccus saxatilis*, taken in size selective fishing gear in Maryland. Chesapeake Science 2:9–36.

Mansueti, R. J. 1961b. Movements, reproduction, and mortality of the white perch, *Roccus americanus*, in the Patuxent estuary, Maryland. Chesapeake Science 2:142–205.

Mansueti, R. J. 1961c. Effects of civilization on striped bass and other estuarine biota in Chesapeake Bay and tributaries. Gulf and Caribbean Fisheries Institute, University of Miami, Proceedings 14:110–136.

Mansueti, R. J. 1962a. Eggs, larvae, and young of the hickory shad, *Alosa mediocris*, with comments on its ecology in the estuary. Chesapeake Science 3:173–205.

Mansueti, R. J. 1962b. Distribution of small, newly metamorphosed sea lampreys, *Petromyzon marinus*, and their parasitism on menhaden, *Brevoortia tyrannus*, in mid-Chesapeake Bay during winter months. Chesapeake Science 3:137–139.

Mansueti, R. J. 1964. Eggs, larvae, and young of the white perch, *Roccus americanus*, with comments on its ecology in the estuary. Chesapeake Science 5:3–45.

Mansueti, R. J., and H. J. Elser. 1953. Ecology, age and growth of the mud sunfish, *Acantharchus pomotis*, in Maryland. Copeia 1953:117–119.

Mansueti, R. J., and H. Kolb. 1953. A historical review of the shad fisheries of North America. Chesapeake Biological Laboratory Publication 97, Solomons, Maryland.

Manville, R. H. 1968. Natural history of Plummers Island, Maryland: XX, annotated list of the vertebrates. Special Publication of the Washington Biologists' Field Club, Washington, D.C.

Marchant, B., and F. Reimherr. 1985. Trout-watching with Jeff Gosse. Rod and Reel (2):22–25, 45–47.

Marcy, B. C. 1968. Age determinations from scales of *Alosa pseudoharengus* (Wilson) and *Alosa aestivalis* (Mitchill), in Connecticut waters. Master's thesis. University of Connecticut, Storrs.

Marcy, B. C. 1969. Age determinations from scales of *Alosa pseudoharengus* (Wilson), and *Alosa aestivalis* (Mitchill), in Connecticut waters. Transactions of the American Fisheries Society 98:622–630.

Marcy, B. C. 1972. Spawning of the American shad in the lower Connecticut River. Chesapeake Science 13:116–119.

Markus, H. C. 1934. Life history of the blackhead minnow (*Pimephales promelas*). Copeia 1934:116–122.

Marshall, H. G. 1979. Lake Drummond: with a discussion regarding its plankton composition. Pages 169–182 *in* P. W. Kirk, editor. The Great Dismal Swamp. University Press of Virginia, Charlottesville.

Marshall, H. G., and W. W. Robinson. 1979. Notes on the overlying substrate and bottom contours of Lake Drummond. Pages 183–187 *in* P. W. Kirk, editor. The Great Dismal Swamp. University Press of Virginia, Charlottesville.

Marshall, N. B. 1939. Annulus formation in scales of the common shiner, *Notropis cornutus chrysocephalus* (Rafinesque). Copeia 1939:148–154.

Marshall, N. B. 1947. Studies on the life history and ecology of *Notropis chalybaeus* (Cope). Quarterly Journal of the Florida Academy of Sciences 9:163–188.

Marshall, N. B. 1965. The life of fishes. Weidenfeld and Nicolson, London.

Martin, F. D. 1984a. Diets of four sympatric species of *Etheostoma* (Pisces: Percidae) from southern Indiana: interspecific and intraspecific multiple comparisons. Pages 37–44 *in* D. G. Lindquist and L. M. Page, editors. Environmental biology of darters. Kluwer Boston, Hingham, Massachusetts. (Also: Environmental Biology of Fishes 11:113–120.)

Martin, F. D. 1984b. Esocoidei: development and relationships. Pages 140–142 *in* Moser et al. (1984).

Martin, F. D., and C. Hubbs. 1973. Observations on the development of pirate perch, *Aphredoderus sayanus* (Pisces: Aphredoderidae) with comments on yolk circulation patterns as a possible taxonomic tool. Copeia 1973:377–379.

Martin, P. S. 1973. The discovery of America. Science 179:969–974.

Martin, R. G. 1953. Game fish survey of the impounded public fishing waters of Virginia. Virginia Commission of Game and Inland Fisheries, Federal Aid in Sport Fish Restoration, Project F-1-R-2, Progress Report, Richmond.

Martin, R. G. 1954. Game fish survey of the impounded public fishing waters of Virginia. Virginia Commission of Game and Inland Fisheries, Federal Aid in Sport Fish Restoration, Project F-1-R-3, Progress Report, Richmond.

Martin, R. G. 1955. Fisheries management investigation of impoundments of Virginia. Virginia Commission of Game and Inland Fisheries, Federal Aid in Sport Fish Restoration, Project F-5-R-1, Progress Report, Richmond.

Martin, R. G. 1961. The pros and cons of brown trout. Virginia Wildlife 22(3):6–7.

Martin, R. G. 1975. Sexual and aggressive behavior, density and social structure in a natural population of mosquitofish, *Gambusia affinis holbrooki*. Copeia 1975:445–454.

Martin, R. G., W. E. Neal, D. L. Shumate, and J. M. Hoffman. 1963. Evaluation of a minimum length on largemouth bass. Virginia Commission of Game and Inland Fisheries, Federal Aid in Sport Fish Restoration, Project F-5-R-9, Job 12, January 1, 1963–December 31, 1963, Progress Report, Richmond.

Martinez, A. M. 1984. Identification of brook, brown, rainbow, and cutthroat trout larvae. Transactions of the American Fisheries Society 113:252–259.

Martof, B. S., W. M. Palmer, J. R. Bailey, J. R. Harrison III, and J. Dermid. 1980. Amphibians and reptiles of the Carolinas and Virginia. University of North Carolina Press, Chapel Hill.

Masnik, M. T. 1971. Correlation of the morphometric variation in the eastern race of *Clinostomus funduloides funduloides* (Girard) with two suspected stream piracies in Virginia. Master's thesis. Virginia Polytechnic Institute and State University, Blacksburg.

Masnik, M. T. 1973. New records of fishes and the distribution of *Cottus baileyi* in the Clinch River system in

Virginia. ASB (Association of Southeastern Biologists) Bulletin 20:68.

Masnik, M. T. 1974. Composition, longitudinal distribution, and zoogeography of the fish fauna of the upper Clinch system in Tennessee and Virginia. Doctoral dissertation. Virginia Polytechnic Institute and State University, Blacksburg.

Masnik, M. T., and W. G. Knollenberg. 1972. A comparison of the fishes in the Clinch and Big Sandy drainages in Tazewell County, Virginia. Virginia Journal of Science 23:113.

Masnik, M. T., J. R. Stauffer, C. H. Hocutt, and J. H. Wilson. 1976. The effects of an oil spill on the macroinvertebrates and fish in a small southwestern Virginia creek. Journal of Environmental Science and Health, A Part 11(4–5):281–296.

Mason, J. C., and S. Machidori. 1976. Populations of sympatric sculpins, *Cottus aleuticus* and *Cottus asper*, in four adjacent salmon-producing coastal streams on Vancouver Island, B.C. U.S. National Marine Fisheries Service Fishery Bulletin 74:131–141.

Massie, F. 1984. The occurrence of smallmouth bass in the lower North Anna River, Va. Virginia Journal of Science 35:117.

Massmann, W. H. 1952. Characteristics of spawning areas of shad, *Alosa sapidissima* (Wilson), in some Virginia streams. Transactions of the American Fisheries Society 81:78–93.

Massmann, W. H. 1957. A checklist of fishes of the Virginia waters of Chesapeake Bay and its tidal tributaries. Virginia Institute of Marine Science, Finfish Progress Report 33, Gloucester Point.

Massmann, W. H., E. C. Ladd, and H. N. McCutcheon. 1952. A biological survey of the Rappahannock River, Virginia. Virginia Institute of Marine Science Special Scientific Report 6.

Massmann, W. H., and A. L. Pacheco. 1961. Movements of striped bass tagged in Virginia waters of Chesapeake Bay. Chesapeake Science 2:37–44.

Matheson, R. E. 1979. Notes on the comparative ecology of *Cottus bairdi* and *Cottus girardi* in Naked Creek, Virginia. Master's thesis. College of William and Mary, Williamsburg, Virginia.

Matheson, R. E., and G. R. Brooks. 1983. Habitat segregation between *Cottus bairdi* and *Cottus girardi*: an example of complex inter- and intraspecific resource partitioning. American Midland Naturalist 110:165–176.

Mathur, D. 1972. Seasonal food habits of adult white crappie, *Pomoxis annularis* Rafinesque, in Conowingo Reservoir. American Midland Naturalist 87:236–241.

Matson, R. H., and R. L. Mayden. 1988. Generic variation in southeastern populations of *Notropis leuciodus*. Page 137 *in* Abstracts of the 68th Annual Meeting of the American Society of Ichthyologists and Herpetologists.

Matta, J. F. 1973. The aquatic Coleoptera of the Dismal Swamp. Virginia Journal of Science 24:199–205.

Matta, J. F. 1979. Aquatic insects of the Dismal Swamp. Pages 200–221 *in* P. W. Kirk, editor. The Great Dismal Swamp. University Press of Virginia, Charlottesville.

Matthews, F. D. 1980. *Cottus girardi* (Pisces: Cottidae), a valid species. Copeia 1980:158–159.

Matthews, F. D., D. A. Cincotta, C. H. Hocutt, and J. R. Stauffer. 1978. Checklist of the fishes and macroinvertebrates of Conochocheague Creek, Pennsylvania and Maryland. Proceedings of the Pennsylvania Academy of Science 52:60–66.

Matthews, W. J. 1984. Influence of turbid inflows on vertical distribution of larval shad and freshwater drum. Transactions of the American Fisheries Society 113: 192–198.

Matthews, W. J. 1985a. Summer mortality of striped bass in reservoirs of the United States. Transactions of the American Fisheries Society 114:62–66.

Matthews, W. J. 1985b. Critical current speeds and microhabitats of the benthic fishes *Percina roanoka* and *Etheostoma flabellare*. Environmental Biology of Fishes 12: 303–308.

Matthews, W. J. 1986a. Fish faunal 'breaks' and stream order in the eastern and central United States. Environmental Biology of Fishes 17:81–92.

Matthews, W. J. 1986b. Geographic variation in thermal tolerance of a widespread minnow *Notropis lutrensis* of the North American mid-west. Journal of Fish Biology 28:407–417.

Matthews, W. J. 1988. North American prairie streams as systems for ecological study. Journal of the North American Benthological Society 7:387–409.

Matthews, W. J. 1990. Spatial and temporal variation in fishes of riffle habitats: a comparison of analytical approaches for the Roanoke River. American Midland Naturalist 124:31–45.

Matthews, W. J., J. Bek, and E. Surat. 1982. Comparative ecology of the darters *Etheostoma podostemone*, *E. flabellare* and *Percina roanoka* in the upper Roanoke River drainage, Virginia. Copeia 1982:805–814.

Matthews, W. J., and D. C. Heins, editors. 1987. Community and evolutionary ecology of North American stream fishes. University of Oklahoma Press, Norman.

Matthews, W. J., and L. G. Hill. 1977. Tolerance of the red shiner, *Notropis lutrensis* (Cyprinidae) to environmental parameters. Southwestern Naturalist 22:89–98.

Matthews, W. J., L. G. Hill, D. R. Edds, and F. P. Gelwick. 1989. Influence of water quality and season on habitat use by striped bass in a large southern reservoir. Transactions of the American Fisheries Society 118:243–250.

Matthews, W. J., J. J. Hoover, and W. B. Milstead. 1985. Fishes of Oklahoma springs. Southwestern Naturalist 30:23–32.

Matthews, W. J., and R. E. Jenkins. 1979. A distinctive madtom catfish (Ictaluridae) from the Dan River, Virginia. ASB (Association of Southeastern Biologists) Bulletin 26:36.

Matthews, W. J., R. E. Jenkins, and J. T. Styron. 1982. Systematics of two forms of blacknose dace, *Rhinichthys atratulus* (Pisces: Cyprinidae) in a zone of syntopy, with a review of the species group. Copeia 1982:902–920.

Matthews, W. J., and J. T. Styron. 1981. Tolerance of headwater vs. mainstream fishes for abrupt physicochemical changes. American Midland Naturalist 105: 149–158.

Maughan, O. E. 1978. Morphometry of sculpins (*Cottus*) in

the Clearwater drainage, Idaho. Great Basin Naturalist 38:115–122.

Mauney, M. 1979. Assessment of the impact of a shallow reservoir on benthic macroinvertebrate and fish communities of a second order stream in the Virginia Piedmont. Doctoral dissertation. Virginia Polytechnic Institute and State University, Blacksburg.

Mauney, M., and O. E. Maughan. 1986. Habitat and diversity of fishes of selected tributaries of Roanoke Creek, on the Virginia Piedmont. Virginia Journal of Science 37:157–165.

Maurakis, E. G., A. F. Horne, R. E. Jenkins, R. W. Watson, and W. S. Woolcott. 1984. The effects of stream order on the longitudinal distribution of fishes in the Rappahannock River, Virginia. ASB (Association of Southeastern Biologists) Bulletin 31:70.

Maurakis, E. G., and J. J. Loos. 1986. Spawning of *Hybopsis rubrifrons* and *Notropis lutipinnis* over a *Nocomis leptocephalus* nest (Pisces: Cyprinidae). ASB (Association of Southeastern Biologists) Bulletin 33:85–86.

Maurakis, E. G., and W. S. Woolcott. 1984. Seasonal occurrence of fishes in a thermally enriched stream. Virginia Journal of Science 35:5–21.

Maurakis, E. G., and W. S. Woolcott. 1989. Phylogeny of pebble-nest building cyprinids based on reproductive behavior. Page 116 *in* Abstracts of the 69th Annual Meeting of the American Society of Ichthyologists and Herpetologists.

Maurakis, E. G., W. S. Woolcott, and R. E. Jenkins. 1987. Physiographic analyses of the longitudinal distribution of fishes in the Rappahannock River, Virginia. ASB (Association of Southeastern Biologists) Bulletin 34:1–14.

Maurakis, E. G., W. S. Woolcott, and J. T. Magee. 1990. Pebble-nests of four *Semotilus* species. Proceedings of the Southeastern Fishes Council 22:7–13.

Maurakis, E. G., W. S. Woolcott, and M. H. Sabaj. 1991. Reproductive behavior of *Exoglossum* species. Bulletin Alabama Museum of Natural History 10:11–16.

May, B. 1969. Observations on the biology of the variegated darter, *Etheostoma variatum* (Kirtland). Ohio Journal of Science 69:85–92.

Mayden, R. L. 1983. Madtoms, America's miniature catfishes. Tropical Fish Hobbyist 31(August):66–73.

Mayden, R. L. 1985a. Biogeography of Ouachita Highland fishes. Southwestern Naturalist 30:195–211.

Mayden, R. L. 1985b. Nuptial structures in the subgenus *Catonotus*, genus *Etheostoma* (Percidae). Copeia 1985: 580–583.

Mayden, R. L. 1987a. Historical ecology and North American highland fishes: a research program in community ecology. Pages 210–222 *in* W. J. Matthews and D. C. Heins, editors. Community and evolutionary ecology of North American stream fishes. University of Oklahoma Press, Norman.

Mayden, R. L. 1987b. Pleistocene glaciation and historical biogeography of North American central-highland fishes. Kansas Geological Survey Guidebook Series 5:141–151.

Mayden, R. L. 1988a. Vicariance biogeography, parsimony, and evolution in North American freshwater fishes. Systematic Zoology 37:329–355.

Mayden, R. L. 1988b. Systematics of the *Notropis zonatus* species group, with description of a new species from the Interior Highlands of North America. Copiea 1988: 153–173.

Mayden, R. L. 1989. Phylogenetic studies of North American minnows, with emphasis on the genus *Cyprinella* (Teleostei: Cypriniformes). University of Kansas Museum of Natural History Miscellaneous Publication 80.

Mayden, R. L., editor. 1992. Systematics, historical ecology, and North American freshwater fishes. Stanford University Press, Stanford, California.

Mayden, R. L., and C. R. Gilbert. 1989. *Notropis ludibundus* (Girard) and *Notropis tristis* (Girard), replacement names for *N. stramineus* (Cope) and *N. topeka* (Gilbert) (Teleostei: Cypriniformes). Copeia 1989:1084–1089.

Mayden, R. L., and B. R. Kuhajda. 1989. Systematics of *Notropis cahabae*, a new cyprinid fish endemic to the Cahaba River of the Mobile basin. Bulletin Alabama Museum of Natural History 9.

Mayden, R. L., and R. H. Matson. 1988. Evolutionary relationships of eastern North American cyprinids: an allozyme perspective. Page 138 *in* Abstracts of the 68th Annual Meeting of the American Society of Ichthyologists and Herpetologists.

Mayden, R. L., and L. M. Page. 1979. Systematics of *Percina roanoka* and *P. crassa*, with comparisons to *P. peltata* and *P. notogramma* (Pisces: Percidae). Copeia 1979:413–426.

Mayden, R. L., and S. J. Walsh. 1984. Life history of the least madtom *Noturus hildebrandi* (Siluriformes: Ictaluridae) with comparisons to related species. American Midland Naturalist 112:349–368.

Mayden, R. L., B. M. Burr, L. M. Page, and R. R. Miller. 1992. The native freshwater fishes of North America. Pages 827–863 *in* Mayden (1992).

Mayhew, D. A. 1983. A new hybrid cross, *Notropis atherinoides* × *Notropis volucellus* (Pisces: Cyprinidae), from the lower Monongahela River, western Pennsylvania. Copeia 1983:1077–1082.

Mayr, E. 1969. Principles of systematic zoology. McGraw-Hill, New York.

Mayr, E. 1981. Biological classification: toward a synthesis of opposing methodologies. Science 214:510–516.

McAfee, W. R. 1966a. Rainbow trout. Pages 192–215 *in* Calhoun (1966).

McAfee, W. R. 1966b. Eastern brook trout. Pages 242–271 *in* Calhoun (1966).

McAllister, D. E. 1963. A revision of the smelt family, Osmeridae. National Museum of Canada Bulletin 191.

McAllister, D. E. 1964. Distinguishing characters for the sculpins *Cottus bairdii* and *C. cognatus* in eastern Canada. Journal of the Fisheries Research Board of Canada 21:1339–1342.

McAllister, D. E. 1965. The collecting and preserving of fishes. National Museum of Canada Bulletin 69:152–170.

McAllister, D. E. 1968. Mandibular pore pattern in the sculpin family Cottidae. National Museum of Canada Contributions to Zoology IV, Bulletin 223:58–69.

McAllister, D. E. 1978. The complete minicomputer cataloging and research system for a museum. Curator 21:63–91.

McAllister, D. E. 1987. Status of the central stoneroller, *Campostoma anomalum*, in Canada. Canadian Field-Naturalist 101:213–218.

McAllister, D. E., and B. W. Coad. 1978. A test between relationships based on phenetic and cladistic taxonomic methods. Canadian Journal of Zoology 56:2198–2210.

McAllister, D. E., P. Jolicoeur, and H. Tsuyuki. 1972. Morphological and myogen comparison of johnny and tessellated darters and their hybrids, genus *Etheostoma*, near Ottawa, Canada. Journal of the Fisheries Research Board of Canada 29:1173–1180.

McAllister, D. E., and C. C. Lindsey. 1961. Systematics of the freshwater sculpins (*Cottus*) of British Columbia. National Museum of Canada Contributions to Zoology (1959), Bulletin 172:66–89.

McAllister, D. E., B. J. Parker, and P. M. McKee. 1985. Rare, endangered and extinct fishes in Canada. Syllogeus 54.

McAtee, W. L., and A. C. Weed. 1915. First list of the fishes of the vicinity of Plummers Island, Maryland. Proceedings of the Biological Society of Washington 28:1–14.

McBath, G. S. 1968. A morphometric description of the Ohio lamprey, *Ichthyomyzon bdellium*. Master's thesis. Pennsylvania State University, University Park.

McBride, F. T., R. I. Jones, and F. A. Harris. 1982. Growth rates and food habits of Roanoke bass in the Eno and Tar Rivers, North Carolina. Proceedings of the Annual Conference Southeastern Association of Fish and Wildlife Agencies 34(1980):341–348.

McBride, S. I., and D. Tarter. 1983. Foods and feeding behavior of sauger, *Stizostedion canadense* (Smith) (Pisces: Percidae), from Gallipolis Locks and Dam, Ohio River. Brimleyana 9:123–134.

McCary, B. C. 1986. Early man in Virginia. Pages 71–78 *in* J. N. McDonald and S. O. Bird, editors. The Quaternary of Virginia—a symposium volume. Virginia Division of Mineral Resources, Publication 75, Charlottesville.

McCaskill, M. L., J. E. Thomerson, and P. R. Mills. 1972. Food of the northern studfish, *Fundulus catenatus*, in the Missouri Ozarks. Transactions of the American Fisheries Society 101:375–377.

McClane, A. J., editor. 1974. McClane's field guide to freshwater fishes of North America. Holt, Rinehart and Winston, New York.

McCormick, F. H., and N. Aspinwall. 1983. Habitat selection in three species of darters. Pages 117–120 *in* D. L. G. Noakes, D. G. Lindquist, G. S. Helfman, and J. A. Ward, editors. Predators and prey in fishes. Dr. W. Junk, The Hague, Netherlands.

McCune, A. R. 1987. Toward the phylogeny of a fossil species flock: semionotid fishes from a lake deposit in the Early Jurassic Towaco Formation, Newark Basin. Peabody Museum of Natural History, Yale University, Bulletin 43.

McCune, A. R., K. S. Thomson, and P. E. Olsen. 1984. Semionotid fishes from the Mesozoic Great Lakes of North America. Pages 27–44 *in* A. A. Echelle and I. Kornfield, editors. Evolution of fish species flocks. University of Maine at Orono Press, Orono.

McDonald, J. N. 1984. The Saltville, Virginia, locality: a summary of research and field trip guide. Symposium on the Quaternary of Virginia, 1984. Virginia Division of Mineral Resources, Charlottesville.

McDonald, J. N. 1986. On the status of Quaternary vertebrate paleontology and zooarcheology in Virginia. Pages 89–104 *in* J. N. McDonald and S. O. Bird, editors. The Quaternary of Virginia—a symposium volume. Virginia Division of Mineral Resources, Publication 75, Charlottesville.

McDonald, J. N., and C. S. Bartlett. 1983. An associated musk ox skeleton from Saltville, Virginia. Journal of Vertebrate Paleontology 2:453–470.

McDonald, M. 1884a. The shad and alewives. Pages 579–588, 594–609 *in* G. B. Goode. The fisheries and fishery industries of the United States: Section I, Natural history of useful aquatic animals. Report of the Commissioner, U.S. Commission of Fish and Fisheries, Washington, D.C.

McDonald, M. 1884b. A new system of fishway-building. Pages 43–52 *in* U.S. Fish Commission Annual Report of the Commissioner of Fish and Fisheries for 1882, Washington, D.C.

McDonald, M. 1886. Report on distribution of fish and eggs by the U.S. Fish Commission for the season of 1885–1886. U.S. Fish Commission Bulletin 6:385–394.

McDonald, M. 1887. The fisheries of Chesapeake Bay and its tributaries. Pages 637–654 *in* G. B. Goode. The fisheries and fishery industries of the United States: Section 5, History and methods of the fisheries, volume 1. Report of the Commissioner, U.S. Commission of Fish and Fisheries, Washington, D.C.

McDonald, M. 1889. Report of operations at the Wytheville station, Virginia, from January 1, 1885 to June 30, 1887. Pages 793–800 *in* Report of the Commissioner for 1886, U.S. Commission of Fish and Fisheries, Part 14, Washington, D.C.

McDowall, R. M., and J. Richardson. 1983. The New Zealand freshwater fish survey: guide to input and output. New Zealand Fisheries Research Division, Information Leaflet 12, Wellington.

McElman, J. F. 1983. Comparative embryonic ecomorphology and the reproductive guild classification of walleye, *Stizostedion vitreum*, and white sucker, *Catostomus commersoni*. Copeia 1983:246–250.

McElman, J. F., and E. K. Balon. 1980. Early ontogeny of white sucker, *Catostomus commersoni*, with steps of saltatory development. Environmental Biology of Fishes 5:191–224.

McFadden, J. T. 1961. A population study of the brook trout, *Salvelinus fontinalis*. Wildlife Monographs 7.

McFadden, J. T., E. L. Cooper, and J. K. Anderson. 1965. Some effects of environment on egg production in brown trout (*Salmo trutta*). Limnology and Oceanography 10:88–95.

McGeehan, L. T. 1985. Multivariate and univariate analyses of the geographic variation within *Etheostoma flabel-*

lare (Pisces: Percidae) of Eastern North America. Doctoral dissertation. Ohio State University, Columbus.

McGowan, M. F., and F. H. Berry. 1984. Clupeiformes: development and relationships. Pages 108–126 *in* Moser et al. (1984).

McGregor, B. A. 1979. Variations in bottom processes along the U.S. Atlantic continental margin. Pages 139–149 *in* J. S. Watkins, L. Montadert, and P. W. Dickerson. Geological and geophysical investigations of continental margins. American Association of Petroleum Geologists Memoir 29, Tulsa, Oklahoma.

McGregor, B. A. 1984. The submerged continental margin. American Scientist 72:275–281.

McHugh, J. J., and E. Steinkoenig. 1980. Northeast Virginia sport fishery study. Virginia Commission of Game and Inland Fisheries, Federal Aid Sport Fish Restoration, Project F-37-R, January 1, 1977–December 31, 1979. Project Completion Report, Richmond.

McIntyre, A., N. G. Kipp, A. W. H. Bé, T. Crowley, T. Kellogg, J. V. Gardner, W. Prell, and W. F. Ruddiman. 1976a. Late Quaternary climatic changes: evidence from deep-sea coves of Norwegian and Greenland seas. Geological Society of America Memoir 145:77–110.

McIntyre, A., N. G. Kipp, A. W. H. Bé, T. Crowley, T. Kellogg, J. V. Gardner, W. Prell, and W. F. Ruddiman. 1976b. Glacial North Atlantic 18,000 years ago: a CLIMAP reconstruction. Geological Society of America Memoir 145:43–76.

McIvor, C. C., and W. E. Odum. 1988. Food, predation risk, and microhabitat selection in a marsh fish assemblage. Ecology 69:1341–1351.

McKeown, P. E., C. H. Hocutt, R. P. Morgan, and J. H. Howard. 1984. An electrophoretic analysis of the *Etheostoma variatum* complex (Percidae: Etheostomatini), with associated zoogeographic considerations. Environmental Biology of Fishes 11:85–95.

McLean, R. B., P. T. Singley, D. M. Lodge, and R. A. Wallace. 1982. Synchronous spawning of threadfin shad. Copeia 1982:952–955.

McMahon, T. E. 1982. Habitat suitability index models: creek chub. U.S. Fish and Wildlife Service Biological Services Program FWS-OBS-82/10.4.

McMillan, V. E. 1972. Mating of the fathead. Natural History 81(5):72–78.

McMillan, V. E., and R. F. J. Smith. 1974. Agonistic and reproductive behavior of the fathead minnow (*Pimephales promelas* Rafinesque). Zeitschrift fuer Tierpsychologie 34:25–58.

McPhail, J. D., and C. C. Lindsey. 1970. Freshwater fishes of northwestern Canada and Alaska. Fisheries Research Board of Canada Bulletin 173.

Meanley, B. 1973. The Great Dismal Swamp. Aubudon Naturalist Society of the Central Atlantic States, Washington, D.C.

Medcof, J. C. 1957. Nuptial or pre-nuptial behavior of the shad, *Alosa sapidissima* (Wilson). Copeia 1957:252–253.

Medland, T. E., and F. W. H. Beamish. 1987. Age validation for the mountain brook lamprey, *Ichthyomyzon greeleyi*. Canadian Journal of Fisheries and Aquatic Sciences 44:901–904.

Medlen, A. B. 1951. Preliminary observations on the effects of temperature and light upon reproduction in *Gambusia affinis*. Copeia 1951:148–152.

Mednikov, B. M., and A. D. G. Akhundov. 1975. Taxonomy of *Salmo* based on molecular hybridization of DNA. Doklady Akademii Nauk SSSR 2222:744–746. (Not seen; cited in Behnke 1979.)

Meehan, W. E. 1910. Experiments in sturgeon culture. Transactions of the American Fisheries Society 39:85–91.

Meffe, G. K., and A. L. Sheldon. 1988. The influence of habitat structure on fish assemblage composition in southeastern blackwater streams. American Midland Naturalist 120:225–240.

Meffe, G. K., and F. F. Snelson, editors. 1989. Ecology and evolution of livebearing fishes (Poeciliidae). Prentice-Hall, Englewood Cliffs, New Jersey.

Mendelson, J. 1975. Feeding interrelationships among species of *Notropis* (Pisces: Cyprinidae) in a Wisconsin stream. Ecological Monographs 45:199–230.

Menhinick, E. F. 1989. Anal ray/gill raker variation in North Carolina catfishes (*Ictalurus* spp.). ASB (Association of Southeastern Biologists) Bulletin 36:106.

Menhinick, E. F., T. M. Burton, and J. R. Bailey. 1974. An annotated checklist of the freshwater fishes of North Carolina. Journal of the Elisha Mitchell Scientific Society 90:24–50.

Menzel, B. W. 1976. Biochemical systematics and evolutionary genetics of the common shiner species group. Biochemical Systematics and Ecology 4:281–293.

Menzel, B. W. 1977. Morphological and electrophoretic identification of a hybrid cyprinid fish, *Notropis cerasinus* × *Notropis c. cornutus*, with implications on the evolution of *Notropis albeolus*. Comparative Biochemistry and Physiology 57B:215–218.

Menzel, B. W. 1978. Three hybrid combinations of minnows (Cyprinidae) involving members of the common shiner species complex (genus *Notropis*, subgenus *Luxilus*). American Midland Naturalist 99:249–256.

Menzel, B. W., and D. M. Green. 1972. A color mutant of the chain pickerel, *Esox niger* Lesueur. Transactions of the American Fisheries Society 101:370–372.

Menzel, B. W., and E. C. Raney. 1973. Hybrid madtom catfish, *Noturus gyrinus* × *Noturus miurus*, from Cayuga Lake, New York. American Midland Naturalist 90:165–176.

Menzel, R. W. 1944. Albino catfish in Virginia. Copeia 1944:124.

Menzel, R. W. 1945. The catfish fishery of Virginia. Transactions of the American Fisheries Society 73:364–372.

Mercer, J. H. 1968. The discontinuous glacio-eustatic fall in Tertiary sea level. Palaeography, Palaeoclimatology, Palaeoecology 5:77–85.

Meredith, W. G., and F. J. Schwartz. 1959. Summer food of the minnow, *Notropis a. ardens*, in the Roanoke River, Virginia. Proceedings of the West Virginia Academy of Science 29–30:23.

Merriner, J. V., W. H. Kriete, and G. C. Grant. 1976. Seasonality, abundance, and diversity of fishes in the Piankatank River, Virginia (1970–1971). Chesapeake Science 17:238–245.

Meseroll, S. 1974. Stock native muskies? Outdoor Life 154(6):31–32.

Messieh, S. N. 1977. Population structure and biology of alewives (*Alosa pseudoharengus*) and blueback herring (*A. aestivalis*) in the St. John River, New Brunswick. Environmental Biology of Fishes 2:195–210.

Metcalf, A. L. 1966. Fishes of the Kansas River system in relation to zoogeography of the Great Plains. University of Kansas Publications, Museum of Natural History 17:23–189.

Mettee, M. F., P. E. O'Neil, J. M. Pierson, and R. D. Suttkus. 1989. Fishes of the western Mobile River basin in Alabama and Mississippi. Geological Survey of Alabama, Atlas 24, Tuscaloosa.

Meyer, W. H. 1962. Life history of three species of redhorse (*Moxostoma*) in the Des Moines River, Iowa. Transactions of the American Fisheries Society 91:412–419.

Meyertons, C. T. 1963. Triassic formations of the Danville Basin. Virginia Division of Mineral Resources, Report of Investigations 6, Charlottesville.

Mickelson, D. M., L. Clayton, D. S. Fullerton, and H. W. Borns. 1983. The late Wisconsin glacial record of the Laurentide ice sheet in the United States. Pages 3–37 *in* H. E. Wright and S. C. Porter, editors. Late Quaternary environments of the United States, volume 1. University of Minnesota Press, Minneapolis.

Mihursky, J. A. 1962. Fishes of the middle Lenapewihittuck (Delaware River) basin. Doctoral dissertation. Lehigh University, Bethlehem, Pennsylvania.

Miles, R. L. 1964. A systematic study of *Etheostoma longimanum* and *Etheostoma podostemone* (Pisces, Percidae). Master's thesis. Virginia Polytechnic Institute and State University, Blacksburg.

Miles, R. L. 1978. A life history study of the muskellunge in West Virginia. American Fisheries Society Special Publication 11:140–145.

Miller, E. E. 1966. White catfish. Pages 430–440 *in* Calhoun (1966).

Miller, G. L. 1983. Trophic resource allocation between *Percina sciera* and *P. ouachitae* in the Tombigbee River, Mississippi. American Midland Naturalist 110:299–313.

Miller, G. L., and S. C. Jorgenson. 1973. Meristic characters of some marine fishes of the western Atlantic ocean. U.S. National Marine Fisheries Service Fishery Bulletin 71:301–312.

Miller, H. C. 1963. The behavior of the pumpkinseed sunfish, *Lepomis gibbosus* (Linneaus), with notes on the behavior of other species of *Lepomis* and the pigmy sunfish, *Elassoma ever... egladei*. Behaviour 22:88–151.

Miller, J., and K. Buss. 1962. The age and growth of the fishes in Pennsylvania. Pennsylvania Fish Commission, Harrisburg.

Miller, R. B. 1957. Have the genetic patterns of fishes been altered by introductions or by selective fishing? Journal of the Fisheries Research Board of Canada 14:797–806.

Miller, R. B., and W. A. Kennedy. 1946. Color change in a sculpin. Copeia 1946:100.

Miller, R. J. 1962a. Reproductive behavior of the stonerol-ler minnow, *Campostoma anomalum pullum*. Copeia 1962:407–417.

Miller, R. J. 1962b. Sexual development and hermaphroditism in the hybrid cyprinid, *Notropis cornutus* × *N. rubellus*. Copeia 1962:450–452.

Miller, R. J. 1963. Comparative morphology of three cyprinid fishes: *Notropis cornutus*, *Notropis rubellus*, and the hybrid *Notropis cornutus* × *Notropis rubellus*. American Midland Naturalist 69:1–33.

Miller, R. J. 1964. Behavior and ecology of some North American cyprinid fishes. American Midland Naturalist 72:313–357.

Miller, R. J. 1967. Nestbuilding and breeding activities of some Oklahoma fishes. Southwestern Naturalist 12:463–468.

Miller, R. J. 1968. Speciation in the common shiner: an alternate view. Copeia 1968:640–647.

Miller, R. J., and H. E. Evans. 1965. External morphology of the brain and lips in catostomid fishes. Copeia 1965:467–487.

Miller, R. J., and H. W. Robison. 1973. The fishes of Oklahoma. Oklahoma State University Press, Stillwater.

Miller, R. R. 1946. Distributional records for North American fishes, with nomenclatorial notes on the genus *Psenes*. Journal of the Washington Academy of Sciences 36:206–212.

Miller, R. R. 1950. A review of the American clupeid fishes of the genus *Dorosoma*. Proceedings of the United States National Museum 100(3267):387–410.

Miller, R. R. 1957. Origin and dispersal of the alewife, *Alosa pseudoharengus*, and the gizzard shad, *Dorosoma cepedianum*, in the Great Lakes. Transactions of the American Fisheries Society 86:97–111.

Miller, R. R. 1959. Origin and affinities of the freshwater fish fauna of western North America. American Association for the Advancement of Science Publication 51:182–222.

Miller, R. R. 1960. Systematics and biology of the gizzard shad (*Dorosoma cepedianum*) and related fishes. U.S. Fish and Wildlife Service Fishery Bulletin 60(173):370–392.

Miller, R. R. 1961. Man and the changing fish fauna of the American southwest. Papers of the Michigan Academy of Science, Arts and Letters: 365–404.

Miller, R. R. 1964. Genus *Dorosoma* Rafinesque 1820. Gizzard shads, threadfin shads. Pages 443–451 *in* Fishes of the western North Atlantic Part 3. Sears Foundation for Marine Research. Yale University, New Haven, Connecticut.

Miller, R. R. 1965. Quaternary freshwater fishes of North America. Pages 569–581 *in* H. E. Wright and D. J. Frey, editors. The Quaternary of the United States. Princeton University Press, Princeton, New Jersey.

Miller, R. R. 1972. Threatened freshwater fishes of the United States. Transactions of the American Fisheries Society 101:239–252.

Miller, R. R. 1976. An evaluation of Seth E. Meek's contributions to Mexican ichthyology. Fieldiana Zoology 69:1–31.

Miller, R. R. 1978. Composition and derivation of the native fish fauna of the Chihuahuan Desert region. U.S.

National Park Service Transactions and Proceedings Series 3:365–381.

Miller, R. R. 1986. Composition and derivation of the freshwater fish fauna of México. Anales de la Escuela Nacional de Ciencias Biologicas, México 30:121–153.

Miller, R. R., and G. R. Smith. 1981. Distribution and evolution of *Chasmistes* (Pisces: Catostomidae) in western North America. Occasional Papers of the Museum of Zoology, University of Michigan 696.

Miller, R. R., and M. L. Smith. 1986. Origin and geography of the fishes of central Mexico. Pages 487–517 *in* Hocutt and Wiley (1986).

Miller, R. R., J. D. Williams, and J. E. Williams. 1989. Extinctions of North American fishes during the past century. Fisheries (Bethesda) 14(6):22–38.

Miller, R. V. 1964. The morphology and function of the pharyngeal organs in the clupeid, *Dorosoma petenense* (Günther). Chesapeake Science 5:194–199.

Miller, R. V. 1967. Food of the threadfin shad, *Dorosoma petenense*, in Lake Chicot, Arkansas. Transactions of the American Fisheries Society 96:243–246.

Miller, R. V. 1968. A systematic study of the greenside darter, *Etheostoma blennioides* Rafinesque (Pisces: Percidae). Copeia 1968:1–40.

Milligan, J. D., and R. J. Ruane. 1978. Analysis of mercury data collected from the North Fork of the Holston River. Tennessee Valley Authority, TVA/EP78/12, Chattanooga, Tennessee.

Milner, J. W. 1874. The progress of fish-culture in the United States. Pages 523–558 *in* U.S. Commission of Fish and Fisheries, Report of the Commissioner for 1872 and 1873, part 2.

Minckley, W. L. 1959. Fishes of the Big Blue River basin, University of Kansas Museum of Natural History, Miscellaneous Publications 11:401–442.

Minckley, W. L. 1963. The ecology of a spring stream Doe Run, Meade County, Kentucky. Wildlife Monographs 11.

Minckley, W. L. 1973. Fishes of Arizona. Arizona Game and Fish Department, Phoenix.

Minckley, W. L., and J. E. Craddock. 1962. A new species of *Phenacobius* (Cyprinidae) from the upper Tennessee River system. Copeia 1962:369–377.

Minckley, W. L., J. E. Craddock, and L. A. Krumholz. 1963. Natural radioactivity in the food web of the banded sculpin, *Cottus carolinae* (Gill). Pages 229–236 *in* V. Schultz and A. W. Klement, editors. Radioecology. Reinhold, New York.

Minckley, W. L., and J. E. Deacon. 1959. Biology of the flathead catfish in Kansas. Transactions of the American Fisheries Society 88:344–355.

Minckley, W. L., and J. E. Deacon. 1968. Southwestern fishes and the enigma of "endangered species." Science 159:1424–1432.

Minckley, W. L., D. A. Hendrickson, and C. E. Bond. 1986. Geography of western North American freshwater fishes: description and relationships to intracontinental tectonism. Pages 519–613 *in* Hocutt and Wiley (1986).

Minckley, W. L., and L. A. Krumholz. 1960. Natural hybridization between the clupeid genera *Dorosoma* and *Signalosa*, with a report on the distribution of *S. petenensis*. Zoologica (New York) 45:171–180.

Minckley, W. L., and S. P. Vives. 1990. Cavity nesting and male nest defense by the ornate minnow, *Codoma ornata* (Pisces: Cyprinidae). Copeia 1990:219–221.

Miner, J. B. 1978. The feeding habits of smallmouth bass and largemouth bass in the Shenandoah River, Virginia. Master's thesis. University of Virginia, Charlottesville.

Ming, A. 1964. Contributions to a bibliography on the construction, development, use, and effects of electrofishing devices. Pages 33–46 *in* Oklahoma Fishery Research Laboratory Semi-Annual Report, January–June 1964, University of Oklahoma, Norman.

Minor, J. D., and E. Crossman. 1978. Home range and seasonal movements of muskellunge as determined by radiotelemetry. American Fisheries Society Special Publication 11:146–153.

Minshall, G. W., and six coauthors. 1983. Interbiome comparison of stream ecosystem dynamics. Ecological Monographs 53:1–25.

Mitchill, S. L. 1814a. Report, in part, of Samuel L. Mitchill; M. D., Professor of natural history, &c. on the fishes of New York. D. Carlisle, New York. (Reprinted *in* Gill 1898.)

Mitchill, S. L. 1814b. The fishes of New York, described and arranged. Transactions of the Literary and Philosophical Society of New York 1:355–492. (Not seen; title cited from Smith 1985; reference cited from Gill 1898 and Smith 1985. Gilbert 1992 cited the year as 1815 but did not list the reference; others have used 1815, but 1814 was used by Jordan and Evermann 1896, Jordan et al. 1930, Vladykov and Greeley 1964, and Robins et al. 1991. The year is equivocal in Gill 1898:vii, 29.

Mitchill, S. L. 1818. Memoir on ichthyology. The fishes of New York, described and arranged. American Monthly Magazine and Critical Review 2(Supplement 2):241–248.

Mittelbach, G. G. 1984. Predation and resource partitioning in two sunfishes (Centrarchidae). Ecology 65:499–513.

Moen, T. 1959. Sexing of channel catfish. Transactions of the American Fisheries Society 88:149.

Moenkhaus, W. J. 1894. Variation of North American fishes: I, the variation of *Etheostoma caprodes* Rafinesque. American Naturalist 28:641–660.

Moffett, J. W., and B. P. Hunt. 1943. Winter feeding habits of bluegills, *Lepomis macrochirus* Rafinesque, and yellow perch, *Perca flavescens* (Mitchill), in Cedar Lake, Washtenaw County, Michigan. Transactions of the American Fisheries Society 73:231–242.

Mohn, L. O., and P. E. Bugas. 1980. Virginia trout stream and environmental inventory. Virginia Commission of Game and Inland Fisheries, Federal Aid in Sport Fish Restoration, Project F-32, Jobs 1–3, January 1, 1976–December 31, 1979, Final Report, Richmond.

Monaghan, J. P. 1985. A study of riverine muskellunge

populations and habitat in North Carolina. North Carolina Wildlife Resources Commission, Federal Aid in Sport Fish Restoration, Project F-24-9, Raleigh.

Mongeau, J.-R., P. Dumont, and L. Cloutier. 1986. La biologie du Suceur cuivré, *Moxostoma hubbsi*, une espèce rare et endémique à la région de Montréal, Québec, Canada. Rapport Technique 06-39. Service de l'aménagement et de l'exploitation de la faune, Direction régionale de Montréal, Québec.

Montgomery, W. L., S. D. McCormick, R. J. Naiman, F. G. Whoriskey, and G. A. Black. 1983. Spring migratory synchrony of salmonid, catostomid, and cyprinid fishes in Rivière à la Truite, Québec. Canadian Journal of Zoology 61:2495–2502.

Moore, C. J., and D. T. Burton. 1975. Movements of striped bass, *Morone saxatilis*, tagged in Maryland waters of Chesapeake Bay. Transactions of the American Fisheries Society 104:703–709.

Moore, G. A. 1968. Fishes. Pages 21–165 *in* W. F. Blair, A. P. Blair, P. Brodkorb, F. R. Cagle, and G. A. Moore. Vertebrates of the United States, 2nd edition. McGraw-Hill, New York.

Moore, G. A., and W. E. Burris. 1956. Description of the lateral-line system of the pirate perch, *Aphredoderus sayanus*. Copeia 1956:18–20.

Moore, G. A., and F. B. Cross. 1950. Additional Oklahoma fishes with validation of *Poecilichthys parvipinnis* (Gilbert and Swain). Copeia 1950:139–148.

Moore, G. A., H. R. Pollock, and D. Lima. 1950. The visual cells of *Ericymba buccata* (Cope). Journal of Comparative Neurology 93:289–295.

Moore, G. A., and J. D. Reeves. 1955. *Hadropterus pantherinus*, a new percid fish from Oklahoma and Arkansas. Copeia 1955:89–92.

Moore, J. P. 1922. Use of fishes for control of mosquitos in northern fresh waters of the United States. U.S. Bureau of Fisheries, Document 923, Washington, D.C.

Moore, J. W., and F. W. H. Beamish. 1973. Food of larval sea lamprey (*Petromyzon marinus*) and American brook lamprey (*Lampetra lamottei*). Journal of the Fisheries Research Board of Canada 30:7–15.

Moore, J. W., and J. M. Mallatt. 1980. Feeding of larval lamprey. Canadian Journal of Fisheries and Aquatic Sciences 37:1658–1664.

Moore, R. H., R. A. Garrett, and P. J. Wingate. 1976. Occurrence of the red shiner, *Notropis lutrensis*, in North Carolina: a probable aquarium release. Transactions of the American Fisheries Society 105:220–221.

Morgan, R. P., II. 1975. Distinguishing larval white perch and striped bass by electrophoresis. Chesapeake Science 16:68–70.

Morgan, R. P., II, W. L. Goodfellow, C. H. Hocutt, and J. R. Stauffer. 1984. Karyotype of *Nocomis micropogon*, *Rhinichthys cataractae* and their supposed hybrid, "*Rhinichthys bowersi*" (Pisces: Cyprinidae). Copeia 1984:990–992.

Morgan, R. P., II, T. S. Y. Koo, and G. E. Krantz. 1973. Electrophoretic determination of populations of the striped bass, *Morone saxatilis*, in the upper Chesapeake Bay. Transactions of the American Fisheries Society 102:21–32.

Morris, M. A., and L. M. Page. 1981. Variation in western logperches (Pisces: Percidae), with description of a new subspecies from the Ozarks. Copeia 1981:95–108.

Morrison, J. K., and C. E. Smith. 1986. Altering the spawning cycle of rainbow trout by manipulating water temperature. Progressive Fish-Culturist 48:52–54.

Morrow, J. E. 1964. Populations of pike, *Esox lucius*, in Alaska and northeastern North America. Copeia 1964:235–236.

Morrow, J. E. 1980. The freshwater fishes of Alaska. Northwest Publishing, Anchorage.

Morton, W. M. 1965. The taxonomic significance of the kype in American salmonids. Copeia 1965:14–19.

Morton, W. M. 1980. Charr or Char: a history of the English name for members of the salmonid genus *Salvelinus*. Pages 4–6 *in* E. K. Balon, editor. Charrs: salmonid fishes of the genus *Salvelinus*. Dr. W. Junk, The Hague, Netherlands.

Moser, G. A. 1989. Endangered and threatened wildlife and plants; endangered status for the Roanoke logperch. Federal Register 54 (18 August 1989):34468–34472.

Moser, G. A. 1991. Roanoke logperch (*Percina rex*) recovery plan, technical draft. U.S. Fish and Wildlife Service, Newton Corner, Massachusetts, and Annapolis, Maryland.

Moser, H. G., W. J. Richards, D. M. Cohen, M. P. Fahay, A. W. Kendall, and S. L. Richardson, editors. 1984. Ontogeny and systematics of fishes. American Society of Ichthyologists and Herpetologists, Special Publication 1.

Moshenko, R. W., and J. H. Gee. 1973. Diet, time and place of spawning, and environments occupied by creek chub (*Semotilus atromaculatus*) in the Mink River, Manitoba. Journal of the Fisheries Research Board of Canada 30:357–362.

Mount, D. I. 1959. Spawning behavior of the bluebreast darter, *Etheostoma camurum* (Cope). Copeia 1959:240–243.

Moyle, P. B. 1973. Ecological segregation among three species of minnows (Cyprinidae) in a Minnesota lake. Transactions of the American Fisheries Society 102:794–805.

Moyle, P. B. 1976. Inland fishes of California. University of California Press, Berkeley.

Moyle, P. B. 1977a. In defense of sculpins. Fisheries (Bethesda) 2:20–23.

Moyle, P. B. 1977b. Are coarse fish a curse? Fly Fisherman 8(5):35–39.

Moyle, P. B. 1986. Fish introductions into North America: patterns and ecological impact. Pages 27–43 *in* H. Mooney and J. Drake, editors. Ecology of biological invasions of North America and Hawaii. Springer-Verlag, New York.

Moyle, P. B., and J. J. Cech. 1982. Fishes: an introduction to ichthyology. Prentice-Hall, Englewood Cliffs, New Jersey.

Moyle, P. B., and H. W. Li. 1979. Community ecology and predator–prey relations in warmwater streams. Pages 171–180 *in* H. Clepper, editor. Predator–prey systems in fisheries management. Sport Fishing Institute, Washington, D.C.

Mulholland, P. J., and D. R. Lenat. 1992. Streams of the southeastern Piedmont, Atlantic drainage. Pages 193–231 in C. T. Hackney, S. M. Adams, and W. H. Martin, editors. Biodiversity of the southeastern United States. Aquatic communities. Wiley, New York.

Mullan, J. W., R. L. Applegate, and W. C. Rainwater. 1968. Food of the logperch (Percina caprodes), and brook silverside (Labidesthes sicculus). Transactions of the American Fisheries Society 97:300–305.

Mulligan, T. J., and R. W. Chapman. 1989. Mitochondrial DNA analysis of Chesapeake Bay white perch, Morone americana. Copeia 1989:679–688.

Muncy, R. J. 1962. Life history of the yellow perch, Perca flavescens, in estuarine waters of Severn River, a tributary of Chesapeake Bay, Maryland. Chesapeake Science 3:143–159.

Mundahl, N. D., and C. G. Ingersoll. 1983. Early autumn movements and densities of johnny (Etheostoma nigrum) and fantail (E. flabellare) darters in a southwestern Ohio stream. Ohio Journal of Science 83:103–108.

Murawski, S. A., and A. L. Pacheco. 1977. Biological and fisheries data on Atlantic sturgeon, Acipenser oxyrhynchus (Mitchill). U.S. National Marine Fisheries Service Technical Series Report 10.

Murdy, E. O., and J. W. E. Wortham. 1980. Contributions to the reproductive biology of the eastern pirate perch, Aphredoderus sayanus. Virginia Journal of Science 31:20–27.

Murphy, B. R. 1981. Genetic evaluation of walleye (Stizostedion vitreum vitreum) stock structure and recruitment in Claytor Lake, Virginia. Doctoral dissertation. Virginia Polytechnic Institute and State University, Blacksburg.

Murphy, B. R. 1990. Evidence for a genetically unique walleye population in the upper Tombigbee River system of northeastern Mississippi. Proceedings of the Southeastern Fishes Council 22:14–16.

Musick, J. A. 1972. Fishes of Chesapeake Bay and the adjacent Coastal Plain. Pages 175–212 in M. L. Wass, editor. A check list of the biota of lower Chesapeake Bay. Virginia Institute of Marine Science Special Scientific Report 65.

Mussey, O. D. 1948. Major storage reservoirs of Virginia. Virginia Conservation Commission, Division of Water Resources and Power, Bulletin 9, Richmond.

Muth, S. E., and D. C. Tarter. 1975. Reproductive biology of the trout perch, Percopsis omiscomaycus (Walbaum), in Beech Fork of Twelvepole Creek, Wayne County, West Virginia. American Midland Naturalist 93:434–439.

Myers, G. S. 1938. Fresh-water fishes and West Indian Zoogeography. Smithsonian Institution Annual Report 1937:339–364.

Myers, G. S. 1940. Cope as an ichthyologist. Copeia 1940:76–78.

Myers, G. S. 1949. Salt-tolerance of fresh-water fish groups in relation to zoogeographical problems. Bijdragen Tot De Dierkunde 28:315–322.

Myers, G. S. 1951. David Starr Jordan, ichthyologist, 1851–1931. Stanford Ichthyological Bulletin 4:2–6.

Myers, G. S. 1964. A brief sketch of the history of ichthyology to the year 1850. Copeia 1964:33–41.

Myers, G. S. 1965. Gambusia, the fish destroyer. Australian Zoologist 13(2):102. (Not seen; cited in Moyle 1976.)

Nagel, J. W. 1980. Life history of the mottled sculpin, Cottus bairdi, in northeastern Tennessee (Osteichthyes: Cottidae). Brimleyana 4:115–121.

Nance, S. 1978. Some aspects of the reproductive biology of the logperch, Percina caprodes (Rafinesque), from East Lynn Lake, Wayne County, West Virginia. Proceedings of the West Virginia Academy of Science 50:25. (Not seen; cited in Page 1983.)

Nash, C. W. 1908. Check list of the vertebrates of Ontario and catalogue of specimens in the biological section of the Provincial Museum: fishes. Department of Education, Toronto. (Not seen; cited in Adams and Hankinson 1928.)

Neal, W. E. 1967. Striped bass study. Virginia Commission of Game and Inland Fisheries, Federal Aid in Sport Fish Restoration, Project F-5-R-11, Job 8, January 1, 1965–June 30, 1966, Job Completion Report, Richmond.

Neal, W. E. Circa 1968. Landlocked striped bass in John H. Kerr Reservoir: a ten-year summary of research and management activities. Virginia Commission of Game and Inland Fisheries, Federal Aid in Sport Fish Restoration, Project Virginia F-5, Richmond.

Neal, W. E. 1971. Striped bass survey, January 1, 1969–April 1, 1970; and age and growth data for 1965–1968. Virginia Commission of Game and Inland Fisheries, Federal Aid in Sport Fish Restoration, Project F-19-1; Project F-5-R-14, Job 8. Progress Report, Richmond.

Neal, W. E. 1973. Landlocked striped bass survey. Virginia Commission of Game and Inland Fisheries, Federal Aid in Sport Fish Restoration Project F-19-4, Jobs 1–6, April 1, 1972–June 30, 1973. Progress Report, Richmond.

Neal, W. E. 1976. Landlocked striped bass survey. Virginia Commission of Game and Inland Fisheries, Federal Aid in Sport Fish Restoration, Project F-19-R, Jobs 1–6, April 1, 1969–June 30, 1974. Project Completion Report, Richmond.

Needham, P. R. 1961. Observations on the natural spawning of eastern brook trout. California Fish and Game 47:27–40.

Needham, R. G. 1965. Spawning of paddlefish induced by means of pituitary material. Progressive Fish-Culturist 27:13–19.

Neff, N. A., and G. R. Smith. 1979. Multivariate analysis of hybrid fishes. Systematic Zoology 28:176–196.

Neill, W. T. 1950. An estivating bowfin. Copeia 1950:240.

Nelson, E. M. 1948. The comparative morphology of the Weberian apparatus of the Catostomidae and its significance in systematics. Journal of Morphology 83:225–251.

Nelson, G. J. 1972. Cephalic sensory canals, pitlines, and the classification of esocoid fishes, with notes on galaxiids and other teleosts. American Museum Novitates 2492.

Nelson, G. J. 1978. From Candolle to Croizat: comments on the history of biogeography. Journal of the History of Biology 11:269–305.

Nelson, G. J., and N. I. Platnick. 1981. Systematics and biogeography; cladistics and vicariance. Columbia University Press, New York.

Nelson, G. J., and M. N. Rothman. 1973. The species of gizzard shads (Dorosomatinae) with particular reference to the Indo-Pacific region. Bulletin of the American Museum of Natural History 150:131–206.

Nelson, J. S. 1968a. Hybridization and isolating mechanisms between *Catostomus commersonii* and *C. macrocheilus* (Pisces: Catostomidae). Journal of the Fisheries Research Board of Canada 25:101–150.

Nelson, J. S. 1968b. Life history of the brook silverside, *Labidesthes sicculus*, in Crooked Lake, Indiana. Transactions of the American Fisheries Society 97:293–296.

Nelson, J. S. 1984. Fishes of the world, 2nd edition. Wiley, New York.

Nelson, J. S., and S. D. Gerking. 1968. Annotated key to the fishes of Indiana. Indiana Aquatic Research Unit, Department of Zoology, Indiana University, Bloomington.

Nelson, J. S., and M. J. Paetz. 1974. Evidence for underground movement of fishes in Wood Buffalo National Park, Canada, with notes on recent collections made in the park. Canadian Field-Naturalist 88:157–162.

Nelson, W. R. 1968a. Reproduction and early life history of sauger, *Stizostedion canadense*, in Lewis and Clark Lake. Transactions of the American Fisheries Society 97:159–166.

Nelson, W. R. 1968b. Embryo and larval characteristics of sauger, walleye, and their reciprocal hybrids. Transactions of the American Fisheries Society 97:167–174. (Not seen; cited in Becker 1983.)

Nelson, W. R. 1974. Age, growth, and maturity of thirteen species of fish from Lake Oahe during the early years of impoundment, 1963–68. U.S. Fish and Wildlife Service Technical Papers 77.

Nemecek, R. J. 1978. Some observations on the feeding habits and the reproductive biology of *Etheostoma variatum*, *E. caeruleum* and *E. zonale*. Abstracts of the 5th Annual Session for Scientific Papers, Rochester Academy of Science, State University of Arts and Science, Geneseo, New York.

Netsch, N. F., and A. W. Witt. 1962. Contributions to the life history of the longnose gar (*Lepisosteus osseus*) in Missouri. Transactions of the American Fisheries Society 91:251–262.

Netzel, J., and E. Stanek. 1966. Some biological characteristics of blueback, *Pomolobus aestivalis* (Mitch.), and alewife, *Pomolobus pseudoharengus* (Wils.), from Georges Bank, July and October, 1964. International Commission for the Northwest Atlantic Fisheries, Research Bulletin 3.

Neves, R. J. 1975. Factors affecting fry production of smallmouth bass (*Micropterus dolomieui*) on South Branch Lake, Maine. Transactions of the American Fisheries Society 104:83–87.

Neves, R. J. 1981. Offshore distribution of alewife, *Alosa pseudoharengus*, and blueback herring, *Alosa aestivalis*, along the Atlantic Coast. U.S. Fish and Wildlife Service Fishery Bulletin 79:473–485.

Neves, R. J. 1983. Distributional history of the fish and mussel fauna in the Kanawha River drainage. Pages 47–67 in Proceedings New River Symposium, April 14–16, 1983, Blacksburg, Virginia. National Park Service, New River Gorge National River, Glen Jean, West Virginia.

Neves, R. J., and P. L. Angermeier. 1990. Habitat alteration and its effects on native fishes in the upper Tennessee River system, east-central U.S.A. Journal of Fish Biology 37 (Supplement A):45–52.

Neves, R. J., and S. L. Brayton. 1985. Reproductive cycle and associated changes in energy content of body tissues in rainbow trout from the South Fork Holston River, Virginia. Proceedings of the Annual Conference Southeastern Association of Fish and Wildlife Agencies 36(1982):358–368.

Neves, R. J., S. L. Brayton, and L. A. Helfrich. 1985. Abundance and production of a self-sustaining population of rainbow trout in the South Fork Holston River, Virginia. North American Journal of Fisheries Management 5:584–589.

Neves, R. J., and L. Depres. 1979. The oceanic migration of American shad, *Alosa sapidissima* along the Atlantic coast. U.S. National Marine Fisheries Service Fishery Bulletin 77:199–212.

Neves, R. J., and G. B. Pardue. 1983. Abundance and production of fishes in a small Appalachian stream. Transactions of the American Fisheries Society 112:21–26.

Neves, R. J., L. R. Weaver, and A. V. Zale. 1985. An evaluation of host fish suitability for glochidia of *Villosa vanuxemi* and *V. nebulosa* (Pelecypoda: Unionidae). American Midland Naturalist 113:13–19.

Neves, R. J., and J. C. Widlak. 1988. Occurrence of glochidia in stream drift and on fishes of the upper North Fork Holston River, Virginia. American Midland Naturalist 119:111–120.

New, J. G. 1966. Reproductive behavior of the shield darter, *Percina peltata peltata*, in New York. Copeia 1966: 20–28.

Newcombe, C. L. 1946. Report of the Virginia Fisheries Laboratory of the College of William and Mary and Commission of Fisheries 1944–1945. Williamsburg, Virginia.

Newell, W. L. 1985. Architecture of the Rappahannock estuary—neotectonics in Virginia. Pages 321–342 in M. Morisawa and J. T. Hack, editors. Tectonic geomorphology. Allen and Unwin, Boston.

Newman, R. M., and T. F. Waters. 1984. Size-selective predation on *Gammarus pseudolimnaeus* by trout and sculpins. Ecology 65:1535–1545.

Ney, J. J. 1978. A synoptic review of yellow perch and walleye biology. American Fisheries Society Special Publication 11:1–12.

Ney, J. J., and M. Mauney. 1981. Impact of a small impoundment on benthic macroinvertebrate and fish communities of a headwater stream on the Virginia Piedmont. Pages 102–112 in L. A. Krumholz, editor. The warmwater streams symposium. American Fisheries Society, Southern Division, Bethesda, Maryland.

Ney, J. J., and L. L. Smith. 1975. First-year growth of the yellow perch, *Perca flavescens*, in the Red Lakes, Minnesota. Transactions of the American Fisheries Society 104:718–725.

Nichols, J. T. 1916. A large *Polyodon* from Iowa. Copeia 34:65.

Nichols, J. T. 1943. The freshwater fishes of China. American Museum of Natural History, New York.

Nichols, P. R. 1958. Effect of New Jersey–New York pound net catches on shad runs of Hudson and Connecticut rivers. U.S. Fish and Wildlife Service Fishery Bulletin 58(143):491–500.

Nichols, P. R. 1966. Comparative study of juvenile American shad populations by fin ray and scute counts. U.S. Fish and Wildlife Service Special Scientific Report— Fisheries 525:1–10.

Nichols, P. R., and W. H. Massmann. 1963. Abundance, age and fecundity of shad, York River, Virginia, 1953–1959. U.S. Fish and Wildlife Service Fishery Bulletin 63:179–187.

Nigro, A. A., and J. J. Ney. 1982. Reproduction and early-life accommodations of landlocked alewives to a southern range extension. Transactions of the American Fisheries Society 111:559–569.

Nist, J. F. 1968. Growth and behavior of ammocoetes of the Ohio lamprey, *Ichthyomyzon bdellium* (Jordan). Doctoral dissertation. Pennsylvania State University, University Park.

Noble, G. K. 1938. Sexual selection among fishes. Biological Reviews of the Cambridge Philosophical Society 13:133–158.

Noble, R. L. 1965. Life history and ecology of western blacknose dace, Boone County, Iowa. Proceedings of the Iowa Academy of Science 72:282–293.

Noble, R. L. 1975. Growth of young yellow perch (*Perca flavescens*) in relation to zooplankton populations. Transactions of the American Fisheries Society 104: 731–741.

Noltie, D. B. 1985. A method for sexing adult rock bass, *Ambloplites rupestris* (Rafinesque), in the field using external genital characteristics. Aquaculture and Fisheries Management 1:299–302.

Noltie, D. B., and M. H. A. Keenleyside. 1986. Correlates of reproductive success in stream-dwelling male rock bass, *Ambloplites rupestris* (Centrarchidae). Environmental Biology of Fishes 17:61–70.

Nord, R. C. 1967. A compendium of fishery information on the upper Mississippi River. Upper Mississippi River Conservation Commission, Rock Island, Illinois. (Not seen; cited in Becker 1983.)

Norden, C. R. 1961. The identification of larval yellow perch, *Perca flavescens* and walleye, *Stizostedion vitreum*. Copeia 1961:282–288.

Norden, C. R. 1967. Age, growth and fecundity of the alewife, *Alosa pseudoharengus* (Wilson), in Lake Michigan. Transactions of the American Fisheries Society 96:387–393.

Norman, J. R., and P. H. Greenwood. 1975. A history of fishes, 3rd edition. Ernest Benn, London.

Norman, M. D. 1972. Southeastern Virginia impoundment survey. Virginia Commission of Game and Inland Fisheries, Federal Aid in Sport Fish Restoration, Project F-24, Study 1, Jobs 1–2; Study 2, Jobs 1–4, July 1970–April 1971. Progress Report, Richmond.

Norman, M. D. 1973. Southeastern Virginia impoundment survey. Virginia Commission of Game and Inland Fisheries, Federal Aid in Sport Fish Restoration, Project F-24, April 1971–July 1972. Progress Report, Richmond.

Norman, M. D. 1974. Southeastern Virginia impoundment survey. Virginia Commission of Game and Inland Fisheries, Federal Aid in Sport Fish Restoration, Project F-24-R-3, Study 1, Jobs 1–2; Study 2, Jobs 1–4, July 1, 1972–June 30, 1973. Progress Report, Richmond.

Norman, M. D. 1981. Reservoir investigations (Back Bay segment). Virginia Commission of Game and Inland Fisheries, Federal Aid in Sport Fish Restoration, Project F-39-P, December 1, 1978–March 31, 1981. Completion Report, Richmond.

Norman, M. D. 1985. Tidewater's treasures. Virginia Wildlife 46(1)8–11.

Norman, M. D., and A. L. LaRoche. 1975. Southeastern Virginia impoundment survey. Virginia Commission of Game and Inland Fisheries, Federal Aid in Sport Fish Restoration, Project F24-R-5, Study 1, Job 1; Study 2, Jobs 1–5, July 1, 1974–June 30, 1975. Richmond.

Norman, M. D., and R. Southwick. 1985. Notes on the species composition, relative abundance and distribution of the fishes collected in the Nottoway River drainage in 1982 and 1984. Virginia Commission of Game and Inland Fisheries, Richmond.

Norris, K. S. 1974. To Carl Leavitt Hubbs, a modern pioneer naturalist on the occasion of his eightieth year. Copeia 1974:581–594.

Norris, T. 1864. The American angler's book. E. H. Butler and Company, Philadelphia.

Norton, V. M., H. Nishimura, and K. B. Davis. 1976. A technique for sexing channel catfish. Transactions of the American Fisheries Society 105:460–462.

Novak, J. K. 1968. Food of *Cottus baileyi* in South Fork Holston River, Virginia during the summer of 1966. Master's thesis. Virginia Polytechnic Institute and State University, Blacksburg.

Novak, J. K., and R. D. Estes. 1974. Summer food habits of the black sculpin, *Cottus baileyi*, in the upper South Fork Holston River drainage. Transactions of the American Fisheries Society 103:270–276.

Oaks, R. Q., and N. K. Coch. 1973. Post-Miocene stratigraphy and morphology, southeastern Virginia. Virginia Division of Marine Resources Bulletin 82.

Oaks, R. Q., N. K. Coch, J. E. Sanders, and R. F. Flint. 1974. Post-Miocene shorelines and sea levels, southeastern Virginia. Pages 53–87 *in* R. Q. Oaks and J. R. DuBar, editors. Post-Miocene stratigraphy, central and southern Atlantic Coastal Plain. Utah State University Press, Logan.

Oaks, R. Q., and J. R. DuBar. 1974. Tentative correlation of post-Miocene units, central and southern Atlantic Coastal Plain. Pages 232–245 *in* R. Q. Oaks and J. R. DuBar, editors. Post-Miocene stratigraphy, central and southern Atlantic Coastal Plain. Utah State University Press, Logan.

Oaks, R. Q., and D. R. Whitehead. 1979. Geologic setting and origin of the Dismal Swamp, southeastern Virginia and northeastern North Carolina. Pages 1–24 *in* P. W. Kirk, editor. The Great Dismal Swamp. University Press of Virginia, Charlottesville.

Occhiogrosso, T., and S. Goodbred. 1981. The bluespotted sunfish. New York State Conservationist 36(1):41.

O'Donnell, J. 1935. Annotated list of the fishes of Illinois. Illinois Natural History Survey Bulletin 20:473–500.

Odum, W. E., T. J. Smith III, J. K. Hoover, and C. C. McIvor. 1984. The ecology of tidal freshwater marshes of the United States East Coast: a community profile. U.S. Fish and Wildlife Service Biological Services Program, FWS-OBS-83/17.

Oehmcke, A. A., L. Johnson, J. Klingbiel, and C. Wistrom. 1958. The Wisconsin muskellunge, its life history, ecology, and management. Wisconsin Conservation Department, Publication 225, Madison.

Ogden, J. C. 1970. Relative abundance, food habits, and age and growth of the American eel, *Anguilla rostrata* (Lesueur), in certain New Jersey streams. Transactions of the American Fisheries Society 99:54–59.

Okazaki, T. 1984. Genetic divergence and its zoogeographic implications in closely related species *Salmo gairdneri* and *Salmo mykiss*. Japanese Journal of Ichthyology 31:297–310.

Oliver, J. 1980. Exploring the basement of the North American continent. American Scientist 68:676–683.

Ollier, C. D. 1981. Tectonics and landforms. Longman, New York.

Ollier, C. D. 1985. Morphotectonics of continental margins with great escarpments. Pages 3–25 *in* M. Morisawa and J. T. Hack, editors. Tectonic geomorphology. Allen and Unwin, Boston.

Olmsted, L. L. and D. G. Cloutman. 1979. Life history of the flat bullhead, *Ictalurus platycephalus*, in Lake Norman, North Carolina. Transactions of the American Fisheries Society 108:38–42.

Olney, J. E., G. C. Grant, F. E. Schultz, C. L. Cooper, and J. Hageman. 1983. Pterygiophore-interdigitation patterns in larvae of four *Morone* species. Transactions of the American Fisheries Society 112:525–531.

Olsen, P. E. 1984. The skull and pectoral girdle of the parasemionotid fish *Watsonulus eugnathoides* from the Early Triassic Sakamena Group of Madagascar, with comments on the relationships of the holostean fishes. Journal of Vertebrate Palentology 4:481–499.

Olsen, P. E., A. M. McCune, and K. S. Thomson. 1982. Correlation of the early Mesozoic Newark Supergroup by vertebrates, principally fishes. American Journal of Science 282:1–44.

Ommanney, F. D. 1964. The fishes. Time, New York.

O'Neill, J. T. 1980. Aspects of the life histories of anadromous alewife and the blueback herring, Margaree River and Lake Ainsle, Nova Scotia, 1978–1979. Master's thesis. Acadia University, Wolfville, Nova Scotia. (Not seen; cited in Fay et al. 1983.)

Ono, R. D., J. D. Williams, and A. Wagner. 1983. Vanishing fishes of North America. Stone Wall Press, Washington, D.C.

Onuschak, E. 1973. Geologic studies, Coastal Plain of Virginia: Pleistocene–Holocene environmental geology. Virginia Division of Mineral Resources Bulletin 83, Charlottesville.

Orth, D. J., and L. A. Helfrich. 1983. Indices of water quality for the New River Gorge National River and its tributaries. Pages 107–121 *in* Proceedings New River Symposium, April 14–16, 1983, Blacksburg, Virginia. National Park Service, New River Gorge National River, Glen Jean, West Virginia.

Ortmann, A. E. 1908. The Alleghenian divide, and its influence upon the freshwater fauna. Proceedings of the American Philosophical Society 52:287–395.

Ortmann, A. E. 1913. The distribution of closely allied species. Science, New Series 27:427–429.

Osborn, H. F. 1931. Cope: master naturalist. Princeton University Press, Princeton, New Jersey. (Reprinted 1978. Arno Press, New York.)

Ottaway, E. M., P. A. Carling, A. Clarke, and N. A. Reader. 1981. Observations on the structure of brown trout, *Salmo trutta* Linnaeus, redds. Journal of Fish Biology 19:593–607.

Otto, R. G., and J. O. Rice. 1977. Responses of a freshwater sculpin (*Cottus cognatus gracilis*) to temperature. Transactions of the American Fisheries Society 106:89–94.

Outten, L. M. 1957. A study of the life history of the cyprinid fish *Notropis coccogenis*. Journal of the Elisha Mitchell Scientific Society 73:68–84.

Outten, L. M. 1958. Studies of the life history of the cyprinid fishes *Notropis galacturus* and *rubricroceus*. Journal of the Elisha Mitchell Scientific Society 74:122–134.

Outten, L. M. 1962. Some observations on the spawning coloration and behavior of *Notropis leuciodus*. Journal of the Elisha Mitchell Scientific Society 78:101–102.

Page, L. M. 1974. The subgenera of *Percina* (Percidae: Etheostomatini). Copeia 1974:66–86.

Page, L. M. 1975. Relations among the darters of the subgenus *Catonotus* of *Etheostoma*. Copeia 1975:782–784.

Page, L. M. 1976a. The modified midventral scales of *Percina* (Osteichthyes; Percidae). Journal of Morphology 148:255–264.

Page, L. M. 1976b. Natural darter hybrids: *Etheostoma gracile* × *Percina maculata*, *Percina caprodes* × *Percina maculata*, and *Percina phoxocephala* × *Percina maculata*. Southwestern Naturalist 21:145–149.

Page, L. M. 1977. The lateralis system of darters (Etheostomatini). Copeia 1977:472–475.

Page, L. M. 1978. Redescription, distribution, variation and life history notes on *Percina macrocephala* (Percidae). Copeia 1978:655–664.

Page, L. M. 1981. The genera and subgenera of darters (Percidae, Etheostomatini). Occasional Papers of the Museum of Natural History University of Kansas 90:1–69.

Page, L. M. 1983. Handbook of darters. Tropical Fish Hobbyist Publications, Neptune City, New Jersey.

Page, L. M. 1985. Evolution of reproductive behaviors in

percid fishes. Illinois Natural History Survey Bulletin 33:275–295.

Page, L. M., and H. L. Bart. 1989. Egg mimics in darters (Pisces: Percidae). Copeia 1989:514–517.

Page, L. M. and E. C. Beckham. 1987. *Notropis rupestris*, a new cyprinid from the middle Cumberland River system, Tennessee, with comments on variation in *Notropis heterolepis*. Copeia 1987:659–668.

Page, L. M., and B. M. Burr. 1979. The smallest species of darter (Pisces: Percidae). American Midland Naturalist 101:452–453.

Page, L. M., and B. M. Burr. 1991. A field guide to freshwater fishes of North America north of Mexico. Houghton Mifflin, Boston.

Page, L. M., and P. A. Ceas. 1989. Egg attachment in *Pimephales* (Pisces: Cyprinidae). Copeia 1989:1074–1077.

Page, L. M., and L. E. Cordes. 1983. Variation and systematics of *Etheostoma euzonum*, the Arkansas saddled darter (Pisces: Percidae). Copeia 1983:1042–1050.

Page, L. M., and K. S. Cummings. 1984. A portable camera box for photographing small fishes. Page 124 *in* D. G. Lindquist and L. M. Page, editors. Environmental biology of darters. Kluwer Boston, Hingham, Massachusetts. (Also: Environmental Biology of Fishes 11: 160.)

Page, L. M., and C. E. Johnston. 1990a. Spawning in the creek chubsucker, *Erimyzon oblongus*, with a review of spawning behavior in suckers (Catostomidae). Environmental Biology of Fishes 27:265–272.

Page, L. M., and C. E. Johnston. 1990b. The breeding behavior of *Opsopoeodus emiliae* (Cyprinidae) and its phylogenetic implications. Copeia 1990:1176–1180.

Page, L. M., W. L. Keller, and L. E. Cordes. 1981. *Etheostoma (Boleosoma) longimanum* and *E. (Catonotus) obeyense*, two more darters confirmed as egg-clusterers. Transactions of the Kentucky Academy of Science 42: 35–36.

Page, L. M., and R. L. Mayden. 1981. The life history of the Tennessee snubnose darter, *Etheostoma simoterum* in Brush Creek, Tennessee. Illinois Natural History Survey Biological Notes 117.

Page, L. M., M. E. Retzer, and R. A. Stiles. 1982. Spawning behavior in seven species of darters (Pisces: Percidae). Brimleyana 8:135–143.

Page, L. M., and D. W. Schemske. 1978. The effect of interspecific competition on the distribution and size of darters of the subgenus *Catonotus* (Percidae: *Etheostoma*). Copeia 1978:406–412.

Page, L. M., and T. P. Simon. 1988. Observations on the reproductive behavior and eggs of four species of darters, with comments on *Etheostoma tippecanoe* and *E. camurum*. Transactions of the Illinois Academy of Science 81:205–210.

Page, L. M., and P. W. Smith. 1970. The life history of the dusky darter, *Percina sciera*, in the Embarras River, Illinois. Illinois Natural History Survey Biological Notes 69.

Page, L. M., and P. W. Smith. 1971. The life history of the slenderhead darter, *Percina phoxocephala*, in the Embar-ras River, Illinois. Illinois Natural History Survey Biological Notes 74.

Page, L. M., and P. W. Smith. 1976. Variation and systematics of the stripetail darter, *Etheostoma kennicotti*. Copeia 1976:532–541.

Page, L. M., and R. L. Smith. 1970. Recent range adjustments and hybridization of *Notropis lutrensis* and *Notropis spilopterus* in Illinois. Transactions of the Illinois State Academy of Science 63:264–272.

Page, L. M., and D. L. Swofford. 1984. Morphological correlates of ecological specialization in darters. Pages 103–123 *in* D. G. Lindquist and L. M. Page, editors. Environmental biology of darters. Kluwer Boston, Hingham, Massachusetts. (Also: Environmental Biology of Fishes 11:139–159.)

Paine, M. D. 1984. Ecological and evolutionary consequences of early ontogenies of darters (Etheostomatini). Pages 21–30 *in* D. G. Lindquist and L. M. Page, editors. Environmental biology of darters. Kluwer Boston, Hingham, Massachusetts. (Also: Environmental Biology of Fishes 11:97–106.)

Paine, M. D., J. J. Dodson, and G. Power. 1982. Habitat and food resource partitioning among four species of darters (Percidae: *Etheostoma*) in a southern Ontario stream. Canadian Journal of Zoology 60:1635–1641.

Paloumpis, A. A. 1958. Measurement of some factors affecting the catch in a minnow seine. Proceedings of the Iowa Academy of Science 65:580–586.

Paloumpis, A. A. 1963. A key to the Illinois species of *Ictalurus* (class Pisces) based on pectoral spines. Transactions of the Illinois State Academy of Science 56:129–133.

Pappantoniou, A., G. Dale, and R. E. Schmidt. 1984a. Aspects of the life history of the cutlips minnow, *Exoglossum maxillingua*, from two eastern Pennsylvania streams. Journal of Freshwater Ecology 2:449–458.

Pappantoniou, A., R. E. Schmidt, and G. Dale. 1984b. Ecology and life history of the cutlips minnow, *Exoglossum maxillingua*, from a southeastern New York stream. Northeastern Environmental Science 3:75–79.

Pardue, G. B. 1993. Life history and ecology of the mud sunfish (*Acantharcus pomotis*). Copeia 1993(2):533–540.

Pardue, G. B., and M. T. Huish. 1981. An evaluation of methods for collecting fishes in swamp streams. Pages 282–290 *in* L. A. Krumholz, editor. The warmwater streams symposium. American Fisheries Society, Southern Division, Bethesda, Maryland.

Pardue, G. B., M. T. Huish, and H. R. Perry. 1975. Ecological studies of two swamp watersheds in northeastern North Carolina—a prechannelization study. University of North Carolina, North Carolina State University, Water Resources Research Institute, Report 105, Raleigh.

Parenti, L. R. 1981. A phylogenetic and biogeographic analysis of cyprinodontiform fishes (Teleostei, Atherinomorpha). Bulletin of the American Museum of Natural History 168:335–557.

Parker, B., and P. McKee. 1984a. Status of the silver shiner, *Notropis photogenis*, in Canada. Canadian Field-Naturalist 98:91–97.

Parker, B., and P. McKee. 1984b. Status of the river redhorse, *Moxostoma carinatum*, in Canada. Canadian Field-Naturalist 98:110–114.

Parker, B. C., H. E. Wolfe, and R. V. Howard. 1975. On the origin and history of Mountain Lake, Virginia. Southeastern Geology 16:213–226.

Parker, H. L. 1964. Natural history of *Pimephales vigilax* (Cyprinidae). Southwestern Naturalist 8:228–235.

Parker, J. B. 1942. Some observations on the reproductive system of the yellow perch (*Perca flavescens*). Copeia 1942:223–226.

Parker, J. C. 1965. An annotated checklist of the fishes of the Galveston Bay system, Texas. Publications of the Institute of Marine Science, University of Texas 10:201–220.

Parker, N. C., and B. A. Simco. 1975. Activity patterns, feeding and behavior of the pirateperch, *Aphredoderus sayanus*. Copeia 1975:572–574.

Parker, P. E. 1968. Geologic investigation of the Lincoln and Bluemont quadrangles, Virginia. Virginia Division of Mineral Resources, Report of Investigations 14, Charlottesville.

Parker, W., and L. Dixon. 1980. Endangered and threatened wildlife of Kentucky, North Carolina, South Carolina and Tennessee. North Carolina Agricultural Extension Services, North Carolina State University, Raleigh.

Parker, W. D. 1971. Preliminary studies on sexing adult largemouth bass by means of an external characteristic. Progressive Fish-Culturist 33:54–55. (Not seen; cited in Carlander 1977.)

Parramore, T. C. 1968. [Biography notes and reprinting of:] John Brickell. 1737. The natural history of North Carolina. Johnson Publishing Company, Murfreesboro, North Carolina.

Parrish, J. D., D. C. Heins, and J. A. Baker. 1991. Reproductive season, clutch parameters and oocyte size in the johnny darter *Etheostoma nigrum* from southwestern Mississippi. American Midland Naturalist 125:180–186.

Parsons, J. W. 1959. Muskellunge in Tennessee streams. Transactions of the American Fisheries Society 88:136–140.

Parsons, J. W., and J. B. Kimsey. 1954. A report on the Mississippi threadfin shad. Progressive Fish-Culturist 16:179–181.

Pasch, R. W., and C. M. Alexander. 1986. Effects of commercial fishing on paddlefish populations. Pages 46–53 *in* J. G. Dillard, L. K. Graham, and T. R. Russell, editors. The paddlefish: status, management and propagation. American Fisheries Society, North Central Division, Special Publication 7, Bethesda, Maryland.

Pasch, R. W., P. A. Hackney, and J. A. Holbrook II. 1980. Ecology of paddlefish in Old Hickory Reservoir, Tennessee, with emphasis on first-year life history. Transactions of the American Fisheries Society 109:157–167.

Pate, P. P. 1972. Life history aspects of the hickory shad, *Alosa mediocris* (Mitchill), in the Neuse River, North Carolina. Master's thesis. North Carolina State University, Raleigh.

Patrick, R. 1961. A study of the numbers and kinds of species found in rivers in eastern United States. Pro-

ceedings of the Academy of Natural Sciences of Philadelphia 113:215–258.

Patten, B. G. 1971. Spawning and fecundity of seven species of northwest American *Cottus*. American Midland Naturalist 85:493–506.

Patterson, C. 1975. The distribution of Mesozoic freshwater fishes. Memoires du Museum National d'Histoire Naturelle Serie A Zoologie 88:156–173.

Patterson, C. 1981. The development of the North American fish fauna—a problem of historical biogeography. Pages 265–281 *in* P. L. Forey, editor. The evolving biosphere. British Museum (Natural History) and Cambridge University Press, London.

Patterson, C. 1982. Morphology and interrelationships of primitive actinopterygian fishes. American Zoologist 22:241–259.

Patterson, C., and A. E. Longbottom. 1989. An Eocene amiid fish from Mali, West Africa. Copeia 1989:827–836.

Patterson, C., and D. E. Rosen. 1989. The Paracanthopterygii revisited: order and disorder. Natural History Museum of Los Angeles County Science Series 32:5–36.

Pavich, M. J. 1985. Appalachian Piedmont morphogenesis: weathering, erosion, and Cenozoic uplift. Pages 299–319 *in* M. Morisawa and J. T. Hack, editors. Tectonic geomorphology. Allen and Unwin, Boston.

Pavol, K. W., and R. M. Davis. 1982. Life history and management of the smallmouth bass in Susquehanna River below Conowingo Dam. Maryland Department of Natural Resources, Wildlife Administration, Project F-29-R, Study II, Annapolis.

Payne, S. L., and W. D. Pearson. 1981. Feeding preferences of postlarval longnose gar (*Lepisosteus osseus*) of the Ohio River. Transactions of the Kentucky Academy of Science 42:119–131.

Pearse, A. S. 1918. The food of the shore fishes of certain Wisconsin lakes. U.S. Bureau of Fisheries Bulletin 35:246–292.

Pearson, W. D., and L. A. Krumholz. 1984. Distribution and status of Ohio River fishes. National Technical Information Service, ORNL/SUB/79-7831/1, Springfield, Virginia.

Pearson, W. D., G. A. Thomas, and A. L. Clark. 1979. Early piscivory and timing of the critical period in postlarval longnose gar at mile 571 of the Ohio River. Transactions of the Kentucky Academy of Science 40:122–128.

Peden, A. E. 1973. Variation in anal spot expression of gambusiin females and its effect on male courtship. Copeia 1973:250–263.

Peden, A. E., and G. W. Hughes. 1988. Sympatry in four species of *Rhinichthys* (Pisces), including the first documented occurrences of *R. umatilla* in the Canadian drainages of the Columbia River. Canadian Journal of Zoology 66:1846–1856.

Peden, A. E., G. W. Hughes, and W. E. Roberts. 1989. Morphologically distict populations of the shorthead sculpin, *Cottus confusus*, and mottled sculpin, *Cottus bairdi* (Pisces, Cottidae), near the western border of

Canada and the United States. Canadian Jounal of Zoology 67:2711–2720.

Peer, D. L. 1966. Relationship between size and maturity in the spottail shiner, *Notropis hudsonius*. Journal of the Fisheries Research Board of Canada 23:455–457.

Peltz, L. R., and O. E. Maughan. 1979. An analysis of fish populations and selected physical and chemical parameters of five strip mine ponds in Wise County, Virginia with implications toward management. U.S. Fish and Wildlife Service FWS-OBS-78/81A.

Pelzman, R. J. 1971. The blue catfish. California Department of Fish and Game, Inland Fisheries Administrative Report 71-11, Sacramento.

PERCIS (Percid International Symposium). 1977. Proceedings of the 1976 Percid International Symposium. Journal of the Fisheries Research Board of Canada 34(10).

Perry, L. G., and B. W. Menzel. 1979. Identification of nine larval cyprinids inhabiting small northern rivers. Pages 141–173 *in* R. Wallus and C. W. Voigtlander, editors. Proceedings of a workshop on freshwater larval fishes. Tennessee Valley Authority, Norris, Tennessee.

Perry, W. G. 1968. Distribution and relative abundance of blue catfish, *Ictalurus furcatus*, and channel catfish, *Ictalurus punctatus*, with relation to salinity. Proceedings of the Annual Conference Southeastern Association of Game and Fish Commissioners 21(1967):436–444. (Not seen; cited from Moyle 1976.)

Perry, W. G. 1973. Notes on the spawning of blue and channel catfish in brackish water ponds. Progressive Fish-Culturist 35:164–166.

Peterson, E. T., and R. A. Drews. 1957. Some historical aspects of the carp with special reference to Michigan. Michigan Department of Conservation, Fish Division, Pamphlet 23, Lansing.

Peterson, M. S., and S. T. Ross. 1987. Morphometric and meristic characteristics of a peripheral population of *Enneacanthus*. Proceedings of the Southeastern Fishes Council 17:1–4.

Petravicz, W. P. 1938. The breeding habits of the black-sided darter, *Hadropterus maculatus* Girard. Copeia 1938:40–44.

Petrimoulx, H. J. 1980. The biology and distribution of the Roanoke bass, *Ambloplites cavifrons* Cope, in Virginia. Master's thesis. Virginia Commonwealth University, Richmond.

Petrimoulx, H. J. 1983. Life history and distribution of the Roanoke bass *Ambloplites cavifrons* Cope, in Virginia. American Midland Naturalist 110:338–353.

Petrimoulx, H. J. 1984. Observations on the spawning behavior of the Roanoke bass. Progressive Fish-Culturist 46:120–125.

Petrimoulx, H. J., and R. E. Jenkins. 1979. The last stand of the Roanoke bass. Virginia Wildlife 40(11):4–6.

Petrosky, C. E., and T. F. Waters. 1975. Annual production by the slimy sculpin population in a small Minnesota trout stream. Transactions of the American Fisheries Society 104:237–244.

Péwé, T. L. 1983. The periglacial environment in North America during Wisconsin time. Pages 157–189 *in* H. E. Wright and S. C. Porter, editors. Late-Quaternary environments of the United States, volume 1. University of Minnesota Press, Minneapolis.

Pfeiffer, R. A. 1955. Studies on the life history of the rosy-face shiner, *Notropis rubellus*. Copeia 1955:95–104.

Pfieffer, W. 1963. The fright reaction in North American fish. Canadian Journal of Zoology 41:69–77.

Pflieger, W. L. 1965. Reproductive behavior of the minnows, *Notropis spilopterus* and *Notropis whipplei*. Copeia 1965:1–8.

Pflieger, W. L. 1966. Reproduction of the smallmouth bass (*Micropterus dolomieui*) in a small Ozark stream. American Midland Naturalist 76:410–418.

Pflieger, W. L. 1971. A distributional study of Missouri fishes. University of Kansas Publications of the Museum of Natural History 20:225–570.

Pflieger, W. L. 1975. The fishes of Missouri. Missouri Department of Conservation, Columbia.

Pflieger, W. L. 1978. Distribution and status of the grass carp (*Ctenopharyngodon idella*) in Missouri streams. Transactions of the American Fisheries Society 107:113–118.

Pflieger, W. L., and O. F. Fajen. 1975. Natural hybridization between the smallmouth bass and spotted bass. Missouri Department of Conservation, Federal Aid in Sport Fish Restoration, Project F-1-R-24. Final Report, Columbia.

Philipp, D. P., W. F. Childers, and G. S. Whitt. 1983. A biochemical genetic evaluation of the northern and Florida subspecies of largemouth bass. Transactions of the American Fisheries Society 112:1–20.

Phillips, G. L., W. D. Schmid, and J. C. Underhill. 1982. Fishes of the Minnesota region. University of Minnesota Press, Minneapolis.

Phillips, G. L., and J. C. Underhill. 1967. Revised distribution records of some Minnesota fishes, with addition of two species to the faunal list. Journal of the Minnesota Academy of Science 34:177–180.

Phillips, G. L., and J. C. Underhill. 1971. Distribution and variation of the Catostomidae of Minnesota. Occasional Papers, Bell Museum of Natural History University of Minnesota 10.

Piavis, G. W., J. H. Howell, and A. J. Smith. 1970. Experimental hybridization among five species of lampreys from the Great Lakes. Copeia 1970:29–37.

Pierson, J. M., and six coauthors. 1989. Fishes of the Cahaba River system in Alabama. Geological Survey of Alabama Bulletin 134, Montgomery.

Ping, C. 1931. Preliminary notes on the fauna of Nanking. Contributions from the Biological Laboratory of the Science Society of China, Nanking (Zoological Series) 7:173–201.

Pistono, R. P. 1975. Life history and habitat requirements of the Ohrid trout. Wyoming Game and Fish Department Administrative Report Project 5574-23-7301.

Popova, O. A., and L. A. Sytina. 1977. Food and feeding behavior of Eurasian perch (*Perca fluviatilis*) and pike-perch (*Stizostedion lucioperca*) in various waters of the USSR. Journal of the Fisheries Research Board of Canada 34:1559–1570.

Porter, S. C. 1983. Introduction. Pages xi–xiv *in* H. E. Wright and S. C. Porter, editors. Late-Quaternary environments of the United States, volume 1. University of Minnesota Press, Minneapolis.

Potter, I. C. 1980a. The Petromyzoniformes with particular reference to paired species. Canadian Journal of Fisheries and Aquatic Sciences 37:1595–1615.

Potter, I. C. 1980b. Ecology of larval and metamorphosing lampreys. Canadian Journal of Fisheries and Aquatic Sciences 37:1641–1657.

Potter, I. C., and J. R. Bailey. 1972. The life cycle of the Tennessee brook lamprey, *Ichthyomyzon hubbsi* Raney. Copeia 1972:470–476.

Potter, I. C., and F. W. H. Beamish. 1977. The freshwater biology of adult anadromous sea lampreys *Petromyzon marinus*. Journal of Zoology (London) 181:113–130.

Potter, J. M., W. A. Potter, H. H. Seagle, and A. C. Hendricks. 1981. Recovery of the ichthyofauna of the South River, Virginia, as a result of pollution abatement. Pages 388–395 *in* L. A. Krumholz, editor. The warmwater streams symposium. American Fisheries Society, Southern Division, Bethesda, Maryland.

Potter, W. A., J. J. Loos, and J. M. Potter. 1980. Development of larval bull chub, *Nocomis raneyi*. U.S. Fish and Wildlife Service Biological Services Program FWS-OBS-80/43:20–24.

Pough, F. H., J. B. Heiser, and W. N. McFarland. 1989. Vertebrate life, 3rd edition. Macmillan, New York.

Poulson, T. L. 1961. Cave adaptation in amblyopsid fishes. Doctoral dissertation. University of Michigan, Ann Arbor.

Poulson, T. L. 1963. Cave adaptation in amblyopsid fishes. American Midland Naturalist 70:257–290.

Poulson, T. L. 1971. Biology of cave and deep sea organisms: a comparison. National Speleological Society Bulletin 33:51–61.

Poulson, T. L., and W. B. White. 1969. The cave environment. Science 165:971–981.

Powell, J. A. 1984. Observations of cleaning behavior in the bluegill (*Lepomis macrochirus*), a centrarchid. Copeia 1984:996–998.

Power, G. 1980. The brook charr, *Salvelinus fontinalis*. Pages 141–203 *in* E. K. Balon, editor. Charrs: salmonid fishes of the genus *Salvelinus*. Dr. W. Junk, The Hague, Netherlands.

Power, M. E., and W. J. Matthews. 1983. Algae-grazing minnows (*Campostoma anomalum*), piscivorous bass (*Micropterus* spp.), and the distribution of attached algae in a small prairie-margin stream. Oecologia (Berlin) 60:328–332.

Powles, P. M., D. Parker, and R. Reid. 1977. Growth, maturation, and apparent and absolute fecundity of creek chub, *Semotilus atromaculatus* (Mitchill), in the Kawartha Lakes region, Ontario. Canadian Journal of Zoology 55:843–846.

Prather, K. W. 1985. Muskellunge streams investigation in the Middle Fork and North Fork Kentucky River drainages and upper Licking River. Kentucky Department of Fish and Wildlife Resources, Fisheries Bulletin 78, Frankfort.

Pratt, R. M. 1967. The seaward extension of submarine canyons of the northeast coast of the United States. Deep-Sea Research 14:409–420.

Price, K. S., and seven coauthors. 1985. Nutrient enrichment of Chesapeake Bay and its impact on the habitat of striped bass: a speculative hypothesis. Transactions of the American Fisheries Society 114:97–106.

Prince, E., and P. Brouha. 1975. Smith Mountain Lake habitat improvement research study. Virginia Commission of Game and Inland Fisheries, Federal Aid in Sport Fish Restoration, Project F-31-1, April 20, 1973–April 20, 1974. Progress Report, Richmond.

Prince, E. E. 1907. The eggs and early life history of the herring, gaspereau, shad and clupeoids. Contributions to Canadian Biology 1902–1905 volume:95–110.

Pritchard, D. W. 1967. What is an estuary: physical viewpoint. American Association for the Advancement of Science, Washington, D.C., Publication 83:3–5.

Probst, W. E., C. F. Rabeui, W. G. Covington, and R. E. Marteney. 1984. Resource use by stream-dwelling rock bass and smallmouth bass. Transactions of the American Fisheries Society 113:283–294.

Prosser, N. S. 1972a. Public fishing lake fertilization study. Virginia Commission of Game and Inland Fisheries, Federal Aid in Sport Fish Restoration, Project F-20-1, July 1969–April 1970. Progress Report, Richmond.

Prosser, N. S. 1972b. Public fishing lake fertilization study. Virginia Commission of Game and Inland Fisheries, Federal Aid in Sport Fish Restoration, Project F-20-3, March 1971–July 1972. Final Report, Richmond.

Prosser, N. S. 1973. Lake Burke creel census survey. Virginia Commission of Game and Inland Fisheries, Federal Aid in Sport Fish Restoration, Project F-23-3, March 1971–July 1972. Final Report, Richmond.

Purkett, C. A. 1958. Growth rates of Missouri stream fishes. Missouri Fish and Game Division, Federal Aid in Sport Fish Restoration, Series Number 1, Project Number Missouri F-1-R. Jefferson City.

Purkett, C. A. 1961. Reproduction and early development of the paddlefish. Transactions of the American Fisheries Society 90:125–129.

Quinn, D. B. 1977. North America from earliest discovery to first settlements: the Norse voyages to 1612. Harper and Row, New York.

Quinn, J. R. 1976. The pirate perch, nature's anatomical wonder. Tropical Fish Hobbyist 24:86–87, 89.

Quinn, J. R. 1988. The best and the brightest: the cosmopolitan *Chaetodon*. Tropical Fish Hobbyist 36:59–68.

Quinn, J. R. 1991. Chasing rainbows: adventures with darters. Tropical Fish Hobbyist 39:130–146.

Quinn, S. 1989. To catch a crossbreed. In-Fisherman 82:122–130.

Quinn, S. P., and M. R. Ross. 1985. Non-annual spawning in the white sucker, *Catostomus commersoni*. Copeia 1985:613–618.

Rabito, F. G., and D. C. Heins. 1985. Spawning behavior and sexual dimorphism in the North American cyprinid fish *Notropis leedsi*, the bannerfin shiner. Journal of Natural History 19:1155–1163.

Radcliffe, L. 1932. Fresh-water game and bait fishes of the District of Columbia and vicinity. Yearbook, Izaak Walton League of America, Washington, D.C., Chapter.

Radcliffe, L., and W. W. Welsh. 1916. A list of the fishes of the Seneca Creek, Montgomery County, Maryland, region. Proceedings of the Biological Society of Washington 29:39–46.

Radonski, G. C., editor. 1985. Striped bass restoration—can we get there from here? Sport Fishing Institute Bulletin 367:1–3.

Radonski, G. C., editor. 1986. Introduction of grass carp deemed safe by USFWS. Sport Fishing Institute Bulletin 371:6.

Radonski, G. C., N. S. Prosser, R. G. Martin, and R. H. Stroud. 1984. Exotic fishes and sport fishing. Pages 313–321 in W. R. Courtenay and J. R. Stauffer, editors. Distribution, biology, and management of exotic fishes. Johns Hopkins University Press, Baltimore.

Rafinesque, C. S. 1820. Ichthyologia Ohiensis or natural history of the fishes inhabiting the River Ohio and its tributary streams, preceded by a physical description of the Ohio and its branches. W. G. Hunt, Lexington, Kentucky (Reprinted 1970. Arno Press, Salem, New Hampshire.)

Rahel, F. J. 1982. Fish assemblages in Wisconsin bog lakes. Doctoral dissertation. University of Wisconsin, Madison. (Not seen; cited in Hastings 1984.)

Raicu, P., E. Taisescu, and P. Banarescu. 1981. Carassius carassius and C. auratus, a pair of diploid and tetraploid representative species (Pisces, Cyprinidae). Cytologia 46:233–240.

Rainboth, W. J., and G. S. Whitt. 1974. Analysis of evolutionary relationships among shiners of the subgenus Luxilus (Teleostei, Cypriniformes, Notropis) with the lactate dehydrogenase and malate dehydrogenase isozyme systems. Comparative Biochemistry and Physiology 49B:241–252.

Raleigh, R. F. 1982. Habitat suitability index models: brook trout. U.S. Fish and Wildlife Service Biological Services Program FWS-OBS-82/10.24.

Raleigh, R. F., D. H. Bennett, L. O. Mohn, and O. E. Maughan. 1978. Changes in fish stocks after major fish kills in the Clinch River near St. Paul, Virginia. American Midland Naturalist 99:1–9.

Raleigh, R. F., T. Hickman, R. C. Solomon, and P. C. Nelson. 1984. Habitat suitability information: rainbow trout. U.S. Fish and Wildlife Service Biological Services Program FWS-OBS-82/10.60.

Ramsey, J. S. 1965. Zoogeographic studies on the freshwater fish fauna of rivers draining the southern Appalachian region. Doctoral dissertation. Tulane University, New Orleans.

Ramsey, J. S. 1975. Taxonomic history and systematic relationships among species of Micropterus. Pages 67–75 in R. H. Stroud and H. Clepper, editors. Black bass biology and management. Sport Fishing Institute, Washington, D.C.

Ramsey, J. S. 1984. Freshwater fishes. Pages 1–14 in R. H. Mount, editor. Vertebrate wildlife of Alabama. Auburn University Agricultural Experiment Station, Auburn, Alabama.

Ramsey, J. S., and R. O. Smitherman. 1972. Development of color pattern in pond-reared young of five Micropterus species of southeastern U.S. Proceedings of the Annual Conference Southeastern Association of Game and Fish Commissioners 25(1971):348–356.

Raney, E. C. 1939a. The breeding habits of the silvery minnow, Hybognathus regius Girard. American Midland Naturalist 21:674–680.

Raney, E. C. 1939b. The breeding habits of Ichthyomyzon greeleyi Hubbs and Trautman. Copeia 1939:111–112.

Raney, E. C. 1939c. Observations on the nesting habits of Parexoglossum laurae Hubbs and Trautman. Copeia 1939:112–113.

Raney, E. C. 1940a. The breeding behavior of the common shiner, Notropis cornutus (Mitchill). Zoologica (New York) 25:1–14.

Raney, E. C. 1940b. Comparison of the breeding habits of two subspecies of black-nosed dace, Rhinichthys atratulus (Hermann). American Midland Naturalist 23:399–403.

Raney, E. C. 1940c. Nests under the water. Bulletin New York Zoological Society 43:127–135.

Raney, E. C. 1940d. Reproductive behavior of a hybrid minnow, Notropis cornutus × Notropis rubellus. Zoologica (New York) 25:361–367.

Raney, E. C. 1940e. Rhinichthys bowersi from West Virginia a hybrid, Rhinichthys cataractae × Nocomis micropogon. Copeia 1940:270–271.

Raney, E. C. 1941. Poecilichthys kanawhae, a new darter from the upper New River system in North Carolina and Virginia. Occasional Papers of the Museum of Zoology, University of Michigan 434.

Raney, E. C. 1942. Propagation of the silvery minnow (Hybognathus nuchalis regius Girard) in ponds. Transactions of the American Fisheries Society 71:215–218.

Raney, E. C. 1943. Unusual spawning habitat for the common white sucker, Catostomus c. commersonnii. Copeia 1943:256.

Raney, E. C. 1947a. Subspecies and breeding behavior of the cyprinid fish Notropis procne (Cope). Copeia 1947:103–109.

Raney, E. C. 1947b. Nocomis nests used by other breeding cyprinid fishes in Virginia. Zoologica (New York) 32:125–133.

Raney, E. C. 1950. Freshwater fishes. Pages 151–194 in M. H. Stow, editor. The James River basin: past, present and future. Virginia Academy of Science, Richmond.

Raney, E. C. 1952a. A new lamprey, Ichthyomyzon hubbsi, from the upper Tennessee River system. Copeia 1952:93–99.

Raney, E. C. 1952b. The life history of the striped bass, Roccus saxatilis (Walbaum). Bulletin of the Bingham Oceanographic Collection, Yale University 14:5–97.

Raney, E. C. 1957a [not 1955]. Natural hybrids between two species of pickerel (Esox) in Stearns Pond, Massachusetts. Supplement to Fisheries Report for some central, eastern, and western Massachusetts lakes, ponds, and reservoirs, 1951–52. Massachusetts Division of Fisheries and Game, Boston.

Raney, E. C. 1957b. Subpopulations of the striped bass Roccus saxatilis (Walbaum), in tributaries of Chesapeake Bay. U.S. Fish and Wildlife Service Special Scientific Report—Fisheries 208.

Raney, E. C. 1965. Some pan fishes of New York. New York State Conservationist 19 (April–May):1–16.

Raney, E. C. 1969a. Minnows of New York, part 1: facts

about some of our chubs and dace. New York State Conservationist 23(April–May):22–29.

Raney, E. C. 1969b. Minnows of New York, part 2: the shiners. New York State Conservationist 23(June–July): 21–29.

Raney, E. C., and D. P. de Sylva. 1953. Racial investigations of the striped bass, *Roccus saxatilis* (Walbaum). Journal of Wildlife Management 17:495–509.

Raney, E. C., and C. L. Hubbs. 1948. *Hadropterus notogrammus*, a new percid fish from Maryland, Virginia, and West Virginia. Occasional Papers of the Museum of Zoology, University of Michigan 512.

Raney, E. C., and E. A. Lachner. 1939. Observations on the life history of the spotted darter, *Poecilichthys maculatus* (Kirtland). Copeia 1939:157–165.

Raney, E. C., and E. A. Lachner. 1942. Studies of the summer food, growth, and movements of young yellow pike-perch, *Stizostedion v. vitreum*, in Oneida Lake, New York. Journal of Wildlife Management 6:1–16.

Raney, E. C., and E. A. Lachner. 1943. Age and growth of johnny darters, *Boleosoma nigrum olmstedi* (Storer) and *Boleosoma longimanum* (Jordan). American Midland Naturalist 29:229–238.

Raney, E. C., and E. A. Lachner. 1946a. Age, growth, and habits of the hog sucker, *Hypentelium nigricans* (Lesueur), in New York. American Midland Naturalist 36:76–86.

Raney, E. C., and E. A. Lachner. 1946b. Age and growth of the rustyside sucker, *Thoburnia rhothoeca* (Thoburn). American Midland Naturalist 36:675–681.

Raney, E. C., and E. A. Lachner. 1946c. *Thoburnia hamiltoni*, a new sucker from the upper Roanoke River system in Virginia. Copeia 1946:218–226.

Raney, E. C., and E. A. Lachner. 1947. *Hypentelium roanokense*, a new catostomid fish from the Roanoke River in Virginia. American Museum Novitates 1333.

Raney, E. C., and W. H. Massmann. 1953. The fishes of the tidewater section of Pamunkey River, Virginia. Journal of the Washington Academy of Sciences 43: 424–432.

Raney, E. C., and R. D. Suttkus. 1948. The subspecies of the shielded darter, *Hadropterus peltatus*. In Abstracts of the 28th Annual Meeting of the American Society of Ichthyologists and Herpetologists.

Raney, E. C., and D. A. Webster. 1942. The spring migration of the common white sucker, *Catostomus c. commersonnii* (Lacepède), in Skaneateles Lake Inlet, New York. Copeia 1942:139–148.

Raney, E. C., and W. S. Woolcott. 1955. Races of the striped bass, *Roccus saxatilis* (Walbaum), in southwestern United States. Journal of Wildlife Management 19: 444–450.

Raney, E. C., W. S. Woolcott, and A. G. Mehring. 1954. Migratory pattern and racial structure of Atlantic Coast striped bass. Transactions of the North American Wildlife Conference 19:376–396.

Rankin, D. W. 1975. The continental margin of eastern North America in the southern Appalachians—The opening and closing of the Proto-Atlantic Ocean. American Journal of Science 275 A:298–336.

Rasmussen, R. P. 1980. Egg and larva development of the brook silversides from the Peace River, Florida. Transactions of the American Fisheries Society 109:407–416.

Rasquin, P. 1949. Spontaneous depigmentation in the catfish *Ameiurus nebulosus*. Copeia 1949:242–251.

Rawson, D. S. 1957. The life history and ecology of the yellow walleye, *Stizostedion vitreum*, in Lac la Ronge, Saskatchewan. Transactions of the American Fisheries Society 86:15–37.

Rawstron, R. R. 1964. Spawning of threadfin shad, *Dorosoma petenense*, at low temperatures. California Fish and Game 50:58.

Ray, L. E. 1971. Fish breeders newsletter 3. Brawley, California. (Not seen; cited in Pelzman 1971.)

Reagan, N. L., and J. L. West. 1984. Life history of the mottled sculpin in a western North Carolina stream. ASB (Association of Southeastern Biologists) Bulletin 31:78.

Reagan, N. L., and J. L. West. 1985. Life history of the mottled sculpin in a western North Carolina stream. Page 112 *in* Abstracts of the 65th Annual Meeting of the American Society of Ichthyologists and Herpetologists.

Reed, J. R. 1964. A racial study of the blueback herring, *Alosa aestivalis* (Mitchill). Master's thesis. Cornell University, Ithaca, New York.

Reed, J. R. 1980. An ecological investigation of the lower North Anna River. James R. Reed Associates, Annual Report January 1–December 31, 1979, to Virginia Electric and Power Company, Richmond.

Reed, J. R., and G. M. Simmons. 1976. Pre-operational environmental study of Lake Anna, Virginia. Final report, March 1972–December 1975 to Virginia Electric and Power Company, Richmond.

Reed, R. J. 1957a. The prolonged spawning of the rosyface shiner, *Notropis rubellus* (Agassiz), in northwestern Pennsylvania. Copeia 1957:250.

Reed, R. J. 1957b. Phases of the life history of the rosyface shiner, *Notropis rubellus*, in northern Pennsylvania. Copeia 1957:286–290.

Reed, R. J. 1958. The early life history of two cyprinids, *Notropis rubellus* and *Campostoma anomalum pullum*. Copeia 1958:325–327.

Reed, R. J. 1959. Age, growth, and food of the longnose dace, *Rhinichthys cataractae*, in northwestern Pennsylvania. Copeia 1959:160–162.

Reed, R. J. 1971. Biology of the fallfish, *Semotilus corporalis* (Pisces, Cyprinidae). Transactions of the American Fisheries Society 100:717–725.

Reed, R. J., and J. C. Moulton. 1973. Age and growth of blacknose dace, *Rhinichthys atratulus* and longnose dace, *R. cataractae* in Massachusetts. American Midland Naturalist 90:206–210.

Reeves, F. 1932. Thermal springs in Virginia. Virginia Geological Survey Bulletin 36.

Regier, G. 1976. The white amur caper. Audubon 78(5): 108–111.

Regier, H. A., V. C. Applegate, and R. A. Ryder. 1969. The ecology and management of the walleye in western Lake Erie. Great Lakes Fishery Commission Technical Report 15.

Reid, W. F. 1972. Utilization of the crayfish *Orconectes limosus* as forage by the white perch (*Morone americana*) in a

Maine lake. Transactions of the American Fisheries Society 101:608–612.

Reighard, J. 1910. Methods of studying the habits of fishes, with an account of the horned dace. U.S. Bureau of Fisheries Bulletin 28(1908):1113–1136.

Reighard, J. 1913. The breeding habits of the log-perch (*Percina caprodes*). Fifteenth Report of the Michigan Academy of Science 15:104–105.

Reighard, J. 1920. The breeding behavior of the suckers and minnows. Biological Bulletin (Woods Hole) 38:1–32.

Reighard, J. 1943. The breeding habits of the river chub, *Nocomis micropogon* (Cope). Papers of the Michigan Academy of Science, Arts and Letters 28:397–423.

Relyea, K. 1983. A systematic study of two species complexes of the genus *Fundulus* (Pisces: Cyprinodontidae). Bulletin of the Florida State Museum Biological Sciences 29:1–64.

Relyea, K., and B. Sutton. 1973. Cave dwelling yellow bullheads in Florida. Florida Scientist 36:31–34.

Renaud, C. B., and D. E. McAllister. 1988. Taxonomic status of the extinct Banff longnose dace, *Rhinichthys cataractae smithi*, of Banff National Park, Alberta. Environmental Biology of Fishes 23:95–113.

Renfro, J. L., and L. G. Hill. 1970. Factors influencing areal breathing and metabolism of gars (*Lepisosteus*). Southwestern Naturalist 15:45–54. (Not seen; cited in Moyle and Cech 1982.)

Reniers, P. 1941. The springs of Virginia: life, love, and death at the waters, 1775–1900. University of North Carolina Press, Chapel Hill.

Reno, H. W. 1969a. A partial nomenclatural review of *Hybopsis*. Proceedings of the Oklahoma Academy of Science 48:65–71.

Reno, H. W. 1969b. Cephalic lateral-line systems of the cyprinid genus *Hybopsis*. Copeia 1969:736–773.

Reno, H. W. 1971. The lateral-line system of the silverjaw minnow, *Ericymba buccata* Cope. Southwestern Naturalist 15:347–358.

Resh, V. C., D. S. White, S. A. Elbert, D. E. Jennings, and L. A. Krumholz. 1976. Vertebral variation in the emerald shiner *Notropis atherinoides* from the Ohio River: an apparent contradiction to "Jordan's Rule." Bulletin Southern California Academy of Sciences 75:76–84.

Rhodehamel, E. C., and C. W. Carlston. 1963. Geologic history of the Teays Valley in West Virginia. Geological Society of America Bulletin 74:251–273.

Rice, S. P., J. R. MacGregor, and W. L. Davis. 1983. Distributional records for fourteen fishes in Kentucky. Transactions of the Kentucky Academy of Science 44:125–128.

Rice, T. E., A. W. Niedorada, and A. P. Pratt. 1976. The coastal process and geology: Virginia barrier islands (Metomkin Island to Fisherman's Island). Virginia coast reserve study: ecosystem description, 1 (part B). Old Dominion University, Norfolk, Virginia, and The Nature Conservancy, Richmond, Virginia.

Richards, C. E., and R. L. Bailey. 1967. Occurrence of *Fundulus luciae*, spotfin killifish, on the seaside of Virginia's eastern shore. Chesapeake Science 8:204–205.

Richards, H. G. 1967. Stratigraphy of Atlantic Coastal Plain between Long Island and Georgia: review. American Association of Petroleum Geologists Bulletin 51:2400–2429.

Richards, H. G. 1974. Structural and stratigraphic framework of the Atlantic Coastal Plain. Pages 11–20 *in* R. Q. Oaks and J. R. DuBar, editors. Post-Miocene stratigraphy, central and southern Atlantic Coastal Plain. Utah State University Press, Logan.

Richards, H. G. 1975. United States—Atlantic Coastal Plain. Pages 531–541 *in* R. W. Fairbridge, editor. The encyclopedia of world regional geology, part 1: Western Hemisphere (including Antarctica and Australia). Dowden, Hutchinson and Ross, Stroudsburg, Pennsylvania.

Richards, H. G., and S. Judson. 1965. The Atlantic Coastal Plain and the Appalachian Highlands in the Quaternary. Pages 129–130 *in* H. E. Wright and D. G. Frey, editors. The Quaternary of the United States. Princeton University Press, Princeton, New Jersey.

Richards, W. J. 1966. Systematics of the percid fishes of the *Etheostoma thalassinum* species group with comments on the subgenus *Etheostoma*. Copeia 1966:823–838.

Richards, W. J., and L. W. Knapp. 1964. *Percina lenticula*, a new percid fish, with a redescription of the subgenus *Hadropterus*. Copeia 1964:690–701.

Richardson, F., and W. C. Carnes. 1964. Survey and classification of the New River and tributaries, North Carolina (with Appendix). North Carolina Wildlife Resources Commission, Federal Aid in Sport Fish Restoration, Project F-14-R, Job I–O. Final Report, Raleigh.

Richardson, L. R. 1939. The spawning behaviour of *Fundulus diaphanus* (Lesueur). Copeia 1939:165–167.

Richmond, N. D. 1940. Nesting of the sunfish, *Lepomis auritus* (Linnaeus), in tidal waters. Zoologica (New York) 25:329–331.

Richter, H.-J. 1989. The redhorse minnow—*Notropis lutrensis*. Tropical Fish Hobbyist 37(8):10–14, 16–17, 21.

Ricker, W. E., editor. 1971. Methods for assessment of fish production in fresh waters, 2nd edition. International Biological Programme Handbook 3. Blackwell Scientific, Oxford, UK.

Riddle, J. W. 1975. Status of the native muskellunge, *Esox masquinongy ohioensis*, of the Cumberland Plateau, Tennessee. Master's thesis. Tennessee Technological University, Cookeville.

Ridgway, M. S., G. P. Goff, and M. H. A. Keenleyside. 1989. Courtship and spawning behavior in smallmouth bass (*Micropterus dolomieui*). American Midland Naturalist 122:209–213.

Riggs, C. D., and G. A. Moore. 1960. Growth of young gar (*Lepisosteus*) in aquaria. Proceedings of the Oklahoma Academy of Science 40:44–46.

Rimsky-Korsakoff, V. N. 1930. The food of certain fishes of the Lake Champlain watershed. Pages 88–104 *in* A biological survey of the Champlain watershed. Supplemental to 19th Annual Report of the New York State Conservation Department, Albany.

Ringler, N. H. 1985. Individual and temporal variation in

prey switching by brown trout, *Salmo trutta*. Copeia 1985:918–926.

Rivas, L. R. 1963. Subgenera and species groups in the poeciliid fish genus *Gambusia* Poey. Copeia 1963:331–347.

Rivas, L. R. 1966. The taxonomic status of the cyprinodontid fish *Fundulus notti* and *F. lineolatus*. Copeia 1966:353–354.

Robbins, W. H., and H. R. MacCrimmon. 1974. The blackbass in America and overseas. Biomanagement Research Enterprises, Sault Ste. Marie, Ontario.

Roberts, J. K. 1928. The geology of the Virginia Triassic. Virginia Geological Survey Bulletin 29.

Roberts, N. J., and H. E. Winn. 1962. Utilization of the senses in feeding behavior of the johnny darter, *Etheostoma nigrum*. Copeia 1962:567–570.

Roberts, T. R. 1982. Unculi (horny projections arising from single cells), an adaptive feature of ostariophysan fishes. Zoologica Scripta 11:55–76.

Robins, C. R. 1954. A taxonomic revision of the *Cottus bairdi* and *Cottus carolinae* species groups in eastern North America (Pisces, Cottidae). Doctoral dissertation. Cornell University, Ithaca, New York.

Robins, C. R. 1961. Two new cottid fishes from the fresh waters of eastern United States. Copeia 1961:305–315.

Robins, C. R., D. M. Cohen, and C. H. Robins. 1979. The eels, *Anguilla* and *Histiobranchus*, photographed on the floor of the deep Atlantic in the Bahamas. Bulletin of Marine Science 29:401–405.

Robins, C. R., and R. R. Miller. 1957. Classification, variation, and distribution of the sculpins, genus *Cottus*, inhabiting Pacific slope waters in California and southern Oregon, with a key to the species. California Fish and Game 43:213–233.

Robins, C. R., and E. C. Raney. 1956. Studies of the catostomid fishes of the genus *Moxostoma*, with descriptions of two new species. Cornell University Agricultural Experiment Station, Memoir 343, Ithaca, New York.

Robins, C. R., and E. C. Raney. 1957. The systematic status of the suckers of the genus *Moxostoma* from Texas, New Mexico and Mexico. Tulane Studies in Zoology 5:291–318.

Robins, C. R., G. C. Ray, J. Douglas, and R. Freund. 1986. A field guide to Atlantic Coast fishes of North America. Houghton Mifflin, Boston.

Robins, C. R., and H. W. Robison. 1985. *Cottus hypselurus*, a new cottid fish from the Ozark uplands, Arkansas and Missouri. American Midland Naturalist 114:360–373.

Robins, C. R., and six coauthors. 1980. A list of common and scientific names of fishes from the United States and Canada, 4th edition. American Fisheries Society Special Publication 12.

Robins, C. R., and six coauthors. 1991. Common and scientific names of fishes from the United States and Canada, 5th edition. American Fisheries Society Special Publication 20.

Robinson, J. M., and B. A. Branson. 1980. The fishes of Marrowbone Creek, Pike County, Kentucky, with notes on the effects of coal mining. Transactions of the Kentucky Academy of Science 41:57–59.

Robinson, J. W. 1966. Observations on the life history, movement, and harvest of the paddlefish, *Polyodon spathula*, in Montana. Proceedings of the Montana Academy of Sciences 26:33–44.

Robison, H. W. 1977. Distribution, habitat notes, and status of the ironcolor shiner, *Notropis chalybaeus* Cope, in Arkansas. Arkansas Academy of Science Proceedings 31:92–94.

Rodgers, J. 1970. The tectonics of the Appalachians. Wiley, New York.

Rogers, J. S., and R. C. Cashner. 1987. Genetic variation, divergence, and relationships in the subgenus *Xenisma* of the genus *Fundulus*. Pages 251–264 *in* W. J. Matthews and D. C. Heins. Community and evolutionary ecology of North American stream fishes. University of Oklahoma Press, Norman.

Rogier, C. G., J. J. Ney, and B. J. Turner. 1985. Electrophoretic analysis of genetic variability in a landlocked striped bass population. Transactions of the American Fisheries Society 114:244–249.

Rohde, F. C. 1974. Percidae—perches. Pages 196–205 *in* A. J. Lippson and R. L. Moran, editors. Manual for identification of early developmental stages of fishes of the Potomac River estuary. Maryland Department of Natural Resources, Power Plant Siting Program Miscellaneous Publication 13, Annapolis.

Rohde, F. C. 1979. Systematics of the American brook lamprey, *Lampetra* (*Lethenteron*) *lamottenii* (Lesueur) (Pisces: Petromyzonidae). Master's thesis. University of North Carolina, Chapel Hill.

Rohde, F. C., and R. G. Arndt. 1981. Life history of a Coastal Plain population of the mottled sculpin, *Cottus bairdi* (Osteichthyes: Cottidae). Brimleyana 7:69–94.

Rohde, F. C., R. G. Arndt, and J. C. S. Wang. 1975. Records of freshwater lampreys, *Lampetra lamottenii* and *Okkelbergia aepyptera*, from the Delmarva Peninsula (East Coast, United States). Chesapeake Science 16:70–72.

Rohde, F. C., R. G. Arndt, and J. C. S. Wang. 1976. Life history of the freshwater lampreys, *Okkelbergia aepyptera* and *Lampetra lamottenii* (Pisces: Petromyzonidae), on the Delmarva Peninsula (East Coast, United States). Bulletin of the Southern California Academy of Sciences 75:99–111.

Rohde, F. C., G. H. Burgess, and G. W. Link. 1979. Freshwater fishes of Croatan National Forest, North Carolina, with comments on the zoogeography of Coastal Plain fishes. Brimleyana 2:97–118.

Rohde, F. C., and S. W. Ross. 1986. Life history of the swampfish, *Chologaster cornuta*, with comments on morphological changes. ASB (Association of Southeastern Biologists) Bulletin 33:83.

Rollwagen, J., and D. Stainken. 1980. Ectoparasites and feeding behavoir of the blacknose dace, *Rhinichthys atratulus* (Cyprinidae: Cypriniformes) Hermann. American Midland Naturalist 103:185–190.

Romer, A. S. 1964. Cope *versus* Marsh. Systematic Zoology 13:201–207.

Rosebery, D. A. 1950a. Game fisheries investigations of

Claytor Lake, a mainstream impoundment of New River, Pulaski County, Virginia, with emphasis on *Micropterus punctulatus* (Rafinesque). Doctoral dissertation. Virginia Polytechnic Institute, Blacksburg.

Rosebery, D. A. 1950b. Fishery management of Claytor Lake, an impoundment on the New River in Virginia. Transactions of the American Fisheries Society 80:194–209.

Rosebery, D. A, and R. R. Bowers. 1952. Under the cover of Lake Drummond. Virginia Wildlife 13(8):21–23.

Rosen, D. E. 1962. Comments on the relationships of the North American cavefishes of the family Amblyopsidae. American Museum Novitates 2109.

Rosen, D. E. 1973. Suborder Cyprinodontoidei, superfamily Cyprinodontoidea, families Cyprinodontidae, Poeciliidae, Anablepidae. Pages 229–262 *in* Fishes of the western North Atlantic, Part 6. Sears Foundation for Marine Research, Yale University, New Haven, Connecticut.

Rosen, D. E. 1974. Phylogeny and zoogeography of salmoniform fishes and relationships of *Lepidogalaxias salamandroides*. Bulletin of the American Museum of Natural History 153:265–326.

Rosen, D. E. 1979. Fishes from the uplands and intermontane basins of Guatemala: revisionary studies and comparative geography. Bulletin of the American Museum of Natural History 162:267–376.

Rosen, D. E. 1985a. An essay on euteleostean classification. American Museum Novitates 2827.

Rosen, D. E. 1985b. Geological hierarchies and biogeographic congruence in the Caribbean. Annals of the Missouri Botanical Garden 72:636–659.

Rosen, D. E., and R. M. Bailey. 1963. The poeciliid fishes (Cyprinodontiformes), their structure, zoogeography, and systematics. Bulletin of the American Museum of Natural History 126:1–176.

Rosen, D. E., P. L. Forey, B. G. Gardiner, and C. Patterson. 1981. Lungfishes, tetrapods, paleontology, and plesiomorphy. Bulletin of the American Museum of Natural History 167:159–275.

Rosen, D. E., and P. H. Greenwood. 1970. Origin of the Weberian apparatus and the relationships of the ostariophysan and gonorynchiform fishes. American Museum Novitates 2428.

Rosen, D. E., and L. R. Parenti. 1981. Relationships of *Oryzias*, and the groups of atherinomorph fishes. American Museum Novitates 2719.

Rosen, D. E., and C. Patterson. 1969. The structure and relationships of the paracanthopterygian fishes. Bulletin of the American Museum of Natural History 141:357–474.

Rosen, R. A., and D. C. Hales. 1981. Feeding of the paddlefish, *Polyodon spathula*. Copeia 1981:441–445.

Ross, D. F. 1974. Tuberculation in the silverjaw minnow, *Ericymba buccata*. Copeia 1974:271–272.

Ross, H. H. 1974. Biological systematics. Addison-Wesley, Reading, Massachusetts.

Ross, M. R. 1976. Nest–entry behavior of female creek chubs (*Semotilus atromaculatus*) in different habitats. Copeia 1976:378–380.

Ross, M. R. 1977a. Function of creek chub (*Semotilus atro-maculatus*) nest-building. Ohio Journal of Science 77:36–37.

Ross, M. R. 1977b. Aggression as a social mechanism in the creek chub (*Semotilus atromaculatus*). Copeia 1977:393–397.

Ross, M. R. 1983. The frequency of nest construction and satellite male behavior in the fallfish minnow. Environmental Biology of Fishes 9:65–70.

Ross, M. R., and T. M. Cavender. 1977. First report of the natural cyprinid hybrid, *Notropis cornutus* × *Rhinichthys cataractae*, from Ohio. Copeia 1977:777–780.

Ross, M. R., and T. M. Cavender. 1981. Morphological analyses of four experimental intergeneric cyprinid hybrid crosses. Copeia 1981:377–387.

Ross, M. R., and R. J. Reed. 1978. The reproductive behavior of the fallfish *Semotilus corporalis*. Copeia 1978:215–221.

Ross, R. D. 1952. Subspecies and races of the cyprinid fish *Campostoma anomalum* (Rafinesque) in eastern United States. Doctoral dissertation. Cornell University, Ithaca, New York.

Ross, R. D. 1958a. Races of the cyprinid fish *Campostoma anomalum pullum* (Agassiz) in eastern United States. Virginia Agricultural Experiment Station Technical Bulletin 136.

Ross, R. D. 1958b. Some taxonomic problems of Shenandoah River fishes. Virginia Agricultural Experiment Station Technical Bulletin 137.

Ross, R. D. 1959a. Game fish streams and records of fishes from the Potomac–Shenandoah River system of Virginia. Virginia Agricultural Experiment Station Technical Bulletin 140.

Ross, R. D. 1959b. A key to the fishes of the Shenandoah River system of Virginia. Virginia Agricultural Experiment Station Technical Bulletin 142.

Ross, R. D. 1959c. Drainage evolution and distribution problems of the fishes of the New (upper Kanawha) River system in Virginia, part 4—key to the identification of fishes. Virginia Agricultural Experiment Station Technical Bulletin 146.

Ross, R. D. 1962. A preliminary report on studies made of the fishes of the southern Appalachians. Report to National Science Foundation, February 21, 1962 (Grant B-8288), Washington, D.C.

Ross, R. D. 1969. Drainage evolution and fish distribution problems in the southern Appalachians of Virginia. Virginia Polytechnic Institute and State University Research Division Monograph 1:277–292.

Ross, R. D. 1972a. The drainage history of the Tennessee River. Virginia Polytechnic Institute and State University Research Division Monograph 4:11–42.

Ross, R. D. 1972b. Fish studies. Pages 21–30 *in* J. Cairns and K. C. Dickson. An ecosystematic study of the South River, Virginia. Virginia Polytechnic Institute and State University Water Resources Research Center Bulletin 54.

Ross, R. D. 1973. Effects of Radford Army Ammunition Plant wastes on the fishes of the New River, Virginia. Virginia Polytechnic Institute and State University Water Resources Research Center Bulletin 57:43–52.

Ross, R. D., and J. E. Carico. 1963. Records and distribution problems of fishes of the North, Middle, and South forks of the Holston River, Virginia. Virginia Agricultural Experiment Station Technical Bulletin 161.

Ross, R. D., and G. E. Lewis. 1969. Stream survey of District II, West Virginia. West Virginia Department of Natural Resources, Federal Aid in Sport Fish Restoration, Project F-10-R-(1-11). Charleston.

Ross, R. D., and M. T. Masnik. 1971. A report of the fishes collected in the Clinch River. ASB (Association of Southeastern Biologists) Bulletin 18:53.

Ross, R. D., and B. D. Perkins. 1959. Drainage evolution and distribution problems of the fishes of the New (upper Kanawha) River system in Virginia, part 3: records of fishes of the New River. Virginia Agricultural Experiment Station Technical Bulletin 145.

Ross, S. T. 1986. Resource partitioning in fish assemblages: a review of field studies. Copeia 1986:352–388.

Ross, S. W., F. C. Rohde, and D. G. Lindquist. 1988. Endangered, threatened and rare fauna of North Carolina, part III: a re-evaluation of the marine and estuarine fishes. Occasional Papers of the North Carolina Biological Survey 1988-7.

Rostlund, E. 1952. Freshwater fish and fishing in native North America. University of California Publications in Geography 9:1–314.

Roth, J. C., and S. E. Neff. 1964. Studies of physical limnology and profundal bottom fauna, Mountain Lake, Virginia. Virginia Agricultural Experiment Station Technical Bulletin 169.

Rothschild, B. J. 1962. The life history of the alewife, *Alosa pseudoharengus* (Wilson) in Cayuga Lake, New York. Doctoral dissertation. Cornell University, Ithaca, New York.

Rothschild, B. J. 1966. Observations on the alewife (*Alosa pseudoharengus*) in Cayuga Lake. New York Fish and Game Journal 13:188–195.

Rounsefell, G. A. 1962. Relationships among North American Salmonidae. U.S. Fish and Wildlife Service Fishery Bulletin 209.

Rouse, P. 1975. Virginia: a pictorial history. Scribner, New York.

Rozas, L. P., and W. E. Odum. 1987a. Use of tidal freshwater marshes by fishes and macrofaunal crustaceans along a marsh stream-order gradient. Estuaries 10:36–43.

Rozas, L. P., and W. E. Odum. 1987b. The role of submerged aquatic vegetation in influencing the abundance of nekton on contiguous tidal fresh-water marshes. Journal of Experimental Marine Biology and Ecology 114:289–300.

Rozas, L. P., and W. E. Odum. 1987c. Fish and macrocrustacean use of submerged plant beds in tidal freshwater marsh creeks. Marine Ecology Progress Series 38:101–108.

Rubec, P. J., and S. U. Qadri. 1982. Comparative age, growth, and condition of brown bullhead, *Ictalurus nebulosus*, in sections of the Ottawa River, Canada. Canadian Field-Naturalist 96:6–18.

Ruelle, R., and P. L. Hudson. 1977. Paddlefish (*Polyodon spathula*): growth and food of young of the year and a suggested technique for measuring length. Transactions of the American Fisheries Society 106:609–613.

Russell, S. C. 1976. The food habits of *Ictalurus natalis*, *Centrarchus macropterus*, and *Perca flavescens* in Lake Drummond in the Dismal Swamp of Virginia. Master's thesis. Old Dominion University, Norfolk, Virginia.

Russell, T. R. 1986. Biology and life history of the paddlefish—a review. Pages 2–20 *in* J. G. Dillard, L. K. Graham, and T. R. Russell, editors. The paddlefish: status, management and propagation. American Fisheries Society, North Central Division, Special Publication 7, Bethesda, Maryland.

Ryder, J. A. 1887. On the development of osseus fishes including marine and freshwater forms. Pages 489–544 *in* U.S. Commission of Fish and Fisheries Report for 1885, Part 13, Appendix 2.

Ryder, J. A. 1890. The sturgeon and sturgeon industries of the eastern coast of the United States, with an account of experiments bearing upon sturgeon culture. U.S. Fish Commission Bulletin 8(1888):231–238.

Ryder, R. A., W. B. Scott, and E. J. Crossman. 1964. Fishes of northern Ontario, north of the Albany River. Royal Ontario Museum, Life Sciences Contribution 60.

Sadzikowski, M. R., and D. C. Wallace. 1976. A comparison of the food habits of size classes of three sunfishes (*Lepomis macrochirus* Rafinesque, *L. gibbosus* (Linnaeus) and *L. cyanellus* Rafinesque). American Midland Naturalist 95:220–225.

Saecker, J. R., and W. S. Woolcott. 1988. The redbreast sunfish (*Lepomis auritus*) in a thermally influenced section of the James River, Virginia. Virginia Journal of Science 39:1–17.

Saga, J. J. 1973. Population dynamics of the cutlips minnow, *Exoglossum maxillingua*, from a hard-water and a soft-water stream. Master's thesis. Pennsylvania State University, University Park. (Not seen; cited in Haase and Haase 1975.)

Sanderson, A. E. 1958. Smallmouth bass management in the Potomac River basin. Transactions of the North American Wildlife Conference 23:248–262.

Sapir, G. L. 1979. "New" world-record brown trout. Field and Stream February:58, 126–130.

Satô, M. 1941. A comparative observation of the hindbrain of fish possessing barbels, with special reference to their feeding habits. Science Reports of the Tôhoku Imperial University, 4th Series (Biology) 16(2):157–164.

Saunders, J. W., and M. W. Smith. 1965. Changes in a stream population of trout associated with increased silt. Journal of the Fisheries Research Board of Canada 22:395–404.

Savage, T. 1962. *Cottus girardi* Robins, a synonym of *Cottus bairdi* Girard. Copeia 1962:848–850.

Savage, T. 1963. Reproductive behavior of the mottled sculpin, *Cottus bairdi* Girard. Copeia 1963:317–325.

Sawara, Y. 1974. Reproduction in the mosquitofish (*Gambusia affinis affinis*), a freshwater fish introduced into Japan. Japanese Journal of Ecology 24:140–146. (Not seen; cited in Hughes 1985.)

Sawyer, P. J. 1960. A new geographic record for the American brook lamprey, *Lampetra lamottei*. Copeia 1960:136–137.

Saylor, C. F., and D. A. Etnier. 1976. Rediscovery of the sharphead darter, *Etheostoma acuticeps* Bailey, in the lower Nolichucky River, Tennessee. ASB (Association of Southeastern Biologists) Bulletin 23:93–94.

Saylor, C. F., D. M. Hill, S. A. Ahlstedt, and A. M. Brown. 1988. Middle Fork Holston River watershed biological assessment summers of 1986 and 1987. Tennessee Valley Authority, Division of Air and Water Resources, TVA/ONRED/AWR-88/20, Chattanooga, Tennessee.

Scarola, J. F. 1973. Freshwater fishes of New Hampshire. New Hampshire Fish and Game Department, Division of Inland and Marine Fisheries, Concord.

Schaefer, S. A., and T. M. Cavender. 1986. Geographic variation and subspecific status of *Notropis spilopterus* (Pisces: Cyprinidae). Copeia 1986:122–130.

Schaeffer, J. S., and F. J. Margraf. 1986. Food of white perch (*Morone americana*) and potential for competition with yellow perch (*Perca flavescens*) in Lake Erie. Ohio Journal of Science 86:26–29.

Schemske, D. W. 1974. Age, length and fecundity of the creek chub, *Semotilus atromaculatus* (Mitchill), in central Illinois. American Midland Naturalist 92:505–509.

Schlee, J. 1957. Upland gravels of southern Maryland. Geological Society of America Bulletin 68:1371–1410.

Schlosser, I. J., and L. A. Toth. 1984. Niche relationships and population ecology of rainbow (*Etheostoma caeruleum*) and fantail (*E. flabellare*) darters in a temporally variable environment. Oikos 42:229–238.

Schmidt, J. 1925. The breeding places of the eel. Annual Report of the Smithsonian Institution 1924:279–316. (Not seen; cited in Robins et al. 1979.)

Schmidt, R. E. 1980. New distribution records of freshwater fishes in North Carolina. Journal of the Elisha Mitchell Scientific Society 96:36–38.

Schmidt, R. E. 1983. Variation in barbels of *Rhinichthys cataractae* (Pisces: Cyprinidae) in southeastern New York with comments on phylogeny and functional morphology. Journal of Freshwater Ecology 2:239–246.

Schmidt, R. E. 1985. Cutlips minnows in the aquarium. American Currents (November):3.

Schmidt, R. E. 1986. Zoogeography of the northern Appalachians. Pages 137–159 *in* Hocutt and Wiley (1986).

Schmidt, R. E., C. L. Smith, and P. R. Warny. 1984. Discovery of the brook lamprey (Pisces: Petromyzontidae) in Long Island's fresh waters. Northeastern Environmental Science 3:73–74.

Schmidt, R. E., and W. R. Whitworth. 1979. Distribution and habitat of the swamp darter (*Etheostoma fusiforme*) in southern New England. American Midland Naturalist 102:408–413.

Schneider, R. W. 1969. Some aspects of the life history of the gizzard shad, *Dorosoma cepedianum*, in Smith Mountain Lake, Virginia. Master's thesis. Virginia Polytechnic Institute and State University, Blacksburg.

Schontz, C. J. 1962. The effects of altitude and latitude on the morphometry, meristics, growth and fecundity of the eastern blacknose dace, *Rhinichthys atratulus atratulus* (Hermann). Doctoral dissertation. University of Pittsburgh, Pittsburgh, Pennsylvania.

Schubel, J. R., and C. F. Zambawa. 1973. Susquehanna River paleochannel connects lower reaches of Chester, Miles and Choptank estuaries. Chesapeake Science 14:58–62.

Schultz, L. P. 1926. Temperature-controlled variation in the golden shiner, *Notemigonus crysoleucas*. Papers of the Michigan Academy of Science, Arts and Letters 7:417–433.

Schultz, L. P. 1939. The fresh-water fishes of Virginia. Pages 55–58 *in* Exploration and field-work of the Smithsonian Institution in 1938. Smithsonian Institution, Washington, D.C.

Schultz, R. J. 1971. Special adaptive problems associated with unisexual fishes. American Zoologist 11:351–360.

Schultze, H. P., and E. O. Wiley. 1984. The neopterygian *Amia* as a living fossil. Pages 153–159 *in* N. Eldredge and S. M. Stanley. Living fossils. Springer-Verlag, New York.

Schumm, S. A. 1965. Quaternary paleohydrology. Pages 783–794 *in* H. E. Wright and D. G. Frey, editors. The Quaternary of the United States. Princeton University Press, Princeton, New Jersey.

Schwartz, F. J. 1958a. The breeding behavior of the southern blacknose dace, *Rhinichthys atratulus obtusus* Agassiz. Copeia 1958:141–143.

Schwartz, F. J. 1958b. Threadfin shad—a new forage fish for West Virginia. West Virginia Conservation June(1958):6–7.

Schwartz, F. J. 1959. Records of the Allegheny brook lamprey *Ichthyomyzon greeleyi* Hubbs and Trautman, from West Virginia, with comments on its occurrence with *Lampetra aeptypera* (Abbott). Ohio Journal of Science 59:217–220.

Schwartz, F. J. 1961. Food, age, growth, and morphology of the blackbanded sunfish, *Enneacanthus c. chaetodon*, in Smithville Pond, Maryland. Chesapeake Science 2:82–88.

Schwartz, F. J. 1963. The fresh-water minnows of Maryland. Maryland Conservationist 40(2):19–29.

Schwartz, F. J. 1964. Natural salinity tolerances of some freshwater fishes. Underwater Naturalist 2(2):13–15.

Schwartz, F. J. 1965a. Densities and ecology of the darters of the upper Allegheny River watershed. Pages 95–103 *in* Tryon, C. A., R. T. Hartman, and K. W. Cummins, editors. Studies on the aquatic ecology of the upper Ohio River system. University of Pittsburgh, Pymatuning Laboratory of Ecology, Special Publication 3, Pittsburgh, Pennsylvania.

Schwartz, F. J. 1965b. The distribution and probable postglacial dispersal of the percid fish, *Etheostoma b. blennioides*, in the Potomac River. Copeia 1965:285–290.

Schwartz, F. J. 1967. Fishes of the headwaters of Shavers Fork. Pages 35–44 *in* E. L. Core, editor. Natural History of the Cass Scenic Railroad. West Virginia University Library, Morgantown.

Schwartz, F. J. Circa 1969. Bull minnows? Maryland Conservationist 44(3):2–5.

Schwartz, F. J. 1972. World literature to fish hybrids with an analysis by family, species, and hybrid. Publications of the Gulf Coast Research Laboratory Museum 3.

Schwartz, F. J. 1981a. World literature to fish hybrids with an analysis by family, species, and hybrid: Supplement 1. NOAA (National Oceanic and Atmospheric Administration) Technical Report, NMFS (National Marine Fisheries Service), SSRF (Special Scientific Report Fisheries)-750.

Schwartz, F. J. 1981b. Effects of freshwater runoff on fishes occupying the freshwater and estuarine coastal watersheds of North Carolina. U.S. Fish and Wildlife Service Biological Services Program FWS-OBS-81/04:282–294.

Schwartz, F. J., and B. W. Dutcher. 1962. Tooth replacement and food of the cyprinid *Notropis cerasinus* from the Roanoke River, Virginia. American Midland Naturalist 68:369–375.

Schwartz, F. J., and P. A. Howland. 1978. Evaluating gear and factors affecting catch and sampling variation. Institute of Marine Science Special Scientific Report, University of North Carolina, Morehead City.

Schwartz, F. J., and R. Jachowski. 1965. The age, growth, and length–weight relationship of the Patuxent River, Maryland ictalurid white catfish, *Ictalurus catus*. Chesapeake Science 6:226–237.

Schwiebert, E. 1983. A centennial of *Salmo trutta*. Trout 24(1):14–26.

Scofield, N. B., and H. C. Bryant. 1926. The striped bass in California. California Fish and Game 12(2):55–74. (Not seen; cited in Hardy 1978b.)

Scopettone, G. G., M. Coleman, and G. A. Wedemeyer. 1986. Life history and status of the endangered cui-ui of Pyramid Lake, Nevada. U.S. Fish and Wildlife Service Fish and Wildlife Research 1.

Scott, D. C. 1949. A study of a stream population of rock bass, *Ambloplites rupestris*. Investigations of Indiana Lakes and Streams 3:169–234.

Scott, W. B. 1956. Wendigo, the hybrid trout. Royal Ontario Museum, Division of Zoology and Paleontology, Toronto.

Scott, W. B. 1967. Freshwater fishes of eastern Canada, 1st edition. University of Toronto Press, Toronto.

Scott, W. B., and W. J. Christie. 1963. The invasion of the lower Great Lakes by the white perch, *Roccus americanus* (Gmelin). Journal of the Fisheries Research Board of Canada 20:1189–1195.

Scott, W. B., and E. J. Crossman. 1964. Fishes occurring in the fresh waters of insular Newfoundland. Royal Ontario Museum Life Sciences Contribution 5.

Scott, W. B., and E. J. Crossman. 1973. Freshwater fishes of Canada. Fisheries Research Board of Canada Bulletin 184.

Seagle, H. H., and A. C. Hendricks. 1979. Evaluation of the impact of E. I. du Pont de Nemours and Company, Inc., effluent on the South River, Virginia. Center for Environmental Studies, Virginia Polytechnic Institute and State University, Blacksburg.

Seagle, H. H., and J. W. Nagel. 1982. Life cycle and fecundity of the American brook lamprey, *Lampetra appendix*, in Tennessee. Copeia 1982:362–366.

Seal, W. P. 1914. *Mesognistius chaetodon*: an account of its breeding and other habits. Aquarium Notes News 1(7). (Reprinted in American Currents July/August 1986.)

Seaman, E. A. 1979. Observations on *Carassius auratus* (Linnaeus) harvesting *Potamogeton foliosus* Raf. in a small pond in northern Virginia. Fisheries (Bethesda) 4:24–25.

Seaman, W. 1968. Distribution and variation of the American cyprinid fish *Notropis hudsonius* (Clinton). Master's thesis. University of Florida, Gainesville.

Seeb, J. E., L. W. Seeb, D. W. Oates, and F. M. Utter. 1987. Genetic variation and postglacial dispersal of populations of northern pike (*Esox lucius*) in North America. Canadian Journal of Fisheries and Aquatic Sciences 44:556–561.

Seifert, M. F. 1963. Some aspects of territorial behavior of the fantail darter. Proceedings of the Iowa Academy of Science 70:224–227.

Settles, W. H., and R. D. Hoyt. 1976. Age structure, growth patterns, and food habits of the southern redbelly dace *Chrosomus erythrogaster* in Kentucky. Transactions of the Kentucky Academy of Science 37:1–10.

Settles, W. H., and R. D. Hoyt. 1978. The reproductive biology of the southern redbelly dace, *Chrosomus erythrogaster* Rafinesque, in a spring-fed stream in Kentucky. American Midland Naturalist 99:290–298.

Setzler, E. M., and eight coauthors. 1980. Synopsis of biological data on striped bass, *Morone saxatilis* (Walbaum). NOAA (National Oceanic and Atmospheric Administration) Technical Report NMFS (U.S. National Marine Fisheries Service) Circular 433.

Sevebeck, K. P., J. H. Kahn, and N. L. Chapman. 1986. Virginia's waters. Virginia Polytechnic Institute and State University Water Resources Research Center, Blacksburg.

Seversmith, H. F. 1953. Distribution, morphology and life history of *Lampetra aepyptera*, a brook lamprey, in Maryland. Copeia 1953:225–232.

Shackleton, N. J., and N. D. Opdyke. 1976. Oxygen-isotope and paleomagnetic stratigraphy of Pacific core V28-239 late Pliocene to latest Pleistocene. Geological Society of America Memoir 145:449–464.

Shackleton, N. J., and N. D. Opdyke. 1977. Oxygen isotope and palaeomagnetic evidence for early Northern Hemisphere glaciation. Nature 270:216–219.

Shaklee, J. B., M. J. Champion, and G. S. Whitt. 1974. Developmental genetics of teleosts: a biochemical analysis of lake chubsucker ontogeny. Developmental Biology 38:356–382. (Not seen; cited in Fuiman 1982c.)

Shapiro, S. 1947. Geographic variation in *Fundulus diaphanus*, a cyprinodont fish. Doctoral dissertation. University of Michigan, Ann Arbor. (Not seen; cited in Lee et al. 1980.)

Shapiro, S. M. 1975. A bibliography of the spottail shiner, *Notropis hudsonius* (Clinton) (Pisces: Cyprinidae). Massachusetts Cooperative Fishery Research Unit, Publication 43, Boston.

Sheldon, A. L. 1988. Conservation of stream fishes: patterns of diversity, rarity, and risk. Conservation Biology 2:149–159.

Shelton, W. L., and B. G. Grinstead. 1973. Hybridization between *Dorosoma cepedianum* and *D. petenense* in Lake Texoma, Oklahoma. Proceedings of the Annual Conference Southeastern Association of Game and Fish Commissioners 26(1972):506–510.

Shepard, T. E., and B. M. Burr. 1984. Systematics, status,

and life history aspects of the ashy darter, *Etheostoma cinereum* (Pisces: Percidae). Proceedings of the Biological Society of Washington 97:693–715.

Sheridan, J. R. 1962. Copper sulphate toxicity study. Virginia Commission of Game and Inland Fisheries, Federal Aid in Sport Fish Restoration, Project F-5-R-8, Job 7, July 1, 1961–June 30, 1962. Job Completion Report, Richmond.

Sheridan, J. 1963. General survey. Virginia Commission of Game and Inland Fisheries, Federal Aid in Sport Fish Restoration, Project F-5-R-8, Job 9, July 1, 1961–December 31, 1962. Job Completion Report, Richmond.

Sheridan, J., B. Domrose, and B. Wollitz. 1960. Striped bass spawning investigations. Virginia Commission of Game and Inland Fisheries, Federal Aid in Sport Fish Restoration, Project F-5-R-6, July 1, 1959–June 30, 1960. Progress Report, Richmond.

Shideler, G. L., J. C. Ludwick, G. F. Oertel, and K. Finkelstein. 1984. Quaternary stratigraphic evolution of the southern Delmarva Peninsula coastal zone, Cape Charles, Virginia. Geological Society of America Bulletin 95:489–502.

Shields, A. R. 1944. Observations on the migration of fishes from the Cherokee Reservoir. Journal of the Tennessee Academy of Science 19:42–44.

Shields, M. A., and C. H. Mayes. 1983. Occurrence and habitat preference of *Fundulus luciae* (Baird) (Pisces: Cyprinodontidae) on a southeastern North Carolina salt marsh. Brimleyana 9:141–144.

Shingleton, M. V. 1985. Life history of the New River shiner *Notropis scabriceps* (Cope), in the East Fork of the Greenbrier River, West Virginia. Master's thesis. Frostburg State College, Frostburg, Maryland.

Shingleton, M. V., C. H. Hocutt, and J. R. Stauffer. 1981. Temperature preference of the New River shiner. Transactions of the American Fisheries Society 110:660–661.

Shireman, J. V. 1984. Control of aquatic weeds with exotic fishes. Pages 302–312 *in* W. R. Courtenay and J. R. Stauffer, editors. Distribution, biology, and management of exotic fishes. Johns Hopkins University Press, Baltimore, Maryland.

Shireman, J. V., and C. R. Smith. 1983. Synopsis of biological data on the grass carp, *Ctenopharyngodon idella* (Cuvier and Valenciennes, 1844). FAO (Food and Agriculture Organization of the United Nations) Fisheries Synopsis 135.

Shireman, J. V., R. L. Stetler, and D. E. Colle. 1978. Possible use of the lake chubsucker as a baitfish. Progressive Fish-Culturist 40:33–34.

Shuber, D. J., and C. A. Sledd. 1981. Lake Chesdin research study. Virginia Commission of Game and Inland Fisheries, Federal Aid in Sport Fish Restoration, Project F-33-R, January 1, 1976–December 31, 1980. Project Completion Report, Richmond.

Shuler, E. W. 1945. Rocks and rivers. Jaques Cattell Press, Lancaster, Pennsylvania.

Shute, J. R. 1984. A systematic evaluation of the Waccamaw darter, *Etheostoma perlongum* (Hubbs and Raney), with comments on relationships within the subgenus *Boleosoma* (Percidae: Etheostomatini). Master's thesis. University of Tennessee, Knoxville.

Shute, J. R., P. W. Shute, and D. G. Lindquist. 1981. Fishes of the Waccamaw River drainage. Brimleyana 6:1–24.

Shute, P. W. 1984. Ecology of the rare yellowfin madtom, *Noturus flavipinnis* Taylor, in Citico Creek, Tennessee. Master's thesis. University of Tennessee, Knoxville.

Shute, P. W., J. R. Shute, and D. G. Lindquist. 1982. Age, growth and early life history of the Waccamaw darter, *Etheostoma perlongum*. Copeia 1982:561–567.

Sideleva, V. G. 1979. Morphological characteristics of the lateral line system in the Eurasian sculpin of the subfamily Cottinae (Cottidae). Journal of Ichthyology 19(3):45–55 .

Sidell, B. D., R. G. Otto, and D. A. Powers. 1978. A biochemical method for distinction of striped bass and white perch larvae. Copeia 1978:340–343.

Siebert, D. J. 1982. Interrelationships of catostomid genera. *In* Abstracts of the 62nd Annual Meeting of the American Society of Ichthyologists and Herpetologists.

Siebert, D. J. 1984. Cyprinoid interrelationships: gill arch structure and vascularization. Page 192 *in* Abstracts of the 64th Annual Meeting of the American Society of Ichthyologists and Herpetologists.

Sigler, W. F. 1948. Determination of sex in the white bass, *Lepibema chrysops*, from external characters. Copeia 1948:299–300.

Simmons, C. E., and R. C. Heath. 1979. Water-quality characteristics of streams in forested and rural areas of North Carolina. U.S. Geological Survey Water Resources Investigations Report 79-108, U.S. Geological Survey, Raleigh, North Carolina.

Simmons, G. M., and S. E. Neff. 1973. Observations on limnetic carbon assimilation rates in Mountain Lake, Virginia during its thermal stratification periods. Virginia Journal of Science 24:206–211.

Simon, T. P., and R. Wallus. 1989. Contributions to the early life histories of gar (Actinopterygii: Lepisosteidae) in the Ohio and Tennessee river basins with emphasis on larval development. Transactions of the Kentucky Academy of Science 50:59–74.

Simon, T. P., R. Wallus, and K. B. Floyd. 1987. Descriptions of protolarvae of seven species of the subgenus *Nothonotus* (Percidae: Etheostomatini) with comments on intrasubgeneric characteristics. American Fisheries Society Symposium 2:179–190.

Simons, A. M. 1991. The phylogenetic relationships of the crystal darter, *Crystallaria asprella*. Copeia 1991:927–936.

Simons, A. M. 1992. Phylogenetic relationships of the *Boleosoma* species group (Percidae: *Etheostoma*). Pages 268–292 *in* Mayden (1992).

Simonson, T. D., and R. J. Neves. 1986. A status survey of the orangefin madtom and Roanoke logperch. Report of the Virginia Cooperative Fish and Wildlife Research Unit, Virginia Polytechnic Institute and State University, Blacksburg, to Virginia Commission of Game and Inland Fisheries, Richmond.

Sirkin, L. A. 1977. Late Pleistocene vegetation and environments in the middle Atlantic region. Pages 206–217 *in* W. S. Newman and B. Salwen, editors. Amerinds and their paleoenvironments in northeastern North America. Annals of the New York Academy of Sciences 288:206–217.

Sirkin, L. A., C. S. Denny, and M. Rubin. 1977. Late Pleistocene environment of the central Delmarva Peninsula, Delaware, Maryland. Geological Society of America Bulletin 88:139–142.

Sisk, M. E. 1966. Unusual spawning behavior of the northern creek chub, *Semotilus atromaculatus* (Mitchill). Transactions of the Kentucky Academy of Science 27: 3–4.

Sledd, C. A., and D. J. Shuber. 1981. Lake Anna research study. Virginia Commission of Game and Inland Fisheries, Federal Aid in Sport Fish Restoration, Project F-33-R, January 1, 1976–December 31, 1980. Completion Report, Richmond.

Small, J. W. 1975. Energy dynamics of benthic fishes in a small Kentucky Stream. Ecology 56:827–840.

Smart, H. J., and J. H. Gee. 1979. Coexistence and resource partitioning in two species of darters (Percidae), *Etheostoma nigrum* and *Percina maculata*. Canadian Journal of Zoology 57:2061–2071.

Smith, A. J., J. H. Howell, and G. W. Piavis. 1968. Comparative embryology of five species of lampreys of the upper Great Lakes. Copeia 1968:461–469.

Smith, A. O. 1971. Some aspects of trophic relations of gizzard shad, *Dorosoma cepedianum*. Doctoral dissertation. Virginia Polytechnic Institute and State University, Blacksburg.

Smith, B. A. 1971. The fishes of four low-salinity tidal tributaries of the Delaware River estuary. Master's thesis. Cornell University, Ithaca, New York. (Not seen; cited in Wang and Kernehan 1979.)

Smith, B. G. 1922. Notes on the nesting habits of *Cottus*. Papers of the Michigan Academy of Science, Arts and Letters 2:221–224.

Smith, C. G. 1977. The biology of three species of *Moxostoma* (Pisces: Catostomidae) in Clear Creek, Hocking and Fairfield counties, Ohio, with emphasis on the golden redhorse, *M. erythrurum* (Rafinesque). Doctoral dissertation. Ohio State University, Columbus.

Smith, C. L. 1983. Going with the flow. Natural History 92:48–57.

Smith, C. L. 1985. The inland fishes of New York State. New York State Department of Environmental Conservation, Albany.

Smith, C. L. 1988. Minnows first, then trout. Fisheries (Bethesda) 13(4):4–8.

Smith, C. L., and R. M. Bailey. 1961. Evolution of the dorsal-fin supports of percoid fishes. Papers of the Michigan Academy of Science, Arts, and Letters 46: 345–363.

Smith, D. G. 1984. Elopiformes, Notacanthiformes and Anguilliformes: relationships. Pages 94–102 *in* Moser et al. (1984).

Smith, E. 1905. *Exoglossum* east of the Delaware basin. Science 22(552):119–120.

Smith, G. R. 1966. Distribution and evolution of the North American catostomid fishes of the subgenus *Pantos-*

teus, genus *Catostomus*. Miscellaneous Publications Museum of Zoology University of Michigan 129.

Smith, G. R. 1973. Analysis of several hybrid cyprinid fishes from western North America. Copeia 1973:395–410.

Smith, G. R. 1975. Fishes of the Pliocene Glenns Ferry formation, southwest Idaho. University of Michigan Museum of Paleontology Papers on Paleontology 14: iv–68.

Smith, G. R. 1981. Late Cenozoic freshwater fishes of North America. Annual Review of Ecology and Systematics 12:163–193.

Smith, G. R. 1992. Phylogeny and biogeography of the Catostomidae, freshwater fishes of Noth America and Asia. Pages 778–826 *in* Mayden (1992).

Smith, G. R., and J. G. Lundberg. 1972. The Sand Draw fish fauna. Bulletin of the American Museum of Natural History 148:40–54.

Smith, G. R., and R. R. Miller. 1985. Taxonomy of fishes from Miocene Clarkia lake beds, Idaho. Pages 75–83 *in* C. J. Smiley, editor. Late Cenozoic history of the Pacific Northwest. Pacific Division, American Association for the Advancement of Science, San Francisco.

Smith, G. R., and R. F. Stearley. 1989. The classification and scientific names of rainbow and cutthroat trouts. Fisheries (Bethesda) 14(1):4–10.

Smith, G. R., J. N. Taylor, and T. W. Grimshaw. 1981. Ecological survey of fishes in the Raisin River drainage, Michigan. Papers of the Michigan Academy of Science, Arts and Letters 13:275–305.

Smith, H. M. 1893. Report on a collection of fishes from the Albemarle region of North Carolina. U.S. Fish Commission Bulletin 11:185–200.

Smith, H. M. 1903. The common names of the basses and sunfishes. Pages 353–366 *in* U.S. Commission of Fish and Fisheries, Report of the Commissioner for 1902, Part 28.

Smith, H. M. 1905. The drumming of the drum-fishes (Sciaenidae). Science 22:376–378.

Smith, H. M. 1907. The fishes of North Carolina. North Carolina Geological and Economic Survey 2:1–453.

Smith, H. M. 1945. The fresh-water fishes of Siam, or Thailand. Bulletin of the United States National Museum 188:1–622.

Smith, H. M., and B. A. Bean. 1899. List of fishes known to inhabit the waters of the District of Columbia and vicinity. U.S. Fish Commission Bulletin 18:179–187.

Smith, M. L., T. M. Cavender, and R. R. Miller. 1975. Climatic and biogeographic significance of a fish fauna from the late Pliocene–early Pleistocene of the Lake Chapala basin (Jalisco, Mexico). Studies on Cenozoic Paleontology and Stratigraphy, University of Michigan, Papers on Paleontology 12:29–38, Ann Arbor.

Smith, O. R. 1935. The breeding habits of the stone roller minnow (*Campostoma anomalum* Rafinesque). Transactions of the American Fisheries Society 65:148–151.

Smith, P., and J. Kauffman. 1982. Age and growth of Virginia's freshwater fishes. Virginia Commission of Game and Inland Fisheries, Richmond.

Smith, P. W. 1971. Illinois streams: a classification based on their fishes and an analysis of factors responsible for disappearance of native species. Illinois Natural History Survey Biological Notes 76.

Smith, P. W. 1979. The fishes of Illinois. University of Illinois Press, Urbana.

Smith, P. W., and N. M. Welch. 1978. A summary of the life history and distribution of the spring cavefish, *Chologaster agassizi* Putnam, with population estimates for the species in southern Illinois. Illinois Natural History Survey Biological Notes 104.

Smith, R. F. 1953. Some observations on the distribution of fishes in New Jersey. New Jersey Fisheries Survey, Division of Fish and Game, Report 2:165–174, Trenton.

Smith, R. J. F. 1982. The adaptive significance of the alarm substance—fright reaction. Pages 327–342 *in* T. J. Hara, editor. Chemoreception in fishes. Elsevier, Amsterdam, Netherlands.

Smith, R. J. F., and B. D. Murphy. 1974. Functional morphology of the dorsal pad in fathead minnows (*Pimephales promelas* Rafinesque). Transactions of the American Fisheries Society 103:65–72.

Smith, S. H. 1970. Species interactions of the alewife in the Great Lakes. Transactions of the American Fisheries Society 99:754–765.

Smith, T. I. J. 1985. The fishery, biology, and management of Atlantic sturgeon, *Acipenser oxyrhynchus*, in North America. Environmental Biology of Fishes 14:61–72.

Smith, T. I. J., D. E. Marchette, and G. F. Ulrich. 1984. The Atlantic sturgeon fishery in South Carolina. North American Journal of Fisheries Management 4:164–176.

Smith, W. B. 1963. Survey and classification of the Chowan River and tributaries, North Carolina (with Appendix). North Carolina Wildlife Resources Commission, Federal Aid in Sportfish Restoration, Project F-14R, Job I–F. Final Report, Raleigh.

Smith, W. B. 1970. A preliminary report on the biology of the Roanoke bass *Ambloplites cavifrons* in North Carolina. Proceedings of the Annual Conference Southeastern Association of Game and Fish Commissioners 23(1969):491–500.

Smith, W. B. 1971. The biology of the Roanoke bass. North Carolina Wildlife Resources Commission, Federal Aid in Sport Fish Restoration, Project F-19:1–18. Final Report, Raleigh.

Smith, W. B., and W. D. Baker. 1965. Survey and classification of the Perquimans–Pasquotank–North rivers and tributaries, North Carolina (with appendix). North Carolina Wildlife Resources Commission, Federal Aid in Sport Fish Restoration, Project F-14-R, Job I–R. Final Report, Raleigh.

Smock, L. A., and E. Gilinsky. 1992. Coastal Plain blackwater streams. Pages 271–313 *in* C. T. Hackney, S. M. Adams, and W. H. Martin, editors. Biodiversity of the southeastern United States. Aquatic communities. Wiley, New York.

Smock, L. A., G. M. Metzler, and J. E. Gladden. 1989. Role of debris dams in the structure and functioning of low-gradient headwater streams. Ecology 70:764–775.

Sneed, K. E., and H. P. Clemens. 1963. The morphology of the testes and accessory reproductive glands of the catfishes (Ictaluridae). Copeia 1963:606–611.

Snelson, F. F. 1968. Systematics of the cyprinid fish *No-*

tropis amoenus, with comments on the subgenus *Notropis*. Copeia 1968:776–802.

Snelson, F. F. 1971. *Notropis mekistocholas*, a new herbivorous cyprinid fish endemic to the Cape Fear River basin, North Carolina. Copeia 1971:449–462.

Snelson, F. F. 1972. Systematics of the subgenus *Lythrurus*, Genus *Notropis* (Pisces: Cyprinidae). Bulletin of the Florida State Museum Biological Sciences 17:1–92.

Snelson, F. F. 1980. Systematic review of the cyprinid fish, *Notropis lirus*. Copeia 1980:323–334.

Snelson, F. F. 1990. Redescription, geographic variation, and subspecies of the minnow *Notropis ardens* (Pisces: Cyprinidae). Copeia 1990:966–984.

Snelson, F. F. 1991. Review of "Phylogenetic studies of North American minnows, with emphasis on the genus *Cyprinella* (Teleostei: Cyprinidae)" by R. L. Mayden. Copeia 1991:258–260.

Snelson, F. F., and W. L. Pflieger. 1975. Redescription of the redfin shiner, *Notropis umbratilus*, and its subspecies in the central Mississippi basin. Copeia 1975:231–249.

Snelson, F. F., and R. D. Suttkus. 1978. A new species of *Semotilus* (Pisces: Cyprinidae) from the Carolinas. Bulletin Alabama Museum of Natural History 3:1–11.

Snyder, D. E. 1979. Myomere and vertebra counts of the North American cyprinids and catostomids. Pages 53–69 *in* R. D. Hoyt, editor. Proceedings of the 3rd symposium on larval fish. Western Kentucky University, Bowling Green.

Snyder, D. E. 1981. Contributions to a guide to the cypriniform fish larvae of the upper Colorado River system in Colorado. Colorado Bureau of Land Management, Biological Sciences Series 3, Denver.

Snyder, D. E., M. B. M. Snyder, and S. C. Douglas. 1977. Identification of golden shiner, *Notemigonus crysoleucas*, spotfin shiner, *Notropis spilopterus*, and fathead minnow, *Pimephales promelas*, larvae. Journal of the Fisheries Research Board of Canada 34:1397–1409.

Soukup, J. F. 1970. Fish kill #70-025, Clinch River, Carbo, Russell County. Memorandum, 25 June 1970, Virginia State Water Control Board, Richmond.

Southwick, R. 1986. Hybrid striped bass: a new fish, a new opportunity. Virginia Wildlife 46(4):30–33.

Southwick, R., and M. D. Norman. 1987. First record of an albinistic margined madtim (*Noturus insignis*). Virginia Journal of Science 38:42.

Spall, R. D. 1970. Possible cases of cleaning symbiosis among freshwater fishes. Transactions of the American Fisheries Society 99:599–600.

Speare, E. P. 1960. Growth of the central johnny darter, *Etheostoma nigrum nigrum* (Rafinesque) in Augusta Creek, Michigan. Copeia 1960:241–243.

Speare, E. P. 1965. Fecundity and egg survival of the central johnny darter (*Etheostoma nigrum nigrum*) in southern Michigan. Copeia 1965:308–314.

Spoor, W. A. 1935. On the sexual dimorphism of *Catostomus commersoni* (Lacepède). Copeia 1935:167–171.

Stagner, M. 1959. Age and growth in two Piedmont minnows, *Notropis cerasinus* and *Notropis albeolus*. Master's thesis. Duke University, Durham, North Carolina.

Starnes, L. B., and A. E. Bogan. 1988. The mussels (Mollusca: Bivalvia: Unionidae) of Tennessee. American Malacological Bulletin 6:19–37.

Starnes, L. B., and W. C. Starnes. 1981. Biology of the blackside dace *Phoxinus cumberlandensis*. American Midland Naturalist 106:360–371.

Starnes, L. B., and W. C. Starnes. 1985. Ecology and life history of the mountain madtom, *Noturus eleutherus* (Pisces: Ictaluridae). American Midland Naturalist 114:331–341.

Starnes, W. C., and D. A. Etnier. 1980. Fishes. Pages B-1 to B-134 *in* D. C. Eager and R. M. Hatcher, editors. Tennessee's rare wildlife, volume 1, the vertebrates. Tennessee Wildlife Resources Agency, Nashville.

Starnes, W. C., and D. A. Etnier. 1986. Drainage evolution and fish biogeography of the Tennessee and Cumberland rivers drainage realm. Pages 325–361 *in* Hocutt and Wiley (1986).

Starnes, W. C., D. A. Etnier, L. B. Starnes, and N. H. Douglas. 1977. Zoogeographic implications of the rediscovery of the percid genus *Ammocrypta* in the Tennessee River drainage. Copeia 1977:783–786.

Starnes, W. C., and R. E. Jenkins. 1988. A new cyprinid fish of the genus *Phoxinus* (Pisces: Cypriniformes) from the Tennessee River drainage with comments on relationships and biogeography. Proceedings of the Biological Society of Washington 101:517–529.

Starnes, W. C., and L. B. Starnes. 1978. A new cyprinid of the genus *Phoxinus* endemic to the upper Cumberland River drainage. Copeia 1978:508–516.

Starnes, W. C., and L. B. Starnes. 1979. Taxonomic status of the percid fish *Etheostoma nigrum susanae*. Copeia 1979:426–430.

Starrett, W. C. 1950a. Distribution of the fishes of Boone County, Iowa, with special reference to the minnows and darters. American Midland Naturalist 43:112–127.

Starrett, W. C. 1950b. Food relationships of the minnows of the Des Moines River, Iowa. Ecology 31:216–233.

Starrett, W. C. 1951. Some factors affecting the abundance of minnows in the Des Moines River, Iowa. Ecology 32:13–27.

Starrett, W. C., and A. W. Fritz. 1965. A biological investigation of the fishes of Lake Chautauqua, Illinois. Illinois Natural History Survey Bulletin 29:1–104.

Starrett, W. C., W. J. Harth, and P. W. Smith. 1960. Parasitic lampreys of the genus *Ichthyomyzon* in the rivers of Illinois. Copeia 1960:337–346.

Stasiak, R. H. 1978. Food, age and growth of the pearl dace, *Semotilus margarita*, in Nebraska. American Midland Naturalist 100:463–466.

Stauffer, J. R., B. M. Burr, C. H. Hocutt, and R. E. Jenkins. 1982. Checklist of the fishes of the central and northern Appalachian Mountains. Proceedings of the Biological Society of Washington 95:27–47.

Stauffer, J. R., R. F. Denoncourt, C. H. Hocutt, and R. E. Jenkins. 1979a. A description of the cyprinid fish hybrid, *Notropis chrysocephalus* × *Notropis photogenis*, from the Greenbrier River, West Virginia. Natural History Miscellanea (Chicago) 204.

Stauffer, J. R., K. L. Dickson, J. Cairns, and D. S. Cherry. 1976. The potential and realized influences of temper-

ature on the distribution of fishes in the New River, Glen Lyn, Virginia. Wildlife Monographs 40:3–40.

Stauffer, J. R., K. L. Dickson, M. T. Masnik, and J. E. Reed. 1975. The longitudinal distribution of the fishes of the East River, West Virginia–Virginia. Virginia Journal of Science 26:121–125.

Stauffer, J. R., C. H. Hocutt, and R. F. Denoncourt. 1979b. Status and distribution of the hybrid *Nocomis micropogon* × *Rhinichthys cataractae*, with a discussion of hybridization as a viable mode of vertebrate speciation. American Midland Naturalist 101:355–365.

Stauffer, J. R., C. H. Hocutt, and R. F. Denoncourt. 1979c. An intergeneric cyprinid hybrid, *Nocomis platyrhynchus* × *Notropis chrysocephalus*, from the Greenbrier River drainage in West Virginia. Copeia 1979:172–173.

Stauffer, J. R., C. H. Hocutt, and D. S. Lee. 1978a. The zoogeography of the freshwater fishes of the Potomac River basin. Pages 44–54 *in* K. C. Flynn and W. T. Mason, editors. The Freshwater Potomac: aquatic communities and environmental stresses. Interstate Commission on the Potomac River Basin, Rockville, Maryland.

Stauffer, J. R., C. H. Hocutt, and S. Pistolas. 1978b. Preliminary comparison of the ichthyofauna of the northern and southern tributaries of the upper Potomac River. Proceedings of the Potomac Chapter of the American Fisheries Society:24–38.

Stauffer, J. R., D. R. Lispi, and C. H. Hocutt. 1984. The preferred temperatures of three *Semotilus* species. Archiv fuer Hydrobiologie. 101:595–600.

Stearley, R. F. 1992. Historical ecology of Salmoninae, with specific reference to *Oncorhynchus*. Pages 622–658 *in* Mayden (1992).

Stearley, R. F., and G. R. Smith. 1993. Phylogeny of the Pacific trouts and salmons (*Oncorhynchus*) and genera of the family Salmonidae. Transactions of the American Fisheries Society 122:1–33.

Stegman, J. L. 1959. Fishes of Kincaid Creek, Illinois. Transactions of the Illinois State Academy of Science 52:25–32.

Stegman, J. L., and W. L. Minckley. 1959. Occurrence of three species of fishes in interstices of gravel in an area of subsurface flow. Copeia 1959:341.

Steinkoenig, E. L. 1975. Northeastern Virginia fisheries survey. Virginia Commission of Game and Inland Fisheries, Federal Aid in Sport Fish Restoration, Project F-28-2, July 1, 1973–June 30, 1974. Progress Report, Richmond.

Stephens, D. E., and K. W. Prather. 1985. The longnose dace, *Rhinichthys cataractae* (Valenciennes), in Kentucky. Transactions of the Kentucky Academy of Science 46:56.

Stephens, R. R. 1985. The lateral line system of the gizzard shad, *Dorosoma cepedianum* Lesueur (Pisces: Clupeidae). Copeia 1985:540–556.

Sternburg, J. G. 1986. Spawning the blackbanded sunfish. American Currents (January):6–7.

Stevens, R. E. 1958. The striped bass of the Santee–Cooper Reservoir. Proceedings of the Annual Conference Southeastern Association of Game and Fish Commissioners 11(1957):253–264. (Not seen; cited in Setzler et al. 1980.)

Stevens, R. E. 1965. A report on the operation of the Moncks Corner striped bass hatchery, 1961–1965. South Carolina Wildlife Resources Department, Columbia.

Stevens, R. E. 1984. Historical overview of striped bass culture and management. Pages 1–15 in J. P. McCraren, editor. The aquaculture of striped bass, a proceedings. University of Maryland, Sea Grant Publication UM-SG-MAP-84-01, College Park.

Stevenson, C. H. 1899. The shad fisheries of the Atlantic Coast of the United States. Pages 101–269 in U.S. Commission of Fish and Fisheries, Report of the Commissioner for 1898, Part 24.

Stewart, D. J., J. F. Kitchell, and L. B. Crowder. 1981. Forage fishes and their salmonid predators in Lake Michigan. Transactions of the American Fisheries Society 110:751–763.

Stewart, N. H. 1926. Development, growth, and food habits of the white sucker, Catostomus commersonii Lesueur. U.S. Bureau of Fisheries Bulletin 42:147–184.

Stiles, R. A. 1972. The comparative ecology of three species of Nothonotus (Percidae—Etheostoma) in Tennessee's Little River. Doctoral dissertation. University of Tennessee, Knoxville.

Stone, F. L. 1947. Notes on two darters of the genus Boleosoma. Copeia 1947:92–96.

Stone, U. B. 1940. Studies on the biology of the satinfin minnows Notropis analostanus and Notropis spilopterus. Doctoral dissertation. Cornell University, Ithaca, New York. (Not seen; cited in Carlander 1969.)

Stoneking, M., D. J. Wagner, and A. C. Hildebrand. 1981. Genetic evidence suggesting subspecific differences between northern and southern populations of brook trout (Salvelinus fontinalis). Copeia 1981:810–819.

Stout, J. F. 1975. Sound communication during the reproductive behavior of Notropis analostanus (Pisces: Cyprinidae). American Midland Naturalist 94:296–325.

St. Pierre, R. A., and J. Davis. 1972. Age, growth, and mortality of the white perch, Morone americana, in the James and York River, Virginia. Chesapeake Science 13:272–281.

St. Pierre, R. A., and W. J. Hoagman. 1975. Drastic reduction of the white perch, Morone americana, population in the James River, Virginia. Chesapeake Science 16:192–197.

Stras, B. W. 1949. History and organization of the Commission of Game and Inland Fisheries. Virginia Wildlife 10(7–8):[July] 5–7, 9, 22, 24; [Aug.] 5–7, 12, 19.

Strauss, R. E. 1980. Genetic and morphometric variation and the systematic relationships of eastern North American sculpins (Pisces: Cottidae). Doctoral dissertation. Pennsylvania State University, University Park.

Strauss, R. E. 1986. Natural hybrids of the freshwater sculpins Cottus bairdi and Cottus cognatus (Pisces: Cottidae): electrophoretic and morphometric evidence. American Midland Naturalist 115:87–105.

Strauss, R. E., and F. L. Bookstein. 1982. The truss: body form reconstruction in morphometrics. Systematic Zoology 31:113–135.

Strawn, K. 1965. Resistance of threadfin shad to low temperatures. Proceedings of the Annual Conference Southeastern Association of Game and Fish Commissioners 17(1963):290–293.

Stroud, R. H. 1948. Notes on growth of hybrids between the sauger and the walleye (Stizostedion canadense canadense × S. vitreum vitreum) in Norris Reservoir, Tennessee. Copeia 1948:297–298.

Stroud, R. H., and H. Clepper, editors. 1975. Black bass biology and management. Sport Fishing Institute, Washington, D.C.

Stuber, R. J., G. Gebhart, and O. E. Maughan. 1982. Habitat suitability index models: green sunfish. U.S. Fish and Wildlife Service, Biological Services Program FWS-OBS-82/10.15.

Stutz, C. A. 1968. A study of quantitative variation in Etheostoma flabellare Rafinesque from the North Fork and the South Fork of the Roanoke River of Virginia. Master's thesis. Virginia Polytechnic Institute and State University, Blacksburg.

Sule, M. J. 1981. First-year growth and feeding of largemouth bass in a heated reservoir. Illinois Natural History Survey Bulletin 32:520–535.

Sule, M. J., J. M. McNurney, and D. R. Halffield. 1981. Food habits of some common fishes from heated and unheated areas of Lake Sangchris. Illinois Natural History Survey Bulletin 32:500–519.

Sule, M. J., and T. M. Skelly. 1985. The life history of the shorthead redhorse, Moxostoma macrolepidotum, in the Kankakee River drainage, Illinois. Illinois Natural History Survey Biological Notes 123.

Sullivan, C. R. 1956. Population manipulation studies on West Virginia smallmouth bass streams. West Virginia Conservation Commission, Federal Aid in Sport Fish Restoration, Project West Virginia F-1-R-(1-5), November 15, 1951–June 30, 1956. Final Report, Charleston.

Summerfelt, R. C., and C. O. Minckley. 1969. Aspects of the life history of the sand shiner, Notropis stramineus (Cope), in the Smoky Hills River, Kansas. Transactions of the American Fisheries Society 98:444–453.

Summers, L. P. 1903. History of southwest Virginia 1746–1786, Washington County, 1777–1870. (Reprinted 1966, Genealogical Publishing Company, Baltimore.)

Sumner, F. B., R. C. Osburn, and L. J. Cole. 1913. A biological survey of the waters of Woods Hole and vicinity: a catalogue of the marine fauna. U.S. Bureau of Fisheries Bulletin 31(2):545–794.

Surat, E. M., W. J. Matthews, and J. R. Bek. 1982. Comparative ecology of Notropis albeolus, N. ardens and N. cerasinus (Cyprinidae) in the upper Roanoke River drainage, Virginia. American Midland Naturalist 107:13–24.

Surber, E. W. 1958. Results of striped bass (Roccus saxatilis) introduction into fresh-water impoundments. Proceedings of the Annual Conference Southeastern Association of Game and Fish Commissioners 11(1957):273–276.

Surber, E. W. 1970. Smallmouth bass stream investigations. Virginia Commission of Game and Inland Fisheries, Federal Aid in Sport Fish Restoration, Project

F-14-R, Job 2-Shenandoah River study, January 1, 1964–June 30, 1969. Final Report, Richmond.

Surber, E. W. 1972. Shenandoah River survey. Virginia Commission of Game and Inland Fisheries, Federal Aid in Sport Fish Restoration, Project F-14-S, [5 jobs], July 1, 1969–June 30, 1972. Progress and Final Report, Richmond.

Suttkus, R. D. 1958. Status of the nominal cyprinid species *Moniana deliciosa* Girard and *Cyprinella texana* Girard. Copeia 1958:307–318.

Suttkus, R. D. 1961. Additional information about blind catfishes from Texas. Southwestern Naturalist 6:55–64.

Suttkus, R. D. 1964. Order Lepisostei. Pages 61–88 *in* Fishes of the western North Atlantic Part 3. Sears Foundation for Marine Research, Yale University, New Haven, Connecticut.

Suttkus, R. D., and R. M. Bailey. 1990. Characters, relationships, distribution, and biology of *Notropis melanostomus*, a recently named cyprinid fish from southeastern United States. Occasional Papers of the Museum of Zoology, University of Michigan 722.

Suttkus, R. D., and J. S. Ramsey. 1967. *Percina aurolineata*, a new percid fish from the Alabama River system and a discussion of ecology, distribution, and hybridization of darters of the subgenus *Hadropterus*. Tulane Studies in Zoology 4:129–145.

Svardson, G. 1949. Note on spawning habits of *Leuciscus erythrophthalmus* (L.), *Abramis brama* (L.) and *Esox lucius* L. Institute of Fresh-Water Research, Drottningholm, Report 29:102–107.

Svetovidov, A. N. 1952. Fauna of the U.S.S.R. Fishes, volume 2, number 1, Clupeidae. Zoologicheskii Institut Akademii Nauk SSSR, New Series 48. (In Russian.) English translation: 1963. Israel Program for Scientific Translations for the National Science Foundation, Washington, D.C.

Svetovidov, A. N., and E. A. Dorofeeva. 1963. Systematics, origin, and history of the distribution of the Eurasian and North American perches and pike-perches (genera *Perca*, *Lucioperca*, and *Stizostedion*). Voprosy Ikhtiologii 3:625–651. (In Russian.) English translation: Ichthyological Laboratory, U.S. National Marine Fisheries Service, Washington, D.C.

Sweeney, E. F. 1972. The systematics and distribution of the centrarchid fish tribe Enneacanthini. Doctoral dissertation. Boston University, Boston.

Swenson, W. A. 1977. Food consumption of walleye (*Stizostedion vitreum vitreum*) and sauger (*S. canadense*) in relation to food availability and physical conditions in Lake of the Woods, Minnesota, Shagawa Lake, and western Lake Superior. Journal of the Fisheries Research Board of Canada 34:1643–1654.

Swift, C. C. 1970. A review of the eastern North American cyprinid fishes of the *Notropis texanus* species group (subgenus *Alburnops*), with a definition of the subgenus *Hydrophlox*, and materials for the revision of the subgenus *Alburnops*. Doctoral dissertation. Florida State University, Tallahassee.

Swift, C. C. 1975. Classification of the American cyprinid fish genus *Notropis*, and application of graph cluster analysis to an exemplar group. Pages 122–123 *in* Ab-

stracts of the 55th Annual Meeting of the American Society of Ichthyologists and Herpetologists.

Swift, C. C., C. R. Gilbert, S. A. Bortone, G. H. Burgess, and R. W. Yerger. 1986. Zoogeography of the freshwater fishes of the southeastern United States: Savannah River to Lake Pontchartrain. Pages 213–265 *in* Hocutt and Wiley (1986).

Swift, C. C., R. W. Yerger, and P. R. Parrish. 1977. Distribution and natural history of the fresh and brackish water fishes of the Ocklockonee River, Florida and Georgia. Bulletin of Tall Timbers Research Station 20.

Swift, D. J. P. 1975. Tidal sand ridges and shoal retreat massifs. Marine Geology 18:105–134.

Swift, D. J. P. 1976a. Coastal sedimentation. Pages 255–310 *in* D. J. Stanley and D. J. P. Swift, editors. Marine sediment transport and environmental management. Wiley, New York.

Swift, D. J. P. 1976b. Continental Shelf sedimentation. Pages 311–350 *in* D. J. Stanley and D. J. P. Swift, editors. Marine sediment transport and environmental management. Wiley, New York.

Swift, D. J. P., J. W. Kofoed, F. P. Saulsbury, and P. Sears. 1972. Holocene evolution of the shelf surface, central and southern Atlantic shelf of North America. Pages 449–574 *in* D. J. P. Swift, O. B. Duane, and D. H. Pilkey, editors. Shelf sediment transport: process and pattern. Dowden, Hutchinson, and Ross, Stroudsburg, Pennsylvania.

Swingle, H. A. 1971. Biology of Alabama estuarine areas—cooperative Gulf of Mexico estuarine inventory. Alabama Marine Resources Bulletin 5. (Not seen; cited in Hardy 1978b.)

Swingle, W. E. 1965. Length–weight relationships of Alabama fishes. Auburn University Agricultural Experiment Station, Zoology–Entomology Department Series, Fisheries 3, Auburn, Alabama.

Symons, P. E. K., J. L. Metcalfe, and G. D. Harding. 1976. Upper lethal and preferred temperatures of the slimy sculpin, *Cottus cognatus*. Journal of the Fisheries Research Board of Canada 33:180–183.

Taber, C. A. 1969. The distribution and identification of larval fishes in the Buncombe Creek arm of Lake Texoma with observations on spawning habits and relative abundance. Doctoral dissertation. University of Oklahoma, Norman.

Tackett, J. H. 1963. Clinch River basin, biological assessment of water quality. Virginia State Water Control Board Report, Richmond.

Tackett, J. H. 1967. Clinch River fish kill—biological investigation—Honaker, Va., to Norris Lake in Tennessee. Memorandum, 3 July 1967, Virginia State Water Control Board, Richmond.

Talbot, G. B., and J. E. Sykes. 1958. Atlantic coastal migrations of American shad. U.S. Fish and Wildlife Service Fishery Bulletin 58:473–490.

Tanyolac, J. 1973. Morphometric variation and life history of the cyprinid fish *Notropis stramineus* (Cope). Occasional Papers of the Museum of Natural History, University of Kansas 12.

Tarter, D. C. 1968. Age and growth of the western blacknose dace, *Rhinichthys atratulus meleagris* Agassiz, in

Doe Run, Meade County, Kentucky. Transactions of the Kentucky Academy of Science 29:23–37.

Tarter, D. C. 1969. Some aspects of reproduction of the western blacknose dace, *Rhinichthys atratulus meleagris* Agassiz, in Doe Run, Meade County, Kentucky. Transactions of the American Fisheries Society 98:454–459.

Tarter, D. C. 1970. Food and feeding habits of the western blacknose dace, *Rhinichthys atratulus meleagris* Agassiz, in Doe Run, Meade County, Kentucky. American Midland Naturalist 83:134–159.

Tatum, W. M., and P. A. Hackney. 1970. Age and growth of river redhorse, *Moxostoma carinatum* (Cope) from the Cahaba River, Alabama. Proceedings of the Annual Conference Southeastern Association of Game and Fish Commissioners 23(1969):255–261.

Taubert, B. D., and M. J. Dadswell. 1980. Description of some larval shortnose sturgeon (*Acipenser brevirostrum*) from the Holyoke Pool, Connecticut River, Massachusetts, USA, and the Saint John River, New Brunswick, Canada. Canadian Journal of Zoology 58:1125–1128.

Taylor, E. 1982. Upstream . . . on Virginia's Appomattox River, part 1. Aquarium 5(12):35–42.

Taylor, E. 1983. Upstream . . . on Virginia's Appomattox River, part 2. Aquarium 6(1):14–18.

Taylor, J., and R. Mahon. 1977. Hybridization of *Cyprinus carpio* and *Carassius auratus*, the first two exotic species in the lower Laurentian Great Lakes. Environmental Biology of Fishes 1:205–208.

Taylor, J. N., W. R. Courtenay, and J. A. McCann. 1984. Known impacts of exotic fishes in the continental United States. Pages 322–373 *in* W. R. Courtenay and J. R. Stauffer, editors. Distribution, biology and management of exotic fishes. Johns Hopkins University Press, Baltimore, Maryland.

Taylor, W. R. 1954. Records of fishes in the John N. Lowe collection from the Upper Peninsula of Michigan. Miscellaneous Publications, Museum of Zoology, University of Michigan 87.

Taylor, W. R. 1969. A revision of the catfish genus *Noturus* Rafinesque with an analysis of higher groups in the Ictaluridae. Bulletin of the United States National Museum 282.

Taylor, W. R., R. E. Jenkins, and E. A. Lachner. 1971. Rediscovery and description of the ictalurid catfish, *Noturus flavipinnis*. Proceedings of the Biological Society of Washington 83:469–476.

Teifke, R. E. 1973. Geologic studies, Coastal Plain of Virginia. Stratigraphic units of the Lower Cretaceous through Miocene series. Virginia Division of Mineral Resources, Bulletin 83:1–78, Charlottesville.

Terwilliger, K. A., coordinator. 1991. Virginia's endangered species. McDonald and Woodward, Blacksburg, Virginia.

Tesch, F.-W. 1977. The eel: biology and management of anguillid eels. (English translation). Chapman and Hall, London.

Thibault, R. E., and R. J. Schultz. 1978. Reproductive adaptations among viviparous fishes (Cyprinodontiformes: Poeciliidae). Evolution 32:320–333.

Thoits, C. F., III. 1958. A compendium of the life history and ecology of the white perch *Morone americana* (Gmelin). Massachusetts Division of Fisheries and Game, Fisheries Bulletin 24, Boston.

Thomas, D. L. 1970. An ecological study of four darters of the genus *Percina* (Percidae) in the Kaskaskia River, Illinois. Illinois Natural History Survey Biological Notes 70.

Thomerson, J. E. 1969. Variation and relationship of the studfishes, *Fundulus catenatus* and *Fundulus stellifer* (Cyprinodontidae, Pisces). Tulane Studies in Zoology and Botany 16:1–21.

Thompson, B. A. 1973a. The relationships of the percid fish *Etheostoma* (*Etheostoma*) *blennius* (Gilbert and Swain) (class Osteichthyes, order Perciformes, family Percidae). ASB (Association of Southeastern Biologists) Bulletin 20:87.

Thompson, B. A. 1973b. Systematics of the wavyband darters, *Percina cymatotaenia* and *Percina* sp. nov. with a discussion of their phylogenetic position (class Osteichthyes, order Perciformes, family Percidae). ASB (Association of Southeastern Biologists) Bulletin 20:87.

Thompson, B. A. 1977. An analysis of three subgenera (*Hypohomus*, *Odontopholis* and *Swainia*) of the genus *Percina* (tribe Etheostomatini, family Percidae). Doctoral dissertation. Tulane University, New Orleans.

Thompson, B. A. 1978. Logperches of southeastern United States (Etheostomatini, *Percina*). ASB (Association of Southeastern Biologists) Bulletin 25:57.

Thompson, B. A. 1985. *Percina jenkinsi*, a new species of logperch (Pisces, Percidae) from the Conasauga River, Tennessee and Georgia. Occasional Papers of the Museum of Zoology, Louisiana State University 61.

Thompson, H. D. 1939. Drainage evolution in the southern Appalachians. Geological Society of America Bulletin 50:1323–1356.

Thompson, S. M. 1989. Radiocarbon dates. Pages 140–148 *in* T. R. Whyte and S. M. Thompson, editors. Archaeological investigations at the Bessemer site (44BO26): a Late Woodland period Dan River and Page component village site on the upper James River, Virginia. James Madison University, Archeological Research Center, Harrisonburg, Virginia.

Thomson, K. S., and A. R. McCune. 1984. Scale structure as evidence of growth patterns in fossil semionotid fishes. Journal of Vertebrate Paleontology 4:422–429.

Thornbury, W. D. 1965. Regional geomorphology of the United States. Wiley, New York.

Thorpe, J. E. 1977. Morphology, physiology, behavior, and ecology of *Perca fluviatilis* L. and *P. flavescens* Mitchill. Journal of the Fisheries Research Board of Canada 34:1504–1514.

Timmons, T. J., J. S. Ramsey, and B. H. Bauer. 1983. Life history and habitat of the blackfin sucker, *Moxostoma atripinne* (Osteichthyes: Catostomidae). Copeia 1983:538–541.

Tin, H. T. 1982a. Family Clupeidae, herrings. Pages 64–73 *in* Auer (1982a).

Tin, H. T. 1982b. Family Ictaluridae, bullhead catfishes. Pages 436–457 *in* Auer (1982a).

Tin, H. T. 1982c. Family Atherinidae, silversides. Pages 487–493 *in* Auer (1982a).

Tin, H. T. 1982d. Family Centrarchidae, sunfishes. Pages 524–580 *in* Auer (1982a).

Tiner, R. W. 1987. Mid-Atlantic wetlands: a disappearing natural treasure. U.S. Environmental Protection Agency, Philadelphia, and U.S. Fish and Wildlife Service, Newton Corner, Massachusetts.

Todd, J. H. 1971. The chemical language of fishes. Scientific American 224:99–108.

Todd, R. D. 1973. Some aspects of the natural history of the tadpole madtom, *Noturus gyrinus*. Proceedings of the Nebraska Academy of Sciences and Affiliated Societies 83:19.

Todd, T. N. 1986. Occurrence of white bass-white perch hybrids in Lake Erie. Copeia 1986:196–199.

Todd, T. N., and G. R. Smith. 1980. Differentiation in *Coregonus zenithicus* in Lake Superior. Canadian Journal of Fisheries and Aquatic Sciences 37:2228–2235.

Todd, T. N., G. R. Smith, and L. E. Cable. 1981. Environmental and genetic contributions to morphological differentiation in ciscoes (Coregoninae) of the Great Lakes. Canadian Journal of Fisheries and Aquatic Sciences 38:59–67.

Todd, T. N., and C. M. Tomcko. 1985. Hybridization of white bass and white perch in the Great Lakes. Pages 132–133 *in* Abstracts of the 65th Annual Meeting of the American Society of Ichthyologists and Herpetologists.

Toewe, E. C. 1966. Geology of the Leesburg Quadrangle, Virginia. Virginia Division of Mineral Resources, Report of Investigations 11, Charlottesville.

Toner, E. D., and G. H. Lawler. 1969. Synopsis of biological data on the pike, *Esox lucius* Linnaeus 1758. FAO (Food and Agriculture Organization of the United Nations) Fisheries Synopsis 30, Revision 1.

Toole, T. W., and R. J. Ruane. 1976. Evaluation of the mercury monitoring program, the North Fork Holston River. Tennessee Valley Authority, E-WQ-76-2, Chattanooga.

Trail, J. G., C. S. Wade, J. G. Stanley, and P. C. Nelson. 1983. Habitat suitability information: fallfish. U.S. Fish and Wildlife Service Biological Services Program FWS-OBS-82/10.48.

Tranquilli, J. A., R. Kocher, and J. M. McNurney. 1981. Population dynamics of the Lake Sangchris fishery. Pages 413–499 *in* R. W. Larimore and J. A. Tranquilli, editors. The Lake Sangchris study: case history of an Illinois cooling lake. Illinois Natural History Survey Bulletin 32.

Trautman, M. B. 1931. *Parexoglossum hubbsi*, a new cyprinid fish from western Ohio. Occasional Papers of the Museum of Zoology, University of Michigan 235.

Trautman, M. B. 1948. A natural hybrid catfish, *Schilbeodes miurus* × *Schilbeodes mollis*. Copeia 1948:166–174.

Trautman, M. B. 1956. *Carpiodes cyprinus hinei*, a new subspecies of carpsucker from the Ohio and upper Mississippi River systems. Ohio Journal of Science 56:33–40.

Trautman, M. B. 1957. The fishes of Ohio with illustrated keys. Ohio State University Press, Columbus.

Trautman, M. B. 1981. The fishes of Ohio with illustrated keys, revised edition. Ohio State University Press, Columbus.

Traver, J. R. 1929. The habits of the black-nosed dace,

Rhinichthys atronasus (Mitchill). Journal of the Elisha Mitchell Scientific Society 45:101–129.

Trendall, J. T. 1982. Covariation of life history traits in the mosquitofish, *Gambusia affinis*. American Naturalist 119:774–783.

Trent, L., and W. W. Hassler. 1966. Feeding behavior of adult striped bass, *Roccus saxatilis*, in relation to stages of sexual maturity. Chesapeake Science 7:189–192.

Trent, L., and W. W. Hassler. 1968. Gill net selection, migration, size and age composition, sex ratio, harvest efficiency, and management of striped bass in the Roanoke River, North Carolina. Chesapeake Science 9:217–232.

Tresselt, E. F. 1952. Spawning grounds of the striped bass or rock, *Roccus saxatilis* (Walbaum), in Virginia. Bulletin of the Bingham Oceanographic Collection, Yale University 14:98–110.

Trial, J. G., J. G. Stanley, M. Batcheller, G. Gebhart, O. E. Maughan, and P. C. Nelson. 1983. Habitat suitability information: blacknose dace. U.S. Fish and Wildlife Service Biological Services Program FWS-OBS-82/10.41.

Truitt, R. V., B. A. Bean, and H. W. Fowler. 1929. The fishes of Maryland. Maryland Conservation Department, Conservation Bulletin 3, Annapolis.

Tsai, C. 1967. A study of the systematics of *Etheostoma zonale* (Cope) and its relatives, and the phylogeny of subgenus *Etheostoma* Rafinesque (Percidae, Teleostei). Doctoral dissertation. Cornell University, Ithaca, New York.

Tsai, C. 1968. Effects of chlorinated sewage effluents on fishes in upper Patuxent River, Maryland. Chesapeake Science 9:83–93.

Tsai, C. 1972. Life history of the eastern johnny darter, *Etheostoma olmstedi* Storer, in cold tailwater and sewage-polluted water. Transactions of the American Fisheries Society 101:80–88.

Tsai, C., and J. A. Fava. 1982. Habitats and distribution of the pearl dace, *Semotilus margarita* (Cope) in the Potomac River drainage. Virginia Journal of Science 33:201–205.

Tsai, C., and G. R. Gibson. 1971. Fecundity of the yellow perch, *Perca flavescens* Mitchill, in the Patuxent River, Maryland. Chesapeake Science 12:270–284.

Tsai, C., and E. C. Raney. 1974. Systematics of the banded darter, *Etheostoma zonale* (Pisces: Percidae). Copeia 1974:1–24.

Tsai, C., and R. B. Zeisel. 1969. Natural hybridization of cyprinid fishes in Little Patuxent River, Maryland. Chesapeake Science 10:69–74.

Turner, C. L. 1921. Food of the common Ohio darters. Ohio Journal of Science 22:41–62.

Turner, J. S., and F. F. Snelson. 1984. Population structure, reproduction and laboratory behavior of the introduced *Belonesox belizanus* (Poeciliidae) in Florida. Environmental Biology of Fishes 10:89–100.

Turner, W. R. 1961. Pre- and post-impoundment surveys: job 2A, fish population studies. Kentucky Department of Fish and Wildlife Resources, Federal Aid in Sport Fish Restoration, Project F-16-R-2, March 31, 1960–April 1, 1961. Progress Report, Frankfort.

TVA (Tennessee Valley Authority). 1970. Tennessee Valley streams: their fish, bottom fauna, and aquatic habitat. Powell River drainage basin, 1968. Division of Forestry, Fisheries, and Wildlife Development, TVA, Norris, Tennessee.

Tweddle, D., D. S. C. Lewis, and N. G. Willoughby. 1979. The nature of the barrier separating the Lake Malaŵi and Zambezi fish faunas. Ichthyological Bulletin of the J. L. B. Smith Institute of Ichthyology 39:i–9.

Twichell, D. C., H. J. Knebel, and D. W. Folger. 1977. Delaware River: evidence for its former extension to Wilmington submarine canyon. Science 195:483–485.

Tyus, H. M. 1970. Spawning of rock bass in North Carolina during 1968. Progressive Fish-Culturist 32:25.

Tyus, H. M. 1973. Artificial intergeneric hybridization of *Ambloplites rupestris* (Centrarchidae). Copeia 1973:428–430.

Tyus, H. M. 1974. Movements and spawning of anadromous alewives, *Alosa pseudoharengus* (Wilson) at Lake Mattamuskeet, North Carolina. Transactions of the American Fisheries Society 103:392–396.

Uchupi, E. 1968. Atlantic Continental Shelf and slope of the United States—physiography. United States Geological Survey Professional Paper 529:C1 to C30.

Uhler, P. R., and O. Lugger. 1876. List of the fishes of Maryland. Report of the Commissioners of Fisheries of Maryland, Annapolis.

Ulrey, L., C. Risk, and W. Scott. 1938. The number of eggs produced by some of our common freshwater fishes. Investigations of Indiana Lakes and Streams 1:73–78. (Not seen; cited in Carlander 1977.)

Ultsch, G. R., H. Boschung, and M. J. Ross. 1978. Metabolism, critical oxygen tension, and habitat selection in darters (*Etheostoma*). Ecology 59:99–107.

Underhill, J. C. 1963. Distribution in Minnesota of the subspecies of the percid fish *Etheostoma nigrum*, and of their intergrades. American Midland Naturalist 70:470–478.

USFC (United States Fish Commission). 1876–1936. Reports of the Commissioner, U.S. Commission of Fish and Fisheries, or Reports of the Bureau of Fisheries. Year of publication (period covered; FY = fiscal year 1 July–30 June): 1876 (1873–1875); 1878 (1875–1876); 1879 (1877); 1882 (1879); 1884a (1881); 1884b (1882); 1885 (1883); 1889 (1 January 1885–30 June 1887); 1892 (FY 1889); 1893 (FY 1890–1891); 1894 (FY 1892); 1895 (FY 1893); 1896a (FY 1894); 1896b (FY 1895); 1898 (FY 1896); 1899 (FY 1898); 1900 (FY 1899); 1901 (FY 1900); 1902 (?); 1904 (FY 1902); 1905a (FY 1903); 1905b (FY 1904); 1917 (FY 1917); 1922 (FY 1921); 1928 (FY 1927); 1929 (FY 1928); 1930 (FY 1929); 1931 (FY 1930); 1932 (FY 1931); 1934 (FY 1933); 1936a (FY 1934); 1936b (FY 1935).

USFWS (U.S. Fish and Wildlife Service). 1983. Slender chub recovery plan. USFWS, Atlanta.

USGS (U.S. Geological Survey). 1965. [Shaded relief map of] State of Virginia, scale 1:500,000. USGS, Washington, D.C.

USGS (U.S. Geological Survey). 1970. The national atlas of the United States of America. USGS, Washington, D.C.

Uyeno, T. 1960. Osteology and phylogeny of the American cyprinid fishes allied to the genus *Gila*. Doctoral dissertation, University of Michigan, Ann Arbor.

Uyeno, T., and R. R. Miller. 1963. Summary of Late Cenozoic freshwater fish records for North America. Occasional Papers of the Museum of Zoology, University of Michigan 631.

Uyeno, T., and G. R. Smith. 1972. Tetraploid origin of the karyotype of catostomid fishes. Science 175:644–646.

Vadas, R. L. 1990. The importance of omnivory and predator regulation of prey in freshwater fish assemblages of North America. Environmental Biology of Fishes 27:285–302.

Van Cleave, H. J., and H. C. Markus. 1929. Studies of the life history of the blunt-nosed minnow. American Naturalist 63:530–539.

Van Den Avyle, M. J. 1983. Species profiles: life histories and environmental requirements (South Atlantic)—Atlantic sturgeon. U.S. Fish and Wildlife Service Biological Services Program FWS-OBS-82/11. (Also: U.S. Army Corps of Engineers TREL-82-4.)

Vandermeer, J. H. 1966. Statistical analysis of geographic variation of the fathead minnow, *Pimephales promelas*. Copeia 1966:457–466.

van Donk, J. 1976. O^{18} record of the Atlantic Ocean for the entire Pleistocene epoch. Geological Society of America Memoir 145:147–163.

Van Duzer, E. M. 1939. Observations on the breeding habits of the cut-lips minnow, *Exoglossum maxillingua*. Copeia 1939:65–75.

Vanicek, D. 1961. Life history of the quillback and highfin carpsuckers in the Des Moines River. Proceedings of the Iowa Academy of Science 58:238–246.

Vannote, R. L., C. W. Minshall, K. W. Cummins, J. R. Sedell, and C. E. Cushing. 1980. The river continuum concept. Canadian Journal of Fisheries and Aquatic Sciences 37:130–137.

Vannote, R. L., and B. W. Sweeney. 1980. Geographic analysis of thermal equilibria: a conceptual model for evaluating the effect of natural and modified regimes on aquatic insect communities. American Naturalist 115:667–695.

Van Oosten, J. 1932. The maximum age of fresh-water fishes. Fisherman 1(11):1–3. (Not seen; cited in Carlander 1969.)

Van Velson, R. C. 1978. The McConaughy rainbow . . . life history and a management plan for the North Platte River Valley. Nebraska Game and Parks Commission, Technical Series 2, Lincoln.

Van Winkle, W., B. L. Kirk, and B. W. Rust. 1979. Periodicities in Atlantic Coast striped bass (*Morone saxatilis*) commercial fisheries data. Journal of the Fisheries Research Board of Canada 36:54–62.

Van Winkle, W., and K. D. Kumar. 1982. Relative stock composition of the Atlantic Coast striped bass population: further analysis. Oak Ridge National Laboratory, Environmental Sciences Division, Publication 1988 (ORNL/TM-8217), Oak Ridge, Tennessee. (Also: U.S. Nuclear Regulatory Commission NUREG/CR-2563.)

Van Winkle, W., K. D. Kumar, and D. S. Vaughan. 1984. Relative contributions of Hudson River and Chesapeake Bay striped bass stocks to the Atlantic Coast population. American Fisheries Society Monograph 4:255–266.

Vasetskiy, S. G. 1971. Fishes of the family Polyodontidae. Journal of Ichthyology 11:18–31.

VBCED (Virginia Board of Conservation and Economic Development). 1970. Water resources in Appalachia, Virginia portion. Division of Water Resources, VBCED, Richmond.

VDCED (Virginia Department of Conservation and Economic Development). 1966–1972. Comprehensive water resources plans [for the river basins of Virginia]. Planning Bulletins 201–264. Basins, number of volumes, and bulletin numbers are: New, 6, 201–206; Tennessee and Big Sandy, 3, 231–233, addendum 262; Potomac–Shenandoah, 5, 207–211, addendum 264; James, 4, 213–216, addendum 269; Rappahannock, 4, 219–222, addendum 266; York, 4, 225–228, addendum 265; Chowan–Dismal Swamp, 3, 237–239, addendum 263; Roanoke and Peedee, 3, 243–246, addendum 270; small coastal and Chesapeake Bay, 4, 249–252, addendum 268.

VDGIF (Virginia Division of Game and Inland Fisheries). 1987. [Virginia endangered species list]. Virginia Register of Regulations 3(26):3045.

VDMR (Virginia Division of Mineral Resources). 1963. Geologic map of Virginia, scale 1:500,000. VDMR, Charlottesville.

VEPCO (Virginia Electric Power Company). 1982. Environmental study of the lower North Anna River. North Anna Power Station Annual Report, January 1–December 31, 1981. Environmental Services Department, VEPCO, Richmond.

VFC (Virginia Fish Commission). 1876–1892. Reports or annual reports (variously titled on individual reports: Fish Commission; Fish Commissioner; Fish Commissioners; Commission of Fisheries; Commissioner of Fisheries; Superintendent of Fisheries; Board of Fisheries). The following refer to the primary individual reports used in this study. Year of publication is regarded as that of printing, as indicated on title page, although in some cases publication likely occurred in the following year. Year of publication (period covered; pages): 1876 (1876; 13), 1877a (1875–76; 75), 1877b (1877; 60), 1878 (1878; 33), 1879 (1879; 23), 1882 (1 Oct. 1879–1 Oct. 1882; 48), 1885 (1 Oct. 1883–30 Sept. 1885; 28), 1892 (1892; 5).

VFC (Virginia Fish Commission). 1916. 17th annual report of the Commission of Fisheries of Virginia. October 1, 1914 to September 30, 1915. Commission of Fisheries of Virginia, Richmond.

Victor, B. C., and E. B. Brothers. 1982. Age and growth of the fallfish Semotilus corporalis with daily otolith increments as a method of annulus verification. Canadian Journal of Zoology 60:2543–2550.

VIMS (Virginia Institute of Marine Science). 1977. Habital development field investigations Windmill Point Marsh development site, James River, Virginia. Contract 76-C-0040, U.S. Army Corps of Engineers, Gloucester Point, Virginia.

Vincent, R. E., and W. H. Miller. 1969. Altitudinal distribution of brown trout and other fishes in a headwater tributary of the South Platte River, Colorado. Ecology 50:464–465.

Vladykov, V. D. 1945. Trois poissons nouveaux pour la province de Quebec. Naturaliste Canadien 72:27–39. (Not seen; cited in R. R. Miller 1964.)

Vladykov, V. D. 1949. Quebec lampreys (Petromyzonidae) 1—list of species and their economic importance. Quebec Department of Fisheries Contribution 26.

Vladykov, V. D. 1950. Larvae of eastern American lampreys (Petromyzonidae), 1—species with two dorsal fins. Naturaliste Canadien 77:73–95. (Reprinted: Quebec Department of Fisheries Contribution 29.)

Vladykov, V. D. 1951. Fecundity of Quebec lampreys. Canadian Fish Culturist 10:1–14.

Vladykov, V. D. 1955. A comparison of Atlantic sea sturgeon with a new subspecies from the Gulf of Mexico (Acipenser oxyrhynchus desotoi). Journal of the Fisheries Research Board of Canada 12:754–761.

Vladykov, V. D. 1956. Fecundity of wild speckled trout (Salvelinus fontinalis) in Quebec lakes. Journal of the Fisheries Research Board of Canada 13:799–841.

Vladykov, V. D. 1960. Description of young ammocoetes belonging to two species of lampreys: Petromyzon marinus and Entosphenous lamottenii. Journal of the Fisheries Research Board of Canada 17:267–288.

Vladykov, V. D. 1963. A review of salmonid genera and their broad geographic distribution. Transactions of the Royal Society of Canada 1:459–504.

Vladykov, V. D. 1964. Quest for the true breeding area of the American eel (Anguilla rostrata Lesueur). Journal of the Fisheries Research Board of Canada 21:1523–1530.

Vladykov, V. D. 1973a. A female sea lamprey (Petromyzon marinus) with a true anal fin, and the question of the presence of an anal fin in Petromyzonidae. Canadian Journal of Zoology 51:221–224.

Vladykov, V. D. 1973b. North American nonparasitic lampreys of the family Petromyzonidae must be protected. Canadian Field-Naturalist 87:235–239.

Vladykov, V. D. 1973c. Macrophthalmia in the American eel (Anguilla rostrata). Journal of the Fisheries Research Board of Canada 30:689–693.

Vladykov, V. D., and W. I. Follette. 1967. The teeth of lampreys (Petromyzonidae): their terminology and use in a key to the Holarctic genera. Journal of the Fisheries Research Board of Canada 24:1067–1075.

Vladykov, V. D., and J. R. Greeley. 1964. Order Acipenseroidei. Pages 24–60 in Fishes of the western North Atlantic Part 3. Sears Foundation for Marine Research, Yale University, New Haven, Connecticut.

Vladykov, V. D., and C. G. Gruchy. 1972. Comments on the nomenclature of some subgenera of Salmonidae. Journal of the Fisheries Research Board of Canada 29:1631–1632.

Vladykov, V. D., and E. Kott. 1976. Is Okkelbergia Creaser and Hubbs, 1922 (Petromyzonidae) a distinct taxon? Canadian Journal of Zoology 54:421–425.

Vladykov, V. D., and E. Kott. 1978. A new nonparasitic species of the Holarctic lamprey genus Lethenteron Creaser and Hubbs, 1922, (Petromyzonidae) from northwestern North America with notes on other species of the same genus. Biological Papers of the University of Alaska 19:1–74.

Vladykov, V. D., and E. Kott. 1979a. Satellite species among the Holarctic lampreys. Canadian Journal of Zoology 57:860–867.

Vladykov, V. D., and E. Kott. 1979b. List of Northern Hemisphere lampreys (Petromyzonidae) and their distribution. Canada Fisheries and Marine Service Miscellaneous Special Publication 42.

Vladykov, V. D., and E. Kott. 1980. Description and key to metamorphosed specimens and ammocoetes of Petromyzonidae found in the Great Lakes region. Canadian Journal of Fisheries and Aquatic Sciences 37:1616–1625.

Vladykov, V. D., and E. Kott. 1982a. Correct scientific names for the least brook lamprey and the American brook lamprey (Petromyzonidae). Canadian Journal of Zoology 60:856–864.

Vladykov, V. D., and E. Kott. 1982b. Comment on Reeve M. Bailey's view of lamprey systematics: Comment. Canadian Journal of Fisheries and Aquatic Sciences 39:1215–1217.

Vladykov, V. D., E. Kott, and S. Pharand-Coad. 1975. A new nonparasitic species of lamprey, genus *Lethenteron* (Petromyzonidae), from eastern tributaries of the Gulf of Mexico, U.S.A. National Museum of Natural Sciences (Ottawa) Publications in Zoology 12:1–36.

Vladykov, V. D., and D. H. Wallace. 1938. Remarks on populations of the shad (*Alosa sapidissima*) along the Atlantic Coast region. Transactions of the American Fisheries Society 67:52–66.

Vladykov, V. D., and D. H. Wallace. 1952. Studies of the striped bass, *Roccus saxatilis* (Walbaum), with special reference to the Chesapeake Bay region during 1936–1938. Bulletin of the Bingham Oceanographic Institute, Yale University 14:132–177.

VMRC (Virginia Marine Resources Commission). 1985–1989. Virginia landings, annual summary. VMRC, Newport News.

VNHP (Virginia Natural Heritage Program). 1989. Fish of special concern in Virginia (ordered by state rank). Department of Conservation and Historic Resources, Richmond.

Vogele, L. W. 1975. The spotted bass. Pages 34–45 *in* R. H. Stroud and H. Clepper, editors. Black bass biology and management. Sport Fishing Institute, Washington, D.C.

Voiers, W. D. 1988. Agonistic and reproductive behavior of the yellowcheek darter *Etheostoma moorei*. Page 185 *in* Abstracts of the 68th Annual Meeting of the American Society of Ichthyologists and Herpetologists.

VPISU (Virginia Polytechnic Institute and State University). 1985a. An ecological investigation of the New River and Bluestone Lake. Report to U.S. Army Corps of Engineers, Huntington, West Virginia.

VPISU (Virginia Polytechnic Institute and State University). 1985b. Development and application of an energy flow model to analyze impacts of navigation changes on the Kanawha River in West Virginia. Report to U.S. Army Corps of Engineers, Huntington, West Virginia.

VSWCB (Virginia State Water Control Board). 1988a. Water supply plans for the river basins of Virginia. Planning Bulletins 336–346, VSWCB, Richmond. Basins and bulletin numbers are: Potomac 336; James 337 (2 parts); Rappahannock 338; Roanoke and Peedee 339; Chowan 340; Tennessee 341; eastern shore 342; York 343; New 344; Shenandoah and Shenandoah appendices 345; Big Sandy 346.

VSWCB (Virginia State Water Control Board). 1988b. Virginia's water supply: statewide summary and technical data. Planning Bulletin 347, VSWCB, Richmond.

Wagner, C. C., and E. L. Cooper. 1963. Population density, growth, and fecundity of the creek chubsucker, *Erimyzon oblongus*. Copeia 1963:350–357.

Wahl, D. H. 1982. Daily ration, feeding periodicity and prey selection of sauger (*Stizostedion canadense*) in the Ohio River. Master's thesis. Virginia Polytechnic Institute and State University, Blacksburg.

Wainwright, P. C., and G. V. Lauder. 1992. The evolution of feeding biology in sunfishes (Centrarchidae). Pages 472–491 *in* Mayden (1992).

Walburg, C. H. 1956. Observations on the food and growth of juvenile American shad, *Alosa sapidissima*. Transactions of the American Fisheries Society 86:302–306.

Walburg, C. H. 1960. Abundance and life history of the shad, St. John's River, Florida. U.S. Fish and Wildlife Service Fishery Bulletin 60:487–501.

Walburg, C. H., and P. R. Nichols. 1967. Biology and management of the American shad and status of the fisheries, Atlantic Coast of the United States, 1960. U.S. Fish and Wildlife Service Special Scientific Report—Fisheries 550.

Walburg, C. H., and J. E. Sykes. 1957. Shad fishery at Chesapeake Bay with special emphasis on the fishery of Virginia. U.S. Fish and Wildlife Service Resource Report 48.

Waldman, J. R. 1986. Diagnostic value of *Morone* dentition. Transactions of the American Fisheries Society 115:900–907.

Walker, B. W. 1952. A guide to the grunion. California Fish and Game 38:409–420.

Wallace, C. R. 1967. Observations on the reproductive behavior of the black bullhead (*Ictalurus melas*). Copeia 1967:852–853.

Wallace, C. R. 1972. Spawning behavior of *Ictalurus natalis* (Lesueur). Texas Journal of Science 24:307–310.

Wallace, D. C. 1971a. Age, growth, year class strength, and survival rates of the white perch, *Morone americana* (Gmelin) in the Delaware River in the vicinity of Artificial Island. Chesapeake Science 12:205–218.

Wallace, D. C. 1971b. The age and growth of the silverjaw minnow, *Ericymba buccata* Cope. American Midland Naturalist 86:116–127.

Wallace, D. C. 1972. The ecology of the silverjaw minnow, *Ericymba buccata* Cope. American Midland Naturalist 87:172–190.

Wallace, D. C. 1973a. The distribution and dispersal of the silverjaw minnow, *Ericymba buccata* Cope. American Midland Naturalist 89:145–155.

Wallace, D. C. 1973b. Reproduction of the silverjaw minnow, *Ericymba buccata* Cope. Transactions of the American Fisheries Society 102:786–793.

Wallace, D. C. 1976. Feeding behavior and developmental, seasonal and diel changes in the food of the silverjaw minnow, *Ericymba buccata* Cope. American Midland Naturalist 95:361–376.

Wallace, J. B., J. R. Webster, and R. L. Lowe. 1992. High-gradient streams of the Appalachians. Pages 133–191 *in* C. T. Hackney, S. M. Adams, and W. H. Martin, editors. Biodiversity of the southeastern United States. Aquatic communities. Wiley, New York.

Wallace, R. K., and J. S. Ramsey. 1981. Reproductive behavior and biology of the bluestripe shiner (*Notropis callitaenia*) in Uchee Creek, Alabama. American Midland Naturalist 106:197–200.

Wallace, R. K., and J. S. Ramsey. 1982. A new cyprinid hybrid, *Notropis lutrensis* × *N. callitaenia*, from the Apalachicola drainage in Alabama. Copeia 1982:214–217.

Wallin, J. E. 1989. Bluehead chub (*Nocomis leptocephalus*) nests used by yellowfin shiners (*Notropis lutipinnis*). Copeia 1989:1077–1080.

Wallus, R., and K. L. Grannemann. 1979. Spawning behavior and early development of the banded sculpin, *Cottus carolinae* (Gill). Pages 200–235 *in* R. Wallus and C. W. Voigtlander, editors. Proceedings of a workshop on freshwater larval fishes. Tennessee Valley Authority, Norris, Tennessee.

Walsh, S. J., and B. M. Burr. 1981. Distribution, morphology and life history of the least brook lamprey, *Lampetra aepyptera* (Pisces: Petromyzontidae), in Kentucky. Brimleyana 6:83–100.

Walsh, S. J., and B. M. Burr. 1984. Life history of the banded pygmy sunfish, *Elassoma zonatum* Jordan (Pisces: Centrarchidae). Bulletin Alabama Museum of Natural History 8:31–52.

Walsh, S. J., and B. M. Burr. 1985. The biology of the stonecat, *Noturus flavus* (Siluriformes: Ictaluridae), in central Illinois and Missouri streams, and comparisons with Great Lakes populations and congeners. Ohio Journal of Science 85:85–96.

Walters, V. 1955. Fishes of western Arctic America and eastern Arctic Siberia. Bulletin of the American Museum of Natural History 106:255–368.

Wang, J. C. S., and R. J. Kernehan. 1979. Fishes of the Delaware estuaries: a guide to the early life histories. E A Communications, Ecological Analysts, Towson, Maryland.

Warburton, B., C. Hubbs, and D. W. Hagen. 1957. Reproductive behavior of *Gambusia heterochir*. Copeia 1957:299–300.

Ward, C. 1960. The fishes of Nolichucky River. A contribution to a pollution survey. Tennessee Game and Fish Commission, Special Report, Nashville.

Ware, F. J. 1975. Progress with *Morone* hybrids in fresh water. Proceedings of the Annual Conference Southeastern Association of Game and Fish Commissioners 28(1974):48–54.

Warfel, H. E., and Y. H. Olsen. 1947. Vertebral counts and the problem of races in the Atlantic shad. Copeia 1947:177–183.

Warren, M. L. 1981. New distributional records of eastern Kentucky fishes. Brimleyana 6:129–140.

Warren, M. L., B. M. Burr, and B. R. Kuhajda. 1986a. Aspects of the reproductive biology of *Etheostoma tippecanoe* with comments on egg-burying behavior. American Midland Naturalist 116:215–218.

Warren, M. L., and R. R. Cicerello. 1983. Drainage records and conservation status evaluations for thirteen Kentucky fishes. Brimleyana 9:97–109.

Warren, M. L., and fourteen coauthors. 1986b. Endangered, threatened, and rare plants and animals of Kentucky. Transactions of the Kentucky Academy of Science 47:83–98.

Washburn, G. N. 1945. Propagation of the creek chub in ponds with artificial raceways. Transactions of the American Fisheries Society 75:336–350.

Washington, B. B., W. N. Eschmeyer, and K. M. Howe. 1984a. Scorpaeniformes: relationships. Pages 438–447 *in* Moser et al. (1984).

Washington, B. B., H. G. Moser, W. A. Laroche, and W. J. Richards. 1984b. Scorpaeniformes: development. Pages 405–428 *in* Moser et al. (1984).

Watkins, W. D. 1974. Age and growth of the troutperch, *Percopsis omiscomaycus* (Walbaum), in Beech Fork of Twelvepole Creek, Wayne County, West Virginia. West Virginia Academy of Science 46:237–246.

Webb, J. F., and D. D. Moss. 1968. Spawning behavior and age and growth of white bass in Center Hill Reservoir, Tennessee. Proceedings of the Annual Conference Southeastern Association of Game and Fish Commissioners 21(1967):343–357.

Webb, J. R., and eight coauthors. 1990. Acidic deposition and the status of Virginia's wild trout resource. Pages 228–233 *in* F. Richardson and R. H. Hamre, editors. Wild trout IV. Trout Unlimited, Vienna, Virginia.

Webb, J. R., B. J. Cosby, J. N. Galloway, and G. M. Hornberger. 1989. Acidification of native brook trout streams in Virginia. Water Resources Research 25:1367–1377.

Webster, D. A. 1942. The life histories of some Connecticut fishes. Pages 122–127 *in* A fishery survey of important Connecticut Lakes. Connecticut State Geological and Natural History Survey, Bulletin 63.

Webster, D. A. 1980. De Witt Clinton's ". . . Fishes of the western waters of the state of New-York" reexamined. Fisheries (Bethesda) 5(2):5–12.

Webster, D. A. 1981. Spawning. Trout 22(4):6–13.

Weed, A. C. 1927. Pike, pickerel and muskalonge. Field Museum of Natural History Zoology Leaflet 9:153–204.

Weems, R. E. 1990. Evidence for the James River headwaters lying west of the Blue Ridge by Late Miocene time. Virginia Journal of Science 41:96.

Wehnes, R. A. 1973. The food and feeding interrelationships of five sympatric darter species (Pisces: Percidae) in Salt Creek, Hocking County, Ohio. Master's thesis. Ohio State University. (Not seen; cited in Page 1983.)

Weisel, G. F. 1962. Comparative study of the digestive tract of a sucker, *Catostomus catostomus*, and a predaceous minnow, *Ptychocheilus oregonense*. American Midland Naturalist 68:334–346.

Weitzman, S. H., and R. P. Vari. 1988. Miniaturization in

South American freshwater fishes: an overview and discussion. Proceedings of the Biological Society of Washington 101:444–465.

Weldon, P. J., and G. M. Burghardt. 1984. Deception divergence and sexual selection. Zeitschrift fuer Tierpsychologie 65:89–102.

Wells, A. W. 1977. Occurrence of the slimy sculpin, *Cottus cognatus*, in the Missouri drainage system. Canadian Field-Naturalist 91:415–416.

Wells, A. W. 1978. Systematics, variation, and zoogeography of two North American cyprinid fishes. Doctoral dissertation. University of Alberta, Edmonton, Canada.

Wells, L., and R. House. 1974. Life history of the spottail shiner (*Notropis hudsonius*) in southeastern Lake Michigan, the Kalamazoo River, and western Lake Erie. Bureau of Sport Fisheries and Wildlife (U.S.) Research Report 78.

Wenner, C. A. 1973. Occurrence of American eels, *Anguilla rostrata*, in waters overlying the eastern North American Continental Shelf. Journal of the Fisheries Research Board of Canada 30:1752–1755.

Wenner, C. A., and J. A. Musick. 1974. Fecundity and gonad observations of the American eel, *Anguilla rostrata*, migrating from the Chesapeake Bay, Virginia. Journal of the Fisheries Research Board of Canada 31:1387–1391.

Wenner, C. A., and J. A. Musick. 1975. Food habits and seasonal abundance of the American eel, *Anguilla rostrata*, from the lower Chesapeake Bay. Chesapeake Science 16:62–66.

Wentworth, C. K. 1930. Sand and gravel resources of the Coastal Plain of Virginia. Virginia Geological Survey Bulletin 32.

Werner, R. G. 1972. Bluespotted sunfish, *Enneacanthus gloriosus*, in the Lake Ontario drainage, New York. Copeia 1972:878–879.

West, F. H. 1983. The antiquity of man in America. Pages 364–382 *in* H. E. Wright and S. C. Porter, editors. Late-Quaternary environments of the United States, volume 1. University of Minnesota Press, Minneapolis.

West, J. L. 1970. The gonads and reproduction of three intergeneric sunfish (family Centrarchidae) hybrids. Evolution 24:378–394.

West, J. L., and F. E. Hester. 1966. Intergeneric hybridization of centrarchids. Transactions of the American Fisheries Society 95:280–288.

Westman, J. R. 1938. Studies on the reproduction and growth of the bluntnosed minnow, *Hyborhynchus notatus* (Rafinesque). Copeia 1938:56–61.

Wheeler, A. 1978. *Ictalurus melas* (Rafinesque, 1820) and *I. nebulosus* (Lesueur, 1819): the North American catfishes in Europe. Journal of Fish Biology 12:435–439.

Whig, R. 1876. The fresh water fish of Virginia. Forest and Stream 6:284.

Whitaker, J. O., R. A. Schlueter, and M. A. Proffitt. 1973. Effects of heated discharges on fish and invertebrates of White River at Petersburg, Indiana. Indiana University, Water Resources Research Center, Report of Investigations 6, Bloomington.

White, B. N., R. J. Lavenberg, and G. E. McGowen. 1984.

Atheriniformes: development and relationships. Pages 355–362 *in* Moser et al. (1984).

White, C. P. 1982. Endangered and threatened wildlife of the Chesapeake Bay region: Delaware, Maryland and Virginia. Tidewater Publishers, Centreville, Maryland.

White, C. P. 1989. Chesapeake Bay. Nature of the estuary. A field guide. Tidewater Publishers, Centreville, Maryland.

White, J. C., editor. 1976. The effects of Surry Power Station operations on fishes of the oligohaline zone, James River, Virginia. Environmental Services Department, Virginia Electric and Power Company, Richmond.

White, J. C., J. B. Bailey, and M. L. Brehmer. 1984. Striped bass: did the James River love bug ever bite above the Fall Line? Virginia Power Company, Richmond (talk presented to Atlantic Estuarine Research Society, 11–13 October 1984).

White, J. C., and eight coauthors. 1972. Young littoral fishes of the oligohaline zone James River, Virginia, 1970–1972. Surry Nuclear Power Station preoperational studies. Virginia Electric and Power Company, Richmond.

White, J. W., W. S. Woolcott, and W. L. Kirk. 1977. A study of the fish community in the vicinity of a thermal discharge in the James River, Virginia. Chesapeake Science 18:161–171.

White, W. A. 1953. Systematic drainage changes in the Piedmont of North Carolina and Virginia. Geological Society of America Bulletin 64:561–580.

White, W. A. 1966. Drainage asymmetry and the Carolina Capes. Geological Society of America Bulletin 77:223–240.

White, W. J. 1970. A study of a population of smallmouth bass *Micropterus dolomieui* (Lacepède) at Baie du Doré, Ontario. Master's thesis. University of Toronto, Toronto. (Not seen; cited in Scott and Crossman 1973.)

Whitehead, D. R. 1972. Developmental and environmental history of the dismal swamp. Ecological Monographs 42:301–315.

Whitehead, D. R., and R. Q. Oaks. 1979. Developmental history of the Dismal Swamp. Pages 25–43 *in* P. W. Kirk, editor. The Great Dismal Swamp. University Press of Virginia, Charlottesville.

Whitehead, P. J. P., and A. C. Wheeler. 1966. The generic names used for the sea basses of Europe and North America (Pisces: Serranidae). Annali del Museo Civico di Storia Naturale Genova 76:23–41. (Not seen; cited in Bailey et al. 1970.)

Whitehurst, D. K. 1981. Seasonal movements of fishes in a North Carolina swamp stream. Pages 182–190 *in* L. A. Krumholz, editor. The warmwater streams symposium. American Fisheries Society, Southern Division, Bethesda, Maryland.

Whitehurst, D. K. 1985. Reservoir investigations, region II, Claytor Lake, 1 April 1984–31 March 1985. Virginia Commission of Game and Inland Fisheries, Richmond.

Whitehurst, D. K., and C. N. Carwile. 1982. Kerr Reservoir striped bass population study. Virginia Commission of Game and Inland Fisheries, Federal Aid in Sport Fish Restoration, Project F-34, Jobs 1–6, January 1, 1976–June 30, 1981. Final Report, Richmond.

Whiteside, L. A., and B. M. Burr. 1986. Aspects of the life history of the tadpole madtom, *Noturus gyrinus* (Siluriformes: Ictaluridae), in southern Illinois. Ohio Journal of Science 86:153–160.

Whitmore, D. H., and T. R. Hellier. 1988. Natural hybridization between largemouth and smallmouth bass (*Micropterus*). Copeia 1988:493–496.

Whitworth, W. R., P. L. Berrien, and W. T. Keller. 1968. Freshwater fishes of Connecticut. Connecticut State Geological and Natural History Survey, Bulletin 101.

Whitworth, W. R., and R. E. Schmidt. 1980. Snorkeling as a means of evaluating fish populations in streams. New York Fish and Game Journal 27:91–94.

Whyte, T. R. 1988. Fish remains recovered from a protohistoric village site on the Jackson River, Bath County, Virginia. Quarterly Bulletin of the Archeological Society of Virginia 43(4):167–170.

Whyte, T. R. 1989. Faunal remains. Pages 214–243 *in* T. R. Whyte and S. M. Thompson, editors. Archaelogical investigations at the Bessemer site (44BO26): a Late Woodland period Dan River and Page component village site on the upper James River, Virginia. James Madison University, Archeological Research Center, Harrisonburg, Virginia.

Wich, K., and J. W. Mullan. 1958. A compendium of the life history and ecology of the chain pickerel *Esox niger* (Lesueur). Massachusetts Division of Fisheries and Game, Fisheries Bulletin 22, Boston.

Widlak, J. C. 1982. The ecology of freshwater mussel-fish host relationships with a description of the life history of the redline darter in the North Fork Holston River, Virginia. Master's thesis. Virginia Polytechnic Institute and State University, Blacksburg.

Widlak, J. C., and R. J. Neves. 1985. Age, growth, food habits, and reproduction of the redline darter, *Etheostoma rufilineatum* (Perciformes: Percidae), in Virginia. Brimleyana 11:69–80.

Wilbur, R. L. 1969. The redear sunfish in Florida. Florida Game and Fresh Water Fish Commission, Fishery Bulletin 5, Tallahassee.

Wiley, E. O. 1976. The phylogeny and biogeography of fossil and recent gars (Actinopterygii: Lepisosteidae). University of Kansas Museum of Natural History Miscellaneous Publication 64.

Wiley, E. O. 1977. The phylogeny and systematics of the *Fundulus nottii* species group (Teleostei: Cyprinodontidae). Occasional Papers of the Museum of Natural History, University of Kansas 66.

Wiley, E. O. 1981. Phylogenetics. Wiley, New York.

Wiley, E. O. 1986. A study of the evolutionary relationships of *Fundulus* topminnows (Teleostei: Fundulidae). American Zoologist 26:121–130.

Wiley, E. O. 1988. Vicariance biogeography. Annual Review of Ecology and Systematics 19:513–542.

Wiley, E. O., and D. D. Hall. 1975. *Fundulus blairae*, a new species of the *Fundulus nottii* complex (Teleostei, Cyprinodontidae). American Museum Novitates 2577.

Wiley, E. O., and R. L. Mayden. 1985. Species and speciation in phylogenetic systematics, with examples from the North American fish fauna. Annals of the Missouri Botanical Garden 72:596–635.

Wiley, E. O., and H.-P. Schultze. 1984. Family Lepisosteidae (gars) as living fossils. Pages 160–165 *in* N. Eldredge and S. M. Stanley, editors. Living fossils. Springer-Verlag, New York.

Wiley, E. O., and J. D. Stewart. 1977. A gar (*Lepisosteus* sp.) from the marine Cretaceous Niobrara Formation of western Kansas. Copeia 1977:761–762.

Wiley, M. L., and B. B. Collette. 1970. Breeding tubercles and contact organs in fishes: their occurrence, structure, and significance. Bulletin of the American Museum of Natural History 143:143–216.

Wiley, M. L., and C. Tsai. 1983. The relative efficiencies of electrofishing vs. seines in Piedmont streams of Maryland. North American Journal of Fisheries Management 3:243–253.

Willers, W. B. 1981. Trout biology. An angler's guide. University of Wisconsin Press, Madison.

Williams, G. C., and R. K. Koehn. 1984. Population genetics of North Atlantic catadromous eels (*Anguilla*). Pages 529–560 *in* B. J. Turner, editor. Evolutionary genetics of fishes. Plenum, New York.

Williams, G. C., R. K. Koehn, and V. Thorsteinsson. 1984. Icelandic eels: evidence for a single species of *Anguilla* in the North Atlantic. Copeia 1984:221–223.

Williams, H. M. 1976. Characteristics for distinguishing white bass, striped bass and their hybrid (striped bass × white bass). Proceedings of the Annual Conference Southeastern Association of Game and Fish Commissioners 29(1975):168–172.

Williams, J. D. 1968. A new species of sculpin, *Cottus pygmaeus*, from a spring in the Alabama River basin. Copeia 1968:334–342.

Williams, J. D. 1975. Systematics of the percid fishes of the subgenus *Ammocrypta*, genus *Ammocrypta*, with descriptions of two new species. Bulletin Alabama Museum of Natural History 1:1–56.

Williams, J. D. 1976. A review of the Endangered Species Act of 1973. ASB (Association of Southeastern Biologists) Bulletin 23:138–141.

Williams, J. D. 1977. Endangered species: yesterday, today, and tomorrow?. Pages 49–55 *in* J. E. Cooper, S. S. Robinson and J. B. Funderberg, editors. Endangered and threatened plants and animals of North Carolina. North Carolina State Museum of Natural History, Raleigh.

Williams, J. D. 1981. Threatened warmwater stream fishes and the endangered species act: a review. Pages 328–337 *in* L. A. Krumholz, editor. The warmwater streams symposium. American Fisheries Society, Southern Division, Bethesda, Maryland.

Williams, J. D., and D. A. Etnier. 1978. *Etheostoma aquali*, a new percid (subgenus *Nothonotus*) from the Duck and Buffalo rivers, Tennessee. Proceedings of the Biological Society of Washington 91:463–471.

Williams, J. D., and D. A. Etnier. 1982. Description of a new species, *Fundulus julisia*, with a redescription of *Fundulus albolineatus* and a diagnosis of the subgenus *Xenisma* (Teleostei: Cyprinodontidae). Occasional Papers of the Museum of Natural History, University of Kansas 102.

Williams, J. D., and D. K. Finley. 1977. Our vanishing

fishes: can they be saved? Frontiers (summer): (unpaginated reprint).

Williams, J. D., and W. M. Howell. 1979. An albino sculpin from a cave in the New River drainage of West Virginia (Pisces: Cottidae). Brimleyana 1:141–146.

Williams, J. D., and D. P. Jennings. 1988. Preliminary summary of biological data on rudd (Scardinius erythrophthalmus). U.S. Fish and Wildlife Service, National Fisheries Research Center, Gainesville, Florida.

Williams, J. D., and R. M. Nowak. 1986. Vanishing species in our own backyard: extinct fish and wildlife of the United States and Canada. Pages 107–139 in L. Kaufman and K. Mallory, editors. The last extinction. MIT Press, Cambridge, Massachusetts.

Williams, J. D., and C. R. Robins. 1970. Variation in populations of the fish Cottus carolinae in the Alabama River system with description of a new subspecies from below the Fall Line. American Midland Naturalist 83: 368–381.

Williams, J. E., and seven coauthors. 1989. Fishes of North America endangered, threatened, or of special concern: 1989. Fisheries (Bethesda) 14(6):2–20.

Williams, J. M. 1985. A mechanism for long distance dispersal of fresh water organisms. ASB (Association of Southeastern Biologists) Bulletin 32:50.

Williams, M. 1989. Americans and their forests. a historical geography. Cambridge University Press, New York.

Williams, S., and J. B. Stoltman. 1965. An outline of southeastern United States prehistory with particular emphasis on the Paleo-Indian era. Pages 669–683 in H. E. Wright and D. G. Frey, editors. The Quaternary of the United States. Princeton University Press, Princeton, New Jersey.

Willis, L. D., and A. V. Brown. 1985. Distribution and habitat requirements of the Ozark cavefish, Amblyopsis rosae. American Midland Naturalist 114:311–317.

Wilson, A. W. G. 1907. Chubs' nests. American Naturalist 41:323–327.

Wilson, M. V. H. 1977. Middle Eocene freshwater fish from British Columbia. Life Sciences Contribution 11B: 1–61. Royal Ontario Museum.

Wilson, M. V. H. 1979. A second species of Libotonius (Pisces: Percopsidae) from the Eocene of Washington State. Copeia 1979:400–405.

Wilson, M. V. H. 1980. Oldest known Esox (Pisces: Esocidae), part of a new Paleocene teleost fauna from western Canada. Canadian Journal of Earth Sciences 17:307–312.

Wilson, M. V. H. 1984. Osteology of the Paleocene teleost Esox tiemani. Palaeontology 27:597–608.

Wilson, M. V. H., and P. Veilleux. 1982. Comparative osteology and relationships of the Umbridae (Pisces: Salmoniformes). Zoological Journal of the Linnean Society 76:321–352.

Winger, P. V. 1981. Physical and chemical characteristics of warmwater streams: a review. Pages 32–44 in L. A. Krumholz, editor. The warmwater streams symposium. American Fisheries Society, Southern Division, Bethesda, Maryland.

Winn, H. E. 1953. Breeding habits of the percid fish Hadropterus copelandi in Michigan. Copeia 1953:26–30.

Winn, H. E. 1958a. Observations on the reproductive habits of darters (Pisces: Percidae). American Midland Naturalist 59:190–212.

Winn, H. E. 1958b. Comparative reproductive behavior and ecology of fourteen species of darters (Pisces—Percidae). Ecological Monographs 28:155–191.

Winn, H. E., and A. R. Picciolo. 1960. Communal spawning of the glassy darter Etheostoma vitreum (Cope). Copeia 1960:186–192.

Winn, H. E., and J. F. Stout. 1960. Sound production by the satinfin shiner, Notropis analostanus, and related fishes. Science 132:222–223.

Winter, R. L. 1983. An assessment of lake chubsuckers (Erimyzon sucetta (Girard)) as forage for largemouth bass (Micropterus salmoides (Lacepede)) in a small Nebraska pond. Master's thesis. University of Nebraska, Lincoln.

Wirth, T. L. 1958. Lake Winnebago freshwater drum. Wisconsin Conservation Bulletin 23(5):30–32. (Not seen; cited in Becker 1983.)

Witt, A. 1960. Length and weight of ancient freshwater drum, Aplodinotus grunniens, calculated from otoliths found in Indian middens. Copeia 1960:181–185.

Witzel, L. D. 1983. The occurrence and origin of tiger trout, Salmo trutta × Salvelinus fontinalis, in Ontario streams. Canadian Field-Naturalist 97:99–102.

Wolcott, L. T. 1990. Coal waste deposition and the distribution of freshwater mussels in the Powell River, Virginia. Master's thesis, Virginia Polytechnic Institute and State University, Blacksburg.

Wolfe, G. W., B. H. Bauer, and B. A. Branson. 1978. Age and growth, length–weight relationships, and condition factors of the greenside darter from Silver Creek, Kentucky. Transactions of the Kentucky Academy of Science 39:131–134.

Wollitz, R. E. 1963. Back Bay Fishery Investigations. Virginia Commission of Game and Inland Fisheries, Federal Aid in Sport Fish Restoration, Project F-5-R-9, Job 10, July 1, 1962–June 30, 1963. Supplement to Final Report, Richmond.

Wollitz, R. E. 1965. Smallmouth bass stream investigations, job 3—Clinch River study. Virginia Commission of Game and Inland Fisheries, Federal Aid in Sport Fish Restoration, Project F-14-R-3, January 1–December 31, 1964. Job Completion Report, Richmond.

Wollitz, R. E. 1967a. Smallmouth bass stream investigations, job 3—Clinch River study. Virginia Commission of Game and Inland Fisheries, Federal Aid in Sport Fish Restoration, Project F-14-R-5, January 1, 1965–June 30, 1966. Job Completion Report, Richmond.

Wollitz, R. E. 1967b. Smallmouth bass stream investigations, job 3—Clinch River study. Virginia Commission of Game and Inland Fisheries, Federal Aid in Sport Fish Restoration, Project F-14-R-5, July 1, 1966–June 30, 1967. Job Completion Report, Richmond.

Wollitz, R. E. 1968a. Smallmouth bass stream investigations, job 1—New River study. Virginia Commission of Game and Inland Fisheries, Federal Aid in Sport Fish

Restoration, Project F-14-R-5, July 1, 1966–December 31, 1967. Final Job Completion Report, Richmond.

Wollitz, R. E. 1968b. Smallmouth bass stream investigations, Clinch River study. Virginia Commission of Game and Inland Fisheries, Federal Aid in Sport Fish Restoration, Project F-14-R-6, January 1, 1964–June 30, 1968. Final Report, Richmond.

Wollitz, R. E. 1970. Southwest Virginia stream fisheries survey, job 1—fish population sampling—Clinch River. Virginia Commission of Game and Inland Fisheries, Federal Aid in Sport Fish Restoration, Project F-22, July 1, 1969–June 30, 1970. Job Completion Report, Richmond.

Wollitz, R. E. 1972. Southwest Virginia stream fisheries survey. Virginia Commission of Game and Inland Fisheries, Federal Aid in Sport Fish Restoration, Project F-22, July 1969–April 1970. Progress Report, Richmond.

Wollitz, R. E. 1973. Southwest Virginia stream fisheries survey. Virginia Commission of Game and Inland Fisheries, Federal Aid in Sport Fish Restoration, Project F-22-3, July 1972–July 1973. Progress Report, Richmond.

Wollitz, R. E. 1975a. Southwest Virginia stream fisheries survey. Virginia Commission of Game and Inland Fisheries, Federal Aid in Sport Fish Restoration, Project F-22-R-6. Progress Report, Richmond.

Wollitz, R. E. 1975b. Southwest Virginia stream fisheries survey. Virginia Commission of Game and Inland Fisheries, Federal Aid in Sport Fish Restoration, Project F-22-R-5. Progress Report, Richmond.

Woodling, J. 1985. Colorado's little fish: a guide to the minnows and other lesser known fishes in the state of Colorado. Colorado Department of Natural Resources Division of Wildlife, Denver.

Woods, L. P., and R. F. Inger. 1957. The cave, spring, and swamp fishes of the family Amblyopsidae of central and eastern United States. American Midland Naturalist 58:232–256.

Woodward, R. L., and T. E. Wissing. 1976. Age, growth, and fecundity of the quillback (*Carpiodes cyprinus*) and highfin (*C. velifer*) carpsuckers in an Ohio stream. Transactions of the American Fisheries Society 105:411–415.

Woodward, S. L., and R. L. Hoffman. 1991. The nature of Virginia. Pages 23–48 *in* K. Terwilliger, coordinator. Virginia's endangered species. McDonald and Woodward, Blacksburg, Virginia.

Woolcott, W. S. 1957. Comparative osteology of serranid fishes of the genus *Roccus* (Mitchill). Copeia 1957:1–10.

Woolcott, W. S. 1962. Infraspecific variation in the white perch, *Roccus americanus* (Gmelin). Chesapeake Science 3:94–113.

Woolcott, W. S., W. L. Kirk, E. G. Maurakis, and J. W. White. 1974. The effects of thermal loading by the Bremo Power Station on a Piedmont section of James River, July 1972–June 1974. Final report, 2 volumes. Virginia Institute for Scientific Research, Richmond.

Woolcott, W. S., and E. G. Maurakis. 1988. A need for clarification of the concept of nest building among cyprinid minnows. Proceedings of the Southeastern Fishes Council 18:3.

Woolman, A. J. 1892. An examination of the rivers of Kentucky, with lists of the fishes obtained. U.S. Fish Commission Bulletin 1890:249–288.

Wooten, M. C., K. T. Scribner, and M. H. Smith. 1988. Genetic variability and systematics of *Gambusia* in the southeastern United States. Copeia 1988:283–289.

Wootton, R. J. 1976. The biology of the sticklebacks. Academic Press, New York.

Wootton, R. J. 1990. Ecology of teleost fishes. Chapman and Hall, New York.

Worth, S. G. 1898. The shad. Pages 133–158 *in* J. J. Brice. A manual of fish culture, based on the methods of the United States Commission of Fish and Fisheries. U.S. Commission of Fish and Fisheries, Report of the Commissioner for 1897, Part 23, Appendix.

Wourms, J. P. 1981. Viviparity: the maternal–fetal relationship in fishes. American Zoologist 21:473–515.

Wrenn, W. B. 1969. Life history aspects of smallmouth buffalo and freshwater drum in Wheeler Reservoir, Alabama. Proceedings of the Annual Conference Southeastern Association of Game and Fish Commissioners 22(1968):479–495.

Wright, F. J. 1934. The newer Appalachians of the South, part I: between the Potomac and New rivers. Denison University Bulletin 34(13), Journal of the Science Laboratory 29, Article 1:1–105, Granville, Ohio.

Wright, H. E., and S. C. Porter, editors. 1983. Preface. Page ix *in* Late-Quaternary environments of the United States, volume 1. University of Minnesota Press, Minneapolis.

Wright, T. D., and A. D. Hasler. 1967. An electrophoretic analysis of the effects of isolation and homing behavior upon the serum proteins of the white bass (*Roccus chrysops*) in Wisconsin. American Naturalist 101:401–413.

Wujtewicz, D. 1982. The feasibility of utilizing minnows as forage in farm ponds, 4: a life history of the black-banded sunfish *Enneacanthus chaetodon*, in Hudson Pond, Delaware. Delaware State College, Natural Resources Report 3, Dover.

Wydoski, R. S., and R. R. Whitney. 1979. Inland fishes of Washington. University of Washington Press, Seattle.

Wynes, D. L., and T. E. Wissing. 1982. Resource sharing among darters in an Ohio stream. American Midland Naturalist 107:294–304.

Wynne-Edwards, V. C. 1932. The breeding habits of the black-headed minnow (*Pimephales notatus* Raf.). Transactions of the American Fisheries Society 62:381–383.

Yant, D. R., R. O. Smitherman, and O. L. Green. 1976. Production of hybrid (blue × channel) catfish and channel catfish in ponds. Proceedings of the Annual Conference Southeastern Association of Game and Fish Commissioners 29(1975):82–86.

Yates, T. L., M. A. Lewis, and M. D. Hatch. 1984. Biochemical systematics of three species of catfish (genus *Ictalurus*) in New Mexico. Copeia 1984:97–101.

Yeager, B. L. 1979. Larval and early development of the striped shiner, *Notropis chrysocephalus* (Rafinesque). Pages 61–91 *in* R. Wallus and C. W. Voigtlander, editors. Proceedings of a workshop on freshwater larval fishes. Tennessee Valley Authority, Norris, Tennessee.

Yeager, B. L. 1981. Early development of the longear sunfish, *Lepomis megalotis* (Rafinesque). Journal of Tennessee Academy of Science 56: 84–88.

Yeager, B. L., and R. T. Bryant. 1983. Larvae of the longnose gar, *Lepisosteus osseus*, from the Little River in Tennessee. Journal of Tennessee Academy of Science 58:20–22.

Yellayi, R. R., and R. V. Kilambi. 1970. Observations on early development of white bass, *Roccus chrysops* (Rafinesque). Proceedings of the Annual Conference Southeastern Association of Game and Fish Commissioners 23(1969):261–265.

Yerger, R. W., and K. Relyea. 1968. The flat-headed bullheads (Pisces: Ictaluridae) of the southeastern United States, and a new species of *Ictalurus* from the Gulf Coast. Copeia 1968:361–384.

Yoder, C. O., and R. A. Beaumier. 1986. The occurrence and distribution of river redhorse, *Moxostoma carinatum* and greater redhorse, *Moxostoma valenciennesi* in the Sandusky River, Ohio. Ohio Journal of Science 86:18–21.

Yonezawa, K. 1958. A study on the three forms of *Sarcocheilichthys variegatus* in Lake Biwa. Japanese Journal of Ichthyology 7:19–23.

Young, R. D., and O. E. Maughan. 1980. Downstream changes in fish species composition after construction of a headwater reservoir. Virginia Journal of Science 31:39–41.

Youson, J. H. 1980. Morphology and physiology of lamprey metamorphosis. Canadian Journal of Fisheries and Aquatic Sciences 37:1687–1710.

Youson, J. H., and I. C. Potter. 1979. A description of the stages in the metamorphosis of the anadromous sea lamprey, *Petromyzon marinus* L. Canadian Journal of Zoology 57:1808–1817.

Zahuranec, B. J. 1962. Range extensions of some cyprinid fishes in southeastern Ohio. Copeia 1962:842–843.

Ziebell, C. D., J. C. Tosh, and R. L. Barefield. 1986. Impact of threadfin shad on macrocrustacean zooplankton in two Arizona lakes. Journal of Freshwater Ecology 3:399–406.

Zolczynski, S. J., and W. D. Davies. 1976. Growth characteristics of the northern and southern subspecies of largemouth bass and their hybrid, and a comparison of catchability between the subspecies. Transactions of the American Fisheries Society 105:240–243.

Zorach, T. 1967. Systematics of the darters of the subgenus *Nothonotus* (*Etheostoma*, Percidae). Doctoral dissertation. Cornell University, Ithaca, New York.

Zorach, T. 1968. *Etheostoma bellum*, a new darter of the subgenus *Nothonotus* from the Green River system, Kentucky and Tennessee. Copeia 1968:474–482.

Zorach, T. 1969. *Etheostoma jordani* and *E. tippecanoe*, species of the subgenus *Nothonotus* (Pisces: Percidae). American Midland Naturalist 81:412–434.

Zorach, T. 1970. The systematics of the percid fish *Etheostoma rufilineatum* (Cope). American Midland Naturalist 84:208–225.

Zorach, T. 1971. Taxonomic status of the subspecies of the tessellated darter, *Etheostoma olmstedi* Storer, in southeastern Virginia. Chesapeake Science 11:254–263.

Zorach, T. 1972. Systematics of the percid fish, *Etheostoma camurum* and *E. chlorobranchium* new species, with a discussion of the subgenus *Nothonotus*. Copeia 1972: 427–447.

Zorach, T., and E. C. Raney. 1967. Systematics of the percid fish, *Etheostoma maculatum* Kirkland, and related species of the subgenus *Nothonotus*. American Midland Naturalist 77:296–322.

Appendix 1

Following each figure are locality data for specimens shown in color plates. The state is given only when it is not Virginia. Lengths are the standard length except when total length (TL) is specified. Most photographs of adults are adult males; most adult males are in nuptial color. Reds and oranges tend to be slightly less intense in the photographs than on the specimens when they were photographed (see *Photography*).

PLATE 9

Ohio lamprey *Ichthyomyzon bdellium* parasitic juvenile 197 mm TL (REJ 1099), Scott County, Clinch River, 5 June 1984.

Mountain brook lamprey *Ichthyomyzon greeleyi* nuptial male 130 mm TL (REJ 1096), Smyth County, Middle Fork Holston River, 4 June 1984.

Longnose gar *Lepisosteus osseus* juvenile 140 mm TL (REJ 1154), Hancock County, Tennessee, Clinch River, 29 June 1985.

PLATE 10

Muskellunge *Esox masquinongy* juvenile 175 mm (NMB 917), Smyth County, Buller Hatchery, 28 August 1984.

Chain pickerel *Esox niger* juvenile female 193 mm (REJ 1084), Craig County, Craig Creek, 17 May 1984.

Redfin pickerel *Esox americanus* adult female 140 mm (REJ 1116), Charlotte County, Twittys Creek, 10 July 1984.

Eastern mudminnow *Umbra pygmaea* adult female 60 mm (REJ 1117), Sussex County, Coppahaunk Swamp, 11 July 1984.

PLATE 11

Golden shiner *Notemigonus crysoleucas* adult 134 mm (REJ 1057), Franklin County, Pigg River, 20 March 1984.

Mountain redbelly dace *Phoxinus oreas* nuptial male 47 mm (REJ 1094), Carroll County, Coal Creek, 4 June 1984.

Rosyside dace *Clinostomus funduloides* nuptial male 68 mm (REJ 1094), Carroll County, Coal Creek, 4 June 1984.

Longnose dace *Rhinichthys cataractae* adult male 81 mm (REJ 1156), Washington County, Whitetop Laurel Creek, 30 June 1985.

Blacknose dace *Rhinichthys atratulus atratulus* nuptial male 50 mm (REJ 1108), Roanoke County, Back Creek, 11 June 1984.

Blacknose dace *Rhinichthys atratulus obtusus* nuptial male 60 mm (REJ 1094), Carroll County, Coal Creek, 4 June 1984.

PLATE 12

Central stoneroller *Campostoma anomalum* nuptial or just postnuptial male 126 mm (REJ 1093), Carroll County, Big Reed Island Creek, 3 June 1984.

Pearl dace *Margariscus margarita* prenuptial male 57 mm (REJ 1064), Augusta County, Mossy Creek, 3 April 1984.

Fallfish *Semotilus corporalis* juvenile male 223 mm (REJ 1109), Craig County, Johns Creek, 12 June 1984.

Creek chub *Semotilus atromaculatus* subadult or adult male 143 mm (REJ 1113), Carroll County, Pauls Creek, 20 June 1984.

Tonguetied minnow *Exoglossum laurae* adult female 93 mm (NMB 914), Wythe County, South Fork Reed Creek, 27 August 1984.

Cutlips minnow *Exoglossum maxillingua* nuptial male 104 mm (REJ 1090), Craig County, Craig Creek, 1 June 1984.

PLATE 13

River chub *Nocomis micropogon* nuptial male 175 mm (REJ 1097), Scott County, Copper Creek, 5 June 1984.

Bull chub *Nocomis raneyi* nuptial male 237 mm (REJ 1109), Craig County, Johns Creek, 12 June 1984.

Bluehead chub *Nocomis leptocephalus* nuptial male, orange-striped form, 160 mm (REJ 1084), Craig County, Craig Creek, 17 May 1984.

PLATE 14

Slender chub *Erimystax cahni* postnuptial male 81 mm (REJ 1154), Hancock County, Tennessee, Clinch River, 29 June 1985.

Streamline chub *Erimystax dissimilis* adult male 91 mm (REJ 1103), Washington County, North Fork Holston River, 6 June 1984.

Blotched chub *Erimystax insignis* adult male 64 mm (REJ 1097), Scott County, Copper Creek, 5 June 1984.

Kanawha minnow *Phenacobius teretulus* nuptial male 72 mm (NMB 868), Floyd County, Little River, 27 April 1984.

Fatlips minnow *Phenacobius crassilabrum* prenuptial male 70 mm (REJ 1079), Washington County, South Fork Holston River, 24 April 1984.

Stargazing minnow *Phenacobius uranops* adult female 71 mm (REJ 1080), Scott County, Copper Creek, 25 April 1984.

PLATE 15

Bigeye chub *Hybopsis amblops* adult male 52 mm (REJ 1080), Scott County, Copper Creek, 25 April 1984.

Highback chub *Hybopsis hypsinotus* nuptial male 63 mm (REJ 1113), Carroll County, Pauls Creek, 20 June 1984.

Whitetail shiner *Cyprinella galactura* nuptial male 109 mm (REJ 1097), Scott County, Copper Creek, 5 June 1984.

Steelcolor shiner *Cyprinella whipplei* adult male 94 mm (REJ 1154), Hancock County, Tennessee, Clinch River, 29 June 1985.

Satinfin shiner *Cyprinella analostana* adult male 54 mm (REJ 1116), Charlotte County, Twittys Creek, 10 July 1984.

Spotfin shiner *Cyprinella spiloptera* adult male 78 mm (REJ 1154), Hancock County, Tennessee, Clinch River, 29 June 1985.

PLATE 16

Warpaint shiner *Luxilus coccogenis* nuptial male 96 mm (REJ 1105), Russell County, Copper Creek, 7 June 1984.

Crescent shiner *Luxilus cerasinus* nuptial male 69 mm (REJ 1108), Roanoke County, Back Creek, 11 June 1984.

White shiner *Luxilus albeolus* prenuptial male 117 mm (REJ 1086), Roanoke County, Roanoke River, 13 May 1984.

Common shiner *Luxilus cornutus* nuptial male 64 mm (REJ 1092), Craig County, Johns Creek, 3 June 1984.

Striped shiner *Luxilus chrysocephalus* nuptial male 128 mm (REJ 1105), Russell County, Copper Creek, 7 June 1984.

PLATE 17

Mountain shiner *Lythrurus lirus* nuptial male 48 mm (REJ 1105), Russell County, Copper Creek, 7 June 1984.

Rosefin shiner *Lythrurus ardens* nuptial male 68 mm (REJ 1089), Roanoke County, Roanoke River, 31 May 1984.

Rosyface shiner *Notropis rubellus* nuptial male 49 mm (REJ 1110), Craig County, Johns Creek, 12 June 1984.

Tennessee shiner *Notropis leuciodus* nuptial male 47 mm (REJ 1106), Washington County, Laurel Creek, 7 June 1984.

Saffron shiner *Notropis rubricroceus* nuptial male 55 mm (REJ 1106), Washington County, Laurel Creek, 7 June 1984.

Redlip shiner *Notropis chiliticus* nuptial male 49 mm (REJ 1113), Carroll County, Pauls Creek, 20 June 1984.

PLATE 18

Silver shiner *Notropis photogenis* adult male 70 mm (REJ 1103), Washington County, North Fork Holston River, 6 June 1984.

Popeye shiner *Notropis ariommus* adult male 72 mm (REJ 1103), Washington County, North Fork Holston River, 6 June 1984.

Telescope shiner *Notropis telescopus* adult female 50 mm (REJ 1103), Washington County, North Fork Holston River, 6 June 1984.

New River shiner *Notropis scabriceps* adult female 59 mm (NMB 868), Floyd County, Little River, 27 April 1984.

PLATE 19

Sawfin shiner *Notropis* sp., nuptial male 49 mm (REJ 1103), Washington County, North Fork Holston River, 6 June 1984.

Mirror shiner *Notropis spectrunculus* nuptial male 56 mm (REJ 1096), Smyth County, Middle Fork Holston River, 4 June 1984. Dark areas of fins carmine in life.

Swallowtail shiner *Notropis procne* adult male 49 mm (REJ 1114), Bedford County, Beaverdam Creek, 9 July 1984.

PLATE 20

Creek chubsucker *Erimyzon oblongus* adult male 215 mm (REJ 1084), Craig County, Craig Creek, 17 May 1984.

Roanoke hogsucker *Hypentelium roanokense* nuptial male 83 mm (REJ 1075), Montgomery County, South Fork Roanoke River, 20 April 1984.

Torrent sucker *Thoburnia rhothoeca* nuptial male 89 mm (REJ 1076), Montgomery County, South Fork Roanoke River, 20 April 1984.

PLATE 21

Black jumprock *Scartomyzon cervinus* adult female 123 mm (REJ 1058), Franklin County, Blackwater River, 20 March 1984.

Bigeye jumprock *Scartomyzon ariommus* adult male 130 mm (REJ 1126), Montgomery County, South Fork Roanoke River, 24 September 1984.

Golden redhorse *Moxostoma erythrurum* juvenile 107 mm (REJ 1116), Charlotte County, Twittys Creek, 10 July 1984.

V-lip redhorse *Moxostoma pappillosum* adult male 250 mm (REJ 1114), Bedford County, Beaverdam Creek, 9 July 1984.

PLATE 22

White catfish *Ameiurus catus* subadult 184 mm (REJ 1114), Bedford County, Beaverdam Creek, 9 July 1984.

Flat bullhead *Ameiurus platycephalus* juvenile 76 mm (REJ 1116), Charlotte County, Twittys Creek, 10 July 1984.

Brown bullhead *Ameiurus nebulosus* juvenile female 134 mm (REJ 1092), Craig County, Johns Creek, 3 June 1984.

Stonecat *Noturus flavus* juvenile 62 mm (REJ 1080), Scott County, Copper Creek, 25 April 1984.

PLATE 23

Orangefin madtom *Noturus gilberti* adult female 62 mm (REJ 1126), Montgomery County, South Fork Roanoke River, 24 September 1984.

Margined madtom *Noturus insignis* adult female 88 mm (REJ 1093), Carroll County, Big Reed Island Creek, 3 June 1984.

Yellowfin madtom *Noturus flavipinnis* adult female 60 mm (NMB 916), Scott County, Copper Creek, 27 August 1984.

Mountain madtom *Noturus eleutherus* adult female 40 mm (REJ 1081), Scott County, Copper Creek, 25 April 1984.

PLATE 24

Brook trout *Salvelinus fontinalis* prenuptial male 183 mm (REJ 1048), Floyd County, Shooting Creek, 7 October 1983.

Brown trout *Salmo trutta* nuptial male 356 mm TL, Henry County, Smith River, November 1976.

Rainbow trout *Oncorhynchus mykiss* adult male 156 mm (REJ 1156), Washington County, Whitetop Laurel Creek, 30 June 1985.

Pirate perch *Aphredoderus sayanus* adult female 47 mm (REJ 1117), Sussex County, Coppahaunk Swamp, 11 July 1984.

Swampfish *Chologaster cornuta* adult male 33 mm (REJ 1117), Sussex County, Coppahaunk Swamp, 11 July 1984.

PLATE 25

Banded killifish *Fundulus diaphanus* adult female 61 mm (REJ 1138), Rockingham County, War Branch, 10 February 1985.

Speckled killifish *Fundulus rathbuni* nuptial male 57 mm (REJ 1115), Halifax County, Powells Creek, 9 July 1984.

Northern studfish *Fundulus catenatus* nuptial male 95 mm (REJ 1105), Russell County, Copper Creek, 7 June 1984.

Lined topminnow *Fundulus lineolatus* nuptial or postnuptial male 39 mm (REJ 1117), Sussex County, Coppahaunk Swamp, 11 July 1984.

PLATE 26

Mottled sculpin *Cottus b. bairdi* nuptial male 64 mm (REJ 1062), Augusta County, Whisky Creek, 3 April 1984.

Black sculpin *Cottus baileyi* nuptial male 54 mm (REJ 1077), Smyth County, Middle Fork Holston River, 24 April 1984.

Black sculpin *Cottus baileyi* adult female 56 mm (REJ 1137), Smyth County, Middle Fork Holston River, 27 January 1985.

Slimy sculpin *Cottus cognatus* nuptial male 51 mm (REJ 1063), Augusta County, Whisky Creek, 3 April 1984.

Holston sculpin *Cottus* sp., adult female 78 mm (REJ 1137), Smyth County, Middle Fork Holston River, 27 January 1985.

Clinch sculpin *Cottus* sp., nuptial male 77 mm (REJ 1184), Tazewell County, Little River, 27 March 1987. Specimen had been nest-guarding in aquarium.

PLATE 27

Bluestone sculpin *Cottus* sp., nuptial male 67 mm (REJ 1140), Tazewell County, Bluestone River, 17 February 1985.

Bluestone sculpin *Cottus* sp., juvenile 43 mm (REJ 1140), Tazewell County, Bluestone River, 17 February 1985.

Banded sculpin *Cottus c. carolinae* adult male 81 mm (REJ 1055), Smyth County, Middle Fork Holston River, 17 March 1984.

Banded sculpin *Cottus c. carolinae* adult male 91 mm (REJ 1141), Tazewell County, Liberty Creek, 17 February 1985.

Potomac sculpin *Cottus girardi* prenuptial male 81 mm (REJ 1138), Rockingham County, War Branch, 10 February 1985.

Potomac sculpin *Cottus girardi* adult female 75 mm (REJ 1138), Rockingham County, War Branch, 10 February 1985.

PLATE 28

Rock bass *Ambloplites rupestris* nuptial male 139 mm (REJ 1086), Roanoke County, Roanoke River, 18 May 1984.

Roanoke bass *Ambloplites cavifrons* subadult or adult male 158 mm (REJ 1032), Lunenburg County, North Meherrin River, 2 September 1983.

Mud sunfish *Acantharchus pomotis* adult male 103 mm (REJ 1117), Sussex County, Coppahaunk Swamp, 11 July 1984.

Flier *Centrarchus macropterus* adult male 93 mm (REJ 1116), Charlotte County, Twittys Creek, 10 July 1984.

Black crappie *Pomoxis nigromaculatus* adult female 107 mm (REJ 1116), Charlotte County, Twittys Creek, 10 July 1984.

Bluespotted sunfish *Enneacanthus gloriosus* adult female 50 mm (REJ 1117), Sussex County, Coppahaunk Swamp, 11 July 1984.

PLATE 29

Blackbanded sunfish *Enneacanthus chaetodon* adult female 51 mm (REJ 1117), Sussex County, Coppahaunk Swamp, 11 July 1984.

Smallmouth bass *Micropterus dolomieu* subadult 151 mm (REJ 1154), Hancock County, Tennessee, Clinch River, 29 June 1985.

Largemouth bass *Micropterus salmoides* subadult 165 mm (REJ 1111), Franklin County, Ferrum College Pond, 19 June 1984.

Warmouth *Lepomis gulosus* adult female 136 mm (REJ 1117), Sussex County, Coppahaunk Swamp, 11 July 1984.

Green sunfish *Lepomis cyanellus* adult male 93 mm (REJ 1116), Charlotte County, Twittys Creek, 10 July 1984.

PLATE 30

Redbreast sunfish *Lepomis auritus* adult male 144 mm (REJ 1116), Charlotte County, Twittys Creek, 10 July 1984.

Hybrid: redbreast sunfish × bluegill, *Lepomis auritus* × *Lepomis macrochirus* adult male 120 mm (REJ 1111), Franklin County, Ferrum College Pond, 19 June 1984.

Bluegill *Lepomis macrochirus* adult male 147 mm (REJ 1084), Craig County, Craig Creek, 17 May 1984.

Longear sunfish *Lepomis megalotis* nuptial male 105 mm (REJ 1105), Russell County, Copper Creek, 7 June 1984.

Pumpkinseed *Lepomis gibbosus* adult male 129 mm (REJ 1084), Craig County, Craig Creek, 17 May 1984.

Redear sunfish *Lepomis microlophus* juvenile male 143 mm (REJ 1111), Franklin County, Ferrum College Pond, 19 June 1984.

PLATE 31

Yellow perch *Perca flavescens* adult male 129 mm (REJ 1116), Charlotte County, Twittys Creek, 10 July 1984.

Dusky darter *Percina sciera* adult female 57 mm (REJ 1154), Hancock County, Tennessee, Clinch River, 29 June 1985.

Sharpnose darter *Percina oxyrhynchus* adult male 91 mm (REJ 1093), Carroll County, Big Reed Island Creek, 3 June 1984.

Blotchside logperch *Percina burtoni* nuptial male 112 mm (NMB 940), Scott County, Copper Creek, 28 April 1985.

Roanoke logperch *Percina rex* nuptial male 101 mm (REJ 1074), Montgomery County, South Fork Roanoke River, 20 April 1984.

Logperch *Percina caprodes* adult male 125 mm (REJ 1099), Scott County, Clinch River, 5 June 1984.

PLATE 32

Stripeback darter *Percina notogramma* adult female 53 mm (REJ 1084), Craig County, Craig Creek, 17 May 1984.

Appalachia darter *Percina gymnocephala* nuptial male 61 mm (NMB 868), Floyd County, Little River, 27 April 1984.

Shield darter *Percina peltata* adult female 71 mm (REJ 1116), Charlotte County, Twittys Creek, 10 July 1984.

Roanoke darter *Percina roanoka* nuptial male 55 mm (REJ 1074-5), Montgomery County, South Fork Roanoke River, 20 April 1984.

PLATE 33

Gilt darter *Percina evides* nuptial male 62 mm (REJ 1099), Scott County, Clinch River, 5 June 1984.

Tangerine darter *Percina aurantiaca* nuptial male 119 mm (REJ 1100), Scott County, Big Moccasin Creek, 6 June 1984.

Channel darter *Percina copelandi* adult female 37 mm (REJ 1099), Scott County, Clinch River, 5 June 1984.

PLATE 34

Ashy darter *Etheostoma cinereum* nuptial male 52 mm (NMB 835), Blount County, Tennessee, Little River, collected 18 February 1984. Photograph taken soon after fish spawned, 9 March.

Swannanoa darter *Etheostoma swannanoa* nuptial male 69 mm (REJ 1149), Tazewell County, Little River, 31 March 1985.

Kanawha darter *Etheostoma kanawhae* nuptial male 66 mm (NMB 869), Floyd County, West Fork Little River, 27 April 1984.

Candy darter *Etheostoma osburni* nuptial male 86 mm (REJ 1082), Giles County, Big Stony Creek, 26 April 1984.

PLATE 35

Greenside darter *Etheostoma blennioides newmanii* nuptial male 84 mm (REJ 1080), Scott County, Copper Creek, 25 April 1984.

Greenside darter *Etheostoma b. blennioides* nuptial male 75 mm (NMB 868), Floyd County, Little River, 27 April 1984.

Banded darter *Etheostoma zonale* adult male 49 mm (REJ 1103), Washington County, North Fork Holston River, 6 June 1984.

Snubnose darter *Etheostoma simoterum* nuptial male 48 mm (REJ 1106), Washington County, Laurel Creek, 7 June 1984.

PLATE 36

Speckled darter *Etheostoma stigmaeum* nuptial male 46 mm (REJ 1080), Scott County, Copper Creek, 25 April 1984.

Longfin darter *Etheostoma longimanum* nuptial male 51 mm (REJ 1083), Roanoke County, Catawba Creek, 26 April 1984.

Riverweed darter *Etheostoma podostemone* nuptial or postnuptial male 54 mm (REJ 1089), Roanoke County, Roanoke River, 31 May 1984.

Johnny darter *Etheostoma nigrum* adult female 44 mm (REJ 1116), Charlotte County, Twittys Creek, 10 July 1984.

Glassy darter *Etheostoma vitreum* nuptial or postnuptial male 59 mm (REJ 1058), Franklin County, Blackwater River, 20 March 1984.

PLATE 37

Bluebreast darter *Etheostoma camurum* nuptial male 61 mm (REJ 1099), Scott County, Clinch River, 5 June 1984.

Redline darter *Etheostoma rufilineatum* prenuptial male 57 mm (REJ 1055), Smyth County, Middle Fork Holston River, 17 March 1984.

Tippecanoe darter *Etheostoma tippecanoe* nuptial or postnuptial male 30 mm (REJ 1154), Hancock County, Tennessee, Clinch River, 29 June 1985.

Sharphead darter *Etheostoma acuticeps* nuptial male 64 mm (REJ 1155), Greene County, Tennessee, Nolichucky River, 29 June 1984.

Wounded darter *Etheostoma vulneratum* prenuptial male 73 mm (REJ 1082), Scott County, Copper Creek, 25 April 1984.

PLATE 38

Fantail darter *Etheostoma flabellare* nuptial male 66 mm (REJ 1094), Carroll County, Coal Creek, 4 June 1984.

Sawcheek darter *Etheostoma serrifer* adult female 45 mm (REJ 1117), Sussex County, Coppahaunk Swamp, 11 July 1984.

PLATE 39

Paddlefish *Polyodon spathula* in Missouri (photograph by William N. Roston).

Bluehead chubs *Nocomis leptocephalus* over gravel-mound nest (REJ 315), Botetourt County, Catawba Creek, 4 May 1969.

PLATE 40

Turquoise shiner *Cyprinella monacha* nuptial male by spawning crevice (REJ 1033), Washington County, North Fork Holston River, 6 June 1984.

Brook silverside *Labidesthes sicculus* mirrored at surface of a Missouri reservoir (photograph by William N. Roston).

White bass *Morone chrysops* spawning in Missouri (photograph by William N. Roston).

Carolina darter *Etheostoma collis* male and female spawning in aquarium (REJ 1145), specimens from Mecklenburg County, Mines Creek, 12 March 1985.

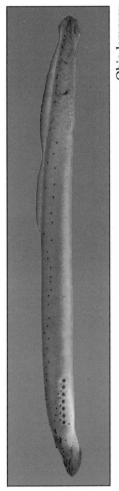

Ohio lamprey

Mountain brook lamprey

Longnose gar

PLATE 9

Chain pickerel

Redfin pickerel

Eastern mudminnow

Muskellunge

PLATE 10

Mountain redbelly dace

Longnose dace

Blacknose dace (subsp. *obtusus*)

Golden shiner

Rosyside dace

Blacknose dace (subsp. *atratulus*)

PLATE 11

Pearl dace

Creek chub

Cutlips minnow

Central stoneroller

Fallfish

Tonguetied minnow

PLATE 12

River chub

Bull chub

Bluehead chub

PLATE 13

Streamline chub

Kanawha minnow

Stargazing minnow

Slender chub

Blotched chub

Fatlips minnow

PLATE 14

Highback chub

Steelcolor shiner

Spotfin shiner

Bigeye chub

Whitetail shiner

Satinfin shiner

PLATE 15

Crescent shiner

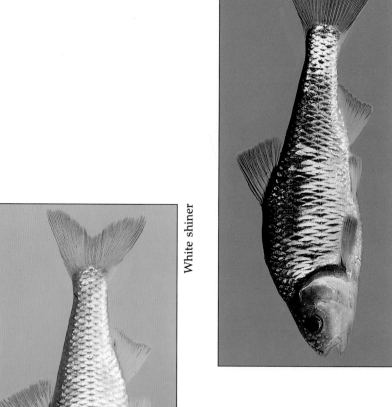

Striped shiner

Warpaint shiner

White shiner

Common shiner

PLATE 16

Rosefin shiner

Tennessee shiner

Redlip shiner

Mountain shiner

Rosyface shiner

Saffron shiner

PLATE 17

Popeye shiner

New River shiner

Silver shiner

Telescope shiner

PLATE 18

Swallowtail shiner

Sawfin shiner

Mirror shiner

PLATE 19

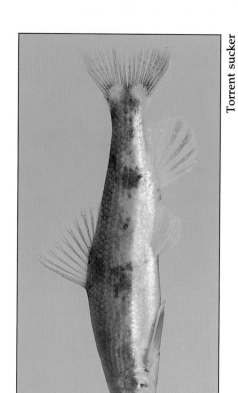

Torrent sucker

Creek chubsucker

Roanoke hogsucker

PLATE 20

Bigeye jumprock

V-lip redhorse

Black jumprock

Golden redhorse

PLATE 21

White catfish

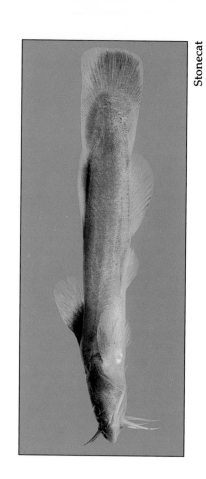

Flat bullhead

Stonecat

Brown bullhead

PLATE 22

Margined madtom

Mountain madtom

Orangefin madtom

Yellowfin madtom

PLATE 23

Brown trout

Rainbow trout

Swampfish

Brook trout

Pirate perch

PLATE 24

Speckled killifish

Lined topminnow

Banded killifish

Northern studfish

PLATE 25

Black sculpin (adult female)

Mottled sculpin

Clinch sculpin

Slimy sculpin

Black sculpin (nuptial male)

Holston sculpin

PLATE 26

Bluestone sculpin (juvenile)

Banded sculpin (adult male)

Potomac sculpin (adult female)

Bluestone sculpin (nuptial male)

Banded sculpin (adult male)

Potomac sculpin (prenuptial male)

PLATE 27

Roanoke bass

Flier

Bluespotted sunfish

Rock bass

Mud sunfish

Black crappie

PLATE 28

Smallmouth bass

Largemouth bass

Green sunfish

Blackbanded sunfish

Warmouth

PLATE 29

Longear sunfish

Pumpkinseed

Redear sunfish

Redbreast sunfish

Hybrid: redbreast sunfish × bluegill

Bluegill

PLATE 30

Dusky darter

Blotchside logperch

Logperch

Yellow perch

Sharpnose darter

Roanoke logperch

PLATE 31

Appalachia darter

Roanoke darter

Stripeback darter

Shield darter

PLATE 32

Gilt darter

Tangerine darter

Channel darter

PLATE 33

Swannanoa darter

Candy darter

Ashy darter

Kanawha darter

PLATE 34

Greenside darter (subsp. *blennioides*)

Snubnose darter

Greenside darter (subsp. *newmanii*)

Banded darter

PLATE 35

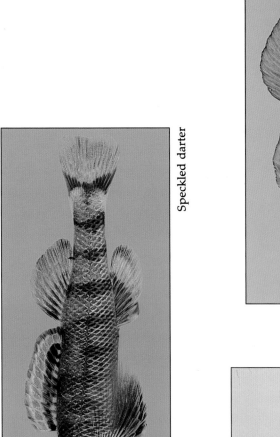

Speckled darter

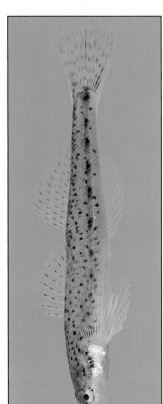

Riverweed darter

Glassy darter

Longfin darter

Johnny darter

PLATE 36

Redline darter

Sharphead darter

Wounded darter

Bluebreast darter

Tippecanoe darter

PLATE 37

Fantail darter

Sawcheek darter

PLATE 38

Paddlefish

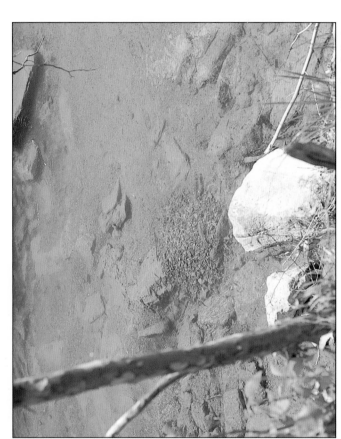

Bluehead chubs

PLATE 39

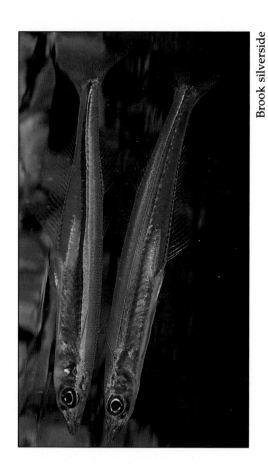

Brook silverside

Carolina darter

Turquoise shiner

White bass

PLATE 40

Appendix 2

DISTRIBUTIONAL DATA
AND SOURCES

DRAINAGE OCCURRENCE STATUS

The faunal data set analyzed in *Biogeography* is summarized in Tables 2 and 3, which update and refine the faunal lists of Ross (1959c), Jenkins et al. (1972, 1975), Stauffer et al. (1982), Hocutt et al. (1986), and Starnes and Etnier (1986). Differences from the most recent lists for each drainage are explained below. Documentation of drainage occurrence status of taxa in Virginia ("Va." in Table 3), of many extralimital populations in Virginia drainages ("non-Va."), and of entire-drainage faunas ("all") is given under *Distribution* in species accounts.

The Virginia drainage occurrence status of the 230 taxa is given in Table 2. For Virginia taxa that are absent in the Virginia section of a drainage, Table 2 also indicates extralimital occurrences in major Atlantic slope drainages from the Potomac to the Roanoke and in the New drainage. These taxa, and extralimital taxa in other drainages (not treated in Table 2), are tallied in Table 3.

Some taxa differ in status between the Virginia and extralimital sections of a drainage, and sometimes a taxon has more than one status in the Virginia or extralimital portion. For example, a species introduced to the Virginia section may be native extralimitally; it is regarded as native (or estuarine or marine, Ma) only on an entire-drainage basis. The format of Table 2 prevents showing all intradrainage differences, and no status shift can be specified by taxon in Table 3; adjustments engendered in Table 3 that are not clearly decipherable from Table 2 are treated below.

Excluded below are the relatively minor, equivocal types of shifts (e.g., N to NI, I to IP) that apply entirely within Virginia or the extralimital section of a

drainage. However, such shifts are specified for taxa whose status differs between the two sections; these cases occur only in the Tennessee drainage. We omit the NP category (probably present, native) that was used by Jenkins et al. (1972), Stauffer et al. (1982), and Hocutt et al. (1986) to denote taxa that almost certainly are or were native in a drainage but have not been found there.

Subspecific intergrades are counted (Table 3) as "taxa" in a drainage in two cases. (1) When two subspecies are represented by intergrades but neither typical (nonintergraded) form is present, the intergrade is counted as two taxa. The one example concerns *Erimystax i. insignis* × *E. i. eristigma* in the Holston and Clinch–Powell systems. (2) When one typical subspecies is present along with a population of intergrades (between that subspecies and one whose typical form lives only in one or more adjacent drainages), again two subspecies are tallied. The three examples here are *Etheostoma olmstedi atromaculatum* and *E. o. olmstedi* × *E. o. atromaculatum* in the Potomac, *E. o. olmstedi* and *E. o. olmstedi* × *E. o. vexillare* in the York, and *Cottus c. carolinae* and *C. c. carolinae* × *C. c. zopherus* in the Clinch–Powell and entire Tennessee drainage. We count certain intergrades as taxa because a presumably typical form; for example, *C. carolinae zopherus*, entered the drainage and its genome remains there (in modified form). Concomitantly, *E. o. vexillare* is not considered endemic to the Rappahannock; it reached the York and intergraded there with *E. o. olmstedi*.

The sequence of taxa for all but one drainage, and within the categories and types of shifts, is that of Table 2, whose sequence is that of the species accounts. The sequence for the Tennessee drainage follows that of Starnes and Etnier (1986).

Changes from Hocutt et al. (1986) for All Pertinent Drainages.—*Dorosoma cepedianum* is regarded as a freshwater fish. *Fundulus heteroclitus* and *Apeltes quadracus* are considered estuarine and are omitted from our lists.

Delmarva Peninsula.—We consider the northern faunal limit of the peninsula to be the Chesapeake and Delaware Canal. The list of non-Virginia species is based largely on Lee et al. (1980, 1981). Excluded are certain species that regionally are typically associated with or limited to the lower Susquehanna drainage: *Acipenser brevirostrum, A. oxyrhynchus, Carpiodes cyprinus, Micropterus dolomieu,* and *Etheostoma sellare.*

Potomac Drainage.—Changes are from Hocutt et al. (1986). Status alterations: N to IP—*Etheostoma blennioides;* NI to IP—*Lepomis gulosus;* NI to I—*Centrarchus macropterus;* IP to NI—*Nocomis leptocephalus.* Additions: I—*Ictalurus furcatus, Pylodictis olivaris,* and *Morone chrysops.* Deletions: formerly N—*Acantharchus pomotis, Enneacanthus obesus;* formerly IP—*Lythrurus ardens* (record uncertain); formerly I, no evidence of persistence—*Leuciscus idus, Tinca tinca, Oncorhynchus nerka, Osmerus mordax,* and *Ictalurus melas. Acipenser brevirostrum,* Ma and Ep, is treated as Ma in Table 3.

Rappahannock Drainage.—Changes are from Hocutt et al. (1986). Status alterations: N to Ep?—*Notropis bifrenatus;* N to IP—*Lepomis gulosus;* NP to N—*Amia calva.* Additions: I—*Dorosoma petenense, Esox lucius,* and *E. masquinongy.* Deletion: formerly NP—*Enneacanthus obesus.*

York Drainage.—Changes are from Hocutt et al. (1986). Status alteration: N to IP—*Lepomis gulosus.* Additions: I—*Esox masquinongy, Ctenopharyngodon idella, Morone chrysops,* and *Pomoxis annularis; Etheostoma olmstedi vexillare* included as intergrade.

James Drainage.—Changes are from Hocutt et al. (1986). Status alterations: N to IP—*Micropterus salmoides;* NI to IP—*Scartomyzon cervinus, Noturus gilberti,* and *Percina roanoka;* IP to N—*Pomoxis nigromaculatus.* Additions: N—*Notropis chalybaeus, Chologaster cornuta, Fundulus lineolatus,* and *Etheostoma serrifer;* NI—*Ameiurus platycephalus;* I—*Carassius auratus, Ctenopharyngodon idella,* and *Pylodictis olivaris.*

Chesapeake Basin.—The basin comprises entire sections of drainages (including the Potomac to the James, above) that flow into the west shore of Chesapeake Bay, the lowermost Susquehanna River and tributaries (upstream to Conowingo Dam), and west-flowing systems on Delmarva. The list is based on our data and Lee et al. (1980, 1981). *Etheostoma olmstedi vexillare* becomes E on a basin level. *Acipenser brevirostrum* (Ma) is extant on a basin level (lower Susquehanna). Non-Virginia taxa are N—*Enneacanthus chaetodon;* E—*Etheostoma sellare.*

Dismal Swamp.—Changes are from Jenkins et al. (1975). Status alteration: N to Ma—*Fundulus diaphanus.* Additions: N—*Lepomis auritus, Etheostoma serrifer,* and (non-Virginia) *Noturus gyrinus;* I—*Micropterus salmoides.* Deletion: *Lepomis microlophus.*

Chowan Drainage.—The Chowan ichthyofauna generally has been combined with the Roanoke drainage fauna, an exception being the list by Jenkins et al. (1975), which is updated (Table 2): N to Ma—*Fundulus diaphanus; Acipenser brevirostrum,* Ma and Ep, is treated as Ma (Table 3).

Roanoke Drainage.—Most changes are from Hocutt et al. (1986). Status alterations: N to E—*Noturus gilberti,* as James population considered IP; N to IP—*Micropterus salmoides;* E to N—*Percina rex,* as Chowan considered a separate drainage; I in Virginia, Ma (and N) in non-Virginia—*Alosa pseudoharengus, A. aestivalis,* and *Morone americana.* Addition in Virginia: IP—*Semotilus corporalis.* Additions in non-Virginia: N—*Elassoma zonatum* and *Etheostoma olmstedi atromaculatum;* I—*Cyprinella lutrensis.* Deletions: formerly N—*Lampetra appendix* and *Notropis bifrenatus* (because of separation of the Chowan fauna; these species unknown in Roanoke); formerly NI—*Fundulus waccamensis* (range in Albemarle basin excludes Roanoke); formerly NP—*Lampetra aepyptera;* formerly E—*Percina peltata* undescribed subspecies (now included in *P. peltata nevisense). Lepomis gulosus* and *Perca flavescens* are NI only in Virginia. *Petromyzon marinus* and *Alosa sapidissima* are counted as Ma and also Ep (and N) in Virginia.

Albemarle Basin.—The list combines those of the Chowan and Roanoke drainages plus *Fundulus waccamensis,* based on Smith (1893), Lee et al. (1980), E. F. Menhinick (in litt.), and our data. *Percina rex* becomes E on a basin basis. Non-Virginia taxa: N—*Elassoma zonatum* and *Etheostoma olmstedi atromaculatum;* NI—*Fundulus waccamensis;* I—*Cyprinella lutrensis;* Ma—*Acipenser brevirostrum* (Ep also), *A. oxyrhynchus, Alosa mediocris,* and *Fundulus diaphanus.*

Pee Dee Drainage.—Changes are from Hocutt et al. (1986). Status alteration: *Cyprinella labrosa* is Ep in

Virginia but extant (N) in North Carolina. Addition, non-Virginia: N—*Moxostoma carinatum*-like. Total taxa in Hocutt et al. (1986: Table 6.2) should have been 110, as 24 are I.

New Drainage.—Changes are from Hocutt et al. (1986). Status alterations: N to E—*Cottus* undescribed species (bluestone sculpin); N to IP—*Luxilus cerasinus*; NI to IP—*Exoglossum maxillingua, Cyprinella galactura, Moxostoma erythrurum, Ameiurus natalis,* and *A. nebulosus*; IP to NI—*Luxilus chrysocephalus* and *Etheostoma simoterum*. Additions: E—*Cottus* undescribed species (albino cave sculpin, recognized here as a species), non-Virginia only; I—*Etheostoma olmstedi,* non-Virginia only; IP—*Scartomyzon cervinus*. Deletion: formerly I—*Esox niger,* Virginia record not supported, establishment unknown in West Virginia. *Nocomis platyrhynchus* is recognized as a species. The ranking of *Thoburnia rhothoeca* as Ep stems from its apparent absence and arbitrary NI status. *Morone saxatilis,* both I and Ma, is counted as I in Table 3.

Holston System of Tennessee Drainage.—Our tally is the first for the entire system. "E" means endemic to the entire Tennessee drainage, not just the Holston system. The two subspecies of *Erimystax insignis* are represented in the Virginia section by an intergrade population (see above). Data for non-Virginia are largely from Lee et al. (1980) and D. A. Etnier (in litt.).

Non-Virginia taxa: N—*Polyodon spathula, Hiodon tergisus, Macrhybopsis aestivalis, Notropis atherinoides, N. stramineus, Moxostoma anisurum, Ictalurus furcatus, Ameiurus melas, Cottus* undescribed species or subspecies (smoky sculpin), *Cottus carolinae* undescribed subspecies (Kanawha sculpin), *Percina sciera, P. squamata, Etheostoma caeruleum,* and *Aplodinotus grunniens*; E—*Erimystax cahni* (also Ep); Ep—*Etheostoma percnurum*; I—*Morone saxatilis* (may extend into Virginia in South Holston Reservoir). Species that are both E and Ep are counted as E—*Noturus flavipinnis* and *Etheostoma stigmaeum jessiae* in Virginia, *Erimystax cahni* in Tennessee.

Possible additions (excluded here) are *Carpiodes carpio, C. velifer, Ictiobus bubalus,* and *Ameiurus melas*.

Clinch–Powell System of Tennessee Drainage.—Our tally is the first for the entire system, including the Emory River subsystem, Tennessee. "E" signifies endemic to the Tennessee drainage, not just the Clinch–Powell. "?" denotes uncertain occurrence or original distributional status in the extreme lower Clinch. Data are largely from Masnik (1974), Etnier et al. (1979), D. A. Etnier (in litt.), Lee et al. (1980), and our investigations. *Erimystax insignis* is represented in the

Virginia and non-Virginia categories by subspecific intergrades.

Non-Virginia taxa: N—*Ichthyomyzon castaneus, Lampetra appendix, Hiodon tergisus, Alosa chrysochloris, Phoxinus erythrogaster* ? (Starnes and Jenkins 1988), *Hemitremia flammea, Macrhybopsis aestivalis, Notropis stramineus, Cycleptus elongatus, Ictiobus bubalus, Carpiodes carpio, C. velifer, Minytrema melanops, Ictalurus furcatus, Fundulus olivaceus, Gambusia affinis, Cottus carolinae zopherus* (as an intergrade), *Morone mississippiensis* ?, *P. squamata, Percina maculata,* and *Etheostoma kennicotti*; NI—*Lepomis gulosus*; E—*Phoxinus tennesseensis, Cyprinella monacha, Noturus stanauli, Etheostoma duryi,* and *E. stigmaeum jessiae*; Ep—*Alosa alabamae, Hybognathus nuchalis* ?, and *Notropis* undescribed species (palezone shiner); I—*Notemigonus crysoleucas* ?, and *Morone saxatilis*.

Status changes from Virginia to "all" reflected in lines 10 and 12 of Table 3: Ep to N—*Etheostoma cinereum*; I to N—*Esox masquinongy*. *Hybognathus hankinsoni* is excluded from the Clinch–Powell list; the single record in Tennessee is a bait-bucket escapee (Starnes and Etnier 1986).

Tennessee Drainage.—The Virginia section of the Tennessee comprises the upper Holston and upper Clinch–Powell systems. Most of the 131 non-Virginia taxa in the drainage are listed by Starnes and Etnier (1986). We interpret "X" of Starnes and Etnier (1986: Table 10.1) to signify native and to comprise our N and NI categories.

Our changes are: *Anguilla rostrata* Ma in all; *Dorosoma petenense* I in Virginia, N in all; *Salmo gairdneri* renamed *Oncorhynchus mykiss*; *Salmo letnica* I in all; *Esox lucius* I in all; *E. masquinongy* I in Virginia, N in all; *Campostoma oligolepis* and *C. pauciradii* N in all; *Clinostomus funduloides* undescribed subspecies N in all (owing to Savannah drainage intergrades); *Ctenopharyngodon idella* I in Virginia and all; *Ericymba buccata* (= *Notropis buccatus*) IP in Clinch–Powell and all; *Notemigonus crysoleucas* I in Virginia, N in all; *Notropis* (= *Luxilus*) *chrysocephalus* regarded a species; *Notropis heterolepis* described as *N. rupestris*; *Phoxinus tennesseensis* (= *P. oreas* in part) described, E in Virginia and all; *P. oreas* IP in Virginia and all; *Pimephales notatus* NI in Virginia, N in all; *P. promelas* IP in Virginia, NI in all; *P. vigilax* NI in Virginia, N in all.

Hypentelium etowanum IP in all; *Ameiurus melas* NI in Virginia, N in all; *A. nebulosus* IP in Virginia, N in all; *Fundulus albolineatus* E and Ex, E counted, in all; *Morone chrysops* NI in Virginia, N in all; *M. saxatilis* unverified in Virginia, I in all; *Lepomis cyanellus* NI in Virginia, N in all; *Lepomis gulosus* I in Virginia, N in all; *Micropterus salmoides* NI in Virginia, N in all; both *Pomoxis* species IP in Virginia, N in all.

Etheostoma cinereum Ep in Virginia, N in all; *E. crossopterum* N in all; *E. flabellare lineolatum* not recognized as a subspecies; *E. flabellare*-like form in all (lower Tennessee) is undescribed; *E. flabellare* undescribed upper Tennessee subspecies, N in Virginia and all; golden snubnose darter *E. flavum* described; "*? E. jessiae*" considered a subspecies of *E. stigmaeum*, E and Ep in Virginia, counted E there and in all; *E. maculatum vulneratum* is a species; *E. neopterum* N in all; *E. nigripinne* N in all; duskytail darter *E. percnurum* described in this book; *E. s. simoterum* N in Virginia and all because New and Big Sandy populations are considered native (NI); *E. stigmaeum* here recognized as the nominate subspecies, restricted in drainage to lower section; *E. stigmaeum meadiae* here regarded provisionally as a subspecies, E in Virginia and all; *E. squamiceps* restricted to other drainages; lowland snubnose darter *E. zonistium* described; *Percina ouachitae* renamed *P. vigil*.

Cottus carolinae zopherus (intergrade) N in all; *C. carolinae* undescribed subspecies (Kanawha sculpin) N in all; *Cottus* undescribed species ("broadband sculpin") divided into Holston sculpin and Clinch sculpin, both E in Virginia and all, Clinch sculpin known only in Virginia; *Cottus* undescribed species or subspecies (smoky sculpin) N in all.

Big Sandy Drainage.—Listed as NP by Hocutt et al. (1986), but excluded here, are the following that may have inhabited the lower drainage: *Ichthyomyzon bdellium*, *I. unicuspis*, *Polyodon spathula*, *Notropis buchanani*, and *Cycleptus elongatus*; the two *Pomoxis* species are IP in Virginia, N (or NI) in all; a Virginia addition is Ep (and NI)—*Salvelinus fontinalis*; non-Virginia additions are N—*Notropis blennius*, I—*Fundulus catenatus* (Burr and Warren 1986), IP—*Rhinichthys cataractae*.

SOURCES OF DATA

The distributional data applied in this study, other than those in published literature and unpublished reports, came from museums or fish collections of academic institutions, governmental agencies, and private consulting firms. Those which furnished Virginia data are listed below; their acronyms (usually those of Leviton et al. 1985) or the collectors' initials are given only when particular specimens are cited in the text or legends. Persons who expedited our study of specimens or access to records are listed in *Acknowledgments*.

Academy of Natural Sciences, Philadelphia—ANSP; American Electric Power Corporation, Hunt-

ington, West Virginia; American Museum of Natural History—AMNH; Aquatic Ecology Associates, Pittsburgh; Army Corps of Engineers, Wilmington—ACE; Auburn University—AU; California Academy of Sciences; Carnegie Museum—CM; Charleston Museum—CHM; Cornell University—CU; D'Appolonia Consulting Engineers, Inc., Pittsburgh; Duke Power Company, Huntersville, North Carolina—DPC; Duke University—DU; Ecological Analysts, Inc., Sparks, Maryland; Field Museum of Natural History—FMNH; George Mason University.

Hayes, Seay, Mattern and Mattern, Inc., Richmond; Henningson, Durham and Richardson, Inc., Norfolk; Illinois Natural History Survey—INHS; James R. Reed and Associates, Inc., Newport News; Lord Fairfax Community College, Virginia; Lynchburg College—LC; Maryland Department of Natural Resources, Thurmont, Maryland; Milwaukee Public Museum—MPM; Museum of Comparative Zoology, Harvard University—MCZ; National Museum of Canada—NMC; North Carolina State Museum—NCSM; Northeast Louisiana University—NLU; Ohio State University, Museum of Zoology; Old Dominion University; Pennsylvania State University—PSU; Potomac Electric Power Company, Washington, D.C.

Roanoke College is designated *RC*; the collection is not cataloged. Series of specimens are identified here and on jar labels by collectors' initials (NMB—Burkhead; REJ—Jenkins; SPM—McIninch; WHH—Haxo; and field numbers; RC is omitted when these series are cited. Initials that directly follow RC in specimen citations denote other collectors who donated material to RC.

Southern Illinois University, Carbondale—SIUC; Stanford University—SU (specimens now at California Academy of Sciences or UMMZ); Summit Engineering, Inc., Grundy; Tennessee Valley Authority, Norris—TVA (specimens at RC); Tulane University—TU; University of Alabama, Tuscaloosa—UAIC; University of Connecticut, Storrs—UCS; University of Florida; University of Kentucky; University of Louisville—UL; University of Maryland, College Park; University of Massachusetts, Amherst; University of Michigan, Museum of Zoology—UMMZ (IU appended for specimens originally at Indiana University).

University of North Carolina at Charlotte—UNCC; University of North Carolina, Institute of Marine Sciences—UNC; University of North Carolina at Wilmington—UNCW; University of Richmond—UR; University of Tennessee, Knoxville—UT; U.S. Fish and Wildlife Service, Annapolis, Atlanta, Cookeville, and Gloucester Point; U.S. Forest Service, Atlanta; U.S.

National Museum of Natural History—USNM; U.S. Soil Conservation Service, Richmond.

Virginia Commonwealth University; Virginia Department of Conservation and Recreation, Richmond; Virginia Department of Game and Inland Fisheries, Chesapeake, Marion Hatchery, Staunton, Vinton, and scientific collectors file in Richmond; Virginia Institute of Marine Science—VIMS; Virginia Institute for Scientific Research, Richmond—VISR; Virginia Polytechnic Institute and State University—VPI (collection formerly in Department of Biology, now at AMNH); Virginia Polytechnic Institute and State University, Fishery Unit—VPIFU; Virginia Power Company, Lake Anna Station and Richmond; Virginia Water Control Board, Roanoke; Wapora, Inc.; and College of William and Mary.

Glossary

GLOSSARY

Many terms and abbreviations used in this book are defined or identified below. Many of these terms are further explained in the *Introduction to Accounts*, topical sections, and associated illustrations that precede the species accounts. Meristic and most morphometric and other taxonomic characters are described only in *Anatomy and Color* and introductions to keys. All hydrographic and geopolitical units with proper names are described or identified only in *Drainages, Biogeography*, Maps 6–12, or species accounts; references to their locations on topographic maps are given by Biggs (1974). Definitions of geological terms are largely from the American Geological Institute (1962); phylogenetic terminology is chiefly from Wiley (1981). Acronyms for fish collections are given in *Appendix 2*.

Italicized terms within definitions (excluding genus and species names) have their own entries elsewhere in the glossary.

Abbreviate heterocercal A caudal fin type in which posterior end of vertebral column is distinctly upturned but short. Same as *hemicercal*. See *heterocercal* and *homocercal*.

Abdomen The ventral area of body between anus and breast; same as belly.

Acidity The capacity to donate protons (H⁺ ions). See *pH* and *alkalinity*.

Acute Sharp, pointed.

Adipose eyelid A fleshy transparent membrane over sides of eye, as in herring family.

Adipose fin A small or medium-sized, fleshy fin lacking both rays and spines and occurring on dorsum between dorsal and caudal fins.

Adipose tissue Fatty tissue.

Adnate Attached, united; refers to condition in madtom catfishes where posterior end of adipose fin is attached to anterodorsal end of caudal fin. Opposite of *adnexed*.

Adnexed With a free edge, not united; refers to adipose fin not being attached to caudal fin, as in bullhead catfishes and trouts. Opposite of *adnate*.

Advanced In reference to a taxonomic character, the character state that evolutionarily originated most recently; same as *apomorphic* and *derived*. Opposite of *primitive*.

Aestivation A form of torpor or inactivity associated with dry environmental conditions.

Air bladder See *gas bladder*.

Alevin An early developmental stage roughly equivalent to a combination of postlarva and early young. Alevins become juveniles when the yolk sac is absorbed. Characteristic of trouts and catfishes.

Alien Introduced, not native to a given area.

Alkalinity The capacity to accept protons (H⁺ ions). Alkalinity usually is imparted by carbonate, bicarbonate, and hydroxide (OH⁻) components. See *pH* and *acidity*.

Allometry Growth pattern of a body part in which the proportion of that part, relative to body length, changes (increases or decreases) with overall growth of the individual. Allometry is particularly typical of early life stages.

Allopatric A distributional relationship or pattern whereby the ranges of two taxa are separate and nowhere in contact. See *parapatric* and *sympatric*.

Allotopic A distributional relationship or pattern whereby species with overlapping ranges do not occur together. See *syntopic*.

Alveolar ridge A bony ridge supporting teeth.

Alveolus A small cavity or pit on a bone, often referring to a tooth socket.

Ammocoete Lamprey larva.

Anadromous A division of *diadromous* referring to species that migrate to spawn in fresh water after spending most of their life in an estuary or ocean. Opposite of *catadromous*.

Anal fin An unpaired median fin on the ventral body just behind the anus; may have spines and rays or rays only.

Ancestral See *extended river* and *primitive*.

Annulus A year mark on a scale or other body part.

Anteriad Toward the head or front.

Anterior The front portion of a fish or a part of a fish.

Antitropical The distribution pattern of species that avoid the tropics.

Anus The terminal opening of digestive tract; sometimes termed vent.

Aphotic Absence of light.

Apomorphic See *advanced*.

Appalachian Plateau The montane physiographic province in the northern spur of southwestern Virginia (and elsewhere; Map 7).

Atrophy To reduce, degenerate.

Attenuate Extended, drawn-out (e.g., a long snout).

Aufwuchs Very small, motile and nonmotile organisms living on substrates. See *periphyton*.

Axillary scale An elongate scale at insertion of pelvic fin (and pectoral fin in Clupeidae).

Backpack shocker An electroshocker mounted on a backpack frame. Especially useful in sampling streams.

Backwater Calm stream habitat at margin of riffle or run; marginal, partly enclosed part of pool.

Band A color marking that is short or moderate in length, or a marking that encircles a body part; may be vertical, oblique, or horizontal.

Bar A color marking that may be long, vertical or oblique, and narrow or wide. Also used for short, horizontal, oblique, or vertical marking about the eye (e.g., *preocular bar*).

Barbed tributary A stream whose upper reach flows in approximately the reverse direction of the lower reach; the area of flow reversal is termed the elbow of capture. Barbed tributaries often are evidence of *stream capture*.

Barbel A slender fleshy protuberance, tiny to long, usually tapered to a point, found on lip, jaw, or elsewhere on head in some fishes ("whiskers" in catfishes); usually taste sensory.

Basad Toward the base of a structure; in reference to an appendage, toward the body.

Basal At or near the base or bottom.

Base color See *ground color*.

Base level The level below which a land surface cannot be eroded by running water; local or temporary base levels include lakes; ultimate base level is sea level.

Base of fin The place of attachment of a fin to the body. The anterior point of base is the origin or anterior insertion; posterior point of base is the posterior insertion.

Basin A major group of drainages interconnected by a (usually large) master river or estuary. See *drainage* and *system*.

Basioccipital The ventral occipital bone; posteroventral portion of cranium; may bear an extension or process that pharyngeal teeth chew against, as in minnows and suckers.

Bathy- (prefix) Regarding depths or deep.

Bedrock A substrate category; unbroken rock strata. See *outcrop*.

Benthic Of the bottom; for example, species that generally inhabit the bottom substrate, infrequently swimming above it.

Benthopelagic Regarding the bottom and water just above; for example, generally free-swimming species that associate closely with the substrate.

Bi- (prefix) Two.

Bicuspid A tooth with two points (cusps) on its upper surface.

Big river A rather large river; for example, the lower freshwater reach of the James River, or the New River at the West Virginia line. In some classifications these reaches would not be placed in the same big-river category with the lower Ohio or Mississippi rivers.

Biogeographic track In *vicariance biogeography*, a line drawn on a map that bounds the range of a monophyletic taxon.

Biogeography The study of the distribution of animals and plants and the factors that influence them.

Biological species See *species*.

Biota The animal and plant species that occupy a given area. See *fauna* and *flora*.

Black-spot parasite An encysted intermediate life stage of strigeid flatworms; the cyst occurs in skin and is covered by black pigment, hence appearing like a spot.

Black water Water strongly darkened by dissolved organic substances; usually acidic, often quite so, and occurs in Coastal Plain, lower Piedmont, and bogs.

Blotch A medium or large, variably shaped but not markedly elongate pigmentary mark.

Blue Ridge The montane–upland physiographic province between the Piedmont and the Valley and Ridge provinces (Map 7).

Body Concerning fishes, the portion between the head and caudal fin. Same as trunk.

Boulder A substrate category; large rocks, 305 mm (12 inches) and larger; nearly synonymous with boulder on the Wentworth Scale—rocks 256 mm (10 inches) and larger.

B.P. (Years) before present, in recent geological time.

Branchial groove The horizontal groove in which a gill opening occurs, in larval lampreys.

Branchial incubation Incubation of fertilized eggs in the branchial (gill) cavity.

Branchiostegal membrane The paired membrane containing branchiostegal rays; located on the posteroventrolateral surface of the head and confluent with the opercular membrane; together the branchiostegal membranes close the lower openings of the gill cavity.

Branchiostegal rays The splintlike bones supporting the branchiostegal membrane.

Breast The ventral body surface between isthmus, branchiostegal–opercular membranes, and bases of pectoral fins (pelvic fin bases if these are located anteriorly).

Breeding tubercle See *tubercle*.

Buccal cavity The mouth or oral cavity.

°C Degrees Celsius (centigrade).

Caecum (plural, caeca) A pouchlike or fingerlike diversion of digestive tract.

Calcareous Containing much calcium. See *dolomite* and *limestone*.

Canine A large conical tooth.

Carbonate rock Rock composed substantially of carbonate—CO_3. See *dolomite* and *limestone*.

Catadromous A division of *diadromous* referring to species that migrate to spawn in salt water after spending most of their life in fresh water. Opposite of *anadromous*.

Caudal fin The tail fin.

Caudal peduncle The part of the body between the posterior insertion of the anal fin and the posterior bony end of the caudal fin base.

Caudal spot An area of dark pigment, usually with sharply defined edges, on the caudal fin base or caudal fin; variably shaped.

Cenozoic era Geologic time from the present to about 66 million years ago; divided into the Quaternary period (with its epochs) and one or more other periods (with epochs).

Cephalic lateralis The system of canals on head; at intervals the canals have pores that open to exterior; canals contain sensory organs (*neuromasts*) that detect displacement of water; sonarlike division of nervous system.

Character An anatomical, physiological, behavioral, or other aspect of species and higher taxa that generally is inferred to have a genetic basis.

Character state One of the different expressions (traits, characteristics) of a character in species and higher taxa; each character has two or more states (one of which may be absence). In a broader sense, each state of a character is considered to be a separate character. See *outgroup* and *polarity*.

Cheek The side of head below and slightly behind eye.

Chin The area between the halves of the lower lip, or in long-jawed species, the anterior part of that area.

Chromatophore A pigment-bearing cell imparting color to tissue.

Chronic Continuously or intermittently persistent.

Circulus A ridgelike ring on scales, concentric to other circuli; by their spacing they often aid in identifying annuli.

Circumoral teeth Teeth surrounding the throat opening in lampreys; excludes supraoral and infraoral plates or laminae.

Circumpolar The distribution pattern in which an organism is widely distributed on all continents or oceans roughly above 60° latitude.

Cirrus A small, branched, featherlike structure; usually elevated from skin.

Clade A branch of an evolutionary lineage or a division of a cladogram. See *cladogram* and *natural taxon*.

Cladistics See *phylogenetics*.

Cladogram A diagram containing taxa whose pattern of branching indicates phylogenetic interrelationships of the taxa. See *clade* and *dendrogram*.

Clay A substrate category; minute particles smaller than silt; may be compacted and termed hardpan.

Cleithrum The largest bone of the pectoral girdle; located just posterior to opercular opening.

Cline Gradual geographic variation of one or more characters in a major part of the range of a species.

cm Centimeter.

Coastal Plain The low-lying easternmost physiographic province of Virginia (Map 7).

Cold water The category for bodies of water that generally do not exceed 20°C in summer; also those species best adapted to or typically occurring in such waters. See *cool water* and *warm water*.

Complementary distribution The distribution pattern whereby two taxa occupy adjacent geographic areas, the ranges having slight or no overlap.

Compressed Flattened laterally (e.g., the body in many sunfishes).

Congeneric Being members of the same genus.

Conspecific Being members of the same species.

Contact organ A tiny, often spinelike dermal outgrowth on scales, fin rays, or body, often in substantial numbers; analogous in some respects to *tubercles* and *unculi*.

Continental Plate The thick crust underlying a continent.

Continental Shelf A plateaulike division of the ocean bottom between the coast and the upper edge of the Continental Slope.

Cool water The category for bodies of water that generally are 20–24°C in summer; also those species best adapted to or typically occurring in such waters. See *cold water* and *warm water*.

Cranium The portion of skull enclosing brain.

Creek A small stream; when stream-size categorization of species is considered, creek denotes waterways of 10 m or less in width. See *river* and *stream*.

Crepuscular Active at dawn or dusk.

Cretaceous period The last period of the Mesozoic era, about 66–144 million years ago.

Cryptic introduction An apparently undocumented introduction of a species to a drainage in which it is not believed to be native.

Cryptic species Species that are very difficult to distinguish from each other; also termed siblings.

Ctenii (singular, ctenium) Minute spines on ctenoid scale.

Ctenoid scale A scale with minute spines (ctenii) on posterior surface.

Cuckoldry An alternative reproductive strategy in some nest-building species in which fertilizations are "stolen" from a sexually dichromatic nest-guarding "parental" male by cuckolder nonnesting males. "Sneakers" are precocial males that dart from hiding while the parental pair is spawning. "Satellites" are males that deceptively mimic females and pair simultaneously with true females and parental males (Gross 1984).

Cumberlandian Pertains to fauna characteristic of, and sometimes unique to, the lower Ohio River basin, particularly the Cumberland and Tennessee drainages.

Cusp A projection on crown of a tooth, or (in lampreys) a pointed division of a tooth.

Cycloid scale A scale lacking ctenii and an enameloid surface.

Declivous Distinctly downsloping, declining.

Deme A subpopulation of a species that differs, usually slightly, from another of the species in morphology or life history; usually less distinct than subspecies and not given formal taxonomic status. See *race* and *stock*.

Dendrogram A diagram portraying taxa whose pattern of branching indicates evolutionary or phenetic interrelationships; if based on phylogenetic principles, the dendrogram is a *cladogram*.

Depauperate In biogeography, a fauna having relatively few species compared with nearby faunas.

Depressed Flattened dorsoventrally (e.g., the flattened head of many catfishes).

Derived See *advanced*.

Di- (prefix) Two.

Diadromous Migrating between fresh water and the sea in order to spawn. See *anadromous* and *catadromous*.

Diagnosis A list of primary traits that best distinguish a taxon from similar taxa; diagnoses are briefer than descriptions.

Dichromatism See *sexual dichromatism*.

Differentiation Becoming different in anatomy, color, physiology, or behavior. Ontogenetically, changes that occur embryonically and postembryonically within an organism. Evolutionarily, changes that occurred in a lineage of organisms. See *evolution, divergence, ontogenetic,* and *speciation*.

Dimorphism See *sexual dimorphism*.

Disjunct Widely separated. See *localized*.

Dispersal The movement of individuals or populations beyond the species range into areas formerly uninhabited by that species.

Distad Away from point of attachment, toward outer edge. Opposite of *proximad*.

Distal At or near outer edge or margin.

Divergence The evolutionary process of branching of lineages. See *evolution, differentiation,* and *speciation*.

Diverse Regarding generic or higher taxa or geographically defined biotas, those having a substantial number of members or a wide range of anatomical or life history traits. See *species richness* and *speciose*. In reference to biotic communities, the distribution of numbers of individuals among the taxa present; higher diversities connote more even representation by each taxon.

Dolomite rock Carbonate rock whose composition approximates the mineral dolomite—$CaMg(CO_3)_2$. Water draining such strata tend to be alkaline and hard.

Dorsal Back or upper body.

Dorsal field See *lateral field* (of scales).

Dorsal fin The median fin(s) on back, supported by spines and rays or rays only; may be partly or entirely divided into an anterior spine-supported fin (the first or spinous dorsal) and posterior soft-ray supported fin (the second, rayed, or soft dorsal). Spinous portion may be termed D_1, the soft part D_2.

Dorsum The back (upper) surface.

Drainage A group of interconnected streams whose main channel enters an ocean, estuary, or the main stem of a basin. See *basin* and *system*.

Drainage occurrence status The original distributional status (native or introduced) of species in a drainage.

Drawdown zone In a reservoir, the shore zone between full pool and normal lower pool levels.

Drowned river A former lowland freshwater river; that is, an *extended river*, that has been inundated by a rise in sea level and is now distinctly estuarine or covered by ocean. See *transgression*.

Earflap See *opercular flap*.

Ecotone The boundary area between two habitats.

Edentulous Lacking teeth.

e.g. For example.

Elaborate Unusually or highly developed, often specialized; for example, very large breeding tubercles or a particularly showy color pattern. See *reduced, rudimentary,* and *vestigial.*

Electroshocker A device consisting of a gasoline-powered generator or an amplified battery circuit used to generate electricity for collecting fish. Current is applied with anode and cathode probes, creating an electrical field which stuns fish.

Elongate A shape of a fish or part of a fish; much longer than wide, particularly compared to the typical form in the group considered.

Emarginate A fin margin with a slight middistal concavity (e.g., caudal fin of most bullheads).

Embedded scales Scales inobvious owing to deep embedment in or full covering by skin.

Endangered A protective status category for taxa threatened with extinction. See *threatened* and *special concern.*

Endemic Native and restricted to a given area. Unless otherwise defined, taxa that are native to only one drainage.

Entire Margin smooth or straight.

Eocene epoch The epoch of the Cenozoic era, 36–58 million years ago, between the Paleocene and Oligocene epochs.

Epi- (prefix) Upon, above.

Epigean Surface dwelling, as opposed to subterranean.

Epilimnion The upper level of a lake when the lake is stratified into thermally distinct layers. See *hypolimnion.*

Epipelagic The upper level of water column away from shore.

Escarpment A steep face that abruptly terminates highlands; for example, the eastern front of the Blue Ridge.

Estuary A partly enclosed body of water that is entirely coastal or reaches inland, that has free connection to an open sea, and within which sea water is measurably diluted by fresh water.

Eu- (prefix) Truly, very.

Eury- (prefix) Widely.

Euryhaline Tolerance of a wide range of salinity.

Eurythermal Tolerance of a wide range of temperature.

Eustasy Worldwide simultaneous change in sea level. See *regression* and *transgression.*

Eutrophic A body of water having a high rate of biological production. Opposite of *oligotrophic.*

Evolution In broadest sense, observable or inferable change. Biological (organic) evolution concerns hereditary changes (mutation and natural selection) that occurs between generations of organisms, including very slight changes within a single lineage and those which constitute divergence (diversification) of taxa. See *divergence, diversification,* and *speciation.*

Evolutionary species See *species.*

Evolutionary tree See *cladogram* and *dendrogram.*

Exclusively shared taxon The occurrence of a species or subspecies in only two drainages.

Exotic Not native, introduced from another country.

Expatriation Wandering or directed movement away from a place normally inhabited. Opposite of *repatriation.*

Extant Still living or present. Opposite of *extinct.*

Extended river The lower reach of a coastal river (and tributaries) that has been lengthened seaward by lowering of sea level; often has prefix "Greater" or "Ancestral" (e.g., the Greater Roanoke River). See *regression*.

Extinct   A taxon no longer living.

Extirpated   Refers to a nonextant population of an extant taxon.

Extralimital   Refers to an area outside of that considered. For example, the lowermost portion of the Roanoke drainage (in North Carolina) is extralimital to Virginia; its species that do not occur in the Virginia portion are extralimital to Virginia.

°F   Degrees Fahrenheit.

Falcate   Refers to fins with a markedly concave or sickle-shaped distal margin.

Fall Line   The eastern edge of the *Fall Zone* (or Piedmont Province); forms the inland boundary of the Coastal Plain (Map 7).

Fall Zone   The relatively narrow belt between the Coastal Plain and Piedmont provinces.

Family   A taxonomic category between order and genus levels; the suffix of animal families is -idae.

Fault   In a rock mass, a fracture or fracture zone along which displacement has occurred.

Fauna   The animal species that occupy a given area. See *biota*.

Fecundity   The reproductive potential of a female in a year; generally based on number of mature ova (eggs) produced.

Fide   According to; used in certain citations.

Filament   A threadlike structure.

Fimbriate   Fringed with numerous small processes or extensions.

First dorsal fin   See *dorsal fin*.

FL   Fork length.

Flora   The plant species that occupy a given area. See *biota*.

Fluvial   Flowing as in streams, or of streams.

Focus   The first-developed area of a scale; usually defined by the innermost circulus of a scale; usually centrally or nearly centrally located.

Fork length (FL)   The distance from the anteriormost point on a fish to the anteriormost point of the notch or indentation of the tail.

Forked   In caudal fin shape, a fin moderately or deeply divided into two lobes; same as *furcate*. Also applied to branching of fin rays.

Form   An informal taxonomic category generally applied to a species, subspecies, race, or some other geographical variant. The term often indicates uncertain taxonomic status. Sometimes termed a *morph*.

Frenum   A bridge of skin-covered tissue binding snout to medial portion of upper lip, making protraction of jaw limited or impossible.

Fulcral scales   Long thick scales along leading ray of certain fins of some primitive fishes (e.g., gars).

Furcate   Forked.

g   Gram.

Ganoid scale   A bony interlocking scale found in gars; often *rhomboid* or diamond-shaped; surfaced with enamel-like substance termed ganoine.

Gape   Mouth width, distance between corners of mouth or lips.

Gas bladder   A thin-walled, saclike, gas-containing organ located dorsally in abdominal cavity of most fishes; used in buoyancy regulation, sound reception, or sound production. Often termed air or swim bladder.

Genealogy   The graphic representation (phylogenetic tree) of the evolutionary descent of one or more taxa from an ancestor. See *phylogenetics*.

Generally distributed   Refers to occurrence of a species at most or all sites having suitable habitat within a given, usually large area.

Genital papilla   A fleshy protuberance bearing the external genital opening; often tubular, extending from body. See *urogenital papilla*.

Genome   The full set of genes (hereditary units) and their alleles in a population or species.

Genus   A taxonomic category between family and species levels.

Geomorphology   See *physiography*.

Gill   A vascularized respiratory (gas exchange) organ located along the posterior edge of a gill arch.

Gill arch   Bony sickle-shaped or angled structures supporting gills in pharyngeal cavity.

Gill filaments   Elongate subdivisions of a gill.

Gill net   A net with mesh large enough to allow passage of the head of a fish, but too small to allow passage of the body.

Gill rakers   Projections along the anterior edge of gill arches.

Gonopodium   Modified elongate anterior anal fin rays in male poeciliid (livebearing) fishes which aid in transmission of sperm to female; also termed an *intromittent organ*.

Gravel   A substrate category; pebbles and small stones, 3–76 mm (0.125–3 inches); essentially comprises pebble and gravel on the Wentworth Scale. Pea gravel is small gravel, usually 3–20 mm.

Gravid A reproductive state of females in which many of the oocytes (developing eggs) present in the ovary are nearly or fully mature (ripe), and the fish is about to spawn or has begun spawning. Gravid females usually appear swollen, rotund ventrally.

Greater river See *extended river* and *regression*.

Ground color Basic background color or shade. Sometimes termed *base color*.

Ground water Water under the surface of land and well below the substrate of a body of water.

Gular area The underside of head just behind chin.

Gular plate The bony plate or splint on underside of head of some primitive fishes.

Gustatory Relating to sense of taste.

Haline Salty or regarding salt content.

Hardpan See *clay*.

Hard water Water with substantial concentrations of dissolved salts of calcium, magnesium, or both; generally found in areas of carbonate rocks such as limestone and dolomite.

Head The anterior portion of a fish including the operculum.

Hemicercal See *abbreviate heterocercal*.

Herpetofauna The amphibian and reptile species of a given area.

Herptile A species of amphibian or reptile.

Heterocercal A primitive caudal fin type in which the vertebral column is upturned and extends well into upper lobe of caudal fin. See *abbreviate heterocercal* and *homocercal*.

Highlands Higher mountains; specifically the Highlands subprovince of the Blue Ridge Province in Virginia and south.

Holarctic The combination of the Nearctic and Palearctic, temperate and higher-latitude, biogeographic realms in the Northern Hemisphere. Holarctic species occur around much of the Northern Hemisphere.

Holocene The current, Recent epoch—the last 10,000 years B.P., following the Pleistocene epoch (first epoch of the Quaternary period).

Homocercal A caudal fin type in which the vertebral column is not distinctly upturned into upper lobe of caudal fin. See *abbreviate heterocercal* and *heterocercal*.

Homonyms Identical names for different taxa of the same higher taxon; for example, with proposed generic merger of *Hybopsis* into *Notropis*, two species each formerly or presently named *rubrifrons* would be in *Notropis*. The first described species would retain the name *rubrifrons*; the other would take a resurrected or newly penned name.

Hours 24-hour clock time when preceded by a four-digit number (e.g., 1500 hours is 3:00 P.M.).

Humeral area The shoulder (*scapular*) area, laterally just behind head.

Hybrid The progeny of crossmating between species. See *intergrade*.

Hyper- (prefix) Highly.

Hypertrophy Highly or overly developed.

Hypo- (prefix) Below, under.

Hypolimnion The lower level of a lake when the lake is stratified into thermally distinct layers. See *epilimnion*.

Hypsi- (prefix) High.

Hypsithermal interval A postglacial period having climate warmer than at present.

Hypurals Flattened splintlike bones at posterior end of vertebral column; they form caudal fin base (hypural plate) which supports caudal fin rays.

Ichthyocide A fish poison; used to collect fish.

Ichthyofauna The fish species of a given area.

ICZN The International Commission of Zoological Nomenclature; publishes a code of nomenclatural rules and resolves disputes of names of family and lower taxa.

i.e. That is.

IGFA The International Gamefish Association, which keeps weight records of fishes.

Igneous rock Rock formed by solidification of hot mobile material termed magma. See *metamorphic* and *sedimentary rocks*.

Illinoian glaciation The next to last Pleistocene glaciation, ending about 125,000 years B.P.; followed by the Sangamonian interglacial and Wisconsinan glaciation.

Imbricate Overlapping, as in roof shingles; refers to pattern of scale positioning.

Immaculate Lacking pigmentation, stippling, or spotting.

Impoundment A lentic body of water created by a dam.

Indigenous Native to a given area.

Inferior mouth Mouth positioned distinctly on underside of head; mouth opens distinctly below horizontal body axis.

Infra- (prefix) Below; among taxonomic categories, the level just below the next highest level (e.g., an infraorder is below a suborder).

Infraorbital canal   The pored canal passing just below eye; part of *cephalic lateralis* system.

Infraspecific   Below the species level (e.g., subspecies). See *intraspecific*.

In litt.   In letter; used to cite unpublished information transmitted to us in written or graphic form, often in a manuscript to be submitted or under review for publication.

In press   Used to cite information from a manuscript that has been accepted for publication.

Insertion   Regarding a fin, the anterior or posterior point of its attachment to the body. See *origin* and *base of fin*.

Insular   Isolated geographically.

Inter- (prefix)   Between.

Intergrade   The progeny of interbreeding of two or more subspecies of the same species. See *hybrid*.

Intermittent   Discontinuous, e.g, headwater stream reaches whose bed surface is dry during part of year.

Internasal   The area of the snout between nasal openings. Same as internarial.

Interradial membranes   Membranes between rays in fins.

Interspinous membranes   Membranes between spines in fins.

Intersticine   Living in small spaces or cavities (interstices) including those between and under stones.

Intra- (prefix)   Within.

Intraspecific   Within, below the species level; for example, intraspecific taxon (subspecies) or intraspecific variation.

Introduced   Non-native distributional status. See *alien*, *exotic*, and *transplant*.

Intromittent organ   A male structure which functions to place sperm within the female. See *gonopodium*.

Invertivore   Feeding on invertebrates.

IO   *Infraorbital canal*.

Iso- (prefix)   Equal, same.

Isobath   A real or imaginary line connecting points of equal depth.

Isotherm   A real or imaginary line connecting points of equal temperature.

Isthmus   The posterior portion of underside of head; just anterior to breast.

Jurassic basin   Analogous to a *Triassic basin*, but formed in the Jurassic period.

Jurassic period   The middle period of the Mesozoic era, about 144–208 million years ago.

K-selection   An ecological model describing the general relationship among reproductive potential, parental investment, longevity, and body size. Species which are K-selected tend to have a low reproductive rate, exhibit parental care, and are long-lived and medium-sized or large (for their group). See *r-selection*.

Keratin   A structural protein forming certain firm or hard (horny) parts (e.g., breeding *tubercles*).

kg   Kilogram.

km   Kilometer.

Labile   Propensity to undergo change.

Lachrymal   The first and usually largest suborbital bone; under skin on side of snout (below naris and anterior to cheek); often spelled lacrimal.

Lachrymal groove   A small groove on lower side of snout, caused by folding of skin under edge of lachrymal bone just above upper lip.

Lacustrine   Refers to lakes and aspects of lakes.

Larva   A developmental stage between hatching and the juvenile (or as herein, the young) stage.

Laterad   Toward the side.

Lateral   The side; between dorsal and ventral.

Lateral field   The areas of a scale between the anterior and posterior fields; "lateral" fields actually are the dorsal and ventral fields; they are dorsoventrally aligned when the scale is oriented as on the body. See Figure 6 caption.

Lateral line   The pored sensory canal along side of body; sometimes incomplete (not reaching tail), interrupted, or absent; connected to *cephalic lateralis* system.

Lateral radii   See *lateral field* and *radii*.

LC   Lateral canal; the horizontal portion of the *cephalic lateralis* system behind the eye.

Lentic   Refers to standing waters (e.g., ponds or lakes).

Limestone rock   Carbonate sedimentary rock composed chiefly of calcium carbonate—$CaCO_3$. Water draining such strata tend to be alkaline and hard.

Limnology   The study of fresh waters.

Lingual lamina   A horny ridge, usually bearing minute teeth, on "tongue" of lampreys; located in throat. The single, but sometimes bilobed transverse lingual lamina is posterior to the two longitudinal lingual laminae.

Lithophilic   Associated with stony substrate.

Littoral   Shore area.

Lobate   Lobed.

Lobulate   Bearing small lobes.

Localized   Refers to a population occupying a small geographic area which is distinctly separated from other populations of the species. See *disjunct*.

Longitudinal zonation   The distribution pattern in streams formed by the occupation by species of particular reaches; sometimes termed linear zonation or linear distribution.

Lot   A sample or *series* of one or more specimens of a single species collected at one site and time. In museums, each lot is contained in a separate jar and assigned a catalog or field number or other identifier.

Lotic   Refers to flowing waters (e.g., creeks).

Lowland   Slightly rolling or virtually flat terrain; as a stream type, characterized by low gradient with runs constituting 10% or less of the length and riffles being very rare or absent. See *montane* and *upland*.

Lumen   An internal space, cavity.

Lunula   The visible, exposed posterior part of a scale when in its natural position.

m   Meter.

Macro- (prefix)   Large.

Mandible   Lower jaw.

Mandibular pores   The series of canal openings on ventral surface of mandible; part of preopercular-mandibular canal of *cephalic lateralis* system.

Marbled   A color pattern; a largely dark area with one or more narrow pale streaks.

Maturation   Becoming an adult, sexually mature, capable of reproducing.

Mean   The arithmetic mean or average.

Medial   Middle or midline.

Melanin   A dark pigment which produces shades of gray to black depending on its concentration.

Melanistic   Quite dark or black.

Melanophore   A color cell bearing melanin; also termed melanocyte.

Mental barbels   Chin barbels.

Meso- (prefix)   Middle.

Mesohaline zone   The section of an estuary where salinity is 5–18‰.

Mesozoic era   Geologic time of about 66–245 million years ago; comprises the Triassic (earliest), Jurassic, and Cretaceous periods.

Metamorphic rock   Rock formed in the solid state in response to pronounced changes of temperature, pressure, and chemical environment, generally taking place below the level of weathering and cementation. See *igneous* and *sedimentary rocks*.

Metamorphosis   The period in which an organism exhibits major change from one form or stage to another, often in preparation for life in a new habitat. Examples include passage from the larval to the juvenile (young) stage in bony fishes, and the transformation of larval lampreys (ammocoetes) to the next stage.

mg   Milligram.

Microphagous   Feeding on small organisms (e.g., plankton).

Migration   A directed movement, often cyclic, for the purpose of breeding, feeding, salinity relations, or other factors. See *diadromous*.

Milt   Gametes and associated fluid released from ripe male; often whitish.

Miocene epoch   The epoch of the Cenozoic era, 5–24 million years ago, between the Oligocene and Pliocene epochs.

mm   Millimeter.

Mode   The value which occurs in the highest frequency.

Molariform   Molarlike; relatively large teeth with flattened or broadly rounded crowns.

Mono- (prefix)   One.

Monogamy   A mating system in which a male and a female mate only with each other.

Monogeneric   A suprageneric taxon having one genus.

Monophyletic group   See *natural taxon, paraphyletic group*, and *polyphyletic group*.

Monospecific   A supraspecific taxon having one species.

Monotypic   A taxon having one member; for example, a genus having one species, or a species lacking subspecies.

Montane   High-relief mountainous terrain; as a stream type, characterized by high gradient, riffles composing 50% or more of the length and pools frequently being runlike. See *lowland* and *upland*.

Morph   See *form*.

Mottled   A pigmentary pattern in which small dark areas are interspersed, usually irregularly, with small pale areas.

m.s.l.   Mean sea level.

Myomeres   Dorsoventrally or obliquely oriented, often angled, bundles of muscle arranged in a series along side of body.

Myoseptum   The juncture between myomeres.

Naked   Lacking scales; applied to a specific area or whole specimen.

Nape   The dorsal area between posterior end of head (occiput) and dorsal fin.

Nares   Nostril openings; naris.

Natal   Refers to birth; for example, natal (birthplace) stream of a fish.

Native   Indigenous to, naturally occurring in a given area. Opposite of *introduced*.

Natural taxon   A species or group of species that exists as a result of a unique history of evolutionary descent. A natural taxon composed of two or more species constitutes a clade or monophyletic group. See *clade, monophyletic group, paraphyletic group,* and *polyphyletic group*.

Naturalized   A self-sustaining population of an *introduced* species.

Nearctic   The biogeographic realm encompassing North America, excluding southern Mexico.

Neuromast   An exposed or semiexposed receptor of the nervous system sensitive to mechanical stimuli such as water movements. See *cephalic lateralis* and *lateral line*.

Nominal form   In name only; a formally named taxon of questionable status.

Nominate subspecies (or nominate form)   Name-bearing taxon; the nominate subspecies has the same subspecific and specific epithets—the oldest valid name for the species (e.g., *Etheostoma olmstedi olmstedi*).

Nonextant   No longer existing; applied to specimens.

Nonindigenous   Not native to a given area.

Nonprotractile jaw   An upper jaw unable to protract (move forward from snout tip) when the mouth is opened. See *frenum*.

Nuptial   Being in reproductive condition; applied, for example, to breeding color and secondary sexual structures such as breeding tubercles. See *contact organ, tubercle,* and *unculi*.

Occiput   The posterodorsal portion of head, immediately anterior to nape.

Ocellus   A round spot surrounded by a circular, differently colored area; often resembling an eye.

Ocular   Refers to the eye or the nearby area (e.g., subocular bar).

Ohioan   Characteristic of, or unique to, the Ohio River basin.

Oligo- (prefix)   Few.

Oligocene epoch   The epoch of the Cenozoic era, 25–36 million years ago, between the Eocene and Miocene epochs.

Oligohaline zone   The section of an estuary where salinity is 0.5–5‰.

Oligotrophic   A body of water having a low rate of biological production.

Oligotypic   A taxon with few members.

Ontogenetic   Refers to development during the embryonic and postembryonic stages—the full life span. See *differentiation*.

Oocyte   A cell that can develop into a mature ovum or egg.

Opercle   The largest bone of the gill cover (*operculum*); posterior to *preopercle*, dorsal to *subopercle*.

Opercular flap   The posterior projection of *operculum* and its membrane; particularly well developed in many sunfishes, in which it is often termed the earflap.

Opercular membrane   The membrane along posterior edge of *operculum*; confluent ventrally with *branchiostegal membrane*.

Opercular spine   A sharp posterior extension of *opercle*.

Operculum   The cover of gill (branchial) chamber; composed of separate bones.

Opportunistic   Taking advantage of unused or little-used resources; also applied to species which flourish soon after being introduced by feeding on abundant food.

Oral disk   The circular mouth area of lampreys, bearing horny teeth in juvenile and adult (disk often preserved in noncircular form).

Orbit   The eye socket.

Order   A taxonomic category between class and family levels; the suffix of many animal orders is -iformes. See also *stream order*.

Origin   Regarding fins, the anterior point of attachment (anterior *insertion*) to the body.

Orogeny   The process of forming mountains, particularly by folding and thrusting.

Ossification   The process of becoming bone.

Otolith   A small stonelike bone located in the inner ear of fishes. Functions in detection of changes in gravitational forces relative to orientation.

Outcrop   Exposed *bedrock* or strata; used here for broken rough-edged strata forming cover for fishes.

Outgroup   One or more species or higher monophyletic taxa, other than those under primary consideration, that are examined in a phylogenetic study to aid in polarization of character states. See *polarization*.

Oviposit   To deposit an egg during spawning.

Ovoid   Round or nearly round.

Palatine teeth Small teeth on paired palatine bones in roof of mouth, just posterior or lateral to medial *vomer* (or *prevomer*) bone.

Palearctic The biogeographic realm encompassing northern Africa, Europe, and northern and central Asia.

Paleocene epoch The first epoch of the Cenozoic era, 58–66 million years ago, between the Mesozoic era and the Eocene epoch.

Paleochannel A former river channel; for example, that of an *extended river* later drowned by an estuary.

Paleozoic era Geologic time of about 245–600 million years ago.

Panmictic population A population in which all members are equally likely to mate.

Papilla A small rounded fleshy protuberance; knob-like or elongate.

Papillose Bearing papillae.

Parapatric A distributional relationship or pattern whereby the ranges of two taxa are separate but are in contact, or may overlap very slightly. See *allopatric* and *sympatric*.

Paraphyletic group A group that includes a common ancestor and some but not all of its descendants. See *natural taxon* and *polyphyletic group*.

Parr A juvenile salmonid; often with large dark bars or blotches (parr marks) on side of body.

Patronym A taxon named after and honoring a person, generally a noted scientist or the collector but not the author (describer) of the taxon.

Parts per thousand (‰) A chemical concentration; the number of parts of a substance dissolved in 1,000 parts of water. Used to express salinity.

Pectoral fin An anteriormost paired fin (when pelvic fin has a posterior position), or dorsalmost paired fin (when pelvic fin is near or under head). Fin is soft-rayed, except catfishes have an anterior spine. May be termed P_1.

Pelagic Open water or of open water; for example, species that live above the substrate and away from the shoreline.

Pelvic fin A paired fin on the ventral surface of the body between the pectoral and anal fins or below the pectoral fin; may have one spine and more than one ray or only rays. May be termed P_2.

Peppered Stippled with dark pigment (*melanophores*).

Periglacial Refers to areas, deposits, or processes that occur near the margin of a glacier. See *proglacial*.

Periphyton Small plantlike organisms, typically algae, growing on a *substrate*. See *aufwuchs*.

Peritoneum The membrane lining the abdominal cavity.

Personal communication Unpublished information verbally transmitted to us.

pH The expression of relative acid-base (H^+:OH^- ions) concentration on a logarithmic scale; water of pH 7.0 is neutral; lesser values are acidic, higher values (pH 14.0 maximum) basic (alkaline). See *acidity* and *alkalinity*.

Pharyngeal arch The bony modified last (posterior) gill arch; term applied when this arch bears definitive teeth, as in minnows and suckers.

Pharyngeal teeth Teeth on the pharyngeal arch.

Phenetics A classification method in which the basis for grouping taxa is overall similarity.

Phenotype All observable anatomical, physiological, and behavioral characteristics of an organism; produced by the genotype and often modified by the environment.

Pheromone A chemical released by an organism to the external environment; functions in the location, attraction, or stimulation of a mate.

Phyletic Refers to lineage of descent. See *phylogeny*.

Phylogenetics A classification method in which the basis for uniting taxa is relative recency of common descent; same as *cladistics*. See *genealogy*.

Phylogenetic tree See *cladogram*.

Phylogeny The evolutionary history of a group of organisms.

Physiographic province A region of similar structure that has had a unified geomorphic history.

Physiography The study of the origin and evolution of land forms; essentially the same as *geomorphology*.

Piedmont The lowland to (and including) upland physiographic province between the Coastal Plain and the Blue Ridge (Map 7).

Plate See *Continental Plate*.

Pleistocene epoch The earlier of the two epochs of the *Quaternary period* (last major division of the Cenozoic era); 10,000 years B.P. to 1.6 million years ago; glacial–interglacial cycles a dominant feature.

Plesiomorphic See *primitive*.

Plicate Having parallel ridges and grooves, appearing pleated or folded, as on lips of certain suckers.

Pliocene epoch The epoch of the Cenozoic era spanning 1.6–5 million years ago, between the Miocene and Pleistocene epochs.

PM (POM) *Preopercular-mandibular canal.*

Polarity Refers to the genealogical position (*advanced* or *primitive*) of a *character state* of a taxonomic character. See *outgroup*.

Polarization The process of determining which states of a character are advanced and which are primitive. See *outgroup*.

Poly- (prefix) Several or many.

Polyandry A mating system in which the male mates with more than one female.

Polygamy Mating in which both sexes mate with more than one other individual.

Polygyny A mating system in which the female mates with more than one male.

Polyhaline zone The section of an estuary where salinity is 18–30‰.

Polymorphic Refers to species having two or more distinct variants in the same population and sex (e.g., color phases); such variants are not recognized taxonomically. Also refers to a character (broad sense) having two or more states. See *character* and *polytypic*.

Polyphyletic group A non-natural taxon; a group that excludes its most recent common ancestor. See *natural taxon* and *paraphyletic group*.

Polyploid The condition in which the number of chromosomes is an integral multiple (greater than 2) of the haploid number. See *triploid* and *tetraploid*.

Polytypic taxon A taxon containing more than one lower taxa or forms. See *polymorphic*.

POM See *PM*.

Pool A stream habitat type characterized by a smooth undisturbed surface, generally slow current (0.1–0.3 m/second), and some moderate or deep water for the size of the stream.

Posteriad Toward the tail.

Posterior The hind or rear portion of a fish or a part of a fish.

Pre- (prefix) Before, in front of.

Precambrian era Geologic time ending about 600 million years ago, at the start of the Paleozoic era.

Premaxilla Anterior paired bones of upper jaw; usually extending distinctly posterior to form much of the side of the lower jaw in fishes with a protractile jaw.

Preocular bar A horizontal or oblique bar, dash, or stripe on the snout in front of eye; often termed preorbital bar.

Preopercle The bone just anterior to the *opercle*, forming the posterior boundary of the *cheek*.

Preopercular-mandibular canal The pored canal coursing along the posterior margin of the *preopercle* to the ventrolateral edge of the *mandible*, terminating on the chin. Part of the *cephalic lateralis* system.

Preterminal barbel A *barbel* attached slightly anterior to the posterior end of the upper lip; usually in groove just above upper lip; often termed a subterminal barbel.

Prevomerine teeth Teeth on the prevomer bone, on the roof of the mouth anteromedially.

Primary radii See *radii*.

Primitive Regarding a taxonomic character, the *character state* that evolutionarily originated first; same as *ancestral* and *plesiomorphic*. Opposite of *advanced*.

Principal ray A ray whose tip reaches the primary distal margin of the fin.

Procurrent ray A small splintlike ray at the origin of a median fin; often same as *rudimentary* ray.

Proglacial Refers to features of glacial origin beyond the limits of the glacier (e.g., meltwater streams). See *periglacial*.

Promiscuous Mating with more than one individual of the opposite sex.

Protocercal tail A caudal fin type in which the vertebral column extends nearly or fully to posterior end of the fish, the tail nonlobed (e.g., in lamprey).

Protractile (protrusile) jaw An upper jaw (*premaxilla*) able to protract from the snout tip when the mouth is opened.

Proximal Toward the point of attachment; same as *basal*. Opposite of *distal*.

Psammophilic Associated with sand substrate.

Pseudobranchium A small patch of vascularized filaments appearing like short *gill filaments*; attached to upper inner surface of gill cover.

Pterygiophore A bony fin support in the body, linking the base of a fin spine or ray to a spine on a vertebral centrum.

Quaternary period The current period of the Cenozoic era, comprising the Pleistocene epoch (duration about 1.6 million years ago to 10,000 years B.P.) and Holocene (Recent) epoch.

r-selection An ecological model describing the general relationship among reproductive potential, parental investment, longevity, and body size. Species which are r-selected tend to have a high potential reproductive rate, exhibit no parental care, and are shortlived and small (for their group). See *K-selected*.

Race An informal taxonomic category generally referring to a geographic or biologically distinctive subset of a species or subspecies; some races have a distinctive phenotype. See *deme* and *stock*.

Radii Lines on scales radiating from the *focus* toward the scale margin. Primary (1°) radii extend nearly or entirely from focus to margin; secondary (2°) radii are about half the length or less of 1° radii.

Range A geographic area occupied by a taxon. See *exotic, introduced, native,* and *naturalized.*

Ray A fin support element that is segmented, bilateral (paired), branched or unbranched, and usually flexible; some rays are spinelike (stiff, the halves fused, and pointed).

Recent (upper case) The current geologic epoch (i.e., the last 10,000 years B.P.); same as *Holocene.*

Recruitment In a biogeographic sense, the recolonization of a place by a species or *fauna.* See *refugium.* Also, the addition of individuals of a species (usually through reproduction) to a preexisting population of that species.

Redd A nest made in gravel (particularly by salmonids); consisting of a depression that is created and then covered.

Reduced A less-developed condition of a structure; reduced *character states* often are *advanced.* See *elaborate, rudiment,* and *vestige.*

Refugium Shelter, a place in which a species or fauna has persisted during changed or adverse conditions; for example, southern regions during glacial periods, or tributaries during a period of toxicity in the main river. See *recruitment* and *repatriation.*

Regenerated scale A scale that has replaced a lost scale; characterized by irregular circuli and a large focus; not suited for age analysis.

Regression The gradual contraction of a shallow sea resulting in emergence of land and seaward extension of rivers, as when sea level falls or land rises. Opposite of *transgression.* See *eustasy* and *extended river.*

Relict group An ancient lineage, usually with one or few extant members.

Relict population A population limited to a small part of the original species range.

Relict species An extant species of an ancient group or, regarding groups of more recent origin, a species that has no obvious close relative.

Repatriation In a biogeographic sense, the return to a place normally inhabited. Opposite of *expatriation.* See *recruitment* and *refugium.*

Rheophilic Associated with moderate or swift current in streams.

Rhomboid scale Same as *ganoid scale.*

Richness See *species richness* and *speciose.*

Riffle A stream habitat type characterized by a broken or choppy surface (white water), moderate or swift current (0.5–2.0 m/second), and relatively shallow depth (usually 0.5 m or less).

Riparian The shore area or the shore of a body of water (e.g., riparian trees).

Ripe The gonadal state of readiness to spawn; applied to both sexes. Running ripe refers to emission of eggs or milt when slight or no pressure is applied to the abdomen.

Riprap Large rocks, broken concrete, or other structure used to stabilize stream banks.

River A large lotic waterway; when stream-size categorization of species is considered, river refers to running waterways of usually 50 m or greater in width. See *big river, creek,* and *stream.*

Riverine Of rivers; generally we use riverine to describe species distributions that are restricted or almost so to medium and larger rivers. See *big river.*

Rkm (upper case) River kilometer; specifies the distance (measured along midstream) that a point in a stream lies above the mouth of that stream (e.g., Rkm 36.2). These were converted from the RM (river miles) determined from detailed maps or the literature. See *rkm.*

rkm (lower case) River kilometers; specifies the entire stream length or the distance (measured along the midstream) between any two points in a stream, e.g, 15 rkm. Determined and converted as for Rkm; usually rounded to nearest rkm.

Roe Fish eggs, often applied to the entire complement in one or both ovaries, and often to their use as human food.

Rostrum Snout; usually applied to a prominently projecting snout, as in sturgeon and paddlefish.

Rotenone An ichthyocide (fish poison), derived from the root of some species of South American plants of the genus *Derris;* used to collect fishes.

Rubble A substrate category; stones of small or medium size, 76–305 mm (3–12 inches) in greatest dimension; nearly synonymous with cobble of the Wentworth scale—64–256 mm (2.5–10 inches). Slab rubble is relatively flat rubble.

Rudimentary Poorly developed or small, often as compared with the analogous or homologous part in a different species or a different ontogenetic stage. See *vestige.*

Run A stream habitat type intermediate between *pool* and *riffle;* characterized by a smooth, often roiled surface, moderate or swift current (0.3–2.0 m/second), and shallow or moderate depth. Also termed raceway or glide.

Run-of-river impoundment An impoundment having a high rate of flushing.

Running ripe See *ripe.*

Saddle   A wide dark pigmentary mark overlying the dorsum. Saddle-band, used in *Cottus*, comprises the saddle proper and its ventral extension.

Salinity   The salt concentration of water. See *parts per thousand*.

Sand   A substrate category; particles smaller than gravel and larger than silt; fragments of rock 0.0626–2 mm (0.0025–0.08 inches) on the Wentworth Scale.

Sangamonian interglacial   The interglacial period about 118,000–125,000 years B.P., between the *Illinoian* and *Wisconsinan glaciations*.

Satellite male   See *cuckoldry*.

Scalation   Same as *squamation*.

Scale   A small or medium-sized, usually flattened structure in the skin. See *ctenoid, cycloid, fulcral, ganoid,* and *rhomboid scales*.

Scale pocket   The envelope of skin in which the anterior portion of a scale is embedded.

Scapula   A bone of the pectoral girdle.

Scapular area   The shoulder (*humeral*) area, anteriormost lateral area of body proper.

Scute   A large, modified, often thick scale or plate.

Second dorsal fin   See *dorsal fin*.

Secondary contact   The zone where ranges of two taxa abut or overlap, following the differentiation in geographic isolation of the taxa from their common ancestor.

Secondary radii   See *radii*.

Sedimentary rock   Rock formed by accumulation of sediment in water or from air; characteristically layered as beds or strata. See *igneous* and *metamorphic rocks*.

Sedimentation   The settling, interbedding, and covering of gravel and larger substrate materials by clay, silt, or sand.

Seine   A net in which each side is tied to a pole (braille). It is drawn through water to collect fishes.

Semelparity   A reproductive strategy of spawning once in a lifetime.

Series   See *lot*.

Serrae   Small pointed toothlike structures.

Serrate   Sawtoothlike, bearing a series of serrae.

Sexual dichromatism   The difference between the sexes in color pattern, hue, or shade.

Sexual dimorphism   The difference between the sexes in anatomy; for example, body size, fin shape, and breeding tubercles. Sexual dichromatism sometimes is included in this term.

Sibling species   See *cryptic species*.

Silt   A substrate category; minute particles, smaller than sand and larger than clay, 0.0039–0.0625 mm (0.0002–0.002 inches) on the Wentworth scale.

Sink   A funnel-shaped depression in the land surface communicating with an underground passage formed by solution; usually occurs in limestone areas and commonly termed a sinkhole.

Sister group   A species or higher monophyletic taxon that is thought to be the closest genealogical relative of a given taxon, exclusive of the ancestral species of both taxa.

SL   Standard length.

S.L.   Sensu lato (i.e., in a broad sense).

Slope   A major region extending from its headwater drainage divide to the sea (e.g., the Atlantic slope).

Sneaker   See *cuckoldry*.

Snout   The anterior part of the head, anterior to eyes and above mouth.

SO   Supraorbital canal; the canal of the *cephalic lateralis* system passing above the eye.

Soft dorsal fin   See *dorsal fin*.

Soft water   Water with a low concentration of dissolved calcium and magnesium salts; tends to be acidic or circumneutral.

sp.   Species; spp. refers to more than one species.

Spate   A heavy rainstorm; a rush or excessive quantity.

Special concern   A protective-status category for taxa of such low abundance or sharp localization that, with substantial further decline, they would be threatened. See *endangered* and *threatened*.

Specialized   Narrowly adapted; for example, having trophic adaptations that allow feeding on only one type of food.

Speciation   The evolutionary process of species formation, involving divergence from an ancestor. See *differentiation, divergence,* and *evolution*.

Species   A lineage that is independent of other lineages in that it may evolve separately, according to the *evolutionary species* concept. Failure to interbreed substantially or at all with any other lineage is the primary criterion for recognition of *biological species*.

Species richness   The number of species in a given area or habitat. See *diversity* and *speciose*.

Speciose   Having a substantial number of species, e.g, a speciose fauna or genus; the terms rich and diverse often are used in this sense.

Spent   Referring to adults that recently completed spawning.

Spine   A fin-support element that is median (unpaired), unsegmented, unbranched, and usually stiff and sharply pointed; soft spines are common in some groups.

Spinous dorsal fin See *dorsal fin*.

Spinulose Bearing tiny spines.

Spiral valve A spiraled fold of the inner wall of the intestine, functioning to increase the surface area.

spm. Specimen.

Squamation The state or an aspect of being scaled.

S.S. Sensu stricto (i.e., in a strict sense).

ST Supratemporal canal; the canal of the *cephalic lateralis* system aligned transversely on the posterodorsal portion of the head.

Stadia Stages; for example, stadia of a glacial period.

Standard length (SL) The distance from the anteriormost point on a fish to the posterior end of the bony caudal fin base (*hypural plate*).

Stellate Star-shaped; that is, having radiating narrow extensions.

Steno- (prefix) Narrow.

Stenohaline Tolerance of or preference for a narrow range of salinity.

Stenothermal Tolerance of or preference for a narrow range of temperature.

Stippled Sparsely pigmented with *melanophores*.

Stitched A pigmentary pattern in which lateral line pores are bordered above and below by a dot or dash of dark pigment, resembling a series of stitches.

Stock To add individuals of a native or nonnative species to a place. Also, a distinctive, informally named subdivision of a species differing from others of that species usually in one or all of growth, foraging area, and spawning area. See *deme* and *race*.

Streaked A pigmentary pattern in fin membranes consisting of dark, sometimes chromatic streaks. Streaks also are linear, short or moderate marks elsewhere on a fish.

Stream A lotic waterway; often applied for stream-size categorization of species to running waterways of 10–50 m in width. See *creek* and *river*.

Stream capture An erosive process by which a stream (the captor or pirate) contacts and takes water from a stream (the captive) on the opposite side of their divide; biota may be exchanged during the period of contact of surface waters and, less often, groundwaters. Same as *stream piracy*. *Theater of capture* is a place where stream capture has occurred. See *barbed tributary*.

Stream order A numerical classification of streams based on their branching pattern. Order 1 streams are the smallest; they lack a tributary; order increases by one when two tributaries of the same order unite. In Virginia, streams of orders 5 and 6 typically are major streams or small rivers.

Stream piracy See *stream capture*.

Stripe A pigmentary streak that is horizontal, long, narrow or wide, and continuous or almost so.

Sub- (prefix) Below, under.

Subadult A juvenile of approximately the size of small adults, often used when maturity (adulthood) is uncertain.

Subgenus A formally named subdivision of a genus that is higher than the species level.

Subocular bar A vertical or slightly oblique dark bar beneath the eye; often termed a suborbital bar.

Subopercle See *opercle*.

subsp. Subspecies; subspp. refers to more than one subspecies.

Subspecies A subdivision of a species, usually formally named.

Substrate Bottom or bottom materials.

Subterminal barbel See *preterminal barbel*.

Subterminal mouth Mouth position in which the anterior end of the mouth (when closed) is just below the tip of the snout; mouth tends to open downward.

Superior mouth Mouth position in which the anterior end of the mouth (when closed) is distinctly above the tip of the snout; mouth opens distinctly above the horizontal body axis.

Supra- (prefix) Above.

Supraoral teeth Teeth, usually 2 or 3 cusps (points), whose bases are united and which occur at anterior margin of throat opening in lampreys.

Supraterminal mouth Mouth position in which the anterior end of the mouth (when closed) is slightly above the tip of the snout; mouth tends to open upward.

Swim bladder See *gas bladder*.

Sympatric A distributional relationship or pattern whereby the ranges occupied by two taxa overlap considerably. See *allopatric* and *parapatric*.

Synonyms Two names applying to the same taxon, as happens, for example, when two species are synonymized (found to be conspecific); generally the first described name is selected unless deemed to be invalid.

Syntopic A distributional relationship or pattern whereby two species commonly occur together. See *allotopic*.

System In the hydrographic sense, a division of a drainage. See *drainage* and *basin*.

Systematics A broad field of study of organismic diversity as that diversity is relevant to some specified kind of relationship thought to exist among populations, species, or higher taxa. Embraces diverse disciplines of biological science. Systematics is singular.

Tactile   Relating to the sense of touch.

Taxon (plural, taxa)   A group of organisms that is given a proper name (e.g., a species or family); or, a group that could be given a proper name but is not named as a matter of convention. See *natural taxon.*

Taxonomy   The theory and practice of describing the diversity of organisms and ordering this diversity into a classification or other system of conveying relationships.

Tectonic   Refers to rock structure and external forms resulting from deformation of the Earth's crust.

Terminal mouth   Mouth position in which the anterior end of the mouth is even with the tip of the snout; mouth tends to open directly forward.

Tessellated   A color pattern of fins created by small, darkly pigmented areas alternating with small, slightly pigmented or unpigmented areas.

Tetraploid   The condition of having twice the normal diploid number of chromosomes, that is, four times (4N) the haploid number; for example, a species with 96 chromosomes whereas related species have 48.

Theater of capture   See *stream capture.*

Thoracic   Refers to *breast* area.

Threatened   A protective status category for taxa at such level of risk that they could easily become endangered. See *endangered* and *special concern.*

TL   Total length.

Total length (TL)   The distance from the anteriormost point on a fish to the posteriormost point of the caudal fin.

Track   See *biogeographic track.*

Transform   See *metamorphosis* regarding lampreys.

Transgression   The gradual expansion of a shallow sea resulting in progressive submergence of land and rivers, as when sea level rises or land subsides. Opposite of *regression.* See *eustasy* and *drowned river.*

Transplanted   In reference to species, those introduced within their native continent to a geographic entity where they are not native.

Triassic basin   An area composed largely of rocks formed from sediments that had been deposited in a large depression that developed in the Triassic period.

Triassic period   The first period of the Mesozoic era, about 208–245 million years ago.

Tricuspid   A tooth with three points (cusps) on its upper surface.

Triploid   The condition of having 1.5 times the normal diploid number of chromosomes; that is, a diploid set and an extra haploid set (3N).

Troglobite   An obligate cave dweller.

Troglophile   A nonobligate, occasional or frequent cave occupant.

Trophic   Refers to nourishment; for example, the productivity of a body of water, or aspects of feeding and digestion in species.

Truncate   Squared-off; for example, the distal margin of a truncate tail.

Tubercle   A small protuberance. Nuptial or breeding tubercles are tiny to medium-sized, usually pointed, keratinized (horny) or nonkeratinized; occur on head, body, or fins, often in large numbers, often in males only, and generally only during breeding period; used in territorial aggression, for sexual stimuli, or to help the sexes to maintain contact while spawning. See *contact organ* and *unculi.*

Tuberculate ridge   Ridge of keratinized tissue in nuptial males of some cyprinids and percids.

Turbid   Water clouded by suspended inorganic particles, usually clay and silt.

TVA   Tennessee Valley Authority.

Ubiquitous   Refers to species that are widely distributed and generally common or abundant in a given area.

Unculi   Minute horny projections derived from single skin-surface cells; generally developed in patches and includes nuptial pad of some minnows; possible functions include mechanical protection of skin, rasping, adhesion, and hydrodynamic effects.

Uni- (prefix)   One.

Unicuspid   A tooth with a single point (cusp) on its upper surface.

Upland   Moderately rolling, hilly, or low-montane terrain, or widened valleys of higher mountains; as a stream type, characterized by moderate gradient, runs and riffles constituting 10–50% of the length. See *lowland* and *montane.*

Urogenital papilla   A fleshy protuberance bearing a common opening of urinary and reproductive tracts; often tubular, extending from body. Often termed *genital papilla.*

USFC   U.S. Fish Commission, now part of U.S. Fish and Wildlife Service.

USFWS   U.S. Fish and Wildlife Service.

Vagile   The propensity to move about.

Valley and Ridge The physiographic province situated just west of the Blue Ridge Province and characterized by long parallel mountain ridges, many U-shaped or wide valleys, and a trellis drainage pattern (Map 7).

Variegated An irregular pattern of small, dark and pale markings, many dark marks interconnected.

VDGIF Virginia Department of Game and Inland Fisheries.

Vent General term for the anus.

Venter Underside.

Ventral Bottom or underside of an organism.

Ventral field See *lateral field* (of scales).

VEPCO Virginia Electric Power Company, recently changed to Virginia Power Company.

Vermiculate A color pattern consisting of wormlike marks.

Vestige A remnant, for example, of a structure that was better developed in an earlier ontogenetic stage or in an ancestor. See *elaborate*, *reduced*, and *rudiment*.

VFC Virginia Fish Commission, now part of the Virginia Department of Game and Inland Fisheries.

Vicariance biogeography A new subdiscipline whose first-order explanation of disjunct distribution of sister groups is that the range of a widespread ancestral species has been fragmented, as opposed to the distribution having developed by dispersal of the ancestor from a center of origin. *Biogeographic tracks* and tenets of *phylogenetics* are stressed.

Villus A small, narrow, fleshy growth.

VIMS Virginia Institute of Marine Science.

Vomerine teeth Teeth on the vomer or prevomer bone, centered on the roof of the mouth anteromedially.

VPISU Virginia Polytechnic Institute and State University.

vs. Versus.

Waif A stray from the principal habitat or geographic range of a species.

Warm water A category for bodies of water that frequently exceed 24°C in summer; also characterizes species best adapted to or typically occurring in such waters. See *cold water* and *cool water*.

Watershed Waters and land, both surface and underground, of a hydrographic unit.

Weberian apparatus In ostariophysan fishes (including minnows, suckers, and catfishes), the modification of the first 4–5 vertebrae and ribs. The chain of ossicles of this apparatus function in transmitting sound and pressure changes from the gas bladder to the inner ear.

Wild Living in nature; or as applied particularly to trout, a fish hatched in nature as a result of the spawning there by its parents.

Wisconsinan glaciation The last Pleistocene glaciation, spanning about 10,000–118,000 years B.P. and having relatively warm stadia; preceded by the Sangamonian interglacial and Illinoian glaciation.

Young The life stage between *larva* and *adult*.

Zooarcheology The study of animal remains from archeological sites.

Zoogeography The division of *biogeography* that concerns animals.

Indexes

TAXONOMIC INDEX

Page numbers in bold type refer to accounts.

SUBJECT INDEX

CONVERSION FACTORS

Multiply	By	To obtain
millimeters (mm)	0.03937	inches (in)
meter (m)	3.281	feet (ft)
kilometer (km)	0.6214	miles (mi)
square kilometers (km^2)	0.3861	square miles (mi^2)
liters (L)	0.2642	gallons
grams (g)	0.03527	ounces
kilograms (kg)	2.205	pounds
Celsius (°C)	1.8 (°C) +32	Farenheit (°F)